International WHO'S WHO in

Poetry

2003

International WHO'S WHO in

2003

Poetry

11th Edition

Routledge
Taylor & Francis Group
LONDON AND NEW YORK

First published 1957 by Europa Publications

Published 2014
by Routledge
2 Park Square, Milton Park, Abingdon, Oxon OX14 4RN

and by Routledge
711 Third Avenue, New York, NY, 10017, USA

Routledge is an imprint of the Taylor & Francis Group, an informa business

ISBN: 978-1-857-43159-9 (hbk)

Consultant Editor: Dennis K. McIntire

Series Editor: Elizabeth Sleeman
Associate Editor: Alison Neale
Freelance Editorial Team: Kate Bomford, Anthony Mannion
Editorial Co-ordinator: Mary Hill

Typeset by Bibliocraft Ltd, Dundee

FOREWORD

The 11th Edition of the INTERNATIONAL WHO'S WHO IN POETRY (formerly the International Who's Who in Poetry and Poets' Encyclopaedia), the first published by Europa Publications, provides biographical information on over 4,000 poets. The biographies include, where available, personal details and information on education, appointments and honours, as well as poets' own publications, their contributions to anthologies, periodicals and, increasingly, to other forms such as online publications and poetry events.

Existing entrants were given the opportunity to make necessary amendments and additions to their biographies. Supplementary research was done by the Consultant Editor and the editorial department in order to ensure that the book is as up to date as possible on publication.

In addition to the biographical information, the appendices, which have been carefully revised and expanded for this edition, provide details of poetry awards and prizes, organizations and publishers, and lists of the Poets Laureate of the United Kingdom and USA. There is an additional appendix of Literary Figures of the Past.

The assistance of the individuals and organizations included in this publication in providing up-to-date material is invaluable, and the editors would like to take this opportunity to express their appreciation.

September 2002

ALPHABETIZATION KEY

The list of names is alphabetical, with the entrants listed under surnames. If part of an entrant's first given name is in parentheses, this will not affect his or her alphabetical listing.

All names beginning Mc or Mac are treated as Mac, e.g. McDevitt before MacDonald.

Names with Arabic prefixes are normally listed after the prefix, except when requested otherwise by the entrant.

In the case of surnames beginning with De, Des, Du, van or von the entries are normally found under the prefix.

Names beginning St are listed as if they began Saint, e.g. St Germain before Salamun.

As a general rule Chinese and Korean names are alphabetized under the first name.

In the case of an entrant whose name is spelt in a variety of ways, who is known by a pseudonym or best known by another name, a cross reference is provided.

CONTENTS

ABBREVIATIONS

AA	Associate in Arts	CD	Compact Disc
AB	Alberta	CD-ROM	compact disc read-only memory
ABC	Australian Broadcasting Corporation	CEO	Chief Executive Officer
Acad.	Academy	Chair.	Chairman, Chairwoman
ACLS	American Council of Learned Societies	Cia	Companhia
ACT	Australian Capital Territory	Cía	Compañía
Admin.	Administrator, Administrative	Cie	Compagnie
AG	Aktiengesellschaft (Joint Stock Company)	circ.	circulation
AIDS	acquired immunodeficiency syndrome	C.M.G.	Companion of (the Order of) St Michael and St George
AK	Alaska		
aka	also known as	CNRS	Centre National de la Recherche Scientifique
AL	Alabama	c/o	care of
ALCS	Authors' Lending and Copyright Society	Co	Company; County
A.O.	Officer of the Order of Australia	CO	Colorado
Apdo	Apartado (Post Box)	Col.	Colonia, Colima
approx.	approximately	COO	Chief Operating Officer
Apt	Apartment	Corpn	Corporation
apto	apartamento	CP	Case Postale; Caixa Postal; Casella Postale (Post Box)
AR	Arkansas		
ASCAP	American Society of Composers, Authors and Publishers	Cres.	Crescent
		Ct	Court
Asscn	Association	CT	Connecticut
Assoc.	Associate	C.V.O.	Commander of the Royal Victorian Order
Asst	Assistant	CWA	Crime Writers' Association
ATD	Art Teacher's Diploma		
Aug.	August	d.	daughter(s)
Avda	Avenida (Avenue)	D.B.E.	Dame Commander of (the Order of) the British Empire
Ave	Avenue		
AZ	Arizona	DC	District of Columbia; Distrito Central
		DD	Doctor of Divinity
b.	born	Dd'ES	Diplôme d'études supérieures
BA	Bachelor of Arts	DE	Delaware
BAFTA	British Academy of Film and Television Arts	Dec.	December
BArch	Bachelor of Architecture	DEd	Doctor of Education
BBC	British Broadcasting Corporation	Dept	Department
BC	British Columbia	D. ès L.	Docteur ès Lettres
BCL	Bachelor of Civil Law	D. ès Sc.	Docteur ès Sciences
BD	Bachelor of Divinity	devt	development
Bdwy	Broadway	DF	Distrito Federal
BE	Bachelor of Engineering; Bachelor of Education	DFA	Doctor of Fine Arts; Diploma of Fine Arts
BEd	Bachelor of Education	DHL	Doctor of Hebrew Literature
BEng	Bachelor of Engineering	DipEd	Diploma in Education
BFA	Bachelor in Fine Arts	DipTh	Diploma in Theology
BFI	British Film Institute	Dir	Director
BJ	Bachelor of Journalism	DJur	Doctor of Law
Bldg	Building	DLitt	Doctor of Letters
BLitt	Bachelor of Letters	DMus	Doctor of Music
BLS	Bachelor in Library Science	DN	Distrito Nacional
Blvd	Boulevard	DPhil	Doctor of Philosophy
BM	Bachelor of Medicine	dpto	departamento
BMus	Bachelor of Music	Dr(a)	Doctor(a)
BP	Boîte postale (Post Box)	Dr.	Drive
BPhil	Bachelor of Philosophy	DSc	Doctor of Science
BS	Bachelor of Science; Bachelor of Surgery	DSocSci	Doctor of Social Science
BSc	Bachelor of Science	DTh	Doctor of Theology
BSE	Bachelor of Science in Engineering (USA)		
BSFA	British Science Fiction Association	E	East(ern)
BTh	Bachelor of Theology	EC	European Community
BTI	British Theatre Institute	Ed.	Editor
		Edif.	Edificio (Building)
c.	circa; child, children	edn	edition
CA	California	e.g.	exempli gratia (for example)
CBC	Canadian Broadcasting Corporation	ENO	English National Opera
C.B.E.	Commander of (the Order of) the British Empire	esq.	esquina (corner)
		etc.	et cetera
CBS	Columbia Broadcasting System	EU	European Union

ABBREVIATIONS

eV	eingetragener Verein
Exec.	Executive
f.	founded
fax	facsimile
Feb.	February
FL	Florida
fmr(ly)	former(ly)
GA	Georgia
Gdns	Gardens
Gen.	General
GmbH	Gesellschaft mit beschränkter Haftung (Limited Liability Company)
GMT	Greenwich Mean Time
Gov.	Governor
GP	General Practitioner
GPO	General Post Office
h.c.	honoris causa
HHD	Doctor of Humanities
HI	Hawaii
HIV	human immunodeficiency virus
HM	His (or Her) Majesty
Hon.	Honorary; Honourable
Hons	Honours
HRH	His (or Her) Royal Highness
HS	Heraldry Society
Hwy	Highway
IA	Iowa
IBA	Independent Broadcasting Authority
ID	Idaho
i.e.	id est (that is to say)
IL	Illinois
IN	Indiana
Inc	Incorporated
incl.	including
IPC	Institute of Professional Critics
ITA	Independent Television Authority
ITN	Independent Television News
ITV	Independent Television
Jan.	January
JD	Doctor of Jurisprudence
JP	Justice of the Peace
Jr	Junior
K.B.E.	Knight Commander, Order of the British Empire
km	kilometre(s)
KS	Kansas
KY	Kentucky
LA	Louisiana
LAMDA	London Academy of Music and Dramatic Art
Lic. en Let.	Licenciado en Letras
L. ès L.	Licenciè és Lettres
L. és Sc.	Licenciè és Sciences
LHD	Doctor of Humane Letters
LLB	Bachelor of Laws
LLD	Doctor of Laws
LL.L	Licentiate of Laws
LLM	Master of Laws
LRCP	Licenciate, Royal College of Physicians, London
Ltd	Limited
LWT	London Weekend Television
m.	married; million
MA	Massachusetts; Master of Arts
Man.	Manager; Managing
MAT	Master of Arts and Teaching
MB	Manitoba
MBA	Master of Business Administration
M.B.E.	Member of (the Order of) the British Empire
MC	master of ceremonies
MD	Maryland

MDiv	Master in Divinity
ME	Maine
MEd	Master in Education
mem.	member
MEngSc	Master of Engineering
MFA	Master of Fine Arts
MHRA	Modern Humanities Research Association
MI	Michigan
MLA	Modern Language Association
MLitt	Master in Letters
MLS	Master in Library Science
MMus	Master of Music
MN	Minnesota
MO	Missouri
MP	Member of Parliament
MPh	Master of Philosophy
MRCS	Member, Royal College of Surgeons of England
MS	Mississippi; Master of Science
MSc	Master of Science
Mt	Mount
MT	Montana
MTh	Master of Theology
MTV	Music Television
N	North(ern)
NB	New Brunswick
NBC	National Broadcasting Company
NC	North Carolina
ND	North Dakota
NDD	National Diploma in Design
NE	Nebraska; North-east(ern)
NEA	National Endowment for the Arts
NF	Newfoundland
NH	New Hampshire
NJ	New Jersey
NM	New Mexico
no.	number
Nov.	November
nr	near
NS	Nova Scotia
NSW	New South Wales
NT	Northwest Territories; Northern Territory
NU	Nunavut Territory
NV	Nevada
NW	North-west(ern)
NY	New York
O.B.E.	Officer of (the Order of) the British Empire
Oct.	October
Of.	Oficina (Office)
OH	Ohio
OK	Oklahoma
ON	Ontario
OR	Oregon
p.	page
PA	Pennsylvania
PBS	Public Broadcasting Service
PE	Prince Edward Island
PEN	Poets, Playwrights, Essayists, Editors and Novelists (Club)
PF	Postfach (Post Box)
PGCE	Post Graduate Certificate of Education
PhB	Bachelor of Philosophy
PhD	Doctor of Philosophy
PhL	Licenciate of Philosophy
Pkwy	Parkway
Pl.	Place
PLC	Public Limited Company
PMB	Private Mail Bag
PO Box	Post Office Box
PR(O)	Public Relations (Officer)
Pres.	President
Prod.	Producer; Produced
Prof.	Professor

ABBREVIATIONS

pt.	part	STD	Doctor of Sacred Theology
Pty	Proprietary	Ste	Sainte
Publ.(s)	Publication(s)	STL	Reader or Professor of Sacred Theology
		STM	Master of Sacred Theology
QC	Québec	str	strasse
Qld	Queensland	SW	South-west(ern); short wave
Q.S.O.	Queen's Service Order		
q.v.	quod vide (to which refer)	tel.	telephone
		TLS	Times Literary Supplement
RADA	Royal Academy of Dramatic Art	TN	Tennessee
Rd	Road	trans.	translated; translation; translator
Rep.	Republic	Treas.	Treasurer
retd	retired	TV	television
rev.ed.	revised edition	TX	Texas
RGS	Royal Geographical Society		
RI	Rhode Island	u.	utca (street)
RNLI	Royal National Life-boat Institution	UK	United Kingdom
RSA	Royal Society of Arts	ul.	ulitsa (street)
RSC	Royal Shakespeare Company	UN	United Nations
RSL	Royal Society of Literature	UNESCO	United Nations Educational, Scientific
RSPB	Royal Society for Protection of Birds		and Cultural Organization
RTS	Royal Television Society	UNICEF	United Nations Children's Fund
		Urb.	Urbanización (urban district)
S	South(ern); San	US(A)	United States (of America)
s.	son(s)	USSR	Union of Soviet Socialist Republics
SA	Société Anonyme, Sociedad Anónima (Limited	UT	Utah
	Company); South Australia		
SC	South Carolina	VA	Virginia
SD	South Dakota	VC	Victoria Cross
SE	South-east(ern)	VI	(US) Virgin Islands
Sec.	Secretary	Vic.	Victoria
Sept.	September	Vol.(s)	Volume(s)
SFWA	Science Fiction and Fantasy Writers of America	VT	Vermont
SK	Saskatchewan		
SL	Sociedad Limitada	W	West(ern)
Sq.	Square	WA	Western Australia; Washington (state)
Sr	Senior	WI	Wisconsin
St	Street; Saint	WV	West Virginia
Sta	Santa	WY	Wyoming
STB	Bachelor of Sacred Theology	YT	Yukon Territory

INTERNATIONAL TELEPHONE CODES

To make international calls to telephone and fax numbers listed in the book, dial the international code of the country from which you are calling, followed by the appropriate code for the country you wish to call (listed below), followed by the area code (if applicable) and telephone or fax number listed in the entry.

	Country code	+ or − GMT*		Country code	+ or − GMT*
Afghanistan	93	+4½	Bulgaria	359	+2
Albania.	355	+1	Burkina Faso	226	0
Algeria	213	+1	Burundi	257	+2
Andorra	376	+1	Cambodia.	855	+7
Angola	244	+1	Cameroon.	237	+1
Antigua and Barbuda.	1 268	−4	Canada.	1	−3 to −8
Argentina.	54	−3	Cape Verde.	238	−1
Armenia.	374	+4	Central African Republic . . .	236	+1
Australia	61	+8 to +10	Chad	235	+1
Australian External Territories:			Chile	56	−4
Australian Antarctic			China, People's Republic. . . .	86	+8
Territory	.672	+3 to +10	Special Administrative Regions:		
Christmas Island.	61	+10	Hong Kong	852	+8
Cocos (Keeling) Islands . . .	61	+10	Macao.	853	+8
Norfolk Island.	672	+11½	China (Taiwan).	886	+8
Austria.	43	+1	Colombia	57	−5
Azerbaijan	994	+5	Comoros.	269	+3
The Bahamas.	1 242	−5	Congo, Democratic Republic .	243	+1
Bahrain	973	+3	Congo, Republic	242	+1
Bangladesh.	880	+6	Costa Rica	506	−6
Barbados	1 246	−4	Côte d'Ivoire.	225	0
Belarus.	375	+2	Croatia.	385	+1
Belgium	32	+1	Cuba	53	−5
Belize.	501	−6	Cyprus	357	+2
Benin	229	+1	'Turkish Republic of		
Bhutan.	975	+6	Northern Cyprus'	90 392	+2
Bolivia	591	−4	Czech Republic.	420	+1
Bosnia and Herzegovina. . . .	387	+1	Denmark	45	+1
Botswana	267	+2	Danish External Territories:		
Brazil.	55	−3 to −4	Faroe Islands	298	0
Brunei	673	+8	Greenland.	299	−1 to −4

	Country code	+ or − GMT*		Country code	+ or − GMT*
Djibouti	253	+3	Haiti	509	−5
Dominica	1 767	−4	Honduras	504	−6
Dominican Republic	1 809	−4	Hungary	36	+1
East Timor	670	+9	Iceland	354	0
Ecuador	593	−5	India	91	+5½
Egypt	20	+2	Indonesia	62	+7 to +8
El Salvador	503	−6	Iran	98	+3½
Equatorial Guinea	240	+1	Iraq	964	+3
Eritrea	291	+3	Ireland	353	0
Estonia	372	+2	Israel	972	+2
Ethiopia	251	+3	Italy	39	+1
Fiji	679	+12	Jamaica	1 876	−5
Finland	358	+2	Japan	81	+9
Finnish External Territory:			Jordan	962	+2
Åland Islands	358	+2	Kazakhstan	7	+6
France	33	+1	Kenya	254	+3
French Overseas Departments:			Kiribati	686	+12
French Guiana	594	−3	Korea, Democratic People's		
Guadeloupe	590	−4	Republic (North Korea)	850	+9
Martinique	596	−4	Korea, Republic		
Réunion	262	+4	(South Korea)	82	+9
French Overseas Collectivités			Kuwait	965	+3
Territoriales:			Kyrgyzstan	996	+5
Mayotte	269	+3	Laos	856	+7
Saint Pierre and Miquelon	508	−3	Latvia	371	+2
French Overseas Territories:			Lebanon	961	+2
French Polynesia	689	−9 to −10	Lesotho	266	+2
Wallis and Futuna Islands	681	+12	Liberia	231	0
French Overseas Country:			Libya	218	+1
New Caledonia	687	+11	Liechtenstein	423	+1
Gabon	241	+1	Lithuania	370	+2
The Gambia	220	0	Luxembourg	352	+1
Georgia	995	+4	Macedonia, former Yugoslav		
Germany	49	+1	Republic	389	+1
Ghana	233	0	Madagascar	261	+3
Greece	30	+2	Malawi	265	+2
Grenada	1 473	−4	Malaysia	60	+8
Guatemala	502	−6	Maldives	960	+5
Guinea	224	0	Mali	223	0
Guinea-Bissau	245	0	Malta	356	+1
Guyana	592	−4	Marshall Islands	692	+12

	Country code	+ or − GMT*		Country code	+ or − GMT*
Mauritania..............	222	0	Qatar..................	974	+3
Mauritius..............	230	+4	Romania...............	40	+2
Mexico................	52	−6 to −7	Russia	7	+2 to +12
Micronesia, Federated States	691	+10 to +11	Rwanda	250	+2
Moldova...............	373	+2	Saint Christopher and		
Monaco................	377	+1	Nevis	1 869	−4
Mongolia	976	+7 to +9	Saint Lucia..............	1 758	−4
Morocco	212	0	Saint Vincent and the		
Mozambique............	258	+2	Grenadines.............	1 784	−4
Myanmar	95	+6½	Samoa	685	−11
Namibia...............	264	+2	San Marino	378	+1
Nauru.................	674	+12	São Tomé and Príncipe	239	0
Nepal.................	977	+5¾	Saudi Arabia	966	+3
The Netherlands..........	31	+1	Senegal	221	0
Netherlands Dependencies:			Seychelles..............	248	+4
Aruba	297	−4	Sierra Leone.............	232	0
Netherlands Antilles	599	−4	Singapore..............	65	+8
New Zealand	64	+12	Slovakia	421	+1
New Zealand's Dependent and			Slovenia	386	+1
Associated Territories:			Solomon Islands	677	+11
Tokelan...............	690	−10	Somalia	252	+3
Cook Islands	682	−10	South Africa.............	27	+2
Niue	683	−11	Spain	34	+1
Nicaragua..............	505	−6	Sri Lanka..............	94	+5½
Niger	227	+1	Sudan.................	249	+2
Nigeria................	234	+1	Suriname	597	−3
Norway................	47	+1	Swaziland..............	268	+2
Norwegian External Territory:			Sweden................	46	+1
Svalbard	47	+1	Switzerland	41	+1
Oman.................	968	+4	Syria	963	+2
Pakistan...............	92	+5	Tajikistan..............	992	+5
Palau	680	+9	Tanzania	255	+3
Palestinian Autonomous			Thailand...............	66	+7
Areas	970	+2	Togo.................	228	0
Panama	507	−5	Tonga.................	676	+13
Papua New Guinea........	675	+10	Trinidad and Tobago	1 868	−4
Paraguay	595	−4	Tunisia................	216	+1
Peru..................	51	−5	Turkey	90	+2
The Philippines	63	+8	Turkmenistan............	993	+5
Poland	48	+1	Tuvalu	688	+12
Portugal...............	351	0	Uganda	256	+3

INTERNATIONAL TELEPHONE CODES

	Country code	+ or − GMT*
Ukraine	380	+2
United Arab Emirates	971	+4
United Kingdom	44	0
United Kingdom Crown		
Dependencies	44	0
United Kingdom Overseas Territories:		
Anguilla	1 264	−4
Ascension Island	247	0
Bermuda	1 441	−4
British Virgin Islands	1 284	−4
Cayman Islands	1 345	−5
Diego Garcia (British		
Indian Ocean Territory . . .	246	+5
Falkland Islands	500	−4
Gibraltar	350	+1
Montserrat	1 664	−4
Pitcairn Islands	872	−8
Saint Helena	290	0
Tristan da Cunha	2 897	0
Turks and Caicos Islands .	1 649	−5
		−5 to −10
United States of America . . .	1	

	Country code	+ or − GMT*
United States Commonwealth Territories:		
Northern Mariana Islands.	1 670	+10
Puerto Rico	1 787	−4
United States External Territories:		
American Samoa	1 684	−11
Guam	1 671	+10
United States Virgin		
Islands	1 340	−4
Uruguay	598	−3
Uzbekistan	998	+5
Vanuatu	678	+11
Vatican City	39	+1
Venezuela	58	−4
Viet Nam	84	+7
Yemen	967	+3
Yugoslavia	381	+1
Zambia	260	+2
Zimbabwe	263	+2

* The times listed compare the standard (winter) times in the various countries. Some countries adopt Summer (Daylight Saving) Time–i.e. +1 hour–for part of the year.

PART ONE

Biographies

A

AALFS, Janet Elizabeth; b. 14 Aug. 1956, Elmira, NY, USA. Writer; Poet; Martial Arts Instructor. *Education:* BA, 1979; MFA, Poetry, 1990; Fifth Degree Black Belt in Karate. *Publications:* Where I Go The Grass Grows Lush, 1984; Against the Odds, 1980; Of Angels and Survivors, 1992; Full Open, 1996; Reach, 1999. Anthologies: Women in Martial Arts, 1992; Martial Arts Teachers on Teaching, 1995; Frauen Kampf Kunst, 1997; Sharp Spear, Crystal Mirror, 1998; Heartbeat of New England, 2000. *Contributions to:* Sinister Wisdom; Evergreen Chronicles; Sarah Lawrence Review; Earth's Daughters; Onion; River Review; Encodings; Women Unlimited; Metis; California State Poetry Quarterly; Sojourner; Common Lives; Peregrine. *Honours:* Alumni Scholar Award, University of Massachusetts, 1978; Finalist, Cleveland State University Press Poetry Prize, 1995; First Prize, Peregrine Poetry Contest, 1996; Woman of Distinction, 1996; Pushcart Prize Nomination, 1996. *Memberships:* Acad. of American Poets; National Writers Union.

AAZIM, Muzaffar; b. 29 April 1934, Kashmir, India. Poet; Writer; Dramatist; Trans.; Educator; Administrator. m. Padshah Jan, 14 Oct. 1956, 2 s. *Education:* BSc, University of Kashmir, 1954; Various administrative courses. *Appointment:* Examiner in Kashmiri, University of Kashmir. *Publications:* Poetry: Zolana, 1964; Man-i-Kaman, 1974. Other: Plays and trans. *Contributions to:* Radio, television, magazines, and periodicals. *Honours:* Best Book of the Year Awards, Jammu and Kashmir Acad. of Art, Culture, and Languages, 1965, 1975. *Memberships:* Brontë Society, England; Kashmir Acad. of Art, Culture, and Languages; National Authors Registry, USA; Sahitya Akademi (National Acad. of Letters), India.

ABALUTA, Constantin; b. 8 Oct. 1938, Bucharest, Romania. Poet; Writer. m. Gabriela Abaluta, 1989. *Education:* Master of Architecture, 1961. *Publications:* Poetry: The Rock, 1968; Objects of Silence, 1979; Air: Directions for Use, 1982; The Cyclops' Solitude, 1995. Other: To Stay Upright, 1986. *Contributions to:* Various Romanian and foreign magazines and journals. *Honours:* Prize, Breve revue, Napoli, 1970; Prix des Poètes Francophones, 1973. *Memberships:* Constantza Haiku Society; Romanian Writers' Union. *Address:* Str Arh D. Hirjeu 76, Sect 2, 73281 Bucharest, Romania.

ABBOTT, Dickon John; b. 9 Jan. 1962, Horsham, England. Social Services Officer; Poet. m. Hazel Dole, 25 July 1992. *Education:* BA, Honours, Modern History, Lincoln College, Oxford, 1984; Postgraduate Certificate in Education, Charlotte Mason College, Ambleside, 1986. *Contributions to:* Poetry Review; Poetry Wales; New Prospects; Westwords; Orbis; Echo Room; Bogg; Pennine Platform; Envoi; Sol; Iota; Resurgence; Staple; Frogmore Papers; Westmorland Gazette. *Honour:* Prize Winner, anthology competition, Lancaster Literature Festival Poetry Competition. *Membership:* Poetry Society. *Address:* 17 Lamb Park, Rosside, Ulverston, Cumbria LA12 7NS, England.

ABBOTT, Keith George; b. 2 Feb. 1944, Tacoma, Washington, USA. Writer; Poet. m. Lani, 1 d. *Appointment:* Asst Prof., Naropa Institute. *Publications:* Harum Scarum, 1984; Mordecai of Monterey, 1985; The First Thing Coming, 1987; Downstream From Trout Fishing in America, 1989; Skin and Bone, 1993; The Last Part, 1991. *Address:* Naropa Institute, Poetics, 2130 Arapahoe, Boulder, CO 80302, USA.

ABBS, Peter Francis; b. 22 Feb. 1942, Cromer, Norfolk, England. Prof. of Creative Writing; Author; Poet; Ed. m. Barbara Beazeley, 10 June 1963, 1 s., 2 d. *Education:* BA, University of Bristol, 1963; DPhil, University of Sussex, 1986. *Appointments:* Lecturer in Education, 1976–85, Reader, 1985–99, Prof. of Creative Writing, 1999–, University of Sussex. *Publications:* English for Diversity: A Polemic, 1969; The Forms of Narrative: A Practical Guide (with John Richardson), 1970; Autobiography in Education, 1974; The Black Rainbow: Essays on the Present Breakdown of Culture (ed.), 1975; Root and Blossom: Essays on the Philosophy, Practice and Politics of English Teaching, 1976; Proposal for a New College (with Graham Carey), 1977; For Man and Islands (poems), 1978; Reclamations: Essays on Culture, Mass-Culture and the Curriculum, 1979; Songs of a New Taliesin (poems), 1979; English Within the Arts: A Radical Alternative, 1982; Living Powers: The Arts in Education (ed.), 1987; A is for Aesthetic: Essays on Creative and Aesthetic Education, 1988; The Symbolic Order: A Contemporary Reader on the Arts Debate (ed.), 1989; The Forms of Poetry: A Practical Guide (with John Richardson), 1991; Icons of Time: An Experiment in Autobiography, 1991; The Educational Imperative, 1994; The Polemics of Imagination: Essays on Art, Culture and Society, 1996; Love After Sappho (poems), 1999; Selected Poems, 2001. *Contributions to:* Scholarly and literary periodicals. *Membership:* New Metaphysical Art, founding mem. *Address:* c/o Graduate Research Centre in the Humanities, Arts Bldg B, University of Sussex, Falmer, Brighton BN1 9QN, England.

ABELL, Carol Louise; b. 25 Sept. 1940, Indiana, USA. Poet. m. Jeno Platthy, 25 Sept. 1976. *Education:* National Institute of America, New York, 1965; PhD, University Asia, 1977; DLitt, University of New York, 1979. *Appointments:* Ed.,

New Muses, 1976–; Permanent Secretary, Federation of International Poetry Asscns, 1976–. *Publications:* Morning Glory World, 1977; Five-Leaf Clover, 1983; Moonflowers, 1985; Mrs Orpheus, 1988; Fleurs de Lune, 1991; Timegraphs, 1993; Shelley Studies, 1998; Wings and Petals, 1999; Inklings, 1999. *Contributions to:* New Muses; Jointure; Festschriften. *Memberships:* International PEN Club; International Poetry Society; Die Literarische Union. *Address:* 961 W Sled Circle, Santa Claus, IN 47579, USA.

ABLEY, Mark; b. 13 May 1955, England. Poet; Journalist. m. Annie Beer, 15 Aug. 1981, 2 d. *Education:* BA, Honours, English, University of Saskatchewan, 1975; BA, Honours, English, St John's College, Oxford, 1977; MA(Oxon), 1983. *Appointments:* Contributing Ed., Saturday Night, 1986–92; Literary Ed., 1989–91, Feature Writer, 1991–, Montreal Gazette. *Publications:* Beyond Forget, 1986; Blue Sand, Blue Moon, 1988; Glasburyon, 1994; Stories From the Ice Storm, 1999; Ghost Cat, 2001. *Contributions to:* TLS; Malahat Review; New Statesman; Encounter; The Listener; Brick; London Review of Books; Quarto; Outposts; Dandelion; Grain; Matrix; Border Crossings; Fiddlehead; Poetry Review. *Honours:* Eric Gregory Award, 1981; Mark Harrison Prize, 1992, 1997. *Memberships:* Writers' Union of Canada; Québec Writers' Federation; PEN. *Address:* 52 Winston Circle, Pointe-Claire, QC H9S 4X6, Canada. *E-mail:* markabley@hotmail.com.

ABSE, Dannie; b. 22 Sept. 1923, Cardiff, Glamorgan, Wales. Physician; Poet; Writer; Dramatist. m. Joan Mercer, 4 Aug. 1951, 1 s., 2 d. *Education:* St Illtyd's College, Cardiff; University of South Wales and Monmouthshire, Cardiff; King's College, London; MD, Westminster Hospital, London, 1950. *Appointments:* Specialist, Chest Clinic, Central Medical Establishment, London, 1954–82; Senior Fellow in Humanities, Princeton University, New Jersey, 1973–74. *Publications:* Poetry: Funland and Other Poems, 1973; Way Out in the Centre, 1981; White Coat, Purple Coat: Collected Poems, 1948–88, 1989; Remembrance of Crimes Past, 1990; On the Evening Road, 1994; Arcadia, One Mile, 1998. Editor: Voices in the Gallery, 1986; The Music Lover's Literary Companion, 1988; The Hutchinson Book of Post-War British Poets, 1989. Fiction: Ash on a Young Man's Sleeve, 1954; Some Corner of an English Field, 1956; O Jones, O Jones, 1970; There Was a Young Man from Cardiff, 2001; The Strange Case of Dr Simmonds and Dr Glas, 2002. Non-Fiction: Goodbye, Twentieth Century: An Autobiography, 2001. *Contributions to:* BBC and various publications in the United Kingdom and USA. *Honours:* Foyle Award, 1960; Welsh Arts Council Literature Prizes, 1971, 1987; Cholmondeley Award, 1985. *Memberships:* Poetry Society, pres., 1979–92; RSL, fellow, 1983; Welsh Acad., fellow, 1990, pres., 1995. *Address:* c/o Peters, Fraser & Dunlop Ltd, 34–43 Russell St, London WC2B 5HA, England.

ACHEBE, (Albert) Chinua(lumogu); b. 16 Nov. 1930, Ogidi, Nigeria. Writer; Poet; Ed.; Prof. m. Christie Chinwe Okoli, 10 Sept. 1961, 2 s., 2 d. *Education:* University College, Ibadan, 1948–53; BA, London University, 1953; Received training in broadcasting, BBC, London, 1956. *Appointments:* Producer, 1954–58, Controller, Eastern Region, Enugu, Nigeria, 1958–61, Founder-Dir, Voice of Nigeria, 1961–66, Nigerian Broadcasting Corpn, Lagos; Senior Research Fellow, 1967–72, Prof. of English, 1976–81, Prof. Emeritus, 1985–, University of Nigeria, Nsukka; Ed., Okike: A Nigerian Journal of New Writing, 1971–; Prof. of English, University of Massachusetts, 1972–75; Dir, Okike Arts Centre, Nsukka, 1984–; Founder-Publisher, Uwa Ndi Igbo: A Bilingual Journal of Igbo Life and Arts, 1984–; Pro-Chancellor and Chair. of the Council, Anambra State University of Technology, Enugu, 1986–88; Charles P. Stevenson Prof., Bard College, New York, 1990–; Visiting Prof. and Lecturer at universities in Canada and the USA. *Publications:* Fiction: Things Fall Apart, 1958; No Longer at Ease, 1960; Arrow of God, 1964; A Man of the People, 1966; Anthills of the Savannah, 1987. Short Stories: The Sacrificial Egg and Other Stories, 1962; Girls at War, 1973. Children's Fiction: Chike and the River, 1966; How the Leopard Got His Claws (with John Iroaganachi), 1972; The Flute, 1978; The Drum, 1978. Poetry: Beware, Soul-Brother and Other Poems, 1971; Christmas in Biafra and Other Poems, 1973. Essays: Morning Yet on Creation Day, 1975; The Trouble With Nigeria, 1983; Hopes and Impediments, 1988; Home and Exile, 2000. Editor: Don't Let Him Die: An Anthology of Memorial Poems for Christopher Okigbo (with Dubem Okafor), 1978; Aka Weta: An Anthology of Igbo Poetry (with Obiora Udechukwu), 1982; African Short Stories (with C. L. Innes), 1984; The Heinemann Book of Contemporary African Short Stories (with C. L. Innes), 1992; Essay and Poems: Another Africa (with Robert Lyons), 1998. *Contributions to:* New York Review of Books; Transition; Callaloo. *Honours:* Margaret Wrong Memorial Prize, 1959; Nigerian National Trophy, 1961; Jock Campbell/New Statesman Award, 1965; Commonwealth Poetry Prize, 1972; Neil Gunn International Fellow, Scottish Arts Council, 1975; Lotus Award for Afro-Asian Writers, 1975; Nigerian National Order of Merit 1979; Order of the Federal Republic of Nigeria, 1979; Commonwealth Foundation Senior Visiting Practitioner Award, 1984; Booker Prize nomination, 1987; Campion Medal, New York, 1996; National Creativity Award, Nigeria, 1999; 36 hon. doctorates,

1972–2002. *Memberships:* American Acad. of Arts and Letters, foreign hon. mem., 1982; Asscn of Nigerian Authors, founder and pres., 1981–86; Vice-pres., Royal African Society, London, 1998; Commonwealth Arts Organization; MLA of America, hon. fellow; RSL, fellow, London, 1981; Writers and Scholars International, London; Nigerian Acad. of Letters, 1999; American Acad. of Arts and Sciences, foreign hon. mem., 2002. *Literary Agent:* David Bolt and Assocs. *Address:* Bard College, Annandale on Hudson, NY 12504, USA.

ACKERMAN, Diane; b. 7 Oct. 1948, Waukegan, IL, USA. Poet; Writer; University Teacher. *Education:* Boston University, 1966–67; BA, English, Pennsylvania State University, 1970; MFA, Creative Writing, 1973, MA, English, 1976, PhD, English, 1978, Cornell University. *Appointments:* Teaching Asst, 1971–78, Lecturer, 1978, Visiting Writer, 1987, Visiting Prof., 1998–2000, Cornell University; Asst Prof., University of Pittsburgh, 1980–83; Writer-in-Residence, College of William and Mary, 1982–83, Ohio University, 1983, New York University, 1986, Columbia University, 1986–87; Writer-in-Residence, 1983–86, Dir, Writers' Program, 1984–86, Washington University; Staff Writer, New Yorker magazine, 1988–94; Visiting Prof., Society for the Humanities, Cornell University, 1998–2000; National Endowment, Humanities Distinguished Prof. of English, University of Richmond, 2001. *Publications:* The Planets: A Cosmic Pastoral, 1976; Wife of Light, 1978; Twilight of the Tenderfoot, 1980; Lady Faustus, 1983; On Extended Wings, 1985; Reverse Thunder, 1988; A Natural History of the Senses, 1990; Jaguar of Sweet Laughter: New and Selected Poems, 1991; The Moon by Whale Light and Other Adventures Among Bats, Crocodilians, Penguins and Whales, 1991; A Natural History of Love, 1994; The Rarest of the Rare, 1995; Monk Seal Hideaway, 1995; A Slender Thread, 1997; Bats: Shadows in the Night, 1997; I Praise My Destroyer, 1998; The Norton Book of Love (ed. with Jeanne Mackin), 1998; Deep Play, 1999; Cultivating Delight: A Natural History of My Garden, 2001. *Contributions to:* Numerous anthologies, books, newspapers, journals and magazines. *Honours:* Abbie Copps Poetry Prize, 1974; National Endowment for the Arts Creative Writing Fellowships, 1976, 1986; Black Warrior Review Poetry Prize, 1981; Pushcart Prize, 1984; Peter I. B. Lavan Award, Acad. of American Poets, 1985; Lowell Thomas Award, 1990; New York Times Book Review Notable Books of the Year, 1991, 1992, and New and Noteworthy Books of the Year, 1993, 1997; Wordsmith Award, 1992; Literary Lion, New York Public Library, 1994; John Burroughs Nature Award, 1997; Art of Fact Award, 2000; Best American Essays Citation, 2001; Molecule named in her honour, Dianeackerone. *Address:* c/oVirginia Barber, William Morris Agency, 1325 Avenue of the Americas, New York, NY 10019, USA.

ACKROYD, Peter; b. 5 Oct. 1949, London, England. Author; Poet; Dramatist; Book Reviewer. *Education:* BA, Clare College, Cambridge, 1971; Mellon Fellowship, Yale University, 1971–73. *Appointments:* Literary Ed., 1973–77, Joint Man. Ed., 1978–82, The Spectator; Chief Book Reviewer, The Times, 1986–. *Publications:* Fiction: The Great Fire of London, 1982; The Last Testament of Oscar Wilde, 1983; Hawksmoor, 1985; Chatterton, 1987; First Light, 1989; English Music, 1992; The House of Doctor Dee, 1993; Dan Leno and the Limehouse Golem, 1994; Milton in America, 1996; The Plato Papers, 1999. Poetry: London Lickpenny, 1973; Country Life, 1978; The Diversions of Purley, 1987. Play: The Mystery of Charles Dickens, 2000. Non-Fiction: Notes for a New Culture, 1976; Dressing Up: Transvestism and Drag: The History of an Obsession, 1979; Ezra Pound and His World, 1980; T. S. Eliot, 1984; Dickens, 1990; Introduction to Dickens, 1991; Blake, 1995; The Life of Thomas More, 1998; London: The Biography, 2000; Dickens: Public Life and Private Passion, 2002; The Collection, 2002; Albion: The Origins of the English Imagination, 2002. *Honours:* Somerset Maugham Award, 1984; W. H. Heinemann Award, RSL, 1985; Whitbread Book of the Year Award for Biography, 1985, and for Fiction, 1986; Guardian Fiction Award, 1986; Hon. doctorates. *Membership:* RSL. *Address:* c/o Anthony Sheil Assocs Ltd, 43 Doughty St, London WC1N 2LF, England.

ADAM, Cornel. See: LENGYEL, Cornel Adam.

ADAMS, Anna Theresa, (Theresa Butt, Anna Butt as painter); b. 9 March 1926, London, England. Writer; Artist; Poet. m. Norman Adams, 18 Jan. 1947, 2 s. *Education:* NDD Painting, Harrow School of Art, 1945; NDD, Sculpture, Hornsey College of Art, 1950. *Appointments:* Teaching at various schools; Designer, Chelsea Pottery, 1953–55; Part-time Art Teacher, Manchester, 1966–70; Art Teacher, Settle High School, 1971–74; Poetry Ed., Green Book, 1989–92. *Publications:* Journey Through Winter, 1969; Rainbow Plantation, 1971; Memorial Tree, 1972; A Reply to Intercepted Mail, 1979; Brother Fox, 1983; Trees in Sheep Country, 1986; Dear Vincent, 1986; Six Legs Good, 1987; Angels of Soho, 1988; Nobodies, 1990; Island Chapters, 1991; Life on Limestone, 1994; Green Resistance: Selected and New Poems, 1996; A Paper Ark, 1996; The Thames: Anthology of River Poems, 1999; London in Poetry and Prose (ed.), 2002; Flying Underwater, 2003. *Contributions to:* Poetry Review; P N Review; The Countryman; 10th Muse; Country Life; Yorkshire Life; Dalesman; Pennine Platform; Western Mail; Stand; Sunday Telegraph; Poetry Durham; Poetry Canada; Poetry Nottingham; Poetry Matters; Encounter; Spokes; Meridian; Acumen; Aquarius; Orbis; Spectator; The North; Yorkshire Journal; Rialto; Scintilla; The Interpreter's House. *Honours:* First Prizes, Yorkshire Poets, 1974, 1976, 1977; First Prize, Arnold Vincent Bowen, 1976; First Prize, Lincoln Open, 1984; First Prize, Rhyme

International, 1986; Second Prize, Cardiff Festival Poetry Competition, 1987. *Memberships:* Poetry Society, London; Committee, Piccadilly Poets. *Address:* (Gainsborough Rd, Chiswick, London W4 1NJ, England.

ADAMS, Barbara, (B. B. Adams); b. 23 March 1932, New York, NY, USA. Prof. of American and English Literature; Poet. m. Elwood Adams, 6 June 1952, deceased 1993, 2 s., 2 d. *Education:* BS, 1962, MA, 1970, State University of New York, New Paltz; PhD, New York University, 1981. *Appointment:* Prof. Dept of English, Pace University, 1984–. *Publications:* Double Solitaire, 1982; Hapax Legomena, 1990; The Enemy Self: Poetry and Criticism of Laura Riding, 1990. *Contributions to:* Nation; Psychoanalytic Review; Confrontation; Antigonish Review; Wooster Review; Negative Capability; Free Assocs; Madison Review; European Judaism. *Memberships:* PEN, 1990; Poetry Society of America; Yeats Society, 1993–. *Address:* Dept of English, Pace University, Pace Plaza, New York, NY 10038, USA.

ADAMS, Deborah; b. 22 Jan. 1956, Tennessee, USA. Writer; Poet. m. 3 c. *Education:* University of Tennessee at Martin; Austin Peay University. *Appointment:* Adjunct Faculty, Nashville State Technical Institute. *Publications:* Fiction: All the Great Pretenders, 1992; All the Crazy Winters, 1992; All the Dark Disguises, 1993; All the Hungry Mothers, 1994; All the Deadly Beloved, 1995; All the Blood Relatives, 1997. Poetry: Propriety, 1976; Looking for Heroes, 1984. *Memberships:* Appalachian Writers' Asscn; Mystery Writers of America; Sisters in Crime. *Address:* Route 4, PO Box 664, Waverly, TN 37185, USA.

ADAMS, Hazard (Simeon); b. 15 Feb. 1926, Cleveland, OH, USA. Prof. of Humanities Emeritus; Writer; Poet; Ed. m. Diana White, 17 Sept. 1949, 2 s. *Education:* BA, Princeton University, 1948; MA, 1949, PhD, 1953, University of Washington. *Appointments:* Instructor, Cornell University, 1952–56; Asst Prof., University of Texas, 1956–59; Assoc. Prof. to Prof., Michigan State University, 1959–64; Fulbright Lecturer, Trinity College, Dublin, 1961–62; Prof., University of California at Irvine, 1964–77, 1990–94; Byron W. and Alice L. Lockwood Prof. of Humanities, 1977–97, Prof. Emeritus, 1997–, University of Washington. *Publications:* Blake and Yeats: The Contrary Vision, 1955; William Blake: A Reading of the Shorter Poems, 1963; The Contexts of Poetry, 1963; The Horses of Instruction: A Novel, 1968; The Interests of Criticism, 1969; The Truth About Dragons: An Anti-Romance, 1971; Lady Gregory, 1973; The Academic Tribes, 1976; Philosophy of the Literary Symbolic, 1983; Joyce Cary's Trilogies: Pursuit of the Particular Real, 1983; Antithetical Essays in Literary Criticism and Liberal Education, 1990; The Book of Yeats's Poems, 1990; The Book of Yeat's Vision, 1995; The Farm at Richwood and Other Poems, 1997; Many Pretty Toys: A Novel, 1999; Home: A Novel, 2001. Editor: Poems by Robert Simeon Adams, 1952; Poetry: An Introductory Anthology, 1968; Fiction as Process (with Carl Hartman), 1968; William Blake: Jerusalem, Selected Poems and Prose, 1970; Critical Theory Since Plato, 1971; Critical Theory Since 1965 (with Leroy Searle), 1986; Critical Essays on William Blake, 1991. *Contributions to:* Numerous poetry, scholarly and critical journals. *Honour:* Guggenheim Fellowship, 1974. *Address:* 3930 NE 157th Pl., Seattle, WA 98155, USA.

ADAMS, Mary Elizabeth Auman; b. 29 Nov. 1940, North Carolina, USA. Teacher; Writer; Poet. m. Richard Chad Adams, 30 March 1962, 1 s., 3 d. *Education:* BS, Pfeiffer College, Misenheimer, North Carolina, 1966. *Appointments:* Elementary School Teacher, Milford Elementary School, Marietta, GA, 1966–67, Kennesaw Elementary School, GA, 1967–68, Robbinsville Elementary School, North Carolina, 1975–88; Educational Dept, North Carolina Zoological Park, Asheboro, 1989–; Adult Education Instructor, Randolph Community College, Asheboro, 1990–. *Publication:* A Collection of Poems by Mary Elizabeth Auman Adams, self published, 1987. *Contributions to:* Various anthologies. *Honours:* Golden Awards, World of Poetry, 1988, 1989, 1990; Poet of Merit, American Poetry Asscn, 1989; Outstanding Poetry Writers Award, National Arts Society, 1990; Caldwell W Nixon Jr Award, North Carolina Poetry Society, 1990. *Memberships:* North Carolina Poetry Society; Southern Poetry Asscn; National Arts Society; Sparrowgrass Poetry Forum; World of Poetry; Great Lakes Poetry Press; American Poetry Asscn. *Address:* 5911 US Highway 220 S, Asheboro, NC 27203, USA.

ADAMS, Perseus; b. 11 March 1933, Cape Town, South Africa. Writer; Journalist; Poet; Teacher (retd). m. 1958. *Education:* BA, University of Cape Town, 1952; Certificate of Education, 1961. *Appointments:* Journalist; English Teacher. *Publications:* The Land at My Door, 1965; Grass for the Unicorn, 1975; Cries and Silences: Selected Poems, 1996. *Contributions to:* Numerous, mostly to Contrast, Cape Town. *Honours:* South Africa State Poetry Prize, 1963; Festival of Rhodesia Prize, 1970; Keats Memorial International Prize, 1971; Bridport Arts Festival Prize, 1984; Co-winner, Writing Section, Bard of the Year, 1993; Nominated for the Forward Prize, 1994–95. *Address:* 21 Mapesbury Rd, Kilburn, London NW2, England.

ADAMS, Wilfried M. G.; b. 23 Nov. 1947, Flanders, Belgium. Poet. 1 s. *Education:* Candidate Law, 1967, Licentiate, Germanic Philosophy, 1972, Catholic University of Louvain. *Publications:* Graafschap, 1970; Dagwaarts Een Woord, 1972; Geen Vogelkreet de Roos, 1975; Ontginning, 1976; Aanspraak, 1981; Lettre de Cachet, 1982; Uw Afwezigheid, 1986; Dicta Dura,

1988; Zayin, 1992; Vll Sirventes, 1993. *Contributions to:* Several Flemish and Dutch literary periodicals. *Honours:* Prys Vlaamse Poeziedagen, 1971; Knokke-Heist, 1976; Provincie Antwerpen, 1988. *Memberships:* Vereiniging van Vloamse Letterkundigen, 1973; Maatschappy der Nederlandse Letterkunde, 1974; Confraria de Recerques. *Address:* c/o Dirk Adams, Bovenbosstraat 78A, 3052 Haasrode, Belgium.

ADAMSON, Donald; b. 15 June 1943, Dumfries, Scotland. Writer; Poet; Ed. *Education:* MA, English Literature, 1965, MLitt, Applied Linguistics, 1975, Edinburgh University. *Appointments:* EFL posts in France, Finland, Iran and Kuwait; Longman EFL Division, Research and Development Unit; Freelance EFL Writer and Ed. *Contributions to:* Lines Review; Orbis; New Writing Scotland. *Honours:* Glasgow University/Radio Clyde Poetry Prize, 1985; Second Prize, Northwords Competition, 1995; Winner, Herald Millennium Poem Competition, 1999. *Address:* 1 St Peter's Ct, Dalbeattie, Scotland.

ADAMSON, Robert (Harry); b. 17 May 1943, Sydney, NSW, Australia. Poet; Writer; Ed.; Publisher. m. (1) Cheryl Adamson, 1973, (2) Juno Adamson, 19 Feb. 1989, 1 s. *Appointments:* Assoc. Ed., 1968–70, Ed., 1970–75, Asst Ed., 1975–77, New Poetry magazine, Sydney; Ed. and Dir, Prism Books, Sydney, 1970–77; Founding Ed. and Dir (with Dorothy Hewett), Big Smoke Books, Sydney, 1979–; Founder (with Michael Wilding), Paper Bark Press, 1988–. *Publications:* Poetry: Canticles on the Skin, 1970; The Rumour, 1971; Swamp Riddles, 1974; Theatre I-XIX, 1976; Cross the Border, 1977; Selected Poems, 1977; Where I Come From, 1979; The Law at Heart's Desire, 1982; The Clean Dark, 1989; Robert Adamson Selected Poems, 1970–1989, 1990; Waving to Hart Crane, 1994; Mulberry Leaves: New and Selected Poems 1970–2001, 2002. Fiction: Zimmer's Essay (with Bruce Hanford), 1974; Wards of the State: An Autobiographical Novella, 1992. Editor: Australian Writing Now (with Manfred Jurgensen), 1988. *Contributions to:* Periodicals. *Honours:* Australia Council Fellowships, 1976, 1977; Grace Leven Prize for Poetry, 1977; Kenneth Slessor Award, 1990; Turnbull-Fox Philips Poetry Prize, 1990; C. J. Dennis Prize for Poetry, 1990. *Memberships:* Australian Society of Authors; Poetry Society of Australia, pres., 1970–80. *Address:* PO Box 59, Brooklyn, NSW 2083, Australia.

ADCOCK, Betty, (Elizabeth S. Adcock); b. 16 Sept. 1938, Fort Worth, Texas, USA. Poet. m. Donald Brandt Adcock, 22 June 1957, 1 d. *Education:* Hockaday Preparatory School, Dallas, Texas, 1954–56; Texas Technical University, 1956–57; North Carolina State University, 1965–67; Goddard College, Vermont, 1967–69. *Appointments:* Visiting Lecturer in Creative Writing, Duke University, 1977; Writer-in-Residence, Kalamazoo College, Michigan, 1983; Kenan Writer-in-Residence, Meridith College, Raleigh, North Carolina, 1984–; Faculty, Warren Wilson MFA Program for Writers, 1999–. *Publications:* Walking Out, 1975; Nettles, 1983; Beholdings, 1988; The Difficult Wheel, 1995; Intervale: New and Selected Poems, 2001. *Contributions to:* Nation; Kenyon Review; Mississippi Review; TriQuarterly; Georgia Review; South Carolina Review; Southern Review; Poetry Northwest; Southern Poetry Review; Chicago Review; American Literary Review. *Honours:* New Writing Award, Great Lakes Colleges Asscn, 1975; Roanoke-Chowan Award, 1984; Zoe Kineaid Brockman Award, 1989; Fellowship in Poetry, National Endowment for the Arts, 1984; Individual Arts Grant, State of North Carolina, 1985; Invitation to read at Library of Congress, Washington, DC, 1989; North Carolina Gov.'s Award for Literature, 1996; Texas Institute of Letters Prize for Poetry, 1996; Guggenheim Fellowship in Poetry, 2002. *Address:* 817 Runnymede Rd, Raleigh, NC 27607, USA.

ADCOCK, Fleur; b. 10 Feb. 1934, Papakura, New Zealand. Poet; Writer; Trans.; Ed. m. (1) Alistair Teariki Campbell, 1952, divorced 1958, 2 s., (2) Barry Crump, 1962, divorced 1966. *Education:* MA, Victoria University of Wellington, 1955. *Appointments:* Northern Arts Fellowship in Literature, Universities of Newcastle upon Tyne and Durham, 1979–81; Eastern Arts Fellowship, University of East Anglia, 1984; Writer-in-Residence, University of Adelaide, 1986. *Publications:* The Eye of the Hurricane, 1964; Tigers, 1967; High Tide in the Garden, 1971; The Scenic Route, 1974; The Inner Harbour, 1979; Below Loughrigg, 1979; The Oxford Book of Contemporary New Zealand Poetry (ed.), 1982; Selected Poems, 1983; The Virgin and the Nightingale: Medieval Latin Poems, 1983; Hotspur: A Ballad for Music, 1986; The Incident Book, 1986; The Faber Book of 20th Century Women's Poetry (ed.), 1987; Orient Express: Poems by Grete Tartler (trans.), 1989; Time Zones, 1991; Letters from Darkness: Poems by Daniela Crasnaru (trans.), 1991; Hugh Primas and the Archpoet (ed. and trans.), 1994; The Oxford Book of Creatures (ed. with Jacqueline Simms), 1995; Looking Back, 1997; Poems 1960–2000, 2000. *Honours:* Buckland Awards, 1967, 1979; Jessie MacKay Awards, 1968, 1972; Cholmondley Award, 1976; New Zealand Book Award, 1984; O.B.E., 1996. *Membership:* Fellow, RSL. *Address:* 14 Lincoln Rd, London N2 9DL, England.

ADHIKARI, Santosh Kumar; b. 24 Nov. 1923, West Bengal, India. College Administrator (retd); Writer; Poet. m. March 1948, 1 s., 2 d. *Education:* Graduated, University of Calcutta, 1943; Diploma, Industrial Finance, Indian Institute of Bankers, Mumbai; Diploma in Management, Indian Institute of Management. *Appointments:* Principal, Staff College, United Bank of India, Calcutta, retd 1983; Vidyasagar Lecturer, University of Calcutta, 1979; Speaker, Bengal Studies Conference, University of Chicago, 1990; Editor,

Spark, 1975–96. *Publications:* Vidyasagar: Educator, Reformer and Humanist; Paari (Bengali poetry); Novels, short stories, biographies, poetry collections and anthologies, 1948–2002. *Contributions to:* All India Radio and major journals. *Honours:* Prasad Puraskar for Poetry, 1986; Hon. title of Bharat Bhasa Bhusan, 1991. *Memberships:* Asiatic Society; Akhil Bharat, Bhasa Sahitya Sammelan; Founder, first Sec., Vidyasagar Research Centre; Former Sec., PEN, West Bengal Branch. *Address:* c/o Vidyasagar Research Centre, 81 Raja Basanta Roy Rd, Calcutta, 700 029, India.

ADNAN, Etel; b. 24 Feb. 1925, Beirut, Lebanon. Poet; Writer; Painter; Tapestry Designer. *Education:* Sorbonne, University of Paris; University of California, Berkeley; Harvard University. *Appointments:* Teacher, Philosophy of Art and Humanities, Dominican College, San Rafael, CA, 1958–72; Cultural Ed., Al-Safa, Lebanon, 1972–79; L'Orient-Le Jour, Lebanon, 1974–79; Paintings exhibited around the world. *Publications:* Poetry: Moonshots, 1966; Five Senses for One Death, 1971; From A to Z, 1982; The Indian Never Had a Horse and Other Poems, 1985; The Arab Apocalypse, 1989; The Spring Flowers Own and the Manifestations of the Voyage, 1990. Novel: Sitt Marie-Rose, 1982. Other: Journey to Mount Tamalpais, 1986; Of Cities and Women, 1993; Paris, When It's Naked, 1993; There, 1995. *Contributions to:* Poems and short stories in many publications. *Honour:* France-Pays-Arabes Prize, 1978. *Membership:* Poetry Center, San Francisco. *Address:* 35 Marie St, Sausalito, CA 94965, USA.

ADOFF, Arnold; b. 16 July 1935, New York, NY, USA. Poet; Writer; Literary Agent. m. Virginia Hamilton, 19 March 1960, 2 c. *Education:* BA, City College of New York, 1956; Columbia University, 1956–58; New School for Social Research Poetry Workshops, New York, 1965–67. *Appointments:* Teacher, New York City Public Schools, 1957–69; Literary Agent, Yellow Springs, OH, 1977–; Distinguished Visiting Prof., Queens College, 1986–87; Guest Lecturer in many US venues. *Publications:* Poetry: Black Is Brown Is Tan, 1973; Make a Circle Keep Us In: Poems for a Good Day, 1975; Big Sister Tells Me That I'm Black, 1976; Tornado!: Poems, 1977; Under the Early Morning Trees, 1978; Where Wild Willie, 1978; Eats: Poems, 1979; I Am the Running Girl, 1979; Friend Dog, 1980; OUTside INside Poems, 1981; Today We Are Brother and Sister, 1981; Birds, 1982; All the Colors of the Race, 1982; The Cabbages Are Chasing the Rabbits, 1985; Sports Pages, 1986; Flamboyan, 1988; Greens, 1988; Chocolate Dreams, 1989; Hard to Be Six, 1990; In for Winter, Out for Spring, 1991. Other: Malcolm X (biography), 1970; MA nDA LA (picture book), 1971. Editor: I Am the Darker Brother: An Anthology of Modern Poems by Negro Americans, 1968; Black on Black: Commentaries by Negro Americans, 1968; City in All Directions: An Anthology of Modern Poems by Black Americans, 1970; Brothers and Sisters: Modern Stories by Black Americans, 1970; It Is the Poem Singing into Your Eyes: An Anthology of New Young Poets, 1971; The Poetry of Black America: An Anthology of the 20th Century, 1973; My Black Me: A Beginning Book of Black Poetry, 1974; Celebrations: A New Anthology of Black American Poetry, 1978. *Contributions to:* Articles and reviews in periodicals. *Honours:* Children's Book of the Year Citations, Child Study Asscn of America, 1968, 1969, 1986; American Library Asscn Notable Book Awards, 1968, 1970, 1971, 1972, 1979; Best Children's Book Citations, School Library Journal, 1971, 1973; Notable Children's Trade Book Citation, Children's Book Council-National Council for Social Studies, 1974; Jane Addams Peace Asscn Special Certificate, 1983; Children's Choice Citation, International Reading Asscn-Children's Book Council, 1985; National Council of Teachers of English Poetry Award, 1988. *Address:* Arnold Adoff Agency, PO Box 293, Yellow Springs, OH 45387, USA.

AFRA, Kwesi. See: THERSON-COFIE, Larweh.

AFTERMAN, Susan; b. 11 May 1947, Melbourne, Vic., Australia. Poet; Architect. m. Allen Afterman, deceased 1992, 4 s. *Education:* BArch, Melbourne University, 1970. *Publications:* Rites, 1978; Rain, 1987. *Contributions to:* Various magazines in Australia and UK. *Honour:* Australian Arts Council Poetry Grant. *Address:* Kfar Clil, D N Ashrat, Israel.

AGEE, Chris(topher Robert); b. 18 Jan. 1956, San Francisco, CA, USA. Educator; Poet. m. Nórín McKinney, 22 Aug. 1990. *Education:* BA, Honours, cum laude, English and American Literature and Language, Harvard University, 1979; MA, English (Irish Writing), Queen's University of Belfast, 1987. *Appointments:* Assoc. Lecturer, Faculty of Social Sciences, Open University in Ireland; Education Adviser, University of East London; Ed., Irish Pages: A Journal of Contemporary Writing. *Publications:* In the New Hampshire Woods, 1992; The Sierra de Zacatecas, 1995; Contemporary Irish Poetry (co-ed.), 1995; Scar on the Stone: Contemporary Poetry from Bosnia (ed.), 1998; First Light, 2003. *Contributions to:* Irish Times; Honest Ulsterman; American Poetry Review; Eire-Ireland; Yale Review; New Statesman; TLS. *Honour:* Award of International Writers' Exchange with Russia, Irish Writers' Centre, 1992; Poetry Book Society Recommendation, 1998. *Membership:* Board of Dirs, Poetry Ireland. *Address:* 102 N Parade, Belfast BT7 2GJ, Northern Ireland.

AGEE, Jonis; b. 31 May 1943, Omaha, NE, USA. Writer; Poet; Prof. m. Paul McDonough, 1 d. *Education:* BA, University of Iowa, 1966; MA, 1969, PhD, 1976, State University of New York at Binghampton. *Appointments:* Teacher, College of St Catherine, St Paul, Minnesota, 1975–95; Literary Consultant,

Walker Arts Center, Minneapolis, 1978–84; Adjunct Teacher, Macalester College, St Paul, Minnesota, 1980–88; Teacher and Ed., Literary Post Program for Senior Citizen Writers, 1986–89; Prof., University of Michigan, 1995–; Many poetry readings. *Publications:* Houses (poem), 1976; Mercury (poems), 1981; Two Poems, 1982; Border Crossings (ed.), 1984; Stiller's Pond (ed.), 1988; Bend This Heart (short stories), 1989; Pretend We've Never Met (short stories), 1989; Sweet Eyes (novel), 1991; Strange Angels (novel), 1993; A .38 Special and a Broken Heart (short stories), 1995; South of Resurrection (novel), 1997. *Contributions to:* Anthologies and periodicals. *Honours:* Minnesota State Arts Board Award, 1977; National Endowment for the Arts Fellowship, 1978; Loft-McKnight Awards, 1987, 1991. *Membership:* Literary Guild. *Address:* 503 S First St, Ann Arbor, MI 48103, USA.

AHARONI, Ada Andree; b. 30 July 1933, Egypt. Writer; Poet; Prof. of Literature and Modern Poetry. m. Chaim Aharoni, 26 March 1951, 1 s., 1 d. *Education:* BA, English and Sociology, 1965, PhD, English Literature, 1975, Hebrew University, Jerusalem; MPhil, English Literature, University of London, 1967. *Appointments:* Lecturer, Dept of English, Haifa University, 1967–77; Senior Lecturer, Dept of General Studies, Technion, Haifa, Israel, 1977–93; Pres., International Friends of Literature Asscn, 1995–; Convenor, IPRA: Pave Peace, Literature and Culture Commission, 1996–98; Ed., Horizon and Poetry Israel, 1997–98. *Publications:* Poems From Israel, 1972; Poems From Israel and Other Poems, 1974; From the Pyramids to Mount Carmel, 1979; Love Poems, 1980; Shin Shalom: Poems, 1984; Shin Shalom: New Poems, English/Hebrew edn, 1986; A Green Week, 1988; Metal et Violettes, 1989; Selected Poems From Israel and Around the World, 1992; Selected Poems: In My Carmel Woods, 1993; In the Curve of Your Palm, 1994; Peace Flower, 1995; Waves of Peace Anthology, in memory of Yitzhak Rabin, 1997; Peace Poems, 1997; Not in Vain: An Extraordinary Life, 1998; You and I Can Change the World: New and Selected Poems, 2000; Culture of Peace Poetry Anthology, 2000; Women Creating a World Beyond War, 2001; The Pomegranate, 2002. *Contributions to:* Poetry Nippon; Jewish Chronicle; Voices; Arc; New Society; International Poetry Review; El Shark, Poet; Ed., various online magazines. *Honours:* British Council Poetry Grant, 1972; Haifa and Bremen Poetry Award, 1975; Pres. of Israel's Literature Award, Keren Amos, 1977; Bank Discount Literary Award, 1979; Boston Forum Prize, 1981; Haifa Culture Poetry Prize, 1984; The Bemaaracha, Jerusalem Poetry Grant, 1987; Pennsylvannia Poetry Award, 1989; Yunus Imri Poetry Award, 1992; Shin Shalom Peace Poetry Award, 1993; International Poetry Prize, 1994; Best of the Planet Award for website, 1998; 100 Global Heroines Award, 1998. *Memberships:* PEN; Galim Writers Asscn; Committee, Hebrew Writers Organization; Chair., International Congress on Conflict Resolution through Poetry, Literature and Culture; IFLAC, Pres., 1999–. *Address:* 57 Horev St, Haifa 34343, Israel.

AHMED, Shafi Uddin Abul Hasnat; b. 1 Jan. 1937, Faridpur, Bangladesh. Marine Engineer; Poet. m. Ruhani Lily Khandkar, 25 Sept. 1960, 2 s. *Education:* RN, Dockyard College, Plymouth, 1952–56; Chartered Engineer, 1970; LLB, 1976; BA, Open University, 1992; European Engineer, 1994. *Publications:* Free Translations From Rabindranath Tagore, 1982; Tagore's Eleven (ten poems and one song), 1985. *Contributions to:* Open University Poetry Society Anthology; Civil Service Poetry Anthology; International Society of Poets Anthology; Bengali Newsweekly Janomot (UK). *Honour:* Peterloo Poet's Award, 1992. *Memberships:* Civil Service Society of Authors; Open University Poetry Society; National Poetry Society; South Asian Literature Society; Bengali Literary Society (UK). *Address:* 100 Western Ave, East Acton, London W3 7TX, England.

Ai, (Florence Anthony); b. 1947, Albany, TX, USA. Poet. *Publications:* Cruelty, 1973; Killing Floor, 1979; Sin, 1986; Fate, 1991; Temporomandibul Joint Dysfunction, 1992; Greed, 1993; Vice, 1999. *Honour:* National Book Award for Poetry, 1999. *Address:* c/o Houghton Mifflin, Trade and Reference Division, Editorial and Sales Offices, 222 Berkeley St, Boston, MA 02116, USA.

AKHMADULINA, Bella (actually Isabella Akhatovna Akhmadulina); b. 10 April 1937, Moscow, Russia. Poet. m. (1) Yevgeny Yevtushenko, 1960, (2) Yury Nagibin, (3) Boris Messerer, 1974. *Education:* Gorky Institute of Literature, Moscow. *Appointment:* Sec., Union of Soviet, (later Russian) Writers, 1986–91. *Publications:* Fire Tree, 1958; The String, 1962; The Rain, 1963; My Ancestry, 1964; Summer Leaves, 1968; The Lessons of Music, 1969; Fever and Other New Poems, 1970; Tenerezza, 1971; Poems, 1975; The Dreams About Georgia, 1977; The Candle, 1978; The Snowstorm, 1978; The Mystery, 1983; The Garden, 1987; The Seaboard, 1991; Selected Works, three vols, 1996; The Ancient Style Attracts Me, 1997; Beautiful Features of My Friends, 1999. *Honours:* USSR State Prize, 1989; Russian Pres.'s Prize, 1998. *Memberships:* American Acad. of Arts and Letters, hon. mem., 1977; Russian PEN Centre, board mem., 1989–92. *Address:* Chernyachovskogo str 4, Apt 37, 125319 Moscow, Russia.

AKMAKJIAN, Alan Paul; b. 18 July 1948, Highland Park, MI, USA. University Teacher; Poet; Writer. *Education:* BA, 1973, MA, 1974, Eastern Michigan University; PhD, University of Texas at Dallas, St John's University, New York, Wayne State University, Detroit, 1979; MA, California State University, San Francisco, 1991. *Appointments:* Teacher, California State University, San Francisco, 1985, St John's University, New York City,

1994–95, University of Texas at Dallas, 1995–; Instructor, Poets in the Schools, CA, 1986–91. *Publications:* Treading Pages of Water, 1992; Let the Sun Go, 1992; California Picnic, 1992; Grounded Angels, 1993; Breaking the Silence, 1994; California Picnic and Other Poems, 1997. *Contributions to:* Anthologies, journals, reviews and magazines. *Honours:* National Endowment for the Arts Grant, 1984; California Arts Council Grant, 1984; St John's University Fellowship, 1994–95; University of Texas Fellowships 1994–95, 1995–96, 1996–97; Texas Public Educational Grant, 1996–97. *Memberships:* Acad. of American Poets; Associated Writing Programs; MLA; PEN; Poetry Society of America. *Address:* 2200 Waterview Pkwy, Apt 2134 Richardson, TX 75080, USA.

ALANAH, Patrica. See: COSENTINO, Patricia Alanah.

ALBARELLA, Joan; b. 22 Sept. 1944, New York, NY, USA. Teacher of English; Poet. *Education:* BS, 1966, MSEd 1971, State University of New York at Buffalo. *Appointments:* Actress, Dir, Indigo Productions, 1973–85; Journalist, Photographer, Western New York Catholic, 1975–88; Assoc. Prof., State University of New York at Buffalo, Educational Opportunity Centre, 1986–. *Publications:* Mirror Me, 1973; Poems for the Asking, 1975; Women, Flowers, Fantasy, 1987; Spirit and Joy, 1993. *Contributions to:* Sunshine Magazine; Buffalo Courier Express; Western New York Catholic; North American Voice of Fatima. *Honours:* Poet of the Year, National Poetry Publications, New York, 1974, 1975, 1976. *Memberships:* Poets and Writers; Niagara Erie Writers. *Address:* c/o State University of New York at Buffalo, Buffalo, NY 14222, USA.

ALBERT, Gwendolyn Hubka; b. 11 Jan. 1967, Oakland, CA, USA. Poet. *Education:* BA Linguistics, University of California, 1989; Fulbright Scholar, Charles Univerity, Prague, 1989–90. *Appointment:* Ed., Je June: America Eats Its Young, 1993–. *Publications:* Dogs, 1991; Green, Green, 1992. *Contributions to:* Berkeley Poetry Review; Blind Date; Byzantium; Carbuncle; CUPS; Cyanosis; East Bay Guardian; Exquisite Corpse; GRIST online; House Organ; MacGuffin; Real Poetik; Sour Grapes. *Honour:* First Prize, Kingfisher Fiction Contest, 1991.

ALBEVERIO MANZONI, Solvejg; b. 6 Nov. 1939, Arogno, Switzerland. Painter; Writer; Poet. m. Sergio Albeverio, 7 Feb. 1970, 1 d. *Education:* Textile Designer, Diploma, Como, Italy, 1960; Art Courses, Zürich, 1969; Drawing and Etching Studies, Oslo, 1972–77. *Appointments:* Exhibitions in many countries. *Publications:* Da stanze chiuse; Il pensatore con il mantello come meteora; Il fiore, il frutto, triandro donna; Frange di solitudine; Spiagge confinanti; La carcassa color del cielo. *Contributions to:* Literary journals and reviews. *Honours:* Premio Ascona, 1987; Pro Helvetia Prize, 1995. *Memberships:* Associazione Scrittori della Svizzera Italiana; PEN; Sculptors and Architects; Swiss Society of Painters; Swiss Society of Writers. *Address:* Liebfrauenweg 5B, 53125 Bonn, Germany.

ALCOSSER, Sandra; b. 3 Feb. 1944, Washington, DC, USA. Poet. m. 10 May 1978. *Education:* Lake Forest Acad.; BA, Purdue University, 1966; MFA, University of Montana, 1982. *Appointments:* Dir, Poets in the Park, Central Park, New York, 1975–77; Writer-in-Residence, Poet in the Schools, Solo Artist for National Endowment for the Arts, 1977–85; Asst Prof., Louisiana State University, 1985–87; Prof., San Diego State University, 1989–. *Publications:* Each Bone a Prayer, 1982; A Fish to Feed All Hunger, 1986; Sleeping Inside the Glacier, 1997; Except by Nature, 1998. *Contributions to:* American Scholar; New Yorker; Paris Review; Poetry; Pushcart Prize VIII; North American Review; Yale Review; American Poetry Review. *Honours:* Guest Ed., Fiction and Poetry, Mademoiselle Magazine, 1966; Dylan Thomas Poetry Award, New School for Social Research, 1976; National University Chapbook Award, 1980; Bread Loaf Scholar, 1983, and Fellow, 1986; American Scholar Poetry Award, 1983; Associated Writing Programs Award, Series Winner in Poetry, 1984; Fellowship, National Endowment for the Arts, 1985, 1991; Syndicated Fiction Project Winner, PEN, 1986; Pushcart Prize for Poetry, 1988; National Poetry Series Recipient, 1997; Acad. of American Poets James Laughlin Award, 1998; Pacific Northwest Booksellers Poetry Award, 1999. *Memberships:* Poets and Writers; Associated Writing Programs. *Address:* 5791 W Countyline, Florence, MT 59833, USA.

ALDERSON, Bill, (William); b. 14 Oct. 1921, New Silksworth, Near Sunderland, England. Poet; Writer. m. Doris Elisha Hart, 11 May 1946. *Education:* Further Education Courses in Management, English and other subjects, Sunderland Technical College. *Publication:* Poems From the Cliff Top, 1990. *Contributions to:* Short stories, Witney Gazette, 1962–64. *Membership:* Warwick Writers Club. *Address:* 25 Chandlers Rd, Whitnash, Leamington Spa, Warwickshire CV31 2LL, England.

ALEGRIA, Claribel; b. 12 May 1924, Esteli, Nicaragua. Writer; Poet. m. Darwin J. Flakoll, 29 Dec. 1947, deceased 1995, 1 s., 3 d. *Education:* BA, George Washington University, Washington, DC, USA. *Publications:* Anillo de silencio, 1948; Suite, 1950; Vigilias, 1953; Acuario, 1955; Huésped de mi tiempo, 1961; Via única, 1965; Aprendizenje, 1972; Pagar a cobrar y otros poemas, 1973; Sobevivo, 1978; Suma y sigue, 1981; Y este poema río, 1989; Luisa en el país de la realidad, 1989; Fugues, 1993; Thresholds, 1996; Sorrow, 1999. *Contributions* to: Many periodicals. *Honours:* Premio Casa de las Americas, Havana, Cuba, 1978; Doctor h.c., University of Eastern Connecticut, 1998. *Address:* Apdo A-36, Managua, Nicaragua.

ALENIER, Karren LaLonde; b. 7 May 1947, Cheverly, Maryland, USA. Poet; Writer; Publisher. m. (1) Howard Scott Alenier, 22 June 1969, divorced 1979, 1 s., (2) James Stuart Rich Jr, 14 Feb. 1999. *Education:* BA, Honours, French, University of Maryland, College Park, 1969. *Publications:* Wandering on the Outside, 1975; The Dancer's Muse, 1981; Whose Woods Are These? (ed.), 1983; Bumper Cars: Gertrude Said She Took Him for a Ride, 1996. *Contributions to:* Mississippi Review; Poet Lore. *Honours:* First Prize, Billee Murray Denny Award, Lincoln College, IL, 1981; Fellow, Virginia Centre for the Creative Arts, 1989, 1990, 1991, 1992; Reading at the Library of Congress, Washington, DC, 1995 and at Viola Café, Prague, Czechoslovakia, 1995. *Memberships:* Poetry Committee, Greater Washington, DC, Area, founder-pres. and chair. of the board, 1986–90; The Word Works, pres. and chair. of the board, 1986–. *Address:* 4601 N Park Ave, No. 301, Chevy Chase, MD 20815, USA.

ALEXANDER, Francis Wesley; b. 3 Nov. 1949, Sandusky, Ohio, USA. Teacher; Poet. 1 s. *Education:* BS, Psychology, Wayne State University, 1973–77; Secondary Provisional Teaching Certificate, Mathematics, Eastern Michigan University, 1985–87. *Appointments:* Teacher, Adult Education, Detroit, Ypsilanti, Michigan, Toledo, Ohio, 1977–; Substitute Teacher, Ann Arbor, Michigan, Pittsburgh, 1981–87. *Contributions to:* Bare Bones; Red Pagoda; Mainichi Daily News, Japan; Dragonfly; Black Bear Review; Haiku Quarterly; Brussels Sprout; Modern Haiku; New Cicada, Japan; Beyond, Ko, Japan; Psychopoetica; Black Bough; Japanophile; Star Line; Scavenger's Newsletter; Haiku Headlines; Starsong; Contemporary Education; Black American Literature Forum; Piedmont Literary Review; Papyrus Writers' Guidelines and News; Xavier Review. *Honours:* Honourable Mention, Mainichi Daily News Annual Haiku Contest, 1989. *Memberships:* Haiku Society of America; Science Fiction Poetry Assscn. *Address:* 1816 Harrison St, Sandusky, OH 44870, USA.

ALEXANDER, Meena; b. 17 Feb. 1951, Allahabad, India. Distinguished Prof. of English and Women's Studies; Poet; Writer. m. David Lelyveld, 1 May 1979, 1 s., 1 d. *Education:* BA, University of Khartoum, 1969; PhD, University of Nottingham, 1973. *Appointments:* Lecturer, 1977–79, Reader, 1979, University of Hyderabad; Asst Prof., Fordham University, 1980–87; Asst Prof., 1987–89, Assoc. Prof., 1989–92, Prof. of English, 1992–99, Distinguished Prof. of English and Women's Studies, 1999–, Hunter College and the Graduate Center, City University of New York. *Publications:* The Poetic Self: Towards a Phenomenology of Romanticism, 1979; Stone Roots (poems), 1980; House of a Thousand Doors (poems and prose), 1988; Women in Romanticism: Mary Wollstonecraft, Dorothy Wordsworth and Mary Shelley, 1989; The Storm: A Poem in Five Parts, 1989; Nampally Road (novel), 1991; Night-Scene: The Garden (poem), 1992; Fault Lines (memoir), 1993; River and Bridge (poems), 1995; The Shock of Arrival: Reflections on Postcolonial Experience (poems and prose), 1996; Manhattan Music (novel), 1997; Notebook (poems), 1999; Illiterate Heart (poems), 2002. *Contributions to:* Books, anthologies and periodicals. *Honours:* Altrusa International Award, 1973; MacDowell Colony Fellow, 1993, 1998; International Writer-in-Residence, Arts Council of England, 1995; Lila Wallace Writer-in-Residence, Asian American Renaissance, Minneapolis, 1995; New York State Foundation for the Arts, Poetry Award, 1999; Poet-in-Residence, National University of Singapore, 1999; Fondation Ledig-Rowohlt Residency, Château de Lavigny, 2001; Commission for Poetry International, Royal Festival Hall, London, 2002; Fulbright Scholar Award, India, 2002; PEN Open Book Award, 2002. *Memberships:* MLA; PEN American Center. *Address:* c/o Graduate School and University Center, City University of New York, 365 Fifth Ave, New York, NY 10016, USA. *E-mail:* malexander@gc.cuny.edu.

ALIESAN, Jody; b. 22 April 1943, Kansas City, Missouri, USA. Poet. *Education:* BA, English and American Literature, Occidental College, 1965; MA, Brandeis University, 1966. *Publications:* Thunder in the Sun, 1971; To Set Free, 1972; Soul Claiming, 1975; As If It Will Matter, 1978; Desire, 1985; Doing Least Harm, 1985; Grief Sweat, 1991; States of Grace, 1992; Desperate for a Clearing, 1998; Loving in Time of War, 1999. *Contributions to:* Wall Street Journal; Los Angeles Times; Portland Review; California Quarterly; Contemporary Quarterly; Negative Capability; Poetry Northwest; Quarry West; Studia Mystica; Calyx; Berkeley Poets Co-operative; Northwest Review; The Advocate; Yellow Silk. *Honours:* Seattle Arts Festival, Written Works Awards, 1973, 1976, 1990, 1992; National Endowment for the Arts Fellowship, 1978; Artist-in-Residence, Seattle Arts Commission, 1983; Thompson Visiting Poet, Babson College, 1988; Grants for Artists, Artists Trust, 1992. *Address:* 5032 22nd Ave NE, Apt E, Seattle, WA 98105, USA.

ALKALAY(-GUT), Karen (Hillary), (Karen Gut, Hillary Keren); b. 29 March 1945, London, England. Lecturer; Writer; Poet. m. (1) Nissim Alkalay, 4 July 1967, (2) Ezra Gut, 26 July 1980, 2 s., 2 d. *Education:* BA, 1966, MA, 1967, PhD, 1975, University of Rochester, New York, USA. *Appointments:* Lecturer, State University of New York, Geneseo, 1967–70, University of the Negev in Beer Sheva, 1972–76, Tel-Aviv University, 1977–. *Publications:* Making Love, 1980; Butter Sculptures (in Hebrew), 1983; Mechitza, 1986; Alone in the Dawn (biography), 1988; Ignorant Armies, 1991; Love and War,

1991; Love Soup, 1992; Harmonies/Disharmonies, 1994; Recipes, 1994; The Love of Clothes and Nakedness, 1999; In My Skin, 2000; High Maintenance, 2001; So Far, So Good, 2002. *Contributions to:* American Voice; Massachusetts Review; Forward; Webster Review; Jerusalem Post; Present Tense; Arc, Israel; Pilgrims, New Zealand; Voices; New Outlook; Rochester Jewish Ledger; International Quarterly; Amelia; Grasslands Review; Lilliput Review; Kerem; Sheila-na-gig. *Honours:* Tel-Aviv Fund, 1980; Shvut Publication Award, Israel Writers' Asscn, 1983; Dulchin, Jewish Agency Award, 1984; First Prize, BBC World Service Poetry Award, 1990; Prairie Schooner Readers' Choice, 1992; Commendation, Arvon Poetry Competition, 1993. *Memberships:* Israel Asscn of Writers in English, founder-chair, 1982–84, 1991–, secretary, 1987–89; Federation of Writers in Israel, vice-chair, 1997–; Poetry Society of America; Voices Israel; American Studies Asscn, Israel, chair, 1991–95; MLA. *Address:* Dept of English, Tel-Aviv University, Ramat Aviv, Israel.

ALLBERY, Debra; b. 3 March 1957, Lancaster, Ohio, USA. Instructor in Creative Writing; Poet. *Education:* Denison University, Granville, Ohio, 1975–77; BA, English, The College of Wooster, Ohio, 1979; MFA, University of Iowa, Iowa City, 1982; University of Virginia, 1991–93. *Appointments:* Writer-in-Residence, Phillips Exeter Acad., Exeter, New Hampshire, 1985–86, Brooks School, North Andover, Massachusetts, 1988, Dickinson College, Carlisle, Pennsylvania; Writer-in-Residence, 1989–90, Creative Writing Instructor, 1990–91, Interlochen Arts Acad. *Publications:* Poems in Anthology of Magazine Verse and Yearbook of American Poetry, 1986–88; Walking Distance, 1991; Pittsburgh Book of Contemporary American Poets, 1993. *Contributions to:* Poetry; Nation; Yale Review; Kenyon Review; Poetry Northwest; Ploughshares; Iowa Review; Western Humanities Review; Ironwood; Crazyhorse. *Honours:* George Bennett Memorial Fellowship, Phillips Exeter Acad., 1985–86; National Endowment for the Arts Fellowships, 1986–87, 1993–94; Discovery, Nation Poetry Prize, 1989; Resident Fellow, MacDowell and Yaddo, 1987, 1990; Fellowships, New Hampshire State Council on the Arts, 1987, 1990; Agnes Lynch Starrett Prize, University of Pittsburgh Press, 1990; Hawthornden Fellowship, 1991. *Memberships:* Acad. of American Poets; Associated Writing Programs. *Address:* 508 N Mulberry St, Clyde, OH 43410-1550, USA.

ALLEN, Blair H.; b. 2 July 1933, Los Angeles, CA, USA. Writer; Poet; Ed.; Artist. m. Juanita Aguilar Raya, 27 Jan. 1968, 1 s., 1 d. *Education:* AA, San Diego City College, 1964; University of Washington, 1965–66; BA, San Diego State University, 1970. *Appointments:* Book Reviewer, Los Angeles Times, 1977–78; Special Feature Ed., Cerulean Press and Kent Publications, 1982–. *Publications:* Televisual Poems for Bloodshot Eyeballs, 1973; Malice in Blunderland, 1974; N/Z, 1979; The Atlantis Trilogy, 1982; Dreamwish of the Magician, 1983; Right Through the Silver Lined 1984 Looking Glass, 1984; The Magical World of David Cole (ed.), 1984; Snow Summits in the Sun (ed.), 1988; Trapped in a Cold War Travelogue, 1991; May Burning into August, 1992; The Subway Poems, 1993; Bonfire on the Beach, by John Brander (ed.), 1993; The Cerulean Anthology of Sci-Fi/Outer Space/Fantasy/Poetry and Prose Poems (ed.), 1995; When the Ghost of Cassandra Whispers in My Ears, 1996; Ashes Ashes All Fall Down, 1997; Around the World in 56 Days, 1998; Thunderclouds from the Door, 1999; Jabberbunglemerkeltoy, 1999; The Athens Café, 2000; The Day of the Jamberee Call, 2001; Assembled I Stand, 2002; Wine of Starlight, 2002. *Contributions to:* Numerous periodicals and anthologies. *Honours:* First Prize for Poetry, Pacificus Foundation Competition, 1992; Various other honours and awards. *Memberships:* Asscn for Applied Poetry; Beyond Baroque Foundation; California State Poetry Society; Medina Foundation. *Address:* PO Box 162, Colton, CA 92324, USA.

ALLEN, Bryan John; b. 27 April 1954, Tynemouth, England. Poet; Author; Journalist. *Appointments:* Regular Recitals on Radio 1 and 2, BBC World Service, Talk Radio UK, Great North Radio, BBC Newcastle, Wear FM, Metro FM, TFM, Radio Tyneside and on all BBC Regional Radio Networks; Appearances on Good Morning Show, BBC1; This Morning Show, ITV; Lifestyle, Cable; Wire TV, Cable; TTTV and BBC North; Organized the 24hr Poetry Charity Marathon Event, 1993; Resident Poet on GNR (Joe Poulters Show) and Radio Tyneside; Co-Presenter and Presenter, Wear in Focus Show, Wear FM. *Publications:* Feelings, 1990; Poetry Marathon Charity (anthology), 1993; Journeys, 1994. *Contributions to:* Mail on Sunday; Sunday Post; Sunday Mirror; Sunday Express; News of the World; People; Evening Chronicle; Journal; Northern Echo; Star Series; Northumberland Gazette; North-East Times Magazine; First Time; Auteur; Link-Up; Northumbrian; Fanzines; Poets Gallery; Charity Magazines; Various anthologies; Bereavement/Comfort Poems used worldwide in CandleLit Services by many support groups and charities; Works used in Undying Heart Requiem, Manchester and London; Works used in greeting cards; Works shown in Poets Gallery; Works translated into French, Italian, German and Spanish. *Memberships:* RSL; Writers Guild of England; Poetry Society; European Asscn for the Promotion of Poetry; British Asscn of Journalists; Broadcasting Press Guild; RTS. *Address:* 16D Clayton St W, Newcastle upon Tyne NE1 5DZ, England.

ALLEN, Edward (Hathaway); b. 20 Oct. 1948, New Haven, CT, USA. Writer; Poet. *Education:* Iowa Writers' Workshop on Poetry, 1975; MA, 1986, PhD, English, Ohio University. *Appointment:* Asst Prof., Rhodes College, Memphis, TN, 1989–91. *Publications:* Fiction: Straight Through the Night, 1989; Mustang

Sally, 1992. *Contributions to:* Newspapers and periodicals. *Memberships:* Acad. of American Poets; Associated Writing Programs; MLA; Poets and Writers; Writers' Guild of America. *Address:* HC 77, PO Box 442421, Pahrump, NV 89041, USA.

ALLEN, Gary; b. 8 Jan. 1959, Ballymena, County Antrim, Northern Ireland. Poet. *Publications:* Irish Notes, 1995; The Farthest Circle, 1996; Mending Churches, 1997; Making Waves, 1998. *Contributions to:* Honest Ulsterman; Edinburgh Review; Orbis; Envoi; Other Poetry; Staple; Teabs in the Fence; Southfields; Seam; Smiths Knoll; West Coast Magazine. *Address:* 1 Riverside Terrace, Toome Rd, Ballymena, County Antrim, Northern Ireland.

ALLEN, Paula Gunn; b. 1939, Cubero, NM, USA. Writer; Poet; University Lecturer. *Education:* BA; MFA; PhD. *Appointments:* Lecturer, San Francisco State University, University of New Mexico, Fort Lewis College, University of California at Berkeley. *Publications:* The Blind Lion, 1974; Sipapu: A Cultural Perspective, 1975; Coyote's Daylight Trip, 1978; A Cannon Between My Knees, 1981; From the Center: A Folio of Native American Art and Poetry (ed.), 1981; Shadow Country, 1982; Studies of American Indian Literature: Critical Essays and Course Designs (ed.), 1983; The Woman Who Owned the Shadows, 1983; The Sacred Hoop: Recovering the Feminine in American Indian Traditions (essays), 1986; Skins and Bones, 1988; Spider Woman's Granddaughters: Traditional Tales and Contemporary Writing by Native American Women (ed.), 1989; Grandmothers of the Light: A Medicine Woman's Sourcebook, 1991; Columbus and Beyond, 1992; Voice of the Turtle, 1994. *Honours:* American Book Award, 1990; Ford Foundation Grant; National Endowment for the Arts Award. *Address:* c/o Diane Cleaver Inc, 55 Fifth Ave, 15th Floor, New York, NY 10003, USA.

ALLISON, Dawn Paula; b. 1 Sept. 1974, Kirkcaldy, Fife, Scotland. Poet; Writer. *Education:* University of Stirling; Fife College; Telford College, Edinburgh. *Publications:* Island Moods and Reflections, 1994; Jewels of the Imagination, 1997. *Contributions to:* Fife Leader; Triumph Herald; Several interviews on local and national radio stations. *Honours:* International Library of Poetry Ed.'s Choice Award, 1997; Awards of Excellence for Short Stories and Poetry Competitions, Meridian Poet and Writers Club. *Membership:* Scottish Fellowship of Christian Writers. *Address:* 160 High St, Dysart, Fife KY1 2YU, Scotland.

ALLISON, Dorothy; b. 11 April 1949, Greenville, SC, USA. Writer; Poet. *Education:* BA, Florida Presbyterian College, 1971; MA, New School for Social Research. *Publications:* Fiction: Trash, 1988; Bastard Out of Carolina, 1992; Cavedweller, 1998. Poetry: The Women Who Hate Me, 1983. Non-Fiction: Skin: Talking About Sex, Class and Literature, 1994; Two or Three Things I Know for Sure, 1995. *Honours:* Lambda Literary Awards for Best Small Press Book and Best Lesbian Book, 1989. *Memberships:* Authors' Guild; PEN; Writers' Union. *Address:* PO Box 136, Guerneville, CA 95446, USA.

ALMON, Bert; b. 29 July 1943, Port Arthur, Texas, USA. Prof. of English; Poet; Writer. m. Olga Costopoulos, 23 Nov. 1984, 1 s., 3 d. *Education:* BA, University of Texas, El Paso, 1965; MA, 1967, PhD, 1971, University of New Mexico. *Appointments:* Prof. of English, University of Alberta, Edmonton, Canada, 1968–. *Publications:* The Return, 1968; Taking Possession, 1976; Poems for the Nuclear Family, 1979; Blue Sunrise, 1980; Deep North, 1984; Calling Texas, 1990; Earth Prime, 1994; Mind the Gap, 1996. *Contributions to:* Chicago Review; Orbis; Malahat Review; Kansas Quarterly; Iron; The North; Poetry Durham; Southern Review. *Honours:* Second Prize, Cardiff Poetry Festival Competition, 1991; Writers' Guild of Alberta Prize for Poetry, 1995. *Memberships:* Writer's Guild of Alberta; Poetry Society, London; Associated Writing Programs; League of Canadian Poets. *Address:* Dept of English, University of Alberta, Edmonton, AB T6G 2E5, Canada.

ALONSO ALVAREZ, Emilio (Andrenio); b. 2 July 1940, Minera de Luna, León, Spain. Naval Architect; Poet; Dramatist. m. Mercedes Pueyo, 29 July 1966, 1 s. *Education:* Naval Architecture, Escuela Técnica Superior de Ingenieros Navales, 1965. *Publications:* Coplas de la transición, de Franco a Tejero (poems), 1986; Octavas reales callejeras sin ton ni son (poems), 1987; An Anonymous Livel Against the Gulf War – El amor petrolero es signo de mal aguro (play), 1991. *Contributions to:* Various publications. *Honour:* Casa Villas Poetry Award, Madrid, 1983. *Address:* Juan Ramón Jiménez 24, 28036 Madrid, Spain.

ALONZO, Anne-Marie; b. 13 Dec. 1951, Alexandria, Egypt. Author; Poet; Dramatist; Journalist; Publisher. *Education:* BA, 1976, MA, 1978, PhD, 1986, University of Montréal. *Appointments:* Co-founder and Vice-Pres., Auto/Graphe theatre and production co, 1981–87; Co-founder, Les Editions Trois, 1985; Co-founder and Dir, Trois review, 1985–99; Founder and Co-ordinator, Festival de Trois, 1989–. *Publications:* Une lettre rouge orange et ocre, 1984; Bleus de mine, 1985; Ecoute, Sultane, 1987; Seul le désir, 1987; Esmai, 1987; Le livre des ruptures, 1988; Lead Blues, 1990; L'Immobile, 1990; Linked Alive (co-author), 1990; Galia qu'elle nommait amour, 1992; Margie Gillis, la danse des marches, 1993; Lettres a Cassandre (with Denise Desautels), 1994; Tout au loin la lumière, 1994; La nuit, 2001. *Contributions to:* Various publications. *Honours:* Prix Emile-Nelligan, 1985; Grand Prix d'excellence artistique en

creation littéraire, 1992; Mem. of the Order of Canada, 1997. *Memberships* Amnesty International; Artistes pour la paix; PEN International; Sociét littéraire de Laval; Society of Composers, Authors and Music Publishers o Canada; Union de écrivaines et écrivains québécois; CEAD. *Address:* 203: Jessop, Laval, QC H7S 1X3, Canada.

ALPHONSO-KARKALA, John B.; b. 30 May 1923, South Kanara, Mysor State, India. Writer; Poet; Prof. of Literature. m. Leena Anneli Hakalehto, 2(Dec. 1964, 3 c. *Education:* BA, 1950, MA, 1953, Mumbai University; University of London, 1954–55; PhD, Columbia University, 1964. *Appointments:* Visiting Lecturer, City College, City University of New York, 1963; Asst Prof., 1964–65 Assoc. Prof., 1965–68, Prof. of Literature, 1969–, State University of New York at New Paltz; Visiting Prof., Columbia University, 1969–70. *Publications:* Indo English Literature in the Nineteenth Century, 1970; Anthology of Indiar Literature (ed.), 1971, revised edn as Ages of Rishis, Buddha, Acharyas Bhaktas and Mahatma, 1987; Bibliography of Indo-English Literature 1800–1966 (ed. with Leena Karkala), 1974; Comparative World Literature Seven Essays, 1974; Passions of the Nightless Night (novel), 1974; Jawaharla Nehru: A Literary Portrait, 1975; When Night Falls (poems), 1980; Vedic Vision (ed.), 1980; Joys of Jayanagara (novel), 1981; Indo-English Literature: Essays (with Leena Karkala), 1994. *Memberships:* American Oriental Society; Asscn for Asian Studies; International Congress of Comparative Literature International Congress of Orientalists; MLA of America. *Address:* 20 Millrock Rd, New Paltz, NY 12561, USA.

ALURISTA; b. 8 Aug. 1947, México, DF, Mexico. Prof. of Spanish, Chicano, Mexican and Latin American Literature and Culture; Poet; Writer. 3 s., 1 d. *Education:* BA, Psychology, San Diego State University, 1970; MA, Spanish Literature, 1979, PhD, Spanish Literature, 1982, University of California, San Diego. *Appointments:* Lecturer of Chicano Studies, University of Texas, Austin, 1974–76; Distinguished Visiting Lecturer of Chicano Literature and Creative Writing, University of Nebraska, Omaha, 1979; Lecturer of Spanish and Chicano Studies, San Diego State University, Calexio Campus, CA, 1976–83; Asst Prof., Romance Languages Dept, Colorado College, Colorado Springs, 1983–86. *Publications:* Floricanto en aztlán, 1971; Nationchild plumaroja, 1972; Timespace huracán, 1976; Z Eros, 1995; Et tú, raza?. Poetry collections: Anque-Collected Works, 1976–1979, 1979; Spik in glyph?, 1981; Return (poems collected and new), 1982. Books for children: Coleccion Tula y Tonan, 9 vols, 1973; Poems in numerous anthologies; Short stories, plays, essays and literary criticism; Audio and video tapes; Numerous edited works; Papers presented to scholarly meetings. *Contributions to:* Many journals, magazines and newspapers. *Honours:* A number of distinguished grants, fellowships and honours. *Memberships:* Asscn of Mexican American Educators; International Acad. of Poets; MLA; National Asscn of Chicano Studies. *Address:* 4112 Calmoor St, National City, CA 91950, USA.

ALVAREZ, Alfred, (Al); b. 5 Aug. 1929, London, England. Poet; Author. m. 7 April 1966, 2 s., 1 d. *Education:* BA, 1952, MA, 1956, Corpus Christi College, Oxford. *Appointments:* Poetry Critic and Ed., Observer, 1956–66; Advisory Ed., Penguin Modern European Poets, 1964–76. *Publications:* The Shaping Spirit, 1958; The School of Donne, 1961; The New Poetry, 1962; Under Pressure, 1965; Beyond All the Fiddle, 1968; Penguin Modern Poets No. 18, 1970; Apparition, 1971; The Savage God, 1971; Beckett, 1973; Hers, 1974; Autumn to Autumn and Selected Poems, 1978; Hunt, 1978; Life After Marriage, 1982; The Biggest Game in Town, 1983; Offshore, 1986; Feeding the Rat, 1988; Rain Forest, 1988; Day of Atonement, 1991; Faber Book of Modern European Poetry, 1992; Night, 1995; Where Did It All Go Right?, 1999; Poker Bets, Bluffs and Bad Beats, 2001; New and Selected Poems, 2002. *Contributions to:* Numerous magazines and journals. *Honours:* Vachel Lindsay Prize for Poetry, 1961; Hon. DLitt, University of East London, 1998; Hon. Fellow, Corpus Christi College, Oxford, 2001. *Address:* c/o Gillon Aitken Asscs, 29 Fernshaw Rd, London SW10 0TG, England.

ALVAREZ, Julia; b. 27 March 1950, New York, NY, USA. Writer: Poet; Assoc. Prof. of English. m. Bill Eichner, 3 June 1989. *Education:* Connecticut College, 1967–69; BA, Middlebury College, 1971; MA, Creative Writing, Syracuse University, 1975; Bread Loaf School of English, 1979–80. *Appointments:* Visiting Asst Prof. of Creative Writing, University of Vermont, 1981–83; Jenny McKean Moore Visiting Writer, George Washington University, 1984–85; Asst Prof. of English, University of Illinois at Urbana-Champaign, 1985–88; Asst Prof. of English, Middlebury College, 1988–91, Assoc. Prof., 1991–93, Prof., 1993–96, Writer-in-Residence, 1996–. *Publications:* Fiction: How the Garcia Girls Lost Their Accents, 1991; In the Time of the Butterflies, 1994; Yo!, 1997; Something to Declare, 1988; In the Name of Salomé, 2000; The Secret Footprints, 2000; How Tía Lola Came to Stay, 2001. Poetry: Old Age Ain't for Sissies (ed.), 1979; The Housekeeping Book, 1984; Homecoming, 1984; The Other Side/El otro lado, 1995; Seven Trees, 1999; A Cafecito Story, 2001; Before We Were Free (children's), 2002. *Contributions to:* Many anthologies and periodicals. *Honours:* La Reina Press Poetry Award, 1982; Robert Frost Poetry Fellowship, Bread Loaf Writers Conference, 1986; National Endowment for the Arts Grant, 1987–88; Ingram Merrill Foundation Grant, 1990; American Library Asscn Notable Book Citation, 1992. *Address:* c/o Susan Bergholz Literary Services, 17 W 10th St, No. 5, New York, NY 10011, USA.

AMABILE, George; b. 29 May 1936, Jersey City, NJ, USA. Prof. of English; Poet; Writer. *Education:* BA, Amherst College, 1957; MA, University of Minnesota, 1961; PhD, University of Connecticut, 1969. *Appointments:* Lecturer, 1963, Asst Prof., 1966–68, 1969–71, Assoc. Prof., 1972–86, Prof. of English, 1987–, University of Manitoba; Visiting Writer-in-Residence, University of British Columbia, 1968–69; Various readings, Manitoba Theatre Centre, radio, and television. *Publications:* Blood Ties, 1972; Open Country, 1976; Flower and Song, 1977; Ideas of Shelter, 1981; The Presence of Fire, 1982; Four of a Kind, 1994; Rumours of Paradise/Rumours of War, 1995. *Contributions to:* Many anthologies, journals, and periodicals. *Honours:* Canada Council Grants, 1968, 1969, 1981, 1982, 1995, 1996; Canadian Authors' Asscn National Prize for Poetry, 1983; Third Prize, CBC National Literary Competition, 1992. *Memberships:* League of Canadian Poets; Western Canadian Publishers' Asscn. *Address:* c/o Dept of English, University of Manitoba, Winnipeg, MB R3T 2N2, Canada.

AMALI, Idris Odumu Onche; b. 6 June 1953, Benue State, Nigeria. Lecturer; Poet. m. Otumenyi Amali, 9 Sept. 1978, 4 s., 2 d. *Education:* BA, Theatre and Drama; MA, PhD in English (Oral Literature). *Appointments:* Chair., Borno State Asscn of Nigerian Authors; Poetry workshop, Vice-Chair., Borno State, ANA; Senior Lecturer and Head of Dept of English, Dir of General Studies, Unimaid. *Publications:* A Week of Broken Pains and Other Poems; Waves Across Maiduguri and Other Poems; A Mountain of Desire; Zaynab Atkali in Focus: Critical Perspectives on Female Voice from Northern Nigeria. *Contributions to:* Kuka; Okike; Postgrats; Liwuram; Voices from Northern Nigeria: An Anthology; Africana Marburgensia; Frankfurter Afrikanische Blätter; Stepping Stone; Nigeria Magazine; Ufahamu; African Theatre Review; Chelsea; Fajar; Voices From the Fringe; ANA Review; Presence Africane; Opon Ifa. *Memberships:* Asscn of Nigerian Authors; Society of Nigerian Theatre Artists; African Literature Asscn; Folklore Society of Nigeria; Borno Museum Asscn; Archaeological Asscn of Nigeria; African Studies Asscn, Washington; Folklore Fellow, Oral Epics, Assoc. Mem. of Folklore Fellows, International Network of Folklorists. *Address:* Dept of English, University of Maiduguri, PMB 1069, Maiduguri, Borno State, Nigeria.

AMB, Daniel. See: ANDERSEN, Baltser.

AMBERT, Alba; b. 10 Oct. 1946, San Juan, Puerto Rico. Writer; Poet. m. Walter McCann, 11 Feb. 1984, 1 d. *Education:* BA, University of Puerto Rico, 1974; MEd, 1975, DEd, 1980, Harvard University. *Appointments:* Bilingual Teacher, Boston Public Schools, 1975–80; Asst Prof. and Dir, Bilingual Special Education Teacher Training Program, University of Hartford, 1980–84; Visiting Scientist, Massachusetts Institute of Technology, 1984–85; Senior Research Scholar, Athens College, Greece, 1985–93; Writer in Residence, Richmond University, 1993–. *Publications:* Fiction: Porque hay silencio, 1989; A Perfect Silence, 1995; The Eighth Continent and Other Stories, 1997; An Inclination of Mirrors, 1997. Poetry: Gotas sobre el columpio, 1980; The Fifth Sun, 1989; Habito tu nombre, 1994; At Dawn We Start Again, 1997. Children's Books: Thunder from the Earth, 1997; Why the Wild Winds Blow, 1997; Face to Sky, 1998. *Honours:* Ford Foundation Fellowship, 1984; Institute of Puerto Rican Literature Award, 1989; Carey McWilliams Award, 1996; Pres.'s Award, Massachusetts Asscn for Bilingual Education, 1997. *Memberships:* Authors' Guild; Writer's Union. *Address:* c/o Richmond University, Queens Rd, Richmond, Surrey TW10 6JP, England.

AMEEN, Mark J.; b. 18 Aug. 1958, Lowell, Massachusetts, USA. Writer; Poet. *Education:* BA, University of Massachusetts, 1980. *Publications:* A Circle of Sirens, 1985; The Buried Body, 1990. *Honour:* Poetry Fellowship, New York Foundation for the Arts, 1989–90. *Address:* 235 E Fourth St, New York, NY 10009, USA.

AMEERUDDIN, Syed; b. 5 Dec. 1942, Guntakal, India. Teacher; Prof.; Poet; Writer. m. Sayeeda Be, 11 April 1968, 1 s. *Education:* BA, 1964; MA, 1966; MPhil, 1980. *Appointment:* Prof. of English, New College, University of Chennai. *Publications:* What the Himalaya Said; Doom to Come; A Lover and A Wanderer; Pe Tallic Love Times; Visioned Summits, poems; Indian Verse in English; Indian Voices; International Voices; International Poets. *Contributions to:* Number of leading Indian and international literary journals. *Honours:* Michael Madhusudan Award; Australia Day Award; Certificate of Merit. *Memberships:* World Poetry Society; United Poets International; Indian Asscn for English Studies; Authors' Guild of India. *Address:* 5 Mohamed Hussain Khan Lane, Royapettah, Chennai 600014, India.

AMIRTHANAYAGAM, Indran; b. 17 Nov. 1960, Sri Lanka. Journalist; Poet. *Education:* BA, Haverford College, 1982; MA, Columbia University, 1985. *Appointments:* Ed., PB Securities; Guest Ed., The Portable Lower East Side; Contributing Ed., Night. *Publication:* The Elephants of Reckoning, 1993. *Contributions to:* Massachusetts Review; Literary Review; Portable Lower East Side; Bomb; Night; Hanging Loose; St Andrews Review; Pivot; Downtown; Dispatch. *Honour:* Pushcart Prize. *Membership:* Poetry Society of America. *Address:* 4810 Mercury Dr., Rockville, MD 20853, USA.

ANANIA, Michael (Angelo); b. 1938, USA. Author; Poet. *Appointments:* Co-ordinator, Council of Literary Magazines; Bibliographer, Lockwood Library;

Ed., 1963–64, Co-Ed., 1963–67, Audit; Instructor, State University of New York, 1964–65, Northwestern University, IL, 1965–68; Literary Ed., Swallow Press, 1968–; Asst Prof., Dept of English, University of Illinois, Chicago, 1970–. *Publications:* New Poetry Anthology; The Color of Dust; Set Sorts; Riversongs; The Red Menace; Constructions/Variations; The Sky at Ashland. *Address:* Dept of English, University of Illinois, Chicago, IL 60680, USA.

ANASTASI, Nerina; b. 24 Dec. 1941, Catania, Sicily, Italy. Poet. m. 1 July 1967. *Education:* Professional Nursing Diploma, Ospedale Vittorio Emanuele, Catania, 1992. *Appointment:* Senator, Sicily, 1998. *Publications:* Canto-D'amore, 1991; I sentieri dell'anima, 1994; Onde sulla scogliera, 1996; Frammenti di passato, 1998. *Contributions to:* Rivista-Storica Siciliana; Ponte Italo Americano; Miscellanea; Oggi Futuro; Il Vastese newspaper; Poetic and bilingual anthologies. *Honours:* Special Prize for Sicily, Vasto, 1993; Special Critics Prize, Accademia Quadrato, Milan, 1993, 1994; Homage to Pirandello International Prize, Rome, 1994; Homage to García Lorca Prize, Rome, 1994; City of Nice Grand Trophy, 1995; Gold Medal, Natale Agropolese, Salerno, 1995, 1996; First Prize, Histonium Competition, Vasto, 1996; Gold Medal, Accademia dei Miceni, 1997; First Prize, Accademia degli Etruschi, Vada Livorno, 1998; Sicily 98 Gold Medal, 1998; City of Prato 2000 Grand Prize, 1998; Poet of the Year, 1998. *Memberships:* Honorary Pres., Accademia Neapolis e Dafni; Accademia di Classe dei Micenei; Accademia di Merito; Acad. of Europe; Accademia gli Etruschi; Senator, Acad. of Sicily, Curriculum Section. *Address:* Via Carnazza 17, 95126 Canalicchio, Catania, Italy.

ANAYA, Rudolfo; b. 30 Oct. 1937, Pastura, NM, USA. Author; Dramatist; Poet; Ed.; Prof. Emeritus. m. Patricia Lawless, 1966. *Education:* Browning Business School, 1956–58; BEd, 1963, MA, English Literature, 1969, MA, Guidance and Counselling, 1972, University of Mexico. *Appointments:* Teacher, Public Schools, Albuquerque, 1963–70; Dir, Counselling Center, 1971–73, Prof., Dept of Language and Literature, 1974–93, Prof. Emeritus, 1993–, University of New Mexico; Lecturer, Universidad Anahuas, México, DF, 1974; Founder-Ed., Blue Mesa Review, 1989–93; Martin Luther King Jr/César Chávez/Rosa Parks Visiting Prof., University of Michigan at Ann Arbor, 1996; Guest Prof., University of Oklahoma, 1997; Assoc. Ed., American Book Review. *Publications:* Fiction: Bless Me, Ultima, 1972; Heart of Aztlan, 1976; Tortuga, 1979; The Legend of La Llorona, 1984; Lord of the Dawn: The Legend of Quetzalcoatl, 1987; Albuquerque, 1992; Zia Summer, 1995; Rio Grande Fall, 1996; Jalamanta: A Message From the Desert, 1996; Isis in the Heart, 1998; Shaman Winter, 1999. Short Stories: The Silence of the Llano, 1982; The Anaya Reader (anthology), 1995. Children's Fiction: The Farolitos of Christmas (picture book), 1995; Maya's Children (picture book), 1997; Farolitos for Abuelo (picture book), 1999; My Land Sings: Stories From the Rio Grande, 1999; Roadrunner's Dance, 2000; Elegy of the Death of César Chávez, 2000. Editor: Voices from the Rio Grande (co-ed.), 1976; Cuentos Chicanos: A Short Story Anthology (co-ed.), 1984; Voces: An Anthology of Nuevo Mexicano Writers, 1987; Atzlan: Essays on the Chicano Homeland (co-ed.), 1989; Tierra: Contemporary Short Fiction of New Mexico, 1989. Other: Cuentos: Tales from the Hispanic Southwest (trans.), 1980; The Adventures of Juan Chicaspatas (epic poem), 1985; A Chicano in China (travel journal), 1986; Descansos: An Interrupted Journey (with Estevan Arellano and Denise Chávez), 1997; Several plays. *Contributions to:* Anthologies, textbooks and literary magazines. *Honours:* Several hon. doctorates; Premio Quinto Sol, 1971; American Book Award, Before Columbus Foundation, 1979; National Endowment for the Arts Fellowship, 1980; New Mexico Governor's Award for Excellence and Achievement in Literature, 1980; W. K. Kellogg Foundation Fellowship, 1983–86; New Mexico Eminent Scholar Award, 1989; Rockefeller Foundation Residency, Bellagio, Italy, 1991; PEN West Award for Fiction, 1993; Excellence in the Humanities Award, New Mexico Endowment for the Humanities, 1995; Tomás Rivera Mexican American Children's Book Awards, 1995, 2000; Distinguished Achievement Award, Western Literature Asscn, 1997; Arizona Adult Authors Award, Arizona Library Asscn, 2000; Wallace Stegner Award, Center of the American West, 2001; National Asscn of Chicano/ Chicana Studies Scholar, 2002. *Address:* 5324 Cañada Vista NW, Albuquerque, NM 87120, USA.

ANDERSDATTER, Karla Margaret, (Margaret Rose, Simetra, Amy Joy, Imogene Love); b. 4 Sept. 1938, San Francisco, USA. Writer; Poet. m. Robert Billings, 17 Sept. 1960, 1 s., 1 d. *Education:* BA, 1959, MA, 1968, University of California at Los Angeles. *Publications:* Spaces, 1972; Witches and Whimsies, 1975; Marissa the Tooth Fairy, 1976; I Don't Know Whether to Laugh or Cry Cause I Lost the Map to Where I Was Going, 1978; Transparencies, Love Poems for the New Age, 1978; Follow the Blue Butterfly; The Rising of the Flesh, 1983; The Girl Who Struggled With Death, 1985; Naked in the Garden, 1988; The Doorway, 1992; The Broken String, 1994; Woman Who Was Wild, 1995; Wild Onions, 1997; White Moon Woman or The Education of Imogene Love, 1999; At the Sacred Pool, 2000; In the Footsteps of a Princess, 2001. *Contributions to:* Anthologies and magazines; New York Times; San Francisco Chronicle; Butterfly Chronicles. *Honour:* California Art Council Grant. *Memberships:* Acad. of American Poets; Marin Poetry Society; PEN West; Poets and Writers. *Address:* PO Box 790, Sausalito, CA 94966, USA.

ANDERSEN, Baltser, (Daniel Amb); b. 3 Jan. 1956, Ribe, Denmark. Schoolteacher; Author; Poet. m. Magdaline Mattak, 26 Dec. 1984, 2 d.

Education: Tonder, 1975; Århus, 1976, 1986–88. *Appointments:* Teacher, Tonder, 1981, Greenland, 1982–87; Leader, Greenlandic Peace Movement, Sorsunnata, 1984–87. *Publications:* Poetry: Interlocking Hands, 1973; To Be Awake, 1974; Grey Asphalt, 1979; Travelling Spaceship, 1992; Angantyr and the Black Sword, 1993. Essay: In the Name of Democracy. *Contributions to:* Many Danish newspapers. *Memberships:* Norse Mythological Circle, Alfheim; Danish Writers' Union; Red-Green Alliance, 1993–.

ANDERSON, Alex; b. 17 June 1932, Liverpool, England. Teacher; Writer; Poet. m. Elizabeth, 16 Sept. 1963, 2 d. *Education:* Liverpool University; Lancaster University; Extensive Travels in North Africa. *Publications:* Hobgoblins Also Dream, 1982; The Apple Tree, 1988; Landscape with Figures, 1989; The Caves of Mali, 1990; Tortoise in the Snow, 1990; Poets are the Priesthood of the World, 1995; Game Over, 1996; African Sequence, 1996; The Land of the Young, 1997. *Membership:* Founder Mem., Cowpat Poetry Society. *Address:* 19 Grosvenor Dr., Wallasey, Wirral, CH45 1LD, England.

ANDERSON, Mark Ransom; b. 3 Sept. 1951, Kansas, USA. Poet; Teacher. m. Susan Aileen Grimes, 29 July 1984, 1 s. *Education:* AB, Cornell University, 1973; MA, University of Minnesota, 1976; MFA, 1977, MA, 1979, PhD, 1983, Cornell University. *Appointments:* Visiting Asst Prof., Emory University, 1984–85; Asst Prof., 1985–91, Assoc. Prof., 1991–, Rhode Island College. *Publications:* The Broken Boat; Serious Joy. *Contributions to:* Poetry; Hudson Review; Poetry Northwest; Epoch; Kansas Quarterly; Cimarron Review; Green Mountains Review; Cumberland Poetry Review; Southern Poetry Review. *Memberships:* Associated Writing Programs; Poetry Society of America; MLA; Acad. of American Poets; National Council of Teachers of English. *Address:* 8 Lake View Dr., Greenville, RI 02828, USA.

ANDERSON, Martin Lawrence; b. 31 Jan. 1948, Essex, England. University Teacher; Poet. Divorced. *Education:* BA, Honours, University of Ulster, 1971; MPhil, University of Stirling, 1991. *Appointments:* Lecturer, Leeds Metropolitan University, University of Grenoble, France, University of Hong Kong; Prof., University of the Philippines, Diliman, Quezon City, 1997. *Publications:* The Kneeling Room, 1981; The Ash Circle, 1986; Heardlanes, 1989; Dried Flowers, 1990; Swamp Fever, 1991; The Stillness of Gardens, 1994. *Contributions to:* Sulfur; Longhouse Anthology; Tamarisk; O Ars; Paper Air; Waves; Prism; Antigonish Review; West Coast Review; Oasis; Palantir; Shearsman; Iron; Kudos; Ninth Decade. *Address:* University of the Philippines, Quezon City, Philippines.

ANDERSON, Steve; b. 8 May 1949, Nairobi, East Africa. Writer; Poet. *Publications:* Bitter Almonds, 1995; Alchemy of Passion, 1998; Working A Way Through, 1999. *Contributions to:* Envoi; Catholic Times; Big Issue; Threads; Krax; Ocular. *Honours:* BSPG First Prize; Manchester Common Word Poetry Winner; Anthology Competition Winner. *Memberships:* Poetry Society; Friends of Arvon. *Address:* 6 Ashbrook Crescent, Wardle, Rochdale OL2 9AJ, England.

ANDOLFI, Brandisio; b. 19 March 1931, Carinola, Italy. Poet. m. Rosa Sacchetti, 10 May 1973, 1 d. *Education:* Degree in Italian Modern Language and Literature, Federico II University of Naples, 1967. *Publications:* Riflusso, 1985; Nel mio tempo, 1986; Oltre la vita, 1988; Ai limiti del silenzio, 1990; Sulla fuga del tempo, 1991; La voce dei giorni, 1992; Aprire la finestra, 1993; Come zampilla l'acqua, 1995; Il diario della sera, 1996; Alberi curvi d'acqua, 1997; Il mondo è la parola, 1998; Dentro la tua presenza, 1999; Muzio Attendolo Sforza, historical essay, 1999; Letture critiche, in press. *Contributions to:* Il Ponte Italo-Americano, USA; Silarus; La Nuova Tribuna Letteraria; Marginalia; Arbol de Fuego, Venezuela: Punto di Vista; Poeti e Poesia; Pagine Lepine. *Honours:* First Prize Alfa, Nordrach, Germany, 1987; First Prize, Augusta Perusia, Perugia, 1990; First Prize, San Benedetto, Norcia, 1992; First Prize, San Francesco, Castiglione del Lago, 1992; First Prize, Il Loggione, Teano, 1997; First Prize, E Frate, Rio Nero Sannitico, Isernia, 1998; Accademico Valentiniano; Accademico Horatio Flacco; Gran Premio Historium d'Oro, Vasto. *Memberships:* F. Nuvolone Cultural Asscn, Caserta; Paideia Group of Artistic Activities, Cassino; Yale Italian Poetry, Yale University. *Address:* Via Ceccano 30, Caserta 81100, Italy.

ANDRE, (Kenneth) Michael; b. 31 Aug. 1946, Halifax, Nova Scotia, Canada. Poet; Ed.; Publisher; Critic. 1 s. *Education:* BA, McGill University; MA, University of Chicago; PhD, Columbia University. *Appointments:* Exec. Dir, Unmuzzled Ox Books and Magazine; Treasurer, Soho Baroque Opera Company. *Publications:* Get Serious; Studying the Ground for Holes; Letters Home; Jabbing the A is High Comedy; It As It; Experiments in Banal Living. *Contributions to:* Little Magazine; Zymergy; Some; Telephone; Mudfish; Abraxas; Spectacular Diseases; Far Point; Canadian Forum. *Memberships:* MLA; Co-ordinating Council of Literary Magazines; Small Press Center. *Address:* 105 Hudson St, No. 311, New York, NY 10013, USA.

ANDRÉE, Alice. See: CLUYSENAAR, Anne.

ANDREWS, Lyman Henry; b. 2 April 1938, Denver, CO, USA. Writer; Poet. *Education:* BA, Brandeis University, 1960. *Appointments:* Asst Lecturer, University of Wales, Swansea, 1964–65; Lecturer, University of Leicester,

1965–88; Poetry Critic, Sunday Times, 1969–78; Visiting Prof., Indiana University, 1978–79. *Publications:* Ash Flowers; Fugitive Visions; The Death of Mayakovsky; Kaleidoscope. *Contributions to:* Times; Sunday Times; Times Higher Educational Supplement; British Book News; San Francisco Examiner; Denver Post; Partisan Review; Encounter; El Corno Empumado; Les Lettres Nouvelles; New Mexico Quarterly; Carolina Quarterly; Transatlantic Review; Anglo Welsh Review; Poetry Quarterly; Root and Branch. *Honours:* Fulbright Fellowship; James Phelan Travelling Fellowship; Woodrow Wilson National Fellowship. *Address:* Flat 4-32, Victoria Centre, Nottingham NG1 3PA, England.

ANDRUKHOVYCH, Yuriy; b. 13 March 1960, Ivano-Frankivsk, Ukraine. Novelist; Poet. *Education:* Graduated, journalism, Ukrainian Institute of Polygraphy, 1982; Maxim Gorky Literary Institute, Moscow, 1989–91. *Appointments:* Military service, 1983–84; Co-Founder, literary performance group, 'Bu-Ba-Bu' (Burlesque-Bluster-Buffoonery), 1985; Literary readings in American universities including: Harvard, Yale, Columbia, Pennsylvania State University, and La Salle University, 1998. *Publications:* Poetry: The Sky and Squares, 1985; Downtown, 1989; Exotic Birds and Plants, 1991. Fiction: Army Stories (short stories), 1989; Recreations, 1992; Moscoviada, 1993; Perversion, 1996. Other: A Military March for an Angel (screenplay), 1989; essays. *Contributions to:* Literary journals. *Honours:* Blahovist, 1993; Helen Shcherban-Lapika Foundation Award, 1996; Novel of the Year Prize, Suchasnist, 1997; Lesia & Petro Kovalev Award, 1998.

ANDRUP, Claus Erik; b. 10 Aug. 1949, Stockholm, Sweden. Public Relations Consultant; Boat Builder; Poet. m. (1) Arabella Patricia Lloyd, 28 July 1978, 1 s., 1 d., (2) Deborah Alice Sharp, 27 April 1989, 1 d. *Education:* Christian Brothers College, Sea Point, Cape Town, South Africa; Diploma in Communications, Advertising and Marketing, London Polytechnic, Metropolitan College. *Publications:* New Nation, 1971; IZWI, 1971; Poems, 1964–74, 1974; Winter Collection, 1991; New Contrast, 1992. *Memberships:* Poetry Society; Chelsea Arts Club.

ANGELIDOU, Klairi; b. 19 Nov. 1932, Ammochostos, Famagu Sta, Cyprus. Minister of Education and Culture; Poet; Trans. m. Nicos Angelides, 1 May 1955, 3 s. *Education:* University of Athens, School of Philosophy. *Appointments:* Teacher to Gymnasium, 1956–61; Asst Headmistress, 1962–80; Headmistress, 1980–91; MP, 1991–93; Minister, 1993. *Publications:* Poiemata, 1967; Tou Xerizomou (Uprooting), 1975; Nostimon Imar, 1982; En Demo Anathountos, 1988; Pentadaktylos, My Son, 1991; The Silence of Statues, 1994. *Contributions to:* Efthini, Greece; Akti, Cyprus; Pnevmatiki Kypros, Cyprus; Aigiopelagitica, Greece; Kypriakos Logos, Cyprus. *Honours:* First Prize, Asscn of Greek Lyceum of Women, 1974; First Prizes, National Asscn of Greek Authors, 1978, 1988. *Memberships:* National Asscn of Greek Authors of Cyprus and Greece; PEN; Greek Asscn of Trans. *Address:* Kimonos 11, Lefkosia, Nicosia, Cyprus.

ANGELOU, Maya; b. 4 April 1928, St Louis, MO, USA. Poet; Writer; Prof. m. (1) Tosh Angelou, divorced, (2) Paul Du Feu, 1973, divorced, 1 s. *Education:* Studied music; Received training in modern dance from Martha Graham, Pearl Primus, and Ann Halprin, in drama from Frank Silvera and Gene Frankel. *Appointments:* Taught modern dance, Rome Opera and Hambina Theater, Tel-Aviv, 1955; Appeared in Off-Broadway plays; Northern Co-ordinator, Southern Christian Leadership Conference, 1959–60; Asst Admin., School of Music and Drama, Institute of African Studies, University of Ghana, 1963–66; Lecturer, University of California at Los Angeles, 1966; Writer-in-Residence, University of Kansas, 1970; Distinguished Visiting Prof., Wake Forest University, 1974, Wichita State University, 1974, California State University at Sacramento, 1974; First Reynolds Prof. of American Studies, Wake Forest University (lifetime appointment), 1981–; Many television appearances in various capacities. *Publications:* Poetry: Just Give Me a Cool Drink of Water 'fore I Die, 1971; Oh Pray My Wings Are Gonna Fit Me Well, 1975; And Still I Rise, 1978; Shaker, Why Don't You Sing?, 1983; Poems: Maya Angelou, 1986; I Shall Not Be Moved, 1990; On the Pulse of Morning, for the inauguration of President Bill Clinton, 1993; The Complete Poems of Maya Angelou, 1994; Phenomenal Woman: Four Poems Celebrating Women, 1995. Fiction: Mrs Flowers: A Moment of Friendship, 1986. Non-Fiction: I Know Why the Caged Bird Sings, 1970; Gather Together In My Name, 1974; Singin' and Swingin' and Gettin' Merry Like Christmas, 1976; The Heart of a Woman, 1981; All God's Children Need Traveling Shoes, 1986; Even the Stars Look Lonesome, 1998; A Song Flung Up to Heaven, 2002. Other: Short stories; stage, film and television plays. *Contributions to:* Many publications. *Honours:* Yale University Fellowship, 1970; Rockefeller Foundation Scholarship for Italy, 1975; Mem., American Revolution Bicentennial Commission, 1975–76; Woman of the Year in Communications, 1976; Matrix Award, 1983; North Carolina Award in Literature, 1987; Distinguished Woman of North Carolina, 1992; Horatio Alger Award, 1992; Grammy Award for On the Pulse of Morning, 1994; National Women's Hall of Fame, 1998. *Memberships:* Dirs' Guild; Harlem Writers' Guild; Women's Prison Asscn, advisory board. *Address:* c/o Dave La Camera, Lordly and Dame Inc, 51 Church St, Boston, MA 02116, USA.

ANGHELAKI-ROOKE, Katerina; b. 22 Feb. 1939, Athens, Greece. Poet; Trans. *Education:* Universities of Nice, Athens, Geneva, 1957–63. *Appointments:* Freelance Trans., 1962–; Visiting Prof. (Fulbright), Harvard

University, 1980; Visiting Fellow, Princeton University, 1987. *Publications:* Wolves and Clouds, 1963; Poems, 1963–69, 1971; The Body is the Victory and the Defeat of Dreams, in English, 1975; The Scattered Papers of Penelope, 1977; The Triumph of Constant Loss, 1978; Counter Love, 1982; The Suitors, 1984; Beings and Things on Their Own, in English, 1986; When the Body, 1988; Wind Epilogue, 1990; Empty Nature, 1993; Trans of Works by Shakespeare, Albee, Dylan Thomas, Beckett, and from Russian: Pushkin, Mayiakorski, Lermontov. *Honours:* Greek National Poetry Prize, 1985; Greek Acad. Ouranis Prize, 2000. *Address:* Synesiou Kyrenes 4, 114 71 Athens, Greece.

ANGLE, Roger; b. 2 Aug. 1938, Kansas, USA. Writer; Poet; Public Relations Consultant. m. Fontelle Slater, 1960, 1 s. *Education:* BA, University of Wichita, KS, 1962; MFA, University of California, 1972. *Appointments:* Copy Ed., The Beacon, Wichita, 1964–67; Investigative Reporter, The Gazette and Daily, 1967–69; Co-ordinator, National Endowment for the Arts, 1973–76; Ed., Reporter, The Newport Ensign, CA, 1979–85; Public Relations, Advertising Consultant, 1986–. *Publications:* The Farm, 1962; Execution, 1963; The Day is Woman, 1966; The Young Girl, 1966; The Hunted Bird, 1975; My Tongue Has Been Everywhere, 1994. Short Fiction and Literary Prose: Moshohoni My Love, 1975; Violence Happens, 1976; Self Portrait at 38, 1976; Whims, 1979; Performance, 1980. Various other screenplays and plays. *Honours:* Several awards in fiction and journalism.

ANGUS, Ken(neth William); b. 13 Aug. 1930, Rhu, Dunbartonshire, Scotland. Veterinary Pathologist; Poet. m. Marna Renwick Redpath, 4 Nov. 1977, 1 s. *Education:* BVMS, Glasgow, 1955; FRCVS, 1976; DVM, Glasgow, 1985. *Publications:* Scotchpotch, 1995; Eechtie-Peechtie-Pandy, 1996; Wrack and Pinion, 1997; Breakfast with Kilroy, 2000; Only the Sound of Sparrows, 2001. *Contributions to:* New Writing Scotland; First Time; Cencrastus; Orbis; Poetry Scotland; Poetry Monthly; Poetry Life; The Herald; Staple; Lallans; Fife Lines; Scarp. *Honour:* Scottish International Poetry Competition, 1998. *Memberships:* Scottish Poetry Library; Poetry Asscn of Scotland. *Address:* 12 Temple Village, Gorebridge, Midlothian EH23 4SQ, Scotland. *E-mail:* kenmarnaintemple@amserve.com.

ANHAVA, Tuomas; b. 5 June 1927, Helsinki, Finland. Poet; Trans. *Publications:* Several vols of poems, including: Runoja, 1953; 36 runoja, 1958; Runoja 1961, 1961; Kuudes kirja, 1966; Runot 1951–1966, 1967; Valitut runot, 1976. *Contributions to:* Periodicals.

ANNAND, James King; b. 2 Feb. 1908, Edinburgh, Scotland. Teacher; Poet. m. Beatrice Lindsay, 1 April 1936, 4 d. *Education:* MA, University of Edinburgh, 1930. *Appointments:* Asst Teacher; Headmaster, Whithorn. *Publications:* Two Voices; Twice for Joy; Poems and Translations; Songs from Carmina Burana; Thrice to Show Ye; Dod and Darier; A Wale and Rhymes. *Contributions to:* Glasgow Herald; Scotsman; Scots Magazine; Burns Chronicle; Lines Review; Voice of Scotland; Saltire Review; Akros; Press and Journal; Chapman; English World Wide. *Honours:* Burns Chronicle Poetry Prize; Scottish Arts Council Special Award. *Membership:* International PEN. *Address:* 173–314 Comely Bank Rd, Edinburgh EH4 1DJ, Scotland.

ANNWN, David, (David James Jones); b. 9 May 1953, Congleton, Cheshire, England. Poet; Critic; Lecturer. m. 26 April 1994. *Education:* Wigan Technical College, 1970–72; BA, English, 1975, PhD, Modern Poetry, 1978, University College of Wales, Aberystwyth; PGCE, Bath University, 1979. *Appointments:* Postgraduate Tutor, Aberystwyth University, 1975–78; Lecturer, 1981–88, Head of English Degree Work, 1988–95, Wakefield College; Lecturer, Tutor, and Examiner, Open University, 1995–96; Lecturer in Creative Writing, Leeds University, 1996. *Publications:* Poetry: Foster the Ghost, 1984; King Saturn's Book, 1986; The Other, 1988; Primavera Violin, 1990; The Spirit/That Kiss, 1993; Dantean Designs, 1995; Danse Macabre, Death and the Printers (with Kelvin Corcoran, Alan Halsey, and Gavin Selerie), 1997. Other: Inhabited Voices: Myth and History in the Poetry of Seamus Heaney, Geoffrey Hill and George Mackay Brown, 1984; Catgut and Blossom: Jonathon Williams in England (ed.), 1989; A Different Can of Words (ed.), 1992; Presence, Spacing Sign: The Graphic Art of Peterjon Skelt, 1993; Hear the Voice of the Bard!: The Early Bards, William Blake and Robert Duncan, 1995; Poetry in the British Isles: Non-Metropolitan Perspectives, 1995; Inner Celtia (with Alan Richardson), 1996; A Breton Herbal: Translations of Poems by Eugene Guillevic, 1998. *Contributions to:* Anthologies: Anglo-Welsh Review; Poetry Wales; Ambit; Iron; Scintilla; David Jones Society Journal. *Honours:* Winner, International Collegiate Eisteddfod, 1975; Prize, Ilkley Arts Festival, 1982; Bursary Award, Yorkshire Arts, 1985; First Prize, Cardiff International Poetry Competition, 1996. *Memberships:* Humanities and Arts Higher Education Network; Northern Asscn of Writers in Education; Welsh Acad. *Address:* 3 Westfield Park, College Grove, Wakefield, West Yorkshire WF1 3RP, England.

ANSEN, Alan; b. 23 Jan. 1922, New York, NY, USA. Poet. *Education:* Woodmere Acad., 1929–38; Harvard College, 1938–42; New School for Social Research, 1946–47. *Appointments:* Secretary to W H Auden, 1948–53; Lecturer, 1969–86. *Publications:* Disorderly Houses; The Old Religion; Various privately printed vols; Contact Highs: Selected Poems; The Table Talk of W H Auden; William Burroughs; The Vigilantes: Fragment of a Novel. *Membership:* PEN America. *Address:* 26 Timoleontos Philimonos, Marasleion, Athens 11521, Greece.

ANTHONY, Frank; b. 6 June 1922, Minnesota, USA. Poet; Teacher; Writer. *Education:* St John's University, 1946–47; BA, University of Minnesota, 1950; University of Iowa, 1951; MA, Dartmouth College, 1984; PhD, Florida State University, 1990. *Appointments:* Ed., Columnist, Beacon Publications; Producer, Vermont Public Radio; Media Consultant, Dartmouth College; Teacher, Cambridge Center, Community College, Vermont, Florida State University. *Publications:* 24 Poems; Vermont Poems; Selected Poems; Collected Poems; That Special Voice; Poetry of the Unconscious; Beyond the Fruited Plain; Terminus; The Amsterdam Papers, 1998; The Brussels Book, 1999; The Conch Chronicle, 2000; Down Gullah, 2001; Evening Vespers, 2002. *Contributions to:* Celebrating T. S. Eliot; Frost in Spring; North of Wakulla; Edgar Allan Poe; Anthology of New England Writers; Dream International Quarterly; Jugglers World; Negative Capability; Northern New England Review; The Sucarnochee Review; Thirteen Poetry Magazine; Northwest Review; American String Teacher; Elk River Review; Life on the Line; Pleiades; A Vermont Scrapbook; Thoughts on High School and Beyond. *Honours:* Grant, Minnesota Council of the Arts; Citation, Dartmouth College. *Memberships:* Acad. of American Poets; National Federation of State Poetry Societies; New England Poetry Club; New England Writers; Vermont Poets Asscn. *Address:* PO Box 483, 151 Main St, Windsor, VT 05089, USA. *E-mail:* newvtpoet@aol.com. *Website:* hometown.aol.com/newvtpoet/myhomepage/profile.html.

ANTHONY, Geneva Jo; b. 10 April 1946, Minden, LA, USA. Poet; Short Story Writer. *Appointments:* Vice-Pres., 1987–90, Installation Officer, 1994, Recording Secretary, Mississippi Poetry Society, South Branch. *Publications:* Five Southern Mississippi Poets; Sweet Southern Dreams. *Contributions to:* Diamonds and Dewdrops; Special People; Poetry Premiere; Voices of the South; Yarn Spinner; XV; Poems of the Great South; Times and Seasons; Poems to Remember, II; Moments in Time; Secrets of Poetic Vision; Poems of Great America; Haiku Happenings; To the Stars; Holiday Gems; The Heritage; The Spirit; Seven Stars Sentinel; Reflections; Omnific; Parnassas; Magnolia Quarterly; Feelings of the Heart; Listen; The Poet; Back Porch; Best Poets of 1987; Moments in Time; The Ultimate Writer; Mississippi Melodies; Mississippi Poetry Society Anthology; Stories published in various magazines. *Honours:* Silver Poet Award, 1989, 1998, Award of Merit, World of Poetry; 4 Blue Ribbon Awards, Southern Poetry Asscn; Several Pres.'s Awards, Runner-up, Poet of the Year, 1988, 1992, 1998, 2000, Mississippi Poetry Society, South Branch; Southern Literature and Southern Poets Officer, United Daughters of the Confederacy; Writers Unlimited Award. *Memberships:* Mississippi Poetry Society; Southern Poetry Asscn. *Address:* 8417 Shady Rest Rd, Vancleave, MS 39565, USA.

ANTHONY, Steve; b. 20 Dec. 1958, Perivale, Middlesex, England. Writer; Poet; Ed.; Tutor. *Education:* BA, English and Philosophy, Hull University, 1983; MPhil, Modern Poetry in English, Stirling University, 1989; Cert Ed in Further Education, Thames Polytechnic, 1990. *Publications:* Take Any Train, Book of Gay Men's Poetry, 1990; The Gregory Anthology 1987–1990, 1990; The Crazy Jig, Lesbian and Gay Writing Scotland 2, 1992; Of Eros and Dust: Poems from the City (ed.), 1992; Language of Water, Language of Fire, 1992; Risk Behaviour, 1993; Jugular Defences: An AIDS Anthology (co-ed.), 1994. *Contributions to:* Author; Clanjamfrie; Encounter; Orbis; Sound Press for the Blind; Ambit; Poetry London Newsletter. *Honours:* Eric Gregory Award, Society of Authors, 1987; Winner, Bloodaxe Poetry Book Competition, 1987; Finalist, Scottish Open Poetry Competition, 1988; Finalist, Kent and Sussex Poetry Competition, 1988; Specially Commended, Lace Poetry Competition, 1990; Runner-up, Skoob/Index on Censorship Poetry Competition, 1992. *Memberships:* Hull University Poetry Society, pres., 1979–80, secretary, 1988; Poetry Society; Oscars Press, editorial panel; Terrible Beauty Poetry Readings, advisory board. *Address:* The Cottage, 40 Chiltern Close, Ickenham, Middlesex UB10 8JT, England.

ANTIN, David; b. 1 Feb. 1932, New York, NY, USA. Prof. of Visual Arts; Poet. m. Eleanor Fineman, 1960, 1 s. *Education:* BA, City College, New York, 1955; MA in Linguistics, New York University, 1966. *Appointments:* Chief Ed. and Scientific Dir, Research Information Service, 1958–60; Curator, Institute of Contemporary Art, Boston, 1967; Dir, University Art Gallery, 1968–72, Asst Prof., 1968–72, Prof. of Visual Arts, 1972–, University of California at San Diego. *Publications:* Definitions, 1967; Autobiography, 1967; Code of Flag Behavior, 1968; Meditiations, 1971; Talking, 1972; After the War, 1973; Talking at the Boundaries, 1976; Who's Listening Out There?, 1980; Tuning, 1984; Poèmes Parlés, 1984; Selected Poems 1963–73, 1991; What it Means to be Avant Garde, 1993; A Conversation with David Antin (with Charles Bernstein), 2002. *Contributions to:* Periodicals. *Honours:* Longview Award, 1960; University of California Creative Arts Award, 1972; Guggenheim Fellowship, 1976; National Endowment for the Humanities Fellowship, 1983; PEN Award for Poetry, 1984; Getty Research Fellow, 2002. *Address:* PO Box 1147, Del Mar, CA 92014, USA.

ANTOINE, Yves; b. 12 Dec. 1941, Port-au-Prince, Haiti. Prof.; Writer; Poet. 1 d. *Education:* MEd, 1972, DLitt, 1988, University of Ottawa. *Publications:* La Veillée, 1964; Témoin Oculaire, 1970; Au gré des heures, 1972; Les sabots de la nuit, 1974; Alliage, 1979; Libations pour le soleil, 1985; Sémiologie et personnage romanesque chez Jacques S. Alexis, 1993; Polyphonie (poems and prose), 1996. *Contributions to:* Une affligeante réalité, Le Droit, Ottawa, 1987; L'indélébile, Symbiosis, Ottawa, 1992; Inventeurs et savants noirs, 1998. *Honour:* Guest, Harambee Foundation Society, 1988; Carter G. Woodward Award, International Council of Outaouais (Québec, Canada), 1999. *Memberships:* Union of Writers, QC; Ligue des Droits et Liberté; Asscn des auteurs de l'Outaouais québécois. *Address:* 200 blvd Cité des Jeunes, apt 403, Hull, QC J8Y 6M1, Canada.

ANTÓNIO, Mário, (Mário António Fernandes de Oliveiro); b. 5 April 1934, Maquela do Zombo, Angola. Poet; Writer; Trans. *Publications:* Many vols of poems, essays, short stories and trans. *Contributions to:* Numerous magazines and journals.

ANYIDOHO, Kofi; b. 1947, Wheta, Ghana. University Lecturer in English; Poet. *Education:* BA, English and Linguistics, University of Ghana. *Appointment:* Lecturer in English, University of Ghana. *Publications:* Elegy for the Revolution, 1978; Our Soul's Harvest (co-ed.), 1978; Earthchild, 1985; The Fate of Vultures: New Poetry of Africa (co-ed.), 1989. *Honour:* BBC Arts and Africa Award. *Address:* c/o Dept of English, University of Ghana, PO Box 25, Legon, Near Accra, Ghana.

ANZRANNII, Avikm Axim, (Vikram Mehta); b. 18 June 1947, Shimla, India. Lecturer in English; Poet. m. 5 May 1979, 1 s., 1 d. *Education:* BSc, Engineering, Delhi College of English, 1966; BA, Economics, SDB College, Shimla, 1968; MA, English, Regional Centre for P G Studies, Shimla, 1970. *Appointment:* Lecturer in English, Head of Dept of Applied Science and Humanities, Government Polytechnic for Women, Kandaghat, India. *Publications:* General English for Polytechnic Students, 1974; The Lover (for private circulation), 1976; Lillian O Ranni: A Love Song, 1987; Prem Geet (Hindi verses), 1990; 55 Love Songs of Anzrannii, 1995. *Contributions to:* Poetcrit; Poet, Chennai; Marande; Durst; Ranchi. *Honours:* DLitt, WAAC, USA, 1990; Diploma of Excellence in Poetry, International Poets Acad., Chennai, 1990. *Memberships:* World Poetry Society, Chennai; Writer's Forum, Ranchi; World Congress of Poets, CA, USA. *Address:* Chail View Palace, Kandaghat HP 173215, India.

AOYAMA, Miyuki; b. 1 Dec. 1954, Ashikaga, Tochigi, Japan. Assoc. Prof; Poet; Trans. m. Toru Arai, 1988, 2 s. *Education:* BA, 1979, MA, 1980, Indiana University of Pennsylvania. *Appointments:* Lecturer, 1989–94, Assoc. Prof., 1994–, Seitoku University. *Publications:* Poetry of Erica Jong (trans.), 1993; A Long Rainy Season: Haiku and Tanka (trans.), 1994; On Love (trans.), 1996; West Wind (poems), 1998; A Zigzag Joy: The Bilingual Anthology of Japanese Contemporary Poetry (trans.), 1998; Collected Linked Quatrains: The Cycle of Passion and Others (anthology), 2002. *Contributions to:* Periodicals. *Honour:* Benjamin Franklin Award, 1995. *Memberships:* American Literary Society of Japan; Emily Dickinson Society of Japan; English Literary Society of Japan. *Address:* 87-1 Takamatsu, Ashikaga, Tochigi, Japan.

APONICK, Kathleen; b. 26 Sept. 1941, Massachusetts, USA. Freelance Writer; Poet. m. Anthony A Aponick, 3 Jan. 1970, 1 s. *Education:* BS, Framlingham State College, 1963; MFA, Warren Wilson College, 1989. *Appointments:* Schoolteacher; Ed., Allyn and Bacon Inc, Boston; Freelance Writer. *Publications:* Merrimack: A Poetry Anthology; Near the River's Edge (chapbook), 1995. *Contributions to:* Tar River Poetry; Worcester Review; Calliope; Seneca Review. *Memberships:* Poetry Society of America; New England Poetry Club. *Address:* 5 Skopelos Circle, Andover, MA 01810, USA.

APPLEMAN, M(arjorie) H(aberkorn); b. Fort Wayne, IN, USA. Dramatist; Poet. m. Philip Appleman. *Education:* BA, Northwestern University; MA, Indiana University; Degré Supérieur, Sorbonne, University of Paris. *Appointments:* Prof. of English and Playwriting, New York University, Columbia University; International Honors Program, Indiana University. *Publications:* Plays: Seduction Duet, 1982; The Commuter, 1985. Other: Over 60 plays given in full productions or staged readings, 1971–2002. Poetry: Against Time, 1994. Opera libretto: Let's Not Talk About Lenny Anymore, 1989. *Contributions to:* Numerous anthologies and journals. *Honours:* Several playwriting awards. *Memberships:* Authors' League of America; Circle East Theater Co; Dramatists' Guild; League of Professional Theatre Women; PEN American Center; Poets and Writers; Acad. of American Poets. *Address:* PO Box 39, Sagaponack, NY 11962, USA.

APPLEMAN, Philip (Dean); b. 8 Feb. 1926, Kendallville, IN, USA. Writer; Poet; Distinguished Prof. of English Emeritus. m. Marjorie Ann Haberkorn, 19 Aug. 1950. Education BS, 1950, PhD, 1955, Northwestern University; MA, University of Michigan, 1951. *Appointments:* Fulbright Scholar, University of Lyon, 1951–52; Instructor to Prof., 1955–67, Prof., 1967–84, Distinguished Prof. of English, 1984–86, Distinguished Prof. Emeritus, 1986–, Indiana University; Dir and Instructor, International School of America, 1960–61, 1962–63; Visiting Prof., State University of New York College at Purchase, 1973, Columbia University, 1974; Visiting Scholar, New York University, University of Southern California at Los Angeles; John Steinbeck Visiting Writer, Long Island University at Southampton, 1992. *Publications:* Fiction: In the Twelfth Year of the War, 1970; Shame the Devil, 1981; Apes and Angels, 1989. Poetry: Kites on a Windy Day, 1967; Summer Love and Surf, 1968; Open

Doorways, 1976; Darwin's Ark, 1984; Darwin's Bestiary, 1986; Let There Be Light, 1991; New and Selected Poems, 1956–1996, 1996. Non-Fiction: The Silent Explosion, 1965. Editor: 1859: Entering an Age of Crisis, 1959; Darwin, 1970; The Origin of Species, 1975; An Essay on the Principle of Population, 1976. *Contributions to:* Numerous publications. *Honours:* Ferguson Memorial Award, Friends of Literature Society, 1969; Christopher Morley Awards, Poetry Society of America, 1970, 1975; Castanola Award, Poetry Society of America, 1975; National Endowment for the Arts Fellowship, 1975; Pushcart Prize, 1985; Humanist Arts Award, American Humanist Asscn, 1994; Friends of Darwin Award, National Center for Science Education, 2002. *Memberships:* Acad. of American Poets; American Asscn of University Profs; Authors' Guild of America; MLA; National Council of Teachers of English; PEN American Center; Poetry Society of America; Poets and Writers. *Address:* PO Box 39, Sagaponack, NY 11962, USA.

AP-THOMAS, Ifan; b. 27 July 1917, Manchester, England. Radiologist (retd) Poet. m. Beti Robinson Owen, 29 March 1958, 1 s., 1 d. *Education:* MB University of Edinburgh, 1939. *Publications:* Journey to the Silverless Island; The Oakwoods of Love. *Membership:* Poetry Society. *Address:* 7 Bryn Estyn Rd, Wrexham LL13 9ND, Wales.

ARAM, Maziar. See: SOLEIMANI, Faramarz.

ARCHIBALD, Mary-Ann; b. 25 Oct. 1963, Truro, Nova Scotia, Canada Writer; Poet. *Education:* BA, Political Science, Acadia University, Wolfville, Nova Scotia. *Publication:* Amethyst Review, 1995. *Contributions to:* Chronicle Herald; Outdoor Canada; Field & Stream; Farm Focus; The Farmer; Truro Magazine; Central Nova Business News; Dunhill. *Memberships:* Nova Scotia Writer's Federation; Periodical Writers of Canada. *Address:* PO Box 1122, Truro, Nova Scotia B2N 5H1, Canada.

ARDEN, Hava. See: TICE, Arden A.

ARENDT, Erica Elisabeth. See: HARVOR, Elisabeth.

ARGUETA, Manilo; b. 24 Nov. 1935, San Miguel, El Salvador. Poet; Novelist. *Education:* Universidad Nacional, San Salvador. *Publications:* Fiction: El valle des hamacas, 1970; Caperucita en la zona rosa, 1977; One Day of Life, 1980; Cuzcatalan, Where the Southern Sea Beats, 1987. Poetry: Poemas, 1967; En el costado de la luz, 1979; El Salvador, 1990. Editor: Poesia de El Salvador, 1983. *Honour:* University of Central America Prize, 1980. *Address:* c/o Chatto and Windus, 20 Vauxhall Bridge Rd, London SW1N 2SA, England.

ARGYLE, Keith; b. 8 Feb. 1951, Worksop, Nottinghamshire, England. Poet. *Education:* City & Guilds Catering, 1978. *Appointments:* Catering Profession; Founder and Chair, White Tower Writers Asscn. *Publications:* The Good, the Fair and the Funny, 1994; A Week at Cleethorps, 1996. *Address:* 33 Wellgate, Conisborough, Doncaster, South Yorkshire DN12 3HN, England.

ARIDJIS, Homero; b. 6 April 1940, Mexico. Poet; Novelist; Playwright. m. Betty Ferber, 1965, 2 d. *Education:* Autonomous University of Mexico, 1961. *Appointments:* Visiting Prof., New York University, Columbia University, University of Indiana; Mexican Ambassador to Netherlands and Switzerland; Founder-Pres., Group 100 environmentalist asscn; Dir, Festival Internacional de Poesia, 1981, 1982, 1987; Nichols Chair in the Humanities and the Public Sphere, University of California at Irvine; International Pres., International PEN, 1997–2003. *Publications:* Poetry: Los ojos desdoblados, 1960; Antes del reino, 1963; Ajedrez-Navegaciones, 1969; Los espacios azules, 1969; Quemar las naves, 1975; Vivir para ver, 1977; Construir la muerte, 1982; Imágenes para el fin del milenio, 1990; Nueva expulsión del paraíso, 1990; El poeta en peligro de extinción, 1992; Tiempo de ángeles, 1994; Ojos de otro mirar, 1998; El ojo de la ballena, 2001. Prose: La tumba de Filidor, 1961; Mirándola dormir, 1964; Perséfone, 1967; El poeta niño, 1971; Noche de independencia, 1978; Espectáculo del año dos mil, 1981; Playa nudista y otros relatos, 1982; 1492 vida y tiempos de Juan Cabezón de Castilla, 1985; El último Adán, 1986; Memorias del nuevo mundo, 1988; Gran teatro del fin del mundo, 1989; La leyenda de los soles, 1993; El Señor de los últimos días: Visiones del año mil, 1994; ¿En quién piensas cuando haces el amor?, 1996; Apocalipsis con figuras, 1997; La montaña de las mariposas, 2000; El silencio de Orlando, 2000; La zona del silencio, 2002; Eyes to See Otherwise: Selected Poems of Homero Aridjis, 2002. *Honours:* Guggenheim Fellowships; Global 500 Award, 1987; Novedades Novela Prize, 1988; Grinzane Cavour Prize for Best Foreign Fiction, 1992; Hon. Doctor of Humane Letters, Indiana University, 1993; Prix Roger Caillois, France, 1997; Presea Generalisimo José María Morelos, City of Morelia, 1998; Environmentalist of the Year Award, Latin Trade Magazine, 1999; John Hay Award, Orion Society, 2000; Forces for Nature Award, Natural Resources Defense Council, 2001; Green Cross Millennium Award for International Environmental Leadership, Global Green, USA, 2002. *Address:* c/o Georges Borchardt Inc, 136 E 57th St, New York, NY 10022, USA.

ARIMA, Takashi Nishida; b. 17 Dec 1931, Kyoto, Japan. Novelist; Poet; Songwriter. m. Yoshiko Oota, 15 Nov 1957, 1 s., 1 d. *Education:* Graduate, Doshisha University, 1954. *Appointments:* Man., Kyoto Bank Branch, 1974–78; Pres., Pegasus Leasing Co Ltd, 1987–; Vice-Chair., Takarabune Corp, 1989–.

Publications: Many poems and songs. *Honour:* International Eminent Poet's Diploma, International Poets Acad., 1993. *Memberships:* Japan PEN Club; Japan Poets' Asscn; Japan Writers' Asscn; Kyoto Contemporary Poetry Asscn; World Acad. of Art and Culture. *Address:* 1-29-103 Izumikawa-cho, Shimogamo, Sakyo-ku, Kyoto 606, Japan.

ARMANTROUT, (Mary) Rae; b. 13 April 1947, Vallejo, CA, USA. College Teacher; Poet. m. Charles Korkegian, 21 Aug. 1971, 1 s. *Education:* AB, University of California, 1970; MA, California State University, San Francisco, 1975. *Appointments:* Teaching Asst, 1972–74; Lecturer, 1978–82; Lecturer, University of California, 1982–. *Publications:* Necromance; Precedence; The Invention of Hungerl Extremities; Made To Seem; The Pretext, 2001; Veil: New and Selected Poems, 2001. *Contributions to:* Partisan Review; Boundary 2; Sulfur; Conjunctions; Canary Islands Review; San Diego Union Newspaper; Best American Poetry of 1988, 2001, 2002. *Honour:* California Arts Council Fellowship. *Address:* 4774 E Mountain View Dr., San Diego, CA 92116, USA.

ARMITAGE, Simon Robert; b. 26 May 1963, Huddersfield, West Yorkshire, England. Poet. m. Alison Tootell, 21 Sept. 1991. *Education:* Portsmouth Polytechnic, 1981–84; BA, Honours, Geography, 1984, MA, Manchester University, 1988. *Appointments:* Probation Officer, Greater Manchester Probation Service, 1988–93; Poetry Ed., Chatto and Windos, 1993–95. *Publications:* Zoom!, 1989; Xanadu, 1992; Kid, 1992; Book of Matches, 1993; The Dead Sea Poems, 1995. *Contributions to:* Sunday Times; TLS; Guardian; Observer; Independent. *Honours:* Eric Gregory Award, 1988; Sunday Times Young Writer of the Year, 1993; Forward Poetry Prize, 1993; Lannan Award, 1994. *Address:* 3 Netherley, Marsden, Huddersfield HD7 6XN, England.

ARMSTRONG, Blair Morton; b. 9 Sept. 1925, Tulsa, Oklahoma, USA. Poet; Artist; Publisher. m. 20 March 1951, 1 s., 3 d. *Education:* Spence School, New York; American Acad. of Dramatic Art; Maryland Institute of Art, Baltimore. *Appointments:* Founder, Mnemosyne Press, AZ, Flagstaff Festival of the Arts; Developer, Mnemosyne Principle for integrating the Arts. *Publications:* Memory of the Mogollon; Arizona Anthem. *Honours:* Ambassador of Honour, Books-Across-the-Sea Programme, 1984; Exhibition of works, Arizona State University, 1992–93. *Memberships:* Arizona Poetry Society; National Society of Arts and Letters. *Address:* 6246 Joshua Tree Lane, Paradise Valley, AZ 85253, USA.

ARMSTRONG, Jeannette Christine; b. 5 Feb. 1948, Canada (Okanagan, mem. of Penticton Indian Band). Educator; Writer; Poet. 1 s., 1 d. *Education:* DFA, Okanagan College, 1975; BFA, University of Victoria, BC, 1978. *Appointment:* Adjunct Prof., Enbwkin School of Writing, University of Victoria, BC, 1989–. *Publications:* Enwhisteetkwa, 1982; Neekna and Chemai, 1984; Slash, 1985; Native Creative Process, 1991; Breath Tracks, 1991; Looking at the Words of Our People, 1993; Whispering in Shadows, 2000; Native Poetry in Canada: A Contemporary Anthology. *Honour:* Children's Book Centre Choice Award, 1983. *Memberships:* PEN International; Writers' Union of Canada. *Address:* c/o Theytus Books, Green Mountain Rd, Lot 45, RR No. 2, Site 50, Comp. 8, Penticton, BC V2A 6J7, Canada.

ARMSTRONG, Keith; b. 25 June 1946, England. Poet; Writer. *Education:* ALA, Newcastle Polytechnic, 1966–67; BA, Honours in Sociology, 1992–95, MA, 1996–98, University of Durham. *Publications:* Tracks From the Span, 1970; Shakespeare and Company, 1975; Giving Blood, 1977; Poets Against Fascism, 1981; Pains of Class, 1982; After the Election, 1983; Wheel Around the World, 1983; Love Poems, 1984; Dreaming North, 1986; Remember What Unites Us, 1986; Jogging to the Falklands, 1987; New Writing From the North, 1988; Modern Poets of Northern England, 1988; Once I Was A Washing Machine, 1989; The Jinglin Geordie, 1990; Sound City, 1991; The Poetry of Percussion, 1991; Poets Voices, 1991; The Brecht Yearbook 20, 1995; Writing for a Change, 1995; Bleeding Sketches, 1995; Darkness Seeping, 1995; Beyond; Imagined Corners. *Contributions to:* Anthologies, periodicals, journals, magazines and newspapers. *Honours:* Kate Collingwood Bursary Award, 1986; Northern Arts Writers' Award and Northern Arts Travel Awards, 1990–91.

ARMSTRONG, Naomi Young, (Gloria Young); b. 17 Oct. 1918, Dermott, AR, USA. Teacher (retd); Actress; Poet. 1 c. *Education:* AA, Wilson Junior College, 1957; BSc in Speech Theatre, Northwestern University, 1961; DDiv, Universal Orthodox College, 1988. *Appointments:* Teacher, Chicago, 1982–83; Actress, 1989–. *Publications:* A Child's Easter, 1971; Expression I, 1973; Expression II, 1976; Naomi's Two-Line Sillies, 1985; Expression V, 1994. *Contributions to:* Anthologies. *Honours:* World Congress of Poets Awards, 1973–79, 1986, 1994; Honorary doctorates. *Memberships:* American Federation of Television and Radio Artists; Centro Studi e Scambi; Chrysopoets Inc, founder-dir; Poetry Society of London; Screen Actors Guild; World Poetry Society. *Address:* c/o American Federation of Television and Radio Artists, 260 Madison Ave, Seventh Floor, New York, NY 10016, USA.

ARMSTRONG, Terry Lee, (Terry Lee, Milo Rosebud); b. 23 Dec. 1949, Elgin, Nebraska, USA. Carpenter; Poet. m. Chris Alvarez, 16 Nov. 1991, 1 d. *Education:* Assoc. in Arts; San Antonio College; North Texas State University; University of Texas at San Antonio. *Appointments:* Ed. and Publisher, Milo Rosebud, Lone Stars Magazine, Armstrong Publishing Company. *Publications:* Call It Love; When the Soul Speaks; Heart Thoughts and I Love Yous. *Contributions to:* National Library of Poetry; Omnific; Poetic Eloquence; My Legacy; Telstar; Moments in Time; Mobius; The Plowman. *Honours:* First Place, Grand Prize, North American Open Poetry Contest, 1990; Poet of the Year, Poetry Break Journal, 1991. *Address:* 4219 Flint Hill, San Antonio, TX 78230, USA.

ARNOLD, Bob; b. 5 Aug. 1952, Adams, Massachusetts, USA. Stonemason; Builder; Ed.; Publisher; Poet. m. Susan Eileen Paules, 28 Aug. 1974, 1 s. *Education:* Graduated, Brewster Acad., 1970. *Appointment:* Ed., Publisher, Longhouse Publishers and Booksellers, 1973–. *Publications:* Rope of Bells, 1974; Along the Way, 1979; Habitat, 1979; Thread, 1980; Self-employed, 1983; Back Road Caller, 1985; Gaze, 1985; Sky, 1986; Go West, 1987; Long Time Together, 1987; Cache, 1987; On Stone, 1988; Souvenir, 1989; Where Rivers Meet, 1990; By Heart, 1991; Our Guardian Angel, 1991; This Romance, 1992; Happy As You Are, 1993; Farm Hand, 1994; American Train Letters, 1995; Tiny Summer Book, 1997; Beautiful Swimmers, 1998; Engine Trouble, 1998; Once in Vermont, 1999. *Contributions to:* Country Journal; Harper's; Poetry East; Coyotes Journal; Falk, West Germany; Edge, Japan; New Letters; Ploughshares; White Pine Journal; Aspect; Flute; Spoor; Heaven Bone; Tel-Let. *Address:* 1604 River Rd, Guilford, VT 05301, USA.

ARNOLD, Eleanor Parsons; b. 4 May 1929, Hendricks County, IN, USA. Ed.; Poet. m. Clarence E Arnold, 26 Dec. 1948, 1 s., 2 d. *Education:* BA in English, Indiana University, 1950. *Publications:* Feeding Our Families, 1983; Party Lines, Pumps and Privies, 1984; Voices of American Homemakers, 1985; Girlhood Days, 1987; Going to Club, 1988; Living Rich Lives, 1990. *Contributions to:* Various publications. *Honour:* Sagamore of the Wabash, State of Indiana. *Memberships:* American Asscn of State and Local History; Indiana Oral History Roundtable; Indianapolis Press Club; National Oral History Asscn. *Address:* 1744 North St, 450 East St, Rushville, IN 46173, USA.

ARRABAL, Fernando; b. 11 Aug. 1932, Melilla, Morocco. Author; Poet; Dramatist. m. Luce Moreau, 1958, 1 s., 1 d. *Education:* University of Madrid. *Appointments:* Political prisoner in Spain, 1967; Co-Founder, Panique Movement. *Publications:* Fiction: Baal Babylone, 1959; L'enterrement de la sardine, 1962; Fêtes et rites de la confusion, 1965; L'extravagante croisade d'un castrat amoureux, 1991; La tueuse du jardin d'hiver, 1994; Le funambule de Dieu, 1998; Porté disparu, 2000; Levitación, 2000. Poetry: La pierre de la folie, 1963; 100 Sonnets, 1966; Humbles paradis, 1983; Liberté couleur de femme, 1993; Arrabalesques, 1994. Other: Numerous plays, screenplays and essays. *Honours:* Société des Auteurs Prize, 1966; Grand Prix du Théâtre, 1967; Grand Prix Humour Noir, 1968; Obie Award, 1976; Premio Nadal, 1983; Officier, Ordre des Arts et des Lettres, France, 1984; World's Theatre Prize, 1984; Medalla de Oro de Bellas Artes, Spain, 1989; Prix du Théâtre, Académie Française, 1993; Premio Internacional de Novela Vladimir Nabokov, 1994; Grand Prix, Société des Gens de Lettres, 1996; Grand Prix de la Méditerranée, 1996; Prix de la Francophonie, 1998; Premio Europa di Alessandro Manzoni, 1999; Satrape du Collège de Pataphysique, 2000. *Address:* 22 rue Jouffroy d'Abbans, 75017 Paris, France.

ARROWSMITH, Pat; b. 2 March 1930, England. Asst Ed. (retd); Poet. *Education:* BA, History, Cambridge University, 1951; University of Ohio, 1952–53; Social Science Certificate, Liverpool University, 1955. *Appointment:* Staff Mem., Amnesty International, 1972–94. *Publications:* Poetry collections: Breakout, 1975; On the Brink, 1980; Thin Ice, 1982; Nine Lives, 1990; Drawing to Extinction, 2001. *Contributions to:* Anthologies, newspapers, magazines and journals. *Honours:* Second Prize, Hornsey, London Competition, 1977; Highly Commended, Westminster, London Competition, 1978; Prize, Ver Poets Competition, 1993. *Memberships:* Ver Poets; London Poetry Society. *Address:* 132C Middle Lane, London, N8 7JP, England.

ARROWSMITH, William; b. 13 April 1924, Orange, New Jersey, USA. Trans.; Educator; Critic; Poet. Divorced, 2 d. *Education:* AB, 1947, PhD, 1954, Princeton University; BA, 1951, MA, 1958, Oxford University. *Appointments:* Visiting Henry McCormick Prof. of Dramatic Literature and Criticism, The Drama School, Yale University, 1976–77; Prof. of Classics and Humanities, Johns Hopkins University, 1977–80; Visiting Presidential Prof., Georgetown University, 1981; Lecturer, The Folger Library, 1981; Visiting David B Kriser Prof. of Humanities, New York University, 1982–84; Robert W Woodruff Prof. of Classics and Comparative Literature, Emory University, 1982–86. *Publications:* General Ed., The Greek Tragedy in New Translations, 33 vols, 1973–; Trans. and introduction, The Alcestis of Euripides, 1974–89; The Poems as Palimpsest: A Dialogue on Eliot's Sweeney Erect, 1981; Eros in Terre Haute: T. S. Eliot's Lune de Miel, 1982; The Occasions by Eugenio Montale (trans.), 1987. *Contributions to:* Arion; Hudson Review; Chimera; The Nation; Harper's; New Yorker; Antaeus; Paris Review; American Poetry Review; Interim; Bostonia; Ploughshares. *Honours:* Landon Trans. Prize, American Acad. of Poets, 1986; Jerome J Shestack Poetry Prize for Trans., 1987; International Eugenio Montale Prize, Parma, Italy, 1990. *Memberships:* PEN; Poetry Society of America. *Address:* Dept of Classical Studies, Boston University, 745 Commonwealth Ave, Boston, MA 02215, USA.

ARROYO-GOMEZ, Mario Vernon; b. 22 April 1948, Gibraltar. Dir; Dancer; Choreographer; Actor; Poet. *Education:* Studied drama, dance, speech, and English, Leeds, 1967–70; Studied dance, Laban School of Dance, London, 1979–80; DipEd, Goldsmith's London University, 1980. *Appointments:* Dir. and choreographer with many youth groups and adults; Pioneered work in modern dance and dance-drama. *Publication:* Profiles... Perflies, 1990. *Honours:* Various achievement awards. *Address:* 16 George Jeger House, Glacis, Gibraltar.

ARTEAGA, Alfred; b. 2 May 1950, Los Angeles, CA, USA. Writer; Poet; University Educator. m. Dec. 1972, divorced 1995, 3 d. *Education:* BA, 1972, MA, 1984, PhD, 1987, University of California, Santa Cruz; MFA, Columbia University, 1974. *Appointments:* Instructor in Mexican-American Studies, San Jose City College, CA, 1977–87; Asst Prof. of English, University of Houston, 1987–90; Asst Prof. of English, University of California, Berkeley, 1990–98. *Publications:* Cantos (poems), 1991; An Other Tongue: Nation and Ethnicity in the Linguistic Borderlands (ed.), 1994; First Words: Origins of the European Nation, 1994; House with the Blue Bed (essays), 1997; Chicano Poetics: Heterotexts and Hybridities, 1997; Love in the Time of Aftershocks (poems), 1998. *Contributions to:* Anthologies including Spivak Reader; Essays and poems to journals including: Stanford Humanities Review; Critical Studies; Baldus; River Styx; Electronic journals. *Honours:* Rockefeller Foundation Fellow, 1993–94; Poetry Fellow, National Endowment for the Arts, 1995. *Address:* c/o Mercury House, 785 Market St, San Francisco, CA 94103, USA. *E-mail:* bluebed@hotmail.com.

ARTHUR, Eagin. See: REIFF, Andrew Edwin.

ARTMANN, H(ans) C(arl); b. 12 June 1921, St Achatz am Walde, Austria. Poet; Author; Trans. *Publications:* Kein pfeffer für czermak, 1954; Reime verse formeln, 1954; Die missglückte luftreise, 1955; XXV epigrammata, in teuschen alexandrinern gesetzt, 1956; Bei überreichung seines herzens, 1958; Hosn rosn baa (with F. Achleitner and G. Rügm), 1959; Verbarium, 1966; Allerleirausch, 1967; Grünverschlossene Botschaft, 1967; Tök ph' rong süleng, 1967; Die Anfangsbuchstaben der Flagge, 1968; Ein lilienweisser brief aus lincolnshire: gedichte aus 21 jahren, 1969; Frankenstein in Sussex, 1969; Die Wanderer, 1978; Grammatik der Rosen: Gesammelte Prosa, three vols, 1979; Die Sonne war ein grünes Ei, 1982; Von der Erschaffung der Welt und ihren Dingen, 1982; Wer dichten kann ist dichtersmann, 1986; Dedichte von der wollust des dichtens in worte gefasst, 1989; Der zerbrochne Krug (adaptation of work by Kleist), 1992. *Honours:* Austrian State Prize, 1974; Literature Prize of the City of Vienna, 1977; Literature Prize of Salzburg, 1981; Büchner Prize, 1997. *Memberships:* Akademie der Künste, Berlin. *Address:* c/o Residenz-Verlag, Salzburg, Austria.

ASANTE, Molefi Kete; b. 14 Aug. 1942, Vaidosta, CA, USA. Prof.; Poet. m. Kariamu Welsh, 1981, 2 s., 1 d. *Education:* BA, Oklahoma Christian University, 1964; MA, Pepperdine University, 1965; PhD, University of California at Los Angeles, 1968. *Appointments:* Prof., University of California at Los Angeles, 1969–73, State University of New York at Buffalo, 1973–84, Temple University, 1984–. *Publications:* Break of Dawn, 1964; Epic in Search of African Kings, 1979; Afrocentricity, 1980; The Afrocentric Idea, 1987; Kemet, Afrocentricity and Knowledge, 1992; Classical Africa, 1992; African American History, 1995; African Intellectual Heritage, 1996; Love Dance, 1997; African American Atlas, 1998. *Contributions to:* Journals. *Honours:* Hon. degrees, citations and awards. *Membership:* African Writers' Union, vice pres., 1994–. *Literary Agent:* Marie Brown Assocs, New York, USA. *Address:* Temple University, Philadelphia, PA 19122, USA.

ASGARI, Mirza Agha; b. 21 March 1951, Assad-Abad, Hamadan, Iran. Poet. m. 1976, 2 s., 1 d. *Education:* Diploma. *Appointments:* Poetry readings at home and abroad. *Contributions to:* Farsi: Ferdusi; Negin; Kyhan; Adineh; Donyay Sochan; Honar V Adabiat; Deutsch: die Brücke; Sowjet Literatur; Together; Kaweh; WDR. *Memberships:* Iranian PEN Center in Exile, 1996; Verband deutscher Schriftsteller, 1991; Verband Iranian Autors, 1975. *Address:* Untere Heide Str 15, 44793 Bochum, Germany.

ASH, John; b. 29 June 1948, Manchester, England. Writer; Poet; Teacher. *Education:* BA, University of Birmingham, 1969. *Publications:* The Golden Hordes: International Tourism and the Pleasure Periphery (with Louis Turner), 1975; Casino: A Poem in Three Parts, 1978; The Bed and Other Poems, 1981; The Goodbyes, 1982; The Branching Stairs, 1984; Disbelief, 1987; The Burnt Pages, 1991. *Contributions to:* Periodicals. *Honours:* Ingram Merrill Foundation Grant, 1985; Writing Foundation Award, 1986.

ASHANTI, Baron James; b. 5 Sept. 1950, New York, NY, USA. Poet; Writer; Ed.; Critic; Lecturer. m. Brenda Cummings, 11 Sept. 1979, 1 s., 1 d. *Appointments:* Literary Ed., Impressions Magazine, 1972–75; City and Third World Ed., Liberation News Service, 1974–79; Contributing Ed., The Paper, 1978; Lecturer; Dir, Arts-in-Education Program, Frederick Douglass Creative Arts Center, New York, 1988–. *Publications:* Nubiana, 1977; Nova, 1990. *Contributions to:* Many periodicals. *Honours:* Killen Prize for Poetry, St Peter's College, 1982; PEN Fellowships, 1985, 1987; Pulitzer Prize in Poetry nomination, 1991. *Address:* 274 W 140th St, Apt No. 45, New York, NY 10030, USA.

ASHBERY, John Lawrence; b. 28 July 1927, Rochester, NY, USA. Prof. of Languages and Literature; Poet; Dramatist; Critic. *Education:* BA, Harvard University, 1949; MA, Columbia University, 1951; Postgraduate Studies, New York University, 1957–58. *Appointments:* Ed., Locus Solus, Lans-en-Vercors, France, 1960–62, Art and Literature, Paris, 1963–66; Art Critic, New York Herald Tribune, Paris, 1960–65, Art International, Lugano, Switzerland, 1961–64, New York Magazine, 1978–80, Newsweek, 1980–85; Exec. Ed., Art News, New York, 1966–72; Prof. of English, 1974–90, Distinguished Prof. 1980–90, Distinguished Prof. Emeritus, 1990–, Brooklyn College; Poetry Ed. Partisan Review, 1976–80; Charles Eliot Norton Prof. of Poetry, Harvard University, 1989–90; Charles P. Stevenson Prof. of Languages and Literature, Bard College, 1990–. *Publications:* Poetry: Turandot and Other Poems, 1953; Some Trees, 1956; The Poems, 1960; The Tennis Court Oath, 1962; Rivers and Mountains, 1966; Selected Poems, 1967; Three Madrigals, 1968; Sunrise in Suburbia, 1968; Fragment, 1969; The Double Dream of Spring, 1970; The New Spirit, 1970; Three Poems, 1972; The Vermont Notebook, 1975; Self-Portrait in a Convex Mirror, 1975; Houseboat Days, 1976; As We Know, 1979; Shadow Train, 1981; A Wave, 1984; Selected Poems, 1985; April Galleons, 1987; Flow Chart, 1991; Hotel Lautreamont, 1992; And the Stars Were Shining, 1994; Can You Hear, Bird, 1995; Wakefulness, 1998; Girls on the Run, 1999; Your Name Here, 2000. Plays: The Heroes, 1952; The Compromise, 1956; The Philosopher, 1963. Novel: A Nest of Ninnies (with James Schuyler), 1969. *Contributions to:* Many anthologies, journals and periodicals. *Honours:* Fulbright Scholarships, 1955–56, 1956–57; Yale Series of Younger Poets Prize, 1956; Poets Foundatioin Grants, 1960, 1964; Ingram Merrill Foundation Grants, 1962, 1972; Harriet Monroe Poetry Awards, 1963, 1975; Guggenheim Fellowships, 1967, 1973; National Institute of Arts and Letters Award, 1969; Pulitzer Prize in Poetry, 1976; National Book Award, 1976; National Book Critics Circle Award, 1976; English-Speaking Union Poetry Award, 1979; Rockefeller Foundation Grant, 1979–80; Mayor's Award, New York, 1983; Charles Flint Kellogg Award, Bard College, 1983; Bollingen Prize in Poetry, Yale University Library, 1985; Lenore Marshall Poetry Prize, 1985; Wallace Stevens Fellow, Yale University, 1985; John D. and Catherine T. MacArthur Foundation Fellowship, 1985–90; Creative Arts Award, Brandeis University, 1989; Ruth Lilly Poetry Prize, 1992; Robert Frost Medal, 1995. *Memberships:* Acad. of American Poets, fellow; American Acad. and Institute of Arts and Letters; American Acad. of Arts and Sciences. *Address:* c/o Dept of Languages and Literature, Bard College, Annandale-on-Hudson, NY 12504, USA.

ASHBY, Jack (Sydney Edward); b. 11 Feb. 1919, Mitcham, Surrey, England. Managing Dir (retd); Poet. m. Ivy Wheatman, 12 Aug. 1944, 2 s. *Education:* Matriculation (university qualification), 1935. *Publications:* Unscrambled Words No. 1, 1992; No. 2, 1992, No. 3, 1992; Anthology of Unscrambled Words, 1992. *Membership:* Poetry Society. *Address:* c/o SEA Publishing Company, 39 Longhill Rd, Ovingdean, Brighton, East Sussex BN2 7BF, England.

ASHOKAMITRAN, Jagadisa Thyagarajan; b. 22 Sept. 1931, Secunderabad, India. Ed.; Writer; Poet. m. Rajeswari, 5 Sept. 1963, 3 s. *Education:* BSc, Mathematics, Physics and Chemistry. *Appointments:* Tutor, Popular Tutorials, Secunderabad, 1950–52; Public Relations Officer, Gemini Studios, Chennai, 1952–66; Exec. Ed., Kanaiyazhi (monthly), 1966–88; Ed., Munril literary journal, 1989–. *Publications:* Karainda Nizhalgal, 1969; Vaazhvilay Oru Murai, 1971; Innum Sila Naatkal, 1972; Thanneer, 1973; Kaalamum 5 Kuzhan Daigalum, 1974; 18th Parallel, 1977; Viduthalai, 1979; Unmai Vetkai, 1979; Akaya Thamarai, 1980; En Payanam, 1981; Vimochanam, 1982; Thanthaikkaka, 1983; Inru, 1984; Muraippen, 1984; Moonru Paarvaigal, 1984; Otran!, 1985; Sila Asiriyargal, Noolgal, 1987; Padaippu Kalai, 1987; Uttara Ramayanam, 1988; Manasarovar, 1989; Oru Gramattu Adyayam, 1990; Appavin Snehidar, 1991; Water and 18th Parallel (in English), 1993; Iruvarukka Podum, 1995; Ellame Sari, 1997; Colours of Evil (in English), 1998; Most Truthful Picture (in English), 1998; Complete Short Stories, 2000; Complete Novellas, 2000; Sila India Mozhigalil Mudal Novelgal, 2001. *Contributions to:* Illustrated Weekly of India; Indian Literature; Poet; Hindu Deccan Herald; India Today. *Honours:* Story of the Month Award, 5 times; Book of the Year Awards, 1977, 1985; Story of the Year Award, 1985; Fiction of the Year Awards, 1985, 1987, 1990; Hon. DLitt, World Acad. of Art and Culture, 1990; Harmony Award, 1995; Agnri Akshara Award, 1996; Sahitya Akademi Award, 1996. *Memberships:* Founder Mem., Ilakkia Sangam (literary forum); Founder Mem., Creative Forum (writers and painters); PEN, India. *Address:* 1A, Ninth Cross Ave, Dandeeswaranagar, Velachery, Chennai 600042, India.

ASHRAF, Allama Syed Waheed; b. 4 Feb. 1933, Kichhauchha, India. Educator; Researcher; Writer; Poet. m. Ale Fatima Farzana, 28 Dec. 1969, 3 s., 1 d. *Education:* BA, 1960, MA, Persian, 1962, PhD, Persian, 1965, AMU Aligarh. *Appointments:* Lecturer in Persian, MS University Baroda, Gujrat, India, 1971–77; Reader in Persian, 1977–85, Prof. of Persian, 1986–, Head of Dept of Arabic, Persian and Urdu, 1986–, University of Chennai, Tamil Nadu, India. *Publications:* Rubai, 1987; Rubai, part II, 1990. *Contributions to:* Anthologies and journals. *Memberships:* Several boards. *Address:* University of Chennai, Tamil Nadu, South India.

ASHWORTH, Anne; b. 24 July 1931, Blackpool, England. Librarian; Poet. m. 3 April 1957, 1 s. *Education:* BA, Open University; ALA, Assoc. of the Library

Asscn. *Appointment:* Librarian, Blackpool Sixth Form College, 1971–92. *Publications:* Mirrorwork, 1989; The Girl Who Runs Backwards, 1997; The Oblique Light, 1998. *Contributions to:* Poetry Review; Orbis; Rialto; Staple; Writing Women; Envoi; Iota; Pennine Platform; Other Poetry; Reform; and others. *Address:* 2 Belle Vue Pl., Blackpool, Lancashire FY3 9EG, England. *E-mail:* anne@poustinia.fsnet.co.uk.

ASHWORTH, James; b. 2 Jan. 1955, Burnley, Lancashire, England. Poet. *Education:* University of Wales, 1980–83; Huddersfield Polytechnic, 1984–85; Nottingham University, 1991–92. *Appointments:* Courtaulds, 1974–76; Works Study Officer, Nelson Public Library, 1977; Local Historian, Padiham Youth Centre, Youth Worker 1984; Lecturer, Keighley Technical College, 1984–87. *Contributions to:* Anthologies: Dreams and Reality, 1994; Joyful Harvest, 1994; Blue and Green, 1996; A Passage in Time, 1996; Whispering Winds, 1997; Gallery of Artistry, 1997; Book of Prayer, 1997; Resurrection, 1998; Friends Together, 1999; Poets around Northern England, 2000; Give a Little Love, 2000; To Be Young Again, 2000; God's Acre: The Spirit of the Churchyard, 2001. *Honours:* Ed.'s Choice Award, International Society of Poets, 1996; Poetry Prize, Poetry Today, 1997; Poet of Merit Award, International Society of Poets, 1997. *Address:* 3 Chapel Close, Trawden, Nr Colne BB8 8QZ, England.

ASNER, Marie A; b. 28 Feb. 1947, Minnesota, USA. Musician; Music Teacher; Journalist; Poet. m. 18 Aug. 1968. *Education:* BS, Music, 1965; MS, Music, 1968; PhD, Music Education, 1982. *Appointments:* Music Teacher, Minnesota School Systems; Private Music Teacher and Journalist, Nebraska; Private Music Teacher, Journalist and Poet, KS, 1982–. *Publications:* Secret Place, 1991; Man of Miracles, 1992; An Inquiring Mind, 1993; Man of Miracles, Part II, 1994; Angels, 1998; Man of Sorrows, 1999. *Contributions to:* Omaha World Herald; Shawnee Journal; Potpourri Literary Journal; Poets; Poets of Now; Encore; Metis; Collage; Chronicle; CSS Publications; Great Bend Poetry Anthology; Poets at Work; Sunflower Petals; Byline; Poets of the Vineyard; Sisyphus; Broken Streets; Prairie Woman; Texture; Writer's Companion; Passages North; Kansas City Star. *Honours:* Winner, CSS Publications National Poetry Contest, 1988; Winner, Jubilee Press National Chapbook Contest, 1989; Second Place Winner, Great Bend Poetry Contest, 1991; Honourable Mention, Poet Magazine Poetry Contest, 1992; Second Place Winner, Minnesota Poet Laureate Contest, 1994; Nominated for Kansas Governor's Art Award, 1995; Grand Prize, Kansas City Christian Writers Conference, 1998. *Memberships:* Poets and Writers; Working Press of America; Kansas State Poetry Society; Missouri State Poetry Society; American Guild of Organists; Women in the Motion Picture Industry; International Women's Writing Guild. *Address:* P O Box 4343, Overland Park, KS 66204-0343, USA.

ASSELINEAU, Roger Maurice, (Maurice Herra); b. 24 March 1915, Orléans, France. Prof. Emeritus of American Literature; Poet; Writer. *Education:* L. ès L., Agrégation, English, 1938, D. ès L., 1953, Sorbonne, Paris. *Publications:* L'Evolution de Walt Whitman, 1954; The Literary Reputation of Mark Twain, 1954; Poésies incomplètes, 1959; E. A. Poe, 1970; Transcendentalist Constant in American Literature, 1980; St John de Crevecoeur: The Life of an American Farmer (with Gay Wilson Allen), 1987; Poésies incomplètes (II), 1989; Poètes anglais de la Grande Guerre, 1991; Poèmes de Guerre 1939–1944, 1991; The Evolution of Walt Whitman, 1999; Miracles et Miettes, 2002. *Contributions to:* Etudes Anglaises; Revue de Littérature Comparée; Forum; Dialogue; Calamus; Walt Whitman Quarterly Review; Diadème; Flammes Vives; Le Bayou; Cahiers du Nouvel Humanisme; Les Hommes Sans Epaule; Iô; Calamus, Oc. *Honours:* Walt Whitman Prize, Poetry Society of America; Hon. Doctorate, University of Poznaé. *Memberships:* Former pres., French Asscn for American Studies; MLA of America, hon. mem.; Hemingway Society; International Asscn of University Profs of English; Société des Gens de Lettres. *Address:* 114 Ave Leon Blum, 92160 Antony, France.

ASTOR, Susan Irene; b. 2 April 1946, New York, NY, USA. Teacher; Writer; Poet. Divorced, 2 d. *Education:* Brandeis University; BA, Postgraduate Studies, Adelphi University; Postgraduate Studies, C. W. Post College. *Appointments:* Poet, various Long Island public schools, 1980–. *Contributions to:* Various anthologies, reviews, quarterlies and journals. *Honours:* Several awards. *Membership:* Poets and Writers. *Address:* 32 Jefferson Ave, Mineola, NY 11501, USA.

ATKINS, John Alfred; b. 26 May 1916, Carshalton, Surrey, England. Teacher (retd); Poet. m. Dorothy Joan Grey, 24 May 1940, 2 d. *Education:* BA, History, University of Bristol, 1938. *Appointments:* Head of English Dept, Higher Teacher Training Institute, Omdurman, Sudan, 1966–68; Senior Lecturer, English Dept, Benghazi University, Libya, 1968–70; Docent in English Literature, Łódź, Poland, 1970–76. *Publications:* Experience of England, 1941; Today's New Poets, 1944; The Pleasure Ground (co-author), 1947; Triad (co-author), 1947. *Contributions to:* New Poetry, PEN; New Poetry, Arts Council; Penguin New Writing; Windmill; Poems of this War; Life and Letters Today; New Saxon Pamphlets; Mercury; Oasis; Australian International Quarterly; Outposts; Writing Today; Gangrel; Variegation; Voices; Million; HPJ (Hartforde Poets Journal); Numerous small magazines; poems featured on www.poetry.com. *Honour:* Eastern Arts Asscn Bursary, 1991. *Membership:* Balkerne Writers, Colchester, 1986–89. *Address:* Braeside Cottage, Mill Lane, Birch, Colchester CO2 0NH, England.

ATKINS, Russell; b. 25 Feb. 1926, Cleveland, Ohio, USA. Composer; Poet. *Education:* Cleveland School of Art, 1943; Cleveland Institute of Music, 1945–46; Private music study in composition with J Harold Bron, 1950–54. *Appointments:* Ed., Free Lance Magazine, 1950–80; Publicity Office Man., Sutphen Music School, 1957–60; Creative Writing Instructor, Karamu Theatre, 1972–86; Writer-in-Residence, Cuyahoga Community College, 1973; Instructor, Ohio Programme in Humanities, 1978. *Publications:* Phenomena, 1961; Objects, 1963; Heretofore, 1968; Podium Presentations, 1969; Here in The, 1976; Whichever, 1978; Beyond the Reef, 1991. *Contributions to:* View; Beloit Poetry Journal; New York Times; Western Review; Botteghe Oscure; Writers Forum; Poetry Now; Coventry Reader; Cornfield Review; Stagebill. *Honours:* Consultant to various conferences and workshops; Karamu Theatre Tribute Award, 1971; Honorary Doctorate, Cleveland State University, 1976; Individual Artists Fellowship, Ohio Arts Council, 1978. *Memberships:* Cleveland State University Poetry Forum; Poets League of Greater Cleveland. *Address:* 6005 Grand Ave, Cleveland, OH 44104, USA.

ATKINS, Timothy Clifford; b. 13 Aug. 1962, London, England. Teacher; Poet. *Education:* BA, Honours, Religious Studies, King's College, London, 1985; MPhil, Poetics, University of Stirling, 1987; RSA Certificate, TEFL London, 1988. *Appointments:* TEFL Teacher, Barcelona, 1989–92, Rio de Janeiro, 1992–93; Creative Writing Teacher, San Francisco, 1993–94, University of London, 1994–. *Contributions to:* Several publications. *Address:* 668B Fulham Rd, London SW6 5RX, England.

ATKINSON, Donald; b. 15 June 1931, Sheffield, England. Poet; Ed. m. (1) 1953, (2) 1973, 1 s., 4 d. *Education:* BA, Honours, 1954, MA, 1957, Cambridge; Chichester Theological College, 1954–56. *Appointments:* Teacher of English; Headmaster of secondary schools; Ed., Spokes magazine, 1990–. *Publications:* St Boniface – A Life in Verse, 1955; A Sleep of Drowned Fathers, 1989; Graffiti for Hard Hearts, 1992; Othello in the Pyramid of Dreams, 1996. *Contributions to:* Guardian; TLS; Poetry Review; Stand; Ambit; Rialto; Lines Review; Writing Ulster; Anthologies: Forward; Blue-Nose; Klaonica; New Writing 5, British Council. *Honours:* Peterloo Poets Competition, 1988; TLS, Cheltenham Festival Competition, 1988; Leek Arts Festival Competition, 1989; Aldeburgh Poetry Festival Prize, 1990; First Prize, Sheffield Thursday Competition, 1994; Writer's Award, Arts Council of England, 1995. *Address:* Casa degli Scrittori, 40 Debden Rd, Saffron Walden, Essex CB11 4AB, England.

ATKINSON, Susan Jane; b. 9 Oct. 1964, Blackburn, Lancashire, England. Artist; Film Technician; Poet. m. Rick Fester, 5 Oct. 1991, 2 d. *Education:* BA, English Literature and Film Studies, Carleton University, Ottawa, Canada, 1986. *Appointment:* Freelance Film Technician, 1987–. *Contributions to:* Amber; Marsh & Maple; Carleton Arts Review; Greens Magazine; Reach Magazine; White Wall Review; Teak International; Focus. *Address:* 305 Indian Grove, Toronto, Ontario M6P 2H6, Canada.

ATLAN, Liliane; b. 14 Jan. 1932, Montpellier, France. Writer; Poet; Dramatist. m. June 1952, divorced 1976, 1 s., 1 d. *Education:* Diploma, Philosophy, Sorbonne, University of Paris, 1953; Studies in Modern Literature, CAPES, 1960. *Publications:* Poetry: Lapsus, 1971; Bonheur mais sur quel ton le dire, 1996; Peuples d'argile, forêts d'etoiles, 2000. Plays: Monsieur Fugue ou le mal de terre, 1967; The Messiahs, 1969; The Little Car of Flames and Voices, 1971; The Musicians, the Migrants, 1976; Lessons in Happiness, 1982; An Opera for Terezin, 1997; The Red Seas, 1998; My Name is No, 1998; Monsieur Fugue, 2000. Other: Videotext; Books to be spoken aloud. *Honours:* Chevalier de l'Ordre des Arts et Lettres, 1984; Prix Villa Medicis, 1992; Prize, Radio SACD, 1999; Prix Mémoire de la Shoah, 1999. *Address:* 70 rue du Javelot, 75645 Paris Cédex 13, France.

ATRE, Madhav V., (M. Angelo); b. 4 Aug. 1938, Nasirabad, Pakistan. Educator (retd); Poet. m. Rekha Atre, 25 Feb. 1968, 1 s., 1 d. *Education:* Visharad, Hindi equivalent to BA, 1958; BA, 1963; B Ed, 1973; MA, English, 1979; PhD, Literature, International University of California, USA. *Appointments:* Clerk, 1956–64; Private Tutor, 1964–66; Teacher, English Medium Secondary School, 1967–80; Principal, English Medium Secondary School, 1981–96. *Publications:* Erotic Eloquence, 1993; Anguished Embers, 1994; Love Bird and Other Selected Poems, 1995; Voyage In Silence (Haiku), 1996; Silent Reach (Haiku), 1997. *Contributions to:* Anthologies and periodicals. *Honours:* Certificate of Merit, The Quest All-India Poetry Contest, 1993; Word Winged Award, International Socio-Literary Foundation, Chennai. *Memberships:* World Poetry Society, Chennai; Poetry Society, New Delhi; International Writers and Artists Asscn, USA; United Writers' Asscn, Chennai, fellow. *Address:* 11-5 The Sewa Samiti Nagar, Sion Koliwada, Mumbai 400 037, India.

ATWOOD, Margaret (Eleanor); b. 18 Nov. 1939, Ottawa, ON, Canada. Poet; Author; Critic. m. Graeme Gibson, 1 d. *Education:* BA, Victoria College, University of Toronto, 1961; MA, Radcliffe College, Cambridge, MA, 1962; Harvard University, 1962–63, 1965–67. *Appointments:* Teacher, University of British Columbia, 1964–65, Sir George Williams University, Montréal, 1967–68, University of Alberta, 1969–70, York University, 1971–72; Writer-in-Residence, University of Toronto, 1972–73, University of Alabama, Tuscaloosa, 1985, Macquarie University, Australia, 1987; Berg Chair, New

York University, 1986. *Publications:* Poetry: Double Persephone, 1961; The Circle Game, 1964; Kaleidoscopes Baroque, 1965; Talismans for Children, 1965; Speeches for Doctor Frankenstein, 1966; The Animals in That Country, 1968; The Journals of Susanna Moodie, 1970; Procedures for Underground, 1970; Oratorio for Sasquatch, Man and Two Androids, 1970; Power Politics, 1971; You Are Happy, 1974; Selected Poems, 1976; Marsh Hawk, 1977; Two-Headed Poems, 1978; True Stories, 1981; Notes Towards a Poem That Can Never Be Written, 1981; Snake Poems, 1983; Interlunar, 1984; Selected Poems II: Poems Selected and New, 1976–1986, 1986; Selected Poems 1966–1984, 1990; Margaret Atwood Poems 1965–1975, 1991; Morning in the Burned House, 1995. Fiction: The Edible Woman, 1969; Surfacing, 1972; Lady Oracle, 1976; Dancing Girls, 1977; Life Before Man, 1979; Bodily Harm, 1981; Encounters With the Element Man, 1982; Murder in the Dark, 1983; Bluebeard's Egg, 1983; Unearthing Suite, 1983; The Handmaid's Tale, 1985; Cat's Eye, 1988; Wilderness Tips, 1991; Good Bones, 1992; The Robber Bride, 1993; Alias Grace, 1996; The Blind Assassin, 2000. Non-Fiction: Survival: A Thematic Guide to Canadian Literature, 1972; Days of The Rebels 1815–1840, 1977; Second Words: Selected Critical Prose, 1982; The Oxford Book of Canadian Verse in English (ed.), 1982; The Best American Short Stories (ed. with Shannon Ravenel), 1989; Strange Things: The Malevolent North in Canadian Literature, 1995; Negotiating With the Dead: A Writer on Writing, 2002. *Contributions to:* Books in Canada; Canadian Literature; Globe and Mail; Harvard Educational Review; The Nation; New York Times Book Review; Washington Post. *Honours:* Guggenheim Fellowship, 1981; Companion of the Order of Canada, 1981; Fellow, Royal Society of Canada; Foreign Hon. Mem., American Acad. of Arts and Sciences, 1988; Order of Ontario, 1990; Centennial Medal, Harvard University, 1990; Commemorative Medal, 125th Anniversary of Canadian Confederation, 1992; Giller Prize, 1996; Author of the Year, Canadian Book Industry Award, 1997; Marian McFadden Memorial Lecturer, Indianapolis-Marion County Public Library Foundation, 1998; Booker Prize, 2000; Hon. degrees. *Memberships:* Writers' Union of Canada, pres., 1981–82; PEN International, pres., 1985–86. *Address:* McClelland & Stewart, 481 University Ave, Suite 900, Toronto, ON M5G 2E9, Canada.

AUBERT, Alvin (Bernard); b. 12 March 1930, Lutcher, LA, USA. Prof. of English Emeritus; Poet. m. (1) Olga Alexis, 1948, divorced, 1 d., (2) Bernardine Tenant, 1960, 2 d. *Education:* BA, Southern University, Baton Rouge, 1959; MA, University of Michigan, 1960; University of Illinois at Urbana-Champaign, 1963–64, 1966–67. *Appointments:* Instructor, 1960–62, Asst Prof., 1962–65, Assoc. Prof. of English, 1965–70, Southern University; Visiting Prof. of English, University of Oregon at Eugene, 1970; Assoc. Prof., 1970–74, Prof. of English, 1974–79, State University of New York at Fredonia; Founder-Ed., Obsidian magazine, 1975–85; Prof. of English, 1980–92, Prof. Emeritus, 1992–, Wayne State University, Detroit. *Publications:* Against the Blues, 1972; Feeling Through, 1975; South Louisiana: New and Selected Poems, 1985; If Winter Come: Collected Poems, 1994; Harlem Wrestler, 1995. *Honours:* Bread Loaf Writers Conference Scholarship, 1968; National Endowment for the Arts Grants, 1973, 1981; Co-ordinating Council of Literary Magazines Grant, 1979; Annual Callaloo Award, 1989. *Address:* 18234 Parkside Ave, Detroit, MI 48221, USA.

AUER, Father Benedict; b. 4 Nov. 1939, Chicago, IL, USA. Priest; Educator; Poet; Writer. *Education:* BSc, Humanities, Loyola University, Chicago, 1962; MA, History, Creighton University, 1964; MDiv, St Meinrad School of Theology, 1980; Doctor of Ministry in Christian Spirituality, San Francisco Theological Seminary, 1993. *Appointments:* Novitiate, 1976, Simple Profession, 1977, Lector, 1978, Acolyte, 1979, Solemn Vows, 1980, Deacon, 1980, Marmion Abbey, Aurora, IL; Priesthood, Annunciation Church, Aurora, Illnois, 1980; Various Pastoral assignments, IL, 1980–88; Dir of Campus Ministry, St Martin's College, Washington, 1988–94; Asst Prof. of Education, then Assoc. Prof., Adjunct in Religious Studies, Speech and Geography, St Martin's College, Lacey, Washington, 1988–; Certification as Campus Minister, National Campus Ministry Asscn, 1993–. *Publications:* Touching Fingers with God, 1986; Priestless People, 1990; Godspeak: Thirteen Characters in Search of an Author, 1993. *Contributions to:* Pastoral Life; New Catholic Review; Priest; Human Development; New Renaissance; American Educator; Momentum; Per Se, Japan; Poetry published in 200 magazines including Lutheran Journal; Inquirer; Croton Review; Blue Buildings; Wind; Daybreak, Canada; Gypsy, Germany; Kansas Quarterly; Bitterroot; Gryphon; Forum; Nexus; Windless Orchard; Short stories in various publications. *Honours:* Poem of the Year, Jubilee Press, FL, 1987; Hon. DH, London Institute for Applied Research, England, 1991; Citation and Award, Medallion of St Andrew, 1993. *Address:* Saint Martin's College/Abbey, Lacey, WA 98503, USA.

AUGUSTINE, Jane; b. 6 April 1931, Berkeley, CA, USA. Poet; Prof. (retd). m. (1) Anthony J Morley, 2 Feb. 1952, 3 s., 1 d., (2) Michael D Heller, 5 March 1979. *Education:* AB, cum laude, Bryn Mawr College, 1952; MA, Washington University, St Louis, Missouri, 1965; PhD, City University of New York, 1988. *Appointment:* Assoc. Prof. of English and Humanities, Pratt Institute, Brooklyn, New York (retd). *Publications:* Lit By the Earth's Dark Blood, 1977; Journeys, 1985; French Windows, 1998; Arbor Vitae, 2002; Transistory, 2002. *Contributions to:* MS; Aphra; Chrysalis; Pequod; Montemora, US; Staple Diet; Figs, UK. *Honours:* Fellowships in Poetry, New York State Council of the Arts, 1976, 1979; HD Fellowship in American Literature, Beinecke Library, Yale

University, 1994–95. *Membership:* International Asscn for Philosophy an Literature. *Address:* PO Box 1289, Stuyvesant Station, New York, NY 10009 USA.

AUGUSTUS, Reuben. See: HALEY, Patricia.

AURA, Alejandro; b. March 1944, México, DF, Mexico. Writer; Poet; Actor. m Carmen Boullosa, 1981, 2 s., 2 d. *Publications:* Poesia joven de Mexico, 1967 Alianza para vivir, 1969; Varios desnudes y dos docenas de naturaleza muertas, 1971; Volver a casa, 1974; Tambor interno, 1976; Hemisferio sur 1982; La patria vieja, 1986; Cinco veces, 1988; Poeta en la manana, 1991 *Contributions to:* Revista Mester; Revista Volatin; Revista de la Universida Nacional Autonoma de Mexico; Sabado; El Nacional; El Semanario d Novedades; La Journado Semanal; Los Universitarios; Revista Vuelta; an others. *Honours:* Grants, Centro Mexicano de Escritores, 1964; Premi Nacional de Poesia, 1973. *Address:* Tiepolo 20, Mixcoac, DF 03710, Mexico.

AUSALA, Margarita Bebrupe Palite; b. 13 July 1919, Smiltene, Latvia Poet; Writer; Ed.; Broadcaster. m. 8 March 1948, 1 s., 2 d. *Education* University of Riga. *Publications:* Poetry: Patiesibasvins, 1965; Agni ur asmeni, 1987. Other: Essays, 2 vols, 1955. *Contributions to:* Anthologies anc periodicals. *Honours:* Various honorary degrees, awards, and memberships *Memberships:* International PEN, fellow; International Poetry Society; United Poets Laureate International. *Address:* 243 Rockingham Rd, Corby Northamptonshire, England.

AUSSANT, Paule Jeannine Louise; b. 27 Oct. 1930, Saint-Vit, France Teacher (retd); Poet. m. Bernard Aussant, 17 May 1956, 2 s. *Education:* BA Teacher Training College, Paris, 1949; Sorbonne, University of Paris, 1952 School of Arts, Paris, 1960; Training in Pedagogy, Paris, 1970. *Publications.* Hirako, 1972; Krizehmurmur, 1980; Poémes d'amour, 1983; Rêve de l'aurore 1986; Testament de l'étrange Planète, 1991; Marcher sur les étoiles, 1993 Visions du routard, 1993; Adieu au Pacifique, 1966. *Contributions to:* Various publications. *Honours:* Many poetry prizes. *Address:* 13 rue du Pont, 25920 Mouthier, Hautepierre, France.

AUSTER, Paul; b. 3 Feb. 1947, Newark, NJ, USA. Writer; Poet. m. (1) Lydia Davis, 6 Oct. 1974, divorced 1979, 1 s., (2) Siri Hustvedt, 16 June 1981, 1 d. *Education:* BA, 1969, MA, 1970, Columbia University. *Appointment:* Lecturer, Princeton University, 1986–90. *Publications:* Fiction: City of Glass, 1985; Ghosts, 1986; The Locked Room, 1986; In the Country of Last Things, 1987; Moon Palace, 1989; The Music of Chance, 1990; Leviathan, 1992; Mr Vertigo, 1994; Timbuktu, 1999. Poetry: Unearth, 1974; Wall Writing, 1976; Fragments from Cold, 1977; Facing the Music, 1980; Disappearances: Selected Poems, 1988; I Thought My Father Was God, 2001. Non-Fiction: White Spaces, 1980; The Invention of Solitude, 1982; The Art of Hunger, 1982; Why Write?, 1996; Translations, 1996; Hand to Mouth, 1997. Editor: The Random House Book of Twentieth-Century French Poetry, 1982. Screenplays: Smoke, 1995; Blue in the Face, 1995; Lulu on the Bridge, 1998. *Contributions to:* Numerous periodicals. *Honours:* National Endowment for the Arts Fellowships, 1979, 1985; Chevalier, l'Ordre des Arts et des Lettres, France; Prix Medicis Étranger, 1993. *Membership:* PEN. *Address:* c/o Carol Mann Agency, 55 Fifth Ave, New York, NY 10003, USA.

AUTUMN. See: KNELL, William.

AVERY, Raymond Kenneth; b. 10 Feb. 1948, Dumfries, Scotland. Poet. m. Gloria, 27 Sept. 1969, 2 d. *Publication:* Self Flagellation, 1993. *Contributions to:* Purple Patch; Disability Arts Magazine; Pot Pourri; Long Islander; Iota; Poetry Nottingham; Kray Desire; Poetry Manchester; Doors; Helicon; Exile; People to People; Dial 174; Dandelion; Banshee. *Address:* 19 Bell Close, Chelmsley Wood, Birmingham B36 0PZ, England.

AVISON, Margaret (Kirkland); b. 23 April 1918, Galt, ON, Canada. Poet; Writer. *Education:* BA, English, Victoria College, University of Toronto, 1940; Indiana University; University of Chicago; Graduate Studies, University of Toronto, 1963–66. *Appointments:* Teacher, Scarborough College, University of Toronto, 1966–68; Writer-in-Residence, University of Western Ontario, 1972–73. *Publications:* Poetry: Winter Sun, 1960; The Dumbfounding, 1966; Sunblue, 1978; No Time, 1989; Margaret Avison: Selected Poems, 1991. Other: A Kind of Perseverance (lectures), 1993. *Honours:* Guggenheim Fellowship, 1956; Gov.-Gen.'s Awards for Poetry, 1960, 1990.

AWOONOR, Kofi; b. 13 March 1935, Wheta, Ghana. Educator; Diplomat; Poet; Writer. 4 s., 1 d. *Education:* BA, University of Ghana, 1960; MA, University of London, 1968; PhD in Comparative Literature, State University of New York at Stony Brook, 1973. *Appointments:* Research Fellow, Institute of American Studies, 1960–64; Dir, Ghana Ministry of Information Film Corpn, 1964–67; Poet-in-Residence, 1968, Asst Prof., 1968–72, Assoc. Prof., 1973–74, Chair, Dept of Comparative Literature, 1974–75, State University of New York; Senior Lecturer, Prof. of Literature, and Dean of the Faculty of Arts, University of Cape Coast, 1977–82; Ghana Ambassador to Brazil, 1984–88, Cuba, 1988–90, United Nations, 1990–. *Publications:* Rediscovery and Other Poems, 1964; Night of My Blood, 1971; This Earth, My Brother, 1972; Ride Me,

Memory, 1973; Guardian of the Sacred Word, 1974; Breast of the Earth (essays), 1974; The House by the Sea, 1978; Until the Morning After: Collected Poems 1963–1985, 1987; Ghana: A Political History, 1990; Comes the Voyage at Last, 1992; Latin American and Caribbean Notebook, 1993. *Honours:* Trans. Award, Columbia University, 1972; Ghana Book Award, 1978; Commonwealth Poetry Prize, 1989; Distinguished Authors Award, Ghana Asscn of Writers, 1992. *Address:* c/o Permanent Mission of Ghana to the United Nations, 19 E 47th St, New York, NY 10017, USA.

AYLEN, Leo (William); b. 15 Feb. 1935, Vryheid, South Africa. Writer; Poet. *Education:* MA, New College, Oxford, 1959; PhD, University of Bristol, 1962. *Appointments:* Producer, BBC TV, London, 1965–70; Poet-in-Residence, Fairleigh Dickinson University, USA, 1972–74; Hooker Distinguished Visiting Prof., McMaster University, Canada, 1982; Numerous appearances as a poet on radio and TV in the UK, USA, and South Africa. *Publications:* Greek Tragedy in the Modern World, 1964; Greece for Everyone, 1976; The Greek Theater, 1985. Poetry: Discontinued Design, 1969; I, Odysseus, 1971; Sunflower, 1976; Return to Zululand, 1980; Jumping-Shoes, 1983; Rhymoceros, 1989; Dancing the Impossible: Selected Poems, 1997. Play: Red Alert: This Is a God Warning, 1981. Children's Opera: The Apples of Youth, 1980. *Contributions to:* 70 anthologies. *Honours:* C Day-Lewis Fellowship, 1979–80; Runner-Up Prizewinner, Arvon International Competition, 1992; Royal Literary Fund Fellow, 1999–2002. *Memberships:* Poetry Society of Great Britain; Poetry Society of America; Writers Guild of Great Britain; Writers Guild of America. *Address:* 165B Bath Rd, Atworth, Melksham, Wiltshire SN12 8JL, England.

AYYANARAPPAN, Kavikkuil Pon; b. 5 May 1945, Arasur, India. Poet; Writer. m. Kamatchi, 6 June 1974, 1 s., 1 d. *Education:* BSc, 1974. *Publications:* Nava Manigal, 1985; Malaithendral, 1985; Kavimurasu, 1990. *Contributions to:* Newspapers and magazines. *Honours:* Several awards and prizes. *Memberships:* All India Tamil Writers Asscn; Federation of World Tamils; Tamil Poetry Asscn; World Congress of Poets, USA; World Literary Acad., founder-dir; World Tamil Poets Asscn. *Address:* E 15 D Postal Telegraphs, Staff Quarters, Anna Nagar, Chennai 600 040, India.

AZAD, Shamim; b. 11 Nov. 1954. Educator; Poet. m. Abul K Azad, 23 April 1972, 1 s., 1 d. *Education:* BA, 1972; MA, 1973. *Publications:* Bhalobashar Kabita, 1981; Sparsher Apekhaya, 1983; Hey Jubak, Tomar Bhabishyat, 1989. *Contributions to:* Overseas Correspondent, Bichitra (national weekly of Bangladesh); New Yorker. *Memberships:* National Education Advisory Board, Primary, Bangladesh; Bangla Acad., Dhaka, Bangladesh; Bangla Shahittayar Parishad, London; Bishwa Shahitya Kendra, Dhaka, Bangladesh. *Address:* 188 Perth Rd, Ilford, Essex IG2 6DZ, England.

AZOFEIFA, Isaac Felipe; b. 11 April 1909, Santo Domingo de Heredia, Costa Rica. Prof. Emeritus; Poet; Writer. m. Clemencia Camacho Mora, 4 Jan. 1936, 4 s., 2 d. *Education:* Pedagogical Institute of Chile, 1933. *Appointments:* Prof. of Literature, Psychology, and Education, 1943–79, Dir of the School of General Studies, 1972–79, Prof. Emeritus, 1980–, University of Costa Rica. *Publications:* Trunca Unidad, 1958; Vigilia en Pie de Muerte, 1961; Cancion, 1964; Estaciones, 1967; Dias y Territorios, 1969; Cima del Gozo, 1974; Cruce de Via, 1982; Ensayo Sobre la Palabra en sele discursos liricos, 1992. *Contributions to:* Various publications. *Honours:* Aquileo Echeverria National Prizes for Poetry, 1964, 1969, 1974; Joaquin Garcia Monge Prize for Cultural Journalism, 1972; Magon National Prize for Culture, 1980. *Memberships:* Several professional organizations. *Address:* Apdo 444-2050, San Pedro de Montes de Oca, Costa Rica.

AZPITARTE ROUSSE, Juan, (Juan Berekiz); b. 27 April 1959, Bilbao, Spain. Writer; Poet. *Education:* Graduated in Philosophy and Theology, University of Deurto, Bilbao. *Appointments:* Pres., Gerekiz Artistic Asscn; Founder-Mem., Graphologic Asscn in Basque Country. *Publications:* La Armonia y El Vitalismo, 1985; El Poeta y el Payaso, 1986; Poemas Raros, 1987; Mi Poesia Para Ti, 1988; Meditaciones en el asfalto, 1988; Sentimentios y Sonidos, 1988; A la Pintura, 1990. *Contributions to:* Gemma; Clarin; Mensajero; Redención; Bilbocio; Club CCC. *Honours:* Prize, Proyecto Hombre de Bizkaia, 1990; Patrocinado por la Asociación Artístiva Vizcaina. *Memberships:* Centro Cultural, Literario e Artistico de Gazeta de Felgueiras, Portugal; International Poetry, USA; Asociación Mundial de Escritores y Centro Cultural, Literario y Artistico Agustin Garcia Alonso-La Penorra 8, Vizcaya, Spain; Asociación Artistica Vizcaina, Spain. *Address:* Avda Zumalacarregui 119-9a C, 48007 Bilbao, Spain.

B

BACHAR, Gregory Paul; b. 3 Dec. 1964, Cheektowaga, New York, USA. Musician; Poet; Ed. *Education:* BA, English/American Studies, University of California, Los Angeles, 1987; MFA, English/Creative Writing, University of Massachusetts, Amherst, 1993. *Appointments:* Ed., Rowhouse Press, Jack Mackerel Magazine, 1992–; Creative Writing Instructor, University of Massachusetts, Amherst, 1992–93; Writing Instructor, Seattle Central, 1994; Curator, Jack Mackerel Art Gallery, Seattle, 1996–. *Publications:* Fragments, 1985; 47 Poems, 1994; The Cage Writings, 1995; Steuben's 47, 1996; Green Clown on a Black Cross, 1996; Permeke's Constant, 1998. *Contributions to:* Conduit; Old Crow; Hawaii Review; Kansas Quarterly; Takahe; Colorado North Review; Portlandia Review of Books. *Address:* P O Box 23134, Seattle, WA 98102, USA.

BADMAN, May Edith, (May Ivimy); b. 10 Nov. 1912, Greenwich, London, England. Poet. m. Raymond Frank Badman, 19 Oct. 1968, 1 s., 1 d. *Appointments:* Former Council Mem. and Hon. Treasurer, The Poetry Society; Founder-Organiser, Ver Poets, 1966–. *Publications:* Night is Another World, 1964; Midway This Path, 1966; Late Swings, 1980; Prayer Sticks, 1980; Parting the Leaves, 1984; Strawberries in the Salad, 1992; The Best Part of the Day, 1992. *Contributions to:* Many anthologies, magazines, and radio. *Honours:* Dorothy Tutin Award, 1983; Howard Sergeant Memorial Award, 1990. *Memberships:* Poetry Society; RSL; St Albans Art Society; Society of Women Writers and Journalists. *Address:* Haycroft, 61/63 Chiswell Green Lane, St Albans, Hertfordshire AL2 3AL, England.

BADOSA, Enrique; b. 16 March 1927, Barcelona, Spain. Writer; Poet. *Education:* Licentiate in Philosophy and Letters. *Appointments:* Literary Critic, El Noticiero Universal Newspaper, Barcelona; Literary Ed., Dept of Spanish, Plaza and Janes Publishing House, Barcelona. *Publications:* Mas alla del viento, 1956; Tiempo de esperar, tiempo de esperanza, 1959; Baladas para la paz, 1963; Arte poetica, 1968; En roman paladino, 1970; Historias en Venecia, 1971; Poesia, 1956–1971, 1973; Dad este escrito a las llamas, 1976; Mapa de Grecia, 1979; Cuadernos de barlovento, 1986; Epigramas confidenciales, 1989. *Contributions to:* ABC; El Noticiero Universal; La Esatfeta Literaria; Papeles de Son Armadans; Insula; Poesia Espanola; Poesia de Espana; Caracola; Cuadernos Hispanoamericanos; Agora; Alamo; Barcarola; Fablas; Camp de l'Arpa; Hora de Poesi; Anfora Nova. *Honours:* Francisco de Quevedo Prize for Poetry, 1986; Poetry Prize of City of Barcelona, 1989; Fastenrath Prize, Real Academia Espanola de la Lengua, 1992. *Memberships:* Asociacion Colegial de Escritores; Asociacion Prometeo de Poesia; Academia Iberoamericana de Poesia. *Address:* Marc Aureli 14, 08006 Barcelona, Spain.

BAILEY, Gordon; b. 22 Feb. 1936, Stockport, Cheshire, England. Chief Exec. of Charity; Poet. m. Corrine, 2 Aug. 1958, 1 s., 3 d. *Education:* BA, Honours, Pastoral Theology. *Publications:* Plastic World, 1971; Mothballed Religion, 1972; Patchwork Quill, 1975; Can a Man Change?, 1979; 100 Contemporary Christian Poets, 1983; I Want to Tell You How I Feel, God, 1983; Stuff and Nonsense, 1989; Mix and Match, 1999. *Address:* The Birches, 9 Wentworth Dr., Blackwell, Worcestershire B60 1BE, England.

BAILEY, Kevin Neil Leroy; b. 16 March 1954, Wallingford-on-Thames, Berkshire, England. Psychologist; Ed.; Poet. Divorced, 1 d. *Education:* Teacher's Certificate, Bulmershe College, University of Reading, 1976; BSc, Honours, Psychology, University of York, 1986; BA, Classics, Open University. *Appointments:* Founder, Day Dream Press; Ed. and Publisher, The Haiku Quarterly. *Publications:* Country Poems 1974–1979, 1979; Blue Ornaments, 1980; Anglo-Saxon Poems, 1980; Sappho, 1983; Poems and Translations, 1987. *Contributions to:* Many anthologies, newspapers, and periodicals. *Memberships:* British Haiku Society; Poetry Society of Japan. *Address:* 39 Exmouth St, Kingshall, Swindon, Wiltshire SN1 3PU, England.

BAILEY, Louise Slagle; b. 26 June 1930, Gainesville, FL, USA. Poet. m. Grayson A Bailey Jr, 1961, divorced, 1 d. *Education:* BA, Honours, 1951, MA, 1953, University of Florida; Doctoral work, University of Tennessee, 1955–59. *Appointments:* Instructor, University of Tennessee, 1959–61; Instructor to Prof. of English Emeritus, 1961–87, Marshall University. *Contributions to:* Many anthologies, journals, and reviews. *Memberships:* Guyandotte Poets Society; West Virginia Poetry Society; West Virginia Writers. *Address:* 1205 Ninth Ave, Huntingdon, WV 25701, USA.

BAIRD, Dorothy Anne Scott; b. 5 March 1960, Edinburgh, Scotland. Teacher; Poet. m. John Philip Shinton, 6 Sept. 1986, 1 s., 2 d. *Publications:* In the Gold of Flesh, 1990; With My Heart in My Mouth (anthology), 1994. *Contributions to:* Acumen; Distaff; Grand Piano; Giant Steps; Spokes; Resurgence. *Membership:* National Poetry Society. *Address:* 117 Lanark Rd W, Currie, Midlothian EH14 5N2, England.

BAISHNAWA, Pradyumna Das; b. 1 April 1928, Saraipali, India. Writer; Poet. m. 10 May 1948, 1 s., 4 d. *Education:* MA, PhD, Ratna, Vidya Vachaspat (Hindi) Srhitya Visharad, Shikshua Visharad. *Publications:* Orissa Ki Adiwas Sanskriti; Mati Ke Bol; Kavita Chowrahe Par; Kabya Chinta; Shabda Bolate Hain; Kavitanjali. *Contributions to:* Bhasha; Rashtra Bharti; Bharat Bharati Madhumati; Shriraja; Harigandha; Rashtra Bhasha; Akshara; Navanit; Anchal Bharati; Karmev Jayate; Punjab Keshari; Nav Vharat; Nav Bharat Times Keral Gharati; Sahitya Sandesh. *Honours:* Pres.'s Award, Central Hindi Directorate, New Delhi, 1995; Award, Hindi Sahitya Sammelan Prayag, 1996; Award, Madhya Pradesh Hindi Bhavan Bhopal, 1996. *Memberships.* Rashtra Bhasha Prachar Gamiti Wardha; Raghtra Shasha Prachar Samiti Hindi Bhawan Bhopal; Hindi Sahitya Sammelan Prayag. *Address:* Rashitra Bhasha Kutir Pajharapali Raipur 493558, India.

BAKER, David (Anthony); b. 27 Dec. 1954, Bangor, Maine, USA. Prof. of English; Poet; Ed. m. Ann Townsend, 19 July 1987. *Education:* BSE, 1976, MA, 1977, Central Missouri State University; PhD, University of Utah, 1983. *Appointments:* Poetry Ed., 1980–81, Ed.-in-Chief, 1981–83, Quarterly West; Visiting Asst Prof., Kenyon College, 1983–84; Asst Ed., 1983–89, Poetry Ed., Consulting Poetry Ed., 1989–94, Poetry Ed., 1994–, Kenyon Review; Asst Prof. of English, 1984–90, Assoc. Prof. of English, 1990–97, Prof. of English, 1997, Denison University; Visiting Telluride Prof., Cornell University, 1985; Contributing Ed., The Pushcart Prize, 1992–; Visiting Assoc. Prof., University of Michigan, 1996; Many poetry readings. *Publications:* Poetry: Looking Ahead, 1975; Rivers in the Sea, 1977; Laws of the Land, 1981; Summer Sleep, 1984; Haunts, 1985; Sweet Home, Saturday Night, 1991; Echo for an Anniversary, 1992; After the Reunion, 1994; Holding Katherine, 1997; Heresy and the Ideal: On Contemporary Poetry, 2000; Changeable Thunder, 2001. Editor: The Soil is Suited to the Seed: A Miscellany in Honor of Paul Bennett, 1986; Meter in English: A Critical Engagement, 1996. *Contributions to:* Anthologies and periodicals. *Honours:* Margaret Bridgman Scholar of Poetry, Bread Loaf, 1982; Outstanding Writer, Pushcart Press, 1982, 1984, 1985, 1986, 1990, 1991, 1994, 1995; James Wright Prize for Poetry, Mid-American Review, 1983; National Endowment for the Arts Fellowship, 1985–86; Bread Loaf Poetry Fellow, 1989; Pushcart Prize, 1992; Mary Carolyn Davies Award, Poetry Society of America, 1995; Thomas B Fordham Endowed Chair in Creative Writing, Denison University, 1996; Ohio Arts Council Fellowship, 2000; Guggenheim Fellowship, 2000–01. *Memberships:* Associated Writing Programs; MLA; National Book Critics Circle; Poetry Society of America; Poets and Writers. *Address:* 135 Granview Rd, Granville, OH 43023, USA.

BAKER, Houston A(lfred Jr); b. 22 March 1943, Louisville, KY, USA. Prof. of English and of Human Relations; Writer; Ed.; Poet. m. Charlotte Pierce-Baker, 10 Sept. 1966, 1 s. *Education:* BA, magna cum laude, Howard University, 1965; MA, 1966, PhD, 1968, University of California at Los Angeles; PhD Studies, University of Edinburgh, 1967–68. *Appointments:* Instructor, Howard University, 1966; Instructor, 1968–69, Asst Prof. of English, 1969–70, Yale University; Assoc. Prof. and Mem., Center for Advanced Studies, 1970–73, Prof. of English, 1973–74, University of Virginia; Prof. of English, 1974–, Dir, Afro-American Studies Program, 1974–77, Albert M Greenfield Prof. of Human Relations, 1982–, Dir, Center for the Study of Black Literature and Culture, 1987–, University of Pennsylvania; Fellow, Center for Advanced Study in the Behavioral Sciences, 1977–78, National Humanities Center, 1982–83; Bucknell Distinguished Scholar, University of Vermont, 1992; Berg Visiting Prof. of English, New York University, 1994; Fulbright 50th Anniversary Distinguished Fellow, Brazil, 1996; Senior Fellow, School of Criticism and Theory, Cornell University, 1996–2002. *Publications:* A Many-Colored Coat of Dreams: The Poetry of Countee Cullen, 1974; The Journey Back: Issues in Black Literature and Criticism, 1980; Blues, Ideology, and Afro-American Literature: A Vernacular Theory, 1984; Modernism and Harlem Renaissance, 1987; Afro-American Poetics: Revisions of Harlem and the Black Aesthetic, 1988; Workings of the Spirit: A Poetics of Afro-American Women's Writing, 1991; Black Studies, Rap, and the Academy, 1993. Poetry: No Matter Where You Travel, You Still Be Black, 1979; Spirit Run, 1982; Blues Journeys Home, 1985. Editor: Various Books. *Contributions to:* Scholarly books and journals. *Honours:* Alumni Award for Distinguished Achievement in Literature and the Humanities, Howard University, 1985; Distinguished Writer of the Year Award, Middle Atlantic Writers Assocn, 1986; Creative Scholarship Award, College Language Assocn of America, 1988; Pennsylvania Governor's Award for Excellence in the Humanities, 1990; Several hon. doctorates. *Memberships:* College Language Assocn; English Institute, board of supervisors, 1989–91; MLA, pres., 1992. *Address:* c/o Center for the Study of Black Literature and Culture, University of Pennsylvania, Philadelphia, PA 19104, USA.

BAKER, June Frankland; b. 27 May 1935, Schenectady, New York, USA. Teacher; Poet. m. David A Baker, 6 July 1962, 2 d. *Education:* AB, State University of New York, Albany, 1957; MA, University of Pennsylvania, 1958.

Appointments: Teacher, 1958–64; Writer, 1964–; Substitute Teacher, Journalism, Columbia Basin College, 1987. *Publication:* Sand Tracks (co-ed., anthology), 1976. *Contributions to:* Christian Science Monitor; Bellingham Review; Berkeley Poetry Review; Blue Unicorn; Commonweal; Crab Creek Review; Crosscurrents, A Quarterly; Gulf Stream Magazine; Kaleidoscope; Kansas Quarterly; Louisville Review; Southern Poetry Review; Three Rivers Poetry Journal; Writers Forum; Poetry Northwest; Poet Lore; Hiram Poetry Review; Calliope; Flyway; Artful Dodge; Woven on the Wind (anthology). *Address:* 614 Lynnwood Ct, Richland, WA 99352, USA.

BAKER, Winona Louise; b. 18 March 1924, Saskatchewan, BC, Canada. Poet. m. Arthur Baker, 9 May 1945, 3 s., 1 d. *Education:* Teaching degree. *Publications:* Clouds Empty Themselves, 1987; Not So Scarlet a Woman, 1987; Moss-hung Trees, 1992; Beyond the Lighthouse, 1992; Even a Stone Breathes, 2000. *Contributions to:* Numerous anthologies and other publications. *Honours:* Shikishi for Haiku in English, 1986; Expo Japan Book Award for Haiku, 1986; Foreign Minister's Prize, World Haiku Contest, 1989; Fundatia Nipponica Societatea Romana de Haiku Commemorative Medal, 1994; First Place, English section, International Hoshi-To-Nori Tanka Contest, 2001. *Memberships:* Canadian, American, European, and Japanese Haiku Asscn; Federation of British Columbia Writers; League of Canadian Poets; Tanka Society of America. *Address:* 606 First St, Nanaimo, BC V9R 1Y9, Canada.

BALABAN, John; b. 2 Dec. 1943, Philadelphia, Pennsylvania, USA. Prof. of English; Writer; Poet; Trans. m. 28 Nov. 1970, 1 d. *Education:* BA, Pennsylvania State University, 1966; AM, Harvard University, 1967. *Appointments:* Instructor in Linguistics, University of Can Tho, South Viet Nam, 1967–68; Instructor, 1970–73, Asst Prof., 1973–76, Assoc. Prof., 1976–82, Prof., 1982–92, of English, Pennsylvania State University; Prof. of English, Dir of Creative Writing, University of Miami, 1992–2000; Prof. of English and Poet-in-Residence, North Carolina State University, Raleigh, 2000–. *Publications:* Vietnam Poems, 1970; Vietnamese Folk Poetry (ed. and trans.), 1974; After Our War (poems), 1974; Letters From Across the Sea (poems), 1978; Ca Dao Vietnam: A Bilingual Anthology of Vietnamese Folk Poetry (ed. and trans.), 1980; Blue Mountain (poems), 1982; Coming Down Again (novel), 1985; The Hawk's Tale (children's fiction), 1988; Three Poems, 1989; Vietnam: The Land We Never Knew, 1989; Words for My Daughter (poems), 1991; Remembering Heaven's Face (memoir), 1991; Vietnam: A Traveler's Literary Companion (ed. with Nguyen Qui Duc), 1996; Locusts at the Edge of Summer: New and Selected Poems and Translations, 1997; Spring Essence: The Poetry of Ho Xuan Huong (trans. and ed.), 2000. *Contributions to:* Anthologies, books, scholarly journals and periodicals. *Honours:* National Endowment for the Humanities Younger Humanist Fellow, 1971–72; Lamont Selection, Acad. of American Poets, 1974; Finalist, National Book Award, 1975, 1997; Fulbright-Hays Senior Lectureship in Romania, 1976–77; Steaua Prize, Romanian Writers Union, 1978; National Endowment for the Arts Fellowships, 1978, 1985; Fulbright Distinguished Visiting Lectureship in Romania, 1979; Vaptsarov Medal, Union of Bulgarian Writers, 1980; National Poetry Series Book Selection, 1990; Pushcart Prize XV, 1990; William Carlos Williams Award, 1997. *Memberships:* American Literary Trans Asscn, pres., 1994–97; National Endowment for the Arts Trans. Panel, chair, 1993–94. *Address:* Dept of English, Box 8105, North Carolina State University, Raleigh, NC 27695, USA.

BALACHANDRAN, Kannaiya, (Crescent Virgo); b. 15 Sept. 1951, Chidambaram, India. Reader in English; Poet. m. Ponni, 3 Sept. 1989, 1 s. *Education:* BA, English, 1971, MA, English, 1974, MPhil, English, 1984, Annamalai University. *Appointments:* Lecturer, 1979–89, Reader, 1989–, in English, Annamalai University. *Publications:* Annai Oru Agal Vilakku, 1975; Longing for You, 1986; For a Future and Heart's Chair, 1988; Oru Puthiya Kathai, 1995; Rusthiyin Veera Deerangal, 1995. *Contributions to:* Magazines and reviews. *Honours:* Several awards, including International Poet of Merit, 1995–96. *Memberships:* American Studies Research Centre; Indian Asscn for American Studies; International Society of Poets; World Acad. of Arts and Culture. *Address:* c/o Annamalai University, Annamalai Nagar 608002, India.

BALAZS, Mary (Elizabeth Webber); b. 2 Aug. 1939, Lakewood, Ohio, USA. Assoc. Prof. of English; Poet. m. Gabriel George Balazs, 18 June 1960, 2 s. *Education:* BA, 1960, MA, 1962, PhD, 1965, Pennsylvania State University. *Appointments:* Assoc. Prof. of English, Virginia Military Institute, 1967–; Poets-in-Schools, National Endowment for the Arts, 1974–. *Publications:* The Voice of Thy Brother's Blood, 1976; The Stones Refuse Their Peace, 1979; Out of Darkness, 1991. *Other:* I That Am Ever Stranger (assoc. ed.), 1974; Puddingstone (ed.), 1975; Touching This Earth (co-ed.), 1977. *Contributions to:* Anthologies, reviews, and magazines. *Honours:* Irene Leache Literary Awards, 1980, 1985; Kansas Quarterly/Kansas Arts Commission Award, 1987; Sam Ragan Poetry Prize, 1987; First Place, 1990, first Honourable Mention, 1994, Third Place, 1995, Jim Wayne Miller Poetry Contest; First and second Place, Kate M Reis Poetry Contest, 1995. *Memberships:* Poetry Society of Virginia; Virginia Asscn of Teachers of English; Virginia Writers' Club. *Address:* 118 W 28th St, Buena Vista, VA 24416, USA.

BALCON, Jill. See: DAY-LEWIS, Jill Angela Henriette.

BALDERSTON, Jean Merrill; b. 29 Aug. 1936, Providence, RI, USA. Psychotherapist; Poet. m. David Chase Balderston, 1 June 1957. *Education:* BA, University of Connecticut, 1957; MA, 1965, DEd, 1968, Teachers College, Columbia University. *Appointments:* Douglass College for Women, Rutgers University, Mountclair State College, New Jersey, Hunter and Queen's Colleges, City University of New York and Teachers College, Columbia University, 1965–70; Psychotherapist in private practice, 1968–. *Contributions to:* Anthologies, reviews and magazines. *Honour:* Co-winner, Writer Magazine / Emily Dickinson Award, Poetry Society of America, 2000. *Memberships:* American Psychological Asscn; Poetry Society of America; American Asscn for Marital and Family Therapy; Emily Dickinson International Society; Acad. of American Poets. *Address:* 1225 Park Ave, New York, NY 10128, USA.

BALDWIN, Michael; b. 1 May 1930, Gravesend, Kent, England. Author; Poet. *Education:* Open Scholar, 1949, Senior Scholar, 1953, St Edmund Hall, Oxford. *Appointments:* Asst Master, St Clement Danes Grammar School, 1955–59; Lecturer, Senior Lecturer, Principal Lecturer, Head of English and Drama Dept, Whitelands College, 1959–78. *Publications:* The Silent Mirror, 1951; Voyage From Spring, 1956; Grandad with Snails, 1960; Death on a Live Wire, 1962; How Chas Egget Lost His Way in a Creation Myth, 1967; Hob, 1972; Buried God, 1973; Snook, 1980; The Way to Write Poetry, 1982; King Horn, 1983; The River and the Downs, 1984; Exit Wounds, 1988; Holofernes, 1989; Ratgame, 1991; The Rape of Oc, 1993; The First Mrs Wordsworth, 1996; Dark Lady, 1998. *Contributions to:* Listener; Encounter; New Statesman; Texas Review; BBC Wildlife Magazine; Outposts. *Honours:* Rediffusion Prize, 1970; Cholmondeley Award, 1984; Fellow, RSL, 1985. *Memberships:* Vice-Chair., Arvon Foundation, 1974–90; Chair., Arvon Foundation at Lumb Bank, 1980–89; CWA; The Athenaeum; The Colony Room. *Address:* 35 Gilbert Rd, Bromley, Kent BR1 3QP, England.

BALK, Christianne; b. 25 Aug. 1952, Oswego, New York, USA. Teacher; Writer; Poet. m. 24 Aug. 1985, 1 d. *Education:* BA, Biology, Grinnell College, 1974; MA, English, MFA, Creative Writing, University of Iowa. *Publications:* Bindweed, 1986; Desiring Flight, 1995. *Contributions to:* New Yorker; Harper's; Crazyhorse; Country Journal; Sonora Review; Pequod; Poetry Northwest; Missouri Review; Cutbank; Minnesota Monthly; Alaska Today; Iowa Journal of Literature Studies; Bellingham Review; Grinnell Magazine; Heartland; New Republic; Ploughshares. *Honours:* Walt Whitman Award, Acad. of American Poets, 1985; Ingram Merrill Foundation Writing Grant, 1988; Verna Emery Award, Purdue University Press, 1995. *Address:* PO Box 15633, Seattle, WA 98115, USA.

BALL, Frank; b. 28 Sept. 1935, Bloxwich, Staffordshire, England. Poet. m. 15 March 1958, 2 s., 1 d. *Appointments:* Soldier, Grenadier Guards, 1953–57; Fire Officer, 1964–87. *Publications:* Fire & Thought, 1983; Verse on Fire, 1985; Fire Our Dreams, 1987; Cats in the Grass, 1989; These Parkinson Times, 1990; Half Penny Pride, 1991; Poets Ghost, 1992. *Contributions to:* Fire Service Magazines; Parkinsons Disease Society Newsletter. *Honour:* First Prize, Young Parkinsons Society, 1990. *Memberships:* Poetry Society; Betjeman Society. *Address:* Allandale, Walsall Rd, Muckley Corner, Lichfield, Staffordshire WS14 0BP, England.

BALL, Richard; b. 25 Dec. 1919, Knighton, Powys, Wales. Poet; Literary Critic; Publisher. m., deceased 2001, 1 d., deceased 1965. *Education:* Advanced French (Army), North Western Polytechnic College, Kentish Town, London, 1938–39; Monastery College, Ampleforth, 1942. *Appointments:* Professional Soldier, First Battalion Grenadier Guards, 1938–46; War Service, Europe; Government Service, 1946–75; Contributing Ed., The Pembroke Magazine, North Carolina, USA, 20 years; Reviewer, The Plowman, Ontario, Canada, 10 years; Publisher. *Publications:* The Last Voyage of the Titanic, 1968; Avalon One, 1968; Avalon Two, 1969; Avalon Three, 1969; In Memory of Dylan Thomas, 1969; Chain, 1974; Silhouette of an Artist Walking, 1974; Mask of Aeschylus, 1981; Parable of the Man-Child, 1988; Anabase en Retard, 1991; Last Ten from the Gulag, 1992; Selected Poems 1933–1993, 1994; Hallowed Journey: New and Selected Poems, 1997; Wife Sleeping (In Memoriam Dorothy Jean), 2001; Homage to the Confessions of St Augustine and Other Poems, 2002. *Contributions to:* Many magazines, journals, newspapers and anthologies. *Honours:* Award Winner, Keats Poetry Prize, London, 1972, 1973; First Prize, An Ode-Prometheus Re-Incarnated, Shelley Society of New York International, 1976; First Prize, Dodman Press Poemcard Competition, 1978; First Prize, 1978, third Prize, 1979, Michael Johnson Memorial Awards International; First Prize, The Plowman Open, 1990; First Prize, Voltage, Crewe and Nantwich International, 1992; Several Diplomas for Excellence, Scottish National Opens, including United Kingdom Section, 1995; Diploma Book Award, Scottish National Open Poetry Competition, 1997–98. *Memberships:* Life Mem., Ver Poets Poetry Society, St Albans. *Address:* Llwyn Huan, Llansantffraid, Ym Mechain, Powys SY22 6AA, North Wales.

BALLARD, Juliet Lyle Brooke; b. 6 Feb. 1913, USA. Poet; Writer; Ed. *Education:* AB, Randolph-Macon Woman's College, 1934; Certificate of Social Case Work, Richmond Professional Institute, 1938. *Appointments:* Assoc. Ed., Asscn for Research and Enlightenment Journal, 1966–70, Asscn for Research and Enlightenment Children's Magazine, 1970; Ed., Treasure Grove, 1971–73.

Publications: Poetry: Under a Tropic Sun, 1945; Winter Has Come, 1945; The Ballad of the Widow's Flag, 1956. Other: The Hidden Laws of Earth, 1979; Treasures From Earth's Storehouse, 1980; The Art of Living, 1982, new edn as Unto the Hills, 1987. *Address:* 2217 Wake Forest St, Virginia Beach, VA 23451, USA.

BALLARD-HARVEY, Margie; b. 12 July 1910, Grand Saline, Texas, USA. Poet. m. W F Harvey, 1933. *Education:* Graduated, Kaufman School, 1930. *Contributions to:* Various anthologies, including: A Treasury of Famous Poems, 1998. *Honours:* Golden Poet Awards, 1985–89; Ed.'s Choice Award, National Library of Poetry, 1995; Award of Recognition for Outstanding Achievement in Poetry, Famous Poets Society, 1998. *Memberships:* International Clover Asscn; Poetry Society of Texas, Life Mem., 1997; World Literary Acad. *Address:* 205 Water St, Seagoville, TX 75159, USA.

BALLEM, John Bishop; b. 2 Feb. 1925, New Glasgow, NS, Canada. Lawyer; Writer; Poet. m. Grace Louise Flavelle, 31 Aug. 1951, 2 s., 1 d. *Education:* BA, 1946, MA, 1948, LLB, 1949, Dalhousie University; LLM, Harvard University, 1950. *Appointments:* Senior and founding Partner, Ballem MacInnes law firm; Queen's Counsel, 1966. *Publications:* Fiction: The Devil's Lighter, 1973; The Dirt Scenario, 1974; The Judas Conspiracy, 1976, new edn as Alberta Alone, 1981; The Moon Pool, 1978; Sacrifice Play, 1981; The Marigot Run, 1983; The Oilpatch Empire, 1985; Death Spiral, 1989; The Barons, 1991; Manchineel, 2000. Poetry: Lovers and Friends, 2000. Non-Fiction: The Oil and Gas Lease in Canada, 1973. *Contributions to:* Various publications. *Honour:* Hon. Doctor of Laws, University of Calgary, 1993. *Memberships:* Calgary Writers' Asscn; Crime Writers of Canada; International Bar Asscn; Law Society of Alberta; Writers' Guild of Alberta; Writers' Union of Canada. *Address:* 350 Seventh Ave SW, Suite 1800, Calgary, AB T2P 3NP, Canada.

BALLENTINE, Lee (Kenney); b. 4 Sept. 1954, Teaneck, NJ, USA. Poet; Writer; Publisher; Ed. m. Jennifer Moore, 20 Aug. 1983, 1 s. *Education:* Harvey Mudd College, 1972–73; University of California at San Diego, 1973; New Mexico State University, 1974; University of Colorado, 1974–75; BSc, State University of New York at Albany, 1976; Postgraduate Studies, University of Colorado, 1976–77, University of California at Berkeley, 1977–78. *Appointments:* Publisher, Ocean View Press, 1981–89, Ocean View books, 1989–; Co-founder and Pres., Ocean View Technical Publication, 1989–91, Professional Book Center, 1991–. *Publications:* Directorial Information, 1981; Basements in the Music Box (poems), 1986; Poly: New Speculative Writing (ed.), 1989; Dream Protocois (poems), 1992; Phase Language (poems), 1995. *Contributions to:* Anthologies and periodicals. *Honours:* Winner, 1989, Finalist, 1993, Readercon Small Press Book Award; Best Scholarly-Limited Book, 1989, Certificate of Merit, 1995, Bookbuilders West; Anatomy of Wonder Best Book, 1995. *Memberships:* American Book Producers Asscn; Bookbuilders West; PEN West; Rocky Mountain Book Publishers Asscn; Science Fiction Poetry Asscn; SFWA; United States Chess Federation. *Address:* Professional Book Center, PO Box 102650, Denver, CO 8-350, USA. *E-mail:* leebal@sni.net.

BALON, Brett John Steven, (Steve Johnson, John Peterson); b. 26 April 1953, Regina, Saskatchewan, Canada. Man.; Poet. *Education:* BA, Honours, Anthropology, Champion College, CDP, 1987, University of Regina; MLS, University of Western Ontario, 1978; CRM, Institute of Certified Records Managers, Prairie Village, KS, 1991; PhD, Information Science, Greenwich University, Hilo, HI. *Appointments:* Senior Branch Supervisor, Southeast Regional Library, 1978–82; Records Management Supervisor, 1982–83; Record Systems Co-ordinator, 1983–88, 1989–90, 1991–, Systems Liaison Officer for Corporate Services, 1988–89, Acting Man., Office Systems, 1990–91, City of Regina; Chair., Board of Dirs, Coreau Books, 1987–88, 1992–93. *Publications:* Anthologies: 100% Cracked Wheat, 1983; Heading Out: The New Saskatchewan Poets, 1986. *Contributions to:* Carillon; Fort Sanity VII; Freelance; Grain; NeWest Review; New Quarterly; Perspectives; Queen's Quarterly; Western People. *Memberships:* Saskatchewan Writers Guild, pres., 1983–84; Western Writers Federation, pres., 1983–84; Weyburn Writers Group, co-founder, 1980, pres., 1980–82.

BAMBER, Juliette Madelaine; b. 21 Aug. 1930, Tidworth, England. Poet; Writer; Occupational Therapist; Counsellor. m. Donald Liddle, 1957, divorced 1995, 2 s. *Education:* Graduated, Psychology, Birkbeck College, 1960. *Publications:* Breathing Space, 1991; On the Edge, 1993; Altered States, 1996; Touch Paper, 1996; The Ring of Words, 1996; The Wasting Game, 1997; The Long Pale Corridor, 1998; Flying Bird, 2000. *Honours:* Blue Nose Poet of the Year, 1998; Houseman Prize, 2000. *Address:* 9 Western Rd, East Finchley, London N2 9JB, England.

BAN, Eva. See: MARTINOVICH BAN, Eva Maria.

BANARASI, Das; b. 16 Oct. 1955, Akorhi, Mirzapur, India. Teacher; Poet. m. Vimala Devi, 10 March 1972, 1 s. *Education:* Sahityacharya (Equivalent to MA in Sanskrit), 1982; BTC, 1988; MA, Hindi Literature, 1993. *Appointments:* Asst Teacher, Government Basic School, Mirzapur, India. *Publications:* Sri Hanumad Vandana, 1982; Sri Vindhyavasinicharitamrit, 1989; Sriashtabhujakathamanjari, 1991; Paryavarankaumudi, 1993; Utsarg, 1995; Hymn to Lord (Hanuman), 1995; Gandhari, 1996; Adyatan, 1997; Silver Poems,

1998. *Contributions to:* Poet International, Anthologised in Poems 96, Worl Poetry, 1996–2000. *Honours:* Sanskrit Literature Award, Uttar Prades] Government Sanskrit Acad., 1995; Gram Ratna Award by Gram Panchaya Akorhi, Mirzapur, 1996; Winged Word Award, International Socio-Literar Foundation, 1997. *Address:* s/o Srimolai, Village-Post Akorhi, District Mirzapur 231307, UP, India.

BANDYOPADHYAY, Prayag, (B. Brayag); b. 19 April 1945, India. Educator Poet. m. Mitali, 16 April 1984, 1 d. *Education:* MA. *Appointments:* Lecturer 1969–74; Senior Asst Prof., 1974–. *Publications:* Prelude; Summer Thoughts Shadows in a Subway; Selected Poems; The Highway Penguins; The Blue Threads; The Voice of a Terror; The Words Upside Down. *Contributions to* Newspapers and journals. *Honours:* First Prize, Fifth World Congress of Poets 1981; Mentioned as Poet Extraordinary in Tokyo; Hon. DLitt. *Membership* Asian Poetry Centre, chair. *Address:* 357/1/12/1, Prince Anwar Shah Rd Calcutta 68, India.

BANG, Mary-Jo; b. 22 Oct. 1946, Waynesville, Missouri, USA. Writing Teacher; Photographer; Poet. 2 s. *Education:* BA, Sociology and English 1972, summa cum laude, MA, 1975, Northwestern University; School of Ar Institute of Chicago, 1984–86; BA, Distinction, Polytechnic of Central London 1989. *Appointments:* Instructor, Dept of English, 1991–, Liberal Arts Dept 1992–, Columbia College, Chicago. *Publication:* Whatever You Desire (ed.) 1990. *Contributions to:* Anthologies and journals. *Honours:* Third Place, Jo Anne Hirshfield Memorial Poetry Prize, 1990; Third Place, The Muse Inc Eighth Annual Poetry Prize, 1990. *Address:* 4247 N Hermitage 1A, Chicago IL 60613, USA.

BANGERTER, Michael; b. Brighton, England. Actor; Playwright; Lecturer. Tutor, Open College of the Arts; Poet. m. Katya Wyeth, 8 May 1971, 1 s., 1 d. *Education:* Graduate Diploma, RADA, Teaching Certificate; MA, Lancaster. *Appointments:* Actor in many television, film and theatre prooductions; Playwright in theatre and radio; Reviewer for various magazines. *Publications:* A Far Line of Hills, 1996; Freezing the Frame, 2001; Eyelines, 2002. *Contributions to:* Envoi; Pause; Iota; Blithe Spirit; Pennine Platform; New Hope International Writing; Others. *Honour:* Award Winner, Kent and Sussex National Open Competition, 1991. *Memberships:* National Poetry Foundation; British Haiku Society. *Address:* Botriphnie Stables, Drummuir, Keith, Banffshire AB55 5JE, England.

BANKS, Brian (Robert); b. 4 Oct. 1956, Carshalton, Surrey, England. Teacher; Writer; Poet. 1 s., 2 d. *Education:* Westminister College; Middlesex Polytechnic. *Publications:* The Image of J-K Huysmans, 1990; Phantoms of the Belle Epoque, 1993; Atmosphere and Attitudes, 1993; Life and Work of Bruno Schulz, 2000. *Contributions to:* Books and journals. *Memberships:* Société de J-K Huysmans, Paris; 1890's Society. *Address:* c/o 4 Meretune Ct, Martin Way, Morden, Surrey SM4 4AN, England.

BANKS, David; b. 10 Oct. 1943, Newcastle, England (British/French citizen). University Lecturer; Poet. m. Christiane Ganchou, 7 July 1973, 2 d. *Education:* BA, 1975, MA, 1979, University of Cambridge; Licence, 1978, Maitrise, 1979, DEA, 1980, Doctorat, 1983, Université de Nantes, France; HDR, Université de Bordeaux 2, 1999. *Appointments:* Exec. Officer, British Civil Service, 1969–72; Asst Lecturer, University of Mosul, Iraq, 1975–76; Lecturer, ENSM, Nantes, 1977–81; Asst, 1981–88, Maitre de Conferences, 1988–99, Prof., 1999–, Université de Bretagne Occidentale, Brest, France. *Publications:* Broken Ice, 1975; The Ones the Censor Didn't See, 1977; Death and Ever After, 1987; Vole File, 1995. *Contributions to:* Ludd's Mill; Ore; Krax; Eureka; Out of Sight; Little Word Machine; Bogg; Star West; Windless Orchard; Poetry North East; Grapeshot; Trends; Pacific Quarterly; Sepia; Iron; Oasis; Orbis. *Address:* 2 Rue des Saules, 29217 Plougonvelin, France. *E-mail:* david.banks@univ-brest.fr.

BARAKA, Amiri. See: JONES, (Everett) LeRoi.

BARAŃCZAK, Stanisław; b. 13 Nov. 1946, Poznań, Poland. Prof. of Polish Language and Literature; Poet; Writer; Ed.; Trans. m., 1 s., 1 d. *Education:* MA, 1969, PhD, 1973, Adam Mickiewicz University, Poznań. *Appointments:* Asst Prof., Adam Mickiewicz University, 1969–77, 1980; Co-founder and mem., KOR, human rights group, 1976–81; Blacklisted for political reasons, 1977–80; Assoc. Prof. of Slavic Languages and Literatures, 1981–84, Alfred Jurzykowski Prof. of Polish Language and Literature, 1984–, Harvard University; Co-Ed., Zeszyty Literackie, 1982–; Assoc. Ed., 1986–87, Ed.-in-Chief, 1987–90, The Polish Review. *Publications:* Poetry: The Weight of the Body (selected poems), 1989; Many other books in Polish. Non-Fiction: Breathing Under Water and Other East European Essays, 1990; Many other books in Polish. Other: Numerous books translated from English into Polish. *Contributions to:* Scholarly books and journals. *Honours:* Alfred Jurzykowski Foundation Literary Award, 1980; Guggenheim Fellowship, 1989; Terrence Des Pres Poetry Prize, 1989; Chivalric Cross of the Order of Polonia Restituta, 1991; Special Diploma for Lifetime Achievement in Promoting Polish Culture Abroad, Polish Minister of Foreign Affairs, 1993; Co-Winner, PEN Best Trans. Award, 1996. *Memberships:* American Asscn for Polish-Jewish Studies; American Asscn for Advancement of Slavic Studies; PEN Polish Center;

Polish Institute of Arts and Sciences in America; Polish Writers' Asscn; Union of Polish Authors; Union of Polish Writers Abroad. *Address:* 8 Broad Dale, Newton Wille, MA 02160, USA.

BARANOW, Joan Marie; b. 10 Oct. 1958, Cincinnati, Ohio, USA. Teacher; Poet. *Education:* BA, English, Hollins College, 1980; MA, English, State University of New York, 1983; PhD, English, Rutgers University, 1992. *Appointments:* Teaching Asst, State University of New York, 1981–83, Rutgers University, 1984–89; Asst Prof., Ashland University, 1989–92. *Publication:* 80 On The 80's: A Decade's History of Verse (co-ed.), 1990. *Contributions to:* USI Worksheets; Sirens; Poetry Miscellany; Pegasus Review; Emily Dickinson: A First Book Affair; Little Magazine; Hollins Critic; Artemis; Window. *Honours:* Award, Acad. of American Poets, 1983; Fellowship, Ohio Arts Council, 1992. *Memberships:* Poets and Writers; Associated Writing Programs; MLA. *Address:* 73 Hillside Ave, Mill Valley, CA 94941, USA.

BARBARESE, Joseph Thomas; b. 18 May 1948, Pennsylvania, USA. Asst Prof. of Creative Writing and Literature; Poet; Writer; Trans. m. Karen Henly, 7 June 1980, 2 s., 1 d. *Education:* BA, English, Franklin and Marshall College, Lancaster, Pennsylvania, 1976; MA, English, 1981, PhD, English, 1994, Temple University, Philadelphia. *Appointments:* Visiting Prof., 1988–92, Asst Prof. of Creative Writing and Literature, 1999, Rutgers University. *Publications:* Under the Blue Moon (poems), 1985; New Science (poems), 1989; The Children of Heracles (trans.), Vol. 4, Complete Works of Euripides, 1999. *Contributions to:* Books and journals. *Honours:* Pennsylvania Council on the Arts Fellowships, 1989, 1994. *Address:* 7128 Cresheim Rd, Philadelphia, PA 19119, USA.

BARBATO, John Allen; b. 4 Sept. 1945, Chicago, IL, USA. Artist; Poet. m. Martha Turner, 11 Nov. 1978, 3 s., 1 d. *Publications:* Commedia dell Arte, 1981; Music Once Made Like Love, 1985; Because I Dreamed of You Last Night, 1990; Face Up On Dash (audio cassette), 1990; Exuberance, Despair, Vision, 1995. *Contributions to:* Deep Valley Review; Childbirth Alternative; Tule Review; Community Endeavour; Glyphs I, II, III; Wild Duck Review; Zyzzyva, 1998. *Membership:* Poets Playhouse.

BARBOSA, Miguel; b. 22 Nov. 1925, Lisbon, Portugal. Writer; Dramatist; Poet; Painter. *Education:* University of Lisbon. *Publications:* Fiction: Trineu do Morro, 1972; Mulher Mancumba, 1973; A Pileca no Poleiro, 1976; As Confissoes de Um Cacador de Dinossauros, 1981; Esta Louca Profissao de Escritor, 1983; Cartas a Um Fogo-Fatuo, 1985. Poetry: Dans un Cri de Couleurs, 1991; Um Gesto no Rosto da Utopia, 1994; Prima del Verbo, 1995; Mare di Illusioni Naufragate, 1995; Preludio Poético de um Vagabundo da Madrugada, 1996; Mouthfuls of Red Confetti and the Hunt for God's Skull, 1996; O Teu Corpo na Minha Alma, 1996. Other: Plays and short stories. *Contributions to:* Various publications. *Honours:* Several for art. *Memberships:* Accademia Internazionale Greci-Marino di Lettere, Arti e Scienze; Society of Portuguese Authors. *Address:* Ave João Crisostomo 91–92, Lisbon 1050, Portugal.

BARBOUR, Douglas (Fleming); b. 21 March 1940, Winnipeg, Manitoba, Canada. Prof. of English; Poet; Writer. m. M Sharon Nicoll, 21 May 1966. *Education:* BA, Acadia University, 1962; MA, Dalhousie University, 1964; PhD, Queen's University, Kingston, Ontario, 1976. *Appointments:* Teacher, Alderwood Collegiate Institute, 1968–69; Asst Prof., 1969–77, Assoc. Prof., 1977–82, Prof. of English, 1982–, University of Alberta. *Publications:* Poetry: Land Fall, 1971; A Poem as Long as the Highway, 1971; White, 1972; Song Book, 1973; He and She and, 1974; Visions of My Grandfather, 1977; Shore Lines, 1979; Vision/Sounding, 1980; The Pirates of Pen's Chance (with Stephen Scobie), 1981; The Harbingers, 1984; Visible Visions: Selected Poems, 1984; Canadian Poetry Chronicle, 1985. Other: Worlds Out of Words: The Science Fiction Novels of Samuel R Delany, 1978; The Maple Laugh Forever: An Anthology of Canadian Comic Poetry (ed. with Stephen Scobie), 1981; Writing Right: New Poetry by Canadian Women (ed. with Marni Stanley), 1982; Tesseracts 2 (ed. with Phyllis Gollieb), 1987; B P Nichol and His Works, 1992; Daphne Marlatt and Her Works, 1992; John Newlove and His Works, 1992; Michael Ondaatje, 1993. *Memberships:* Asscn of Canadian University Teachers; League of Canadian Poets, co-chair., 1972–74. *Address:* c/o Dept of English, University of Alberta, Edmonton, AB T6G 2E5, Canada.

BARDWELL, (Constan Olive) Leland; b. 25 Feb. 1928, India. Writer; Poet; Novelist; Playwright. m. Michael Bardwell, April 1947, 4 s., 2 d. *Education:* Extra Mural, London University, 1949–50. *Appointments:* Teacher, Kilquhanity House School, 1947–49; Various jobs as Teacher in Vocational Studies in Creative Writing. *Publications:* The Mad Cyclist, 1970; The Fly and the Bedbug, 1984; Dostoyevsky's Grave, 1991; The White Beach: New and Selected Poems, 1998. *Contributions to:* Cyphers; Aquarius; Poetry Ireland; Arena; Irish Times; Translated into French, German, Hungarian and Hebrew. *Honours:* Arts Council Bursary, 1979–80; Elected Mem., Aosdána, 1982–; Marten Toonder Award for Literature, 1992. *Memberships:* Irish Writers' Union; Society of Irish Playwrights. *Address:* Cloonagh, Cloughboley, Ballinfull, County Sligo, Ireland.

BARGEN, Walter; b. 20 July 1948, Fort Bragg, North Carolina, USA. Poet. m. Mary Bobette Rose, 1 s., 1 d. *Education:* BA, cum laude, Philosophy, 1970, MEd, English Education, 1990, University of Missouri. *Publications:* Fields of Thenar, 1980; Yet Other Waters, 1990; Mysteries in the Public Domain, 1990; Rising Waters, 1994; The Vertical River, 1996; At the Dead Center of Day, 1997; Water Breathing Air, 1999; Harmonic Balance, 2001. *Contributions to:* Denver Quarterly; Kansas Quarterly; New Letters; Puerto del Sol; New Mexico Humanities Review; Webster Review; Spoon River Quarterly; Georgia Review; Laurel Review; Iowa Review; Witness; Missouri Review; South Dakota Review. *Honours:* National Endowment for the Arts Writing Fellowship, 1991; St Louis Poetry Centre Open Competition Prizes, 1991, 1992; Quarter After Eight Prose Prize, 1996; Chester H Jones Foundation Award, 1997. *Address:* PO Box 19, Ashland, MO 65010, USA. *Website:* www.walterbargen.com.

BARKER, Howard; b. 28 June 1946, London, England. Dramatist; Poet. *Education:* MA, University of Sussex, 1968. *Appointment:* Resident Dramatist, Open Space Theatre, London, 1975–75. *Publications:* Over 30 plays, including Collected Plays, Vol. I, 1990; Poetry. *Address:* c/o Judy Daish Assocs, 83 Eastbourne Mews, Brighton, Sussex, England.

BARLOW, Lolete Falck; b. 23 Aug. 1932, Mobile, AL, USA. Writer; Poet. m. John Woodman Bryan Barlow, 13 May 1952, 2 d. *Education:* Florida State University, 1950–51. *Appointment:* Poetry Ed., The Pen Woman Magazine, 1992–. *Publication:* Unheard Melodies, 1996. *Contributions to:* Books, newspapers and journals. *Honours:* Della Crowder Miller Memorial Award, 1979; First Place, Midwest Poetry Gala, 1987; Midwest Poetry Honoured Poet Award, 1988; Third Place, National Library of Poetry, 1990. *Memberships:* National League of American Pen Women; Poetry Society of Virginia. *Address:* 8902 Bay Ave, Box 754, North Beach, MD 20714, USA.

BARNARD, Keith; b. 26 Oct. 1950, London, England. Composer; Poet; Teacher of Music and English. *Education:* AMus, Trinity College of Music, London, 1971; Diplomas, International Writers Asscn, 1989, International Poets Acad., Chennai, India, 1990. *Publications:* Outer World Poems, 1982; The Sacred Cup, 1982; The Legend of Bran, 1982; The Legend of Fonn, 1983; The Adventures of Fionn Mac Chumail, 1984; Heroes and Rituals, 1984; Dreams of Wisdom, 1986; Visions, 1988; Perspectives, 1989; Dream Soul, 1990; Kingdoms, 1991. *Contributions to:* East-West Voices; Rising Stars; Samvedana-Creative Bulletin; Poet International; Souvenir Tribute to Prof. Saidhana; Canopy, Indian Literary Journal. *Memberships:* Performing Rights Asscn; Musicians' Union; New Age Music Asscn. *Address:* 13 Platts Lane, London NW3 7NP, England.

BARNES, Bruce; b. 3 March 1948, Leytonstone, London, England. Legal Advice Worker; Poet. *Education:* LLB, University of London External, 1973; PGCE, University of Keele, 1975. *Appointments:* Advice Worker, London Borough of Waltham Forest, 1983–90, London Borough of Islington, 1990–92, Nucleus Legal Advice Centre, 1992–96. *Publications:* Four Ways (anthology representing work of 4 poets), 1985; The Love Life of the Absent Minded, 1993. *Contributions to:* Poetry magazines and journals. *Honours:* Runner-up, Poetry Business Competition, 1988; Hornsey Library Campaign Competition, 1992; Runner-up, Newcastle Brown/Poetry Society Competition, 1993; First Prize, Arrival Press Football Poem Competition, 1996; Runner-up, Yorkshire Open Competition, 1996. *Membership:* Poetry Society. *Address:* 37 Wilmer Rd, Heaton, Bradford BD9 4RX, England.

BARNES, Dick, (Richard Gordon Barnes); b. 5 Nov. 1932, San Bernardino, CA, USA. Prof. of English Emeritus; Poet; Writer; Dramatist; Rubboardist. m. Patrica Casey, 30 July 1982, 5 s., 4 d. *Education:* BA, Pomona College, 1954; AM, Harvard University, 1955; PhD, Claremont Graduate School, 1959. *Appointments:* Part-Time Instructor, 1956–58, Instructor, 1961–62, Asst Prof., 1962–67, Assoc. Prof., 1967–72, Prof., 1972–98, Prof. Emeritus, 1998–, Pomona College; Numerous poetry readings. *Publications:* Poetry: A Lake on the Earth, 1982; The Real Time Jazz Band Song Book, 1990; Few and Far Between, 1994. Chapbooks: The Complete Poems of R. G. Barnes, 1972; Thirty-One Views of San Bernardino, 1975; Hungry Again the Next Day, 1978; Lyrical Ballads, 1979; All Kinds of Tremendous Things Can Happen, 1982; A Pentecostal, 1985. Plays: Nacho, 1964; A Lulu for the Lively Arts, 1965; San Antonio Noh, 1966; The Cucamonga Wrapdown, 1967; The Eighth Avatar, 1970; The Death of Buster Quinine, 1972; Purple, 1973; The Detestable Life of Alfred Furkeisar, 1975; The Bradford and Barnes Poverty Circus, 1977; Tenebrae, 1979; Come Sunday, 1982; A New Death of Buster Quinine, 1994; The Sand Mirror, 1998. Other: Trans, films and recordings. *Contributions to:* Many anthologies and magazines. *Address:* 434 W Seventh St, Claremont, CA 91711, USA.

BARNES, Jim Weaver; b. 22 Dec. 1933, Summerfield, OK, USA. Writer; Poet; Teacher. m. Carolyn, 22 Nov. 1973, 2 s. *Education:* BA, Southeastern Oklahoma State University, 1964; MA, 1966, PhD, 1972, University of Arkansas. *Publications:* Fish on Poteau Mountain, 1980; American Book of the Dead, 1982; Season of Loss, 1985; La Plata Canata, 1989; Sawdust War, 1992; Paris, 1997; On Native Ground, 1997; Numbered Days, 1999; On a Wing of the Sun, 2001. *Contributions to:* Poetry Chicago; Nation; American Scholar; Georgia Review; Poetry Northwest; Quarterly West; Prairie Schooner; Mississippi

Review; Plus 400. *Honours:* National Endowment for the Arts Fellowship, 1978; Oklahoma Book Award, 1993; Camargo Foundation Fellowships, 1996, 2001; American Book Award, 1998. *Memberships:* PEN Center West; Assoc. Writing Programs. *Address:* 914 Pine St, Macon, MO 63525, USA.

BARNES, Kate; b. 9 April 1932, Boston, Massachusetts, USA. Poet; Writer. Divorced, 2 s., 2 d. *Publications:* Talking in Your Sleep, 1987; Poems (co-author), 1992. *Contributions to:* Anthologies and periodicals. *Honour:* First Poet Laureate of Maine, 1995. *Address:* RR 1, PO Box 1390, Union, ME 04862, USA.

BARNES, Mary Jane; b. 23 April 1913, Kentucky, USA. Writer; Poet. m. (1) Howard A Beattie, 11 Nov. 1930, deceased, (2) Paul E Barnes, deceased, 3 s., (3) Alexander G Lawson, 1993, deceased 8 March 2002. *Education:* AB, Morehead State University; MA, University of Arizona, Tempe; Diploma of Proficiency, Rome, Italy. *Appointments:* Teacher, Arizona, Kentucky, and California; Co-Owner, Publisher, and Ed., Bay Area Publications Inc, 1990–; Co-Organizer, Readers' Theater, Yuma, AZ, 1992, Yuma Live Poets Society, 1994. *Publications:* Poetry: Delta Portraits, 1962; Rising Tides of Splendour, 1976; Shadows on April's Hills, 1981; Songs From an Islander, 1982; Naomi and Ruth, 1984; Images, 1988; Another View of Paradise, 1990; Ring of Peace, 1990; Ring of Peace II, 1991; Living Forest and Oceanside, 1999. *Contributions to:* Anthologies, periodicals, radio, and television. *Honours:* Hon. DLitt, World Acad. of Arts and Culture, 1988; Golden Crown World Poetry Award, World Poetry Research Institute, Korea, 1990; Woman of the Year, Berkeley Branch, National League of American Pen Women, CA, 1993; Poet of the Year, 1996, Mary Jane Barnes Poet's Award for Excellence in Poetry, Yuma Live Poets Society; Certificate of Recognition for Accomplishments in Poetry and Life, State of California Senate, 2002. *Memberships:* National League of American Pen Women; Kentucky State Poetry Society, judge; Arizona State Poetry Society, judge; California State Poetry Society; Ina Coolbrith Poetry Society. *Address:* 4603 Balfour Rd, No. 36, Brentwood, CA 94513, USA.

BARNETT, Anthony (Peter John); b. 10 Sept. 1941, London, England. Writer; Poet; Publisher. *Education:* MA, University of Essex. *Appointments:* Editorial Dir, Allardyce, Barnett, Publishers; Ed., Fable Bulletin: Violin Improvisation Studies, 1993–2000, online 2000–. *Publications:* Poetry: Blood Flow, 1975; Fear and Misadventure, 1977; The Resting Bell: Collected Poems, 1987. Prose and Poetry: Carp and Rubato, 1995; Anti-Beauty, 1999. Prose: Lisa Lisa, 2000. Other: Desert Sands: The Recordings and Performances of Stuff Smith, 1995; Black Gypsy, The Recordings of Eddie South, 1999. *Contributions to:* New Grove Dictionary of Music and Musicians; New Grove Dictionary of Jazz; Anthologies, journals and periodicals. *Address:* c/o Allardyce, Barnett, Publishers, 14 Mount St, Lewes, East Sussex BN7 1HL, England. *Website:* www.abar.net.

BARNETT SCHARF, Lauren Ileene; b. 9 May 1956, Chicago, IL, USA. Ed.; Publisher; Poet. m. Craig Allen Scharf, 8 April 1979. *Education:* BA, State of Connecticut Board for State Academic Awards, 1980. *Appointments:* Ed., Publisher, Lone Star Publications, 1981–. *Publications:* Stand Up Poems, 1975; The Multi-Billion Dollar Blues, 1990. *Contributions to:* Numerous books and periodicals. *Memberships:* Asscn of Comedy Artists; Society of Professional and Ethical Publishers of Literature.

BARNIE, John Edward; b. 27 March 1941, Abergavenny, Gwent, Wales. Ed.; Writer; Poet. m. Helle Michelsen, 28 Oct. 1980, 1 s. *Education:* BA, Honours, 1963, MA, 1966, PhD, 1971, Birmingham University; Dip Ed, Nottingham University, 1964. *Appointments:* Lecturer, English Literature, University of Copenhagen, 1969–82; Asst, then Ed., Planet: The Welsh International, 1985–. *Publications:* Borderland, 1984; Lightning Country, 1987; Clay, 1989; The Confirmation, 1992; Y Felan a Finnau, 1992; The City, 1993; Heroes, 1996; No Hiding Place, 1996; The Wine Bird, 1998; Ice, 2001. *Contributions to:* American Poetry Review; Critical Quarterly; Poetry Wales; New Welsh Review; Anglo-Welsh Review; Kunapipi; Juke Blues. *Honour:* Welsh Arts Council Prize for Literature, 1990. *Memberships:* Yr Academi Gymreig; Harry Martinson-Sällskapet; Welsh PEN. *Address:* Greenfields, Comins Coch, Aberystwyth, SY23 3BG, Ceredigion, Wales.

BARNSTONE, Willis; b. 13 Nov. 1927, Lewiston, ME, USA. Scholar; Poet; Novelist; Prof. of Comparative Literature. 2 s., 1 d. *Education:* BA, cum laude, French and Philosophy, Bowdoin College, 1948; MA, English and Comparative Literature, Columbia University, 1956; PhD, Comparative Literature, Yale University, 1960. *Appointments:* Asst Prof. of Romance Languages, Wesleyan University, 1959–62; Prof. of Comparative Literature, Spanish and Portuguese, Indiana University, 1966–; Visiting Prof., various universities, 1967–73; Senior Fulbright Prof., English Literature, Instituto Superior del Profesorado, Profesorado de Lenguas Vivas, Buenos Aires, 1975–76; Senior Fulbright Prof., English and American Literature, Peking Foreign Studies University, 1984–85. *Publications:* From This White Island, 1959; A Sky of Days, 1967; A Day in the Country, 1971; China Poems, 1976; Stickball on 88th Street, 1978; Overheard, 1979; Ten Gospels and a Nightingale, 1981; The Alphabet of Night, 1984; Five AM in Beijing, 1987; With Borges on an Ordinary Evening in Buenos Aires, 1992; ABC of Translating Poetry (illustrated), 1993; The Poetics of Translation, 1993; Funny Ways of Staying Alive: Poems and Ink Drawings,

1993; Sunday Morning in Facist Spain: A European Memoir (1948–1953), 1995; The Secret Reader: 501 Sonnets, 1996; The Poems of Sappho: A New Translation, 1997; The Literatures of Asia, Africa and Latin America (co-ed with Tony Barnstone), 1998; To Touch the Sky: Spiritual, Mystical and Philosophical Poems in Translation, 1999; Algebra of Night: New and Selected Poems, 1948–1998, 1998; The Apocalypse (Revelation): A New Translation with Introduction, 2000; The New Covenant: The Four Gospels and Apocalypse. Newly Translated from the Greek and Informed by Semitic Sources, 2002; Literatures of the Middle East (ed. with Tony Barnstone), 2002; Literatures of Latin America (ed.), 2002. *Honours:* Pulitzer Prize nominations for Poetry, 1960, 1977, 2000; Cecil Hemley Memorial Award, 1968, Lucille Medwick Memorial Awards, 1978, 1982, Gustav Davidson Memorial Awards, 1980, 1988, Emily Dickinson Award, Poetry Society of America, 1985; W. H. Auden Award, New York State Arts Council, 1986; National Poetry Competition Award, Chester H. Jones Foundation, 1988. *Memberships:* PEN; Poetry Society of America. *Address:* Dept of Comparative Literature, Indiana University, Bloomington, IN 47405, USA.

BARON, Emilio; b. 21 March 1954, Almeria, Spain. Prof.; Poet; Critic. *Education:* BA, 1975, MA, 1976, PhD, 1982, University of Montréal. *Appointments:* Asst Prof., University of Waterloo, Canada, 1982–83, Queen's University, Kingston, Canada, 1983–90, Universidad de Granada, Spain, 1990–93, Universidad de Almeria, 1993–. *Publications:* Cuenco de Soledad, 1974; La Soledad, La Lluvia, Los Caminos, 1977; De Este Lado, 1983; Poemas, 1974–1986, 1987; Llegan los Años, 1993; Los Dias (poems 1978–1999), 2000; Poemas al margen, 2002. *Contributions to:* Many books (on Cernuda, Lorca, T. S. Eliot, Manuel Machado, Laforgue, and others) journals and periodicals. *Honour:* Access First, Premio Jorge Guillen, 1979. *Membership:* Asociacion de Escritores Espanoles. *Address:* Dept de Filologia Inglesa y Alemana, Universidad de Almeria, 04120 Almeria, Spain.

BARR, Marylin Lytle; b. 11 Aug. 1920, USA. Poet; Writer. m. Orlando Sydney Barr, 6 Nov. 1942, deceased, 2000, 1 s., 2 d. *Education:* BA, Beecher College, 1942; MA, Bank Street College of Education, 1967; Graduate courses, Syracuse University, Cambridge University, New York University, 1969–77. *Appointments:* Teacher, Glen Parkway School, New Haven, CT; The Chelsea School, New York Board of Education. *Publications:* Drawn from the Shadows, 1991; Concrete Considerations, 1993; Unexpected Light, 1999. *Contributions to:* Oxalis; Outloud; Piedmont Literary Review; Catskill Life; Tucumcari Literary Review; Pegasus Review; Poet's Gallery; Zephyr; Poetry Peddler; Confetti; Echoes; Apple Blossom Connection; Poet; S S Calliope; Messages; Implosion; Times Herald Almanac; Glens Falls Review; Mohawk Valley USA; Still Night Writings; Blue Light Review; Wide Open; Anthologies and various collections. *Honours:* Recognition in poetry contests with publication by Hudson Valley Writers Asscn, 1988; Stone Ridge Poetry Society, 1990; First Prize, North Shore Poets Forum, 1998, 2001. *Memberships:* Alchemy Club; Poetry Society of America; Poets and Writers; Massachusetts State Poetry Society; Greater Haverhill Poetry Society; North Shore Poets' Forum; Catskill Reading Society; International Women's Writing Guild; New Hampshire State Poetry Society. *Address:* PO Box 75, Grahamsville, NY 12740, USA.

BARRETT, Cathlene Gillespie; b. 14 Aug. 1962, Utah, USA. Poet; Publisher; Ed. m. Kevin Barrett, 29 Aug. 1981, 1 s., 1 d. *Education:* College. *Appointment:* Publisher, Ed., Midge Literary Magazine, 1991–. *Contributions to:* Anthologies and periodicals. *Honours:* Golden Poet Award; Honorable Mention, Poet of the Year, Utah State Poetry Society. *Membership:* Utah State Poetry Society. *Address:* 2330 Tierra Rose Dr., West Jordan, UT 84084, USA.

BARRIERE, William J., (Vassillil Vidor); b. 15 Feb. 1936, Canada. Writer; Poet. *Education:* Loyola College, Montréal; New York Institute of Finance. *Contributions to:* Scimitar; Song; Vermont Life; American Poetry Journal. *Honour:* World of Poetry Honorable Mention, National Library of Poetry. *Address:* Drawer G, Angel Fire, NM 87710, USA.

BARRINGTON, Judith Mary; b. 7 July 1944, Brighton, England. Poet; Memoirist; Critic. *Education:* BA, 1978; MA, 1980. *Appointments:* West Coast Ed., Motheroot Journal, 1985–93; Poet-in-the-Schools, Oregon, and Washington, 1986–2000; Dir, The Flight of the Mind Writing Workshops, 1984–2000; Pres., Soapstone Inc, a writing retreat. *Publications:* Deviation, 1975; Why Children (co-author), 1980; Trying to Be an Honest Woman, 1985; History and Geography, 1989; An Intimate Wilderness (ed.), 1991; Writing the Memoir: From Truth to Art, 1997; Lifesaving: A Memoir, 2000. *Contributions to:* Anthologies, journals, and magazines. *Honours:* Fairlie Place Essay Prize, 1963; Jeanette Rankin Award for Feminist Journalism, 1983; Oregon Institute of Literary Arts Fellowships, 1989, 1992, 1999; Andres Berger Award in Creative Non-Fiction, 1996; Dulwich Festival Poetry Prize, 1996; Stuart H Holbrook Award, Literary Arts Inc, 1997; Lambda Literary Award, 2001. *Memberships:* National Writers Union; Poetry Society of America. *Address:* 622 SE 29th Ave, Portland, OR 97214, USA. *Website:* www.judithbarrington.com.

BARROW, Jedediah. See: BENSON, Gerard John.

BARRY, Sebastian; b. 5 July 1955, Dublin, Ireland. Writer; Dramatist; Poet. *Education:* BA, Trinity College, Dublin, 1977. *Appointments:* Writer-in-Asscn and Dir of the Board, Abbey Theatre, Dublin, 1989–90. *Publications:* Inherited Boundaries, 1984; The Engine of Owl-Light, 1987; Boss Grady's Boys, play, 1989; Fanny Hawke Goes to the Mainland Forever (verse), 1989; The Steward of Christendom, 1997; Prayers of Sherkin, 1997; White Woman Street, 1997; The Only True History of Lizzie Finn, 1997; Our Lady of Sligo, 1998; The Whereabouts of Eneas McNulty, 1998; The Water Colourist, 1998; The Rhetorical Town: Poems, 1999; Annie Dunne, 2002. *Contributions to:* Periodicals. *Honours:* Arts Council Bursary, 1982; Iowa International Writing Fellowship, 1984; Hawthornden International Fellowships, 1985, 1988; BBC/ Stewart Parker Award, 1989. *Memberships:* Aosdana; Irish Writers' Union. *Address:* c/o Curtis Brown Ltd, 28–29 Haymarket, London SW1Y 4SP, England.

BARTLE, Rajarajeswari; b. 11 Dec. 1943, Chennai, India. Poet. *Education:* BA, Panjab University, 1968; MA, University of Delhi, 1970. *Appointment:* Lecturer, Reader in Political Science, Jesus and Mary College for Women, University of Delhi, 1971–94. *Publication:* Poetic Outflow Part I, 1998. *Contributions to:* Anthologies and journals including: Merverse Muse; Millennium Peace, 2001. *Membership:* Shakespeare Society of India; United Writers' Asscn, Chennai, fellow; Poetry Club of India, New Delhi. *Address:* A 5B/113B DDA Flats, Janakpuri, New Delhi 110058, India.

BARTLETT, Elizabeth; b. 28 April 1924, Deal, Kent, England. Poet. *Appointment:* Lecturer, Workers Education Asscn, Burgess Hill, 1960–63. *Publications:* A Lifetime of Dying, 1979; Strange Territory, 1983; The Czar is Dead, 1986; Look, No Face, 1991; Instead of a Mass, 1991; Two Women Dancing, 1994; Appetites of Love, 2001. *Honours:* Cheltenham Poetry Competition Prize, 1982; Arts Council Bursary, 1985; Cholmondeley Award, Society of Authors, 1996. *Address:* 17 St John's Ave, Burgess Hill, West Sussex RH15 8HJ, England.

BARTLETT, Elizabeth R.; b. 20 July 1921, New York, NY, USA. Educator; Poet; Ed.; Literary Dir. m. 19 April 1943, 1 s. *Education:* BS, New York Teacher's College, 1941; Graduate Studies, Columbia University, 1941–42. *Appointments:* Instructor, Speech and Theatre, Southern Methodist University, 1946–49; Dir, Creative Writers Asscn, New School for Social Research, New York City, 1955; Asst Prof. of English, San Jose State University, 1960–61; Assoc. Prof., University of California at Santa Barbara, 1962–64; Poetry Ed., ETC, 1963–76; Prof. of Creative Writing, San Jose State University, 1979, 1981; Poetry Ed., Crosscurrents, 1983–88; Ed./Dir, International Anthology, Literary Olympians, 1992. *Publications:* Poems of Yes and No, 1952; Behold This Dreamer, 1959; Poetry Concerto, 1961; It Takes Practice Not To Die, 1964; Threads, 1968; Twelve-tone Poems, 1968; Selected Poems, 1970; The House of Sleep, 1975; In Search of Identity, 1977; Dialogue of Dust, 1977; Address in Time, 1979; A Zodiac of Poems, 1979; Memory is No Stranger, 1981; The Gemini Poems, 1984; Candles, 1987; Around the Clock, 1989. *Contributions to:* Harper's Bazaar; Saturday Review; New York Times; Literary Review; Virginia Quarterly; National Forum; Queen's Quarterly; Windsor Review; Dalhousie Review; Tamarack Review; Antigonish Review; Fiddlehead; Canadian Forum; Times; Orbis; Outposts; Candelabrum; Prospice; Delhi-London Poetry Journal; Westwords. *Honours:* Writing Fellowships, 1959, 1960, 1961, 1970, 1977, 1979, 1985; Syndicated Fiction Awards, 1983, 1985. *Memberships:* Poetry Society of America; PEN International; Author's Guild; International Women's Writing Guild. *Address:* 2875 Cowley Way, No. 1302, San Diego, CA 92110, USA.

BARTOLOMÉ, Efraín; b. 15 Dec. 1950, Ocosingo, Chiapas, Mexico. Poet. m. Guadalupe Belmontes Stringel, July 1986, 1 s., 1 d. *Education:* Psychotherapy, University of Mexico. *Publications:* Poetry: Ojo de jaguar, 1982; Ciudad bajo el relámpago, 1983; Música solar, 1984; Cuadernos contra el ángel, 1987; Mínima animalia, 1991; Cantos para la joven concubina y otros poemas dispersos, 1991; Música lunar, 1991; Agua lustral (Poetry 1982–1987), 1994; Corazón del monte, 1995; Trozos de sol, 1995; Ocosingo: Diario de guerra y algunas voces, 1995; La Poesía, 1996; Partes un verso a la mitad y sangra, 1997; Avellanas, 1997; Anima mundi, 1999; La casa sola, 1999; Oficio: Arder (Collected Poems 1982–1997), 1999. Other: Recordings, including: La palabra del poeta Efraín Bartolomé, poems from Ojo de jaguar, 1991; Efraín Bartolomé: Música lunar (La voz del poeta y el canto extático de los Derviches), 1996. *Contributions to:* Vuelta; México en el Arte; Universidad de México; Proceso; Casa del Tiempo; Siempre!; Periódico de Poesía; La Jornada Semanal; La palabra y el Hombre; Mandorla; The Café Review; First Intensity!; Many Latin American anthologies. *Honours:* Mexico City Prize; Aguascalientes National Poetry Prize; Carlos Pellicer National Poetry Book of the Year Prize; Gilberto Owen National Literature Prize; Jaime Sabines International Poetry Prize; Mexican Government, National Forestry and Wildlife Excellence Award in the field of Culture; Chiapas Art Award; National System of Creators of Art Fellowship; Ledig Rowolht Fellowship; Legacy Award in Literary Arts; International Latino Arts Award for a 'Lifetime of Achievement and Contribution to the Arts'. *Memberships:* PEN Club; International Acad. of Latino Artists. *Address:* Conkal 266, Torres de Padierna, 14200 México, DF, Mexico. *E-mail:* efrainbartolome@hotmail.com.

BARTOSY, Francisca Judith, (Judy Bartosy); b. 29 Oct. 1929, Budapest, Hungary. Poet; Writer; Trans. m. Francis Michael Bartosy, 2 s., 1 d. *Education:* Budapest; Bavaria; Deakin University, 1985. *Publications:* Poetry: Island Roses (co-author), 1975; Pebbles (bilingual, English/Hungarian), 1990; From Silver Pines to Blue Gums, 1997. *Contributions to:* Anthologies and periodicals, including: Translations in The Australian Literary Trans' Journal and regular contributions to Poetry Monash, a Monash University publication. *Honours:* Commendation, 1990, Medallion of Achievement, 1991, Melbourne Poetry Society; First Prize, Coolum J Interstate Writers Asscn Competition, 1991; 2 Certificates of Merit, Coolum Writers, 1991; Best Poem Award, Society of Women Writers, Australia, 1991; Runner-up, Robert Burns Poetry Competition, Nairn, Scotland, 1996. *Memberships:* Australian Literary Trans' Asscn; Fellowship of Australian Writers; Society of Women Writers, Australia; Thursday Poets; Victorian Writers Centre. *Address:* 73 Church Rd, Carrum, Vic. 3197, Australia.

BARUA, Bhaben; b. 27 Nov. 1941, Jhaji, Assam, India. Poet. m. Mamata Barua, 12 Dec. 1970, 2 s. *Education:* BA, Calcutta University, 1960; MA, Delhi University, 1963. *Appointments:* Staff, English Dept, Punjabi University, Punjab, and Guwahati University, Assam. *Publications:* Collected Poems, 3 vols, 1996 et seq. *Honours:* Assam Publication Board Award, 1978; Sahitya Akademie Award, 1979. *Address:* Flat No. 402, Swati Apartments, G S Rd, Guwahati, India.

BASINGER, William Daniel; b. 14 Feb. 1952, Washington, DC, USA. Computer Specialist; Poet. m. Mary Basinger, 11 June 1988. *Education:* BA, University of Maryland, 1974; MS, Georgetown University, 1977; MS, Johns Hopkins University, 1989. *Appointments:* Computer Programmer and Analyst, various companies, 1977–89, George Washington University, 1989–. *Publications:* Logistic Resource Analysis of Causes of Downtime, 1986; Chemical Element Distribution of Sediments from Kane Basin, 1994. Poems: Voice of the Earth; The Infinite Cosmos; Of Time and Tide; Moonlight Sonnet. *Memberships:* Several professional organizations. *Address:* 11342 Cherry Hill Rd, T-203, Bettsville, MD 20705, USA.

BASLER, Sabra Jane; b. 6 July 1950, Sacramento, CA, USA. Registrar; Poet. Divorced, 1 d. *Education:* BA, University of California, 1977; MA, California State University, Sacramento, 1984. *Appointments:* Dir, Tooth of Time Books; Registrar, Rare Books and Poetry Collections, University of California, Davis. *Publications:* Men of Mind, 1990; AH!, 1990; Cycladic Code, 1991; Opening the Gate, 1992. *Contributions to:* Coyote's Journal; Quercus; Wind Chimes; Poet News; Sierra Journal; Nexus; Colt Drill; Valley Spirit. *Memberships:* Poets and Writers; Associated Writing Programs; Council for Creative Projects. *Address:* 1920 Gold Southeast, Albuquerque, NM 87106, USA.

BASS, Clara May Overy, (Clara May Overy); b. 11 May 1910, Grimsby, England. Writer; Poet; Musician; Artist; Teacher. m. Donald Lesley Bass, 27 July 1937, 1 s. *Education:* Training in music, ballet, and voice production. *Publications:* Dreams of a Singer, 1963; Living Poetry, 1968; Major and Minor, 1975; Reflections, 1985. *Contributions to:* Anthologies, magazines, and journals. *Honours:* Several medals, diplomas, and trophies. *Memberships:* Centre Studi e Scambi, Rome; International Poetry Society, founder-fellow; Poetry Society of Great Britain; Writers Guild of Great Britain. *Address:* 68 Lestrange St, Cleethorpes, South Humberside DN35 7HL, England.

BASS, Ellen; b. 16 June 1947, Philadelphia, Pennsylvania, USA. Poet; Writer; Educator. 1 s., 1 d. *Education:* BA, Goucher College, 1968; MA, Boston University. *Appointments:* National Educator in child sexual abuse and healing; Co-founder, Survivors Healing Centre. *Publications:* No More Masks: An Anthology of Poems by 20th Century Women (co-ed.), 1973; I'm Not Your Laughing Daughter, 1973; Of Separateness and Merging, 1977; For Earthly Survival, 1980; I Never Told Anyone: Writings by Women Survivors of Child Sexual Abuse (co-author), 1983; Our Stunning Harvest, 1985; The Courage to Heal: A Guide for Women Survivors of Child Sexual Abuse (co-author), 1988; Free Your Mind: The Book for Gay, Lesbian and Bisexual Youth and Their Allies (co-author), 1996. *Contributions to:* Atlantic Monthly; Ms; Calyx; Conditions; Sinister Wisdom; Nimrod; Sojourner; Ploughshares. *Honours:* Finalist, William Carlos Williams Award, Poetry Society of America, 1978; Elliston Poetry Award, University of Cincinnati, 1980. *Membership:* National Writers Union. *Address:* PO Box 5296, Santa Cruz, CA 95060, USA.

BASSO, Eric; b. 29 June 1947, Baltimore, Maryland, USA. Novelist; Dramatist; Poet; Essayist; Artist; Photographer; Trans. *Education:* Catonsville Community College, 1965–67; BSc, Towson State University, 1970. *Publications:* The Beak Doctor: Short Fiction, Vol. One, 1974–75, 1987; A History in Smallwood Cuts, 1990; Equus Caballus, 1991; The Golem Triptych, 1994; Bartholomew Fair, 1997. *Contributions to:* Chicago Review; Asylum; Central Park; Mr Cogito; Nocturne; Open; Oyez; Cold-drill; Vice Versa; Archer; Amputated Fingers. *Address:* 3623 Templar Rd, Randallstown, MD 21133, USA.

BASU, Krishnabasu; b. 17 Nov. 1917, Chandernagore, West Bengal, India. College Teacher; Poet. m. Aparajito Basu, 22 July 1969, 1 d. *Education:* MA, 1973; PhD, 1986. *Appointments:* Lecturer; Senior Lecturer. *Publications:*

Sabder Sarir, 1976; Jaler Saralve, 1982; Kardigane Kusum Prastab, 1986; Narsicus Fute Aache, Eka, 1988; Jal Batase Andhakare, 1990. *Contributions to:* Deshi; Ananda Bazar Patrika; Parichay; Jugantar; Aajkal; Bivab; Prama; Kritibas; Pratikhan; Maha Nagar; Amrita; Ananda Mela; Basumati. *Honour:* Pratishruti Puraskar, 1981. *Address:* B 16/8 Kalindi Housing Estate, Calcutta 700 089, India.

BATE, John Leonard; b. 27 Dec. 1919, London, England. Librarian; Poet. m. Margaret Mary Banks, 6 June 1945, 6 s., 6 d. *Education:* Fellow, Library Asscn (FLA), 1953; MA, 1961, Dip Ed, 1962, St Andrews University. *Appointment:* Chief Librarian, Napier Polytechnic, Edinburgh, 1964–85. *Publications:* Damaged Beauty Needs a New Design, 1981; Florence Nightingale: A Dramatic Poem, 1983; Pictures of Edinburgh, 1984; Tablet-ed: a poem sheet, 1985; Title Deeds: a poem sheet, 1988; The Ballad of Gwen John, 1988; Glimpses of a School Year, 1990; Meditations on Simple Themes, 1991; No Stones, No Scorpions, 1993; At the Time of My Beginning, 1998; English Haiku, 2001– in preparation. *Contributions to:* Tribune; Poetry Review; Orbis; Outposts; The Tablet; The Month. *Honour:* M.B.E., 1982. *Membership:* School of Poets, Edinburgh, secretary, 1981–82. *Address:* 15 Bowness Ave, Oxford OX3 0AJ, England.

BATEMAN, David (Robert); b. 26 Aug. 1957, River Hill, Kent, England. Performance Poet; Comedian; Writer; Tutor. *Education:* BSc, Honours, Social Studies, Teesside Polytechnic, 1979; Diploma in Psychology, 1981, and in Landscape Interpretation, 1990, University of Liverpool. *Appointments:* Co-Writer and Performer, Magix Ox outdoor theatre company; Co-Writer and Vocalist, Petra and the Probes poetry and music band; Lecturer in Creative Writing, University of Liverpool. *Publications:* The Ideal God Competition, 1989; David Bateman's Golden Treasury of Dinosaurs, 1993; From Jellybeans to Reprobation, 1996; Curse of the Killer Hedge, 1996. *Contributions to:* BBC, journals, and magazines. *Honour:* First Prize, Edinburgh Performance Poetry Competition. *Membership:* Evil Dead Poets Society, co-founder; Dead Good Poets Society, chair. *Address:* Flat 7, 7 Gambier Terrace, Liverpool L1 7BG, England.

BATES, Scott; b. 13 June 1923, Evanston, IL, USA. Prof.; Poet. m. 17 April 1948, 4 s. *Education:* BA, Carleton College, 1947; PhD, University of Wisconsin, 1954. *Appointments:* Prof. of French Prof., 1954–87, Prof. of Film, 1970–, University of the South, Sewanee, TN. *Publications:* Guillaume Apollinaire, 1967, 1989; Poems of War Resistance, from 2300 BC to the Present, 1969; Petit Glossaire des mots libres d'Apollinaire, 1975; The ABC of Radical Ecology, 1982; Lupo's Fables, 1983; Merry Green Peace, 1991; Songs for the Queen of the Animals, 1992; The ZYX of Political Sex, 1999; The ZYX of Biblical Sex, 2002. *Contributions to:* New Yorker; Furioso; Sewanee Review; Partisan Review; New Republic; Southern Poetry Review; Tennessee Poetry Journal; Lyric; Quixote; Mountain Summer; Diliman Review; Delos. *Honour:* American Literary Anthology Prize, 1970. *Address:* Box 1263, 735 University Ave, Sewanee, TN 37383, USA.

BATSTONE, Patricia, (Annette Collins); b. 8 July 1941, West Hartlepool, England. Poet; Writer. m. Geoffrey Batstone, 17 July 1965, 2 s. *Education:* BA in Theology; MEd, RE and Literature, PGCE, University of Hull; University of Exeter; PhD, RE and Literature. *Publications:* Messages of Devon, 1991; Farewell to Wincolmlee, 1994; Time and the Gospel, 1995; A World of Love, 1996; Memo to God, 1998; Still Dancing, 1998; Candles in the Darkness, 1998; In Debt to C. S. Lewis, 1999; Meeting Jesus, 2000; Daughters of Eve: Characterisation, Authenticity and Poetic Licence in Bible-based Narrative Poetry, 2001; Happy in Hospital (co-ed. with Daphne Ayles), 2000. *Contributions to:* Springboard; Dial 174; Areopagus; One; Triumph Herald; Poetry Church Anthology; Feather Books and others. *Honour:* Areopagus Open, 1996; Highly Commended, Julia Cairns Poetry Competition, 1998. *Memberships:* Methodist Retreat Group; Society of Women Writers and Journalists. *Address:* 5 Foxglove Close, Dunkeswell, Devon EX14 4QE, England.

BATSTONE, Stephanie; b. 22 Dec. 1922, Croydon, Surrey, England. Poet. *Publications:* Poems of the Second World War, 1985; More Poems of the Second World War, 1989; Change at Peckham Rye, 1992; Wren's Eye View, 1994; Poems, 1998; Wren's Eye View, 2001. *Address:* 39 Beechwood Ct, West Street Lane, Carshlaton, Surrey SM5 2QA, England.

BATTILANA, Maria Giuseppina, (Marilla Battilana); b. 26 Sept. 1932, Milan, Italy. Poet; Writer. m. Igor P. Shankovsky, 19 March 1973, divorced 1989. *Education:* Interpreter in French and English degree, Interpreter School of Milan, 1956; Studied painting, Venice, 1956–67; Degree in Foreign Literature and Languages, Ca'Foscari, Venice, 1968. *Appointments:* Lecturer in English Literature and Language, Ca'Foscari, 1968; Fulbright Lecturer, Southern Illinois University, Carbondale, 1971–73; Assoc. Prof. of English Literature and Language, Ca'Foscari, Venice, 1973–81; Prof. of North American Literature, Padua University, 1980–96. *Publications:* L'erba rompe le pietre, 1960; Valore Zero Valore, 1968; Telefonare al boss, 1979; Yo, el Rey, visual poetry, a portfolio, 1981; Occhiodiamante, 1989; La corona d'oro, 1992. *Contributions to:* La battana; Lettera; Galleria; Contrappunto; Zeta; Quinta generazione; Laboratorio; L'ozio; La Nuova Tribuna Letteraria; Poesia.

Honours: First Prize, Proposta di Poesia, Abano Terme, PD, 1970; Finalist, Premio XXa Regione, 1978; Finalist, Premio Natura-Siena, 1977; Represented Italy at Writers 20th Conference in Belgrade, Yugoslavia, 1983; Represented Italy as poet and critic at Struga Festival, Macedonia, 1984; Nantopoesia Prize (Vicenza) for her whole poetic and literary production, 1994. *Memberships:* Ateneo Veneto, Venice; European Asscn American Studies; Societa Italiana di Comparatistica Letteraria; Centro Interuniversitario per la Ricerca sul Viaggio in Italia; Hon. Mem., Dante Alighieri Society. *Address:* Via Garda, 57 Selvazzano, Padova 35030, Italy.

BAUER, Steven (Albert); b. 10 Sept. 1948, Newark, New Jersey, USA. Prof. of English; Writer; Poet. m. Elizabeth Arthur, 19 June 1982. *Education:* BA, Trinity College, Hartford, CT, 1970; MFA, University of Massachusetts, Amherst, 1975. *Appointments:* Instructor, 1979–81, Asst Prof., 1981–82, Colby College, Waterville, Maine; Asst Prof., 1982–86, Assoc. Prof., 1986–96, Prof., 1996–, of English, Dir of Creative Writing, 1986–96, Internal Dir of Creative Writing, 1996–2001, Miami University, Oxford, Ohio. *Publications:* Satyrday (novel), 1980; The River (novel), 1985; Steven Spielberg's Amazing Stories, 2 vols, 1986; Daylight Savings (poems), 1989; The Strange and Wonderful Tale of Robert McDoodle (Who Wanted to be a Dog), children's book, 1999; A Cat of a Different Color (novel for children), 2000. *Contributions to:* Essays, stories and poems in many periodicals. *Honours:* Strousse Award for Poetry, Prairie Schooner, 1982; Master Artist Fellowship Award, Indiana Arts Council, 1988; Peregrine Smith Poetry Prize, 1989; Parents' Choice Recommended Writer, 2000. *Address:* 14100 Harmony Rd, Bath, IN 47010, USA.

BAUMAN, Ann R. See: MENEBROKER, Ann Reynolds.

BAUMEL, Judith; b. 9 Oct. 1956, New York, NY, USA. Poet. m. David Ghitelman, 4 July 1985. *Education:* BA, Harvard University, 1977; MA, Johns Hopkins University, 1978. *Publications:* The Weight of Numbers, 1988; Now, 1996. *Contributions to:* Periodicals. *Honours:* Walt Whitman Award, Acad. of American Poets, 1987; New York Foundation for the Arts Fellowship in Poetry, 1987. *Membership:* Poetry Society of America. *Address:* 3530 Henry Hudson Pkwy, No. 12M, New York, NY 10463, USA.

BAWER, Bruce; b. 31 Oct. 1956, New York, NY, USA. Poet; Critic. *Education:* BA, English, 1978, MA, English, 1982, PhD, English, 1983, State University of New York at Stony Brook. *Appointment:* Literary Ed., Arrival Magazine, 1986–87. *Publication:* Innocence, 1988. *Contributions to:* Poetry; Paris Review; New Criterion; Hudson Review; American Scholar; Poetry East; Poetry Northwest; Boulevard; Chelsea; Pequod; Agni; Crosscurrents; Verse; 2 Plus 2; Arizona Quarterly; Kansas Quarterly; Wall Street Journal. *Honour:* Residency, Djerassi Foundation, 1987. *Memberships:* Poetry Society of America; PEN; National Book Critics Circle, board of dirs, 1989–. *Address:* 425 E 65th St, No. 26, New York, NY 10021, USA.

BAXTER, Charles; b. 13 May 1947, Minneapolis, Minnesota, USA. Prof. of English; Author; Poet. m. Martha Hauser, 1 s. *Education:* BA, Macalester College, 1969; PhD, State University of New York at Buffalo, 1974. *Appointments:* Asst Prof., 1974–79, Assoc. Prof., 1979–85, Prof. of English, 1985–89, Wayne State University; Faculty, Warren Wilson College, 1986; Visiting Faculty, 1987, Prof. of English, 1989–, University of Michigan. *Publications:* Fiction: Harmony of the World, 1984; Through the Safety Net, 1985; First Light, 1987; A Relative Stranger, 1990; Shadow Play, 1993; Believers, 1997; The Feast of Love, 2000. Non-Fiction: Burning Down the House, 1997. Poetry: Chameleon, 1970; The South Dakota Guidebook, 1974; Imaginary Paintings and Other Poems, 1990. *Contributions to:* Numerous anthologies, journals, reviews, and newspapers. *Honours:* National Endowment for the Arts Grant, 1983; Guggenheim Fellowship, 1985–86; Arts Foundation of Michigan Award, 1991; Lila Wallace-Reader's Digest Foundation Fellowship, 1992–95; Michigan Author of the Year Award, 1993; American Acad. of Arts and Letters Award in Literature, 1997. *Address:* 1585 Woodland Dr., Ann Arbor, MN 48103, USA.

BAYLISS, Timothy. See: BAYBARS, Taner.

BEACH, Eric; b. 1947, New Zealand. Poet; Writer. *Publications:* St Kilda Meets Hugo Ball, 1974; In Occupied Territory, 1977; A Photo of Some People in a Football Stadium, 1978; Weeping for Lost Babylon, 1996. *Contributions to:* Anthologies. *Address:* c/o HarperCollins, 10 E 53rd St, New York, NY 10022, USA.

BEAM, Jeffrey Scott; b. 4 April 1953, Concord, North Carolina, USA. Poet; Ed. *Education:* Bachelor, Creative Arts in Poetry, University of North Carolina, Charlotte, 1975. *Appointment:* Poetry Ed., Oyster Boy Review, 1997–. *Publications:* The Golden Legend, 1981; Two Preludes for the Beautiful, 1981; Midwinters Fire, 1990; The Fountain, 1992; Visions of Dame Kind, The Jargon Society, 1995; Submergences, 1997; Little, 1997; Light and Shadow, 1998; Aperture; An Elizabethan Bestiary: Retold, 1999; What We Have Lost: New and Selected Poems 1977–2001, enhanced CDs, 2001; Life of the Bee (song cycle with Lee Hoiby, 2002). Anthologies: Son of The Male Muse; Black Men/White Men; Sparks of Fire; Blake in a New Age; Yellow Silk: 10th Anniversary

Anthology. *Contributions to:* Carolina Quarterly; Yellow Silk; Dreamworks; Mouth of The Dragon; James White Review; Asheville Poetry Review; The Double Dealer Redux. *Honours:* Mary Duke Biddle Foundation Grant, 1998–99; Best Book Citations, American Institute of Graphic Arts, 1999, Independent Publisher Magazine, 1999; University of North Carolina at Chapel Hill Provost's Award for Public Service, 2000. *Memberships:* Poets and Writers; North Carolina Writers Network. *Address:* Golgonooza at Frog Level, 3212 Arthur Minnis Rd, Hillsborough, NC 27278, USA. *E-mail:* jeffbeam@email.unc.edu. *Website:* www.unc.edu/~jeffbeam/index.html.

BEARDSLEY, J(ohn) Douglas; b. 27 April 1941, Montréal, QC, Canada. Writer; Poet; Ed.; Reviewer; Teacher. *Education:* BA, University of Victoria, BC, 1976; MA, York University, Toronto, Ontario, 1978. *Appointments:* Chief Ed., Gregson Graham Ltd, 1980–82; Senior Instructor, Dept of English, University of Victoria, 1981–; Writer, Ed. and Graphic Designer, 1982–85, Writer, Ed. and Proofreader, 1985–, Beardsley and Assocs, Victoria. *Publications:* Going Down into History, 1976; The Only Country in the World Called Canada, 1976; Six Saanich Poems, 1977; Play on the Water: The Paul Klee Poems, 1978; Premonitions and Gifts (with Theresa Kishkan), 1979; Poems (with Charles Lillard), 1979; Pacific Sands, 1980; Kissing the Body of My Lord: The Marie Poems, 1982; Country on Ice, 1987; A Dancing Star, 1988; The Rocket, the Flower, the Hammer and Me (ed.), 1988; Free to Talk, 1992; Inside Passage, 1994; Wrestling with Angels (Selected Poems, 1960–1995), 1996; My Friends the Strangers, 1996; Our Game (ed.), 1998; No One Else is Lawrence! (with Al Purdy), 1998; The Man Who Outlived Himself (with Al Purdy), 2000. *Contributions to:* Anthologies, newspapers, magazines and periodicals. *Honours:* Canada Council Arts Award, 1978; British Columbia Book Prize for Poetry Nomination, 1989; British Columbia Millennium Book Award, 2000. *Address:* 1074 Lodge Ave, Victoria, BC V8X 3A8, Canada.

BEASLEY, Bruce; b. 20 Jan. 1958, Thomaston, GA, USA. Poet; Prof. of English. m. Suzanne Paola Beasley, 7 Aug. 1992, 1 c. *Education:* BA, Oberlin College, 1980; MFA, Columbia University, 1982; PhD, University of Virginia, 1993. *Appointment:* Prof. of English, Western Washington University, Bellingham, 1992–. *Publications:* Spirituals, 1988; The Creation, 1994; Summer Mystagogia, 1996; Signs and Abominations, 2000. *Contributions to:* Periodicals. *Honours:* National Endowment for the Arts Fellowship, 1992; Ohio State University Press-The Journal Award, 1993; Colorado Prize, 1997. *Literary Agent:* Wesleyan University Press, 110 Mt Vernon St, Middletown, CT 06457, USA. *Address:* Dept of English, Western Washington University, Bellingham, WA 98225, USA.

BEASLEY, Joan Helen Ostrom; b. 27 April 1941, Seattle, Washington, USA. Teacher; Poet; Writer. m. Jon Steven Beasley, 16 July 1965. *Education:* BA, 1962, MA, 1963, University of Washington; MA, California State University at Long Beach, 1971; PhD, University of Denver, 1985. *Appointments:* Various teaching positions, 1963–94; Adjunct Faculty, Arapahoe Community College, Castle Rock, CO, 1994–. *Publications:* Over 20 poems, 1994–98. Other: Sagebrush Cache, 1996. *Honours:* Several awards and honorable mentions for poetry. *Address:* 8902 Thunderbird Ct, PO Box 4070, Parker, CO 80134, USA.

BEATTIE, Ann; b. 7 Sept. 1947, Washington, DC, USA. Writer; Poet. *Education:* BA, American University, Washington, DC, 1969; MA, University of Connecticut, 1970. *Publications:* Secrets and Surprises, 1978; Where You'll Find the Other Stories, 1986; What Was Mine and Other Stories, 1991; With This Ring, 1997; My Life, Starring Dara Falcon, 1998; Park City: New and Selected Stories, 1998; New and Selected Poems, 1999; Perfect Recall, 2001; The Doctor's House, 2002. *Contributions to:* Various publications. *Address:* c/o Janklow and Nesbit, 445 Park Ave, New York, NY 10022, USA.

BEAUMONT, Jeanne Marie; b. 15 June 1954, Darby, Pennsylvania, USA. Teacher; Ed.; Poet. *Education:* BA, English, magna cum laude, Eastern College, St Davids, Pennsylvania, 1978; MFA, Writing, Columbia University School of the Arts, 1989. *Appointments:* Resident Faculty, The Frost Place Annual Festival of Poetry, 1991–94; Ed., Co-Publisher, American Letters & Commentary, 1992–99; Part-time Lecturer, Rutgers University, New Brunswick, NJ, 1998–. *Publication:* Placebo Effects, 1997. *Contributions to:* Poetry; The Nation; Harper's; Antioch Review; Boulevard; New American Writing; Poetry East; Seneca Review; Boston Review; Verse; Gettysburg Review; Many others. *Honours:* Winner, Benjamin T. Burns Poetry Contest, 1989; Honorable Mentions, Billee Murray Denny Poetry Awards, 1992, 1993; Winner, National Poetry Series, 1996. *Membership:* PEN; AWP; Poets House, New York. *Address:* 120 W 70th St, New York, NY 10023, USA. *E-mail:* jeanne.beaumont@att.net.

BEAUSOLEIL, Claude; b. 1948, Montréal, QC, Canada. Poet; Writer; Trans.; Ed.; Prof. *Education:* BA, Collège Sainte-Marie, University of Montréal; Bac Specialisé, MA, Université du Québec a Montréal; PhD, Sherbrooke University. *Appointments:* Prof. of Québec Literature, Collège Edouard-Montpetit, Longueuil, 1973–; Ed., Livrès urbaines. *Publications:* Intrusion ralentie, 1972; Journal mobile, 1974; Promenade modern style, 1975; Sens interdit, 1976; La surface du paysage, 1979; Au milieu du corps l'attraction s'insinue, 1980; Dans la matière revant comme une émeute, 1982; Le livre du voyage, 1983; Concrete City: Selected Poems 1972–82, 1983; Une certaine fin de siècle,

two vols, 1983, 1991; Les livres parlent, 1984; Il y a des nuits que nous habitons tous, 1986; Extase et déchirure, 1987; Grand hotel des étrangers, 1988; Fureur de Mexico, 1992; Montréal une vill de poèmes vous savez, 1992; L'Usage du temps, 1994. *Honours:* Prix Emile-Nelligan, 1980; Ordre des francophones d'Amérique, 1989. *Address:* c/o Union des écrivaines et écrivains québécois, La Maison des Écrivains, 3492 Ave Laval, Montréal H2X 3C8, Canada.

BEAVER, Bruce (Victor); b. 14 Feb. 1928, Sydney, NSW, Australia. Journalist; Writer; Poet. m. Brenda Bellam, 30 Sept. 1963. *Publications:* Under the Bridge, 1961; Seawall and Shoreline, 1964; The Hot Spring, 1965; You Can't Come Back, 1966; Open at Random, 1967; Letters to Live Poets, 1969; Lauds and Plaints, 1968–72, 1974; Odes and Days, 1975; Death's Directives, 1978; As It Was: Selected Poems, 1979; Prose Sketches, 1986; Charmed Lives, 1988; New and Selected Poems, 1960–90, 1991. *Contributions to:* Periodicals. *Honours:* Poetry Society of Australia Awards, 1983; Christopher Brennan Award, Fellowship of Australian Writers, 1983; New South Wales State Literary Awards Special Citation, 1990; AM Award, 1991. *Membership:* Australian Society of Authors. *Address:* 14 Malvern Ave, Manly, NSW 2095, Australia.

BEBEK, Robert; b. 19 Jan. 1968, Rijeka, Yugoslavia. Ed.; Reviewer; Writer; Poet. *Education:* Graduated, University of Rijeka, 1997. *Publications:* Lamp at Dawn, 1994; The Shapes of Emptiness, 1997; Into Infinity, 1998. *Contributions to:* Anthologies, newspapers and periodicals worldwide. *Honours:* Yomiuri Award, Japan, 1992; Honorable Mention, Itoen Contest, Japan, 1993; Award and Special Recognition, Haiku Headlines, USA, 1995; Prize, New Zealand Poetry Society, 1996. *Membership:* Croatian Writers' Asscn. *Address:* Franje Mladenica 6A, 51000 Rijeka, Croatia.

BECATOROS, Stefanos; b. 23 Sept. 1946, Athens, Greece. Librarian; Poet; Writer. m. Mary, 30 April 1977, 1 s. *Education:* Chemistry, University of Athens; Librarianship, Technological Institute of Athens, 1982–85. *Appointment:* Librarian, Municipal Library of Athens, 1975–. *Publications:* Terra Rossa, 1968; Knowing of One's Fatherland, 1972; Limited Space, 1975; Knowing of One's Fatherland: Collected Poems 1969–1981, 1985; Kithathineon Street, 1991; Wheel with Sky, 1994; The Sky is the Soil, 1998. *Contributions to:* Dentro; Letters and Arts; Planodion; Porphiras; Graphi; Enteuctirion; Parateretes; Nea Hestix, Anti, Themata Logotechnics. *Membership:* Union of Greek Librarians. *Address:* 69a Hippocrates St, 10680 Athens, Greece.

BECK, Al(bert); b. 4 April 1931, Scranton, PA, USA. Artist; Poet; Writer; Educator. m. Carmen Federowich, 2 s., 1 d. *Education:* BA, Art, Northwestern University, 1952; US Army Administrative School, 1952; Graduate Studies, Sorbonne, University of Paris, 1957; MFA, Clayton University, St Louis, 1977. *Appointments:* Dean of Students, Kansas City Art Institute, Missouri, 1967–68; Assoc. Prof. of Art and Head of Art Dept, 1968–96, Artist-in-Residence, 1996–97, Culver-Stockton College; Dir, Pyrapod Gallery, 1996–. *Publications:* Gnomes and Poems, 1992; Sight Lines, 1996; Songs from the Rainbow Worm, 1997; Beaucoup Haiku, 1999; God is in the Glove Compartment, 2000; Survival Weapons, 2001. *Contributions to:* Professional journals. *Honours:* Various painting and poetry awards. *Memberships:* Missouri Arts Council; Missouri Writers' Guild. *Address:* 5987 County Rd 231, Monroe City, MO 63456, USA. *E-mail:* abeck@marktwain.net.

BECK, Tatyana; b. 21 April 1949, Moscow, Russia. Poet; Writer. *Education:* Diploma in Literary Editing, Moscow State University, 1972. *Publications:* Skvoreshniky, 1974; Snegir, 1980; Zamysel, 1987. Poetry: Mixed Forest, 1993. *Contributions to:* Various journals. *Memberships:* Russian PEN Center, secretary; Writers Union. *Address:* Krasnoarmelskaya St, House No. 23, Apartment 91, Moscow 125319, Russia.

BECKER, Jürgen; b. 10 July 1932, Cologne, Germany. Poet; Writer; Dramatist. m. (1) Marie, 1954, divorced 1965, 1 s., (2) Rango Bohne, 1965, 1 step-s., 1 step-d. *Education:* University of Cologne, 1953–54. *Appointments:* Writer, Westdeutscher Rundfunk, Cologne, 1959–64; Reader, Rowohlt Verlag, 1964–66; Reader, Suhrkamp Verlag, 1973–74; Head, Dept of Drama, Deutschlandfunk, Cologne, 1974–93. *Publications:* Felder, 1964; Ränder, 1968; Umgebungen, 1970; Schnee, 1971; Das Ende der Landschaftsmalerei, 1974; Erzahl mir nichts vom Krieg, 1977; In der verbleibenden Zeit, 1979; Erzählen bis Ostende, 1981; Gedichte 1965–1980, 1981; Odenthals Küste, 1986; Das Gedicht von der wiedervereinigten Landschaft, 1988; Das englische Fenster, 1990; Foxtrott im Erfurter Stadion, 1993; Korrespondenzen mit Landschaft (with Rango Bohne), 1996; Der fehlende Rest, 1997; Aus der Geschichte der Trennungen, 1999. Other: Various radio plays. *Honours:* Literature Prize, Cologne, 1968; Literature Prize, Bavarian Acad. of Fine Arts, Munich, 1980; Critics' Prize, 1981; Literature Prize, Bremen, 1986; Peter Huchel Prize, 1994; Literature Prize, Berlin, 1994; Heinrich Böll Prize, 1995. *Memberships:* Akademie der Künste, Berlin-Brandenburg; Deutsche Akademie für Sprache und Dichtung eV, Darmstadt; PEN Centre, Federal Republic of Germany. *Address:* Am Klausenberg 84, 51109 Cologne, Germany.

BECKWITH, Merle Ray; b. 16 July 1942, East Grand Rapids, Michigan, USA. Writer: Poet. m. 19 June 1982. *Education:* BA, Political Science, Western Michigan University, 1964; Graduate Student, Anthropology and Education,

University of California at Los Angeles, 1966–68. *Appointments:* Teaching positions. *Publications:* Nature, 1980; Nature and Love, 1980; Meditations: A Collection of Contemplative Reflections, 1991. *Contributions to:* Many journals and periodicals. *Honours:* Golden Poetry Awards, World of Poetry, 1985, 1986, 1987. *Memberships:* American Society of Composers, Authors, and Publishers; California Chaparral Poets; California State Poetry Society; Christian Writers League. *Address:* 3732 Monterey Pine, No. A109, Santa Barbara, CA 93105, USA.

BECTON, Henry Jr, (H. B. Kamau); b. 21 Nov. 1953, Chicago, IL, USA. Poet; Playwright; Publisher; Television and Radio Producer. *Education:* Antioch College, 1971–74; Kennedy-King City College of Chicago, 1983–84. *Appointments:* Creative Writing Instructor, Cultural Arts Project, Baltimore, 1977–78, Hyde Park YMCA, Chicago, 1979; Artist-in-Residence, Chicago Council on Fine Arts, 1979–80; Co-ordinator, Writers' Seminar and Poetry Festival, DuSable Museum of African American History, Chicago, 1983; Producer and Host, Chicago Renaissance, Radio Station WHPK, University of Chicago, 1986–87; Host, Book Break, Chicago Access Corpn (cable tv), 1988–. *Publication:* Where Men Gather (ed.), 1982. *Contributions to:* Anthologies, newspapers and journals. Chatham-Southeast Citizen Newspaper; Chicago Defender. *Honours:* Barbara Broome Literary Scholarship for Poetry, Chicago, 1978; Finalist, Walt Whitman Award, Acad. of American Poets, 1980. *Memberships:* American Poetry Society; International Black Writers' Conference; The Perspectivist; The Triumverate, chair. *Address:* 935 E 50th St, Chicago, IL 60615, USA.

BEDOLACH, Hanna; b. 15 April 1931, Israel. Dyslexic Children's Teacher; Poet. m. Mr Epshtein, 9 Sept. 1949, 2 s., 1 d. *Education:* Senior Teacher, 1967; BA, Literature, 1980. *Publications:* My Flower-Bed River, 1983; Secure Space, 1986; The Cactus Scheme, 1989; Slow Motion, 1993; Imprisoned City, 1996. *Contributions to:* Newspapers and literary magazines. *Honours:* Creators and Researchers Asscn Prizes, 1986–96; Encouragement Award, Literature Art Research Asscn, 1993; Amos Fund Award, 1996. *Memberships:* Hebrew Writers Asscn; Literature Fans Asscn; Music Asscn; Poets and Composers Asscn. *Address:* 3 Aharon St, Givat-Shmuel 54019, Israel.

BEECHING, Jack; b. 8 May 1922, Hastings, Sussex, England. Writer; Poet. *Publications:* Fiction: Let Me See Your Face, 1958; The Dakota Project, 1967; Death of a Terrorist, 1982; Tides of Fortune, 1988. Non-Fiction: The Chinese Opium Wars, 1975; An Open Path: Christian Missionaries 1515–1914, 1979; The Galleys at Lepanto, 1982. Poetry: Aspects of Love, 1950; The Polythene Maidenhead, in Penguin Modern Poets, 1969; Twenty-Five Short Poems, 1982; The View From the Balloon, 1990; The Invention of Love, 1996; Poems 1940–2000, 2000. *Address:* c/o Tessa Sayle Agency, 11 Jubilee Pl., London SW3 3CE, England.

BEER, Hilda Doreen; b. 29 Jan. 1934, Thorverton, Nr Exeter, Devon, England. Poet. m. Wilfred Beer, 7 Sept. 1957, 2 d. *Publications:* Poems From a Devon Village, 1977; Poems of the English Countryside, 1996. *Contributions to:* Express and Echo; Mid Devon Gazette; This England Magazine and Calenders; Local Focus; Spotlight South West TV; Graham Danton Radio Devon; Review Devon Life; The Golden Book of Poetry; Poetry of the World; Poetry Galaxy; Poetry Now; The South West; Under a Southern Sky; Anthologies; UK 2000 Magazine; Poetry Digest. *Address:* 10 Broadlands, Thorverton, Nr Exeter, Devon, England.

BEESON, Diane Kay; b. 3 Sept. 1949, Boulder, CO, USA. Teacher; Writer; Poet; Trans. *Education:* BA, Lindenwood College, 1972; MA, Middlebury College, 1974; TOEFL Certificate, Fundación Ponce de León, Madrid, 1981; Diploma, Trans., Institute of Linguists, England, 1987. *Appointments:* Dir, English Classes, Grupo Anaya, 1983–92; Staff, Linguacentre Acad., 1984–89; Faculty, University of Delaware at University of Madrid, 1988-89, British Institute for Young Learners, British Council, Madrid, 1994; Prof., University of Cluny of Paris in Madrid, 1992–93; Acting Dir, Tulane-Newcombe Spanish Year Abroad 1999–; Prof., Trinity Diploma Programme, British Council, Madrid, 1999–2000. *Publications:* Eight books (co-author); Trans., four books. *Contributions to:* Anthologies, journals, and periodicals. *Honours:* Joyce Kilmer Contest, CO, 1982; Hon. citations. *Memberships:* American Asscn of University Women; Asscn of Teachers of Spanish and Portuguese; Institute of Linguists; MLA; National League of American Pen Women; Teachers of English to Speakers of Other Languages, Spain. *Address:* Escosura 21, Bajoh, 28015 Madrid, Spain.

BEEVERS, Mark (Busy); b. 29 Jan. 1955, Carlton, North Yorkshire, England. Writer; Poet; Dramatist. *Appointment:* Founder, Saltburn Scene, literary magazine, 1992. *Publications:* A Cuckoo in the Coop, 1988; CHRYME, 1988; Ball and Chain, 1988; Black Sheep, 1988; Dark Angel, 1988; Death is My Lady, 1988; Heathen Heart, 1989; Savage Soul, 1989; Turning Over an Old Leaf, 1989; Blank, Broker and Best of Beevers?, 1989; Behind These Shades, 1989; Vicously Fair, 1989; A Lone Wolf's Whistle, 1989; Poetry Partisan, 1989; Driven by Daemons, 1990; Mirroring Madness, 1990; Pagan Pages, 1990; Bards, Bandits, Bohemians, 1990; Jester Years, 1990; Punch Lines, 1990; Unmasked, 1990; Lion of Love, 1991; A Double-Edged Sword, 1991; Both Barrels Blazing, 1991; Scallywag, 1991; De Sade Serenade, 1991; Bewitched,

Bemused, Bedevilled and Beguiled, 1991; Hermit's Hot Pot, 1992; Pyrat Potshots, 1992; Gunning for Gurus, 1992; The Dead and the Divine, 1992 Pen Pages, 1992; Sorcery Sauce, 1993. Other: Punch Daze (plays), 1992 *Contributions to:* Evening Gazette; Outlet; Purple Patch; Psychopoetica Rapture; Top Copy; Peace and Freedom; Welcome; Super Trouper; Thurdays Krax, White Rose; Exile; Third Half; ET; Tops; Something for Nothing Gardengate News; Write Around (Cleveland anthology); Radio Cleveland BBC2 Open Space (television). *Honour:* First Prize, Outlet Magazine Competition. *Address:* Glenside Cottage, Saltburn, Cleveland, England.

BEGUHN, Sandra Eleta; b. 3 Nov. 1942, Kirksville, Missouri, USA. m. Lynn 29 June 1963, 1 s., 1 d. *Education:* Mary Crest College, Davenport, IA *Contributions to:* Capper's Weekly; Literary Iowa; Michigan Poetry Society Durango Cowboy Gathering; Western Poetry; The National Library of Poetry *Honours:* Ed.'s Choice Awards, 1997, 1998, 1999, 2000; Famous Poets Society Outstanding Achievement, Excellence in Poetry, 2000. *Memberships:* Nationa Library of Poetry; Famous Poets Society; Sparrow Grass Poetry; Acad. o American Poets; Creative Artists in Science; Iowa Poetry Society; Poetry Guild. *Address:* 2115 W 34th St, Davenport, IA 52806, USA.

BÉGUIN, Louis-Paul; b. 31 March 1923, Amiens, France. Writer; Poet. *Education:* BA, Sorbonne, University of Paris. *Publications:* Miroir de Janus 1966; Impromptu de Québec, 1974; Un homme et son langage, 1977; Problèmes de langage, 1978; Idoles et Paraboles, 1982; Yourcenar, 1982; Poèmes et pastiches, 1985; Parcours paralleles, 1988; Ange Pleureur, 1991; Poèmes depuis la tendre enfance, 1995; The Weeping Angel, 1996; Écrits des trois pignans, 1998. *Contributions to:* Newspapers and magazines. *Honours:* Poetry Award, 1967; Prix Montcalm, 1974. *Memberships:* PEN, Québec; Québec Writers Union. *Address:* 1800 rue Bercy, Apt 1218, Montréal, QC H2K 4K5, Canada.

BEHAR, Ruth; b. 12 Nov. 1956, Havana, Cuba. Prof. of Anthropology; Poet; Writer. m. David Frye, 6 June 1982, 1 s. *Education:* Wesleyan University, 1977; MA, 1981, PhD, 1983, Princeton University. *Appointments:* Asst Prof., 1986–89, Assoc. Prof., 1989–94, Prof. of Anthropology, 1994–, University of Michigan at Ann Arbor. *Publications:* Santa Maria del Monte: The Presence of the Past in a Spanish Village, 1986, revised edn as The Presence of the Past in a Spanish Village: Santa Maria del Monte, 1991; Translated Woman: Crossing the Border with Esperanza's Story, 1993; Bridges to Cuba (Puentes a Cuba) (ed.), 1995; Las Visiones de una Bruja Guachichil en 1599: Hacia una Perspectiva Indígena Sobre la Conquista de San Luis Potosal, 1995; Women Writing Culture (co-ed.), 1995; The Vulnerable Observer: Anthropology That Breaks Your Heart, 1996. *Contributions to:* Anthologies, scholarly journals and literary periodicals. *Honours:* John D. and Catherine T. MacArthur Foundation Fellowship, 1988–93; Guggenheim Fellowship, 1995–96. *Address:* c/o Dept of Anthropology, University of Michigan, 1020 LSA Bldg, Ann Arbor, MI 48109, USA.

BEHERA, Bhagaban; b. 3 Feb. 1953, Pathuria, Nayagarh, Orissa, India. Broadcaster; Poet. m. Angali Behera. *Education:* MA, Political Science, Delhi University; PhD, Jawaharlal Nehru University, New Delhi. *Appointments:* Research Scholar, Jawaharlal Nehru University, New Delhi; News Reader and Trans., Oriya Unit, All India Radio. *Publications:* 2 books in English, 1 in Oriya. *Contributions to:* Newspapers and journals. *Membership:* Kalinga Poetry Society, founder, 1996. *Address:* 1-171 Garnali Monalla, Laxmi Nagar, Delhi 110092, India.

BEHLEN, Charles (William); b. 29 Jan. 1949, Slaton, Texas, USA. Poet. 1 d. *Education:* New Mexico Junior College, 1968–70. *Publications:* Perdition's Keepsake; Three Texas Poets; Dreaming at the Wheel; Uirsche's First Three Decades; The Voices Under the Floor; Texas Weather. *Contributions to:* Bloomsbury Review; Cedar Rock; New Mexico Humanities Review; Poetry Now; Puerto del Sol; The Smith; Texas Observer; Borderlands; New Texas '91; New Texas '95. *Honours:* Pushcart Prize (nominee); Ruth Stephan Reader; Manuscripts Displayed and Placed in Time Capsule by San Antonio Museum of Art; Guest Poet, Tenth Annual Houston Poetry Fest; Dobie-Paisano Fellowship in Poetry (1995–96); The Frank Waters Foundation Fellowship, 1996. *Address:* 501 W Industrial Dr., Apartment 503-B, Sulphur Springs, TX 75482, USA. *E-mail:* cwbehlen@yahoo.com.

BEISSEL, Henry (Eric); b. 12 April 1929, Cologne, Germany. Poet; Dramatist; Writer; Trans.; Ed.; Teacher. m. (1) Ruth Heydasch, 2 d., (2) Arlette Francière, 3 April 1981, 1 d. *Education:* University of London, 1949; BA, 1958, MA, 1960, University of Toronto. *Appointments:* Teacher, University of Edmonton, 1962–64, University of Trinidad, 1964–66; Faculty, 1966–96, Prof. of English Emeritus, 1997–, Distinguished Emeritus Prof., 2000–, Concordia University, Montréal; Founder-Ed., Edge Journal, 1963–69. *Publications:* Poetry: Witness the Heart, 1963; New Wings for Icarus, 1966; The World is a Rainbow, 1968; Face on the Dark, 1970; The Salt I Taste, 1975; Cantos North, 1980; Season of Blood, 1984; Poems New and Selected, 1987; Ammonite, 1992; Dying I Was Born, 1992; Stones to Harvest, 1993; The Dragon and the Pearl, 2002. Plays: Inook and the Sun, 1974; Goya, 1978; Under Coyote's Eye, 1980; The Noose, 1989; Improvisations for Mr X, 1989; Inuk, 2000. Other: Kanada: Romantik und Wirklichkeit, 1981; Raging Like a Fire: A

Celebration of Irving Layton (ed. with Joy Bennett), 1993; Trans of poetry and plays. *Contributions to:* Journals. *Honours:* Epstein Award, 1958; Davidson Award, 1959; Deutscher Akademischer Austauschdienst Fellowship, 1977; Walter-Bauer Literaturpreis, Germany, 1994. *Memberships:* League of Canadian Poets, pres., 1980–81; PEN; Playwrights Canada; Writers Union of Canada. *Address:* Box 339, Alexandria, Ontario K0C 1A0, Canada. *E-mail:* beifran@glen-net.ca.

BEJERANO, Maya; b. 23 Feb. 1949, Haifa, Israel. Librarian; Teacher; Poet; Writer. m. Oct. 1983, divorced 1988, 1 d. *Education:* BA, 1973, 1974, MA, 1978, Bar-Ilan University and Hebrew University of Jerusalem. *Appointment:* Librarian, Main Public Library, Tel-Aviv. *Publications:* Ostrich, 1978; The Heat and the Cold, 1981; Data Processing, 1982; The Song of Birds, 1985; Selected Poems, 1987; Voice, 1987; Whale, 1990. *Contributions to:* Newspapers and journals. *Honours:* Hary Harshon Prize, 1976; Levi Eschol Prize, 1986; Bernstein Prize for Poetry, 1989.

BEKRI, Tahar; b. 7 July 1951, Gabès, Tunisia. Writer; Poet. m. Annick Le Thoër, 16 Jan. 1987. *Education:* Licence, French Literature, University of Tunisia, 1975; PhD, French Literature, Sorbonne, University of Paris, 1981. *Appointment:* Maître de conférences, University of Paris X, Nanterre. *Publications:* Le Laboureur du soleil, 1983; Le Chant du roi errant, 1985; Malek Haddad, 1986; Le coeur rompu aux océans, 1988; Les Chapelets d'attache, 1994; Littératures de Tunisie et du Maghreb, 1994; Poèmes à Selma, 1996; Les Songes impatients, 1997; Journal de neige et de feu, 1997; Le pêcheur de lunes, 1998; Inconnues Saisons/Unknown Seasons, 1999; De la littérature tunisienne et maghrébine, 1999; Marcher sur l'oubli, 2000. *Contributions to:* Various publications. *Honour:* Officier Mérite Culturel, Tunisia, 1993. *Address:* 32 Rue Pierre Nicole, 75005 Paris, France.

BELITT, Ben; b. 2 May 1911, New York, NY, USA. Prof. of Literature and Languages; Poet; Writer. *Education:* BA, 1932, MA, 1934, Postgraduate Studies, 1934–36, University of Virginia. *Appointments:* Asst Literary Ed., The Nation, 1936–37; Faculty Mem. to Prof. of Literature and Languages, Bennington College, Vermont, 1938–. *Publications:* Poetry: Wilderness Stair, 1955; The Enemy Joy: New and Selected Poems, 1964; Nowhere But Light: Poems, 1964–1969, 1970; The Double Witness: Poems, 1970–1976, 1977; Possessions: New and Selected Poems, 1938–1985, 1986; Graffiti, 1990. Other: School of the Soldier, 1949; Adam's Dream: A Preface to Translation, 1978; The Forged Feature: Toward a Poetics of Uncertainty, 1994; Ed. and trans. of several vols. *Contributions to:* Books. *Honours:* Shelley Memorial Award in Poetry, 1936; Guggenheim Fellowship, 1947; Brandeis University Creative Arts Award, 1962; National Institute of Arts and Letters Award, 1965; National Endowment for the Arts Grant, 1967–68; Ben Belitt Lectureship Endowment, Bennington College, 1977; Russell Loines Award for Poetry, American Acad. and Institute of Arts and Letters, 1981; Rockefeller Foundation Residency, Bellagio, Italy, 1984; Williams/Derwood Award for Poetry, 1986. *Memberships:* Authors Guild; PEN; Vermont Acad. of Arts and Sciences, fellow. *Address:* PO Box 88, North Bennington, VT 05257, USA.

BELL, Antoinette; b. 25 Jan. 1938, Los Angeles, CA, USA. Poet. m. Raymond J Bell, 24 Dec. 1971, 1 s., 1 d. *Education:* University of California at Los Angeles; University of California at Berkeley. *Publication:* The Edge of Vision, 1995; Amber Man, chapbook. *Contributions to:* Many periodicals. *Honours:* 8 Golden Poets Awards, 1985–92; Eleanor Cox Award, California Federation of Chaparral Poets, 1993; Grand Prize, Pipers Collection, 1995; Certificate of Merit, Shakespeare Sonnet, US, 1996; 2 First Place Prizes, US Poets, Napa, CA. *Memberships:* Acad. of American Poets; California Federation of Chaparral Poets; Ina Coolbrith Circle; Library of Congress Assocs; Poets of the Vineyards; United States Poets; New Horizons Poetry Society; Poetry Society of America. *Address:* 2884 Cypress Way, Fairfield, CA 94533, USA.

BELL, Charles Greenleaf; b. 31 Oct. 1916, Greenville, Mississippi, USA. Teacher Emeritus; Author. m. (1) Mildred Chiathan, 1939, divorced, (2) Diana Mason, 1949, 5 d. *Education:* BS, University of Virginia, 1936; BA, 1938, LittB, 1939, MA, 1966, University of Oxford, England. *Publications:* Fiction: The Married Land, 1962; The Half Gods, 1968. Poetry: Songs for a New America, 1953; Delta Return, 1955; Five Chambered Heart, 1986. Other: The Spirit of Rome (film), 1965; Symbolic History: Through Sight and Sound (40 slide tape/ video dramas, also on digital CD-ROM). *Contributions to:* Numerous magazines. *Honours:* Ford Foundation Fellowship; Rhodes Scholarship; Rockefeller Foundation Grant; Fulbright Fellowship. *Address:* 1260 Canyon Rd, Santa Fe, NM 87501, USA.

BELL, Marvin (Hartley); b. 3 Aug. 1937, New York, NY, USA. Prof. of Letters; Poet; Writer. m. Dorothy Murphy, 2 s. *Education:* BA, Alfred University, 1958; MA, Literature, University of Chicago, 1961; MFA, Literature, University of Iowa, 1963. *Appointments:* Faculty, Writers Workshop, 1965–, Flannery O'Connor Prof. of Letters, 1986–, University of Iowa; Distinguished Visiting Prof., University of Hawaii, 1981; Visiting Prof., University of Washington, 1982; Lila Wallace-Reader's Digest Writing Fellow, University of Redlands, 1991–93; Woodrow Wilson Visiting Fellow, Saint Mary's College of California, 1994–95, Pacific University, 1996–97, Nebraska-Wesleyan University, 1996–97, Hampden-Sydney College, 1998–99, West Virginia Wesleyan College, 2000–01, Birmingham Southern College, 2000–01; Series Poetry Ed., Pushcart Prize, 1997–; First Poet Laureate of the State of Iowa, 2000–. *Publications:* Poetry: Things We Dreamt We Died For, 1966; A Probable Volume of Dreams, 1969; The Escape Into You, 1971; Residue of Song, 1974; Stars Which See, Stars Which Do Not See, 1977; These Green-Going-to-Yellow, 1981; Segues: A Correspondence in Poetry (with William Stafford), 1983; Drawn by Stones, by Earth, by Things That Have Been in the Fire, 1984; New and Selected Poems, 1987; Iris of Creation, 1990; The Book of the Dead Man, 1994; Ardor: The Book of the Dead Man, Vol. 2, 1997; Poetry for a Midsummer's Night, 1998; Wednesday: Selected Poems 1966–1997, 1998; Nightworks: Poems 1962–2000, 2000. Other: Old Snow Just Melting: Essays and Interviews, 1983; A Marvin Bell Reader: Selected Prose and Poetry, 1994. *Contributions to:* Many anthologies and periodicals. *Honours:* Lamont Award, Acad. of American Poets, 1969; Guggenheim Fellowship, 1977; National Endowment for the Arts Fellowships, 1978, 1984; American Poetry Review Prize, 1982; Senior Fulbright Scholar, 1983, 1986; Hon. Doctorate of Letters, Alfred University, 1986; American Acad. of Arts and Letters Award in Literature, 1994. *Address:* 1416 E College St, Iowa City, IA 52245, USA.

BELL, Robin; b. 4 Jan. 1945, Dundee, Scotland. Writer; Poet; Broadcaster. 2 d. *Education:* MA, St Andrews University, Scotland; MS, Columbia University, New York, USA. *Publications:* Sawing Logs, 1980; Strathinver: A Portrait Album, 1984; Radio Poems, 1989; Scanning the Forth Bridge, 1994; Le Château des Enfants, 2000; Chapeau!, 2002. Editor: The Best of Scottish Poetry, 1989; Collected poems of the Marquis of Montrose, 1990; Bittersweet Within My Heart, The Collected Poems of Mary, Queen of Scots, 1992. *Honours:* Best Documentary Television and Radio Industries of Scotland Award, 1984; Sony Award for Best British Radio Feature, 1985. *Membership:* General Secretary, Poetry Asscn of Scotland, 1983–99. *Address:* The Orchard Muirton, Auchterarder, Perthshire PH3 1ND, Scotland.

BELL, Sy(lvia) M(arie Dobbs); b. 16 Aug. 1952, Harrodson County, Mississippi, USA. Poet; Writer; Photographer. m. 24 Nov. 1968, 2 s. *Education:* Diploma, Cumberland Acad. *Publications:* Memories, 1988; Thorns and Roses, 1990. *Contributions to:* Various periodicals. *Honours:* Numerous awards, including 5 Golden Poetry Awards, 1987–91, World of Poetry Awards, and Writers Unlimited Awards. *Memberships:* Gulf Coast Writer's Asscn; National Federation of State Poetry Societies; Southern Poetry Asscn. *Address:* 1419 Georgia Pl., Gulfport, MS 39507, USA.

BELLAMY, Joe David; b. 29 Dec. 1941, Cincinnati, Ohio, USA. Prof. of English; Writer; Poet. m. Connie Sue Arendsee, 16 Sept. 1964, 1 s., 1 d. *Education:* Duke University, 1959–61; BA, Literature, Antioch College, 1964; MFA, English and Creative Writing, University of Iowa, 1969. *Appointments:* Instructor, 1969–70, Asst Prof., 1970–72, Mansfield State College, Pennsylvania; Publisher and Ed., Fiction International magazine and press, 1972–84; Asst Prof., 1972–74, Assoc. Prof., 1974–80, Prof. of English, 1980–, St Lawrence University, Canton, New York; Program Consultant in American Literature, Divisions of Public Programs and Research Programs, National Endowment for the Humanities, 1976–90; Pres. and Chair, Board of Dirs, Co-ordinating Council of Literary Magazines, 1979–81, and Associated Writing Programs, 1990; Distinguished Visiting Prof., George Mason University, 1987–88; Dir, Literature Program, National Endowment for the Arts, 1990–92; Whichard Distinguished Prof. in the Humanities, East Carolina University, 1994–96. *Publications:* Apocalypse: Dominant Contemporary Forms, 1972; The New Fiction: Interviews with Innovative Writers, 1974; Superfiction, or the American Story Transformed, 1975; Olympic Gold Medallist (poems), 1978; Moral Fiction: An Anthology, 1980; New Writers for the Eighties: An Anthology, 1981; Love Stories/Love Poems: An Anthology (with Roger Weingarten), 1982; American Poetry Observed: Poets on Their Work, 1984; The Frozen Sea (poems), 1988; Suzi Sinzinnati (novel), 1989; Atomic Love (stories), 1993; Literary Luxuries: American Writing at the End of the Millennium, 1995. *Contributions to:* Books, anthologies, journals and magazines. *Honours:* Bread Loaf Scholar-Bridgman Award, 1973; National Endowment for the Humanities Fellowship, 1974; Fels Award, 1976; Co-ordinating Council of Literary Magazine Award for Fiction, 1977; Kansas Quarterly-Kansas Arts Commission Fiction Prize, 1982; Pushcart Prize Nominations and Listings, 1983 et seq.; New York State Council on the Arts Grant in Fiction, 1984; National Endowment for the Arts Fellowship for Creative Writers, 1985; Eds' Book Award, 1989. *Membership:* National Book Critics Circle. *Address:* 1145 Lawson Cove, Virginia Beach, VA 23455, USA.

BELLI, Gioconda; b. 9 Dec. 1949, Managua, Nicaragua. Poet; Author. m. (2) Charles Castaldi, 10 April 1987, 4 c. *Education:* Advertising and Journalism, Charles Morris Price School, Philadelphia; Advertising Management, INCAE (Harvard University School of Business Administration in Central America); Philosophy and Literature, Georgetown University, Washington, DC. *Appointments:* Mem., Political-Diplomatic Commission, 1978–79, International Press Liaison, 1982–83, Exec. Secretary and Spokesperson for the Electoral Campaign, 1983–84, Sandinista National Liberation Front; Dir of Communications and Public Relations, Ministry of Economic Planning, 1979–82; Foreign Affairs Secretary, Nicaragua Writer's Union, 1983–88; Managing Dir, Sistema Nacional de Publicidad, 1984–86. *Publications:* Poetry: Sobre la Grama, 1972, English trans. as On the Grass; Línea de

Fuego, 1978, English trans. as Line of Fire; Truenos y Arco Iris, 1982; Amor Insurrecto (anthology), 1985; De la Costilla de Eva, 1987, English trans. as From Eve's Rib; El Ojo de la Mujer, 1991; Sortilegio contral el Frío (erotic collection), 1992; Apogeo, 1997. Fiction: La mujer Habitada, 1988, English trans. as The Inhabited Woman, 1994; Sofia de los Presagios, 1990; Waslala, 1996. Other: The Workshop of the Butterflies (children's story), 1994. *Contributions to:* Anthologies and periodicals. *Honours:* National University Poetry Prize, Nicaragua, 1972; Casa de las Americas Poetry Prize, Cuba, 1978; Friedrich Ebhert Foundation Booksellers, Eds and Publishers Literary Prize, Germany, 1989; Anna Seghers Literary Fellowship, Germany, 1989. *Address:* 1842 Union St, San Francisco, CA 94123, USA.

BELLOTTI, Antonio; b. 20 May 1959, Algeciras, Spain. Sculptor; Poet. m. Feb. 1983, 1 s., 1 d. *Education:* BA, Honours, Essex, 1987; MA, University of Cambridge. *Publication:* The Established Order of Words and Things, 1991. *Contributions to:* Rialto; North; Oxford Poetry; Smiths Knoll; Odyssey; Spoils Anthology; Bradford Poetry; Staple. *Membership:* Poetry Society, London. *Address:* 101 High St, Cherry Hinton, Cambridge CB1 4LU, England.

BELLUOMINI, Ronald Joseph; b. 19 July 1946, Chicago, IL, USA. Teacher; Poet. m. Marilyn Naselli, 27 Sept. 1969, 2 s. *Education:* BS, Education, MA, Geography, Chicago State University. *Publication:* The Thirteenth Labor, 1985. *Contributions to:* Menagerie, 1985; Rhino, 1986; Menagerie, 1989; FOC Review, 1990; Autumn Harvest, 2001. *Honour:* Robert and Hazel Ferguson Memorial Award, Friends of Literature, 1986. *Membership:* Poetry Society of America. *Address:* 2179 Spruce Pointe Ct, Gurnee, IL 60031-6350, USA.

BELOOF, Robert Lawrence; b. 30 Dec. 1923, Wichita, KS, USA. University Prof.; Poet. m. Ruth M La Barre, 14 June 1946, divorced 1972, 4 s. *Education:* BA, Friends University, 1946; MA, Middlebury College, 1948; MA, 1948, PhD, 1954, Northwestern University. *Appointments:* Asst Prof., Assoc. Prof., Prof., University of California, Berkeley, 1948–89; Fulbright Prof. of American Literature, Instituto Orientale, 1960–61; Chair., Dept of Rhetoric, 1964–69. *Publications:* The One-Eyed Gunner, 1956; Good Poems, 1973; The Children of Venus and Mars, 1974. *Contributions to:* Poetry, Chicago; Saturday Review of Literature; Humanist; Poetry Review; Recurrence; Variegation; University of Kansas City Review; Arena; Western Humanities Review; Poetry Quarterly; Shenandoah; Perspective; Dalhousie Review; Window; Contact; Listen; New Departures. *Honours:* Atlantic Monthly Scholarship, 1946; Elinor Frost Scholarship, 1947; Committee for Creative Arts, Fellowship, 1963. *Address:* 1613 Josephine St, Berkeley, CA 94703, USA.

BELSKY, Robert William; b. 14 March 1952, New York, NY, USA. Poet; Writer. *Education:* Nassau County School of Practical Nursing, 1979; Portland Community College, 1982. *Publications:* An Autumn's Day, 1984; At the End of the Rainbow, 1984; A Step Into the Land of Thought, 1985. *Contributions to:* Anthologies and other publications. *Honours:* Golden Poetry Award, 1988; Silver Poetry Award, 1989. *Memberships:* Acad. of American Poets; New Hampshire Writer's Asscn; PEN; Poetry Society of New Hampshire. *Address:* 5 C St, Hudson, NH 03051, USA.

BEN JELLOUN, Tahar; b. 1 Dec. 1944, Fes, Morocco. Writer; Poet; Dramatist. m. Aicha Ben Jelloun, 8 Aug. 1986, 2 s., 2 d. *Education:* University of Rabat, 1963–68; PhD, University of Paris, 1975. *Publications:* Fiction: Harrouda, 1973; La Réclusion solitaire, 1976, English trans. as Solitaire, 1988; Moha le fou, Moha le sage, 1978; La Prière de l'absent, 1981; Muha al-ma'twah, Muha al-hakim, 1982; L'Écrivain public, 1983; L'Enfant de sable, 1985, English trans. as The Sand Child, 1987; La Nuit sacreé, 1987, English trans. as The Sacred Night, 1989; Jour de silence à Tanger, 1990, English trans. as Silent Day in Tangier, 1991; Les Yeux baissés, 1991; Corruption, 1995; Le Premier Amour et Toujours le Dernier, 1995; La Nuit de l'erreur, 1997; Cette aveuglante absence de lumière, 2001. Poetry: Hommes sous linceul de silence, 1970; Cicatrices du soleil, 1972; Le Discours du chameau, 1974; La Memoire future: Anthologie de la nouvelle poésie du Maroc, 1976; Les Amandiers sont morts de leurs blessures, 1976; A l'insu du souvenir, 1980; Sahara, 1987; La Remontée des cendres, 1991; Poésie Complète (1966–1995), 1995. Plays: Chronique d'une solitude, 1976; Entretien avec Monsieur Said Hammadi, ouvrier algerien, 1982; La Fiancée de l'eau, 1984. Non-Fiction: La Plus Haute des solitudes: Misere sexuelle d'emigres nord-africains, 1977; Haut Atlas: L'Exil de pierres, 1982; Hospitalité française: Racisme et immigration maghrebine, 1984; Marseille, comme un matin d'insomnie, 1986; Giacometti, 1991; Le racisme expliqué à ma fille, 1998. *Honours:* Prix de l'Amitie Franco-Arabe, 1976; Chevalier des Arts et des Lettres, 1983; Prix Goncourt, 1987; Chevalier de la Légion d'Honneur, 1988; Prix des Hemispheres, 1991. *Address:* 27 Rue Jacob, 75 Paris 6, France.

BENDON, Chris(topher Graham); b. 27 March 1950, Leeds, Yorkshire, England. Poet; Writer; Critic. m. Sue Moules, 30 Aug. 1979, 1 d. *Education:* BA, English, St David's University College, Lampeter, 1980. *Appointments:* Ed., Spectrum Magazine, 1983–88. *Publications:* In Praise of Low Music, 1981; Software, 1984; Matter, 1986; Cork Memory, 1987; Ridings Writings - Scottish Gothic, 1990; Constructions, 1991; Perspective Lessons, Virtual Lines..., 1992; Jewry, 1995; Crossover, 1996; Novella, 1997. Chapbooks: Testaments, 1983; Quanta, 1984; Aetat 23, 1985; The Posthumous Poem, 1988; A Dyfed Quartet,

1991. *Contributions to:* Anthologies, magazines and journals. *Honours:* Hugh MacDiarmid Memorial Trophy, First Prize, Scottish Open Poetry Competition 1988; £1000 Prize, Guardian/WWF Poetry Competition, 1989. *Memberships* Welsh Acad.; Welsh Union of Writers. *Address:* 14 Maesyderi, Lampeter Ceredigion SA48 7EP, Wales.

BENEDICT, Elinor; b. 4 June 1931, Chattanooga, Tennessee, USA. Writer Poet; Ed. m. Samuel S Benedict, 3 Oct. 1953, 2 s., 1 d. *Education:* BA, Duke University, 1953; MA, Wright State University, 1977; MFA, Vermont College 1983. *Appointments:* Staff, Times Publications, Kettering, Ohio, 1969–76; Part time Instructor, Writers Workshop, Bay de Noc Community College, 1977–86 Ed., Passages North, 1979–89. *Publications:* Landfarer, 1978; A Bridge to China, 1983; Passages North Anthology (ed.), 1990; The Green Heart, 1995 Chinavision, 1995; The Tree Between Us, 1997. *Contributions to:* Many periodicals and reviews. *Honours:* American Asscn of University Women Grant, 1983; Michigan Council for the Arts Creative Artist Award, 1985; Illinois Writers Inc Chapbook Award, 1993; Co-Winner, Sandburg-Livesay Award, 1997. *Memberships:* Acad. of American Poets; Poetry Society of America; Poets and Writers. *Address:* 8627 S Lakeside Dr., Rapid River, M 49878, USA.

BENEDIKT, Michael; b. 26 May 1935, New York, NY, USA. Writer; Poet; Critic; Ed. *Education:* BA, New York University, 1956; MA, Columbia University, 1961. *Appointments:* Professorships in Literature and Poetry, Bennington College, 1968–69, Sarah Lawrence College, 1969–73, Hampshire College, 1973–75, Vassar College, 1976–77, Boston University, 1977–79; Contributing Ed., American Poetry Review, 1973–; Poetry Ed., Paris Review 1974–78. *Publications:* The Body (verse), 1968; Sky (verse), 1970; Mole Notes (prose poems), 1971; Night Cries (prose poems), 1976; The Badminton at Great Barrington or Gustav Mahler and the Chattanooga Choo-Choo (poems), 1980. Anthologies: Modern French Theatre: The Avant-Garde, Dada and Surrealism (with George E Wellwarth), 1964, in the UK as Modern French Plays: An Anthology from Jarry to Ionesco, 1965; Post-War German Theatre (with George E Wellwarth), 1967; Modern Spanish Theatre (with George E Wellwarth), 1968; Theatre Experiment, 1968; The Poetry of Surrealism, 1975; The Prose Poem: An International Anthology, 1976. *Contributions to:* Agni Review; Ambit; Art International; Art News; London Magazine; Massachusetts Review; New York Quarterly; Paris Review; Partisan Review; Poetry. *Honours:* Guggenheim Fellowship, 1968–69; Bess Hokin Prize, 1969; National Endowment for the Arts Prize, 1970; Benedikt: A Profile (critical monograph/Festschrift), 1978; National Endowment for the Arts Fellowship, 1979–80; Retrospective, Library of Congress, videotape, 1986. *Memberships:* PEN Club of America; Poetry Society of America. *Address:* 315 W 98th St, No. 6 A, New York, NY 10025, USA.

BENGTSON, (John) Erik (Robert); b. 21 July 1938, Degerfors, Sweden. Teacher; Poet; Novelist. m. Peggy Lundberg, 26 July 1963, 2 d. *Education:* MA, Uppsala University, 1964. *Appointments:* Teacher, Sundstagymnasiet, Karlstad. *Publications:* I somras, 1963; Orfeus tolv sanger, 1963; Som en a, 1964; Pep Talk, 1977; 10 novels. *Honours:* Various literary prizes. *Address:* Hantverkaregatan 12, 654 60 Karlstad, Sweden.

BENJAMIN, David. See: SLAVITT, David R(ytman).

BENNETT, John M(ichael); b. 12 Oct. 1942, Chicago, IL, USA. Poet; Librarian. m. C Mehrl Bennett, 3 c. *Education:* BA, cum laude, Spanish and English, 1964, MA, Spanish, 1966, Certificate of Competence in Latin American Studies, 1966, Washington University, St Louis; PhD, Spanish, University of California, Los Angeles, 1970; Certified Poetry Therapist, National Asscn for Poetry Therapy, 1985. *Appointments:* Ed., Lost and Found Times, 1974–; Ed.-Publisher, Luna Bisonte Productions, 1974–; Latin American Bibliographic Asst and Ed., 1976–98, Curator, Avant Writing Collector, 1998–, Ohio State University. *Publications:* White Screen, 1976; Nips Poems, 1980; Jerks, 1980; Blender, 1983; Antpath, 1984; No Boy, 1985; Cascade, 1987; Stones in the Lake, 1987; Twitch, 1988; Swelling, 1988; Milk, 1990; Was Ah, 1991; Fenestration, 1991; Somation, 1992; Blind on the Temple, 1993; Wave, 1993; Blanksmanship, 1994; Just Feet, 1994; Infused, 1994; Eddy, 1995; Spinal Speech, 1995; Fish, Man, Control, Room, 1995; Prime Sway, 1996; Ridged Poeta, 1996; Milky Floor (with Sheila E Murphy), 1996; Door Door, 1997; The Seasons, 1997; Clown Door, 1997; Cul Lit, 1997; Know Other, 1998; Luggage, 1998; Loose Watch, 1998; Sendero Luminoso in Context, 1998; Mailer Leaves Ham, 1999; Rolling Combers, 2001; Chac Prostibulario (with Ivan Argüelles), 2001; Yr Cream Dip (with Reed Altemus), 2001; The Chapters, 1980–2001 (with Robin Crozier), 2002. *Contributions to:* Poetry, word art, graphics, articles, reviews and trans to numerous publications. *Honours:* 20 Ohio Arts Council Awards, 1979–2002. *Address:* 137 Leland Ave, Columbus, OH 43214, USA.

BENNETT, Louise (Simone); b. 7 Sept. 1919, Kingston, Jamaica. Lecturer; Poet. m. Eric Coverley. *Education:* RADA, London. *Appointments:* Resident Artist, BBC (West Indies section) 1945–46, 1950–53; Residencies in Coventry, Huddersfield and Amersham, United Kingdom; Drama Specialist, Jamaica Social Welfare Commission, 1955–60; Lecturer, Drama and Jamaican Folklore, University of the West Indies, Kingston, 1959–61; Lecturer, television and radio commentator in Jamaica. *Publications:* Dialect Verses,

1940; Jamaican Dialect Verses, 1942; Jamaican Humour in Dialect, 1943; Miss Lulu Sez, 1948; Anancy Stories and Dialect Verses, 1950; Laugh with Louise, 1960; Jamaica Labrish, 1966; Anancy and Miss Lou, 1979; Selected Poems, 1982; Aunt Roachy Seh, 1993. Other: Various recordings of Jamaican songs and poems. *Honours:* Order of Jamaica; M.B.E.; Silver Musgrave Medal, Institute of Jamaica; Norman Manly Award of Excellence, University of the West Indies, 1982. *Address:* Enfield House, Gordon Town, St Andrew, Jamaica.

BENNETT, Paul (Lewis); b. 10 Jan. 1921, Gnadenhutten, Ohio, USA. Prof. of English (retd); Poet; Writer; Gardener; Orchardist. m. Martha Jeanne Leonhart, 31 Dec. 1941, deceased 1995, 2 s. *Education:* BA, Ohio University, 1942; AM, Harvard University, 1947. *Appointments:* Instructor, Samuel Adams School of Social Studies, Boston, 1945–46; Teaching Asst, Harvard University, 1945–46; Instructor in English, University of Maine, Orono, 1946–47; Instructor to Prof. of English, 1947–86, Poet-in-Residence, 1986–, Denison University; Gardener and Orchardist, 1948–; Consultant, Aerospace Laboratories, Owens-Corning Fiberglass Corp, 1964–67, Ohio Arts Council, 1978–81, Ohio Board of Regents, 1985–86. *Publications:* Poetry: A Strange Affinity, 1975; The Eye of Reason, 1976; Building a House, 1986; The Sun and What It Says Endlessly, 1995; Appalachian Mettle, 1997. Fiction: Robbery on the Highway, 1961; The Living Things, 1975; Follow the River, 1987; Fact Book: Max: The Tail of a Waggish Dog, 1999. *Contributions to:* Many periodicals. *Honours:* National Endowment for the Arts Fellowship, 1973–74; Significant Achievement Award, Ohio University, 1992. *Address:* 1281 Burg St, Granville, OH 43023, USA.

BENSLEY, Connie; b. 28 July 1929, London, England. Poet; Writer. m. J A Bensley, 2 Aug. 1952, 2 s. *Education:* Diploma, Social Sciences, University of London, 1962. *Appointment:* Poetry Ed., PEN Magazine, 1984–85. *Publications:* Progress Report, 1981; Moving In, 1984; Central Reservations, 1990; Choosing to be a Swan, 1994; The Back and the Front of It, 2000. *Contributions to:* Observer; Poetry Review; Spectator; TLS. *Honours:* First Place, TLS Poetry Competition, 1986; Second Place, Leek Poetry Competition, 1988; Prizewinner, Arvon/Observer Poetry Competition, 1994; Second Place, Tate Gallery Poetry Competition, 1995. *Memberships:* Poetry Society. *Address:* 49 Westfields Ave, Barnes, London SW13 0AT, England.

BENSON, Gerard John, (Jedediah Barrow); b. 9 April 1931, London, England. Poet; Writer; Ed. m. (2) 1 s., 1 d. *Education:* Rendcomb College; Exeter University; Diplomas, Distinction, Drama and Education, Central School of Speech and Drama, University of London; IPA. *Appointments:* Resident Tutor, Arvon Foundation and Taliesen Centre; Senior Lecturer, Central School of Speech and Drama; Co-originator and Administrator of Poems on the Underground, 1986–; Arts Council Poet-in-Residence, Dove Cottage, Wordsworth Trust, 1994–; British Council Poet -in-Residence, Cairo and Alexandria, 1997; British Council Writer-in-Residence, Stavanger and Kristiansand, 1998; Poetry in Practice, Poet-in-Residence, Ashwell Medical Centre, Bradford, 2000–01. *Publications:* Name Game, 1971; Gorgon, 1983; This Poem Doesn't Rhyme (ed.), 1990; Tower Block Poet: Sequence of 15 poems commissioned by BBC Radio, 1990; Co-ed. of the ten Poems on the Underground anthologies, 1991–2001; The Magnificent Callisto, 1993; Does W Trouble You? (ed.), 1994; Evidence of Elephants, 1995; In Wordsworth's Chair, 1995; Love Poems on the Underground, 1996; Bradford and Beyond, 1997; Help! (15 poems with woodcuts by Ros Cuthbert), 2001; The Poetry Business, 2002; To Catch an Elephant (poems for children), 2002. *Contributions to:* Newspapers, journals, reviews, and the Internet. *Honours:* Signal Award for Poetry, 1991; Carnegie Medal Nominee, 1996. *Memberships:* Barrow Poets; Quaker Arts Network; Poems on the Underground; Poetry Society, education advisory panel; National Asscn of Writers in Education, chair., 1992. *Address:* 46 Ashwell Rd, Manningham, Bradford, West Yorkshire BD8 9DU, England.

BENSON, Judi (Lamar Parish); b. 20 Dec. 1947, Coronado, CA, USA. Poet; Artist; Ed. m. Ken Smith, 6 July 1981, 1 s. *Education:* BA, Literature and Communications, University of North Florida; MA, Creative Writing, Antioch University, London. *Appointments:* Public Relations Dir, Jacksonville Symphony Orchestra, 1975–78; Asst Dir and Creative Writing Tutor, Antioch University, London, 1980–87; Freelance Writer and Artist, 1987–; Ed., Foolscap Magazine, 1987–96; Writer-in-Schools, Huddersfield, World Poetry Festival, 1995. *Publications:* Making the Family Again, 1987; Somewhere Else, 1990; In the Pockets of Strangers, 1993; Call It Blue, 2000; Klaonica: Poems for Bosnia (co-ed.), 1993; What Poets Eat (ed.), 1994; The Long Pale Corridor (co-ed.), 1996. *Contributions to:* Kalliope; Atlantic Review; Ambit; Orbis; Writing Women; The Rialto; Iron; Neon Clouds; Harry's Hand; Foolscap; Sunk Island Review; Bete Noire; Staple; Slow Dancer; Affirming Flame, anthology; Broadsheet Series; Arts Assembler; Time for Verse, BBC Radio 4 broadcast; Stanza; Poetry Please. *Honours:* First Prize, Jacksonville Arts Festival, 1976; Reader's Choice, Orbis Magazine, 1986; Honourable Mention, Staple Competition, 1989. *Address:* 78 Friars Rd, East Ham, London E6 1LL, England.

BENSON, Steve; b. 14 June 1949, Princeton, New Jersey, USA. Proofreader; Poet. *Education:* BA, Yale College, 1971; MFA, University of California at Irvine, 1973; MA, The Wright Institute. *Publications:* As Is, 1978; The Busses, 1980; Blindspots, 1980; Dominance, 1984; Briarcombe Paragraphs, 1984; Blue

Book, 1989; Reverse Order, 1990. *Contributions to:* Oblek; Poetics Journal; Temblor; Avec; Tasted Screens and Parallels; New American Review; Writing; Raddle Moon. *Honour:* National Endowment for the Arts Poetry Fellowship, 1990. *Address:* 507 Cottekill Rd, Stone Ridge, NY 12484, USA.

BENTOIU, Annie Maria Alice; b. 1 May 1927, Bucharest, Romania. Writer; Poet; Trans. m. Pascal Bentoiu, 8 Jan. 1949, 1 d. *Education:* Faculty of Law, Bucharest, 1945–48; Institut Français de hautes études, 1946–47. *Publications:* Poèmes I; Poèmes II; Dix méditations sur une rose; Phrases pour la vie quotidienne; Voyage en Moldavie. Other: Trans; Memoirs. *Contributions to:* Anthologies, periodicals, journals and magazines. *Honours:* Trans. Prizes, Writers Union of Romania, 1979, 1983, 1991. *Memberships:* PEN; Writers' Union of Romania. *Address:* Aleea Parva 5, App 60, Bloc D 23B, Scara F 77429 Bucharest, Romania.

BENZING, Rosemary Anne; b. 18 Sept. 1945, South India. Teacher; Counsellor; Freelance Journalist; Poet. m. Richard Benzing, 5 April 1969, 1 s., 1 d. *Education:* BA, Honours, English and Philosophy, University College of North Wales, Bangor, 1968; Diploma in Education, 1969; Diploma in Counselling, 1990. *Appointments:* Teacher, Edward Shelley High School, Walsall, 1968–71; Supply Teacher, Shropshire LEA, 1980–; Counsellor, SRCC, 1988–98. *Contributions to:* Hybrid; Foolscap; Folded Sheets; Smoke; Borderlines; Envoi; First Time; Purple Patch; Shropshire Magazine; Plowman; White Rose; Poetry Nottingham; Symphony; Psycho Poetica; Third Half; Krax; Bare Wires; Housewife Writers' Forum. *Honour:* Anglo Welsh Poetry Competition, 1986. *Membership:* Poetry Society. *Address:* Roden House, Shawbury, Shrewsbury, Shropshire, England.

BEOBIDE, Isabel; b. 12 June 1942, Barcelona, Spain. Poet. 3 s., 3 d. *Appointment:* Pres., European Arts Acad. *Publications:* Donner sa Main, 1974; Poétes Face à La Vie, 1976; Cuaderno Literario Azor, 1981; Poétes sans Frontières, 1987. *Contributions to:* Books, newspapers, and journals. *Honours:* Hon. Academic Award, Hispanic Cultural Centre, 1981; Silver Medal, 1990, Gold Medal, 1991, AEA, Paris; Gold Medal, AEA, Luxembourg, 1991; Silver Medal, AEA, Belgium, 1992. *Memberships:* AEA; Agustin Garcia Alonso Centro Cultural Literario y Artistico, Spain; Poetry Writers Asscn. *Address:* Klieverink 814, 1104 KC Amsterdam, Netherlands.

BEREKIZ, Juan. See: AZPITARTE ROUSSE, Juan.

BERESFORD, Anne. See: HAMBURGER, Anne (Ellen).

BERG, Stephen (Walter); b. 2 Aug. 1934, Philadelphia, Pennsylvania, USA. Poet; Writer; Ed. m. Millie Lane, 1959, 2 d. *Education:* University of Pennsylvania; Boston University; BA, University of Iowa, 1959; Indiana University. *Appointments:* Teacher, Temple University, Philadelphia, Princeton University, Haverford College, Pennsylvania; Prof., Philadelphia College of Art; Poetry Ed., Saturday Evening Post, 1961–62; Founding Ed. (with Stephen Parker and Rhoda Schwartz), American Poetry Review, 1972–. *Publications:* Poetry: Berg Goodman Mezey, 1957; Bearing Weapons, 1963; The Queen's Triangle: A Romance, 1970; The Daughters, 1971; Nothing in the Word: Versions of Aztec Poetry, 1972; Grief: Poems and Versions of Poems, 1975; With Akmatova at the Black Gates: Variations, 1981; In It, 1986; First Song, Bankei, 1653, 1989; Homage to the Afterlife, 1991; New and Selected Poems, 1992; Oblivion: Poems, 1995. Editor: Naked Poetry: Recent American Poetry in Open Forms (with Robert Mezey), 1969; Between People (with S J Marks), 1972; About Women (with S J Marks), 1973; The New Naked Poetry (with Robert Mezey), 1976; In Praise of What Persists, 1983; Singular Voices: American Poetry Today, 1985. Other: Sea Ice: Versions of Eskimo Songs, 1988. *Contributions to:* Periodicals. *Honours:* Rockefeller-Centro Mexicano de Escritores Grant, 1959–61; National Trans. Center Grant, 1969; Frank O'Hara Prize, Poetry magazine, 1970; Guggenheim Fellowship, 1974; National Endowment for the Arts Grant, 1976; Columbia University Trans. Center Award, 1976. *Address:* 2005 Mt Vernon St, Philadelphia, PA 19130, USA.

BERGAN, Brooke; b. 6 Dec. 1945, Indianapolis, IN, USA. Writer; Ed.; Poet. *Education:* BA, English, Marian College, Indianapolis, 1967; MA, English, 1973; PhD, English, 1989, University of Illinois, Chicago. *Appointments:* Technical Writer, 1973–76, Senior Ed., 1976–82, Managing Ed., 1982–86, Exec. Ed., 1986–94, Assoc. Dir of Publications, 1994–, University of Illinois, Chicago; Lecturer, Newberry Library, Chicago, 1989–; Literary Ed., Private Arts, 1992–. *Publications:* Windowpane, 1974; Distant Topologies, 1976; Storyville: A Hidden Mirror, 1994. *Contributions to:* Periodicals. *Honours:* Illinois Arts Council Literary Award, 1975, Writer-in-Residence, 1976–78 and Fellowship, 1986; Runner-up, George Bogin Memorial Award, Poetry Society of America, 1991. *Address:* 1150 N Lake Shore Dr., 19F, Chicago, IL 60611, USA.

BERGÉ, Carol; b. 4 Oct. 1928, New York, NY, USA. Writer; Poet; Ed.; Publisher; Antiques Dealer. m. Jack Henry Berge, June 1955, 1 s. *Education:* New York University; New School for Social Research, New York City. *Appointments:* Ed., 1970–84, Publisher, 1991–93, CENTER Magazine and Press; Distinguished Prof. of Literature, Thomas Jefferson College, Allendale, Michigan, 1975–76; Instructor, Goddard College, 1976; Teacher, University of

California Extension Program, Berkeley, 1976–77; Assoc. Prof., University of Southern Mississippi, 1977–78; Ed., Mississippi Review, 1977–78; Visiting Prof., University of New Mexico, 1978–79, 1987; Visiting Lecturer, Wright State University, Dayton, Ohio, 1979, State University of New York at Albany 1980–81; Proprietor, Blue Gate Gallery of Art and Antiques, 1988–. *Publications:* Fiction: The Unfolding, 1969; A Couple Called Moebius, 1972; Acts of Love: An American Novel, 1973; Timepieces, 1977; The Doppler Effect, 1979; Fierce Metronome, 1981; Secrets, Gossip and Slander, 1984; Zebras, or, Contour Lines, 1991. Poetry: The Vulnerable Island, 1964; Lumina, 1965; Poems Made of Skin, 1968; The Chambers, 1969; Circles, as in the Eye, 1969; An American Romance, 1969; From a Soft Angle: Poems About Women, 1972; The Unexpected, 1976; Rituals and Gargoyles, 1976; A Song, A Chant, 1978; Alba Genesis, 1979; Alba Nemesis, 1979. Editor: Light Years: The New York City Coffeehouse Poets of the 1960's, 2001. Reportage: The Vancouver Report, 1965. *Contributions to:* Anthologies and periodicals. *Honours:* New York State Council on the Arts CAPS Award, 1974; National Endowment for the Arts Fellowship, 1979–80. *Memberships:* Authors League; MacDowell Fellows Asscn; National Press Women; Poets & Writers. *Address:* 2070 Calle Contento, Santa Fe, NM 87505, USA.

BERGER, François; b. 16 May 1950, Neuchâtel, Switzerland. Barrister; Poet; Writer. *Education:* Licence Degree in Law, Neuchâtel University, 1977; Barrister, Neuchâtel. *Publications:* Poetry: Mémoire d'anges, 1981; Gestes du veilleur, 1984; Le Pré, 1986, Italian trans., 1996; Les Indiennes, 1988; Le Repos d'Ariane, 1990. Fiction: Le jour avant, 1995; Le voyage de l'Ange, 1999. *Contributions to:* L'Express Feuille d'Avis de Neuchâtel. *Honours:* Louise Labé Prize, Paris, 1982; Citation of Distinction, Schiller Foundation, Zürich, 1985; Auguste Bachelin Prize, Neuchâtel, 1988. *Memberships:* Asscn des écrivains de langue française; Asscn des écrivains neuchâtelois et jurassiens; Canton of Neuchâtel, literature committee pres.; Société suisse des écrivains. *Address:* 28, Rebatte, CH-2068 Hauterive (Neuchâtel), Switzerland.

BERGER, John (Peter); b. 5 Nov. 1926, London, England. Author; Dramatist; Poet; Art Critic. m. twice, 3 c. *Education:* Central School of Art, London; Chelsea School of Art, London. *Appointments:* Painting exhibitions, Wildenstein, Refern and Leicester Galleries, London; Art Critic, Tribune, New Statesman; Many television appearances; Visiting Fellow, BFI, 1990–. *Publications:* A Painter in Our Time, 1958; Marcel Frishman, 1958; Permanent Red, 1960; The Foot of Clive, 1962; Corker's Freedom, 1964; The Success and Failure of Picasso, 1965; A Fortunate Man: The Story of a Country Doctor (with J. Mohr), 1967; G, 1972; The Seventh Man, 1975; About Looking, 1980; Another Way of Telling (with J. Mohr), 1982; Question of Geography (with Nella Bielshi), 1984; The White Bird, 1985; Francisco Goya's Last Portrait (with Nella Bielski), 1989; Once in Europa, 1989; Lilac and Flag, 1991; Keeping a Rendezvous, 1992; To the Wedding, 1995; Photocopies, 1996; Pages of the Wound; Poems, Drawings, Photographs, 1955–96, 1996; King: A Street Story, 1999. *Honours:* Booker Prize, 1972; James Tait Black Memorial Prize, 1972; Guardian Fiction Prize, 1973; New York Critics' Prize, 1976; George Orwell Memorial Prize, 1977; Barcelona Film Festival Europa Award, 1989. *Address:* Quincy, Mieussy, 74440 Taninges, France.

BERGHASH, Rachel; b. 14 Nov. 1935, Jerusalem, Israel. Teacher; Poet. m. Mark Berghash, 21 Jan. 1962, 2 s. *Education:* Rubin Acad. of Music, Jerusalem, 1955–59; MSW, Yeshiva University, 1991. *Appointments:* Producer, A World Elsewhere, programme featuring poets and writers, WBAI-FM, New York, 1983–87. *Contributions to:* Images; Chicago Review; Pulp; Blue Unicorn; Bitterroot; Jewish Frontier; Waterways; Anima. *Membership:* Poets and Writers. *Address:* 7 E 20th St, New York, NY 10003, USA.

BERGMAN, David; b. 13 March 1950, Fitchburg, Massachusetts, USA. Prof. of English; Poet. *Education:* BA, Kenyon College, 1972; MA, 1974, PhD, 1977, Johns Hopkins University. *Appointments:* Prof. of English, Towson University, 1978–; Editorial Board, Kenyon Review, American Literary History. *Publications:* Cracking the Code, 1985; Gaiety Transfigured, 1991; Care and Treatment of Pain, 1994; Heroic Measures, 1998. *Contributions to:* American Scholar; New Criterion; New Republic; Poetry; Paris Review; Raritan; Yale Review. *Honours:* Donor Award, American Society for Arts and Letters, 1982; Towson State Prize for Literature, 1985; George Elliston Poetry Prize, 1985. *Memberships:* MLA; Poetry Society of America. *Address:* 3024 N Calvert St, Apt C5, Baltimore, MD 21218, USA.

BERGONZI, Bernard; b. 13 April 1929, London, England. Author; Poet; Prof. of English Emeritus. *Education:* BLitt, 1961, MA, 1962, Wadham College, Oxford. *Appointments:* Senior Lecturer, 1966–71, Prof. of English, 1971–92, Prof. Emeritus, 1992–, University of Warwick, Coventry. *Publications:* The Early H G Wells, 1961; Heroes' Twilight, 1965; Innovations: Essays on Art and Ideas, 1968; T S Eliot: Four Quartets: A Casebook, 1969; The Situation of the Novel, 1970; T S Eliot, 1972; The Turn of a Century, 1973; H G Wells: A Collection of Critical Essays, 1975; Gerard Manley Hopkins, 1977; Reading the Thirties, 1978; Years: Sixteen Poems, 1979; Poetry 1870–1914, 1980; The Roman Persuasion (novel), 1981; The Myth of Modernism and Twentieth Century Literature, 1986; Exploding English, 1990; Wartime and Aftermath, 1993; David Lodge, 1995; War Poets and Other Subjects, 1999. *Address:* 19 St Mary's Crescent, Leamington Spa CV31 1JL, England.

BERKSON, Bill, (William Craig Berkson); b. 30 Aug. 1939, New York, NY, USA. Poet; Critic; Ed.; Prof. m. (1) Lynn O'Hare, 1975, divorced, 1 s., 1 d., (2) Constance Lewallen, 1998. *Education:* Brown University, 1957–59; Columbia University, 1959–60; New School for Social Research, New York City, 1959–61; New York University Institute of Fine Arts, 1960–61. *Appointments:* Instructor, New School for Social Research, 1964–69; Marin Community College, 1983–84; Ed. and Publisher, Big Sky magazine and books, 1971–78; Adjunct Prof., Southampton College, Long Island University, 1980; Assoc. Prof., California College of Arts and Crafts, 1983–84; Prof. and Co-ordinator of Public Lectures Programme, 1984–, Dir, Letters and Science, 1994–, San Francisco Art Institute; Visiting Artist/Scholar, American Acad. in Rome, 1991. *Publications:* Saturday Night: Poems, 1960–1961, 1961; Shining Leaves, 1969; Two Serious Poems and One Other (with Larry Fagin), 1972; Recent Visitors, 1973; Hymns of St Bridget (with Frank O'Hara), 1975; Enigma Variations, 1975; Ants, 1975; 100 Women, 1975; The World of Leon (with Ron Padgett, Larry Fagin and Michael Brownstein), 1976; Blue is the Hero: Poems, 1960–1975, 1976; Red Devil, 1983; Lush Life, 1983; Start Over, 1984; Serenade, 2000; Fugue State, 2001. Other: Ed. or co-ed. of several books. *Contributions to:* Anthologies, periodicals, quarterlies and journals. *Honours:* Dylan Thomas Memorial Award, 1959; Poets Foundation Grant, 1968; Yaddo Fellowship, 1968; National Endowment for the Arts Fellowship, 1980; Briarcombe Fellowship, 1983; Artspace Award, 1990; Fund for Poetry Award, 1995. *Address:* 25 Grand View Ave, San Francisco, CA 94114, USA.

BERLANDT, Herman Joseph; b. 7 May 1923, Chelm, Poland. Writer; Poet; Ed.; Publisher; Administrator. m. 27 Sept. 1967, 1 s., 2 d. *Education:* AA, University of California; Self-Educated. *Appointments:* Programme Dir, International Festivals Inc, New York, 1965–67; Dir, 16 Poetry-Film Festivals, 1975–91; Ed., Poetry, USA, 1985–90; Publisher and Ed., Mother Earth International. *Publications:* I Spent One Lifetime Dancing, 1972; Poems from the Delphi EpiCentre, 1978; The Street Vendor, 1979; Yu-Me Love Songs, 1986; A Musical Offering, 1990; Soviet Poetry Since Glasnost (ed.), 1990; Uniting the World Through Poetry, 1991; A Hippie Garden of Verses, 1992; In Praise of The Muses, 1994; Suicide Meditations, 1995. *Contributions to:* Poetry; Poetry Flash; Three Penny Poets; The Folio. *Honours:* Ambassador for Poetry, Medallion, Artists Embassy Annual Award, 1990; Marin Arts Council Grant, 1995. *Memberships:* National Poetry Asscn, founding chair., 1987–93; PEN, Oakland; Artists Embassy International; Commonwealth Club. *Address:* c/o National Poetry Asscn, Fort Mason Centre, Building D, San Francisco, CA 94123, USA.

BERLIND, Bruce; b. 17 July 1926, New York, NY, USA. Prof. of English Emeritus; Writer; Poet. m. (1) 2 s., 3 d., (2) Jo Anne Pagano, 17 Jan. 1985. *Education:* AB, Princeton University, 1947; MA, 1950, PhD, 1958, Johns Hopkins University. *Appointments:* Instructor to Prof., 1954–88, Charles A Dana Prof. of English Emeritus, 1988–, Colgate University. *Publications:* Bred in the Bone: An Anthology of Verse (co-ed.), 1945; Three Larks For a Loony, 1957; Ways of Happenings, 1959; Companion Pieces, 1971; Selected Poems of Agnes Nemes Nagy (trans.), 1980; Birds and Other Relations: Selected Poetry of Dezso Tandori (trans.), 1987; Through the Smoke: Selected Poetry of Istvan Vas (co-trans.), 1989; Imre Oravecz's When You Became She (trans.), 1994; Ottó Orbán's The Journey of Barbarus (trans.), 1997; Charon's Ferry: Fifty Poems of Gyula Illyés (trans.), 2000. *Contributions to:* Encounter; London Magazine; Stand; New Letters; Poetry; Transatlantic Review; TriQuarterly; Chicago Review; Paris Review; Grand Street; New England Review; Kenyon Review; Translation Review; Honest Ulsterman; Massachusetts Review; American Poetry Review. *Honours:* Fulbright Award for Trans., 1984; Hungarian PEN Memorial Medal, 1986. *Memberships:* Poetry Society of America; PEN American Centre; American Literary Trans' Asscn. *Address:* Box 237, Hamilton, NY 13346, USA.

BERMAN, Cassia; b. 5 April 1949, New York, NY, USA. Writer; Poet; Teacher. *Education:* BA, Sarah Lawrence College, 1970; Certified Qi Healer, Qi Gong Therapist, Chinese Healing Arts Center, 1991, 1994. *Appointments:* New York City CETA Arts Project; Poet-in-Residence, many community organizations. *Publication:* Divine Mother Within Me, 1995. *Contributions to:* American Poetry Review; Divine Mosaic; Women's Images of the Sacred; Mothers of the Universe; Visions of the Goddess; Tantric Hymns of Enlightenment. *Address:* 11 1/2 Tannery Brook Rd, Woodstock, NY 12498, USA.

BERNARD, Chris; b. 26 Jan. 1943, Lyon, France. Teacher; Poet. m. Gabrielle Farge, 2 Aug. 1969, 2 s. *Education:* Baccalauréat, University of Lyon, 1961. *Publications:* Le Vol des Abeilles, 1986; Le Poéte Sourire, 1988; La Maison de N, 1991; Poèmes d'Azur, 1992; Respirs, 1994. *Contributions to:* Various publications. *Honours:* Grand Poetry Prize, Festival de Nyons, 1988; Gold Medal de l'Education Sociale, 1989; Gold Medal, Internationale d'Arts et Lettres, 1992; Many other prizes. *Memberships:* Académie International de Lutece; Society of French Poets. *Address:* Le Theron, 84110 Puymeras, France.

BERNARD, Oliver (Owen); b. 6 Dec. 1925, Chalfont St Peter, Buckinghamshire, England. Poet; Trans. 2 s., 2 d. *Education:* BA, Goldsmiths College, 1953; ACSD, Central School of Speech and Drama, 1971. *Appointments:* Teacher of English, Suffolk and Norfolk, 1964–74; Advisory Teacher of Drama, Norfolk Education Committee, 1974–81. *Publications:*

Country Matters, 1960; Rimbaud: Collected Poems (translating ed.), 1961; Apollinaire: Selected Poems (trans.), 1965; Moons and Tides, 1978; Poems, 1983; Five Peace Poems, 1985; The Finger Points at the Moon (trans.), 1989; Salvador Espriu: Forms and Words, 1990; Getting Over It (autobiography), 1992; Quia Amore Langueo (trans.), 1995; Verse Etc, 2001. *Contributions to:* Various publications. *Honour:* Gold Medal for Verse Speaking, Poetry Society, 1982. *Memberships:* British Actors' Equity Asscn; Speak-a-Poem, committee mem.; William Morris Society. *Address:* 1 E Church St, Kenninghall, Norwich NR16 2EP, England.

BERNSTEIN, Charles; b. 4 April 1950, New York, NY, USA. Prof. of Poetry and Poetics; Poet; Writer; Ed. m. Susan Bee Laufer, 1977, 1 s., 1 d. *Education:* AB, Harvard College, 1972. *Appointments:* Freelance writer in the medical field, 1976–89; Visiting Lecturer in Literature, University of California at San Diego, 1987; Lecturer in Creative Writing, Princeton University, 1989, 1990; David Gray Prof. of Poetry and Letters, State University of New York at Buffalo, 1990–. *Publications:* Poetry: Asylums, 1975; Parsing, 1976; Shade, 1978; Poetic Justice, 1979; Senses of Responsibility, 1979; Legend (with others), 1980; Controlling Interests, 1980; Disfrutes, 1981; The Occurrence of Tune, 1981; Stigma, 1981; Islets/Irritations, 1983; Resistance, 1983; Veil, 1987; The Sophist, 1987; Four Poems, 1988; The Nude Formalism, 1989; The Absent Father in Dumbo, 1990; Fool's Gold (with Susan Bee), 1991; Rough Trades, 1991; Dark City, 1994; The Subject, 1995; Republics of Reality: Poems 1975–1995, 2000; With Strings, 2001. Essays: Content's Dream: Essays 1975–1984, 1986; A Poetics, 1992; My Way: Speeches and Poems, 1999. Editor: L=A=N=G=U=A=G=E Book, with Bruce Andrews, 4 vols, 1978–81; The L=A=N=G=U=A=G=E Book, with Bruce Andrews, 1984; The Politics of Poetic Form: Poetry and Public Policy, 1990; Close Listening: Poetry and the Performed Word, 1998. *Contributions to:* Numerous anthologies, collections, and periodicals. *Honours:* William Lyon Mackenzie King Fellow, Simon Fraser University, 1973; National Endowment for the Arts Fellowship, 1980; Guggenheim Fellowship, 1985; University of Auckland Foundation Fellowship, 1986; New York Foundation for the Arts Fellowships, 1990, 1995; American Society of Composers, Authors and Publishers Standard Award, 1993; Roy Harvey Pearce/Archive for New Poetry Prize, 2000. *Address:* Poetics Program, Dept of English, 438 Clemens Hall, State University of New York at Buffalo, Buffalo, NY 14260, USA.

BERROA, Rei; b. 11 March 1949, Dominican Republic. Prof. of Spanish Literature; Poet. *Education:* Diploma, Consejo Superior de Investigaciones Cientificas, Madrid, 1977–78; MA, 1977, Middlebury College, Vermont and Madrid, Spain; MA, 1980, PhD, 1983, University of Pittsburgh, Pennsylvania. *Appointments:* Asst Prof. of Spanish and Latin American Literature, Humboldt State University, CA, 1982–83, Blackburn College, IL, 1983–84; Assoc. Prof. of Modern Spanish Literature, Stylistics and Literary Criticism, George Mason University, Virginia, 1984–; Poet-in-Residence, Cincinnati Conference of Literature and Oklahoma State University, 1985; Vice-Ed. for Creative Writing, Discurso Literario, 1988–. *Publications:* Retazos para un traje de tierra, 1979; En el reino de la ausencia, 1979; Los otros, 1983; Libro de los fragmentos, 1989; Book of Fragments, 1992. *Contributions to:* Compass; El Arco y la Lira; Isla Abierta; Cuadernos de Poetica; Cuadernos Americanos; Ahora!; Discurso Literario; Revista de Poeticas; Revista Mexicana de Cultura; Mundo; Problemas y Confrontaciones; Cuadernos Hispanoamericanos; Insula. *Honours:* Recorded a selection of his poetic works for the Library of Congress Poetry Archives, 1987; Readings at several councils, libraries and universities. *Memberships:* Poetry Society of America, 1991–; Latin American Writers Institute, New York, 1990–. *Address:* 3505 Spring Lake Terrace, Fairfax, VA 22030, USA.

BERRY, Francis; b. 23 March 1915, Ipoh, Malaysia. Poet; Writer; Prof. Emeritus. m. (1) Nancy Melloney Graham, 4 Sept. 1947, 1 s., 1 d., (2) Eileen Marjorie Lear, 9 April 1970. *Education:* University College of the South West, 1937–39, 1946–47; BA, University of London, 1947; MA, University of Exeter, 1949. *Appointments:* Prof. of English Literature, University of Sheffield, 1967–70; Prof. of English, Royal Holloway, University of London, 1970–80. *Publications:* Gospel of Fire, 1933; Snake in the Moon, 1936; The Iron Christ, 1938; Fall of a Tower, 1943; The Galloping Centaur, 1952; Murdock and Other Poems, 1955; Poets' Grammar, 1958; Morant Bay and Other Poems, 1961; Poetry and the Physical Voice, 1962; Ghosts of Greenland, 1966; The Shakespeare Inset, 1966; I Tell of Greenland, 1977; From the Red Fort, 1984; Collected Poems, 1994. *Contributions to:* Periodicals; BBC. *Membership:* Fellow, RSL. *Address:* 4 Eastgate St, Winchester, Hampshire SO23 8EB, England.

BERRY, Ila; b. 9 June 1922, USA. Poet; Writer. *Education:* AA, Fullerton College, CA; BA, John F Kennedy University, Orinda, CA; MA, English and Creative Writing, San Francisco State University, 1985. *Publications:* Poetry: Come Walk With Me, 1979; Rearranging the Landscape, 1986; Rowing in Eden, 1987; Behold the Bright Demons, 1993. *Contributions to:* Periodicals. *Honours:* Jessamyn West Creative Award, 1969; Woman of Distinction, Fullerton College, 1969. *Memberships:* California Federation of Chaparral Poets, Robert Frost Chapter; California State Poetry Society; California Writers Club; Ina Coolbrith Circle, pres., 1977–79; National League of American Pen Women. *Address:* 761 Sequoia Woods Pl., Concord, CA 94518, USA.

BERRY, Jake; b. 16 June 1959, Florence, AL, USA. Ed.; Poet. *Education:* Northwest Alabama Junior College; University of North Alabama; International Bible College. *Appointments:* Ed., Outre, Anomaly, and The Experioddicist journals. *Publications:* The Pandemonium Spirit, 1986; Idiot Menagerie, 1987; Hairbone Stew, 1988; Psyclsomp, 1989; Unnon Theories, 1989; The Tongue Bearer's Daughter, 1990; Equations, 1991; Brambu Drezi, 1994; Phaseostrophes, 1995; Species of Abandoned Light, 1995. *Contributions to:* Magazines and reviews. *Address:* PO Box 2113, Florence, AL 35630, USA.

BERRY, James; b. 1925, Fair Prospect, Jamaica. Poet; Writer; Ed. *Publications:* Bluefoot Traveller: An Anthology of West Indian Poets in Britain (ed.), 1976; Fractured Circles, 1979; News for Babylon: The Chatto Book of West Indian-British Poetry (ed.), 1984; Chain of Days, 1985; The Girls and Yanga Marshall (stories), 1987; A Thief in the Village and Other Stories, 1988; Don't Leave an Elephant to Go and Chase a Bird, 1990; When I Dance (poems), 1991; Ajeema and His Son, 1992. *Honours:* C Day-Lewis Fellowship; Poetry Society Prize, 1981; Boston Globe/Horn Book Award, 1993. *Address:* c/o Hamish Hamilton Ltd, 27 Wrights Lane, London W8 5TZ, England.

BERRY, Wendell (Erdman); b. 5 Aug. 1934, Henry County, KY, USA. Writer; Poet; Prof. m. Tanya Amyx Berry, 29 May 1957, 1 s., 1 d. *Education:* BA, 1956, MA, 1957, University of Kentucky. *Appointments:* Instructor, Georgetown College, 1957–58; E H Jones Lecturer in Creative Writing, 1959–60, Visiting Prof. of Creative Writing, 1968–69, Stanford University; Asst Prof., New York University, 1962–64; Faculty Mem., 1964–77, Prof., 1987–93, University of Kentucky; Elliston Poet, University of Cincinnati, 1974; Writer-in-Residence, Centre College, 1977, Bucknell University, 1987. *Publications:* Fiction: Nathan Coulter, 1960; A Place on North, 1967; The Memory of Old Jack, 1974; The Wild Birds, 1986; Remembering, 1988; The Discovery of Kentucky, 1991; Fidelity, 1992; A Consent, 1993; Watch With Me, 1994; A World Lost, 1996. Poetry: The Broken Ground, 1964; Openings, 1968; Findings, 1969; Farming: A Handbook, 1970; The Country of Marriage, 1973; Sayings and Doings, 1975; Clearing, 1977; A Part, 1980; The Wheel, 1982; Collected Poems, 1985; Sabbaths, 1987; Sayings and Doings and an Eastward Look, 1990; Entries, 1994; The Farm, 1995. Non-Fiction: The Long-Legged House, 1969; The Hidden Wound, 1970; The Unforseen Wilderness, 1971; A Continuous Harmony, 1972; The Unsettling of America, 1977; Recollected Essays 1965–1980, 1981; The Gift of Good Land, 1981; Standing by Words, 1983; Home Economics, 1987; What Are People For?, 1990; Harlan Hubbard: Life and Work, 1990; Standing on Earth, 1991; Sex, Economy, Freedom and Community, 1993; Another Turn of the Crank, 1995; Life is a Miracle: An Essay Against Modern Superstition, 2000. *Honours:* Guggenheim Fellowship, 1962; Rockefeller Fellowship, 1965; National Institute of Arts and Letters Award, 1971; Jean Stein Award, American Acad. of Arts and Letters, 1987; Lannan Foundation Award for Non-Fiction, 1989; T S Eliot Award, Ingersoll Foundation, 1994; Award for Excellence in Poetry, The Christian Century, 1994; Harry M Caudill Conservationist Award, Cumberland Chapter, Sierra Club, 1996. *Address:* Lanes Landing Farm, Port Royal, KY 40058, USA.

BERTOLINO, James; b. 4 Oct. 1942, Hurley, Wisconsin, USA. Poet; Writer; University Teacher. m. Lois Behling, 29 Nov. 1966. *Education:* BS, University of Wisconsin, 1970; MFA, Cornell University, 1973. *Appointments:* Teacher, Washington State University, 1970–71, Cornell University, 1971–74, University of Cincinnati, 1974–84, Washington Community Colleges, 1984–91, Chapman University, 1989–96, Western Washington University, 1991–96. *Publications:* Poetry: Employed, 1972; Soft Rock, 1973; The Gestures, 1975; Making Space for Our Living, 1975; The Alleged Conception, 1976; New & Selected Poems, 1978; Precint Kali, 1982; First Credo, 1986; Snail River, 1995. Chapbooks: Drool, 1968; Day of Change, 1968; Stone Marrow, 1969; Becoming Human, 1970; Edging Through, 1972; Terminal Placebos, 1975; Are You Tough Enough for the Eighties?, 1979; Like a Planet, 1993. *Contributions to:* Poetry in 27 anthologies; Prose in 3 anthologies; Poetry, stories, essays, and reviews in periodicals. *Honours:* Hart Crane Poetry Award, 1969; Discovery Award, 1972; National Endowment for the Arts Fellowship, 1974; Quarterly Review of Literature International Book Awards, 1986, 1995; Djerassi Foundation Residency, 1987; Bumbershoot Big Book Award, 1994. *Address:* 533 Section Ave, Anacortes, WA 98221, USA.

BESWICK, Zanna; b. 15 Oct. 1952, London, England. Television Drama Ed.; Lecturer in Dramatic Literature; Poet. m. Andy Paterson, 3 June 1989. *Education:* BA, Drama, Bristol University, 1971–75. *Appointments:* Theatre Designer and Script Reader; BBC Script Ed. in drama series, serials; Thames TV Ed. of Young People's Drama Dept; Producer, comedy series, The Faint Hearted Feminist, BBC; Thames TV Series Ed., The Bill; Lecturer in Drama, Wake Forest University, USA. *Publication:* And for the Footsteps, 1984. *Contributions to:* Camden Voices; Resurgence; Writing Women; 3 X 4; Niai; Second Shift; Female Eye; Kindred Spirit; Caduceus; The Independent; Daily Telegraph. Anthologies: In the Gold of Flesh, 1990; Mirror Image, 1995; The Upper Hand, 1995; Earth Ascending, 1996; The Ring of Words, 1999. *Membership:* Poetry Society. *Address:* 18 Cardigan Rd, Richmond, Surrey TW10 6BJ, England.

BETAKI, Vassily; b. 29 Sept. 1930, Rostov on Don, Russia. Poet; Trans. of Poetry; Literary Critic; Architectural Historian. 2 d. *Education:* MA, Institute of Literature, Moscow. *Appointments:* Teacher, high school, 1950–55; Science Dir, Pavlovsk Palace Museum, 1956–62; Critic, Radio Liberty, Munich-Paris, 1973–88. *Publications:* Earth Flame, 1965; Short Circuit of Time, 1974; The Island of Europe, 1981; The Fifth Horseman, 1985; In Kitezh Town, 1991; Selected Poems, 1992; Poems 1990–1993, 1994; The Results of Romanticism, 1997; Selected Poems, 1998; Collected Poems, 2001. Translations: Brel and Brassens: Songs, 1985; Kipling: Poems, 1986; Lina Kostenko: Selected Poems, 1988, Marmion, 1998; Old Possum's Book of Practical Cats, 1999; Sylvia Plath: Poems, 2000. *Contributions to:* Zvezda; Avrora; Grani; Kontinent; Strelets; Den Poezii; Neva. *Honour:* Trans. Competition Prize for the major works of Edgar Allan Poe, Moscow, 1971. *Address:* 4 rue Michel Vignaud, 92360 Meudon-la-Foret, France. *E-mail:* kassel@free.fr.

BETLEJ, Bronislawa; b. 26 Aug. 1928, Dominikowice, Poland. Writer; Poet. m. Bronislaw Betlej, 15 July 1950, 2 s., 1 d. *Education:* College of Philology, Gorlice, 1945–47; Teachers College, Gorlice, 1947–48; College of Biology, Krosno, 1948–50. *Publications:* Przeciw swiatu, English trans. as Against the World, 1989; Zatrzymac jeszcze wiatr, English trans. as Stop Only the Wind, 1990; Oto moja godzina, English trans. as This is My Time, 1991; Slowa na niepogode, 1991; Pióro tanczcego ptaka, English trans. as The Feather Dancing Bird, 1991; Moje krajobrazy, English trans. as My Landscape, 1992; Cnoty i niecnoty, 1992; Los zapisany westchnieniem, 1993; Mój malenki swiat, English trans. as My Small World, 1993; Slowo wobec Boga, 1993; Bac sie nie trzeba, 1993; Posluchaj starych drzew, 1994; Ty który w oczach masz wiosne, English trans. as You, With the Spring in Your Eyes, 1995; Jakie jest imie ciszy, English trans. as What is the Name of Silence, 1995; Gorlice, Brosza serca, 1995; Taniec woskowych figur, 1996; Modlitwa Pielgrzyma, 1996; Psalmy mojego zycia, 1996; Z wiard ojcow w nowe tysiaclecie, 1997; Pozwótkie spiewac dzieciom, 1997; Pozoldle karty historii odwracam, 1998; Stan skupienia, 1998; Gwiezdna obietnica, 1998; Mala Ojczyzna-Jedlicze, 1999; To tylko mysli (It's Only Thoughts), 2000. *Contributions to:* Magazines and newspapers. *Honours:* Woman of the Year, Literature na swiecie, 1995; Golden Pen Award, Polish Writers Asscn, 1997; Golden Order of Merit, Pres. of Poland; Freeman of the Town of Jedlicze, 50th Anniversary of Literary Work. *Memberships:* Polish Writers Asscn; Warsaw Writers Club; Literary and Artistic Club, Krosno; Civitas Christiana, Krosno; Union of Polish Men of Letters, Warsaw. *Address:* ul Jesionowa 23, Krosno Wojewodz Podkerpeckie, 38-460 Jedlicze, Poland.

BETTARINI, Mariella; b. 31 Jan. 1942, Florence, Italy. Writer; Poet; Teacher. *Education:* Teacher's Diploma, 1964. *Appointments:* Elementary School Teacher; Co-Founder, Ed. and Publisher, Salvo Imprevisti, 1973. *Publications:* Il pudore e l'effondersi, 1966; Il leccio, 1968; La rivoluzione copernicana, 1970; Terra di tutti e altre poesie, 1972; Dal vero, 1974; In bocca alla balena, 1977; Storie d'Ortensia: Romanza, 1978; Felice di essare: Scritti sulla condizione della donna e sulla sessualità, 1978; Diario fiorentino, 1979; Chi è il poeta? (co-ed.), 1980; Ossessi oggetti-Spiritate materie, 1981; Il viaggio-Il corpo, 1982; La nostra gioventù: 18 gennaio 1976, 1982; Poesie vegetali, 1982; Psicografia, 1982; Vegetali figure: 1978–82, 1983; I Guerrieri di Riace di Mario Grasso, 1984; Tre lustri ed oltre: Antologia poetica 1963–1981, 1986; Amorosa persona, 1989. *Address:* c/o Salvatore Sciascia Editori, Corso Umberto 1111, 93100 Caltanissetta, Italy.

BETTENCOURT-PINTO, Eduardo; b. 23 April 1954, Gabela, Angola. Accountant; Poet. m. Rosa Pinto, 17 Dec. 1980, 2 s. *Education:* Post Secondary Education in Commercial and Accounting, Labor Law, 1975. *Publications:* Emoçao, 1978; Poemas, c/Jorge Arrimar, 1979; Razoes, 1979; Mao Tardia, 1981; Emersos Vestigios, 1985; Deusa da Chuva, 1991. *Contributions to:* Correio dos Agores; Diario Insular; Gavea Brown Magazine; Prism International Suplemento Agoriano de Cultura. *Honours:* Contexto, Poetry Award, 1981; Portuguese Cultural Asscn, France, 1986. *Membership:* Portuguese Writers' Asscn. *Address:* 11528-198 St, Pitt Meadows, BC V3Y 1N9, Canada.

BEVAN, Alistair. See: ROBERTS, Keith (John Kingston).

BEVERIDGE, Judith Helen; b. 3 Aug. 1956, London, England. Poet. m. Surinder Singh Joson, 4 Aug. 1990, 1 s. *Education:* BA, Communications, University of Technology, Sydney. *Publication:* The Domesticity of Giraffes, 1987. *Contributions to:* Poetry Australia; Meanjin; Island Magazine; New Poetry; Southerly; Sydney Morning Herald; The Age; Penguin Book of Modern Australian Poetry; Oxford Book of Australian Poetry; Compass; P76; *Phoenix Review.* *Honours:* Dame Mary Gilmore Award, 1988; New South Wales State Literary Award for Poetry, 1988; Victorian Premier's Literary Award for Poetry, 1988; Short-listed for South Australian Premier's Award, 1988, Commonwealth Poetry Prize for a First Book, 1989. *Membership:* Poets Union. *Address:* 12 Cobham Ave, West Ryde, NSW 2114, Australia.

BEZNER, Kevin; b. 21 March 1953, Bainbridge, Maryland, USA. Poet. m. Lili Corbus, 16 Nov. 1980, 1 s. *Education:* BA, American Studies, Roger Williams College, 1975; MA, American Studies, 1976, MA, English, 1989, University of Maryland; PhD, English, Ohio University, 1991. *Appointments:* Florida Community College, Jacksonville, 1986–88; Humanities, University of Montana, 1991–93; English, Idaho State University, 1994–95; Livingstone College, Salisbury, North Carolina, 1995–96. *Publications:* About Water 1993; In the City of Troy, 1994; The Wilderness of Vision: On the Poetry o John Haines (co-ed.), 1996; The Tools of Ignorance, 1997. *Contributions to:* Bi Scream; Calapooya Collage; Cincinnati Poetry Review; Elf; Eclectic Literar Forum; On the Bus; Snowy Egret; Turning Wheel. *Memberships:* PEN West Poetry Society of America. *Address:* 4710 Walker Rd, Charlotte, NC 28211 USA.

BHARTI, Dharmvir; b. 1926, India. Novelist; Poet; Ed. *Education:* MA University of Allahabad, 1947. *Appointments:* Founder-Ed., Charmayu magazine; Ed., Alocha quarterly. *Publications:* Fiction: The Village of the Dead, 1946; The God of Sins, 1949; The Seventh House of the Sun God, 1952 Immortal Son, 1952; The Moon and Broken People, 1965. Poetry: Cold Iron 1952; The Beloved of Krishna, 1959; Seven Years of Lyrics, 1959. *Address:* c/c Dharmayug, Bennett, Coleman & Co, Times Building, Dr D B Rd, Mumbai 400001, India.

BHATIA, H. S.; b. 15 Aug. 1936, Lala Musa, Pakistan. Senior Lecturer ir English (retd); Poet. m. Sita Bhatia, 18 Nov. 1962, 2 s. *Education:* BA, Panjab University, Chandigarh, 1961; MA, English Literature, Meerut University, Meerut, 1970. *Appointments:* School Teacher, Jalandhar, 1955; Accounts Official, 1955–70; College Lecturer, degree classes, Panjab University, Chandigarh, 1970–94. *Publications:* Modern Trends in Indo-Anglian Poetry (ed.), 1982–83; Prevalent Aspects of Indian English Poetry (ed.), 1983–84; Burning Petals (poems), 1983–84; The Necklace Wild (poems), 1994; Social Reality in Indian English Poetry, 1994. *Contributions to:* Poetry Times; Poet; Homeros, Turkey; Skylark; Poetcrit; Eureka; Commonwealth Quarterly; Kavita India; Journal of Indian Writing in English; Youth Age; Canopy; Creative Forum; Bharat Protiva. *Address:* B 4-301 Nandi Colony, Chandigarb Rd, Khanna, Punjab 141401, India.

BHATNAGAR, Om Prakash; b. 30 May 1932, Agra, India. University Teacher of English; Writer; Poet. m. Parvati Bhatnagar, 21 Oct. 1959, 1 s., 1 d. *Education:* MA, 1954; MA, 1956; DLitt, 1959; PhD, 1991. *Appointments:* University Teacher of English; Editorial Board, Indian Journal of English Studies, 1979–86. *Publications:* Thought Poems; Angles of Retreat; Oneiric Visions; Shadows in Floodlights; Audible Landscape; Perspectives on Indian Poetry in English; Studies in Indian Drama in English. *Contributions to:* Many literary and research publications. *Memberships:* Indian Asscn for English Studies; University English Teachers Asscn. *Address:* Rituraj, Camp, Amravati 444 602, India.

BHATTACHARJYA, Hiren; b. 28 July 1932, Jorhat, India. Writer; Poet. m. Parul, 6 Dec. 1973, 1 s., 1 d. *Education:* BA, Guwahati University. *Publications:* Mor Desh Mor Premor Kabita, 1972; Bivinna Dinar Kabita, 1974; Kabita Road, 1976; Sugandhi Pakhila, 1981; Sashyor Pathar Manuh, 1991; Jonakimon O Annyanya, 1991. *Contributions to:* Assamese Daily; Periodicals. *Honours:* Raghunath Chowdhury Poetry Award, 1976; Bishnu Rava Award, 1985; Rajaji Literary Award, 1986; Soviet Land Nehru Award, 1988–89. *Memberships:* All India Progressive Writers Asscn; Progressive Writers and Artists Asscn. *Address:* Sheha Tirtha, RG Barua Rd, Guwahati 781003, India.

BHATTACHARYA, Indrajit; b. 22 March 1960, India. College English Teacher; Poet. m. Chandana Bhattacharya, 20 Feb. 1992. *Education:* BA, Honours, Economics, Calcutta, 1980; MA, English Literature, 1983, PhD, Modern American Poetry, 1991, Ravishankar University. *Publications:* Song of the Morrow, 1988; Bubbles, 1991; Hattali, 1991. *Contributions to:* Literary journals and periodicals. *Memberships:* American Studies Research Centre, Hyderabad; Comparative Literature Asscn of India; Indian Asscn for Canadian Studies; United Writers' Asscn; PEN All India Centre; Indian Asscn for Commonwealth Literature and Language Studies. *Address:* Dept of Applied Sciences and Humanities, Shaheed Bhagat Singh College of Engineering and Technology, Post Box 20, Ferozepur 152 001, Punjab, India.

BHIMANNA, Boyi; b. 19 Sept. 1911, Mamidi Kuduru, India. Writer; Poet. *Education:* Double Graduation, 1935, 1940. *Appointments:* Journalist, 1936–55; Teacher, 1942–45; Dir, Trans, Government of Andhra Pradesh, 1955–66; Mem., Legislative Council, Andhra Pradesh, 1978–84; Mem., Senate, Andhra and Osmania Universities, 1940–71; Mem., Syndicate, S. K. University, 1983. *Publications:* A Farm Boy, 1940; The Labour King, 1947; The Parliament of Lights, 1955; The Seventh Season, 1964; Raaga Vysaakhi, 1965; Fight for Social Justice, 1968; Raabhilu, 1971; The Huts are on Fire, 1973; The Photo, 1975; Janmantara Vyram, 1980; Ambedkara Suprabhatam, 1984; Salvation is My Birth Right, 1987; Idigo, Idee Bhagavadgita, 1990; Paatalalo Ambedkar, 1992; Drug Addicts, 1993; How Deep the Darkness and How Many the Lights, 1994; The Great Harijan and Girijan Personalities of Puranic Age, 1995. *Contributions to:* Numerous newspapers, magazines and journals. *Honours:* Awarded title Maha Kavi at Kakinada, 1968; Hon. Doctorate, Kalaa Prapoorna, Andhra University, 1971; Awards of Padma Shri, Pres. of India, 1973; National Award, Central Saahitya Akademi for Poetry, 1975; Hon. DLitt, Kashi Vidyapeeth, Vaarnai, 1976; Rajalakshmi Literary Award, 1991; Telugu University Visishta Puraskaram, 1992; Hon. Doctorate, Nagarjuna University, 1993; Sahasra Poorna Chandra Darsanotsavan, 1994; B N Reddy Literary Award, 1995; Telugu Aatma Gourava Award, 1996. *Address:* 1C 85, Irrum Manzil Colony, Hyderabad 500 082, Andhra Pradesh, India.

BIANCHI, Herman, (Thomas Cashet); b. 14 Dec. 1924, Rotterdam, Netherlands. Prof. of Law (retd); Poet. 1 s. *Education:* LLD, Legal Studies, 1956. *Appointments:* Prof. of Law, Free University, Amsterdam, 1960–89. *Publication:* A Breviary of Torment, 1991. *Membership:* Maatschappij der Nederlandse Letterkunde, Leiden. *Address:* Albrecht Dürerstraat 48, 1077 MB Amsterdam, Netherlands.

BIARUJIA, Javant; b. 8 Aug. 1955, Melbourne, Vic., Australia. Ed.; Poet; Writer. *Appointments:* Founder-Ed., Nosukumo, 1982–96, Labassa Quarterly, 1995–97; Ed., Australian-Indonesian Asscn News, Victoria, 1995–98; Writer-in-Residence, University of Indonesia, Jakarta, 1998. *Publications:* Fallen Angels, 1980; Warrior Dolls, 1981; Thalassa Thalassa, 1983; Eye in the Anus, 1985; Autumn Silks, 1988; Gakai, 1989; Calqueneaux, 1989; This is a Table, 1989; Ra, 1991; Low/Life, 2002; Calques, 2002. *Contributions to:* Anthologies, literary journals and magazines in Australia, Japan, England and the USA. *Honours:* First Place in HIV/AIDS Radio Plays, 1991; First Prize in the inaugural Irene Mitchell Award for short plays, 1996; Australia Council Grant, 1998; Robert Duncan Poetry Prize, 1998. *Memberships:* Society of Eds; Fellowship of Australian Writers; Imago; Carringbush Writers, co-founder, 1981. *Address:* GPO Box 994-H, Melbourne, Vic. 3001, Australia.

BIBBY, Peter Leonard; b. 21 Dec. 1940, London, England. Poet; Writer; Dramatist; Screenwriter; Ed. m. 15 April 1967, 2 s., 2 d. *Education:* BA, University of Western Australia; DipEd, Murdoch University. *Appointments:* Ed., Fellowship of Australian Writers, and Bagabala Books. *Publication:* Island Weekend, 1960. *Contributions to:* Various anthologies and journals. *Honours:* Tom Collins Literary Awards, 1978, 1982; Lyndall Hadow National Short Story Award, 1983; Donald Stuart National Short Story Award, 1985. *Memberships:* Australian Film Institute; Australian Writers Guild; Computer Graphics Asscn; Fellowship of Australian Writers. *Address:* c/o PO Box 668, Broome, WA, Australia.

BIBERGER, Erich Ludwig; b. 20 July 1927, Passau, Germany. Poet; Writer; Ed. *Education:* Passau. *Appointments:* Founder-Dir, Internationale Regensbürger Literaturtage, 1967–94, Internationale Jungautoren-Wettbewerbe, 1972–94; Founder-Ed., RSG Studio International, 1973–, RSG Forum 15/25, 1977–. *Publications:* Dreiklang der Stille (poems), 1955; Rundgang über dem Norlicht (prose), 1958; Die Traumwelle (novel), 1962; Denn im Allsein der Welt (poems), 1966; Gar mancher (satirical verses), 1967; Anthology Quer, 1974; Anthology 3, 1979; Andere Wege bis Zitterluft (poems), 1982; Nichts als das Meer (poems), 1984; Zwei Pfund Morgenduft (feuilletons), 1987; Drei Millimeter Erd-Kugel, Trei Milimetristerapamanteasca (poems), 1997; Fantasieschutzgebiet, Imaginationis hortulus (haiku), 1998. *Honours:* Several, including establishment of the Erich-und-Maria-Biberger Preises für Verdienste um die Literatur, 1995. *Memberships:* Regensburg Asscn of Authors, chair., 1960–, hon. pres., 1995–; Humboldt-Gesellschaft für Wissenschaft und Kunst, 1993–; Bayerischer Kulturrat, 1998–. *Address:* Altmühlstrasse 12, 93059 Regensburg, Germany.

BICKERSTAFF, Patsy Anne; b. 7 Jan. 1940, Virginia, USA. Attorney; Poet. m. Wilson Lee Seay, 7 Jan. 1988, 3 s., 1 d. *Education:* BA, English, 1963, JD, 1978, University of Richmond. *Publications:* City Rain, 1989; Chained to a Post, 1994. *Contributions to:* Anthologies, reviews, and journals. *Honours:* First Prize, International Shakespearean Contest, 1985; Hackney Literary Award, 1986; Virginia Highlands Festival Award, 1986; Poetry Society of Virginia Awards, 1987–2001; American Pen Women Award, 1988; Black Hills Writers Group Prize, 1988; New York Poetry Forum Award, 1988; Fifth Place, Writer's Digest, 1994; Robert Penn Warren Award, First Place, 1995; Second Place, Raintown Review, 2001; Nominated for Poet Laureate, Commonwealth of VA, 2002. *Memberships:* Poetry Society of Virginia, exec. board; Virginia Writers Club, first vice-pres., 1998, pres., 1999–2000. *Address:* PO Box 156, Weyers Cave, VA 24486, USA.

BIDEL, F. See: SOLEIMANI, Faramarz.

BIDGOOD, Ruth; b. 20 July 1922, Seven Sisters, Glamorgan, Wales. Writer; Poet. m. David Edgar Bidgood, 31 Dec. 1946, 2 s., 1 d. *Education:* BA, 1943, MA, 1947, Oxford University. *Appointments:* Coder, WRNS; Sub-Ed., Chambers Encyclopaedia. *Publications:* The Given Time, 1972; Not Without Homage, 1975; The Print of Miracle, 1978; Lighting Candles, 1982; Kindred, 1986; Selected Poems, 1992; The Fluent Moment, 1996; Singing to Wolves, 2000. *Contributions to:* Literary reviews, magazines and journals. *Honours:* Welsh Arts Council Award, 1975; Runner-up, Welsh Book of the Year, 1993, 1997. *Membership:* Fellow, Academi Gymreig, English Speaking Section. *Address:* Tyhaearn, Abergwesyn, Llanwrtyd Wells, Powys, Wales.

BIELAWA, Michael Joseph; b. 12 June 1960, Amsterdam, New York, USA. Library Dir; Poet. 1 s. *Education:* AA, Housatonic Community College; BA, Southern Connecticut State College, 1982; AA, Sacred Heart University, 1990; MLS, Southern Connecticut State University, 1993. *Contributions to:* Orphic Lute; Stratford Magazine; Trumbull Arts Festival; Bean Feast; Rycenda Symposiuml; Alura; Stratford Life, Section of Bridgeport Post; Polish-American Journal; BEI Compass; Vytis; Poetry for Peace. *Honour:* First

Place, Stratford, Connecticut's 350th Anniversary Poetry Contest, 1989. *Memberships:* Connecticut Poetry Society; National Hawthorne Society. *Address:* 38 William St, Ansonia, CT 906401, USA.

BIELBY, John Nicholas Lyne; b. 4 June 1939, London, England. Lecturer; Poet; Writer. m. Sheila Marland, 22 Aug. 1964, 1 s., 1 d. *Education:* BA, 1961; MA, 1963; Dip Primary Ed, 1972; Dip Psych and Sociology of Ed, 1973. *Appointments:* Lecturer, St John's College, Agra, India; Teacher, Bradley Junior School, Huddersfield; Lecturer, Senior Lecturer, Bradford and Ilkley Community College; Lecturer, Leeds University. *Publications:* Three Early Tudor Poets, 1976; An Invitation to Supper, 1978; Making Sense of Reading, 1994; How to Teach Reading, 1998. *Contributions to:* Pennine Platform; New Poetry; Orbis; Honest Ulsterman; Poetry & Audience; English; Poetry Reviewing, Times Educational Supplement. *Honours:* Awards from New Poetry, Lancaster (3 times) and Yorkshire Open; Rhyme International, 1989; Runner-up, Arvon, 1991. *Memberships:* Pennine Poets; Bradford and Baildon Poetry Society; Gowland Poets. *Address:* Frizingley Hall, Frizinghall Rd, Bradford BD9 4LD, West Yorkshire, England.

BIELSKI, Alison Joy Prosser; b. 24 Nov. 1925, Newport, Gwent, Wales. Poet; Writer; Lecturer. m. (1) Dennis Ford Treverton Jones, 19 June 1948, (2) Anthony Edward Bielski, 30 Nov. 1955, 1 s., 1 d. *Appointment:* Lecturer, Writers on Tour, Welsh Arts Council. *Publications:* The Story of the Welsh Dragon, 1969; Across the Burning Sand, 1970; Eve, 1973; Flower Legends of the Wye Valley, 1974; Shapes and Colours, 1974; The Lovetree, 1974; Mermaid Poems, 1974; Seth, 1980; Night Sequence, 1981; Eagles, 1983; The Story of St Mellons, 1985; That Crimson Flame, 1996; The Green-Eyed Pool, 1997. *Contributions to:* Anthologies and journals. *Honours:* Premium Prize, Poetry Society, 1964; Anglo-Welsh Review Poetry Prize, 1970; Arnold Vincent Bowen Poetry Prize, 1971; Third Place, Alice Gregory Memorial Competition, 1979; Orbis Poetry Prize, 1984; Second Prize, Julia Cairns Trophy, Society of Women Writers and Journalists, 1984, 1992. *Memberships:* Gwent Poetry Society; Society of Women Writers and Journalists; Welsh Acad.; Welsh Union of Writers. *Address:* 64 Glendower Ct, Velindre Rd, Whitchurch, Cardiff CF4 7JJ, Wales.

BIERMANN, Wolf; b. 15 Nov. 1936, Hamburg, Germany. Poet; Songwriter; Musician. m. Christine Bark, 2 s. *Education:* Humboldt University, Berlin, 1959–63. *Appointments:* Asst Dir, Berliner Ensemble, 1957–59; Song and guitar performances throughout Germany. *Publications:* Die Drahtharfe: Balladen, Gedichte, Lieder, 1965; Mit Marx-und Engelszungen, 1968; Der Dra-Dra (play), 1970; Für meine Genossen, 1972; Deutschland: Ein Wintermärchen, 1972; Nachlass I, 1977; Wolf Biermann; Poems and Ballads, 1977; Preussicher Ikarus, 1978; Verdrehte welt das seh'ich gerne, 1982; Und als ich von Deutschland nach Deutschland: Three Contemporary German Poets, 1985; Affenels und Barrikade, 1986; Alle Lieder, 1991; Ich hatte viele Bekümmernis: Meditation on Cantata No. 21 by J S Bach, 1991; Vier Neue Lieder, 1992. *Honours:* Büchner Prize, 1991; Möricke Prize, 1991; Heine Prize, 1993. *Address:* c/o Verlag Kiepenheuer und Witsch, Rondorferstrasse 5, 5000 Colonge-Marienurg, Germany.

BIGGS, Margaret Annette, (Margaret Key Biggs); b. 26 Oct. 1933, Needmore, AL, USA. Writer; Poet. m. 1 March 1956. *Education:* BS, Troy State University, 1954; MA, California State University, 1979. *Publications:* Swampfire, 1980; Sister to the Sun, 1981; Magnolias and Such, 1982; Petals from the Womanflower, 1983; Plumage of the Sun, 1986. *Contributions to:* Anthologies, journals, and reviews. *Honours:* Numerous awards. *Memberships:* Alabama State Poetry Society; National Federation of State Poetry Societies; National League of American Pen Women. *Address:* PO Box 2600, County Rd 852, Heflin, AL 36264, USA

BILSON, Rodney Eric; b. 9 Nov. 1939, Northampton, England. Leather Manufacturer; Poet. m. Olive Bilson, 6 Nov. 1971, 2 s., 1 d. *Publications:* Awaken to a Dream, 1997; Rhyme and Reason, 1997; Diana Princess of Wales, 1998; This Vanishing World, 1998; A Celebration of Poets Showcase Edition, 1998. *Honours:* Ed.'s Choice Award, 1997; Best Poem of 1997. *Membership:* Endless Time United Society of Poets, 1997. *Address:* 203 High Barns, Ely, Cambridgeshire CB7 4RN, England.

BIMGO. See: MARGOLIS, William J.

BINNS, John; b. 12 Nov. 1947, Bradford, West Yorkshire, England. Poet. *Publication:* A Phoenix Rising, 1991. *Contributions to:* Rialto; Purple Patch; Third Half; Roads; Momentum; Peace and Freedom; Kissing the Sky; Barddoni; Songs; Dream Cell; Exile; Wire; Pennine Platform; Bare Wires; Poetry Nottingham; Wayfarers; Enigma; US magazines: Omnific; Minotaur; Nocturnal Lyric; Irreversible Man, anthology; Make Mine Canine, anthology. *Honours:* Runner-up, Mosaic Competition, 1990. *Address:* 14 Silver Royd Close, Wortley, Leeds LS12 4QZ, England.

BIRD, Polly; b. 30 Sept. 1950, London, England. Poet; Writer. m. Dr J M Bird, 27 July 1974, 2 s., 1 d. *Education:* BEd, Cantab, 1973, Certificate, Field Archaeology, University of London, 1978. *Contributions to:* Various anthologies and periodicals. *Honours:* First Prize, C J Poetry Competition,

1987; Second Prize, Speakeasy Poetry Competition, 1991. *Memberships:* Poetry Society; Society of Authors. *Address:* 49 Oakhurst Grove, East Dulwich, London SE22 9AH, England.

BISHOP, Michael (Lawson); b. 12 Nov. 1945, Lincoln, Nebraska, USA. Writer; Poet; Ed. m. Jeri Whitaker, 7 June 1969, 1 s., 1 d. *Education:* BA, 1967, MA, 1968, University of Georgia. *Appointment:* Writer-in-Residence, LaGrange College, 1997–. *Publications:* Fiction: A Funeral for the Eyes of Fire, 1975, revised edn as Eyes of Fire, 1980; And Strange at Ecbatan the Trees, 1976; Stolen Faces, 1977; A Little Knowledge, 1977; Transfigurations, 1979; Under Heaven's Bridge (with Ian Watson), 1981; No Enemy but Time, 1982; Who Made Steve Cry?, 1984; Ancient of Days, 1985; The Secret Ascension, or, Philip K Dick Is Dead, Alas, 1987; Unicorn Mountain, 1988; Apartheid, Superstrings and Mordecai Thubana, 1989; Count Geiger's Blues, 1992; Brittle Innings, 1994; Would It Kill You to Smile? (with Paul Di Filippo), 1998; Muskrat Courage (with Paul di Filippo), 2000. Short Stories: Catacomb Years, 1979; Blooded on Arachne, 1982; One Winter in Eden, 1984; Close Encounters with the Deity, 1986; Emphatically Not SF, Almost, 1990; At the City Limits of Fate, 1996; Brighten to Incandescence, 2003. Poetry: Windows and Mirrors, 1977; Time Pieces, 1999; Novella Collection: Blue Kansas Sky, 2000. Editor: Changes (anthology with Ian Watson), 1982; Light Years and Dark (anthology), 1984; Nebula Awards: SFWA's Choices for the Best Science Fiction and Fantasy, vols 23–25, 1989–91. *Contributions to:* Anthologies and periodicals. *Honours:* Phoenix Award, 1977; Clark Ashton Smith Award, 1978; Rhysling Award, Science Fiction Poetry Asscn, 1979; Nebula Awards, SFWA, 1981, 1982; Mythopoetic Fantasy Award, 1988; Locus Award for Best Fantasy Novel, 1994; Hon. LHD, LaGrange College, 2001. *Memberships:* SFWA; Science Fiction Poetry Asscn. *Address:* Box 646, Pine Mountain, GA 31822, USA.

BISHOP, Patricia Julia Rose; b. London, England. Poet. m. 4 s. *Education:* Cert Ed. *Appointments:* Civil Servant; Teacher; Smallholder. *Publications:* Double Exposure, 1988; All Wings & Bones (co-author Spacex), 1992; Aubergine is a Gravid Woman, 1993. *Contributions to:* New Welsh Review; Planet International; Envoi; Ostinato; Odyssey; Writing Women; Rialto; Radio 4; Radio Cornwall; Radio Stoke; Long Pale Corridor; Bloodaxe Anthology. *Honours:* Joint Second Place, National Poetry Competition, 1994; Arts Council/BBC North Award, Write Out Loud, 1996. *Address:* Newburn, Cockwells, Nr Penzance, Cornwall TR20 8DB, England.

BISHOP, Pike. See: OBSTFELD, Raymond.

BISHOP, Robert Gregory; b. 23 Sept. 1936, London, England. Teacher; Poet; Writer; Trans. *Education:* BA, London, 1968; Certificate of Education, University of Leeds, 1972. *Appointments:* Library Staff, London Evening News, 1959–62; Guardian Library, 1962–64; English Teacher, Munich, 1968–69, Watford College of Further Education; Trans., Lecturer and Teacher at various companies in Munich, 1972–. *Publications:* Other Moments, 1999; Poems of Ludwig II of Bavaria (trans.), 1998. *Contributions to:* Numerous publications worldwide. *Honours:* Special Commendation, Poetry Society, 1992, and English Explorer Magazine, 1992; Joint Fourth Prize, Kent and Sussex Society, 1995. *Membership:* Poetry Society of Great Britain. *Address:* Paschstr 56, 80637 Munich, Germany. Telephone and Fax: (89) 1577627. *Website:* www.rgbishop.com.

BISHOP, Wendy; b. 13 Jan. 1953, Japan. Prof. of English; Writer; Poet. m. (1) Marvin E Pollard Jr, 1 s., 1 d., (2) Conrad Dean Newman. *Education:* BA, English, 1975, BA, Studio Art, 1975, MA, English, Creative Writing, 1976; MA, English, Teaching Writing, 1979, University of California at Davis; PhD, English, Rhetoric and Linguistics, Indiana University of Pennsylvania, 1988. *Appointments:* Bayero University, Kano, Nigeria, 1980–81; Northern Arizona University, 1981–82; Chair, Communications, Humanities, and Fine Arts, Navajo Community College, Tsaile, AZ, 1984–85; Asst Prof. of English, University of Alaska, Fairbanks, 1985–89; Prof. of English, Florida State University, Tallahassee, 1989–; Chair, Conference on College Composition and Communication, 2001. *Publications:* Released into Language: Options for Teaching Creative Writing, 1990; Something Old, Something New: College Writing Teachers and Classroom Change, 1990; Working Words: The Process of Creative Writing, 1992; The Subject in Writing: Essays by Teachers and Students in Writing, 1993; Colors of a Different Horse (ed. with Hans Ostrom), 1994; Water's Night (poems with Hans Ostrom), 1994; Genres of Writing: Mapping the Territories of Discourse (ed. with Hans Ostrom), 1997; Mid-Passage (poems), 1997; Teaching Lives: Essays and Stories, 1997; Touching Liliana (poems), 1998; Ethnographic Writing Research-Writing it Down, Writing It Up and Reading It, 1999; When We Say We're Home: A Quartet of Place and Memory (co-author), 1999; Metro: Journeys in Writing Creatively (co-author), 2000; In Praise of Pedagogy: Poetry, Flash Fiction and Essays on Composing (co-ed.), 2000; The Subject is Reading: Essays by Teachers and Students (ed.), 2000; Thirteen Ways of Looking for a Poem: A Guide to Writing Poetry, 2000. *Contributions to:* Poems, fiction, and essays in various reviews and journals. *Honours:* Joseph Henry Jackson Award, 1980; Several fellowships; Many literary awards. *Memberships:* Associated Writing Programs; MLA; National Council of Teachers of English; National Writing Centres Asscn; Poetry Society of America. *Address:* c/o Dept of English, Florida State University, Tallahassee, FL 32306, USA.

BISSETT, Bill; b. 23 Nov. 1939, Halifax, Nova Scotia, Canada. Poet; Artist. *Education:* Dalhousie University, 1956–57; University of British Columbia, 1963–65. *Appointment:* Ed., Printer, Blewointmentpress, Vancouver, 1962–83. *Publications:* The Jinx Ship and other Trips: Poems-drawings-collage, 1966; We Sleep Inside Each Other All, 1966; Fires in the Temple, 1967; Where Is Miss Florence Riddle, 1967; What Poetiks, 1967; Gossamer Bed Pan, 1967; Lebanon Voices, 1967; Of the Land/Divine Service Poems, 1968; Awake in the Red Desert, 1968; Killer Whale, 1969; Sunday Work?, 1969; Liberating Skies, 1969; The Lost Angel Mining Company, 1969; The Outlaw, 1970; Blew Trewz, 1970; Nobody Owns the Earth, 1971; Air 6, 1971; Dragon Fly, 1971. Four Parts Sand: Concrete Poems, 1972; The Ice Bag, 1972; Poems for Yoshi, 1972; Drifting into War, 1972; Air 10-11-12, 1973; Pass the Food, Release the Spirit Book, 1973; The First Sufi Line, 1973; Vancouver Mainland Ice and Cold Storage, 1973; Living with the Vishyan, 1974; What, 1974; Drawings, 1974; Medicine My Mouths on Fire, 1974; Space Travel, 1974; You Can Eat it at the Opening, 1974; The Fifth Sun, 1975; The Wind up Tongue, 1975; Stardust, 1975; An Allusyun to Macbeth, 1976; Plutonium Missing, 1976; Sailor, 1978; Beyond Even Faithful Legends, 1979; Soul Arrow, 1980; Northern Birds in Color, 1981; Parlant, 1982; Seagull on Yonge Street, 1983; Canada Geese Mate for Life, 1985; Animal Uproar, 1987; What we Have, 1989; Hard 2 Beleev, 1990; Incorrect Thoughts, 1992; Vocalist with the Luddites, Dreaming of the Night, 1992; The Last Photo of the Human Soul, 1993; th Influenza uv Logik, 1995; loving without being vulnrabul, 1997; Offthroad (cassette), 1998; Skars on the Seehors, 1999; b leev abul char ak trs, 2000; Offthroad (with CD), 2000; rainbow mewsick (ed.), 2002; peter among th towring boxes, 2002; unmatching phenomena I (with CD), 2002. *Address:* Box 272, Str F, Toronto, Ontario M4Y 2L7, Canada.

BIXBY, Robert J.; b. 9 Nov. 1952, Michigan, USA. Ed.; Poet. m. Kathleen Mae Beal, 1971, 1 s., 1 d. *Education:* BS, Central Michigan University, 1978; MSW, Western Michigan University, 1980; MFA. University of North Carolina, 1992. *Appointments:* Social Worker, 1980–87; Ed., General Media, 1987–96; Ed./Publisher, March Street Press and Ed./Publisher, Parting Gifts; Webmaster, Koz. Com, 1996–. *Contributions to:* Gypsy; Abbey; Aleron; Albany Review; Amelia; Blue Light Review; Caroline Quarterly; Celery; Chrysalis; Connecticut River Review; Green River Review; Greensboro Review; Impetus; Lucky Star; Magic Changes; Omni; Open 24 Hours; Passages North; Poetic Space; Prophetic Voices; Pulpsmith; Redbiik; Slipstream; South Coast Review; Cathartic; Thirteen Touchstone; Verse and Universe; Wooster Review; Xanadu. *Address:* 3413 Wilshire, Greensboro, NC 27408, USA.

BJELKHAGEN, Teresa Grace; b. 28 June 1951, Poland. Linguist; Poet. *Education:* BA, English and Russian, 1974; MA, Applied Linguistics, 1977; Diploma in Applied, Descriptive and Theoretical Linguistics, Exeter University, England, 1982. *Appointments:* Lecturer, Applied Linguistics, University of South Africa, 1987; Trans., Stockholm University, 1995–. *Publications:* Poetry: Why Once Again, 1988; The Laughing Jacaranda, 1988; Fleurs de la Cote d'Azur, 1988; All That's You is Light, 1988; Engele, 1989; Encounters, 1989; Posh Array, 1989; Life's Perverse Cabooze, 1990; Lips of Scarlet, 1992; Squeezeling, 1992; Your Phantom of the Night, 1992; Chirping Like a Bird, 1993; I Look in Long Mirrors, 1994. *Contributions to:* Pasque Petals. *Membership:* South Dakota State Poetry Society, USA. *Address:* Hälsingegatan 8, 11323 Stockholm, Sweden.

BLACK, David Macleod; b. 8 Nov. 1941, Cape Town, South Africa (British citizen). Poet; Trans. *Education:* MA, University of Edinburgh, 1966; MA, Religious Studies, University of Lancaster, 1971. *Appointments:* Teacher, Chelsea Art School, London, 1966–70; Lecturer and Supervisor, Westminster Pastoral Foundation, London, 1972–2000. *Publications:* Rocklestrakes, 1960; From the Mountain, 1963; Theory of Diet, 1966; With Decorum, 1967; A Dozen Short Poems, 1968; Penguin Modern Poets 11, 1968; The Educators, 1969; The Old Hag, 1972; The Happy Crow, 1974; Gravitations, 1979; Collected Poems 1964–1987, 1991; A Place for Exploration, 1991. *Contributions to:* Modern Poetry in Translation, 1998, 2000; Other periodicals and journals; Anthologies. *Honours:* Arts Council of Great Britain Bursary, 1968; Scottish Arts Council Prize, 1968, and Publication Award, 1991. *Address:* 30 Cholmley Gardens, Aldred Rd, London NW6 1AG, England. *Website:* www.dmblack.co.uk.

BLACK, Matt(hew); b. 26 Oct. 1956, Oxford, England. Poet. 2 s. *Education:* BA, English Literature, University of Sheffield, 1988. *Publications:* Now We Are Twenty-Six, 1984; The Scent of Sweat, 1985; Soft Fruit Centre, 1987; In The Kitchen with the Candlestick, 1990; The Sofa or On Liberty, 1991; The Garden, 1993; Squeezing Lemons, 1994. *Contributions to:* Over 500 performances. *Honours:* First Prize, Avon Poetry Competition, 1984; Oppenheim John-Downes Memorial Award, 1990; Arts Council/YHA Writers' Award, 1998; Writers Award, Yorkshire and Humberside Arts, 1998. *Membership:* Poetry Society of Great Britain. *Address:* 51 Pearson Pl., Sheffield S8 9DE, England.

BLACKBURN, Kim Lorraine; b. 25 Oct. 1961, Takapuna, Auckland, New Zealand. Poet. *Education:* Auckland Institute of Technology. *Publications:* Lizards in Love, 1987; Dreaming in the White Room, 1987; Feel, 1997; Strawberries for Argentina, 1997. *Contributions to:* Anthologies, magazines and the Internet. *Membership:* Group of Auckland Poets. *Address:* PO Box 331050, Takapuna AK9, Auckland, New Zealand.

BLACKBURN, Michael Anthony; b. 8 March 1954, Newton Aycliffe, County Durham, England. Writer; Poet; Publisher. m. Sylvia Dann, 14 July 1990, 1 step-s., 1 step-d. *Education:* MA, English, Leeds University, 1977. *Publications:* The Constitutions of Things, 1984; Why Should Anyone Be Here and Singing?, 1987; Backwards into Bedlam, 1987; The Lean Man Shaving, 1988; The Prophecy of Christos, 1992. *Contributions to:* The North; Hubbub, USA; Stand; Tribune; Pen; Noorus; Estonia; Echo Room; Wide Skirt; Joe Soap's Canoe. *Address:* Sunk Island Publishing, PO Box 74, Lincoln LN1 1QG, England.

BLACKHALL, Sheena Booth, (Sheena Middleton, Sìne Nic Theàrlaich); b. 18 Aug. 1947, Aberdeen, Scotland. Poet; Writer; Scots Ballad Singer; Illustrator. Divorced, 2 s., 2 d. *Education:* Gray's School of Art, Aberdeen, 1964–65; Diploma in Primary Education, College of Education, Aberdeen, 1965–68; BSc, Honours, Psychology, Open University, 1995; M. Litt, Aberdeen University, 2000. *Appointment:* Creative Writing Fellow in Scots, Elphinstone Institute, University of Aberdeen, 1998–. *Publications:* Poetry: The Cyard's Kist, 1984; The Spik o' the Lan, 1986; Hamedrauchtit, 1987; Nor'East Neuk, 1989; Fite-Doo/Black Crow, 1989; A Toosht o' Whigmaleeries, 1991; Back o' Bennachie, 1993; Druids, Drachts, Drochles, 1994; Stagwyes (poems), 1995; Lament for the Raj, 1996; The Life-Bluid o' Cromar, 1997; Gliong Gliong, 1997; Death, Demons, Perfume and Pearls (co-author), 1999; The Heilanman's Sporran, 1999; Millennium Blues, 1999; The Twa B's (co-author), 2000; The Singing Bird, 2000; Dancing with Maenads, 2000; The Telepathic Butcher's Boy (co-author), 2000; Skin Balaclava (co-author), 2000; Spik Nae Evil (co-author), 2000; Bringing up the Tail (co-author), 2001. Short Stories: Nippick o' Nor'East Tales, 1989; Reets, 1991; A Hint o' Granite, 1992; Braeheid, A Fairm an its Fowk, 1993; A Kenspeckle Creel, 1995; Wittgenstein's Web, 1996; The Bonsai Grower, 1998; The Fower Quarters, 2002. Other: The Elphinstone Kist (co-ed.); Stories and plays for radio and television. *Honours:* Robert McClellan Silver Tassies for Best Scots Short Story, 1988, 1990, 1998, 2001; Best Scots Short Story, Doric Festival, 1988, 1995, 1996, 1997, 1999; Prizewinner, Scottish International Open Competition, 1989; Hugh MacDiarmid Silver Tassies for Best Scots Poem, 1990, 2000, 2001; Joint Winner, Sloane Competition for Scots Writing, St Andrews University, 1993; Bennachie Baillie Award, Best Scots Narrative Ballad, 1993; Best Female Traditional Singer and Best Song Written in the Traditional Style, Joe Leonard Trophy, Press and Journal Cup, 2001, 2002. *Memberships:* Scottish Poetry Library; Scots Language Society; Aberdeen Artists' Society; Limousine Bull Artists Collective; Scots Language Resource Centre. *Address:* c/o G. K. B. Books, 3A Skene Pl., Dyce, Aberdeen AB21 7AY, Scotland. *Website:* www.gkbenterprises.org.uk.

BLACKMAN, Roy Alfred Arthur, (Arthur Peasmair); b. 15 May 1943, Burnham, England. Poet; Ed. m. Jillian Frances, 11 Dec. 1965, 1 s., 1 d. *Education:* BSc Honours, Zoology with Geology, University of Bristol, 1964; PhD, Marine Zoology, University of Newcastle upon Tyne, 1971; BA, Open University, 1990. *Appointments:* Senior Scientific Officer, Ministry of Agriculture, Fisheries and Food, 1971–92; Co-Ed., Smiths Knoll, 1991–. *Publication:* As Lords Expected, 1996. *Contributions to:* Stand; Staple; The Rialto; Outposts; Other Poetry; Thames Poetry; Foolscap; Spokes; Slow Dancer; New Welsh Review; Grand Piano; Margin; Poetry Nottingham; Pennine Platform; Envoi; Frogmore Papers; Odyssey; The Honest Ulsterman; Seam; Lines Review; The North; The Interpreter's House; Acumen; Bridport Prize Anthology, 1996; Poetic Art, 1997; Oxford Magazine; New Writer; Third Way; Brando's Hat; Boomerang; The Shop; Obsessed with Pipework; Eclipse; Links; Crabbe Memorial Anthology, 1998; Staple 50 Anthology, 2001; Soundings; BBC Radio 4. *Honour:* Hawthornden Fellow, 1993. *Address:* 49 Church Rd, Little Glemham, Woodbridge, Suffolk IP13 0BJ, England.

BLAINE, Julien; b. 19 Sept. 1942, Rognac, France. Poet; Ed.; Writer; Actor. m. Catherinne Poitevin, 1 Dec. 1962, 1 s., 2 d. *Education:* Faculté des Lettres, Aix-en-Provence. *Appointments:* Co-Organiser and Co-ordinator, Polyphonix, 1979–94; Co-Founder, Festival of Poetry, Cogolin, 1984; International Poetry Meetings, Tarascon, 1988, Venezia Poesia, 1996. *Publications:* 10 vols, 1992–98. *Contributions to:* Anthologies, reviews, recordings, festivals, exhibitions, and meetings. *Address:* Le Moulin de Ventabren, 13122 Ventabren, France.

BLAIS, Marie-Claire; b. 5 Oct. 1939, Québec, QC, Canada. Writer; Dramatist; Poet. *Education:* Courses in literature and philosophy, Laval University. *Publications:* Fiction: La Belle Bete, 1959, English trans. as Mad Shadows, 1960; Tete blanche, 1960, English trans., 1961; Le Jour est noir, 1962, English trans. as The Day is Dark, 1966; Une saison dans la vie d'Emmanuel, 1965, English trans. as A Season in the Life of Emmanuel, 1966; L'imsoumise, 1966, English trans. as The Fugitive, 1991; David Sterne, 1967, English trans., 1972; Manuscrits de Pauline Archange, 1968, and Vivre! Vivre!, 1969, both in English trans. as Manuscripts of Pauline Archange, 1970; Les Apparences, 1971, English trans. as Durer's Angel, 1976; Le Loup, 1972, English trans. as The Wolf, 1974; Un Joualonais, sa Joualonie, 1973, English trans. as St Lawrence Blues, 1975; Une liaison parisienne, 1975, English trans. as A Literary Affair, 1979; Les Nuits de l'Underground, 1978, English trans. as Nights in the Underground, 1979; Le Sourd dans la ville, 1980, English trans. as Deaf to the City, 1980; Visions d'Anna, 1982, English trans. as Anna's World, 1984; Pierre ou La Guerre du printemps 81, 1984; L'Ange de la solitude, 1989, English trans. as Angel of Solitude, 1993; Pierre, 1991, English trans., 1993;

Soifs, 1995. Poetry: Pays voiles, 1964; Existences, 1964. Autobiography: Parcours d'un écrivain notes américaines, 1993. *Honours:* Prix de la Langue française, 1961; Guggenheim Fellowship, 1963; Prix France-Québec, Paris, 1966; Prix Médicis, Paris, 1966; Governor-General of Canada Prizes, 1969, 1979, 1996; Order of Canada, 1975; Prix Belgique-Canada, Brussels, 1976; Prix Athanase-David, Québec, 1982; Prix de l'Académie Française, Paris, 1983; Commemorative Medal for the 125th Anniversary of the Confederation of Canada, 1982; Ordre National du Québec, 1995. *Membership:* Académie Royale de langue et de littérature françaises de Belgique, Brussels. *Address:* 4411 Rue St Denis, Apt 401, Montréal, QC H2J 2L2, Canada.

BLAKE, Jennifer. See: MAXWELL, Patricia Anne.

BLANCHARD, Enrique Daniel; b. 14 Dec. 1944, Buenos Aires, Argentina. Writer; Poet; Prof. m. Elisa Ruiz-Toranzo, 3 July 1975, Education: Literature, University of Buenos Aires and University del Salvador, Buenos Aires, scriptwriting at University of La Plata, Buenos Aires, and Museology at Town Hall of Buenos Aires. *Appointments:* Ed.-in-Chief, Nuevo Milenio, publishing house specialising in poetry; Prof., University of Buenos Aires; Dir of literary workshops. *Publications:* El Fantasma y Su Límite, 1982; Silveta de Polvo, 1982; El Disfraz del Cuerpo, 1982; Función del Ventrílocuo, 1984; Idolo de Niebla, 1984; Reo de Redes, 1986; El Locutor Físico, 1989; Retrato de Antifaz, 1990; Desnudo de Espectro, 1991; Viajero de una Mano, 1994; Escenas en las Estaciones Terminales, 1994; Physicus Loquutor I, 1995; Physicus Loquutur II, 1997. *Contributions to:* Newspapers and literary magazines, including: Lost and Found Times; Droomschaar; Norte; Calandrajas; Nicolau. *Honour:* Best Book of the Year, Buenos Aires Lawyers Assocn, 1986. *Address:* Casilla de Correo 2847, 1000 Correo Central, Buenos Aires, Argentina.

BLAND, Peter; b. 12 May 1934, Scarborough, Yorkshire, England. Poet; Reviewer; Actor; Dramatist. m. Beryl Matilda Connolly, 27 April 1956, 1 s., 2 d. *Education:* English, Victoria University of Wellington, New Zealand. *Appointments:* Journalist and Talks Producer, New Zealand Broadcasting Corp, 1960–64; Co-Founder, Dir, Actor and Dramatist, Downstage Theatre, Wellington, 1964–68; Actor, West End plays and numerous television productions, London; Leading role, Came a Hot Friday (New Zealand film), 1985. *Publications:* Poetry: My Side of the Story, 1964; The Man with the Carpet Bag, 1972; Mr Maui, 1976; Stone Tents, 1981; The Crusoe Factor, 1985; Selected Poems, 1987; Paper Boats, 1991; Selected Poems, 1998. Plays: Father's Day, 1967; George the Mad Ad Man, 1967. *Contributions to:* Anthologies and periodicals. *Honours:* Macmillan-Brown Prize for Creative Writing, Victoria University of Wellington, 1958; Melbourne Arts Festival Literary Award, 1960; Queen Elizabeth II Arts Council Drama Fellowship, 1968; Cholmondeley Award for Poetry, 1977; Best Film Actor Award, Guild of Film and Television Arts, New Zealand, 1985; Poetry Book Society Recommendation, 1987. *Address:* 2 Westrow, Putney SW15 6RH, England.

BLANDIANA, Ana, (Otila Valeria Rusan); b. 25 March 1942, Timişoara, Romania. Poet; Writer. m. Romulus Rusan. *Education:* Graduated, University of Cluj, 1967. *Appointments:* Columnist, Romania literary magazine, 1974–88; Librarian, Institute of Fine Arts, Bucharest, 1975–77. *Publications:* Poetry: 50 Poems, 1972; The Hour of Sand: Selected Poems, 1969–89, 1989; The Architecture of the Waves, 1990; 100 Poems, 1991; The Morning After the Death, 1996. Fiction: The Drawer with Applause (novel), 1992; Imitation of a Nightmare (short stories), 1995. Other: Several essays. *Honours:* Romanian Writers' Union Poetry Prizes, 1969, 2000; Romanian Acad. Poetry Prize, 1980; Herder Prize, Austria, 1982; National Poetry Prize, 1996. *Memberships:* Romanian PEN Center, pres.; Civic Acad., pres. *Address:* Academia Civica, Piata Amzei 13 et 2, CP 22-216, Bucharest, Romania.

BLASER, Robin (Francis); b. 18 May 1925, Denver, CO, USA. Prof. of English; Poet. *Education:* MA, 1954, MLS, 1955, University of California at Berkeley. *Appointments:* Prof. of English, Centre for the Arts, Simon Fraser University, Burnaby, BC, Canada, 1972–86. *Publications:* The Moth Poem, 1964; Les Chimères, 1965; Cups, 1968; The Holy Forest Section, 1970; Image-nations 1-12 and The Stadium of the Mirror, 1974; Image-nations 13–14, 1975; Suddenly, 1976; Syntax, 1983; The Faerie Queene and the Park, 1987; Pell Mell, 1988; The Holy Forest, 1993. *Honours:* Poetry Society Award, 1965; Canada Council Grant, 1989–90; Fund for Poetry Award, New York, 1995. *Address:* 1636 Trafalgar St, Vancouver, BC V6K 3R7, Canada.

BLASING, Randy; b. 27 July 1943, Minneapolis, Minnesota, USA. Prof. of English; Poet. m. Mutlu Konuk, 21 Aug. 1965, 1 s. *Education:* BA, Carleton College, 1965; MA, University of Chicago, 1966. *Appointments:* Instructor in English, Randolph Macon College, 1966–67, College of William and Mary, 1967–69; Instructor in English, 1969–72, Asst Prof. of English, 1972–77, Assoc. Prof. of English, 1979–88, Prof. of English, 1988–, Community College of Rhode Island; Lecturer in English, Pomona College, 1977–79; Ed., Copper Beech Press, 1983–. *Publications:* Light Years, 1977; To Continue, 1983; The Particles, 1983; The Double House of Life, 1989; Graphic Scenes, 1994. *Contributions to:* Poetry; Paris Review; The Nation; Yale Review; Sewanee Review; Southern Review; The New Criterion; Virginia Quarterly Review; Southwest Review; Michigan Quarterly Review. *Honours:* National Endowment for the Arts Fellowship, 1981–82; Ingram Merrill Poetry Fellowship, 1989. *Address:* 44 Benefit St, Providence, RI 02904, USA.

BLAZEK, Joseph Lawrence, (Larry Blazek, Johanny Nightrider); b. 19 July 1957, Valparaiso, IN, USA. Farmer; Poet. *Publications:* Occult Memmories, 1988; Dark Passages, 1986; In the Mind; Composite Dreams; Earsore; Corksore. *Contributions to:* Numerous anthologies, journals, reviews, periodicals, quarterlies, magazines and newspapers. *Honours:* Prize, White Rose Poetry Contest; Hon. Mention, Ilaid Poetry Contest; Pres.'s Award for Literary Excellence. *Address:* 5094 N Country Rd 750E, Orleans, IN 47452, USA.

BLITZER, (Ilse) Hanna; b. 9 April 1915, Beuthen, Germany. Poet. m. S Blitzer, 31 July 1934, deceased, 2 s., 1 d. *Education:* Matriculation, Cambridge Proficiency in English Language, 1964. *Publications:* Staub und Sterne (Dust and Stars), 1982; Hánna Blitzer Lyrics, 1984; Noch ein Akkord (Another Accord), 1987; Od Akkord, Hebrew version, 1988; Ein Zeichen Setzen (To Set a Mark), 1991; Worte die Leben Sagen (Words That Say Life), 1994; On the Search of the Milky Way, 1997. *Contributions to:* Das Neue Israel; Die Stimme; Israel Nachrichten; Gauke's Jahrbuch; Anthology Auf dem Weg; Mnemosyne; Impressum; Feuerprobe; Kaleidoscope Israel; Anthology Spurenlese; Silhouette; Frauen Erinnern. *Memberships:* International Writers Asscn, Regensburg, Germany; German Writers Asscn in Israel; Else Lasker-Schueler Asscn, Wuppertal. *Address:* Kehilat-Sofia 14, 69018 Tel-Aviv, Israel.

BLOCH, Chana; b. 15 March 1940, New York, NY, USA. Prof. of English; Poet; Trans.; Critic; Essayist. m. Ariel Bloch, 26 Oct. 1969, divorced, 2 s. *Education:* BA, Cornell University, 1961; MA, 1963, MA, 1965, Brandeis University; PhD, University of California at Berkeley, 1975. *Appointments:* Instructor of English, Hebrew University, Jerusalem, 1964–67; Assoc. in Near Eastern Studies, University of California at Berkeley, 1967–69; Instructor, 1973–75, Asst Prof., 1975–81, Assoc. Prof., 1981–87, Chair., Dept of English, 1986–89, Prof. of English, 1987–, Dir, Creative Writing Program, 1993–2001, Mills College, Oakland, CA. *Publications:* Poetry: The Secrets of the Tribe, 1981; The Past Keeps Changing, 1992; Mrs Dumpty, 1998. Literary Criticism: Spelling the Word: George Herbert and the Bible, 1985. Translator: Dahlia Ravikovitch: A Dress of Fire, 1978; Yehuda Amichai: The Selected Poetry (with Stephen Mitchell), 1986; Dahlia Ravikovitch: The Window: New and Selected Poems (with Ariel Bloch), 1989; The Song of Songs: A New Translation, Introduction and Commentary (with Ariel Bloch), 1995; Open Closed Open, by Yehuda Amichai (with Chana Kronfeld), 2000. *Contributions to:* Poetry, trans, criticism and essays in various anthologies and periodicals. *Honours:* Discovery Award, Poetry Centre, New York, 1974; Trans. Award, Columbia University, 1978; National Endowment for the Humanities Fellowship, 1980; Book of the Year Award, Conference on Christianity and Literature, 1986; Writers Exchange Award, Poets and Writers, 1988; Yaddo Residencies, 1988, 1990, 1993, 1994, 1995, 1996, 1997, 1999, 2001; MacDowell Colony Residencies, 1988, 1992, 1993, 2000; Djerassi Foundation Residencies, 1989, 1991; National Endowment for the Arts Fellowships, 1989–90, 1999; Felix Pollak Prize, 1998; California Book Award Silver Medal in Poetry, 1999; PEN Award for Poetry in Trans., 2001. *Memberships:* PEN; Poetry Society of America; MLA. *Address:* c/o Dept of English, Mills College, Oakland, CA 94613, USA.

BLOOM, Harold; b. 11 July 1930, New York, NY, USA. Prof. of Humanities; Writer. m. Jeanne Gould, 8 May 1958, 2 s. *Education:* BA, Cornell University, 1951; PhD, Yale University, 1955. *Appointments:* Faculty, 1955–65, Prof. of English, 1965–77, DeVane Prof. of Humanities, 1974–77, Prof. of Humanities, 1977–83, Sterling Prof. of Humanities, 1983–, Yale University; Visiting Prof., Hebrew University, Jerusalem, 1959, Bread Loaf Summer School, 1965–66, Cornell University, 1968–69; Visiting University Prof., New School for Social Research, New York City, 1982–84; Charles Eliot Norton Prof. of Poetry, Harvard University, 1987–88; Berg Prof. of English, New York University, 1988–. *Publications:* Shelley's Mythmaking, 1959; The Visionary Company, 1961; Blake's Apocalypse, 1963; Commentary to Blake, 1965; Yeats, 1970; The Ringers in the Tower, 1971; The Anxiety of Influence, 1973; A Map of Misreading, 1975; Kabbalah and Criticism, 1975; Poetry and Repression, 1976; Figures of Capable Imagination, 1976; Wallace Stevens: The Poems of Our Climate, 1977; The Flight to Lucifer: A Gnostic Fantasy, 1979; Agon: Towards a Theory of Revisionism, 1981; The Breaking of the Vessels, 1981; The Strong Light of the Canonical, 1987; Freud: Transference and Authority, 1988; Poetics of Influence: New and Selected Criticism, 1988; Ruin the Sacred Truths, 1988; The Book of J, 1989; The American Religion, 1990; The Western Canon, 1994; Omens of Millennium: The Gnosis of Angels, Dreams and Resurrection, 1996; Shakespeare: The Invention of the Human, 1998; How to Read and Why, 2000; Stories and Poems for Extremely Intelligent Children of All Ages, 2000. *Contributions to:* Scholarly books and journals. *Honours:* Fulbright Fellowship, 1955; Guggenheim Fellowship, 1962; Newton Arvin Award, 1967; Melville Caine Award, 1970; Zabel Prize, 1982; John D and Catherine T MacArthur Foundation Fellowship, 1985; Christian Gauss Prize, 1989; Hon. Doctorates, University of Bologna, 1997, St Michael College, 1998, University of Rome, 2000; Gold Medal for Criticism, American Acad. of Arts and Letters, 1999. *Membership:* American Acad. of Arts and Letters. *Address:* 179 Linden St, New Haven, CT 06511, USA.

BLOOMFIELD, Lawrence E(dward), (Larry Bloomfield); b. 5 Oct. 1956, Wheeling, West Virginia, USA. Poet; Writer. m. (1) 1 s., 3 d., (2) Norma Jean Scott, 29 Nov. 1980. *Education:* Certificate in Graphic Arts, McKinley Vocational Technical Centre, 1974; Classes, West Virginia Career College, Belmont Technical College, Northern Community College, 1978–83. *Appointment:* Columnist, Poet's Ink, 1991–93. *Publications:* All My Own Poems by Lawrence E Bloomfield; Over 70 poems published. *Contributions to:* Various magazines and periodicals. *Honours:* Several awards in poetry competitions. *Memberships:* Parnassus of World Poets; West Virginia Poetry Society, state treasurer, 1995–. *Address:* PO Box 617-A, Boggs Run Rd, Benwood, WV 26031, USA.

BLOSSOM, Laurel; b. 9 June 1943, Washington, DC, USA. Poet; Writer. Divorced, 1 d. *Education:* BA, Radcliffe College, 1966. *Publications:* An Minute, 1979; What's Wrong, 1987; The Papers Said, 1993. *Contributions to:* Poetry; Paris Review; Pequod; New York Quarterly; Confrontation; Carolina Quarterly; American Poetry Review; Columbia; Harper's. *Honours:* Scholar, Bread Loaf Writers Conference, 1976; Fellow, Squaw Valley Community of Writers, 1977; Elliston Book Award Finalist, 1979; Yaddo Residency, 1979; Fellow, Ohio Arts Council, 1980–81; Nomination, Pushcart Prize, 1983, 1984, 1985, 1992; Finalist, National Poetry Series, 1985; Fellow, National Endowment for the Arts, 1987; Fellow, New York Foundation for the Arts, 1988; Assoc., Atlantic Centre for the Arts, 1989. *Memberships:* Chair, Programme Committee, National Writer's Voice Project, 1990–95; Founder, The Writers Community, 1976. *Address:* 920 Park Ave, No. 2B, New York, NY 10028, USA.

BLOUNT, Roy (Alton) Jr, (Noah Sanders, C R Ways); b. 4 Oct. 1941, Indianapolis, IN, USA. Writer; Poet; Screenwriter. m. (1) Ellen Pearson, 6 Sept 1964, divorced March 1973, 1 s., 1 d., (2) Joan Ackermann, 1976, divorced 1990. *Education:* BA, magna cum laude, Vanderbilt University, 1963; MA, Harvard University, 1964. *Appointments:* Staff, Decatur-DeKalb News, GA, 1958–59, Morning Telegraph, New York City, 1961, New Orleans Times-Picayune, 1963, Reporter, Editorial Writer, Columnist, Atlanta Journal, 1966–68; Staff Writer, 1968–74, Assoc. Ed., 1974–75, Sports Illustrated; Contributing Ed., Atlantic Monthly, 1983–. *Publications:* About Three Bricks Shy of a Load, 1974, revised edn as About Three Bricks Shy–and the Load Filled Up: The Story of the Greatest Football Team Ever, 1989; Crackers: This Whole Many-Sided Thing of Jimmy, More Carters, Ominous Little Animals, Sad-Singing Women, My Daddy and Me, 1980; One Fell Soup, or, I'm Just a Bug on the Windshield of Life, 1982; What Men Don't Tell Women, 1984; Not Exactly What I Had in Mind, 1985; It Grows on You: A Hair-Raising Survey of Human Plumage, 1986; Soupsong/Webster's Ark, 1987; Now, Where Were We?, 1989; First Hubby, 1990; Camels Are Easy, Comedy's Hard, 1991; Roy Blount's Book of Southern Humor, 1994; Be Sweet: A Conditional Love Story, 1998; If Only You Knew How Much I Smell You, 1998; I Am Puppy, Hear Me Yap, 2000; Am I Pig Enough For You Yet?, 2001. *Contributions to:* Many anthologies and periodicals. *Address:* c/o Atlantic Monthly, 77 N Washington St, Suite 5, Boston, MA 02114, USA.

BLUMENTHAL, Michael Charles; b. 8 March 1949, Vineland, New Jersey, USA. Writer; Poet; Prof. 1 s. *Education:* BA, Philosophy, State University of New York at Binghampton, 1969; JD, Cornell University, 1974. *Appointments:* Bingham Distinguished Poet-in-Residence, University of Louisville, 1982; Briggs-Copeland Lecturer, Asst Prof. of Poetry, 1983–88, Assoc. Prof. of English, Dir of Creative Writing, 1988–93, Harvard University; Senior Fulbright Lecturer in American Literature, Eötvös Lorand University, Budapest, 1992–95; Distinguished Visiting Writer-in-Residence, Boise State University, 1996; Assoc. Prof. of English, University of Haifa, 1996; Visiting Writer, Southwest Texas State University, 1997–98; Distinguished Visiting Poet-in-Residence, Wichita State University, 1999; Distinguished Writer-in-Residence, Santa Clara University, CA, 2001; Lecturer in Creative Non-Fiction, American University of Paris, 2001–02; Distinguished Visiting Prof. of American Literature, Université Jean Monnet, Saint-Etienne, France, 2001–. *Publications:* Sympathetic Magic, 1980; Days We Would Rather Know, 1984; Laps, 1984; Against Romance, 1987; The Wages of Goodness, 1992; To Wed & To Woo: Poets on Marriage (ed.), 1992; Weinstock Among the Dying, 1993; When History Enters the House: Central European Essays, 1998; Dusty Angel, 1999; All My Mothers and Fathers, 2002. *Contributions to:* Reviews, quarterlies and journals. *Honours:* First Book Prize, Water Mark Poets of North America, 1980; Juniper Prize, University of Massachusetts, 1984; Lavan Younger Poets Prize, Acad. of American Poets, 1986; Guggenheim Fellowship, 1989; Harold U Ribelow Prize for Jewish Fiction, Hadassah magazine, 1994. *Memberships:* Associated Writing Programs; PEN American Center; Poetry Society of America; Poets and Writers. *Address:* 28 rue Thubaneau, 13001, Marseille, France. *E-mail:* mcblume@attglobal.net.

BLY, Robert (Elwood); b. 23 Dec. 1926, Madison, Minnesota, USA. Poet; Trans.; Ed.; Publisher. m. (1) Carolyn McLean, 1955, divorced 1979, (2) Ruth Counsell, 1980, 2 s., 2 d. *Education:* St Olaf College, 1946–47; AB, Harvard University, 1950; MA, University of Iowa, 1956. *Appointments:* Publisher and Ed., 1958–; Various writing workshops. *Publications:* Poetry: The Lion's Tail and Eyes: Poems Written Out of Laziness and Silence (with William Duffy and James Wright), 1962; Silence in the Snowy Fields, 1962; The Light Around the Body, 1967; Chrysanthemums, 1967; Ducks, 1968; The Morning Glory: Another Thing That Will Never Be My Friend, 1969; The Teeth Mother Naked at Last, 1971; Poems for Tennessee (with William Stafford and William Matthews),

1971; Christmas Eve Service at Midnight at St Michael's, 1972; Water Under the Earth, 1972; The Dead Seal Near McClure's Beach, 1973; Sleepers Joining Hands, 1973; Jumping Out of Bed, 1973; The Hockey Poem, 1974; Point Reyes Poems, 1974; Old Man Rubbing His Eyes, 1975; The Loon, 1977; This Body is Made of Camphor and Gopherwood, 1977; Visiting Emily Dickinson's Grave and Other Poems, 1979; This Tree Will Be Here for a Thousand Years, 1979; The Man in the Black Coat Turns, 1981; Finding an Old Ant Mansion, 1981; Four Ramages, 1983; The Whole Moisty Night, 1983; Out of the Rolling Ocean, 1984; Mirabai Versions, 1984; In the Month of May, 1985; A Love of Minute Particulars, 1985; Selected Poems, 1986; Loving a Woman in Two Worlds, 1987; The Moon on a Fencepost, 1988; The Apple Found in the Plowing, 1989; What Have I Ever Lost By Dying?: Collected Prose Poems, 1993; Gratitude to Old Teachers, 1993; Meditations on the Insatiable Soul, 1994; Morning Poems, 1997; This Body is Made of Eating the Honey of Words: New and Selected Poems, 1999; The Night Abraham Called to the Stars, 2001. Editor: Various books. Translator: Over 35 books. Other: Talking All Morning: Collected Conversations and Interviews, 1980; The Eight Stages of Translation, 1983; American Poetry: Wildness and Domesticity, 1990; Remembering James Wright, 1991; The Sibling Society, 1996. Honours: Fulbright Grant, 1956–57; Lowell Travelling Fellowship, 1964; Guggenheim Fellowships, 1964, 1972; American Acad. of Arts and Letters Grant, 1965; Rockefeller Foundation Fellowship, 1967; National Book Award, 1968. Memberships: American Acad. and Institute of Arts and Letters; Asscn of Literary Magazines of America, exec. committee. Address: 1904 Girard Ave S, Minneapolis, MN 54403, USA.

BOBYSHEV, Dmitry (Vasilievich); b. 11 April 1936, Russia. Asst Prof.; Poet; Writer. Education: Diploma of Engineer, Leningrad Technological Institute, 1959. Appointments: Lecturer, Dept of Slavic Languages and Literatures, University of Wisconsin at Milwaukee, 1982–85; Asst Prof., Dept of Slavic Languages and Literatures, University of Illinois, Urbana-Champaign, 1985–. Publications: Ziianiia, 1979; Zveri Sv Antoniia, 1989; Polnota Vsego, 1992; Russkie Tertsiny, 1992; Angely i Sily, 1997. Contributions to: USA periodicals: AGNI; TriQuarterly; Visions; Cumberland Poetry Review; Cream City Review; Clockwatch Review; Lucky Star; Poetry from the Russian Underground; Russian Poetry; The Modern Period; Contemporary Russian Poetry; USSR Periodicals: Yunost; Den' poezil; Molodoi Leningrad; Zvezda; Znamia; Smena; Petropol; Leningradskii rabochii; Leningradskii universitet; Russian emigre periodicals: Kontinent; Grani; Russkaia Mysl; 22; Novyi Zhurnal; Perekriostki; Russki Al'manakh; Vstrechi; Vestnik RSKD; Streletz. Honour: Anna Akhmatova dedicated her poem Piataia rosa (The Fifth Rose) to him as a poet. Memberships: MLA; American Asscn of Teachers of East European Languages; Beast Fable Society; Writers Union, St Petersburg; Acad. of American Poets. Address: University of Illinois, Dept of Slavic, 3092 FLB, 707 S Mathews Ave, Urbana-Champaign, IL 61801, USA.

BOCCHORITANO, A. S. See: SEGUI BENNASSAR, Antoni.

BOCCIA, Edward; b. 22 June 1921, Newark, New Jersey, USA. Prof. Emeritus of Fine Arts; Poet. m. Madeleine Wysong, 14 July 1945, 1 d. Education: BS, MA, Columbia University; Art Students League, New York, 1938–46; Pratt Institute, New York, 1939–42. Appointments: Dean, Columbus Art School, 1948–51; Asst Dean, 1951–54, Prof. of Fine Arts, 1954–86, School of Fine Arts, Washington University, St Louis. Publications: Moving the Still Life, 1993; No Matter How Good the Light Is, 1998; A Light in the Grapes, 2000; The Magic Fish, 2002. Contributions to: River King Poetry Press; Rockhurst Review; Pudding Magazine; Graffiti Rag Anthology; Live Poets Society; Negative Capability Press; Rhino; Blue Unicorn; 'Flash!Point', 2002. Memberships: National Society of Arts and Letters, chair. of fine arts, 1995–99; St Louis Artists Guild. Address: 600 Harper Ave, Webster Groves, MO 63119, USA.

BOCEK, Alois. See: VANICEK, Zdenek.

BOGEN, Don; b. 27 May 1949, Wisconsin, USA. Prof. of English; Poet. m. Cathryn Jeanne Long, 5 Sept. 1976, 1 s., 1 d. Education: AB, 1971, MA, 1974, PhD, 1976, University of California at Berkeley. Appointments: Asst Prof. of English, 1976–82, Assoc. Prof. of English, 1982–97, Prof. of English, 1997, University of Cincinnati. Publications: After the Splendid Display, 1986; The Known World, 1997. Contributions to: New Republic; Nation; Paris Review; Poetry; Yale Review; Partisan Review; Kenyon Review; Ploughshares; Shenandoah; Stand; American Poetry Review. Honours: Edwin Markham Award, Eugene V Debs Foundation, 1976; Grand Prize, Associated Writing Programs Anniversary Awards, 1982; Individual Artists Fellowships, Ohio Arts Council, 1985, 1999; Ingram Merrill Foundation Grant, 1989; National Endowment for the Arts Fellowship, 1989; Camargo Foundation Fellowship, 1993; The Writer/Emily Dickinson Award, Poetry Society of America, 1997. Membership: Associated Writing Programs. Address: 362 Terrace Ave, Cincinnati, OH 45220, USA.

BOGLIUN, Loredana; b. 18 Jan. 1955, Pula-Pola, Croatia. Social Psychologist; Prof.; Poet. m. Dino Bogliun, 2 Sept. 1978, 1 s., 1 d. Education: Laurea in Psychology, 1978; Master in Psychology, 1986; PhD, Social Psychology, 1992. Appointments: University Prof., 1991–; Vice-Pres., Istrian Region, Croatia, 1993–; International Poetry Festival, Colombia, 1998; International Biennal of Poetry, 1998. Publications: Poesie, 1988; Vorbind

Despre Noi, 1989; Mazere, 1993; Istarskite Zidista, 1996; La Peicia, 1996; La Trasparenza, 1996; Soun La Poiana, 2000. Contributions to: La Battana; Istra; Alfabeta; Il Territorio; Diverse Lingue; Balcanica; Republica; Issimo; Razgledi; Erasmus; Vilenica; Sodobnost; Corrispondenze; Approdi; Istria Nobilissima; Voci Nostre; Flowers of Peace; Mundial Fotofestival. Honours: Istria Nobilissima, 1977, 1979, 1983, 1987, 1988, 1989, 1991, 1995; Trofeo Del Buonconsiglio, Trento, 1987; Premio Drago Gervais, Rijeka-Fiume, 1989. Address: Rudine 20, 52460 Buje-Buie, Istria, Croatia.

BOGOJEVICH, Dejan; b. 4 July 1971, Valjevo, Yugoslavia. Teacher; Poet. Education: College for Teachers, Belgrade University. Appointments: Ed., Society of Writers, Valjevo, 1995; Writer, Painter, Designer, Editor, Lotus International Haiku Magazine, Greedy Nostril Strip Magazine, Black Lime Art Magazine; Literature Youth of Serbia, pres., 1996–97. Publications: Somewhere at the End, 1991; Palms of Ground From Hills, 1995; Letters From Fields of Moss, 1996; Griots, 1998; Abolla, 1998; In Street XI, 1998; In the Sky Mirror (Serbian and English), 1999; The Shadows Undulate, 1999. Contributions to: National and international journals and magazines. Honours: St Sava Prize, Club for Literature, 1997; Alexandar Nejgebauer Prize, Haiku Club, 1998; Ratkovic's Nights of Poetry Prize, 1998. Memberships: Society of Writers, Valjevo, 1989; Haiku Club, Belgrade, 1996; Society of Serbian Writers, Belgrade, 1997; Club of Writers, Zemun, 1997; Club of Writers, Belgrade, 1999. Address: 14202 Rajkovic, Valjevo, Yugoslavia.

BOISVERT, France, (Marguerite de Nevers); b. 10 June 1959, Sherbrooke, QC, Canada. French Teacher; Writer; Poet. 1 s. Education: MLitt, 1986; DD, French Literature, 2001. Publications: Les Samourailles (fiction), 1987; Li Tsing-tao ou Le grand avoir (fiction), 1989; Massawippi (poem), 1992; Comme un vol de gerfauts (poem), 1993; Les Vents de l'Aube (prose), 1997; Le Voyageur aux yeux d'onyx (prose), 2002. Contributions to: Liberté; La Presse; Le Devoir. Honours: Bursaries, Minister of Culture, Québec, 1989, 1990, 1991. Memberships: Union des Écrivains du Québec; Asscn internationale des Études québécoises; Élue au Conseil d'administration de l'UNEQ (1992–93, 1995). Address: A/S UNEQ Maison des Écrivains, 3492 Ave Laval, Montréal, QC H2X 3C8, Canada. E-mail: france59boisvert@yahoo.ca.

BOLAM, Robyn, (Marion Lomax); b. 20 Oct. 1953, Newcastle upon Tyne, England. Prof. of Literature; Poet; Ed. m. Michael Lomax, 29 Aug. 1974, divorced 1999. Education: BA, Librarianship, 1974, BA, English and American Studies, 1979, University of Kent; DPhil, University of York, 1983. Appointments: Part-time Lecturer, King Alfred's College, 1983–86; Creative Writing Fellow, University of Reading, 1987–88; Lecturer, Senior Lecturer in English, 1988–95, Prof. of Literature, 1995–98, St Mary's College, Strawberry Hill, Middlesex; Writer-in-Residence, University of Stockholm, 1998–. Publications: Poetry: The Peepshow Girl, 1989; Raiding the Borders, 1996. Non-Fiction: Stage Images and Traditions: Shakespeare to Ford, 1987. Editor: Time Present and Time Past: Poets at the University of Kent 1965–1985, 1985; Four Plays by John Ford, 1995; The Rover, by Alpha Behn, 1995; Out of the Blue (with Steven Harman), 1998. Contributions to: Collections of essays, anthologies and periodicals. Honours: E. C. Gregory Award, Society of Authors, 1981; First Prize, Cheltenham Festival Poetry Competition, 1981; Hawthornden Fellowship, 1993. Memberships: National Asscn for Writers in Education; Poetry Society; Society of Authors. Address: c/o Bloodaxe Books, Highgreen, Tarset, Nothumberland NE48 1RP, England.

BOLAND, Eavan (Aisling); b. 24 Sept. 1944, Dublin, Ireland. Poet; Writer. m. Kevin Casey, 1969, 2 d. Education: BA, Trinity College, Dublin, 1966; University of Iowa, 1979. Appointments: Lecturer, Trinity College, Dublin, 1967–68, School of Irish Studies, Dublin, 1968–. Publications: 23 Poems, 1962; New Territory (poems), 1967; W. B. Yeats and His World (with Michael MacLiammoir), 1971; The War Horse (poems), 1975; In Her Own Image (poems), 1980; Night Feed (poems), 1982; The Journey and Other Poems, 1987; Selected Poems, 1989; A Kind of Scar: The Woman Poet in a National Tradition, 1989; Outside History: Selected Poems, 1980–1990, 1990; In a Time of Violence (poems), 1994; A Dozen Lips, 1994; Collected Poems, 1995; Object Lesson: The Life of the Woman and the Poet in Our Time, 1995; Code (poems), 2001. Contributions to: Anthologies, newspapers and journals. Honours: Irish Arts Council Macauley Fellowship, 1967; Irish American Cultural Award, 1983; Poetry Book Society Choice, 1987. Membership: Irish Acad. of Letters. Address: c/o School of Irish Studies, Dublin, Ireland.

BOLAND, Michael (John); b. 14 Nov. 1950, Kingston, Surrey, England. Poet; Civil Servant. Appointment: Ed., The Arcadian, poetry magazine. Publication: The Midnight Circus; The Trout... Minus One (co-author), 1993. Contributions to: Envoi; Purple Patch; Weyfarers; Firing Squad; Various anthologies. Honours: Patricia Chown Sonnet Award. Memberships: PEN; Society of Civil Service Authors; Keats-Shelley Memorial Asscn; Wordsworth Trust; Friends of Coleridge; MIAP. Address: 11 Boxtree Lane, Harrow Weald, Middlesex HA3 6JU, England.

BOLD, Alan (Norman); b. 20 April 1943, Edinburgh, Scotland. Writer; Poet. m. 29 June 1963, 1 d. Education: Edinburgh University, 1961–64. Appointments: Journalist, Times Educational Supplement, 1965–66; Reviewer, The Scotsman, 1970–88, Glasgow Herald, 1989–. Publications:

Society Inebrious, 1965; To Find the New, 1967; The Voyage, 1968; A Perpetual Motion Machine, 1969; Penguin Modern Poets 15, 1969; The State of the Nation, 1969; The Auld Symie, 1971; He Will Be Greatly Missed, 1971; A Century of People, 1971; A Pint of Bitter, 1971; Scotland, Yes, 1978; This Fine Day, 1979; In This Corner, 1983; Summoned by Knox, 1985; Bright Lights Blaze Out, 1986; MacDiarmid, 1988; A Burns Companion, 1991; East is West, 1991; Rhymer Rab: An Anthology of Poems and Prose by Robert Burns, 1993. *Contributions to:* New York Times; TLS; London Review of Books; New Statesman; Glasgow Herald; Scotsman; 2 Plus 2; Poetry Review; Stand. *Honours:* McVitie's Prize, Scottish Writer of the Year, 1989; Arts Award, Royal Philosophical Society, 1990; Auchinleck Boswell Society, hon. pres., 1992. *Memberships:* Scotish Poetry Library; Society of Authors; Society of Scottish Artists. *Address:* Balbirnie Burns East Cottage, Nr Markinch, Glenrothes, Fife KY7 6NE, Scotland.

BOLEK, Juliusz Erazm; b. 25 Nov. 1963, Warsaw, Poland. Poet; Writer of Short Stories; Literary and Arts Critic; Journalist. *Education:* Faculty of Journalism and Political Sciences, University of Warsaw, 1985–91. *Appointments:* Ed.-in-Chief, Enigma (magazine for young intellectuals), 1987–; Owner, I'm God Sent Enterprise (publishing house), 1990–91; Dir, Studio-Kineo Arts Gallery, Warsaw, 1991–. *Publications:* Poetry: Teksty, 1985; Nago, 1986; Miniatury, 1987; Prywatne Zagrozenie, 1989; Skroty Szalenstwa, 1991; Serge Btyskawicy, 1995. *Contributions to:* Radar; Razem; Walka Mlodych Przeglad Tygodniowy; Tygodnik Kulturalny; Kierunki; Zycie Literackie; Namietnosci; Cherwell, Oxford University Weekly; Miesiecznik Literacki; Nurt; Okolice; Miraz Premiera; Missland; Slowo Powszechne; Trybuna; Sztandar Mlodych; Ekran; Ekran; Dziennik Polski (Polish Daily, London). *Membership:* Polish Journalists Asscn; Polish Writers' Asscn. *Address:* ul Chmielna 35 m 199, 00-117 Warsaw, Poland.

BOLGER, Dermot; b. 6 Feb. 1959, Finglas, Ireland. Novelist; Dramatist; Poet; Ed. m. Bernadette Bolger, 1988, 2 c. *Education:* Beneavin College Secondary School. *Appointments:* Founder-Ed., Raven Arts Press, 1979–92; Exec. Ed., New Island Books, 1992–. *Publications:* Fiction: Night Shift, 1985; The Woman's Daughter, 1987; The Journey Home, 1990; Emily's Shoes, 1992; A Second Life, 1994; Father's Music, 1997; Finbar's Hotel (collaborative novel), 1997; Ladies Night at Finbar's Hotel (collaborative novel), 1999; Temptation, 2000; The Valparaiso Voyage, 2001. Plays: The Lament for Arthur Cleary, 1989; Blinded by the Light, 1990; In High Germany, 1990; The Holy Ground, 1990; One Last White Horse, 1991; The Dublin Bloom, 1994; April Bright, 1995; The Passion of Jerome, 1999; Consenting Adults, 2000. Poetry: The Habit of Flesh, 1979; Finglas Lilies, 1980; No Waiting America, 1981; Internal Exiles, 1986; Leinster Street Ghosts, 1989; Taking My Letters Back: New and Selected Poems, 1998. Editor: The Dolmen Book of Irish Christmas Stories, 1986; The Bright Wave: Poetry in Irish Now, 1986; 16 on 16: Irish Writers on the Easter Rising, 1988; Invisible Cities: The New Dubliners: A Journey through Unofficial Dublin, 1988; Invisible Dublin: A Journey through Its Writers, 1992; The Picador Book of Contemporary Irish Fiction, 1993; 12 Bar Blues (with Aidan Murphy), 1993; The New Picador Book of Contemporary Irish Fiction, 2000; Druids, Dudes and Beauty Queens: The Changing Face of Irish Theatre, 2001. *Contributions to:* Anthologies. *Honours:* A E Memorial Prize, 1986; Macauley Fellowship, 1987; A Z Whitehead Prize, 1987; Samuel Beckett Award, 1991; Edinburgh Fringe First Awards, 1991, 1995; Stewart Parker BBC Award, 1991; Playwright in Asscn, Abbey Theatre, Dublin, 1998. *Address:* c/o A P Watt, 20 John St, London WC1N 2DR, England.

BOLTON, Ken; b. 24 June 1949, Sydney, NSW, Australia. Poet; Art Critic. *Education:* BA, University of Sydney, 1974. *Publications:* Selected Poems, 1992; Two Poems - A Drawing of the Sky; The Ferrara Poems (co-author); Talking to You; Blazing Shoes; Sestina to the Centre of the Brain; Airborne Dogs (co-author); Notes for Poems; Blonde & French; Four Poems. *Contributions to:* Scripsi; Otis Rush; Salt; Meanjin; Ear in the Wheatfield; Overland. *Honour:* Michel Wesley Wright Award, Melbourne University, 1990. *Address:* PO Box 21, North Adelaide, SA 5006, Australia.

BOND, Edward; b. 18 July 1934, London, England. Dramatist; Dir; Poet; Trans. m. Elisabeth Pablé, 1971. *Appointment:* Resident Theatre Writer, University of Essex, 1982–83. *Publications:* Plays, 4 vols, 1977–92; Theatre Poems and Songs, 1978; Collected Poems, 1978–85, 1985; Notes on Post-Modernism, 1990; Selected Letters, 5 vols, 1994–2000; Selected Notebooks, 2 vols, 2000–01; The Hidden Plot: Notes on Theatre and the State, 2000. Other: Libretti for Henze's operas We Come to the River, 1976, and The English Cat, 1983; Trans. *Honour:* George Devine Award, 1968; John Whiting Award, 1968; Hon. DLitt, Yale University, 1977; Northern Arts Literary Fellow, 1977–79. *Address:* c/o Casarotto Ramsay, National House, 60–66 Wardour St, London W1V 3HP, England.

BOND, Harold; b. 2 Dec. 1939, Boston, Massachusetts, USA. Poet; Teacher; Ed. *Education:* AB, English and Journalism, Northeastern University, 1962; MFA, Creative Writing, University of Iowa, 1967. *Appointments:* Instructor, Center for Adult Education, Cambridge, Massachusetts, 1968–; Copy Ed., Boston Globe, 1969–71; Ed., 1969–70, Editorial Board, 1971–, Ararat magazine; Various teaching positions, adult education, poetry, Poet-in-Schools, Massachusetts; Founder, Dir, Seminars in Poetry Writing, Belmont, Massachusetts, 1978–. *Publications:* Poetry: The Northern Wall, 1969; Dancing

on Water, 1970; The Way It Happens to You, 1979; Other Worlds. *Contribution to:* Numerous anthologies and journals. *Honours:* Awards and fellowships *Address:* 11 Chestnut St, Melrose, MA 02176, USA.

BOND, Katherine L.; b. 7 June 1949, Sardis, Mississippi USA. Poet Transcriptionist. m. John R Bond IV, 27 July, 1969, 2 d. *Contributions to* Over 10 anthologies and many journals. *Honours:* Several awards from poetr groups. *Memberships:* International Society of Authors and Artists International Society of Poets; National Authors Registry; National Poet' Asscn; Poet's Guild. *Address:* 316 Notre Dame Ave, Joliet, IL 60436, USA.

BONDE, Heidi; b. 27 May 1954, Oslo, Norway. Author; Poet. m. Eitna Kleppe, 8 Aug. 1975, 1 s. 1 d. *Education:* Cand Mag, University of Oslo *Publications:* Lucifers Munn, 1988; J Dette Rom Planter Jeg En Hegg, 1990 September, 1991; Svommeskolen, 1994; Oktobermusikantene, 1995; Detaljene diktatur (novel), 1996; Qvelse i det Soleklare, 1997; Flamingohøsten ha begynt, 1997; Fortellingen om Fregatten Felicita (novel), 1998; Fabelaktig forhold (poems), 1999; Marsipangrisen (novel), 2000. Translations: Annerledes 1995; Selected Poems from 'Quaderno di quattro anni' and 'Altn versi e poesi disperse' by Eugenio Montale. *Contributions to:* Aftenposten; Dagbladet Klassekampen; Vinduet; Lyrikkmagastnet. *Membership:* The Norwegiar Author's Union. *Address:* Vestengsvingen 54, 1182 Oslo, Norway.

BONNEFOY, Yves Jean; b. 24 June 1923, Tours, France. Poet; Author Trans.; Prof. m. Lucille Vine, 1968, 1 d. *Education:* Philosophy degree University of Paris. *Appointments:* Assoc. Prof., University of Nice, 1973–76 University of Aix-en-Provence, 1979–81; Prof., Collège de France, Paris, 1981–93. *Publications:* Poetry: Du mouvement et de l'immobilitè de Douve, 1953, English trans. as On the Motion and Immobility of Douve, 1968; Peintures murales de la France gothique, 1954; Hier régnant desert, 1958; L'Improbable, 1959; La Seconde Simplicité, 1961; Rimbaud par lui-même, 1961, English trans. as Rimbaud, 1973; Anti-Plato, 1962; Mirò, 1964, English trans. 1967; Pierre écrite, 1965, English trans. as Words in Stone, 1976; Un rêve fait à Mantoue, 1967; La Poésie française et le principe d'identité, 1967; Selected Poems, 1968; Rome 1630: L'horizon du premier baroque, 1970; L'arrière-pays, 1972; L'Ordalie, 1975; Dans le leurre du seuil, 1975; Terre seconde, 1976; Rue traversière, 1977; Le Nuage rouge, 1977; Poèmes, 1978, English trans. as Poems, 1959–1975, 1985; The Origin of Language, 1980; Entretiens sur la poésie, 1980; La Presence et l'Image, 1983; Things Dying, Things Newborn, 1986; La Vérité de Parole, 1988; The Act and the Place of Poetry: Selected Essays, 1989; In the Shadow's Light, 1990; Early Poems, 1947–1959, 1991; Alberto Giacometti: A Biography of His Work, 1991; Mythologies, 2 vols, 1991; Roman and European Mythologies, 1992; Greek and Egyptian Mythologies, 1992; Asian Mythologies, 1993; American, African, and European Mythologies, 1993; New and Selected Poems, 1995; Dessin, Couleur, et Lumière, 1995; La Vie errante, 1995; The Lure and the Truth of Painting: Selected Essays on Art, 1995; Shakespeare et Yeats, 1998; Lieux et destins de l'image: Un cours de poétique au Collège de France, 1981–93; La Communauté des traducteurs, 2000; Giacometti (trans.), 2002. *Contributions to:* Many reviews and journals. *Honours:* Prix de l'Express, 1958; Cecil Hamly Award, 1967; Prix des Critiques, 1971; Prix Montaigne, 1978; Grand Prix de Poesie, Académie Française, 1981; Grand Prix, Société des gens de Lettres, 1987; Bennet Award, Hudson Review, 1988; Bourse Goncourt, 1991; Prix Balzac, 1995; Prix national de Poesie, 196; Mutsuoko Shiki Prize, 2000; Many hon. doctorates. *Address:* 63 Rue Lepic, 75018 Paris, France.

BONTRIDDER, Albert; b. 4 April 1921, Brussels, Belgium. Poet; Architect. m. Olga Dohnalova, 17 Sept. 1953, 1 s., 1 d. *Education:* Diploma in Architecture, 1942. *Publications:* Hoog Water, 1951; Dood Hout, 1955; Bagatelle, 1962; Open Einde, 1967; Zelfverbranding, 1971; Gedichten, 1942–1972, 1973; Huizen vieren haat, 1979; Een oog te veel, 1983; Poésie Flamande d'aujourd'hui, 1986; Groeten van Mijnheer en Mevrouw Ledepop, 1990. *Contributions to:* Tijd En Mens; Kentering; Architecture. *Honours:* Arkpreis Van het Vrije Woord, 1957; Prix de la Province du Brabant, 1960; Prix de la ville Heist-Duinbergen, 1969; Prix Dirk Martens, 1970; Prix Jan Campert, 1972; Prix SABAM for La Traduction, 1990. *Memberships:* PEN Club International, Belgium; Académie Royale des Sciences, des Lettres et des Beaux-Arts de Belgique; European Asscn for the Promotion of Poetry, Louvain. *Address:* Ave Lequime 16a, 1640 Rhode-Saint-Genèse, Belgium.

BOOTH, Philip; b. 8 Oct. 1925, Hanover, New Hampshire, USA. Prof. of English (retd); Poet. m. Margaret Tillman, 1946, 3 d. *Education:* AB, Dartmouth College, 1948; MA, Columbia University, 1949. *Appointments:* Asst Prof., Wellesley College, 1954–61; Assoc. Prof., 1961–65, Prof. of English and Poet-in-Residence, 1965–85, Syracuse University. *Publications:* Letter from a Distant Land, 1957; The Islanders, 1961; North by East, 1966; Weathers and Edges, 1966; Margins: A Sequence of New and Selected Poems, 1970; Available Light, 1976; Before Sleep, 1980; Relations: Selected Poems, 1950–85, 1986; Selves, 1990; Pairs: New Poems, 1994; Trying to Say It: Outlooks and Insights on How Poems Happen, 1996; Lifelines: New and Selected Poems 1950–1999, 1999. *Honours:* Guggenheim Fellowships, 1958, 1965; Theodore Roethke Prize, 1970; National Endowment for the Arts Fellowship, 1980; Acad. of American Poets Fellowship, 1983; Rockefeller Fellowship, 1986; Maurice English Poetry Award, 1987. *Address:* PO Box 330, Castine, ME 04421, USA.

BOOTHROYD, Christine; b. 31 March 1934, Batley, Yorkshire, England. Linguist; Poet. m. Don Brinkley, 10 April 1982, 1 step-s., 1 step-d. *Education:* Leeds College of Commerce, 1951–52; Teachers Certificate, University College of Wales, Aberystwyth, 1966; Diplomas in Italian, Perugia and Florence. *Appointments:* Teacher of French/Italian, Leeds, 1963–65; Lecturer in charge of Modern Languages, North Oxfordshire Technical College, 1966–77; Part-time Lecturer, French/Italian, Banbury and Harrogate. *Publications:* The Floating World, 1975; The Snow Island, 1982; The Lost Moon, 1992. *Contributions to:* Arts Council Anthology 3; Workshop New Poetry; Orbis; Glasgow Magazine; Writers in Concert; Doors; Krax; Moorlands Review; Envoi; Penniless Press; Links; Dalesman; Poetry Nottingham International; Yorkshire Journal. *Membership:* Harrogate Writers' Circle; Italian Cultural Institute. *Address:* 35 St George's Rd, Harrogate, North Yorkshire HG2 9BP, England.

BORDEN, William (Vickers); b. 27 Jan. 1938, Indianapolis, IN, USA. Prof. of English Emeritus; Writer; Poet; Dramatist; Novelist; Ed. m. Nancy Lee Johnson, 17 Dec. 1960, 1 s., 2 d. *Education:* AB, Columbia University, 1960; MA, University of California at Berkeley, 1962. *Appointments:* Instructor, 1962–64, Asst Prof., 1966–70, Assoc. Prof., 1970–82, Prof. of English, 1982–90, Chester Fritz Distinguished Prof. of English, 1990–97, Prof. Emeritus, 1998–, University of North Dakota; Fiction Ed., North Dakota Quarterly, 1986–2002. *Publications:* Fiction: Superstoe (novel), 1967; Many short stories. Poetry: Slow Step and Dance (chapbook), 1991; Eurydice's song, 1999. Other: Numerous plays, including the full-length plays: The Last Prostitute, 1980; Tap Dancing Across the Universe, 1981; Loon Dance, 1982; The Only Woman Awake is the Woman Who Has Heard the Flute, 1983; Makin' It, 1984; The Consolation of Philosophy, 1986; When the Meadowlark Sings, 1988; Meet Again, 1990; Turtle Island Blues, 1991; Don't Dance Me Outside, 1993; Gourmet Love, 1996; Bluest Reason, 2001. Musical Drama: Sakakawea, 1987. Also Screenplays, radio plays, and video scripts. *Contributions to:* Many anthologies and periodicals. *Honours:* North Dakota Centennial Drama Prize, 1989; American Society of Composers, Authors and Publishers Awards, 1990, 1991, 1992; Burlington Northern Award, University of North Dakota, 1990; Minnesota Distinguished Artist Award, 1992; Minnesota State Arts Board Career Opportunity Grant, 1996. *Memberships:* American Society of Composers, Authors and Publishers; Authors League of America; Dramatists Guild; PEN. *Address:* 10514 Turtle River Lake Rd NE, Bemidji, MN 56601, USA.

BORDIER, Roger; b. 5 March 1923, Blois, France. Author; Dramatist; Poet. m. Jacqueline Bouchaud. *Publications:* Fiction: La cinquième saison, 1959; Les blés, 1961; Le mime, 1963; L'Entracte, 1965; Un âge d'or, 1967; Le tour de ville, 1969; Les éventails, 1971; L'océan, 1974; Demain l'éte, 1977; La grande vie, 1981; Les temps heureux, 1983; La longue file, 1984; 36 La fête, 1985; La belle de mai, 1986; Les saltimvanques de la révolution, 1989; Vel d'hib, 1989; Les fusils du 1er Mai, 1991; Chroniques de la cité joyeuse, 1995; L'interrogatoire, 1998. Poetry: Les épicentres, 1951. Other: Several plays. *Contributions to:* Journals, radio and television. *Honours:* Prix Renaudot, 1961; Officier Ordre des Arts et des Lettres. *Address:* 8 rue Geoffroy St Hilaire, 75005 Paris, France.

BOREL, Jacques; b. 17 Dec. 1925, Paris, France. Author; Poet; Trans. m. Christine Idrac, 1948, 1 s., 4 d. *Education:* Lycée Henri IV, Paris; University of Paris. *Appointments:* Teacher, Lycée de Clermont-Ferrand, 1952–56, Lycée Rodin, Paris, 1956–67; Literary Adviser, Gallimard, 1969–75, Balland, 1978–82; Cultural Attaché, French Embassy, Belgium, 1984–86; Various visiting professorships. *Publications:* Fiction: L'adoration, 1965; Le retour, 1970; Histoire de mes vieux habits, 1979; Le déferlement, 1993. Poetry: Sur les murs du temps, 1990. Non-Fiction: Marcel Proust, 1972; La d'épossession, 1973; Commentaires, 1974; Un voyage ordinaire, 1975; Poésie et nostalgie, 1979; Petite histoire de mes rêves, 1981; L'Aven Différé, 1997; Sur les poètes, 1998. Other: Trans. *Contributions to:* Many periodicals and journals. *Honours:* Prix Goncourt, 1965; Chevalier, 1971, Officier, 1986, Ordre des Arts et des Lettres; Grand Prix, Société des Gens de Lettres, 1993. *Address:* 22 rue Charles de Gaulle, 91440 Bures-sur-Yvette, Essonne, France.

BORLAND, Betty Jean; b. 17 Oct. 1919, Oil City, Pennsylvania, USA. Poet. *Education:* Graduated, High School, Dubois, Pennsylvania, 1937. *Publications:* Treasures From the Heart, 3 vols, 1988, 1991, 1999. *Contributions to:* Anthologies. *Honours:* Award of Merit Certificates, 1988, 1990; Golden Poet Award, 1990. *Membership:* National League of American Pen Women. *Address:* 1311 Delaware Ave SW, No. 445, Washington, DC 20024, USA.

BORN, Anne; b. 9 July 1930, Cooden Beach, Sussex, England. Poet; Reviewer; Trans. m. Povl Born, 1 June 1950, 3 s., 1 d. *Education:* MA, University of Copenhagen, 1955; MLitt, University of Oxford, 1978. *Appointments:* Writer-in-Residence, Barnstaple, 1983–85, Kingsbridge, 1985–87, Buckinghamshire, 1996. *Publications:* 12 poetry collections, four history books, 35 translated books. *Contributions to:* TLS; Ambit; Rialto; Green Book; Scratch; Cimarron Review; Tears in the Fence; The Frogmore Papers; Other Poetry; The Rialto; Salzbury Poetry Review; Troubleshare; Oasis; Links; Seam; Odyssey. *Honours:* Over 20 prizes and commendations. *Memberships:* Society of Authors; Trans' Assen, chair., 1987, 1993–95; University Women's Club; Fellow of Hawthornden Castle. *Address:* Oversteps, Froude Rd, Salcombe, South Devon TQ8 8LH, England. *Fax:* (1548) 844384. *E-mail:* overstep@globalnet.co.uk.

BORSON, Roo, (Ruth Elizabeth Borson); b. 20 Jan. 1952, Berkeley, CA, USA. Poet; Writer. *Education:* University of California at Santa Barbara, 1969–71; BA, Goddard College, 1973; MFA, University of British Columbia, 1977. *Appointments:* Writer-in-Residence, University of Western Ontario, 1987–88, Concordia University, 1993; Green College, University of British Columbia, 2000. *Publications:* Landfall, 1977; Rain, 1980; In the Smoky Light of the Fields, 1980; A Sad Device, 1982; The Whole Night, Coming Home, 1984; The Transparence of November/Snow (with Kim Maltman), 1985; Intent, or the Weight of the World, 1989; Night Walk: Selected Poems, 1994; Water Memory, 1996; Introduction to the Introduction to Wang Wei (with Kim Maltman and Andy Patten), 2000. *Contributions to:* Many anthologies and periodicals. *Honours:* MacMillan Prize for Poetry, University of British Columbia, 1977; First Prize, 1982, Third Prize, 1989, for Poetry, and Third Prize for Personal Essay, 1990, Canadian Broadcasting Corporation; Governor-General's Award Nominations for Poetry, 1984, 1994. *Memberships:* International PEN; Pain Not Bread; Writer's Union of Canada. *Address:* c/o Writer's Union of Canada, 24 Ryerson Ave, Toronto, Ontario M5T 2P3, Canada.

BOSLEY, John E.; b. 26 Aug. 1937, Stevenage, Hertfordshire, England. Writer; Poet; Counsellor. Divorced, 2 s., 2 d. *Education:* BA, 1961, PGCE, 1962, Manchester; MSc, Bradford, 1982. *Contributions to:* Bogg; X-Calibre; Envoi; Foolscap; Iota; Klik; North; Odyssey; Pennine Platform; Psychopoetica; Scratch; Sepia; The Wide Skirt; Local radio and buses (Yorkshire Rider). *Honour:* Second Prize, Huddersfield Poetry Competition, 1990. *Membership:* Poetry Society. *Address:* 9 Wheatroyd Lane, Huddersfield HD5 8XS, England.

BOSLEY, Keith Anthony; b. 16 Sept. 1937, Bourne End, Buckinghamshire, England. Poet; Trans. m. Satu Salo, 27 Aug. 1982, 3 s. *Education:* Universities of Reading, Paris, and Caen, 1956–60; BA, Honours, French. *Appointments:* Staff, BBC, 1961–93; Visiting Lecturer, BBC and British Council, Middle East, 1981. *Publications:* The Possibility of Angels, 1969; And I Dance, 1972; Dark Summer, 1976; Mallarmé: The Poems (trans.), 1977; Eino Leino: Whitsongs (trans.), 1978; Stations, 1979; The Elek Book of Oriental Verse, 1979; From the Theorems of Master Jean de La Ceppède (trans.), 1983; A Chiltern Hundred, 1987; The Kalevala (trans.), 1989; I Will Sing of What I Know (trans.), 1990; Luis de Camões: Epic and Lyric (trans.), 1990; The Kanteletar (trans.), 1992; The Great Bear (trans.), 1993; Aleksis Kivi: Odes (trans.), 1994; André Frénaud: Rome the Sorceress (trans.), 1996; Eve Blossom has Wheels: German Love Poetry, 1997; Skating on the Sea: Poetry from Finland, 1997; An Upton Hymnal, 1999. *Contributions to:* Many newspapers, reviews, magazines and journals. *Honours:* Finnish State Prize for Trans, 1978; First Prize, British Comparative Literature Asscn Trans. Competition, 1980; First Prize, Goethe Society Trans. Competition, 1982; Knight, First Class, Order of the White Rose of Finland, 1991; Pension, Royal Literary Fund, 2001. *Membership:* Finnish Literature Society, Helsinki, corresponding mem. *Address:* 108 Upton Rd, Upton-cum-Chalvey, Slough SL1 2AW, England.

BOSTON, Bruce; b. 16 July 1943, Chicago, IL, USA. Writer; Poet; Book Designer. *Education:* BA, 1965, MA, 1967, University of California at Berkeley. *Appointment:* Prof. of Creative Writing, John F Kennedy University, Orinda, CA, 1979–83. *Publications:* All the Clocks Are Melting, 1984; Alchemical Texts, 1985; Nuclear Futures, 1987; Time, 1988; The Nightmare Collector, 1988; Faces of the Beast, 1990; Cybertexts, 1992; Chronicles of the Mutant Rain Forest, 1992; Accursed Wives, 1993; Specula, 1993; Sensuous Debris, 1995; Conditions of Sentient Life, 1996; Cold Tomorrows, 1998. *Contributions to:* Asimov's Science Fiction Magazine; Amazing Stories; Science Fiction Age; Weird Tales; Year's Best Fantasy and Horror; Nebula Awards Anthology. *Honours:* Rhysling Awards for Speculative Poetry, 1987, 1988, 1993, 1995, 1996; Asimov Readers Choice Awards, 1989, 1993, 1996. *Memberships:* SFWA; Science Fiction Poetry Asscn. *Address:* 1819 Ninth St, Apt 3, Berkeley, CA 94710, USA.

BOSVELD, Jennifer Miller, (Jennifer DeRhodes, Jennifer Groce, Jennifer Welch); b. 24 Jan. 1945, Columbus, Ohio, USA. Poet; Writer; Publisher; Writing Centre Dir; Teacher of Poetry; Career Counsellor; Consultant. m. (1) Raoul DeRhodes, 1963, 1 s., (2) Richard Groce, 1971, 1 s., (3)1981, (4) 1986. *Education:* Ohio State University, School of Social Work. *Appointments:* Publisher, Pudding House Publications and Pudding Magazine, International Journal of Applied Poetry, The Poetry Publishing Workshop and The Poetry Writing Workshop. *Publications:* Earthdays, 1976; Magic House, 1979; The Pulling, 1981; Free With the Purchase of a Spaghetti Fork, 1981; Topics for Getting in Touch: A Poetry Therapy Songbook, 1981; Criminal Hands, 1985; Jazz Kills the Paperboy, 1995; The Unitarian Universalist Poets: A Contemporary American Survey (ed.), 1996. *Contributions to:* Hiram Poetry Review; Negative Capability; Amelia; Christian Science Monitor; Smackwarm; Pteranadon; Chiron Review; Bottomfish; Cornfield Review; Wind; Pig Iron; Maryland Poetry Review; Coffeehouse Poems, An Anthology, 1996; Over 400 others. *Honour:* Ohio Arts Council Individual Artist Fellowship, 1995; Pioneer Award, National Asscn for Poetry Therapy, 1996. *Address:* Pudding House, 60 N Main St, Johnstown, OH 43031, USA.

BOSWORTH, J(ames) A(lfred); b. 16 Feb. 1936, Hastings, Sussex, England. Poet. m. Anne Elizabeth Moran, 19 Dec. 1960, 5 s. *Education:* BA, Open University, 1994. *Publications:* Neknus and Other Poems, 1984; Clouds of Glory and Other Poems, 1985; Natural Memories, 1992; A Theory for Art, 1993; Prefaces, 1994; Helvetian Harmonics. *Contributions to:* Numerous periodicals. *Memberships:* Poetry Society; British Society of Aesthetics; Open University Poets; New-Tradition Movement, founder-mem. *Address:* c/o Cite Du Castel A/10, 1482 Cugy (FR), Switzerland.

BOULANGER, Daniel; b. 24 Jan. 1922, Compiègne, Oise, France. Author; Poet; Dramatist. m. (2) Clémence Dufour, 4 s., 3 d. *Education:* Petit Séminaire Saint-Charles, Chauny. *Publications:* Fiction: Les noces du merle, 1963; Retouches, 1969; Vessies et lanternes, 1971; Fouetter cocher, 1974; La confession d'Omer, 1991; Un eté à la diable, 1992; Ursacq, 1993; A la courte paille, 1993; Le retable wasserfall et etiquettes, 1994; Caporal supérieur, 1994; Le miroitier, 1995; Taciturnes, 1995; Tombeau d'héraldine, 1997; Talbard, 1998; Le ciel de bargetal, 1999. Other: Numerous plays and screenplays; Several poetry collections. *Honours:* Prix de la Nouvelle, 1963; Prix Max Jacob, 1970; Prix de l'Académie française, 1971; Prix Goncourt, 1974; Prix Pierre de Monaco, 1979; Prix Kléber Haedens, 1983; Officier, Légion d'honneur; Officier, Ordre Nationale du Mérite Commandeur des Arts et des Lettres. *Membership:* Académie Goncourt, 1983–. *Address:* 22 rue du Heaume, 60300 Senlis, France.

BOUVARD, Marguerite Anne, (Marguerite Guzman Bouvard); b. 10 Jan. 1937, Trieste, Italy. Prof.; Writer; Poet. m. Jacques Bouvard, 25 Nov. 1959, 1 s., 1 d. *Education:* BA, Northwestern University, 1958; MA, Political Science, Radcliffe College, 1960; PhD, Political Science, Harvard University, 1965; MA, Creative Writing, Boston University, 1977. *Appointment:* Prof. of Political Science and English, Regis College, 1966–. *Publications:* Journeys Over Water, 1980; Landscape and Exile (ed.), 1985; Voices From An Island, 1985; Of Light and Silence, 1990; With the Mothers of the Plaza de Mayo, 1993. *Contributions to:* Ploughshares; Partisan Review; Ohio Journal; Mid-West Quarterly; West Branch; Southern Humanities Review; Sojourner; Yarrow; Radcliffe Quarterly; Literary Review; Centennial Review; Caesura; San Jose Studies; Christian Science Monitor. *Honours:* Scholarship in Poetry, Bread Loaf Writers' Conference, 1976; Residencies, MacDowell Colony, Leighton Arts Colony Banff, Yaddo, Virginia Centre for Creative Arts, Djerassi Foundation, Villa Montalvo, Cottages at Hedgebrook, 1978–90. *Memberships:* New England Poetry Club; PEN; Poetry Society of America. *Address:* 6 Brookfield Circle, Wellesley, MA 02181, USA.

BOWDEN, Roland Heywood; b. 19 Dec. 1916, Lincoln, England. Poet; Dramatist. m. 2 Jan. 1946, 1 s., 1 d. *Education:* School of Architecture, Liverpool University, 1934–39. *Publications:* Poems From Italy, 1970; Every Season is Another, 1986. Plays: Death of Paolini, 1980; After Neruda, 1984; The Fence, 1985. *Contributions to:* Arts Review: London Magazine; Panurge; Words International. *Honours:* Arts Council Drama Bursary, 1978; Cheltenham Festival Poetry Prize, 1982; First Prize, All-Sussex Poets, 1983. *Membership:* National Poetry Secretariat. *Address:* 2 Roughmere Cottage, Lavant, Chichester, West Sussex PO18 0BG, England.

BOWER, Susan; b. 9 Aug. 1969, Sydney, NSW, Australia. Poet; Ed. *Education:* BA, Australian Literature, MA, Creative Writing, University of Sydney. *Publication:* Factory Joker. *Contributions to:* Many periodicals. *Honour:* Winner, University of Sydney Union Poetry Prize, 1996. *Address:* c/o University of Sydney Union, Level 1, Manning Building, 24 Booth St, Arncliffe 2205, NSW, Australia.

BOWERING, George; b. 1 Dec. 1936, Penticton, BC, Canada. Author; Poet; Dramatist; University Teacher. m. Angela Luoma, 14 Dec. 1963, 1 d. *Education:* Victoria College; MA, University of British Columbia, 1963; University of Western Ontario. *Appointments:* Teacher, University of Calgary, 1963–66, Simon Fraser University, 1972–; Writer-in-Residence, 1967–68, Teacher, 1968–71, Sir George Williams University. *Publications:* Fiction: Mirror on the Floor, 1967; A Short Sad Book, 1977; Burning Water, 1980; En eaux troubles, 1982; Caprice, 1987; Harry's Fragments, 1990; Shoot!, 1994; Parents From Space, 1994; Piccolo Mondo, 1998. Stories: Flycatcher & Other Stories, 1974; Concentric Circles, 1977; Protective Footwear, 1978; A Place to Die, 1983; The Rain Barrel, 1994; Diamondback Dog, 1998. Poetry: Sticks & Stones, 1963; Points on the Grid, 1964; The Man in Yellow Boots/El hombre de las botas amarillas, 1965; The Silver Wire, 1966; Rocky Mountain Foot, 1969; The Gangs of Kosmos, 1969; Touch: Selected Poems 1960–1969, 1971; In the Flesh, 1974; The Catch, 1976; Poem & Other Baseballs, 1976; The Concrete Island, 1977; Another Mouth, 1979; Particular Accidents: Selected Poems, 1981; West Window: Selected Poetry, 1982; Smoking Poetry, 1982; Smoking Mirrow, 1982; Seventy-One Poems for People, 1985; Delayed Mercy & Other Poems, 1986; Urban Snow, 1992; George Bowering Selected: Poems 1961–1992, 1993; Blonds on Bikes, 1997; His Life: A Poem, 2000. Non-Fiction: Al Purdy, 1970; Three Vancouver Writers, 1979; A Way with Words, 1982; The Mask in Place, 1983; Craft Slices, 1985; Errata, 1988; Imaginary Hand, 1988; The Moustache: Remembering Greg Curnoe, 1993; Bowering's B.C., 1996; A Magpie Life, 2001. Other: Chapbooks, plays, and edns of works by other authors. *Honours:* Governor-General's Award for Poetry, 1969, and for Fiction, 1980; bp Nichol

Chapbook Awards for Poetry, 1991, 1992; Canadian Authors' Asscn Award for Poetry, 1993; Hon. DLitt, University of British Columbia, 1994. *Address:* 249 W 37th Ave, Vancouver, BC V6M 1P4, Canada.

BOWERING, Marilyn (Ruthe) b. 13 April 1949, Winnipeg, Ontario, Canada. Poet; Writer. m. Michael S Elcock, 3 Sept. 1982, 1 d. *Education:* University of British Columbia, 1968–69; BA, 1971, MA, 1973, University of Victoria; University of New Brunswick, 1975–78. *Appointments:* Writer-in-Residence, Aegean School of Fine Arts, Paris, 1973–74; Visiting Lecturer, 1978–82, Lecturer in Creative Writing, 1982–86, 1989, Visiting Assoc. Prof. of Creative Writing, 1993–96, University of Victoria, BC; Faculty, 1992, Writer-in-Residence, 1993–94, Banff Centre, Alberta, Memorial University of Newfoundland, 1995. *Publications:* Poetry: The Liberation of Newfoundland 1973; One Who Became Lost, 1976; The Killing Room, 1977; Third/Child Zian 1978; The Book of Glass, 1978; Sleeping with Lambs, 1980; Giving Back Diamonds, 1982; The Sunday Before Winter, 1984; Anyone Can See I Love You, 1987; Grandfather was a Soldier, 1987; Calling All the World, 1989; Love As It Is, 1993; Human Bodies: New and Collected Poems, 1987–99, 1999 Fiction: The Visitors Have All Returned, 1979; To All Appearances a Lady 1990. Editor: Many Voices: An Anthology of Contemporary Canadian Indian Poetry (with David A Day), 1977; Guide to the Labor Code of British Columbia 1980. *Contributions to:* Anthologies and journals. *Honours:* Many Canada Council Awards for Poetry; Du Maurier Award for Poetry, 1978; National Magazine Award for Poetry, 1989; Long Poem Prize, Malahat Review, 1994 *Memberships:* League of Canadian Poets; Writers Union of Canada. *Address:* c/o League of Canadian Poets, 54 Wolseley St, Third Floor, Toronto, ON M5T 1AS, Canada.

BOWERS, Fleur(ette E.); b. 8 Nov. 1918, Jamaica. Poet. m. Donald Thomas Bowers, 31 July 1944, deceased, 1 s., 1 d. *Education:* Assoc. Student in 20th Century Poetry, Open University, 1980. *Appointment:* Ed., Publisher, Kites Anthology, 1977–84. *Publications:* The Golden Thread, 1979; Breaking the Silence, 1993; Facing Daylight, 1997. *Contributions to:* Anthologies and magazines. *Honours:* Second Prize, Dorothy Tutin, Hastings, 1990; First Prize, Local Library Support Group, 1992. *Memberships:* Arts Council Poetry Library; Highgate Poets; Highgate Society, 1970–; Ver Poets. *Address:* Longholm, East Bank, Sutton Bridge, Spalding PE12 9YS, England.

BOWMAN, Roberta Pipes; b. 1 July 1915, USA. Writer; Poet; Painter. m. Elton Nuel Bowman, 24 Jan. 1948, 2 s. *Education:* Business College, 1941; Texas Christian University, 1942–48. *Publications:* Make Room for Joy, 1942; In This Our Times, 1977; Writing That Certain Poem, 1988; Poems for Christmas, 1990; Wind, Be Still, 1992; C & W Poems, 1995; Welcome to Today, 1995; Light and Shadows, 1998. *Contributions to:* Anthologies, newspapers and journals. *Honours:* 17 Poetry Society of Texas Awards, 1956–2001; National Poetry Day, 1966, 1970, 1990, 1995; Chas Hanna Awards, 1985, 1990; Composers, Authors and Artists Mason Sonnet Awards, 1986, 1990, 1996; Lucidity Chapbook Contest, 1995; Hilton Ross Greer Service Award, Poetry Society of Texas, 1998. *Memberships:* Poetry Society of America; Poetry Society of Texas; Poets of Tarrant County; Composers, Authors and Artists of America; National Composers, Authors and Artists Asscn. *Address:* 3521 Eastridge Dr., Fort Worth, TX 76117, USA.

BOYD, Megan E.; b. 19 Aug. 1956, New Mexico, USA. Poet. m. Scott Chaskey, 3 June 1982, 2 s., 1 d. *Education:* BA, Bennington College, 1980; MA, Lesley College, 1981. *Publications:* Blue is the Color that Made the World, 1969; Heartwood, 1980; Gathering to Deep Water, 1988. *Contributions to:* Anthologies and periodicals. *Honours:* Acad. of American Poets Poetry Prize, 1980; Hamptons International Poetry Prize, 1989. *Address:* PO Box 27, Sag Harbor, NY 11963, USA.

BRACKENBURY, Alison; b. 20 May 1953, Gainsborough, Lincolnshire, England. Poet. *Education:* BA, English, St Hugh's College, Oxford, 1975. *Publications:* Journey to a Cornish Wedding, 1977; Two Poems, 1979; Dreams of Power and Other Poems, 1981; Breaking Ground and Other Poems, 1984; Christmas Roses and Other Poems, 1988; Selected Poems, 1991; 1829, 1994; After Beethoven, 1999. Radio play: The Country of Afternoon, 1985. *Honours:* Eric Gregory Award, 1982; Cholmondeley Award, 1997.

BRACKENBURY, Rosalind; b. 14 May 1942, London, England. Writer; Poet. 1 s., 1 d. *Education:* MA, History, Cambridge University, 1963; PGCE with distinction, London University, 1964. *Appointments:* Leicester University Extra-Mural Dept, 1975–82; Edinburgh University Extra-Mural Dept, 1982–86; Writer-in-Residence, Dumfries and Galloway, 1989. *Publications:* Telling Each Other It Is Possible, 1986; Making for the Secret Places, 1989; Coming Home the Long Way Round the Mountain, 1993. *Contributions to:* Stand; Other Poetry; Writing Women; Chapman; Cencrastus; Poetry Now; Lines Review; Meanjin (Australia); Adelaide Review; Green Book; Resurgence; Anthologies: Sleeping With Monsters; Frankestein's Daughter; Small School Anthology. *Memberships:* Shore Poets, Eith, Scotland, founder-mem., 1991–; Key West Poets' Guild, FL, USA, 1992.

BRADBURY, Ray (Douglas); b. 22 Aug. 1920, Waukegan, IL, USA. Writer; Poet; Dramatist. m. Marguerite Susan McClure, 27 Sept. 1947, 4 d. *Education:* Public Schools. *Publications:* Fiction: The Martian Chronicles, 1950; Dandelion Wine, 1957; Something Wicked This Way Comes, 1962; Death is a Lonely Business, 1985; A Graveyard for Lunatics, 1990; Green Shadows, White Whale, 1992. Short-Story Collections: Dark Carnival, 1947; The Illustrated Man, 1951; The Golden Apples of the Sun, 1953; Fahrenheit 451, 1953; The October Country, 1955; A Medicine for Melancholy, 1959; The Ghoul Keepers, 1961; The Small Assassin, 1962; The Machineries of Joy, 1964; The Vintage Bradbury, 1965; The Autumn People, 1965; Tomorrow Midnight, 1966; Twice Twenty-Two, 1966; I Sing the Body Electric!, 1969; Bloch and Bradbury: Ten Masterpieces of Science Fiction (with Robert Bloch), 1969; Whispers From Beyond (with Robert Bloch), 1972; Harrap, 1975; Long After Midnight, 1976; To Sing Strange Songs, 1979; Dinosaur Tales, 1983; A Memory of Murder, 1984; The Toynbee Convector, 1988; Kaleidoscope, 1994; Quicker Than the Eye, 1996; Driving Blind, 1997. Poetry: Old Ahab's Friend, and Friend to Noah, Speaks His Piece: A Celebration, 1971; When Elephants Last in the Dooryard Bloomed: Celebrations for Almost Any Day in the Year, 1973; That Son of Richard III: A Birth Announcement, 1974; Where Robot Mice and Robot Men Run Round in Robot Towns, 1977; Twin Hieroglyphs That Swim the River Dust, 1978; The Bike Repairman, 1978; The Author Considers His Resources, 1979; The Aqueduct, 1979; The Attic Where the Meadow Greens, 1979; The Last Circus, 1980; The Ghosts of Forever, 1980; The Haunted Computer and the Android Pope, 1981; The Complete Poems of Ray Bradbury, 1982; The Love Affair, 1983; Forever and the Earth, 1984; Death Has Lost Its Charm for Me, 1987. Plays: The Meadow, 1960; Way in the Middle of the Air, 1962; The Anthem Sprinters and Other Antics, 1963; The World of Ray Bradbury, 1964; Leviathan 99, 1966; The Day it Rained Forever, 1966; The Pedestrian, 1966; Dandelion Wine, 1967; Christus Apollo, 1969; The Wonderful Ice-Cream Suit and Other Plays, 1972; Madrigals for the Space Age, 1972; Pillars of Fire and Other Plays for Today, Tomorrow, and Beyond Tomorrow, 1975; That Ghost, That Bride of Time: Excerpts from a Play-in-Progress, 1976; The Martian Chronicles, 1977; Farenheit 451, 1979; A Device Out of Time, 1986; Falling Upward, 1988. Non-Fiction: Teacher's Guide: Science Fiction, 1968; Zen and the Art of Writing, 1973; Mars and the Mind of Man, 1973; The Mummies of Guanajuato, 1978; Beyond, 1984: Remembrance of Things Future, 1979; Los Angeles, 1984; Orange County, 1985; The Art of Playboy, 1985; Yestermorrow: Obvious Answers to Impossible Futures, 1991; Ray Bradbury on Stage: A Chrestomathy of His Plays, 1991; Journey to Far Metaphor: Further Essays on Creativity, Writing, Literature, and the Arts, 1994; The First Book of Dichotomy, The Second Book of Symbiosis, 1995. Other: Television and film scripts. *Honours:* O Henry Prizes, 1947, 1948; National Institute of Arts and Letters Award, 1954; Writers Club Award, 1974; Balrog Award for Best Poet, 1979; PEN Body of Work Award, 1985; Hon. Medal, National Book Foundation, 2000. *Memberships:* SFWA; Screen Writers Guild of America; Writers Guild of America. *Address:* 10265 Cheviot Dr., Los Angeles, CA 90064, USA.

BRADHURST, Jane; b. 28 Oct. 1926, Sydney, NSW, Australia. Writer; Dramatist; Poet. m. Colin Russell-Jones, deceased, 2 s., 1 d. *Education:* MSc, University of Sydney, 1954; DipEd, 1969, BA, 1977, University of Canberra; Assoc. Dip, Theatre Practice, Goulburn CAE, 1979. *Publications:* The Flowers of the Snowy Mountains, 1977; Document of Our Day: Women of the Pre-Pill Generation, 1986; Three One Act Plays, 1987; Duet String Trio Quartet, 1987; Animalia in Australia, 1992; 100 Poems, 1993; The BD II, 1995; Love in a Hot Climate, 1996; Three Festival Plays, 1998; Summertime (musical), 1998; There is no Mystery (anthology), 1999; Mystery in Manhattan, 2000. *Honours:* Several drama awards. *Memberships:* Australian Capital Territory Writers Centre; Australian Writers Guild. *Address:* PO Box 9009, Deakin, ACT 2600, Australia.

BRADING, Tilla; b. 3 June 1945, Devon, England. Poet; Review Ed.; Teacher. m. David Brading, 24 July 1969, 2 s., 1 d. *Education:* Teachers Certificate, Rachel McMillan College of Education, 1963–66; SEN, Bristol Polytechnic, 1989; MA, Creative Writing, Plymouth University, 1996–. *Appointments:* ILEA Teacher of Special Needs, 1967–73; Teacher of Special Needs, Somerset and Devon, 1982–97. *Publications:* Pirates and Buccaneers, 1974; Pirates, 1976; Possibility of Inferno, 1998; Autumnal Jour, 1998. *Contributions to:* Irish Democrat; Times Educational Supplement; Lady; Shearsman; Oasis; Terrible Work; Phoenix; Memes; Ramraid; Extraordinaire. *Memberships:* Pentameters; Poetry Society; Drama Board. *Address:* Coleridge Cottage, 35 Lime St, Nether Stowey, Somerset TA5 1NQ, England.

BRADLEY, George; b. 22 Jan. 1953, Roslyn, New York, USA. Writer; Poet. m. Spencer Boyd, 8 Sept. 1984. *Education:* BA, Yale University, 1975; University of Virginia, 1977–78. *Publications:* Terms to Be Met, 1986; Of the Knowledge of Good and Evil, 1991; The Fire Fetched Down, 1996; The Yale Younger Poets Anthology (ed.), 1998. *Contributions to:* Periodicals. *Honours:* Acad. of American Poets Prize, 1978; Yale Younger Poets Prize, 1985; Lavan Younger Poets Award, 1990; Witter Bynner Prize, 1992. *Address:* 82 W Main St, Chester, CT 06412, USA.

BRADLEY, Marjorie; b. 22 May 1916, Portsmouth, Hampshire, England. Civil Servant (retd); Poet. m. Reuben Stephen Bradley, 22 June 1938, 3 s. *Education:* Municipal College, Portsmouth. *Publication:* Coffee Spoons. *Contributions to:* Envoi; Writer; London Calling; Purple Patch; Civil Service

Author; Focus; Weyfarers; Success Magazine. *Honours:* Civil Service Authors, Herbert Spencer Competition; Open Poetry Competition; Envoi Magazine Open Competition; Salopian Poetry Competition; Success and Springboard Magazine Competitions. *Memberships:* Society of Civil Service Authors; Patchway Writers Group. *Address:* 88 Oak Close, Little Stoke, Bristol BS12 6RD, England.

BRADY, Adrienne Sophia; b. 23 Aug. 1936, Maymyo, Burma. Teacher; Poet. Widow, 1 s., 3 d. *Education:* BA, Honours, English and History, University of London, 1983; MA, Creative Writing, University of Lancaster, 1985. *Appointments:* Head of English, Ursuline High School, Brentwood, 1985; Humanities Tutor, Singapore, 1987–89; English Language Instructor, Brunei, Borneo, 1990–92, Language Training Institute, Marsa El Brega, Libya, 1993–96; Co-Ordinator of English, Cambridge High School, Abu Dhabi, 1996–99. *Publications:* Summer Comes Barefoot Now (general ed.), 1989; Quintet, 1993. *Contributions to:* Anthologies and journals. *Honours:* Late Aske Memorial Award, 1984; Third Prize, Basil Bunting Poetry Competition, 1984; Second Prize, Surrey Poetry Competition, 1985; Runner-up, 1989, First Prize, 1992, Leek Arts Festival; Fourth Prize, Greenwich Festival, 1990. *Memberships:* Poetry Society; Schools Poetry Asscn, committee, 1982–84. *Address:* 34 Parklands, Billericay, Essex CM11 1AS, England.

BRADY, Philip; b. 15 Aug. 1955, New York, NY, USA. Assoc. Prof. of English; Poet. *Education:* BA, Buckwell University, 1977; MA, University of Delaware, 1980; MA, San Francisco State University, 1984; PhD, State University of New York at Binghamton, 1990. *Appointments:* Prof. of English, University of Lubumbashi, Zaire; Tutor, University College Cork, Ireland; Assoc. Prof. of English, Youngstown State University. *Contributions to:* Belfast Literary Supplement; Honest Ulsterman; Poetry Northwest; Massachusetts Review. *Honours:* Thayer Fellowship, 1990; Yaddo Residency, 1992; Ohio Arts Fellowship, 1993. *Membership:* Associated Writing Programs. *Address:* English Dept, Youngstown State University, Youngstown, PA 44555, USA.

BRAMHARAJAN. See: RAJARAM, A.

BRAND, Alice Glarden; b. 8 Sept. 1938, New York, NY, USA. Poet; Writer; Prof. of English. m. Ira Brand, 10 April 1960, 3 c. *Education:* University of Rochester, 1965–58; BA, City College of New York, 1960; MEd, 1973, DEd, 1979, Rutgers University. *Appointments:* Asst Prof., 1980–86, Assoc. Prof. of English, 1987, University of Missouri at St Louis; Visiting Scholar, University of California at Berkeley, 1982–83; Assoc. Prof. of English and Dir of Writing, Clarion University of Pennsylvania, 1987–89; Assoc. Prof., 1989–91, Dir of Composition, 1989–93, Prof. of English, 1992–99, State University of New York at Brockport; Many workshops, lectures and readings. *Publications:* Poetry: As it Happens, 1983; Studies on Zone, 1989. Other: Therapy in Writing: A Psycho-Educational Enterprise, 1980; The Psychology of Writing: The Affective Experience, 1989; Presence of Mind: Writing and the Domain Beyond the Cognitive (ed. with Richard L. Graves), 1994; Court of Common Pleas, 1996; Writing in the Majors: A Guide to Disciplinary Faculty, 1998. *Contributions to:* Numerous anthologies and periodicals. *Honours:* New Jersey State Council on the Arts Fellowship in Poetry, 1981; Residencies, Yaddo Artist's Colony, 1986, 1987, 1991; Wildwood Poetry Prize, 1988; Hon. Mention, National Writers' Union National Poetry Competition, 1993. *Memberships:* Acad. of American Poets; MLA; National Council of Teachers of English; Poetry Society of America; Poets and Writers. *Address:* 1235 N Astor St, No. 2, Chicago, IL 60610, USA.

BRANDI, John; b. 5 Nov. 1943, USA. Poet; Painter. *Education:* BFA, California State University at Northridge. *Publications:* A Question of Journey; Weeping the Cosmos; Shadow Play; Hymn for a Night Feast; In the Desert We Do Not Count the Days; That Back Road In; Diary from a Journey to the Middle of the World; That Crow That Visited Was Flying Backwards; Narrow Gauge to Riobamba; Desde Alla; Zulekah's Book; Heartbeat Geography: Poems 1966–1994, 1995. *Contributions to:* Atlantic; Denver Post; LA Free Press; Blue Mesa Review; Chelsea; IO; River Styx; Kyoto Journal. *Honour:* National Endowment for the Arts Fellowship for Poetry, 1980. *Address:* Holy Cow! Press, PO Box 3170, Mt Royal Station, Duluth, MN 55803, USA.

BRANDT, Di(ana Ruth); b. 31 Jan. 1952, Winkler, Manitoba, Canada. Poet; Writer. m. Les Brandt, 1971, divorced 1990, 2 d. *Education:* BTh, Canadian Mennonite Bible College, 1972; BA, Honours, 1975, PhD, 1993, University of Manitoba; MA, English, University of Toronto, 1976. *Appointments:* Faculty, University of Winnipeg, 1986–95; Writer-in-Residence, University of Alberta, 1995–96; Research Fellow, University of Alberta, 1996–97; Assoc. Prof. of English and Creative Writing, University of Windsor, 1997–. *Publications:* Poetry: questions i asked my mother, 1987; Agnes in the sky, 1990; mother, not mother, 1992; Jerusalem, beloved, 1995. Other: Wild Mother Dancing: Maternal Narrative in Canadian Literature, 1993; Dancing Naked: Narrative Strategies for Writing Across Centuries, 1996. *Contributions to:* Various publications. *Honours:* Gerald Lampert Award for Best First Book of Poetry in Canada, 1987; McNally Robinson Award for Manitoba Book of the Year, 1990; Silver National Magazine Award, 1995; Canadian Authors' Asscn National Poetry Award, 1996. *Memberships:* Canadian PEN; League of

Canadian Poets; Manitoba Writers' Guild; Writers' Union of Canada. *Address:* c/o Writers' Union of Canada, 24 Ryerson Ave, Toronto, Ontario M5T 2P3, Canada.

BRANDT, Per Aage; b. 26 April 1944, Buenos Aires, Argentina. Prof. in Semiotics; Poet. m. Mette Brudevold, 1966, divorced 1983, 1 d. *Education:* MA, University of Copenhagen, 1971; Doctorate d'Etat, Semiolinguistics, Sorbonne, Paris, 1987. *Appointments:* Lecturer, Roskilde Universitetscenter, Denmark, 1972–75; Lecturer, 1975–88, Prof. (docentur), 1988, University of Åarhus; Co-Founder and Teacher, School of Writers, Copenhagen, 1987–; Research Prof., 1996–98; Prof., 1998–. *Publications:* Poesi I, II, 1969; Pamplona, 1971; Wie die Zeit vergeht, 1973; Dødshjælp, 1977; Beskyttelse, 1978; Indsigt i det nodvendige, 1979; Det skulle ikke være sådan, 1982; Ondskab, 1982; Livet i himlen, 1985; Fraværsmusik, 1986; Credo, 1988; Ostinato, 1989; Ingen kan vaagne, 1990; Rubato, 1991; Physis, 1992; Largo, 1994; Ups and downs, 1996; Fisk, 1997; Night and Day, 1999; Om noget og hoad deraf følger, 2001. Numerous trans of Borges, Jabès, Roubaud, Bataille, Sade, Lorca, Calderón, Molière, Koltès. *Contributions to:* Periodicals, including: Action Poétique; Poesie; Banana Split. *Honours:* Danish Ministry of Culture Prizes, 1971, 1994; Emil Aarestrup Medal, 1993.

BRASFIELD, James; b. 19 Jan. 1952, Savannah, GA, USA. University Senior Lecturer; Poet. m. 7 March 1983, 1 s. *Education:* BA, English, Armstrong State College, 1975; MFA, Columbia University, 1979. *Appointments:* Editorial Asst, Paris Review, 1981–82; Asst Prof., Western Carolina University, 1984–87; Senior Lecturer, Pennsylvania State University, University Park, 1987–. *Publications:* Inheritance and Other Poems (chapbook), 1983; The Selected Poems of Oleh Lysheha (trans. with Oleh Lysheha), 1999. *Contributions to:* Agni; American Scholar; Antaeus; Black Warrior Review; Chicago Review; College English; Colorado Review; Columbia; Iowa Review; Poetry East; Poetry Wales; Prairie Schooner; Quarterly West; Seattle Review; New Virginia Review; Glas: New Russian Writing; Other literary magazines. *Honours:* Fulbright Creative Arts Award to Ukraine, 1993–94; Fulbright Award to Ukraine, 1999; American Asscn for Ukrainian Studies Prize for Trans., 1999; PEN Award for Poetry in Trans., 2000; Creative Writing Fellowship in Poetry, National Endowment for the Arts, 2001–02; Pushcart Prize, Best of the Small Presses for Trans. *Memberships:* Associated Writing Program; PEN American Centre. *Address:* Dept of English, 119 Burrowes Building, Pennsylvania State University, University Park, PA 16802, USA.

BRASS, Perry M.; b. 15 Sept. 1947, Savannah, GA, USA. Writer; Poet. *Education:* BS, Art Education, New York University, 1974. *Publications:* 7 books, including: Sex-Charge, 1991. *Contributions to:* Christopher Street; Amethyst; Everard Review; Anthologies: The Penguin Book of Homosexual Verse; The Columbia University Press Book of Gay Literature; The Male Muse; Angels of the Lyre; The Bad Boy Book of Erotic Poetry; The Lover of My Soul, 1998. *Honours:* Jane Chambers International Gay Playwriting Contest, 1985; Nominated, Lambda Literary Award, 1992 (twice), 1998. *Membership:* The Publishing Triangle, New York, secretary, 1994–95. *Address:* 2501 Palisade Ave, Apt A1, Bronx, NY 10463, USA.

BRATA, Sasthi, (Sasthibrata Chakravarti); b. 16 July 1939, Calcutta, India. Writer; Poet. m. Pamela Joyce Radcliffe, divorced. *Education:* University of Calcutta. *Appointment:* London Columnist, Statesman, 1977–80. *Publications:* Eleven Poems, 1960; Confessions of an Indian Woman Eater, 1971; She and He, 1973; Encounter (short stories), 1978; The Sensorous Guru: The Making of a Mystic President, 1980. *Address:* 33 Savernake Rd, London NW3 2JU, England.

BRATHWAITE, Edward Kamau; b. 11 May 1930, Bridgetown, Barbados. Prof. of Social and Cultural History; Poet; Writer; Ed. m. Doris Monica Welcome, 1960, 1 s. *Education:* Harrison College, Barbados; BA, History, 1953, CertEd, 1954, Pembroke College, Cambridge; DPhil, University of Sussex, 1968. *Appointments:* Education Officer, Ministry of Education, Ghana, 1955–62; Tutor, Extramural Dept, University of the West Indies, St Lucia, 1962–63; Lecturer, 1963–76, Reader, 1976–82, Prof. of Social and Cultural History, 1982–, University of the West Indies, Kingston; Founding Secretary, Caribbean Artists Movement, 1966; Ed., Savacou magazine, 1970–; Visiting Fellow, Harvard University, 1987; Several visiting professorships. *Publications:* Poetry: Rights of Passage, 1967; Masks, 1968; Islands, 1969; Penguin Modern Poets 15 (with Alan Bold and Edwin Morgan), 1969; Panda No. 349, 1969; The Arrivants: A New World Trilogy, 1973; Days and Nights, 1975; Other Exiles, 1975; Poetry '75 International, 1975; Black + Blues, 1976; Mother Poem, 1977; Soweto, 1979; Word Making Man: A Poem for Nicolas Guillen, 1979; Sun Poem, 1982; Third World Poems, 1983; X-Self, 1987; Sappho Sakyi's Meditations, 1989; Shar, 1990. Other: Folk Culture of the Slaves in Jamaica, 1970; The Development of Creole Society in Jamaica, 1770–1820, 1971; Caribbean Man in Space and Time, 1974; Contradictory Omens: Cultural Diversity and Integration in the Caribbean, 1974; Our Ancestral Heritage: A Bibliography of the Roots of Culture in the English-Speaking Caribbean, 1976; Wars of Respect: Nanny, Sam Sharpe, and the Struggle for People's Liberation, 1977; Jamaica Poetry: A Checklist 1686–1978, 1979; Barbados Poetry: A Checklist, Slavery to the Present, 1979; Kumina, 1982; Gods of the Middle East, 1982; National Language Poetry, 1982; The Colonial Encounter:

Language, 1984; History of the Voice: The Development of a Nationa Language in Anglophone Caribbean Poetry, 1984; Jah Music, 1986; Roots 1986. Editor: Iouanaloa: Recent Writing from St Lucia, 1963; New Poets fron Jamaica, 1979; Dream Rock, 1987. *Honours:* Arts Council of Great Britai Bursary, 1967; Camden Arts Festival Prize, 1967; Cholmondeley Award, 197 Guggenheim Fellowship, 1972; Bussa Award, 1973; Casa de las Américas Prize 1976; Fulbright Fellowships, 1982–83, 1987–88; Musgrave Medal, Institute c Jamaica, 1983. *Address:* c/o Dept of History, University of the West Indie Mona, Kingston 7, Jamaica.

BRAUD, Janice L.; b. 22 Oct. 1941, Corpus Christi, Texas, USA. Compute Analyst; Business Owner; Poet. m. Nolan J Braud, 23 Feb. 1963, 3 d. *Education* BA, Psychology, University of Houston, 1972; ASM, Business, 1984, BSBA Business Data Processing, 1987, Thomas A Edison College, New Jersey *Appointment:* Owner/Pres., Cypress Systems Company Inc, 1978– *Publications:* Through a Glass Darkly, 1994. *Contributions to:* Bellowing Ark Catharsis; Color Wheel; Orphic Lute; Touchstone; Poetic Page; Feelings Lucidity; Opus; Poet; Many Voices; Writer's Journal; Sophomore Jinx; Poetr Society of Texas Yearbooks. *Honours:* Several awards. *Memberships:* Poetr Society of Texas; National Federation of State Poetry Societies; Poets at Work *Address:* 30103 Bashaw Dr., Spring, TX 77386, USA.

BRAULT, Jacques; b. 29 March 1933, Montréal, QC, Canada. Poet; Writer Critic; Teacher. Education; MA, University of Montréal, 1958; University o Paris; University of Poitiers. *Appointments:* Teacher, Institut des Sciences Médiévales; Faculty of Letters, University of Montréal. *Publications:* Poetry La poésie et nous (with others), 1958; Mémoire, 1965; La poésie ce matin, 1971; L'en dessous, l'admirable, 1972, English trans. as Within the Mystery, 1986; Poèmes des quartre côtés, 1975; Trois fois passera, 1981; Moments fragiles, 1981, English trans., 1985; Il n'y a plus de chemin, 1990, English trans. as On the Road No More, 1993; Au petit matin (with Robert Melancon), 1993. Fiction: Nouvelles (short stories), 1963; Trois partitions (plays), 1972; Agonie (novel), 1984, English trans. as Death-watch, 1987. Other: Alain Grandbois, 1968; Miron le magnifique, 1969; Chemin faisant, 1975; La poussiere de chemin, 1989; Ô saison, ô châteaux, 1991; Que la vie est quotidienne, 1993; Au fond du jardin, 1996. *Contributions to:* Periodicals. *Honours:* Prix France-Canada, 1968; Gov.-Gen.'s Literary Award, 1971; Prix Duvernay, 1979; Prix du Athanse-David, 1986. *Address:* 231 Chemin Saint-Armand, Saint-Armand ouest, QC J0J 1T0, Canada.

BRAUN, Richard Emil; b. 22 Nov. 1934, Detroit, Michigan, USA. Prof. of Latin; Poet; Trans. 1 s. *Education:* AB, 1956, AM, Latin, 1957, University of Michigan; PhD, Classical Languages, University of Texas, 1969. *Appointments:* Lecturer, 1962–64, Asst Prof., 1964–69, Assoc. Prof., 1969–76, Prof., 1976–, University of Alberta, Edmonton, Canada. *Publications:* Children Passing, 1962; Bad Land, 1971; The Foreclosure, 1972; Last Man In, 1990. Translations: Sophocles' Antigone, 1973; Euripides' Rhesos, 1978; Persius's Satires, 1984. *Contributions to:* Grosseteste Review; Modern Poetry Studies; Prism; Poetry Now; University of Georgia Review; Others. *Honours:* Pres.'s Medal, Western Ontario, 1965; Robert Frost Fellowship, 1968. *Address:* University of Alberta, Dept of Classics, Edmonton, AB T6G 2E5, Canada.

BRAUN, Volker; b. 7 May 1939, Dresden, Germany. Author; Poet; Dramatist. *Education:* Philosophy, University of Leipzig, 1960–64. *Appointments:* Asst Dir, Deutschen Theater, Berlin, 1972–77, Berlin Ensemble, 1979–90. *Publications:* Prose: Unvollendete Geschichte, 1977; Hinze-Kunze-Roman, 1985; Bodenloser Satz, 1990; Der Wendehals: Eine Enterhaltung, 1995; Das Wirklichgewollte, 2000. Essays: Verheerende Folgen magnelnden Anscheins innerbetrieblicher Demokratie, 1988. Poetry: Gegen die symmetrische Welt, 1974; Training des aufrechten Gangs, 1979; Langsamer knirschender Morgen, 1987; Der Sotff zum Leben, 1990; Lustgarten Preussen, 1996. Plays: Grosser Frieden, 1979; Dmitri, 1982; Die Ubergangsgesellschaft, 1987; Lenins Tod, 1988; Transit Europa: Der Ausflug der Toten, 1988; Böhmen am Meer, 1992. *Honours:* Heinrich Mann Prize, 1980; Bremen Literature Prize, 1986; National Prize, First Class, 1988; Berlin Prize, 1989; Schiller Commemorative Prize, 1992; Büchner Prize, 2000. *Membership:* Akademie der Künste, Berlin. *Address:* Wolfshagenerstrasse 68, 13187, Berlin, Germany.

BRAUNE, Beverliey, (Beverley E. Brown); b. 25 Feb. 1954, Kingston, Jamaica. Poet; Essayist. m. Thoran Mark Braune, 12 May 1985, 1 d. *Education:* BA, 1977; Master of Philosophy, English, 1981, University of the West Indies; Doctor of Creative Arts, University of Wollongong, Australia, 1999. *Appointments:* Co-Ed., Arts Review, University of the West Indies, 1978; Lecturer, Cultural Training Centre, 1981–82; Guest Lecturer, School of English, University of New South Wales, Australia, 1998; Poetry Ed., LiNQ, 1999; Guest writer online in literature, Tennessee State University, 1999, Cogswell College, 2001. *Publications:* Dream Diary, 1982; Camouflage, 1998. *Contributions to:* Academic books, reviews, journals and periodicals. *Honours:* Silver and Bronze Medals, Jamaican Festival Awards for Poetry, 1976; Academic Research Scholarships, 1978, 1983, 1997. *Membership:* Poets Union Inc, NSW, pres., 1998–99; PEN Australia. *Address:* PO Box 164, Glebe, NSW 2037, Australia. *E-mail:* poets_brave@hotmail.com.

BRAVERMAN, Kate; b. 2 May 1949, Philadelphia, Pennsylvania, USA. Prof. of Creative Writing; Poet; Writer. m. Alan Goldstein, 15 June 1991, 1 d. *Education:* BA, Anthropology, 1971; MA, English, 1986. *Appointment:* Prof. of Creative Writing, California State University at Los Angeles. *Publications:* Milk Run (poems), 1977; Lithium for Medea (novel), 1979; Lullaby for Sinners (poems), 1980; Hurricane Warnings (poems), 1987; Palm Latitudes (novel), 1988; Postcard From August (poems), 1990; Squandering the Blue (stories), 1990. *Contributions to:* Periodicals. *Memberships:* PEN Los Angeles West; National Book Critics Circle. *Address:* c/o Dept of English, California State University at Los Angeles, Los Angeles, CA 90032, USA.

BRAWN, M. A. See: MINEO, Melani.

BRAX, Najwa Salam; b. 3 Sept. 1948, Aley, Lebanon. Poet; Writer. m. Ghazi Brax, 24 June 1981. *Education:* BA, 1974, MA, 1983, Lebanese University; MA, English, Queen's College, New York. *Appointment:* Teacher of Arabic Literature, 1972–86. *Publications:* (in English) Dr Dahesh: A Great Writer and His Literary Works, 1981; Halim Dammous and Spirituality in His Writings, 1984; Wings, 1993; Zephyrus Wings, 1994; Daring Wings, 1996; Growing Wings, 1998; Ethereal Wings, 1999; Dahesh as I Knew Him. *Contributions to:* Over 150 US, Canadian, Italian, Indian and British publications. *Honours:* More than 160 poetry awards, 1990–. *Address:* 150-16 60th Ave, Flushing, NY 11355, USA.

BRAXTON, Joanne M(argaret); b. 25 May 1950, Washington, DC, USA. Poet; Critic; Prof. 1 d. *Education:* BA, Sarah Lawrence College, 1972; MA, 1974, PhD, 1984, Yale University. *Appointments:* Lecturer, University of Michigan, 1979; Asst Prof., 1980–86, Assoc. Prof., 1986–89, Prof. of English, 1989–, College of William and Mary. *Publications:* Sometimes I Think of Maryland (poems), 1977; Black Women Writing Autobiography: A Tradition Within a Tradition, 1989; Wild Women in The Whirlwind: The Renaissance in Contemporary Afro-American Writing (ed. with Andree N McLaughlin), 1990; The Collected Poems of Paul Laurence Dunbar (ed.), 1993. *Contributions to:* Books, anthologies, journals, and periodicals. *Honours:* Outstanding Faculty Award, State Council for Higher Education for Virginia, 1992; Fellowships and grants. *Memberships:* American Studies Asscn; College Language Asscn; MLA. *Address:* c/o Dept of English, St George Tucker Hall, College of William and Mary, Williamsburg, VA 23185, USA.

BRAY, J(ohn) J(efferson); b. 16 Sept. 1912, Adelaide, SA, Australia. Barrister; Chief Justice (retd); Poet. *Education:* LLB, 1932, LLB, Honours, 1933, LLD, 1937, University of Adelaide. *Appointments:* Admitted to South Australian Bar, 1933; Chief Justice of South Australia, 1967–78; Chancellor, University of Adelaide, 1968–83. *Publications:* Poems, 1962; Poems 1961–71, 1972; Poems 1972–79, 1979; The Bay of Salamis and Other Poems, 1986; Satura: Selected Poetry and Prose, 1988; The Emperor's Doorkeeper (occasional addresses), 1988; Seventy Seven (poems), 1990. *Contributions to:* Periodicals. *Honour:* South Australian Non-Fiction Award, Adelaide Festival of the Arts, 1990. *Memberships:* Australian Society of Authors; Friendly Street Poets, Adelaide. *Address:* 39 Hurtle Sq., Adelaide, SA 5000, Australia.

BRAYAG, B. See: BANDYOPADHYAY, Prayag.

BRAYBROOKE, Neville (Patrick Bellairs); b. 30 May 1923, London, England. Writer; Poet; Dramatist. *Publications:* London Green: The Story of Kensington Gardens, Hyde Park, Green Park and St James' Park, 1959; The Idler (novel), 1960; The Delicate Investigation (play), 1969; Four Poems for Christmas, 1986; Dialogue With Judas (poem), 1989; Two Birthdays (poem), 1996; Life of Olivia Manning (with Isobel English), 2001. *Contributions to:* Periodicals. *Address:* 29 Castle Rd, Cowes PO31 7QZ, Isle of Wight.

BRECKENRIDGE, Jill; b. 23 Oct. 1938, Idaho, USA. Writer; Poet; Writing Consultant. Divorced, 3 s. *Education:* BA, University of Minnesota, 1972; MA, St Mary's College, Winona, 1987; MFA, Goddard College, Vermont, 1980. *Appointments:* Teacher, workshops and seminars; Writing Consultant; Writer in the Schools; Teacher; Judge. *Publications:* How to be Lucky; Civil Blood; Three Women Poets; Poems in Milweed Chronicle; Moons and Lion Tailes; Steelhead; 25 Minnesota Poets. *Honours:* Loft McKnight Writers Award; Minnesota State Arts Board Grants; Bush Foundation Individual Artist Fellowship; Lake Superior Regional Writers Contest; Ragdale Writing Fellowship. *Address:* 42 S St Albans, No. 3, St Paul, MN 55105, USA.

BREEDEN, David; b. 23 March 1958, Illinois, USA. Prof. of English; Poet. m. Joan Bishop-Breeden, 15 Oct. 1983, 2 s., 1 d. *Education:* BA, 1981; MFA, 1985; PhD, 1988. *Appointment:* Faculty, Schreiner University. *Publications:* Picnics, 1985; Hey, Schlieman, 1990; Double-Headed End Wrench, 1992; Building a Boat, 1995; The Guiltless Traveler, 1996. *Contributions to:* Poet Lore; Mid-American Review; Quarterly; North Atlantic Review; Literary Review; Paragraph. *Memberships:* PEN Center USA West; Poets and Writers; Associated Writing Programs. *Address:* 1424 Fifth St, Kerrville, TX 78028, USA.

BREMNER, Betty Avice; b. 12 Feb. 1921, Christchurch, New Zealand. Freelance Journalist; Poet. m. William Laohlan Bremner, 26 Jan. 1946,

deceased, 1 d. *Education:* Canterbury University, Christchurch; BA, Victoria University of Wellington, 1989. *Publication:* The Scarlet Runners, 1991–92. *Contributions to:* Sport; Kapiti Poems, III-VI; King's Cross Poets; Dominion; MsCellany. *Memberships:* Women Writer's Society; PEN International; L'Alliance Française; Poetry Society. *Address:* 20 Dowse Dr., Maungaraki, Lower Hutt, New Zealand.

BRENNAN, Matthew Cannon; b. 18 Jan. 1955, Richmond Heights, Missouri, USA. Prof. of English; Poet. m. (1) Laura L Fredendall, 13 Aug. 1977, divorced 1987, 1 s., (2) Beverley Simms, 21 May 1994. *Education:* AB, Grinnell College, 1977; MA, 1980, PhD, 1984, University of Minnesota. *Appointments:* Visiting Asst Prof. of English, University of Minnesota, 1984–85; Asst Prof. of English, 1985–88, Assoc. Prof. of English, 1988–92, Prof. of English, 1992–, Indiana State University, Terre Haute. *Publications:* Seeing in the Dark, 1993; The Music of Exile, 1994. *Contributions to:* Poetry magazines and journals. *Honours:* Indiana State University Grant, 1993; Indiana Arts Commission Master Fellowship in Poetry, 1994–95; Resident Fellow, Mary Anderson Center for the Arts, 1998; Thomas Merton Centre Poetry Prize, 1999. *Memberships:* Poets and Writers; Writers' Center of Indianapolis. *Address:* Dept of English, Indiana State University, Terre Haute, IN 47809, USA.

BRENTON, Howard; b. 13 Dec. 1942, Portsmouth, England. Playwright; Poet. *Education:* BA, St Catherine's College, Cambridge, 1965. *Appointments:* Resident Dramatist, Royal Court Theatre, London, 1972–73; Resident Writer, University of Warwick, 1978–79; Granada Artist-in-Residence, University of California, Davis, 1997; Arts and Humanities Research Board Fellow, Birmingham University, 2000–03. *Publications:* Notes from a Psychotic Journal and Other Poems, 1969; Revenge, 1969; Scott of the Antarctic (or what God didn't see), 1970; Christie in Love and Other Plays, 1970; Lay By (co-author), 1972; Plays for Public Places, 1972; Hitler Diaries, 1972; Brassneck (with David Hare), 1973; Magnificence, 1973; Weapons of Happiness, 1976; The Paradise Run (television play), 1976; Epsom Downs, 1977; Sore Throats, with Sonnets of Love and Opposition, 1979; The Life of Galileo (adaptor), 1980; The Romans in Britain, 1980; Plays for the Poor Theatre, 1980; Thirteenth Night and A Short Sharp Shock, 1981; Danton's Death (adaptor), 1982; The Genius, 1983; Desert of Lies (television play), 1983; Sleeping Policemen (with Tunde Ikoli), 1984; Bloody Poetry, 1984; Pravda (with David Hare), 1985; Dead Head (television series), 1987; Greenland, 1988; H.I.D. (Hess is Dead), 1989; Iranian Night (with Tariq Ali), 1989; Diving for Pearls (novel), 1989; Moscow Gold (with Tariq Ali), 1990; Berlin Bertie, 1992; Playing Away (opera libretto), 1994; Hot Irons (essays and diaries), 1995; Adaptation of Goethe's Faust, 1996; Plays I, 1996; Plays II, 1996; In Extremis, 1997; Ugly Rumours (with Tariq Ali), 1998; Collateral Damage (with Tariq Ali and Andy de la Tour), 1999; Snogging Ken (with Tariq Ali and Andy de la Tour), 2000; Kit's Play, 2000; Democratic Demons, 2000 . *Honour:* Hon. Doctorate, University of North London, 1996. *Address:* c/o Casarotto Ramsay Ltd, National House, 60–66 Wardour St, London W1V 3HP, England.

BREW, (Osborne Henry) Kwesi; b. 27 May 1928, Cape Coast, Ghana. Ambassador (retd); Poet. *Education:* BA, University College of the Gold Coast, Legon, 1953. *Appointments:* Former Ghanian Ambassador to Britain, India, France, USSR, Germany and Mexico. *Publications:* The Shadows of Laughter, 1968; African Panorama and Other Poems, 1981. *Contributions to:* Anthologies and periodicals. *Honour:* British Council Prize. *Address:* c/o Greenfield Review Press, PO Box 80, Greenfield Center, NY 12833, USA.

BREWER, Derek Stanley; b. 13 July 1923, Cardiff, Wales. Prof. of English Emeritus; Writer; Poet; Ed. m. Lucie Elisabeth Hoole, 17 Aug. 1951, 3 s., 2 d. *Education:* BA, 1941–42, MA, 1945–48, Magdalen College, Oxford; PhD, University of Birmingham, 1956; DLitt, University of Cambridge, 1980. *Appointments:* Asst Lecturer, then Lecturer, 1949–56, Senior Lecturer, 1958–64, University of Birmingham; Prof., International Christian University, Tokyo, 1956–58; Lecturer, 1965–76, Reader, 1976–83, Prof., 1983–90, Prof. Emeritus, 1990–, University of Cambridge; Fellow, 1965–77, Master, 1977–90, Life fellow, 1990–, Emmanuel College, Cambridge. *Publications:* Chaucer, 1953; Proteus, 1958; Chaucer and His World, 1978; Symbolic Stories, 1980; English Gothic Literature, 1983; Medieval Comic Tales (ed.), 1996; A Critical Companion to the Gawain-poet (ed.), 1996; A New Introduction to Chaucer, 1998; Seatonian Exercises and Other Verses, 2000; The World of Chaucer, 2000. *Contributions to:* Scholarly books and journals. *Honours:* Several hon. doctorates; Seatonian Prizes for Poetry, 1969, 1972, 1979, 1980, 1983, 1986, 1988, 1992, 1994, 1999; Hon. Mem., 1981, Medal, 1997, Japan Acad.; Corresponding Fellow, Medieval Society of America, 1987. *Address:* c/o Emmanual College, Cambridge CB2 3AP, England.

BREWSTER, Elizabeth (Winifred); b. 26 Aug. 1922, Chipman, New Brunswick, Canada. Prof. Emeritus of English; Poet; Novelist. *Education:* BA, University of New Brunswick, 1946; MA, Radcliffe College, Cambridge, Massachusetts, 1947; BLS, University of Toronto, 1953; PhD, Indiana University, 1962. *Appointments:* Faculty, Dept of English, University of Victoria, 1960–61; Reference Librarian, Mt Allison University, 1961–65; Visiting Asst Prof. of English, University of Alberta, 1970–71; Asst Prof., 1972–75, Assoc. Prof., 1975–80, Prof., 1980–90, Prof. Emeritus, 1990–, of English, University of Saskatchewan. *Publications:* East Coast, 1951;

Lillooet, 1954; Roads, 1957; Passage of Summer: Selected Poems, 1969; Sunrise North, 1972; In Search of Eros, 1974; The Sisters, 1974; It's Easy to Fall on the Ice, 1977; Sometimes I Think of Moving, 1977; Digging In, 1982; Junction, 1982; The Way Home, 1982; A House Full of Women, 1983; Selected Poems of Elizabeth Brewster, 1944–1984, 1985; Entertaining Angels, 1988; Spring Again, 1990; The Invention of Truth, 1991; Wheel of Change, 1993; Footnotes to the Book of Job, 1995; Away from Home (autobiography), 1995; Garden of Sculpture, 1998; Burning Bush, 2000. *Honours:* E J Pratt Award for Poetry, University of Toronto, 1953; Pres.'s Medal for Poetry, University of Western Ontario, 1980; Hon. LittD, University of New Brunswick, 1982; Canada Council Award, 1985; Lifetime Award for Excellence in the Arts, Saskatchewan Arts Board, 1995; Short-listed, Gov.-Gen.'s Award for Poetry, 1996; Mem., Order of Canada, 2001. *Memberships:* League of Canadian Poets; Writers' Union of Canada; Saskatchewan Writers' Guild; PEN. *Address:* 206, 910 Ninth St E, Saskatoon, Saskatchewan S7H 0N1, Canada.

BREYTENBACH, Breyten; b. 16 Sept. 1939, Bonnievale, South Africa. Poet; Writer. *Education:* Graduated, University of Cape Town, 1959. *Publications:* And Death White as Words: Anthology, 1978; In Africa Even the Flies Are Happy: Selected Poems, 1964–77, 1978; Mouroir: Mirrornotes of a Novel, 1984; End Papers, 1986; All One Horse, 1990; The Memory of Birds in Times of Revolution (essays), 1996. *Honour:* Rapport Prize, 1986. *Address:* c/o Faber Ltd, 3 Queen Sq., London WC1N 3AU, England.

BRIDGES, Lee Norris; b. 31 May 1927, Thomasville, GA, USA. Poet. m. Grietje Antjy Boontje, 4 May 1973, 1 s. *Education:* Detroit Institute of Arts, Music, 1952–54; City College of New York. *Publications:* The Rhythm Man, 1987; The Blue Bird Sings, 1989. *Contributions to:* Asscn for the Study of Afro-American Life and History; Presense Africain; Black Scholar; Third Half Literary Magazine; Tucumari Literary Review. *Honours:* Fine Points Area Youth Festival Award, Performance, New York, 1979; Poetalk Quarterly Awards, Certificate for Excellence, 1991. *Membership:* Poets and Writers, New York. *Address:* Postbox 1346, 1000 BH Amsterdam, Netherlands.

BRIDLE, Joyce; b. 26 Feb. 1941, Keighley, West Yorkshire, England. Poet. 1 s. *Education:* Stroud College of Further Education. *Appointments:* Lifelong Oblate, Order of Saint Benedict. *Publications:* Several anthologies. *Contributions to:* Gloucestershire Citizen; The Citizen; Stroud News and Journal; Triumph Herald Winter Edn; Roundabout Ruscombe Summer Edn. *Honours:* Semi Finalist for Poetry, Cheltenham Festival of Literature, 1994, 1995, 1996; Prize for Poetry, Stroud College of Further Education, 1996. *Memberships:* Friends of Cheltenham Festival of Literature; Friends of Ledbury Festival; Friends of Nailsworth Festival. *Address:* Poet's Place, 42 Victory Rd, Whiteshill, Stroud, Gloucestershire GL6 6BD, England. *Website:* www.poets.com.

BRIGHAM, Faith Elizabeth Huckabone, (Fay Huckabone, Faith Mairee); b. 14 May 1953, Pittsburgh, Pennsylvania, USA. Poet. m. John Jefferson Brigham, 20 Dec. 1980. *Contributions to:* Many anthologies and periodicals. *Honours:* Golden Poet Awards, 1988–90, Honourable Mention, 1988–91, World of Poetry; Blue Ribbon Award, Southern Poetry Asscn. *Memberships:* International Society for the Advancement of Poetry; Poet's Guild; Southern Poetry Asscn. *Address:* 6725 Corto Rd, Cocoa, FL 32927, USA.

BRIN, Herb; b. 17 Feb. 1915, Chicago, IL, USA. Poet; Journalist. 3 s. *Education:* Mem., Great Book Series, University of Chicago. *Appointments:* Feature Writer, Los Angeles Times; Publisher, Heritage Publications of California. *Publications:* Poetry: Wild Flowers, 1965; Justice, Justice, 1967; Conflicts, 1971; My Spanish Years and Other Poems, 1985. *Memberships:* American Poetry Society; Acad. of American Poets. *Address:* 1101 E Loma Alta Dr., Alradena, CA 91001, USA.

BRINGHURST, Robert; b. 16 Oct. 1946, Los Angeles, CA, USA. Poet; Writer. 1 d. *Education:* Massachusetts Institute of Technology, 1963–64, 1970–71; University of Utah, 1964–65; Defense Language Institute, 1966–67; BA, Comparative Literature, Indiana University, 1973; MFA, University of British Columbia, 1975. *Appointments:* General Ed., Kanchenjunga Poetry Series, 1973–79; Reviews Ed., Canadian Fiction Magazine, 1974–75; Visiting Lecturer, 1975–77, Lecturer, 1979–80, University of British Columbia; Poet-in-Residence, Banff School of Fine Arts, 1983, Ojibway and Cree Cultural Centre Writers' Workshops, 1985–86, University of Western Ontario, 1998–99; Adjunct Lecturer, 1983–84, Adjunct Prof., Frost Centre for Native Studies and Canadian Studies, 1998–, and Centre for Studies in Publishing, 2000–, Simon Fraser University; Lecturer, 1984, Ashley Fellow, 1994, Trent University; Contributing Ed., Fine Print: A Review for the Arts of the Book, 1985–90; Writer-in-Residence, University of Edinburgh, 1989–90. *Publications:* The Shipwright's Log, 1972; Cadastre, 1973; Bergschrund, 1975; The Stonecutter's Horses, 1979; Tzuhalem's Mountain, 1982; The Beauty of the Weapons: Selected Poems 1972–82, 1982; Visions: Contemporary Art in Canada, 1983; The Raven Steals the Light, 1984; Ocean, Paper, Stone, 1984; Tending the Fire, 1985; The Blue Roofs of Japan, 1986; Pieces of Map, Pieces of Music, 1986; Conversations with Toad, 1987; The Black Canoe, 1991; The Elements of Typographic Style, 1992; The Calling: Selected Poems, 1970–95, 1995; Elements, 1995; Native American Oral Literatures and the Unity of the

Humanities, 1998; A Story as Sharp as a Knife: The Classical Haid Mythtellers and Their World, 1999; A Short History of the Printed Word 1999; The Book of Silences, 2001. Translations: Nine Visits to the Mythworl (by Ghandl of the Qayahl Llaanas), 2000; Being in Being: The Collected Work of Skaay of the Qquuna Qiighawaay, 2001. *Contributions to:* Many anthologies Honours: Macmillan Prize, 1975; Alcuin Society Design Awards, 1984, 1985 Canadian Broadcasting Corporation Poetry Prize, 1985; Guggenheim Fellowship, 1987–88. *Address:* Box 357, 1917 W Fourth Ave, Vancouver, BC V6J 1M7, Canada.

BRINKLOW, Win(nie Melvin); b. 1 Jan. 1941, Fearn, Ross-shire, Scotland Poet. m. 20 Sept. 1957, 1 s., 1 d. *Publications:* She Thought It Was Naughty an Other Poems, 1990; Anthology: O' Mice & Men, 1992; Tartan Custard *Contributions to:* Writers News; Poetry Digest. *Honour:* First Prize, Dornoch Firth Bridge Poetry Competition, Sutherland, 1991. *Address:* Gneiss House Invershin, By Lairg, Sutherland IV27 4ET, Scotland.

BRISSETT, Linda May; b. 16 Aug. 1940, Kingston, Jamaica. Registered Nurse; Certified Midwife; Poet; Writer. m. Louis Floyd Brissett, 19 June 1971, 1 s. *Education:* Diploma in Short-Story Writing and Journalism Registered General Nurse, 1960; Certified Midwife, 1962; Certificate in Nursing Unit Administration, 1971; Effective Supervision Certificate, 1975 *Appointments:* Head Nurse, Neonatal Unit, Henderson General Hospital Hamilton, Ontario, Canada, 1965–93; Pres., Briss Books Inc. *Publications:* In Fields of Dreams and Other Poems, 1991; Sunshine in the Shadows, 1993; Give Us This Day, 1995; Ingots (anthology with 5 other poets), 1996; Carols of Christmases Past, 1996; Naked Frailties, 1999; Linda's Culinary Cuisine Jamaican Cookery, 1999; Canadianizing Jamaican Patois, 2001. *Contributions to:* Various publications. *Honours:* Second Prize, Quills, 1990; Certificate of Merit, National Library of Poetry, 1993. *Memberships:* Canadian Authors Asscn; Canadian Poetry Asscn. *Address:* 58 Skyview Dr., Hamilton, ON L9B 1X5, Canada. E-mail:linbri7@hotmail.com.

BRITO, Casimiro de; b. 14 Jan. 1938, Algarve, Portugal. Writer; Poet; Bank Dir. *Education:* Graduated in Commercial Studies. *Appointments:* Ed. Cadernos do Meio-Dia, 1956–58, Cadernos de Poesia, 1971–72, Loreto 13, 1975–77. *Publications:* Poemas da Solidao Imperfeita, 1957; Carta a Pablo Picasso, 1958; Telegramas, 1959; Canto Adolescente, 1961; Poemas Orientais (trans.), 1963; Jardins de Guerra, 1966; Mesa do Amor, 1970; Negaçao da Morte, 1974; Corpo Sitiado, 1976; Labyrinthus, 1981; Ode & Ceia - Collected Poems 1955–84, 1985; Ni Maître, Ni Serviteur, 1986; Onde se acumula o po, 1987; Arte de Respiraçao, 1988; Duas Aguas, Um Rio, 1989; Subitamente o Silencio, 1991; Opus Affettuso, 1993; Intensidades, 1995. *Contributions to:* Many publications in several countries. *Honours:* Ministry of Culture Prize; Writers' Asscn Prize; Versilia-Viareggio Prize. *Membership:* Portuguese PEN. *Address:* Rua Prof Prado Coelho, Lote 16, 6ø frente, 1600 Lisbon, Portugal.

BROADHURST, Valorie Anne. See: WOERDEHOFF, Valorie Anne Breyfogle.

BROBST, Richard Alan; b. 13 May 1958, Sarasota, FL, USA. Teacher; Poet; Writer; Ed. m. Pamela Millace, 27 Dec. 1986, 2 s., 1 d. *Education:* BA, University of Florida, 1988. *Appointments:* Co-founder and Ed., Albatross Poetry Journal, 1986–99; Resident Poet, Charlotte County Schools, 1989–. *Publications:* Inherited Roles, 1997; Dancing With Archetypes, 1998; Songs From the Lost Oaks, 1999; The Cody Star, 2000. *Contributions to:* Anthologies and periodicals. *Honour:* Winner, Duanne Locke Chapbook Series, 1997. *Address:* 17145 Urban Ave, Port Charlotte, FL 33954, USA. *E-mail:* aliasd13@aol.com.

BROCK, James; b. 2 Dec. 1958, Boise, ID, USA. Educator; Poet; Writer. m. Annette Sisson, 13 Oct. 1984, divorced March 1993, 1 s. *Education:* BA, College of Idaho, 1981; MFA, 1984, PhD, 1992, Indiana University. *Appointments:* Assoc. Instructor, Indiana University, 1982–83; Ed., Indiana Review, 1985–87; Asst Prof., Belmont University, 1988–93; Visiting Asst Prof., Idaho State University, Pocatello, 1993–96; Instuctor, East Stroudsburg University, 1996–97. *Publication:* The Sunshine Mine Disaster (poems), 1995. *Contributions to:* Anthologies, quarterlies, reviews and journals. *Honours:* Acad. of American Poets Award, 1985; National Endowment for the Arts Creative Writing Fellowship, 1990; Alex Haley Fellow, Tennessee Arts Commission, 1991; Poetry Fellow, Idaho Commission for the Arts, 1996. *Memberships:* Associated Writing Programs; Popular Culture Asscn. *Address:* PO Box 419, Analomink, PA 18320, USA.

BROCK, Randall J.; b. 24 Nov. 1943, Colfax, Washington, USA. Poet. *Education:* BA, History, BA, Education, Eastern Washington University, 1970; MFA, University of Oregon, 1973. *Publications:* Mouse Poems, 1971; Poems and Photographs, 1979; I Am Poems, 1982; Shadows of Seclusion, 1983; The Goat Poems, 1984; Solid Blue, 1985; Stranger to the Stars, 1986; Cold Fire Poems, 1988; Inside and Out, 1988; Lost Voices, 1988; Seven Zen Meditations, 1990; inside i Am, 1991; variations, 1994; Weave, 1994; A Message From the Other Side, 1995; Images in Stone, 1995; Love and Other Secrets of the Sea, 1995; Concrete, 1996; Pieces from the Valley, 1998. Anthologies: The Abraxas/ Five Anthology, 1972; Encore Encore Anthology, 1976; Deep Down Things, 1990. *Contributions to:* Numerous publications. *Memberships:* Poets and

Writers; MLA; Associated Writing Programs; Piedmont Literary Society; PEN West, USA; Spokane Open Poetry Asscn; Volume II Poets. *Address:* PO Box 1673, Spokane, WA 99210, USA.

BROCK, Van(dall) K(line); b. 31 Oct. 1932, Boston, Geogia, USA. Poet; Writer; Ed. 2 s., 2 step-d. *Education:* BA, Emory University, 1954; MA, 1963, MFA, 1964, PhD, 1970, University of Iowa. *Appointments:* Asst Prof., Oglethorpe University, 1964–68; Asst Prof., 1970–75, Assoc. Prof., 1975–78, Prof., 1978–87, Florida State University. *Publications:* Final Belief, 1972; Weighing the Penalties, 1977; Spelunking, 1978; The Window, 1981; Ossabow Tabby, 1990; A Conversation with Martin Heidegger, 1990. *Contributions to:* Anthologies and periodicals. *Honours:* Six Resident Fellowships; Borestone Mountain Poetry Awards; Best Poem, Pacific Books, Palo Alto, 1965, 1972; First Prize, Florida Poetry Contest, Florida Review, 1977; First Creative Writing Award, 1977, Individual Artist's Award, 1982–83, Fine Arts Council, FL; First featured poet, Poets in the South, 1977; Rockefeller Fellowship, Centre for Study of Southern Culture, 1978–79. *Memberships:* Poetry Society of America; Associated Writing Programs. *Address:* c/o Dept of English, Florida State University, Tallahassee, FL 32306, USA.

BROCKWAY, James Thomas; b. 21 Oct. 1916, Birmingham, England. Writer; Poet; Trans. *Education:* London School of Economics. *Publications:* No Summer Song, 1949; A World Beyond Myself, 1991; A Way of Getting Through, 1995; Singers Behind Glass: Eight Modern Dutch Poets, 1995; Two-in-One Poems, 1997. *Contributions to:* Literary periodicals. *Honours:* Belgian Government Trans' Award, 1965; Martinus Nijhoff Prize, the Netherlands, 1966; Dutch knighthood, 1997. *Address:* Riouwstraat 114, The Hague, The Netherlands.

BRODSKY, Louis Daniel; b. 17 April 1941, St Louis, Missouri, USA. Poet. m., 1 s., 1 d. *Education:* BA magna cum laude, Yale University, 1963; MA, English Literature, Washington University, St Louis, 1967; MA, Creative Writing, San Francisco State University, 1968. *Appointments:* Instructor in Creative Writing, Mineral Area Junior College, Flat River, Missouri, 1980–89; Curator, Brodsky Faulkner Collection, Southeast Missouri State University, Cape Girardeau, 1984–. *Publications:* Poetry: Five Facets of Myself, 1967; The Easy Philosopher, 1967; 'A Hard Coming of It' and Other Poems, 1967; The Foul Rag-and-Bone Shop, 1967; Points in Time, 1971; Taking the Back Road Home, 1972; Trip to Tipton and Other Compulsions, 1973; 'The Talking Machine' and Other Poems, 1974; Tiffany Shade, 1974; Trilogy: A Birth Cycle, 1974; Monday's Child, 1975; Cold Companionable Streams, 1975; Monday's Child, 1975Preparing for Incarnations, 1975; The Kingdom of Gewgaw, 1976; Point of Americas II, 1976; La Preciosa, 1977; Stranded in the Land of Transients, 1978; The Uncelebrated Ceremony of Pants-Factory Fatso, 1978; Birds in Passage, 1980; Résumé of a Scrapegoat, 1980; A Mississippi Trilogy: Vol. 1, Mississippi Vistas, 1983, Vol. 2, Mistress Mississippi, 1992, Vol. 3, Disappearing in Mississippi Latitudes, 1994; You Can't Go Back, Exactly, 1988; The Thorough Earth, 1989; Four and Twenty Blackbirds Soaring, 1989; Falling from Heaven: Holocaust Poems of a Jew and a Gentile (co-author), 1991; Forever, for Now: Poems for a Later Love, 1991; A Gleam in the Eye: Poems for a First Baby, 1992; Gestapo Crows: Holocaust Poems, 1992; The Capital Café: Poems of Redneck, USA, 1993; Paper-Whites for Lady Jane: Poems of a Midlife Love Affair, 1995; The Complete Poems of Louis Daniel Brodsky: Vol. 1, 1963–1967, 1996, Vol. 2, 1967–1976, 2001; Three Early Books of Poems by Louis Daniel Brodsky 1967–1969, 1997; The Eleventh Lost Tribe: Poems of the Holocaust, 1998; Toward the Torah, Soaring: Poems of the Renascence of Faith, 1998; Voice Within the Void: Poems of Homo supinus, 2000; Rabbi Auschwitz: Poems Touching the Shoah, 2000; The Swastika Clock: Endlösung Poems, 2001; Shadow War: Poems of September 11 and Beyond, Vol. 1, 2001, Vol. 2, 2002, Vol. 3, 2003. *Contributions to:* Anthologies, reviews, quarterlies and journals. *Address:* 10411 Clayton Rd, Suites 201–203, St Louis, MO 63131, USA.

BROGAARD-PEDERSEN, Berit Oskar; b. 28 Aug. 1970, Copenhagen, Denmark. PhD Researcher; Writer; Poet. *Education:* MSc, Biochemistry, 1989–94; BA, Danish Literature and Theatre, 1994–96. *Publications:* Danskere til Salg, 1991; Livet I Iysthuset, 1992; Solnedgangens Orange Born, 1994; Handen der fandt ud af livets gade; Marcos. *Contributions to:* Pseudo-Pop Magazine, 1995; Kritik, 1995. *Membership:* Dansik Writers Union. *Address:* Attika Strandlejen 429, 2930 Klampenborg, Gyldendal, Denmark; Klareboderne 3, 1001 Copenhagen, Denmark.

BROGGER, Suzanne; b. 18 Nov. 1944, Copenhagen, Denmark. Writer; Poet; Dramatist. m. Keld Zeruneith, 1991. *Education:* University of Copenhagen. *Publications:* 4 novels; 8 poetry books; 1 play. *Honour:* Gabor Prize, 1987. *Address:* Knudstrup Gl Skole, 4270 Hong, Denmark.

BROHL, Ted; b. 18 Feb. 1924, Pittsburgh, Pennsylvania, USA. Poet. m. Ellie D Johnes, 27 June 1948, 1 s., 2 d. *Education:* New York University, 1944. *Publications:* Ted Brohl's Gargoyles and Other Muses, 1990; In A Fine Frenzy Rolling, 1992; A Simple Grace, 1994; I Don't Talk Down to Kids, 1996; Make a Joyful Noise, 1996; Spectacular!, 1998. *Contributions to:* National Poets Asscn Market Letter; Oatmeal & Poetry; News Report; Courier Post; Beachcomber News; Maturity Today; Gloucester County Times; New Jersey Legionnaire; Press of Atlantic City; Poetry in Motion; Hopscotch for

Girls. *Honours:* Poet of Merit, American Poetry Asscn, 1990; Poet Laureate, Gloucester County, Poet Laureate, Washington Township, 1991; Authors Award, New Jersey Writer's Conference, 1993; Pres.'s Award for Literary Excellence, 1998. *Memberships:* Poetry Society of America; International Society of Poets; Walt Whitman Cultural Arts Center, 1990–. *Address:* 812 Saratoga Terrace, Turnersville, NJ 08012, USA.

BROLL, Brandon William; b. 18 Aug. 1960, Johannesburg, South Africa. Journalist; Ed.; Writer; Poet. *Education:* Graduated, Natural Science, University of Cape Town, 1980; Studies in Media Practice, University of London, 1995–96. *Appointments:* Senior Writer, 1991–2000, Web Ed., 2000–, Science Photo Library, London; Freelance journalist, 2000–. *Publication:* Not Merely White-South African poems, 1986–88. *Contributions to:* Numerous anthologies and periodicals. *Memberships:* Poetry Library, London; Poetry Society, London. *Address:* 50A N View Rd, London N8 7LL, England.

BROMIGE, David (Mansfield); b. 22 Oct. 1933, London, England (Naturalized Canadian citizen, 1961). Poet; Writer; Prof. of English. m., 1 s., 1 d. *Education:* BA, University of British Columbia, 1962; MA, 1964, ABD, 1969, University of California at Berkeley. *Appointments:* Poetry Ed., Northwest Review, 1962–64; Instructor, University of California at Berkeley, 1965–69; Lecturer, California College of Arts and Crafts, 1969, University of San Francisco, 2000–; Prof. of English, Sonoma State University, CA, 1970–93; Contributing ed., Avec, Penngrove, 1986–, Kaimana, Honolulu, 1989–. *Publications:* The Gathering, 1965; Please, Like Me, 1968; The Ends of the Earth, 1968; The Quivering Roadway, 1969; Threads, 1970; Ten Years in the Making, 1973; Three Stories, 1973; Birds of the West, 1974; Out of My Hands, 1974; Spells and Blessings, 1974; Tight Corners and What's Around Them, 1974; Credences of Winter, 1976; Living in Advance, 1976; My Poetry, 1980; P-E-A-C-E, 1981; In the Uneven Steps of Hung Chow, 1982; It's the Same Only Different, 1984; The Melancholy Owed Categories, 1984; You See, 1985; Red Hats, 1986; Desire, 1988; Men, Women and Vehicles, 1990; Tiny Courts in a World Without Scales, 1991; They Ate, 1992; The Harbormaster of Hong Kong, 1993; A Cast of Tens, 1994; Romantic Traceries, 1994; From the First Century, 1995; Piccolomondo, 1998; Establishing, 1999; Authenticizing, 2000. Contributions to Anthologies and periodicals. *Honours:* Macmillan Poetry Prize, 1957–59; Poet Laureate, University of California (all campuses), 1965; Discovery Award, 1969, Poetry Fellowship, 1980, National Endowment for the Arts; Canada Council Grant in Poetry, 1976–77; Pushcart Prize in Poetry, 1980; Western States Arts Federation Prize in Poetry, 1988; Gertrude Stein Award in Innovative Writing, 1994; Living Treasure Award, Sonoma County, 1994; Award, Fund for Poetry, 1998. *Address:* Dept of English, University of San Francisco, San Francisco, CA 94117, USA.

BRONNUM, Jakob; b. 16 April 1959, Copenhagen, Denmark. Author; Poet; m. Anette Bronnum, 12 Aug. 1995. *Education:* MA, Theology, 1992. *Publications:* Skyggedage (prose), 1989; Europadigte (poems), 1991; Den Lange Sondag (novel), 1994; Morke (novel), 1996; Sjaelen og Landskaberne (poems), 1997. *Contributions to:* Literaturnaja Gazetta; Parnasso, Finland. *Memberships:* Danish Writers' Asscn. *Address:* Draabydalen 30, 8400 Ebeltoft, Denmark.

BROOKENS, Diane; b. 29 May 1952, Raleigh, NC, USA. Teacher; Poet; Writer. *Education:* BEd, Education and Drama, London University, 1979; MA, Linguistics and Its Applications, Hertfordshire University, 1998. *Appointments:* Founder-Dir, Naturama School of Drama, 1985; Appearances on radio and television, including poetry readings on BBC Radio, Lancashire, 1992–2001. *Publications:* The Artistic Value of the American Musical, 1977; Timothy Earler and Other Poems for Children, 1986; Poems from a Chrysalis, 1997; Across the Atlantic: Memories of America, 2000; Back to Blackpool: The Lancashire Poems, 2001. *Contributions to:* Poetry magazines and reviews; Television and radio appearances. *Memberships:* Asscn of Lamda Teachers; Piccadilly Poets; Poetry Society; Writers' Guild of Great Britain. *Address:* 42 Pinner Ct, Pinner Rd, Pinner, Middlesex HA5 5RJ, England.

BROOKS, Katherine Elizabeth Howes; b. 14 Oct. 1922, Framingham, Massachusetts, USA. Poet. m. Wendell C Brooks, 1 Aug. 1943, 2 d. *Education:* BA, Colby College, Waterville, Maine, 1944. *Publications:* The Nine Lives of Frank and Natalie, 1995; Off Limits, 1995; Unsung Creatures from A to Z, 1996; The Last Dinosaur, 1996. *Contributions to:* Poets' Review; Apropos; Omnific; Feelings; Cliff Island Seagull; Anterior Bitewing; Poets' Pouch; Ellery Queen; Housewife's Humor; Poetpourri. *Honours:* Numerous first places, 1985–96; Joan Brown Award for Humorous Poetry, Poetpourri, 1989; Poet of the Year, Poets' Review, 1992, 1994. *Address:* 25 Fessenden St, Portland, ME 04103, USA.

BROSMAN, Catharine Savage; b. 7 June 1934, Denver, CO, USA. Prof. of French Emerita; Poet; Writer. m. Paul W Brosman Jr, 21 Aug. 1970, divorced 1993, 1 d. *Education:* BA, 1955; MA, 1957; PhD, 1960. *Appointments:* Instructor, Rice University, 1960–62; Asst Prof. of French, Sweet Briar College, 1962–63; University of Florida, 1963–66; Assoc. Prof. of French, Mary Baldwin College, 1966–68; Assoc. Prof. of French, 1968–72, Prof. of French, 1972–92, Kathryn B Gore Prof. of French, 1992–96, Prof. Emerita, 1997–, Tulane University; De Velling and Willis Visiting Prof., University of Sheffield, 1996. *Publications:* Watering, 1972; Abiding Winter, 1983; Jean-Paul

Sartre, 1983; Journeying from Canyon de Chelly, 1990; The Shimmering Maya and Other Essays, 1994; Dictionary of Twentieth-century Culture, Vol. 2: French Culture 1900–1975, 1995, Vol. 3: Hispanic Culture of South America, 1995, Vol. 4: Hispanic Culture of Mexico, Central America and the Caribbean, 1995, Vol. 5, 1996; Passages, 1996; Visions of War in France, 1999; The Swimmer and Other Poems, 2000; Places in Mind, 2000; Literary Masters: Albert Camus, 2000. *Contributions to:* Southern Review; Sewanee Review; Southwest Review; New England Review; Georgia Review; Shenandoah; Critical Quarterly; Interim; American Scholar. *Honour:* Third Place Award, Best Poems of 1973. *Address:* 1550 Second St, Suite 7-I, New Orleans, LA 70130, USA. *E-mail:* cbrosman@tulane.edu.

BROSSARD, Nicole; b. 27 Nov. 1943, Montréal, QC, Canada. Poet; Novelist. *Education:* Licence ès Lettres, 1968, Scolarité de maîtrise en lettres, 1972, Université de Montréal; Bacc. spécialisé en pédagogie, Université du Québec à Montréal, 1971. *Publications:* Poetry: Mécanique jongleuse, 1973, English trans. as Daydream Mechanics, 1980; Le centre blanc, 1978; The Story So Far 6 (ed.), 1978; Amantes, 1980, English trans. as Lovhers, 1986; Double Impression, 1984; Mauve, 1984; Character/Jeu de lettres, 1986; Sous la langue/ Under Tongue (bilingual edn) 1987; A tout regard, 1989; Installations, 1989; Langues obscures, 1991; Anthologie de la poésie des femmes au Québec (ed.), 1991; La Nuit verte du parc labyrinthe (trilingual edn), 1992; Vertige de l'avant-scène, 1997; Musée de l'os et de l'eau, 1999; Poèmes a dire la francophonie, 2002. Fiction: Un livre, 1970, English trans. as A Book, 1976; Sold-Out, 1973; French Kiss, 1974; L'amèr, 1977, English trans. as These Our Mothers, or, The Disintegrating Chapter, 1983; Le Sens apparent, 1980, English trans. as Surfaces of Sense, 1989; Picture Theory, 1982; Le Désert mauve, 1987, English trans. as Mauve Desert, 1990; Baroque d'aube, 1995, English trans. as Baroque at Dawn, 1997; Hier, 2001; Au présent des veines, 1999; Journal intime. Essays: La Lettre aérienne, 1985, English trans. as The Aerial Letter, 1988. *Contributions to:* Numerous anthologies. *Honours:* Gov.-Gen. Prizes, 1974, 1984; Chapbook Award, Therafields Foundation, 1986; Grand Prix de Poésie, Foundation Les Forges, 1989, 1999; Prix Athanase-David, 1991; Hon. doctorates, Universities of Western Ontario, 1991, Sherbrooke, 1997. *Membership:* l'Académie des Lettres du Québec, 1993–; Académie mondiale de la poesis, 2001. *Address:* 34 Ave Robert, Outremont, QC H3S 2P2, Canada.

BROSTROM, Kerri Rochelle; b. 22 July 1961, Minneapolis, Minnesota, USA. Publicist; Poet. m. Peter Masters, 29 March 1996, 1 s., 2 d. *Education:* St Cloud State University; University of Minnesota. *Contributions to:* Over 30 periodicals, reviews, and journals. *Address:* 2512 E 125th St, Burnsville, MN 55337, USA.

BROUGHTON, James; b. 10 Nov. 1913, USA. Poet; Filmmaker. m. Suzanne Hart, 6 Dec. 1962, 1 s., 1 d. *Education:* BA, Stanford University, 1936. *Appointments:* Assoc. Prof., San Francisco State University; Special Instructor, San Francisco Art Institute. *Publications:* Making LIght of it; The Androgyne Journal; Special Deliveries; Hooplas; 75 Lifelines; A to Z; Ecstasies; Graffiti for the Johns of Heaven; Hymns to Hermes; A Long Undressing; High Kukas; Tidings; True & False Unicorn; Musical Chairs; The Playground; Making Light of It, 1992; Coming Unbuttoned, 1993. *Contributions to:* Credences; Exquisite Corpse; Saturday Review; New Yorker; Beatitude; Vortex; City Lights Review; Zyzzva; Several anthologies. *Honours:* Distinguished Service Award; Lifetime Achievement Award. *Membership:* Poetry Society of America. *Address:* PO Box 1330, Port Townsend, WA 98368, USA.

BROUMAS, Olga; b. 6 May 1949, Hermoupolis, Greece. Poet; Trans. m. Stephen Edward Bangs, 1973, divorced 1979. *Education:* BA, University of Pennsylvania, 1970; MFA, University of Oregon at Eugene, 1973. *Appointments:* Instructor, University of Oregon, 1972–76; Visiting Assoc. Prof., University of Idaho, 1978; Poet-in-Residence, Goddard College, Plainfield, Vermont, 1979–81, Women Writers Center, Cazenovia, New York, 1981–82; Founder-Assoc. Faculty, Freehand Women Writers and Photographers Community, Provincetown, Massachusetts, 1982–87; Visiting Assoc. Prof., Boston University, 1988–90; Fanny Hurst Poet-in-Residence, 1990, Dir Creative Writing, 1995–, Brandeis University. *Publications:* Restlessness, 1967; Caritas, 1976; Beginning with O, 1977; Soie Sauvage, 1980; Pastoral Jazz, 1983; Black Holes, Black Stockings, 1985; Perpetua, 1989; Sappho's Gymnasium, 1994; Eros, Eros, Eros (trans.), 1998; Rave: Poems 1975–1999, 1999. *Honours:* Yale Younger Poets Award, 1977; National Endowment for the Arts Grant, 1978; Guggenheim Fellowship, 1981–82. *Address:* 162 Mill Pond Dr., Brewster, MA 02631, USA.

BROWN, Barbara Marie; b. 6 Dec. 1934, London, England. Secretary; Poet. m. Philip Brown, 30 March 1954, deceased, 1 s., 1 d. *Publication:* First Time, 1992. *Contributions to:* Brighton Festival, 1992; National Poetry Society; Ouse Valley Poetry; Hastings Festival, 1992. *Membership:* Poetry Society. *Address:* 22 London Prospect, Oakwood Dr., Central Hill, Upper Norwood, London SE19, England.

BROWN, Beverley E. See: BRAUNE, Beverliey.

BROWN, James Willie, Jr. See: KOMUNYAKAA, Yusef.

BROWN, John Gracen; b. 8 Oct. 1936, Martinsburg, West Virginia, USA. Writer; Poet; Dramatist. *Education:* BS, 1961, MS, 1962, Southern Illinoi University. *Publications:* Variation in Verse, 1975; A Sojourn of the Spirit 1981; Passages in the Wind, 1985; Eight Dramas, 1991; The Search, 1994 *Honours:* Lyrics used worldwide by over 200 composers. *Membership:* America Society of Composers, Authors and Publishers. *Address:* 430 Virginia Ave Martinsburg, WV 25401, USA.

BROWN, Rita Mae; b. 28 Nov. 1944, Hanover, Pennsylvania, USA. Write Poet. *Education:* University of Florida; AA, Broward Junior College, 1965; BA New York University, 1968; Cinematography Certificate, New York School c the Visual Arts, 1968; PhD, Institute for Policy Studies, Washington, DC, 1973 *Appointments:* Writer-in-Residence, Cazenovia College, New York, 1977–78 Pres., American Artists Inc, 1981–; Visiting Instructor, University of Virginia 1992. *Publications:* The Hand that Cradles the Rock (poems), 1971; Babyfru Jungle, 1973; Songs to a Handsome Woman (poems), 1973; In Her Day, 1976; A Plain Brown Rapper (essays), 1976; Six of One, 1978; Southern Discomfor 1982; Sudden Death, 1983; High Hearts, 1986; The Poems of Rita Mae Brown 1987; Starting from Scratch: A Different Kind of Writer's Manual, 1988; Bingo 1988; Wish You Were Here, 1990; Rest in Pieces, 1992; Venus Envy 1993;Dolley: A Novel of Dolley Madison in Love and War, 1994; Murder a Monticello, or, Old Sins, 1994; Pay Dirt, or, Adventures at Ash Lawn, 1995 Murder, She Meowed, 1996; Riding Shotgun, 1996; Rita Will: Memoir of Literary Rabble-Rouser, 1997; Murder on the Prowl, 1998; Cat on the Scene 1998; Loose Lips, 1999; Sneaky Pie's Cookbook for Mystery Lovers, 1999 Outfoxed, 2000; Pawing Through the Past, 2000. Other: Screenplays teleplays. *Contributions to:* Anthologies. *Honours:* National Endowment fo the Arts Grant, 1978; Co-Winner, Writers guild of America Award, 1983 New York Public Library Literary Lion, 1987; Hon. Doctorate, Wilso College, 1992. *Memberships:* International Acad. of Poets; PEN Internationa Poets and Writers. *Address:* c/o American Artists Inc, PO Box 4671 Charlottesville, VA 22905, USA.

BROWN, Rosellen; b. 12 May 1939, Philadelphia, Pennsylvania, USA. Writer Poet; Assoc. Prof. m. Marvin Hoffman, 16 March 1963, 2 d. *Education:* BA Barnard College, 1960; MA, Brandeis University, 1962. *Appointments* Instructor, Tougaloo College, Mississippi, 1965–67; Staff, Bread Loaf Writer' Conference, Middlebury, Vermont, 1974, 1991, 1992; Instructor, Goddard College, Plainfield, Vermont, 1976; Visiting Prof. of Creative Writing, Bosto University, 1977–78; Assoc. Prof. in Creative Writing, University of Houston 1982–85, 1989–. *Publications:* Some Deaths in the Delta and Other Poems 1970; The Whole World Catalog: Creative Writing Ideas for Elementary and Secondary Schools (with others), 1972; Street Games: A Neighborhood (stories) 1974; The Autobiography of My Mother (novel), 1976; Cora Fry (poems), 1977 Banquet: Five Short Stories, 1978; Tender Mercies (novel), 1978; Civil Wars: A Novel, 1984; A Rosellen Brown Reader: Selected Poetry and Prose, 1992; Befor and After (novel), 1992; Cora Fry's Pillow Book (poems), 1994; Half a Heart 2000. *Contributions to:* Books, anthologies and periodicals. *Honours:* Woodrov Wilson Fellow, 1960; Howard Foundation Grant, 1971–72; Nationa Endowment for the Humanities Grants, 1973–74, 1981–82; Radcliff Institute Fellow, 1973–75; Great Lakes Colleges New Writers Award, 1976 Guggenheim Fellowship, 1976–77; American Acad. and Institute of Arts and Letters Award, 1988; Ingram Merrill Grant, 1989–90. *Address:* c/o Creative Writing Program, University of Houston, Houston, TX 77204, USA.

BROWN, Stewart; b. 14 March 1951, Lymington, Hampshire, England University Lecturer in African and Caribbean Literature; Writer; Poet; Ed m. Priscilla Margaret Brant, 1976, 1 s., 1 d. *Education:* BA, Falmouth School o Art, 1978; MA, University of Sussex, 1979; PhD, University of Wales, 1987 *Appointments:* Lecturer in English, Bayero University, Kano, Nigeria, 1980–83 Reader in African and Caribbean Literature, University of Birmingham, 1988– *Publications:* Mekin Foolishness (poems), 1981; Caribbean Poetry Now, 1984 Zinder (poems), 1986; Lugard's Bridge (poems), 1989; Voiceprint: An Anthology of Oral and Related Poetry from the Caribbean (ed. with Mervyn Morris and Gordon Rohler), 1989; Writers from Africa: A Readers' Guide, 1989; New Wave The Contemporary Caribbean Short Story, 1990; The Art of Derek Walcott: A Collection of Critical Essays, 1991; The Art of Kamau Brathwaite: A Collection of Critical Essays, 1992; The Heinemann Book of Caribbean Poetry (with Ian McDonald), 1992; The Pressures of the Text: Orality, Texts and the Telling o Tales, 1995; Caribbean New Voices I, 1996; The Oxford Book of Carribbean Short Stories (with John Wickham), 1998; African New Voices, 1999 Elsewhere: New and Selected Poems, 1999; All are Involved: The Art o Martin Carter, 2000; Kiss and Quarrell: Youba/English, Strategies o Mediation, 2000. *Contributions to:* Anthologies and periodicals. *Honours:* Eric Gregory Award, 1976; Southwest Arts Literature Award, 1978; Hon. Fellow Centre for Caribbean Studies, University of Warwick, 1990. *Memberships* Welsh Acad.; Welsh Union of Writers. *Address:* Centre of West African Studies, University of Birmingham, Edgbaston, Birmingham B15 2TT England.

BROWN, William Imray; b. 11 May 1929, Aberdeen, Scotland. Teacher Lecturer; Poet. m. Roma Learmonth Robertson, 22 Dec. 1951, 3 s. *Education.*

University of Aberdeen, 1946–50; MA, Aberdeen College of Education, 1962. *Appointments:* Teacher, Glasgow Schools, 1952–53; Dufftown, Banffshire, 1953–57; Principal Teacher, Benwick High School, 1957–62; Senior Lecturer, Aberdeen College of Education, 1962–78. *Publications:* Pools Cycle; Langstene Nou and Syne. *Contributions to:* Acumen; Iota; Orbis; Apostrophe; Iron; Ore; Celtic Dawn; Isthmus; Outposts; Chapman; Lallans; Pennine Platform; Spokes; Envoi; Lines Review; Poetry Nottingham; Programore Papers; New Hope International Poetry Digest; Staple; Gairm; New Prospects. *Honours:* Nottingham Poetry Society; Open University Poets; Poetry Digest General Competition; Scottish International Competition; Yeats Club. *Address:* The Coach House, Huntly Pl., Aboyne, Aberdeenshire AB34 5HD, Scotland.

BROWNE, Michael Dennis; b. 28 May 1940, Walton-on-Thames, England (Naturalized US citizen, 1978). Prof.; Writer; Poet. m. Lisa Furlong McLean, 18 July 1981, 1 s., 2 d. *Education:* BA, Hull University, 1962; Oxford University, 1962–63; Ministry of Education Teacher's Certificate, 1963; MA, University of Iowa, 1967. *Appointments:* Visiting Lecturer, University of Iowa, 1967–68; Instructor, 1967, 1968, Visiting Adjunct Asst Prof., 1968, Columbia University; Faculty, Bennington College, Vermont, 1969–71; Visiting Asst Prof., 1971–72, Asst Prof., 1972–75, Assoc. Prof., 1975–83, Prof., 1983–, University of Minnesota. *Publications:* The Wife of Winter, 1970; Sun Exercises, 1976; The Sun Fetcher, 1978; Smoke From the Fires, 1985; You Won't Remember This, 1992; Selected Poems 1965–1995, 1997. *Contributions to:* Numerous anthologies and journals. Other: Texts for various musical compositions. *Honours:* Fulbright Scholarship, 1965–67; Borestone Poetry Prize, 1974; National Endowment for the Arts Fellowships, 1977, 1978; Bush Fellowship, 1981; Loft-McKnight Writers' Award, 1986; Minnesota Book Award for Poetry, 1993, 1998. *Memberships:* The Loft; Poetry Society of America. *Address:* 2111 E 22nd St, Minneapolis, MN 55404, USA.

BROWNJOHN, Alan (Charles); b. 28 July 1931, London, England. Poet; Novelist; Critic. *Education:* BA, 1953, MA, 1961, Merton College, Oxford. *Appointments:* Lecturer, Battersea College of Education, 1965–76, Polytechnic of the South Bank, 1976–79; Visiting Lecturer, University of North London, 2001–; Poetry Critic, New Statesman, 1968–76, Encounter, 1978–82, Sunday Times, 1990–. *Publications:* Poetry: Travellers Alone, 1954; The Railings, 1961; The Lions' Mouths, 1967; Sandgrains on a Tray, 1969; Penguin Modern Poets 14, 1969; First I Say This: A Selection of Poems for Reading Aloud, 1969; Brownjohn's Beasts, 1970; Warrior's Career, 1972; A Song of Good Life, 1975; A Night in the Gazebo, 1980; Collected Poems, 1982; The Old Flea-Pit, 1987; The Observation Car, 1990; In the Cruel Arcade, 1994; The Cat Without E-Mail, 2001. Fiction: To Clear the River, 1964; The Way You Tell Them, 1990; The Long Shadows, 1997; A Funny Old Year, 2001. Other: Philip Larkin, 1975; Meet and Write, 1985–87; The Gregory Anthology, 1990. Translations: Torquato Tasso (play), Goethe, 1985; Horace (play), Corneille, 1996. *Memberships:* Arts Council of Great Britain Literature Panel, 1968–72; Poetry Society, chair., 1982–88; Writers' Guild of Great Britain; Society of Authors. *Address:* 2 Belsize Park, London NW3, England.

BROWNSTEIN, Michael H.; b. 17 July 1953, Evanston, IL, USA. Teacher; Writer; Poet; Ed.; Publisher. m. Deborah Wymbs, 10 Oct. 1988, 2 s., 2 d. *Education:* BA, Elementary Education, Northern Illinois University, 1974; MA, Curriculum and Development, National College of Education, 1988. *Appointments:* Writer, Publisher, Ed., Paper Bag Press, 1988–; Ed., Wymbs Broadside, 1989–91; Contributing Ed., Letter X, 1992–95; Educational Columnist, South Street Journal, 1994–. *Publications:* The Shooting Gallery, 1988; Poems From the Body Bags, 1989; Reflections, 1991; The Principal of Things, 1994; Recessions & Other Poems, 1998. *Contributions to:* Over 400 publications. *Honours:* Omation Press Chapbook First Prize, 1989; Triton College of International Poetry First Place, 1991, 1992, 1993, 1994, 1996, 1999, 2000, 2002; YAR Award to produce poetry, Community Arts Grant for poetry, IASA State of Illinois Poetry Workshops. *Address:* PO Box 268805, Chicago, IL 60626, USA.

BRUCE, Lennart; b. 21 Feb. 1919, Stockholm, Sweden. Writer; Poet. m. Sonja Wiegandt, 22 July 1960, 1 s., 1 d. *Education:* College and university studies. *Appointment:* International financier, 1945–64. *Publications:* In English: Making the Rounds, 1967; Observations, 1968; Moments of Doubt, 1969; Mullioned Windows, 1970; The Robot Failure, 1971; Exposure, 1972; Letter of Credit, 1973; Subpoemas, 1974; The Broker, 1984. In Swedish: En Sannsaga, 1982; Utan Synbar Anledning, 1988; Forskingringen, 1990; En Nasares Gang, 1993; Kafferepet, 1995. Translations: Instructions for Undressing the Human Race (with Matthew Zion), 1968; Agenda, 1976; The Second Light, 1986; Speak to Me, 1989; The Ways of a Carpetbagger, 1993. *Contributions to:* Many US and Swedish literary magazines. *Honour:* Royal Swedish Acad. of Letters Awards, 1978, 1988. *Memberships:* PEN American Centre; Poetry Society of America; Swedish Writers Union. *Address:* 31 Los Cerros Pl., Walnut Creek, CA 94598, USA.

BRUCHAC, Joseph; b. 16 Oct. 1942, Saratoga Springs, New York, USA. Author; Poet; Storyteller; Publisher; Ed. m. Carol Worthen, 12 June 1964, 2 s. *Education:* AB, Cornell University, 1965; MA, Syracuse University, 1966; Graduate Studies, State University of New York at Albany, 1971–73; PhD, Union Institute, Ohio, 1975. *Appointments:* Co-Founder, Dir, Greenfield Review

Press, 1969–; Ed., Greenfield Review literary magazine, 1971–90; Visiting Scholar and Writer-in-Residence at various institutions; Mem., Dawnland Singers, 1993–. *Publications:* Fiction and Poetry: Indian Mountain and Other Poems, 1971; Turkey Brother and Other Iroquois Folk Tales, 1976; The Dreams of Jesse Brown (novel), 1977; Stone Giants and Flying Heads: More Iroquois Folk Tales, 1978; The Wind Eagle and Other Abenaki Stories, 1984; Iroquois Stories, 1985; Walking With My Sons and Other Poems, 1986; Near the Mountains: New and Selected Poems, 1987; Keepers of the Earth (stories), 1988; The Faithful Hunter: Abenaki Stories, 1988; Long Memory and Other Poems, 1989; Return of the Sun: Native American Tales from the Northeast Woodlands, 1989; Hoop Snakes, Hide-Behinds and Side-Hill Winders: Tall Tales from the Adirondacks, 1991; Keepers of the Animals (with Michael Caduto) (stories), 1991; Thirteen Moons on Turtle's Back (with Jonathan London) (poems and stories), 1992; Dawn Land (novel), 1993; The First Strawberries, 1993; Flying With the Eagle, Racing the Great Bear (stories), 1993; The Girl Who Married the Moon (with Gayle Ross) (stories), 1994; A Boy Called Slow, 1995; The Boy Who Lived With Bears (stories), 1995; Dog People (stories), 1995; Long River (novel), 1995; The Story of the Milky Way (with Gayle Ross), 1995; Beneath Earth and Sky, 1996; Children of the Long House (novel), 1996; Four Ancestors: Stories, Songs and Poems from Native North America, 1996. Other: Survival This Way: Interviews with Native American Poets, 1987; The Native American Sweat Lodge: History and Legends, 1993; Roots of Survival: Native American Storytelling and the Sacred, 1996. Editor: Over 15 books. *Contributions to:* Many anthologies, books and periodicals. *Honours:* National Endowment for the Arts Fellowship, 1974; Rockefeller Foundation Humanities Fellowship, 1982–83; American Book Award, 1985; Notable Children's Book in the Language Arts Award, 1993; Scientific American Young Readers Book Award, 1995; Parents Choice Award, 1995; American Library Asscn Notable Book Award, 1996; Knickerbocker Award for Juvenile Literature, New York Library Asscn, 1996. *Memberships:* National Asscn for the Preservation and Perpetuation of Storytelling; PEN; Poetry Society of America. *Address:* PO Box 308, Greenfield Center, NY 12833, USA.

BRUIN, John. See: BRUTUS, Dennis (Vincent).

BRUTUS, Dennis (Vincent), (John Bruin); b. 28 Nov. 1924, Salisbury, Rhodesia. Prof.; Poet; Writer. m. May Jaggers, 14 May 1950, 4 s., 4 d. *Education:* BA, University of the Witwatersrand, Johannesburg, South Africa, 1947. *Appointments:* Prof. at universities in Pittsburgh, Austin, Dartmouth, and Boston. *Publications:* Sirens, Knuckles, Boots, 1963; Letters to Martha and Other Poems from a South African Prison, 1968; Poems from Algiers, 1970; Thoughts Abroad, 1970; A Simple Lust: Selected Poems, 1973; China Poems, 1975; Stubborn Hope, 1978; Strains, 1982; Salutes and Censures, 1984; Airs and Tributes, 1988; Still the Sirens, 1993. *Contributions to:* Periodicals. *Honours:* Paul Robeson Award; Langston Hughes Award. *Memberships:* African Literature Asscn; American Civil Liberties Union; Amnesty International; PEN; Union of Writers of African Peoples.

BRUUN, Mette Tine; b. 5 April 1956, Copenhagen, Denmark. Writer; Poet. m. L Bohm, 16 June 1984, 1 s., 3 d. *Education:* Nurse, 1980. *Publications:* De Betydningsfulde Kvinder, 1992; Natmasker, 1995. *Membership:* Dansk Forfatter Forening. *Address:* Skipper Clements Alle 5 1, 2300 Copenhagen S, Denmark.

BRYAN, Sharon; b. 10 Feb. 1943, Salt Lake City, Utah, USA. Poet; Writer. *Education:* BA, Philosophy, University of Utah, 1965; MA, Anthropology, Cornell University, 1969; MFA, Poetry, University of Iowa, 1977. *Appointments:* Adjunct Faculty, University of Washington, 1987–93; Assoc. Prof., Memphis State University, 1987–93; Visiting Prof., Dartmouth College, University of Houston, 1993–. *Publications:* Salt Air, 1983; Objects of Affection, 1987; Flying Blind, 1996. *Contributions to:* Atlantic; Georgia Review; Ploughshares; Poetry Northwest; Nation; Southern Review; Quarterly West; Seattle Review; Tar River Poetry. *Honours:* Acad. of American Poets Prize, 1977; Discovery, The Nation, 1977; Arvon Foundation Prize, 1985; Governor's Award, Washington, 1985; National Endowment for the Arts Grant, 1987; Tennessee Arts Fellowship, 1991. *Memberships:* Poetry Society of America; Acad. of American Poets; Poets and Writers; Associated Writing Programs. *Address:* 1254 W St, 1000 North St, Salt Lake City, UT 84116, USA.

BUCHAN, Tom; b. 19 June 1931, Glasgow, Scotland. Poet. *Education:* MA, University of Glasgow, 1953. *Appointments:* Lecturer in Scotland, including Senior Lecturer in English and Drama, Clydebank Technical College, Glasgow, 1967–70; Dir, theatre ensembles. *Publications:* Ikons, 1958; Dolphins at Cochin, 1969; Exorcism, 1972; Poems 1969–72, 1972; Forwards, 1978. *Honours:* Scottish Arts Council Awards. *Address:* Scoraig, Dundonnell, Wester Ross IV23 2RE, Scotland.

BUCHER, Werner; b. 19 Aug. 1938, Zürich, Switzerland. Poet; Writer; Journalist; Ed. m. Josiane Fidanza, 2 May 1968. *Publications:* Nicht Solche Aengste, du... (poems), 1974; Zeitzünder 3: Dank an den Engel, 1987; Was ist mit Lazarus?, 1989; Einst & Jetzt & Morgen (poems), 1989; Ein anderes Leben: Versuch, sich einem Unbekannten anzunahern; De Wand: Roman; Eigentlich wunderbar, das Leben...: Tagtag-Gedichte und Nachtnacht-Nachrichten; Das bessere Ende: Gedichte; Mouchette (poem), 1995; Wegschleudern die Brillen, die Lügen (poems), 1995; Unruhen, 1997; Wenn der zechpreller gewinnt (poems), 1997; Urwaldhus, Tierhag, Ochsenhutte & Co, Die Schonsten Ostschweizer Beizen, 1997; Im Schatten des Campanile, 2000; Weitere Stürme sind angesagt (poems), 2002. *Contributions to:* Entwürfe; Tobel und Hoger; Listerarisches aus dem Appenzellerland, 2001. *Membership:* Swiss Writers' Union. *Address:* Rest, Kreuz, 9427 Zelg-Wolfhalden, Switzerland. *Website:* www.wernerbucher.ch.

BUCK, Heather; b. 6 April 1926, Kent, England. Writer; Poet. m. Hadley J Buck, 23 May 1952, 1 s., 1 d. *Publications:* The Opposite Direction, 1971; At the Window, 1982; The Sign of the Water Bearer, 1987; Psyche Unbound, 1995; Waiting for the Ferry, 1998. *Contributions to:* Acumen; Agenda; Critical Quarterly; Encounter; English; Poetry Review; Rialto; Pen New Poems 1976–77; New Poetry 7; Interactions; Understanding & Response; The Independent; The Month; Anthologies: Sixty Women Poets; Completing the Picture. *Memberships:* Poetry Society; English Asscn. *Address:* 14 High St, Lavenham, Suffolk CO10 9PT, England.

BUCK, Lilli Lee; b. 25 Feb. 1950, Butler, PA, USA. Teacher; Poet; Astrologer. *Education:* BA, Anthropology, 1972; MEd, Special Education, 1984; College of William and Mary. *Contributions to:* Anthologies and magazines including: American Poetry Annual, Best Poems and Poets of 2001, The Poet's Domain. *Honours:* Third Place, World of Poetry Contest, 1983; Excellence in Poetry Award, Fine Arts Press, 1985; Ed.'s Choice Award, National Library of Poetry, 1994; Ed.'s Choice Award, Poetry.com, Sept. 2001; International Poet of Merit, International Society of Poets, 2002. *Memberships:* Asscn for Research and Enlightenment; Poetry Society of Virginia. *Address:* 7000 Reedy Creek Rd, Bristol, VA 24202, USA. *E-mail:* astrolog7000@aol.com.

BUCKHOLTS, Claudia; b. 29 Dec. 1944, Ardmore, OK, USA. Poet; Writer. m. Thomas Glannon, 19 Sept. 1987. *Education:* Matthew Vassar Scholar, Vassar College; BA, History, University of Michigan, 1967. *Appointments:* Editorial Asst, Houghton Mifflin Company, 1968, 1969; Dir, Cambridge Poets Workshop, 1973–83; Ed., Gargoyle poetry magazine, 1975–82, Harvard University Press, 1979–. *Publications:* Bitterwater, 1975; Travelling Through the Body, 1979. *Contributions to:* Autumn Harvest; Green Mountains Review; Harvard Magazine; Southern Poetry Review; Alaska Quarterly Review; Connecticut Poetry Review; Kansas Quarterly; Midwest Quarterly; Minnesota Review; Paintbrush; Prairie Schooner; Sojourner; Soundings East; Hiram Poetry Review; Indiana Review; Dark Horse; Gargoyle; Shadowgraphs; Night House Anthology; 48 Younger American Poets; Provincetown Poets; Polis; Zeugma; Noise; Sri Chinmoy Awards Anthologies. *Honours:* Hopwood Awards, 1965, 1967; Grolier Poetry Prize, 1976; Sri Chinmoy Poetry Awards, 1977, 1978; Ed.'s Choice, Best Poems of 1980; Massachusetts Artists' Foundation Fellowship, 1981; National Endowment for the Arts Fellowship, 1988. *Membership:* Acad. of American Poets. *Address:* 15 Clarendon Ave, Somerville, MA 02144, USA.

BUCKLEY, William K.; b. 14 Nov. 1946, San Diego, CA, USA. Prof.; Writer; Poet. m. Mary Patricia, 25 Nov. 1969, 1 s. *Education:* BA, University of San Diego, 1969; MA, 1972, MA, 1975, California State University at San Diego; PhD, Miami University, Oxford, Ohio, 1980. *Appointments:* Instructor, San Diego Community Colleges, 1972–90; Co-Founder and Co-Ed., Recovering Literature, 1972–; Dir, Learning Skills Center, California State University at San Diego, 1974–75; Teaching Fellow, Miami University, Oxford, Ohio, 1975–79; Visiting Asst Prof., Hanover College, 1979–82; Visiting Asst Prof., 1982–84, Prof., 1985–, Indiana University Northwest, Gary, IN. *Publications:* A Half-Century of Céline, co-author, 1983; Critical Essays on Louis-Ferdinand Céline, ed., 1989; Senses' Tender: Recovering the Novel for the Reader, 1989; New Perspectives on the Closing of the American Mind, co-ed., 1992; Lady Chatterley's Lover: Loss and Hope, 1993. Poetry: Meditation on the Grid, 1995; By the Horses Before the Rains, 1996; Heart Maps, 1997; Images Entitled to Their Recoil From Utopia, 1998; 81 Mygrations, 1998; Athena in Steeltown, 1999; Sylvia's Bells, 2002. *Honour:* Best Chapbook of the Year, Modern Poetry, 1997. *Membership:* Acad. of American Poets. *Address:* c/o Dept of English, Indiana University Northwest, 3400 Broadway, Gary, IN 46408, USA.

BUCKNER, Sally (Beaver); b. 3 Nov. 1931, Statesville, North Carolina, USA. College Teacher; Poet. m. Robert Lynn Buckner, 21 Aug. 1954, 2 s., 1 d. Education, AB, English, 1953; MA, English, 1970; PhD, English Education, 1980. *Appointments:* Public School Teacher, Gastonia, NC, 1954–55; Kindergarten Teacher, Goldsboro, 1962–65; Journalist, Raleigh Times, 1966–68; Teaching Asst, North Carolina State University, 1968–70; English Faculty, Peace College, 1970–98; Co-Dir, Capital Area Writing Project, 1983–95. *Publication:* Strawberry Harvest, 1986; Our Words, Our Ways: Reading and Writing in North Carolina (ed.), 1991; Word and Witness: 100 Years of North Carolina Poetry (ed.), 1999. *Contributions to:* Christian Century; Woman's Day; Southern Poetry Review; Pembroke Review; Crab Creek Review; Embers; Sunrust; Uwharrie Review; Crucible. *Honours:* Crucible First Award, 1976; San Ragan Prizes, 1986, 1989; Nostalgia Second Prize, 1989; Chester Jones Special Merit, 1989. *Memberships:* North Carolina Writers Conference; North Carolina Poetry Society; North Carolina Women Writers Conference. *Address:* 3231 Birnamwood Rd, Raleigh, NC 27607, USA.

BUDBILL, David; b. 13 June 1940, Cleveland, OH, USA. Writer; Poet; Dramatist. *Education:* BA, Philosophy, minor Art History, Muskingum College, New Concord, Ohio, 1962; Philosophy, Columbia University, 1961; MDiv, Theology, Literature, Union Theological Seminary, New York, 1967. *Appointments:* Poet-in-Residence, Niagara Erie Writers, Buffalo, New York, 1984, Jamestown Community College, Jamestown, New York, 1986, 1987. *Publications:* Barking Dog, 1968; The Chain Saw Dance, 1977; Pulp Cutters' Nativity, 1981; From Down to the Village, 1981; Why I Came to Judevine, 1987; Judevine: The Complete Poems, 1991; Danvis Tales: Selected Stories by Rowland Robinson (ed.), 1995; Little Acts of Kindness, 1995; Moment to Moment, 1999. Play: Two for Christmas, 1996. *Contributions to:* Many anthologies and periodicals. *Honours:* Williamstown Repertory Theatre Playwright's Fellowship, 1965; Publication Grant, American Studies Institute, 1967; Poetry Fellowships, Vermont Council on the Arts, 1973, 1977, 1979; Kirkus Reviews Best Books, 1974, 1976; Guggenheim Fellowship, 1982–83; Playwriting Fellowship, National Endowment for the Arts, 1991; San Francisco Bay Area Critics' Circle Award, 1991. *Memberships:* PEN; Dramatists' Guild. *Address:* 4592 E Hill Rd, Wolcott, VT 05680, USA.

BUDDEE, Paul (Edgar); b. 12 March 1913, Western Australia, Australia. Author; Poet. m. Elizabeth Vere Bremner, 1944, 1 s., 1 d. *Education:* Claremont Teachers College. *Publications:* Stand to and Other War Poems, 1943; The Oscar and Olga Trilogy, 1943–47; The Unwilling Adventurers, 1967; The Mystery of Moma Island, 1969; The Air Patrol Series, 1972; The Ann Rankin Series, 1972; The Escape of the Fenians, 1972; The Peter Devlin Series, 1972; The Escape of John O'Reilly, 1973; The Call of the Sky, 1978; The Fate of the Artful Dodger, 1984; Poems of the Second World War, 1986. *Contributions to:* Many periodicals. *Honours:* Australia Commonwealth Literary Board Grants, 1977, 1978, 1984; OAM, 1989. *Memberships:* Australian Society of Authors; Fellowship of Writers; PEN International. *Address:* 2 Butson Rd, Leeming, WA 6149, Australia.

BUEHLER, Evelyn Judy; b. 18 March 1953, Chicago, IL, USA. Poet; Writer. m. Henry Eric Buehler, 23 Aug. 1985, 1 s., 1 d. *Education:* Harold Washington College. *Contributions to:* Short stories in: Millennium the Alpha the Omega 2000; Silver Words and Golden Thoughts, 2000; The Best Writers of the Decade, 2000; Envoy Collection, 2000; Treasure Thoughts, 2000; Windows on the World (CD-ROM), 2001; Poems in: Silver Words and Golden Thoughts, 2000; In-Between Days, 2000; Where Words Haven't Spoken, 2000; The Falling Rain, 2000; Time After Time, 2000; Nature's Echoes, 2000; The Best Poets of the Decade, 2000; Poetry 2000: Our Century's Best Famous Poems, 2001; Poetry's Elite: The Best Poets of 2000, 2001; The Sound of Poetry (audio) 2001; Treasures in Your Heart, 2001; Windows on the World (CD-ROM), 2001; The Sex of Poetry (CD-ROM), 2001; The Silence Within, 2001. *Honours:* Seven Golden Poet Awards, World of Poetry, 1985–91; Ed.'s Choice Awards, International Society of Poets, 1993, 1994 (twice). *Membership:* International Society of Poets. *Address:* 5658 S Normal Blvd, Chicago, IL 60621, USA.

BUI, Khoi Tien, (Huy-Luc); b. 23 Dec. 1937, Binh-dinh, Viet Nam. College Counsellor; Poet Laureate. m. Yen Kim Nguyen, 7 Dec. 1962, 3 c. *Education:* BS, Law; MS, Business Management; National Planner Training, 1963–71. *Appointments:* Founder, Moderator, radio programme The Voice of Free Vietnam, 1980–; Oriental Culture Adviser, Rice University and University of Houston, 1980–; Oriental Culture Lecturer, University of Texas, University of Houston, 1982–. *Publications:* 7 poetry books. *Contributions to:* Vietnamese and English magazines. *Honours:* Many medals and decorations, Govenment of the Republic of Viet Nam, 1965–75; National Literature Prize, 1966; Houston's Poet Laureate Award, 1984; Golden Poet Award, 1985. *Memberships:* PEN Vietnamese Centre, exec. mem., 1960–75; PEN American Centre, 1982–; Galaxy Verse; American Poetry Society. *Address:* PO Box 720236, Houston, TX 77272, USA.

BUKHARAEV, Ravil; b. 18 Oct. 1951, Russia. Writer; Poet. m. L. Grigorieva. *Education:* Degree, Mathematics, Kazan State University; Postgraduate Studies, Computer Science, Moscow University. *Appointments:* Consultant, Writers' Union of Russia, 1980–82; Prof. of Literary Trans., Moscow Literary Institute, 1988–89; Prod., BBC, 1992–. *Publications:* Poetry: An Apple Tied Up to the Branch, 1977; The Thin Rain, 1979; The Sign of August, 1981; The Time of Flowers, 1985; The Snow Crane, 1986; Commentaries to Love, 1986; Around Tukai, 1986; Sober Feasts, 1990; Vad Szonettek Koszoruja, 1993; Quest, 1993. Prose: Disclosure of Uncertainties (novel), 1989; The Road to God Knows Where (novel), 1996; The Model of Tatarstan, 1999; Islam in Russia: The Four Seasons, 2000; Historical Anthology of Kazan Tatar Verse (with D. J. Matthews), 2000. Plays: The Litte Daisy Star, 1985; The Magic Dreams of Apush, 1986. Other: Trans. of religious and philosophical books; The Kayum Nasiri Street (television series). *Contributions to:* Russian and Islamic studies; Television films; Newsletters, journals and reviews. *Honours:* Golden Pen Award, Moscow, 1982; Jalil Prize of the Republic of Tatarstan, 1986. *Memberships:* Union of Writers, Russia and Hungary; PEN Centers of Hungary and USA; European Society of Culture, Venice, Italy; Acad. of Arts and Culture; World Congress of Poets, Taiwan, USA; International Poets' Acad., Madras, India; Asscn of Finno-Ugric Writers, Helsinki, Finland. *Address:* 65 Crescent Wood Rd, Dulwich, London, England.

BULLEY, Anne. See: MAIER, Anne Winifred.

BULLOCK, Kenneth Jr; b. 17 Aug. 1950, New Orleans, LA, USA. Writer; Poet. 2 d. *Education:* Assoc. of Arts, Jones County Junior College. *Appointments:* Served in US Marine Rifle Company (Seventh Marines), Viet Nam, 1970 (awarded Purple Heart). *Contributions to:* Fuel; Alternative Press; Night Roses; Prutea Poetry; Context South; Mobius; Journal Poetry Forum; Poetry Motel; Riverrun; Lost Creek Letters; Nexus; Dream International Quarterly; Press of the Third Mind; Plowman Press (Chapbook); Wayne Literary Review; Poet Magazine; Pokeday Sticks; Minature; Sanscrity; Oyez Review; White Wall; Muddy River Poetry Review. *Address:* 1113 Parker Dr., Laurel, MS 39440, USA.

BULLOCK, Michael; b. 19 April 1918, London, England. Prof. Emeritus; Poet; Dramatist; Writer; Trans. *Education:* Hornsey College of Art. *Appointments:* Commonwealth Fellow, 1968, Prof. of Creative Writing, 1969–83, Prof. Emeritus, 1983–, University of British Columbia, Vancouver, Canada; McGuffey Visiting Prof. of English, Ohio University, Athens, Ohio, 1969; New Asia Ming Yu Visiting Scholar, 1989, Writer-in-Residence, 1996, New Asia College, Chinese University of Hong Kong; Adviser, New Poetry Society of China, 1995–. *Publications:* Poetry: Transmutations, 1938; Sunday is a Day of Incest, 1961; World Without Beginning Amen, 1963; Two Voices in My Mouth/ Zwei Stimmen in meinem Mund, 1967; A Savage Darkness, 1969; Black Wings White Dead, 1978; Lines in the Dark Wood, 1981; Quadriga for Judy, 1982; Prisoner of the Rain, 1983; Brambled Heart, 1985; Dark Water, 1987; Poems on Green Paper, 1988; The Secret Garden, 1990; Avatars of the Moon, 1990; Labyrinths, 1992; The Walled Garden, 1992; The Sorcerer with Deadly Nightshade Eyes, 1993; The Inflowing River, 1993; Moons and Mirrors, 1994; Dark Roses, 1994; Stone and Shadow, 1996; Der Grüne Mond, 1997; Sonnet in Black and Other Poems, 1998; Nocturnes: Poems of Night, 2000; Wings of the Black Swan: Poems of Love and Loss, 2001. Fiction: Sixteen Stories as They Happened, 1969; Green Beginning Black Ending, 1971; Randolph Cranstone and the Pursuing River, 1975; Randolph Cranstone and the Glass Thimble, 1977; The Man with Flowers Through His Hands, 1985; The Double Ego, 1985; Randolph Cranstone and the Veil of Maya, 1986; The Story of Noire, 1987; Randolph Cranstone Takes the Inward Path, 1988; The Burning Chapel, 1991; The Invulnerable Ovoid Aura, Stories and Poems, 1995. Other: Selected Works, 1936–1996 (co-eds Peter Loeffler and Jack Stewart), 1998. *Contributions to:* Many anthologies. *Honours:* Schlegel-Tieck German Trans. Prize, 1966; British New Fiction Society Book of the Month, 1977; Canada Council French Trans. Award, 1979; San Francisco Review of Books Best Book List, 1982; San Jose Mercury News Best Booklist, 1984; Okanagan Short Fiction Award, 1986. *Address:* Suite 103, 3626 W 28th Ave, Vancouver, BC V6S 1S4, Canada.

BULMAN, Aaron E.; b. 12 Jan. 1948, Lawrence, Massachusetts, USA. Corporate Man.; Poet. m. Rachelle L Schwartzman, 29 Aug. 1971, 2 s., 2 d. *Education:* BA, Yeshiva University, 1969; BA, City College of the City University of New York, 1970; Rabbi Isaac Elchonow Theological Seminary, 1969–71. Contributions to Ten Jewish American Poets; Christian Science Monitor; Voices International; Home Planet News; Images; Jewish Currents; Paris Review; Partisan Review; Small Pond. *Membership:* Poets and Writers. *Address:* 15 Magaw Pl., Apt 1-B, New York, NY 10033, USA.

BUNCH, Richard Alan; b. 1 June 1945, Honolulu, HI, USA. College Instructor; Poet; Writer. m. Rita Anne Glazar, 11 Aug. 1990, 1 s., 1 d. *Education:* AA, Napa Valley College, 1965; BA, Stanford University, 1967; MA, University of Arizona, 1969; MDiv, 1970, DD, 1971, Graduate Studies, Philosophy, 1972–75, Vanderbilt University; Graduate Studies, Asian Religions, Temple University, 1975–76; JD, University of Memphis, 1980; Teaching Credential, Sonoma State University, 1988. *Appointments:* Instructor in Philosophy, Belmont University, 1973–74, Chapman University, 1986–87; Instructor in Law, University of Memphis, 1982–83; Instructor in Humanities, Napa Valley College, 1985–, Diablo Valley College, 1991–94, 1997; Instructor in Law, 1986–87, and in Philosophy, 1990–91, Sonoma State University. *Publications:* Poetry: Summer Hawk, 1991; Wading the Russian River, 1993; A Foggy Morning, 1996; Santa Rosa Plums, 1996; South by Southwest, 1997; Rivers of the Sea, 1998; Sacred Space, 1998; Greatest Hits: 1970–2000, 2001. Prose: Night Blooms, 1992. Play: The Russian River Returns, 1999. *Contributions to:* Many reviews. *Honours:* Pushcart Prize Nominations, 1988, 1996, 1997; Grand Prize, Ina Coolbirth National Poetry Day Contest, 1989; Jessamyn West Prize, 1990; Nominee, Poet Laureate of California, 2002. *Memberships:* Acad. of American Poets; Ina Coolbirth Poetry Circle. *Address:* 248 Sandpiper Dr., Davis, CA 965616, USA.

BUNTON, Hope; b. 11 Jan. 1921, Willingham, Cambridgeshire, England. Poet; Short Story Writer. m. John Bunton, 15 July 1961, divorced. *Education:* University of London, 1939–42; International Language School, London, 1971. *Publications:* Until All Is Silence; Beyond Silence; Through My Eyes. *Contributions to:* Envoi; Writer's Voice; Lancashire Life; Cambridgeshire Life; Lincolnshire Writers; Liverpool Echo; Viewpoint; Breakthru; Bedsitter; Lantern Light; Journal of Indian Writing in English; Anthology of Peace Poems for Lancashire Literature Festival; Haiku magazine; Radio Merseyside; Radio Lancashire; Poetry Now; New Hope International; Parnassus of World Poets; Darius Anthology; Railway Anthology, 1996;

Countryside Tales; Acorn Magazine; Imagine Writing Group. *Honours:* Second Prize, Religious Section, Third Prize, Topical Section, Chorley Arts Poetry Competition. *Address:* 10 Clifton St, Preston, Lancashire PR1 8EE, England.

BURACK, Alexandra; b. 13 Jan. 1960, Boston, Massachusetts, USA. Poet; Ed.; Teacher. *Education:* BA, Sociology, Manhattanville College, Purchase, New York, 1982; MFA, Writing, Sarah Lawrence College, Bronxville, NY, 2002. *Appointment:* Founder-Exec. Dir, Boris Burack Memorial Poetry Reading Series, Middletown, CT, 1996–. *Publication:* On the Verge, 1997. *Contributions to:* Anthologies and periodicals. *Honours:* Co-Winner, Brush Hill Press Poetry Competition, 1984; Honourable Mention, Connecticut Poetry Society, 1987; Commendation, UK Poets-of-the-Year Competition, 1994; Pushcart Prize Nomination, 1996; Ludwig Vogelstein Foundation Grant, 1996; CT Commission on the Arts, Artist Fellow in Poetry, 1999. *Memberships:* Acad. of American Poets, assoc. mem.; Brick Walk Poets Collective, West Hartford, CT, founding mem.; Poetry Society of America; Poets House. *Address:* PO Box 99, Higganum, CT 06441, USA.

BURCH, Claire; b. 19 Feb. 1925, New York, NY, USA. Writer; Poet; Filmmaker. m. Bradley Bunch, 14 April 1944, deceased, 1 s., deceased, 2 d. *Education:* BA, Washington Square College, 1947. *Publications:* Stranger in the Family, 1972; Notes of a Survivor, 1972; Shredded Millions, 1980; Goodbye My Coney Island Baby, 1989; Homeless in the Eighties, 1989; Solid Gold Illusion, 1991; You Be the Mother Follies, 1994; Homeless in the Nineties, 1994; Stranger on the Planet: The Small Book of Laurie, 1996. *Contributions to:* Periodicals. *Honours:* Carnegie Awards, 1978, 1979; California Arts Council Grants, 1991, 1992, 1993, 1994; Seva Foundation Award, 1996. *Membership:* Writer's Guild. *Address:* c/o Regent Press, 6020A Adeline, Oakland, CA 94808, USA.

BURDICK, Carol; b. 8 Aug. 1928, Salem, West Virginia, USA. Educator; Writer; Poet. m. Robert Hudson, 19 June 1949, divorced 1970, 2 s., 1 d. *Education:* BA, Milton College, 1949; MS, State University of New York at Geneseo, 1963. *Appointments:* Teacher, Alfred University, 1974; Co-Dir, Ossabaw Island Project, 1979–82. *Publications:* Destination Unknown, 1968; Stop Calling Me Mr Darling, 1989; Woman Alone: A Farmhouse Journal, 1990. *Contributions to:* Maine Times; Maine Edition; Alfred Review; Poet Lore; Down East; Maine Sunday Paper; English Journal; Journal of Academic Medicine; Lyrics for songs by Klaus Roy, Tom Benjamin, Jeffrey Ryan. *Honours:* First Prize, Chautauqua Institution, 1988; Distinguished Teaching Award, 1996; Outstanding Faculty Leader Award, 1998; Abigail Allen Award, 1999; Hon. Alumni, Alfred University, 1999. *Memberships:* Asscn for the Study of Literature and Environment; Society for Values in Higher Education; MacDowell Colony Fellow. *Address:* Pondhouse, Alfred Station, NY 14803, USA.

BURGESS, Craig Edward; b. 8 Oct. 1944, Camden, NJ, USA. Teacher. *Education:* BA, Rutgers University, 1967; Teaching Fellowship in Spanish, 1967–68, MS, Education, University of Pennsylvania, 1971. *Appointments:* Chair., Foreign Language Dept, 1970–76; Foreign Language Representative to District Instructional Council, Cherry Hill Public Schools, 1971–72; Consultant, Heinle & Heinle Publishers, 1991–92; Advisory Panel, International Society of Poets, 1993–; Consultant, New Jersey Education Asscn, 1994–; Public Relations Representative, Living Arts Repertory Theatre, 1995–2001; Continental Gov., American Biographical Institute Research Asscn, 1998–; Free Public Library of Audubon, 1998. *Publications:* Life and Living: Thoughts and Perspectives, 1989; Once Upon a Lifetime: A Teacher's Eye View of Living in the World Today, 1994; Dueling Poets, 1996; Travels Across America, 1997; Travel Images and Impressions, 1997; The Best of the Audubon Poets, 1998; The Green Wave and the Navy: The History of the USS BENFOLD DDG-65, 1999; September 11, 2002; The Audebon Poets, Vol. II: The Journey Continues, 2002. *Contributions to:* Newspapers and magazines. *Honours:* Fifth Place Award, America's Best Amateur Poets, Johnson Publishing Company, 1985; Golden Poetry Award, World of Poetry, 1985, 1986, 1987; Semi-Finalist, International Society of Poets' Symposium, Washington, DC, 1995, 1996; Grand Winner, Silver Bowl in Poetry, 167th Annual Convention, International Platform Speakers' Asscn, Washington, DC, 1998; Applause Award for Literature, 2001. *Memberships:* International Society of Poets; New Jersey Poetry Society; Audubon Poets, founder, facilitator. *Address:* 327 Washington Terrace, Audubon, NJ 08106-2148, USA.

BURNETT, Alfred David; b. 15 Aug. 1937, Edinburgh, Scotland. University Librarian; Poet; Critic; Trans. *Education:* MA, Honours, English Language and Literature, University of Edinburgh, 1959; ALA, University of Strathclyde, 1964. *Appointments:* Library Asst, Glasgow University Library, 1959–64; Asst Librarian, Durham University Library, England, 1964–90. *Publications:* Mandala, 1967; Diversities, 1968; A Ballad Upon a Wedding, 1969; Columbaria, 1971; Shimabara, 1972; Fescennines, 1974; **Thirty Snow Poems,** 1973; Hero and Leander, 1975; **He and She, 1976;** The Heart's Undesign, 1977; Figures and Spaces, 1978; Jackdaw, 1980; **Thais,** 1981; Romans, 1983; Vines, 1984; Autolycus, 1987; Kantharos, 1989; Lesbos, 1990; Mirror and Pool (trans from Chinese, with John Cayley), 1992; Nine Poets, 1993; The Island, 1994; Twelve Poems, 1994; Something of Myself, 1994; Six

Poems, 1995; Transfusions, trans from French, 1995; Hokusai, 1996; Marina Tsvetaeva, 1997; Chesil Beach, 1997; Akhmatova, 1998; Butterflies, 1999; Cinara, 2001; Evergreens, 2002; Quoins for the Chase, 2002. Editor: Anthologies. *Contributions to:* Numerous publications. *Honours:* Essay Prize, 1956, Patterson Bursary in Anglo-Saxon, 1958, University of Edinburgh; Kelso Memorial Prize, University of Strathclyde, 1964; Essay Prize, Library Asscn, 1966; Sevensma Prize, International Federation of Library Asscns, 1971; Hawthornden Fellowships, 1988, 1992, 2002; Panizzi Medal, British Library, 1991; Fellow, British Centre for Literary Trans., Norwich, 1994. *Memberships:* Poetry Book Society; Fine Press Book Asscn; Private Libraries Asscn. *Address:* 33 Hastings Ave, Merry Oaks, Durham DH1 3QG, England. *Telephone:* (191) 384-3039.

BURNS, Jim; b. 19 Feb. 1936, Preston, Lancashire, England. Writer; Poet. *Education:* BA Honours, Bolton Institute of Technology, 1980. *Appointments:* Ed., Move, 1964–68; Palantir, 1976–83; Jazz Ed., Beat Scene, 1990–. *Publications:* A Single Flower, 1972; The Goldfish Speaks from Beyond the Grave, 1976; Fred Engels bei Woolworth, 1977; Internal Memorandum, 1982; Out of the Past: Selected Poems 1961–1986, 1987; Confessions of an Old Believer, 1996; The Five Senses, 1999; As Good a Reason As Any, 1999; Beats, Bohemians and Intellectuals, 2000. *Contributions to:* London Magazine; Stand; Ambit; Jazz Journal; Critical Survey; The Guardian; New Statesman; Tribune; New Society; Penniless Press; Prop; Verse; Others. *Address:* 11 Gatley Green, Gatley, Cheadle, Cheshire SK8 4NF, England.

BURNS, Ralph; b. 8 June 1949, Norman, OK, USA. Poet; Ed.; Prof. m. Candace Wilson Calhoun, 10 Oct. 1974, 1 s. *Education:* MFA, University of Montana, 1977. *Appointments:* Prof., University of Arkansas at Little Rock, 1985–; Ed., Crazyhorse magazine. *Publications:* Us, 1983; Any Given Day, 1985; Mozart's Starling, 1991; Swamp Candles, 1996. *Honours:* Two National Endowment for the Arts Fellowships; Iowa Poetry Prize, 1996. *Address:* 315 Linwood Ct, Little Rock, AR 72205, USA.

BURNSHAW, Stanley; b. 20 June 1906, New York, NY, USA. Publisher; Poet; Writer. m. Lydia Powsner, 2 Sept. 1942, deceased, 1 d. *Education:* BA, University of Pittsburgh, 1925; University of Poitiers, France, 1927; University of Paris, 1927; MA, Cornell University, 1933. *Appointments:* Pres. and Ed.-in-Chief, The Dryden Press, 1937–58; Program Dir, Graduate Institute of Book Publishing, New York University, 1958–62; Vice-Pres., Holt, Rinehart and Winston, publishers, 1958–67; Regents Visiting Lecturer, University of California, 1980; Visiting Distinguished Prof., Miami University, 1989. *Publications:* Poems, 1927; The Great Dark Love, 1932; Andre Spire and His Poetry, 1933; The Iron Land, 1936; The Bridge, 1945; The Revolt of the Cats in Paradise, 1945; Early and Late Testament, 1952; Caged in an Animal's Mind, 1963; The Hero of Silence, 1965; In the Terrified Radiance, 1972; Mirages: Travel Notes in the Promised Land, 1977; Robert Frost Himself, 1986; A Stanley Burnshaw Reader, 1990; The Seamless Web, 1991. *Contributions to:* Many periodicals. *Honours:* National Institute of Arts and Letters Award, 1971; Hon. Doctorate of Humane Letters, Hebrew Union College, 1983; Hon. Doctorate of Letters, City University of New York, 1996. *Address:* 250 W 89th St, No. PH2G, New York, NY 10024, USA.

BURNSIDE, John; b. 19 March 1955, Dunfermline, Fife, Scotland. Poet. *Publications:* Physical Diagnosis, 1981; The Hoop, 1988; Common Knowledge, 1991; Feast Days, 1992; The Myth of the Twin, 1994; Swimming in the Flood, 1995; The Dumb House, 1997; A Normal Skin, 1997; Sense Data, 1998; The Mercy Boys, 1999; Love for Love, 2000; Burning Elvis, 2000; The Asylum Dance, 2000; The Locust Room, 2001; The Light Trap, 2002; The Forest of Beguilement, 2003; The Shifting Stars, 2003; Antimony, 2003. *Contributions to:* Newspapers, journals and periodicals. *Honours:* Scottish Arts Council Book Awards, 1988, 1991; Geoffrey Faber Memorial Prize, 1994. *Address:* c/o Jonathon Cape, 20 Vauxhall Bridge Rd, London SW1V 2SA, England.

BURROWAY, Janet (Gay); b. 21 Sept. 1936, Tucson, AZ, USA. Prof.; Writer; Poet. m. (1) Walter Eysselinck, 1961, divorced 1973, 2 s., (2) William Dean Humphries, 1978, divorced 1981, (3) Peter Ruppert, 1993, 1 step-d. *Education:* University of Arizona, 1954–55; AB, Barnard College, 1958; BA, 1960, MA, 1965, Cambridge University; Yale School of Drama, 1960–61. *Appointments:* Instructor, Harpur College, Binghamton, New York, 1961–62; Lecturer, University of Sussex, 1965–70; Assoc. Prof., 1972–77, Prof., 1977–, MacKenzie Prof. of English, 1989–95, Robert O Lawson Distinguished Prof., 1995–, Florida State University; Fiction Reviewer, Philadelphia Enquirer, 1986–90; Reviewer, New York Times Book Review, 1991–; Essay-Columnist, New Letters: A Magazine of Writing and Art, 1994–. *Publications:* Fiction: Descend Again, 1960; The Dancer From the Dance, 1965; Eyes, 1966; The Buzzards, 1969; The Truck on the Track, 1970; The Giant Jam Sandwich, 1972; Raw Silk, 1977; Opening Nights, 1985; Cutting Stone, 1992. Poetry: But to the Season, 1961; Material Goods, 1980. Other: Writing Fiction: A Guide to Narrative Craft, 1982. *Contributions to:* Numerous journals and periodicals. *Honours:* National Endowment for the Arts Fellowship, 1976; Yaddo Residency Fellowships, 1985, 1987; Lila Wallace-Reader's Digest Fellow, 1993–94; Carolyn Benton Cockefaire Distinguished Writer-in-Residence, University of Missouri, 1995; Woodrow Wilson Visiting Fellow, Furman University, Greenville, South Carolina, 1995; Visiting Writer, Erskine College, Due West,

South Carolina, 1997, Drury College, Springfield, IL, 1999. *Memberships:* Associated Writing Programs; Authors' Guild. *Literary Agent:* Gail Hochman, Brandt & Brandt, 1501 Broadway, New York 10036, USA. *Address:* 240 De Soto St, Tallahassee, FL 32303, USA.

BURROWS, Edwin Gladding; b. 23 July 1917, Dallas, Texas, USA. Poet. m. Beth Elpern, 7 Dec. 1972, 3 s. *Education:* BA, Yale University, 1938; MA, University of Michigan, 1940. *Appointments:* Man., University Michigan Radio Stations, 1945–70; Dir, Centre for Audio Research, University of Wisconsin, 1970–73. *Publications:* The Arctic Tern; Man Fishing; The Crossings; Kiva; On the Road to Baileys; Properties; The House of August; Handsigns for Rain; The Birds Under the Earth, 1997. *Contributions to:* American Poetry Review; Atlantic Monthly; Ascent; Gettysburg Review; Hawaii Review; Massachusetts Review; Michigan Quarterly Review; Paris Review; Poetry; Poetry Northwest; Seattle Review; Virginia Quarterly Review; Wilderness Magazine. *Honours:* John Masefield Award; Major Hopwood Award; Ohio State Award; First Poetry Prize Ascent; Nominated for National Book Award. *Address:* 20319 92nd Ave W, Edmonds, WA 98020, USA.

BURROWS, Michael James; b. 4 March 1962, Cheltenham, Gloucester, England. Poet. *Education:* Diploma in Higher Education, English and Theology, Leeds University, 1990. *Appointments:* Ed. and (occasional) Creative Writing Tutor, Poetry Magazine, 1993–. *Publication:* Flexham's Shadow, 1996. *Contributions to:* Smoke; Poetry and Audience; T O P S; First Time; A Hairshirt of Words; Snapshot Poems; Under the Asylum Tree; Ripon Gazette; Big Plug; Still Waters; Cliff Hanger; Merseyside Poets CD.

BURTON, Gabrielle; b. 21 Feb. 1939, Lansing, MI, USA. Writer; Poet. m. Roger V. Burton, 18 Aug. 1962, 5 d. *Education:* BA, Marygrove College Michigan, 1960; MFA, American Film Institute, Los Angeles, 1997. *Appointments:* Teacher, Fiction in the Schools, Writers in Education Project, New York, 1985; Various prose readings and workships. *Publications:* I'm Running Away From Home But I'm Not Allowed to Cross the Street, 1972; Heartbreak Hotel, 1986; Manna From Heaven (screenplay, filmed), 2000. *Contributions to:* Numerous publications. *Honours:* MacDowell Colony Fellowships, 1982, 1987, 1989; Yaddo Fellowship, 1983; Maxwell Perkins Prize, 1986; Great Lakes Colleges Asscn Award, 1987; Bernard De Voto Fellow in Non-Fiction, Bread Loaf Writer's Conference, 1994; Mary Pickford Foundation Award for First Year Screenwriter, 1996; First Prize, Austin Film Festival Screenwriting Contest, 1999; Nicholl Fellow, 2000. *Address:* 211 LeBrun Rd, Eggetsville, NY 14226, USA.

BURTON, Michael Hedley; b. 20 July 1955, New Zealand. Speech Artist; Teacher; Reciter; Poet. *Education:* BA, Waikato University, 1977; Diploma in Drama, Auckland University, 1977; Diploma in Speech, Goetheanum, Basel, Switzerland, 1987. *Publications:* In the Light of a Child; 1989; In Celebration of Being Human, 1990; Songs of a Washing Machine and Other Loony Poems, 1992; The Very Old Donkey, 1995. *Contributions to:* New Zealand School Journal. *Address:* 2 Lower St, Ruscombe, Stroud, Gloucestershire GL6 6BU, England.

BUSACCA, Helle Fathma; b. 21 Dec. 1915, San Piero-Patti, Sicily, Italy. Teacher; Poet; Writer; Painter. *Education:* PhD, University of Milan, 1938. *Appointments:* Teacher of Languages and the Arts. *Publications:* 8 poetry books, 1949–94, 1 novel, 1987, and 1 collection of short stories, 1991. *Contributions to:* Anthologies and periodicals. *Honours:* Over 15 prizes, 1950–95. *Memberships:* Several professional organisations.

BUSH, Duncan (Eric); b. 6 April 1946, Cardiff, Wales. Poet; Writer; Teacher. m. Annette Jane Weaver, 4 June 1981, 2 s. *Education:* BA, in English and European Literature, Warwick University, 1978; Exchange Scholarship, Duke University, USA, 1976–77; DPhil, Research in English Literature, Wadham College, Oxford, 1978–81. *Appointments:* European ed., The Kansas Quarterly and Arkansas Review; Writing Tutor with various institutions. *Publications:* Aquarium, 1983; Salt, 1985; Black Faces, Red Mouths, 1986; The Genre of Silence, 1987; Glass Shot, 1991; Masks, 1994; The Hook, 1997; Midway, 1998. Editor: On Censorship, 1985. *Contributions to:* BBC and periodicals. *Honours:* Eric Gregory Award for Poetry, 1978; Barbara Campion Memorial Award for Poetry, 1982; Welsh Arts Council Prizes for Poetry; Arts Council of Wales Book of the Year, 1995. *Memberships:* Welsh Acad.; Society of Authors. *Literary Agent:* Peters, Fraser & Dunlop, London, England. *Address:* Godre Waun Oleu, Brecon Rd, Ynyswen, Penycae, Powys SA9 1YY, Wales.

BUSHE, Paddy; b. 18 Aug. 1948, Dublin, Ireland. Writer; Poet. m. Fiona Ni Chinnsealaigh, 26 Dec. 1970, 1 d. *Education:* BA, University College Dublin, 1969. *Publications:* Poems with Amergin, 1989; Teanga, 1990; Counsellor, 1991. *Contributions to:* Cyphers; Poetry Ireland Review; Great Book of Ireland; Arvon International Anthology; Irish University Review; Labour Party Congress Journal; Steeple Salmon; others. *Honours:* Specially Commended, Arvon Competition, 1987; Runner-up, Patrick Kavanagh Award, 1988; Poetry Prize, Listowel Writers' Week, 1990. *Memberships:* Poetry Ireland; Irish Writers' Union; Poetry Society, London. *Address:* Cliff Rd, Waterville, Co Kerry, Ireland.

BUSHNO, Lila Joan Goyer; b. 9 Aug. 1931, Pomona, MO, USA. Poet. m. John J. Bushno, 1954, 3 s., 4 d. *Education:* AA, 1980, AS, 1989, Black Hawk College. *Contributions to:* Many anthologies, newspapers and magazines. *Honours:* Golden Poets Awards, 1985–90; Ed.'s Choice, 1988; Poet of Merit, 1988; Poet of the Year, International Society of Poets; World Parnassian Guild International, hon. mem.; Ed.'s Choice Award, National Library of Poetry. *Address:* 714 E Fifth St, Kewanee, IL 61443, USA.

BUTLER, Allen Todd, (Cool Al); b. 6 May 1961, Portsmouth, Virginia, USA. Poet; Songwriter. *Education:* BS, Norfolk State University, 1985. *Contributions to:* Anthologies, reviews, and magazines. *Honours:* Golden Poet Awards, 1989–91. *Memberships:* Creative Writers Club, vice-pres.; National Writers Club. *Address:* 1273 W 27th St, Norfolk, VA 23508, USA.

BUTLER, Michael David; b. 18 Sept. 1931, London, England. Poet. m. Veronica Helen Freudenberg, 15 May 1971, 1 s., 2 d. *Education:* MA, English Literature, Jesus College, Oxford, 1953. *Appointments:* Mem. of Order of Friars Minor Capuchin, 1955–69; Ordained Priest, 1963; Worker Priest, Layman, 1966–73; Part-time Teacher of English Literature, The City Lit, London, 1973–76; Part-time Teacher of English as a Foreign Language, then Adult Literacy, Holloway AEI, 1974–79. *Publication:* Street and Sky, 1980. *Contributions to:* Orbis; Iron; Stride; Voices; South; Doors. *Membership:* Poetry Society. *Address:* 29 Cattistock Rd, Maiden Newton, Dorchester, Dorset DT2 0AG, England.

BUTLER, Michael Gregory; b. 1 Nov. 1935, Nottingham, England. Prof. of Modern German Literature; Writer; Poet. m. Jean Mary Griffith, 31 Dec. 1961, 1 s., 1 d. *Education:* BA, 1957, MA, 1960, Cambridge University; DipEd, Oxford University, 1958; FIL, 1967; PhD (CNAA), 1974; Litt.D., Cambridge University, 1998. *Appointments:* Asst Master, King's School, Worcester, 1958–61, Reuchlin Gymnasium, Pforzheim, Germany, 1961–62; Head of German, Ipswich School, England, 1962–70; Lecturer in German, 1970–80, Senior Lecturer, 1980–86, Head, Dept of German Studies, 1984, Prof. of Modern German Literature, 1986–, Head, School of Modern Languages, 1988–93, Public Orator, 1997–, University of Birmingham. *Publications:* Nails and Other Poems, 1967; Samphire (co-ed.), 3 vols, 1968–83; The Novels of Max Frisch, 1975; Englische Lyrik der Gegenwart (ed. with Ilsabe Arnold Dielewicz), 1981; The Plays of Max Frisch, 1985; Frisch: 'Andorra', 1985; Rejection and Emancipation - Writing in German-speaking Switzerland 1945–1991 (ed. with M Pender), 1991; The Narrative Fiction of Heinrich Böll (ed.), 1994; The Making of Modern Switzerland, 1948–1998 (ed.) 2000; The Challenge of German Culture (ed.), 2000. *Contributions to:* Migrant; Mica (California); Poetry Review; BBC; Sceptre Press; Vagabond (Munich); Universities Poetry. *Honour:* Taras Schevchenko Memorial Prize, 1961; Cross of the Order of Merit, Federal Republic of Germany, 1999. *Address:* 45 Westfields, Catshill, Bromsgrove B61 9HJ, England.

BUTLIN, Ron; b. 17 Nov. 1949, Edinburgh, Scotland. Poet; Writer. m. Regula Staub, 18 June 1993. *Education:* MA, DipCDAE, University of Edinburgh. *Appointments:* Writer-in-Residence, University of Edinburgh, 1983, 1985, Midlothian Region, 1990–91, Craigmillar Literary Trust, 1997–98, University of St Andrews, 1998–; Writer-in-Residence, 1993, Examiner in Creative Writing, 1997–, Stirling University. *Publications:* Creature Tamed by Cruelty, 1979; The Exquisite Instrument, 1982; The Tilting Room, 1984; Ragtime in Unfamiliar Bars, 1985; The Sound of My Voice, 1987; Faber Book of Twentieth Century Scottish Poetry (ed.), 1992; Histories of Desire, 1995; Night Visits, 1997; When We Jump We Jump High! (ed.), 1998; Our Piece of Good Fortune, 2002; Panther Book of Scottish Short Stories (ed.). *Contributions to:* Reviews, periodicals and journals. *Honours:* Writing Bursaries, 1977, 1987, 1990, 1994; Scottish Arts Council Book Awards, 1982, 1984, 1985; Scottish-Canadian Writing Fellow, 1984; Poetry Book Society Recommendation, 1985. *Membership:* Scottish Arts Council, literature committee, 1995–96. *Address:* 7W Newington Pl., Edinburgh EH9 1QT, Scotland.

BUTOR, Michel (Marie François); b. 14 Sept. 1926, Mons-en-Baroeul, Nord, France. Author; Poet; Prof. m. Marie-Josephe Mas, 22 Aug. 1958, 4 d. *Education:* Licence en philosophie, 1946, Diplôme d'études supérieures de philosophie, 1947, Sorbonne, University of Paris; Docteur es Lettres, Université of Tours, 1972. *Appointments:* Assoc. Prof., University of Vincennes, 1969, University of Nice, 1970–73; Prof. of Modern French Language and Literature, University of Geneva, 1973–91; Visiting Professorships in the USA. *Publications:* Passage de Milan, 1954; L'Emploi du temps, 1956, English trans. as Passing Time, 1960; La Modification, 1957, English trans. as Change of Heart, 1959; La Génie du lieu, 5 vols, 1958, 1971, 1978, 1988, 1995; Degrés, 1960, English trans. as Degrees, 1961; Répertoire, 5 vols, 1960, 1964, 1968, 1974, 1982; Histoire extraordinaire: Essai sur un rêve de Baudelaire, 1961, English trans. as Histoire extraordinaire: Essay on a Dream of Baudelaire's, 1969; Mobile: Étude pour une representation des Etats-Unis, 1962, English trans. as Mobile: Study for a Representation of the United States, 1963; Description de San Marco, 1963, English trans. as Description of San Marco, 1983; Illustrations, 4 vols, 1964, 1969, 1973, 1976; 6,810,00 litres d'eau par seconde: Étude stéréophonique, 1965, English trans. as Niagara, 1969; Essai sur 'Les Essais', 1968; La Rose des vents: 32 rhumbs pour Charles Fourier, 1970; Matière de rêves, 5 vols, 1975, 1976, 1977, 1981, 1985; Improvisations sur Flaubert, 1984; Improvisations sur Henri Michaux, 1985; Improvisations sur Rimbaud, 1989; Improvisations sur Michel Butor, 1994; L'Utilité Poétique, 1995; Gyroscope, 1996; Ici et là, 1997; Improvisations sur Balzac, 1998; Entretiens, 1999; Many other vols of fiction, poetry and essays. *Honours:* Chevalier de l'Ordre National du Mérite; Chevalier des Arts et des Lettres; Several literary prizes. *Address:* à l'Ecart, 216 pl. de l'église, 74380 Lucinges, France.

BUTT, Theresa. See: ADAMS, Anna Theresa.

BUTTACI, Salvatore (Amico) M.; b. 12 June 1941, New York, NY, USA. English Teacher; Poet; Document Examiner; Entrepreneur. *Education:* BA, Communication Arts, Seton Hall University, 1965; MBA Marketing, Rutgers Graduate School of Management, 1981; Total Certification in Psychology of Handwriting, Felician College, 1989; Graduate Handwriting Analyst (GHA), highest level handwriting analyst. *Appointments:* English Teacher, 1966–68, 1971–80; Vice-Principal, 1968–70; Principal, 1970–71; Marketing Exec., 1980–91; Document Examiner, 1989–; Teacher, 1992–; Former Ed., New Worlds Unlimited, showcase for new and established poets. *Publications:* Stops and Pauses on the Scrapbook Express, 1974; Grandpa: Memory Poems, 1976; Bread and Tears and 35 other poems, 1986; Promising the Moon, 1998; A Family of Sicilians: Stories and Poems, 1998; Greatest Hits: 1970–2000, 2001. *Contributions to:* Poetry magazines and journals. *Memberships:* Poets and Writers; New Jersey Poetry Society; American Society of Composers, Authors and Publishers; Songwriters' Guild; National Writers' Club. *Address:* 124 Garfield Ave, Lodi, NJ 07644, USA. *E-mail:* sambpoet@yahoo.com.

BYARD, Olivia Elizabeth; b. 23 April 1946, Newport, Gwent, Wales. Writer; Poet; Creative Writing Tutor. m. Aug. 1980, 2 s. *Education:* BA, Queen's University, Kingston, Canada. *Publication:* Peterloo Poets, 1997. *Membership:* Poetry Society. *Address:* Oxford, England. *E-mail:* docbyard@ntl.world.com.

BYRD, Robert James, (Bobby Byrd); b. 15 April 1942, Memphis, Tennessee, USA. Poet; Publisher. m. Lee Merrill Byrd, 2 Dec. 1967, 2 s., 1 d. *Education:* BA, University of Arizona, Tucson, 1965; MA, University of Washington, Seattle, 1967. *Appointment:* Faculty, State University of New York at Albany. *Publications:* Places Is and Memphis Poems, 1971; Here, 1975; Pomegranates, 1984; Get Some Fuses for the House, 1987; On the Transmigration of Souls in El Paso, 1993. *Contributions to:* Blue Mesa Review; Puerto del Sol; Exquisite Corpse; Io; Cayote's Journal; Rolling Stock; Rio Grande Review; From a Window; Longhouse; Bombay Gin; New Dog II; Aethlon: A Journal of Sports Literature; Talking from the Heart; Dead Tree; Starving Artist Times; Truck; The Spirit That Wants Me. *Honours:* National Endowment for the Arts Fellowship, 1990; D H Lawrence Fellowship, 1990. *Memberships:* PEN West; Rio Grande Writers' Asscn, pres., 1984. *Address:* c/o Dept of English, State University of New York at Albany, 1400 Washington, Albany, NY 12222, USA.

C

CABRAL DEL HOYO, Roberto; b. 7 Aug. 1913, Mexico. Poet. m. Alicia Bowling, 1944, 3 s., 2 d. *Education:* Bachillerato, Instituto de Ciencias, Zacatecas. *Appointments:* Various positions, cultural programmes, radio and TV stations; Editorial positions, Fondo de Cultura Economica and Reader's Digest of Mexico. *Publications:* De tu amor y de tu olvido y otros poemas, 1948; Por merecer la gracia, 1950; Contra el oscuro viento, 1959; Tres de sus palabras, 1962; Palabra, 1964; Potra de nacar, 1966; De mis raices en la tierra, 1968; Rastro en la arena, 1970; Poetic Works, 1940–80, 1980; Estas cosas que escribo, 1988; Camino caminado, 1991; Codicilos, 1992. *Contributions to:* Various national newspapers and magazines, including Excelsior, El Universal, El Nacional, Novedades, Universitarios. *Honours:* Various prizes, national literary competitions. *Membership:* PEN Mexico. *Address:* Cerrada do Calyecac 19-4, Campestre, San Angel, México, DF 01040, Mexico.

CABRAL (KURTZ), Olga (Marie); b. 14 Sept. 1909, Trinidad. Poet; Writer. m. Aaron Samuel Kurtz, 27 June 1951, deceased. *Education:* Several art courses, New School for Social Research, New York, 1961–62. *Appointments:* Co-Owner, Little Art Centre, Brooklyn, New York, 1950–56; Owner and Man., French-American Art Gallery, Long Beach, New York, 1958–66. *Publications:* Cities and Deserts, 1959; The Evaporated Man, 1968; Tape Found in a Bottle, 1971; Occupied Country, 1976; The Darkness in My Pockets, 1976; In the Empire of Ice, 1980; The Green Dream, 1990; Voice/Over: Selected Poems, 1993. *Contributions to:* 36 anthologies in the US and Europe, including: We Believe in Humanity; A Geography of Poets; We Become New; Poems by Contemporary American Women; For Neruda, For Chile; From the Belly of the Shark; Imaginative Literature; Also 40 literary journals. *Honours:* Emily Dickinson Award, 1971; Lucille Medwick Award, 1976, Poetry Society of America. *Memberships:* Poetry Society of America; Authors Guild; Authors League of America. *Address:* 463 West St, Apt H-523, New York, NY 10014, USA.

CABRINETY, Patricia Ann Butler; b. 4 Sept. 1932, Earlville, New York, USA. Writer; Poet; Illustrator; Inventor; Teacher; Company Pres. m. Lawrence P Cabrinety, 20 Aug. 1955, 1 s., 2 d. *Education:* BS, Education and Music; AS, Paralegal. *Publications:* Charis Series; Songs. *Contributions to:* World of Poetry; Editor's Desk; Vantage Press; All Seasons of Poetry; Poetry Centre; American Press; WPBS Poetry. *Honours:* 5 Golden Poet Awards; 2 Vantage Press International Awards; Numerous Honorable Mentions with Award of Publication; 2 Awards, Parnassus of Parnassus of World Poets, India. *Memberships:* American Management Asscn; American Professional and Executive Women; National Writers Asscn of University Women; National Writers Asscn; National Female Executives; Computer History Institute for the Preservation of Software; National Notary Asscn; National Asscn of Legal Assts. *Address:* 925 Pearl Hill Rd, Fitchburg, MA 01420, USA.

CADDEL, Richard Ivo; b. 13 July 1949, Bedford, England. Librarian; Poet; Writer; Critic. Ed. m. Ann Barker, 31 Aug. 1971, 1 s., deceased, 1 d. *Education:* BA, University of Newcastle, 1971; Newcastle Polytechnic, 1971–72; ALA, 1974. *Appointments:* Staff, University of Durham Library, 1972–2000; Dir, Pig Press, 1973–2001, Basil Bunting Poetry Centre, 1989–. *Publications:* Sweet Cicely, 1983; Uncertain Time, 1990; 26 New British Poets (ed.), 1991; Basil Bunting: Uncollected Poems (ed.), 1991; Basil Bunting: Three Essays, 1994; Basil Bunting: Complete Poems (ed.), 1994; Ground, 1994; Sharp Study and Long Toil (ed.), 1995; Basil Bunting: A Northern Life (with Anthony Flowers), 1997; Larksong Signal, 1997; British and Irish Poetry since 1970 (ed. with Peter Quartermain), 1998; Underwriter, 1999; For the Fallen, 2000; Magpie Words: Selected Poems 1970–2000, 2002. *Contributions to:* Poems and criticism in numerous magazines and periodicals. *Honours:* Northern Arts Writers Awards, 1985, 1988, 1990; Fund for Poetry Award, 1992, 2000; Northern Writers Award, 2002. *Address:* 7 Cross View Terrace, Nevilles Cross, Durham, DH1 4JY, England.

CAHILL, Mike. See: NOLAN, William F(rancis).

CAHIT, Neriman; b. 21 May 1937, Kirni, Cyprus. Journalist; Writer; Poet. m. Ahmet Gursel, 6 Sept. 1959, divorced 1980, 1 s., 1 d. *Education:* Diploma, Teachers Training Centre, 1957. *Publications:* Distress That is Knotted, 1988; KTOS Struggle History (The history of the Turkish Cypriot Teachers' Trade Union), 2 vols 1988–91; Our Children and Sexuality, 1990; Subject Woman, 1990; Aysefari (A Journey to the Moon): Poems, 1995; Ziya Rizki (biography), 1996; A Journey to Death (biography), 1996; Walking for Independence, 1998; Anasu: Motherly Soul (poems), 2000; Guldamlasi: The Deep Side of Women, 2001; Old Nicosia Coffees, 2001. *Contributions to:* Nacak; Soz; Halkin Sesi; Bozkurt; Kibris Postasi; Ortam; Besparmak; 502; Poet; World Poetry; Newspapers and magazines. *Honours:* Nine prizes in journalism and/or literature. *Memberships:* Cyprus Turkish Artist and Writers Union; World Acad. of Arts and Culture; Teacher's Trade Union; Women Research Centre, Founder; Journalists' Asscn; Greenpeace; Conflict Resolution Studies, Cyprus.

Address: 51 Ogretmenler Cad, Ogretmen Evleri, Ortakoxy Lefkosa, Mersin 10 Turkey.

CAIMBEUL, Maoilios MacAonghais; b. 23 March 1944, Isle of Skye Scotland. Writer; Poet. m. Margaret Hutchison, 2 Dec. 1971, 1 s. *Education* BA, Edinburgh University; Teaching Diploma, Jordanhill College, Glasgow 1978. *Publications:* Eileanan, 1980; Bailtean, 1987; A Caradh an Rathaid, 1988 An Aghaidh na Siorraidheachd (anthology with 7 other Gaelic poets), 1991 *Contributions to:* Gairm; Lines Review; Chapman; Cencrastus; Orbis; Poetry Ireland Review; Comhar; Gairfish; Baragab; Weekend Scotsman; West Highland Free Press; Anthologies: Air Ghleus 2, 1989; Twenty of the Best 1990; The Patched Fool, 1991; Somhairle, Dain is Deilbh, 1991. *Honours* Award, Gaelic Books Council Poetry Competition, 1978–79; Poetry/Fiction Prize, Gaelic Books Council, 1982–83. *Membership:* Scottish PEN. *Address* 12 Na Dunanan, Stamhain, An t-Eilean Sgitheanach IV51 9HZ, Scotland.

CAIRD, Janet Hinshaw; b. 24 April 1913, Livingstonia, Malawi. Poet. m James Bowman Caird, 19 July 1938, 2 d. *Education:* MA Honours, English Literature, University of Edinburgh, 1935; University of Grenoble and Sorbonne, University of Paris, 1935–36; St George's College, Edinburgh 1935–36. *Publications:* Some Walk a Narrow Path, 1977; Distant Urn, 1983 John Donne You Were Wrong, 1988. *Contributions to:* Glasgow Herald; Lines Review; Chapman. *Memberships:* Poetry Society, London; Scottish Poetry Library; Asscn of Scottish Literary Studies; Society of Antiquaries of Scotland. *Address:* 1 Drummond Crescent, Inverness IV2 4QW, Scotland.

CALCAGNO, Anne; b. 14 Nov. 1957, San Diego, CA, USA. Assoc. Prof. of English; Writer; Poet. m. Leo, 1986, 1 s., 1 d. *Education:* BA, English, Williams College, 1979; MFA, Fiction and Poetry, University of Montana, 1984. *Appointments:* Part-time Lecturer, North Park College and American Conservatory of Music, Chicago, 1989–91; Teacher, School of the Art Institute of Chicago, 1990–93; Artist-in-Education, Illinois Arts Council, 1992–93; Lecturer, 1992–93, Assoc. Prof. of English, 1993–, DePaul University. *Publications:* Pray for Yourself (short stories), 1993; Travelers Tales, Italy (ed.), 1998. *Contributions to:* Anthologies and periodicals. *Honours:* National Endowment for the Arts Creative Writing Fellowship, 1989; Illinois Arts Council Artists Fellowship, 1993; James D. Phelan Literary Award, San Francisco Foundation, 1993; Silver Medal, ForeWord Travel Book of the Year, 1999; Ed.'s Choice Award, Journey Woman, 1999. *Memberships:* Associated Writing Programs; Authors' Guild; Poets and Writers. *Address:* c/o Dept of English, DePaul University, 802 W Belden Ave, Chicago, IL 60614-3214, USA.

CALDER, Angus Lindsay Ritchie; b. 5 Feb. 1942, Sutton, Surrey, England. Writer; Poet. m. (1) Jenni Daiches, (2) Kate Kyle, 2 s., 2 d. *Education:* MA, King's College, Cambridge, 1960–63; DPhil, University of Sussex, 1963–68. *Appointments:* Lecturer in Literature, University of Nairobi, 1968–71; Staff Tutor in Arts, Open University in Scotland, 1979–93; Visiting Prof. of English, University of Zimbabwe, 1992; Ed., Journal of Commonwealth Literature. *Publications:* The People's War: Britain, 1939–1945, 1969; Russia Discovered: Nineteenth Century Fiction, 1976; Revolutionary Empire: The Rise of the English - Speaking Empires, 1981; The Myth of the Blitz, 1991; Revolving Culture: Notes From the Scottish Republic, 1994; Waking in Waikato (poems), 1997; Horace in Tollcross (poems), 2000; Scotlands of the Mind, 2002; Colours of Grief (poems), 2002. *Contributions to:* Cencrastus; Chapman; Herald; London Review of Books; New Statesman; Scotland on Sunday. *Honours:* Eric Gregory Award, 1967; John Llewellyn Rhys Memorial Prize, 1970; Scottish Arts Council Book Awards, 1981, 1994; Scottish Arts Council Writer's Bursary, 2002. *Membership:* Scottish PEN. *Address:* 15 Spittal St, Edinburgh EH3 9DY, Scotland.

CALDER, Robert Russell; b. 22 April 1950, Burnbank, Scotland. Writer; Poet; Ed.; Critic. *Education:* Glasgow University, 1967–71; Edinburgh University, 1972–74; MA, Philosophy, History, 1973. *Appointments:* Co-Ed., 1973–76, Assoc. Ed., 1988–, Chapman; Ed., Lines Review, 1976–77. *Publications:* Il Re Giovane, 1972; Serapion, 1996. *Contributions to:* PN Review; NER; Edinburgh Review; Poetry Ireland; Chapman; Others. *Address:* 23 Glenlee St, Burnbank, Hamilton, Lanarkshire ML3 9JB, Scotland.

CALDWELL, Grant; b. 6 March 1947, Melbourne, Vic., Australia. Writer; Poet; Teacher. *Appointments:* Ed.-Publisher, MEUSE art and literature magazine. 1980–82; Teacher, Victoria College of the Arts, University of Melbourne, 1995–2000. *Publications:* Poetry: The Screaming Frog That Ralph Ate, 1979; The Bells of Mr Whippy, 1982; The Nun Wore Sunglasses, 1984; The Life of a Pet Dog, 1993; You Know What I Mean, 1996. Other: The Revolt of the Coats (short stories), 1988; Malabata (autobiography), 1991. *Contributions to:* Anthologies, newspapers and magazines. *Honour:* Short-listed for Book of the

Year, The Age, 1996. *Address:* c/o Hale and Iremonger, 19 Eve St, Erskineville, NSW 22043, Australia.

CALDWELL, Robert Francis; b. 7 March 1931, Greenwich, CT, USA. Government Civil Servant (retd); Minister; Poet. *Education:* DPsy, 1961; MsD, 1965; Dip of Naturopathy, 1967; PhD, 1968. *Publication:* A Poet's Reflections, 1993. *Contributions to:* Anthologies and periodicals. *Honours:* Several awards, honorable mentions, and certificates. *Memberships:* International Society of Poets, life mem.; National Asscn of Retd Federal Employees; National Authors Registry; Poets and Writers; South Florida Poetry Institute. *Address:* Griffwood Mobile Home Park, Picciola Rd 03896-132, Fruitland Park, FL 34731, USA.

CALIBAN. See: KNELL, William.

CALLAGHAN, Barry; b. 5 July 1937, Toronto, Ontario, Canada. Writer; Poet; Ed.; Publisher; Trans.; College Teacher. 1 s. *Education:* BA, 1960, MA, 1962, St Michael's College, University of Toronto. *Appointments:* Teacher, Atkinson College, York University, Toronto, 1965–; Literary Ed., Telegram, Toronto, 1966–71; Host and Documentary Producer, Weekend, CBC-TV, 1969–72; Founder-Publisher, Exile, 1972–, Exile Editions, 1976–; Writer-in-Residence, University of Rome, 1987. *Publications:* Poetry: The Hogg Poems and Drawings, 1978; As Close As We Came, 1982; Stone Blind Love, 1987; Hogg: The Poems and Drawings, 1997; Hogg, Seven Last Words, 2001. Fiction: The Black Queen Stories, 1982; The Way the Angel Spreads Her Wings, 1989; When Things Get Worst, 1993; A Kiss is Still a Kiss, 1995. Non-Fiction: Barrelhouse Kings, 1998. Editor: Various anthologies and books. *Honours:* Many National Magazine Awards; Gold Medal, University of Western Ontario, 1979; Co-Winner, International Authors Festival Award, Harbourfront, Toronto, 1986; Toronto Arts Award, 1993; Hon. Doctor of Letters, State University of New York, 1999. *Address:* 20 Dale Ave, Toronto, Ontario M4W 1K4, Canada.

CALLAWAY, Kathy J; b. 19 Feb. 1943, Springfield, Massachusetts, USA. Writer; Poet; Educator. 1 s. *Education:* BA, 1978, MFA, 1979, University of Montana. *Appointments:* Writer-in-Residence, Asst Prof. of English, Mankato State University, Minnesota, 1982–84; Asst Prof. of English, Moorhead State University, Minnesota, 1987–88; Visiting Asst Prof. of English, University of Alaska/Fairbanks, Nome, AK, 1989–90, 1993; Soros Foundation Fellow to Tartu, Estonia, 1993–94; United Nations Volunteer, Graduate Teacher-Training, North East Agricultural University, Harbin, China, 1995. *Publications:* Heart of the Garfish, (poems), 1982; The Bloodroot Flower (novel), 1982. *Contributions to:* Antaeus; Iowa Review; Ploughshares; Nation; Crazyhorse; Parnassas; Pushcart Prize: V Anthology. *Honours:* PEN New Writer, 1980; Loring Williams Prize for Poetry, 1980; Pushcart Prize, 1982; Agnes Lynch Starrett Award for Poetry, 1982; National Endowment for the Arts Fellowships, 1984, 1990. *Membership:* Poets and Writers.

CAMERON, Esther Beatrice; b. 10 Sept. 1941, New York, NY, USA. Trans.; Poet; Lawyer. *Education:* BA, University of Wisconsin, 1964; MA, 1966, PhD, 1973, University of California at Berkeley; University of Wisconsin Law School, 1993. *Appointment:* Assoc. Prof. of German, State University of New York at Buffalo, 1969–71. *Publications:* A Gradual Light, in Hebrew Translation, 1983; Various collections distributed privately, including: Here and There, 1992. *Contributions to:* Poetry Northwest; Primavera; Gryphon; Jewish Spectator; Ma'Ariv; 'Al Ha-Mishmar; B'Or Hatorah; Seven Gates; Lyris; Orbis; Wisconsin Poets' Calendar; Arc. *Honours:* Peter Schwiefert Poetry Prize, 1985; Orbis Rhyme International Contest, First Prize in Formal Poetry Category, 1990. *Memberships:* Israel Asscn of Writers in English; Voices Group, Jerusalem. *Address:* 4414 Rolla Lane, Madison, WI 53711, USA.

CAMERON, Lori Michelle; b. 18 March 1965, Valdosta, GA, USA. English Prof.; Ed.; Poet. m. Brian S Cameron, 30 July 1994. *Education:* AA, Religion, 1986; BA, Writing, 1988; MA, English, 1992. *Appointments:* English Instructor, Chaffey College, 1992–94; English Prof., DeVry Institute of Technology, 1995–; Ed., Penwood Review, 1996–. *Contributions to:* Spring Harvest; Thalia: Studies in Literary Humor; At Water's Edge; Best Poems of 1996. *Honours:* Third Place, National Library of Poetry Annual Contest, 1995; Ed.'s Choice Awards, National Library of Poetry, 1995, 1996. *Address:* 3910 Howard Ave, Los Alamitos, CA 90720, USA.

CAMNER, Howard; b. 14 Jan. 1957, Miami, FL, USA. English Teacher; Writer; Poet. m., 2 c. *Education:* BA, English, Florida International University, 1982. *Appointments:* English Teacher; Screen Writer; Producer and Host of cable TV talk show; New York Performance Poet. *Publications:* Notes From the Eye of a Hurricane, 1979; Transitions, 1980; Scattered Shadows, 1980; Road Note Elegy, 1980; A Work in Progress, 1981; Poetry From Hell to Breakfast, 1981; Midnight at the Laundromat and Other Poems, 1983; Hard Times on Easy Street, 1987; Madman in the Alley, 1989; Stray Dog Wail, 1991; Banned in Babylon, 1993; Jammed Zipper, 1994; Bed of Nails, 1995; Brutal Delicacies, 1996; Hiss, 2000. *Contributions to:* Howling Mantra; New York Magazine; Poet's Voice; Without Halos; Poetry Journal; The Diversifier; Amanda Blue; Eleventh MUSE; Louder Than Bombs; Cuthbert's Treasury; Gathering Stars; Poetpourri; Palmetto Review; Perceptions; Florida in Poetry; Poems That Thump In the Dark; Tributary; Security Blanket; Fluid Ink Press;

Steel Point Quarterly; Melic Review; Facets; Pedestal Magazine; Poetry: An American Heritage; After the Meeting on Elbe; American Poets 1990's; The Bristol Banner Anthology Series: Report to Hell, 1996, Graffiti off the Asylum Walls, 1996, Crescendo, 1997, Office Chronicles, Obstacles and Laments, 1997. *Honours:* Works included in 100 prominent literary collections worldwide; Nominated for Poet Laureate of Florida, 1980; Inducted into the Last Poets, Hon. Mem., 1980; Fine Arts Press Poetry Award, 1988; Golden Poet Award, 1988; Silver Poet Award, 1989; Inducted into the Homer Honour Society of International Poets, 1992. *Memberships:* Poets and Writers; Acad. of American Poets; Poetry Society of America; South Florida Poetry Institute; Writers' Exchange; National Writers Asscn; Authors Guild. *Address:* 10440 SW 76th St, Miami, FL 33173, USA.

CAMPBELL, Alistair Te Ariki; b. 25 June 1925, Rarotonga, New Zealand. Writer; Poet; Dramatist. m. (1) Fleur Adcock, 1952, (2) Meg Andersen, 1958, 3 s., 2 d. *Education:* BA, Victoria University of Wellington, 1953; Diploma of Teaching, Wellington Teachers' College, 1954. *Appointments:* Senior Ed., New Zealand Council for Educational Research, 1972–87; Writer's Fellow, Victoria University of Wellington, 1992. *Publications:* Poetry: Mine Eyes Dazzle, 1950; Sanctuary of Spirits, 1963; Wild Honey, 1964; Blue Rain, 1967; Kapiti: Selected Poems, 1972; Dreams, Yellow Lions, 1975; The Dark Lord of Savaiki, 1980; Collected Poems, 1981; Soul Traps, 1985; Stone Rain: The Polynesian Strain, 1992; Death and the Tagua, 1995; Pocket Collected Poems, 1996; Gallipoli and Other Poems, 1999; Maori Battalion, 2001. Fiction: The Frigate Bird, 1989; Sidewinder, 1991; Tia, 1993; Fantasy with Witches, 1998. Autobiography: Island to Island, 1984. Plays: The Suicide, 1965; When the Bough Breaks, 1970. *Contributions to:* Landfall; New Zealand Listener; Poetry New Zealand; New Zealand Poetry Yearbook; Comment; Poetry Australia. *Honours:* Gold Medal for TV documentary, La Spezia International Film Festival, 1974; New Zealand Book Award for Poetry, 1982; Pacific Islands Artists Award, 1998; Hon. D.Litt, 1999. *Membership:* PEN International, New Zealand Centre. *Address:* 4B Rawhiti Rd, Pukerua Bay, Wellington, New Zealand.

CAMPBELL, Donald; b. 25 Feb. 1940, Caithness, Scotland. Poet; Dramatist. m. Jean Fairgrieve, 1966, 1 s. *Appointments:* Writer-in-Residence, Edinburgh Education Dept, 1974–77, Royal Lyceum Theatre, 1981–82. *Publications:* Poetry: Poems, 1971; Rhymes 'n Reasons, 1972; Murals: Poems in Scots, 1975; Blether: A Collection of Poems, 1979; A Brighter Sunshine, 1983; An Audience for McGonagall, 1987; Selected Poems 1870–90, 1990. Other: Plays for stage, radio and television. *Address:* 85 Spottiswood St, Edinburgh EH9 1BZ, Scotland.

CAMPBELL, George; b. 26 Dec. 1916, Panama (Jamaican citizen). Poet. m. Odilia Crane, 1948, 4 d. *Education:* St George's College, Kingston. *Publications:* First Poems, 1945; Earth Testament, 1983. *Address:* c/o Garland Publishing, 136 Madison Ave, New York, NY 10016, USA.

CAMPBELL, Rona Mary; b. 7 Oct. 1945, Chichester, England. Poet; Singer. m. (1) 1967, divorced 1970, 2 s., 1 d., (2) Roderick Campbell, 1972, divorced 1992. *Education:* Finals in Singing, Theory and General Musicianship, Cardiff College of Music and Drama, 1963–68; Studied Drama, Spanish, Italian, some German. *Appointments:* Principal Soprano, Metropolitana Opera de Caracas, Venezuela; Dir, The Third Room, Performance, Poetry Venue, Everyman Bistro, Everyman Theatre, 1988–91; Singing Teacher, Natural Health Centre, Liverpool, 1992; Founder, Dir, Central Acad. of Singing, Liverpool, 1994, Voice Link, Liverpool, 1994. *Publications:* The Hedge, 1988. Contributions to anthologies, radio, television and periodicals. *Honour:* Runner-up (from 44,000 entrants), Sotheby's International Poetry Competition, 1982. *Memberships:* Poetry Society; Aldeburgh Poetry; Friend of the Arvon Foundation; Asscn of Teachers of Singing; Voicecare Network UK. *Address:* 19 Elmsley Rd, Mossley Hill, Liverpool L18 8AY, England.

CAMPEDELLI, Giancarlo, (Rudy de Cadaval); b. 1 Jan. 1933, Verona, Italy. Writer; Poet. m. Grazia Corsini, 31 March 1962, 1 s., 1 d. *Publications:* Over 10 poetry collections, 1959–2000. *Contributions to:* Various publications in Europe and the USA. *Honours:* 10 national poetry prizes, 1959–90; Four international poetry prizes, 1959–94; Knight, Grand Officer of the Order of Merit, Republic of Italy, 1989; Knight Commander, Sovereign Order of St John of Jerusalem, 1990. *Memberships:* Several Italian and foreign literary organizations. *Address:* G. Gioacchina Belli 2, 37124 Verona, Italy.

CAMPION, Dan(iel Ray); b. 23 Aug. 1949, Oak Park, IL, USA. Ed.; Poet; Literary Critic. Companion of JoAnn E Castagna. *Education:* AB, University of Chicago, 1970; MA, University of Illinois, Chicago, 1975; PhD, University of Iowa, 1989. *Appointments:* Production Ed., Encyclopaedia Britannica Inc, Chicago, IL, 1972–74; Children's Book Ed., Follett Publishing Company, Chicago, 1977–78; Teaching and Research Asst, University of Iowa, Iowa City, 1978–84; Test Specialist, Senior Ed., ACT Inc, Iowa City, 1984–. *Publications:* Walt Whitman: The Measure of his Song (co-ed.), 1981; Calypso (poems), 1981; Peter De Vries and Surrealism, 1995. *Contributions to:* Poetry and articles to periodicals, including: College English; Literary Magazine Review; The Writer's Chronicle; Hispanic Journal; Rolling Stone; Chicago Tribune; Chicago Reader; Ascent; Poet Lore; English Journal; Poetry. *Honours:* Festival of the Arts Poetry Award, University of Chicago, 1967; All-

Nations Poetry Contest Award, Triton College, River Grove, IL, 1975; Poetry Award, Illinois Arts Council, 1979. *Memberships:* Authors' Guild; MLA; Midwest MLA; National Council of Teachers of English; Society for the Study of Midwestern Literature. *Address:* 1700 E Rochester Ave, Iowa City, IA 52245, USA.

CANALES, Jacque; b. 18 July 1932, Uncastillo, Zaragoza, Spain. Writer; Poet. m. Manuel Galdeano, 29 March 1962, 2 s., 2 d. *Publications:* Un viento en el espejo, 1985; Entre la transparencia y la música, 1985; Ese perfume de la puerta sellada, 1985; En la piel de la palabra, 1986; La noche y sus sandalias, 1986; Un largo pez de plata, 1987; Nietzsche también se rie, 1987; Colón, presencia entre dos olas, 1987; Safo, 1987; Tiempo de sed, 1988; De vita et moribus, 1989; Urgentes amapolas, 1991. *Contributions to:* Anthologies, newspapers and Journals. *Honours:* Many Spanish and foreign prizes and medals. *Memberships:* Spanish Writers' and Artists' Asscn; National Union of Spanish Writers; Worthy Mem. ad honorem, Cultural Literary and Artistic Centre of Felgueiras, Portugal; Latin-American Acad. of Poetry, general secretary; Nemesis Literary Social Group, co-founder; World Acad. of Arts and Culture, CA. *Address:* c/o Fernando Gabriel, 18-80-E, 28017 Madrid, Spain.

CANAN, Janine; b. 2 Nov. 1942, Los Angeles, CA, USA. Poet. *Education:* BA, Stanford University 1963; University of California, 1963–66; New York University, 1972–76. *Appointments:* Private Psychiatrist, Berkeley, CA, 1979–. *Publications:* Of Your Seed; The Hunger; Daughter; Who Buried the Breast of Dreams; Shapes of Self; Her Magnificent Body; She Rises Like the Sun; Invocation of the Goddess. *Contributions to:* Colorado North Review; Caprice; California Quarterly; Tree Kalliope; New Directions; Conditions; Synapse; Exquisite Corpse; Earth's Daughters; Thesmophoria; Manhattan Poetry Review; No Apologies; We Moon. *Honour:* Swan Koppelman Award. *Membership:* Poetry Society of America. *Address:* 466 Cascade Dr., Fairfax, CA 94930, USA.

CANDEIAS, Marcolino; b. 28 Aug. 1952, Cinco Riberas, Terceira, Azores, Portugal. Exec. Secretary; Poet. m. Valdeci Purim, 22 Sept. 1990, 1 s., 1 d. *Education:* Bachelor in Romanic Philology, University of Coimbra, Portugal, 1978; Grade of Licenciate in Modern Languages and Literatures, Portuguese and French Branch, University of Coimbra, Portugal. *Appointments:* Asst Prof., Linguistics, University of Azores, Portugal, 1979–80; Linguistics, University of Coimbra, Portugal, 1980–86; Lecturer, Portuguese and Brazilian Culture and Portuguese Language, University of Montréal, QC, Canada, 1986–90; Exec. Secretary, General Direction and Board of Dirs, Caisse d'économie des Portugais de Montréal, Montréal, Canada. *Publications:* Por ter escrito Amor, 1971; Na distância deste tempo, 1984. *Contributions to:* Antologia de Poesia Açoriana do Séc, 1975; Antologia de Poesia Açoriana; Sempre disse tais coisas esperançado na vulcanologia; The Sea Within; Pai sua bênçao; Os Nove Rumores do Mar; Cadernos de Literatura; Vértice; New Canadian Review; Correio dos Açores; Diário Insular; A Uniao. *Membership:* Instituto Açoriano de Cultura. *Address:* 4132 Hillcrest, Pierrefonds, QC H9J 1W3, Canada.

CANNELLA, Vincent; b. 19 May 1927, Tampa, FL, USA. Poet; Illustrator. *Education:* Museum of Modern Art School; Janice Franklyn School of Art; Art Student League of New York. *Contributions to:* American Poetry Asscn; Poetry Anthology; Ed.'s Choice; Days of Future Past; Quill Books Chasing Rainbows; Dan River Anthology; American Anthology of Midwestern Poetry; Voices of the South; Tabula Rasa Magazine; Lucidity Quarterly; First Time Publications; Poetry Forum; Kola; Riverun Fall; Wide Open Magazine; Se La Vie Writer's Journal, Aug. 1995. *Address:* 953 E 211th St, New York, NY 10469, USA.

CANNON, Frank. See: MAYHAR, Ardath.

CANNON, Janet; b. 8 Oct. 1945, USA. Poet. 1 d. *Education:* BA, University of Iowa, 1970; MA (clearance), 1972. *Publications:* The Last Night in New York; Percipience. *Contributions to:* Literary journals, pamphlets and periodicals. *Honours:* Honorable Mention, Rio Grande Writers' Asscn Poetry Contest; Kimo Theatre Writing Contest; Honourable Mention, Minimuse Poetry Contest; ASCAP Award. *Memberships:* Poetry Society of America; ASCAP.

CANTALUPO, Charles; b. 17 Oct. 1951, Orange, New Jersey, USA. Prof. of English; Poet; Writer. m. (1) Catherine Musello, 21 Aug. 1976, deceased 1983, 1 s., deceased, (2) Barbara Dorosh, 29 Oct. 1988, 1 s., 3 d. *Education:* University of Kent at Canterbury, 1972; BA, Washington University, St Louis, 1973; MA, 1978, PhD, 1980, Rutgers University. *Appointments:* Teaching Asst, 1973–76, Instructor, 1977–79, Rutgers University; Instructor, 1980–81, Asst Prof., 1981–89, Assoc. Prof., 1989–96, Prof. of English, 1996–, Pennsylvania State University, Schuylkill Haven. *Publications:* The Art of Hope (poems), 1983; A Literary Leviathan: Thomas Hobbe's Masterpiece of Language, 1991; The World of Ngugi wa Thiong'o (ed.), 1995; Poetry, Mysticism, and Feminism: From th' Nave to the Chops, 1995; Ngugi wa Thiong'o: Text and Contexts (ed.), 1995; Anima/l Wo/man and Other Spirits (poems), 1996. *Contributions to:* Books, anthologies, scholarly journals and periodicals. *Honour:* American Acad. of Poets Prize, 1976. *Address:* c/o Dept of English, Pennsylvania State University, 200 University Dr., Schuylkill Haven, PA 17972, USA.

CAO, Xuan Tu; b. 1 Jan. 1943, Hué, Viet Nam. Writer; Trans.; Poet. 1 d. *Education:* BSc, Syracuse University, 1964; MSc, Boston University, 1981. *Publications:* Y Thu Vuon Xuan, English trans. as Autumn Thoughts in Spring Garden, 1965; Vang, English trans. as Gold, 1996; En Traag Vloeit de Rivier, English trans. as And Slowly Flows the River, 1997; Een Ogenblik English translation as Momentarily, 2002. Other: Trans of Dutch authors including Anne Frank, Harry Mullisch, Cees Nooteboom and Helle Haasse into Vietnamese. *Contributions to:* Van Hoc; The KY 21; Hop Luu; Vietnam Review; New Edinburgh Review; De Tweede Ronde; Deus Ex Machina; Onze Wereld. *Honour:* Dunya Prize, Netherlands, 1995. *Membership:* Netherland Union of Writers and Trans. *Address:* Lange Leidsedwarstraat 119, 1017 N. Amsterdam, Netherlands. *E-mail:* caoxuantu@hetnet.nl.

CARDENAL, (Martínez) Ernesto; b. 20 Jan. 1925, Granada, Nicaragua Roman Catholic Priest; Poet. *Education:* University of Mexico, 1944–48; Columbia University, New York, 1948–49. *Appointments:* Roman Catholic Priest, 1965–; Minister of Culture, 1979–90. *Publications:* Proclama del conquistador, 1947; Gethsemani, Ky., 1960; La hora O, 1960; Epigramas Poemas, 1961; Oracion por Marilyn Monroe and Other Poems, 1965; E. estrecho dudoso, 1966; Poemas, 1967; Psalms of Struggle and Liberation, 1967; Mayapan, 1968; Poemas reunidos 1949–69, 1969; Homage to the American Indians, 1969; Zero Hour and Other Documentary Poems, 1971; Poemas, 1971; Canto nacional, 1973; Oraculo sobre Managua, 1973; Poesia escogida, 1975; Apocalypse and Other Poems, 1977; Canto a un pais que nace, 1978; Nueva antologia poetica, 1979; Waslala, 1983; Poesia dela nueva Nicaragua, 1983; Flights of Victory, 1984; With Walker in Nicaragua and Other Early Poems 1949–54, 1985; From Nicaragua with Love: Poems 1976–1986, 1986; Golden UFOS: The Indian Poems, 1992; Cosmic Canticle, 1993. *Honour:* Premio de la Paz Grant, 1980. *Address:* Apartado Postal A-252, Managua, Nicaragua.

CAREW, Jan (Rynveld); b. 24 Sept. 1925, Agricola, Guyana. Prof. Emeritus; Writer; Poet. *Appointments:* Lecturer in Race Relations, University of London Extra-Mural Dept, 1953–57; Writer and Ed., BBC Overseas Service, London, 1954–65; Ed., African Review, Ghana, 1965–66; CBC Broadcaster, Toronto, 1966–69; Senior Fellow, Council of Humanities and Lecturer, Dept of Afro-American Studies, Princeton University, 1969–72; Prof., Dept of African-American Studies, Northwestern University, 1972–87; Visiting Clarence J Robinson Prof. of Caribbean Literature and History, George Mason University, 1989–91; Visiting Prof. of International Studies, Illinois Wesleyan University, 1992–93. *Publications:* Streets of Eternity, 1952; Black Midas, 1958, US edn as A Touch of Midas; 1958; The Last Barbarian, 1961; Green Winter, 1964; University of Hunger, 1966; The Third Gift, 1975; The Origins of Racism and Resistance in the Americas, 1976; Rape of the Sun-people, 1976; Children of the Sun, 1980; Sea Drums in My Blood, 1981; Grenada: The Hour Will Strike Again, 1985; Fulcrums of Change, 1987. *Address:* Dept of African-American Studies, Northwestern University, Evanston, IL 60208, USA.

CARLILE, Henry (David); b. 6 May 1934, San Francisco, CA, USA. Prof. of English; Poet; Writer. 1 d. *Education:* AA, Grays Harbor College, 1958; BA, 1962, MA, 1967, University of Washington. *Appointments:* Instructor, 1967–69, Asst Prof., 1969–72, Assoc. Prof., 1972–78, Prof. of English, 1980–, Portland State University; Visiting Lecturer, Writers Workshop, University of Iowa, 1978–80. *Publications:* The Rough-Hewn Table, 1971; Running Lights, 1981; Rain, 1994. *Contributions to:* Many anthologies, reviews, and journals. *Honours:* National Endowment for the Arts Discovery Grant, 1970, and Fellowship in Poetry, 1976; Devins Award, 1971; PEN Syndicated Fiction Awards, 1983, 1986; Ingram Merrill Poetry Fellowship, 1985; Helen Foundation Award, 1986; Pushcart Prizes, 1986, 1992; Poetry Award, Crazyhorse, 1988; Oregon Arts Commission Literary Fellowship, 1994. *Address:* c/o Dept of English, Portland State University, PO Box 751, Portland, OR 97207, USA.

CARLIN, Vuyelwa Susan; b. 13 Sept. 1949, South Africa. Poet. m. Brian Wigston, 8 March 1969, 1 s., 1 d. *Education:* BA, Bristol University, 1972. *Publications:* Midas' Daughter, 1991; How We Dream of the Dead, 1995. *Contributions to:* Anthologies and periodicals. *Honours:* Third Prize, Cardiff International Poetry Competition, 1988; Prize, National Poetry Competition, 1988. *Memberships:* Poetry Society; Out of Bounds Poetry Group; Anglo-Welsh Poetry Society. *Address:* c/o Seren Books, First Floor, 2 Wyndham St, Bridgend, Mid Glamorgan CF31 1EF, Wales.

CARMEN, Marilyn Elain; b. 23 Nov. 1941, USA. Writer; Poet; Prof. 2 s., 2 d. *Education:* MA, Iowa State University, 1987. *Appointment:* Prof., Community College of Philadelphia, 1991–. *Publication:* Born of the Wind, 1997. *Contributions to:* Paterson Literary Review, 1997. *Honour:* Fellowship, Pennsylvania State Council on the Arts, 1990. *Address:* Community College of Philadelphia, 17th and Springgarden Streets, Philadelphia, PA 19130, USA.

CARMI, T. See: CHARNY, Carmi.

CARMICHAEL, Jack B(lake); b. 31 Jan. 1938, Ravenswood, West Virginia, USA. Writer; Poet; Ed. m. Julie Ann Carmichael, 2 Oct. 1981, 4 d. *Education:* BA, Ohio Wesleyan University, 1959; PhD, Michigan State University, 1964;

Postdoctoral Studies, University of Oregon, 1966–67. *Appointment:* Ed. and Publisher, Dynamics Press, 1990–. *Publications:* Fiction: A New Slain Knight, 1991; Black Knight, 1991; Tales of the Cousin, 1992; Memoirs of the Great Gorgeous, 1992; The Humpty Boys in Michigan, 1996; Here Me America, with other poems and short stories, 1999. *Contributions to:* Poems in anthologies and journals. *Honour:* Outstanding Achievement Award, American Poetry Asscn, 1990. *Membership:* Acad. of American Poets. *Address:* c/o Dynamics Press, 519 S Rogers St, Mason, MI 48854, USA.

CARON, Louis; b. 1942, Sorel, QC, Canada. Author; Poet; Dramatist. *Publications:* L'illusionniste suivi de Le guetteur, 1973; L'emmitouflé, 1977, English trans. as The Draft-Dodger, 1980; Bonhomme sept-heures, 1978; Le canard de bois, 1981; La corne de brume, 1982; Le coup de poing, 1990; La tuque et le béret, 1992; Le bouleau et l'epinette, 1993. Other: Many radio and television plays. *Honours:* Prix Hermes, France, 1977; Prix France-Canada, 1977; Prix Ludger-Duvernay, Société Saint-Jean-Baptiste, Montréal, 1984. *Membership:* Académie des lettres de Québec, 1995–. *Address:* c/o Union des écrivaines et écrivains québécois, La Maison des écrivains, 3492 Ave Laval, Montréal, QC H2X 3C8, Canada.

CARPATHIOS, Neil Emmanuel; b. 4 March 1961, Columbus, Ohio, USA. English Teacher; Adjunct Prof.; Poet. m. Danielle Marie Cacioppo, 28 Dec. 1989. *Education:* BA, Ohio State University, 1983; MFA, University of Iowa, 1986; University of Akron, 1988. *Publications:* Its Own Kind of Beauty, 1989; I the Father, 1993. *Contributions to:* Kansas Quarterly; Sun; South Coast Poetry Journal; Stone Country; Plain Song; Albany Review; Ohio Journal; Poetry Magazine. *Honours:* Pushcart Prize; Ohio Arts Council Community of Poets Award; Ohio Arts Council, Poetry in the Park. *Address:* 7954 Daytona NW, Masillon, OH 44646, USA.

CARPENTER, Carol Maureen; b. 9 Nov. 1943, Highland Park, Michigan, USA. Writer; Poet; Instructional Designer. m. Mack L Carpenter, 5 April 1963, 1 s., 1 d. *Education:* BS, 1966, MEd, 1972, DEd, 1984, Wayne State University. *Appointments:* English Teacher, Detroit Public School, 1966–71; English Instructor, Oakland Community College, 1971–73; Program Co-Ordinator, Instructor, Detroit Institute of Technology, 1974–80; Curriculum Developer, Oakland University, 1980–81; Creative Man., Planning, Sandy Corp, 1982–85; Founder, Owner, Pres., The High Performance Group Inc, 1985–99. *Contributions to:* Wisconsin Review; Indiana Review; Bellingham Review; Writer's Forum; Cape Rock. *Honours:* Tompkins Awards, Graduate Division, 1979, 1980; First Place, Poetry, Writers Digest Annual Competition, 1992. *Address:* 10005 Berwick, Livonia, MI 48150, USA.

CARPENTER, John Randell; b. 14 April 1936, Cambridge, Massachusetts, USA. Writer; Poet; Trans.; Ed.; Teacher. m. Bogdana Maria-Magdalena Chetkowska, 15 April 1963, 1 s., 1 d. *Education:* BA, Harvard College, 1958; Sorbonne, University of Paris, 1962–66. *Publications:* Gathering Water; Egret; Pebble, Cedar, Star; Trans. of poetry. *Contributions to:* New York Times; The New Yorker; The New York Review of Books; Quarterly Review of Literature; Southwest Review; Minnesota Review; Epoch; Perspective; Mister Cogito; Penny Dreadful; Cafe Solo; Slant; Embers; Poet Lore; The Humanist. *Honours:* Writter Bynner Poetry Award; Islands and Continents Trans. Award; Andrew Mellon Foundation Award; National Endowment for the Arts Fellowships. *Memberships:* Acad. of American Poets; PEN; Poets and Writers. *Address:* 1606 Granger Ave, Ann Arbor, MI 48104, USA.

CARPENTER, Lucas; b. 23 April 1947, Elberton, GA, USA. Prof. of English; Writer; Poet; Ed. m. Judith Leidner, 2 Sept. 1972, 1 d. *Education:* BS, College of Charleston, 1968; MA, University of North Carolina at Chapel Hill, 1973; PhD, State University of New York at Stony Brook, 1982. *Appointments:* Instructor, State University of New York at Stony Brook, 1973–78; Instructor, 1978–80, Assoc. Prof. of English, 1980–85, Suffolk Community College; Editorial Consultant, Prentice-Hall Inc, 1981–; Assoc. Prof. of English, 1985–94, Prof. of English, 1994–, Charles Howard Candler Prof. of English, 2000, Oxford College of Emory University. *Publications:* A Year for the Spider (poems), 1972; The Selected Poems of John Gould Fletcher (ed. with E Leighton Rudolph), 1988; The Selected Essays of John Gould Fletcher (ed.), 1989; John Gould Fletcher and Southern Modernism, 1990; The Selected Correspondence of John Gould Fletcher (ed. with E Leighton Rudolph), 1996; Perils of the Affect (poems), 2002. *Contributions to:* Anthologies, scholarly journals, and periodicals. *Honours:* Resident Fellow in Poetry and Fiction Writing, Hambidge Center for the Creative Arts, 1991; Oxford College Prof. of the Year Awards, 1994, 1996; Fulbright Distinguished Scholar, Belgium, 1999. *Memberships:* National Council of Teachers of English; Poetry Atlanta; Poetry Society of America; Southeast MLA. *Address:* c/o Dept of English, Oxford College of Emory University, Oxford, GA 30267, USA.

CARPENTER, William; b. 31 Oct. 1940, USA. Writer; Teacher; Poet. 2 s. *Education:* BA, Dartmouth College, 1962; PhD, University of Minnesota, 1969. *Appointments:* Asst Prof., University of Chicago, IL, 1967–72; Faculty Mem., College of the Atlantic, 1972–. *Publications:* The Hours of Morning; Rain; Speaking Fire At Stones; A Keeper of Sheep; The Wooden Nickel, 2002. *Contributions to:* American Poetry Review; Poetry; New England Review. *Honours:* Associated Writing Programs Award; National Endowment for the

Arts Fellowship; Samuel French Morse Prize. *Address:* Box 1297, Stockton Springs, ME 04981, USA.

CARR, Sally; b. 5 Feb. 1948, Runcorn, Cheshire, England. Poet. m. Michael Carr, 15 Aug. 1970, 1 s., 1 d. *Education:* BA, English and American Literature, University of Kent, 1969; Dip Ed, University of Bath, 1970. *Publications:* Electrons on Bonfire Night, 1997; Handing on the Genes, 2002. *Contributions to:* Periodicals. *Memberships:* Poetry Society; Friends of Arvon. *Address:* Glebe House, Grittleton, Chippenham, Wilts SN14 6AP, England.

CARRIER, Roch; b. 13 May 1937, Sainte-Justine-de-Dorchester, QC, Canada. Author; Dramatist; Poet. m. Diane Gosselin, 1959, 2 d. *Education:* Collège Saint-Louis; BA, MA, University of Montréal; Doctoral Studies, Sorbonne, University of Paris. *Appointments:* Secretary-General, Théatre du Nouveau Monde, Montréal; Teacher, Collège Militaire, St-Jean; Dir, Canada Council, until 1997. *Publications:* Fiction: Jolis deuils, 1964; La guerre, yes sir!, 1968, English trans., 1970; Floralie, ou es-tu?, 1969, English trans. as Floralie, Where Are You?, 1971; Il est par la le soleil, 1970, English trans. as Is it the Sun, Philibert?, 1972; Le deux-millième é'tage, 1973, English trans. as They Won't Demolish Me!, 1974; Le jardin des délices, 1975, English trans. as The Garden of Delights, 1978; Les enfants du bonhomme dans la lune, 1979, English trans. as The Hockey Sweater and Other Stories, 1979; Il n'y a pas de pays sans grand-père, 1979, English trans. as No Country Without Grandfathers, 1981; Les fleurs vivent-elles ailleurs que sur la terre, 1980; La dame qui avait des chaines aux cheville, 1981; De l'amour dans la feraille, 1984, English trans. as Heartbreaks Along the Road, 1987; La fleur et autres personnages, 1985; Prières d'un enfant très très sage, 1988; L'homme dans le placard, 1991; Fin, 1992; The Longest Home Run, 1993; Petit homme tornade, 1996. Plays: La celeste bicyclette, 1980, English trans. as The Celestial Bycycle, 1982; Le cirque noir, 1982; L'ours et le kangourou, 1986. Other: Various poems. *Honours:* Prix Littéraire de la Province de Québec, 1965; Grand Prix Littéraire de la Ville de Montréal, 1980; Québec Writer of the Year, 1981. *Address:* c/o Canada Council, 350 Albert St, PO Box 1047, Ottawa, ON K1P 5V8, Canada.

CARRIER, Warren (Pendleton); b. 3 July 1918, Cheviot, Ohio, USA. University Chancellor (retd); Writer; Poet. m. (1) Marjorie Jane Regan, 3 April 1947, deceased, 1 s., (2) Judy Lynn Hall, 14 June 1973, 1 s. *Education:* Wabash College, 1938–40; AB, Miami University, Oxford, Ohio, 1942; MA, Harvard University, 1948; PhD, Occidental College, 1962. *Appointments:* Founder-Ed., Quarterly Review of Literature, 1943–44; Assoc. Ed., Western Review, 1949–51; Asst Prof., University of Iowa, 1949–52; Assoc. Prof., Bard College, 1953–57; Faculty, Bennington College, 1955–58; Visiting Prof., Sweet Briar College, 1958–60; Prof., Deep Springs College, CA, 1960–62, Portland State University, Oregon, 1962–64; Prof., Chair., Dept of English, University of Montana, 1964–68; Assoc. Dean, Prof. of English and Comparative Literature, Chair., Dept of Comparative Literature, Livingston College, Rutgers University, 1968–69; Dean, College of Arts and Letters, San Diego State University, 1969–72; Vice-Pres., Academic Affairs, University of Bridgeport, CT, 1972–75; Chancellor, University of Wisconsin at Platteville, 1975–82. *Publications:* City Stopped in Time, 1949; The Hunt, 1952; The Cost of Love, 1953; Reading Modern Poetry (co-ed.), 1955; Bay of the Damned, 1957; Toward Montebello, 1966; Leave Your Sugar for the Cold Morning, 1977; Guide to World Literature (ed.), 1980; Literature from the World (co-ed.), 1981; The Diver, 1986; Death of a Chancellor, 1986; An Honorable Spy, 1992; Murder at the Strawberry Festival, 1993; An Ordinary Man, 1997; Death of a Poet, 1999; Risking the Wind, 2000; Justice at Christmas, 2000. *Contributions to:* Periodicals. *Honours:* Award for Poetry, National Foundation for the Arts, 1971; Collady Prize for Poetry, 1986. *Address:* 69 Colony Park Circle, Galveston, TX 77551, USA.

CARROLL, Paul (Donnelly Michael); b. 15 July 1927, Chicago, IL, USA. Prof. of English; Poet; Writer. m. Maryrose Carroll, June 1979, 1 s. *Education:* MA, University of Chicago, 1952. *Appointments:* Poetry Ed., Chicago Review, 1957–59; Ed., Big Table Magazine, 1959–61, Big Table Books, Follett Publishing Company, 1966–71; Visiting Poet and Prof., University of Iowa, 1966–67; Prof. of English, University of Illinois, 1968–. *Publications:* Edward Dahlberg Reader (ed.), 1966; The Young American Poets, 1968; The Luke Poets, 1971; New and Selected Poems, 1978; The Garden of Earthly Delights, 1986; Poems, 1950–1990, 1990. *Contributions to:* Periodicals. *Address:* 1682 N Ada St, Chicago, IL 60622, USA.

CARRUTH, Hayden; b. 3 Aug. 1921, Waterbury, CT, USA. Poet; Writer; Prof. Emeritus. m. (1) Sara Anderson, 14 March 1943, 1 d., (2) Eleanor Ray, 29 Nov. 1952, (3) Rose Marie Dorn, 28 Oct. 1961, 1 s., (4) Joe-Anne McLaughlin, 29 Dec. 1989. *Education:* AB, University of North Carolina, 1943; MA, University of Chicago, 1948. *Appointments:* Ed.-in-Chief, Poetry magazine, 1949–50; Assoc. Ed., University of Chicago Press, 1950–51; Project Administrator, Intercultural Publications Inc, New York City, 1952–53; Poet-in-Residence, Johnson State College, Vermont, 1972–74; Adjunct Prof., University of Vermont, 1975–78; Poetry Ed., Harper's magazine, 1977–83; Prof., 1979–85, 1986–91, Prof. Emeritus, 1991–, Syracuse University; Prof., Bucknell University, 1985–86. *Publications:* Poetry: The Crow and the Heart, 1946–1959, 1959; In Memoriam: G V C, 1960; Journey to a Known Place, 1961; The Norfolk Poems: 1 June to 1 September 1961, 1962; North Winter, 1964; Nothing for Tigers: Poems,

1959–1964, 1965; Contra Mortem, 1967; For You, 1970; The Clay Hill Anthology, 1970; From Snow and Rock, From Chaos: Poems, 1965–1972, 1973; Dark World, 1974; The Bloomingdale Papers, 1975; Loneliness: An Outburst of Hexasyllables, 1976; Aura, 1977; Brothers, I Loved You All, 1978; Almanach du Printemps Vivarois, 1979; The Mythology of Dark and Light, 1982; The Sleeping Beauty, 1983; If You Call This Cry a Song, 1983; Asphalt Georgics, 1985; Lighter Than Air Craft, 1985; The Oldest Killed Lake in North America, 1985; Mother, 1985; The Selected Poetry of Hayden Carruth, 1986; Sonnets, 1989; Tell Me Again How the White Heron Rises and Flies Across the Nacreous River at Twilight Toward the Distant Islands, 1989; Collected Shorter Poems, 1946–1991, 1992; Collected Longer Poems, 1994; Scrambled Eggs and Whiskey: Poems, 1991–1995, 1995; Dr Jazz, 2001. Other: Appendix A (novel), 1963; After 'The Stranger': Imaginary Dialogues with Camus, 1964; Working Papers: Selected Essays and Reviews, 1981; Effluences from the Sacred Caves: More Selected Essays and Reviews, 1984; Sitting In: Selected Writings on Jazz, Blues, and Related Topics, 1986; Beside the Shadblow Tree (memoir), 2000. Editor: A New Directions Reader (with James Laughlin), 1964; The Voice That is Great Within Us: American Poetry of the Twentieth Century, 1970; The Bird/Poem Book: Poems on the Wild Birds of North America, 1970. Contributions to: Various periodicals. Honours; Bess Hokin Prize, 1954; Vachel Lindsay Prize, 1956; Levinson Prize, 1958; Harriet Monroe Poetry Prize, 1960; Bollingen Foundation Fellowship, 1962; Helen Bullis Award, 1962; Carl Sandburg Award, 1963; Emily Clark Balch Prize, 1964; Eunice Tietjens Memorial Prize, 1964; Guggenheim Fellowships, 1965, 1979; Morton Dauwen Zabel Prize, 1967; National Endowment for the Humanities Fellowship, 1967; Governor's Medal, Vermont, 1974; Sheele Memorial Award, 1978; Lenore Marshall Poetry Prize, 1978; Whiting Writers Award, 1986; National Endowment for the Arts Senior Fellowship, 1988; Ruth Lilly Poetry Prize, 1990; National Book Critics Circle Award in Poetry, 1993; National Book Award for Poetry, 1996. Address: RR 1, Box 128, Munnsville, NY 13409, USA.

CARSON, Anne; b. 21 June 1950, Toronto, ON, Canada. Prof. of Classics; Poet; Writer. Education: BA, 1974, MA, 1975, PhD, 1980, University of Toronto. Appointments: Prof. of Classics, University of Calgary, 1979–80, Princeton University, 1980–87, Emory University, 1987–88, McGill University, 1988–. Publications: Eros the Bittersweet: An Essay, 1986; Short Talks, 1992; Plainwater, 1995; Glass, Irony and God, 1995; Autobiography of Red, 1998; Economy of the Unlost, 1999; Men in the Off Hours, 2000; The Beauty of the Husband, 2001; Sophocles Electra 2001. Contributions to: Anthologies and journals. Honours: Lannan Literary Award, 1996; Pushcart Prize for Poetry, 1997; Guggenheim Fellowship, 1999; John D. and Catherine T. MacArthur Foundation Fellowship, 2001; T. S. Eliot Prize, 2002. Address: 5900 Esplanade Ave, Montréal, QC H2T 3A3, Canada.

CARSON, Ciaran; b. 9 Oct. 1948, Belfast, Ireland. Arts Administrator; Poet. m. Deidre Shannon, 16 Oct. 1982, 2 s., 1 d. Education: BA, Queen's University, Belfast. Appointments: Traditional Arts Officer, Arts Council of Northern Ireland, 1975–. Publications: The New Estate; The Irish For No; Belfast Confetti. Contributions to: TLS; New Yorker; Irish Review; Honest Ulsterman; London Review of Books. Honours: Gregory Award; Alice Hunt Bartlett Award; Irish Times/Her Lingus Award. Address: Arts Council of Northern Ireland, 181A Stranmillis Rd, Belfast BT9 5DU, Ireland.

CARSON, Timotheu; b. 8 June 1933, Little Rock, AR, USA. Instructor; Poet. m. Lillian B Carson, 21 Dec. 1957, 1 s. Education: BA, Butler University; Indiana University-Purdue University at Indianapolis; Sorbonne, University of Paris. Publication: Selected Poetry of T H Carson, 1994. Contributions to: Anthologies and journals. Honours: Several awards, citations, and honorable mentions. Memberships: National Authors Registry; National Poetry Registry. Address: 2020 W Farwell, Box 502, Chicago, IL 60645, USA.

CARTER, Cassandra June; b. 10 June 1945, Doncaster, Yorkshire, England. Poet; Scriptwriter; Ed. m. Colin Vancad, 31 July 1975, deceased. Education: BA, University of Queensland, Australia, 1967; MA, Bryn Manor College, 1969; Fulbright Scholar, 1967–69. Contributions to: Maker; Kindred Spirits Quarterly; Moonstone; Age; Australian. Honour: University of Queensland Poetry Prize. Membership: Australian Writers Guild. Address: 12 Diamond St, East Preston, Vic. 3072, Australia.

CARTER, Jared; b. 10 Jan. 1939, Elwood, IN, USA. Poet. m. Diane Haston, 21 June 1979, 1 d. by previous marriage. Education: Yale University; AB, Goddard College, 1969. Publications: Early Warning, 1979; Work, for the Night is Coming, 1981; Fugue State, 1984; Pincushion's Strawberry, 1984; Millennial Harbinger, 1986; The Shriving, 1990; Situation Normal, 1991; Blues Project, 1991; After the Rain, 1993; Sphinx, 1995; Les Barricades Mystérieuses, 1999. Contributions to: Many anthologies and periodicals. Honours: Walt Whitman Award, 1980; Bridgman Fellowship, Bread Loaf Writers Conference, 1981; National Endowment for the Arts Fellowships, 1981, 1991; Great Lakes Colleges Asscn New Writers Award, 1982; Guggenheim Fellowship, 1983; Governor's Arts Award, IN, 1985; New Letters Literary Award for Poetry, 1992; The Poets' Prize, 1995. Membership: PEN American Center. Address: 1220 N State Ave, Indianapolis, IN 46201-1162, USA. E-mail: jaredrcarter@hotmail.com.

CARTER, Mavis; b. 9 March 1939, London, England. Teacher; Poet. m. Edwi Carter, 3 s., 3 d., 2 foster d. Education: Digby Stuart Training College, 1957–5? Publications: Seasonal Change, 1986; Turning Up the Volume, 199 Contributions to: Distaff; Fatchance; Froghore Papers; Orbis; Outpost Poetry Nottingham; Smiths Knoll; Thursdays; Westwords; Hepworth, Celebration, anthology; Chayns, a Cornish Anthology. Memberships: Arvo Centres Ltd; Taliesin Trust. Address: West Barn, Tarlton, Cirencester Gloucestershire GL7 6PA, England.

CARTWRIGHT, Emma-Louise; b. 29 Jan. 1976, Sutton Coldfield Birmingham, England. Actor; Writer; Artist. Education: BA, English Language and Literature, University of Hull; Diplomas in Newspape Journalism and Professional Acting. Publication: It's for Joy, 2000 Contributions to: Magazines, reviews and periodicals. Honours: Thomas Gre Prize; Joseph Henry Noble Award for Academic Achievement; Philip Larki Prize, Literary Merit, Hull University, 1997. Address: 18 Summer Lane Minworth, Sutton Coldfield, Birmingham B76 9AU, England. E-mai elcartist@hotmail.com. Website: www.emma-louise.com.

CASE, Angelo; b. 16 Dec. 1936, Locarno, Switzerland. Poet. m. Elen Uehlinger Pianista, 20 Oct. 1962. Education: Teaching Certificate, Teache Training College, Locarno, 1955. Publications: Poetry: Il Silos, 1960; Compagni Del Cribbio, 1965; Le Precarie Certezze, 1976; Die Rote Piazza 1976; Al Dunque, 1986. Contributions to: Newspapers, journals and radic Honours: Premio Schiller due volte, 1966, 1976. Address: Via San Quirico 11 6648 Minusio (Ticino), CH, Switzerland.

CASEY, Michael; b. 1947, Lowell, Massachusetts, USA. Civil Servant; Poet Ed. m. Kathleen Davey, 26 July 1975. Education: BS, Lowell Technologica Institute, 1968; MA, State University of New York at Buffalo, 1973 Appointments: Editorial Adviser, Alice James Press, Cambridge Massachusetts, 1972–; Civil Servant, 1974. Publications: Obscenities, 1972 On Scales, 1972; My Youngest That Tall, 1972; My Brother-in-Law and Me 1974; The Company Pool, 1976. Contributions to: New York Times; Nation Quarterly; Rolling Stone; Araet. Honour: Younger Poet Award, Yale University 1972. Address: c/o Ashod Press, PO Box 1147, Madison Sq. Station, New York NY 10159, USA.

CASHET, Thomas. See: BIANCHI, Herman.

CASSELLS, Cyrus Curtis; b. 16 May 1957, Dover, DE, USA. Poet; Teacher Trans. Education: BA, Stanford University, 1979. Publications: The Mud Actor 1982; Soul Make a Path Through Shouting, 1994; Beautiful Signor, 1997. Contributions to: Southern Review; Callaloo; Translation; Seneca Review Quilt; Sequoia. Honours: Acad. of American Poets Prize, 1979; Nationa Poetry Series Winner, 1982; Bay Area Book Reviewers Asscn Awar Nominee, 1983; Callaloo Creative Writing Award, 1983; Massachusetts Artists Foundation Fellowship, 1985; National Endowment for the Arts Fellowship, 1986; Lavan Younger Poets Award, 1992; Lannan Award, 1993; William Carlos Williams Award, 1994; Finalist, Lenore Marshall Prize, 1995. Memberships: PEN; Poetry Society of America. Address: c/o Mary Cassells, 2190 Belden Pl., Escondido, CA 92029, USA.

CASTELLIN, Philippe; b. 26 June 1948, Isle sur Sorgnes, Vaucluse, France. Writer; Poet; Fisherman; Publisher. 3 s. Education: Arege de Philosophie, ENS; DLitt, Sorbonne, University of Paris. Publications: René Char, Traces, 1988; Paesine, 1989; Livre, 1990; Vers la Poesie Totale, 1992; HPS, 1992. Contributions to: Periodicals. Honour: Charge de Mission, 1990. Membership: Société des Gens de Lettres. Address: c/o Akenaton Docks, 20 rue Bonaparte, 20000 Ajaccio, France.

CASTRO, Jan Garden; b. 8 June 1945, St Louis, Missouri, USA. Writer; Poet; Lecturer; Ed.; Arts Consultant. Education: BA, English, University of Wisconsin, 1967; Publishing Certificate, Radcliffe College, 1967; MAT, 1974, MA, 1994, Washington University, St Louis; Dir, Big River Asscn, St Louis, 1975–85; Ed., River Styx magazine, 1975–86; Lecturer, Lindenwood College, 1980–; Founder and Dir, River Styx PM Series, St Louis, 1981–83; Arts Consultant, Harris-Stowe State College, 1986–87. Publications: Mandala of the Five Senses, 1975; The Art and Life of George O'Keeffe, 1985; Margaret Atwood: Vision and Forms (co-ed.), 1988; Seeking St. Louis: Voices from a River City, 1670–2000 (co-ed.), 2000; The Last Frontier (poems), 2001. Contributions to: Various reviews and television. Honours: Arts and Letters Award, St Louis Magazine, 1985; Co-ordinating Council of Literary Magazines Award, 1986; Leadership Award, Young Women's Christian Asscn, St Louis, 1988; National Endowment for the Humanities Fellowships, 1988, 1990; Camargo Foundation Fellow, 1996. Memberships: Margaret Atwood Society, founder; MLA. Address: 7420 Cornell Ave, St Louis, MO 63130, USA.

CASTRO, Michael; b. 28 July 1945, New York, NY, USA. Prof. of Humanities; Poet; Ed. m. Adelia Parker, 2 s., 1 d. Education: BA cum laude, English, State University of New York at Buffalo, 1967; MA, American Literature, 1971, PhD, English, 1981, Washington University at St Louis. Appointments: Senior and Founding Ed., River Styx Magazine, 1975–; Asst Prof., 1980–86, Assoc. Prof., 1987–92, Prof. of Humanities, 1992–, Lindenwood College, St Charles,

Missouri; Dir, River Styx at Duffs Poetry Series, 1986–; Host, Poetry Beat Radio Programme, 1989–. *Publications:* The Kokopilau Cycle, 1975; Ghost Hiways and Other Homes, 1976; Cracks, 1977. *Contributions to:* Edge; World's Edge, Japan; Sagarin Review; Tampa Review; Mississippi Valley Review; Printed Matter, Japan; Not a Single Answer; Literati Internazionale; Visions; Shadows Project; River Styx; Noctiluca. *Honour:* First Prize for Poetry, Visions Magazine/Art Barn of Washington, DC, 1987. *Address:* LCIE, Lindenwood College, 209 N Kingshighway, St Charles, MO 63301, USA.

CASTRO SOTOMAYOR, Maria Cristina; b. 4 Aug. 1931, Rancagua, Chile. Teacher of English; Poet. *Education:* BA, University of Chile, 1951. *Appointments:* Various teaching positions, 1958–80; Dir, own private acad. for adults, 1980–92. *Publications:* Regreso a la Esperanza, 1952; Poemas, 1989; En Familia, 1992; Epistolario, 1993. *Contributions to:* Chilean and foreign newspapers, magazines and anthologies. *Honours:* Several awards. *Address:* Casilla 308, San Felipe, Aconcagua, Chile.

CATES, Edward William; b. 11 March 1952, New Hampshire, USA. Social Worker; Poet. *Education:* BA, Boston University, 1974. *Appointments:* Co-ordinator, Boston Poetry Film Festival, 1973–77, First Night Poetry Event, 1979. *Publications:* Geopolitics; Remember Your Dreams; The Gypsy's Bible: Selected Poems of John Tuwim, trans. from Polish. *Contributions to:* Small Moon; Door no. 3; Noctiluca; Miscellaneous; Boston Literary Review; Modularist Review; Moody Street Review; Words; Imagine. *Honour:* Massachusetts Artist Foundation Fellowship. *Membership:* New England Poetry Club. *Address:* 72 Moreland St, First Floor, Somerville, MA 02145, USA.

CAULFIELD, Lotti Lota Carlotta; b. 16 Jan. 1953, Havana, Cuba. Ed.; Publisher; Poet. 1 s. *Education:* MA, University of Havana, 1979; MA, San Francisco State University, 1986; PhD, Tulane University, 1991. *Appointments:* Ed., Publisher, El Gato Tuerto, 1984–; Lecturer, San Francisco State University, 1984–86, Tulane University, 1988–. *Publications:* Fanaim; Oscuridad Divine; Sometimes I Call Myself Childhood; El Tiempo Es Una Mujer Que Espera; 34th Street and Other Poems; Angel Dust. *Contributions to:* Visions; Haight Ashbury Literary Journal; Poetry San Francisco; Lyra; Mairena; Termino Magazine; La Papirola; Codice; El Faro; Le Nuez; Linden Lane Magazine. *Honours:* Honourable Mention, Mairena International Poetry Competition; Ultimo Novecento International Prize; Honourable Mention, La Torre do Calafuria; Cintas Fellowship. *Memberships:* Internazionale Accademia di Lettura, Pisa; Libera Accademia Galileo Galilei; MLA; PEN; American Asscn of Teachers of Spanish and Portuguese. *Address:* Box 5028, Tulane University Station, New Orleans, LA 70118, USA.

CAUNT, Lorna Margaret; b. 30 Nov. 1927, England. Poet. m. Tony Caunt, 27 Feb. 1954, 2 s., 1 d. *Education:* BSc, Zoology, London University, 1949. *Publications:* Keeping Company, 1989; No Sense of Grandeur, 1991; No One About, 1993. *Contributions to:* Outposts; Envoi; Weyfarers; Iota; Staple; Pause; First Time; Doors; Poetry Nottingham; Poet's England; The Countryman; Spokes; Vision On (Ver); Ver Poets' Voices; Arcadian; Psychopoetica; Success Magazine. *Honours:* Second prize, Arts Council/David bookshops, 1985, 1987, 1988; Ver Poets International Competitions, 1988 twice, 1990, 1991, 1992 twice; Various mentions. *Memberships:* Ver Poets; Welwyn Garden City Literary Society; Ware Poetry Reading Group. *Address:* 1 Templewood, Welwyn Garden City, Hertfordshire AL8 7HT, England.

CAUSLEY, Charles (Stanley); b. 24 Aug. 1917, Launceton, Cornwall, England. Poet; Dramatist; Ed. *Education:* Launceston College. *Appointment:* Teacher, Cornwall, 1947–76. *Publications:* Survivors Leave, 1953; Union Street, 1957; Johnny Alleluia, 1961; Penguin Modern Poets 3, 1962; Underneath the Water, 1968; Pergamon Poets 10, 1970; Timothy Winters, 1970; Six Women, 1974; Ward 14, 1974; St Martha and the Dragon, 1978; Collected Poems, 1951–75, 1975; Secret Destinations, 1984; 21 Poems, 1986; The Young Man of Cury, 1991; Bring in the Holly, 1992; Collected Poems for Children, 1996; Penguin Modern Poets 6, 1996; Collected Poems, 1951–97, 1997. Other: Several plays: Libretto for William Mathias's opera Jonah, 1990. *Contributions to:* Various publications. *Honours:* Queen's Gold Medal for Poetry, 1967; Hon. DLitt, University of Exeter, 1977; Hon. MA, Open University, 1982; C.B.E., 1986; T S Eliot Award, Ingersoll Foundation, USA, 1990. *Address:* 2 Cyprus Well, Launceston, Cornwall PL15 8BT, England.

CAWS, Ian; b. 19 March 1945, Bramshott, Hants, England. Poet; Writer. m. Hilary Walsh, 20 June 1970, 3 s., 2 d. *Education:* Certificate in Social Work, 1970; Certificate for Social Workers with the Deaf, 1973. *Publications:* Looking for Bonfires, 1975; Bruised Madonna, 1979; Boy with a Kite, 1981; The Ragman Totts, 1990; Chamomile, 1994; The Feast of Fools, 1994; The Playing of the Easter Music (with Martin C Caseley and B L Pearce), 1996; Herrick's Women, 1996; Dialogues in Mask, 2000. *Contributions to:* Acumen Magazine; London Magazine; New Welsh Review; Observer; Poetry Review; Scotsman; Spectator; Stand Magazine; Swansea Review. *Honours:* Eric Gregory Award, 1973; Poetry Book Society Recommendation, 1990. *Membership:* Poetry Society. *Address:* 9 Tennyson Ave, Rustington, West Sussex BN16 2PB, England.

CECIL, Richard; b. 14 March 1944, Baltimore, Maryland, USA. Poet. m. Maura Stanton, 10 April 1971. *Education:* BA, University of Maryland, 1966;

MA, University of Iowa, 1972; MFA, Indiana University, 1985. *Appointments:* Visiting Asst Prof., Lockham University, 1986–87; Visiting Asst Prof., 1987–88, Asst Prof., 1989–, Indiana University, Bloomington; Asst Prof., Rhodes College, 1988–89. *Publications:* Einstein's Brain, 1986; Alcatraz, 1992; In Search of the Great Dead, 1999. *Contributions to:* Poetry; American Poetry Review; Southern Review; Crazy Horse; Virginia Quarterly Review; Chelsea; Louisville Review; Georgia Review; Ohio Review; New England Review; Antioch Review; Sycamore Review; Carolina Quarterly. *Honour:* Verna Emory Prize. *Membership:* Associated Writing Programs. *Address:* Dept of English, Indiana University, Bloomington, IN 47405, USA.

CEDERING, Siv; b. 5 Feb. 1939, Sweden. Writer; Poet; Artist. 1 s., 2 d. *Publications:* Mother Is, 1975; The Juggler, 1977; The Blue Horse, 1979; Oxen, 1981; Letters from the Floating Worlds, 1984. *Contributions to:* Harper's; Ms; New Republic; Paris Review; Partisan Review; New York Times; Goergia Review; Fiction Interntional Shenandoah; Confrontation; Over 80 anthologies and textbooks. *Honours:* New York Foundation Fellowships, 1985, 1992. *Memberships:* Co-ordinating Council of Literary Magazines; PEN; Poetry Society of America; Poets and Writers. *Address:* PO Box 800, Amagansett, NY 11930, USA.

CERVANTES, James V.; b. 2 April 1941, Houston, Texas, USA. Prof. of English; Poet; Writer. 3 d. *Education:* BA, English, Writing, University of Washington, 1972; MFA, Poetry, University of Iowa, 1974. *Appointments:* Instructor in Humanities, Community College of Vermont, 1974–77; Lecturer in Creative Writing, Arizona State University, 1978–81; Instructor in English, Northern Arizona University, 1985–88; Asst Prof. of Learning Skills and English, California State University at Sacramento, 1988–92; Prof. of English, Mesa Community College, Arizona, 1992–. *Publications:* The Fires in Oil Drums, 1980; The Year is Approaching Snow, 1981; The Headlong Future, 1990; Fever Dreams: Contemporary Arizona Poetry (co-ed.), 1997. *Contributions to:* Southwest; Pacific Review; Hayden's Ferry Review; Telescope; Northwest Review; Nebraska Review; Seattle Review; Cincinnati Poetry Review; Michigan Quarterly Review; Western Humanities Review; Christian Science Monitor; Tumblewords: Writers Reading the West; Blue Mesa Review; Lucid Stone; Gruene Street; Thin Air. *Honours:* Poetry Fellowship, Arizona Commission on the Arts, 1981; Capricorn Award, 1987. *Memberships:* Associated Writing Programs; The Writer's Voice. *Address:* 448 North Matlock, Mesa, AZ 85203, USA.

CHAARITHRA. See: VIJAY BHANU, A. K.

CHAKRAVARTI, Sasthibrata. See: BRATA, Sasthi.

CHAMBERLAIN, Franklin Fred; b. 24 Dec. 1948, Rutland, Vermont, USA. Artist; Writer; Poet. 4 s., 1 d. *Publications:* Light in the Window (chapbook); Light at the Top of the Stairs (poems). *Honours:* Emmy Lou Cole Awards, World of Poetry, 1987–90; Numerous awards, Library of Poetry, 1988–98.

CHAMBERLAIN, Velma. See: RICHESON, C(ena) G(older).

CHAMBERS, Alan; b. 6 Sept. 1929, Manchester, England. Educator; Poet. *Education:* BA (Admin), MEd, Dip Ed, Manchester University. *Appointments:* Primary School Teacher, Manchester; Lecturer in Education, Furzedown College; Head of Education, Battersea College, later amalgamated into South Bank Polytechnic. *Publications:* A Gregarious Creature?, 1988; Your Voice on My Ear. *Contributions to:* Outposts; Brentford Poets; Cobweb. *Memberships:* Poetry Society, London; Wooden Lambs; Founder, Poets at Questors and Mattock Press. *Address:* Flat L, Mattock Lane, Ealing, London W5 5BG, England.

CHAMBIAL, D. C.; b. 29 Sept. 1950, Bajrol, India. Teacher; Poet. m. Kanta, 5 March 1975, 2 s. *Education:* BSc, 1970; BEd, 1971; MA, 1975; MPhil, 1976; PhD, 1994. *Appointments:* School Teacher, 1971–87; School Lecturer, 1987–89; College Lecturer, 1989–; Ed., Poetcrit, an international journal of poetry and criticism. *Publications:* Broken Images, 1983; Cargoes of Bleeding Hearts, 1984; Poetry of Himachal, 1985; Perceptions, 1986; A Cobweb of Words, 1990; Gyrating Hawks and Sinking Roads, 1996. *Contributions to:* Tribune; Indian Express; Poet; Poetry; Poetry Time; Indian Literature; JIWE; Quest; Bharat Protiva; Commonwealth Quarterly; Byword; Poeterit. *Honours:* Trans-Word Poetry Expo Medal, 1987; Seventh Poetry Day Australia Medal, 1988; Michael Madhusudan Acad. Award, 1995. *Memberships:* Poetry Society of America; Poetry Society of India; Rachna. *Address:* Chambial Niwas, Maranda 176 102, India.

CHAMPAGNE, Lenora Louise; b. 13 Dec. 1951, Louisiana, USA. Theatre Artist; Dramatist; Poet; Teacher. m. Robert C Lyons, 17 Aug. 1991, 1 d. *Education:* BA, English, Louisiana State University, 1972; MA, Drama, 1975, PhD, Performance Studies, 1980, New York University. *Appointments:* Faculty, Gallatin School of Individualized Study, New York University, 1981–; State University of New York at Purchase, 1990–95; Visiting Artist, Trinity College, 1985–89. *Publication:* Out From Under: Texts by Women Performance Artists (ed. and contributor), 1990. *Contributions to:* Heresies; Benzene; Between C & D; Poetry Project Newsletter; Blatant Artifice; Iowa Review. *Honour:* Native

Voice Visions Prize, Louisiana State University, 1993. *Memberships:* New Dramatists, 1993–; Dramatists Guild. *Address:* 3 Horatio St, New York, NY 10014, USA.

CHAN, Stephen; b. 11 May 1949, Auckland, New Zealand. Prof. in International Relations and Ethics; Writer; Poet. *Education:* BA, 1972, MA, 1975, University of Auckland; MA, King's College, London, 1977; PhD, University of Kent, Canterbury, 1992. *Appointments:* International Civil Servant, Commonwealth Secretariat, 1977–83; Lecturer in International Relations, University of Zambia, 1983–85; Faculty, University of Kent, 1987–96; Prof. in International Relations and Ethics, Head of International Studies, Dean of Humanities, Nottingham Trent University, 1996–. *Publications:* The Commonwealth Observer Group in Zimbabwe: A Personal Memoir, 1985; Issues in International Relations: A View from Africa, 1987; The Commonwealth in World Politics: A Study of International Action, 1965–85, 1988; Exporting Apartheid: Foreign Policies in Southern Africa, 1978–1988, 1990; Social Development in Africa Today: Some Radical Proposals, 1991; Kaunda and Southern Africa: Image and Reality in Foreign Policy, 1991; Twelve Years of Commonwealth Diplomatic History: Commonwealth Summit Meetings, 1979–1991, 1992; Mediation in South Africa (ed. with Vivienne Jabri), 1993; Renegade States: The Foreign Policies of Revolutionary States (ed. with Andrew Williams), 1994; Towards a Multicultural Roshamon Paradigm in International Relations, 1996; Portuguese Foreign Policy in Southern Africa (with M. Venancio), 1996; Theorists and Theorising in International Relations (ed. with Jarrold Wiener), 1997; War and Peace in Mozambique (with M. Vanancio), 1998; Giving Thought: Currents in International Relations (ed. with Jarrold Wiener), 1998; Twentieth Century International History (ed. with Jarrold Wiener), 1998; Zambia and the Decline of Kaunda 1984–1998, 2000; Security and Development in Southern Africa, 2001. Poetry: Postcards from Paradise (with Rupert Glover and Merlene Young), 1971; Arden's Summer, 1975; Songs of the Maori King, 1986; Crimson Rain, 1991. *Honours:* Visiting fellowships; Hon. LittD, WAAC, Istanbul; Hon. Prof., University of Zambia, 1993–95. *Address:* c/o Dept of International Studies, Nottingham Trent University, Clifton Lane, Nottingham NG11 8NS, England.

CHANCE, Jane; b. 26 Oct. 1945, Neosho, Missouri, USA. Prof. of English; Writer; Poet; Ed. m. (1) Dennis Carl Nitzsche, June 1966, divorced 1967, 1 d., (2) Paolo Passaro, 30 April 1981, 2 s., divorced 2002. *Education:* BA, English, Purdue University, 1967; AM, English, 1968, PhD, English, 1971, University of Illinois. *Appointments:* Lecturer, 1971–72, Asst Prof. of English, 1972–73, University of Saskatchewan; Asst Prof., 1973–77, Assoc. Prof., 1977–80, Prof. of English, 1980–, Rice University; Hon. Research Fellow, University College London, 1977–78; Mem., Institute for Advanced Study, Princeton, New Jersey, 1988–89; General Ed., Library of Medieval Women, 1988–; Visiting Research Fellow, Institute for Advanced Studies in the Humanities, University of Edinburgh, 1994; Eccles Research Fellow, University of Utah, Humanities Centre, 1994–95; Various guest and plenary lectures. *Publications:* The Genius Figure in Antiquity and the Middle Ages, 1975; Tolkien's Art: A 'Mythology for England', 1979; Woman as Hero in Old English Literature, 1986; Tolkien's Lord of the Rings: The Mythology of Power, 1992; Medieval Mythography, two vols, 1994, 2000; The Mythographic Chaucer: The Fabulation of Sexual Politics, 1995. Editor: Various books. *Contributions to:* Scholarly books and journals. *Honours:* Hon. Research Fellow, University College, London, 1977–78; National Endowment for the Humanities Fellowship, 1977–78; Guggenheim Fellowship, 1980–81; Rockefeller Foundation Residency, Bellagio, Italy, 1988; South Central MLA Best Book Award, 1994. *Memberships:* American Asscn of University Profs; Authors Guild; Christine de Pizan Society; International Asscn of Neo-Latin Studies; International Society in Classical Studies; Medieval Acad. of America; MLA; South Central MLA. *Address:* Dept of English MS-30, Rice University, PO Box 1892, Houston TX 77251-1892, USA.

CHANDLER, Rose Wiley; b. 3 Oct. 1921, Kentucky, USA. Teacher; Antique Collector and Dealer; Poet. m. Claude Chandler, 31 May 1942, deceased, 2 d. *Education:* Eastern State Teachers College, 1939–40; Music Course, 1959; University of Kentucky, 1962; Writers Digest Writing School, 1989. *Publications:* A Gypsy's Delight, 1971; Moonlight Mystique, 1988; Traveling Through Atlanta at Night in the Rain, 1996; Symphony (chapbook), 1997. *Contributions to:* Lucidity Poetry Journal, 1999; Anthologies and newspapers. *Honours:* Golden Poet Award; Prize, Kentucky State Poetry Society Contest; Prize, Ocala Chapter, National League of American Pen Women, 1995. *Memberships:* National Society of Poetry; National Library of Poetry; National League of American Pen Women, Chair, Finance Committee, 1998. *Address:* 10962 SW 79th Terrace, Ocala, FL 34476, USA.

CHANDRA SEKHAR, K., (Srivatsa); b. 3 Dec. 1925, Mysore City, India. Linguist; Poet. *Education:* BSc, 1951, DLitt, 1980, University of Arizona, USA. *Appointments:* Several teaching positions. *Publications:* Several poetry books. *Contributions to:* Anthologies and periodicals. *Membership:* Poetry International Organisation. *Address:* 637, 11th Main Rd, HAL Second Stage, Indiranagar, Bangalore 560008, India.

CHANDRASEKARAN, S.; b. 8 Aug. 1953, Salem, India. Teacher; Poet. m. Maheswari, 27 April 1978, 1 s., 1 d. *Education:* BA, English, 1980; BEd, English, 1983; MA, English, 1987. *Appointments:* Teacher, 1974–95; Warden, Government College Boys Hostel, 1995–. *Contributions to:* Poet; World Poetry Metverse Muse; Poems-96; Kamakoti Vani. *Honours:* Second Prize, Poetic Competition, Sri Sankaracharya Swamigal of Kanchi Kamakoti Mutt, 1991. *Memberships:* Metverse Muse and Tradverse and Friends; Poet. *Address:* Iswaramurthi Palayam, Via Mangalapuram, Salem District 636202, Tamilnadu, India.

CHAO, Patricia; b. 9 July 1955, Carmel-by-the-Sea, CA, USA. Writer; Poet. *Education:* BA, Creative Writing, Brown University, 1979; MA, English, New York University, 1992. *Appointments:* Creative Writing Teacher, Sarah Lawrence College, Bronxville, NY; Ed., Global City Review special issue, 1996. *Publications:* Fiction: Monkey King, 1997. Children's Fiction: On the Silk Road; Mimi and the Tea Ceremony; The Lost and Found Twins. *Contributions to:* Periodicals and books. *Honours:* Rose Low Memorial Poetry Prize, Brown University, 1978; Fellowship, New York University Master's Programme in Creative Writing, 1990–92; Dean's Fiction Prize, New York University, 1992; Finalist, Barnes and Noble, Discover Great New Writers, 1997; New York Foundation for the Arts, 2002; New Voice Award for Poetry, The Writer's Voice, 1996; Several residencies. *Address:* 55 W 14th St, No. 11M, New York, NY 10011, USA.

CHAPLIN, Jenny, (Tracie Telfer, Wendy Wentworth); b. 22 Dec. 1928, Glasgow, Scotland. Ed.; Publisher; Writer; Poet. m. J. McDonald Chaplin, 21 April 1951, 1 d. *Education:* Jordanhill College of Education, 1946–49. *Appointments:* Founder, Ed., Publisher, International: The Writers Rostrum, 1984–93. *Publications:* Tales of a Glasgow Childhood, 1994; Alone in a Garden, 1994; Happy Days in Rothesay, 1995; From Scotland's Past, 1996; Childhood Days in Glasgow, 1996; Thoughts on Writing (with Fay Goldie and V. Cuthbert), 1996; An Emigrant's Farewell, in A Scottish Childhood, Vol. II, anthology of memoirs from famous Scottish people, 1998; We Belonged to Glasgow, 2001. *Contributions to:* The Scots Magazine; The Highlander Magazine; Scottish Memories; The Scottish Banner; Anthologies. *Honour:* Proclaimed Champion Poet of Largs, Ayrshire, 2000; Fellow, Society of Antiquaries, Scotland, 2000. *Address:* Tigh na Mara Cottage, 14 Ardbeg Rd, Rothesay, Bute PA20 0NJ, Scotland.

CHAPMAN, David Charles, (Charles Davies); b. 15 April 1944, Williamsport, Pennsylvania, USA. Maintenance Mechanic; Poet. m. Carol Jane Livermore, 23 May 1964, 2 d. *Education:* Lincoln University, 1964–70; Penn College, 1979–81. *Publication:* Lavander Moments. *Contributions to:* Grit Publishing Company; American Anthology of Contemporary Poetry. *Honour:* Golden Poet Award. *Address:* 1217 Race St, Williamsport, PA 17701, USA.

CHAPMAN, Janice Noreen; b. 25 Dec. 1941, Woodward, Oklahoma, USA. Poet. m. (1) Donald Plain, divorced 1968, 1 s., 2 d., (2) Donald Cleve Johns, Nov. 1968, divorced 2 s., 1 deceased, 1 d., (3) Leon Sylvan Chapman Jr, 4 Dec. 1985, divorced 19 Sept. 1997, 3 step-s., 3 step-d. *Appointment:* Owner, Lucky Lady Publishing Company; Proprietor, Rising Stars paper. *Publication:* Hello Out There, 1999. *Contributions to:* Various anthologies and other publications, 1985–99. *Honours:* Ed.'s Choice Award, National Library of Poetry, 1995; Accomplishment of Merit Award, Creative Arts and Sciences, 1995; Ed.'s Choice Award, J Mark Press, 1998; Pres.'s Recognition for Literary Excellence, National Author's Registry, 1999. *Membership:* International Society of Poets. *Address:* 2914 N Fifth St, Enid, OK 73701, USA.

CHAPPELL, Fred (Davis); b. 28 May 1936, Canton, North Carolina, USA. University Teacher; Poet; Writer. m. Susan Nicholls, 2 Aug. 1959, 1 s. *Education:* BA, 1961, MA, 1964, Duke University. *Appointments:* Teacher, University of North Carolina at Greensboro, 1964–; Poet Laureate, North Carolina, 1997–2003. *Publications:* Poetry: The World Between the Eyes, 1971; River, 1975; The Man Twiced Married to Fire, 1977; Bloodfire, 1978; Awakening to Music, 1979; Wind Mountain, 1979; Earthsleep, 1980; Driftlake: A Lieder Cycle, 1981; Midquest, 1981; Castle Tzingal, 1984; Source, 1985; First and Last Words, 1989; C: 100 Poems, 1993; Spring Garden: New and Selected Poems, 1995; Poetry Collection: Family Gathering, 2000. Fiction: It is Time, Lord, 1963; The Inkling, 1965; Dagon, 1968; The Gaudy Place, 1972; I Am One of You Forever, 1985; Brighten the Corner Where You Are, 1989; Farewell, I'm Bound to Leave You, 1996; Look Back All the Green Valley, 1999. Short Fiction: Moments of Light, 1980; More Shapes Than One, 1991. Collection: The Fred Chappell Reader, 1987. Other: Plow Naked: Selected Writings on Poetry, 1993; A Way of Happening: Observations of Contemporary Poetry, 1998. *Honours:* Rockefeller Grant, 1967–68; National Institute of Arts and Letters Award, 1968; Prix de Meilleur des Livres Étrangers, Académie Française, 1972; Sir Walter Raleigh Prize, 1972; Roanoke-Chowan Poetry Prizes, 1972, 1975, 1979, 1980, 1985, 1989; North Carolina Award in Literature, 1980; Bollingen Prize in Poetry, 1985; World Fantasy Awards, 1992, 1994; T S Eliot Prize, Ingersoll Foundation, 1993; Aiken Taylor Award in Poetry, 1996. *Address:* 305 Kensington Rd, Greensboro, NC 27403, USA.

CHARLES, Nicholas J. See: KUSKIN, Karla (Seidman).

CHARLES, Tony; b. 4 April 1947, Birmingham, England. Writer; Poet. 1 s., 1 d. *Education:* Cert Ed (Drama), Bretton Hall, 1969; BA, Open University, 1984. *Appointments:* Teacher; Writer-in-Residence, Bishops Castle, 1991, Yeovil, 1992, Barrow-in-Furness, 1993. *Publications:* The Wonderful Rubbish Tip, 1976; The Bear and Ragged Staff, 1984; Wake, 1992. *Contributions to:* Acumen; Agenda; Bull; Candelabrum; Cobweb; Country Life; Ecologist; Envoi; Folio International; Foolscap; Interactions; Iron; Issue One; Odyssey; Outposts; Poetry Express; Prospice; Sepia; Spokes; Thursdays; Westwards; Wide Skirt. *Memberships:* Poetry Society; Friends of Arvon. *Address:* 33 Lillebonne Close, Wellington, Somerset TA21 9EX, England.

CHARNEY, Lena London; b. 26 Jan. 1919, Symiatycze, Poland. Poet. m. Roy L Charney, 10 Nov. 1955, 1 s. *Education:* BA, cum laude, Hunter College, New York City, 1941; MA, Clark University, Worcester, Massachusetts, 1942; PhD, ABD, Columbia University, 1947–53. *Contributions to:* Various anthologies, reviews, magazines, and journals; Many poetry readings. *Honours:* Finalist, Verve Poetry Competition, 1990; Honorable Mention, Nostalgia Poetry Contest, 1991; Finalist, Greenburgh Poetry Competition, 1993; Diamond Homer Awards, Famous Poets Poetry Contest, 1996, 1998, 1999; Featured poet, Mount Pleasant Public Library, Pleasantville, NY, 2001. *Memberships:* Hudson Valley Writers Center; National Writers Union; Acad. of American Poets; Society of American Poetry. *Address:* PO Box 145, Mohegan Lake, NY 10547, USA.

CHARNY, Carmi, (T. Carmi); b. 31 Dec. 1925, New York, NY, USA (Naturalized Israeli citizen). Poet; Ed.; Teacher. m. Lilach Peled, 3 s. *Education:* BA, Yeshiva University, 1946; Graduate Studies, Columbia University, 1946, Sorbonne, University of Paris, 1946–47, Hebrew University, 1947, 1949–51. *Appointments:* Ziskind Visiting Prof. of Humanities, Brandeis University, 1969–70; Adjunct Assoc. Prof., University of Tel-Aviv, 1971–73; Visiting Fellow, Oxford Centre for Postgraduate Hebrew Studies, 1974–76; Visiting Prof., Hebrew Union College, Jerusalem, 1978–, Stanford University, 1979, Yale University, 1986, New York University, 1986, University of Texas at Austin, 1987. *Publications:* Poetry: As T Carmi: Mum Vahalom, 1951; Eyn Prahim Shehorim, 1953; Sheleg Birushalayim, 1955; Hayam Ha'aharon, 1958; Nehash Hanehoshet, 1961, English trans. as The Brass Serpent, 1964; Ha'unicorn Mistakel Bamar'ah, 1967; Tevi'ah, 1967; Davar Aher/Selected Poems, 1951–1969, 1970; Somebody Likes You, 1971; Hitnatslut Hamehaber, 1974; T Carmi and Dan Pagis: Selected Poems (with Dan Pagis), 1976; El Erets Aheret, 1977; Leyad Even Hato'im, 1981, English trans. as At the Stone of Losses, 1983; Hatsi Ta'avati, 1984; Ahat Hi Li, 1985; Shirim Min Ha'azuva, 1989; Emet Vehova, 1993. Editor: As T Carmi: The Modern Hebrew Poem Itself (with Stanley Burnshaw and Ezra Spicehandler), 1965; The Penguin Book of Hebrew Verse, 1981. Other: Trans of plays into Hebrew. *Contributions to:* Periodicals. *Honours:* Brenner Prize for Literature, 1972; Prime Minister's Awards for Creative Writing, 1973, 1994; Guggenheim Fellowship, 1987–88; Bialik Prize, 1990; Hon. Doctor of Humane Letters, Hebrew Union College, Jewish Institute of Religion, 1993. *Memberships:* Acad. for the Hebrew Language; Writers Assocaition of Israel. *Address:* Hebrew Union College, Jewish Institute of Religion, 13 King David St, Jerusalem 94101, Israel.

CHATERGIE, Annand. See: SHEINFELD, Ilan.

CHATTARJI, Chandak; b. 17 Aug. 1935, India. Teacher; Poet. m. Rina Banerjee, 8 Dec. 1961, 1 s., 1 d. *Education:* BA, Viswa Bharati University, 1955; MA, Calcutta University, 1957; Assoc. of the College Preceptors, London, 1970. *Appointments:* English Teacher, La Martiniere College, Lucknow; English Teacher, Housemaker, Sainik School, Rewa; Senior English Master, Housemaker, Tashi Namgyal Acad., St Paul's School, Darjeeling; Principal, Dr Virendra Swarup Public School, Kanpur, Air Force School, Kanpur. *Publication:* Another Dorian Gray. *Contributions to:* Telegraph; Poetry India; Poet. *Membership:* World Poetry Society. *Address:* Air Force School, 402 Air Force Station, Chakeri, Kanpur 208008, Udra Pradesh, India.

CHATTERJEE, Debjani; b. 21 Nov. 1952, Delhi, India. Poet; Writer; Ed.; Trans. m. Brian D'Arcy, 20 July 1983. *Education:* BA, American University in Cairo, 1972; MA, University of Kent, Canterbury, 1973; PhD, University of Lancaster, 1977; PGCE, Sheffield City Polytechnic, 1981. *Publications:* Peaces; Poems for Peace, 1987; Whistling Still: Bloody Lyres, 1989; I Was That Woman, 1989; Northern Poetry, Vol. II, 1991; The Sun Rises in the North, 1993; A Little Bridge, 1997; Albino Gecko, 1998; Songs in Exile (trans.), 1999; Cette-Femme La. . ., 2000; The Redbeck Anthology of British South Asian Poetry, 2000; Animal Antics, 2000; My Birth Was Not in Vain: Selected Poems by Seven Bengali Women, 2001. Other: The Role of Religion in A Passage to India, 1984; The Elephant-Headed God and Other Hindu Tales, 1989; Barbed Lines, 1990; Sweet and Sour, 1993; The Parrot's Training (trans.), 1993; The Monkey God and Other Hindu Tales, 1993; Sufi Stories from Around the World, 1994; Nyamia and the Bag of Gold, 1994; Home to Home, 1995; The Most Beautiful Child, 1996; Album (trans.), 1997; The Message of Thunder and Other Plays, 1999; The Snake Prize and Other Folk Tales from Bengal, 1999; Just Faith, 2002. *Honours:* Shankars International Children's Competition Poetry Prize; Lancaster LitFest Poems Competition Winner; Peterloo Poets Open Poetry Competition Afro-Caribbean/Asian Prize; Southport Writers' Circle Poetry Competition, second prize; Artrage Annual Literature Award; Raymond

Williams Community Publishing Prize, 1990; Yorkshire and Humberside Arts Writer's Award, 1995; Raymond Williams runner-up prize, 2001. *Memberships:* Poetry Society, India, UK; National Assen of Writers in Education; Arts Council of England, Literature Advisory Group, 1996–99; Mini Mushaira, 1996–; Bengali Women's Support Group and Book Project, 1985–. *Address:* 11 Donnington Rd, Sheffield S2 2RF, England.

CHAUDHARY, Ajit Kumar Shankar, (Ajit Kumar); b. 9 June 1933, Lucknow, Udra Pradesh, India. Educator; Poet. m. Snehmayi Chaudhary, 20 May 1959, 1 s. *Education:* MA, Hindi, Allahabad University, India, 1952. *Appointments:* Lecturer in Hindi, D A V College, Kanpur, 1953–56; Hindi Trans., Ministry of External Affairs, New Delhi, 1956–62; Lecturer, then Reader in Hindi, Kirorimal College, Delhi University, 1962–. *Publications:* Akele Kanth Ki Pukar, 1958; Ankit Hone Do, 1962; Ye Phool Nahin, 1970; Gharonda, 1987; Hirni Ke Liye, 1993. *Contributions to:* Numerous journals and symposiums. *Honours:* Several prizes. *Memberships:* Hindi Advisory Board, National Book Trust, New Delhi; Advisory Board, Sahitya Kala Parishad, Delhi Administration, Delhi; Numerous selection committees for central and state awards. *Address:* Kirorimal College, Delhi University, Delhi 110007, India.

CHAWLA, Jasbir; b. 20 June 1953, Etawah, India. Government Servant; Poet; Writer. m. Ravinder Kaur, 15 Oct. 1980, 1 s., 2 d. *Education:* Diploma, Russian, 1974, French, 1991; BTech, 1970; MBA, 1990. *Publications:* Chernobyl, 1989; Reti Ki Gandh, 1990; Eh Nahin Awaz Khalistan Ki, 1991; Niche Wali Chitkhani, 1992; Punjab: Dararen Aurdalal, 1992; Janta Jaan Gayi, 1992. *Contributions to:* Journals and periodicals. *Memberships:* Authors Guild of India; Indian Institute of Medals; Institution of Engineers; PEN. *Address:* 247 Defence Colony, Jalandhar City 144001, India.

CHEDID, Andrée; b. 20 March 1920, Cairo, Egypt. Author; Poet; Dramatist. m. Louis A. Chedid, 23 Aug. 1942, 1 s., 1 d. *Education:* BA, American University, Cairo, 1942. *Publications:* Fiction: Le Sommeil délivré, 1952, English trans. as From Sleep Unbound, 1983; Jonathan, 1955; Le Sixième Jour, 1960, English trans. as The Sixth Day, 1988; Le Survivant, 1963; L'Autre, 1969; La Cité fertile, 1972; Nefertiti et le rêve d'Akhnaton, 1974; Les Marches de sable, 1981; La Maison sans racines, 1985, English trans. as The Return to Beirut, 1989; L'Enfant multiple, 1989, English trans. as The Multiple Child, 1995; Lucy: La femme verticale, 1998; Le Message, 2000. Poetry: Numerous books, including: Textes pour un poème, 1949–1970, 1987; Poèmes pour un texte, 1970–1991, 1991; Selected Poems of Andrée Chedid, 1995; Fugitive Suns: Selected Poetry, 1999. Other: Short-story collections, plays, essays and children's books. *Honours:* Prix Louise Labe, 1966; L'aigle d'or de la poésie, 1972; Grand Prix des Lettres Françaises, l'Académie Royale de Belgique, 1975; Prix de l'Afrique Méditerranéenne, 1975; Prix de l'Académie Mallarmé, 1976; Prix Goncourt, 1979; Prix de Poésie, Société des Gens de Lettres, 1991; Prix de PEN Club International, 1992; Prix Paul Morand, l'Academie Française, 1994; Prix Albert Camus, 1995; Prix Poésie de la SALEH, 1999. *Address:* c/o Flammarion, 26 rue Racine, 75006 Paris, France.

CHERKOVSKI, Neeli, (Neeli Cherry); b. 1945, Los Angeles, CA, USA. Writer; Poet; Ed. Partner, Jesse Guinto Cabrera, 1983. *Education:* San Bernardino Community College; BA, California State University, 1967; Hebrew Union College, Jewish Institute of Religion. *Publications:* Poetry: Anthology of Los Angeles Poets, (co-ed.), 1972; Don't Make a Move, 1973; Public Notice, 1975; The Waters Reborn, 1975; Love Proof, 1981; Clear Wind, 1983; Ways in the Wood, 1993; Animal, 1996; Elegy for Bob Kaufman, 1996. Other: Ferlinghetti: A Life, 1979; Whitman's Wild Children, 1988; Hank: The Life of Charles Bukowski, 1991. *Address:* c/o Sun Dog Publishing, Silver City, NM 88061, USA.

CHERRY, Kelly; b. Baton Rouge, LA, USA. Prof.; Writer; Poet. m. Jonathan B. Silver, 23 Dec. 1966, divorced 1969. *Education:* Du Pont Fellow, University of Virginia, 1961–63; MA, University of North Carolina, 1967; Visiting Lecturer, 1977–78, Prof., 1978–79, Asst Assoc. Prof., 1979–82, Prof. 1982–83, Romnes Prof. of English, 1983–88, Evjue-Bascom Prof. in the Humanities, 1993–, Eudora Welty Prof. of English, 1997–, University of Wisconsin at Madison; Writer-in-Residence, Southwest State University, Marshall, MN, 1974, 1975; Visiting Prof. and Distinguished Writer-in-Residence, Western Washington University, 1981; Faculty, MFA Program, Vermont College, 1982, 1983; Distinguished Visiting Prof., Rhodes College, TN, 1985. *Publications:* Fiction: Sick and Full of Burning, 1974; Augusta Played, 1979; Conversion, 1979; In the Wink of an Eye, 1983; The Lost Traveller's Dream, 1984; My Life and Dr Joyce Brothers, 1990; The Society of Friends, 1999. Poetry: Lovers and Agnostics, 1975; Relativity: A Point of View, 1977; Songs for a Soviet Composer, 1980; Natural Theology, 1988; Benjamin John, 1993; God's Loud Hand, 1993; Time Out of Mind, 1994; Death and Transfiguration, 1997. Other: The Exiled Heart: A Meditative Autobiography, 1991; Writing the World (essays and criticism), 1995; History, Passion, Freedom, Death and Hope: Prose about Poetry, 1999. Translations: Octavia, by Seneca; Antigone, by Sophocles. *Contributions to:* Anthologies and periodicals. *Honours:* Canaras Award, 1974; Bread Loaf Fellow, 1975; Yaddo Fellow, 1979, 1989; National Endowment for the Arts Fellowship, 1979; Romnes Fellowship, 1983; Wisconsin Arts Board Fellowships, 1984, 1989, 1994; Hanes Prize for Poetry, Fellowship of Southern Writers, 1989; Wisconsin Notable Author, 1991; Hawthornden

Fellowship, Scotland, 1994; E. B. Coker Visiting Writer, Converse, 1996; Leidig Lectureship in Poetry, 1999. *Membership:* Associated Writing Programs, board of dirs, 1990–93. *Address:* c/o Dept of English, University of Wisconsin at Madison, Madison, WI 53706, USA.

CHESSA, Charles E; b. 16 Feb. 1955, Warren, ME, USA. Poet; Writer. *Publications:* Chapbooks: Ink River, 1994; Poetry 9-4-8-4, 1996. *Contributions to:* Writers World, 1995; The Long Islander, Walts Corner, 1993; GRIT, 1994; Just Write, 1995; Cat's Magazine, 1995; Westbury Anthology, 1995; The Pointed Circle, 1995; Scroll Magazine, 1998; The Poetry Church, 1998; Homemakers Monthly, 1998; Up South, 1998; Stepping Stones Magazine, 1998; The Sounds of Poetry, Coffee Cup Limited Edition, 1998; Teak Roundup, 1998, 1999. *Honours:* Runner-up, Scottish International Open Poetry Competition, Scotland, 1995; Pres.'s Award for Literary Excellence, 1994. *Address:* PO Box 520, No. 6, McIntosh TP, Bar Harbor, ME 04609, USA.

CHESSEX, Jacques; b. 1 March 1934, Payerne, France. Novelist; Poet. *Education:* Graduated, University of Lausanne, 1961. *Publications:* La Tête ouverte, 1962; La Confession du pasteur Burg, 1967; A Father's Love, 1973; L'Ardent Royaume, 1975; Le Séjour des morts, 1977; Les Yeux jaunes, 1979; Où vont mourir les oiseaux, 1980; Judas le transparent, 1983; Jonas, 1987; Morgane Madrigal, 1990; Sosie d'un saint, 2000; Monsieur, 2001. Poetry: Le Jour proche, 1954; Chant du printemps, 1955; Une Voix la nuit, 1957; Batailles dans l'air, 1959; Le Jeûne de huit nuits, 1966; L'Ouvert obscur, 1967; Elégie, soleil du regret, 1976; La Calviniste, 1983; Feux d'orée, 1984; Comme l'os, 1988. Non-Fiction: Maupassant et les autres, 1981; Mort d'un cimetière, 1989; Flaubert, ou, le désert en abîme, 1991; Notes sur Saura, 2001. *Honour:* Prix Goncourt, 1973; Commandeur Ordre des Arts et des Lettres, 1984; Légion d'honneur, 2002. *Address:* Editions Grasset, 61 Rue des Sts-Pères, 75006 Paris, France.

CHESTERFIELD, Reginald Alan; b. 8 Nov. 1925, Exeter, Devon, England. Poet. m. Patricia Mary, 14 July 1951, 2 s. *Education:* Royal College of Physicians, 1949; Royal College of Surgeons, 1950. *Publications:* Requiem for Innocence; A Lovely Slice of Bread; Sampler, 1990; It Gets Late Early Now, 1995; Table for One, 2001. *Contributions to:* Oribs; Pause; Staple; BBC Radio; Television; Countryman; Farmers Weekly; Poetry Now; Others. *Honours:* First Prize, Forward Press, 2000. *Membership:* Company of Poets. *Address:* South Hayne, Bishops Nympton, South Molton, Devon EX36 3QR, England.

CHEUNG, Judy Hardin; b. 3 Feb. 1945, USA. Teacher (retd); Poet. m. Benjamin Szeshing Cheung, 16 Aug. 1990, 2 s. *Education:* BA, Sonoma State University, 1966; MA, University of San Francisco, 1981. *Appointment:* Teacher, Special Education, Sonoma Development Center, 1972–2001. *Publications:* Welcome to the Inside; Captions; Flying on the Wings of a Dragon; Phoenix and the Dragon. *Contributions to:* Numerous publications. *Honours:* Silver Pegasus Award; Poets of the Vineyard Award. *Memberships:* California Federation of Chaparral Poets; Ina Coolbirth Circle; Poets of the Vineyard; Artists Embassy International; Redwood Empire Chinese Asscn. *Address:* 704 Brigham Ave, Santa Rosa, CA 95404, USA.

CHEYNEY-COKER, Syl; b. 28 June 1945, Freetown, Sierra Leone. Senior Lecturer; Poet. *Education:* Universities of Oregon, 1967–70, California, 1970, and Wisconsin, 1971–72. *Appointments:* Visiting Prof. of English, University of the Philippines, Quezon City, 1975–77; Senior Lecturer, University of Maiduguri, Nigeria, 1979–. *Publications:* Concerto for an Exile, 1973; The Graveyard Also Has Teeth, 1974; The Blood in the Desert's Eyes: Poems, 1990. *Address:* Dept of English, University of Maiduguri, PMB 1069, Maiduguri, Nigeria.

CHIANG, Robert; b. 5 July 1963, New York, NY, USA. Physician; Poet. *Education:* BA, Augustana College, Rock Island, 1985; MD, Rush Medical College, Chicago, 1990. *Contributions to:* SAGA; American Anthology of Mid Western Poetry; American Anthology of Southern Poetry. *Memberships:* American Acad. of Ophthalmology; American Society of Cataract and Refractive Surgery. *Address:* 10406 Owensmouth Ave, Chatsworth, CA 91311, USA.

CHIBEAU, Edmond; b. 20 Oct. 1947, New York, NY, USA. Video Producer; Poet. m. Amy Reusch, 20 June 1987. *Education:* BA, Long Island University, 1973; University of California at Santa Barbara, 1973; MA, University of Pennsylvania, 1992; PhD, Northwestern University, 1996. *Appointments:* Asst Prof., Pace University; Video Producer, Time Warner, Manhattan; Video Curator, Children's Museum of Manhattan. *Contributions to:* Nation; Santa Barbara News Press; California Quarterly; Ear; Glants Play Well; Red Weather; Shuttle; Flute; Assembling; Gallery Works; Pan Arts; The Fly. *Honours:* Ace Award; New York State Foundation for the Arts. *Memberships:* Authors League of America; Poets and Writers. *Address:* 7522 NE Lake Terrace, Chicago, IL 60626, USA.

CHILDERS, Joanne; b. 5 Sept. 1926, Ohio, USA. Ed. (retd); Poet. m. 20 Aug. 1951, 3 s. *Education:* BA, University of Cincinnati, 1948; MA University of Florida, 1952. *Publications:* The Long Distance, 1989; Moving Mother Out, 1992. *Contributions to:* Sewannee Review; Massachusetts Review; College

English; Commonwealth; Carolina Quarterly; Forum; Kentucky Poetry Review; Cumberland Poetry Review. *Honour:* Individual Artist Grant Florida State of the Arts, 1988. *Address:* 3504 NW Seventh Pl., Gainesville FL 32607, USA.

CHILDISH, Billy; b. 1959, Chatham, Kent, England. Poet; Painter Songwriter. Poems from the Barrier Block, 1984; Monks Without God, 1986 Companions in a Death Boat, 1987; To the Quick, 1988; Girl in the Tree, 1988 Maverick Verse, 1988; Admissions to Strangers, 1989; Death of a Wood, 1989 The Silence of Words (short stories), 1989; The Deathly Flight of Angels, 1990 Like a God I Love All Things, 1990; Child's Death Letter, 1990; The Hart Rises 1991; Poems of Laughter and Violence: Selected Poetry 1981–86, 1992; Poem to Break the Harts of Impossible Princesses, 1994; Days With a Hart Like a Dog, 1994; Big Hart and Balls, 1995; Messerschmitt Pilot's Severed Hand 1996; My Fault (novel), 1996; Billy Childish and His Famous Headcoat, 1997 Notebooks of a Naked Youth (novel), 1997; I'd Rather You Lied: Selected Poems 1980–1998, 1999; Chatham Town Welcomes Desperate Men, 2001. *Address:* c/o Hangman Books, 11 Boundary Rd, Chatham, Kent ME4 6TS, England. Website www.billychildish.com.

CHILTON, Joan Shaw; b. 27 May 1917, York, England. Poet. *Education* Midland Agricultural College, 1935–37; Leicester University, 1937–39 Diploma in Christian Studies, Southampton University, 1992–95 *Publication:* Various Poems. *Contributions to:* Selsey Chronicle; Selsey Parish Magazine; Anthology, 1992. *Honour:* Certificate for 30 years work with the blind in West Sussex (voluntary). *Memberships:* National Poetry Society Poetry Now Society; Selsey Poetry Society; Society of the Sisters of Bethany. *Address:* 1 Selsey Ct, Hillfield Rd, Selsey, Chichester, West Sussex PO20 0LD England.

CHI-LUNG WANG, (Luti); b. 1 Jan. 1942. Publisher; Poet. m. Sun Xiao-Zhen, 12 March 1980, 1 s., 4 d. *Education:* BA, Tam King University, 1954; PhD, Chinese Literature, Guan-Da College, Hong Kong. *Appointments:* Ed., The Gale Literary Monthly, 1961–68; Publisher, The Nymph, 1972–92; Secretary-General, Chinese Poetry Society, Taipei, 1984–92; Ed., The Long Song Press, Taipei; Vice-Pres., Treasurer, World Acad. of Arts and Culture, 1994–. *Publications:* Blue Star, 1962; Green Statue, 1963; Wind and Castle, 1991; Ladder in the Clouds; Anchor; Admiring the Origin of Breezes. *Contributions to:* Anthologies and periodicals. *Honours:* Hon. Doctor of Literature, World Acad. of Arts and Culture, 1987; Poetry Education Award, Ministery of Education, China, 1989. *Memberships:* Chinese Poetry Society, pres.; Dow Fang Art Centre, secretary general. *Address:* PO Box 14-57, Taipei, China (Taiwan).

CHISHOLM, Alison (Fiona Williams); b. 25 July 1952, Liverpool, England. Teacher, Writer, Poet. m. Malcolm Chisholm, 10 July 1971, 2 d. *Education:* ATCL, 1969; FLCM, 1971; LLAM, 1973. *Appointments:* Teacher, Oxford Acad. of Speech and Drama, Middlesbrough; Principal, Richmond Acad. of Speech, Southport; Poetry and Creative Writing Tutor, Southport College; Poetry Consultant, BBC Radio Merseyside, 1996–2001. *Publications:* Alone No More (co-author), 1977; Flying Free, 1985; The Need for Unicorns, 1987; Single Return, 1988; Paper Birds, 1990; The Craft of Writing Poetry, 1992; A Practical Poetry Course, 1994; How to Write 5-Minute Features, 1996; Daring the Slipstream, 1997; How to Write About Yourself (co-author), 1999; Writing Competitions: The Way to Win (co-author), 2001. *Contributions to:* Envoi; Outposts; Doors; Orbis; Smoke; Staple; Acumen; Poetry Now; Poetry Nottingham Int; The Formalist; Various anthologies and children's anthologies; BBC Radio Merseyside and Network Northwest; Articles on poetry in numerous writers' magazines. *Honours:* Prizes, Mary Wilkins Memorial Competition (twice), Success Open, Grey Friars, Rhyme International, Lace, KQBX, Wells Literature Festival, Chester, Banstead, Lake Aske, Envoi, Julia Cairns, Ouse Valley, Sefton, New Prospects and Yorkshire Competitions, and US competitions in various categories of World Order of Narrative and Formalist Poets and National Federation of State Poetry Societies, Ohio Poetry Day Competitions. *Memberships:* Society of Women Writers and Journalists; Poetry Society; Ohio Poetry Asscn; Asscn of Christian Writers; Southport Writers' Circle; Society of Authors. *Address:* 53 Richmond Rd, Birkdale, Southport, Merseyside PR8 4SB, England.

CHISM-PEACE, Yvonne, (Yvonne); b. 23 Jan. 1945, Philadelphia, Pennsylvania, USA. Poet; Essayist; Filmmaker. *Education:* BA, Rosemont College, 1966; MA, New York University, 1968; MS, Bank Street College of Education, 1998. *Appointments:* Poetry Ed., MS Magazine, 1973–86; Adjunct Prof. of English, City University of New York, 1977–86; Writer-in-Residence, Poets in the Schools, 1979–86, Bronx Council on the Arts, 1982–84; Independent Filmmaker, 1983–; Adjunct Prof. of English, 1996–97, Board of Trustees, 1998–, Rosemont College. *Publications:* IWILLA/Soil, 1985; IWILLA/Scourge, 1986; IWILLA/Rise, 1999. *Contributions to:* MS Magazine; Daily Fare; The Third Woman; We Become New; Callaloo; Pushcart Press; Catholic Girls; Bless Me Father. *Honours:* National Endowment for the Arts (twice); Mary Roberts Rinehart Fellowship; Creative Artists in Public Service; Brio Award. *Memberships:* Poetry Society of America; Poets and Writers; Bronx Council on the Arts; Schomburg Center; American Asscn of University Women; MLA, 1995–; Germantown Historical Society, 1997–. *Address:* Greene St Artists Corporation, 5225 Greene St, No. 16, Philadelphia, PA 19144, USA.

CHIUNG JUNG HO, (Pai Chiu); b. 8 June 1937, Taichung, China (Taiwan). Businessman; Poet. m. 1 April 1962, 1 s., 3 d. *Education:* Graduate, Taichung Junior College of Commerce, 1956. *Publications:* Death of the Moth, 1959; Rose of the Wind, 1965; The Sky Symbol, 1969; Pai Chiu Anthology, 1971; Chansons, 1972; Poetry Square, 1984; The Wind Blowing, You Feel a Tree's Existence, 1989; Cherish, 1990; Images From Observation and Measurement, 1991. *Contributions to:* Various publications. *Honours:* First National Literary Award for Poetry, 1955; Taiwan Kong-How Award for Poetry, 1994. *Address:* 198-1, Sec 4, Tian Jin Rd, Taichung, China (Taiwan).

CHO, Kwungsoo; b. 4 March 1958. Poet. *Education:* Graduated, National Railroad High School, 1977. *Appointment:* Locomotive Repair and Maintenance Engineer, 1977–. *Publications:* Poem I, 1990; Poem II, 1992; A Collection of Poems, The Aroma of a Cup of Tea, 1994; Tout le monde: 2, 1995; la azalée: 8, 1995; la galaxie: 12, 1995; le zéro: 4, 1996; le chemin du retour: 1996; le vide à vie: 10, 1996; le labyrinthe à vie: 7, 1997; la mort à vie: 12, 1999. *Honours:* Poet of the Millennium, India, 2000; Dove in Peace, Millennium Poet, Australia, 2001; International Poets Acad. Award, 2001. *Address:* B Dong 905 Ho, Life Mi-Sung Apartment, Shinnae-Dong 487, Jungrang-ku, Seoul, 131 - 130, Korea. *E-mail:* chok@netsgo.com.

CHOATE, Alec Herbert; b. 5 April 1915, High Barnet, Hertfordshire, England. Writer; Poet. m. 26 Feb. 1943, 1 s., 2 d. *Appointments:* Surveyor, 1945–75. *Publications:* Gifts Upon the Water, 1978; A Marking of Fire, 1986; Schoolgirls at Borobudur, 1990; Mind in Need of a Desert, 1995; The Wheels of Hama: Collected War Poems, 1997; Ashes To Water (poems), 2000; My Days Were Fauve (verse autobiography), 2002. *Contributions to:* Fremantle Arts Review; Habitat Australia; Patterns; Quadrant; Salt; Southerly; Westerly. *Honours:* Tom Collins Poetry Prize; Western Australia Week Literary Award; Patricia Hackett Prize; Western Australian Premier's Book Award, 1997. *Memberships:* Fellowship of Australian Writers; International PEN; Perth PEN Centre. *Address:* 11A Joseph St, West Leederville, WA 6007, Australia.

CHONG RUIZ, Eustorgio Antonio; b. 21 Feb. 1934, Los Santos, Panamá. Poet. *Education:* BS, University of Panamá, 1958. *Appointments:* Dir, Felix E Oller High School, 1958–62; High School Teacher, 1962–92; Asst Prof., University of Panamá, 1965–68. *Publications:* Canción del Hombre en la Ventana; Yaya; Y Entonces tu; Del mar y la Selva; A La Luz del Fogón; Detrás de la Noche; Otra vez, Pueblo; Techumbres, Guijarros y Pueblo; Después del Manglar; Diario de una noche de camino; Los chinos en la sociedad panameña; Gente Común; Poemas. *Contributions to:* Revista Boreal; Revista Amancer; Revista Pliego de Murmurios; Revista Puerto Norte Sur; Revista Galaxia 71; Periódico El Sol de Azuero; Revista China hoy; Parnassus of World Poets. *Honour:* Poetry Award. *Memberships:* Sociedad Bolivariana de Panamá; Academia Panaména de la Historia; Asociación de Professores de la República de Panamá; Sociedad Amigos Museo Afro Antillano. *Address:* Apartado 6507, Panamá 5, Panamá.

CHOON WOO. See: DEOK KY JEON.

CHORLTON, David; b. 15 Feb. 1948, Spittal-an-der-Drau, Austria. Writer; Poet; Artist. m. Roberta Elliott, 21 June 1976. *Education:* Stockport College, 1966–69. *Publications:* Without Shoes, 1987; The Village Painters, 1990; Measuring Time, 1990; Forget the Country You Came From, 1992; Outposts, 1994; The Insomniacs, 1994. *Contributions to:* Many reviews and journals. *Memberships:* PEN West; Writer's Voice. *Address:* 118 W Palm Lane, Phoenix, AZ 85003, USA.

CHOROSINSKI, Eugene Conrad; b. 1 Jan. 1930, Sienno, Poland. Poet; Writer. *Education:* LLB, Blackstone School of Law, 1968. *Publications:* Through the Years, 1995; Days Remembered, 1999. *Contributions to:* Anthologies, periodicals and journals. *Honours:* 10 Ed.'s Choice Awards, 1994–97; Award of Recognition for Outstanding Achievement in Poetry, Famous Poets Society, 1998; Poet of the Millennium Award, 2000. *Membership:* International Society of Poets, life mem. *Address:* 131 Madrona Dr., Eustis, FL 32726, USA.

CHOUDHURI, Pradip; b. 5 Feb. 1943, Bengal, India. Teacher; Poet; Ed. m. Gouri Choudhuri, 29 May 1967, 1 s. *Education:* MA in English; PG Diploma, Teaching of English; Diploma in French. *Appointments:* Teacher, English Language and English Poetry; Ed., numerous poetry journals. *Publications:* My Rapid Activities; Skin Disease; Poetry, Religion; 64 Ghosts Ferry; A Few Concepts to be Abandoned in Poetry; The Black Hole. *Contributions to:* Second Aeon; Cosmos; Robot; Swakal; Alpha Beat Soup; The Blue Jacket; Décharge; Rimbaud Revue; An Amzer; La Toison d'Or; Press-Stances; Art et Poésie de Touraine; L'écriture; Noréal; Inédit, Bouillabaisse; Tamanoir; Lieux d'Asile, Lieux d'Exil. *Memberships:* Le Club Kerouac; Nimporte quelle Route. *Address:* 73 Regent Estate, Second Floor, Apt 6, Calcutta, 700 092 India.

CHOWDHRY, Maya; b. 1964, Edinburgh, Scotland. Playwright; Image Maker; Poet. *Education:* MA, Scriptwriting for film and television, Northern School of Film and Television, Leeds Metropolitan University, 1994; Short courses, Arvon Foundation. *Appointments:* Administrator, Edinburgh Fringe Film Festival, 1986; Producer, Dir, Sheffield Film Co-operative, 1987–91; Tutor, Manchester Writing Festival, 1993, 1994; Resident Dramatist, Red Ladder Theatre Company, 1994. *Publication:* Putting in the Pickle Where the Jam Should Be, 1989. *Contributions to:* Anthologies, periodicals, and radio. *Honour:* Cardiff International Poetry Competition, 1992. *Membership:* Black Arts Alliance. *Address:* 18 Vickers Rd, Sheffield S5 6UZ, England.

CHOYCE, Lesley; b. 21 March 1951, Riverside, New Jersey, USA (Naturalized Canadian citizen). Prof.; Writer; Poet; Ed. m. Terry Paul, 19 Aug. 1974, 2 d. *Education:* BA, Rutgers University, 1972; MA, Montclair State College, 1974; MA, City University of New York, 1983. *Appointments:* Ed., Pottersfield Press, 1979–; Prof., Dalhousie University, 1986–. *Publications:* Adult Fiction: Eastern Sure, 1981; Billy Botzweiler's Last Dance, 1984; Downwind, 1984; Conventional Emotions, 1985; The Dream Auditor, 1986; Coming Up for Air, 1988; The Second Season of Jonas MacPherson, 1989; Magnificent Obsessions, 1991; Ectasy Conspiracy, 1992; Margin of Error, 1992; The Republic of Nothing, 1994; The Trap Door to Heaven, 1996; Beautiful Sadness, 1997; Dance the Rocks Ashore, 1998; World Enough, 1998. Young Adult Fiction: Skateboard Shakedown, 1989; Hungry Lizards, 1990; Wavewatch, 1990; Some Kind of Hero, 1991; Wrong Time, Wrong Place, 1991; Clearcut Danger, 1992; Full Tilt, 1993; Good Idea Gone Bad, 1993; Dark End of Dream Street, 1994; Big Burn, 1995; Falling Through the Cracks, 1996. Poetry: Re-Inventing the Wheel, 1980; Fast Living, 1982; The End of Ice, 1985; The Top of the Heart, 1986; The Man Who Borrowed the Bay of Fundy, 1988; The Coastline of Forgetting, 1995; Beautiful Sadness, 1998. Non-Fiction: An Avalanche of Ocean, 1987; December Six: The Halifax Solution, 1988; Transcendental Anarchy (autobiography), 1993; Nova Scotia: Shaped by the Sea, 1996. Editor: Chezzetcook, 1977; The Pottersfield Portfolio, 7 vols, 1979–85; Visions from the Edge (with John Bell), 1981; The Cape Breton Collection, 1984; Ark of Ice: Canadian Futurefiction, 1992. *Honours:* Event Magazine's Creative Nonfiction Competition Winner, 1990; Dartmouth Book Awards, 1990, 1995; Ann Connor Brimer Award for Children's Literature, 1994; Authors Award, Foundation for the Advancement of Canadian Letters, 1995. *Address:* 83 Leslie Rd, East Lawrencetown, Nova Scotia B2Z 1P8, Canada.

CHRISCADEN. See: HINDS, Sallie A.

CHRISTENSEN, Paul; b. 18 March 1943, Pennsylvania, USA. Prof.; Poet. m. Catherine Anne Tensing, 20 Aug. 1969, 2 s., 2 d. *Education:* William and Mary College, 1967; University of Cincinnati, 1970; University of Pennsylvania, 1975. *Appointments:* Instructor, 1974–75, Asst Prof., 1975–79, Assoc. Prof., 1979–83, Prof., 1983–, Texas A&M University. *Publications:* In Seven Poets; Old and Lost Rivers; Signs of the Whelming; Weights and Measures; Where Three Roads Meet, 1996; West of the American Dream: An Encounter with Texas, 2001; Blue Alleys, 2001; Hard Country, 2001. *Contributions to:* Washington Post; Los Angeles Times; American Statesman; Sulfur; Parnassus; Southwest Review; Temblor; Madison Review; Quarter After Eight; Antioch Review, Connecticut Review; Waterstone. *Honours:* Writer's Grant, National Endowment for the Arts; Best Short Fiction, Texas Institute of Letters, 1995; Distinguished Prose Award, Antioch Review 1999; Writers' League Prize in Creative Non-Fiction, 2001; William Bronk Fellowship, 2001. *Memberships:* MLA; Texas Institute of Letters; Great Plains Institute, assoc. fellow. *Address:* Dept of English, Texas A&M University, College Station, TX 77843, USA.

CHRISTIAN, Dudley Noel; b. 15 Nov. 1944, Port of Spain, Trinidad. Chief Engineer; Inventor; Poet; Writer. m. Grace Sujkowski, 18 Sept. 1967, 2 s., 1 d. *Education:* Fourth Class, 1980, Second Class, 1987, Engineering. *Publications:* Poets Pen, 1971; Only Children of the Universe Are We, 1973; Sonnets of Life-Love-Racism and Hate, 1973; Inside a Heart, 1974; Judge Me Not Without a Trial, 1975; Legends, Lives and Loves Along the Inside Passage, 1976; That We Too Free May Live, 1980; Love's Reflections, 1983; The Seelaats, 1988; Short Stories for Guidance of Children, 1992. *Contributions to:* Various anthologies and other publications. *Honours:* Royal Patronage Status Title, 1995; Various certificates and acknowledgements. *Memberships:* Burnaby Arts Club; Fraser Valley Poets Potpourri and Pause for Poetry; Vancouver Poetry Asscn. *Address:* 8573 McEwan Terrace, Mission, BC V2V 6R2, Canada.

CHRISTOPHER, Nicholas; b. 28 Feb. 1951, New York, NY, USA. Poet; Writer. m. Constance Barbara Davidson, 20 Nov. 1980. *Education:* AB, Harvard College, 1973. *Appointments:* Adjunct Prof. of English, New York University; Lecturer, Columbia University. *Publications:* On Tour with Rita (poems), 1982; A Short History of the Island of Butterflies (poems), 1986; The Soloist (novel), 1986; Desperate Characters (poems), 1988; Under 35: The New Generation of American Poets (ed.), 1989; In the Year of the Comet (poems), 1992; 5 Degrees and Other Poems, 1994; Walk and Other Poems, 1995; Veronica (novel), 1996; Somewhere in the Night: Film Noir and the American City, 1997. *Contributions to:* Anthologies and periodicals. *Honours:* New York Foundation for the Arts Fellowship, 1986; National Endowment for the Arts Fellowship, 1987; Peter I B Lavan Award, Acad. of American Poets, 1991; Guggenheim Fellowship, 1993; Melville Cane Award, 1994. *Address:* c/o Janklow & Nesbit Assocs, 445 Park Ave, New York, NY 10022, USA.

CHRISTY, Ana; b. 13 Nov. 1948, Greece. Poet. m. David Christy, 26 Aug. 1993, 1 s., 2 d. *Publications:* Beatnik Blues, 1992; Concrete Bologna, 1992; Real Junkies Don't Eat Pie, 1994; Adnavsem, 1995; Trebor and Trevor, 1997; Kudzu,

1998. *Contributions to:* Connections; Lucid Moon; Cherotic Review; Alpha Beat Soup; Cokefish; Lilliput Review. *Address:* 31 Waterloo St, New Hope, PA 18938, USA.

CHRISTY, Dave; b. 28 Jan. 1952, Philadelphia, Pennsylvania, USA. Ed.; Publisher; Poet. m. Ana Christy, 26 Aug. 1993, 1 s., 1 d. *Publication:* Loose Stones, 1983. *Contributions to:* Connections; Quelle Route; Blue Jacket; Lucid Moon; Lullabye Jesus; Gypsy. *Address:* 31 Waterloo St, New Hope, PA 18938, USA.

CHRYSTOS, Christina, (Singingarrow-Smith); b. 7 Nov. 1946, San Francisco, CA, USA. Poet; Performer. *Education:* Self-educated. *Appointments:* Numerous poetry readings, 1977–. *Publications:* Not Vanishing, 1988; Dream On, 1991; Fugitive Colors, 1994; Fire Power, 1995; Reinventing the Enemy's Language: Anthology, 1996. *Contributions to:* Anthologies and periodicals. *Honours:* Barbara Demming Memorial Award, 1988; National Endowment for the Arts Grant, 1990; Freedom of Expression Award, Human Rights Fund, 1991; Lannan Foundation Poetry Grant, 1991. *Memberships:* Northwest Native Writers; Poets and Writers; Returning the Gift. *Address:* 3900 Pleasant Beach Dr. NE, Bainbridge Island, WA 98110, USA.

CHULA, Margaret; b. 10 Oct. 1947, Vermont, USA. Writer; Poet; Small Press Owner. *Education:* Diploma, 1961–65, AS cum laude, 1965–67, Bay Path College; Northeastern University, 1967–69. *Appointments:* Teacher, Kyoto Seika College, Kyoto, Japan, 1982–92; Doshisha Women's College, Kyoto, Japan, 1983–92; Owner, Katsura Press, 1992–. *Publications:* Grinding My Ink, 1993; This Moment, 1995; Shadow Lines, 1999; Always Filling, Always Full, 2001. *Contributions to:* Anthologies and periodicals. *Honours:* Second Prize, Japan Airlines National Haiku Contest, 1987; First Prize, International English Tanka Contest, 1993, 2000; Haiku Society of America's National Book Awards, 1994, 2000; First Prize, Kansai Time Out Seventh Annual Writing Contest, 1994; Oregon Literary Arts Fellowship, 1998. *Memberships:* PEN West; Haiku Society of America; Poetry Society of Japan; Asian Art Council, Board of Dirs; International Asscn of Japanese Gardens, Board of Dirs. *Address:* 206 Southwest Carey Lane, Portland, OR 97219, USA.

CHURCH, Avery Grenfell; b. 21 Feb. 1937, North Wilkesboro, North Carolina, USA. Educator (retd); Scientist (retd); Poet. m. Dora Ann Creed, 1991. *Education:* University of North Carolina; BA, Baylor University, 1962; MA, University of Colorado, 1965. *Appointments:* Asst Prof., Memphis State University, Tennessee, 1965–66, 1969–72; Lecturer, University of South Alabama, 1972–83; Vice-Chair. of Anthropology, 1975–76, Vice-Pres., 1976–77, Exec. Committee, 1975–77, Alabama Acad. of Science; Various positions with educational, business and humanitarian organisations, 1984–95. *Publications:* Rainbows of the Mind; Patterns of Thought; Waves of Life, 1995. *Contributions to:* Anthologies and journals. *Honours:* Lloyd Frank Merrell Award, Bardic Echoes, 1977; Poets Hall of Fame, Parnassus Literary Journal, 1982; September Prize, Pasque Petals, 1989; Hon. Doctor of Humanities, London Institute for Applied Research, 1993; several others. *Address:* 2749 Park Oak Dr., Clemmons, NC 27012, USA.

CHURCH, David Randall; b. 20 Jan. 1947, Providence, RI, USA. Poet; Ed. Divorced, 1 s., 5 d. *Education:* Christian Brothers Acad., Providence, RI, 1961–65. *Publications:* Cool Earth, 1977; Blue Balls, 1995; Straight Up, 1996; Under the Influence, 1999; Roadie, 1999; What do you Want to Call This Thing?, 1999; Eternal Hmmmmm, 2000; A Good Life it is These Days, 2001; Hack Job: A Novella, 2002. *Contributions to:* Newport Review; Poets Press; Cer-Ber-Us; Spoken Word Anthology of Providence Poets, 1993; Paris / Atlantic; Rattle; Sunspot Press; Chiron Review; Atom Mind; Nedge. *Address:* 30 Forest St, Providence, RI 02906, USA.

CHUTE, Robert Maurice; b. 13 Feb. 1926, Naples, Maine, USA. Prof. Emeritus; Poet. m. Virginia Hinds, 24 June 1946, 1 s., 1 d. *Education:* BA, University of Maine, 1950; ScD, Johns Hopkins University, 1953. *Appointments:* Instructor, Asst Prof., Middlebury College; Asst Prof., San Fernando Valley State College; Assoc. Prof., Lincoln University; Prof., Prof. Emeritus, 1993–, Bates College. *Publications:* Quiet Thunder; Uncle George; Voices Great and Small; Thirteen Moons; Samuel Sewall Sails for Home; When Grand Mother Decides to Die; The Crooked Place; Androscoggin Too, 1997. *Contributions to:* Kansas Quarterly; Beloit Poetry Review; Bitterroot; South Florida Poetry Review; North Dakota Review; Cape Rock; Fiddlehead; Greenfield Review; Literary Review. *Honours:* Maine Humanities Chapbook Award; Beloit Poetry Journal Chad Walsh Award, 1997. *Memberships:* Acad. of American Poets; American Asscn for the Advancement of Science, fellow. *Address:* 85 Echo Cove Lane, Poland, ME 04274, USA.

CIMINO, Lorenzo; b. 26 May 1938, Trani, Italy. Psychologist; Writer; Poet. m. Maria Peduzzi, 28 June 1975. *Education:* Piano Diploma, 1957; PhD, 1966. *Publications:* Four poetry books, 1989–98. *Contributions to:* Various magazines. *Honour:* Città di Leonforte, 1998. *Memberships:* Authors' Society, Rome; Psychologists' Society. *Address:* Nosee 4, 22020 Schignano, Italy.

CINGOLANI, Charles L; b. 18 Jan. 1933, Butler, Pennsylvania, USA. Teacher; Poet. m. Roswitha V. Volkmann, 12 July 1969, 1 s., 1 d. *Education:* BA, Stonehill College, 1955; MA, Duquesne University, 1966; PhD, University of Basel, 1972. *Appointment:* Point Park College, Pittsburgh, Pennsylvania. *Publications:* In the Wheat; The Butler Pennsylvania Poems; Thomas Merton in Auschwitz. *Contributions to:* Poetry Quarterly; Coal City Review; New Hope International Quartos Magazine; Lundian; New Europe; Purple Patch; Foolscap. *Address:* Waldshuterstrasse 6, 79862 Hoechenschwand, Germany. *E-mail:* clcing@web.de. *Website:* www.geocities.com/clcing/.

CIRINO, Leonard John; b. 11 Sept. 1943, USA. Teacher; Writer; Ed.; Painter; Musician. *Education:* BA, Sonoma State University, 1977. *Appointment:* Instructor, Mendocino Branch, College of the Redwoods, CA, 1980–88. *Publications:* Poems After the Spaniards of 27, 1992; Sweeney Everyman, 1992; Poems From Some Latins, 1992; Rocking Over Dawn: Selected Poems 1988–1991, 1992; Waiting For the Sun to Fill With Courage (prose, poems), 1994; Henry's Will: A Tribute to John Berryman, 1995; The Terrible Wilderness of Self, 1998; 96 Sonnets Facing Conviction, 1999. *Contributions to:* Amelia; Anderson Valley Advertiser; Blue Unicorn; The Cape Rock; Plains Poetry Journal; Paper Radio; Paragraph; Canada Poetry Review; Fiddlehead; West Branch; New Settler Interview; Arts and Entertainment; Sisters Today; Epiphany; Exquisite Corpse. *Address:* PO Box 7097, Eureka, CA 95506, USA.

CISNEROS, Antonio; b. 27 Dec. 1942, Lima, Peru. Teacher of Literature; Poet. *Education:* Catholic and National universities, Lima; PhD, 1974. *Appointment:* Teacher of Literature, University of San Marcos, 1972–. *Publications:* Destierro, 1961; David, 1962; Comentarios reales, 1964; The Spider Hangs Too Far From the Ground, 1970; Aqua que no has de beber, 1971; Come higuera en un campo de golf, 1972; El libro de Dios y los hungaros, 1978; Cuatro poetas (with others), 1979; Helicopters in the Kingdom of Peru, 1981; La crónica del Niño Jesús de Chilca, 1981; At Night the Cats, 1985; Land of Angels, 1985; Monologo de la casta Susana y otros poemas, 1986; Propios como agenos poesia 1962–88, 1989; El arte de envolver pescado, 1990; Poesia, una historia de locos: 1962–1986, 1990. *Honour:* Casa de las Americas Prize, 1968. *Address:* c/o Dept of Literature, Universidad Nacional de San Marcos de Lima, Avda Republica de Chile 295, Of 506, Casilla 454, Lima, Peru.

CISNEROS, Sandra; b. 20 Dec. 1954, Chicago, IL, USA. Writer; Poet. *Education:* BA, Loyola University, 1976. *Publications:* Bad Boys, 1980; The House on Mango Street, 1983; The Rodrigo Poems, 1985; My Wicked, Wicked Ways, 1987; Woman Hollering Creek and Other Stories, 1991; Hairs-Pelitos, 1994; Loose Women, 1994. *Contributions to:* Periodicals. *Honours:* National Endowment for the Arts Fellowships, 1982, 1987; American Book Award, 1985; Lannan Foundation Award, 1991; John D. and Catherine T. MacArthur Foundation Fellowship, 1995. *Address:* c/o Susan Bergholz Literary Services, 17 W 10th St, Suite 5, New York, NY 10011, USA.

CLAIRE, William; b. 4 Oct. 1935, Northampton, Massachusetts, USA. Consultant; Poet. m. Sedgley Mellon Schmidt, divorced, 1 s. *Education:* BA, Columbia College, Columbia University, 1958; MLS, Georgetown University, 1979. *Appointments:* Dir, Washington Office, American Paper Institute, Washington Office, State University of New York; Pres., Senior Partner, Washington Resources; Founding Ed., Publisher, Voyages: A National and International Literary Magazine, 1967–73. *Publications:* Poems from a Southern France Notebook; Strange Coherence of Our Dreams. *Contributions to:* New York Times; American Scholar; The Nation; Chelsea; Carleton Miscellany; New York Quarterly; West Coast Review. *Honours:* National Endowment for the Arts Grant; Yaddo Fellowship; Rockefeller Foundation Grant. *Memberships:* PEN America; Cosmos Club; National Press Club. *Address:* 138 Jefferson Ave, Lewes, DE 19958, USA. *E-mail:* voyagesbks@aol.com.

CLANCY, Joseph Patrick Thomas; b. 8 March 1928, New York, NY, USA. College Teacher; Writer; Poet. m. Gertrude Wiegand, 31 July 1948, 4 s., 4 d. *Education:* BA, 1947, MA, 1949, PhD, 1957, Fordham University. *Appointments:* Faculty, 1948, Prof., 1962, Marymount Manhattan College. *Publications:* The Odes and Epodes of Horace, 1960; Medieval Welsh Lyrics, 1965; The Earliest Welsh Poems, 1970; 20th Century Welsh Poems, 1982; Gwyn Thomas: Living a Life, 1982; The Significance of Flesh: Poems, 1950–83, 1984; Bobi Jones: Selected Poems, 1987. *Contributions to:* Poetry Wales; Planet; Anglo Welsh Review; Book News from Wales; Epoch; College English; America. *Honours:* American Philosophical Society Fellowships, 1963, 1968; National Trans. Centre Fellowship, 1968; Welsh Arts Council, Literature Award, 1971; Major Bursary, 1972; National Endowment for the Arts Trans. Fellowship, 1983; St Davids Society of New York Annual Award, 1986. *Memberships:* American Literary Trans' Asscn; Dramatists' Guild; Yr Academi Gymreig; Eastern States Celtic Asscn; St Davids Society of New York. *Address:* 1549 Benson St, New York, NY 10461, USA.

CLARK, Douglas George Duncan; b. 3 Oct. 1942, Darlington, England. Poet. *Education:* BSc, Honours, Mathematics, Glasgow University, 1966. *Publications:* The Horseman Trilogy in 4 books: Troubador, 1985; Horsemen, 1988; Coatham, 1989; Disbanded, 1991; Dysholm, 1993; Selected Poems, 1995; Cat Poems, 1997; Wounds, 1997; Kitten Poems, 2002; Lynx: Poetry from Bath (ed.), 1997–2000. *Contributions to:* Lines Review; Cencrastus; Avon Literary Intelligencer; Outposts; Acumen; Sand Rivers Journal; Rialto; Completing the Picture: Exiles, Outsiders and Independents; Poet's Voice; Mount Holyoke News; Isibongo; Agnieszka's Dowry; Recursive Angel; Octavo; Perihelion; Autumn Leaves; Scriberazone. *Address:* 69 Hillcrest Dr., Bath, Avon BA2 1HD, England. *E-mail:* d.g.d.clark@bath.ac.uk. *Website:* www.bath.ac.uk/ ~exxdgdc.

CLARK, Gary Osgood; b. 14 Nov. 1945, Norfolk, Massachusetts, USA. Library Asst; Poet. m. Dawn McClain, 24 March 1979, divorced 1991, 1 s. *Education:* BA, English, California State University, San Jose, CA, 1975. *Appointments:* Publishing, 1979–; Poetry readings in Sacramento area; Hosted a poetry series, Davis Art Center, 1985–87. *Publications:* Letting the Eye to Wonder, 1990; 7 Degrees of Something, 1999; A Box Full of Alien Skies, 2001. *Contributions to:* Tales of the Unanticipated; Indigenous Fiction; ZYZZYVA; Star*Line (poems and book reviews); Asimov's Sci Fi; Star Trek - The Poems; Sonoma Mandala; Manhattan Poetry Review; Vincent Brothers Review; Phase & Cycle; Wormwood Review; Next Phase; Pirate Writings; South Coast Poetry Journal. *Honour:* Asimov's Reader's Award, 2000. *Membership:* Science Fiction Poetry Asscn. *Address:* 79 Broken Circle, Davis, CA 95616, USA.

CLARK, John(son) Pepper; b. 3 April 1935, Kiagbodo, Nigeria. Poet; Writer; Dramatist. m. Ebunoluwa Bolajoko Odutola, 1 s., 3 d. *Education:* Government College, Ughelli; University College, Ibadan; BA, Princeton University, 1960. *Appointments:* Research Fellow, Institute of African Studies, 1963–64; Lecturer, 1965–69, Senior Lecturer, 1969–72, Prof. of English, 1972–80, University of Lagos; Ed., Black Orpheus journal, 1965–78; Visiting Distinguished Fellow, Wesleyan University, 1975–76; Visiting Research Prof., University of Ibadan, 1979–80; Distinguished Visiting Prof. of English and Writer-in-Residence, Lincoln University, PA, 1989; Visiting Prof. of English, Yale University, 1990. *Publications:* Poetry: Poems, 1962; A Reed in the Tide, 1965; Casualties, 1970; A Decade of Tongues, 1981; State of the Union, 1985; Mandela and Other Poems, 1988; A Lot From Paradise, 1997. Other: America, Their America, 1964; The Example of Shakespeare, 1970; The Hero as a Villain, 1978. *Honour:* Nigerian Academy of Letters Foundation Fellow, 1996. *Membership:* National Council of Laureates. *Address:* PO Box 1668, Marina, Lagos, Nigeria.

CLARK, Marjorie Russell McMillan, (Lisa Russell McMillan); b. 23 March 1925, Edinburgh, Scotland. Plant Pathologist (retd); Poet. *Education:* BSc, Honours, 1947, PhD, 1949, University of Edinburgh. *Appointment:* Plant Pathologist, West of Scotland Agricultural College, 1949–85. *Publication:* Organisms. Other: Inspired by Nature (BBC tape), 1995. *Contributions to:* Periodicals. *Honour:* Runner-up, BBC Wildlife Poet of the Year, Scottish Open Poetry Competition. *Membership:* Asscn of Applied Biologists. *Address:* Woodlands, Gattonside, Melrose, Roxburghshire, Scotland.

CLARK, Patricia Denise, (Claire Lorrimer, Patricia Robins, Susan Patrick); b. 1 Feb. 1921, Hove, Sussex, England. Writer; Poet. *Publications:* As Claire Lorrimer: A Voice in the Dark, 1967; The Shadow Falls, 1974; Relentless Storm, 1975; The Secret of Quarry House, 1976; Mavreen, 1976; Tamarisk, 1978; Chantal, 1980; The Garden (a cameo), 1980; The Chatelaine, 1981; The Wilderling, 1982; Last Year's Nightingale, 1984; Frost in the Sun, 1986; House of Tomorrow (biography), 1987; Ortolans, 1990; The Spinning Wheel, 1991; Variations (short stories), 1991; The Silver Link, 1993; Fool's Curtain, 1994; Beneath the Sun, 1996; Connie's Daughter, 1997; The Reunion, 1997; The Woven Thread, 1998; The Reckoning, 1998; Second Chance, 1998; An Open Door, 1999; Never Say Goodbye, 2000; Search for Love, 2000; For Always, 2001; The Faithful Heart, 2002. As Patricia Robins: To the Stars, 1944; See No Evil, 1945; Three Loves, 1949; Awake My Heart, 1950; Beneath the Moon, 1951; Leave My Heart Alone, 1951; The Fair Deal, 1952; Heart's Desire, 1953; So This is Love, 1953; Heaven in Our Hearts, 1954; One Who Cares, 1954; Love Cannot Die, 1955; The Foolish Heart, 1956; Give All to Love, 1956; Where Duty Lies, 1957; He Is Mine, 1957; Love Must Wait, 1958; Lonely Quest, 1959; Lady Chatterley's Daughter, 1961; The Last Chance, 1961; The Long Wait, 1962; The Runaways, 1962; Seven Loves, 1962; With All My Love, 1963; The Constant Heart, 1964; Second Love, 1964; The Night is Thine, 1964; There Is But One, 1965; No More Loving, 1965; Topaz Island, 1965; Love Me Tomorrow, 1966; The Uncertain Joy, 1966; The Man Behind the Mask, 1967; Forbidden, 1967; Sapphire in the Sand, 1968; Return to Love, 1968; Laugh on Friday, 1969; No Stone Unturned, 1969; Cinnabar House, 1970; Under the Sky, 1970; The Crimson Tapestry, 1972; Play Fair with Love, 1972; None But He, 1973; Fulfilment, 1993; Forsaken, 1993; Forever, 1993; The Legend, 1997. *Memberships:* Society of Authors; Romantic Novelists' Asscn. *Address:* Chiswell Barn, Marsh Green, Edenbridge, Kent TN8 5PR, England.

CLARK, Thomas Willard; b. 1 March 1941, Oak Park, IL, USA. Poet. m. Angelica Heinegg, 22 March 1968, 1 d. *Education:* BA, University of Michigan, 1963; MA, Cambridge University, England, 1965. *Appointments:* Poetry Ed., The Paris Review, 1963–74; Instructor in American Poetry, University of Essex, 1966–67; Core Faculty in Poetics, New College of California, 1987–. *Publications:* Stones, 1969; Air, 1970; When Things Get Tough on Easy Street, 1978; Paradise Resisted, 1984; Disordered Ideas, 1987; Easter

Sunday, 1987; Fractured Karma, 1990; Sleepwalker's Fate, 1992; Junkets on a Sad Planet: Scenes from the Life of John Keats, 1993; Like Real People, 1995; Empire of Skin, 1997. *Contributions to:* New Statesman; Kulchur; The Listener; TLS; Encounter; Poetry, Chicago; The Nation. *Honours:* Hopwood Award, 1963; Bess Hokin Prize for Poetry, 1966; George Dillon Memorial Prize for Poetry, 1968; Rockefeller Fellow, 1968; Guggenheim Fellow, 1970; Poets Foundation Award, 1978; National Endowment for the Arts Grant, 1985; Jerome Shestack Award for Poetry, 1992. *Address:* 1740 Marin Ave, Berkeley, CA 94707, USA.

CLARK (BEKEDEREMO), J(ohn) P(epper); b. 6 April 1935, Kiagaboo, Nigeria. Dramatist; Poet; Writer. m. Ebun Odutola Clark, 1 s., 3 d. *Education:* Warri Government College, 1948–54; University of Ibadan, 1955–60; BA, Princeton University, 1960. *Appointments:* Information Officer, Government of Nigeria, 1960–61; Head of Features and Editorial Writer, Lagos Daily Express, 1961–62; Research Fellow, 1964–66; Prof. of African Literature, 1966–85, University of Lagos; Co-Ed., Black Orpheus, 1968–. *Publications:* Poems, 1962; A Reed in the Tide: A Selection of Poems, 1965; Casualties: Poems 1966–68, 1970; Urhobo Poetry, 1980; A Decade of Tongues: Selected Poems 1958–68, 1981; State of the Union, 1985; Mandela and Other Poems, 1988. Other: Plays and other publications. *Address:* c/o Curtis Brown Ltd, Haymarket House, 28–29 Haymarket, London SW1Y 4SP, England.

CLARKE, Gillian; b. 8 June 1937, Cardiff, Glamorgan, Wales. Poet; Ed.; Trans.; Tutor of Creative Writing. *Education:* BA, University College, Cardiff, 1958. *Appointments:* Lecturer, Gwent College of Art and Design, Newport, 1975–82; Ed., Anglo-Welsh Review, 1976–84; Pres., Ty Newydd (Welsh creative writers' house), Gwynedd, 1993–. *Publications:* Poetry: Snow on the Mountain, 1971; The Sundial, 1978; Letter From a Far Country, 1982; Selected Poems, 1985; Letting in the Rumour, 1989; The King of Britain's Daughter, 1993; Collected Poems, 1997; Five Fields, 1998; The Animal Wall, 1999; Nine Green Gardens, 2000. Editor: The Poetry Book Society Anthology, 1987–88, 1987; The Whispering Room, 1996; I Can Move the Sea (anthology), 1996. Other: Trans. *Honours:* Fellow, University of Wales, Cardiff, 1984; Hon. Fellow, University of Wales, Aberystwyth, 1995–, University of Wales, Swansea, 1996; Cholmondeley Award for Poetry, 1997; Owain Glyndwr Award for Outstanding Contribution to Arts in Wales, 1999. *Membership:* Welsh Acad., chair, 1988–93. *Address:* Blaen Cwrt, Talgarreg, Llandysul, Ceredigion SA44 4EU, Wales.

CLARKE, Patrick John Harrison; b. 7 March 1926, Portishead, Somerset, England. University Teacher (retd); Poet. m. Ailsa Mary Clarke, 31 July 1962, deceased, 4 s., 1 d. *Education:* MA, University of Cambridge, 1955; Post-Graduate Certificate of Education, University of London, 1959; DipEd, Exeter University, 1970; MA Education, University of Durham, 1973. *Appointments:* East African Man., Henry Hope and Sons Ltd, Nairobi, Kenya, 1951–58; Lecturer, Kagumo Teachers College, Nyeri, Kenya, 1959–64; Senior Geography Teacher, Bishop Fox's School, Taunton, Somerset, 1965–70; On secondment, Principal, Bishop Kitching Teacher Training College, Uganda, 1966–68; Lecturer, Senior Lecturer, Dept of Education, University of Malawi, 1970–72; Head of Dept, 1973–81, Deputy Dir, Scottish Centre for Education Overseas, 1981–91, Moray House, Edinburgh Education Dept; Consultant to Overseas Development Administration, India and Africa, 1981–91. *Publications:* Poems: The Flowers of Crete, 1998; Snowfall Near the Ochils, 1998; Selected Poems by Patrick Clarke, 1998; She, 1999. *Contributions to:* Reach magazine; Parkinson's Disease Society; The Countryman magazine. *Membership:* Erskine Writers Group. *Address:* The Annexe, Middle Stoford, West Buckland, Wellington, Somerset, TA21 9LS4 The Glebe, Dollar, Clackmannanshire FK14 7AN, Scotland.

CLARRICOATES, Katherine Mary; b. 23 July 1953, Knaresborough, North Yorkshire, England. Social Anthropologist; Poet; Writer. Partner, Graham Clarricoates, 2 s., 1 d. *Education:* BA, Sociology and Anthropology, 1976, PhD, Social Anthropology, 1984, University of Hull. *Publications:* Anti-social woman, 1998; Crestfallen, 1998; The Written Word, 1998; Stealing Time, 1998; Temptation, 1998; Move Over, I'm Fighting Back, 1998; Catching The Light of the Low-winter Sun, 1998; Road Accident, 1998; Sweet Sleep, 1998; Young and On The Margins, 1998; Unfinished Business, 1998; Moving House Again, 1998; Real Men at War, 1999; Ordinary Happinesses, 1999; Japan Next Year? (short story); As Rare as a Purple Giraffe; Bless Me. *Contributions to:* Various publications. *Honours:* Honours: Third Place, Partners in Poetry National Poetry Competition, 1998; Highly Commended, Viewpoint Literary Competition, 1998; Samaritans Poetry Competition, 1998; Special Commendation, Hilton House Poetry of the Year Competition, 1998. *Address:* c/o 22 Water Lane, South Cave, Brough, East Yorkshire HU15 2HJ, England.

CLEARY, Brendan; b. 6 June 1958, County Antrim, Ireland. Part Time Lecturer; Performance Poet; Stand Up Comic. *Education:* BA, 1980; MA, 1985. *Appointments:* Co-Ed., Stand Magazine, 1981–82; Founder, Ed., Eclto Room Machine, 1985. *Publications:* Tears in the Burger Store; Expecting Cameras; Late Night Bouts; The Parties Upstairs; Newcastle is Benidorm; Crack; White Bread and ITV; The Irish Card. *Contributions to:* New Younger Irish Poets; Blackstaff; 12 Bar Blues; New Statesman; New England Review; Stand; Sunk Island Review; Tribune; The North; The Wipe Skirt; Salmon; The Echo Room. *Honour:* Basil Bunting Award. *Membership:* Morden Tower

Readings. *Address:* c/o 45 Bewick Ct, Princes Sq., Newcastle upon Tyne, Tyne & Wear NE1 8EG, England.

CLEVERLY, Henry David; b. 20 Nov. 1962. Poet. *Publications:* Walking Willacome Well; Render My Heart. *Address:* 2 Pantile Cottages, Kettlestone Rd, Little Snoring, Norfolk NR21 0JE, England.

CLIFTON, (Thelma) Lucille; b. 27 June 1936, Depew, NY, USA. Poet; Writer; University Prof. m. Fred James Clifton, 10 May 1958, deceased 10 Nov. 1984, 2 s., 4 d. *Education:* Howard University, 1953–55; Fredonia State Teachers College, 1955. *Appointments:* Poet-in-Residence, Coppin State College, 1974–79; Poet Laureate of Maryland, 1974–85; Prof. of Literature and Creative Writing, University of California at Santa Cruz, 1985–89; Distinguished Prof. of Literature, 1989–91, Distinguished Prof. of Humanities, 1991–, Hilda C. Landers Endowed Chair in the Liberal Arts, 2000–, St Mary's College of Maryland; Blackburn Prof. of Creative Writing, Duke University, 1998–. *Publications:* Poetry: Good Times, 1969; Good News about the Earth: New Poems, 1972; An Ordinary Woman, 1974; Two-Headed Woman, 1980; Good Woman: Poems and a Memoir, 1969–1980, 1987; Next: New Poems, 1987; Ten Oxherding Pictures, 1988; Quilting: Poems, 1987–1990, 1991; The Book of Light, 1993; The Terrible Stories, 1998; Blessing the Boats: New and Selected Poems, 1988–2000, 2000. Other: Generations: A Memoir, 1976. Children's Books: Over 20 books, 1970–2001. *Contributions to:* Anthologies and periodicals. *Honours:* National Endowment for the Arts Awards, 1969, 1970, 1972; Juniper Prize, University of Massachusetts, 1980; Coretta Scott King Award, American Library Asscn, 1984; Andrew White Medal, Loyola College in Maryland, 1993; Named, Maryland Living Treasure, 1993; Lannan Literary Award for Poetry, 1997; Inducted, National Literature Hall of Fame for African-American Writers, 1998; Lenore Marshall Poetry Prize, 1998; Los Angeles Times Poetry Prize, 1998; Lila Wallace/ Reader's Digest Award, 1999; National Book Award for Poetry, 2001; Pushcart Prize, 2001. *Memberships:* Acad. of American Poets, chancellor, 1999–; Authors' Guild; Authors' League of America; International PEN; Poetry Society of America. *Address:* c/o Marc Apter, Public and Media Relations, St Mary's College of Maryland, 107 Calvert Hall, St Mary's City, MD 20686, USA.

CLIMENHAGA, Joel Ray; b. 9 April 1922, Rhodesia. Writer; Poet; Teacher. m. Zoe Lenore Motter, 21 Dec. 1955, 1 s., 3 d. *Education:* AA, Chaffey College, Ontario, CA, 1949; BA, 1953, MA, 1958, University of California at Los Angeles. *Publications:* The Month of the Shadow On My Heart, 1990; Hawk and Chameleon, 1990; Report on the Progress of the Bearded One's Homework, 1990; Preliminary Walk into the Sweat of Dying, 1991; Tomb of the Snake, 1992; The Treachery of Innocence, 1994; Moan of Raping Bees, 1996; One Candle is Light Enough Forever, 1996; Exploration of the Great Northwest While Traveling With the Fat Man, 1996; Fragmented Rhythm Becomes Whole Again, 1997; A Peculiar Oleander Blooms, 1997; White Flower Unfeeling, 1997; Cold Flowers of the Night, 1998; Early on in the Dance of Dying, 1998; Osmosis for the Unborn, 1998; The Murdering Hand of God, 1998; Death of Desire Along an Ancient Beach, 1998; The Sign for Myself is Infinity, 1998; Blood in the Air, 1998; Shadow of This Red Rock, 1998. *Honours:* McIntosh Cup, 1980; Distinguished Alumnus Award, Alumni Asscn of Pottstown High School, 1989. *Address:* 2068 S Barnett Rd, Bisbee, AZ 85603-6514, USA.

CLINE, Charles William; b. 1 March 1937, Waleska, GA, USA. Prof.; Poet. m. Sandra Lee Williamson, 11 June 1966, 1 s. *Education:* AA, Reinhardt College, 1957; University of Cincinnati, 1957–58; BA, 1960, MA, 1963, Vanderbilt University. *Appointments:* Asst Prof., Shorter College, 1963–64; Instructor, West Georgia College, 1964–68; Manuscript Procurement Ed., 1968, Assoc. Prof., 1969–75, Prof., 1975–, Kellogg Community College. *Publications:* Forty Salutes to Michigan Poets (ed.); Crossing the Ohio; Questions for the Snow; Ultima Thule; Wholeness of Dreams (co-author). *Contributions to:* Poet; Voices International; New Laurel Review; Great Lakes Review; Green River Review; Wind Literary Journal; SouWester; Orbis; Ocarina; World Institute of Achievement Newsletter; Bardic Echoes; Modus Operandi; North American Mentor Magazine; Invictus; New Europe; New Muses. *Honours:* LittD, World University, 1981; International Acad. of Poets Award; Medallion for Distinguished Participation, 20th International Congress on Arts and Communications, 1993; Silver Sceptre Award, Accademia Internazionale di Pontzen di Lettere, Scienze ed Arti, Naples, Italy, 1998. *Memberships:* World Poetry Society; Tagore Institute of Creative Writing; Acad. of American Poets; Poetry Society of America; Wordsworth-Coleridge Asscn; Asscn of Literary Scholars and Critics; MLA. *Address:* 9866 S Westnedge Ave, Portage, MI 49002, USA.

CLINTON, (Lloyd) DeWitt; b. 29 Aug. 1946, Topeka, KS, USA. Prof.; Poet. m. 14 July 1973, 1 step-d. *Education:* BA, Southwestern College, 1968; MA, Wichita State University, 1972; MFA, 1975, PhD, 1981, Bowling Green State University. *Appointments:* Lecturer, 1981–85, Asst Prof., 1985–88; Assoc. Prof., 1988–95, Prof., 1995–, University of Wisconsin at Whitewater. *Publications:* Conquistador, Dog Texts; The Rand McNally Poems; Coyot, Dog Texts; Das Illustrite Mississippithal Revisited; Night Jungle Bird Life; Active Death: Unholy Rhymes. *Contributions to:* Journal of Reform Judaism; Kenyon Review; Great River Review; Wisconsin Review; Birmingham Poetry Review;

Apalachee Quarterly; Eleven Wisconsin Poets; Heartland II: Poets of the Midwest; Southern California Quarterly; Abiko Quarterly; Cross Currents: Religion and Intellectual Life; Louisiana Literature; Image: A Jounal of the Arts and Religion; Oxford University Press Anthology. *Honours:* Ann Stanford Poetry Prize, University of Southern California, 1994; Summer Enhancement Grant, University of Wisconsin at Whitewater, 1994; Milwaukee County Individual Artist Fellowship, 1997. *Memberships:* Associated Writing Programs; Wisconsin Fellowship of Poets. *Address:* 3567 N Murray Ave, Shorewood, WI 53211, USA.

CLITHEROE, Frederic; b. 25 Sept. 1941, Bury, Lancashire, England. Librarian; Poet. m. Catherine Eyre, 1 July 1971, 1 s., 1 d. *Education:* BA English, University of Exeter, 1966–69; ALA, 1970. *Appointments:* University of Sussex, 1970–71; Asst Librarian, University of Keele, 1971–90; Freelance Writer, 1990–. *Publications:* Ellipsis, 1961; Poems, 1968; Meerbrook, 1979; Forsbrook, 1981; Countess Torsy, 1989; Harecastle Mint, 1993; That Velvet Smile, 2002. *Contributions to:* Anthologies and periodicals. *Honours:* Dunn Wilson Prize, 1966; Award from Beanica Foundation, 1981. *Address:* Greenfields, Agger Hill, Finney Green, Newcastle, Staffordshire ST5 6AA, England.

CLOUDSLEY, Timothy; b. 18 Sept. 1948, Cambridge, England. University Lecturer; Poet; Writer. m. Rhona Cleugh, 18 July 1987, 2 s. *Education:* BA Honours, Cantab, 1971; MA, 1974; Postgraduate Research, Durham University, 1972–74. *Appointments:* Lecturer, Sociology, Newcastle University, 1972–74; Napier University, Edinburgh, 1974–76, Heriot-Watt University, Edinburgh, 1976–77; Glasgow Caledonian University, 1977–. *Publications:* Poems to Light (Through Love and Blood), 1980; Mair Licht (anthology), 1988; The Construction of Nature (social philosophy), 1994; Coincidence (anthology), 1995; Incantations From Streams of Fire, 1997; Poems, 1998. *Contributions to:* Northlight Poetry Review; Understanding Magazine; Interactions; Romantic Heir; The People's Poetry; Cadmium Blue Literary Journal; Le Journal des Poètes. *Membership:* Open Circle (Arts and Literature Organization), Glasgow, literary secretary, 1990–96. *Address:* 31 Hamilton Dr., Glasgow G12 8DN, Scotland.

CLOUTIER, Cécile; b. 13 June 1930, Québec, QC, Canada. Poet; Writer; Prof. Emerita. m. Jerzy Wojciechowski, 27 Dec. 1966, 2 d. *Education:* BA, Collège de Sillery, 1951; Licence-ès-Lettres, 1953, Diplôme d'Etudes Supérieures, 1954, Université Laval; Doctorat en Esthétique, Université de Paris, 1962; MA, McMaster University, 1978; MA, University of Toronto, 1981; Doctorat en Psychologie, Université de Tours, 1983. *Appointments:* Prof. of French and Québec Literature, University of Ottawa, 1958–64; Prof. of Aesthetics and French and Québec Literature, 1964–95, Prof. Emerita, 1995–, University of Toronto. *Publications:* Mains de sable, 1960; Cuivre et soies, 1964; Cannelles et craies, 1969; Paupières, 1970; Câblogrammes, 1972; Chaleuils, 1979; Springtime of Spoken Words, 1979; Près, 1983; Opuscula Aesthetica Nostra: Essais sur L'Esthétique, 1984; La Girafe, 1984; L'Echangeur, 1985; L'Ecouté, 1986; Solitude Rompue, 1986; Lampées, 1990; Périhélie, 1990; La poésie de l'Hexagone, 1990; Ancres d'Encre, 1993; Ostraka. *Contributions to:* Various publications. *Honours:* Medal, Société des Ecrivains de France, 1960; Centennial Medal, Canada, 1967; Governor-General's Award for Poetry, 1986; Medal Société des Poètes Français, 1994. *Memberships:* Asscn des Ecrivains de Langue Française; PEN Club de France; Société des Ecrivains; Société des Gens de Lettres de Paris; Union des Ecrivains Québécois. *Address:* 44 Farm Greenway, Don Mills, Ontario, Canada M3A 3M2.

CLOVIS, Donna Lucille; b. 22 Aug. 1957, East Orange, New Jersey, USA. Educator; Writer; Poet. 2 s., 1 d. *Education:* BA, Trenton State College, 1978. *Appointments:* Teacher, 1981–. *Publications:* Metamorphosis: Survival Through These Hard Times; Struggles for Freedom, 1994. *Contributions to:* Instructor Magazine; True Love Magazine; Black Masks Magazine. *Honours:* New Jersey Institute of Technology Writers Award for Poetry; ESL Success Award; Blue Ribbon Award. *Memberships:* Poets and Writers Guild; Southern Jersey Poetry Asscn; New Jersey Poetry Society; National Council of Teachers of English. *Address:* PO Box 0741, Princeton Junction, NJ 08550, USA.

CLUYSENAAR, Anne, (Alice Andrée); b. 15 March 1936, Brussels, Belgium (Naturalized Irish citizen). Lecturer; Poet; Songwriter; Librettist; Painter. m. Walter Freeman Jackson, 30 Oct. 1976. *Education:* BA, Trinity College, Dublin, 1957; Diploma in General Linguistics, University of Edinburgh, 1962. *Appointments:* Asst Lecturer, University of Manchester, 1957–58; Reader to (blind) critic and novelist, Percy Lubbock, 1959; Librarian, Chester Beatty Library of Oriental Manuscripts, Dublin; Lecturer, King's College, Aberdeen, 1963–65, University of Lancaster, 1965–71, Huddersfield Polytechnic, 1972, University of Birmingham, 1973–76, Sheffield City Polytechnic, 1976–89; Part-time Lecturer, University of Wales, Cardiff, 1990–2002. *Publications:* A Fan of Shadows, 1967; Nodes, 1971; Introduction to Literary Stylistics, 1976; Selected Poems of James Burns Singers (ed.), 1977; Poetry Introduction 4, 1978; Double Helix, 1982; Timeslips: New and Selected Poems, 1997. *Contributions to:* Various publications. *Memberships:* Co-founder and Secretary, Usk Valley Vaughan Asscn, 1995–; Founding General Ed., now Poetry Ed., U.V.V.A journal, Scintilla; Fellow, Welsh Acad., 2001–; Verbal Arts Asscn, chair, 1983–86. *Address:* Little Wentwood Farm, Llantrisant, Usk, Gwent NP15 1ND, Wales. *E-mail:* anne.cluysenaar@virgin.net.

COBB, David Jeffery; b. 12 March 1926, Harrow, Middlesex, England. Writer; Poet. m. Pannee Siripongpreeda, 10 July 1979, 2 s., 3 d. *Education:* BA, 1954; PGCE, 1955. *Appointments:* German Teacher, Nottinghamshire, 1955–58; Programme Officer, UNESCO Institute of Education, Hamburg, 1958–62; English Teacher, British Council, Bangkok, 1962–68; Asst Prof., Asian Institute of Technology, Bangkok, 1968–72; Man., RDU, Longman Group Ltd, 1972–84. *Publications:* A Leap in the Light; Mounting Shadows; Jumping From Kiyomizu; Chips off the Old Great Wall; The Shield-Raven of Wittenham; The Cuckoo Pen; The Spring Journey to the Saxon Shore; The Iron Book of British Haiku; A Bowl of Sloes; The Genius of Haiku, Readings From R H Blyth; The British Museum Haiku; Palm. *Contributions to:* Rialto; Blithe Spirit; Modern Haiku; Frogpond; HQ; Snapshots; Tundra. *Honours:* First Prize, Cardiff International Haiku Competition, 1991; Second Prize, HSA Merit Book Award, 1997–2002; First Prize, Itoen International Contest, Japan, 1993; Third Prize, Hobo, Australia, 1998. *Memberships:* British Haiku Society, pres., 1997–; Haiku Society of America; John Clare Society. *Address:* Sinodun, Shalford, Braintree, Essex CM7 5HN, England. E-mail:dcobb@cosi.fsnet.co.uk.

COBBING, Bob; b. 30 July 1920, Enfield, Middlesex, England. Poet; Writer; Ed. *Education:* Teacher's Certificate, Bognor Training College, 1949. *Appointments:* Co-ordinator, Asscn of Little Presses, 1971–92; Co-Ed., Poetry and Litte Press Information, 1980–92. *Publications:* Collected Poems, 16 edns, 1977–99; Concerning Concrete Poetry (with Peter Mayer), 1978; A Short History of London (with Jeremy Adler), 1979; Domestic Ambient Noise (with Lawrence Upton), 300 issues, 1994–2000; Koh Bok: Selected Poems, 1948–99, 1999. *Address:* 89A Petherton Rd, London N5 2QT, England.

COCCO-ANGIOY, Marisa; b. 18 Dec. 1938, Benevento, Italy. Educator; Writer; Poet. *Education:* University studies. *Publications:* Tramenta il Sole, 1990; I Morti di Palermo, 1993; El Amor, 1994. *Contributions to:* Various publications. *Honour:* Premio, San Valentino, 1990. *Address:* Via Pisacane, 17-16129 Genoa, Italy.

CODRESCU, Andrei; b. 20 Dec. 1946, Sibiu, Romania (Naturalized US citizen, 1981). Prof. of English; Author; Poet; Ed.; Radio and Television Commentator. m. Alice Henderson, 12 Sept. 1969, divorced 1998, 2 s. *Education:* BA, University of Bucharest, 1965. *Appointments:* Prof. of English, Louisiana State University, 1966–; Commentator, All Things Considered, National Public Radio; Ed., Exquisite Corpse, literary journal. *Publications:* Fiction: The Repentence of Lorraine, 1994; The Blood Countess, 1995; Messiah, 1999–. Poetry: Comrade Past and Mister Present, 1991; Belligerence, 1993; Alien Candor: Selected Poems, 1970–1995, 1996. Essays: Raised by Puppets Only to be Killed by Research, 1987; Craving for Swan, 1988; The Disappearance of the Outside: A Manifesto for Escape, 1990; The Hole in the Flag: A Romanian Exile's Story of Return and Revolution, 1991; Road Scholar: Coast to Coast Late in the Century, 1993; The Muse is Always Half-Dressed in New Orleans, 1995; Zombification: Essays from NPR, 1995; The Dog With the Chip in His Neck: Essays from NPR & Elsewhere, 1996; Ay, Cuba! A Socio-Erotic Journey, 1999. Editor: American Poetry Since 1970: Up Late, 1988; The Stiffest of the Corpse: An Exquisite Corpse Reader, 1983–1990, 1990; American Poets Say Goodbye to the 20th Century, 1996. Film: Road Scholar, Public Broadcasting Service, 1994. *Honours:* George Foster Peabody Award, 1995; Freedom of Speech Award, American Civil Liberties Union, 1995; Literature Prize, Romanian Cultural Foundation, 1996. *Address:* 1114 Peniston, New Orleans, LA 70115, USA.

CODRESCU, Ion; b. 16 Dec. 1951, Cobadin, Constanza, Romania. Art Teacher; Poet. m. Mihaela Codrescu, 17 Aug. 1977. *Education:* Graduated, Dept of Drawing, 1973, History of Art Dept, 1982, Fine Arts Acad., Bucharest; First Degree of Training. *Appointments:* Teacher, Art, 1973–, Art History, 1982–; Founder, Ed., Albatross, English-Romanian haiku magazine, 1992–; Founder, Organiser, Constantza International Haiku Festival, 1992, 1994, Mamaia National Haiku Conference, 1993, 1995, 1997; Corresponding Academician, Accademia Internazionale Greci-Marino, Accademia del Verbano di Lettere, Arti e Scienze, Vercelli, Italy. *Publications:* Drawings Among Haiku, 1992; Constantza Haiku Anthology, 1992; L'abricotier change de visage, 1994; Round the Pond (haiku anthology), 1994; Unsold Flowers, 1995; Foreign Guest, 1999. *Contributions to:* Anthologies, magazines and other periodicals. *Honours:* Museum of Haiku Literature Award, Tokyo, 1991; Merited Book Award, 1992, First Prize, 1994, Special Award, Ed. of Poetry Books, 1997, Haiku Society of America; Grand Prize, Renku Contest, USA, 1996; Diploma, 1997, Best Haiku Books in the World from 1992–98 Award for Drawings, Croatian Haiku Asscn; Nagoya City Prize for Haiku, 1998; Third Prize, First International Poetry Competition, Nis, Yugoslavia, 1998; Kokushikan University Medal for Poetry, Tokyo, 1998; Tyrone Guthrie Scholarship, Ireland, 1998. *Memberships:* Haiku Society of America, 1991–; Founder, Pres., Constantza Haiku Society, 1992–; Haiku International Asscn, Japan, 1994–; Romanian Writers' Asscn, 1995–; Renku Asscn of Japan, 1998–. *Address:* Str Soveja nr 25, Bl V2, sc B, ap 31, 8700 Constantza, Romania.

COEN, Christiana; b. 18 Dec. 1943, Shanghai, China. Teacher; Poet. m. Massimo A Tosini, 28 Dec. 1992. Educatioin: Degree in Literature and Philosophy, University of Genoa. *Publications:* Qualcosa Che Ritorna, 1966; Storia di Ingrid La Viaggiatrice, 1995. *Contributions to:* L'Incantiere, poetry review. *Honours:* Finalist, Lerici-Pea Award, 1966, National Lorenzo Montano Award, 1996. *Membership:* Baobab, sound poets asscn. *Address:* Via Casale 7, 20144, Milan, Italy.

COFFEY, Marilyn J(une); b. 22 July 1937, Alma, Nebraska, USA. Writer; Poet; Assoc. Prof. of Creative Writing. m. 15 April 1961, divorced, 1 s. *Education:* BA, University of Nebraska, 1959; MFA, Brooklyn College, 1981. *Appointments:* Faculty, Pratt Institute, New York, 1966–69, 1973–90; Adjunct Communication Instructor, St Mary's College, Lincoln, Nebraska, 1990–92; Assoc. Prof. of Creative Writing, Ft Hays State University, 1992–. *Publications:* Marcella (novel), 1973; Great Plains Patchwork (non-fiction), 1989; A Cretan Cycle: Fragments Unearthed From Knossos (poems), 1991; Creating the Classic Short Story: A Workbook, 1995; Delicate Footsteps: Poems About Real Women, 1995. *Contributions to:* Anthologies, journals, reviews, and newspapers. *Honours:* Pushcart Prize, 1976; Master Alumnus, University of Nebraska, 1977; Winner, Newark Public Library Competitions, New Jersey, 1985, 1987–88; Several grants. *Memberships:* E A Burnett Society, charter mem.; Poets and Writers. *Address:* c/o Dept of English, Fort Hays State University, Hays, KS 67601, USA.

COGSWELL, Frederick William; b. 8 Nov. 1917, East Centreville, New Brunswick, Canada. Prof. Emeritus; Author; Poet; Ed.; Trans. m. (1) Margaret Hynes, 3 July 1944, deceased 2 May 1985, 2 d., (2) Gail Fox, 8 Nov. 1985. *Education:* BA, 1949, MA, 1950, University of New Brunswick; PhD, University of Edinburgh, 1952. *Appointments:* Asst Prof., 1952–57, Assoc. Prof., 1957–61, Prof., 1961–83, Prof. Emeritus, 1983–, University of New Brunswick; Ed., Fiddlehead Magazine, 1952–66, Humanities Asscn Bulletin, 1967–72. *Publications:* The Stunted Strong, 1955; The Haloed Tree, 1956; Testament of Cresseid, 1957; Descent from Eden, 1959; Lost Dimensions, 1960; A Canadian Anthology, 1960; Five New Brunswick Poets, 1962; The Arts in New Brunswick, 1966; Star People, 1968; Immortal Plowman, 1969; In Praise of Chastity, 1970; One Hundred Poems of Modern Québec, 1971; The Chains of Liliput, 1971; The House Without a Door, 1973; Against Perspective, 1979; A Long Apprenticeship: Collected Poems, 1980; Pearls, 1983; The Edge to Life, 1987; The Best Notes Merge, 1988; Black and White Tapestry, 1989; Unfinished Dreams: Contemporary Poetry of Acadie, 1990; Watching an Eagle, 1991; When the Right Light Shines, 1992; In Praise of Old Music, 1992; In My Own Growing, 1993; As I See It, 1994; In Trouble With Light, 1996. *Honours:* Order of Canada; Medals; Awards. *Memberships:* League of Canadian Poets; PEN; Writers Federation of New Brunswick. *Address:* Comp A6, Site 6, RR4, Fredericton, New Brunswick E3B 4X5, Canada.

COHEN, Helen Degen; b. 19 Nov. 1934, USA. Writer; Poet. m. Arnold L Cohen, 4 March 1956, divorced, 2 s., 1 d. *Education:* BS, University of San Antonio; MA, University of Illinois, 1977. *Appointments:* School Teacher, 1958–60; Instructor, Roosevelt University, 1979–84; Artist in Education, Illinois Arts Council, 1983–90. *Contributions to:* Partisan Review; Spoon River Quarterly; The House in Via Gambito; Concert at Chapins House; Another Chicago Magazine; Outerbridge. *Honours:* National Endowment for the Arts; Literary Award, Illinois Arts Council; First Prize, Stand Magazine; First Prize, Korone; Special Award, Indiana University Writer's Conference. *Memberships:* Poetry Forum; Poetry Society of America; Illinois Writers Inc. *Address:* 1166 Osterman, Deerfield, IL 60015, USA.

COHEN, Leonard (Norman); b. 21 Sept. 1934, Montréal, QC, Canada. Poet; Singer; Songwriter; Author. *Education:* BA, English, McGill University, 1955. *Appointments:* Many poetry readings; Various concert appearances in Canada and abroad. *Publications:* Let Us Compare Mythologies, 1956; The Spice-Box of Earth, 1961; The Favourite Game, 1963; Flowers for Hitler, 1964; Beautiful Losers, 1966; Parasites of Heaven, 1966; Selected Poems 1956–1968, 1968; The Energy of Slaves, 1972; Death of a Lady's Man, 1978; Book of Mercy, 1984; Stranger Music: Selected Poems and Songs, 1993. Other: Various songs and recordings. *Honours:* William Harold Moon Award, Recording Rights Organizatioin of Canada Ltd, 1984; Juno Hall of Fame, 1991. *Address:* c/o Kelley Lynch, 419 N Larchmont Blvd, Suite 91, Los Angeles, CA 90004, USA.

COHN, Jim; b. 17 April 1953, Illinois, USA. Poet; Scholar. *Education:* BA, University of Colorado; Jack Kerouac Fellowship, Naropa Institute; MSEd, University of Rochester and National Technical Institute for the Deaf. *Publications:* Green Sky; Mangrove; Divine April; Prairie Falcon. *Contributions to:* Rolling Stone; Brief; Heaven Bone; Napalm Health Spa; Nada Anthology; The Temple of Baseball; Nice to See You: Talking with Tranquility; Sign Language Studies; Akwesasne Notes. *Honour:* Walt Whitman Award. *Memberships:* Poets and Writers; Writers and Books. *Address:* Birdsfoot Farm, Star Route, Box 138, Canton, NY 17617, USA.

COLAUTTI FOCARDI, Rosa; b. 5 Oct. 1918, Tarcento, Italy. Poet. m. Vincenzo Focardi, 16 Dec. 1950, 1 s., 1 d. *Publications:* Diario Poetico, 1974. *Contributions to:* Anthologies, periodicals, journals and magazines. *Honours:* Numerous. *Memberships:* Accademia Internazionale Artistico Letteraria Citta' di Boretto, 1987; Accademia Internazionale Della Rosa Azzurra; Associazione Accademica Amica Dell'Umbria. *Address:* Viale della Liberta 41, Chianciano Terme SI, Italy.

COLBY, Beulah M Wadsworth; b. 10 May 1941, Maine, USA. Housewife; Town Clerk; Columnist; Poet. 1 s., 4 d. *Contributions to:* Republican Journal; Golden Treasury of Great Poems. *Honours:* Golden Poet Award; Silver Poet Award. *Address:* HCR 80, Box 4, Liberty, ME 04949, USA.

COLDWELL, John Walter; b. 10 April 1950, London, England. Teacher; Poet. m. Rosemary John, 19 April 1982, 2 s. *Appointments:* Bank Clerk, 1967–74; Teacher, Temple Boys School, 1974–86; Head of English, Hoo Middle School, 1986–89; Teacher, St Georges High School, 1989–. *Publications:* Hoo Sir, Me Sir; More Lasting Than a Fish Supper; Well, Well; Daleks on Ramsey Street; Beast in the Bedroom; The Bees Knees; The Slack Jawed Camel; Thunder Clap; Bees Sneeze. *Contributions to:* Issue One; Brandos Hat; The North; Working Titles; The Third Half; The Rialto; Ioata; Foolscap; Poetry Now; Terrible Work; Purple Patch; Brian Moor's Head; Sol; Smoke; Children's Anthologies. *Honours:* Runner-up, BBC Wildlife Poet of the Year, 2000. *Memberships:* Salford Poems, Swop Scheme; Margate Poetry Festival, Vice Chair. *Address:* 11 Park Rd, Ramsgate, Kent CT11 7QN, England.

COLE, Barry; b. 13 Nov. 1936, Woking, Surrey, England. Writer; Poet. m. Rita Linihan, 1959, 3 d. *Appointments:* Northern Arts Fellow in Literature, Universities of Durham and Newcastle upon Tyne, 1970–72. *Publications:* Blood Ties, 1967; Ulysses in the Town of Coloured Glass, 1968; A Run Across the Island, 1968; Moonsearch, 1968; Joseph Winter's Patronage, 1969; The Search for Rita, 1970; The Visitors, 1970; The Giver, 1971; Vanessa in the City, 1971; Pathetic Fallacies, 1973; Dedications, 1977; The Edge of the Common, 1989; Inside Outside: New and Selected Poems, 1997; Lola and the Train, 1999; Ghosts Are People Too, 2002. *Contributions to:* Many periodicals. *Address:* 68 Myddelton Sq., London EC1R 1XP, England.

COLE, Eugene Roger, (Peter E Locre); b. 14 Nov. 1930, Cleveland, Ohio, USA. Writer; Ed.; Researcher; Poet. *Education:* BA, 1954; MDiv, 1958; AB, 1960; MA, 1970. *Appointments:* Ordained Roman Catholic Priest, 1958; Newman Moderator, Central Washington University, 1958–59; English Instructor, Dept Chair., Schools of Northwest, 1959–69; Poetry Critic, National Writers' Club, 1969–72; Founder, Dir, Godspeople Inc, 1985–. *Publications:* Which End; Spring as Ballet; Have You; Woman, You: Falling Up; Act and Potency; Ding An Sich; Uneasy Camber. *Contributions to:* Saturday Review; Northwest Review; International Poetry Review; Cape Rock Journal; Laurel Review; Discourse; Numerous others. *Honours:* Poetry Broadcast Award; Danae International Poetry Award; Distinguished Service to Poetry Award. *Memberships:* Authors' Guild; National Writers' Club; Friends of the Lilly Society.

COLE, Henri; b. 9 May 1956, Japan. Poet; Teacher; Ed. *Education:* BA, College of William and Mary, 1978; MA, University of Wisconsin, 1980; MFA, Columbia University, 1982. *Appointments:* Exec. Dir, Acad. of American Poets, 1982–88; Visiting Lecturer, Yale College, 1989; Assoc. Prof., Columbia University, 1989; Visiting Writer, University of Maryland, 1990; Briggs-Copeland Lecturer in Poetry, Harvard University, 1993–. *Publications:* The Zoo Wheel of Knowledge; The Marble Queen. *Contributions to:* Antaeus; Atlantic Monthly; Boulevard; Gettysburg Review; Grand Street; Hudson Review; Nation; New Yorker; Ontario Review; Paris Review; Poetry; Southern Review; Yale Review. *Honours:* Pushcart Prize; Ingram Merrill Foundation Fellowship; Amy Lowell Poetry Travelling Scholarship; New York Foundation for the Arts Fellowship; National Endowment for the Arts Fellowship. *Memberships:* Acad. of American Poets; PEN; Poetry Society of America.

COLE-EARNEY, Beverly. See: EARNEY, Beverly (Verna).

COLEMAN, Jane Candia; b. 1 Jan. 1939, Pittsburgh, PA, USA. Writer; Poet. m. Bernard Coleman, 27 March 1965, divorced 1989, 2 s. *Education:* BA, Creative Writing, University of Pittsburgh. *Publications:* No Roof But Sky (poems), 1990; Stories From Mesa Country, 1991; Discovering Eve (short stories), 1993; Shadows in My Hands (memoir), 1993; The Red Drum (poems), 1994; Doc Holliday's Woman (novel), 1995; Moving On (short stories), 1997; I, Pearl Hart (novel), 1998; The O'Keefe Empire (novel), 1999; Doc Holliday's Gone (novel), 1999; Borderlands (short stories), 2000; Desperate Acts (novel), 2001; The Italian Quartet (novel), 2001; Mountain Time (memoir), 2001; Country Music (short stories), 2002; Wives and Lovers (short stories), 2002. *Contributions to:* Periodicals. *Honours:* Western Heritage Awards, 1991, 1992, 1994. *Memberships:* Authors' Guild; Women Writing the West. *Address:* 1702 E Lind Rd, Tucson, AZ 85719, USA.

COLEMAN, Mary Ann; b. 3 Jan. 1928, USA. Writer; Poet. m. Oliver McCarter Coleman, 4 March 1955. *Education:* Indiana University, 1945–49; BSEd, Auburn University, 1950. *Appointments:* Teacher of Poetry Workshops, 1970–. *Publications:* Disappearances; Secret Passageway; Recognizing the Angel; The Dreams of Hummingbirds: Poems from Nature. *Honours:* Poetry Society of America Consuelo Ford Memorial Award; Anhinga Press Cynthia Cahn Memorial Award; Hororable Mention, International Sri Chinmoy Contest. *Memberships:* Poetry Society of America; National League of American Penwomen; Poetry Atlanta; Society of Children's Book Writers; Georgia State Poetry Society. *Address:* 205 Sherwood Dr., Athens, GA 30606, USA.

COLEMAN, Wanda; b. 13 Nov. 1946, Los Angeles, CA, USA. Poet; Writer. *Publications:* Mad Dog Black Lady, 1979; Imagoes, 1983; Heavy Daughte: Blues: Poems and Stories, 1968–1986, 1987; A War of Eyes and Othe: Stories, 1988; Women for All Seasons: Poetry and Prose About th: Transitions in Women's Lives (ed. with Joanne Leedom-Ackerman), 1988; Dicksboro Hotel and Other Travels, 1989; African Sleeping Sickness: Storie: and Poems, 1990; Hand Dance, 1993; Native in a Strange Land: Trials & Tremors, 1996; Bathwater Wine, 1998; Mambo Hips & Make Believe: A Novel 1999. *Contributions to:* Anthologies and periodicals. *Honours:* Fellowships Lenore Marshall Poetry Prize, Acad. of American Poets, 1999.

COLES, Donald Langdon; b. 12 April 1928, Woodstock, Ontario, Canada Prof.; Poet. m. 28 Dec. 1958, 1 s., 1 d. *Education:* BA, Victoria College; MA University of Toronto; MA (Cantab), 1954. *Appointments:* Fiction Ed., The Canadian Forum, 1975–76; Dir, Creative Writing Programme, York University, 1979–85; Poetry Ed., May Studio, Banff Centre for the Fine Arts 1984–93. *Publications:* Sometimes All Over, 1975; Anniversaries, 1979; The Prinzhorn Collection, 1982; Landslides, 1986; K in Love, 1987; Little Bird 1991; Forests of the Medieval World, 1993; Someone Has Stayed in Stockholm Selected and New Poems, 1994; Kurgan, 2000. *Contributions to:* Saturday Night; Canadian Forum; London Review of Books; Poetry (Chicago); Globe and Mail; Arc; Ariel. *Honours:* CBC Literary Competition, 1980; Gold Medal for Poetry, National Magazine Awards, 1986; Gov.-Gen.'s Award for Poetry Canada, 1993; Trillium Prize, Ontario, 2000. *Membership:* PEN International. *Address:* 122 Glenview Ave, Toronto, Ontario M4R 1P8, Canada

COLES, Robert (Martin); b. 12 Oct. 1929, Boston, Massachusetts, USA Physician; Prof. of Psychiatry and Medical Humanities; Writer; Poet. m. Jane Hallowell, 3 s. *Education:* AB, Harvard College, 1950; MD, Columbia University of Physicians and Surgeons, 1954; Internship, University of Chicago Clinics, 1954–55; Psychiatric Residency, Massachusetts General Hospital, 1955–56, McLean Hospital, 1956–57. *Appointments:* Research Psychiatrist, Health Services, 1963–, Lecturer on General Education, 1966–, Prof. of Psychiatry and Medical Humanities, 1977–, Harvard University; Contributing Ed., New Republic, 1966–, American Poetry Review, 1972–, Aperture, 1974–, Literature and Medicine, 1981–, New Oxford Review, 1981–; Visiting Prof. of Public Policy, Duke University, 1973–; Ed., Children and Youth Services Review, 1978–; Visiting Prof. of Psychiatry, Dartmouth College, 1989. *Publications:* Children of Crisis, 5 vols, 1967, 1972, 1978; The Middle Americans, 1970; The Geography of Faith, 1971; The Old Ones of New Mexico, 1973; William Carlos Williams, 1975; Walker Percy, 1978; Flannery O'Connor's South, 1980; The Moral Life of Children, 1986; The Political Life of Children, 1986; Simone Weil, 1987; Dorothy Day, 1987; The Call of Stories: Teaching and the Moral Imagination, 1989; Rumors of Another World, 1989; The Spiritual Life of Children, 1990; Anna Freud: The Dream of Psychoanalysis, 1992; Collected Essays: Omnibus, 1993; The Call of Service: A Witness to Idealism, 1993; The Story of Ruby Bridges, 1995; The Moral Intelligence of Children, 1997; Old and On Their Own, 1998. *Contributions to:* Numerous books, journals, reviews, magazines, and periodicals. *Honours:* McAlpin Medal, National Asscn of Mental Health, 1972; Pulitzer Prize in General Non-Fiction, 1973; Weatherford Prize, Berea College and Council of Southern Mountains, 1973; Lillian Smith Award, Southern Regional Council, 1973; MacArthur Prize Fellow, 1981; Sarah Josepha Hale Award, 1986; Christopher Medals, 1989, 1991; Gold Medal, College of Physicians and Surgeons, Columbia University, 1991; US Presidential Medal of Freedom, 1998; Numerous hon. doctorates. *Memberships:* American Acad. of Arts and Sciences, fellow; American Orthopsychiatric Asscn; American Psychiatric Asscn; Institute of Society, Ethics, and Life Sciences, fellow. *Address:* 81 Carr Rd, Concord, MA 01742, USA.

COLLIER, Michael (Robert); b. 25 May 1953, Phoenix, AZ, USA. Prof. of English; Poet; Writer; Ed. m. Katherine A. Branch, 2 May 1981, 2 s. *Education:* BA, Interdisciplinary Studies, Connecticut College, 1976; MFA, Creative Writing, University of Arizona, 1979. *Appointments:* Lecturer in English, George Mason University, 1982, Trinity College, Washington, DC, 1982–83; Writing Staff, The Writer's Center, Bethesda, MD, 1982–85; Visiting Lecturer, 1984–85, Adjunct Instructor, 1985–86; Asst Prof. of English, 1986–90, Prof. of English, 1995–, University of Maryland at College Park; Visiting Prof., Johns Hopkins University, 1986–89; Yale University, 1990, 1992; Teacher, Warren Wilson College, 1991–93, 1996; Assoc. Staff, 1992–94, Dir, 1994–, Bread Loaf Writers' Conference, Middlebury College. *Publications:* Poetry: The Clasp and Other Poems, 1986; The Folded Heart, 1989; The Neighbor, 1995; The Ledge, 2000. Editor: The Wesleyan Tradition: Four Decades of American Poetry, 1993; The New Bread Loaf Anthology of Contemporary American Poetry (with Stanley Plumly), 1999; The New American Poets: A Bread Load Anthology, 2000. *Contributions to:* Anthologies, journals and magazines. *Honours:* Writing Fellow, Fine Arts Work Center, Provincetown, 1979–80; 'Discovery' The Nation Award, 1981; Margaret Bridgeman Scholar in Poetry, 1981, Theodore Morrison Fellow in Poetry, 1986, Bread Loaf Writers' Conference; National Endowment for the Arts Creative Writing Fellowships, 1984, 1994; Alice Faye di Castagnola Award, Poetry Society of America, 1988; Fellow, Timothy Dwight College, Yale University, 1992–96; Guggenheim Fellowship, 1995–96; Maryland Arts Council Grant, 2000; Poet Laureate of Maryland, 2001. *Memberships:* Acad. of American Poets; Poetry Society of America. *Address:* 111 Smithwood Ave, Catonsville, MD 21228, USA.

COLLINS, Annette. See: BATSTONE, Patricia.

COLLINS, Billy; b. 22 March 1941, New York, NY, USA. Poet; Writer; Distinguished Prof. m. Diane Collins, 21 Jan. 1979. *Education:* BS, English, Holy Cross College, 1963; PhD, University of California at Riverside, 1971. *Appointments:* Prof., 1969–2001, Distinguished Prof., 2001–, Lehman College of the City University of New York; Visiting Writer, Poets House, Northern Ireland, 1993–96, Lenoir-Rhyne College, 1994, Ohio State University, 1998; Resident Poet, Burren College of Art, Ireland, 1996, Sarah Lawrence College, 1998–2000; Adjunct Prof., Columbia University, 2000–01; Poet Laureate of the United States, 2001–02; Numerous poetry readings. *Publications:* Pokerface, 1977; The Video Poems, 1980; The Apple That Astonished Paris, 1988; Questions About Angels, 1991; The Art of Drowning, 1995; Picnic, Lightning, 1998; Taking Off Emily Dickinson's Clothes: Selected Poems, 2000; Sailing Alone Around the Room: New and Selected Poems, 2001. *Contributions to:* Books and journals. *Honours:* New York Foundation for the Arts Poetry Fellowship, 1986; National Endowment for the Arts Creative Writing Fellowship, 1998; National Poetry Series Competition Winner, 1990; Bess Hokin Prize, 1991; Frederick Bock Prize, 1992; Guggenheim Fellowship, 1993; Levinson Prize, 1995; Paterson Poetry Prize, 1999; J. Howard and Barbara M. J. Wood Prize, 1999; Pushcart Prize, 2002. *Address:* c/o Dept of English, Lehman College of the City University of New York, Bronx, NY 10468, USA.

COLLINS, Martha; b. 25 Nov. 1940, Omaha, Nebraska, USA. Prof.; Writer; Poet. m. Theodore M Space, 6 April 1991. *Education:* AB, Stanford University, 1962; MA, 1965, PhD, 1971, University of Iowa. *Appointments:* Asst Prof., Northeast Missouri University, 1965–66; Prof., University of Massachusetts, Boston, 1966–97, Oberlin College, 1997–. *Publications:* The Catastrophe of Rainbows; The Arrangement of Space; A History of Small Life on a Windy Planet, 1993; Some Things Words Can Do, 1998. *Contributions to:* Magazines and journals. *Honours:* Gordon Barber Memorial Award; National Endowment for the Arts Fellowship; Alice Fay Di Castagnola Award; Peregrine Poetry Prize; Ingram Merrill Fellowship; Pushcart Prize; Mary Carolyn Davies Award; Bunting Fellowship. *Memberships:* Poetry Society of America; Associated Writing Programs; New England Poetry Club. *Address:* Creative Writing, Oberlin College, Oberlin, OH 44074, USA.

COLOMBO, John (Robert); b. 24 March 1936, Kitchener, ON, Canada. Writer; Poet; Ed.; Trans.; Consultant. m. Ruth Florence Brown, 11 May 1959, 2 s., 1 d. *Education:* Waterloo College, 1956–57; BA, 1959, Graduate Studies, 1959–60, University of Toronto. *Appointments:* Asst Ed., Ryerson Press, 1960–63; Consulting Ed., McClelland & Stewart, 1963–70; Gen. Ed., The Canadian Global Almanac, 1992–2000. *Publications:* Author, ed. or trans. of over 153 titles, including collections of quotations, anthologies, poetry, mysteries, folklore. *Contributions to:* Periodicals; Radio and TV programmes. *Honours:* Centennial Medal, 1967; First Writer-in-Residence, Mohawk College, 1979–80; Hon. DLitt, York University, 1998; Various prizes and awards including: Harbourfront Literary Award. *Address:* 42 Dell Park Ave, Toronto, ON M6B 2T6, Canada. *E-mail:* jrc@inforamp.net. *Website:* www.colombo.ca.

COMBS, Maxine; b. 14 June 1937, Dallas, Texas, USA. Teacher; Writer; Poet. m., 1 s., 1 d. *Education:* BA, Mills College, 1958; MA, Wayne State University, 1961; PhD, University of Oregon, 1967. *Appointments:* Instructor, Idaho State University, 1963–65, Howard University, 1998, 1990; Lecturer, Lane Community College, 1966–69, American University, 1970–74; Instructor, 1972–77, 1981–88, Asst Prof., 1990–, University of the District of Columbia; Asst Prof., George Mason University, 1979–80. *Publications:* Swimming Out of the Collective Unconscious; The Foam of Perilous Seas. *Contributions to:* South Florida Poetry Review; Backbone; Ariel; Up Against the Wall; Poets' Domain; Echoes; Finding the Name; Round Table; Iris. *Honours:* Honourable Mention, National League of American Pen Women, Finalist, Signpost Press Chapbook Contest; Semi-finalist, The Nation Chapbook Contest; Larry Neal Award in Fiction. *Memberships:* Writers' Center; Acad. of American Poets. *Address:* 2216 King Pl. NW, Washington, DC 20007, USA.

COMPTON, Suzette Childeroy; b. 27 Oct. 1922, India. Poet. m. (1) Eric Burn, divorced, (2) Alfred Busiel, deceased, 1 d., (3) Angus Mackintosh, divorced, (4) Roddy Wilson, divorced. *Publications:* Debrett's Book of Antiques; Christmas Cards for The Collector. *Contributions to:* Parnassus Book of World Poets, 1995; Anchor Poets of the Southeast, England; Kettleshill Press Anthology; Blue Dragon Press Anthology; Over 70 poems, illustrated with paintings by Michael Garady; Phoenix Poets; Lings Greetings Cards, Paintings and Poetry Series. *Honours:* Dame of the Order of St Michael of The Wing. *Memberships:* London Writers Circle; Phoenix Poets. *Address:* 9 The Hoo, Church St, Old Willingdon, Eastbourne, East Sussex BN20 9HR, England.

CONLEY, Robert J(ackson); b. 29 Dec. 1940, Cushing, OK, USA. Writer; Poet. m. Evelyn Snell, March 1978. *Education:* BA, 1966, MA, 1968, Midwestern State University. *Appointments:* Instructor in English, Northern Illinois University, 1968–71, Southwest Missouri State University, 1971–74; Co-ordinator of Indian Culture, Eastern Montana College, 1975–77; Dir of Indian Studies, 1979–86, Assoc. Prof. of English, 1986–90, Morningside College. *Publications:* Twenty-One Poems, 1975; Adawosgi: Swimmer Wesley Snell, A Cherokee Memorial, 1980; Echoes of Our Being (ed.), 1982; The

Rattlesnake Band and Other Poems, 1984; Back to Malachi, 1986; The Actor, 1987; Killing Time, 1988; Wilder and Wilder, 1988; The Witch of Goingsnake and Other Stories, 1988; Colfax, 1989; The Saga of Henry Starr, 1989; Quitting Time, 1989; Go-ahead Rider, 1990; Ned Christie's War, 1990; Strange Company, 1991; Mountain Windsong: A Novel of the Trail of Tears, 1992; The Way of the Priests, 1992; Nickajack, 1992; Border Line, 1993; The Dark Way, 1993; The Long Trail North, 1993; The White Path, 1993; The Long Way Home, 1994; Geronimo: An American Legend (with John Milius and Larry Gross), 1994; To Make a Killing, 1994; Crazy Snake, 1994; The Way South, 1994; Zeke Proctor: Cherokee Outlaw, 1994; The Dark Island, 1995; Captain Dutch, 1995; Outside the Law, 1995; The War Trail North, 1995; War Woman: A Novel of the Real People, 1997; The Meade Solution, 1998; The Peace Chief: A Novel of the Real People, 1998; Incident at Buffalo Crossing, 1998; Brass, 1999; Cherokee Dragon: A Novel of the Real People, 2000; Barjack, 2000; Fugitive's Trail, 2000; Broke Loose, 2000; The Gunfighter, 2001; A Cold Hard Trail, 2001; Spanish Jack: A Novel of the Real People, 2001. *Contributions to:* Anthologies and periodicals. *Honours:* Spur Awards, Western Writers of America, 1992, 1995; Inducted, Oklahoma Professional Writers Hall of Fame, 1996; Oklahoma Writer of the Year, University of Oklahoma Professional Writing Program, 1999; Cherokee Medal of Honor, Cherokee Honor Society, 2000. *Memberships:* International Poetry Society; Western Writers of America. *Address:* PO Box 1871, Tahlequah, OK 74464, USA.

CONN, Jeanne Emily Louise; b. 18 Dec. 1931, Ilford, Essex, England. Ed.; Poet; Writer. m. Victor William Amos Conn, 5 April 1956. *Education:* University of Leicester. *Appointments:* Ed., Connections, Literary Quarterly. *Contributions to:* Kerouac Connection; Atlantean; Sol; Global Tapestry; Alpha Beat Soup; Connections; Matrix. *Memberships:* Goldsmiths Literary Society; Luciad, Leicester University Literary Magazine. *Address:* 165 Domonic Dr., New Eltham, London SE9 3LE, England.

CONN, Stewart; b. 5 Nov. 1936, Glasgow, Scotland. Poet; Playwright. *Appointments:* Radio Producer, Glasgow, 1962–77, Head of Radio Drama, Edinburgh, 1977–92, BBC; Literary Adviser, Royal Lyceum Theatre, Edinburgh, 1972–75. *Publications:* Poetry: Thunder in the Air, 1967; The Chinese Tower, 1967; Stoats in the Sunlight, 1968, US edn as Ambush and Other Poems; An Ear to the Ground, 1972; PEN New Poems, 1973–74 (ed.), 1974; Under the Ice, 1978; In the Kibble Palace: New and Selected Poems, 1987; The Luncheon of the Boating Party, 1992; In the Blood, 1995; At the Aviary, 1995; The Ice Horses (ed.), 1996; Stolen Light: Selected Poems, 1999. Plays: The Aquarium and Other Plays, 1976; Thistlewood, 1979; The Burning in Scots Plays of the 70's, 2000. Prose and Poetry: Distances, 2001. *Contributions to:* Anthologies, journals, and radio. *Honours:* E C Gregory Award, 1964; Scottish Arts Council Awards and Poetry Prize, 1968, 1978, 1992; English-Speaking Union Travel Scholarship, 1984; Scottish Arts Council Playwrights Bursary, 1995; Society of Authors Travel Bursary, 1996. *Memberships:* Knight of Mark Twain; Royal Scottish Acad. of Music and Drama, fellow; Pres., Shore Poets; Scottish Society of Playwrights. *Literary Agent:* Lemon Unna & Durbridge Ltd, 24 Pottery Lane, Holland Park, London W11 4LZ, England. *Address:* 1 Fettes Row, Edinburgh EH3 6SF, Scotland.

CONNELL, Evan S(helby), Jr; b. 17 Aug. 1924, Kansas City, MO, USA. Author; Poet. *Education:* Dartmouth College, 1941–43; BA, University of Kansas, 1947; Graduate Studies, Stanford University, 1947–48, Columbia University, 1948–49, San Francisco State College. *Appointment:* Ed., Contact magazine, 1960–65. *Publications:* Fiction: The Anatomy Lesson and Other Stories, 1957; Mrs Bridge, 1959; The Patriot, 1960; At the Crossroads: Stories, 1965; The Diary of a Rapist, 1966; Mr Bridge, 1969; The Connoisseur, 1974; Double Honeymoon, 1976; St Augustine's Pigeon, 1980; The Alchymist's Journal, 1991; The Collected Stories of Evan S. Connell, 1995; Deus Lo Volt!: Chronicle of the Crusades, 2000. Poetry: Notes From a Bottle Found on the Beach at Carmel, 1963; Points for a Compass Rose, 1973. Non-Fiction: A Long Desire, 1979; The White Lantern, 1980; Son of the Morning Star: Custer and the Little Bighorn, 1984; Mesa Verde, 1992; The Aztec Treasure House, 2001. *Contributions to:* Periodicals. *Honours:* Eugene F. Saxton Fellow, 1953; Guggenheim Fellowship, 1963; Rockefeller Foundation Grant, 1967; California Literature Silver Medal, 1974; Los Angeles Times Book Award, 1985; American Acad. of Arts and Letters Award, 1987; Lannan Foundation Lifetime Achievement Award, 2000. *Membership:* American Acad. of Arts and Letters. *Address:* c/o Fort Marcy 13, 320 Artist Rd, Sante Fe, NM 87501, USA.

CONNERS, Logan T. See: MASON, H(enry) C(onner).

CONNOR, Joan; b. 21 Jan. 1954, Holyoke, MA, USA. Writer; Poet; Educator. m. Nils Wessell, separated, 1 s. *Education:* BA cum laude, Mount Holyoke College, 1976; MA, Middlebury College, 1984; MFA, Vermont College, 1995. *Appointments:* Assoc. Fiction Ed., Chelsea, 1994–96; Visiting Prof., 1995–96, Asst Prof. of English, 1996–, Ohio University, Athens. *Publications:* Here on Old Route 7, 1997; We Who Live Apart, 2000. *Contributions to:* Anthologies and periodicals. *Honours:* Fellow, Vermont Studio Colony, 1990, MacDowell Colony, 1992, Virginia Center for the Creative Arts, 1993, Yaddo Colony, 1993. *Memberships:* Associated Writing Programs; Young Writers' Institute. *Address:* 328 Carroll Rd, Athens, OH 45701, USA. *E-mail:* connor@oak.cats.ohiou.edu.

CONNOR, Margaret Lamorna; b. 10 Sept. 1929, Bedford, England. Teacher (retd); Collage Artist; Poet; Writer. *Education:* Ripon College of Education, 1952–54. *Publications:* Introducing Fabric Collage, 1969; Pilgrimage (poems), 1995: B H Latrobe Architect, (pamphlet), 1995. *Contributions to:* Many anthologies, journals, and newspapers. *Honours:* 17 collage exhibitions; Third Prize, Society of Teachers of Speech and Drama, 1985; Runner-up, Yorkshire Television Poetry Competition, 1985; Co-Winner, First Prize in Poetry, Swarthmore Creative Writing Competition, 1995; Second Prize, Yorkshire Journal Poetry Competition, 2000. *Membership:* Brontë Society. *Address:* 13 Fulneck, Pudsey, West Yorkshire LS28 8NT, England.

CONNOR, Tony; b. 16 March 1930, Manchester, England. Prof. of English; Poet. m. Frances Foad, 1961. *Appointments:* Prof. of English, Wesleyan University, CT, 1971–. *Publications:* With Love Somehow, 1962; Lodgers, 1965; 12 Secret Poems, 1965; Kon in Springtime, 1968; In the Happy Valley, 1971; The Memoirs of Uncle Harry, 1974; Twelve Villanelles, 1977; New and Selected Poems, 1982; Spirits of the Place, 1987; Metamorphic Adventures, 1996. *Address:* 44 Brainerd Ave, Middletown, CT 06457, USA.

CONQUEST, (George) Robert (Acworth); b. 15 July 1917, Malvern, Worcestershire, England. Historian; Writer; Poet. m. (1) Joan Watkins, 1942, divorced 1948, 2 s., (2) Tatiana Mihailova, 1948, divorced 1962, (3), Caroleen Macfarlene, 1964, divorced 1978, (4) Elizabeth Neece, 1 Dec. 1979. *Education:* University of Grenoble, France, 1935–36; Magdalen College, Oxford, 1936–39. *Appointments:* Mem., Foreign Service, 1946–56; Fellow, London School of Economics and Political Science, 1956–58, Columbia University, 1964–65, Woodrow Wilson International Center, 1976–77, Hoover Institution, 1977–79, 1981–; Visiting Fellow, University of Buffalo, 1959–60; Literary Ed., The Spectator, 1962–63; Distinguished Visiting Scholar, Heritage Foundation, 1980–81; Research Assoc., Harvard University, 1982–83; Adjunct Fellow, Center for Strategic and International Studies, 1983–; Jefferson Lecturer in Humanities, 1993. *Publications:* Poems, 1955; A World of Difference, 1955; New Lines (ed.), 1956; Common Sense About Russia, 1960; Power and Policy in the USSR, 1961; Courage of Genius, 1962; Between Mars and Venus, 1962; New Lines II (ed.), 1963; The Egyptologists (with Kingsley Amis), 1965; Russia After Khrushchev, 1965; The Great Terror, 1968; Arias from a Love Opera, 1969; The Nation Killers, 1970; Lenin, 1972; Kolyma, 1978; The Abomination of Moab, 1979; Present Danger, 1979; Forays, 1979; We and They, 1980; What to Do When the Russians Come, 1984; Inside Stalin's Secret Police, 1985; The Harvest of Sorrow, 1986; New and Collected Poems, 1988; Tyrants and Typewriters, 1989; Stalin and the Kirov Murder, 1989; The Great Terror Reassessed, 1990; Stalin: Breaker of Nations, 1991; Reflections on a Ravaged Century, 1999; Demons Don't, 1999. *Contributions to:* Various publications. *Honours:* O.B.E., 1955; MA, 1972, DLitt, 1975, Oxon; Companion of the Order of St Michael and St George, 1996. *Memberships:* British Acad., corresponding fellow, 1994; RSL, fellow, 1972. *Address:* 52 Peter Coutts Circle, Stanford, CA 94305, USA.

CONRADI-BLEIBTREU, Ellen, (Ellen Schmidt-Bleibtreu); b. 11 June 1929, Heidelberg, Germany. Author; Poet. m. Bruno Schmidt-Bleibtreu, 5 June 1956, 1 s., 1 d. *Education:* English, Spanish, Philosophy, History, University of Mainz. *Publications:* Jahre m FJ, 1950; Kraniche, 1970; Fragmente, 1973; Ruhestorung (stories), 1975; Unter dem Windsegel, 1978; Im Schatten des Genius, Schillers Kinder, 1981; Die Schillers, Schillers Lebem (novel), 1986; Zeitzeichen I, 1988; Klimawechsel, 1989; Begegnung über Grenzen hinweg(stories), 1993 Zeitzeichen II, 1999; Die Kuhlmanns im Woundel der Zeiten (novel), 2000. *Contributions to:* Newspapers and periodicals. *Honours:* Urban Prize, 1976; Hon. Prize, Literary Union, 1977; World Culture Prize, Accademia Italia, 1984; Prof., honoris causa, Istitute Europe di Cultura, 1989. *Memberships:* Gedok, 1967; Die Kogge European Authors Union, 1973; Humboldt-Gesellschaft, 1993. *Address:* Pregelstrasse 5, 53127 Bonn, Germany.

CONRAN, Tony, (Anthony Conran); b. 7 April 1931, Kharghpur, India. Poet; Dramatist; Trans.; Critic. *Education:* BA, 1953, MA, 1956, University of Wales. *Appointments:* Research Asst, 1957–66, Research Fellow and Tutor in English, 1966–80, University of Wales, Bangor. *Publications:* Formal Poems, 1960; Metamorphoses, 1961 Stalae, 1966; Poems 1951–67, 4 vols, 1965–67, combined edn, 1974; The Penguin Book of Welsh Verse, 1967; Claim, Claim, Claim, 1969; Spirit Level, 1974; Life Fund, 1979; The Cost of Strangeness: Essays on the English Poets of Wales, 1982; Welsh Verse, 1987; Bloddeuwedd and Other Poems, 1989; Castles, 1993; The Angry Summer by Idris Davies (ed.), 1993; All Hallows: A Symphony in Three Movements, 1995; Visions and Praying Mantids: The Angelogical Notebooks, 1997; The Peacemakers, by Waldo Williams (trans.), 1997; Frontiers in Anglo Welsh Poetry, 1997; A Theatre of Flowers: Collected Pastorals, 1998; Eros Proposes a Toast, 1998; A Gwynedd Symphony, 1999. *Contributions to:* Numerous magazines and journals. *Honours:* Welsh Arts Council Prize, 1960, 1989; Second Prize, BBC Wales Writer of the Year Award, 1993; Welsh Union of Writers, Tony Conran Festival, Bangor, 1995; Hon. Fellow, Welsh Acad., 1995; Hon. DLitt, University of Wales, 1997. *Memberships:* Welsh Acad., 1970; British Pteridological Society; English Folk Dance and Song Society; SIEF Ballad commission; Welsh Union of Writers; Ascn for the Study of Welsh Writers in English. *Address:* Min Menai, Siliwen Rd, Bangor Gwynedd LL57 2BS, Wales.

CONSTABLE, Geoffrey David; b. 7 Aug. 1958, Prestwood, Buckinghamshire, England. Poet; Musician. *Education:* BA, English, 1989, Information Technology course, 1992, St David's University College of Wales. *Publications:* The Island of Storms, 1981; Leavings, 1985; The Prophetic Tapes, 1995. *Contributions to:* Poetry Review; Ostinato; Poetry Now; Poetry Business; CND Cymru. *Honours:* Third Prize, CND National Poems for Peace Competition, 1983; Third Prize, Poetry Society National Competition, 1990 Runner-up Prize, First Cardiff International Poetry Competition, 1990 Runner-up Prize, Poetry Business Competition, 1990. *Memberships:* Poetry Society; Welsh Union of Writers; Early English Texts Society; Founder Mem. Leader, New Age Christian Movement. *Address:* 78 Hastoe Pk, Aylesbury Bucks HP20 2AA, England.

CONSTANTINE, David (John); b. 4 March 1944, Salford, Lancashire, England. Fellow in German; Poet; Writer; Trans. m. Helen Frances Best, 9 July 1966, 1 s., 1 d. *Education:* BA, 1966, PhD, 1971, Wadham College, Oxford. *Appointments:* Lecturer to Senior Lecturer in German, University of Durham, 1969–81; Fellow in German, Queen's College, Oxford, 1981–2000. *Publications:* Poetry: A Brightness to Cast Shadows, 1980; Watching for Dolphins, 1983; Mappi Mundi, 1984; Madder, 1987; Selected Poems, 1991; Caspar Hauser, 1994; Sleeper, 1995; The Pelt of Wasps, 1998; Something for the Ghosts, 2002. Fiction: Davies, 1985; Back at the Spike, 1994. Non-Fiction: The Significance of Locality in the Poetry of Friedrich Hölderlin, 1979; Early Greek Travellers and the Hellenic Ideal, 1984; Hölderlin, 1988; Friedrich Hölderlin, 1992; Fields of Fire: A Life of Sir William Hamilton, 2001. Translator: Hölderlin: Selected Poems, 1990; Henri Michaux: Spaced, Displaced (with Helen Constantine), 1992; Philippe Jaccottet: Under Clouded Skies/Beauregard (with Mark Treharne), 1994; Goethe: Elective Affinities, 1994; Kleist: Selected Writings, 1998; Hölderlin's Sophocles, 2001. Editor: German Short Stories 2, 1972. *Honours:* Alice Hunt Bartlett Prize, 1984; Runciman Prize, 1985; Southern Arts Literature Prize, 1987; European Poetry Trans. Prize, 1998. *Memberships:* Poetry Society; Society of Authors. *Address:* 1 Hilltop Rd, Oxford OX4 1PB, England.

CONTOGENIS, Constantine; b. 21 June 1947, New York, NY, USA. Teacher; Poet. *Education:* BA, City College of the City University of New York, 1973. *Publication:* Brief Songs of the Kisang. *Contributions to:* Ironwood; Poetry New York; TriQuarterly; Grand Street; Chicago Review; Nimrod; Beloit Poetry Journal; Pulpsmith; New England Review; Bread Loaf Quarterly; Poetry East; Pequod. *Honours:* Poetry Grants, Edward Albee Foundation, Ragdale Foundation, Hélène Wurlitzer, Korean Arts and Culture Foundation. *Membership:* Poetry Society of America.

COOK, Christopher (Paul); b. 24 Jan. 1959, Great Ayton, North Yorkshire, England. Artist; Poet; Reader in Painting. m. Jennifer Jane Mellings, 1982, 2 s. *Education:* University of Exeter; Royal College of Art. *Appointments:* Italian Government Scholar, Accademia di Belle Arti, Bologna, 1986–89; Fellow in Painting, Exeter College of Art, 1989–90; Visiting Fellow, Ruskin School, University of Oxford, 1992–93; Distinguished Visiting Artist, California State University at Long Beach, 1994; Reader in Painting, University of Plymouth, 1997–; Many solo exhibitions. *Publications:* Dust on the Mirror, 1997; For and Against Nature, 2000. *Honours:* Prizewinner, John Moores Liverpool XXI, 1999; Arts Council of England Award, 2000. *Address:* 12 Archibald Rd, Exeter EX1 1SA, England.

COOK, Geoffrey Arthur; b. 9 April 1946, Cleveland, Ohio, USA. Scholar; Artist; Writer; Poet. *Education:* Kenyon College, 1964–67; BA, University of California, 1982; MA, 1987; PhD. *Publications:* Tolle Lege; A Basket of Chestnuts: From the Miscellanea of Venantius Fortunatus; Love and Hate; Azrael; The Heart of the Beast. *Contributions to:* Nation; West Coast Poetry Review; Invisible City; Isthmus; Took; West Consciousness Review; Berkeley Review of Books; Minotaur; Poetry USA; Hartford Courant; Androgyny; Free Lance; Zahir; India Currents; Global Tapestry Journal; Buddhist Third Class Junkmail Oracle; Orbis; Kings Review; Fiction International; Forum on Political Correctness. *Memberships:* PEN; Asscn of Asian Studies; Indo-British Historical Society; Independent Scholars of South Asia; American Council on Southern Asian Art. *Address:* PO Box 4233, Berkeley, CA 94704, USA. *E-mail:* gcook69833@aol.com.

COOK, Robert Leslie; b. 2 May 1921, Edinburgh, Scotland. Poet. m. Janet Ritchie, 28 Oct. 1942, deceased, 1997, 2 d. *Education:* Edinburgh University, 1952–57. *Publications:* Hebrides Overture and Other Poems; Within the Tavern Caught; Sometimes a Word; Time With a Drooping Hand; The Daylight Lingers; World Elsewhere; Voices From Ithaca; Waiting for the End. *Contributions to:* Antioch Review; Candelabrum; Countryman; Linq; Negative Capability; New English Weekly; Nimrod; Orbis; Outposts; Poetry Review; Prairie Schooner; etc. Several anthologies. *Honour:* Grierson Verse Prize. *Memberships:* Scottish Asscn for the Speaking of Verse; Edinburgh University Poetry Society, National Fancy Rat Society. *Address:* 4 Whitecraigs, Kinnesswood, Kinross KY13 9JN, Scotland.

COOK, Stanley; b. 12 April 1922, Austerfield, Yorkshire, England. Lecturer (retd); Poet. m. Kathleen Mary Daly, 1 s., 2 d. *Education:* BA, Christ Church, Oxford, 1943. *Appointments:* Lecturer, Huddersfield Polytechnic, 1969–81; Ed.,

Poetry Nottingham, 1981–85. *Publications:* Form Photograph, 1971; Sign of Life, 1972; Staff Photograph, 1976; Alphabet, 1976; Woods Beyond a Cornfield, 1981; Concrete Poems, 1984; Barnsdale, 1986; Selected Poems, 1972–86, 1986; The Northern Seasons, 1988. Other: Children's poems. *Honour:* Cheltenham Festival Competition Prize, 1972. *Address:* 600 Barnsley Rd, Sheffield, South Yorkshire S5 6UA, England.

COOKE, William; b. 27 Dec. 1942, Stoke-on-Trent, Staffordshire, England. Lecturer; Poet. *Education:* BA, 1964; MA, 1966; PhD, 1969. *Appointments:* Teacher, Thistley Hough Grammar School; Tutor, Sixth Form College, City of Stoke-on-Trent; Lecturer, Stoke-on-Trent College. *Publications:* Builder; Small Ads; Edward Thomas: A Critical Biography, 1970; Business English, 1990; Edward Thomas: Everyman Poetry (ed.), 1997. *Contributions to:* Critical Quarterly; Anglo Welsh Review; Poetry Wales; Outposts; English; New Poetry 1, 2 and 4; BBC Radio 3. *Honour:* Writer's Bursary. *Membership:* West Midland Arts, literature advisory panel. *Address:* 17 Stuart Ave, Trentham, Stoke-on-Trent ST4 8BG, England.

COOKSON, William George; b. 8 May 1939, London, England. Ed.; Publisher; Poet. m. Margaret Elizabeth Craddock, 20 July 1985, 1 d. *Education:* New College, Oxford, 1960–63. *Appointment:* Ed., Agenda Magazine, 1959–. *Publications:* Ezra Pound - Selected Prose 1909–1965 (ed.), 1973; Dream Traces, a sequence, 1975; A Guide to the Cantos of Ezra Pound, 1985; Spell, 1986; Vestiges, 1987; Vestiges and Versions- Poems 1955–1997, 1997. *Address:* 5 Cranbourne Ct, Albert Bridge Rd, London SW11 4PE, England.

COOL AL. See: BUTLER, Allen Todd.

COOLEY, Peter John; b. 19 Nov. 1940, Detroit, Michigan, USA. Prof.; Poet. m. Jacqueline Marks, 12 June 1965, 1 s., 2 d. *Education:* AB, Shimer College, 1962; MA, University of Chicago, 1969; PhD, University of Iowa, 1970. *Appointments:* Asst Prof., Assoc. Prof., University of Wisconsin, 1970–75; Assoc. Prof., Prof., Tulane University, 1975–. *Publications:* The Company of Strangers; The Room Where Summer Ends; Night Seasons; The Van Gogh Notebook; The Astonished Hours; Sacred Conversations, 1998; A Place Made of Starlight, 2001. *Contributions to:* New Yorker; Atlantic; Poetry; Harper's; Nation; New Republic. *Honours:* Pushcart Prize; Robert Frost Fellowship; Bread Loaf Writers' Conference. *Memberships:* PEN; Poets and Writers; Poetry Society of America. *Address:* Tulane University, New Orleans, LA 70118, USA.

COOLIDGE, Clark; b. 26 Feb. 1939, Providence, RI, USA. Poet. m. Susan Hopkins, 1 d. *Education:* Brown University, 1956–58. *Publications:* Flag Flutter and US Electric, 1966; Poems, 1967; Ing, 1969; Space, 1970; The So, 1971; Moroccan Variations, 1971; Suite V, 1973; The Maintains, 1974; Polaroid, 1975; Quartz Hearts, 1978; Own Face, 1978; Smithsonian Depositions, and Subjects to a Film, 1980; American Ones, 1981; A Geology, 1981; Research, 1982; Mine: The One That Enters the Stories, 1982; Solution Passage: Poems, 1978–1981, 1986; The Crystal Text, 1986; Mesh, 1988; At Egypt, 1988; Sound as Thought: Poems, 1982–1984, 1990; The Book of During, 1991; Odes of Roba, 1991; Baffling Means, 1991; On the Slates, 1992; Lowell Connector: Lines and Shots from Kerouac's Town, 1993; Own Face, 1994; Registers: (People in All), 1994; The ROVA Improvisations, 1994. *Honours:* National Endowment for the Arts Grant, 1966; New York Poets Foundation Award, 1968. *Address:* c/o The Figures, 5 Castle Hill, Great Barrington, MA 01230, USA.

COONEY, Anthony Paul; b. 3 July 1932, Liverpool, England. Poet. m. 12 April 1958, 2 d. *Education:* Gregg Commercial College, Liverpool, 1948–50; Ethel Wormald College of Education, 1968–70; Open University. *Appointments:* Asst Master, 1971–91. *Publications:* Georgian Sequence; The Wheel of Fire; Germinal; Inflections; Mersey Poems; Personations; Land of My Dreams; Bread in the Wilderness; The Story of St George. *Contributions to:* Various small press magazines. *Address:* Rose Cottage, 17 Hadassah Grove, Lark Lane, Liverpool L17 8XH, England.

COONS, Susan Anderson; b. 21 June 1937, Minnesota, USA. Poet. Divorced, 1 s., 1 d. *Education:* BA, College of Wooster, Ohio; Sonons State University. *Appointments:* Teacher; Freelance Writer; Insurance Agent; Publisher. *Publications:* Harnassing Motion; Party in the Fields; Wine Song; What Did Slena Do. *Contributions to:* Poet; Blue Unicorn; Rooftops. *Honours:* Ina Coolbrith Golden Award; Poets of Vineyard World of Poetry. *Membership:* California Writers Club.

COOPER, Jane (Marvel); b. 9 Oct. 1924, Atlantic City, NJ, USA. Prof. (retd); Poet. *Education:* BA, University of Wisconsin, 1946; MA, University of Iowa, 1954. *Appointments:* Faculty, Sarah Lawrence College, 1950–87; Visiting Prof., Graduate Writing Division, Columbia University School of the Arts, 1979, 1987–88, 1990, University of Iowa, 1980–81. *Publications:* The Weather of Six Mornings, 1969; Maps and Windows, 1974; Scaffolding: New and Selected Poems, 1984, second edn, 1993; Green Notebook, Winter Road, 1994; The Flashboat: Poems Collected and Reclaimed, 2000. *Contributions to:* American Poetry Review; American Voice; Iowa Review; Kenyon Review; New Yorker; Paris Review; Ploughshares. *Honours:* Lamont Award, 1968; Shelley Award,

1978; Award in Literature, American Acad. of Arts and Letters, 1995; New York State Poet, 1995–97. *Memberships:* PEN; Poets House, Poets' Advisory Board. *Address:* 545 W 111th St, Apt 8K, New York, NY 10025, USA.

COOPER, John Charles, (Charles Greene); b. 3 April 1933, Charleston, South Carolina, USA. Prof. of Philosophy and Religion; Lutheran Pastor; Poet. 4 s., 2 d. *Education:* AB, University of South Carolina, 1955; MA, 1964, PhD, 1966, University of Chicago; MDiv, Lutheran Seminary, Columbia; STM, Lutheran Seminary, Chicago. *Appointments:* Prof. of Philosophy and Religion, Newberry College, Eastern Kentucky University, Winebrenner Theological Seminary, Susquehanna University, Asbury College, University of Kentucky; Pastor, Faith Lutheran Church, Tampa, All Saints Lutheran Church, Nicholasville, KY, Lord of the Seas Lutheran Church, Big Pine Key, FL. *Publications:* Over 40 books on religion, sociology and philosophy, including: The Unexamined Life, 1975; Vickie's Lake, KY, 1989; Four Quartets (poems), 1991; Cast a Single Shadow (novel), 1995; The Spiritual Presence in the Theology of Paul Tillich. *Contributions to:* Christianity Today; Christian Century; Time of Singing; Carolina Review; Wind; Merton Seasonal; Scripset. *Honours:* Euphrosynean Award, University of South Carolina, 1955; Second Prize, Time of Singing, 1992. *Memberships:* American Acad. of Religion; Sören Kierkegaard Society. *Address:* 70 E Cahill Ct, Big Pine Key, FL33043, USA.

COOPER, Marti(ne Linda); b. 29 Nov. 1955, Sheffield, England. Poet. 1 s., 1 d. *Education:* BA, Leeds University, 1977. *Publications:* Contemporary Yorkshire Poetry; Poems for Peace; Poetry Now Political. *Contributions to:* Staple; Weyfarers; Counterpoint; Aireings; Pennine Platform; New Hope International. *Honour:* Winner, Pontefract Liquorice Festival Poetry Competition, 2000. *Address:* 10 Sheepwalk Lane, Castleford, West Yorkshire WF10 3HP, England.

COOPER, Thomas (Edward); b. 12 July 1932, Ashton under Lyne, Lancashire, England. Social Worker (retd); Poet. *Education:* BA, Social Work, North Lancashire Polytechnic, 1967–70. *Publications:* Tameside Tales, 1992; Cheshire Odes, 1993; Fenland Fables, 1995. *Contributions to:* Newspapers and periodicals. *Honours:* Honourable mentions in many competitions in local and national newspapers and periodicals. *Address:* St Thomas Pl., Ely, Cambridgeshire CB7 4GG, England.

COOPER FRATRIK, Julie; b. 8 Dec. 1941, Philadelphia, Pennsylvania, USA. Poet. 4 d. *Education:* BA, 1980; MFA, 1983; MA. *Publication:* Where Our Voices Lie. *Contributions to:* Louisville Review; Texas Review; Tondril. *Honour:* Bucks County, Pennsylvania Poet. *Memberships:* Acad. of American Poets; Poetry Society of America; Pennsylvania Arts Commission; Poets and Writers. *Address:* 6144 Upper Mountain Rd, New Hope, PA 18938, USA.

COOVER, Robert (Lowell); b. 4 Feb. 1932, Charles City, IA, USA. Writer; Dramatist; Poet; University Teacher. m. Maria del Pilar Sans-Mallagre, 3 June 1959, 1 s., 2 d. *Education:* Southern Illinois University; BA, Indiana University, 1953; MA, University of Chicago, 1965. *Appointments:* Teacher, Bard College, 1966–67, University of Iowa, 1967–69, Princeton University, 1972–73, Brown University, 1980–; Various guest lectureships and professorships. *Publications:* The Origin of the Brunists, 1966; The Universal Baseball Asscn, J. Henry Waugh, Prop., 1968; Pricksongs & Descants (short fictions), 1969; A Theological Position (plays), 1972; The Public Burning, 1977; A Political Fable (The Cat in the Hat for President), 1980; Spanking the Maid, 1982; Gerald's Party, 1986; A Night at the Movies, 1987; Whatever Happened to Gloomy Gus of the Chicago Bears?, 1987; Pinocchio in Venice, 1991; John's Wife, 1996; Briar Rose, 1997. *Contributions to:* Plays, poems, fiction, trans, essays and criticism in various publications. *Honours:* William Faulkner Award for Best First Novel, 1966; Rockefeller Foundation Grant, 1969; Guggenheim Fellowships, 1971, 1974; Obie Awards, 1972–73; American Acad. of Arts and Letters Award, 1976; National Endowment for the Arts Grant, 1985; Rhode Island Gov.'s Arts Award, 1988; Deutscher Akademischer Austauschdienst Fellowship, Berlin, 1990. *Memberships:* American Acad. and Institute of Arts and Letters; PEN International. *Address:* c/o Dept of English, Brown University, Providence, RI 02912, USA.

COPE, Wendy Mary; b. 21 July 1945, Erith, Kent, England. Poet; Ed. *Education:* BA, History, St Hilda's College, Oxford, 1966; Diploma in Education, 1967. *Publications:* Across the City, 1980; Hope and the 42, 1984; Making Cocoa for Kingsley Amis, 1986; Poem from a Colour Chart of Housepaints, 1986; Men and Their Boring Arguments, 1988; Does She Like Wordgames?, 1988; Twiddling Your Thumbs, 1988; The River Girl, 1990; Serious Concerns, 1992. Editor: Is That the New Moon?: Poems by Women Poets, 1989; The Orchard Book of Funny Poems, 1993; The Funny Side, 1998; The Faber Book of Bedtime Stories, 2000; If I Don't Know, 2001; Heaven on Earth: 101 Happy Poems, 2001. *Contributions to:* Newspapers and reviews. *Honours:* Cholmondeley Award, 1987; Michael Braude Award for Light Verse, American Acad. of Arts and Letters, 1995. *Memberships:* RSL, fellow, 1993; Society of Authors, management committee, 1992–95. *Address:* c/o Peters, Fraser and Dunlop, Fifth Floor, The Chambers, Chelsea Harbour, Lots Rd, London SW10 0XF, England.

CORBEN, Beverly Balkum; b. 6 Aug. 1926, USA. Educator (retd); Poet; Writer; Artist. m. Herbert Charles Corben, 25 Oct. 1957, 1 stepson, 2 step-d. *Education:* AA, Santa Monica College, 1950; BA with honours, University of California, Los Angeles, 1960; MA, Case Western Reserve University, 1972. *Appointments:* Teaching Asst, 1972–73, Dir of Writing Laboratory, 1973–78, 1980–82, Scarborough College, University of Toronto, Canada; Visiting Scholar, 1978–80, Scholar-in-Residence, 1982–88, Harvey Mudd College. *Publication:* On Death and Other Reasons for Living (poems), 1972. *Contributions to:* Poetic Justice; Texas Review; Voices International; Prophetic Voices; Modern Haiku; Old Hickory Review. *Honours:* Cleveland State University Hon. Alumna, 1971; More than 60 awards for poetry and fiction nationwide, 1989–. *Memberships:* Mississippi Poetry Society; Gulf Coast Writers Asscn; Writers Unlimited, pres., 1991, 1992; Acad. of American Poets. *Address:* 4304 O'Leary Ave, Pascagoula, MS 39581, USA.

CORBETT, Peter George; b. 13 April 1952, Rossett, Wales. Poet; Artist. *Education:* Foundation, Fine Art, Liverpool College of Art and Design, 1971; BA, Manchester Regional College of Art and Design, 1974. *Publications:* In Anthologies: Undercurrents, 1990; Poets, 1993; On the Other Side of the Mirror, 1996; Awaken to the Dream, 1996; The Star Laden Sky, 1997; Quantum Leap Poetry Magazine, 1997; The Best Poems of 1997; Aural Images, 1997; Parnassus of World Poets, 1997, 1998, 2000; Mountains and Memories, 1998; New Humanity Journal, 1998; A Call from Beyond, 1998; Wonderment of Words, 1998; Mountains, Memories and Mersey Ferries, 1998; Light Through Dimensions, 1998; Honoured Poets of 1998, 1998; Lasting Treasures, 1998; A Celebration of Poets, 1999; Open Minds, 1999; The Spirit of Nature, 1999; Poetry Now Northern England, 2000, 2001; Time and Tide, 2000; The Inner Voice, 2000; Chasing Dreams, 2000; Prominent Voices, 2000; Memories of the Millennium, 2000; Sanctuary, 2000; Then and Now, 2000; A Flash of Inspiration, 2000; Heartfelt Symphonies, 2001; Tales from Erewhon: (Select Poems 1980–2000), 2001. *Honours:* Two Eds' Awards for Outstanding Achievement in Poetry, 1997; International Scottish Open Poetry Competition, 1998; The International German Art Prize, St Lukas Acad., Memmelsdorf, Germany, 1998; Hon. Prof., St Lukas Acad., Memmelsdorf, Germany, 1998. *Memberships:* Maison Internationale des Intellectuals, Paris; Hon. Prof. of the Academie des Sciences Universelles, Paris; Lifelong Fellow and Hon. Prof. in Fine Arts, University of Co-ordinated Research, Vic., Australia; Life Mem., Design and Artist's Copyright Society. *Address:* 7 Gambier Terrace, Hope St, Liverpool L1 7BJ, England.

CORBETT-FIACCO, Christopher; b. 2 April 1961, Albany, New York, USA. Writer; Poet. *Appointment:* Publisher, Ed., Sisyphus 1990–. *Publication:* Pieces of Eight (anthology), 1992. *Contributions to:* American Poetry Annual, Amherst Society; Archer; Chiron Review; Fennel Stalk; Frugal Chariot; Hemispheres; Kana; Pegasus; Plowman; Renovated Lighthouse; Vandeloecht's Fiction Magazine. *Address:* 8 Asticou Rd, Boston, MA 02130, USA.

CORBLUTH, Elsa; b. 2 Aug. 1928, Beckenham, Kent, England. Writer; Photographer. m. David Boadella, divorced 1987, 1 s., 1 d., deceased 1980. *Education:* BA, Combined Creative Arts, Alsager College, 1982; MA, Creative Writing, Lancaster University, 1984. *Publications:* St Patrick's Night; The Planet Iceland, 2002. Other: Various booklets, including: Stone Country; Brown Harvest; I Looked for You; Wilds; Group of seven poems in SW Arts Proof Series of small books, 1998. *Contributions to:* Poetry Review; Outposts; The Rialto; TLS; Anthologies. *Honours:* First Prizes, South-West Arts Competition, Bridport, 1979–1981; Joint First Prize, Cheltenham Festival Competition, 1981; First Prize, Sheffield Competition, 1981; First Prize, ORBIS Rhyme Revival, 1986, 1993, 1995; First Prize and Gold Medal, Poetry Digest Competition, 1994; First Prize, Yorkshire Poetry Competition, 1997. *Membership:* Harbour Poets, Weymouth. *Address:* Hawthorn Cottage, Rodden, Near Weymouth, Dorset DT3 4JE, England.

CORDANI, Albert; b. 15 July 1947, Torrington, CT, USA. Poet. m. 3 Feb. 1979, 1 s., 1 d. *Contributions to:* Various anthologies and other publications. *Honours:* Silver Poetry Award; Best Poet of the 90s citation. *Address:* 28 Hoffman St, Torrington, CT 06790-6224, USA.

CORDELLI, Franco; b. 20 Feb. 1943, Rome, Italy. Critic; Writer; Poet. *Education:* Modern American Literature, University of Urbino, 1971. *Appointments:* Theatre Critic, 1968–89, Europeo, 1986; Vice-Dir, Nuovi Argomenti, 1990–. *Publications:* Fuoco Celeste; Il Pubblico della Poesia; Il Poeta Postumo; Pro Prieta Perduta. *Contributions to:* Nuovi Argomenti; Poesia; Russian and Swedish anthologies. *Honours:* Teatrale Award; Sila Opera Prima; Sila; Brutium; Villa; Fondi. *Memberships:* Jury of Mondello Literary Prize; Colosseo Theatre; Teatro delle Arti; International Poetry Festival of Rome. *Address:* Via Francesco Mengotti 39, 00191 Rome, Italy.

CORDER, Louise Pugh; b. 24 April 1936, Asheboro, NC, USA. School Media Co-ordinator; Poet. m. Leo D Corder, 16 Aug. 1958, 3 s. *Education:* BA, summa cum laude, High Point College, 1958; MEd, University of North Carolina at Greensboro, 1972. *Appointments:* High School Teacher, 1958–62; School Media Co-ordinator, 1976–99. *Contributions to:* Various anthologies and periodicals. *Honours:* First Place Winner, Burlington Writers Club Annual Contests, North Carolina Poetry Society Contests, Christian Writers Fellowship International

Contest and Robert Ruark Contests. *Membership:* North Carolina Poetr Society. *Address:* 2713 Bruce Pugh Rd, Franklinville, NC 27248, USA.

COREY, Stephen Dale; b. 30 Aug. 1948, Buffalo, New York, USA. Poe Literary Ed.; Essayist. m. Mary Elizabeth Gibson, 28 Jan. 1970, 4 d *Education:* BA, English, 1971; MA, English, 1974; PhD, English, 197S *Appointments:* Instructor of English, University of Florida, 1979–80; Ass Prof. of English, University of South Carolina, 1980–83; Asst Ed., 1983–86 Assoc. Ed., 1986–, The Georgia Review. *Publications:* Synchronized Swimming 1985, reissued, 1993; The Last Magician, 1981, reissued, 1987; All These Land You Call One Country, 1992; Greatest Hits: 1980–2000, 2000. Poetr Chapbooks: Fighting Death, 1983; Gentle Iron Lace, 1984; Attacking th Pieta, 1988; Mortal Fathers and Daughters, 1999. *Contributions to:* Poetry American Poetry Review; Kenyon Review; New Republic; Yellow Silk; Laure Review. *Honours:* Writing Fellowships from the state arts councils of Florida 1978–79, South Carolina, 1981–82 and Georgia, 1985–86, 1988–89; Wate Mark Poets First Book Award, 1981, Swallow's Tale Press Poetry Award 1984; Author of the Year in Poetry, Georgia Writers Inc, 1992, 1993, 2000 *Address:* 357 Parkway Dr., Athens, GA 30606, USA.

CORKHILL, Annette Robyn, (Annette Robyn Vernon); b. 10 Sept. 1955 Brisbane, Australia. Writer; Poet; Trans. m. Alan Corkhill, 18 March 1977, 2 s 1 d. *Education:* BA, 1977; DipEd, 1978; MA, 1985; PhD, 1993. *Publications:* Th Jogger: Anthology of Australian Poetry, 1987; Destination, Outrider, 1987 Mangoes Encounter – Queensland Summer, 1987; Age 1, LINQ, 1987; Tw Soldiers of Tiananmen, Earth Against Heaven, 1990; Australian Writing Ethnic Writers 1945–1991, 1994; The Immigrant Experience in Australiar Literature, 1995. *Contributions to:* Outrider; Australian Literary Studies *Honour:* Hon. Mention, The Creativity Centre, Harold Kesteven Poetry Prize 1987. *Address:* 5 Wattletree Pl., The Gap, Qld 4061, Australia.

CORMAN, Cid, (Sidney Corman); b. 29 June 1924, Boston, MA, USA. Poet; Writer; Trans. m. Shizumi Konishi. *Education:* BA, Tufts College, 1945. University of Michigan, 1946–47; University of North Carolina, 1947; Fulbright Scholar, Sorbonne, University of Paris, 1954–55. *Appointments:* Ed., Origin, 1951–71; Part-time teacher, various colleges and universities. *Publications:* Many poetry collections, including: Thanksgiving Eclogue, 1954; Livingdying, 1970; Aegis, 1984; And the Word, 1987. Other: Essays; Translations from the Japanese. *Contributions to:* Numerous anthologies, books, reviews, quarterlies, journals and videos. *Honours:* Many. *Address.* Fujuoji Cho, 80 Utano, Ukyo Ku, Kyoto 616-8208, Japan. *E-mail:* aad40080@pop01.odn.ne.jp.

CORN, Alfred; b. 14 Aug. 1943, Bainbridge, GA, USA. Poet; Writer; Critic; Trans. m. Ann Jones, 1967, divorced 1971. *Education:* BA, Emory University, 1965; MA, Columbia University, 1967. *Appointments:* Poet-in-Residence, George Mason University, 1980, Blaffer Foundation, New Harmony, IN, 1989, James Thurber House, 1990; Humanities Lecturer, New School for Social Research, New York City, 1988; Ellison Chair in Poetry, University of Cincinnati, 1989; Bell Distinguished Visiting Prof., University of Tulsa, 1992; Hurst Residency in Poetry, Washington University, St Louis, 1994; Numerous college and university seminars and workshops; Many poetry readings. *Publications:* Poetry: All Roads at Once, 1976; A Call in the Midst of the Crowd, 1978; The Various Light, 1980; Tongues on Trees, 1980; The New Life, 1983; Notes from a Child of Paradise, 1984; An Xmas Murder, 1987; The West Door, 1988; Autobiographies, 1992; Present, 1997. Novel: Part of His Story, 1997. Criticism: The Metamorphoses of Metaphor, 1987; Incarnation: Contemporary Writers on the New Testament (ed.), 1990; The Pith Helmet, 1992; A Manual of Prosody, 1997. *Contributions to:* Books, anthologies, scholarly journals, and periodicals. *Honours:* Woodrow Wilson Fellow, 1965–66; Fulbright Fellow, Paris, 1967–68; Ingram Merrill Fellowships, 1974, 1981; National Endowment for the Arts Fellowships for Poetry, 1980, 1991; Gustav Davidson Prize, Poetry Society of America, 1983; American Acad. and Institute of Arts and Letters Award, 1983; New York Foundation for the Arts Fellowships, 1986, 1995; Guggenheim Fellowship, 1986–87; Acad. of American Poets Prize, 1987; Yaddo Corporation Fellowship in Poetry, 1989; Djerassi Foundation Fellowship in Poetry, 1990; Rockefeller Foundation Fellowship in Poetry, Bellagio, Italy, 1992; MacDowell Colony Fellowships in Poetry, 1994, 1996. *Memberships:* National Book Critics Circle; PEN; Poetry Society of America. *Address:* 350 W 14th St, Apt 6A, New York, NY 10014, USA.

CORNISH, Sam(uel James); b. 22 Dec. 1935, Baltimore, Maryland, USA. Poet; Writer; Teacher. m. Jean Faxon, 1967. *Education:* Goddard College, Vermont; Northwestern University. *Appointments:* Teacher of Creative Writing, Highland Park Free School, Roxbury, Massachusetts; Instructor in Afro-American Studies, Emerson College, Boston. *Publications:* Poetry: In This Corner: Sam Cornish and Verses, 1961; People Beneath the Window, 1962; Angles, 1965; Winters, 1968; Short Beers, 1969; Generations, 1971; Streets, 1973; Sometimes: Ten Poems, 1973; Sam's World, 1978; Songs of Jubilee: New and Selected Poems, 1969–1983, 1986; Folks Like Me, 1993. Other: Your Hand in Mine, 1970; My Daddy's People Were Very Black, 1976; 1935: A Memoir, 1990. Editor: Chicory: Young Voices from the Black Ghetto (with Lucian W Dixon), 1969; The Living Underground: An Anthology of Contemporary American Poetry (with Hugh Fox), 1969. *Honour:* National Endowment for the Arts Grants, 1967, 1969. *Address:* c/o Dept of English, Emerson College, 100 Beacon St, Boston, MA 02116, USA.

CORR, John Franz; b. 29 May 1937, New York, NY, USA. Reader to Blind; Poet. m. Ruth Immerwahr, Sept. 1972, 1 s. *Education:* BA, English, Whitman College, Walla Walla, Washington, 1959; Teaching Certificate, Western Washington State College, Bellingham, Washington, 1965. Publication; Woodfrogs in Chaos (anthology), 1996. *Contributions to:* Seattle Post Intelligencer. *Memberships:* 19th Draft, Auburn's Literary Arts Society. *Address:* 304 15th St SE, No. 7, Auburn, WA 98002, USA.

CORSERI, Gary Steven; b. 31 March 1946, New York, NY, USA. Writer; Poet. m. May 1982. *Education:* BA, University of Florida, 1967; MAT, Harvard University, 1969; PhD, Florida State University, 1988. *Publication:* Random Desert, 1989. *Contributions to:* Poetry Northwest; Poetry Lore; Florida Review; Buffalo Spree Magazine; Southern Humanities Review; International Poetry Review; Harvard Advocate; Florida Quarterly; West Branch; Atlantic Gazette; Premiere; Pyramid; University of Tampa Poetry Review; Woodrider; Your Place; Your Grace. *Honours:* First Prize, Stephen Vincent Benét Narrative Poem Contest, 1972; First Prize, Florida Poetry Contest, 1975; Co-winner, Georgia Poetry Circuit, 1989; Tennessee Williams Scholarship, 1990. *Membership:* Poetry Society of America. *Address:* c/o Pat Kenning, 2732 Williams, Denver, CO 80205, USA.

CORTI, Doris Joyce; b. 29 Dec. 1928, Plaistow, London, England. Poet; Writer. m. Arthur George Stump, 6 Aug. 1949. *Education:* RSA, English Literature, Grove-Russell Central School, 1942; GCE, A Level, English Literature and Language, Havering College of Further Education. *Publications:* Poetry: The Space Between, 1982; New Moves, 1987; Rituals and Reminders, 1991; The Moon is a Letter C, 1995. Other: Writing Poetry, 1994. *Contributions to:* Books, anthologies, and periodicals. *Honours:* Second Prize, Brentwood Poetry Group, 1980; Third Prize, Stamford Literature Festival, 1990; First Prize, 1994, Second Prize, 1995, Poetry, Centenary Competition, Society of Women Writers and Journalists. *Address:* 52 Poors Lane, Hadleigh, Essex SS7 2LN, England.

COSCIA, Patricia Denise, (Mary Palace); b. 20 Dec. 1963, New York, NY, USA. Teacher; Poet. *Education:* BA, English, Wagner College, Staten Island, New York. *Appointments:* Teacher, Spanish-American Institute, New York, 1985–91; Tutor, Hoboken, 1994–; Hoboken Public Library, 1996–. *Publications:* Free Focus, 1984; Ostentatious Mind, 1987. *Contributions to:* Poets Market; Sparrow Press; Harper and Row. *Address:* Box 7415, New York, NY 10116-7415, USA.

COSENTINO, Patricia Alanah, (Patricia Alanah); b. 6 June 1925, USA. Poet. m. David A Cosentino, 28 June 1990, 2 s. *Education:* MEd, Regis College, 1984. *Appointments:* Dir, Learning Laboratory, Newton College, 1967–70; Asst Dir, MAT, Harvard School of Education, 1970–72; Teacher, Wellesley, Massachusetts, 1972–90. *Publications:* Always Being Born, 2002; Tapestries (anthology, ed.). *Contributions to:* Anthologies and reviews. *Honours:* First Honours and Honorable Mention, Kentucky State Poetry Society; Mary F Lindsley Award and First Honours, New York Poetry Forum. *Memberships:* Acad. of American Poets; Poetry Society of America. *Address:* 33 Leo Dr., Gardner, MA 01440-1211, USA. *E-mail:* daupat@myexcel.com.

COSMOS, Eddie. See: THERSON-COFIE, Larweh.

COSTANZA, Mary S(carpone); b. 14 May 1927, Berwyn, PA, USA. Artist; Writer; Poet; Lecturer. m. John Costanza, 1 Sept. 1951, 1 s., 1 d. *Education:* BFA, BS, Tyler School of Fine Arts, Temple University, 1950. *Appointments:* Dir, Costanza Art Gallery; Painting exhibitions. *Publications:* Kaddish/Six Million, 1978; The Living Witness: Art in the Concentration Camps and Ghettos, 1982; Shoah (poems), 1997; Country Cousins (short stories), 1999. *Honours:* Grants and awards. *Memberships:* American-Italian Historical Asscn; Authors' Guild; Holocaust Memorial Museum. *Address:* 737 Polo Rd, Bryn Mawr, PA 19010, USA.

COSTLEY, Bill, (William Kirkwood Costley Jr); b. 21 May 1942, Salem, Massachusetts, USA. Journalist; Writer; Poet; Dramatist. m. 6 June 1964, 1 s., 1 d. *Education:* BA, English, Boston College (Arts and Sciences), 1963; MFA coursework, Boston University, 1967–. *Publications:* Knosh 1 Cir: Selected Poems 1964–75, 1975; R(A)G(A)S, 1978; A(Y)S(H)A, 1988; Terrazzo, 1992; Siliconia, 1995. *Contributions to:* Anthologies and periodicals. *Honour:* Honourable Mention, Poetry Society Anthology, UK, 1985. *Memberships:* Scottish Poetry Library Asscn, Edinburgh; National Writers Union; Robinson Jeffers Asscn, Santa Clara University. *Address:* 1 Sunset Rd, Wellesley, MA 02482-4615, USA. *E-mail:* billcostley@yahoo.com.

COTTINGHAM, Valery Jean, (Countesse de Cassellet, Baroness, Lady of Camster); b. 4 Sept. 1934, Kingston-upon-Hull, Yorkshire, England. Poet; Writer. m. George Cottingham, 28 Dec. 1965, deceased 1991. *Publications:* Memories, poems and short stories, three vols. *Contributions to:* Modern Poetry 1–8, 1981, 1982, 1983, 1984; Poetry for Everyone, United Kingdom, 1983; Winter Gold, 1991; New Beginnings, 1993; Writers' World Anthology,

Australia, 1995; New Dimensions, special edn, Australia, 1995. *Honours:* Certificate of Merit, Writers' World Publishers, Australia; Certificate of Merit, CA, USA; DLitt, 2000. *Address:* 58 Colliers Close, Horsell, Woking, Surrey GU21 3AW, England.

COTTON, John; b. 7 March 1925, Hackney, London, England. Poet. m. Peggy Midson, 27 Dec. 1948, 2 s. *Education:* BA, Honours, English, London University, 1956. *Appointments:* Ed., Priapus magazine, 1967–72, The Private Library journal, 1969–79; Headmaster, Highfield Comprehensive, Hemel Hempstead, 1963–85. *Publications:* Fourteen Poems, 1967; Outside the Garden of Eden and Other Poems, 1969; Old Movies and Other Poems, 1971; Roman Wall, 1973; Photographs, 1973; Kilroy Was Here, 1975; Powers, 1977; A Letter for a Wedding, 1980; Somme Man, 1980; The Totleigh Riddles, 1981; Daybook Continued, 1982; The Storyville Portraits, 1984; The Crystal Zoo, 1984; Oh Those Happy Feet, 1986; The Poetry File, 1989; Two by Two (with Fred Sedgwick), 1990; Here's Looking at You Kid: New and Selected Poems, 1992; Oscar the Dog, 1994; This is the Song, 1996; The Ammonites Revenge (with Fred Sedgwick), 2000; Poems From and About the Past, 2000; Out There in Rows, 2002. *Contributions to:* Newspapers and journals. *Honours:* Art Council Publication Award, 1971; Deputy Lieutenant of the Country of Hertfordshire, 1989. *Memberships:* Poetry Society, chair., 1972–74, 1977, treasurer, 1986–89; Toddington Poetry Society, pres.; Ver Poets, pres. *Address:* 37 Lombardy Dr., Berkhamstead, Hertfordshire HP4 2LQ, England.

COUPER, John Mill; b. 7 Sept. 1914, Dundee, Scotland. University Lecturer in English Literature (retd); Poet. m. Katharine Boyd, 17 July 1940, 2 s., 1 d. *Education:* MA, 1936, PhD, 1948, Aberdeen University. *Appointments:* Lecturer, University of Queensland, Australia, 1951–54; Headmaster, Knox Grammar School, 1954–55; Lecturer, University of New South Wales, 1958–67; Senior Lecturer, Assoc. Prof., Macquarie University, 1968–78. *Publications:* East of Living, 1967; The Book of Bligh, 1969; In From the Sea, 1974; The Lee Shore, 1979; Canterbury Folk, 1984. *Contributions to:* Sydney Morning Herald; Australian; The Bulletin; Meanjin; Southerly; Melbourne Age. *Honour:* Moomba Prize, 1970. *Address:* 9 Dudley St, Asquith, NSW 2077, Australia.

COURT, Wesli. See: TURCO, Lewis Putnam.

COUTO, Nancy Vieira; b. 11 June 1942, New Bedford, Massachusetts, USA. Poet. m. Joseph A Martin, 13 Aug. 1988. *Education:* BS, Education, Bridgewater State College, 1964; MFA, English, Cornell University, 1980. *Appointments:* Subsidiary Rights Man., Cornell University Press, 1982–94; Lecturer, Dept of English, Cornell University, 1994–2001; Consultant and Ed., Leatherstocking Literary Services, 1994–. *Publication:* The Face in the Water, 1990. *Contributions to:* Gettysburg Review; Epoch; American Poetry Review; Hudson Review; Iowa Review; Milkweed Chronicle; Poetry Northwest; Prairie Schooner; American Voice; Black Warrior Review; Shenandoah. *Honours:* New York State CAPS Fellowship, 1982–83; National Endowment for the Arts Fellowship, 1987; Agnes Lynch Starrett Prize, 1989; Gettysburg Review Award, 1994; American Antiquarian Society Creative and Performing Artists and Writers Fellowship, 1995; Constance Saltonstall Foundation for the Arts Grant, 1998; National Endowment for the Arts Fellowship, 1999; Community Arts Partnership Fellowship, 2002. *Membership:* Associated Writing Programs; Community Arts Partnership of Tompkins County. *Address:* 508 Turner Pl., Ithaca, NY 14850, USA. *E-mail:* nvcouto@juno.com.

COUZYN, Jeni; b. 26 July 1942, South Africa (Naturalized Canadian citizen). Poet; Psychotherapist; Lecturer; Broadcaster. *Education:* BA, University of Natal, 1963. *Appointment:* Writer-in-Residence, University of Victoria, BC, 1976; Founder and Dir, Bethesda Arts Centre, Nieu Bethesda, South Africa, 1999–. *Publications:* Flying, 1970; Monkeys' Wedding, 1972; Christmas in Africa, 1975; House of Changes, 1978; The Happiness Bird, 1978; Life by Drowning, 1983; In the Skin House, 1993; Homecoming, 1998; A Time to Be Born, 1999; Selected Poems, 2000. Editor: Bloodaxe Book of Contemporary Women Poets, 1985; Singing Down the Bones, 1989. Other: Children's books and edns of poetry. *Honours:* Arts Council of Great Britain Grants, 1971, 1974; Canada Council Grants, 1977, 1983. *Memberships:* Guild of Psychotherapists; Poetry Society, general council, 1968–75. *Literary Agent:* Andrew Mann, 1 Old Compton St, London W1V 5PH, England. *Address:* c/o Bloodaxe Books, PO Box 1SN, Newcastle upon Tyne NE99, England.

COVARRUBIAS ORTIZ, Miguel; b. 27 Feb. 1940, Monterrey, Mexico. Writer; Poet; Prof. m. Silvia Mijares, 18 March 1967, 2 d. *Education:* Licenciado en letras, 1973, Maestria en letras espagnolas (pasantia), 1987, Universidad Autónoma de Nuevo León, Monterrey. *Appointments:* Dir, Centre for Literary and Linguistic Research, 1976–79, and Institute of Fine Arts, 1976–79, Co-ordinator, Creative Writing Workshop, 1981–, Universidad Autónoma de Nuevo León, Monterrey. *Publications:* Fiction: La raiz ausente, 1962; Custodia de silencios, 1965; Minusculario, 1966. Poetry: El poeta, 1969; El segundo poeta, 1977; Pandora, 1987. Essays: Papeleria, 1970; Olavide o Sade, 1975; Nueva papeleria, 1978; Papeleria en tramite, 1997. **Editor:** Antologia de autores contemporáneos, 1972, 1974, 1975, 1979, 1980; Desde el Cerro de la Silla, 1992; Traduction: El traidor, 1993; Conversations: Junto a una taza de café, 1994. *Contributions to:* Various publications. *Honours:* Second Place, Story, Xalapa Arts Festival, 1962; Arts Prize, Literature, Universidad

Autónoma de Nuevo León, Monterrey, 1989; Medal of Civic Merit in Literature and Arts, Gobierno del Estado du Nuevo León, 1993; Poetry Trans. Prize, National Institute of Fine Arts, Mexico, 1993. *Memberships:* Deslinde (culture review), dir, 1985–; Sociedad General de Escritores de Mexico. *Address:* Kant 2801, Contry-La Silla, Guadalupe, NL, México, DF, 67170, Mexico.

COWEN, Athol Ernest; b. 18 Jan. 1942, Corbridge, Hexham, England. Writer; Poet; Publisher. *Publications:* Word Pictures (Brain Soup), 1989; Huh!, 1991. *Contributions to:* Various anthologies. *Memberships:* Publishers' Asscn; Poetry Society; Writers' Guild of Great Britain; Musicians' Union; Guild of International Songwriters and Composers. *Address:* 40 Gibson St, Wrexham LL13 7TS, Wales.

COWLAN, Paul Francis; b. 7 June 1950, Farnborough, Kent, England. Songwriter/Performer; Peripatetic Tutor/Lecturer; Poet. *Education:* BEd, Hons. *Contributions to:* Stand; Orbis; Tabla; Envoi; Poetry Life; Still; Scintilla; Psychopoetica; Housmann Anthology; Helicon; Open University Sonnet Society; Resurgence; South West Arts Review; Trewithen Chapbook; TOPS; A Handful of Care; Vision On; Poetry Digest; Devon Life. *Honours:* Joint Third Place, Envoi Competition 100, 1991; Second Place, Poetry Digest Bard of the Year, 1994; First Place, Envoi Competition 111, 1995; First Place, Poetry Life Eighth Competition, 1996; Runner-up, Writers News Country Poem Competition, 1998; Third Place, Trewithen Poetry Prize, 1998; Runner-up, Stand International Poetry Competition, 1998; Commended, Daily Telegraph/Arvon International Poetry Competition, 1998; First Place, Tabla Poetry Competition, 1998; Second Place, Scintilla Open Poetry Competition, 2001; Fourth Place, Peterloo Poets Open Poetry Competition, 2002. *Address:* Hainerweg 3, 60599 Frankfurt am Main, Germany. *Website:* www.paulcowlan.co uk.

COWLIN, Dorothy. See: WHALLEY, Dorothy.

COX, (Charles) Brian; b. 5 Sept. 1928, Grimsby, Lincolnshire, England. Prof. Emeritus of English Literature; Writer; Poet; Ed. *Education:* BA, 1952, MA, 1955, MLitt, 1958, Pembroke College, Cambridge. *Appointments:* Lecturer, Senior Lecturer, University of Hull, 1954–66; Co-Ed., Critical Quarterly, 1959–; Prof. of English Literature, 1966–93, Prof. Emeritus, 1993–, Pro-Vice Chancellor, 1987–91, University of Manchester; Visiting Prof., King's College, London, 1994; Hon. Fellow, Westminster College, Oxford, 1994; Mem., Arts Council, 1996–98. *Publications:* The Free Spirit, 1963; Modern Poetry (with A E Dyson), 1963; Conrad's Nostromo, 1964; The Practical Criticism of Poetry (with A E Dyson), 1965; Poems of This Century (ed. with A E Dyson), 1968; Word in the Desert (ed. with A E Dyson), 1968; The Waste Land: A Casebook (ed. with A P Hinchliffe), 1968; The Black Papers on Education (ed. with A E Dyson), 1971; The Twentieth Century Mind (ed. with A E Dyson), 3 vols, 1972; Conrad: Youth, Heart of Darkness and The End of the Tether (ed.), 1974; Joseph Conrad: The Modern Imagination, 1974; Black Paper 1975 (ed. with R Boyson), 1975; Black Paper 1977 (ed. with R Boyson), 1977; Conrad, 1977; Every Common Sight (verse), 1981; Two Headed Monster (verse), 1985; Cox on Cox: An English Curriculum for the 1990's, 1991; The Great Betrayal: Autobiography, 1992; Collected Poems, 1993; The Battle for the English Curriculum, 1995; African Writers (ed.), 1997; Literacy is Not Enough (ed.), 1998; Emeritus (poems), 2001. *Honours:* C.B.E., 1990; Fellow, RSL, 1993 DLitt, De Montfort University, 1999. *Membership:* Chair, North West Arts Board, 1994–2000. *Address:* 20 Park Gates Dr., Cheadle Hulme, Stockport SK8 7DF, England.

COX, Dorothy Gene; b. 25 March 1923, Dallas, Texas, USA. Poet; Writer. m. Jesse Vernon Cox, 1944, deceased 1974, 1 s. *Education:* BSc, Nursing, Texas Woman's University, Denton, 1979; MSc, Human Relations and Business, Amber University, Garland, Texas, 1985. *Publications:* To Up From Down, 1994; Continuing Up, 1995; On the Freeway, 1996; The Dreamer, 1998; Soap-Box Salad (short stories), 2000. *Contributions to:* Anthologies. *Honour:* Certificate of Merit, Writer's Digest, 1995. *Memberships:* International Society of Poets; Poetry Society of Texas.

COY, David Lavar; b. 24 April 1951, Powell, Wyoming, USA. Prof. of English and Creative Writing; Poet. m. 19 Nov. 1975, 1 s., 1 d. *Education:* BA, English Literature, University of Wyoming, 1975; MFA, Creative Writing, University of Arkansas, Fayetteville, 1983. *Appointments:* Graduate Asst, University of Arkansas, 1979–83; Instructor, 1983–87, Asst Prof., 1987–88, Southwest Missouri State University; Prof., Dir of Writing School, Arizona Western College, 1988–. *Publication:* Rural News, 1991. *Contributions to:* Antioch Review; Aracne; Colorado North Review; Intro; Jumping Pond; Plainsong; Poetry NOW; Slant; Sow's Ear; Spoon River Quarterly; Widener Review. *Honour:* Acad. of American Poets Prize, University of Arizona, 1982. *Membership:* Associated Writing Programs.

CRAIG, Shawna Anne Hudson; b. 1 July 1955, Vancouver, Washington, USA. Researcher; Poet. m. Patrick Naughtin, 31 Jan. 1955, Vancouver, WA, USA. Researcher; Poet. m. Patrick Naughtin, 31 Jan. 1992, 2 d. *Education:* AAS, Anthropology, 1980; BA, cum laude, Anthropology, 1982; MA, Anthropology, 1984. *Contributions to:* Anthologies and journals. *Honours:* Honourable mentions. *Membership:* International Society for the Advancement of Poetry. *Address:* 303 White Oak Dr., Austin, TX 78753, USA.

CRAIG, Timothy, (Theresa Mullholland, Janet Turpin); b. 22 July 194♦ USA. Librarian; Garden Designer; Poet. m. Sarah Brewster Coy, 20 Aug., 199♦ 1 s. *Education:* BA, University of Maryland, 1962; MA, New York University 1963; PhD, 1972; DLitt, Trinity College, Cambridge, 1974. *Appointments:* Ass Prof., City University of New York; Asst Keeper, British Museum; Editoria Asst, Wellesley Index; Curator, Mansell Collection. *Publications:* Heart Slum Everything in Its Path; Knots and Fans; Advice to the Rain; One If By Lan♦ *Contributions to:* Xanadu; Plains Poetry Review; Pale Fire Review; Romanti♦ Thirteen; Lyric; Prairie Light. *Memberships:* MLA; Hidden Chiefs. *Address:* P♦ Box 784, Salem, NY 12865, USA.

CRAM, David; b. 5 April 1945, Sutton-on-Sea, Lincolnshire, England. Lecture in General Linguistics; Poet. *Education:* BA, Oxford University, 1967; PhI Cornell University, 1973. *Appointments:* Aberdeen University 1974–88; Jesu♦ College, Oxford, 1988–. *Publication:* Heinrich Heine (verse trans.), 199♦ *Contributions to:* Aberdeen Evening Express; Acta Victoriana; Ambit; Hone♦ Ulsterman; Light Year; Literary Review; London Magazine; Oxford Magazine Spectator. *Address:* Jesus College, Oxford OX1 3DW, England.

CRAMER, Steven; b. 24 July 1953, Orange, New Jersey, USA. Lecturer; Poe♦ Book Reviewer. m. Hilary Rao, 20 Sept. 1987. *Education:* Antioch College 1972–76; BA, University of Iowa, 1978. *Appointments:* Poetry Ed., David ♦ Godine, Publisher; Instructor, Massachusetts Institute of Technology; Sta♦ Ed., Atlantic Monthly; Lecturer, Boston University, Tufts University *Publications:* The Eye That Desires to Look Upward; The World Boo♦ *Contributions to:* Antioch Review; Atlantic; Iowa Review; Nation; Ne♦ England Review; New Republic; North American Review; Ohio Review; Par♦ Review; Partisan Review; Ploughshares; Poetry. *Honours:* Stanley Youn♦ Fellowship; National Endowment for the Arts Fellowship. *Memberships* Associated Writing Programs; Poetry Society of America. *Address:* Englis♦ Dept, Tufts University, Medford, MA 02155, USA.

CRANE, R. H.; b. 1937, USA. Poet. *Appointment:* Founder, Ed., Veery Journal 1991–. *Publication:* Crossed Silver: Poems in Poetry, Drawing, and Geometr♦ 1992. *Honours:* Letter of Honour, Renate Princess of Windisch-Graet♦ Generalkonsulat der Bundesrepublik Deutschland, 1998. *Membership* American Philosophical Asscn, 1997–. *Address:* c/o Milne, McKinnon, an♦ Christie, Suite 2032, 333 N Michigan Ave, Chicago, IL 60601, USA.

CRASE, Douglas; b. 5 July 1944, Battle Creek, Michigan, USA. Poet *Education:* AB, Princeton University, 1966. *Appointment:* Fellow, New Yor♦ Institute for the Humanities, 1983–86. *Publication:* The Revisionist, 1981 *Contributions to:* New Yorker; Poetry; American Poetry Review; Partisan Review; Paris Review; Nation; Oxford Poetry; Spazio Umano. *Honour♦ Witter Bynner Prize, American Acad. and Institute of Arts and Letters, 1983 Guggenheim Fellowship, 1984; Whiting Writers Award, 1985; John D. an♦ Catherine T. MacArthur Fellowship, 1987–92. *Address:* 470 W 24th St, Apt 6D New York, NY 10011, USA.

CRATE, Joan, (Louise Imida); b. 15 June 1953, Yellowknife, Northwes♦ Territories, Canada. University English Instructor; Poet; Writer. 3 s., 1 d *Education:* Certificate of Communications Media; BA; MA. *Appointments* Instructor, University of Calgary, 1988, Lakeland College, Cold Lake, AB 1988–, Red Deer College, Alberta, 1991–; Writer-in-Residence, Calgary Publi♦ Library 1992. *Publications:* Pale as Real Ladies (poems), 1989; Breathin♦ Water (novel), 1989; Foreign Homes (poems), 2001. Anthologies: Nativ♦ Writers and Canadian Writing, 1990; Literature in English: Writers an♦ Styles From Anglo-Saxon Times to the Present, 1992. *Contributions to* Grain; Dandelion; Fiddlehead; Subterrain; Orbis; Quarry; Canadia♦ Literature; Amethyst Review; Ariel; Sanscrit; Arc; Canadian Author an♦ Bookman; Canadian Forum; Newest Review; Calgary Herald; CBC Radio *Honours:* Third Place, Kalamalka New Writers Poetry Competition, 1987 Bliss Carmen Award for Poetry, 1988. *Memberships:* Alberta Writers Guild Dandelion Society. *Address:* 71 Marion Crescent, Red Deer, AB T4R 1N1 Canada.

CRAWFORD, John W(illiam); b. 2 Sept. 1936, Ashdown, AR, USA. Poet Writer; Prof. of English Emeritus. m. Kathryn Bizzell, 17 June 1962, 1 s., 1 d *Education:* AA, Texarkana College, 1956; BA, BSE, Ouachita Baptist College 1959; MSE, Drake University, 1962; DEd, Oklahoma State University, 1968 *Appointments:* Instructor in English, Clinton Community College, 1962–66 Asst Prof., 1967–68, Assoc. Prof., 1968–73, Prof. of English, 1973–97, Chair. Dept of English, 1977–86, Prof. Emeritus, 1997–, Henderson State University *Publications:* Poetry: Making The Connection, 1989; I Have Become Acquainte♦ With the Rain, 1997. Non-Fiction: Shakespeare's Comedies: A Guide, 1968 Shakespeare's Tragedies: A Guide, 1968; Steps to Success: A Study Skill♦ Handbook, 1976; Discourse: Essays on English and American Literature 1978; Romantic Criticism of Shakespearean Drama, 1978; Earl♦ Shakespearian Actresses, 1984; The Learning, Wit and Wisdom o♦ Shakespeare's Renaissance Women, 1997. *Contributions to:* Anthologies reviews, quarterlies, journals, etc. *Honours:* Sybil Nash Abrams Prizes, 1982 1995; Merit Award, Poets' Roundtable of Arkansas, 1988; Arkansas Haik♦ Society Award, 1998. *Memberships:* Arkansas Philological Asscn; College

English Asscn; Poets' Roundtable of Arkansas; South Central MLA. *Address:* PO Box 1813 Walnut, Arkadelphia, AR 71923, USA.

CRAWFORD, Robert; b. 23 Feb. 1959, Bellshill, Scotland. University Prof. of English; Writer; Poet. m. Alice Wales, 2 Sept. 1988. *Education:* MA, 1981; DPhil, 1985. *Appointments:* Elizabeth Wordsworth Junior Research Fellow, Oxford, 1984–87; British Acad. Postdoctoral Fellow, Glasgow University, 1987–89; Lecturer, 1989–95, Prof. of English, 1995–, Modern Scottish Literature, University of St Andrews. *Publications:* Poetry: A Scottish Assembly, 1990; Sharawaggi (with W. N. Herbert), 1990; Talkies, 1992; Masculinity, 1996; Spirit Machines, 1999; The Tip of My Tongue, 2003. Prose: The Savage and the City in the Work of T. S. Eliot, 1987; Devolving English Literature, 1992; Identifying Poets: Self and Territory in Twentieth Century Poetry, 1993; The Modern Poet, 2001. *Contributions to:* Anthologies, including: Other Tongues, 1990; The Penguin Book of Poetry from Britain and Ireland since 1945 (ed. with Simon Armitage), 1998; The New Penguin Book of Scottish Verse (with Mick Imlah), 2000; Scottish Religious Poetry (ed. with Meg Bateman and James McGonigal), 2000. *Honours:* Gregory Award; Poetry Book Society Recommendations; Selected for Arts Council of Great Britain's New Generation Poets, 1994; Scottish Arts Council Book Award. *Memberships:* Society of Authors; English Asscn; Royal Society of Edinburgh. *Literary Agent:* David Godwin, 55 Monmouth St, London WC2H 9DG, England. *Address:* School of English, University of St Andrews, Fife KY16 9AL, Scotland.

CREELEY, Robert White; b. 21 May 1926, Arlington, Massachusetts, USA. Writer; Poet; Prof. of English. m. (1) Ann McKinnon, 1946, divorced 1955, 2 s., 1 d., (2) Bobbie Louise Hall, 1957, divorced 1976, 4 d., (3) Penelope Highton, 1977, 1 s., 1 d. *Education:* BA, Black Mountain College, 1954; MA, University of New Mexico, 1960. *Appointments:* Prof., 1967–78, David Gray Prof., Poetry, Letters, 1978–89, Samuel P Capen Prof., Poetry, Humanities, 1989, Dir, Poetics Programme, 1991–92, State University of New York, Buffalo; Advisory Ed., American Book Review, 1983–; Sagetrieb, 1983–, New York Quarterly, 1984–; Board of Chancellors, Acad. of American Poets, 1999–. *Publications:* Poetry: For Love, Poems 1950–60, 1962; Words, 1967; Pieces, 1969; A Day Book, 1972; Selected Poems, 1976; Hello, 1978; Later, 1979; Mirrors, 1983; Collected Poems 1945–75, 1983; Memory Gardens, 1986; Windows, 1990; Echoes, 1994; Life and Death, 1998. Prose: The Island, 1963; The Gold Diggers, 1965; Mabel: A Story, 1976; The Collected Prose, 1984; Tales Out of School, 1993. Criticism: A Quick Graph, 1970; Was That a Real Poem and Other Essays, 1976; Collected Essays, 1989. Autobiography, 1990. Editor: Selected Writings of Charles Olson, 1967; Whitman, Selected Poems, 1973; The Essential Burns, 1989; Charles Olson, Selected Poems, 1993. *Honours:* Guggenheim Fellowships, 1964, 1967; Rockefeller Grantee, 1965; Shelley Memorial Award, 1981, Frost Medal, 1987, Poetry Society of America; National Endowment for the Arts Grantee, 1982; Berlin Artists Programme Grants, 1983, 1987; Leone d'Oro Premio Speziale, 1984; Distinguished Fulbright Award, Bicentennial Chair of American Studies, University of Helsinki, 1988; Distinguished Prof., State University of New York, 1989; Walt Whitman Citation, State Poet of New York, 1989–91; Horst Bienek Preis für Lyrik, Munich, 1993; Hon. DLitt, University of New Mexico, 1993; America Award in Poetry, 1995; Fulbright Award, University of Auckland, 1995; Lila Wallace-Reader's Digest Writer's Award, 1995. *Memberships:* American Acad. and Institute of Arts and Letters; PEN American Center. *Address:* 64 Amherst St, Buffalo, NY 14207, USA.

CREMONA, John Joseph; b. 6 Jan. 1918, Gozo, Malta. Chief Justice (retd); Prof. Emeritus of Criminal Law; Historian; Poet. m. Marchioness Beatrice Barbaro of St George, 20 Sept. 1949, 1 s., 2 d. *Education:* BA, 1939, LLD, cum laude, 1942, University of Malta; DLitt, University of Rome, 1939; BA, 1946, PhD, Law, 1951, University of London. *Appointments:* Crown Counsel, 1947; Lecturer in Constitutional Law, Royal University of Malta, 1947–65; Attorney General, 1957–64; Prof. of Criminal Law, 1959–65, Prof. Emeritus, 1965–, Pro-Chancellor, 1971–74, University of Malta; Crown Advocate-General, 1964–65; Vice-Pres., Constitutional Court and Court of Appeal, 1965–71; Judge, 1965–92, Vice-Pres., 1986–92, European Court of Human Rights; Chief Justice and Pres., Constitutional Court, Court of Appeal, and Court of Criminal Appeal, 1971–81; Judge, 1986–92, Vice-Pres., 1986–92, European Tribunal in Matters of State Immunity. *Publications:* Non-Fiction: The Treatment of Young Offenders in Malta, 1956; The Malta Constitution of 1835, 1959; The Legal Consequences of a Conviction in the Criminal Law of Malta, 1962; The Constitutional Development of Malta, 1963; From the Declaration of Rights to Independence, 1965; Human Rights Documentation in Malta, 1966; Selected Papers, 1946–89, 1990; The Maltese Constitution and Constitutional History, 1994; Malta and Britain: The Early Constitutions, 1996. Poetry: Eliotropi, 1937; Songbook of the South, 1940; Limestone 84 (with others), 1978; Malta Malta, 1992. *Contributions to:* Law reviews. *Honours:* Many, including: Knight of Magisterial Grace, Sovereign Military Order of Malta; Companion of the National Order of Merit of Malta; Chevalier, Legion d'honneur, France; Knight of the Grand Cross, Order of Merit, Italy; Hon. Fellow, London School of Economics and Political Science. *Memberships:* Royal Historical Society, fellow; Human rights and environmental organizations. *Address:* Villa Barbaro, Main St, Attard, Malta.

CRIPPS, Joy Beaudette, (H. E. Nobless); b. 13 June 1923, Melbourne, Australia. Poet; Writer. m. Charles John Cripps, 2 s. *Appointments:* Founder,

Melbourne Poetry Society, 1981; Founder, Poetry Day Australia, 1981; Founder, Dove in Peace Award, 1993; Representative of Australia at international poetry events, festivals and congresses; Pres., Board of Govs, Ansted University, British Virgin Islands, 2000–. *Publications:* Magpie Bridge, Poems on Chinese Mythology, 1981; Actinia Collection, 1983; Getting Published, 1983; Celebration International Anthology, 1984; Tatters of Hessian, 1985; Poetry Day Australia Anthology, 1985; Beneath the Southern Cross, Book 1 (poems), Book 2 (poems and papers), 1988; India: Where Life Revolves Around the Well, 1989; Poetry of Journey (trans. with Zaio Luo), 1989; Poetry, Joy Beaudette Cripps, 1990; Doves of Peace, 1990; Tanabata, 1992; Thailand, 1992; India WLRAT Well (English trans.), 2000. *Contributions to:* Poetry reviews, newsletters, magazines. *Honours:* Life Fellow, International Acad. of Poets, 1983; Hon. doctorates, 1986; International Poet Laureate, Eminent Poet, Chennai, 1986; Dame Commander, Order Souberaine Militaire de la Mailice du St Sepulcre, 1988; Dame Grand, Noble Religious Order of St Tatjana, 1991; Baroness, Royal Order of Bohemian Crown, Netherlands, 1994; Nobless of Humanity, Sovereign Order of White Cross; Poet Olympian, Order of Pegasus, Lady of Olympoetry, 1994; Accademia Internazionale di Pontzen 1997, Accademico di Merito, Palme Aureate, Naples; United Poets Laureate, Children's Peace Poetry Award, 2000; Poet of the Millennium, International Poets Acad., 2000; Voice of Kolkata Award, International Poetry Society of Kolkata, 2001. *Address:* 3 Mill St, Aspendale 3195, Australia.

CRISTIENS, Sara. See: STEIN, Clarissa Ingeborg.

CROFT, Andy; b. 13 June 1956, Handforth, Cheshire, England. Poet; Writer. m. Nikki Wray, 4 s., 2 d. *Education:* BA, 1978, PhD, 1986, University of Nottingham. *Appointment:* Full-time Lecturer, University of Leeds, 1983–96; Writer-in-Residence, Great North Run, 2000, HMP Holme House, 2000–. *Publications:* Red Letter Days, 1990; Out of the Old Earth, 1994; The Big Meeting, 1994; Nowhere Special, 1996; Gaps Between Hills, 1996; A Weapon in the Struggle, 1998; Selected Poems of Randall Swingler, 2000; Just as Blue, 2001; Great North, 2001; Headland, 2001. *Contributions to:* The Guardian; The Independent; London Magazine; Marxism Today; Labour History Review; The Listener; The New Statesman. *Membership:* Chair., Artistic Dir, Write Around Festival, 1989–99. *Address:* c/o Cleveland Arts, Gurney House, Gurney St, Middlesbrough TS1 1JL, England.

CRONIN, Anthony; b. 23 Dec. 1928, Enniscorthy, County Wexford, Ireland. Author; Poet. m. Thérèse Campbell, 1955, 2 d. *Education:* BA, University College, Dublin, 1948. *Appointments:* Visiting Lecturer, University of Montana, 1966–68; Poet-in-Residence, Drake University, 1968–70; Columnist, Irish Times, 1973–86; Cultural Adviser, Irish Prime Minister, 1980–83, 1987–92. *Publications:* Poems, 1957; Collected Poems, 1950–73, 1973; Reductionist Poem, 1980; RMS Titanic, 1981; 41 Sonnet Poems, 1982; New & Selected Poems, 1982; Letter to an Englishman, 1985; The End of the Modern World, 1989. Fiction: The Life of Riley, 1964; Identity Papers, 1979. Biography: No Laughing Matter: The Life and Times of Flann O'Brian, 1989. Memoir: Dead as Doornails, 1976. Essays: Heritage Now, 1983; An Irish Eye, 1985; Samuel Beckett: The Last Modernist, 1996. *Honour:* Marten Toonder Award, 1983. *Address:* 9 Rainsford Ave, Dublin 8, Ireland.

CROOKER, Barbara Poti; b. 21 Nov. 1945, Cold Spring, NY, USA. College Instructor; Writer; Poet. m. Richard McMaster Crooker, 26 July 1975, 1 s., 3 d. *Education:* BA, Douglass College, Rutgers University, 1967; MS Education, Elmira College, 1975. *Appointments:* Instructor, County College of Morris, 1978–79, Women's Center, Cedar Crest College, 1982–85, Lehigh Community College, 1993, Cedar Crest College, 1999–; Asst Prof., Northampton County Area Community College, 1980–82; Artist-in-Education (poet in the schools), 1989–93. *Publications:* Writing Home, 1983; Starting from Zero, 1987; Looking for the Comet Halley, 1987; The Lost Children, 1989; Obbligato, 1992; Moving Poems; In the Late Summer Garden, 1998. *Contributions to:* Anthologies, reviews, quarterlies, journals and magazines. *Honours:* Nominee, Pushcart Prize, 1978, 1989, 1998, 1999, 2001; Pennsylvania Council on the Arts Fellowships, 1985, 1989, 1993; Winner, Passages North and National Endowment for the Arts Emerging Writers Competition, 1987; Phillips Award, Stone Country, 1988; Virginia Center for the Creative Arts Fellowships, 1990, 1992, 1994, 1995, 1997, 1998, 2000, 2001; First Prize, Karamu Poetry Contest, 1997; Hon. Mention and Special Mention, Comstock Prize, 1998; First Place, Y2K Writing Prize, New Millennium Writings, 2000; Grand Prize Winner, Dancing Poetry Contest, 2000; Winner, Byline Chapbook Competition, 2001. *Membership:* Poetry Society of America; Acad. of American Poets. *Address:* 7928 Woodsbluff Run, Fogelsville, PA 18051, USA.

CROSHAW, Michael; b. 12 March 1943, Warwick, England. Poet. m. Theresa Belt, 6 June 1970, divorced 1976, 2 s. *Appointments:* British Telecom, 1973–91; Assoc. Ed., Orbis Magazine, 1980–87. *Publications:* Alum Rock, 1992; A Harmony of Lights, 1993. *Contributions to:* Acumen; Babel; Bogg; Bradford Poetry Quarterly; Bull; Chapman; Completing the Picture; Core; Emotional Geology; Envoi; Envoi Book of Quotes on Poetry; The Interpreter's House; Jennings; Manhattan Poetry Review; Mercia Poets, 1980; The Mouth; Moorlands Review; New Hope International; Orbis; Ore; Other Poetry; Outposts Poetry Quarterly; Pennine Platform; Poetry Australia; Poetry

Business Anthology, 1987–88; Poetry Nottingham; Poet's Voice; Psychopoetica; Stride; Vigil; Wayfarers. *Address:* Queen's Rd, Nuneaton, Warwickshire CV11 5ND, England.

CROSS, Beryl Mary; b. 5 Oct. 1929, London, England. Journalist; Poet. *Education:* Exemption from Matriculation, 1945, GCE, Advanced Level, English Economic History, Economics, 1953, London University; Diploma in Economics and Political Science, Oxford University, 1955. *Appointments:* Ed., several journals. *Publications:* A Colour That is Not a Colour (collected poetry), 1997; Picking Raspberries in December, 2000. *Contributions to:* Anthologies and periodicals. *Honours:* Certificate of Distinction and Seal of Achievement Certificate, W B Yeats Club International. *Memberships:* Phoenix Poets, chair.; Society of Women Writers and Journalists, chair., 1996–98. *Address:* 32 Silver Cres., Gunnersbury, London W4 5SE, England.

CROSSLEY-HOLLAND, Kevin (John William); b. 7 Feb. 1941, Mursley, Buckinghamshire, England. Prof.; Poet; Writer; Ed.; Trans. m. (1) Caroline Fendall Thompson, 1963, 2 s., (2) Ruth Marris, 1972, (3) Gillian Paula Cook, 1982, 2 d., (4) Linda Marie Waslien, 1999. *Education:* MA, St Edmund Hall, Oxford. *Appointments:* Fiction and Poetry Ed., Macmillan & Co, 1962–69; Lecturer in English, Tufts-in-London Programme, 1967–78; Gregory Fellow in Poetry, University of Leeds, 1969–71; Talks Producer, BBC, 1972; Editorial Dir, Victor Gollancz, 1972–77; Lecturer in English Language and Literature, University of Regensburg, 1979–80; Editorial Consultant, Boydell and Brewer, 1983–89; Arts Council Fellow in Writing, Winchester School of Art, 1983, 1984; Visiting Prof. of English and Fulbright Scholar-in-Residence, St Olaf College, MN, 1987–89; Endowed Chair in Humanities and Fine Arts, University of St Thomas, St Paul, MN, 1991–95. *Publications:* Poetry: The Rain-Giver, 1972; The Dream-House, 1976; Between My Father and My Son, 1982; Time's Oriel, 1983; Waterslain, 1986; The Painting-Room, 1988; East Anglian Poems, 1989; New and Selected Poems, 1991; The Language of Yes, 1996; Poems from East Anglia, 1997; Selected Poems, 2001. Children's Fiction: Havelok the Dane, 1964; King Horn, 1965; The Green Children, 1966; The Callow Pit Coffer, 1968; Wordhoard (with Jill Paton Walsh), 1969; The Pedlar of Swaffham, 1971; The Sea Stranger, 1973; Green Blades Rising, 1974; The Fire-Brother, 1974; The Earth-Father, 1976; The Wildman, 1976; The Dead Moon, 1982; Beowulf, 1982; The Mabinogion (with Gwyn Thomas), 1984; Axe-Age, Wolf-Age, 1985; Storm, 1985; The Fox and the Cat: Animal Tales from Grimm (with Susanne Lugert), 1985; British Folk Tales, 1987; The Quest for the Olwen (with Gwyn Thomas), 1988; Boo!: Ghosts and Graveyards, 1988; Dathera Dad: Fairy Tales, 1988; Small Tooth Dog: Wonder Tales, 1988; Piper and Pooka: Boggarts and Bogles, 1988; Wulf, 1988; Under the Sun and Over the Moon, 1989; Sleeping Nanna, 1989; Sea Tongue, 1991; Tales from Europe, 1991; Long Tom and the Dead Hand, 1992; The Tale of Taliesin (with Gwyn Thomas), 1992; The Labours of Herakles, 1993; The Old Stories: Tales From East Anglia and the Fen Country, 1997; Short!, 1998; The King Who Was and Will Be, 1998; Arthur: The Seeing Stone, 2000; Enchantment, 2000; The Ugly Duckling, 2001; Arthur: At the Crossing Places, 2001. Non-Fiction: Pieces of Land: A Journey to Eight Islands, 1972; The Norse Myths, 1980; The Stones Remain (with Andrew Rafferty), 1989. Editor: Running to Paradise, 1967; Winter's Tales for Children 3, 1967; Winter's Tales 14, 1968; New Poetry 2 (with Patricia Beer), 1976; The Faber Book of Northern Legends, 1977; The Faber Book of Northern Folk-Tales, 1980; The Riddle Book, 1982; Folk-Tales of the British Isles, 1985; The Oxford Book of Travel Verse, 1986; Northern Lights, 1987; Medieval Lovers, 1988; Medieval Gardens, 1990; Peter Grimes by George Crabbe, 1990; The Young Oxford Book of Folk-Tales, 1998; The New Exeter Book of Riddles, 1999. Drama: The Wuffings (with Ivan Cutting), 1997. Other: Individual poems; Trans from Old English; Opera Libretti; Programmes for television and radio. *Contributions to:* Numerous journals and magazines. *Honours:* Arts Council Awards, Best Book for Young Children, 1966–68; Poetry Book Society Choice, 1976, and Recommendation, 1986; Carnegie Medal, 1986; Fellow, RSL, 1998; Bronze Medal, Nestlé Smarties Prize, 2000; Guardian Children's Fiction Award, 2001; Tir na n-Og Award, 2001; Silver Medal, Spoken Awards, 2001. *Memberships:* Dir, Minnesota Composers Forum, 1993–97; Steering Committee, King's Lynn Festival, 1997; Co-founder and Chair., Poetry-next-to-the-Sea, 1997–. *Literary Agent:* Rogers, Coleridge and White, 20 Powis Mews, London W11 1JN, England. *Address:* Clare Cottage, Burnham Market, Norfolk PE31 8HE. *E-mail:* kevincrossleyholland@cc702.fsnet.

CROSSWAIT, Helen Goodwin Moorhouse; b. 19 Nov. 1930, White River, South Dakota, USA. Poet. m. Bruce Crosswait, divorced 1984, 2 s., 1 d. *Education:* South Dakota State University, Brookings; South Dakota Black Hills State College, Spearfish; Wesleyan University; BA, Arts and Science, University of Nebraska, 1985. *Publications:* Riot in a Parrot Shop and Other Eruptions, 1991; Reflections of a Paleface From the Rosebud, 1992; Taming of the Rose. *Contributions to:* South Dakota Magazine; Husker Magazine; Deadwood Magazine; Moon Willow Poetry Series; UNL Laurus; South Dakota University Literary Journal. *Honours:* Several. *Address:* 333 Pine St, Chadron, NE 69337, USA.

CROW, Mary; b. 14 July 1933, Mansfield, Ohio, USA. Poet; Prof. of English. Divorced, 2 s. *Education:* BA, College of Wooster, 1955; MA, Indiana University, 1963; Writers' Workshop, University of Iowa. *Appointments:* Faculty Mem., 1964–, Prof. of English, Colorado State University, Ft Collins;

Poet Laureate of Colorado. *Publications:* Poetry: Going Home, 1979; The Business of Literature, 1980; Borders, 1989; I Have Tasted the Apple, 1996. Other: Trans of Latin American poetry. *Contributions to:* American Poetry Review; Ploughshares; Prairie Schooner; Literary Review; Beloit Poetry Review; New Letters; Massachusetts Review; Quilt; Three Rivers Poetry Journal. *Honours:* Poetry Fellowship, National Endowment for the Arts 1984; Fulbright Creative Writing Award to Yugoslavia, 1988; Colorado Book Award, 1992; Poetry Fellowship, Colorado Council on the Arts, 2000. *Memberships:* Poetry Society of America; PEN; Associated Writing Programs. *Address:* English Dept, Colorado State University, Fort Collins, CO 80523 USA.

CROWDEN, James Pascoe; b. 27 Jan. 1954, Plymouth, Devon, England. Shepherd; Woodman; Anthropologist; Poet. m. Olivia Joan Sanders, 6 July 1985, 1 d. *Education:* BSc, Civil Engineering. *Appointment:* 2nd Lieutenant, Royal Engineers. *Publications:* Blood, Earth and Medicine, 1991; In Time of Flood, 1996; Cider: The Forgotten Miracle, 1999; Bridgwater: The Parrett's Mouth, 2000; The Wheal of Hope - South Crofty and Cornish Tin Mining, 2000; Working Women of Somerset, 2001. *Contributions to:* Whitehorse Star; Yukon; Country Living. *Address:* Forge House, Fore St, Winsham, Chard, Somerset TA20 4DY, England.

CROWE, Thomas Rain; b. 23 Aug. 1949, Chicago, IL, USA. Writer; Poet; Ed.; Publisher; Trans. Partner, Nan Watkins, 1 s. *Education:* BA, Furman University, 1972. *Appointments:* Ed., Beatitude Press, San Francisco, CA, 1974–78; Founder-Dir, San Francisco International Poetry Festival, 1976; Founder-Ed., Katuah Journal, Asheville, NC, 1983–87; Publisher, New Native Press, Cullowhee, NC, 1988–; Master Class Instructor, South Carolina Gov.'s School for the Arts, 1989, 1990; Ed.-at-Large, Asheville Poetry Review, 1994–2001; Founder-Prod., Fern Hill Records, 1994–; Founder-Performer, The Boatrockers, 1996. *Publications:* Learning to Dance (poems), 1985; Poems of Che Guevara's Dream, 1991; The Sound of Light (poems and music), 1991; Night Sun (poems), three vols, 1993; The Laugharne Poems, 1997; Writing the Wind: A Celtic Resurgence (co-ed. and trans.), 1997. Other: Several translations, 1991–2001. *Honours:* Thomas E. McDill Poetry Prize, 1980; International Merit Award, Atlanta Review, 1996; Publishers' Book of the Year Award, Appalachian Writers Asscn, 1997. *Memberships:* Amnesty International; Foundation for Global Sustainability. *Address:* 407 Canada Rd, Tuskaseegee, NC 28783, USA. *E-mail:* newnativepress@hotmail.com.

CROZIER, Andrew; b. 1943, England. Poet; Senior Lecturer in English. *Education:* MA, University of Cambridge; PhD, University of Essex. *Appointment:* Senior Lecturer in English, University of Sussex. *Publications:* Poetry: Love Litter of Time Spent, 1967; Train Rides: Poems from '63 and '64, 1968; Walking on Grass, 1969; In One Side and Out the Other (with John James and Tom Phillips), 1970; Neglected Information, 1973; The Veil Poem, 1974; Printed Circuit, 1974; Seven Contemporary Sun Dials (with Ian Potts), 1975; Pleats, 1975; Duets, 1976; Residing, 1976; High Zero, 1978; Were There, 1978; Utamaro Variations, 1982; All Where Each Is, 1985; Ghosts in the Corridor (with Donald Davie and C H Sisson), 1992. Other: A Various Art (ed. with Tim Longville), 1987. *Address:* c/o University of Sussex, Falmer, Brighton, Sussex BN1 9RH, England.

CROZIER, Lorna; b. 24 May 1948, Swift Current, Saskatchewan, Canada. Assoc. Prof.; Poet. *Education:* BA, University of Saskatchewan, 1969; MA, University of Alberta, 1980. *Appointments:* Creative Writing Teacher, Saskatchewan Summer School of the Arts, Fort San, 1977–81; Writer-in-Residence, Cypress Hills Community College, Swift Current, 1980–81, Regina Public Library, Saskatchewan, 1984–85, University of Toronto, 1989–90; Broadcaster and Writer, CBC Radio, 1986; Guest Instructor, Banff School of Fine Arts, Alberta, 1986, 1987; Special Lecturer, University of Saskatchewan, 1986–91; Assoc. Prof., University of Victoria, BC, 1991–. *Publications:* Inside is the Sky, 1976; Crow's Black Joy, 1978; No Longer Two People (with Patrick Lane), 1979; Animals of Fall, 1979; Humans and Other Beasts, 1980; The Weather, 1983; The Garden Going On Without Us, 1985; Angels of Flesh, Angels of Silence, 1988; Inventing the Hawk, 1992; Everything Arrives at the Light, 1995; A Saving Grace: The Collected Poems of Mrs Bentley, 1996; What the Living Won't Let Go, 1999. Editor: A Sudden Radiance: Saskatchewan Poetry (with Gary Hyland), 1987; Breathing Fire: The New Generation of Canadian Poets (with Patrick Lane), 1995. *Honours:* CBC Prize, 1987; Gov.-Gen.'s Award for Poetry, 1992; Canadian Author's Award for Poetry, 1992; Pat Lowther Awards, League of Canadian Poets, 1992, 1996; National Magazine Award Gold Medal, 1996. *Membership:* Saskatchewan Writers' Guild. *Address:* c/o McClelland and Stewart Inc, 481 University Ave, Suite 900, Toronto, Ontario M5G 2E9, Canada.

CRUCEFIX, Martyn; b. 11 Feb. 1956, Trowbridge, Wiltshire, England. Teacher; Lecturer; Poet. m. Louise Tulip, 24 July 1992. *Education:* BA, English, University of Lancaster, 1979; DPhil, English, Worcester College, Oxford, 1985. *Publications:* The Gregory Poems Anthology, 1985; Beneath Tremendous Rain, 1990; At The Mountjoy Hotel, 1993; On Whistler Mountain, 1994; A Madder Ghost, 1998. *Contributions to:* Anthologies, reviews, quarterlies and journals. *Honours:* E. C. Gregory Award, 1984;

Hawthornden Fellowship, 1991; Second Place, Arvon/Observer Competition, 1991; Joint Winner, Sheffield Thursday Poetry Competition, 1993. *Memberships:* Poetry Society, gen. council; Blue Nose, founding mem.; Shadowork performance quartet. *Address:* 10 Topsfield Rd, London N8 8SN, England. *E-mail:* martyncrucefix@aol.com.

CSOÓRI, Sándor; b. 3 Feb. 1930, Zámoly, Hungary. Poet; Writer. *Education:* Lenin Institute, Budapest, 1951. *Appointments:* Ed., Uj hang journal, 1955–56; Active in the opposition movement from 1980; Founding mem., 1987, Presidium mem., 1988–92, Hungarian Democratic Forum; Chair., Illyés Gyula Foundation, 1990–94; Pres., World Federation of Hungarians, 1991–. *Publications:* (in English trans.) Poetry: Wings of Knives and Nails, 1981; Memory of Snow, 1983; Barbarian Prayer: Selected Poems, 1989; Selected Poems of Sándor Csoóri, 1992. Other: Fiction, non-fiction, and screenplays. *Contributions to:* Various publications. *Honours:* Attila József Prize, 1954; Cannes Film Festival Prizes, 1964, 1968; Herder Prize, Vienna, 1981; Kossuth Prize, 1990; Eeva Joenpelto Prize, 1995. *Address:* Benczúr u. 15, 1068 Budapest, Hungary.

CUBA, Ivan; b. 1920, Nottingham, England. Poet; Writer; Artist. *Education:* University of Auckland. *Publication:* Gold Medal Poems: Poems by Ivan Cuba, 1990. *Contributions to:* Several publications. *Honours:* Greek Gold Medal for Military Services, 1941; Poet Laureate, Gold Medal, Rome, 1979; DLitt, World Acad. of Arts and Culture, 1988; Michael Madhusudan Award, India, 2000. *Memberships:* Various academies in Australasia, India, Europe, and the USA. *Address:* PO Box 5199, Auckland, New Zealand.

CUMBERLEGE, Marcus (Crossley); b. 23 Dec. 1938, Antibes, France. Poet; Trans. m. (1) Ava Nicole Paranjoti, 11 Dec. 1965, divorced 1972, (2) Maria Lefever, 9 Nov. 1973, 1 d. *Education:* BA, St John's College, Oxford, 1961. *Appointments:* Lecturer, Universities of Hilversum and Lugano, 1978–83. *Publications:* Oases, 1968; Poems for Quena and Tabla, 1970; Running Towards a New Life, 1973; Bruges, Bruges (with Owen Davis), 1975; Firelines, 1977; The Poetry Millionaire, 1977; La Nuit Noire, 1977; Twintig Vriendelijke Vragen (with Horst de Blaere), 1977; Northern Lights, 1981; Life is a Flower, 1981; Vlaamse Fables, 1982; Sweet Poor Hobo, 1984; Things I Cannot Change, 1993; The Best Is Yet To Be, 1997; The Moon, the Blackbird and the Falling Leaf, 1999; Once I Had a Secret Love, 2000; Angels at Work, 2002. *Contributions to:* Shin Buddhist and 30 others. *Honour:* Eric Gregory Award, 1967. *Address:* Eekhoutstraat 42, 8000 Brugge, Belgium.

CUNNING, Alfred. See: HOLLIDAY, David John Gregory.

CUNNINGHAM, Michael; b. 25 April 1950, Liverpool, England. Accountant; Legal Cashier; Poet. *Education:* BA, Honours, Class II, History of Art, Manchester University, 1971; Certificate in Education, Manchester Polytechnic, 1972. *Contributions to:* Magazines and radio. *Memberships:* Dead Good Poets Society; Evil Dead Poets Society; Poetry Society. *Address:* 162 Booker Ave, Liverpool L18 9TB, England.

CURRY, Duncan Charles; b. 5 Oct. 1957, Southall, Middlesex, England. Teacher; Poet. *Education:* BA, 1979; PGCE, 1984; MA, 1993. *Publications:* Contemporary Yorkshire Poetry, 1984; Oranges, 1986; Against the Grain, 1989; The Darts and the Commentary, 1996. *Contributions to:* Orbis; Iron; Rialto; Harry's Hand; The Wide Skirt; North; Outposts; Poetry and Audience; Poetry Nottingham; Bradford Poetry Quarterly; English in Education. *Honours:* Prizewinner, Louth Writer's Circle Poetry Competition, 1985; Second Prize, Stamford Poetry Festival Competition, 1990. *Address:* 79 School St, Moldgreen, Huddersfield HD5 8AX, England.

CURRY, Elizabeth; b. 31 Jan. 1934, Evanston, IL, USA. Prof. of English and Women's Studies; Poet. m. Stephen J Curry, 10 June 1958, 1 s. *Education:* BA, Northwestern University, 1956; PhD, University of Wisconsin at Madison, 1963. *Appointment:* Prof. of English and Women's Studies, Slippery Rock University, Pennsylvania. *Publications:* 27 chapbooks, 1985–91; Earth Against Heaven: A Tianamen Square Anthology, 1990; Thinking About Your Creative Writing, 1995. *Contributions to:* Many journals, reviews, and magazines, including Poetry, Interim. *Honours:* First Prize, Southern California Poets PEN Contest, 1987; Second Prize, Macomb College, 1987; Second Prize, K-Bar of California, 1987; Finalist, Negative Capability Eve of St Agnes Contest, 1989; Finalist, Central Pennsylvania Council of the Arts Competition, 1989; Atlanta Review Merit Award, International Poetry Contest, 2001. *Address:* c/o Dept of English, Slippery Rock University, Slippery Rock, PA 16057, USA.

CURTIS, David; b. 21 Feb. 1946, Providence, RI, USA. Assoc. Prof. of English; Poet. m. Elaine B Davis, 6 Jan. 1990, 3 s. *Education:* AB, Rhode Island College,

1968; PhD, Brown University, 1977. *Appointments:* Asst Prof., English, Wilkes College, 1977–78; Assoc. Prof., English, Sacred Heart University, 1981–. *Publication:* Updade from Pahrump, 1992. *Contributions to:* Dalhousie Review; Poem; Four Quarters; Coe Review; Karamu; Midwest Poetry Review; Plains Poetry Journal; Shorelines; Candelabrum; Literature and Film Quarterly. *Honours:* Honourable Mention, Quarterly Poetry Review, 1987; Third Prize, North American Open Poetry Competition, 1990. *Membership:* Poetry Society of America. *Address:* 126 Ardmore Rd, Milford, CT 06460, USA.

CURTIS, Linda Lee, (Herren); b. 18 April 1950, Stafford, KS, USA. Poet; Writer. m. Ronald Benson Curtis, 8 June 1979. *Education:* AA, Barton County Community College, Great Bend, KS, 1978. *Appointments:* Ed., Publisher, Winter Wheat Newsletter, 1985–; Founder, Pres., Poems Against Pushers, 1990–. *Publications:* Midnight Echoes, 1976; Sonnets and Sunbonnets, 1976; The Cheater's Almanac, 1976; Smoke Rings, 1977; More Than My Share, 1979; Intermissio, 1982; Ghetto Rain, 1990; When I Wear Red, 1990; Head Shots, 1993. *Contributions to:* Over 1,000 poems to anthologies and other publications. *Honours:* Soundboard Poet of the Year Award, 1984; Arizona Women's Partnership Songwriting Award, 1985; The Poets' Voice Best Poem of the Issue Award, 1994. *Membership:* Poets and Writers, New York. *Address:* 1919 W Adams, Phoenix, AZ 85009, USA.

CURTIS, Tony; b. 26 Dec. 1946, Carmathen, Wales. Prof. of Poetry; Poet. m. Margaret Blundell, 1970, 1 s., 1 d. *Education:* BA, University College of Swansea, 1968; MFA, Goddard College, Vermont, 1980. *Appointment:* Prof. of Poetry, University of Glamorgan. *Publications:* Poetry: Walk Down a Welsh Wind, 1972; Home Movies, 1973; Album, 1974; The Deerslayers, 1978; Carnival, 1978; Preparations: Poems, 1974–79, 1980; Letting Go, 1983; Selected Poems, 1970–85, 1986; The Last Candles, 1989; Taken for Pearls, 1993. Other: Islands (radio play), 1975; Out of the Dark Wood: Prose Poems, Stories, 1977; Dannie Abse, 1985; The Art of Seamus Heaney (ed.), 1986; How to Study Modern Poetry, 1990; How Poets Work (ed.), 1996. *Honours:* National Poetry Competition Winner, 1984; Dylan Thomas Prize, 1993; Cholmondeley Award, 1997. *Address:* Pentwyn, 55 Colcot Rd, Barry, South Glamorgan CF6 8BQ, Wales.

CUTHBERT, Valerie; b. 30 Oct. 1923, London, England. Writer; Journalist; Poet. m. 27 Nov. 1965. *Education:* Various teaching certificates. *Publications:* The Great Siege of Fort Jesus, 1970; Yusuf Bin Hasan, 1972; Jomo Kenyatta: The Burning Spear, 1982; Dust and the Shadow, 1988. *Contributions to:* Various anthologies and other publications. *Honours:* Second Prize, Short Story Competition, Writers Asscn of Kenya, 1993; Placing, International Society of Poets Competition, UK, 1996. *Membership:* Writers Asscn of Kenya. *Literary Agent:* International Press Agency (Pty) Ltd, PO Box 67, Howard Pl., South Africa. *Address:* PO Box 82727, Mombasa, Kenya.

CZAJKOWSKI, Jerzy Stanisław; b. 13 Jan. 1931, Oscislowo, Mazowsze, Poland. Poet; Essayist; Novelist. *Education:* History and Sociology, 1961–68; MA, Cultural Sociology, 1968. *Appointments:* Senior Ed., Artistic and Film Publishing House, 1961–67, State Scientific Publishing House, 1968–71, Polish Contemporary Poetry Series, 1974–80, Kiw Publishing House, 1980–89; Literary consultant. *Publications:* Poetry, essays, and novels, 1958–98. *Contributions to:* Anthologies and journals. *Honours:* Writer's and Ed.'s awards. *Address:* ul Swietojerska 4–10 m 57, 00-236 Warsaw, Poland.

CZCIBOR-PIOTROWSKI, Andrzej. See: PIOTROWSKI, Andrzej Stanisław.

CZERNIAWSKI, Adam; b. 20 Dec. 1934, Warsaw, Poland. Writer; Poet; Trans. m. Ann Christine Daker, 27 July 1957, 1 s., 1 d. *Education:* BA, English, 1955, BA, Philosophy, 1967, London University; MA, Philosophy, Sussex University, 1968; BPhil, Philosophy, Oxford University, 1970. *Appointments:* Lecturer in Philosophy; Trans.-in-Residence, Asst Dir, British Centre for Literary Trans., University of East Anglia; Administrator, Hawthornden Castle. *Publications:* Poetry, essays and trans. *Contributions to:* Reviews and journals. *Honours:* Woursell Foundation Fellowship, 1966–70; Koscielski Foundation Prize, 1971; Rockefeller Foundation Fellowship, 1993; Turzaéski Foundation Prize for Lifetime's Achievement, 1999. *Address:* 1 Monkswell Rd, Monmouth NP25 3PF, Wales.

CZIGANY, György; b. 12 Aug. 1931, Budapest, Hungary. Poet. m. Erika Jámbor, 10 Oct. 1960, 2 s., 1 d. *Education:* Pianist, Acad. of Music, 'Liszt Ferenc' Budapest, 1956. *Appointment:* Hungarian Television, 1956–94. *Publications:* Aszfaltfolyók; Házat; Álmok Ninivéből; Augusztus tárgyai; Csak a derü óráit számolom; Lacrimosa; Mozarttal vacsorázok; Három gyertya; Fények e vizen; Itt van Pompeji; Ima. Fél perc nyár; Vàndorèvek. *Contributions to:* Various publications. *Address:* Zöldlomb utca 32, 1025, Budapest, Hungary.

D

DABYDEEN, Cyril; b. 15 Oct. 1945, Guyana. Poet; Writer. *Education:* BA Honours, Lakehead University, Thunder Bay, Ontario, 1973; MA, 1974; MPA, Queen's University, Kingston, Ontario. *Appointments:* Juror, Neustadt International Prize for Literature, 2000; Juror, Governor General's Award for Literature, 2000; Speaker, Reader, across Canada, USA, UK, Europe, India, Cuba, Caribbean and South America. *Publications:* Poetry; Distances, 1977; Goatsong, 1977; Heart's Frame, 1979; This Planet Earth, 1980; Islands Lovelier Than a Vision, 1988; Coastland: New and Selected Poems, 1989; Dark Swirl, 1989; Stoning the Wind, 1994; Born in Amazonia, 1996; Discussing Columbus, 1997. Fiction: Still Close to the Island, 1980; To Monkey Jungle, 1986; The Wizard Swami, 1989; Dark Swirl, 1989; Jogging in Havana, 1992; Sometimes Hard, 1994; Berbice Crossing (stories), 1996; Black Jesus and Other Stories, 1997; My Brahmin Days and Other Stories, 2000; North of the Equator (stories), 2001. Editor: A Shapely Fire: Changing the Literary Landscape, 1987; Another Way to Dance: Asian-Canadian Poetry, 1990. *Contributions to:* Canadian Forum; Canadian Fiction Magazine; Fiddlehead; Dalhousie Review; Antigonish Review; World Literature Today; The Atlanta Journal; The Critical Quarterly; Wascana Review; Literary Review; Globe and Mail; Caribbean Quarterly; Kunapipi. *Honours:* Sandbach Parker Gold Medal; A J Seymour Lyric Poetry Prize; Poet Laureate of Ottawa; Okanagan Fiction Award; Recipient, Canada Council, Ontario Arts Council, Ottawa-Carleton Region Literary Awards; Certificate of Merit for the Arts; Honoured for work in race relations, City of Ottawa and the Federation of Canadian Municipalities. *Memberships:* US Asscn of Commonwealth Language and Literature Studies; PEN International. *Address:* 106 Blackburn, Ottawa, Ontario K1N BA7, Canada.

DABYDEEN, David; b. 9 Dec. 1955, Guyana. Poet; Writer; Prof. of Literature. *Education:* BA, Cambridge University, 1978; PhD, London University, 1982. *Appointments:* Junior Research Fellow, Oxford University, 1983–87; Prof. of Literature, Warwick University, 1987–. *Publications:* Slave Song, 1984; Coolie Odyssey, 1988; The Intended, 1991; Disappearance, 1993; Turner, 1994; The Counting House, 1996; Across the Dark Waters: Indian Identity in the Caribbean, 1996; A Harlot's Progress, 1999. *Contributions to:* Various periodicals. *Honours:* Commonwealth Poetry Prize, 1984; Guyana Literature Prize, 1992. *Memberships:* Arts Council of Great Britain, literature panel, 1985–89; RSA, fellow; Guyana's Ambassador to UNESCO, 1997. *Address:* c/o Warwick University, Coventry CV4 7AL, England.

DACEY, Philip; b. 9 May 1939, St Louis, Missouri, USA. Poet; Teacher. m. Florence Chard, 1963, divorced 1986, 2 s., 1 d. *Education:* BA, St Louis University, 1961; MA, Stanford University, 1967; MFA, University of Iowa, 1970. *Appointments:* Instructor in English, University of Missouri at St Louis, 1967–68; Faculty, Dept of English, Southwest State University, Marshall, Minnesota, 1970–; Distinguished Writer-in-Residence, Wichita State University, 1985. *Publications:* Poetry: The Beast with Two Backs, 1969; Fist, Sweet Giraffe, The Lion, Snake, and Owl, 1970; Four Nudes, 1971; How I Escaped from the Labyrinth and Other Poems, 1977; The Boy Under the Bed, 1979; The Condom Poems, 1979; Gerard Manley Hopkins Meets Walt Whitman in Heaven and Other Poems, 1982; Fives, 1984; The Man with Red Suspenders, 1986; The Condom Poems II, 1989; Night Shift at the Crucifix Factory, 1991. Editor: I Love You All Day: It is That Simple (with Gerald M Knoll), 1970; Strong Measures: Contemporary American Poetry in Traditional Forms (with David Jaus), 1986. *Honours:* Woodrow Wilson Fellowship, 1961; New York YM-YWHA Discovery Award, 1974; National Endowment for the Arts Fellowships, 1975, 1980; Minnesota State Arts Board Fellowships, 1975, 1983; Bush Foundation Fellowship, 1977; Loft-McKnight Fellowship, 1984; Fulbright Lecturer, 1988. *Address:* Route 1, Box 89, Lynd, MN 56157, USA.

DAELMAN, Jos (Walter Zone); b. 1 Aug. 1937, Zwijndrecht, Belgium. Librarian; Poet. m. Yolanda Stroobant, 24 Nov. 1959, 1 d. *Education:* Graduate in Library Science, 1970; Graduate in Scientific and Technical Documentation, 1972. *Appointments:* Branch Librarian, 1958; Teacher, Library School, Antwerp, 1973; Head, Reference Dept, 1982, Head, Psycho-Pedagogical Dept, Central Public Library, Antwerp, 1987; Prof. of Poetry, Acad. of Creative Writing, Antwerp, 1995. *Publications:* Land tussen Zee en Aarde, 1974; Vacuum, (with Cel Overberghe), 1977; De Stilte toewaarts, 1979; De Landschapstuin, 1980; De zwarte Wandelaar (with Cel Overberghe), 1982; Buiten de Roedel, 1983; Het Verlangzamen, 1986; Een Haas in Winterkoren, 1989; Letters from Sark and Other Places, 1992; Huiswaarts, 1994; Herdersuur, 1996; Beperkte Toegang, 2000. *Contributions to:* Nieuw Vlaams Tijdschrift; Deus Ex Machina; Gieriek; Journal of Contemporary Anglo-Scandinavian Poetry. *Honour:* Award for Poetry, Province of Antwerp, 1984. *Membership:* Vereniging voor Vlaamse Letterkundigen; PEN. *Address:* Oostvaart 42, 9180 Moerbeke-Waas, Belgium.

D'AGUIAR, Fred; b. 2 Feb. 1960, London, England. Poet; Writer; Dramatist; Trans.; Prof. of English. *Education:* BA, Honours, University of Kent, 1985.

Appointments: Writer-in-Residence, London Borough of Lewisham, 1986–8 Birmingham Polytechnic, 1988–89; Instructor in Writing, Arvon Foundatio 1986–; Visiting Fellow, Cambridge University, 1989–90; Northern Ar Literary Fellow, Newcastle and Durham universities, 1990–92; Visitir Writer, Amherst College, Massachusetts, 1992–94; Asst Prof. of Englisl Bates College, Lewiston, Maine, 1994–95; Prof. of English, University Miami at Coral Gables, FL, 1995–. *Publications:* Poetry: Mama Dot, 198 Airy Hall, 1989; British Subjects, 1993; Bill of Rights, 1996. Fiction: Th Longest Memory, 1994; Dear Future, 1996; Feeding the Ghosts, 1997. Play: Jamaican Airman Forsees His Death, 1995. Co-Editor: The New British Poetr 1988. *Contributions to:* Journals, magazines, radio and television. *Honour* BBC Race in the Media Award, 1992; Most Innovative Film Award, Britis Film Institute, 1993; David Higham First Novel Award, 1995; Whitbread Firs Novel Award, 1995. *Address:* c/o Curtis Brown, Haymarket House, 28–2 Haymarket, London SW1Y 4SP, England.

DALAL, Suresh; b. 11 Oct. 1932, Mumbai, Thane, India. Prof.; Poet. n Sushila, 11 May 1960, 2 d. *Education:* MA, Gujarati, 1955, PhD, Gujarat 1969, University of Mumbai. *Appointments:* Lecturer, K. C. Arts and Scienc College, 1956–64, H. R. College of Commerce, 1960–64; Prof. and Head, Dept Gujarati, K. J. Somaiya College, 1964–73; Prof. and Head, Dept of Gujarat 1973–92, Dir, Dept of Post-graduate Studies and Research, 1981–92, SND Women's University; Ed., Kavita magazine; Joint Ed., Kavilok magazin Vivechan magazine; Man. Dir, Image Publications Pvt. Ltd, Mumba *Publications:* Poetry: Ekant, 1966; Astitva, 1973; Kastakshar, 1977; V Sangati, 1980; Gharzurapo, 1981; Kavyasrushti, 1986; Mayapravesh, 198 Layna Pravasman, 1990; Vibrations, 1989. Children's Poetry: Ittakitta, 196 Chakamchhalo, 1977. Children's Fiction: Hathibhai Dantwala, 1985. Sho Stories: Pin Cushion, 1978. Essays: Mari Bariathi, 1975; Maro Aaspasn Rasto, 1981; Amne Tadko Aapo, 1987. Criticism: Apeksha, 1958; Impression 1984; Walt Whitman, 1985; Kavi Parichay, 1986. Other: Trans; Ed. of man titles; Interviews. *Contributions to:* Journals and periodicals. *Honours:* Bes Teacher's Award, Government of Maharashtra, 1980–81; National Lecturer fc the Year, University Grants Commission, 1982–83; Ranjitram Gold Medal fc Creative Writing, Gujarat Government, 1983; Sri Auribindo Ghosh Gold Meda for Creative Writing; Maha Kavi Nhanalal Award for Creative Writing; Kak Kalelkar Award for Creative Writing; Narmad Medal; Bhasa Parishad Awarc *Address:* 133 Hassa Mahal, Dalamal Park, Cuffe Parade, Mumbai 400 00§ India.

DALE, Peter John; b. 21 Aug. 1938, Addlestone, Surrey, England. Poe Writer; Trans. m. Pauline Strouvelle, 29 June 1963, 1 s., 1 d. *Education:* B/ Honours, English, St Peter's College, Oxford, 1963. *Appointments:* Teacher Secondary Schools, 1963–93; Co-Ed., Agenda, 1972–96; Editorial Dir, Betwee the Lines, 1997–; Poetry Ed., Oxford Today, 1999–. *Publications:* Poetry: Wal from the House, 1962; The Storms, 1968; Mortal Fire, 1976; One Anothe (sonnet sequence), 1978; Too Much of Water, 1983; A Set of Darts (epigram with W. S. Milne and Robert Richardson), 1990; Earth Light: New Poems, 199 Edge to Edge: Selected Poems, 1996; Da Capo (poem sequence), 1997; Unde the Breath, 2002. Prose: Michael Hamburger in Conversation with Peter Dak 1998; An Introduction to Rhyme, 1998; Anthony Thwaite in Conversation wit Peter Dale and Ian Hamilton, 1999; Richard Wilbur in Conversation with Pete Dale, 2000; Peter Dale in Conversation with William Bedford, 2002. Translato Selected Poems of François Villon, 1978; Poems of Jules Laforgue, 1986; Th Divine Comedy, terza rima version, 1996; Poems of Jules Laforgue, 2001; Poems c François Villon, 2001. *Contributions to:* Journals and periodicals. *Honour:* Art Council Bursary, 1970. *Membership:* Society of Authors; Trans Asscn. *Address* 10 Selwood Rd, Sutton, Surrey SM3 9JU, England.

DALEY, Terence; b. 7 Feb. 1932, Pontypridd, South Wales. Poet. m. Dian Daley, 29 June 1957, 2 s., 1 d. *Education:* ONC; HNC Drawing; Art an Creative Writing. *Appointment:* Project Engineer, 1973. *Publications:* Lasting Calm, 1997; Light of the World, 1997; The Star Laden Sky, 199? The Sweetest Thing, 1997; Natural Tranquility, 1997; Meaningful Words, 1997 Bats in the Belfry, 1997; Web of Thoughts, 1997; A Celebration of Poets, 1997; Quiet Storm, 1997; My Regards to You, 1997; Perceptions, 1997; Time t Reflect, 1997; A Picture of Life, 1998; A Sense of Sussex, 1998; Poeti Visions, 1998; The World Versus Humans, 1999; Timeless Emotions, 1999 Labour of Love, 1999; In Those Days, 1999; Solitary Christmas, 1999; God's Gif to Me, 1999; Poets in Focus, 1999. *Contributions to:* Anthologies, journals reviews, quarterlies and periodicals. *Honour:* Inclusion in Forward Press's To 100 Poets. *Address:* 36 Constable Rd, Rugby, Warwickshire CV21 4DF England.

D'ALFONSO, Antonio; b. 6 Aug. 1953, Montréal, QC, Canada. Writer; Poe Ed. m. Julia Mary Gualtieri, 8 Sept. 1990. *Education:* BA, Communication Art Loyola College, Montréal, 1975; MSc, Communications in Semiology of Film Université de Montréal, 1979. *Appointments:* Teacher, 1974–79; Ed.-in-Chie

Guernica Editions, Montréal, 1979–. *Publications:* La Chanson du Shaman Sedna, 1973; Queror, 1979; Black Tongue, 1983; The Other Shore, 1986; L'Autre Rivage, 1987; L'Amour panique, 1987; Avril ou l'anti-passion, 1990; Panick Love, 1992; Lettre a Julia, 1992. *Contributions to:* Le Devoir; The Gazette; La Presse. *Membership:* Union des écrivains, Québec. *Address:* Guernica Editions, PO Box 633, Station NDG, Montréal, QC H4A 3R1, Canada.

DALIBARD, Jill E. Dawson; b. 24 July 1936, Long Melford, Suffolk, England. Social Worker; Poet. *Education:* BA, Bristol University, 1958; MSW, McGill University, Montréal, 1969; MA, Concordia University, Montréal, 1988. *Appointments:* Lecturer in English, Concordia University; Social Worker, Royal Victoria Hospital, Montréal; Dir of Hospital Services, Ville Marie Social Service Centre, Montréal. *Publication:* Deed of Gift, 1995. *Contributions to:* Waves; Canadian Forum; Antigonish Review; Wascana Review; Poetry Canada Review; League of Canadian Poets Annual Anthology. *Memberships:* British Poetry Society; National Asscn for Poetry Therapy, USA. *Address:* 3550 Ridgewood Ave, Apt 34, Montréal, QC H3V 1C2, Canada.

DALLAS, Ruth. See: MUMFORD, Ruth.

DALY, Padraig John; b. 25 June 1943, Dungarvan, County Waterford, Ireland. Priest of the Order of St Augustine; Poet. *Education:* BA, 1967, H Dip Ed, 1973, University College, Dublin; BD, Gregorian, Pontifical University, Rome, 1969. *Appointments:* Prior, St John's Priory, Dublin 1981–85, St Augustine's, Ballyboden 1985–89; Parish Priest, Ballyboden 1989–; Prior, Good Counsel College, New Ross, Co Wexford, 1997–. *Publications:* Nowhere But in Praise, 1978; This Day's Importance, 1981; Dall' Orlo Marino Del Mondo, 1981; A Celibate Affair, 1984; Poems, Selected and New, 1988; Out of Silence, 1993; The Voice of the Hare, 1997; Libretto (from the Italian of Eduardo Sanguineti), 1998; The Last Dreamers, 1999. *Contributions to:* Books, magazines and journals in Ireland. *Memberships:* Poetry Ireland; Irish Writers Union. *Address:* Good Counsel College, New Ross, Co Wexford, Ireland.

D'AMBRA, Adrian Lewis; b. 15 Dec. 1957, Melbourne, Vic., Australia. Secondary English and Literature Teacher; Freelance Travel Journalist; Poet. *Education:* BA 1984, Dip Ed 1985, University of Melbourne. *Publications:* The Flowers of Impotence, 1983; Cavafy's Room, chapbook, 1987. *Contributions to:* Journals and magazines. *Memberships:* Australian Education Union; European Council of International Schools. *Address:* 37 Venice St, Mornington, Vic. 3931, Australia.

DAMYANOV, Damyan Petrov; b. 18 Jan. 1935, Sliven, Bulgaria. Writer; Poet. m. Nadejda Zacharieva, 23 Aug. 1964, 2 s., 1 d. *Education:* Graduated, Sofia State University, 1960. *Appointments:* Literary Consultant, 1957–61; Ed., 1964–68. *Publications:* More than 60 books including: If There Was Not a Fire, 1959; Waiting, 1960; Lyric, 1963; Poem of the Happiness, 1964; Like a Grass, 1965; Kneeling Before You, 1966; Walls, 1966; Live in Such a Way that..., 1967; And the Summer is Passing Away, 1968; You are Like my Tear Drop, 1970; Gladness, Blue and Light, 1971; A Prayer to the World, 1973; A First Name of the Happiness, 1974; Farewell, I am in a Hurry, 1982; The Way I had Passed, 1983; There is a Beauty in Every Day, 1985; Be Alive my Fiction Love, 1985; Call me Love, 1992; Still Alive, 1993; Soul in Knot, 1998. *Contributions to:* All Bulgarian literary magazines. *Honours:* Dimitrov Literary Award, 1971; Tchintolov Literary Award, 1972; Love's Lyric Award, 1978; Golden Orpheus Award, 1998; Ivan Vazov Award, 1998. *Membership:* Bulgarian Union of Writers. *Address:* 24 Tzarigradsko Shosse, Bl 22, Entr B, 1113 Sofia, Bulgaria.

DANA, Robert (Patrick); b. 2 June 1929, Allston, Massachusetts, USA. Emeritus Prof. of English; Poet. m. (1) Mary Kowalke, 2 June 1951, divorced 1973, 3 c., (2) Margaret Sellen, 14 Sept. 1974. *Education:* AB, Drake University, 1951; MA, University of Iowa, 1954. *Appointments:* Asst Prof., Assoc. Prof., Prof. of English, Cornell College, Mount Vernon, IA, 1953–94; Distinguished Visiting Poet, University of Florida, 1975–76, Wayne State University, 1978–79, University of Idaho, 1980, Wichita State University, 1982, Stockholm University, 1996; Ed., Hillside Press, Mount Vernon, 1957–67; Ed., 1964–68; Contributing Ed., 1991–; North American Review; Contributing Ed., American Poetry Review, 1973–88, New Letters, 1980–83. *Publications:* My Glass Brother and Other Poems, 1957; The Dark Flags of Waking, 1964; Journeys from the Skin: A Poem in Two Parts, 1966; Some Versions of Silence: Poems, 1967; The Power of the Visible, 1971; In a Fugitive Season, 1980; What the Stones Know, 1984; Blood Harvest, 1986; Against the Grain: Interviews with Maverick American Publishers, 1986; Starting Out for the Difficult World, 1987; What I Think I Know: New and Selected Poems, 1990; Wildebeest, 1993; Yes, Everything, 1994; Hello, Stranger: Beach Poems, 1996; A Community of Writers: Paul Engle and The Iowa Writers' Workshop, 1999; Summer, 2000. *Contributions to:* New Yorker; New York Times; Poetry; Georgia Review; Manoa. *Honours:* Rainer Maria Rilke Prize, 1984; National Endowment for the Arts Fellowships, 1985, 1993; Delmore Schwartz Memorial Poetry Award, 1989; Carl Sandburg Medal for Poetry, 1994; Pushcart Prize, 1996. *Memberships:* Acad. of American Poets; PEN; Associated Writing Programs; Poetry Society of America. *Address:* 1466 Westview Dr., Coralville, IA 52241, USA.

DANIEL, Colin. See: WINDSOR, Patricia.

DANIEL, Geoffrey Peter, (Peter Thorne); b. 5 March 1955, Bedford, England. Teacher; Poet. m. Iseabal Flora MacDonald, 12 July 1980, 1 s., 1 d. *Education:* Kings Canterbury, 1968–72; St Andrews University, 1973–77; Durham University, 1977–78; Hamilton College of Education, 1980. *Appointments:* Head of Drama, Kamuzu Acad., Malawi; Glenalmond College, Perthshire; Head of English, later Sixth Form, Reeds School, Surrey; Deputy Rector, Dollar Acad.; Poetry Adviser, Asscn of Christian Writers. *Publication:* Gripping the Perch, 1999. *Contributions to:* Books, magazines and journals. *Honour:* International Haiku. *Memberships:* British Haiku Society; Asscn of Christian Writers; Society of Antiquaries, Scotland, fellow. *Address:* Dollar Acad., Dollar, Clackmannanshire FK14 7DU, Scotland.

DANIELEWSKA, Lucja Zofia, (Lucja Wrzos, Julia Tarczyn); b. 6 Nov. 1932, Poznań, Poland. Poet; Writer; Trans.; University Lecturer. m. Jerzy Danielews, 26 Dec. 1951, 2 s. *Education:* MA, Croatian and Serbian Philology, Adam Mickiewicz University, Poznań. *Appointments:* Deputy Pres., Poznań Branch, Polish Writers Asscn, 1987–89, 1989–92; Mem., National Council of Culture, 1986–, Literature Fund Council, 1989–; University Lecturer, 1995–. *Publications:* Short Noon Shadow, 1972; Bar Antiphons, 1975; Home Antiphons, 1977; Raspberry Antiphons, 1977; Korkonosze Lyrics, 1977; Epigrams, 1977; Paradise Yard, 1979; Home, 1980; Epigrams on Polish Women, 1980; In the Heart, 1980; Swallow's Songs, 1982; Adam's Rib, 1983; Fair Play, 1986; Flower Motif Poems, 1987; Like a Bird, 1989; Fluorescence, 1989; Flower Poems Dedicated to All Who Love Flowers, 1990; From the South, 1990; Herbal Epigrams, 1990; Dream: Reality, 1992; Request for Silence, 1993; Space Eyes, 1994; She is Looking, 1995; Lively Source: Anthology of Modern Croatian Poetry, 1996; Sea Rose, 1998. Other: Prose; Poetry trans. *Contributions to:* Newspapers, reviews, magazines, journals and periodicals, at home and abroad. *Honours:* First Prize, Polish Radio, 1974; Jan Kasprowicz Prize, Poznań, 1986; Pegasus Prize, Red Rose Contest, Gdańsk, 1988; Prize, 11th International Poetic, Poznań, 1988; Prize, 19th Warsaw Poetry Autumn, Warsaw Polish Writers Asscn. *Address:* PO Box, Skrytka Pocztowa 256.60-967, Poznań 9, Poland.

DANIELS, Peter John; b. 20 July 1954, Cambridge, England. Librarian; Indexer; Poet. *Education:* BA, English, Reading University, 1978; Postgraduate Diploma in Librarianship, Birmingham Polytechnic, 1981. *Appointment:* Asst Librarian, Religious Society of Friends. *Publications:* Breakfast in Bed, 1987; Take Any Train: A Book of Gay Men's Poetry (ed.), 1990; Peacock Luggage (co-author), 1992. *Contributions to:* Magazines. *Honours:* Runner-up, National Poetry Competition, 1990; Winner, Poetry Business Pamphlet Competition, 1991. *Membership:* Oscars (gay poetry group), treasurer, 1986–. *Address:* c/o Oscars Press, B M Oscars, London WC1N 3XX, England.

DANTE, Robert; b. 12 Feb. 1953, Lytham St Annes, Lancashire, England. Writer; Poet. *Education:* BA, University of Houston, 1992. *Appointments:* Writer; Ed.; Theatre Critic; Poet; Publisher, Boudoir Noir Magazine. *Publication:* Silent Command, 1993. *Contributions to:* Stone Drum; Aileron; Cincinnati Poetry Review; En Passant; Phosphene; Harvest. *Memberships:* International Asscn of Theatre Critics; Canadian Magazine Publishers Asscn; Canadian Eds Asscn. *Address:* PO Box 5, Station F, Toronto, Ontario M4Y 2L4, Canada.

DAOUST, Jean-Paul; b. 30 Jan. 1946, Valleyfield, QC, Canada. Writer; Poet; Teacher; Ed. *Education:* MA, University of Montréal, 1976. *Appointments:* Prof., Cegep Edouard-Montpetit, Québec; Mem., Editorial Board, magazine Estuaire. *Publications:* Poetry: Oui, cher: Récit, 1976; Chaises longues, 1977; Portrait d'intérieur, 1981; Poèmes de Babylone, 1982; Taxi, 1984; Dimanche après-midi, 1985; La peau du coeur et son opéra, 1985; Les garçons magiques, 1986; Suite contemporaine, 1987; Les Cendres bleues, 1990; Rituels d'Amérique, 1990; Les Poses de la lumière, 1991; L'Amérique, 1993; Poèmes faxés (co-author), 1994; 111, Wooster Street, 1996; Taxi pour Babylone, 1996; Les Chambres de la Mer, 1991; Les Saisons de L'Ange, Tome I, 1997, Tome II, 1999; Blue Ashes, 1999; Les versets amoureux, 2001; Lèvres ouvertes, 2001; Roses labyrinthes, 2002. Other: Soleils d'acajou (novel), 1983; Le Désert Rose (novel), 2000. *Honour:* Gov.-Gen.'s Literary Award in Poetry, 1990. *Membership:* Union des Ecrivains Québecois. *Address:* 151 chemin Champoux, Ste Mélanie, QC J0K 3A0, Canada.

DARBYSHIRE, Alan. See: HIRST, John Alan.

DARDEN, Kathryn E.; b. 19 Dec. 1958, Nashville, Tennessee, USA. Publisher; Poet. *Education:* MA, David Lipscomb University. *Appointments:* Pres., Darden and Assocs, 1982–; Publisher, 1988–; Teacher, Nashville Christian School, 1990–95. *Contributions to:* Anthologies. *Honours:* Ed.'s Choice Awards; International Woman of the Year Citations, 1995, 1996. *Address:* PO Box 210182, Nashville, TN 37221, USA.

DARDEN-SMITH, Patricia; b. 21 Dec. 1955, Savannah, GA, USA. Poet. m. DeWitt Smith, 5 Oct. 1981, 1 s. *Education:* In a Different Light, 1991; Language of the Soul, 1991; Impressions, 1995; Freedom, 1995; Endless Harmony, 1995; The Rainbow's End, 1996; Mirrors of the Mind, 1996; Crossings, 1996; Sweetheart, 1997. *Contributions to:* Anthologies and periodicals. *Honours:*

Famous Poet, Famous Poets' Society, Hollywood, 1996; Several honorable mentions and other awards. *Memberships:* Georgia State Poetry Society; International Society of Authors and Artists; National Poets Asscn. *Address:* PO Box 1637, Vidalia, GA 30475, USA.

DARRAGH, Simon Timothy; b. 12 June 1944, Walmer, Kent, England. Plumber; Poet; Trans. *Education:* BA, Honours, Philosophy, University College, London, 1971. *Contributions to:* Anthologies and periodicals. *Honour:* Second Prize, Literary Review Poetry Competition, 1988. *Address:* Alonnisos, Sporades, Greece.

DARUWALLA, K(eki) N(asserwanji); b. 24 Jan. 1937, Lahore, India. Poet; Writer. m. Khorshed Keki Daruwalla, 10 May 1965. *Education:* MA, English, Punjab University, Chandigarh. *Appointment:* Visiting Fellow, Queen Elizabeth House, Oxford, 1980–81. *Publications:* Poetry: Under Oion, 1970; Apparition in April, 1971; Crossing of Rivers, 1976; Winter Poems, 1980; The Keeper of the Dead, 1982; Landscapes, 1987; A Summer of Tigers, 1995. Fiction: Sword and Abyss, 1979. Editor: Two Decades of Indian Poetry, 1960–80, 1981; The Minister for Permanent Unrest, 1996. *Contributions to:* Anthologies, journals, and periodicals. *Honours:* Sahitya Akademi Award, 1984; Commonwealth Poetry Award, Asia Region, 1987. *Memberships:* Sahitya Akademi, advisory board for English, 1983–87. *Address:* 79 Mount Kailash, Pocket-A, SFS Apartments, New Delhi 110065, India.

DARWISH, Mahmoud; b. 1942, Birwa. Poet; Politician; Journalist. *Education:* Moscow University, USSR. *Appointments:* Journalist, Haifa, Israel; Chief Ed., Al-Karmil periodical, Al-Ittihad newspaper; Left Israel for exile in Lebanon, 1971; Ed., Shu'un Filistiniyya (Palestinian Affairs), 1972; Dir, Palestinian Liberation Organization Research Centre, Beirut, 1975–82. *Publications:* Asafir Bila Ajniha (Bird Without Wings), 1960; Awraq al-Zaytun (Olive Leaves), 1964; Ashiq Min Filastin (A Lover from Palestine), 1966; Uhibbuki aw la Uhibikki (I Love You, I Love You Not), 1972; Qasidat Bayrut (Ode to Beirut), 1982; Madih al-Zill al-Ali (A Eulogy for the Tall Shadow), 1983; Sareer El Ghariba (Bed of a Stranger), 1988; Why Did You Leave the Horse Alone?, 1994. *Honours:* Lotus Prize, Union of Afro-Asian Writers, 1969; Mediterranean Prize, 1980; Ibn Sina Prize, 1982; Lenin Peace Prize, 1983. *Membership:* Palestinian Liberation Organization, Exec., 1987–93. *Address:* c/o Kegan Paul, PO Box 256, London WC1B 3SW, England.

DAS, Jagannath Prasad; b. 26 April 1936, Orissa, India. Writer; Poet; Researcher. m. Mitra, 7 May 1960, 1 d. *Education:* MA; PhD. *Publications:* First Person, 1976; Love Is a Season, 1978; Timescapes, 1980; Silences, 1989; Lovelines, 2001; 9 collections of poems in Oriya language. *Contributions to:* Illustrated Weekly of India; Indian Literature; Poetry Society Journal. *Honour:* Sahitya Akademi Award, 1991. *Membership:* Pres., Poetry Society of India. *Address:* 305-SFS, Hauz Khas, New Delhi 110016, India.

DAS, Kamala; b. 31 March 1934, Malabar, South India. Poetry Ed.; Poet; Writer. m. K Madhava Das, 1949, 3 s. *Education:* Private. *Appointment:* Poetry Ed., Illustrated Weekly of India, Mumbai, 1971–79. *Publications:* Poetry: Summer in Calcutta: Fifty Poems, 1965; The Descendants, 1967; The Old Playhouse and Other Poems, 1973; Tonight This Savage Rite: The Love Poetry of Kamala Das and Pritish Nandy, 1979; Collected Poems, 1987. Fiction: Alphabet of Lust, 1977; Manomi, 1987; The Sandalwood Tree, 1988. *Honours:* Kerala Sahitya Acad. Award for Fiction, 1969; Asian World Prize for Literature, 1985. *Address:* Sthanuvilas Bungalow, Sastgamangalam, Trivndrum 10, Kerala, India.

DAS, Sisir Kumar; b. 7 Nov. 1936, Calcutta, India. Educator; Poet. m. 11 Aug. 1960, 2 s., 1 d. *Education:* MA, 1957, Calcutta; PhD, 1963, Calcutta and London. *Appointments:* Lecturer in Bengali, SOAS, University of London, 1960–63; Reader in Bengali, 1963–80, Tagore Prof., 1980–, University of Delhi. *Publications:* In Bengali Language: Jama Lagna, 1956; Hayto Daroja Ache, 1986; Abalupta Chaturtha Charan, 1986; Baj Pakhir Sange, 1992. *Memberships:* Comparative Literature Asscn of India, pres., 1977–87, vice-pres., 1989–. *Address:* Dept of Modern Indian Language, University of Delhi, Delhi 110007, India.

DASGUPTA, Buddhadeb; b. 11 Feb. 1944, Anara, India. Film Dir; Poet. m. 27 June 1975, 2 d. *Education:* MA, Economics, University of Calcutta. *Appointment:* Prof., Economics, Calcutta, 1969–76. *Publications:* Govir Aerialey, 1962; Coffin Kimba Suitcase, 1971; Himjug, 1978; Chatakahini, 1982; Roboter Gan, 1986; Srestha Kobita, 1990; Bhomboler Ashchorjo Kahini, 1992; Unki Mare Nil Armstrong, 1994. *Contributions to:* Krittibash; Shotobhisha; Alinda; Desh; Ananda Bazar Patrika. *Address:* 32-1F Gariahat Rd S, Flat 3A, Calcutta 700031, India. *E-mail:* bdggupta@cal2.vsnl.net.in.

DASH, Braja Kishore; b. 25 Sept. 1958, Kaladia, Namouza, Cutlack, India. Teacher; Poet; Writer. *Education:* ISC, BA, with distinction; BEd, First Class; MA, First Class. *Appointments:* Teacher, Government High School, Machkund, Koraput, India. *Publications:* Love; My Livelong Here Peace of Dove; Truth; My Life Is Your Eternal Game; I Am Potentially Divine; Meditation; Oriya Poem Collection. *Contributions to:* Poetry 96; Poet; Poetry Time; Poetcrit; Poetry; Heaven; Triveni; Kavita India; Vedic Light; Skylark; Genadaishi. *Honours:*

World Congress of Poetry; Bharat Chakra Memorial Award, Sambalpu University; Gem of Oriental Knowledge, Kalikrishna, Jeypore, Koraput Certificate, Bhakta Charan Charitable Trust; Gem of Oriental Knowledge Kali Krishna. *Address:* Government High School, Machkund, Koraput, Orissa 764 040, India.

DASH, Brusaketu, (Kuna); b. 1 Feb. 1962, Buguda, India. Headmaster Writer; Poet. m. 9 March 1991. *Education:* HSC, BSE, Orissa, 1978 Intermediate Arts, 1980, BA, 1982, MEd, 1983, MEd, 1984, MA, English 1987, Berhampur University. *Appointments:* Ed., Premika literary monthly Reporter, Sambad, Sun Times; Headmaster, Budhagiri Bidyapitha, B D Pur *Publications:* Pasu Pakshyenka Kahani (children's fiction), 1989; Nadi Nare Namaskar (short story), 1990; Rutu O'Rati (poems), 1991. *Contributions to* Periodicals and magazines. *Honours:* Jadumani Sahitya Sansad, Udayapur 1988; Palli Shree Poetry Awards, 1990. *Memberships:* Yuba Lekhaka Samilana General Secretary, Chinta O'Chetana, Orissa; General Secretary, Ossta Buguda Zone; Darnik Asha Sahitya Ashara; Secretary, Sakala Sahitya Sansad. *Address:* Buguda 761118, Gianjam, Orissa 761118, India.

DASSANOWSKY, Robert von; b. 28 Jan. 1960, New York, NY, USA. Writer; Poet; Ed.; University Prof.; Film Producer. *Education:* Graduate, American Acad. of Dramatic Arts, Pasadena, CA, 1977–78; American Film Institute Conservatory Program, Los Angeles, 1979–81; BA, 1985, MA, 1988, PhD, 1992, University of California at Los Angeles. *Appointments:* Founding Ed., Rohwedder: International Magazine of Literature and Art, 1986–93; Corresponding Ed., Rampike, 1991–; Editorial Board, Osiris, 1991–, Poetry Salzbury Review, 2002; Visiting Asst Prof. of German, University of California, 1992–93; Asst Prof. of German, 1993–99, Assoc. Prof. of German and Film, 1999–, Chair, Dept of Languages and Cultures, 2001–, Interim Chair, Dept of Visual and Performing Arts, 2001–, University of Colorado at Colorado Springs; Editorial Board, Modern Austrian Literature, 1997–2000; Co-Head, Bevedere Film, 1999–; Board mem., LA Flickapalooza film festival, 2001–. *Publications:* Phantom Empires: The Novels of Alexander Lernet-Holenia and the Question of Postimperial Austrian Identity, 1996; Hans Raimund: Verses of a Marriage (trans.), 1996; Telegrams from the Metropole: Selected Poetry, 1999; Alexander Lernet-Holenia: Mars in Aries (trans.), 2002. Other: Several plays and television scripts. Film Production: Exec. Producer: Semmelweis, 2001; Epicure, 2001; The Nightmare Stumbles Past, 2002; Wilson Chance, 2002. *Contributions to:* Contributing Ed., Gale Encyclopedia of Multicultural America, 1999; Editorial Board and Contributor, International Dictionary of Films and Filmmakers, 2000; Poetry and articles in periodicals and anthologies. *Honours:* Academico h.c., Academia Culturale d'Europa, Italy, 1989; University of Colorado Pres.'s Fund for the Humanities Grants, 1996, 2001; Outstanding Teaching Award, University of Colorado, 2001; Elected Mem., European Acad. of Arts and Sciences, 2001. *Memberships:* MLA; PEN/ USA West; Austrian PEN; Poet and Writers; American Federation of Film Producers; Society for Cinema Studies; Screen Actors Guild; Founder and Vice-Pres., International Alexander Lernet-Holenia Society 1997–; Founder and Vice-Pres., Austrian American Film Asscn. 1998–; PEN Colorado, founding-pres., 1994–99, 2001–. *Address:* c/o Dept of Languages and Cultures, University of Colorado, Colorado Springs, CO 80933, USA.

DATTA, Bidhan; b. March 1948, Akherpur, India. Poet; Lyricist; Writer. m. June 1975, 1 d. *Publications:* Over 1,000 songs; Several poems. *Contributions to:* Anthologies and other publications. *Honours:* World Poet Award, 1986; Bangladesh Tribuj Parisad, 1994. *Membership:* Michael Madhusudan Acad. *Address:* 284 MNK Rd (N), (BJF) PO Alalmbazar, Calcutta, 700035, India.

DAUER, Lesley; b. 10 Aug. 1965, Mountain View, CA, USA. Poet; Educator. *Education:* BA, Middlebury College, 1987; MFA, University of Massachusetts at Amherst, 1992; MEd, Harvard University, 1993. *Appointments:* Instructor in English and Creative Writing, University of Massachusetts at Amherst, 1989–91; Instructor in English and Creative Writing, Foothill College, 1996–; Instructor, Cabrillo College, 1996–97. *Publications:* The Fragile City, 1996. *Contributions to:* Anthologies and journals. *Honour:* Bluestem Award, Bluestem Press, 1996. *Membership:* Associated Writing Programs. *Address:* 488 University Ave, No. 310, Palo Alto, CA 94301, USA.

DAUNT, Jon; b. 1 March 1951, Columbus, Ohio, USA. Poet. m. 16 Dec. 1979, 2 s. *Education:* BA, Stanford University, 1973; MA, University of California, 1983. *Contributions to:* California Quarterly; Cincinnati Poetry Review; Connecticut Poetry Review; Denver Quarterly; Descant; Louisiana Literature; Malahat Review; Mississippi Review; Nimrod; Prairie Schooner; Shenandoah; South Carolina Review; South Dakota Review. *Honours:* Acad. of American Poets Award, 1984; Alice Sherry Memorial Prize, Poetry Society of Virginia, 1985; Wildwood Poetry Prize, 1985–86; Black Bear Poetry Awards, 1985–86, 1988–89; Fulbright-Hays Grant, 1987–88. *Memberships:* Poetry Society of America; Philological Asscn of the Pacific Coast. *Address:* 609 D St, Davis, CA 95616, USA.

DAVEY, Frank(land Wilmot); b. 19 April 1940, Vancouver, BC, Canada. Prof. of Canadian Literature; Writer; Poet; Ed. m. (1) Helen Simmons, 1962, divorced 1969, (2) Linda McCartney, 1969, 1 s., 1 d. *Education:* BA, 1961, MA, 1963, University of British Columbia, Vancouver; PhD, University of Southern

California at Los Angeles, 1968. *Appointments:* Lecturer, 1963–67, Asst Prof., 1967–69, Royal Roads Military College, Victoria, BC; Writer-in-Residence, Sir George Williams University, Montréal, 1969–70; Asst Prof., 1970–72, Assoc. Prof., 1972–80, Prof. of English, 1980–90, Chair, Dept of English, 1985–88, 1989–90, York University, Toronto; Carl F Klinck Prof. of Canadian Literature, University of Western Ontario, London, 1990–. *Publications:* Poetry: D-Day and After, 1962; City of the Gulls and Sea, 1964; Bridge Force, 1965; The Scarred Hill, 1966; Four Myths for Sam Perry, 1970; Weeds, 1970; Griffon, 1972; King of Swords, 1972; L'An Trentiesme: Selected Poems 1961–70, 1972; Arcana, 1973; The Clallam, 1973; War Poems, 1979; The Arches: Selected Poems, 1981; Capitalistic Affection!, 1982; Edward and Patricia, 1984; The Louis Riel Organ and Piano Company, 1985; The Abbotsford Guide to India, 1986; Postcard Translations, 1988; Popular Narratives, 1991; Cultural Mischief: A Practical Guide to Multiculturalism, 1996. Criticism: Five Readings of Olson's 'Maximus', 1970; Earle Birney, 1971; From There to Here: A Guide to English-Canadian Literature Since 1960, 1974; Louis Dudek and Raymond Souster, 1981; The Contemporary Canadian Long Poem, 1983; Surviving the Paraphrase: 11 Essays on Canadian Literature, 1983; Margaret Atwood: A Feminist Poetics, 1984; Reading Canadian Reading, 1988; Post-National Arguments: The Politics of the Anglophone-Canadian Novel Since 1967, 1993; Reading 'KIM' Right, 1993; Canadian Literary Power: Essays on Anglophone-Canadian Literary Conflict, 1994; Karla's Web: A Cultural Examination of the Mahaffy-French Murders, 1994. *Contributions to:* Books and journals. *Honours:* Macmillan Prize, 1962; Dept of Defence Arts Research Grants, 1965, 1966, 1968; Canada Council Fellowships, 1966, 1974; Humanities Research Council of Canada Grants, 1974, 1981; Canadian Federation for the Humanities Grants, 1979, 1992; Social Sciences and Humanities Research Council Fellowship, 1981. *Membership:* Asscn of Canadian College and University Teachers of English, pres., 1994–96. *Address:* 499 Dufferin Ave, London, Ontario N6B 2A1, Canada.

DAVEY, William; b. 20 March 1913, New York, NY, USA. Poet; Writer. m. (7) Susan Steenrod, 19 Nov. 1965. *Education:* Princeton University; University of California at Berkeley; New York University; Sorbonne, University of Paris. *Appointments:* Commando, First Special Service Force, Canadian-American Elite Unit, World War II; Contributing and Foreign Language Ed., The Long Story magazine, 1991–97. *Publications:* Dawn Breaks the Heart (novel), 1932; Arms, Angels, Epitaphs (poems); The Angry Dust (novel), 1995; Trial of Pythagoras and Other Poems, 1996; Lost Adulteries and Other Stories, 1998; Bitter Rainbow and Other Stories, 1999. *Contributions to:* Anthologies, periodicals and magazines. *Honour:* Nominated four times for Literary Prizes. *Memberships:* Poetry Society of America; Poetry Society of Virginia; World Congress of Poets. *Address:* Lions Watch Farm, PO Box 129, Keene, VA 22946, USA.

DAVID, Adele; b. 12 Dec. 1937, Manchester, England. Jungian Analyst; Astrologer; Poet; Artist. m. 1959, divorced 1971, 2 d. *Education:* National Diploma of Art, Painting Special, 1962. *Appointments:* Lecturer in Drawing, Chelsea College of Art, 1962–63; Lecturer in Drawing and Painting, Plymouth College of Art, 1964–65; Lecturer in Creative Writing and Literature, Enfield College of Higher Education, 1974–83; Private Practice as Analyst and Lecturer in Psychology, 1985–; Supervisor and Lecturer, Centre for Psychological Astrology, 1985–96, Training Analyst and Training Supervisor, 1993–. *Publications:* Becoming, 1980; The Moon's Song, 2001. *Contributions to:* Anthologies, newspapers and journals. *Honours:* Prize, Caernarvon Festival, 1978; Appleby Cup, Cheltenham Open Competitive Festival, 1993. *Memberships:* Asscn of Jungian Analysts; International Asscn of Jungian Analysts; UKCP. *Address:* 5 Raleigh St, London N1 8NW, England.

DAVIDSON, Michael; b. 18 Dec. 1944, Oakland, CA, USA. Prof. of Literature; Poet; Writer. m. (1) Carol Wikarska, 1970, divorced 1974, (2) Lois Chamberlain, 1988, 2 c. *Education:* BA, San Francisco State University, 1967; PhD, State University of New York at Buffalo, 1971; Post-doctoral Fellow, University of California at Berkeley, 1974–75. *Appointments:* Visiting Lecturer, San Diego State University, 1973–76; Curator, Archive for New Poetry, 1975–85, Prof. of Literature, 1977–, University of California at San Diego. *Publications:* Poetry: Exchanges, 1972; Two Views of Pears, 1973; The Mutabilities, and the Foul Papers, 1976; Summer Letters, 1977; Grillwork, 1980; Discovering Motion, 1980; The Prose of Fact, 1981; The Landing of Rochambeau, 1985; Analogy of the Ion, 1988; Post Hoc, 1990. Other: The San Francisco Renaissance: Poetics and Community at Mid-Century, 1989. *Contributions to:* Periodicals. *Honour:* National Endowment for the Arts Grant, 1976. *Address:* c/o Dept of Literature, University of California at San Diego, La Jolla, CA 92093, USA.

DAVIDSON, Phebe Elizabeth; b. 25 March 1944, Summit, New Jersey, USA. Prof. of English; Writer; Poet. m. Stephen Davidson, 29 May 1968, 2 s. *Education:* BA, English, Trenton State College, 1967; MA, English, 1987; PhD, English, 1991, Rutgers University. *Appointments:* English Teacher, High School, 1967–76; Writing Instructor, Rutgers University, 1990–91; Asst Prof. of English, 1991–96, Assoc. Prof. of English, 1996–, University of South Carolina. *Publications:* Milk and Brittle Bone, 1991; Two Seasons, 1993; The Silence and Other Poems, 1995; The Artists' Colony, 1996; Dreameater, 1998. *Contributions to:* Kenyon Review; Calliope; Literary Review; Confluence; Elephants & Other Gods; Poetry East; South East Poetry Journal; Southern

Poetry Review. *Honours:* Amelia Award, 1988; Lester Cash Short Poem Award, 1991; H R Roberts Foundation Award, 1992; Joanna Burgoyne Prize, 1993; Society Prize, Poetry Society of South Carolina, 1998. *Memberships:* Associated Writing Programs; South Carolina Poetry Society; South Carolina Writer's Workshop. *Address:* Dept of English, University of South Carolina at Aiken, Aiken, SC 29801, USA.

DAVIES, Charles. See: CHAPMAN, David Charles.

DAVIES, Josie Ennis; b. 8 Dec. 1928, Coventry, Warwickshire, England. School Teacher and College Lecturer (retd); Poet. m. Harold Henry Davies, 26 Dec. 1967. *Education:* Teaching Diploma, 1952, 1964. *Publications:* Waiting for Hollyhocks; Shadows on the Lawn; The Tuning Tree; Marmalade and Mayhem; Miscellany; Understanding Stone, 1994; A Press of Nails, 1996; Grief Like A Tiger, 1996; Journey to Ride, 1997; Daisies in December, 1999; For All Seasons, 2001; Wanting Rainbows, 2002. *Contributions to:* Folio International; Pennine Platform; Iota; Periaktos; Poetry Nottingham; Spokes; Success; The Countryman; Weyfarers; The Writers Voice; The Lady; Vigil; Haiku Quarterly; Period Piece and Paperback; Envoi; Poetry Digest. *Membership:* National Poetry Foundation. *Address:* 349 Holyhead Rd, Coventry, Warwickshire CV5 8LD, England.

DAVIES, Piers (Anthony David); b. 15 June 1941, Sydney, NSW, Australia. Barrister; Solicitor; Screenwriter; Poet. m. Margaret Elaine Haswell, 24 Aug. 1973, 1 d. *Education:* LLB, University of Auckland, 1964; Diploma, English and Comparative Law, City of London College, 1967. *Appointments:* Barrister and Solicitor, Jordan, Smith and Davies, Auckland, New Zealand; Chair., Short Film Fund, New Zealand Film Commission, 1987–91; Mem., Cultural Heritage Law Committee of the International Law Asscn, 1997–. *Publications:* East and Other Gong Songs, 1967; Day Trip from Mount Meru, 1969; Diaspora, 1974; Bourgeois Homage to Dada, 1974; Central Almanac (ed.), 1974; Jetsam, 1984. Screenplays: The Life and Flight of Rev Buck Shotte (with Peter Weir), 1969; Homesdale (with Peter Weir), 1971; The Cars That Ate Paris (with Peter Weir), 1973; Skin Deep, 1978; The Lamb of God, 1985; A Fair Hearing, 1995. Other: R. V. Huckleberry Finn (documentary), 1979; Olaf's Coast (documentary), 1982. *Contributions to:* Anthologies and periodicals. *Address:* 16 Crocus Pl., Remuera, Auckland 5, New Zealand.

DAVIES, William Thomas Pennar; b. 12 Nov. 1911, Aberpennar, Glamorgan, Wales. Author; Poet. m. Rosemarie Wolff, 26 June 1943, 4 s., 1 d. *Education:* BA, University of Wales, 1932; BLitt, University of Oxford, 1938; PhD, Yale University, 1943. *Publications:* Fiction: Anadl o'r Uchelder, 1958; Caregel Nwyf, 1966; Meibion Darogan, 1968; Llais y Durtur, 1985. Poetry: Cinio'r Cythraul, 1946; Naw Wfft, 1957; Yr Efrydd o lyn Cynon, 1961; Y Tlws yn y Lotws, 1971; Llef, 1987. Non-Fiction: Cudd fy Meiau, 1957; Rhwng Chwedl a Chredo, 1966. *Contributions to:* Reviews and periodicals. *Honours:* Commonwealth Fund Fellow, 1936–38; Fellow, 1938–40, Fellow Honoris Causa, 1986, Hon. DD, 1987, University of Wales; Hon. Fellow, Welsh Acad., 1989. *Address:* 10 Heol Grosvenor, Sgeti, Abertawe, Swansea SA2 0SP, Wales.

DAVIS, Albert (Joseph Jr), (Albert Belisle Davis); b. 23 June 1947, Houma, LA, USA. Distinguished Service Prof. of Languages and Literature; Author; Poet. m. (1) Carol Anne Campbell, 24 Feb. 1968, divorced 1992, 1 s., (2) Mary Archer Freet, 31 Dec. 1994, 1 d. *Education:* BA, English and History, Nicholls State University, 1969; MA, Creative Writing, Colorado State University, 1974. *Appointments:* Novelist-in-Residence, 1991–, Distinguished Service Prof. of Languages and Literature, 1994–, Assoc. Dean, College of Arts and Sciences, 1999–2001, Nicholls State University. *Publications:* What They Wrote on the Bathhouse Walls (poems), 1989; Leechtime (novel), 1989; Marquis at Bay (novel), 1992; Virginia Patout's Parish (poems), 1999. *Contributions to:* Anthologies and literary journals. *Honours:* Ione Burden Award for the Novel, 1983; John Z. Bennet Award for Poetry, 1984; Louisiana Division of the Arts Creative Writing Fellowship, 1989. *Memberships:* Acad. of American Poets; Associated Writing Programs; Louisiana Asscn of Educators; Louisiana Division of the Arts, literary panel, 1995–97; National Education Asscn; PEN American Center. *Address:* c/o Dept of General Studies, Nicholls State University, PO Box 2106, Thibodaux, LA 70310, USA.

DAVIS, Dick; b. 18 April 1945, Portsmouth, Hampshire, England. Assoc. Prof. of Persian; Poet. m. Afkham Darbandi, 1974, 2 d. *Education:* BA, King's College, Cambridge, 1966; PhD, University of Manchester, 1988. *Appointments:* Asst Prof., 1988–93, Assoc. Prof. of Persian, 1993–, Ohio State University. *Publications:* Shade Mariners, 1970; In the Distance, 1975; Seeing the World, 1980; The Selected Writings of Thomas Traherne (ed.), 1980; Visitations, 1983; The Covenant, 1984; What the Mind Wants, 1984; Lares, 1986; Devices and Desires: New and Selected Poems, 1967–87, 1989; The Rubaiyat of Omar Khayyam, trans. by Edward Fitzgerald (ed.), 1989; A Kind of Love: New & Selected Poems, 1991; Epic & Sedition: One Case of Ferdonzi's Shahnameh, 1992. Translations: The Conference of the Birds, 1984; The Legend of Seyavash, 1992. *Honour:* RSL Heinemann Award, 1981. *Address:* Dept of Near Eastern Languages, Ohio State University, 190 N Oval Mall, Columbus, OH 43210, USA.

DAVIS, Eunice Christine; b. 5 July 1914, Brooklyn, Mississippi, USA. Teacher (retd); Poet. m. George Vernon Barnes, 17 July 1949. *Education:* BS, University of South Mississippi, 1935. *Appointments:* Various teaching positions, 1935–49. *Publications:* To the Stars, 1992; Autumn Leaves, 1994; Dreams Wander, 1994; Haiku Happenings, 1995. *Contributions to:* Many publications. *Honours:* Several. *Memberships:* Mississippi Poetry Society; Southern Poetry Asscn; Writers Unlimited. *Address:* 712 Irving St, Pascagoula, MS 39567, USA.

DAVIS, Jack (Leonard); b. 11 March 1917, Perth, WA, Australia; Poet; Dramatist; Writer. m. Madelon Jantine Wilkens, 12 Dec. 1987, 1 d. *Appointment:* Writer-in-Residence, Murdoch University, 1982. *Publications:* The First Born and Other Poems, 1968; Jagardoo Poems from Aboriginal Australia, 1978; The Dreamers (play), 1983; Kullark (play), 1983; John Pat and Other Poems, 1988; Burungin (Smell the Wind) (play), 1989; Plays From Black Australia, 1989. *Contributions to:* Identity. *Honours:* Human Rights Award, 1987; BHP Award, 1988; Australian Artists Creative Fellowship, 1989; Hon. doctorates. *Memberships:* Aboriginal Writers Oral Literature and Dramatists Asscn; Australian Writers Guild; PEN International. *Address:* 3 Little Howard St, Fremantle, WA, Australia.

DAVIS, Jon E(dward); b. 28 Oct. 1952, New Haven, CT, USA. Poet; Writer; Prof. of Creative Writing and Literature. m. Terry Lynne Layton, 8 Jan. 1978, 1 d. *Education:* University of Bridgeport, 1978–80; BA, High Honours, English, 1984, MFA, Creative Writing, 1985, University of Montana. *Appointments:* Ed., CutBank, 1982–85; Managing Ed., Shankpainter, 1986–87; Fellow, 1986–87, Co-ordinator, Writing Program, 1987–88, Fine Arts Work Center, Provincetown, Massachusetts; Visiting Asst Prof., Salisbury State University, Maryland, 1988–90; Prof. of Creative Writing and Literature, Institute of American Indian Arts, Santa Fe, New Mexico, 1990; Co-Ed., Countermeasures, 1993–. *Publications:* Poetry: West of New England, 1983; Dangerous Amusements, 1987; The Hawk, The Road, The Sunlight After Clouds, 1995; Local Color, 1995; Scrimmage of Appetite, 1995. *Contributions to:* Anthologies, reviews, quarterlies and journals. *Honours:* Winner, Connecticut Poetry Circuit Competition, 1980; Acad. of American Poets Prize, 1985; INTRO Award for Fiction, 1985; National Endowment for the Arts Fellowship, 1986; Richard Hugo Memorial Award, CutBank, 1988; Maryland Arts Council Fellowship, 1990; Winner, Owl Creek Press Chapbook Contest, 1994; Palanquin Press Chapbook Contest, 1995.

DAVIS, Melody D.; b. 19 Sept. 1959, Harrisburg, Pennsylvania, USA. Writer; Poet; Photographer. m. Shahan Islam, 29 Jan. 1983. *Education:* BA, Columbia University, 1981; MA, State University of New York at Stony Brook, 1989. *Appointments:* Pres., Founder, Poetlink, 1989–93; Adjunct Prof., State University of New York at Stony Brook, 1989, 1993, Montclair State College, 1990. *Publications:* The Center of Distance; The Male Nude in Contemporary Photography. *Contributions to:* Anthologies, journals and periodicals. *Honours:* First Place, Alice Moser Claudel Poetry Contest; Amy Loveman Prize for Poetry; Lenore Marshall Prize for Poetry; National Endowment for the Arts Fellowship in Poetry, 1995; Fellowship in American Art, Henry Luce Foundation, ACLS. *Memberships:* Poetlink; Poets and Writers; New Orleans Poetry Forum. *Address:* 24 Childsworth Ave, Bernardsville, NJ 07924, USA.

DAVIS, Owen; b. 27 Jan. 1939, Kuala Lumpur, Malaysia. Poet. m. 30 Jan. 1986, 2 s., 1 d. *Appointment:* Ed., South West Review, 1979–81. *Publications:* Ace of Fools, 1980; The Reflective Arrangement, Galloping Dog, 1982; One Plus One (with Jeremy Hilton), 1986; Two Stones, One Bird (with Paul Mathews), 1989. *Contributions to:* Magazines and anthologies. *Honour:* South West Arts Writer's Bursary, 1975. *Address:* 15 Argyle Rd, Swanage, Dorset BH19 1HZ, England.

DAVIS, Selwyn Sylvester, (Niwles Sivad); b. 18 Sept. 1945, Trinidad and Tobabo. Town Planner; Martial Arts Instructor; Poet; Dramatist; Writer. m. Violet Nidali Nyasoka Sakala, 3 Jan. 1992, 1 s., 1 d. *Education:* BA, Honours, Geography, 1969, Postgraduate Diploma, City Planning, 1977, University of Manitoba; Advanced Reading Dynamics Certificate, Evelyn Wood Institute, Halifax, 1976; Postgraduate Diploma, Financial Management, Conductor Ltd, Toronto, 1980. *Appointments:* Chief Town Planner, Lusaka City Council, Zambia; Environment Research Consultant, UN Centre for Regional Development, Nagoya, Japan; Dir, International Tae Kwon Do Federation, Vienna. *Contributions to:* Various books, anthologies and periodicals. *Honours:* Best 1-Act Play, Lusaka Theatre Club, 1988; Several honorable mentions in poetry. *Memberships:* Canadian Authors Asscn; Lusaka Press Club; Lusaka Theatre Club; Poetry Society, National Poetry Centre, London; Zambian National Asscn of Writers. *Address:* PO Box 835, 36 Adelaide St, Toronto, Ontario M5C 2K1, Canada.

DAVIS, Sonia. See: WILLIAMS, Alberta Norine.

DAVIS, William (Virgil); b. 26 May 1940, Canton, Ohio, USA. Prof. of English; Writer; Poet. m. Carol Demske, 17 July 1971, 1 s. *Education:* AB, English and American Literature, 1962, MA, English and American Literature, 1965, PhD, American Literature, 1967, Ohio University; MDiv, Pittsburgh Theological Seminary, 1965. *Appointments:* Teaching Fellow, 1965–67, Asst Prof. of

English, 1967–68, Consultant, Creative Writing Program, 1992–98, Ohio University; Asst Prof. of English, Central Connecticut State University, 1968–72, University of Illinois, Chicago, 1972–77; Assoc. Prof. of English, 1977–79, Prof. of English and Writer-in-Residence, 1979–, Centennial Prof 2002–, Baylor University; Guest Prof., University of Vienna, 1979–80, 1989–90, 1997, University of Copenhagen, 1984; Visiting Scholar-Guest Prof., University of Wales, Swansea, 1983; Writer-in-Residence, University of Montana, 1983; Adjunct MFA Faculty, Southwest Texas State University, 1990–98; Adjunct Mem., Graduate Faculty, Texas Christian University, 1992–96. *Publications:* George Whitefield's Journals, 1737–1741 (ed.), 1969; Theodore Roethke: A Bibliography (contributing ed.), 1973; One Way to Reconstruct the Scene 1980; The Dark Hours, 1984; Understanding Robert Bly, 1988; Winter Light 1990; Critical Essays on Robert Bly (ed.), 1992; Miraculous Simplicity: Essays on R S Thomas (ed.), 1993; Robert Bly: The Poet and His Critics, 1994 *Contributions to:* Articles in scholarly journals and poems in numerous anthologies and other publications. *Honours:* Scholar in Poetry, 1970, John Atherton Fellow in Poetry, 1980, Bread Loaf Writers' Conference; Ordained Minister, Presbyterian Church in the USA, 1971; Yale Series of Younger Poets Award, 1979; Lilly Foundation Grant, 1979–80; Calliope Press Chapbook Prize 1984; Outstanding Faculty Mem., Baylor University, 1989; Nominations, Pushcart Prize, 1991, 1992, 1993, 1995; James Sims Prize in American Literature, 2002; Fellowship in Creative Writing, Poetry, Writers' League of Texas, 2002. *Memberships:* Acad. of American Poets; International Asscn of University Profs of English; MLA; PEN; Poetry Society of America; Poets and Writers; Texas Asscn of Creative Writing Teachers; Texas Institute of Letters, councilor, 1993–97. *Address:* 2633 Lake Oaks Rd, Waco, TX 76710, USA.

DAVISON, Peter (Hubert); b. 27 June 1928, New York, NY, USA. Poet; Writer; Ed. m. (1) Jane Truslow, 7 March 1959, deceased 1981, 1 s., 1 d., (2) Joan Edelman Goody, 11 Aug. 1984. *Education:* AB, Harvard College, 1949; Fulbright Scholar, St John's College, Cambridge University, 1949–50. *Appointments:* Asst Ed., Harcourt, Brace and Co, 1950–51, 1953–55; Asst to Dir, Harvard University Press, 1955–56; Assoc. Ed., 1956–59, Exec. Ed., 1959–64, Dir, 1964–79, Senior Ed., 1979–85, Atlantic Monthly Press; Poetry Ed., The Atlantic Monthly, 1972–; Ed., Peter Davison imprint, Houghton Mifflin Co, 1985–98. *Publications:* Poetry: The Breaking of the Day, 1964; The City and the Island, 1966; Pretending to Be Asleep, 1970; Walking the Boundaries, 1974; A Voice in the Mountain, 1977; Barn Fever, 1981; Praying Wrong: New and Selected Poems, 1959–84, 1984; The Great Ledge: New Poems, 1989; The Poems of Peter Davison, 1957–95, 1995; Breathing Room, 2000. Prose: Half Remembered: A Personal History, 1973; One of the Dangerous Trades: Essays on the Work and Workings of Poetry, 1991; The Fading Smile: Poets in Boston 1955–60, 1994. *Contributions to:* Many journals, reviews and periodicals. *Honours:* Yale Series of Younger Poets Award, 1963; American Acad. of Arts and Letters Award, 1972; James Michener Prizes, 1981, 1985; New England Booksellers Award for Literary Excellence, 1995; Massachusetts Book Award, 2001. *Address:* 70 River St, No. 2, Boston, MA 02108, USA.

DAVITT, Michael; b. 20 April 1950, Cork, Ireland. Poet. *Education:* BA, Celtic Studies, 1971, University College, Cork. *Publications:* Gleann Ar Ghleann, 1982; Bligeard Sraide, 1983; An Tost A Scagadh, 1993; Sruth Na Maoile (ed.), 1993; Scuais, 1998; Selected Poems with English Translations, 2000. *Contributions to:* Anthologies, reviews, and journals. *Honours:* Arts Council Writing Bursaries, Ireland, 1980, 1990; Oireachtas Award, 1981; Butler Award for Literature, Irish-American Cultural Institute, 1994. *Memberships:* Aosdána; National Union of Journalists. *Address:* 29 Elgin Wood, Bray, Co Wicklow, Ireland.

DAWE, (Donald) Bruce; b. 15 Feb. 1930, Fitzroy, Vic., Australia. Assoc. Prof.; Poet; Writer. m. (1) Gloria Desley Blain, 27 Jan. 1964, deceased 30 Dec. 1997, 2 s., 2 d., (2) Ann Elizabeth Qualtiough, 9 Oct. 1999. *Education:* BA, 1969, MLitt, 1973, MA, 1975, PhD, 1980, University of Queensland. *Appointments:* Lecturer, 1971–78, Senior Lecturer, 1978–83, DDIAE; Writer-in-Residence, University of Queensland, 1984; Senior Lecturer, 1985–90, Assoc. Prof., 1990–93, School of Arts, Darling Heights, Toowoomba. *Publications:* No Fixed Address, 1962; A Need of Similar Name, 1964; Beyond the Subdivisions, 1968; An Eye for a Tooth, 1969; Heat-Wave, 1970; Condolences of the Season: Selected Poems, 1971; Just a Dugong at Twilight, 1974; Sometimes Gladness: Collected Poems, 1978; Over Here Harv! and Other Stories, 1983; Towards Sunrise, 1986; This Side of Silence, 1990; Bruce Dawe: Essays and Opinions, 1990; Mortal Instruments: Poems 1990–1995, 1995; A Poets' People, 1999. *Contributions to:* Various periodicals. *Honours:* Myer Poetry Prizes, 1966, 1969; Ampol Arts Award for Creative Literature, 1967; Dame Mary Gilmore Medal, Australian Literary Society, 1973; Braille Book of the Year, 1978; Grace Leven Prize for Poetry, 1978; Patrick White Literary Award, 1980; Christopher Brennan Award, 1984; Order of Australia, 1992; Australian Arts Council Emeritus Writers Award, 2000. *Memberships:* Australian Asscn for Teaching English, hon. life mem.; Centre for Australian Studies in Literature; Victorian Asscn for Teaching of English, hon. life mem. *Address:* c/o Pearson Education, 95 Coventry St, South Melbourne 32059, Australia.

DAWE, Gerald Chartres; b. 22 April 1952, Belfast, Northern Ireland. Poet; College Lecturer. m. Dorothea Melvin, 28 Oct. 1979, 1 s., 1 d. *Education:* BA,

Honours, University of Ulster; MA, University College, Galway. *Appointments:* Tutor in English, Asst Lecturer, University College, Galway, 1978–87; Lecturer, 1987–, Dir, MPhil in Creative Writing, 1997–, Lecturer in English and Dir of the Oscar Wilde Centre for Irish Writing, 1999–, Trinity College, Dublin. *Publications:* Poetry: Sheltering Places, 1978; The Lundy Letter, 1985; Sunday School, 1991; Heart of Hearts, 1995; The Morning Train, 1999. Criticism: Across a Roaring Hill: The Protestant Imagination in Modern Ireland, with Edna Longley, 1985; How's the Poetry Going?: Literary Politics and Ireland Today, 1991; The Poet's Place, with John Wilson Foster, 1991; A Real Life Elsewhere, 1993; False Faces: Poetry, Politics and Place, 1994; Against Piety: Essays in Irish Poetry, 1995; The Rest is History, 1998; Stray Dogs and Dark Horses (selected essays), 2000. Editor: The Younger Irish Poets, 1982; Krino (anthology with Jonathan Williams), 1986–96; The Younger Irish Poets, 1991; The Ogham Stone (anthology with Michael Mulreany), 2001. *Contributions to:* Newspapers, reviews and journals. *Honours:* Major State Awards, 1974–77; Arts Council Bursary for Poetry, 1980; Macaulay Fellowship in Literature, 1984; Hawthornden International Writers Fellowship, 1988; Ledwig-Rowholt Fellowship, 1999. *Memberships:* International Asscn for the Study of Irish Literature; Irish Writers Union; Poetry Ireland. *Address:* c/o Oscar Wilde Centre, School of English, Trinity College, Dublin 2, Ireland. *E-mail:* gdawe@tcd.ie.

DAWSON, Jill Dianne; b. 1962, England. Writer; Poet; Ed.; Teacher. 1 s. *Education:* BA, American Studies, University of Nottingham, 1983; MA, Sheffield Hallam University, 1995. *Publications:* School Tales, 1990; How Do I Look? (non-fiction), 1991; Virago Book of Wicked Verse, 1992; Virago Book of Love Letters, 1994; White Fish with Painted Nails (poems), 1994; Trick of the Light, 1996; Magpie, 1998; Fred and Edie, 2001. *Contributions to:* Anthologies and periodicals. *Honours:* Major Eric Gregory Award, 1992; Second Prize, London Writers Short Story Competition, 1994; Blue Nose Poet of the Year, 1995; London Arts Board New Writers, 1998. *Memberships:* National Asscn of Writers in Education; Society of Authors. *Address:* 38 Lockhurst St, London E5 0AP, England.

DAY-LEWIS, Jill Angela Henriette, (Jill Balcon); b. 3 Jan. 1925, London, England. Actress; Broadcaster; Ed. m. C Day-Lewis, 27 April 1951, deceased 1972, 1 s., 1 d. *Education:* Gold Medal, Central School of Speech and Drama, London. *Publications:* Editor: A Lasting Joy, 1973; Posthumous Poems of C Day-Lewis, 1979; The Pity of War, 1985; Complete Poems of C Day-Lewis, 1992; Alec: An 80th Birthday Present for Alec Guinness (with Christopher Sinclair-Stevenson), 1994. *Honour:* Hon. Degree, Open University, 1992. *Memberships:* Poetry Society, vice-pres.; RSL, hon. fellow; Society of Teachers of Speech and Drama, pres.; Thomas Hardy Society, vice-pres.; Wilfred Owen Asscn, vice-pres. *Address:* Vine Cottage, Steep, Petersfield, Hampshire GU32 2DP, England.

DAYTON, Irene Catherine; b. 6 Aug. 1922, Lake Ariel, Pennsylvania, USA. Poet; Novelist. m. Benjamin B Dayton, 16 Oct. 1943, 2 s. *Education:* Assoc. Degree, Robert Wesleyan College, 1942. *Appointments:* Poetry Consultant, 1971–73, Poet-in-Residence, 1972–73, New York State Arts Council, Rochester, New York; Instructor, Modern Poetry Writing, Adult Education, Blue Ridge Community College, Flat Rock, North Carolina, 1978–85. *Publications:* Poetry: The Sixth Sense Quivers, 1970; The Panther's Eye, 1974; Seven Times the Wind, 1977; In Oxbow of Time's River, 1978; The Falcon's Flight, 2000. Novel: Sobs of the Violins. Historical Fiction: Vercors Mts France – Resistance. *Contributions to:* Anthologies and magazines. *Honours:* Finalist, Yale Series of Younger Poets, 1958; First Prize Awards, Rochester Festival of Religious Art, 1959, 1960; Guinness Award, Cheltenham Festival of Literature, 1963; Distinguished Submission Award, Shenandoah Valley Acad. of Literature, 1979. *Memberships:* Rochester New York Poetry Society, hon. life mem.; Poetry Society of America, life mem.; North Carolina Poetry Society, life mem.; International Acad. of Poets, founder-fellow; Assoc. mem., Acad. of American Poets. *Address:* 209 S Hillandale Dr., East Flat Rock, NC 28726-2609, USA.

DE BIASE, Angela Maria Rocha, (Monica de Oliveira Moulin); b. 12 Dec. 1949, Muniz Freire-Espirito Santo, Brazil. Lawyer; Attorney; Poet. *Education:* Law School, University of São Paulo, 1968–72; Master degree,. FADUSP, 1973–75; Courses in legal area and international private law seminars. *Appointments:* Attorney, Municipality of São Paulo, 1977; Chief Attorney, 1981–87; Legal Counsel, Regional Administration Office, 1987–88; Dir, Property Dept, General Law Office, Municipality of São Paulo, 1989–90; Mem., Legal Studies Centre, General Law Office, São Paulo, 1990–. *Publications:* Cantos do Encontrar, 1986; International Poetry Year Book, 1988; International Poetry, 1990, 1991, 1992; Cahiers Jaions, 1992. *Contributions to:* Pan Artes. *Honours:* Citation, Mulheres entre Linhas, State Culture Office, São Paulo, 1985; Golden Crown of World Poets Award, World Poetry Research Institute, Korea, 1992. *Memberships:* World Poetry Research Institute, Cheong Ju, Korea; Interdisciplinary Law Studies Institute, São Paulo. *Address:* Avenida Silvio Sciumbata, No. 595, Interlagos, São Paulo, SP, CEP 04789-010, Brazil.

DE CADAVAL, Rudy. See: CAMPEDELLI, Giancarlo.

DE CAMP, L(yon) Sprague; b. 27 Nov. 1907, New York, NY, USA. Writer; Poet. m. Catherine Adelaide Crook, 12 Aug. 1939, 2 s. *Education:* BS, Aeronautical Engineering, California Institute of Technology, 1930; MS, Engineering and Economics, Stevens Institute of Technology, 1933. *Publications:* Over 130 books, including science fiction, fantasy, historical novels, history, biography, textbooks, and children's books among others. *Contributions to:* Numerous stories, articles and poems in anthologies, periodicals and other publications. *Honours:* International Fantasy Award, 1953; Grandmaster Fantasy Award, 1976; Nebula Award, 1978; World Fantasy Conference Award, 1984. *Memberships:* Authors Guild; History of Science Society; SFWA; Society for the History of Technology. *Address:* 3453 Hearst Castle Way, Plano, TX 75025, USA.

DE FRANCE, Stephen David, (Steve De France); b. 29 Dec. 1939, Denver, CO, USA. College Prof.; Writer; Poet. *Education:* BA, English; BA, Theatre Arts; MEd; MA, English Literature; Postgraduate Work, University of Southern California. *Appointments:* Actor, motion pictures and television; Businessman; Tenured Prof., Literature, Writing, Los Angeles Trade Technical College, CA. *Publications:* Voices at the Way Station, 1968; Another Night in the Dog Breath Cafe, 1974; Angel's Flight: L A Poems, 1980; Lost in Hollywood, 1989; To the Eye it Seems Not to Move, 1991; Poems of Ordinary Anger, 1993. *Contributions to:* Trellis; Hornspoon; Community of Friends; Jesture Magazine; Cardinal Poetry Quarterly; Orbis; Apostrophe; California State Poetry Quarterly. *Address:* 2125 E Ocean Blvd, Suite 3B, Long Beach, CA 90803, USA.

DE KOK, Ingrid Jean; b. 4 June 1951, South Africa. Educator; Poet. 1 s. *Education:* BA, English, Political Science, Witwatersrand University; BA, Honours, English, University of Cape Town; MA, English, Queen's University, Canada. *Appointments:* Junior Lecturer, English Dept, University of Cape Town; Research Asst, Dept of Film Studies, Queen's University, Kingston, Canada; Planning Co-ordinator, Khanya College, SACHED Trust, South Africa; Dir, Extra-Mural Studies, Dept of Adult Education, University of Cape Town, 1988–. *Publications:* Familiar Ground, 1988; Transfer, 1997; Terrestrial Things, 2002. *Contributions to:* Anthologies including, The Best American Poetry, 1996; The Lava of the Land, 1997; Reviews and periodicals. *Memberships:* PEN; Amnesty International. *Address:* Centre for Extra-Mural Studies, University of Cape Town, Rondebosch 7701, South Africa.

DE LINT, Charles (Henri Diederick Hoefsmit); b. 22 Dec. 1951, Bussum, Netherlands (Naturalized Canadian citizen, 1961). Ed.; Writer; Poet; Musician. m. MaryAnn Harris, 15 Sept. 1980. *Appointments:* Owner-Ed., Triskell Press; Writer-in-Residence, Ottawa and Gloucester Public Libraries, 1995. *Publications:* Drink Down the Moon: A Novel of Urban Faerie, 1990; Death Leaves an Echo, 1991; Dreaming Place, 1992; From a Whisper to a Scream, 1992; Dreams Underfoot: The Newford Collection, 1993; Memory and Dream, 1994; The Ivory and the Horn, 1995; Trader, 1997; Someplace to be Flying, 1998; Moonlight and Vines, 1999; Forests of the Heart, 2000. *Contributions to:* Anthologies and periodicals. *Honours:* Various awards. *Memberships:* SFWA; Science Fiction Writers of Canada. *Address:* PO Box 9480, Ottawa, Ontario K1G 3V2, Canada.

DE NAPOLI, Francesco; b. 15 June 1954, Potenza, Italy. Librarian; Writer; Poet. m. Assunta Cardile, 5 Dec. 1987, 2 d. *Education:* Maturità Classica, 1973; Addottorato in Science Sociali, 1981. *Appointments:* Prof. Onorario di Letteratura Italiana, Brussels, 1993; Dir, Istituto 'A Labriola', Cassino; Pres. di Giuria Premio Letterario Internazionale 'Succisa Virescit'. *Publications:* Noùmeno e realtà, 1979; Fernfahrplan, 1980; La dinamica degli eventi, 1983; L'attesa, 1987; Il pane di siviglia, 1989; Contagi, 1991; Urna d'amore, 1992; Dialogo serale, 1993; Poesie per urbino, 1996; Nel tempo a zenja, 1998; Carte da gioco, 1999; Giogo/forza 2000; La casa del porto, 2002. Anthologies: Dossier poesia, 1993; Poeti di paideia, 1994; Omaggio a Montale, 1996; Il fiore del deserto, 1998; Ritmo Cassinese, 2000. Essays: La letteratura di protesta del novecento in Europa e in America, 1990; Breve profilo della poesia Italiana del secondo novecento, 1993; Cesare Pavese e il suo tempo, 2000; Graffiti poetici, 2000. *Contributions to:* Various publications. *Honours:* Premio Cultura della Presidenza del Consiglio dei Ministri; Premio Casentino; Premio Monferrato; Premio Firenze Capitale Europea della Cultura; Premio Città di Valletta; Premio David; PhD, h.c., Lettre Moderne, Paris, 1994; PhD, h.c., Philosophy, Massachusetts, 1995. *Address:* Via Parini 9, 03043 Cassino (FR), Italy.

DE OLIVEIRA MOULIN, Monica. See: DE BIASE, Angela Maria Rocha.

DE PAZZI, E(llen) E(ugenia Bosley); b. 7 April 1915, Elcador, IA, USA. Poet; Writer; Artist. m. Passino de Pazzi (Marchese), 17 Aug. 1940, 2 s. *Education:* Design Studies, Indiana University, 1934–37; Art Student, Atelier Caterina Baratelli, Rio de Janeiro, 1949–52; Degree, Fine Arts, Suffolk Community College, 1987. *Appointments:* Frequent guest poetry readings, radio stations, college campuses and bookstores. *Contributions to:* Anthologies and magazines. *Honours:* Poetry Prizes, Soundwave Magazine, 1983, 1986. *Membership:* Westhampton Library Poetry Group. *Address:* 11 Maple St, Westhampton Beach, NY 11978, USA.

DE REGNIERS, Beatrice Schenk, (Tamara Kitt); b. 16 Aug. 1914, Lafayette, IN, USA. Children's Writer; Poet; Dramatist. m. Francis de Regniers, May 1953. *Education:* University of Illinois, 1931–33; PhD, 1935, Graduate Studies, 1936–37, University of Chicago; MEd, Winnetka Graduate Teachers College, 1941. *Publications:* Over 50 children's books. *Memberships:* Authors Guild; Dramatists Guild; PEN; Society of Children's Book Writers and Illustrators. *Address:* 4530 Connecticut Ave NW, Apt 302, Washington, DC 20008, USA.

DE ROSA, Antonio; b. 1 Jan. 1953, Altavilla, Ikpina, Italy. Poet. m. Bruno Alba, 22 Feb. 1981, 1 s. *Education:* Diploma. *Publications:* Amari Grappoli di Poesia, 1985; Linquietudine, 1990; Il Capo, 1993; Riflessi di Vita, 1995. *Contributions to:* Journals and magazines. *Honours:* Premio Roma Città Eterna; Gli Allori del Palatino. *Address:* Via Bolzano 11, 20024 Garbagnate, Milaneses MI, Italy.

DE SOUZA, Eunice; b. 1 Aug. 1940, Poona, India. Reader in English; Poet; Writer. *Education:* BA, 1960, PhD, 1988, University of Mumbai. *Appointments:* Reader in English, 1969–, Head, Dept of English, 1990–, St Xavier's College, Mumbai. *Publications:* Folk Tales from Gujarat, 1975; Himalayan Tales, 1978; Fix, 1979; Women in Dutch Painting, 1988; Ways of Belonging: Selected Poems, 1990; Selected and New Poems, 1994; Nine Indian Women Poets (ed.), 1997; Talking Poems, 1999. Other: Several children's books. *Honour:* Poetry Book Society Recommendation, 1990. *Address:* c/o Dept of English, St Xavier's College, Mumbai 400 001, India.

DEAHL, James Edward; b. 5 Dec. 1945, Pittsburgh, Pennsylvania, USA. Author; Poet; Ed.; Teacher. m. Gilda L Mekler, 23 May 1982, 3 d. *Appointments:* Ed., Poemata; Managing Partner, Mekler & Deahl, publishers. *Publications:* In the Lost Horn's Call, 1982; No Cold Ash, 1984; Blue Ridge, 1985; Geschriebene Bilder, 1990; Opening the Stone Heart, 1992; Heartland, 1993; Even This Land Was Born of Light, 1993; Under the Watchful Eye, 1995; Tasting the Winter Grapes, 1995. *Honour:* Mainichi Award, 1985. *Memberships:* International PEN; League of Canadian Poets; Haiku Canada; Poetry Society, UK; Acad. of American Poets, USA. *Address:* 237 Prospect St S, Hamilton, Ontario LM8 2Z6, Canada.

DEAL, Susan Strayer; b. 21 Feb. 1948, Lincoln, Nebraska, USA. Poet. *Education:* BA, Kearney State College, 1973; MA, University of Lincoln, 1980. *Appointments:* Teacher; Adjunct Prof. *Publications:* No Moving Parts, 1980; The Dark is a Door, 1984; Sometimes So Easy, 1991. *Contributions to:* Bay Windows; Northwest Review; Sows Ear; Prairie Schooner; Black Warrior Review; Mid America Review; En Passant; Abraxas; Blue Unicorn; Potato Eye; Oxford Magazine; Oxlis; Anemone; Sandhills Press. *Honours:* Pushcart Prize, 1974; Triton Poetry Contest, 1978; Mississippi Poetry Contest, 1984; Writers Choice, 1984; Poetry on the Buses, 1984. *Address:* 3825 Woods Blvd, Lincoln, NE 68502, USA.

DEAN, Melfyn; b. 31 Oct. 1943, Caerphilly, Wales. Poet. m. Inga Jordis, 29 Nov. 1986. *Education:* St Loyes College, Exeter; Catering Diploma, 1968; Telephonist Diploma, 1969. *Publications:* Poems and Things, 1995; White Tower Relics and Jewels, 1996; Two Steps Together, 1997. *Contributions to:* Anthologies, books, periodicals and radio. *Address:* Dursona Dhys, 28 Maidwell Way, Laceby Acres, Grimsby DN34 5UP, England.

DEAN-RICHARDAS, Wayne; b. 3 Sept. 1961, England. Lecturer in English; Poet; Writer. 2 s., 1 d. *Education:* BA, Honours, Creative Arts, University of Nottingham, 1983; PGCE, University of Wolverhampton, 1994. *Publications:* Poems By Two Fat Men, 1986; Tea and Biscuits for Two, 1996; Spouting Forth: The Anthology, 1997; Thicker than Water, 1998. *Contributions to:* New Yorker; Colorado Review; Understanding; People to People; Heartthrob; Chronicles of Disorder; Vigil; Scratch; Helix; Art Review. *Address:* 191 Pound Rd, Oldbury, Warley, West Midland B68 8NF, England.

DEANE, Seamus (Francis); b. 9 Feb. 1940, Derry City, Northern Ireland. Prof. of Irish Studies; Writer; Poet. m. Marion Treacy, 19 Aug. 1963, separated, 3 s., 2 d. *Education:* BA, 1961, MA, 1963, Queen's University, Belfast; PhD, Cambridge University, 1966. *Appointments:* Visiting Fulbright and Woodrow Wilson Scholar, Reed College, Oregon, 1966–67; Visiting Lecturer, 1967–68, Visiting Prof., 1978, University of California at Berkeley; Prof. of Modern English and American Literature, University College, Dublin, 1980–93; Walker Ames Prof., University of Washington, Seattle, 1987; Julius Benedict Distinguished Visiting Prof., Carleton College, Minnesota, 1988; Keough Prof. of Irish Studies, University of Notre Dame, IN, 1993–. *Publications:* Fiction: Reading in the Dark, 1996. Poetry: Gradual Wars, 1972; Rumours, 1977; History Lessons, 1983; Selected, 1988. Non-Fiction: Celtic Revivals: Essays in Modern Irish Literature, 1880–1980, 1985; A Short History of Irish Literature, 1986, reissued, 1994; The French Revolution and Enlightenment in England, 1789–1832, 1988; Strange Country: Ireland, Modernity and Nationhood, 1790–1970, 1997. Editor: The Adventures of Hugh Trevor by Thomas Holcroft, 1972; The Sale Catalogues of the Libraries of Eminent Persons, Vol. IX, 1973; Nationalism, Colonialism and Literature, 1990; The Field Day Anthology of Irish Writing, 3 vols, 1991; Penguin Twentieth Century Classics: James Joyce, 5 vols, 1993. *Honours:* AE Memorial for Literature,

1973; American-Irish Fund, Literature, 1989; Guardian Fiction Prize, 199▨ Irish Times International Fiction Award, 1997; Irish Times Fiction Awar▨ 1997; London Weekend Television South Bank Award for Literature, 199▨ Ruffino Antico-Fattore International Literature Award, Florence, 199▨ *Memberships:* Aosdána (Irish Artists' Council); Field Day Theatre an▨ Publishing Company, dir; Royal Irish Acad. *Address:* c/o Sonya Land, She▨ Land Assocs Ltd, 43 Doughty St, London WC1N 2LF, England.

DECKER, Donna; b. 15 Aug. 1956, Staten Island, New York, USA. Asst Pro▨ of English; Poet. *Education:* BA, Honours, English, College of Staten Islan▨ 1981; MA, English, City College of New York, 1984; PhD, English, Florida Stat▨ University, 1990. *Appointments:* Adjunct Instructor, Pace University, Ne▨ York and College of Staten Island, New York, 1985–86; Teaching Ass▨ English, Florida State University, 1986–90; Asst Prof., English, University ▨ Wisconsin, Stevens Point, 1990–. *Publications:* Three Thirds (with N Rashee▨ and C Acuna-Gomez), 1984; North of Wakulla (ed. with Mary Jane Ryals), 199▨ *Contributions to:* IKON; Apalachee Quarterly; Genre; Sundog. *Honou▨* Outstanding Creative Writing Award to Graduate Student, Florida Stat▨ University, 1987. *Memberships:* Poets and Writers; M & D Harbor Serie▨ Associated Writing Programs. *Address:* 317 Sixth Ave, Stevens Point, W▨ 54481, USA.

DEEMER, Bill; b. 4 March 1945, Norfolk, Virginia, USA. Poet. m. Toby Jo▨ Murray. *Publications:* Poems, 1964; Diana, 1966; The King's Bounty, 1968; ▨ Few for Lew, 1972; A Few for Lew and Other Poems, 1974; All Wet, 1975; Thi▨ is Just to Say, 1981; Subjects, 1984. *Contributions to:* Coyote's Journa▨ Longhouse. *Honour:* National Endowment for the Arts Award, 1968. *Address▨* 92400 River Rd, Junction City, OR 97448, USA.

DEEN, Cheryl Ann; b. 24 Jan. 1943, Pomona, CA, USA. Floral Designe▨ (retd); Poet. m. Jack Deen, 14 May 1966, 2 s., 2 d. *Education:* University of Sa▨ Francisco. *Publications:* Moments More to Go, 1990; The Fountain, 199▨ Something for Everyone, 1991; Urania, 1991. *Contributions to:* Anthologies▨ reviews and periodicals. *Honours:* Silver Poet Award, 1989, Golden Poet Awar▨ 1990, World of Poetry; Bronze Quill Award, International Society for th▨ Advancement of Poetry, 1990; Various honourable mentions. *Membership▨* International Society for the Advancement of Poetry; Mile High Poetr▨ Society. *Address:* 4040 E Piedmont, No. 375, Highland, CA 92346, USA.

DEGUY, Michel; b. 23 May 1930, Paris, France. Poet; Writer; Ed. *Education▨* Philosophy Studies, Paris. *Appointment:* Ed., Poésie, 1972–; University Prof▨ Paris. *Publications:* Les Meurtrières, 1959; Fragments du cadastre, 196▨ Poèmes de la presqu'ile, 1961; Approche de Hölderlin, 1962; Le Monde d▨ Thomas Mann, 1963; Biefs, 1964; Actes, 1966; Oui-dire, 1966; Histoire de▨ rechutes, 1968; Figurations, 1969; Tombeau de Du Bellay, 1973; Poème▨ 1960–1970, 1973; Reliefs, 1975; Jumelages suivi de Made in U.S.A., 197▨ Donnant, donnant, 1981; La Machine matrimoniale ou Marivaux, 198▨ René Girard et le problème du mal (with J-P Dupuy), 1982; Gisants, 198▨ Poèmes II; 1970–1980, 1986; Brevets, 1986; Choses de la poésie et affair▨ culturelle, 1986; Le Comité: Confessions d'un lecteur de grande maison, 198▨ La Poésie n'est pas seule: Court traité de Poétique, 1988; Arrets fréquent▨ 1990; Aux heures d'affluence, 1993; A ce qui n'en finit pas, 1995; L'Energie d▨ Desespoir, 1998; La Raison Poétique, 2000; L'Impair, 2000; Spleen de Pari▨ 2001; Poémes en pensée, 2001. *Honour:* Grand Prix national de Poésie, 198▨ *Address:* 26 rue Las-Cases, Paris 75007, France.

DELEANU, Daniel; b. 12 Sept. 1972, Sibiu, Romania. Teacher; Poet▨ *Education:* BA, English and Romanian, 1995, MA, English, 1996, M▨ Romanian, 1997, University of Sibiu. *Appointments:* Teacher of Englis▨ Romanian and World Literature, Christian High School, Sibiu, 1995▨ Teaching Asst, University of Sibiu, 1996. *Publications:* Efigiile Himerei, 199▨ Taci, 1993; The Sunset at Sundown, 1993; Self-Portraits and Other Visionar▨ Indiscretions, 1995; Mythopoems/Mitopoeme, 1999. Translations: Sr▨ Isopanisad (from Sanskrit to English and Romanian), 1999; Cormoran▨ Fishing: An Anthology of Basho's haikus (from Japanese to English), 199▨ Herbarium of Words: Ten Romanian Poets (from Romanian to English), 199▨ *Contributions to:* Luceafarul; Euphorion; Tribuna; Saeculum; Art Panoram▨ North Words; Psychopoetica; 100 Words; Back to Godhead; Anthologies: ▨ Break in the Clouds, 1993; The Sound of Poetry, 1993. *Honours:* Internationa▨ Poet of Merit, 1995; Nominated as 'Poet of the Year', International Society o▨ Poets, 1995. *Address:* Str George Cosbuc 30, Sibiu 2400, Jud Sibiu, Romania.

DELIUS, Anthony, (Ronald Martin); b. 11 June 1916, Simonstown, Sout▨ Africa. Writer; Poet; Dramatist. *Education:* BA, Rhodes University▨ Grahamstown, 1938. *Appointment:* Writer, BBC Africa Service, Londo▨ 1968–77. *Publications:* Fiction: The Young Traveller in South Africa, 194▨ The Long Way Round, 1956; Upsurge in Africa, 1960; Border, 1963; The Da▨ Natal Took Off: A Satire, 1963. Poetry: An Unknown Border, 1954; The La▨ Division, 1959; A Corner of the World: Thirty-Four Poems, 1962; Black Sout▨ Easter, 1966. Play: The Fall: A Play About Rhodes, 1957. *Honour:* CN▨ Literary Award, 1977. *Address:* 30 Graemesdyke Ave, London SW14 7B▨ England.

DEMARIA, Robert; b. 28 Sept. 1928, New York, NY, USA. Prof. of English Emeritus; Author; Poet. m. (1) Maddalena Buzeo, (2) Ellen Hope Meyer, 3 s., 1 d. *Education:* BA, 1948, MA, 1949, PhD, 1959, Columbia University. *Appointments:* Instructor, University of Oregon, 1949–52; Asst Prof., Hofstra University, 1952–61; Assoc. Dean, New School for Social Research, New York City, 1961–64; Prof. of English, 1965–97, Prof. Emeritus, 1997–, Dowling College; Ed. and Publisher, The Mediterranean Review, 1969–73. *Publications:* Fiction: Carnival of Angels, 1961; Clodia, 1965; Don Juan in Lourdes, 1966; The Satyr, 1972; The Decline and Fall of America, 1973; To Be a King, 1976; Outbreak, 1978; Blowout, 1979; The Empress, 1980; Secret Places, 1981; A Passion for Power, 1983; Sons and Brothers, 2 vols, 1985; Stone of Destiny, 1986; That Kennedy Girl, 1999; The White Road, 2000. Textbooks: The College Handbook of Creative Writing, 1991; A Contemporary Reader for Creative Writing, 1995. *Contributions to:* Fiction, poetry, and articles in numerous publications. *Address:* 106 Vineyard Pl., Port Jefferson, NY 11777, USA.

DEMETILLO, Ricaredo; b. 2 June 1920, Dumangas, Philippines. Prof. of Humanities (retd); Poet; Writer. *Education:* AB, Silliman University, 1947; MFA, University of Iowa, 1952. *Appointments:* Asst Prof., 1959–70, Chair., Dept of Humanities, 1961–62, Assoc. Prof., 1970–75, Prof. of Humanities, 1975–86, University of the Philippines. *Publications:* Poetry: No Certain Weather, 1956; La Via: A Spiritual Journey, 1958; Daedalus and Other Poems, 1961; Barter in Panay, 1961; Masks and Signature, 1968; The Scare-Crow Christ, 1973; The City and the Thread of Light, 1974; Lazarus, Troubadour, 1974; Sun, Silhouttes and Shadow, 1975; First and Last Fruits, 1989. Novel: The Genesis of a Troubled Vision, 1976. Play: The Heart of Emptiness is Black, 1973. Non-Fiction: The Authentic Voice of Poetry, 1962; Major and Minor Keys, 1986. *Address:* 38 Balacan St, West Ave, Quezon City, Philippines.

DEMING, Alison Hawthorne; b. 13 July 1946, USA. Writer; Poet. 1 d. *Education:* MFA, Vermont College, 1983; Stegner Fellow, Stanford University, 1987–88. *Appointment:* Dir, 1990–, Assoc. Prof., Dept of English, 1998, University of Arizona. *Publications:* Science and Other Poems, 1994; Temporary Homelands, 1994; The Edges of the Civilized World, 1994; The Monarchs: A Poem Sequence, 1998; Poetry of the American West, 1996; Writing the Sacred into the Real, 2001. *Contributions to:* Georgia Review; Denver Quarterly; Sierra; Orion; Wilderness; Alaska Quarterly; Third Coast. *Honours:* Pablo Neruda Prize, 1983; National Endowment for the Arts Fellowships, 1990, 1995; Gertrude Claytor Award, Poetry Society of America, 1991; Walt Whitman Award, Acad. of American Poets, 1993; Bayer Award in Science Writing, 1998. *Memberships:* Acad. of American Poets; Poetry Society of America; Asscn for the Study of Literature and the Environment. *Address:* University of Arizona, Dept of English, PO Box 210067, Tucson, AZ 85721, USA. *E-mail:* aldeming@aol.com.

DENIORD, Richard (Chard) Newnham; b. 17 Dec. 1952, New Haven, CT, USA. Teacher; Poet. m. 20 June 1971, 1 s., 1 d. *Education:* BA, 1975; MDiv, Yale University, 1978; MFA, University of Iowa, 1985. *Appointments:* Psychotherapist, Connecticut Mental Health Centre 1978–82; Teacher, The Gunnery, 1985–89, The Putney School, 1989–. *Publication:* Asleep in the Fire. *Contributions to:* Iowa Review; Ploughshares; Denver Review; North American Review; Bad Henry Review; Agni; Quarterly West; Mississippi Review; Poetry East; Graham House Review; Antioch Review. *Honour:* Emily Dickinson Award. *Membership:* Poetry Society of America. *Address:* RR4, Box 929, Putney, VT 05346, USA.

DENNIS, Carl; b. 17 Sept. 1939, St Louis, MO, USA. Poet; Writer; Prof. of English. *Education:* Oberlin College, 1957–58; University of Chicago, 1958–59; BA, University of Minnesota, 1961; PhD, University of California at Berkeley, 1966. *Appointments:* Prof. of English, State University of New York at Buffalo, 1966–; Sometime faculty mem., Writing Program, Warren Wilson College. *Publications:* Poetry: A House of My Own, 1974; Climbing Down, 1976; Signs and Wonders, 1979; The Near World, 1985; The Outskirts of Troy, 1988; Meetings with Time, 1992; Ranking the Wishes, 1997; Practical Gods, 2001. Other: Poetry as Persuasion, 2001. *Contributions to:* Many anthologies, quarterlies, reviews and journals. *Honours:* Guggenheim Fellowship; National Endowment for the Arts Fellowship; Fellow, Rockefeller Study Center, Bellagio, Italy; Ruth Lilly Prize, 2000; Pulitzer Prize in Poetry, 2002. *Membership:* PEN. *Address:* 49 Ashland Ave, Buffalo, NY 14222, USA.

DENNISTON, Edward Connor; b. 13 Nov. 1956, Longford, Ireland. Teacher of English, Drama and Media Studies; Poet. m. Gillian Doonan, 26 July 1980, 2 d. *Education:* BA, H Dip Ed, Trinity College, Dublin. *Appointments:* Asst Head Teacher, 1980; Head of English, 1983. *Contributions to:* Fortnight, Belfast; Poetry Ireland; Honest Ulsterman; Riverine; Salmon Magazine; Belfast Review. *Memberships:* Poetry Society; Poetry Ireland; Poetry Wales. *Address:* 11 Alder Grove, Mt Pleasant, Waterford, Ireland.

DENOO, Joris; b. 6 July 1953, Torhout, Belgium. Author; Poet. m. Lut Vandemeulebroecke, 23 July 1976, 1 s., 2 d. *Education:* Graduate, German Philology, University of Louvain, 1975; Aggregation PHO, 1976. *Publications:* Poetry: Binnenscheepvaart, 1988; Staat van Medewerking, 1988; Voltooid Verwarmde Tijd, 1992. Prose: Repelsteel in Bourgondie, 1986; Verkeerde Lieveheer, 1993; Vallen en Opstaan: Diary of an Epileptic Child, 1996; Het Kind van de Rekening: A Christmas Story; Rode Blossen: A Story for Children, 1999. Other: Essays and children's stories. *Contributions to:* Many Flemish and Dutch magazines and periodicals. *Honours:* Vlaamse Klub Prize, Brussels, 1979; Premies West-Vlaanderen, 1983, 1991; Prijs Tielt Boekenstad, 1992; Essay Prize, Royal Acad. for Dutch Language and Literature, 1996; Poetry Prize, Keerbergen, 1998; Guido Gezelle Poetry Prize, 1999; Essay Prize Ambrozijn, 2000. *Membership:* SABAM, Belgium. *Address:* Oude Ieperseweg 85, 8501 Heule, Belgium.

DEOK KY JEON, (Choon Woo); b. 15 Oct. 1933, Jinan, Jeonrabookdo, Korea. Publishing Man. m. Sung Ki Yoon, 2 s., 2 d. *Education:* Complet Korean Literature, Dept of DukSung University, 1955–56; Complet Creative Literature, Dept of Serabal University, 1956–57; Graduate, Social Work, Dept of KangNam University, 1967–69; Complet LifeLong Education of Ewa University, Majoring in Infant Education and Administration, 1984–85; Complet University of South Carolina, MSW Postgraduate Course, 1996–98. *Appointments:* Public Official of the Welfare Ministry, Man. of Infant Education. *Publications:* A Grassland of not coming down a dew, 1971; A Wild Goose's Four Seasons, 1983; Spring Rain, 1989; This one Day of being Permitted, 1992; Let's ease the Concern, 1995; Making a light at the Soul Wick, 1995; The Road to that Earth, 1996; A Silver Colored Sand which picked up my Working Life, 1996; A Spring Rain is Diging Up Dead Leaves, 1998; Mind of being Opened and Closed, 2000; Contributions to newspapers, magazines and journals. *Honours:* Korean Poems Great Prizes, 1991; Distinguished Service Prizes of the Modern Korea Poetry Asscn, 1991; Nosan Literature Prizes, 1992; Korea Christian Literature Prizes, 1998; Poem and Poetics Prizes, 1998. *Memberships:* Dir, Korea Modern Poets Asscn; Dir, Korea Christian Literary Men's Asscn; Dir, Korea Literary Women's Asscn; Korea Literary Men's Asscn; Korea International Pen Club. *Address:* 132-848, 106-303 Sindonga, Apartment 513, Banghak4Dong DoBonggoo, Seoul, Korea. *E-mail:* sinjisungsa@hanmail.net.

DEPAOR, Louis; b. 27 June 1961, Cork, Ireland. Writer; Poet. m. Shirley Bourke, 1 s., 4 d. *Education:* University College, Cork, 1978–81; PhD, 1986. *Appointments:* Asst Lecturer, University College, Cork, 1984–85, Thomond College, 1985–87; Visiting Prof., University of Sydney. *Publications:* Próca Solais is Luatha; 30 Dán; Aimsir Bhreicneach/Freckled Weather; Gobán Cré is Cloch/Sentences of Earth and Stone. *Contributions to:* Innti; Comhar; Stet; Australian Short Stories; Modern Writing; Meanjin; Melbourne Age; Melbourne Times; Chapman. *Honours:* Duais Sheáin Uí Ríordáin, 1988, 1992; Writers Project Grants, 1990, 1991; Short-listed, Victoria Premier's Prize, 1994; Australia Council Fellowship, 1995. *Membership:* Flann O'Brien Society. *Address:* 117 Shaftsbury St, Coburg 3058, Australia.

DEPESTRE, René; b. 29 Aug. 1926, Jacmel, Haiti (Naturalized French citizen). Poet; Author. m. Nelly Campano, 1962. *Education:* Sorbonne, University of Paris, 1946–51. *Appointment:* Attaché, Office of Culture, UNESCO, Paris, 1982–86. *Publications:* Poetry: Etincelles, 1945; Gerbe de sang, 1946; Minerai noir, 1956; Un arc-en-ciel pour l'occident chrétien, 1967; Journal d'un animal marin (selected poems, 1956–90), 1990; Au matin de la négritude, 1990; Anthologie personnelle, 1993. Fiction: Alléluia pour une femme jardin, 1973; Le Mat de cocagne, 1979; Hadriana dans tous mes reves, 1988; Eros dans un train chinois: Neuf histories d'amour et un conte sorcier, 1990. Non-Fiction: Pour la révolution, pour la poésie, 1969; Bonjour et adieu a la négritude, 1980. *Honours:* Prix Goncourt, 1982; Prix Renaudot, 1988. *Address:* 31 bis, Route de Roubia, 11200 Lezignan-Corbières, France.

DERHODES, Jennifer. See: BOSVELD, Jennifer Miller.

DERRICOTTE, Toi; b. 11 April 1941, Hamtramck, Michigan, USA. Prof. of English; Poet; Author. m. C Bruce Derricotte, 30 Dec. 1967, 1 s. *Education:* BA, Special Education, Wayne State University, 1965; MA, English Literature and Creative Writing, New York University, 1984. *Appointments:* Master Teacher and Poet in the Schools, New Jersey State Council on the Arts and Maryland State Council on the Arts, 1973–88; Assoc. Prof. of English Literature, Old Dominion University, 1988–90; Commonwealth Prof., George Mason University, 1990–91; Assoc. Prof., 1991–97, Prof. of English, 1998–, University of Pittsburgh; Visiting Prof., New York University, 1992; Many poetry readings around the world. *Publications:* The Empress of the Death House, 1978; Natural Birth, 1983; Creative Writing: A Manual for Teachers (with Madeline Bass), 1985; Captivity, 1989; Tender, 1997; The Black Notebooks, 1997. *Contributions to:* Numerous anthologies and journals. *Honours:* MacDowell Colony Fellowship, 1982; New Jersey State Council on the Arts Poetry Fellowship, 1983; Lucille Medwick Memorial Award, Poetry Society of America, 1985; National Endowment for the Arts Creative Writing Fellowships, 1985, 1990; Pushcaft Prizes, 1989, 1998; Poetry Committee Book Award, Folger Shakespeare Library, Washington, DC, 1990; Yaddo Residency, 1997; Anisfield-Wolf Book Award for Non-Fiction, 1998; Award in Non-Fiction, Black Caucus, American Library Asscn, 1998; Paterson Poetry Prize, 1998. *Memberships:* Acad. of American Poets; Associated Writing Programs; MLA; PEN; Poetry Society of America. *Address:* c/o Dept of English, University of Pittsburgh, Pittsburgh, PA 15260, USA.

DESAUTELS, Denise; b. 1945, Montréal, QC, Canada. Poet; Writer. *Education:* Collège Basile-Moreau; MA, University of Montréal, 1980. *Publications:* Comme miroirs en feuilles, 1975; Marie, trout s'éteignait en moi, 1977; La promeneuse et l'oiseau suivi de journal de la promeneuse, 1980; L'écran, précéde de, aires du tempts, 1983; Leçons de Venise, 1990; Mais la menace est une belle extravagance suivi de le signe discret, 1991; La saut de l'ange, 1992; Lettres à Cassandre (with Anne-Marie Alonzo), 1994. *Honour:* Gov.-Gen.'s Award for Poetry, 1993. *Address:* c/o Editions de Noirot, 1835 blvd des Hauteurs, St Hippolyte, QC J0R 1P0, Canada.

DESCHOEMAEKER, Frans; b. 8 Sept. 1954, Belgium. Government Education Official; Poet. *Education:* Institute for Psychical and Social Training, Kortrijk, 1973–74. *Publications:* Down the River; Autumn's Halls of Mirrors; The Chuckle of the Country Squire; Elements of Archaeology. *Contributions to:* De Periscoop; Diogenes; The Critical Lexicon of Dutch Literature After 1945; Dietsche Warande & Belfort; Kreatief; De Vlaamse Gids; Elseviers Magazine. *Honours:* Poetry Prize, Flemish Club, Brussels; Poetry Prize, West Flanders; Maurice Gilliams Prize, Royal Acad. of Dutch Linguistics and Literature, 1995. *Memberships:* Diogenes; Nieuwe Stemmen; Filter. *Address:* Vontstraat 61, 9700 Oudenaarde, Belgium.

DESHPANDE, Renukadas Yeshwant; b. 17 April 1931, Maharashtra, India. Prof.; Poet; Writer. m. Suniti, 9 June 1962, 1 s. *Education:* MSc, Physics, 1955. *Appointments:* Research Scientist, Tata Institute of Fundamental Research, Mumbai, Bhabha Atomic Research Centre, Mumbai, Lawrence Radiation Laboratory, Berkeley, USA; Sri Aurobindo International Centre of Education, Pondicherry; Assoc. Ed., Mother India, Pondicherry. *Publications:* Poetry: The Rhododendron Valley, 1988; All is Dream-Blaze, 1992; Under the Raintree, 1994; Paging the Unknown, 2000. Prose: Nirodbaran: Poet and Sadhak; Amal-Kiran: Poet and Critic; The Ancient Tale of Savitri; Satyavan Must Die; Vyasa's Savitri; Sri Aurobindu and the New Millennium; Perspectives of Savitri, two vols; The Wager of Amrbosia; Nagin-bhai Tells Me. *Contributions to:* Mother India; Sri Aurobindo Circle; Sri Aurobindo Action; POET; Bridge-in-Making. *Address:* Sri Aurobindo International Centre of Education, Pondicherry 605002, India.

DEVAPOOJITHAYA, Arikkady Srisha; b. 11 Dec. 1944, Kasaragod, India. Prof. of English (retd); Poet. m. B V Usharani, 26 April 1969, 1 s., 1 d. *Education:* MA, English Language, 1966; MA, Kannada, 1971; MA, Sanskrit, 1973; MA, Hindi, 1975. *Appointments:* Prof. of English, 1966–, Head, Dept of English, 1988–, Head, Postgraduate Dept of English, 1998–99, Government College, Kasaragod, Kerala; Regular Broadcast of Poems, All India Radio. *Publications:* Kasaragodina Kavithegalu, 1978; Idu Varthamana, 1979; Thappenu, 1987; Kavi Goshthi, 1994; Banjaru Bhoomi, 1996. *Contributions to:* Udayavani; Thushara; Mallige; Navabharatha; Tainudi; Hosa Digantha; Suguna Digest. *Honour:* Muddana Kavya Rajya Prashasthi. *Memberships:* Navya Sahithya Sangha; Kasaragodu Jilla Lekhakara Sangha, exec. committee; Kasaragod; Kerala Government College Teachers' Asscn. *Address:* Srinivas Compound, Navakana, Badiaka, PO Perdala, PIN 671551, Kerala, India.

DEVARAJ, Ramasamy; b. 4 Dec. 1941, Sankaralingapuram, India. Physics Teacher; Poet; Dramatist. m. Rukmani, 16 Sept. 1973, deceased, 1 s., 2 d. *Education:* MSc, Physics, 1969, MPhil, Physics, 1977, BL, 1982, Chennai University; MEd, Annamalai University, 1984. *Appointments:* Assitant Prof. of Physics, Chennai Christian College; Teacher of Physics, Government Model Higher Secondary School, Government College of Education, Saidapet, Chennai. *Publications:* Lamps of Lightning (poems), 1990; Poems of Ramasamy Devaraj, 1991; One Hundred Love Poems, 1991; The People of the Hoaxama Islands (plays and poetry), 1993; Songs of Good Hope, 1995. Other: Books in Tamil and trans. *Contributions to:* Periodicals and magazines. *Membership:* World Parnassians Guild International, Chennai, founder-pres. *Address:* K-13, Todhunter Nagar, Saidapet, Chennai 600015, India.

DEVEREAUX, Emily. See: LEWIS-SMITH, Anne Elizabeth.

DEVIDE, Vladimir; b. 3 May 1925, Zagreb, Croatia. Prof. of Mathematics (retd); Poet. m. Yasuyo Hondo, 26 Dec. 1981, 1 s. *Education:* Diploma, Civil Engineering, 1951; DSc, Mathematics, 1956. *Appointment:* Prof. of Mathematics, University of Zagreb, retd 1990. *Publications:* Eight books of poetry in Croatian, English, and/or German, 1970, 1985, 1987, 1988, 1989, 1992, 1995, 1999. *Contributions to:* Periodicals and Haiku publications in Croatia, Japan and USA. *Honours:* Encouragement Prizes, Japanese International Haiku Contests, 1991, 1993, 1994, 1997; Order of the Sacred Treasure, Japan; Rugjer Boskovic Prize, Croatia. *Memberships:* Croatian Acad. of Sciences and Arts; Croatian PEN Club; Haiku International Asscn, Japan; Union of Croatian Writers; Asscn of Croatian Haiku Poets, hon. pres.; World Haiku Asscn, USA; German Haiku Asscn, hon. mem. *Address:* Vinogradska 10, 10000 Zagreb, Croatia.

DEVILLE, Edward Samuel; b. 31 Aug. 1950, Hertford, England. Poet. m. Deborah Marie Booty, 18 April 1992. *Publication:* A Bone to Pick With the Sea, 1970. *Contributions to:* Telegraph Magazine; Outposts; Poetry Review. *Honour:*

Cheltenham Festival, 1981. *Membership:* Poetry Society. *Address:* 74 Fordwic Rise, Hertford SG14 2DE, England.

DEWDNEY, Christopher; b. 9 May 1951, London, Ontario, Canada. Poe Writer. m. (1) Suzanne Dennison, 1971, divorced 1975, 1 d., (2) Lise Downe 1977, divorced 1990, 1 s., (3) Barbara Gowdy. *Education:* South an Westminster Collegiate Institutes, London, Ontario; H B Beal Art Anne London, Ontario. *Appointments:* Assoc. Fellow, Winters College, Yor University, Toronto, 1984; Poetry Ed., Coach House Publishing, Toront 1988; Academic Adviser, Columet College, York University, 1997– *Publications:* Poetry: Golders Green, 1972; A Paleozoic Geology of Londor Ontario, 1973; Fovea Centralis, 1975; Spring Trances in the Control Emeral Night, 1978; Alter Sublime, 1980; The Cenozoic Asylum, 1983; Predators of th Adoration: Selected Poems 1972–1982, 1983; Permugenesis, 1987; The Radiar Inventory, 1988; Demon Pond, 1994. Other: The Immaculate Perception, 198(Recent Artifacts from the Institute of Applied Fiction, 1990; Concordar Proviso Ascendant: A Natural History of Southwestern Ontario, Book II 1991; The Secular Grail, 1993; Demon Pond, 1994; Last Flesh, 1998; Signa Fires, 2000; The Natural History, 2002. *Contributions to:* Periodicals. *Honour* Design Canada Award, 1974; CBC Prize, 1986; Fellow, Columet College, Yor University; Fellow, McLuhen Program in Culture and Technology. *Address:* c/ McClelland and Stewart Inc, 481 University Ave, Suite 900, Toronto, Ontari M5G 2E9, Canada.

DEWHIRST, Ian; b. 17 Oct. 1936, Keighley, Yorkshire, England. Librariar (retd); Writer; Poet. *Education:* BA Honours, Victoria University c Manchester, 1958. *Appointment:* Staff, Keighley Public Library, 1960–9! *Publications:* The Handloom Weaver and Other Poems, 1965; Scar Top an Other Poems, 1968; Gleanings From Victorian Yorkshire, 1972; A History c Keighley, 1974; Yorkshire Through the Years, 1975; Gleanings from Edwardia Yorkshire, 1975; The Story of a Nobody, 1980; You Don't Remember Bananas 1985; Keighley in Old Picture Postcards, 1987; In the Reign of the Peacemake 1993; Down Memory Lane, 1993; Images of Keighley, 1996; A Century c Yorkshire Dialect (co-ed.), 1997. *Contributions to:* Yorkshire Riding Magazine; Lancashire Magazine; Dalesman; Cumbria; Pennine Magazine Transactions of the Yorkshire Dialect Society; Yorkshire Journal. *Honour* Hon. Doctor of Letters, University of Bradford, 1996; M.B.E., 199! *Memberships:* Yorkshire Dialect Society; Brontë Society; Edward Thoma Fellowship; Assoc. of the Library Asscn; Fellow, RSA, 2000. *Address:* 1 Raglan Ave, Fell Lane, Keighley, West Yorkshire BD22 6BJ, England.

DEWITT, Genevieve Judice Didier. See: JUDICE, Genevieve

DEY, Richard Addison, (Richard Morris Dey); b. 28 Nov. 1945, USA Writer; Poet. 2 s. *Education:* Harvard College, BA, 1973. *Appointments* Freelance Journalist; Commercial Fisherman; Yacht Captain; Instructo Maritime History and Literature Seamaster Programme, Long Islan University. *Publications:* The Beguia Poems, 1988; In the Way of Adventure 1989. *Contributions to:* Poetry; New Republic; Harvard Advocate; Harvar Magazine; Sail; Country Journal; Indian Express; Lokmat Times; Nagpu Florescence; Haryana; Poets and Writers; Light. *Memberships:* Poets an Writers; New England Poetry Society. *Address:* 178 Gardner St, Hingham MA 02043, USA.

DEY, Tapati; b. 13 Sept. 1957, Gwahati, Assam, India. Poet; Writer *Education:* MA, English Literature, 1980. *Contributions to:* Hitavada Nagpur; Tribune, New Delhi and Chandigarh; Telegraph, Calcutta; All Indi Radio, Nagpur; Telecom Journals, New Delhi and Mumbai. *Honours:* Secon Prize in Poetry (English), All India Posts and Telegraphs Literary Competition 1983; Selected amongst Accomplished Writers of the Year, All India Radi Annual Journal, 1983–84; Consolation Prizes for Fiction, Hitavada newspaper magazine, 1986, 1987, 1988; Best Writer and Best Article Award, 199(Commendation, British Council through Poetry Society of India, 200(*Address:* Munmun, 32 Yogendra Nagar, Nagpur 440013, Maharashtra, India.

DHOOMKETU, Kaviraj. See: DWIVEDI, Suresh Chandra.

DI CICCO, Pier Giorgio; b. 5 July 1949, Arezzo, Italy. Roman Catholic Priest Poet. *Education:* BA, 1972, BEd, 1973, Master of Divinity, 1990, University o Toronto; Bachelor of Sacred Theology, St Paul's University, 199(*Appointments:* Founder-Poetry Ed., Poetry Toronto Newsletter, 1976–77 Assoc. Ed., Books in Canada, 1976–79; Co-Ed., 1976–79, Poetry Ed., 1980–82 Waves; Ordained Roman Catholic Priest and Assoc. Pastor, St Anne's Church Brampton, Ontario, 1993–. *Publications:* We Are the Light Turning, 1975; Th Sad Facts, 1977; The Circular Dark, 1977; Dancing in the House of Cards, 1977 A Burning Patience, 1978; Roman Candles: An Anthology of 17 Italo-Canadiar Poets (ed.), 1978; Dolce-Amaro, 1979; The Tough Romance, 1979; A Straw Ha for Everything, 1981; Flying Deeper into the Century, 1982; Dark to Light Reasons for Humanness: Poems 1976–1979, 1983; Women We Never Se Again, 1984; Twenty Poems, 1984; Post-Sixties Nocturne, 1985; Virgi Science: Hunting Holistic Paradigms, 1986; The City of Hurried Dreams 1993. *Honours:* Canada Council Awards, 1974, 1976, 1980; Carleto University Italo-Canadian Literature Award, 1979. *Address:* PO Box 34 King City, Ontario L0G 1K0, Canada.

DI MICHELE, Mary; b. 6 Aug. 1949, Lanciano, Italy (Naturalized Canadian citizen). Poet; Author; Assoc. Prof. Divorced, 1 d. *Education:* BA, University of Toronto, 1972; MA, University of Windsor, 1974. *Appointments:* Poetry Ed., Toronto Life, 1980–81, Poetry Toronto, 1982–84; Writer-in-Residence, University of Toronto, 1985–86, Metro Reference Library, Toronto, 1986, Regina Public Library, 1987–88; Writer-in-Residence, 1990, then Assoc. Prof., Creative Writing Programme, Concordia University. *Publications:* Poetry: Tree of August, 1978; Bread and Chocolate, 1980; Mimosa and Other Poems, 1981; Necessary Sugar, 1984; Immune to Gravity, 1986; Luminous Emergencies, 1990; Stranger in You: Selected Poems & New, 1995; Debriefing the Rose, 1998. Novel: Under My Skin, 1994. Editor: Anything is Possible, 1984. *Contributions to:* Anthologies and periodicals. *Honours:* First Prize for Poetry, CBC Literary Competition, 1980; Silver Medal, DuMaurier Poetry Award, 1982; Air Canada Writing Award, 1983. *Memberships:* Italian-Canadian Writers Asscn; Writers Union. *Address:* c/o Dept of English, Concordia University, 1455 de Maisonneuve Blvd W, Montréal, QC H3G 1M8, Canada.

DI PASQUALE, Emanuel; b. 25 Jan. 1943, Sicily, Italy. Prof. of English; Poet. m. (1) Marie, 11 Feb. 1965, divorced 1 June 1990, (2) Mary, 3 Oct. 1995, 1 d. *Education:* BA, English, Adelphi University, 1965; MA, English, New York University. *Appointments:* Faculty, Elizabeth City State University, North Carolina, Middlesex County College, Edison, New Jersey. *Publication:* Genesis, 1989. *Contributions to:* Newspapers, reviews and journals. *Honour:* Bordighera Poetry Prize, 1998; Raiziss/de Palchi Fellowship, Acad. of American Poets, 2000. *Address:* c/o Dept of English, Middlesex County College, Edison, NJ 08818, USA.

DI PIERO, William Simone; b. 3 Dec. 1945, Philadelphia, PA, USA. Teacher. *Education:* BA, St Joseph's College, 1969; MA, San Francisco State College, 1971. *Appointments:* Instructor, Louisiana State University, Northwestern University; Prof., Stanford University. *Publications:* The First Hour, 1982; The Only Dangerous Thing, 1983; Early Light, 1985; The Dog Star, 1989; The Restorers, 1992; Shadows Burning, 1995; Skirts and Slacks, 2001. *Contributions to:* New Yorker; Threepenny Review; Partisan Review; Hudson Review; TriQuarterly. *Honour:* Guggenheim Fellowship, 1985. *Address:* 225 Downey St, No. 5, San Francisco, CA 94117, USA.

DI PRIMA, Diane; b. 6 Aug. 1934, New York, NY, USA. Poet; Writer; Dramatist; Trans.; Publisher; Artist. m. (1) Alan S Marlowe, 1962, divorced 1969, (2) Grant Fisher, 1972, divorced 1975, 2 s., 3 d. *Education:* Swarthmore College, 1951–53. *Appointments:* Co-Founder, New York Poets Theater, 1961–65; Co-Ed. (with LeRoi Jones), 1961–63, Ed., 1963–69, Floating Bear magazine; Publisher, Poets Press, 1964–69, Eidolon Editions, 1974–; Faculty, Naropa Institute, 1974–97, New College of California, San Francisco, 1980–87; Co-Founder, San Francisco Institute of Magical and Healing Arts, 1983–91; Senior Lecturer, California College of Arts and Crafts, Oakland, 1990–92; Visiting Faculty, San Francisco Art Institute, 1992; Adjunct Faculty, California Institute of Integral Studies, 1994–95; Master Poet in Residence, Columbia College, Chicago, 2000. *Publications:* This Kind of Bird Flies Backward, 1958; Ed., Various Fables from Various Places, 1960; Dinners and Nightmares, 1961, 1998; The New Handbook of Heaven, 1962; Translator, The Man Condemned to Death, 1963; Poets Vaudeville, 1964; Seven Love Poems from the Middle Latin, 1965; Haiku, 1966; New Mexico Poem, 1967; Earthsong, 1968; Hotel Albert, 1968; Ed., War Poems, 1968; Memoirs of a Beatnik, 1969, 1988; LA Odyssey, 1969; The Book of Hours, 1970; Kerhonkson Journal 1966, 1971; Revolutionary Letters, 1971; The Calculus of Variation, 1972; Loba, Part 1, 1973; Ed., The Floating Bear: a Newsletter, 1973; Freddie Poems, 1974; Brass Furnace Going Out, 1975; Selected Poems 1956–1975, 1975; Loba, Part 2, 1976; Loba as Eve, 1977; Loba, Parts 1–8, 1978; Wyoming Series, 1988; The Mysteries of Vision, 1988; Pieces of a Song: Selected Poems, 1990; Seminary Poems, 1991; The Mask is the Path of the Star, 1993; Loba, Parts 9–16, 1998; Recollections of My Life as a Woman, 2001. *Contributions to:* Over 300 literary and popular magazines and newspapers; Work appeared in over 100 anthologies. *Honours:* National Endowment for the Arts Grants, 1966, 1973; Co-ordinating Council of Little Magazines Grants, 1967, 1970; Lapis Foundation Awards, 1978, 1979; Institute for Aesthetic Development Award, 1986; Lifetime Service Award, National Poetry Asscn, 1993; Hon. Doctor of Literature, St Lawrence University, Canton, New York, 1999. *Literary Agent:* Sandra Dijkstra, PO Box 4500, Del Mar, CA 92014, USA. *Address:* 78 Niagara Ave, San Francisco, CA 94112, USA.

DICKENSON, George Therese; b. 23 Oct. 1951, California, USA. Writer; Poet. *Education:* BA, 1976. *Appointments:* Proofreader, Copy Ed., 1977; Dir, Founder, Incisions Arts, 1978–88; Senior Ed., New York Magazine, 1982–88; Ed., Freelance 1988–; Writer, Freelance, 1990–. *Publications:* Transducing Segue; Striations. *Contributions to:* Big Allis; Assassin; Baltimore Sun; Black Rose; Body Politic; Blues 10; Gay Community News; The News and the Weather; The World; Artzone; Ahnoi; Pegasus; Contact 11; Dream Helmut. *Honours:* American Acad. of Poets Award; Wellesley Entrant to Glassioch Poetry Contest; Massachusetts Arts and Humanities Foundation. *Membership:* Poets and Writers. *Address:* 65 Second Ave, No. 2H, New York, NY 10003, USA.

DICKEY, Phillip, (Philo); b. 9 June 1948, Cincinnati, Ohio, USA. Actor; Poet; Playwright; Metaphysicist. Phenomenologist; Multi-media Artist. *Education:* BA, 1975; Further Studies, Ohio University. *Publications:* Front Seat Revelations, 1972; Feng Shui, 1982; Quod Scipsi, Scripsi, 1989; Wordsmith (play), 1992; 1-900 (play), 1994; Butch and His Buddies: Growing-up in Mid-America, Mid-Century, 2000. Other: Multi-media works. *Contributions to:* Anthologies, including: The Astral Valentine. *Honours:* Several awards and prizes. *Address:* PO Box 541, Chillicothe, OH 45601-0541, USA.

DICKEY, R(obert) P(reston); b. 24 Sept. 1942, Flat River, Missouri, USA. Prof. of English (retd); Poet. *Education:* BA, 1967, MA, 1969, PhD, 1975, University of Missouri. *Appointments:* Instructor in English, University of Missouri, 1964–69; Asst Prof. of English, University of Southern Colorado, 1969–74, Pima College, 1974–80. *Publications:* Running Lucky, 1969; Acting Immortal, 1970; Concise Dictionary of Lead River, Missouri, 1972; The Basic Stuff of Poetry, 1972; Life-Cycle of Seventy Songs, 1984; The Poetica Erotica of R P Dickey, 1989; The Little Book on Racism and Politics, 1990; Ode on Liberty, 1996; The Lee Poems, 1998; Self-Liberation, 1998; Exercise Anytime (with Mary K O'Brien), 1998; Collected Poems, 1999. *Contributions to:* Poetry; New Yorker; Atlantic; Harper's; Sewanee Review; Poetry Northwest; Hudson Review; Western Review; New York Times; American Poetry Review; Salmagundi; Poetry Bag; Black Bear Review; Poet (India); Revue Moderne (France); Chicago Review; Big Table; Southern Review. *Address:* PO Box 87, Ranchos de Taos, NM 87557, USA.

DIEZ SERRANO, Isabel; b. 13 Feb. 1940, Sevilla, Spain. Reflexotherapist; Poet. m. Antonio Martínez, 30 May 1963, 1 s., 1 d. *Education:* English and French, Assimil School, 1958–63; Psychology, Complutense University, 1980–82; Reflexotherapy, Martpo Center, 1984. *Appointment:* Pres., Asociación Prometeo de Poesía, 1997–98, 1999–2000. *Publications:* El último espejo, 1987; En el principio de la carne, 1988; Alimentando lluvias, 1990; De mis noches con Juan, 1991; Y el sueño se hizo voz, 1994; Marcada por tres fuegos, 1995; Ecos de prensa I, 1995; Ecos de prensa II, 1996; La palabra es la sombra de las cosas, 1997; Via crucis, 1998; Las horas detenidas, 1998. *Contributions to:* Anthologies, reviews, journals and periodicals. *Honours:* Alhoja de Plata, 1985; Placa Antonio Machado, 1986; Sanchez Brun, 1986; Peliart and Menciou Honour in Asoc Promete o de Poesía, 1987; Llave de Plata, 1988; Flor Natural, 1990; Pluma de Plata, 1993; Feria del Libro del Buen Retiro, 1994; Trofeo Reina Amalia, 1994; Two Jorge Manrique Awards; Mario Angel Marrodan, 1996; Maria del Villar, 1996; Iaccesit Fernando Poesía Mistica, 1996. *Address:* Decoradores 1-1, 28037 Madrid, Spain.

DIGGES, Deborah; b. 6 Feb. 1950, Jefferson, MO, USA. Writer; Poet. m. (1) Charles Digges, 1969, divorced 1980, (2) Stanley Plumly, 1985, divorced 1993, 2 s. *Education:* BA, University of California at Riverside; MA, University of Missouri; MFA, Iowa Writers' Workshop. *Publications:* Vesper Sparrows, 1986; Late in the Millennium, 1989; Fugitive Spring: Coming of Age in the 50's and 60's, 1992; Ballad of the Blood: The Poems of Maria Elena Cruz Varela (co-ed. and co-trans.), 1996; The Star Dust Lounge, 2001. *Address:* c/o Alfred A. Knopf Inc, 299 Park Ave, New York, NY 10171, USA.

DILLARD, R(ichard) H(enry) W(ilde); b. 11 Oct. 1937, Roanoke, Virginia, USA. Prof. of English; Writer; Poet; Ed. m. (1) Annie Doak, 1965, divorced 1972, (2) Cathy Hankla, 1979. *Education:* BA, Roanoke College, Salem, Virginia, 1958; MA, 1959, PhD, 1965, University of Virginia. *Appointments:* Instructor, Roanoke College, 1961, University of Virginia, 1961–64; Asst Prof., 1964–68, Assoc. Prof., 1968–74, Prof. of English, 1974–, Hollins College, Virginia; Contributing Ed., Hollins Critic, 1966–77; Ed.-in-Chief, Children's Literature, 1992–. *Publications:* Fiction: The Book of Changes, 1974; The First Man on the Sun, 1983; Omniphobia, 1995. Poetry: The Day I Stopped Dreaming About Barbara Steele and Other Poems, 1966; News of the Nile, 1971; After Borges, 1972; The Greeting: New and Selected Poems, 1981; Just Here, Just Now, 1994. Non-Fiction: Horror Films, 1976; Understanding George Garrett, 1988. Editor: The Experience of America: A Book of Readings (with Louis D Rubin Jr), 1969; The Sounder Few: Essays from 'The Hollins Critic' (with George Garrett and John Rees Moore), 1971. *Contributions to:* Periodicals. *Honours:* Acad. of American Poets Prize, 1961; Ford Foundation Grant, 1972; O B Hardison, Jr Poetry Award, Folger Shakespeare Library, Washington, DC, 1994. *Address:* Box 9671, Hollins College, CA 24020, USA.

DILLON, Enoch (LaRoy); b. 18 Oct. 1925, Hillsboro, Oregon, USA. Government Official (retd); Poet. m. Jean Marie Lang, 3 Feb. 1951, 2 s., 4 d. *Education:* BS, Economics, Pacific University, 1948; MA, Economics, Catholic University of America, 1952. *Appointments:* Public Administration Specialist, 1948–51, 1952–55; Budget Specialist, Exec. Office of the Pres. of the US, 1955–71; Exec. Asst, Budgets, National Science Foundation, 1971–80. *Publications:* The Bicentennial Blues, 1988; Love, from the ends of the earth, 1990. *Contributions to:* Poet Lore; Visions; Poultry; Gryphon; San Fernando Poetry Journal; Odyssey; Federal Poet; Country Cottage Poetry Journal; Light; Deus ex Machina; Heaven Bone. *Memberships:* Writers Center, Bethesda, Maryland; Federal Poets, Washington, DC. *Address:* 6310 Hollins Dr., Bethesda, MD 20817, USA.

DILSAVER, Paul; b. 8 Dec. 1949, Colorado, USA. Poet; Writer; Ed. *Education:* BA, Philosophy, University of Southern Colorado, 1972; MA, English, 1973, Additional Graduate Studies, 1974, 1975, Colorado State University; MFA, Creative Writing, Bowling Green State University, Ohio, 1979; BS, Accounting, State University of New York, 1996. *Appointments:* Instructor, Laramie County Community College, Cheyenne, Wyoming, 1973–74; Casper College, Wyoming, 1974–77, Western Illinois University, Macomb, 1979–81; Poetry Ed., Rocky Mountain Creative Arts Journal and Chapbook Series, 1974–78; Poet-in-Residence, Wyoming Arts Council, 1977–78; Ed., Blue Light Books, 1979–, Blue Light Review, 1983–91; Asst Prof. of English, Carroll College, Helena, Montana, 1981–84; Lecturer in English, University of Southern Colorado, 1986–91; Visiting Instructor of English, Anoka-Ramsey College, Coon Rapids, Minnesota, 1991–92. *Publications:* Malignant Blues (poems), 1976; Words Wyoming (anthology), 1976; A Brutal Blacksmith: An Anvil of Bruised Tissue (poems), 1979; Encounters with the Antichrist (prose poems), 1982; Character Scatology (poems), 1984; Stories of the Strange (fiction), 1985; Nurtz! Nurtz! (novel), 1989; A Cure for Optimism (poems), 1993; The Toilet Papers (anthology), 1994; Medi-Phoria, 1999; Hardcore Haiku, 2000. *Contributions to:* Various anthologies and periodicals. *Address:* PO Box 1621, Pueblo, CO 81002, USA.

DIMIT, Emma; b. 24 Nov. 1922, Johnstown, Pennsylvania, USA. Poet. m. Robert Morgan Dimit, 15 June 1946, 3 s., 1 d. *Education:* BS, Home Economics, Indiana University of Pennsylvania, 1944; Ohio State University, 1962–63; South Dakota State University, 1976–79. *Publication:* In Black and White, 1989. *Contributions to:* Anthologies and magazines. *Honours:* Numerous, South Dakota State Poetry Society, 1977–92; First Prize, Peteranodon Magazine, 1980; National Federation of State Poetry Societies Prizes, 1981, 1986; Centennial Poet and Poet of the Year, State of South Dakota, 1989; League of Minnesota Poets Award, 1989. *Memberships:* National Federation of State Poetry Societies; South Dakota State Poetry Society. *Address:* 330 Marian Ave, Brookings, SD 57006, USA.

DINSMORE, Danika; b. 17 Feb. 1968, Glendale, CA, USA. Teacher; Writer; Poet. m. David Johnson, 12 June 1993. *Education:* BA, English, 1990; MFA, Writing and Poetics, 1993; Certificate, Screenwriting, 1996. *Appointments:* Ed.-in-Chief, Morning Glory, 1988–90; Co-Ed., Bombay Gin, 1991–92, Iiyena, 1992–94. *Publication:* Traffic, 1996. *Contributions to:* Anthologies and periodicals. *Honours:* Helicon Award, 1990; IPIPP Creative Community Organizing Award, 1996. *Address:* 28915 NE 34th Ct, Redmond, WA 98053, USA.

DIOMEDE, Matthew; b. 8 June 1940, Yonkers, New York, USA. Educator; Poet. m. Barbara Diomede, 29 June 1968. *Education:* BA, Fordham College; MS, Fordham University; MA, Long Island University; PhD, St Louis University, 1992. *Appointments:* Teacher, Connecticut, New York, 1962–79; Lecturer, Co-ordinator, University of Missouri, St Louis, 1979–82; Lecturer, Asst Prof., English, Parks College, St Louis University, 1982–92; English Instructor, St Louis Community College, Forest Park, 1992–95, University of South Florida, Tampa and University of Tampa, 1995–. *Publication:* Pietro Di Donato, 1995. Anthologies: Poetry of Our Time; A Yearbook of Modern Poetry, 1971; Black Cat Bone; Outstanding Contemporary Poetry, 1971; International Who's Who in Poetry Anthology, 1972; National Poetry Anthology, 1972, 1973. *Contributions to:* Journals and magazines. *Honours:* Bronze Medal of Honour, Centre Studi e Scambi Internazionali, 1972; Graduate Poetry Award, Long Island University, 1975; Award Finalist, Virginia Commonwealth University Contemporary Poetry Series, 1975; Long Island University Alumni Poetry Award, 1978; Special Merit, IVA Mary Williams Inspirational Poetry Competition, 1990; Poetry Scholarship, Rope Walk Writers Retreat, 1990. *Memberships:* MLA; National Council of Teachers of English; Poets and Writers; Asscn of Literary Scholars and Critics. *Address:* 815 Bourbon Red Dr., Des Peres, MO 63131, USA.

DISCH, Thomas M(ichael), (Leonie Hargrave, Dobbin Thorpe); b. 2 Feb. 1940, Des Moines, IA, USA. Writer; Poet; Dramatist; Librettist; Lecturer. *Education:* Cooper Union, New York; New York University. *Appointments:* Lecturer at colleges and universities; Artist-in-Residence, College of William and Mary, 1996. *Publications:* Fiction: The Genocides, 1965; Mankind Under the Leash, 1966; The House That Fear Built (with John Sladek), 1966; Echo Round His Bones, 1967; Black Alice (with John Sladek), 1968; Camp Concentration, 1968; The Prisoner, 1969; 334, 1974; Clara Reeve, 1975; On Wings of Song, 1979; Triplicity, 1980; Neighboring Lives (with Charles Naylor), 1981; The Businessman: A Tale of Terror, 1984; Amnesia 1985; The M.D.: A Horror Story, 1991; The Priest: A Gothic Romance, 1995. Poetry: The Right Way to Figure Plumbing, 1972; ABCDEFG HIJKLM NOPQRST UVWXYZ, 1981; Orders of the Retina, 1982; Burn This, 1982; Here I Am, There You Are, Where Were We, 1984; Yes, Let's: New and Selected Poetry, 1989; Dark Verses and Light, 1991; The Dark Old House, 1995. Criticism: The Castle of Indolence, 1995; The Dreams Our Stuff is Made of: How Science Fiction Conquered the World, 1998. Other: Short story collections; plays; opera libretti; Children's books. *Contributions to:* Many anthologies and periodicals. *Honours:* O Henry Prizes, 1975, 1979; John W Campbell Memorial Award, 1980; BSFA Award, 1981. *Memberships:* National Book Critics Circle; PEN; Writers Guild. *Address:* Box 226, Barryville, NY 12719, USA.

DITTA, Joseph Michael; b. 12 May 1943, New York, NY, USA. Prof.; Poet Writer. m. Joann Diaz, 2 June 1968, 1 s., 1 d. *Education:* BA, Adelphi Suffolk College, 1969; MFA, University of Iowa, 1971; PhD, University of Missouri at Columbia, 1982. *Appointments:* Visiting Prof., Kyushu Institute of Technology 1972–74; Prof., Dakota Wesleyan University, 1983–. *Publications:* San Gimignano, 1995; The Philodendron and How Eagles Shape the Future, 1996; The Children Coming Home From School on a Spring Afternoon, 1996 Abjecto Scuto, Animus Abjectior, 1996; the Journey, 1996; The News and the Weather, Snow, and The Realist, 1996; The Door, 1996; Custom of the House, Early Snow, and In Linear Time, 1996; On Fiction and Poetry, and Hiding Out With Words, 1996; Still Life: A Pot of Frozen Flowers, 1997; On Once Being Romantic, 1997; On Cleaning Out the Closet, 1997; The City After Snowfall, Cold Morning and In Dead Winter, 1997. *Contributions to:* Anthologies, reviews, quarterlies and journals. *Honour:* Artists Fellowship in Literature-Poetry, South Dakota Arts Council. *Address:* English Dept, Dakota Wesleyan University, Mitchell, SD 57301, USA.

DIVOK, Mario J.; b. 22 Sept. 1944, Benus, Czechoslovakia. Real Estate Broker; Investments Exec.; Poet; Dramatist. m. Eva Pytlova, 6 Oct. 1990, 1 d. *Education:* MA, Pedagogic Institute, Martin, Czechoslovakia, 1967; MPA, California State University, Long Beach, 1977; Management, University of California at Irvine, 1995. *Publications:* The Relations, 1975; The Voice, 1975; The Wind of Changes, 1978; Equinox, 1978; The Collection, 1978; I Walk the Earth, 1980; The Blind Man, 1980; Looking for the Road to the Earth, 1983; The Birthday, 1984; Stranger in the Land, 1989; Selected Works, 1992. *Contributions to:* Various periodicals. *Honours:* Schlossar Award, Hall Publishers, Switzerland, 1980; American Poetry Asscn Award, 1988; World of Poetry Award, 1990. *Memberships:* American Asscn of Poets; American Playwrights Asscn. *Address:* 5 Misty Meadow Dr., Irvine, CA 92612, USA.

DIXON, Alan (Michael); b. 15 July 1936, Waterloo, Lancashire, England. Poet. m. Josephine Stapleton, 13 Aug. 1960. *Education:* Studied Art, Goldsmiths College, University of London, 1956–63; University of London Diploma in Visual Arts. *Appointment:* Teacher of Art, Schools in London and Peterborough, England, 1959–87. *Publications:* Snails and Reliquaries, 1964; The Upright Position, 1970; The Egotistical Decline, 1978; The Immaculate Magpies, 1982; The Hogweed Lass, 1991; A Far-Off Sound, 1994; Transports, 1996. *Contributions to:* Poetry; Partisan Review; The Observer; TLS; The Listener; New Statesman; London Review of Books; The Nation; London Magazine; Encounter; The Spectator; Prairie Schooner; The Scotsman. *Address:* 51 Cherry Garden Rd, Eastbourne, BN20 8HG, England.

DIXON, Peter; b. 6 April 1937, London, England. Senior Lecturer in Art and Education; Poet; Radio and TV Writer/Presenter. m. Marion Blades, 8 Aug. 1964, 1 s., 1 d. *Education:* Qualified as a Teacher, 1960. *Appointments:* Teacher, primary and secondary schools, 1960–70; Lecturer in Art and Education, Saffron Walden, 1970–75; Senior Lecturer in Art and Education, King Alfred College, Winchester, 1975–. *Publications:* Grow Your Own Poems, 1988; I Heard a Spider Sobbing, 1989; Big Billy, 1990; Matt, Wes, Pete, 1996; Lost Property Box; Peter Dixon's Grand Prix of Poetry, 1999; Juggler, 2000; Penguin in the Fridge, 2001; The Colour of My Dreams, 2002. *Contributions to:* Times Newspapers; Learning magazine, USA; Parents magazine, UK. *Membership:* National Poetry Society, London. *Address:* 30 Cheriton Rd, Winchester, Hampshire SO22 5AX, England.

DJEBAR, Assia, (Fatima-Zohra Imalayen); b. 4 Aug. 1936, Cherchell, Algeria. Author; Poet; Dramatist; Trans.; Filmmaker; Prof. m. (1) Ahmed Ould-Rouïs, 1958, divorced, (2) Malek Alloula, 1980. *Education:* Lycée Fénélon, Paris, 1954; École Normale Supérieure de Sèvres, France, 1955–56. *Appointments:* Faculty, University of Algiers; Prof. and Dir, Center for French and Francophone Studies, Louisiana State University, 1997–. *Publications:* La soif, 1957, English trans. as The Mischief, 1958; Les impatients, 1958; Women of Islam, 1961; Les enfants du nouveau monde, 1962; Les alouettes naïves, 1967; Poèmes pour l'Algérie heureuse, 1969; Rouge l'aube (with Walid Garn), 1969; La nouba des femmes du Mont Chenoua, 1969; Les femmes d'Alger dans leur appartement, 1980, English trans. as Women of Algiers in Their Apartment, 1992; L'amour, la fantasia, 1985, English trans. as Fantasia: An Algerian Cavalcade, 1993; In ombre sultane, 1987, English trans. as Far from Medina, 1994; Chronique d'un été algérien, 1993; Le blanc de l'Algérie, 1995, English trans. as Algerian White, 2001; Vaste est la prison, 1995, English trans. as So Vast the Prison, 1999; Oran, langue morte, 1997; Les nuits de Strasbourg, 1997; Ces voix qui m'assiègent, 1999. Other: Films: La nouba des femmes du Mont Chenoua, 1979; La zerda ou les chants d'oubli, 1982. *Honours:* International Critics' Prize, Venice Film Festival, 1979; Prix Maurice Maeterlinck, 1995; Neustadt International Prize for Literature, 1996; Yourcenar Prize, 1997; Friedenspreis des Deutschen Buchhandels, 2000. *Address:* c/o Center for French and Francophone Studies, Louisiana State University, Baton Rouge, LA 70803, USA.

DJERASSI, Carl; b. 29 Oct. 1923, Vienna, Austria. Prof. of Chemistry; Author; Playwright. m. Diane Wood Middlebrook, 20 June 1985, 1 s. *Education:* AB summa cum laude, Kenyon College, 1942; PhD, University of Wisconsin, 1945. *Appointments:* Assoc. Prof., 1952–53, Prof. of Chemistry, 1953–59, Wayne State University; Prof. of Chemistry, Stanford University, 1959–. *Publications:*

Optical Rotatory Dispersion, 1959; Steroid Reactions, 1963; Mass Spectrometry of Organic Compounds (with H Budzikiewicz and D H Williams), 1967; The Politics of Contraception, 1979; The Futurist and Other Stories, 1988; Cantor's Dilemma (novel), 1989; Steroids Made It Possible, 1990; The Clock Runs Backward (poems), 1991; The Pill, Pygmy Chimps, and Degas' Horse (autobiography), 1992; The Bourbaki Gambit (novel), 1994; From the Lab into the World (collected essays), 1994; Marx, Deceased (novel), 1996; Menachem's Seed (novel), 1997; NO (novel), 1998; This Man's Pill (memoir), 2001; Unpublished Plays: An Immaculate Misconception, 1998; Oxygen (with Roald Hoffmann), 2000. *Contributions to:* Kenyon Review; Southern Review; Grand Street; New Letters; Exquisite Corpse; Michigan Quarterly Review; South Dakota Review; Frank; Midwest Quarterly. *Honours:* National Medal of Science, 1973; National Medal of Technology, 1991. *Memberships:* National Acad. of Sciences; American Acad. of Arts and Sciences; Swedish, German, Brazilian and Mexican Academies of Science; Royal Society of Chemistry. *Address:* Dept of Chemistry, Stanford University, Stanford, CA 94305-5080, USA. *Website:* www.djerassi.com.

DJURDJEVICH, Milos; b. 2 Aug. 1961, Rab, Yugoslavia. Critic; Ed.; Trans.; Poet. *Education:* BA, Philosophy and Comparative Literature, 1991, MA, Literature, 1997, University of Zagreb. *Appointments:* Literary Critic, Radio 101, Radio Zagreb; Literary Critic and Trans., Croatian Radio; Poetry Ed., Vijenac magazine. *Publications:* Landscapes or Circling for Words, 1989; In the Mirror, 1994; Harvest, 1997. *Contributions to:* Journals, reviews and periodicals. *Memberships:* Croatian Asscn of Writers; International PEN. *Address:* 1 Ferenscica 27, 10000 Zagreb, Croatia.

DOANE, Myrtle Caroline; b. 19 May 1914, Lynn, Massachusetts, USA. Schoolteacher (retd); Writer; Poet. m. Alfred M Doane, 6 Nov. 1959, 1 step-s., 2 d., 1 adopted. *Education:* Bachelor of General Studies, University of New Hampshire, Durham, 1975. *Publications:* Lyrical Echoes of Freedom, 1961; Sounds of Maine, 1970; Think Ecology with Haiku, 1972; Sounds of Arkansas, 1978; Sounds of Heaven, 1978; Sounds of Liberty, 1979; Sounds of New Hampshire, 1980; Treasures of Laughter, 1983; Sounds of Bethlehem, 1988; My Father's World, 1990. *Contributions to:* Anthologies, magazines and periodicals. *Honours:* Poetry on Trees Awards, State of Maine Writers Conference, 1960–90; George Washington Medals for Poetry, Freedoms Foundation, Valley Forge, Pennsylvania, 1961, 1972; Arkansas Poetry Day Contest, 1988. *Memberships:* Various poetry societies. *Address:* PO Box 567, Bethlehem, NH 03574, USA.

DOBAI, Péter; b. 12 Aug. 1944, Budapest, Hungary. Author; Poet; Screenwriter. m. (1) Donatella Failioni, 1972, (2) Maria Mate, 1992. *Education:* Teacher's Diploma, University of Budapest, 1970. *Publications:* Fiction: Csontmolnárok, 1974; Tartozó élet, 1975; Lavina, 1980; Vadon, 1982; Háromszögtan, 1983; A birodalom ezredese, 1985; Iv, 1988; Lendkerék, 1989. Short Stories: Játék a szobákkal, 1976; Sakktábla két figurával, 1978. Poetry: Kilovaglás egy öszi erödböl, 1973; Egy arc módosulásai, 1976; Hanyatt, 1978; Az éden vermei, 1985 Válogatott versek, 1989; Vitorlák emléke, 1994; Onmultszád, 1996. Other: 15 screenplays, 1971–95. *Honours:* József Attila Prize, 1976; Several Awards, Hungarian Literary Foundation and Minister of Culture; Various screenplay awards. *Memberships:* Hungarian Acad. of Artists; Hungarian Writers' Asscn, Exec. Board; PEN Club, Hungary. *Address:* Közraktár u 12/B, 1093 Budapest, Hungary.

DOBSON, Rosemary (de Brissac); b. 18 June 1920, Sydney, NSW, Australia. Poet; Ed. m. A T Bolton, 1951, 2 s., 1 d. *Education:* Frensham, Mittagong, NSW. *Publications:* In a Convex Mirror, 1944; The Ship of Ice & Other Poems, 1948; Child with a Cockatoo and Other Poems, 1955; Poems, 1963; Cock Crow, 1965; Songs for all Seasons, 1968; Focus on Ray Crooke, 1972; Selected Poems, 1973; Greek Coins: A Sequence of Poems, 1977; Australian Voices, 1978; Over the Frontier, 1978; The Three Fates and Other Poems, 1984; Collected Poems, 1991; Untold Lives: A Sequence of Poems, 1992. *Honours:* Patrick White Award, 1984; Officer, Order of Australia, 1987; Hon. DLitt, Sydney University, 1996; Emeritus Award, Literature Fund of the Australia Council, 1996. *Address:* 61 Stonehaven Crescent, Deakin, Canberra, ACT 2600, Australia.

DOBYNS, Stephen; b. 19 Feb. 1941, Orange, New Jersey, USA. Prof. of Creative Writing; Poet; Writer. m., 3 c. *Education:* Shimer College, Mount Carroll, IL, 1959–60; BA, Wayne State University, 1964; MFA, University of Iowa, 1967. *Appointments:* Instructor, State University of New York College at Brockport, 1968–69; Reporter, Detroit News, 1969–71; Visiting Writer, University of New Hampshire, 1973–75, University of Iowa, 1977–79, Boston University, 1978–79, 1980–81, Syracuse University, 1986; Faculty, Goddard College, Plainfield, Vermont, 1978–80, Warren Wilson College, Swannanoa, North Carolina, 1982–87; Prof. of Creative Writing, Syracuse University, New York, 1987–. *Publications:* Poetry: Concurring Beasts, 1972; Griffon, 1976; Heat Death, 1980; The Balthus Poems, 1982; Black Dog, Red Dog, 1984; Cemetery Nights, 1987; Body Traffic, 1991; Velocities: New and Selected Poems, 1966–1992, 1994; Common Carnage, 1996; Pallbearers Envying the One Who Rides, 1999. Fiction: A Man of Little Evils, 1973; Saratoga Longshot, 1976; Saratoga Swimmer, 1981; Dancer with One Leg, 1983; Saratoga Headhunter, 1985; Cold Dog Soup, 1985; Saratoga Snapper, 1986; A Boat Off the Coast, 1987; The Two Deaths of Señora Puccini, 1988; Saratoga Bestiary, 1988; The

House of Alexandrine, 1989; Saratoga Hexameter, 1990; After Shocks/Near Escapes, 1991; Saratoga Haunting, 1993; The Wrestler's Cruel Study, 1993; Saratoga Backtalk, 1994; Saratoga Fleshpot, 1995; Saratoga Trifecta, 1995; The Church of Dead Girls, 1997; Saratoga Strongbox, 1998; Boy in the Water, 1999; Eating Naked, 2000. *Honours:* Lamont Poetry Selection Award, 1971; MacDowell Colony Fellowships, 1972, 1976; Yaddo Fellowships, 1972, 1973, 1977, 1981, 1982; National Endowment for the Arts Grants, 1974, 1981; Guggenheim Fellowship, 1983; National Poetry Series Prize, 1984. *Address:* 208 Brattle Rd, Syracuse, NY 13203, USA.

DOCHERTY, Brian; b. 19 Aug. 1953, Glasgow, Scotland. Lecturer in English and American Literature, Poet. m. Rosemary Docherty, 4 Aug. 1984. *Education:* BA, Humanities, Middlesex Polytechnic; MA, American Poetry, University of Essex; PGCE, London University Institute of Education. *Appointment:* Part-time Tutor in Literature, Birkbeck College of Extra-Mural Studies. *Publications:* Suspended Sentence and Other Poems, 1998; Armchair Theatre, 1999. *Contributions to:* ABSA Annual Report, 1990; Smith's Knoll; Echo Room; Foolscap; Verse; Gairfish; Poetry Ireland Review. *Membership:* Poetry Society. *Address:* 10A Dickenson Rd, London N8 9ET, England.

DODD, Wayne (Donald); b. 23 Sept. 1930, Clarita, OK, USA. Poet; Writer; Ed.; Prof. Emeritus. m. (1) Betty Coshow, 7 June 1958, divorced 12 Nov. 1980, (2) Joyce Barlow, 27 June 1981, 2 c. *Education:* BA, 1955, MA, 1957, PhD, 1963, University of Oklahoma. *Appointments:* Instructor, 1960–64, Asst Prof. of English, 1964–68, University of Colorado at Boulder; Fellow, Center for Advanced Studies, Wesleyan University, 1964; Assoc. Prof., 1968–73, Prof. of English, 1973–94, Edwin and Ruth Kennedy Distinguished Prof. of Poetry, 1994–2001, Prof. Emeritus, 2001–, Ohio University; Ed., Ohio Review, 1971–2001. *Publications:* Poetry: We Will Wear White Roses, 1974; Made in America, 1975; The Names You Gave It, 1980; The General Mule Poems, 1981; Sometimes Music Rises, 1986; Echoes of the Unspoken, 1990; Of Desire and Disorder, 1994; The Blue Salvages, 1998. Fiction: A Time of Hunting, 1975. Other: Poets on the Line (ed.), 1987; Toward the End of the Century: Essays into Poetry, 1992; Art and Nature: Essays by Contemporary Writers (ed.), 1993; Mentors (ed.), 1994. *Contributions to:* Anthologies, reviews, quarterlies and journals. *Honours:* ACLS Fellowship, 1964–65; Ohio Arts Council Fellowship, 1980, 1989, 1998; National Endowment for the Arts Fellowship in Poetry, 1982; Krout Award for Lifetime Achievement in Poetry, Ohioana Library Foundation, 1991; Rockefeller Foundation Achievement in Poetry, Ohioana Library Foundation, 1991; Rockefeller Foundation Fellowship, 1995; Ohio Gov.'s Award for the Arts, 2001. *Membership:* Associated Writing Programs. *Address:* 11292 Peach Ridge Rd, Athens, OH 45701, USA.

DOHERTY, Berlie; b. 6 Nov. 1943, Liverpool, England. Writer; Dramatist; Poet. m. Gerard Doherty, 17 Dec. 1966, divorced 1996, 1 s., 2 d. *Education:* BA, Honours, English, Durham University, 1964; Postgraduate Certificate, Social Studies, Liverpool University, 1965; Postgraduate Certificate, Education, Sheffield University, 1976. *Publications:* Fiction: Requiem, 1991; The Vinegar Jar, 1994. Children's Books: How Green You Are, 1982; The Making of Fingers Finnigan, 1983; White Peak Farm, 1984; Children of Winter, 1985; Granny Was a Buffer Girl, 1986; Tilly Mint Tales, 1986; Tilly Mint and the Dodo, 1988; Paddiwak and Cosy, 1988; Tough Luck, 1988; Spellhorn, 1989; Dear Nobody, 1990; Snowy, 1992; Big, Bulgy, Fat Black Slug, 1993; Old Father Christmas, 1993; Street Child, 1993; Walking on Air (poems), 1993; Willa and Old Miss Annie, 1994; The Snake-Stone, 1995; The Golden Bird, 1995; Dear Nobody (play), 1995; The Magical Bicycle, 1995; Our Field, 1996; Morgan's Field (play), 1996; Daughter of the Sea, 1996. *Contributions to:* Periodicals. *Honours:* Boston Globe-Horn Book Award, 1987; Burnley Children's Book of the Year Award, 1987; Carnegie Medals, 1987, 1991; Writer's Guild of Great Britain Children's Play Award, 1994. *Membership:* Arvon Foundation, Lumb Bank, chair., 1988–93. *Address:* 222 Old Brompton Rd, London, England.

DOLIS, John; b. 25 April 1945, St Louis, Missouri, USA. Prof.; Writer; Poet. *Education:* BA, English, St Louis University, 1967; MA, English, 1969; PhD, English, 1978, Loyola University, Chicago. *Appointments:* Teaching Asst, 1967–69, 1970–73, Lecturer, 1974–75, 1978–80, Loyola University, Chicago; Instructor, Columbia College, 1970–71, Northeastern Illinois University, 1978–80, University of Kansas, 1981–85; Fulbright Lecturer, University of Turin, 1980–81; Asst Prof., 1985–92, Assoc. Prof., 1992–, Pennsylvania State University, Scranton; Senior Fulbright Lecturer, University of Bucharest, 1989–90; Visiting Prof. of American Culture and Literature, Bilkent University, Ankara, 1995–96. *Publications:* The Style of Hawthorne's Gaze: Regarding Subjectivity, 1993; Bl( )nk Space, 1993; Time Flies: Butterflies, 1999. *Contributions to:* Articles in scholarly journals; Poems in anthologies and magazines. *Honours:* National Endowment for the Humanities Fellowships, 1979–88; Pharmakon Research International Award for Excellence in Scholarly Activities, Pennsylvania State University, 1991; Various grants. *Memberships:* American Culture Asscn; American Literature Asscn; American Philosophical Asscn; Asscn for Applied Psychoanalysis; International Asscn for Philosophy and Literature; International Husserl and Phenomenological Research Society; International Society for Phenomenology and the Human Sciences; International Society for Phemomenology and Literature; MLA; Nathaniel Hawthorne Society; National Social Science Asscn; Society for the Advancement of American Philosophy; Society for Phenomenology and

Existential Philosophy; Society for Philosophy and Psychiatry; Society for Romanian Studies; Thoreau Society; World Phenomenology Institute. *Address:* 711 Summit Pointe, Scranton, PA 18508, USA.

DONOVAN, Katie Susan; b. 20 June 1962, Dublin, Ireland. Journalist; Writer; Poet. *Education:* BA, Trinity College, Dublin, 1984; MA, University of California at Berkeley, 1986. *Appointments:* Teacher of English, Rakocsi Gimnazium, Sarospatak, Hungary, 1987–88; Teacher of Creative Writing and Literature, Bray Adult Education Centre, Ireland, 1988–90; Journalist, The Irish Times, 1990–. *Publications:* Watermelon Man, 1993; Ireland's Women: Writings Past and Present (ed. with Brendan Kennelly and A Norman Jeffares), 1994; Entering the Mare, 1997; Day of the Dead, 2002. *Contributions to:* The Southern Review; Seneca Review; Verse; Poetry Ireland Review; Cyphers; The Irish Times; Force 10; The Independent; Readings on BBC Radio 4, BBC Radio 3, RTE Radio 1. *Membership:* Irish Writers' Union. *Address:* An Tigh Thuas, Torca Rd, Dalkey, Co Dublin, Ireland.

DOOLEY, Maura; b. 18 May 1957, Cornwall, England. Arts Administrator; Poet. *Education:* University of York, 1975–78; University of Bristol, 1980–81. *Appointments:* Centre Dir, Arvon Foundation, 1982–87; Head of Literature, Royal Festival Hall, 1987–93; Dir of UK Year of Literature, 1993; Freelance Literature Consultant, 1994–; Script Consultant Jim Henson Films, 1997–2000; Advisory Dir to Performing Arts Labs (New Theatre for Young Audiences), 1994–; Convenor of MA in Creative Writing at Goldsmiths College, University of London, 2000–. *Publications:* Ivy Leaves and Arrows; Turbulence; Explaining Magnetism; Kissing a Bone; Sound Barrier; How Novelists Work (ed.); Making for Planet Alice (ed.); The Honey Gatherers: Love Poems (ed.). *Contributions to:* Poetry Review; Observer; Critical Quarterly; North; Southern Review; Independent. *Honours:* Major Eric Gregory Award; short-listed for T. S. Eliot Award, Forward Prize; Poetry Book Society Recommendation. *Memberships:* Arvon Foundation; Poetry Books Society; Southern Arts Literature Panel; PEN; London Arts Board. *Address:* c/o Bloodaxe Books, PO Box 1SN, Newcastle upon Tyne NE99 1SN, England.

DOORTY, John; b. 7 Feb. 1959, County Clare, Ireland. Teacher; Ed.; Poet. *Education:* BA, Higher Diploma in Education, 1981, National University of Ireland; Postgraduate Diploma in Computing, University of Limerick, 1989. *Appointments:* Teacher of Creative Writing and Complementary Studies, Co Act College of Art, Commerce and Technology, Limerick, 1983–90; Co-ordinator, Ennistymon 84 Visual Arts Project, 1984; Founder-Ed., Departures literary journal, 1987–95; Teacher of English Language, Valencia, Spain, 1990–96. *Publication:* Into the Heart of It: Daley Dialogues and Other Poems, 1997. *Contributions to:* Bellingham Review; Flaming Arrows; Dal of Cais; Departures; North-Clare Writers Workshop Collection; Visions International; Café Review. *Honour:* Third Prize, Ripost Reader's Choice, 1997. *Membership:* Writers Union. *Address:* Carrowkeal, Kilshanny, County Clare, Ireland.

DOR, Moshe; b. 9 Dec. 1932, Tel-Aviv, Palestine. Poet; Journalist; Ed. m. Ziona Dor, 29 March 1955, 2 s. *Education:* Hebrew University of Jerusalem, 1949–52; BA, Political Science, University of Tel-Aviv, 1956. *Appointments:* Counsellor for Cultural Affairs, Embassy of Israel, London, England, 1975–77; Distinguished Writer-In-Residence, American University, Washington, DC, 1987. *Publications:* From the Outset, 1984; On Top of the Cliff (in Hebrew), 1986; Crossing the River, 1989; From the Outset (selected poems in Dutch trans.), 1989; Crossing the River (selected poems in English trans.), 1989; Love and Other Calamities (poems in Hebrew), 1993; Khamsin (memoirs and poetry in English trans.), 1994; The Silence of the Builder (poems in Hebrew), 1996; Co-ed., English anthologies of Israeli Hebrew poetry: The Burning Bush, 1977; The Stones Remember, 1991; After the First Rain, 1997. Other books of poetry, children's verse, literary essays, interviews with writers, trans of poetry and literature from English into Hebrew. *Honours:* Honourable Citation, International Hans Christian Andersen Prize for Children's Literature, 1975; Holon Prize for Literature, 1981; Prime Minister's Award for Creative Writing, 1986; Bialik Prize for Literature, 1987. *Memberships:* Asscn of Hebrew Writers, Israel; National Federation of Israel Journalists; Israel Pen Centre, pres., 1988–90. *Address:* 6623 Fairfax Rd, Chevy Chase, Maryland 20815, USA.

DORCAS. See: WILDHAGEN, Dorothy Mabel.

DORESKI, William; b. 10 Jan. 1946, Stafford, CT, USA. Prof. of English; Writer; Poet. m. Carole Doreski, 17 June 1981. *Education:* BA, 1975, MA, 1977, Goddard College; PhD, Boston University, 1983; Postdoctoral Studies, Princeton University, 1987, Dartmouth College, 1994. *Appointments:* Writer-in-Residence, Emerson College, 1973–75; Instructor in Humanities, Goddard College, 1975–80; Asst Prof., 1982–87, Assoc. Prof., 1988–91, Prof. of English, 1992–, Keene State College, New Hampshire. *Publications:* The Testament of Israel Potter, 1976; Half of the Map, 1980; Earth That Sings: The Poetry of Andrew Glaze, 1985; How to Read and Interpret Poetry, 1988; The Years of Our Friendship: Robert Lowell and Allen Tate, 1990 Ghost Train, 1991; The Modern Voice in American Poetry, 1995; Sublime of the North and Other Poems, 1997; Pianos in the Woods, 1998; Shifting Colors: The Public and the Private in the Poetry of Robert Lowell, 1999. *Contributions to:* Books, journals, reviews, quarterlies, and magazines. *Honours:* Poet Lore Trans. Prize, 1975; Black Warrior Prize, 1979; National Endowment for the Humanities Grants, 1987,

1995; Whiting Foundation Fellowship, 1988; Clay Potato Fiction Prize, 1997 Frith Press Poetry Award, 1997. *Memberships:* American Studies Asscn Associated Writing Programs; Asscn of Scholars and Critics; MLA; New Hampshire Writers' Project; Robert Frost Society; Wallace Stevens Society *Address:* c/o Dept of English, Keene State College, Keene, NH 03435, USA.

DORET, Michel; b. 5 Jan. 1938, Petion-Ville, Haiti. Architect; Artist; Writer Poet. m. Liselotte Bencze, 30 Nov. 1970. *Education:* BA, Pace University, 1970 MA, New York University, 1972; BS, State University of New York, 1978 MPhil, 1980, PhD, 1982, George Washington University. *Appointments* Founder and Dir, Les Editions Amon Ra, 1982–97. *Publications:* Isolement 1979; La Poésie francophone, 8 vols, 1980; Panorama de la poésie feminine Suisse Romande, 1982; Panorama de la poésie feminine francophone, 1984; La negritude dans la poésie haitienne, 1985; Poétesses Genevoises francophones 1985; Haiti en Poésie, 1990; Les Mamelles de Lutèce, 1991; Lyrisme du Moi 1992; The History of the Architecture of Ayiti, 2 vols, 1995. *Contributions to* Numerous books, journals, reviews and other publications. *Honours:* Variou medals, diplomas, and honorable mentions. *Memberships:* Several literary organizations. *Address:* 26 Mellow Lane, Westbury, NY 11590, USA. *E-mai* mdor26@aol.com. *Website:* www.michelddoret.org.

DORFMAN, Ariel; b. 6 May 1942, Buenos Aires, Argentina (Naturalized Chilean citizen). Research Prof. of Literature and Latin; Author; Dramatist Poet. *Education:* Graduated, University of Chile, Santiago, 1967. *Appointment* Walter Hines Page Research Prof. of Literature and Latin, Center fo International Studies, Duke University, Durham, North Carolina, 1984– *Publications:* Fiction: Hard Rain, 1973; My House is On Fire, 1979; Widows 1983; Dorando la pildora, 1985; Travesia, 1986; The Last Song of Manuel Sendero, 1986; Mascara, 1988; Konfidenz, 1996; Blake's Therapy, 2001; The Rabbit's Rebellion, 2001. Poetry: Last Waltz in Santiago and Other Poems o Exile and Disappearance, 1988. Plays: Widows, 1988; Death and the Maiden 1991; Reader, 1992; Who's Who (with Rodrigo Dorfman), 1997. Films: Death and the Maiden, 1994; Prisoners in Time, 1995; My House is on Fire, 1997; In Case of Fire in a Foreign Land, 2002. Non-Fiction: How to Read Donald Duck (with Armand Mattelart), 1971; The Empire's Old Clothes, 1983; Some Write to the Future, 1991; Heading South, Looking North: A Bilingual Journey, 1998 Exorcising Terror: The Incredible Ongoing Trial of General Augusto Pinochet 2002. *Honours:* Olivier Award, London 1991; Time Out Award, 1991; Literary Lion, New York Public Library, 1992; Dora Award, 1994; Charity Randal Citation, International Poetry Forum, 1994; Best Film for Television, Writers Guild of Great Britain, 1996; Fellow, American Acad. of Arts and Sciences 2001; ALDA Prize, Denmark, 2002. *Address:* c/o Center for International Studies, Duke University, PO Box 90404, Durham, NC 27708, USA.

DORN, Alfred; b. 9 Dec. 1929, New York, NY, USA. Prof. (retd); Poet. m. Anita Lorenz, 11 Sept. 1971. *Education:* BS, cum laude, 1953, MA, 1956, PhD, 1966 New York University. *Appointments:* Graduate Asst, New York University 1956–60; English Instructor, Rider College, 1963–64; Queensborough Community College, City University of New York, 1966–91. *Publications:* A Formalist Quartet, 1991; From Cells to Mindspace, 1997; Voices from Rooms 1997. *Contributions to:* Amelia; Blue Unicorn; Edge City Review; Ekphrasis Formalist; Hellas; Hudson Review; Light; Sparrow; Writer's Digest; Nassau Review; American Poets and Poetry; Poetry Digest; Wings. *Honours:* Travelling Fellowship, 1966, First Prize, National Awards, 1979, Poetry Society of America; Third Prize, National Federation of State Poetry Societies, 1987 First Prize, 1998, Third Prize, 1999, Newburyport Art Asscn Contest *Memberships:* Poetry Society of America, 1958–, governing board, 1963–66 vice-pres., 1969–70, 1971–72; World Order of Narrative and Formalist Poets dir, 1980–. *Address:* PO Box 580174, Station A, Flushing, NY 11358, USA.

DORN, Ed(ward Merton); b. 2 April 1929, Villa Grove, IL, USA. Poet; Writer Trans.; Anthropologist; Ethnologist; Prof. m. Jennifer Dunbar, 1969 *Education:* University of Illinois at Urbana-Champaign, 1949–50; BA, Black Mountain College, 1954. *Appointments:* Lecturer, Idaho State University Pocatello, 1961–65; Co-Ed., Wild Dog, Pocatello, 1964–65; Visiting Prof. University of Kansas, Lawrence, 1968–69; Fulbright Lecturer in American Literature, Mem., English Dept, 1969–70, 1974–75, University of Essex Colchester, England; Regent's Lecturer, University of California at Riverside 1973–74; Writer-in-Residence, University of California at San Diego, La Jolla 1976; Prof., University of Colorado at Boulder, 1977–. *Publications:* Poetry: The Newly Fallen, 1961; Hands Up!, 1964; From Gloucester Out, 1964; Idaho Out 1965; Geography, 1965; The North Atlantic Turbine, 1967; Gunslinger I, 1968 II, 1969; The Midwest Is That Space Between the Buffalo Statler and the Lawrence Eldridge, 1969; The Cosmology of Finding Your Spot, 1969; Twenty-Four Love Songs, 1969; Songs: Set Two, A Short Count, 1970; Spectrum Breakdown: A Microbook, 1971; By the Sound, 1971; The Cycle, 1971; A Poem Called Alexander Hamilton, 1971; The Hamadyas Baboon at the Lincoln Park Zoo, 1972; Gunslinger, Book III: The Winterbook, Prologue to the Great Book IV Kornerstone, 1972; Recollections of Gran Apacheria, 1974 Manchester Square (with Jennifer Dunbar), 1975; Collected Poems: 1956–1974 1975; Hello, La Jolla, 1978; Selected Poems, 1978; Abhorrences, 1989. Fiction Some Business Recently Transacted in the White World (short stories), 1971 Non-Fiction: What I See in the Maximum Poems, 1960; Prose 1 (with Michael Rumaker and Warren Tallamn), 1964; The Rites of Passage: A Brief History,

1965; The Shoshoneans: The People of the Basin-Plateau, 1966; Way West: Essays and Verse Accounts 1963–1993, 1993. Translations: Our Word: Guerilla Poems From Latin America (with Gordon Brotherston), 1968; Tree Between Two Walls (with Gordon Brotherston), 1969; Selected Poems of Cesar Vallejo, 1976. Honour: D. H. Lawrence Fellow, 1969. Address: 1035 Mapleton, Boulder, CO 80302, USA.

DORSEY, John Victor; b. 27 Nov. 1976, Honolulu, HI, USA. Poet; Ed. Education: Westmoreland County Community College. Appointments: Ed., Traditionalist Poetry Review, 1994–95, Heaven Train, 1996–. Publications: When It's Over and Other Poems, 1995; The Ghost of Helen Keller, 2000. Contributions to: MOON Magazine; Poet's Fantasy; Stretchmarks; Report to Hell; Twisted Nipples; Lines 'N' Rhymes; The Laureate Letter. Honour: Ed.'s Choice Award Winner, National Library of Poetry, 1994. Address: Rd 1, Box 858, Greensburg, PA 15601, USA.

DOSAL, Carmen; b. 10 Oct. 1928, Santander, Spain. Painter; Art Journalist; Poet. Education: Diploma, Museo Arte Moderno, Barcelona. Publications: Paloma Rosa del amor (poems), 1973–82; Mareas, 1983; Viajero del Viento, 1991. Contributions to: Anthologies and journals. Honours: Diploma of Honour, Palme d'Or des Beaux Arts, Monte Carlo; Hon. DLitt, World Acad. of Arts and Culture; Academician of Merit with Silver Palm, Accademia Internazionale di Pontzen, Italy, 1992. Memberships: Accademia Internazionale di Pontzen, Italy; Asociacion de Poesiam, Madrid; Instituto Literario y Cultural Hispanico; World Acad. of Arts and Culture.

DOTY, Mark; b. 10 Aug. 1953, Maryville, Tennessee, USA. Writer; Poet; Prof. Education: BA, Drake University, 1978; MFA, Goddard College, 1980. Appointments: Faculty, MFA Writing Program, Vermont College, 1981–94; Writing and Literature, Goddard College, 1985–90; Guest Faculty, Sarah Lawrence College, 1990–94, 1996; Fannie Hurst Visiting Prof., Brandeis University, 1994; Visiting Faculty, University of Iowa, 1995, 1996; Columbia University, 1996; Prof., Creative Writing Program, University of Utah, 1997–. Publications: Turtle, Swan, 1987; Bethlehem in Broad Daylight, 1991; My Alexandria, 1993; Atlantis, 1995; Heaven's Coast (memoir), 1996; Firebird (memoir), 1999; Source, 2001. Contributions to: Many anthologies and journals. Honours: Theodore Roethke Prize, 1986; National Endowment for the Arts Fellowships in Poetry, 1987, 1995; Pushcart Prizes, 1987, 1989; Los Angeles Times Book Prize, 1993; Ingram Merrill Foundation Award, 1994; National Book Critics Circle Award, 1994; Guggenheim Fellowship, 1994; Whiting Writers Award, 1994; Rockefeller Foundation Fellowship, Bellagio, Italy, 1995; New York Times Notable Book of the Year, citations, 1995, 1996; American Library Asscn Notable Book of the Year, 1995; T S Eliot Prize, 1996; Bingham Poetry Prize, 1996; Ambassador Book Award, 1996; Lambda Literary Award, 1996. Address: c/o Creative Writing Program, University of Utah, Salt Lake City, UT 84112, USA.

DOUGLAS, George William; b. 9 May 1952, Corbridge, Northumberland, England. Local Government Officer; Poet. Contributions to: Anthologies and journals. Honour: Hon. Mem., World Parnassians Guild International, 1995. Membership: Friends of the Dymock Poets, Herefordshire, England. Address: 14 Barnes Rd, Farncombe, Godalming, Surrey GU7 3RG, England.

DOVE, Rita (Frances); b. 28 Aug. 1952, Akron, Ohio, USA. Poet; Writer; Prof. m. Fred Viebahn, 23 March 1979, 1 d. Education: BA, summa cum laude, Miami University, Oxford, Ohio, 1973; Postgraduate Studies, University of Tübingen, 1974–75; MFA, University of Iowa, 1977. Appointments: Asst Prof., 1981–84, Assoc. Prof., 1984–87, Prof. of English, 1987–89, Arizona State University, Tempe; Writer-in-Residence, Tuskagee Institute, 1982; Assoc. Ed., Callaloo, 1986–; Adviser and Contributing Ed., Gettysburg Review, 1987–, TriQuarterly, 1988–, Georgia Review, 1994, Bellingham Review, 1996–; Prof. of English, 1989–93, Commonwealth Prof., 1993–, University of Virginia; Poet Laureate of the USA, 1993–95; Special Consultant in Poetry, Library of Congress, Washington, DC, 1999. Publications: Poetry: Ten Poems, 1977; The Only Dark Spot in the Sky, 1980; The Yellow House on the Corner, 1980; Mandolin, 1982; Museum, 1983; Thomas and Beulah, 1986; The Other Side of the House, 1988; Grace Notes, 1989; Selected Poems, 1993; Lady Freedom Among Us, 1994; Mother Love, 1995; On the Bus with Rosa Parks, 1999. Other: Fifth Sunday (short stories), 1985; Through the Ivory Gate (novel), 1992; The Darker Face of Earth (verse play), 1994; The Poet's World (essays), 1995. Contributions to: Numerous magazines and journals. Honours: Fulbright Fellow, 1974–75; National Endowment for the Arts Grants, 1978, 1989; Portia Pittman Fellow, Tuskegee Institute, 1982; Guggenheim Fellowship, 1983–84; Peter I B Lavan Younger Poets Award, Acad. of American Poets, 1986; Pulitzer Prize in Poetry, 1987; General Electric Foundation Award for Younger Writers, 1987; Rockefeller Foundation Residency, Bellagio, Italy, 1988; Ohio Governor's Award, 1988; Mellon Fellow, National Humanities Center, 1988–89; Fellow, Center for Advanced Studies, University of Virginia, 1989–92; NAACP Great American Artist Award, 1993; Renaissance Forum Award, Folger Shakespeare Library, 1994; Charles Frankel Prize, 1996; National Medal in the Humanities, 1996; Heinz Award in the Arts and Humanities, 1996; Sara Lee Frontrunner Award, 1997; Barnes and Noble Writers Award, 1997; Levinson Prize, 1998; Ohioana Library Book Award, 2000; Literary Lion, New York Public Library, 2000; Many hon. doctorates.

Memberships: Acad. of American Poets; Associated Writing Programs; Poetry Society of America; Poets and Writers. Address: Dept of English, PO Box 400121Bryan Hall, University of Virginia, Charlottesville, VA 22904-4121, USA.

DOVRING, Karin Elsa Ingeborg; b. 5 Dec. 1919, Stenstorp, Sweden (Naturalized US citizen, 1968). Writer; Poet; Dramatist. m. Folke Dovring, 30 May 1943. Education: Graduated, College of Commerce, Göteborg, 1936; MA, 1943, PhD, 1951, Lund University; PhilLic, Göteborg University, 1947. Appointments: Journalist, 1940–60; Research Assoc., Harold D Lasswell, Yale University, 1953–78, University of Illinois at Urbana-Champaign, 1968–69; Visiting Lecturer, many universities and colleges. Publications: Songs of Zion, 1951; Road of Propaganda, 1959; Land Reform as a Propaganda Theme, third edn, 1965; Optional Society, 1972; Frontiers of Communication, 1975; No Parking This Side of Heaven (short stories), 1982; Harold D Lasswell: His Communication with a Future, 1987; Heart in Escrow (novel), 1990; Faces in a Mirror (poems), 1995; Shadows on a Screen (poems), 1996; Whispers on a Stage (poems), 1996; English as Lingua Franca, 1997; Changing Scenery (poems), 2002; In the Service of Persuasion: English as Lingua Franca across the Globe, 2001. Other: Film and television plays. Contributions to: Anthologies and professional journals. Honour: International Poetry Hall of Fame, 1996; Hon. Lifetime Mem., Société Jean Jacques Rousseau, Geneva, 1997; Nominated Poet of the Year, 2000, 2001. Membership: International Society of Poets, USA. Address: 613 W Vermont Ave, Urbana, IL 61801, USA.

DOWDEN, Kaviraj George (Duncan Jr); b. 15 Sept. 1932, USA. Poet; Writer. m. (1) Pauline Chatterton, 11 June 1965, divorced 1971, (2) Nancy Roncati, 11 Oct. 1995. Education: BA, Bucknell University, 1957; MA, New York University, 1960. Appointments: Graduate Asst, New York University, 1959; English Teacher, Brooklyn College, 1960–63, 1966–67. Publications: Flight from America, 1965; Renew Jerusalem, 1969; Earth Incantations-Body Chants, 1976; A Message to Isis, 1977; from the stone through you, and White Faces, 1978; The Moving I, 1987; Great Love Desiderata, 1988; Flowers of Consciousness, 1991; The Deepening, 1994; Behold: Woman!, 1997; Being Somewhere Saying Something, 1999; The Eternities of Shiva, 2000. Contributions to: Anthologies and magazines. Address: Top Flat, 82 Marine Parade, Brighton, East Sussex BN2 1AJ, England.

DOWNEY, Martin M., (A. A. Martin, Andy Martin); b. 1958, Melbourne, Vic., Australia. Insurance Assessor; Poet. 2 s., 1 d. Education: Intermediate Degree, St Joseph's Technical College, 1974; Technical Degree, Mastery of Metalwork, Brunswick Technical College, 1978. Publications: Going Down Swinging, 1996; Poetry on Paper, 1997; Sidewalk, 1998; Homebrew, 1998; Core, 1998; Ampersand, 1998. Other: Many recitals. Contributions to: Anthologies, including: Scribe's Corner; Redlamp; Vernacular; Centoria; Micropress Oz; Four W; Mod-Piece; The Mozzie; Illness; A Journal of Personal Experience; Micropress New Zealand; Poam; Famous Reporter; Why See This; Wetkiss; Pigeon Milk; Periodicals. Honour: Highly Commended, Melbourne Poets National Poetry Competition, 1996. Membership: Melbourne Poets' Union. Address: c/o Arnwater Arts Agency, Unit 1, 23 Wingate Ave, Ascot Vale, Vic. 3032, Australia.

DOWNIE, Mary Alice Dawe (née Hunter); b. 12 Feb. 1934, Alton, IL, USA. Writer. m. John Downie, 27 June 1959, 3 d. Education: BA, English Language and Literature, Trinity College, University of Toronto. Appointment: Book Review Ed., Kingston Whig-Standard, 1973–78. Publications: The Wind Has Wings: Poems from Canada (with Barbara Robertson), 1968; Scared Sarah, 1974; Dragon on Parade, 1974; The Last Ship, 1980; Jenny Greenteeth, 1981; A Proper Acadian (with George Rawlyk), 1982; The Wicked Fairy-Wife, 1983; Alison's Ghost (with John Downie), 1984; Stones and Cones (with Jillian Gilliland), 1984; The New Wind Has Wings: Poems from Canada (with Barbara Robertson), 1984; The Window of Dreams: New Canadian Writing for Children, 1986; The Well-Filled Cupboard (with Barbara Robertson), 1987; How the Devil Got His Cat, 1988; The Buffalo Boy and the Weaver Girl, 1989; Doctor Dwarf and Other Poems for Children, 1990; Cathal the Giant-Killer and the Dun Shaggy Filly, 1991; Written in Stone: A Kingston Reader (with M. A. Thompson), 1993; The Cat Park, 1993; Snow Paws, 1996; Bright Paddles, 1999; Danger in Disguise (with John Downie), 2000. Contributions to: Hornbook Magazine; Pittsburgh Press; Kingston Whig-Standard; Ottawa Citizen; Globe and Mail; United Church Observer; OWL Magazine; Chickadee; Crackers. Memberships: Writers' Union of Canada; PEN. Address: 190 Union St, Kingston, ON K7L 2P6, Canada.

DOYLE, Charles Desmond, (Mike Doyle); b. 18 Oct. 1928, Birmingham, England. Prof. Emeritus of English; Author; Poet. m. (1) Helen Merlyn Lopdell, 1952, deceased, (2) Doran Ross Smithells, 1959, divorced, (3) Rita Jean Brown, 1992, 3 s., 1 d. Education: Diploma of Teaching, 1956, BA, 1957, MA, 1959, University of New Zealand; PhD, University of Auckland, 1968. Appointments: Assoc. Prof., 1968–76, Prof. of English, 1976–93, Prof. Emeritus, 1993–, University of Victoria, BC, Canada. Publications: A Splinter of Glass, 1956; The Night Shift: Poems on Aspects of Love (with others), 1957; Distances, 1963; Messages for Herod, 1965; A Sense of Place, 1965; Quorum-Noah, 1970; Abandoned Sofa, 1971; Earth Meditations, 1971; Earthshot, 1972; Preparing for the Ark, 1973; Pines (with P K Irwin), 1975; Stonedancer, 1976; A Month

Away from Home, 1980; A Steady Hand, 1982; The Urge to Raise Hats, 1989; Separate Fidelities, 1991; Intimate Absences: Selected Poems 1954–1992, 1993; Trout Spawning at the Lardeau River, 1997. Non-Fiction: R. A. K. Mason, 1970; James K Baxter, 1976; William Carlos Williams and the American Poem, 1982; William Carlos Williams: The Critical Heritage (ed.), 1982; The New Reality (co-ed.), 1984; Wallace Stevens: The Critical Heritage (ed.), 1985; After Bennett (co-ed.) 1986; Richard Aldington: A Biography, 1989; Richard Aldington: Reappraisals (ed.), 1990. *Contributions to:* Journals, reviews, and periodicals. *Honours:* UNESCO Creative Arts Fellowship, 1958–59; ACLS Fellowship, 1967–68. *Memberships:* New Canterbury Literary Society; Writers Union of Canada; PEN Canada. *Address:* 641 Oliver St, Victoria, BC V8S 4W2, Canada.

DOYRAN, Turhan; b. 20 June 1926, Ankara, Turkey. Poet; Writer; Photographer. m. Madeleine Ménager, 17 Aug. 1953, 1 d. *Education:* Diploma, University of Ankara, 1948; Ansaldi Acad., Paris, 1950; Institute Hautes Études International, Paris, 1950; Diploma of Filmologie, Sorbonne, Paris, 1957; Photography, Conservatory of Arts and Trades, Paris, 1962. *Publications:* Poetry: The Town Ankara, 1959; Partir, 1962; One Cannot Do Without It, 1962; Le Jour, 1962; Il faut bien, 1962; Comme Autrefois, 1964; The Tree, 1967; Je ne suis pas de Bologne, 1967; The Way, 1975; The Mirror, 1975; The Rain, 1986; RUE, 1998; We Were All Born at the Seaside, 1999. *Contributions to:* Anthologies, periodicals and journals. *Honours:* Prize, Leonardo da Vinci, Rome, 1962; Pale d'Oro Academiche, Rome, 1968; Prize, Comite Européen Arts et Culture, 1985; Artist of the Year, Turkey, 1987. *Address:* 8 rue du Cambodge, 75020 Paris, France.

Dr G. See: GLYNN, Martin Roy.

DRAGSETH, Terje; b. 26 June 1955, Kristiansand, Norway. Writer; Poet. m. Lise Dedenroth, 6 Aug. 1994, 2 d. *Education:* National Film School, Copenhagen, Denmark, 1983–87. *Appointments:* Readings in Festivals. *Publications:* Offerfesten, 1980; Jeg tenker, lik en pike som tar sin kjole av, 1982; Hymner & Hypnoser, 1985; Ennå Allerede, 1987; Nå er alle steder, 1989; Kjaerligheten er som doden, 1991; VAEKST; Den Sovende, 1995; DU, 1996; Den Amerikanske Turisten, 1997. *Contributions to:* Periodicals, journals and magazines. *Membership:* Norwegien Writers Union. *Address:* Setesdalsvn 229, 4618 KR Sand, Norway.

DRAKE, Albert Dee; b. 26 March 1935, Portland, Oregon, USA. Prof. Emeritus of English; Writer; Poet. m. 28 Dec. 1960, divorced 1985, 1 s., 2 d. *Education:* Portland State College, 1956–59; BA, English, 1962, MFA, English, 1966, University of Oregon. *Appointments:* Research Asst, 1965, Teaching Asst, 1965–66, English Dept, University of Oregon; Asst Prof., English, 1966–70, Assoc. Prof., English, 1970–79, Prof., English, 1979–91, Prof. Emeritus, English, 1995, Michigan State University; Dir, Clarion Science Fiction and Fantasy Workshop, 1983, 1988–90. *Publications:* Michigan Signatures (ed.), 1969; 3 Northwest Poets, 1970; Poems, 1972; Assuming the Position, 1972; Riding Bike, 1972; By Breathing In and Out, 1974; Cheap Thrills, 1975; Returning to Oregon, 1975; Roadsalt, 1976; Reaching for the Sun, 1979; Garage, 1980; Homesick, 1988; Hot Rodder, 1993; Flat Out, 1994; Fifties Flashback, 1998. *Contributions to:* Poetry Northwest; Poetry Now; Northwest Review; Shenandoah; South Dakota Review; Arts in Society; Wormwood Review; West Coast Poetry Review; Windsor Review; Midwest Quarterly; Assembling; TransPacific; December. *Honours:* Poetry Prize, St Andrews Review, 1974; National Endowment for the Arts Grants, 1975, 1984; Michigan Council for the Arts Grant, 1981. *Address:* 9727 SE Reedway, Portland, OR 97266, USA.

DRAKE, Barbara (Ann); b. 13 April 1939, Abilene, KS, USA. Prof. of English; Poet; Writer. m. (1) Albert Drake, 28 Dec. 1960, divorced 1985, 1 s., 2 d., (2) William Beckman, 1986. *Education:* BA, 1961, MFA, 1966, University of Oregon. *Appointments:* Instructor, Michigan State University, 1974–83; Prof. of English, Linfield College, 1983–. *Publications:* Poetry: Narcissa Notebook, 1973; Field Poems, 1975; Love at the Egyptian Theatre, 1978; Life in a Gothic Novel, 1981; What We Say to Strangers, 1986; Bees in Wet Weather, 1992; Space before A, 1996. Other: Peace at Heart: An Oregon Country Life (memoir), 1998. *Contributions to:* Many books, anthologies, reviews, quarterlies and journals. *Honours:* Northwest Arts Foundation Grant, 1985; National Endowment for the Arts Fellowship, 1986; Edith Green Distinguished Prof. Award, Linfield College, 1993; Finalist, Oregon Book Award, 1999. *Address:* c/o Linfield College, 900 SE Baker St, mcMinnville, OR 97128, USA.

DREW, Bettina; b. 23 April 1956, New York, NY, USA. Writer; Poet; Teacher. *Education:* BA, Philosophy, University of California, Berkeley, 1977; MA, Creative Writing, City College of New York, 1983; MA, American Studies, Yale University, 1995. *Appointments:* Lecturer in English, College of New York; Lecturer in Humanities, New York University, 1990–93; Part-time Acting Instructor, Yale University, 1995–97. *Publications:* Nelson Algren: A Life on the Wild Side, 1989; The Texas Stories of Nelson Algren (ed.), 1995; Crossing the Expendable Landscape, 1997. *Contributions to:* Boulevard; The Writer; Chicago Tribune; Threepenny Review; Washington Post Book World; Chicago Tribune Book World; Ms; Black American Literature Forum; Michigan Quarterly Review; Poems to various magazines. *Memberships:* PEN American Center; Biography Seminar, New York University. *Literary Agent:*

Theresa Park, Sanford J Greenberg Assocs, 55 Fifth Ave, New York, NY 10003 USA. *Address:* 87 Olive St, New Haven, CT 06511, USA.

DREYER, Inge; b. 12 June 1933, Berlin, Germany. Writer; Poet. *Education:* Abitur, 1951; First State Examination, 1955, Second State Examination, 1959 University College of Education. *Publications:* Achtung Stolperstelle, 1982 Schule mit Dachschaden, 1985; Toenende Stille, 1985; Die Streuner vor Pangkor, 1987. *Contributions to:* Anthologies and journals. *Honours:* Rektorin, 1968; World Poets Award Golden Crown, 1990; Hon. Doctor of Literature, London, 1992; Hon. Prof. of Literature, Paris, 1992; International Cultural Diploma of Honour, 1995. *Memberships:* World Acad. of Arts and Culture; World Poetry Society; Neue Gesellschaft für Literatur. *Address:* Winkler Strasse 4A, 14193 Berlin, Grunewald, Germany.

DRISCOLL, Mary Harris; b. 6 June 1928, Worcester, Massachusetts, USA. Poet. m. Joseph F Driscoll, 21 June 1952, 3 s., 6 d. *Education:* AB, magna cum laude, Smith College, 1949; MA, Romance Languages and Literature, Wellesley College, 1952. *Publications:* In Formal Gardens, 1980; Brief Lightning, 1981. *Contributions to:* Journals and periodicals. *Address:* 206 W Main St, Milbury, MA 01527, USA.

DRIVER, Charles Jonathan, (Jonty); b. 19 Aug. 1939, Cape Town, South Africa. Writer; Poet; Schools Consultant. m. Ann Elizabeth Hoogewerf, 1967, 2 s., 1 d. *Education:* BA, BEd, University of Cape Town, 1958–62; MPhil, Trinity College, Oxford, 1967. *Appointments:* The Master, Wellington College, Crowthorne, Berkshire, 1989–2000; Ed., Conference and Common Room, 1993–2000. *Publications:* Elegy for a Revolutionary, 1968; Send War in Our Time, O Lord, 1970; Death of Fathers, 1972; A Messiah of the Last Days, 1974; I Live Here Now (poems), 1979; Occasional Light (poems, with Jack Cope), 1979; Patrick Duncan (biography), 1980, paperback, 2000; Hong Kong Portraits (poems), 1985; In the Water-Margins (poems), 1994; Holiday Haiku (poems), 1996; Requiem (poems), 1998. *Contributions to:* Numerous magazines and journals. *Honour:* RSA, fellow. *Address:* Apple Yard Cottage, Mill Lane, Northiam, nr Rye, Sussex, TN31 6JU, England.

DROOGENBROODT, Germain; b. 11 Sept. 1944, Belgium. Trans.; Poet; Ed. m. Liliane Leroy, 8 June 1968, 1 s., 1 d. *Education:* Languages, 1967. *Appointments:* Pres., TTI Belgium, 1969–88; Pres., Chief Ed., Point, 1984–. *Publications:* Appearances; Forty at the Wall; Do You Know the Country?, Poems; Waves, What Shall I Do; When The Dark Blue Night Smashes Down. Other: Trans. *Contributions to:* Spectator; Argus; Revolver; Point; Marina D'Art; Trenc D'Alba; Aiguadolc; Kruispunt; Vlaanderen. *Honours:* Literature Award; Poetry Award; Hon. Degree of Doctor of Literature; Hawthornden International Retreat for Writers Fellowship. *Address:* Ithaca, Camino Monte Molar 69, E03590 Altea, Alicante, Spain.

DROR, Shlomo. See: SHEINFELD, Ilan.

DROZDIK, Ladislav; b. 3 March 1930, Nova Bana, Czechoslovakia. Assoc. Prof.; Poet. m. Jarmila Sikova, 21 Sept. 1953, 2 s., 1 d. *Education:* BA, 1953; Dr, 1967; Habilitation thesis, 1979. *Appointments:* Asst Prof., 1953–79; Assoc. Prof., 1979–92; Prof., 1992–. *Publications:* High Shade Celebration; The Close Orbit; Tormenting Passion of the Sun; Selections from the Love Poetry of Nizar Qabbani; Homeless Poems. *Honour:* National Jan Holly Prize. *Memberships:* Slovak Oriental Society; Linguistic Society of America. *Address:* Zahrebska 6, 81105 Bratislava, Czech Republic.

DRURY, Finvola Margaret; b. 7 Aug. 1926, Cleveland, Ohio, USA. Poet; Teacher. m. George Drury, 28 Aug. 1948, 1 s., 1 d. *Education:* BA, State University of New York, 1976; MA, 1984. *Appointments:* Lecturer, Toledo Museum of Art, 1946–48; Visiting Prof., Rochester Institute of Technology, 1990. *Publications:* Casualties of War; Elegy for Joric Ross; Burning the Snow. *Contributions to:* Poetry Magazine; AD; Social Text; 60's Without Apology; Conservatory of American Letters Anthology; New Rivers Irish American Anthology. *Memberships:* Miles Modern Poetry Committee; Writers and Books Literary Center. *Address:* RR 1 Box 96A, Brooksville, ME 04617, USA.

DU PLESSIS, Nancy Ellen; b. 20 Aug. 1954, Hartford, CT, USA. Writer; Poet; Performer; Teacher. *Education:* State University of New York, College at Purchase, 1972–74; BA, Urban Design Studies, Journalism, New York University, Washington Square College, 1975–77; Institut des Études Théâtrales, 1987–89; Dept of Theatre, l'Université de Paris VIII, 1989–92; Diploma, Études Supérieures Universitaires, 1992; TOEFL Certificate, WICE, Paris, 1992. *Publications:* Bud, 1981; Notes From The Moroccan Journals, and Art New York, bilingual edn of two texts, 1995. *Contributions to:* Women and Performance Journals; La Tribune Internationale des Langues Vivantes; River Styx; Home Planet News; The Tie That Binds, anthology. *Memberships:* Poets and Writers, New York; Société des Auteurs et Compositeurs Dramatiques, Paris. *Address:* Kyreinstrasse 11, 81371 Munich, Germany.

DU, Yunxie, (Jin Wu, Dahan Wu); b. 17 March 1918, Sitiawan, Malaysia. Ed.; Trans.; Poet; Teacher. m. Li Lijun, 22 April 1982, 2 s., 4 d., 2 step-s. *Education:* Trinity College, Fuzhou, 1934–37; Xiamen University, 1938–39; BA,

Southwest Associated University, 1945. *Publications:* Forty Poems; Nine Leaves Anthology; Late Paddies; Sitiawan, You Are My First Beloved; Selected 100 Poems of Du Yunxie, 1995; Questing on the Road Between Sea and Wall: Selected Poems and Prose of Du Yunxie, 1998; Sixty Years of Poems by Du Yunxie: 1940–2000. *Contributions to:* Ta Kung Pao; Wen Ju Magazine; Chinese New Poetry; Renaissance; Poetry Magazine; Chinese Poets; People's Daily. *Memberships:* Chinese Writers Asscn; PEN; Dongqing Literature Society; China Poetry Institute, council mem. *Address:* Flat 8-6, Building 17, 3 Yangfangdian Rd, Beijing 100038, China.

DUBE, Marcel; b. 3 Jan. 1930, Montréal, QC, Canada. Dramatist; Author; Poet; Trans. m. Nicole Fontaine, April 1956. *Education:* BA, Collège Sainte-Marie, 1951; University of Montréal; Theatre schools, Paris, 1953–54. *Publications:* Over 30 plays, including: Zone, 1955, English trans., 1982; Un simple soldat, 1958; Le temps des lilas, 1958, English trans. as Time of the Lilacs, 1990; Florence, 1958; Bilan, 1968; Les beaux dimanches, 1968; Au retour des oies blanches, 1969, English trans. as The White Geese, 1972; Hold-up! (with Louis-George Carrier), 1969; Un matin commes les autres, 1971; Le neufrage, 1971; De l'autre coté du mur, 1973; L'impromptu de Québec, ou Le testament, 1974; L'été s'appelle Julie, 1975; Le réformiste, ou L'honneur des hommes, 1977; Le trou, 1986; L'Amérique a sec, 1986. Other: Television series. Poetry: Poèmes de sable, 1974. Non-Fiction: Textes et documents, 1968; La tragédie est un acte de foi, 1973; Jean-Paul Lemieux et le livre, 1988; Andrée Lachapelle: Entre ciel et terre, 1995. *Honours:* Prix Victor-Morin, Saint-Jean-Baptiste Society, 1966; Prix David, Québec, 1973; Molson Prize, Canada Council, 1984; Académie canadienne-française Medal, 1987. *Memberships:* Académie canadienne-française, fellow; Federation of Canadian Authors and Artists, pres., 1959; Royal Society of Canada, fellow. *Address:* c/o Société professionnalle des auteurs et des compositeurs du Québec, 759 Sq. Victoria, No. 420, Montréal, QC H2Y 2J7, Canada.

DUBERSTEIN, Helen Laura; b. 3 June 1926, New York, NY, USA. Writer; Dramatist; Poet. m. 10 April 1949, 2 d. *Publications:* The Shameless Old Lady, 1995; Shadow Self and Other Tales, 1996; Roma; A Thousand Wives Dancing, 2002. *Contributions to:* Periodicals and journals. *Honours:* Awards and grants. *Memberships:* Dramatists Guild; League of Professional Theatre Women; PEN; Poetry Society of America. *Address:* 463 West St, No. 904 D, New York, NY 10014, USA. *E-mail:* ghohelz@aol.com.

DUBH, Crom. See: O'RUAIRC, Micheál.

DUBIE, Norman (Evans Jr); b. 10 April 1945, Barre, Vermont, USA. Prof. of English; Writer; Poet. *Education:* BA, Goddard College, 1969; MFA, University of Iowa, 1971. *Appointments:* Teaching Asst, Goddard College, 1967–69; Teaching Asst, 1969–70, Writing Fellow, 1970–71, Distinguished Lecturer and Mem. of the Graduate Faculty, 1971–74, University of Iowa; Poetry Ed., Iowa Review, 1971–72, Now Magazine, 1973–74; Asst Prof., Ohio University, 1974–75; Lecturer, 1975–76, Dir, Creative Writing, 1976–77, Assoc. Prof., 1978–81, Prof. of English, 1982–, Arizona State University. *Publications:* The Horsehair Sofa, 1969; Alehouse Sonnets, 1971; Indian Summer, 1973; The Prayers of the North American Martyrs, 1975; Popham of the New Song, 1975; In the Dead of Night, 1975; The Illustrations, 1977; A Thousand Little Things, 1977; Odalisque in White, 1978; The City of the Olesha Fruit, 1979; Comes Winter, the Sea Hunting, 1979; The Everlastings, 1980; The Window in the Field, 1982; Selected and New Poems, 1983; The Springhouse, 1986; Groom Falconer, 1989; Radio Sky, 1991; The Clouds of Magellan, 1991; The Choirs of June and January, 1993. *Contributions to:* Anthologies and periodicals. *Honours:* Bess Hokin Prize, 1976; Guggenheim Fellowship, 1977–78; Pushcart Prize, 1978–79; National Endowment for the Arts Grant, 1986; Ingram Merrill Grant, 1987. *Address:* c/o Dept of English, Arizona State University, Tempe, AZ 85281, USA.

DUBOIS, Frédéric (Julien Dunilac); b. 24 Sept. 1923, Neuchâtel, Switzerland. Diplomat (retd); Writer; Poet. m. Lydia Induni, 14 April 1947, 1 s., 2 d. *Education:* Classics, Neuchâtel; Social Sciences, Paris. *Publications:* La Vue Courte, 1952; La Part du Feu, 1954; Corps et Biens, 1957; Les Mauvaises Tetes, 1958; Passager clandestin, 1962; Futur mémorable, 1970; L'Un, 1974; La Passion alon Belle, 1985; Plein ciel, 1985; Mythologiques, 1987; Précaire Victoire, 1991; Le Coup de grâce, 1998; Garden-party, 2000; Le dos au mur, 2001; La Méduse, 2002. *Contributions to:* Various publications and radio. *Memberships:* Société Ecrivains neuchâtelois et jurassiens; Société Suisse des Ecrivains; Société Suisse des Auteurs. *Address:* Rue des Parcs 5, CH 2000 Neuchâtel, Switzerland.

DUBOIS, Jean; b. 4 Jan. 1926, Denver, CO, USA. Writer; Poet. m. Edward N Dubois, 21 Aug. 1947, 1 s., 2 d. *Education:* BA, University of Wyoming, 1947; MA, Pennsylvania State University, 1963. *Publications:* Silent Stones, Empty Passageways, 1992; The Same Sweet Yellow, 1994. *Contributions to:* Poets On; Thema; Modern Haiku; Brussels Sprout; Wall Street Journal; Mayfly. *Membership:* Haiku Society of America, Address: P O Box 1430, Golden, CO 80402, USA.

DUBOIS, Rochelle Holt. See: HOLT, Rochelle Lynn.

DUCHARME, Mark Edward; b. 27 Oct. 1960, Detroit, Michigan, USA. Project Man.; Poet. m. Lori S Cushman, 31 Dec. 1989, 1 d. *Education:* BA, Communication, University of Michigan, 1982; MFA, Writing and Poetics, Naropa Institute, 1992. *Publications:* Life Could Be a Dream, 1990; Emphasis, 1993; i, a series, 1995; 4 sections from Infringement, 1996; Contracting Scale, 1996; Three Works, Invasive Map, 1998; Desire Series, 1999; Near To, 1999; Cosmopolitan Tremble, 2002; Anon (chapbook, co-author), 2001. *Contributions to:* Talisman; Lingo; New American Writing; First Intensity; ACM; Washington Review; Situation; Big Allis; Torque; B City; Ribot; Mirage # 4 Period(ical); Juxta; The Impercipient; Texture; Lost and Found Times. *Address:* 2965 13th St, Boulder, CO 80304, USA.

DUCKER, Carolyn; b. 15 Oct. 1968, Cirencester, Gloucestershire, England. Florist; Poet; Trans. *Education:* St Anne's College, Oxford, 1987–92. *Contributions to:* Envoi; Frogmore Papers; Hybrid; Journal of Refugee Studies; Memes; Cascando; Angel Exhaust. *Address:* 7 Northmoor Pl., Northmoor Rd, Oxford OX2 6XB, England.

DUEMER, Joseph; b. 31 May 1951, San Diego, CA, USA. Assoc. Prof. of Humanities; Poet; Writer. m. Carole A Mathery, 31 Dec. 1987. *Education:* BA, University of Washington, 1978; MFA, University of Iowa, 1980. *Appointments:* Lecturer, Western Washington University, 1981–83, San Diego State University, 1983–87; Assoc. Prof. of Humanities, Clarkson University, 1987–; Poet-in-Residence, St Lawrence University, 1990. *Publications:* Poetry: Fool's Paradise, 1980; The Light of Common Day, 1985; Customs, 1987; Static, 1996; Primitive Alphabets, 1998. Editor: Dog Music (with Jan Simmerman), 1996. *Contributions to:* Reference books, anthologies, reviews, journals, magazines and radio. *Honours:* National Endowment for the Arts Creative Writing Fellowships, 1984, 1992, and National Endowment for the Humanities Grants, 1985, 1995. *Membership:* Associated Writing Programs, board of dirs, 1998–2002. *Address:* c/o Clarkson University, Potsdam, NY 13699, USA.

DUFFIELD, Jeremy; b. 25 June 1946, Alfreton, Derbyshire, England. Chartered Textile Technologist; Poet. m. Andrea Bramley, 7 Sept. 1968, 1 d. *Education:* Derby and District College of Art and Technology, 1963–69; Associateship of Textile Institute (ATI). *Publication:* Danced By the Light of the Moon, 1993. *Contributions to:* Poetry Nottingham; Poetry Digest; Envoi; Iota; She; Countryman; Nottingham Topic; Poetry Society Newsletter. *Honours:* First Prize, Open Section, CISWO Mining Poems Competition, 1988; First Prize, Swanage Arts Festival Poetry Group, 1991; First Prize, Queenie Lee Poetry Competition, 1993. *Memberships:* Nottingham Poetry Society; Poetry Society, London; Nottingham Writers' Club; Robert Louis Stevenson Club, Edinburgh; Herrick Society, Leicestershire. *Address:* 71 Saxton Ave, Heanor, Derbyshire DE75 7PZ, England.

DUFFY, Carol Ann; b. 23 Dec. 1955, Glasgow, Scotland. Poet; Dramatist. *Education:* BA, Honours, Philosophy, University of Liverpoool, 1977. *Publications:* Standing Female Nude, 1985; Selling Manhattan, 1987; The Other Country, 1990; The World's Wife, 2000. Other: Plays. *Contributions to:* Numerous magazines and journals. *Honours:* C Day-Lewis Fellowships, 1982–84; Eric Gregory Award, 1985; Scottish Arts Council Book Awards of Merit, 1985, 1987; Somerset Maugham Award, 1988; Dylan Thomas Award, 1990; C.B.E., 2002. *Address:* c/o Liz Graham, 4 Camp View, London SW19 4VL, England.

DUFFY, Maureen Patricia; b. 21 Oct. 1933, Worthing, Sussex, England. Writer; Poet. *Education:* BA, Honours, English, King's College, University of London, 1956. *Publications:* That's How It Was, 1962; The Microcosm, 1966; Lyrics for the Dog Hour, 1968; Rites, 1969; Wounds, 1969; Love Child, 1971; The Venus Touch, 1971; The Erotic World of Faery, 1972; I Want to Go to Moscow, 1973; A Nightingale in Bloomsbury Square, 1974; Capital, 1975; Evesong, 1975; The Passionate Shepherdess, 1977; Housespy, 1978; Memorials for the Quick and the Dead, 1979; Illuminations, 1992; Occan's Razor, 1992; Henry Purcell, 1994; Restitution, 1998; England: The Making of the Myth From Stonehenge to Albert Square, 2001. *Memberships:* Copyright Licencing Agency, chair., 1996; European Writers Congress, vice-pres.; RSL, fellow; Writer's Action Group, co-founder; Writer's Guild of Great Britain. *Literary Agent:* Jonathan Clowes Ltd, 10 Ironbridge House, Bridge Approach, London NW1 8BD, England. *Address:* 18 Fabian Rd, London SW6 7TZ, England.

DUGAN, Alan; b. 12 Feb. 1923, New York, NY, USA. Poet. m. Judith Shahn. *Education:* Queens College; Olivet College; BA, Mexico City College. *Appointments:* Teacher, Sarah Lawrence College, 1967–71, Fine Arts Work Center, Provincetown, Massachusetts, 1971–. *Publications:* General Prothalamion in Populous Times, 1961; Poems, 1961; Poems 2, 1963; Poems 3, 1969; Collected Poems, 1969; Poems 4, 1974; Sequence, 1976; New and Collected Poems, 1961–1983, 1983; Poems 6, 1989; Poems 7: New and Complete Poems, 2001. *Contributions to:* Several magazines, periodicals. *Honours:* Yale Series of Younger Poets Award, 1961; National Book Award, 1961; Pulitzer Prizes in Poetry, 1962, 1967; Rome Fellowship, American Acad. of Arts and Letters, 1962–63; Guggenheim Fellowship, 1963–64; Rockefeller Foundation Fellowship, 1966–67; Levinson Poetry Prize, 1967. *Address:* Box 97, Truro, MA 02666, USA.

DUHIG, Robert Ian; b. 9 Feb. 1954, London, England. Homelessness Worker; Poet. m. Jane Vincent, 1 s. *Education:* BA, Postgraduate Certificate in Education, Leeds University. *Publication:* The Bradford Count, 1991. *Contributions to:* Irish Review; TLS; New Statesman; Society; Honest Ulsterman; Arion; Bottlenose Review. *Honours:* First Prize, British National Poetry Competition, 1987; Short-listed, Whitbread Poetry Prize, 1991. *Address:* c/o Bloodaxe Books, PO Box 1SN, Newcastle upon Tyne NE99 1SN, England.

DULING, Paul; b. 14 Nov. 1916, Spokane, Washington, USA. Writer; Poet. m. Helen Julia Pendexter, 5 Jan. 1946, 2 d. *Education:* BA, University of Washington, 1939. *Publications:* Lunch Hour Girls/Lunch Hour Man, 1979; Love Until the Sun Goes Down, 1984; Whispering Without Walls, 1990. *Contributions to:* Saturday Evening Post; Poet Lore; Euterpe; Connecticut River Review; Wings Press; Greens; Embers; Bean Feast; Connecticut Artists; San Fernando Poetry Journal; Small Pond; Fair Press. *Memberships:* Connecticut Poetry Society; World Poetry Day, state chair. *Address:* 49 Taquoshe Pl., Fairfield, CT 06430, USA.

DUNCAN, Andrew A(itken); b. 7 July 1912, St Andrews, Fife, Scotland. Poet. m. Constance May Godfrey, 1 s., 1 d. *Education:* Madras College, St Andrews, Fife; Daniel Stewart's College, Edinburgh. *Publications:* Jist A Wee Mixter-Maxter O Scots and English Verse (anthology), 1993; A Wheen Mair O Scots and English Verse (anthology), 1996; My Best 100 Scots Poems', 1999. *Contributions to:* First Time; Poetry Now; Wits' End; The Peoples Poetry; Staple; Areopagus; Lallans; The Scots Magazine; Iota; Dandelion; Northwords; The Broken Fiddle; Acorn; Voice and Verse; Anchor and Triumph House. *Honours:* Second Place, The Writers Rostrum, 1991, Third Prize and Commended, Southport Writers Circle Competition. *Address:* Lanesmeet, Brompton Terrace, Perth PH2 7DH, Scotland.

DUNCAN, Andrew Charles Maitland; b. 26 Nov. 1956, Leeds, Yorkshire, England. Engineer; Poet. *Publications:* Cut Memories and False Commands, 1991; Sound Surface, 1992; Alien Skies, 1992. *Contributions to:* Ochre; Eduofinality; Grosseteste Review; Memes; First Offence. *Address:* Flat 6, Avon Ct, Holden Rd, London N12 8HR, England.

DUNCAN, Stephen Thomas; b. 19 March 1952, London, England. Writer; Poet; Artist. m. Marilyn Rogers, 1981, 2 s., 1 d. *Education:* BA, Fine Art, 1974, Wimbledon School of Art; Postgraduate Certificate, Royal Acad. of Art, 1977; Postgraduate studies, Accademia di Belle Arti, Rome, 1979; Award in Sculpture, British School at Rome, 1993. *Appointments:* Part-time Lecturer in Creative Writing, Fine Art and Cultural Studies Depts, number of colleges and universities; Readings and competition judging, workshops and lectures including the Arts Council, Peterloo Press, Arvon Foundation. *Contributions to:* Anthologies, reviews, and periodicals. *Honours:* First Prize, 1981, Second Prize, 1987, Wandsworth London Writers Competition; First Prize, Greenwich Festival Poetry Competition, 1985; Second Prize, TLS/Cheltenham Festival Poetry Competition, 1986; Second Prize, Bridport Literary Competition, 1989; Second Prize, Jewish Quarterly National Poetry Competition, 1994; Arts Council Writers Award, 1994; Fourth Prize, Cardiff International Poetry Competition, 1995, 1996; Fourth Prize, Arvon International Poetry Competition, 2000. *Membership:* Poetry Society, UK. *Address:* 56 Mervan Rd, London SW2 1DU, England.

DUNKERLEY, Hugh David; b. 30 July 1963, Surrey, England. College Lecturer; Poet. m. Alison MacLeod, 6 April 1991. *Education:* BA, Christchurch College, 1985; University of Bristol, 1986–87; BA, University of Lancaster, 1988. *Appointment:* Lecturer, West Sussex Institute of Higher Education. *Contributions to:* Orbis; Westmords; Giant Steps; Stand; Experience of Poetry. *Honours:* Lancaster Literary Festival Poetry Competition Prizewinner; Eric Gregory Award. *Address:* 68 Oving Rd, Chichester, West Sussex PO19 4EW, England.

DUNMORE, Helen; b. 1952, Yorkshire, England. Poet; Novelist. m. 1 s., 1 d., 1 step-s. *Education:* BA, York University, 1973. *Publications:* Poetry: The Apple Fall, 1983; The Sea Skater, 1986; The Raw Garden, 1988; Short Days, Long Nights: New & Selected Poems, 1991; Secrets, 1994; Recovering a Body, 1994; Bestiary, 1997; Out of the Blue: New and Selected Poems, 2001. Fiction: Going to Egypt, 1992; Zennor in Darkness, 1993; In the Money, 1993; Burning Bright, 1994; A Spell of Winter, 1995; Talking to the Dead, 1996; Your Blue-Eyed Boy, 1998; With Your Crooked Heart, 1999; The Siege, 2001. Short Stories: Love of Fat Men, 1997; Ice Cream, 2000. *Honours:* Poetry Book Society Choice, 1988; Poetry Book Society Recommendation, 1991; Signal Award for Poetry, 1994; Alice Hunt Bartlett Award; Orange Prize, 1996. *Membership:* Fellow, RSL. *Address:* c/o Caradoc King, A. P. Watt Ltd, 20 John St, London WC1N 2DR, England.

DUNN, Douglas (Eaglesham); b. 23 Oct. 1942, Inchinnan, Scotland. Prof. of English; Writer; Poet. m. Lesley Jane Bathgate, 10 Aug. 1985, 1 s., 1 d. *Education:* BA, University of Hull, 1969. *Appointments:* Writer-in-Residence, University of Hull, 1974–75, Duncan of Jordanstone College of Art, Dundee District Library, 1986–88; Writer-in-Residence, 1981–82, Hon. Visiting Prof., 1987–88, University of Dundee; Fellow in Creative Writing, 1989–91, Prof. of English, 1991–, Head, School of English, 1994–99, University of St Andrews;

Dir, St Andrews Scottish Studies Institute, 1993–. *Publications:* Terry Street 1969; The Happier Life, 1972; Love or Nothing, 1974; Barbarians, 1979; S Kilda's Parliament, 1981; Europea's Lover, 1982; Elegies, 1985; Secret Villages 1985; Selected Poems, 1986; Northlight, 1988; New and Selected Poems, 1989 Poll Tax: The Fiscal Fake, 1990; Andromache, 1990; Scotland: An Anthology (ed.), 1991; The Faber Book of 20th Century Scottish Poetry (ed.), 1992; Dante' Drum-Kit, 1993; Boyfriends and Girlfriends, 1994; The Oxford Book of Scottish Short Stories (ed.), 1995; Norman MacCaig: Selected Poems (ed.), 1997; The Donkey's Ears, 2000; 20th Century Scottish Poems (ed.), 2000; The Year' Afternoon, 2000. *Contributions to:* Newspapers, reviews, and journals *Honours:* Somerset Maugham Award, 1972; Geoffrey Faber Memorial Prize 1975; Hawthornden Prize, 1982; Whitbread Poetry Award, 1985; Whitbread Book of the Year Award, 1985; Hon. LLD, University of Dundee, 1987 Cholmondeley Award, 1989; Hon. DLitt, University of Hull, 1995 *Membership:* Scottish PEN. *Address:* c/o School of English, University of St Andrews, St Andrews, Fife KY16 9AL, Scotland.

DUNN, Stephen; b. 24 June 1939, New York, NY, USA. Poet; Writer. m. Lois Kelly, 1964, 2 d. *Education:* BA, History, Hofstra University, 1962; New School for Social Research, New York City, 1964–66; MA, Creative Writing, Syracuse University, 1970. *Appointments:* Asst Prof., Southwest Minnesota State College, Marshall, 1970–73; Visiting Poet, Syracuse University, 1973–74, University of Washington at Seattle, 1980; Assoc. Prof. to Prof., 1974–90, Stockton State College, New Jersey; Adjunct Prof. of Poetry, Columbia University, 1983–87. *Publications:* Poetry: Five Impersonations, 1971; Looking for Holes in the Ceiling, 1974; Full of Lust and Good Usage, 1976; A Circus of Needs, 1978; Work and Love, 1981; Not Dancing, 1984; Local Time, 1986; Between Angels, 1989; Landscape at the End of the Century, 1991; New and Selected Poems, 1974–1994, 1994; Loosestrife, 1996; Riffs and Reciprocities, 1998; Different Hours, 2000. Other: Walking Light: Essays and Memoirs, 1993. *Contributions to:* Periodicals. *Honours:* Acad. of American Poets Prize, 1970; National Endowment for the Arts Fellowships, 1973, 1982, 1989; Bread Loaf Writers Conference Robert Frost Fellowship, 1975; Theodore Roethke Prize, 1977; New Jersey Arts Council Fellowships, 1979, 1983; Helen Bullis Prize, 1982; Guggenheim Fellowship, 1984; Levinson Prize, 1988; Oscar Blumenthal Prize, 1991; James Wright Prize, 1993; American Acad. of Arts and Letters Award, 1995; Pulitzer Prize in Poetry, 2001. *Address:* 445 Chestnut Neck Rd, Port Republic, NJ 08241, USA.

DUNNETT, Alan David Michael; b. 7 July 1953, London, England. Playwright; Poet; Theatre Dir. *Education:* English Degree, Trinity College, Oxford University, 1971–74. *Appointments:* Creative Writing Tutor, Aspley Library, Nottingham, 1989–90; Writer-in-Residence, Ashwell Prison, 1991–92. *Publications:* In the Savage Gap, 1989; Hurt Under Your Arm, 1991. *Contributions to:* New Poetry 6; Rialto; Prospice; Smoke; Pennine Platform; Orbis; Grand Piano; Staple; Stepping Out; Zenos; Weyfarers; Poetry Nottingham; Iota; Frogmore Papers; Skoob Occult Review; Envoi; Methuen Book of Theatre Verse; Stand; Outposts; Interpreter's House; Links; Other Poetry. *Honour:* East Midlands Arts Literature Bursary, 1989. *Address:* 43 Bolivar Terrace, Glasgow, G42 9AT, Scotland.

DUNNETT, Denzil Inglis; b. 21 Oct. 1917, Sirsa, India. Diplomat (retd); Poet. m. Ruth Rawcliffe, 20 March 1946, 2 s., 1 d. *Education:* Edinburgh Acad., 1922–35; MA Lit Hum, Corpus Christi College, Oxford, 1939. *Appointments:* Editorial Staff, The Scotsman, 1946–47; Diplomatic posts, Bulgaria, Paris, Buenos Aires, Congo, Madrid, Mexico, Senegal, 1946–77. *Publication:* Bird Poems, 1989; The Weight of Shadows, poems descriptive and religious, 2001. *Contributions to:* Scottish Review; Scottish Bookman; Satire Review; Anthology of the Anarhyme. *Address:* 11 Victoria Grove, London W8 5RW, England.

DURCAN, Paul; b. 16 Oct. 1944, Dublin, Ireland. Poet. m. Nessa O'Neill, 8 May 1969, 2 d. *Education:* BA, Honours, Archaeology and Mediaeval History, University College, Cork. *Appointment:* Writer-in-Residence, Trinity College, Dublin. *Publications:* Endsville, 1967; O Westport in the Light of Asia Minor, 1975; Teresa's Bar, 1976; Sam's Cross, 1978; Jesus, Break His Fall, 1980; Ark of the North, 1982; Jumping the Train Tracks With Angela, 1983; The Selected Paul Durcan, 1985; The Berlin Wall Cafe, 1985; Going Home to Russia, 1987; In the Land of Punt, 1988; Jesus and Angela, 1988; Daddy, Daddy, 1990; Crazy About Women, 1991; A Snail in My Prime, 1993; Give Me Your Hand, 1994. *Contributions to:* Irish Press; Irish Times; Hibernia; Magill; Cyphers; Honest Ulsterman; Gorey Detail; Cork Examiner; Aquarius. *Honours:* Patrick Kavanagh Poetry Award, 1974; Arts Council of Ireland Bursaries for Creative Writing, 1976, 1980–81; Poetry Book Society Choice 1985; Irish-American Cultural Institute Poetry Award, 1989; Whitbread Poetry Award, 1990; Heinemann Award, 1995. *Membership:* Aosdána. *Address:* 14 Cambridge Ave, Ringsend, Dublin 4, Ireland.

DURGA, Kanaka; b. 22 Jan. 1968, Mumbai, India. Poet; Children's author. *Education:* SSC, Mumbai Board of Education; PCT, FSBT, Society of Business Teachers, London. *Publication:* Voices of Peace. *Contributions to:* Anthologies and other publications. *Honours:* International Eminent Poet and Hon. Fellowship, International Poets Acad., Chennai, 1991; Hon. Fellowship, United Writers' Asscn, Chennai, 1991; Wing-Word Poetry Award, Indo-Socio-Literary Foundation of India, 1997. *Memberships:* Chetana Literary Group;

Haiku Society of India, trustee and gen. sec.; International Socio-Literary Foundation, Karnataka State, hon. dir; Poet-Chennai, India; Poets International, India; World Poetry Intercontinental, India. *Address:* PO Box 26611, Matunga Post Office, Matunga (C/Rly), Mumbai 400 019, India.

DÜRRSON, Werner; b. 12 Sept. 1932, Schwenningen am Neckar, Germany. Poet; Writer; Dramatist; Trans. *Education:* Music Studies, Trossingen, 1953; German and French Literature Studies, Tübingen, Munich, 1957; PhD, 1962. *Publications:* Schubart (play), 1980; Stehend bewegt (poem), 1980; Der Luftkünstler (prose), 1983; Wie ich lese? (essay), 1986; Ausleben (poems of 12 years), 1988; Abbreviaturen (aphorisms), 1989; Werke (works: poetry and prose), 4 vols, 1992; Ausgewählte Gedichte (poems), 1995; The Kattenhorn Silence (trans. by Michael Hamburger), 1995; Stimmen aus der Gutenberg-Galaxis (essays of literature), 1997; Der verkaufte Schatten, Romanian elegies and Romanian diary, 1997; Wasserspiele (poems), 1999; Pariser Spitzen (poems), 2001. Several works in co-operation with painters (Klaus Staeck, Erich Heckel, HAP Grieshaber, Jonny Friedlaender) and musicians (Klaus Fessmann and others); Trans of authors including Guillaume d'Aquitaine, Marguerite de Navarre, Stéphane Mallarmé, Arthur Rimbaud, Yvan Goll, René Char, and Henri Michaux. *Contributions to:* Anthologies and radio. *Honours:* Lyric Poetry Prize, South West German Press, 1953; German Awards for Short Stories, 1973, 1983; Literary Prize, Stuttgart, 1978; Literary Prize, Überlingen, 1985; Bundesverdienstkreuz, 1993; Prize of the Schiller Foundation, Weimar, 1997; Eichendorff Literary Prize, 2001. *Memberships:* Asscn Internationale des Critiques littéraires, Paris; Asscn of German Writers; PEN. *Address:* Schloss Neufra, 88499 Riedlingen, Germany.

DUTTA, Amal Kumar, (Amalananda); b. 7 March 1944, Bangladesh. Audit Officer; Poet. m. 20 April 1984, 2 s. *Education:* BCom, 1968, BA, 1971, Calcutta University; Diploma in Homoeopathy, 1986 and Magneto Therapy, 1987, Mavelil Homoeo Mission, Trivandram, India. *Appointments:* Audit Officer, Tata Tea Ltd. *Publications:* Over 300 poems in English and Bengali; The Puppet Songs of Life (collected poems). *Contributions to:* Asian Age; Poet; Quest; Bridge-in-Making; Voice. *Honours:* First Prize, Bengal Poetry Competition; Awards, National Library of Poetry, 1997, 1998, 1999. *Address:* c/o Tata Tea Ltd, Bishop Lefroy Rd, Calcutta 700020, India.

DUTTON, G(eoffrey) J(ohn) F(raser); b. 30 Dec. 1924, Chester, England. Emeritus Prof.; Scientist; Poet. m. Elizabeth Caird, 22 Sept. 1957, 2 s., 1 d. *Education:* BSc, 1949, PhD, 1954, University of Edinburgh; DSc, University of Dundee, 1968. *Appointment:* Emeritus Prof. of Biochemistry, University of Dundee. *Publications:* Camp One, 1978; Squaring the Waves, 1986; The Concrete Garden, 1991; Harvesting the Edge, 1995; The Bare Abundance, 2002. *Contributions to:* Periodicals. *Honours:* Scottish Arts Council Awards, 1979, 1988, 1995; Poetry Book Society Recommendation, 1991, 2002; Hon. doctorates; Royal Society of Edinburge, fellow. *Address:* Druimchardain, Bridge of Cally, Blairgowrie PH10 7JX, Scotland.

DWIVEDI, Suresh Chandra, (Kaviraj Dhoomketu); b. 29 March 1950, Ballia, Uttar Pradesh, India. Prof. of English; Poet. m. Prabha Dwivedi, 14 June 1975, 1 s., 2 d. *Education:* BA, 1967; MA, English, 1969; PhD, 1976; DLitt, 1988. *Appointments:* IUGC Fellow, Kashi Vidyapith Varanasi, 1969–72; Lecturer in English, Allahabad Degree College, 1972–84, Shri Aurobindo College, Delhi University, 1975; Reader in English, 1984–96, Prof. of English, 1996–, Allahabad University, India. *Publications:* Ek Aur Sabera, 1978; Haira Pipar Kabahun Na Dole, 1988. *Honours:* Rahul Sankrityayan Award, Uttar Prasdesh Hindi Sansthan, 1986; George Abrahim Grierson Award, Akhil Bharatiya Bhojpuri Bhasha Parishad, 1988; Hon. DLitt, World Acad. of Arts and Letters, USA, 1988; Janapadiya Samman, 1989; Rastra Kavi, 1995; Vani Ratna Award, 1996. *Memberships:* American Studies Research Centre,

Hyderabad; Indian Asscn for English and American Studies; Bharatiya Sahitya Sansthan; World Bhojpuri Asscn, pres.; Samagra Dharma, founder. *Address:* Poet's Corner 125-3, Ome Gayatri Nagar, PO Teliarganj, Allahabad 211004, India.

DWYER, Deirdre Diana; b. 18 June 1958, Liverpool, Nova Scotia, Canada. Poet; Teacher. m. Hans von Hammerstein, 12 Oct. 1992. *Education:* MA, English and Creative Writing; BA, Philosophy, Studio Writing I & II, Banff Centre for the Arts. *Contributions to:* Event; Canadian Literature; Poetry Canada Review. *Honours:* Various Scholarships and Grants. *Memberships:* Writer's Federation of Nova Scotia; League of Canadian Poets. *Address:* 2375 June St, Halifax, Nova Scotia B3K 4K3, Canada.

DYBEK, Stuart; b. 10 April 1942, Chicago, IL, USA. Poet; Writer; Prof. of English. m. Caren Bassett, 1966, 1 s., 1 d. *Education:* BS, 1964, MA, 1967, Loyola University; MFA, University of Iowa, 1973. *Appointments:* Teaching Asst, 1970–72, Teaching and Writing Fellow, 1972–73, University of Iowa; Prof. of English, Western Michigan University, 1973–; Guest Writer and Teacher, Michigan Council for the Arts' Writer in the Schools Program, 1973–92; Faculty, Warren Wilson MFA Program in Creative Writing, 1985–89; Visiting Prof. of Creative Writing, Princeton University, 1990, University of California, Irvine, 1995; University of Iowa Writers' Workshop, 1998; Numerous readings, lectures and workshops. *Publications:* Brass Knuckles (poems), 1979; Childhood and Other Neighbourhoods (stories), 1980; The Coast of Chicago (stories), 1990; The Story of Mist (short fiction and prose poems), 1994. *Contributions to:* Many anthologies and magazines. *Honours:* Award in Fiction, Society of Midwest Authors, 1981; Cliffdwellers Award for Fiction, Friends of American Literature, 1981; Special Citation, PEN/Hemingway Prize Committee, 1981; Michigan Council for the Arts Grants, 1981, 1992; Guggenheim Fellowship, 1982; National Endowment for the Arts Fellowships, 1982, 1994; Pushcart Prize, 1985; First Prize, O Henry Award, 1985; Nelson Algren Prize, 1985; Whiting Writers Award, 1985; Michigan Arts Award, Arts Foundation of Michigan, 1986; American Acad. of Arts and Letters Award for Fiction, 1994; PEN/Malamud Award, 1995; Rockefeller Residency, Bellagio, Italy, 1996; Lannan Writers Award, 1998. *Address:* 310 Monroe, Kalamazoo, MI 49006, USA.

DYER, Bernadette Elaine; b. 19 April 1946, Kingston, Jamaica. Library Asst; Poet. m. Terry Dyer, 15 May 1971, 2 s., 1 d. *Education:* Art College Diploma, 1968. *Appointments:* Display Artist; Library Worker. *Publications:* Bite to Eat Place, 1995; An Invisible Accordian, 1995. *Contributions to:* Jones Ave; Alpha Beat Soup; Word Up; Poemata; Paper Plates; Artery; Next Exit; Egorag. *Honour:* Winner, League of Canadian Black Artists Competition, 1995. *Membership:* Canadian Poetry Asscn. *Address:* PO Box 22571, St George Postal Station, Toronto, Ontario M5S 1U0, Canada.

DYKEMAN, Therese (Marie) B(oos); b. 11 April 1936, Iowa, USA. Adjunct Prof.; Writer; Poet. m. King John Dykeman, 7 Feb. 1959, 1 s., 2 d. *Education:* BS, Creighton University, 1958; MA, Loyola University; PhD, Union Institute, Ohio, 1980. *Appointments:* Adjunct Prof., Loop City College, Chicago, 1965–67; Housatonic Community College, 1970–80, University of Bridgeport, 1980–90, Fairfield University, CT, 1990–. *Publications:* Eleven Voices, 1990; American Women Philosophers 1650–1930: Six Exemplary Thinkers, 1993; The Neglected Canon: Nine Women Philosophers, 1st to the 20th Century, 1999. *Contributions to:* Western Voice, 1987–89. *Honour:* Honourable Mention, Connecticut Poetry Society, 1988. *Memberships:* Connecticut Poetry Society; Centre for Independent Study, pres., 1989–91; Rhetoric Society of America; MLA; Danforth Assocs of New England, pres., 1992–93. *Address:* 47 Woods End Rd, Fairfield, CT 06430, USA.

E

EARLEY, Thomas Powell; b. 13 Sept. 1911, South Wales. Poet. m. 13 April 1939, 2 d. *Education:* Trinity College, Carmathen. *Appointments:* Senior English Master; Headmaster, Preparatory School. *Publications:* Welshman in Bloomsbury, 1968; The Sad Mountain, 1970; Rebel's Progress, 1979; All These Trees, 1992. *Contributions to:* New Statesman; Tribune; Poetry Wales; Anglo-Welsh Review; Planet; Welsh Nation; London Welshman; Western Mail; Second Aeon; Country Quest; Breakthrough; Poet; Outposts; Anthologies: Lilting House; Oxford Book of Welsh Verse; Voices of Today; London Lines; Anglo-Welsh Poetry. *Honours:* Poems discussed on BBC and read on several radio channels; Film of life work shown on television, 1970. *Memberships:* Welsh Acad. of Writers; Welsh Union of Writers; Poetry Society. *Address:* 21 Bloomsbury Sq., London WC1A 2NS, England.

EARNEY, Beverly (Verna), (Beverly Cole-Earney); b. 15 Aug. 1951, Auckland, New Zealand. Poet. m. Michael David Frederick Earney, 9 Aug. 1980, 2 s., 1 d. *Education:* Diploma in German, Auckland Goethe Society, 1967; Hamilton Teachers' College, New Zealand; University of Waikato, New Zealand. *Publication:* Beneath the Southern Cross, 1988. *Contributions to:* Earwig; Parnassus of World Poets, 1994, 1995; V Anthology of Olympoetry, 1995–96; World Poetry Anthology, 1996. *Honours:* Commendation, Poetry Day Competition, 1987; Melbourne Poetry Society Haiku Selections, 1989; Poetry Day Manuscripts Certificate, 1991. *Membership:* Melbourne Poetry Society. *Address:* 17 Vandeven Ct, Ferntree Gully 3156, Vic., Australia.

EATON, Charles Edward; b. 25 June 1916, Winston-Salem, NC, USA. Poet; Writer. m. Isabel Patterson, 1950. *Education:* Duke University, 1932–33; BA, University of North Carolina at Chapel Hill, 1936; Princeton University, 1936–37; MA in English, Harvard University, 1940. *Appointments:* Instructor in Creative Writing, University of Missouri, 1940–42; Vice Consul, American Embassy, Rio de Janeiro, 1942–46; Prof. of Creative Writing, University of North Carolina, 1946–52. *Publications:* Poetry: The Bright Plain, 1942; The Shadow of the Swimmer, 1951; The Greenhouse in the Garden, 1956; Countermoves, 1963; On the Edge of the Knife, 1970; The Man in the Green Chair, 1977; Colophon of the Rover, 1980; The Thing King, 1983; The Work of the Wrench, 1985; New and Selected Poems 1942–1987, 1987; A Guest on Mild Evenings, 1991; The Country of the Blue, 1994; The Fox and I, 1996; The Scout in Summer, 1999; The Jogger by the Sea, 2000. Fiction: A Lady of Pleasure, 1993. Short Stories: Write Me From Rio, 1959; The Girl From Ipanema, 1972; The Case of the Missing Photographs, 1978; New and Selected Stories 1959–1989, 1989. *Contributions to:* Magazines and journals. *Honours:* Bread Loaf Writers' Conference Robert Frost Fellowship, 1941; Ridgely Torrence Memorial Award, 1951; Gertrude Boatwright Harris Award, 1955; Arizona Quarterly Awards, 1956, 1975, 1977, 1979, 1982; Roanoke-Chowan Awards, 1970, 1987, 1991; Oscar Arnold Young Award, 1971; O. Henry Award, 1972; Alice Faye di Castagnola Award, 1974; Arvon Foundation Award, 1980; Hollins Critic Award, 1984; Brockman Awards, 1984, 1986; Kansas Quarterly Awards, 1987; North Carolina Literature Award, 1988; Fortner Award, 1993; Hon. DLitt, St Andrews College, NC, 1998. *Membership:* American Acad. of Poets. *Address:* 808 Greenwood Rd, Chapel Hill, NC 27514, USA.

EBERHART, Richard (Ghormley); b. 5 April 1904, Austin, MN, USA. Prof. of English Emeritus; Poet; Writer. m. Helen Elizabeth Butcher, 1941, 1 s., 1 d. *Education:* Dartmouth College, 1926; BA, 1929, MA, 1933, St John's College, Cambridge, England; Harvard University, 1932–33. *Appointments:* Founder-Pres., Poets' Theater, Cambridge, MA, 1951; Visiting Prof. of English and Poet-in-Residence, University of Washington, 1952–53, Wheaton College, Norton, MA, 1954–55, Prof. of English, University of Connecticut, 1953–54; Resident Fellow in Creative Writing and Christian Gauss Lecturer, Princeton University, 1955–56; Prof. of English, 1956–70, Poet-in-Residence, 1956–, Prof. Emeritus, 1970–, Dartmouth College; Consultant in Poetry, Library of Congress, Washington, DC, 1959–61; Distinguished Visiting Prof., 1974–75, Visiting Prof., 1975–86, University of Florida at Gainesville; Adjunct Prof., Columbia University, 1975; Regents' Prof., University of California at Davis, 1975. *Publications:* A Bravery of Earth, 1930; Reading the Spirit, 1937; Song and Idea, 1942; Poems New and Selected, 1944; Burr Oaks, 1947; Brotherhood of Men, 1949; An Herb Basket, 1950; Selected Poems, 1951; Undercliff, 1953; Great Praises, 1957; Collected Poems, 1930–1960, 1960; Collected Verse Plays, 1962; The Quarry, 1964; Selected Poems, 1930–1965, 1965; New Directions, 1965; Thirty-One Sonnets, 1967; Shifts of Being, 1968; Fields of Grace, 1972; Collected Poems, 1930–1976, 1976; Poems to Poets, 1976; Survivors, 1979; Of Poetry and Poets, 1979; Ways of Light, 1980; New Hampshire: Nine Poems, 1980; Four Poems, 1980; A Celebration, 1980; Chocorua, 1981; Florida Poems, 1981; The Long Reach, 1984; Collected Poems, 1930–1986, 1986; Negative Capability, 1986; Maine Poems, 1988; New and Collected Poems, 1990. *Contributions to:* Books and periodicals. *Honours:* Hon. doctorates; Harriet Monroe Memorial Prize, 1950; Shelley Memorial Prize, 1951; Bollingen Prize, 1962; Pulitzer Prize in Poetry, 1966; National Book Award, 1977; Poet Laureate of New Hampshire, 1979; Sarah

Josepha Hale Award, 1982; Robert Frost Medal, Poetry Society of America, 1986. *Memberships:* Acad. of American Poets, fellow; American Acad. of Arts and Letters; American Acad. of Arts and Sciences. *Address:* 80 Lyme Rd, Apt 161, Hanover, NH 03755, USA.

EBERT, Tibor; b. 14 Oct. 1926, Bratislava, Czechoslovakia. Writer; Poet; Dramatist. m. Eva Gati, 11 Feb. 1968, 1 d. *Education:* BA, Music, Ferenc Liszt Acad. of Music, 1952; Law, Philosophy, Literature Studies, Dept of Law and Philosophy, Eötvös Lóránd University, Budapest, 1951–53. *Appointments:* Dramaturg, József Attila Theatre, Budapest, 1984–85; Ed.-in-Chief, Agora Publishers, Budapest, 1989–92; Ed., Hirvivo Literary Magazine, 1990–92. *Publications:* Mikrodrámák, 1971; Rosarium, 1987; Kobayashi, 1989; Legenda egy fúvószenekarról, 1990; Jób könyve, 1991; Fagyott Orpheusz (poems), 1993; Esö, 1996; Egy város glóriája, 1997; Bartók, 1997; Eredök, 1998; Éltem, 1998; Drámák, 2000; Bolyongás, 2001; Vecseruye, 2001; Kaleidoszlnóp, 2002; Álmomban, 2002. Other: Several plays performed on stage including: Les Escaliers; Musique de Chambre; Demosthenes; Esterházy. *Contributions to:* Numerous short stories, poems, dramas and essays to several leading Hungarian literary journals and magazines. *Honours:* Hon. mem., Franco-Hungarian Society, 1980–; Bartók Prize, 1987; Commemorative Medal, City of Pozsony-Pressburg-Bratislava, 1991; Esterházy Prize, 1993; Order of Hungarian Republic, 1996. *Memberships:* PEN Club; Asscn of Hungarian Writers; Literary Asscn Berzsenyi. *Address:* Csévi u 15c, 1025 Budapest, Hungary.

ECKLES, Arden. See: TICE, Arden A.

ECONOMOU, George; b. 24 Sept. 1934, Great Falls, Montana, USA. Prof. Emeritus of English; Poet; Trans. m. Rochelle Owens, 17 June 1962. *Education:* AB, Colgate University, 1956; MA, 1957, PhD, 1967, Columbia University. *Appointments:* Long Island University, Brooklyn Center, 1961–83; University of Oklahoma, 1983–2001. *Publications:* The Georgics, 1968; Landed Natures, 1969; Poems for Self Therapy, 1972; Ameriki: Book One and Selected Earlier Poems, 1977; Philodemos: His Twenty-Nine Poems Translated into English, 1983; Voluntaries, 1984; Harmonies and Fits, 1987; William Langland's Pier Plowman, The C-Version, A Translation into Modern English, 1996; Century Dead Center and Other Poems, 1997. *Contributions to:* Reviews, periodicals and magazines. *Honours:* New York State CAPS Fellow in Poetry, 1975; National Endowment for the Arts Fellow in Poetry, 1988; Rockefeller Fellow, Bellagio, 1993; National Endowment for the Arts Fellow in Poetry, 1999. *Address:* 1401 Magnolia St, Norman, OK 73072-6827, USA.

EDLOSI, Mario. See: LEIH, Grace Janet.

EDMOND, Murray (Donald); b. 1949, New Zealand. Poet. *Appointments:* Dir, Actor and Writer with the Town and Country Players, Wellington. *Publications:* Entering the Eye, 1973; Patchwork, 1978; End Wall, 1981; Letters and Paragraphs, 1987; From the Word Go, 1992; The Switch, 1994; Names Manes, 1996. Co-Editor: The New Poets of the 80's: Initiatives in New Zealand Poetry, 1987. *Address:* c/o University of Auckland, Private Bag 92019, Auckland, New Zealand.

EDSON, Russell; b. 9 April 1935, USA. Poet; Writer. m. Frances Edson. *Education:* Art Students' League, New York; New School for Social Research, New York; Columbia University; Black Mountain College, NC. *Publications:* Poetry: Appearances: Fables and Drawings, 1961; A Stone is Nobody's: Fables and Drawings, 1964; The Boundry, 1964; The Very Thing That Happens: Fables and Drawings, 1964; The Brain Kitchen: Writings and Woodcuts, 1965; What a Man Can See, 1969; The Childhood of an Equestrian, 1973; The Calm Theatre, 1973; A Roof with Some Clouds Behind It, 1975; The Intuitive Journey and Other Works, 1976; The Reason Why the Closet-Man is Never Sad, 1977; Edson's Mentality, 1977; The Traffic, 1978; The Wounded Breakfast: Ten Poems, 1978; With Sincerest Regrets, 1981; Wuck Wuck Wuck!, 1984; The Wounded Breakfast, 1985; Tick Tock, 1992; The Tunnel: Selected Poems, 1994. Fiction: Gulping's Recital, 1984; The Song of Percival Peacock, 1992. *Honours:* Guggenheim Fellowship, 1974; National Endowment for the Arts Grant, 1976, and Fellowship, 1982; Whiting Foundation Award, 1989. *Address:* 29 Ridgeley St, Darien, CT 06820, USA.

EDWARDS, F. E. See: NOLAN, William F(rancis).

EDWARDS, Rebecca Jane; b. 4 April 1969, Batlow, NSW, Australia. Writer; Poet; Artist. 1 d. *Education:* BA, Japanese Language and Culture, University of Queensland, 1992. *Appointment:* Writer-in-Residence, James Cook University, Townsville, Qld, 1996. *Publications:* Eating the Experience, 1994; Eat the Ocean (contributor), 1996. *Contributions to:* Anthologies and journals. *Honours:* Red Earth Award, Northern Territories Section, 1989; Ford Memorial Medals, University of Queensland, 1991, 1992; Fifth Regional

Illustrated Poetry Competition, 1995. *Memberships:* Fellowship of Australian Writers; New South Wales Poets' Union; Queensland Artworkers' Alliance; Queensland Writers' Centre.

EGAN, Desmond; b. 15 July 1936, Athlone, Ireland. Poet; Writer; Trans. m. Vivienne Abbott, 13 Aug. 1981, 2 d. *Education:* MA and Higher Diploma, University College, Dublin. *Publications:* Midland, 1972; Leaves, 1974; Siege!, 1977; Woodcutter, 1978; Athlone?, 1980; Seeing Double, 1983; Collected Poems, 1983–84; Poems for Peace, 1986; A Song for my Father, 1989; Peninsula, 1992; Selected Poems (ed. by Hugh Kenner), 1992; In the Holocaust of Autumn, 1994; Poems for Eimear, 1994; Elegies, 1972–96, 1996; Famine, 1997; Music, 1999; The Hill of Allen, 2001. Translations: Medea, Euripides, 1997; Philoctetes, Sophocles, 1997. Other: Documentary video, USA, 1999. *Contributions to:* Numerous publications. *Honours:* National Poetry Foundation Award, USA, 1983; Citation, Osaka University, Japan, 1986; Chicago Haymarket Literary Award, 1987; Farrell Literary Award, 1988; Pilgrim's Progress Prize, Stanford, 1993; Hon. DLitt, Washburn University, Topeka, KS, USA, 1996; Bologna Literary Award, Italy, 1998. *Address:* c/o The Arts Council, 79 Merrion Sq., Dublin 2, Ireland.

EGLINTON, Edna Mary; b. 26 Oct. 1924, London, England. Poet. m. George Arthur Eglinton, 12 Jan. 1946, 1 s., 1 d. *Publications:* Pisgah, 1977; Holiday Viewing, 1982; Listen to Us (1 of 6 poets), 1983; Hands Together (with David Santer), 1994; How Are Your Spirits, 2001; Forever Panto, 2001. *Contributions to:* Magazines and anthologies for children and adults. *Honours:* Prizes in competitions. *Memberships:* Friends of the Arvon Foundation; Asscn of Christian Writers. *Address:* 9 North St, North Tawton, Devon EX20 2DE, England.

EHRET, Terry; b. 12 Nov. 1955, San Francisco, CA, USA. Poet; University Lecturer. m. Donald Nicholas Moe, 7 April 1979, 3 c. *Education:* BA, Stanford University, 1977; Chapman College, 1979–81; MA, San Francisco State University, 1984. *Appointments:* Instructor in English, Santa Rosa Junior College, 1991–; Lecturer in Poetry, Sonoma State University, 1994–, San Francisco State University, 1995–99; Many poetry readings and lectures. *Publications:* Suspensions (with Steve Gilmartin and Susan Herron Sibbet), 1990; Lost Body, 1993; Travel/How We Go on Living, 1995; Translations from the Human Language, 2001. *Contributions to:* Reviews and journals. *Honours:* National Poetry Series Award, 1992; California Commonwealth Club Book Award for Poetry, 1994; Pablo Neruda Poetry Prize, Nimrod magazine, 1995. *Memberships:* Acad. of American Poets; Associated Writing Programs; California Poets in the Schools; Poets and Writers. *Address:* 924 Sunnyslope Rd, Petaluma, CA 94952, USA.

EIBEL, Deborah; b. 25 June 1940, Montréal, QC, Canada. Poet. *Education:* BA, McGill University, 1960; MA, Radcliffe College, 1962; MA, Johns Hopkins University, 1971. *Publications:* Kayak Sickness, 1972; Streets Too Narrow for Parades, 1985; Making Fun of Travellers, 1992; Gold Rush, 1996; Purple Passages, 1998; A Poet's Notebook, 1999. *Contributions to:* Anthologies and periodicals. *Honours:* Arthur Davison Ficke Sonnet Award, Poetry Society of America, 1965; Arts Bursary, Canada Council, 1967; Residency, Leighton Artists' Colony, 1988. *Memberships:* League of Canadian Poets; Poetry Society of America. *Address:* 6657 Wilderton Ave, Montréal, QC H3S 2L8, Canada.

EINBOND, Bernard Lionel; b. 19 May 1939, New York, NY, USA. Prof. of English; Poet. m. Linda Saxe, 20 Feb. 1977, 1 s., 1 d. *Education:* AB, 1958, AM, 1960, PhD, 1966, Columbia University. *Appointments:* Prof. of English, Lehman College, 1968–; Adjunct Prof. of English, Columbia University, New York City, 1989–90. *Publications:* The Coming Indoors and Other Poems, 1979; The Tree As It Is, 1994. *Contributions to:* Bogg; Modern Haiku; Sunbury; Frogpond. *Honours:* Keats Poetry Prize, 1975; Grand Prize Winner, Japan Air Lines Haiku Competition, 1988; Mirrors International Tanka Award, 1990. *Membership:* Haiku Society of America, pres., 1975. *Address:* PO Box 307, Fort George Station, New York, NY 10040, USA.

ELDER, Karl; b. 7 July 1948, Beloit, WI, USA. Poet; Writer; Ed.; Prof. of Creative Writing. m. Brenda Kay Olson, 23 Aug. 1969, 2 s. *Education:* BS, 1971, MS, 1974, Northern Illinois University; MFA, Wichita State University, 1977. *Appointments:* Instructor, Southwest Missouri State University, 1977–79; Faculty, 1979–89, Jacob and Lucile Fessler Prof. of Creative Writing, 1990–, Lakeland College. *Publications:* Poetry: Can't Dance an' It's Too Wet to Plow, 1975; The Celibate, 1982; Phobophobia, 1987; A Man in Pieces, 1994; Locutions, 2001. Editor: What Is the Future of Poetry?, 1991. *Contributions to:* Many anthologies, reviews, quarterlies and journals. *Honours:* Lucien Stryk Award for Poetry, 1974; Illinois Arts Council Award, 1975, and Grant, 1977; Outstanding Teacher Award, Lakeland College, 1987; Robert Schuricht Endowment, 1993; Pushcart Prize for Poetry, 2000. *Address:* c/o Creative Arts Division, Lakeland College, PO Box 359, Sheboygan, WI 53082, USA.

ELFICK, Hilary Margaret; b. 25 April 1940, Warwickshire, England. Poet; Writer. m. Richard Elfick, 15 March 1968, 1 s., 2 d. *Education:* BA, History and English Language, Diploma in Education, University of Keele, 1962. *Appointments:* BBC Studio Man., Radio, 1962; BBC Prod., Radio 4, 1964–68;

Teacher, Head of English and Sixth Form Tutor, Danes Hill Prep School, 1988–92; Freelancer for Settlement of Vietnamese and Bosnian Refugees, 1979–89, for the Hospice Movement, 1983–; International Co-ordinator, Voices for Hospices, 1992–97; Trustee, Princess Alice Hospice, Esher, 1983–; Broadcasts on local, national and international radio and TV; Poetry workshops in UK, Australia, New Zealand. *Publications:* Folk and Vision, 1971; The Horse Might Sing, 1990; Unexpected Spring, 1992; Going Places, 1994; The Sleeping Warrior, 1999; Bush Track, 1999; Harpoon the Breeze, 1999; The Wedding Poem, 2002. *Contributions to:* Sydney Morning Herald; The Tablet; The Shop; Envoi. Reviews for Orbis, BBC World Service, TLS, Times Educational Supplement. *Honours:* Highly Commended, Twice in Weyfarers, 1998, and Three Times in Envoi International Poetry Competitions, 1996; Hon. Life Mem., Hospice Africa, Uganda; Hon. Life Mem., Hibiscus Coast Hospice, New Zealand. *Memberships:* Surrey Poets (Weyfarers); National Poetry Society; Riverhouse Writers; Aldeburgh Festival. *Address:* Wybarton, Moles Hill, Oxshott, Surrey KT22 0QB, England.

ELKAYAM, (Rachel) Shelley; b. 18 Nov. 1955, Haifa, Israel. Ed.; Poet; Writer; Counsellor. m. Sorin Sandor. *Education:* BA, Haifa University, 1980; MA, Hebrew University, Jerusalem, 1980–86; MA, University of Liverpool, 2001. *Appointments:* Spokesperson, East for Peace, 1983; Chair, World Conference on Religion and Peace, Israel, 1987–95; Chief Ed., Taril, Israel Defence Forces Literature Publishing House, 1991; Ed., Publications of Hebrew Writers' Asscn, 1993–95; Ed., Platform of the Poetess, 1993–95; Ed., First Poetess Festival, Jerusalem, 1995; Pres., Israeli Women's Federation for World Peace, 1996–2001. *Publications:* Six books of poetry, 1981–87. Other: Radio and television. *Contributions to:* Anthologies, reviews and journals, including: Poetry International; One World Poetry. *Honour:* Keren Adler Young Poet's Prize, Haifa University, 1980. *Memberships:* Hebrew Writers' Asscn; Israeli Asscn of Educational Counsellors. *Address:* Malkha, Jerusalem 96901, Israel. *Fax:* (2) 6794636. *E-mail:* shelley_elk@yahoo.com.

ELKIN, Roger James; b. 14 March 1943, Congleton, Cheshire, England. Curriculum Dir in Continuing Education; Poet. m. Eileen Baddley, 22 Aug. 1965, 1 s., 1 d. *Education:* BA, Honours, History, 1965; PGCE, 1966; MA, Keele University, 1982. *Appointment:* Curriculum Dir in Continuing Education, Leek College of Further Education, Staffordshire. *Publications:* Pricking Out, 1988; Points of Reference, 1996; Home Ground, 2001. *Contributions to:* Poetry Canada; Outposts; Orbis; Staple; Tees Valley Writer; Green Book; Prospice; Weyfarers; Acumen; Envoi; Poetry Nottingham; Resurgence; Psychopoetica; Tribune; Poetry Wales; Purple Patch. *Honours:* Lake Aske Memorial Awards, 1982, 1987; Douglas Gibson Memorial Award, 1986; Sylvia Plath Award, 1986; Howard Sergeant Memorial Award for Services to Poetry, 1987; Writers' Rostrum Poet of the Year, 1991. *Address:* 44 Rudyard Rd, Biddulph Moor, Stoke-on-Trent, Staffordshire ST8 7JN, England.

ELLIOT, Alistair; b. 13 Oct. 1932, Liverpool, Lancashire, England. Poet; Trans.; Ed.; Librarian (retd). m. 1956, 2 s. *Education:* Fettes College, Edinburgh; BA, MA, Christ Church, Oxford. *Appointments:* Librarian, Kensington Public Library, London, 1959–61, Keele University, 1961–65, Pahlavi University, Iran, 1965–67, Newcastle University, 1967–82. *Publications:* Air in the Wrong Place, 1968; Contentions, 1977; Kisses, 1978; Talking to Bede, 1982; Talking Back, 1982; On the Appian Way, 1984; My Country: Collected Poems, 1989; Turning the Stones, 1993; Facing Things, 1997. Editor: Poems by James I and Others, 1970; Virgil, The Georgics with John Dryden's Translation, 1981. Editor and Translator: French Love Poems (bilingual), 1991; Italian Landscape Poems (bilingual), 1993. Translator: Alcestis, by Euripides, 1965; Peace, by Aristophanes, 1965; Femmes Hombres, by Paul Verlaine, 1979; The Lazarus Poems, by Heinrich Heine, 1979; Medea, by Euripides, 1993; La Jeune Parque, by Paul Valéry, 1997. *Contributions to:* Many journals, reviews and magazines. *Honours:* Arts Council of Great Britain Grant, 1979; Ingram Merrill Foundation Fellowships, 1983, 1989; Prudence Farmer Awards, New Statesman, 1983, 1991; Djerassi Foundation Fellowship, 1984; Cholmondeley Award, Society of Authors, 2000. *Literary Agent:* Peters, Fraser and Dunlop. *Address:* 27 Hawthorn Rd, Newcastle upon Tyne NE3 4DE, England.

ELLIOT, Bruce. See: FIELD, Edward.

ELLISON, Lee. See: HARVEY, Marshall L.

ELLSON, Peter Kenneth; b. 22 July 1937, Surrey, England. Poet; Painter; Publisher. m. (1) Barbara Norman, 1966, deceased 1972, (2) Anke Kornmuller, 1978, divorced 1993. *Publications:* Poems, 1978; Halde, 1983. *Contributions to:* Tuba Magazine; New Leaf. *Address:* Route des Vans, La Republique, 30160 Bordezac-Gard, France.

ELMSLIE, Kenward Gray; b. 27 April 1929, New York, NY, USA. Poet; Librettist. *Education:* BA, Harvard University, 1950. *Publications:* Poetry: The Champ, 1968; Album, 1969; Circus Nerves, 1971; Motor Disturbance, 1971; The Orchid Stories, 1972; Tropicalism, 1976; The Alphabet Work, 1977; Communications Equipment, 1979; Moving Right Along, 1980; Bimbo Dirt, 1981; 26 Bars, 1986; Sung Sex, 1989; Pay Dirt (with Joe Brainard), 1992; Champ Dust, 1994; Bare Bones, 1995; Routine Disruptions: Selected Poems and Lyrics, 1998; Cyberspace (with Trevor Winkfield), 2000; Blast from the Past, 2000; Nite Soil, 2000; Snippets, 2002; Opera Libretti: Lizzie Borden, 1966; Miss Julie, 1966; The Sweet Bye and Bye, 1973; The Seagull, 1974; Washington Square, 1976; Three Sisters, 1986. Play: City Junket, 1987. Musical Plays: The Grass Harp, 1971; Lola, 1982; Postcards on Parade, 1993. Contributions to: Many anthologies, reviews and journals. Honour: Frank O'Hara Poetry Award, 1971. Membership: American Society of Composers, Authors and Publishers. Address: PO Box 38, Calais, VT 05648, USA. Website: www.kenwardmslie.com.

ELSBERG, John William; b. 4 Aug. 1945, New York, NY, USA. Ed.; Poet. m. Constance Waeber, 17 June 1967, 1 s. Education: BA, Columbia College, 1967; MA, University of Cambridge, England, 1973. Appointments: Ed.-in-Chief, US Army Centre of Military History; Adjunct Prof., University of Maryland; Lecturer, Northern Virginia Community College; Fiction Ed., Gargoyle Magazine, 1977–80; Ed., Bogg Magazine, 1980–. Publications: Cornwall and Other Poems, 1972; Poems by Lyn Lifshin and John Elsberg, 1979; The Price of Reindeer, 1979; Walking as a Controlled Fall, 1980; Home-style Cooking on Third Avenue, 1982; Limey and the Yank, 1982; Torn Nylon Comes with the Night, 1987; 10 or Less, 1989; The Affair, 1991; Father Poems, 1993; Offsets, 1994; The Randomness of E, 1995; Family Values, 1996; Broken Poems for Evita, 1997; A Week in the Lake District, 1998; Small Exchange, 1999; Sailor, 1999. Contributions to: Poetry Now; Gargoyle; Tribune; Orbis; Cambridge Review; Maryland Poetry Review; Amelia; Real Poetry; New Hope International; Outposts; Hanging Loose; Lost and Found Times; Printed Matter; Wind; Tight; Atom Mind; Beltway; Modern Haiku; American Tanka; New Orleans Review; Score; Artemis; RawNervz; Membrane; Blue Unicorn. Memberships: Writers' Centre, Bethesda, Maryland; Poets and Writers; Washington Poetry Committee; Poetry Society of America. Address: 422 N Cleveland St, Arlington, VA 22201, USA.

ELTON, William R.; b. 15 Aug. 1921, New York, NY, USA. Prof. of English Literature; Poet. m. Mary Elizabeth Bowen, 1970, divorced 1974. Education: Columbia University; University of London; PhD, Ohio State University, 1956. Appointments: Prof., University of California, Riverside, 1955–69; Prof. of English Literature, Graduate School, City University of New York, 1969–. Publication: Wittgenstein's Trousers: Poems, 1991. Contributions to: Partisan Review; Poetry New York; Denver Quarterly; Christian Science Monitor; Medicinal Purposes; Experiment. Address: c/o PhD Program in English, Graduate School, City University of New York, 33 W 42nd St, New York, NY 10036, USA.

EMANUEL, James Andrew; b. 15 June 1921, Nebraska, USA. Prof. of English (retd); Poet. m. Mattie Etha Johnson, divorced 1974, 1 s., deceased. Education: BA summa cum laude, Howard University, Washington, DC, 1950; MA, Northwestern University, Evanston, IL, 1953; PhD, Columbia University, New York, 1962. Appointments: Lecturer through to Prof. of English, City College of the City University of New York, 1957–84; Fulbright Prof., Universities of Grenoble, 1968–69, Warsaw, 1975–76; Visiting Prof., University of Toulouse, 1971–73, 1979–81. Publications: The Treehouse and Other Poems, 1968; Panther Man, 1970; Black Man Abroad: The Toulouse Poems, 1978; A Chisel in the Dark, 1980; A Poet's Mind, 1983; The Broken Bowl, 1983; Deadly James and Other Poems, 1987; The Quagmire Effect, 1988; Whole Grain: Collected Poems, 1958–89, 1991; De la Rage au Coeur, 1992; Blues in Black and White (with Godelieve Simons), 1992; Reaching for Mumia: 16 Haiku, 1995. Contributions to: Kenyon Review; New York Times; Phylon; Negro Digest/Black World; Freedomways; Afro American History Bulletin; African American Review; Freelance; Interculture; Midwest Quarterly; Ararat; Negative Capability; La Vague á l'Ame; Inédit; Les Elytres du Hanneton; Jubilarni Sarajevski Dani Poezije; Change; La Traductière; Obaje; II Tarocco; Rovesnik. Honours: John Hay Whitney Foundation Fellowship, 1952–54; Flame Magazine Citation of Merit, 1958; Eugene F Saxton Memorial Trust Fellowship, 1965; Black American Literature Forum Special Distinction Award, 1978; Sidney Bechet Creative Award, 1996. Memberships: Asscn Festival Franco-Anglais de Poésie, Paris; Assocation Grenier Jane Tony, Brussels. Address: Boite Postale 339, 75006 Paris Cedex 06, France.

EMBERSON, Ian McDonald; b. 29 July 1936, Hove, Sussex, England. Librarian (retd); Poet; Artist. m., 2 c. Publications: Doodles in the Margins of My Life, 1981; Swallows Return, 1986; Pirouette of Earth (novel in verse), 1995; Natural Light, 1998; The Comet of 1811 and Other Prose Poems, 2001. Contributions to: Pennine Platform; Envoi; Orbis; New Hope International; Bradford Poetry Quarterly; Dalesman; Countryman; Acumen; Poets Voice; Aireings; Pennine Ink. Honour: William Alwyn International Poetry Society Award, 1981. Memberships: Pennine Poets; Brontë Society; Gaskell Society. Address: Eastroyd, 1 Highcroft Rd, Todmorden, Lancashire OL14 5LZ, England.

EMMOTT, Stewart Earl; b. 6 Oct. 1950, Manchester, England. Archivist; Poet; Writer. 1 s. Education: Part 1 English Literature, Drama, Hull University Teachers' Training College, 1971–73. Appointment: Founder, Archive of Modern Poetry, Fylde Coast. Publications: Poetical Offerings, 1970; Plaintive Poems, 1973; The Frailest Flowers, 1975; Burnt Leaves, 1976; Little Verses, 1978; Fading Innocence, 1980; A College Romance (play), 1981; The Northern

Romantic, 1981; Particles of Rain, 1985; Patterns of Life, 1986; Catching the Rain, 1987; Hidden Worlds, 1990; The Dark Harvest, 1991. Contributions to: The Parnassus of World Poets' Anthology, 1994; Viking Gifts, 1996; Poems; Dalesman; Cumbria Life; Lancashire Life; Record; Preston Arts News; Gothic Society Magazine. Membership: Cumbria Trust for Nature Conservation. Address: 15 Bolton Ave, Carleton, Poulton le Fylde, Lancashire FY6 7TW, England.

EMRICK, Ernestine Hoff; b. 25 Oct. 1918, Chicago, IL, USA. Teacher (retd). Poet. m. Leland B Emrick, 31 May 1941, 1 s. Education: BS, Music, 1940. Publications: Look to the Light, 1954; His Kingdom in My Kitchen, 1955; Tall Thoughts, 1997; Heaven Along the Way, 1997. Contributions to: Various anthologies and periodicals. Honours: National Federation of State Poetry Societies Awards, 1975–94; Theme Poem, 1976, Golden Pegasus Award, 1988, Archie Rosenhouse Memorial Award, 1988, Beth Martin Haas Memorial Award, 1995, California Federation of Chaparral Poets. Memberships: California Federation of Chaparral Poets; California State Poetry Society. Address: 2780 Hillcrest Dr., La Verne, CA 91750-4332, USA.

ENEKWE, Onuora Osmond; b. 12 Nov. 1942, Afa, Nigeria. Researcher; Lecturer; Poet. m. Josephine Chioma Adinde, 9 April 1974, 1 s., 6 d. Education: BA, Honours, English, University of Nigeria, 1971; MFA, Creative Writing, 1974, MPhil, Theatre, 1977, PhD, Theatre, 1982, Columbia University. Appointments: Asst Ed., 1978–87, Ed., 1987–, Okike: An African Journal of New Writing; Senior Lecturer, 1980–84, Assoc. Prof., 1984, Co-ordinator, Dept of Dramatic Arts, 1986–89, Assoc. Dean, Faculty of Arts, 1989–91, University of Nigeria. Publication: Broken Pots, 1977. Contributions to: Mundus Artium: Selection of African Writers and Artists, 1977; Aftermath (anthology), 1977; Rhythms of Creation, 1978; Jungle Muse, 1987; Anthill Annual, 1989; Literary Review, 1991; Echoes of the Sunbird: An Anthology of Contemporary African Poetry, 1993; Parnassus of World Poets, 1997; English for Senior Secondary Schools; Daily Times; Weekend Concord. Honour: Commonwealth Poetry Prize Nomination, 1978. Membership: Asscn of Nigerian Authors. Address: Dept of Dramatic Arts, University of Nigeria, Nsukka, Nigeria.

ENG, Stephen Richard; b. 31 Oct. 1940, San Diego, CA, USA. Biographer; Poet; Literary Journalist; Scholar. m. Anne Jeanne Kangas, 15 May 1969, 2 s., 2 d. Education: BA, English Literature, George Washington University, Washington, DC, 1963; MS, Education (Counselling), Portland State University, Oregon, 1973. Appointments: Poetry Ed., The Diversifier, 1977–78; Assoc. Ed., Triads, 1985; Dir and Ed., Nashville House, 1991–; Staff Book Reviewer, Nashville Banner, 1993–98. Publications: Elusive Butterfly and Other Lyrics (ed.), 1971; The Face of Fear and Other Poems (ed.), 1984; The Hunter of Time: Gnomic Verses (ed.), 1984; Toreros: Poems (ed.), 1990; Poets of the Fantastic (co-ed.), 1992; A Satisfied Mind: The Country Music Life of Porter Wagoner, 1992; Jimmy Buffett: The Man From Margaritaville Revealed, 1996; Yellow Rider and Other Lyrics, 2000. Contributions to: Lyric; Night Cry; Journal of Country Music; Tennessee Historical Quarterly; Bookpage; Nashville Banner; Music City Blues; Space & Time. Honours: American Poets' Fellowship Society Certificate of Merit, 1973; Co-Winner, Rhysling Award, Science Fiction Poetry Asscn, 1979; Best Writer, 1979, 1983, Special Achievement, 1985, Small Press Writers and Artists Organization. Memberships: Broadcast Music Inc, 1972–; Syndic, F. Marion Crawford Memorial Society, 1978–; Country Music Asscn, 1990–; Science-Fiction Poetry Asscn, 1990–. Address: PO Box 111864, Nashville, TN 37222, USA.

ENGELHARDT, Robert Michael; b. 19 Sept. 1964, Albany, New York, USA. Writer; Poet. Education: College of Saint Rose, 1984. Publications: Release..., 1992; Sacred Days, 1994; Hearse, 1995. Contributions to: Atlier; Mobius; The Charles Bukowski Newsletter #10; Delirium; Pumpkinhead; Chronicles of Disorder; Happy Kitty; Mertz! Times Union; Source; Metroland; Volume. Membership: Hudson Valley Writers Guild. Address: 25 McNutt Ave, Albany, NY 12205, USA.

ENGELS, Deen, (Bert Fermin); b. 7 Dec. 1926, Indonesia. Teacher (retd); Poet. m. Cili van Neer, 1 March 1958, 1 s., 4 d. Education: Diploma Teachers Training, Heerlen, 1957; Diploma Teachers Training Special Education, Tilburg, 1961. Appointments: Schools for Retarded Children, 1958–64; Gipsy Children's School, 1964–66; School for Children with Difficulties in Learning and Education, Maastricht, 1966–68; School for Children with Difficulties in Hearing and Speech, Hoensbroek, 1968–90. Publications: Poems by Ulrich Bouchard and Deen Engels, 1980; Don't Blow, 1981; Kicking Occiput, 1983; Together in the Holes, 1986; Menu for Surviving, 1987; The Tricks of the Death, 1988; The Snares of Existence, 1989; Abiding in the Fridge, 1991; The Flowers Shark, 1992; Whitehaven, 1994; Vehicles, 2000; Cosmetics, 2000. Contributions to: Appel; Gist; Concept; Vlam; WeL; In zekere zin; Horizon; Karree; Vlaanderen; Nieuw Vlaams Tijdschrift-Gierik; International Poetry. Honours: Poetry Prize, Sint-Truiden, 1979; Secundo Precio en la Categoria Prosa y Poesia, Consulado de Costa Rica, The Hague, 1990. Membership: Vereniging van Limburgse Auteurs. Address: Mauritslaan 1, 6371 ED Landgraaf, Netherlands.

ENGELS, John (David); b. 19 Jan. 1931, South Bend, IN, USA. Prof. of English; Poet; Writer. m. Gail Jochimsen, 1957, 4 s., 2 d. *Education:* BA, University of Notre Dame, 1952; University College, Dublin, 1955; MFA, University of Iowa, 1957. *Appointments:* Instructor, Norbert College, West De Pere, Wisconsin, 1957–62; Asst Prof., 1962–70, Prof. of English, 1970–, St Michael's College, Winooski Park, Vermont; Visiting Lecturer, University of Vermont, 1974, 1975, 1976; Slaughter Lecturer, Sweet Briar College, 1976; Writer-in-Residence, Randolph Macon Women's College, 1992. *Publications:* Poetry: The Homer Mitchell Place, 1968; Signals from the Safety Coffin, 1975; Blood Mountain, 1977; Vivaldi in Early Fall, 1981; The Seasons in Vermont, 1982; Weather-Fear: New and Selected Poems 1958–1982, 1983; Cardinals in the Ice Age, 1987; Walking to Cootehill: New and Selected Poems 1958–1992, 1993; Big Water, 1995. Other: Writing Techniques (with Norbert Engels), 1962; Experience and Imagination (with Norbert Engels), 1965; The Merrill Checklist of William Carlos Williams (ed.), 1969; The Merrill Studies in Paterson (ed.), 1971. *Honours:* Bread Loaf Writers' Conference Scholarship, 1960, and Robert Frost Fellowship, 1976; Guggenheim Fellowship, 1979. *Address:* c/o Dept of English, St Michael's College, Winooski Park, VT 05404, USA.

ENGLAND, Gerald; b. 21 Dec. 1946, Ackworth, England. Financial Adviser (retd); Poet; Ed.; Webmaster. m. Christine Ann Smedley, 22 June 1974, 2 s. *Education:* Strathclyde University, 1964–66; Leeds College of Technology, 1967–68; HNC Chemistry, Sheffield Polytechnic, 1969–71; Open University, 1973–74. *Appointments:* Technician, Sheffield University, 1969–74; Ed., Headland, 1969–79, New Hope International, 1980–, Aabye, 1998–2001; Agent, Britannic Assurance, 1974–1998. *Publications:* Poetic Sequence for Five Voices, 1966; Mousings, 1970; The Wine, the Women and the Song, 1972; For Her Volume One, 1972; Meetings at the Moors Edge, 1976; The Rainbow, 1980; Daddycation, 1982; Futures (with Christine England), 1986; Stealing Kisses, 1992; Limbo Time, 1998. *Contributions to:* Bogg; Candelabrum; Crooked Roads; Envoi; Folio; Green's Magazine; Haiku Quarterly; Hybrid; Inkshed; International Journal on World Peace; Krax; Legend; Lo Straniero; Moorlands Review; New Wave; Owen Wister Review; Pennine Ink; Periaktos; Pididdle; Prophetic Voices; Radio Void; Verve; Waterways; Wormwood Review; Z Miscellaneous. *Memberships:* Yorkshire Dialect Society, Council Mem.; Pennine Poets; Wordwizards; Ukku; Paradoxist Movement; International Writers' and Authors' Asscn. *Address:* 20 Werneth Ave, Gee Cross, Hyde, Cheshire SK14 5NL, England. *E-mail:* nhi@clara.net. *Website:* www.nhi.clara.net/gehome.htm.

ENGLER, Robert Klein; b. 20 May 1948, Chicago, IL, USA. Tutor; Writer; Poet. *Education:* Divinity Degree, University of Chicago, 1976. *Appointments:* Chair., Social Sciences Dept, Richard J Daley College, Chicago. *Publication:* Sonnets by Degree, 1986. *Contributions to:* Christopher Street; James Wright Review; Tribe. *Honour:* Illinois Arts Council Award for Poetry, 1989. *Address:* Richard J Daley College, 7500 S Polaski, Chicago, IL 60652, USA.

ENGLISH, June Vincent; b. 16 June 1936, Dover, Kent, England. Writer; Poet; Teacher. m. (1) Alan E John, 9 May 1959, 1 s., (2) John Brian English, 7 July 1979, 1 s. *Education:* BA, English and History, University of Kent, 1989; MA, Humanities, Christchurch, England, 1992. *Contributions to:* Acumen; Psychopoetica; Poetry Digest; Peace & Freedom; Dam; Hen House. *Memberships:* Poetry Society. *Address:* Four Winds, Pommeus Lane, Ripple, Nr Deal, Kent CT14 8HZ, England.

ENRIGHT, D(ennis) J(oseph); b. 11 March 1920, Leamington, Warwickshire, England. Writer; Poet; Ed. m. Madeleine Harders, 3 Nov. 1949, 1 d. *Education:* BA, 1944, MA, 1946, Downing College, Cambridge; DLitt, University of Alexandria, Egypt, 1949. *Appointments:* Prof. of English, Far East, 1947–70; Co-Ed., Encounter, 1970–72; Dir, Chatto and Windus Publishers, 1974–82. *Publications:* The Laughing Hyena and Other Poems, 1953; Academic Year, 1955; Bread Rather Than Blossoms, 1956; Some Men are Brothers, 1960; Selected Poems, 1969; Memoirs of a Mendicant Professor, 1969; Daughters of Earth, 1972; The Terrible Shears: Scenes From a Twenties Childhood, 1974; Sad Ires and Others, 1975; Paradise Illustrated, 1978; A Faust Book, 1979; The Oxford Book of Death (ed.), 1983; A Mania for Sentences, 1983; The Alluring Problem, 1986; Collected Poems, 1987; Fields of Vision, 1988; The Faber Book of Fevers and Frets (ed.), 1989; Selected Poems, 1990; Under the Circumstances, 1991; The Oxford Book of Friendship (ed. with David Rawlinson), 1991; The Way of the Cat, 1992; Old Men and Comets, 1993; The Oxford Book of the Supernatural (ed.), 1994; Interplay: A Kind of Commonplace Book, 1995; The Sayings of Goethe (ed.), 1996; Collected Poems 1948–1998, 1998; Play Resumed: A Journal, 1999; Signs and Wonders: Selected Essays, 2001. *Contributions to:* Journals, reviews, and magazines. *Honours:* Cholmondeley Award, 1974; Queen's Gold Medal for Poetry, 1981; Hon. Doctorates, University of Warwick, 1982, University of Surrey, 1985; O.B.E., 1991; Companion of Literature, 1998. *Membership:* RSL, Fellow. *Literary Agent:* Watson Little Ltd, Capo di Monte, Windmill Hill, London NW3 6RJ, England. *Address:* 35A Viewfield Rd, London SW18 5JD, England.

ENSLIN, Theodore (Vernon); b. 25 March 1925, Chester, PA, USA. Poet; Writer. m. (1) Mildred Marie Stout, 1945, divorced 1961, 1 s., 1 d., (2) Alison Jane Jose, 1969, 1 s. *Education:* Studied composition with Nadia Boulanger. *Appointment:* Columnist, The Cape Codder, Orleans, MA, 1949–56.

Publications: Poetry: The Work Proposed, 1958; New Sharon's Prospect, 1962; The Place Where I Am Standing, 1964; To Come to Have Become, 1966; The Diabelli Variations and Other Poems, 1967; 2/30–6/31: Poems 1967, 1967; The Poems, 1970; Forms, five vols, 1970–74; The Median Flow: Poems 1943–73, 1974; Ranger, Ranger 2, two vols, 1979, 1980; Music for Several Occasions, 1985; Case Book, 1987; Love and Science, 1990; A Sonare, 1994. Fiction: 2 + 12 (short stories), 1979. Play: Barometric Pressure 29.83 and Steady, 1965. Other: Mahler, 1975; The July Book, 1976. *Honours:* Nieman Award for Journalism, 1955; National Endowment for the Arts Grant, 1976. *Address:* RFD Box 289, Kansas Rd, Milbridge, MA 04658, USA.

ENZENSBERGER, Hans Magnus; b. 11 Nov. 1929, Kaufbeuren, Germany. Author; Poet; Dramatist; Trans.; Ed.; Publisher. m. (1) Dagrun Christensen, 1 d., (2) Maria Makarowa, (3) Katharina Bonitz, 1 d. *Education:* German Literature, Philosophy, and Linguistics, Universities of Erlangen, Hamburg, Freiburg im Breisgau, Sorbonne, Paris, 1949–54; DPhil, 1955. *Appointments:* Mem., Gruppe 47, 1955; Lecturer, Hochschule für Gestaltung, Ulm, 1956–57; Literary Consultant, Suhrkamp publishers, 1960–; Hon. Lecturer, University of Frankfurt am Main, 1964–65; Ed., 1965–75, Publisher, 1970–90, Kursbuch periodical; Ed., TransAtlantik periodical, 1980–82; Ed.-Publisher, Die Andere Bibliothek, 1985–; Artistic Dir, Renaissance Theatre, Berlin, 1995–. *Publications:* Verteidigung der wölfe (poems), 1957; Landessprache (poems), 1957; Museum der modernen Poesie (ed. and trans.), 1960; Clemens Brentanos Poetik (essay), 1961; Einzelheiten, 1964; Blindenschrift (poems), 1964; Politik und Verbrechen, 1964; Das Verhör von Habana (play), 1970; Klassenbuch (co-ed.), three vols, 1972; Der kurze Sommer der Anarchie: Buenaventura Durrutis Leben und Tod (novel), 1972; Gespräche mit Marx und Engels (ed.), 1973; Mausoleum: Siebenunddreissig Balladen aus der Geschichte des Fortschritts (poems), 1975; Der Untergang der Titanic (epic poem), 1978; Die Furie des Verschwindens (poems), 1980; Politische Brosamen (essays), 1982; Der Menschenfeind (play), 1984; Gedichte 1950–1985 (collected poems), 1986; Ach Europa!: Wahrnehmungen aus sieben Ländern (essays), 1987; Mittelmass und Wahn: Gesammelte Zerstreuungen (essays), 1988; Requiem für eine romantische Frau: Die Geschichte von Auguste Bussmann und Clemens Brentano (novel), 1988; Zukunftsmusik (poems), 1991; Die Grosse Wanderung: 33 Markierungen (essays), 1992; Aussichten des Bürgerkriegs (essay), 1993; Kiosk (poems), 1995; Der Zahlenteufel, 1997; Wo warst du, Robert (novel), 1998, English trans. as Where Were You, Robert?, 2000; Leichter als Luft: Moralische Gedichte (poems), 1999; Zickzack, 1999; Einladung zu einem Poesie-Automaton, 2000; Die Elixiere der Wissenschaft, 2002. *Honours:* German Critics' Literature Prize, 1962; Georg Büchner Prize, 1963; Cultural Prize of the City of Nuremberg, 1967; Premio Pasolino, 1982; Heinrich Böll Prize, 1985; Bavarian Acad. of Fine Arts Literature Award, Munich, 1987; Erich Maria Remarque Peace Prize, Osnabrück, 1993; Cultural Prize of the City of Munich, 1994; Orden pour le mérite für Wissenschaften und Künste, 2000; Premio Principe de Asturias, 2002. *Address:* c/o Suhrkamp Verlag, Lindenstr 29–35, 60325 Frankfurt am Main, Germany.

ERBA, Luciano; b. 18 Sept. 1922, Milan, Italy. Poet; Trans.; Writer; Prof. of French Literature (retd). *Education:* PhD, Catholic University, Milan, 1947. *Appointments:* Prof. of Comparative Literature, Rutgers University, NB, USA, 1964–65; Prof. of Italian and French Literature, University of Washington at Seattle, USA, 1965–66; Prof. of French Literature, University of Padua, 1973–82, University of Verona, 1982–87, Catholic University, Milan, 1987–97. *Publications:* Linea K, 1951; Il bel paese, 1956; Il prete di Ratanà, 1959; Il male minore, 1960; Il prato più verde, 1977; Il nastro di Moebius, 1980; Il cerchio aperto, 1983; L'ippopotamo, 1989; L'ipotesi circense, 1995; Negli spazi intermedi, 1998; Nella terra di mezzo, 2000. Other: Françoise (novel), 1982; Radio plays; Trans. *Honours:* Viareggio Prize, 1980; Bagutta Prize, 1988; Librex-Guggenheim Eugenio Montale Prize, 1989; Italian PEN Club Prize, 1995. *Address:* Via Giason del Maino 16, 20146 Milan, Italy.

ERDRICH, (Karen) Louise; b. 7 June 1954, Little Falls, MN, USA. Writer; Poet. m. Michael Anthony Dorris, 10 Oct. 1981, deceased 1997, 7 c. *Education:* BA, Dartmouth College, 1976; MA, Johns Hopkins University, 1979. *Appointments:* Visiting Poet and Teacher, North Dakota State Arts Council, 1977–78; Writing Instructor, Johns Hopkins University, 1978–79; Communications Dir and Ed. of Circle of the Boston Indian Council, 1979–80. *Publications:* Fiction: Love Medicine, 1984; The Beet Queen, 1986; Tracks, 1988; The Crown of Columbus (with Michael Anthony Dorris), 1991; The Bingo Palace, 1994; The Bluejay's Dance, 1995; Tales of Burning Love, 1996; The Antelope Wife, 1998; The Birchbark House, 2000; The Last Report on the Miracles at Little No Horse, 2001. Poetry: Jacklight, 1984; Baptism of Desire, 1989. Other: Imagination (textbook), 1980. *Contributions to:* Anthologies; American Indian Quarterly; Atlantic; Frontiers; Kenyon Review; Ms; New England Review; New York Times Book Review; New Yorker; North American Review; Redbook; Others. *Honours:* MacDowell Colony Fellowship, 1980; Yaddo Colony Fellowship, 1981; Dartmouth College Visiting Fellow, 1981; National Magazine Fiction Awards, 1983, 1987; National Book Critics Circle Award for Best Work of Fiction, 1984; Virginia McCormick Scully Prize for Best Book of the Year, 1984; Best First Fiction Award, American Acad. and Institute of Arts and Letters, 1985; Guggenheim Fellowship, 1985–86; First

Prize, O. Henry Awards, 1987. *Address:* c/o Andrew Wylie Agency, 250 W 57th St, Suite 2114, New York, NY 10107, USA.

ERICKSON, Rollie; b. 17 Jan. 1953, Madison, Wisconsin, USA. Artist; Painter; Poet. m. Cass Erickson, 4 July 1992. *Education:* BFA, State University of New York at Purchase, 1981. *Contributions to:* Wordimage; Asheville Poetry Review. *Address:* PO Box 867, Weaverville, NC 28787, USA.

ESBER, Ali Ahmad Said, (Adonis); b. 1930, Oassabin, Syria. Poet; Educator. *Education:* BA, University of Damascus, 1954; PhD, University of St Joseph, Beirut, 1973. *Appointments:* Prof. of Arabic Literature, Lebanese University, Beirut, 1971–85; PhD Advisor, University of St Joseph, Beirut, 1971–85; Visiting Lecturer, Collège de France, Paris, 1983, Georgetown University, Washington, DC, 1985; Assoc. Prof. of Arab Poetry, University of Geneva, 1989–95. *Publications:* Poetry in French: Chants de Mihyar le Damascene, 1983; Tombeau pour New York suivi de Prologue a l'histoire des rois des ta'ifa et de Ceci est mon nom, 1986; Le Temps les Villes, 1990; Célébrations, 1991; Chronique des branches, 1991; Mémoire du vent (anthology), 1991; Soleils Seconds, 1994; Singuliers, 1995. In English: An Introduction to Arab Poetics, 1990; The Pages of Day and Night, 1994. Other: Poetry in Arabic. *Honours:* Prix des Amis du Livre, Beirut, 1968; Syria-Lebanon Award, International Poetry Forum, 1971; National Prize for Poetry, Lebanon, 1974; Officier des Arts et des Lettres, France, 1993; Grand Prix des Biennales Internationales de la Poésie de Liège, Belgium, 1986; Prix Jean Malrieu-Étranger, Marseille, 1991; Feronia-Cita di Fiano, Rome, 1993; Nazim Hikmat Prize, Istanbul, 1994; Prix Méditerranée-Étranger, France, 1995. *Memberships:* Académie Stéphane Mallarmé, Paris; Haut Conseil de Réflexion du Collège International de Philosophie, Paris. *Address:* 1 Sq. Henri Regnault, 92400 Courbevoie, France.

ESCANDELL, Noemi; b. 27 Sept. 1936, Havana, Cuba. Prof. of Spanish Language and Literature; Poet. m. Peter Knapp, 1 June 1957, divorced 1972, 2 s., 2 d. *Education:* BLitt, Instituto de la Vibora, 1955; BA, Queens College of the City University of New York, 1968; MA, 1971, PhD, 1976, Harvard University. *Appointments:* Asst Prof., Bard College, 1976–83; Language Programme Dir, Nuevo Instituto de Centroamerica, Esteli, Nicaragua, 1987–88; Prof. of Spanish, Westfield State College, 1983–93; Dir, Afterschool Programme, Ross School, Washington, DC, 1995–96. *Publications:* Cuadros, 1982; Ciclos, 1982; Palabras/Words, 1986. *Contributions to:* Anthologies and periodicals. *Honours:* Poet-in-Residence, Millay Colony for the Arts, Austerlitz, New York, 1983, 1991; Special Mention, Certamen Poetico Federico García Lorca Poetry Contest, 1995; First Prize in Poetry, XXXII Certamen Literario International Odon Betanzos Palacio, 1996. *Membership:* Acad. Iberoamericana de Poesia, Washington, DC, Chapter. *Address:* 1525 Q St NW, No. 11, Washington, DC 20009, USA.

ESH, Eshed. See: SHEINFELD, Ilan.

ESHLEMAN, Clayton; b. 1 June 1935, Indianapolis, IN, USA. Prof. of English; Poet; Writer; Trans. m. (1) Barbara Novak, 1961, divorced 1967, 1 s., (2) Caryl Reiter, 1969. *Education:* BA, Philosophy, 1958, MA, Creative Writing, 1961, Indiana University. *Appointments:* Ed., Folio, 1959–60; Instructor, University of Maryland Eastern Overseas Division, 1961–62, New York University American Language Institute, 1966–68; Publisher, Caterpillar Books, 1966–68; Founder-Ed.-Publisher, Caterpillar magazine, 1967–73; Faculty, School of Critical Studies, California Institute of the Arts, Valencia, 1970–72; Dreyfuss Poet-in-Residence and Lecturer, California Institute of Technology, Pasadena, 1979–84; Visiting Lecturer in Creative Writing, Universities of California at San Diego, Los Angeles, Santa Barbara, and Riverside, 1979–86; Reviewer, Los Angeles Times Book Review, 1979–86; Founder-Ed., Sulfur magazine, 1981–; Prof. of English, Eastern Michigan University, 1986–. *Publications:* Mexico & North, 1962; Brother Stones, 1968; Indiana, 1969; The House of Ibuki, 1969; Altars, 1971; A Caterpillar Anthology: A Selection of Poetry and Prose from Caterpillar Magazine (ed.), 1971; Coils, 1973; The Gull Wall, 1975; Grotesca, 1975; On Mules Sent from Chavin, 1977; What She Means, 1977; Our Lady of the Three-Pronged Devil, 1977; Nights We Put the Rock Together, 1980; Hades in Manganese, 1981; Fracture, 1983; The Name Encanyoned River: Selected Poems, 1960–85, 1986; Hotel-Cro-Magnon, 1989; Antiphonal Swing: Selected Prose, 1962–87, 1989; Novices: A Study of Poetic Apprenticeship, 1989; Under World Arrest, 1994; Nora's Roar, 1996; From Scratch, 1998. Translations: 13 books, 1962–95. *Contributions to:* Numerous anthologies, magazines, and newspapers. *Honours:* PEN Trans. Prize, 1977; Guggenheim Fellowship, 1978; National Book Award for Trans., 1979; National Endowment for the Arts Fellowship, 1979; National Endowment for the Humanities Grant, 1980, and Fellowships, 1981, 1988; Michigan Arts Council Grant, 1988; Eastern Michigan University Research Grants, 1990, 1997. *Address:* 210 Washtenaw Ave, Ypsilanti, MI 48197, USA.

ESPOSITO, Nancy (Giller); b. 1 Jan. 1942, Dallas, TX, USA. Poet; Writer; Ed.; Asst Prof. *Education:* University of Wisconsin; BA, English, MA, English, New York University. *Appointments:* Assoc. Prof., Illinois Central College, East Peoria, 1968–70; Instructor, Harvard University, 1976–80, 1981–84, Wellesley College, 1980; Lecturer, Tufts University, 1986–93, Boston College, 1994; Asst Prof., Bentley College, 1986–; CIEE Seminar, Viet Nam, 2002. *Publication:* Changing Hands, 1984. *Contributions to:* Anthologies: Two Decades of New

Poets, 1984, Ixok-Amar-Go, 1987, Quarterly Review of Literature 50th Anniversary Anthology, 1993, and Poetry from Sojourner, 1999; Reviews, journals, and periodicals. *Honours:* Discovery/The Nation Award, 1979; Virginia Center for the Creative Arts Fellow, 1979–80, 1981, 1990; Yaddo Fellow, 1981; Colladay Award, 1984; MacDowell Colony Fellow, 1986–87; Gordon Barber Memorial Award, Poetry Society of America, 1987; Fulbright-Hays Grant, Egypt, 1988; Publishing Award, 1988, Faculty Development Fund Grant, Bentley College, 1997; Ragdale Foundation Fellow, 1990; Bentley College Faculty Grant, Viet Nam, 1999–2000. *Memberships:* Acad. of American Poets; Associated Writing Programs; Poetry Society of America; Poets and Writers. *Address:* 34 Trowbridge St, Belmont, MA 02478, USA.

ESTRELLA. See: GRESS, Esther Johanne.

ETTER, Dave, (David Pearson Etter); b. 18 March 1928, Huntington Park, CA, USA. Poet; Writer; Ed. m. Margaret A. Cochran, 8 Aug. 1959, 1 s., 1 d. *Education:* BA, History, University of Iowa, 1953. *Appointments:* Promotion Dept, Indiana University, 1959–60; Rand McNally Publishing Co, 1960–61; Ed., Northwestern University Press, 1962–63; Asst Ed., Encyclopaedia Britannica, Chicago, 1964–73; Ed., Northern Illinois University Press, 1974–80; Freelance Writer, Poet and Ed., 1981–. *Publications:* Go Read the River, 1966; The Last Train to Prophetstown, 1968; Well You Needn't, 1975; Central Standard Time, 1978; Open to the Wind, 1978; Riding the Rock Island Through Kansas, 1979; Cornfields, 1980; West of Chicago, 1981; Boondocks, 1982; Alliance, IL, 1983; Home State, 1985; Live at the Silver Dollar, 1986; Selected Poems, 1987; Midlanders, 1988; Electric Avenue, 1988; Carnival, 1990; Sunflower County, 1994; How High the Moon, 1996; The Essential Dave Etter, 2001. *Contributions to:* Poetry; Nation; Chicago Review; Kansas Quarterly; Prairie Schooner; Poetry Northwest; TriQuarterly; Massachusetts Review; North American Review; Ohio Review; New Letters; Shenandoah; Beloit Poetry Journal; El Corno Emplumado; San Francisco Review; New Mexico Quarterly; Mark Twain Journal; Slow Dancer (England), among others. *Honours:* Society of Midland Authors Poetry Prize, 1967; Friends of Literature Poetry Prize, 1967; Bread Loaf Writers' Conference Fellowship in Poetry, 1967; Illinois Sesquicentennial Poetry Prize, 1968; Theodore Roethke Poetry Prize, 1971; Carl Sandburg Poetry Prize, 1982. *Address:* 628 E Locust St, Lanark, IL 61046, USA.

ETTY, Robert; b. 6 Nov. 1949, Waltham, Lincolnshire, England. Schoolteacher; Poet. m. Anne Levison, 3 April 1975, 1 s., 1 d. *Education:* BA. *Publications:* Hovendens Violets, 1989; New Pastorals, 1992; Marking Places, 1994; A Selection, 1997; Small Affairs on the Estate, 2000; The Blue Box, 2001. *Contributions to:* Poetry Review; The North; Spectator; Outposts; Rialto; Staple; Stand; Verse; The Independent. *Honours:* Lake Aske Award, Nottingham Poetry Society, 1990; First Prize, Wykeham Poetry Competition, 1991; First Prize, Kent and Sussex Open Poetry Competition, 1992. *Address:* Evenlode, Church Lane, Keddington, Louth, Lincolnshire LN11 7HG, England.

EVANS, Aled Lewis; b. 9 Aug. 1961, Machynlleth, Wales. Poet; Teacher; Broadcaster. *Education:* BA, Welsh and English, University College of North Wales, Bangor. *Publications:* Border Town, 1983; Whispers, 1986; Waves, 1989; Can I Have a Patch of Blue Sky?, 1991; Between Two September Tides, 1994. *Contributions to:* Barn; Chester Poets Anthologies; Golwg; Tu Chwith. *Honour:* National Eisteddfod of Wales Award for Poetry, 1991. *Memberships:* Chester Poets; Gorsedd Bards. *Address:* 28 Jubilee Rd, Pentrefelin, Wrexham, Clwyd LL13 7NN, Wales.

EVANS, Donald; b. 12 June 1940, Cardiganshire, Wales. Poet. m. Pat Thomas, 29 Dec 1972, 1 s. *Education:* BA, Welsh, 1962, Diploma, Education, 1963, University College of Wales, Aberystwyth. *Publications:* Egin, 1976; Haidd, 1977; Grawn, 1979; Y Flodeugerdd O Gywyddau (ed.), 1981; Machlud Canrif, 1983; Cread Crist, 1986; O'r Bannau Duon, 1987; Iasau, 1988; Seren Poets 2 (with others), 1990; The Life and Work of Rhydwen Williams, 1991; Wrth Reddf, 1994; Asgwrn Cefen, 1997; Y Cyntefig Cyfoes, 2000. *Contributions to:* Several publications. *Honours:* National Eisteddfod Crown and Chair, 1977, 1980; Welsh Arts Council Poetry Prizes, 1977, 1983, 1989; Welsh Academy Literary Award, 1989. *Memberships:* Welsh Acad.; Welsh Poetry Society. *Address:* Y Plas, Talgarreg, Llandysful, Co of Ceredigion SA44 4XA, Wales.

EVANS, Mari; b. 16 July 1923, Toledo, Ohio, USA. Poet; Writer. Divorced, 2 s. *Education:* University of Toledo. *Appointments:* Writer, Producer and Dir, The Black Experience television programme, Indianapolis, 1968–73; Writer-in-Residence and Instructor in Black Literature, Indiana University-Purdue University at Indianapolis, 1969–70; Asst Prof. of Black Literature and Writer-in-Residence, Indiana University, 1970–78, Purdue University, 1978–80; Writer-in-Residence and Visiting Asst Prof., Northwestern University, 1972–73; Visiting Prof., Washington University, 1980, Cornell University, 1981–84, University of Miami, Coral Gables, 1989; Assoc. Prof., State University of New York, Albany, 1985–86; Writer-in-Residence, Spelman College, Atlanta, 1989–90. *Publications:* Poetry: Where Is All the Music?, 1968; I Am a Black Woman, 1970; Whisper, 1979; Nightstar, 1981; A Dark and Splendid Mass, 1992. Other: Rap Stories, 1973; J D, 1973; I Look at Me, 1974; Singing Black, 1976; Jim Flying High, 1979; Black Women Writers 1950–1980: A Critical Evaluation (ed.), 1984. *Honours:* John Hay Whitney Fellowship,

1965; Woodrow Wilson Foundation Grant, 1968; Black Acad. of Arts and Letters Award, 1971; MacDowell Fellowship, 1975; Copeland Fellowship, 1980; National Endowment for the Arts Award, 1981; Yaddo Fellowship, 1984. *Address:* PO Box 483, Indianapolis, IN 46206, USA.

EVANS, Martina Mary Lelia; b. 11 Aug. 1961, Cork, Ireland. Radiographer; Poet. m. Declan Evans, 5 Oct. 1985, 1 d. *Education:* BA, Open University, 1991. *Contributions to:* Poetry Ireland Review; Celtic Dawn; Scratch; Rialto; Iota; Hybrid; Brandos Hat; Third Half; Symphony; Cobweb; New Hope International; Fat Chance; Bound Spiral; New Irish Writing; New Virago Poets. *Honours:* Frances Martin College Prize; Hennessy Award Nomination, 1992.

EVANS, Richard Rowland; b. 26 May 1936, Tabor, Dolgellau, Wales. Writer; Poet. m. Bronwen Edwards, 21 Aug. 1965, 1 d. *Education:* Teacher's Certificate, 1958; Diploma, Bilingual Education, 1964; BEd, University College of Wales, 1980; BA, University of Wales, 1998. *Appointment:* Welsh Ed., The Normalite/Y Normalydd, 1957–58. *Publication:* Mynd i'r Lleuad, 1973. *Contributions to:* Dalen, Godre'r Gader; The Normalite/Y Normalydd; Y Cyfnod; Y Dydd. *Honour:* Bardic Chair, 1988. *Membership:* Welsh Academy/Yr Academi Gymreig. *Address:* Brithdir, 93 Ger-y-llen, Penrhyn coch, Aberystwyth, Ceredigion SY23 3HQ, Wales.

EVERETT, Graham; b. 23 Dec. 1947, Oceanside, NY, USA. Prof.; Poet; Writer. m. Elyse Arnow, 27 Dec. 1981, 1 s. *Education:* BA, English, Canisius College, 1970; MA, English, 1987, PhD, English, 1994, State University of New York at Stony Brook. *Appointments:* Ed. and Publisher, Street Press and Magazine, 1972–86. *Publications:* Trees, 1978; Strange Coast, 1979; Paumanok Rising: An Anthology of Eastern Long Island Aesthetics (co-ed.), 1981; Sunlit Sidewalk, 1985; Minus Green, 1992; Minus Green Plus, 1995; Corps Calleux, 2000. *Contributions to:* Anthologies, reviews, quarterlies, and journals. *Memberships:* MLA; National Council of Teachers of English. *Address:* PO Box 772, Sound Beach, NY 11789, USA.

EYTHORSDOTTIR, Sigridur; b. 21 Aug. 1940, Selvogur, Iceland. Teacher; Writer; Poet; Dramatist. m. Jon Laxdalarnalds, 24 Aug. 1963, 1 s., 1 d. *Education:* Diploma in Drama, 1968; Professional Skills in Special Education; Diploma in Teaching, University of Teaching. *Publications:* Gunnar Eignast Systur, 1979; Lena Sol, 1983. Other: Stage plays, radio dramas, short stories and poems. *Contributions to:* Several publications. *Honours:* Malog Menning Award, 1982; Kramhusio Award, 1992; Ibbx Award, 1996. *Membership:* Writers' Asscn of Iceland. *Address:* Asvallagata 26, 101 Reykjavík, Iceland.

EZEKIEL, Nissim; b. 16 Dec. 1924, Mumbai, India. Prof. of English (retd); Poet. m. Daisy Jacob, 1952, 1 s., 2 d. *Education:* MA, University of Mumbai, 1947. *Appointments:* Reader, 1972–81, Prof., 1981–85, English, University of Mumbai; Writer-in-Residence, National University of Singapore, 1988–89. *Publications:* A Time to Change and Other Poems, 1952; Sixty Poems, 1953; The Third, 1958; The Unfinished Man: 1959, 1960; The Exact Name, 1960–64, 1965; A Martin Luther King Reader (ed.), 1969; Pergamon Poets 9, 1970; Hymns in Darkness, 1976; Collected Poems, 1952–88, 1990. *Honours:* National Acad. Award, 1983; Padma Shree, 1988. *Address:* 18 Kala Niketan, Sixth Floor, 47C, Bhulabhai Desai Rd, Mumbai 400 026, India.

F

FABILLI, Mary; b. 16 Feb. 1914, USA. Poet; Artist. *Education:* BA, University of California at Berkeley, 1941. *Appointment:* Assoc. Curator of History, Oakland Museum, CA, 1949–77. *Publications:* The Old Ones, 1966; Aurora Bligh and Early Poems, 1968; The Animal Kingdom, 1975; Poems, 1976–81, 1981; Winter Poems, 1983; Simple Pleasures, 1987; Shingles and Other Poems, 1990; Aurora Bligh, 2000; Pious Poems, (illustrated by author), 2001. *Contributions to:* New Directions; Experimental Review; Talisman; Various books. *Address:* 2445 Ashby Ave, Berkeley, CA 94705, USA.

FABRI, Peter; b. 21 Dec. 1953, Budapest, Hungary. Writer; Poet; Librettist. m. (1) 1 s., (2) Kriszta Kovats, 7 June 1986, 1 d. *Education:* Eötvös Lorand University, Budapest, 1973–78. *Publications:* Folytatasos Regeny, 1981; Napfordulo, 1987; Bameszkodasaim Konyve, 1991; Kolumbusz, Az Orult Spanyol, 1992. Other: Librettos for musicals; Lyrics for songs. *Contributions to:* Periodicals. *Honour:* Emerton Prize, Best Lyricist of the Year, 1990. *Membership:* Hungarian PEN. *Address:* Rippl Ronai u 27, 1068 Budapest, Hungary.

FACOS, James; b. 28 July 1924, Lawrence, Massachusetts, USA. Prof. (retd); Writer; Poet. m. Cleo Chigos, 1 Dec. 1956, 1 s., 2 d. *Education:* AB, Bates College, 1949; MA, Florida State University, 1958; DHL, Norwich Univerity, 1989. *Appointments:* Prof., Vermont College and Norwich University, 1958–89. *Publications:* The Piper O The May, 1962; Morning's Come Singing, 1981. *Contributions to:* Poetry; Saturday Evening Post; Lyric; Christian Science Monitor. *Honours:* Walter Peach Award, 1962; Corinne Davis Award, 1970. *Address:* 333 Elm St, Montpelier, VT 05602, USA.

FAES, Urs; b. 13 Feb. 1947, Aarau, Switzerland. Author; Poet; Dramatist. *Education:* MA, University of Zürich. *Appointments:* Journalist, 1979–81; Dramatist, 1982–86; Writer, 1982–. *Publications:* Eine Kerbe im Mittag (poems), 1975; Heidentum und Aberglaube (essay), 1979; Regenspur (poems), 1979; Webfehler (novel), 1983; Zugluft (play), 1983; Der Traum vom Leben (short stories), 1984; Kreuz im Feld (play), 1984; Bis ans Ende der Erinnerung (novel), 1986; Wartzimmer (play), 1986; Partenza (radio play), 1986; Sommerwende (novel), 1989; Alphabet des Abschieds, 1991; Eine andere Geschichte (radio play), 1993; Augenblicke im Paradies (novel), 1994; Ombra (novel), 1997; Und Ruth (novel), 2001. *Honours:* Prize, City of Zurich, 1986; Prize for Literature, 1991; Literary Prize, Kanton Soluthurn, 1999. *Memberships:* Swiss Authors' Group; PEN. *Address:* Urs Faes, Sirius Str 4, 8044 Zürich, Switzerland.

FAGLES, Robert; b. 11 Sept. 1933, Philadelphia, PA, USA. Prof.; Trans.; Poet. m. Marilyn Fagles, 17 June 1956, 2 c. *Education:* AB, summa cum laude, Amherst College, 1955; MA, 1956, PhD, 1959, Yale University. *Appointments:* Instructor, Yale University, 1959–60; Instructor, 1960–62, Asst Prof., 1962–65, Assoc. Prof., 1965–70, Dir, Program in Comparative Literature, 1966–75, Prof., 1970–, Chair., Dept of Comparative Literature, 1976–94, Princeton University. *Publications:* Translator: Complete Poems, by Bacchylides, 1961; The Oresteia, by Aeschylus, 1975; The Three Theban Plays, by Sophocles, 1984; The Iliad, by Homer, 1990; The Odyssey, by Homer, 1996. Poetry: I, Vincent: Poems from the Pictures of Van Gogh, 1978. Co-Editor: Homer: A Collection of Critical Essays, 1962; Pope's Iliad and Odyssey, 1967. *Contributions to:* Books and journals. *Honours:* Harold Morton Landon Trans. Award, Acad. of American Poets, 1991; American Acad. of Arts and Letters Award, 1996; PEN/Ralph Manheim Medal for Life-time Achievement in Trans., 1997; Commander, Order of the Phoenix, Hellenic Republic, 1999. *Memberships:* American Acad. of Arts and Letters; American Acad. of Arts and Sciences; American Philosophical Society. *Address:* c/o Dept of Comparative Literature, Princeton University, Princeton, NJ 08540, USA.

FAHEY, Diane Mary; b. 2 Jan. 1945, Melbourne, Vic., Australia. Writer; Poet. *Education:* BA, 1966, Dip Ed, 1972, MA, 1975, University of Melbourne; PhD, Creative Writing, University of Western Sydney. *Appointments:* Teacher, Humanities, Box Hill Technical College, 1973; English Tutor, Burwood Teacher's College, 1976–79; Lecturer, Literary Studies, University of South Australia, Salisbury Campus, 1986; Teacher, Professional Writing and Editing Course, Centre for Adult Education, Melbourne, 2002–. *Publications:* Voices from the Honeycomb, 1986; Metamorphoses, 1988; Turning the Hourglass, 1990; Mayflies in Amber, 1993; The Body in Time, 1995; Listening to a Far Sea, 1998; The Sixth Swan, 2001. *Contributions to:* The Age; Canberra Times; Island; Meanjin; Overland; Scripsi; Southerly; Southern Review; Voices; Westerly; Ambit; Modern Painters; Poetry Review; Resurgence; New Welsh Review; Planet; Poetry Wales; Ariel; Kunapipi; Poetry Ireland; Poetry (Chicago). *Honours:* Mattara Poetry Prize, 1985; Wesley Michael Poetry Prize, 1987; John Shaw Neilson Prize, 1989; Wesley Michel Wright Poetry Prize, 1987; Three Writers Fellowships and 3-Year New Work Grant, Literature Fund of the Australia Council. *Memberships:* Victorian Writers Centre; New South Wales Writers Centre; Fellowship of Australian Writers.

Address: 12 Noble St, Barwon Heads, Vic. 3227, Australia. *E-mail:* difay@swift.net.au.

FAINLIGHT, Ruth (Esther); b. 2 May 1931, New York, NY, USA. Writer; Poet; Trans.; Librettist. m. Alan Sillitoe, 19 Nov. 1959, 1 s., 1 d. *Education:* Colleges of Arts and Crafts, Birmingham, Brighton. *Appointment:* Poet-in-Residence, Vanderbilt University, 1985, 1990. *Publications:* Poetry: Cages, 1966; To See the Matter Clearly, 1968; The Region's Violence, 1973; Another Full Moon, 1976; Sibyls and Others, 1980; Climates, 1983; Fifteen to Infinity, 1983; Selected Poems, 1987; The Knot, 1990; Sibyls, 1991; This Time of Year, 1994; Sugar-Paper Blue, 1997; Burning Wire, 2002. Translator: All Citizens Are Soldiers, from Lope de Vega, 1969; Navigations, 1983; Marine Rose Selected Poems of Sophia de Mello Breyner, 1988. Short Stories: Daylife and Nightlife, 1971; Dr Clock's Last Case, 1994. Libretti: The Dancer Hotoke, 1991; The European Story, 1993; Bedlam Britannica, 1995; Poemas, 2000; Bleue Papier-Sucre, 2000. *Contributions to:* Atlantic Monthly; Critical Quarterly; English; Hudson Review; Lettre Internationale; London Magazine; London Review of Books; New Yorker; Poetry Review; Threepenny Review; TLS. *Honours:* Cholmondeley Award for Poetry, 1994; Hawthornden Award for Poetry, 1994. *Memberships:* PEN; Writers in Prison Committee. *Address:* 14 Ladbroke Terrace, London W11 3PG, England.

FAIRBRASS, Graham John; b. 14 Jan. 1953, Meopham, Kent, England. Traveller; Writer; Poet; Painter. *Education:* BA, Arts, Open University, 1991; Coleg Harlech, 1995–96; Diploma, University of Wales, 1996; Norwich School of Art and Design, 1996–99. *Publication:* Conquistadors Shuffle Moon, 1989. *Contributions to:* Poetry Now, 1994; Anthology South East; Parnassus of World Poets, 1994, 1995, 1997; Poetry Club Anthology, Vol. 1, 1995; Birdsuit, 1997–99; Parnassus of World Poets, 2002; Inspirations From the South, 2002; Perceptions of Reality. *Address:* 6 Hornfield Cottages, Harvel, Gravesend, Kent DA13 0BU, England.

FAIRFAX, John; b. 9 Nov. 1930, London, England. Writer; Poet. 2 s. *Appointments:* Co-Founder and Mem. of Council of Management, Arvon Foundation; Dir, Phoenix Press, Arts Workshop, Newbury; Poetry Ed., Resurgence. *Publications:* The Fifth Horseman of the Apocalypse, 1969; Double Image, 1971; Adrift on the Star Brow of Taliesin, 1974; Bone Harvest Done, 1980; Wild Children, 1985; The Way to Write, 1981; Creative Writing, 1989; Spindrift Lp, 1981; 100 Poems, 1992; Zuihitsu, 1996; Poem Sent to Satellite E2F3, 1997; Poem on Sculpture, 1998; Poem in Hologram, 1998; Commissioned poems: Boots Herbal Garden, engraved on glass for several institutes, 1999, 2000; Poems for dance and art films, 2001–02. *Contributions to:* Most major literary magazines. *Membership:* The Arvon Foundation, co-founder, 1968. *Address:* The Thatched Cottage, Eling, Hermitage, Newbury, Berkshire RG16 9XR, England.

FALCK, (Adrian) Colin; b. 14 July 1934, London, England. Assoc. Prof.; Writer; Poet. 1 d., 1 s. *Education:* BA, 1957, MA, 1986, University of Oxford; PhD, University of London, 1988. *Appointments:* Lecturer in Sociology, London School of Economics and Political Science, 1961–62; Assoc. Ed., The Review, 1962–72; Lecturer in Literature, Chelsea College, 1964–84; Poetry Ed., The New Review, 1974–78; Assoc. Prof., York College, Pennsylvania, 1989–99. *Publications:* The Garden in the Evening, 1964; Promises, 1969; Backwards into the Smoke, 1973; Poems Since 1900: An Anthology (ed. with Ian Hamilton), 1975; In This Dark Light, 1978; Robinson Jeffers: Selected Poems (ed.), 1987; Myth, Truth and Literature, 1989; Edna St Vincent Millay: Selected Poems (ed.), 1991; Memorabilia, 1992; Post-Modern Love, 1997. *Contributions to:* Many professional journals and general periodicals. *Literary Agent:* John Johnson Ltd, Clerkenwell House, 45–47 Clerkenwell Green, London EC1R 0HT, England. *Address:* 20 Thurlow Rd, London NW3 5PP, England.

FALLON, Peter; b. 26 Feb. 1951, Osnabrück, Germany (Naturalized Irish citizen). Ed.; Poet. 2 c. *Education:* BA, 1975, H Dip Ed, 1976, MA, 1979, Trinity College, Dublin. *Appointments:* Founder, Ed., Gallery Press, Dublin, 1970–; Poet-in-Residence, Deerfield Acad., MA, 1976–77, 1996–97; International Writer-in-Residence at various Indiana Schools, 1979; Fiction Ed., O'Brien Press, Dublin, 1980–85; Teacher, Contemporary Irish Poetry, School of Irish Studies, Dublin, 1985–89; Writing Fellow, Poet-in-Residence, Trinity College, Dublin, 1994; Heimbold Prof. of Irish Studies, Villanova University, PA. *Publications:* Among the Walls, 1971; Co-incidence of Flesh, 1972; The First Affair, 1974; Finding the Dead, 1978; The Speaking Stones, 1978; Winter Work, 1983; The News and Weather, 1987; The Penguin Book of Contemporary Irish Poetry (ed. with Derek Mahon), 1990. Other: Eye to Eye, 1992; News of the World: Selected and New Poems, 1998, 1999. *Contributions to:* Poetry anthologies, periodicals and journals. *Honours:* Irish Arts Council Bursary, 1981; National Poetry Competition, England, 1982; Meath Merit Award, Arts and Culture, 1987; O'Shaughnessy Poetry Award, 1993. *Address:* Gallery Press, Loughcrew, Oldcastle, County Meath, Ireland.

FAMA, Maria; b. 3 March 1951, Philadelphia, Pennsylvania, USA. Writer; Poet; Educator; Researcher. *Education:* BA, 1971, MA, 1973, Temple University. *Appointments:* Teacher, 1972–79; Research Writer, Temple University School of Dentistry, 1979–87; Bibliographic Asst, Charles L Blockson, Afro-American Collection, 1987–89; Public Services Co-ordinator, Temple University, 1990–. *Publications:* Current, 1988; Fig Tree in the Yard, and Sneakers, 1989; Identification, 1991; Italian Notebook, 1995. *Contributions to:* Pearl; Piedmont Literary Review; South Street Star; Cardinal Review; Sons of Italy Times; La Bella Figura; City Paper of Philadelphia; Labyrinth; Hyacinths and Biscuits; Giornale di Matera; In the Public Eye; Heat; Modern Haiku; Poetry; Poet; Philadelphia Poets; La Bella Figura; A Choice, 1993; Via: Voices in Italian Americana; Laurel Leaves; North Star Poets; Joy and Tears; Seven Arts Magazine; Labyrinth, American Writing; Footwork – The Paterson Literary Review; Italian American and Italian Canadian Poets: An Anthology; Phati'tude, 1997; Hey!, 1998; Identity Lessons, 1999; Curaggia, 1999. *Honours:* Philadelphia Writers Conference Poetry Awards, 1976, 1977, 1990; Read work on radio as part of Philadelphia Writers Series, 1990; Allen Ginsberg Poetry Awards, honorable mentions, 1994, 1995, 1998. *Memberships:* American Poetry Center; Penn Laurel Poets, pres., 1997–99; Philadelphia Writers Organization and Writers Conference. *Address:* 1322 Sigel St, Philadelphia, PA 19148, USA.

FANNING, Micheal, (O. Fionnain); b. 3 March 1954, Ireland. Writer; Poet; Medical Doctor. *Publications:* The Love Letters of Daniel O'Connell, 1983; Tombolo, 1994; Deithe an t Solais, 1994. *Contributions to:* Ulsterman; Envoi; Acumen; Comhar. *Address:* The Wood, Dingle, County Kerry, Ireland.

FANTHORPE, U(rsula) A(skham); b. 22 July 1929, Kent, England. Writer; Poet. Partner, R. V. Bailey. *Education:* BA, MA, Oxford University. *Appointments:* Writer-in-Residence, St Martin's College, Lancaster, 1983–85; Northern Arts Literary Fellow, Universities of Durham and Newcastle, 1987–88. *Publications:* Side Effects, 1978; Standing To, 1982; Voices Off, 1984; Selected Poems, 1986; A Watching Brief, 1987; Neck Verse, 1992; Safe as Houses, 1995; Penguin Modern Poets 6, 1996; Double Act (audiobook with R V Bailey), 1997; Poetry Quartets 5 (audiobook), 1999; Consequences, 2000. *Contributions to:* TLS; Encounter; Outposts; Firebird; Bananas; South West Review; Quarto; Tribune; Country LIfe; Use of English; Poetry Review; Poetry Book Society Supplement; Writing Women; Spectator; BBC. *Honours:* Travelling Scholarship, Society of Authors, 1983; Hawthornden Scholarships, 1987, 1997, 2002; Fellow, RSL, 1988; Arts Council Writers Award, 1994; Chomondeley Award, Society of Authors, 1995; Hon. DLitt, the West of England, 1995; Hon. PhD, University of Gloucestershire, 2000; C.B.E., 2001. *Membership:* PEN. *Address:* Culverhay House, Wotton-under-Edge, Gloucestershire GL12 7LS, England. *E-mail:* fanthorpe.bailey@virgin.net.

FARAGHER, E(ric) S(teven); b. 23 April 1957, Liverpool, England. Librarian; Poet. *Education:* Diploma of Higher Education, 1988; BA, Honours, Humanities, 1989; Postgraduate Diploma, Information and Library Studies, 1990–91. *Contributions to:* Several anthologies and various journals, reviews and magazines. *Memberships:* Library Asscn; Liverpool Writers' Club, chair., 1981–82. *Address:* 31 Tudor St, Liverpool L6 6AG, England.

FARHI, Musa Moris; b. 5 July 1935, Ankara, Turkey. Novelist; Poet. m. Nina Ruth Gould, 2 July 1978, 1 step-d. *Education:* BA, Humanities, Istanbul American College, 1954; Diploma, RADA, London, 1956. *Publications:* The Pleasure of Death, 1972; Voices Within the Art: The Modern Jewish Poets, 1980; The Last of Days, 1983; Journey Through the Wilderness, 1989; Children of the Rainbow, 1999. *Contributions to:* Menard Press; Men Cards; European Judaism; Modern Poetry in Translation; Frank; Jewish Quarterly; Steaua (Romania); Confrontation (USA); North Atlantic Review (USA); Reflections on the Universal Declaration of Human Rights. *Honours:* MBE, Services to Literature; RSL, fellow. *Memberships:* Society of Authors; Writers Guild; PEN. *Address:* 11 North Sq., London NW11 7AB, England.

FARLEY, Joseph Michael; b. 28 Dec. 1961, Philadelphia, PA, USA. Ed.; Publisher; Writer; Poet. m. Juan Xu, 25 Aug. 1988. *Education:* BA, English, St Joseph's University, Philadelphia, 1983; MA, English and Creative Writing, Temple University, Philadelphia, 1988. *Appointments:* Ed., Axe Factory, 1986–; Poetry Chain Letter, 1994–99; Paper Airplane, 1995–; Holy Rollers, Low Budget Science Fiction, Low Budget Adventure Stories and Cynic Book Reviews, 2001–. *Publications:* January, 1985; Beat Ballad Blues, 1995; Souvenir or Evolution, 1996; Suckers, 1998; Wolf Poems, 2000; For the Birds (short stories), 2001. *Contributions to:* The Next Parish Over: Collection of Irish-American Writing; Painted Bride Quarterly; Pearl Magazine; Bogg Magazine; Wayfarers; Iota. *Address:* 2653 Sperry St, Philadelphia, PA 19152, USA.

FARMER, Rod; b. 9 June 1947, Carthage, Missouri, USA. Prof. of Education and History; Poet. m. Margaret Eastman Farmer, 8 Aug. 1986. *Education:* BS, Social Science, 1968, MA, History, 1972, Central Missouri State University; PhD, Social Science Education, University of Missouri at Columbia, 1978; Postgraduate Study in History, University of Maine, 1984–85. *Appointment:* Prof. of Education and History, University of Maine at Farmington, 1978–. *Publication:* Universal Essence, 1986. *Contributions to:* Over 700 poems published in journals. *Membership:* Maine Writers and Publishers Alliance.

Address: Franklin Hall, 252 Main St, University of Maine at Farmington, Farmington, ME 04938, USA.

FARNSWORTH, Robert Lambton; b. 8 April 1954, Boston, Massachusetts, USA. College Prof.; Poet. m. Georgia N Nigro, 28 Aug. 1977, 2 s. *Education:* AB, English, Brown University, 1976; MFA, Columbia University, 1979. *Appointments:* Visiting Asst Prof., Ithaca College, Colby College and Bates College; Poetry Ed., The American Scholar, 1997–. *Publications:* Three or Four Hills and a Cloud, 1982; Honest Water, 1989. *Contributions to:* American Poetry Review; Poetry; Missouri Review; New England Review; Poetry Northwest; Ironwood; Ploughshares; Michigan Quarterly Review; Antioch Review. *Honour:* National Endowment for the Arts Fellowship in Poetry, 1989–90. *Address:* 19 Ware St, Lewiston, ME 04240, USA.

FARRELL, Michael John; b. 7 July 1964, Ashton under Lyne, Lancashire, England. Poet; Artist. *Education:* BA, English Literature, Sunderland University, 1984; Studying Life, Foundation in Fine Art, Bilston, Wolverhampton, 1992. *Appointment:* Ed., The Memo Bowl literary journal, 1992. *Publications:* Ghosts on Glass, 1983; Christmas Box, 1991. *Contributions to:* Ambit 119; Iron 62; several dozen small presses. *Honour:* A Reading in Chester, 1983–84. *Memberships:* Poetry Society; Dances With Wolves Fan Club. *Address:* 45 Heantun Rise, Francis St, Wolverhampton WV1 4RE, England.

FARRELL, Pamela Barnard; b. 11 Oct. 1943, Mt Holly, New Jersey, USA. Writer; Poet; Teacher. m. Joseph Donald Farrell, 1 Sept. 1969. *Education:* BA, English, Radford College, 1965; MS, English, Radford University, 1975; MA, Writing, Northeastern University, 1988. *Appointments:* Ed., The Grapevine, Northeastern University Writing Program Newsletter, 1986–90; Poetry Teacher, Consultant, Geraldine R Dodge Foundation, 1986–; Editorial Board, Computers and Composition, 1987–90, The Writing Center Journal, 1988–; Caldwell Chair of Composition, The McCallie School, 1991–. *Publications:* Waking Dreams (poems), 1989; The High School Writing Center: Establishing and Maintaining One, 1989; Waking Dreams II (poems), 1990; National Directory of Writing Centres, 1992. *Contributions to:* Anthologies, books and journals. *Honours:* Woodrow Wilson National Fellowship Foundation Fellow, 1985; Golden Poet Award, 1986. *Memberships:* Assembly of Computer in English, treasurer; MLA; National Writing Center Asscn. *Address:* The McCallie School, 2850 McCallie Ave, Chattanooga, TN 37404, USA.

FARUQI, Moeen; b. 2 Feb. 1958, Karachi, Pakistan. Educator; Art Critic; Artist; Poet. 2 s. *Education:* BSc, Physics, California State University, 1981; MEd, University of Wales College of Cardiff, Wales, 1992. *Appointments:* School Administrator, Modern Education Society, 1983–; Art Critic, Pakistan Press International, 1986–. *Contributions to:* UK: Orbis; Verse; Iron; Rialto; Cyphers; Poetry Society Journal, India; Rattle, USA. *Memberships:* International Asscn of Art Critics; Commonwealth Council of Educational Administration. *Address:* 17-B/1, 12th Central St, Phase-2, DHA, Karachi 75500, Pakistan.

FASEL, Ida; b. 9 May 1909, Portland, Maine, USA. Prof. Emeritus of English; Poet. m. Oskar A Fasel, 24 Dec. 1946. *Education:* BA, 1931, MA, 1945, Boston University; PhD, University of Denver, 1963. *Appointments:* University of Connecticut, New London; Midwestern University, Wichita Falls, Texas; Colorado Woman's College, Denver, University of Colorado, Denver, 1962–77; Prof. Emeritus of English, 1977. *Publications:* On the Meanings of Cleave, 1979; Where is the Center of the World?, 1998; All Real Living is Meeting, 1999; The Difficult Inch, 2000; Journey of a Hundred Years, 2002. Chapbooks: Thanking the Flowers, 1981; West of Whitecaps, 1982; All of Us, Dancers, 1984; Amphora Full of Light, 1985; Available Light, 1988; Basics, 1988; Where Is the Center of the World?, 1991; Air, Angels and Us, 2002; Aureoles, 2002; A Prairie Year, 2002. *Contributions to:* Renaissance and Baroque Lyrics; Study and Writing of Poetry; Anthology of Magazine Verse; Yearbook of American Poetry; Clap Hands and Sing; Cape Rock; Ekphrasis; Poet Lore; Creeping Bent; Blue Unicorn. *Honours:* Faculty Fellowship, University of Colorado, 1967; Collegium of Distinguished Alumni, Boston University, 1979; First Prizes, Boston University Poetry Competition, 1986, 1990. *Memberships:* Poetry Society of America; Milton Society of America; Friends of Milton's Cottage; Conference on Christianity and Literature; Denver Women's Press Club; Colorado Centre for the Book; Asscn of Literary Scholars and Critics. *Address:* 165 Ivy St, Denver, CO 80220, USA.

FATCHEN, Maxwell Edgar; b. 3 Aug. 1920, Adelaide, SA, Australia. Author; Poet. m. Jean Wohlers, 15 May 1942, 2 s., 1 d. *Appointments:* Journalist, Feature Writer, Adelaide News, 1946–55; Special Writer, 1955, 1981–84, Literary Ed., 1971–81, The Advertiser. *Publications:* The River Kings, 1966; Conquest of the River, 1970; The Spirit Wind, 1973; Chase Through the Night, 1977; Closer to the Stars, 1981; Wry Rhymes, 1987; A Country Christmas, 1990; Tea for Three, 1994. *Contributions to:* Denver Post; Sydney Sun; Regional South Australian Histories. *Honours:* Mem. of the Order of Australia, 1980; Advance Australia Award for Literature, 1991; AMP-Walkley Award for Journalism, 1996; SA Great Award for Literature, 1999. *Memberships:* Australian Society of Authors; Australian Fellowship of Writers; South Australian Writers Centre; Media Alliance. *Address:* 15 Jane St, Box 6, Smithfield, SA 5114, Australia.

FATT CHEE GOON; b. 8 Jan. 1924, China. Educator (retd); Poet. m. Phuah Guay Kee, 12 Jan. 1955, 1 s., 1 d. *Education:* Teacher's Training, Penang Free School, Malaysia, 1949; BA Honours, London University. *Appointments:* Teacher, 1946–64; Curriculum and Textbook Officer, Statistician, Ministry of Education, Malaysia, 1965–69; Principal: Clifford Secondary School, Kuala Kangsar, 1969–71, Cochrane Road School, Kuala Lumpur, 1971–74, Penang Free School, 1974–79. *Publications:* Tatarakyat Menengah Baru 4, 1977; Modern Civics for Secondary Schools, book 4, 1978; The Role of the Principal in Malaysia, 1980. *Contributions to:* Poet; World Poetry; Eminent Poets; Dawn of a New Era; Dance on the Horizon; Parnassus of World Poets; Best Poems of 1996; Metverse Muse. *Honours:* Fulbright Scholarship, 1966–67; Title of PKT conferred by Governor of Penang; Cultural Doctorate in Literature, World University, AZ, 1987; International Poetry Competition, 1989. *Memberships:* World Poetry Society Intercontinental; World University, international advisory board. *Address:* 85 Jalan Durian, Taman Cheras, 56100 Kuala Lumpur, Malaysia.

FAUX, Elizabeth Christine, (Liz Faux); b. 14 April 1953, Buckinghamshire, England. Special Needs Teacher; Poet. m. 2 s. *Education:* BA, Honours, Humanities, Hatfield Polytechnic; Certificate, Education, Hertfordshire College of Higher Education, 1982; Advanced Diploma, Special Needs Education, 1995. *Appointment:* Lecturer in Special Needs, Oaklands College, St Albans. *Publication:* Between the Islands, 1994. *Contributions to:* Anthologies and journals. *Honours:* First Prize, 1990, First Prize, 1991, VER Poets Open Competition; Highly Commended and Commended, Ripley Open Poetry Competition, 1992; First Prize, Specialist Category, Barnet Open Competition, 1994; Joint Winner, Blue Nose Poetry Competition, 1996. *Memberships:* Poetry Society; Toddington Poetry Society.

FECSKE, Csaba; b. 10 March 1948, Szögliget, Hungary. Poet. 1 s., 1 d. *Publications:* Halo Round the Faces, 1978; Neither Rhyme Not Reason, 1980; Blind Spot/Poems, 1987; In Moonlight, 1992; Cricket Tales, 1993; A Kind of Message, 1994; Where Was I, 1996; Somewhere Else (poems), 1998; The Little Herd (tales), 1999; The World Bought by Dreams (children's poems), 2000; Everything has Passed That Still Could be Here (poems), 2001; Representing my Disappearing (poems), 2002. *Contributions to:* Anthologies, periodicals, journals and quarterlies. *Honour:* Szabo Lörinc Prize, 1994. *Memberships:* Society of Hungarian Artists; Literary Society of Hungarian Writers. *Address:* 3529 Miskolc, Gesztenyes u 10, Hungary.

FEDERICI, Tersilla; b. 15 June 1956, Mantua, Italy. Poet. *Education:* University of Parma. *Contributions to:* Anthologies and reviews. *Honours:* International Competition of Poetry Prizes, Mantua, 1981, 1984, 1985, 1986; City of Mantua Poetry Prize, 1983; S Bettinelli International Prize, 1983; Federico García Lorca Honour Diploma, Rome, 1986; Golden Plate, City of Sabbioneta International Poetry Prize, 1990; Lions Club Viadana-Ogliopo Prize, 1996. *Address:* 46010 Commessaggio Inf, Mantua, Italy.

FEDERMAN, Raymond; b. 15 May 1928, Paris, France. Distinguished Prof.; Novelist; Poet; Trans. m. Erica Hubscher, 14 Sept. 1960, 1 d. *Education:* BA cum laude, Columbia University, 1957; MA, 1958, PhD, 1963, University of California at Los Angeles. *Appointments:* Asst Prof., University of California at Los Angeles, 1960–64; Assoc. Prof. of French and Comparative Literature, 1964–68, Prof. of Comparative Literature, 1968–73, Prof. of English and Comparative Literature, 1973–90, Distinguished Prof., 1990–, State University of New York at Buffalo. *Publications:* Fiction: Double or Nothing, 1971; Amer Eldorado, 1974; Take It or Leave It, 1976; The Voice in the Closet, 1979; The Twofold Vibration, 1982; Smiles on Washington Square, 1985; To Whom It May Concern, 1990. Non-Fiction: Journey to Chaos, 1965; Samuel Beckett, 1970; Surfiction, 1976; Critifiction, 1992; The Supreme Indecision of the Writer, 1996. Poetry: Temporary Landscapes, 1965; Among the Beasts, 1967; Me Too, 1975; Duel, 1989; Autobiographic Poems, 1991. *Contributions to:* Reviews, journals, and magazines. *Honours:* Guggenheim Fellowship, 1966–67; Frances Steloff Fiction Prize, 1971; Panache Experimental Prize, 1972; American Book Award, 1986. *Memberships:* American PEN Centre; Fiction Collective, board mem., 1988–, dir, 1989–94. *Address:* 46 Four Seasons West, Eggertsville, NY 14226, USA.

FEI MA. See: MARR, William Wei-Yi.

FEINSTEIN, Elaine Barbara; b. 24 Oct. 1930, Bootle, Lancashire, England. Poet. 3 s. *Education:* Newnham College, Cambridge, 1949–52. *Appointments:* Editorial Staff, Cambridge University Press, 1960–62; Lecturer, Bishops Stortford College, 1963–66; Asst Lecturer, University of Essex, 1967–70. *Publications:* In a Green Eye, 1966; The Circle, 1970; The Magic Apple Tree, 1971; At the Edge, 1972; The Celebrants and Other Poems, 1973; The Glass Alembic, 1973; The Children of the Rose, 1974; The Ecstasy of Miriam Garner, 1976; Some Unease and Angels: Selected Poems, 1977; The Silent Areas, 1980; The Feast of Euridice, 1980; The Survivors, 1982; The Border, 1984; Badlands, 1987; Bessie Smith, 1985; A Captive Lion: The Life of Marina Tsvetayeva, 1987; Mother's Girl, 1988; All You Need, 1989; City Music, 1990; Loving Brecht, 1992; Lawrence's Women, 1993; Dreamers, 1994; Selected Poems, 1994; Daylight, 1997; Gold, 2000; Dark Inheritance, 2001; Ted Hughes: The Life of a Poet, 2001; Collected Poems and Translations, 2002. *Contributions to:* Periodicals.

Honours: Fellow, RSL, 1980; Chomondeley Award, 1990; Hon. DLitt Leicester University, 1990. *Address:* c/o Rogers, Coleridge and White, 2 Powis Mews, London W11, England.

FEINSTEIN, Robert N.; b. 10 Aug. 1915, Milwaukee, Wisconsin, USA. Biochemist; Poet. m. Betty J Greenbaum, 5 May 1941, 2 d. *Education:* BS Chemistry, 1937, MS, Biochemistry, 1938, PhD, Physiological Chemistry, 1940 University of Wisconsin. *Appointments:* Resident Asst, Michael Reese Hospital Chicago; Resident Assoc., May Institute for Medical Research, Cincinnati, Ohio Assoc. Prof., University of Chicago; Senior Biochemist, Argonne National Laboratory. *Publications:* Oysters in Love, 1984; Son of an Oyster, 1989 Oyster's Last Stand, 1994. *Contributions to:* Lyric; Light year; Light; Plain Poetry Journal; Saturday Evening Post; Wall Street Journal; Christian Science Monitor. *Honours:* Prize, Individual Magazines, Erew, 1981, Lyric, 1987 Archer, 1987, 1988, Heartland Journal, 1989, Amelia, 1991, Parnassur, 1995 *Address:* 200 Village Dr., Apt 227, Downers Grove, IL 60516, USA.

FEINSTEIN, Sascha; b. 13 March 1963, New York, NY, USA. Poet Anthologist; Ed.; Educator. m. Marleni Rajakrishnan, 3 June 1989, 2 c *Education:* BA magna cum laude, University of Rochester, 1985; MFA Poetry, 1990, PhD, American Literature, 1993, Indiana University *Appointments:* Asst Prof., 1995–98, Co-Dir, Creative Writing Program, 1996– Assoc. Prof., 1998–, Lycoming College, Williamsport, Pennsylvania; Founding Ed., Brilliant Corners: A Journal of Jazz and Literature, 1996–. *Publications:* Summerhouse Piano, chapbook, 1989; The Jazz Poetry Anthology, co-ed., 1991. Christmas Eve, chapbook, 1994; The Second Set: The Jazz Poetry Anthology Vol. Two, co-ed., 1996; Blues Knowledge of Departure, chapbook, 1997; Jazz Poetry: From the 1920s to the Present, 1997; A Bibliographic Guide to Jazz Poetry, 1998; Misterioso, 2000. *Contributions to:* Literary journals including: American Poetry Review; Southern Review; Missouri Review; North American Review; New England Review. *Honours:* Writers' Exchange Program Award, 1995; Hayden Carruth Award, 1999. *Address:* Dept of English, Lycoming College, Williamsport, PA 17701, USA. *E-mail:* feinstei@lycoming.edu.

FELDMAN, Alan Grad; b. 16 March 1945, New York, NY, USA. Writer; Poet; Teacher. m. Nanette Hass, 22 Oct. 1972, 1 s., 1 d. *Education:* AB, Columbia College, 1966; MA, Columbia University, 1969; PhD, State University of New York, Buffalo, 1973. *Publications:* The Household, 1966; The Happy Genius, 1978; Frank O'Hara, 1978; The Personals, 1982; Lucy Mastermind, 1985; Anniversary, 1992. *Contributions to:* New Yorker; Atlantic; Kenyon Review; Mississippi Review; Ploughshares; North American Review; Threepenny Review; Boston Review; Tendril; College English. *Honours:* Award for Best Short Story in a College Literary Magazine, Saturday Review-National Student Asscn, 1965; Elliston Book Award for Best Book of Poems by a Small Press in US, 1978. *Address:* 399 Belknap Rd, Framingham, MA 01701, USA.

FELDMAN, Irving (Mordecai); b. 22 Sept. 1928, New York, NY, USA. Prof. of English; Poet. m. Carmen Alvarez del Olmo, 1955, 1 s. *Education:* BS, City College, New York City, 1950; MA, Columbia University, 1953. *Appointments:* Teacher, University of Puerto Rico, Rio Piedras, 1954–56, University of Lyons, France, 1957–58, Kenyon College, Gambier, Ohio, 1958–64; Prof. of English, State University of New York at Buffalo, 1964–. *Publications:* Poetry: Work and Days and Other Poems, 1961; The Pripet Marshes and Other Poems, 1965; Magic Papers and Other Poems, 1970; Lost Originals, 1972; Leaping Clear, 1976; New and Selected Poems, 1979; Teach Me, Dear Sister, and Other Poems, 1983; All of us Here and Other Poems, 1986; Beautiful False Things, 2000. Other: The Life and Letters, 1994. *Honours:* Kovner Award, Jewish Book Council of America, 1962; Ingram Merrill Foundation Grant, 1963; American Acad. of Arts and Letters Grant, 1973; Guggenheim Fellowship, 1973; Creative Artists Public Service Grant, 1980; Acad. of American Poets Fellowship, 1986; John D. and Catherine T. MacArthur Foundation Fellowship, 1992. *Address:* c/ o Dept of English, State University of New York at Buffalo, Buffalo, NY 14260, USA.

FENECH, Raymond Mario Paul; b. 6 Jan. 1958, St Julians, Malta. Writer; Ed. m. Angela Azzopardi, 12 Dec. 1987. *Education:* Diploma in Journalism, Freelance Writing and Creative Writing. *Appointments:* Malta Delegate for European Union Asscn for the Promotion of Poetry, Brussels, Belgium, 1995–97; Malta Delegate for the National Poetry Centre, Ghent, Belgium. Ed., Living 2000 magazine, 1998–99; Ed., The Globe Trotter Travel Magazine, 1999–2001. *Publications:* Within the Edges of Immortality (poems), 1992; Expressions (poems on cassette), 1992; A Tapestry of Thoughts, 1998; Poignant Voices (poems on Internet), 1999; Broken Innocence (poems), 2000; research on ghosts of Malta International Directory of Haunted Places, 2000. *Contributions to:* The Affectionate Punch; Poetry Now; B.A.D.; Flaming Arrows; Times; Sunday Times; The People; Democrat; Micro Press; Atlanta Review; Writers Gazette; Verses; Poets' Paradise; Poemata; The Globe Trotter. *Honours:* First Prize, Poetry Network Newsletter 1993 Poetry Competition; Third Prize, Triumph House Publishers Ed.'s Choice Poetry Award, 1997; Several commendations, runner-up awards, merit awards and pres' awards. *Memberships:* Canadian Poetry Asscn; Poeziecentrum, Ghent, Belgium; Poezija Plus, Malta; National Authors Registry, USA; Poetry Society, UK; Freelance Press Services, UK; The Poetry Society UK. *Address:* 2 Carmen Flats, C Von Brockdorff St, Msida MSD02, Malta. *E-mail:* writer@camline.net.mt.

FENTON, James (Martin); b. 25 April 1949, Lincoln, England. Prof. of Poetry; Poet; Writer. *Education:* MA, Magdalen College, Oxford, 1970. *Appointments:* Asst Literary Ed., 1971, Editorial Asst, 1972, Political Columnist, 1976–78, New Statesman; Freelance Correspondent, Indo-China, 1973–75; German Correspondent, Guardian, 1978–79; Theatre Critic, Sunday Times, 1979–84; Chief Book Reviewer, Times, 1984–86; Far East Correspondent, 1986–88, Columnist, 1993–95, Independent; Prof. of Poetry, University of Oxford, 1994–99. *Publications:* Our Western Furniture, 1968; Terminal Moraine, 1972; A Vacant Possession, 1978; A German Requiem, 1980; Dead Soldiers, 1981; The Memory of War, 1982; Rigoletto, by Giuseppe Verdi (trans.), 1982; You Were Marvellous, 1983; The Original Michael Frayn, 1983; Children in Exile, 1984; Poems 1968–83, 1985; Simon Boccanegra, by Giuseppe Verdi (trans.), 1985; The Fall of Saigon, 1985; The Snap Revolution, 1986; Cambodian Witness: The Autobiography of Someth May (ed.), 1986; Partingtime Hall (poems with John Fuller), 1987; All the Wrong Places: Adrift in the Politics of Asia, 1988; Manila Evelope, 1989; Underground in Japan, by Rey Ventura (ed.), 1992; Out of Danger (poems), 1993; Leonardo's Nephew: Essays on Art and Artists, 1998; The Strength of Poetry: Oxford Lectures, 2001; An Introduction to English Poetry, 2002. *Honours:* Fellow, RSL; Hon. Fellow, Magdalen College, Oxford, 1999. *Address:* c/o Peters Fraser and Dunlop, Drury House, 34–43 Russell St, London WC2B 5HA, England.

FERGUSON, Joseph (Francis); b. 11 Feb. 1952, Yonkers, New York, USA. Critic; Writer; Poet. m. Janice Robinson, 30 July 1986, 1 s. *Education:* BA, State University of New York at New Paltz, 1979; MS (not completed), Pace University. *Appointment:* Critic for various publications. *Contributions to:* Fiction and poetry in many anthologies and other publications; Articles and columns in numerous publications. *Honours:* Honorable Mention, American Poetry Asscn Contest, 1989; Finalist, American Book Series, San Diego Poets Press, 1990; Honorable Mention, World of Poetry Contest, 1990; Golden Poet, World of Poetry, 1990; Distinguished Poet of America, 1993; Semi-Finalist, North American Open Poetry Contest, 1993. *Address:* 26 Bank St, Cold Spring, NY 10516, USA.

FERGUSON, William (Rotch); b. 14 Feb. 1943, Fall River, Massachusetts, USA. Assoc. Prof. of Spanish; Writer; Poet. m. Nancy King, 26 Nov. 1983. *Education:* BA, 1965, MA, 1970, PhD, 1975, Harvard University. *Appointments:* Instructor, 1971–75, Asst Prof., 1975–77, Boston University; Visiting Prof., 1977–79, Asst Prof., 1979–83, Assoc. Prof. of Spanish, 1983–, Adjunct Prof. of English, 1989–, Chair., Foreign Languages, 1990–98, Clark University, Worcester, Massachusetts; Visiting Lecturer in Spanish Renaissance Literature, University of Pennsylvania, 1986–87; Assoc. Ed., Hispanic Review, 1986–87. *Publications:* Dream Reader (poems), 1973; Light of Paradise (poems), 1973; La versificación imitativa en Fernando de Herrera, 1981; Freedom and Other Fictions (stories), 1984. *Contributions to:* Scholarly journals, anthologies, periodicals and magazines. *Memberships:* American Asscn of University Profs; International Institute in Spain; MLA. *Address:* 1 Tahanto Rd, Worcester, MA 01602, USA.

FERLINGHETTI, Lawrence (Monsanto); b. 24 March 1920, Yonkers, New York, USA. Poet; Writer; Dramatist; Publisher; Ed.; Painter. m. Selden Kirby-Smith, April 1951, divorced, 1 s., 1 d. *Education:* AB, University of North Carolina, 1941; MA, Columbia University, 1948; Doctorat (with honours), Sorbonne, University of Paris, 1951. *Appointments:* Co-Owner, City Lights Pocket Bookshop, later City Lights Books, San Francisco, 1953–; Founder-Ed., City Lights Books, publishing, San Francisco, 1955–; Many poetry readings; Participation in many national and international literary conferences; Retrospective exhibition of paintings, Palazzo delle Esposizione, Rome, Italy, 1996. *Publications:* Poetry: Pictures of the Gone World, 1955; A Coney Island of the Mind, 1958; Berlin, 1961; Starting from San Francisco, 1961; Where is Vietnam?, 1965; An Eye on the World: Selected Poems, 1967; After the Cries of the Birds, 1967; The Secret Meaning of Things, 1969; Tyrannus Nix?, 1969; Back Roads to Far Places, 1971; Open Eye, Open Heart, 1973; Who Are We Now?, 1976; Landscapes of Living and Dying, 1979; A Trip to Italy and France, 1980; Endless Life: Selected Poems, 1984; Over All the Obscene Boundaries: European Poems and Transitions, 1985; Inside the Trojan Horse, 1987; When I Look at Pictures, 1990; These Are My Rivers: New and Selected Poems, 1955–1993, 1993. Fiction: Her, 1960; Love in the Days of Rage, 1988. Other Writings: The Mexican Night: Travel Journal, 1970; Northwest Ecolog, 1978; Literary San Francisco: A Pictorial History from the Beginning to the Present (with Nancy J Peters), 1980; The Populist Manifestos, 1983; Seven Days in Nicaragua Libre, journal, 1985. Editor: Beatitude Anthology, 1960; City Lights Anthology, 1974; City Lights Review, No. 1, 1987, and No. 2, 1988. Plays: Unfair Arguments with Existence: Seven Plays for a New Theatre, 1963; Routines (13 short plays), 1964. *Contributions to:* Numerous books and periodicals. *Honours:* National Book Award Nomination, 1970; Notable Book of 1979 Citation, Library Journal, 1980; Silver Medal for Poetry, Commonwealth Club of California, 1986, 1998; Poetry Prize, City of Rome, 1993; First Poet Laureate of San Francisco, 1998; Lifetime Achievement Award, Los Angeles Times Book Expo, 2001. *Address:* c/o City Lights Books, 261 Columbus Ave, San Francisco, CA 94133, USA.

FERMIN, Bert. See: ENGELS, Deen.

FERNANDEZ, Antonio J. Ruiz; b. 1 March 1929, Fonelas, Guadix, Granada, Spain. Poet; Writer. m. Vida Maria Sàez Carcelén, 1 s., 3 d. *Education:* High School Graduate. *Publications:* Several collections of poems and stories. *Contributions to:* Anthologies and reviews. *Honours:* Various certificates and diplomas. *Memberships:* Marcilla; International Writers and Artists Asscn; World Asscn of Cultural Congresses. *Address:* Magnolia 1-2-2, 18015 Granada, Spain.

FERNANDEZ, Querubin D. Jr, (Efren Banez Nuqui, Quefer, Quick Desert Fox); b. 30 Jan. 1936, Manila, Philippines. Writer; Poet. m. Victoria S Talens, 20 July 1964, 2 s., 2 d. *Education:* BA, English, 1969, BSc, Education, 1970, Angeles University. *Appointments:* Managing Ed., Columnist, The Voice, 1968–73; Ed.-in-Chief, Pampanga Times, 1970–71; High School Instructor, Angeles University Foundation, 1970–72; Municipal Secretary, 1973–79; Asst Municipal Assessor, Mabalacat, Pampanga Municipal Government, 1979–2001. *Publications:* History of Mabalacat, 1976; Bulung Dutung, 1982; Yamut Dikut, 1991; Bakas Panas, 1997; Himno ning Mabalacat, 1997. *Contributions to:* Books, magazines and journals. *Honours:* Poet Laureate, Agtaka, 1973; Alternate Poet Laureate, Emerme, 1975; First Place, Don Gonzalo Puyat Memorial Awards for Pampango Literature, 1980; Most Outstanding Alumnus in Literature, Angeles University, 1983; First Prize, Foundation Day, Pampanga, 1990; Most Outstanding Citizen in Literature, Mabalacat, Pampanga, 1996; Most Outstanding Kampanangan in Literature, 426th Pampanga Day, 1997. *Memberships:* Aguman Talasulat Kapampangan, secretary, 1978–82; Aguman Poeta, Taladalit Ning Amanung Siswan, vice-pres., 1990–94. *Address:* 502 Washington Ave, El Rosario Village, Mabiga, Mabalacat, Pampanga, 2010 Philippines.

FERNANDEZ DE LA PUENTE, Amando Jesús, (Amando Fernandez); b. 16 March 1949, Havana, Cuba. College Instructor; Poet. *Education:* BA, 1983, MSc, Modern Language Education, 1984, MA, Hispanic Studies, 1988, Florida International University. *Publications:* Herir at Tiempo, 1986; Perfil de la Materia, 1986; Azar en Sombra, 1987; Pentagrama, 1987; El Ruiseñor y la Espada, 1988; Materia y Forma, 1990; Los Siete Circulos, 1991. *Honours:* First Prizes for Poetry, José Maria Heredia, 1986, 1987; Mairena Prize, 1986; Agustín Acosta Prize, 1987; Jaén de Poesía, 1987; Odon Betanzos Prize, 1987; Luis de Gongora Prize, 1987; Antonio González de Lama Prize, 1988; Ciudad de Badajoz, 1989. *Address:* 4803 NW Seventh St, Apt 302, Miami, FL 33126, USA.

FERRARA, Ranieri Walter; b. 17 June 1954, Naples, Italy. Poet. *Publications:* Ritrattazioni, 1988; La correzione, 1990; La sostituzione, 1993. *Contributions to:* Quinta Generazione; Visionario; Offerta Speciale; Anterem; Mito; Ballyhoo-Letterature; Annales; Gemma; Pliego de Murmurios; Escamotage; Presencias; Anthologies: International Poetry, 1990; World Poetry, 1992; La Poésie des Palmipedes, 1992. *Membership:* World Acad. of Arts and Culture, USA. *Address:* Via Saverio Altamura 22, 80128 Naples, Italy.

FERRETT, Mabel, (MF, Mrs Wuzzle); b. 30 April 1917, Leeds, Yorkshire, England. Teacher (retd); Writer; Poet; Ed. m. Harold Ferrett, 7 Aug. 1947, 1 s. *Education:* Teacher's Certificate, Ripon Teaching College. *Appointments:* Teacher, Leeds; Ed., Pennine Platform, 1973–76, Orbis, 1978–80. *Publications:* The Lunx-Eyed Strangers, 1956; The Angry Men, 1965; The Tall Tower, 1970; Years of the Right Hand, 1975; A Question of Menhirs, 1984; Humber Bridge: Selected Poems, 1955–85, 1986; The Taylors of the Red House, 1987; The Bontës in the SpenValley, 1978, extended 1997; Scathed Earth, 1996. *Contributions to:* Anthologies, journals, reviews and radio. *Honours:* First Prize, Kirklees Festival, 1975; Special Prize, Phoenix Anag-rhyme Competition, 1975; First Prize, Julian Cairns Award, Society of Women Writers and Journalists, 1976; Yorkshire Arts Asscn Bursaries, 1979, 1983. *Memberships:* Pennine Poets; Spen Valley Historical Society, life pres.; Partner, Fighting Cock Press. *Address:* 2 Vernon Rd, Heckmondwike, West Yorkshire WF16 9LU, England.

FERRY, David (Russell); b. 5 March 1924, Orange, NJ, USA. Prof. of English Emeritus; Poet; Writer; Trans. m. Anne Elizabeth Davidson, 22 March 1958, 1 s., 1 d. *Education:* BA, Amherst College, 1948; MA, 1949, PhD, 1955, Harvard University. *Appointments:* Instructor, 1952–55, Asst Prof., 1955–61, Assoc. Prof., 1961–67, Prof. of English, 1967–71, Sophie Chautal Hart Prof. of English, 1971–89, Prof. Emeritus, 1989–, Wellesley College; Fannie Hurst Visiting Poet, Washington University, St Louis, 1999. *Publications:* The Limits of Mortality: An Essay on Wordsworth's Major Poems, 1959; On the Way to the Island (poems), 1960; British Literature (co-ed.), two vols, 1974; Strangers: A Book of Poems, 1983; Gilgamesh: A New Rendering in English Verse, 1992; Dwelling Places: Poems and Translations, 1993; The Odes of Horace: A Translation, 1997; The Eclogues of Virgil: A Translation, 1999; Of No Country I Know: New and Selected Poems and Translations, 1999; The Epistles of Horace: A Translation, 2001. *Contributions to:* Literary journals. *Honours:* Pushcart Prize, 1988; Ingram Merrill Award for Poetry and Translation, 1993; Teasdale Prize for Poetry, 1995; Hon. Fellow, Acad. of American Poets, 1995; Hon. Fellow, Acad. of American Poets, 1995; Guggenheim Fellowship, 1996–97; William Arrowsmith Translation Prize, AGNI, 1999; Bingham Poetry Prize, Boston Book Review, 2000; Lenore Marshall Poetry Prize, 2000; Rebekah Johnson Bobbitt National Prize for Poetry, Library of Congress, 2000; American Acad. of Arts and Letters Award for Literature, 2001. *Memberships:* Fellow, Acad. of American Poets, 1994; Fellow, American Acad. of Arts and Sciences, 1998. *Address:* 8 Ellery St, Cambridge, MA 02138, USA. *E-mail:* dferry@wellesley.edu.

FIEDLER, Leslie A(aron); b. 8 March 1917, Newark, New Jersey, USA. Prof. of English; Writer; Poet. m. (1) Margaret Ann Shipley, 7 Oct. 1939, divorced 1972, 3 s., 3 d., (2) Sally Andersen, 1973, 2 step-s. *Education:* BA, New York University, 1938; MA, 1939, PhD, 1941, University of Wisconsin; Postgraduate Studies, Harvard University, 1946–47. *Appointments:* Instructor to Assoc. Prof., 1941–53, Prof. of English, 1953–64, Chair., Dept of English, State University of New York at Buffalo, 1965–; Various visiting professorships. *Publications:* Waiting for God (with S Weil), 1952; Leaves of Grass: 100 Years After (with others), 1955; An End to Innocence, 1955; The Art of the Essay, 1959; The Image of the Jew in American Fiction, 1959; Love and Death in the American Novel, 1960; Pull Down Vanity (short stories), 1962; The Second Stone (novel), 1963; The Continuing Debate (with J. Vinocur), 1964; Waiting for the End, 1964; Back to China, 1965; The Girl in the Black Raincoat (with others), 1966; The Last Jew in America, 1966; The Return of the Vanishing American, 1967; O Brave New World (with A Zeiger), 1967; Nude Croquet and Other Stories, 1969; Being Busted, 1970; Collected Essays, 1971; The Stranger in Shakespeare, 1972; The Messengers Will Come No More, 1974; In Dreams Awake, 1975; Freaks, 1977; A Fiedler Reader, 1977; The Inadvertent Epic, 1979; Olaf Stapledon, 1982; Fiedler on the Roof, 1991; Stranger in a Strange Land (collected essays), 1994; Tyranny of the Normal, 1996; A New Fiedler Reader, 1999. *Contributions to:* Many journals, reviews, and magazines. *Honours:* Furioso Prize for Poetry, 1951; Christian Gauss Lecturer, 1956; Guggenheim Fellowship, 1970–71; Lifetime Achievement Award, National Book Critics Circle, 1998. *Memberships:* American Acad. of Arts and Letters; American Asscn of University Profs; Dante Society of America; MLA; PEN. *Address:* c/o Dept of English, Clemens Hall, State University of New York at Buffalo, Buffalo, NY 14260, USA.

FIELD, Edward, (Bruce Elliot); b. 7 June 1924, New York, NY, USA. Writer; Poet. *Education:* New York University, 1946–48. *Publications:* Stand Up, Friend, With Me, 1963; Variety Photoplays, 1967; Eskimo Songs and Stories, 1973; A Full Heart, 1977; A Geography of Poets (ed.), 1979, revised edn as A New Geography of Poets, 1992; New and Selected Poems, 1987; Counting Myself Lucky, 1992; A Frieze for a Temple of Love, 1998; Magic Words, 1998; The Villagers, 2000. *Contributions to:* Reviews, journals, and periodicals. *Honours:* Lamont Award, 1963; Shelley Memorial Award, 1978; Lambda Award, 1993. *Memberships:* American Acad. of Rome, Fellow. *Address:* 463 West St, A323, New York, NY 10014, USA.

FIELD, Simon; b. 21 Nov. 1955, Cookham, Berkshire, England. Nurse; Poet. *Education:* BA, Philosophy, Leicester University, 1979. *Contributions to:* Rialto; Orbis; Staple; New Hope International; Mildred; Southern Review; Bogg; Poetry New Zealand; Takalie; and others. *Membership:* Auckland Poetry Workshop, New Zealand. *Address:* 55 Finch St, Morningside, Auckland, New Zealand.

FIELDING, Amber. See: MONEYSMITH, Carol Louise Giesbrecht.

FINALE, Frank (Louis); b. 10 March 1942, New York, NY, USA. Ed.; Poet. m. Barbara Long, 20 Oct. 1973, 3 s. *Education:* BS, Education, Ohio State University, 1964; MA, Human Development, Fairleigh Dickinson University, 1976. *Appointments:* Founding-Ed., 1983, Ed.-in-Chief, 1985–95, Without Halos; Poetry Ed., The New Renaissance, 1996–. *Publications:* Under a Gull's Wing: Poems and Photographs of the Jersey Shore (co-ed.), 1996; To the Shore Once More: A Portrait of the Jersey Shore, Prose, Poetry and Works of Art, 1999. *Contributions to:* Various anthologies, reviews, and journals. *Honour:* Literacy Award, International Reading Asscn and Ocean County Reading Council, 1993. *Memberships:* Poetry Society of America; National Education Asscn; New Jersey Education Asscn; Ocean County Poets Collective. *Address:* 19 Quail Run, Bayville, NJ 08721, USA.

FINCH, Annie Ridley Crane; b. 31 Oct. 1956, New Rochelle, New York, USA. Poet; Ed.; Critic; Prof. m. Glen Brand, 6 Dec. 1985, 1 s. *Education:* BA, Yale University, 1979; MA, University of Houston, 1986; PhD, Stanford University, 1990. *Appointments:* Asst Prof., University of North Iowa, 1992–95, Miami University of Ohio, 1995–. *Publications:* The Encyclopedia of Scotland, 1982; Catching the Mermother, 1997; Eve, 1997. *Contributions to:* Hudson Review; Partisan Review; Paris Review; Agni; Many Mountains Moving; PMCA; Legacy. *Honours:* Sparrow Sonnet Prize; Nomination, Pushcart Prize, 1997; Finalist, National Poetry Series, Yale Series of Younger Poets. *Memberships:* Acad. of American Poets; Poetry Society of America. *Address:* Dept of English, Miami University, Oxford, OH 45056, USA.

FINCH, Peter; b. 6 March 1947, Cardiff, Wales. Poet; Writer. 2 s., 1 d. *Education:* Glamorgan Polytechnic. *Appointment:* Ed., Second Aeon, 1966–75. *Publications:* Wanted, 1967; Pieces of the Universe, 1968; How to Learn Welsh, 1977; Between 35 and 42 (short stories), 1982; Some Music and a Little War, 1984; How to Publish Your Poetry, 1985; Reds in the Bed, 1986; Selected Poems, 1987; How to Publish Yourself, 1988; Make, 1990; Poems for Ghosts, 1991; Five Hundred Cobbings, 1994; The Spe Ell, 1995; The Poetry

Business, 1995; Antibodies, 1997; Useful, 1997; Food, 2001. *Contributions to* Magazines and journals. *Memberships:* Welsh Acad.; Welsh Union of Writers *Address:* 19 Southminster Rd, Roath, Cardiff CF23 5AT, Wales. *E-mail* peter@peterfinch.co.uk. Website; www.peterfinch.co.uk.

FINCH, Roger; b. 17 April 1937, Pittsburgh, Pennsylvania, USA. Prof. of English and Linguistics; Writer; Poet. *Education:* BA, Music Theory, George Washington University, 1968; PhD, Near Eastern Language and Literature Harvard University, 1977. *Appointments:* Lecturer, Sophia University, Tokyo 1978–; Prof., Surugadai University, Saitama, 1990–. *Publications:* What I Written in the Wind; According to Lilies, 1993. *Contributions to:* PN Review London Magazine; Beloit; Michigan Quarterly; Horam Poetry Review; Poe Lore; Wormwood; Prairie Schooner; Cimarron Review; Clockwatch Review; Sa Jose Studies; Waascana Review; Antigonish Review; Windsor Review. *Honour* First Prize, Bridport Arts Centre, 1988. *Address:* O-Aza Kitagawa 176-Hanno-shi, Saitama, Japan.

FINCKE, Gary (William); b. 7 July 1945, Pittsburgh, Pennsylvania, USA Prof. of English; Poet; Writer. m. Elizabeth Locker, 17 Aug. 1968, 2 s., 1 d *Education:* BA, Thiel College, 1967; MA, Miami University, 1969; PhD, Ken State University, 1974. *Appointments:* Instructor in English, Pennsylvania State University of Monaca, 1969–75; Chair, Dept of English, LeRoy Centra School, New York, 1975–80; Administrator, 1980–93, Prof. of English and Dir o the Writers' Institute, 1993–, Susquehanna University; Ed., The Apprentice Writer, 1982–98; Syndicated Columnist, 1996–. *Publications:* Poetry: Breath 1984; The Coat in the Heart, 1985; The Days of Uncertain Health, 1988 Handing the Self Back, 1990; Plant Voices, 1991; The Public Talk of Death 1991; The Double Negatives of the Living, 1992; Inventing Angels, 1994; The Technology of Paradise, 1998; The Almanac for Desire, 2000. Fiction: For Keepsies, 1993; Emergency Calls, 1996; The Inadvertent Scofflaw, 1999 Blood Ties, 2002. *Contributions to:* Many anthologies, reviews, quarterlies journals, and magazines. *Honours:* Various grants and fellowships; Beloi Fiction Journal Short-Story Prize, 1990; Bess Hokin Prize, Poetry Magazine 1991; Book-of-the-Month, Vietnam Veteran's Magazine, 1993; Notable Fiction Book of the Year, Dictionary of Literary Biography, 1993; Pushcart Prize, 1995 Rose Lefcowitz Prize, Poet Lore, 1997. *Address:* 3 Melody Lane, Selinsgrove, PA 17870, USA.

FINK-JENSEN, Jens; b. 19 Dec. 1956, Copenhagen, Denmark. Poet; Writer Photographer; Composer; Architect. 1 d. *Education:* MAA, 1986, Multimedia Design, 1997, Royal Academy of Fine Arts, Copenhagen. *Publications:* Poetry The World is an Eye, 1981; Travels in Sorrow, 1982; Dancing Under the Gallows, 1983; Near the Distance, 1988; The Sea of Change, 1995. Other: The Beasts (short stories), 1986; Jonas and the Conch Shell (children's book), 1994; Jonas and the Sky Tent (children's book), 1998. *Contributions to:* Periodicals worldwide. *Honours:* Danish Arts Foundation, 1982; The Ministry of Culture's Commission for the Illustrated Danish Book, 1992; The Danish Literature Council, 1997, 1998. *Memberships:* Danish PEN; The Danish Writers' Asscn. *Address:* Holger Danskes Vej 56 2tv, 2000 Frederiksberg, Denmark.

FINKEL, Donald; b. 21 Oct. 1929, New York, NY, USA. Poet; University Teacher (retd). m. Constance Urdang, 1956, 1 s., 2 d. *Education:* BA, 1952, MA, 1953, Columbia University. *Appointments:* Teacher, University of Iowa, 1957–58, Bard College, 1958–60; Faculty, 1960–92, Poet-in-Residence, 1965–92, Poet-in-Residence Emeritus, 1992–, Washington University, St Louis; Visiting Lecturer, Bennington College, 1966–67, Princeton University, 1985, University of Missouri-St Louis, 1998–99, Webster University, 1999–2000. *Publications:* The Clothing's New Emperor and Other Poems, 1959; Simeon, 1964; A Joyful Noise, 1966; Answer Back, 1968; The Garbage Wars, 1970; Adequate Earth, 1972; A Mote in Heaven's Eye, 1975; Going Under, and Endurance: An Arctic Idyll: Two Poems, 1978; What Manner of Beast, 1981; The Detachable Man, 1984; Selected Shorter Poems, 1987; The Wake of the Electron, 1987; Beyond Despair, 1994; A Question of Seeing, 1998. *Honours:* Helen Bullis Prize, 1964; Guggenheim Fellowship, 1967; National Endowment for the Arts Grants, 1969, 1973; Ingram Merrill Foundation Grant, 1972; Theodore Roethke Memorial Prize, 1974; Morton Dauwen Zabel Award, American Acad. of Arts and Letters, 1980; Dictionary of Literary Biography Yearbook Award, 1994. *Address:* 2051 Park Ave, Apt D, St Louis, MO 63104, USA.

FINNEY, Frank Jr; b. 28 Feb. 1956, Massachusetts, USA. Lecturer in British and American Literature; Writer; Poet. m. Piyachat Ruengviseth, 1 d. *Education:* BA, magna cum laude, University of Massachusetts; MA, English, MPhil, English, Simmons College School of Graduate Studies. *Appointments:* Lecturer in English and American Literature, Thammasat University, Bangkok, Thailand. *Publications:* Fragments from the Smoked-Glass Elephant Bank, 1990; The Dissolution of the Sparkling Bridge, 1997. *Contributions to:* Bone and Flesh; Great Midwestern Quarterly; Green Hills Literary Lantern; Green Mountains Review; Haiku Quarterly; Iota; The MacGuffin; The Maryland Poetry Review; Medicinal Purposes; Midwest Poetry Review; Orbis; Positively Poetry; Staple; The Starving Poets' Cookbook; Verandah; Weyfarers; The Nation; T. U. Journal of Liberal Arts. *Honours:* Poetpourri Special Merit Award for Poetry, 1994; Nomination for

Pushcart Prize for Poetry, 1995, 1996; Staple Open Poetry Competition Prize, England, 1997; Scottish International Open Poetry Competition; Diploma Award, International section, 1998. *Membership:* International Order of Merit. *Address:* Thammasat University, Faculty of Liberal Arts, Dept of Language and Literature, Tha Prachan, Bangkok, 10200, Thailand.

FIRER, Susan; b. 14 Oct. 1948, Milwaukee, Wisconsin, USA. Adjunct Asst Prof. of English; Poet. 1 s., 2 d. *Education:* BA, 1973, MA, 1982, University of Wisconsin at Milwaukee. *Appointments:* Teaching Asst, 1981–82, Lecturer, 1982, Adjunct Asst Prof. of English, 1988–, University of Wisconsin at Milwaukee. *Publications:* My Life with the Tsar and Other Poems, 1979; The Underground Communion Rail, 1992; The Lives of the Saints and Everything, 1993. *Contributions to:* Numerous anthologies, reviews, journals, and magazines. *Honours:* Acad. of American Poets Prize, University of Wisconsin at Milwaukee, 1977; Best American Poetry, 1992; Cleveland State University Poetry Center Prize, 1992; Wisconsin Council of Writers Posner Poetry Award, 1993; First Place, Writer's Place Literary Awards, 1995; Milwaukee County Artist Fellowship, 1996; Work included in Midwest Express Center, 1998. *Address:* 1514 E Kensington, Milwaukee, WI 53211, USA.

FIRTH, A. Lee; b. 22 May 1962, Pontefract, Yorkshire, England. Charity Dir; Poet. *Publications:* Undue Vibrations (co-author), 1989; Snapshots, 2 vols, 1991–92; Poems 1988–92, 1992. *Contributions to:* Envoi Summer 1991 Anthology; Poetry Now; North West Anthology, 1992; Guardians of the State Anthology, 1992; Numerous poetry magazines. *Address:* 109 High St, Thurnscoe, Rotherham, Yorkshire S63 0QZ, England.

FISHER, Allen; b. 1 Nov. 1944, Norbury, Surrey, England. Painter; Poet; Art Historian. *Education:* BA, University of London; MA, University of Essex. *Appointment:* Head of Art, Professor of Poetry and Art, University of Surrey Roehampton. *Publications:* Over 100 books including: Place Book One, 1974; Brixton Fractals, 1985; Unpolished Mirrors, 1985; Stepping Out, 1989; Future Exiles, 1991; Fizz, 1994; Civic Crime, 1994; Breadboard, 1994; Now's the Time, 1995; The Topological Shovel (essays), 1999. *Contributions to:* Various magazines and journals. *Honour:* Co-Winner, Alice Hunt Bartlett Award, 1975. *Address:* 14 Hopton Rd, Hereford HR1 1BE, England.

FISHER, Leona. See: KERR, Kathryn Ann.

FISHER, Lynn Helen; b. 2 June 1943, Red Wing, Minnesota, USA. Writer; Poet; Ed.; Inventor. *Education:* College Studies; Doctor of Genius Degree, 1986. *Appointments:* Ed., Genius Newsletter, 1990–; Welcome Neighbor Newsletter, 1995–. *Publications:* The 1, 2, 4 Theory: A Synthesis, 1971; Sexual Equations of Electricity, Magnetism and Gravitation, 1971; Human Sexual Evolution, 1971; Middle Concept Theory, 1972; A Revised Meaning of Paradox, 1972; Unitary Theory, 1973; An Introduction to Circular or Fischerian Geometry, 1976; Two Four Eight Theory, 1976; Fischer's Brief Dictionary of Sound Meanings, 1977; Introducing the Magnetic Sleeve: A Novel Sexual Organ, 1983; The Expansion of Duality, 1984; The Inger Poems, 1987; Circular Geometry, 1990; The Four Inventions, 1990; The Expansion of Dualism: A 2 4 8 System, 1990; The Early Poems of Musical Lynn, 1990; The Musical Lynn Song Lyrics, 1991; The Musical Lynn Essays, 1992; Caveman Talk, 1992; The Three in One Ring (and) The Magnetic Woman, 1992; Apple Skies, 1993; A Triversal Woman, 1997. *Membership:* National Asscn for Female Executives. *Address:* 1415 E 22nd St, Apt 1108, Minneapolis, MN 55404, USA.

FISHER, Roy; b. 11 June 1930, Birmingham, England. Poet; Musician. *Education:* BA, 1951, MA, 1970, Birmingham University. *Publications:* City, 1961; Interiors, 1966; The Ship's Orchestra, 1967; The Memorial Fountain, 1968; Matrix, 1971; Cut Pages, 1971; Metamorphoses, 1971; The Thing About Joe Sullivan, 1978; A Furnace, 1986; The Left-Handed Punch, 1987; Poems 1955–1987, 1988; Birmingham River, 1994; The Dow Low Drop: New and Selected Poems, 1996; Interviews Through Time, 2000. *Contributions to:* Numerous journals and magazines. *Honours:* Andrew Kelus Prize, 1979; Cholmondeley Award, 1981; Hamlyn Award, 1997; Hon. DLitt, University of Keele, 1999. *Memberships:* Musicians Union; Society of Authors. *Address:* Four Ways, Earl Sterndale, Buxton, Derbyshire SK17 0EP, England.

FISHMAN, Charles (Munro); b. 10 July 1942, Oceanside, NY, USA. Prof. Emeritus; Poet; Writer; Ed. m. Ellen Marci Haselkorn, 25 June 1967, 2 d. *Education:* BA, English Literature, 1964, MA, English Literature, 1965, Hofstra University; DA, Creative Writing, State University of New York at Albany, 1982. *Appointments:* Founder-Dir, Visiting Writers Program, 1979–97, Distinguished Service Prof., 1989–97, Prof. Emeritus, 1997–, State University of New York at Farmingdale; Founder-Ed., Xanadu, 1975–78; Poetry Ed., Gaia, 1993–95, The Genocide Forum, 1997–99, the Cistercian Studies Quarterly, 1998–99, Journal of Genocide Research, 1999; Assoc. Ed., The Drunken Boat, 1999–2001. *Publications:* An Index to Women's Magazines and Presses (ed.), 1977; Mortal Companions, 1977; The Death Mazurka, 1989; Zoom, 1990; Catlives, by Sarah Kirsch (trans. with Marina Roscher), 1991; Blood to Remember: American Poets on the Holocaust (ed.), 1991; As the Sun Goes Down in Fire, 1992; Nineteenth-Century Rain, 1994; The Firewalkers, 1996; An Aztec Memory, 1997. *Contributions to:* Many anthologies and over 300 periodicals. *Honours:* Gertrude B Claytor Memorial Award, Poetry Society of

America, 1987; Outstanding Academic Book of the Year, American Library Asscn, 1989; Firman Houghton Poetry Award, New England Poetry Club, 1995; New York Foundation for the Arts Fellowship in Poetry, 1995; Winner, Anabiosis Press Chapbook Competition, 1996; Ann Stanford Poetry Prize, Southern California Anthology, 1996; Eve of St Agnes Poetry Prize, 1999. *Memberships:* Associated Writing Programs; PEN; Poetry Society of America; Poets and Writers. *Address:* 56 Wood Acres Rd, East Patchogue, NY 11772, USA.

FISHMAN, Lisa; b. 14 Dec. 1966, Michigan, USA. Asst Prof.; Poet. m. Henry Morren, 31 July 1992. *Education:* BA, English, Michigan State University, 1988; MFA, Creative Writing, Western Michigan University, 1992; PhD, English, University of Utah, 1998. *Appointment:* Asst Prof., Beloit College, 1998–. *Publication:* The Deep Heart's Core is a Suitcase, 1996. *Contributions to:* Reviews and journals. *Address:* c/o English Dept, Beloit College, Beloit, WI 53511, USA.

FITZGERALD, Judith (Ariana); b. 11 Nov. 1952, Toronto, Ontario, Canada. Poet; Critic. *Education:* BA, Honours, 1976, MA, 1977, York University. *Appointments:* Teacher, Erindale College, 1978–81; Prof., Laurentian University, 1981–83; Poetry Ed., Black Moss Press, 1981–87; Entertainment Journalist, The Globe, 1983–84; Poetry Critic, The Toronto Star, 1984–88; Writer-in-Residence, University of Windsor, 1993–94; Creator, Today's Country, Satellite Radio Network, 1993–; Prof. of English, Université Canadienne en France, 1994–95. *Publications:* Poetry: City Park, 1972; Journal Entries, 1975; Victory, 1975; Lacerating Heartwood, 1977; Easy Over, 1981; Split/Levels, 1983; Heart Attacks, 1984; Beneath the Skin of Paradise, 1984; Given Names, 1985; Diary of Desire, 1987; Rapturous Chronicles, 1991; Ultimate Midnight, 1992; Walkin' Wounded, 1993; River, 1995; AKA Paradise, 1996. Children's Poetry: My Orange Gorange, 1985; Whale Waddleby, 1986. Editor: Un Dozen: Thirteen Canadian Poets, 1982; Sp/Elles: Poetry by Canadian Women/Poesie de femmes canadiennes, 1986; First Person Plural, 1988. *Contributions to:* Various anthologies and other publications. *Honours:* Fiona Mee Award, 1983; Writers' Choice Award, 1986; Short-listed, Gov.-Gen.'s Award for Poetry, 1991; Several grants. *Memberships:* League of Canadian Poets; Society of Composers, Authors and Music Publishers of Canada. *Address:* c/o League of Canadian Poets, 54 Wolseley St, Third Floor, Toronto, Ontario M5T 1AS, Canada.

FITZMAURICE, Gabriel John; b. 7 Dec. 1952, Moyvane, County Kerry, Ireland. Primary Teacher; Poet. m. Brenda Downey, 17 Aug. 1981, 1 s., 1 d. *Education:* Leaving Certificate, Honours, St Michael's College, Listowel, County Kerry, 1970; Diploma, Primary Teaching, Mary Immaculate College, Limerick, 1972. *Appointments:* Asst Teacher, Avoca National School, County Wicklow, 1972–74; Teacher, Christ the King National School, Limerick City, 1974–75; Moyvane National School, 1975–. *Publications:* Poetry in English: Rainsong, 1984; Road to the Horizon, 1987; Dancing Through, 1990; The Father's Part, 1992; The Space Between: New and Selected Poems 1984–92, 1993; The Village Sings, 1996; A Wrenboy's Carnival: Poems 1980–2000, 2000; I and the Village, 2002. Poetry in Irish: Nocht, 1989; Ag Síobshíul Chun An Rince, 1995; Giolla na nAmhrán: Dánta 1988–1998, 1998. Essays: Kerry on My Mind, 1999. Other: Children's poetry in English and Irish. Translator: The Purge, by Mícheál Ó hAirtnéide, 1989; Poems I Wish I'd Written, 1996. Editor: The Flowering Tree, 1991; Between the Hills and Sea: Songs and Ballads of Kerry, 1991; Con Greaney: Traditional Singer, 1991; Homecoming/An Bealach 'na Bhaile: Selected Poems of Cathal Ó Searcaigh (Cló Iar-Chonnacnta, 1993; Irish Poetry Now: Other Voices, 1993; Kerry Through Its Writers, 1993; The Listowel Literary Phenomenon: North Kerry Writers – A Critical Introduction, 1994; Rusty Nails and Astronauts: A Wolfhound Poetry Anthology, 1999; 'The Boro' and 'The Cross': The Parish of Moyvane-Knockanure (with Áine Cronin and John Looney), 2000; The Kerry Anthology, 2000. *Contributions to:* Newspapers, reviews, and journals. *Honours:* Represented Ireland, Europees Poeziefestival, Leuven, Belgium, 1987, 1991; Award Winner, Gerard Manley Hopkins Centenary Poetry Competition, 1989. *Address:* Applegarth, Moyvane, County Kerry, Ireland.

FITZSIMMONS, Thomas; b. 21 Oct. 1926, Lowell, Massachusetts, USA. Poet; Writer; Trans.; Ed.; Publisher; Prof. Emeritus of English and Comparative Literature. m. Karen Hargreaves, 2 s. *Education:* Fresno State College, 1947–49; Sorbonne and Institut de Sciences Politiques, Paris, 1949–50; BA, English Literature and Creative Writing, Stanford University, 1951; MA, English and Comparative Literature, Columbia University, 1952. *Appointments:* Writer and Ed., The New Republic magazine, 1952–55; Research Team Chair., 1955–56, Dir of Research for Publication, 1956–58, Dir and Ed., 1958–59, HRAF Press, Yale University; Asst Prof., 1959–61, Assoc. Prof., 1961–66, Prof. of English and Comparative Literature 1966–89, Prof. Emeritus, 1989–, Oakland University, Rochester, Michigan; Fulbright Lecturer, Tokyo University of Education, 1962–64, Tsuda University, Tokyo, 1962–64, University of Bucharest, 1967–68, University of Nice, 1968; Visiting Lecturer, Japan National Women's University, Tokyo, 1973–75, Keio University, Tokyo, 1973–75, Detroit Institute of Arts, 1986; Visiting Prof., Tokyo University of Education, 1973–75, Kyushu National University, Fukuoka, 1979; Visiting Poet and Scholar, Sophia University, Tokyo, 1988–89; Ed.-Publisher, Katydid Books. *Publications:* Poetry: This Time This

Place, 1969; Mooning, 1971; Meditation Seeds, 1971; With the Water, 1972; Playseeds, 1973; The Big Huge, 1975; The Nine Seas and the Eight Mountains, 1981; Rocking Mirror Daybreak, 1982; Water Ground Stone (poems and essays), 1994; The Dream Machine, 1996; Fencing the Sky, 1998; Iron Harp, 1999; The One-Eyed Boy Tries to Grow Another Eye, 2002. Other: Author, ed. or trans. of over 60 vols, 1955–98. *Honours:* National Endowment for the Arts Fellowships, 1967, 1982, 1989–90, and Grants, 1984, 1986; Oakland University Research Fellowship, 1982; Japan-US Friendship Foundation Grant, 1983; Michigan Council for the Arts Award, 1986; Fulbright Research Fellowship, Japan, 1988–89. *Address:* 1 Balsa Rd, Santa Fe, NM 87505, USA.

FLEISCHMAN, Paul; b. 5 Sept. 1952, Monterey, CA, USA. Children's Writer and Poet. m. Becky Mojica, 15 Dec. 1978, 2 s. *Education:* University of California at Berkeley; BA, University of New Mexico. *Publications:* The Birthday Tree, 1979; The Half-a-Moon Inn, 1980; Graven Images, 1982; Path of the Pale Horse, 1983; Finzel the Farsighted, 1983; Coming-and-Going Men, 1985; I Am Phoenix: Poems for Two Voices, 1985; Rondo in C, 1988; Joyful Noise: Poems for Two Voices, 1989; Saturnalia, 1990; Shadow Play, 1990; The Borning Room, 1991; Time Train, 1991. *Honours:* Silver Medal, Commonwealth Club of California, 1980; Newberry Medals, American Library Asscn, 1983, 1989; Parents Choice Award, 1983; Numerous citations by Society of Children's Book Writers, American Library Asscn, New York Times. *Memberships:* Authors' Guild; Society of Children's Book Writers. *Address:* 855 Marin Pines, Pacific Grove, CA 93950, USA.

FLETCHER, Harvey Dupree; b. 28 Feb. 1936, Spartanburg, South Carolina, USA. US Marine (retd); Poet. *Education:* University of South Carolina, 1977–79. *Appointments:* US Marine Corps, 1952–71; Veteran of Korea, 1953; Veteran of Vietnam, 1964, 1967–68, 1970–71; TV shows, 1987–89; Lecturer, University of South Carolina, 1989. *Publications:* Visions of NAM, 4 vols, 1987–91. *Address:* 4189 Sheppard Crossing Way, Stone Mountain, GA 30083, USA.

FLORSHEIM, Stewart; b. 14 Nov. 1952, New York, NY, USA. Company Dir; Poet. m. Judy Rosloff, 24 May 1987, 2 d. *Education:* BA, Journalism and Philosophy, Syracuse University, 1974; MA, English, San Francisco State University, 1978. *Publications:* Ghosts of the Holocaust, 1989; Unsettling America, 1994; And What Rough Beast, 1999; Bittersweet Legacy, 2001. *Contributions to:* Berkeley Poets Co-operative; Dremples; Round Table; Dimension; Blue Unicorn; Syracuse Poems; Yoga Journal; DoubleTake; Slipstream; Rattle; 88; Seattle Review. *Honours:* Hon. Mention, Whiffen Prize, Syracuse University, 1974; Honorable Mentions, Judah Magnes Poetry Prize, 1991, 1993, 1996, 1999. *Address:* 170 Sandringham Rd, Piedmont, CA 94611, USA. *E-mail:* stewjay@pacbell.net.

FLORY, Sheldon; b. 28 June 1927, USA. Episcopal (Anglican) Priest (retd); Poet. 3 c. *Education:* AB, French, Middlebury College, Vermont, 1950; MA English and Comparative Literature, Columbia University, New York City, 1952; MDiv, General Theological Seminary, New York, 1958. *Appointments:* Fellow and Tutor, General Theological Seminary 1958–60; Rector, St Margaret's Church, Belfast, Maine, 1960–63; Rector, Trinity Church, Geneva, New York, 1963–69; Chaplain, Brown University, Rhode Island School of Design, Providence, RI, 1969–74; Chaplain, English Teacher and Dean of Faculty, Darrow School, New Lebanon, New York, 1974–90; Part-time Priest-in-Charge, St Peter's Church, Bloomfield, New York, 1991–96; Chaplain, Ontario-Yates Hospice, 1994–97. *Publications:* A Winter's Journey, 1979. *Contributions to:* New Yorker; Poetry; Epoch; Iowa, Seneca, and Northern Reviews; Lamp in the Spine; Williwaw; Separate Doors; London Sunday Observer; Anglican Theological Review; Zone 3; Gulf Coast Mangrove; European Judaism; Puckerbrush Review; Pivot; Graffiti Rag; Anthologies: Dan River; Words of Wisdom. *Honours:* Honourable Mention, 1988, First Prize, 1989, Williwaw Competition; Judge, Arvon International Poetry Competition, 1991; Constance Saltonstall Fellowship Award, 1999. *Address:* 6981 Route 21, Naples, NY 14512, USA.

FLYNN, (John) David; b. 4 April 1948, Jackson, Tennessee, USA. Teacher; Writer; Poet. Divorced, 1 d. *Education:* BA, BJ, University of Missouri, 1971; MA, University of Denver, 1972; MA, Boston University, 1980; PhD, University of Nebraska, 1984. *Contributions to:* 71 poems published in professional publications. *Honours:* Several residencies. *Membership:* Poets and Writers. *Address:* 303 Crestmeade Dr., Nashville, TN 37221, USA.

FLYNN, Sharon Washburn; b. 14 Jan. 1949, Winchester, Massachusetts, USA. Bursar; Poet. m. Bill Flynn, 10 Dec. 1977, 2 s., 2 d. *Education:* Institute of Children's Literature, 1988–90; External Studies, Creative Writing, Poetry, University of Wisconsin, 1990–91. *Publications:* Lions, Lizards and Lady Bugs, 1989; Bears, Bunnies and Bees, 1990; A Voyage to Remember, 1996. *Contributions to:* Anthologies and magazines. *Honours:* Honorable Mention, Writer's Digest Writing Competition, 1992; Commendable Award, New England Writers-Vermont Poets Free Verse, 1992. *Memberships:* Acad. of American Poets; New England Writers-Vermont Poets Asscn. *Address:* 106 Lang St, Springfield, MA 01104, USA.

FOERSTER, Richard Alfons; b. 29 Oct. 1949, New York, NY, USA. Ed.; Writer; Poet. m. Valerie Elizabeth Malinowski, 28 Oct. 1972, divorced 1985. *Education:* BA, English, Fordham University, 1971; MA, English, University of Virginia, 1972; Teacher's Certificate, Manhattanville College, 1975. *Appointments:* Asst Ed., Clarence L Barnhart Inc, 1973–75; Ed., Prentice Hall Inc, 1976–78; Assoc. Ed., 1978–94, Ed., 1994–2001, Chelsea Magazine. *Publications:* Transfigured Nights, 1990; Sudden Harbor, 1992; Patterns of Descent, 1993; Trillium, 1998; Double Going, 2002. *Contributions to:* Boulevard; Epoch; Kenyon Review; Nation; New Criterion; Poetry; Shenandoah; Southern Review; Southwest Review. *Honours:* Discovery/The Nation Award, 1985; Bess Hokin Prize, 1992; Hawthornden Fellow, 1993; National Endowment for the Arts Creative Writing Fellowship, 1995; Maine Arts Commission Individual Artist Fellowship, 1997; Amy Lowell Poetry Travelling Scholarship, 2000–01; Hobart City International Writer-in-Residence, 2002. *Memberships:* Acad. of American Poets; Maine Writers and Publishers Alliance; Poetry Society of America; Society for the Arts, Religion and Contemporary Culture. *Address:* PO Box 1040, York Beach, ME 03910, USA.

FOGDEN, Barry; b. 28 June 1948, Sussex, England. Ed.; Poet. m. Celia Marjorie Avard, 16 Sept. 1980. *Education:* BSc, Psychology, University of Surrey, 1980; BA Humanities, The Open University, 1981; MA, Philosophy University of Sussex, 1981. *Publications:* Displaced Person, 1989; De Fordrevne, 1990; Swede, 1993; In the Darkroom, An Exploding Still, 1994; Utan Identitet, 1994; A Chalk Stream in Sussex, 1995; The Black Heralds, 1995. *Contributions to:* South; Acumen; Downlander; Wessex Poets 1 and 2; Vision On; Orbis; Envoi; Staple; Psychopoetica; Iron; Foolscap; Iota; Skoob Review; Index on Censorship; Verse; Hippo; Parting Gifts; Ambit; ELF; Poet's Market; New York Echoes. *Honours:* Sussex Poet of the Year, 1987; Skoob Index of Censorship International Competition Winner, 1989; Leek Arts Festival Competition, 1990; Surrey Open Competition, 1990. *Membership:* Poetry Society. *Address:* 27 Bradbourne Park Rd, Sevenoaks, Kent TN13 3LJ, England.

FOLEY, Jack, (John Wayne Harold Foley); b. 9 Aug. 1940, Neptune, New Jersey. Poet; Writer; Ed.; Radio Personality. m. Adelle Joan Abramowitz, 23 Dec. 1961, 1 s. *Education:* BA, English, Cornell University, 1963; MA, 1965. Continuing graduate studies, 1960s, 1970s, University of California, Berkeley. *Appointments:* Host, Exec. Producer in charge of Poetry Programme, KPFA FM, Berkeley, CA, 1988–; Guest Ed., Poetry: San Francisco, 1988–89; Ed.-in Chief, Poetry USA, Oakland, CA, 1990–95; Contributing Ed., Poetry Flash, 1992–; Resident Artist, Djerassi Program, 1994; Performs poetry with wife. *Publications:* Poetry: Letters/Lights – Words for Adelle, 1987; Gershwin, 1991; Adrift, 1993; Exiles, 1996; Bridget, 1997; New Poetry from California: Dead Requiem (with Ivan Argüelles), 1998; Some Songs by Georges Brassens (trans.), 2002. Prose: Inciting Big Joy, monograph, 1993; O Her Blackness Sparkles! – The Life and Times of the Batman Art Gallery, San Francisco, 1960–63, 1995; O Powerful Western Star (criticism), 2000; Foley's Books (criticism), 2000; The 'Fallen Western Star' Wars (criticism, ed.), 2001. *Contributions to:* Journals including: Barque; Beloit Poetry Journal; Berkeley Poetry Review; Blue Beetle Press Magazine; Cafe Review; The Experioddicist; Exquisite Corpse; Galley Sail Review; Inkblot; MaLLife; Malthus; Meat Epoch; New York Quarterly; NRG; Outre; Talisman; Tight; Transmog; Wet Motorcycle; ELH; Heaven Bone; Konch; Linden Lane Magazine; Lower Limit Speech; Multicultural Review; Open Letter; Poetry Flash; Prosodia; Seattle Literary Quarterly; W'Orcs; Bright Lights; Journal of Popular Film; Artweek; East Bay Express; Poetry Flash; Anthologies, including: Poly: New Speculative Writing; The Love Project; Online column (criticism) at The Alsop Review (www.alsopreview.com). *Honours:* Full Scholarship to Cornell University, 1958–63; Woodrow Wilson Fellowship, University of California, 1963–65; Yang Poetry Prize, University of California at Berkeley, 1971; Poetry Grantee, Oakland Arts Council, 1992–95; The Artists Embassy Literary Cultural Award, 1998–2000. *Memberships:* MLA; Poets and Writers; National Poetry Asscn; PEN, Oakland, CA, Programme Dir, 1990–97. *Address:* 2569 Maxwell Ave, Oakland, CA 94601-5521, USA. *E-mail:* jasfoley@aol.com.

FOOTE, Arthur Dawson; b. 19 March 1931, Toxteth, Liverpool, England. Asst Minister (retd); Poet. *Education:* MA, Balliol College, Oxford, 1953; Diploma, Theology, Manchester College, Oxford, 1956. *Publications:* Angla Antologio, 1952; Esperanto Anthology, 1958; The House Not Right in the Head, 1986; The Sunken Well, 1988. *Contributions to:* Various publications. *Address:* Flat 1/A, 12 Peddie St, Dundee DD1 5LS, Scotland.

FOQUÉ, Richard K. V.; b. 21 Nov. 1943, Willebroek, Belgium. Prof.; Architect; Poet. 2 s., 1 d. *Education:* Engineer-Architect, University of Leuven, 1967; Postgraduate Diploma, Hochschule für Gestaltung, Ulm, 1968; MSc, Design Technology, University of Manchester, 1969. *Appointment:* Co-Founder, Dichters in het Elzenveld international poetry event, Antwerp, 1988–89, 1993–95. *Publications:* Alleen Kringen, 1967; De Dieren Komen, 1969; Poetical Functions, 1969; De Mekanische Priester, 1971; Drie Millivolt voor Oneindig, 1972. *Contributions to:* Many magazines. *Memberships:* Flemish Literary Society; International Acad. of Poets; World Literary Acad., fellow. *Address:* Hortside, Bruinstraat 14, 2275 Lille, Belgium.

FORBES, Calvin; b. 6 May 1945, Newark, NJ, USA. Poet; Writer; Assoc. Prof. *Education:* New School for Social Research; Rutgers University; MFA, Brown University, 1978. *Appointments:* Asst Prof. of English, Emerson College, 1969–73, Tufts University, 1973–74, 1975–77; Asst Prof. of Creative Writing, Washington College, 1988–89; Assoc. Prof., Art Institute of Chicago, 1991–. *Publications:* Poetry: Blue Monday, 1974; From the Book of Shine, 1979; The Shine Poems, 2001. *Contributions to:* Many anthologies. *Honours:* Bread Loaf Writers' Conference Fellowship, 1973; Yaddo Residency, 1976–77; National Endowment for the Arts Fellowship, 1982–83; District of Columbia Commission on the Arts Fellowship, 1984; Illinois Arts Council Fellowship, 1999. *Memberships:* College Language Asscn; MLA of America. *Address:* c/o School of the Art Institute of Chicago, 37 S Wabash Ave, Chicago, IL 60603, USA.

FORBES, John; b. 1 Sept. 1950, Melbourne, Vic., Australia. Poet; Writer. *Education:* BA, University of Sydney, 1973. *Appointment:* Ed., Surfer's Paradise, 1974–83. *Publications:* Tropical Skiing, 1976; On the Beach, 1977; Drugs, 1980; Stalin's Holidays, 1981; The Stunned Mullet and Other Poems, 1988; New and Selected Poems, 1992. *Contributions to:* Newspapers and magazines. *Honours:* New Poetry Prize, 1973; Southerly Prize, 1976; Grace Leverson Prize, 1993. *Membership:* Australian Society of Authors. *Address:* 54 Morris St, Summerhill, NSW, Australia.

FORCHE, Carolyn (Louise); b. 28 April 1950, Detroit, Michigan, USA. Poet; Writer; Assoc. Prof. m. Henry E Mattison, 27 Dec. 1984, 1 s. Education BA, Michigan State University, 1972; MFA, Bowling Green State University, 1975. *Appointments:* Visiting Lecturer in Poetry, Michigan State University, Justin Morrill College, East Lansing, 1974; Visiting Lecturer, 1975, Asst Prof., 1976–78, San Diego State University; Journalist and Human Rights Activist, El Salvador, 1978–80; Visiting Lecturer, 1979, Visiting Assoc. Prof., 1982–83, University of Virginia; Asst Prof., 1980, Assoc. Prof., 1981, University of Arkansas at Fayetteville; Visiting Writer, New York University, 1983, 1985, Vassar College, 1984; Adjunct Assoc. Prof., Columbia University, 1984–85; Visiting Assoc. Prof., University of Minnesota, 1985; Writer-in-Residence, State University of New York at Albany, 1985; Assoc. Prof., George Mason University, 1994–. *Publications:* Poetry: Gathering the Tribes, 1976; The Country Between Us, 1981; The Angel of History, 1994. Non-Fiction: Women in the Labor Movement, 1835–1925: An Annotated Bibliography (with Martha Jane Soltow), 1972; Women and War in El Salvador (ed.), 1980; El Salvador: The Work of Thirty Photographers (with others), 1983. Other: Claribel Alegria: Flowers from the Volcano (trans.), 1982; Against Forgetting: Twentieth-Century Poetry of Witness (ed.), 1993. *Contributions to:* Anthologies and periodicals. *Honours:* Devine Memorial Fellowship in Poetry, 1975; Yale Series of Younger Poets Award, 1975; Tennessee Williams Fellowship in Poetry, Bread Loaf Writers Conference, 1976; National Endowment for the Arts Fellowships, 1977, 1984; Guggenheim Fellowship, 1978; Emily Clark Balch Prize, Virginia Quarterly Review, 1979; Alice Fay di Castagnola Award, Poetry Society of America, 1981; Lamont Poetry Selection Award, Acad. of American Poets, 1981; Los Angeles Times Book Award for Poetry, 1994. *Memberships:* Acad. of American Poets; Amnesty International; Associated Writing Programs; PEN American Centre; Poetry Society of America. *Address:* c/o Dept of English, George Mason University, 4400 University Dr., Fairfax, VA 22030, USA.

FORD, Charles Henri; b. 10 Feb. 1913, Brookhaven, Mississippi, USA. Poet. *Publications:* Poetry: A Pamphlet of Sonnets, 1936; The Garden of Disorder, 1938; ABC's, 1940; The Overturned Lake, 1941; Poems for Painters, 1945; The Half-Thoughts, The Distances of Pain, 1947; Sleep in a Nest of Flames, 1949; Spare Parts, 1966; Silver Flower Coo, 1968; Flag of Ecstasy, 1972; Om Krishna l, 1979, ll, 1981, lll, 1982; Haiku and Imprints, 1984; Handshakes from Heaven, 1985, ll, 1986; Emblems of Arachne, 1986; Out of the Labyrinth, 1991; Water From a Bucket, 1997. Editor: Blues 10, A Special Issue of Un Muzzled Ox Magazine; I Will Be What I Am; Exhibitions: From Dali to Mapplethorpe, Portrait Photographs, Akehurst Gallery, London, 1993. Novel: The Young and Evil, 1993. *Address:* 1 W 72nd St, New York, NY 10023, USA.

FORD, Robert A(rthur) D(ouglass); b. 8 Jan. 1915, Ottawa, Ontario, Canada. Diplomat (retd); Poet; Writer. m. Maria Thereza Gomes, 27 June 1946, deceased. *Education:* BA, Honours, English and History, University of Western Ontario, 1938; MA, History, Cornell University, 1939. *Appointments:* Diplomatic Service, Canada, 1940–83, including Ambassador to Colombia, 1957–59, Yugoslavia, 1959–61, Egypt, 1961–63, USSR, 1964–80; Governor, International Institute of Geopolitics, 1980–88. *Publications:* Poetry: A Window on the North, 1956; The Solitary City, 1969; Holes in Space, 1979; Needle in the Eye, 1983; Doors, Words and Silence, 1985; Dostoyevsky and Other Poems, 1988; Coming From Afar: Selected Poems, 1990. Translator: Russian Poetry: A Personal Anthology, 1984. Non-Fiction: Our Man in Moscow: A Diplomat's Reflection on the Soviet Union from Stalin to Brezhnev, 1989; A Moscow Literary Memoir Among the Great Artists of Russia from 1946 to 1980, 1993. *Contributions to:* Journals, reviews and magazines. *Honours:* Gov.-Gen.'s Award for Poetry, 1956; Hon. DLitt, 1965, Award of Merit, 1988, University of Western Ontario; Companion of the Order of Canada, 1971; Gold Medal, Professional Institute of Public Service of Canada, 1971; Hon. LLD, University of Toronto, 1987. *Memberships:* Asscn of Bourbonnais Writers; Canada-France Asscn of the Bourbonnais, hon. pres. *Address:* La Poivrière, St-Sylvestre-Pragoulin, 63310 Randan, France.

FORD-CHOYKE, Phyllis May; b. 25 Oct. 1921, Buffalo, New York, USA. Ed.; Poet. m. Arthur Davis Choyke Jr, 18 Aug. 1945, 2 s. *Education:* BS, summa cum laude, Northwestern University, 1942. *Appointment:* Founder-Dir, Harper Square Press, 1966–. *Publications:* Apertures to Anywhere, 1979. Editor: Gallery Series One: Poets, 1967; Gallery Series Two: Poets – Poems of the Real World, 1968; Gallery Series Three: Poets: Levitations and Observations, 1970; Gallery Series Four: Poets, I Am Talking About Revolution, 1973; Gallery Series Five: Poets, To An Aging Nation, 1977. *Honour:* Bonbright Scholar, 1942. *Memberships:* Daughters of the American Revolution; Society of Midland Authors, board of dirs, 1988–96, treasurer, 1987–93, pres., 1994–95; Mystery Writers of America; Chicago Press Veterans Asscn; Arts Club, Chicago; John Evans Club of Northwestern University. *Address:* 29 E Division St, Chicago, IL 60610, USA.

FORELLE, Helen. See: LEIH, Grace Janet.

FOREST, Jody; b. 11 Jan. 1949, Summerland, CA, USA. Poet; Writer. *Education:* Santa Barbara City College, 1969–72; Medieval Metaphysics, Miskatonic University, 1972–76. *Publications:* Strange Days in Spookville; Outsiders, 1971; Bring Me the Head of Bozo the Clown, 1998; Homages to Xena, 2001. *Contributions to:* Santa Barbara News and Review; Tales of Lovecraftian Horror; Cemetery Dance; Rouge et Noir; Surrealist Toiler; Firesignal; Scavenger's; Santa Barbara Independent. *Honours:* Salvador Dali Fan Club Poet of Year, 1971; Busby Berkley Memorial Award, 1972; Jim Morrison Award for Poetry, 1977; Killer Frog Award, 1986. *Memberships:* Clark Ashton Smith Fan Club; Sci-Fi Poetry Society; Viet Nam Veteran's Against War. *Address:* PO Box 666, Summerland, CA 93067, USA.

FORSHAW, Cliff; b. 20 July 1953, Liverpool, England. Poet; Writer. *Education:* Liverpool Art College, 1971–72; BA, Honours, English and European Literature, Warwick University, 1972–75. *Publications:* Spectra, 1977; Bombed Out, 1979; Himalnan Fish, 1991; Esau's Children, 1991. *Contributions to:* London Poetry Quarterly; Envoi; Heaven Bone; Not Otherwise; Orbis; Outposts; Poetry Wales; Prospice; Quartz; Rialto; Resurgence; Poetry Nottingham. *Honours:* Several Prizes. *Membership:* Writers' Guild. *Address:* 341 Victoria Park Rd, London E9 5DX, England.

FORSYTH, Sheila Constance; b. 5 Sept. 1938, Irvington, New Jersey, USA. Poet. *Education:* Graduate, Irvington High School, New Jersey. *Contributions to:* Anthologies, reviews, magazines and journals. *Honours:* Honorable Mention, Writers' Digest Magazine Contest, 1979, 1983, 1985; Second Prize, Hawaii Education Asscn, 1980; First Place in Haiku, Arizona State Poetry Society, 1980; First Prize, Louisiana State Poetry Society, 1982; Third Prize, International Contest, 1984, Silver Poet Award, 1986, World of Poetry; Honourable Mention, World Order of Narrative Poets, 1985, 1987; First Prize, Indiana State Poetry Contest, 1993; University of Baltimore Passager Contest Winner, 1995. *Membership:* Suburban Poets Guild. *Address:* 1207 Clinton Ave, Irvington, NJ 07111, USA.

FORT, Gary W.; b. 23 July 1956, St Louis, Missouri, USA. Writer; Poet. m., 1 d. *Education:* BA, Communications, University of Missouri, 1990. *Appointments:* Teacher; Advertisement Writer. *Publication:* In the Writers Mind, 1991. *Contributions to:* Essence Magazine; World of Poetry; Poet's Forum; Quill Press; Poetry Magiz; Warner Press; and others. *Honours:* Golden Poet Awards, World of Poetry, 1985–89; Certificate of Achievement, Hollywood Song Jubilee, 1987; Music City Song Festival Award, 1989. *Memberships:* Society of American Poets; Acad. of American Poets; Midwest Writer's Asscn; Writer's World International; International Society of Poets; Songwriters and Lyricist Club; America's Songwriter Club; Poets Page Literary Club. *Address:* 4735 Lewis Pl., St Louis, MO 63113, USA.

FORTH, John; b. 15 June 1950, Bethnal Green, London, England. Teacher of English; Poet. m. 30 July 1977, 2 d. *Education:* BEd, 1975, MEd, 1980, West London Institute of Higher Education. *Appointments:* Head of English, Feltham School; Kingswood School; East Midlands Arts New Voices Tour, 1994. *Publication:* Malcontents, 1994. *Contributions to:* London Magazine; Poetry Durham; Verse; Owl; Outposts; A Sense of Place, East Midlands Arts; Spoils, Poetry Business Anthology; New Prospects; North; Risk Behaviour, Poetry Business Anthology; Envoi. *Honour:* East Midlands Arts Development Award for Work on Second Collection. *Membership:* Poetry Society. *Address:* 32 High St, Gretton, Northamptonshire, England.

FOSS, Phillip; b. 20 Oct. 1950, Portland, Oregon, USA. Writer; Poet. m. Joyce Begay, 1 s., 1 d. *Education:* BA, English, 1973; MEA, Writing, 1977. *Appointments:* Dir, Creative Writing Programme, Institute of American Indian Arts, 1979–89; Publishing Dir, Recursos de Santa Fe, 1989–92; Dir, Pedernal Inc, 1991–. *Publications:* Roaring Fork Passage, 1977; Grace, The Snakes and the Dogs, 1978; Yana, 1978; House of Eagles, 1979; Somata, 1982; The Composition of Glass, 1988; The Excesses, the Caprices, 1990; Courtesan of Seizure, 1992. *Contributions to:* Conjunctions; Sulfur; Tyuonyi; Shearsman; Esquire. *Honour:* National Endowment for the Arts Fellowship in Poetry, 1987. *Address:* PO Box 23266, Santa Fe, NM 87502, USA.

FOSSE, Jon; b. 29 Sept. 1959, Haugesund, Norway. Author; Dramatist; Poet. *Education:* Cand philol, Comparative Literature, University of Bergen. *Appointments:* Teacher of Creative Writing, Acad. of Writing, Bergen, 1987–93; Professional Writer, 1993–. *Publications:* Fiction: Raudt, svart, 1983; Stengd gitar, 1985; Naustet, 1989; Flaskesamlaren, 1991; Bly og vatn, 1992; Melancholia I, 1995; Melancholia II, 1996; Morgen og kveld, 2000. Shorter prose: Blod. Steinen er. Forteljing, 1987; To forteljingar, 1993; Prosa frå ein oppvekst. Kortprosa, 1994; Eldre kortare prosa, 1997. Books of poems: Engel med vatn i augene, 1986; Hundens bevegelsar, 1990; Hund og engel, 1992; Nye dikt, 1997. Plays: Og aldri skal vi skiljast, 1994; Namnet, 1995; Nokon kjem til å komme, 1996; Barnet, Mor og barn, Sonen: Tre skodespel, 1997; Natta syng sine songar, Ein sommars dag: To skodespel, 1998; Draum om hausten, 1999; Besak, Vinter, Ettermiddag. Treskodespel, 2000; Vakkert, 2001; Dadsvariasjonar, 2002. Essays: Frå telling via showing til writing, 1989; Gnostiske essays, 1999. Other: Books for children. *Honours:* Noregs Mållags Prize for Children's Books, 1990; Andersson-Rysst Fondet, 1992; Prize for Literature in New Norwegian, 1993; Samlags Prize, 1994; Ibsen Prize, 1996; Sunnmoers Prize, 1996; Melsom Prize, 1997; Aschoug Prize, 1997; Dobloug Prize, 1999; Gyldendal Prize, 2000; Nordic Prize for Dramatists, 2000; Nestroy Prize, 2001; Scandinavian National Theatre Prize, 2002. *Memberships:* Norwegian Society of Authors; Norwegian Society of Dramatists; Norwegian Actors' Society, hon. mem. Literary Agents: For books: Samlaget, Boks 4672 Sofienberg, 0506 Oslo, Norway; For plays: Colombine Teaterförlag, Gaffelgränd 1A, 11130 Stockholm, Sweden.

FOSTER, Edward (Halsey); b. 17 Dec. 1942, Northampton, Massachusetts, USA. Poet; Publisher; Ed.; Teacher. Divorced, 1 s., 1 d. *Education:* AB, Columbia College, 1965; MA, 1966, PhD, 1970, Columbia University. *Appointments:* Asst Prof., Assoc. Prof., Prof., Stevens Institute of Technology, 1985–; Visiting Prof., Ankara University, 1978–79, University of Istanbul, 1985–86, Drew University, 1990, 1992, 1994, 1996; Poetry Ed., MultiCultural Review, 1991–95; Ed., Talisman: A Journal of Contemporary Poetry and Poetics, 1988–; Pres., Talisman House Publishers, 1993–. *Publications:* The Space Between Her Bed and Clock, 1993; The Understanding, 1994; All Acts Are Simple Acts, 1995; Adrian as Song, 1996; Boy in the Key of E, 1998. *Contributions to:* Five Fingers Review; Bombay Gin; American Letters and Commentary; MultiCultural Review; New Jersey History; Rendezvous; Hudson Valley Review; Ararat: A Quarterly Small Press, Western American Literature; Journal of The West; The Greenfield Review; Sagetrieb; American Book Review; Double Eye; Exact Change; First Intent; Poetry New York; Poetry USA. *Memberships:* MLA; PEN. *Address:* Talisman House Publishers, PO Box 3157, Jersey City, NJ 07303-3157, USA.

FOSTER, John Louis, (Derek Stuart); b. 12 Oct. 1941, Carlisle, Cumbria, England. Educator; Poet; Ed. m. Christine Eileen Paul, 2 April 1966, 2 s. *Education:* Denstone College, 1954–60; BA, Brasenose College, Oxford, 1963; DipEd, 1965, MA, Oxon. *Appointments:* Teacher; Vice-Principal, Lord William's School, Thame, 1977–88. *Publications:* Four O'Clock Friday, 1991; Standing on the Sidelines, 1995; You Little Monkey, 1996; Making Waves, 1997; Lollipops, 1998; Climb Aboard the Poetry Plane, 2000; Word Wizard, 2001. Editor: Numerous poetry anthologies, 1986–. *Contributions to:* BBC Radio and TV. *Membership:* Poetry Society. *Address:* 58 Abingdon Rd, Standlake, Witney, Oxon, OX29 7RQ, England.

FOSTER, Linda Nemec; b. 29 May 1950, Garfield Heights, Ohio, USA. Poet; Writer; Teacher. m. Anthony Jesse Foster, 26 Oct. 1974, 1 s., 1 d. *Education:* BA, Aquinas College, Grand Rapids, 1972; MFA, Goddard College, Plainfield, Vermont, 1979. *Appointments:* Teacher of Creative Writing and Poetry, Michigan Council for the Arts, 1980–; Instructor of English Composition, Ferris State University, 1983–84; Dir of Literature Programming, Urban Institute for Contemporary Arts, Grand Rapids, 1989–95; Lecturer in Poetry, Aquinas College, 1999–; Guest Lecturer and Speaker, various schools, colleges, and conferences. *Publications:* A History of the Body, 1987; A Modern Fairy Tale: The Baba Yaga Poems, 1992; Trying to Balance the Heart, 1993; Living in the Fire Nest, 1996. *Contributions to:* Reviews, journals, and magazines. *Honours:* Creative Artist Grants in Poetry, Michigan Council for the Arts, 1984, 1990, 1996; Grand Prize, American Poetry Asscn, 1986; Honourable Mention, Writers' Digest, 1987; Prizewinner, McGuffin Poetry Contest, 1987, 1994; Passages North National Poetry Competition, 1988; Poetry/Visual Art Selections, Sage College, New York, 1994, 1995; Arts Foundation of Michigan Fellowship in Poetry, 1996; Fellowship, National Writer's Voice Project, 1999; Nomination, James Laughlin Award, 2000. *Memberships:* Acad. of American Poets; Detroit Women Writers; Poetry Resource Center of Michigan; Urban Institute for Contemporary Arts; Poetry Society of America. *Address:* 2024 Wilshire Dr. SE, Grand Rapids, MI 49506, USA.

FOSTIERIS, Antonis; b. 16 May 1953, Athens, Greece. Ed.; Poet. m. 1991. *Education:* Degree, Law, Athens University; MPhil, History of Law, University of Paris. *Appointment:* Co-Ed. and Dir, He Lexi (The Word), literary magazine, 1981–. *Publications:* The Long Journey, 1971; Interiors, or The Twenty, 1973; Poetry Within Poetry, 1977; Dark Eros, 1977; The Devil Sang in Tune, 1981; The Shall and the Must of Death, 1987. *Contributions to:* Anthologies and periodicals in Greece and abroad. *Membership:* Greek Writers' Asscn. *Address:* Dionyssiou Aiginitou 46, 115 28 Athens, Greece.

FOURIE, Jeanette Beatrice; b. 22 March 1949, Springs, South Afric: Trans.; Poet. *Education:* JMB, Vereeniging, South Africa, 1966; B: University of South Africa, 1981; Teacher's Diploma, Yoga, Amsterdam, 198' *Publication:* The Haunted Heart, 1992. *Contributions to:* Anthologie *Membership:* Netherlands Society of Trans. *Address:* Ymertstraat 8, 1611 B Bovenkarspel, Netherlands.

FOWLER, Alastair (David Shaw); b. 17 Aug. 1930, Glasgow, Scotland. Prc of English; Writer; Ed. m. Jenny Catherine Simpson, 23 Dec. 1950, 1 s., 1 : *Education:* MA, University of Edinburgh, 1952; MA, 1955, DPhil, 1957, DLit 1972, University of Oxford. *Appointments:* Junior Research Fellow, Queen College, Oxford, 1955–59; Instructor, Indiana University, 1957; Lecture University College, Swansea, 1959–61; Fellow and Tutor in Englis Literature, Brasenose College, Oxford, 1962–71; Visiting Prof., Columbi University, 1964; Mem., Institute for Advanced Study, Princeton, Ne Jersey, 1966, 1980; Visiting Prof., 1969, 1979, 1985–90, Prof. of Englis 1990–98, University of Virginia; Regius Prof. of Rhetoric and Englis Literature, 1972–84, Prof. Emeritus, 1984–, University Fellow, 1985–8; University of Edinburgh; Advisory Ed., New Literary History, 1972–; Visitir Fellow, Council of the Humanities, Princeton University, 1974, Humanitie Research Centre, Canberra, 1980, All Souls College, Oxford, 1984; General Ed Longman Annotated Anthologies of English Verse, 1977–80; Mem., Editoria Board, English Literary Renaissance, 1981–, Word and Image, 1984–9; 1992–97, The Seventeenth Century, 1986–, Connotations, 1990–99, Englis Review, 1990–, Translation and Literature, 1990–. *Publications:* De re poetic: by Richard Wills (ed. and trans.), 1958; Spenser and the Numbers of Tim 1964; Spenser's Images of Life, by C. S. Lewis (ed.), 1967; The Poems of Joh Milton (ed. with John Carey), 1968; Triumphal Forms, 1970; Silent Poetry (ed 1970; Topics in Criticism (ed. with Christopher Butler), 1971; Seventeen, 197: Conceitful Thought, 1975; Catacomb Suburb, 1976; Edmund Spenser, 197; From the Domain of Arnheim, 1982; Kinds of Literature, 1982; A History c English Literature, 1987; The New Oxford Book of Seventeenth Century Vers (ed.), 1991; The Country House Poem, 1994; Time's Purpled Masquers, 1996 Milton: Paradise Lost (ed.), 1998. *Contributions to:* Scholarly books an journals. *Membership:* Fellow, British Acad., 1974. *Address:* 11 E Claremon St, Edinburgh EH7 4HT, Scotland.

FOWLES, John (Robert); b. 31 March 1926, Leigh-on-Sea, Essex, England Writer; Poet; Dramatist. m. (1) Elizabeth Whitton, 1956, deceased 1990, (2 Sarah Smith, 1998. *Education:* University of Edinburgh, 1949; BA, Honours French, New College, Oxford, 1950. *Appointments:* Lecturer in English University of Poitiers, France, 1950–51; Teacher, Anargyrios College Spetsai, Greece, 1951–52, and London, 1953–63. *Publications:* The Collector 1963; The Aristos, 1965; The Magus, 1966; The French Lieutenant's Woman 1969; Poems, 1973; The Ebony Tower, 1974; Shipwreck, 1975; Daniel Martin 1977; Islands, 1978; The Tree, with Frank Horvat, 1979; John Aubrey': Monumenta Britannica (ed.), Parts 1 and 2, 1980, Part 3 and Index, 1982 The Enigma of Stonehenge, 1980; Mantissa, 1982; Thomas Hardy's England 1984; Land, 1985; A Maggot, 1985; Wormholes, 1998; Lyme Worthies, 2000 *Honours:* Silver Pen Award, PEN English Centre, 1969; W H Smith Award 1970; Hon. Fellow, New College, Oxford, 1997. *Address:* Anthony Sheil, Gillor Aitken Assocs, 29 Fernshaw Rd, London, SW10 0TG, England.

FOX, Hugh (Bernard); b. 12 Feb. 1932, Chicago, IL, USA. Prof.; Author; Poet; Dramatist. m. (1) Lucia Alicia Ungaro, 9 June 1957, divorced 1969, 1 s., 2 d., (2) Nona W Werner, June 1970, 1 s., 2 d., (3) Maria Bernadette Costa, 14 Apri 1988. *Education:* BS, Humanities, 1955, MA, 1956, Loyola University, Chicago PhD, University of Illinois, Urbana-Champaign, 1958. *Appointments:* Prof. o American Literature, Loyola Marymount University, Los Angeles, 1958–68; Fulbright Prof., Mexico, 1961, Venezuela, 1964–66, Brazil, 1978–80; Ed., Ghost Dance: The International Quarterly of Experimental Poetry, 1968–95; Prof. Michigan State University, 1968–99; Lecturer, Spain, Portugal, 1975–76. *Publications:* Fiction: Honeymoon/Mom, 1978; Leviathan, 1980; Shaman, 1993; The Last Summer, 1995. Poetry: The Face of Guy Lombardo, 1975; Almazora 42, 1982; Jamais Vu, 1991; The Sacred Cave, 1992; Once, 1995; Techniques, 1997. Non-Fiction: Henry James, 1968; Charles Bukowski: A Critical and Bibliographical Study, 1969; The Gods of the Cataclysm, 1976; First Fire: Central and South American Indian Poetry, 1978; Lyn Lifshin: A Critical Study, 1985; The Mythological Foundations of the Epic Genre: The Solar Voyage as the Hero's Journey, 1989; Stairway to the Sun, 1996. *Contributions to:* Many journals, reviews, quarterlies, and periodicals. *Honours:* John Carter Brown Library Fellowship, Brown University, 1968; Organization of American States Grants, Argentina, 1971, Chile, 1986. *Address:* 815 Seymour, Lansing, MI 48906, USA

FRANCE, Linda; b. 21 May 1958, Newcastle upon Tyne, England. Poet; Tutor in Adult Education; Writer. 2 s. *Education:* BA, English/History, University of Leeds, 1979. *Publications:* Acts of Love, 1990; Red, 1992; Acknowledged Land, 1993; Sixty Women Poets (ed.), 1993; The Gentleness of the Very Tall, 1994; Storyville, 1997; The Simultaneous Dress, 2002. *Contributions to:* Anthologies: New Women Poets, 1990; Wordworks, 1992; Making for Planet Alice, 1997; The Firebox, 1998; Magazines: North; Rialto; Iron; Stand; London Magazine; Poetry Durham; Writing Women; Wide Skirt and others. *Honours:* Basil Bunting Awards, 1988, 1990; Northern Arts Writers' Awards, 1989, 1995; Tyrone

Guthrie Award, 1990; Author's Foundation Award, 1993; Arts Foundation Poetry Fellowship, 1993; Fellowship, Fine Arts Center, Provincetown, 1997; Hawthornden Fellowship, 1999. *Address:* c/o Bloodaxe Books, PO Box 1SN, Newcastle upon Tyne NE99 1SN, England.

FRANCISCO, Nia; b. 2 Feb. 1952, Fort Defiance, AZ, USA. Poet. m. Dec. 1975, 5 c. *Education:* Institute of American Indian Arts, 1970–71; Navajo Community College, 1971–77; Fort Lewis College, 1994–97. *Publications:* Blue Horses for Navajo Women, 1988; Carried Away by the Black River, 1994. *Contributions to:* Anthologies. *Honours:* Arizona Commission on the Arts Grant; National Endowment for the Arts Grant; New York Commission on the Arts Grant. *Membership:* Arizona Commission on Humanities, 1978–79. *Address:* PO Box 794, Navajo, NM 87328, USA.

FRANCO, Tomaso; b. 23 May 1933, Bologna, Italy. Poet; Writer. divorced, 2 s. *Education:* Classical Studies, 1952; Doctorate in Law, 1959; Art Studies. *Publications:* Poetry: Uno Scatto dell'Evoluzione, 1984; Parole d'Archivio, 1986; Il Libro dei Torti, 1988; Casa di Frontiera, 1990. Novel: Soldato dei Sogni, 1995. Essays: Sila-Torino, 1961; Lettere a un Fuoruscito, 1988. *Contributions to:* Various anthologies, newspapers, and journals. *Honours:* First Award, Clemente Rèbora, Milan, 1986; Gold Medal, City of Como, 1990; First Award, National, Associazione Promozione Cultura in Toscana, 1992. *Address:* Via San Domenico 2, 36100 Vicenza, Italy.

FRANK, John Frederick; b. 7 Sept. 1917, Milwaukee, Wisconsin, USA. Poet. m. L Page Gooch, 8 March 1944, 1 d. *Education:* BS, Northwestern University, IL, 1939; MA, Johns Hopkins University, 1953; ABD, University of Pennsylvania, 1961; Full Prof., Aeronautics Acad., 1966. *Appointments:* Asst Instructor, Pennsylvania State University, 1953; Instructor, University of North Carolina, 1958–60; Lecturer in Writing, Southern Illinois University, 1960–63; Asst Prof., Kutztown State University, 1963–65; Lecturer in English, City University of New York, 1965–66. *Publication:* Johnny Appleseed, 1989. *Contributions to:* Several anthologies; Poetry; Voices; New Quarterly of Poetry; Pennsylvania Literary Magazine; New York Poetry Forum; Poet. *Honours:* Writers Conference Award, 1941; S. V. Benét Award, Pasadena Playhouse, 1945; Analects, 1960; Award, World Literature, University of Rome, 1969; Concorso Internazionale di Poesia, Italy, 1983; Fellow, International Poets Acad. Award, 1987; Premier Poet, 1993, 1995; Best Poems of 1996. *Memberships:* World Poetry Society; New York Poetry Forum; MLA; American Asscn of University Profs; Acad. of American Poets. *Address:* 7903 Fishel Creek Rd, Seven Valleys, PA 17360, USA.

FRANK, Niels; b. 25 Feb. 1963, Braedstrup, Denmark. Writer; Poet. m. Alvarado Gerardo, 6 Oct. 1989. *Education:* MA, University of Åarhus, Denmark, 1987. *Publications:* Ojeblikket, 1985; Digte i kim, 1986; Genforltryllelsen, 1988; Yucatan, 1993; Tabernakel, 1996; Livet I troperne, 1998. *Contributions to:* Newspapers, anthologies and literary journals. *Honours:* 3 year stipend, Danish Art Foundation, 1988–90; Steffens – Studienstipendium, FVS zu Hamburg, 1992; Aarestrup Medallion, Danish Writers' Union, 1995. *Address:* Strandboulevarden 97, 2100 Copenhagen J, Denmark.

FRANKLIN, Walt; b. 19 June 1950, Schwabach, Germany. Poet; Writer. m. Leighanne Parkins, 4 Sept. 1982, 1 s., 1 d. *Education:* BS, Psychology, 1973, Elementary Education Teaching Certificate, 1975, Alfred University. *Appointments:* Publisher and Ed., Great Elm Press, Greenwood, New York, 1984–92. *Publications:* Talking to the Owls, 1984; Topographies, 1984; The Glass Also Rises, 1985; Little Water Company, 1986; Ekos: A Journal Poem, 1986; The Ice Harvest, 1988; Instrument, 1988; Rootwork and Other Poems, 1988; The Wild Trout, 1989; Uplands Haunted by the Sea, 1992; The Flutes of Power, 1995; Letters from Susquehannock, 1995. *Contributions to:* About 350 publications. *Honours:* Numerous small press awards, including Abacus and Rose, 1988. *Memberships:* Poets Theatre, Hornell, New York; Appalachian Writers Asscn; Poets and Writers. *Address:* 1205 Co Rt 60, Rexville, NY 14877, USA.

FRASER, Kathleen; b. 22 March 1937, Tulsa, Oklahoma, USA. Prof.; Poet. m. Jack Marshall, 1961, divorced 1970, 1 s. *Education:* BA, Occidental College, Los Angles, 1959; Columbia University, 1960–61; New School for Social Research, New York City, 1960–61; Doctoral Equivalency in Creative Writing, San Francisco State University, 1976–77. *Appointments:* Visiting Prof., University of Iowa, 1969–71; Writer-in-Residence, Reed College, Portland, Oregon, 1971–72; Dir, Poetry Center, 1972–75, Assoc. Prof., 1975–78, Prof., 1978–92, San Francisco State University. *Publications:* Poetry: Change of Address and Other Poems, 1966; In Defiance of the Rains, 1969; Little Notes to You from Lucas Street, 1972; What I Want, 1974; Magritte Series, 1978; New Shoes, 1978; Each Next, 1980; Something (Even Human Voices) in the Foreground, A Lake, 1984; Notes Preceding Trust, 1987; Boundayr, 1988; Giotto, Arena, 1991; When New Time Folds Up, 1993; Wing, 1995; Il Cuore: The Heart, New and Selected Poems 1970–95, 1997; Translating the Unspeakable (essays), 1999. *Editor:* Feminist Poetics: A Consideration of Female Construction of Language, 1984. *Honours:* YMM-YWHA Discovery Award, 1964; National Endowment for the Arts Grant, 1969, and Fellowship, 1978; Guggenheim Fellowship in Poetry, 1981. *Address:* 1936 Leavenworth St, San Francisco, CA 94133, USA.

FRAZEUR, Gisele Barling; b. 16 Jan. 1961, Rochester, New York, USA. Actress; Poet; Playwright; Journalist. *Education:* BA, State University of New York at Fredonia. *Contributions to:* Anthologies, journals and magazines. *Honour:* Ed.'s Choice Award, National Library of Poetry. *Address:* 418 N Lima, Sierra Madre, CA 91024, USA.

FRAZEUR, Joyce Jaeckle; b. 17 Jan. 1931, Lewisburg, Pennsylvania, USA. Poet; Writer. m. Theodore C Frazeur Jr, 24 July 1954, 1 s., 2 d. *Education:* BA, William Smith College, 1952. *Publications:* Poetry: A Slip of Greenness, 1989; The Bovine Affliction, 1991; Flower Soup, 1993; Chirruping, 1994; Cycles, 1996. Novel: By Lunar Light, 1995. *Contributions to:* Newspapers, reviews, magazines, and journals. *Address:* 390 Juniper Dr., Sedona, AZ 86336, USA.

FREET, Paul Irvin; b. 16 Sept. 1943, Concord, Pennsylvania, USA. Poet. *Education:* Courses in Writing, Famous Writers School, Westport, CT; Poetry Courses, Shippensburg University. *Publications:* Reflections on a Clear Stream, 1993; Bridge into Time, 1998. *Contributions to:* Midwest Poetry Review; Apprise; Poetic Page; Patriot; Apropos; Rhyme Time. *Honour:* 2 Top Awards, Midwest Poetry Review, 1994; Two First Place Awards, Poetic Page, 1995, 1996. *Membership:* Acad. of American Poets. *Address:* 728 Brookens Rd, Fayetteville, PA 17222, USA.

FREIBERG, Stanley Kenneth; b. 26 Aug. 1923, Wisconsin, USA. Teacher (retd); Poet; Writer. m. Marjorie Ellen Speckhard, 29 June 1947, 1 s., 1 d. *Education:* BA, 1948, MA, 1949, PhD, 1957, University of Wisconsin. *Appointments:* Chair., English Dept, Cottey Cottage, Nevada, Missouri, 1954–58; Chair., Board of Foreign Language Studies, University of Baghdad, 1964–65. *Publications:* The Baskets of Baghdad: Poems of the Middle East, 1968; Plumes of the Serpent: Poems of Mexico, 1973; The Caplin-Crowded Seas: Poems of Newfoundland, 1975; The Hidden City: A Poem of Peru, 1988. *Contributions to:* Redlands Review; Christian Century; Dalhousie Review; Queen's Quarterly; Ariel; Parnassus of World Poets, 1994. *Honour:* Canada Council Award, 1978. *Address:* 1523 York Pl., Victoria, BC V8R 5X1, Canada.

FREISINGER, Randall R(oy); b. 6 Feb. 1942, Kansas City, Missouri, USA. Prof. of Rhetoric, Literature and Creative Writing; Poet. m., 2 s. *Education:* BJ, Journalism, 1962, MA, English Literature, 1964, PhD, English Literature, 1975, University of Missouri. *Appointments:* Instructor, Jefferson College, 1964–68; Resident Lecturer, University of Maryland Overseas Program, 1968–69, 1975–76; Asst Prof., Columbia College, 1976–77; Asst. Assoc. Prof., 1977–93, Prof. of Rhetoric, Literature and Creative Writing, 1993–, Michigan Technological University; Assoc. Ed., Laurel Review, 1989–. *Publications:* Running Patterns, 1985; Hand Shadows, 1988; Plato's Breath, 1997. *Contributions to:* Anthologies, journals, reviews, and quarterlies. *Honours:* Winner, Flume Press National Chapbook Competition, 1985; 4 Pushcart Prize Nominations, 1985–97; May Swenson Poetry Award, 1996. *Memberships:* Associated Writing Programs; National Council of Teachers of English. *Address:* 200 Prospect St, Houghton, MI 49931, USA.

FRENCH, Wendy Rowena, (Rowena Morgan-Jones); b. 4 Sept. 1945, Neath, Wales. Teacher; Poet. m. William Marshall, 3 Jan. 1992, 2 s., 2 step-d. *Education:* Certificate, Education, 1967; BA, Open University, 1983; Certificate, Counselling and Psychotherapy, 1989. *Contributions to:* Various anthologies and periodicals. *Honour:* Third Prize, Envoi Competition, 1990. *Memberships:* Dulwich Poetry Group; Poetry Society, London; Ripley Poetry Society. *Address:* 4 Myton Rd, West Dulwich, London SE21 8EB, England.

FRESTA, Maria Catina; b. 24 Aug. 1952, Tully, Qld, Australia. Teacher; Writer; Poet. 1 s., 1 d. *Education:* BEd, 1975. *Appointments:* Research Officer, Water Management, Norfolk Island; Teacher, Shalom College, Bundaberg, Australia. *Publications:* An Australian Mix, 1992; Mix Don't Blend, 1993. *Contributions to:* Linq; Quadrant; Rebout; Imago; Ulitarra; Hecate; Idiom 25; North of Capricorn; Social Alternatives; The Guide; Range Writers; Heartland; Northern Perspective; From all Walks of Life; Courier Mail; Canberra Times. *Honours:* Eaglehawk Dahlia Award, 1992; Queensland Government Literary Grants, 1992, 1994; Numerous Second and Third Prizes and Highly Commended Awards around Australia and Overseas. *Memberships:* Australian Society of Authors; Queensland Writers Centre; Regional Poets Society; Victorian Writers Society. *Address:* 2/90 Boundary St, Bundaberg, Qld 4670, Australia.

FRIAR, Will. See: MARGOLIS, William J.

FRIED, Philip Henry; b. 8 Jan. 1945, Georgia, USA. Ed.; Poet. m. Lynn Saville, 5 Oct. 1985. *Education:* BA, English, Antioch College, 1966; MFA, Poetry, University of Iowa Writers Workshop, 1968; PhD, English, State University of New York, 1978. *Appointments:* Ed., Holt, Rinehart and Winston, 1984–86; Prentice Hall, 1986–; Founder and Ed., Manhattan Review; Founder, National Poetry Initiative, 1994. *Publications:* Mutual Trespasses, 1988; Acquainted with the Night (ed.), 1997; Quantum Genesis, 1997. *Contributions to:* Beloit Poetry Journal; Chicago Review; Partisan Review; Paris Review; Poetry Northwest; Cream City Review; Maryland Poetry Review; Orim; Poet and Critic; Sequoia; Raccoon; Southern Poetry Review; Poet Lore; Magazine of Speculative Poetry, among others. *Honour:* Grant, Council of Literary Magazines and Presses, 1984. *Memberships:* Council of Literary Magazines and Presses; Poets House; National Writers Union; Poets and Writers; Poetry Society of America; PEN. *Address:* c/o Manhattan Review, 440 Riverside Dr., No. 38, New York, NY 10027, USA.

FRIEDMAN, Debbie (Dina); b. 13 June 1957, Takoma Park, Maryland, USA. Writer; Poet. m. Shef Horowitz, 9 Oct. 1983, 1 s., 1 d. *Education:* BA, English, Cornell University, 1978; MSW, University of Connecticut, 1985. *Appointments:* Workshop Leader, private workshops and through Amherst Writers and Artists; Instructor, Holyoke Community College and University of Massachusetts; Co-Dir, Accurate Writing and More. *Contributions to:* Pacific Poetry and Fiction Review; Calyx; Peregrine; Slant; Jewish Currents; Permafrost; Black Bean Review; Pig Iron; Rhino; Hurricane Alice. *Address:* PO Box 1164, Northampton, MA 01061, USA.

FRIEDMAN, Norman; b. 10 April 1925, Boston, Massachusetts, USA. Writer; Poet; Psychotherapist. m. Zelda Nathanson, 7 June 1945, 1 s., 1 d. *Education:* AB, 1948, AM, 1949, PhD, 1952, Harvard University; MSW, Adelphi University, 1978. *Appointments:* Teaching Fellow, Harvard University, 1950–52; Instructor, Assoc. Prof., University of Conneticut, 1952–63; Assoc. Prof., Prof., Queens College of the City University of New York, 1963–88; Fulbright Lecturer, Universities of Nantes and Nice, France, 1966–67, New School, New York City, 1966–69, 1993. *Publications:* The Magic Badge: Poems 1953–84, 1984; The Intrusions of Love: Poems, 1992. *Contributions to:* New Mexico Quarterly; Georgia Review; Northwest Review; Nation; Texas Quarterly. *Honours:* NWR Annual Poetry Prize, 1963; Borestone Mt Poetry Awards, 1964, 1967; Fourth, All Nations Poetry Contest. *Membership:* MLA. *Address:* 33–54 164th St, Flushing, NY 11358, USA. *E-mail:* nfriedman18@aol.com.

FRIEDRICH, Paul (William); b. 22 Oct. 1927, Cambridge, Massachusetts, USA. Prof. of Anthropology, Linguistics, and Social Thought; Writer; Poet. m. (1) Lore Bucher, 6 Jan. 1950, divorced Jan. 1966, 1 s., 2 d., (2) Margaret Hardin, 26 Feb. 1966, divorced June 1974, (3) Deborah Joanna Gordon, 9 Aug. 1975, divorced Nov. 1996, 2 d., (4) Domnica Radulescu, 10 Nov. 1996, 1 s. *Education:* Williams College, 1945–46; BA, Harvard College, 1951; MA, Harvard University, 1951; PhD, Yale University, 1957. *Appointments:* Asst Prof., University of Pennsylvania, 1959–62; Visiting Asst Prof., University of Michigan, 1960, 1961; Assoc. Prof., 1962–67, Prof. of Anthropology, Linguistics, Social Thought, 1992–, University of Chicago; Visiting Prof., Indiana University, 1964, Georgetown University, 1998, 1999, 2000, Washington and Lee University, 1999; Visiting Prof., University of Virginia, 2002. *Publications:* Proto-Indo-European Trees, 1970; The Tarascan Suffices of a Locative Space: Meaning and Morphotactics, 1971; A Phonology of Tarascan, 1973; On Aspect Theory and Homeric Aspect, 1974; Proto-Indo-European Syntax: The Order of Meaningful Elements, 1975; Neighboring Leaves Ride This Wind (poems), 1976; The Meaning of Aphrodite, 1978; Bastard Moons (poems), 1978; Language, Context, and the Imagination: Essays by Paul Friedrich (edited by A S Dil), 1979; Redwing (poems), 1982; The Language Parallax: Linguistic Relativity and Poetic Indeterminacy, 1986; The Princes of Naranja: An Essay in Anthrohistorical Method, 1987; Sonata (poems), 1987; Russia and Eurasia: Encyclopedia of World Cultures, Vol. 6 (co-ed.), 1994; Music in Russian Poetry, 1998. *Contributions to:* Books and journals. *Honours:* Ford Foundation Grant, 1957; Social Science Research Council Grant, 1966–67; National Endowment for the Humanities Grant, 1974–76; Guggenheim Fellowship, 1982–83. *Memberships:* Acad. of American Poets; American Acad. of Arts and Sciences; American Anthropological Asscn; American Assn for Teachers of Slavic and East European Languages; American Assn for the Advancement of Science; Linguistic Society of America, life mem.; Linguistic Society of India, life mem.; MLA; Poetry Society of America. *Address:* c/o Committee on Social Thought, University of Chicago, 1130 E 59th St, Chicago, IL 60637, USA.

FRIGGIERI, Oliver; b. 27 March 1947, Floriana, Malta. Author; Poet; Critic; Prof. m. Eileen Cassar, 6 April 1972, 1 d. *Education:* BA, 1968, MA, 1975, PhD, 1978, University of Malta. *Appointments:* Prof. and Head, Dept of Maltese, University of Malta, 1987–; Presenter, many television and radio cultural programmes. *Publications:* Il-Gidba (novel), 1977; La cultura italiana a Malta: Storia e influenza letteraria e stilistica attraverso l'opera di Dun Karm (criticism), 1978; Storja tal-letteratura Maltija (criticism), 1979; L-Istramb (novel), 1980, English trans. as A Turn of the Wheel, 1987; L'esperienza leopardiana di un poeta maltese: Karmenu Vassallo (criticism), 1983; Fil-Parlament ma Jikbrux Fjuri (novel), 1986; Stejjer ghal Qabel Jidlam (short stories), two vols, 1986; Storia della letteratura maltese (criticism), 1986; Il-Kuxjenza Nazzjonali Maltija (criticism), 1995; Dissjunarju ta' Termini Letteraji, revised edn, 1996; Gizimin li qatt ma jiftah (novel), 1998; Poeziji (poems), 1998; It-tfal jigu bil-vapuri (novel), 2000; Il-Poeziji Migbura, 2002. *Contributions to:* Many journals. *Honours:* Premio Internazionale Mediterraneo, Palermo, 1988; Malta Government Literary Awards, 1988, 1996, 1997, 1999; National Order of Merit, Malta Government, 1999. *Memberships:* Academia Internationale Mihai Eminescu, Graiova, founder-mem., 1995; Asscn Internationale des Critiques Littéraire, Paris; PEN Club, Switzerland. *Address:* c/o Faculty of Arts, Dept of Maltese, University of Malta, Msida-Malta.

FRIMAN, Alice (Ruth); b. 20 Oct. 1933, New York, NY, USA. Prof. of English; Poet; Writer. m. (1) Elmer Friman, 3 July 1955, 2 s., 1 d., (2) Marshall Bruce Gentry, 24 Sept. 1989. *Education:* BA, Brooklyn College, 1954; Indiana University, 1964–66; MA, English, Butler University, 1971. *Appointments:* Lecturer of English, Indiana University-Purdue University of Indianapolis, 1971–74; Faculty, 1971–90, Prof. of English, 1990–, University of Indianapolis; Visiting Prof. of Creative Writing, Indiana State University, 1982, Ball State University, 1996; Writer-in-Residence, Curtin University, Perth, Australia, 1989. *Publications:* A Question of Innocence, 1978; Song to My Sister, 1979; Loaves and Fishes: A Book of Indiana Women Poets (ed.), 1983; Reporting from Corinth, 1984; Insomniac Heart, 1990; Driving for Jimmy Wonderland, 1992; Inverted Fire, 1997; Zoo, 1999. *Contributions to:* Several anthologies and numerous reviews, quarterlies, and journals. *Honours:* Virginia Center for the Creative Arts Fellowships, 1983, 1984, 1993, 1996, 2000; Consuelo Ford Award, 1988, Cecil Hemley Memorial Award, 1990, Lucille Medwick Memorial Award, 1993, Poetry Society of America; Midwest Poetry Award, Society for the Study of Midwestern Literature, 1990; Erika Mumford Prize, 1990, Firman Houghton Award, 1996, Sheila Margaret Molton Prize, 2001, New England Poetry Club; Millay Colony for the Arts Fellowship, 1990; Yaddo Fellowship, 1991; Teacher of the Year Award, University of Indianapolis, 1993; First Prize, Abiko Quarterly International Poetry Contest, 1994; Individual Artist Fellowship, Indiana Arts Commission, 1996–97; Ezra Pound Poetry Award, Truman State University, 1998; Creative Renewal Fellowship, Arts Council of Indianapolis, 1999–2000; James Boatwright Third Prize for Poetry, Shenandoah, 2001; Georgia Poetry Circuit, 2001–02. *Memberships:* Associated Writing Programs; MLA; Poetry Society of America; Writers' Center of Indiana, board mem., 1984–89, hon. life mem., 1993–. *Address:* 6312 Central Ave, Indianapolis, IN 46220, USA.

FRITH, Roger Crispian; b. 4 April 1936, Wanstead, Essex, England. Poet; Writer. *Appointments:* Poet-in-Residence, Keele University Summer School, 1969, Ohio State University Summer School, New College, Oxford, 1979–89. *Publications:* The Serving Boy, 1969; Immortality Farm, 1978; Dreams and Realities, 1980; No Man's Land and Other Poems, 1984; Black Tern, 1984; Waiting for Nightingales, 1996; Darkness, 2001. *Contributions to:* Tribune; Ecologist; Poetry Now; BBC Radio 3; John Clare Society Journal; Richard Jefferies' Society Review. *Address:* Crix Lodge, Hatfield Peverel, Chelmsford, Essex CM3 2EU, England.

FRITZ, Leah Hurwit; b. 31 May 1931, New York, NY, USA. Poet; Writer. m. Howard William Fritz, 25 Dec. 1955, 2 d. *Publications:* Poetry: From Cookie to Witch is an Old Story, 1987; Somewhere en Route: Poems 1987–92, 1992; The Way to Go, 1999. Other: Thinking Like a Woman (essays), 1975; Dreamers and Dealers: An Intimate Appraisal of the Women's Movement, 1979. Editor: Touching the Sun: Poems in Memory of Adam Johnson, 1995. *Contributions to:* Anthologies, reviews and magazines. *Memberships:* PEN, English Centre; Poetry Society. *Address:* 47 Regent's Park Rd, London NW1 7SY, England. *E-mail:* leah@fritz.fsworld.co.uk.

FRITZ, Walter Helmut; b. 26 Aug. 1929, Karlsruhe, Germany. Author; Poet. *Education:* Literature and Philosophy, University of Heidelberg, 1949–54. *Publications:* Achtsam sein, 1956; Veranderte Jahre, 1963; Umwege, 1964; Zwischenbemerkungen, 1965; Abweichung, 1965; Die Verwechslung, 1970; Aus der Nahe, 1972; Die Beschaffenheit solcher Tage, 1972; Bevor uns Horen und Sehen Vergeht, 1975; Schwierige Uberfahrt, 1976; Auch jetzt und morgen, 1979; Gesammelte Gedichte, 1979; Wunschtraum alptraum, 1981; Werkzeuge der Freiheit, 1983; Cornelias Traum und andere Aufzeichnungen, 1985; Immer einfacher, immer schwieriger, 1987; Zeit des Sehens, 1989; Die Schlüssel sind vertauscht, 1992; Gesammelte Gedichte 1979–94, 1994; Das offene Fenster, 1997; Zugelassen im Leben, 1999. *Contributions to:* Journals and periodicals. *Honours:* Literature Prize, City of Karlsruhe, 1960; Prize, Bavarian Acad. of Fine Arts, 1962; Heine-Taler Lyric Prize, 1966; Prize, Culture Circle, Federation of German Industry, 1971; Literature Prize, City of Stuttgart, 1986; Georg Trakl Prize, 1992. *Memberships:* Acad. for Sciences and Literature; Bavarian Acad. of Fine Arts; German Acad. for Speech and Poetry; PEN; Union of German Writers. *Address:* Kolbergerstrasse 2a, 76139 Karlsruhe, Germany.

FROEHLICH, Joey, (W. J. Stephens); b. 13 Nov. 1954, Honolulu, HI, USA. Poet; Ed.; Publisher. *Education:* BA, English and Political Science, Brescia College. *Publication:* The Fuel of Tender Years (poems), 1996. *Contributions to:* Various anthologies, magazines and newsletters. *Honours:* Several award nominations. *Address:* PO Box 155, Frankfort, KY 40602, USA.

FROST, Jason. See: OBSTFELD, Raymond.

FROST, Richard; b. 8 April 1929, Palo Alto, CA, USA. Poet; Writer; Prof. of English. m. (1) Frances Atkins, 2 Sept. 1951, 1 s., 2 d., (2) Carol Kydd, 23 Aug. 1969, 2 s. *Education:* BA, 1951, MA, 1957, San Jose State College. *Appointments:* Instructor in English, San Jose State College, 1956–57, Towson State College, 1957–59; Asst Prof., 1959–64, Assoc. Prof., 1964–71, Prof. of English, 1971–, State University of New York College at Oneonta. *Publications:* The Circus Villains, 1965; Getting Drunk With the Birds, 1971; Neighbor Blood, 1996. *Contributions to:* Magazines, reviews, quarterlies and journals. *Honours:* Danforth Fellow, Bread Loaf Writers' Conference, 1961;

Resident Fellow, Yaddo, 1979, 1981, 1983; Gustav Davidson Memorial Award, Poetry Society of America, 1982; National Endowment for the Arts Creative Writing Fellowship, 1992. *Address:* c/o Dept of English, State University of New York College at Oneonta, Oneonta, NY 13820, USA.

FRUCHTMANN, Benno; b. 5 Sept. 1913, Meuselwitz, Germany. Writer; Poet; Dramatist. m. Mirjam David, 2 Nov. 1951, 2 s. *Publications:* Poetry in anthologies in German and Hebrew trans.; short stories; ballads; metric prose. Other: Radio plays. *Contributions to:* German and Hebrew newspapers and periodicals. *Honours:* Stipend Atelierhaus, Worpswede, Germany, 1986; Participant, International Colloquium of Jewish Authors, Osnabrück, 1991. *Memberships:* Asscn of German Writers; Israel Writers Asscn. *Address:* 10 Liesin St, 62977, Tel-Aviv, Israel.

FRUMKIN, Gene; b. 29 Jan. 1928, New York, NY, USA. Poet; Prof. m. Lydia Samuels, 3 July 1955, 1 s., 1 d. *Education:* BA, English, University of California, Los Angeles. *Appointments:* Prof., University of New Mexico; Ed., Coastlines Literary Magazine, 1958–62; Guest Ed., New Mexico Quarterly, 1969; Visiting Prof., Modern Literature, State University of New York, Buffalo, 1975; Co-Ed., San Marcos Review, 1978–83; Exchange Prof., 1980–81, 1984–85, Writer-in-Residence, 1989, University of Hawaii. *Publications:* Hawk and the Lizard, 1963; Orange Tree, 1965; Rainbow-Walker, 1969; Dostoyevsky and Other Nature Poems, 1972; Locust Cry: Poems 1958–65, 1973; Mystic Writing-Pad, 1977; Indian Rio Grande: Recent Poems from three Cultures (co-ed.), anthology, 1977; Clouds and Red Earth, 1982; Lover's Quarrel With America, 1985; Sweetness in the Air, 1987; Comma in the Ear, 1991; Saturn Is Mostly Weather, 1992. *Contributions to:* Paris Review; Prairie Schooner; Yankee; Conjunctions; Sulfur; Poetry; Saturday Review; Nation; Evergreen Review; Dacotah Territory; Malahat Review; Minnesota Review. *Honour:* First Prize for Poetry, Yankee magazine, 1979. *Memberships:* Past Pres., Rio Grande Writers' Asscn; Hawaii Literary Arts Council; PEN West. *Address:* 3721 Mesa Verde NE, Albuquerque, NM 87110, USA.

FRY, Christopher; b. 18 Dec. 1907, Bristol, England. Dramatist. m. Phyllis Marjorie Hart, 1936, deceased 1987, 1 s. *Education:* Bedford Modern School. *Publications:* The Boy with a Cart, 1939; The Firstborn, 1946; A Phoenix too Frequent, 1946; The Lady's Not for Burning, 1949; Thor, with Angels, 1949; Venus Observed, 1950; A Sleep of Prisoners, 1951; The Dark is Light Enough, 1954; The Lark, 1955; Tiger at the Gates, 1955; Duel of Angels, 1958; Curtmantle, 1961; Judith, 1962; A Yard of Sun, 1970; Peer Gynt, 1970. Television Plays: The Brontës of Haworth, 1973; Sister Dora, 1977; The Best of Enemies, 1977; Can You Find Me: A Family History, 1978; Selected Plays, 1985; Genius, Talent and Failure, 1986; One Thing More or Caedmon Construed, 1987; A Journey into Light, 1992. Films: The Queen is Crowned, 1953; The Beggar's Opera, 1953; Ben Hur, 1958; Barabbas, 1960; The Bible: In the Beginning, 1962. *Honours:* Fellow, RSL, 1950; Queen's Gold Medal for Poetry, 1962; Hon. Fellow, Manchester Metropolitan University, 1988; Hon. doctorates, Lambeth University, 1988, University of Sussex, 1994, De Montfort University, 1994; RSL Benson Medal, 2000. *Membership:* Garrick Club. *Address:* The Toft, East Dean, Chichester, West Sussex PO18 0JA, England.

FRYM, Gloria; b. 28 Feb. 1947, New York, NY, USA. Writer; Poet. m. Jeffrey J Carter, 1 d. *Education:* BA, 1968, MA, 1973, University of New Mexico. *Appointments:* Core Faculty, Poetics Programme, New College of California; Instructor, Creative Writing, San Francisco State University. *Publications:* Impossible Affection, 1979; Back to Forth, 1982; By Ear, 1990; How I Learned, 1992; Distance No Object, 1999. *Honour:* San Francisco State University Poetry Center Book Award, 1983. *Address:* 2119 Eunice St, Berkeley, CA 94709, USA.

FULLER, Cynthia Dorothy; b. 13 Feb. 1948, Isle of Sheppey, England. Poet; Adult Education Tutor. Divorced, 2 s. *Education:* BA, English, Sheffield University, 1969; Postgraduate Certificate of Education, Oxford University, 1970; MLitt, Aberdeen University, 1979. *Appointments:* Teacher of English, Redborne School, 1970–72; Freelance in Adult Education, University Depts at Durham and Newcastle Universities, also Open University and Workers' Education Asscn. *Publications:* Moving Towards Light, 1992; Instructions for the Desert, 1996; Only a Small Boat, 2001. *Contributions to:* Poems in various magazines including: Other Poetry; Iron; Poetry Durham; Literary Review. *Honour:* Northern Arts Financial Assistance. *Address:* 28 South Terrace, Esh Winning, Co Durham DH7 9PR, England.

FULLER, Jean Violet Overton; b. 7 March 1915, Iver Heath, Bucks, England. Author; Poet. *Education:* Brighton High School, 1927–31; RADA, 1931–32; BA, University of London, 1945; University College of London, 1948–50. *Publications:* The Comte de Saint Germain, 1988; Blavatsky and Her Teachers, 1988; Dericourt: The Chequered Spy, 1989; Sickert and the Ripper Crimes, 1990; Cats and Other Immortals, 1992; Espionage as a Fine Art, 2002; Krishnamurti and the Wind, 2002. *Honour:* Writers Manifold Poems of the Decade, 1968. *Membership:* Society of Authors. *Address:* Fuller D'Arch Smith Ltd, 37B New Cavendish St, London, England.

FULLER, John Leopold; b. 1 Jan. 1937, Ashford, Kent, England. Poet; Writer. m. Cicely Prudence Martin, 20 July 1960, 3 d. *Education:* BA, BLitt, MA, New College, Oxford, 1957–62. *Publications:* Fairground Music, 1961; The Tree That Walked, 1967; Cannibals and Missionaries, 1972; The Sonnet, 1972; Epistles to Several Persons, 1973; Penguin Modern Poets 22, 1974; The Mountain in the Sea, 1975; Lies and Secrets, 1979; The Illusionists, 1980; The Dramatic Works of John Gay (ed.), 1983; The Beautiful Inventions, 1983; Flying to Nowhere, 1983; The Adventures of Speedfall, 1985; Selected Poems, 1954–82, 1985; The Grey Among the Green, 1988; Tell it Me Again, 1988; The Burning Boys, 1989; Partingtime Hall (with James Fenton), 1989; The Mechanical Body and Other Poems, 1991; Look Twice, 1991; The Worm and the Star, 1993; The Chatto Book of Love Poetry, 1994; Stones and Fires 1996; Collected Poems, 1996; A Skin Diary, 1997; W. H. Auden: A Commentary, 1998; W. H. Auden: Poems Selected by John Fuller, 2000; The Oxford Book of Sonnets (ed.), 2000; The Memoirs of Laetitia Horsepole, 2001; Now and for a Time, 2002. *Contributions to:* Periodicals, reviews, and journals. *Honours:* Newdigate Prize, 1960; Richard Hillary Award, 1962; E C Gregory Award, 1965; Geoffrey Faber Memorial Prize, 1974; Southern Arts Prize, 1980; Whitbread Prize, 1983; Short-listed, Booker Prize, 1983; Forward Prize, 1996. *Memberships:* Fellow, RSL; Fellow, Magdalen College, Oxford. *Address:* 4 Benson Pl., Oxford OX2 6QH, England.

FULTON, Alice; b. 25 Jan. 1952, Troy, New York, USA. Prof. of English; Poet. m. Hank De Leo, 1980. *Education:* BA, Empire State College, Albany, New York, 1978; MFA, Cornell University, 1982. *Appointments:* Asst Prof., 1983–86, Willam Willhartz Prof., 1986–89, Assoc. Prof., 1989–92, Prof. of English, 1992–, University of Michigan; Visiting Prof. of Creative Writing, Vermont College, 1987, University of California at Los Angeles, 1991. *Publications:* Anchors of Light, 1979; Dance Script with Electric Ballerina, 1983; Palladium, 1986; Powers of Congress, 1990; Sensual Math, 1995; Feeling as a Foreign Language: The Good Strangeness of Poetry, 1999; Felt, 2001. *Honours:* Macdowell Colony Fellowships, 1978, 1979; Millay Colony Fellowship, 1980; Emily Dickinson Award, 1980; Acad. of American Poets Prize, 1982; Consuelo Ford Award, 1984; Rainer Maria Rilke Award, 1984; Michigan Council for the Arts Grants, 1986, 1991; Guggenheim Fellowship, 1986–87; Yaddo Colony Fellowship, 1987; Bess Hokin Prize, 1989; Ingram Merrill Foundation Award, 1990; John D. and Catherine T. MacArthur Foundation Fellowship, 1991–96; Elizabeth Matchett Stover Award, 1994. *Address:* 2370 Le Forge Rd, RR2, Ypsilanti, MI 48198, USA.

FULTON, Robin; b. 6 May 1937, Arran, Scotland. Poet; Writer; Trans.; Ed. *Education:* MA, Hons, 1959, PhD, 1972, University of Edinburgh. *Appointment:* Ed., Lines Review, 1967–76. *Publications:* Poetry: Instances, 1967; Inventories, 1969; The Spaces Between the Stones, 1971; The Man with the Surbahar, 1971; Tree-Lines, 1974; Following a Mirror, 1980; Selected Poems, 1963–78, 1980; Fields of Focus, 1982; Coming Down to Earth and Spring is Soon, 1990. Criticism: Contemporary Scottish Poetry: Individuals and Contexts, 1974; Iain Crichton Smith: Selected Poems, 1955–80, 1982; Robert Garioch: The Complete Poetical Works with Notes, 1983; Robert Garioch: A Garioch Miscellany, Selected Prose and Letters, 1986; The Way the Words are Taken, Selected Essays, 1989. Translator: An Italian Quartet, 1966; Five Swedish Poets, 1972; Lars Gustafsson, Selected Poems, 1972; Gunnar Harding: They Killed Sitting Bull and Other Poems, 1973; Tomas Transtromer: Selected Poems, 1974; Östen Sjöstrand: The Hidden Music & Other Poems, 1975; Toward the Solitary Star: Selected Poetry and Prose, 1988; Werner Aspenström: 37 Poems, 1976; Tomas Transtromer: Baltics, 1980; Werner Aspenström: The Blue Whale and Other Prose Pieces, 1981; Kjell Espmark: Béla Bartók Against the Third Reich and Other Poems, 1985; Olav Hauge: Don't Give Me the Whole Truth and Other Poems, 1985; Tomas Transtromer: Collected Poems, 1987; Stig Dagerman: German Autumn, 1988; Pär Lagervist: Guest of Reality, 1989; Preparations for Flight, and other Swedish Stories, 1990; Four Swedish Poets (Kjell Espmark, Lennart Sjögren, Eva Ström & Tomas Transtromer), 1990; Olav Hauge: Selected Poems, 1990; Hermann Starheimsaeter: Stone-Shadows, 1991; Five Swedish Poets (Werner Aspenström, Kjell Espmark, Lennart Sjögren, Eva Ström, Staffan Söderblom), 1997; Tomas Transtromer, New Collected Poems, 1997. *Contributions to:* Various journals and magazines. *Honours:* Gregory Award, 1967; Writers Fellowship, University of Edinburgh, 1969; Scottish Arts Council Writers Bursary, 1972; Arthur Lundquist Award for Trans. from Swedish, 1977; Swedish Acad. Award, 1978. *Address:* Postboks 467, N 4002, Stavanger, Norway.

FUNKHOUSER, Erica; b. 17 Sept. 1949, Cambridge, Massachusetts, USA. Poet. m. Thaddeus Beal, 1 Sept. 1973, divorced, 1 s., 1 d. *Education:* BA, English, Vassar College, 1971; MA, English, Stanford University, 1973. *Appointments:* Lecturer in English, Lesley College, Massachusetts; Dramaturg, Revels Inc, Cambridge, Massachusetts; Lecturer in Poetry, Massachusetts Institute of Technology, 1998–99. *Publications:* Natural Affinities, 1983; Sure Shot, 1992; The Actual World, 1997; Pursuit, 2002. *Contributions to:* Anthologies, reviews and magazines. *Honours:* Sylvia Plath Poetry Contest Winner, 1979; Fellowship, The Artists Foundation, Massachusetts Council on the Arts and Humanities, 1982, The MacDowell Colony, 1994; Consuelo Ford Award, Poetry Society of America, 1989. *Memberships:* Poetry Society of America; Acad. of American Poets. *Address:* 179 Southern Ave, Essex, MA 01929, USA.

G

GABRIEL, Stella; b. 2 June 1921, England. Senior Lecturer and Student Counsellor (retd); Poet. Divorced. *Education:* BA Honours, Manchester University, 1969. *Appointments:* Ed., then Asst Personnel Man. and Staff Trainer, House Magazine, Liverpool, 1953–64; Teacher, English and Russian, 1970–73; Teacher-Trainer and Lecturer in English, 1973–80; Senior Lecturer, Student Counsellor, 1980–86. *Contributions to:* Poetry Now; Brando's Hat. *Membership:* Manchester Poet. *Address:* 1 Brayton Ave, Didsbury, Manchester M20 0LP, England.

GAGE, Maura (Liebman); b. 27 April 1963, Pittsburgh, PA, USA. Assoc. Prof. of English; Writer; Poet. m. (1) Dennis Gage, 19 Aug. 1990, divorced 1993, (2) Robert N. Funk, 1996. *Education:* BA, English, California University of Pennsylvania, 1984; MA, English, Colorado State University, 1987; PhD, English, University of South Florida, 1997. *Appointments:* English Instructor, Pasco-Hernando Community College, 1988–89; Teaching Asst, English, 1989–, Student Support Services Programme, 1995–97, University of South Florida; Instructor of English and Creative Writing, Hillsborough Community College, Tampa, FL, 1993–97; Asst Prof. of English, Limestone College, 1997–98; Asst Prof. of English, 1998–2001, Assoc. Prof. of English, 2001–, Louisina State University at Eunice. *Publications:* Jackets (chapbook), 1991; Spun From the Gold in David's Hair (chapbook), 1994; Sweet Man of Morning, 1994; On Edge: Country Visions Between Skyscrapers and Corner Dives, 1996; Poetry and the Universal Complaint, 1996; Blossoming Field, Burgeoning Problems, Germinal Solutions, 1998; Make Me Spring and Other Poems, 2002. *Contributions to:* Many periodicals. *Honours:* Winner, Florida Suncoast Writers' Conference Poetry Contest, 1990; Estelle J. Zbar, Poetry Award, 1991; First Prize, Sparrowgrass Poetry Forum, 1992; Acadiana Arts Council and Louisiana Decentralized Grants, 1999, 2000, 2001. *Memberships:* Distinguished Mem., International Society of Poets, 1996; Louisiana Asscn for Developmental Education, pres., 1998–99; Mississippi Philogical Asscn, pres., 1999–2000; Louisiana Asscn of College Composition, pres., 1999–2000; Poetry Area, chair. *Address:* 1499 E Lovell St, Crowley, LA 70526-6012, USA.

GAGNON, Madeleine; b. 27 July 1938, Amqui, QC, Canada. Author; Poet. Divorced, 2 s. *Education:* BA, Literature, Université Saint-Joseph du Nouveau-Brunswick, 1959; MA, Philosophy, University of Montréal, 1961; PhD, Literature, Université d'Aix-en-Provence, 1968. *Appointments:* Teacher of Literature, Université du Québec à Montréal, 1969–82; Various guest professorships and writer-in-residencies. *Publications:* Les morts-vivants, 1969; Pour les femmes et tous les autres, 1974; Poélitique, 1975; La venue à l'écriture (with Hélène Cixous and Annie Leclerc), 1977; Retailles (with Denise Boucher), 1977; Antre, 1978; Lueur: Roman archéologique, 1979; Au coeur de la lettre, 1981; Autographie 1 and 2: Fictions, 1982; Les fleurs du catapla, 1986; Toute écriture est amour, 1989; Chant pour un Québec lointain, 1991; La terre est remplie de langage, 1993; Les cathédrales sauvages, 1994; Le vent majeur, 1995; Le Deuil du Soleil, 1998; Rêve de Pierre, 1999; Les Femmes et la Guerre, 2000. *Contributions to:* Many periodicals. *Honours:* Grand Prize, Journal de Montréal, 1986; Governor-General's Award for Poetry, 1991. *Memberships:* Union des écrivaines et écrivains Québecois; Académie des Lettres du Québec; PEN Canada, Québec section. *Address:* c/o Union des écrivaines et écrivains québecois, La Maison des écrivains, 3492 Ave Laval, Montréal, QC H2X 3C8, Canada.

GALANES, Miguel. See: JIMENEZ DE LOS GALANES Y DE LA FLOR, Miguel.

GALING, Ed; b. 1 June 1917, New York USA. Poet. m. Esther, 6 Feb. 1938, 2 s. *Education:* Temple University, 1936. *Appointment:* Poet Laureate of Hatboro, 1996–. *Publications:* Words of Wisdom, 1996; Pipe Dreams, 1997; Rhymes and Reasons, 1997; Old Age is Not for Sissies, 1998; Stepping Stones, 1998; Snapshots, 1998; Blowin in the Wind, 1998; Tales of South Philly, 2000; Raising the Roof, 2002; Senior Centre, 2002. *Contributions to:* 60 literary magazines. *Address:* 3435 Mill Rd, Hatboro, PA 19040, USA.

GALIOTO, Salvatore; b. 6 June 1925, Italy. Prof. of Humanities (retd); Poet. m. Nancy Morris, 8 July 1978, 1 s. *Education:* BA, University of New Mexico, 1952; MA, University of Denver, 1955; John Hay Fellow, Yale University, 1959–60; Catskill Area Project Fellow, Columbia University, 1961–62; Mediaeval and Renaissance Doctoral Programme, University of New Haven. *Publications:* The Humanities: Classical Athens, Renaissance Florence and Contemporary New York, 1970; Bibliographic Materials on Indian Culture, 1972; Let Us Be Modern (poems), English, Italian, 1985; INAGO Newsletter (poems), 1988; Is Anybody Listening? (poems), English, 1990; Flap Your Wings (poems), 1992; Rosebushes and the Poor (poems), Italian, 1993. *Contributions to:* Anthologies and periodicals. *Honours:* Purple Heart, Bronze Star, 1944; John Hay Fellowship, 1958–59; Asian Studies Fellow, 1965–66; First Prize, Chapbook Competition, The Poet, 1985, 1986; Gold Medal, Istituto Carlo Capodieci, 1987; INAGO Newspaper Poet, 1989. *Memberships:* Long Island

Historians' Society; Asian Society; California State Poetry Society; Poets and Writers of America; International Society of Poets.

GALLAGHER, Katherine; b. 7 Sept. 1935, Maldon, Vic., Australia. Teacher Poet; Writer. m. 8 April 1978, 1 s. *Education:* BA, 1962, DipEd, 1963, University of Melbourne. *Appointments:* Teacher of English as a Second Language, Paris 1971–78; Part-time Secondary Teacher, London Borough of Haringey, 1982–; Teacher of Creative Writing, London, Australia, 1984–, Open College of the Arts, 1990–, Barnet College, 1991–; Writer-in-Residence, Railway Fields. *Publications:* The Eye's Circle, 1974; Tributaries of the Love-Song, 1978; Passengers to the City, 1985; Fish-Rings on Water, 1989; Finding the Prince, 1993; Shifts, 1997; Tigers on the Silk Road, 2000. Translator: The Sleepwalker with Eyes of Clay, by Jean-Jacques Celly, 1994. *Contributions to:* Many anthologies, reviews, journals and periodicals. *Honours:* Australian Literature Board Fellowship, 1978; Warana Poetry Prize, Brisbane, 1981 Runner-Up, She Magazine Poetry Competition, UK, 1985; Short-listed, Australian National Poetry Award, 1986; Runner-up, Stand International Poetry Competition, 2000; Royal Literary Fund Bursary, 2000; Writers Inc Blue Nose Education Officer for Haringey Arts Council, July–Oct. 2002. *Address:* 49 Myddleton Rd, Wood Green, London N22 8LZ, England. *E-mail:* katherine_gallagher@compuserve.com. *Website:* ourworld.compuserve.com homepages.katherine_gallagher.

GALLAGHER, Tess; b. 21 July 1943, Port Angeles, Washington, USA. Poet; Writer. m. (1) Lawrence Gallagher, 1963, divorced 1968, (2) Michael Burkard, 1973, divorced 1977, (3) Raymond Carver, 1988, deceased. *Education:* BA, 1969, MA, 1970, University of Washington, Seattle; MFA, University of Iowa, 1974. *Appointments:* Instructor, St Lawrence University, Canton, New York, 1974–75; Asst Prof., Kirkland College, Clinton, New York, 1975–77; Visiting Lecturer, University of Montana, 1977–78; Asst Prof., University of Arizona, Tucson, 1979–80; Prof. of English, Syracuse University, 1980–89; Visiting Fellow, Williamette University, Salem, Oregon, 1981; Cockefair Chair Writer-in-Residence, University of Missouri, Kansas City, 1994; Poet-in-Residence, Trinity College, Hartford, CT, 1994; Edward F Arnold Visiting Prof. of English, Whitman College, Walla Walla, Washington, 1996–97; Guest, Bucknell University, 1998. *Publications:* Poetry: Stepping Outside, 1974; Instructions to the Double, 1976; Under Stars, 1978; Portable Kisses, 1978; On Your Own, 1978; Willingly, 1984; Amplitude: New and Selected Poems, 1987; Moon Crossing Bridge, 1992; The Valentine Elegies, 1993; Portable Kisses Expanded, 1994; My Black Horse: New and Selected Poems, 1995. Short Stories: The Lover of Horses, 1986; At the Owl Woman Saloon, 1997. Non-Fiction: A Concert of Tenses: Essays on Poetry, 1986; Ten More Years with Ray, 2000. Translator: The Sky Behind the Forest, by Liliana Ursu (with Liliana Ursu and Adam Sorkin), 1997. Other: Screenplay: Dostoevsky (with Raymond Carver); Many introductions to the works of Raymond Carver, 1988–2000. *Contributions to:* Many anthologies. *Honours:* Elliston Award, 1976; National Endowment for the Arts Grants, 1977, 1981, 1987; Guggenheim Fellowship, 1978; American Poetry Review Award, 1981; Washington State Governor's Awards, 1984, 1986, 1987, 1993; New York State Arts Grant, 1988; Maxine Cushing Gray Foundation Award, 1990; American Library Asscn Most Notable Book List, 1993; Lyndhurst Prize, 1993; Trans. Award, 1997; Hon. DHL, Whitman College, Walla Walla, Washington, 1998; Pryor Award for Literary Excellence, 1999. *Memberships:* Writers Union; PEN; American Poetry Society; Poets and Writers. *Address:* c/o International Creative Management, 40 W 57th St, New York, NY 10019, USA.

GALLAS, John Edward; b. 11 Jan. 1950, Wellington, New Zealand. Teacher in Student Support Service; Poet. *Education:* Nelson College, New Zealand, 1961–67; BA, Honours, English, Otago University, Dunedin, New Zealand, 1968–71; MPhil, English Literature, 1100–1400, Merton College, Oxford, 1972–74; PGCE, North Staffs Polytechnic, 1980–81. *Publications:* Practical Anarchy, 1989; Flying Carpets Over Filbert Street, 1993; Grrrrr, 1997; Resistance is Futile, 1999. *Contributions to:* PN Review; Landfall; Thames Poetry; Staple; Outposts; Stand; Rialto; Envoi; Poetry London Newsletter, Poetry Ireland. *Honours:* Rutland Poetry Prize, 1984; Runner-up, National Poetry Prize, 1985; East Midlands Arts Bursary, 1986; Charnwood Poetry Prize, 1987; New Voices Midlands Reading Tour, 1990; Surrey Poetry Centre Prize, 1992; Bernet Poetry Prize, 1997. *Address:* 40 London Rd, Coalville, Leicestershire LE67 3JA, England.

GALLETTI DE MASTRANGELO, Irma; b. 11 Dec. 1928, Argentina. Poet. m. Hugo Mastrangelo, 1 July 1950, 1 s., 1 d. *Education:* First and Adult Level Teaching Qualifications; Assessor, Centre of Educational Investigations. *Contributions to:* Various anthologies and other publications. *Honour:* Special Mention, Poesia Argentina Contemporanea. *Membership:* Argentine Society of Writers. *Address:* Zelarrayan 317 p10 Dpto 6, 8000 Bahia Blanca, Buenos Aires, Argentina.

GALVIN, Brendan; b. 20 Oct. 1938, Everett, Massachusetts, USA. Prof. of English; Poet. m. Ellen Baer, 1968, 1 s., 1 d. *Education:* BS, Boston College, 1960; MA, Northeastern University, 1964; MFA, 1967, PhD, 1970, University of Massachusetts. *Appointments:* Instructor, Northeastern University, 1964–65; Asst Prof., Slippery Rock State College, 1968–69; Asst Prof., 1969–74, Assoc. Prof., 1974–80, Prof. of English, 1980–, Central Connecticut State University; Visiting Prof., Connecticut College, 1975–76; Ed. (with George Garrett), Poultry: A Magazine of Voice, 1981–; Coal Royalty Chairholder in Creative Writing, University of Alabama, 1993. *Publications:* The Narrow Land, 1971; The Salt Farm, 1972; No Time for Good Reasons, 1974; The Minutes No One Owns, 1977; Atlantic Flyway, 1980; Winter Oysters, 1983; A Birder's Dozen, 1984; Seals in the Inner Harbour, 1985; Wampanoag Traveler, 1989; Raising Irish Walls, 1989; Great Blue: New and Selected Poems, 1990; Early Returns, 1992; Saints in Their Ox-Hide Boat, 1992; Islands, 1993; Hotel Malabar, 1998. *Honours:* National Endowment for the Arts Fellowships, 1974, 1988; Connecticut Commission on the Arts Fellowships, 1981, 1984; Guggenheim Fellowship, 1988; Sotheby Prize, Arvon International Foundation, 1988; Levinson Prize, Poetry magazine, 1989; O B Hardison Jr Poetry Prize, Folger Shakespeare Library, 1991; Charity Randall Citation, International Poetry Forum, 1994. *Address:* c/o Dept of English, Central Connecticut State University, New Britain, CT 06050, USA.

GALVIN, James; b. 8 May 1951, Chicago, IL, USA. Poet. *Education:* BA, Antioch College; MFA, University of Iowa. *Appointments:* Prof.; Ed., Crazyhorse, 1979–81. *Publications:* Imagining Timber, 1980; God's Mistress, 1984; Elements, 1988. *Contributions to:* New Yorker; Nation; Antioch Review; Poetry Now; Antaeus; Sewanee Review. *Honours:* Discovery Award, Nation/ Young Men's Hebrew Asscn, 1977; Co-Winner, National Poetry Series Open Competition, 1984. *Address:* Iowa Writers' Workshop, University of Iowa, 436 EPB, Iowa City, IA 52242, USA.

GALVIN, Patrick (Joseph); b. 1927, Cork, Ireland. Dramatist; Poet. m. Diana Ferrier, 2 s. *Education:* Cork schools. *Appointments:* Resident Dramatist, Lyric Theatre, Belfast, 1974–77; Writer-in-Residence, West Midlands Arts Asscn, 1979–80. *Publications:* Plays: And His Stretched, 1960; Cry the Believers, 1961; Nightfall to Belfast, 1973; The Last Burning, 1974; We Do It For Love, 1976; The Devil's Own People, 1976; Collected Plays and Letters, 1986. Poetry: Heart of Grace, 1957; Christ in London, 1960; Two Summers, 3 parts, 1970; By Nature Diffident, 1971; Lon Chaney, 1971; The Woodburners, 1973; Man on the Porch, 1980; Collected Poems and Letters, 1985; Let the Seahorse Take Me Home and Other Poems, 1986. *Honour:* Leverhulme Fellowship, 1974–76. *Address:* c/o Martin, Brian and O'Keefe, 78 Coleraine Rd, Blackheath, London SE3, England.

GAMSON, Leland Pablo; b. 30 Dec. 1950, Minneapolis, Minnesota, USA. Social Worker; Poet. m. Bonnie Lou Campbell, 24 Aug. 1985. *Education:* BA, Religion, Hiram College, 1973; MEd, American University, 1974; MSW, Catholic University of America, 1981. *Appointments:* Ed., As Is, 1975–79; Economics Asst, US Dept of Labor, 1977–79; Veterans Administration Social Worker, 1981–; Ed., Bacon and Eggs News, 1982–. *Publication:* Sinia and Olympus, 1977. *Contributions to:* Friends Journal; Gargoyle; American Magazine; As Is; Higgison Journal of Poetry; Federal Poet; James Whitcomb Riley Celebration Anthology; Bacon and Eggs; Edgar Allan Poe Celebration Anthology; Quaker Life; Parnassus of World Poets. *Address:* 607 W Spencer, Marion, IN 46952, USA.

GANDER, Forrest; b. 21 Jan. 1956, Barstow, CA, USA. Prof.; Poet; Ed. m. C D Wright, 1983, 1 s. *Appointments:* Co-Ed., Lost Road Publishers, 1982–; Prof., Dir of graduate programme in literary arts, Brown University. *Publications:* Rush to the Lake, 1988; Eggplants and Lotus Root, 1991; Lynchburg, 1993; Mouth to Mouth: Poems by 12 Contemporary Mexican Women (ed.), 1993; Deeds of Utmost Kindness, 1994; Science of Steepleflower, 1998; Torn Awake, 2001; Immanent Visitor: Selected Poems of Jaime Saenz (trans. with Kent Johnson), 2001. *Memberships:* Associated Writing Programs; PEN. *Address:* 351 Nayatt Rd, Barrington, RI 02806, USA. *Website:* www.brown.edu/ Departments/English/Writing/people/gander/.

GANGOPADHYAY, Rabi, (Aranyak Singha); b. 26 Feb. 1946, Bankura, West Bengal, India. Teacher; Poet. m. Reba Gangopadhyay, 8 May 1969, 1 s., 2 d. *Education:* BA, Honours in Philosophy, Christian College, Bankura; MA in Philosophy, University of Calcutta; MA in Bengali Language and Literature, University of Burdwan, 1978; BEd, University of Burdwan, 1983. *Appointments:* Asst Teacher of Philosophy and Bengali Language and Literature. *Publications:* Bhalobasay Abhimane, 1976; Kabitar Kachhakachhi Eka, 1981; Bristir Megh, 1982; Arshi Tawar, 1991; Kojagar, 1994. *Contributions to:* Desh; Anandabazar; Sananda; Krittibas; Amrit; kalkata Kabi O Kabita; Dhrupadi; Chintabhabna. *Honours:* Nikhil Banga Sahitya Pratiyogita First Prize, 1963 (twice); Several regional honours. *Address:* 73/5 Nutanchati, Bankura 722101, West Bengal, India.

GANNELLO, Alfreda Mavis; b. 17 Nov. 1926, London, England. Poet; Writer. m. Charles Carmelo Gannello, 2 Jan. 1954. *Education:* College and Postgraduate Studies. *Publication:* Meet Carmelo, 1988. *Contributions to:* Various anthologies, reviews and journals. *Honours:* Numerous awards,

honourable mentions and certificates of merit, 1987–91; Browning Poetry Award, 1994; Ed.'s Choice Award, 1997; Poet of the Year, 1998. *Memberships:* International Society for the Advancement of Poetry; National Audubon Society. *Address:* PO Box 2272, Oak Park, IL 60302, USA.

GARCIA-SIMMS, Michael. See: SIMMS, Michael Arlin.

GARDNER, Mariana Carmen Zavati; b. 20 Jan. 1952, Bacau, Romania. Poet. m. John Edward Gardner, 8 Aug. 1980, 1 s., 1 d. *Education:* Baccalauréat, 1971; MSc, Philology, Alexandru Ioan Cuza University, Iaêi, 1975; Postgraduate Certificate, Education, University of Leeds, 1987; Postgraduate Studies, Goethe Institute, Rosenheim, Germany, 1991, L'École Normale Supérieure, Auxerre, France, 1991. *Appointments:* Teacher, Modern Languages, var HS, 1975–99; Part-time Asst Lecturer, University of Iaêi, 1975, 1976; Asst Lecturer, University of Bacau, 1979. *Publications:* Poetry: Whispers; The Journey; Watermarks; Travellers; Calatori; The Spinning Top; Snapshot Poems; Pilgrims; Pelerini; The Remains of the Dream Catcher. Other: Trans. of Cerul Meu de Hartie (My Paper Sky), by Al Florin Tene. *Contributions to:* Anthologies, including: Between a Laugh and a Tear; Light of the World; The Sounds of Silence; The Secret of Twilight; A Blossom of Dreams; The Lyre's Song; Honoured Poets of 1998; Last Good-Byes; A Celebration of Poets; The Definitive Version; Sunrise and Soft Mist; Lifelines; Antologia Padurii; Eastern Voices 2001; Memories of the Millennium; Nature's Orchard; International Notebook of Poetry, 2000, 2001, 2002; Journal of the American Romanian Academy of Arts and Sciences; Family Ties; Sunkissed; Reflections of Time. *Honours:* Ed.'s Choice Award, International Society of Poets, 1996; Ed.'s Choice Award, International Library of Poetry, 1997; Ed.'s Choice Award, National Library of Poetry, 1998; Bronze Medal, North American Poetry Competition, 1998; American Romanian Acad. Award, 2001, Ionel Jianu Award for Arts, 2001, American Romanian Acad. of Arts and Sciences. *Memberships:* International Society of Poets; American Romanian Acad. of Arts and Sciences; LiterArt XXI. *Address:* 14 Andrew Goodall Close, East Dereham, Norfolk NR19 1SR, England.

GARDNER, Stephen Leroy; b. 8 April 1948, South Carolina, USA. Prof. of English; Poet; Ed. m. Mignon P W Derrick. *Education:* BA, English, Honours, 1970, MA, English, 1972, University of South Carolina; PhD, English and Creative Writing, Oklahoma State University, 1979. *Appointments:* Teaching Fellow, 1970–72, Co-ordinator, 1975–81, Asst, Assoc., Prof. of English, 1972–84, Prof. of English and Chair, Division of Arts and Letters, 1984–86, Dean, College of Humanities and Social Sciences, 1986–93, University of South Carolina at Aiken; Ed., The Devil's Millhopper Press, 1986–. *Publication:* This Book Belongs to Eva, 1996. *Contributions to:* Anthologies, reviews and journals. *Honours:* Honourable Mention, Hollins Critic Poetry Contest, 1972; Best Poem, Borestone Mountain Poetry Awards, 1976; First Prize, Oklahoma State University Acad. of American Poets Competition, 1978; University of South Carolina Grants, 1982, 1983; Selected for South Carolina Arts Commission Approved Artists List, 1989–; Eyster Prize for Poetry, 1994. *Memberships:* Aiken Center for the Arts, board of governors, 1992–96; Associated Writing Programs; Council of Colleges of Arts and Sciences; Hemingway Society; South Carolina Acad. of Authors, treasurer, board of governors, 1993–96, pres., 1996–97; Walt Whitman Asscn. *Address:* PO Box 40, Ballentine, SC 29002, USA.

GARDONS, S. S. See: SNODGRASS, W. D.

GARFINKEL, Patricia Gail; b. 15 Feb. 1938, New York, NY, USA. Poet; Writer. 2 s. *Education:* BA, New York University. *Publications:* Ram's Horn (poems), 1980; From the Red Eye of Jupiter (poems), 1990; Making the Skeleton Dance, 2000. *Contributions to:* Numerous anthologies and other publications. *Honours:* Poetry in Public Places Award for New York State, 1977; First Prize, Lip Service Poetry Competition, 1990; Book Competition, Washington Writers Publishing House, 1990. *Membership:* Poets and Writers. *Address:* 900 N Stuart St, Suite 1001, Arlington, Virginia, 22203, USA.

GARFITT, Roger; b. 12 April 1944, Melksham, Wiltshire, England. Poet; Writer. *Education:* BA, Honours, Merton College, Oxford, 1968. *Appointments:* Arts Council Creative Writing Fellow, University College of North Wales, Bangor, 1975–77, and Poet-in-Residence, Sunderland Polytechnic, 1978–80; Ed., Poetry Review, 1977–82; Welsh Arts Council Poet-in-Residence, Ebbw Vale, 1984; Poet-in-Residence, Pilgrim College, Boston, 1986–87; Blyth Valley Disabled Forum, 1992. *Publications:* Caught on Blue, 1970; West of Elm, 1974; The Broken Road, 1982; Rowlstone Haiku (with Frances Horovitz), 1982; Given Ground, 1989; Border Songs, 1996. *Contributions to:* Journals, reviews, and magazines. *Honours:* Guinness International Poetry Prize, 1973; Gregory Award, 1974. *Memberships:* National Asscn of Writers in Education: Poetry Society; Welsh Acad. *Address:* c/o Jane Turnbull, 13 Wendell Rd, London W12 9RS, England.

GARLICK, Raymond; b. 21 Sept. 1926, London, England. Poet; Lecturer (retd). m. Elin Jane Hughes, 1948, 1 s., 1 d. *Education:* BA, University College of North Wales, Bangor, 1948. *Appointment:* Principal Lecturer, Trinity College, Carmarthen, 1972–86. *Publications:* Poetry: Poems from the Mountain-House, 1950; Requiem for a Poet, 1954; Poems from Pembrokeshire,

1954; The Welsh-Speaking Sea, 1954; Blaenau Observed, 1957; Landscapes and Figures: Selected Poems, 1949–63, 1964; A Sense of Europe: Collected Poems, 1954–68, 1968; A Sense of Time: Poems and Antipoems, 1969–72, 1972; Incense: Poems, 1972–75, 1975; Collected Poems, 1946–86, 1987; Travel Notes: New Poems, 1992. Other: An Introduction to Anglo-Welsh Literature, 1970; Anglo-Welsh Poetry, 1480–1980 (ed.), 1982. *Honours:* Welsh Arts Council Prizes; Hon. Fellow, Trinity College, Carmarthen; Fellow, Welsh Acad.; DLitt, Central University, Pella, IA, 1998. *Address:* 26 Glannant House, College Rd, Carmarthen SA31 3EF, Wales.

GARNER, Van Dee; b. 25 Jan. 1933, Sherwood, TN, USA. Disabled Veteran; Poet. m. Helen Lively, 18 Nov. 1967. *Publications:* Deep Within, 1987; Special Edition of the Poems of Van Garner, 1989; The Collected Works of Van Garner, 1990; Mountain Echoes, 1995; Wanderlust, 2000; My Catharsis, 2001; Remembering Seasons, 2002. *Contributions to:* Jean's Journal; Veteran's Voices Magazine. *Honours:* Delaware Heritage Bill of Rights Award, 1991; International Poet of Merit, 1995. *Memberships:* International Society of Poets; World of Poetry. *Address:* 3725 Jarren Dr., Chattanooga, TN 37415, USA.

GARRETT, Evvy; b. 28 Jan. 1946, Kansas City, Missouri, USA. Poet; Writer. 1 s., 1 d. *Contributions to:* New York Quarterly; Poetic Space; Anemone; Riverrun; Pearl; Chicago Street; Rapping Paper; San Diego Lesbian Press; Journal; AKA; Poetic Space First Anthology; The Shadows Project; Cappers; Copper Hill Quarterly; Rant; Radiant Woman; We Accept Donations; Writer's Info; Psychopoetica; Alura; December Rose. *Address:* PO Box 7155, San Diego, CA 92167, USA.

GARRETT, George (Palmer Jr); b. 11 June 1929, Orlando, FL, USA. Prof. of English; Writer; Poet; Ed. m. Susan Parrish Jackson, 1952, 2 s., 1 d. *Education:* BA, 1952, MA, 1956, PhD, 1985, Princeton University. *Appointments:* Asst Prof., Wesleyan University, 1957–60; US Poetry Ed., Transatlantic Review, 1958–71; Visiting Lecturer, Rice University, 1961–62; Assoc. Prof., 1962–67, Hoyns Prof. of English, 1984–, University of Virginia; Writer-in-Residence, Princeton University, 1964–65, Bennington College, Vermont, 1979, University of Michigan, 1979–80, 1983–84; Prof. of English, Hollins College, Virginia, 1967–71; Prof. of English and Writer-in-Residence, University of South Carolina, 1971–73; Senior Fellow, Council of the Humanities, Princeton University, 1974–78; Adjunct Prof., Columbia University, 1977–78. *Publications:* Fiction: The Finished Man, 1959; Which Ones Are the Enemy?, 1961; Do, Lord, Remember Me, 1965; Death of the Fox, 1971; The Succession: A Novel of Elizabeth and James, 1983; Poison Pen, or, Live Now and Pay Later, 1986; Entered from the Sun, 1990; The Old Army Game, 1994; The King of Babylon Shall Not Come Against You, 1996. Short Stories: King of the Mountain, 1958; In the Briar Patch, 1961; Cold Ground Was My Bed Last Night, 1964; A Wreath for Garibaldi and Other Stories, 1969; The Magic Striptease, 1973; To Recollect a Cloud of Ghosts: Christmas in England, 1979; An Evening Performance: New and Selected Short Stories, 1985. Poetry: The Reverend Ghost, 1957; The Sleeping Gypsy and Other Poems, 1958; Abraham's Knife and Other Poems, 1961; For a Bitter Season: New and Selected Poems, 1967; Welcome to the Medicine Show: Postcards, Flashcards, Snapshots, 1978; Luck's Shining Child: A Miscellany of Poems and Verses, 1981; The Collected Poems of George Garrett, 1984; Days of Our Lives Lie in Fragments, 1998. Other: James Jones, 1984; Understanding Mary Lee Settle, 1988; The Sorrows of Fat City, 1992; Whistling in the Dark, 1992; My Silk Purse and Yours, 1993; Bad Man Blues, 1998; Going to See the Elephant, 2002. Editor: 18 books, 1963–93. *Honours:* American Acad. in Rome Fellowship, 1958; Sewanee Review Fellowship in Poetry, 1958; Ford Foundation Grant, 1960; National Endowment for the Arts Grant, 1967; Guggenheim Fellowship, 1974; American Acad. of Arts and Letters Award, 1985; Cultural Laureate of Virginia, 1986; T. S. Eliot Award, 1989; PEN/Malamud Award for Short Fiction, 1989; Aiken Taylor Award for Poetry, 2000; Commonwealth of Virginia Gov.'s Award for the Arts, 2000. *Membership:* Fellowship of Southern Letters. *Address:* 1845 Wayside Pl., Charlottesville, VA 22903, USA.

GARRISON, Deborah; b. 12 Feb. 1965, Ann Arbor, MI, USA. Ed.; Poet. m. Matthew C. Garrison, 10 Aug. 1986, 2 d. *Education:* BA, Brown University, 1986; MA, English, New York University, 1992. *Appointments:* Editorial Asst to Senior Ed., New Yorker, 1986–2000; Poetry Ed., Alfred A. Knopf, 2000–; Senior Ed., Pantheon Books, 2000–. *Publication:* A Working Girl Can't Win and Other Poems, 1998. *Contributions to:* Elle; Slate; New York Times; New Yorker. *Address:* c/o Alfred A. Knopf, 299 Park Ave, New York, NY 10171, USA.

GARSTON, Maureen Beatrice Courtnay, (Maureen Weldon); b. 4 Oct. 1940, Leicester, England. Poet. 1 d. *Education:* Diploma, Royal Acad. of Dancing, London, 1973; Chester College, Cheshire. *Appointments:* Ballet Dancer; Ballet Teacher; Poetry Readings. *Publications:* Poems From the Back Room, 1991; Leap, 1992. *Contributions to:* About 500 poems in numerous publications. *Membership:* Society of Women Writers and Journalists. *Address:* 16 Glastonbury Ave, Off St James Ave, Upton by Chester, Cheshire CH2 1NG, England.

GASS, William H(oward); b. 30 July 1924, Fargo, North Dakota, USA. Distinguished Prof. in the Humanities; Author; Critic. m. (1) Mary Pat O'Kelly, 1952, 2 s., 1 d., (2) Mary Henderson, 1969, 2 d. *Education:* AB,

Philosophy, Kenyon College, 1947; PhD, Philosophy, Cornell University 1954. *Appointments:* Instructor in Philosophy, College of Wooster, 1950–54 Asst Prof., 1955–58, Assoc. Prof., 1960–65, Prof. of Philosophy, 1966–69 Purdue University; Visiting Lecturer in English and Philosophy, University of Illinois, 1958–59; Prof. of Philosophy, 1969–78, David May Distinguished Prof. in the Humanities, 1979–2001, Dir, International Writers Centre 1990–2001, Washington University. *Publications:* Fiction: Omensetter's Luck 1966; Willie Masters' Lonesome Wife, 1968; The Tunnel, 1995. Stories: In the Heart of the Heart of the Country, 1968; Cartesian Sonata, 1998. Essays Fiction and the Figures of Life, 1971; On Being Blue, 1976; The World Within the Word, 1978; The Habitations of the Word, 1984; Finding a Form, 1996 Cartesian Sonata, 1998; Tests of Time, 2002. Editor: The Writer in Politics (with Lorin Cuoco), 1996. Translator: Reading Rilke, 1999. *Contributions to* Essays, criticism, poems, stories, and trans in various publications. *Honours* Longview Foundation Prize for Fiction, 1959; Rockefeller Foundation Grant 1965–66; Guggenheim Fellowship, 1970–71; American Acad. and Institute of Arts and Letters Award, 1975, and Medal of Merit, 1979; Pushcart Prizes, 1976 1983, 1987, 1992; National Book Critics Circle Awards, 1985, 1996; Getty Scholar, 1991–92; American Book Award, Before Columbus Foundation 1996; Lannan Lifetime Achievement Award, 1997; PEN-Nabokov Prize, 2000. *Memberships:* American Acad. of Arts and Letters; American Acad. of Arts and Sciences. *Address:* 6304 Westminster Pl., St Louis, MO 63130, USA.

GATENBY, Greg; b. 5 May 1950, Toronto, Ontario, Canada. Artistic Dir; Poet *Education:* BA, English Literature, York University, 1972. *Appointments:* Ed. McClelland and Stewart, Toronto, 1973–75; Artistic Dir, Harbourfront Reading Series and concomitant festivals, 1975–, Humber College School of Creative Writing, 1992–93. *Publications:* Imaginative Work: Rondeaus for Erica, 1976 Adrienne's Blessing, 1976; The Brown Stealer, 1977; The Salmon Country 1978; Growing Still, 1981. Anthologies: 52 Pickup, 1977; Whale Sound, 1977 Whales: A Celebration, 1983; The Definitive Notes, 1991; The Wild Is Always There, 1993; Toronto Literary Guide, 1999. Translator: Selected Poems, by Giorgio Bassani, 1980; The Wild Is Always There, Vol. 2, 1995; The Very Richness of that Past, 1995. *Honours:* City of Toronto Arts Award for Literature, 1989; League of Canadian Poets Hon. Lifetime Mem., 1991; Jack Award for Lifetime Promotion of Canadian Books, 1994; E J Pratt Lifetime Fellow, 1995. *Memberships:* PEN, Canadian Centre; Writers Union of Canada. *Address:* 235 Queen's Quay W, Toronto, Ont M5J 2G8, Canada.

GATTI, Pietro; b. 29 Oct. 1928, Pavia, Italy. Public Servant (retd); Poet; Writer. m. Maria Teresa Lambri, 28 April 1960, 1 s., 1 d. *Education:* Diploma, Expert in Commerce; Diploma, Poet, Accademia Internazionale I Principi, Genoa; Academician, Istituto Studi Superiori Tiberino, Rome. *Appointments:* Hon. Inspector of Archives, Lombardy, 1992–97; Inventor, blank verse metrical schemes; Organiser, literary and artistic events; Poetry readings. *Publications:* Poetry: Sprazzi di Poesia, 1971; Vagabondaggio poetico, 1973; Poesie d'amore, 1976; Riflessi d'armonia, 1979; Luce del duemila (co-author), 1992; Voce nel vento; Poesia italiana armonermetica, 1995. *Contributions to:* Periodicals and magazines, mostly published in Italy, but also in USA, Brazil and Germany. *Honours:* Knight, 1969, Officer, 1978, Commander, 1982, Order of Merit of the Italian Republic; Cultural Prize of the Cabinet Council, Rome, 1975, 1978, 1982; Silver Medal, Haute Académie Internationale de Lutèce, Paris, 1976; Winner, numerous prizes in national and international competitions; Many diplomas and certificates of merit. *Memberships:* Accademia Internazionale Leonardo da Vinci, Rome, 1977; Academia Azteca de Artes, Ciencias y Letras, Spain, 1977–; Accademia Ferdinandea, Catania, 1989–; Accademia Internazionale Padre Pio, Trinitapoli, 1998–; Hon. Mem., Cenacolo Artistico Culturale de Il Tizzone, Rieti; Many others. *Address:* Via Verdi 44, 27058 Voghera, Pavia, Italy.

GEDDES, Gary; b. 9 June 1940, Vancouver, BC, Canada. Distinguished Prof. of Canadian Culture; Writer; Poet. m. (1) Norma Joan Fugler, 1963, divorced 1969, 1 d., (2) Jan Macht, 2 May 1973, 2 d. *Education:* BA, University of British Columbia, 1962; Diploma in Education, University of Reading, 1964; MA, 1966, PhD, 1975, University of Toronto. *Appointments:* Lecturer, Carleton University, Ottawa, Ontario, 1971–72, University of Victoria, BC, 1972–74; Writer-in-Residence, 1976–77, Visiting Assoc. Prof., 1977–78, University of Alberta, Edmonton; Visiting Assoc. Prof., 1978–79, Prof. of English, 1979–98, Concordia University, Montréal, QC; Distinguished Prof. of Canadian Culture, Western Washington University, 1999–2001. *Publications:* Poetry: Poems, 1971; Rivers Inlet, 1972; Snakeroot, 1973; Letter of the Master of Horse, 1973; War and Other Measures, 1976; The Acid Test, 1980; The Terracotta Army, 1984; Changes of State, 1986; Hong Kong, 1987; No Easy Exit/Salida dificil, 1989; Light of Burning Towers, 1990; Girl By the Water, 1994; Perfect Cold Warrior, 1995; Active Trading: Selected Poems 1970–95, 1996; Flying Blind, 1998. Short Stories: The Unsettling of the West, 1986. Non-Fiction: Letters from Managua: Meditations on Politics and Art, 1990; Sailing Home: A Journey Through Time, Place and Memory, 2001. Play: Les Maudits Anglais, 1984. Criticism: Conrad's Later Novels, 1980. Translator: I Didn't Notice the Mountain Growing Dark, by Li Bai and Du Fu (with George Liang), 1986. Editor: 20th Century Poetry and Poetics, 1969; 15 Canadian Poets (with Phyllis Bruce), 1970, fourth edn as 15 Canadian Poets x 3, 2001; Skookum Wawa: Writings of the Canadian Northwest, 1975; Divided We Stand, 1977; Chinada: Memoirs of the Gang of Seven, 1983; The Inner Ear: An Anthology of New

Canadian Poets, 1983; Vancouver: Soul of a City, 1986; Compañeros: Writings about Latin America, 1990; The Art of Short Fiction: An International Anthology, 1992. *Honours:* E. J. Pratt Medal; National Poetry Prize, Canadian Authors Assocn; America's Best Book Award, 1985; Commonwealth Poetry Competition; Writers Choice Award; National Magazine Gold Award; Archibald Lampman Prize; Gabriela Mistral Prize, 1996; Poetry Book Society Recommendation, 1996. *Memberships:* League of Canadian Poets; Writers' Union of Canada; Playwright's Union of Canada. *Address:* 975 Seaside Dr., RR 2, Sooke, BC V0S 1N0, Canada.

GEIER, Joan Austin; b. 6 March 1934, New York, NY, USA. Writer. m. Walter Geier, 15 Sept. 1956, 2 s., 1 d. *Education:* BS, Humanities, Hunter College. *Publications:* Garbage Can Cat, 1976; Mother of Tribes, 1987; A Formal Feeling Comes, 1994. *Contributions to:* Good Housekeeping; Christian Science Monitor; New York Newsday; Catholic Digest; Poetry Society of America Quarterly; SPSM&H; A Formal Feeling Comes; The Lyric; Poetpourri; Negative Capability; Hiram Poetry Review. *Honours:* Poetry Awards, World Order of Narrative Poets, 1980, 1987, 1990, 1992; Gustav Davidson Award, Poetry Society of America, 1982; John Masefield Award, World Order of Narrative Poets, 1983; Amelia Special Award for Haiku, 1985. *Memberships:* Brooklyn Poetry Circle; Poetry Society of America. *Address:* 556 H 102 Main St, Roosevelt Island, NY 10044, USA.

GELDMAN, Mordechai; b. 16 April 1946, Germany. Clinical Psychologist; Poet. *Education:* MA, Clinical Psychology. *Appointments:* Psychotherapist; Literary Critic. *Publications:* Sea Time Land Time, 1970; Bird, 1975; Window, 1980; 66-83 (poems), 1983; Milano, 1988; Eye, 1993; Dark Mirror, 1995; Book of Ask, 1997; Time, 1997; Literature and Psychoanalysis, 1998; Oh My Dear Walls, 2000; Eats Fire, Drinks Fire, 2002 . *Contributions to:* Ha'aretz; Iediot Acharonot; Siman Kri'a; Achshav; Eton 77; Hadarim; Moznaiim; Shvo; Alpaiim. *Honours:* Homsky Prize for Poetry, Hebrew Writers Asscn, 1983; Prime Minister's Prize, 1995; Brener Prize, Hebrew Writers Asscn, 1998. *Memberships:* Hebrew Writers Asscn; Society of Hebrew Writers. *Address:* 73 Shlomtzion Hamalka St, Tel-Aviv 62266, Israel.

GELLIS, Willard; b. 9 June 1936, New York, NY, USA. Poet; Writer. m. Shirley Routten, 23 Aug. 1981, 1 d. *Education:* AB, Hofstra University, 1958; MA, University of Maryland, 1961; PhD, New York University, 1970. *Appointments:* Asst Prof. of English, Lockhaven College, Pennsylvania; Assoc. Prof. of English, Purdue University, IN, New York Institute of Technology; Visiting Prof., English Literature, State University of New York, Farmingdale, 1989. *Publications:* Moon inna Baad House, 1984; Ballad a Jim Fidley, 1985; Making Nightmares Pay, 1987; Sin and Hoodoo Memory, 1987; Satan's Suckhole, 1987; Old Sparky, 1987; Death Makes Ya Horny, 1987; The Bigfoot Songbook, 1989; St Joe Road, 1989; Satan's Suckhole Trilogy, 1990; Bamboo and Cotton, 1991; Go Slow Swift of Heart, 1991; Hard Dick and Bubblegum, 1991; Hard Leg, 1991; Popped, 1992; Bronco Junky, 1994; Dark Transit, 1995; Black Sheep Finder, 1995; Wayless Way, 1996; Die Metal, 1996; NamJam, 1996; Testament, 1996; East Baltimore Street, 1996; Fire Rat, 1998; Tramping Dirtyside, 1999; Under Algol, 2000; Old Sparky (revised stage version), 2000. Other: CDs, videos and audiocassettes. *Contributions to:* Analecta; Hanging Loose; Goodly Co; New American and Canadian Poetry; Mountain Ways; North America Book; Long Shot; Best of The Penny Dreadful Review. *Memberships:* Poets and Writers; Westhampton Cultural Consortium; Alliance for Community Media. *Address:* 57 Seafield Lane, Bay Shore, NY 11706, USA.

GENSLER, Kinereth Dushkin; b. 17 Sept. 1922, New York, NY, USA. Poet. Widow, 2 s., 1 d. *Education:* BA, University of Chicago, 1943; MA, Columbia University, 1946. *Appointment:* Ed., Alice James Books, 1976–99. *Publications:* Threesome Poems, 1976; The Poetry Connection (co-author), 1978; Without Roof, 1981; Journey Fruit, 1997. *Contributions to:* Anthologies, books, journals, and periodicals. *Honours:* Members Award, Poetry Society of America, 1969; Power Dalton Award, New England Poetry Club, 1971; Borestone Mountain Award, 1973; Residency, Ragdale, 1981; Residency, MacDowell Colony, 1982, 1983. *Memberships:* Acad. of American Poets; Alice James Poetry Co-operative Society; Poetry Society of America. *Address:* 221 Mt Auburn St, Cambridge, MA 02138, USA.

GENTRY, Mary E.; b. 19 Oct. 1933, California, USA. Poet. m. Harlan C. Gentry, 21 Feb. 1964, deceased, 1 s., 3 d. *Education:* Simmons Institute, 1959. *Publications:* Hearts on Fire: A Treasury of Poems of Love, 1983; These Too Shall Be Heard, 1991; Down Peaceful Paths, 1991; Listen With Your Heart, 1992; An Ever-Growing Wonder, 2001; Letters From the Soul, 2002. Other: The Sound of Poetry (audio), three vols, 1992, 2001, 2002. *Contributions to:* Anthologies. *Honours:* Awards of Merit, 1987, 1988, Golden Poet, 1987, 1988, Silver Poet, 1990, World of Poetry. *Address:* 7045 Molokai Dr., Paradise, CA 95969, USA.

GEORGALAS, Robert Nicholas; b. 11 Nov. 1951, New York, NY, USA. Prof. of English; Poet. m. Joanne Pepe, 5 Sept. 1981. *Education:* AA, Bronx Community College, 1970; BA, Herbert H Lehman College, 1972; MA, City College of New York, 1974. *Appointments:* Adjunct Lecturer, Herbert Lehman College, 1974–77; Adjunct Prof. of English, Marymount Manhattan College, 1979–88; Prof. of English, College of DuPage. *Contributions to:* Anthologies and

periodicals. *Honours:* Second Prize, Chicagoland Poetry Contest, 1989; Third Prize, Autumn Harvest Poetry Festival, 1989; Ed.'s Choice Awards, National Library of Poetry, 1993, 1994. *Memberships:* MLA; National Council of Teachers of English. *Address:* 360 E Randolph, Apt 1407, Chicago, IL 60601, USA.

GEORGE, Etty (Elsa); b. 5 July 1937, Cochin, Kerala, India. Educator; Poet. m. Abraham George, 15 July 1979. *Education:* MA, English Literature, 1960; DLitt, 1980. *Appointments:* Faculty, MG University, BCM College. *Contributions to:* Anthologies and other publications. *Honour:* International Eminent Poet Award and Honours Fellow, International Acad. of Poets. *Memberships:* Christian Society of Poets, USA; Society of Poets, Australia; World of Poetry Society Intercontinental. *Address:* c/o BCM College, Kottayam, Kerala, India.

GEORGE, Victor André Gilles Joseph; b. 27 Oct. 1937, Bois-et-Borsu, Belgium. Teacher; Poet. *Publications:* Adju K'pagnon, 1963; Gris Pwin, 1965; In Paradisum, 1978; Recineyes, 1979; Totes les Ameurs de Monde, 1983; Tchonson d'a ci qu'a passe l'Baye. *Contributions to:* Les Cahiers Wallons; La Vie Wallonne; Dialectes de Wallonie. *Honours:* Prix des Critiques Wallons, 1963; Prix Biennal de la Ville de Liège, 1965; Prix Durbuy, Huy, 1966; Prix Michaux, Namur, 1978; Prix du Ministere de la Communaute Française, 1982. *Memberships:* Société de Langue et de Litterature Wallonnes, Liège; Relis Namurwes, Namur. *Address:* Tier Laurent 6, 4560 Bois-et-Borsu, Belgium.

GERALD, John Bart; b. 25 Sept. 1940, New York, NY, USA. Writer; Poet; Trans.; Publisher. m. Julie Maas, 3 Oct. 1970. *Education:* AB, Harvard College, 1962. *Publications:* Plainsongs, 1985; Country Poems, 1991; 37 Poems, 1998; Poems from a River City, 2000. Other: Stories and trans. *Contributions to:* Periodicals. *Memberships:* PEN Canada; League of Canadian Poets. *Address:* 206 St Patrick St, Ottawa, ON K1N 5K3, Canada. *E-mail:* jbgerald@achilles.net. *Website:* www.nightslantern.ca.

GERARD, David; b. 19 Oct. 1923, Glasgow, Scotland. Librarian (retd); Poet. *Education:* BA, London, 1955; BA, Dunelm, 1985. *Appointments:* Deputy City Librarian, Exeter, 1955–57, Nottingham, 1957–64, City Librarian, Nottingham, 1964–68; Senior Lecturer, College of Librarianship, Wales, 1968–82. *Publications:* Personalia, 1983; Revenants, 1985; Piano Piano, 1988; This Year, Next Year, 1991; Aller Retour, 1993; Lifelines, 1999; Some Words Before Tomorrow, 2002. *Honour:* Churchill Fellow, 1967. *Membership:* Library Asscn, fellow. *Address:* 153A Woodlands Ave, Eastcote, Ruislip, Middlesex HA4 9QX, England.

GERAS, Adele Daphne; b. 15 March 1944, Jerusalem, Palestine. Writer; Poet. m. Norman Geras, 7 Aug. 1967, 2 d. *Education:* BA, Honours, Modern Languages, St Hilda's College, Oxford, 1966. *Publications:* Up on the Roof (with Pauline Stainer), 1987; Sampler, 1991; Voices From the Doll's House, 1994. *Contributions to:* Anthologies, reviews and journals. *Honours:* Winner, Smith-Doorstop Pamphlet Competition, 1987; Jewish Quarterly Poetry Prize, 1993; Arts Council Award, 2000; A. E. Housman Poetry Award, 2000. *Memberships:* National Asscn of Writers in Education; Poetry Society; Society of Poets; VER Poets. *Address:* 10 Danesmoor Rd, Manchester M20 3JS, England.

GEREIGHTY, Andrea (Ann) S(aunders); b. 20 July 1938, New Orleans, LA, USA. Public Opinion Pollster; Poet. m. Dennis Anthony Gereighty Jr, 9 May 1959, deceased, 1 s., 2 d. *Education:* BA, English Education, 1974, MA, English, 1978, University of New Orleans. *Contributions to:* Many quarterlies, reviews and journals. *Honours:* English-Speaking Union Scholarship, Exeter College, England, 1972; First Place, Deep South Literary Award for Poetry, 1973; Honourable Mention, Poetry Award, Deep South Writers, 1983; First Place, National League of American Pen Women, 1984; First Runner-Up, Gibbons Award for Poetry, 1984; Second Place, Nuyorican Poetry Competition, New York City, 1994. *Memberships:* Deep South Literary Society; New Orleans Poetry Forum. *Address:* 257 Bonnabel Blvd, Metairie, LA 70005, USA.

GEROLD, Charles, (Charles Perdu, Carlos Perdido); b. 21 Feb. 1927, Chicago, IL, USA. Poet. m. Adriana Youssif, 15 June 1967, 3 s., 1 d. *Education:* BA, 1949; MA, 1953; PhD, 1983. *Publications:* Echoes of Valor, 1993; Idylls Hymns Dirges, 2002. *Contributions to:* American Poetry Anthology, 1990. *Honour:* Alden Award for Drama, Dramatists Alliance, San Francisco. *Address:* 17 Woodford Dr., Moraga, CA 94556, USA.

GERSTLER, Amy; b. 24 Oct. 1956, San Diego, CA, USA. Poet; Writer. *Education:* BA, Pitzer College. *Publications:* Poetry: Yonder, 1981; Christy's Alpine Inn, 1982; White Marriage/Recovery, 1984; Early Heavens, 1984; The True Bride, 1986; Bitter Angel, 1990; Nerve Storm, 1993; Crown of Weeds, 1997; Medicine, 2000. Fiction: Martine's Mouth, 1985; Primitive Man, 1987. Other: Past Lives (with Alexis Smith), 1989. *Contributions to:* Magazines. *Honour:* National Book Critics Circle Award, 1991. *Address:* c/o Viking Penguin, 375 Hudson St, New York, NY 10014, USA.

GERVAIS, Charles Henry Martin; b. 20 Oct. 1946, Windsor, Ontario, Canada. Poet; Writer; Ed. m. Donna Wright, 1968, 2 s., 1 d. *Education:* BA, University of Guelph, 1971; MA, University of Windsor, 1972. *Appointments:*

Staff, Toronto Globe and Mail, 1966, Canadian Press, Toronto, 1967; Reporter, Daily Commercial News, Toronto, 1967, Chatham Daily News, 1972–73; Teacher of Creative Writing, St Clair College, Windsor, 1969–71; Publisher, Black Moss Press, Windsor, 1969–; Ed., Sunday Standard, Windsor, 1972; General News Reporter, 1973–74, 1976–81, Bureau Chief, 1974–76, Religion Ed., 1979–80, Book Ed., 1980–, Entertainment Writer, 1990–, Windsor Star. *Publications:* Poetry: Sister Saint Anne, 1968; Something, 1969; Other Marriage Vows, 1969; A Sympathy Orchestra, 1970; Bittersweet, 1972; Poems for American Daughters, 1976; The Believable Body, 1979; Up Country Lines, 1979; Silence Comes with Lake Voices, 1980; Into a Blue Morning: Selected Poems, 1982; Public Fanatasy: The Maggie T Poems, 1983; Letters From the Equator, 1986; Autobiographies, 1989; Playing God: New Poems, 1994. Other: The Rumrunners: A Prohibition Scrapbook, 1980; Voices Like Thunder, 1984; The Border Police: One Hundred and Twenty-Five Years of Policing in Windsor, 1992; Seeds in the Wilderness: Profiles of World Religious Leaders, 1994; From America Sent: Letters to Henry Miller, 1995. Editor: The Writing Life: Historical and Critical Views of the Tish Movement, 1976. Children's Books: How Bruises Lost His Secret, 1975; Doctor Troyer and the Secret in the Moonstone, 1976; If I Had a Birthday Everyday, 1983. *Honours:* Western Ontario Newspaper Awards, 1983, 1984, 1987. *Address:* 1939 Alsace Ave, Windsor, Ontario N8W 1M5, Canada.

GERY, John Roy Octavius; b. 2 June 1953, Reading, PA, USA. Research Prof. of English; Poet. *Education:* BA, Princeton University, 1975; MA, English, University of Chicago, 1976; MA, Creative Writing, Stanford University, 1978. *Appointments:* Lecturer, Stanford University and San Jose State University, 1977–79; Instructor, 1979–84, Asst Prof., 1984–88, Assoc. Prof., 1988–95, Prof. of English, 1995–2000, Research Prof. of English, 2000–, University of New Orleans; Founding Dir, Ezra Pound Center for Literature, Brunnenburg, Italy, 1990–; Visiting Prof., University of Iowa, 1991–92. *Publications:* Charlemagne: A Song of Gestures, 1983; The Burning of New Orleans, 1988; Three Poems, 1989; The Enemies of Leisure, 1995; Nuclear Annihilation and Contemporary American Poetry, 1996; For the House of Torkom (co-trans.), 1999; American Ghost: Selected Poems, 1999; Davenport's Version, 2002. *Contributions to:* Reviews and journals. *Honours:* Deep South Writers Poetry Award, 1987; Charles William Duke Long Poem Award, 1987; Wesleyan Writers' Conference Poetry Fellowship, 1989; National Endowment for the Arts Creative Fellowship, 1992–93; Critics' Choice Award for Poetry, 1996; European Award Circle Franz Kafka, 2000; Louisiana Artist Fellowship, 2002. *Memberships:* Acad. of American Poets; Assoc. Writing Programs; MLA; Poets and Writers. *Address:* c/o Dept of English, University of New Orleans, New Orleans, LA 70148, USA.

GEVIRTZ, Susan; b. 27 Oct. 1955, Los Angeles, CA, USA. Poet; Writer. m. David Delp, 15 Aug. 1992. *Education:* BA, Literature, Cultural Theory, Poetics, Evergreen State College, 1977; MA, Classical Literature, Philosophy, St John's Graduate Institute, Santa Fe, New Mexico, 1980; PhD, History of Consciousness, University of California at Santa Cruz, 1990. *Appointments:* Teaching Asst, University of California at Santa Cruz, 1983–87; Teacher-Poet, California Poets in the Schools, San Francisco, 1984–86; Teacher, Aegean College of Fine Arts, Paros, Greece, 1985; Assoc. Ed., HOW(ever) journal, 1985–90; Instructor, University of San Francisco, 1988–89, California College of Arts and Crafts, Oakland, 1989–91; Asst Prof., Hutchins School of Liberal Studies, Sonoma State University, Rohnert Park, CA, 1989–98. *Publications:* Poetry: Korean and Milkhouse, 1991; Domino: Point of Entry, 1992; Linen minus, 1992; Taken Place, 1993; Prosthesis: Caesarea, 1994; Black Box Cutaway, 1998. Other: Feminist Poetics: A Consideration of the 'Female' Construction of Language (assoc. ed.), 1984; Narrative's Journey: The Fiction and Film Writing of Dorothy Richardson, 1995. *Contributions to:* Anthologies, journals, and magazines. *Honours:* Awards, grants, and fellowships. *Address:* 1939 Jones St, San Francisco, CA 94133, USA.

GHIGNA, Charles Vincent; b. 25 Aug. 1946, New York, NY, USA. Poet; Children's Writer. m. Debra Ghigna, 2 Aug. 1975, 1 s., 1 d. *Education:* BA, English; MEd, English and Education. *Appointments:* Poetry Ed., English Journal for the National Council of Teachers of English, Poet-in-Residence, Alabama School of Fine Arts; Correspondent, Writer's Digest Magazine; Nationally Syndicated Writer of Snickers Feature; Speaker, schools, colleges, book fairs and conferences. *Publications:* Returning to Earth, 1989; Good Dog/Bad Dog, 1992; Good Cat/Bad Cat, 1992; Tickle Day: Poems from Father Goose, 1994; Riddle Rhymes, 1995; Speaking in Tongues: New and Selected Poems 1974–1995, 1995; Plastic Soup: Dream Poems, 1999; Mice Are Nice, 1999; See the Yak Yak, 1999; The Animal Trunk, 1999; Christmans is Coming, 2000; One Hundred Shoes, 2002; The Alphabet Parade, 2002; Halloween Poems, 2003; Animal Tracks, 2003; Poems for Boys who Hate Poems, 2002. *Contributions to:* Harper's; Playboy; McCall's; New York Quarterly; Writer's Digest; Artist's Magazine; Writer; Rolling Stone; Saturday Evening Post; Ladies Home Journal; Good Housekeeping; Guideposts; Wall Street Journal; Village Voice; Christian Science Monitor; Highlights for Children; Ranger Rick; Child Life; Humpty Dumpty; Jack and Jill; Children's Digest; Children's Playmate; Turtle; Lollipops. *Honours:* Alabama Poet-in-Residence Schools Program Grant, 1974; Pulitzer Prize Nomination, 1989. *Address:* 204 W Linwood Dr., Homewood, AL 35209, USA.

GHOSE, Zulfikar; b. 13 March 1935, Sialkot, Pakistan (Naturalized British citizen). Prof. of English; Poet; Writer. *Education:* BA, Keele University, 1959. *Appointment:* Prof. of English, University of Texas at Austin, 1969–. *Publications:* Poetry: The Loss of India, 1964; Jets from Orange, 1967; The Violent West, 1972; A Memory of Asia, 1984; Selected Poems, 1991. Fiction: The Contradictions, 1966; The Murder of Aziz Khan, 1967; The Incredible Brazilian the Native, 1972; The Beautiful Empire, 1975; Crump's Terms, 1975; A Different World, 1978; Hulme's Investigations into the Bogan Script, 1981; A New History of Torments, 1982; Don Bueno, 1983; Figures of Enchantment, 1986; The Triple Mirror of the Self, 1992. Criticism: Hamlet, Prufrock and Language, 1978; The Fiction of Reality, 1983; The Art of Creating Fiction, 1991; Shakespeare's Mortal Knowledge, 1993; Veronica and the Góngora Passion, 1998. Autobiography: Confessions of a Native-Alien, 1965. *Address:* c/o Dept of English, University of Texas at Austin, Austin, TX 78712, USA.

GIANNINI, David; b. 19 March 1948, USA. Poet. *Publications:* Opens, 1970; Stories, 1974; Fourfield, 1976; Close Packet, 1978; Three, 1978; Stem, 1982; Antonio and Clara, 1992; Keys, 1992; Fist, 1997; Lines, 1997; Arizona Notes, 1998; RIM, 1998. *Contributions to:* Sonora Review; Longhouse; Shadowplay; Tel-Let; Talisman; Room; George Mason Review; Shearsman, Malaysia; MJP, Canada. *Honours:* Osa and Lee Mays Award for Poetry, 1970; Massachusetts Artists Foundation Fellowship Award, 1990; University of Florida Award, 1991. *Address:* PO Box 630, Otis, MA 01253, USA.

GIBBONS, (William) Reginald (Jr); b. 7 Jan. 1947, Houston, Texas, USA. Prof. of English; Poet; Writer; Trans. m. Cornelia Maude Spelman, 18 Aug. 1983, 1 step-s., 1 step-d. *Education:* AB, Spanish and Portuguese, Princeton University, 1969; MA, English and Creative Writing, 1971, PhD, Comparative Literature, 1974, Stanford University. *Appointments:* Lecturer, Livingston College, Rutgers University, 1975–76, Princeton University, 1976–80, Columbia University, 1980–81; Ed., TriQuarterly magazine, 1981–97; Prof. of English, Northwestern University, 1981–; Core Faculty, MFA Program for Writers, Warren Wilson College, 1989–. *Publications:* Poetry and Fiction: Roofs Voices Roads (poems), 1979; The Ruined Motel (poems), 1981; Saints (poems), 1986; Maybe It Was So (poems), 1991; Five Pears or Peaches (short stories), 1991; Sweetbitter (novel), 1994; Sparrow: New and Selected Poems, 1997; Homage to Longshot O'Leary (poems), 1999; It's Time (poems), 2002. Other: Criticism in the University (ed. with Gerald Graff), 1985; The Writer in Our World (ed.), 1986; Writers from South Africa (ed.), 1988; William Goyen: A Study of the Short Fiction, 1991; Thomas McGrath: Life and the Poem (ed. with Terrence Des Pres), 1991; New Writings from Mexico (ed. and principal trans.), 1992; Selected Poems of Luis Cernuda (trans.), 2000; Euripides' Bakkhai (trans.), 2001. *Contributions to:* Many journals, reviews, quarterlies, and magazines. *Honours:* Fulbright Fellowship, Spain, 1971–72; Co-Winner, Denver Quarterly Trans. Award, 1977; Guggenheim Fellowship, 1984; National Endowment for the Arts Fellowship, 1984–85; Texas Institute of Letters Short Story Award, 1986; Illinois Arts Council Fellowship, 1987; John Masefield Memorial Award, Poetry Society of America, 1991; Carl Sandburg Award, Friends of the Chicago Public Library, 1992; Anisfield-Wolf Book Award, 1995; Pushcart Prize XXII, 1997; Thomas H Carter Prize, Shenandoah magazine, 1998; Balcones Poetry Prize, 1998. *Memberships:* Associated Writing Programs; The Guild Complex, co-founder; PEN American Center; Poetry Society of America; Texas Institute of Letters; Society of Midland Authors. *Address:* 1428 Crain St, Evanston, IL 60202, USA.

GIBSON, Grace Evelyn Loving; b. 29 Oct. 1919, Drakes Branch, Virginia, USA. Educator; Poet. m. Alton Brooks Gibson, 16 Dec. 1944, 3 s. *Education:* BA, University of North Carolina, Greensboro, 1940; MA, English, Duke University, Durham, 1943. *Appointments:* Instructor in English, St Andrews College, 1963–65; Asst, then Assoc. Prof., Communicative Arts Dept, Pembroke State University, 1966–86; Adjunct Prof., English Literature, St Andrews College, 1986–. *Publications:* Home in Time, 1977; Drakes Branch, 1982; Wind Burial (co-trans.), 1990; The Pocket John Charles McNeill (ed.), 1990; By Reason of Strength, by Gerald W Johnson (ed.), 1994; Frayed Edges (poems), 1995. *Contributions to:* Pembroke Magazine; St Andrews Review; Crucible; Arts Journal; Cape Rock International Poetry Review; Pilot. *Honours:* Fartner Writer and Community Award, 1989; Sam Ragan Award, 1992. *Memberships:* North Carolina Poetry Society; North Carolina Writers' Network, nominating committee, 1994–96. *Address:* 709 McLean St, Laurinburg, NC 28352, USA.

GIBSON, Keiko Matsui; b. 4 Sept. 1953, Kyoto, Japan. University Prof.; Poet. m. Morgan Gibson, 14 Sep 1978, 1 s. *Education:* BA, English, Kwansei Gakvin University, Japan, 1976; MA, Comparative Literature, University of Illinois, 1983; PhD, Indiana University, 1992. *Appointments:* Instructor, Japanese, Northwestern Michigan College, 1980; Assoc. Instructor, Comparative Literature, Indiana University, 1984–85; Instructor, 1991–92, Asst Prof., 1992–93, Comparative Literature, Pennsylvania State University; Assoc. Prof., British-American Studies, Kanda University of International Studies, Chiba, Japan, 1993–. *Publications:* Tremble of Morning, 1979; Kokora: Heart-Mind, 1981; Stir Up the Precipitable World, 1983. *Contributions to:* Other Side River; Anthology of Magazine Verse and Yearbook of American Poetry; for Rexroth; Passages North; Vajradhattu Sun; Sackbut Review; Nexus; New Letters; Crosscurrents; Kyoto Review; Ao; Kansai Time Out; Blue Jacket; Jandararin; Edge. *Honour:* Kenneth Rexroth Special Award for Poetry,

Kyoto, Japan. *Memberships:* Japan, American and International Comparative Literature Asscns. *Address:* Dept of English, Kanda Gai University of International Studies, 1-4-1 Wakaba, Mihama-ku, Chiba-Shi, Chiba-Ken 261, Japan.

GIBSON, Margaret; 2 Feb. 1944, Philadelphia, Pennsylavania, USA. Poet. m. David McKain. *Education:* Hollins College, University of Virginia. *Publications:* Lunes, 1973; On the Cutting Edge, 1976; Signs, 1979; Long Walks in the Afternoon, 1982; Memories in the Future: The Daybooks of Tina Modotti, 1986; Out in the Open, 1989; The Vigil: A Poem in Four Voices, 1993; Earth Elegy: New and Selected Poems, 1997. *Honours:* Lamont Poetry Selection, 1982; Melville Cane Award, 1986; Finalist, National Book Award in Poetry, 1993. *Address:* c/o Louisiana State University Press, PO Box 25053, Baton Rouge, LA 70894, USA.

GIBSON, Morgan; b. 6 June 1929, Cleveland, Ohio, USA. Prof.; Poet; Writer. m. (1) Barbara Gibson, 1950, divorced 1972, 2 d., (2) Keiko Matsui Gibson, 14 Sept. 1978, 1 s. *Education:* BA, English Literature, Oberlin College, 1950; MA, English and American Literature and Creative Writing, 1952, PhD, 1959, University of Iowa. *Appointments:* Asst, then Assoc. Prof. of English, University of Wisconsin at Milwaukee, 1961–72; Chair, Graduate Faculty, Goddard College, Vermont, 1972–75; Osaka University, 1975–79; Visiting Prof., Michigan State University, 1979, University of Illinois, 1982, Knox College, 1989–91; Prof., Chukyo University, 1987–89, Japan Women's University, Tokyo, 1993–96, Kanda University of International Studies, 1997–; Lecturer, Pennsylvania State University, 1991–93. *Publications:* Stones Glow Like Lovers' Eyes, 1970; Crystal Sunlake, 1971; Kenneth Rexroth, 1972; Dark Summer, 1977; Wakeup, 1978; Speaking of Light, 1979; Kokoro: Heart-Mind, 1979; The Great Brook Book, 1981; Revolutionary Rexroth: Poet of East-West Wisdom, 1986, and online, 2000; Among Buddhas in Japan, 1988; Winter Pilgrim, 1993. Editor: Several books and journals. *Contributions to:* Anthologies, books, journals and reviews. *Honours:* Awards and grants. *Address:* 3-17-604 Sakashita-cho, Isogo-ku, Yokohama-shi, 235-0003, Japan.

GIBSON, William; b. 13 Nov. 1914, New York, NY, USA. Dramatist; Writer; Poet. m. (1), divorced, (2) Margaret Brenman, 6 Sept. 1940, 2 s. *Education:* College of the City of New York. *Publications:* Plays (with dates of production and publication): I Lay in Zion, 1943, 1947; A Cry of Players, 1948, 1969; The Ruby, 1955; The Miracle Worker, 1957, 1957; Two for the Seesaw, 1958, 1960; Dinny and the Witches, 1959, 1960; Golden Boy (with Clifford Odets), 1964, 1965; John and Abigail, 1969, 1972; The Body and the Wheel, 1974, 1975; The Butterfingers Angel, Mary and Joseph, Herod the Nut, and the Slaughter of 12 Hit Carols in a Pear Tree, 1974, 1975; Golda, 1977, 1977; Goodly Creatures, 1980, 1986; Monday After the Miracle, 1982, 1983; Handy Dandy, 1984, 1986; Raggedy Ann: The Musical Adventure, 1985, 1986. Novel: The Cobweb, 1954. Poetry: Winter Crook, 1948; A Mass for the Dead, 1968. Criticism: Shakespeare's Game, 1978. *Contributions to:* Magazines. *Honours:* Harriet Monroe Memorial Prize for Poetry, 1945; Sylvania Award, 1957. *Memberships:* Authors League of America; Dramatists Guild; PEN. *Address:* c/o Flora Roberts, 157 W 57th St, New York, NY 10022, USA.

GIFFORD, Terry; b. 28 June 1946, Cambridge, England. Poet. 1 s., 1 d. *Education:* BEd, 1973, PhD, 1992, Lancaster University; MA, Sheffield University, 1978. *Appointment:* Reader in Literature and Environment, University of Leeds. *Publications:* The Stone Spiral, 1987; Ten Letters to John Muir, 1990; Outcrops, 1991; The Rope, 1996; Whale Watching with a Boy and a Goat, 1998. *Contributions to:* Poetry Wales; North; Alpine Journal; Pennine Platform; Cencrastus; Climbing Art, USA; High; Critical Quarterly. *Honours:* Lancaster Literature Festival Anthology, 1982, 1983, 1985; First Prize, South Yorkshire Literary Competition, 1983; South Yorkshire Mike Hayward Award, 1986. *Memberships:* ASLE UK, sec.; International Festival of Mountaineering Literature, dir. *Address:* 56 Conduit Rd, Sheffield S10 1EW, England. *E-mail:* t.gifford@leeds.ac.uk. *Website:* www.terrygifford.co.uk.

GIL, Lourdes; b. 14 Dec. 1951, Havana, Cuba. Writer; Ed.; Poet. m. Ariel Rodriguez, 20 Nov. 1983, 1 s. *Education:* Certificate, University of Madrid, Spain, 1973; BA, Fordham University, 1974; ABD, MA, 1978, New York University. *Appointments:* Ed., Romanica Journal, New York University, 1975–82, Lyra Quarterly, New Jersey, 1987–; Trans., Hearst Publishers, New York, 1977–83; Pres., Giralt Publishers Co, New York, 1984–. *Publications:* Pneumas, 1977; Manuscrito Nina Avsente, 1980; Vencido Fuego Especie, 1983; Blanca Aldaba Preludes, 1989. *Contributions to:* Linden Lane Magazine; Romanica Journal; EN/ACE Review; Inti; Kantil Review; Spectrum; Latino Stuff Review; Gato Tuerto; Michigan Literary Quarterly; Poesia Venezuela; Hudson Literary Quarterly. *Honours:* Cintas Fellowship, United Nations, 1979, 1991; Alenco-Barcelona, Venezuela, 1982. *Memberships:* Americas Society; Poetry Society of America; Latin American Writers Institute; Friends of PEN; Asscn of Hispanic Arts; Pan-American Literary Circle; Lyra Society for the Arts, pres. *Address:* Lyra Society for the Arts Inc, PO Box 3188, Guttenberg, NJ 07093, USA.

GILBERT, Ilsa; b. 27 April 1933, New York, NY, USA. Poet; Playwright; Librettist; Lyricist. *Education:* University of Michigan, 1951–52; BA, Brooklyn College, 1955. *Publications:* Pardon the Prison, 1976; Survivors and Other New York Poems, 1985. Other: Numerous productions, staged readings, verse plays, musicals, concert pieces, etc. *Contributions to:* Numerous magazines. *Honours:* Honourable Mention, Atlantic Monthly College Poetry Contest, 1955; Best Subjective Poem, Poet Lore, 1968; Writers Colony Residencies, Dorset, Vermont, 1982, 1986–87. *Memberships:* Authors League of America; Dramatists Guild; PEN American Center; Pentangle Literary Society; Poets and Writers; Women's Salon. *Address:* 203 Bleecker St, Apt 9, New York, NY 10012, USA.

GILBERT, Jack; b. 17 Feb. 1925, Pittsburgh, Pennsylvania, USA. Poet; Writer. *Education:* BA, University of Pittsburgh, 1954; MA, San Francisco State University, 1962. *Appointments:* University of California at Berkeley, 1958–59, San Francisco State University, 1962–63, 1965–67, 1971, Syracuse University, 1982–83, University of San Francisco, 1985; Prof., Kyoto University, Tokyo, 1974–75; Chair, Creative Writing, University of Alabama, Tuscaloosa, 1986. *Publications:* Poetry: Views of Jeopardy, 1962; Monolithos, 1982; The Great Fires: Poems, 1982–1992, 1994. *Contributions to:* Various reviews, journals, and periodicals. *Honours:* Yale Younger Poet Award, 1962; Guggenheim Fellowship, 1964; National Endowment for the Arts Award, 1974; First Prize, American Poetry Review, 1983; Stanley Kunitz Prize, 1983; Lannan Award, 1995. *Address:* 136 Montana St, San Francisco, CA 94112, USA.

GILBERT, Marie; b. 27 Jan. 1924, Florence, South Carolina, USA. Poet. m. Richard A Gilbert, 1 s., 1 d. *Education:* Dual Major, BA, Psychology and Theatre Arts, Sullivan Medallion at graduation, Rollins College. *Appointments:* Board of Visitors, St Andrews Presbyterian College, instrumental in establishing Creative Writing Chair for college. *Publications:* From Comfort, 1981; The Song and the Seed, 1983; Forever New, 1987; Myrtle Beach Back When, 1989; Connexions, 1994; Brookgreen Oaks, 1999. *Contributions to:* Magazines and journals. *Honours:* Sam Ragan Poet Laureate Award, 1994; Second Place, State Contests. *Memberships:* North Carolina Writer's Network, 1985–2001; North Carolina Poetry Society. *Address:* 2 Saint Simons Sq., Greensboro, NC, USA. *E-mail:* ragmrgworldnet.att.net.

GILBERT, Virginia; b. 19 Dec. 1946, Elgin, IL, USA. Assoc. Prof. of English; Poet; Writer. *Education:* BA, English, Iowa Wesleyan College, 1969; MFA, Creative Writing and Poetry, University of Iowa, 1971; PhD, Creative Writing, Poetry and English, University of Nebraska, 1991. *Appointments:* Instructor, College of Lake County, IL, 1979; Teaching Asst, University of Nebraska, 1984–87; Asst Prof., 1990–92, Assoc. Prof., 1992–, of English, Alabama A&M University. *Publications:* To Keep at Bay the Hounds, 1985; The Earth Above, 1993. That Other Brightness, 1996. *Contributions to:* Anthologies: Wordlens, Ordinary and Sacred as Blood, Claiming the Spirit Within: A Source Book of Women's Poetry; Journals, reviews, and quarterlies. *Honours:* National Endowment for the Arts Fellowship, 1976–77; Second Place, Hackney Awards, 1990; First Place, Sakura Festival Haiku Contest, 1992; Fulbright Fellow to China, 1993; Nominated Book of the Year, Alabama Poetry Society, 1995 First Place Alabama State Poetry Society's Poetry Slam, 1998. *Memberships:* Associated Writing Programs; MLA; Peace Corps Volunteer Asscn; Peace Corps Volunteer Readers and Writers Asscn; Poetry Society of America; Poets and Writers. *Address:* c/o Dept of English, Alabama A & M University, Box 453, Normal, AL 35762, USA.

GILCHRIST, Ellen; b. 20 Feb. 1935, Vicksburg, Mississippi, USA. Author; Poet. *Education:* BA, Millsaps College, Jackson, Mississippi, 1967; Postgraduate Studies, University of Arkansas, 1976. *Publications:* The Land Surveyor's Daughter (poems), 1979; The Land of Dreamy Dreams (stories), 1981; The Annunciation (novel), 1983; Victory Over Japan: A Book of Stories, 1984; Drunk With Love (stories), 1986; Riding Out the Tropical Depression (poems), 1986; Falling Through Space: The Journals of Ellen Gilchrist, 1987; The Anna Papers (novel), 1988; Light Can Be Both Wave and Particle: A Book of Stories, 1989; I Cannot Get You Close Enough (3 novellas), 1990; Net of Jewels (novel), 1992; Anabasis: A Journey to the Interior, 1994; Starcarbon: A Meditation on Love, 1994; An Age of Miracles (stories), 1995; Rhoda: A Life in Stories, 1995; Sarah Conley, 1997. *Contributions to:* Many journals and periodicals. *Honours:* National Endowment for the Arts Grant in Fiction, 1979; Pushcart Prizes, 1979–80, 1983; Louisiana Library Asscn Honor Book, 1981; Mississippi Acad. of Arts and Sciences Awards, 1982, 1985; Saxifrage Award, 1983; American Book Award for Fiction, 1984; J William Fulbright Award for Literature, University of Arkansas, 1985; Mississippi Institute of Arts and Letters Literature Award, 1985. *Memberships:* Authors Guild; Authors League of America. *Address:* 834 Eastwood Dr., Fayetteville, AR 72701, USA.

GILL, David Lawrence William; b. 3 July 1934, Chislehurst, Kent, England. Poet; Writer. m. Irene Henry, 5 July 1958, 2 s., 1 d. *Education:* BA, Honours, German, University College, London, 1955; Certificate in Education, Birmingham University, 1958; BA, Honours, English, London External, 1970. *Appointments:* Lecturer, 1971–79, Senior Lecturer, 1979–87, Newland Park College of Education, later incorporated into Bucks College of Higher Education. *Publications:* Men Without Evenings, 1966; The Pagoda and Other Poems, 1969; In the Eye of the Storm, 1975; The Upkeep of the Castle, 1978; Karel Klimsa, by Ondra Lysohorsky (trans.), 1984; One Potato, Two

Potato (with Dorothy Clancy), 1985; Legends, Please, 1986; The White Raven, 1989; The New Hesperides, 1991. *Contributions to:* Many journals, reviews, and magazines. *Address:* 38 Yarnells Hill, Botley, Oxford OX2 9BE, England.

GILL, Stephen Matthew; b. 25 June 1932, Sialkot, Pakistan. Poet; Author; Ed. m. Sarala Gill, 17 Feb. 1970, 1 s., 2 d. *Education:* BA, Punjab University, 1956; MA, Meerut College, Agra University, 1963; University of Ottawa, 1967–70; University of Oxford, 1971. *Appointments:* Ed., Canadian World Federalist, 1971–73, 1977–79, Writer's Lifeline, 1982–; Pres., Vesta Publications Ltd, 1974–90. *Publications:* Poetry: Reflections and Wounds, 1978; Moans and Waves, 1989; The Dove of Peace, 1989; The Flowers of Thirst, 1991; Songs for Harmony, 1992; Flashes, 1994; Aman Di Ghuggi, 1994; Divergent Shades, 1995; Shrine, 1999. Fiction: Life's Vagaries (short stories), 1974; Why, 1976; The Loyalist City, 1979; Immigrants, 1982. Non-Fiction: Six Symbolist Plays of Yeats, 1974; Discovery of Bangladesh, 1975; Scientific Romances of H G Wells, 1975; English Grammar for Beginners, 1977; Political Convictions of G B Shaw, 1980; Sketches of India, 1980. Editor: Various anthologies. *Contributions to:* Over 250 publications. *Honours:* Hon. DLitt, World University, 1986; World Acad. of Arts and Culture, 1990; International Eminent Poet, International Poets Acad., Chennai, 1991; Pegasus International Poetry for Peace Award, Poetry in the Arts, Austin, Texas, 1991; Laureate Man of Letters, United Poets Laureate International, 1992; Poet of Peace Award, Pakistan Asscn, Orleans, Ontario, 1995; Mawaheb Culture Friendship Medal, Mawaheb Magazine, 1997; Sahir Award of Honour, 1999. *Memberships:* Christian Cultural Asscn of South Asians, vice-pres.; International Acad. of Poets, fellow; PEN International; World Acad. of Arts and Culture; World Federalists of Canada; Amnesty International; Writers Union of Canada. *Address:* PO Box 32, Cornwall, ON K6H 5R9, Canada. *E-mail:* stefgill@hotmail.com.

GILLAN, Maria Mazziotti; b. 12 March 1940, Paterson, New Jersey, USA. Poet; Poetry Centre Dir. m. Dennis Gillan, 30 June 1964, 1 s., 1 d. *Education:* BA, English, Seton Hall University, 1961; MA, English, New York University, 1963; Postgraduate Studies, Drew University, 1977–80. *Appointments:* Exec. Dir, Poetry Centre, Passaic County Community College, 1980–; Dir, Creative Writing Program, Binghamton University, State University of New York Ed., Footwork: The Paterson Literary Review, 1980–; Geraldine R Dodge Foundation Poetry Teacher, 1986–; Numerous readings/workshops. *Publications:* Winter Light, 1985; Lice D'Inverno, 1989; Cries of the Spirit, 1990; Taking Back My Name, 1991; Unsettling America: Contemporary Ethnic Poetry (co-ed.), 1994; Where I Come From: Selected and New Poems, 1995; Things My Mother Told Me, 1998; Italian Women in Black Dresses, 2002. Anthologies: International Women Poets Anthology, 1990; Literature Across Cultures: A Reader in Writing, 1994; I Feel a Little Jumpy Around You, 1995. Co-Editor: Unsettling America: Contemporary Ethnic American Poetry, 1994; Identity Lessons: Growing Up Ethnic in America (ed. with Jennifer Gallon). *Contributions to:* Anthologies and professional journals. *Honours:* Fellow in Poetry, New Jersey State Council on The Arts, 1981, 1985; Sri Chinmoy Awards, 1981, 1982, 1983; American Literary Trans Award, 1987; National Poetry Competition Commendation, Chester H Jones Foundation, 1990; Semifinalist, PEN Syndicated Fiction Competition, 1994; May Sarton Award, 1998. *Memberships:* PEN America; Poets and Writers; Poetry Society of America. *Address:* 40 Post Ave, Hawthorne, NJ 07506, USA.

GILLIARD, Emile; b. 12 April 1928, Malonne, Namur, Belgium. Librarian (retd); Poet. m. Jeanine Schmitz, 27 Nov. 1957, 1 s. *Education:* Diploma, Baccalaureate, Greco-Latin, 1948; Certificate of Philosophy, 1951; Certificate of Librarian, 1959. *Appointments:* Teacher, College du Sacré-Coeur, Profondeville, 1954–57; Secretary, 1957–59, Librarian and Dir of Library, 1960–93, Les Comtes de Hainaut, Mons, Hainaut, Belgium. *Publications:* Chîmagrawes, 1955; Pâtèrs Po Tote One Sôte Di Djins, 1959; Vias d'Mârs, 1961; Rukes di Têre, 1966; Li Dêrene Saison, 1976; Silicose Valley, 1989; Paurt èt R'Vindje, 1989; A Ipe, 1992; Vicadje, 1992; Li Navia dèl Pîrète, 1992; Come dès Gayes Su On Baston, 1995. *Contributions to:* Les Cahiers Wallons, Namur; Vers L'Avenir, Namur; Micromania, Châtelet. *Honours:* J Durbuy Prize, 1952; Ville de Liège Prize, 1959; Prize of Government, 1970; G Michaux Prize, Ville de Namur, 1980. *Memberships:* Société de Langue et de Littérature Wallones, Liège, pres., 1995–; Rèlis Namurwès, Namur, 1953–. *Address:* 321 Rue Saint Laurent, 4000 Liège, Belgium.

GILLIES, Valerie; b. 4 June 1948, Edmonton, AB, Canada (Naturalized British citizen). Poet; Writer. m. William Gillies, 24 June 1972, 1 s., 2 d. *Education:* MA, 1970, MLitt, 1974, University of Edinburgh. *Appointments:* Writer-in-Residence, Duncan of Jordanstone College of Art, Dundee, 1988–90, University of Edinburgh, 1995–98. *Publications:* Trio: New Poets from Edinburgh, 1971; Each Bright Eye: Selected Poems, 1977; Bed of Stone, 1984; Leopardi: A Scottish Quair, 1987; Tweed Journey, 1989; The Chanter's Tune, 1990; The Jordanstone Folio, 1990; The Ringing Rock, 1995. *Contributions to:* Radio, television, reviews, and journals. *Honours:* Scottish Arts Council Bursary, 1976, and Book Award, 1996; Eric Gregory Award, 1976. *Membership:* Society of Authors, Scotland, fellow.

GILLILAND, Brian Keith, (Martin Musick); b. 1 May 1959, Wichita, KS, USA. Poet. m. Linda Lee Miller. *Education:* GED, State of Arkansas, 1977;

North Arkansas Community College, 1978–79. *Publications:* Sex With a Barren Landscape, 1986; Sea of Thirst, 1997; Neutrino Gilliland, 2001. *Contributions to:* Midwest Poetry Review; Riverfront Times. *Address:* 1661 Vassier Ave, St Louis, MO 63133, USA.

GILLON, Adam; b. 17 July 1921, Poland. Prof. of English Emeritus; Writer; Poet. m. Isabella Zamojre, 1946, 1 s., 1 d. *Education:* MA, Hebrew University of Jerusalem, 1949; PhD, English and Comparative Literature, Columbia University, 1954. *Appointments:* Prof. of English, Acadia University, Nova Scotia, 1957–62, University of Haifa, 1979–84; Prof. of English and Comparative Literature, 1962–81, Prof. Emeritus, 1981–, State University of New York at New Paltz. *Publications:* Poetry: Selected Poems and Translations, 1962; In the Manner of Haiku: Seven Aspects of Man, 1967; Daily New and Old: Poems in the Manner of Haiku, 1971; Strange Mutations in the Manner of Haiku, 1973; Summer Morn... Winter Weather: Poems 'Twist Haiku and Senryu, 1975; The Withered Leaf: A Medley of Haiku and Snryu, 1982. Fiction: A Cup of Fury, 1962; Jared, 1986. Non-Fiction: The Eternal Solitary: A Study of Joseph Conrad, 1960; Joseph Conrad: Commemorative Essays (ed.), 1975; Conrad and Shakespeare and Other Essays, 1976; Joseph Conrad, 1982; Joseph Conrad: Comparative Essays, 1994. Other: Trans, radio plays, and screenplays. *Contributions to:* Journals, reviews, and periodicals. *Honours:* Alfred Jurzykowski Foundation Award, 1967; Joseph Fels Foundation Award, 1970; National Endowment for the Humanities Grant, 1985; Gold Award, Worldfest International Film Festival, 1993. *Memberships:* Haiku Society of America; Joseph Conrad Society of America; MLA; Polish Institute of Arts and Sciences. *Address:* Lake Illyria, 490 Route 299 W, New Paltz, NY 12561, USA.

GIOIA, (Michael) Dana; b. 24 Dec. 1950, Los Angeles, CA, USA. Writer; Poet. m. Mary Hiecke, 23 Feb. 1980, 3 s., 1 deceased. *Education:* BA, English, 1973, MBA, 1977, Stanford University; MA, Comparative Literature, Harvard University, 1975. *Publications:* The Ceremony and Other Stories, 1984; Daily Horoscope, 1986; Mottetti: Poems of Love (trans.), 1990; The Gods of Winter, 1991; Can Poetry Matter?, 1992; An Introduction to Poetry, 1994; The Madness of Hercules (trans. of Seneca), 1995; Interrogations at Noon (poems), 2001; Nosferatu (opera libretto), 2001; The Barrier of a Common Language: Essays on Contemporary British Poetry, 2002. Editor: Poems from Italy (with William Jay Smith), 1985; New Italian Poets (with Michael Palma), 1991; Formal Introductions: An Investigative Anthology, 1994; Certain Solitudes: Essays on the Poetry of Donald Justice (with William Logan), 1997; The Longman Anthology of Short Fiction: Stories and Authors in Context (with R. S. Gwynn), 2001; An Introduction to Poetry (with X. J. Kennedy), 2002; An Introduction to Fiction (with X. J. Kennedy), 2002; Literature: An Introduction to Fiction, Poetry and Drama (with X. J. Kennedy), 2002. *Contributions to:* Reviews, journals, and periodicals. *Honours:* Best of New Generation Award, Esquire, 1984; Frederick Bock Prize for Poetry, 1985. *Memberships:* Poetry Society of America, board; Wesleyan University Writers Conference. *Address:* 7190 Faught Rd, Santa Rosa, CA 95403, USA.

GIOSEFFI, Daniela; b. 12 Feb. 1941, Orange, New Jersey, USA. Poet; Writer. m. (1) Richard J Kearney, 5 Sept. 1965, divorced 1982, 1 d., (2) Lionel B Luttinger, 1986. *Education:* BA, Montclair State College; MFA, Drama, Catholic University of America. *Appointments:* Editorial Board, VIA, magazine of literature and culture at Purdue University; Skylands Writers Asscn Inc, pres.; Wise Womans Web, ed.-in-chief: Electronic magazine of Literature and Graphics; Ed. literary websites: njpoets.com, poetsusa.com, italianamericanwriters.com, gioseffi.com. *Publications:* The Great American Belly Dance (novel), 1977; Eggs in the Lake (poems), 1979; Earth Dancing: Mother Nature's Oldest Rite, 1980; Women on War, 1990; On Prejudice: A Global Perspective, 1993; Words, Wounds and Flowers, 1995; Dust Disappears by Carilda Oliver Labra, (trans.), 1995; In Bed With the Exotic Enemy: Stories and Novella, 1997; Going On (poems), 2000; Symbiosis (poems), 2002. *Contributions to:* Nation; Chelsea; Ambit; Poetry Review; Modern Poetry Studies; Anteus; The Paris Review; American Book Review; The Hungry Mind Review; Prairie Schooner; Independent publishers; Poetry East; The Cortland Review; Big City Lit. *Honours:* New York State Council on the Arts Award Grants in Poetry, 1972, 1977; American Book Award, 1990; PEN American Centre Short Fiction Award, 1990. *Memberships:* PEN; Acad. of American Poets; National Book Critics Circle; Poetry Society of America; Poets House, NYC. *Address:* 57 Montague St, 8G, Brooklyn Heights, New York, NY 11201, USA.

GIOVANNI, Nikki, (Yolande Cornelia Giovanni); b. 7 June 1943, Knoxville, Tennessee, USA. Poet; Writer; Prof. of Creative Writing. 1 s. *Education:* BA, Fisk University, 1967; School of Social Work, University of Pennsylvania, 1967; Columbia University, 1968. *Appointments:* Asst Prof., Queens College of the City University of New York, 1968; Assoc. Prof., Livingston College, Rutgers University, 1968–72; Founder-Publisher, Niktom Publishers, 1970–74; Visiting Prof., Ohio State University, 1984; Prof. of Creative Writing, College of Mount St Joseph on the Ohio, 1985–87; Prof., Virginia Polytechnic Institute and State University, 1987–. *Publications:* Poetry: Black Judgement, 1968; Black Feeling, Black Talk, 1968; Re: Creation, 1970; Poem for Angela Yvonne Davis, 1970; My House, 1972; The Women and the Men, 1975; Cotton Candy on a Rainy Day, 1978; Those Who

Ride the Night Winds, 1983; Blues: For All the Changes, 1999. Children's Poetry: Spin a Soft Black Dog, 1971; Ego Tripping and Other Poems for Young Readers, 1973; Vacation Time, 1980; Knoxville, Tennessee, 1994; Blues: For All the Changes, 1999. Non-Fiction: Gemini: An Extended Autobiographical Statement on My First Twenty-Five Years of Being a Black Poet, 1971; A Dialogue: James Baldwin and Nikki Giovanni, 1973; A Poetic Equation: Conversations Between Nikki Giovanni and Margaret Walker, 1974; Sacred Cows... and Other Edibles, 1988; Conversations with Nikki Giovanni, 1992; Racism 101, 1994. Editor: Night Comes Softly: An Anthology of Black Female Voices, 1970; Appalachian Elders: A Warm Hearth Sampler (with Cathee Dennison), 1991; Grandmothers: Poems, Reminiscences, and Short Stories About the Keepers of Our Traditions, 1994. Honours: Ford Foundation Grant, 1968; National Endowment for the Arts Grant, 1969; Hon. doctorates. Address: c/o Dept of English, Virginia Polytechnic Institute and State University, Blacksburg, VA 24063, USA.

GISCOMBE, C. S.; b. 30 Nov. 1950, Dayton, OH, USA. Poet; Writer; Prof. of English. m. Katharine Wright, 10 Aug. 1975, 1 d. Education: BA, State University of New York at Albany, 1973; MFA, Cornell University, 1975. Appointments: Faculty, Syracuse University, 1977, Cornell University, 1980–89; Prof. of English, Illinois State University, 1989–98, Pennsylvania State University, 1998–. Publications: Poetry: Postcards, 1977; Here, 1994; Giscombe Road, 1998; Two sections from 'Practical Geography: Five Poems', 2000; Inland, 2001. Other: Intro and Out of Dislocation, 2000. Contributions to: Periodicals. Honours: Creative Artists Public Service Fellowship, 1981–82; National Endowment for the Arts Fellowship, 1986–87; New York Foundation for the Arts Fellowship, 1988; Carl Sandburg Award for Poetry, 1998. Membership: Poets and Writers. Address: c/o Dept of English, Pennsylvania State University, State College, PA 16804, USA.

GITIN, David; b. 19 Dec. 1941, Buffalo, New York, USA. Teacher; Poet. Education: BA, Philosophy, State University of New York, Buffalo; MA, English, San Francisco State University; Further studies in English, University of Wisconsin-Madison. Appointments: Teacher at various universities and colleges. Publications: Guitar Against the Wall, 1972; City Air, 1974; Ideal Space Relations, 1976; Legwork, 1977; This Once: New and Selected Poems, 1965–1978, 1979; Vacuum Tapestries: Poems From Haight Ashbury Notebooks, 1967–69, 1981; Fire Dance, 1989. Contributions to: Over 200 periodicals. Honours: Arx Foundation Award, 1970; Doris Green Award, 1975. Address: PO Box 505, Monterey, CA 93942, USA.

GIULIANI, Marilyn Kay; b. 16 March 1948, Missoula, Montana, USA. Teacher; Poet. Education: BA, Education; MEd, University of Montana. Publication: In the Shadow of Your Wings. Contributions to: Silver Wings; Poetic Eloquence; National Library of Poetry; Cappers Magazine; Montana Poet Magazine; The Apostolic Crusade. Membership: Society of American Poets. Address: PO Box 1812, Missoula, MT 59806, USA.

GIUSTI, Mariangela; b. 26 Aug. 1951, Empoli, Italy. Teacher; Journalist; Poet. m. 8 Dec. 1973, 1 s., 2 d. Education: Science Degree, Philosophy, 1975, Master's Degree, 1977, University of Florence. Appointments: Teacher of Italian Literature, Secondary Upper School, 1980–88; Teacher, Dept of Science Education, University of Florence, 1989–. Publications: Fare on Non Fare, 1975; Ripartire la Successione, 1977; Il Tempo non E'Uno, 1982; Il Cavaliere, 1983; Poeti Della Toscana, 1985; Poesie di Dogana, 1988. Contributions to: Lettera; Silarus; Collettivo; Erba D'Arno; Poesia Nuova; Ann Magazine. Honours: Honourable Mention, Acad. of Science, Turin, 1980; Second Prize, Letterasio Trinita, 1981; Premio Estate Locridea, 1986; Premil il Portone Pisa, 1988; Premio Naz e Montale, Rome, 1988. Membership: International Centre Eugenio Monale, Rome. Address: Viale Giotto 12, 50053 Empoli, Florence, Italy.

GIVANS, Raymond John; b. 20 July 1951, Portadown, County Armagh, Northern Ireland. Secondary School Teacher; Poet. m. Eileen Watt, 2 Aug. 1978, 2 s. Education: BEd, Queen's University, Belfast, 1974; MEd, University of Bath, Avon, England, 1977. Contributions to: Poetry Ireland; Studies: An Irish Quarterly; Irish Press; Cyphers; Connacht Tribune; Salmon; Threshold; Orbis; Acumen; Other Poetry; Poetry Nottingham; Poetry Post; Germination, Canada. Memberships: Poetry Ireland, Dublin; Postal, Vers Poets, St Albans, England. Address: 26 Kingsland Park, Dundonald, Belfast BT5 7FB, Northern Ireland.

GJESSING, Ketil; b. 18 Feb. 1934, Oslo, Norway. Gunvor. Poet. Education: Magister artium and candidatus philologiae; University of Oslo, 1965. Appointments: Teacher, Atlantic College (now United World College of the Atlantic), 1965–66; Dramaturg at the Radio Drama Dept, Norwegian Broadcasting Corp, 1966–99; Adviser, Klassisk Musikkmagasion, 2001. Publications: 10 collections of poetry including: Dans på roser og glass (Dance on Roses and Glass), 1996. Contributions to: Aftenposten (newspaper); Vinduet; Samtiden (magazines); others. Honour: Gyldendals Prize, 1983; Språklig Samlings Litteraturpris, 1996. Memberships: Norwegian Authors' Asscn; Norwegian Authors' Centre; Norwegian Trans' Asscn. Address: Dannevigsvn 12, 0463 Oslo, Norway.

GJUZEL, Bogomil; b. 9 Feb. 1939, Cacak, Yugoslavia. Poet. m. (1) Alexandra Judith Rainsford, 24 Dec. 1966, divorced 1987, 1 d., (2) 1 s. Education: BA, English, University of Skopje, 1963; University of Edinburgh, 1965. Appointments: Dramaturgist, Dramski Theatre, Skopje, 1966–70, 1985–99; Programme Dir, 1971–73, Acting Dir, 1999–, Struga Poetry Evenings; Mem., International Writing Programme, Iowa City, 1972–73; Ed.-in-Chief, Nase pismo, 1995–. Publications: Mead, 1962; Alchemical Rose, 1963; Libation Bearers, 1965; Odysseus in Hell, 1969; The Well in Time, 1972; The Wheel of the Year, 1977; Reality is All, 1980; A State of Siege, 1981; The Empty Space, 1982; Darkness and Milk, 1986; Destroying the Wall, 1989; Selected Poems, 1991; Naked Life, 1994; Chaos, 1998; She/It, 2000; A Bundle (essays), 2002; Survival, 2003. Honours: Brothers Miladinov Awards, Best Book of the Year in Macedonian, 1965, 1972; Aleksa Santic Yugoslav Award, 1985–88. Memberships: Macedonian PEN; Macedonian Writers Union; Independent Writers of Macedonia, first chair. Address: Ivan Cankar 113a, Vlae, 1000 Skopje, Republic of Macedonia. E-mail: stpoetry@unet.com.mk.

GLANG, Gabriele; b. 18 July 1959, Arlington, Virginia, USA. Ed.; Graphic Designer; Poet. m. Rudi Ebert, 21 May 1992, 2 s. Education: BA, English, George Mason University, 1979; Certificate, Publications Specialist Program, George Washington University, 1982. Publications: Roundelay, 1981; Free State: A Harvest of Maryland Poets, 1989; Stark Naked on a Cold Irish Morning, 1990; Wem ich eines Vorschlag machen dürfte, 1996. Contributions to: Anthologies, reviews and journals. Honours: Dr Antonio J Waring Jr Memorial Prize, 1978; John Ciardi Memorial Prize for Poetry, National Society of Arts and Letters, 1987; Eve of St Agnes' Poetry Prize, Negative Capability, 1987; Virginia Center for the Creative Arts Fellowship, 1988. Address: Schwarzwiesenstrasse 48, D 73312 Geislingen, Germany.

GLASER, Elton Albert II; b. 13 Jan. 1945, New Orleans, LA, USA. Distinguished Prof. Emeritus of English; Poet; Ed. m. Helen Christensen, 14 Aug. 1968, 1 s., 1 d. Education: BA, English, 1967, MA, English, 1969, University of New Orleans; MFA, Creative Writing, University of California, Irvine, 1972. Appointments: Instructor of English, Western Michigan University, 1968–70; Instructor, Prof. of English, University of Akron, 1972–99; Dir, University of Akron Press, 1993–99; Ed., Akron Poetry Series. Publications: Relics, 1984; Tropical Depressions, 1988; Color Photographs of the Ruins, 1992; Winter Amnesties, 2000; Pelican Tracks, 2003. Contributions to: Poetry; Georgia Review; Iowa Review; Poetry Northwest; North Dakota Quarterly; Southern Poetry Review; Parnassus; Poems in The Best American Poetry, 1995, 1997, 2000. Honours: Theodore Roethke Award, Poetry Northwest, 1979; Hart Crane Memorial Poetry Award, Icon, 1981; Ohio Arts Council Fellowships, 1983, 1987, 1995, 2000; National Endowment for the Arts Grants, 1983, 1990; Iowa Poetry Prize, 1987; Poetry Prize, Louisiana Literature, 1989; Nancy Dasher Award, College English Asscn of Ohio, 1990; Randall Jarrell Poetry Prize, North Carolina Writers' Network, 1990; Sarah Henderson Hay Prize, Pittsburgh Quarterly, 1995; Poetry Prize, Sow's Ear Poetry Review, 1996; Poetry Prize, Louisiana Literature, 1996; Ohioana Poetry Award, 1996; Poetry Award, The Ledge, 1996; Ed.'s Award in Poetry, Florida Review, 1998; Crab Orchard Award, 2002. Address: Dept of English, University of Akron, Akron, OH 44325, USA.

GLASER, Isabel Joshlin; b. 7 June 1929, Birmingham, AL, USA. Writer; Former Teacher. m. M W Glaser, 7 Nov. 1953, 1 s., 1 d. Education: BA, Peabody College, Vanderbilt University, 1951; Postgraduate Work, several universities and colleges. Publications: Old Visions... New Dreams, 1977; Deams of Glory: Poems Starring Girls, 1995. Contributions to: Southern Poetry Review; Wind Literary Magazine; Cricket; Cicada. Honours: Hungry Mind Review's Children's Book of Distinction Finalist; Poetry Society of Tennessee, Poet Laureate, 1990–91; Golden Owl Award, Pen Women. Membership: Society for Children's Writers and Illustrators. Address: 5383 Mason Road, Memphis, TN 38120-1707, USA. Telephone: (901) 685-5597. E-mail: isajglaser@yahoo.com.

GLASER, Michael Schmidt; b. 20 March 1943, Chicago, IL, USA. Prof. of English; Poet. m. 8 May 1976, 3 s., 2 d. Education: BA, Denison University, 1965; MA, 1967, PhD, 1971, Kent State University. Appointments: Asst, Assoc., Full Prof., Dir of Festival and Poets and Poetry, Co-ordinator of Oxford Programme, St Mary's College of Maryland; Chair., Division of Arts and Letters; Poet-in-the-School, Maryland State Arts Council. Publications: Marmalade, 1976; On Being a Father, 1987; A Lover's Eye, 1991; In the Men's Room and Other Poems, 1997. Editor: The Cooke Book: A Seasoning of Poems, 1987; Weavings 2000: The Maryland Millennial Anthology, 2000. Contributions to: Periodicals and newspapers, including: American Scholar; New Letters; Prairie Schooner; Christian Science Monitor; First Things; Anthologies, including: Unsettling America; Outsiders; Light Gathering Poems. Honours: Chester H. Jones National Poetry Prize Competition, 1983; Publications Prize, 1987; Columbia Merit Award for Service to Poetry, 1995; Winner, Painted Bride Quarterly Competition, 1996; Homer Dodge Endowed Award for Excellence in Teaching; Individual Artist's Award in Poetry, Maryland State Arts Council, 1997. Memberships: Writers Centre, Bethesda; Poets and Writers; Ebenezer Cooke Poetry Society. Address: PO Box 1, St Mary's City, MD 20686, USA.

GLASGOW, Eric; b. 10 June 1924, Leeds, Yorkshire, England. University Teacher (retd); Poet. *Education:* MA, St John's College, Cambridge, 1948; PhD, Victoria University of Manchester, 1951. *Appointments:* Teacher, 1954–70; Tutor in History, Open University, 1974–78; Tutor in History and English, London University External Students, 1984–2002. *Publications:* Liverpool People, 1992; Some Liverpool Lives, 1996. *Contributions to:* Contemporary Review; Year's Poetry; Library Review; Library History; Biblio; Victorians Institute Journal. *Address:* Flat 37 Clairville, 21 Lulworth Rd, Birkdale, Southport, Merseyside PR8 2FA, England.

GLASSCOTT, Alison Julia; b. 25 May 1973, Reading, Berkshire, England. Creative Writing Tutor; Poet. 1 s., deceased 1993, 1 d. *Education:* St Joseph's, Reading, 1983–91. *Appointment:* Creative Writing Tutor, Chiltern Edge Adult Education Centre, Oxfordshire, 1991–92. *Publication:* The Fragile Continent, 1991. *Contributions to:* Rialto; Bare Bones; Weyfarers; Haiku Quarterly; Editions of Word for Word; Shell Young Poet of The Year Collection, 1990. *Honours:* Joint Second Prize, Shell Young Poet of the Year Award, 1990; Joint First Prize, Charterhouse International Poetry Competition, 1991. *Memberships:* Berkshire Literature Festival, steering committee, 1990–92; Thin Raft Poetics, co-leader, 1990–92; National Poetry Society. *Address:* Omey Island, Claddaghduff, County Galway, Ireland.

GLEE, Glenna; b. 1 Feb. 1918, Anderson, IN, USA. Poet. m. Robert Paul Williamson, 24 Dec. 1939, 2 s. *Education:* General, 1970, Master, 1972, International Graphonanalysis Society. *Publications:* Kerosene Lamp, 1978; A Bard's Eye View of Graphoanalysis, 1981; Mindwind, 1983; After All, 1990; Poems from a Hospital Bed, 1997. *Contributions to:* Anthologies and periodicals. *Honour:* Poet Laureate, Indiana State Federation of Poetry Clubs, 1980–81. *Memberships:* Anderson Poetry Corner; Indiana State Federation of Poetry Clubs, pres., 1998–99; Kentucky State Poetry Society; Poets Study Club of Terre Haute. *Address:* 808 E 32nd St, Anderson, IN 46016, USA.

GLEN, Duncan Munro; b. 11 Jan. 1933, Cambuslang, Lanarkshire, Scotland. Prof. (retd); Poet; Writer. m. Margaret Eadie, 4 Jan. 1958, 1 s., 1 d. *Education:* Edinburgh College of Art. *Appointments:* Lecturer to Principal Lecturer, South Lancashire University, 1965–78; Prof. and Head of the Dept of Visual Communication, Nottingham Trent University, 1972–87; Ed., Akros, 1965–83, Zed 2 O, 1991–. *Publications:* Hugh MacDiarmid and the Scottish Renaissance, 1964; Selected Essays of Hugh MacDiarmid (ed.), 1969; In Appearances: A Sequence of Poems, 1971; The Individual and the Twentieth Century Scottish Literary Tradition, 1971; Buits and Wellies: A Sequence of Poems, 1976; Gaitherings (poems), 1977; Realities (poems), 1980; The Turn of the Earth: A Sequence of Poems, 1985; The Autobiography of a Poet, 1986; Tales to Be Told, 1987; European Poetry in Scotland (ed.), 1990; Selected Poems, 1965–90, 1991; The Poetry of the Scots, 1991; Hugh MacDiarmid: Out of Langhoom and Into the World, 1992; Echoes: Frae Classical and Italian Poetry, 1992; The Bright Writers' Guides to Scottish Culture, 1995; A Nation in a Parish: A New Historical Prospect of Scotland, 1995; Splendid Lanarkshire, 1997; Selected New Poems 1987–1996, 1998; Illustrious Fife, 1998; A New History of Cambuslang, 1998; Selected Scottish and Other Essays, 1999; Scottish Literature: A New History from 1299 to 1999, 1999; Printing Type Designs: A New History from Gutenburg to 2000, 2001; Winter: A Poem , and Other Verses by James Thomson (ed.), 2002; Historic Fife Murders, 2002. *Contributions to:* Numerous journals and magazines. *Honours:* Special Award for Services to Scottish Literature, Scottish Arts Council, 1975; Howard Sergeant Poetry Award, 1993; Hon. Doctorate, Paisley University, 2000. *Membership:* Chartered Society of Designers, fellow. *Address:* 33 Lady Nairn Ave, Kirkcaldy, Fife KY1 2AW, Scotland.

GLISSANT, Édouard; b. 21 Sept. 1928, Sainte-Marie, Martinique. Distinguished Prof.; Writer; Dramatist; Poet. *Education:* DPhil, 1953, State Doctorate, 1977, Sorbonne, Université de Paris; Musée de l'homme, Paris. *Appointments:* Instructor in Philosophy, Lycée des Jeunes Filles, Fort-de-France, Martinique, 1965; Founder, 1967, Dir, 1967–78, Institut Martiniquais d'Etudes, Fort-de-France; Co-Founder, ACOMA Review, 1970; Ed., UNESCO, Paris, France, 1981–88; Distinguished Prof. and Dir of Center for French and Francophone Studies, Louisiana State University, Baton Rouge, USA, 1988–. *Publications:* Poetry: Un champ d'îles, 1953; La terre inquiète, 1954; Les Indes: Poèmes de l'une et l'autre terre, 1955; Le sel noir, 1959; Le sang rivé, 1960; Poèmes, 1963; Boises, 1979; Pays rêvé, pays réel, 1985; Fastes, 1992. Non-Fiction: Soleil de la conscience, 1956; L'intention poétique, 1969; Le discours antillais, 1981, English trans. as Caribbean Discourse: Selected Essays, 1989; Poétique de la relation, 1990. Fiction: La Lézarde, 1958; Le quatrième siècle, 1964; Malemort, 1975; La case du commandeur, 1981; Mahagony, 1987; Tout-monde, 1993. Play: Monsieur Toussaint, 1961, revised version, 1978. *Honours:* Ordre des Francophones d'Amérique, Québec; Prix Rénaudot, 1958; Prix Charles Veillon, 1965; Award, 12th Putterbaugh Conference, Norman, Oklahoma, 1989; Hon. LittD, York University, 1989; Roger Callois International Prize, 1991. *Address:* 213 Prescott, Baton Rouge, LA 70803, USA.

GLOVER, Jon Martin; b. 13 May 1943, Sheffield, Yorkshire, England. Prof.; Poet. m. Elaine Alice Shaver, 3 Oct. 1965, 2 d. *Education:* BA, English and Philosophy, 1965, MPhil, Philosophy, 1969, University of Leeds. *Appointment* Prof. and Head of Division of Humanities, Bolton Institute of Higher Education *Publications:* The Grass's Time, 1970; The Wall and the Candle, 1982; Ou Photographs, 1986; The Penguin Book of First World War Prose (co-ed.), 198 To the Niagara Frontier (poems), 1994. *Contributions to:* Stand; PN Revie Acumen; Poet's Voice; Notes and Queries. *Address:* 3 Lightburne Ave, Bolto Lancashire, England.

GLÜCK, Louise (Elisabeth); b. 22 April 1943, New York, NY, USA. Autho Poet; Prof. m. (1) Charles Hertz, divorced, (2) John Dranow, 1 Jan. 197 divorced 1996, 1 s. *Education:* Sarah Lawrence College, 1962; Columb University, 1963–66, 1967–68. *Appointments:* Artist-in-Residence, 1971–7 Faculty Mem., 1973–74, Goddard College, Plainfield, Vermont; Poet-i Residence, University of North Carolina at Greensboro, 1973; Visiting Pro University of Iowa, 1976–77, Columbia University, 1979, University California at Davis, 1983; Ellison Prof. of Poetry, University of Cincinnat 1978; Faculty Mem., Board Mem., MFA Writing Program, Warren Wilso College, Swannoa, North Carolina, 1980–84; Holloway Lecturer, University California at Berkeley, 1982; Scott Prof. of Poetry, 1983, Senior Lecturer i English, part-time, 1984–97, Parrish Prof., 1997–, Williams College Williamstown, MA; Regents Prof. of Poetry, University of California at L Angeles, 1985–88; Phi Beta Kappa Poet, 1990, Visiting Prof., 1995, Harvar University; Hurst Prof., Brandeis University, 1996; Special Consultant i Poetry, Library of Congress, Washington, DC, 1999–2000; Board Chancellors, Acad. of American Poets, 1999–. *Publications:* Poetry: Firstborr 1968; The House on the Marshland, 1975; The Garden, 1976; Descendin Figure, 1980; The Triumph of Achilles, 1985; Ararat, 1990; The Wild Iri 1992; Proofs and Theories: Essays on Poetry, 1994; The First Four Book Poems, 1995; Meadowlands, 1996; Vita Nova, 1999; The Seven Ages, 200 *Contributions to:* Many anthologies and periodicals. *Honours:* Acad. American Poets Prize, 1967; Rockefeller Foundation Grant, 1968–6 National Endowment for the Arts Fellowships, 1969–70, 1979–80, 1988–8 Eunice Tietjens Memorial Prize, 1971; Guggenheim Fellowships, 1975–7 1987–88; Vermont Council for the Arts Grant, 1978–79; American Acad. an Institute of Arts and Letters Award, 1981; National Book Critics Circle Awar 1985; Melville Cane Award, Poetry Society of America, 1985; Sara Teasda Memorial Prize, Wellesley College, 1986; Co-recipient, Bobbitt National Priz 1992; Pulitzer Prize in Poetry, 1993; William Carlos Williams Award, 199 LLD, Williams College, 1993; Poet Laureate of Vermont, 1994; PEN/Marth Albrand Award, 1995; LLD, Skidmore College, 1995; LLD, Middlebury Colleg 1996; New York Magazine Award in Poetry, 1999; Ambassador Award, Englis Speaking Union, 1999; Bollingen Prize, 2001. *Memberships:* American Acad. Arts and Sciences, fellow; PEN; American Acad. and Institute of Arts an Letters; Acad. of American Poets, board of chancellors, 1999–. *Address:* 1 Ellsworth Park, Cambridge, MA 02139, USA.

GLYNN, Martin Roy, (Dr G); b. 26 July 1957, Nottingham, England. Write Poet. 2 d. *Education:* Certificate of Education. *Appointment:* Literatur Development Office, Nottingham, 1989–90. *Publications:* Poetic Vibration 1981; Fuel, 1982; True Reflections, 1983; Subtle Racist Top 10, 1984; D Rachet a Talk, 1985; So You Say, 1989; Angola, 1990; Rage/Warzone, 199 *Contributions to:* You'll Love This Stuff, 1986; Dub Poetry, 1986; Too Littl Toffee, 1989; Poem Street, 1990. *Memberships:* Board, East Midlands ALT! Equity Actors Union. *Address:* 195 Rock St, Pitsmoor, Sheffield, Yorkshire, S 9JF, England.

GODBERT, Geoffrey Harold; b. 11 June 1937, Manchester, England. Poet. s., 1 d. *Education:* Royal Manchester College of Music, Performanc *Publications:* Ides of March, 1975; The Lover Will Dance Incredibly, 198 Still Lifes (co-author), 1983; Journey to the Edge of Light, 1985; The Brookl Bridge, 1985; The Theatre of Decision, 1985; For Now (co-author), 1991; Ar You Interested in Tattooing?, 1996; I Was Not, Was Not, Mad Today, 199 *Contributions to:* Anthologies and magazines. *Address:* 5 Berners Mansion 34–36 Berners St, London W1P 3DA, England.

GODBOUT, Jacques; b. 27 Nov. 1933, Montréal, QC, Canada. Author; Poe Filmmaker. m. Ghislaine Reiher, 31 July 1954, 2 c. *Education:* BA, 1953, MA 1954, University of Montréal. *Appointments:* Lecturer, 1969, Writer-in Residence, 1991–92, University of Montréal; Visiting Lecturer, University c California at Berkeley, 1985. *Publications:* Fiction: L'aquarium, 1962; L couteau sur la table, 1965, English trans. as Knife on the Table, 1968; Salu Galarneau!, 1967, English trans. as Hail Galarneau!, 1970; D'Amour, PQ, 1972 L'île au dragon, 1976, English trans. as Dragon Island, 1979; Les tetes Papineau, 1981; Une histoire americaine, 1986, English trans. as a American Story, 1988; Le temps des Galarneau, 1993. Poetry: Carton-pate 1956; Les pavés secs, 1958; La chair est un commencement, 1959; C'est l chaude loi des hommes, 1960; La grande muraille de Chine (with J R Colombo 1969. Essays: Le réformiste, 1975; Le murmure marchand, 1984; L'écran d bonheur, 1990; Journal: Ecrivain de province, 1991. Other: Many films Honours: Prix France-Canada, 1962; Prix de l'Académie Française, 196 Governor-General's Award for Fiction, 1968; Various film prizes. *Address:* 81 Pratt, Montréal, QC H2V 2T7, Canada.

GODEL, Vahé; b. 16 Aug. 1931, Switzerland. Poet. 2 s. *Education:* Licencié es Lettres, University of Geneva. *Publications:* Signes Particuliers, 1969; Cendres Brûlantes, 1970; L'Oeil Étant la Fenêtre de L'Ame, 1972; Poussières, 1977; Du Même Désert à la Même Nuit, 1978; Obscures Besognes, 1979; Qui Parle? Que Voyez-vous?, 1982; Faits et Gestes, 1983; L'Heure d'Or, 1985; Les Frontières Naturelles, 1986; Quelque Chose Quelqu'un, 1987; Exclu Inclus, 1988; La Chute des Feuilles, 1989; Vous, 1990; Ov, 1992; Le Goût de la Lecture, 1992; De plus Belle, 1993; Arthur Autre, 1994; Le Congrès d'Automne, 1995; P.S., 1995; Un Homme errant, 1997; Zones frontieres, 1998; L'Errance la Dérive la Trace, 1998; Ruelle des Oiseaux, 1999; Ici (Ailleurs), 2000; Fragments d'une Chronique (Genève-Paris-Arménie, 2001; Le Sentiment de la Nature, 2002. *Contributions to:* Ecritures; Présages; Revue de Belles-Lettres; Europe; Cahiers de la Différence; Cahiers du Centre International d'Etude Poétiques; Le Journal des Poètes. *Memberships:* Maison Internationale de la Poésie; Groupe d'Olten; World Acad. of Arts and Culture; Société Civile des Auteurs Multimedia; PEN Club. *Address:* 25 Ave des Cavaliers, 1224 Chêne Bougeries, Geneva, Switzerland.

GOEDICKE, Patricia (Patricia Ann McKenna); b. 21 June 1931, Boston, Massachusetts, USA. Prof. of Creative Writing; Poet. m. Leonard Wallace Robinson, 3 June 1971. *Education:* BA, Middlebury College, 1953; MA, Ohio University, 1965. *Appointments:* Lecturer in English, Ohio University, 1963–68, Hunter College, 1969–71; Assoc. Prof. of Creative Writing, Instituto Allende, 1972–79; Visiting Writer-in-Residence, Kalamazoo College, 1977; Guest Faculty, Writing Programme, Sarah Lawrence College, 1980; Visiting Poet-in-Residence, 1981–83, Assoc. Prof., 1983–90, Prof. of Creative Writing, 1990–, University of Montana. *Publications:* Between Oceans, 1968; For the Four Corners, 1976; The Trail That Turns on Itself, 1978; The Dog That Was Barking Yesterday, 1980; Crossing the Same River, 1980; The King of Childhood, 1984; The Wind of Our Going, 1985; Listen Love, 1986; The Tongues We Speak: New and Selected Poems, 1989; Paul Bunyan's Bearskin, 1992; Invisible Horses, 1996; As Earth Begins to End, 2000. *Contributions to:* Reviews, journals, and periodicals. *Honours:* National Endowment for the Arts Fellowship, 1976; Pushcart Prize, 1977–78; Honourable Mention, Arvon International Poetry Competition, 1987; Honourable Award, Memphis State Review, 1988; Research Grant, 1989, Distinguished Scholar, 1991, University of Montana; Residency, Rockefeller Center, Bellaggio, Italy, 1993; Distinguished Alumna, Ohio University, 2002; Ohioana Poetry Award, 2002. *Memberships:* Acad. of American Poets; Associated Writing Programs; Poetry Society of America. *Address:* 310 McLeod Ave, Missoula, MT 59801, USA.

GOING, Dale Frances; b. 5 Jan. 1953, Troy, New York, USA. Poet; Book Artist. m. Philip Going, 23 June 1979. *Education:* BA, English, Manhattanville College, 1975; MA, English and Creative Writing, San Francisco State University, 1993. *Appointments:* Proprietor, Em Press, 1990–; Co-Founder, Rooms, quarterly literary magazine, 1993–. *Publications:* As/Of the Whole, 1990; Or Less, 1991; She Pushes With Her Hands, 1992; The View They Arrange, 1994. *Contributions to:* How; Rooms; Talisman; Active in Airtime; Lyric and Poetry Flash; Volt; Fish Dance; Ink; Artists Dialogue. *Honours:* San Francisco State University Poetry Chapbook Competition, 1990; Diane Wood Middlebrook Fellowship, 1994; California Arts Council Fellowship, 1997. *Address:* 541 Ethel Ave, Mill Valley, CA 94941, USA.

GOLDBARTH, Albert; b. 31 Jan. 1948, Chicago, IL, USA. Poet; Writer; Asst Prof. of Creative Writing. *Education:* BA, University of Illinois, 1969; MFA, University of Iowa, 1971; University of Utah, 1973–74. *Appointments:* Instructor, Elgin Community College, IL, 1971–72, Central YMCA Community College, Chicago, 1971–73, University of Utah, 1973–74; Asst Prof., Cornell University, 1974–76; Visiting Prof., Syracuse University, 1976; Asst Prof. of Creative Writing, University of Texas at Austin, 1977–. *Publications:* Poetry: Under Cover, 1973; Coprolites, 1973; Opticks: A Poem in Seven Sections, 1974; Jan. 31, 1974; Keeping, 1975; A Year of Happy, 1976; Comings Back: A Sequence of Poems, 1976; Curve: Overlapping Narratives, 1977; Different Flashes, 1979; Eurekas, 1980; Ink Blood Semen, 1980; The Smugglers Handbook, 1980; Faith, 1981; Who Gathered and Whispered Behind Me, 1981; Goldbarth's Book of Occult Phenomena, 1982; Original Light: New and Selected Poems 1973–1983, 1983; Albert's Horoscope Almanac, 1986; Arts and Sciences, 1986; Popular Culture, 1989; Delft: An Essay Poem, 1990; Heaven and Earth: A Cosmology, 1991; Across the Layers: Poems Old and New, 1993; The Gods, 1993. Fiction: Marriage and Other Science Fiction, 1994. Essays: A Sympathy of Souls, 1990; Great Topics of the World: Essays, 1994. Editor: Every Pleasure: The 'Seneca Review' Long Poem Anthology, 1979. *Honours:* Theodore Roethke Prize, 1972; Ark River Review Prizes, 1973, 1975; National Endowment for the Arts Grants, 1974, 1979; Guggenheim Fellowship, 1983. *Address:* c/o Dept of English, University of Texas at Austin, Austin, TX 78712, USA.

GOLDBERG, Barbara June; b. 26 April 1943, Wilmington, DE, USA. Writer; Poet; Ed. m. (1) J. Peter Kiers, 1963, divorced 1970, (2) Charles Goldberg, 1971, divorced 1990, 2 s. *Education:* BA, Mt Holyoke College, 1963; MA, Yeshiva University, 1969; MEd, Columbia University, 1971; MFA, American University, 1985. *Appointments:* Dir, Editorial Board, The World Works publishers, 1987–; Exec. Ed., Poet Lore, 1990–. *Publications:* Berta Broad Foot and Pepin the Short; Cautionary Tales; The Stones Remember.

Contributions to: American Scholar; Antioch Review; New England Review; Bread Loaf Quarterly. *Honours:* Work in Progress Grant; National Endowment for the Arts Fellowship; Armand G. Erpf Award; Writter Bynner Foundation Award. *Memberships:* Poetry Society of America; Poets and Writers; Poetry Committee, Greater Washington Area. *Address:* 6623 Fairfax Rd, Chevy Chase, MD 20815, USA.

GOLDENBERG, Iosif Sukharovich; b. 1 May 1927, Ukraine. Poet. *Education:* PhD, Philology, Karkov State University, 1949. *Publications:* Tavolga; Nad Propast'yu v Tishi; Zalozhniki Zaveta; Izbrannoe; 1996 God; Svet I Ten'; Serdoliki; Iz Pushchino s Lyubov'yu; Kashtanovye Svechi. *Contributions to:* Galilee, 1998; Raduga, 2001. *Address:* Building AB-1, Apt 43, 142292 Pushchino, Moscow Region, Russia.

GOLDENSOHN, Barry Nathan; b. 26 April 1937, New York, NY, USA. Prof. of English; Poet; Writer. m. Lorraine Goldensohn, 5 Aug. 1956, 1 s., 1 d. *Education:* BA, Philosophy, Oberlin College, 1957; MA, English Literature, University of Wisconsin, 1959. *Appointments:* Teacher, Goddard College, 1965–77; Visiting Prof., Iowa Writers' Workshop, 1970–72; Dean, School of Humanities and Arts, 1977–81, Prof. of Literature and Writing, 1980–82, Hampshire College; Prof. of English, Skidmore College, 1982–. *Publications:* Gulliver's Travels, 1961; Saint Venus Eve, 1972; Uncarving the Block, 1978; The Marrano, 1988; Dance Music, 1992; East Long Pond, 1997; The Work of Ending (online), 2002. *Contributions to:* Poetry; Agenda; Salmagundi; Yale Review; Massachusetts Review; Southern Review; New Republic. *Honours:* MacDowell Fellowships; Vermont Council for the Arts Poetry Award, 1977; 6 Faculty Research Grants, Skidmore College; Residency Fellowships, MacDowell, Millay and Djerassi Foundations; Poetry Award, New York Foundation for the Arts, 1985. *Address:* 11 Seward St, Saratoga Springs, NY 12866, USA. *Website:* www.skidmore.edu/academics/english/bgoldens.

GOLDIE, Joyce Marion (Ortolan); b. 11 Feb. 1930, London, England. Poet. m. Derek George Goldie, 8 Aug. 1953, 3 d. *Contributions to:* 6 anthologies, 1990–96, and other publications; Channel 4 TV, 1991, 1993. *Honours:* Runner-Up, York and District Poetry Competition, 1990; First Prize, Kym Whybrow Memorial Competition; Certificate of Merit, London Calling. *Address:* Ivy Cottage, Portloe, Truro, Cornwall TR2 5RG, England.

GOLDLEAF, Steven; b. 18 June 1953, New York, NY, USA. Prof.; Writer; Poet. m. Carolyn Yalkut, 23 Aug. 1981, divorced 1996, 2 d. *Education:* AB, Columbia University, 1976; MA, Johns Hopkins University, 1980; PhD, University of Denver, 1985. *Appointments:* Asst Prof., Le Moyne College; Lecturer, State University of New York, Albany; Asst Prof., Assoc. Prof., 1998–, Pace University. *Contributions to:* Denver Quarterly; Spitball; Northeast Journal. *Honours:* American Acad. of Poets Award, 1984; Spitball Honorable Mention, 1985. *Address:* Dept of English, Pace University, 1 Pace Plaza, NY 10038, USA.

GOLDSCHMIDT, Allan David; b. 7 July 1944, USA. Poet; Artist. *Education:* AAS, Bronx Community College, 1965; BA, Social Work, Empire State College, State University of New York, 1985. *Appointments:* Staff Art Ed., Asst Ed., Medicinal Purposes; Asst Poetry Ed., New Press. *Publications:* Of Sun and Wind, 1994; Wood Winds, 1996. *Contributions to:* Reviews, journals and quarterlies. *Honours:* Second Place, French Poetry Recital Contest, Bronx Community College, 1964; Talent Contest Winner in Poetry and Flute, New York University, 1994; Honourable Mention, Tom Catterson's Stop Short Poetry Contest, 1996. *Address:* 33-06 34th Ave 2A, Long Island, NY 11106, USA.

GOLDSTEIN, Laurence (Alan); b. 5 Jan. 1943, Los Angeles, CA, USA. Prof. of English; Writer; Poet; Ed. m. Nancy Jo Copeland, 28 April 1968, 2 s. *Education:* BA, University of California at Los Angeles, 1965; PhD, Brown University, 1970. *Appointments:* Instructor, Brown University, 1968–70; Asst Prof., 1970–78, Assoc. Prof., 1978–85, Prof. of English, 1985–, University of Michigan; Ed., Michigan Quarterly Review, 1977–. *Publications:* Ruins and Empire: The Evolution of a Theme in Augustan and Romantic Literature, 1977; Altamira, 1978; The Automobile and American Culture (ed. with David L Lewis), 1983; The Flying Machine and Modern Literature, 1986; The Three Gardens, 1987; Writers and Their Craft: Short Stories and Essays on the Narrative (ed. with Nicholas Delbanco), 1991; Seasonal Performances: A Michigan Quarterly Review Reader (ed.), 1991; The Female Body: Figures, Styles, Speculations (ed.), 1992; The American Poet at the Movies: A Critical History, 1994; The Male Body: Features, Destinies, Exposures (ed.), 1994; Cold Reading, 1995; The Movies: Texts, Receptions, Exposures (ed. with Ira Konigsberg), 1996; Robert Hayden: Essays on the Poetry (ed. with Robert Chrisman), 2001. *Contributions to:* Books, anthologies, reviews, and journals. *Honours:* Distinguished Service Award, University of Michigan, 1977; University of Michigan Press Book Award, 1995. *Address:* c/o Dept of English, University of Michigan, Ann Arbor, MI 48109, USA.

GOLDSTEIN-JACKSON, Kevin Grierson; b. 2 Nov. 1946, Windsor, Berkshire, England. Writer; Poet. m. Mei Leng Ng, 6 Sept. 1975, 2 d. *Education:* BA, Reading University; MPhil, Southampton University. *Contributions to:* Hampshire Poets; Sandwiches; Bogg; Isthmus; Bare Bones;

Contemporary Poets; Doors; Envoi; Haiku Quarterly; Iota; Krax; Ellery Queen's Mystery Magazine; Kangaroo; Tidepool; New England Review; Presence. *Memberships:* Writers' Guild; Society of Authors; Poetry Society. *Address:* c/o Alcazar, 18 Martello Rd, Branksome Park, Poole, Dorset BH13 7DH, England.

GOLDSTONE, Tim John; b. 2 June 1958, Hertford, England. Writer; Poet. *Education:* BA, English and History, St David's University College, Lampeter, Wales. *Contributions to:* Reviews, journals, radio and television. *Honours:* Radio Times Comedy Award, 1991; Runner-Up, Bridport Prize, 1994. *Address:* Clifton House, Penllyn, Cilgerran, Cardigan, Pembrokeshire SA43 2RZ, Wales.

GOLDSWORTHY, Peter; b. 12 Oct. 1951, Minlaton, SA, Australia. Poet; Writer. m. Helen Louise Whardall, 1972, 1 s., 2 d. *Education:* BMed, BSurg, 1974, University of Adelaide. *Publications:* Number Three Friendly Street: Poetry Reader (co-ed.), 1979; Readings from Ecclesiastes, 1982; This Goes With This, 1988; Maestro (novel), 1989; This Goes With That: Poems 1974–2001, 2001. *Honours:* Commonwealth Poetry Prize, 1982; South Australia Poetry Award, 1988.

GOMBOS, Susan; b. 11 Dec. 1952, New York, NY, USA. Family Therapist; Poet. m. 6 Aug. 1972, 1 s., 1 d. *Education:* Masters in Social Work, 1975; Advanced Certificate, Family Therapy, 1989. *Appointments:* Clinical Private Practice; New York City Board of Education; Jewish Board of Family and Children's Services. *Publication:* Twilight, Afternoon, Night, 1997. *Contributions to:* Visions International; Feelings; Reflections; Womens' News, Westchester County. *Honour:* First Place, Town of Greenburgh Poetry Contest, 1992. *Memberships:* Hudson Valley Writers Center; Poetry Society of America. *Address:* 22 Treetop Lane, Dobbs Ferry, NY 10522, USA.

GOMEZ, Jewelle Lydia; b. 11 Sept. 1948, Boston, Massachusetts, USA. Writer; Poet. *Education:* BA, Northeastern University, 1971; MS, Columbia Graduate School of Journalism, 1973. *Appointments:* Assoc., 1984–91, Dir of Literature, 1991–93, New York State Council on the Arts; Adjunct Prof., New College of California, 1994, Menlo College, CA, 1994; Writer-in-Residence, California Arts Council, 1995–96. *Publications:* The Gilda Stories, 1991; Forty-Three Septembers, 1993; Oral Tradition, 1995. *Contributions to:* Various publications. *Memberships:* American Center of Poets and Writers; PEN. *Address:* c/o Frances Goldin Literary Agency, 57 E 11th St, New York, NY 10003, USA.

GOMEZ, Mercedes Estíbaliz; b. 24 Sept. 1932, Santurce, Vizcaya, Spain. Housewife. m. Mario Angel Marrodán, 1 s., 1 d. *Education:* Colegio Santa Ana de Portugalete; Artistic Studies, private acad. *Publications:* Poetry: Estrofas de una mujer; El alma iluminada; El limbo dorado; El parnaso intimo; Los dones del azar; Los caudales del leudo. Contributons to: Numerous poetry journals in Spain and abroad; Various anthologies; Trans into Italian. *Honours:* Poetry Prizes; Abanto y Zierbana; Amigos de Galicia (de Sestao); Poesía Mínima (de Baracalo). *Memberships:* Asociación Artística Vizcaina; A Garibaldi, Portugal; Asociación Colegial de Escritore de España; AGA. *Address:* Cristóbal Mello 7-20, Izqda Apdo 16, 48920 Portugalete, Vizcaya, Spain.

GONZALEZ, Anson (John); b. 21 Aug. 1936, Trinidad and Tobago. Educator; Poet; Ed. m. Sylvia Figuero, 6 Aug. 1961, 2 d. *Education:* Teachers Diploma, 1959; BA, 1971; MPhil, 1982. *Appointments:* Primary School Teacher, 1953–71; Teachers College Lecturer, 1971–72; Educational Publisher, 1972–86; School Supervisor, 1986–89; University Lecturer, 1988; Sixth Form School Principal, 1991–96. *Publications:* Score (with V D Duestel), 1972; Love Song of Boysie, 1974; Collected Poems 1969–1979, 1979; Postcards and Haiku, 1984; Moksha: Poems of Light and Sound, 1988; Merry-Go-Round and Other Poems, 1992. *Contributions to:* The New Voices; Bim; Now; Guardian; Express; Caribbean Poetry Now; West Indian Poetry; Crossing Water; Lion Book of Christian Poetry; Education Journal. *Honours:* Writer of the Year, 1988; Wutt Award for Services to Poetry Day, 1990; Certificate of Merit, University of Miami Caribbean Writers Institute, 1996. *Memberships:* International Poetry Society, fellow; World Literary Acad., life fellow; Writers Union of Trinidad and Tobago, founding mem. and pres., 1988–92. *Address:* PO Box 3254, Diego Martin, Trinidad and Tobago.

GONZALEZ-MARINA, Jacqueline; b. 19 Feb. 1935, Madrid, Spain (British citizen). Lecturer; Poet; Writer; Ed. m. (1), 2 s., 1 d., (2) Desmond Savage, 22 Dec. 1982. *Education:* BA, Modern Philology, 1959, MA, Modern Philology, 1962, University of Barcelona. *Appointments:* Lecturer, University of Barcelona, 1960–68, St Godrics College, London, 1970–91; Ed., Dandelion Magazine, 1979–, Fern Publications, 1979–, The Student Magazine; Lecturer in Modern Languages, American Intercontinental University, London, 1994–; Interpreter, Artist and Designer for Network Arts, Northampton, and Northamptonshire Council. *Publications:* Dieciocho Segundos, 1953; Tijeras Sin Filo, 1955; Antología de Temas, 1961; Short Stories, 1972; Brian Patten, 1975; A Survival Course, 1975; Once Poemas, 1977; Poesía Andaluza, 1977; Adrian Henri, 1980; Historias y conversaciones, 1995; Mediterranean Poetry (bilingual anthology), 1997; Conversaciones en Español, 1998; Historias de ayer y de hoy, 2002. *Contributions to:* Anthologies, including The Millennium Anthology, and international magazines and newspapers. *Honour:* Royal

Academician, Royal Acad. of St Telmo, Malaga, Spain, 1975. *Memberships:* Society of Women Writers and Journalists, London; Historical Assoc Saxoferreo, Córdoba, Spain, 1997–; ATENEO, Alicante; Spanish Trans Society, Madrid, 1995. *Address:* 'Casa Alba', 24 Frosty Hollow, Eas Hunsbury, Northants NN4 0SY, England.

GOODALL, David Arthur; b. 3 May 1945, England. Teacher (retd); Poet. m Vivien Ann, 15 Feb. 1975, 3 d. *Education:* BA, 1966; Diploma in Education 1967; Fellow, College of Preceptors, 1976; ACP Diploma, 1983. *Appointments* Teacher of History and English, Rhyddings School, Oswaldtwistle, Lancs 1967–77; Head of History, Willingdon School, East Sussex, 1977–92 *Contributions to:* Education Today; Odyssey; New Hope International; Staple Outposts; Envoi; Acumen; Frogmore Papers; Pennine Platform; Symphony Third Half; Moonstone; First Time; Poetry Nottingham; Poetry Monthly; Exile Iota; Nutshell; Cobweb; Aeirings; Purple Patch; White Rose; Poetry Digest Hybrid; Peace and Freedom; Eastern Rainbow; Pause; Firing Squad; Poetry Nottingham International; BBC Radio and TV. *Address:* 64 Hawkswood Dr. Hailsham, East Sussex BN27 1UR, England.

GOODISON, Lorna (Gaye); b. 1 Aug. 1947, Kingston, Jamaica. Poet; Painter Writer. *Education:* Art schools, Kingston and New York, 1967–69 *Appointments:* Teacher of Creative Writing, USA and Canada. *Publications* Poetry: Poems, 1974; Tamarind Season, 1980; I Am Becoming My Mother 1986; Heartease, 1988; To Us All Flowers Are Roses, 1992; Selected Poems 1992. Short Stories: Baby Mother and the King of Swords, 1989. *Honours* Institute of Jamaica Centenary Prize, 1981; Commonwealth Poetry Prize, 1986 *Address:* 8 Marley Close, Kingston 6, Jamaica.

GOODMAN, Jonathan; b. 17 Jan. 1931, London, England. Author; Poet Publisher; Ed. *Appointments:* Theatre Dir and Television Prod., various companies, United Kingdom, 1951–64; Dir, Anmbar Publications Ltd London, 1967–; Gen. Ed., Celebrated Trials Series, David & Charles (Publishers) Ltd, Newton Abbott, Devon, 1972–. *Publications:* Martinee Idylls (poems), 1954; Instead of Murder (novel), 1961; Criminal Tendencies (novel) 1964; Hello Cruel World Goodbye (novel), 1964; The Killing of Julia Wallace 1969; Bloody Versicles, 1971; Posts-Mortem, 1971; Trial of Ian Brady and Myra Hindley (ed.), 1973; Trial of Ian Ruth Ellis (ed.), 1975; The Burning of Evelyn Foster, 1977; The Last Sentence (novel), 1978; The Stabbing of George Harry Storrs, 1982; Pleasure of Murder, 1983; Railway Murders, 1984; Who-He, 1984 Seaside Murders, 1985; The Crippen File (ed.) 1985; The Underworld (with I Will), 1985; Christmas Murders (ed.) 1986; The Moors Murders, 1986; Acts of Murder, 1986; Murder in High Places, 1986; The Slaying of Joseph Bowne Elwell, 1987. *Address:* 43 Ealing Village, London W5 2LZ, England.

GOONERATNE, Malini Yasmine; b. 22 Dec. 1935, Colombo, Sri Lanka Writer; Poet; Ed.; Emeritus Prof. m. Brendon Gooneratne, 31 Dec. 1962, 1 s. 1 d. *Education:* BA, Ceylon, 1959; PhD, English Literature, Cambridge University, 1962; DLitt, English and Commonwealth Literature, Macquarie University, Australia, 1981. *Appointments:* Dir, Post-Colonial Literature and Language Research Centre, 1988–93, Personal Chair in English Literature 1991–99, Emeritus Prof., 1999–, Macquarie University. *Publications:* English Literature in Ceylon 1815–1878: The Development of an Anglo-Ceylonese Literature, 1968; Jane Austen, 1970; Word Bird, Motif, 53 Poems, 1971; The Lizard's Cry and Other Poems, 1972; Alexander Pope, 1976; Diverse Inheritance: A Personal Perspective on Commonwealth Literature, 1980 6000 Foot Death Dive (poems), 1981; Silence, Exile, and Cunning: The Fiction of Ruth Prawer Jhabvala, 1983; Relative Merits (memoir), 1986 Celebrations and Departures (poems), 1991; A Change of Skies (novel), 1991 The Pleasures of Conquest (novel), 1995; This Inscrutable Englishman: Sir John S'Oyly 1774–1824 (co-author), 1999; Masterpiece and Other Stories, 2002 Celebrating Sri Lankan Women's English Writing, 2002. *Contributions to* Various publications. *Honours:* Order of Australia, 1990; Marjorie Barnard Literary Award for Fiction, 1992; Several research and travel grants. *Memberships:* Australian Society of Authors; Fédération Internationales des Langues et Littératures Modernes, vice-pres., 1990–96; International Asscn of University Prof.s of English; Jane Austen Society of Australia, patron; New South Wales Writers Centre; South Asian Studies Asscn of Australia. *Address:* c/o Dept of English, College of Humanities, Macquarie University, North Ryde, NSW 2109, Australia.

GOORHIGIAN, Martin; b. 1 July 1932, New York, NY, USA. Teacher; Poet. m. Louise Zarifian, 23 June 1963, 1 s., 1 d. *Education:* BA, University of Connecticut, 1954; MS, University of Bridgeport, 1966. *Publications:* Ani, 1989; Between Ice Floes, 1990; The Road Narrows, 1991. *Contributions to:* Meriden Record Journal; High Tide; Sound and Waves of West Haven; Laurels; Hob Nob; Prophetic Voices; Parnassus; Night Roses; Wide Open; Plowman; Tucumcari. *Honour:* Fourth Prize for Poetry, Sparrowgrass Poetry Forum, 1991. *Address:* 12 Cardinal Dr., Milford, CT 06460, USA.

GORDON, Coco; b. 16 Sept. 1938, Italy. Artist; Poet; Publisher. 1 s., 2 d. *Publications:* Raw Hands and Bagging, 1978; Water Mark Papers, 1979; Loose Pages (co-author), 1983; Opaque Glass (co-author), 1985; Things in Loops and Knots I Pick From the Ground Become a Small Italian Opera, 1987; Acquaterra, MetaEcology and Culture, 1995; New Observations May, 1995;

SuperSky Woman: La Caduta (V-idea), 1995. *Contributions to:* Various anthologies, reviews and magazines. *Honours:* Residencies, Banff Centre, 1991, Djerassi Foundation, 1996; Grant, Harvestworks, 1993. *Address:* 138 Duane St, New York, NY 10013, USA.

GORRELL, Dena Ruth; b. 8 June 1932, Loyal, Oklahoma, USA. Writer; Poet. m. John S Gorrell, 14 Nov. 1953, 1 s., 1 d. *Education:* Assoc. in Commerce, Oklahoma State University, 1952; Diploma, Institute of Children's Literature, 1989. *Publications:* Truths, Tenderness and Trifles, 1986; Sunshine and Shadow, 1989. *Contributions to:* Edmond Sun; Living Streams; Poets at Work; Muse; Wide Open Magazine; Odessa Poetry Review; Independent Review. *Honours:* Grand Prize, 1989, Second Prize, 1989, International Society for the Advancement of Poetry; First Prize, Creative Endeavors Spring Contest, 1990, Cimarron Valley Writers, 1990, Poets at Work, 1990, Tulsa Tuesday Writers, 1990; Second Prize, Poetry Press, 1990. *Memberships:* Poetry Society of Oklahoma; Acad. of American Poets; International Society for the Advancement of Poetry; National Federation of State Poetry Societies; National League of American Pen Women. *Address:* 14024 Gateway Dr., Edmond, OK 73013, USA.

GORZELSKI, Roman; b. 12 April 1934, Luck, Poland. Journalist; Writer; Poet; Dramatist; Trans. *Education:* College, Łódź, 1954; University of Warsaw, 1962. *Publications:* Three Blueses, 1964; Metamorphosis, 1973; The Town and the Poem, 1975; Pronunciation of Words, 1977; Stadium Full of Sun, 1980; Return to the Point, 1981; The Bitter Man, 1982; The Pichna River, 1986; The Warta River, 1988; The Grain of Anxiety, 1991; The Thoughts in Section, 1995; The Fears of Cupido, 1996; Self-Portrait from Memory, 1999. Other: Plays, aphorisms, trans, etc. *Contributions to:* Various publications. *Honours:* Nike Warszawska Award, 1969; Polish Culture Award of Merit, 1977; Award of Merit, Łódź. *Memberships:* Asscn of Authors and Composers; Polish Society of Authors; Union of Polish Writers. *Address:* ul Chodkiewicza 6, 94-028 Łódź, Poland.

GOTO, Takahiko, (Naoya Shibasawa); b. 8 Dec. 1940, Japan. Poet. m. Yasuko, 18 Nov. 1966, 1 d. *Education:* BA, Education, University of Gifu, 1963. *Publications:* The Summer I Found, 1965; The Jumper Over the Butterfly, 1985; A Crawfish in the Rain, 1993. *Contributions to:* Mainichi; Shi to Shisoh. *Honour:* International Poets Acad. Award, 1995. *Membership:* International Writers and Artists Asscn, USA. *Address:* 1512-50 Masaki, Gifu City 502-0857 Japan.

GOUDGE, John Barnaby; b. 9 July 1921, India. Trans.; Poet. m. 20 Sept. 1952, 2 d. *Education:* MA Honours, Modern History, Trinity College, Oxford, 1946–48; Barrister at Law, Middle Temple, 1957. *Publications:* Selected Poems of Baudelaire (trans.), 1979; October Sun, 1985. Translator: Le Crève-Coeur, 1990, Les Yeux d'Elsa, 1992; Le Nouveau Crève-Coeur, 1994; Le Christ aux Oliviers and Les Chimères, 1996, Les Fleurs du Mal, 1998. *Contributions to:* Outposts; TLS; Orbis; Envoi; South East Arts Review; Poetry World; Oxford; The Oldie. *Honours:* First Prize for Verse Trans., Yeats Club, 1987; Skoob Books Index on Censorship Poetry Competition, 1988; First Prize for a Rhymed Poem, Envoi, 1991; First Prize, Oldie Competition, 1995. *Address:* Capers, Mutton Hill, Dormansland, Lingfield, Surrey RH7 6NP, England.

GOULD, Alan David; b. 22 March 1949, London, England. Poet; Novelist. m. Anne Langridge, 17 Jan. 1984, 2 s. *Education:* BA, Honours, 1971; DipEd, 1974. *Appointments:* Creative Fellow, Australian National University, 1978; Writer-in-Residence, Geelong College, 1978, 1980, 1982, 1985, Australian Defence Forces Acad., 1986, Lincoln Humberside Arts Centre, 1988. *Publications:* Poetry: Icelandic Solitaries, 1978; Astral Sea, 1981; The Pausing of the Hours, 1984; The Twofold Place, 1986; Years Found in Likeness, 1988; Former Light (selected poems), 1992; Momentum, 1992; Mermaid, 1996; Dalliance and Scorn, 1999; A Fold in the Light, 2001. Fiction: The Man Who Stayed Below, 1984; The Enduring Disguises, 1988; To The Burning City, 1991; Close Ups, 1994; The Tazyrik Year, 1998; The Schoonermaster's Dance, 2000. Essays: The Totem Ship, 1996. *Contributions to:* Various Australian publications. *Honours:* New South Wales Premier's Prize for Poetry, 1981; Prizes for Fiction, 1985, 1992; Philip Hodgins Memorial Medal, 1999; Royal Blind Society Audio Book of the Year, 1999; Co-winner, Courier-Mail Book of the Year, 2001; Co-winner, A.C.T. Book of the Year, 2001. *Address:* 6 Mulga St, O'Connor, ACT 2602, Australia.

GOUMAS, Yannis; b. 20 Oct. 1935, Athens, Greece. Poet. *Education:* Hove College, 1946–49; Seaford College, 1949–53; University of Southampton School of Navigation, 1953–54. *Publications:* Take One, 1967; Sorry, Wrong Number, 1973; Athens Blues, 1974; Signing On, 1977; Thorns in Each Other's Flesh, 1977; Athenians Go to Work, 1978; Past the Tollgate, 1983; The Silence of Others, 1990. *Contributions to:* Poetry Review; London Magazine; Mundus Artium; Malahat Review; Prism International; Tribune; Shenandoah; Iron; Prospice; Contemporary Literature in Translation; Waves; Samphire; Sycamore Review; Oasis; Verse; Second Aeon; Xenia; Eureka; Kudos; Poesie Vivante; Roots; and others. *Membership:* Poetry Society. *Address:* J G Goumas Shipping Co SA, 1–3 Filellinon St, GR 185-36 Piraeus, Greece.

GOURLAY, Caroline; b. 10 Aug. 1939, London, England. Poet. m. Simon Gourlay, 17 May 1967, 3 s. *Education:* Royal Acad. of Music, 1957–60; LRAM, 1960. *Appointment:* Ed., Blithe Spirit, Journal of the British Haiku Society, 1998–2000. *Publications:* Crossing the Field, 1995; Through the Café Door, 1999; Reading All Night, 1999; Against the Odds, 2000. *Contributions to:* Envoi; Poetry Wales; New Welsh Review; Iron; Haiku Quarterly; Outposts; Blithe Spirit, Journal of the British Haiku Society, Tanka Splendor. *Honour:* James Hackett Award, 1996. *Membership:* Writers Union of Wales. *Address:* Hill House Farm, Knighton, Powys LD7 1NA, Wales. *E-mail:* gourlay@maryvale.wyenet.co.uk.

GOWLAND, Mary Lee, (Mary Lee); b. 6 May 1949, Los Angeles, CA, USA. Poet. *Publications:* Tender Bough, 1969; Hand in Hand, 1971; The Guest, 1973; Snow Summits in the Sun, 1989; Remembering August, 1994. *Contributions to:* Poetry LA; Sierra Star; Mountain Times; Blue Window; Onthebus; Women in Photography; Brentwood Bla Bla; Poetry Motel; Fat Tuesday; B-City; Impetus; Random Weirdness. *Memberships:* California Poets in the Schools; Presenting Arts to Children in Elementary School. *Address:* 49386 Cavin Lane, Coarsegold, CA 93614, USA.

GRABILL, James Roscoe; b. 29 Nov. 1949, Ohio, USA. Teacher; Poet; Essayist; Ed. *Education:* National Presbyterian Scholar, College of Wooster, 1967–70; BFA, Bowling Green State University, 1974; MA, Graduate Fellow, 1984, MFA, Graduate Fellow, 1988, Colorado State University. *Appointments:* Producer, Radio Transmissions, 1979–80; Ed., Leaping Mountain Press, 1985–89; Poetry Co-Ordinator, Power Plant Arts Centre, 1986–88; Dir, Oregon Writers' Workshop, 1990–91; Educator, Clackamas Community College. *Publications:* One River, 1974; Clouds Blowing Away, 1976; To Other Beings, 1981; In the Coiled Light, 1985; The Poem Rising Out of the Earth and Standing Up in Someone, 1994; Through the Green Fire, 1994; Through the Green Fire (essays), 1995; Listening to the Leaves Form (poems), 1997; An Indigo Scent After the Rain (poems), 2002. *Contributions to:* East West Journal; Sun; A Magazine of Ideas; Kayak; Granite; Momentum; Caliban; Another Chicago Magazine; Mid-American Review; Poetry Northwest; New Letters; NRG; Intro; Bloomsbury Review; Colorado Review; Germination; Ed.'s Choice II; Writers' Forum; Willamette Week; Quartet; New Orleans Review; Common Review; South Dakota Review; Barnabe Mountain Review; Willow Springs; Talking River Review; Pemmican. *Honour:* Oregon Book Award for Poetry, 1995. *Address:* 9835 SW 53rd Ave, Portland, OR 97219, USA. *E-mail:* jimg@clackamas.cc.or.us.

GRABOWSKA-STEFFEN, Alicja Wanda. See: PATEY-GRABOWSKA, Alicja Wanda.

GRACE, Eugene Vernon; b. 12 Dec. 1927, Jackson, Tennessee, USA. Physician; Poet. Divorced, 1 s., 3 d. *Education:* BS, MD, University of Michigan, Ann Arbor; Ophthalmology Speciality, University of North Carolina. *Appointments:* Private Practice in Ophthalmology; Foreign Expert, American Poetry and Literature, Guangzhou Teachers College, China, 1988–89. *Publications:* The Most Beautiful Love Poetry in the English Language, 1984; Sonnets from the Portuguese, 1984; Mash, 1985; Central America, 1985; Poetry of a Bible Reader, 1985; Vision of Job, 1985; Life's Too Short and the Weeks are Too Long, 1986; Wildness, 1986; From These Stones, 1986; Cave, 1988; American Sonnets, The First Century, 1989; The China Chronicle, 1990. *Contributions to:* Poetry Under the Stars, 1988; England and Roanoke, A Collection of Poems, 1548–1987; Durham Morning Herald; People's Daily, Beijing; Inkling; Writer's Journal; Parnassus; Z Miscellaneous; Corradi. *Memberships:* North Carolina Poetry Society; North Carolina Writers Conference, pres., 1976; Friday Noon Poets, founder, 1978. *Address:* 911 Broad St, Durham, NC 27705, USA.

GRAHAM, Henry; b. 1 Dec. 1930, Liverpool, England. Lecturer; Poet. *Education:* Liverpool College of Art, 1950–52. *Appointment:* Poetry Ed., Ambit, London, 1969–. *Publications:* Good Luck to You Kafka/You'll Need It Boss, 1969; Soup City Zoo, 1969; Passport to Earth, 1971; Poker in Paradise Lost, 1977; Europe After Rain, 1981; Bomb, 1985; The Very Fragrant Death of Paul Gauguin, 1987; Jardin Gobe Avions, 1991; The Eye of the Beholder, 1997; Kafka in Liverpool, 2002. *Contributions to:* Ambit; Transatlantic Review; Prism International Review; Evergreen Review; Numerous anthrologies worldwide. *Honours:* Arts Council Literature Awards, 1969, 1971, 1975. *Address:* Flat 5, 23 Marmion Rd, Liverpool L17 8TT, England.

GRAHAM, Jorie; b. 9 May 1951, New York, NY, USA. Poet; Teacher. m. James Galvin. *Education:* BFA, New York University, 1973; MFA, University of Iowa, 1978. *Appointments:* Poetry Ed., Crazy Horse, 1978–81; Asst Prof., Murray State University, KY, 1978–79, Humboldt State University, Arcata, CA, 1979–81; Instructor, Columbia University, 1981–83; Staff, University of Iowa, 1983–. *Publications:* Hybrids of Plants and of Ghosts, 1980; Erosion, 1983; The End of Beauty, 1987; The Best American Poetry (ed. with David Lehman), 1990; Region of Unlikeness, 1991; Materialism, 1993; The Dream of the Unified Field, 1995; Errancy, 1997; Swarm, 1999. *Honours:* American Acad. of Poets Award, 1977; Young Poets Prize, Poetry Northwest, 1980; Pushcart Prizes, 1980, 1982; Ingram Merrill Foundation Grant, 1981; Great Lakes Colleges Asscn Award, 1981; American Poetry Review Prize, 1982; Bunting

Fellow, Radcliffe Institute, 1982; Guggenheim Fellowship, 1983–84; John D. and Catherine T. MacArthur Foundation Fellowship, 1990; Pulitzer Prize in Poetry, 1996. *Address:* c/o Dept of Creative Writing, University of Iowa, Iowa City, IA 52242, USA.

GRAHN, Judy, (Judith Rae Grahn); b. 28 July 1940, Chicago, IL, USA. Poet; Writer. *Education:* BA, San Francisco State University. *Appointments:* Teacher, Stanford University, New College of California; Lecturer and Poetry Reader, many US colleges and universities. *Publications:* The Common Women Poems, 1969; Edward the Dyke and Other Poems, 1971; A Woman is Talking to Death, 1974; She Who, 1977; The Work of a Common Woman, 1978; The Queen of Wands, 1982; The Queen of Swords, 1987; March to the Mother Sea, 1990. *Contributions to:* Many anthologies and other publications. *Honours:* Poem of the Year, American Poetry Review, 1979; National Endowment for the Arts Grant, 1980; American Book Award, 1983; Ed.'s Choice, 1984. *Address:* c/o Beacon Press, 25 Beacon St, Boston, MA 01208, USA.

GRANT, James Russell; b. 14 Dec. 1924, Bellshill, Scotland. Physician; Poet. m. (1) Olga Zarb, 23 March 1955, divorced, 1 s., (2) Susan Tierney, 22 April 1994. *Education:* Medal in English, Hamilton Acad., 1941; MB CHb, University of Glasgow, 1951; Institute of Psychiatry, University of London, 1954–55. *Appointments:* Various medical posts. *Publications:* Hyphens, 1959; Poems, 1959; The Excitement of Being Sam, 1977; Myths of My Age, 1985; In the '4 Cats', 1997; Jigsaw and the Art of Poetry, 2002. *Contributions to:* Glasgow University Magazine; Botteghe Oscure; Saltire Review; Prism International; Fiddlehead; Chapman; Ambit; BBC; CBC; Agenda; Edinburgh Review; Anthologies: Oxford Book of Travel Verse, 1985; Christian Poetry, 1988; Book of Machars, 1991. *Honours:* Third Prize, Scottish Open Poetry Competition, 1976; Third Prize, UK National Poetry Competition. *Memberships:* National Poetry Society; British Medical Asscn. *Address:* 255 Creighton Ave, London N2 9BP, England.

GRASS, Günter (Wilhelm); b. 16 Oct. 1927, Danzig, Germany (now Gdańsk, Poland). Author; Dramatist; Poet; Artist. m. (1) Anna Schwartz, 1954, divorced 1978, 3 s., 1 d., (2) Utte Grunert, 1979. *Education:* Conradinum, Danzig; Kunstakademie, Düsseldorf; Höchschule für Bildende Künste, Berlin. *Publications:* Beritten, hin und zurück (play), 1954; Hochwasser (play), 1954; Die Vorzüge der Windhühner (poems, prose and drawings), 1956; Die bösen Köche (play), 1957; Noch zehn Minuten bis Buffalo (play), 1957; Onkel, Onkel (play), 1958; Die Blechtrommel (novel), 1959, English trans. as The Tin Drum, 1962; Gleisdreieck (poems and drawings), 1960; Katz und Maus (novella), 1961, English trans. as Cat and Mouse, 1963; Hundejahre (novel), 1963, English trans. as Dog Years, 1965; Die Plebejer proben den Aufstand: Ein Deutsches Trauerspiel (play), 1966; Ausgefragt (poems and drawings), 1967; Örtlich betäubt (novel), 1969; Aus dem Tagebuch einer Schnecke, 1972; Der Butt (novel), 1977, English trans. as The Flounder, 1978; Das Treffen in Telgte (fiction), 1979, English trans. as The Meeting in Telgte; Kopfgeburten oder Die Deutschen sterben aus (novel), 1980, English trans. as Headbirths, or the Germans Are Dying Out; Die Rättin (novel), 1986; Zungezeigen (diary), 1987; Werkausgabe, 10 vols, 1987–; Die Gedichte, 1955–1986, 1988; Deutscher Lastenausgleich: Wider das dumpfe Einheitsgebot, 1990; Vier Jahrzehnte: Ein Werkstattbericht (drawings and notes), 1991; Rede vom Verlust: Über den Niedergang der politischen Kultur im geiinten Deutschland, 1992; Unkenrufe (fiction), 1992, English trans. as The Call of the Toad, 1992; Studienausgabe, 12 vols, 1994; Ein weites Feld, 1995, English trans. as Too Far Afield, 2000; Fundsachen für Nichtleser (poems), 1997; Mein Jahrhundert, 1999, English trans. as My Century, 1999; Im Krebsgang: Eine Novelle, 2002. Other: Dokumente zur politischen Wirkung, 1972; Aufsätze zur Literatur, 1980; Zeichen und Schreiben, 1982; Widerstand lernen-Politische Gegenreden, 1980–83, 1984; On Writing and Politics, 1967–1983, 1985; Two States – One Nation?, 1990. *Honours:* Lyric Prize, Süddeutscher Rundfunk, 1955; Group 47 Prize, 1959; Literary Prize, Asscn of German Critics, 1960; Georg Büchner Prize, 1965; Hon. doctorates, Kenyon College, 1965, Harvard University, 1976; Theodor Heuss Prize, 1969; International Feltrinelli Prize, 1982; Karel Čopek Prize, 1994; Sonning Arts Prize, 1996; Thomas Mann Prize, 1996; Nobel Prize for Literature, 1999; Premio Príncipe de Asturias, 1999. *Memberships:* Akademie der Künste, Berlin, pres., 1983–86; American Acad. of Arts and Sciences. *Address:* Glockengiesserstr 21, 23552 Lübeck, Germany.

GRAVES, Michael David; b. 21 March 1951, New York, NY, USA. College Instructor; Poet. *Education:* BA, English, Hunter College, 1978; MA, English, Temple University, 1984. *Appointments:* Instructor, English, Pennsylvania State University, University Park State College, 1986–88; Adjunct Instructor, City University of New York, 1988–90, Borough of Manhattan Community College, 1988–92, Touro College, 1992–95. *Publication:* Outside St Jude's, 1990. *Contributions to:* Journal of Irish Literature; James Joyce Quarterly; Classical Outlook; European Judaism; Hollins Critic; Poetry Newsletter; Wind; Green's Magazine; Writer's Forum. *Membership:* Poetry Society of America. *Address:* 462 83rd St, New York, NY 11209, USA.

GRAVES, Roy Neil; b. 2 Feb. 1939, Medina, Tennessee, USA. Prof. of English; Poet; Writer. m. Sue Lain Hunt, 5 June 1965, divorced July 1982, 1 s., 2 d. *Education:* BA, Honours, English, Princeton University, 1961; MA, English, Duke University, 1964; DA, English, University of Mississippi, 1977.

Appointments: Asst Prof. of English, Lynchburg Branch, University of Virginia, 1965–67; Asst Prof., 1967–68, Assoc. Prof. of English, 1968–69, Central Virginia Community College, Lynchburg; Asst Prof., 1969–77, Assoc Prof., 1977–82, Prof. of English, 1982–, University of Tennessee at Martin. *Publications:* River Region Monographs: Reports on People and Popular Culture (ed.), 1975; 'Medina' and Other Poems, 1976; Hugh John Massey of the Royal Hall: The Lost Master Poet of Forteenth-Century England and the Lost Runes, 1977; Out of Tennessee: Poems, with an Introduction, 1977; The Runic 'Beowulf' and Other Lost Anglo-Saxon Poems, Reconstructed and Annotated, 1979; Shakespeare's Lost Sonnets: The 154 Runic Poems Reconstructed and Introduced, 1979; Somewhere on the Interstate (poems) 1987; Shakespeare's Sonnets Upside Down, 1995; Always at Home Here: Poems and Insights from Six Tennessee Poets (edited by Ernest Lee), 1997. *Contributions to:* Articles in reference works and scholarly journals; Poems in anthologies and periodicals. *Honours:* National Endowment for the Humanities Grant, 1975; Cunningham Teacher/Scholar Award, University of Tennessee at Martin, 1997; First Place, Southern Poets over 50 Competition, Kennesaw State University, 2002. *Address:* c/o Dept of English, University of Tennessee at Martin, Martin, TN 38238, USA. *E-mail:* ngraves@utm.edu. *Website.* www.utm.edu/ngraves.

GRAY, Alice Wirth; b. 29 April 1934, Chicago, IL, USA. Writer; Poet. m. Ralph Gareth Gray, 16 July 1954, 2 d. *Education:* BA, 1956, MA, 1960, University of California. *Publication:* What the Poor Eat, 1993. *Contributions to:* Reviews, journals and magazines. *Honours:* Illinois Arts Council Literary Award; Gordon Barber Memorial Award; Duncan Lawrie Award. *Memberships:* PEN Center USA West; Poetry Society of America. *Address:* 1001 Merced St, Berkeley, CA 94707, USA.

GRAY, James Martin; b. 30 Nov. 1930, Harrow, Middlesex, England (Canadian citizen). Poet. m. Hilary Parr, 1 Sept. 1961, 2 d. *Education:* MA, 1952, PhD, 1961, University of Edinburgh; Auditor (non-credit), University of Toronto, Canada, 1984–87. *Appointments:* Taught at McMaster University; University of Saskatchewan, Saskatoon; University of Guelph; University of Calgary; Simon Fraser University; Royal Roads Military College. *Publications:* Poems, 1958; Thro' the Vision of the Night (on Tennyson's Idylls of the King), 1980; Ed Tennyson's Idylls, 1983; Death of Villeneuve, 1992; Modigliani, 1997; Blues for Bird, 2001;. *Contributions to:* All About Jazz; Beatlick News; The Blindman's Rainbow; Cer*ber*us; Bouillabaisse; Event; Heeltap; Heliotrope; Home Planet News; The Iconoclast; Iota; Iota; Journal of Canadian Poetry; Lines Review; Links; Long Shot; Outposts; Poetry Canada Review; Poetry Monthly; Talus and Scree; Writer's Muse. *Honour:* First Prize, Seventh International Reuben Rose Poetry Competition, Tel-Aviv, Israel, 1996. *Membership:* Tennyson Society; League of Canadian Poets. *Address:* 918 Collinson St No. 305, Victoria, BC V8V 4V5, Canada.

GREALY, Lucy; b. 1963, Dublin, Ireland. Writer; Poet. *Education:* BA, Sarah Lawrence College, Bronxville, NY; MFA, University of Iowa. *Publications:* Autobiography of a Face, 1994, UK edn as In the Mind's Eye, 1994; As Seen on TV: Provocations, 2000. *Contributions to:* Periodicals. *Honours:* Fine Arts Work Centre Fellow, Provincetown, MA, 1993; National Magazine Award, 1994. *Address:* c/o Houghton Mifflin Co, 2 Park St, Boston, MA 02107, USA.

GREEN, Fay; b. 30 Jan. 1954, Kent, England. Solicitor; Poet; Breeder of Rare Sheep. *Education:* Law Society Examinations, Honours, 1978. *Publications:* Pure Green, 1990; Colours, 1991; No Telegrams, 1992; Fragile Ground, 1994; Poems-in-Law, 1995. *Contributions to:* Kent and Sussex Poetry Society Folio Competition Winners Anthologies; Law Society's Gazette; Angels of the Heart Anthology, 1992; Heart and Soul Anthology, 1996; Kentish Poems, 1996. *Honours:* Kent and Sussex Poetry Society, Commendations, 1992, 1994. *Membership:* Kent and Sussex Poetry Society; Federation of Kent Writers, committee, 1994–. *Address:* Charity Farmhouse, Pilgrims Way, Hollingbourne, Kent ME17 1RB, England.

GREENBERG, Alvin (David); b. 10 May 1932, Cincinnati, Ohio, USA. Prof. of English; Poet; Writer. m. (1), 2 s., 1 d., (2) Janet Holmes, 1993. *Education:* BA, 1954, MA, 1960, University of Cincinnati; PhD, University of Washington, 1964. *Appointments:* Faculty, University of Kentucky, 1963–65; Prof. of English, 1965–, Chair, Dept of English, 1988–93, Macalester College; Fulbright Lecturer, University of Kerala, India, 1966–67; Ed., Minnesota Review, 1967–71. *Publications:* Poetry: The Metaphysical Giraffe, 1968; The House of the Would-Be Gardner, 1972; Dark Lands, 1973; Metaform, 1975; In/ Direction, 1978; And Yet, 1981; Heavy Wings, 1988; Why We Live with Animals, 1990. Fiction: The Small Waves, 1965; Going Nowhere, 1971; The Invention of the West, 1976. Short Stories: The Discovery of America and Other Tales of Terror, 1980; Delta q, 1983; The Man in the Cardboard Mask, 1985; How the Dead Live, 1998. Play: A Wall, 1971. Opera Libretti: Horspfal, 1969; The Jealous Cellist, 1979; Apollonia's Circus, 1994. *Contributions to:* Many reviews, journals, and quarterlies. *Honours:* National Endowment for the Arts Fellowships, 1972, 1992; Bush Foundation Artist Fellowships, 1976, 1981; Associated Writing Programs Short Fiction Award, 1982; Nimrod/Pablo Neruda Prize in Poetry, 1988; Loft-McKnight Poetry Award, 1991, and Distinction in Poetry Award, 1994; Chelsea Award for Poetry, 1994; Minnesota State Arts Board Fellowship, 1996. *Address:* 1113 Lincoln Ave, St Paul, MN 55105, USA.

GREENBERG, Barbara (Levenson); b. 27 Aug. 1932, Boston, Massachusetts, USA. Poet; Writer; Teacher. 2 s. *Education:* BA, Wellesley College, 1953; MA, Simmons College, 1973. *Appointments:* Teacher of Creative Writing at various colleges and universities. *Publications:* Spoils of August (poems), 1974; Fire Drills (stories), 1982; The Never-Not Sonnets, 1989. *Address:* 770 Boylston St, No. 6-1, Boston, MA 02199, USA.

GREENE, Charles. See: COOPER, John Charles.

GREENE, Jeffrey; b. 22 May 1952, Norwalk, CT, USA. Prof. of English; Poet. *Education:* BA, Goddard College, 1975; MFA, University of Iowa, 1977; PhD, University of Houston, 1986. *Appointments:* Asst Prof., Assoc. Prof. of English, University of New Haven. *Publications:* To the Left of the Worshipper, 1991; Glimpses of the Invisible World in New Haven, 1995; American Spirituals, 1998; French Spirits, 2002. *Contributions to:* New Yorker; Nation; American Scholar; Iowa Review; Antioch Review; Sewanee Review; Ploughshares; Missouri Review; Prairie Schooner; Indiana Review; Seneca Review; Ohio Review; Denver Quarterly. *Honours:* Discovery, The Nation Award; Mary Roberts Rinehart Grant; Brazos Prize in Poetry; Second Prize, National Poetry Competition; Connecticut Commission on the Arts Grant; Randall Jarrell Prize, 1996; National Endowment for the Arts Fellowship, 1996; Samuel French Morse Prize, 1998. *Memberships:* Associated Writing Programs; Poetry Society of America. *Address:* 42 rue du Cherche Midi, 75006 Paris, France. *E-mail:* jeffrey.greene@wanadoo.fr.

GREENE, Jonathan (Edward); b. 19 April 1943, New York, NY, USA. Poet; Writer; Ed.; Publisher; Book Designer. m. (1) Alice-Anne Kingston, 5 June 1963, divorced, 1 d., (2) Dobree Adams, 23 May 1974. *Education:* BA, Bard College, 1965. *Publications:* The Reckoning, 1966; Instance, 1968; The Lapidary, 1969; A 17th Century Garner, 1969; An Unspoken Complaint, 1970; The Poor in Church, by Arthur Rimbaud (trans.), 1973; Scaling the Walls, 1974; Glossary of the Everyday, 1974; Peripatetics, 1978; Jonathan Williams: A 50th Birthday Celebration (ed.), 1979; Once a Kingdom Again, 1979; Quiet Goods, 1980; Idylls, 1983; Small Change for the Long Haul, 1984; Trickster Tales, 1985; Les Chambres des Poètes, 1990; The Man Came to Haul Stone, 1995; Of Moment, 1998; Inventions of Necessity: Selected Poems, 1998; Incidents of Travel in Japan, 1999; A Little Ink in the Paper Sea, 2001; Book of Correspondences, 2002. *Contributions to:* Anthologies, reviews, quarterlies, and journals. *Honours:* National Endowment for the Arts Fellowships, 1969, 1978; Southern Federation of State Arts Agencies Fellowship, 1977. *Address:* PO Box 475, Frankfort, KY 40602-0475, USA.

GREENHALGH, Christopher David; b. 17 March 1963, Bury, Lancashire, England. Poet. *Education:* BA, English, 1984, PhD, 1993, University of Hull; PGCE, English, University of East Anglia, 1987. *Appointment:* English Teacher, International School, Athens, 1987–90. *Contributions to:* Bete Noire Magazine; BBC Radio 4. *Honours:* First Prize, Thetford Open Poetry Competition, 1987; Gregory Award Winner, 1992. *Membership:* Poetry Society, 1990–. *Address:* 17 Kew Gardens, Penwortham, Preston, Lancashire PR1 0DR, England.

GREENING, John David; b. 20 March 1954, London, England. Teacher of English; Poet. m. Jane Woodland, 29 April 1978, 2 d. *Education:* BA, Honours, English, University College of Swansea, 1975; University of Mannheim, Germany, 1975–76; MA, Drama, University of Exeter, 1977. *Appointments:* Clerk to Hans Keller, BBC Radio 3; EFL Teacher in Aswan, Upper Egypt and then to Vietnamese Boat People in North-east Scotland; Teacher of English, Kimbolton School, Huntingdon. *Publications:* Westerners, 1982; Winter Journeys, 1984; Boat People, 1988; The Tutankhamun Variations, 1991; Fotheringhay and Other Poems, 1995; The Coastal Path, 1996; The Bocase Stone, 1996; Nightflights: New and Selected Poems, 1998; Gascoignes Egg, 1999. *Contributions to:* Observer; Spectator; Encounter; World and I; Stand; Poetry Review; Bananas; Rialto; Poetry Wales; Outposts; Poetry Durham; Oxford Poetry; Cumberland Poetry Review; PBS Anthology; Gregory Anthology. *Honours:* First prize, Alexandria International Poetry Prize, 1981; Scottish Arts Council Writer's Bursary, 1982; Top Prizes, Arvon/Sotheby's International Poetry Competition, 1987, 1989. *Membership:* Poetry Society. *Address:* 27 Hatchet Lane, Stonely, Huntingdon, Cambridgeshire PE18 0EG, England.

GREENLAW, Lavinia; b. 30 July 1962, London, England. Poet. *Education:* BA Honours, English, Kingston Polytechnic, 1983; Diploma in Printing and Production, London College of Printing, 1985. *Appointments:* British Council Fellow in Writing, Amherst College, Massachusetts, USA, 1995; Writer-in-Residence, Science Museum, London, 1995, Wellington College, 1996, Mishcon de Reya, solicitors, 1997–98; Fellow in Writing, Sevenoaks School, 1997. *Publications:* The Cost of Getting Lost in Space (pamphlet), 1991; Love from a Foreign City (pamphlet), 1992; Night Photograph, 1993; A World Where News Travelled Slowly, 1997. *Contributions to:* TLS; London Review of Books; New Yorker; Paris Review; Poetry Review; Verse; New Statesman; The Observer; American Poet. *Honours:* Eric Gregory Award, 1990; Arts Council of England Writers Award, 1995; Forward Prize for Best Poem of the Year, 1997. *Address:* c/o Faber and Faber, 3 Queen Sq., London, WC1N 3AU, England.

GREENWALD, Roger (Gordon); b. Neptune, New Jersey, USA. University Teacher; Poet; Writer; Trans. *Education:* BA, English, City College, New York City, 1966; Graduate Studies, English, New York University, 1966–67; MA, English, 1969, PhD, English, 1978, University of Toronto. *Appointments:* Tutor, Senior Lecturer, 1969–, Dir of Creative Writing, 1973–94, Dir of the Writing Centre, 1994–, Innis College, University of Toronto; Founder-Ed., WRIT Magazine, Toronto, 1970–95. *Publications:* Poetry: A Mustard Sandwich (co-author), 1980; Connecting Flight, 1993; The Silence Afterwards: Selected Poems of Rolf Jacobsen (trans., ed.), 1985; Stone Fences by Paal-Helge Haugen (co-trans.), 1986; Mickey's View-Master (trans.), 1987; Ten Poems by Pia Tafdrup (co-trans.), 1989; The Time in Malmö on the Earth by Jacques Werup (trans.), 1989; Our Lives as Dogs: Scandinavian Literature in the Marketplace (ed.), 1990; A Story about Mr Silberstein by Erland Josephson (trans.), 1995; Wintering with the Light by Paal-Helge Haugen (trans.), 1997; Did I Know You? by Rolf Jacobsen (trans., ed.), 1997; I Miss You, I Miss You!, by Peter Pohl and Kinna Gieth (trans.), 1999; Through Naked Branches: Selected Poems of Tarjei Vesaas (trans., ed.), 2000; North in the World: Selected Poems of Rolf Jacobsen (trans., ed.), 2002. *Contributions to:* Anthologies, books, journals, reviews, and magazines. *Honours:* Winner, Poetry, Norma Epstein National Writing Competition, 1977; Trans. Center Award, Columbia University, 1983; Co-Winner, Richard Wilbur Trans. Prize, 1985; F R Scott Trans. Prize, League of Canadian Poets, 1986; National Endowment for the Arts Trans. Fellowship, 1988; American-Scandinavian Foundation Trans. Prize, 1990, 1996; Inger Sjöberg Trans. Prize, 1995; Winner, Poetry, CBC Radio/ Saturday Night Literary Competition, 1994; Finalist, PEN Award for Poetry in Trans., 2001. *Memberships:* American Literary Trans' Asscn; Asscn for the Advancement of Scandinavian Studies in Canada; PEN American Center. *Address:* Innis College, University of Toronto, 2 Sussex Ave, Toronto, M5S 1J5, Canada. *E-mail:* roger@chass.utoronto.ca. *Website:* www.chass.utoronto.ca/~roger/.

GREENWAY-WHITE, Melanie Robin; b. 30 May 1956, Carlisle, Pennsylvania, USA. Artist; Poet. m. Randy Dee White, 17 Dec. 1979, 2 s., 3 d. *Education:* Assoc. Degree, Ricks College, Rexburg, ID, 1976; BSc, Brigham Young University, Provo, Utah, 1978. *Publication:* Afterthoughts, 1996. *Contributions to:* Ensign; Northwest Herald. *Membership:* Northwest Area Arts Council. *Address:* 3810 Tecoma Dr., Crystal Lake, IL 60012, USA.

GREGERSON, Linda; b. 5 Aug. 1950, USA. Poet; Scholar; Educator. m. Steven Mullaney, 26 July 1980, 2 d. *Education:* BA, Oberlin College, 1971; MA, Northwestern University, 1972; MFA, University of Iowa, 1977; PhD, Stanford University, 1987. *Appointments:* Staff Ed., Atlantic Monthly, Boston, 1982–87; Asst Prof., 1987–94, Assoc. Prof., 1994–2001, Prof., 2001–, University of Michigan at Ann Arbor. *Publications:* Fire in the Conservatory, 1982; The Woman Who Died in Her Sleep, 1996; Negative Capability: Contemporary American Poetry, 2001; Waterborne, 2002. *Contributions to:* The Atlantic Monthly; Poetry; Partisan Review; Yale Review; TriQuarterly; Antaeus; Virginia Quarterly Review; New England Review; Many other journals. *Honours:* National Endowment for the Arts Fellowship, 1985, 1992; Levinson Prize for Poetry, 1991; Consuelo Ford Award, Poetry Society of America, 1992; Arts Foundation of Michigan Grant, 1994; Finalist, Lenore Marshall Prize, 1997; Finalist, The Poets Prize, 1998; Guggenheim Fellowship, 2000; Award in Literature, American Acad. of Arts and Letters, 2002. *Memberships:* MLA, Exec. Division for Renaissance Literature, 1995–99; Spenser Society, Exec. Board, 1998–2000; Milton Society; Renaissance Society of America; Shakespeare Asscn of America. *Address:* Dept of English, University of Michigan, Ann Arbor, MI 48109, USA. *E-mail:* gregerso@umich.edu.

GREGOR, Arthur; b. 18 Nov. 1923, Vienna, Austria. Writer; Poet; Teacher; Ed. *Education:* BS, New Jersey Institute of Technology, 1945. *Appointments:* Senior Ed., Macmillan Company, 1962–70; Prof. of English, 1974–88, Poet in Residence, 1988, Hofstra University. *Publications:* Octavian Shooting Targets, 1954; Declensions of a Refrain, 1957; Basic Movements, 1966; Figure in the Door, 1968; A Bed By the Sea, 1970; Selected Poems, 1971; The Past Now, 1975; Embodiment and Other Poems, 1982; Secret Citizen, 1989; The River Serpent, 1995. *Contributions to:* New Yorker; Nation; New Republic; New York Times; New York Herald Tribune; Saturday Review; Esquire; Harper's; Commentary; Commonweal; Poetry; Sewanee Review; Kenyon Review; Hudson Review; Botteghe Oscura; New World Writing; Quarterly Review of Literature; Southern Review; Minnesota Review; Michigan Quarterly. *Honours:* First Appearance Prize, Poetry, Chicago, 1948; Palmer Award, Poetry Society of America, 1962. *Memberships:* Poetry Society of America; PEN; Authors' Guild.

GREGORY, Joan. See: POULSON, Joan.

GREGORY, R. G.; b. 6 Jan. 1928, Southampton, Hampshire, England. Language Worker; Arts Writer; Poet. *Education:* BA, English, London, 1952; Diploma in Drama, Institute of Education, Newcastle, England, 1972. *Appointments:* Teacher, English/Drama, Hampshire, Uganda, Shropshire, 1952–72; Founder, Word and Action, Language Arts Organisation, Dorset, 1972–. *Publication:* Glimpses of Dorset, 1996. *Contributions to:* Outposts; New Poetry; Ambit. *Address:* 77 Wimborne Rd, Colehill, Wimborne, Dorset BH21 2RP, England.

GRENIER, Arpine Konyalian; b. 29 June 1943, Beirut, Lebanon. Poet. 1 s. *Education:* BSc, 1965; MSc, 1967; MFA, 1997. *Appointments:* Research in Veterinary Medicine, University of California, Davis, 1967–70; Medical Research, Huntington Medical Research Institute, 1973–90; Financial Research Analyst, Southern California Edison Company, 1980–93. *Publications:* St Gregory's Daughter, 1991; Whores From Samarkand, 1993. *Contributions to:* Ararat; Sulfur; Chiron Review; Columbia Review; California Quarterly; Asbarez. *Membership:* Acad. of American Poets. *Address:* 990 S Marengo Ave, Pasadena, CA 91106, USA.

GRENNAN, Eamon; b. 13 Nov. 1941, Dublin, Ireland. Prof.; Poet. 1 s., 2 d. *Education:* BA, 1963, MA, 1964, University College, Dublin; PhD, Harvard University, 1973. *Appointments:* Lecturer in English, University College, Dublin, 1966–67; Asst Prof., Herbert Lehman College, City University of New York, 1971–74; Asst Prof., 1974–83, Assoc. Prof., 1983–89, Prof., 1989–, Vassar College. *Publications:* Wildly for Days, 1983; What Light There Is, 1987; Twelve Poems, 1988; What Light There Is and Other Poems, 1989; As If It Matters, 1991; So It Goes, 1995; Selected Poems of Giacomo Leopardi (trans.), 1995; Relations: New and Selected Poems, 1998; Facing the Music: Irish Poetry in the 20th Century, 1999; Still Life with Waterfall, 2001. *Contributions to:* Anthologies and periodicals. *Honours:* National Endowment for the Humanities Grant, 1986; National Endowment for the Arts Grant, 1991; Guggenheim Fellowship, 1995. *Address:* c/o Dept of English, Vassar College, Poughkeepsie, NY 12604, USA.

GRESIN, Gad. See: SINGER, Gali-Dana.

GRESS, Esther Johanne, (Estrella); b. 20 Aug. 1921, Copenhagen, Denmark. Publisher; Ed.; Poet. *Education:* Degrees in Commerce. *Appointments:* Publisher; Ed. of encyclopedias and other publications; Radio, film, and theatre columnist. *Publications:* Skal, 1974; Liv, 1977; Ville vejen i vejen, 1979; Det sker maske, 1982; Det gik, 1983; Raise, 1984; En ny begyndelse, 1993; Let Us, 1995; Hvad du gor mod andre, 1997. *Contributions to:* Numerous anthologies, newspapers, and magazines around the world. *Honours:* Danish Acad. Consul for the Accadmia d'Europ, Naples, 1982; Grand Dame, Knights of Malta, 1984; Dr Amado Yuzon Medal for Exemplary Services for World Brotherhood and Peace, Rome, 1988; Grand Prix, Mediterranee d'Europe Trofeo, Italia, 1989; Numerous other awards. *Memberships:* Acad. of Arts and Culture; International Poets Acad., co-founder and international regent, India; World Congress of Poets, pres., 1997. *Address:* Ny Strandvej 27, 3050 Humlebaek, Denmark.

GRESSER, Sy; b. 9 May 1926, Baltimore, Maryland, USA. Stone Sculptor; Writer; Poet. 3 s., 1 d. *Education:* BS, 1949, MA, 1972, Zoological Sciences, English and American Literature, University of Maryland; Institute of Contemporary Arts, Washington, DC, 1949–50. *Appointments:* Publications Consultant for various firms, 1960–; Teacher, 1965–70; Private Students. *Publications:* Stone Elegies, 1955; Coming of the Atom, 1957; Poems From Mexico, 1964; Voyages, 1969; A Garland for Stephen, 1971; A Departure for Sons, 1973; Fragments and Others, 1982; Hagar and Her Elders, 1989. *Contributions to:* Poetry Quarterly; Stand; Antioch Review; Western Humanities Review; Johns Hopkins Review; Atavist Magazine; New York Times Book Review. *Address:* 1015 Ruatan St, Silver Spring, MD 20903, USA.

GREY, Eilonwy. See: LLOYD-JONES, Jenafer.

GREY, John Anthony; b. 14 Aug. 1949, Brisbane, Australia. Data Processor; Poet. m. Gale Grey, 12 Jan. 1980. *Publications:* First, 1989; Devil in the River, 1990; Chainsaw Massacre Suite and Other Poems of Psychotic Bliss, 1991; Dance to the Window, 1993. *Contributions to:* Paintbrush; Osiris; Sequoia; Greensboro Review; Wisconsin Poetry Review; Spoon River Quarterly; Miocoro Review; Green Mountains Review; Bugg; Seams; Cape Rock; Birmingham Poetry Review; Roanoke Poetry Review; Seattle Review; Louisville Review. *Honours:* Poet of the Year Awards, Small Press Writers of America, 1990, 1991. *Memberships:* Small Press Writers of America; Science Fiction Poetry Asscn. *Address:* 72 Fruit Hill Ave, Providence, RI 02909, USA.

GRIEDER, Ted; b. 25 Feb. 1926, USA. Rare Books Curator (retd); Poet. *Education:* BA, University of Southern California, 1948; MA, 1950, PhD, 1958, Stanford University; MLS, University of California at Berkeley, 1962. *Appointments:* Chief Bibliographer, University of California at Santa Barbara, 1962–63; University of California at Davis, 1963–66; Chief Bibliographer, 1966–70, Assoc. Curator to Curator, Rare Books, 1970–82, New York University. *Publications:* Corpus, 1967; I Shall Come to You, 1973; The High Country, 1985; Williamsburg Ramble, 1988; The Broken Country, 1990; Coastlands, 1993. *Contributions to:* Nexus. *Honour:* Hon. Poet Laureate, Flagler County, FL, 1989–. *Memberships:* MLA; Poetry Society of America; Grolier Club. *Address:* 276 Ocean Palm, Flagler Beach, FL 32136, USA.

GRIFFIN, Ted, (Edward Francis Griffin); b. 1939, Pinner, Middlesex, England. Journalist; Poet. m. *Education:* BA, Honours, Open University, 1987. *Appointments:* Poetry Reviewer, Topical Books, 1990–93; Ed., The Betjemanian Journal, 1991–94; Occasional Reviewer for Orbis, Envoi and Outposts Poetry Quarterly. *Contributions to:* Outposts Poetry Quarterly;

Acumen; Poetry Nottingham; Spokes; Openings; Folio International; BBC Radio. *Memberships:* Open University Poets, chair., 1985–88; Francis Bret Young Society. *Address:* Manor Farm House, Steeple Claydon Buckinghamshire MK18 2QF, England.

GRIFFITHS, Bill, (Brian William Bransom Griffiths); b. 20 Aug. 1948, London, England. Publisher; Researcher; Writer; Poet. *Education:* BA Honours, Medieval and Modern History, University College, London, 1969 MA, 1983, PhD, 1987, Old English, King's College, London. *Appointments:* Artist-in-Residence, Westfield College, London, 1984–85; Eric Motran Archivist, King's College, London, 1997–99; Visting Fellow, Northumbria University, 2002. *Publications:* War With Windsor, 1974; Tract Against the Giants, 1984; Alfred's Metres of Boethius (ed.), 1991; Nomad Sense (poems) 1998; Ushabtis (poems), 2001; Durham and Other Sequences (poems), 2002 *Contributions to:* Figs; Fragmente; Poetry Review; Talus. *Honour:* Joint Winner, Alice Hunt Bartlett Award, Poetry Society, 1974. *Address:* 21 Alfred St, Seaham Harbour, County Durham SR7 7LH, England. Webwite www.billygriff.co.uk.

GRIFO, Lionello See: VAGGE, Ornello.

GRINKER, Morton; b. 19 May 1928, Paterson, New Jersey, USA. Writer, Poet. m. Lynn Grinker, 28 June 1963. *Education:* BA, English, University of Idaho, 1952. *Publications:* To the Straying Aramaean, 1972; The Gran Phenician Rover, 6 vols, 1996. *Contributions to:* Shig's Review; S-B Gazette; Perspectives; Or; Dust; Manhattan Review; Work; Tampa Poetry Review; Amphora; Buffalo Stamps; Hyperion; Illuminations Reader; Poems Read in the Spirit of Peace and Gladness; San Francisco Bark. *Address:* 1367 Noe St, San Francisco, CA 94131, USA.

GROCE, Jennifer. See: BOSVELD, Jennifer Miller.

GROCH, Erik; b. 25 April 1957, Kosice, Czechoslovakia. Journalist; Ed.; Poet. m. Monika Torok, 2 s. *Publications:* Sukromne hodiny smutku (Private Lessons in Sadness), 1989; Baba Jaga: Zalospevy (Baba Yaga: Elegies), 1991; Bratsestra (Brothersister), 1992. *Contributions to:* Kulturny Zivot; Slovenske Pohlady; Romboid; Dotyky; Ticha Voda; Fragment K; Inostrannaya Literatura, Russia; Prairie Schooner, USA. *Honour:* Ivan Krasko Prize for Best Debut of the Year, 1989. *Membership:* Obec Spisovatelov Slovenska, PEN Club. *Address:* Tomasikova 19, 04001 Kosice, Slovakia.

GROLLMES, Eugene E.; b. 9 Nov. 1931, Seneca, KS, USA. University Administrator; Poet. *Education:* AB, MA, St Louis University, 1961; PhD, Boston College, 1969; Harvard University Divinity School, 1969–70. *Appointments:* Asst Dean of Arts and Sciences, 1974–93, Consultant to the Provost, 1993–, St Louis University. *Publication:* At the Vietnam Veterans Memorial, Washington, DC: Between the Lines, 1988. *Contributions to:* Reviews, quarterlies, and journals. *Membership:* Acad. of American Poets. *Address:* 3601 Lindell Blvd, St Louis, MO 63108, USA.

GRONDAHL, Cathrine; b. 4 May 1969, Oslo, Norway. Poet. *Education:* Studies in Philosophy, Psychology and Comparative Religion, University of Oslo; Legal Studies. *Publications:* Riv Ruskende Rytmer, 1994; I Klem Mellom Natt og Dag, 1996; Det Har Ingenting Med Kjaerlighet å Gjore, 1998. *Contributions to:* Vagant; Vinduet. *Honours:* Tarjei Vesaas Debutant Pris, 1994; Anders Jahres Pris, 1997. *Membership:* Norwegian Authors Union.

GROSS, Natan; b. 16 Nov. 1919, Kraków, Poland. Film Dir; Journalist; Trans.; Poet. m. Shulamit Lifszyc, 1 s., 1 d. *Education:* Law and Art Studies; Diploma, Film Directing, Polish Film Institute, 1946. *Appointment:* Film Critic, Al Hamishmar, 1962–82. *Publications:* Over 15 books, including poetry, anthologies, monographs, criticism, and trans, 1945–99. *Contributions to:* Journals and magazines. *Honours:* Numerous Israeli and international film festivals and literary awards. *Memberships:* Film and Television Dirs Guild of Israel; Israel Federation of Writers; Israeli Film Union, secretary, 1951–71; Israel Journalists Asscn. *Address:* 14 Herzog St, Givatayim 53586, Israel.

GROSS, Philip (John); b. 27 Feb. 1952, Delabole, England. Author; Poet; Tutor in Creative Writing. *Education:* BA, Honours, University of Sussex, 1973; Postgraduate Diploma in Librarianship, Polytechnic of North London, 1977. *Appointments:* Numerous residencies and teaching posts. *Publications:* Familiars, 1983; The Ice Factory, 1984; Cat's Whisker, 1987; The Air Mines of Mistila, 1988; Manifold Manor, 1989; The Song of Gail and Fludd, 1991; The Son of the Duke of Nowhere, 1991; The All-Nite Café, 1993; I.D. (poems), 1994; The Wind Gate, 1995; Scratch City (poems), 1996; Psylicon Beach, 1998; The Wasting Game (poems), 1998; Changes of Address: Poems 1980–98, 2000. *Contributions to:* Numerous magazines and journals. *Honours:* Eric Gregory Award, 1981; Poetry Book Society Choice, 1988; Arts Council Bursary for Writing for Young People, 1990; Signal Award for Children's Poetry, 1994; Short-listed, Whitbread Poetry Prize, 1998. *Address:* 40 York Rd, Bristol BS6 5QF, England.

GROVES, Gene; b. 14 Aug. 1951, Prestatyn, North Wales. Teacher; Poet. m. Richard Geoffrey Groves, 2 s. *Education:* Certificate of Education, Elizabeth

Gaskell College of Education, Manchester, 1974; Qualified in Social Work, University of Northumbria, 1993–95. *Contributions to:* Flambard New Poets 2; New Welsh Review; Iron; Staple; Foolscap; Poetry Nottingham; Tees Valley Writer; Tidelines Anthology. *Address:* 3 Turners Way, Morpeth, Northumberland NE61 2YE, England.

GROVES, Paul Raymond; b. 28 July 1947, Gloucester, England. Teacher; Poet. m. Annette Kelsall, 1 June 1972, 2 d. *Education:* Teaching Certificate, Caerleon College of Education, 1969. *Appointments:* Schoolmaster, 1970–87; College Lecturer in Creative Writing, 1989–; Tutor, Open College of the Arts, 1999–. *Publications:* Poetry Introduction 3, 1975; Academe, 1988; Ménage à Trois, 1995; Eros and Thanatos, 1999; Wowsers, 2002. *Contributions to:* Critical Quarterly; Literary Review; London Magazine; New Statesman; Outposts Poetry Quarterly; Poetry Review; Poetry Wales; Dalhousie Review; Oxford Poetry; Stand; Spectator; TLS; Wascana Review. *Honours:* Eric Gregory Award, 1976; First Prizes, TLS/Cheltenham Festival, 1986, Green Book, 1986, Yeats Club, 1987, Surrey Poetry Group, 1987, 1988, 1991, Charterhouse International, 1989, 1990, Rainforest Trust, 1991, Orbis International, 1992, Bournemouth Festival, 1994, Cotswold Writers, 1995, Wilkins Memorial, 1997. *Membership:* Poetry Society. *Address:* 4 Cornford Close, Osbaston, Monmouth NP25 3NT, Wales.

GRUFFYDD, Peter; b. 12 April 1935, Liverpool, England. Writer; Poet; Trans.; Actor. m. (1), 1 s., 1 d., (2) Susan Soar, 28 Dec. 1974, 2 s. *Education:* BA, Honours, University of Wales, Bangor, 1960. *Publications:* Triad, 1963; Welsh Voices, 1967; Poems, 1969; The Lilting House, 1970; Poems, 1972; The Shivering Seed, 1972; On Censorship, 1985; Environmental Teletex, 1989; Damned Braces, 1993. *Contributions to:* Anthologies and periodicals. *Honours:* Eric Gregory Trust, 1963; Second Prize, Young Poets Competition, Welsh Arts Council, 1969; First Prizes, 1984, 1994, Third Prizes, 1986, 1991, 1993, Aberystwyth Open Poetry Competitions; Duncan Lawrie Prize, Arvon-Observer International Poetry Competition, 1993. *Memberships:* Equity; PEN International, founder-mem., Welsh Branch, 1993; Welsh Union of Writers; Yr Academi Gymraeg. *Address:* 21 Beech Rd, Norton, Stourbridge, West Midlands DY8 2AS, England.

GRUMBACH, Doris (Isaac); b. 12 July 1918, New York, NY, USA. Author; Critic; Prof. of English (retd). m. Leonard Grumbach, 15 Oct. 1941, divorced, 1972, 4 d. *Education:* AB, Washington Square College, 1939; MA, Cornell University, 1940. *Appointments:* Assoc. Ed., Architectural Forum, 1942–43; Teacher of English, Albany Acad. for Girls, New York, 1952–55; Instructor, 1955–58, Asst Prof., 1958–60, Assoc. Prof., 1960–69, Prof. of English, 1969–73, College of Saint Rose, Albany; Visiting University Fellow, Empire State College, 1972–73; Literary Ed., New Republic, 1973–75; Adjunct Prof. of English, University of Maryland, 1974–75; Prof. of American Literature, American University, Washington, DC, 1975–85; Columnist and reviewer for various publications, radio, and television. *Publications:* The Spoil of the Flowers, 1962; The Short Throat, the Tender Mouth, 1964; The Company She Kept (biography of Mary McCarthy), 1967; Chamber Music, 1979; The Missing Person, 1981; The Ladies, 1984; The Magician's Girl, 1987; Coming Into the End Zone, 1992; Extra Innings: A Memoir, 1993; Fifty Days of Solitude, 1994; The Book of Knowledge: A Novel, 1995; The Presence of Absence, 1998; The Pleasure of Their Company, 2000. *Contributions to:* Books and periodicals. *Membership:* PEN. *Address:* c/o Maxine Groffsky, 2 Fifth Ave, New York, NY 10011, USA.

GRUMMAN, Robert Jeremy; b. 2 Feb. 1941, Norwalk, CT, USA. Poet; Critic. *Education:* BA, English, California State University, Northridge, 1982. *Publications:* An April Poem, 1989; Of Manywhere-at-Once, 1990; Spring Poem, 1990; Mathemaku 1–5, 1992; Mathemaku 6–12, 1994; Of Poem, 1995; Poems, 1996. *Contributions to:* Score; Kaldron; New Orleans Review; Poetry USA; Generator; Sub Bild, Germany; Freie Zeit Art, Austria; Offerta Speciale, Italy; Central Park; Sticks. *Memberships:* National Coalition of Independent Scholars; National Book Critics Circle. *Address:* 1708 Hayworth Rd, Port Charlotte, FL 33952-4529, USA.

GUBERMAN, Jayseth; b. 4 April 1960, Bridgeport, CT, USA. Writer; Poet. *Education:* BA, History, Sacred Heart University, Fairfield, CT, 1981; Arabic and Islamic Studies, Yale University Graduate School, 1983–84; MA, Near East Studies, New York University, 1985. *Appointments:* Asst Prof., Adjunct, Political Science, Sacred Heart University, Fairfield, CT, 1987. *Contributions to:* Jewish Spectator; Jewish Currents; Judaism; Orim; A Jewish Journal at Yale; Israel Horizons; Response; Reconstructionist; New Zealand Jewish Chronicle; Black Buzzard Review; Prophetic Voices; Plowman Anthologies; Voices Israel; European Judaism; Martydom and Resistance. *Memberships:* Writers and Artists for Peace in the Middle East; International Society for Yad Va-Shem; Poets and Writers; New Zealand Asscn for the Study of Jewish Civilization, corresponding mem. *Address:* 294 S Quaker Lane, West Hartford, CT 06119, USA.

GUDMUNDSDOTTIR, Kristjana Emilia; b. 23 April 1939, Stykkishólmur, Iceland. Writer; Poet. m. 10 June 1957, 3 s., 3 d. *Education:* Journeyman's Certificate, Bookbinding, 1985. *Publications:* Ljódnálar, 1982; Ljódspeglar, 1989; Ljódblik, 1993; Ljódgeislar, 1995; Ljód Dagsins, 1995; Gluggi, 1996;

Lífid Sjálft, 1996; The Icelandic Art Festival Book of Poems, 1996. *Contributions to:* Newspapers. *Address:* Borgarholtsbraut 27, 200 Kópavogur, Iceland.

GUENTHER, Charles John; b. 29 April 1920, St Louis, Missouri, USA. Teacher; Poet; Writer. m. Esther Laura Klund, 11 April 1942, 1 s., 2 d. *Education:* AA, Harris Teachers College, St Louis, 1940; BA, 1973, MA, 1974, Webster University. *Appointments:* US Army Engineers; US Air Force Aero Chart and Information Service; Adjunct Prof. or Instructor, various US colleges and universities. *Publications:* Modern Italian Poets, 1961; Phrase-Paraphrase, 1970; Paul Valery in English, 1970; The Pluralism of Poetry, 1973; Voices in the Dark, 1974; High Sundowns, by Juan Ramón Jiménez (trans.), 1974; Jules Laforgue: Selected Poems (trans.), 1984; The Hippopotamus: Selected Translations, 1945–85, 1986; Moving the Seasons: Selected Poems, 1994. *Contributions to:* Reviews, anthologies, and journals. *Honours:* Commander, Order of Merit, Italy, 1973; James Joyce Award, 1974, Witter Bynner Poetry Trans. Grant, 1979, Poetry Society of America; Missouri Library Asscn Literary Award, 1974; PhD Fellow, St Louis University, 1976–79; Hon. Doctor of Humane Letters, Southern Illinois University, 1979; Missouri Writers Guild Poetry Awards, 1983, 1986, 1993, 1996, 1998; Walter Williams Awards, 1987, 1995; Missouri Arts Award, 2001; St Louis A&E Arts Award, 2001. *Memberships:* Acad. of American Poets; Missouri Writers Guild; Poetry Society of America, Midwest vice-pres., 1976–90; St Louis Poetry Center; St Louis Writers Guild; Special Libraries Asscn. *Address:* 9877 Allendale Dr., St Louis, MO 63123, USA.

GUESS, Jim; b. 23 Sept. 1970, Long Beach, CA, USA. Exporter; Poet. *Education:* Bachelor Degree, California State University at Long Beach, 1996. *Appointment:* Ed.-in-Chief, Black Cross Journal of Heavy Poetry and Art, 1995–. *Publication:* Verbal Eyesore, 1997. *Contributions to:* Rip Rap; Chiron Review; Celery/Inky Blue; Calfironia Poetry Calendar; Poetry Calendar; Sheila-na-gig; Poet; Bender; Poetry Motel; Huma's Eclipse; Succulent; Poetry Superhighway; Liquid Ohio; Iconoclast; Damaged Goods. *Honours:* Winner, Best On-Line Poetry Magazine, 1997. *Address:* 3121 Corto Pl., No. 2, Long Beach, CA 90803, USA.

GUEST, Barbara; b. 6 Sept. 1920, Wilmington, North Carolina, USA. Writer; Poet; Novelist; Biographer. m. (1) Stephen, Lord Haden-Guest, 1948, divorced, (2) Trumbull Higgins, 1955, deceased, 1 s., 1 d. *Education:* BA, University of California, Berkeley, 1943. *Publications:* The Location of Things, 1960; Poems, 1963; The Blue Stairs, 1968; Moscow Mansions, 1973; Quilts, 1974; The Countess from Minneapolis, 1976; Seeking Air (novel), 1978; The Turler Losses, 1980; Biography, 1980; Herself Defined: H.D. The Poet and Her World (biography), 1984; Musicality, 1989; Fair Realism, 1989; The Altos (with Richard Tuttle), 1991; Defensive Rapture, 1993; Selected Poems, 1995; Stripped Tales (with Anne Dunn), 1995; Symbiosis (with Laurie Reid), 2000; Miniatures and Other Poems, 2002; Forces of the Imagination: Selected Essays, 2002. *Contributions to:* Conjunctions; O-blek; New American Writing; American Poetry Review; Pembroke; Hambone; Art in America; Art News; Paris Review; Blue Mesa Review; Denver Quarterly; Iowa Review; New American Letters; Arshile; Chelsea Review; Inprint Magazine. *Honours:* Longview Award, 1960; Laurence Lipton Award for Literature, University of Southern California, 1989; Poetry Award, San Francisco State University, 1995; Robert Frost Medal for Distinguished Lifetime Work in Poetry, 1999. *Memberships:* Poetry Society of America; PEN. *Address:* 1301 Milvia St, Berkeley, CA 94709, USA.

GUEST, Harry, (Henry Bayly Guest); b. 6 Oct. 1932, Glamorganshire, Wales. Poet; Writer. m. Lynn Doremus Dunbar, 28 Dec. 1963, 1 s., 1 d. *Education:* BA, Trinity Hall, Cambridge, 1954, DES, Sorbonne, University of Paris, 1955. *Appointments:* Lecturer, Yokohama National University, 1966–72; Head of Modern Languages, Exeter School, 1972–91; Teacher of Japanese, Exeter University, 1979–95. *Publications:* Arrangements, 1968; The Cutting-Room, 1970; Post-War Japanese Poetry (ed. and trans.), 1972; A House Against the Night, 1976; Days, 1978; The Distance, the Shadows, 1981; Lost and Found, 1983; The Emperor of Outer Space (radio play), 1983; Lost Pictures, 1991; Coming to Terms, 1994; Traveller's Literary Companion to Japan, 1994; So Far, 1998; The Artist on the Artist, 2000. *Contributions to:* Reviews, quarterlies, and journals. *Honours:* Hawthornden Fellow, 1993; Hon. Research Fellow, Exeter University, 1994–; Hon. Doctor of Letters, Plymouth University, 1998. *Membership:* Poetry Society, General Council, 1972–76. *Address:* 1 Alexandra Terrace, Exeter, Devon EX4 6SY, England.

GUETHE, M. Baugher; b. 21 Feb. 1951, Lafayette, IN, USA. Medical Technologist; Poet. m. Richard Guethe, 18 May 1984, 1 s., 1 d. *Education:* Completed Lafayette Home Hospital Medical Technologist Program, 1970; Certification, 1971; Upgraded Certification, 1981. *Contributions to:* Dream International Quarterly; Feelings; Capper's Poetry Explosion Newsletter; The Plowman; Tight; Penny Dreadful Review; Ralph's Review; One Earth, Scotland; En Plein Air, Switzerland; Sivullinen, Finland; First Time, England. *Membership:* Acad. of American Poets. *Address:* 1905 E Oak St, New Albany, IN 47150, USA.

GUGLIELMI, Joseph Julien; b. 30 Dec. 1929, Marseille, France. Teacher (retd); Poet. m. Therese Bonnelalbay, deceased, 2 s., 1 d. *Education:*

Baccalaureat Philosophie-Lettres, 1950; Propedentique lettres classiques, 1952; Primary School Teacher's Certificate, 1960. *Publications:* La Preparation des Titres, 1980; Aube, 1984; Fins de vers, 1986; Le Mouvement de la mort, 1988; Joe's Bunker, 1991; Principe de paysage, 1991. *Contributions to:* Many publications. *Address:* 6 allee du Parc, 94200 Ivry sur Seine, France.

GUGLIELMO, Dolores; b. 29 Aug. 1928, Corona, Long Island, New York, USA. Poet. *Education:* BA, English, Queen's College, 1983; Master's Degree, St John's University, Jamaica, New York, 1986. *Publications:* Comet Racer, 1994; Black Picasso, 1994; He Was Mike, 1994; Ballad of Uriah Cabe, 1994; Heatwave, 1995; In a Japanese Tea Room, 1995; Shapes, 1995; The Forest, 1995; Truckline Cafe, 1995. *Contributions to:* Paper Salad; US Poets; Mobious; Summer Soliloquy; Echoes; Howling Dog; Weyfarers; Hammers; Uprising; Firewater Press; Vigil; Poetry Motel; At Last; Tears in the Fence; Poetry Depth Quarterly; Paris/Atlantic; The Poets' Voice; Pulsar; Offerings; Seam; Fire; Aabye; Offerta; Flarestack; Studio One; Sepia; Poetry Nottingham. *Honours:* Winner, International Poetry Contest, Seven Magazine, 1967; Writers Club Award for Excellence in Poetry, Queenborough Community College, 1992; Finalist, Boxcar Poetry Competition, 1996. *Membership:* World Poetry Society. *Address:* 43–44 Kissena Blvd, Flushing, NY 11355, USA.

GUHA, Ananya Sankar; b. 18 Feb. 1957, Shillong, India. Academic Administrator; Poet. m. Punam Guha, 9 March 1995. *Education:* MA, English Literature, 1980, PhD, North Eastern University, Shillong, 1992. *Appointments:* Lecturer, Senior Lecturer, Dept of English, St Edmund's College, Shillong, 1981–92; Asst Regional Dir, National Open University, Shillong 1992–; Regional Dir, IGNOU, Shillong. *Publications:* What Else Is Alive, 1988; In This My Land, 1989; Ananya Sankau Guhar, 1997. *Contributions to:* Indian and foreign publications. *Honours:* First Prize, All India Poetry Festival, Mumbai, 1979; Michael Madhusudan Prize for Poetry, Michael Madhusudan Acad., Calcutta. *Memberships:* Various cultural groups in Shillong and North East India; National Institute of Research in Indian English Literature. *Address:* 'Mitali', Latumkhrah, Shillong 793003, Meghalaya, India.

GUHA, R. P.; b. 23 June 1929, Calcutta, India. Poet. m. Anima Datta, 17 Feb. 1960, 1 s., 1 d. *Education:* DLitt, 1980; MHM, 1985; PhD, Law, USA. *Publications:* A Bouquet, 1975; A Winsome Marrow, 1976; The World, 1978; The Philosophy of Life, 1982; Life, 2001; Life II, 2002; A Collection of Poems, 2002. *Contributions to:* Poet; World of Poetry; American Poetry Anthology; Metverse Muse; Brainwave; Art and Poetry Today; Bridge-in-Making; Heaven; Poets International. *Honours:* Michael Madhusudan Acad. Award for Literature, 1997; Bharat Pathik Award, USIS Prize. *Memberships:* Poets International; World Poetry Society; Metverse Muse; Fellow, United Writers' Asscn. *Address:* Patratu School of Economics, PO Patratu Thermal Power Station, 829119 PB, Hazaribagh, India.

GUIDA, George; b. 17 Nov. 1967, New York, NY, USA. College Instructor; Poet. *Education:* BA, Columbia College, 1989; MA, 1994, MPhil, 1995, City University of New York. *Appointments:* Instructor, City College, 1989–91, Hunter College, 1991–95, Barnard College, 1995–. *Publications:* In Low Italian, 1995; Stiletto Tongues, 1995. *Contributions to:* Voices in Italian American; Footwork: Patterson Literary Review; Poetry New York; Dream International Quarterly; Upstart; Columbia Guide to New York. *Membership:* Italian American Writers Asscn. *Address:* 120 W 44th St, No. 1404, New York, NY 10036, USA.

GUINANE, Alison Maria; b. 22 May 1948, Manchester, England. Teacher (retd); Poet. 1 d. *Education:* BA, Honours, English, University of York, 1969; PGCE (Primary), University of Manchester, 1977; MA with Distinction, Creative Writing, University of Lancaster, 1993. *Appointments:* Teacher of English, 1977–94. *Publication:* Through the Railings, 1991. *Contributions to:* Anthologies and other publications. *Membership:* Poetry Society. *Address:* Quince Cottage, 26 Upcast Lane, Wilmslow, Cheshire SK9 6EH, England.

GUJRAL, Shiela, (Shiela); b. 24 Jan. 1924, Lahore, India. Poet; Writer. m. I K Gujral, 26 May 1945, 2 s. *Education:* MA, Economics, 1943; Diploma, Journalism, 1945; Diploma, Montessori Training, 1946. *Publications:* Jagi Janata, 1963; Ghungat Ke Pat, 1974; Sagar Tat Par, 1980; Two Black Cinders, 1985; Anunad, 1986; Amar Vel, 1986; Niara Hindustan, 1989; Nishwas, 1989; Signature of Silence, 1991; Mahak, 1992; Tapovan Mae Bawander, 1992; Throttled Dove, 1995; Jab Mai Na Rahun, 1995; Sangli, 1995; Canvas of Life, 1995; Barf Ke Chehre, 1997; My Years in the USSR, 2002; Sparks, 2002. Other: Children's books. *Contributions to:* Poetry and literary journals. *Honours:* Nirala Award, 1989; Golden Poets Awards, 1989, 1990; Hon. DLitt, World Acad. of Arts and Culture, 1992; Huh Nansolhoen Poetry Award, Korea, 1997; Soka Gokkai University Award, Japan, 1997; Shiromani Sahitkar Award, Punjab, 1997; Delhi Ratan Award, All India Intellectuals, 1998. *Memberships:* Authors Guild; Indian Poetry Society; Lekhika Sangh (Women Writers Asscn), Pres., 1981–86; PEN. *Address:* 5 Janpath, New Delhi 110011, India.

GULDAGER, Katrine Marie; b. 29 Dec. 1966, Maglegaard, Copenhagen, Denmark. Writer. *Education:* Candidate Phil in Danish Literature, 1994.

Publications: Days Are Changing Hands, 1994; Crash, 1995; Blank, 1996; The Green Eye, 1998; Arrival, Husumgade, 2001; Kicdollgimikk, 2002. *Honours:* Prize for Days Are Changing Hands, 1994; Travel Grant to Southern Africa, 1994; 3 Year Working Grant, 1995; The Humour Prize, 1996; Henri Nathansens Memory Grant, 1996; Danish Acad. Debutant Prize 1996; Gyldendals Boglegat, 1997; Morten Nielscus Middelegat, 1999; Peder Kjaergaards Forfatterlegat, 2001. *Address:* c/o Gyldendal, Klareboderne 3, 1001 Copenhagen N, Denmark.

GUNDERSON, Keith Robert; b. 29 Aug. 1935, New Ulm, Minnesota, USA. Prof. of Philosophy; Writer; Poet. m. (1), 3 s., (2) Sandra Riekki, 28 July 1979. *Education:* BA, Philosophy, Macalester College, St Paul, Minnesota, 1957; BA Philosophy, Worcester College, University of Oxford, 1959; PhD, Philosophy Princeton University, 1963. *Appointments:* Instructor of Philosophy, Princeton University, 1962–64; Asst Prof., University of California at Los Angeles 1964–67; Assoc. Prof., 1967–70, Prof., 1971–, Philosophy, University of Minnesota. *Publications:* A Continual Interest in the Sun and Sea, 1971; 3142 Lyndale Avenue So, Apt 24, 1974; To See a Thing, 1975; A Continual Interest in the Sun and Sea and Inland, Missing the Sea, 1976. *Contributions to:* Western Humanities Review; Prairie Schooner; Massachusetts Review; American Poetry Review; North Stone Review; Milkweed; Chronicle; South and West; Burning Water; Trace; New Mexico Quarterly; Epoch; Black Flag; Chelsea; Various poems set to music by composers, Sydney Hodkinson and Eric Stokes. *Honours:* National Endowment for the Arts Grant for Poetry, 1974; Minnesota State Arts Board Grant, 1979. *Membership:* Los Angeles Incognoscent, 1964–. *Address:* 1212 Lakeview Ave S, Minneapolis, MN 55416, USA.

GUNESEKERA, Romesh; b. 1954, Colombo, Sri Lanka. Writer; Poet. *Publications:* Monkfish Moon, 1992; Reef, 1995; The Sandglass, 1998; Heaven's Edge, 2002. *Honours:* Notable Book of the Year, New York Times, 1993; Best First Work Award, Yorkshire Post, 1994; Short-listed, Booker Prize, 1994; Premio Mondello, 1997. *Address:* c/o Granta USA Ltd, 250 W 57th St, 13th Floor, New York, NY 10107, USA.

GUNN, Thom(son William); b. 29 Aug. 1929, Gravesend, England. Poet. *Education:* Trinity College, Cambridge. *Appointments:* Taught English, 1958–66; Lecturer, 1977–, Senior Lecturer, 1988–, University of California, Berkeley, USA. *Publications:* Fighting Terms, 1954; The Sense of Movement, 1957; My Sad Captains, 1961; Positives (with Ander Gunn), 1966; Touch, 1967; Moly, 1971; Jack Straw's Castle, 1976; Selected Poems, 1979; The Passages of Joy, 1982; The Occasions of Poetry (prose), 1982; The Man with Night Sweats, 1992; Collected Poems, 1993; Shelf Life (prose), 1993; Boss Cupid, 2000. *Honours:* Levinson Prize, 1955; Somerset Maugham Prize, 1959; National Institute of Arts and Letters Grant, 1964; Rockefeller Foundation, 1966; Guggenheim Fellowship, 1972; Lila Wallace/ Reader's Digest Fund Award, 1991; Forward Poetry Prize, 1992; MacArthur Fellowship, 1993; Lenore Marshall Prize, 1993. *Address:* 1216 Cole St, San Francisco, CA 94117, USA.

GUNNARSDOTTIR, (Asta) Berglind; b. 5 Dec. 1953, Reykjavík, Iceland. Writer; Poet; Ed.; Teacher of Spanish. 3 d. *Education:* Commercial College of Iceland; BA, Spanish and Linguistics, University of Iceland, including one year at Universidad de Complutense, Madrid, Spain. *Publications:* Ljod Fyrir Lifi, 1983; Ljodsott, 1986; Ljosbrot i Skuggann, 1990; Flugfiskur, 1992; Allsherjargodinn, 1992; Bragd Af Eilifd, 1995; Ljódvissa, 1999. *Contributions to:* Timarit Mals og Menningar; Lesbok Morgunbladsins; Andvari; Sky; Bjartur og Fru Emilia; Arbok, 1988. *Membership:* Rithöfundasamband Islands (Writer's Union of Iceland). *Address:* Holtsgata 37, 101 Reykjavík, Iceland.

GUNTON DEAL, Kathleen; b. 12 Oct. 1946, Santa Monica, CA, USA. Writer; Poet; Teacher. m., 2 s., 1 d. *Education:* AA, Orange Coast College, 1978; BA, California State University, Long Beach, 1982. *Contributions to:* America; Lyric; Christian Science Monitor; California State Poetry Quarterly; The Rectangle; Abbey; Vintage 45. *Honours:* Prof. Foote Writing Award, California State University, Long Beach, 1982; UFCW Writing Award, 1986; Honourable Mentions, Writer's Digest, 1988, 1989, 1990; Robert Frost Gold Award, San Mateo, 1989; Edna St Vincent Millay, San Mateo, 1990. *Membership:* California State Poetry Society.

GUSTAFSSON, Lars; b. 17 May 1936, Västeras, Sweden. Writer; Poet; Dramatist; Prof. *Education:* Licentiate, Philosophy, 1960, DPhil, 1978, University of Uppsala. *Appointments:* Assoc. Ed., 1960–65, Ed.-in-Chief, 1965–72, Bonniers Litterära Magasin; Deutscher Akademischer Austauschdienst Fellow, Berlin, 1972–73; Research Fellow, Bielefeld Institute of Advanced Studies, Germany, 1981–82; Adjunct Prof. of German Studies, 1982–98, Jamail Distinguished Prof., 1998–, University of Austin at Texas; Aby Warburg Foundation Prof., Warburg Stiftung, Hamburg, 1997. *Publications:* Over 50 works, including fiction, non-fiction, poetry, and drama, 1957–99. *Contributions to:* Various publications. *Honours:* Swedish Novel Prize, 1979; Prix International Charles Veillon des Essais, 1983; Officier de l'Ordre des Arts et des Lettres, France, 1986; Heinrich Steffens Prize, Germany, 1986; Kommendör des Bundesverdienstzeichens, Germany, 1988; Bellman Prize, Royal Swedish Acad., 1990; Poetry Prize, Swedish Broadcasting Corp, 1993; Guggenheim Fellowship, 1994; Pilot Prize, Sweden, 1996.

Memberships: Akademie der Künste, Berlin; Akademie der Wissenschaften und der Literatur, Mainz; Akademie der Schönen Künste, Munich Royal Swedish Acad. of Engineering; Authors' Guild of America; PEN International, Sweden. *Address:* 2312 Tower Dr., Austin, TX 78703, USA.

GUT, Karen. See: ALKALAY-GUT, Karen Hillary.

GUTIERREZ VEGA, Hugo; b. 11 Feb. 1934, Mexico. Diplomat; Lecturer; Poet. m. 21 Nov. 1960, 3 d. *Education:* Degrees in Law, Mexico, Italian Literature, Rome, and English Literature, London. *Appointments:* Dean, University of Queretaro, Mexico; Dir of Cultural Extension, National University of Mexico; Diplomat in Rome, Italy, Moscow, London, Madrid, Washington and Rio de Janeiro; Ambassador of Mexico in Greece, Lebanon, Cyprus, Romania and Moldova; Lecturer, National University, Mexico. *Publications:* Buscado Amor, 1965; Des de Inglaterra, 1969; Cantos de Plasencia; Resistencia de Particulares, 1976; Cuando el Placer Termine, 1976; Meridiano 8-0, 1980; Antologia, 1980; Cantos de Tomelloso, 1982; Las Peregrinaciones del Deseo, Poesia Revnida, 1965–86; Audar En Brasil, 1985; Los Soles Griegos, 1986; Cantos del Despotado de Morea, 1991. *Contributions to:* Cuadernos Hispano Americanos; Siglo XX; Estafeta; TLS; Vuelta; Nexos. *Honours:* National Prize for Poetry, Mexico, 1976; Order of Alfonso X Elsabio, Isabel la Catolica, and Commendatore. *Membership:* PEN Club, Mexico. *Address:* Mexican Embassy, Diamandidou 73, Paleo Psychico, Athens 15452, Greece.

GUTTERIDGE, Don(ald George); b. 30 Sept. 1937, Sarnia, Ontario, Canada. Poet: Author; Prof. of English Methods Emeritus. m. Anne Barnett, 30 June 1961, 1 s., 1 d. *Education:* Chatham College Institute, Ontario, 1956; BA, Honours, University of Western Ontario, London, 1960. *Appointments:* Asst Prof., 1968–75, Assoc. Prof., 1975–77, Prof. of English Methods, 1977–93, Prof. Emeritus, 1993–, University of Western Ontario. *Publications:* Poetry: Riel: A Poem for Voices, 1968; The Village Within, 1970; Death at Quebec and Other Poems, 1972; Saying Grace: An Elegy, 1972; Coppermine: The Quest for North, 1973; Borderlands, 1975; Tecumseh, 1976; A True History of Lambton County, 1977; God's Geography, 1982; The Exiled Heart: Selected Narratives, 1986; Love in the Wintertime, 1982; Flute Music in the Cello's Belly, 1997; Bloodlines, 2001. Fiction: Bus-Ride, 1974; All in Good Time, 1980; St Vitus Dance, 1986; Shaman's Ground, 1988; How the World Began, 1991; Summer's Idyll, 1993; Winter's Descent, 1996; Bewilderment, 2001. *Honours:* Pres.'s Medal, University of Western Ontario, 1971; Canada Council Travel Grant, 1973. *Address:* 114 Victoria St, London, Ontario N6A 2B5, Canada.

GUTTMAN, Naomi; b. 10 July 1960, Montréal, QC, Canada. Teacher; Poet. m. Jonathan Mead, 6 July 1986. *Education:* BFA, Concordia University, 1985; MFA, Warren Wilson College, 1988; MA, English, Loyola Marymount University, Los Angeles, 1992. *Publication:* Reasons for Winter, 1991. *Contributions to:* Malahat Review; Matrix. *Honours:* Bliss Carman Award for Poetry, Banff School of Fine Arts, 1989; QSpell Award for Poetry, 1992. *Address:* 356 N Spaulding Ave, Los Angeles, CA 90036, USA.

GUY, Scott; b. 26 Nov. 1958, Chicago, IL, USA. Television and Film Writer; Poet. *Education:* BS, magna cum laude, Northwestern University, 1979; MFA,

University of California at Los Angeles, 1981. *Appointments:* Artistic Dir, Passage Theatre; Head Writer, NBC's Our Place, Flying Whales and Peacock Tales; Collaborations with Milcho Leviev, Ed Zelnis, Ken Nevfeld and John Vorhaus. *Publications:* Poetry: The Loot of Loma, 1979; Hugh Selwyn Mauberley (after Pound), 1980; Edward ll, 1980; Our Place, 1986; Flying Whales and Peacock Tales, 1987; A Christmas Warning, 1989; The Pooblies, 1991; The Green House, 1991; Kensington Gardens, 1992; Der Curmudgeon Lieder, 1992; The Coming of Madness, 1993; Outcasts of the Dark Boneyard, 1993. *Contributions to:* Passage Theatre; Children's Classical Theatre; Urban Gateways; Encino Playhouse; Performing Tree; Los Angeles Jazz Choir; NBC; C and K Productions, Xanadu Theatre. *Honours:* Illinois Arts Council Individual Artist Grant, 1981; Rosenbaum Foundation Musical Comedy Grant, 1986; California Arts Council Screenwriting Fellowship, 1992; Los Angeles Cultural Affairs Dept Fellowship, 1992; Finalist, Eugene O'Neill Musical Theatre Conference, 1993. *Address:* 6650 Hayvenhurst, No. 229, Van Nuys, CA 91406, USA.

GUZMAN BOUVARD, Marguerite. See: BOUVARD, Marguerite Anne.

GWYN, Richard; b. 22 July 1956, Pontypool, Wales. Poet; Writer; Lecturer. m. Rosemary Pallot, 2 June 1992, 2 d. *Education:* London School of Economics, 1975–77; MA, 1991, PhD, 1997, University of Cardiff. *Appointment:* Lecturer, University of Cardiff, 1996–. *Publications:* Defying Gravity (poems), 1992; One Night in Icarus Street (poems), 1995; Stone Dog, Flower Red (poems), 1995; Walking on Bones (poems), 2000; Being in Water (poems), 2001; Discourse, Health and Illness (prose), 2001. *Contributions to:* Literary and medical journals. *Memberships:* Welsh Academi; Welsh Union of Writers. *Address:* c/o School of English, Communication and Philosophy, University of Wales, Cardiff, Cardiff, Wales.

GYARFAS, Endre; b. 6 May 1936, Szeged, Hungary. Poet; Novelist; Dramatist. m. Edit Kincses, 7 Dec. 1963, 1 s. *Education:* Hungarian and English Literature, Elte University, Budapest, 1961. *Publications:* Partkozelben (poems), 1964; Pazarlo Skotok (travel book), 1970; Apaczai (novel), 1978; Varazslasok (poems), 1984; Hosszu Utnak Pora (novel), 1988; Zsuzsanna Kertje (novel), 1989; Zoldag-Parittya (poems), 1990; Cowboyok, Aranyasok, Csavargok (Folk Poetry of North America), 1992; Szölöhegyi varazslat (novel), 1995; Erdotanitvany (poems), 1999; Der Zauberkloss (novel), 1999; Gulliver utolsó utazása (satirical novel), 2001; Édes Öcsém (novel), 2002. *Honours:* Gold Medal for Children's Literature, 1976; Fulbright Grant, 1988. *Memberships:* PEN Club of Hungary; Union of Hungarian Writers. *Address:* 1 Attila ut 133, Budapest 1012, Hungary.

GYÖRI, Ladislao Pablo; b. 13 July 1963, Buenos Aires, Argentina. Engineer; Writer; Poet. *Education:* Graduated as Electronic Engineer, National Technological University of Buenos Aires, 1989. *Publication:* Estiajes, Creator of Virtual Poetry, 1994. *Contributions to:* Dimensao; Teraz Mowie; PO Box; Piel de Leopardo; Visible Language; Luz en Arte & Literatura. *Memberships:* Argentinian Society of Writers; Argentinian Tevat Group for the Research and Diffusion of Poetry and Arts and New Technology, co-founder. *Address:* Ave Federico Lacroze 3814 2do 10 (1427), Buenos Aires, Argentina.

H

HA JIN, (real name, Xuefei Jin); b. 21 Feb. 1956, Jinzhou, China. Author; Poet. m. Lisah Bian, 6 July 1982, 1 c. *Education:* BA, Heilongjian University, Harbin, 1981; MA, Shangdong University, Quingdao, 1984; PhD, Brandeis University, 1992. *Appointment:* Faculty, Dept of English, Emory University, 1993–. *Publications:* Fiction: Ocean of Words: Army Stories, 1996; Under the Red Flag, 1997; In the Pond, 1998; Waiting, 1999; Quiet Desperation, 2000. Poetry: Between Silences, 1990; Facing Shadows, 1996; Wreckage, 2001. *Honours:* PEN/Hemingway Award, 1997; Flannery O'Connor Award, 1997; National Book Award, 1999; PEN/Faulkner Award, 2000. *Address:* c/o Dept of English, Emory University, 302 N Callaway, Atlanta, GA 30322, USA.

HAAVIKKO, Paavo (Juhani); b. 25 Jan. 1931, Helsinki, Finland. Poet; Author; Dramatist; Publisher. m. (1) Marja-Liisa Vartio, 1955, deceased 1966, 1 s., 1 d., (2) Ritva Rainio, 1971. *Appointments:* Literary Dir, Otava Publishing Co, 1967–83; Publisher, Art House Publishing Group, 1983–. *Publications:* Tiet etäisyyksiin, 1951; Tuuliönä, 1953; Synnyinmaa, 1955; Lehdet lehtiä, 1958; Talvipalatsi, 1959; Yksityisiä Asioita, 1960; Toinen taivas ja maa, 1961; Runot, 1962; Vuodet, 1962; Lasi Claudius Civiliksen salaliittolaisten pöydällä, 1964; Puut, kaikki heidän vihreytensä, 1966; Selected Poems, 1968; Neljätoista hallitsijaa, 1970; Puhua vastata opettaa, 1972; Runoja matkalta salmen ylitse, 1973; Kaksikymmentä ja yksi, 1974; Runot 1949–1974, 1975; Runoelmat, 1975; Viiniä, Kirjoitusta, 1976; Kansakuninan linja, 1977; Yritys omaksikuvaksi, 1987; Toukokuu, ikuinen, 1988; Prospero, 1967–1995, 1996. *Honours:* Six Finnish State Prizes for Literature; Pro Finlandia Medal; Neustadt International Prize for Literature, 1984. *Membership:* Finnish Writers' Asscn, board mem., 1962–66. *Address:* c/o Art House Publishing Group, Blvd 19C, 00120 Helsinki, Finland.

HACKER, Marilyn; b. 27 Nov. 1942, New York, NY, USA. Poet; Writer; Critic; Ed.; Teacher. 1 d. *Education:* BA, Romance Languages, New York University, 1964. *Appointments:* Ed., Quark: A Quarterly of Speculative Fiction, 1969–71, The Kenyon Review, 1990–94; Jenny McKean Moore Chair in Writing, George Washington University, 1976–77; Mem., Editorial Collective, 1977–80, Ed.-in-Chief, 1979, The Little Magazine; Teacher, School of General Studies, Columbia University, 1979–81; Visiting Artist, Fine Arts Work Center, Provincetown, Massachusetts, 1981; Visiting Prof., University of Idaho, 1982; Ed.-in-Chief, Thirteenth Moon: A Feminist Literary Magazine, 1982–86; Writer-in-Residence, State University of New York at Albany, 1988, Columbia University, 1988; George Elliston Poet-in-Residence, University of Cincinnati, 1988; Distinguished Writer-in-Residence, American University, Washington, DC, 1989; Visiting Prof. of Creative Writing, State University of New York at Binghamton, 1990, University of Utah, 1995, Barnard College, 1995, Princeton University, 1997; Fannie Hurst Poet-in-Residence, Brandeis University, 1996. *Publications:* Presentation Piece, 1974; Separations, 1976; Taking Notice, 1980; Assumptions, 1985; Love, Death and the Changing of the Seasons, 1986; The Hang-Glider's Daughter: New and Selected Poems, 1990; Going Back to the River, 1990; Selected Poems: 1965–1990, 1994; Winter Numbers, 1994; Edge (trans. of poems by Claire Malroux), 1996; Squares and Courtyards, 2000; A Long-Gone Sun, by Claire Malroux (trans.), 2000; Here There Was Once a Country, by Vénus Khoury-Ghata (trans.), 2001. *Contributions to:* Numerous anthologies and other publications. *Honours:* National Endowment for the Arts Grants, 1973–74, 1985–86, 1995; National Book Award in Poetry, 1975; Guggenheim Fellowship, 1980–81; Ingram Merrill Foundation Grant, 1984–85; Robert F Winner Awards, 1987, 1989, John Masefield Memorial Award, 1994, Poetry Society of America; Lambda Literary Awards, 1991, 1995; Lenore Marshall Award, Acad. of American Poets, 1995; Poets' Prize, 1995. *Address:* 230 W 105th St, New York, NY 10025, USA.

HACKNEY, Frances Marie Veda; b. 14 July 1917, Sydney, NSW, Australia. Botanist; General and Human Biologist; Writer; Poet. m. Walter Frederick Frohlich, 19 March 1949, 3 s., 3 d. *Education:* BSc, 1938, MSc, 1940, DSc, 1949, Sydney University; Postgraduate Studies in Zoology, Human Histology. *Appointments:* Various positions, Sydney University, University of New South Wales, Macquarie University, 1964–81. *Publications:* Bread and Butter Moon, 1956; Australian Science (essays), 1964; For All I Have Loved (poems), 1994. *Contributions to:* Anthologies and periodicals. *Honours:* Australian Women's Weekly Poetry Prize, 1965; Australia Day Council's Medals for Achievement, 1987, 1991, Gold Medal, 1989; First Prizes, Melbourne Poetry Society, 1987, 1991; Writing Fellow, Fellowship of Australian Writers, 1993; Citizenship's Award for Services to Music and the Arts, 1996. *Memberships:* Fellowship of Australian Writers; Fellow Mem., International Poets Acad.; Society of Women Writers; RSA, fellow; International Writers and Artists Asscn; The Writers' Forum. *Address:* 78 Kenneth St, Longueville, NSW 2066, Australia.

HADAS, Rachel; b. 8 Nov. 1948, New York, NY, USA. Prof. of English; Poet; Writer. m. (1) Stavros Kondilis, 7 Nov. 1970, divorced 1978, (2) George Edwards, 22 July 1978, 1 s. *Education:* BA, Classics, Radcliffe College, 1969; MA, Poetry, Johns Hopkins University, 1977; PhD, Comparative Literature, Princeton University, 1982. *Appointments:* Asst Prof., 1982–87, Assoc. Prof. 1987–92, Prof. of English, 1992–, Rutgers University; Adjunct Prof., Columbia University, 1992–93; Visiting Prof., Princeton University, 1995, 1996. *Publications:* Starting From Troy, 1975; Slow Transparency, 1983; A Son from Sleep, 1987; Pass It On, 1989; Living in Time, 1990; Unending Dialogue, 1991; Mirrors of Astonishment, 1992; Other Worlds Than This, 1994; The Empty Bed, 1995; The Double Legacy, 1995; Halfway Down the Hall (New and Selected Poems), 1998; Merrill, Cavafy, Poems and Dreams, 2000; Indelible, 2001. *Contributions to:* Periodicals. *Honours:* Ingram Merrill Foundation Fellowship, 1976–77; Guggenheim Fellowship, 1988–89; American Acad. and Institute of Arts and Letters Award, 1990; O B Hardison Award, 2000; Scholars and Writers, New York Public Library, 2000–01. *Memberships:* American Acad. of Arts and Sciences, fellow; Modern Greek Studies Asscn; MLA; PEN; Poetry Society of America. *Address:* 838 West End Ave, No. 3A, New York, NY 10025, USA.

HAGEN, Edna (Sue); b. 9 April 1957, Sandpoint, ID, USA. Poet; Songwriter. m. Curtis Hagen, 3 Aug. 1992. *Education:* Kalispell College. *Publications:* Satin and Lace, 1989; Selected Poetry, 1995; April's Song, 1996. *Contributions to:* Anthologies and periodicals. *Honours:* Golden Poetry Award, Library of Poets, 1991; Blue Ribbon, Southern Poetry Asscn, 1994; Top Writer Award, Song Writers Asscn, 1995; Certificate of Excellence, National Poetry Asscn, 1995; Special Certificate, New Voices, 1996. *Memberships:* Kalispell Poetry Asscn; National Poetry Asscn. *Address:* 526 Fourth St W, Kalispell, MT 59901, USA.

HAGGARD, Edward Roy; b. 24 June 1946, Chicago, IL, USA. Poet; Publisher. Divorced. *Education:* BA, Ripon College, Wisconsin, 1964–68; Lincoln College, Oxford University, 1968; Northern Illinois University, 1968–70. *Appointments:* Workshops: University of Chicago, 1998; Gotham Writers' Workshop, 1998; Harvard University, 1999. *Publications:* Heroines, 1988. *Contributions to:* Reviews and journals. *Honour:* First Place, Jim Wayne Miller Prize, Green River Writers, 1998. *Memberships:* Poetry Society of America; Acad. of American Poets; Modern Poetry Asscn. *Address:* c/o Lakes and Prairies Enterprises, Inc, Orland Park, IL 60462-4766, USA.

HAGGER, Nicholas Osborne; b. 22 May 1939, London, England. British Poet; Verse Dramatist; Short Story Writer; Lecturer; Author; Man of Letters; Philosopher; Cultural Historian. m. (1) Caroline Virginia Mary Nixon, 16 Sept. 1961, 1 d., (2) Madeline Ann Johnson, 22 Feb. 1974, 2 s. *Education:* MA English Literature, Worcester College, Oxford, 1958–61. *Appointments:* Lecturer in English, University of Baghdad, 1961–62; Prof. of English Literature, Tokyo University of Education and Keio University, Tokyo, 1963–67; Lecturer in English, University of Libya, Tripoli, 1968–70; Freelance Features for Times, 1970–72. *Publications:* The Fire and the Stones: A Grand Unified Theory of World History and Religion, 1991; Selected Poems: A Metaphysical's Way of Fire, 1991; The Universe and the Light: A New View of the Universe and Reality, 1993; A White Radiance: The Collected Poems 1958–93, 1994; A Mystic Way: A Spiritual Autobiography, 1994; Awakening to the Light: Diaries, Vol. 1, 1958–67, 1994; A Spade Fresh with Mud: Collected Stories, Vol. 1, 1995; The Warlords: From D-Day to Berlin, A Verse Drama, 1995; A Smell of Leaves and Summer: Collected Stories, Vol. 2, 1995; Overlord, The Triumph of Light 1944–1945: An Epic Poem, Books 1–2, 1995, Books 3–6, 1996, Books 7–9, 10–12, 1997; The One and the Many, 1999; Wheeling Bats and a Harvest Moon: Collected Stories, Vol. 3, 1999; Prince Tudor, A Verse Drama, 1999; The Warm Glow of the Monastery Courtyard: Collected Stories, Vol. 4, 1999. *Address:* Otley Hall, Otley, Nr Ipswich, IP6 9PA, England.

HAGHDOUST, Derakhshandeh. See: NOORIALA, Partow.

HAHN, Susan; b. 11 Nov. 1947, Chicago, IL, USA. Poet; Writer; Ed. m. Frederic L. Hahn, 26 March 1967, 1 s. *Appointments:* Staff, 1980–, Ed., 1997–, TriQuarterly literary magazine; Co-Founder/Co-Ed., TriQuarterly Books, 1988–. *Publications:* Harriet Rubin's Mother's Wooden Hand, 1991; Incontinence, 1993; Melancholia et cetera, 1995; Confession, 1997; Holiday, 2001; Mother in Summer, 2002. *Contributions to:* Many reviews, quarterlies and journals. *Honours:* Illinois Arts Council Literary Awards, 1985, 1990, 1996, 1997; Society of Midland Authors Award for Poetry, 1994; Pushcart Prize for Poetry, 2000; George Kent Prize, Poetry magazine, 2000. *Address:* 1377 Scott Ave, Winnetka, IL 60093, USA.

HAHN (GARCES), Oscar (Arturo); b. 5 July 1938, Iquique, Chile (Naturalized US citizen). Poet; Writer; Assoc. Prof. of Spanish-American Literature. m. Nancy Jorquera, 1971, 1 d. *Education:* Graduated, University of Chile, 1963; MA, University of Iowa, 1972; PhD, University of Maryland at College Park, 1977. *Appointments:* Prof. of Hispanic Literature, University of Chile, 1965–73; Instructor, University of Maryland at College Park, 1974–77;

Asst Prof., 1977–79, Assoc. Prof. of Spanish-American Literature, 1979–, University of Iowa. *Publications:* Esta rosa negra (poems), 1961; Agua final (poems), 1967; Arte de morir (poems), 1977, English trans. as The Art of Dying, 1987; El cuento fantástico hispanoamericano en el siglo XIX, 1978; Mal de amor, 1981, English trans. as Love Breaks, 1991; Imagenes nucleares, 1983; Texto sobre texto, 1984; Tratado de sortilegios, 1992; Antología poética, 1993; Antología virtual, 1996; ¿Qué hacia yo el once de septiembre de 1973? (with Matias Rivas and Roberto Merino), 1997; Antología retroactiva, 1998; Versos robados/Stolen Verses and Other Poems, 2000. *Contributions to:* Literary journals. *Honours:* Premio Alerce, 1961; Poetry Award, University of Chile, 1966; Hon. Fellow, International Writing Program, 1972. *Memberships:* Instituto Internacional de Literatura Iberoamericana; MLA of America. *Address:* c/o Dept of Spanish, University of Iowa, Iowa City, IA 52240, USA.

HAIG, Margaret Jane Darrah; b. 7 Dec. 1919, Gambusnethan, Strathclyde, Scotland. Poet. m. James Peacock Haig, 15 Dec. 1964, 1 s. *Education:* ASCT, 1956; FSCT, 1964; AIST, 1965; WHO, 1967. *Appointments:* Head, Dept of Cardiological Technicians; Reader of English, University of Parma; Co-Dir, London School of English, Parma. *Publications:* Fragmentary Thoughts of Time Place and Space, 1990; Beyond the Frontiers, 1991; Along the Banks of Time, 1992. *Contributions to:* James Joyce Quarterly Journal, USA; Plowman International Journal of Poetry, Canada; Eavesdropper Journal of Poetry, London. *Honours:* 1990 Xth International Award for Literature; Colombini Cenelli Award. *Memberships:* National Poetry Society, London; Poetry Society, Palma; Eavesdropper Society, London.

HAINES, Brian William; b. 24 Jan. 1918, Devonport, Devon, England. Writer; Poet; Researcher. *Appointments:* Solicitor and Barrister, Supreme Court, Vic., Australia, 1967. *Publications:* Four Winds, 1948; A Book of Epigrams, 1950; Lark in the Morning, 1952; Block Towers, 1960; Other publications include technical writing, short stories and novels. *Contributions to:* Poetry and reviews: Daily Herald; News Chronicle. *Membership:* Poetry Society, life mem. *Address:* 9a Sharpleshall St, London NW1 8YN, England.

HAINES, John Francis; b. 30 Nov. 1947, Chelmsford, Essex, England. Government Official; Poet. m. Margaret Rosemary Davies, 19 March 1977. *Education:* Padgate College of Education, 1966–69; ONC in Public Administration, Millbank College of Commerce, 1972. *Appointments:* General Asst; Payments Asst. *Publications:* Other Places, Other Times, 1981; Spacewain, 1989; After the Android Wars, 1992; Orders from the Bridge, 1996. *Contributions to:* Dark Horizons; Fantasy Commentator; First Time; Folio; Idomo; Iota; Macabre; New Hope International; Not To Be Named; Overspace; Purple Patch; Sandor; The Scanner; Simply Thrilled Honey; Spokes; Star Line; Stride; Third Half; Yellow Dwarf; A Child's Garden of Olaf; A Northern Chorus; Ammonite; Boggers All; Eldritch Science; Foolscap; Heliocentric Net; Lines of Light; Ore; Pablo Lennis; Pleiade; Premonitions; Mentor; Rampant Guinea Pig; Zone; Positively Poetry; What Poets Eat; Mexicon 6 – The Party; Terrible Work; Xenophilia. *Memberships:* Science Fiction Poetry Asscn; British Fantasy Society; The Eight Hand Gang, founder-mem. *Address:* 5 Cross Farm, Station Rd, Padgate, Warrington WA2 0QG, England.

HAINES, John (Meade); b. 29 June 1924, Norfolk, Virginia, USA. Poet; Writer; Teacher. m. (1) Jo Ella Hussey, 10 Oct. 1960, (2) Jane McWhorter, 23 Nov. 1970, divorced 1974, (3) Leslie Sennett, Oct. 1978, divorced, 4 c. *Education:* National Art School, Washington, DC, 1946–47; American University, 1948–49; Hans Hoffman School of Fine Art, New York City, 1950–52; University of Washington, 1974. *Appointments:* Poet-in-Residence, University of Alaska, 1972–73; Visiting Prof. in English, University of Washington, 1974; Visting Lecturer in English, University of Montana, 1974; Writer-in-Residence, Sheldon Jackson College, 1982–83, Ucross Foundation, 1987, Montalvo Center for the Arts, 1988, Djerassi Foundation, 1988; Visiting Lecturer, University of California at Santa Cruz, 1986, Wordsworth Conference, Grasmere, England, 1996; Visting Writer, The Loft Mentor Series, 1987, George Washington University, 1991–92; Visiting Prof., Ohio University, 1989–90; Elliston Fellow in Poetry, University of Cincinnati, 1992; Chair in Creative Arts, Austin Peay State University, Clarksville, Tennessee, 1993. *Publications:* Poetry: Winter News, 1966; Suite for the Pied Piper, 1968; The Legend of Paper Plates, 1970; The Mirror, 1970; The Stone Harp, 1971; Twenty Poems, 1971; Leaves and Ashes, 1975; In Five Years, 1976; Cicada, 1977; In a Dusty Light, 1977; The Sun on Your Shoulder, 1977; News From the Glacier: Selected Poems, 1960–80, 1982; New Poems: 1980–1988, 1990; Rain Country, 1990; The Owl in the Mask of a Dreamer, 1993. Non-Fiction: Minus Thirty-One and the Wind Blowing: Nine Reflections About Living on the Land (with others), 1980; Living Off the Country: Essays on Poetry and Place, 1981; Other Days, 1982; Of Traps and Snares, 1982; Stories We Listened To, 1986; You and I and the World, 1988; The Stars, the Snow, the Fire, 1989; Fables and Distances: New and Selected Essays, 1996; A Guide to the Four-Chambered Heart, 1996. *Contributions to:* Periodicals. *Honours:* Guggenheim Fellowships, 1965–66, 1984–85; National Endowment for the Arts Grant, 1967–68; Amy Lowell Scholarship, 1976–77; Governor's Award for lifetime contributions to the arts in Alaska, 1982; Hon. LD, University of Alaska, 1983; Ingram Merrill Foundation Grant, 1987; Lenore Marshall Nation Award, 1991; Literary Award, American Acad. of Arts and Letters, 1995. *Memberships:* Acad. of

American Poets; Alaska Conservation Society; Natural Resources Defense Council; PEN American Center; Poetry Society of America; Sierra Club; Wilderness Society. *Address:* PO Box 103431, Anchorage, AL 99510, USA.

HAKIM, Seymour, (Sy Hakim); b. 23 Jan. 1933, New York, NY, USA. Poet; Writer; Artist; Educator. m. Odetta Roverso, 18 Aug. 1970. *Education:* AB, Eastern New Mexico University, 1954; MA, New York University, 1960; Postgraduate work, various universities. *Appointments:* Consultant Ed., Poet Gallery Press, New York, 1970; Ed., Overseas Teacher, 1977. *Publications:* The Sacred Family, 1970; Manhattan Goodbye (poems), 1970; Under Moon, 1971; Museum of the Mind, 1971; Wine Theorem, 1972; Substituting Memories, 1976; Iris Elegy, 1979; Balancing Act, 1981; Birth of a Poet, 1985; Eleanor, Goodbye, 1988; Michaelangelo's Call, 1999. Other: Exhibits with accomanying writings: 1970, 1973, 1982–83, 1985. *Contributions to:* Overseas Educator; California State Poetry Quarterly; American Writing; Dan River Anthology; Its On My Wall; Older Eyes; Art Exhibition and Reading, New York, 1999; Life Shards, 2000; Artwork/readings NYC, 2000. *Memberships:* Asscn of Poets and Writers; National Photo Instructors' Asscn; Italo-Brittanica Asscn. *Address:* Via Chiesanuova No. 1, 36023 Langare, VI 36023, Italy.

HALEY, Patricia, (Reuben Augustus, Rosie Lee); b. 17 Jan. 1951, Waxahachie, Texas, USA. Therapist; Teacher; Poet; Writer. *Education:* BA, Texas Woman's University, 1973; MEd, University of North Texas, 1994; Licensed Professional Counselor. *Appointment:* Founder-Ed.-Publisher, Poetic Perspective Inc, 1988–. *Publications:* Family Tributes, 1989; Therapeutic Poetry, 1990; Heroes: A Poetic Perspective, 1991. *Contributions to:* Anthologies and other publications. *Honours:* Poet of Merit, American Poet Asscn, 1989; Honourable mentions. *Memberships:* American Counseling Asscn; Galaxy of Verse Foundation; National Asscn of Poetry Therapy; Poetry Society of America; Poetry Society of Texas; Texas Counseling Asscn. *Address:* 110 Onieda St, Waxahachie, TX 75165, USA.

HALIM, Huri. See: OFFEN, Yehuda.

HALL, Bernadette Mary; b. 6 Dec. 1945, Alexandra, South Island, New Zealand. Secondary School Teacher; Poet. m. John Hall, 13 Jan. 1968, 2 s., 1 d. *Education:* MA, Honours, Otago University, 1968. *Publications:* Heartwood, 1989; Of Elephants, etc. 1990; The Persistent Leviator, 1994; Still Talking, 1997; Settler Dreaming, 2001. *Contributions to:* Soho Square; Landfall; Sport; Poetry New Zealand; Contemporary New Zealand Poetry; Vital Writing; Carcanet; Takahe magazine. *Honours:* Writer-in-Residence, University of Canterbury, Christchurch, 1991; Robert Burns Fellowship, Otago University, Dunedin, 1996; New Zealand Representative at the International Writing Programme, IA, USA, 1997. *Membership:* New Zealand Society of Authors. *Address:* 19 Bryndwr Rd, Fendalton, Christchurch 5, New Zealand.

HALL, Daniel; b. 1952, USA. Poet. *Publications:* Hermit With Landscape, 1990; Strange Relation, 1996. *Honours:* Yale Younger Poets Competition Prize, 1989; National Poetry Series Competition Prize, 1995. *Address:* c/o Penguin Books, 375 Hudson St, New York, NY 10014, USA.

HALL, David, (David Iveson); b. 30 Dec. 1946, England. Teacher; Poet. m. Valerie E Walters, 19 May 1984, 1 d. *Education:* BA, Honours, English, London University. *Publications:* A Bit of England, 1990; Birds of Passage, 1991. *Contributions to:* Ore; Orbis; Scratch; North; Odyssey; Foolscap. *Address:* 54 Poll Hill Rd, Heswall, Wirral, Merseyside L60 7SW, England.

HALL, Donald (Andrew Jr); b. 20 Sept. 1928, New Haven, CT, USA. Poet; Writer; Prof. of English (retd). m. (1) Kirby Thompson, 1952, divorced 1969, 1 s., 1 d., (2) Jane Kenyon, 1972, deceased 1995. *Education:* BA, Harvard University, 1951; BLitt, Oxford University, 1953; Stanford University, 1953–54. *Appointments:* Poetry Ed., Paris Review, 1953–62; Asst Prof., 1957–61, Assoc. Prof., 1961–66, Prof. of English, 1966–75, University of Michigan. *Publications:* Poetry: Poems, 1952; Exile, 1952; To the Loud Wind and Other Poems, 1955; Exiles and Marriages, 1955; The Dark Houses, 1958; A Roof of Tiger Lilies, 1964; The Alligator Bride: Poems New and Selected, 1969; The Yellow Room: Love Poems, 1971; A Blue Wing Tilts at the Edge of the Sea: Selected Poems 1964–1974, 1975; The Town of Hill, 1975; Kicking the Leaves, 1978; The Toy Bone, 1979; The Twelve Seasons, 1983; Brief Lives, 1983; Great Day at the Cows' House, 1984; The Happy Man, 1986; The One Day: A Poem in Three Parts, 1988; Old and New Poems, 1990; The One Day and Poems (1947–1990), 1991; The Museum of Clear Ideas, 1993; The Old Life, 1996; Without, 1998; The Painted Bed, 2000. Short Stories: The Ideal Bakery, 1987. Other: Henry Moore: The Life and Work of a Great Sculptor, 1966; Marianne Moore: The Cage and the Animal, 1970; The Gentleman's Alphabet Book, 1972; Writing Well, 1973; Remembering Poets: Reminiscences and Opinions – Dylan Thomas, Robert Frost, T S Eliot, Ezra Pound, 1978; Goatfoot Milktongue Twinbird: Interviews, Essays and Notes on Poetry 1970–76, 1978; To Read Literature: Fiction, Poetry, Drama, 1981; The Weather for Poetry: Essays, Reviews and Notes on Poetry 1977–81, 1982; Poetry and Ambition: Essays 1982–1988, 1988; Anecdotes of Modern Art (with Pat Corrigan Wykes), 1990; Here at Eagle Pond, 1990; Their Ancient Glittering Eyes, 1992; Life Work, 1993; Death to Death of Poetry, 1994; Principal Products of Portugal, 1995. *Honours:* Edna St Vincent Millay Memorial Prize, 1956; Longview Foundation Award, 1960; Guggenheim

Fellowships, 1963, 1972; Sarah Josepha Hale Award, 1983; Poet Laureate of New Hampshire, 1984–89; Lenore Marshall Award, 1987; National Book Critics Circle Award, 1989; Los Angeles Times Book Award, 1989; Robert Frost Silver Medal, Poetry Society of America, 1991; Lifetime Achievement Award, New Hampshire Writers and Publishers Project, 1992; New England Book Award for Non-Fiction, 1993; Ruth Lilly Prize for Poetry, 1994; Hon. doctorates. *Address: Eagle Pond Farm, 24 US Route 4, Wilmot, NH 03287-4438, USA.*

HALL, Fiona Jane; b. 15 July 1955, Swinton, England. Teacher; Poet. 2 d. *Education:* BA, Honours, St Hugh's College, Oxford, 1976; Postgraduate Certificate in Education, Oxford Polytechnic, 1977. *Contributions to:* Anthologies and journals. *Honours:* Bloodaxe/Evening Chronicle Edward Boyle Prize for Most Promising New Poet, 1988, Runner-up, 1990, 1991; Northern Arts Bursary, 1989; Northern Arts Tyrone Guthrie Award, 1990; First Prize, Durham Litfest Competition, 1992. *Membership:* Poetry Society. *Address:* The School House, Whittingham, Alnwick, Northumberland NE66 4UP, England.

HALL, Floriana Frances; b. 2 Oct. 1927, Pittsburgh, PA, USA. m. Robert E. Hall, 31 Dec. 1948, 2 s., 3 d. *Education:* Akron University. *Publications:* Small Change (children's non-fiction), 1997; The Sands of Rhyme (poems), 1998; Through Our Eyes: Poems of Beautiful Northeast Ohio (ed.), 1999; Daddy Was a Bad Boy (non-fiction), 2001; Poet's Nook Potpourri (ed.), 2001. Other: 20 stories; 300 poems in various books and magazines in USA, England and India. *Honours:* Seven Eds' Choice Awards, National Library of Poetry, 1995–99; Various other prizes. *Membership:* Distinguished Mem., National Library of Poetry; Honored Writer, Poets League of Greater Cleveland, 1998; Famous Poets Society, 1998. *Address:* 1232 Clifton Ave, Akron, OH 44310, USA. *E-mail:* Floriana102@aol.com. *Website:* www.expage.com/flossiesbooknook.

HALL, James B(yron); b. 21 July 1918, Midland, Ohio, USA. Author; Poet; University Provost Emeritus. m. Elizabeth Cushman, 14 Feb. 1946, 1 s., 4 d. *Education:* Miami University, Oxford, Ohio, 1938–39; University of Hawaii, 1938–40; BA, 1947, MA, 1948, PhD, 1953, University of Iowa; Postgraduate Studies, Kenyon College, 1949. *Appointments:* Writer-in-Residence, Miami University, Oxford, Ohio, 1948–49; University of North Carolina at Greensville, 1954, University of British Columbia, 1955, University of Colorado, 1963; Instructor, Cornell University, 1952–54; Asst Prof., 1954–57, Assoc. Prof., 1958–60, Prof. of English, 1960–65, University of Oregon; Prof. of English and Dir, Writing Center, University of California at Irvine, 1965–68; Provost, 1968–75, Provost Emeritus, 1983–88, University of California at Santa Cruz. *Publications:* Fiction: Not by the Door, 1954; Racers to the Sun, 1960; Mayo Sergeant, 1968. Short Story Collections: 15 x 3 (with Herbert Gold and R V Cassill), 1957; Us He Devours, 1964; The Short Hall, 1980; I Like It Better Now, 1992. Poetry: The Hunt Within, 1973; Bereavements (collected and selected poems), 1991. Non-Fiction: Perspectives on William Everson (co-ed.), 1992; Art and Craft of the Short Story, 1995; The Extreme Stories +3. *Contributions to:* Anthologies and other publications. *Honours:* Octave Thanet Prize, 1950; Rockefeller Foundation Grant, 1955; Oregon Poetry Prize, 1958; Emily Clark Balch Fiction Prize, 1967; Chapelbrook Award, 1967; James B Hall Gallery named in his honour, University of California Regents, 1985; James B Hall Traveling Fellowship founded in his honour, University of California at Santa Cruz, 1985. *Memberships:* Associated Writing Programs, pres., 1965–66; American Asscn of University Profs; National Writers' Union; Oregon Book Awards, trustee, 1992–2001. *Address:* 1413 Oak St, Lake Oswego, OR 97034, USA.

HALL, Jane Anna; b. 4 April 1959, New London, CT, USA. Writer; Poet; Artist. *Education:* Professional Model, Barbizon School, 1976; Graduate, Westbrook High School, 1977. *Appointment:* Founder-Ed., Poetry in Your Mailbox Newsletter, 1989–. *Publications:* Cedar and Lace, 1986; Satin and Pinstripe, 1987; Fireworks and Diamonds, 1988; Stars and Daffodils, 1989; Sunrises and Stonewalls, 1990; Mountains and Meadows, 1991; Moonlight and Water Lilies, 1992; Sunset and Beaches, 1993; Under Par Recipes, 1994; New and Selected Poems 1986–1994, 1994; Poems for Children 1986–1995, 1995; Butterflies and Roses, 1996; Hummingbirds and Hibiscus, 1997; Swans and Azaleas, 1998; Damselflies and Peonies, 1999; Egrets and Cattails, 2000; Doves and Rhododendron, 2001; Bluebirds and Mountain Laurel, 2002; The Full Moon Looks Like (children's book)), 2002. *Contributions to:* Several publications. *Honours:* Second Prizes, Connecticut Poetry Society Contest, 1983, 1986; Various certificates. *Memberships:* Romance Writers of America; Connecticut Poetry Society. *Address:* PO Box 629, Westbrook, CT 06498, USA.

HALL, J(ohn) C(live); b. 12 Sept. 1920, London, England. Poet. *Education:* Oriel College, Oxford. *Appointments:* Staff, Encounter Magazine, 1955–91; Ed., Literary Executor of Keith Douglas. *Publications:* Poetry: Selected Poems, 1943; The Summer Dance and Other Poems, 1951; The Burning Hare, 1966; A House of Voices, 1973; Selected and New Poems 1939–84, 1985. Other: Collected Poems of Edwin Muir, 1921–51 (ed.), 1952; New Poems (co-ed.), 1955; Edwin Muir, 1956. *Address:* 9 Warwick Rd, Mount Sion, Tunbridge Wells, Kent TN1 1YL, England.

HALL, Rodney; b. 18 Nov. 1935, Solihull, Warwickshire, England. Writer; Poet. m. Bet MacPahil, 3 d. *Education:* BA, University of Queensland, Brisbane, 1971. *Appointments:* Poetry Ed., The Australian, 1967–78; Creative Arts Fellow, Australian National University, 1968–69. *Publications:* Fiction: The Ship on the Coin, 1972; A Place Among People, 1975; Just Relations, 1982; Kisses of the Enemy, 1987; Captivity Captive, 1988; The Second Bridegroom, 1991; The Grisly Wife, 1993; The Island in the Mind, 1998; The Day We Had Hitler Home, 2000; The Owner of My Face, 2002. Poetry: Penniless Till Doomsday, 1962; The Law of Karma: A Progression of Poems, 1968; A Soapbox Omnibus, 1973; Selected Poems, 1975; Black Bagatelles, 1978; The Most Beautiful World: Fictions and Sermons, 1981; Journey Through Australia, 1989. *Contributions to:* Newspapers, magazines, reviews, and journals. *Honours:* Grace Leven Prize for Poetry, 1973; Miles Franklin Awards, 1982, 1994; Order of Australia, 1990. *Address:* PO Box 7, Bermagui South, NSW 2546, Australia.

HALPERN, Daniel; b. 11 Sept. 1945, Syracuse, New York, USA. Assoc. Prof. Poet; Writer; Ed. m. Jeanne Catherine Carter, 31 Dec. 1982, 1 d. *Education:* San Francisco State College, 1963–64; BA, California State University at Northridge, 1969; MFA, Columbia University, 1972. *Appointments:* Founder-Ed., Antaeus literary magazine, 1969–95; Instructor, New School for Social Research, New York City, 1971–76; Ed.-in-Chief, Ecco Press, 1971–; Visiting Prof., Princeton University, 1975–76, 1987–88, 1995–96; Assoc. Prof., Columbia University, 1976–. *Publications:* Poetry: Traveling on Credit, 1978; Seasonal Rights, 1982; Tango, 1987; Foreign Neon, 1991; Selected Poems, 1994; Antaeus 1970, 1996; Something Shining, 1998. Other: The Keeper of Height, 1974; Treble Poets, 1975; Our Private Lives: Journals, Notebooks and Diaries, 1990; Not for Bread Alone: Writers on Food, Wine, and the Art of Eating, 1993; The Autobiographical Eye, 1993; Holy Fire: Nine Visionary Poets and the Quest for Enlightenment, 1994. Editor: Borges on Writing (co-ed.), 1973; The American Poetry Anthology, 1975; The Antaeus Anthology, 1986; The Art of the Tale: An International Anthology of Short Stories, 1986; On Nature, 1987; Writers on Artists, 1988; Reading the Fights (with Joyce Carol Oates), 1988; Plays in One Act, 1990; The Sophisticated Cat (with Joyce Carol Oates), 1992; On Music (co-ed.), 1994. *Contributions to:* Various anthologies, reviews, journals, and magazines. *Honours:* Jesse Rehder Poetry Award, Southern Poetry Review, 1971; YMHA Discovery Award, 1971; Great Lakes Colleges National Book Award, 1973; Borestone Mountain Poetry Award, 1974; Robert Frost Fellowship, Bread Loaf, 1974; National Endowment for the Arts Fellowships, 1974, 1975, 1987; Pushcaft Press Prizes, 1980, 1987, 1988; Carey Thomas Award for Creative Publishing, Publishers Weekly, 1987; Guggenheim Fellowship, 1988; PEN Publisher Citation, 1993. *Address:* c/o The Ecco Press, 100 W Broad St, Hopewell, NJ 08525, USA.

HALSE, Frank Adams Jr; b. 3 May 1927, Troy, New York, USA. Clergyman (retd); Poet. m. Joyce Holcomb, 7 June 1952, 2 d. *Education:* AB, Psychology and Religion, 1955; STM, Psychology and Religion, 1958; MA, Family Studies, 1974. *Publications:* Poems of the Spirit, 1962; Sidewalks of Fog, 1981; View from the Catacombs, 1988; A Portable Ark, 1989. *Contributions to:* Frying Pan; Lake Effect; Daily Change. *Membership:* Poetry Society of America. *Address:* 506 Third St, Brandon, FL 33511, USA.

HALSEY, Alan; b. 22 Sept. 1949, Croydon, Surrey, England. Bookseller; Poet. *Education:* BA, Honours, London. *Publications:* Yearspace, 1979; Another Loop in Our Days, 1980; Present State, 1981; Perspectives on the Reach, 1981; The Book of Coming Forth in Official Secrecy, 1981; Auto Dada Cafe, 1987; A Book of Changes, 1988; Five Years Out, 1989; Reasonable Distance, 1992; The Text of Shelley's Death, 1995; A Robin Hood Book, 1996; Fit to Print (with Karen McCormack), 1998; Days of '49 (with Gavin Selerie), 1999; Wittgenstein's Devil: Selected Writings, 1978–98, 2000; Sonatas and Preliminary Sketches, 2000; Dante's Barber Shop, 2001. *Contributions to:* Critical Quarterly; Conjunctions; North Dakota Quarterly; Writing; Ninth Decade; Poetica; South West Review; Poetry Wales; Poesie Europe; O Ars; Figs; Interstate; Prospice; Reality Studios; Fragmente; Screens and Tasted Parallels; Avec; Purge; Grille; Acumen; Shearsman; Oasis; New American Writing; Agenda; Colorado Review; Talisman; PN Review; Resurgence; West Coast Line; The Gig; Boxkite; The Paper; Chicago Review; Envelope; Ecorché. *Membership:* Thomas Lovell Beddoes Society; David Jones Society. *Address:* 40 Crescent Rd, Nether Edge, Sheffield S7 1HN, England. *E-mail:* alan@nethedge.demon.co.uk.

HALTER, Aloma; b. 25 Nov. 1954, London, England. Poet; Ed. *Education:* BA, Honours, Newnham College, Cambridge, 1978. *Appointments:* English Correspondent to Minister of Science and Technology; Literary Critic, Jerusalem Post; Bureau Man., Baltimore Sun, Jerusalem; Asst to Dir, Jerusalem Film Archive; Literary Critic, Jerusalem Post, 1983–; Asst Ed., Ariel, Israel Review of Arts and Letters, 1985–. *Publication:* The Mosaic Press. *Contributions to:* Ambit; Tel-Aviv Review; Jewish Chronicle; Jerusalem Quarterly; Jerusalem International Poetry Festival; European Judaism. *Address:* c/o Ariel, 214 Jaffa St, Jerusalem 91130, Israel.

HAMBURGER, Anne (Ellen), (Anne Beresford); b. 10 Sept. 1928, Redhill, Surrey, England. Poet; Writer; Actress; Teacher. m. Michael Hamburger, 28 July 1951, 1 s., 2 d. *Education:* Central School of Dramatic Art, London, 1944–46. *Appointments:* Actress, various repertory companies, 1946–48, BBC

Radio, 1960–78; Teacher; General Council, Poetry Society, 1976–78; Committee Mem., 1989, Adviser on Agenda, Editorial Board, 1993–96, Aldeburgh Poetry Festival. *Publications:* Poetry: Walking Without Moving, 1967; The Lair, 1968; The Courtship, 1972; Footsteps on Snow, 1972; The Curving Shore, 1975; Songs a Thracian Taught Me, 1980; The Songs of Almut, 1980; The Sele of the Morning, 1988; Charm with Stones (Lyrik im Hölderlinturm), 1993; Landscape With Figures, 1994; Selected and New Poems, 1997; No Place for Cowards, 1998; Hearing Things, 2002. Other: Struck by Apollo, radio play (with Michael Hamburger), 1965; The Villa, radio short story, 1968; Alexandros Poems of Vera Lungu (trans.), 1974; Duet for Three Voices, dramatized poems for Anglia TV, 1982; Snapshots from an Album, 1884–1895, 1992. *Contributions to:* Periodicals. *Address:* Marsh Acres, Middleton, Saxmundham, Suffolk IP17 3NH, England.

HAMBURGER, Michael (Peter Leopold); b. 22 March 1924, Berlin, Germany (Naturalized British citizen). Poet; Writer; Trans.; Ed. m. Anne Ellen File, 28 July 1951, 1 s., 2 d. *Education:* MA, Christ Church, Oxford, England. *Appointments:* Asst Lecturer in German, University College, London, 1952–55; Lecturer, then Reader in German, University of Reading, 1955–64; Florence Purington Lecturer, Mount Holyoke College, South Hadley, Massachusetts, 1966–67; Visiting Prof., State University of New York at Buffalo, 1969, and at Stony Brook, 1971, University of South Carolina, 1973, Boston University, 1975–77; Visiting Fellow, Wesleyan University, Middletown, CT, 1970; Regent's Lecturer, University of California at San Diego, 1973; Prof. (part-time), University of Essex, 1978. *Publications:* Poetry: Flowering Cactus, 1950; Poems 1950–51, 1952; The Dual Site, 1958; Weather and Season, 1963; Feeding the Chickadees, 1968; Penguin Modern Poets (with A Brownjohn and C Tomlinson), 1969; Travelling, 1969; Travelling I-V, 1973; Ownerless Earth, 1973; Travelling VI, 1975; Real Estate, 1977; Moralities, 1977; Variations, 1981; Collected Poems, 1984; Trees, 1988; Selected Poems, 1988; Roots in the Air, 1991; Collected Poems, 1941–94, 1995; Late, 1997; Mr Littlejoy's Rattlebag for the New Millennium, 1999; Intersections: Shorter Poems, 1994–2000, 2000; From a Diary of Non-Events, 2002. Prose: Reason and Energy, 1957; From Prophecy to Exorcism, 1965; The Truth of Poetry, 1970; A Mug's Game (memoirs), 1973, revised edn as String of Beginnings, 1991; Hugo von Hofmannsthal, 1973; Art as a Second Nature, 1975; A Proliferation of Prophets, 1983; After the Second Flood: Essays in Modern German Literature, 1986; Testimonies: Selected Shorter Prose 1950–1987, 1989; Michael Hamburger in Conversation with Peter Dale, 1998; The Take-Over (fiction), 2000; Philip Larkin: A Retrospect (memoir), 2002. Translator: Many books, including: Poems of Hölderin, 1943, revised edn as Hölderlin: Poems, 1952; JCF Hölderin: Selected Verse, 1961; H von Hofmannsthal: Poems and Verse Plays (with others), 1961; H von Hofmannsthal: Selected Plays and Libretti (with others), 1964; J C F Hölderlin: Poems and Fragments, 1967; The Poems of Hans Magnus Enzenberger (with others), 1968; The Poems of Günter Grass (with C Middleton), 1969; Paul Celan: Poems, 1972, revised edn as Poems of Paul Celan, 1988; Kiosk, 1997; Günter Grass: Selected Poems, 1998. *Contributions to:* Numerous publications. *Honours:* Bollingen Foundation Fellow, 1959–61, 1965–66; Trans. Prizes, Deutsche Akademie für Sprache und Dichtung, Darmstadt, 1964, Arts Council of Great Britain, 1969; Medal, Institute of Linguistics, 1977; Schlegel-Tieck Prizes, 1978, 1981; Goethe Medal, 1986; Austrian State Prize for Literary Trans., 1988; Hon. LittD, University of East Anglia, 1988; European Trans. Prize, 1990; O.B.E., 1992; Hon. DPhil, Technical University, Berlin, 1995; Cholmondeley Award for Poetry, 2000; Horst Bienek Prize, Munich, 2001. *Address:* c/o John Johnson Ltd, Clerkenwell House, 45–47 Clerkenwell Green, London EC1 0HT, England.

HAMBY, James Allan; b. 16 May 1943, Oakland, CA, USA. University Administrator; Poet; Writer. m. Laura A Roche, 30 July 1988, 3 d. *Education:* BS, 1965, MA, 1970, Southern Oregon State College. *Appointments:* Asst, Southern Oregon State College, 1965–66; Dir, Oregon Museum of Natural History, 1966–67; Faculty, Medford (Oregon) High School System, 1967–70; Instructor, Utah State University, 1970–71; Administrator, Humboldt State University, 1971–. *Publication:* Collection: Lake Ice Splitting. *Contributions to:* Forum; The Old Red Kimono; Driftwood East Quarterly; Transactions of the Pacific Circle; Poem; Lowlands Review; Pandora; Song; Waters; Western Poetry; Toyon; New Mexico Magazine; Idaho Heritage; Bitterroot Review; South Dakota Review; Hartford Courant; Quartet; University of Portland Review; Pacifica; Descant; Cardinal Poetry Quarterly; Above Ground Review; New Laurel Review; Western Review; Oyez!; Energy West; Bardic Echoes; Humboldt Journal of Social Relations; The Mainstreeter; El Viento. *Honours:* Poetry Award, Utah Fine Arts Institute, 1971; Various Ed's Choice Citations. *Memberships:* Acad. of American Poets; Poets and Writers. *Address:* PO Box 1124, Arcata, CA 95521, USA.

HAMELIN, Claude; b. 25 Aug. 1943, Montréal, QC, Canada. Poet; Writer; Scientist. m. Renée Artinian, 11 Sept. 1970, 1 s., 1 d. *Education:* BPed, 1965; BSc, 1970; MSc, 1972; PhD, 1975. *Publications:* Poetry: Fables des quatre-temps, 1990; Lueurs froides, 1991; Nef des fous, 1992; Néant bleu/Nada azul/Blue Nothingness, 1994. Novel: Roman d'un quartier, 1993. *Contributions to:* Anthologies and journals. *Address:* 4630 Ave Lacombe, Montréal, QC H3W 1R3, Canada.

HAMEL-MICHAUD, Susanne; b. 10 Aug. 1928, Ancienne-Lorette, QC, Canada. Poet; Writer. m. Andre Michaud, deceased, 2 step-s. *Education:* BSD, Laval University, 1951. *Publications:* Réséda et Capucine (poems), 1986; Hublots (poems), 1987; La Chambre aux Miroirs (poems), 1989; L'innommable erectile voltigeant (poems), 1991; Chant, Echo du Coeur de Pablo (poems), 1994; Glenn Gould, mon bel et tendre amour (essay, narration and poems), 1995; Poudreries d'etoiles mes dunes (poems), 1997; Histoire d'une retraite correspondance Père Léger (essay, narration and poems), 1998; Variations pour un archet de velours (poems), 2001. *Contributions to:* Journals and magazines. *Memberships:* Société des Écrivians Canadiens; Union des Écrivains Québecois. *Address:* c/o Union des Écrivains Québecois, La Maison des écrivains, 3492 ave Laval, Montréal, QC H2X 3C8, Canada.

HAMER, Forrest; b. 31 Aug. 1956, Goldsboro, North Carolina, USA. Psychologist; Poet. *Education:* BA, Yale University, 1978; PhD, University of California at Berkeley, 1987. *Publication:* Call and Response, 1995. *Contributions to:* Best American Poetry, 1994; Kenyon Review; TriQuarterly; ZYZZYVA; Washington Post Book World. *Honour:* Beatrice Howley Award, 1995. *Address:* 5275 Miles Ave, Oakland, CA 94618, USA.

HAMILL, Sam P(atrick); b. 9 May 1943, California, USA. Poet; Publisher; Ed.; Trans. m. (1) Nancy Larsen, 1964, divorced, 1 d., (2) Tree Swenson, 1973, divorced, (3) Gray Foster. *Education:* Journalism, Los Angeles Valley College, 1966–69; English Literature, University of California at Santa Barbara, 1970–72. *Appointments:* Co-Founder, Copper Canyon Press, 1972–; Writer-in-Residence, Reed College, University of Alaska, South Utah State University, South Oregon College, Austin College, Trinity College, 1974–, Dept of Correction, Washington, Alaska, California, 1976–88; Columnist, Port Townsend Leader, 1990–93. *Publications:* Poetry: Heroes of the Teton Mythos, 1973; Petroglypics, 1975; Uintah Blue, 1975; The Calling Across Forever, 1976; The Book of Elegaic Geography, 1978; Triada, 1978; Animae, 1980; Fatal Pleasure, 1984; The Nootka Rose, 1987; Passport, 1988; A Dragon in the Clouds, 1989; Mandala, 1991; Destination Zero: Poems 1970–1995, 1995. Essays: At Home in the World, 1980; Basho's Ghost, 1989; A Poet's Work: The Other Side of Poetry, 1990. Ed. or co-ed., anthologies, selected poems, collections, including: Endless River: Li Po and Tu Fu: A Friendship in Poetry, 1993; Love Poems from the Japanese, 1994; Twenty-Five Years of Poetry from Copper Canyon Press, 1996. Trans. or co-trans. of Chinese, Estonian, Latin, Japanese and ancient Greek works. *Contributions to:* Poetry, essays and trans to numerous anthologies and literary magazines. *Honours:* College Ed.'s Award, Best College Journal, Co-ordinating Council of Literary Magazines, 1972; Washington Gov.'s Arts Awards to Copper Canyon Press, 1975, 1990; National Endowment for the Arts Fellowship, 1980; Pacific Northwest Booksellers' Award, 1980; Guggenheim Fellowship, 1983; Pushcart Prizes, 1989, 1996; Lila Wallace-Reader's Digest Writing Fellowship, 1992–93. *Memberships:* PEN American Center; Poetry Society of America; Acad. of American Poets. *Address:* PO Box 468, Port Townsend, WA 98368, USA.

HAMILTON, Carol Jean Barber; b. 23 Aug. 1935, Enid, Oklahoma, USA. Writer; Poet; Educator. Divorced, 2 s., 1 d. *Education:* BS, Phillips University, 1957; MA, University of Central Oklahoma, 1978. *Appointments:* English Prof., Rose State College; Prof. in Creative Studies, University of Central Oklahoma. *Publications:* Children's Books: The Dawn Seekers, 1987; Legends of Poland, 1993; The Mystery of Black Mesa, 1995. Other: Dancing the Wind, 1988; Once the Dust, 1992. *Contributions to:* Christian Science Monitor; Common Weal; New York Quarterly; Christian Century; Arizona Quarterly; Hawaii Review; Midwest Quarterly Review; Oklahoma Today; Kansas Quarterly; Arkansas Review; Chariton Review; Windsor Review. *Honours:* Oklahoma Book Award for Poetry, 1992; Byline Literary Award for Poetry, 1994; Pegasus Award, 1995; Poet Laureate of Oklahoma, 1995–97. *Memberships:* Poetry Society of Oklahoma; Individual Artists of Oklahoma; Mid Oklahoma Writers. *Address:* 9608 Sonata Ct, Midwest City, OK 73130, USA.

HAMMIAL, Philip R.; b. 10 Jan. 1937, Detroit, Michigan, USA. Writer; Poet; Artist. m. Anne Welch, 15 Dec. 1991, 1 d. *Education:* BA, English Literature and Philosophy, Ohio University, Athens. *Publications:* Foot Falls & Notes, 1976; Chemical Cart, 1977; Mastication Poems, 1977; Hear Me Eating, 1977; More Bath, Less Water, 1978; Swarm, 1979; Squeeze, 1985; Vehicles (with Anthony Mannix), 1985; Pell Mell, 1988; Outsider Art in Australia (co-ed.), 1989; Travel/Writing (with Ania Walwicz), 1989; With One Skin Less, 1994; Just Deserts, 1995; Blackmarket, 1996; Bread, 2000. *Contributions to:* Anthologies, magazines, newspapers and journals. *Honour:* Rothmans Poetry Prize, 1988; Senior Writer's Fellowship, 1996; Short-listed, NSW Premier's Award, 2001. *Address:* 29 Park Rd, Woodford, NSW 2778, Australia. *E-mail:* isphaw@hermes.net.au. *Website:* www.geocities.com/memnom/phammialindex.html.

HAMMICK, Georgina; b. 24 May 1939, Hampshire, England. Writer; Poet. m. 24 Oct. 1961, 1 s., 2 d. *Education:* Academie Julian, Paris, 1956–57; Salisbury Art School, 1957–59. *Publications:* A Poetry Quintet (poems), 1976; People for Lunch, 1987; Spoilt (short stories), 1992; The Virago Book of Love and Loss (ed.), 1992; The Arizona Game, 1996. *Contributions to:* Journals and periodicals. *Membership:* Writers Guild. *Address:* Bridgewalk House, Brixton, Deverill, Warminster, Wiltshire BA12 7EJ, England.

HAMMOND, Clifford; b. 16 Sept. 1915, Epping, Essex, England. Life Assurance Official (retd); Poet. *Education:* Fellow, Chartered Insurance Institute, 1954. *Publications:* Reflections, 1977; Further Reflections, 1987; One Hundred Aphorisms, 1992. *Contributions to:* Envoi; Orbis; Southern Evening Echo. *Address:* 38 Hocombe Dr., Chandlers Ford, Hampshire SO5 1QE, England.

HAMMOND, Karla Marie; b. 26 April 1949, Middletown, CT, USA. Consultant; Poet. *Education:* BA, English, Goucher College, 1971; MA, English, Trinity College, 1973. *Contributions to:* Over 185 publications in USA, Canada, England, Sweden, Italy, Japan, Australia and Greece. *Honour:* Nominated for Pushcart Prize. *Address:* 12 West Dr., East Hampton, CT 06424, USA.

HAMMOND, Mary Stewart; b. Richmond, Virginia, USA. Poet. m. Arthur Yorke Allen, 22 May 1971. *Education:* BA with Honours in Poetry, Goucher College. *Appointments:* Poet-in-Residence, Writer's Community, 1992; Teacher, Advanced Poetry, Writers's Voice, 1992–2001. *Publication:* Out of Canaan, W W Norton, 1991. *Contributions to:* New Yorker; Atlantic Monthly; New Criterion; Yale Review; American Voice; Gettysberg Review; New England Review and Bread Loaf Quarterly; Paris Review; American Review; Boulevard; Field. *Honours:* First Prize, 1985, Finalist, 1986, 1990, Narrative Poem Contest, New England Review and Bread Loaf Quarterly; 1992 Winner, Best First Collection of Poetry Award, Great Lakes Colleges' Asscn; MacDowell Colony Fellowship, 1985; Yaddo Fellowship, 2000. *Memberships:* Acad. of American Poets; Poetry Society of America; Poets' House Century Asscn. *Address:* 1095 Park Ave, Apt 4A, New York, NY 10128, USA.

HAMRI, Thorsteinn Fra. See: JONSSON, Thorsteinn.

HAN YEPING. See: YANXIANG SHAO.

HANDKE, Peter; b. 6 Dec. 1942, Griffen-Altenmarkt, Austria. Writer; Dramatist; Poet. 1 d. *Education:* Law Studies, University of Graz. *Publications:* Die Hornissen, 1966; Publikumsbeschimpfung, 1966; Der Hausierer, 1967; Kaspar, 1968, English trans. as Kaspar and Other Plays, 1969; Deutsche Gedichte, 1969; Die Innenwelt der Aussenwelt der Innenwelt, 1969, English trans. as The Innerworld of the Outerworld of the Innerworld, 1974; Die Angst des Tormanns beim Elfmeter, 1970, English trans. as The Goalie's Anxiety at the Penalty Kick, 1972; Ich bin ein Bewohner des Elfenbeinturms, 1972; Der kurze Brief zum langen Abschied, 1972, English trans. as Short Letter, Long Farewell, 1974; Stücke, 2 vols, 1972–73; Wunschloses Unglück, 1972, English trans. as A Sorrow Beyond Dreams, 1975; Als das Wünschen noch geholfen hat, 1974, English trans. as Nonsense and Happiness, 1976; Falsche Bewegung, 1975; Der Rand der Wörter, 1975; Die linkshändige Frau, 1975, English trans. as The Left-Handed Woman, 1978; Die Stunde der wahren Empfindung, 1975, English trans. as A Moment of True Feeling, 1977; Das Ende des Flanierens, 1977; Das Gewicht der Welt: Ein Journal, 1977; Langsame Heimkehr, 1979; Die Lehre der Sainte-Victoire, 1980; Kindergeschichte, 1981; Über die Dörfer, 1981; Die Geschichte des Bleistifts, 1982; Der Chinese des Schmerzes, 1983; Die Wiederholung, 1986; Die Abwesenheit, 1987, English trans. as Absence, 1990; Nachmittag eines Schriftstellers, 1987; Versuch über die Müdigkeit, 1989; Noch einmal für Thukydides, 1990; Versuch über die Jukebox, 1990; Versuch über den geglückten Tag: Ein Wintertagtraum, 1991; Abschied des Träumers von Neunten Land: Eine Wirklichkeit, die vergangen ist: Erinnerung an Slowenien, 1991; Langsam in Schatten: Gesammelte Verzettelungen 1980–91, 1992; Theaterstücke in einem Band, 1992; Mein Jahre in der Niemandsbucht, 1994; Eine winterliche Reise zu den Flüssen Donau, Save, Morawa und Drina oder Gerechtigkeit für Serbien, 1996, English trans. as A Journey to the Rivers: Justice for Serbia, 1997; Die Fahrt im Einbaum, oder, Das Stück zum Film vom Krieg, 1999. *Honours:* Gerhart Hauptmann Prize, 1967; Peter-Rosegger-Literary-Prize, 1972; Schiller Prize, Mannheim, 1972; Büchner Prize, 1973; Prix Georges Sadoul, 1978; Kafka Prize, 1979; Salzburg Literary Prize, 1986; Great Austrian (state) Prize, 1987; Bremen Literary Prize, Hamburg, 1991; Franz Grillparzer Prize, Hamburg, 1991; Drama Prize, Goethe, Institute, Munich, 1993; Prize of Honour of the Schiller Memorial Prize, 1995. *Address:* c/o Suhrkamp Verlag, Lindenstrasse 29, 60325 Frankfurt am Main, Germany.

HANDLIN, James P.; b. 14 Nov. 1943, Boston, Massachusetts, USA. Educator; Poet. m. Diane Rubin, 14 Nov. 1981, 1 s., 2 d. *Education:* BA, Iona College, 1965; MS, Bank Street College of Education, 1985; DEd, Columbia University, 1988. *Appointments:* Head of Upper School, Pingry School, Martinsville; Head of School, Brooklyn Friends' School, New York. *Publications:* Where the Picture Book Ends, 1979; The Distance in a Door, 1980; The Haiku Anthology, 1986; Blue Stones and Salt Hay: An Anthology of New Jersey Writers, 1990; Ed.'s Choice III, 1992. *Contributions to:* Poetry; Prairie Schooner; Lips; Patterson Review; Footwork. *Honours:* Dylan Thomas Award, New School for Social Research, 1979; Gusto Press Discovery Award, 1979; Gusto Press Haiku Award, 1980; Grant, 1985, Awards, 1988, 1995, New Jersey State Council of the Arts; First Prize, Passaic County College Poetry Award, 1986. *Address:* 969 Cedarbrook Rd, Plainfield, NJ 07060, USA.

HANF, James Alphonso, (James Wildwood); b. 3 Feb. 1923, Chehalis, Washington, USA. Naval Architect Technician; Poet. m. 16 Aug. 1947, 1 d. *Education:* Graduate, Centralia Junior College, Washington, 1943. *Appointments:* Poetry Ed., Coffee Break Magazine, 1977–82; Lecturer, new Americana version of Haiku (originator), 1977; Lecturer, Haiku and Siamese poetry to professional and civic groups. *Contributions to:* Numerous literary journals, anthologies and popular magazines. *Honours:* Poet Laureate, Outstanding Poet of the Year, Inky Trails, 1978; Grand Prize, World Poetry Society Convention, 1985–86; Golden Poet Award, World of Poetry, CA, 1985–88; Grand Prize Winner, Las Vegas World Poetry Convention, 1990. *Memberships:* Stella Woodall Poetry Society, hon. mem.; World Poet Resource Centre; California Federation of Chaparral Poets; Ina Coolbrith Circle; Literarische Union; New York Poetry Forum; Illinois State Poetry Society; Western World Haiku Society; International Poetry Society, India. *Address:* PO Box 374, Bremerton, WA 98337, USA.

HANFORD BRUCE, Mary, (Mary Hanford, June Minim); b. 18 June 1940, Washington, DC, USA. Prof. of English; Poet. m. Guy Steven Bruce, 23 March 1991, 2 s. *Education:* BA, University of Texas, Arlington, 1965; MA, Southern Methodist University, 1968; PhD, Arizona State University, 1986. *Appointments:* Instructor in English, Arizona State University, Tempe, 1981–85; Prof. of English, Monmouth College, IL, 1985–; Senior Scholar in American Literature, Fulbright Prof. of American Literature, École Normale Supérieure, Yaoundé, Cameroon, Africa, 1988–90. *Publications:* Swamproot featuring Mary Hanford's African Poetry, 1989; Holding to the Light, 1991; Zimbabwe on the Cheap: Transitions Abroad, 1995; Voodoo Faust, 1995; Dr Ayuk's Funeral, 1996; Twin Beads, 1996; C'est le Parfum, 1997. *Contributions to:* Waves of Peace Anthology, 1997; Poetry View; New Earth Review; Mockingbird; Poetry Scope; Cedar Rock; Louisville Review; KMCR Anthology; Bisbee Times; Prickly Pear; Slipstream; Brush Fire; New Kauri; Signalfire; Visions; Oasis; Bisbee Observer; The Carillon; Spoon River Quarterly; Embassy Echo; Huskyn News; Spectrum; Poems Across Our Land; Jane's Stories; World Parnassus of Poets; The Lucid Stone. *Honours:* Prize, Arizona Poetry Society, 1983; Runner-up, Jonquil Trevor Sonnet Contest, 1984; Runner-up, Flume Press National Chapbook Contest, 1990. *Memberships:* Acad. of American Poets; American Asscn of University Profs; Warren County Writers' Bloc; Free Fall, Monmouth College; Illinois Writers Asscn. *Address:* 511 E Boston, Monmouth, IL 61462, USA.

HANSEN, Clayton Kenneth; b. 31 May 1964, Brisbane, Qld, Australia. School Principal; Poet. m. Lisbeth Robinson, 19 Sept. 1992, 1 s., 1 d. *Education:* Diploma of Teaching, Brisbane College of Advanced Education, 1984; BEd, 1987, Master of Educational Administration, 1992, University of Queensland. *Appointments:* Teracher, 1985, Principal 1987, Cordelia State School; Principal, Freestone State School, 1989, Warwick Central State School, 1995–. *Contributions to:* Northern Perspectives; Westerly; Riding Out; Contemporary Writing. *Address:* c/o Warwick Central State School, PO Box 217, Warwick, Qld 4370, Australia.

HANSEN, Jefferson; b. 8 Feb. 1965, Sturgeon Bay, Wisconsin, USA. Poet; Teacher. m. Elizabeth Burns, 19 Oct. 1991, 2 d. *Education:* BA, Beloit College, 1987; MA, State University of New York, Buffalo, 1992. *Appointments:* Teacher of English, Albany Acad., New York, 1993–95, Blake School, Minneapolis, Minnesota, 1995–. *Publications:* Gods to the Elbows, 1991; Red Streams of George Through Pages, 1993; The Dramatic Monologues of Joe Blow Only Artsy, 1994; A Particular Pluralist Poem, 1996. *Contributions to:* Sulfur; O-blek; Avec; Washington Review; B-City; Abacus; Writers from the New Coast, anthology. *Address:* 2510 Highway 100 S, No. 333, St Louis Park, MN 55416, USA.

HAO ZHU; b. 27 May 1969, Shanghai, China. Playwright; Poet. *Education:* Shi Xi Senior Middle School, 1981–87; Shanghai Drama Institute, 1987–91. *Publication:* First Frost. *Contributions to:* Shanghai Literature; Modern Haiku; Frogpond; Windchimes; Mainchi Daily News; Ko Haiku Magazine. *Honours:* Honorable Mention, Haiku in English Contest; Ko Haiku Magazine Award. *Membership:* Haiku Societies of America. *Address:* Lane 906, No. 5, Xinzha Rd, Shanghai 200041, China.

HARALDSDOTTIR, Ingibjörg; b. 21 Oct. 1942, Reykjavík, Iceland. Writer; Trans.; Poet. 1 s., 1 d. *Education:* Diploma, Feature Film Dir; MA, All Union State Institute of Cinematography, Moscow, 1969. *Publications:* Thangad vil eg fljuga, 1974; Ordspor daganna, 1983; Nu eru adrir timar, 1989; Ljód (collected poems), 1991; Höfud konunnar, 1995. *Contributions to:* Timarit Mals og Menningar; Skirnir. *Honours:* Nominations, Icelandic Literature Award, 1990, Nordic Literature Prize, 1993. *Membership:* Writers' Union of Iceland, chairperson, 1994–98. *Address:* Drápuhlid 13, 105 Reykjavík, Iceland.

HARBOUR, Josephine, (Singleton Harbour); b. 22 Jan. 1923, Goody Hills, Cumberland, England. Poet. m. Stanley Harbour, 8 Feb. 1946, 2 s., 1 d. *Publications:* Everyday Poems, 1982; Second Everyday Poems, 1983; My World, 1986; Verse from the Bible, 1986; In Search of a Dream, 1986; Treasured Thoughts, 1987; Of Changing Scienes, 1988; Bob's Story, 1989; Peals in Words, 1991. *Contributions to:* Christian Herald; The Lady; Writers Rostrum; Woman's Own, magazine; Third Half; Folio; Ploughman, Canada;

White Rose. *Honours:* First prize, local competition, 1985; Runner-up, White Rose Competition, 1991. *Address:* 65 Moorgate Rd, Dereham, Norfolk NR19 1NU, England.

HARDARSON, Hrafn Andres; b. 9 April 1948, Kopavogur, Iceland. Librarian; Poet. m. Anna S Einarsdottir, Oct. 1969, 1 s., 1 d. *Education:* Chartered Librarian, UK, 1972; Fellow, Library Asscn, UK, 1994. *Appointments:* Asst Librarian, 1968–72, Branch Librarian, 1973–76, City Library, Reykjavík; Chief Librarian, Kopavogur Town Library, 1976–. *Publications:* Fyrrvera, 1982; Thrileikur Ad Ordum, 1990; Tonmyndaljod, 1992; Tone-Picture-Poems, 1993; Hafid Brennur (trans. of Vizma Belsevica), 1994; Hler, 1995; Mylsna, 1995. *Contributions to:* Morgunbladid-Lesbok; Andblaer; TMM; Lystraeninginn. *Honour:* Second Prize, Eyjafjardarsveit, 1995. *Membership:* Writers Union of Iceland. *Address:* Medalbr 2, 200 Kopavogur, Iceland.

HARDY, Alan William; b. 10 March 1951, Luton, Bedfordshire, England. Teacher; Poet. m. Sibylle Mory, 24 Aug. 1985, 1 d. *Education:* BA, English and Italian Literature, 1973, MA, Comparative Literature, 1976, Warwick University; Dip TEFL, Christ Church College, Kent University, 1983. *Appointments:* English Teacher, Sir Joseph Williamson's Mathematical School, Rochester, Kent; English Language Teacher, Whitehill Estate School of English, Flamstead, Hertfordshire. *Publication:* Wasted Leaves, 1996. *Contributions to:* Envoi; Iota; New Hope International; Poetry Nottingham; The Interpreter's House; Weyfarers; South. *Honour:* Second Prize, Hastings National Poetry Competition, 1994. *Address:* Whitehill Estate School of English, Flamstead, St Albans, Hertfordshire AL3 8EY, England.

HARGRAVE, Leonie. See: DISCH, Thomas M(ichael).

HARJO, Joy; b. 9 May 1951, Tulsa, Oklahoma, USA. Poet; Author; Educator; Musician. 1 s., 1 d. *Education:* BA, University of New Mexico, 1976; MFA, University of Iowa, 1978; Anthropology Film Center, 1982. *Appointments:* Instructor, Institute of American Indian Arts, 1978–79, 1983–84, Santa Fe Community College, 1983–84; Lecturer, Arizona State University, 1980–81; Asst Prof., University of Colorado at Boulder, 1985–88; Assoc. Prof., University of Arizona at Tucson, 1988–90; Prof., University of New Mexico, 1991–97, UCLA, 2001–. *Publications:* The Last Song, 1975; What Moon Drove Me To This?, 1980; She Had Some Horses, 1983; Secrets From the Center of the World (with Stephen Strom), 1989; In Mad Love and War, 1990; Fishing, 1992; The Woman Who Fell From the Sky, 1994; Reinventing the Enemy's Language, 1997; A Map to the Next World, 2000; The Good Luck Cat, 2000; How We Became Human, 2002; Joy Harjo and Poetic Justice: Letter from the End of the 20th Century (CD). *Contributions to:* Many anthologies, magazines, and recordings. *Honours:* National Endowment for the Arts Creative Writing Fellowships, 1978, 1992; Pushcart Prize, Poetry XIII, 1987–88, and Poetry Anthology XV, 1990; Arizona Commission on the Arts Poetry Fellowship, 1989; American Indian Distinguished Achievement in the Arts Award, 1990; American Book Award, Before Columbus Foundation, 1991; Delmore Schwartz Memorial Award, New York University, 1991; Mountains and Plains Booksellers Award for Best Book of Poetry, 1991; William Carlos Williams Award, Poetry Society of America, 1991; Hon. Doctorate, Benedictine College, 1992; Woodrow Wilson Fellowship, 1993; Witter Bynner Poetry Fellowship, 1994; Lifetime Achievement Award, Native Writers Circle of the Americas, 1995; Oklahoma Book Arts Awards, 1995; Governor's Award for Excellence in the Arts, State of New Mexico, 1997; Lila Wallace-Reader's Digest Writers Award, 1998–2000. *Membership:* PEN, advisory board; National Council of the Arts. *Address:* c/o Mekko Productions Inc, 1140 Alewa Dr., Honolulu, HI 96817, USA.

HARPER, Albert William John; b. 25 July 1917, Fullarton, ON, Canada. Teacher (retd); Poet. *Education:* BA, Psychology and Philosophy, University of Western Ontario, 1949; MA, Philosophy, University of Toronto, 1952; PhD, Philosophy, Mellen University, Lewiston, New York, 1996. *Publications:* Adventures in Ideas, 1985; Poems of Reflection, 1995; The Philosophy of Time, 1997. *Contributions to:* Poemata, Canadian Poetry Asscn; Reach Magazine, HI. *Membership:* Canadian Poetry Asscn. *Address:* 59 Victor St, London, ON N6C 1B9, Canada.

HARPER, Michael S(teven); b. 18 March 1938, New York, NY, USA. Prof. of English; Poet. m. 3 c. *Education:* BA, 1961, MA, 1963, California State University at Los Angeles; MA, University of Iowa Writers Workshop, 1963; ad eundem, Brown University, 1972. *Appointments:* Visiting Prof., Lewis and Clark College, 1968–69, Reed College, 1968–69, Harvard University, 1974–77, Yale University, 1976; Prof. of English, Brown University, 1970–; Benedict Distinguished Prof., Carleton College, 1979; Elliston Poet and Distinguished Prof., University of Cincinnati, 1979; National Endowment for the Humanities Prof., Colgate University, 1985; Distinguished Minority Prof., University of Delaware, 1988, Macalester College, 1989; First Poet Laureate of the State of Rhode Island, 1988–93; Phi Beta Kappa Visiting Scholar, 1991; Berg Distinguished Visiting Prof., New York University, 1992. *Publications:* Dear John, Dear Coltrane, 1970; History is Your Own Heartbeat, 1971; History as Apple Tree, 1972; Song: I Want a Witness, 1972; Debridement, 1973; Nightmare Begins Responsibility, 1975; Images of Kin, 1977; Chant of Saints

(co-ed.), 1979; Healing Song for the Inner Ear, 1985; Songlines: Mosaics, 1991; Every Shut Eye Ain't Asleep, 1994; Honorable Admendments, 1995; Collected Poems, 1996. *Honours:* Black Acad. of Arts and Letters Award, 1972; National Institute of Arts and Letters Grants, 1975, 1976, 1985; Guggenheim Fellowship, 1976; Melville Cane Award, Poetry Society of America, 1978; Governor's Poetry Award, Rhode Island Council of the Arts, 1987; Robert Hayden Memorial Poetry Award, United Negro College Fund, 1990; Literary Lion, New York Public Library, 1992; Hon. doctorates. *Membership:* American Acad. of Arts and Sciences. *Address:* c/o Dept of English, Brown University, Providence, RI 02912, USA.

HARRIS, Edna Beulah Mae Warren, (End); b. 28 Feb. 1950, Milford, Deleware, USA. Writer; Poet. m. A Harris, 7 Feb. 1970, 2 s., 1 d. *Education:* BS, Education, 1982; MA, Educational Psychology, 1982, ANU; Delaware Technical Community College in Nursing; Certificate in Human Service Work I and II. *Publication:* Talking About All Kinds of Things. *Contributions to:* American Poetry Asscn; National LIbrary of Poetry; Watermark Press; World of Poetry. *Honours:* Golden Poet Award, 1985–89; Silver Poet Award, 1990; Ed.'s Choice Award, 1985–89; Certificates of Merit, 1984–86; Royal Award, 1995. *Memberships:* American Poetry Asscn; Amherst Society; National Library of Poetry; Watermark Press; Hon. Mem., World Parnassians' Guild International, 1995. *Address:* PO Box 272, Route 1, Lincoln, DE 19960, USA.

HARRIS, Jana; b. 21 Sept. 1947, San Francisco, CA, USA. Writer; Poet; Instructor. m. Mark Allen Bothwell. *Education:* BS, University of Oregon, 1969; MA, San Francisco State University, 1972. *Appointments:* Instructor, Creative Writing, New York University, 1980, University of Washington, 1986–, Pacific Lutheran University, 1988; Founder, Ed., Switch-on Gutenberg, cyberspace poetry journal. *Publications:* This House That Rocks with Every Truck on the Road, 1976; Pin Money, 1977; The Clackamas, 1980; Alaska (novel), 1980; Who's That Pushy Bitch?, 1981; Running Scared, 1981; Manhattan as a Second Language, 1982; The Sourlands: Poems by Jana Harris, 1989; Oh How Can I Keep on Singing: Voices of Pioneer Women (poems), 1993; The Dust of Everyday Life (poems); The Pearl of Ruby City (novel), 1998. *Contributions to:* Periodicals. *Honours:* Berkeley Civic Arts Commemoration Grant, 1974; Washington State Arts Council Fellowship, 1993. *Memberships:* Feminist Writers' Guild; Assoc. Writing Programs; Women's Salon; PEN; Poetry Society of America; National Book Critics Circle. *Address:* 32814 120th St SE, Sultan, WA 98294, USA.

HARRIS, Marie; b. 7 Nov. 1943, New York, NY, USA. Poet; Writer. m. Charter Weeks, 4 Nov. 1977, 3 s. *Education:* BA, Goddard College, 1971. *Appointments:* Freelance Writer; Partner, Isinglass Marketing. *Publications:* Raw Honey, 1975; Interstate, 1980; Weasel in the Turkey Pen, 1993; Your Sun, Manny, 1999; G is for Granite: A New Hampshire Alphabet. *Contributions to:* Poet Lore; Sojourner; Bluefish; Hanging Loose; Longhouse. *Honours:* National Endowment for the Arts Fellowship, 1976; New Hampshire Council on the Arts Fellowship, 1981; New Hampshire Poet Laureate, 1999–2003. *Memberships:* National Writers Union; Poetry Society of America; Alice James Poetry Co-operative. *Address:* PO Box 203, Barrington, NH 03825, USA.

HARRIS, Roy Nevitt; b. 12 Jan. 1954, Adelaide, SA, Australia. Teacher; Poet. m. Hazel Catherine Forrester, 14 Feb. 1987, 2 d. *Education:* BEd, Graduate Diploma in Religious Education, MEd Studies. *Appointments:* Poet-in-Residence in various educational institutions; Curriculum Co-ordinator, English and the Arts, St Paul's College, Adelaide. *Publications:* Over the Outrow, 1982; From the Residence, 1984; Snapshots From a Moving Train, 1988; 16 Poems, 1994; Uncle Jack and Other Poems, 1997; Waterline, 1999. *Contributions to:* Literary journals. *Membership:* South Australian Writers Centre. *Address:* 154 Esplanade, Largs Bay, SA 5016, Australia.

HARRIS, (Theodore) Wilson; b. 24 March 1921, New Amsterdam, British Guiana. Poet; Novelist. m. (1) Cecily Carew, 1945, (2) Margaret Whitaker, 1959. *Education:* Graduated, Queen's College, Georgetown, 1939. *Appointments:* Visiting Lecturer, State University of New York, Buffalo, 1970; Writer-in-Residence, University of the West Indies, Jamaica, Scarborough College, University of Toronto, 1970, University of Newcastle, NSW, 1979; Commonwealth Fellow in Caribbean Literature, Leeds University, Yorkshire, 1971; Visiting Prof., University of Texas, Austin, 1972, 1981–82, University of Mysore, 1978, Yale University, 1979; Regents Lecturer, University of California, Santa Cruz, 1983. *Publications:* Poetry: Fetish, 1951; The Well and the Land, 1952; Eternity to Season, 1954. Fiction: The Guyana Quartet, 1960–63; Tumatumari, 1968; Black Marsden, 1972; Companions of the Day and Night, 1975; Da Silva's Cultivated Wilderness, 1977; Genesis of the Clowns, 1977; The Tree of the Sun, 1978; The Angel at the Gate, 1982; The Carnival Trilogy, 1985–90; Resurrection at Sorrow Hill, 1993; The Dark Jester, 2001. Other: Short stories and other publications. *Address:* c/o Faber and Faber Ltd, 3 Queen Sq., London WC1N 3AU, England.

HARRISON, James. See: LIGHTFOOT, David James.

HARRISON, James (Thomas); b. 11 Dec. 1937, Grayling, Michigan, USA. Author; Poet. m. Linda May King, 10 Oct. 1959, 2 d. *Education:* BA, 1960, MA,

1964, Michigan State University. *Appointment:* Instructor, State University of New York at Stony Brook, 1965–66. *Publications:* Fiction: Wolf: A False Memoir, 1971; A Good Day to Die, 1973; Farmer, 1976; Legends of the Fall, 1979; Warlock, 1981; Sundog, 1984; Dalva, 1988; The Woman Lit by Fireflies, 1990; Sunset Limited, 1990; Julip, 1994; The Road Home, 1998. Poetry: Plain Song, 1965; Locations, 1968; Walking, 1969; Outlyer and Ghazals, 1971; Letters to Yesinin, 1973; Returning to Earth, 1977; New and Selected Poems, 1961–81, 1982; The Theory and Practice of Rivers, 1986; Country Stores, 1993. Screenplays: Cold Feet (with Tom McGuane), 1989; Revenge (with Jeffrey Fishkin), 1990; Wolf (with Wesley Strick), 1994. Non-Fiction: Just Before Dark, 1991. *Honours:* National Endowment for the Arts Grant, 1967–69; Guggenheim Fellowship, 1968–69. *Address:* PO Box 135, Lake Leelanau, MI 49653, USA.

HARRISON, Jeffrey Woods; b. 10 Oct. 1957, Cincinnati, Ohio, USA. Poet; University Teacher. m. Julie Wells, 28 Nov. 1981, 1 s., 1 d. *Education:* BA cum laude, Columbia University, 1980; MFA, English, University of Iowa, 1984; Stegner Fellowship in Creative Writing, Stanford University, 1985–86. *Appointments:* English Teacher, Berlitz Schools, Japan, 1980–81; Researcher and Writer, H W Wilson Publishing Co, 1981–82; Teaching Asst, University of Iowa, 1983–84; Museum Asst, Researcher, The Phillips Collection, 1985–87; Instructor, Johns Hopkins University, 1989; Lecturer, George Washington University, Washington, DC, 1990–92; Roger E Murray Chair in Creative Writing, Phillips Acad., Andover, Massachusetts, 1997–2000. *Publications:* The Singing Underneath, 1988; Sign of Arrival, 1996; Feeding the Fire, 2001. *Contributions to:* Poets of the New Century; A Bread Loaf Anthology of Contemporary American Poetry; Sixty Years of American Poetry; New Yorker; Poetry; New Republic; Hudson Review; Yale Review; Paris Review; Partisan Review; Kenyon Review; Sewanee Review; Nation; Gettysburg Review; Ploughshares; Double Take; TriQuarterly; Shenandoah; New Criterion; Southern Review. *Honours:* McAfee Discovery Prize, Missouri Review, 1986; Ingram Merrill Foundation Fellowship, 1988; Amy Lowell Fellowship, 1988–89; Peter I B Lavan Younger Poets Award, Acad. of American Poets, 1989; National Endowment for the Arts Fellowship, 1992; Ingram Merrill Foundation Fellowship, 1995; Howard Foundation Merit Award, 1998; Pushcart Prize, 1998; Guggenheim Fellowship, 1999. *Memberships:* Acad. of American Poets; Poetry Society of America. *Address:* 77 Haven St., Dover, MA 02030, USA.

HARRISON, Pamela Alice; b. 16 Aug. 1946, USA. Poet; Teacher. m. Dennis M. McCullough, 12 June 1971, 1 d. *Education:* BA, English Literature, Smith College, 1968; Special Student, Philosophy, University of Western Ontario, 1973–75; MFA, Vermont College, 1983. *Appointments:* Instructor, University of New Hampshire system, 1987–94; Dartmouth College, 1995, 1997, Franklin Pierce College, 1998. *Publication:* Noah's Daughter, 1988. *Contributions to:* Numerous reviews, quarterlies and journals. *Honours:* Winner, Panhandler Chapbook Competition, 1988; MacDowell Colony Fellowship, 1998. *Memberships:* Acad. of American Poets; Associated Writing Programs; Poetry Society of America. *Address:* PO Box 1106, Norwich, VT 05055, USA.

HARRISON, Tony; b. 30 April 1937, Leeds, England. Poet; Dramatist. *Publications:* Earthworks, 1964; Aikin Mata (play with J Simmons), 1965; Newcastle is Peru, 1969; The Loiners, 1970; Voortrekker, 1972; The Misanthrope (trans. of Molière's play), 1973; Poems of Palladas of Alexandria (ed. and trans.), 1973; Phaedra Britannica (trans. of Racine's Phèdre), 1975; Bow Down (music theatre), 1977; The Passion (play), 1977; The Bartered Bride (libretto), 1978; From the 'School of Eloquence' and Other Poems, 1978; Continuous, 1981; A Kumquat for John Keats, 1981; The Oresteia (trans.), 1981; US Martial, 1981; Selected Poems, 1984; Dramatic Verse, 1973–1985, 1985; The Fire-Gap, 1985; The Mysteries, 1985; V, 1985; Theatre Works, 1973–1985, 1986; Loving Memory, 1987; The Blasphemers' Banquet, 1989; The Trackers of Oxyrhynchus, 1990; V and Other Poems, 1990; A Cold Coming: Gulf War Poems, 1991; The Common Chorus, 1992; The Gaze of the Gorgon, 1992; Square Rounds, 1992; Black Daisies for the Bride, 1993; Poetry or Bust, 1993; A Maybe Day in Kazakhstan, 1994; The Shadow of Hiroshima, 1995; Permanently Bard, 1995; The Prince's Play, 1996; The Labourers of Herakles, 1996; The Kaisers of Carnuntum, 1996; Prometheus, 1998; Plays One: The Mysteries, 1999; Laureate's Block and Other Poems, 2000. *Address:* c/o 2 Crescent Grove, London, SW4 7AH, England.

HARROW, Ian; b. 27 Jan. 1945, Bamburgh, Northumberland, England. Poet. *Publications:* PEN New Poems 1977–78; Adam's Dream, 1980; Hume's Study, 1986. *Contributions to:* English; Grand Piano; Literary Review; London Magazine; Poetry and Audience; Poetry Wales; The Rialto; Stand; Hungarian Quarterly; Magyar PEN; Polemos.

HARROWER, Jennifer Hilary, (Jenny Johnson); b. 2 Nov. 1945, Bristol, England. Poet; Writer. m. Noel David Harrower, 28 April 1990, 1 s. *Publications:* Poetry: The Wisdom Tree, 1993; Neptune's Daughters, 1999. *Contributions to:* Periodicals. *Honours:* Four Literary Awards, Southwest Arts, 1978–82. *Address:* 'Culross', 11 The Crescent, Woodthorpe, Nottingham NG5 4FX, England.

HARRY, J. S.; b. 1939, Adelaide, SA, Australia. Poet. *Appointments:* Writer-in Residence, Australian National University, Canberra, 1989, Narrabunda College, Canberra, 1995. *Publications:* The Deer Under the Skin, 1970; Ho for a Little While, and Turn Gently, 1979; A Dandelion for Van Gogh, 1985; Th Life on Water and the Life Beneath, 1995; Selected Poems, 1995. *Honour* Harri Jones Memorial Prize, 1971; PEN International Lynne Phillips Priz 1987; Kenneth Slessor Poetry Prize, 1996. *Memberships:* Australian Society Authors, NSW Writers' Centre; Poets' Union. *Address:* PO Box 184, Randwic NSW 2031, Australia.

HARSENT, David; b. 9 Dec. 1942, Devonshire, England. Poet; Writer. m. (1 divorced, 2 s., 1 d., (2), 1 d. *Appointments:* Fiction Critic, TLS, London, 1965–7 Poetry Critic, Spectator, London, 1970–73. *Publications:* Poetry: Tonight Lover, 1968; A Violent Country, 1969; Ashridge, 1970; After Dark, 197; Truce, 1973; Dreams of the Dead, 1977; Mister Punch, 1984; Selected Poem 1989; Storybook Hero, 1992; News From the Front, 1993; Playback, 199 Sprinting from the Graveyard, 1997; A Bird's Idea of Flight, 1998. Nove From an Inland Sea, 1985. Libretto: Gawain (for Harrison Birtwistle's opera 1991. Music Theatre: Serenade the Silkie (music by Julian Grant), 1989; Th Woman and the Hare (music by Harrison Birtwistle), 1998. Editor: New Poetr 7, 1981; Poetry Book Society Supplement, 1983; Savremena Britanska Poezij 1988; Another Round at the Pillars, a festschrift for Ian Hamilton, 1999. Othe The Sorrow of Sarajevo (trans. of poems by Goran Simic). *Honours:* Er Gregory Award, 1967; Cheltenham Festival Prize, 1968; Arts Counc Bursaries, 1969, 1984; Geoffrey Faber Memorial Prize, 1978; Society Authors Travel Fellowship, 1989; Fellow, RSL, 1998. *Address:* c/o Jonatha Clowes Literary Agency, 10 Iron Bridge House, Bridge Approach, London NW 8BD, England.

HART, Kevin; b. 5 July 1954, London, England (Naturalized Australia citizen). Prof. of English; Poet. *Education:* Australian National Universit Stanford University, CA, and University of Melbourne; PhD, 198 *Appointments:* Lecturer in English, Melbourne University, Australi 1986–87; Lecturer in Literary Studies, Deakin University, Victoria, 1987–9: Senior Lecturer to Assoc. Prof., 1991–95, Prof. of English, 1995–2002, Monas University; Foundation Prof. of Australian and New Zealand Studie Georgetown University, Washington, DC, 1996–97; Visiting Prof., Villanov University, 2001; Prof. of English, University of Notre Dame, IN, 2002– *Publications:* Nebuchadnezzar, 1976; The Departure, 1978; The Lines of th Hand: Poems 1976–79; Your Shadow, 1984; The Trespass of the Sign, 1989 Peniel, 1990; The Buried Harbour (trans.), 1990; A D Hope, 1992; The Oxfor Book of Australian Religious Verse (ed.), 1994; New and Selected Poems, 199 Dark Angel, 1996; Samuel Johnson and the Culture of Property, 1999; Wicke Heat, 1999; Flame Tree: Selected Poems, 2002. *Contributions to:* Aren Journal, The Critical Review, Boxkite, Heat, Verse. *Honours:* Australia Literature Board Fellowship, 1977; New South Wales Premier's Award, 198 Victorian Premier's Award for Poetry, 1985; Grace Levin Awards for Poetry 1991, 1995; Christopher Brennan Award for Poetry, 1999. *Memberships:* Vic Pres., Johnson Society of Australia; Fellow, Australian Acad. of th Humanities. *Address:* Dept of English, University of Notre Dame, Notr Dame, IN 46556, USA.

HÄRTLING, Peter; b. 13 Nov. 1933, Chemnitz, Germany. Author; Poet; Criti m. Mechthild Maier, 1959, 2 s., 2 d. *Education:* Grammar School, Nürtinge *Appointments:* Ed. and Co-Publisher, Der Monat, 1967–70; Ed. and Managin Dir, S Fischer Verlag, Frankfurt am Main, 1968–74; Prof. of Poetry, Universit of Frankfurt am Main, 1984. *Publications:* Yamins Stationen, 1955; Spielgeis Spielgeist, 1962; Niembsch oder Der Stillstand: Eine Suite, 1964; Janek Porträt einer Erinnerung, 1966; Das Familienfest oder Das Ende eine Geschichte, 1969; Neue Gedichte, 1972; Zwettl: Nachprüfung eine Erinnerung, 1973; Eine Frau, 1974; Hölderlin, 1976; Hubert oder Di Rückkehr nach Casablanca, 1978; Meine Lekture: Literatur als Widerstand 1980; Nachgetragene Liebe, 1980; Die dreifache Maria, 1982; Vorwarnung 1983; Sätze von Liebe, 1983; Das Windrad, 1983; Ich rufe die Wörte zusammen, 1984; Der spanische Soldat oder Finden und Erfinden Frankfurter Poetik-Vorlesungen, 1984, 1984; Die Mörsinger Pappel, 1987 Waiblingers Augen, 1987; Gedichte 1953–1987, 1989; Herzwand: Mei Roman, 1990; Zwischen Untergang und Aufbruch: Aufsätze, Reden Gespräche, 1990; Brüder und Schwestern: Tagebuch eines Synodalen, 1991 Schubert, 1992; Bozena, 1994; Schumanns Schatten, 1996; Grosse, klein Schwester, 1998; Hoffmann oder Die vielfältige Liebe, 2000. *Honours* Literary Prize, German Critics' Asscn, 1964; Gerhart Hauptmann Prize 1971; Friedrich Hölderlin Prize, 1987; Andreas Gryphius Prize, 1990; Lio Feuchtwanger Prize, Acad. of Arts, Berlin, 1992; Hon. Prof., Stuttgart, 1994 Grand Cross of Merit, Federal Republic of Germany, 1995; Eichendorff Prize 2000. *Memberships:* Acad. of Arts, Berlin; Acad. of Science and Literature Mainz; Deutsche Akademie für Sprache und Dichtung eV, Darmstadt; PEN *Address:* Finkenweg 1, 46546 Mörfelden-Walldorf, Germany.

HARTNETT, David William; b. 4 Sept. 1952, London, England. Writer; Poet Ed. m. Margaret R N Thomas, 26 Aug. 1976, 1 s., 1 d. *Education:* Scholarship English Language and Literature, 1971, Honour Moderations, 1973, BA English Language and Literature, 1975, MA, 1981, DPhil, 1987, Oxfor University. *Appointments:* Co-Ed., Poetry Durham magazine; Dir

Contributing Ed., Leviathan Publishing Ltd, Leviathan Quarterly. *Publications:* Poetry: A Signalled Love, 1985; House of Moon, 1988; Dark Ages, 1992; At the Wood's Edge, 1997. Fiction: Black Milk, 1994; Brother to Dragons, 1998. *Contributions to:* TLS. *Honour:* TLS/Cheltenham Festival Poetry Competition, 1989. *Literary Agent:* David Higham Assocs, 5–8 Lower John St, Golden Sq., London W1R 4HA, England. *Address:* c/o Jonathan Cape, 20 Vauxhall Bridge Rd, London SW1V 2SA, England.

HARTNETT, Michael; b. 18 Sept. 1941, Co Limerick, Ireland. Poet. *Education:* University College and Trinity College, Dublin. *Appointment:* Teacher of Physical Education, National College, Limerick. *Publications:* Anatomy of a Cliche, 1968; Selected Poems, 1971; Culuide: The Retreat of Ita Cagney, 1975; A Farewell to English and Other Poems, 1975; Poems in English, 1977; Prisoners, 1978; Collected Poems, two vols, 1985, 1987; A Necklace of Wrens: Poems in English and Irish, 1987; House of Moon, 1989. *Address:* c/o Gallery Press, Loughcrew, Oldcastle, Co Meath, Ireland.

HARTSHORN, Willard L(ansing), (Bud Hartshorn); b. 28 Sept. 1922, Waterbury, CT, USA. Poet. m. Mary Eugenie Ruda, 30 Jan. 1942, 3 s., 2 d. *Education:* University of Connecticut, 1957; US Civil Service Rating, 1966; Qualification, Live Literature Program, New England Foundation for the Arts, 1984. *Publications:* Poems by Willard L Hartshorn, 1973; What Spilled When the Door of Life Was Left Ajar, 1991. Other: As I See It (audio tape, 75 poems), 1988; On Borrowed Time: 60 Poems, 1998. *Contributions to:* Anthologies, newspapers, and magazines. *Honours:* First Prize, artists and Writers of Connecticut, 1972; First Prize, Connecticut Poetry Society, 1984; Fourth Prize, Golden Poet Award, 1988, Fifth Prize, Silver Poet Award, 1989, Overall Standing Award, Silver Poet Award, 1990, World of Poetry. *Memberships:* Artists and Writers of Connecticut; Connecticut Poetry Society; National Acad. of Repertory Poetry; National Federation of State Poetry Societies. *Address:* 1256 Summit Rd, Cheshire, CT 06410, USA.

HARVEY, Anne (Berenice); b. 27 April 1933, London, England. Actress; Writer; Poet; Ed. m. Alan Harvey, 13 April 1957, 1 s., 1 d. *Education:* Guildhall School of Music and Drama, London, 1950–54. *Publications:* A Present for Nellie, 1981; Poets in Hand, 1985; Of Caterpillars, Cats and Cattle, 1987; In Time of War: War Poetry, 1987; Something I Remember (selected poetry of Eleanor Farjeon), 1987; A Picnic of Poetry, 1988; The Language of Love, 1989; Six of the Best, 1989; Faces in the Crowd, 1990; Headlines from the Jungle (with Virginia McKenna), 1990; Occasions, 1990; Flora's Red Socks, 1991; Shades of Green, 1991; Elected Friends (poems for and about Edward Thomas), 1991; He Said, She Said, They Said (conversation poems, ed.), 1993; Solo Audition: Speeches for Young Actors, 1993; Criminal Records: Poetry of Crime (ed.), 1994; Methuen Book of Duologues, 1995; Starlight, Starbright: Poems of Night, 1995; Swings and Shadows: Poems of Times Past and Present, 1996; Words Aloud, two vols (ed.), 1998; Eleanor Farjeon, The Last Four Years (ed.); Blackbird Has Spoken: Selected Poems of Eleanor Farjeon (ed.), 1999; Eleanor Farjeon, Come Christmas (ed.), 2000; Adlestrop Revisited (ed.), 2000; When Christmas Comes (anthology, ed.), 2002. Series Editor: Poetry Originals, 1992–95. *Contributions to:* Radio, journals, and magazines. *Honour:* Signal Poetry Award, 1992. *Memberships:* Poetry Society; Friends of the Dymock Poets; Eighteen Nineties Society; Imaginative Book Illustration Society; Walter de la Mare Society, founder mem.; Wilfred Owen Society; John Masefield Society; Edward Thomas Fellowship; Charlotte Mary Yonge Fellowship. *Address:* 37 St Stephen's Rd, Ealing, London W13 8HJ, England.

HARVEY, Francis; b. 13 April 1925, Enniskillen, Ireland. Poet. m. Marie A Gormley, 22 June 1955, 5 d. *Education:* University College, Dublin. *Publications:* In the Light on the Stones, 1978; The Rainmakers, 1988; The Boa Island Janus, 1996. *Contributions to:* Anthologies, reviews, and magazines. *Honours:* Irish Times-Yeats International Summer School Poetry Prize, 1977; Worldwide Fund for Nature Hutchinson-Guardian Prize, 1989; Peterloo Poets Prize, 1990. *Memberships:* Irish Writers' Union; Poetry Ireland; Poetry Society, London; Society of Irish Playwrights. *Address:* Trienna, Upper Main St, Donegal Town, Co Donegal, Ireland.

HARVEY, John Barton; b. 21 Dec. 1938, London, England. Writer; Poet. *Education:* Goldsmith College, University of London; Hatfield Polytechnic; University of Nottingham. *Publications:* What About It, Sharon?, 1979; Lonely Hearts, 1989; Rough Treatment, 1990; Cutting Edge, 1991; Off Minor, 1992; Ghosts of a Chance (poems), 1992; Wasted Years, 1993; Cold Light, 1994; Living Proof, 1995. Other: Numerous radio and television scripts. *Website:* www.mellotone.co.uk.

HARVEY, Marshall L., (Lee Ellison, Thomas Norman); b. 23 Aug. 1950, New Mexico, USA. Teacher; Technical Writer; Poet. m. Virginia, 28 Dec. 1972, 1 d. *Education:* BA, cum laude, Williams College, 1972; MA, Indiana University, 1974; PhD, University of Chicago, 1979. *Appointments:* Instructor, English, Columbia College; Technical Writer, Digital Engineering Corp; Writer, Converse Technology Inc. *Publications:* Painted Light, 1994; Iambic Pentameter from Shakespeare to Browning, 1996. *Contributions to:* Berkeley Poetry Review; Hawaii Review; NRG; Impetus; Boston Poet; Next Exit. *Honour:* Bay Area Poetry Coalition; Wallace Stevens Journal. *Membership:* Poetry

Society of New Hampshire, 1983–. *Address:* 59 Boulder Dr., Londonderry, NH 03053, USA.

HARVEY, Pamela Ann; b. 15 Oct. 1934, Bush Hill Park, Edmonton, London, England. Writer; Poet. *Education:* Edmonton County Grammar; RSA Diploma. *Publications:* Poetry, 1994; Quiet Lines, 1996; The Wellspring (with Anna Franklin), 2000. *Contributions to:* The People's Poetry; Romantic Heir; Cadmium Blue Literary Journal; Pendragon; Keltria, USA; Celtic Connections; Silver Wheel; Sharkti Laureate; Time Haiku; Azami, Japan. *Memberships:* Enfield Writers Group; New Renaissance Poets Society. *Address:* 21 Blakesware Gdns, Edmonton, London N9 9HX, England.

HARVEY, Steven; b. 9 June 1949, Dodge City, KS, USA. Prof. of English; Writer; Poet. m. Barbara Hupfer, 8 May 1971, 2 s., 2 d. *Education:* BA, Wake Forest University, 1971; MA, Writing Seminars, Johns Hopkins University, 1973; MA, Literature, Middlebury College, 1984; PhD, University of Virginia, 1989. *Appointments:* Prof. of English, Young Harris College, GA, 1976–; Instructor in Writing, John C. Campbell Folk School, 1995–. *Publications:* Powerlines (poems), 1976; A Geometry of Lilies (non-fiction), 1993; Lost in Translation (non-fiction), 1997; In a Dark Wood: Personal Essays by Men on Middle Age, 1997; Bound for Shady Grove (non-fiction), 2000. *Contributions to:* Periodicals. *Honour:* MacDowell Colony Fellowship, 1994. *Membership:* Associated Writing Programs. *Address:* PO Box 356, Young Harris, GA 30582, USA. *E-mail:* sharvey@yhc.edu.

HARVOR, Elisabeth, (Erica Elisabeth Arendt); b. 26 June 1936, Saint John, NB, Canada. Poet; Writer. m. Stig Harvor, 16 Nov. 1957, divorced 1977, 2 s. *Education:* MA, Concordia University, 1986. *Appointments:* Teacher, various creative writing programs; Writer-in-Residence, Ottawa Public Library, 1993. *Publications:* Women and Children, 1973, revised edn as Our Lady of All the Distances, 1991; If Only We Could Drive Like This Forever, 1988; Fortress of Chairs, 1992; Let Me Be the One, 1996; The Long Cold Green Evenings of Spring, 1997; A Room at the Heart of Things (ed.), 1998. *Honours:* League of Canadian Poets' National Poetry Prize, 1989, 1991; Malahat Long Poem Prize, 1990; Gerald Lampert Memorial Award, 1992; Finalist, Gov.-Gen.'s Literary Award, 1996. *Address:* c/o The Writers' Union of Canada, 24 Ryerson Ave, Toronto, ON M5T 2P3, Canada.

HARWOOD, Edmund Donald; b. 9 Jan. 1924, Cannes, France. Royal Navy Officer (retd); Poet. m. Penelope Ann St Clair Morford, 2 April 1949, 1 s., 1 d. *Education:* Naval Trans. in German, 1949, Norwegian, 1969. *Appointments:* Naval Officer, retiring as Commander, 1942–72; Freelance Trans., 5 languages, 1972–. *Publications:* A Clutch of Words, 1980; A Flight of Words, 1985. *Contributions to:* Acumen; Argo; Country Life; Countryman; Envoi; Field; Iron; Orbis; Outposts; Pennine Platform; Poetry Nottingham; Rialto; Spokes; Stand; Staple; Weyfarers; Doors; Global Tapestry; Iota; Sepia; South. *Honours:* Rhyme Revival, 1983; Stanza, 1984; Chester, Staple, 1986; Surrey Competition, 1988; Queenie Lee Competition, 1989; Ver Poets Open, 1990; Ouse Valley Poetry Competition, 1992; Christchurch Poetry Competition, 1992; LACE Competition, 1994; Balwest Competition, 1996; Martello Competitions, 1996, 1997; Open University Sonnet Competition, 1996; Swanage Competition, 1996; Christchurch Competition, 1998, 1999, 2000; Torbay Open Poetry Competition. *Address:* Wadswell, Haythorne Common, Horton, Wimborne, Dorset BH21 7JG, England.

HARWOOD, Lee; b. 6 June 1939, Leicester, England. Poet; Writer; Trans. Divorced, 2 s., 1 d. *Education:* BA, Honours, English, Queen Mary College, University of London, 1961. *Publications:* Title Illegible, 1965; The Man with Blue Eyes, 1966; The White Room, 1968; The Beautiful Atlas, 1969; Landscapes, 1969; The Sinking Colony, 1970; Penguin Modern Poets 19 (with John Ashbery and Tom Raworth), 1971; The First Poem, 1971; New Year, 1971; Captain Harwood's Log of Stern Statements and Stout Sayings, 1973; Freighters, 1975; H.M.S. Little Fox, 1976; Boston-Brighton, 1977; Old Bosham Bird Watch and Other Stories, 1977; Wish You Were Here (with A Lopez), 1979; All the Wrong Notes, 1981; Faded Ribbons, 1982; Wine Tales (with Richard Caddel), 1984; Crossing the Frozen River: Selected Poems 1965–1980, 1984; Monster Masks, 1985; Dream Quilt (stories), 1985; Rope Boy to the Rescue, 1988; The Empty Hill: Memories and Praises of Paul Evans 1945–1991 (ed. with Peter Bailey), 1992; In the Mists: Mountain Poems, 1993. Other: Trans of works by Tristan Tzara. *Contributions to:* Journals, reviews, and magazines. *Honours:* Poetry Foundation Award, New York, 1966; Alice Hunt Bartlett Prize, Poetry Society, London, 1976. *Memberships:* National Poetry Secretariat, Chair., 1974–76; Poetry Society, London, Chair., 1976–77. *Address:* 2 Ivy Pl., off Waterloo St, Hove, Sussex BN3 1AP, England.

HASELMANN, Ralph Jr; b. 4 Oct. 1965, Union, New Jersey, USA. Poet; Publisher. *Education:* BFA in Graphic Design, Mason Gross School of Arts, Rutgers, New Brunswick, 1990. *Publication:* Wounded Heart, Naked Soul, 2001; Scattershot Haze, 2001. *Contributions to:* Magazines. *Honour:* Ed. of the Year, Cedar Hill Review. *Address:* 67 Norma Rd, Hampton, NJ 08827, USA. *Website:* www.lucidmoonpoetry.com.

HASHMI, (Aurangzeb) Alamgir; b. 15 Nov. 1951, Lahore, Pakistan. Prof.; Poet; Writer; Ed.; Broadcaster. m. Beatrice Stoerk, 15 Dec. 1978, 2 s., 1 d.

Education: MA, University of Louisville, 1977. *Appointments:* Lecturer, Forman Christian College, Lahore, 1973–74, University of Berne, University of Basel, 1982; Davidson International Visiting Scholar from Pakistan, University of North Carolina, 1974–75; Lecturer in English, University of Louisville, 1975–78, University of Zürich and Volkshochschule, Zürich, 1980–85; Asst Prof. of English, University of Bahawalpur, Pakistan, 1979–80; Assoc. Prof. of Englsh, International Islamic University, Islamabad, 1985–86; Prof. of English and Comparative Literature, Pakistan Futuristics Institute, Islamabad, 1990. *Publications:* Poetry: The Oak and Amen: Love Poems, 1976; America is a Punjabi Word, 1979; An Old Chair, 1979; My Second in Kentucky, 1981; This Time in Lahore, 1983; Neither This Time/Nor That Place, 1984; Inland and Other Poems, 1988; The Poems of Alamgir Hashmi, 1992; Sun and Moon and Other Poems, 1992; Others to Sport with Amaryllis in the Shade, 1992. Other: Pakistani Literature (ed.), 2 vols, 1978, second edn as Pakistani Literature: The Contemporary English Writers, 1987; Commonwealth Literature, 1983; The Commonwealth, Comparative Literature and the World, 1988; Pakistani Short Stories in English (ed.), 1992; Encyclopedia of Post-Colonial Literatures (co-ed.), 1994; Where Coyotes Howl and Wind Blows Free (ed. with Alexandra Haslam), 1995; The Great Tejon Club Jubilee, 1996. *Contributions to:* Many books, journals, and periodicals. *Honours:* Hon. DLitt, Centre Universitaire de Luxembourg, 1984, San Francisco State University, 1984; Patras Bokhari Award, Pakistan Acad. of Letters, 1985; Rockefeller Foundation Fellow, 1994; Roberto Celli Memorial Award, 1994. *Memberships:* Associated Writing Programs; Asscn for Asian Studies; Commonwealth Club; Asscn for Commonwealth Literature and Language Studies; International Asscn of University Profs of English; International Centre for Asian Studies, fellow; International PEN, fellow; MLA of America. *Address:* House 162, St 64, Ramna 8/1, Islamabad, Pakistan.

HASLUCK, Nicholas (Paul); b. 17 Oct. 1942, Canberra, ACT, Australia. Writer; Poet. *Education:* University of Western Australia, 1960–63; Oxford University, 1964–66. *Appointments:* Barrister, Solicitor, Supreme Court of Western Australia, 1968; Deputy Chair., Australia Council, 1978–82; Chair., Literature Board, 1998–2001. *Publications:* Fiction: Quarantine, 1978; The Blue Guitar, 1980; The Hand that Feeds You: A Satiric Nightmare, 1982; The Bellarmine Jug, 1984; The Country without Music, 1990; The Blosseville File, 1992; Offcuts From a Legal Literary Life, 1993; A Grain of Truth, 1994; Our Man K, 1999. Stories: The Hat on the Letter O and Other Stories, 1978. Poetry: Anchor and Other Poems, 1976; On the Edge, 1980; Chinese Journey, 1985. *Honours:* Age Book of the Year Award, 1984; Mem. of the Order of Australia, 1986. *Address:* 14 Reserve St, Claremont, WA 6010, Australia.

HASS, Robert (Louis); b. 1 March 1941, San Francisco, CA, USA. Poet; Writer; Trans.; Ed.; Prof. m. Earlene Joan Leif, 1 Sept. 1962, divorced 1986, 2 s., 1 d. *Education:* BA, St Mary's College of California, 1963; MA, 1965, PhD, 1971, Stanford University. *Appointments:* Asst Prof., State University of New York, Buffalo, 1967–71; Prof. of English, St Mary's College of California, 1971–89, University of California, Berkeley, 1989–; Visiting Lecturer, University of Virginia, 1974, Goddard College, 1976, Columbia University, 1982, University of California, Berkeley, 1983; Poet-in-Residence, The Frost Place, Franconia, New Hampshire, 1978; Poet Laureate of the USA, 1995–97. *Publications:* Poetry: Field Guide, 1973; Winter Morning in Charlottesville, 1977; Praise, 1979; The Apple Tree at Olema, 1989; Human Wishes, 1989; Sun under Wood, 1996. Other: Twentieth Century Pleasures: Prose on Poetry, 1984; Into the Garden – A Wedding Anthology: Poetry and Prose on Love and Marriage, 1993. Translations: Czesław Miłosz's The Separate Notebooks (with Robert Pinsky), 1983; Czesław Miłosz's Unattainable Earth (with Czesław Miłosz), 1986; Czesław Miłosz's Collected Poems, 1931–1987 (with Louis Iribane and Peter Scott), 1988. Editor: Rock and Hawk: A Selection of Shorter Poems by Robinson Jeffers, 1987; The Pushcart Prize XII (with Bill Henderson and Jorie Graham), 1987; Tomaz Salamun: Selected Poems (with Charles Simic), 1988; Selected Poems of Tomas Tranströmer, 1954–1986 (with others), 1989; The Essential Haiku: Versions of Basho, Buson and Issa, 1994. *Contributions to:* Anthologies and other publications. *Honours:* Woodrow Wilson Fellowship, 1963–64; Danforth Fellowship, 1963–67; Yale Series of Younger Poets Award, Yale University Press, 1972; US-Great Britain Bicentennial Exchange Fellow in the Arts, 1976–77; William Carlos Williams Award, 1979; National Book Critics Circle Award, 1984; Award of Merit, American Acad. of Arts and Letters, 1984; John D. and Catherine T. MacArthur Foundation Grant, 1984. *Address:* PO Box 807, Inverness, CA 94937, USA.

HASTINGS, Jennifer Sue; b. 31 Oct. 1965, Cincinnati, Ohio, USA. Poet. *Education:* BA, International Business, Muskingum College, 1987; Diploma, Institute of Children's Literature, 1991. *Contributions to:* Anthologies and other publications. *Honours:* Third Place, Poetry, National French Creative Writing Contest, 1981; Poet of Merit, American Poetry Asscn, 1989, 1990; Golden Poet, World of Poetry, 1989, 1990. *Memberships:* Acad. of American Poets; American Poetry Asscn; Night Writers; World of Poetry.

HATHAWAY, Michael; b. 20 Sept. 1961, El Paso, Texas, USA. Poet. *Publications:* Shadows of Myself, 1980; Inconspicuous, 1988; Excerpt, 1989; Come Winter and Other Poems, 1989; God Poems, 1991. *Contributions to:* Fire!; Calliopes Corner; Waterways; Manna; Golden Isis; RFD; Up Against the Wall,

Mother; Raw Bone; Nothing Sinister; ArtiMag; Psychopoetica; Forum fo Universal Spokesmen; Clock Radio; New Sins; Daring Poetry Quarterly Thirteen; River Rat Review; Silver Wings; Parnassus Literary Journal Gypsy; Impetus; Anemone; Pididdle; Cats Eye; Off My Fare; Poet Perspective; Proof Rock; Heigh-Ashbury Literary Journal; Cat Fancy; Pearl Ransom; Poet; Abbey. *Honour:* First Place, Jubilee Press Contest, 1987 *Address:* 1514 Stone, Great Bend, KS 67530, USA.

HATOUM, Milton; b. 19 Aug. 1952, Manaus, Brazil. Prof. of French Literature; Poet; Writer; Trans. *Education:* Diploma in Urban Architecture State University of São Paulo; MA, Sorbonne, University of Paris, 1983 *Appointment:* Prof. of French Literature, University of Amazonas Manaus 1983–. *Publications:* Um rio entre ruinas (poems), 1978; Relato de um Certo Oriente (novel), 1989, English translation as The Tree of the Seventh Heaven 1994; Dois Irmãos (novel), 2000, English trans. as The Brothers, 2002. Other Trans. into Portuguese: La Croisade des enfants, Marcel Schwob; Trois Contes Gustave Flaubert; Representations of the Intellectual, Edward Said *Contributions to:* Periodicals. *Honour:* Jabuti Award, 2000. *Address:* Rua D Veiga Filho, 83/131, 012229-001, São Paulo, SP, Brazil. *E-mail* mhatoum@uol.com.br.

HAUGEN, Paal-Helge; b. 26 April 1945, Valle, Norway. Poet; Writer Dramatist. *Appointments:* Chair., Norwegian State Film Production Board 1980–85, Board of Literary Advisers, Asscn of Norwegian Authors, 1984–88 International Pegasus Prize Committee, 1988. *Publications:* 30 books including: Anne (novel), 1968; Stone Fences, 1986; Meditasjonar over Georges de la Tour (poems), 1990; Sone O (poems), 1992; Wintering with the Light 1995; Poesi: Collected Poems, 1965–1995, 1995. Other: Plays for stage, radio and television; Opera libretti. *Contributions to:* Professional journals. *Honours* Dobloug Prize, 1986; Richard Wilbur Prize, USA, 1986; Norwegian Literary Critics Prize, 1990; Norwegian National Brage Prize, 1992; Grieg Prize for texts set to music, 2000. *Address:* Skrefjellv 5, 4645 Nodeland, Norway. E-mail:phaugen@online.no.

HAUGOVA, Mila, (Mila Srnková); b. 14 June 1942, Budapest, Hungary. Ed.; Poet. m. (1) Edgar Haug, 16 Sept. 1967, divorced, 1 d., (2) Ladislav Kvasz, 1993. *Education:* Degree, Agronomy Engineer, Nitra, 1965. *Appointment:* Ed., Romboid literary magazine. *Publications:* Rusty Earth, 1980; Variable Surface, 1981; Possible Tenderness, 1984; Clean Days, 1990; Prime Love, 1991; Nostalgia, 1992; Lady with Unicorn, 1995. *Contributions to:* Radio, television, and periodicals. *Honours:* Prize, Literary Foundation, 1981; Poetry Prize, Slovensky Spisovatel Publishing House, 1992. *Memberships:* Club of Independent Writers; PEN Slovak Centre, secretary. *Address:* Nejedlého 27, 84102 Bratislava, Slovakia.

HAVIARAS, Stratis; b. 28 June 1935, Nea Kios, Greece. Librarian; Poet; Writer; Ed. m. Heather E Cole, 30 March 1990, 1 d. *Education:* BA, 1973, MFA, 1976, Goddard College. *Appointments:* Librarian, Harvard University Library; Ed., Harvard Review, 1990–. *Publications:* Poetry: 4 books in Greek, 1963, 1965, 1967, 1972; Crossing the River Twice, 1976. Fiction: When the Tree Sings, 1979; The Heroic Age, 1984. Editor: Seamus Heaney: A Celebration, 1996. *Contributions to:* Newspapers and magazines. *Honours:* National Book Critics Circle Awards. *Memberships:* PEN New England; Signet; Societe Imaginaire. *Address:* c/o Poetry Room, Harvard University Library, Cambridge, MA 02138, USA.

HAWKESWORTH, Pauline Mary; b. 28 April 1943, Portsmouth, England. Poet. m. Rex Hawkesworth, 25 Oct. 1961, 2 d. *Publications:* 2 books, 82 poems. Anthologies: Parents Enitharmon, 2000; Spirit of Wilfred Owen, 2001. *Contributions to:* Envoi; South; Interpreters House; Script; Iota; Poetry Nottingham International; Frogmore Press; Others. *Honours:* First Prize, Short Story, Portsmouth Polytechnic, 1981; First Prize, South Wales Miners Eisteddfod, 1990; First Prize, Hastings Open Poetry Competition, 1993; Runner-Up, Redbeck Competition, 1996; First Prize, Tavistock and North Dartmoor, 2000; First Prize, Newark and Sherwood Millennium Project, 2001. *Membership:* Vice-Pres., Portsmouth Poetry Society. *Address:* 4 Rampart Gardens, Hilsea, Portsmouth PO3 5LR, England.

HAWKINS, Hunt; b. 23 Dec. 1943, Washington, DC, USA. Prof. of English; Poet. m. Elaine Smith, 4 Sept. 1976, 1 s., 1 d. *Education:* BA, Williams College, 1965; MA, 1969, PhD, 1976, Stanford University. *Appointments:* Instructor, Texas Southern University, 1968–70; Asst Prof., University of Minnesota, 1977–78; Asst Prof., 1978–83, Assoc. Prof., 1983–94, Prof. of English, 1994–, Florida State University, Tallahassee. *Publication:* The Domestic Life, 1994. *Contributions to:* Poetry: Southern Review; Georgia Review; Tri-Quarterly; Carleton Miscellany; Poetry Northwest; Beloit Poetry Journal; Harvard Magazine; Minnesota Review; Kayak; Wormwood Review; Kansas Quarterly; Yankee Magazine; Bellingham Review; Florida Review; Southern Poetry Review; Apalachee Quarterly. *Honours:* Acad. of American Poets Prizes, 1963, 1965, 1973; Agnes Lynch Starrett Poetry Prize, 1992; Florida Individual Artist Fellowship, 1993–94; Florida Individual Artists Fellowship, 1993–94, 1998–99. *Memberships:* MLA; South Atlantic MLA; Joseph Conrad Society; Mark Twain Circle. *Address:* English Dept, Florida State University, Tallahassee, FL 32306, USA.

HAWKINS, Loretta; b. 1 Jan. 1942, Winston-Salem, NC, USA. Writer; Dramatist; Poet; Teacher. m. 3 d. *Education:* BS, Education, Illinois Teachers College, 1965; MA, Literature, 1977, MA, African Cultures, 1978, Governors State University; MLA, Humanities, University of Chicago, 1998. *Appointments:* Teacher, Chicago Public Schools, 1967–; Lecturer, Chicago City Colleges, 1987–90. *Contributions to:* Numerous periodicals. *Honours:* Several grants; First Place, James H. Wilson Full-Length Play Award, 1993; Zora Neale Hurston-Bessie Head Fiction Award, 1993; Third Place, Fiction, Feminist Writers Contest, 1993. *Memberships:* American Asscn of University Women; Dramatists' Guild of America; International Women's Writing Guild; National Council of Teachers of English; Women's Theatre Alliance. *Address:* 8928 S Oglesby, Chicago, IL 60617, USA.

HAWTHORNE, Susan; b. 30 Nov. 1951, Wagga Wagga, NSW, Australia. University Lecturer; Publisher; Poet; Writer. *Education:* Diploma, Primary Teaching, Melbourne Teachers College, 1972; BA, Honours, Philosophy, La Trobe University, 1976; MA, Prelim, Classics, University of Melbourne, 1981. *Appointments:* Tutor, Koori Teacher Education Programme, Deakin University, 1986; Ed. and Commissioning Ed., Penguin Books, Australia, 1987–91; Publisher, Spinifex Press, 1991–; Lecturer, Dept of Communication and Language Studies, Victoria University of Technology, 1995–. *Publications:* Difference (ed.), 1985; Moments of Desire, 1989; The Exploring Frangipani, 1990; Angels of Power, 1991; The Falling Woman, 1992; The Language in My Tongue: Four New Poets, 1993; The Spinifex Quiz Book, 1993; Australia for Women (co-ed.), 1994; Car Maintenance, Explosives and Love (co-ed.), 1997; CyberFeminism (co-ed.), 1999; Bird, 1999. *Contributions to:* Journals, reviews, and periodicals. *Memberships:* Australian Society of Authors; Fellowship of Australian Authors; PEN International; Victoria Writers Centre. *Address:* c/o Spinifex Press, 504 Queensbury St, North Melbourne, Vic. 3051, Australia.

HAXTON, Brooks; b. 1 Dec. 1950, Greenville, Mississippi, USA. Teacher; Poet. m. 5 June 1983, 1 s. *Education:* BA, Beloit College, Wisconsin; MA, Syracuse University. *Appointments:* Resident Poet, Warren Wilson College, 1990–, Syracuse University, 1993–. *Publications:* The Lay of Eleanor and Irene, 1985; Dominion, 1986; Traveling Company, 1989; Dead Reckoning, 1989. *Contributions to:* American Poetry Review; Atlantic; Beloit Poetry Journal; Kenyon Review; Missouri Review; Southern Review; Tri-Quarterly Review. *Honours:* Fellowships, Syracuse University, 1979–81, Council for the Arts, Washington, DC, 1984, Ingram Merrill Foundation, 1985, National Endowment for the Arts, 1987, New York Foundation for the Arts, 1988. *Membership:* Poetry Society of America. *Address:* 21 Bloomingdale Rd, White Plains, NY 10605, USA.

HAYES, Ann Louise; b. 13 May 1924, Los Angeles, CA, USA. Prof. of English; Poet. *Education:* AB summa cum laude, English, 1948, MA, English, 1950, Stanford University. *Appointments:* Acting Instructor, Stanford University, 1950; Teaching Assoc., Indiana University, 1953–55; Instructor, Coe College, 1955–57; Instructor, 1957–60, Asst Prof., 1960–65, Carnegie Institute of Technology; Assoc. Prof., 1965–74, Prof. of English, 1974–, Carnegie Mellon University, Pittsburgh. *Publications:* For Sally Barnes, 1963; Amo Ergo Sum, Amo Ergo Est, 1969; The Dancer's Step, 1973; The Living and the Dead, 1975; Witness How All Occasions..., 1977; Progress, Dancing, 1986; Circle of the Earth, 1990; Letters at Christmas and Other Poems, 1995. *Contributions to:* New Mexico Quarterly Review; City Lights; American Scholar; Southern Review; Virginia Quarterly Review; Carnegie Review; Three Rivers Poetry Journal; Oakland Review; Cloud Chamber; Fountain; Focus; Poema Convidada; New England Journal of Medicine; Hudson Review; Confrontation; Maryland Review; The Epigrammatist; La Fontana. *Honours:* Irene Hardy Poetry Award, 1943; Ina Coolbrith Award, 1943; Clarence Urmy Poetry Prizes, 1943, 1947, 1950; Honourable Mention, James D Phelan Award in Poetry, 1947; Borestone Mountain Poetry Award, 1968; Best Poems of 1969. *Address:* Dept of English, Baker Hall 259, Carnegie Mellon University, Pittsburgh, PA 15213, USA.

HAZARA, Singh; b. 30 Nov. 1922, Sheikhupura District, Punjab, India. University Teacher (retd); Poet. m. Phool Kaur, 13 March 1949, 2 s., 2 d. *Education:* BA, Punjab University, Lahore, 1945; MA, 1950, LLB, 1955, Punjab University, Chandigarh. *Appointments:* Lecturer of English, Khalsa College, Amritsar, 1950–53; Asst Prof. of English, Government Agricultural College, Ludhiana, 1954–66; Assoc. Prof. of English, 1966–84, Head, Dept of Journalism, Languages and Culture, 1977–82, Punjab Agricultural University, Ludhiana; Sec. to Vice-Chancellor, Guru Nanak Dev University, Amritsar, 1985–88. *Publications:* Aspirations, 1980; Yearnings, 1987; Expectations, 1999. *Contributions to:* 20 anthologies, 1980–96, and other publications. *Memberships:* Indian Society of Authors; World Poetry International; Punjabi Sahitya Acad., Ludhiana. *Address:* 3-C Udham Singh Nagar, Ludhiana 141 001, India.

HAZO, Samuel (John); b. 19 July 1928, Pittsburgh, Pennsylvania, USA. Prof. of English; Writer; Poet. *Education:* BA, University of Notre Dame, 1948; MA, Duquesne University, 1955; PhD, University of Pittsburgh, 1957. *Appointments:* Faculty, 1955–65, Dean, College of Arts and Sciences, 1961–66, Prof. of English, 1965–, Duquesne University; Dir, International Forum, 1966–; State Poet, Commonwealth of Pennsylvania. *Publications:*

Discovery and Other Poems, 1959; The Quiet Wars, 1962; Hart Crane: An Introduction and Interpretation, 1963, revised edn as Smithereened Apart: A Critique of Hart Crane, 1978; The Christian Intellectual Studies in the Relation of Catholicism to the Human Sciences (ed.), 1963; A Selection of Contemporary Religious Poetry (ed.), 1963; Listen With the Eye, 1964; My Sons in God: Selected and New Poems, 1965; Blood Rights, 1968; The Blood of Adonis (with Ali Ahmed Said), 1971; Twelve Poems (with George Nama), 1972; Seascript: A Mediterranean Logbook, 1972; Once for the Last Bandit: New and Previous Poems, 1972; Quartered, 1974; Inscripts, 1975; The Very Fall of the Sun, 1978; To Paris, 1981; The Wanton Summer Air, 1982; Thank a Bored Angel, 1983; The Feast of Icarus, 1984; The Color of Reluctance, 1986; The Pittsburgh That Starts Within You, 1986; Silence Spoken Here, 1988; Stills, 1989; The Rest is Prose, 1989; Lebanon, 1990; Picks, 1990; The Past Won't Stay Behind You, 1993; The Pages of Day and Night, 1995; The Holy Surprise of Right Now, 1996; As They Sail, 1999; Spying for God, 1999; Mano a Mano: The Life of Manolete, 2001. *Address:* 785 Somerville Dr., Pittsburgh, PA 15243, USA.

HEANEY, Seamus (Justin); b. 13 April 1939, County Londonderry, Northern Ireland. Poet; Writer; Prof. m. Marie Devlin, 1965, 2 s., 1 d. *Education:* St Columb's College, Derry; BA, Queen's University, Belfast, 1961. *Appointments:* Teacher, St Thomas's Secondary School, Belfast, 1962–63; Lecturer, St Joseph's College of Education, Belfast, 1963–66, Queen's University, Belfast, 1966–72, Carysfort College, 1975–81; Senior Visiting Lecturer, 1982–85, Boylston Prof. of Rhetoric and Oratory, 1985–97, Ralph Waldo Emerson Poet-in-Residence, 1998–, Harvard University; Prof. of Poetry, Oxford University, 1989–94. *Publications:* Eleven Poems, 1965; Death of a Naturalist, 1966; Door Into the Dark, 1969; Wintering Out, 1972; North, 1975; Field Work, 1979; Selected Poems, 1965–1975, 1980; Sweeney Astray, 1984, revised edn as Sweeney's Flight, 1992; Station Island, 1984; The Haw Lantern, 1987; New Selected Poems, 1966–1987, 1990; Seeing Things, 1991; The Spirit Level, 1996; Opened Ground: Selected Poems, 1966–1996, 1998; Electric Light, 2000. Prose: Preoccupations: Selected Prose, 1968–1978, 1980; The Government of the Tongue, 1988; The Place of Writing, 1989; The Redress of Poetry: Oxford Lectures, 1995; Finders Keepers: Selected Prose 1971–2001, 2001. Other: Beowulf: A New Verse Translation, 1999. *Honours:* Somerset Maugham Award, 1967; Cholmondeley Award, 1968; W H Smith Award, 1975; Duff Cooper Prize, 1975; Whitbread Awards, 1987, 1996; Nobel Prize for Literature, 1995; Whitbread Book of the Year Awards, 1997, 1999. *Memberships:* Royal Irish Acad.; British Acad.; American Acad. of Arts and Letters. *Address:* c/o Faber & Faber, 3 Queen Sq., London WC1N 3AU, England.

HEARLE, Kevin (James); b. 17 March 1958, Santa Ana, CA, USA. University Lecturer; Poet; Writer. m. Elizabeth Henderson, 26 Nov. 1983. *Education:* AB, English, Stanford University, 1980; MFA, University of Iowa, 1983; MA, Literature, 1990; PhD, Literature, 1991, University of California at Santa Cruz. *Appointments:* Poetry Co-Ed., Quarry West, 1988–92; Instructor, 1991, Lecturer, 1993, 1998, University of California at Santa Cruz; Lecturer, San Jose State University, 1992–94, California State University at Los Angeles, 1995–96, Santa Clara University, 1999; Instructor, University of California at Los Angeles Extension, 1995–96. *Publication:* Each Thing We Know Is Changed Because We Know It, and Other Poems, 1994. *Contributions to:* Books, reviews, quarterlies and reviews. *Honours:* Peninsula Community Foundation Individual Artist Grants, 1986, 1999; Millay Colony for the Arts Residency, 1990. *Memberships:* American Literature Asscn; International John Steinbeck Society; Western Literature Asscn. *Address:* 102 Hobart Ave, San Mateo, CA 94402, USA.

HEATH, Desmond Butterworth; b. 27 Feb. 1927, London, England. Violinist; Teacher; Poet. m. Sylvia Noel Putterill, 21 June 1952, 1 s., 2 d. *Education:* ARCM, Royal College of Music, 1942–47. *Appointments:* Violinist, BBC Symphony Orchestra, 1948–57, Philharmonia, 1961–70; Freelance Player, English Baroque Soloists, London Classical Players, Acad. of Ancient Music and others; Violin Teacher, Eton and Westminster (peripatetic). *Publications:* After This Sky, 1968; Chiaroscuro, 1985; Country Night and Other Poems, 1990; Roden Noel: A Wide Angle, 1996. *Contributions to:* New Hope International Writing; Poetry Wales; Iota; Breakthru; Poetry Nottingham; Envoi; Outposts; Equinox. *Honours:* Highly Commended, Lake Aske Competition, 1983; First Prize, Queenie Lee Memorial Competition, 1986; Merit Award, Queenie Lee Poetry Competition, 1991. *Address:* 60 Esmond Rd, Bedford Park, London W4 1JF, England.

HEATHERLEY, A. Celeste. See: MORGAN, Ariel Celeste Heatherley.

HEATH-STUBBS, John (Francis Alexander); b. 9 July 1918, London, England. Poet; Writer; Trans.; Ed. *Education:* Worcester College for the Blind; Queen's College, Oxford. *Appointments:* English Master, Hall School, Hampstead, 1944–45; Editorial Asst, Hutchinson's 1945–46; Gregory Fellow in Poetry, University of Leeds, 1952–55; Visiting Prof. of English, University of Alexandria, 1955–58, University of Michigan, 1960–61; Lecturer in English Literature, College of St Mark and St John, Chelsea, 1963–73. *Publications:* Poetry: Wounded Thammuz, 1942; Beauty and the Beast, 1943; The Divided Ways, 1946; The Swarming of the Bees, 1950; A Charm Against the Toothache,

1954; The Triumph of the Muse, 1958; The Blue Fly in His Head, 1962; Selected Poems, 1965; Satires and Epigrams, 1968; Artorius, 1973; A Parliament of Birds, 1975; The Watchman's Flute, 1978; Mouse, the Bird and the Sausage, 1978; Birds Reconvened, 1980; Buzz Buzz, 1981; Naming the Beasts, 1982; The Immolation of Aleph, 1985; Cat's Parnassus, 1987; Time Pieces, 1988; Collected Poems, 1988; A Partridge in a Pear Tree, 1988; A Ninefold of Charms, 1989; Selected Poems, 1990; The Parson's Cat, 1991; Sweetapple Earth, 1993; Chimeras, 1994; Galileo's Salad, 1996; The Torriano Sequences, 1997; The Sound of Light, 2000. Play: Helen in Egypt, 1958. Autobiography: Hindsights, 1993. Criticism: The Darkling Plain, 1950; Charles Williams, 1955; The Pastoral, 1969; The Ode, 1969; The Verse Satire, 1969. Translator: Hafiz of Shiraz (with Peter Avery), 1952; Leopardi: Selected Prose and Poetry (with Iris Origo), 1966; The Poems of Anyte (with Carol A Whiteside), 1974; The Rubaiyat of Omar Khayyam (with Peter Avery), 1979; Sulpicia, 2000. Editor: Several books, including: Faber Book of Twentieth Century Verse (with David Wright), 1953; Poems of Science (with Phillips Salman), 1984. Honours: Queen's Gold Medal for Poetry, 1973; Oscar Williams/Jean Durwood Award, 1977; O.B.E., 1989; Commonwealth Poetry Prize, 1989; Cholmondeley Award, 1989; Howard Sargeant Award, 1989; Cross of St Augustine, 1999; Fellow, English Asscn, 1999. Membership: RSL, Fellow. Address: 22 Artesian Rd, London W2 5AR, England.

HECHT, Anthony (Evan); b. 16 Jan. 1923, New York, NY, USA. Poet; Prof. m. (1) Patricia Harris, 27 Feb. 1954, divorced 1961, 2 s., (2) Helen D'Alessandro, 12 June 1971, 1 s. Education: BA, Bard College, 1944; MA, Columbia University, 1950. Appointments: Teacher, Kenyon College, 1947–48, State University of Iowa, 1948–49, New York University, 1949–56, Smith College, 1956–59; Assoc. Prof. of English, Bard College, 1961–67; Faculty, 1967–68, John D Deane Prof. of English of Rhetoric and Poetry, 1968–85, University of Rochester, New York; Hurst Prof., Washington University, St Louis, 1971; Visiting Prof., Harvard University, 1973, Yale University, 1977; Faculty, Salzburg Seminar in American Studies, 1977; Consultant in Poetry, Library of Congress, Washington, DC, 1982–84; Prof., Georgetown University, 1985–93; Andrew Mellon Lecturer in Fine Arts, National Gallery of Art, Washington, DC, 1992. Publications: A Summoning of Stones, 1954; The Seven Deadly Sins, 1958; A Bestiary, 1960; The Hard Hours, 1968; Millions of Strange Shadows, 1977; The Venetian Vespers, 1977; Obbligati: Essays in Criticism, 1986; The Transparent Man, 1990; Collected Earlier Poems, 1990; The Hidden Law: The Poetry of W H Auden, 1993; On the Laws of the Poetic Art, 1995; The Presumption of Death, 1995; Flight Among the Tombs, 1996; The Darkness and the Light, 2001. Co-Author and Co-Editor: Jiggery-Pokery: A Compendium of Double Dactyls (with John Hollander), 1967. Editor: The Essential Herbert, 1987. Translator: Seven Against Thebes (with Helen Bacon), 1973. Contributions to: Many anthologies; Hudson Review; New York Review of Books; Quarterly Review of Literature; Transatlantic Review; Voices. Honours: Prix de Rome Fellowship, 1950; Guggenheim Fellowships, 1954, 1959; Hudson Review Fellowship, 1958; Ford Foundation Fellowships, 1960, 1968; Acad. of American Poets Fellowship, 1969; Bollingen Prize, 1983; Eugenio Montale Award, 1983; Harriet Monroe Award, 1987; Ruth Lilly Award, 1988; Aiken Taylor Award, Sewanee Review, 1988; National Endowment for the Arts Grant, 1989. Memberships: Acad. of American Poets, hon. chancellor, 1971–97; American Acad. of Arts and Sciences; American Acad. of Arts and Letters. Address: 4256 Nebraska Ave NW, Washington, DC 20016, USA.

HECKLER, Jonellen; b. 28 Oct. 1943, Pittsburgh, Pennsylvania, USA. Writer; Poet. m. Lou Heckler, 17 Aug. 1968, 1 s. Education: BA, English Literature, University of Pittsburgh, 1965. Publications: Safekeeping, 1983; A Fragile Peace, 1986; White Lies, 1989; Circumstances Unknown, 1993; Final Tour, 1994. Contributions to: Numerous poems and short stories in Ladies Home Journal Magazine, 1975–83. Membership: Authors Guild. Address: 5562 Pernod Dr. SW, Ft Myers, FL 33919, USA.

HEDIN, Mary Ann; b. 3 Aug. 1929, Minneapolis, MN, USA. Writer; Poet. m. Roger Willard Hedin, 3 s., 1 d. Education: BS, University of Minnesota; MA, University of California. Appointments: Fellow, Yaddo, 1974; Writer-in-Residence, Robinson Jeffers Town House Foundation, 1984–85. Publications: Fly Away Home, 1980; Direction, 1983. Contributions to: Anthologies and journals. Honours: John H. McGinnis Memorial Award, 1979; Iowa School of Letters Award for Short Fiction, 1979. Memberships: Authors Guild; PEN; American Poetry Society. Address: 182 Oak Ave, San Anselmo, CA 94960, USA.

HEENAN, Anthony Peter, (Tony Heenan); b. 13 May 1950, Wallasey, Merseyside, England. Divorced, 1 d. Publications: Idyllic Thoughts, 1997; By the Light of the Moon, 1997; Inspired Lines, 1998; Passionate Thoughts, 1998; A Quiet Storm, 1998; Love, 1998; Ottersway, 1998; A Blossom of Dreams, 1998; Voices of the Heart, 1998; Autumn, 1998. Honour: Ed.'s Choice Award, 1998.

HEFFERNAN, Michael; b. 20 Dec. 1942, Detroit, Michigan, USA. Prof.; Poet. m. (1) Kathleen Spigarelli, 9 Aug. 1975, divorced 1994, 3 s., (2) Anna Monardo, Sept. 1995. Education: AB, University of Detroit, 1964; MA, 1967, PhD, 1970, University of Massachusetts. Appointments: Instructor, Oakland University, Michigan, 1967–69; Prof., Pittsburg State University, KS, 1969–86, University of Arkansas, Fayetteville, 1986–. Publications: The Cry of Oliver Hardy, 1979; To the Wreakers of Havoc, 1984; The Man at Home, 1988; Love's Answer, 1994;

The Back Road to Arcadia, 1994. Contributions to: American Poetry Review; Georgia Review; Gettysburg Review; Iowa Review; Shenandoah; Quarterly; TriQuarterly. Honours: Bread Loaf Scholarship, 1977; National Endowment for the Arts Fellowships, 1978, 1987, 1993. Membership: Poetry Society of America 1975–. Address: c/o University of Arkansas, Fayetteville, AR, USA.

HEFFERNAN, Thomas (Patrick Carroll); b. 19 Aug. 1939, Hyannis Massachusetts, USA. American and English Studies Educator; Writer; Poet m. Nancy E Iler, 15 July 1972, divorced 1977. Education: AB, Boston College 1961; MA, English Literature, University of Manchester, England, 1963 Universita per Stranieri, Perugia, Italy, 1965; PhD, English Literature Sophia University, Tokyo, 1990. Appointments: Poet in Schools, North Carolina Dept of Public Instruction, Raleigh, 1973–77; Visiting Artist, Poetry North Carolina Dept of Community Colleges, 1977–81, South Carolina Arts Commission, 1981–82; Co-Ed., The Plover (Chidori), bilingual haiku journal Japan, 1989–92; Prof. of English, Kagoshima Prefectural University, Japan. Publications: Mobiles, 1973; A Poem is a Smile You Can Hear (ed.), 1976; A Narrative of Jeremy Bentham, 1978; The Liam Poems, 1981; City Renewing Itself, 1983; Art and Emblem: Early Seventeenth Century English Poetry of Devotion, 1991; Gathering in Ireland, 1996. Contributions to: Anthologies and other publications. Honours: National Endowment for the Arts Fellowship, 1977; Gordon Barber Memorial Award, 1979; Portfolio Award, 1983; Roanoke Chowan Prize, 1982. Memberships: MLA; Japan English Literary Society; Japan American Literary Society. Address: Kagoshima Prefectural University, 1-52-1 Shimo-Ishiki-cho, Kagoshima-shi, 890-0005, Japan.

HEGI, Ursula (Johanna); b. 23 May 1946, Büderich, Germany. Prof. of English; Writer; Poet; Critic. 2 s. Education: BA, 1978, MA, 1979, University of New Hampshire. Appointments: Instructor, University of New Hampshire, 1980–84; Book Critic, Los Angeles Times, New York Times, Washington Post, 1982–; Asst Prof., 1984–89, Assoc. Prof., 1989–95, Prof. of English, 1995–, Eastern Washington University; Visiting Writer, various universities. Publications: Fiction: Intrusions, 1981; Unearned Pleasures and Other Stories, 1988; Floating in My Mother's Palm, 1990; Stones from the River, 1994; Salt Dancers, 1995; The Vision of Emma Blau, 1999; Hotel of the Saints (short stories), 2001. Non-Fiction: Tearing the Silence: On Being German in America, 1997. Contributions to: Anthologies, newspapers, journals and magazines. Honours: Indiana Fiction Award, 1988; National Endowment for the Arts Fellowship, 1990; New York Times Best Books Selections, 1990, 1994; Pacific Northwest Booksellers Asscn Award, 1991; Governor's Writers Awards, 1991, 1994. Memberships: Associated Writing Programs; National Book Critics Circle, board of dirs, 1992–94. Address: c/o Dept of English, Eastern Washington University, Cheney, WA 99004, USA.

HEIGHTON, (John) Steven; b. 14 Aug. 1961, Toronto, ON, Canada. Writer; Poet; Ed.; Trans. Education: BA, 1985, MA, 1986, Queen's University. Appointment: Ed., Quarry Magazine, 1988–94. Publications: Fiction: Flight Paths of the Emperor, 1992; On Earth As It Is, 1995; The Shadow Boxer, 2000. Non-Fiction: The Admen Move on Lhasa (writing and culture in a virtual world), 1997. Poetry: Stalin's Carnival, 1989; Foreign Ghosts, 1989; The Ectasy of Skeptics, 1994. Honours: Air Canada Award, 1988; Gerald Lampert Award, 1990; Gold Medal for Fiction, National Magazine Awards, 1991; Finalist, Trillium Award, 1993; Finalist, Gov.-Gen.'s Award, 1995; Petra Kenney Prize, 2002. Memberships: League of Canadian Poets; PEN; Writers' Union of Canada. Address: PO Box 383, Kingston, ON K7L 4W2, Canada.

HEIM, Scott; b. 26 Sept. 1966, Hutchinson, KS, USA. Writer; Poet. Education: BA, 1989, MA, 1991, University of Kansas; MFA, Columbia University, 1993. Publications: Saved from Drowning: Poems, 1993; Mysterious Skin (novel), 1995; In Awe (novel), 1997. Honours: William Herbert Carruth Award for Poetry, 1991; Edna Osborne Whitcomb Fiction Prize, 1991. Address: c/o Harper Collins, 10 E 53rd St, New York, NY 10022, USA.

HEINRICH, Peggy; b. 20 Feb. 1929, USA. Writer; Poet. m. Martin R Heinrich, 4 April 1952, deceased 1976, 2 d. Education: BA, Hunter College, New York City, 1949. Appointment: Ed., Connecticut River Review, 1985–87. Publications: Haiga Haiku (with artist Barbara Gray), 1982; A Patch of Grass, 1984; Sharing the Woods, 1992; Forty-four Freckles, 1995. Contributions to: Periodicals, including: Acorn Connecticut Artist; Blue Unicorn; Footwork; Calliope; Poet Lore; Frogpond; Connecticut River Review; The New Renaissance; Mainichi (Tokyo) Daily News; Embers; San Fernando Poetry Journal; DeKalb Literary Arts Journal; Z Misc; Passager; Iconoclast; World Haiku Asscn website; Poetry in the Light website; Anthologies, including: Basho Festival; Women and Death; Red Moon; Ridge Whisperings. Honours: Sri Chinmoy Award, Committee for Spiritual Poetry, 1980; Second Prize, North Carolina Haiku Society, 1984; Medal for Literary Achievement, State of Connecticut, 1985; Third Prize, Henderson Award, Haiku Society of America, 1994; First Prize, Hawaii Education Asscn International Haiku Contest, 1996; Second Prize, International Kusamakura Haiku Competition, 1998; Ashiya International Haiku Festival Prize, 1998; Second Prize and Hon. Mention, Hawaii Education Asscn, 1999; Hon. Mention, Henderson Award, Haiku Society of America, 2000. Memberships: Poetry Society of America; Acad. of American Poets; Poets and Writers; Dramatists' Guild; Haiku Society of America; Connecticut Poetry Society. Address: 625 Gilman St, Bridgeport, CT 06605, USA.

HEINZ, Evelyn M.; b. 24 Oct. 1939, Streator, IL, USA. Writer; Poet. m. John C Heinz, 7 June 1958, 3 s., 4 d. *Education:* Institute of Children's Literature, Redding Ridge, CT. *Publications:* Reflections, 1989; Nature's Beckoning, 1995. *Contributions to:* Various anthologies and periodicals. *Honours:* Numerous Honourable Mentions and Golden Poet Awards, 1985–90. *Membership:* International Society of Poets, Washington, DC. *Address:* 3707 W Bradley Ct, McHenry, IL 60050, USA.

HEJINIAN, Lyn; b. 17 May 1941, Alameda, CA, USA. Poet; Writer. m. (1) John P Hejinian, 1961, divorced 1972, 1 s., 1 d., (2) Larry Ochs, 1977. *Education:* BA, Harvard University, 1963. *Appointments:* Founder-Ed., Tuumba Press, 1976–84; Co-Founder and Co-Ed., Atelos; Prof., Dept of English, University of California at Berkeley. *Publications:* A Great Adventure, 1972; A Thought is the Bride of What Thinking, 1976; A Mask of Motion, 1977; Gesualdo, 1978; Writing is an Aid to Memory, 1978; My Life, 1980; The Guard, 1984; Redo, 1984; Individuals, 1988; Leningrad: American Writers in the Soviet Union (with Michael Davidson, Ron Silliman, and Barrett Watten), 1991; The Hunt, 1991, revised edn as Oxota: A Short Russian Novel, 1991; The Cell, 1992; The Cold of Poetry, 1994; Two Stein Talks, 1995; Guide, Grammar, Watch and the Thirty Nights, 1996; The Little Book of a Thousand Eyes, 1996; Wicker (with Jack Collom), 1996; The Traveler and the Hill and the Hill (with Emilie Clark), 1998; Sight, 1999; Sunflower (with Jack Collom), 2000; Chartings, 2000; Happily, 2000; The Beginner, 2000; The Language of Enquiry, 2000; A Border Comedy, 2001; Slowly, 2002. *Contributions to:* Journals. *Membership:* Fellow, Acad. of American Poets. *Address:* 2639 Russell St, Berkeley, CA 94705, USA.

HELER, Ziv. See: SHEINFELD, Ilan.

HELLER, Janet Ruth; b. 8 July 1949, Milwaukee, Wisconsin, USA. Asst Prof.; Poet. m. Michael A Krischer, 13 June 1982. *Education:* Oberlin College, 1967–70; BA, Honours, 1971, MA, 1973, University of Wisconsin at Madison; University of Chicago, 1973–75; PhD, English Literature, 1987. *Appointments:* Instructor, Northern Illinois University, 1982–88; Asst Prof., Nazareth College, 1989–90, Grand Valley State University, 1990–. *Publication:* Coleridge, Lamb, Hazlitt and the Reader of Drama, 1990. *Contributions to:* Anthologies, reviews, quarterlies, journals and periodicals. *Honours:* Finalist, Poetry Press, 1977; Winner, Friends of Poetry Contest, 1989. *Memberships:* MLA; Byron Society; Michigan College English Asscn; National Council of Teachers of English; Society for the Study of Midwestern Literature; Council of Writing Program Administrators. *Address:* c/o Dept of English, Grand Valley State University, Allendale, MI 49401, USA.

HELLER, Michael; b. 11 May 1937, New York, NY, USA. Poet; Writer; Teacher. m. (1) Doris Whytal, 1962, divorced 1978, (2) Jane Augustine, 5 March 1979, 1 s. *Education:* BS in Engineering, Rensselaer Polytechnic Institute, 1959; MA in English, New York University, 1986. *Appointments:* Faculty, 1967, Acting Dir, 1986–87, Academic Co-ordinator, 1987–91, American Language Institute, New York University; Poet and Teacher, New York State Poets in the Schools, 1970–. *Publications:* Two Poems, 1970; Accidental Center, 1972; Figures of Speaking, 1977; Knowledge, 1979; Marble Snows, Origin, 1979; Conviction's Net of Branches: Essays on the Objectivist Poets and Poetry, 1985; Marginalia in a Desperate Hand, 1986; In the Builded Place, 1990; Carl Rakosi: Man and Poet (ed.), 1993; Wordflow: New and Selected Poems, 1997; Living Root: A Memoir, 2000. *Contributions to:* Anthologies, reference books, and journals. *Honours:* Coffey Poetry Prize, New School for Social Research, 1964; Poetry in Public Places Award, 1975; New York State Creative Artists Public Service Fellowship in Poetry, 1975–76; National Endowment for the Humanities Grant, 1979; Di Castagnola Award, Poetry Society of America, 1980; Outstanding Writer Citations, Pushcart Press, 1983, 1984, 1992; New York Fellowship in the Arts, 1989. *Memberships:* American Acad. of Poets; MLA; New York State Poets in Public Service; PEN; Poetry Society of America; Poets House. *Address:* PO Box 1289, Stuyvesant Station, New York, NY 10009, USA.

HELLERSTEIN, Kathryn A.; b. 27 July 1952, Cleveland, OH, USA. Senior Lecturer of Yiddish and Jewish Studies; Trans. of Yiddish Poetry; Poet. 1 s., 1 d. *Education:* BA, magna cum laude, English, Brandeis University, 1974; MA, Creative Writing, English, 1976, PhD, English and American Literature, 1981, Stanford University. *Appointments:* Asst Prof. of English, Wellesley College, 1982–86; Visiting Asst Prof. of English, Haverford College, 1988–90; Adjunct Asst Prof. of Yiddish, University of Pennsylvania, 1991–93; Visiting Asst Prof. of Judaic Studies, University of Washington, 1992; Lecturer in Yiddish, University of Pennsylvania, 1993–. *Publications:* Yiddish Poems of Moyshe-Leyb Halpern (trans.), 1982; American Yiddish Poetry: A Bilingual Anthology (contributor, trans.), 1986; Paper Bridges: Selected Poems of Kadya Molodowsky (trans.), 1999; Jewish American Literature: A Norton Anthology (co-ed.), 2001. *Contributions to:* Poetry; Kenyon Review; New York Review of Books; Partisan Review; Bridges; Midstream. *Honours:* Edith Mirrielees Fellowship in Creative Writing, Poetry, Stanford University, 1974–75; National Endowment for the Arts Literature Program Fellowship for Trans Grant, 1986–87; Honourable Mention for Group of Poems, Anna Davidson Rosenberg Poetry Award, 1987; Marie Syrkin Fellowship, 1991; Guggenheim Fellowship, 1999–2000. *Memberships:* MLA; Asscn of Jewish Studies; Yivo

Institute for Jewish Research. *Address:* Dept of Germanic Languages, 745 Williams Hall, University of Pennsylvania, PA 19104-6305, USA.

HELMES, Leslie Scott; b. 27 Oct. 1945, Fort Snelling, Minnesota, USA. Architect; Graphic Designer; Photographer; Poet. m. Julie Holbrook Williams, 15 Sept. 1967, divorced 1974. *Education:* BArch, University of Minnesota, Minneapolis, 1968. *Publications:* Autistext, 1987; Our Bodies, Our Icons, 1991; Red Letters, 1991; Xpos, 1991; Postcards from the Back of the Eye, 1991; Archaeology Structures, 1992; Mental Activities, 1992; Rubber Stamp Art, 1999; Dictionary of the Avant-Garde, 2001. *Contributions to:* Paris Review; Clown War; Kaldron; Scope; O; White Walls; Interstate; Tam-Tam; Shishi News; Aticus Review; Lost and Found; NRG; Mosumumo; Anterum; Eleven; Oars; Lake Street Review; Pigiron. *Honour:* First Prize, Concrete Poetry Contest, Gamut Magazine, 1982. *Memberships:* Ampersand Club of Minnesota; Minnesota Center for Book Arts. *Address:* 862 Tuscarora, St Paul, MN 55102, USA.

HELWIG, David (Gordon); b. 5 April 1938, Toronto, Ontario, Canada. Poet; Writer; Ed. m. Nancy Keeling, 1959, 2 d. *Education:* Graduated, Stamford Collegiate Institute, 1956; BA, University of Toronto, 1960; MA, University of Liverpool, 1962. *Appointments:* Faculty, Dept of English, Queen's Unversity, Kingston, Ontario, 1962–80; Co-Ed., Quarry magazine. *Publications:* Poetry: Figures in a Landscape, 1967; The Sign of the Gunman, 1969; The Best Name of Silence, 1972; Atlantic Crossings, 1974; A Book of the Hours, 1979; The Rain Falls Like Rain, 1982; Catchpenny Poems, 1983; The Hundred Old Names, 1988; The Beloved, 1992; Telling Stories, 2001. Fiction: The Day Before Tomorrow, 1971; The Glass Knight, 1976; Jennifer, 1979; The King's Evil, 1981; It Is Always Summer, 1982; A Sound Like Laughter, 1983; The Only Son, 1984; The Bishop, 1986; A Postcard From Rome, 1988; Old Wars, 1989; Of Desire, 1990; Blueberry Cliffs, 1993; Just Say the Words, 1994; Close to the Fire, 1999. Editor: Fourteen Stories High: Best Canadian Stories of 71 (with Tom Marshall), 1971; 72, 73, 74 and 75: New Canadian Stories (with Joan Harcourt), 4 vols, 1972–75; Words From Inside, 1972; The Human Elements: Critical Essays, 2 vols, 1978, 1981; Love and Money: The Politics of Culture, 1980; 83, 84, 85 and 86: Best Canadian Stories (with Sandra Martin), 4 vols, 1983–86; Coming Attractions 1983, 1984, 1985, and 1986 (with Sandra Martin), 4 vols, 1983–86; Coming Attractions 1987 and 1988 (with Maggie Helwig), 2 vols 1987, 1988; 87, 88, 89, and 91: Best Canadian Stories (with Maggie Helwig), 4 vols, 1987–91. *Honour:* CBC Literary Prize, 1983. *Address:* c/o Viking Penguin, 375 Hudson St, New York, NY 10014, USA.

HENDERSON, Neil Keir; b. 7 March 1956, Glasgow, Scotland. Poet; Writer. *Education:* MA, English Language, English Literature and Scottish Literature, University of Glasgow, 1977. *Publications:* Maldehyde's Discomfiture, or A Lady Churned, 1997; Fish-Worshipping: As We Know It, 2001. *Contributions to:* Anthologies, including: Mystery of the City; Loveable Warts: A Defence of Self-Indulgence, Chapman 87, 1997; Mightier Than the Sword: The Punch-Up of the Poses, Chapman 91, 1998; The Red Candle Treasury, Chapman 91, 1998; Haggis: The Thinking Man's Buttock, Chapman 98, 2001. *Address:* 46 Revoch Dr., Knightswood, Glasgow G13 4SB, Scotland.

HENDREN, Harriet. See: MEANLEY, Deborah Ann.

HENDRIKS, A(rthur) L(emiere); b. 7 April 1922, Kingston, Jamaica. Poet; Writer. *Education:* Open University. *Publications:* The Independence Anthology of Jamaican Literature (ed. with C Lindo), 1962; On This Mountain and Other Poems, 1965; These Green Islands, 1971; Muet, 1971; Madonna of the Unknown Nation, 1974; The Islanders and Other Poems, 1983; Archie and the Princess and the Everythingest Horse (for children), 1983; The Naked Ghost and Other Poems, 1984; Great Families of Jamaica, 1984; To Speak Slowly: Selected Poems, 1961–86, 1988. *Address:* Box 265, Constant Spring, Kingston 8, Jamaica.

HENDRY, Diana (Lois); b. 2 Oct. 1941, Meols, Wirral, Cheshire, England. Poet; Children's Writer. m. George Hendry, 9 Oct. 1965, divorced 1981, 1 s., 1 d. *Education:* BA, Honours, 1984, MLitt, 1986, University of Bristol. *Appointments:* Asst to Literature Ed., Sunday Times, London, 1958–60; Reporter and Feature Writer, Western Mail, Cardiff, 1960–65; Freelance journalist, 1965–80; Part-time English Teacher, Clifton College, 1984–87; Part-time Lecturer, Bristol Polytechnic, 1987; WEA, Modern Poets Course, 1987–; Tutor, Open University, 1991–92; Part-time Tutor, Creative Writing, University of Bristol, 1993–1997; Writer-in-Residence, Dumfries and Galloway Royal Infirmary, 1997–98. *Publications:* Midnight Pirate, 1984; Fiona Finds Her Tongue, 1985; Hetty's First Fling, 1985; The Not Anywhere House, 1989; The Rainbow Watchers, 1989; The Carey Street Cat, 1989; Christmas on Exeter Street, 1989; Sam Sticks and Delilah, 1990; A Camel Called April, 1990; Double Vision, 1990; Harvey Angell, 1991; Kid Kibble, 1992; The Thing-in-a-Box, 1992; Wonderful Robert and Sweetie-Pie Nell, 1992; Back Soon, 1993; Making Blue, 1995; Strange Goings-on, 1995; The Awesome Bird, 1995; The Thing on Two Legs, 1995; Harvey Angell and the Ghost Child, 1997; Minders, 1998; Borderers, 2001; Harvey Angell Beats Time, 2001. *Contributions to:* Anthologies and periodicals. *Honours:* Stroud Festival International Poetry Competition, 1976; Third Prize, 1991, Second Prize, 1993, Peterloo Poetry Competition; Whitbread Award for children's novel, 1991; First Prize,

Housman Poetry Society competition, 1996; Scottish Arts Council Children's Book Award, 2001. *Memberships:* Society of Authors; PEN. *Address:* 23 Dunrobin Pl., Edinburgh, EH3 5HZ, Scotland.

HENDRY, Joy McLaggan; b. 3 Feb. 1953, Perth, Scotland. Ed.; Writer; Poet; Dramatist; Broadcaster. m. Ian Montgomery, 25 July 1986. *Education:* MA, Honours, Mental Philosophy, 1976, Diploma, Education, 1977, University of Edinburgh. *Appointments:* Ed., Chapman magazine, 1972–; Radio Critic, The Scotsman newspaper, 1987–97; Chair, Scottish Actors Studio, 1994–2000; Lecturer in Drama, Queen Margaret University College, Edinburgh; Lecturer in Periodical Journalism, Napier University, Edinburgh. *Publications:* Scots: The Way Forward, 1981; Poems and Pictures by Wendy Wood (ed.), 1985; Critical Essays on Norman MacCaig (ed. with Raymond J. Ross), 1991. Plays: Gang down wi' a Sang, 1990; The Wa' at the World's End, 1993; Diehard, 1995. *Contributions to:* Newspapers, journals, periodicals, radio, and television. *Memberships:* Advisory Council for the Arts in Scotland; National Union of Journalists; Scottish PEN. *Address:* 4 Broughton Pl., Edinburgh EH1 3RX, Scotland.

HERMAN, Grace Gales; b. 12 May 1926, Lawrence, New York, USA. Physician (retd); Poet. m. (1) Roland B Herman, 22 July 1945, divorced 1981, 2 d., (2) Marvin A Bregman, 15 Aug. 1993. *Education:* Diploma, High School of Music and Art, New York City, 1942; BA, Honours, Cornell University, 1945; MD, College of Physicians and Surgeons, Columbia University, 1949. *Appointments:* Intern, 1949–50, Cancer Researcher, 1962–65, Mount Sinai Hospital, New York City; Pathology Resident, White Plains Hospital, New York, 1950–51; Cancer Researcher, Gynaecology, College of Physicians and Surgeons, Columbia University, 1957–62; Examining Physician, Employee Health, Metropolitan Life Insurance Co, 1969–88. *Publications:* Set Against Darkness, 1992. *Contributions to:* Reviews, quarterlies, and journals; Anthologies, including: Blood and Bone – Poems by Physicians; Jewish Women's Literary Annual. *Honours:* Second Prize, Dir's Prize, Chautauqua Institute Poetry Center, 1990; Finalist, National Awards Editions, Poetpourri, 1991, 1992. *Membership:* Poetry Society of America, chairperson, peer workshop, 1982–92. *Address:* 370 First Ave, 9C, New York, NY 10010, USA.

HERMAN-SEKULICH, Maya (Marija), (Maja Herman); b. 17 Feb. 1949, Belgrade, Yugoslavia. Essayist; Poet; Trans. m. Milosh Sekulich. *Education:* MA, Belgrade University, 1977; PhD, Princeton University, 1986. *Appointments:* Fulbright Visiting Lecturer, Rutgers University, 1982–84; Lecturer, Princeton University, 1986, 1987–88. *Publications:* Micromegas Modern Yugoslav Poetry (guest ed.), 1985; Camerography (poems), 1990; Catography (poems), 1992; Sketches for Portraits (essays), 1992; Trans, introductions in 10 books and 3 anthologies. *Contributions to:* Paris Review; Printed Matter; Antaeus; Confrontation; Night; Knjizevne Novine, Irene, Belgrade. *Honours:* Fellowship, Princeton University, 1980–85; American Asscn of University Women, 1981–82; Fulbright Fellowship, 1982–84. *Memberships:* American PEN Center, New York; Serbian PEN Centre, Belgrade; Poetry Society of America; Serbian Writers' Asscn; MLA.

HERRA, Maurice. See: ASSELINEAU, Roger Maurice.

HERREN. See: CURTIS, Linda Lee.

HERREWEGHEN, Hubert F. A. van; b. 16 Feb. 1920, Pamel, Belgium. Television Exec.; Poet. m. Maria B Botte, 18 July 1946, 2 s., 3 d. *Appointment:* Ed., Dietsche Warande en Belfort, 1947–. *Publications:* Het Jaar der Gedachtenis, 1943; Liedjes van de Liefde en van de Dood, 1949; Gedichten, 1953; Gedichten II, 1958; Gedichten III, 1961; Gedichten IV, 1968; Gedichten V, 1977; Verzamelde Gedichten, 1977, 1986; Kort Dag, 1988; Twee Fazanten, 1988; Korf en Trog, 1993; Karakol, 1995; Bloemlezing uit de Gedichten van Hubert van Herreweghen, 1999; Een Brussels Tuintje, 1999; Kornoeljebloed, 2000; Een Kortwoonst in de Heuvels, 2002. *Honours:* Staatsprijs voor Poezie, 1962; Prijs de Standaard, 1985; Prize, SABAM. *Memberships:* Koninklijke Academie voor Nederlandse Taal en Letterkunde, Gent, Belgium; Maatschappij der Nederlandse Letterkunde, Leiden, Netherlands. *Address:* Grilstraat 4, 1080 Brussels, Belgium.

HERSVEINN, Gunnar. See: SIGURSTEINSSON, Gunnar Hersveinn.

HERTZ, Dalia; b. 19 May 1942, Palestine. Lecturer; Poet; Writer. *Education:* Philosophy, Oxford, England, 1964–68; BA, Philosophy, 1974, MA, Philosophy, 1978, University of Tel-Aviv. *Appointments:* Ed. and Presenter, Literary Programmes, Israeli Radio; Teacher of Philosophy, University of Tel-Aviv; Dir, Creative Writing, Hebrew University of Jerusalem; Mem., Drama Dept, Israeli TV. *Publications:* Quartet, 1962; The Tel-Aviv Poets (co-ed.), 1990; Ir-Shirim, City of Poems, 1990. *Contributions to:* Various publications. *Honours:* Israeli Publishers' Prize, 1991; Several grants. *Memberships:* ACUM (Society of Authors, Composer, and Music Publishers); PEN; Union of Hebrew Writers. *Address:* c/o Union of Hebrew Writers, Beit Ha-Sofez, Kaplan 6, Tel-Aviv, Israel.

HERZBERG, Judith; b. 4 Nov. 1934, Amsterdam, Netherlands. Poet; Playwright. *Education:* Graduated, Montessori Lyceum, 1952. *Appointments:*

Teacher at film schools in Netherlands and Israel. *Publications:* Slow Boat 1964; Meadow Grass, 1968; Flies, 1970; Grazing Light, 1971; 27 Love Songs 1973; Botshol, 1980; Remains of the Day, 1984; Twenty Poems, 1984; But What Selected Poems, 1988; The Way, 1992; What She Meant to Paint, 1998; Small Catch, 1999. Plays: Near Archangel, 1971; It Is Not a Dog, 1973; That Day May Dawn, 1974; Lea's Wedding, 1982; The Fall of Icarus, 1983; And/Or, 1984; The Little Mermaid, 1986; Scratch, 1989; Lulu (adaptation of Wedekind), 1989; A Good Head, 1991; Rijgraad, 1995; The Nothing-factory, 1997; Wie Is Van Wie 1999; Simon, 2002. Other: Texts for the stage and film, 1972–88; Screenplays and television plays; Trans, including The Trojan Women, by Euripides, and Ghosts, by Ibsen. *Honours:* Netherlands-Vlaamse Drama Prize, 1989 Constantijn Huyens Prize, 1995; P C Hooft Prize for Poetry, 1997. *Address:* c o De Harmonie, PO Box 3547, 1001 AH Amsterdam, Netherlands.

HESKETH, Phoebe; b. 29 Jan. 1909, Preston, Lancashire, England. Lecturer (retd); Poet; Writer. *Appointments:* Lecturer, Bolton Women's College, 1967–69; Teacher of Creative Writing, Bolton School, 1977–79. *Publications:* Poetry: Lean Forward, Spring, 1948; No Time for Cowards, 1952; Out of the Dark, 1954; Between Wheels and Stars, 1956; The Buttercup Children, 1958; Prayer for Sun, 1966; A Song of Sunlight, 1974; Preparing to Leave, 1977; The Eighth Day, 1980; A Ring of Leaves, 1985; Over the Brook, 1985; Netting the Sun: New and Collected Poems, 1989; Sundowner, 1992; The Leave Train, New and Selected Poems, 1994; A Box of Silver Birch, 1997. Prose: My Aunt Edith, 1966; Rivington: The Story of a Village, 1972; What Can the Matter Be?, 1985; Rivington: Village of the Mountain Ash, 1989. *Honour:* Hon. Fellow, University of Central Lancashire, 1992. *Address:* 10 The Green, Heath Charnock, Chorley, Lancashire PR6 9JH, England.

HESTER, Alan William Walter; b. 3 Nov. 1957, Reading, Berkshire, England. Civil Servant; Poet. m. Eunice Hester, 11 July 1987, 1 s., 1 d. *Education:* BA, Honours, English Literature, University College, Cardiff, 1979. *Contributions to:* Rialto; Orbis; Acumen; Iron; Spokes; Grand Piano; Wide Skirt; Echo Room; Envoi; Weyfarers; Inkshed; South Coast Poetry Journal, CA; Hybrid; Anthologies: Poems for Peace; Grovoi Summer Anthology, 1988, 1989, 1990, 1991. *Honour:* Second Prize, Ver Poets Open Poetry Competition, 1985. *Address:* 67 Skilton Rd, Tilehurst, Reading, Berkshire RG3 6SA, England.

HEWETT, Dorothy (Coade); b. 21 May 1923, Perth, WA, Australia. Poet; Writer; Dramatist. *Education:* BA, 1961, MA, 1963, University of Western Australia. *Publications:* Bobbin Up (novel), 1959; What About the People? (poems with Merv Lilly), 1962; The Australians Have a Word for It (stories), 1964; Windmill Country (poems), 1968; The Hidden Journey (poems), 1969; The Chapel Perilous, or The Perilous Adventures of Sally Bonner, 1971; Sandgropers: A Western Australian Anthology, 1973; Rapunzel in Suburbia (poems), 1975; Miss Hewett's Shenanigans, 1975; Greenhouse (poems), 1979; The Man from Mukinupin (play), 1979; Susannah's Dreaming (play), 1981; The Golden Oldies (play), 1981; Selected Poems, 1990; Wild Card (autobiography), 1990. *Honour:* Mem. of the Order of Australia, 1986. *Address:* 195 Bourke St, Darlinghurst, NSW 2011, Australia.

HEWITT, Bernard (Robert); b. 11 Feb. 1927, Greenwich, NSW, Australia; Environmental Engineering Consultant (retd); Poet; Writer. m. Betty Lorna Mills, 2 Jan. 1956, divorced 1975, 3 d. *Education:* BA, Queensland University, 1961; MPhil, Hull University, 1977. *Appointments:* Various university and government positions, 1950–90. *Publications:* Numerous poems and stories. *Contributions to:* Many periodicals. *Honours:* Over 100 literary prizes, 1984–93.

HEYEN, William (Helmuth); b. 1 Nov. 1940, New York, NY, USA. Prof. of English; Poet; Writer. m. Hannelore Greiner, 7 July 1962, 1 s., 1 d. *Education:* BS, Education, State University of New York College at Brockport, 1961; MA, English, 1963, PhD, English, 1967, Ohio University. *Appointments:* Asst Prof. to Prof. of English and Poet-in-Residence, State University of New York College at Brockport, 1967–2000; Senior Fulbright Lecturer in American Literature, 1971–72; Visiting Creative Writer, University of Wisconsin at Milwaukee, 1980; Visiting Writer, Hofstra University, 1981, 1983, Southampton College, 1984, 1985; Visiting Prof. of English, University of Hawaii, 1985. *Publications:* Depth of Field, 1970; Noise in the Trees: Poems and a Memoir, 1974; American Poets in 1976 (ed.), 1976; The Swastika Poems, 1977; Long Island Light: Poems and a Memoir, 1979; The City Parables, 1980; Lord Dragonfly: Five Sequences, 1981; Erika: Poems of the Holocaust, 1984; The Generation of 2000: Contemporary American Poets (ed.), 1984; Vic Holyfield and the Class of 1957: A Romance, 1986; The Chestnut Rain: A Poem, 1986; Brockport, New York: Beginning with 'And', 1988; Falling From Heaven (co-author), 1991; Pterodactyl Rose: Poems of Ecology, 1991; Ribbons: The Gulf War, 1991; The Host: Selected Poems 1965–1990, 1994; With Me Far Away: A Memoir, 1994; Crazy Horse in Stillness: Poems, 1996; Pig Notes and Dumb Music: Prose on Poetry, 1998; Diana, Charles and the Queen: Poems, 1998; September 11, 2001: American Writers Respond, 2002; The Hummingbird Corporation: Stories, 2002; Home: Autobiographies, Etc., 2002. *Contributions to:* Many books, chapbooks, journals and magazines. *Honours:* Borestone Mountain Poetry Prize, 1965; National Endowment for the Arts Fellowships, 1973–74, 1984–85; American Library Asscn Notable American Book, 1974; Ontario Review Poetry Prize, 1977; Guggenheim Fellowship, 1977–78; Eunice

Tietjens Memorial Award, 1978; Witter Bynner Prize for Poetry, 1982; New York Foundation for the Arts Poetry Fellowship, 1984–85; Lillian Fairchild Award, 1996; Small Press Book Award for Poetry, 1997. *Address:* c/o Dept of English, State University of New York College at Brockport, Brockport, NY 14420, USA.

HICKOK, Gloria Vando. See: VANDO (HICKOK), Gloria.

HIEMSTRA, Marvin R.; b. 27 July 1939, Iowa, USA. Poet; Scholar; Drollist. *Education:* BA (Hons), Creative Writing and Literature, State University of Iowa, 1962; MA, English Literature and Folklore, Indiana University, Bloomington, 1966. *Publications:* MRH, 1960; I'd Rather Be a Phoenix!, 1976; Sun Cat, 1986; Jasmine, Opera Libretto about Tahiti, 1987; Golden Gate Treasure, 1987; Cats in Charge, 1989; Dream Tees, Poems from Dreams, 1991; San Francisco Cats, 1991; 26 Compliments, 1991; Redwood Burl, 1992; Seasons, 1993; Star Molen, 1994; Snow on Golden Bamboo, 1995; Kiku, 1997; A Turquoise Coyote Under Your Pillow one person performance video, 1998; Autobiography of a Teardrop, 2001; Two-Way Zipper, 2002. *Contributions to:* North American Review; Abstract; Knickerbocker; Microbibliophile; www.poetrymagazine.com. *Honours:* Browning Society Award, 1975; American Poetry Society, 1982; Villa Montalvo Poetry Competition, 1985; Villa Montalvo Solo Reading Performance, 1986; Lilly Library, Poetry in Performance, 1986; Glendale Public Library, Poetry Cats, 1990; Miniature Book Society, Distinguished Book Award for Golden Gate Treasure, 1990; Dream Tees- Pulitzer Prize in Poetry Nomination, 1991; In Deepest USA, performance with music by Doni Harvey for CD, 1996; Carmel Performing Arts Festival, 1998; Edinburgh Festival Fringe, 1999. *Memberships:* The Poetry Society of America; The Dramatists Guild; Miniature Book Society Inc; The Acad. of American Poets. *Address:* c/o Juniper Von Phitzer Press, 166 Bonview St, San Francisco, CA 94110-5147, USA.

HIGGINBOTHAM, Patricia; b. 19 Oct. 1941, Pittsburgh, Pennsylvania, USA. Teacher; Poet. m. S Roy Higginbotham, 8 May 1963, 1 s., 1 d. *Education:* BA, English, University of Florida, 1963; MA, English Education, University of South Florida, 1988. *Appointments:* Teacher, Tampa schools; Co-Ed., Florida English Journal, 1990–93. *Contributions to:* Numerous journals. *Membership:* Acad. of American Poets. *Address:* 3211 Swann Ave, Apt 310, Tampa, FL 33609, USA.

HIGSON, Philip (John Willoughby); b. 21 Feb. 1933, Newcastle-under-Lyme, Staffordshire, England. Poet; Trans.; Ed.; Historian; Art Historian; Playwright; Author. *Education:* BA, 1956, MA, 1959, PhD, 1971, Liverpool University; PGCE, Keele University, 1972. *Appointments:* Lecturer, Senior Lecturer in History, 1972–89, Visiting Lecturer, 1989–90, University College, Chester; Chair., Pres., Anthology Ed., Chester Poets, 1974–92; Pres., La Société Baudelaire, Chester and Paris, 1992–. *Publications:* Poems of Protest and Pilgrimage, 1966; To Make Love's Harbour..., 1966; The Riposte and Other Poems, 1971; Sonnets to My Goddess, 1983; Maurice Rollinat's Les Névroses: Selected English Versions (trans.), 1986; A Warning to Europe: The Testimony of Limouse (co-author), 1992; The Complete Poems of Baudelaire with Selected Illustrations by Limouse (ed. and principal trans.), 1992; Limouse Nudes, 1994; Childhood in Wartime Keele: Poems of Reminiscence, 1995; Poems on the Dee, 1997; Inner City Love-Revolt: Footage from a Fifties Affair, 2000; A Poet's Pilgrimage: The Shaping of a Creative Life, 2000; Ut Pictura Poesis: Pictorial Poems, 2002; Poems of Sauce and Satire, 2002; The Jewelled Nude: A Play About Baudelaire and Queen Pomaré, 2002; The Girl With Gorgeous Hips: An Inner City Love-Story, 2002. *Contributions to:* Books; Historical articles to journals, including: Oxford Dictionary of National Biography; Antiquaries Journal; Genealogists' Magazine; Coat of Arms; Poems to journals, including: Critical Quarterly; Candelabrum; Red Candle Treasury; Lexikon. *Honours:* First Prize for an Established Poet, The Eclectic Muse, Vancouver, 1990; David St John Thomas Poetry Publication Prize, 1996; Prizewinner, Lexikon Poetry Competition, 1996. *Memberships:* Society of Antiquaries of London, fellow; Royal Historical Society, fellow; RSA, fellow; Society of Authors. *Address:* 1 Westlands Ave, Newcastle-under-Lyme, Staffordshire ST5 2PU, England.

HILDEBIDLE, John; b. 2 Feb. 1946, Hartford, CT, USA. Poet; Writer; Asst Prof. of Literature. m. Nichola Gilsdorf, 27 May 1978, 1 s., 1 d. *Education:* BA, 1967, MA, 1969, PhD, 1981, Harvard University. *Appointments:* Lecturer in English and American Literature, 1980–83, Mem., Extension Faculty, 1981–, Harvard University; Asst Prof. of Literature, Massachusetts Institute of Technology, 1983–. *Publications:* Poetry: The Old Chore, 1981; One Sleep, One Waking, 1994; Defining Absence, 1999. Other: Modernism Reconsidered (ed. with Robert J. Kiely), 1983; Thoreau: A Naturalist's Liberty, 1983; Stubborness: A Field Guide, 1986; Five Irish Writers: The Errand of Keeping Alive, 1989; A Sense of Place: Poetry from Ireland (with Dorys Crow Grover and Michael D. Riley), 1995. *Contributions to:* Anthologies and periodicals. *Honours:* Book Award, San Francisco Poetry Center, 1982; Katherine Anne Porter Prize, Tulsa Arts and Humanities Council, 1984; Anniversary Award for Poetry, Associated Writing Programs, 1984; John Gardner Short Fiction Prize, 1987. *Memberships:* MLA of America; National Council of Teachers of English; Thoreau Society. *Address:* c/o Dept of Humanities, Massachusetts Institute of Technology, Cambridge, MA 02139, USA.

HILL, David Anthony; b. 22 Aug. 1952, Walsall, West Midlands, England. English Teaching Adviser; Poet. *Education:* CEd, BEd, St Paul's College, Cheltenham, 1970–74; DipEd, English Language Teaching (Exeter), College of St Mark and St John, Plymouth, 1980; MPhil, Applied Linguistics, Exeter University, 1987. *Appointments:* Primary Teacher: Aston, Oxfordshire, 1974–75, Swindon, Wiltshire, 1975–77; Teacher, English as a Foreign Language, Riva, Italy, 1977–79; British Council Lektor, Prizren, 1980–82, Nis, 1982–86, Yugoslavia; Dir of Studies, 1986–87, English Teaching Adviser, 1987–, British Council, Milan, Italy. *Publications:* The Eagles and the Sun, 1986; The Judas Tree, 1993. *Contributions to:* Poetry Review; Relations, trans from Serbo-Croat; Knjizene Novine, in trans.; Knjizevna Rec, in trans.; Mediaeval and Renaissance Serbian Poetry (language ed., trans.); The Pre-Raphaelitism of Ezra Pound, 1995. *Honour:* Competition Winner, Poetry Review. *Memberships:* William Morris Society; Poetry Society; Poetry Book Society; International Asscn of Teachers of English as a Foreign Language; Teaching English to Speakers of Other Languages.

HILL, Geoffrey (William); b. 18 June 1932, Bromsgrove, Worcestershire, England. Prof. of Literature and Religion; Poet; Writer. m. (1) Nancy Whittaker, 1956, divorced 1983, 3 s., 1 d., (2) Alice Goodman, 1987, 1 d. *Education:* BA, 1953, MA, 1959, Keble College, Oxford. *Appointments:* Staff, 1954–76, Prof. of English Literature, 1976–80, University of Leeds; Churchill Fellow, University of Bristol, 1980; University Lecturer in English and Fellow, Emmanuel College, Cambridge, 1981–88; Clark Lecturer, Trinity College, Cambridge, 1986; University Prof. and Prof. of Literature and Religion, Boston University, 1988–. *Publications:* Poetry: Poems, 1952; For the Unfallen: Poems, 1952–58, 1959; Preghiere, 1964; King Log, 1968; Mercian Hymns, 1971; Somewhere is Such a Kingdom: Poems 1952–72, 1975; Tenebrae, 1978; The Mystery of the Charity of Charles Péguy, 1983; New and Collected Poems 1952–92, 1994; Canaan, 1996; Speech! Speech!, 2000. Criticism: The Lords of Limit, 1984; The Enemy's Country, 1991. Other: Brand (adaptation of Henrik Ibsen's play), 1978. *Honours:* Gregory Award, 1961; Hawthornden Prize, 1969; Alice Hunt Bartlett Award, 1971; Geoffrey Faber Memorial Prize, 1971; Whitbread Award, 1971; Duff Cooper Memorial Prize, 1979; Hon. Fellow, Keble College, Oxford, 1981, Emmanuel College, Cambridge, 1990; Loines Award, American Acad. and Institute of Arts and Letters, 1983; Ingram Merrill Foundation Award, 1988; Hon. DLitt, University of Leeds, 1988. *Memberships:* RSL, fellow; American Acad. of Arts and Sciences, fellow. *Address:* The University Profs, Boston University, 745 Commonwealth Ave, Boston, MA 02215, USA.

HILL, Harriet. See: TURNER, Stella.

HILL, Jane (Bowers); b. 17 Oct. 1950, Seneca, SC, USA. Asst Prof.; Ed.; Writer; Poet. m. Robert W. Hill, 16 Aug. 1980, 1 d. *Education:* BA, 1972, MA, 1978, Clemson University; PhD, University of Illinois, 1985. *Appointments:* Assoc. Ed., Peachtree Publishers, 1986–88; Senior Ed., Longstreet Press, 1988–91; Dir, Kennesaw Summer Writers' Workshop, 1988–92; Asst Prof., West Georgia College, 1992–. *Publications:* Gail Godwin, 1992. Editor: An American Christmas: A Sampler of Contemporary Stories and Poems, 1986; Our Mutual Room: Modern Literary Portraits of the Opposite Sex, 1987; Songs: New Voices in Fiction, 1990; Cobb County: At the Heart of Change, 1991. *Contributions to:* Numerous stories, poems, essays and reviews. *Honours:* Frank O'Connor Prize for Fiction, 1989; Syvenna Foundation Fellow, 1991; Monticello Fellowship for Female Writers, 1992. *Membership:* MLA. *Address:* 1419 Arden Dr., Marietta, GA 30060, USA.

HILL, Selima (Wood); b. 13 Oct. 1945, London, England. Poet. 2 s., 2 d. *Education:* New Hall College, Cambridge. *Appointments:* Writing Fellow, University of East Anglia, 1991; Writer-in-Residence, Exeter and Devon Arts Centre, 1996; Poet-in-Residence, Royal Festival Hall, 1998; Reader-in-Residence, South Bank Centre, 1998–. *Publications:* Saying Hello at the Station, 1984; My Darling Camel, 1988; The Accumulation of Small Acts of Kindness, 1989; A Little Book of Meat, 1993; Trembling Hearts in the Bodies of Dogs, 1994; My Sister's Horse, 1996; Violet, 1997; Paradise for Sale, 1998; Bunny, 1999. *Honours:* Cholmondeley Prize, 1986; Arvon Observer Poetry Competition Prize, 1988; Arts Council Writers Bursary, 1993; H K Travel Scholarship to Mongolia, 1994; Judge, Kent, Exeter, 1995, Bournemouth, 1996; Nominated for T. S. Eliot, Whitbread, Forward Prizes, 1998. *Address:* c/o Bloodaxe Books, PO Box 1SN, Newcastle upon Tyne, NE99 1SN, England.

HILLES, Robert (Edward); b. 13 Nov. 1951, Kenora, Ontario, Canada. Poet; Writer; Senior Prof. m. Rebecca Susan Knight, 16 Aug. 1980, 2 c. *Education:* BA, 1976, MSc, 1984, University of Calgary. *Appointments:* Prof. of Computer Programming, 1983–, Senior Prof., 1994–, DeVry Institute of Technology, Calgary, AB. *Publications:* Look the Lovely Animal Speaks, 1980; The Surprise Element, 1982; An Angel in the Works, 1983; Outlasting the Landscape, 1989; Finding the Lights On, 1991; A Breath at a Time, 1992; Cantos From a Small Room, 1993; Raising of Voices, 1993; Near Morning, 1995; Kissing the Smoke, 1996; Nothing Vanishes, 1996; Breathing Distance, 1997. *Contributions to:* Anthologies and periodicals. *Honours:* Gov.-Gen.'s Literary Award for Poetry, 1994; Best Novel Award, Writers' Guild of Alberta, 1994. *Memberships:* League of Canadian Poets; Writers' Union of Canada; Writers'

Guild of Alberta. *Address:* c/o League of Canadian Poets, 54 Wolseley St, Third Floor, Toronto, Ontario M5T 1AS, Canada.

HILLIS, Rick; b. 3 Feb. 1956, Nipawin, Saskatchewan, Canada. Writer; Poet; Teacher. m. Patricia Appelgren, 29 Aug. 1988, 1 s., 1 d. *Education:* University of Victoria, 1977–78; BEd, University of Saskatchewan, 1979; Graduate Studies, Concordia University, 1983; MFA, University of Iowa, 1984; Stanford University, 1988–90. *Appointments:* Stegner Fellow, 1988–90, Jones Lecturer, 1990–92, Stanford University; Lecturer, California State University at Hayward, 1990; Chesterfield Film Writer's Fellowship, 1991–92; Visiting Asst Prof. of English, Reed College, 1992–96. *Publications:* The Blue Machines of Night (poems), 1988; Coming Attractions (co-author), 1988; Canadian Brash (co-author), 1990; Limbo Stories, 1990. *Contributions to:* Anthologies and periodicals. *Honours:* Canada Council Grants, 1985, 1987, 1989; Drue Heinz Literature Prize, 1990. *Address:* c/o Dept of English, Lewis and Clark College, Portland, OR 97202, USA.

HIND, Steven; b. 24 Feb. 1943, Emporia, KS, USA. Teacher of Writing and Literature; Poet. m. Annabeth Dall, 10 July 1965, 1 s., 1 d. *Education:* BSE, Kansas State Teachers College, 1965; MSE, Emporia State University, 1968; MA, English, University of Kansas, 1970. *Appointments:* English Teacher, Topeka High School, 1965–69; Teacher of Writing and Literature, Hutchinson Community College, 1970–. *Publications:* Familiar Ground, 1980; That Trick of Silence, 1990; A Place with No Map, 1997. *Contributions to:* Anthologies and periodicals. *Honours:* Scholarship Winner, Colorado Writers Conference, Boulder, 1977, and Kansas Quarterly Award Winner, 1977. *Address:* 503 Monterey Place, Hutchinson, KS 67502, USA.

HINDS, Sallie A., (Chriscaden); b. 8 June 1930, Saginaw, Michigan, USA. Poet. m. James F Hinds, 25 Aug. 1951, 2 d. *Education:* MacMurray College for Women, 1948–49; Michigan State University. *Appointment:* Treasurer, Sims Township, 1980–92; City of East Tawas Planning Commission. *Publications:* Bits and Pieces of Nature's Seasons, 1986; Simple Words... Quiet Thoughts, 1994; Halcyon Days, 2000. *Contributions to:* Various anthologies, journals, and magazines. *Honours:* Silver Poet Award, 1986, Golden Poet Awards, 1987–92, World of Poetry; First Place Blue Ribbon, Arenac County Fair, 1990; Ed.'s Choice Award, National Library of Poetry, 1995; Ed.'s Choice Award, Poets Guild, 1998; First Prizes, 1998, 2000, 2002, Second Prize, 1999, GFWC Michigan Poetry Awards; GFWC Short Story Award, 2000; International Poet of Merit Award, 2002. *Memberships:* East Tawas Ladies Literary Club, treasurer; Writers Club; International Library of Poetry, life mem.; National Library of Poetry; Northeast Michigan Arts Council; World of Poetry. *Address:* 1216 E Lincoln, East Tawas, MI 48730, USA.

HINE, (William) Daryl; b. 24 Feb. 1936, Burnaby, BC, Canada. Poet; Writer; Trans. *Education:* McGill University, 1954–58; MA, 1965, PhD, 1967, University of Chicago. *Appointments:* Asst Prof. of English, University of Chicago, 1967–69; Ed., Poetry magazine, Chicago, 1968–78. *Publications:* Poetry: Five Poems 1954; The Carnal and the Crane, 1957; The Devil's Picture Book, 1960; Heroics, 1961; The Wooden Horse, 1965; Minutes, 1968; Resident Alien, 1975; In and Out: A Confessional Poem, 1975; Daylight Saving, 1978; Selected Poems, 1980; Academic Festival Overtures, 1985; Arrondissements, 1988; Postscripts, 1992. Novel: The Prince of Darkness and Co, 1961. Other: Polish Subtitles: Impressions from a Journey, 1962; The 'Poetry' Anthology 1912–1977 (ed. with Joseph Parisi), 1978. Translator: The Homeric Hymns and the Battle of the Frogs and the Mice, 1972; Theocritus: Idylls and Epigrams, 1982; Ovid's Heroines: A Verse Translation of the Heroides, 1991; Hesiod's Works, 2000; Puerilities from the Greek Anthology, 2001. *Honours:* Canada Foundation-Rockefeller Fellowship, 1958; Canada Council Grants, 1959, 1979; Ingram Merrill Foundation Grants, 1962, 1963, 1983; Guggenheim Fellowship, 1980; American Acad. of Arts and Letters Award, 1982; John D. and Catherine T. MacArthur Foundation Fellowship, 1986. *Address:* 2740 Ridge Ave, Evanston, IL 60201, USA.

HINO, Seiji; b. 8 Dec. 1927, Tokyo, Japan. Teacher (retd); Poet. m. Yamagata-Shi, 31 Oct. 1959, 1 s., 1 d. *Education:* MA, Western Philosophy, Tohoku University, 1956. *Publications:* Nikogori (Frozen Dishes), 1984; Letters to Young Friends, 1989. *Contributions to:* Shinto no Tomo, monthly; Poet, monthly, India; Parnassus, India; Heaven, India. *Honours:* Michael Madhusudan Acad. Award, 1994. *Memberships:* Research for Modern Poetry; World Poetry Research Institute, Pres., Kim Joung Woong, Korea; Poet; International Poets Acad., Chennai, India. *Address:* 1-4-33 Kiyozumi-cho, Yamagata-shi, 990-0834 Japan.

HINRIKSSON, Larus; b. 28 Feb. 1956, Reykjavík, Iceland. Writer; Poet. m. Freyja Baldursdottir, Aug. 1982, 1 s., 1 d. *Education:* Industrial School of Iceland. *Publications:* Enigma Well, 1993; The Lupin, 1994; Echo of Time, Broken Glass (poems), 1995. *Membership:* Writers' Union of Iceland. *Address:* Box 410, 602 Akureyri, Iceland.

HIRSCH, Edward (Mark); b. 20 Jan. 1950, Chicago, IL, USA. Prof. of English; Poet; Writer. m. Janet Landay, 29 May 1977, 1 s. *Education:* BA, Grinnell College, 1972; PhD, University of Pennsylvania, 1979. *Appointments:* Teacher, Poetry in the Schools Program, New York and Pennsylvania, 1976–78;

Asst Prof., 1978–82, Assoc. Prof. of English, 1982–85, Wayne State Universit Assoc. Prof., 1985–88, Prof. of English, 1988–, University of Housto *Publications:* For the Sleepwalkers, 1981; Wild Gratitude, 1986; The Nig Parade, 1989; Earthly Measures, 1994; Transforming Vision (ed.), 1994; C Love, 1998; How to Read a Poem and Fall in Love with Poetry, 199 Responsive Reading, 1999. *Contributions to:* Many anthologies, book journals, and periodicals. *Honours:* Awards, 1975–77, Peter I B Lava Younger Poets Award, 1983, Acad. of American Poets; Ingram Merr Foundation Award, 1978; ACLS Fellow, 1981; National Endowment for th Arts Fellowship, 1982; Delmore Schwartz Memorial Poetry Award, New Yo University, 1985; Guggenheim Fellowship, 1986–87; Texas Institute of Lette Award in Poetry, 1987; National Book Critics Circle Award, 1987; Rome Priz American Acad. and Institute of Arts and Letters, 1988; Robert and Haz Ferguson Memorial Award for Poetry, Friends of Chicago Literature, 1990; Li Wallace-Reader's Digest Writing Fellow, 1993; Woodrow Wilson Fellow, 199 1995; Lyndhurst Prize, 1994–96. *Memberships:* Authors Guild; MLA; PEl Poetry Society of America; Texas Institute of Letters. *Address:* 1528 Sul Ros Houston, TX 77006, USA.

HIRSCHFIELD, Theodore H.; b. 25 May 1941, Nordenburg, East Prussi Germany. Asst Prof. of English; Poet. m. Margaret Allen, 26 Jan. 1963, 1 *Education:* BA, English, Ottawa University, KS, 1963; MA, Creative Writin Hollins College, Virginia, 1964; 23 hours towards PhD in English, Souther Illinois University at Carbondale, 1964–65, 1977–79; 60 hours toward PhD i English, Vanderbilt University, 1970–73. *Appointments:* Instructor of Englis 1965–74, Asst Prof. of English, 1974–, Southeast Missouri State University Cape Girardeau. *Publications:* After Dürer: Knight, Death and the Devil, 196 The Cape Rock, 1965; A Poem for My Wife, 1966; Human Weather, 199 German Requiem, 1993; Orbiting God, 1993. *Contributions to:* Cape Roc. Today; Hollins Critic; Cargoes; Ariel; LIT; Ottawa University Campu Literary Supplement; Tauy Talk. *Membership:* MLA. *Address:* 158 Lexington, Cape Girardeau, MO 63701, USA.

HIRSCHMAN, Jack; b. 13 Dec. 1933, New York, NY, USA. Poet; Trans. n Ruth Epstein, 1954, 1 s., 1 d. *Education:* BA, City College of New York, 195 AM, 1957, PhD, 1961, Indiana University. *Publications:* Poetry: Fragment 1952; Correspondence of Americans, 1960; Two, 1963; Interchange, 1964; Klin Sky, 1965; Yod, 1966; London Seen Directly, 1967; Wasn't Like This in th Woodcut, 1967; William Blake, 1967; A Word in Your Season (with As Benveniste), 1967; Ltd Interchangeable in Eternity: Poems Jackruthdavidcelia Hirschman, 1967; Jerusalem, 1968; Aleph, Benoni an Zaddik, 1968; Jerusalem Ltd, 1968; Shekinah, 1969; Broadside Golem, 196 Black Alephs: Poems 1960–68, 1969; NHR, 1970; Scintilla, 1970; Soledet 1971; DT, 1971; The Burning of Los Angeles, 1971; HNYC, 1971; Les Vidange 1972; The R of the Ari's Raziel, 1972; Adamnan, 1972; K'wai Sing: The Origin the Dragon, 1973; Cantillations, 1973; Aur Sea, 1974; Djackson, 197 Cockroach Street, 1975; The Cool Boyetz Cycle, 1975; Kashtaniya Segodnyah, 1976; Lyripol, 1976; The Arcanes of Le Comte de St Germai 1977; The Proletarian Arcane, 1978; The Jonestown Arcane, 1979; Th Caliostro Arcane, 1981; The David Arcane, 1982; Class Questions, 198 Kallatumba, 1984; The Necessary Is, 1984; The Bottom Line, 1988; Sunson 1988; The Tirana Arcane, 1991; The Satin Arcane, 1991; Endless Threshold 1992; The Back of a Spoon, 1992; The Heartbeat Arcane, 1993; The Xibalb Arcane, 1994. Editor: Artaud Anthology, 1965; Would You Wear My Eyes: Tribute to Bob Kaufman, 1989. Translator: Over 25 vols, 1970–95. *Address:* P Box 26517, San Francisco, CA 94126, USA.

HIRSHFIELD, Jane; b. 24 Feb. 1953, New York, NY, USA. Poet; Writer; Ed Lecturer. *Education:* AB magna cum laude, Princeton University, 197 *Appointments:* California Poet in the Schools, 1980–85; Faculty, variou writers conferences, 1984–; Lecturer, University of San Francisco, 1991– Visiting Poet-in-Residence, University of Alaska, Fairbanks, 1993; Adjunc Prof., Northern Michigan University, 1994; Assoc. Faculty, Bennington College, 1995; Visiting Assoc. Prof., University of California at Berkeley 1995; Core Faculty, Bennington College, MFA Writing Seminars, 1999– Elliston Visiting Poet, University of Cincinnati, 2000. *Publications:* Poetry Alaya, 1982; Of Gravity and Angels, 1988; The October Palace, 1994; The Live of the Heart, 1997; Given Sugar, Given Salt, 2001. Other: The Ink Dark Moor Poems by Ono no Komachi and Izumi Shikibu (trans. with Aratani), 1988 Women in Praise of the Sacred: 43 Centuries of Spiritual Poetry by Wome (ed.), 1994; Nine Gates: Entering the Mind of Poetry (essays), 1997 *Contributions to:* Many anthologies, journals, and reviews. *Honours:* Yadd Fellowships, 1983, 1985, 1987, 1989, 1992, 1996; Guggenheim Fellowship 1985; Joseph Henry Jackson Award, San Francisco Foundation, 1986 Columbia University Trans. Center Award, 1987; Poetry Society of Americ Awards, 1987, 1988; Artist-in-Residence, Djerassi Foundation, 1987–90 Pushcart Prize, 1988; Commonwealth Club of California Poetry Medals 1988, 1994; Dewar's Young Artists Recognition Award in Poetry, 1990 MacDowell Colony Fellowship, 1994; Bay Area Book Reviewers Awards 1994, 2001; Poetry Center Book Award, 1995; Rockefeller Foundatio Fellowship, Bellagio Study Center, Italy, 1995; Finalist, National Boo Critics Circle Award, 2001. *Memberships:* Associated Writing Programs Authors Guild; Djerassi Resident Artist Program, board mem., 1996–

Lindisfarne Asscn, fellow, 1995–; PEN American Center. *Address:* c/o Michael Katz, 367 Molino Ave, Mill Valley, CA 94941, USA.

HIRST, Joanna. See: HIRST, John Alan.

HIRST, John Alan, (Alan Darbyshire, Joanna Hirst); b. 14 Oct. 1953, Chesterfield, Derbyshire, England. Poet. m., 4 s., 1 d. *Education:* DIP, Retail Excellence, 1984. *Publications:* Nite-Lites, three vols, 1997, 1998, 1999; Visions and Versions, 1999; Perceptions are Reality, 1999; Sweet 'n' Sour, 2001. *Contributions to:* Numerous magazines and journals. *Honours:* Several. *Memberships:* The Gallery Writers, Solihull; Survivors Poetry. *Address:* 37 Micklehill Dr., Shirley, Solihull B90 2PU, England. *E-mail:* johnalanhirst@ukonline.co.uk.

HOBSBAUM, Hannah, (Hannah Kelly); b. 27 July 1937, Poona, India. Poet; Ed. m. Philip Hobsbaum, 1957, divorced 1966. *Education:* Violin, Trinity College of Music, London; English, Birkbeck College, University of London, 1966–71. *Publications:* Prelude, 1974; A Game of Cards, 1981; The Butterfly, 1985; The Promised Land, 1991; Before the Cock Crows (with Sumra Green), 1997; The Road from Israel to Rome, 1998. Ed.: Various anthologies, including The Silver Snake, Camden Anthology (with Roy Batt), 1994; The Memory-Link, Camden Anthology (ed. with Colin Holcombe), 1997; The Human Tide, Camden Anthology (ed. with Rachel Silbert), 2000; Years of Plenty, Camden Anthology (ed. with Judith Miller and Rachel Silbert), 2002. *Contributions to:* Several publications. *Honour:* Citation of Meritorious Achievement for Services to Literature, 1994. *Memberships:* Belfast Poetry Group; Birkbeck Poetry Workshop; Poets' Workshop, London; Camden Poetry Group, chair. *Address:* 64 Lilyville Rd, London SW6 5DW, England.

HOBSBAUM, Philip (Dennis); b. 29 June 1932, London, England. Writer; Poet; Emeritus Prof. of English Literature. m. (1) Hannah Hobsbaum, 1957, divorced 1968, (2) Rosemary Phillips, 20 July 1976. *Education:* BA, 1955, MA, 1961, Downing College, Cambridge; Licentiate, Royal Acad. of Music, London, 1956, Guildhall School of Music, 1957; PhD, University of Sheffield, 1968. *Appointments:* Ed., Delta, 1954–55; Co-Ed., Poetry from Sheffield, 1959–61; Lecturer in English, Queen's University, Belfast, 1962–66; Lecturer, 1966–72, Senior Lecturer, 1972–79, Reader, 1979–85, Prof. of English Literature, 1985–97, Hon. Professorial Research Fellow, 1997–, University of Glasgow. *Publications:* A Group Anthology (ed. with E Lucie-Smith), 1963; The Place's Fault and Other Poems, 1964; Snapshots, 1965; In Retreat and Other Poems, 1966; Ten Elizabethan Poets (ed.), 1969; Coming Out Fighting, 1969; Some Lovely Glorious Nothing, 1969; A Theory of Communication: A Study of Value in Literature, 1970; Women and Animals, 1972; A Reader's Guide to Charles Dickens, 1973; Tradition and Experiment in English Poetry, 1979; A Reader's Guide to D H Lawrence, 1981; Essentials of Literary Criticism, 1983; A Reader's Guide to Robert Lowell, 1988; Wordsworth: Selected Poetry and Prose (ed.), 1989; Channels of Communication (ed. with P Lyons and J McGhie), 1993; Metre, Rhythm and Verse Form, 1996. *Contributions to:* Anthologies, journals, reviews, and magazines. *Honours:* Hon. DLitt, University of Glasgow, 1994, University of Sheffield, 2003. *Address:* c/o Dept of English Literature, University of Glasgow, Glasgow G12 8QQ, Scotland.

HOCHHUTH, Rolf; b. 1 April 1931, Eschwege, Germany. Dramatist; Writer; Poet; Critic. m. 3 s. *Education:* Extramural Studies, University of Heidelberg, University of Munich. *Appointment:* Chief Cultural Correspondent, Die Welt newspaper, Berlin, 1989–. *Publications:* Der Stellvertreter, 1963; Die Berliner Antigone, 1966; Soldaten, 1967; Guerrillas, 1970; Die Hebamme, 1971; Lysistrate und die NATO, 1973; Tod eines Jägers, 1976; Eine Liebe in Deutschland, 1978; Juristen, 1979; Arztinnen, 1980; Spitze des Eisbergs: Ein Reader, 1982; Judith, 1984; Atlantik, 1985; Der Berliner Antigone: Erzählungen und Gedichte, 1986; War hier Europa?: Reden, Gedichte, Essays, 1987; Tater und Denker: Profile und Probleme von Cäaser bis Jünger, 1987; Unbefleckte Empfängnis: Ein Kreidekreis, 1988; Sommer 14: Ein Totentan, 1989; Alle Dramen, 2 vols, 1991; Panik im Mai: Sämtliche Gedichte und Erzählungen, 1991; Wessis in Weimar: Szenen aus einem besetzten Land, 1993; Julia oder Weg zur Macht, 1994. *Honours:* Gerhart Hauptmann Prize, 1962; Berlin Art Prize, 1963; Basel Art Prize, 1976; Literature Prize, City of Munich and Asscn of Bavarian Publishers, 1980; Lessing Prize, Hamburg, 1981; Jacob Burckhardt Prize, 1991. *Memberships:* Acad. of Fine Arts; PEN Club. *Address:* c/o Die Welt, Kochstrasse 50, 10069 Berlin, Germany.

HODDINOTT, Allyson Gray, (Allyson G Scott); b. 17 Feb. 1961, Singapore. Legal Secretary; Poet. m. Jeremy C Hoddinott, 20 Aug. 1997, 1 s. *Education:* University of Glasgow, 1978–82; MA, English Literature and Moral Philosophy, Hammersmith and West London College, 1988; RSA, Typing and Business Communications, Souters Exclusive College, 1993; Legal Secretarial Diploma, Part 1, 1998, Part 2 Studies, 1999–, Institute of Legal Executives. *Contributions to:* Anthologies, including: The Cream of the Troubadour Coffee House, 1990; Poem in Songs of Senses, 1999; The Sounds of Poetry (cassette); Periodicals, including: Response newspaper; Scallywag magazine. *Membership:* Life Mem., Goldsmith's Society, University of London.

HOFF, Kay; b. 15 Aug. 1924, Neustadt, Holstein, Germany. Writer; Poet. m. Marianne Schilling, 12 Jan. 1951, 3 s., 1 d. *Education:* DPhil, University of Kiel, 1949. *Appointments:* Ed., Neues Rheinland, 1958–67; Publisher, Guido Hildebrandt Verlag, 1965–72; Dir, German Cultural Centre, Tel-Aviv, Israel, 1969–73. *Publications:* In Babel zuhaus, 1958; Zeitzeichen, 1962; Skeptische Psalmen, 1965; Netzwerk, 1969; Zwischen zeilen, 1970; Bestandsaufnahme, 1977; Gegen den Stundenschlag, 1982; Zur Zeit, 1987; Zeitgewinn, Gesammelte Gedichte, 1953–1989, 1989; Fruehe Gedichte 1951–52, 1994; Zur Neige, Gedichte 1989–1998, 1999. *Contributions to:* Frankfurter Allgemeine Zeitung; Suddeutsche Zeitung; Die Welt; Frankfurter Hefte; Neue Deutsche Hefte; Neue Rundschau. *Honours:* Poetry Prize, Young Authors Competition, Schleswig-Holstein, 1952; Second Prize, Radio Play Competition, South German Radio, 1957; North Rhein-Westphalian Award of Achievement, 1960; Ernst Reuter Prize, 1965; Georg Mackensen Prize, 1968; Guest of Honour, Villa Massimo, Rome, 1994. *Membership:* PEN International. *Address:* Stresemannstrasse 30, 23564 Lübeck, Germany.

HOFFMAN, Barbara A.; b. 19 Dec. 1941, Rochester, New York, USA. Prof. of English; Poet. *Education:* AB, D'Youville College, 1963; MA, Catholic University of America, 1965; ABD, Duquesne University, 1969. *Appointment:* Prof. of English, Marywood College, 1969–. *Publication:* Cliffs of Fall, 1979. *Contributions to:* Studin Mystreu; Endless Mountain Review; Best Sellers; Scanlou's Poetry Journal. *Memberships:* Mulberry Poets and Writers Asscn; Lambda Iota Tau. *Address:* 1749 Jefferson Ave, Dunmore, PA 18509, USA.

HOFFMAN, Daniel (Gerard); b. 3 April 1923, New York, NY, USA. Prof. of English Emeritus; Poet; Writer. m. Elizabeth McFarland, 1948, 2 c. *Education:* AB, 1947, MA, 1949, PhD, 1956, Columbia University. *Appointments:* Visiting Prof., University of Dijon, 1956–57; Asst Prof., 1957–60, Assoc. Prof., 1960–65, Prof. of English, 1965–66, Swarthmore College; Elliston Lecturer, University of Cincinnati, 1964; Lecturer, International School of Yeats Studies, Sligo, Ireland, 1965; Prof. of English, 1966–83, Poet-in-Residence, 1978–, Felix E Schelling Prof. of English, 1983–93, Prof. Emeritus, 1993–, University of Pennsylvania; Consultant in Poetry, 1973–74, Hon. Consultant in American Letters, 1974–77, Library of Congress, Washington, DC; Poet-in-Residence, Cathedral of St John the Divine, New York City, 1988–; Visiting Prof. of English, King's College, London, 1991–92. *Publications:* Poetry: An Armada of Thirty Whales, 1954; A Little Geste and Other Poems, 1960; The City of Satisfactions, 1963; Striking the Stones, 1968; Broken Laws, 1970; Corgi Modern Poets in Focus 4 (with others), 1971; The Center of Attention, 1974; Able Was I Ere I Saw Elba: Selected Poems 1954–1974, 1977; Brotherly Love, 1981; Hang-Gliding from Helicon: New and Selected Poems 1948–1988, 1988; Middens of the Tribe, 1995. Other: The Poetry of Stephen Crane, 1957; Form and Fable in American Fiction, 1961; Barbarous Knowledge: Myth in the Poetry of Yeats, Graves and Muir, 1967; Poe Poe Poe Poe Poe Poe Poe, 1972. Others: Shock Troops of Stylistic Change, 1975; 'Moonlight Dries No Mittens': Carl Sandburg Reconsidered, 1979; Faulkner's Country Matters: Folklore and Fable in Yoknapatawpha, 1989; Words to Create a World: Interviews, Essays and Reviews of Contemporary Poetry, 1993. Editor: Several books. *Honours:* Yale Series of Younger Poets Award, 1954; Ansley Prize, 1957; ACLS Fellowships, 1961–62, 1966–67; Columbia University Medal for Excellence, 1964; American Acad. of Arts and Letters Grant, 1967; Ingram Merrill Foundation Grant, 1971; National Endowment for the Humanities Fellowship, 1975–76; Hungarian PEN Medal, 1980; Guggenheim Fellowship, 1983; Hazlett Memorial Award, 1984; Paterson Poetry Prize, 1989. *Membership:* Acad. of American Poets, chancellor, 1973–97, chancellor emeritus, 1997–. *Address:* c/o Dept of English, University of Pennsylvania, Philadelphia, PA 19104, USA.

HOFFMANN, Roald; b. 18 July 1937, Zloczow, Poland. Chemist; Poet. m. Eva Borjesson, 30 April 1960, 1 s., 1 d. *Education:* BA, Columbia University, 1958; PhD, Harvard University, 1962. *Appointments:* Junior Fellow, Society of Fellows, Harvard University, 1962–65; Assoc. Prof. to John A Newman Prof. of Physical Science, Cornell University, 1965–. *Publications:* The Metamict State, 1987; Gaps and Verges, 1990; Memory Effects, 1997; Soliton, 2002. *Contributions to:* Paris Review; Literaturnaya Gazeta; Prairie Schooner; New England Review; Bread Loaf Quarterly; Lyrikvännen; TriQuarterly. *Honour:* Pergamon Press Fellowship in Literature, Djerassi Foundation, 1988. *Address:* Dept of Chemistry, Cornell University, Ithaca, NY 14853, USA.

HOFMANN, Michael; b. 25 Aug. 1957, Freiburg, Germany. Poet; Dramatist; Trans. *Education:* BA, Magdalene College, Cambridge, 1979. *Appointments:* Visiting Assoc. Prof., Creative Writing Dept, University of Michigan, Ann Arbor, 1994; Visiting Distinguished Lecturer, University of Florida, Gainesville, 1994–. *Publications:* Nights in the Iron Hotel, 1983; Acrimony, 1986; K S in Lakeland: New and Selected Poems, 1990; Corona, Corona, 1993; After Ovid: New Metamorphoses (co-ed. with James Lasdun), 1994; Penguin Modern Poets 13, 1998; Approximately Nowhere, 1999; Behind the Lines, 2002. Plays: The Double Bass (adaptation of a play by Patrick Suskind), 1987; The Good Person of Sichuan (adaptation of a play by Brecht), 1989. Other: Trans. *Contributions to:* The London Review of Books; TLS. *Honours:* Cholmondeley Award, 1984; Geoffrey Faber Memorial Prize, 1988; Schlegel Tieck Prizes, 1988, 1992; Arts Council Writers Bursary, 1997–98; PEN/Book of the Month Club Trans. Prize, 1999; Helen and Kurt Wolff Prize, 2000. *Address:* c/o Faber and Faber, 3 Queen Sq., London WC1N 3AU, England.

HOGAN, Linda Chickasaw Nation; b. 16 July 1947, Denver, CO, USA. Poet: Novelist; Essayist; Prof. of English. m. Pat Hogan, divorced, 2 d. *Education:* MA, University of Colorado at Boulder, 1978. *Appointments:* Assoc., Rocky Mountain Women's Institute, University of Denver, 1979–80; Poet-in-the-Schools, Colorado and Oklahoma, 1980–84; Asst Prof., Tribes Program, Colorado College, 1982–84; Assoc. Prof. of American and American Indian Studies, University of Minnesota, 1984–89; Prof. of English, University of Colorado at Boulder, 1989–. *Publications:* Poetry: Calling Myself Home, 1979; Eclipse, 1983; Seeing Through the Sun, 1985; Savings, 1988; The Book of Medicines, 1993. Fiction: That Horse, 1985; Mean Spirit, 1990; Solar Storms, 1995; Power, 1998. Other: A Piece of Moon (play), 1981; The Stories We Hold Secret: Tales of Women's Spiritual Development (ed. with Carol Bruchac and Judith McDaniel), 1986; Dwellings: A Spiritual History of the Natural World, 1995; Intimate Nature: The Bond Between Women and Animals, 1998. *Honours:* Guggenheim Fellowship; Lannan Award for Poetry; National Endowment for the Arts Grant; American Book Award, 1986; Oklahoma Book Award for Fiction, 1990; Colorado Book Awards, 1994, 1997. *Memberships:* Authors Guild; MLA; National American Studies Program; National Council of Teachers of English; PEN West; Writers Guild. *Address:* c/o Dept of English, University of Colorado at Boulder, Boulder, CO 80302, USA.

HOGGARD, James (Martin); b. 21 June 1941, Wichita Falls, Texas, USA. Prof. of English; Poet; Writer; Trans. m. Lynn Taylor Hoggard, 23 May 1976, 1 s., 1 d. *Education:* BA, Southern Methodist University, 1963; MA, University of Kansas, 1965. *Appointments:* Teaching Asst, University of Kansas, 1963–65; Instructor to Prof. of English, Midwestern State University, 1966–; Guest Prof., Instituto Allende, San Miguel de Allende, Mexico, 1977, 1978; University of Mosul, Iraq, 1990; Exchange Prof., Instituto Tecnologico de Estudias Superiores de Monterrey, Chihuahua, Mexico, 1993. *Publications:* Poetry: Eyesigns: Poems on Letters and Numbers, 1977; The Shaper Poems, 1983; Two Gulls, One Hawk, 1983; Breaking an Indelicate Statue, 1986; Medea in Taos, 2000; Rain In A Sunlit Sky, 2000. Fiction: Trotter Ross, 1981; Riding the Wind and Other Tales, 1997. Non-Fiction: Elevator Man, 1983. *Contributions to:* Anthologies, reviews, quarterlies, journals, and magazines. *Honours:* Soeurette Diehl Fraser Award; Stanley Walker Award; Brazos Bookstore (Houston) Short Story Award; Grants and citations. *Memberships:* American Literary Trans Asscn; American Studies Asscn of Texas; PEN; Conference of College Teachers of English; Texas Institute of Letters, pres., 1994–98. *Address:* c/o Dept of English, Midwestern State University, Wichita Falls, TX 76308, USA.

HOGUE, Cynthia Anne; b. 26 Aug. 1951, Moline, IL, USA. Prof. of English; Poet. m. Jon Jaukur Ingimundarson, 17 July 1983. *Education:* BA, 1973; Master of Arts and Humanities, 1975; PhD, English, 1990. *Publications:* Touchwood, 1978; Where the Parallels Cross, 1983; The Woman in Red, 1989. *Contributions to:* American Poetry Review; American Poetry; Central Park; Cut Bank; Fiction International; Field; Hayden's Ferry; How(ever); Ironwood; Negative Capability; Passages North; Ploughshares; Quarterly West; Sequoia; University Publishing; Willow Springs; Women's Quarterly Review. *Honours:* Fulbright-Hayes Fellowship, 1979–80; Judith Siegel Pearson Award in Poetry, 1987; National Endowment for the Arts Fellowship, 1990. *Memberships:* MLA; Associated Writing Programs; National Council of Teachers of English; Freedom Writers' Asscn (associated with Amnesty International); Poets and Writers, USA. *Address:* Dept of English, University of New Orleans, Lakefront, LA 70148, USA.

HOLBROOK, David (Kenneth); b. 9 Jan. 1923, Norwich, England. Author; Poet. m. 23 April 1949, 2 s., 2 d. *Education:* BA, Honours, English, 1946, MA, 1951, Downing College, Cambridge. *Appointments:* Fellow, King's College, Cambridge, 1961–65; Senior Leverhulme Research Fellow, 1965, Leverhulme Emeritus Research Fellow, 1988–90; Writer-in-Residence, Dartington Hall, 1972–73; Fellow and Dir of English Studies, 1981–88, Emeritus Fellow, 1988, Downing College. *Publications:* English for Maturity, 1961; Imaginings, 1961; Against the Cruel Frost, 1963; English for the Rejected, 1964; The Secret Places, 1964; Flesh Wounds, 1966; Children's Writing, 1967; The Exploring Word, 1967; Object Relations, 1967; Old World New World, 1969; English in Australia Now, 1972; Chance of a Lifetime, 1978; A Play of Passion, 1978; English for Meaning, 1980; Selected Poems, 1980; Nothing Larger than Life, 1987; The Novel and Authenticity, 1987; A Little Athens, 1990; Edith Wharton and the Unsatisfactory Man, 1991; Jennifer, 1991; The Gold in Father's Heart, 1992; Where D H Lawrence Was Wrong About Women, 1992; Creativity and Popular Culture, 1994; Even If They Fail, 1994; Tolstoy, Women and Death, 1996; Wuthering Heights: A Drama of Being, 1997; Getting it Wrong with Uncle Tom, 1998; Bringing Everything Home (poems), 1999; A Study of George MacDonald and the Image of Woman, 2000; Lewis Carroll: Nonsense Against Sorrow, 2001. *Contributions to:* Numerous professional journals. *Honour:* Festschrift, 1996. *Memberships:* English Asscn, founding fellow, 2000; Society of Authors. *Address:* 1 Tennis Court Terrace, Cambridge CB2 1QX, England.

HOLDEN, Kim Michelle; b. 29 Jan. 1970, Edmonton, AB, Canada. Special Needs Child Care Worker; Poet. *Education:* Licenced Nurses Aid Graduate with Distinction, 1992. *Publications:* Whispers in the Wind, 1991; Dawn Peaceful Paths, 1992; Apex One, 1992; I'm Only Shaken not Stirred, 1995.

Contributions to: Quill Book Anthology; Daily Courier; Kelowna BC; Plowmen Quarterly Publication. *Honour:* Caprice Poetry Award, 1994. *Address:* 235 Marshall Rd, No. 2, Kelowna, BC V1Z1E9, Canada.

HOLDT, David M.; b. 12 May 1941, Cleveland, Ohio, USA. Teacher; Writer Poet. m. Sandra B Wood-Holdt, 26 June 1976, 1 s., 1 d. *Education:* BA, 1963 CAS, 1993, Wesleyan University; MA, Duke University. *Publications:* Sun Through Trees, 1972; Rivers Edge, 1985; Waterscapes, 1987. *Contributions to:* Northwoods Journal; Chelsea; Maine Life; Cambric Poetry I, II, III; Just Pulp; Spectrum; Pastiche; Poet; Firelands Review; Connecticut River Review; Stone Country; Poets On; Embers; Clearwater Navigator; Amelia Connecticut Writer; Blueline; Lake Effect; River of Dreams. *Honour:* Second Prize, Connecticut Writers League, 1987. *Memberships:* Poets and Writers Teachers and Writers Collaborative. *Address:* 3 Orchard Hill Rd, Canton, CT 06019, USA.

HOLENDER, Barbara D.; b. 15 March 1927, Buffalo, New York, USA. Poet. m. H William Holender, 8 May 1949, deceased, 1 s., 1 d. *Education:* Cornell University, 1944–46; BA, University of Buffalo, 1948. *Appointments:* Instructor in English, University of Buffalo, 1973–76; New York State Poets in the Schools, 1976. *Publications:* Shivah Poems: Poems of Mourning, 1986; Ladies of Genesis, 1991; Is This the Way to Athens?, 1996. *Contributions to:* New York Times; Christian Science Monitor; Literary Review; Prairie Schooner; Helicon Nine; Anthologies: New York Times Book of Verse, 1970; Sarah's Daughters Sing, 1990; 80 on the 80's, 1990; Helicon Nine Reader, 1990; Scarecrow Poetry, 1994; Lifecycles, Vol. I, 1994, Vol. II, 1997. *Honours:* Hans S Bodenheimer Award for Poetry, 1984; Western New York Writers in Residence Award, 1988. *Memberships:* Acad. of American Poets; Poets and Writers. *Address:* 263 Brantwood Rd, Snyder, NY 14226, USA.

HOLLANDER, John; b. 28 Oct. 1929, New York, NY, USA. Prof. of English; Poet; Critic; Ed. m. (1) Anne Loesser, 15 June 1953, divorced, 2 d., (2) Natalie Charkow, 17 Dec. 1982. *Education:* AB, 1950, MA, 1952, Columbia University; PhD, Indiana University, 1959. *Appointments:* Lecturer, Connecticut College, 1957–59; Poetry Ed., Partisan Review, 1959–65; Instructor to Assoc. Prof., 1959–66, Prof. of English, 1977–86, A Bartlett Giametti Prof. of English, 1986–95, Sterling Prof. of English, 1995–, Yale University; Christian Gauss Seminarian, Princeton University, 1962; Visiting Prof., 1964, Patten Lecturer, 1986, Fellow, Institute for Advanced Study, 1986, Indiana University; Prof. of English, Hunter College and the Graduate Center of the City University of New York, 1966–77; Elliston Prof. of Poetry, University of Cincinnati, 1969. *Publications:* Poetry: A Crackling of Thorns, 1958; Movie-Going and Other Poems, 1962; Visions from the Ramble, 1965; Types of Shape, 1968; The Night Mirror, 1971; Town and Country Matters, 1972; Selected Poems, 1972; Tales Told of the Fathers, 1975; Reflections on Espionage, 1976; Spectral Emanations: New and Selected Poems, 1978; Blue Wine, 1979; Flowers of Thirteen, 1983; In Time and Place, 1986; Harp Lake, 1988; Selected Poetry, 1993; Tesserae, 1993; Figurehead and Other Poems, 1999; War Poems, 1999; Sonnets, 2000. Criticism: The Untuning of the Sky, 1960; Images of Voice, 1970; Vision and Resonance, 1975; The Figure of Echo, 1981; Rhyme's Reason, 1981; Melodious Guile, 1988; William Bailey, 1990; The Gazer's Spirit, 1995; The Work of Poetry, 1997; The Poetry of Everyday Life, 1998; Figurehead, 1998. Editor: The Wind and the Rain (with Harold Bloom), 1961; Jiggery-Pokery (with Anthony Hecht), 1966; Poems of Our Moment, 1968; Modern Poetry: Essays in Criticism, 1968; The Oxford Anthology of English Literature (with Frank Kermode, Harold Bloom, J B Trapp, Martin Price and Lionel Trilling), 1973; Nineteenth-Century American Poetry, 2 vols, 1993; Committed to Memory, 1997; The Best American Poetry, 1998. Other: The Death of Moses (libretto for Alexander Goehr's opera), 1992. *Honours:* Poetry Chapbook Award, 1962; Melville Cane Award, 1990, Poetry Society of America; National Institute of Arts and Letters Award, 1963; National Endowment for the Humanities Senior Fellowship, 1973–74; Levinson Prize, 1974; Washington Monthly Prize, 1976; Guggenheim Fellowship, 1979–80; Mina P Shaughnessy Award, MLA, 1982; Bollingen Prize, 1983; Shenandoah Prize, 1985; John D. and Catherine T. MacArthur Foundation Fellowship, 1990–95; Robert Penn Warren-Cleanth Brooks Award, 1998. *Memberships:* Acad. of American Poets, board of chancellors, 1980–2000; American Acad. of Arts and Letters, sec., 2000–; Asscn of Literary Scholars and Critics, pres., 2000–01. *Address:* c/o Dept of English, Yale University, PO Box 208302, New Haven, CT 06520, USA.

HOLLIDAY, David John Gregory, (Alfred Cunning, William Speaker); b. 20 Aug. 1931, Isleworth, Middlesex, England. Poet; Ed.; Adjudicator. m. Ruth Brick, 29 Feb. 1960, 1 s., 1 d. *Appointments:* Joint Ed., Deuce, 1956–61; Ed., Scrip, 1961–73, Iota, 1988–2002. *Publications:* Pictures from an Exhibition (with Patrick Snelling), 1959; Compositions of Place, 1961; Jerusalem, 1982; The Abbot Speaks, 1995. *Contributions to:* Various publications. *Honour:* Founder-Fellow, International Poetry Society, 1976. *Memberships:* Nottingham Poetry Society, past chair.; Wensley Poetry Group, past chair. *Address:* 67 Hady Crescent, Chesterfield, Derbyshire S41 0EB, England.

HOLLINGHURST, Alan; b. 26 May 1954, Stroud, Gloucestershire, England. Writer; Poet; Trans. *Education:* BA, 1975, MLitt, 1979, Magdalen College, Oxford. *Appointments:* Asst Ed., 1982–84, Deputy Ed., 1985–90, Poetry Ed., 1991–95, TLS. *Publications:* Fiction: The Swimming-Pool Library, 1988; The

Folding Star, 1994; The Spell, 1998. Poetry: Confidential Chats with Boys, 1982. Translator: Bajazet, by Jean Racine, 1991. *Honours:* Somerset Maugham Award, 1988; E. M. Forster Award, 1990; James Tait Black Memorial Prize, 1995. *Membership:* Fellow, RSL. *Address:* c/o Antony Harwood, 109 Riverbank House, 1 Putney Bridge Approach, London SW6 3JD, England.

HOLLO, Anselm; b. 12 April 1934, Helsinki, Finland. Prof. of Poetry, Poetics, and Trans.; Poet; Writer; Trans.; Ed. m. Jane Dalrymple-Hollo. *Education:* Modern Languages and Literature, University of Helsinki, University of Tübingen. *Appointments:* Visiting Prof., State University of New York at Buffalo, 1967, University of Iowa, 1968–73, Bowling Green State University, Ohio, 1971–73, Hobart and William Smith Colleges, Geneva, New York, 1973–75, Southwest Minnesota State College, Marshall, 1977–78; Distinguished Visiting Poet, Michigan State University, 1974; Assoc. Prof. of Literature and Creative Writing, University of Maryland, 1975–77; Margaret Bannister Distinguished Writer-in-Residence, Sweet Briar College, 1978–81; Poet-in-Residence, 1981, Visiting Lecturer, 1985–89, Kerouac School of Poetics, Boulder; Visiting Lecturer in Poetics, New College of California, San Francisco, 1981–82; Book Reviewer, Baltimore Sun, 1983–85; Distinguished Visiting Prof. of Poetry, University of Colorado at Boulder, 1985; Contributing Ed., The New Censorship, 1989–; Assoc. Prof. of Poetry, Poetics and Trans., Naropa University, Boulder, 1989–. *Publications:* Poetry: Sojourner Microcosms: New and Selected Poems, 1959–77, 1978; Finite Continued, 1981; Pick Up the House: New and Selected Poems, 1986; Outlying Districts: New Poems, 1990; Near Miss Haiku, 1990; Blue Ceiling, 1992; High Beam: 12 Poems, 1993; West is Left on the Map, 1993; Survival Dancing, 1995; Corvus: New Poems, 1995; Hills Like Purple Pachyderms, 1997; AHOE: And How on Earth, 1997; Rue Wilson Monday, 2000; Notes on the Possibilities and Attractions of Existence: New and Selected Poems, 1965–2000, 2001. Prose: Caws and Causeries: Around Poetry and Poets, 1999. *Honours:* Yaddo Residency Fellowship, 1978; National Endowment for the Arts Fellowship in Poetry, 1979; PEN/American-Scandinavian Foundation Award for Poetry in Trans., 1980; American-Scandinavian Foundation Award for Poetry in Trans., 1989; Fund for Poetry Award for Contributions to Contemporary Poetry, 1989, 1991; Stein Award in Innovative American Poetry, 1996; Grez-sur-Loing Foundation Fellowship, 1998; Baltic Centre for Writers and Trans Residency Fellowship, 2002. *Address:* 3336 14th St, Boulder, CO 80304, USA.

HOLLOWAY, Glenna Preston; b. 7 Feb. 1928, USA. Artist; Poet. m. Robert Wesley Holloway, 20 Feb. 1948, deceased 1997. *Education:* Ward Belmont College; Specialist in Enamelling, Silversmithing, and Lapidary. *Contributions to:* Anthologies, 1971–99, and numerous reviews, journals, and periodicals. *Honours:* Daniel Whitehead Hicky Award, 1984; Best of the Best, Chicago Poets and Patrons, 1984, 1986–89, 1991, 1997, and National League of American Penwomen, 1985–2000; Grand Prize, National Federation of State Poetry Societies, 1986; Hart Crane Memorial Award, Kent State University, 1988; Ragdale Foundation Fellow, 1989; Edward D Vickers Award, 1994; Winchell Award, 1995; Bartlet College Award, 1998; Abbie Copps Award, Olivet College, 1998; Dorfman Award, Rome Art Centre, New York, 1999; Pushcart Prize, 2000; Pushcart Anthology, 25th Anniversary Edn, 2001. *Memberships:* Illinois State Poetry Society, pres., 1991–94; National Federation of State Poetry Societies; National League of American Penwomen. *Address:* 913 E Bailey Rd, Naperville, IL 60565, USA.

HOLLOWAY, John; b. 1 Aug. 1920, Croydon, Surrey, England. Prof. of Modern English (retd); Writer; Poet. m. (1) Audrey Gooding, 1946, 1 s., 1 d., (2) Joan Black, 1978. *Education:* BA, Modern Greats, New College, Oxford, 1941; DPhil, Oxon, 1947. *Appointments:* Temporary Lecturer in Philosophy, New College, Oxford, 1945; Fellow, All Souls College, Oxford, 1946–60; Lecturer in English, University of Aberdeen, 1949–54, University of Cambridge, 1954–66; Fellow, 1955–82, Life Fellow, 1982–, Queens' College, Cambridge; Reader, 1966–72, Prof. of Modern English, 1972–82, University of Cambridge; Various visiting lectureships and professorships. *Publications:* Language and Intelligence, 1951; The Victorian Sage, 1953; Poems of the Mid-Century (ed.), 1957; The Charted Mirror (essays), 1960; Selections from Shelley (ed.), 1960; Shakespeare's Tragedies, 1961; The Colours of Clarity (essays), 1964; The Lion Hunt, 1964; Widening Horizons in English Verse, 1966; A London Childhood, 1966; Blake: The Lyric Poetry, 1968; The Establishment of English, 1972; Later English Broadside Ballads (ed. with J Black), 2 vols, 1975, 1979; The Proud Knowledge, 1977; Narrative and Structure, 1979; The Slumber of Apollo, 1983; The Oxford Book of Local Verses (ed.), 1987. Poetry: The Minute, 1956; The Fugue, 1960; The Landfallers, 1962; Wood and Windfall, 1965; New Poems, 1970; Planet of Winds, 1977; Civitatula: Cambridge, the Little City, 1994. *Contributions to:* Professional journals. *Membership:* RSL, fellow, 1956. *Address:* c/o Queens' College, Cambridge CB3 9ET, England.

HOLLOWAY, Patricia, (Patricia Pogson); b. 8 March 1944, Rosyth, Scotland. Yoga Teacher; Poet. m. (1) 1 s., 1 d., (2) Geoffrey Holloway, 27 Aug. 1977, deceased 1997. *Education:* National Diploma in Design, 1964; Teaching Certificate, 1971; Diploma, British Wheel of Yoga, 1987. *Appointments:* Draughtswoman Restorer, Ashmolean Museum, Oxford, 1964–66; Part-time Yoga Teacher; Poetry Tutor, Schools and Writing Centres, Libraries. *Publications:* Before the Road Show, 1983; Snakeskin, Belladonna, 1986;

Rattling the Handle, 1991; A Crackle from the Larder, 1991; The Tides in the Basin, 1994; Holding, 2002. *Contributions to:* Anthologies, journals, reviews and magazines. *Honours:* First Prize, York Open Competition, 1985; Third Prize, Manchester Open Competition, 1989; Second Prize, National Poetry Competition, 1989; First Prize, BBC Kaleidoscope Competition, 1990. *Memberships:* Brewery Poets, Brewery Arts Centre, Kendal; Keswick Poetry Group. *Address:* 4 Gowan Crescent, Staveley, nr Kendal, Cumbria LA8 9NF, England.

HOLM, Peter Röwde; b. 5 April 1931, Oslo, Norway. Author; Poet. m. Nina Stang-Lund, 1954, 1 s., 1 d. *Education:* Graduate, St Gallen, Switzerland, 1953; Certificate of Proficiency in English, Cambridge, 1955. *Publications:* Skygger rundt en virkelighet, 1955; Din sang om noe annet, 1957; Men natten kommer senere, 1959; Innvielse ved havet, 1960; Stentid, 1962; Det plutselige landskapet, 1963; Öyeblikkets forvandlinger, 1965; Befrielser, 1966; Diabas, 1968; Synslinjer, 1970; Sanndrömt, 1971; Isglimt, glödepunkt, 1972; Reisens formler, 1974; Portrettalbum, 1975; Tegnene tydes, 1976; I disse bilder, 1977; Vinden stiger, 1978; I båten om hösten, 1979; Langsom musikk, 1991; Sangen om Aral, 1993, Canadian edn as The Song of Aral, 1999; Collected Poems, 1996. *Contributions to:* Dagbladet; Aftenposten; Morgenbladet; Verdens Gang; Vinduet; Various periodicals abroad. *Honours:* Sarpsborg Literary Prize, 1957; Mads Wiel Nygaard Prize, Aschehoug, 1962; Dagbladets Poetry Prize, 1964; Norwegian Cultural Council Prize, 1966; Literary Critics Prize, 1966; Riksmaals Prize, 1977; Oslo City Prize, 1983; Literary Prize, Norwegian Acad., 1996. *Memberships:* Norwegian Union of Authors; Norwegian Authors Centre; Johnson Society (Societas Johnsoniana); Artists Society; De Niderton. *Address:* Östre Holmensvingen 4, 0774 Oslo, Norway.

HOLMES, Clyde; b. 20 Oct. 1940, Barnet, London, England. Landscape Painter; Poet. m. Annette Charpentier, 27th Sept. 2000, 1 s., 4 d. *Education:* BA, Hornsey School of Art, St Martin's School of Art, London, 1965. *Publications:* Cwm Hesgin, 1977; Standing Stone, 1978; In Season, 1988; Skywalls, 1998. *Contributions to:* Anthologies, reviews, magazines, radio, and television. *Honours:* New Poetry Prize, 1976; Michael Johnson Memorial Prizes, 1977, 1979; Diploma Winner, Scottish Open Poetry Competitions, 1977, 1978, 1979; Special Commendation, Welsh Arts Council New Poets Competition, 1978; Edmund Blunden Prize, 1979. *Membership:* International Poetry Society. *Address:* Cwm Hesgin, Capel Celyn, Frongoch, Y Bala, Gwynedd LL23 7NY, North Wales.

HOLMES, John. See: SOUSTER, (Holmes) Raymond.

HOLMES, Richard (Gordon Heath); b. 5 Nov. 1945, London, England. Writer; Poet; Prof. of Biographical Studies. *Education:* BA, Churchill College, Cambridge. *Appointments:* Reviewer and Historical Features Writer, The Times, London, 1967–92; Earnest Jones Memorial Lecturer, British Institute of Psycho-Analysis, 1990; John Keats Memorial Lecturer, Royal College of Surgeons, 1995; Visiting Fellow, Trinity College, Cambridge, 2000; Prof. of Biographical Studies, University of East Anglia, 2001–. *Publications:* Thomas Chatterton: The Case Re-Opened, 1970; One for Sorrows (poems), 1970; Shelley: The Pursuit, 1974; Shelley on Love (ed.), 1980; Coleridge, 1982; Nerval: The Chimeras (with Peter Jay), 1985; Footsteps: Adventures of a Romantic Biographer, 1985; Mary Wollstonecraft and William Godwin (ed.), 1987; Kipling: Something Myself (ed. with Robert Hampson), 1987; Coleridge: Early Visions, 1989; Dr Johnson and Mr Savage, 1993; Coleridge: Selected Poems (ed.), 1996; The Romantic Poets and Their Circle, 1997; Coleridge: Darker Reflections, 1998; Sidetracks: Explorations of a Romantic Biographer, 2000. *Honours:* Somerset Maugham Award, 1977; Whitbread Book of the Year Prize, 1989; O.B.E., 1992; James Tait Black Memorial Prize, 1994; Duff Cooper Prize, 1998; Hon. doctorates, University of East Anglia, 2000, Tavistock Institute, 2001. *Membership:* RSL, fellow. *Address:* c/o HarperCollins, 77 Fulham Palace Rd, London W6 8JB, England.

HOLMES, Stewart Quentin; b. 25 Dec. 1929, London, England. Actor; Journalist; Poet. *Education:* RSA Credits, English-Typewriting, Pitman's Shorthand, 1950; Mandarin Chinese, Hong Kong University, 1971–72. *Appointments:* BBC Correspondent, Tehran, Iran, 1971; Features Ed., Hong Kong Standard, 1971–72; London Correspondent, International Press Bureau and Union Jack newspaper, 1981. *Publications:* Odes and Ends, 1985; Once Upon a Rhyme, 1987. *Contributions to:* Outpost; British MENSA Magazine; Union Jack newspaper. *Honour:* Golden Poet, World of Poetry, CA, 1990. *Memberships:* London Poetry Society; Stanza Poets; British MENSA; British Actors Equity; Chartered Institute of Journalists; Foreign Press Assocn, London. *Address:* 106 Clarence Gate Gardens, Baker St, London NW1 6AL, England. *Telephone:* (7703) 115182. *Fax:* (20) 7925-0469. *E-mail:* holmessq@hotmail.com.

HOLT, Rochelle Lynn, (Rochelle Holt Dubois); b. 17 March 1946, Chicago, IL, USA. Writer; Poet; Dramatist. *Education:* BA, English, University of Illinois, Chicago, 1967; MFA, English, University of Iowa, 1970; PhD, English and Psychology, Columbia Pacific University, 1980. *Appointments:* Adjunct Teacher, Union College, Westfield, NJ, 1983–86; Kean College of New Jersey, 1988–92; Writer-in-Residence and Teacher of English, Elizabeth High School, NJ, 1988–94; Instructor in Fiction, Writer's Digest School, 1989–99. *Publications:* Two Plus One, 1984; Extended Family, 1986; Uno-Duo, 1988;

Bushels of Broken Glass, 1989; Chords, 1990; Above-Underground Anthology (ed.), 1990; Author's Choice, 1991; Warm Storm, 1991; Panes: Fiction As Therapy, 1993; The River's Shadow, 1993; Jokers are Wild: 39 Plays to Ruffle Your Lover, 1994; Caution: Child at Play, 2000. *Contributions to:* Numerous magazines and periodicals. *Honours:* Several grants; National Endowment for the Arts Writer-in-Residence, 1976, 1977; Poet-in-the-Schools, Virginia, 1977; Willow Bee Publishing House Literature Award, 1986. *Memberships:* Acad. of American Poets; Associated Writing Programs; Feminist Writers' Guild; International Women Writers' Guild; Poetry Society of America; Women for Freedom of the Press. *Address:* c/o Olga G. Holt, 5111 N 42nd Ave, Phoenix, AZ 85019, USA.

HOLTON, John Clark; b. 14 April 1959, Washington, DC, USA. Ed.; Poet. *Education:* Atlantic College, 1975–77; American University, 1980–82. *Appointments:* Ed., Acclaim, 1977, Creative Expressions, 1983, Swinging Light, Voyager 83, 1996. *Publication:* Cry of the Invisible, 1991. *Contributions to:* Tropos; The Pearl; Influence; Expressions. *Address:* 2633 Guilford Ave, Baltimore, MD 21218, USA.

HONIG, Edwin; b. 3 Sept. 1919, New York, NY, USA. Prof. of English and of Comparative Literature (retd); Poet; Writer; Dramatist; Trans. m. (1) Charlotte Gilchrist, 1 April 1940, deceased 1963, (2) Margot Dennes, 15 Dec. 1963, divorced 1978, 2 s. *Education:* BA, 1939, MA, 1947, University of Wisconsin at Madison. *Appointments:* Poetry Ed., New Mexico Quarterly, 1948–52; Instructor, Claremont College, CA, 1949; Faculty, 1949–57, Asst Prof. of English, Harvard University; Faculty, 1957–60, Prof. of English, 1960–82, Prof. of Comparative Literature, 1962–82, Brown University; Visiting Prof., University of California at Davis, 1964–65; Mellon Prof., Boston University, 1977. *Publications:* Poetry: The Moral Circus, 1955; The Gazabos: 41 Poems, 1959; Survivals, 1964; Spring Journal, 1968; Four Springs, 1972; At Sixes, 1974; Shake a Spear with Me, John Berryman, 1974; Selected Poems 1955–1976, 1979; Interrupted Praise, 1983; Gifts of Light, 1983; The Imminence of Love: Poems 1962–1992, 1993. Stories: Foibles and Fables of an Abstract Man, 1979. Non-Fiction: García Lorca, 1944; Dark Conceit: The Making of Allegory, 1959; Calderón and the Seizures of Honor, 1972; The Poet's Other Voice: Conversations on Literary Translation, 1986. Plays: Ends of the World and Other Plays, 1984. Translations: Over 10 books, 1961–93. *Contributions to:* Books, anthologies, reviews, journals, and periodicals. *Honours:* Guggenheim Fellowships, 1948, 1962; National Acad. of Arts and Letters Grant, 1966; Amy Lowell Traveling Poetry Fellowship, 1968; Rhode Island Governor's Award for Excellence in the Arts, 1970; National Endowment for the Humanities Fellowship, 1975, and Grants, 1977–80; National Endowment for the Arts Fellowship, 1977; Trans. Award, Poetry Society of America, 1984; National Award, Columbia University Trans. Center, 1985; Decorated by the Portuguese Pres. for trans. of Pessoa, 1989; Decorated by the King of Spain for trans. of Calderón, 1996. *Memberships:* Dante Society of America; Poetry Society of America. *Address:* 229 Medway St, Apt 305, Providence, RI 02906, USA.

HOOKER, Jeremy (Peter); b. 23 March 1941, Warsash, Hampshire, England. Lecturer in English; Poet; Writer. *Education:* BA, 1963, MA, 1965, University of Southampton. *Appointments:* Arts Council Creative Writing Fellow, Winchester School of Art, 1981–83; Lecturer in English, Bath College of Higher Education, 1988–. *Publications:* The Elements, 1972; Soliloquies of a Chalk Giant, 1974; Solent Shore: New Poems, 1978; Landscape of the Daylight Moon, 1978; Englishman's Road, 1980; Itchen Water, 1982; Poetry of Place, 1982; A View from the Source: Selected Poems, 1982; Master of the Leaping Figures, 1987; The Presence of the Past, 1987; In Praise of Windmills, 1990; Their Silence a Language (with Lee Grandjean), 1994; Writers in a Landscape, 1996; Our Lady of Europe, 1997; Groundwork (with Lee Grandjean), 1998. *Contributions to:* Reviews and journals. *Honours:* Eric Gregory Award, 1969; Welsh Arts Council Literature Prize, 1975. *Memberships:* Fellow, Academi Gymreig, 2000; Richard Jefferies Society, pres., 1999. *Address:* Old School House, 7 Sunnyside, Frome, Somerset BA11 1LD, England.

HOOVER, Paul (Andrew); b. 30 April 1946, Harrisonburg, VA, USA. Poet; Writer; Ed.; Educator. m. Maxine Chernoff, 5 Oct. 1974, 2 s., 1 d. *Education:* BA, English, Manchester College, 1968; MA, English, University of Illinois, 1973. *Appointments:* Ed., OINK!, 1971–78; Founder-Mem., 1974, Mem., Board of Dirs, 1974–87, Pres., 1975–78, School of the Art Institute of Chicago; Poet-in-Residence, Columbia College, 1974–; Co-Founder and Ed., New American Writing, 1986–; Fellow, Simon's Rock of Bard College, 1988–; Lecturer in Creative Writing, San Francisco State University, 1999–2000. *Publications:* Harpin Turns (poems), 1973; The Monocle Thugs, 1977; Letter to Einstein Beginning Dear Albert (poems), 1979; Somebody Talks a Lot (poems), 1983; Nervous Songs (poems), 1986; Idea (poems), 1987; Saigon, Illinois (novel), 1988; The Novel: A Poem, 1990; Postmodern American Poetry: A Norton Anthology (ed.), 1993; Viridian (poems), 1997; Totem and Shadow: New and Selected Poems, 1999; Rehearsal in Black, 2001; Winter (Mirror), 2002. *Contributions to:* Numerous anthologies, reviews, quarterlies and journals. *Honours:* National Endowment for the Arts Poetry Fellowship, 1980; Illinois Arts Council Artist's Fellowships, 1983, 1984, 1986; General Electric Foundation Award for Younger Writers, 1984; Carl Sandburg Award, Friends of the Chicago Public Library, 1987; Gwendolyn Brooks Poet Laureate Award, 1988; Shifting Foundation

Grants, 1990, 1991; Gertrude Stein Award in Innovative American Poetry 1994–95; Winner, Contemporary Poetry Series Competition, University o Georgia, 1997; San Francisco Literary Laureate Award, Friends of the Sar Francisco Public Library, 2000. *Memberships:* Associated Writing Programs Co-ordinating Council of Literary Magazines; MLA of America. *Address:* 36ξ Molino Ave, Mill Valley, CA 94941, USA. *Website:* www.previewport.com.

HOPE, Akua Lezli; b. 7 June 1957, New York, NY, USA. Writer; Poet. *Education:* BA, Williams College, 1975; MSJ, 1977, MBA, 1978, Columbia University. *Appointment:* Ed., New Heat, 1989–. *Publications:* Lovecycles 1977; Shard, 1989; Sister Fire, 1994; Embouchure, 1995. *Contributions to.* Obsidian II; Ikon; Hambone; Contact II; Black American Literature Forum Erotique Noire, An Anthology of Erotic Writing by Black Writers, 1992 Confirmation, An Anthology of Afrikan American Women Writers; Extended Outlooks, An Anthology of American Women Writers. *Honours:* Sterling Brown Award, 1975; Finalist, Walt Whitman Prize, 1983; Poetry Fellowship, New York Foundation for the Arts, 1987–88; Finalist, MacDonalds Literary Achievement Award Competition, 1989; Creative Writing Fellowship, National Endowment for the Arts, 1990; Finalist, Barnard New Women Poets Series, 1990; US-Africa Fellowship, Ragdale Foundation, 1993. *Memberships:* Poetry Society of America; Science Fiction Poetry Asscn; Teachers and Writers; Poets and Writers; New Renaissance Writers' Guild, founding mem. *Address:* PO Box 33, Corning, NY 14830, USA.

HOPMAN, Ellen Evert; b. 31 July 1952, Salzburg, Austria. Author; Poet; Herbalist; Lay Homeopath. *Education:* MEd, Mental Health Counseling, University of Massachusetts, 1990. *Publications:* Tree Medicine, Tree Magic, 1992; A Druid's Herbal For the Sacred Earth Year, 1994; People of the Earth: The New Pagans Speak Out (co-author), 1995, revised edn as Being a Pagan: Druids, Wiccans and Witches Today, 2001; Walking the World in Wonder – A Children's Herbal, 2000. Other: Gifts from the Healing Earth, two vols (video); The Herbal and Magical Powers of Trees (cassette); The Druid Path: Herbs and Festivals (cassette); Celtic Goddesses and Gods (cassette). *Memberships:* American Herbalists' Guild; Nature Conservancy; Druid Order of the White Oak (Ord Na Darach Gile). *Address:* PO Box 219, Amherst, MA 01004, USA.

HORIUCHI, Toshimi; b. 5 Sept. 1931, Fukushima, Japan. Writer. m. Yoshiko Takayama, 25 March 1958. *Education:* BA, Tohoku Gakuin College, 1952–56; Saint John's University, Minnesota, USA, 1981–82, 1984–85; Exeter College, Oxford, 1992. *Appointments:* Prof., English Dept, 1987, Head, English Dept, 1994, Sendai Shirayuri Junior College. *Publications:* Drops of Rainbow, 1979; Minnesota Songs, 1982; Journey to the Fire Flower, 1990; Oasis in the Heart, 1995; Mental Coins (A Pocketful of Short Pieces), 2002. *Contributions to:* Poetry Nippon; Ko; Sakura; Mainichi Daily News; Japan Times. *Honours:* Nagoya City Prize for Haiku in English, Japan, 1987; Aichi Prefecture Prize for Haiku in English, Japan, 1989; Special Merit Book Award, Haiku Society of America, 1991. *Memberships:* Poetry Nippon; Poetry Society of Japan, 1972; Poetry Reading Circle of Tokyo, 1974. *Address:* 1-42-1-106 Asahigaoka, Aoba-ku, Sendai-shi 981-0904, Japan.

HOROVITZ, Michael; b. 4 April 1935, Frankfurt am Main, Germany. Writer; Poet; Ed.; Publisher. *Education:* BA, 1959, MA, 1964, Brasenose College, Oxford. *Appointments:* Ed. and Publisher, New Departures International Review, 1959–; Founder, Co-ordinator, and Torchbearer, Poetry Olympics Festivals, 1980–. *Publications:* Europa (trans.), 1961; Alan Davie, 1963; Declaration, 1963; Strangers: Poems, 1965; Poetry for the People: An Essay in Bop Prosody, 1966; Bank Holiday: A New Testament for the Love Generation, 1967; Children of Albion (ed.), 1969; The Wolverhampton Wanderer: An Epic of Football, Fate and Fun, 1970; Love Poems, 1971; A Contemplation, 1978; Growing Up: Selected Poems and Pictures 1951–1979, 1979; The Egghead Republic (trans.), 1983; A Celebration of and for Frances Horovitz, 1984; Midsummer Morning Jog Log, 1986; Bop Paintings, Collages and Drawings, 1989; Grandchildren of Albion (ed.), 1992; Wordsounds and Sightlines: New and Selected Poems, 1994; Grandchildren of Albion Live (ed.), 1996; The POW! Anthology, 1996; A New Waste Land: Britain at the Millennium, 1998. *Address:* c/o New Departures International Review, Mullions, Bisley, Stroud, Gloucestershire GL6 7BU, England.

HORVATH, Elemer G.; b. 15 April 1933, Hungary. Poet; Writer. m. 29 May 1968. *Education:* University of Budapest, 1953–56; University of Florence, Italy, 1957–61. *Publications:* A mindennapok arca, 1962; Egy feher neger naplojabol, 1976; A homokora nyaka, 1980; Maya tukor, 1982; A szelrozsa gyokerei (selected poems), 1990; Scaliger Rosa (poems), 1995. *Contributions to:* Almost all major Hungarian language literary magazines abroad; Literary magazines, Hungary, 1978–. *Honours:* Robert Graves Award, 1992; Book of the Year Award, 1995; József Attila Award, 1997; Ady Endre Award, 1998; First Milan Award, 2000. *Memberships:* International PEN Club; Poetry Society of America; Hungarian Writers Asscn. *Address:* 209 Bullet Hole Rd, Mahopac, NY 10541, USA.

HOTHERSALL, Patricia Ann; b. 23 June 1942, Burnley, Lancashire, England. Teacher; Poet. m. Colin Hothersall, 28 Dec. 1963, 2 s. *Education:* Cert Ed; MA; PhD. *Publications:* And on the 8th Day, 1978; Images & Illusions, 1986; Occasional Reflections (with Robert Hothersall), 1990. *Contributions to:*

Poets Voice; Periaktos; Weyfarers; Success; Counterpoint; Outrigger; TOPS; Others. *Honours:* Minor competitions and in small magazines; Prize, The Writer. *Address:* Middlen, 23 Churchill Rd, Thetford, Norfolk IP24 2JW, England.

HOUGHTON, Timothy Dane; b. 1 March 1955, Dayton, Ohio, USA. Prof. of English and Creative Writing; Poet. m. Cynthia Moore, 18 Aug. 1990. *Education:* BA, English, Psychology, Sociology, University of Pennsylvania; MA, English, Creative Writing, San Francisco State University, 1979; PhD, English, Creative Writing, University of Denver, 1984. *Appointment:* Prof. of English and Creative Writing, University of Houston. *Publications:* High Bridges, 1989; Below Two Skies, 1993. *Contributions to:* Greensboro Review; College English; Poet Lore; Denver Quarterly; Stand Magazine; Carolina Quarterly; Brooklyn Review; Arizona Quarterly. *Honours:* Residencies, Artist Colonies, Yaddo, 1990, Virginia Center for the Creative Arts, 1990, 1991, 1992, Helene Wurlitzer Foundation, 1993. *Membership:* Creative Writing Programs. *Address:* Creative Writing Program, English Dept, University of Houston, Houston, TX 77204, USA.

HOUSTON, Libby. See: JEWELL, Elizabeth Maynard.

HOWARD, Catherine Audrey; b. 5 Feb. 1953, Huddersfield, England. Poet; Writer. m. Leslie Howard, 3 April 1987. *Education:* Harold Pitchforth School of Commerce; Ashlar and Spen Valley Further Education Institute; RSA Diplomas. *Publications:* Elland in Old Picture Postcards, 1983; Down By the Old Mill Stream, 1993; The Flamborough Longsword Dance, 1994; Sacrifice for Christianity, 1994; My Pennine Roots, 1994; The Old and the New, 1994; Having Faith, 1994; The Might of the Meek, 1995; Tough as Old Boots, 1995; Portrait of All Hallows, 1996; Childhood Memories, 1996; Old Ways in Modern Days, 1996; Northern Cornucopia, 1996; A Glimpse of Spring, 1998; Poetry From Yorkshire, 1999. *Contributions to:* Visions in Verse (anthology); Mercedes-Benz Gazette. *Honours:* National Poet of the Year Commendations, 1996; National Open Competition Commendations, 1996, 1997; Robert Bloomfield Memorial Awards Commendation, 1998. *Address:* 17 Woodlands Close, Bradley Grange, Bradley, Huddersfield, West Yorkshire HD2 1QS, England.

HOWARD, David Andrew; b. 20 Aug. 1959, Christchurch, New Zealand. Writer; Poet; Designer; SFX Pyrotechnician; Ed. 1 s. *Education:* Diploma in Cabaret, Christchurch Acad., 1989; Certificate in Hazardous Substances, 1995. *Appointments:* Mem., The Curtainless Window Theatre Co, 1988; Partner, Takahe Publishing Collective, 1989–; Poetry Ed., Takahe literary quarterly, 1989–93; Ed., Firebrand, 1997–. *Publications:* In the First Place: Poems 1980–1990, 1991; Holding Company, 1995; Complete with Instructions (video), 1995; Shebang: Collected Poems, 1980–2000, 2001; How To Occupy Our Selves (with Fiona Perdington), 2002. *Contributions to:* Chelsea; Descant; Landfall; New Zealand Listener; Poet Lore; Poetry Australia; Poetry New Zealand; Anthologies, including: The Bird Catcher's Song, Australia, 1992; Catching the Light, New Zealand, 1992; The Oxford Anthology of New Zealand Love Poems, 2001; Snapshots on the Journey, 2002. *Honours:* First Prize, Gordon and Gotch Poetry Award, 1984; First Prize, New Zealand Poetry Society International Competition, 1987. *Memberships:* New Zealand Society of Authors; New Zealand Book Council; New Zealand Writers Guild; Canterbury Poets' Collective; New Zealand Guild of Design. *Address:* 142 Avonside Dr., Christchurch, New Zealand.

HOWARD, Noni H. E.; b. 26 Dec. 1949, Montréal, QC, Canada. Publisher; Educator; Writer; Poet. *Education:* BA, English, Religion, Bishop's University, Lennoxville, QC; MA, English, University of Alberta, 1972; PhD, Creative Writing, University of British Columbia, 1974. *Appointments:* Consulting Ed., The Phoenix, 1971–80; Staff Writer, Vancouver City Magazine, Gay Tide, 1972–74; Staff Teacher, Vancouver Free University, 1972–74; Orpheus Alternative University, San Francisco, 1974–80; Ed.-in-Chief, Publisher, New World Press, Daly City, CA, 1974–; Consulting Ed., Catlin Press, Vancouver, 1978–85, Women Talking-Women Listening, 1979–80; Poetry readings, Canada, England, Mexico, USA. *Publications:* I Think of You, I Thought of You, I Will Think of You, 1967; A Transparent Quiet Sea, 1971; Politics of Separation, 1974; Almost Like Dancing; Anthology of First Annual Women's Poetry Festival of San Francisco, 1977; The Politics of Love: Selected Poems 1970–1996, 1996. *Contributions to:* Many publications. *Honours:* First Prize, many Honourable Mentions, Alberta Poetry Contests, 1965–71; Kind Ed. Award, Poetry Organization of Women, CA, 1980; Grants. *Memberships:* League of Canadian Poets; Poets and Writers; Poetry Organization of Women, CA; Asscn of American Publishers; Women's Choice; Feminist Literary Guild; World Parnassians' Guild International, hon. mem.; Bay Area Poets' Coalition; Olympoetry Movement Committee. *Address:* 744 Stoneyford Dr., Daly City, CA 94015, USA.

HOWARD, Richard (Joseph); b. 13 Oct. 1929, Cleveland, Ohio, USA. Poet; Critic; Ed.; Trans. Educator: BA, 1951, MA, 1952, Columbia University; Postgraduate Studies, Sorbonne, University of Paris, 1952–53. *Appointments:* Lexicographer, World Publishing Co, 1954–58; Poetry Ed., New American Review, New Republic, Paris Review, Shenandoah; Rhodes Prof. of Comparative Literature, University of Cincinnati. *Publications:* Poetry:

Quantities, 1962; The Damages, 1967; Untitled Subjects, 1969; Findings, 1971; Two-Part Inventions, 1974; Fellow Feelings, 1976; Misgivings, 1979; Lining Up, 1984; Quantities/Damages, 1984; No Traveller, 1989; Like Most Revelations: New Poems, 1994. Criticism: Alone With America, 1969; Passengers Must Not Ride on Fenders, 1974. Editor: Preferences: Fifty-One American Poets Choose Poems from Their Own Work and from the Past, 1974; The War in Algeria, 1975. Translator: Over 65 books. *Contributions to:* Magazines and journals. *Honours:* Guggenheim Fellowship, 1966–67; Harriet Monroe Memorial Prize, 1969; Pulitzer Prize in Poetry, 1970; Levinson Prize, 1973; Cleveland Arts Prize, 1974; American Acad. and Institute of Arts and Letters Medal for Poetry, 1980; American Book Award for Trans., 1984; PEN American Center Medal for Trans., 1986; France-American Foundation Award for Trans., 1987; National Endowment for the Arts Fellowship, 1987. *Address:* c/o Alfred A. Knopf Inc, 299 Park Ave, New York, NY 10171, USA.

HOWARD, Roger; b. 19 June 1938, Warwick, England. Dramatist; Poet; Author; Senior Lecturer in Literature. m. Anne Mary Zemaitis, 13 Aug. 1960, 1 s. *Education:* RADA, London, 1956–57; University of Bristol, 1958; MA, University of Essex, 1976. *Appointments:* Teacher, Nankai University, Tientsin, China, 1965–67; Lecturer, University of Beijing, 1972–74; Fellow in Creative Writing, University of York, 1976–78; Writing Fellow, University of East Anglia, 1979; Lecturer, 1979–93, Founder-Dir, Theatre Underground, 1979–, Ed., New Plays series, 1980–, Senior Lecturer in Literature, 1993–, University of Essex. *Publications:* A Phantastic Satire (novel), 1960; From the Life of a Patient (novel), 1961; To the People (poems), 1966; Praise Songs (poems), 1966; The Technique of the Struggle Meeting, 1968; The Use of Wall Newspapers, 1968; New Plays I, 1968; Fin's Doubts, 1968; Episodes from the Fighting in the East, 1971; The Hooligan's Handbook, 1971; Slaughter Night and Other Plays, 1971; Method for Revolutionary Writing, 1972; Culture and Agitation: Theatre Documents (ed.), 1972; Contemporary Chinese Theatre, 1977; Mao Tse-tung and the Chinese People, 1978; The Society of Poets, 1979; A Break in Berlin, 1980; The Siege, 1981; Partisans, 1983; Ancient Rivers, 1984; The Speechifier, 1984; Contradictory Theatres, 1985; Senile Poems, 1988; The Tragedy of Mao and Other Plays, 1989; Britannia and Other Plays, 1990; Selected Poems 1966–96, 1997. *Contributions to:* Anthologies, newspapers and journals. *Address:* c/o Theatre Underground, Dept of Literature, University of Essex, Wivenhoe Park, Colchester, Essex CO4 3SQ, England.

HOWARD, Sherwin Ward; b. 19 Feb. 1936, Safford, AZ, USA. College Administrator; Poet. m. Annette Mina Shoup, 30 June 1960, 3 s., 1 d. *Education:* BS, Mathematics, 1960, MA, Theatre, Music, 1963, Utah State University; MFA, Playwriting, Yale University; PhD, Higher Education Administration, University of Wisconsin, 1980. *Appointments:* Asst to Provost, Ohio University, 1966–69; Asst to Pres., Lawrence University, 1969–80; Dean, Arts and Humanities, Weber State University, 1980–. *Publication:* Sometime Voices, 1988. *Contributions to:* Dialogue; Redneck Review; Weber Studies; Ensign Magazine. *Honours:* Dialogue Prize for Best Poetry of the Year, 1987; Utah Poet of the Year, 1988. *Memberships:* Utah Poetry Society; Ben Lomond Poets. *Address:* 5150 Shawnee, Ogden, UT 84403, USA.

HOWE, Fanny; b. 15 Oct. 1940, Buffalo, New York, USA. Prof. of Writing and American Literature; Author; Poet; Dramatist. 1 s., 2 d. *Education:* Stanford University, 1958–61. *Appointments:* Lecturer, Tufts University, 1968–71, Emerson College, 1974, Columbia University Extension and School of the Arts, 1975–78, Yale University, 1976, Harvard University Extension, 1977, Massachusetts Institute of Technology, 1978–87; Prof. of Writing and American Literature, University of California at San Diego, 1987–; Assoc. Dir, Study Center, University College, London, 1993–95; Distinguished Visiting Writer-in-Residence, Mills College, 1996–97. *Publications:* Fiction: Forty Whacks, 1969; First Marriage, 1975; Bronte Wilde, 1976; Holy Smoke, 1979; The White Slave, 1980; In the Middle of Nowhere, 1984; Taking Care, 1985; The Lives of a Spirit, 1986; The Deep North, 1988; Famous Questions, 1989; Saving History, 1992; Nod, 1998. Young Adult Fiction: The Blue Hills, 1981; Yeah, But, 1982; Radio City, 1983; The Race of the Radical, 1985. Poetry: Eggs, 1980; The Amerindian Coastline Poem, 1976; Poem from a Single Pallet, 1980; Alsace Lorraine, 1982; For Erato, 1984; Introduction to the World, 1985; Robeson Street, 1985; The Vineyard, 1988; The Quietist, 1992; The End, 1992; O'Clock, 1995; One Crossed Out, 1997; Q, 1998. *Contributions to:* Many anthologies, reviews, quarterlies, journals, and magazines. *Honours:* MacDowell Colony Fellowships, 1965, 1990; National Endowment for the Arts Fellowships in Fiction, 1969, and in Poetry, 1991; Bunting Institute Fellowship, 1974; St Botolph Award for Fiction, 1976; Writer's Choice Award for Fiction, 1984; Village Voice Award for Fiction, 1988; California Council on the Arts Award for Poetry, 1993; Lenore Marshall Poetry Prize, Acad. of American Poets, 2001. *Address:* 5208 La Jolla Hermosa, La Jolla, CA 92037, USA.

HOWE, Susan; b. 10 June 1937, USA. Poet; Prof. of English. *Education:* BFA, Painting, Museum of Fine Arts, Boston, 1961. *Appointments:* Butler Fellow in English, 1988, Prof. of English, 1991–, State University of New York at Buffalo; Visiting Scholar and Prof. of English, Temple University, Philadelphia, 1990, 1991; Visiting Poet and Leo Block Prof., University of Denver, 1993–94; Visiting Brittingham Scholar, University of Wisconsin at Madison, 1994; Visiting Poet,

University of Arizona, 1994; Visiting Prof., Stanford University, 1998. *Publications:* Poetry: Hinge Picture, 1974; The Western Borders, 1976; Secret History of the Dividing Line, 1978; Cabbage Gardens, 1979; The Liberties, 1980; Pythagorean Silence, 1982; Defenestration of Prague, 1983; Articulation of Sound Forms in Time, 1987; A Bibliography of the King's Book, or Eikon Basilike, 1989; The Europe of Trusts: Selected Poems, 1990; Singularities, 1990; The Nonconformist's Memorial, 1993; Frame Structures: Early Poems 1974–1979, 1996; Pierce-Arrow, 1999; Bad-Hangings, 2000. Other: My Emily Dickinson, 1985; Incloser, 1990; The Birthmark: Unsettling the Wilderness in American Literary History, 1993. *Honours:* Before Columbus Foundation American Book Awards, 1980, 1986; New York State Council of the Arts Residency, 1986; Pushcart Prize, 1987; New York City Fund for Poetry Grant, 1988; Roy Harvey Pearce Award, 1996; Guggenheim Fellowship, 1996–97; Distinguished Fellow, Stanford Humanities Centre, 1998. *Memberships:* Acad. of American Poets, board of chancellors, 2000–; American Acad. of Arts and Sciences. *Address:* 115 New Quarry Rd, Guilford, CT 06437, USA.

HOWELL, Anthony; b. 20 April 1945, London, England. Poet; Writer; Ed. *Education:* Leighton Park School; Royal Ballet School, London. *Appointments:* Lecturer, Grenoble University, Cardiff School of Art; Ed., Softly, Loudly Books, London, Grey Suit. *Publications:* Poetry: Inside the Castle, 1969; Femina Deserta, 1971; Oslo: A Tantric Ode, 1975; The Mekon, 1976; Notions of a Mirror: Poems Previously Uncollected, 1964–82, 1983; Winter's Not Gone, 1984; Why I May Never See the Walls of China, 1986; Howell's Law, 1990; Near Cavalry: Selected Poems of Nick Lafitte (ed.), 1992. Fiction: In the Company of Others, 1986; First Time in Japan, 1995. *Honour:* Welsh Arts Council Bursary, 1989. *Address:* 21 Augusta St, Adamsdown, Cardiff CF2 1EN, Wales.

HOWELL, Elmo; b. 5 Aug. 1918, Tremont, Mississippi, USA. English Teacher (retd); Poet. *Education:* BA, University of Mississippi, 1940; MA, 1948, PhD, 1955, University of Florida. *Appointments:* Jackson State College, Jacksonville, AL, 1955–57; Memphis State University, 1957–83. *Publications:* Winter Verses, 1989; The Apricot Tree, and Other Poems, 1993; I Know a Planted Field, 1995; Have You Been to Shubuta?, 1996; Tuesday's Letter, 2000; Mount Pleasant, 2001. *Membership:* Mississippi Poetry Society. *Address:* 3733 Douglass Ave, Memphis, TN 38111, USA.

HOYLAND, Michael (David); b. 1 April 1925, Nagpur, India. Art Lecturer (retd); Author; Poet. m. Marette Nicol Fraser, 21 July 1948, 2 s., 2 d. *Appointments:* School Teacher, 1951–63; Lecturer, 1963–65, Senior Lecturer in Art, 1963–80, Kesteven College of Education. *Publications:* Introduction Three, 1967; Art for Children, 1970; Variations: An Integrated Approach to Art, 1975; A Love Affair with War, 1981; The Bright Way In, 1984; Dominus-Domina (play); Poems in journals and a collection; 6 Short Stories. *Contributions to:* Reviewing for Ore; Jade. *Memberships:* Stamford Writers Group; PEN; Welland Valley Art Society; East Anglian Potters Asscn. *Address:* Foxfoot House, South Luffenham, Nr Oakham Rutland, Leicestershire LE15 8NP, England.

HRABAL, Milan; b. 10 Jan. 1954, Varnsdorf, Czechoslovakia. Writer; Poet. m. Libuse Vohankova, 10 July 1976, 1 s., 2 d. *Education:* Acad. of Economics, 1973. *Publications:* Sólo vetru, English trans. as A Solo For Wind, 1981; Cas pospichá, English trans. as Hurrying Time, 1985; Nepretrzité zitrky, English trans. as The Continuous Tommorrows, 1989; Zrcadlo pro Quijoty, English trans. as The Mirror for Quijotes, 1990; Nepokoje, English trans. as Disturbances, 1994; Kamenná kridla, English trans. as Stone Wings, 1996; Noci jen pro nás, English trans. as Nights Only for Us, 1996; Hanka Krawcec, 1996; Cokoli promenlivého, English trans. as Whatever Changeable, 1997; Prázdniny ve Zvatlánsku, English trans. as Holidays in Chatterland, 1997; Láska mezi paneláky, English trans. as Love Among Prefabs, 1999; Erotikon, 2000; Na svatbu k Chagallém, English trans. as To Chagall's Wedding, 2000; Kdyby nehráli Rolling Stones, English trans. as If the Rolling Stones Don't Play, 2001. Other: Trans fro Upper Sorbian and Polish. *Contributions to:* Anthologies, journals, quarterlies and periodicals. *Honours:* Zlaty Olomoucky Tvaruzek, 1989; O Kridlo Ikarovo, 1996; Turniej Jednego Wiersza, 1987; International Warsaw Prize, Autumn of Poetry, 1999. *Memberships:* Czech Writers Society; North Bohemian Writers Club; International PEN. *Address:* Varnsdorf 3, 407 47, Komenskeho 2321/9, Czech Republic. *E-mail:* okvdf@interdata.cz.

HUBBARD, Thomas Frederick; b. 6 Nov. 1950, Kirkcaldy, Fife, Scotland. Poet; Writer; Lecturer. m. 3 April 1982, 2 s., 1 d. *Education:* MA, 1973, PhD, 1982, University of Aberdeen; Diploma, Distinction, Libarianship, University of Strathclyde, 1978. *Appointments:* Senior Library Asst, University of Edinburgh Library, 1980–82; Librarian, Scottish Poetry Library, 1984–92; Lecturer, University of Grenoble, France, 1993; Visiting Asst Prof., University of Connecticut, 1993–94, University of North Carolina at Asheville, 1996–98. *Contributions to:* Books, anthologies, reviews, and journals. *Honour:* Scottish Arts Council Writer's Bursary, 1992. *Membership:* International PEN Scottish Centre. *Address:* 4 Asquith St, Kirkcaldy, Fife KY1 1PW, Scotland.

HUCKABONE, Fay. See: BRIGHAM, Faith Elizabeth Huckabone.

HUDDLE, David; b. 11 July, 1942, Ivanhoe, VA, USA. Prof. of English; Writer; Poet. m. Lindsey M. Huddle, 2 d. *Education:* BA, Foreign Affairs, University of Virginia, 1968; MA, English, Hollins College, 1969; MFA, Writing, Columbia Unversity, 1971. *Appointments:* Faculty, Warren Wilson College, 1981–85; Prof. of English, University of Vermont, 1982–; Ed., New England Review, 1993–94. *Publications:* A Dream With No Stump Roots In It, 1975; Paper Boy, 1979; Only the Little Bone, 1986; Stopping by Home, 1988; The High Spirits, 1992; The Writing Habit: Essays on Writing, 1992; The Nature of Yearning, 1992; Intimates, 1993; Tenormen, 1995; Summer Lake: New and Selected Poems, 1999; The Story of a Million Years, 1999; Not: A Trio – A Novella and Two Stories, 2000; La Tour Dreams of the Wolf Girl, 2002. *Contributions to:* Esquire; Harper's; New York Times Book Review; Kentucky Poetry Review; Texas Quarterly; Poetry; Shenandoah; American Poetry Review. *Honours:* Hon Doctorate of Humanities, Shenandoah College and Conservatory, Virginia 1989; Bread Loaf School of English Commencement Speaker, 1989; Robert Frost Prof. of American Literature, 1991. *Address:* Dept of English, University of Vermont, Burlington, VT 05405, USA.

HUDGINS, Andrew (Leon Jr); b. 22 April 1951, Killeen, Texas, USA. Prof. of English; Poet; Writer. *Education:* BA, Huntingdon College, 1974; MA, University of Alabama, 1976; Postgraduate Studies, Syracuse University, 1976–78; MFA Writers' Workshop, University of Iowa, 1981–83. *Appointments:* Adjunct Instructor, Auburn University, 1978–81; Teaching-Writing Fellow, University of Iowa, 1981–83; Lecturer, Baylor University, 1984–85; Prof. of English, University of Cincinnati, 1985–. *Publications:* Poetry: Saints and Strangers, 1985; After the Lost War: A Narrative, 1988; The Never-Ending: New Poems, 1991; The Glass Hammer: A Southern Childhood, 1994; Babylon in a Jar, 1998. Non-Fiction: The Glass Anvil (essays), 1997. *Contributions to:* Numerous journals. *Honours:* Wallace Stegner Fellow in Poetry, Stanford University, 1983–84; Yaddo Fellowships, 1983, 1985, 1987, 1988, 1991; Acad. of American Poets Award, 1984; MacDowell Colony Fellowship, 1986; National Endowment for the Arts Fellowships, 1986, 1992; Ingram Merrill Foundation Grant, 1987; Poets' Prize, 1988; Witter Bynner Award, American Acad. and Institute of Arts and Letters, 1988; Alfred Hodder Fellow, Princeton University, 1989–90; Poetry Award, Texas Institute of Letters, 1991; Ohioana Poetry Award, 1997. *Membership:* Texas Institute of Letters. *Address:* c/o Dept of English, ML 69, University of Cincinnati, Cincinnati, OH 45221, USA.

HUDSON, Louise Deborah; b. 2 Dec. 1958, London, England. Writer; Poet. 2 s. *Education:* Certificate in Recreational Arts for the Community. *Appointments:* Acting Education Officer, Publicity Secretary, Poetry Society; Arts Co-ordinator, Halton Borough Council; Centre Dir, Arvon Foundation, Devon; Literature Education Development Worker, Isle of Wight, 1996. *Publications:* Four Ways, 1985; Some People, 1989; Intimate Relations, 1993. *Contributions to:* Rialto; Slow Dancer; Orbis; Iron; Smoke; Foolscap; Wide Skirt. *Membership:* Company of Poets, founder mem. *Address:* Elm Ct, East St, Sheepwash, Beaworthy, Devon EX21 5NL, England.

HUDSON, Rosamund; b. 23 Sept. 1940, Escrick, York, England. Writer; Poet. m. Noel, 1 June 1963, 1 s., 1 d. *Publications:* A Lasting Calm, 1997; Talking Whispers, 1997; Tigress First Anthology, 1997; Poetic Thoughts, 1997; A Quiet Storm, 1997; Everlasting Dreams, 1997; The Path of Life, 1998; Earth in Our Hands, 1998; Tigress Second Anthology, 1998; Poet of the Year Awards, 1998; Poetic Visions, 1998. *Contributions to:* Malton Gazette and Herald; Escrick Surgery Newsletter; Yorkshire Evening Press. *Honours:* Ed.'s Choice Award, 1997, Third Prize, 1997, International Library of Poetry; Commendation, Hilton House Publishers, 1997, 1998; Finalist, Yorkshire Evening Press, 1998. *Memberships:* Poetry Now; Tigress Publications. *Address:* Holly-Dene, Moreby, Escrick, York YO19 6HN, England.

HUDSON, Thomas Cyril; b. 25 Aug. 1910, Cowes, Isle of Wight, England. Chief Engineering Estimator and Planning Engineer (retd); Poet; Writer; Playwright. *Publication:* Kairos, 1960; The Hounds of Cridmore and other Isle of Wight poems, 2000. *Contributions to:* Many anthologies and other publications. *Honours:* First Prizes, 1971, 1972, Margery Hume Cups, 1972–73, 1979, 1982, 1984–90, 1992, 1994–96, 1998– 2000, W G and S F Tillyard Cup, 1974, Isle of Wight Writers Circle; First Prize, Isle of Wight Arts Council, 1983; 33 Cups for stories, articles and one-act plays. *Address:* Wyvern, 250 Newport Rd, Cowes, Isle of Wight, England.

HUDSON-SAVAGE, Ruth. See: SAVAGE, Ramona Ruth.

HUERTA PALACIOS, Encarnación; b. 12 Feb. 1940, Madrid, Spain. Writer; Poet. m. Simeón Martín, 25 Feb. 1959, 2 s. *Publications:* Alerta del alma inmortal, 1980; Mis naipes en otoño, 1983; Raíz de mi aliento, 1984; El teclado de lázaro, 1986; Amor, vivo en tu lluvia, 1987; Desde que adán lloró, 1987; Des-concierto, 1989; Voces que me cantan, 1990; El atrio de la mariposa, 1996. *Contributions to:* Turia; Poesía Nueva; Alisma; Manxa; Alaluz; Litoral. *Honours:* Dama de Elche, 1985; Queen Amalia, 1986; Finalist, Fernando Rielo International Competition, 1986; Odón Betanzos Prize, 1988; Named El Prometeo, Best Woman's Poetic Work in Castilian Spanish, 1990. *Memberships:* Asociación Prometeo, 1980; Colegial des Escritores, 1983; Escritores y Artistas, 1983. *Address:* Arturo Soria 31p, 28033 Madrid, Spain.

HUFANA, Alejandrino; b. 22 Oct. 1926, San Fernando, Philippines. Ed.; Writer; Poet; Dramatist. *Education:* AB, 1952, MA, 1961, University of the Philippines; University of California at Berkeley, 1957–58; MS, Columbia University, 1969. *Appointments:* Co-Founding Ed., Signatures Magazine, 1955, Comment Magazine, 1956–67; Co-Founding Ed., 1967–68, Literary Ed., 1987–, Heritage Magazine; Dir, Cultural Center of the Philippines Library, 1970–85; Prof., 1975, Dir, Creative Writing Center, 1981–85, University of the Philippines. *Publications:* 13 Kalisud, 1955; Man in the Moon, 1956; Sickle Season, 1948–58, 1959; Poro Point, 1955–60, 1961; Curtain Raisers: First Five Plays, 1964; A Philippine Cultural Miscellany, 1970; The Wife of Lot and Other New Poems, 1971; Notes on Poetry, 1973; Sieg Heil, 1975; Philippine Writing, 1977; Shining On, 1985; Dumanon, 1994; No Facetious Claim: Notes on Writers and Writing, 1995; Enuegs, 1999; Survivor, 1999; Kaputt, 1999. *Address:* c/o Heritage Magazine, 20218 Tajauta Ave, Carson, CA 90746, USA.

HUFFSTICKLER, Albert, (Albert Huff); b. 17 Dec. 1927. Library Asst (retd); Poet. *Education:* BA, English, Southwest Texas State University, San Marcos, 1961. *Publications:* Night Diner, 1986; Walking Wounded, 1989; Working on My Death Chant, 1991; City of the Rain, 1993. *Contributions to:* Nimrod; Abraxas; Poetry East; New Mexico Humanities Review; Pig Iron; Journal of Anthroposophy; Poetry Motel. *Honours:* Austin Book Award, 1989; Senate Resolution, State of Texas honouring his contribution to Texas Poetry, 1989. *Address:* 312 E 43rd St 103, Austin, TX 78751, USA.

HUGHES, Annie. See: SNUGGS, Olive.

HUGHES, Glyn; b. 25 May 1935, Middlewich, Cheshire, England. Author; Poet. 1 s. *Education:* Regional College of Art, Manchester, 1952–56; Qualified Art Teacher, 1959. *Appointments:* Teacher, Lancashire and Yorkshire, 1956–72; Arts Council Fellow, Bishop Grosseteste College, Lincoln, 1979–81; Southern Arts Writer-in-Residence, Farnborough, 1982–84; Arts Council Writer-in-Residence, D H Lawrence Centenary Festival, 1985. *Publications:* Fiction: Where I Used to Play on the Green, 1982; The Hawthorne Goddess, 1984; The Antique Collector, 1990; Roth, 1992; Brontë, 1996; Autobiography: Millstone Grit, 1975; Fair Prospects, 1976. Poetry: Neighbours, 1970; Rest the Poor Struggler, 1972; Best of Neighbours, 1979. Plays: Mary Hepton's Heaven, 1984; Pursuit, BBC Radio 4, 1999; Mr Lowry's Loves, BBC Radio 4, 2001; Glorious John, BBC Radio 4, 2002. Various plays for BBC school broadcasts on radio and television. *Honours:* Welsh Arts Council Poets Prize, 1970; Guardian Fiction Prize, 1982; David Higham Fiction Prize, 1982. *Literary Agent:* Mic Cheetham Agency, 11–12 Dover St, London W1X 3PH, England. *Address:* Mors House, 1 Mill Bank Rd, Mill Bank, Sowerby Bridge, West Yorkshire HX6 3DY, England. *E-mail:* glyn-hughes@novelist-poet.freeserve.co.uk. *Website:* www.novelist-poet.freeserve.co.uk.

HUGHES, Gwyneth; b. 10 May 1929, Berkeley, CA, USA. Poet. m. Henri Lasry, 13 Oct. 1951, 2 s., 1 d. *Education:* BA, University of California, Berkeley, 1949. *Contributions to:* Orbis; Outposts; Envoi; Staple; Pennine Platform; Iota; Writing Women; Wayfarers; Poetry Nottingham; Fatchance; Smiths Knoll; Cardiff Poet; Sphinx; Writer; Poet Lore; Cyclotron; New Athenean. *Memberships:* Theatre Writers' Union; New Playwrights' Trust; Women Writers' Network; Magdalena Project; Welsh Union of Writers; Poetry Society; Dramatists' Guild, USA; Poetry Society of America. *Address:* c/o Lasry, 106 Blvd Diderot, 75012 Paris, France.

HUGHES, Ian. See: PATERSON, Alistair (Ian).

HUGHES, Richard (Edward); b. 31 Oct. 1950, Los Angeles, CA, USA. Writer; Poet; Teacher. m. Dalcy Beatriz Camacho, 24 June 1989, 1 c. *Education:* BA, California State University, 1982; MEd, University of Hawaii, 1985. *Appointments:* Prof. of English as a Second Language, American Samoa Community College, Pago Pago, 1984–86; Instructor in English, Cambria English Institute, Los Angeles, 1986–88; Freelance Writer, 1988–. *Publications:* Isla Grande (novel), 1994; Legends of the Heart (novel), 1997. *Contributions to:* Poems to magazines and anthologies. *Honour:* Henri Coulette Award for Poetry, Acad. of American Poets, 1981. *Memberships:* PEN; Poets and Writers. *Address:* 4902 E Montecito St, Tucson, AZ 85711, USA.

HUGHES, Sophie; b. 24 Sept. 1927, Houlton, Maine, USA. Art Teacher; Artist; Poet. *Education:* BA, English Literature, Barnard College, Columbia University, 1949; MA, Fine Arts, Columbia Teachers' College, 1951; 32 postgraduate credits, various New York colleges. *Appointments:* Asst to Librarian, Columbia College Library, New York City, 1952–55; Art Teacher, Goddard Neighborhood Center, New York City, 1954–58; Painting Teacher, Adult Classes, YMCA, New York City, 1958; Art Teacher, Lexington School for the Deaf, New York City, 1958–83. *Contributions to:* Anthology of Magazine Verse-Yearbook of American Poetry, 1986–88; Art-Life; Candelabrum Chelsea; Confrontation; Cotton Boll-Atlanta Review; Exquisite Corpse; Hollins Critic; Interim; New York Quarterly; Poem; Princeton Spectrum; Sing Heavenly Muse!; Tea Leaves; Writers' Forum. *Membership:* Poets and Writers. *Address:* 49 W 12th St, Apt 2H, New York, NY 10011, USA.

HUGHEY, David Vaughn; b. 19 Jan. 1944, Henderson, Nevada, USA. College Prof.; Poet. *Education:* BA, Sociology, Kent State University, 1967; PhD, Anthropology, University of Pittsburgh, 1977; BS, Business, International College of the Cayman Islands, 1987. *Appointments:* Instructor, Faculty Adviser, Duquesne Magazine, Duquesne University, 1978; Visiting Asst Prof., Santa Clara University, 1979–80; Faculty Mem., 1981–83; Assoc. Prof., 1983–87, Prof., 1992–2001, International College of the Cayman Islands, Grand Cayman; Asst Prof., National-Louis University, Atlanta, GA, 1991–92. *Contributions to:* Driftwood East; CSP World News, Canada; Quintessence; New Earth Review; Bardic Echoes; Feelings; Adventures in Poetry Magazines; Bitterroot; Green Fuse; Hyperion; Journal of Contemporary Poets; McLean County Poetry Review; Orphic Lute; Parnassus Literary Review; Piedmont Literary Review. *Membership:* Poets and Writers. *Address:* 1242 23rd Ave, Longview, WA 98632, USA. *E-mail:* caymanprof@yahoo.com.

HULL, Coral Eileen; b. 12 Dec. 1965, Sydney, NSW, Australia. Poet. *Education:* Bachelor, Creative Arts, University of Wollongong, NSW, Australia, 1987; MA, Deakin University, Vic., Australia, 1994. *Publications:* In the Dog Box of Summer, 1995; William's Mongrels, 1996. *Contributions to:* Hecate; Island; Voices; Poetrix; Scratch; Fine Line; Poetry on Paper; Northern Perspective; Top Dog Journal; Women and Survival; Numerous others. *Honours:* Eaglehawk Dahila Arts Festival Literary Competition, 1985; Philip Larkin Poetry Prize, Wollongong University, 1987; H. M. Butterfly – F. Earle Hooper Award, English Asscn, Sydney Branch, University of Sydney, 1993; Highly Commended, Red Earth Poetry (Open) Category, Northern Territory Literary Awards, Darwin, 1995.

HULLAH, Paul William; b. 26 June 1963, Ripon, England. University Lecturer; Poet. m. Hitomi, 18 May 1996. *Education:* MA, English Language and Literature, Edinburgh University, 1985; PhD, Edinburgh University, 1992. *Appointment:* Foreign Lecturer in English, Okayama University, Japan, 1992–. *Publication:* And Here's What You Could Have Won, 1997. *Contributions to:* Agenda; Thumbscrew; Ibid; Understanding. *Honour:* Shimyaku Poetry Award for Original Poetry in English, Japan, 1997. *Membership:* Iris Murdoch Society of Japan, senior committee mem. *Address:* c/o Faculty of Letters, Okayama University, Tsushimanaka 2-1-1, Okayama 700, Japan.

HULSE, Michael (William); b. 12 June 1955, Stoke-on-Trent, Staffordshire, England. Poet; Writer; Translator; Ed.; Publisher. *Education:* MA, German, University of St Andrews, 1977. *Appointments:* Lecturer, University of Erlangen-Nuremberg, 1977–79, Catholic University of Eichstätt, 1981–83; Part-time Lecturer, University of Cologne, 1985–95; Trans., Deutsche Welle TV, Cologne, 1986–2000; Assoc. Ed., Littlewood Arc, Todmorden, 1992–98; Visiting Lecturer, University of Zürich, 1994; Founder-Editorial Dir, Leviathon publishing house, Amsterdam, 2000–. *Publications:* Poetry: Monochrome Blood, 1980; Dole Queue, 1981; Knowing and Forgetting, 1981; Propaganda, 1985; Eating Strawberries in the Necropolis, 1991; Monteverdi's Photographs, 1995. Other: The New Poetry (with David Kennedy and David Morley), 1993; Numerous trans. *Contributions to:* Anthologies. *Honours:* First Prize, National Poetry Competition, 1978; Second Prize, TLS/Cheltenham Literature Festival Poetry Competition, 1987; First Prizes, Bridport Poetry Competition, 1988, 1994; Hawthornden Castle Fellowship, 1991. *Memberships:* Poetry Society; Society of Authors. *Address:* c/o Leviathan, Amsterdam, Netherlands.

HUMPHREY, Paul; b. 14 Jan. 1915, New York, NY, USA. Poet; Writer. m. Eleanor Nicholson, 22 Feb. 1941, 2 s., 1 d. *Education:* Graduate, DeVeaux Military Acad., 1936; Graduate, 1940, MA, 1948, University of Rochester. *Publications:* Poetry: Burnt Toast, 1977; Surburban Briefs, 1986; Ballad Bar, 1991; The Lighter Touch, 1992. Other: Several prose vols. *Contributions to:* Newspapers, reviews, journals, and magazines. *Honour:* First Prize, Humour, Writers Digest, 1988. *Memberships:* Authors League, New York City; Poets and Writers; Rochester Poets, pres., 1955–88. *Address:* 2329 S Union St, Spencerport, NY 14559, USA.

HUMPHREYS, Emyr Owen; b. 15 April 1919, Clwyd, Wales. Author; Poet. m. Elinor Myfanwy, 1946, 3 s., 1 d. *Education:* University College, Aberystwyth; University College, Bangor. *Publications:* The Little Kingdom, 1946; The Voice of a Stranger, 1949; A Change of Heart, 1951; Hear and Forgive, 1952; A Man's Estate, 1955; The Italian Wife, 1957; A Toy Epic, 1958; The Gift, 1963; Outside the House of Baal, 1965; Natives, 1968; Ancestor Worship, 1970; National Winner, 1971; Flesh and Blood, 1974; Landscapes, 1976; The Best of Friends, 1978; The Kingdom of Bran, 1979; The Anchor Tree, 1980; Pwyll a Riannon, 1980; Miscellany Two, 1981; The Taliesin Tradition, 1983; Salt of the Earth, 1985; An Absolute Hero, 1986; Open Secrets, 1988; The Triple Net, 1988; Bonds of Attachment, 1990; Outside Time, 1991; Unconditional Surrender, 1996; The Gift of a Daughter, 1998; Collected Poems, 1999; Dal Pen Rheswm, 1999; Ghosts and Strangers, 2001; Conversations and Reflections, 2002. *Honours:* Somerset Maugham Award, 1953; Hawthornden Prize, 1959; Society of Authors Travel Award, 1978; Welsh Arts Council Prize, 1983; Hon. DLitt, University of Wales, 1990; Welsh Book of the Year, 1992, 1999; Hon. Prof. of English, University College of North Wales, Bangor. *Membership:* Fellow, RSL, 1991. *Address:* Llinon, Penyberth, Llanfairpwll, Ynys Môn, Gwynedd LL61 5YT, Wales.

HUMPHRIES, Martin Charles; b. 5 April 1955, Bristol, England. Museum Dir; Poet; Ed. *Education:* Assoc., Guildhall School of Music and Drama, London, 1976; BEd, University of London, 1977. *Appointments:* Administrator, Oval House Arts Education Centre; Man., Ronald Grant Archive; Dir, The Cinema Museum. *Publications:* Mirrors, 1980; Searching for a Destination, 1982; Salt and Honey (co-author), 1989. Editor: Not Love Alone: A Modern Gay Anthology, 1985; The Sexuality of Men (co-ed.), 1985; So Long Desired: Poems by James Kirkup and John McRae, 1986; Dreams and Speculations: Poems by Paul Binding and John Horder, 1986; Heterosexuality (co-ed.), 1987; Three New York Poets, 1988; Tongues Untied: 5 Black Gay Poets, 1988. *Contributions to:* Anthologies and other publications. *Address:* 7 Meru Close, London NW5 4AQ, England. *E-mail:* Martin.Humphries@dial.pipex.co.

HUNT, Laird Burnau; b. 3 Sept. 1968, Singapore. Poet; Writer. *Education:* BA, Indiana University, 1990; Naropa Institute, Boulder; MFA, Writing and Politics, 1996; Licencié ès Lettres Modernes, Sorbonne, University of Paris, 1996. *Appointment:* Founder-Publisher, Psalm 51, literary biannual. *Publications:* Canon, 1993; Pieces, 1994; Snow Country, 1995; T.E.L., 1996. *Contributions to:* Various publications. *Honour:* Marianne Moore Scholarship for Poetry and Editing, 1994. *Address:* 3 Rue Ruhmkorff, 75017, Paris, France.

HUNT, Sam; b. 4 July 1946, Auckland, New Zealand. Poet. *Publications:* Between Islands, 1964; A Fat Flat Blues, 1969; Selected Poems, 1965–69, 1970; A Song About Her, 1970; Postcard of a Cabbage Tree, 1970; Bracken Country, 1971; Letter to Jerusalem, 1971; Bottle Creek Blues, 1971; Bottle Creek, 1972; Beware the Man, 1972; Birth on Bottle Creek, 1972; South into Winter, 1973; Roadsong Paekakariki, 1973; Time to Ride, 1976; Drunkards' Garden, 1978; Collected Poems, 1963–80, 1980; Three Poems of Separation, 1981; Running Scared, 1982; Approaches to Paremata, 1985; Selected Poems, 1987. *Address:* PO Box 1, Mana, Wellington, New Zealand.

HURCOT, Jason. See: EVERS, Jason Harvey.

HURFORD, Christopher R.; b. 10 Oct. 1965, Bristol, England. Solicitor's Representative; Poet. *Education:* BA, Honours, English, St John's College, Cambridge, 1988; MA, Creative Writing, Lancaster University, 1989. *Appointments:* Lecturer in English, Catholic University, Lublin, Poland; Harper-Wood Scholar for Poetry, 1991–92; Overseas Aid Worker. *Publications:* Love/Hate (co-author), 1991; Heroes, 1993; Tiger Book of Popular Verse, 1994; Erotic Verse (ed.), 1995. *Contributions to:* Verse; Rialto; Orbis; Contra-Flow; The North; BIS; TLS; Brulion. *Honours:* Master's Prize, Cambridge, 1988; Harper-Wood Scholar, 1991–92. *Address:* 1 Font Lane, West Coker, Yeovil, Somerset BA22 9BP, England.

HURKOVA, Klára; b. 15 Feb. 1962, Prague, Czechoslovakia. Poet. *Education:* PhD, Charles University, Prague, 1986; MA, English Literature and Art, University of Aachen, 1996. *Publications:* Verse z Hor, 1994; Fusspuren auf dem Wasser, 1994; A Season of Blue-Grey Thoughts, 1999; Vor der Sonnenwende, 2002. *Contributions to:* Anthologies, journals and magazines. *Honours:* Two special commendations, Poet of the Year Awards, Hilton House, 1998. *Address:* Svobody 347, 362 35 Abertamy, Czech Republic.

HURLEY, Maureen; b. 24 Nov. 1952, San Francisco, CA, USA. Writer; Poet; Journalist; Photojournalist. *Education:* AA, Arts, College of Marin, 1973; BA, Art, 1975, BA, Expressive Arts, 1981, MA, Creative Writing (Poetry), Sonoma State University. *Appointments:* Artist-in-Residence, various organizations and institutions; Numerous poetry readings. *Publications:* Co-Author: Falling to Sea Level, 1986; Dream Vessels, 1993; We Are Not Swans, 1993. Editor: Several books. *Contributions to:* Various anthologies, reviews, and journals. *Honours:* San Francisco Arts Commission Achievement Award, 1986; National Endowment for the Arts Fellowships, 1990, 1992; Chester H Jones National Poetry Prize, 1992; Anna Davidson Rosenberg Poetry Award on the Jewish Experience, 1994. *Memberships:* California Confederation of the Arts; California Poets in the Schools; National Poetry Asscn; Poets and Writers; Russian River Writers' Guild. *Address:* 7491 Mirable Rd, No. 5, Forestville, CA 95436, USA.

HURST, Frances. See: MAYHAR, Ardath.

HUSSEY, Charlotte Anne; b. 20 Dec. 1945, Portland, Maine, USA. Educator Poet. m. Spiro Arriotis, 21 April 1991, 1 d. *Education:* BA, Wheaton College Norton, Massachusetts, 1968; MA, Concordia University, Montréal, 1979 MFA, Warren Wilson College, Swannanod, North Carolina, 1991 *Appointments:* Co-ordinator, Teacher, Centre for Continuing Education an Creative Writing Programmes, McGill University, Montréal; Prof., Creative Writing Programme, Concordia University; Literary Critic, Montreal Gazette *Publication:* Rue Sainte Famille, 1990. *Contributions to:* Anthologies, review and journals. *Memberships:* League of Canadian Poets; Maine Writers an Publishers' Alliance; Women and Words/Les Femmes et les Mots, Writin Workshop; Montréal's Tuesday Night Group. *Address:* c/o League o Canadian Poets, 24 Ryerson Ave, Toronto, Ontario M5T 2P3, Canada.

HUTTERLI, Kurt; b. 18 Aug. 1944, Bern, Switzerland. Writer; Poet; Artist. m Marianne Büchler, 7 July 1966, 1 s., 1 d. *Education:* Secondary School Teache Diploma, University of Bern, 1966. *Publications:* Aber, 1972; Herzgrün, 1974 Felsengleich, 1976; Die Faltsche, 1977; Das Matterköpfen, 1978; Ein Hausmann, 1980; Finnlandisiert, 1982; Überlebenslust, 1986; Elchspur 1986; Baccalà, 1989; Gaunerblut, 1990; Mir kommt kein Tier ins Haus, 1991 Stachelflieder, 1991; Katzensprung, 1993; Die sanfte Piratin, 1994; In Fischbauch, 1998; Hotel Goldtown, 2000; Der Clown im Mond, 2000; Arche Titanic, 2000; Das Centovalli Brautgeschenk, 2002. *Contributions to:* Der Bund Stuttgarter Zeitung; Drehpunkt; Einspruch. *Honours:* Poetry Prize, City of Bern, 1971; Book Prizes, City of Bern, 1972, 1978; Theatre Awards, 1976, 1982 1987. *Memberships:* PEN Switzerland; Autorengruppe Olten; Berne Schriftsteller-Verein. *Address:* RR2, S53/C9, Oliver, BC V0H 1T0, Canada.

HUY-LUC. See: BUI, Khoi Tien.

HYDE, Lewis; b. 16 Oct. 1945, Boston, MA, USA. Prof. of Creative Writing Author; Poet; Ed.; Trans. m. Patricia Auster Vigderman, 27 Nov. 1981, 1 step-s. *Education:* BA, Sociology, University of Minnesota, 1967; MA, Comparative Literature, University of Iowa, 1972. *Appointments:* Instructor in Literature, University of Iowa, 1969–71; Lecturer in Expository Writing, 1983–85, Briggs-Copeland Asst Prof. of English, 1985–89, Dir, Creative Writing Programme, 1988–89, Harvard University; Henry R. Luce Prof. of Art and Politics, 1989–2001, Richard L. Thomas Prof. of Creative Writing, 2001–, Kenyon College. *Publications:* Twenty Poems of Vicente Aleixandre (ed. and trans. with Robert Bly), 1977; A Longing for the Light: Selected Poems of Vicente Aleixandre (ed. and trans. with others), 1979; World Alone, by Vicente Aleixandre (trans. with David Unger), 1982; The Gift: Imagination and the Erotic Life of Property, 1983; On the Work of Allen Ginsberg (ed.), 1984; Alcohol and Poetry: John Berryman and the Booze Talking, 1986; This Error is the Sign of Love (poems), 1988; Trickster Makes This World: Mischief, Myth, and Art, 1998; Selected Essays of Henry D. Thoreau (ed. and annotator), 2002. *Contributions to:* Numerous journals, quarterlies, reviews, etc. Honours; Acad. of American Poets Prize, 1966; National Endowment for the Arts Creative Writing Fellowships, 1977, 1982, 1987; Columbia University Trans. Center Award, 1979; National Endowment for the Humanities Fellowship for Independent Study and Research, 1979; Massachusetts Council on the Arts and Humanities Fellowship In Poetry, 1980; MacDowell Colony Fellowships, 1989, 1991, 1996, 1999, 2000; Scholar-in-Residence, Rockefeller Study and Conference Center, Bellagio, Italy, 1991; John D. and Catherine T. MacArthur Foundation Fellowship, 1991–96; Getty Scholar, 1993–94; Hon. DFA, San Francisco Art Institute, 1997; Osher Fellow, 1998. *Address:* PO Box 613, Gambier, OH 43022, USA.

HYLAND, Paul Robert; b. 15 Sept. 1947, Poole, Dorset, England. Poet; Travel Writer. *Education:* BSc, Honours, Bristol University, 1968. *Publications:* Purbeck: The Ingrained Island, 1978; Wight: Biography of an Island, 1984; The Black Heart, 1988; Indian Balm, 1994; Backwards Out of the Big World, 1996; Discover Dorset: Isle of Purbeck, 1998. Poetry: Poems of Z, 1982; The Stubborn Forest, 1984; Getting into Poetry, 1992; Kicking Sawdust, 1995. *Honours:* Eric Gregory Award, 1976; Alice Hunt Bartlett Award, 1985; Authors Foundation, 1995. *Memberships:* Society of Authors; Poetry Society; PEN. *Literary Agent:* David Higham Assocs Ltd. *Address:* 32 Colliton St, Dorchester, Dorset DT1 1XH, England.

I

IBSEN, Arni. See: THORGEIRSSON, Arni Ibsen.

IDDINGS, Kathleen; b. 25 June 1945, West Milton, Ohio, USA. Poet; Writer; Ed.; Publisher. Divorced, 1 s., 3 d. *Education:* BS, Education: Miami University, Oxford, Ohio, 1968; University of California at San Diego; Napa College; Mira Costa College. *Appointments:* Ed. and Publisher, San Diego Poets Press, La Jolla Poets Press. *Contributions to:* Hundreds of poems in anthologies and other publications. *Honours:* National Endowment for the Arts Fellowship, 1986; PEN America Writer's Grant, 1989; Djerassi Arts Colony Residency, 1990. *Memberships:* Acad. of American Poets; Asscn of Women Poets; Independent Scholars, San Diego; PEN America; World Poetry Society. *Address:* PO Box 8638, La Jolla, CA 92038, USA.

IGLESIAS SERNA, Amalia; b. 8 Jan. 1962, Menaza, Palencia, Spain. Writer; Poet; Journalist. *Education:* Licentiate, Philosophy and Letters, University of Deusto, Bilbao. *Publications:* Un lugar para el fuego, 1985; Memorial de Amauta, 1988; Mar en sombra, 1989. *Contributions to:* Anthologies and magazines. *Honours:* Adonais Prize, 1984; Alonso de Ercilla del Gobierno Vasco Prize, 1987. *Address:* c/o Constanilla de Santiago 2, 4° iqda, 28013 Madrid, Spain.

IKEDA, Daisaku; b. 2 Jan. 1928, Tokyo, Japan. Buddhist Philosopher; Writer; Poet. m. Kaneko Shiraki, 1952, 2 s. *Education:* Fuji College. *Appointments:* Pres., Soka Gakkai Institute, 1975–; Founder, Soka University, Soka University of America, Soka Women's College, Tokyo, Kansai Soka Schools, Soka Kindergartens, Makiguchi Foundation for Education, Institute of Oriental Philosophy, Boston Research Center for the 21st Century, Toda Institute for Global Peace and Policy Research, Tokyo, Shizuoka Fuji Art Museum, Min-On Concert Asscn, Victor Hugo House of Literature, Komeito Party. *Publications:* The Human Revolution, five vols, 1972–99; Choose Life: A Dialogue with Arnold Toynbee, 1976; The Living Buddha, 1976; Buddhism: The First Millennium, 1977; Songs From My Heart, 1978; Glass Children and Other Essays, 1979; La nuit appelle l'aurore, 1980; Letters of Four Seasons, 1980; A Lasting Peace, two vols, 1981, 1987; Life: An Enigma, a Precious Jewel, 1982; Before it is too Late, 1984; Buddhism and the Cosmos, 1985; The Flower of Chinese Buddhism, 1986; Human Values in a Changing World (with Bryan Wilson), 1987; Unlocking the Mysteries of Birth and Death, 1988; The Snow Country Prince, 1990; A Lifelong Quest for Peace (with Linus Pauling), 1992; Choose Peace (with Johan Galtung), 1995; A New Humanism: The University Addresses of Daisaku Ikeda, 1996; The Wisdom of the Lotus Sutra (in Japanese), four vols, 1996–2000; The Way of Youth, 2000; For the Sake of Peace, 2000; Soka Education, 2001; Dialogue pour la paix, 2001; The World is Yours to Change, 2002. *Other:* Writings on Buddhism, civilization, life and peace. *Contributions to:* Newspapers, magazines and books. *Honours:* Poet Laureate, World Acad. of Arts and Culture, 1981; UN Peace Award, 1983; Kenya Oral Literature Award, 1986; World Poet Laureate Award, World Poetry Society, 1995; Tagore Peace Award, 1997; Hon. doctorates, Moscow State University, 1975, University of Sofia, 1981, University of Buenos Aires, 1990, University of the Philippines, 1991, University of Glasgow, 1994, University of Hong Kong, 1996, University of Havana, 1996, University of Ghana, 1996, University of Delhi, 1999, Queen's College, City University of New York, 2000, Morehouse College, 2002; Hon. Profs, National University of San Marcos, 1981, University of Beijing, 1984. *Memberships:* Brazilian Acad. of Letters, non-resident mem.; Pan-African Writers' Asscn, hon. founding-mem.; European Acad. of Sciences and Arts, hon. senator; International Poetry for Peace Asscn, hon. mem.; Writers' Asscn of Kenya, hon. mem. *Address:* 32 Shinano-machi, Shinjuku-ku, Tokyo 160-8583, Japan. *Telephone:* (3) 5360-9831. *Fax:* (3) 5360-9885. *Website:* www.sgi.org.

IKEDA, Kazuyosi; b. 15 July 1928, Fukuoka, Japan. Prof. Emeritus of Theoretical Physics; Poet; Writer. m. Mieko Ikeda, 20 Nov. 1956, 1 s., 1 d. *Education:* Graduated, 1951, Postgraduate Studies, 1951–56, DSc, 1957, Dept of Physics, Kyushu University. *Appointments:* Asst, 1956–60, Assoc. Prof., 1960–65, Kyushu University; Assoc. Prof., 1965–68, Prof. of Theoretical Physics, 1968–89, Prof. of Theoretical and Mathematical Physics, 1989–92, Prof. Emeritus, 1992–, Osaka University; Prof., 1992, Pres., 1995–, International Earth Environment University, Japan; Board Mem. of Advisory Council, Ansted University, 1999. *Publications:* Serialized Poems of Fixed Form in Seven and Five Syllable Metre (subjects including Migratory Birds, Fierce Animals, Marine Animals, Fierce Birds, Fishing Implements, Mountains), 1979–; Bansyoo Hyakusi (A Hundred Poems on All Creation), 1986; A Physicist's Modern Poems, 1989–91; The World of God, Creation and Poetry, 1991; Intercultural Communication in Poetry, 1993; Poems on the Hearts of Creation, 1993; International Intercourse Among Poets, 1995; Mountains, 1995; North, South, East and West, 1996; Poems on Love and Peace, 1998; Poetry on the Animate and the Inanimate, 1998; Hearts of Myriad Things in the Universe, 1998; Songs of the Soul, 1999; Hearts of Innumerous Things in Heaven and Earth, 2000; The World of Hearts, 2002; Kazuyosi's Poems on

Myriad Things, 2002. *Other:* Over 100 scientific papers; numerous scientific books; Trans of Shakespeare's Sonnets into Japanese Poems of Fixed Form, 1994. *Contributions to:* Periodicals, including: Chishiki magazine; Osaka University newspaper; Mainichi Shimbun newspaper; World Poetry; Modern Poetry; Shintenchi magazine; Poets International Journal; Poet Journal; Samvedana; Anthologies, including: Olympic Anthologies; The First 100; Barcelona '92; The Relay of Opinions; Olympoetry '94. *Honours:* International Cultural Diploma of Honor, 1989; Grand Ambassador of Achievement, 1989; International Order of Merit, 1990; Chevalier Grand Cross, 1991; Golden Acad. Award for Lifetime Achievement, 1991; International Honors Cup, 1992; Silver Shield of Valour, 1992; Award of International Eminent Poet, 1993; Prize Catania e il suo Vulcano, 1994; Prize Catania Duomo, 1995; Hon. DLitt, 1995; Knight of Year, International Writers and Artists Asscn, 1995; Knight of Templar Order, Lofsensic Ursinus Order, Holy Grail Order, Universal Knights Order, San Ciriaco Order, 1995; Albert Einstein Acad. Award for Outstanding Achievement, 1998; World Laureate, 1999; Cult. Dr Poet. Lit., 1999; Best World Poet of the Year, 1999; Poet of Millennium, 2000; Gran Premio d'Autore, 2000; N. S. Chandra Bose National Award for Excellence, 2001; Companion of Honour, 2001; Knight Commander, 2001; Ambassador of Grand Eminence, 2002. *Memberships:* United Writers Asscn; World Literary Acad.; International Poets Acad.; World Congress of Poets; World Acad. of Arts and Culture; World Institute of Achievement; Hon. Founder, Olympoetry Movement; Academician of Honour, Accademia Ferdinandea di Scienze, Lettere ed Arti; Charter Mem., Order of International Fellowship; Hon. Dir, World Parnassians Guild International; Board Mem., Modern Poets Society; Senator, Maison Internationale des Intellectuels; Founding Mem., London Diplomatic Acad.; Founding Charter Mem., Leading Intellectuals of the World; Chief Exec., Michael Madhusudan Acad.; Founder, American Order of Excellence; Founder, Scientific Faculty of Cambridge; Senator, Minister Plenipotentiary for Japan, International Parliament for Safety and Peace; Senator, Minister Plenipotentiary for Asian States, Council of the States for Protection of Life. *Address:* Nisi-7-7-11 Aomadani, Minoo-si, Osaka 562-0023, Japan.

ILLO, Maria; b. 6 July 1949, New York, NY, USA. Writer; Poet. *Education:* PhD, Philosophy, Columbia University, 1979. *Publications:* Mirrors for the Unnamed Flower, 1976; Songs of Flight and Song of the Lute, 1980; The Way of the Soul, 1990. *Contributions to:* Reviews and magazines. *Honours:* First Award, National Federation of State Poetry Societies, 1979; First Prize, California State Poetry Society, 1979; Grand International Prize, IFTO, 1986; Delong Prizes, 1987, 1988, 1989; First Prize, Tokyo Literary Society, 1988; Second Place, National Writers Club, 1989; First Prize, Southern Rose Review, 1990; First Prize, Poetic Page, 1992; First Prize, PN Magazine, 1992. *Address:* 1000 Jackson Keller, No. 3101, San Antonio, TX 78213, USA.

IMALAYEN, Fatima-Zohra. See: DJEBAR, Assia.

IMIDA, Louise. See: CRATE, Joan.

INDERMILL, Marilyn, (Marcus Ivan Windorquill); b. 8 Aug. 1948, CO, USA. Poet. *Education:* Alliance Française, Paris, 1969–70; BA, English Literature, University of Colorado, 1971. *Publications:* Tales of Ancient Trees, 1979; The Asboo Bampin Forest and Other Places I Have Known, 1985; A Photographic Essay, 1986; Quill on the Wind, 1986; Land of the Quick Draw Howdy, 1987; Asboo Bampin Forest Books for a Better Future: The Magical World, 1990. *Contributions to:* Anthologies and other publications. *Honours:* Golden Poet Awards, World of Poetry, 1989, 1990. *Address:* 787 18th St, Boulder, CO 80302, USA. *E-mail:* marilyni1@juno.com.

INDU. See: SRINIVASAN, Indira.

INEZ, Colette; b. 23 June 1931, Brussels, Belgium. Poet; Teacher. m. Saul Stadtmauer, 26 July 1964. *Education:* BA, English Literature, Hunter College, USA, 1961. *Appointments:* Faculty, The New School, New York City, 1973–83; Poetry Instructor, Kalamazoo College, 1975, 1976, 1978, 1985, 1989, State University of New York, Stony Brook, 1975; Visiting Prof., Kalamazoo College, 1978; Instructor, Writing Programme, Columbia University, 1983–; Visiting Prof., Ohio University, 1990; Poet-in-Residence, Bucknell University, 1992; Visiting Prof., Cornell University, 1998, Colgate University, 2000. *Publications:* The Woman Who Loved Worms, 1972; Alive and Talking Names, 1977; Eight Minutes from the Sun, 1983; Family Life, 1988; Getting Underway: New and Selected Poetry, 1993; Naming the Moons, 1993; For Reasons of Music, 1994; Clemency, 1998. *Contributions to:* Anthologies and periodicals, including: Nation; Partisan Review; Hudson Review; Poetry; New Republic; Yale Review; Ohio Review; Beloit Poetry Journal; Harvard Magazine; Antioch Review; Chicago Review; Poetry Northwest; Ms Magazine; Texas Quarterly Review; American Voice; Prairie Schooner; Poetry; American Poetry Review; Michigan Quarterly Review; Humanist; Virginia Quarterly

Review; Poetry Australia; Yankee; Helicon Nine; Antaes. *Honours:* Reedy Memorial Award, 1973, Kreymborg Award, 1976, Poetry Society of America; National First Book Award, Great Lakes Colleges Asscn, 1973; Fellowships, National Endowment for the Arts, 1974, 1988, New York State CAPS, 1975, Yaddo, 1980, 1986, 1988, 1989, 1990, Rockefeller, 1980, Ragdale, 1982, 1984, Virginia Colony for the Creative Arts, 1983, 1986, 1987, 1988, Guggenheim, 1985–86, Leighton Art Center, Banff, Canada, 1986, Blue Mountain Center, 1988–93, Djerassi Foundation, 1989, New York State Foundation for the Arts, 1994, Medway Institute, 2002; Pushcart Prizes, 1986–98; Norma Millay honoree, Millay Colony, 1991. *Memberships:* Poetry Society of America; PEN American Center; Poet's Prize. *Address:* 5 W 86th St, New York, NY 10024, USA.

INSINGEL, Mark; b. 3 May 1935, Antwerp, Belgium. Poet; Author. *Education:* Koninklijk Vlaams Muziekconservatorium, Antwerp; Drama Studies, 1954–57; French Literature, Sorbonne, University of Paris, 1957–59. *Publications:* Drijfhout, 1963; Een Kooi Van Licht, 1966; Perpetuum Mobile, 1969; Modellen, 1970; Reflections (novel), 1971; Posters, 1974; Dat Wil Zeggen, 1975; A Course of Time (novel), 1977; Gezwel Van Wortels, 1978; Het Is Zo Niet Zo Is Het, 1978; When a Lady (prose), 1982; My Territory (novel), 1985; Een Meisje Nam de Tram, 1983; Jij Noemt Stom Wat Taal Is, 1986; In Elkanders Armen, 1990; De Een En de Ander, 1991; De Druiven Die Te Hoog Hangen, 1993; Eenzaam Lichaam, 1996. *Contributions to:* Books and journals. *Honours:* Tweejaarlijkse Prijs van De Vlaamse Gids, 1970; Arthur Merghelynckprijs van de Koninklijke Academie voor Nederlandse Letterkunde, 1974; Visser-Neerlandiaprijs, 1974; Dirk Martensprijs, 1978. *Memberships:* PEN Centre, Belgian-Dutch speaking; Maatschappij voor Nederlandse Letterkunde te Leiden. *Address:* Rucaplein 205, 2610 Antwerp, Belgium

IOANNOU, Susan; b. 4 Oct. 1944, Toronto, Ontario, Canada. Writer; Poet. m. Lazaros Ioannou, 28 Aug. 1967, 1 s., 1 d. *Education:* BA, 1966, MA, 1967, University of Toronto. *Appointments:* Managing Ed., Coiffure du Canada, 1979–80; Assoc. Ed., Cross-Canada Writers' Magazine, 1980–89; Poetry Ed., Arts Scarborough Newsletter, 1980–85; Poetry Instructor, Toronto Board of Education, 1982–94, University of Toronto, 1989–90; Dir, Wordwrights Canada, 1985–. *Publications:* Spare Words, 1984; Motherpoems, 1985; The Crafted Poem, 1985; Familiar Faces, Private Griefs, 1986; Ten Ways to Tighten Your Prose, 1988; Writing Reader-Friendly Poems, 1989; Clarity Between Clouds, 1991; Read-Aloud Poems: For Students from Elementary through Senior High School, 1993; Polly's Punctuation Primer, 1994; Where the Light Waits, 1996; A Real Farm Girl, 1998; A Magical Clockwork: The Art of Writing the Poem, 2000. *Honours:* Arts Scarborough Poetry Award, 1987; Media Club of Canada Memorial Award, 1990; Okanagan Short Story Award, 1997. *Memberships:* League of Canadian Poets; Writers' Union of Canada; Arts and Letters Club of Toronto; Canadian Poetry Asscn. *Address:* c/o Wordwrights Canada, PO Box 456, Station O, Toronto, Ontario M4A 2P1, Canada.

IRANI, Rustom Bailty; b. 1 Aug. 1962, London, England. Poet; Television Journalist. *Education:* Selwyn College, Cambridge, 1981–84; MA, Theology and Religious Studies, Cambridge University; Postgraduate Diploma in Journalism, City University, London, 1984–85. *Contributions to:* Grass Roots (anthology of new poets); Magazines including: Outposts; Speaking in Tongues. *Address:* 1 Queensborough Terrace, Queensway, London W2, England.

IRBY, Kenneth (Lee); b. 18 Nov. 1936, Bowie, TX, USA. Writer; Poet; Teacher. *Education:* BA, Univerity of Kansas; MA, 1960, PhD, 1962–63, Harvard University; MLS, University of California, 1968. *Appointment:* Assoc. Prof. of English, University of Kansas, Lawrence. *Publications:* The Roadrunner Poem, 1964; Kansas-New Mexico, 1965; Movements/Sequences, 1965; The Flower of Having Passed Through Paradise in a Dream, 1968; Relation, 1970; To Max Douglas, 1971; Archipelago, 1976; Catalpa, 1977; Orexis, 1981; Riding the Dog, 1982; A Set, 1983; Call Steps, 1992; Antiphonal and Fall to Fall, 1994. *Contributions to:* Anthologies and magazines. *Address:* N-311 Regency Pl., Lawrence, KS 66049, USA.

IRELAND, Allen Lee; b. 10 Oct. 1969, Quakertown, Pennsylvania, USA. Poet. *Education:* BA, English, 1990; Teacher Certification, 1992, MA, English, University of North Carolina, Greensboro. *Contributions to:* Lyric; Breakthrough!; Candelabrum; Parnassus Literary Journal; Eclectic Muse; Tucumcari Literary Review. *Honours:* Second Honourable Mention, Archibald Rutledge Contest, Poetry Council of North Carolina, 1989; Runner-up, Second Annual Poetry Contest, Eclectic Muse, 1992. *Address:* 2005 Spring Garden St, Greensboro, NC 27403, USA.

IRELAND, Kevin Mark; b. 18 July 1933, Auckland, New Zealand. Writer; Poet. m. Phoebe Caroline Dalwood, 2 s. *Appointments:* Writer-in-Residence, Canterbury University, 1986; Sargeson Fellow, 1987, Literary Fellow, 1989, Auckland University. *Publications:* Poetry: Face to Face, 1964; Educating the Body, 1967; A Letter From Amsterdam, 1972; Poems, 1974, A Grammar of Dreams, 1975; Literary Cartoons, 1978; The Dangers of Art: Poems 1975–80, 1980; Practice Night in the Drill Hall, 1984; The Year of the Comet, 1986; Selected Poems, 1987; Tiberius at the Beehive, 1990; Skinning a Fish, 1994; Anzac Day: Selected Poems, 1997; Fourteen Reasons for Writing, 2001. Other: Sleeping with the Angels (stories), 1995; Blowing My Top (novel), 1996; The Man Who Never Lived (novel), 1997; Under the Bridge and Over the Moon (memoir), 1998; The Craymore Affair (novel), 2000; Backwards to Forwards (memoir), 2002. *Honours:* New Zealand National Book Award for Poetry, 1979; Commemorative Medal, 1990; O.B.E., 1992; Montana Award for History and Biography, 1999; Hon. DLitt, 2000. *Membership:* NZSA (PEN). *Address:* 8 Domain St, Devonport, Auckland 9, New Zealand.

IRION, Mary Jean; b. 6 Nov. 1922, Newport, KY, USA. Writer; Poet. m. Paul Irion, 29 Aug. 1944, 1 s., 1 d. *Education:* BA, Millersville State College, 1966. *Appointments:* English Teacher, Lancaster Country Day School, Pennsylvania, 1968–73; Visiting Lecturer, Theology, Literature, Lancaster Theological Seminary, Lancaster, 1985–; Founder, Dir, The Writers Center, Chautauqua, New York, 1988–97. *Publications:* Holding On. *Contributions to:* Poetry; Prairie Schooner; Yankee; New England Review; Western Humanities Review; Southern Humanities Review; The Christian Century; Southwest Review; Poet Lore; Poet and Critic; Ladies' Home Journal; The Literary Review; Others. *Honours:* First Place, Unicorn Award, 1976, Third Prize, Wisconsin Award, 1985, National Federation of State Poetry Societies; Prize, Chautauqua Poetry Workshop, 1976, 1977, 1978; Honourable Mention, Lucille Medwick Award, 1983; Honourable Mention, Wildwood Poetry Festival, 1988; Ruth Lake Memorial Award, Poetry Society of America, 1993. *Memberships:* Fellow, Society for the Arts and Religion in Contemporary Culture; Poets and Writers; Acad. of American Poets; Poetry Society of America. *Address:* 149 Kready Ave, Millersville, PA 17551, USA.

ISSAIA, Nana; b. 1 Oct. 1934, Athens, Greece. Poet; Essayist; Writer; Trans.; Painter; Broadcaster. *Education:* Secretarial Course, Denson Secretarial College, London; First Pitman Diploma, 1953; Studied Painting, Free Workshop of Fine Arts, 1958–62. *Appointments:* Private Secretary to Prime Minister Karamanlis, 1958–63; Broadcasting, Fourth National Programme, ERA 4, 1989. *Publications:* Poems, 1969; Six Poets, collective edn, 1971; Persona, 1972; One Glance, 1974; Nights and Days of No Importance, 1977; Alice in Wonderland, 1977; Form, 1980; The Tactics of Passion (prose and poetry), 1982; Realization of Forgetting, 1982. Fiction: The Various Aspects of the Game, 1990; The Only Possible Adventure, 1994; The Story Then and Now, 1997; The Unknown Adventure of the Soul, 1998; An Affair Variating Another, 2001. *Contributions to:* Anthologies, newspapers, journals and magazines, including To Bima. *Honour:* State Prize for Poetry, 1981. *Memberships:* Society of Greek Writers; Greek Society of World Trans of Literature; Greek PEN Club. *Address:* Iridanou 3, GR 115 28 Athens, Greece.

IVANOVA, Mirela Tsvetkova; b. 11 May 1962, Sofia, Bulgaria. Writer; Poet; Ed. *Education:* German Language School, 1981; Plovdiv St Paissii Hilendarski University, 1985. *Appointments:* Ed., Literaturen Front, weekly, Detsa, Izkoustvo, Knigi, bimonthly. *Publications:* Stone Wings, 1985; Whispers, 1990; Lonely Game, 1990; Memory for Details, 1992. *Contributions to:* Literaturen Vestnik; Plamak; Septemvri; Savremennik; Poetry Review; Litfass; Sunk Island Review; Scratch; Textura. *Honour:* Poetry Award, Union of Bulgarian Writers, 1992. *Membership:* Union of Bulgarian Writers. *Address:* Mladost II, blvd 221-A, apt 19, Sofia 1799, Bulgaria.

IVENS, Michael William, (Yorick); b. 15 March 1924, England. Writer; Poet. m. (1) Rosalie Turnbull, (2) Katherine Laurence, 5 s., 1 d. *Appointments:* Ed., Twentieth Century; Dir, STD Telephone and Cable, Aims of Industry, Foundation for Business Responsibilities; Yorick Column, Time and Tide; Free Nation. *Publications:* Another Sky, 1963; Last Waltz, 1964; Private and Public, 1968; Born Early, 1975; No Woman is An Island, 1983; New Divine Comedy, 1990. *Contributions to:* Poetry Review; Outposts; Oxford Book of Twentieth Century Verse; New Poetry of the Commonwealth; After a War; Poetry and Business Life. *Honour:* C.B.E., 1983. *Address:* 2 Mulgrave Rd, London NW10 1BT, England.

IVESON, David. See: HALL, David.

IVIMY, May. See: BADMAN, May Edith.

J

JABBOURI, Youssif A. B. D. Al-Jabbar al-; b. 1 July 1951, Thekar, Iraq. Poet; Writer. m. 16 Feb. 1978, 1 s., 2 d. *Appointments:* Ed.-in-Chief, Atlas, 1993; Exec. General Man., Ed.-in-Chief, Tuqus, 1998. *Publications:* Thabaht al wardan, 1977; Sakhab tur Moshaksh, 1978; Olmpead al Luga of Maaglh, 1980; Lash Urasm Fawasl, 1980; Nyskhat al Thahub al Ola, 1988; Al Imbaratur, 1995; Tayran fawq al Nahar, 1995; Al taalif Ban tabakot Al Layl, 1997. *Contributions to:* Various publications. *Memberships:* Arab Writers Union; Dansk Writers Union. *Address:* Blegdammen 10 D 1, 4000 Roskilde, Denmark.

JACCOTTET, Philippe; b. 30 June 1925, Moudon, Switzerland. Poet. *Education:* Graduated, University of Lausanne, 1946. *Publications:* Poetry: Requiem, 1947; L'Effraie et autres poésies, 1953; L'ignorant: Poèmes 1952–56. Airs: Poèmes 1961–64; Poésie 1946–67; Leçons, 1969; Chants d'en bas, 1974; Breathings, 1974; Pensées sous les nuages, 1983; Selected Poems, 1987; Cahier de verdure, 1990; Libretto, 1990. Other: Through the Orchard, 1975; Des Histoires de passage: Prose 1948–78; Autres Journées, 1987; Trans. of works by Robert Musil, Thomas Mann, Leopardi, Homer and Hölderlin. *Honour:* Larbaud Prize, 1978. *Address:* c/o Editions Gallimard, 5 rue Sebastien-Bottin, 75007 Paris, France.

JACKOWSKA, Nicki; b. 6 Aug. 1942, Brighton, Sussex, England. Poet; Novelist; Writer; Teacher. m. Andrzej Jackowski, 1 May 1970, divorced, 1 d. *Education:* ANEA Acting Diploma, 1965; BA, 1977, MA, 1978, University of Sussex. *Appointments:* Founder-Tutor, Brighton Writing School; Writer-in-Residence at various venues; Readings; Radio and television appearances. *Publications:* The House That Manda Built, 1981; Doctor Marbles and Marianne, 1982; Earthwalks, 1982; Letters to Superman, 1984; Gates to the City, 1985; The Road to Orc, 1985; The Islanders, 1987; News from the Brighton Front, 1993; Write for Life, 1997; Lighting a Slow Fuse, New and Selected Poems, 1998. *Contributions to:* Various publications. *Honours:* Winner, Stroud Festival Poetry Competition, 1972; Continental Bursary, South East Arts, 1978; C. Day-Lewis Fellowship, 1982; Arts Council Writer's Fellowship, 1984–85; Arts Council of England Writer's Bursary, 1994. *Membership:* Poetry Society. *Address:* c/o Judy Martin Agency, 94 Goldhurst Terrace, London, NW6 3HS, England.

JACKSON, Alan; b. 6 Sept. 1938, Liverpool, Lancashire, England. Poet. m. Margaret Dickson, 1963, 2 s. *Education:* Edinburgh University, 1956–59, 1964–65. *Appointments:* Founding Dir, Kevin Press, Edinburgh, 1965; Dir, Live Readings, Scotland, 1967–. *Publications:* Under Water Wedding, 1961; Sixpenny Poems, 1962; Well Ye Ken Noo, 1963; All Fall Down, 1965; The Worstest Beast, 1967; Penguin Modern Poets, 1968; The Grim Wayfarer, 1969; Idiots are Freelance, 1973; Heart of the Sun, 1986; Salutations: Collected Poems, 1960–89, 1990. *Honours:* Scottish Arts Council Bursaries. *Address:* c/o Polygon, 22 George Sq., Edinburgh EH8 9LF, Scotland.

JACKSON, Andrew John; b. 27 Oct. 1962, Winchester, Hampshire, England. Poet. *Education:* BA, Honours, History/English, College of Ripon and York St John, 1985–89. *Contributions to:* Poetry Now Anthology: Love Lines, 1995; Poetry Now Anthology: Book of Traditional Verse, 1995; Poetry Now: Indelible Ink (anthology), 1995; Poetry Now magazine; Rivet magazine. *Address:* 100 Priors Dean Rd, Harestock, Winchester, Hampshire SO22 6LA, England.

JACKSON, Richard Paul; b. 17 Nov. 1946, Lawrence, Massachusetts, USA. Writer; Poet; College Prof.; Ed. m. Theresa Harvey, 19 June 1999, 1 d. *Education:* BA, Merrimack College, 1969; MA, Middlebury College, 1972; PhD, Yale University, 1976. *Appointments:* Journal Ed., University of Tennessee at Chattanooga; Faculty, Vermont College, MFA, 1988–. *Publications:* Part of the Story, 1983; Acts of Mind, 1983; Worlds Apart, 1987; Dismantling Time in Contemporary Poetry, 1989; Alive All Day, 1993; Heart's Bridge, 1999; Heartwall, 2000; Half Lives, 2001. *Contributions to:* Georgia Review; Antioch Review; North American Review; New England Review. *Honours:* National Endowment for the Humanities Fellowship, 1980; National Endowment for the Arts Fellowship, 1985; Fulbright Exchange Fellowships, 1986, 1987; Agee Prize, 1989; CSU Poetry Award, 1992; Juniper Prize, 2000; 4 Pushcart Prizes. *Memberships:* Sarajevo Committee of Slovene PEN; Associated Writing Programs. *Address:* 3413 Alta Vista Dr., Chattanooga, TN 37411, USA.

JACKSON, Rueben M.; b. 1 Oct. 1956, Augusta, GA, USA. Archivist; Poet. m. Jacquelyn Carrie Kathleen Hunter, 24 Sept. 1983. *Education:* BA, English Literature, 1978, Goddard College, Plainfield, Vermont; MLS Library and Information Science, 1984, University of the District of Columbia. *Appointments:* Library Technician, Smithsonian Institution Libraries, 1983–85; Asst Librarian, Museum of African Art, 1985–87; Children's Librarian, District of Columbia Public Library, 1987–89; Archivist, Smithsonian Institution's Duke Ellington Collection, 1989–. *Publication:*

Fingerin the Keys, 1991. *Contributions to:* Indiana Review; Plum Review; Black American Literature Forum; Christian Science Monitor; Visions; Washington Review; Folio; Catalyst; Washington Post; Processed World; Painted Bride Quarterly; Chelsea; Washington City Paper; Lip Service; Tryst; Library Journal; Washington Post. *Honours:* Runner-up, Grolier Poetry Prize, Cambridge, Massachusetts, 1986; Honourable Mention, Visions Magazine Poetry Competition, 1989; Runner-up, Larry Neal Award, Washington, DC, 1992. *Address:* 519 Powhatan Pl. NW, Washington, DC 20011, USA.

JACKSON, William David; b. 15 July 1947, Liverpool, England. Freelance Journalist; Trans.; Poet. m. Christa Antonie Range, 3 June 1972, 1 s., 1 d. *Education:* BA, Honours, English Language and Literature, St Catherine's College, Oxford, 1968. *Contributions to:* Acumen; Babel; The Dark Horse; Iron; Leviathan Quarterly; Metre; Modern Poetry in Translation; Orbis; Outposts; Oxford Poetry; Pennine Platform; Poetry Review; Poetry Wales; Stand; Staple; Rialto; Then and Now, Vol. I, 2002. *Address:* Clemensstrasse 66, 80796 Munich, Germany.

JACOB, Thekkalthyparampil Samuel; b. 2 Oct. 1941, Keezhuvaipur, Kerala, India. Teacher; Writer; Poet. m. Thankamma Jacob, 21 Nov. 1971, 1 s., 1 d. *Education:* BA, 1968; MA, 1970. *Appointments:* Clerk, Mandle District Collector's Office, MP India, 1962; Postal Clerk, Indian Postal Dept, 1963–70; Mem., Exec. Body, Kerala Cultural Asscn, Indore, 1968–70; High School Teacher, Uganda, 1972; Headmaster, Pro-High School Ungma, Nagaland, India, 1973–75; Lecturer, M T College, Wokha, Nagaland, India, 1976–; Guest Ed., Gruha Deepam magazine, Deepam Book Club, Vennikulam, Kerala, India, 1994; Editorial Board Mem., Hon. Dir, International Socio Literary Foundation, Karnataka State, India, 1996–; Vice-Pres., Michael Madhusudhana Acad., Calcutta, 1996–. *Publications:* Celestial Melody, 1991; Memorable Moments, 1995; Ikeda First: Rest Nowhere Review of Poet Ikeda: An Assessment of His Unique Poetry, 1994; Fiction: The Preferential Genre of Literature, 1996; Represented in anthologies: Samvedana; Poet; Rising Stars: A World of Anthology of Poetry; East West Voices; World Poetry, 1990, 1992. *Contributions to:* Poems included in World Poetry, 1990–1992, 1994–96; Mosaic by Writers Forum, Ranchi, 1994 & 1995. *Honours:* Hon. PhD, International University California, USA, 1993; Merit Certificate, Writers Forum, Ranchi, 1994; Hon. DLitt, World Acad. of Art and Culture, Japan, 1996; Winged Word Award, International Sociolit Foundation, India, 1996. *Memberships:* Chetana Literary Group, Mangalore; United Writers Asscn, Chennai; World Poetry Society, Chennai; Writers Club of India; Michael Madhusudhana Acad., vice-pres., 1996–. *Address:* PB No. 16, Wokha 797 111, Nagaland, India.

JACOBIK, Jane Gray; b. 21 May 1944, Newport News, Virginia, USA. Poet; Prof. m. Bruce N Gregory, 4 Jan. 1983, 1 s., 1 d. *Education:* BA, Goddard College, Plainfield, Vermont, 1976; MA, British and American Literature, 1985, PhD, British and American Literature, 1990, Brandeis University. *Appointments:* Asst Prof., English, Eastern Illinois University, Charleston, 1989–91; Assoc. Prof., 1991–98, Prof., 1998–, Eastern Connecticut State University. *Publications:* Jane's Song, 1976; Paradise Poems, 1978; Sandpainting, 1980; The Double Task, 1998; The Surface of Last Scattering, 1999. *Contributions to:* Ploughshares; Georgia Review; Kenyon Review; Prairie Schooner, Ontario Review; South Dakota Review; Cream City Review; Hollin's Critic; American Literary Review; Hiram Poetry Review; Alaska Quarterly Review; North American Review; Poetry East; Tar River Review. *Honours:* Juniper Prize, 1992; X J Kennedy Poetry Prize, 1998; The Best American Poetry, 1997, 1999. *Memberships:* Poetry Society of America; New England Poetry Club; Worcester Country Poetry Asscn. *Address:* 86 Fox Hill Rd, Pomfret Center, CT 06259, USA.

JACOBS, Alan John Lawrence; b. 9 Sept. 1929, London, England. Art Dealer (retd); Poet. *Publications:* The Pearl Fishers, 1994; Element Book of Mystical Verse (ed.); Poetry of the Spirit, 2002; The Bhagrad Yita: A Translation, 2002. *Contributions to:* Reflections; Self Enquiry; Mountain Path. *Membership:* Keats-Shelley Memorial Asscn. *Address:* 53 Broadfield, Broadhurst Gardens, London NW6 3BN, England.

JACOBS, Ruth Harriet; b. 15 Nov. 1924, Boston, Massachusetts, USA. Sociologist; Gerontologist; Writer; Poet. m. Neal Jacobs, 18 July 1948, divorced, 1 s., 1 d. *Education:* BS, 1964, Boston University, 1969, Brandeis University. *Appointments:* Prof., Boston University, 1969–82; Prof., 1982–89, Dept Chair, 1982–87, Clark University; Senior Lecturer, Regis College, 1988–. *Publications:* Button, Button Who Has the Button, 1987; Out of Their Mouths, 1988; Be an Outrageous Older Woman A RASP, 1991; We Speak for Peace (ed.), 1993; Women Who Have Touched My Life, 1996; Three prose books. *Contributions to:* Anthologies and reviews. *Honours:* Poetry Writing Fellowships; Grants. Women Writers Guild. *Address:* 75 High Ledge Ave, Wellesley, MA 02181, USA.

JAEGER, Sharon Ann; b. 15 Jan. 1945, Douglas, AZ, USA. Writer; Poet; Ed.; Prof.; Trans. *Education:* BA, summa cum laude, University of Dayton; MA, in English, Boston College, 1971; DA, in English, State University of New York at Albany, 1982; PhD, Comparative Literature and Literary Theory, University of Pennsylvania, 1995. *Appointments:* Visiting Prof., University of Pennsylvania, 1986–95; Visiting Scholar, University of Pennsylvania, 1996–. *Publications:* Keeping the Lowest of Profiles, 1983; Filaments of Affinity, 1989; The Chain of Dead Desire, 1990; Why the Planets Do Not Speak, 1996; Looking Back, Moving On, 1999. Co-Translator: Duino Elegies, by Rilke, 1991. *Honours:* Chaminade Award for Excellence, University of Dayton, 1966; Austrian Government Scholarship for German Study, Universität Salzburg, 1966; Presidential Fellowship, State University of New York at Albany, 1979–82; Fulbright Lectureship, Portugal, 1983–84; Honorable Mentions, 1988, 1991, 1994, 1995; First Place, 1992, William Carlos Williams Awards, Poetry, University of Pennsylvania; Dean's Award for Distinguished Teaching, University of Pennsylvania, 1992. *Memberships:* Pen Center USA West; Acad. of American Poets; Small Press Center; American Medical Writers Asscn; American Comparative Literature Asscn. *Address:* 2633 E 17th Ave, Anchorage, AK 99508-3207, USA.

JAGGI, Satya Dev; b. 15 Jan. 1937, Punjab, Pindigheb, India. University Senior Lecturer; Poet; Writer. m. 3 March 1974. *Education:* BA, Honours, English, 1958; MA, Philosophy, 1960; MA, English, 1963, PhD, English, 1977. *Publications:* Coleridge's and Yeats' Theory of Poetry, 1966; Homewards and Other Poems, 1966; No More Words, 1966; End of Hunger, 1968; The Point of Light, 1968; The Earthrise, 1969; The Moon Voyagers, 1970; One Looks Earthward Again, 1970; Our Awkward Earth, 1970; Readiness is All, 1970; Obscure Goodbyes, 1970; A City Within a City, 1983; Far in Maiduguri, 1983; Lead No One by the Nose (play), 1983; Our Concern with Poetry, 1983; A Passage to London, 1983; The Poet's Plenty, 1983; The Poet's Proposition, 1984; I A Richards on Poetic Truth, 1985; The Language of Poetry, 1990. *Contributions to:* Newspapers, quarterlies, and journals. *Honour:* Third Prize, BBC Poetry Competition, 1990. *Memberships:* Falcon Poetry Society, Delhi, chair.; Indian Writers in English, chair., Delhi. *Address:* 8258, B-XI, Vasant Kunj, New Delhi 110070, India.

JAINS, Jessica. See: RICHESON, C(ena) G(older).

JAMES, Anthony Stephen; b. 27 Oct. 1956, Penllergaer, South Wales. Writer; Poet. m. Penny Windsor, 24 May 1987, divorced 1994, 1 d. *Education:* BA, University College of Swansea, 1991. *Publications:* Novel: A House with Blunt Knives. Poetry: All That the City Has to Offer; Introducing Kivi; We Rescued a Dog Called Gordon, 1997. As Antonia James: The Serpent in April. *Contributions to:* Numerous publications. *Honour:* Eileen Illtyd David Award, 1983. *Membership:* Literature for More than One Year Group. *Address:* 16 Buckingham Rd, Bonymaen, Swansea SA1 7AL, Wales.

JAMES, Clive (Vivian Leopold); b. 7 Oct. 1939, Kogarah, NSW, Australia. Writer; Poet; Broadcaster; Journalist; Lyricist. *Education:* BA, University of Sydney, 1960; MA, Pembroke College, Cambridge, 1967. *Appointments:* Asst Ed., Morning Herald, Sydney, 1961; Television Critic, 1972–82, Feature Ed., 1972–, The Observer, London; Dir, Watchmaker Productions, 1994–. Various television series and documentaries. *Publications:* Poetry: Peregrine Prykke's Pilgramage Through the London Literary World, 1974; The Fate of Felicity Fark in the Land of the Media, 1975; Britannia Bright's Bewilderment in the Wilderness of Westminster, 1976; Fan-Mail, 1977; Charles Charming's Challenges on the Pathway to the Throne, 1981; Poem of the Year, 1983; Other Passports: Poems, 1958–1985, 1986. Fiction: Brilliant Creatures, 1983; The Remake, 1987; Brrm! Brrm!, 1991; The Dreaming Swimmer, 1992; The Silver Castle, 1996; The Speaker in Ground Zero, 1999. Non-Fiction: The Metropolitan Critic, 1974; Visions Before Midnight, 1977; At the Pillars of Hercules, 1979; First Reactions, 1980; Unreliable Memoirs, three vols, 1980, 1985, 1990; The Crystal Bucket, 1981; From the Land of Shadows, 1982; Glued to the Box, 1982; Flying Visits, 1984; Snakecharmers in Texas, 1988; Fame in the 20th Century, 1993; Clive James on Television, 1993; Even As We Speak: New Essays, 1993–2001, 2001; Reliable Essays: The Best of Clive James, 2001. *Contributions to:* Commentary; Encounter; Listener; London Review of Books; Nation; New Review; New Statesman; New York Review of Books; New Yorker; TLS; Others. *Address:* c/o The Observer, 8 St Andrew's Hill, London EC4V 5JA, England.

JAMIE, Kathleen; b. 13 May 1962, Johnston, Renfrewshire, Scotland. Poet. *Education:* MA, Philosophy, University of Edinburgh. *Appointment:* Lecturer in Creative Writing, University of St Andrews. *Publications:* Mr & Mrs Scotland are Dead: Selected Poems, 1980–94; Jizzen, 1999; Among Muslims: Meetings at the Frontiers of Pakistan, 2002. *Honours:* Somerset Maugham Award, 1994; Geoffrey Faber Awards, 1996, 2000; Creative Scotland Award, 2001. *Address:* c/o Triple PA, 15 Connaught Gdns, Forest Hall, Newcastle upon Tyne NE12 8AT, England. *E-mail:* Triplepa@cableinet.co.uk.

JANABI, Hatif; b. 27 July 1952, Kadisia, Iraq. Poet; Critic; Trans.; Lecturer. m. Shaza, 23 Aug. 1996, 1 s. *Education:* BA, Arabic Language and Literature, University of Baghdad, 1972; MA, Polish Language and Literature, 1979, PhD, Drama, 1983, University of Warsaw. *Appointments:* Lecturer, Arabic Literature and Drama, University of Tizi-Ouzu, Algeria, 1985–88; Lecturer, Arabi Language and Literature and Culture, University of Warsaw, Poland, 1988– Visiting Scholar, Indiana University, Bloomington, USA, 1993–94 *Publications:* Study on Arabic Theatre and Drama: Roots, History and Quest 1995; Questions and their Retinue: Selected Poems 1972–1994, 1996; Wislaw Szymborska, Al-Shair wa al-alam (Poet and the World), 1997; Paradises Deer and Militaries, 1998; Tadeusz Rozewicz, Matha Yahduth Li-Nnijum (What' Happening to the Stars) (poems), 1998; Babilon Poszukuje Babilonu (Babylon Seeking Babylon) (poems), 1998; Czeslaw Milosz, Madih at-Tair (Praise of the Bird) (poems), 2002; W. Szymborska, An-Nihaya WA Al-Bidaya (The End an the Beginning) (poems), 2002. *Honours:* University of Arkansas-Press Annual Award for Arabic Literature, 1995; Fellowship, Polish Ministry of Culture and Art, 1997–98, 2000–02; Award, Metafora Review in Literature for 1997 (fo poetry), Poland; First Poetry Collection Prize, Miedzynarodowy Listopa Poetycki-Poznan, Poland, 1991. *Membership:* Polish PEN Club, board, 1996– Polish Oriental Asscn; Middle East Studies Asscn of North America; Union c Polish Writers. *Address:* 00 950 Warsaw, PO Box 685, Poland.

JANES, Adrian Clive; b. 8 May 1958, Kingston, Surrey, England. Librarian Poet. *Education:* BA, Honours, English, St David's University College Lampeter, 1982; Postgraduate Diploma, Library and Information Studies Ealing College of Higher Education, 1987. *Appointments:* Library Asst Kingston Polytechnic, 1985–86; Library Asst/Asst Librarian, Roehampton Institute, 1988; Asst Librarian, 1989–95, Senior Asst Librarian, 1995–, L E Havering. *Publications:* Failing Light, 1985; Attempted Communication, 1988 *Contributions to:* Orbis; Resurgence; Rouska; Spectrum; Digger's Magazine Memes; Purple Patch. *Honour:* Assoc. of Library Asscn, 1992. *Memberships* Blake Society; Library Asscn, 1985–.

JANKIEWICZ, Leo. See: YANKEVICH, Leo.

JÁNOSHÁZY, György; b. 20 June 1922, Cluj, Romania. Ed. m. Annamária Biluska, 2 Feb. 1980, 1 s. *Education:* LLB, Bolyai University, Cluj, 1946; Acad of Dramatic Arts, Tg Mures, 1952; Studies in Aesthetics and History of Arts, Bolyai University. *Appointments:* Journalist, 1945–48; Art Secretary, Stage Man., Hungarian Opera, Cluj, 1949–59; Ed., Korunk, monthly, 1958–63, Igaz Szó, monthly, 1963–90, Deputy General Ed., 1969–. *Publications:* Lepkék szekrényben, English trans. as Butterflies in a Glass Case, 1994; Innen semerre, English trans. as From Here In No Direction, 1995; Böllérek miséje, English trans. as Butchers' Mass, 1999; Úszó sziget, English trans. as Floating Island, 2002. Other: Numerous trans; Essays on literature and the arts. *Contributions to:* Anthologies, reviews and journals. *Honours:* Order of Labour, 1968; Prize, Tg Mures Writers' Asscn, 1974; Cultural Merit Medal, 1981; Prize, Látó, monthly, 1992, 1999; Prize, Szentgyörgyi Albert Society, 1995; Gold Merit Cross of the Republic of Hungary, 1997; Prize, Writers' Union of Romania, 2000. *Memberships:* Writers' Union of Romania; Tg Mures Asscn, secretary, 1981–90; Hungarian Writers' Union. *Address:* Str Parangului 24/9, 4300 Tg Mures, Romania.

JANOWITZ, Phyllis; b. 3 March 1940, New York, NY, USA. Poet. Divorced, 1 s., 1 d. *Education:* BA, Queens College; MFA, University of Massachusetts, Amherst, 1970. *Appointments:* Hodder Fellow in Poetry, Princeton University, 1979–80; Assoc. Prof. in English, then Prof., Cornell University, 1980–. *Publications:* Rites of Strangers, 1978; Visiting Rites, 1982; Temporary Dwellings, 1988. *Contributions to:* Poems to New Yorker; Atlantic; Nation; New Republic; Paris Review; Ploughshares; Radcliffe Quarterly; Prairie Schooner; Esquire; Andover Review; Harvard Magazine Backbone; Literary Review; Mid-Atlantic Review. *Honour:* National Endowment for the Arts Fellowship, 1989. *Address:* Dept of English, Cornell University, Ithaca, NY 14853, USA.

JANSEN, Garfield (Auburn Mariano), (Mar iananda); b. 15 Aug. 1967, Coimbatore, India. Monk; Writer; Poet. *Education:* BA, Psychology, PSG College of Arts and Science, Coimbatore, 1989; PhD, Mariology, 1997, DD, 1998, DEd, 1999, DPhil, 1999, STD, 2000, International University of California. *Publications:* Assumption of Our Lady Mary, 1994; Mary: Mother and Queen, 1995; Hail Mary: Full of Grace, 1996; Mystic Woman, 1997; Fragrance of Modelling; In Love; Jacqueline; Mother Euphrasia and the Blessed Virgin Mary; My Book of Poor Christ. *Contributions to:* Many publications. *Honours:* May Ash Prize, 1986; Winged Word Award, 1996; Michael Madhusudhan Award, 1999. *Memberships:* International Socio-Literary Foundation; Stop the Killing, Indian Chapter, pres.; United Writers Asscn. *Address:* 1275 Trichy Rd, Near Screepathy Theatre, Coimbatore 641018, Tamil Nadu, India.

JARMAN, Mark (Foster); b. 5 June 1952, Mt Sterling, KY, USA. Prof. of English; Poet. m. Amy Kane Jarman, 28 Dec. 1974, 2 d. *Education:* BA, University of California at Santa Cruz, 1974; MFA, University of Iowa, 1976. *Appointments:* Teacher and Writing Fellow, University of Iowa, 1974–76; Instructor, Indiana State University, Evansville, 1976–78; Visiting Lecturer, University of California at Irvine, 1979–80; Asst Prof., Murray State University, KY, 1980–83; Asst Prof., 1983–86, Assoc. Prof., 1986–92, Prof. of English, 1992–, Vanderbilt University. *Publications:* Poetry: North Sea, 1978; The Rote Walker, 1981; Far and Away, 1985; The Black Riviera, 1990; Iris,

1992; Questions for Ecclesiastes, 1997. Other: The Reaper Essays (with Robert McDowell), 1996; Rebel Angels: 25 Poets of the New Formalism (ed. with David Mason), 1996. *Contributions to:* Journals, periodicals, and magazines. *Honours:* Joseph Henry Jackson Award, 1974; Acad. of American Poets Prize, 1975; National Endowment for the Arts Grants, 1977, 1983, 1992; Robert Frost Fellowship, Bread Loaf Writers' Conference, 1985; Guggenheim Fellowship, 1991–92; Finalist, National Book Critics Circle Award in Poetry, 1997; Lenore Marshall Poetry Prize, 1998. *Memberships:* Associated Writing Programs; MLA; Poetry Society of America; Poets Prize Committee. *Address:* 509 Broadwell Dr., Nashville, TN 37220, USA.

JAYANATHAN, T. K.; b. 20 April 1933, Trichur, Kerala, India. Banker; Poet. m. M Arya, 7 Feb. 1956, 1 s., 2 d. *Education:* BA, Statistics, 1957; CAIIB, 1966. *Contributions to:* Various anthologies in Malayalam and English, newspapers, reviews, and periodicals. *Membership:* International Poets Acad., fellow. *Address:* Kadalasseri, PO Vallachira 680 562, Trichur District, Kerala, India.

JELENKOVIC, Sasa; b. 8 Aug. 1964, Zajecar, Yugoslavia. Poet; Writer; Ed. *Education:* Comparative Literature, University of Belgrade, 1990. *Appointments:* Ed.-in-Chief, Znak (Sign) magazine, 1988–90; Poetry Ed., Knjizevna rec (Literary Word) magazine, 1992–94, Rec (Word) magazine, 1994–. *Publications:* Neprijatna Geometrija (Unpleasant Geometry), 1992; Ono sto ostaje (What Remains Behind), 1993; Heruvimske tajne (Cherub's Secrets), 1994. *Contributions to:* Magazines. *Honours:* Matic's Scarf Award, 1992; Milan Rakic Award, Serbian Writers Asscn, 1993. *Membership:* Serbian Writers Asscn. *Address:* Cara Dusana 7/26, 11000 Belgrade, Yugoslavia.

JELINEK, Elfriede; b. 20 Oct. 1946, Mürzzuschlag, Austria. Author; Dramatist; Poet. m. Gottfried Hüngsberg. *Education:* Piano and Organ, Vienna Conservatory; Theatre and Art History, University of Vienna. *Publications:* Lisas Schatten, 1967; Wir sind lockvögel baby!, 1970; Michael: Ein Jugendbuch für die Infantilgesell-schaft, 1973; Die Liebhaberinnen, 1975; Bukolit, 1979; Ende: gedichte, 1966–1968, 1980; Die Ausgesperrten, 1980; Die Klavierspielerin, 1983; Burgtheater, 1984; Clara S, 1984; Was geschah, nachdem Nora ihren Mann verlassen hatte oder Stützen der Gesellschaft, 1984; Oh Wildnis, oh Schutz vor ihr, 1985; Krankeit oder Moderne Frauen, 1987; Lust, 1989; Wolken: Heim, 1990; Malina, 1991; Totenauberg, 1991; Die Kinder der Toten, 1995; Gier, 2000. *Honours:* Prize for Poetry and Prose, Innsbrucker Jugendkulturwoche, 1969; National Scholarship for Writers, Austria, 1972; Roswitha von Gandersheim Memorial Medal, 1979; Drehbuchpreis, Ministry of the Interior, Austria, 1979; Heinrich Böll Prize, 1986; Styrian Literature Prize, 1987; Bremen Prize for Literature, Rudolf Alexander Schroder Foundation, 1996; Büchner Prize, 1998; Dramatist of the Year, Festival of Theatre of Muelheim and der Ruhr, 2002. *Membership:* Graz Writers' Asscn. *Address:* Sendlingerstr 43, 80331 Munich, Germany; Jupiterweg 40, 1140 Vienna, Austria.

JENKINS, Catherine Anne May; b. 18 Feb. 1962, Hamilton, ON, Canada. Writer; Poet. *Education:* BA, 1984, MA, 1996, Trent University, Peterborough, ON. *Publications:* Submerge, 1997; Written in the Skin (anthology, contributor), 1998; Blood, Love and Boomerangs (co-author), 1999; Swimming in the Ocean (novel), 2002. *Contributions to:* Descant; Lichen; Rampike; Queen Street Quarterly; Room of One's Own; Blood and Aphorisms; Carleton Arts Review; Quill and Quire; The Toronto Star; The Globe and Mail; Dream Catcher; Magma Poetry Magazine; Poetry Croydon. *Memberships:* The Writers' Union of Canada; PEN Canada; Eds' Asscn of Canada. *E-mail:* scripted@hotmail.com. *Website:* www.catherinejenkins.com.

JENNERMANN, Donald; b. 20 Dec. 1939, Ladysmith, Wisconsin, USA. Prof.; Writer; Poet. m. Gretchen Bauer, 7 Oct. 1976, 2 s., 2 d. *Education:* BA, MA, University of Wisconsin; PhD, Indiana University. *Appointment:* Prof., Indiana State University, 1964–. *Publications:* Born of a Cretan Spring, 1981; Bearing North, 1996; The Insistent Sound, 1999. *Contributions to:* Esparavel; Cali, Colombia; Indiana Writes; Stone Drum; South Dakota Review; Wisconsin Review; Hellas. *Membership:* Indianapolis Writer's Center. *Address:* University Honors Program, Indiana State University, Terre Haute, IN 47809, USA.

JENSEN, Laura Linnea; b. 16 Nov. 1948, Tacoma, Washington, USA. Poet. *Education:* BA, University of Washington, 1972; MFA, University of Iowa, 1974. *Appointments:* Occasional Teacher; Visiting Poet, Oklahoma State University, 1978. *Publications:* After I Have Voted, 1972; Anxiety and Ashes, 1976; Bad Boats, 1977; Tapwater, 1978; The Story Makes Them Whole, 1979; Memory, 1982; Shelter, 1985; A Sky Empty of Orion, 1985. *Contributions to:* Periodicals. *Honours:* National Endowment for the Arts Fellowship, 1980–81; Ingram Merrill Foundation Grant, 1983; Theodore Roethke Award, 1986; Guggenheim Fellowship, 1989–90; Lila Wallace-Reader's Digest Writers Award, 1993. *Memberships:* Acad. of American Poets; Associated Writing Programs; Poets and Writers. *Address:* 302 N Yakima, No. C3, Tacoma, WA 98403, USA.

JEPSON, Edwin Keith, (Eddie Jepson); b. 6 March 1938, Mansfield, Nottinghamshire, England. Poet. m. May Cave, 23 Sept. 1961, 1 s., 4 d. *Education:* Mansfield Technical College. *Publications:* Island Moods and Reflections, 1995; Sunlight and Shadows, 1995; A Moment in Time, 1996; As Time Passes, 1998; Legacy of Life, 1998; A Passage to Creation, 1998; Book of Rondeaux, 1998; Shadows of My Mind, 1998; Dawn's First Light, 1998; Twins, 1999. *Contributions to:* Chad; Evening Post; Poetry Now Magazine; Orbis; Outposts; Retford Writers; Exile First Time; Splizz; Poetry Church White Tower. *Honours:* Excellence Certificate, Poetry in Print, 1996; Four certificates, three First Places and one Second Place, White Tower Writers Asscn; Runner-Up Prize, Evening Post, Nottingham, 1997; Third Prize, National Poetry Competition, 1998. *Membership:* White Tower Writers Asscn. *Address:* 1 Mount St, Mansfield, Nottinghamshire NG19 7AT, England.

JESSENER, Stephen, (Desney Weild); b. 28 Dec. 1966, Wanstead, London, England. Special Needs Teacher; Poet; Ed. *Education:* English Degree, North London Polytechnic, 1989; PGCE, Brentwood College, 1991. *Appointments:* Teacher, Handsworth Primary School, 1991–93; Special Needs Teacher, Chapel Primary School, 1994–; Staff Poet, Bad Poetry Quarterly, 1994–95; Ed., Zimmerframepileup, 1995–96. *Address:* 54 Hillcrest Rd, Walthamstow, London E17 4AP, England.

JESSUP, Frances; b. 29 July 1936, England. Novelist; Poet; Playwright. m. Clive Turner, 1960, divorced 1996, 1 s., 3 d. *Education:* BA, Honours, Philosophy, King's College, University of London, 1958. *Appointments:* Organiser, Theatre Writing, Haslemere, UNA, 1992; Programme Secretary, Wey Poets, 2000; Healthy Planet Poems, Electric Theatre, 2001; Signing the Charter, Haslemere UNA Branch Theatre. *Publications:* The Fifth Child's Conception, 1970; Deutsch Penguin, 1972; The Car: A Fable for Voices, 1999. *Contributions to:* Anthologies and magazines. *Honours:* First Prize for Fiction and Poetry, Moor Park College, 1972; UNA Trust Award, 1988; University of Surrey Arts Committee Literary Festival Award, 1991. *Membership:* PEN. *Address:* 20 Heath Rd, Haslemere, GU27 3QN England.

JEWELL, Elizabeth Maynard, (Libby Houston); b. 9 Dec. 1941, North London, England. Poet. m. Mal Dean, 21 May 1966, deceased, 1 s., 1 d. *Education:* BA, Honours, English Language and Literature, 1963, MA, 1987, Lady Margaret Hall, Oxford; Certificate in Science Biology, University of Bristol, 1986. *Appointments:* Research Asst, Botany Dept, University of Bristol, 1989–; Legal Co-Worker, Berry's Legal Services Co-operative, 1992–. *Publications:* A Stained Glass Raree Show, 1967; Plain Clothes, 1971; At the Mercy, 1981; Necessity, 1988; A Little Treachery, 1990; All Change (children's poems), 1993. *Contributions to:* Anthologies, periodicals and radio. *Address:* c/o 120 Grosvenor Rd (Berry's), St Pauls, Bristol BS2 8YA, England.

JEWELL, Terri L.; b. 4 Oct. 1954, Louisville, KY, USA. Freelance Writer and Book Reviewer; Poet. *Education:* BS, Montclair State College, Upper Montclair, New Jersey, 1979. *Appointments:* Poetry Ed., Shooting Star Review, Pittsburgh, Pennsylvania, 1992; Creative Writers Grant Review Panel Mem., Arts Foundation of Michigan, 1994–; Poet-in-Residence, Oak Park Public Library, Michigan, 1994. *Publications:* The Black Woman's Gumbo Ya-Ya: Quotations by Black Women, 1993; Succulent Heretic, 1994. *Contributions to:* African American Review; American Voice; International Poetry Review; Midland Review; Negative Capability; When I Grow Old I Shall Wear Purple, 1986; Kentucky Poetry Review; Bloomsbury Review; Black Scholar; Small Press Review; Poetry Flash; Chicago Magazine. *Honours:* Pushcart Prize Nomination, 1989; Residency, Wolf Pen Women Writers Colony, Prospect, KY, 1990; Individual Creative Artist Grant, Arts Foundation of Michigan, 1993–94; Prism Award for Literature and Activism, Lansing, 1994. *Memberships:* Michigan Creative Writers-in-the-Schools Program; Teachers and Writer's Collaborative, New York. *Address:* PO Box 23154, Lansing, MI 48909, USA.

JI HUA. See: JIANHUA CHEN.

JI HUN. See: KWOK YIN WOO.

JIANHUA CHEN, (Ji Hua, You Chen); b. 16 July 1947, Shanghai, China. Poet; Scholar. m. Wei Xing Wang, 26 April 1981, 1 s. *Education:* Fudan University, 1982; PhD, 1988. *Appointments:* Teacher, College of Liberal Arts, Shanghai University, 1982–85; Lecturer, Fudan University, 1988–90; Academic Consultant, Chinese Great Dictionary Publishing House, 1988–90; Visiting Scholar, University of California at Santa Cruz, 1988–. *Publications:* Poetry and Death; The Literature of Jiangsu and Zhejiang in the Ming Dynasty; Hua Jian Ji. *Contributions to:* Journals and periodicals. *Honours:* Academic Award, Fudan University; Zhao Jingshen Chinese Classics Award. *Memberships:* Classical Drama Asscn of China; American Asscn for Asian Studies; International Center for Asian Studies, Hong Kong. *Address:* 220 Miller Ct, Santa Cruz, CA 95060, USA.

JILES, Paulette; b. 1943, Salem, Missouri, USA. Poet; Writer. *Education:* BA, University of Missouri, 1968. *Appointments:* Teacher, David Thompson University, Nelson, BC, 1984–85; Writer-in-Residence, Phillips Acad., Andover, Massachusetts, 1987–. *Publications:* Poetry: Waterloo Express, 1973; Celestial Navigation, 1983; The Jesse James Poems, 1987; Flying Lessons: Selected Poems, 1995. Other: Sitting in the Club Car Drinking Rum & Karma-Kola, 1986; The Late Great Human Roadshow, 1986; Blackwater,

1988; Song to the Rising Sun, 1989; Cousins, 1991; North Spirit, 1995; Enemy Women, 2001. *Honours:* Governor-General's Award, 1984; Gerald Lampert Award, 1984; Pat Lowther Award, 1984; ACTRA Award for Best Original Drama, 1989. *Membership:* Writers' Union of Canada. *Address:* c/o Writers' Union of Canada, 24 Ryerson Ave, Toronto, Ontario M5T 2P3, Canada.

JIMENEZ DE LOS GALANES Y DE LA FLOR, Miguel, (Miguel Galanes); b. 5 Jan. 1951, Daimiel, Cuidad Real, Spain. Teacher of Literature and Spanish Language; Critic; Poet. m. Esperanza Diaz Martin, 26 Nov. 1973, 1 s., 1 d. *Education:* BA, Spanish Literature. *Appointments:* Critic, El Sol and El Mundo, journals. *Publications:* Inconexiones, 1979; Urgencias sin nombre, 1981; Opera ingenua para Isabel Maria, 1983; Condicion de una musica inestable, 1984; La Demencia consciente, 1987; Los restos de la juerga, 1991. *Contributions to:* Journals and periodicals. *Membership:* Creador del movimiento poetico El Sensismo. *Address:* c/o Pedro Rico, No. 31 10 E, 28029 Madrid, Spain.

JIPING DONG; b. 13 Aug. 1962, Chongqing, China. Teacher; Poet. *Education:* Sichuan Tourism School, 1979–81. *Publications:* Octavio Paz: Selected Poems; Maple Leaves in Four Seasons. *Contributions to:* Orbis; Salmon; Scripsi; Westerly; Indigo; Prism International; Footwork; Paterson Literary Review; Contemporary Poetry; Poetry Press Monthly; Modern Chinese Poetry. *Honours:* International Canadian Studies Award; International Writing Program and International Visitor Program, USA, 1993. *Memberships:* Haiku Society of America; World Poetry Society; Chinese Prose Poetry Society; Asscn for International Canadian Studies; Centre for Studies in Australian Literature. *Address:* 6 Yizijie St, Central District, Chongqing 630012, China.

JOHANSSON-BACKE, Karl Erik; b. 24 Nov. 1914, Stockholm, Sweden. Teacher (retd); Writer; Dramatist; Poet. m. Kerstin Gunhild Bergquist, 21 Nov. 1943, 1 s., 3 d. *Education:* High School Teacher's Degree. *Publications:* Fiction: A Pole in the River, 1950; Daybreak, 1954; The Mountain of Temptation, 1983; The Tree and the Bread, 1987; King of the Mountains, 1993. Poetry: Lust and Flame, 1981. *Honours:* Many literary awards, 1961–93. *Memberships:* Swedish Authors Federation; Swedish Playwrights Federation, hon. mem.

JOHN, Roland; b. 14 March 1940, England. Ed.; Poet; Writer. *Appointment:* Ed., Outposts Poetry Quarterly, 1986–. *Publications:* Report from the Desert, 1974; Boundaries, 1976; The Child Bride's Diary (from the Chinese), 1980; Believing Words are Real, 1985; To Weigh Alternatives, 1992; A Reader's Guide to the Cantos of Ezra Pound, 1995. *Contributions to:* Agenda; Acumen; Envoi; Prospice; Poetry Review; South Coast Poetry Journal, USA; Printed Matter, Japan; Litteratura, Zagreb; Word and Image, Amsterdam; Outposts; Scripsi, Australia. *Address:* 22 Whitewell Rd, Frome, Somerset BA11 4EL, England.

JOHNSON, Charles; b. 1 Jan. 1942, Erdington, Birmingham, England. Poet. m. Rosalind Mora MacInnes, 15 July 1977, 1 d. *Education:* Newcastle upon Tyne College of Commerce, 1964–65. *Publication:* A Box of Professional Secrets: Poems, 1995. *Contributions to:* Anthologies, journals, and periodicals. *Memberships:* Droitwich Poetry Groups; Redditch Poets Workshop, founder; St John's Poetry Workshop. *Address:* 41 Buckleys Green Alvechurch, Birmingham B48 7NG, England.

JOHNSON, Darren; b. 31 Jan. 1970, Rome, New York, USA. Journalist; Writer; Poet. m. Eileen Murphy, 18 Oct. 1995. *Education:* BA, English and Pre-Law, Southampton College, New York, 1992; Graduate work, State University of New York, Stony Brook. *Appointment:* Ed., Publisher, Rocket Literary Quarterly, New York, literary magazine of poetry and fiction. *Publications:* Novel: I Do Not Prefer to Have Sex. Chapbooks: Kayla, 1994; Clits in My Mouth Make Me Happy, 1995; Jazz Poems. *Contributions to:* Rocket Literary Quarterly; Plastic Tower; Alpha Beat Press; Impetus; Tight. *Address:* PO Box 672, Water Mill, NY 11976, USA.

JOHNSON, Denis; b. 1949, Munich, Germany. Writer; Poet. *Publications:* Poetry: The Man Among the Seals, 1969; Inner Weather, 1976; The Incognito Lounge and Other Poems, 1982; The Veil, 1987; The Throne of the Third Heaven of the Nations Millennium General Assembly: Poems Collected and New, 1995. Other: Angels, 1983; Fiskadoro, 1985; The Stars at Noon, 1986; Resuscitation of a Hanged Man, 1991; Jesus' Son, 1993; Already Dead: A Californian Gothic, 1997; The Name of the World, 2000; Seek: Reports from the Edges of America & Beyond, 2001. *Honours:* Whiting Writers' Award, 1986; American Acad. of Arts and Letters Literature Award, 1993; Several grants. *Address:* c/o Robert Cornfield, 145 W 79th St, New York, NY 10024, USA.

JOHNSON, Halvard; b. 10 Sept. 1936, Newburgh, New York, USA. Teacher; Writer; Poet. m. Lynda Schor, 10 Sept. 1990, 2 step-s., 1 step-d. *Education:* BA, Ohio Wesleyan University, 1958; MA, University of Chicago, 1960. *Appointments:* Lecturer, Wright Junior College, Chicago, University of Maryland; Instructor, University of Texas at El Paso, New York University; Asst Prof., University of Puerto Rico; Visiting Part-time Lecturer, Rutgers University, Newark. *Publications:* Transparencies and Projections, 1969; The Dance of the Red Swan, 1971; Eclipse, 1974; Winter Journey, 1979. *Contributions to:* West Coast Review; Latitudes; El Corno Emplumado; Monk's Pond; Sou'Wester; Gosis; Stony Brook; Cafe Solo; Sumac; For Review;

Dacotah Territory; Poetry Now; Eureka; Puerto Del Sol; Ironwood; Arx; Images; Maryland Poetry Review; Pearl; Mudfish; Gulf Stream; Saint Andrews Review. *Honours:* National Endowment for the Arts Grant, 1990; Baltimore City Arts Grants, 1991, 1992. *Memberships:* Poets and Writers; PEN; Associated Writing Programs; Writer's Centre, Bethesda, Maryland. *Address:* 118 S Collington Ave, Baltimore, MD 21231, USA.

JOHNSON, J. Chester; b. 28 Sept. 1944, Chattanooga, TN, USA. Poet. m. (1) 1 s., 1 d., (2) Freda Stern, 7 May 1989. *Education:* Harvard College, 1962–65; BSE, University of Arkansas, 1968. *Appointments:* Senior Analyst, Moody's Investors Service; Head, Public Finance Research and Advisory Group, Morgan Guaranty Trust; Deputy Asst Sec., US Treasury dept; Chair., Government Finance Assocs Inc. *Publications:* Oh America! and January 1967, 1975; Family Ties, Intervecine Interregnum, 1981; For Conduct and Innocents, 1982; Shorts: On Reaching Forty, 1985; It's a Long Way Home and An American Sequence, 1985; Shorts: For Fun, Not for Instruction, 1985; Exile/Martin, 1986; The Professional Curiosity of a Martyr, 1987; Freda's Appetite, 1991; Lazarus, Come Forth and Plain Bob (Unbeh Aved), 1993. *Contributions to:* New York Times; Chicago Tribune; Choice; International Poetry Review; Parnassus; Pegasus; Southern Poetry Review; Potpourri; The Iconoclast; Literary Times; Taproot; Broken Streets. *Honour:* Retrans. (with W. H. Auden) of the Psalms in the Book of Common Prayer, Episcopal Church. *Memberships:* Poetry Society of America; American Acad. of Poets; Poets and Writers. *Address:* 315 E 86th St, Apt 16GE, New York, NY 10028, USA. *E-mail:* jchester.gfa@prodigy.net.

JOHNSON, Linton Kwesi; b. 1952, Chapeltown, Jamaica. Poet; Writer. *Education:* BA, Sociology, Goldsmith's College, University of London, 1973. *Publications:* Voices of the Living and the Dead, 1974; Dread, Beat, and Blood, 1975; Inglan is a Bitch, 1980; Tings an Times: Selected Poems, 1991; Mi Revalue Shanary Fren: Selected Poems, 2002. *Contributions to:* Recordings and television. *Honours:* C. Day-Lewis Fellowship, 1977; Assoc. Fellow, Warwick University, 1985; Hon. Fellow, Wolverhampton Polytechnic, 1987; Italian literary awards, 1990, 1998; Hon. Fellowship, Goldsmith's College, University of London, 2002. *Address:* PO Box 623, Herne Hill, London SE24 0LS, England.

JOHNSON, Nancy; b. 11 July 1948, Bethlehem, PA, USA. Poet. m. Arthur Y. Bryant, 17 Aug. 1991, 1 s. *Education:* BA, Randolph-Macon College, 1970; MEd, Lehigh University, 1972; MA, Johns Hopkins University, 1987; MFA, University of Arizona, 1989. *Publication:* Zoo and Cathedral (poems), 1996. *Address:* 3612 Newark St NW, Washington, DC 20016, USA. *E-mail:* nkjohnson@mindspring.com.

JOHNSON, Peter Martin; b. 22 Feb. 1951, Buffalo, New York, USA. Prof.; Poet. m. Genevieve Allaire, 1 s. *Education:* PhD, University of New Hampshire. *Appointments:* Prof. of English, Providence College, RI, 1985–; Ed., The Prose Poem: An International Journal, 4 vols. *Publications:* Pretty Happy!: Prose Poems, 1997; I'm A Man (fiction), 1997; Love Poems for the Millennium (prose poems), 1998. *Contributions to:* Over 60 poems in 40 different journals including: Verse, Epoch, Iowa Review and Field. *Honour:* National Endowment for the Arts Fellowship in Creative Writing, 1999. *Membership:* Acad. of American Poets. *Address:* c/o Dept of English, Providence College, Providence, RI 02918, USA.

JOHNSON, Steve. See: BALON, Brett John Steven.

JOHNSTON, Allan James; b. 25 Oct. 1949, San Diego, CA, USA. Instructor; Ed.; Poet. m. Guillemette Claude Johnston, 28 Nov. 1980. *Education:* BA, English, California State University, Northridge, 1973; MA, Creative Writing, 1980, PhD, English, 1988, University of California, Davis. *Appointments:* Lecturer, University of California, Davis; Ed., Great Books Foundation, Chicago; Lecturer and Instructor, Northeastern Illinois University, Chicago; Loyola University, Chicago; Lecturer, Oakton Community College, DePaul University, Chicago, Columbia College, Chicago. *Publication:* Tasks of Survival (selected poems 1970–90), 1996. *Contributions to:* Poetry; Americas Review; Androgyne; Arts and Academe; Ariel; Asylum; Black Mountain II Review; California Quarterly; Dickinson Review; Green Fuse; Orbis; Rhino; Riverrun; South Florida Poetry Review; Weber Studies; Z Miscellaneous; Stick; MacGuffin; Psychopoetica; Pig Iron; Pacific International; Lazy Bones Review; Strong Coffee; Wisdom; CQ; Black Bear Review; Black River Review; 20th Century Literature; Review of Contemporary Fiction; McNeese Review. *Honours:* First Prize, Second Prize, Fairfax Folio, 1980; Honourable Mentions, C T Wright Poetry Contest, 1980, 1981, Flying Colors Anthology, 1980; September Achievement in Poetry, Z Miscellaneous, 1987; Second Prize, Riverrun Poetry Contest, 1989; Finalist, Roberts Writing Awards, 1991. *Membership:* Midwest Philosophy of Education Society. *Address:* 1105 Asbury, Evanston, IL 60202, USA.

JOHNSTON, George (Benson); b. 7 Oct. 1913, Hamilton, Ontario, Canada. Poet; Trans. m. Jeanne McRae, 1944, 3 s., 3 d. *Education:* BA, 1936, MA, 1945, University of Toronto. *Appointments:* Faculty, Dept of English, Mount Allison University, Sackville, New Brunswick, 1947–49, Carleton College, later University, Ottawa, 1949–79. *Publications:* Poetry: The Cruising Auk, 1959; Home Free, 1966; Happy Enough: Poems 1935–1972, 1972; Between, 1976;

Taking a Grip, 1979; Auk Redivivus: Selected Poems, 1981; Ask Again, 1984; Endeared by Dark: The Collected Poems, 1990; What is to Come: Selected and New Poems, 1996. Prose: Carl: Portrait of a Painter, 1986. Translator: Over 10 vols, 1963–94. Honours: Hon. doctorates. Address: PO Box 1706, Huntingdon, QC J0S 1H0, Canada.

JOINES, Mary Elizabeth; b. 30 July 1911, Madison, KS, USA. Poet. m. Glenn V. Joines, 7 June 1934, 1 s., 2 d. Education: BS, cum laude, Home Economics, Kansas State University, 1933. Publications: Of Home and Other Hazards, 1986; Echoes in the Wind, 2001. Contributions to: Anthologies and periodicals. Honours: Over 300 prizes since 1949; Plaque, In Appreciation of Service, Kansas Authors' Club, 1981. Memberships: Ionian Literary Society; Midwest Federation of Chaparral Poets; National League of American Pen Women; Poetry Society of Colorado; Kentucky State Poetry Society. Address: 8905 Oakwood St, Westminster, CO 80030, USA.

JONAS, Ann; b. 15 July 1919, Joplin, Missouri, USA. Poet. m. Walter H Jonas, 30 March 1944, 1 d. Education: Graduated, Goodman Theatre, Chicago, 1939. Publication: So Small, This Arc, 2002. Contributions to: Anthologies, reviews, journals and quarterlies. Honours: Fellowship, Yaddo, 1968; Cecil Hemley Award in Poetry, Poetry Society of America, 1972; Henry Rago Memorial Award, New York Poetry Forum, 1972; Finalist, Eleanor B North Award, International Poetry Society, England, 1975; First Prize in Poetry, Caddo National Writing Center, 1982; Fellowship, Virginia Center for the Creative Arts, 1993. Memberships: Centro Studie e Scambi Internazionali, hon. vice-pres.; International Poetry Society, fellow; Poetry Society of America. Address: 2425 Ashwood Dr., Louisville, KY 40205, USA.

JONAS, Edward Joseph; b. 30 Sept. 1966, Wharton, Texas, USA. Poet; Writer. m. Leira Laken-Lee Jonas, 1 d. Education: United States Air Force. Contributions to: Various anthologies and other publications. Honours: Several poetry awards and certificates of merit. Address: 3321 Turnabout Loop, Cibolo, TX 77108, USA.

JONES, Brian; b. 1938, London, England. Poet; Writer. Publications: Poems, 1966; A Family Album, 1968; Interior, 1969; The Mantis Hand and Other Poems, 1970; For Mad Mary, 1974; The Spitfire on the Northern Line, 1975; The Island Normal, 1980; The Children of Separation, 1985; Freedom John, 1990. Honours: Cholmondeley Award, 1967; Eric Gregory Award, 1968. Address: c/o Carcanet Press, 208–212 Corn Exchange Buildings, Manchester M4 3BQ, England.

JONES, David James. See: ANNWN, David.

JONES, Douglas Gordon; b. 1 Jan. 1929, Bancroft, Ontario, Canada. Prof. (retd); Poet. Education: MA, Queen's University, Kingston, Ontario, 1954. Appointment: Prof., University of Sherbrooke, Québec, 1963–94. Publications: Poetry: Frost on the Sun, 1957; The Sun Is Axeman, 1961; Phrases from Orpheus, 1967; Under the Thunder the Flowers Light Up the Earth, 1977; A Throw of Particles: Selected and New Poems, 1983; Balthazar and Other Poems, 1988; The Floating Garden, 1995; Wild Asterisks in Cloud, 1997; Grounding Sight, 1999. Other: Butterfly on Rock: A Study of Themes and Images in Canadian Literature, 1970. Honours: Pres.'s Medal, University of Western Ontario, 1976; Gov.-Gen.'s Award for Poetry, 1977, and for Trans., 1993; Hon. DLitt, Guelph University, 1982. Address: 120 Houghton St, North Hatley, QC J0B 2C0, Canada.

JONES, Emory Davis; b. 30 March 1944, Starkville, Mississippi, USA. Instructor of English; Poet. m. Glenda Lynn Broughton, 14 Aug. 1966, 2 d. Education: BAE, 1965, MA, 1966, PhD, 1981, University of Mississippi. Appointment: Instructor of English, Northeast Mississippi Community College, Booneville. Publications: Magic Medicine Show and Other Poems, 1987; Lodestone and Other Poems, 1989. Contributions to: Anthologies and reviews. Honours: Bela Egydi Awards, 1983, 1984. Memberships: Mississippi Community College Creative Writing Asscn, founder-pres.-historian; North Branch, Mississippi Poetry Society Inc. Address: 608 N Pearl St, Iuka, MS 38852, USA.

JONES, Evan (Lloyd); b. 20 Nov. 1931, Preston, Vic., Australia. Poet; Writer. m. (1) Judith Anne Dale, 1954, 1 s., (2) Margot Sanguinetti, 1966, 3 d. Education: BA, History, MA, History, University of Melbourne; AM, Creative Writing, Stanford University. Publications: Poetry: Inside the Whale, 1960; Understandings, 1967; Recognitions, 1978; Left at the Post, 1984. Other: Kenneth Mackenzie, 1969; The Poems of Kenneth Mackenzie (ed. with Geoffrey Little), 1972. Contributions to: Innumerable essays and reviews in venues ranging from learned journals to newspapers, on topics ranging from literature to physics. Address: PO Box 122, North Carlton, Vic. 3054, Australia.

JONES, (Everett) LeRoi, (adopted the name Amiri Baraka, 1968); b. 7 Oct. 1934, Newark, New Jersey, USA. Prof. of Africana Studies; Poet; Dramatist; Writer. m. (1) Hettie Robert Cohen, divorced 1965, 2 d., (2) Sylvia Robinson, 1967, 6 c. and 2 step-d. Education: Rutgers University, 1951–52; BA, English, Howard University, 1954. Appointments: Founder-Dir, Yugen magazine and Totem Press, New York, 1958–62; Co-Ed., Floating Bear

magazine, New York, 1961–63; Teacher, New School for Social Research, New York City, 1961–64, 1977–79, State University of New York at Buffalo, 1964, Columbia University, 1964, 1980; Founder-Dir, Black Arts Repertory Theatre, Harlem, New York, 1964–66, Spirit House, Newark, 1966–; Visiting Prof., San Francisco State College, 1966–67, Yale University, 1977–78, George Washington University, 1978–79; Chair, Congress of Afrikan People, 1972–75; Asst Prof., 1980–82, Assoc. Prof., 1983–84, Prof. of Africana Studies, 1985–, State University of New York at Stony Brook. Publications: Poetry: April 13, 1959; Spring and Soforth, 1960; Preface to a Twenty Volume Suicide Note, 1961; The Disguise, 1961; The Dead Lecturer, 1964; Black Art, 1966; A Poem for Black Hearts, 1967; Black Magic: Collected Poetry 1961–67, 1970; It's Nation Time, 1970; In Our Terribleness: Some Elements and Meaning in Black Style (with Billy Abernathy), 1970; Spirit Reach, 1972; African Revolution, 1973; Hard Facts, 1976; Selected Poetry, 1979; AM/TRAK, 1979; Spring Song, 1979; Reggae or Not!, 1982; Thoughts for You!, 1984; The LeRoi Jones/Amiri Baraka Reader, 1993. Plays: A Good Girl is Hard to Find, 1958; Dante, 1961; The Toilet, 1964; Dutchman, 1964; The Slave, 1964; The Baptism, 1964; Jello, 1965; Experimental Death Unit #1, 1965; A Black Mass, 1966; Arm Yrsell or Harm Yrsell, 1967; Slave Ship: A Historical Pageant, 1967; Madheart, 1967; Great Goodness of Life (A Coon Show), 1967; Home on the Range, 1968; Police, 1968; The Death of Malcolm X, 1969; Rockgroup, 1969; Insurrection, 1969; Junkies Are Full of (SHHH...), 1970; BA-RA-KA, 1972; Black Power Chant, 1972; Columbia the Gem of the Ocean, 1973; A Recent Killing, 1973; The New Ark's a Moverin, 1974; The Sidnee Poet Heroical, 1975; S-1, 1976; The Motion of History, 1977; What Was the Relationship of the Lone Ranger to the Means of Production?, 1979; At the Dim'cracker Convention, 1980; Boy and Tarzan Appear in a Clearing, 1981; Weimar 2, 1981; Money: A Jazz Opera (with George Gruntz), 1982; Primitive World, 1984; General Hag's Skeezag, 1992. Fiction: The System of Dante's Hell (novel), 1965; Tales (short stories), 1967. Other: Selected Plays and Prose, 1979; Daggers and Javelins: Essays 1974–1979, 1984; The Autobiography of LeRoi Jones/Amiri Baraka, 1984; The Artist and Social Responsibility, 1986; The Music: Reflections on Jazz and Blues (with Amina Baraka), 1987; A Race Divided, 1991; Conversations with Amiri Baraka, 1994. Honours: Obie Award, 1964; Guggenheim Fellowship, 1965; Yoruba Acad. Fellowship, 1965; Dakar Festival Prize, 1966; Grant, 1966, Award, 1981, National Endowment for the Arts; DHL, Malcolm X College, Chicago, 1972; Rockefeller Foundation Grant, 1981; American Book Award, Before Columbus Foundation, 1984. Membership: Black Acad. of Arts and Letters. Address: c/o Dept of Africana Studies, State University of New York at Stony Brook, Stony Brook, NY 11794, USA.

JONES, Frederick Malcolm Anthony; b. 14 Feb. 1955, Middlesex, England. University Lecturer in Classics and Ancient History; Writer; Poet. m. Christina Jones, 2 s. Education: BA, Classics, University of Newcastle upon Tyne, 1977; MA, Medieval Studies, University of Leeds, 1979; PhD, St Andrews University, 1987. Appointments: Asst Lecturer, University of Cape Town, 1982–86; Teacher of Classics, Cobham Hall, Kent, 1987–89; Lecturer in Classics and Ancient History, University of Liverpool, 1989–. Publication: Congreve's Balsamic Elixir, 1995. Contributions to: Journals, reviews, and periodicals. Honours: 1 of 10 joint winners, Northern Poetry Competition, 1991; Felicia Hemans Prize for Lyrical Poetry, 1991. Memberships: Cambridge Philological Society; Society for the Promotion of Roman Studies. Address: c/o Dept of Classics and Ancient History, University of Liverpool, Liverpool L69 3BX, England.

JONES, (Glyn) Martin; b. 3 June 1937, Surbiton, Surrey, England. Examiner; Poet. m. 1 April 1966, 1 s., 1 d. Education: BA, History, 1962, Postgraduate Certificate in Education, 1963, London University. Appointment: Co-Ed., Weyfarers. Publication: The Pink Shiny Raincoat, 1992; Guildford Poems, 2001. Contributions to: Outposts; New Poetry; Poetry South-East; Samphire; Weyfarers; Envoi; Poetry Nottingham. Membership: Surrey Poetry Centre, Guildford. Address: 1 Mountside, Guildford, Surrey GU2 4JD, England.

JONES, Huw Griffith; b. 5 Feb. 1955, England. Teacher of Religious Education and Welsh; Poet. m. Janice Dixon, 28 July 1978, 2 d. Education: BD, United Theological College, University College of Wales, Aberystwyth, 1977; PGCE, University College of Wales, 1978. Appointment: Reviews Ed., Anglo-Welsh Review 1985–88. Publications: A Small Field, 1985; Lleuad y Bore, 1994. Contributions to: Poetry Wales; Taliesin; The Bright Field (anthology), 1991. Honour: Second Prize, Welsh Arts Council's New Poets Competition, 1983. Membership: Welsh Acad. Address: 5 Ffordd Coed Mawr, Bangor, Gwynedd LL57 4TB, Wales.

JONES, Jill Patricia; b. 13 Oct. 1951, Sydney, NSW, Australia. Poet; Reviewer. Education: BA, Honours, University of Sydney; Graduate Diploma, Communications, New South Wales Institute of Technology; MA, University of New South Wales. Publications: The Mask and the Jagged Star, 1992; Flagging Down Time, 1993; A Parachute of Blue: First Choice of Australian Poetry (co-ed.). Contributions to: Australia: Age Monthly Review; Australian; Bulletin; Island; Meanjin; Overland; Poetry Australia; Southerly; Sydney Morning Herald; Westerly; UK; Oasis; Slow Dancer; Echo Room; USA: Antipodes; Visions; Canada: Prism International; Antignaton Review; New Zealand: Takahe. Honours: Writer' Project Grant, Australia Council, 1992; Highly Commended, Fellowship of Australian Writers' Anne Elder Award, 1992; Mary Gilmore Award, 1993; Category B Writers' Fellowship, 1995.

Memberships: Australian Society of Authors; Poets Union of New South Wales; Fellowship of Australian Writers; Writers Centre of New South Wales.

JONES, Paul McDonald; b. 5 Feb. 1950, Hickory, North Carolina, USA. Poet; Research Computing Development Man. m. Sally Greene. *Education:* BS, Computer Science, North Carolina State University, 1972; MFA, Poetry, Warren Wilson College, 1992. *Publication:* What the Welsh and Chinese Have in Common, 1990. *Contributions to:* Thinker Review; Southern Humanities Review; Ohio Review; Georgia Review; Carolina Quarterly; American Literary Review; St Andrews Review; Ironwood; Pembroke Magazine; Crescent Review; Plainsong; Loblolly; Lyricist; Poet Lore; Hampden-Sydney Review; Crucible; Cold Moutain Review; Brix; Turning Dances. *Honours:* North Carolina Quarterly Poetry Prize, 1979; North Carolina Arts Council Fellowship, 1981; Theodore Christian Hoefner Award, 1987; North Carolina Writers' Network Chapbook Award, 1990; Second Place, Guy Owen-Tom Walters Poetry Prize, 1992. *Memberships:* North Carolina Writers' Network, vice-pres., 1984–87; Art Centre of Carrboro, poetry dir, 1978–90; Acad. of American Poets; Poets and Writers; North Carolina Writers' Conference. *Address:* 5526 Hideaway Dr., Chapel Hill, NC 27516, USA.

JONES, Richard (Andrew III); b. 8 Aug. 1953, London, England. Prof. of English; Poet; Writer; Ed. *Education:* BA, English, 1975, MA, English, 1976, University of Virginia; MFA, Poetry, Vermont College, 1987. *Appointments:* Production Ed., CBS Books, 1978–80; Ed., Poetry East, 1979–, Scandinavian Review, 1982–83; Adjunct Faculty, Piedmont College, 1981–82; Dir of Publications, American-Scandinavian Foundation, 1982–83; Lecturer, University of Virginia, 1982–86; Teaching Fellow, Vermont College, 1985–87; Asst Prof., Ripon College, 1986–87; Prof. of English, DePaul University, 1987–. *Publications:* Windows and Walls, 1982; Innocent Things, 1985; Walk On, 1986; Country of Air, 1986; Sonnets, 1990; At Last We Enter Paradise, 1991; A Perfect Time, 1994; The Abandoned Garden, 1997; 48 Questions, 1998; The Stone It Lives On, 1999; The Blessing: New and Selected Poems, 2000. Editor: Of Solitude and Silence: Writings on Robert Bly (with Kate Daniels), 1982; Poetry and Politics, 1984; The Inward Eye: The Photographs of Ed Roseberry (with S Margulies), 1986; The Last Believer in Words, 1998. *Contributions to:* Numerous publications. *Honours:* Many grants; Swedish Writers Union Excellence Prize, 1982; Co-ordinating Council of Literary Magazines Eds' Award, 1985, and Citation of Special Commendation, 1988; Posner Award for Best Book of Poetry, Council for Wisconsin Writers, 1986; Illinois Artists Fellowship, 1990–91; Illinois Arts Council Awards, 1991, 1995, 1996, 1997, 2000, 2002; Society of Midland Authors Award for Best Book of Poetry, 2000; Via Sapentia Lifetime Achievement Award, 2000. *Memberships:* Co-ordinating Council of Literary Magazines; Poetry Society of America. *Address:* c/o Dept of English, DePaul University, 802 W Belden Ave, Chicago, IL 60614, USA.

JONES, Rodney; b. 11 Feb. 1950, Hartselle, AL, USA. Poet; Writer. m. (1) Virginia Kremza, 1972, divorced 1979, (2) Gloria Nixon de Zepeda, 21 June 1981, 2 c. *Education:* BA, University of Alabama, 1971; MFA, University of North Carolina at Greensboro, 1973. *Publications:* Going Ahead, Looking Back, 1977; The Story They Told Us of Light, 1980; The Unborn, 1985; Transparent Gestures, 1989; Apocalyptic Narrative and Other Poems, 1993. *Contributions to:* Periodicals. *Honours:* Lavan Younger Poets Award, Acad. of American Poets, 1986; Younger Writers Award, General Electric Foundation, 1986; Jean Stein Prize, American Acad. and Institute of Arts and Letters, 1989; National Book Critics Circle Award, 1989. *Memberships:* Associated Writing Programs; MLA. *Address:* c/o Houghton Mifflin Co, 222 Berkeley St, Boston, MA 02116, USA.

JONES, Tom, (Thomas Claburn Jones Jr); b. 4 May 1941, Chicago, IL, USA. Attorney-at-Law; Poet; Trans.; Teacher. m. Karin K Krueger, 29 Nov. 1980, 2 s., 3 d. *Education:* BA cum laude, Harvard University, 1965; JD cum laude, Columbia University School of Law, 1968; MFA, George Mason University, 1992. *Appointments:* Attorney, Amnesty International, USA, 1972–79; District Attorney, Greenlake County, Wisconsin, 1983–84; Visiting Prof. of Poetry, Visua Bharati University, West Bengal, India, 1990; Private Practice, Passim, Navajo-Hopi Legal Services, 1992–. *Publications:* Songbook of Absences, by Miguel Hernandez (trans.), 1972; No Prisoners, 1976; Footbridge to India, 1990; Madmen and Bassoons, 1992. *Contributions to:* Greenfield Review; International Poetry Review; Kansas Quarterly; Nation; New Republic; Poet Lore; Southern Poetry Review; Wind Literary Journal; Wisconsin Review; Wisconsin Trails; Yale Review. *Memberships:* Acad. of American Poets; Associated Writing Programs; Poetry Society of America; MLA. *Address:* c/o Navajo-Hopi Legal Services, PO Box 2990, 117 Main St, Tuba City, AZ 86045, USA.

JONES, Volcano. See: MITCHELL, Adrian.

JONG, Erica (Mann); b. 26 March 1942, New York, USA. Author; Poet. m. (1) Michael Werthmann, 1963, divorced 1965, (2) Allan Jong, 1966, divorced, 1975, (3) Jonathan Fast, 1977, divorced 1983, 1 d., (4) Kenneth David Burrows, 1989. *Education:* BA, Barnard College, 1963; MA, Columbia University, 1965. *Appointments:* Lecturer in English, City College, New York, 1964–65, 1969–70; Lecturer in English, University of Maryland Overseas Division 1967–69; Mem., Literary Panel, NY State Council on Arts, 1972–74; Faculty,

Bread Loaf Writers Conference, Middlebury, VT, 1982; Faculty, Salzburg Seminar, Austria, 1993. *Publications:* Poetry: Fruits and Vegetables, 1971, reissued, 1997; Half Lives, 1973; Loveroot, 1975; At the Edge of the Body, 1979; Witches, 1981; Ordinary Miracles, 1983; Becoming Light: Poems New and Selected, 1992. Fiction: Fear of Flying, 1973; How to Save Your Own Life, 1977; Fanny: Being the True History of Fanny Hackabout-Jones, 1980; Parachutes and Kisses, 1984; Serenissima: A Novel of Venice, 1987, revised edn as Shylock's Daughter; A Novel of Love in Venice; Any Woman's Blues, 1990; The Devil at Large: Erica Jong on Henry Miller, 1993; Fear of Fifty: A Midlife Memoir, 1994; Composer Zipless: Songs of Abandon from the Erotic Poetry of Erica Jong, 1995; Inventing Memory: A Novel of Mothers and Daughters, 1997; What Do Women Want? Bread. Roses. Sex. Power., 1998. *Honours:* Acad. of American Poets Prize, 1971; New York State Council on the Arts Grants, 1971; Woodrow Wilson Fellow; Recipient Bess Hokin Prize Poetry Magazine, 1971; Alice Faye di Castagnola Award, Poetry Society of America 1972; National Endowment of the Arts Grant, 1973; Named Mother of the Year, 1982; Hon. Fellow, Welsh College of Music and Drama, 1994; Prix Littéraire Deuville Film Festival, 1997. *Literary Agent:* Ed Victor Ltd. *Address:* c/o Kenneth D. Burrows, 425 Park Ave, New York, NY 10019, USA; 6 Bayley St, Bedford Sq., London WC1B 3HB, England.

JONSSON, Thorsteinn, (Thorsteinn Fra Hamri); b. 15 March 1938, Hamar, Iceland. Poet; Writer. *Publications:* I Svortum Kufli, 1958; Tannfe Handa Nyjum Heimi, 1960; Lifandi Manna Land, 1962; Langnaetti a Kaldadal, 1964; Jorvik, 1967; Vedra Hjalmur, 1972; Fidrid ur Saeng Daladrottningar, 1977; Spjotalog a Spegil, 1982; Ny Ljod, 1985; Urdargaldur, 1987; Vatns Gotur og Blods, 1989; Saefarinn Sofandi, 1992; Thad Talar I Trjanum, 1995; Ritsafn (collected works), 1998; Medan thu Vaktir, 1999; Vetrarmyndin, 2000. Other: Three novels. *Contributions to:* Various Icelandic and Scandinavian newspapers and magazines. *Honours:* Award, Writers Fund of the State Radio, 1962; Award, Ari Josefsson Memorial Fund, 1968; Cultural Award, Dagbladid newspaper, Reykjavík, 1981; Children's Book Literary Award for Trans., Reykjavík, 1981; Thorbergur Thordarson's Literary Prize, 1991; Icelandic Literary Prize, 1992. *Memberships:* Writers' Asscn of Iceland; PEN. *Address:* Smaragata 2, 101 Reykjavík, Iceland.

JOPE, Norman Francis; b. 28 May 1960, Plymouth, Devon, England. Administrator; Poet. *Education:* BA, Honours, Philosophy, University of Wales, 1982. *Appointments:* Various public sector administrative positions; Ed., Memes, 1989–94. *Publications:* Spoil, 1989; Tors, 1990; In the Absence of a Summit, 1992; Zones of Impulse, 1994; Francis, 1995; Time Over, 1995; Air, 1995; For the Wedding Guest, 1997; Terra Fabulosa, 1999. *Contributions to:* Anthologies and numerous magazines. *Membership:* The Language Club, Plymouth. *Address:* c/o 38 Molesworth Rd, Plympton, Plymouth, Devon PL7 4NT, England.

JORDAN, Andrew; b. 17 July 1959, Norfolk, England. Ed.; Poet. *Appointments:* Ed., Publisher, 10th Muse Magazine. *Publications:* Living in the Shadow of the Weather, 1984; Ancestral Deaths, 1985; St Catherine's Buried Chapel, 1987; Decoded Chronicles, 1987; The Invisible Children, 1991; The Mute Bride, 1996. *Contributions to:* Acumen; Orbis; Stand; PN Review; Tabla; Oasis; Shearsman; Angel Exhaust. *Address:* 33 Hartington Rd, Southampton SO14 0EW, England.

JORDAN, June; b. 9 July 1936, New York, NY, USA. Prof. of African-American Studies; Poet; Writer. m. Michael Meyer, 5 April 1955, divorced 1966, 1 s. *Education:* Barnard College, 1953–55, 1956–57; University of Chicago, 1955–56. *Appointments:* Faculty, City College of the City University of New York, 1967–69, Sarah Lawrence College, 1969–70, 1973–74; Prof. of English, State University of New York at Stony Brook, 1978–79; Visiting Poet-in-Residence, MacAlester College, 1980; Chancellor's Distinguished Lecturer, 1986, Prof. of Afro-American Studies and Women's Studies, 1989–93, Prof. of African-American Studies, 1994–, University of California at Berkeley; Playwright-in-Residence, 1987–88, Poet-in-Residence, 1988, New Dramatists, New York City; Visiting Prof., University of Wisconsin at Madison, 1988; Poet-in-Residence, Walt Whitman Birthplace Asscn, 1988. *Publications:* Who Look at Me, 1969; Soulscript, 1970; The Voice of the Children, 1970; Fannie Lou Hamer, 1971; His Own Where, 1971; Dry Victories, 1972; New Days: Poems of Exile and Return, 1974; New Life: New Room, 1975; Passion: New Poems 1977–80, 1980; Civil Wars: Selected Essays 1963–80, 1981; Kimako's Story, 1981; Things I Do in the Dark: Selected Poems 1954–77, 1981; Living Room: New Poems 1980–84, 1985; On Call: New Political Essays, 1981–85, 1985; Lyrical Campaigns: Selected Poems, 1989; Moving Towards Home: Selected Political Essays, 1989; Naming Our Destiny: New and Selected Poems, 1989; Technical Difficulties: New Political Essays, 1992; The Haruko/Love Poetry of June Jordan, 1993; I Was Looking at the Ceiling and Then I Saw the Sky, 1995; Affirmative Acts: New Political Essays, 1998; Soldier, A Poet's Childhood, 2000. *Contributions to:* Professional journals and magazines. *Honours:* Rockefeller Foundation Grant, 1969; Prix de Rome, 1970; CAPS Grant in Poetry, 1978; Yaddo Fellow, 1979, 1980; National Endowment for the Arts Fellowship, 1982; Achievement Award for International Reporting, National Asscn of Black Journalists, 1984; New York Foundation for the Arts Fellowship, 1985; MADRE Award for Leadership, 1989; Freedom to Write Award, PEN West, 1991; Lila Wallace/Reader's Digest Writers Award, 1995; Lifetime Achievement

Award, National Black Writers' Conference, 1998. *Memberships:* American Writers Congress; PEN American Center; Poets and Writers. *Address:* Dept of African American Studies, University of California at Berkeley, Berkeley, CA 94720-2572, USA.

JORIS, Pierre; b. 14 July 1946, Strasbourg, France. Poet; Trans.; Assoc. Prof. Companion, Nicole Peyrafitte, 2 s. *Education:* BA, Bard College, 1969; MA, Essex University, 1975; PhD, State University of New York at Binghamton, 1990. *Appointments:* Ed., Sixpack Magazine, 1972–77; Teacher, University of Constantine, Algeria, 1976–79; Visiting Writer, University of Iowa, 1987, University of California, 1990–92; Assoc. Prof., State University of New York, Albany, 1992–. *Publications:* Breccia (Selected Poems 1972–1986), 1987; Janus, 1988; The Irritation Ditch, 1991; Turbulence, 1991; Winnetou Old, 1994. *Contributions to:* Numerous professional journals, magazines, reviews and newspapers. *Honours:* Fonds Cultural National Writers Grant, Luxembourg, 1987; Co-Winner, PEN Center West Awards, USA, 1994, 1996. *Memberships:* Luxembourg Writers Union, founding mem., 1986–; PEN American Center. *Address:* 6 Madison Pl., Albany, NY 12202, USA.

JOSEPH, Jenny; b. 7 May 1932, Birmingham, England. Writer; Poet; Lecturer. m. C A Coles, 29 April 1961, deceased 1985, 1 s., 2 d. *Education:* BA, Honours, English, St Hilda's College, Oxford, 1953. *Publications:* The Unlooked-for Season, 1960; Warning, 1961; Boots, 1966; Rose in the Afternoon, 1974; The Thinking Heart, 1978; Beyond Descartes, 1983; Persephone, 1986; The Inland Sea, 1989; Beached Boats, 1991; Selected Poems, 1992; Ghosts and Other Company, 1995; Extended Smiles, 1997 Warning, 1997; All the Things I See (poems for children), 2000. Other: 6 children's books. *Contributions to:* Anthologies and magazines. *Honours:* Eric Gregory Award, 1962; Cholmondeley Award, 1974; Arts Council of Great Britain Award, 1975; James Tait Black Memorial Prize for Fiction, 1986; Society of Authors Travelling Scholarship, 1995; Forward Prize, 1995. *Memberships:* Centre for the Spoken Word, patron; National Poetry Society of Great Britain, council, 1975–78; Fellow, RSL. *Literary Agent:* John Johnson Ltd, London, England. *Address:* 17 Windmill Rd, Minchinhampton, Gloucestershire GL6 9DX, England.

JOSEPH, Lawrence; b. 10 March 1948, Detroit, Michigan, USA. Poet; Essayist; Critic; Prof. of Law. m. 10 April 1976. *Education:* BA 1970, JD 1975, University of Michigan; BA 1972, MA 1976, University of Cambridge. *Appointments:* Law Clerk, Michigan Supreme Court, Justice G Mennen Williams; Litigator, Shearman Sterling, New York City; Creative Writing Prof., Princeton University, New Jersey; Prof. of Law, St John's University School of Law, Jamaica, New York, 1987–. *Publications:* Shouting at No One, 1983; Curriculum Vitae, 1988; Before Our Eyes, 1993; Lawyerland: What Lawyers Talk about When They Talk about Law, 1997. *Contributions to:* Paris Review; Nation; Village Voice; Partisan Review; Poetry; Boulevard; Kenyon Review. *Honours:* Hopwood Award for Poetry, 1970; Agnes Lynch Starrett Poetry Prize, 1982; National Endowment for the Arts Poetry Award, 1984; Fellowship, Cambridge University. *Memberships:* PEN American Centre; Poetry Society of America; Poets House; National Writers Voice. *Address:* c/o Law School, St John's University, Jamaica, NY 11439, USA.

JOSHY, George Joseph; b. 30 May 1967, Meloor, India. Artist; Musician; Poet. *Education:* BSc. *Appointments:* Exhibitions of paintings, sculptures, and pencil sketches. *Contributions to:* Poems in several publications. *Honours:* Poetry awards. *Memberships:* Poetry Society of India; Socio-Literary Foundation, hon. dir, World Poetry Society. *Address:* Shee's International Art Centre, Meloor, PO 680311 CKDY-TCR, Kerala, India.

JOURDAN, Pat; b. 19 Oct. 1939, Liverpool, England. Artist; Poet. Divorced, 2 s. *Education:* NDD, Painting, Liverpool College of Art, 1961. *Appointments:* Various poetry readings. *Publications:* The Bedsit Girl, 1968; The Common Thread (ed.), 1989. *Contributions to:* Anthologies and periodicals. *Honours:* Borestone Mountain Poetry Award, 1969; Second Prize, Norwich Writers Circle, 1982. *Membership:* Norwich Poetry Group. *Address:* 5 Onley St, Unthank Rd, Norwich, Norfolk NR2 2EA, England.

JOY, Amy. See: ANDERSDATTER, Karla Margaret.

JOYCE, Veronica Dolores; b. 4 Feb. 1939, New York, NY, USA. Poet. *Education:* BS, 1963, MA, 1965, Fordham University; PhD, New York University, 1978. *Contributions to:* Anthologies and journals. *Honour:* Honourable Mention, California Quarterly Poetry Competition, 1990. *Memberships:* Poetry Society of America; South Florida Poetry Society. *Address:* PO Box 5634, Sun City Center, FL 33571, USA.

JOYETTE, Anthony; b. 21 Feb. 1949, St Vincent. Painter; Illustrator; Poet. m. 24 Sept. 1977, 2 d. *Education:* Bishop's College, Kingstown, St Vincent, 1969; Diplome d'Etudes Collegiales, Marie Victorian College, Québec, 1991. *Publications:* Germination of Feeling, 1980; Vincentian Poets 1950–1980, 1990. *Contributions to:* Kola, Québec; Bim, Barbados; Vince World, St Vincent; Matrix, Québec. *Honour:* World of Poetry Award, 1989. *Memberships:* Québec Black Writers Guild; Canadian Poetry Ass
cn; World of Poetry. *Address:* PO Box 1381, St Laurent, QC H4L 4X3, Canada.

JUANITA, Judy; b. 19 July 1946, Berkeley, CA, USA. College Instructor; Poet. 1 s. *Education:* BA, Psychology 1969, MFA, Creative Writing 1993, San Francisco State University. *Appointments:* San Francisco State University, 1969–71, 1992–93; Poet-in-the-Schools, New Jersey State Arts Council, 1982–88; Lecturer, Writing and Literature, Laney College, Oakland, 1993–, Holy Names College, 1996. *Publications:* Heaven's Hold, 1993; Knocked Up, 1994–95. *Contributions to:* 13th Moon; Painted Bride Quarterly; Croton Review; Lips; Passaic Review; Aquarian Weekly Rock Magazine; Bergen Poets; Rare Form; Rooms. *Honours:* New Jersey State Council on the Arts Fellowships for Poetry, 1982, 1986. *Address:* 6645 Eastlawn St, Oakland, CA 94621, USA.

JUDICE, Genevieve, (Genevieve Judice Didier DeWitt); b. 21 Oct. 1925, Lafayette, LA, USA. Homemaker; Poet. m. (1) Clyde P Didier Sr, 24 Aug. 1946, deceased, 1982, 5 s., 2 d., (2) Robert E DeWitt, 18 Feb. 1995. *Education:* BS, Business Administration, 1945. *Publications:* Captured Moments, 1993; False River Moods, 1996; Love Notes, 1996; Together We Sing (with Robert E DeWitt), 1998. *Contributions to:* Anthologies and newsletters. *Honours:* Numerous. *Memberships:* National Federation of State Poetry Societies; Louisiana State Poetry Society; Southern Poetry Asscn; Florida State Poets Asscn. *Address:* PO Box 77721, Baton Rouge, LA 70879-7721, USA.

JUDSON, John; b. 9 Sept. 1930, Stratford, CT, USA. Educator; Ed.; Writer; Poet. *Education:* BA, Colby College, 1958; University of Maine, 1962–63; MFA, University of Iowa, 1965. *Appointments:* Ed., Juniper Press, Northeast/Juniper Books, literary magazine and chapbook series, 1961–; Prof. of English, University of Wisconsin, La Crosse, 1965–93. *Publications:* Two From Where It Snows (co-author), 1963; Surreal Songs, 1968; Within Seasons, 1970; Voyages to the Inland Sea, six vols, 1971–76; Finding Worlds in Winter; West of Burnam South of Troy, 1973; Ash Is the Candle's Wick, 1974; Roots from the Onion's Dark, 1978; A Purple Tale, 1978; North of Athens, 1980; Letters to Jirac II, 1980; Reasons Why I Am Not Perfect, 1982; The Carrabassett Sweet William Was My River, 1982; Suite for Drury Pond, 1989; Muse(sic), 1992; The Inardo Poems, 1996. *Address:* 1310 Shorewood Dr., La Crosse, WI 54601, USA.

JUNKINS, Donald (Arthur); b. 19 Dec. 1931, Saugus, Massachusetts, USA. Poet; Writer; Prof. of English Emeritus. m. (1), 2 s., 1 d., (2) Kaimei Zheng, 18 Dec. 1993, 1 step-s. *Education:* BA, University of Massachusetts, 1953; STB, 1956, STM, 1957, AM, 1959, PhD, 1963, Boston University. *Appointments:* Instructor, 1961–62, Asst Prof., 1962–63, Emerson College, Boston; Asst Prof., Chico State College, CA, 1963–66; Asst Prof., 1966–69, Assoc. Prof., 1969–74, Dir, Master of Fine Arts Program in English, 1970–78, 1989–90, Prof. of English, 1974–95, Prof. Emeritus, 1995–, University of Massachusetts, Amherst. *Publications:* The Sunfish and the Partridge, 1965; The Graves of Scotland Parish, 1969; Walden, One Hundred Years After Thoreau, 1969; And Sandpipers She Said, 1970; The Contemporary World Poets (ed.), 1976; The Uncle Harry Poems and Other Maine Reminiscences, 1977; Crossing By Ferry: Poems New and Selected, 1978; The Agamenticus Poems, 1984; Playing for Keeps: Poems, 1978–1988, 1989; Andromache, by Euripides (trans.), 1998; Journey to the Corrida, 1998; Lines from Bimini Waters, 1998. *Contributions to:* Longman Anthology of American Poetry: Colonial to Contemporary; reviews, journals and magazines. *Honours:* Bread Loaf Writers Conference Poetry Scholarship, 1959; Jennie Tane Award for Poetry, 1968; John Masefield Memorial Award, 1973; National Endowment for the Arts Fellowships, 1974, 1979. *Memberships:* PEN; Hemingway Society; Fitzgerald Society. *Address:* 63 Hawks Rd, Deerfield, MA 01342, USA.

JUNLAKAN, Lesley Diane; b. 24 May 1955, Manchester, England. University English Teacher; Poet. m. Wilat Junlakan, 10 March 1988. *Education:* BA, Honours, 1976, MA, 1977, University of Manchester. *Appointments:* Tutor, College of Adult Education, Manchester, 1981–85; Lecturer, Thammasat University, Bangkok, Thailand, 1985–88; Srinakarinwirod University, Thailand, 1988–89, NIFS, Kanoya, Kagoshima, Japan, 1989–. *Publications:* Japanese Fan, Western Fingers, 1990; Plum Blossom and Persimmons. *Contributions to:* Azami; Haiku in English; Shi Miyaku; Katahira. *Memberships:* Azami, Osaka; National Poetry Foundation, England; Poetry Society, England. *Address:* Kimotsuki Cottage, Otemachi 12-15, Kanoya-shi, Kagoshima-ken 893, Japan.

JUSTICE, Donald (Rodney); b. 12 Aug. 1925, Miami, FL, USA. Prof. (retd); Poet; Writer. m. Jean Catherine Ross, 22 Aug. 1947, 1 s. *Education:* BA, University of Miami, 1945; MA, University of North Carolina, 1947; Postgraduate Studies, Stanford University, 1948–49; PhD, University of Iowa, 1954. *Appointments:* Instructor, University of Miami, 1947–51; Asst Prof., Hamline University, 1956–57; Lecturer, 1957–60, Asst Prof., 1960–63, Assoc. Prof., 1963–66, Prof., 1971–82, University of Iowa; Prof., Syracuse University, 1966–70, University of Florida at Gainesville, 1982–92. *Publications:* Poetry: The Summer Anniversaries, 1960; Night Light, 1967; Departures, 1973; Selected Poems, 1979; The Sunset Maker, 1987; A Donald Justice Reader, 1992; New and Selected Poems, 1995. Other: The Collected Poems of Weldon Kees (ed.), 1962; Platonic Scripts (essays), 1984; Oblivion: On Writers and Writing, 1998; Orpheus Hesitated Beside the Black River, 1998. *Contributions to:* Journals and magazines. *Honours:* Rockefeller Foundation Fellowship, 1954; Lamont Award, 1959; Ford Foundation Fellowship, 1964; National Endowment for the Arts Grants, 1967, 1973, 1980, 1989; Guggenheim

Fellowship, 1976; Pulitzer Prize in Poetry, 1980; Acad. of American Poets Fellowship, 1988; Co-Winner, Bollingen Prize, 1991; Lannan Literary Award, 1996. *Memberships:* Acad. of American Poets, board of chancellors, 1997–; American Acad. of Arts and Letters. *Address:* 338 Rocky Shore Dr., Iowa City, IA 52246, USA.

JUTEAU, Monique; b. 8 Jan. 1949, Montréal, QC, Canada. Poet; Author. *Education:* MA, French Literature, 1987. *Publications:* Poetry: La Lune Aussi, 1975; Regard Calligraphes, 1986; Trop Plein D'Angles, 1990; Des jours de chemins perdus et retrouvés, 1997. Fiction: En Moins de Deux, 1990; L'Emporte-Clé, 1994; La Fin des Terres, 2001. *Contributions to:* Various publications. *Honours:* Prix Gerald-Godin, 1998; Télé-Québec Prix Daring, 2002; Second Prize, Grands Prix Littéraires, Radio-Canada, 2002. *Memberships:* Société des Écrivains de la Mauricie; Union des Écrivains du Québec. *Address:* 19200 Forest, Becancour, QC G9H 1P9, Canada. *E-mail:* monique_juteau@uqtr.uquebec.ca.

K

KABADI, Dwarakanath; b. 17 Feb. 1936, Bangalore City, India. Auditor and Advocate (retd); Poet. m. Smt Chandrakantha Kabadi, 24 May 1962, 3 s. *Education:* BCom, 1958; BL, 1963. *Publications:* Symphony of Skeletons, 1985; Ruptured Senses, 1985; Geetha Gangothri, 1987; Minchina Butti, 1988; Tender Wings (children's poems), 1988; Melting Moments, 1990; Swapna Sopana, 1993; Naguva Mallige, 1994; Kabadi's Glimmericks, 1994; A Tear on a Pancake, 1995; Kolminchina Daariyalli, 1996; Golden Glimmers, 1997; Heegu ondu Ithihasa, 1998; Shimmering Waves, 2000; Snail-Pace Street, 2000; Sharana Kirana, 2000; Belakabimbadali, 2001; Chariot of Dreams, 2002. *Contributions to:* Various publications. *Honours:* Chancellor of the Congress and Bronze Plaque, World Congress of Poets, Baltimore, 1976; Diploma of Merit, Universite delle Arte, Italy, 1982; Medallion of Honour, Melbourne Poetry Society, 1988; Michael Madhusudan International Poetry Award, 1988; Hon. degrees. *Memberships:* Federation of International Poetry Asscns; Garden of World Poets, founder-pres.; Poets International Organization, founder-pres.; World Poetry Society, life fellow. *Address:* No. 80, Fifth Cross, Eighth Block, First Main, BDA Layout, RMV Second Stage, Bangalore 560 094, India.

KADARÉ, Ismail; b. 28 Jan. 1936, Gjirokastër, Albania. Writer; Poet. m. Elena, 2 d. *Education:* University of Tirana; Gorky Institute of World Literature, Moscow. *Publications:* Fiction: Gjenerali i ushtërisë së vdekur, 1963. English trans. as The General of the Dead Army, 1971; Kështjella, 1970, English trans. as The Castle, 1974; Kronikë në gur, 1971, English trans. as Chronicle in Stone, 1987; Ura më tri harque, 1978, English trans. as The Three-Arched Bridge, 1995; Kush e solli doruntinen, 1980, English trans. as Doruntine, 1988; Prilli i thyer, 1980, English trans. as Broken April, 1990; Nëpunësi i pallatit të ëndrrave, 1980, English trans. as The Palace of Dreams, 1993; Nje dosje per Homerin, 1980, English trans. as The File on H, 1998; Koncert në fund të dimrit, 1988, English trans. as The Concert, 1994; Piramida, 1992, English trans. as The Pyramid, 1996; Oeuvres, 1993–97, 5 vols, 1997; Il a fallu ce deuil pour se retrouver, 2000. Poetry: Six vols, 1954–80. Other: Short stories, criticism, essays, etc. *Address:* c/o Librairie Artheme Fayard, 75 rue des Saints-Pères, 75006 Paris, France.

KADMON, Jean Ball Kosloff; b. 1 Aug. 1922, Denver, CO, USA. Poet; Novelist; Painter. m. 18 Aug. 1945, 2 s. *Education:* BA, University of Alberta, 1943; Graduate Studies, Anthropology, University of Chicago, 1944–46. *Appointments:* Anthropologist, International Centre for Community Development, Haifa, Israel, 1964–65; Sociologist, Jewish Agency, Israel, 1966–68. *Publications:* Moshav Segev, 1972; Clais and Clock, 1988; Peering Out, 1996; MacKenzie Breakup, 1997. *Contributions to:* Anthologies and periodicals. *Honour:* Second Prize, New Zealand International Writers Workshop, 1981. *Membership:* Israel Asscn of Writers in English. *Address:* 12 Zerubbabel St, Jerusalem 93505, Israel.

KADOTA, Teruko; b. 9 April 1935, Fukuoka, Japan. Poet. m. Yasusuke Kadota, 9 Nov. 1960, 2 c. *Publications:* Pilgrimage, 1979; The Front of Allergy, 1989; Fare Well!, 1992; Responses From the Past, 1995; An Embrace, 1996. *Honours:* Poet of Fukuoka Prefecture, 1997; Shizuo Ito Prize, 2001. *Memberships:* Four Seasons of Tokyo; Japan Poets Club; Japan Modern Poets Asscn; Japan Literary People's Asscn. *Address:* 4-38-5 Hiigawa, Jonan-ku, Fukuoka-City, 814-0153, Japan.

KAHN, Sy; b. 15 Sept. 1924, New York, NY, USA. Prof. Emeritus; Writer; Poet. m. Janet Baker, 1 s. *Education:* BA, Honours, University of Pennsylvania, 1948; MA, University of Connecticut, 1951; PhD, University of Wisconsin, 1957. *Appointments:* Asst Prof., Beloit College, 1955–60, University of South Florida, 1960–63; Fulbright Prof. of American Literature, University of Salonika, Greece, 1958–59, University of Warsaw, 1966–67, University of Vienna, 1970–71, University of Porto, Portugal, 1985–86; Prof. of English and Humanities, Raymond College, 1963–68; Prof. of Drama and English, 1968–86, Chair., Dept of Drama, 1970–81, Prof. Emeritus, 1986–, University of the Pacific. *Publications:* Our Separate Darkness, 1963; Triptych, 1964; The Fight is With Phantoms, 1966; A Later Sun, 1966; Another Time, 1968; Facing Mirrors, 1981; Devour the Fire: Selected Poems of Harry Crosby (ed.), 1984; Between Tedium and Terror: A Soldier's World War II Diary, 1993. *Contributions to:* Various anthologies, journals, reviews and quarterlies. *Honours:* Gardner Writing Awards, University of Wisconsin, 1954, 1955; Crosby Writing Fellowships, 1962, 1963; Borestone Poetry Award, 1964; Promethean Lamp Prize, 1966; Grand Prize in Poetry, University of the Pacific, 1985. *Membership:* MLA. *Address:* Ravenshill House, 1212 Holcomb St, Port Townsend, WA 98368, USA.

KAMANDA, Kama; b. 11 Nov. 1952, Luebo, Belgian Congo. Poet; Writer; Critic; Lecturer. *Education:* Political Science Degree, University of Kinshasa, 1973; Law Degrees, University of Liège, 1981, University of Strasbourg, 1988. *Publications:* Chants de brumes, 1986; Les Résignations, 1986; Éclipse

d'étoiles, 1987; La Somme du néant, 1989; L'Exil des songes, 1992; Les Myriades des temps vécus, 1992; Les Vents de l'épreuve, 1993; Lointaine sont les rives de destin, 1994; Quand dans l'âme les mers s'agitent, 1994; L'Étreinte des mots, 1995; Oeuvre Poétique, 1999; Les contes du crépuscule, 2000. *Honours:* Paul Verlaine Award, 1987; Théophile Gautier Award, 1993, Académie Française; Silver Medals, Institut de France, 1987, 1993; Melina Mercouri Award, Asscn of Greek Writers and Poets, 1999; Poet of the Millennium Award, International Poets Acad., India, 2000. *Address:* 18 Am Moul, 7418 Buschdorf, Luxembourg.

KAMERER, Jocelyne Maria; b. 6 Sept. 1950, Pont-a-Moussons, France. Poet. *Education:* Upsala College, East Orange, New Jersey. *Publications:* Reflections, 1990; Life Within. *Contributions to:* Periodicals. *Honours:* Gold Quill Award, 1990; Robert Bennett's Viewpoint Award of Poetic Excellence, 1990; Sparrowgrass Anthology Writer of the Month, 1990; Imagination Golden Poet, 1990; Silver Quill Award, 1991; First Place, Plowman, 1991; 4 Blue Ribbon Awards, Southern Poetry Asscn, 1991; Poets of Now Award, World of Poetry, 1992; Third Place, Khepera, 1994. *Memberships:* National Asscn. *Address:* 2816 Airport Rd, No. 122, Colorado Springs, CO 80910, USA.

KANE, Julie; b. 20 July 1952, Boston, Massachusetts, USA. Poet; Writer. *Education:* BA, Distinction, English, Cornell University, 1974; MA, Creative Writing, Boston University, 1975; Louisiana State University. *Appointment:* Writer-in-Residence, Phillips Exeter Acad., New Hampshire, 1975–76. *Publications:* Two into One, 1982; Body and Soul, 1987; The Bartender Poems, 1991. *Contributions to:* Anthologies, reviews, journals, and magazines. *Honours:* Honourable Mention, Boston University Graduate Poetry Contest, 1990; National Merit Award, Poetry Atlanta Prize, 1990; Acad. of American Poets Prize, 1993. *Memberships:* New Orleans Gulf South Booksellers Asscn, assoc. mem.; New Orleans Poetry Forum; Poets and Writers. *Address:* 7111 Walmsley Ave, New Orleans, LA 70125, USA.

KANE, Paul; b. 23 March 1950, Cobleskill, New York, USA. Poet; Critic; Prof. of English. m. Christine Reynolds, 21 June 1980. *Education:* BA, 1973, MA, 1987, MPhil, 1988, PhD, 1990, Yale University; MA, University of Melbourne, 1985. *Appointments:* Instructor, Briarcliff College, 1975–77; Assoc., Institute for World Order, 1982; Dir of Admissions and Instructor, Wooster School, 1982–84; Part-time Instructor, Yale University, 1988–90; Prof. of English, Vassar College, 1990–. *Publications:* The Farther Shore, 1989; A Hudson Landscape (with William Cliff), 1993; Ralph Waldo Emerson: Collected Poems and Translations, 1994; Poetry of the American Renaissance, 1995; Australian Poetry: Romanticism and Negativity, 1996; Emerson: Essays and Poems, 1996; Drowned Lands, 2000. *Contributions to:* Articles, poems, and reviews in New Republic; Paris Review; Poetry; Sewanee Review; Partisan Review; Raritan; Antipodes; The New Criterion. *Honours:* Fulbright Scholar, 1984–85; National Endowment for the Humanities Grant, 1998; Guggenheim Fellowship, 1999. *Memberships:* Acad. of American Poets; PEN; Poetry Society of America. *Address:* 8 Big Island, Warwick, NY 10990, USA.

KANG, Shin Il; b. 1 April 1943, Samye, Jeonbuk, Korea. Teacher; Poet. m. Sun-Deok Jeon, 7 Feb. 1971, 2 s., 1 d. *Education:* BA, 1967, MEd, 1985, Jeonbuk National University. *Appointment:* Sec.-Gen., World Poetry Research Institute, 1993–97. *Publications:* Getting Off the Last Step of the Four Seasons, 1991; In the Place Where Colours of Solitude and Love Remain, 1995. *Contributions to:* Anthologies and magazines. *Honours:* New Poet Prize, Moonyesajo, 1990; Kaya Gold Crown World Poets Award, World Poetry Research Institute, 1996. *Memberships:* Korea Literary Men's Asscn; International PEN; Jeonbuk Literary Men's Asscn; Korea Free Poets Asscn; Korea Literary Space Poets' Asscn; Jeonbuk Catholic Literary Asscn, pres.; Iksan Literary Men's Asscn, pres. *Address:* 957-1 Samye-Ri, Samye-Eub, Wanju-Kun, Jeonbuk 565-802, Republic of Korea. *Telephone:* (63) 291-2280. *E-mail:* jb43@netian.com.

KANNAN, Lakshmi (Kaaveri); b. 13 Aug. 1947, Mysore, India. Writer; Poet. m. L. V. Kannan, 2 s. *Education:* BA, MA, PhD, English. *Appointment:* Writer-in-Residence, University of Kent at Canterbury, 1993. *Publications:* Glow and the Grey, 1976; Exiled Gods, 1985; Rhythms, 1986; India Gate, 1993; Going Home, 1999. Other: Books in Hindi and Tamil. *Honour:* Hon. Fellow in Writing, University of Iowa. *Memberships:* American Studies Research Centre, Hyderabad; Indian International Centre, Delhi, life mem.; Indian Asscn for American Studies; Poetry Society, India, founder-mem. and treasurer, 1986–. *Address:* B-11/8193, Vasant Kunj, New Delhi 110030, India.

KANTARIS, Sylvia; b. 9 Jan. 1936, Grindleford, Derbyshire, England. Poet; Writer; Teacher. m. Emmanuel Kantaris, 11 Jan. 1958, 1 s., 1 d. *Education:* Diplome d'Etudes Civilisation Française, Sorbonne, University of Paris, 1955; BA, Honours, 1957, CertEd, 1958, Bristol University; MA, 1967, PhD, 1972, University of Queensland, Australia. *Appointments:* Tutor, University of Queensland, Australia, 1963–66, Open University, England, 1974–84; Extra-Mural

Lecturer, Exeter University, 1974–. *Publications:* Time and Motion, 1975; Stocking Up, 1981; The Tenth Muse, 1983; News From the Front (with D M Thomas), 1983; The Sea at the Door, 1985; The Air Mines of Mistila (with Philip Gross), 1988; Dirty Washing: New and Selected Poems, 1989; Lad's Love, 1993. *Contributions to:* Many anthologies, newspapers, and magazines. *Honours:* National Poetry Competition Award, 1982; Hon. Doctor of Letters, Exeter University, 1989; Major Arts Council Literature Award, 1991; Society of Authors Award, 1992. *Memberships:* Poetry Society of Great Britain; South West Arts, literature panel, 1983–87, literary consultant, 1990–. *Address:* 14 Osborne Parc, Helston, Cornwall TR13 8PB, England.

KANTOR, Peter; b. 5 Nov. 1949, Budapest, Hungary. Poet. *Education:* MA, English and Russian Literature, 1973, MA, Hungarian Literature, 1980, Budapest ELTE University. *Appointment:* Literary Ed., Kortars magazine, 1984–86; Poetry Ed., Élet és Irodalom, magazine, 1997–2000. *Publications:* Kavics, 1976; Halmadar, 1981; Sebbel Lobbal, 1982; Gradicsok, 1985; Hogy no az eg, 1988; Naplo, 1987–89, 1991; Font lomb, lent avar, 1994; Mentafü (selected poems), 1994; Bucsu és Megérkezés, 1997. *Contributions to:* Various publications. *Honours:* George Soros Fellowship, 1988–89; Wessely Laszlo Award, 1990; Dery Tibor Award, 1991; Fulbright Fellowship, 1991–92; Fust Milan Award, 1992; József Attila Award, 1994; George Soros Award, 1999. *Memberships:* Hungarian Writers Union; International PEN Club. *Address:* Stollar Bela u 3/a, Budapest 1055, Hungary.

KAPLAN, Susan Robin; b. 13 Dec. 1958, Philadelphia, Pennsylvania, USA. Asst Prof. of English Literature; Poet. *Education:* BA, Religion, Temple University, 1980; MA, English, University of Southern Mississippi, 1982; PhD, English, Creative Writing, University of Houston, 1987. *Appointments:* Instructor, University of Southern Mississippi; Asst Ed., Mississippi Review; Asst Prof. of English Literature, Virginia Military Institute, Lexington. *Contributions to:* Poetry; New Orleans Review; Boulevard. *Honours:* Acad. of American Poets Award, 1986; Ruth Lake Memorial Award, Poetry Society of America, 1989. *Memberships:* Associated Writing Programs; Poetry Society of America. *Address:* Dept of English, Virginia Military Institute, Lexington, VA 24450, USA.

KAPODISTRIAS, Panagiotis; b. 16 Nov. 1961, Zakynthos, Greece. Hellenic Orthodox Priest; Prof.; Poet. m. Fotini Papantoni, 5 Sept. 1982, 2 s., 1 d. *Education:* University of Athens. *Appointments:* General Vicar, Holy Metropolis of Zakynthos, 1987; Parish Priest, Banato Church, Zakynthos, 1987–; Prof., School of Music, Zakynthos, 1992–98; Prof., First High School, Zakynthos, 1998–. *Publications:* As If Painting on Glass, 1987; Translucent Waters, 1992; When the Cave-Owner Cometh, 1995; Outlines for a Eulogy for Odysseus Elytis, 1997; Dream with Dome, 1999; The Last Friend, 2001. *Honour:* Haiku Poetry Prize, Japanese Embassy, Athens, 1993. *Memberships:* Parnassos Literature Society, 1998; National Asscn of Greek Authors, 2000; Zakynthos Public Library, governing committee. *Address:* Banato, GR 291 00 Zakynthos, Greece. *E-mail:* kap61@otenet.gr. *Website:* genesis.ee.auth.gr/dimakis/archilochos/pk/orthostasia.html.

KAPSALIS, John; b. 27 Jan. 1927, Mytelene, Greece. Poet. m. Athena, 2 Sept. 1956, 2 d. *Education:* BS, 1954; MS, 1955; PhD, 1959; Postdoctoral Studies, Ohio University, 1959. *Publications:* The Odds, 1972; Twentyeth and Other Centuries, 1974; The Saga of Chrysodontis Pappas, 1994; Tales of Pergamos, 1999. *Contributions to:* Dark Horse; Bitterroot; Northeast Journal; Nebraska Review. *Honour:* Massachusetts Artists Foundation Poetry Award, 1985. *Memberships:* American Poets and Fiction Writers; Acad. of American Poets. *Address:* 5776 Deauville Lake Circle No. 308, Naples, FL 34112, USA.

KARAHLIOU-TOKA, Melita; b. 17 June 1940, Thessaloniki, Greece. Poet; Writer. m. Konstantinos Karahalios, 1 s., 1 d. *Education:* Degree, French Philology. *Publications:* Passages, 1980; Wandering, 1983; Ideograms, 1995; The Night is Born Liquid, 1997; Phaeô, the Sleeplessness of the Open Sea, 1999. *Contributions to:* Periodicals. *Honours:* Giovanni Gronchi, 1998; Special Award, Poets and Authors Society, Nîmes, 1998; French-speaking Poet's Award, Allauch, 1999; First Prize for French-speaking Poet, Marseille, 2000. *Membership:* Thessaloniki Literary Society. *Address:* 5 Kapetan Dogra St, Malakopi, Thessaloniki 54352, Greece.

KARAMBA, Evangelia, (Lina Karamba); b. 12 April 1942, Larissa, Greece. Journalist; Poet. m. Thrasky Karambas, 1 Dec., 2 s. *Publications:* Kykloi, 1972; Diastaseis, 1974; Synola, 1978; Fasma, 1985; Alpha, 1988; Laas, 1998. *Contributions to:* Various Greek magazines. *Address:* 42 Alolou St, Larissa 41221, Greece.

KARARACH, Auma; b. 20 May 1965, Gulu, Uganda. Development Economist; Poet. *Education:* BA, Makerere University, 1989; MA, 1991, PhD, Leeds University, England. *Publications:* A Feast of Poison, 1986; The Pains of Our Heart, 1988. *Contributions to:* Lobo Mews; Dowing Magazine; Radio Uganda Writers Club Programme. *Honour:* Acoli Young Poets Award, 1987. *Memberships:* Poetry Society, London; Acoli Writing Club; Royal Economic Society. *Address:* Flat 5, 20 Kelso Rd, Leeds LS2 9PR, England.

KARASEK, Krzysztof; b. 19 Feb. 1937, Warsaw, Poland. Ed.; Literary Critic Poet. 1 d. *Education:* Philosophy, University of Warsaw. *Appointments:* Co Founder, Ed., Nowy Wyraz Literary Monthly, 1972–76; Ed., Poetry Section Polish Radio, 1976–82, Essays, Literature Monthly, 1983–92, Poetry, Przedswit Publishing House, 1992–; Vice-Dir and Deputy in Chief, II Program, Polish Radio. *Publications:* Godzina Jastrzebi, 1970; Drozd i inne wiersze, 1972 Poezje, 1974; Prywatna historia ludzkosci, 1978; Trzy poematy, 1982 Wiersze i poematy, 1982; Sceny z Grottgera i Inne wiersze, 1984; Poezje wybrane, 1986; Swierszcze, 1987; Lekcja biologi i Inne wiersze, 1990; Poeta nie spoznia sie ne poemat, 1991; Poezje, 1994; Czerwone jabluszko, 1994 *Contributions to:* Polish and foreign periodicals and magazines. *Honours:* Czerwona Roza Prize, 1969; Prize, Best Poetry Book of Year, Literature 1990. *Memberships:* Polish PEN; Society of Polish Writers. *Address:* Walbrzyska 15-402, 02-739 Warsaw, Poland.

KARAVIA, Lia Headzopoulou; b. 27 June 1932, Athens, Greece. Writer Poet; Dramatist. m. Vassillis Karavias, 20 Sept. 1953, 2 s. *Education:* Diploma English Literature, Pierce College, Athens, 1953; Diploma, French Literature Institute of France, Athens, 1954; Diploma, Acting School, Athens, 1962 Classical Literature, University of Athens, 1972; Doctorat Nouveau Regime Comparative Literature, Paris, 1991. *Publications:* 10 novels; 10 poetry collections; Stage and radio plays; Television scripts. *Contributions to:* Anthologies, journals, and magazines. *Honours:* Menelaos Loudemis Prize, 1980; Michaela Averof Prize, 1981; Prizes for plays for Young People, 1986, 1987, 1988; National Prize for Best Play for Young People, 1989; National Playwrights Prizes, 1990, 1991. *Memberships:* International Theatre Institute, Greek Centre, secretary general; Maison Internationale de la Poésie, Liège: Society of Greek Writers; Union of Greek Playwrights; Greek Centre of IBBY. *Literary Agent:* Wendy Gresser, 24 Pottery Lane, Holland Park, London W11 4LZ, England. *Address:* 51 Aghiou Polycarpou St, Nea Smyrni 17124, Athens, Greece.

KARIM, Fawzi; b. 1 July 1945, Baghdad, Iraq. Poet; Writer; Ed.; Publisher. m. 31 Dec. 1980, 2 s. *Education:* BA, Arabic Literature, College of Arts, Baghdad, 1967. *Appointment:* Ed.-in-Chief and Publisher, Al-Lahda Al-Shiriya quarterly, London. *Publications:* Where Things Begin, 1968; I Raise My Hand in Protest, 1973; Madness of Stone, 1977; Stumbling of a Bird, 1985; We Do Not Inherit the Earth, 1988; Schemes of Adam, 1991; Pestilential Continents, 1995; Selected Poems, 1968–95, 1995; Collected Poems, in two vols, 2000. Other: From Exile to Awareness, 1972; City of Copper, 1995; The Emperor's Clothes, 2000; The Musical Values, 2002; Essays and short stories. *Contributions to:* Reviews and periodicals. *Memberships:* Poetry Society, England; Union of Iraqi Writers. *Address:* 81 Hill Rise, Greenford, Middlesex UB6 8PE, England. *E-mail:* fawzi46@hotmail.com.

KAROL, Pamala Marie, (La Loca); b. 29 March 1950, Los Angeles, CA, USA. Legal Secretary; Poet. *Education:* University of California, Berkeley, 1967–71; First Teaching Certificate in French, Sorbonne, University of Paris, 1973; BA, Communication Arts, Columbia College, 1974; Graduate Studies, Film, Loyola Marymount University; Poetry Workshop with Ron Koertge, Pasadena City College. *Publications:* The Mayan, 1988; Adventures on the Isle of Adolescence, 1989. *Contributions to:* Threepenny Review; Steaua; Kozmik Blues; Gridlock; Los Angeles Times; Poetry Australia; Jacaranda Review; City Lights Review; Pretext; Endless Party; Inscape; Sierra Madre Review. *Honours:* Fellowship for Graduate Studies in Film, Acad. of Motion Picture Arts and Sciences, 1974, 1976; College Prize, Acad. of American Poets, 1986; Official US Representative, Winter Olympic Writers Festival, Calgary, Canada, 1988; Artists Fellowship in Literature, California Arts Council, 1988–89; National Endowment for the Arts Fellowship in Literature, 1994. *Memberships:* PEN Center USA West; Poetry Society of America; Acad. of American Poets; National Writers Union. *Literary Agent:* Carol Lees Management. *Address:* 1608 N Cahuenga Blvd No. 562, Los Angeles, CA 90028, USA.

KARR-KIDWELL, P. J.; b. 15 July 1952, Ludlow, Massachusetts, USA. University Prof.; Writer; Poet. m. David Casey Kidwell, 10 Aug. 1980. *Education:* BA, University of New Hampshire, 1974; MA, 1975, PhD, 1976, Ohio State University. *Appointments:* Prof., Texas Woman's University, 1977–. *Publication:* Youth and Adolescence: The Rising Generation, Subcultures and Contemporary Society, 1981. *Contributions to:* Journals, anthologies and periodicals. *Honours:* Over 55 professional awards. *Address:* 3804 Red Oak Dr., Route 4, Corinth, TX 76208, USA.

KASISCHKE, Laura; b. 5 Dec. 1961, Lake Charles, LA, USA. Poet; Writer; Teacher. m. William Abernethy, Aug. 1994, 1 s. *Education:* BA, 1984, MFA, 1987, University of Michigan; Graduate Studies, Columbia University. *Appointments:* Instructor in Writing, South Plains College, Levelland, Texas, 1987–88; Visiting Lecturer in Creative Writing and Literature, Eastern Michigan University, 1989–90; Instructor in Creative Writing and Literature, Washtenaw Community College, Ann Arbor, 1990–; Assoc. Prof., University of Nevada, Las Vegas, 1994–95. *Publications:* Poetry: Brides, Wives, and Widows, 1990; Wild Brides, 1992; Housekeeping in a Dream, 1995. Fiction: Suspicious River, 1996; The Life Before Her Eyes, 2001. *Contributions to:* Numerous periodicals. *Honours:* Michael Gutterman Poetry Award, 1983; Marjorie Rapaport Poetry Award, 1986; Michigan Council for the Arts Individual

Artist Grant, 1990; Ragdale Foundation Fellowships, 1990–92; Elmer Holmes Bobst Award for Emerging Writers, 1991; Bread Loaf Fellow in Poetry, 1992; MacDowell Colony Fellow, 1992; Creative Artists Award, Arts Foundation of Michigan, 1993; Alice Fay DiCastagnola Award, 1993; Pushcart Prize, 1993; Barbara Deming Memorial Award, 1994; National Endowment for the Arts Fellowship, 1994; Poets & Writers Exchange Fellowship, 1994. *Address:* 2997 S Fletcher Rd, Chelsea, MI 48118, USA.

KASPER, Stanley Frank; b. 11 May 1920, Erie, Pennsylvania, USA. Writer; Poet. m. Rita Marina Komiskey, 25 March 1944, 1 s., 2 d. *Education:* BA, 1972, MA, 1974, Goddard College, Vermont. *Publications:* Poems of Life, 1985; Slices of Life, 1988; Images of Life, 1990. *Contributions to:* Norristown Times Herald; Byline; Creative Enterprises; Poet's Review; Poetry Press; Fine Arts Press; Poetic Page; New York Poetry Foundation; Piper Calling; Lucidity; Cambridge Collection; Apropos; Suwanne Poetry. *Honour:* Best Valentine's Poem, Poet's Review, 1991. *Memberships:* Pennsylvania Poetry Society; Philadelphia Writers Conference; St David's Christian Writers Conference. *Address:* 2803 Curtis Lane, Lansdale, PA 19446, USA.

KASPER, Wayne Lee; b. 17 Oct. 1956, Columbia, Missouri, USA. Poet; Poetry Ed.; Naturalist. 1 s., 2 d. *Education:* BA, English, 1989, MA, English, 1991, Central Missouri State University. *Appointment:* Poetry Ed., Gray. *Contributions to:* Amherst Society, 1989, 1990; Trellis; Protea; Green Fuse; Poetry Explosion Newsletter: Pen; Minotaur; Old Hickory Review; Potpourri; Word and Image; Tin Wreath; Feelings; Reflections; Plowman; Onionhead; Portable Wall; Long Islander; My Legacy; Tandava; IaZer; World of Poetry. *Address:* 18212 Westwood Dr., Sterling, CO 80751, USA.

KATZ, Bobbi; b. 2 May 1933, Newburgh, New York, USA. Poet; Author; Ed. m. H D Katz, 1956, divorced 1979, 1 s., deceased, 1 d. *Education:* BA, Goucher College, 1954. *Appointment:* Ed., Books for Young Readers, Random House, New York City, 1982–94. *Publications:* Books for children, including picturebooks; A biography of Nelson Mandela; Professional books for teachers; Poetry anthologies; 10 collections of poetry, including We the People. *Contributions to:* Anthologies of poetry and essays. *Memberships:* Authors' Guild; PEN International. *Address:* 65 W 96th St, 21H, New York, NY 10025, USA. *E-mail:* bobbikatz@aol.com.

KATZ, Steve; b. 14 May 1935, New York, NY, USA. Writer; Poet; Screenwriter; Prof. m. Patricia Bell, 10 June 1956, divorced, 3 s. *Education:* BA, Cornell University, 1956; MA, University of Oregon, 1959. *Appointments:* English Language Institute, Lecce, Italy, 1960; Overseas Faculty, University of Maryland, Lecce, Italy, 1961–62; Asst Prof. of English, Cornell University, 1962–67; Lecturer in Fiction, University of Iowa, 1969–70; Writer-in-Residence, 1970–71, Co-Dir, Projects in Innovative Fiction, 1971–73, Brooklyn College, City University of New York; Adjunct Asst Prof., Queens College, City University of New York, 1973–75; Assoc. Prof. of English, University of Notre Dame, 1976–78; Assoc. Prof. of English, 1978–82, Prof. of English, 1982–, University of Colorado at Boulder. *Publications:* Fiction: The Lestriad, 1962; The Exagggerations of Peter Prince, 1968; Posh, 1971; Saw, 1972; Moving Parts, 1977; Wier and Pouce, 1984; Florry of Washington Heights, 1987; Swanny's Ways, 1995. Short Stories: Creamy and Delicious: Eat my Words (in Other Words), 1970; Stolen Stories, 1985; 43 Fictions, 1991. Poetry: The Weight of Antony, 1964; Cheyenne River Wild Track, 1973; Journalism, 1990. Screenplay: Grassland, 1974. *Honours:* PEN Grant, 1972; Creative Artists Public Service Grant, 1976; National Educational AsscnGrants, 1976, 1982; GCAH Book of the Year, 1991; America Award in Fiction, 1995. *Memberships:* Authors' League of America; PEN International; Writers' Guild. *Address:* 669 Washington St, No. 602, Denver, CO 80203, USA.

KATZ, Vincent; b. 4 June 1960, New York, NY, USA. Poet; Trans.; Critic. m. Vivien Bittencourt, 16 Nov. 1987, 2 s. *Education:* BA, Music, Classics, University of Chicago, 1982; BA, MA, Classics, Oxford University, England, 1985. *Appointments:* Assoc. Ed., The Print Collectors Newsletter, New York City, 1988–90. *Publications:* Rooms, 1978; A Tremor in the Morning, 1986; Cabal of Zealots, 1988; New York Hello!, 1990; Charm, by Propertius (trans.), 1995; Boulevard Transportation, 1997; Pearl, 1998; Understanding Objects, 2000. *Contributions to:* World; New American Writing; Exquisite Corpse; Broadway; Fred; Tranfer; New Censorship; Poetry Project Newsletter; Caffeine Destiny; Can We Have Our Ball Back?; Conjunctions; The East Village; Milk; Shampoo. *Honours:* Billings Fiske Poetry Prize, University of Chicago, 1982; Selected by Kenneth Koch to read at PEN Young Writers Series, 1988; John Guail Writer's Fund Rome Prize Fellowship, American Acad., Rome. *Membership:* Poets and Writers; PEN International. *Address:* 211 W 19th St, No. 5, New York, NY 10011, USA. *E-mail:* vincent@elnet. *Website:* www.vincentkatz.com.

KAUFMAN, Alan; b. 12 Jan. 1952, New York, NY, USA. Writer; Poet; Ed. m. Diane Spencer, 1 d. *Education:* BA, City College of the City University of New York, 1975; Columbia University, 1986–87. *Appointments:* Founder-Ed., Jewish Arts Quarterly, 1974–75; Jewish Cultural Revolution, 1996–97; TATTOOJEW.COM, 1998–2001; Many poetry performances. *Publications:* The End of Time (short stories), 1985; The New Generation: Fiction for Our Time from America's Writing Programs (ed.), 1987; Who Are We? (poems),

1997; The Outlaw Bible of American Poetry (ed.), 1999; Jew Boy: A Memoir, 2000. *Contributions to:* Anthologies and periodicals. *Honour:* Firecracker Alternative Book Award, 2000. *Address:* 1126 Bush St, Apt 605, San Francisco, CA 94109, USA.

KAUFMAN, Shirley; b. 5 June 1923, Seattle, WA, USA. Poet; Trans. m. (1), 3 d., (2) Hillel Daleski, 19 June 1974. *Education:* BA, University of California at Los Angeles, 1944; MA, California State University, San Francisco, 1967. *Appointments:* Visiting Lecturer, University of Massachusetts, Amherst, 1974; Visiting Prof., University of Washington, Seattle, 1977, Hebrew University, Jerusalem, 1983–84; Poet-in-Residence, Oberlin College, OH, 1979, 1989. *Publications:* The Floor Keeps Turning, 1970; Gold Country, 1973; From One Life to Another, 1979; Looking at Henry Moore's Elephant Skull Etchings in Jerusalem During the War, 1977; Claims, 1984; Rivers of Salt, 1993; Roots in the Air: New and Selected Poems, 1996; Threshold, 2003. Other: Several trans. *Contributions to:* American Poetry Review; Atlantic; Field; Harper's; Iowa Review; Nation; New Republic; New Yorker; Poetry; Western Humanities Review; Paris Review. *Honours:* First Prize, Acad. of American Poets, San Francisco State University, 1964; Discovery Award, Poetry Center, YM-YWHA, New York, 1967; US Award, International Poetry Forum, Pittsburgh, 1969; Fellowship, National Endowment for the Arts, 1979; Cecil Hemley Memorial Award, 1985; Columbia University Trans. Award, 1988; Alice Fay Di Castagnola Award, 1989, Shelley Memorial Award, 1991, Poetry Society of America; Charity Randall Citation, International Poetry Forum, 1998. *Memberships:* Poetry Society of America; PEN, Israel. *Address:* 7 Rashba St, 92264 Jerusalem, Israel.

KAUFMAN-KIERCE, Diana Faye, (Diana Kierce); b. 3 Oct. 1935, Oakland, CA, USA. Poet. m. 2 Sept. 1951, 4 s., 3 d. *Education:* Degree in Nursing, Lincoln School of Nursing, 1965. *Publications:* The Golden Gate Bridge; The Poem for San Francisco; The Official City Song for Clayton, California; Song of the Black Diamond Mines. *Contributions to:* Anthologies and newspapers. *Honours:* Awards; Certificates of Honour; Recognitions; Trophies. *Memberships:* World of Poetry; American Poetry Asscn; Lupus Foundation of America. *Address:* 208 Towers Dr., Pacheco, CA 94553, USA.

KAUL, Madan Lel; b. 11 Aug. 1923, Srmagar, Kashmir, India. College Teacher; Poet. m. Srat Gange Kaul, 9 May 1955, 2 s., 1 d. *Education:* MA, English and Political Science; Bachelor of Teaching, 1950. *Appointments:* Teacher, 1948–49; Headmaster, High School, Fazilka; Government School Lecturer, 1950–58; College Prof., 1960–81. *Publications:* The Home Coming, 1992–93; The Pilgrimage, 1994–95. *Contributions to:* The Tribune; Indian Express; Poetcrit. *Address:* Taraniwas Depot, Bazar, Dharamasala, Humaschal Pradesh, India.

KAVANAGH, P(atrick) J(oseph); b. 6 Jan. 1931, Worthing, Sussex, England. Poet; Writer; Ed. m. (1) Sally Philipps, 1956, deceased, (2) Catherine Ward, 1965, 2 s. *Education:* MA, Merton College, Oxford. *Appointments:* Columnist, The Spectator, 1983–96, TLS, 1996–. *Publications:* Poetry: One and One, 1960; On the Way to the Depot, 1967; About Time, 1970; Edward Thomas in Heaven, 1974; Life Before Death, 1979; Selected Poems, 1982; Presences: New and Selected Poems, 1987; An Enchantment, 1991; Collected Poems, 1992. Fiction: A Song and Dance, 1968; A Happy Man, 1972; People and Weather, 1978; Scarf Jack: The Irish Captain, 1978; Rebel for Good, 1980; Only By Mistake, 1980. Non-Fiction: The Perfect Stranger, 1966; People and Places, 1988; Finding Connections, 1990; Voices in Ireland: A Traveller's Literary Companion, 1994. Editor: The Collected Poems of Ivor Gurney, 1982; The Oxford Book of Short Poems (with James Michie), 1985; The Bodley Head G K Chesterton, 1985; Selected Poems of Ivor Gurney, 1990; A Book of Consolations, 1992. *Honours:* Richard Hillary Prize, 1966; Guardian Fiction Prize, 1968; Cholmondeley Poetry Prize, 1993. *Membership:* Fellow, RSL. *Address:* c/o A D Peters, Drury House, 34–43 Russell St, London WC2B 5HA, England.

KAVOUNAS, Alice Juno; b. 7 July 1945, New York, NY, USA. Writer; Poet. m. Frederick Taylor, 20 May 1988, 1 step-s., 2 step-d. *Education:* BA, English Literature, Vassar College, 1966. *Publication:* The Invited (poems), 1995. *Contributions to:* Anthologies, quarterlies, reviews, magazines, and radio. *Memberships:* Poetry Society, London; Society of Authors. *Address:* Vallier, Travalsoe, St Keverne, Cornwall TR12 6NU, England.

KAWIŃSKI, Wojciech; b. 22 May 1939, Poland. Poet. m. Helena Lorenz, 17 April 1964, 1 s., 1 d. *Education:* MA, 1964. *Publications:* Odległości Posłuszne, 1964; Narysowane We Wnetrzu, 1965; Ziarno Rzeki, 1967; Pole Widzenia, 1970; Śpiew Bezimienny, 1978; Pod Okiem Słońca, 1980; Listy Do Ciebie, 1982; Miłość Nienawistna, 1985; Ciemna strona jasności, 1989; Wieczorne śniegi, 1989; Czysty zmierzch, 1990; Pamieć zywa, 1990; Zwierciadło sekund, 1991; Srebro Liści, 1993; Zelazna rosa, 1995; Planeta Ognia, 1997. *Contributions to:* Numerous journals and magazines. *Honours:* Prize, City of Kraków, 1985; Red Rose Prize for Poetry, Gdańsk, 1985; Prize Kl. Janicki, Bydgoszcz, 1995. *Membership:* Polish Writers Asscn. *Address:* ul Stachiewicza 22a, 31-303 Kraków, Poland.

KAY, Jackie; b. 9 Nov. 1961, Edinburgh, Scotland. Writer; Poet; Arts Administrator. 1 s. *Education:* BA Honours, English. *Appointments:* Writer-in-Residence, Hammersmith, London, 1988–90; Literature Touring Co-ordinator, Arts Council, 1990–92. *Publications:* The Adoption Papers, 1991; Two's Company, 1992. *Contributions to:* Poetry Review; Spare Rib; Conditions; Poetry Wales; Chapman; Rialto; Poetry Matters; London Poetry Newsletter; City Limits. *Honours:* Eric Gregory Society of Authors Award, 1991; Book Award, Scottish Arts Council. *Memberships:* Poetry Society; Writers Guild. *Address:* 62 Kirkton Rd, London N15 5EY, England.

KAZANTZIS, Judith; b. 14 Aug. 1940, Oxford, England. Poet; Novelist. 1 d., 1 s. *Education:* Degree, Modern History, Oxford, 1961. *Publications:* Minefield, 1977; The Wicked Queen, 1980; Touch Papers (co-author), 1982; Let's Pretend, 1984; Flame Tree, 1988; A Poem for Guatemala (pamphlet), 1988; The Rabbit Magician Plate, 1992; Selected Poems 1977–92, 1995; Swimming Through the Grand Hotel, 1997; The Odysseus Papers: Fictions on the Odyssey of Homer, 1999; In Cyclop's Cave (trans. of book IX of The Odyssey), 2002; Of Love and Terror (novel), 2002. *Contributions to:* Anthologies and periodicals. *Memberships:* Society of Authors; English PEN; Palestine Solidarity Campaign; Nicaragua Solidarity Campaign. *Address:* 32 St Anne's Cres., Lewes BN7 1SB, England.

KEARNS MORALES, Rick; b. 3 Feb. 1958, Harrisburg, Pennsylvania, USA. Writer; Poet; Teacher. m. Ziza Almeido, 15 Oct. 1989. *Education:* BA, Spanish, Millersville University of Pennsylvania, 1984; MS, Journalism, Columbia University School of Journalism, 1986. *Appointments:* Instructor, Creative Writing, Pennsylvania School of Art and Design, 1992–95; Political Reporter, El Hispano Newspaper, 1994–; Instructor, Poetry of Protest of Latin America, Rutgers University, New Jersey, 1995–. *Publications:* Street of Knives, 1993; ALOUD – Voices from the Nuyorican Poets Cafe (anthology), 1995; In Defense of Mumia (anthology), 1996. *Contributions to:* Chicago Review; Massachusetts Review; Drum Voices; On the Bus. *Memberships:* Paper Sword Writers Organization, co-ordinator, 1988–94; Harrisburg Artists Factory, board mem., 1995–. *Address:* 3022 N Fifth St, Harrisburg, PA 17110, USA.

KEELEY, Edmund (Leroy); b. 5 Feb. 1928, Damascus, Syria (Naturalized US citizen). Prof. of English and Creative Writing Emeritus; Author; Trans. m. Mary Stathatos-Kyris, 18 March 1951. *Education:* BA, Princeton University, 1949; DPhil, University of Oxford, 1952. *Appointments:* Instructor, Brown University, 1952–53; Fulbright Lecturer, University of Thessaloniki, 1953–54, 1986; Instructor, 1954–57, Asst Prof., 1957–63, Assoc. Prof., 1963–70, Prof. of English and Creative Writing, 1970–92, Charles Branwell Straut Class of 1923 Prof. of English, 1992–94, Prof. Emeritus, 1994–, Princeton University; Visiting Lecturer, University of Iowa, 1962–63, University of the Aegean, 1988; Writer-in-Residence, Knox College, 1963; Visiting Prof., New School for Social Research, New York, 1980, Columbia University, 1981; King's College, University of London, 1996; Fulbright Lecturer, 1985, and Research Fellow, 1987, University of Athens; Senior Assoc. Mem., St Antony's College, Oxford, 1996. *Publications:* Fiction: The Libation, 1958; The Gold-Hatted Lover, 1961; The Impostor, 1970; Voyage to a Dark Island, 1972; A Wilderness Called Peace, 1985; School for Pagan Lovers, 1993; Some Wine for Remembrance, 2001. Non-Fiction: Cavafy's Alexandria, 1976; Modern Greek Poetry: Voice and Myth, 1982; The Salonika Bay Murder: Cold War Politics and the Polk Affair, 1989; Albanian Journal: The Road to Elbasan, 1996; George Seferis and Edmund Keeley: Correspondence, 1951–1971, 1997; Inventing Paradise: The Greek Journey, 1937–1947, 1999; On Translation: Reflections and Conversations, 2000. Translator: George Seferis: Collected Poems (with Philip Sherrard), 1967; Odysseus Elytis: The Axion Esti (with George Savidis), 1974; C. P. Cavafy: Collected Poems (with Philip Sherrard and George Savidis), 1975; Angelos Sikelianos: Selected Poems (with Philip Sherrard), 1979; Odysseus Elytis: Selected Poems (with Philip Sherrard), 1981; Yannis Ritsos: Repetitions, Testimonies, Parentheses, 1991; A Greek Quintet (with Philip Sherrard), 1992. *Contributions to:* Books and journals. *Honours:* Rome Prize Fellow, 1959–60, Award in Literature, 1999, American Acad. of Arts and Letters; Guggenheim Fellowships, 1959–60, 1973; Columbia University Trans. Center-PEN Award, 1975; Harold Morton Landon Trans. Award, 1980; National Endowment for the Arts Fellowships, 1981, 1988–89; Rockefeller Foundation Scholar, Bellagio Study Center, Italy, 1982, 1989; Research Fellow, Virginia Center for the Creative Arts, 1983, 1984, 1986, 1990; Pushcart Prize Anthology, 1984; First European Prize for Trans. of Poetry, 1987; Hon. Doctorate, University of Athens, 1994; PEN-Ralph Manheim Medal for Trans., 2000; Commander, Order of the Phoenix (Greece), 2001. *Memberships:* American Acad. of Arts and Sciences; Acad. of Athens; American Literary Trans Asscn; Authors Guild; Modern Greek Studies Asscn, pres., 1969–73, 1982–84; PEN American Center, pres., 1991–93; Poetry Society of America. *Address:* 140 Littlebrook Rd, Princeton, NJ, USA.

KEEN, Suzanne Parker; b. 10 April 1963, Bethlehem, Pennsylvania, USA. Prof. of English; Poet. m. Francis MacDonnell, 7 June 1992. *Education:* AB, English, Studio Art, 1984, AM, Creative Writing, 1986, Brown University; PhD, English and American Literature, Harvard University, 1990. *Appointments:* Asst Prof. of English, Yale University, 1990–95; Assoc. Prof., Washington and Lee University, 1995–, Prof., 2001–. *Publication:* Victorian Renovations of the Novel: Narrative Annexes and the Boundaries of Representation, 1998; Romances of the Archive in Contemporary British Fiction, 2001. *Contributions to:* Anthologies, reviews, and journals. *Honours:* Pawtucket

Arts Council Prize, 1985; Kim Ann Arstark Poetry Prize, Brown University, 1985; Acad. of American Poets Prize, 1987; Second Prize, New England Poetry Competition, 1991; Individual Artist Fellowship, Virginia Commission for the Arts, 1998; National Endowment for the Humanities Fellowship, 1999. *Memberships:* MLA; Society for the Study of Narrative Literature. *Address:* c/o Dept of English, Washington and Lee University, Lexington, VA 24450, USA.

KEENE, Dennis; b. 10 July 1934, London, England. Prof. of English Literature (retd); Poet; Writer; Trans. m. Keiko Kurose, 5 May 1962. *Education:* BA, Honours, English Literature and Language, 1957, MA, 1961, DPhil, Oriental Studies, 1973, University of Oxford. *Appointments:* Asst Lecturer in English Literature, University of Malaya, 1958–60; Lecturer in English Language and Literature, Kyoto University, 1961–63; Invited Prof. of English Literature, Haile Selassie I University, Ethiopia, 1964–65; Lecturer in English Literature, Kyushu University, 1965–69; Asst Prof., 1970–76, Prof. of English Literature, 1976–81, 1983–93, Japan Women's University. *Publications:* Poetry: Surviving, 1980; Universe and Other Poems, 1984. Prose: Problems in English, 1969; Yokomitsu Riichi, Modernist, 1980; Wasurerareta Kuni, Nippon, 1995. Editor: Selected Poems of Henry Howard, Earl of Surrey, 1985. Translator: Grass For My Pillow (trans. of novel by Saiichi Maruya), 2002; Over 10 books of Japanese poems, novels and short stories, 1974–2002. *Honours:* Independent Foreign Fiction Special Award, 1990; Noma Trans. Prize, 1992. *Address:* 77 Staunton Rd, Headington, Oxford OX3 7TL, England.

KEENEY, Patricia; b. 21 June 1943, England. Poet; Writer; Ed.; Critic; Teacher of Creative Writing. *Education:* BA, McGill University; MA, Sir George Williams University; Doctoral Work, University of Sussex. *Appointments:* Poetry Ed. and Features Writer, Cross Canada Writers Quarterly and the Canadian Forum; Columnist, Canadian Poetry Review. *Publications:* Swimming Alone, 1988; New Moon, Old Mattress, 1990; The New Pagans, 1991; The Book of Joan, 1994; The Incredible Shrinking Wife (novel), 1995; Selected Poems, 1996; Global Warnings, 1999; Vocal Braiding: An Experiment in Poetry and Theatre. *Contributions to:* Anthologies and periodicals. *Memberships:* League of Canadian Poets; The Writers' Union of Canada. *Address:* c/o Dept of Thr, York University, York, Ontario M3J 1P3, Canada. *E-mail:* patdon@yorku.ca.

KEIN, Sybil; b. 29 Sept. 1939, New Orleans, LA, USA. Prof. of English; Poet; Dramatist; Musician. m. Felix Provost, 1960, divorced 1969, 1 s., 2 d. *Education:* BS, Xavier University, 1964; Aspen School of Arts, 1964; MA, Louisiana State University, 1972; PhD, University of Michigan, 1975. *Appointments:* Instructor, 1972–75, Asst Prof., 1975–78, Assoc. Prof., 1979–88, Prof. of English, 1988–, University of Michigan at Flint. *Publications:* Bessie, Bojangles and Me, 1975; Visions from the Rainbow, 1979; Gombo People: Poésies Créoles de la Nouvelle Orleans, 1981; Delta Dancer, 1984; An American South, 1997. *Contributions to:* Anthologies and journals. *Honours:* Several teaching awards; Creative Artist Awards for Poetry, Michigan Council for the Arts, 1981, 1984, 1989; Chercheur Associé, Centre d'Etudes Afro-Americaines, Université de la Sorbonne Nouvelle, 1990. *Address:* PO Box 15246, New Orleans, LA 70175-5426, USA. *E-mail:* sybkein@aol.com.

KEITH, W(illiam) J(ohn); b. 9 May 1934, London, England (Naturalized Canadian citizen, 1974). Prof. of English Emeritus; Literary Critic. m. Hiroko Teresa Sato, 26 Dec. 1965. *Education:* BA, Jesus College, Cambridge, 1958; MA, 1959, PhD, 1961, University of Toronto. *Appointments:* Lecturer, 1961–62, Asst Prof., 1962–66, McMaster University; Assoc. Prof., 1966–71, Prof. of English, 1971–95, Prof. Emeritus, 1995–, University of Toronto; Ed., University of Toronto Quarterly, 1976–85. *Publications:* Richard Jefferies: A Critical Study, 1965; Charles G D Roberts, 1969; The Rural Tradition, 1974; Charles G D Roberts: Selected Poetry and Critical Prose (ed.), 1974; The Poetry of Nature, 1980; The Arts in Canada: The Last Fifty Years (co-ed.), 1980; Epic Fiction: The Art of Rudy Wiebe, 1981; A Voice in the Land: Essays by and About Rudy Wiebe (ed.), 1981; Canadian Literature in English, 1985; Regions of the Imagination, 1988; Introducing The Edible Woman, 1989; A Sense of Style: Studies in the Art of Fiction in English-Speaking Canada, 1989; An Independent Stance: Essays on English-Canadian Criticism and Fiction, 1991; Echoes in Silence (poems), 1992; Literary Images of Ontario, 1992; The Jefferies Canon, 1995; In the Beginning and Other Poems, 1999; Canadian Odyssey: A Reading of Hugh Hood's The New Age/Le nouveau siècle, 2002. *Contributions to:* Journals. *Honour:* Fellow, Royal Society of Canada, 1979. *Membership:* Richard Jefferies Society, hon. pres., 1974–91. *Address:* University College, University of Toronto, Toronto, ON M5S 3H7, Canada.

KEJIA YUAN; b. 18 Sept. 1921, Cixi, China. Prof. of English and American Literature (retd); Poet; Writer; Trans.; Ed. m. Cheng Qi Yun, 20 Jan. 1955, 2 d. *Education:* BA, English Literature, National South-West Associated University, 1946. *Appointments:* Asst Researcher, 1957–78, Assoc. Researcher and Assoc. Prof., 1979–82, Prof. of English and American Literature, 1983–90, Research Institute of Foreign Literature. *Publications:* On the Modernization of Chinese Poetry, 1988; Source Materials for the Study of Modernist Literature (ed.), 1989; A Study of Western Modernist Literature, 1992; An Anthology of Modern Western Poetry (ed.), 1992; Poems and Essays, 1941–1991, 1994. Translator: Several vols. *Contributions to:* Books, journals, and magazines.

Honours: Second Class Prize, 1991, First Class Prize, 1994, Foreign Books Award. *Memberships:* All China Society for Literary and Art Theories, advisory board; Chinese Trans.'s Asscn, council mem.; Chinese Writers' Union. *Address:* c/o Research Institute of Foreign Literature, 5 Jian Guo Men Nei Da Jie, Beijing 100732, China.

KELL, Richard (Alexander); b. 1 Nov. 1927, Youghal, County Cork, Ireland. Senior Lecturer in English (retd); Poet; Ed. m. Muriel Adelaide Nairn, 31 Dec. 1953, 2 s., 2 d. *Education:* BA, 1952, Higher Diploma in Education, 1953, University of Dublin. *Appointments:* Lecturer in English, Isleworth Polytechnic, England, 1960–70; Senior Lecturer in English, Newcastle upon Tyne Polytechnic, 1970–83; Joint Ed., Other Poetry, 1994. *Publications:* Poems, 1957; Control Tower, 1962; Six Irish Poets, 1962; Differences, 1969; Humours, 1978; Heartwood, 1978; The Broken Circle, 1981; Wall (with others), 1981; In Praise of Warmth, 1987; Rock and Water, 1993; Collected Poems, 2001. *Contributions to:* Newspapers and magazines. *Address:* 18 Rectory Grove, Gosforth, Newcastle upon Tyne NE3 1AL, England.

KELLER, David (Michael); b. 26 May 1941, Berkeley, CA, USA. Poet. m. Eloise F Bruce, 7 Aug. 1994. *Education:* AB, Harvard College, 1964; Iowa State University, 1961–62; University of Iowa, 1963; PhD, University of Wisconsin, 1974. *Appointments:* Dir of Admissions, Frost Place Festival of Poetry, Franconia, New Hampshire, 1980–; Asst Poetry Co-ordinator, Geraldine R Dodge Foundation, 1986–90; American Guest Poet, Poets' House, Islandmagee, Northern Ireland, 1991–95; Teacher, University of Vermont, 1995, College of New Jersey, 1997. *Publications:* Circling the Site, 1982; A New Room, 1987; Land That Wasn't Ours, 1989; Trouble in History, 2000. *Contributions to:* 11 anthologies, 1981–2000, and various journals and magazines. *Honours:* Prize for Best Poem, Indiana Review, 1985; Artistic Merit Grant for Poetry, 1985, Fellowship for Poetry, 1991, New Jersey State Council on the Arts; Colladay Award, Quarterly Review of Literature, 1987; Lucille Medwick Memorial Award, Poetry Society of America, 1993; Carolyn Kizer Prize, Poetry Northwest, 1993. *Memberships:* Frost Place, Franconia, New Hampshire, advisory board, 1994–; Poetry Society of America, board of governors, 1989–92; Poets' House, Islandmagee, Northern Ireland, advisory board, 1993–; Roosevelt Arts Project, New Jersey, board of dirs, 1988–. *Address:* 151 Hughes Ave, Lawrenceville, NJ 08648, USA.

KELLER, Johanna; b. 26 April 1955, Ahoskie, North Carolina, USA. Writer; Poet; Librettist. *Education:* MMus, Honours, University of Colorado, 1977; MA, Creative Writing/Poetry, Antioch University, 1996. *Appointments:* Workshop Teacher, The Writers Voice, New York, Northern Westchester Center, Mount Kisco, Putnam Valley Schools and Newport Writers Conference. *Publications:* Poetry: Moose, 1995. Other: Libretto: The War Prayer, adaptation of Mark Twain (with David Sampson), 1995. *Contributions to:* Dark Horse (Scotland); Voices (Israel); US journals: Southwest Review; Chelsea; Plum Review; Pivot; Nimrod; Negative Capability; Connecticut Review; Reviewer for Antioch Review. *Honours:* Grand Prize, Green River Writers National Contest, 1994; Grand Prize, Community Writers Asscn National Contest, 1995; Finalist, Randall Jarrell Poetry Prize, Ireland, 1996; Artist Fellowship, New York Foundation for the Arts, 1997; Ludwig Vogelstein Foundation Grant, 1997; Annual Ed.'s Award, Florida Review, 1997; Residency Fellowship, Ragdale Foundation, 1997. *Address:* c/o Howard Morhaim Literary Agency, 841 Broadway, No. 604, New York, NY 10003, USA.

KELLEY, Alita, (C. A. de Lomellini); b. 19 Nov. 1932, Bradford, West Yorkshire, England. Teacher; Poet; Trans. m. (1) Carlos de Luchi Lomellini, 17 Sept. 1951, (2) Alec E Kelley, 29 May 1970, 2 d. *Education:* BA, 1981, MA, 1986, PhD, 1992, University of Arizona. *Appointments:* Teacher of English, British Council, Lima, Peru, 1962–68; Teacher of Italian, US Embassy, Lima, Peru, 1967–68; Commercial Trans. and Office Man., Wiesman & Co, Tucson, AZ, 1969–92; Asst Prof. of Spanish and French, 1992–96, Assoc. Prof., 1996–, Pennsylvania State University, Delaware County Campus, Media, PA. *Publications:* Shared Images, 1981; Dreams of Samarkand, 1982; Ineffable Joys, 1983; Antimacassars, 1984; Target Practice, 1994. Other: Trans. *Contributions to:* Aireings; Ambit; Outposts; Haravec (Lima, Peru); Tribune (London); Writing Women; Poetry Nottingham; Global Tapestry; Pennine Platform; Fiction International (Puerto del Sol). *Memberships:* American Literary Trans. Asscn; Latin American Indian Literature Asscn. *Address:* 1086 King Rd, MP-215, Malvern, PA 19355, USA.

KELLY, Jeanne Lin Smith; b. 4 Feb. 1945, Corinth, Mississippi, USA. Teacher; Poet. m. 13 Aug. 1966, 2 s. *Education:* BA, 1966, MEd, 1981, Mississippi College; Additional coursework, University of Southern Mississippi, Auburn University, University of Mississippi. *Publications:* Scrapbook (chapbook), 1995; From Sunrise to Sunset (chapbook), 2002. *Contributions to:* Southern Poetry Review; Decision; Home Life; Living with Teenagers; Mississippi Poetry Journal; National Federation of State Poetry Societies Contest Journal, 2002; Grandmother's Earth VIII, 2002. *Honours:* Recognition, Spring Contests, Mississippi Poetry Society, 1986–2002. *Membership:* Mississippi Poetry Society, state sec., 2000–2002. *Address:* 315 Church St, Madison, MS 39110, USA. *E-mail:* jkelly@holmes.cc.ms.uk.

KELLY, M(ilton) T(errence); b. 30 Nov. 1946, Toronto, Ontario, Canada. Writer; Poet; Dramatist. *Education:* BA, York University, 1970; BEd, University of Toronto, 1976. *Appointments:* Reporter, Moose Jaw Times Harald, 1974–75; Columnist, Globe and Mail, 1979–80; Teacher of Creative Writing, York University, 1987–92, 1995; Writer-in-Residence, North York Public Library, 1992, Metropolitan Toronto Reference Library, 1993. *Publications:* Fiction: I Do Remember the Fall, 1978; The More Loving One, 1980; The Ruined Season, 1982; A Dream Like Mine, 1987; Breath Dances Between Them, 1990; Out of the Whirlwind, 1995; Save Me, Joe Louis, 1998. Poetry: Country You Can't Walk In, 1979; Country You Can't Walk In and Other Poems, 1984. Other: The Green Dolphin (play), 1982; Wildfire: The Legend of Tom Longboat (screenplay), 1983. *Contributions to:* Many anthologies, reviews, quarterlies, and journals. *Honours:* Canada Council Grants; Ontario Arts Council Grants; Toronto Arts Council Award for Poetry, 1986; Governor-General's Award for Fiction, 1987; Award for Journalism, 1995. *Memberships:* International PEN; Writers' Union of Canada. *Address:* 60 Kendal, Toronto, Ontario M5R 1L9, Canada.

KELLY, Robert; b. 24 Sept. 1935, New York, NY, USA. Prof. of Literature; Poet; Writer. *Education:* AB, City College, New York City, 1955; Columbia University, 1955–58. *Appointments:* Ed., Chelsea Review, 1957–60, Matter magazine and Matter publishing, 1964–, Los 1, 1977; Lecturer, Wagner College, 1960–61; Founding Ed. (with George Economou), Trobar magazine, 1960–64, Trobar Books, 1962–65; Instructor, 1961–64, Asst Prof., 1964–69, Assoc. Prof., 1969–74, Porfessor of English, 1974–86, Dir, Writing Programme, 1980–93, Asher B Edelman Prof. of Literature, 1986–, Bard College; Asst Prof., State University of New York at Buffalo, 1964; Visiting Lecturer, Tufts University, 1966–67; Poet-in-Residence, California Institute of Technology, Pasadena, 1971–72, University of Kansas, 1975, Dickinson College, 1976. *Publications:* Poetry: Armed Descent, 1961; Her Body Against Time, 1963; Round Dances, 1964; Tabula, 1964; Entasy, 1964; Matter/Fact/Sheet/1, 1964; Matter/Fact/Sheet/2, 1964; Lunes, 1964; Lectiones, 1965; Words in Service, 1966; Weeks, 1966; Songs XXIV, 1967; Twenty Poems, 1967; Devotions, 1967; Axon Dendron Tree, 1967; Crooked Bridge Love Society, 1967; A Joining: A Sequence for H D, 1967; Alpha, 1968; Finding the Measure, 1968; From the Common Shore, Book 5, 1968; Songs I-XXX, 1969; Sonnets, 1969; We Are the Arbiters of Beast Desire, 1969; A California Journal, 1969; The Common Shore, Books I-V: A Long Poem About America in Time, 1969; Kali Yuga, 1971; Flesh: Dream: Book, 1971; Ralegh, 1972; The Pastorals, 1972; Reading Her Notes, 1972; The Tears of Edmund Burke, 1973; Whaler Frigate Clippership, 1973; The Bill of Particulars, 1973; The Belt, 1974; The Loom, 1975; Sixteen Odes, 1976; The Lady of, 1977; The Convections, 1978; The Book of Persephone, 1978; The Cruise of the Pnyx, 1979; Kill the Messenger Who Brings the Bad News, 1979; Sentence, 1980; The Alchemist to Mercury, 1981; Spiritual Exercises, 1981; Mulberry Women, 1982; Under Words, 1983; Thor's Thrush, 1984; Not This Island Music, 1987; The Flowers of Unceasing Coincidence, 1988; Oahu, 1988; A Strange Market, 1992; Mont Blanc, 1994. Fiction: The Scorpions, 1967; Cities, 1971; Wheres, 1978; A Transparent Tree: Ten Fictions, 1985; Doctor of Silence, 1988; Cat Scratch Fever: Fictions, 1990; Queen of Terrors: Fictions, 1994. Other: A Controversy of Poets: An Anthology of Contemporary American Poetry (ed. with Paris Leary), 1965; Statement, 1968; In Time, 1971; Sulphur, 1972; A Line of Sight, 1974. *Honours:* Los Angeles Times Book Prize, 1980; American Acad. of Arts and Letters Award, 1986. *Address:* c/o Dept of English, Bard College, Annandale-on-Hudson, NY 12504, USA.

KELLY, Tom; b. 22 May 1947, Jarrow, Tyne and Wear, England. College Lecturer; Poet. m. (1) Carol Kelly, 20 Dec. 1969, deceased 1992, 1 d., (2) Linda Kelly, 1 Sept. 1995. *Education:* BA, Honours. *Appointment:* Lecturer, Further Education College. *Publications:* The Gibbetting of William Jobling, 1972; Still With Me, 1986; John Donne in Jarrow, 1993; Their Lives, 1993; Riddle of Pain, 1995. *Contributions to:* Stand; Iron; Orbis; Rialto; Staple; Hybrid; Samphire; Working Titles; Purple Patch; Oasis; Sepia; First Time; Exile; Intoprint; Tees Valley Writer; Krax; Harry's Hand; Foolscap; Eavesdroppper; Here Now; Tourism; Reid Review; Iota; Pennine Platform; Poetry Nottingham; Westwords; Third Half; Overspill. *Address:* Thorneyholme, 11 Thorneyholme Terrace, Blaydon, Tyne and Wear NE21 4PS, England.

KEMP, Harry Vincent; b. 11 Dec. 1911, Singapore. Poet; Mathematician. m. Alix Eiermann, 9 July 1941, 1 s., 1 d. *Education:* Clare College, Cambridge, 1931–34. *Publications:* The Left Hersey (with Laura Riding and Robert Graves), 1939; Ten Messengers (with Witold Kawalec), 1977; Verses for Heidi, 1978; Poems for Erato, 1980; Collected Poems, 1985; Poems for Mnemosyne, 1993. *Address:* 6 Western Villas, Western Rd, Crediton, Devon EX17 3NA, England.

KEMP, Jan; b. 12 March 1949, Hamilton, New Zealand. University Teacher of English; Poet. *Education:* BA, 1970, MA, Honours, 1974, University of Auckland; Diploma of Teaching, Auckland Teachers' College, 1972; RSA Certificate, British Council, Hong Kong, 1984. *Appointments:* Teacher of English, University of Papua, New Guinea, 1980–82, University of Hong Kong, 1982–85, National University of Singapore, 1985–. *Publications:* Against the Softness of Woman, 1976; Diamonds and Gravel, 1979; Ice-Breaker Poems, 1980; The Other Hemisphere, 1991. *Contributions to:* Various publications. *Honours:* Four Poets Tour, New Zealand, 1979; Queen Elizabeth II Arts Council Poetry Representative, South Pacific Festival of the

Arts, Papua, New Guinea, 1980; PEN/Stout Centre Fellowship, Victoria University of Wellington, New Zealand, 1991. *Memberships:* PEN International, New Zealand Centre; PEN International, Writers in Exile Centre, USA.

KENDALL, Tina; b. 6 Jan. 1958, Bradford, West Yorkshire, England. Poet; Writer. 2 s., 1 d. *Education:* BA, Honours, Modern Languages; BA, English; MA, French; MA, English; MA, Scriptwriting for Film and TV. *Appointments:* Ed., Spare Rib Magazine; University Teacher; Equal Opportunities Officer; Writer-in-Residence. *Contributions to:* Beautiful Barbarian; Naming the Wares; Feminist Arts News; Peterloo Poets; Hambone 10; Language of Water, Language of Fire; Onlywomen Press; Virago. *Address:* c/o Sheba Feminist Press, 10a Bradbury St, London N16 8JN, England.

KENNEDY, John Hines; b. 1 Nov. 1925, Washington, DC, USA. Cardiothoracic Surgeon (retd); Physiologist; Poet. m. (1), 2 s., 2 d., (2) Shirley Angela Josephine Watson. *Education:* Princeton University, 1943–45; MD, Harvard Medical School, 1945–49; FACS, 1957; MPhil, Imperial College, London, 1990. *Publications:* Carnet Parisien, 1987; Vieux Colombier, 1987–88; Les Images, 1991. *Contributions to:* Books and journals. *Honours:* Medal of Vishnevsky, Moscow, 1962; Medal, Un Liège, Belgium, 1978. *Memberships:* Cercle de l'Union Interslièe, Paris; PEN Club. *Address:* Old Court, Clare, Sudbury, Suffolk CO10 8NP, England.

KENNEDY, Joseph Charles, (X. J. Kennedy); b. 21 Aug. 1929, Dover, New Jersey, USA. Poet; Writer. m. Dorothy Mintzlaff, 31 Jan. 1962, 4 s., 1 d. *Education:* BSc, Seton Hall University, 1950; MA, Columbia University, 1951; University of Paris, 1956. *Appointments:* Teaching Fellow, 1956–60, Instructor, 1960–62, University of Michigan; Poetry Ed., The Paris Review, 1961–64; Lecturer, Women's College of the University of North Carolina, 1962–63; Asst Prof. to Prof., Tufts University, 1963–79. *Publications:* Nude Descending a Staircase, 1961; An Introduction to Poetry (with Dana Gioia), 1968; The Bedford Reader, 1982; Cross Ties, 1985; Dark Horses, 1992. *Contributions to:* Newspapers and journals. *Honours:* Lamont Award, 1961; Los Angeles Times Book Award, 1985. *Memberships:* Authors Guild; John Barton Wolgamot Society; MLA; PEN. *Address:* 4 Fern Way, Bedford, MA 01730, USA.

KENNEDY, Margaret Mary Downing; b. 13 July 1933, Stourbridge, Worcestershire, England. Poet. m. James Kennedy, 2 Nov. 1963, 3 d. *Education:* Secretarial College, 1950–51. *Contributions to:* John L. London's Weekly; BBC Poetry Programmes; Orbis. *Membership:* John Clare Society. *Address:* 22 Bridlington Rd, Ferryvale, Nigel, Transvaal, South Africa.

KENNEDY, X. J. See: KENNEDY, Joseph Charles.

KENNELLY, Laura B.; b. 28 July 1941, Denton, Texas, USA. Writer. m. (1) Kevin Kennelly, 26 Aug. 1961, divorced 1996, (2) Robert Mayerovitch, 6 Sept. 1996, 4 s., 1 d. and 2 step-d. *Education:* BA, 1961, MA, 1969, PhD, 1975, University of North Texas. *Appointments:* Adjunct Prof., University of North Texas, 1976–94, Texas Woman's University, 1995; Ed., Grasslands Review, 1989. *Publications:* The Passage of Mrs Jung, 1990; A Certain Attitude, 1995. *Contributions to:* San Jose Studies; Studies in Contemporary Satire; Exquisite Corpse; New Mexico Humanities Review; Australian Journal of Communication. *Honours:* First Place, North Central Texas College Poetry Contest, 1988; First Place, University of North Texas Centennial Poem Award, 1990. *Membership:* Texas Asscn of Creative Writing Teachers, pres., 1993–95. *Address:* PO Box 626, Berea, OH 44017, USA.

KENNELLY, Louise; b. 2 Nov. 1964, Hartford, CT, USA. Writer; Poet. m. Adam Curtis, 21 Dec. 1990. *Education:* BA, Yale University, 1986; MS, Columbia University Graduate School of Journalism, 1989; MFA, University of North Carolina, 1994. *Appointments:* Instructor, Eastern New Mexico University, Roswell; Asst to the writer John Hersey, 1989; Writing Asst to Mrs Robert F Kennedy, 1990–91; Book Reviewer for English Literature in Transition. *Publication:* Tracking God in Italy, 1995. *Contributions to:* Northwest Review; Greensboro Review; Alaska Quarterly Review. *Honours:* Amon Liner Prize for Poetry; Greensboro Scholarship for Poetry. *Address:* PO Box 1894, Jamestown, NC 27282, USA.

KENNELLY, (Timothy) Brendan; b. 17 April 1936, Ballylongford, County Kerry, Ireland. Prof. of Modern Literature; Senior Fellow; Poet; Author; Dramatist. *Education:* BA, English and French, 1961, MA, 1963, PhD, 1966, Trinity College, Dublin. *Appointments:* Prof. of Modern Literature and Senior Fellow, Trinity College, Dublin, 1973–. *Publications:* Poetry: Cast a Cold Eye (with Rudi Holzapfel), 1959; The Rain, The Moon (with Rudi Holzapfel), 1961; The Dark About Our Loves (with Rudi Holzapfel), 1962; Green Townlands: Poems (with Rudi Holzapfel), 1963; Let Fall No Burning Leaf, 1963; My Dark Fathers, 1964; Up and At It, 1965; Collection One: Getting Up Early, 1966; Good Souls to Survive, 1967; Dream of a Black Fox, 1968; Selected Poems, 1969; A Drinking Cup: Poems From the Irish, 1970; Bread, 1971; Love Cry, 1972; Salvation, the Stranger, 1972; The Voices, 1973; Shelley in Dublin, 1974; A Kind of Trust, 1975; New and Selected Poems, 1976; Islandman, 1977; The Visitor, 1978; A Girl: 22 Songs, 1978; A Small Light, 1979; In Spite of the Wise,

1979; The Boats Are Home, 1980; The House That Jack Didn't Build, 1982; Cromwell: A Poem, 1983; Moloney Up and At It, 1984; Selected Poems, 1985; Mary: From the Irish, 1987; Love of Ireland: Poems From the Irish, 1989; A Time for Voices: Selected Poems 1960–1990, 1990; The Book of Judas: A Poem, 1991; Breathing Spaces: Early Poems, 1992; Poetry My Arse, 1995; The Man Made of Rain, 1998; The Singing Tree, 1998; Begin, 1999; Glimpses, 2001; The Little Book of Judas, 2002. Fiction: The Crooked Cross, 1963; The Florentines, 1967. Plays: Medea, 1991; The Trojan Women, 1993; Antigone, 1996; Blood Wedding, 1996. Criticism: Journey into Joy: Selected Prose, 1994. Anthologies: The Penguin Book of Irish Verse, 1970; Landmarks of Irish Drama, 1988; Joycechoyce: The Poems in Verse and Prose of James Joyce (with A Norman Jeffares), 1992; Irish Prose Writings: Swift to the Literary Renaissance (with Terence Brown), 1992; Between Innocence and Peace: Favourite Poems of Ireland, 1993; Dublines (with Katie Donovan), 1994; Ireland's Women Writings Past and Present (with Katie Donovan and A Norman Jeffares), 1994. Other: Real Ireland, 1984; Ireland Past and Present (ed.), 1985. *Honours:* AE Monorial Prize for Poetry, 1967; Fellow, Trinity College, Dublin, 1967; Critics' Special Harveys Award, 1988; American Ireland Funds Literary Award, 1999. *Address:* c/o School of English, Trinity College, Dublin 2, Ireland.

KENNET, Lady. See: YOUNG, Elizabeth Ann.

KENNEY, Richard Laurence; b. 10 Aug. 1948, USA. Poet; Teacher. m. Mary F Hedberg, 4 July 1982, 2 s. *Education:* BA, Dartmouth College, 1970. *Appointment:* Asst Prof. to Assoc. Prof. to Prof., University of Washington, 1987–. *Publications:* The Evolution of the Flightless Bird, 1983; Orrery, 1984; The Invention of the Zero, 1993. *Contributions to:* New Yorker; Poetry; New England Review; Yale Review. *Honours:* Yale Series of Younger Poets Prize, 1982; Guggenheim Fellowship, 1984; Rome Prize in Literature, 1986; MacArthur Fellowship, 1987–92; Lannan Literary Award, 1994. *Address:* c/o Dept of English Box 354330, University of Washington, Seattle, WA 98195, USA.

KENNY, Adele; b. 28 Nov. 1948, Perth Amboy, New Jersey, USA. Poet; Writer; Ed.; Consultant. *Education:* BA, English, Kean University, 1970; MS, Education, College of New Rochelle, 1982. *Appointments:* Artist-in-Residence, Middlesex County Arts Council, 1979–80; Poetry Ed., New Jersey ArtForm, 1981–83; Assoc. Ed., Muse-Pie Press, 1988–; Dir; Carriage House Poetry Reading Series, 1998–99. *Publications:* An Archeology of Ruins, 1982; Illegal Entries, 1984; The Roses Open 1984; Between Hail Marys, 1986; Migrating Geese, 1987; The Crystal Keepers Handbook, 1988; Counseling Gifted, Creative and Talented Youth Through the Arts, 1989; Castles and Dragons, 1990; Questi Momenti, 1990; Starship Earth, 1990; We Become By Being, 1994; Staffordshire Spaniels, 1997; At the Edge of the Woods, 1997; Staffordshire Animals, 1998. *Contributions to:* Periodicals. *Honours:* Writer's Digest Award, 1981; New Jersey State Council on the Arts Fellowships, 1982, 1987; Merit Book Awards, 1983, 1986, 1987, 1991; Henderson Award, 1984; Roselip Award, 1988; Haiku Quarterly Award, 1989; Allen Ginsberg Poetry Award, 1993. *Memberships:* Haiku Society of America, pres., 1987–88, 1990; Poetry Society of America; Poets and Writers Inc. *Address:* 207 Coriell Ave, Fanwood, NJ 07023, USA.

KENT, (Alice) Jean (Cranley); b. 30 Aug. 1951, Chinchilla, Qld, Australia. Psychologist; Poet. m. Martin Kent, 8 Jan. 1974. *Education:* BA, University of Queensland, 1971. *Appointment:* Counsellor, Dept of Technical and Further Education, New South Wales, 1977–79, 1983–89. *Publications:* Verandahs, 1990; Practising Breathing, 1991; The Satin Bowerbird, 1998. *Contributions to:* Anthologies, newspapers, reviews, and journals. *Honours:* John Shaw Neilson Prizes, 1980, 1991; Patricia Hackett Prizes, 1981, 1990; Anne Danckwerts Memorial Prize, 1986; Joint Winner, National Library Award, 1988; Henry Kendall Awards, 1988, 1989; Anne Elder Award, 1990; Mary Gilmore Award, 1991; Wesley Michel Wright Prize, 1998. *Membership:* Australian Society of Authors. *Address:* c/o Hale & Iremonger, 19-21 Eve St, Erskineville, NSW 2043, Australia.

KEREN, Hillary. See: ALKALAY-GUT, Karen Hillary.

KERR, Kathryn Ann, (Leona Fisher, Willi Red Bear); b. 15 Aug. 1946, St Louis, Missouri, USA. Writer; Poet; Ed. m. Thomas A Palmer, 7 July 1990, 2 d. *Education:* BA, Southern Illinois University, 1971; MS, Eastern Illinois University, 1984. *Publications:* First Frost; Equinox; Coneflower. *Contributions to:* Another Chicago Magazine; Ascent; Great River Review; Spoon River Quarterly; Thema; Illinois Writers Review, River Styx, Crab Orchard Review; Tamagua. *Honours:* Pushcart Foundation Writer's Choice; Illinois Wesleyan Univerity Poetry Prize; Illinois Arts Council Fellowship; Illinois Arts Council Poetry Award; Eastern Illinois University Poetry Award. *Memberships:* Red Herning Poets; Illinois Writers. *Address:* 11947 Deer Run Rd, Marion, IL 62959, USA.

KERR-SMILEY, Justin Robert; b. 25 April 1965. Poet; Journalist. *Education:* BA Honours, University of Newcastle upon Tyne, 1987; Postgraduate Diploma, TV and Radio Journalism, London College of Printing, 1990; Bursary, BBC South and East. *Appointments:* Reporter, ABC Radio 2BL, Sydney, NSW, Australia, 1990–91, Associated Press, London,

England, 1991–. *Publication:* Love, Loss and Other Seasons. *Contributions to:* Hourglass; Frogspawn; Courier; Sociedad de Poesia; Palabras y Letras; Lengua. *Membership:* Poetry Society. *Address:* 2A Newby St, London SW8 3BG, England.

KERRIGAN, Thomas Sherman; b. 15 March 1939, Los Angeles, CA, USA. Lawyer; Drama Critic; Poet. m. Victoria Elizabeth Thompson, 31 Jan. 1980, 2 s., 4 d. *Education:* University of California at Berkeley, 1957–61; Loyola University, 1964. *Appointments:* Deputy Attorney General, CA, 1965–69; Ed., Hierophant Press, 1969–74; Assoc., 1970–74, Partner, 1974–, McLaughlin and Irvin law firm; Drama Critic, 1993–. *Contributions to:* Reviews, quarterlies, and journals. *Memberships:* American Bar Asscn; Augustan Society; California Bar Asscn; Irish-American Bar Asscn; Yeats Society.

KERSHAW, Peter. See: LUCIE-SMITH, (John) Edward (McKenzie).

KESSLER, Jascha (Frederick); b. 27 Nov. 1929, New York, NY, USA. Prof.; Poet; Writer; Dramatist. m. 17 July 1950, 2 s., 1 d. *Education:* BA, University of Heights College of New York University, 1950; MA, 1951, PhD, 1955, University of Michigan. *Appointments:* Faculty, University of Michigan, 1951–54, New York University, 1954–55, Hunter College, 1955–56, Hamilton College, 1957–61; Prof. of English and Modern Literature, University of California at Los Angeles, 1961–. *Publications:* Poetry: Whatever Love Declares, 1969; After the Armies Have Passed, 1970; In Memory of the Future, 1976, revised edn as Collected Poems, 2000. Fiction: An Egyptian Bondage (short stories), 1967; Death Comes for the Behaviorist (short stories), 1983; Classical Illusions (short stories), 1985; Transmigrations: 18 Mythologemes, 1985; Siren Songs and Classical Illusions (short stories), 1992; Rapid Transit 1948: An Unsentimental Education (novel), 1998. Plays: Selected Plays, 1998; Christmas Carols and Other Plays, 1998. Other: The Anniversary (opera libretto); Trans. *Honours:* National Endowment for the Arts Fellowship, 1974; Rockefeller Foundation Fellowship, 1979; Hungarian PEN Club Memorial Medal, 1979; George Soros Foundation Prize, 1989; California Arts Council Fellowship, 1993–94; Many trans. prizes. *Memberships:* Asscn of Literary Scholars and Critics; ASCAP; Poetry Society of America. *Address:* c/o Dept of English, University of California at Los Angeles, Los Angeles, CA 90095, USA.

KHAIR, Tabish; b. 21 March 1966, Ranchi, India. Journalist; Poet; Writer. *Education:* BA, Honours, 1988; Diploma, Journalism, 1988; MA, 1992; PhD, 1999. *Appointments:* Part-time Teacher, Nazareth Acad., 1986; District Correspondent, 1986–87, Staff Correspondent, 1990–92, Times of India; Co-Ed., Cultural Acad., Gaya, 1987–89. *Publications:* My World, 1991; A Reporter's Diary, 1993; The Book of Heroes, 1995; An Angel in Pyjamas (novel), 1996; Where Parallel Lines Meet, 2000; Babu Fictions, 2001. *Contributions to:* The Telegraph; Indian PEN; Debonair; Times of India; Eonomic Times; Journal of the Poetry Society of India; Skylark; Mirror; Hindustan Times; Poetry Chronicle; London Magazine; The Independent; Stand; Metre; Planet; The Rialto; Thumbscrew; Iron Lines Review; Orbis; PN Review; Wasafiri; Other international magazines and anthologies. *Honour:* British Council's All India Prize, 1996. *Membership:* Poetry Society of India. *Address:* Raadmand Steins Alle 33, -46, Sal. 4, 2000 Frederiksberg, Denmark.

KHALIL, Muhammad. See: LANGE, Eugene Samuel.

KHALVATI, Mimi; b. 28 April 1944, Tehran, Iran. Poet; Writer. 1 s., 1 d. *Education:* University of Neuchâtel, Switzerland, 1960–62; Drama Centre, London, 1967–70; University of London, 1991. *Appointments:* Lecturer, Goldsmith's College, University of London, 1995; Dir, The Poetry School, 1997–; Lecturer, Middlesex University, 1998. *Publications:* Persian Miniatures, 1990; In White Ink, 1991; Mirrorwork, 1995; Entries on Light, 1997; Selected Poems, 2000; The Chine, 2002; Tying the Song (co-ed.), 2000. *Contributions to:* Anthologies, reviews and journals. *Honours:* Joint Winner, Poetry Business Pamphlet Competition, 1989; Joint Winner, Afro Caribbean-Asian Prize, Peterloo Poets, 1990; Writer's Award, Arts Council of England, 1994. *Address:* 130C Evering Rd, London N16 7BD, England.

KHARRAT, Edwar al-; b. 16 March 1926, Alexandria, Egypt. Writer; Poet. m., 2 s. *Education:* LLB, University of Alexandria, 1946. *Publications:* High Walls, 1959; Hours of Pride, 1972; Ramah and the Dragon, 1980; Suffocations of Love and Mornings, 1983; The Other Time, 1985; City of Saffron, 1986; Girls of Alexandria, 1990; Waves of Nights, 1991; Bobello's Ruins, 1992; Penetrations of Love and Perdition, 1993; My Alexandria, 1993; The New Sensibility, 1994; From Silence to Rebellion, 1994; Transgeneric Writing, 1994; Ripples of Salt Dreams, 1994; Fire of Phantasies, 1995; Hymn to Density, 1995; 7 Interpretations, 1996; Wings of Your Bird Struck Me, 1996; Why?: Extracts of a Love Poem, 1996; Soaring Edifices, 1997; The Certitude of Thirst, 1998; Cry of the Unicorn, 1998; Throes of Facts and Madness, 1998; Beyond Reality, 1998; Voices of Modernity in Arabic Fiction, 1999; Seven Clouds, 2000; Boulders of Heaven, 2001; Way of the Eagle, 2002. *Contributions to:* Many Arab literary magazines. *Honours:* Arts and Letters Medal, 1972; Franco-Arab Friendship Award, 1989; Cavafy Prize, 1998; State Merit Award for Literature, 2000. *Memberships:* Egyptian Writers' Union; Egyptian PEN Club; High Council of

Culture Committee on Fiction. *Address:* 45 Ahmed Hishmat St, Zamalak 11211, Cairo, Egypt.

KHATCHADOURIAN, Haig; b. 22 July 1925, Old City, Jerusalem, Palestine. Emeritus Prof. of Philosophy; Writer; Poet. m. Arpiné Yaghlian, 10 Sept. 1950, 2 s., 1 d. *Education:* BA, MA, American University of Beirut, Lebanon; PhD, Duke University, USA. *Appointments:* American University of Beirut, Lebanon, 1948–49, 1951–67; Prof. of Philosophy, University of Southern California at Los Angeles, 1968–69; Prof. of Philosophy, 1969–94, Emeritus Prof., 1994–, University of Wisconsin at Milwaukee. *Publications:* The Coherence Theory of Truth: A Critical Evaluation, 1961; Traffic with Time (co-author, poems), 1963; A Critical Study in Method, 1967; The Concept of Art, 1971; Shadows of Time (poems), 1983; Music, Film and Art, 1985; Philosophy of Language and Logical Theory: Collected Papers, 1996; The Morality of Terrorism, 1998; Community and Communitarianism, 1999; The Quest for Peace Between Israel and the Palestinians, 2000. *Contributions to:* Numerous professional and literary journals including Armenian Mind. *Memberships:* Fellow, Royal Society for the Encouragement of Arts, Manufacture and Commerce; Foreign Mem., Armenian Acad. of Philosophy; Founding Mem., International Acad. of Philosophy. *Address:* Dept of Philosophy, University of Wisconsin, Milwaukee, WI 53201, USA.

KHERDIAN, David; b. 17 Dec. 1931, Racine, Wisconsin, USA. Author; Poet. m. (1) Kato Rozeboom, 1968, divorced 1970, (2) Nonny Hogrogian, 17 March 1971. *Education:* BS, University of Wisconsin, 1965. *Appointments:* Founder-Ed., Giligia Press, 1966–72, Press at Butterworth Creek, 1987–88, Fork Roads: Journal of Ethnic American Literature, 1995–96; Rare Book Consultant, 1968–69, Lecturer, 1969–70, Fresno State College; Poet-in-the-Schools, State of New Hampshire, 1971; Dir, Two Rivers Press, 1978–86; Founder, Ed., Stopinder: A Gurdjieff Journal for our Time, 2000. *Publications:* On the Death of My Father and Other Poems, 1970; Homage to Adana, 1970; Looking Over Hills, 1972; The Nonny Poems, 1974; Any Day of Your Life, 1975; Country Cat, City Cat, 1978; I Remember Root River, 1978; The Road from Home: The Story of an Armenian Girl, 1979; The Farm, 1979; It Started With Old Man Bean, 1980; Finding Home, 1981; Taking the Soundings on Third Avenue, 1981; The Farm Book Two, 1981; Beyond Two Rivers, 1981; The Song of the Walnut Grove, 1982; Place of Birth, 1983; Right Now, 1983; The Mystery of the Diamond in the Wood, 1983; Root River Run, 1984; The Animal, 1984; Threads of Light: The Farm Poems Books III and IV, 1985; Bridger: The Story of a Mountain Man, 1987; Poems to an Essence Friend, 1987; A Song for Uncle Harry, 1989; The Cat's Midsummer Jamboree, 1990; The Dividing River/The Meeting Shore, 1990; On a Spaceship with Beelzebub: By a Grandson of Gurdjieff, 1990; The Great Fishing Contest, 1991; Junas's Journey, 1993; Asking the River, 1993; By Myself, 1993; Friends: A Memoir, 1993; My Racine, 1994; Lullaby for Emily, 1995. Editor: Several books. Other: Various trans. *Honours:* Jane Addams Peace Award, 1980; Banta Award, 1980; Boston Globe/Horn Book Award, 1980; Lewis Carroll Shelf Award, 1980; Newbery Honor Book Award, 1980; Friends of American Writers Award, 1982. *Membership:* PEN. *Address:* 3860 Elmran Dr., West Linn, OR 97068, USA.

KHETAN, Gulab; b. 3 Nov. 1946, Kathmandu, Nepal. Ed.; Writer; Poet; Lyricist; Trans. m. Vimala Khetan, 1 d. *Education:* BCom, 1964. *Appointments:* Chief Ed., Anmol Gyan Sangalo monthly, Vishleshan weekly; Deputy Ed., Aarth-Jagat fortnightly. *Publications:* Various short stories, poems, and essays. *Contributions to:* Many publications. *Honours:* Numerous literary awards and titles. *Memberships:* Many business organizations. *Address:* Gyaneshwar, PO Box 2975, Kathmandu, Nepal.

KHWAJA, Waqas Ahmad; b. 14 Oct. 1952, Lahore, Pakistan. Asst Prof. of English; Lawyer; Writer; Poet; Ed. m. Maryam Khurshid, 6 Nov. 1978, 4 c. *Education:* BA, Government College, Lahore, 1971; LLB, 1974; MA, 1979; MA, PhD, Emory University, 1995. *Appointments:* Visiting Prof., Quaid-e-Azam Law College, 1988–91, Punjab Law College, 1988–92; Visiting Faculty, Lahore College for Arts and Sciences, 1989–90, Punjab University, 1990–91; Asst Prof. of English, Agnes Scott College, 1995–. *Publications:* Cactus: An Anthology of Recent Pakistani Literature (ed. and trans.), 1984; Six Geese from a Tomb at Medum (poems), 1987; Mornings in the Wilderness (ed. and trans.), 1988; Writers and Landscapes (prose and poems), 1991; Miriam's Lament and Other Poems, 1992; Short Stories from Pakistan (ed. and trans.), 1992. *Contributions to:* Newspapers and magazines. *Honours:* Ansley Miller Scholar, Emory University, 1981; International Writing Fellowship, US Information Agency and University of Iowa, 1988; Hon. Fellow, University of Iowa, 1988; Commemorative Medal, Islamic Philosophic Society, Lahore, 1991. *Memberships:* MLA of America; Writers Group, Lahore, Founder, 1984, convener and gen. ed., 1984–92. *Address:* 2923 Evans Wood Dr., Atlanta, GA 30040, USA.

KIDMAN, Fiona (Judith); b. 26 March 1940, Hawera, New Zealand. Writer; Poet. m. Ernest Ian Kidman, 20 Aug. 1960, 1 s., 1 d. *Publications:* Fiction: A Breed of Women, 1979; Mandarin Summer, 1981; Paddy's Puzzle, 1983, US edn as In the Clear Light, 1985; The Book of Secrets, 1987; True Stars, 1990; Ricochet Baby, 1996; The House Within, 1997; The Best of Fiona Kidman's Short Stories, 1998. Poetry: Honey and Bitters, 1975; On the Tightrope, 1978; Going to the Chathams, Poems: 1977–1984, 1985; Wakeful Nights: Poems

Selected and New, 1991. Other: Search for Sister Blue (radio play), 1975; Gone North (with Jane Ussher), 1984; Wellington (with Grant Sheehan), 1989; Palm Prints, 1994. *Contributions to:* Periodicals. *Honours:* Scholarships in Letters, 1981, 1985, 1991, 1995; Mobil Short Story Award, 1987; Queen Elizabeth II Arts Council Award for Achievement, 1988; O.B.E., 1988; Victoria University Writing Fellowship, 1988; Pres. of Honour, New Zealand Book Council, 1997; Distinguished Companion of the New Zealand Order of Merit, 1998; A. W. Reed Award for Lifetime Achievement, 2001. *Memberships:* International PEN; New Zealand Book Council, pres., 1992–95; Patron, Cambodia Trust Aotearoa. *Address:* 28 Rakau Rd, Hataitai, Wellington 3, New Zealand.

KIERCE, Diana. See: KAUFMAN-KIERCE, Diana Faye.

KIGHTLY, Ross; b. 29 Sept. 1945, Melbourne, Vic., Australia. Teacher; Poet. m. Carol Ann Stoker, 20 Dec. 1986, 3 s., 2 d. *Education:* BA, Honours, 1966, Diploma in Education, 1967, Monash University. *Contributions to:* Scratch; Oennine Ink; Inshed; Pennine Platform; Weyfarers; Acumen; Iota; Poetry Nottingham; Orbis. *Honours:* Third Prize, Orbis-Rhyme International Poetry Competition, 1991; Third Prize, Southport Writers Circle Poetry Competition, 1992. *Address:* 1 Heathy Ave, Holmfield, Halifax, West Yorkshire HX2 9UP, England.

KIKEL, Rudy; b. 23 Feb. 1942, New York, NY, USA. Ed.; Writer; Poet. *Education:* BA, St John's University, Jamaica, New York, 1963; MA, Pennsylvania State University, 1965; PhD, Harvard University, 1975. *Publications:* Lasting Relations, 1984; Long Division, 1993; Gents, Bad Boys and Barbarians: New Gay Male Poetry (ed.), 1994; Period Pieces, 1997. *Contributions to:* Kenyon Review; Massachusetts Review; Shenandoah; Ploughshares and other periodicals. *Honour:* Grolier Poetry Prize, 1977. *Address:* 154 W Newton St, Boston, MA 02118, USA.

KILKA, Adel. See: SINGER, Gali-Dana.

KILLDEER, John. See: MAYHAR, Ardath.

KILLEEN, Kevin; b. 31 Oct. 1966, London, England. Writer; Poet; English Teacher. *Education:* Philosophy, Liverpool University, 1984–87. *Publication:* Evictions from the Nursery, 1989. *Contributions to:* Prague Post; Lidova Npveny; Ambit; Poetry Now. *Membership:* Prague Radio Poets Everyman Poetry Society, organiser. *Address:* 116 Empire Ave, London N18 1AG, England.

KILLICK, (Edward) John; b. 18 July 1936, Southport, Merseyside, England. Teacher in Further, Adult and Prison Education; Poet. m. Carole Lesley Forrow, 5 Oct. 1963, 1 s., 2 d. *Education:* Teacher's Certificate, Garnett College, 1965; BA, General Arts, Open University, 1979. *Appointments:* Vice-Principal for Adult Education, Swale Division of Kent, 1976–79; Deputy Education Officer, HMP Canterbury, 1979–80; Education Officer, HMDC Buckley Hall, Rochdale, 1980–83, HMP Drake Hall, Stafford, 1983–90; Ed., Littlewood Press, 1982–90, Littlewood Arc Press, 1990–92; Writer-in-Residence, HMP New Hall, Wakefield, 1990–92, Westminster Health Care, 1992–; Research Fellow, University of Stirling, 1998–. *Publications:* Continuous Creation, 1979; A Pennine Chain, 1983; Things Being Various, 1987; Singular Persons, 1988; The Times of Our Lives, 1994; Between the Lines Between the Bars, 1994; Would You Please Give Me Back My Personality, 1994; Wind-Horse, 1996; Coming of Age, 1996; You Are Words: Dementia Poems, 1997; Writing for Self Discovery (with Myra Schneider), 1998. *Contributions to:* TLS; Scotsman; Lines Review; Poetry Review; PN Review; London Magazine; Green Book; North; Journal of Dementia Care. *Memberships:* National Asscn of Writers in Education; Poetry Book Society. *Address:* 5 Slater Bank, Hebden Bridge, West Yorkshire HX7 7DY, England.

KILLINGLEY, Siew-Yue; b. 17 Dec. 1940, Kuala Lumpur. University Teacher; Publisher. m. Dermot Hastings Killingley, 20 July 1963, 1 d. *Education:* BA, English, MA, Linguistics, 1966, University of Malaya; PhD, Linguistics, University of London, 1972. *Appointments:* Teacher of English and Linguistics, Malaysian Schools and University of Malaya, 1961–67; Tutoral Asst in Linguistics and Phonetics, School of English, University of Newcastle upon Tyne, 1970–72; Lecturer, Senior Lecturer, English and Linguistics, St Mary's College of Education, Newcastle upon Tyne, 1972–80; Visiting Lecturer, Linguistics, Dept of Speech, University of Newcastle upon Tyne, 1978–82; Founder, Ed., Sole Proprietor, Grevatt & Grevatt, 1981–; Tutor, Community Interpreting and Bilingual Skills, College of Arts and Technology, Newcastle upon Tyne, 1987–88; Tutor, Linguistics and Chinese, Centre for Continuing Education, University of Newcastle upon Tyne, 1988–; Ed., British Linguistic Newsletter, 1991–96. *Publications:* Song-Pageant From Christmas to Easter, With Two Settings, 1981; Where No Poppies Blow: Poems of War and Conflict, 1983; In Sundry Places: Views of Durham Cathedral, 1987; Sound, Speech and Silence: Selected Poems, 1995; Lent and Easter Cycle: Poems for Meditation, 1998; Other Edens: Poems of Love and Conflict, 2000; The Pilgrim's Progress (drama adaptation), 2002. *Contributions to:* Reviews, anthologies, periodicals and journals. *Honour:* Second Prize, Durham Cathedral Ninth Centenary Poetry Competition, 1982. *Address:* c/o Grevatt & Grevatt, 9 Rectory Dr., Newcastle upon Tyne

NE3 1XT, England. *E-mail:* siew-yue.killingley@ncl.ac.uk. *Website:* grevatt grevatt.freeservers.com/index.htm.

KIM, Unsong, (William Soo); b. 1 Sept. 1924, Seoul, Korea. Prof. of Molecular Biology (retd); Writer; Poet; Trans. m. Sue Kim, 17 Jan. 1947, 4 s. *Education:* BS, Seoul University, 1949; MS, 1956, PhD, 1958, University of Wisconsin. *Appointments:* Asst Prof., Michigan State University, 1958–59; Fellow, NASA Ames Research Centre, 1962–66, Max Planc Institute, Germany, 1966–69; Prof., Yonsei University, Seoul, 1970–83. *Publications:* Search of Life, 1987; Modern Sijo, 1996. Translator: Over 10 books of poetry trans. into English including: Classical Korean Poems (Sijo) 1986–1987; Hyangga, the Oldest Korean Songs, 1988; Lao Tzu's Tao Teaching, 1990; Anthology of Korean Poets in China, 1993; Poetry of Mao Tse Tung, 1994; Sijo by Korean Poets in China, 1996. *Contributions to:* Anthologies and periodicals. *Honour:* Hon. DLitt, World Acad. of Arts and Culture, 1991. *Memberships:* California Federation of Chaparral Poets; International Poets Acad.; World Congress of Poets; World Poetry Society. *Address:* 120 Lassen Dr., San Bruno, CA 94066, USA.

KIMM, Robert; b. 15 Aug. 1941, Wenatchee, Washington, USA. Poet. m. Beki Sue Biefeld, 1976, 1 s., 1 d. *Education:* BA, San Francisco University, 1967; MA, University of Washington, 1971; PhD, DePaul University, 1976. *Appointments:* Army language school, 1960; Trans., US Army in Germany, 1961–62. *Publication:* Going Nowhere Sunday, 1996. *Honour:* Phatin Fellowship, 1973–75. *Address:* RR02, Marcellus, NY 13108-9623, USA.

KIND, Anne; b. , 16 May 1922, Berlin, Germany. Poet; Writer. m. Robert William Kind, 26 July 1943, 1 s., 1 d. *Education:* Northern Polytechnic; Holloway, London, 1938–39; Kettering General Hospital, 1941–43. *Publications:* View in a Rear Mirror: Selective Memories; Come and See This Folks (biography of Jack Otter), 1994; Footprints (poems), 1999. *Contributions to:* Various publications. *Honours:* Third Prize, Long Eaton Festival, 1982; Runner-up, Staple Competition, 1986; Winner, Millennium Poetry Competition, Leicester Mercury, 2000; O.B.E., 1990. *Memberships:* Leicester Poetry Society; Poetry Society. *Address:* 8 Ridge Way, Oadby, Leicester, LE2 5TN, England.

KING, Joy Rainey; b. 5 Aug. 1939, Memphis, Tennessee, USA. Poet. m. Guy T King, 24 Dec. 1956, 1 s., 1 d. *Publications:* Four collections of poetry. *Contributions to:* Numerous anthologies, magazines and periodicals; Radio; Song lyrics. *Honours:* Ed.'s Choice Awards, National Library of Poetry, 1993, 1994, 1995, 1996; Pres.'s Recognition of Literary Excellence, National Authors Registry, 1999, 2000, 2001, 2002; Author of the Year, International Board of Examiners, Italy, 1999. *Memberships:* International Poetry Hall of Fame; International Society of Poets; Poet's Guild; Southern Illinois Writer's Guild. *Address:* 3029 Willow Branch, Herrin, IL 62948, USA.

KING, Robert W.; b. 6 Dec. 1937, Denver, CO, USA. Prof. of English; Poet. Divorced, 1 s., 2 d. *Education:* BA, 1959, PhD, 1965, University of Iowa; MA, Colorado State University, 1961. *Appointments:* Asst Prof., University of Alaska, 1965–68; Assoc. Prof., 1968–72, Prof. of English, 1972–, University of North Dakota; Visiting Prof., University of Nebraska, 1997. *Publications:* Standing Around Outside, 1979; A Circle of Land, 1990. *Contributions to:* Anthologies, quarterlies, and reviews. *Address:* c/o Dept of English, University of North Dakota, Box 7029, University Station, Grand Forks, ND 58202, USA.

KING, Thomas; b. 24 April 1943, Sacramento, CA, USA. Assoc. Prof. of English; Writer; Dramatist; Poet. m. Kristine Adams, 1970, divorced 1980, 2 s., 1 d. *Education:* BA, English, 1970, MA, English, 1972, Chico State University; PhD, University of Utah, 1986. *Appointments:* Dir, Native Studies, 1971–73, Co-ordinator, History of the Indians of the Americas Program, 1977–79, University of Utah; Assoc. Dean, Student Services, Humboldt State University, 1973–77; Asst Prof. of Native Studies, 1978–89, Chair, Native Studies, 1985–87, University of Lethbridge; Assoc. Prof. of American Studies/Native Studies, 1989–95, Chair, Native Studies, 1991–93, University of Minnesota; Assoc. Prof. of English, University of Guelph, 1995–. *Publications:* The Native in Literature: Canadian and Comparative Perspectives (ed. with Helen Hoy and Cheryl Calver), 1987; An Anthology of Short Fiction by Native Writers in Canada (ed.), 1988; All My Relations: An Anthology of Contemporary Canadian Native Fiction (ed.), 1990; Medicine River, 1990; A Coyote Columbus Story, 1992; Green Grass, Running Water, 1993; One Good Story, That One, 1993; Coyote Sings to the Moon, 1998; Truth and Bright Water, 1999; Coyote's Suit, 2002. Other: Films and radio and television dramas. *Contributions to:* Reference works, books, anthologies, reviews, quarterlies and journals. *Honours:* Best Novel Award, Writers' Guild of Alberta, 1991; Josephine Miles Award, Oakland PEN, 1991; Candian Authors Award for Fiction, 1994; American Library Asscn Notable Book Citation, 2001. *Address:* 7 Ardmay Crescent, Guelph, ON N1E 4L4, Canada.

KING-HELE, Desmond George; b. 3 Nov. 1927, Seaford, Sussex, England. Scientist; Author; Poet. m. Marie Therese Newman, 1954, separated 1992, 2 d. *Education:* BA, Mathematics, 1948, MA, 1952, Trinity College, Cambridge. *Appointments:* Staff, 1948–68, Deputy Chief Scientific Officer, Space Dept, 1968–88, Royal Aircraft Establishment; Ed., Notes and Records of the Royal

Society, 1989–96; Various lectureships. *Publications:* Shelley: His Thought and Work, 1960; Satellites and Scientific Research, 1960; Erasmus Darwin, 1963; Theory of Satellite Orbits in an Atmosphere, 1964; Space Research V (ed.), 1965; Observing Earth Satellites, 1966; Essential Writings of Erasmus Darwin (ed.), 1968; The End of the Twentieth Century?, 1970; Poems and Trixies, 1972; Doctor of Revolution, 1977; Letters of Erasmus Darwin (ed.), 1981; The RAE Table of Earth Satellites (ed.), 1981; Animal Spirits, 1983; Erasmus Darwin and the Romantic Poets, 1986; Satellite Orbits in an Atmosphere: Theory and Applications, 1987; A Tapestry of Orbits, 1992; John Herschel (ed.), 1992; A Concordance to the Botanic Garden (ed.), 1994; Erasmus Darwin: A Life of Unequalled Achievement, 1999; Antic and Romantic (poems), 2000; Charles Darwin's Life of Erasmus Darwin (ed.), 2002. *Contributions to:* Numerous scientific and literary journals. *Honours:* Eddington Medal, Royal Astronomical Society, 1971; Charles Chree Medal, Institute of Physics, 1971; Lagrange Prize, Académie Royale de Belgique, 1972; Hon. Doctorates, Universities of Aston, 1979, and Surrey, 1986; Nordberg Medal, International Committee on Space Research, 1990; Society of Authors Medical History Prize, 1999. *Memberships:* British National Committee for the History of Science, Medicine and Technology, chair., 1985–89; Institute of Mathematics and Its Applications, fellow; Royal Astronomical Society, fellow; Royal Society, fellow; Bakerian Lecturer, Royal Society, 1974. *Address:* 7 Hilltops Ct, 65 North Lane, Buriton, Hampshire GU31 5RS, England.

KINGSOLVER, Barbara; b. 8 April 1955, Annapolis, Maryland, USA. Author; Poet. m. (1) Joseph Hoffmann, 1985, divorced 1993, 1 d., (2) Steven Hopp, 1995, 1 d. *Education:* BA, DePauw University, 1977; MS, University of Arizona, 1981. *Appointments:* Research Asst, Dept of Physiology, 1977–79, Technical Writer, Office of Arid Land Studies, 1981–85, University of Arizona, Tucson; Journalist, 1985–87; Author, 1987–; Founder, Bellwether Prize to recognize a first novel of social significance, 1997. *Publications:* The Bean Trees (novel), 1988; Homeland and Other Stories, 1989; Holding the Line: Women in the Great Arizona Mine Strike of 1983 (non-fiction), 1989; Animal Dreams (novel), 1990; Pigs in Heaven (novel), 1993; Another America (poems), 1994; High Tide in Tucson: Essays from Now or Never, 1995; The Poisonwood Bible (novel), 1998; Prodigal Summer (short stories), 2000; Small Wonder (essays), 2002. *Contributions to:* Many anthologies and periodicals. *Honours:* Feature-Writing Award, Arizona Press Club, 1986; American Library Asscn Awards, 1988, 1990; PEN Fiction Prize, 1991; Edward Abbey Ecofiction Award, 1991; Los Angeles Times Book Award for Fiction, 1993; PEN Faulkner Award, 1999; American Booksellers Book of the Year, 2000; National Humanities Medal, 2000. *Address:* c/o Frances Goldin, Suite 513, 57 E 11th St, New York, NY 10003, USA.

KINLOCH, David; b. 21 Nov. 1959, Glasgow, Scotland. University Senior Lecturer; Poet; Ed. *Education:* MA, University of Glasgow, 1982; DPhil, Balliol College, Oxford, 1986. *Appointments:* Junior Research Fellow, St Anne's College, Oxford, 1985–87; Research Fellow, University of Wales, 1987–89; Lecturer, University of Salford, 1989–90; Lecturer, 1990–94, Senior Lecturer, 1994–, University of Strathclyde; Ed., Southfields Magazine; Founder/Co-Ed., Verse Poetry Magazine. *Publications:* Other Tongues (co-author), 1990; Dustie-Fute, 1992; Paris-Forfar, 1994; Un Tour d'Ecosse, 2001. *Contributions to:* Reviews, journals and magazines. *Address:* c/o Dept of Modern Languages, University of Strathclyde, Glasgow, Scotland.

KINNELL, Galway; b. 1 Feb. 1927, Providence, RI, USA. Poet; Writer; Prof. of Creative Writing. m. Inés Delgado de Torres, 1965, 1 s., 2 d. *Education:* MA, Princeton University. *Appointments:* Dir, Writing Program, 1981–84, Samuel F. B. Morse Prof. of Arts and Sciences, 1985–92, Erich Maria Remarque Prof. of Creative Writing, 1992–, New York University; Vermont State Poet, 1989–93. *Publications:* Poetry: What a Kingdom It Was, 1960; Flower Herding on Mount Monadnock, 1963; Body Rags, 1966; The Book of Nightmares, 1971; The Avenue Bearing the Initial of Christ into the New World, 1974; Mortal Acts, Mortal Words, 1980; Selected Poems, 1982; The Past, 1985; When One Has Lived a Long Time Alone, 1990; Imperfect Thirst, 1994; The Essential Rilke, 1999; New Selected Poems, 2000. Other: The Poems of François Villon (trans.), 1965; Black Light (novel), 1966; On the Motion and Immobility of Douve, 1968; The Lackawanna Elegy, 1970; Interviews: Walking Down the Stairs, 1977; How the Alligator Missed Breakfast (children's story), 1982; The Essential Whitman (ed.), 1987. *Honours:* National Institute of Arts and Letters Award, 1962; Cecil Hemley Poetry Prize, 1969; Medal of Merit, 1975; Pulitzer Prize in Poetry, 1983; National Book Award, 1983; John D. and Catherine T. MacArthur Foundation Fellowship, 1984. *Memberships:* PEN; Poetry Society of America; MLA; Acad. of Arts and Letters; Acad. of Arts and Sciences; Acad. of American Poets, board of chancellors, 2001–. *Address:* RR 2 Box 138, Sheffield, VT 05866, USA.

KINSELLA, John; b. 1963, Perth, WA, Australia. Poet; Writer; Ed.; Publisher. *Education:* University of Western Australia. *Appointments:* Writer-in-Residence, Churchill College, Cambridge, 1997; Ed., Salt literary journal; Publisher, Ed., Folio (Salt) Publishing. *Publications:* Poetry: The Frozen Sea, 1983; Night Parrots, 1989; The Book of Two Faces, 1989; Eschatologies, 1991; Full Fathom Five, 1993; Syzygy, 1993; The Silo: A Pastoral Symphony, 1995; Erratum/Frame(d), 1995; The Radnoti Poems, 1996; Anathalamion, 1996; The Undertow: New and Selected Poems, 1996; Lightning Tree, 1996; Poems: 1980–1994, 1997; The Hunt and Other Poems, 1998; Visitants, 1999; Fenland Pastorals, 1999; The Hierarchy of Sheep, 2000; Auto, 2001; Zoo (with Coral Hull), 2001; Outside the Panopticon, 2002; Four Australian Poets (with others), 2003. Editor: The Bird Catcheris Song, 1992; A Salt Reader, 1995; Graphology, 1997; The Benefaction, 1997; Authenticities, 1998; Directions in Contemporary Australian Poetry, 1998; The May Anthologies, 1999; Landbridge: An Anthology of Contempory Australian Poetry, 1999; Vanishing Points Vol. 1 (with Rod Mengham), 2002. Other: Genre (novel), 1997; Grappling Eros (short stories), 1998; Crop Circles (play in verse); From Poetry to Politics and Back Again, 2000; Peter Porter in Conversation with John Kinsella (with Peter Porter), 2003. *Contributions to:* Newspapers and journals. *Honours:* Western Australian Premier's Award for Poetry, 1993; Harri Jones Memorial Prize for Poetry; John Bray Poetry Award, Adelaide Festival, 1996; Senior Fellowships, Literature Board of the Australia Council; Young Australian Creative Fellowship. *Address:* PO Box 202, Applecross, WA 6153, Australia.

KINSELLA, Thomas; b. 4 May 1928, Dublin, Ireland. Poet; Trans.; Ed.; Prof. of English (retd). m. Eleanor Walsh, 27 Dec. 1955, 1 s., 2 d. *Appointments:* Irish Civil Service, 1946–65; Artist-in-Residence, 1965–67, Prof. of English, 1967–70, Southern Illinois University; Prof. of English, Temple University, Philadelphia, 1970–90. *Publications:* Poetry: Poems, 1956; Another September, 1958; Downstream, 1962; Nightwalker and Other Poems, 1968; Notes From the Land of the Dead, 1972; Butcher's Dozen, 1972; A Selected Life, 1972; Finistere, 1972; New Poems, 1973; Selected Poems, 1956–68, 1973; Song of the Night and Other Poems, 1978; The Messenger, 1978; Fifteen Dead, 1979; One and Other Poems, 1979; Poems, 1956–73, 1980; Peppercanister Poems, 1972–78, 1980; One Fond Embrace, 1981; Songs of the Psyche, 1985; Her Vertical Smile, 1985; St Catherine's Clock, 1987; Out of Ireland, 1987; Blood and Family, 1988; Personal Places, 1990; Poems From Centre City, 1990; Madonna, 1991; Open Court, 1991; From Centre City, 1994; Collected Poems, 1956–94, 1996; The Pen Shop, 1997; The Familiar, 1999; Godhead, 1999; Citizen of the World, 2000; Littlebody, 2000. Other: The Tain (trans. from Old Irish), 1970; Selected Poems of Austin Clarke (ed.), 1976; An Duanaire: Poems of the Dispossessed (trans.), 1981; The New Oxford Book of Irish Verse (ed. and trans.), 1986; The Dual Tradition: An Essay on Poetry and Politics in Ireland, 1995. *Honours:* Guinness Poetry Award, 1958; Denis Devlin Memorial Awards, 1966, 1969, 1988, 1994; Guggenheim Fellowships, 1968–69, 1971–72; Hon. PhD, National University of Ireland, 1984. *Memberships:* Irish Acad. of Letters; American Acad. of Arts and Sciences. *Address:* 639 Addison St, Philadelphia, PA 19147, USA.

KINSELLA, W(illiam) P(atrick); b. 25 May 1935, Edmonton, AB, Canada. Author; Poet. m. (1) Myrna Salls, 28 Dec. 1957, divorced 1963, 3 d., (2) Mildred Irene Clay-Heming, 10 Sept. 1965, divorced 1978, (3) Ann Ilene Knight, 30 Dec. 1978, divorced, (4) Barbara L. Turner, 1999. *Education:* BA, University of Victoria, 1974; MFA, University of Iowa, 1978. *Publications:* Dance Me Outside, 1977; Scars, 1978; Shoeless Joe Jackson Comes to Iowa, 1980; Born Indian, 1981; Shoeless Joe, 1982; The Ballad of the Public Trustee, 1982; The Moccasin Telegraph, 1983; The Thrill of the Grass, 1984; The Alligator Report, 1985; The Iowa Baseball Confederacy, 1986; The Fencepost Chronicles, 1986; Five Stories, 1987; Red Wolf, Red Wolf, 1987; The Further Adventures of Slugger McBatt: Baseball Stories, 1987, revised edn as Go The Distance, 1995; The Miss Hobbema Pageant, 1988; The Rainbow Warehouse (poems with Ann Knight), 1989; Two Spirits Soar: The Art of Allen Sapp, 1990; Box Socials, 1991; A Series for the World, 1992; The Dixon Cornbelt League and Other Baseball Stories, 1993; Even at This Distance (poems with Ann Knight), 1994; Brother Frank's Gospel Hour, 1994; The Winter Helen Dropped By, 1995; If Wishes Were Horses, 1996; Magic Time, 1998. *Contributions to:* Many anthologies and periodicals. *Honours:* Houghton Mifflin Literary Fellowship, 1982; Books in Canada First Novel Award, 1982; Canadian Authors' Asscn Award for Fiction, 1982; Writers' Guild of Alberta Awards for Fiction, 1982, 1983; Vancouver Award for Writing, 1987; Stephen Leacock Medal Humor, 1987; Canadian Booksellers' Asscn Author of the Year, 1987. *Address:* PO Box 3067, Sumas, WA 98295, USA.

KINZIE, Mary; b. 30 Sept. 1944, Montgomery, AL, USA. Prof. of English; Poet; Critic; Ed. *Education:* BA, Northwestern University, 1967; Graduate Studies, Free University of Berlin, 1967–68; MA, 1970, MA, 1972, PhD, 1980, Johns Hopkins University. *Appointments:* Exec. Ed., TriQuarterly magazine, 1975–78; Instructor, 1975–78, Lecturer, 1978–85, Assoc. Prof., 1985–90, Martin J and Patricia Koldyke Outstanding Teaching Prof., 1990–92, Prof. of English, 1990–, Dir of Creative Writing Program, 1999–, Northwestern University. *Publications:* Poetry: The Threshold of the Year, 1982; Summers of Vietnam, 1990; Masked Women, 1990; Autumn Eros and Other Poems, 1991; Ghost Ship, 1996. Non-Fiction: The Cure of Poetry in an Age of Prose: Moral Essays on the Poet's Calling, 1993; The Judge is Fury: Dislocation and Form in Poetry, 1994; A Poet's Guide to Poetry, 1979. *Contributions to:* Various books, anthologies, reviews, quarterlies, journals, and magazines. *Honours:* Illinois Arts Council Awards, 1977, 1978, 1980, 1982, 1984, 1988, 1990, 1993, and Artist Grant, 1983; DeWitt Wallace Fellow, MacDowell Colony, 1979; Devins Award for a First Vol. of Verse, 1982; Guggenheim Fellowship, 1986; Elizabeth Matchett Stover Memorial Award in Poetry, Southwest Review, 1987; Celia B Wagner Award, Poetry Society of America, 1988; Pres.'s Fund for the Humanities Research Grant, 1990–91. *Memberships:* PEN; Poetry Society of America; Society of Midland Authors. *Address:* c/o College of Arts and Sciences, Dept of English, Northwestern University, University Hall 215, Evanston, IL 60208-2240, USA.

KIRK, Pauline Marguerite; b. 14 April 1942, Birmingham, England. Writer; Poet. m. Peter Kirk, 4 April 1964, 1 s., 1 d. *Education:* Nottingham University, 1960–63; Sheffield University, 1963–64; Monash University, 1966–70; MA, Bretton Hall College, Leeds University, 1999. *Appointments:* Teacher, Methodist Ladies College, 1965–66; Teaching Fellow, Monash University, 1965–69; Tutor-Counsellor, Asst Senior Counsellor, Open University, 1971–88; Senior Officer, Leeds Dept of Social Service, 1988–95; Partner, Fighting Cock Press, 1996–. *Publications:* Fiction: Waters of Time, 1988; The Keepers, 1996. Poetry: Scorpion Days, 1982; Red Marl and Brick, 1985; Rights of Way, 1990; Travelling Solo, 1995; Return to Dreamtime, 1996; No Cure in Tears, 1997. Criticism: Brian Merrikin Hill: Poet and Mentor, 1999. Editor: A Survivor Myself: Experiences of Child Abuse, 1994; Local history booklets for Leeds City Council. Poetry Collections: Dunegrass, Brakken City, 1997; Chernobyls Cloud, Natural Light, Kingfisher Days, 1998; The Imaginator, 2000; Imaginary Gates, 2001. *Contributions to:* Anthologies and other publications. *Honours:* Yorkshire and Humberside Arts New Beginnings Award, 1994. *Memberships:* Aireings, Partner, Fighting Cock Press, 1997–; Pennine Poets; Society of Authors. *Address:* 8 Dale Park Rise, Cookridge, Leeds LS16 7PP, England.

KIRKUP, James (Falconer); b. 23 April 1918, South Shields, Tyne and Wear, England. Poet; Author; Dramatist; Trans. *Education:* BA, Durham University. *Appointments:* Gregory Fellow in Poetry, University of Leeds, 1950–52; Visiting Poet and Head of the Dept of English, Bath Acad. of Art, Corsham, 1953–56; Prof. of English, University of Salamanca, 1957–58, Tohoku University of Malaya, Kuala Lumpur, 1961–62, Japan Women's University, Tokyo, 1963–70; Literary Ed., Orient/West Magazine, Tokyo, 1963–64; Prof. of English Literature, Nagoya University, 1969–72; Prof. of Comparative Literature, Kyoto University of Foreign Studies, 1976–88. *Publications:* Poetry: The Drowned Sailor and Other Poems, 1947; The Submerged Village and Other Poems, 1951; A Correct Compassion and Other Poems, 1952; The Spring Journey and Other Poems of 1952–53, 1954; the Descent Into the Cave and Other Poems, 1957; The Prodigal Son: Poems 1956–59, 1959; Refusal to Conform: Last and First Poems, 1963; Paper Windows: Poems from Japan, 1968; White Shadows, Black Shadows: Poems of Peace and War, 1970; A Bewick Bestiary, 1971; The Body Servant: Poems of Exile, 1971; Cold Mountain Poems, 1979; To the Ancestral North: Poems for an Autobiography, 1983; The Sense of the Visit: New Poems, 1984; Fellow Feelings, 1986; Throwback: Poems Towards the Autobiography, 1992; Shooting Stars, 1992; Strange Attractors, 1995; Counting to 9,999, 1995; Noems, Koans and a Navel Display, 1995; Collected Longer Poems, 2 vols, 1995, 1997; Selected Shorter Poems, 1995; Broad Daylight, 1996; Figures in a Setting, 1997; The Patient Obituarist, 1997; One-Man Band: Poems Without Words, 1998; Burning Giraffes, 1998; Tank Alphabet, 2000; Tokonoma, 2000; A Tiger in Your Tanka, 2000; Shields Sketches: Poems about Tyneside, 2002; An Island in the Sky: Poems for Andorra, 2002. Fiction: The Love of Others, 1962; Insect Summer, 1971; Gaijin on the Ginza, 1991; Queens Have Died Young and Fair, 1993. Non-Fiction: The Only Child: An Autobiography of Infancy, 1957; Sorrows, Passions, and Alarms: An Autobiography of Childhood, 1959; I, Of All People: An Autobiography of Youth, 1988; Object Lessons, 1990; A Poet Could Not But Be Gay: Some Legends of My Lost Youth, 1991; Me All Over: Memoirs of a Misfit, 1993; Child of the Tyne, 1997. Other: Travel books, essays, plays and trans. *Contributions to:* Various publications. *Honours:* Many awards and prizes. *Memberships:* RSL, fellow; British Haiku Society. *Literary Agent:* Curtis Brown, New York, USA. *Address:* c/o British Monomarks, Box 2780, London WC1N 3XX, England; Atic D, Edifici les Bons, Avinguda de Rouillac 7, Les Bons, Encamp, Andorra. Telephone and Fax: 831-065.

KIRSCH, Sarah; b. 16 April 1935, Limlingerode, Germany. Author; Poet. m. Rainer Kirsch, 1958, divorced 1968, 1 s. *Education:* Diploma, University of Halle, 1959; Johannes R Becher Institute, Leipzig, 1963–65. *Publications:* Landaufenthalt, 1967; Die Vögel signen im Regen am Schönsten, 1968; Zaubersprüche, 1973; Es war der merkwürdigste Sommer, 1974; Musik auf dem Wasser, 1977; Rückenwind, 1977; Drachensteigen, 1979; Sieben Häute: Ausgewählte Gedichte 1962–79, 1979; La Pagerie, 1980; Erdreich, 1982; Katzenleben, 1984; Hundert Gedichte, 1985; Landwege: Eine Auswahl 1980–85, 1985; Irrstern, 1986; Allerlei-Rauh, 1988; Schneewärme, 1989; Die Flut, 1990; Spreu, 1991; Schwingrasen, 1991; Sic! natur!, 1992; Erlkönigs Tochter, 1992; Das simple Leben, 1994; Winternachtigall, 1995; Ich Crusoe, 1995; Nachtsonnen, 1995; Bodenlos, 1996. *Honours:* Petrarca Prize, 1976; Austrian State Prize for Literature, 1981; Austrian Critics Prize, 1981; Gandersheim Literary Prize, 1983; Hölderlin Prize, Bad Homburg, 1984; Art Prize, Schleswig-Holstein, 1987; Author-in-Residence, City of Mainz, 1988; Heinrich-Heine-Gesellschaft Award, Düsseldorf, 1992; Peter Huchel Prize, 1993; Konrad Adenauer Foundation Literature Prize, 1993; Büchner Prize, 1996. *Address:* Eiderdeich 22, 25794 Tielenhemme, Germany.

KIRSTEN-MARTIN, Diane; b. 29 March 1950, Bronx, New York, USA. Poet; Writer. m. 2 Oct. 1976, 1 s. *Education:* BA, University of Rochester, 1972; MA, San Francisco State University, 1986. *Contributions to:* Hayden's Ferry Review; Yellow Silk; Zyzzyua; On the Bus; Bellingham Review; Gomimomo; Torncat; Blue Mesa Review; Santa Clara Review. *Honour:* Second Prize, National Writers Union Competition, 1992. *Address:* 68 Ashton Ave, San Francisco, CA 94112, USA.

KISS, Iren; b. 25 Sept. 1947, Budapest, Hungary. Writer; Poet; Dramatist; University Prof. m. Laszlo Tabori, 10 June 1988. *Education:* PhD, History of Literature, University of Budapest, 1992. *Publications:* Szelcsend (poems) 1977; Allokep (novel), 1978; Arkadiat Tatarozxzak (poems), 1979 Maganrecept (cycle), 1982; Kemopera (plays), 1988. *Contributions to:* Variou publications. *Honours:* Yeats Club Award, 1987; Gold Medal, Brianza Worl Competition in Poetry, Italy, 1988. *Memberships:* Asscn of Hungarian Writers Hungarian PEN. *Address:* Somloi ut 60/B, Budapest 1118, Hungary.

KIZER, Carolyn Ashley; b. 10 Dec. 1925, Spokane, Washington, USA. Poet Prof. *Education:* BA, Sarah Lawrence College, 1945; Postgraduate studies Columbia University, 1946–47; Studied poetry with Theodore Roethke University of Washington, 1953–54. *Appointments:* Founder-Ed., Poetry North West, 1959–65; First Dir, Literature Programs, National Endowment for the Arts, 1966–70; Poet-in-Residence, University of North Carolina at Chapel Hill, 1970–74; Hurst Prof. of Literature, Washington University, St Louis, 1971; Lecturer, Barnard College, 1972; Acting Dir, Graduate Writing Program, 1972, Prof., School of Arts, 1982, Columbia University; Poet-in Residence, Ohio University, 1974; Prof., University of Maryland, 1976–77 Poet-in-Residence, Distingusihed Visiting Lecturer, Centre College, KY, 1979 Distinguished Visiting Poet, East Washington University, 1980; Elliston Prof of Poetry, University of Cincinnati, 1981; Bingham Distinguished Prof. University of Louisville, 1982; Distinguished Visiting Poet, Bucknell University, 1982; Visiting Poet, State University of New York at Albany 1982; Prof. of Poetry, Stanford University, 1986. *Publications:* Poetry: The Ungrateful Garden, 1961; Knock Upon Silence, 1965; Midnight Was My Cry 1971; Mermaids in the Basement: Poems for Women, 1984; Yin: New Poems, 1984; Carrying Over, 1988; Harping On: Poems, 1985–1995, 1996. Prose: On Poems and Poets, 1993; Picking and Choosing: Prose on Prose, 1996. *Contributions to:* Poems and articles in various journals including The Paris Review; Antaeus; Michigan Quarterly. *Honours:* Governor's Awards, State of Washington, 1965, 1985, 1995, 1998; Pulitzer Prize in Poetry, 1985; American Acad. and Institute of Arts and Letters Award, 1985; San Francisco Arts Commission Award in Literature, 1986; Silver Medal, Commonwealth Club, 1998. Memberships; American Civil Liberties Union; American Poets; Amnesty International; PEN; Acad. of American Poets, chancellor; Poetry Society of America; Associated Writing Programs, dir. *Address:* 19772 Eighth St E, Sonoma, CA 95476, USA.

KLAPPERT, Peter; b. 14 Nov. 1942, Rockville Center, New York, USA. Prof.; Poet; Writer. *Education:* BA, Cornell University, 1964; MA, Honours, Renaissance English Literature, 1967, MFA, Poetry, 1968, University of Iowa. *Appointments:* Instructor, Rollins College, 1968–71; Briggs-Copeland Lecturer, Harvard University, 1971–74; Visiting Lecturer, New College, 1972; Writer-in-Residence, 1976–77, Asst Prof., 1977–78, College of William and Mary; Asst Prof., 1978–81, Dir, Graduate Writing Program, 1979–81, 1985–88, Assoc. Prof., 1981–91, Prof., 1991–, Dir, MFA Degree Program in Poetry, 1995–98, George Mason University. *Publications:* On a Beach in Southern Connecticut, 1966; Lugging Vegetables to Nantucket, 1971; Circular Stairs, Distress in the Mirrors, 1975; Non Sequitur O'Connor, 1977; The Idiot Princess of the Last Dynasty, 1984; '52 Pick-Up: Scenes From the Conspiracy, A Documentary, 1984; Chokecherries: New and Selected Poems 1966–1999, 2000. *Contributions to:* Many anthologies, books, journals, and magazines. *Honours:* Yale Series of Younger Poets Prize, 1970; Yaddo Resident Fellowships, 1972, 1973, 1975, 1981; MacDowell Colony Resident Fellowships, 1973, 1975; National Endowment for the Arts Fellowships, 1973, 1979; Lucille Medwick Award, Poetry Society of America, 1977; Virginia Center for the Creative Arts Resident Fellowships, 1978, 1979, 1981, 1983, 1984, 1987, 1993, 1995; Millay Colony for the Arts Resident Fellowship, 1981; Ingram Merrill Foundation Grant, 1983; Klappert-Ai Poetry Award established in his honour by Gwendolyn Brooks, George Mason University, 1987; Poet-Scholar, American Library Asscn-National Endowment for the Humanities Voices and Visions Project, 1988. *Memberships:* Acad. of American Poets; Associated Writing Programs; Asscn of Literary Scholars and Critics; PEN; Poetry Society of America; Writers' Center, Bethesda, Maryland. *Address:* 2003 Klingle Rd NW, Washington, DC 20010, USA. *E-mail:* petermail@earthlink.net.

KLEEFELD, Carolyn Mary; b. 1935, London, England. Poet; Writer; Painter. *Education:* University of California at Los Angeles. *Publications:* Climates of the Mind, 1979; Satan Sleeps with the Holy, Word Paintings, 1982; Lovers in Evolution, 1983; Songs of Ecstasy, 1990; The Alchemy of Possibility: Reinventing Your Personal Mythology, 1998. *Contributions to:* Several publications. *Memberships:* Amnesty International, board of dirs; The New Forum, co-founder. *Address:* PO Box 128, Big Sur, CA 93920, USA.

KLEINSCHMIDT MAYES, Edward Joseph; b. 29 Oct. 1951, Winona, Minnesota, USA. Assoc. Prof. of English; Poet. m. Frances Mayes, 1998. *Education:* BA, St Mary's College, 1974; MA, Hollins College, 1976. *Appointments:* Poet-in-the-Schools Program, CA, 1979–82; Lecturer in English, De Anza College, 1980–82, Stanford University, 1981–82; Lecturer, 1981–89, Asst Prof., 1990–93, Assoc. Prof. of English, 1994–, Santa Clara University. *Publications:* Magnetism, 1987; First Language, 1990; To Remain, 1990; Bodysong: Love Poems, 1999; Works & Days, 1999; Speed of

Life, 1999. *Contributions to:* Reviews and journals. *Honours:* Juniper Prize, Bay Area Book Reviewers Award; Gesù Award, 1990. *Memberships:* Associated Writing Programs; PEN; Poetry Society of America. *Address:* c/o Dept of English, Santa Clara University, 500 Camino Real, Santa Clara, CA 95053, USA.

KLEINZAHLER, August; b. 10 Dec. 1949, Jersey City, NJ, USA. Poet; Writer. *Education:* University of Wisconsin at Madison, 1967–70; University of Victoria, 1973. *Appointment:* Visiting Holloway Lecturer, University of California at Berkeley, 1987. *Publications:* A Calendar of Airs, 1978; News and Weather: Seven Canadian Poets (ed.), 1982; Storm Over Hackensack, 1985; On Johnny's Time, 1988; Earthquake Weather, 1989; Red Sauce, Whiskey and Snow, 1995; Live from the Hong Kong Nile Club: Poems, 1975–1990, 2000. *Contributions to:* Newspapers and magazines. *Honours:* Guggenheim Fellowship, 1989; Lila Wallace-Reader's Digest Writers' Award, 1991–94. *Membership:* Poetry Society of America. *Address:* PO Box 842, Fort Lee, NJ 07024, USA.

KLIKOVAC, Igor; b. 16 May 1970, Bosnia. Poet. *Education:* General Literture and Librarianship, University of Sarajevo, 1989–92. *Appointments:* Ed., Literary Review, Sarajevo, 1991–92; Ed., Stone Soup Magazine, London, 1995–. *Publications:* Last Days of Peking (poems), 1996. *Contributions to:* Literary Review; Echo; Bridge; Transitions; Stone Soup; New Iowa Review. *Address:* 37 Chesterfield Rd, London W4 3HQ, England.

KNELL, William, (Autumn, Caliban, Sparrow, Von Wernich); b. 5 March 1927, New York, NY, USA. Prof. of English Emeritus; Poet. m. 27 Aug. 1977, 1 s. *Education:* BA, Highlands University, 1952; MA, Adelphi University, 1965. *Appointments:* Staff, New York Mirror, 1953–60, Santa Fe New Mexican, 1960–65; Prof. of English, 1965–91, Prof. Emeritus, 1991–, New Mexico Highlands University. *Contributions to:* Newspapers, reviews, quarterlies, and journals. *Memberships:* Rio Grande Writers Asscn; Squares; World Poetry Society. *Address:* 862 Sperry Dr., Las Vegas, NM 87701, USA.

KNIGHT, Arthur Winfield; b. 29 Dec. 1937, San Francisco, CA, USA. Prof. of English; Writer; Poet; Film Critic. m. Kit Duell, 25 Aug. 1976, 1 d. *Education:* AA, Santa Rosa Junior College, 1958; BA, English, 1960, MA, Creative Writing, 1962, San Francisco State University. *Appointments:* Prof. of English, California University of Pennsylvania, 1966–93; Film Critic, Russian River News, Guerneville, CA, 1991–92, Anderson Valley Advertiser, Boonville, CA, 1992–, Potpourri, Prairie Village, KS, 1993–95; Part-time Prof., University of San Francisco, 1995. *Publications:* A Marriage of Poets (with Kit Knight), 1984; King of the Beatniks, 1986; The Beat Vision (co-ed.), 1987; Wanted!, 1988; Basically Tender, 1991; Cowboy Poems, 1993, retitled Outlaws, Lawmen and Bad Women; Tell Me An Erotic Story, 1993; The Darkness Starts Up Where You Stand, 1996; The Secret Life of Jesse James, 1996; The Cruelest Month, 1997; Johnnie D. (novel), 1999. *Contributions to:* Reviews, quarterlies, and journals. *Honour:* First Place, Joycean Lively Arts Guild Poetry Competition, 1982. *Membership:* Western Writers of America. *Literary Agent:* Nat Sobel, Sobel Weber Assocs Inc, 146 E 19th St, New York, NY 10003-2404, USA. *Address:* 544 Citrus Heights, CA 956ll, USA.

KNIGHT, Cranston Sedrick; b. 10 Sept. 1950, Chicago, IL, USA. Historian; Poet; Writer; Dramatist. m. Joyce Anderson, 5 Aug. 1977, 2 s., 1 d. *Education:* BA, History, Southern Illinois University, 1977; MA, History, Northeastern Illinois University, 1990; Doctoral Studies, History, Loyola University, Chicago. *Appointments:* Literary Consultant, Black Open Lab Theater, Southern Illinois University, 1975–77, Mystic Voyage theatre group, Carbondale, IL, 1977–80; Columnist, Chicago Daily Defender newspaper, 1987–; Dramatis (Historian), National Passtime Theatre, Chicago, 1996; Poet-in-Residence, Loyola University, Chicago, 1996. *Publications:* Poetry: Freedom Song, 1988; In the Garden of the Beast, 1989, second edn as In the Garden of the Beast: Vietnam Cries a Love Song, 1996; I, 1996; On the Borders of Hiroshima: I Heared a Rumor of War, 1998. Play: When Silence Cries, 1998. Other: Tour of Duty: Vietnam in the Words of Those Who Were There (ed.), 1986. *Contributions to:* Anthologies, journals, and magazines. *Honours:* Benjamin Henry Matchett Foundation Grant, 1989; Illinois Arts Council Writers Grants, 1996, 1998; Illinois Humanities Plaque, 1998. *Honour:* Humanities and Letters Award, 1997. *Memberships:* Associated Writing Programs; Asscn for Asian Studies; Illinois Writers Inc; Japan Society of America; Joint Center for Political Studies; Midwest Asian Asscn; National Asscn for Developmental Educators; West Side Writers Guild. *Address:* 5935 N Magnolia, No. 1, Chicago, IL 60660, USA.

KNIGHT, Edith Joan; b. 18 May 1932, Great Houghton, Barnsley, England. Teacher (retd); Poet. Widow. *Education:* Certificate in Education, Huddersfield College of Education, 1969. *Contributions to:* Anthologies, including: This Moment in Time, 2001; Sweet Memories, 2002; The Prime of Life, 2002; Magazines. *Honour:* Bronze Medallion, International Society of Poets, 1997. *Honour:* Bronze Medallion, International Society of Poets, 1997. *Membership:* Retford Writers. *Address:* 20 Thurnscoe Lane, Great Houghton, Barnsley, South Yorkshire S72 0DY, England.

KNIGHT, Kit; b. 21 Sept. 1952, North Kingston, RI, USA. Writer; Poet. m. Arthur Winfield Knight, 25 Aug. 1976, 1 d. *Education:* BA, Communications, California University of Pennsylvania, 1975. *Appointments:* Co-Ed., Unspeakable Views of the Individual, 1976–88; Poet and Columnist, Russian River News, Guerneville, CA, 1988–92; Poet/columnist, film critic, Russian River Times, Monte Rio, CA, 1997–99; Reviewer, Citizens Echo, CA, 2000–; Film critic, City Times, Fair Oaks Times, Gold River News, Citrus Heights, CA, 2002–. *Publications:* A Marriage of Poets (with Arthur Winfield Knight), 1984; Women of Wanted Men, 1994. *Contributions to:* Periodicals. *Honour:* Perry Award for Best Achievement in Poetry, 1994. *Address:* PO Box 544, Citrus Heights, CA 95611, USA. *E-mail:* tens178295@aol.com.

KNOPP, Lisa; b. 4 Sept. 1956, Burlington, IA, USA. Asst Prof.; Writer; Poet. m. Colin Ramsay, 4 Sept. 1990, divorced 1996, 1 s., 1 d. *Education:* BA, Iowa Wesleyan College, 1981; MA, Western Illinois University, 1986; PhD, University of Nebraska, Lincoln, 1993. *Appointments:* Teaching Asst, 1988–93, Lecturer, 1994–95, University of Nebraska, Lincoln; Asst Prof., Southern Illinois University, 1995. *Publication:* Field of Vision (essays), 1996. *Contributions to:* Anthologies, newspapers and periodicals. *Honours:* Frank Vogel Scholar in Non-Fiction, Bread Loaf Writers Conference, 1992; Second Place, Society of Midland Authors, 1996. *Memberships:* Associated Writing Programs; Asscn for the Study of Literature and the Environment; Western Literature Asscn. *Address:* c/o Dept of English, Southern Illinois University, Carbondale, IL 62901-4503, USA.

KNOX, Ann B.; b. 31 Jan. 1926, Buffalo, New York, USA. Writer; Ed.; Teacher. 3 s., 2 d. *Education:* BA, Vassar College, 1946; MA, Catholic University of America, 1970; MFA, Warren Wilson College, 1981. *Appointment:* Ed.-in-Chief, Antietam Review, 1984–. *Publications:* Stone Crop (poems), 1988; Signatures; Late Summer Breath (stories), 1995; Staging is Nowhere, 1996. *Contributions to:* Poetry; Negative Capability; New York Quarterly; Berkeley Review; Nimrod Poets; Soundings East; Blueline; Poet Love; Maryland Poetry Review. *Honours:* Washington Writers Publishing House Winner; Pennsylvania Council on the Arts Grant; Virginia Center for Creative Arts Fellowship; Atlantic Centre for the Arts Fellowships, 1994, 1996; Ucross Foundation Fellowship, 1997. *Memberships:* Poets and Writers; Acad. of American poets; Writers Center; Associated Writing Program; International Womens Writing Guild; Poetry Society of America. *Address:* Box 65, Hancock, MD 21750, USA.

KOESTENBAUM, Phyllis; b. 16 Sept. 1930, New York, NY, USA. Poet; University Scholar. m. (1) Peter Koestenbaum, 29 June 1952, divorced 1986, (2) Aaron Goldman, 16 July 1989, 3 s., 1 d. *Education:* BA, Radcliffe College, 1952; MA, San Francisco State University, 1979. *Appointments:* Instructor, West Valley Community College; Lecturer, Santa Clara University, San Francisco State University; Affiliated Scholar, Institute for Research on Women and Gender, Stanford University, 1984–. *Publications:* Crazy Face, 1980; oh I can't she says, 1980; Hunger Food, 1980; That Nakedness, 1982; 14 Criminal Sonnets, 1984; Necessary Mistake, 1995; Criminal Sonnets, 1998. *Contributions to:* Anthologies, reviews and quarterlies. *Honours:* National Endowment for the Arts Fellowship; Honorable Mention, Annual Book Award, San Francisco State University Poetry Center; First Prize, Acad. of American Poets Contest. *Memberships:* Authors Guild; National Writers Union. *Address:* 982-E La Mesa Terrace, Sunnyvale, CA 94086, USA.

KOESTENBAUM, Wayne; b. 20 Sept. 1958, San Jose, CA, USA. Prof. of English; Poet; Writer; Critic. *Education:* BA, magna cum laude, English, Harvard College, 1980; MA, Creative Writing, Johns Hopkins University, 1981; PhD, English, Princeton University, 1988. *Appointments:* Assoc. Prof. of English, Yale University, 1988–97; Co-Ed., The Yale Journal of Criticism, 1991–96; Prof. of English, City University of New York, 1997–. *Publications:* Double Talk: The Erotics of Male Literary Collaboration, 1989; Ode to Anna Moffo and Other Poems, 1990; The Queen's Throat: Opera, Homosexuality, and the Mystery of Desire, 1993; Rhapsodies of a Repeat Offender, 1994; Jackie Under My Skin: Interpreting an Icon, 1995; The Milk of Inquiry, 1999; Cleavage: Essays on Sex, Stars and Aesthetics, 2000; Andy Warhol, 2001. Other: Jackie O (libretto for the opera by Michael Daugherty), 1997. *Contributions to:* Anthologies, books, newspapers, reviews, quarterlies, and journals. *Honours:* Whiting Fellowship in the Humanities, 1987–88; Twentieth Century Literature Prize in Literary Criticism, 1988; Co-Winner, Discovery/The Nation Poetry Contest, 1989; Morse Fellowship, Yale University, 1990–91; New York Times Book Review Notable Book, 1993; Whiting Writer's Award, 1994; Finalist, National Book Critics Circle Award, 1993. *Address:* c/o English Program, City University of New York Graduate School, 365 Fifth Ave, New York, NY 10016, USA.

KOGAWA, Joy (Nozomi); b. 6 June 1935, Vancouver, BC, Canada. Writer; Poet. m. David Kogawa, 2 May 1957, divorced 1968, 1 s., 1 d. *Education:* University of Alberta, 1954; Anglican Women's Training College, 1956; University of Saskatchewan, 1968. *Appointment:* Writer-in-Residence, University of Ottawa, 1978. *Publications:* Poetry: The Splintered Moon, 1967; A Choice of Dreams, 1974; Jericho Road, 1977; Woman in the Woods, 1985. Fiction: Obasan, 1981; Naomi's Road, 1986; Itsuka, 1992; The Rain Ascends, 1995. *Contributions to:* Canadian Forum; Chicago Review; Prism International; Quarry; Queen's Quarterly; West Coast Review; Others. *Honours:* First Novel

Award, Books in Canada, 1982; Book of the Year Award, Canadian Authors Assen, 1982; American Book Award, Before Columbus Foundation, 1982; Best Paperback Award, Periodical Distributors, 1982; Notable Book Citation, American Library Assen, 1982; Mem. of the Order of Canada; Doctor of Laws, Honoris Causa, 1991, 1993; Doctor of Letters, Honoris Causa, 1992. *Memberships:* Canadian Civil Liberties Assen, dir; Canadian Tribute to Human Rights, patron; League of Canadian Poets; PEN International; Writers Union of Canada. *Address:* c/o Writers Union of Canada, 24 Ryerson, Toronto, Ontario M5T 2P3, Canada.

KOLLER, James; b. 30 May 1936, Oak Park, IL, USA. Writer; Poet; Artist. Divorced, 2 s., 4 d. *Education:* BA, North Central College, Naperville, IL, 1958. *Publications:* Poetry: Two Hands, 1965; Brainard and Washington Street Poems, 1965; The Dogs and Other Dark Woods, 1966; Some Cows, 1966; I Went To See My True Love, 1967; California Poems, 1971; Bureau Creek, 1975; Poems for the Blue Sky, 1976; Messages-Botschaften, 1977; Andiamo, 1978; O Didn't He Ramble-O ware er nicht unhergezogen, 1981; Back River, 1981; One Day at a Time, 1981; Great Things Are Happening-Grossartoge Dige passieren, 1984; Give the Dog a Bone, 1986; Graffiti Lyriques (with Franco Beltrametti), graphics and texts, 1987; Openings, 1987; Fortune, 1987; Roses Love Sunshine, 1989; This Is What He Said (graphics and texts), 1991; In the Wolf's Mouth, Poems 1972-88, 1995; The Bone Show, 1996; Iron Bells, 1999; Close to the Ground, 2000. Other: Messages, 1972; Working Notes 1960-82, 1985; Gebt dem alten Hund'nen Knochen (Essays, Gedichte and Prosa 1959-85), 1986; The Natural Order (essay and graphics), 1990; Like It Was (selected poems, prose and fiction), 2000. Fiction: If You Don't Like Me You Can Leave Me Alone, 1974; Shannon Who Was Lost Before, 1975; The Possible Movie, 1997. *Address:* PO Box 629, Brunswick, ME 04011, USA.

KOLUMBAN, Nicholas; b. 17 June 1937, Budapest, Hungary. College Instructor; Poet. m. 11 June 1967, 1 d. *Education:* BA, 1962, MA, 1966, Pennsylvania State University. *Appointments:* Instructor, Virginia Polytechnic Institute and State University, Blacksburg, 1965-70, Raritan Valley Community College, Somerville, NJ, 1997-; German Teacher, High School, Bridgewater, NJ, 1971-84; English Teacher, High School, Paterson, NJ, 1985-96. *Publications:* In Memory of My Third Decade, 1981; Reception at the Mongolian Embassy, 1987; The Porcelain Balloon, 1992; Surgery on My Soul, 1996; Tangled But Accurate: An Anthology of 20th Century Hungarian Verse (ed. and trans.), 1999. *Contributions to:* Another Chicago Magazine; Artful Dodge; Chariton Review; Hawaii Review; Hitel, Hungary; Michigan Quarterly Review; Mudfish; New Letters; Poetry East; Poetry Review. *Honours:* Poetry Prize, New Jersey State Arts Council, 1984-85; Literary Merit Award of the Republic of Hungary, 1997. *Membership:* Hungarian Writers' Assen. *Address:* 150 W Summit St, Somerville, NJ 08876, USA.

KOMUNYAKAA, Yusef, (James Willie Brown Jr); b. 29 April 1947, Bogalusa, LA, USA. Prof. of Creative Writing; Poet. m. Mandy Sayer, 1985. *Education:* BA, University of Colorado, 1975; MA, Colorado State University, 1979; MFA, University of California at Irvine, 1980. *Appointments:* Visiting Prof., 1985, Assoc. Prof. of Afro-American Studies, 1987-96, Indiana University; Prof. of Creative Writing, Princeton University, 1997-; Board of Chancellors, Acad. of American Poets, 1999; Many poetry readings. *Publications:* Dedications and Other Darkhorses, 1977; Lost in the Bonewheel Factory, 1979; Copacetic, 1984; I Apologize for the Eyes in My Head, 1986; Dien Cai Dau, 1988; The Jazz Poetry Anthology (ed. with Sascha Feinstein), 1991; Magic City, 1992; Neon Vernacular: New and Selected Poems, 1993; Thieves of Paradise, 1998; Talking Dirty to the Gods (poems), 2000; Pleasure Dome: New and Collected Poems, 2001. *Contributions to:* Anthologies and periodicals. *Honours:* Pulitzer Prize in Poetry, 1994; Kingsley Tufts Poetry Award, 1994; Union League Civic Arts and Poetry Prize, Chicago, 1998; Ruth Lilly Poetry Prize, 2001. *Address:* c/o Dept of English, Princeton University, Princeton, NJ 08544, USA.

KOONTZ, Thomas Wayne; b. 9 July 1939, Fort Wayne, IN, USA. Poet. m. (1), 5 d., (2) Nina B Marshall 30 Aug. 1998. *Education:* BA, Miami University, 1961; MA, 1965, PhD, 1970, Indiana University. *Appointments:* Instructor, George Washington University, 1965-67; Prof., Ball State University, 1967-. *Publications:* To Begin With, 1983; Charms, 1983; In Such a Light, 1997; Rice Paper Sky, 1999. *Contributions to:* Spoon River Quarterly; Asylum; Cicada; Frog Pond; Black Fly Review; Blue Unicorn; Forum; Indiannual; Windless Orchard. *Membership:* Associated Writing Programs. *Address:* 2700 S Whitney Rd, Selma, IN 47383, USA.

KOOSER, Ted, (Theodore Kooser); b. 25 April 1939, Ames, IA, USA. Poet; Teacher; Company Vice-Pres. m. (1) Diana Tresslar, 1962, divorced 1969, 1 s., (2) Kathleen Rutledge, 1977. *Education:* BS, Iowa State University, 1962; MA, University of Nebraska, 1968. *Appointments:* Underwriter, Bankers Life Nebraska, 1965-73; Part-Time Instructor in Creative Writing, 1970-, Senior Underwriter, 1973-84, Vice-Pres., 1984-98, Lincoln Benefit Life; Visiting Prof., University of Nebraska;. *Publications:* Poetry: Official Entry Blank, 1969; Grass County, 1971; Twenty Poems, 1973; A Local Habitation, and a Name, 1974; Shooting a Farmhouse: So This is Nebraska, 1975; Not Coming to be Barked At, 1976; Hatcher, 1978; Old Marriage and New, 1978; Cottonwood County (with William Kloefkorn), 1979; Sure Signs: New and Selected Poems,

1980; One World at a Time, 1985; The Blizzard Voices, 1986; Weather Central, 1994; Winter Morning Walks, 2000; 100 Postcards to Jim Harrison, 2000; Loca Wonders, 2002; Seasons in the Bohemian Alps, 2002. Editor: The Windflowe Home Almanac of Poetry, 1980; As Far as I Can See: Contemporary Writers o the Middle Plains, 1989. *Honours:* Prairie Schooner Prizes, 1975, 1978 National Endowment for the Arts Fellowships, 1976, 1984; Poetry Award Society of Midland Authors, 1980; Stanley Kunitz Prize, 1984; Governor's Art Award, Nebraska, 1988; Richard Hugo Prize, 1994. *Address:* 1820 Branched Oak Rd, Garland, NE 68360-9393, USA.

KOPPANY, Zsolt; b. 20 Aug. 1955, Budapest, Hungary. Writer; Poet Dramatist. m. Aranka Hegyesi, 15 Aug. 1981. *Publications:* 14 books including short stories, essays, poetry and drama, 1988-2002. *Contributions to:* Various publications. *Honours:* Josef Lengyel Grant, 1985; 'For Budapest Prize, 1990; Ottó Major Art Prize, 2000. *Membership:* Hungarian Writers Assen. *Address:* Fadrusz utca. 2 IV/7, Budapest 1114, Hungary.

KOPS, Bernard; b. 28 Nov. 1926, London, England. Poet; Writer; Dramatist. m. Erica Gordon, 1956, 4 c. *Appointments:* Lecturer, Spiro Institute, 1985-86, Surrey Education Authority, Ealing Education Authority, Inner London Education Authority, Arts Educational School/Acting Co, 1989-90, Cith Literary Institute, 1990-93. *Publications:* Poetry: Poems, 1955; Poems and Songs, 1958; Anemone for Antigone, 1959; Erica, I Want to Read You Something, 1967; For the Record, 1971; Barricades in West Hampstead, 1988; Grandchildren and Other Poems, 2000. Other: Awake for Mourning, 1958; Motorbike, 1962; Autobiography, The World is a Wedding, 1963; Yes From No Man's Land, 1965; By the Waters of Whitechapel, 1970; The Passionate Past of Gloria Gaye, 1971; Settle Down Simon Katz, 1973; Partners, 1975; On Margate Sands, 1978. Plays: The Hamlet of Stepney Green, 1958; Goodbye World, 1959; Change for the Angel, 1960; Stray Cats and Empty Bottles, 1961; Enter Solly Gold, 1962; The Boy Who Wouldn't Play Jesus, 1965; More Out Than In, 1980; Ezra, 1981; Simon at Midnight, 1982; Some of These Days, 1990; Sophie: Last of the Red Hot Mamas, 1990; Playing Sinatra, 1991; Androcles and the Lion, 1992; Dreams of Anne Frank, 1992; Who Shall I Be Tomorrow?, 1992; Call in the Night, 1995; Green Rabbi, 1997; Cafe Zeitgeist, 1998; Collected Plays, two vols, 1998, 2000; Shalom Bomb, 2000. *Honours:* Arts Council Bursaries, 1957, 1979, 1985, and Award, 1991; C. Day-Lewis Fellowship, 1981-83; London Fringe Award, 1993; Writer's Guild of Great Britain Best Radio Play Award, 1995. *Literary Agent:* John Rush, Sheil Land Assocs, 43 Doughty St, London, England. *Address:* 41B Canfield Gdns, London NW6 3JL, England.

KORFIS, Tasos. See: ROMBOTIS, Anastasios.

KORNFELD, Robert Jonathan; b. 3 March 1919, Newtonville, MA, USA. Dramatist; Writer; Poet. m. Celia Seiferth, 23 Aug. 1945, 1 s. *Education:* BA, Harvard University, 1941; Attended, Columbia University, Tulane University, New York University, New School for Social Research, Circle-in-the-Square School of Theatre, Playwrights' Horizons Theatre School and Laboratory. *Appointment:* Playwright-in-Residence, University of Wisconsin, 1998. *Publications:* Plays: Great Southern Mansions, 1977; A Dream Within a Dream, 1987; Landmarks of the Bronx, 1990; Music For Saint Nicholas, 1992; Hot Wind From the South, 1995; The Hanged Man, 1996. Plays Produced: Father New Orleans, 1997; The Queen of Carnival, 1997; The Celestials, 1998; Passage in Purgatory, Shanghai, China, 2000; The Gates of Hell, 2002. Other: Fiction and poetry. *Contributions to:* Various publications. *Honours:* Numerous awards and prizes; Visiting Artist, American Acad., Rome, 1996. *Memberships:* Authors' League; Dramatists' Guild; National Arts Club; New York Drama League; PEN; Theater for the New City, board mem., 2002. *Address:* The Withers Cottage, 5286 Sycamore Ave, Riverdale, NY 10471, USA.

KOSTELANETZ, Richard (Cory); b. 14 May 1940, New York, NY, USA. Writer; Poet; Critic; Artist; Composer. *Education:* AB, Honours, Brown University, 1962; Graduate Studies, King's College, London, 1964-65; MA, Columbia University, 1966; Study in music and theatre, Morley College, London, and New School for Social Research, New York. *Appointments:* Literary Dir, Future Press, New York, 1976-; Sole Proprietor, R K Editions, New York, 1978-; Contributing Ed. to various journals; Guest lecturer and reader at many colleges and universities; Numerous exhibitions as an artist. *Publications:* Poetry: Visual Language, 1970; I Articulations/Short Fictions, 1974; Portraits From Memory, 1975; Numbers: Poems and Stories, 1976; Rain Rains Rain, 1976; Illuminations, 1977; Numbers Two, 1977; Richard Kostelanetz, 1980; Turfs/Arenas/Fields/Pitches, 1980; Arenas/Fields/Pitches/ Turfs, 1982; Fields/Pitches/Turfs/Arenas, 1990; Solos, Duets, Trios, and Choruses, 1991; Wordworks: Poems Selected and New, 1993; Paritions, 1993; Repartitions, 1994; More Wordworks, 2002. Fiction: In the Beginning (novel), 1971; Constructs, 5 vols, 1975-91; One Night Stood (novel), 1977; Tabula Rasa: A Constructivist Novel, 1978; Exhaustive Parallel Intervals (novel), 1979; Fifty Untitled Constructivist Fictions, 1991; 3-Element Stories, 1998; Many others. Non-Fiction: Recyclings: A Literary Autobiogrphy, 2 vols, 1974, 1984; The End of Intelligent Writing: Literary Politics in America, 1974; Metamorphosis in the Arts, 1980; The Old Poetries and the New, 1981; The Grants-Fix: Publicly Funded Literary Granting in America, 1987; The Old Fictions and the New, 1987; On Innovative Music(ian)s, 1989; Unfinished Business: An Intellectual

Nonhistory, 1990; The New Poetries and Some Old, 1991; Published Encomia, 1967–91, 1991; On Innovative Art(ist)s, 1992; A Dictionary of the Avant-Gardes, 1993; On Innovative Performance(s), 1994; Fillmore East: 25 Years After: Recollections of Rock Theatre, 1995; An ABC of Contemporary Reading, 1995; Crimes of Culture, 1995; Radio Writings, 1995; John Cage (Ex)plain(ed), 1996; Thirty Years of Critical Engagement with John Cage, 1996; One Million Words of Booknotes, 1958–1993, 1996; Political Essays, 1999; Three Canadian Geniuses, 2001; Thirty-Five Years of Visile Writing, 2002. Plays: Vocal Shorts: Collected Performance Texts, 1998. Editor: Various books. Other: Films; Videotapes; Radio Scripts; Recordings. Contributions to: Many anthologies; Numerous poems, articles, essays, reviews in journals and other publications. Honours: Woodrow Wilson Fellowship, 1962–63; Fulbright Fellowship, 1964–65; Pulitzer Fellowship, 1965–66; Guggenheim Fellowship, 1967; One of Best Books, American Institute of Graphic Arts, 1976; Pushcart Prize, 1977; Deutscher Akademischer Austauschdienst Stipend, Berlin, 1981–83; American Society of Composers, Authors, and Publishers Awards, 1983–91. Memberships: American PEN; American Society of Composers, Authors, and Publishers; Artist Equity; International Asscn of Art Critics; National Writers Union; Others. Address: PO Box 444, Prince St Station, New York, NY 10012-0008 USA. E-mail: richardkostelanetz.com.

KOTIKALAPUDI, Venkata Suryanarayana Murti, (K V S Murti); b. 9 May 1925, Parlakhemundi, Orissa, India. Prof. of English (retd); Writer; Poet. Education: MA, English Language and Literature, 1963, PhD, English, 1972, Andhra University, Visakhapatnam; Intensive course in Linguistics and Phonetics, Central Institute of English and Foreign Languages, Hyderabad, 1969. Appointments: Lecturer to 1980, Asst Prof., 1980–85, Prof. of English, 1986–87, MMA Law College, Chennai; Many international seminars and lectures; Various poetry readings. Publication: Poetry in Telugu: Ihamlo Param, 1979; Liilaahela, 1981; Pranavamtho Pranayam, 1994. Poetry in English: Allegory of Eternity, 1975; Triple-Light, 1975; Sparks of the Absolute, 1976; Spectrum, 1976; Symphony of Discords, 1977; Araku, 1982; Comic and Absolute, 1995; Convex-Image and Concave Mirror, 1995; Glimpses and Grandeur, 1997. Criticism: Waves of Illumination, 1978; Sword and Sickle: Critical Study of Mulk Raj Anand's Novels, 1983; Kohinoor in the Crown: Critical Studies in Indian English Literature, 1987; Old Myth and New Myth: Letters from MRA to KVS, 1993. Contributions to: Many national and international publications. Honours: Fellow, International Acad. of Poets, England, 1976; Hon. DLitt, Free University of Asia, 1976, World University, Tucson, AZ, 1977; Several merit certificates and honours. Memberships: Authors Guild of India; Indian PEN; World University Round Table. Address: 43-21-9A Venkataraju Nahar, Visakhapatnam 530 016 AP, India.

KOUL, Chaman Lal, (Shakhtinternational); b. 27 July 1938, Kashmir, India. Senior Lecturer; Poet. m. Sarlabhan Ritajee, 26 May 1967, 1 s., 1 d. Education: MA, Hindi and English; Diplomas, Journalism and Direction. Publications: Several poetry works. Contributions to: Anthologies and other publications. Honours: Second Prize, Poetry, Hindi Institute, Agra; Semi-Finalist, World Poetry Competition. Memberships: Bombay English Asscn, life mem.; Indian PEN, life mem.; Poetry Society of India, life mem.; World Poetry Society. Address: Interesteller, Shakhtinternational, PO Gangiyal, Jammu 1800 10, India.

KOULENTIANOS, Denis; b. 7 June 1935, Piraeus, Greece. Journalist; Writer; Poet. m. Toula Conomos, 10 Sept. 1960, 2 s. Education: College St Paul, Piraeus; Certificate in Philosophy, 1962; Postgraduate Center of Public Relations, Athens, 1967. Publications: Lyric Agonies, 1956; Thus Jesus Spoke, 1959; Bowings, 1962; The Bridge, 1965; D K: An Anthology, 1972; Aphorisms, 1976; Essence, 1979; In the Zodiac of Twins, 1981; Kytherian Yearnings, 1987; Violets and Stilettos, 1989; Pictures, 1992; My Debt to Poetry, 1994; Greek Smiles, 1996; IX2, English-Spanish, 1996; Five Women Poets of India, 1996; 10 Poems of Love, Greek-Spanish, 1997; Pages of Acquaintance, 1998; Denis Koulentianos, 1998; For Africa with Love, 2000; Anthology of World Love, 2002. Contributions to: Anthologies and periodicals. Honours: Hon. DLitt, World Acad. of Arts and Culture, 1988; International Eminent Poet, International Poets Acad., 1991; Medaille d'Or Academie de Lutece, 1995. Memberships: International Poets Acad., fellow; Panhellenic Union of Writers; Society of Kytherian Studies; United Poets Laureate International, hon. vice-pres. Address: 28a Xenophon St, 181 20 Korydallos, Greece.

KOWIT, Steve; b. 30 June 1938, New York, NY, USA. Poet; Teacher. m. Mary Petrangelo. Education: BA, Brooklyn College, 1965; MA, San Francisco State College, 1967; MFA, Warren Wilson College, 1991. Appointments: Instructor, San Diego State University, 1975–89, Southwestern College, 1989–; Visiting Prof., University of California, San Diego, 1978–79; Prof., US International University, 1979–80. Publications: Cutting Our Losses, 1984; Lurid Confessions, 1985; Heart in Utter Confusion, 1986; Passionate Journey, 1988; Pranks, 1990; In the Palm of Your Hand: The Poet's Portable Workshop; The Dumbbell Nebula, 1999. Contributions to: Anthologies, newspapers, and journals. Honour: Fellowship in Poetry, National Endowment for the Arts, 1985. Address: PO Box 184, Potrero, CA 91963, USA.

KOZAK, Henryk (Jozef); b. 15 July 1945, Krasna, Poland. Writer; Poet. m. Maria Tomasiewicz, 1 July 1967, 2 s. Education: MA, History, University of Marie Curie-Sklodowskiej, 1969. Publications: Various novels and books of poetry. Contributions to: Numerous journals and magazines. Honours: Josef Czechowicz Literary Awards, 1980, 1987. Membership: Society of Polish Writers. Address: ul Paryska 7 m 6, 20 854 Lublin, Poland.

KOZER, José; b. 28 March 1940, Havana, Cuba. Prof. of Spanish Literature and Language (retd); Poet; Writer. m. Guadalupe Kozer, 15 Dec. 1974, 2 d. Education: BA, New York University, 1965; MA, PhD Equivalent, 1983, Queens College of the City University of New York. Appointment: Prof. of Spanish Literature and Language, Queens College of the City University of New York, 1960–97. Publications: Poetry: 13 chapbooks, 1974–96. Other: 15 books, 1972–97. Contributions to: Numerous poetry magazines, literary journals, and newspapers in North and South America, and Spain. Honours: CINTAS Foundation Award, 1973; Julio Tovar Poetry Prize, 1974; City University of New York/PSC Foundation Award, 1991. Address: 6937 Bay Dr., No. 511, Miami Beach, FL 33141, USA.

KRAMER, Aaron; b. 13 Dec. 1921, New York, NY, USA. Prof. of English Emeritus; Author; Poet. m. Katherine Kolodny, 10 March 1942, 2 d. Education: BA, 1941, MA, 1951, Brooklyn College; PhD, New York University, 1966. Appointments: Instructor, 1961–63, Asst Prof., 1963–66, Adelphi University; Lecturer, Queens College, Flushing, New York, 1966–68; Assoc. Prof., 1966–70, Prof. of English, 1970–91, Prof. Emeritus, 1991–, Dowling College, Oakdale, New York. Publications: The Glass Mountain, 1946; Poetry and Prose of Heine, 1948; Denmark Vesey, 1952; The Tinderbox, 1954; Serenade, 1957; Tune of the Calliope, 1958; Moses, 1962; Rumshinsky's Hat, 1964; Rilke: Visions of Christ, 1967; The Prophetic Tradition in American Poetry, 1968; Poetry Therapy (co-author), 1969; Melville's Poetry, 1972; On the Way to Palermo, 1973; Poetry the Healer (co-author), 1973; The Emperor of Atlantis, 1975; O Golden Land, 1976; Death Takes a Holiday, 1979; Carousel Parkway, 1980; The Burning Bush, 1983; In the Suburbs, 1986; A Century of Yiddish Poetry, 1989; Indigo, 1991; Life Guidance Through Literature (co-author), 1991; Dora Teitelboim: Selected Poems (ed. and trans.), 1995. Contributions to: Professional journals. Honours: Hart Crane Memorial Award, 1969; Eugene O'Neill Theatre Center Prize, 1983; National Endowment for the Humanities Grant, 1993; Festschrift published in his honour, 1995. Memberships: American Society of Composers, Authors and Publishers; Asscn for Poetry Therapy; Edna St Vincent Millay Society; e. e. Cummings Society; International Acad. of Poets; PEN; Walt Whitman Birthplace Asscn, exec. board, 1969–85. Address: 96 Van Bomel Blvd, Oakdale, NY 11769, USA.

KRAMER, Lotte Karoline; b. 22 Oct. 1923, Mainz, Germany. Poet; Painter. m. Frederic Kramer, 20 Feb. 1943, 1 s. Education: Art; History of Art. Publications: Poetry: Scrolls, 1979; Ice Break, 1980; Family Arrivals, 1981; A Lifelong House, 1983; The Shoemaker's Wife, 1987; The Desecration of Trees, 1994; Earthquake and Other Poems, 1994; Selected and New Poems, 1980–1997; The Phantom Lane, 2000. Contributions to: Anthologies, newspapers, reviews, quarterlies and journals. Honours: Second Prize, York Poetry Competition, 1972; Bursary, Eastern Arts Board, 1999. Memberships: Decorative and Fine Arts Society; PEN; Peterborough Museum Society; Poetry Society; Ver Poets; Writers in Schools. Address: 4 Apsley Way, Longthorpe, Peterborough PE3 9NE, England.

KRASILOVSKY, Alexis; b. 5 July 1950, Alaska, USA. Writer; Poet; Film Maker. 1 s. Education: BA, Yale University, 1971; MFA, California Institute of the Arts, 1984. Appointments: Prof., California State University at Northridge, 1987–; Co-ordinator, Etheridge Knight's West Coast Tour, 1987; Several poetry readings. Publications: Some Women Writers Kill Themselves, 1983; Some Men, 1986; Abuse of Privacy, 1990; What Memphis Needs, 1990; The Earthquake Haggadah, 1995; Camp Terezin, 1999. Contributions to: Agenda; Approches; Filmnotes; Caffeine; Southern Exposure. Honours: Prizes, San Francisco Poetry Film Festival, James River Festival of Moving Image, Jewish Video Competition. Memberships: Poetry Film Workshops. Address: Dept of Cinema and Television Arts, California State University at Northridge, Northridge, CA 91330-8317, USA.

KRATT, Mary; b. 7 June 1936, Beckley, West Virginia, USA. Writer; Poet. m. Emil F. Kratt, 29 Aug. 1959, 1 s., 2 d. Education: BA, Agnes Scott College, 1958; MA, University of North Carolina at Charlotte, 1992. Publications: Southern Is, 1985; Legacy: The Myers Park Story, 1986; The Imaginative Spirit: Literary Heritage of Charlotte and Mecklenburg County, 1988; A Little Charlotte Scrapbook, 1990; A Bird in the House, 1991; The Only Thing I Fear is a Cow and a Drunken Man (poems and prose), 1991; Charlotte: Spirit of the New South, 1992; On the Steep Side (poems), 1993; Small Potatoes (poems), 1999; Valley (poems), 2000; Remembering Charlotte: Postcards from a New South City 1905–50, 2000; New South Women, 2001. Contributions to: Newspapers, reviews, and magazines. Honours: Lyricist Prize, 1982; Oscar Arnold Young Award for Best Original Poetry Book by a North Carolinian, 1983; Sidney Lanier Award, North Carolina Poetry Society, 1985; St Andrews Writer and Community Award, 1994; Distinguished Alumnae Writer Award, Agnes Scott College, 1994; MacDowell Colony Residency, 1996; Brockman Poetry Book Award, 2000. Memberships: North Carolina Writers Conference, chair., 1991–92; North Carolina Writers Network, board mem.; Poets and Writers. Address: 3328 Providence Plantation Lane, Charlotte, NC 28270, USA.

KRATZ, Steve; b. 14 May 1935, New York, NY, USA. Prof.; Poet. 3 s. *Education:* AB, Cornell University, 1956; MA, University of Oregon. *Appointments:* Asst Prof., Cornell University; Assoc. Prof., University of Notre Dame; Prof., University of Colorado. *Publications:* The Weight of Antony, 1966; Cheyenne River Wild Tract, 1972; Journalism, 1990. *Contributions to:* Periodicals. *Memberships:* PEN International; Writers' Guild. *Address:* 3060 8th St, Boulder, CO 80304, USA.

KRAUSE, Nina; b. 11 Aug. 1932, Delta, Ohio, USA. Writer; Poet. m. William Krause, 5 March 1955, 1 s., 1 d. *Education:* BA, Bowling Green State University, Ohio, 1954. *Appointments:* Various Writing and Editorial Work. *Contributions to:* Kentucky Poetry Review; Connecticut River Review; Dream Shop; Kentucky Book; Modern Lyrics Anthology; Contemporary Kentucky Poetry; Louisville Courier Journal Magazine. *Memberships:* Poetry Society of America; Acad. of American Poets. *Address:* 1704 E Hunter Ave, Bloomington, IN 47401, USA.

KRAUSHAAR, Keith Conrad Francis; b. 1 Sept. 1928, Hendon, London, England. Actor; Writer; Poet. *Education:* Studied Singing at the Guildhall School of Music and Drama. *Publications:* Thirty Two Poems, 1992; Twenty Six Poems for the Nineties, 1994. *Contributions to:* Comic Heritage, 1997; Beyond the Boundary, 1998. *Address:* c/o CADS Management, 48 Light Woods, Hill Bearwood, Smethwick, West Midlands B67 5EB, England.

KRAUSS, Beatrice Joy; b. 26 Dec. 1943, Portland, Oregon, USA. Principal Investigator; Poet; Writer. m. Herbert H Krauss, 28 Aug. 1965, 2 s. *Education:* BMus, Northwestern University; MA, University of Kansas; PhD, City University of New York. *Appointments:* Dir of Research, Community School District, Brooklyn, 1978–79; Asst to Assoc. Prof., College of New Rochelle, 1979–90; Senior Research Assoc., Memorial Sloan Kettering Cancer Centre, 1990–93; Principal Investigator, National Development and Research Institute, 1993–, and Institutes, 1995–. *Contributions to:* Blue Unicorn; River Run; Small Pond Magazine. *Memberships:* Hudson Valley Writer's Center; Poetry Society of America. *Address:* 6 Downing Ct, Irvington, NY 10533, USA.

KREITER-FORONDA, Carolyn; b. 20 Dec. 1946, Farmville, Virginia, USA. Teacher; Poet. m. Patricio Gomez-Foronda, 28 March 1991. *Education:* MEd, 1973; MA, 1979; DAE, 1983; PhD, 1995. *Appointment:* Teacher of English and Creative Writing, Fairfax County Public Schools, Virginia, 1969–. *Publications:* Contrary Visions, 1988; Gathering Light, 1993; Death Comes Riding, 1999. *Contributions to:* Anthologies and reviews. *Honours:* Virginia Commission on the Arts-in-Education Grants, 1986–88; Arts on the Road Poetry Winner, 1989; Cultural Laureate Award, Virginia, 1991; First Place Poetry Award, Poetry Society of Virginia, 1993. *Memberships:* Associated Writing Programs; Poetry Committee, Greater Washington, DC, Area. *Address:* 5966 Annaberg Pl., Burke, VA 22015, USA.

KREITMAN, Norman; b. 5 July 1927, London, England. Physician; Poet. m. 26 March 1957, 1 s., 1 d. *Education:* MBBS, London; MD, London. *Publications:* Touching Rock, 1987; Against Leviathan, 1989; Butterfly Brown, Yellow, 1999. *Contributions to:* Acumen; Lines Review; Chapman; New Writing Scotland; Others. *Membership:* Chair., Poetry Asscn of Scotland. *Address:* 24 Lauder Rd, Edinburgh EH9 2JF, Scotland.

KREMERS, Carolyn Sue; b. 2 Nov. 1951, Denver, CO, USA. University Lecturer; Poet; Writer. *Education:* BA, English, Humanities with Honours, Stanford University, 1973; BA, Flute Performance, summa cum laude, Metropolitan State College, Denver, 1981; MFA, Creative Writing, University of Alaska, Fairbanks, 1991. *Appointment:* Lecturer, University of Alaska, Fairbanks, 1993–. *Publications:* Poems; Essays. *Contributions to:* Anthologies, reviews, quarterlies and journals. *Honour:* Individual Artist Fellowship, Alaska State Council on the Arts, 1992. *Memberships:* Associated Writing Programs; MLA; Wordcraft Circle of Native Writers and Storytellers. *Address:* c/o Creative Writing Program, Eastern Washington University, 705 W First Ave, Mail Stop 1, Spokane, WA 99201, USA.

KRESH, David; b. 13 March 1940, New York, NY, USA. Librarian; Poet. m. Diane Elizabeth Nester, 16 May 1986, 3 s., 1 d. *Education:* BA, Swarthmore College, 1962; MSLS, Drexel University, 1966. *Appointment:* Reference Specialist in Poetry, Library of Congress, 1967–; Assoc. Ed., Slow Dancer, 1988–93; Poet-in-Residence, Capitol Hill Day School, 1996–. *Publications:* Bloody Joy; Sketches After Pete's Beer. *Contributions to:* Poetry; Chicago Review; Salmagundi; Mississippi Review; Ironwood; Slow Dancer; High Plains Literary Review. *Address:* 601 North Carolina Ave SE, Washington, DC 20003, USA.

KRISTENSEN, Lise Lotte; b. 13 May 1961, Frederiksberg, Denmark. Writer; Poet. *Education:* University of Copenhagen. *Publications:* Immediately But Flowing, 1989; The Time it Takes Being God, 1991; Southern Balm, 1994. *Contributions to:* Various publications. *Memberships:* Buddhist Forum; Committee for World Peace; Danish Writers Union. *Address:* Toldbodgade 14B 1 Tv, 1253 Copenhagen, Denmark.

KROLL, Jeri; b. 7 Oct. 1946, New York, NY, USA. Writer; Poet; Lecturer. m. Jeff Chilton, 1 s. *Education:* BA, cum laude, Smith College, USA, 1967; MA English, University of Warwick, Coventry, England, 1968; PhD, English Columbia University, USA, 1974. *Appointments:* Instructor, University of Maine, Presque Isle, 1974–75; Asst Prof., Dickinson College, 1975–77; Tutor, 1978–81, Senior Lecturer in English, Flinders University, Australia. *Publications:* Death as Mr Right, 1982; Indian Movies, 1984; The Electrolux Man and Other Stories, 1987; Monster Love, 1990; House Arrest, 1993. Children's Books: You Be the Witch; Sunny Faces; Swamp Soup (poems); What Goes with Toes?; Beaches. *Contributions to:* Poetry Australia; Southerly; Canberra Times; Overland; Bulletin; Southern Review; Quadrant. *Honours:* Third Prize, Grand Prize Competition, National Federation of State Poetry Societies, USA, 1977; Prize, Pennsylvania State Poetry Society Competition, 1978; First Prize, Esso Literary Competition, 1980; First Prize, Artlook National Poetry Contest, 1981; Second Prize, Anne Elder Award, 1982; Highly Commended, ABC Bicentennial Literary Awards, 1988. *Membership:* South Australian Writers' Centre. *Address:* 29 Methuen St, Fitzroy, Adelaide, SA 5082, Australia.

KRONENFELD, Judy Z.; b. 17 July 1943, New York, NY, USA. University Lecturer; Poet; Writer. m. David Brian Kronenfeld, 21 June 1964, 1 s., 1 d. *Education:* BA, summa cum laude, Smith College, 1964; MA, 1966, PhD, 1971, Stanford University; University of Oxford, 1968–69. *Appointments:* Lecturer, 1971, 1984–, Visiting Scholar, 1977–78, 1981–83, Instructor, 1978, Visiting Asst Prof., 1980–81, 1988–89, University of California at Riverside; Lecturer, 1972–73, 1978–79, Visiting Lecturer, 1984, 1985–86, Visiting Assoc. Prof., 1987, University of California at Irvine; Asst Prof., Purdue University, 1976–77. *Publications:* Shadow of Wings (poems), 1991; King Lear and the Naked Truth: Rethinking the Language of Religion and Resistance, 1998. *Contributions to:* Articles in scholarly books and journals; Poems in anthologies, reviews, quarterlies, and magazines. *Honours:* Leverhulme Trust Fund Fellowship, 1968–69; Squaw Valley Community of Writers Scholarship, 1983; Non-Senate Academic Distinguished Researcher Award, University of California at Riverside, 1996–97. *Address:* 3314 Celeste Dr., Riverside, CA 92507, USA.

KUEI-SHIEN LEE; b. 19 June 1937, Taipei, China (Taiwan). Patent Agent; Chemical Engineer; Corporation Pres.; Poet; Essayist; Trans. m. Huei-uei Wang, 1965, 1 s., 1 d. *Education:* Chemical Engineering, Taipei Institute of Technology, 1958; German Literature, European Language Center, Ministry of Education, 1964. *Publications:* (in Chinese): Poetry: 14 works, 1963–2001. Essays: 20 works, 1971–2002. Translator: 25 works, 1969–2001. *Contributions to:* Anthologies and other publications. *Honours:* Hon. PhD, Chemical Engineering, Marquis Giuseppe Scicluna International University Foundation, 1985; Albert Einstein International Acad. Foundation Alfred Nobel Medal for Peace, 1991; Poetic Creation Award, Le Poetry Society, 1994; Secretary General, Asian Poets Conference, 1995; Best World Poet of the Year, 1997, 1998; Poet of the Millennium Award, 2000; New Millennium Michael Madhusudan Award, 2002; Taiwan Premier Culture Award, 2002. *Memberships:* International Acad. of Poets, founder-fellow; Li Poetry Society; Rilke Gesellschaft; Taiwan PEN, pres., 1995. *Address:* Room 705, Asia Enterprise Center, No. 142 Minchuan E Rd, Sec 3, Taipei 105, China (Taiwan).

KUEPPER, Philip Watson; b. 14 Aug. 1948, Burlington, IA, USA. Poet; Writer. *Education:* BA, St Francis College, 1982. *Contributions to:* The Washingtonian, 1975; Currents, 1997. *Contributions to:* Anthologies, including: American Poetry Annual, 2000. *Honours:* Golden Poet Awards, World of Poetry, 1987–91. *Memberships:* Poets and Writers; Amherst Society. *Address:* 233 Bouton St W, Stamford, CT 06907, USA.

KUHNER, Herbert; b. 29 March 1935, Vienna, Austria. Writer; Poet; Trans. *Education:* BA, Columbia University. *Publications:* Broadsides and Pratealls; Will the Stars Fall?, 1995; Love of Austria, 1995. *Contributions to:* Dimension; European Judaism; Malahat Review; Confrontation; Poetry Australia; Skylark; Negative Capability; PEN International; Die Ziehharmonika. *Honours:* Golden Pen for Trans.; Hon. Professorship, Austrian Ministry of Art and Science. *Memberships:* PEN; Poetry Society of America. *Address:* Gentzgasse 14/4, 1180 Vienna, Austria.

KUIPER, Koenraad; b. 22 Feb. 1944, Hanover, Germany. Assoc. Prof. in Linguistics; Poet. m. Alison Clare Wylde, 11 May 1968, 3 d. *Education:* MA, Honours, Victoria University of Wellington, 1967; PhD, Simon Fraser University, 1972; DSc, University of Canterbury, 2001. *Appointments:* Master, Riccarton High School; Master, Burnside High School; Lecturer and Senior Lecturer, University of Canterbury. *Publications:* Signs of Life, 1981; Mikrokosmos, 1990; Time Pieces, 1999. *Contributions to:* Comment; Islands; Landfall; West Coast Review; Works; Tuatara; Untold; Takahe; Plainwraps; Poetry New Zealand. *Honours:* Award Winner, Whitireia Poetry Competition, 1990, 1991, 1992; Runner-up, PEN Best First Book Award, 1991; Runner-up, New Zealand Poetry Society Annual Competition, 1991. *Memberships:* New Zealand Society of Authors; Linguistic Society of America. *Address:* 16 Tui St, Christchurch 4, New Zealand.

KUKUO, Tani. See: NAKAJIMA, Hojo.

KUMAR, Ajit. See: CHAUDHARY, Ajit Kumar Shankar.

KUMAR, Khan Singh; b. 1 Nov. 1966, Hillingdon, West London, England. Teacher; Poet. 1 d. *Education:* BA, MA, English, Royal Holloway and Bedford New College. *Appointments:* Series of teaching posts in secondary schools. *Publications:* Several poems. *Contributions to:* Rialto; Staple; Krax; Poetry London Newsletter; Markings; Sepia; Iota; Peer; Prop; Yellow Crane; The Magazine; Bad; Connections. *Honours:* Runner-Up, London Writers Competition, 1998; Recognised in Peer Poetry, 1998; Commendation in Viewpoint Manuscript Service, 1998; Grateful Mention, Surrey Poetry Competition, 1998. *Address:* 18 Burket Close, Norwood Green, Middlesex UB2 5NR, England.

KUMAR, Shiv K(umar); b. 16 Aug. 1921, Lahore, Punjab, India. Prof. of English (retd); Poet. *Education:* PhD, Fitzwilliam College, Cambridge, 1956. *Appointment:* Prof. of English, Osmania University, 1959–86. *Publications:* Articulate Silences, 1970; Cobwebs in the Sun, 1974; Subterfuges, 1976; Woodpeckers, 1979; Trapfalls in the Sky, 1986. Editor: British Romantic Poets: Recent Revelations, 1966; Indian Verse in English, 1970, 1971. *Honour:* Fellow, RSL, 1978. *Address:* 2-F/Kakatiya Nagar, PO Jamia Osmania, Hyderabad 500 007, India.

KUMIN, Maxine; b. 6 June 1925, Philadelphia, Pennsylvania, USA. Poet; Writer; Teacher. m. Victor M Kumin, 29 June 1946, 1 s., 2 d. *Education:* AB, 1946, MA, 1948, Radcliffe College. *Appointments:* Instructor, 1958–61, Lecturer in English, 1965–68, Tufts University; Lecturer, Newton College of the Sacred Heart, Massachusetts, 1971; Visiting Lecturer, Prof., and Writer, University of Massachusetts, Amherst, 1972, Columbia University, 1975, Brandeis University, 1975, Washington University, St Louis, 1977, Princeton University, 1977, 1979, 1982, Randolph-Macon Women's College, Lynchburg, Virginia, 1978, Bucknell University, 1983, Atlantic Center for the Arts, New Smyrna Beach, FL, 1984, University of Miami, 1995. *Publications:* Poetry: Halfway, 1961; The Privilege, 1965; The Nightmare Factory, 1970; Up Country: Poems of New England, New and Selected, 1972; House, Bridge, Fountain, Gate, 1975; The Retrieval System, 1978; Our Ground Time Here Will Be Brief, 1982; Closing the Ring, 1984; The Long Approach, 1985; Nurture, 1989; Looking for Luck, 1992; Connecting the Dots, 1996; Selected Poems 1960–1990, 1997; The Long Marriage, 2001. Fiction: Through Dooms of Love, 1965; The Passions of Uxport, 1968; The Abduction, 1971; The Designated Heir, 1974; Why Can't We Live Together Like Civilized Human Beings?, 1982. Other: In Deep: Country Essays, 1987; To Make a Prairie: Essays on Poets, Poetry, and Country Living, 1989; Women, Animals, and Vegetables: Essays and Stories, 1994; Quit Monks or Die!, 1999; Inside the Halo and Beyond (memoir), 2000; Always Beginning (essays), 2000. For Children: Various books. *Contributions to:* Numerous magazines and journals. *Honours:* Lowell Mason Palmer Award, 1960; National Endowment for the Arts Grant, 1966; National Council on the Arts Fellowship, 1967; William Marion Reedy Award, 1968; Eunice Tietjens Memorial Prize, 1972; Pulitzer Prize in Poetry, 1973; American Acad. of Arts and Letters Award, 1980; Acad. of American Poets Fellowship, 1985; Levinson Award, 1987; Poet Laureate, State of New Hampshire, 1989; Sarah Josepha Hale Award, 1992; Poet's Prize, 1994; Aiken Taylor Poetry Award, 1995; Centennial Award, Harvard Graduate School, 1996; Ruth Lilly Poetry Prize, 1999; Various hon. doctorates. *Memberships:* PEN; Poetry Society of America; Writers Union. *Literary Agent:* Giles Anderson Agency, New York, USA. *Address:* 40 Harriman Lane, Warner, NH 03278, USA.

KUMMINGS, Donald D.; b. 28 July 1940, Lafayette, IN, USA. Prof. of English; Poet; Writer. Divorced 18 Aug. 1978, m. 21 March 1987, 2 s. *Education:* BA, 1962, MA, 1964, Purdue University; PhD, English and American Studies, Indiana University, 1971. *Appointments:* Instructor, Adrian College, Michigan, 1964–66; Assoc. Instructor, Indiana University, 1966–70; Asst Prof., 1970–75, Prof. of English, 1974–76, 1991–94, Assoc. Prof., 1975–85, Prof. of English, 1985–, University of Wisconsin, Parkside; Book Review Ed., The Mickle Street Review, 1983–90. *Publications:* Walt Whitman, 1940–1975: A Reference Guide, 1982; The Open Road Trip: Poems, 1989; Approaches to Teaching Whitman's Leaves of Grass, 1990; The Walt Whitman Encyclopedia (ed. with J R LeMaster), 1998. *Contributions to:* Anthologies, reviews, quarterlies, and journals. *Honours:* Acad. of American Poets Prize, 1969; Posner Poetry Prize, Council for Wisconsin Writers, 1990; Wisconsin Prof. of the Year, Carnegie Foundation for the Advancement of Teaching, 1997. *Address:* c/o Dept of English, University of Wisconsin, Parkside, Kenosha, WI 53141, USA.

KUNDERA, Milan; b. 1 April 1929, Brno, Czechoslovakia (Naturalized French citizen). Prof.; Writer; Dramatist; Poet. m. Vára Hrabánková, 1967. *Education:* Film Faculty, Acad. of Music and Dramatic Arts, Prague. *Appointments:* Asst to Asst Prof., Film Faculty, Acad. of Music and Dramatic Arts, Prague, 1958–69; Prof., University of Rennes, 1975–80, École des hautes études en sciences sociales, Paris, 1980–. *Publications:* Fiction: The Joke, 1965; Laughable Loves (short stories), 1968/69; Life is Elsewhere, 1969/70; The Farewell Waltz (earlier trans. as Party), 1970/71; The Book of Laughter and Forgetting, 1978; The Unbearable Lightness of Being, 1982; Identity, 1996; La Ignorancia (in Spanish), 2000. Plays: The Owner of the Keys, 1962; Two Ears, Two Weddings (Slowness), 1968; The Blunder, 1969; Jaques and His Master,

1971. Poetry: Man: A Broad Garden, 1953; The Last May, 1954–1955, 1961; Monologues, 1957–1964, 1965. Essays: About the Disputes of Inheritance, 1955; The Art of the Novel, 1960; The Czech Deal, 1968; Radicalism and Exhibitionism, 1969; The Stolen West or the Tragedy of Central Europe, 1983; The Art of the Novel (in seven parts), 1985; Immortality, 1990; Slowness, 1995; Testaments Betrayed (in nine parts), 1992. *Honours:* States prize of the CSSR, 1964; Union of Czechoslovak Writer's Prize, 1968; Czechoslovak Writers' Publishing House Prize, 1969; Prix Médicis, 1973; Premio Letterario Mondello, 1978; Commonwealth Award, 1981; Prix Europa-Littérature, 1982; Hon. Doctorate, University of Michigan, 1983; Los Angeles Times Prize, 1984; Jerusalem Prize, 1985; Prix de la critique de l'Académie Française, 1987; Prix Nelly Sachs, 1987; Austrian State Prize for European Literature, 1987; Officier, Légion d'honneur, 1990; The Independent foreign literature prize, 1991; Aujourd'hui Prize, France, 1993; Jaroslav-Seifert-Prize, 1994; Medal of Merit, Czech Republic, 1995; Herder Prize, Austria, 2000. *Address:* c/o École des hautes études en sciences sociales, 54 Blvd Raspail, Paris 75006, France.

KUNERT, Günter; b. 6 March 1929, Berlin, Germany. Poet; Author; Dramatist. m. Marianne Todten. *Education:* Hochschule für angewandte Kunst, Berlin-Weissensee. *Publications:* Poetry: Wegschilder und Mauerinschriften, 1950; Erinnerung an einen Planeten: Gedichte aus Fünfzehn Jahren, 1963; Der ungebetene Gast, 1965; Verkündigung des Wetters, 1966; Warnung vor Spiegeln, 1970; Im weiteren Fortgang, 1974; Unterwegs nach Utopia, 1977; Abtötungsverfahren, 1980; Stilleben, 1983; Berlin beizeiten, 1987; Fremd daheim, 1990; Mein Golem, 1996; Nachtvorstellung, 1999. Novel: Im Namen der Hüte, 1967. Other: Der ewige Detektiv und andere Geschichten, 1954; Kramen in Fächen: Geschichten, Parabeln, Merkmale, 1968; Die Beerdigung findet in aller Stille statt, 1968; Tagträume in Berlin und andernorts, 1972; Gast aus England, 1973; Der andere Planet: Ansichten von Amerika, 1974; Warum schreiben?: Notizen ins Paradies, 1978; Ziellose Umtriebe: Nachrichten von Reisen und Daheimsein, 1979; Verspätete Monologe, 1981; Leben und Schreiben, 1983; Vor der Sintflut: Das Gedicht als Arche Noah, 1985; Die letzten Indianer Europas, 1991; Erwachsenenspiele (autobiography), 1997. *Honours:* Heinrich Mann Prize, 1962; Heinrich Heine Prize, Düsseldorf, 1985; Hölderlin Prize, 1991; Georg-Trakl Prize, Austria, 1997. *Memberships:* Deutsche Akademie für Sprache und Dichtung eV, Darmstadt. *Address:* Schulstrasse 7, 25560 Kaisborstel, Germany.

KUNIHIRO, Kei (Yoshihide); b. 11 Dec. 1961, Harajuku, Tokyo, Japan. Poet; Writer; Actor; Singer. 1 d. *Education:* Graduated, Law School, Hosei University, 1985. *Appointment:* Founder, Straight Edge Poetry System and Hard Core Reading Machine. *Publications:* Poet and Killer, 1993; Poetic Assassin, 1995; Poet and Killer Chronicles, 1995. *Contributions to:* Various publications. *Address:* 3-33-19 Sakuragaoka Setagaya-ku, Tokyo 156, Japan.

KUNITZ, Stanley (Jasspon); b. 29 July 1905, Worcester, Massachusetts, USA. Poet; Ed.; Essayist; Educator. m. (1) Helen Pearce, 1930, divorced 1937, (2) Eleanor Evans, 21 Nov. 1939, divorced 1958, 1 d., (3) Elise Asher, 21 June 1958. *Education:* AB, summa cum laude, 1926, MA, 1927, Harvard University. *Appointments:* Ed., Wilson Library Bulletin, 1928–43; Teacher, Bennington College, 1946–49; Prof. of English, Potsdam State Teachers College, New York, 1949–50; Lecturer, New School for Social Research, New York City, 1950–57; Visiting Prof. of Poetry, University of Washington, Seattle, 1955–56, Yale University, 1970, Rutgers University at Camden, New Jersey, 1974; Visiting Prof. of English, Queens College, New York City, 1956–57, Brandeis University, 1958–59; Lecturer, 1963–66, Adjunct Prof. in Writing, Graduate School of the Arts, 1967–85, Columbia University; Consultant on Poetry, 1974–76, Hon. Consultant in American Letters, 1979–83, Library of Congress, Washington, DC; Visiting Prof. and Senior Fellow in Humanities, Princeton University, 1978, Vassar College, 1981; Poet Laureate of the USA, 2000–01; Numerous poetry readings and lectures. *Publications:* Poetry: Intellectual Things, 1930; Passport to the War: A Selection of Poems, 1944; Selected Poems, 1928–1958, 1958; The Testing Tree: Poems, 1971; The Terrible Threshold: Selected Poems, 1940–70, 1974; The Coat Without a Seam: Sixty Poems, 1930–72, 1974; The Lincoln Relics, 1978; Poems of Stanley Kunitz: 1928–78, 1979; The Wellfleet Whale and Companion Poems, 1983; Next-to-Last Things: New Poems and Essays, 1985; Passing Through: The Later Poems, 1995; The Collected Poems, 2000. Non-Fiction: Robert Lowell: Poet of Terribilità, 1974; A Kind of Order, a Kind of Folly: Essays and Conversations, 1975; Interviews and Encounters, 1993. Editor: British Authors of the Nineteenth Century (with Howard Haycraft), 1936; American Authors, 1600–1900: A Biographical Dictionary of American Literature (with Howard Haycraft), 1938; Twentieth Century Authors: A Biographical Dictionary (with Howard Haycraft), 1942, first supplement, 1955; British Authors before 1800: A Biographical Dictionary (with Howard Haycraft), 1952; European Authors, 1000–1900: A Biographical Dictionary of European Literature (with Vineta Colby), 1967; The Essential Blake, 1987; The Wild Card, Selected Poems of Karl Shapiro (with David Ignatow), 1998. *Contributions to:* Many anthologies, books and periodicals. *Honours:* Garrison Medal for Poetry, Harvard University, 1926; Oscar Blumenthal Prize, 1941; Guggenheim Fellowship, 1945–46; Amy Lowell Travelling Fellowship for Poetry, 1953–54; Levinson Prize for Poetry, 1956; Harriet Monroe Award, University of Chicago, 1958; Ford Foundation Grant, 1958–59; National Institute of Arts and Letters Grant, 1959; Pulitzer Prize in

Poetry, 1959; Brandeis University Creative Arts Award, 1964; Lenore Marshall Award for Poetry, 1980; National Endowment for the Arts Senior Fellow, 1984; Bollingen Prize, 1987; Walt Whitman Award, 1987; State Poet of New York, 1987–88; Montgomery Fellow, Dartmouth College, 1991; Centennial Medal, Harvard University, 1992; National Medal of Arts, 1993; Shelley Memorial Award, 1995; National Book Award for Poetry, 1995; Medal for Distinguished Service in the Arts, Fine Arts Work Center, Provincetown, 1997–; Robert Frost Medal, 1998. *Memberships:* American Acad. and Institute of Arts and Letters, 1968–; Acad. of American Poets, chancellor, 1970–95; Founding Mem., Board of Dirs, Fine Arts Work Center, Provincetown, 1968–; Poets House, New York, founding pres., 1985–90. *Address:* 37 W 12th St, New York, NY 10011, USA.

KUNZ, Carol Ann; b. 22 March 1940, Zanesville, Ohio, USA. Nurse; Writer; Poet; Teacher. m. Robert J Kunz, 11 March 1976, 3 s., 2 d. *Education:* Weatherford College of Nursing, Texas; BA, English, Journalism, Carleton State University, Stephenville, Texas, 1995. *Contributions to:* Anthologies, periodicals and other publications. *Honours:* Prizes and honourable mentions. *Memberships:* Dublin Shamrock Writers; International Society of Poets; Wordrunners Writing Group. *Address:* Route 5, Box 258, Dublin, TX 76446, USA.

KUNZE, Reiner; b. 16 Aug. 1933, Oelsnitz, Germany. Poet; Author. m. Elisabeth Mifka, 1 s., 1 d. *Education:* University of Leipzig, 1951–55. *Publications:* Poetry: Vögel über dem Tau, 1959; Widmungen, 1963; Sensible wege, 1969; Zimmerlautstärke, 1972; Auf eigene hoffnung, 1981; Gespräch mit der amsel, 1984; Eines jeden einziges leben, 1986; Wohin der Schlaf sich schlafen legt, 1991; Ein tag auf dieser erde, 1998; Gedichte, 2000. Other: Der Löwe Leopold, 1970; Die wunderbaren Jahre, 1976; Das weisse Gedicht, 1989; Mensch ohne Macht, 1991; Am Sonnenhang, 1992; wo Freiheit ist, 1994; Steine und Lieder, 1996; Bindewort deutsch, 1997. *Honours:* German Children's Book Prize, 1971; Literary Prize, Bavarian Acad. of Fine Arts, Munich, 1973; Georg Trakl Prize, Salzburg, 1977; Georg Büchner Prize, 1977; Bavarian Film Prize, 1979; Eichendorff Literature Prize, 1984; Federal Cross of Merit, First Class, Germany, 1984; Upper Bavarian Cultural Prize, 1988; Freemasons' Prize for Culture, Chemnitz, 1993; Europapreis für Poesie, Serbien, 1998; Friedrich-Hölderlin-Preis, 1999; Christian Ferber Ehrengabe, 2000; Hans-Sahl-Literaturpreis, 2001; Bayerischer Maximiliansorden für Kunst und Wissenschaft, 2001; Kunstpreis zur deutsch-tschechischen Verständigung, 2002. *Memberships:* Bavarian Acad. of Fine Arts, Munich; Deutsche Akademie für Sprache und Dichtung, Darmstadt. *Address:* Am Sonnenhang 19, 94130 Obernzell, Germany.

KUPKA, Valerij; b. 23 Dec. 1962, Khomut, Ukraine. Poet. m. Ivana, 7 Aug. 1993, 1 s., 1 d. *Education:* PhD, 1988; Diploma in Russian Language and History. *Publications:* Inconstancy, 1994; Skomoroshina, 1995; A Fly in the Ear, 1998. *Contributions to:* Ticha Voda; Tvorba; Gumanitarny Fond; Romboid; Cirk; Olme. *Membership:* Slovak Writers Community. *Address:* Vazecka 12, 080 05 Presov, Slovakia.

KUPPNER, Frank; b. 1951, Glasgow, Scotland. Writer; Poet. *Education:* University of Glasgow. *Publications:* Fiction: Ridiculous! Disgusting!, 1989; A Very Quiet Street, 1989; A Concussed History of Scotland, 1990; Something Very Like Murder, 1994. Poetry: A Bad Day for the Sung Dynasty, 1984; The Intelligent Observation of Naked Women, 1987; Everything is Strange, 1994. *Address:* c/o Polygon, 22 George Sq., Edinburgh EH8 9LF, Scotland.

KUSHNER, Aleksandr Semyonovich; b. 14 Sept. 1936, Leningrad, Russia. Poet. m. Elena Vsevologovna Nevzgliadova, 21 July 1984, 1 s. *Education:* Graduate, Leningrad Pedagogical Institute, 1959. *Appointment:* Ed.-in-Chief, Biblioteka Poeta, publishing house. *Publications:* First Impression, 1962; Omens, 1969; Letter, 1974; Voice, 1978; The Tavrichesky Garden, 1984; The Hedgerow, 1988; A Night Melody, 1991; Apollo in the Snow (essays and memoirs), 1991; On a Clouded Star, 1994. *Contributions to:* Novii Mir; Znamya; Zvezda; Unost; Voprosi Literaturi. *Honours:* Severnaya Palmira Award, 1995; Russian State Award, 1996. *Memberships:* Union of Writers; PEN Club. *Address:* Kaluzhsky Pereulok 9, Apt 48, St Petersburg 193015, Russia.

KUSHWAHA, Tejnarayan; b. 24 April 1933, Singhandi, India. Teacher (retd); Poet. 3 s., 1 d. *Education:* BA, 1958, MA, Hindi, 1960, MA, Sanskrit, PhD, 1971; Diploma in Education, 1971, Bhagalpuruni University. *Appointment:* Asst Teacher, Secondary School, Eshipur, 1960–94. *Publications:* OMA, 1963; Savarna, 1984; Geet Chirayeenke, 1992; Devata, 1993. *Contributions to:* Anthologies, newspapers, and journals. *Honours:* Several literary awards. *Address:* At-Gandhi Nagar Po Eshipur D1-Bhagalpur (Bihar), Pin 813206, India.

KUSKIN, Karla (Seidman), (Nicholas J. Charles); b. 17 July 1932, New York, NY, USA. Writer and Illustrator of Children's Fiction and Verse. m. (1) Charles M Kuskin, 4 Dec. 1955, divorced Aug. 1987, 1 s., 1 d., (2) William L Bell, 24 July 1989. *Education:* Antioch College, 1950–53; BFA, Yale University, 1955. *Appointments:* Illustrator for several publishers; Conductor of poetry and writing workshops. *Publications:* Roar and More, 1956; James and the Rain, 1957; In the Middle of the Trees, 1958; The Animals and the Ark, 1958; Just Like Everyone Else, 1959; Which Horse is William?, 1959; Square As a House, 1960; The Bear Who Saw the Spring, 1961; All Sizes of Noises, 1962; Alexander Soames: His Poems, 1962; How Do You Get From Here to There?, 1962; ABCDEFGHIJKLMNOPQRSTUVWXYZ, 1963; The Rose on My Cake, 1964; Sand and Snow, 1965; Jane Anne June Spoon and Her Very Adventurous Search for the Moon, 1966; The Walk the Mouse Girls Took, 1967; Watson, the Smartest Dog in the USA, 1968; In the Flaky Frosty Morning, 1969; Any Me I Want To Be: Poems, 1972; What Did You Bring Me?, 1973; Near the Window Tree: Poems and Notes, 1975; A Boy Had a Mother Who Brought Him a Hat, 1976; A Space Story, 1978; Herbert Hated Being Small, 1979; Dogs and Dragons, Trees and Dreams: A Collection of Poems, 1980; Night Again, 1981; The Philharmonic Gets Dressed, 1982; Something Sleeping in the Hall, 1985; The Dallas Titans Get Ready for Bed, 1986; Jerusalem, Shining Still, 1987; Soap Soup, 1992; A Great Miracle Happened Here: A Chanukah Story, 1993; Patchwork Island, 1994; The City Dog, 1994; City Noise, 1994; Paul, 1994; James and the Rain, 1995; The Upstairs Cat, 1997; The Sky is Always in the Sky (poems), 1998; I Am Me, 2000. *Contributions to:* Magazines and periodicals. *Honours:* Book Show Awards, American Institute of Graphic Arts, 1955–60; Children's Book Award, International Reading Asscn, 1976; Children's Book Council Showcase Selections, 1976–77; National Council of Teachers of English Award for Poetry, 1979; Children's Science Book Award, New York Acad. of Sciences, 1980; American Library Asscn Awards, 1980, 1982, 1993; School Library Journal Best Book, 1987; John S. Burrough Science Award, 1992. *Address:* 96 Joralemon St, New York, NY 11201, USA.

KUZNETSOV, Sergei Leonidovich; b. 10 June 1963, Moscow, Russia. Poet; Writer; Journalist; Publisher. m. Elena Kuznetsova, 1 s., 1 d. *Education:* Master of Science, Forest University, 1982. *Appointments:* Correspondent, Moscow and regional newspapers, 1982–94; Publisher, Washington DC, 1994–; Publisher and Ed.-in-Chief, Greater Washington (journal in Russian), 1996–. *Publications:* Shot Poet (poems), 1983; A Life Behind the Iron Curtain (novel), 1986; Otkrovenie (poems), 1999. *Contributions to:* The Capital & Vicinity; Novoe Russkoe Slovo; Interesting Paper; World; Television and Radio programmes. *Memberships:* Moscow Literature Union, Vesyi; Washington Literature Club, Nadejda, pres.; International Pushkin Committee; American-Russian Asscn, Washington Russian Connection; New York Russian Writers Club; Olympoetry Movement. *Address:* 436 Girard St, No. T-2, Gaithersburg, MD 20877, USA

KWANG-CHUNG YU; b. 9 Sept. 1928, China. Prof.; Poet; Essayist; Trans. m. Fan Wo-chun, 1956, 4 d. *Education:* BA, National Taiwan University; MFA, University of Iowa. *Appointments:* Visiting Fulbright Prof., USA, 1964–66, 1969–71; Prof., National Taiwan Normal University, 1966–72, National Chengchi University, 1972–74; Reader, Chinese University of Hong Kong, 1974–85; Dean, College of Liberal Arts, National Sun Yat-sen University, Kaohsiung, Taiwan, 1985–91. *Publications:* 17 poetry collections, 1960–98; 12 prose works, 1968–98. *Contributions to:* Reviews, quarterlies, journals, and periodicals. *Honours:* Australian Cultural Award, 1972; Golden Tripod Awards for Lyrics, 1981, 1984; Wu San-lien Award for Prose, 1983; China Times Poetry Award, 1985; National Literary Award for Poetry, 1990; Hon. Fellowship, Hong Kong Trans. Society, 1991. *Memberships:* Blue Stars Poetry Society, founder; International PEN. *Address:* c/o Institute of Foreign Languages and Literature, National Sun Yat-sen University, Kaohsiung, China (Taiwan).

KWOK YIN WOO, (Ji Hun); b. 20 Oct. 1946, Hong Kong. Educator; Poet. m. Li Sook Ling, 11 Nov. 1972, 1 s., 2 d. *Education:* BA, 1969, MA, 1972, Diploma in Education, 1974, University of Hong Kong; PhD Candidate, University of Suzhou, China, 1999. *Appointments:* Lecturer, Hong Kong Institute of Education, 1997–99; Principal, Confucian Ho Kwok Pui Chan College, 1997–; Sec.-Gen., Confucian Acad., 2000–; Mem., Election Committee, HKSAR, 2001–; Ed., Poetry Network Bi-monthly, 2002–. *Publications:* A Vision Revealed, 1964; Blue Beast, 1970; Three Acquaintances, 1976; Broken Spear, 1978; Just Before the Gust Blows, 1987; The Racing Poet, 1980; When the Hill is Still Creeping, 1990; Lest I Fall Asleep Before Dawn, 1991; Unconventional Essays, 1993; One Poem a Week, 1995; Collection of Essays on Modern Chinese Poetry of Hong Kong, 1997; Collection of Modern Chinese Poems from Hong Kong from the Last 50 Years, 2001. *Contributions to:* Undergrad; Shih Feng Monthly; Shi Bi-Monthly; Poetry Network Bi-monthly, 2002–. Hong Kong Literature Monthly; Chinese Students Weekly; One Ninth Poetry Journal; Sing Tao Daily; Ming Pao; Blue Stars Poetry Quarterly; Epoch Poetry Quarterly; United Daily News; Chung Hua Daily News; Overseas Digest; Sun Poetry Press; Zhong Yuan Bi-Monthly; Plough Literature; Singapore Literature; Stratosphere; Asian Chinese Writers Magazine; The Independence Daily; The Overseas Chinese Daily. *Honours:* Writer-in Residence, Hong Kong Urban Council, 1997; Merit Award of Chinese Modern Poetry; Adjudicators of Various Literary Awards. *Memberships:* Shih Feng Asscn; Singapore Literary Society; Shi Bi-Monthly Asscn; Australian Chinese Writers Asscn; Poets Union Inc of Australia; Professional Teachers Union, Australia. *Address:* Flat D, 12/F, Tower 6, Uptown Plaza, TaiPo, Hong Kong. *E-mail:* kpcwky@chkpcc.edu.hk.

L

LA FORTUNE, Knolly Stephen; b. 2 Jan. 1920, Trinidad. Teacher (retd); Poet; Writer. m. Catherine Searle, 28 Aug. 1971, 1 s., 1 d. *Education:* Trinidad Teachers College, 1943–45; ACP, College of Preceptors, London, 1954; ATC, Goldsmith's College, University of London, 1956; BA, Open University, 1977; PhD, International University, 1985. *Publications:* Several poems. *Contributions to:* Anthologies, newspapers and magazines. *Honours:* International Acad. of Poets Award; Fellow, RGS, 1976. *Memberships:* Acad. of Poets; Caribbean Art Society. *Address:* 68 Arthurdon Rd, Brockley, London SE4 1J0, England.

LA GATTUTA, Margo; b. 18 Sept. 1942, Detroit, Michigan, USA. Poet; Teacher. m. Stephen La Gattuta, 14 Nov. 1964, divorced June 1988, 3 s. *Education:* BA, Honours, English, Oakland University, Rochester, Michigan, 1980; MFA, Writing, Vermont College, 1984. *Publications:* Diversion Road, 1983; Noedgelines, 1986; The Dream Givers, 1990; Video, 1992; Embracing the Fall, 1994; The Heart Before the Course, 1999. *Contributions to:* Anthologies, reviews, journals and magazines. *Honours:* Several poetry awards and prizes. *Address:* 2134 W Gunn Rd, Rochester, MI 48306, USA.

LA LOCA. See: KAROL, Pamala Marie.

LABERGE, Marie; b. 29 Nov. 1950, Québec, Canada. Dramatist; Author; Poet; Ed. *Education:* Université Laval, 1970–72; Conservatoire d'art dramatique de Québec, 1972–75. *Appointments:* Pres., Centre d'essai des auteurs dramatiques, 1987–89; Theatre Ed., Editions du Boréal, 1991–. *Publications:* Avec l'hiver qui s'en vient, 1981; Ils étaient venus pour…, 1981; C'était avant la guerre à l'Anse à Gilles, 1981, English trans. as Before the War, Down at l'Anse à Gilles, 1986; Jocelyne Trudelle trouvée morte dans ses larmes, 1983; Deux tangos pour toute une vie, 1985; L'homme gris, 1986, English trans. as Night, 1988; Le Night Cap Bar, 1987; Oublier, 1987, English trans. as Forgetting, 1988; Aurélie, ma soeur, 1988, English trans. as Aurélie, My Sister, 1989; Le Blanc, 1989; Juillet, 1989; Quelques adieux, 1992; Pierre, ou, La consolation, 1992; Annabelle, 1996; Le gout du bonheur, 2000. *Contributions to:* Film, radio, television and various publications. *Honours:* Gov.-Gen.'s Award for Drama, 1982; Croix de Chevalier de l'Ordre des Arts et des Lettres, France, 1989; Prix des Lectrices de Elle-Québec, 1992. *Address:* c/o Editions du Boréal, 447 rue Saint-Denis, Montréal, QC H2J 2L2, Canada.

LABOMBARD, Joan; b. 2 July 1920, San Francisco, CA, USA. Poet. m. Emerson H LaBombard, 17 July 1943, 1 d. *Education:* BA, University of California at Los Angeles, 1943. *Publications:* Calendar, 1985; The Counting of Grains, 1990; The Winter Watch of the Leaves, 1993. *Contributions to:* Atlantic; Chicago Tribune; Colorado Review; Poetry; Poetry Northwest; Nation; Prairie Schooner; Virginia Quarterly Review; several anthologies. *Honours:* Borestone Mountain Poetry Awards Annual Vols, First Prizes, 1958, 1969; Poetry Society of America Reedy Award, 1971; Lucile Medwick Award, 1974; Consuela Ford Wagner Award, 1977; American Book Award, 1989. *Memberships:* Acad. of American Poets; Poetry Society of America; Associated Writing Programs; PEN Center USA West. *Address:* 814 Teakwood Rd, Los Angeles, CA 90049, USA.

LACZKOWSKI, Zdzislaw Tadeusz, (Tadeusz Seweryn); b. 27 Oct. 1926, Zawiercie, Katowice, Poland. Novelist; Dramatist; Poet. *Education:* Law Faculty, Jagiellonian University, 1948–49; Actor School, 1948–49; Catholic University of Lublin. *Appointments:* Art Ed., Slowo Powszechne, 1952–92, Slowo-Dziennik Katolicki, 1992–95. *Publications:* Poems and Poetical Prose; Novels; Plays. *Honours:* Wlodzimierz Pietrzak Literary Awards; Kierunki Magazine Award; International Giorgio La Pira Award. *Memberships:* European Culture Asscn; Dramaturgists and Stage Composers Asscn. *Address:* Falecka 5/7 m 65, 02-547 Warsaw, Poland.

LAIBI, Shaker; b. 21 March 1955, Iraq. Writer; Poet; Painter. *Education:* MA, Baghdad, 1977; Diploma, École Superieur d'Art Visuel, Geneva, 1982. *Publications:* Eloquence, 1988; Menga, la pastorale, 1996; Soufisme et art visuel, iconographie de Sacré, 1996. Other: Several works in Arabic. *Contributions to:* Various publications. *Membership:* Société Suisse des Écrivaines et Écrivains. *Address:* 77 bd Carl-Vogt, 1205 Geneva, Switzerland.

LAIR, Helen Humphrey; b. 3 Jan. 1918, Indiana, USA. Poet; Artist; Art Teacher. m. Marvin Lair, 2 July 1966, 1 s., 2 d. *Education:* Anderson College; Herron School of Art; Wisconsin University; Gloucester School of Art. *Publication:* Earth Pilgrim and Lair of the Four Winds. *Contributions to:* Best Loved Contemporary Poems; Adventures in Poetry; Hibiscus Press; National Society of Art and Literature; Premier Poets; Poets of India; Poetry Review; The Criterion, 1994–95. *Honours:* Clover International Award; Bicentennial Poetry Award; Farnell Award; Miller Award; Golden Poet Award; Campbell Historical Award; National Federation of Poets Award; Hibiscus Press Award. *Memberships:* New York Poetry Forum; Raintree Writers; California

Chaparrel Poets; World Congress of Poets; Acad. of American Poets; International Platform Asscn; Indiana Federation of Poets; National Federation of Poets. *Address:* 741 Kenwood Ave, Fort Wayne, IN 46805, USA.

LAITER, Saloman; b. 16 July 1937, México, DF, Mexico. Poet; Film Dir; Painter. 4 s. *Education:* School of Architecture; MGM Studio, England. *Publications:* Several poems. *Contributions to:* Uno Mas Uno; Siempre; Revista De Bellas Artes; Excelsior. *Memberships:* Society of Mexican Authors; Dirs Guild. *Address:* Montanas Rocallasas Pte 210, Lomas de Chapultepec, Mexico 11000, DF Mexico.

LALLY, Michael David; b. 25 May 1942, Orange, New Jersey, USA. Poet; Actor. m. Jaina Flynn, 10 June 1997, 2 s., 1 d. *Education:* BA, 1968, MFA, 1969, University of Iowa. *Publications:* What Withers, 1970; Stupid Rabbits, 1971; The South Orange Sonnets, 1972; Sex/The Swing Era, 1975; Dues, 1975; Rocky Dies Yellow, 1975; Charisma, 1976; Just Let Me Do It, 1978; In the Mood, 1978; White Life, 1980; Attitude, 1982; Hollywood Magic, 1982; Can't Be Wrong, 1996; Of, 1999. *Contributions to:* Washington Post; TriQuarterly; American Review; Partisan Review; Massachusetts Review. *Honours:* New York Poetry Center's Discovery Award, 1972; Poets Foundation Award, 1974; National Endowment for the Arts Poetry Award, 1974–81; Pacificus Foundation Literary Award, 1997; PEN Oakland Josephine Miles Award, 1997. *Membership:* PEN. *Address:* 2102 Neilson Way, Santa Monica, CA 90405, USA.

LAM, Cecil Justin; b. 16 Dec. 1957, Hong Kong. Poet; Painter; Performer. 1 s. *Education:* University degrees. *Publications:* Several poems. *Contributions to:* Various anthologies, newspapers, reviews, journals and magazines. *Honours:* Ed.'s Choice and First Prize Awards. *Memberships:* Canadian League of Poets; Canadian Poetry Asscn; United Nation of Canadian Assocs. *Address:* PO Box 22127, Thorncliffe PO Station, Toronto, Ontario M4H 1N9, Canada.

LAMANTIA, Philip; b. 23 Oct. 1927, San Francisco, CA, USA. Poet. *Education:* University of California, Berkeley, 1947–49. *Publications:* Erotic Poems, 1946; Narcotica: I Demand Extinction of Laws Prohibiting Narcotic Drugs, 1959; Ekstasis, 1959; Destroyed Works, 1962; Touch of the Marvelous, 1966; Selected Poems 1943–1966, 1967; Penguin Modern Poets 13 (with Charles Bukowski and Harold Norse), 1969; The Blood of the Air, 1970; Becoming Visible, 1981; Meadowland West, 1986. *Address:* c/o City Lights Books, 261 Columbus Ave, San Francisco, CA 94133, USA.

LAMB, Elizabeth Searle; b. 22 Jan. 1917, Topeka, KS, USA. Poet; Writer; Ed. m. F Bruce Lamb, 11 Dec. 1941, deceased 1992, 1 d. *Education:* BA, 1939, BMus, 1940, University of Kansas. *Appointments:* Ed., Frogpond, 1984–90, 1994; Co-Ed., Haiku Southwest, 1993–94. *Publications:* Pelican Tree and Other Panama Adventures (co-author), 1953; Today and Every Day, 1970; Inside Me, Outside Me, 1974; In This Blaze of Sun, 1975; Picasso's Bust of Sylvette, 1977; 39 Blossoms, 1982; Casting Into a Cloud, 1985; Lines for My Mother, Dying, 1988; The Light of Elizabeth Lamb: 100 American Haiku, 1993; Ripples Spreading Out, 1997; Platek Irysa (Petals of Iris), 1998; Across the Windharp, 1999. *Contributions to:* Many anthologies, journals, and magazines. *Honours:* Cicada Awards, Canada, 1977, 1980; Henderson Awards, 1978, 1981, 1982, 1991, 1993; Dellbrook Poetry Award, 1979; HSA Merit Book Awards, 1979, 1983, 1987; Yuki Teikei, 1981, 1982, 1989, 1994; Certificate of Achievement, Haiku Society of America, 1995; Hon. Curator, American Haiku Archive, California State Library, Sacramento, 1996–97; 55th Basho Festival English Haiku Special Award, Japan. *Memberships:* Haiku Society of America; Haiku International, Japan; Asscn of International Renku, Japan; Haiku Canada; Poetry Society of America. *Address:* 970 Acequia Madre, Sante Fe, NM 87505, USA. *E-mail:* eslamb@earthlink.net.

LAMBOVSKI, Boyko Panov; b. 13 March 1960, Sofia, Bulgaria. Poet; Writer. m. Liudmila Kirilova Koteva, 13 May 1992. *Education:* Maxim Gorky Literary Institute, Moscow, 1982–87. *Publications:* Poetry and prose in Bulgarian. *Contributions to:* Anthologies, reviews and journals. *Honours:* Vladimir Bashev National Prize for Poetry, 1987; Achievement in the Arts Prize, Svoboden Narod, 1992. *Memberships:* Union of Bulgarian Writers; Friday the 13th, co-founder. *Address:* Shipchenski Prokhod 7-11, BI 228-A, Ap 65, Sofia 1111, Bulgaria.

LAMMON, Martin; b. 19 June 1958, Wilmington, OH, USA. Prof. of English; Poet. m. Frances Elizabeth Davis, 17 Aug. 1996. *Education:* BA, Wittenberg University, 1980; MA, 1982, PhD, 1991, Ohio University. *Appointments:* Visiting Instructor in English, Juniata College, Huntingdon, Pennsylvania, 1988–91; Asst Prof., then Assoc. Prof. of English, Fairmont State College, West Virginia, 1991–97; Co-Founder and Co-Ed., Kestrel: A Journal of Literature and Art, 1992–97; Prof. of English and Fuller E. Callaway Endowed Flannery O'Connor Chair in Creative Writing, Georgia College and State University, Milledgeville, 1997–. *Publications:* Written in Water, Written in Stone: Twenty Years of Poets on Poetry (ed.), 1996; News From Where I Live: Poems, 1998. *Contributions to:* Periodicals. *Honours:* Fellow, West Virginia Commission on the Arts, 1994; Arkansas Poetry Award, University of Arkansas Press, 1997; Neruda Prize for Poetry, Nimrod International Journal, 1997. *Membership:* Associated Writing Programs. *Address:* 620 N Columbia Terrace, Milledgeville, GA 31061, USA. *E-mail:* mlammon@mail.gac.peachnet.edu.

LANCASTER, William John; b. 18 April 1946, England. Writer; Poet; Teacher. m. Barbara Milligan, 2 s. *Education:* BA, 1967, MA, 1970, University of Sheffield. *Appointments:* Lecturer in Creative Writing, University of Huddersfield and Open College of the Arts. *Publications:* Effects of War, 1986; Spilt Shift (with Geoff Hattersley), 1990. *Contributions to:* Poetry Review; London Magazine; TLS; Ambit; Iron; Encounter; Rialto; Wide Skirt; Echo Room; Pennine Platform; Slow Dancer; Orbis; Scratch; Verse; Aquarius; North; English In Education. *Honours:* Second Prize, National Poetry Competition, 1979; Writer's Award, Yorkshire Arts, 1983. *Membership:* National Asscn of Writers in Education. *Address:* 32 Thornhill Rd, Edgerton, Huddersfield, Yorkshire HD3 3DD, England.

LANCE, Betty Rita Gomez; b. 28 Aug. 1923, Costa Rica. Prof. Emeritus; Writer; Poet. 2 s. *Education:* Teaching Diploma, Universidad Nacional, Costa Rica, 1941; BA, Central Missouri State University, Warrensburg, 1944; MA, University of Missouri, Columbia, 1947; PhD, Washington University, St Louis, 1959. *Appointment:* Prof. Emeritus of Romance Languages and Literatures, Kalamazoo College. *Publications:* La actitud picaresca en la novela española del siglo XX, 1969; Vivencias, 1981; Bebiendo luna, 1983; Vendimia del tiempo, 1984; Hoy hacen corro las ardillas (short story), 1985; Alas en el alba, 1987; Siete cuerdas, 1996. *Contributions to:* Americas; Letras Femeninas; Caprice. *Memberships:* Poets and Writers of America; Asociación de Escritores de Costa Rica; Asociación Prometeo de Poesía, Madrid; Academia Iberoamericana de Poesia, Madrid. *Address:* Kalamazoo College, Kalamazoo, MI 49006; 1562 Spruce Dr., Kalamazoo, MI 49008, USA.

LANDERT, Walter; b. 3 Jan. 1929, Zürich, Switzerland. Writer; Poet. m. Elsy Weber, 15 April 1954, 3 s., 1 d. *Education:* Neuchâtel; London. *Publications:* Manager auf Zeit (novel), 1968; Selbstbefragung (poems), 1969; Entwurf Schweiz (literary essay), 1970; Koitzsch (novel), 1971; Traum einer besseren Welt (short stories and poems), 1980; Unkraut im helvetischen Kulturgartchen (literary essays), 1981; Meine Frau baut einen Bahnof (short stories), 1982; Klemms Memorabilien: Ein Vorspiel (novel), 1989; Umwerfende Zeiten: Ein Prozess (novel), 1990; Treffpunkt: Fondu Bourguignonne (novel), 1993. *Contributions to:* Newspapers. *Honours:* Artemis Jubilee Prize, 1969; Literary Union Poetry Prize, Saarbrücken, 1977. *Membership:* Swiss Authors Group, Olten. *Address:* Lendikonerstrasse 54, CH 8484 Weisslingen/ZH, Switzerland.

LANE, M. Travis, (Millicent Elizabeth Travis); b. 23 Sept. 1934, San Antonio, Texas, USA (Naturalized Canadian citizen, 1973). Poet; Writer. m. Lauriat Lane, 26 Aug. 1957, 1 s., 1 d. *Education:* BA, Vassar College, 1956; MA, 1957, PhD, 1967, Cornell University. *Appointments:* Assistantships, Cornell University, University of New Brunswick; Poetry Reviewer, Fiddlehead Magazine. *Publications:* Five Poets: Cornell, 1960; An Inch or So of Garden, 1969; Poems 1969–72, 1973; Homecomings, 1977; Divinations and Shorter Poems, 1973–78, 1980; Walking Under the Nebulae, 1981; Reckonings: Poems 1979–83, 1988; Solid Things: Poems New and Selected, 1993; Temporary Shelter, 1993; Night Physics, 1994; Keeping Afloat, 2001. *Contributions to:* Reviews, quarterlies and journals. *Honours:* Hon. Research Assoc., University of New Brunswick; Pat Lowther Prize, League of Canadian Poets, 1980. *Memberships:* Canadian Poetry Asscn; League of Canadian Poets; Writers Federation of New Brunswick. *Address:* 807 Windsor St, Fredericton, New Brunswick E3B 4G7, Canada.

LANE, Patrick; b. 26 March 1939, Nelson, BC, Canada. Writer; Poet. 4 s., 1 d. *Education:* University of British Columbia. *Appointments:* Ed., Very Stone House, Publishers, Vancouver, 1966–72; Writer-in-Residence, University of Manitoba, Winnepeg, 1978–79, University of Ottawa, 1980, University of Alberta, Edmonton, 1981–82, Saskatoon Public Library, 1982–83, Concordia University, 1985, Globe Theatre Co, Regina, Saskatchewan, 1985–. *Publications:* Letters From the Savage Mind, 1966; For Rita: In Asylum, 1969; Calgary City Jail, 1969; Separations, 1969; Sunflower Seeds, 1969; On the Street, 1970; Mountain Oysters, 1971; Hiway 401 Rhapsody, 1972; The Sun Has Begun to Eat the Mountain, 1972; Passing into Storm, 1973; Beware the Months of Fire, 1974; Certs, 1974; Unborn Things: South American Poems, 1975; For Riel in That Gawdam Prison, 1975; Albino Pheasants, 1977; If, 1977; Poems, New and Selected, 1978; No Longer Two People (with Lorna Uher), 1979; The Measure, 1980; Old Mother, 1982; Woman in the Dust, 1983; A Linen Crow, a Caftan Magpie, 1985; Milford and Me, 1989; Winter, 1990; Mortal Remains, 1992; Too Spare, Too Fierce, 1995; Selected Poems, 1978–1997, 1997; The Bare Plum of Winter Rain, 2000. *Contributions to:* Most major Canadian magazines, American and English journals. *Honour:* Governor-General's Award for Poetry, 1979; Canadian Authors' Asscn Award, 1985; British Columbia Book Award, 1997. *Memberships:* League of Canadian Poets; Writer's Union of Canada; PEN, Canada. *Address:* c/o Writer's Union of Canada, 24 Ryerson Ave, Toronto, Ontario M5T 2P3, Canada.

LANGE, Eugene Samuel, (Muhammad Khalil); b. 7 July 1955, Liverpool England. Teacher; Performance Artist; Freelance Performance Poet. 1 d. *Education:* Youth and Community Work, North East Wales, 1979–81 Millbrook College, 1988. *Publications:* Numerous poems. *Contributions to* Various anthologies and other publications. *Honour:* Black Penmanship Award. *Address:* Flat 321, Belvedere Rd, Liverpool L8 3TF, England.

LANGFORD, Gary (Raymond); b. 21 Aug. 1947, Christchuch, New Zealand Writer; Dramatist; Poet; Senior Lecturer. 1 d. *Education:* BA, 1969, MA Honours, History, 1971, MA, Honours, English, 1973, University of Canterbury; Diploma of Teaching Drama, Christchurch Secondary Teachers College, 1973. *Appointments:* Senior Lecturer in Creative Writing, University of Western Sydney, 1986; Writer-in-Residence, University of Canterbury, 1989. *Publications:* Over 20 books, including novels and poetry. Other: Plays and scripts for stage, radio, and television. *Contributions to:* Anthologies and other publications. *Honours:* Australia Council Young Writers Fellowship, 1976; Alan Marshall Award, 1983. *Address:* c/o Curtis Brown Pty Ltd, Box 19, Paddington, NSW 2021, Australia.

LANGLAND, Joseph Thomas; b. 16 Feb. 1917, Spring Grove, Minnesota, USA. Prof. Emeritus; Writer. m. Judith Gail Wood, 26 June 1943, 2 s., 1 d. *Education:* AA, Santa Ana College, 1936; BA, 1940, MA, 1941, Graduate Studies, 1946–48, University of Iowa; Harvard University, Columbia University, 1953–54. *Appointments:* Instructor, Dana College, 1941–42, University of Iowa, 1946–48; Asst, then Assoc. Prof., University of Wyoming, 1948–49; Assoc. Prof. to Prof., 1959–80, Prof. Emeritus, 1980–, University of Massachusetts. *Publications:* A Dream of Love, 1986; Twelve Poems, 1991; Selected Poems, 1992. *Contributions to:* Reviews, quarterlies, journals, and magazines. *Honours:* Ford Foundation Faculty Fellowship; Amy Lowell Poetry Fellowship; New England Living Legend; Chancellor's Prize. *Address:* 18 Morgan Circle, Amherst, MA 01002, USA.

LANGTON, Daniel Joseph; b. 6 Sept. 1927, New Jersey, USA. College Prof.; Poet. m. 1 Feb. 1949, 1 s. *Education:* San Francisco State College; University of California. *Appointments:* High School Teacher, 1963–67; College Teacher, 1967–. *Publications:* Querencia; The Hogarth-Selkirk Letters; The Inheritance; Life Forms. *Contributions to:* Periodicals. *Honours:* London Prize; Browning Award; Devins Award. *Memberships:* Poetry Society of America; Acad. of American Poets. *Address:* Box 170012, San Francisco, CA 94117, USA.

LANNERS, Paul; b. 25 June 1948, Luxembourg. Adult Educator; Poet. *Education:* Licence in Classical Philology, Catholic University of Louvain, Belgium, 1973; Licence in Catholic Theology, University of Strasbourg, France, 1988. *Publications:* Point de Convergence, Poèmes de 1967 à 1980, 1983. *Contributions to:* Anthologies, journals and magazines. *Address:* 28 rue Charles-Arendt, 1134 Luxembourg.

LANTAY, Patricia; b. 6 March 1946, New York, NY, USA. Office Administrator; Poet. 2 d. *Education:* BA, Marymount College, 1982. *Appointments:* Ed., St Bartholomew's Review, 1972; Historian, New York Poetry Forum, 1974. *Contributions to:* Anthologies and reviews. *Honours:* Sylvia Plath Award, World Narrative of Poets, 1980; Eva Ban Award, 1983; Annette Feldman Award, New York Poetry Forum, 1983; Massachusetts State Poetry Society Award, 1994; Miller Award, Green Rivers Writers, 1994; Jessee Poet Award, 1995. *Memberships:* Acad. of American Poets; National Federation of State Poetry Societies; New York Poetry Forum. *Address:* 333 E 43rd St, New York, NY 10017, USA.

LAPERLE, P(atricia) J(oan Karr); b. 4 Jan. 1943, Springfield, Massachusetts, USA. Author; Poet. m. Donald A Laperle, 10 Oct. 1981, 1 s., 4 step-s., 2 step-d. *Education:* Barrington College, 1960–62. *Publications:* Under His Wings; Land of Living Waters. *Contributions to:* World of Poetry Press; Odessa Poetry Review; Sparrow Grass Poetry; National Arts Society; Poetry; Caring Connection – John Milton Society for the Blind Publications. *Honours:* Golden Poet Award; Silver Poet Award; Apa Poet of Merit Award; Christian Writers Fellowship International Koala Book Award. *Memberships:* Poetry Society of America; National Arts Society; Massachusetts State Poetry Society; National Federation of State Poetry Societies; Christian Writers Fellowship International. *Address:* 59 Kingsley St, Southbridge, MA 01550, USA.

LAPIERRE, Matthew Scott; b. 9 Oct. 1968, Augusta, Maine, USA. Poet. *Education:* BA, Colby College, 1990; MFA, University Massachusetts, Amherst, 1993. *Contributions to:* Atom Mind; Chiron Review; Midwest Quarterly; Daedalus Anthology of Kinky Verse; Cokefish; Poetry Motel; Sheila-Na-Gig. *Honours:* Third Place, Chiron Review Poetry Contest, 1995; Winner, Rocket Press Poetry Contest, 1995; Pushcart Prize Nomination, 1996. *Address:* PO Box 7615, Portland, ME 04112, USA.

LAPIERRE, Pierre; b. 16 Jan. 1932, Elisabethville, Belgian Congo. Poet; Playwright. Divorced, 1 s., 5 d. *Education:* BSc, University of Cape Town, 1954; BA, Honours, Drama, French, 1979, PhD, 1993, UKC. *Publications:* Poster Poems; Celebration of Summer; State of the Kingdom; Ducks; Signs of Life.

Honours: Radio Medway Second Prize; Herbert Read Gallery. *Membership:* Poetry Society of Great Britain. *Address:* 160 Old Dover Rd, Canterbury, Kent CT1 3EX, England.

LAPOLT, Eda Marie; b. 11 March 1956, Monticello, New York, USA. Personal Care Aid; Poet. *Education:* AAS Degree, Secretarial Science with Word Processing, Orange County Community College, 1983. *Publication:* Expressions from the Heart, 1998. *Contributions to:* National Library of Poetry; Poetry in Motion; Poet's Corner; True Romance Magazine. *Honours:* Five Ed.'s Choice Awards, National Library of Poetry. *Memberships:* National Poet's Asscn; International Society of Poets. *Address:* 7 Nelshore Dr., Monticello, NY 12701, USA.

LARGE, Timothy Stoker; b. 11 Sept. 1972, Iowa City, IA, USA. Ed.; Poet. *Education:* BA, English, Balliol College, Oxford, 1992. *Appointments:* Ed., Corroboree. *Publications:* Wonderland and Other Poems, 1991; Wonderland and Thy Hand, 1992. *Contributions to:* Hybrid; Purple Patch; Poems; Others. *Honour:* First Prize, Under-19 Section, Charterhouse International Poetry Competition, 1991. *Memberships:* Poetry Society; Society of Lunatics, Lovers and Poets, pres. *Address:* 78 Windsor Rd, Cambridge CB4 3JN, England.

LARSEN, Jeanne (Louise); b. 9 Aug. 1950, Washington, DC, USA. Prof. of English; Writer; Poet; Trans. m. Thomas Hugh Mesner, 13 Aug. 1977, 1 step-s., 1 step-d. *Education:* BA, Oberlin College, 1971; MA, Hollins College, 1972; Graduate Research Certificate, Nagasaki University, 1980; PhD, University of Iowa, 1983. *Appointments:* Lecturer, Tunghai University, 1972–74; Asst Prof., 1975, 1980–86, Assoc. Prof., 1986–92, Prof. of English, 1992–98, Hollins College; Prof. of English, Hollins University, 1998–. *Publications:* Fiction: Silk Road, 1989; Bronze Mirror, 1991; Manchu Palaces, 1996. Poetry: James Cook in Search of Terra Incognita: A Book of Poems, 1979. Other: Brocade River Poems: Selected Works of the Tang Dynasty Courtesan Xue Tao (trans. and ed.), 1987; Engendering the Word: Feminist Essays in Psychosexual Poetics (ed. with others), 1989. *Contributions to:* Scholarly books, anthologies, learned journals and periodicals. *Honours:* First Selection, Associated Writing Programs' Annual Poetry Book Competition, 1979; Resident Fellowships, Virginia Center for the Creative Arts, 1982, 1986, 1987, 1989, 1990, 1995; John Gardner Fellowship in Fiction, Bread Loaf Writers' Conference, 1990; William L Crawford Award for Year's Best New Novelist, International Asscn for the Fantastic in the Arts, 1990; National Endowment for the Arts Fellowship in Trans., 1995. *Memberships:* Asscn for Asian Studies; Authors Guild; International Asscn for the Fantastic in the Arts; PEN; Poets and Writers. *Address:* c/o Dept of English, Hollins University, Roanoke, VA 24020, USA.

LARSEN, Marianne; b. 27 Jan. 1951, Kalundborg, Denmark. Poet. *Publications:* Several vols of poems, 1971–; Free Compositions, 1991. *Contributions to:* Many Danish and foreign magazines. *Honours:* Adam Oehelagers Prize, 1980; Emil Aarestrup Prize, 1982; Beatrice Prize, 1989; Martin Andersen Nexø Prize, 1990; Egmont Fond Prize, 1991. *Membership:* Danish Ministry of Cultural Affairs Committee for Rewarding Poets and Writers with State Aid. *Address:* Worsaesvej 20, 2 tv, 1972 Frederiksbourg C, Denmark.

LARSON, Edna (Doris) Miner; b. 3 June 1928, Cedar Rapids, IA, USA. Poet; Writer. m. Ted A Larson, 13 Aug. 1974. *Education:* Coe College, 1949–53. *Contributions to:* Numerous publications. *Honour:* Iowa Lyrical. *Memberships:* Iowa Poetry Asscn; Midwest Federation of Chaparral Poets; National League of American Pen Women. *Address:* 1611 Second Ave Southeast, Cedar Rapids, IA 52403, USA. *E-mail:* edinalars@aol.com.

LARSON, Rosamond Winterton; b. 10 Dec. 1932, Los Angeles, CA, USA. Poet. m. Robert Patten Larson, 16 May 1977, 3 s., 4 d. *Education:* St Joseph Hospital School of Nursing, 1950–52; Palomar Junior College, 1965–66. *Contributions to:* Various anthologies and other publications. *Membership:* Amnesty International, USA. *Address:* PO Box 11912, Zephyr Cove, NV 89448, USA.

LASKEY, Michael; b. 15 Aug. 1944, Lichfield, Staffordshire, England. Teacher; Poet. m. Kay Osler, 23 April 1974, 3 s. *Education:* Open Exhibitioner, English, 1962–65, BA, English, 1965, St John's College, Cambridge. *Appointments:* Teacher of English; Poetry Correspondent, BBC, Radio Suffolk; Co-Ed., Smiths Knoll Poetry Magazine. *Publications:* Cloves of Garlic, 1989; Thinking of Happiness, 1991; In the Fruit Cage, 1997; The Tightrope Wedding, 1999. *Contributions to:* Anthologies, reviews, and magazines. *Honours:* Co-Winner, Poetry Business Pamphlet Competition, 1988; Poetry Book Society Recommendations, 1991, 1999. *Memberships:* Aldeburgh Poetry Trust, hon. secretary, chair., trustee; Aldeburgh Poetry Festival, founding co-ordinator; East Suffolk Poetry Workshop, founding mem. *Address:* Goldings, Goldings Lane, Leiston, Suffolk IP16 4EF, England.

LASSELL, Michael John; b. 15 July 1947, New York, NY, USA. Writer; Poet; Ed.; Journalist. *Education:* AB, Colgate University, 1969; MFA, School of Drama, Yale University, 1976. *Appointments:* Articles Dir, Metropolitan Home; Exec. Ed., SI Magazine; Managing Ed., Interview, LA Style.

Publications: Poems for Lost and Un-Lost Boys, 1985; Decade Dance, 1990; The Hard Way, 1995; The Name of Love, 1995; Eros in Boystown, 1996; A Flame for the Touch that Matters, 1998; Certain Ecstasies, 1999. *Contributions to:* Anthologies, reviews and quarterlies. *Honour:* Lamda Literary Award, 1991. *Memberships:* PEN American Centre; Poets and Writers; National Lesbian and Gay Journalists Asscn; Publishing Triangle; American Society of Magazine Eds. *Address:* PO Box 236, Radio City Station, New York, NY 10101-0236, USA.

LATHBURY, Roger, (Roger Lewis); b. 9 Sept. 1945, New York, NY, USA. University Prof.; Poet. m. Begona, 6 Aug. 1986. *Education:* Indiana University, 1968. *Appointment:* Assoc. Prof., George Mason University. *Publication:* The Carbon Gang. *Address:* Orchises Press, PO Box 20602, Alexandria, VA 22320, USA.

LAU, Evelyn; b. 1970, Canada. Poet; Writer. *Publications:* Poetry: You Are Not Who You Claim, 1990; Oedipal Dreams, 1993; In the House of the Slaves, 1993. Fiction: Fresh Girls, and Other Stories, 1993; Other Women, 1995. Non-Fiction: Runaway: Diary of a Street Kid, 1989. *Contributions to:* Periodicals. *Honour:* Air Canada Award, 1989. *Address:* c/o Coach House Press, 50 Prince Arthur Ave, Suite 107, Toronto, Ontario M5R 1B5, Canada.

LAURENT-CATRICE, Nicole; b. 8 April 1937, France. Poet. m. Loeiz Laurent, 1963, 4 s., 1 d. *Education:* Diplome d'Etudes Supérieures d'Espagnol, Sorbonne, University of Paris, 1963. *Publications:* Paysages Intérieurs, 1980; Deuil M'Est Seuil, 1987; Liturgie Des Pierres, 1989; La Sans Visage, 1996; Métacuisine, 1998. *Contributions to:* Many French poetry reviews; Le Journal des Poèts (Belgium); Poesía Sempre (Brazil); Poesia (Mexico); Litté Réalité (Canada); Metai (Lithuania); Prometeo (Colombia). *Address:* La Branche Rouge, 35760 Montgermont, France.

LAUTURE, Denizé; b. 11 May 1946, Haiti. Asst Prof.; Poet; Writer. m. 2 s. *Education:* BA, 1977, MA, 1981, City College of the City University of New York. *Appointment:* Asst Prof., St Thomas Aquinas College, Sparkill, New York. *Publications:* When the Denizen Weeps, 1989; Father and Son, 1993; Running the Road to ABC, 1996. *Contributions to:* Anthologies and periodicals. *Memberships:* American Asscn of Teachers of French; Poetry Society of America; Poets and Writers. *Address:* c/o St Thomas Aquinas College, Route 340, Sparkill, NY 10976, USA.

LAUWEREYNS, Johan Marc José, (Jan Lauwereyns); b. 13 May 1969, Berchem, Belgium. Scientist; Poet. m. Shizuka Sakurai, 24 Oct. 1998. *Education:* PhD in Psychology, University of Leuven, Belgium, 1998. *Appointments:* Postdoctoral Fellow, Dept of Physiology, Juntendo University, Tokyo, Japan, 1998–. *Publication:* Nagelaten Sonnetten, English trans. as Sonnets Left Behind, 1999. *Contributions to:* Dietsche Warande & Belfort; Yang; De Brakke Hond.

LAVIN, S. R.; b. 2 April 1945, Springfield, Massachusetts, USA. Poet; Writer. 2 s., 4 d. *Education:* AIC, BA, 1967; MA, Literature, Trinity College, 1970. *Appointments:* Poet-in-Residence, Clark University, Worcester, Massachusetts, 1972; Prof. of English, Castleton State College, Vermont, 1987–99. *Publications:* Poetry: The Stonecutters at War with the Cliff Dwellers, 1972; Cambodian Spring, 1973; Let Myself Shine, 1979. Fiction: Metacomet. Translation: I and You, by Martin Buber. *Contributions to:* Cold Drill; Hiram; I.P.R.; Mandrake; Stand; Vermont Literary Magazine; Chinese Poetry International. *Address:* c/o Parchment Press, 52 S River St, Coxsackie, NY 12051, USA.

LAVOIE, Steven Paul; b. 9 Oct. 1953, Minnesota, USA. Librarian; Poet; Writer. *Education:* AB, Humanities, 1975, Master of Library and Information Studies, 1986, University of California at Berkeley. *Appointments:* Librarian, Marin Independent Journal, CA, 1986–89; Librarian, 1989–96, Columnist, Editorial Writer, 1991–96, Oakland Tribune, CA; Consultant, Oakland Museum of California, 1996–; Faculty, Armstrong University, 1998–. *Publications:* Snoring Practice, 1982; On the Way, 1982; Erosion Surface, 1984; Birth of a Brain (with Dave Morke), 1984; Plastic Rulers, 1984; Nine Further Plastics, 1985; Lipsynch, 1986; Harbour of Light: An Illustrated History of Oakland, 1999. *Contributions to:* Anthologies, journals, and magazines. *Honours:* Winner, Sonoma State University Poetry Festival, 1971; Doris Green Award, 1982; Mark Twain Prize, 1984; Partners in Preservation, 1996. *Memberships:* Black Bart Poetry Society, co-founder; Pacific Center for the Book Arts; Society for American Baseball Research. *Address:* 4085 B Lincoln Ave, Oakland, CA 94602, USA.

LAWRENCE, Christina. See: LOOTS, Barbara Kuntz.

LAWSON, David Douglas Alexander; b. 20 June 1965, London, England. Writer; Poet. *Education:* Trinity College, Glenalmond, Scotland, 1979–83; Trinity College, Cambridge, 1984–87; Trinity College, Oxford, 1987–90. *Contributions to:* Haiku Hundred. *Honour:* Powell Prize. *Memberships:* School of Poets, Edinburgh. *Address:* Pittarow, Perth Rd, Abernethy, Tayside PH2 9LW, Scotland.

LAWSON, Sarah (Anne); b. 4 Nov. 1943, Indianapolis, IN, USA. Writer; Poet; Trans. m. Alastair Pettigrew, 8 April 1969, deceased 20 Sept. 1992. *Education:* BA, Indiana University, 1965; MA, University of Pennsylvania, 1966; PhD, University of Glasgow, 1971. *Publications:* New Writers and Writing 16, 1979; The Treasure of the City of Ladies, by Christine de Pisan (trans.), 1985; Dutch Interiors (poems), 1985; Poetry Introduction 6 (with others), 1986; A Foothold in Florida, by René de Laudonniere (trans.), 1992; Down Where the Willow is Washing Her Hair (poems), 1995; A Fado for My Mother, 1996; Below the Surface (poems), 1996; El Si de las Ninas, by Leandro Fernandez de Moratín (trans.), 1998; Twelve Scenes of Malta, 2000; Jacques Prévert, Selected Poems (trans.), 2002. *Contributions to:* Anthologies, reviews, quarterlies and journals. *Honour:* C. Day-Lewis Fellowship, 1979–80. *Memberships:* English PEN; Poetry Society; RSL; Society of Authors; Trans' Asscn. *Address:* 186 Albyn Rd, London SE8 4JQ, England.

LAYTON, Irving (Peter); b. 12 March 1912, Neamt, Romania. Poet; Author. m. (1) Faye Lynch, 13 Sept. 1938, divorced 1946, (2) Betty Frances Sutherland, 1 s., 1 d., (3) Aviva Cantor, 1 s., (4) Harriet Bernstein, divorced 1983, 1 d., (5) Anna Pottier. *Education:* BSc, Macdonald College, 1939; MA, McGill University, 1946. *Appointments:* Poet-in-Residence, University of Guelph, 1969; Visiting Prof., 1978, Adjunct Prof., 1988, 1989, Writer-in-Residence, 1989, Concordia University; Writer-in-Residence, University of Toronto, 1981. *Publications:* Poetry: Numerous vols, including: The Collected Poems of Irving Layton, 1971; The Darkening Fire: Selected Poems, 1945–68, 1975; The Unwavering Eye: Selected Poems, 1969–75; Uncollected Poems, 1935–59, 1976; A Wild Peculiar Joy: Selected Poems, 1945–82, 1982; Final Reckoning: Poems 1982–86, 1987; Fornalux: Selected Poems, 1928–90, 1992. Other: Engagements: The Prose of Irving Layton, 1972; Taking Sides: The Collected Social and Political Writings, 1977; Waiting for the Messiah: A Memoir, 1985; Wild Gooseberries: The Selected Letters of Irving Layton, 1989; Irving Layton and Robert Creeley: The Complete Correspondence, 1953–78, 1990. Editor: Various anthologies. *Contributions to:* Many publications. *Honours:* Governor-General's Award for Poetry, 1959; First Prize, Prix Litteraire de Québec, 1963; Centennial Medal, 1967; Doctor of Civil Laws, Bishop's University, 1970; Officer of the Order of Canada, 1976; DLitt, Concordia University, 1976, York University, Toronto, 1976; Canada Council Arts Award, 1979–81; Petrarch Award for Poetry, Italy, 1993. *Address:* c/o McClelland & Stewart, 481 University Ave, Toronto, Ontario M5G 2E9, Canada.

LAZARUS, Arnold (Leslie); b. 20 Feb. 1914, Revere, Massachusetts, USA. Writer; Poet. m. Keo Felker, 24 July 1938, 2 s., 2 d. *Education:* BA, University of Michigan, 1935; BS, Middlesex Medical School, 1937; MA, 1939, PhD, 1957, University of California, Los Angeles. *Publications:* Entertainments and Valedictions, 1970; Harbrace Adventures in Literature (ed. with R Lowell and E Hardwick), 1970; Modern English (ed. with others), 1970; A Suit of Four, 1973; The Indiana Experience, 1977; Beyond Graustark (with Victor H Jones), 1981; Glossary of Literature and Composition (ed. with H Wendell Smith), 1983; Best of George Ade (ed.), 1985; Some Light: New and Selected Verse, 1988; A George Jean Nathan Reader (ed.), 1990. *Contributions to:* Numerous periodicals. *Honours:* Ford Foundation Fellow, 1954; Kemper McComb Award, 1976. *Memberships:* Acad. of American Poets; American Society for Theatre Research; Comparative Literature Asscn; MLA; Poetry Society of America. *Address:* 709 Chopin Dr., Sunnyvale, CA 94087, USA.

LAZARUS, Henry. See: SLAVITT, David R(ytman).

LE GUIN, Ursula K(roeber); b. 21 Oct. 1929, Berkeley, CA, USA. Writer; Poet. m. Charles A Le Guin, 1953, 3 c. *Education:* BA, Radcliffe College, 1951; MA, Columbia University, 1952. *Publications:* Fiction: Rocannon's World, 1966; Planet of Exile, 1966; City of Illusion, 1967; A Wizard of Earthsea, 1968; The Left Hand of Darkness, 1969; The Tombs of Atuan, 1970; The Lathe of Heaven, 1971; The Farthest Shore, 1972; The Dispossessed: An Ambiguous Utopia, 1974; The Word for World is Forest, 1976; Very Far Away From Anywhere Else, 1976; Malafrena, 1979; The Beginning Place, 1980; The Eye of the Heron, 1983; Always Coming Home, 1985; Tehanu: The Last Book of Earthsea, 1990; The Telling, 2000. Story Collections: The Wind's Twelve Quarters, 1975; Orsinian Tales, 1976; The Compass Rose, 1982; Buffalo Gals, 1987; Searoad, 1991; A Fisherman of the Inland Sea, 1994; Four Ways to Forgiveness, 1995; Unlocking the Air, 1996. Poetry: Wild Angels, 1974; Walking in Cornwall, 1976; Tillai and Tylissos (with Theodora Kroeber), 1979; Hard Words, 1981; In the Red Zone, 1983; Wild Oats and Fireweed, 1988; No Boats, 1992; Blue Moon Over Thurman Street, 1993; Going Out with Peacocks, 1994; The Twins, The Dream/Las Gemelas, El Sueno (with Diana Bellessi), 1997; Sixty Odd, 1999. Non-Fiction: Dancing at the Edge of the World, 1989; The Language of the Night, revised edn, 1992; Steering the Craft, 1998. Editor: Nebula Award Stories XI, 1977; Interfaces (with Virginia Kidd), 1980; Edges (with Virginia Kidd), 1980; The Norton Book of Science Fiction (with Brian Attebery and Karen Fowler), 1993. Other: Lao Tzu: Tao Te Ching: A Book About the Way and the Power of the Way (trans.), 1977; 12 children's books, 1979–2000. *Honours:* Boston Globe-Horn Book Award, 1968; Hugo Awards, 1969, 1973, 1974, 1975, 1988; Nebula Awards, 1969, 1975, 1975, 1990, 1996; Newbery Silver Medal, 1972; National Book Award, 1972; Locus Awards, 1973, 1984, 1995, 1996; Jupiter Awards, 1975, 1976; Lewis Carroll Shelf Award, 1979; Gandalf Award, 1979; Janet Heidinger Kafka Prize, 1986; Prix Lectures – Jeunesse,

1987; International Fantasy Award, 1989; Pushcart Prize, 1991; Harold Versell Award, American Acad. and Institute of Arts and Letters, 1991; H. L. Davis Readers Award, 1992; Asimov's Readers Award, 1995; Theodore Sturgeon Award, 1995; James Triptree Jr Awards, 1995, 1996, 1997; Robert Kirsch/Los Angeles Times Award, 2000. *Address:* PO Box 10541, Portland, OR 97296, USA.

LE HEGARAT, Irene; b. 25 Dec. 1923, Halden, Norway. Poet. *Education:* University of Götebirgm 1964–66; Foreningen Nordens Institute, 1966–69. *Publications:* Stenspiror/Stone Spires; In the World; Under Vintergatan; Tunnlarna. *Contributions to:* Anthologies and periodicals. *Memberships:* Parnassus of World Poets, hon. dir; Swedish Writers Foundation.

LE PLASTRIER, Robert. See: WARNER, Francis.

LEADER, Mary; b. 9 Jan. 1948, Pawnee, OK, USA. Poet. m. Neal Leader, divorced, 1 s., 1 d. *Education:* BA, 1975, JD, 1980, University of Oklahoma; MFA, Warren Wilson College, 1991; ABD, Brandeis University. *Publication:* Red Signature, 1997. *Contributions to:* Reviews, quarterlies and journals. *Address:* 916 Oakbrooke Dr., Norman, OK 73072, USA.

LEALE, B(arry) C(avendish); b. 1 Sept. 1930, Ashford, Middlesex, England. Poet. *Publications:* Under a Glass Sky, 1975; Preludes, 1977; Leviathan and Other Poems, 1984; The Colours of Ancient Dreams, 1984. *Contributions to:* Anthologies and periodicals. *Address:* Flat E10, Peabody Estate, Wild St, London WC2B 4AH, England.

LEALMAN, Brenda; b. 12 June 1939, West Yorkshire, England. Religious Educator; Poet. *Education:* BA, University of Birmingham; University of London. *Appointments:* Religious Education Teacher, Staffordshire, 1963–69; Head of Dept, Collegiate School, Leicester, 1970–79; National Religious Education Adviser, Christian Education Movement, 1979–92; Fellow, 1990–92, Warden, 1992–96, Westhill College, Birmingham; School Inspector, 1994–. *Publications:* The Image of Life; Knowing and Unknowing; The Mystery of Creation; Nought at the Pole, 1997. *Contributions to:* Envoi Summer Anthology; Studia Mystica. *Honours:* First Prize, Resurgence Writing Competition; Guest Lecturer, Theological College, Pangnirtung, Baffin Island, 1987; Prize, Bridport Poetry Competition, 1998; Runner-Up, Staple Open Poetry Competition, 1998. *Membership:* Poetry Society. *Address:* Flat 5, 158 London Rd, Leicester LE2 1ND, England.

LEBIODA, Dariusz Thomas, (Michael Podhorodecki, Marek Rosenbaum); b. 23 April 1958, Bydgoszcz, Poland. University Teacher; Writer; Poet. m. Danuta Futyma, 25 June 1983, 1 s. *Education:* MA, Higher Pedagogical School, 1984; PhD, University of Gdańsk, 1994. *Appointment:* Teacher, Higher Pedagogical School, 1985–. *Publications:* Sucides from Under the Charles River, 1980; The Newest Testament, 1983; A Moment Before the End of the World, 1988; Cry, My Generation, 1990; Mysteries of the Life of Karol Wojtyla, 1991; The Land of Swallow, 1995; Mickiewicz: Imagination and Element, 1996. *Contributions to:* Art; Misiecznik Literacki; Literature Life; Culture; Poetry. *Honours:* Andrzej Bursa Prize; Red Rose Prize; Ianicius Prize; Stanislav Wyspianski Prize; Best Poetical Book in Poland Prize. *Memberships:* Adam Mickiewicz Literary Society; Henryk Sienkiewicz Literary Society; Polish Writers Union. *Address:* ul Osiedlowa 18/16, 85-794 Bydgoszcz, Poland.

LEBOW, Jeanne; b. 29 Jan. 1951, Richmond, Virginia, USA. Writer; Poet; Teacher; Photographer. m. (1) Howard Lebow, 1975, divorced 1981, (2) Steve Shepard, 1985. *Education:* AB, English, College of William and Mary, 1973; MA, Liberal Arts, Hollins College, 1982; PhD, English, University of Southern Mississippi, 1989; Master Naturalist Program, 1998–. *Appointments:* Instructor, Memphis State University, 1982–84; Teaching Asst, University of Southern Mississippi, 1984–87; Fulbright Lecturer in American Studies, University of Ouagadougou, Burkina Faso, 1987–88; Asst Prof., Northeast Missouri State University, 1988–92; Freelance Nature Columnist, 1991–; Adjunct Prof., 1992–93, 1994–95, Visiting Prof., 1993–94, University of Southern Mississippi. *Publication:* The Outlaw James Copeland and the Champion-Belted Empress (poems), 1991. *Contributions to:* Anthologies, books, reviews, and journals. *Honours:* National Award, Georgia State Poetry Society, 1983; Runner-up, Norma Farber First Book Award, 1991; Mississippi Humanities Council Grants, 1994, 1995. *Address:* PO Box 1295, Gautier, MS 39553, USA. *E-mail:* shepart@datasync.com.

LECKNER, Carole; b. 13 Jan. 1946, Montréal, QC, Canada. Writer; Poet; Consultant. *Education:* MA, English and Creative Writing, Concordia University, 1979. *Appointments:* Publisher, Ed., Rufanthology, 1974–80; Ed., Viewpoints magazine, 1980–81; Poet-in-the-Schools, League of Canadian Poets, 1984–; Educator, Writing Seminars, Paradigm Communications, 1984–; Faculty, School of Continuing Studies, University of Toronto, 1986–92, 1997–; Writer-in-Residence, Simon Fraser University, 1987. *Publications:* Daisies on a Whale's Back, 1972; Seasons in Transition, 1980; Cityheart, 1988; Fire Your Creativity in Action, 1997; Geometry of Life: Birth in the Eye of Creation, 1998. Other: This Time Forever (film), 1977; The Hour Has Come, choral symphony (poet-librettist), 1988. *Contributions to:* Anthologies, reviews and journals. *Honours:* Awards and grants. *Memberships:* Alliance of Canadian Cinema, Television, and Radio Artists; League of Canadian Poets; PEN; Society of Composers, Authors, and Music Publishers of Canada; Writers' Guild of Canada. *Address:* 1-270 Beatrice St, Toronto, ON M6G 3G1, Canada.

LEE, Amy Freeman; b. 3 Oct. 1914, USA. Poet. *Appointments:* Lifetime Chair., Young Pegasus Poetry Contest, San Antonio Public Library, 1984–. *Publications:* Remember Pearl Harbor, 1943; Ipso Facto, 1976; Inkwell Echoes, 1985; Parnassus of World Poetry, 1994. *Contributions to:* American Poetry Magazine; Writing Teacher Magazine; EarthKind. *Honours:* Hon. Mem., San Antonio Poets Asscn, 1985; Art and Letters Award, Friends of the San Antonio Public Library, 1985; Award for 50 Years of Service, 1991, 60 Years of Service, 2001, Young Pegasus Poetry Contest, San Antonio Public Library, 1991; Library Champion Award, San Antonio Public Library, 1996; Medal, San Antonio Chapter, National Society of Arts and Letters, 2001. *Memberships:* Poetry Society of America, 1940–; Poetry Society of Texas, 1991–; Texas Watercolor Society; Southwestern Watercolor Society; National Watercolor Society; International Art Critics Asscn; Texas Committee for the Humanities; Texas Art Education Asscn; International Women's Forum, New York. *Address:* 127 Canterbury Hill, San Antonio, TX 78209, USA.

LEE, Ann; b. 9 Aug. 1923, Idaho, USA. Librarian (retd); Poet. m. Thomas S Lee, 25 Feb. 1946, 1 s., 1 d., deceased. *Education:* BA, Scripps College, 1944; MA, University of Chicago, 1951; MA, University of California, 1966. *Publication:* Mornings. *Contributions to:* Epoch; First the Blade; Spring Harvest; Creative Writing; Michigan Quarterly Review; Encore; Christian Century; Small Pond; Mongoose; Poet Lore; Writer; Poetry Today; Stone Country; Herald Press Publications. *Memberships:* Acad. of American Poets; Valley Poets; California State Poetry Society; Chaparral Poets. *Address:* 520 W Colorado Ave, No. 13, Glendora, CA 91740, USA.

LEE, Byung Suk; b. 30 May 1938, Korea. Buddhist Priest; Poet. *Education:* Korea Air and Correspondence University; Dong University. *Appointments:* Received Commandments of Buddhism; Resident Priest, Yon Kook Sa Temple. *Publications:* Korea Buddhist Priests Poems, Vols I-IV; A Stone of the World Beyond; A Dream Lane to the Moon. *Contributions to:* Modern Literature; Poetic Literature; Modern Poetic Science; Monthly Literature; South Poems; Friends; Album of International Poets; World Poetry; Laurel Leaves Asiatic Poems Collections. *Memberships:* Korean Literature Asscn; Korean Buddhist Monk Poets Asscn; Pusan Korea Affairs of UPLI; Tagore Institute of Creative Writing International. *Address:* Chun Ryong Sa Temple, 130 Cho Jang Dong, Pusan 602 040, Korea.

LEE, Dennis Beynon; b. 31 Aug. 1939, Toronto, Ontario, Canada. Poet; Writer. m. (1), 1 s., 1 d., (2) Susan Perly, 1985. *Education:* BA, 1962, MA, 1965, University of Toronto. *Appointments:* Lecturer, University of Toronto, 1963–67; Ed., House of Anasi Press, 1967–72; Consulting Ed., Macmillan of Canada, 1972–78; Poetry Ed., McClelland and Stewart, 1981–84. *Publications:* Poetry: Kingdom of Absence, 1967; Civil Elegies, 1972; The Gods, 1979; The Difficulty of Living on Other Planets, 1998; Riffs, 1993; Nightwatch: New and Selected Poems, 1968–96, 1996. Children's Poetry: Wiggle to the Laundromat, 1970; Alligator Pie, 1974; Nicholas Knock, 1974; Garbage Delight, 1977; Jelly Belly, 1983; Lizzy's Lion, 1984; The Ice Cream Store, 1991. Non-Fiction: Savage Fields, 1977. *Contributions to:* Journals and magazines. *Honours:* Governor-General's Award for Poetry, 1972; Mem. of the Order of Canada, 1994. *Memberships:* PEN, Canada; Writers' Union of Canada. *Address:* c/o Westwood Creative Artists, 10 St Mary St, No. 510, Toronto, Ontario M4Y 1P9, Canada.

LEE, Hamilton; b. 10 Oct. 1921, Zhouxian, Shandong, China. Prof. Emeritus; Poet; Writer. m. Jean C Chang, 24 Aug. 1945, 1 s., 3 d. *Education:* BS, Beijing Normal University, 1948; MA, University of Minnesota, 1958; DEd, Wayne State University, Detroit, 1964. *Appointments:* Teacher of English, High Schools, Taiwan, 1948–56; Research Assoc., Wayne State University, Detroit, 1958–64; Visiting Prof. of Chinese Literature, Seton Hall University, summer, 1964; Asst Prof., Moorhead State University, 1964–65; Visiting Scholar, Harvard University, 1965 and Summer 1966; Assoc. Prof., University of Wisconsin at La Crosse, 1965–66; Prof., 1966–84, Prof. Emeritus, 1984–, East Stroudsburg University, Pennsylvania; Visiting Fellow, Princeton University, 1976–78. *Publications:* Readings in Instructional Technology, 1970; Relection (poems), 1989; Revelation (poems), 1991. *Contributions to:* Numerous anthologies, journals, and literary magazines. *Honours:* Many poetry contest awards; Ed.'s Choice, National Library of Poetry, 1994. *Memberships:* Acad. of American Poets; Distinguished Mem., Mem. of Advisory Panel, International Society of Poets; Poetry Society of America; Pennsylvania Poetry Society; World Literary Acad.; fellow, World Future Society. *Address:* 1141 Kelvington Way, Lilburn, GA 30047, USA.

LEE, James Alan; b. 4 Oct. 1958, Windber, Pennsylvania, USA. Writer; Poet; Ed. *Education:* University of Pittsburgh at Johnstown, 1976–78. *Appointments:* Contributing or Asst Ed., Scavengers NL, 1988–, Pillow Talk, 1989, Dark Side, 1990. *Contributions to:* Anthologies and magazines. *Memberships:* Pennwriters; Southern Alleghenies Writers Guild, secretary-treasurer. *Address:* 801 26th St, Windber, PA 15963, USA.

LEE, Jin Ho, (Cheon-Dung); b. 5 April 1937, Choong Joo, Korea. Prof.; Poet. m., 2 s., 1 d. *Education:* Dept of Korean Language and Linguistics, Cheong Joo University, 1964. *Appointments:* Elementary School Teacher, various schools, 1957–99; Principal, Noo Won Elementary School, Seoul, 1999–. *Publications:* Flower Festival, 1972; Longitude and Latitude, 1974; In My Thought, 1976; Better, Much Better, 1978; New Mind, 1980; A Child Revolving the Earth, 1986; What are in the Rooms?, 2000. *Contributions to:* The Monthly Children's Literature; Literature 21; So-Nyum-Hankwk-Ibo. *Honours:* Han Jung Don Children's Literature Award, 1979; Korea Children's Literature Writer's Award, 1989; Korea Children's Culture Award, 1997; Grand Prix of Korea Children's Song, 2000. *Memberships:* International PEN Club; Pres., Central Children's Literature; Pres., Teacher Literature; Board Mem., Korean Language Education. *Address:* 415 38 Beon Dong, Gan Book Goo, Seoul, Korea.

LEE, Lance (Wilds); b. 25 Aug. 1942, New York, NY, USA. Dramatist; Poet; Writer; Ed. m. Jeanne Barbara Hutchings, 30 Aug. 1962, 2 d. *Education:* Boston University; BA, Brandeis University, 1964; MFA, Playwriting and Dramatic Literature, Yale School of Drama, 1967. *Appointments:* Lecturer, University of Bridgeport, 1967–68; Asst Prof., University of California at Los Angeles, 1971–73, California State University at Northridge, 1981–; Instructor, Southern Connecticut State College, 1968; Senior Lecturer, Asst Prof., University of Southern California at Los Angeles, 1968–71. *Publications:* Fox, Hound and Huntress (play), 1973; Time's Up (play), 1979; The Understructure of Screenwriting (with Ben Brady), 1988; Wrestling with The Angel (poems), 1990; A Poetics for Screenwriters, 2001; Second Chances (novel), 2001; Time's Up and Other Plays, 2001; Becoming Human (poems), 2001. *Contributions to:* Reviews, quarterlies, journals, and periodicals, in England and the US. *Honours:* Arts at the Theatre Foundation Fellowship, 1967; University of Southern California Research and Publication Grants, 1970, 1971; Rockefeller Foundation Grant, Office for Advanced Drama Research, 1971; Theatre Development Fund Grant, 1976; National Endowment for the Arts Fellowship, 1976; Squaw Valley Scholarships in Poetry, 1982, 1983; Port Townsend Writers Conference Scholarship in Poetry, 1985. *Memberships:* Acad. of American Poets; Poetry Society of America; PEN. *Address:* c/o Reece Halsey Agency, 8733 Sunset Blvd, Los Angeles, CA 90069, USA.

LEE, Li-Young; b. 19 Aug. 1957, Jakarta, Indonesia. Poet. m. Donna Lee, 25 Nov. 1978, 2 c. *Education:* University of Pittsburgh, 1975–79; University of Arizona, 1979–80; State University of New York at Brockport, 1980–81. *Publications:* Rose, 1986; The City in Which I Love You, 1990; The Winged Seed: A Remembrance, 1995. *Honours:* Delmore Schwartz Memorial Poetry Award, New York University, 1986; Ludwig Vogelstein Foundation Fellowship, 1987; Mrs Giles Whiting Foundation Writer's Award, 1988; Lamont Poetry Selection, Acad. of American Poets, 1990. *Address:* c/o Simon and Schuster, 1230 Avenue of the Americas, New York, NY 10020, USA.

LEE, Mary. See: GOWLAND Mary Lee.

LEE, Paul; b. 23 Feb. 1950, Yesan, Choongnam, Korea (Naturalized US citizen, 1986). Electrical Engineer; Poet; Writer; Trans.; Publisher; Ed. m. Lisa Park, 28 May 1994, 1 d. *Education:* BS, Electrical Engineering, 1975, Graduate Studies, 1978–80, Inha University; University of Southern California at Los Angeles, 1981; University of California at Los Angeles, 1981, 1989; Fullerton College, 1983–84; BA, English, California State University at Los Angeles, 1995. *Appointments:* Electrical Engineer, California Dept of Transportation, 1981–; Principal, Korean School of Southern California, Peninsula, 1986–88; Pres., Eastwind Press, 1991–; Publisher and General Ed., Modern Poetry, 1996–. *Publications:* Desert Moon, 1989; Opening a New Horizon, 1989; Korea's Freedom Poetry, 1989; Literature/LA, 1990; Overseas Land, 1990; The Power of a Flower, 1993; Looking at Hanbit Tower, 1996. Other: Several trans. *Contributions to:* Many anthologies, reviews, journals, and periodicals. *Honours:* Korean-American Christian Literature Award in Poetry, 1986; Echo Literary Prizes in Poetry, 1987, 1989; Ed.'s Choice Award, North American Open Poetry Contest, 1989; Mona O'Connor Memorial Poetry Prizes, 1989, 1991. *Memberships:* Acad. of American Poets; Korean-Writers' Asscn; Korean Literary Writers' Asscn; Modern Poetry Asscn; Modern Poets Asscn; Poetry Society of America; Sijo Society of America; Taejon Literary Writers' Asscn. *Address:* c/o Modern Poetry/Eastwind Press, PO Box 348, Los Angeles, CA 90053, USA.

LEE, Rosie. See: HALEY, Patricia.

LEE, Terry. See: ARMSTRONG, Terry Lee.

LEE, (William) David; b. 13 Aug. 1944, Matador, Texas, USA. Poet; Prof. of English. m. Jan M Lee, 13 Aug. 1971, 1 s., 1 d. *Education:* BA, Colorado State University, 1967; Idaho State University, 1970; PhD, University of Utah, 1973. *Appointments:* Prof. of English, 1971–, Chair, 1973–82, Acting Chair, 1984–85, Dept of English, Head, 1987–, Dept of Language and Literature, Southern Utah University; Poetry Ed., Weber Studies, 1986–; John Neihardt Distinguished Lectureships, State of Nebraska, 1990, 1996; First Poet Laureate, State of Utah, 1997. *Publications:* The Porcine Legacy, 1978; Driving and Drinking, 1979; Shadow Weaver, 1984; The Porcine Canticles, 1984; Paragonah Canyon, Autumn, 1990; Day's Work, 1990; My Town, 1995; Covenants, 1996; The Fish,

1997; The Wayburne Pig, 1998; A Legacy of Shadows: Poems 1979–1999, 1999. *Contributions to:* Many anthologies, reviews, quarterlies, journals, and magazines. *Honours:* National Endowment for the Arts Fellowship, 1985; First Place, Poetry, Creative Writing Competition, 1988, Publication Prize, 1989, Utah Arts Council; Outstanding Utah Writer, Utah Endowment for the Humanities and National Council of Teachers of English, 1990; Governor's Award for Lifetime Achievement, Utah, 1994; Western States Book Award, 1995; Mountain and Plain Booksellers Award, 1995; Gov.'s Award in the Humanities, 2001; Bronze Minuteman Award for Lifetime Service to State and Nation, 2000. *Memberships:* National Foundation for Advancement of the Arts, board of dirs, 1996–; Western States Foundation; Writers at Work, board of advisers, 1993–. *Address:* c/o Dept of Language and Literature, Southern Utah University, Cedar City, UT 84720, USA.

LEGAGNEUR, Serge; b. 10 Jan. 1937, Jeremie, Haiti. Prof. of French Literature; Writer; Poet. *Publications:* Textes Interdits; Textes en croix; Le Crabe; Inalterable Glyphes; Dialogue d'île en île, 1996; Poèmes Choisis, 1997. *Contributions to:* Lettres et Ecritures; Passe Partout; Estuaire; Nouvelle Optique; Possibles; Mot pout Mot; Nouvelliste; Haiti Litteraire; Le Matin; Sapriphage; Encres Vagabondes. *Honour:* Gov.-Gen.'s Literary Awards Finalist, 1997. *Memberships:* Haiti Litteraire; Québec Writers Union; PEN International. *Address:* 3320 Blvd Gouin E, Apt 401, Montréal, QC H1H 5P3, Canada.

LEGGETT, Andrew Alfred George; b. 25 April 1962, Brisbane, Qld, Australia. Psychiatrist; Poet; Writer. 1 s., 1 d., 1 step-s. *Education:* MBBS, Queensland; FRANZCP. *Publications:* Old Time Religion and Other Poems, 1998. *Contributions to:* Numerous reviews, quarterlies, journals and magazines in Australia, the UK and USA. *Honour:* Mem., Queensland State of Origin performance poetry team, 1993–95. *Memberships:* Fellowship of Australian Writers; Poetry Society, UK; Poets' Union, Australia; Queensland Writers Centre. *Address:* PO Box 5389, West End, Qld 4101, Australia.

LEHMAN, David (Cary); b. 11 June 1948, New York, NY, USA. Writer; Poet; Ed. m. Stefanie Green, 2 Dec. 1978, 1 s. *Education:* BA, 1970, PhD, 1978, Columbia University; BA, MA, 1972, University of Cambridge. *Appointments:* Instructor, Brooklyn College of the City University of New York, 1975–76; Asst Prof., Hamilton College, Clinton, New York, 1976–80; Fellow, Society for the Humanities, Cornell University, 1980–81; Lecturer, Wells College, Aurora, New York, 1981–82; Book Critic and Writer, Newsweek, 1983–89; Series Ed., The Best American Poetry, 1988–, Poets on Poetry, 1994–; Editorial Adviser in Poetry, W W Norton & Co, 1990–93. *Publications:* Some Nerve, 1973; Day One, 1979; Beyond Amazement: New Essays on John Ashbery (ed.), 1980; James Merrill: Essays in Criticism (ed.), 1983; An Alternative to Speech, 1986; Ecstatic Occasions, Expedient Forms: 65 Leading Contemporary Poets Select and Comment on Their Poems (ed.), 1987; Twenty Questions, 1988; The Perfect Murder: A Study in Detection, 1989; Operation Memory, 1990; The Line Forms Here, 1992; Signs of the Times: Deconstruction and the Fall of Paul de Man, 1992; The Best American Poetry (ed. with Charles Simic), 1992; The Best American Poetry (ed. with Louise Glück), 1993; The Big Question, 1995; Valentine Place, 1996. *Contributions to:* Anthologies, newspapers, reviews and journals. *Honours:* Acad. of American Poets Prize, 1974; Ingram Merrill Foundation Grants, 1976, 1982, 1984; National Endowment for the Humanities Grant, 1979; National Endowment for the Arts Fellowship, 1987; American Acad. of Arts and Letters Fellowship, 1990; Lila Wallace-Reader's Digest Fund Writers Award, 1991–94. *Address:* 900 West End Ave, No. 14E, New York, NY 10025, USA.

LEHMAN, Geoffrey (John); b. 20 June 1940, Sydney, NSW, Australia. Lawyer; Poet. m. 1981, 3 s., 2 d. *Education:* BA, LLM, University of Sydney. *Appointments:* Partner, Price Waterhouse; Lecturer in Law, University of New South Wales. *Publications:* The Ilex Tree (with Les Murray), 1967; A Voyage of Lions and Other Poems, 1970; Conversation with a Rider, 1972; Selected Poems, 1975; Ross' Poems, 1978; Children's Games, 1990; Spring Forest, 1992. Other: Ed. or Co-Ed., anthologies. *Contributions to:* Various publications. *Honours:* Grace Levin Prizes, 1967, 1981. *Membership:* Australia Council Literature Board, 1982–85. *Address:* c/o Curtis Brown Pty Ltd, 27 Union St, Paddington, NSW 2021, Australia.

LEIH, Grace Janet, (Mario Edlosi, Helen Forelle); b. 27 Jan. 1936, USA. Poet; Writer; Publisher. m. John Maxwell Jeffords, 2 Dec. 1955, divorced 1968, 1 s., 2 d. *Education:* New York State College for Teachers; Augustana College, Sioux Falls, South Dakota; Memphis State University. *Publications:* The Pasque Petals Index, 1987; Publication Indexing: A Writer's Guide to Inventory (pamphlet), 1989; When Medicine Failed, 1998; As Mario Edlosi: Which Way the Wind Blows, 1979, Shouting to the Wind, 1996, The Windmill, three vols, 1996; As Helen Forelle: The Story of Mortimer Troll (children's poems), 1981; Conversations in a Clinic (pamphlet), 1981; If Men Got Pregnant, Abortion Would be a Sacrament, 1982; Pearls Among the Swine (poems), 1990; A Classical Garden (poems), 1996; Under the Gun (poems), 1997. *Contributions to:* Various publications. *Honour:* Several honourable mentions. *Memberships:* Poet's House; South Dakota Poetry Society. *Address:* PO Box 164, Canton, SD 57013, USA.

LEITHAUSER, Brad; b. 27 Feb. 1953, Detroit, Michigan, USA. Poet; Writer m Mary Jo Salter, 1980, 1 d. *Education:* BA, 1975, JD, 1980, Harvard University. *Appointments:* Research Fellow, Kyoto Comparative Law Center 1980–83; Visiting Writer, Amherst College, 1984–85; Lecturer, Mount Holyoke College, 1987–88. *Publications:* Poetry: Hundreds of Fireflies, 1982; A Seaside Mountain: Eight Poems from Japan, 1985; Cats of the Temple, 1986; Between Leaps: Poems 1972–1985, 1987; The Mail from Anywhere: Poems, 1990. Fiction: The Line of Ladies, 1975; Equal Distance, 1985; Hence, 1989 Seaward, 1993. Non-Fiction: Penchants & Places: Essays and Criticism, 1995. Editor: The Norton Book of Ghost Stories, 1994; No Other Book, 1999. *Honours:* Harvard University-Acad. of American Poets Prizes, 1973, 1975; Harvard University McKim Garrison Prizes, 1974, 1975; Amy Lowell Traveling Scholarship, 1981–82; Guggenheim Fellowship, 1982–83; Lavan Younger Poets Award, 1983; John D. and Catherine T. MacArthur Foundation Fellowship, 1983–87. *Address:* c/o Alfred A. Knopf Inc, 299 Park Ave, New York, NY 10171, USA.

LEMASTER, J(immie) R(ay); b. 29 March 1934, Pike County, Ohio, USA. Prof. of English; Poet; Writer; Ed. m. Wanda May Ohnesorge, 21 May 1966, 1 s., 2 d. *Education:* BS, English, Defiance College, 1959; MA, English, 1962, PhD, English, 1970, Bowling Green State University, Ohio. *Appointments:* Faculty, Defiance College, 1962–77; Prof. of English and Dir of American Studies, Baylor University, 1977–; Assoc. Ed., 1988–90, Ed., 1992–96, JASAT (Journal of the American Studies Asscn of Texas). *Publications:* Poetry: The Heart is a Gypsy, 1967; Children of Adam, 1971; Weeds and Wildflowers, 1975; First Person, Second, 1983; Purple Bamboo, 1986; Journey to Beijing, 1992. Other: Jesse Stuart: A Reference Guide, 1979; Jesse Stuart: Kentucky's Chronicler-Poet, 1980; The New Mark Twain Handbook (with E Hudson Long), 1985. Editor: Poets of the Midwest, 1966; The World of Jesse Stuart: Selected Poems, 1975; Jesse Stuart: Essays on His Work (with Mary Washington Clarke), 1977; Jesse Stuart: Selected Criticism, 1978; Jesse Stuart on Education, 1992; The Mark Twain Encyclopedia (with James D Wilson), 1993; Walt Whitman: An Encyclopedia (with Donald D Kummings), 1998. *Honours:* South and West Inc Publishers Award, 1970; Ohio Poet of the Year, 1976; Hon. Doctor of Letters, Defiance College, 1988; Outstanding Reference Source Citation, American Library Asscn, 1993. *Memberships:* American Studies Asscn; Conference of College Teachers of English; Jesse Stuart Foundation, board of dirs, 1989–99; Mark Twain Circle of America; MLA. *Address:* 201 Harrington Ave, Waco, TX 76706, USA.

LENGYEL, Cornel Adam, (Cornel Adam); b. 1 Jan. 1915, Fairfield, CT, USA. Historian; Poet; Ed. m. Teresa Murphy Delaney, 10 July 1933, 3 s., 1 d. *Education:* DLitt, Taiwan. *Appointments:* Visiting Prof., California State University of Sacramento, 1962–63; Guest Lecturer, Hamline University, 1968–69, Massachusetts Institute of Technology, 1969; Founder-Exec. Ed., Dragons Teeth Press, 1969–. *Publications:* Various poems. *Contributions to:* Anthologies and other publications. *Honours:* Albert M Bender Award; Maritime Poetry Award; Maxwell Anderson Award; Castagnola Award; National Endowment for the Arts Award. *Memberships:* American Asscn of University Profs; MLA; PEN; Poetry Society of America. *Address:* El Dorado National Forest, 7700 Wentworth Springs Rd, Georgetown, CA 95634, USA.

LENHART, Gary; b. 15 Oct. 1947, Newark, Ohio, USA. Poet; Writer. m. Louise Hamlin, 1 d. *Education:* BA, Siena College, 1969; MA, University of Wisconsin, 1973. *Publications:* One at a Time, 1983; Light Heart, 1991; Father and Son Night, 1999. *Contributions to:* Anthologies and other publications. *Address:* 166 Beaver Meadow Rd, Norwich, VT 05055, USA.

LENIER, Sue; b. 9 Oct. 1957, Birmingham, England. Playwright; Poet; Solicitor. Education: MA, Clare College, Cambridge University, 1980; University of California, 1981–82; Drama Studio, London, 1982–83. *Publications:* Swansongs; Rain Following. *Contributions to:* Lines Review; Staple; New Prospects; Washington Post; New York Times. *Honours:* Harkness Fellowship; London Writers Competition Winner. *Memberships:* Playwrights Co-operative; New Playwrights Trust. *Address:* 24 Hunter Close, East Boldon, Tyne and Wear NE36 OTB, England.

LEON BASCUR, Maria Del Carmen; b. 14 Aug. 1944, Cabildo, Chile. Newsreader; Poet; Ed. m. 20 Aug. 1973, 1 s., 2 d. *Publications:* Several anthologies. *Contributions to:* Anthologies and other publications. *Honours:* Several First Place Awards in Poetry; Ruben Dario Medal; Gabriela Mistral Medal. *Membership:* Sociedad de Escritores de Chile. *Address:* Avda Santa Rosa 8171, Apto 207, Santiago, Chile.

LEONARD, Tom, (Thomas Anthony Leonard); b. 22 Aug. 1944, Glasgow, Scotland. Writer; Poet. m. Sonya Maria O'Brien, 24 Dec. 1971, 2 s. *Education:* MA, Glasgow University, 1976. *Appointments:* Writer-in-Residence, Renfrew District Libraries, 1986–89, Glasgow University/Strathclyde University, 1991–92, Bell College of Technology, 1993–94. *Publications:* Intimate Voices (writing), 1965–83, 1984; Situations Theoretical and Contemporary, 1986; Radical Renfrew (ed.), 1990; Nora's Place, 1990; Places of the Mind: The Life and Work of James Thomson 'BV' Cafe, 1993; Reports From the Present: Selected Works 1982–94, 1995. *Contributions to:* Edinburgh Review. *Honour:*

Joint Winner, Saltire Scottish Book of the Year Award, 1984. *Address:* 56 Eldon St, Glasgow G3 6NJ, Scotland.

LEONG, Choy Yin, (Simon Leong); b. 5 Dec. 1938, Kuala Lumpur, Malaysia. Poet. m. Teoh Kim Lean, 3 Feb. 1966, 2 s. *Education:* University of Cambridge. *Publications:* As I See the World Today, 1994; We Are The World, 1997. *Contributions to:* Anthologies and periodicals. *Honours:* Ed.'s Choice Awards, National Library of Poetry, 1993–96. *Memberships:* International Society of Poets; Poetry Society. *Address:* 56 Jln 35-26 Timn Sri Tampal, Rampal Court J Blk, Setapak 53300 Kuala Lumpur, Malaysia.

LEONG, Russell, (Wallace Lin); b. 7 Sept. 1950, San Francisco, CA, USA. Writer; Poet; Ed. *Education:* BA, San Francisco State College, 1972; Graduate Studies, National Taiwan University, 1973–74; MFA, University of California at Los Angeles, 1990. *Appointments:* Asian American Studies Center, University of California at Los Angeles; Ed., Amerasia Journal. *Publications:* Fiction: Phoenix Eyes and Other Stories, 2000. Poetry: The Country of Dreams and Dust, 1993. Non-Fiction: A History Reclaimed: An Annotated Bibliography of Chinese Language Materials on the Chinese of America (ed. with Jean Pang Yip), 1986; Frontiers of Asian American Studies; Writing, Research, and Criticism (ed. with G. Nomura, R. Endo and S. Sumida), 1989; Moving the Image: Independent Asian Pacific American Media Arts, 1970–1990 (ed.), 1991; Los Angeles—Struggle toward Multiethnic Community: Asian America, African America, and Latino Perspectives (ed. with Edward T. Chang), 1995; Asian American Sexuality: Dimensions of the Gay and Lesbian Experience, 1996. *Contributions to:* Anthologies and periodicals. *Address:* c/o Asian American Studies Center, University of California at Los Angeles, Los Angeles, CA 90024, USA.

LEONHARDT, Joyce LaVon; b. 17 Dec. 1927, Aurora, Nebraska, USA. Poet. *Education:* BS, Union College, Lincoln, 1952. *Appointments:* High School Teacher, 1952–76; Junior College Instructor, 1981–90. *Contributions to:* Several books of poems. *Honours:* Honourable Mention Certificates; Golden Poet; Silver Poet. *Membership:* World of Poetry. *Address:* 1824 Atwood St, Longmont, CO 80501, USA.

LEOTTA, Guido; b. 2 May 1957, Faenza, Italy. Writer; Poet; Publisher. *Education:* Accountant's Diploma. *Appointments:* Pres., Tratti/Mobydick Cultural Co-operative and Publishing House, 1987; Author and Co-ordinator, Tratti Folk Festival, 1989–2000. *Publications:* Sacsaphone (collected novels), 1981; Anatre (short stories), 1989; Strategie di Viaggio Nel Non Amore (poems), 1992; Il Bambino Ulisse (children's stories), 1995; Passo Narrabile (novel), 1997; Leviatamo (poems), 1999; Doppio Diesis (novel), 2000. *Contributions to:* Anthologies and magazines. *Honours:* Premio Leonforte for Children's Stories, 1991; Laoghaire Poetry Prize, Ireland, 1994; Premio Selezione Bancarellino, 1996. *Address:* Corso Mazzini, 85 48018 Faenza RA, Italy.

LERNER, Arthur; b. 10 Jan. 1915, Chicago, IL, USA. Prof. (retd); Psychologist; Poet; Writer. m. Matilda Fisher. *Education:* Roosevelt University, Chicago, 1942; Northwestern University, 1946; University of Southern California at Los Angeles, 1953, 1968. *Appointments:* Prof., Los Angeles City College, 1957–83; Lecturer, University of California at Los Angeles, 1970–74; Dir, Poetry Therapy, Woodview Calabasas Hospital, 1971–86. *Publications:* Several poems. *Contributions to:* Various reviews and journals. *Memberships:* Authors Guild; PEN; Poetry Society of America. *Address:* 520 S Burnside Ave, No. 11C, Los Angeles, CA 90036, USA.

LERNER, Laurence (David); b. 12 Dec. 1925, Cape Town, South Africa (British citizen). Prof. (retd); Poet; Writer. m. Natalie Winch, 15 June 1948, 4 s. *Education:* MA, University of Cape Town, 1945; BA, Pembroke College, Cambridge, 1949. *Appointments:* Lecturer, University College of the Gold Coast, 1949–53; Queen's University, 1953–62; Lecturer to Prof., University of Sussex, 1962–84; Kenan Prof., Vanderbilt University, Nashville, Tennessee, 1985–95; Several visiting professorships. *Publications:* Poems, 1955; Domestic Interior and Other Poems, 1959; The Directions of Memory: Poems 1958–63, 1964; Selves, 1969; A.R.T.H.U.R.: The Life and Opinions of a Digital Computer, 1974; The Man I Killed, 1980; A.R.T.H.U.R. and M.A.R.T.H.A., or, The Loves of the Computer, 1980; Chapter and Verse: Bible Poems, 1984; Selected Poems, 1984; Rembrandt's Mirror, 1987. Fiction: The Englishmen, 1959; A Free Man, 1968; My Grandfather's Grandfather, 1985. Play: The Experiment, 1980. Non-Fiction: The Truest Poetry, 1960; The Truthtellers: Jane Austen, George Eliot, Lawrence, 1967; The Uses of Nostalgia, 1973; An Introduction to English Poetry, 1975; Love and Marriage: Literature in its Social Context, 1979; The Frontiers of Literature, 1988; Angels and Absences, 1997; Wandering Prof., 1999. *Contributions to:* Newspapers, reviews, journals, and magazines. *Honours:* South-East Arts Literature Prize, 1979; Fellow, RSL, 1986. *Address:* Abinger, 1-B Gundreda Rd, Lewes, East Sussex BN7 1PT, England.

LESSER, Rika; b. 21 July 1953, New York, NY, USA. Poet; Trans. *Education:* BA, Yale University, 1974; University of Göteborg, 1974–75; MFA, Columbia University, 1977. *Appointments:* Visiting Lecturer, Yale University, 1976, 1978, 1987–88; Baruch College of the City University of New York, 1979; Poetry Workshop Instructor, Young Men's and Young Women's Hebrew Assocn, New York, 1982–85; Jenny McKean Moore Visiting Lecturer in English, George

Washington University, 1985–86; Master Artist-in-Residence, Atlantic Center for the Arts, New Smyrna Beach, FL, 1998; Adjunct Assoc. Prof. of Trans., Columbia University, 1998–. *Publications:* Poetry: Etruscan Things, 1983; All We Need of Hell, 1995; Growing Back: Poems, 1972–1992, 1997. Translations: 11 books, 1975–96. *Honours:* Ingram Merrill Foundation Award, 1978–79; Harold Morton Landon Trans. Prize for Poetry, Acad. of American Poets, 1982; Batchelder Award, 1990; American-Scandinavian Foundation Trans. Prize, 1992; George Bogin Memorial Award, Poetry Society of America, 1992; Swedish Writers' Foundation Award, 1995; Swedish Acad. Poetry Trans. Prize, 1996; Fulbright-Hays Senior Scholar Award, 1999; National Endowment for the Arts Fellowship, 2001. *Memberships:* Acad. of American Poets; American PEN; ASCAP; Associated Writing Programs; Poets and Writers. *Address:* 133 Henry St, Apt 5, New York, NY 11201, USA.

LESSING, Doris (May); b. 22 Oct. 1919, Kermanshah, Persia. Author. m. (1) Frank Charles Wisdom, 1939, dissolved 1943, 1 s., 1 d., (2) Gottfried Anton Nicholas Lessing, 1945, dissolved 1949, 1 s. *Publications:* Fiction: The Grass is Singing, 1950; This Was the Old Chief's Country, 1951; Martha Quest, 1952; Five, 1953; A Proper Marriage, 1954; Retreat to Innocence, 1956; Going Home, 1957; The Habit of Loving, 1957; A Ripple from the Storm, 1958; In Pursuit of the English, 1960; The Golden Notebook, 1962; A Man and Two Women, 1963; African Stories, 1964; Landlocked, 1965; The Four-Gated City, 1969; Briefing for a Descent into Hell, 1971; The Story of a Non-Marrying Man, 1972; The Summer Before the Dark, 1973; The Memoirs of a Survivor, 1974; Collected Stories, two vols, 1978; Canopus in Argos: Archives: Re Planet 5, Shikasta, 1979; The Marriages Between Zones Three, Four and Five, 1980; The Sirian Experiments, 1981; The Making of the Representative for Planet 8, 1982; Documents Relating to the Sentimental Agents in the Volyen Empire, 1983; The Diary of a Good Neighbour (as Jane Somers), 1983; If the Old Could... (as Jane Somers), 1984; The Good Terrorist, 1985; The Fifth Child, 1988; Doris Lessing Reader, 1990; London Observed, 1992; Love, Again, 1996; Playing the Game, 1996; Play With a Tiger and Other Plays, 1996; Mara and Dann: An Adventure, 1999; Ben, in the World, 2000; The Sweetest Dream, 2002. Poetry: Fourteen Poems, 1959. Non-Fiction: Under My Skin: Volume One of My Autobiography to 1949, 1994; Walking in the Shade: Volume Two of My Autobiography 1949–1962, 1997. *Honours:* Somerset Maugham Award, 1954; Austrian State Prize for European Literature, 1981; Shakespeare Prize, Hamburg, 1982; W. H. Smith Literary Award, 1986; Palermo Prize, 1987; James Tait Black Memorial Prize, 1995; Los Angeles Times Book Prize, 1995; Premio Internacional, Cataluña, 1999; Companion of Hon., 1999; Premio Príncipe de Asturias, 2001; David Cohen British Literature Prize, 2001; Hon. doctorates. *Address:* c/o Jonathan Clowes Ltd, Iron Bridge House, Bridge Approach, London NW1 8BD, England.

LETKO, Ken; b. 8 May 1953, Ashland, Wisconsin, USA. Prof. of English; Poet. *Education:* BS, University of Wisconsin at Stevens Point, 1975; MFA, 1983, MA, 1988, Bowling Green State University. *Appointments:* Lecturer, then Prof. of English, Bowling Green State University; Foreign Expert, Xian Foreign Languages University, China; Instructor in Writing and Literature, College of the Redwoods. *Publications:* Wisconversation, 1979; Shelter for Those Who Need It, 1985; All This Tangling, 1995. *Contributions to:* Greenfield Review; Cottonwood; Permafrost; Gambit. *Memberships:* Associated Writing Programs; Acad. of American Poets. *Address:* College of the Redwoods, 883 W Washington Blvd, Crescent City, CA 95531, USA.

LEVENDOSKY, Charles (Leonard); b. 4 July 1936, New York, NY, USA. Journalist; Poet. *Education:* BS, Physics, 1958, BA, Mathematics, 1960, University of Oklahoma; MA, Secondary Education, New York University, 1963. *Appointments:* Asst Prof. of English, New York University, 1967–71; Visiting Poet, Poetry-in-the-Schools Program, New York State, Georgia, New Jersey, 1971–72; Poet-in-Residence, Wyoming Council on the Arts, 1972–82; Editorial Page Ed., Casper Star-Tribune, Wyoming; Columnist, New York Times; Poet Laureate of Wyoming, 1988–96. *Publications:* Perimeters, 1970; Small Town America, 1974; Words and Fonts, 1975; Aspects of the Vertical, 1978; Distances, 1980; Wyoming Fragments, 1981; Nocturnes, 1982; Hands and Other Poems, 1986; Circle of Light, 1995. *Contributions to:* Numerous magazines and journals. *Honours:* National Endowment for the Arts Fellowship, 1974; Wyoming Governor's Award for the Arts, 1983; Silver Gavel Award, American Bar Assocn, 1994; H. L. Mencken Award, Baltimore Sun, 1994; First Amendment Award, Society of Professional Journalists, 2000. *Memberships:* Freedon to Read Foudation, American Library Assocn, 1993–2002; Citizens for the Constitution; Wyoming Centre for the Book, advisory board, 1995–98. *Address:* 714 E 22nd St, Casper, WY 82601, USA.

LEVENSON, Christopher; b. 13 Feb. 1934, London, England (Naturalized Canadian citizen, 1973). Poet; Ed.; Trans.; Educator. *Education:* University of Cambridge; University of Bristol; MA, University of Iowa, 1970. *Appointments:* Teacher, University of Münster, 1958–61, Carleton University, Ottawa, 1968–99; Ed.-in-Chief, ARC magazine, 1978–88; Founder-Dir, ARC Reading Series, Ottawa, 1981–91; Series Ed., Harbinger Poetry Series, 1995–99; Poetry Ed., Literary Review of Canada; Poetry Ed., Literary Review of Canada, 1997. *Publications:* Poetry: In Transit, 1959; Cairns, 1969; Stills, 1972; Into the Open, 1977; The Journey Back, 1978; Arriving at Night, 1986; The Return, 1986; Half Truths, 1990; Duplicities: New and Selected Poems, 1993; The Bridge, 2000;

Belvédère (trans.), 2002. Other: Seeking Heart's Solace (trans.), 1981; Light of the World (trans.), 1982; Reconcilable Differences: The Changing Face of Poetry by Canadian Men Since 1970 (ed.), 1994. *Contributions to:* Various anthologies, reviews, quarterlies, and journals. *Honours:* Eric Gregory Award, 1960; Archibald Lampman Award, 1987. *Membership:* League of Canadian Poets. *Address:* 333 St Andrew St, Ottawa, ON K1N 5G9, Canada. *E-mail:* clevenson@rogers.com.

LEVETT, John Anthony; b. 30 Oct. 1950, London, England. Librarian; Poet. m. Wendy Dawn Peters, 1 July 1972, 1 s., 1 d. *Education:* Assoc., Library Asscn, 1974. *Appointments:* Librarian, Greenwich and London; Stock Ed., Bexley Libraries, London; Service Man., Bromley Libraries. *Publications:* Changing Sides, 1983; Skedaddle, 1987; Their Perfect Lives, 1994. *Contributions to:* Periodicals, including: Encounter; Guardian; London Magazine; London Review of Books; Literary Review; New Statesman; Orbis; Poetry Review; TLS; BBC Radio; Spectator; Anthologies, including: The Droon Foundation Poetry Anthology, 1980; The Gregory Awards, 1980; The Orange Dove of Fyi, 1989; The Poetry Book Society Anthology, 1989; The Forward Book of Poetry, 1999; Scarring the Century, 1999; Poems of the Decade, 2001. *Honours:* New Statesman Prudence Farmer Award, 1982; Joint Winner, National Poetry Competition, Poetry Society of Great Britain, 1991; Short-listed, Whitbread Poetry Award, 1994; Also prizes in a number of International Poetry Competitions including Cheltenham, Stroud and York. *Address:* 321 Halfway St, Avery Hill, Kent DA15 8DP, England.

LEVI, Steven, (Warren Sitka); b. 9 Dec. 1948, Chicago, IL, USA. Poet; Writer. *Education:* BA, History, University of California at Davis, 1970; Teaching Credential, 1972; MA, History, San Jose State College, 1973. *Publications:* Alaskan Phantasmagoria, 1978; The Last Raven, 1979; The Phantom Bowhead, 1979; We Alaskans, 1980; Fish-Fed Maize, 1981; Our National Tapestry, 1986; A Destiny Going Sour, 1991. *Contributions to:* Numerous publications. *Address:* 8512 E Fourth St, Anchorage, AK 99504, USA.

LEVINE, Philip; b. 10 Jan. 1928, Detroit, Michigan, USA. Poet; Writer; Prof. of English (retd). m. Frances Artley, 12 July 1954, 3 s. *Education:* BA, 1950, AM, 1955, Wayne State University; MFA, University of Iowa, 1957; Studies with John Berryman, 1954. *Appointments:* Instructor, 1958–69, Prof. of English, 1969–92, California State University at Fresno; Elliston Prof. of Poetry, University of Cincinnati, 1976; Poet-in-Residence, National University of Australia, Canberra, 1978; Visiting Prof. of Poetry, Columbia University, 1978, 1981, 1984, New York University, 1984, 1991, Brown University, 1985; Chair., Literature Panel, National Endowment for the Arts, 1985; Various poetry readings. *Publications:* Poetry: On the Edge, 1961; Silent in America: Vivas for Those Who Failed, 1965; Not This Pig, 1968; 5 Detroits, 1970; Thistles: A Poem of Sequence, 1970; Pili's Wall, 1971; Red Dust, 1971; They Feed, They Lion, 1972; 1933, 1974; New Season, 1975; On the Edge and Over: Poems Old, Lost, and New, 1976; The Names of the Lost, 1976; 7 Years from Somewhere, 1979; Ashes: Poems New and Old, 1979; One for the Rose, 1981; Selected Poems, 1984; Sweet Will, 1985; A Walk with Tom Jefferson, 1988; New Selected Poems, 1991; What Work Is, 1991; The Simple Truth: Poems, 1994; The Mercy, 1995. Non-Fiction: Don't Ask (interviews), 1979; Earth, Stars, and Writers (with others), lectures, 1992; The Bread of Time: Toward an Autobiography, 1994. *Contributions to:* Many anthologies and reviews. *Honours:* Joseph Henry Jackson Award, San Francisco Foundation, 1961; National Endowment for the Arts Grants, 1969, 1976, 1981, 1987; Frank O'Hara Prizes, 1973, 1974; Award of Merit, American Acad. of Arts and Letters, 1974; Levinson Prize, 1974; Guggenheim Fellowships, 1974, 1981; Harriet Monroe Memorial Prize for Poetry, University of Chicago, 1976; Leonore Marshall Award for Best American Book of Poems, 1976; American Book Award for Poetry, 1979; National Book Critics Circle Prize, 1979; Notable Book Award, American Library Asscn, 1979; Golden Rose Award, New England Poetry Society, 1985; Ruth Lilly Award, 1987; Elmer Holmes Bobst Award, New York University, 1990; National Book Award for Poetry, 1991; Silver Medal in Poetry, Commonwealth Club of California, 1992, 2000; Pulitzer Prize in Poetry, 1995. *Memberships:* American Acad. of Arts and Letters; Acad. of American Poets, chancellor, 2000–. *Address:* 4549 N Van Ness Blvd, Fresno, CA 93704, USA.

LEWIN, Peter Carrigue; b. 28 May 1946, Lancaster, Lancashire, England. Restaurateur; Poet. m. Carolyn Ann Gee, 3 June 1967, 2 d. *Education:* Teacher's Certificate. *Appointments:* Chef and Owner, The Olde Ship Inn, Pilling; Bennet's French Bistro, Lytham St Annes. *Contributions to:* Pennine Platform 25th Anniversary Edition, 1991; Iota Magazine, 1991; Lancashire Life; Radio Lancashire; Radio Mersey; GMR; Radio Cumbria. *Membership:* Northern Asscn of Writers in Education. *Address:* Flat 2, Heeley Rd, Lytham St Annes, Lancashire FY8 2JY, England.

LEWIN, Roger A.; b. 22 Jan. 1946, Cleveland, OH, USA. Psychiatrist; Teacher; Writer; Poet. m. (1) Julia Vandivort, 11 June 1977, deceased 1988, 1 d., (2) Joan Lilienthal, 3 May 1990. *Education:* BA, magna cum laude, Harvard University; MD, Wright State University, 1981. *Appointments:* Resident, 1981–85, Psychiatrist, 1985–91, Teacher, Supervisor, 1991–, Sheppard and Enoch Pratt Hospital, Towson, Maryland; Private Practice of Psychiatry,

1981–. *Publications:* Losing and Fusing (co-author), 1992; Compassion, 1996; New Wrinkles (poems), 1996; Creative Collaboration in Psychotherapy, 1997. *Honours:* Ford Foundation Grant, 1965; Ginsburg Fellow, Group for the Advancement of Psychiatry, 1981–85. *Address:* 504 Club Lane, Towson, MD 21286, USA. *E-mail:* oaktree@home.com.

LEWIS, Bill. See: LEWIS, William Edward.

LEWIS, D(esmond) F(rancis); b. 18 Jan. 1948, Colchester, Essex, England. Poet; Writer. m. Denise Jean Woolgar, 23 May 1970, 1 s., 1 d. *Education:* BA Honours, English, Lancaster University, 1969. *Contributions to:* Hundreds of prose poems and stories in various UK and USA publications. *Address:* 7 Lloyd Ave, Coulsdon, Surrey CR5 2QS, England.

LEWIS, Elizabeth (Burton); b. 16 Nov. 1916, Toledo, IA, USA. Teacher (retd); Librarian. m. Leslie B Lewis, 6 Sept. 1939, 3 s., 2 d. *Education:* BA, Huron College, 1963; Graduate work, Mankato University, Minnesota, Minnesota University of South Dakota at Vermillion. *Appointments:* Teacher, Librarian, 1952–84. *Publications:* Songs From the Plains, 1990; Between Tears and Laughter, 1999. *Contributions to:* Anthologies and magazines. *Honours:* Great Poet, Iowa State Poet of the Year, Iowa Poetry Day, 1970; Winner, Federal Womens Club, 1978; Numerous prizes at South Dakota State Fair. *Membership:* Iowa Poetry Day Society, vice-pres. *Address:* 1018 W Ninth St, Yankton, SD 57078, USA.

LEWIS, Roger. See: LATHBURY, Roger.

LEWIS, William Edward, (Bill Lewis); b. 1 Aug. 1953, Maidstone, Kent, England. Poet; Writer; Ed.; Storyteller; Mythographer. m. Ann Frances Morris, 17 Oct. 1981. *Appointment:* Writer-in-Residence, Brighton Festival, 1985. *Publications:* Poems, 1975–83, 1983; Night Clinic, 1984; Communion, 1986; Rage Without Anger, 1987; Skyclad Christ, 1992; Paradigm Shift (ed.), 1992; Coyote Cosmos (short stories), 1994; Translation Women, 1996; The Book of North Kent Writers (co-ed.), 1996; The Wine of Connecting (poems), 1996; Intellect of the Heart, 1997; Shattered English: Complete North Kent Poems, 1998; Leaving the Autoroute (stories), 1999; Beauty is the Beast (poems), 2000. *Contributions to:* Best Horror and Fantasy, 1997, 1998; Jungewelt; Anthologies, review, and journals. *Membership:* Medway Poets, founder mem.; Stuckist Group, founder mem. *Address:* 66 Glencoe Rd, Chatham, Kent ME4 5QE, England.

LEWIS-SMITH, Anne Elizabeth, (Emily Devereaux, A McCormick, Quilla Slade); b. 14 April 1925, London, England. Poet; Writer; Ed.; Publisher. m. Peter Lewis-Smith, 17 May 1944, 1 s., 2 d. *Appointments:* Asst Ed., 1967–83, Ed., 1983–91, Envoi; Ed., Aerostat, 1973–78, British Asscn of Friends of Museums Yearbook, 1985–91; Publisher, Envoi Poets Publications, 1986–. *Publications:* Seventh Bridge, 1963; The Beginning, 1964; Flesh and Flowers, 1967; Dandelion Flavour, 1971; Dinas Head, 1980; Places and Passions, 1986; In the Dawn, 1987; Circling Sound, 1996; Feathers, Fancies and Feelings, 2000. *Contributions to:* Newspapers and magazines. *Honours:* Tissadier Diploma for Services to International Aviation; Debbie Warley Award for Services to International Aviation; Dorothy Tutin Award for Services to Poetry. *Membership:* PEN, fellow. *Address:* Pen Ffordd, Newport, Pembrokeshire SA42 0QT, Wales.

LI, Leslie; b. 21 Nov. 1945, New York, NY, USA. Writer; Dramatist; Poet. *Education:* BA, University of Michigan, 1967; Sème dégré, Alliance Francaise, 1970. *Publications:* Bittersweet, 1992; The Magic Whip, 1995. *Contributions to:* Books, newspapers, and periodicals. *Honour:* Leo Maitland Fellowship, 1992. *Address:* c/o Witherspoon Assocs, 157 W 57th St, New York, NY 10019, USA.

LI YAN; b. 28 Aug. 1954, Beijing, China. Poet; Painter; Sculptor; Publisher; Ed. *Publication:* Selected Poetry, 1990. *Contributions to:* Anthologies, reviews, quarterlies, journals, and newspapers. *Honour:* First Prize for Poetry, Assocation of Modern Chinese Literature and the Arts of North America. *Memberships:* First Line Poetry Society; Star Art Group; Today Literary Society.

LIARDET, Tim; b. 26 Sept. 1949, London, England. Poet; Critic; Tutor. m. Alison Liardet, 23 Jan. 1983, 1 s. *Education:* BA, History, University of York; PhD Studies. *Publications:* Clay Hill, 1988; Fellini Beach, 1994; Competing with the Piano Tuner, 1998. *Contributions to:* Anthologies, reviews, journals, and quarterlies in the UK and USA. *Honour:* Poetry Society Special Commendation, 1998. *Address:* 2 Powis Pl., Oswestry, Shropshire SY11 1JU, England.

LIDDY, James (Daniel Reeves); b. 1 July 1934, Dublin, Ireland. Prof. of English; Poet; Writer. *Education:* BA, 1956, MA, 1959, English Language and Literature, National University of Ireland; Barrister-at-Law, King's Inns, Dublin, 1961. *Appointments:* Visiting Lecturer, San Francisco State College, 1967–68; Visiting Asst Prof., State University of New York at Binghamton, 1969, University of Wisconsin at Parkside, 1972–73; Visiting Lecturer, Lewis and Clark College, Portland, Oregon, 1970, University College, Galway, 1973–74; Asst Prof., Denison University, Ohio, 1970–71; Lecturer, Delgado

Community College, New Orleans, 1975; Visiting Asst Prof., 1976, Lecturer and Poet-in-Residence, 1976–80, Asst Prof., 1981–82, Assoc. Prof., 1982–88, Prof. of English, 1988–, University of Wisconsin at Milwaukee. *Publications:* Poetry: In a Blue Smoke, 1964; Blue Mountain, 1968; A Life of Stephen Dedalus, 1968; A Munster Song of Love and War, 1969; Orpheus in the Ice Cream Parlour, 1975; Corca Bascin, 1977; Comyn's Lay, 1979; Moon and Starr Moments, 1982; At the Grave of Father Sweetman, 1984; A White Thought in a White Shade, 1987; In the Slovak Bowling Alley, 1990; Art is Not for Grownups, 1990; Trees Warmer Than Green: Notes Towards a Video of Avondale House, 1991; Collected Poems, 1994; Epitaphery, 1997; Gold Set Dancing, 2000. Other: Esau My Kingdom for a Drink, 1962; Patrick Kavanagh: An Introduction to His Work, 1971; Baudelaire's Bar Flowers (trans.), 1975; You Can't Jog for Jesus: Jack Kerouac as a Religious Writer, 1985; Young Men Go Walking (novella), 1986. *Contributions to:* Books and journals. *Honours:* University of Wisconsin at Parkside Teaching Award, 1973; Council of Wisconsin Writers Prize for Poetry, 1995. *Membership:* Aosdána, Irish Acad. of Arts and Letters. *Address:* c/o Dept of English and Comparative Literature, University of Wisconsin at Milwaukee, PO Box 413, Milwaukee, WI 53201, USA.

LIDDY, John; b. 11 April 1954, Ireland. Poet; Teacher. m. Pilar Gutierrez de Los Rios, 2 s. *Education:* Librarianship, University of Wales. *Appointments:* Curator's Asst, Hunt Museum, Limerick; Teacher/Librarian, Instituto Británica Madrid-Jóvenes, 1987–2001. *Publications:* Boundaries; The Angling Cot; Song of the Empty Cage; Wine and Hope/Vino y Esperanza. *Contributions to:* Irish, English, American and Spanish journals. *Memberships:* Poetry Ireland; Irish Writers Union; Irish Hispanic Society. *Address:* Archione Editorial, Ferraz 29, 1 Ext. Dcha, 28008 Madrid, Spain.

LIE, Arvid Torgeir; b. 18 Aug. 1938, Skafsaa, Norway. Poet; Writer. m. Liv Greaker, 3 s. *Education:* University of Oslo, 1959–62. *Publications:* Several works in Norwegian. *Contributions to:* Anthologies and periodicals, domestic and foreign. *Membership:* Norwegian Author's Union, literary council. *Address:* Vestlia 7, 1820 Spydeberg, Norway.

LIEBERMAN, Laurence; b. 16 Feb. 1935, Detroit, Michigan, USA. Prof. of English and Creative Writing; Poet; Writer; Ed. m. Bernice Braun, 17 June 1956, 1 s., 2 d. *Education:* BA, 1956, MA, 1958, University of Michigan; Doctoral Program, University of California, 1958–60. *Appointments:* Assoc. Prof. of English, College of the Virgin Islands, 1964–68; Assoc. Prof. of English, 1968–70, Prof. of English and Creative Writing, 1970–, University of Illinois at Urbana-Champaign; Poetry Ed., University of Illinois Press, 1971–. *Publications:* The Unblinding (poems), 1968; The Achievement of James Dickey, 1968; The Osprey Suicides (poems), 1973; Unassigned Frequencies: American Poetry in Review, 1964–77, 1977; God's Measurements, 1980; Eros at the World Kite Pageant: Poems, 1979–83, 1983; The Mural of Wakeful Sleep (poems), 1985; The Creole Mephistopheles (poems), 1990; New and Selected Poems: 1962–92, 1993; The St Kitts Monkey Feuds (poem), 1995; Beyond the Muse of Memory: Essays on Contemporary American Poets, 1995; Dark Songs: Slave House and Synagogue, 1996; Compass of the Dying (poems), 1998; The Regatta in the Skies: Selected Long Poems, 1999; Flight from the Mother Stone, 2000. *Contributions to:* Anthologies, reviews, journals, and magazines. *Honours:* Yaddo Foundation Fellowship, 1964; Illinois Arts Council Fellowship, 1981; National Endowment for the Arts Fellowship, 1986–87; Jerome J. Shestack Poetry Prize, American Poetry Review, 1986–87; Runner-up, William Carlos Williams Award, Poetry Society of America, 1997. *Memberships:* Acad. of American Poets; Associated Writing Programs; Poetry Society of America. *Address:* 1304 Eliot Dr., Urbana, IL 61801, USA.

LIEBLER, M(ichael) L(ynn); b. 24 Aug. 1953, Detroit, Michigan, USA. University Senior Lecturer; Poet. m. Pamela Mary Liebler, 5 Nov. 1976, 1 s., 1 d. *Education:* BA, 1976, MAT, 1980, Oakland University, Rochester, Michigan. *Appointments:* Part-time Instructor, Henry Ford Community College, 1980–86; Lecturer, 1981–92, Senior Lecturer, 1992–, Wayne State University; Detroit Dir, National Writers' Voice Project, 1995–; Arts and Humanities Dir, YMCA of Metro Detroit. *Publications:* Measuring Darkness, 1980; Breaking the Voodoo: Selected Poems, 1990; Deliver Me, 1991; Stripping the Adult Century Bare, 1995; Brooding the Heartlands, 1998. *Contributions to:* Rattle; Exquisite Corpse; Cottonwood Review; Relix Magazine; Christian Science Monitor; Detroit Sunday Journal; Review of Contemporary Fiction; American Book Review. *Memberships:* American Asscn of University Profs; Associated Writing Programs; MLA; National Council of Teachers of English; National Writers Voice Project; National Writers Corp Program; Poetry Resource Center of Michigan, pres., 1987–93; Popular Culture Asscn. *Address:* PO Box 120, Roseville, MI 48066, USA.

LIFSHIN, Lyn (Diane); b. 12 July 1944, Burlington, Vermont, USA. Poet; Teacher. *Education:* BA, Syracuse University, 1960; MA, University of Vermont, 1963. *Appointments:* Instructor, State University of New York at Cobleskill, 1968, 1970; Writing Consultant, New York State Mental Health Dept, Albany, 1969, Empire State College of the State University of New York at Saratoga Springs, 1973; Poet-in-Residence, Mansfield State College, Pennsylvania, 1974, University of Rochester, New York, 1986, Antioch's Writers' Conference, Ohio, 1987. *Publications:* Poetry: Over 75 collections, including: Upstate Madonna: Poems, 1970–74, 1975; Shaker House Poems,

1976; Some Madonna Poems, 1976; Leaning South, 1977; Madonna Who Shifts for Herself, 1983; Kiss the Skin Off, 1985; Many Madonnas, 1988; The Doctor Poems, 1990; Apple Blossoms, 1993; Blue Tattoo, 1995; The Mad Girl Drives in a Daze, 1995. Editor: Tangled Vines: A Collection of Mother and Daughter Poems, 1978; Ariadne's Thread: A Collection of Contemporary Women's Journals, 1982; Unsealed Lips, 1988. *Contributions to:* Many books and numerous other publications, including journals. *Honours:* Hart Crane Award; Bread Loaf Scholarship; Yaddo Fellowships, 1970, 1971, 1975, 1979, 1980; MacDowell Fellowship, 1973; Millay Colony Fellowships, 1975, 1979; Jack Kerouac Award, 1984; Centennial Review Poetry Prize, 1985; Madeline Sadin Award, New York Quarterly, 1986; Footwork Award, 1987; Esterscefiler Award, 1987. *Address:* 2142 Appletree Lane, Niskayuna, NY 12309, USA.

LIGHTFOOT, David James, (James Harrison); b. 7 April 1941, Wrexham, Wales. Teacher (retd); Poet. m. Valerie Elizabeth Lightfoot, 23 Oct. 1965, 1 s., 1 d. *Education:* BA, 1962, MA, 1964, University of Wales; PhD, University of Leicester, 1980. *Appointments:* Head of Classics, St Margaret's, Liverpool, Boston Grammar School; Education Officer, Kenya; Head of English, Monks Dyke School; Deputy Head, St Peter and Paul School, London. *Publications:* Down Private Lanes, 1991; Last Round, 1991; Correcting Fluid, 1993; Wounds Heal, 1996; David Lightfoot: A Selection, 1996. *Contributions to:* Various publications. *Honours:* Rosemary Arthur Award; Runner-up, Orbis Rhyme Revival, 1993. *Address:* 1 Horncastle Rd, Louth, Lincolnshire LN11 9LB, England.

LIM, Shirley Geok-lin; b. 27 Dec. 1944, Malacca, Malaya. Prof. of English and Women's Studies; Author; Poet. m. Dr Charles Bazerman, 27 Nov. 1972, 1 s. *Education:* BA, English Literature, 1967, MA Studies, 1967–69, University of Malaya; MA, 1971, PhD, 1973, English and American Literature, Brandeis University. *Appointments:* Lecturer and Teaching Asst, University of Malaya, 1967–69; Teaching Fellow, Queens College, City University of New York, 1972–73; Asst Prof., Hostos Community College, City University of New York, 1973–76; Lecturer, Universiti Sains, Penang, Malaysia, 1974; Assoc. Prof., State University of New York College at Westchester, 1976–90; Writer-in-Residence, University of Singapore, 1985, East West Center, Honolulu, 1988; Prof. of Asian American Studies, 1990–93, Prof. of English and Women's Studies, 1993–, University of California at Santa Barbara; Fulbright Distinguished Lecturer, Nanyang Technological University, 1996; Chair, Prof. of English, University of Hong Kong, 1999–. *Publications:* Crossing the Peninsula and Other Poems, 1980; Another Country and Other Stories, 1982; No Man's Grove and Other Poems, 1985; Modern Secrets: New and Selected Poems, 1989; Nationalism and Literature: Literature in English from the Philippines and Singapore, 1993; Monsoon History: Selected Poems, 1994; Writing Southeast/Asia in English: Against the Grain, 1994; Life's Mysteries: The Best of Shirley Lim, 1995; Among the White Moon Faces: An Asian-American Memoir of Homelands, 1996; Two Dreams: Short Stories, 1997; What the Fortune Teller Didn't Say, 1998. Editor: The Forbidden Stitch: An Asian American Women's Anthology, 1989; Reading the Literatures of Asian America, 1992; One World of Literature, 1993; Asian American Literature: An Anthology, 2000; Joss and Gold, 2001. *Contributions to:* Anthologies, books, reviews, quarterlies, and journals. *Honours:* Numerous grants and fellowships; Fulbright Scholarship, 1969–72; Commonwealth Poetry Prize, 1980; American Book Awards, 1990, 1997. *Memberships:* American Studies; Asscn for Asian American Studies; Asscn for Commonwealth Languages and Literatures; MLA; Multi-Ethnic Literatures of the United States; National Women's Studies Asscn; PEN; Popular Culture Asscn. *Address:* c/o Women's Studies Program, University of California at Santa Barbara, Santa Barbara, CA 93106, USA.

LIMA, Robert; b. 7 Nov. 1935, Havana, Cuba. Prof. Emeritus of Spanish and Comparative Literature; Writer; Poet; Dramatist; Ed.; Trans. m. Sally Murphy, 27 June 1964, 2 s., 2 d. *Education:* BA, English, Philosophy, and History, 1957, MA, Theatre and Drama, 1961, Villanova University; PhD, Romance Languages and Literatures, New York University, 1968. *Appointments:* Lecturer, Hunter College, New York City, 1962–65; Asst Prof., 1965–69, Assoc. Prof., 1969–73, Prof. of Spanish and Comparative Literature, 1973–, Pennsylvania State University. *Publications:* Reader's Encyclopedia of American Literature (co-ed.), revised edn, 1962; The Theatre of García Lorca, 1963; Borges the Labyrinth Maker (ed. and trans.), 1965; Ramón del Valle-Inclán, 1972; An Annotated Bibliography of Ramón del Valle-Inclán, 1972; Dos ensayos sobre teatro espanol de los veinte (co-author), 1984; Valle-Inclán: The Theatre of His Life, 1988; Savage Acts: Four Plays (ed. and trans.), 1993; Borges and the Esoteric (ed. and contributor), 1993; Valle-Inclán: El teatro de su vida, 1995; Dark Prisms: Occultism in Hispanic Drama, 1995; Homenaje a/Tribute to Martha T Halsey (co-ed. and contributor), 1995; Ramón del Valle-Inclán, An Annotated Bibliography, Vol. I: The Works, 1999; The Alchemical Art of Leonora Carrington, Special Issue of Cauda Pavonis, Studies in Hermeticism (ed. and contributor), 2001. *Contributions to:* Many books, reference works, anthologies, newspapers, reviews, quarterlies, and journals. *Honours:* Fellowships; Awards; Enxebre Ordre da Vieira, 2002; Distinguished Alumnus Medal, College of Arts and Sciences, Villanova University, 1999. *Memberships:* Poetry Society of America; International PEN; American Center; Institute for the Arts and Humanistic Studies, fellow emeritus; Academia Norteamericana de la Lengua Española, academician; Real Academia Española, corresponding mem. *Address:* c/o Dept of Spanish, Italian, and Portuguese, Pennsylvania State University, 352 N Burrowes Building, University Park, PA 16802, USA.

LIN, Wallace. See: LEONG, Russell.

LIN SONG; b. 20 Jan. 1959, China. Teacher; Poet. m. Valerie Tehio, 5 June 1991, 1 s. *Education:* Master of Chinese Language and Literature, East China Normal University, 1983. *Publication:* Citadins. *Contributions to:* Today; Poetry Magazine; Shanghai Literature; New Spring; Yellow River; Guandong Literature; Harvest. *Honours:* Poetry Prizes: Beijing University, 1986; Poetry International, Rotterdam, 1990.

LINDAL, Tryggvi V(altyr); b. 3 May 1951, Reykjavík, Iceland. Journalist; Writer; Poet. *Education:* BA, Anthropology, University of Toronto, 1978; Graduate Studies, Cultural Anthropology, University of Manitoba, 1980; Teacher's Certificate, University of Iceland, 1984. *Publications:* Naeturvordurinn, 1989; Tromet og fiol, 1992; Lindal og Lorca, 1997; An Icelandic Poet, 1998; Hetjuljod og sogur, 2001; Astarljod og stridssogur, 2002. *Contributions to:* Anthologies, newspapers and journals. *Honours:* Jean Monnet Prize for Poetry, 1998. *Memberships:* Iceland-Canada Friendship Society, pres., 1995–; Writers Union of Iceland; Ethnologist's Society of Iceland. *Address:* Skeggjagata 3, 105 Reykjavik, Iceland.

LINDE, Nancy; b. 21 Dec. 1949, New York, NY, USA. College Lecturer; Writer; Poet. m. Stephan A. Khinoy, 1980, divorced 1990. *Education:* BA, 1971, MA, 1972, City University of New York. *Appointments:* Lecturer, College of Staten Island, 1978–85, 1988–; Mem., Board of Dirs, Woodstock Writers Worskhop, 1980–. *Publication:* The Orange Cat Bistro (novel), 1996. Other: Arabesque (screenplay), 1969. *Contributions to:* Periodicals. *Honour:* Poetry Prize, City University of New York, 1970. *Membership:* American Aikido Federation. *Address:* 29 Four Corners Rd, Staten Island, NY 10304, USA.

LINDEMAN, Jack; b. 31 Dec. 1924, Philadelphia, Pennsylvania, USA. Prof. Emeritus; Poet; Writer. *Education:* West Chester State College, Pennsylvania, 1949; University of Pennsylvania, 1949; University of Mississippi, 1949–50; Villanova University, 1973. *Appointments:* Ed., Whetstone, 1955–61; Faculty, Lincoln University, Pennsylvania, 1963–64, Temple University, 1964–65; Faculty, 1969–85, Prof. Emeritus, 1985–, Kutztown University, Pennsylvania; Poetry Ed., Time Capsule, 1981–83, Appleseed Hollow, 2001. *Publications:* Twenty-One Poems; The Conflict of Convictions; Appleseed Hollow, 2001. *Contributions to:* Anthologies, quarterlies, reviews, journals and magazines, including: Apocalypse; Bellowing Ark; Beloit Poetry Journal; Blueline; Blue Unicorn; California Poetry Quarterly; California Quarterly; Christian Science Monitor; Colorado Quarterly; Commonweal; Dickinson Review; Eureka Literary Magazine; Harper's Bazaar; High Plains Review; Hollins Critic; Kansas Quarterly; Massachusetts Review; Nation; New World Writing; Oregon East; Poetry; Prairie Schooner; Rocky Mountain Review; Slant; South Carolina Review; Southern Poetry Review; Southwest Review; Calapooya, Chiron Review, Poetry Motel, The Poet's Page, San Fernando Poetry Journal. *Membership:* Poets and Writers. *Address:* 133 S Franklin St, Fleetwood, PA 19522-1810, USA.

LINDEN, Eddie (Sean); b. 5 May 1935, Northern Ireland. Poet; Writer; Ed. *Education:* Holy Family, Mossend; St Patrick's, New Stevenson; Catholic Workers College, Oxford. *Appointment:* Founder-Ed., Aquarius literary magazine. *Publications:* The Chameleon Poet: A Life of George Parker, 2002. *Contributions to:* Anthologies and other publications. *Membership:* Poetry Society. *Address:* Flat 4, Room B, 116 Sutherland Ave, London W9, England.

LINDNER, Carl Martin; b. 31 Aug. 1940, New York, NY, USA. Prof. of English; Poet. 1 s., 1 d. *Education:* BS, 1962, MA, 1965, City College of the City University of New York; PhD, University of Wisconsin at Madison, 1970. *Appointments:* Asst Prof., 1969–74, Assoc. Prof., 1974–87, Prof. of English, 1987–, University of Wisconsin at Parkside. *Publications:* Vampire, 1977; The Only Game, 1981; Shooting Baskets in a Dark Gymnasium, 1984; Angling into Light, 2001; Eat and Remember, 2001. *Contributions to:* Reviews, journals and periodicals. *Honours:* Wisconsin Arts Board Creative Writing Fellowship for Poetry, 1981; Stella C. Gray Teaching Excellence Awards, 1990–91, 2000–01; University of Wisconsin at Parkside Award for Excellence in Research and Creative Activity, 1996. *Address:* c/o Dept of English, University of Wisconsin at Parkside, PO Box 2000, Wood Rd, Kenosha, WI 53141, USA.

LINDOP, Grevel (Charles Garrett); b. 6 Oct. 1948, Liverpool, England. Prof. Emeritus of Romantic and Early Victorian Studies; Poet; Writer; Ed. m. Amanda Therese Marian, 4 July 1981, 1 s., 2 d. *Education:* Liverpool College; MA, BLitt, Wadham College, Oxford. *Appointments:* Lecturer, 1971–84, Senior Lecturer, 1984–93, Reader in English Literature, 1993–96, Prof. of Romantic and Early Victorian Studies, 1996–2001, University of Manchester; Dir, Temenos Acad.; Ed., Temenos Acad. Review. *Publications:* Poetry: Against the Sea, 1970; Fools' Paradise, 1977; Moon's Palette, 1984; Tourists, 1987; A Prismatic Toy, 1991; Selected Poems, 2000. Prose: British Poetry Since 1960 (with Michael Schmidt), 1971; The Opium-Eater: A Life of Thomas De Quincey, 1981; A Literary Guide to the Lake District, 1993; The Path and the Palace: Reflections on the Nature of Poetry, 1996. Editor: Selected Poems, by Thomas Chatterton, 1971; Confessions of an English Opium-Eater and Other Writings, by Thomas De Quincey, 1985; The White Goddess, by Robert Graves, 1997; Complete Works, of Thomas De Quincey, 21 vols, 1999–2001. *Contributions to:*

Poetry Nation Review; TLS; Other publications. *Honour:* Lake District Book of the Year Award, 1993. *Memberships:* Temenos Acad., fellow; Buddhist; Wordsworth Museum and Library, Dove Cottage, Grasmere, trustee. *Address:* 216 Oswald Rd, Chorton-cum-Hardy, Manchester, M21 9GW, England.

LINDSAY, (John) Maurice; b. 21 July 1918, Glasgow, Scotland. Poet; Writer; Ed. m. 3 Aug. 1946, 1 s., 3 d. *Education:* Glasgow Acad., 1928–36; Scottish National Acad. of Music, 1936–39. *Appointments:* Programme Controller, Border Television, 1959–62, Chief Interviewer, 1962–67; Dir, The Scottish Civic Trust, 1967–83; Ed., Scottish Review, 1975–85; Pres., Asscn for Scottish Literary Studies, 1982–83. *Publications:* The Advancing Day, 1940; Predicament, 1942; No Crown for Laughter, 1943; The Enemies of Love: Poems, 1941–45, 1946; Selected Poems, 1947; At the Wood's Edge, 1950; Ode for St Andrew's Night and Other Poems, 1951; The Exiled Heart: Poems, 1941–56, 1957; Snow Warning and Other Poems, 1962; One Later Day and Other Poems, 1964; This Business of Living, 1971; Comings and Goings, 1971; Selected Poems, 1942–72, 1973; The Run from Life: More Poems, 1942–72, 1975; Walking Without an Overcoat: Poems, 1972–76, 1977; Collected Poems, 2 vols, 1979, 1993; A Net to Catch the Wind and Other Poems, 1981; The French Mosquitoe's Woman and Other Diversions, 1985; Requiem for a Sexual Athlete and Other Poems and Diversions, 1988; The Scottish Dog (with Joyce Lindsay), 1989; The Theatre and Opera Lover's Quotation Book (with Joyce Lindsay), 1993; News of the World: Last Poems, 1995; Speaking Likenesses, 1997; The Burns Quotation Book (with Joyce Lindsay), 1999; Worlds Apart (poems), 2000; Glasgow: Fabric of a City, 2000. Other: Edns of poetry, plays, etc. *Honours:* Terretorial Decoration; C.B.E., 1979; DLitt, University of Glasgow, 1982. *Memberships:* Asscn of Scottish Literary Studies; Hon. Fellow, Royal Incorporation of Architects in Scotland. *Address:* Park House, 104 Dumbarton Rd, Bowling, G60 5BB, Scotland.

LINDSAY, Graham Boyd; b. 16 Sept. 1952, Wellington, New Zealand. Writer; Poet. *Education:* BA; Diploma in Teaching. *Publications:* Thousand-Eyed Eel, 1976; Public, 1980; Big Boy, 1986; Return to Earth, 1991. Editor: Morepork 1–3, 1979–80; The Subject, 1994. *Contributions to:* New Quarterly Cave; Islands; Spleen; Climate; Pilgrims; Parallax; Landfall; Splash; Untold; OUSA Review; Canta Critic; Frame; Metro; Takahe; Listener; Edge; Span; Poetry New Zealand; Plainwraps; Sport; Literary Half-Yearly; Origin; Quote Unquote; New Zealand Books; Printout. *Membership:* New Zealand Society of Authors. *Address:* 100 Main South Rd, Christchurch 4, New Zealand.

LINEBARGER, James Morris; b. 6 July 1934, Abilene, Texas, USA. Prof.; Poet. m. Lillian Tillery, 1958, divorced, 2 s. *Education:* AB, Columbia University, 1952; MA, 1957; PhD, Emory University, 1963. *Appointments:* Instructor, Asst Prof., Georgia Tech, 1957–62; Asst Prof., 1963–65, Assoc. Prof., 1965–70, Full Prof., 1970–, Poet-in-Residence, 1989–, University of North Texas. *Publications:* The Worcester Poems, 1991; Anecdotal Evidence, 1993. *Contributions to:* Southwest Review; Laurel Review; Descant; Cross Timbers Review; Southern Humanities Review; Pebble; Midwestern University Quarterly; Arts and Letters; Vanderbilt Review. *Memberships:* Poetry Society of America.

LIS, Ketty Alejandrina; b. 15 Oct. 1946, Santa Fe, Argentina. Poet; Writer. m. Abraham Lis, 13 Aug. 1971. *Publications:* Imaginaciones (poems), 1987; Poesía contemporánea: Conflicto y contenido (opuscule), 1990; Un genio llamado Wolfgang Amadeus Mozart (opuscule), 1991; Adiós al poeta Alfredo Veiravé (article), 1991; Cartas para Adriana (poems), 1992; La poesía, esa lámpara incorruptible (opuscule), 1993; ¿Quiénes leen poesía hoy? (opuscule), 1994; Alejandra Pizarnik, una muñeca de huesos de pájaro (opuscule), 1994; Juan L. Ortiz, Localismo y universalidad (opuscule), 1995; Piedra Filosofal (poems), 1997, English trans. as The Philosopher's Stone; La mujer y su escasa presencia en la historia de la literatura: Una revisión a lo largo de los siglos (opuscule), 1998, English trans. as The Woman: From Slavery to the Nobel Prize; Situación de la poesía en el mundo actual (opuscule), 1999; Poesía y conocimiento (opuscule), 2000; El ser, ese enigma (opuscule), 2001; La zona (poems); Líneas de fuga (poems). Other: Ed. of online Antología de la poesía argentina (antologiapoetica.com.ar/poesia) and Antología de la Poesia Universal (www.poeticas.com.ar). *Contributions to:* Various publications. *Honours:* Special Award, 1991, Sash of Honour, 1993, Sociedad Argentina de Escritores, Filial Oeste; Carlos J. Corbella Plaque for contribution to culture, Fundación Héctor I. Astengo, 1994; Second Prize, Illustrated Poem competition, Fundación El Libro, 1994; Hon. Mention, Lions Club of Buenos Aires, 1997. *Memberships:* Mozarteum Argentino; Lorenzo de Medicis Group; Co-founder, Mozart Fund. *Address:* Avda de la Libertad 8, 1°, 2000 Rosario, Argentina. *E-mail:* kettylis@citynet.net.ar.

LISTER, Richard Percival; b. 23 Nov. 1914, Nottingham, England. Author; Poet; Painter. m. Ione Mary Wynniatt-Husey, 24 June 1985. *Education:* BSc, Manchester University. *Publications:* Fiction: The Way Backwards, 1950; The Oyster and the Torpedo, 1951; Rebecca Redfern, 1953; The Rhyme and the Reason, 1963; The Questing Beast, 1965; One Short Summer, 1974. Poetry: The Idle Demon, 1958; The Albatross, 1986. Travel: A Journey in Lapland, 1965; Turkey Observed, 1967; Glimpses of a Planet, 1997. Biography: The Secret History of Genghis Khan, 1969; Marco Polo's Travels, 1976; The Travels of

Herodotus, 1979. Short Stories: Nine Legends, 1991; Two Northern Stories, 1996. *Contributions to:* Punch; New Yorker; Atlantic Monthly. *Honour:* RSL, fellow, 1970. *Membership:* International PEN. *Address:* Flat H, 81 Ledbury Rd, London W11 2AG, England.

LITHERLAND, Sheila Jacqueline; b. 18 Sept. 1936, Birmingham, England. Poet; Creative Writing/Literature Tutor. Divorced, 1 s., 1 d. *Education:* Regent Street Polytechnic, 1955; Ruskin College, Oxford, 1986; BA, University College, London, 1989. *Publications:* The Long Interval; Fourpack; Half Light; Modern Poets of Northern England; New Women Poets; The Poetry of Perestroika; Flowers of Fever. *Contributions to:* Iron Magazine; Writing Women Magazine; Oxford Magazine; Green Book. *Honour:* Annaghmakerrig Residence, 1994. *Memberships:* Colpitts Poetry; Poetry Society. *Address:* 6 Waddington St, Durham City DH1 4BG, England.

LITT, Iris; b. 18 March 1928, New York, NY, USA. Writer; Poet. m. Gilbert Burris, 11 July 1948, 2 s. *Education:* BA, Ohio State University, 1948. *Publication:* Word Love (poems), 1994. *Contributions to:* Anthologies, reviews, journals, and magazines. *Honours:* Several poetry awards. *Membership:* Poetry Society of America. *Address:* 252 W 11th St, New York, NY 10014, USA. *E-mail:* irislitt@aol.com.

LITTLE, Geraldine Clinton; b. 20 Sept. 1925, Portstewart, Ireland. Poet; Writer. m. Robert Knox Little, 26 Sept. 1953, 3 s. *Education:* BA, Goddard College, 1971; MA, Trenton State College, 1976. *Appointment:* Adjunct Prof. of English. *Publications:* Hakugai: Poem from a Concentration Camp, 1983; Seasons in Space, 1983; A Well-Tuned Harp, 1988; Beyond the Boxwood Comb, 1988; Heloise and Abelard: A Verse Play, 1989; Star-Mapped, 1989. *Contributions to:* Journals. *Honours:* Associated Writing Programs' Anniversary Award, 1986; Pablo Neruda Award, 1989; Grants. *Memberships:* Haiku Society of America; PEN; Poetry Society of America. *Address:* 1200 Campus Dr., Mt Holly, NJ 08060, USA.

LITTLEJOHN, Joan Anne; b. 20 April 1937, London, England. Poet. *Education:* Royal College of Music, 1955–59; Postgraduate Study, Howells and Others; LRAM, 1957; GRSM, 1958. *Appointments:* Freelance Composer, Musicologist, Photographer, 1959–; Administrative Staff, Royal College of Music, 1960–83; Piano Teacher, Harrow School, 1972–73. *Publications:* Numerous poems. *Contributions to:* Envoi; Country Life; Exmoor Review. *Honours:* Honorable Mention, New Poetry Magazine Competition, 1979; Award of Merit, Golden Poet Award, 1985, Silver Poet Award, 1986, World of Poetry. *Membership:* Brontë Society. *Address:* Shepherd's Delight, 49 Hamilton Lane, Exmouth, Devon EX8 2LW, England.

LIU, Timothy; b. 2 Oct. 1965, San Jose, CA, USA. Poet; Writer; Asst Prof. *Education:* BA, Brigham Young University, 1989; MA, University of Houston, 1991. *Appointments:* Asst Prof., Cornell College, 1994–98, William Paterson University, 1998–. *Publications:* A Zipper of Haze, 1988; Vox Angelica: Poems, 1992; Burnt Offerings, 1995; Say Goodnight, 1998; Word of Mouth: An Anthology of Gay American Poets, 2000; Hard Evidence, 2001. *Contributions to:* Reviews, quarterlies and journals. *Honours:* Norma Farber First Book Award, Poetry Society of America, 1992; John Ciardi Fellowship, Bread Loaf Writers' Conference, 1993; Holloway Lecturer, University of California at Berkeley, 1997; Judge's Choice Award, Bumbershoot Festival, 1998. *Memberships:* Associated Writing Programs; PEN American Center. *Address:* c/o William Paterson University, 300 Pompton Rd, Wayne, NJ 07470, USA.

LIVON GROSMAN, Ernesto L.; b. 2 March 1956, Buenos Aires, Argentina. Prof.; Poet. *Education:* Poetic Fellowship, English Dept, State University of New York at Buffalo, 1993; MA, Humanities, 1994, Doctoral Candidate in Latin American Literature, New York University. *Appointment:* Senior Lecturer, Dept of Spanish and Portuguese, Yale University, 1994–. *Publications:* Xul (anthology of Argentine poetry), 1996; Charles Olson (anthology in Spanish), 1996. *Contributions to:* American Poetry Review; Rift; Xul; Exact Change; Mandorla. *Address:* 19 Off Twin Lake Rd, North Branford, CT 06471, USA.

LIYONG, Taban; b. 1939, Kajo Kaji, Sudan. Lecturer; Poet. *Education:* BA, Howard University, Washington, DC, 1966. *Appointments:* Lecturer in Nairobi, Tanzania and New Guinea. *Publications:* Eating Chiefs: Lwo Culture from Lolwe to Malkal, 1970; Frantz Fanon's Uneven Ribs: With Poems More and More, 1971; Another Nigger Dead, 1972; Ballads of Underdevelopment: Poems and Thoughts, 1974; To Still a Passion, 1977. *Address:* Literature Unit, College of Education, University of Juba, PO Box 82, Juba, Sudan.

LLOYD-JONES, Jenafer, (Eilonwy Grey, Greya Locke); b. 16 June 1971, Joplin, Missouri, USA. Opera Singer; Poet. *Education:* BM, Conservatory of Music, Cincinnati. *Publication:* The Babblings of an Insane Mind. *Contributions to:* Spectrum; Seven Hills Review. *Membership:* Poetry Society of America. *Address:* 1122 White Pine Ct, Cincinnati, OH 45255, USA.

LOBO PRABHU, Louella; b. 27 Dec. 1942, Mangalore, India. Ed.; Publisher; Poet; Writer; Broadcaster. m. J M Lobo Prabhu, 12 May 1964, 1 d. *Education:* BA, Literature, University of Mumbai, 1963. *Appointments:* Ed.-Publisher, Insight, 1964–; Partner, Lobo Prabhu Enterprises; Dir, Elite Cultural Centre.

Publications: A Musical Credo, 1987; The Grammar of Politics in Verse, 1988; My Temple of the Arts, 1991; My India is One India, 1992; The Heart of Eve, 1993; The Ascent of Mount Carmel, 1994; Tiaha, 1995–96. *Contributions to:* Books, journals, radio, and television. *Honours:* Sandesha Media Award for the Arts, 1991; New Leader Award, 1994; Michael Mudhusudan Dutt Award, 1995; Bethany Award for Guest Editing, 1996. *Memberships:* All India Women's Ed.'s Asscn; Indo-African Society, New Delhi, fellow; United Writers Asscn of India, fellow. *Address:* Chateau De Lou, Light House Hill Rd, Mangalore 575 001, Karnataka, India.

LOCHHEAD, Douglas (Grant); b. 25 March 1922, Guelph, Ontario, Canada. Poet; Writer; Prof. of Canadian Studies Emeritus. m. Jean St Clair, 17 Sept. 1949, deceased, 2 d. *Education:* BA, 1943, BLS, 1951, McGill University; MA, University of Toronto, 1947. *Appointments:* Librarian, Victoria College, BC, 1951–52, Cornell University, Ithaca, New York, 1952–53, Dalhousie University, Halifax, Nova Scotia, 1953–60, York University, Toronto, 1960–63; Librarian and Fellow, Massey College, 1963–75; Prof. of English, University College, University of Toronto, 1963–75; Davidson Prof. of Canadian Studies and Dir of the Centre for Canadian Studies, 1975–87, Prof. Emeritus, 1987–, Mount Allison University, Sackville, New Brunswick; Visiting Prof., University of Edinburgh, 1983–84. *Publications:* The Heart is Fire, 1959; It is all Around, 1960; Millwood Road Poems, 1970; The Full Furnace: Collected Poems, 1975; A & E, 1980; Battle Sequence, 1980; High Marsh Road, 1980; The Panic Field, 1984; Tiger in the Skull: New and Selected Poems, 1959–85, 1986; Dykelands, 1989; Upper Cape Poems, 1989; Black Festival: A Long Poem, 1991; Homage to Henry Alline & Other Poems, 1992; Breakfast at Mel's and Other Poems of Love and Places, 1997; All Things Do Continue (poems), 1997; Cape Enragé: Poems on a Raised Beach, 2000; Weathers: New and Selected Poems, 2002; Orkney: October Diary, 2002. *Contributions to:* Various publications. *Honours:* Golden Dog Award, 1974; Fellow, Royal Society of Canada, 1976; Hon. DLitt, St Mary's University, 1987; Hon. LLD, Dalhousie University, 1987. *Memberships:* League of Canadian Poets, life mem.; Bibliographical Society of Canada. *Address:* 9 Quarry Lane, Sackville, NB E4L 4G3, Canada.

LOCHHEAD, Liz; b. 26 Dec. 1947, Motherwell, Scotland. Poet; Playwright; Screenwriter; Teacher. *Education:* Diploma, Glasgow School of Art, 1970. *Appointments:* Art teacher in Glasgow and Bristol schools; Lecturer, University of Glasgow. *Publications:* Poetry: Memo for Spring, 1972; The Grimm Sisters, 1981; Dreaming of Frankenstein and Collected Poems, 1984; True Confessions and New Clichés, 1985; Bagpipe Muzak, 1991; Cuba / Dog House (with Gina Moxley), 2000. Plays: Blood and Ice, 1982; Silver Service, 1984; Dracula (adaptation), 1989; Mary Queen of Scots Got Her Head Chopped Off, 1989; Moliere's Tartuffe (Scots trans. in rhyming couplets); Perfect Days, 1998; Medea (adaptation), 2000; Misery Guts (adaptation), 2002. Unpublished Plays: Disgusting Objects; Rosaleen's Baby; Red Hot Shoes; Same Difference; Shanghaied; Fancy You Minding That; Sweet Nothings; True Confessions; Complete Alternative of the World, Part One. Screenplay: Now and Then, 1972. For Television: Damages (BBC). *Contributions to:* Anthologies, including: Penguin Modern Poets Vols 3 and 4; Shouting It Out, 1995. *Honours:* BBC Scotland Prize, 1971; Scottish Arts Council Award, 1972. *Address:* 11 Kersland St, Glasgow G12 8BW, Scotland.

LOCKE, Greya. See: LLOYD-JONES, Jenafer.

LOCKETT, Reginald Franklin, (Tahid); b. 5 Nov. 1947, Berkeley, CA, USA. Instructor of English; Poet. m. Faye West, 18 Jan. 1983, 1 d. *Education:* BA, English Literature, 1971, MA, English Literature, 1972, San Francisco State University. *Appointments:* Instructor of English, Peralta Community College District, 1973–76, San Jose City College, 1990–; Lecturer in Creative Writing, San Francisco State University, 1976–78, City College of San Francsico, 1982–90. *Publications:* Good Times & No Bread, 1978; Where the Birds Sing Bass, 1995. *Contributions to:* Negro Digest; Iowa Review; Konceptualizations; Journal of Black Poetry; Visions Across the Americas; Thresholds; Black Dialogue; Soul Book; Black Fire; Quitt; Genetic Dancers. *Honour:* Josephine Miles Literary Award, 1996. *Memberships:* National Poetry Asscn, board mem.; PEN, Oakland. *Address:* 211 Hanover Ave No. 6, Oakland, CA 94606, USA.

LOCKLIN, Gerald (Ivan); b. 17 Feb. 1941, Rochester, NY, USA. Author; Poet; Dramatist; Literary Critic; Prof. of English. m. (1) Mary Alice Keefe, 1 s., 2 d., (2) Maureen McNicholas, 2 s., (3) Barbara Curry, 1 s., 1 d. *Education:* BA, St John Fisher College, 1961; MA, 1963, PhD, 1964, University of Arizona. *Appointments:* Instructor in English, California State College at Los Angeles, 1964–65; Assoc. Prof. to Prof. of English, California State University at Long Beach, 1965–. *Publications:* Sunset Beach, 1967; The Toad Poems, 1970; Poop and Other Poems, 1973; Toad's Europe, 1973; Locked In, 1973; Son of Poop, 1974; Tarzan and Shane Meet the Toad (with others), 1975; The Chase: A Novel, 1976; The Criminal Mentality, 1976; The Four-Day Week and Other Stories, 1977; Pronouncing Borges, 1977; A Weekend on Canada, 1979; The Cure: A Novel for Speed Readers, 1979; Two Summer Sequences, 1979; Two Weeks on Mr Stanford's Farm, 1980; The Last of Toad, 1980; Two for the Seesaw and One for the Road, 1980; Scenes from a Second Adolescence, 1981; A Clear and Present Danger to Society, 1981; By Land, Sea, and Air, 1982; Why Turn a Perfectly Good Toad into a Prince?, 1983; Fear and Paternity in the Pauma Valley, 1984; The Ensenada Poems (with Ray Zepada), 1984; The Case of the Missing Blue Volkswagen, 1984; The Phantom of the Johnny Carson Show, 1984; We Lose L.A. (with Ray Zepeda), 1985; The English Mini-Tour, 1987; Gringo and Other Poems, 1987; Gerald Haslam, 1987; A Constituency of Dunces, 1988; Children of a Lesser Demagogue, 1988; On the Rack, 1988; Lost and found, 1989; The Treasure of the Sierra Faulkner, 1989; The Gold Rush and Other Stories, 1989; The Rochester Trip, 1990; The Conference, 1990; The Illegitimate Son of Mr Madman, 1991; The Firebird Poems, 1992; A New Geography of Poets (ed. with Edward Field and Charles Stetler), 1992; The Old Mongoose and Other Poems, 1994; Big Man on Canvas, 1994; The Cabo Conference, 1995; Charles Bukowski: A Sure Bet, 1996; The Pittsburgh Poems, 1996; The Macao/Hong Kong Trip, 1996; The Hospital Poems, 1998; Two Novellas (with Donna Hilbert), 1998; Down and Out: A Novel for Adults, 1999; Hemingway Colloquium: The Poet Goes to Cuba, 1999; Candy Bars, 2000; A Simpler Time, a Simpler Place: Three Mid-Century Stories, 2000; The Iceberg Theory, 2000; Four Jazz Women, 2000; Art and Life, 2000; The Sixth Jazz Chapbook, 2001; Familiarities, 2001; The Life Force Poems, 2002; The Mystical Exercycle, 2002. Contributions to: Periodicals. Memberships: Associated Writing Programs; e. e. cummings Society; Hemingway Society; PEN; Western Literature Asscn. Address: c/o Dept of English, California State University at Long Beach, Long Beach, CA 90840, USA.

LOCRE, Peter E. See: COLE, Eugene Roger.

LOFTON, Ramona, (Sapphire); b. 4 Aug. 1950, Fort Ord, CA, USA. Literacy Educator; Poet; Writer. Education: BFA cum laude, City University of New York, 1983; MFA, Brooklyn College, 1995. Appointment: Writer, Writing Project of Teachers College, Columbia University, 1992–93. Publications: American Dreams, 1994; Push, 1996. Contributions to: Anthologies, newspapers and magazines. Honours: Amaranth Review Prize, 1991; Harvest Works/Audio Arts, Artist-in-Residence Award, 1991; MacArthur Scholarship for Poetry, Brooklyn College, 1994; Millay Colony Fellow, 1996; Sundance Theatre Laboratory Fellow, 1997; Mind Book of the Year Award, UK, 1997; Black Caucus of the American Library Asscn's First Novelist Award, 1997; Book of the Month Club Stephen Crane First Fiction Award, 1997; Yaddo, Catherine T. MacArthur Foundation Residency, 1998. Address: PO Box 975, Manhattanville Station, New York, NY 10027, USA.

LO-FU MO; b. 11 May 1928, Hunan, China. Chief Ed; Poet. m. C. F. Chen, 10 Oct. 1961, 1 s., 1 d. Education: English Dept, Tamkang University, 1968–73; AB, Tamkang University, 1973. Appointments: Commander, Chinese Navy, 1953–73; Lecturer, Soochow University, 1974–77. Publications: Spiritual River; Poems of Beyond; Clamoring of Time; Because of the Wind; Angels Nirvana; Death of Stone Cell; Songs of a Wizard; The Wine-brewing Rocks; The Dialectics of Love; Moonlight House; Bury me in Snow; Poems of Hidden Titles; The Poet's Mirror; Echoes in Solitude; Metaphysical Game; Silent Snow; Lo Fu's Selected Poems from the Twentieth Century; Driftwood; Falling Leaves Pondering in the Fire. Contributions to: United Daily News; China Times; Central Daily News; China News; Epoch Poetry Quarterly; Blue Star Poetry Quarterly; Modern Poetry; Free China Review; Chinese PEN. Honours: China Times Literary Award; Sun Yat Sen Memorial Literary Award; Wu San-Lien Literary Award; Chinese National Literary and Art Award; Annual Poetry Award, 2001. Membership: Epoch Poetry Society. Address: 7428 Ludlow Pl., Richmond, BC V7C 2Z6, Canada.

LOGGHE, Joan Slesinger; b. 23 Aug. 1947, Pittsburgh, Pennsylvania, USA. Poet; Ed.; Writing Teacher. m. Michael Logghe, 2 Aug. 1971, 1 s., 2 d. Education: BA, magna cum laude as Class Poet, Tufts University, 1969. Publications: Twenty Years in Bed with the Same Man, 1995; Another Desert: Jewish Poetry of New Mexico, 1999; Blessed Resistance, 1999. Contributions to: Anthologies, reviews, and magazines. Honours: National Acad. of Poets College Award, 1966; National Endowment for the Arts Fellowship, 1992; Mabel Dodge Lujan Internship; Barbara Deming/Money for Women Fund Award. Membership: PEN. Address: 12C Eckards Way, Espanola, NM 87532, USA. E-mail: jlogghe@espanola.com. Website: www.espanola.com/metaphor.

LOGUE, Christopher (John); b. 23 Nov. 1926, Portsmouth, Hampshire, England. Poet; Writer; Dramatist. m. Rosemary Hill, 1985. Education: Prior College, Bath. Publications: Poetry: Wand and Quadrant, 1953; Devil, Maggot and Son, 1954; The Weakdream Sonnets, 1955; The Man Who Told His Love: 20 Poems Based on P Neruda's 'Los Cantos d'amores', 1958; Songs, 1960; Songs from 'The Lily-White Boys', 1960; The Establishment Songs, 1966; The Girls, 1969; New Numbers, 1970; Abecedary, 1977; Ode to the Dodo, 1981; War Music: An Account of Books 16 to 19 of Homer's Iliad, 1981; Fluff, 1984; Kings: An Account of Books 1 and 2 of Homer's Iliad, 1991; The Husbands: An Account of Books 3 and 4 of Homer's Iliad, 1994; Selected Poems (edited by Christopher Reid), 1996; Logue's Homer: War Music, 2001. Plays: The Lily-White Boys (with Harry Cookson), 1959; The Trial of Cob and Leach, 1959; Antigone, 1961; War Music, 1978; Kings, 1993. Screenplays: Savage Messiah, 1972; The End of Arthur's Marriage, 1965; Crusoe (with Walter Green), 1986. Other: Lust, by Count Plamiro Vicarion, 1955; The Arrival of the Poet in the City: A Treatment for a Film, 1964; True Stories, 1966; The Bumper Book of True Stories, 1980. Editor: Count Palmiro Vicarion's Book of Limericks, 1959; The Children's Book of Comic Verse, 1979; London in Verse, 1982; Sweet & Sour: An Anthology of

Comic Verse, 1983; The Children's Book of Children's Rhymes, 1986. Honour: First Wilfred Owen Award, 1998. Address: 41 Camberwell Grove, London SE5 8JA, England.

LOMAS, Herbert; b. 7 Feb. 1924, Yorkshire, England. Poet; Critic; Trans. m. Mary Marshall Phelps, 29 June 1968, 1 s., 1 d. Education: BA, 1949, MA, 1952, University of Liverpool. Appointments: Teacher, Spetsai, Greece, 1950–51; Lecturer, Senior Lecturer, University of Helsinki, 1952–65; Senior Lecturer, 1966–72, Principal Lecturer, 1972–82, Borough Road College. Publications: Chimpanzees are Blameless Creatures, 1969; Who Needs Money?, 1972; Private and Confidential, 1974; Public Footpath, 1981; Fire in the Garden, 1984; Letters in the Dark, 1986; Trouble, 1992; Selected Poems, 1995; A Useless Passion, 1998. Translations: Territorial Song, 1991; Contemporary Finnish Poetry, 1991; Fugue, 1992; Wings of Hope and Daring, 1992; The Eyes of the Fingertips are Opening, 1993; Black and Red, 1993; Narcissus in Winter, 1994; The Year of the Hare, 1994; Two Sequences for Kuhmo, 1994; In Wandering Hall, 1995; Selected Poems, Eeva-Lisa Manner, 1997; Three Finnish Poets, 1999; A Tenant Here, 1999. Contributions to: Reviews, journals, and magazines. Honours: Prize, Guinness Poetry Competition; Runner-up, Arvon Foundation Poetry Competition; Cholmondeley Award; Poetry Book Society Biennial Trans. Award; Knight First Class, Order of the White Rose of Finland, 1991: Finnish State Prize for Trans., 1991. Memberships: Society of Authors; Finnish Acad.; Finnish Literary Society; Pres., Suffolk Poetry Society, 1999–. Address: North Gable, 30 Crag Path, Aldeburgh, Suffolk IP15 5BS, England. E-mail: herbert@hlomas.freeserve.co.uk.

LOMAX, Marion. See: BOLAM, Robyn.

LOMBARDO, Gian; b. 24 Sept. 1953, Hartford, CT, USA. Poet. m. Margaret Soussloff, 28 April 1991. Education: BA, Trinity College, 1980; MA, Boston University, 1981. Publications: Between Islands, 1984; Standing Room, 1989; Before Arguable Answers, 1993; Sky Open Again, 1997. Contributions to: Lift; Prose Poem International; Agni; Denver Quarterly; Talisman; Iowa Review. Membership: Associated Writing Programs. Address: 781 E Guinea Rd, Williamsburg, MA 01096, USA.

LOMELLINI, C. A. de. See: KELLEY, Alita.

LONG, Robert Hill; b. 23 Nov. 1952, Raleigh, North Carolina, USA. Senior Lecturer in Creative Writing; Poet; Writer. m. Sandra Morgen, 22 March 1980, 1 s., 1 d. Education: BA, Honours Studies, Comparative Literature, Davidson College, 1975; MFA, Program for Writers, Warren Wilson College, 1983. Appointments: Visiting Lecturer, Clark University, University of Hartford, Smith College, University of Connecticut at Torrington, 1987–91; Senior Lecturer in Creative Writing, University of Oregon, 1991–. Publications: The Power to Die (poems), 1987; The Work of the Bow (poems), 1997; The Effigies (fiction), 1998. Contributions to: Various anthologies and journals. Honours: Aspen Writers' Conference Poetry Fellowship, 1981; First Prize, North Carolina Poetry Award, 1986; Grand Prize, A Living Culture in Durham Anthology, 1986; North Carolina Arts Council Literary Fellowship, 1986; National Endowment for the Arts Fellowship, 1988; Cleveland State University Poetry Center Prize, 1995; Oregon Arts Commission Literary Fellowship, 1997. Membership: Associated Writing Programs. Address: c/o Program in Creative Writing, University of Oregon, Eugene, OR 97403, USA.

LONGCHAMPS, Renaud; b. 5 Nov. 1952, St Ephrem, QC, Canada. Poet; Writer. m. Charlotte Poulin, 29 July 1973, 1 s., 2 d. Education: François Xavier Garneau College. Publications: Several works. Contributions to: Various reviews, journals, and magazines. Membership: Union des Écrivains Québecois. Address: 24 Blvd Chartier, ST Ephrem, Comte de Beauce, QC G0M 1R0, Canada.

LONGLEY, Michael; b. 27 July 1939, Belfast, Northern Ireland. Poet; Arts Administrator. m. Edna Broderick, 1964, 1 s., 2 d. Education: BA, Trinity College, Dublin, 1963. Appointments: Asst Master, Avoca School, Blackrock, 1962–63, Belfast High School and Erith Secondary School, 1963–64, Royal Belfast Academical Institution, 1964–69; Dir, Literature and the Traditional Arts, Arts Council of Northern Ireland, Belfast, 1970–. Publications: Poetry: Ten Poems, 1965; Room To Rhyme (with Seamus Heaney and David Hammond), 1968; Secret Marriages: Nine Short Poems, 1968; Three Regional Voices (with Barry Tebb and Ian Chrichton Smith), 1968; No Continuing City: Poems, 1963–1968, 1969; Lares, 1972; An Exploded View: Poems, 1968–72, 1973; Fishing in the Sky, 1975; Man Lying on a Wall, 1976; The Echo Gate: Poems 1975–1978, 1979; Selected Poems, 1963–1980, 1980; Patchwork, 1981; Poems 1963–1983, 1985; Gorse Fires, 1991; The Weather in Japan, 2001. Editor: Causeway: The Arts in Ulster, 1971; Under the Moon, Over the Stars: Young People's Writing from Ulster, 1971; Selected Poems by Louis MacNeice, 1988; The Ghost Orcid, 1995; Selected Poems, 1998. Contributions to: Periodicals. Honours: Eric Gregory Award, Society of Authors, 1965; Commonwealth Poetry Prize, 1985; Hon. DLitt, Queen's University, Belfast, 1995; Hawthornden Prize; T. S. Eliot Prize, 2000; Irish Times Poetry Prize, 2001; Queen's Gold Medal for Poetry, 2001. Address: 32 Osborne Gardens, Malone, Belfast 9, Northern Ireland.

LONSFORD, Florence Hutchinson; b. 7 Jan. 1914, Lebanon, IN, USA. Artist; Designer; Poet; Writer. m. Graydon Lee Lonsford, 18 Dec. 1938. *Education:* BS, Purdue University, 1936; Postgraduate Studies, National Acad. of Fine Arts, 1956–58, John Herron Art Institute, Indianapolis, 1963; MA, Hunter College, New York City, 1963. *Appointments:* Teacher of Fine Arts, New York Public Schools, 1960–80; Owner-Operator, Greeting Card Design Business, 1966–69. *Publications:* Poems and books. *Contributions to:* Newspapers and periodicals. *Honours:* Exhibitions of works; First Prize, Print Making, Indiana State Fair, 1995; Merit Award, Water Color Society of Indiana, 1995. *Memberships:* Indiana Artists; Metropolitan Portrait Society; National Art League; National Society of Independent Scholars; Poetry Society of America. *Address:* 311 E 72nd St, New York, NY 10021, USA.

LOONEY, George; b. 22 March 1959, Cincinnati, Ohio, USA. University Instructor; Poet; Writer. m. Mairi Meredith, 25 Aug. 1984. *Education:* BFA, Art Education, University of Cincinnati, 1981; MFA, Creative Writing, Bowling Green State University, 1984. *Appointments:* Intern Instructor to Instructor in Creative Writing, Bowling Green State University. *Publication:* Animals Housed in the Pleasure of Flesh (poems), 1995. *Contributions to:* Various anthologies, reviews, quarterlies, journals, and magazines. *Honours:* Charles Angoff Award, Literary Review, 1990; Ohio Arts Council Individual Artists Fellowship, 1992; Bluestem Award, 1995. *Address:* 325 Wallace, Bowling Green, OH 43402, USA.

LOOTS, Barbara Kuntz, (Christina Lawrence); b. 30 Sept. 1946, Kansas City, Missouri, USA. Poet; Writer; Ed. m. Larry Rolfe Loots, 20 July 1969. *Education:* BA, Winthrop College, 1967; MLA, Baker University, 1993. *Publications:* Several poems. *Contributions to:* Anthologies, journals, and magazines. *Honour:* Second Award, Hanks Competition. *Memberships:* Piedmont Literary Society; Poetry Society of America; Poets and Writers. *Address:* 7943 Charlotte, Kansas City, MO 64131, USA.

LOPATE, Phillip; b. 16 Nov. 1943, New York, NY, USA. Prof. of English; Writer; Poet; Ed. m. Cheryl Cipriani, 31 Dec. 1990, 1 c. *Education:* BA, Columbia College, 1964; PhD, Union Institute, 1979. *Appointments:* Assoc. Prof. of English, University of Houston, 1980–88; Assoc. Prof. of Creative Writing, Columbia University, 1988–90; Prof. of English, Bennington College, 1990, Hofstra University, 1991–; Ed., The Anchor Essay Annual, 1997–99. *Publications:* Fiction: Confessions of Summer, 1979; The Rug Merchant, 1987. Poetry: The Eyes Don't Always Want to Stay Open, 1972; The Daily Round, 1976. Other: Being with Children (memoir), 1975; Bachelorhood (essays), 1981; Against Joie de Vivre (essays), 1989; Portrait of My Body (essays), 1996; Totally, Tenderly, Tragically (film criticism), 1998. Editor: Journal of a Living Experiment, 1979; The Art of the Personal Essay, 1994; Writing New York, 1998. *Contributions to:* Anthologies, newspapers, reviews, quarterlies, journals, and magazines. *Honours:* Guggenheim Fellowship; National Endowment for the Arts Grants; New York Foundation for the Arts Grants; Christopher Medallion; Texas Institute of Letters Award. *Address:* 402 Sackett St, New York, NY 11231, USA.

LOPEZ, Tony; b. 5 Nov. 1950, London, England. University Reader in Poetry; Poet; Writer. m. Sara Louise Banham, 19 Oct. 1985, 1 s., 1 d. *Education:* BA Literature University of Essex, 1980; PhD, English, Gonville & Caius College, Cambridge. *Appointments:* Lecturer in English, University of Leicester, 1986–87, University of Edinburgh, 1987–89; Lecturer to Reader in Poetry, University of Plymouth, 1989–. *Publications:* Snapshots, 1976; Change, 1978; The English Disease, 1979; A Handbook of British Birds, 1982; Abstract and Delicious, 1983; The Poetry of W S Graham, 1989; A Theory of Surplus Labour, 1990; Stress Management, 1994; Negative Equity, 1995; False Memory, 1996. *Contributions to:* Anthologies and periodicals. *Honours:* Blundel Award, 1990; Wingate Scholarship, 1996. *Address:* c/o MBA Literary Agents Ltd, 45 Fitzroy St, London W1P 5HR, England.

LOPEZ ANGLADA, Luis; b. 13 Sept. 1919, Ceuta, Spain. Poet. m. Maria Guerra Vozmediano, 26 Nov. 1946, 3 s., 7 d. *Education:* University of Valladolid. *Publications:* Poemas Americanos y Otros Poemas, 1966; Arte de Amar, 1968; Los Amantes, 1972. *Contributions to:* Journals. *Honours:* Numerous literary awards and prizes, including National Prizes for Literature, 1961, 1983. *Memberships:* Several literary organizations. *Address:* Call de Aviacion Espanola num 5, 28003 Madrid, Spain.

LORENC, Kito; b. 4 March 1938, Schleife, Germany. Poet; Writer; Ed. *Education:* Sorbian/Russian Pedagogical Exam, University of Leipzig, 1961. *Appointment:* Ed., Serbska poezija (Sorbian poetry series), 1973–; Sorbisches Lesebuch, 1981. *Publications:* Poetry: Struga, 1967; Flurbereinigung, 1973; Die Rasselbande im Schlamassellande (children's poems), 1983; Wortland, 1984; Rymarej a dyrdomdej (children's poems), 1985; Gegen den grossen Popanz, 1990; Suki w zakach, 1998. Other: Die wendische Schiffahrt, 1994; Kim Broiler, 1996. *Honours:* Heinrich Heine Prize, 1974; Heinrich Mann Prize, 1991. *Membership:* Sächsische Akademie der Künstei; PEN Zentrum Deutschland. *Address:* 02627 Wuischke bei Hochkirch 4, Germany.

LORRIMER, Claire. See: CLARK, Patricia Denise.

LOVE, Imogene. See: ANDERSDATTER, Karla Margaret.

LOVEDAY, John; b. 1926, England. Headmaster (retd); Poet. *Publications:* Particularities, 1977; Bones and Angels (with Shirley Toulson), 1978; The Agricultural Engineer, 1982; From the Old Foundary, 1983; Particular Insights, 1986. *Address:* c/o Headland, 38 York Ave, West Kirby, Wirral, Merseyside L48 3JF, England.

LOVELOCK, Yann Rufus; b. 11 Feb. 1939, Birmingham, England. Writer; Poet; Trans. m. Ann Riddell, 28 Sept. 1961. *Education:* BA, English Literature, St Edmund Hall, Oxford, 1963. *Appointments:* Various Writer-in-Residencies. *Publications:* The Vegetable Book, 1972; The Colour of the Weather (ed. and trans.), 1980; The Line Forward, 1984; A Vanishing Emptiness (ed. and part trans.), 1989; A Townscape of Flanders, Versions of Grace by Anton von Wilderode (trans.), 1990; Landscape with Voices, Poems 1980–95, 1995; In the Pupil's Mirror (ed. and trans.), 1997; Some 25 other books of poems, experimental prose, anthologies and trans. *Contributions to:* Periodicals and anthologies. *Honour:* Silver Medal, Haute Académie d'Art et de Littérature de France, 1986. *Memberships:* Freundkreis Poesie Europe, asst dir; La Société de Langue et de la Littérature Wallonnes, corresponding mem. *Address:* 80 Doris Rd, Birmingham, West Midlands B11 4NF, England.

LOW(-WESO), Denise; b. 9 May 1949, Emporia, KS, USA. Poet; Writer; University Instructor of Humanities. m. Thomas F Weso, 2 s. *Education:* BA, English, 1971, MA, English, 1974, PhD, English, 1997, University of Kansas; MFA, Creative Writing, Wichita State University, 1984. *Appointments:* Asst Instructor, 1970–72, Lecturer, 1977–84, Visiting Lecturer, 1988, University of Kansas; Temporary Instructor, Kansas State University, 1975–77; Part-time Instructor, Washburn University, Topeka, 1982–84; Instructor of Humanities, Haskell Indian Nations University, Lawrence, KS, 1984–. *Publications:* Dragon Kite, 1981; Quilting, 1984; Spring Geese and Other Poems, 1984; Learning the Language of Rivers, 1987; Starwater, 1988; Selective Amnesia: Stiletto I, 1988; Vanishing Point, 1991; Tulip Elegies: An Alchemy of Writing, 1993; Touching the Sky: Essays, 1994; New and Selected Poems: 1980–99, 1999. *Contributions to:* Anthologies, books, reviews, quarterlies, journals, and magazines. *Honours:* Several grants and fellowships. *Memberships:* Associated Writing Programs; MLA; Poets and Writers. *Address:* c/o Haskell Indian Nations University, Lawrence, KS 66046, USA.

LOWBURY, Edward (Joseph Lister); b. 6 Dec. 1913, London, England. Physician; Poet; Writer. m. Alison Young, 12 June 1954, 3 d. *Education:* BA, 1936, BM and BCh, 1939, University College, Oxford; MA; London Hospital Medical College, 1940; DM, Oxford University, 1957. *Appointments:* Bacteriologist, Medical Research Council Burns Research Unit, Birmingham Accident Hospital, 1949–79; Founder-Hon. Dir, Hospital Infection Research Laboratory, Birmingham, 1966–79. *Publications:* Poetry: Over 20 collections, including: Time for Sale, 1961; Daylight Astronomy, 1968; The Night Watchman, 1974; Poetry and Paradox: Poems and an Essay, 1976; Selected Poems, 1978; Selected and New Poems, 1990; Collected Poems, 1993; Mystic Bridge, 1997. Non-Fiction: Thomas Campion: Poet, Composer, Physician (with Alison Young and Timothy Salter), 1970; Drug Resistance in Antimicrobial Therapy (with G A Ayliffe), 1974; Hallmarks of Poetry (essays), 1994; To Shirk No Idleness: A Critical Biography of the Poet Andrew Young (with Alison Young), 1998. Editor: Control of Hospital Infection: A Practical Handbook (with others), 1975; The Poetical Works of Andrew Young (with Alison Young), 1985. *Contributions to:* Numerous medical, scientific, and literary publications, including reference works and journals. *Honours:* Newdigate Prize, 1934; Hon. Research Fellow, Birmingham University; John Keats Memorial Lecturer Award, 1973; Everett Evans Memorial Lecturer Award, 1977; DSc, Aston University, 1977; A B Wallace Memorial Lecturer and Medal, 1978; Hon. Prof. of Medical Microbiology, Aston University, 1979; LL D, Birmingham University, 1980; O.B.E., 1980. *Memberships:* British Medical Asscn; Fellow, Royal College of Pathologists; RSL; Founder Mem. and First Pres. of Hospital Infection Society; Hon. Fellow, Royal College of Physicians; Royal College of Surgeons. *Address:* 79 Vernon Rd, Birmingham B16 9SQ, England.

LOWERY, Martyn John; b. 8 July 1961, Rochdale, Lancashire, England. College Lecturer; Poet. *Education:* BA, Honours, English, 1982, MA, English, 1984, PhD, English, 1990, University of Exeter. *Appointments:* Lecturer in English, Salford University, 1989, Worthing Sixth Form College, 1991. *Publication:* The Dignity of Labour, 1984. *Contributions to:* Anthologies, reviews, journals, and magazines. *Address:* Hollies, 16 Wordsworth Rd, Worthing, West Sussex BN11 3NH, England.

LOWITZ, Leza; b. 12 Feb. 1962, San Francisco, CA, USA. Poet; Writer; Ed.; Trans. m. Oketani Shogo, Feb. 1995. *Education:* BA, English Literature, University of California at Berkeley, 1984; MA, English, Creative Writing, San Francisco State University, 1988. *Appointments:* Lecturer, San Francisco State University, 1989, Rikkyo University, Tokyo, 1991–92, University of Tokyo, 1992–94. *Publications:* Long Rainy Season (ed. and co-trans.), 1994; Other Side River Winds (ed. and co-trans.), 1995; Old Ways to Fold/New Paper, 1996. *Contributions to:* Various publications. *Honours:* University of California at Berkeley and Young Poetry Award, 1984; Browning Society Poetry Awards, 1986, 1987; PEN Syndicate Fiction Award, 1989; Printed Matter Poetry Award,

1993; National Endowment for the Humanities Award, 1994; Benjamin Franklin Award, 1995; Ministry of Arts Grant, Austria, 1995. *Memberships:* Acad. of American Poets; PEN, Freedom to Write Committee; San Francisco Women Writers Workshop.

LOYDELL, Rupert Michael; b. 7 July 1960, London, England. Poet; Writer; Ed.; Publisher; Artist. m. Susan Callaghan, 3 Sept. 1983, 1 d. *Education:* BA, Creative Arts, 1988, MA Creative Writing, 2002. *Appointments:* Founder-Managing Ed., Stride Publications, 1979–; Jazz Ed. and Art Ed., 1987–92, Ed., 1988–89, Event South West; Design Ed., Third Way Magazine, 1989–93; Arts Development Officer, Exeter Arts Council, 1994–96; Reviews Ed., Orbis, 1997–; Arts Council Visiting Fellow in Poetry, Warwick University, 2001–03, Royal Literary Fund Fellow, 2002–03. *Publications:* Fill These Days, 1990; Pitched at Silence, 1991; Between Dark Dreams, 1992; Timbers Across the Sun, 1993; The Giving of Flowers, 1994; Stone Angels: Prose 1979–1993, 1995; Trajectories, 1995; Fool's Paradise, 1995; Frosted Light: 14 Sequences, 1978–88, 1996; Sirens Singing in the Grey Morning, 1998; Background Noise I-III, 1999; Home All Along, 1999; A Hawk Into Everywhere, 2001; The Museum of Improvisation, 2002; The Museum of Light, 2002. Editor: How the Net is Gripped, 1992; Ladder to the Next Floor, 1993; The Stumbling Dance, 1994; A Curious Architecture, 1995. *Contributions to:* Reviews and journals. *Address:* c/o Stride Publications, 11 Sylvan Rd, Exeter, Devon EX4 6EW, England. *E-mail:* editor@stridebooks.co.uk. *Website:* www.stridebooks.co.uk.

LTAIF, Nadine; b. 19 July 1961, Cairo, Egypt. Poet. *Education:* MA, French Literature, University of Montréal, 1986. *Publications:* Les Métamorphoses d'Ishtar, 1987; Entre les Fleuves, 1991; Vestige d'Un Jardin, 1993; Elegies du Levant, 1995; Le Livre des dunes, 1999. *Contributions to:* Various publications. *Address:* 2004 St Laurent, 303, Montréal, QC H2X 2T2, Canada.

LUBWA P'CHONG, Cliff; b. 20 Aug. 1946, Gulu, Uganda. Educator; Poet. m. (1), 1 d., (2) Pat Hope Keshubi, 30 June 1992. *Education:* Diploma in Education, 1968; BA, 1976; MA, 1987; MEd, 1991. *Appointment:* Faculty, Institute of Teacher Education, Kampala. *Publication:* Words of My Groaning, 1976. *Contributions to:* Many anthologies. *Honours:* Runner-up, BBC Arts and Africa Poetry Award, 1982; Fellow in Creative Writing, University of Iowa, 1987. *Address:* c/o Institute of Teacher Education, PO Box 1, Kyambogo, Kampala, Uganda.

LUCAS, Dennis Michael; b. 23 Sept. 1968, Catskill, New York, USA. Musician; Poet. *Education:* BA, English, Brooklyn College, 1991. *Publications:* Haiku for Harry, 1989; Thirteen Ways of Looking at a Crow, 1992; Poetic License, 1996. *Contributions to:* Reviews and periodicals. *Address:* PO Box 263, Hunter, NY 12442, USA.

LUCAS, John; b. 26 June 1937, Exeter, Devon, England. Prof. of English; Poet; Writer; Publisher. m. 30 Sept. 1961, 1 s., 1 d. *Education:* BA, Philosophy and English Literature, 1959, PhD, 1965, University of Reading. *Appointments:* Asst Lecturer, University of Reading, 1961–64; Lecturer, Senior Lecturer, Reader, University of Nottingham, 1964–77; Visiting Prof., University of Maryland and Indiana University, 1967–68; Prof. of English, Loughborough University, 1977–; Reasearch prof., Nottingham Trent University, 1996–; Lord Byron Visiting Prof., University of Athens, 1984–85; Publisher, Shoestring Press, 1994–. *Publications:* About Nottingham, 1971; A Brief Bestiary, 1972; Egils Saga: Versions of the Poems, 1975; The Days of the Week, 1983; Studying Grosz on the Bus, 1989; Flying to Romania, 1992; One for the Piano, 1997; The Radical Twenties, 1997; On the Track: Poems, 2000; A World Perhaps: New and Selected Poems, 2002. *Contributions to:* Anthologies, newspapers, reviews; BBC Radio 3 and 4. *Honour:* Poetry Prize for Best First Full Vol. of Poetry, Aldeburgh Festival, 1990. *Memberships:* John Clare Society; Poetry Book Society, chair., 1988–92; RSA, fellow; William Morris Society. *Address:* 19 Devonshire Ave, Beeston, Nottingham NG9 1BS, England.

LUCIE-SMITH, (John) Edward (McKenzie), (Peter Kershaw); b. 27 Feb. 1933, Kingston, Jamaica. Art Critic; Poet; Journalist; Broadcaster. *Education:* MA, Honours, Modern History, Merton College, Oxford. *Publications:* A Tropical Childhood, 1961; Confessions and Histories, 1964; Penguin Modern Poets 6 (with Jack Clemo and George MacBeth), 1964; Penguin Book of Elizabethan Verse (ed.), 1965; What is a Painting?, 1966; The Liverpool Scene (ed.), 1967; A Choice of Browning's Verse (ed.), 1967; Penguin Book of Satirical Verse (ed.), 1967; Thinking About Art, 1968; Towards Silence, 1968; Movements in Art Since 1945, 1969; British Poetry Since 1945 (ed.), 1970; A Primer of Experimental Verse (ed.), 1971; French Poetry: The Last Fifteen Years (ed. with S W Taylor), 1971; A Concise History of French Painting, 1971; Symbolist Art, 1972; Eroticism in Western Art, 1972; The First London Catalogue, 1974; The Well Wishers, 1974; The Burnt Child (autobiography), 1975; The Invented Eye, 1975; World of the Makers, 1975; How the Rich Lived (with Celestine Dars), 1976; Joan of Arc, 1976; Work and Struggle (with Celestine Dars), 1977; Fantin-Latour, 1977; The Dark Pageant (novel), 1977; Art Today, 1977; A Concise History of Furniture, 1979; Super Realism, 1979; Cultural Calendar of the Twentieth Century, 1979; Art in the Seventies, 1980; The Story of Craft, 1981; The Body, 1981; A History of Industrial Design, 1983; Art Terms: An Illustrated Dictionary, 1984; Art in the Thirties, 1985; American

Art Now, 1985; Lives of the Great Twentieth Century Artists, 1986; Sculpture Since 1945, 1987; The New British Painting (with Carolyn Cohen and Judith Higgins), 1988; Art in the Eighties, 1990; Art Deco Painting, 1990; Fletcher Benton, 1990; Jean Rustin, 1991; Harry Holland, 1992; Art and Civilization, 1992; The Faber Book of Art Anecdotes (ed.), 1992; Andres Nagel, 1992; Wendy Taylor, 1992; Alexander, 1992; British Art Now, 1993; Race, Sex and Gender: Issues in Contemporary Art, 1994; Elisabeth Frink: A Portrait (with Elisabeth Frink), 1994; American Realism, 1994; Art Today, 1995; Visual Arts in the Twentieth Century, 1996; As Erotica, 1997; Lyn Chadwick, 1997; Adam, 1998; Zoo, 1998; Women and Art (with Judy Chicago), 1999; Judy Chicago, 2000; Flesh and Stone (photographs), 2000. *Contributions to:* Many newspapers and journals. *Membership:* RSL, fellow. *Address:* c/o Rogers, Coleridge and White, 20 Powis Mews, London W11 1JN, England.

LUMSDEN, Robert James; b. 7 Aug. 1914, London, England. Teacher (retd); Poet; Writer. m. 8 June 1940, 1 s. *Education:* BA, Queen Mary College, 1949. *Publications:* Letter to Tennyson and Other Poems, 1992; A Deal of Wonder, 1995. *Contributions to:* Reviews, quarterlies, and journals. *Honours:* Several prizes. *Memberships:* Enfield Writers Workshop; Farringford Tennyson Society; Isle of Wight Poetry Society. *Address:* Spindrift, Heathfield Rd, Freshwater, Isle of Wight PO40 9SH, England.

LUNDE, David (Eric); b. 14 Oct. 1941, Berkeley, CA, USA. Prof. of English; Poet. m. (1) Mary Lee Brannock, 1967, divorced 1981, (2) Marilyn C. Masiker, 1983, divorced 1996, 1 s., 1 d. *Education:* BA, Knox College, 1963; MFA, University of Iowa, 1967. *Appointments:* Instructor, Asst Prof., 1969–72, Assoc. Prof., 1972–78, Prof. of English, 1978–, State University of New York at Fredonia; Poetry Ed., Riverside Quarterly, 1968–75; Ed.-Publisher, Basilisk Press, 1970–85; Contributing Ed., Escarpments, 1982–84. *Publications:* Sludge Gulper 1, 1971; Calibrations, 1981; Blues for Port City, 1995. *Honours:* Acad. of American Poets Prize, University of Iowa, 1967; Rhysling Award for Best Science Fiction Poem of the Year, Science Fiction Poetry Asscn, 1992, 1995. *Memberships:* Acad. of American Poets; Science Fiction Poetry Asscn; SFWA. *Address:* 252 King Rd, Forestville, NY 14062, USA.

LUPPINO, Vincent; b. 10 July 1937, New Britain, CT, USA. Poet. *Education:* BS, CCSC, 1959; MA, Trinity College, 1970. *Contributions to:* Tunxis Poetry Review; World of Poetry Anthologies; Poetry Press Anthology. *Honours:* State of Connecticut Medal for Literary Achievement; Gold Poet Award; Silver Poet Award. *Membership:* Connecticut Poetry Society. *Address:* 43 Lawlor St, New Britain, CA 06051, USA.

LUTHER, Susan Militzer; b. 28 May 1946, Lincoln, Nebraska, USA. Literary Scholar; Ed.; Teacher; Poet. m. Robert N Luther, 18 July 1971. *Education:* BA, Louisiana State University, 1969; MA, University of Alabama, 1976; PhD, Vanderbilt University, 1986. *Appointments:* Asst/Assoc. Ed., Poem, 1985–98; Faculty Mem., Dept of English, University of Alabama in Huntsville, 1986–92. *Publications:* 'Christabel' as Dream Reverie, 1976; Poems on the Line, 1992. *Contributions to:* Malahat Review; Negative Capability; Kansas Quarterly; Slow Dance; Kalliope Waterways; MacGuffin; Poem; Wordsworth Circle; Slant; Cumberland Poetry Review; Piedmont Lterary Review; Hellas Frontiers; California State Poetry Quarterly; Sonoma Mardala. *Honours:* Fellowship, Vermont Studio Center; Finalist, Half Tones Jubilee Poetry Contest; Finalist, Anhinga Prize. *Memberships:* MLA; Alabama State Poetry Society; Alabama Writers' Forum; National Coalition of Independent Scholars; Friends of Coleridge; National Asscn for Poetry Therapy; North American Society for the Study of Romanticism; National Council of Teachers of English. *Address:* Huntsville, AL, USA.

LUX, Thomas; b. 10 Dec. 1946, Northampton, Massachusetts, USA. Poet; Teacher. m. Jean Kilbourne, 1983, 1 d. *Education:* BA, Emerson College, Boston, 1970; University of Iowa, 1971. *Appointments:* Managing Ed., Iowa Review, 1971–72; Ploughshares, 1973; Poet-in-Residence, Emerson College, 1972–75; Faculty, Sarah Lawrence College, 1975, Warren Wilson College, 1980–, Columbia University, 1980–. *Publications:* The Land Sighted, 1970; Memory's Handgrenade, 1972; The Glassblower's Breath, 1976; Sunday, 1979; Like a Wide Anvil From the Moon the Light, 1980; Massachusetts, 1981; Tarantulas on the Lifebuoy, 1983; Half Promised Land, 1986; Sunday: Poems, 1989; The Drowned River, 1990; A Boat in the Forest, 1992; Pecked to Death by Swans, 1993; Split Horizon, 1994; The Sanity of Earth and Grass (ed. with Jane Cooper and Sylvia Winner), 1994. *Honours:* Bread Loaf Scholarship, 1970; MacDowell Colony Fellowships, 1973, 1974, 1976, 1978, 1980, 1982; National Endowment for the Arts Grants, 1976, 1981, 1988; Guggenheim Fellowship, 1988; Kingsley Tufts Poetry Award, 1995. *Address:* 67 Temple St, West Newton, MA 02164, USA.

LUZA, Rad(omir Jr); b. 7 Dec. 1963, Vienna, Austria. Poet; Writer; Actor; Comedian. *Education:* BA, English, Tulane University, 1985. *Publications:* Harahan Journal, 1991; This n'That: Handwritings from a Wounded Heart, 1993; Porch Light Blues, 1995; Broken Headlights, 1997; Airports and Railroads, 1997. *Contributions to:* Reviews, quarterlies, and magazines. *Memberships:* Acad. of American Poets; Poetry Society of America; Poets and Writers. *Address:* 18 Golf Club Dr., Langhorne, PA 19047, USA.

LYKIARD, Alexis (Constantine); b. 2 Jan. 1940, Athens, Greece. Poet; Writer; Trans. *Education:* BA, 1962, MA, 1966, King's College, Cambridge. *Appointments:* Creative Writing Tutor, Arvon Foundation, 1974–; Writer-in-Residence, Sutton Central Library, 1976–77, Loughborough Art College, 1982–83, Tavistock, Devon Libraries, 1983–85, HMP Channings Wood, 1988–89, HMP Haslar, 1993–94. *Publications:* Lobsters, 1961; Journey of the Alchemist, 1963; The Summer Ghosts, 1964; Wholly Communion (ed.), 1965; Zones, 1966; Paros Poems, 1967; A Sleeping Partner, 1967; Robe of Skin, 1969; Strange Alphabet, 1970; Best Horror Stories of J Sheridan Le Fanu (ed.), 1970; Eight Lovesongs, 1972; The Stump, 1973; Greek Images, 1973; Lifelines, 1973; Instrument of Pleasure, 1974; Last Throes, 1976; Milesian Fables, 1976; A Morden Tower Reading, 1976; The Drive North, 1977; New Stories 2 (ed.), 1977; Scrubbers, 1983; Cat Kin, 1985; Out of Exile, 1986; Safe Levels, 1990; Living Jazz, 1991; Beautiful is Enough, 1992; Selected Poems, 1956–96, 1997; Jean Rhys Revisited, 2000. Other: Many French trans. *Membership:* Society of Authors. *Address:* 77 Latimer Rd, Exeter, Devon EX4 7JP, England.

LYMAN, Harlan; b. 3 Dec. 1975, Petersburg, Virginia, USA. Poet. *Publication:* Miles to Go Before I Sleep, 1996; The Glistening Stars, 1997; Reach to Other Worlds, 1997; Dream Quest, 1997; Pathways, 1997; Visions, 1997. *Contributions to:* Slug Fest; LTA; Mojo Risin; Small Press Review; Silent But Deadly; Blindman's Rainbow; Chance Magazine; Transcendent Visions. *Honours:* Honorable Mentions, Quill Books, 1997, Iliad Press, 1998. *Address:* Route 3, Box 221, Cumberland, VA 23040, USA.

LYNCH, Annette Peters; b. 23 Oct. 1922, Marion, IN, USA. College Prof. (retd); Poet. m. Thomas Millard Lynch, 24 Aug. 1949, 2 s., 2 d. *Education:* BA, Indiana University, 1944; MA, 1945, PhD, Occidental College, Los Angeles, 1960. *Appointments:* Instructor, Indiana University, 1945–49, Glendale College, 1949–50, Occidental College, 1950–55, Mount San Antonio College, 1955–93. *Publication:* Ways Around the Heart. *Contributions to:* Alderbaran; Athena Incognito; California State Poetry Quarterly; Calapooya Collage; Christian Science Monitor; Facet; Galley Sail Review; Inside English; Maryland Poetry Review; Toyon; Underpass; Wisconsin Review; Blue Unicorn; Cloverdale Review; Forum; Gaia; New Los Angeles Poets; Onthebus; Psychopoetica; Tempo; Voices; Christman Blues (anthology). *Honours:* Anthology of Magazine Verse, 1986–88; Second Prize, Annual California Quarterly National Contest, 1992; Outstanding Faculty Emeritus, Mount San Antonio College, 1993. *Memberships:* Acad. of American Poets; Poetry Society of America; California State Poetry Society. *Address:* 833 Garfield Ave, South Pasadena, CA 91030, USA. **LYNCH, Thomas;** b. 16 Oct. 1948, Detroit, MI, USA. Writer; Poet; Funeral Dir. 4 c. *Publications:* Skating with Heather Grace (poems), 1986; Grimalkin and Other Poems, 1994; The Undertaking: Life Studies from the Dismal Trade (non-fiction), 1997; Still Life in Milford (poems), 1998; Bodies in Motion and at Rest (poems), 2000. *Address:* 404 E Liberty, Milford, MI 48381, USA. *E-mail:* thoslynch@aol.com.

LYON, Martin; b. 10 Feb. 1954, Romford, Essex, England. Librarian; Poet. *Education:* BA, 1976. *Appointments:* Principal Library Asst, University of London. *Contributions to:* Acumen; Agenda; Orbis; Outposts Poetry Quarterly; Pen International; Spokes. *Honour:* Lake Aske Memorial Award. *Address:* 63 Malford Ct, The Dr., South Woodford, London E18 2HS, England.

LYON, Richard Woodward; b. 24 Oct. 1953, Puerto Rico. Poet. *Education:* MFA, Columbia University; BA, Boston University. *Publication:* Bell 8, 1994. *Contributions to:* Agni Review; American Poetry Review; Ironwood; Kansas Quarterly; Massachusetts Review; Nation and Partisan Review; Missouri Review. *Honours:* Yaddo Residency; Connecticut Commission on the Arts Fellowship; Discovery/The Nation Award of 92nd Street YM-YWHA; Writer-in-Residence, Camargo Foundation, Cassis, France, 1995; Residency, MacDowell Colony, 1996. *Address:* 29 Pratt St, Essex, CT 06426, USA.

M

MAC LOW, Jackson; b. 12 Sept. 1922, Chicago, IL, USA. Poet; Composer; Painter; Multimedia Performance Artist. m. Anne Tardos. *Education:* Chicago Musical College, 1927–32; Northwestern University School of Music, 1932–36; AA, University of Chicago, 1941; BA, Brooklyn College, 1958. *Appointments:* Teacher, New York University, 1966–73, Mannes College of Music, 1966, Naropa University, 1975, 1991, 1994, 1999, State University of New York at Albany, 1984, at Binghamton, 1989, and at Buffalo, 1990, 1997, Temple University, 1989; Schule für Dichtung, Vienna, 1992, 1993, Bard College, 1994, Brown University, 1994; Regents Lecturer, University of California at San Diego, 1990; Distinguished Visiting Writer, Saint Mary's College, Moraga, CA, 2000. *Publications:* 26 books, including: The Twin Plays: Port-au-Prince and Adams County Illinois, 1963; The Pronouns: A Collection of 40 Dances – For the Dancers, 1964; August Light Poems, 1967; 22 Light Poems, 1968; Stanzas for Iris *Lezak*, 1972; 21 Matched Asymmetries, 1978; A Dozen Douzains for Eve Rosenthal, 1978; Asymmetries 1-260, 1980; From Pearl Harbor Day to FDR's Birthday, 1982; French Sonnets, 1984; The Virginia Woolf Poems, 1985; Representative Works, 1938–1985, 1986; Words and Ends from Ez, 1989; Twenties: 100 Poems, 1991; Pieces o' Six: Thirty-Three Poems in Prose, 1992; 42 Merzgedichte in Memorian Kurt Schwitters, 1994; Barnesbook, 1996; 20 Forties, 1999; Struggle Through, 2001; Les Quarantains; Doings: An Assortment of Performance Pieces, 1955–2002, 2002; 154 Forties, 2002. *Contributions to:* Various publications. *Honours:* Creative Artists Public Service Fellowship in Multimedia, 1973–74, and in Poetry, 1976–77; National Endowment for the Arts Fellowship, 1978; Guggenheim Fellowship, 1985; New York Foundation for the Arts Fellowship, 1988; Wallace Stevens Award, Acad. of American Poets, 1999. *Memberships:* PEN American Centre; Poetry Society of America; Poets Advisory Committee, New York. *Address:* 42 N Moore St, New York, NY 10013, USA.

MACADAMS, Lewis; b. San Angelo, TX, USA. Poet; Journalist; Film Producer; Political Activist. m. JoAnne Klabin, 2 c. *Education:* Princeton University, NJ, 1966. *Appointments:* Freelance Journalist, Rolling Stone, Actuel, LA Weekly, Los Angeles Times Magazine, Men's Journal, and others; Founder, Friends of the Los Angeles River. *Publications:* Poetry: News from Niman Park, 1976; Africa and the Marriage of Walt Whitman and Marilyn Monroe, 1983. Prose: The River: Books One and Two; Birth of the Cool: Beat, Bebop, and the American Avant-Garde, 2001. Film Documentaries: What Happened to Jack Kerouac?, 1986; Eric Bogosian's Funhouse, 1987; The Battle of the Bards. *Honours:* Numerous journalism awards. *Address:* c/o Simon and Schuster Inc, 1230 Avenue of the Americas, New York, NY 10017, USA.

MCALPINE, Katherine; b. 31 Oct. 1948, Plainfield, New Jersey, USA. Singer; Voice Teacher; Poet; Writer. 1 s. *Education:* Private; Voice with Leon Kurzer, Vienna. *Contributions to:* Anthologies, reviews, journals, and magazines. *Honours:* Eva Le Fevre Award, 1988; Fluvanna Award, 1989; Galbraith Award, 1990; The Nation/Discovery Award, 1992; Judith's Room Award for Emerging Women Poets, 1992. *Address:* 11 Mitchell St, Eastport, ME 04631, USA.

MCALPINE, Rachel Phyllis; b. 24 Feb. 1940, Fairlie, New Zealand. Poet; Writer. m. Grant McAlpine, 19 Dec. 1959, divorced, 2 s., 2 d. *Education:* BA, University of Canterbury, 1960; DipEd, Massey University, 1973; BA, Honours, Victoria University of Wellington, 1977. *Appointments:* Writer-in-Residence, University of Canterbury, 1986; Visiting Scholar, Doshisha Women's College of Liberal Arts, Kyoto, Japan, 1993–94. *Publications:* Lament for Ariadne, 1975; Stay at the Dinner Party, 1977; Fancy Dress, 1978; House Poems, 1980; Recording Angel, 1983; Thirteen Waves, 1986; Selected Poems, 1988; Kiwi in Kyoto, 1993. *Contributions to:* Periodicals. *Honours:* New Zealand-Australia Writers Exchange, 1982; New Zealand Scholarship in Letters, 1990. *Memberships:* New Zealand Writers Guild; PEN, New Zealand.

MCAULEY, James J(ohn); b. 8 Jan. 1936, Dublin, Ireland. Prof.; Poet. m. Deirdre O'Sullivan, 1982. *Education:* University College Dublin; University of Arkansas, Fayetteville. *Appointments:* Ed., Dolmen Press, Dublin, 1960–66; Prof., Eastern Washington University, Cheney, 1978–; Dir, Eastern Washington University Press, 1993. *Publication:* Observations, 1960; A New Address, 1965; Draft Balance Sheet, 1970; Home and Away, 1974; After the Blizzard, 1975; The Exile's Recurring Nightmare, 1975; Recital, Poems, 1975–80, 1982; The Exile's Book of Hours, 1982; Coming and Going: New and Selected Poems, 1968–88, 1989. Play: The Revolution, 1966. Libretto: Praise, 1981. *Honours:* National Endowment for the Arts Grant, 1972; Washington Governor's Award, 1976. *Address:* Eastern Washington University Press, MS No. 14, Eastern Washington University, Cheney, WA 99004, USA.

MCCAFFERY, Stephen; b. 24 Jan. 1947, Sheffield, England. Poet; Critic. m. Karen MacCormack, 22 Jan. 1998. *Education:* BA, Honours, Hull University, 1968; MA Programme, York University, Toronto, 1969; PhD, State University

of New York at Buffalo, 1998. *Appointments:* Lecturer, Queen's University, Kingston, Ontario, Canada, 1993–95; John Logan Fellow in Poetics, State University of New York at Buffalo, 1996–97; Assoc. Prof., Temple University Philadelphia, 1998–. *Publications:* Dr Sadhu's Muffins, 1974; 'Ow's Waif, 1975 Intimate Distortions, 1978; Knowledge Never Knew, 1983; Panopticon, 1984 Evoba, 1987; The Black Debt, 1989; Theory of Sediment, 1991; The Cheat o Words, 1996. *Contributions to:* Avec; Boundary 2; Writing; West Coastline; Temblor; Parnassus Poetry in Review; Common Knowledge; Iowa Review Chain; Canadian Forum. *Honours:* Diploma of Merit, Università della Arti, Salsmaggiore, Italy, 1982; Gertrude Stein Awards in Innovative Poetry, 1994, 1995. *Memberships:* MLA; International James Joyce Foundation. *Address:* Temple University, Dept of English, Anderson Hall, 1114 W Berks St, Philadelphia, PA 19122-6090, USA.

MCCALLISTER, Weslynn; b. 18 May 1949, Evansville, IN, USA. Poet; Writer. m. R A Holway, deceased, 2 s., 1 d. *Education:* Liberal Arts; Fine Arts; Real Estate. *Publications:* The Looking Glass of Yesterday, 1993; Reflections, 1995; Apache Springs; Prophecy of the Ancients; The Sorcerer's Android; As Wes Alistair: Romancing the Zodiac. *Contributions to:* Quarterlies and magazines. *Honour:* Poet and Pen Quarterly Award, 1990. *Memberships:* Romance Writers of America; National Writers' Asscn; Florida Writers' Asscn, founding mem. *Address:* 7350 S Tamiami Trail, No. 229, Sarasota, FL 34231, USA. *E-mail:* wmccal6734@aol.com. *Website:* www.weslynn.com.

MCCALLUM-PETERS, Yvonne Veronica; b. 21 May 1944, Guyana. Teacher; Poet. m. Dereck George McCallum, 7 Nov. 1964, 3 s., 1 d. *Education:* Teachers College, 1971; BA, 1979, Further Studies, 1983, University of Guyana; Brooklyn College of the City University of New York, 1986–89; Teachers College, Columbia University, New York City, 1990. *Contributions to:* Anthologies. *Honours:* Several poetry awards. *Address:* 568 Powell St, New York, NY 11212, USA.

MCCARRON, Daniel Peter; b. 14 Dec. 1933, Canada. Journalist; Ed.; Publisher; Poet. m. (1) Jessie Drysdale, 2 s., 3 d., (2) Diane Arsenault, 31 Dec. 1993. *Education:* Arts, Journalism, St Mary's University, Halifax, Nova Scotia, 1957. *Appointments:* Editorial positions, various publications, 1957–96; Founder-Ed., The Strait News, and Ordinary Times. *Contributions to:* Periodicals. *Honour:* Journalist of the World Contest Citation, International City of Poets, 1995. *Address:* 2–15 Falconwood Rd, Charlottetown, PE C1A 6B6, Canada.

MCCARTHY, Joanne; b. 18 March 1935, Missoula, Montana, USA. College Teacher (retd); Poet. Divorced, 4 s., 2 d. *Education:* BA, English, University of Montana, 1955; MA, English, University of Puget Sound, 1969. *Appointments:* Teaching Fellow, University of Puget Sound, 1965–68; Faculty, Tacoma Community College, 1969–96. *Publication:* Shadowlight, 1989. *Contributions to:* Anthologies, reviews, and magazines. *Honours:* Winner, Writers' Omnibus Poetry Competition, 1980; Fulbright Exchange Fellow, Nuremberg, Germany, 1984–85; Poetry Selection, New American Writing International Tour, 1989; Brodie Herndon Memorial Award, Poetry Society of Virginia, 1994. *Address:* 1322 N Cascade, Tacoma, WA 98406, USA.

MCCASLIN, Susan Elizabeth; b. 3 June 1947, Indianapolis, IN, USA. College Instructor in English; Poet. m. Mark Haddock, 9 Aug. 1979, 1 d. *Education:* BA, University of Washington, 1969; MA, Simon Fraser University, 1973; PhD, University of British Columbia, 1984. *Appointments:* Teaching Asst, Simon Fraser University, 1969–71; Sessional Lecturer, University of Victoria, 1973–74; Instructor, English Dept, Trinity Western College, 1974–77; Sessional Lecturer, 1977–79, 1984–85, Teaching Asst, 1980–82, University of British Columbia; Asst Prof., English Dept, Trent University, Peterborough, Ontario, 1984; Instructor in English, Douglas College, New Westminster, BC, 1984–. *Publications:* Conversing with Paradise, 1986; Locutions, 1995; Light Housekeeping, 1997; Veil/Unveil, 1997; Letters to William Blake, 1997; Oracular Heart, 1999; Into the Open, 1999; Flying Wounded, 2000; The Altering Eye, 2000; Common Longing, 2001; The Fit of Song, 2002. *Contributions to:* West Coast Review; Littack; Crux; Bellowing Ark; White Wall Review; Scrivener; Christianity and Literature; Carleton Arts Review; Kore; Anima; Journal of Human Experience; Journal of Feminist Studies in Religion; Canadian Woman Studies; Literature and Belief; Contemporary Verse 2; Ariel; New Quarterly; Grain; Pottersfield Portfolio; Vox Feminarum. *Honours:* Honourable Mention, William Stafford Award, 1986; Second Place for Poem, Cecilia Lament Literary Contest, 1994; First Place, Annual Poetry Contest, Burnaby Writers' Society, 1995. *Memberships:* Burnaby Writers' Society; Federation of British Columbia Writers; Canadian Authors' Asscn; League of Canadian Poets. *Address:* 21 Brackenridge Pl., Port Moody, BC V3H 4G4, Canada.

MCCLANE, Kenneth (Anderson Jr); b. 19 Feb. 1951, New York, NY, USA. Prof.; Poet; Writer. m. Rochelle Evette Woods, 22 Oct. 1983. *Education:* AB, 1973, MA, 1974, MFA, 1976, Cornell University. *Appointments:* Instructor, Colby College, 1974–75; Luce Visiting Prof., Williams College, 1983; Assoc. Prof., 1983–89, Prof., 1989–93, W. E. B. DuBois Prof., 1993–, Cornell University; Visiting Prof., Wayne State University, 1987, University of Michigan, 1989, Washington University, 1991. *Publications:* Take Five: Collected Poems, 1988; Walls: Essays 1985–90, 1991. *Contributions to:* Journals. *Honours:* George Harmon Coxe Award, 1973; Corson Morrison Poetry Prize, 1973. *Memberships:* Associated Writing Programs; Poets and Writers. *Address:* c/o Dept of English, Cornell University, Rockefeller Hall, Ithaca, NY 14853, USA.

MCCLATCHY, J(oseph) D(onald Jr); b. 12 Aug. 1945, Bryn Mawr, Pennsylvania, USA. Poet; Writer; Ed. *Education:* AB, Georgetown University, 1967; PhD, Yale University, 1974. *Appointments:* Instructor, LaSalle College, Philadelphia, 1968–71; Assoc. Ed., Four Quarters, 1968–72; Asst Prof., Yale University, 1974–81; Poetry Ed., 1980–91, Ed., 1991–, The Yale Review; Lecturer in Creative Writing, Princeton University, 1981–93. *Publications:* Anne Sexton: The Artist and Her Critics, 1978; Scenes from Another Life (poems), 1981; Stars Principal (poems), 1986; James Merrill: Recitative: Prose (ed.), 1986; Kilim (poems), 1987; Poets on Painters: Essays on the Art of Painting by Twentieth-Century Poets (ed.), 1988; White Paper: On Contemporary American Poetry, 1989; The Rest of the Way (poems), 1990; The Vintage Book of Contemporary American Poetry (ed.), 1990; Woman in White: Selected Poems of Emily Dickinson (ed.), 1991; The Vintage Book of Contemporary World Poetry (ed.), 1996; Ten Commandments (poems), 1998; Twenty Questions (essays), 1998. *Contributions to:* Anthologies and magazines. *Honours:* Woodrow Wilson Fellowship, 1967–68; O Henry Award, 1972; Ingram Merrill Foundation Grant, 1979; Michener Award, 1982; Gordon Barber Memorial Award, 1984, Melville Cane Award, 1991, Poetry Society of America; Eunice Tietjens Memorial Prize, 1985, Oscar Blumenthal Prize, 1988, Levinson Prize, 1990, Poetry Magazine; Witter Bynner Poetry Prize, 1985, Award in Literature, 1991, American Acad. of Arts and Letters; National Endowment for the Arts Fellowship, 1986; Guggenheim Fellowship, 1988; Acad. of American Poets Fellowship, 1991. *Memberships:* American Acad. of Arts and Letters; International PEN; Acad. of American Poets, chancellor, 1996–. *Address:* 15 Grand St, Stonington, CT 06378, USA.

MCCLOSKEY, Phil(omena Mary), (Yvonne Somerville); b. 11 May 1940. Poet. m. Patrick Daniel McCloskey, 5 Sept. 1959, 2 s., 2 d. *Education:* Drake Business School, 1959; NDEC, Dublin City University, 1995–2001. *Publication:* Revelations of an Ant, 2000. *Contributions to:* Several publications. *Honours:* John Player Trophy; Second Prize, McGill Poetry Competition; Donegal Poet of the Year; Highly Commended Certificate, Gerard Manley Hopkins Poetry Competition; I. C. A. Magnier Cup for Art, 2001. *Memberships:* Killybegs Literary Society; Killybegs Writers Workshop; National Poetry Foundation. *Address:* Fintra, Killybegs, County Donegal, Ireland.

MCCLURE, Michael (Thomas); b. 20 Oct. 1932, Marysville, KS, USA. Prof.; Poet; Dramatist; Writer. m. Joanna Kinnison, 1954, 1 d. *Education:* University of Wichita, 1951–53; University of Arizona, 1953–54; BA, San Francisco State College, 1955. *Appointments:* Asst Prof., 1962–77, Assoc. Prof., 1977–78, Prof., 1978–, California College of Arts and Crafts, Oakland; Playwright-in-Residence, American Conservatory Theatre, San Francisco, 1975; Assoc. Fellow, Pierson College, Yale University, 1982. *Publications:* Poetry: Passage, 1956; For Artaud, 1959; Hymns to St Geryon and Other Poems, 1959; The New Book: A Book of Torture, 1961; Dark Brown, 1961; Ghost Tantras, 1964; 13 Mad Sonnets, 1964; Hail Thee Who Play, 1968; The Sermons of Jean Harlow and the Curses of Billy the Kid, 1969; Star, 1971; The Book of Joanna, 1973; Rare Angel (writ with raven's blood), 1974; September Blackberries, 1974; Jaguar Skies, 1975; Antechamber and Other Poems, 1978; The Book of Benjamin, 1982; Fragments of Perseus, 1983; Selected Poems, 1986; Rebel Lions, 1991; Simple Eyes and Other Poems, 1994. Plays: The Growl, in Four in Hand, 1964; The Blossom, or, Billy the Kid, 1967; The Beard, 1967; The Shell, 1968; The Cherub, 1970; Gargoyle Cartoons (11 plays), 1971; The Mammals, 1972; The Grabbing of the Fairy, 1973; Gorf, 1976; General Gorgeous, 1975; Goethe: Ein Fragment, 1978; The Velvet Edge, 1982; The Beard and VKTMs: Two Plays, 1985. Fiction: The Mad Club, 1970; The Adept, 1971. Other: Meat Science Essays, 1963; Freewheelin' Frank, Secretary of the Angels, as Told to Michael McClure by Frank Reynolds, 1967; Scratching the Beat Surface, 1982; Specks, 1985; Lighting the Corners: On Art, Nature, and the Visionary: Essays and Interviews, 1993. *Honours:* National Endowment for the Arts Grants, 1967, 1974; Guggenheim Fellowship, 1971; Magic Theatre Alfred Jarry Award, 1974; Rockefeller Foundation Fellowship, 1975; Obie Award, 1978. *Address:* 264 Downey St, San Francisco, CA 94117, USA.

MCCONNELL, Will. See: SNODGRASS, W. D.

MCCORKLE, James Donald Bruland; b. 6 Feb. 1954, St Petersburg, FL, USA. College Prof.; Poet; Writer. m. Cynthia Jane Williams, 16 July 1989. *Education:* BA, Hobart College, 1976; MA, 1977, MFA, 1981, PhD, 1984, University of Iowa. *Appointments:* Teaching Asst, 1979–84, Visiting Asst Prof., 1986–87, Asst Prof., Hobart College, 1987–92; Visiting Asst Prof.,

Keuka College, 1995–96. *Publications:* The Still Performance; Conversant Essays. *Contributions to:* Many reviews, quarterlies and journals. *Honour:* Ingram Merrill Foundation Fellowship; National Endowment for the Arts Fellowship, 1997–98. *Memberships:* Poetry Society of America; Associated Writing Programs; MLA; Elizabeth Bishop Society. *Address:* 790 S Main St, Geneva, NY 14456, USA.

MCCORMACK, William John. See: MAXTON, Hugh.

MCCORMICK, A. See: LEWIS-SMITH, Anne Elizabeth.

MCCRORIE, Edward Pollitt; b. 19 Nov. 1936, Central Falls, RI, USA. Prof. of English; Poet; Trans. m. 27 May 1995. *Education:* PhD, Brown University, 1970. *Appointment:* Prof. of English, Providence College, RI. *Publications:* After a Cremation (poems), 1974; The Aeneid of Virgil (trans.), 1995. *Contributions to:* Journals. *Address:* c/o Dept of English, Providence College, Providence, RI 02918, USA.

MCCROSSAN, Eamon; b. 12 Dec. 1963, Belfast, Northern Ireland. Civil Servant; Journalist; Poet. *Education:* A Level Evening Education. *Publications:* After Rain; Snow Queen; Evacuated to Coalisland. *Contributions to:* Orbis; Northern Women; Ulster Tatler; Cyphers; Universe; Belfast Review; Poetry Ireland. *Address:* 24 La Salle Dr., Belfast BT12 6DB, Northern Ireland.

MCCULLOUGH, Ken(neth); b. 18 July 1943, Staten Island, New York, USA. Poet; Writer; Teacher. *Education:* BA, University of Delaware, 1966; MFA, University of Iowa, 1968. *Appointments:* Teacher, Montana State University, 1970–75, University of Iowa, 1983–95, Kirkwood Community College, Cedar Rapids, 1987, St Mary's University, Winona, Minnesota, 1996; Writer-in-Residence, South Carolina ETV Network, 1975–78; Participant, Artist-in-the-Schools Program, Iowa Arts Council, 1981–96. *Publications:* Poetry: The Easy Wreckage, 1971; Migrations, 1972; Creosote, 1976; Elegy for Old Anna, 1985; Travelling Light, 1987; Sycamore Oriole, 1991; Walking Backwards, 1997. *Contributions to:* Numerous publications. *Honours:* Acad. of American Poets Award, 1966; Second Place, Ark River Awards, 1972; Helene Wurlitzer Foundation of New Mexico Residencies, 1973, 1994; National Endowment for the Arts Fellowship, 1974; Second Prize, Sri Chinmoy Poetry Awards, 1980; Writers' Voice Capricorn Book Award, 1985; Second Place, Pablo Neruda Award, Nimrod magazine 1990; Third Prize, Kudzu Poetry Contest, 1990; Ucross Foundation Residency, Wyoming, 1991; Witter Bynner Foundation for Poetry Grant, 1993; Iowa Arts Council Grants, 1994, 1996. *Memberships:* Associated Writing Programs; Asscn of American University Profs; National Asscn of College Academic Advisers; Renaissance Artists and Writers Asscn and Renaissance International; Rocky Mountain MLA; SFWA. *Address:* 372 Center St, Winona, MN 55987, USA.

MACDONALD, Alastair A.; b. 24 Oct. 1920, Aberlour, Scotland. Prof. of English Emeritus; Poet; Writer. *Education:* MA, University of Aberdeen, 1948; BLitt, Christ Church, Oxford, 1953; Senior Studentship in Arts, 1953–55, PhD, 1956, University of Manchester. *Appointments:* Temporary Senior English Master, King William's College, Isle of Man, 1953; Prof. of English, 1955–87, Prof. Emeritus, 1992–, Memorial University, NF, Canada; Various poetry readings. *Publications:* Poetry: Between Something and Something, 1970; Shape Enduring Mind, 1974; A Different Lens, 1981; Towards the Mystery, 1985; A Figure on the Move, 1991; Landscapes of Time: New, Uncollected, and Selected Poems, 1994; If More Winters, Or This the Last. Novel: Flavian's Fortune, 1985. Other: Prose and criticism. *Contributions to:* Various anthologies, reviews, journals and magazines. *Honours:* Best Poem, Canadian Author and Bookman, 1972; New Voices in American Poetry, 1973; First Prize for Poetry, 1976, Hon. Mention, 1978, Second Prize for Poetry, 1982, Newfoundland Government Arts and Letters Competition. *Memberships:* League of Canadian Poets; Scottish Poetry Library Asscn; Writers' Alliance of Newfoundland and Labrador. *Address:* c/o Dept of English, Arts and Administration Bldg, Memorial University, St John's, NF AC1 5S7, Canada.

MACDONALD, Cynthia; b. 2 Feb. 1928, New York, NY, USA. Poet; Lecturer. m. E. C. Macdonald, 1954, divorced 1975, 1 s., 1 d. *Education:* BA, Bennington College, Vermont, 1950; Graduate Studies, Mannes College of Music, New York City, 1951–52; MA, Sarah Lawrence College, 1970. *Appointments:* Asst Prof., 1970–74, Assoc. Prof. and Acting Dean of Studies, 1974–75, Sarah Lawrence College; Prof., Johns Hopkins University, 1975–79; Consultant, 1977–78, Co-Dir, Writing Program, 1979–, University of Houston; Guest Lecturer at various universities, colleges, seminars, etc. *Publications:* Amputations, 1972; Transplants, 1976; Pruning the Annuals, 1976; (W)holes, 1980; Alternate Means of Transport, 1985; Living Wills: New and Selected Poems, 1991; I Can't Remember, 1997. *Contributions to:* Anthologies and other publications. *Honours:* MacDowell Colony Grant, 1970; National Endowment for the Arts Grants, 1973, 1979; Yaddo Foundation Grants, 1974, 1976, 1979; CAPS Grant, 1976; American Acad. and Institute of Arts and Letters Award, 1977; Rockefeller Foundation Fellow, 1978. *Memberships:* American Society of Composers, Authors, and Publishers; Associated Writing Programs. *Address:* c/o Alfred A. Knopf Inc, 299 Park Ave, New York, NY 10171, USA.

MCDONALD, Ian (A.); b. 18 April 1933, St Augustine, Trinidad. Poet; Writer; Dramatist; Ed. m. Mary Angela Callender, 1984, 3 s. *Education:* Queen's Royal College, Trinidad; University of Cambridge, 1951–55. *Appointments:* CEO, Sugar Asscn of the Caribbean; Dir, Theatre Co of Guyana, Georgetown, 1981–; Ed., Kyk-Over-Al, West Indian literary journal, 1984–; Chair., Demerana Publishers, 1988–. *Publications:* The Tramping Man (play), 1969; The Humming Bird Tree (novel), 1969; Selected Poems, 1983; Mercy Ward, 1988; Essequibo, 1992; Jaffo the Calypsonian (poems), 1994; The Heinemann Book of Caribbean Poetry (co-ed.), 1994. *Honours:* Fellow, RSL, 1970; Guyana National Award, 1987; Hon. DLitt, University of the West Indies, 1997. *Address:* c/o Demerara Sugar Terminal, River View, Ruimveldt, Georgetown, Guyana. *Fax:* (2) 2665054. *E-mail:* dstrsc@guyana.net.gy.

MCDONALD, Paul John; b. 1 May 1961, Walsall, West Midlands, England. Poet; Lecturer; Reviewer. *Education:* Arts, Open University, 1983–86; BA, English, Birmingham Polytechnic, 1989; PhD Candidate, Central England University, 1990–94. *Appointments:* Lecturer, Central England University, 1990–; Book Reviewer, The Birmingham Post; Ed., Publisher, Read This Poetry Broadsheet; Lecturer in American Literature, University of Wolverhampton, 1994–. *Publications:* Circles, 1992; First Communion, 1993; A Funny Old Game, 1994. *Contributions to:* Reviews, journals and magazines. *Address:* 70 Walstead Rd, Delves, Walsall, West Midlands WS5 4LX, England.

MCDONALD, Walter R(obert); b. 18 July 1934, Lubbock, TX, USA. Prof. of English; Poet; Writer. m. Carol Ham, 28 Aug. 1959, 2 s., 1 d. *Education:* BA, 1956, MA, 1957, Texas Technological College; PhD, University of Iowa, 1966. *Appointments:* Faculties, US Air Force Acad., University of Colorado, Texas Tech University; Paul W. Horn Prof. of English and Poet-in-Residence, Texas Tech University, Lubbock. *Publications:* Poetry: Caliban in Blue, 1976; One Thing Leads to Another, 1978; Anything, Anything, 1980; Working Against Time, 1981; Burning the Fence, 1981; Witching on Hardscrabble, 1985; Flying Dutchman, 1987; After the Noise of Saigon, 1988; Rafting the Brazos, 1988. Fiction: A Band of Brothers: Stories of Vietnam, 1989; Night Landings, 1989; The Digs in Escondido Canyon, 1991; All That Matters: The Texas Plains in Photographs and Poems, 1992; Where Skies Are Not Cloudy, 1993; Counting Survivors, 1995. *Contributions to:* Numerous journals and magazines. *Honours:* Poetry Awards, Texas Institute of Letters, 1976, 1985, 1987; George Elliston Poetry Prize, 1987; Juniper Prize, 1988; Western Heritage Awards for Poetry, National Cowboy Hall of Fame, 1990, 1992; 1993. *Memberships:* Texas Asscn of Creative Writing Teachers; PEN; Poetry Society of America; Assoc. Writing Programs; Texas Institute of Letters, councillor; Conference of College Teachers of English of Texas. *Address:* Dept of English, Texas Tech University, Lubbock, TX 79409, USA.

MCDONOUGH, William J.; b. 5 May 1971, Pell City, AL, USA. Brick Mason; Poet. *Education:* Southern Union State College, Wadley, AL. *Publications:* Voyage to Remember, 1996. *Contributions to:* Anthologies and other publications. *Honours:* Ed.'s Choice Award, National Library of Poetry, 1996; Honorable Mention, Iliad Press, 1996. *Memberships:* International Society of Poets; National Author's Registry. *Address:* PO Box 1267, Ashland, AL 36251, USA.

MCELROY, Colleen J(ohnson); b. 30 Oct. 1935, St Louis, MO, USA. Prof.; Poet; Writer. Divorced, 1 s., 1 d. *Education:* BS, 1958, MS, 1963, Kansas State University; PhD, University of Washington, Seattle, 1973. *Appointments:* Ed., Dark Waters, 1973–79; Prof., University of Washington, Seattle, 1973–. *Publications:* Music From Home, 1976; The Halls of Montezuma, 1979; The New Voice, 1979; Winters Without Snow, 1979; Lie and Say You Love Me, 1981; Queen of the Ebony Isles, 1984; Jesus and Fat Tuesday, 1987; What Madness Brought Me Here, 1990. *Contributions to:* Various journals. *Address:* c/o Creative Writing Program, Dept of English, University of Washington, Seattle, WA 98195, USA.

MACER-STORY, Eugenia; b. 20 Jan. 1945, Minneapolis, MN, USA. Writer; Dramatist; Poet. m. Leon A. Story, 1970, divorced 1975, 1 s. *Education:* BS, Speech, Northwestern University, 1965; MFA, Playwriting, Columbia University, 1968. *Publications:* Congratulations: The UFO Reality, 1978; Angels of Time: Astrological Magic, 1981; Du Fu Man Chu Meets the Lonesome Cowboy: Sorcery and the UFO Experience, 1991; Legacy of Daedalus, 1995; Cattle Bones and Coke Machines (anthology), 1995; The Dark Frontier, 1997; Crossing Jungle River (poems), 1998; Troll: Other Interdimensional Invasions (short stories), 2000; Vanishing Questions (poems), 2000; Carrying Thunder, 2002; Doing Business in the Adrondocks (metaphysical travelogue), 2002. Plays: Meister Hemmelin, 1994; Double or Nothing, 1994; Radish, 1995; Conquest of the Asteroids, 1996; Mister Shooting Star, 1997; Wild Dog Casino, 1998; Holy Dragonet, 1998–99; Old Gaffer from Boise, 2000; Redecoration According to Currier, 2000; Ars Chronicon Sylvestre, 2002. *Contributions to:* Numerous publications. *Honour:* Shubert Fellowship, 1968. *Memberships:* Dramatists' Guild; US Psychotronics Asscn; Poet's House, New York; American Society for Psychical Research. *Address:* Magick Mirror Communications, PO Box 741, JAF Bldg, New York, NY 10116, USA.

MCEWEN, Christian; b. 21 April 1956, London, England. Poet; Writer; Teacher. *Education:* BA, English Literature, Social Anthropology, University

of Cambridge, 1979; MA, English Literature, Creative Writing, University o California at Berkeley, 1982. *Appointments:* Reader, Virago, Press, 1983–86 Writer, Teachers & Writers Collaborative, 1988–; Lecturer, Parsons an Eugene Lang, New School for Social Research, New York City, 1992–94 Lesley University, Cambridge, MA. *Publications:* Jo's Girls: Tomboy Tales o High Adventure; The Alphabet of the Trees: A Guide to Nature Writing (co-ed with Mark Statman). *Contributions to:* Anthologies and periodicals. *Honours:* Several residencies; Fulbright Scholarship, 1979; Lambda Literary Award 1989; Fund for Poetry Grant, 1991; Quadrangle Award for Poetry, Springfield Libraries and Museums, 2002. *Membership:* National Writers Union. *Address* 41 Kopkind Rd, Guilford, VT 05301, USA. *E-mail:* christianmcewan@aol.com.

MCFADDEN, Roy; b. 14 Nov. 1921, Belfast, Northern Ireland. Poet *Publications:* Swords and Ploughshares; Flowers for a Lady; The Hearts Townland; Elegy for the Dead of the Princess Victoria; The Garryowen Verifications; A Watching Brief; The Selected Roy McFadden; Letters to the Hinterland; After Seymour's Funeral; Collected Poems 1943–95. *Address:* 1: Shrewsbury Gardens, Belfast BT9, Northern Ireland.

MCFADDEN, Tom; b. 20 Sept. 1945, Lancaster, PA, USA. Poet. m. Loretta Yasson, 15 July 1967, 3 d. *Education:* BA, Pennsylvania State University, 1967 *Contributions to:* Many reviews, quarterlies and journals. *Address:* 11704 Running Fox Trail, Austin, TX 78759, USA.

MCFARLAND, Ron(ald Earl); b. 22 Sept. 1942, Bellaire, Ohio, USA. Prof. o English; Poet; Writer. m. Elsie Roseland Watson, 29 Jan. 1966, 1 s., 2 d. *Education:* AA, Brevard Junior College, 1962; BA, 1963, MA, 1965, Florida State University; PhD, University of Illinois, 1970. *Appointments:* Teaching Asst, Florida State University, 1964–65, University of Illinois, 1967–70; Instructor, Sam Houston State College, 1965–67; Asst Prof., Assoc. Prof. 1970–79, Prof. of English, 1979–, University of Idaho; Idaho State Writer-in-Residence, 1984–85; Exchange Prof., Ohio University, 1985–86. *Publications:* Poetry: Certain Women, 1977; Composting at Forty, 1984; The Haunting Familiarity of Things, 1993; Stranger in Town, 2000; The Hemingway Poems, 2000; The Mad Waitress Poems, 2000; Ballygloves, 2000. Fiction: Catching First Light (short stories), 2001. Non-Fiction: The Villanelle: Evolution of a Poetic Form, 1988; David Wagoner, 1989; Norman Maclean, 1993; Tess Gallagher, 1995; The World of David Wagoner, 1997; Understanding James Welch, 2000. Editor: Eight Idaho Poets, 1979; James Welch, 1987; Norman Maclean (with Hugh Nichols), 1988; Idaho's Poetry: A Centennial Anthology (with William Studebaker), 1988; Deep Down Things: Poems of the Inland Pacific Northwest (with Franz Schneider and Kornel Skovajsa), 1990. *Contributions to:* Scholarly books and journals, poetry anthologies, reviews, quarterlies, and periodicals. *Honours:* National Endowment for the Arts Grant, 1978; Asscn for the Humanities in Idaho Grant, 1983; Burlington-Northern Faculty Achievement Award, 1990; Alumni Award for Faculty Excellence, 1991; Distinguished Alumnus, Brevard Community College, 1996; University of Idaho Faculty Award for Creative Excellence, 2002. *Memberships:* Acad. of American Poets; Hemingway Society; Pacific Northwest American Studies Asscn. *Address:* 857 East St, Moscow, ID 83843, USA.

MCFERREN, Martha Dean; b. 25 April 1947, Henderson, Texas, USA. Librarian; Poet. m. Dennis Scott Wall, 21 May 1977. *Education:* BS, 1969, MLS, 1971, North Texas State University; MFA, Warren Wilson College, 1988. *Publications:* Four books; Several poems. *Contributions to:* Reviews, quarterlies, and journals. *Honours:* Marianne Moore Poetry Prize; National Endowment for the Arts Fellowship; Yaddo Fellowship; Deep South Poetry Prize; Louisiana Artist Fellowship. *Memberships:* Poetry Society of America; Poets and Writers. *Address:* 2679 Verbena St, New Orleans, LA 70122, USA.

MCGILL, Nicole Grace; b. 16 Oct. 1978, St Louis Park, USA. Nursing Asst; Poet. *Education:* Public schools. *Publication:* Poems. *Honour:* Ed.'s Choice Award, National Library of Poetry. *Address:* 3440 Placer Ave, Anoka, MN 55303, USA.

MCGONIGAL, James; b. , 20 May 1947, Dumfries, Scotland. Educator; Poet. m. Mary Alexander, 1 Aug. 1970, 1 s., 3 d. *Education:* MA, 1970, MPhil, 1974, PhD, 1978, University of Glasgow. *Appointments:* High School English Teacher, 1971–84; College Lecturer, 1985–91; Head, Dept of English, 1991–92, Dept of Language and Literature, 1992–, St Andrew's College of Education, Glasgow. *Publications:* A Sort of Hot Scotland: New Writing Scotland 12 (with A L Kennedy), 1994; Last Things First: New Writing Scotland 13 (with A L Kennedy), 1995; Sons of Ezra: British Poets and Ezra Pound (with M Alexander), 1995; Full Strength Angels: New Writing Scotland 14 (with K Jamie), 1996; Driven Home: Selected Poems, 1998; Across the Water: 'Irishness' in Contemporary Scottish Literature (co-ed.), 2000; Scottish Religious Poems: From Columba to the Present (co-ed.), 2000; The Star You Steer By: Basil Bunting and British Modernism (co-ed.), 2000. *Contributions to:* Aquarius; The Dark Horse; New Blackfriars; New Edinburgh Review; Temenos; various others. *Membership:* Council, Asscn for Scottish Literary Studies. *Address:* c/o Dept of Curriculum Studies, Faculty of Education, University of Glasgow, Duntocher Rd, Bearsden, Glasgow G61 4QA, Scotland.

MCGOUGH, Roger; b. 9 Nov. 1937, Liverpool, England. Poet. m. (1) Thelma Monaghan, 1970, divorced 1980, (2), 20 Dec. 1986, 3 s., 1 d. *Education:* St Mary's College, Crosby; BA and Graduate Certificate of Education, Hull University. *Appointments:* Fellow of Poetry, University of Loughborough, 1973–75; Writer-in-Residence, West Australian College of Advanced Education, Perth, 1986. *Publications:* The Mersey Sound (with Brian Patten and Adrian Henri), 1967; Strictly Private (ed.), 1982; An Imaginary Menagerie, 1989; Blazing Fruit (selected poems 1967–87), 1990; Pillow Talk, 1990; The Lighthouse That Ran Away, 1991; You at the Back (selected poems 1967–87, Vol. 2), 1991; My Dad's a Fire Eater, 1992; Defying Gravity, 1992; The Elements, 1993; Lucky, 1993; Stinkers Ahoy!, 1994; The Magic Fountain, 1995; The Kite and Caitlin, 1996; Sporting Relations, 1996; Bad, Bad Cats, 1997; Until I Met Dudley, 1997; The Spotted Unicorn, 1998; The Ring of Words (ed.), 1998; The Way Things Are, 1999; Everyday Eclipses, 2002; Good Enough to Eat, 2002; Dotty Inventions, 2002; Moonthief, 2002; What on Earth, 2002; Wicked Poems (ed.), 2002. *Honours:* BAFTA Awards, 1984, 1992; Signal Awards, 1984, 1998; Hon. Prof., Thames Valley University, 1993; O.B.E., 1997; Cholmondeley Award, 1998; Hon. MA, Nene College, 1998; Fellow, John Moores University, 1999; Freeman, City of Liverpool, 2001. *Address:* c/o The Peters, Fraser and Dunlop Group Ltd, Drury House, 34–43 Russell St, London WC2B 5HA, England.

MCGRATH, Campbell; b. 1962, Chicago, IL, USA. Poet. *Education:* University of Chicago; MFA, Columbia University, 1988. *Publications:* Capitalism, 1990; American Noise, 1993; Spring Comes to Chicago, 1996. *Honours:* Pushcart Prize; Acad. of American Poets Prize; Kingsley Tufts Poetry Award, 1997. *Address:* c/o Ecco Press, 100 W Broad St, Hopewell, NJ 08525, USA.

MCGRORY, Edward; b. 6 Nov. 1921, Stevenston, Ayrshire, Scotland. Poet. m. Mary McDonald, 20 Nov. 1948, 1 s., 1 d. *Education:* BA, Open University, 1985. *Publications:* Selected Poems, 1984; Plain and Coloured, 1985; Pied Beauty, 1986; Orchids and Daisies, 1987; Light Reflections – Mirror Images, 1988; Chosen Poems by Celebrities: Eddie McGrory's Poems, 1988; Masks and Faces, 1989; Illuminations, 1990; Letters from Flora, 1991; Candles and Lasers, 1992. *Memberships:* Various literary societies. *Address:* 41 Sythrum Crescent, Glenrothes, Fife KY7 5DG, Scotland.

MCGUCKIAN, Medbh; b. 12 Aug. 1950, Belfast, Northern Ireland. Poet; Teacher. m. John McGuckian, 1977, 3 s., 1 d. *Education:* BA, 1972, MA, 1974, Queen's University, Belfast. *Appointments:* Teacher, Dominican Convent, Fortwilliam Park, Belfast, 1974; Instructor, St Patrick's College, Knock, Belfast, 1975–; Writer-in-Residence, Queen's University, Belfast, 1986–88. *Publications:* Poetry: Single Ladies: Sixteen Poems, 1980; Portrait of Joanna, 1980; Trio Poetry (with Damian Gorman and Douglas Marshall), 1981; The Flower Master, 1982; The Greenhouse, 1983; Venus and the Rain, 1984; On Ballycastle Beach, 1988; Two Women, Two Shores, 1989; Marconi's Cottage, 1991; The Flower Master and Other Poems, 1993; Captain Lavender, 1994; Drawing Ballerinas, 2001. Editor: The Big Striped Golfing Umbrella: Poems by Young People from Northern Ireland, 1985. *Honours:* National Poetry Competition Prize, 1979; Eric Gregory Award, 1980; Rooney Prize, 1982; Ireland Arts Council Award, 1982; Alice Hunt Bartlett Award, 1983; Cheltenham Literature Festival Poetry Competition Prize, 1989. *Address:* c/o Gallery Press, Oldcastle, County Meath, Ireland.

MCGUINNESS, Frank; b. 29 July 1953, Buncrana, Donegal, Ireland. Dramatist; Writer; Poet; University Lecturer in English. *Education:* BA, 1976, MPh, University College, Dublin. *Appointments:* Lecturer in English, University of Ulster, Coleraine, 1977–79; University College, Dublin, 1979–80, 1997–, St Patrick's College, Maynooth, 1984–97; Dir, Abbey Theatre, Dublin, 1992–96. *Publications:* Plays: The Factory Girls, 1982; Observe the Sons of Ulster Marching Towards the Somme, 1985; Borderlands, 1988; Baglady, 1988; Carthaginians, 1988; Mary Lizzie, 1989; Peer Gynt (adaptation of Ibsen's play), 1990; Three Sisters (adaptation of Chekov's play), 1990; Someone Who'll Watch Over Me, 1992; Plays One, 1996; A Doll's House (adaptation of Ibsen's play), 1997; Mutabilitie, 1997; Electra (adaptation of Sophocles' play), 1997; Miss Julie (adaptation of Strindberg's play), 2000. Other: In Loving Memory (poems), 1989; Booterstown (poems), 1994; The Dazzling Dark: New Irish Places, 1996; Dancing at Lughnasa (screenplay), 1998; Dolly West's Kitchen, 1999; The Sea With No Ships (poems), 1999. *Honours:* Rooney Prize, 1985; Harvey's Award, 1985; Most Promising Playwright Award, Evening Standard, 1986; Plays and Players Award, 1986; Cheltenham Prize, 1989; Charrington Award, 1987; Ewart-Biggs Peace Prize, 1987; Edinburgh Fringe First Award, 1988; Prix des Journalists, Prague, 1989; Irish-American Literary Prize, 1992; Best Play, Independent on Sunday, 1992; New York Drama Critics' Award, 1993; Writers' Guild Award, 1993; Tony Award for Best Revival, 1997; Officier des Arts et des Lettres, France. *Membership:* Aosdána. *Address:* 32 Booterstown Ave, Dublin, Ireland.

MACHAN, Katharyn Howd; b. 12 Sept. 1952, Woodbury, CT, USA. College Prof.; Poet. m. Eric Machan Howd, 20 June 1991, 1 s., 1 d. *Education:* BA, College of Saint Rose, 1974; MA, University of Iowa, 1975; PhD, Northwestern University, 1984. *Appointments:* Teacher of Writing, Literature, Speech and Performance, Tompkins Cortland Community College, Ithaca College, Cornell University, Northwestern University. *Publications:* Sixteen collections, including, Belly Words, 1994. *Contributions to:* Yankee; Seneca Review; Poets On; South Coast Poetry Journal; Zone 3; Kalliope. *Honours:* Poetry Society of America Awards, 1981, 1983; Several grants for poetry. *Memberships:* Feminist Women's Writing Workshops, board dir. *Address:* PO Box 456, Ithaca, NY 14851, USA.

MCHUGH, Heather; b. 20 Aug. 1948, San Diego, CA, USA. Prof. of English; Poet; Writer; Trans. m. Nikolai Popov. *Education:* BA, Harvard University, 1969–70; MA in English Literature, University of Denver, 1972. *Appointments:* Assoc. Prof., State University of New York at Binghamton, 1974–83; Core Faculty, MFA Program for Writers, Goddard College, later Warren Wilson College, 1976–; Milliman Distinguished Writer-in-Residence and Prof. of English, University of Washington, 1984–; Holloway Lecturer in Poetry, University of California at Berkeley, 1987; Visiting Prof., University of Iowa, 1991–92, 1995, University of California at Los Angeles, 1994, University of California at Irvine, 1994; Coal-Royalty Chair in Poetry, University of Alabama, Tuscaloosa, 1992; Elliston Prof. of Poetry, University of Cincinnati, 1993; Visiting Lecturer, University of Bergen, Norway, 1994. *Publications:* Poetry: Dangers, 1977; A World of Difference, 1981; To the Quick, 1987; Shades, 1988; Hinge & Sign: Poems 1968–1993, 1994; The Father of the Predicaments (Poems 1993–1998), 1999. Essays: Broken English: Poetry and Partiality, 1993. Translator: D'Apres Tout: Poems by Jean Follain, 1981; Because the Sea is Black: Poems by Blaga Dimitrova (with Niko Boris), 1989. Other: Where Are They Now? (with Tom Phillips), 1990; Glottal Sytop: 101 Poems by Paul Celan (with Nikolai Popov). *Contributions to:* Many anthologies and journals. *Honours:* National Endowment for the Arts Grants, 1974, 1979, 1981; Pushcart Prizes, 1978 et seq; Guggenheim Fellowship, 1989; Woodrow Wilson National Poetry Fellow, 1992–93; Daniel A Pollack Prize, Harvard University and Harvard College Library, 1995; Bingham Prize, Boston Book Review, 1995; TLS International Book of the Year List, 1995; Lila Wallace/ Reader's Digest Writing Award, 1996–99; O D Hardison Award, 1998; PEN Voelker Prize, 2000. *Memberships:* Acad. of American Poets, board of chancellors, 1999–; American Acad. of Arts and Sciences, 2000. *Address:* c/o Dept of English, Box 354330, University of Washington, Seattle, WA 98195, USA.

MCILVANNEY, William; b. 25 Nov. 1936, Kilmarnock, Ayrshire, Scotland. Author; Poet. *Education:* MA, University of Glasgow, 1959. *Publications:* Fiction: Remedy is None, 1966; A Gift from Nessus, 1968; Docherty, 1975; Laidlaw, 1977; The Papers of Tony Veitch, 1983; The Big Man, 1985; Walking Wounded (short stories), 1989. Poetry: The Long Ships in Harbour, 1970; Landscapes and Figures, 1973; Weddings and After, 1984. *Address:* c/o John Farquharson Ltd, 162–168 Regent St, London W1R 5TB, England.

MACINNES, Mairi (Clare); b. 5 Jan. 1925, Norton on Tees, England. Writer; Poet. m. John McCormick, 4 Feb. 1954, 2 s., 1 d. *Education:* BA, MA, University of Oxford. *Publications:* Splinters, 1953; Herring, Oatmeal, Milk and Salt, 1982; The House on the Ridge Road, 1987; Elsewhere and Back, 1993; The Ghostwriter, 1999; The Pebble: Old and New Poems, 2000; Clearances: A Memoir, 2002. *Contributions to:* New Yorker; Spectator; Ploughshares; Massachusetts Review; Literary Review; Nation; TriQuarterly Review; Prairie Schooner; Quarterly Review of Literature; Canto; Stand; Ontario Review; New Statesman; PN Review; Noble Savage; Lines; New Republic; Columbia; TLS; Poetry Wales; Threepenny Review; Hudson Review; Yale Review. Honours; Witter Bynner Fellowship; New Jersey Council of the Arts Grant; National Endowment for the Arts Fellowship; Ingram Merrill Fellowship. *Membership:* Poetry Society. *Address:* Hovingham Lodge, Hovingham, York YO6 4NA, England.

MCKAY, Don(ald Fleming); b. 25 June 1942, Owen Sound, Ontario, Canada. Poet; Writer; Ed. divorced, 1 s., 1 d. *Education:* Bishop's University; BA, 1965, MA, 1966, University of Ontario; PhD, University College, Swansea, Wales, 1971. *Appointments:* Teacher, University of New Brunswick, 1990–96; Ed., The Fiddlehead. *Publications:* Air Occupies Space, 1973; Long Sault, 1975; Lependu, 1978; Lightning Ball Bait, 1980; Birding, or Desire, 1983; Sanding Down This Rocking Chair on a Windy Night, 1987; Night Field, 1991; Apparatus, 1997; Another Gravity, 2000. *Contributions to:* Periodicals. *Honours:* Canadian Authors' Asscn Award for Poetry, 1983; Governor-General's Award for Poetry, 1991; National Magazine Award for Poetry, 1991. *Memberships:* League of Canadian Poets; PEN; Writers' Union of Canada. *Address:* 434 Richmond Ave, Victoria, BC V8S 3Y4, Canada.

MCKEE, Lois Hester Grace; b. 15 June 1938, Belfast, Northern Ireland. Administrative Officer; Poet. m. 14 July 1961, 3 s., 1 d. *Contributions to:* Belfast Telegraph; Scottish Poetry Society; Orbis. *Honour:* Prize Winner, Scottish Poetry Society. *Memberships:* Orbis; Civil Service Author. *Address:* 49 Downpatrick Rd, Clough BT30 8NL, Northern Ireland.

MCKEE, Louis; b. 31 July 1951, Philadelphia, PA, USA. Poet; Writer; Ed. m. Christine Caruso, 19 Aug. 1978, divorced 1982. *Education:* BA, LaSalle College, 1973; Temple University, 1973–75. *Appointments:* Ed., Painted Bride Quarterly, 1984–88, One Trick Pony, 1997–; Co-Ed., Axe Factory Review, 1984–. *Publications:* Schuylkill Country, 1982; The True Speed of Things,

1984; Safe Water, 1986; No Matter, 1987; Oranges, 1989; Angelus, 1990; Three Poems, 1993; River Architecture: Poems from Here and There: Selected Poems, 1973–1993, 1999; Right as Rain, 2000; Near Occasions of Sin, 2000. *Contributions to:* Anthologies, reviews, quarterlies and journals. *Memberships:* Acad. of American Poets; PEN; Poetry Society of America; Poets and Writers. *Address:* 8460 Frankford Ave, Philadelphia, PA 19136, USA.

MCKEEHAN, Mildred Hope, (Hope Scott); b. 5 July 1926, Miami, FL, USA. Poet. m. (1) Thomas W Scott, 19 Dec. 1958, 1 s., 1 d., (2) Emory A McKeehan, 12 April 1998. *Education:* Eastern Nazarene College, 1954–55; Bachelor of Bible Theology, International Bible Institute and Seminary, 1982. *Publications:* The Empty Chair, 2000. *Contributions to:* Our Forgotten Graces, 1999; Timepieces, 1999; American Poetry Annual, 1999; A Time To Be Free, 1999; The Sunlit Path, 2000; Bouquet of Love, 2000; Best Short Poems, 2000. *Honours:* Medal for poetry, Greater Miami Women's Club, 1941; Ed.'s Choice Award for Outstanding Achievement in Poetry, International Library of Poetry, 1999. *Memberships:* National Authors Registry; Newspaper Institute of America; International Society of Poets; ASCAP. *Address:* 3714 NW 12th Ave, Miami, FL 33127-3009, USA. *E-mail:* floridapoet@yahoo.com.

MCKENNA, Patricia Ann. See: GOEDICKE, Patricia.

MACKENZIE, Ginny; b. 20 Sept. 1945, Clearfield, Pennsylvania, USA. Writer; Poet; Prof. m. Jake Berthot, 1 s. *Education:* MFA, Goddard College, 1981. *Publications:* By Morning, 1984; New York/Beijing, 1988. *Contributions to:* New Letters; Boulevard; Ploughshares; Iowa Review; Threepenny Review; Nation; Shenandoah; Agni Review; Pequod; Madison Review; Mid-American Review; Poetry East; Seneca Review. *Honours:* Winner, Crab Orchard Review's Annual Contest and Korone Women's Voices Annual Contest, 1998. *Memberships:* PSA; AAP; Poets and Writers. *Address:* 66 Grand St, New York, NY 10013, USA.

MCKEOWN, Tom S.; b. 29 Sept. 1937, Evanston, IL, USA. Poet; Writing Consultant. m. Patricia Haebig, 22 April 1989, 1 s., 1 d. *Education:* BA, 1961, MA, 1962, University of Michigan; MFA, Vermont College, 1989. *Appointments:* Writer-in-Residence, Stephens College, 1968–74; Poet-in-Residence, Savannah College of Art and Design, 1982–83; University of Wisconsin, Oshkosh, 1983–87, University of Wisconsin at Madison, 1989–94. *Publications:* The Luminous Revolver, 1973; The House of Water, 1974; Driving to New Mexico, 1974; Certain Minutes, 1978; Circle of the Eye, 1982; Three Hundred Tigers, 1994. *Contributions to:* Newspapers, reviews, and magazines. *Honours:* Avery Hopwood Award, 1968; Wisconsin Arts Fellowship, 1980. *Address:* 1220 N Gammon Rd, Middleton, WI 53562, USA.

MCKERNAN, Llewellyn McKinnie; b. 12 July 1941, Hampton, AR, USA. Poet; Children's Writer. m. John Joseph McKernan, 3 Sept. 1967, 1 d. *Education:* BA, English, Hendrix College, 1963; MA, English, University of Arkansas, 1966; MA, Creative Writing, Brown University, 1976. *Appointments:* Instructor of English, Georgia Southern College, 1966–67; Adjunct Prof. of English, Marshall University, 1980–86, 1991; Prof. of English, St Mary's College, 1989. *Publications:* Short and Simple Annals, 1979; More Songs of Gladness, 1987; Bird Alphabet, 1988; Many Waters, 1993; This is the Day and This is the Night, 1994. *Contributions to:* Reviews and journals. *Honours:* Third Prize, Chester H Jones National Poetry Competition, 1982; West Virginia Humanities Artist Grant, 1983; Second Prize, National Founders Award Contest, National Federation of State Poetry Societies, 1994. *Memberships:* West Virginia Writers; Poetry Society of West Virginia; Society of Children's Book Writers and Illustrators. *Address:* Route 10, Box 4639B, Barboursville, WV 25504, USA.

MACKEY, Mary; b. 21 Jan. 1945, Indianapolis, IN, USA. Author; Poet; Prof. of English. m. Rob Colwell, Dec. 1965, divorced, partner Angus Wright. *Education:* BA, Radcliffe College, 1966; MA, 1967, PhD, Comparative Literature, 1970, University of Michigan. *Appointments:* Asst Prof., 1972–76, Assoc. Prof., 1976–80, Prof. of English, 1980–, California State University at Sacramento. *Publications:* Fiction: Immersion, 1972; McCarthy's List, 1979; The Last Warrior Queen, 1983; A Grand Passion, 1986; The Kindness of Strangers, 1988; Season of Shadows, 1991; The Year the Horses Came, 1993; The Horses at the Gate, 1996; The Fires of Spring, 1998; October at Fools Hope, 2001. Poetry: Split Ends, 1974; One Night Stand, 1977; Skin Deep, 1978; The Dear Dance of Eros, 1987. Other: Chance Music (ed. with Mary MacArthur), 1977. *Contributions to:* Periodicals. *Honours:* Woodrow Wilson Fellowship, 1966–67; Virginia Center for the Creative Arts Fellowship, 1999. *Memberships:* Feminist Writers' Guild; National Book Critics Circle; PEN American Center West, pres., 1989–92; Writers' Guild of America. *Address:* c/o Dept of English, California State University at Sacramento, Sacramento, CA 95819, USA. *E-mail:* mackeym@mindspring.com. *Website:* csus.edu/indiv/m/mackeym.

MACKEY, Nathaniel; b. 25 Oct. 1947, Miami, FL, USA. Prof.; Poet; Writer; Ed. m. Pascale Gaitet, 1991, 1 d., 1 step-s. *Education:* AB in English, Princeton University, 1969; PhD in English and American Literature, Stanford University, 1975. *Appointments:* Asst Prof., University of Wisconsin at Madison, 1974–76; Ed., Hambone, literary magazine, 1974–; Asst Prof. and

Dir of Black Studies, University of Southern California at Los Angeles, 1976–79; Visiting Prof., Occidental College, 1979; Asst Prof., 1979–81, Assoc. Prof., 1981–87, Prof., 1987–, Board of Studies in Literature and American Studies Program, University of California at Santa Cruz; Writer-in-Residence, Washington, DC, Project for the Arts, 1986, Institute of American Indian Arts, Santa Fe, New Mexico, 1987, 1988, Brown University, 1990, Intersection for the Arts, San Francisco, 1991; Faculty, Naropa Institute, Boulder, summers 1991, 1993; Visiting Foreign Artist, Kootenay School of Writing, Vancouver, BC, 1994. *Publications:* Poetry: Four for Trane, 1978; Septet for the End of Time, 1983; Eroding Witness, 1985; Outlandish, 1992; School of Udhra, 1993; Song of the Andoumboulou: 18–20, 1994; Whatsaid Serif, 1998. Fiction: From a Broken Bottle Traces of Perfume Still Emanate, Vol. I, Bedouin Hornbook, 1986, Vol. II, Djbot Baghostus's Run, 1993. Non-Fiction: Discrepant Engagement: Dissonance, Cross-Culturality and Experimental Writing, 1993. Other: Moment's Notice: Jazz in Poetry and Prose (ed. with Art Lange), 1993. Other: Strick: Song of the Andoumboulon 16–25 (poems with musical accompaniment), 1995. *Contributions to:* Anthologies, scholarly journals and magazines. *Honours:* Co-ordinating Council of Literary Magazines Ed.'s Grant, 1985; Whiting Writer's Award, 1993. *Membership:* Acad. of American Poets, board of chancellors, 2001–. *Address:* c/o Kresge College, University of California at Santa Cruz, Santa Cruz, CA 95064, USA.

MACKIE, Peter George; b. 6 Jan. 1957, Perth, Scotland. Poet. *Education:* Higher National Diploma, Data Processing, 1987. *Publications:* All the Words Under the Sun, 1973; The Madhouse of Love, 1992; Epicycles of Sinking Time, 1997; The Last Thing Before the Apocalypse, 2002. *Contributions to:* Various publications. *Memberships:* Asscn of Little Presses; Small Press Center, New York; Small Press Group, Great Britain; Society of Young Publishers, assoc. mem. *Address:* c/o Tetrahedron Books, 30 Birch Crescent, Blairgowrie, Perthshire PH10 6TS, Scotland.

MCKINLEY, Hugh; b. 18 Feb. 1924, Oxford, England. Poet. m. Deborah Waterfield, 15 Sept. 1979. *Appointments:* Literary Ed., Athens Daily Post, 1966–77; European Ed., Poet, India, 1967–91; Editorial Panel, Bitterroot, USA, 1980–89. *Publications:* Starmusic, 1976; Transformation of Faust, 1977; Poet in Transit, 1979; Exulting for the Light, 1983; Skylarking, 1994. *Contributions to:* Various publications worldwide. *Honours:* Pres. Marcos Medal, Philippines, 1967; Hon. DLitt, International Acad. of Leadership, 1967, Free University of Asia, Karachi, 1973; Directorate, Academia Pax Mundi, Israel, 1978. *Memberships:* Baha'i World Faith, life mem.; Suffolk Poetry Society. *Address:* Owl's Hoot, 10 The Glebe, Lawshall, Bury St Edmunds, Suffolk IP29 4PW, England.

MACKLIN, Elizabeth (Jean); b. 28 Oct. 1952, Poughkeepsie, New York, USA. Poet. m. Francis Gerald Macklin Jr, 12 Jan. 1974, divorced March 1979. *Education:* BA in Spanish, State University of New York at Potsdam, 1973; Graduate School of Arts and Sciences, New York University, 1975–78. *Appointment:* Poetry Ed., Wigwag Magazine, 1989–91. *Publication:* A Woman Kneeling in the Big City, 1992; You've Just Been Told (poems), 2000. *Contributions to:* Nation; New Republic; New York Times; New Yorker; Paris Review; Threepenny Review. *Honours:* Ingram Merrill Foundation Award in Poetry, 1990; Guggenheim Fellowship, 1994; Amy Lowell Poetry Travelling Scholarship, 1998–99. *Memberships:* Authors Guild; PEN American Center, exec. board, 1995–96. *Address:* 207 W 14th St, 5F, New York, NY 10011, USA.

MACKMIN, Michael; b. 20 April 1941, London, England. Psychotherapist; Poet; Ed. Divorced, 2 d. *Education:* BA, 1963; MA, 1965. *Appointment:* Ed., The Rialto. *Publications:* The Play of Rainbow; Connemara Shore. *Address:* PO Box 309, Aylsham, Norwich NR11 6LN, England. *Website:* www.therialto.co.uk.

MCKUEN, Rod; b. 29 April 1933, Oakland, CA, USA. Poet; Composer; Writer. *Appointments:* Many concert, film, and television appearances. *Publications:* Poetry: And Autumn Came, 1954; Stanyan Street and Other Sorrows, 1966; Listen to the Warm, 1967; Lonesome Cities, 1968; Twelve Years of Christmas, 1968; In Someone's Shadow, 1969; A Man Alone, 1969; With Love, 1970; Caught in the Quiet, 1970; New Ballads, 1970; Fields of Wonder, 1971; The Carols of Christmas, 1971; And to Each Season, 1972; Pastorale, 1972; Grand Tour, 1972; Come to Me in Silence, 1973; America: An Affirmation, 1974; Seasons in the Sun, 1974; Moment to Moment, 1974; Beyond the Boardwalk, 1975; The Rod McKuen Omnibus, 1975; Alone, 1975; Celebrations of the Heart, 1975; The Sea Around Me, 1977; Hand in Hand, 1977; Coming Close to Earth, 1978; We Touch the Sky, 1979; Love's Been Good to Me, 1979; Looking for a Friend, 1980; The Power Bright and Shining, 1980; Too Many Midnights, 1981; Rod McKuen's Book of Days, 1981; The Beautiful Strangers, 1981; The Works of Rod McKuen, Vol. 1 (poems), 1950–82, 1982; Watch for the Wind..., 1982; Rod McKuen: 1984 Book of Days, 1983; The Sound of Solitude, 1986; Intervals, 1987. Prose: Finding My Father: One Man's Search for Identity, 1976; An Outstretched Hand, 1980. Other: Various classical, film, and television scores. *Honours:* 41 Gold and Platinum Records Awards; Grand Prix du Disque, Paris, 1966, 1974, 1975, 1982; Grammy Award, 1969. *Address:* PO Box 2783, Los Angeles, CA 90078, USA.

MCLAUGHLIN, Joseph (David); b. 24 Sept. 1940, Canton, Ohio, USA. Prof. of English (retd); Poet. m. Anna Franz, 2 Dec. 1961, 3 s., 1 d. *Education:* AA,

1974, BA, 1977, University of New York; MA, Vermont College, 1983. *Publications:* Dream Frames, 1978; Zen in the Art of Golf, 1991; Memory, In Your Country, 1996; Golf is the Devil's Game, 1997; Greatest Hits: 1970–2000, 2001. *Contributions to:* Southern Poetry Review; Hiram Poetry Review; Confrontation. *Address:* 186 Pegasus Dr. NW, Dover, OH 44622, USA.

MACLEAN, Alasdair; b. 16 March 1926, Glasgow, Scotland. Poet. *Publications:* From the Wilderness, 1973; Waking the Dead, 1976; Night Falls on Ardnamurchan: The Twilight of a Crofting Family, 1984. *Honour:* Cholmondeley Award, 1974. *Address:* c/o Victor Gollancz Ltd, 14 Henrietta St, London WC2E 8QJ, England.

MCLEMORE, Monita Prine; b. 7 June 1927, Avera, Mississippi, USA. Adjunct College Teacher of Music; Harpist; Poet. m. Harry Kimbrell McLemore, 9 March 1952, 1 s., 1 d. *Education:* BMus, 1949, MMus, 1951, PhD, 2000, University of Southern Mississippi. *Publications:* Poems by Monita, 1985; More Poems, 1987; Still More Poems, 1989; Ripples From the Edge, 1992; A Tapestry of Nature, 1993; Haiku Happenings, 1995; Fingerprints in Rhyme, 1996. *Contributions to:* Various publications. *Honours:* Numerous poetry competition awards; Poet of the Year, South Chapter, Mississippi Poetry Society, 1994. *Memberships:* Mississippi Poetry Society; National Federation of State Poetry Societies; Writers Unlimited. *Address:* 110 Winchester Dr., Ocean Springs, MS 39564, USA. *E-mail:* hkm@bellsouth.net.

MACLENNAN, Ian Alexander; b. 22 Aug. 1924, London, England. Prof. (retd). Poet. m. Vivien Margery, 26 April 1974. *Education:* MSc, University of London, 1958; MA, University of Oxford, 1964. *Appointments:* Asst Prof., Mathematics, University of King's College, 1947–53; Assoc. Prof., Philosophy, Dalhousie University, 1956–79. *Publications:* Winter Apples, 1987; In Celebration, 1991; Images, 1991. *Contributions to:* Dalhousie Review; Kansas Quarterly; Psychopoetica; Möbius; Whetstone Poetry; Poetry WLU; Canadian Author and Bookman; The Eclectic Muse; Colorado North Review. *Honours:* Second Prize, North American Poetry Competition, National Library of Poetry, USA, 1994; Second Prize, Sparrowgrass Poetry Forum, 1997. *Address:* Apt 310, Fort Massey Apts, 1263 Queen St, Halifax, Nova Scotia B3J 3L4, Canada.

MACLEOD, Iris Jean; b. 18 May 1927, Calgary, AB, Canada. Musician; Poet. divorced, 2 s. *Education:* BA, English, Philosophy, San Jose State University, 1961; Graduate Studies, English, 1962; BA, Music, California State University, Hayward, 1982. *Publications:* Chord or Nonchord (music and poems), 1977; A Masque for All-Souls Eve (miniature music drama), 1982; Seven Sonnets From Notes of a Winter Voyageur, 1989. *Contributions to:* Various publications. *Honours:* Several poetry prizes; International Order of Merit in Music, 1991; International Honours Cup for Poetry and Music, 1992; Hon. DLitt, 1993. *Memberships:* World Poetry Society; Dame des Lofsensischen Ursinius-Orden. *Address:* 1332 Paloma Ave, Belmont, CA 94002, USA.

MACLEOD, N(orma) J(ean), (Normajean MacLeod, Cass Peru); b. 27 Feb. 1929, Indiana, USA. Data Systems Co-ordinator (retd); Poet; Writer; Ed. m. John C MacLeod, 13 Sept. 1947, 1 s. *Education:* Motel Management School, Santa Barbara, CA, 1973. *Publications:* Poetica Erotica; Womanclature; The Queen Bee Syndrome. *Contributions to:* Various anthologies and other publications. *Honours:* Literary prizes and awards; Hon. degrees. *Memberships:* Indiana State Federation of Poetry Clubs; International Womens Writing Guild; National Federation of State Poetry Societies; United Poets Laureate International. *Address:* 1403 N Jackson Branch Ridge Rd, Nashville, IN 47448, USA.

MCLOUGHLAND, Beverly; b. 13 May 1946, Newark, New Jersey, USA. Poet; Writer. m. Keith F McLoughland, deceased. *Education:* Seton Hall University, Newark, 1963–65; BA, Early Childhood Education, Kean College, Union, New Jersey, 1973. *Publication:* A Hippo's a Heap and Other Animal Poems, 1993. *Contributions to:* Many anthologies, elementary school textbooks, and periodicals. *Membership:* Society of Children's Book Writers and Illustrators. *Address:* c/o Boyd Mills Press, 815 Church St, Honesdale, PA 18431, USA.

MCMANUS, James; b. 22 March 1951, New York, NY, USA. Poet; Writer; Teacher. m. Jennifer Arra, 9 July 1992, 1 s., 1 d. *Education:* BA, 1974, MA, 1977, University of Illinois at Chicago. *Appointment:* Faculty, School of the Art Institute, Chicago, 1981–. *Publications:* Several works. *Contributions to:* Many publications. *Honour:* Guggenheim Fellowship, 1994–95. *Memberships:* Associated Writing Programs; PEN. *Address:* c/o School of the Art Institute, 37 S Wabash, Chicago, IL 60603, USA.

MCMASTER, Susan, (S. M. Page); b. 11 Aug. 1950, Toronto, ON, Canada. Poet; Ed. m. Ian McMaster, 5 July 1969, 2 d. *Education:* BA, English, 1970, Graduate Studies, Journalism, 1975–80, Carleton University: Teaching Certificate, Ottawa Teachers' College, 1971. *Appointments:* Founding Ed., Branching Out Magazine, 1973–75; Senior Book Ed., National Gallery of Canada, 1989–98, 2002–; Ed.-in-Chief, Vernissage, 1999–2002. *Publications:* Pass This Way Again (co-author), 1983; Dark Galaxies, 1986; North/South (co-author), 1987; Dangerous Graces (ed.), 1987; Women and Language (ed.), 1990; Two Women Talking, Erin Mouré and Bronwen Wallace, 1991; Illegitimate Positions (ed.), 1991; The Hummingbird Murders, 1992; Learning to Ride, 1994;

Dangerous Times, 1996; Uncommon Prayer, 1997; Siolence: Poets on Violence and Silence (ed.), 1998. Other: Wordmusic (with First Draft), 1987; Audio tape (with Sugarbeat), 1997; Sugar Beat music and poetry (CD), 1999; Geode music and poetry (CD), 2000. *Contributions to:* Magazines, journals and anthologies. *Honours:* Various awards from Canada Council for the Arts, Ontario Arts Council, Regional Municipality of Ottawa Carleton. *Memberships:* League of Canadian Poets; PEN. *Address:* 43 Belmont Ave, Ottawa, ON K15 0T9, Canada.

MACNAB, Arden. See: TICE, Arden A.

MACNAB, Roy Martin; b. 17 Sept. 1923, Durban, South Africa. Diplomat (retd); Writer; Poet. m. Rachel Heron-Maxwell, 6 Dec. 1947, 1 s., 1 d. *Education:* Hilton College, Natal, South Africa; MA, Jesus College, Oxford, 1955; DLitt et Phil, University of South Africa, 1981. *Publications:* The Man of Grass and Other Poems, 1960; The French Colonel, 1975; Gold Their Touchstone, 1987; For Honour Alone, 1988. Co-Editor: Oxford Poetry, 1947; Poets in South Africa, 1958; Journey Into Yesterday, 1962. Editor: George Seferis: South African Diary, 1990; The Cherbourg Circles, 1994. *Contributions to:* TLS; Spectator; Poetry Review; History, Today. *Honour:* Silver Medal, RSA, 1958. *Address:* 9/18 Elm Park Gdns, London SW10 9PD, England.

MCNAIR, Wesley; b. 19 June 1941, Newport, New Hampshire, USA. Prof.; Poet. m. Diane Reed McNair, 24 Dec. 1962, 3 s., 1 d. *Education:* BA, English, Keene State College, 1963; MA, English, 1968, MLitt, American Literature, 1975, Middlebury College. *Appointments:* Assoc. Prof., Colby Sawyer College, 1968–87; Senior Fulbright Prof., Catholic University of Chile, 1977–78; Visiting Prof., Dartmouth College, 1984, Colby College, 2000–01; Assoc. Prof. to Prof., University of Maine at Farmington, 1987–98. *Publications:* The Town of No, 1989; Twelve Journeys in Maine, 1992; My Brother Running, 1993; Talking in the Dark, 1998; Mapping the Heart: Reflections on Place and Poetry, 2002; Fire: Poems, 2002. *Contributions to:* Anthologies, reviews, quarterlies, and journals. *Honours:* National Endowment for the Arts Fellowships, 1980, 1990; Devins Award, 1984; Eunice Tietjens Prize, 1984; Guggenheim Fellowship, 1986; Pushcart Prize, 1986; New England Emmy Award, 1991; Rockefeller Residency, Bellagio, Italy, 1993; Theodore Roethke Prize, 1993; Yankee Magazine Poetry Prize, 1995; Sarah Josepha Hale Medal, 1997. *Address:* c/o Dept of Humanities, University of Maine at Farmington, Farmington, ME 04938, USA.

MCNALLY, Marcy Ada; b. 29 Dec. 1951, Tucson, AZ, USA. Poet; Writer; Artist. *Education:* University of Arizona, Tucson. *Publications:* Over 20 poems. *Honours:* Several poetry awards, 1995–96. *Memberships:* Arizona State Poetry Society; International Society of Poets; National Authors Registry; National Federation of State Poetry Societies; National Writers Union. *Address:* 5326 E Sixth St, Tucson, AZ 85711, USA.

MCNAMARA, Eugene Joseph; b. 18 March 1930, Oak Park, IL, USA. Prof.; Ed.; Poet; Writer. m. Margaret Lindstrom, 19 July 1952, 4 s., 1 d. *Education:* BA, MA, DePaul University; PhD, Northwestern University, 1964. *Appointments:* Ed., University of Windsor Review, 1965–, Mainline, 1967–72, Sesame Press, 1973–80; Prof. of English, University of Windsor. *Publications:* Poetry: For the Mean Time, 1965; Outerings, 1970; Dillinger Poems, 1970; Love Scenes, 1971; Passages, 1972; Screens, 1977; Forcing the Field, 1980; Call it a Day, 1984. Short Stories: Salt, 1977; Search for Sarah Grace, 1978; Spectral Evidence, 1985; The Moving Light, 1986. *Contributions to:* Queens Quarterly; Saturday Night; Chicago; Quarry; Denver Quarterly. *Address:* 166 Randolph Pl., Windsor, Ontario N9B 2T3, Canada.

MCNAMARA, Robert (James); b. 28 March 1950, New York, NY, USA. University Lecturer in English; Poet. 1 d. *Education:* BA, Amherst College, 1971; MA, Colorado State University, 1975; PhD, University of Washington, Seattle, 1985. *Appointments:* Founder-Ed., L'Epervier Press, 1977; Senior Lecturer in English, University of Washington, Seattle, 1985–. *Publication:* Second Messengers, 1990. *Contributions to:* Anthologies, reviews, quarterlies, and journals. *Honours:* National Endowment for the Arts Fellowship, 1987–88; Fulbright Grant, Jadavpur University, Calcutta, 1993. *Memberships:* Acad. of American Poets; PEN West. *Address:* c/o Dept of English, Box 354330, University of Washington, Seattle, WA 98195, USA.

MACNAUGHTAN, Maureen; b. 31 Aug. 1945, Glasgow, Scotland. Ceramic Artist; Poet. m. Gordon MacNaughtan, 4 June 1966, 1 s., 2 d. *Education:* Open University, 1985–87; University of Aberdeen, 1992. *Contributions to:* Numerous anthologies, reviews, quarterlies, and journals. *Honours:* Scottish Arts Bursary; Dorothy Dunbar Trophy; Bobby Aiken Memorial Prize; Diplomas of Excellence. *Memberships:* Poetry Society; Scottish Poetry Library; World Development Asscn. *Address:* 122 Oldany Rd, Glenrothes, Fife KY7 6RF, Scotland.

MACNEACAIL, Aonghas; b. 7 June 1942, Uig, Isle of Skye, Scotland. Writer; Poet. m. Gerda Stevenson, 21 June 1980, 1 s. *Education:* University of Glasgow. *Appointments:* Writing Fellowships, The Gaelic College, Isle of Skye, 1977–79, An Comunn Gaidhealachm Oban, 1979–81, Ross-Cromarty District Council, 1988–90. *Publications:* Poetry Quintet, 1976; Imaginary Wounds, 1980; **Sireadh Bradain Sicir/Seeking Wise Salmon**, 1983; **An Cathadh Mor/The Great Snowbattle**, 1984; **An Seachnadh/The Avoiding**, 1986; **Rocker and Water**,

1990. *Contributions to:* Many publications. *Honours:* Grampian TV Gaelic Poetry Award; Diamond Jubilee Award, Scottish Asscn for the Speaking of Verse, 1985; An Comunn Gaidhealach Literary Award, 1985. *Membership:* Scottish Poetry Library Asscn, council mem., 1984–. *Address:* 1 Roseneath Terrace, Marchmont, Edinburgh EH9 1JS, Scotland.

MCNEIL, Florence (Ann); b. 8 May 1940, Vancouver, BC, Canada. Poet; Children's Author. m. David McNeal, 3 Jan. 1973. *Education:* BA, 1960, MA, 1965, University of British Columbia. *Appointments:* Instructor, Western Washington University, 1965–68; Prof., University of Calgary, 1968–73; Prof., 1973–76, Visiting Lecturer, 1989–90, University of British Columbia. *Publications:* The Rim of the Park, 1972; Walhachin, 1972; Emily, 1975; Ghost Towns, 1975; A Balancing Act, 1979; When is a Poem: Creative Ideas for Teaching Poetry Collected from Canadian Poets, 1980; Miss P and Me, 1982; The Overlanders, 1982; Here is a Poem (ed.), 1983; Barkerville, 1984; Catriona's Island, 1988; Do Whales Jump at Night?: Poems for Kids (ed.), 1990; Swimming Out of History, 1991; Breathing Each Other's Air, 1994. *Contributions to:* Anthologies, journals and magazines. *Honours:* Many Canada Council Grants; Thea Koerner Award, 1963; MacMillan Prize, 1963; National Magazine Award for Poetry, 1980; Sheila A Egoff Prize for Children's Literature, 1989. *Memberships:* British Columbia Writers Federation; Canadian Society of Children's Authors, Illustrators, and Performers; Canadian Writers Union; League of Canadian Poets. *Address:* 20 Georgia Wynd, Delta, BC V4M 1A5, Canada.

MCNEILL, Christine; b. 4 April 1953, Vienna, Austria. Poet. m. Ralph McNeill, 24 May 1975, divorced 21 Oct. 1992. *Education:* English as a Foreign Language Teaching Certificate, London, 1976; German Teaching Certificate, London, 1976; English as a Second Language Teaching Certificate, London, 1977. *Appointment:* Language Tutor. *Publication:* Kissing the Night, 1993. *Contributions to:* Reviews, quarterlies, and journals. *Honour:* Co-Winner, Richard Ellmann Award, 1993. *Membership:* National Poetry Society. *Address:* 31 Burnt Hills, Cromer, Norfolk NR27 9LW, England.

MCPHERSON, Sandra Jean; b. 2 Aug. 1943, San Jose, CA, USA. Prof. of English; Poet. m. (1) Henry D Carlile, 24 July 1966, divorced 1985, 1 d., (2) Walter D Pavlich, 3 Jan. 1995. *Education:* BA, San Jose State University, 1965; Postgraduate Studies, University of Washington, 1965–66. *Appointments:* Visiting Lecturer, University of Iowa, 1974–76, 1978–80; Holloway Lecturer, University of California, Berkeley, 1981; Teacher, Oregon Writers Workshop, Portland, 1981–85; Prof. of English, University of California, Davis, 1985–; Ed. and publisher, Swan Scythe Press, 1999–. *Publications:* Elegies for the Hot Season, 1970; Radiation, 1973; The Year of Our Birth, 1978; Patron Happiness, 1983; Streamers, 1988; The God of Indeterminacy, 1993; Edge Effect, 1996; The Spaces Between Birds, 1996; A Visit to Civilisation, 2002. *Contributions to:* Periodicals. *Honours:* Ingram Merrill Foundation Grants, 1972, 1984; National Endowment for the Arts Grants, 1974, 1980, 1985; Guggenheim Fellowship, 1976; Oregon Arts Commission Fellowship, 1984; American Acad. and Institute of Art and Letters Award, 1987. *Address:* c/o Dept of English, University of California at Davis, CA 95616, USA.

MCQUEEN, (Pris)Cilla (Muriel); b. 22 Jan. 1949, Birmingham, England. Poet; Artist. m. Ralph Hotere, 1974, divorced 1986, 1 d. *Education:* MA, Otago University, Dunedin, New Zealand, 1970. *Publications:* Homing In, 1982; Anti Gravity, 1984; Wild Sweets, 1986; Benzina, 1988; Berlin Diary, 1990; Crikey, 1994. *Contributions to:* Various publications. *Honours:* New Zealand Book Awards for Poetry, 1983, 1989, 1991; Fulbright Visiting Writers Fellowship, 1985; Robert Burns Fellowships, 1985, 1986; Australia-New Zealand Exchange Writers' Fellowship, 1987; Goethe Institute Scholarship, Berlin, 1988. *Memberships:* Australasian Performing Rights Asscn; PEN. *Address:* 33 Skibo St, Kew, Dunedin, New Zealand.

MACTHÒMAIS, Ruaraidh. See: THOMSON, Derick S(mith).

MCWHIRTER, George; b. 26 Sept. 1939, Belfast, Northern Ireland. Writer; Poet; Trans.; Prof. m. Angela Mairead Coid, 26 Dec. 1963, 1 s., 1 d. *Education:* BA, Queen's University; MA, University of British Columbia. *Appointments:* Co-Ed.-in-Chief, 1977, Advisory Ed., 1978–, Prism International Magazine; Prof., 1970–, Head of Creative Writing, 1983–93, University of British Columbia. *Publications:* Catalan Poems, 1971; Bodyworks, 1974; Queen of the Sea, 1976; God's Eye, 1981; Coming to Grips with Lucy, 1982; Fire Before Dark, 1983; Paula Lake, 1984; Cage, 1987; The Selected Poems of José Emilio Pacheco (ed. and trans.), 1987; The Listeners, 1991; A Bad Day to be Winning, 1992; A Staircase for All Souls, 1993; Incubus: The Dark Side of the Light, 1995; Musical Dogs, 1996; Fab, 1997; Where Words Like Monarchs Fly (ed. and trans.), 1998; Ovid in Saskatchewan, 1998; Eyes to See Otherwise: The Selected Poems of Homero Aridjis, 1960–2000 (co-ed. and trans.), 2001; The Book of Contradictions (poems), 2002. *Contributions to:* Numerous magazines and journals. *Honours:* McMillan Prize, 1969; Commonwealth Poetry Prize, 1972; F R Scott Prize, 1988; Ethel Wilson Fiction Prize, 1988; Killan Prize for Teaching, University of British Columbia, 1998. *Memberships:* League of Canadian Poets; Writers' Union of Canada; PEN; Literary Trans Asscn of Canada. *Address:* 4637 W 13th Ave, Vancouver, BC V6R 2V6, Canada.

MADDEN, David; b. 25 July 1933, Knoxville, Tennessee, USA. Educator; Writer; Critic; Ed.; Poet; Dramatist. m. Roberta Margaret Young, 6 Sept. 1956, 1 s. *Education:* BS, University of Tennessee, 1957; MA, San Francisco State College, 1958; Postgraduate Studies, Yale Drama School, 1959–60. *Appointments:* Faculty, Appalachian State Teachers College, Boone, North Carolina, 1957–58, Centre College, 1964–66, Ohio University, 1966–68; Asst Ed., Kenyon Review, 1964–66; Writer-in-Residence, 1968–92, Dir, Creative Writing Program, 1992–94, and US Civil War Center, 1992–99, Alumni Prof. 1994, Louisiana State University; Donald and Veliva Crunbley Prof. of Creative Writing, 2000. *Publications:* Fiction: The Beautiful Greed, 1961; Cassandra Singing, 1969; The Shadow Knows, 1970; Brothers in Confidence, 1972; Bijou, 1974; The Suicide's Wife, 1978; Pleasure-Dome, 1979; On the Big Wind, 1980; The New Orleans of Possibilities, 1982; Sharpshooter, 1995. Non-Fiction: Wright Morris, 1964; The Poetic Image in 6 Genres, 1969; James M Cain, 1970; Creative Choices: A Spectrum of Quality and Technique in Fiction, 1975; Harlequin's Stick: Charlie's Cane: A Comparative Study of Commedia dell' arte and Silent Slapstick Comedy, 1975; A Primer of the Novel: For Readers & Writers, 1980; Writer's Revisions (with Richard Powers), 1981; Cain's Craft 1986; Revising Fiction, 1988; The World of Fiction, 1990; The Fiction Tutor 1990; Eight Classic American Novels, 1990; A Pocketful of Prose: Vintage, 1992; A Pocketful of Prose: Contemporary, 1992. Editor: Proletarian Writers of the Thirties, 1968; Tough Guy Writers of the Thirties, 1968; American Dreams, American Nightmares, 1970; Rediscoveries, 1971; The Popular Culture Explosion (with Ray B Browne), 1972; The Contemporary Literary Scene (assoc. ed.), 1973; Nathanael West: The Cheaters and the Cheated, 1973; Remembering James Agee, 1974; Studies in the Short Story, fourth to sixth edns, 1975–84; Rediscoveries II (with Peggy Bach), 1988; Classics of Civil War Fiction, 1991; Beyond the Battlefield (ed.). *Contributions to:* Poems, essays and short stories in various publications. *Honours:* John Golden Fellow in Playwriting, 1959; Rockefeller Foundation Grant in Fiction, 1969; National Council on the Arts Award, 1970. *Memberships:* Associated Writing Programs; Authors League. *Address:* 614 Park Blvd, Baton Rouge, LA 70806, USA.

MADGETT, Naomi Long; b. 5 July 1923, Norfolk, Virginia, USA. Poet; Publisher; Prof. of English Emeritus. m. Leonard P Andrews Sr. *Education:* BA, Virginia State College, 1945; MEd, English, Wayne State University; PhD, International Institute for Advanced Studies, 1980. *Appointments:* Research Assoc., Oakland University; Lecturer in English, University of Michigan; Assoc. Prof. to Prof. of English Emeritus, Eastern Michigan University; Publisher; Ed., Lotus Press. *Publications:* Songs to a Phantom Nightingale, 1941; One and the Many, 1956; Star by Star, 1965; Pink Ladies in the Afternoon, 1972; Exits and Entrances, 1978; Phantom Nightingale, 1981; A Student's Guide to Creative Writing, 1990. *Contributions to:* Numerous anthologies and journals. *Address:* 16886 Inverness Ave, Detroit, MI 48221, USA.

MADU, Ladi; b. 28 June 1960, Lagos, Nigeria. Writer; Journalist; Poet. m. Ida Heidemans Madu, 6 April 1987, 1 s. *Education:* Diploma, D'Etudes Françaises, 1983; London School of Journalism, 1991. *Contributions to:* Poetry Nottingham; Orbis; Folio International; Prophetic Voices; Parallel; Barddowi; Songs. *Address:* 32 Witte Van Haemstedestraat, 3021 SZ Rotterdam, Netherlands.

MAGEE, Wes(ley Leonard Johnston); b. 20 July 1939, Greenock, Scotland. Poet; Writer. m. Janet Elizabeth Parkhouse, 10 Aug. 1967, 1 s., 1 d. *Education:* Teaching Certificate, Goldsmith's College, University of London, 1967; Advanced Certificate in Education, University of Bristol, 1972. *Publications:* Over 40 books for children, 1972–98. *Contributions to:* Reviews and journals. *Honours:* New Poets Award, 1972; Poetry Book Society Recommendation, 1978; Cole Scholar, FL, 1985. *Memberships:* Poetry Society of Great Britain; Philip Larkin Society. *Address:* Crag View Cottage, Thorgill, Rosedale, North Yorkshire YO18 8SG, England.

MAGER, Donald Northrop; b. 24 Aug. 1942, Santa Rita, New Mexico, USA. Assoc. Prof.; Poet; Writer; Trans. m. Barbara Feldman, divorced, 2 s., partner William McDowell. *Education:* BA, Drake University, 1964; MA, Creative Writing, Syracuse University, 1966; PhD, English Literature, Wayne State University, 1986. *Appointments:* Instructor, Syracuse University; Assoc. Prof., Johnson C Smith University. *Publications:* Poetry: To Track the Wounded One: A Journal, 1988; Glosses: Twenty-four Preludes and Etudes, 1995; That Which is Owed to Death, 1998; Borderings, 1998. *Contributions to:* Anthologies, books, reviews, quarterlies, journals, and magazines. *Honours:* First Prize, Hallmark Competition, 1965; Approach Magazines Award, 1978; Tompkings Award First Prize for Poetry, Wayne State University, 1986; First Prize, The Lyricist Statewide Poetry Competition, Campbell University, 1992; Assoc. Artist Residency, Atlantic Center for the Arts, New Smyrna Beach, FL, 1994; Winner, Union County Writers Club Chapbook Contest, 1998. *Membership:* MLA. *Address:* c/o Johnson C Smith University, UPO 2441, Charlotte, NC 28216, USA.

MAGLIOCCO, Peter; b. 26 Oct. 1948, Glendale, CA, USA. Ed.; Poet; Writer. *Education:* BA, Fine Arts, California State University at Northridge, 1975. *Appointments:* Ed., Writer, Limited Editions Press, Northridge, 1982–85, Las Vegas, 1985–. *Publications:* Among a Godly Few, 1982; Poetica Rex, 1994; In a Land of Techno-Rave, 1994; Non-Parables, 1996; Kiss of Space, 1997. *Address:* 552 Sierra Vista Dr., Apt 41, Las Vegas, NV 89109-3748, USA.

MAGNUSDOTTIR, Thorunn Magnea; b. 10 Nov. 1945, Reykjavík, Iceland. Actress; Theatre Dir; Poet. 2 s. *Education:* Icelandic College of Arts and Crafts, Reykjavík, 1959–60; Private acting school, 1959–62; National Theatre School, Reykjavík, 1962–64; Jacques Lecocq Ecole de Mime et Théatre, Paris, 1964–66. *Appointments:* Actress and Dir, National Theatre, Reykjavík; Film, radio, and television appearances. *Publications:* Morgunregn, 1962; Islanske dikt, 1975; Laerebok i islandsk, 1976; Ljo asafn, 1980; Dikt av islanske kvinner, 1985; Ljo spor, 1988. Other: Various trans. *Contributions to:* Newspapers and magazines. *Memberships:* Actors Union; Alliance Francaise, Iceland; Writers Union. *Address:* Laufasveg 6, Reykjavik, Iceland.

MAGNUSSON, Sigurdur A.; b. 31 March 1928, Reykjavik, Iceland. Writer; Poet. m. (1), divorced, (2), divorced, 2 s., 3 d. *Education:* University of Iceland, 1948–50; University of Copenhagen, 1950–51; University of Athens, 1951–52; University of Stockholm, 1952–53; BA, New School for Social Research, New York, 1955. *Appointments:* Literary and Drama Critic, Morgunbladid, 1956–67; Ed.-in-Chief, Samvinnan, 1967–74; Mem., International Writing Programme, University of Iowa, 1976, 1977; Mem., International Artists' Programme, West Berlin, 1979–80; Mem., Jury, Nordic Council Prize for Literature, 1990–98. *Publications:* In English: Northern Sphinx: Iceland and the Icelanders from the Settlement to the Present, 1977; Iceland: Country and People, 1978; The Iceland Horse, 1978; The Postwar Poetry of Iceland, 1982; Icelandic Writing Today, 1982; Iceland Crucible: A Modern Artistic Renaissance, 1985; The Icelanders, 1990; Iceland: Isle of Light, 1995. Other: 31 books in Icelandic; 28 trans into Icelandic from English, Danish, German and Greek. *Contributions to:* Professional journals. *Honours:* Golden Cross of Phoenix, Greece, 1955; Cultural Council Prize for Best Play, 1961, and Best Novel, 1980; European Jean Monnet Prize for Literature, 1995. *Memberships:* Amnesty International, chair., 1988–89, 1993–95; Greek-Icelandic Society, chair., 1985–88; Society of Icelandic Drama Critics, chair., 1963–71; Writers' Union of Iceland, chair., 1971–78. *Address:* Barónsstig 49, 101 Reykjavík, Iceland.

MAGORIAN, James; b. 24 April 1942, Palisade, Nebraska, USA. Poet; Writer. *Education:* BS, University of Nebraska, 1965; MS, Illinois State University, 1969; Graduate Studies, Oxford University, 1972, Harvard University, 1973. *Publications:* Poetry: Hitchhiker in Hall County, 1968; The Garden of Epicurus, 1971; Safe Passage, 1977; Phases of the Moon, 1978; Tap Dancing on a Tightrope, 1981; Taxidermy Lessons, 1982; The Walden Pond Caper, 1983; The Emily Dickinson Jogging Book, 1984; Weighing the Sun's Light, 1985; The Hideout of the Sigmund Freud Gang, 1987; Borderlands, 1992; The Yellowstone Meditations, 1996; Haymarket Square, 1998. Fiction: America First, 1992; The Man Who Wore Layers of Clothing in the Winter, 1994; Hearts of Gold, 1996; Souvenir Pillows From Mars, 1996. Other: Children's books. *Contributions to:* Reviews, quarterlies, and journals. *Address:* 1224 N 46th St, Lincoln, NE 68503, USA.

MAGRADZE, David; b. 28 June 1962, Tbilisi, Georgia. Ed.; Poet. m. Tsitsishuili Nestar, 12 Nov. 1983, 2 d. *Education:* Philology, Tbilisi State University. *Appointments:* Ed., Tsiskhari literary journal; Minister of Culture of Georgia. *Publications:* Poems, 1984; Marula, 1987; Shandlis asuli, 1990; Poems, 1994. *Contributions to:* Newspapers and journals. *Honour:* Newspaper Prize for Best Poems, 1996. *Memberships:* International PEN; Writers' Union of Georgia. *Address:* c/o Writers' Union of Georgia, 13 Machabeli St, 380004 Tbilisi, Georgia.

MAHAPATRA, Jayanta; b. 22 Oct. 1928, Cuttack, Orissa, India. Poet; Writer; Ed. Trans. m. Jyotsna Rani Das, 16 Jan. 1951, 1 s. *Education:* University of Cambridge, 1941; BSc, Utkal University, 1946; MSc, Patna University, 1949. *Appointments:* Lecturer, Reader, 1950–86; Poet-in-Residence, Rockefeller Foundation Conference Center, Bellagio, Italy, 1986; Poetry Ed., The Telegraph, Calcutta, 1994–98; Ed., Lipi, 1998. *Publications:* Close the Sky, 1971; Svayamvara and Other Poems, 1971; A Rain of Rites, 1976; Waiting, 1979; Relationship, 1980; The False Start, 1980; Life Signs, 1983; Dispossessed Nests, 1984; Selected Poems, 1987; Burden of Waves and Fruit, 1988; Temple, 1989; A Whiteness of Bone, 1992; The Best of Jayanta Mahapatra, 1995; Shadow Space, 1997; The Green Gardener, 1997; Bare Face, 2001. Other: Various children's stories and trans; Ed., Chandrabhaga magazine, 2000–. *Contributions to:* Reviews, quarterlies, and journals. *Honours:* Jacob Glatstein Memorial Award, Chicago, 1975; National Acad. of Letters Award, New Delhi, 1981; El consejo nacional para la cultura y las artes, Mexico, 1994; Gangadhar National Award for Poetry, 1994; Jaidayal Harmony Award, 1994. *Address:* Tinkonia Bagicha, Cuttack 753 001, Orissa, India. *Telephone:* (671) 617434.

MAHAPATRA, Laxmi Narayan; b. 20 April 1942, Phasi, India. Advocate; Poet. m. Binodina Mahapatra, 15 May 1964, 2 s., 1 d. *Education:* LLB, 1962; MA, 1963. *Publications:* Rita and Other Poems; Lone Boatman; Bhuma; Dead River; Night without Moon; The Shadowed Sun. *Contributions to:* Illustrated Weekly of India; India Literature; International Poetry; World Poetry; Selected Writings; Prophetic Voices. *Honours:* Nehru Award; International Literature Award. *Membership:* International Writers Asscn. *Address:* Gliri Rd, Benhampuz 760005, Orissa, India.

MAHASHWETA, Chaturvedi; b. 2 Feb. 1950, Etawah, Uttar Pradesh, India. College Lecturer; Poet; Ed. m. Uma Kamt Chaturvedi, 11 Dec. 1970, 2 s., 1 d. *Education:* MA, English, 1966; MA, Sanskrit, 1969; MA, Hindi, 1978; PhD, 1983; DLitt, 1991; LLB, 1993. *Appointments:* Lecturer, RPPG College, Meerganj, Bareilly, 1984–; Ed., Mandakini, Hindi-English magazine. *Publications:* Several poetry books in English, including: Voice of Agony, 1985; Roaming Aroma, 1994; Waves of Joy, 1997; Way of Melody, 1997; Eternal Pilgrim, 1997; Immortal Wings, 1998; Back to the Vedas, 1998; 20 books in Hindi. *Contributions to:* Various publications. *Honours:* Certificate for Poetry, Melbourne Poetry, Australia, 1986; Sahitya Bharti, 1994; Gold Medal in Poetry, 1995; Michael Madhusudan Award, 1995; Subhadra Kumari Chauhan Padak, 1995. *Memberships:* Authors Guild of India; International Poets Acad.; Hindi Sahitya Sammelan. *Address:* c/o Professors' Colony, Shyam Ganj, Bareilly 243 005, Uttar Pradesh, India.

MAHER, Mary Geraldine Kennedy; b. 29 Oct. 1937, Yorkshire, England. Teacher; Poet. m. Kenneth Maher, 6 April 1978, 1 d. *Education:* Diploma, Paget Gorman Sign System, 1974; Postgraduate Diploma, Special Education, 1978. *Publications:* Several poems. *Contributions to:* Reviews and magazines. *Honour:* South West Arts Literary Award. *Memberships:* Company of Poets; Poetry Society. *Address:* Pippins, Hillhead, Chittlehampton, Umberleigh, North Devon EX37 9RG, England.

MAHON, Derek; b. 23 Nov. 1941, Belfast, Northern Ireland. Critic; Ed.; Poet. *Education:* BA, Belfast Institute; BA, Trinity College, Dublin, 1965. *Appointments:* Drama Critic, Ed., Poetry Ed., New Statesman, 1981–; Poet-in-Residencies. *Publications:* Twelve Poems, 1965; Night-Crossing, 1968; Lives, 1972; The Man Who Built His City in Snow, 1972; The Snow Party, 1975; Light Music, 1977; The Sea in Winter, 1979; Poems 1962–1978, 1979; Courtyards in Delft, 1981; The Hunt by Night, 1982; A Kensington Notebook, 1984; Antarctica, 1986; Selected Poems, 1991. Editor: Modern Irish Poetry, 1972; The Penguin Book of Contemporary Irish Poetry, 1990. *Address:* c/o Rogers, Coleridge & White Ltd, 20 Powis Mews, London W11 1JN, England.

MAHY, Margaret; b. 21 March 1936, Whakatane, New Zealand. Writer; Poet. *Education:* BA, University of New Zealand, 1958. *Appointments:* Writer-in-Residence, Canterbury University, 1984, College of Advanced Education, WA, 1985. *Publications:* Some 50 books for children, 1969–95. *Honours:* Several. *Address:* Rd No. 1, Lyttelton, New Zealand.

MAIDEN, Jennifer (Margaret); b. 7 April 1949, Penrith, NSW, Australia. Poet; Writer. m. David Toohey, 14 July 1984, 1 d. *Education:* BA, Macquarie University, 1974. *Publications:* Tactics, 1974; The Occupying Forces, 1975; The Problem of Evil, 1975; Birthstones, 1978; The Border Loss, 1979; For the Left Hand, 1981; The Terms, 1982; The Trust, 1988; Play with Knives, 1990; Selected Poems of Jennifer Maiden, 1990; Acoustic Shadow, 1993. *Contributions to:* Many newspapers and magazines. *Honours:* Several Australia Council Fellowships and Grants; Grenfell Henry Lawson Award, 1979; New South Wales Premier's Prize, 1991; Victorian Premier's Prize, 1991. *Membership:* Australian Society of Authors. *Address:* PO Box 4, Penrith, NSW 2751, Australia.

MAIER, Anne Winifred, (Anne Bulley); b. 15 April 1922, Grayshott, England. Potter (retd); History Researcher; Poet. m. 31 March 1947, 2 s., 2 d. *Education:* St Anne's College, Oxford, 1946. *Publications:* Selected Poems, 1980; Free Mariner, 1992; Bombay County Ships, 1999; The Distaff Dimension, 1999. *Contributions to:* Anthologies and other publications. *Membership:* Art Workers Guild. *Address:* 28 Caledonian Rd, Chichester, West Sussex PO19 7PO, England.

MAIETTA, Diane Marie; b. 24 April 1957, Pittsburgh, Pennsylvania, USA. Poet; Writer. Divorced, 1 d. *Education:* BA, Point Park College, Pittsburgh; Indiana University. *Contributions to:* Several publications. *Honours:* Ed.'s Choice Award, National Library of Poetry; Golden Poet Award; Honorable Mentions. *Membership:* International Society of Poets. *Address:* PO Box 265, Apollo, PA 15613, USA.

MAILLARD, Keith; b. 28 Feb. 1942, Wheeling, WV, USA (Naturalized Canadian citizen, 1976). Writer; Poet; Assoc. Prof. m., 2 d. *Education:* West Virginia University; Vancouver Community College. *Appointments:* Instructor, 1980–89, Asst Prof., 1989–94, Assoc. Prof., 1994–, University of British Columbia. *Publications:* Fiction: Two Strand River, 1976; Alex Driving South, 1980; The Knife in My Hands, 1981; Cutting Through, 1982; Motet, 1989; Light in the Company of Women, 1993; Hazard Zones, 1995; Gloria, 1999. Poetry: Dementia Americana, 1994. *Contributions to:* Newspapers, reviews and journals. *Honours:* Ethel Wilson Fiction Prize, 1990; Gerald Lampert Prize for Best First Book of Poetry, League of Canadian Poets, 1995. *Membership:* Federation of British Columbia Writers. *Address:* c/o University of British Columbia, Vancouver, BC V6T 121, Canada.

MAIN, Gordon Ian, (Kendric Ross); b. 11 Aug. 1954, Dundee, Scotland. Writer; Poet. m. Bernadette Martin, 6 Oct. 1983, 2 s. *Education:* BSc, Honours, Chemistry, Heriot-Watt University, Edinburgh, 1980; Diploma in Industrial Administration, Napier University, Edinburgh, 1981. *Publications:* Classic

Children's Games From Scotland, 1996; Kaleidoscope, 1998. *Contributions to:* Scottish newspapers and magazines; Quantum Leap; Linkway; The Fireside Book (anthology), 2001. *Honours:* Commended, Stafford Arts Festival, 1997; Commended, Poetry Today, 1998. *Memberships:* Poetry Society; Writers in Education; Society of Authors. *Address:* 10 Manse Rd, Linlithgow EH49 6AL, Scotland. *E-mail:* kendricross@aol.com.

MAIREE, Faith. See: BRIGHAM, Faith Elizabeth Huckabone.

MAJA-PEARCE, Adewale; b. 3 June 1953, London, England. Researcher; Consultant; Writer; Poet. *Education:* BA, University of Wales, Swansea, 1975; MA, School of Oriental and African Studies, London, 1986. *Appointments:* Researcher, Index on Censorship, London, 1986–; Consultant, Heinemann International, Oxford, 1986–94. *Publications:* Christopher Okigbo: Collected Poems (ed.), 1986; In My Father's Country: A Nigerian Journey (non-fiction), 1987; Loyalties (stories), 1987; How Many Miles to Babylon? (non-fiction), 1990; The Heinemann Book of African Poetry in English (ed.), 1990; Who's Afraid of Wole Soyinka?: Essays on Censorship, 1991; A Mask Dancing: Nigerian Novelists of the Eighties, 1992. *Contributions to:* Various periodicals. *Memberships:* PEN; Society of Authors. *Address:* 33 St George's Rd, Hastings, East Sussex TN34 3NH, England.

MAJOR, André; b. 22 April 1942, Montréal, QC, Canada. Writer; Poet. m. Ginette Lepage, June 1970, 1 s., 1 d. *Education:* Collège de Montréal; Collège des Eudistes. *Publications:* Fiction: Nouvelles, 1963; Le Cabochon, 1964; La chair de poule, 1965; Le Vent du diable, 1968; L'Épouvantail, 1974, English trans. as The Scarecrows of Saint-Emmanuel, 1977; L'Épidéme, 1975, English trans. as Inspector Therrien, 1980; Les Rescapés, 1976, English trans. as Man on the Run, 1984; La folle d'Elvis, English trans. as Hooked on Elvis, 1983; L'hiver au coeur, 1987, English trans. as The Winter of the Heart, 1989; La vie provisoire, 1995, English trans. as A Provisional Life, 1997. Poetry: Le froid se meurt, 1961; Holocauste à 2 voix, 1961; Poèmes pour durer, 1969. Other: Journal: Le Sourire d'Anton ou l'adieu au roman (1975–92), 2001. *Honours:* Gov.-Gen.'s Literary Award, 1977; Prix Canada-Communauté française de Belgique, 1991; Prix Études françaises, 2001. *Address:* 10595 Rue Tanguay, Montréal, QC H3L 3G9, Canada.

MAJOR, Clarence; b. 31 Dec. 1936, Atlanta, GA, USA. Poet; Writer; Artist; Prof. m. (1) Joyce Sparrow, 1958, divorced 1964, (2) Pamela Ritter. *Education:* BS, State University of New York at Albany, 1976; PhD, Union Graduate School, 1978. *Appointments:* Ed., Coercion Review, 1958–66, Writer-in-Residence, Center for Urban Education, New York, 1967–68, Teachers and Writers Collaborative-Teachers College, Columbia University, 1967–71, Aurora College, IL, 1974, Albany State College, GA, 1984, Clayton College, Denver, 1986, 1987; Assoc. Ed., Caw, 1967–70, Journal of Black Poetry, 1967–70; Lecturer, Brooklyn College of the City University of New York, 1968–69, 1973, 1974–75, Cazenovia Collge, New York, 1969, Wisconsin State University, 1969, Queens College of the City University of New York, 1972, 1973, 1975, Sarah Lawrence College, 1972–75, School of Continuing Education, New York University, 1975; Columnist, 1973–76, Contributing Ed., 1976–86, American Poetry Review; Asst Prof., Howard University, 1974–76, University of Washington, 1976–77; Visiting Asst Prof., University of Maryland at College Park, 1976, State University of New York at Buffalo, 1976; Assoc. Prof., 1977–81, Prof., 1981–89, University of Colorado at Boulder; Ed., 1977–78, Assoc. Ed., 1978–, American Book Review; Prof., 1989–, Dir, Creative Writing, 1991–, University of California at Davis. *Publications:* Poetry: The Fires That Burn in Heaven, 1954; Love Poems of a Black Man, 1965; Human Juices, 1965; Swallow the Lake, 1970; Symptons and Madness, 1971; Private Line, 1971; The Cotton Club: New Poems, 1972; The Syncopated Cakewalk, 1974; Inside Diameter: The France Poems, 1985; Surfaces and Masks, 1988; Some Observations of a Stranger in the Latter Part of the Century, 1989; Parking Lots, 1992; Configurations: New and Selected Poems 1958–1998, 1998; Waiting for Sweet Betty, 2002. Fiction: All-Night Visitors, 1969; NO, 1973; Reflex and Bone Structure, 1975; Emergency Exit, 1979; My Amputations, 1986; Such Was the Season, 1987; Painted Turtle: Woman with Guitar, 1988; Fun and Games, 1990; Dirty Bird Blues, 1996. Non-Fiction: Come By Here: My Mother's Life, 2002. Other: Dictionary of Afro-American Slang, 1970; The Dark and Feeling: Black American Writers and Their Work, 1974; Juba to Jive: A Dictionary of African-American Slang, 1994; Necessary Distance, 2001. Editor: Writers Workshop Anthology, 1967; Man is Like a Child: An Anthology of Creative Writing by Students, 1968; The New Black Poetry, 1969; Calling the Wind: Twentieth Century African-American Short Stories, 1993; The Garden Thrives: Twentieth Century African-American Poetry, 1995. *Honours:* Fulbright-Hays Exchange Award, 1981–83; Western States Book Award, 1986; Pushcart Prize, 1989. *Address:* c/o Dept of English, University of California at Davis, Davis, CA 95616, USA.

MAJUMDER, Pronab Kumar; b. 3 Jan. 1941, Khulna, East Benegal. Civil Servant; Poet. m. 23 Jan. 1973, 1 s. *Education:* Graduate, University of Calcutta. *Publications:* Poetry collections in Bengali, 1973–93, in English, 1993, 1995. *Contributions to:* Various publications. *Memberships:* Poetry Society of India; Writers Forum, Ranchi, India. *Address:* P233, Block B, Lake Town, Calcutta 700089, India.

MAKARSKI, Henryk; b. 17 Aug. 1946, Biala Podlaska, Poland. Writer; Poet. m. Maria Anna Koziolkiewicz, 24 July 1971, 1 s., 1 d. *Education:* MA, Polish Philology, Marie Curie-Sktodowska University of Lublin, 1969. *Publications:* 7 vols of fiction; 5 vols of poetry; various essays of literary criticism, etc. *Honours:* Numerous awards. *Membership:* Polish Writers Asscn, Lublin. *Address:* u. Radzynska 18 m 23, 20-850 Lublin, Poland.

MAKEPEACE, Eleanor Maria; b. 8 Nov. 1946, Bishop Auckland, County Durham, England. Teacher; Poet; Artist. *Education:* Certificate of Education, Oxford, 1969; BEd, University of Newcastle upon Tyne, 1976. *Publications:* Our Unofficial Tourist Guide, 1972; A Little Lower Than the Angels, 1978; Uprooting, 1981; Tynes, 1986; Contradictions, 1990. *Contributions to:* Various publications.

MAKERS, Rikki. See: DENSON, William Alan.

MAKOTO, Ryu. See: STROUD, Drew McCord.

MALASCHAK, Dolores M.; b. 19 March 1923, Illmo, MO, USA. Educator (retd); Writer; Poet. m. (1) Anthony Malaschak, deceased 17 May 1941, 3 s., 2 d., (2), deceased 4 June 1989. *Education:* BA, Secondary Education, Southern Illinois University, Edwardsville, 1972. *Publications:* Run in the Morning, 1968; The Prodigal, 1987; Rainbow in My Hand, 1984; Garden Years, 1990; Greenwood Days, 1990; Harvest Time, 1990; Midnight in The Study, 1992; Holy Stone, 2001. *Contributions to:* Imprints Quarterly; Poetry Australia; The Poet (India); Bitterroot; Alura Quarterly – Anthology; Cyclo Flame; Bell's Letters; Castalian Springs; Sunflower Dream; Footprints; Mature Years. *Membership:* National League of American Pen Women, Metro East Branch. *Address:* 105 Hoffman Ave, Gilman City, MO 64642, USA.

MALIK, Keshav; b. 5 Nov. 1934, Srinagar, India. Ed.; Art Critic; Poet. m. 7 Aug. 1969. *Education:* BA, 1949; Italian and French Government Cultural Scholarships, 1950–55. *Publications:* Several poetry vols. *Contributions to:* Reviews, quarterlies, and journals. *Honours:* Padma Shri National Award; Potlasch Award, USA. *Membership:* Poetry Society; Poetry Club of India, pres. *Address:* 5/90P Connaught Circus, New Delhi 110 001, India.

MALITO, Giovanni, (John Malito); b. 30 May 1957, Toronto, ON, Canada. Chemist; Lecturer; Poet. m. 16 Sept. 1993, 1 d., 1 s. *Education:* BSc, University of Toronto, 1981; MSc, 1987, PhD, 1989, University of Guelph. *Appointments:* Lecturer, Chemistry Dept, Cork Institute of Technology; Editorial Board, Tableaux Networks. *Publications:* Why I Don't Read Newspapers, 1994; Unnatural Science, 1995; Touching the Moon, 1997; Poetry for Joe, 1997; Animal Crackers, 1997; Notes of a Physics Teacher, 1999; To Be the Fourth Wise Man, 2001; A Poets' Manifesto, 2002; Slingshot, 2002. *Contributions to:* Queen's Quarterly; Windsor Review; Books Ireland; Carousel; Envoi; Bellowing Ark; Whetstone; Taproot; Irish Times; Pottersfield Portfolio. *Honours:* Several. *Address:* 96 Albert Rd, Cork, Ireland.

MALLINSON, John David; b. 14 April 1939, Oldham, Lancashire, England. Teacher (retd); Poet. m. Catharine Tillman Williams, 11 July 1970, 1 s., 2 d. *Education:* St Cassian's College, 1952–55; London School of Economics and Political Science, 1957–60; Institute of Linguists. *Publications:* Spirit of Place; By North West; Composition of a European City, 1996. *Contributions to:* Various publications and BBC Radio. *Honour:* North West Arts Publication Grant, 1989. *Address:* 8 Norwich Ave, Oldham, Lancashire OL9 0BA, England.

MALLORY, Lee; b. 16 March 1946, San Mateo, CA, USA. Prof. of English; Poet. m., 2 d. *Education:* AA, Orange Coast College, 1967; BA, University of California at Santa Barbara, 1969; MA, California University at Long Beach, 1978. *Publications:* Beach House Poems, 1969; Oatmeal Candy, 1970; 91739, 1973; I Write Your Name, 1990; Full Moon, Empty Hands, 1994; Holiday Sheer, 1997; Impacts: Creativity and the Word, 1998. *Contributions to:* Invisible City; Wisconsin Review; Smith; Oink; Talisman; Beyond Baroque; California Quarterly; South; Desperado; Mojo Navigator. *Honours:* Award, Celebrity Centre International Guild of Poets; Faculty Lecturer Award, Rancho Santiago Community College. *Address:* c/o English Dept, Santa Ana College, 17th at Bristol, Santa Ana, CA 92706, USA.

MALONE, Joseph L(awrence); b. 2 July 1937, New York, NY, USA. Emeritus Prof. of Linguistics; Writer; Poet; Trans. m. 31 Jan. 1964, 2 s. *Education:* AB, 1963, PhD, 1967, University of California at Berkeley. *Appointments:* Instructor, University of California Extension, San Francisco, 1965; Instructor, 1967–68, Chair., Dept of Linguistics, 1967–2002, Asst Prof., 1968–71, Assoc. Prof., 1971–75, Prof. of Linguistics, 1975–2002, Prof. Emeritus, 2002–, Barnard College at Columbia University; Academic American at Grolier Multimedia Encyclopedia, 1977–; Editorial Board, Hellas, 1990–. *Publications:* The Science of Linguistics in the Art of Translation: Some Tools from Linguistics for the Analysis and Practice of Translation, 1988; Tiberian Hebrew Phonology, 1993; Carmina Gaiana, 1998; As Light Rises, 1999; Above the Salty Bay, 2001. *Contributions to:* Numerous publications. *Memberships:* American Oriental Society; Linguistic Society of America; North American Conference on Afro-Asiatic Linguistics. *Address:* 169 Prospect St, Leonia, NJ 07605, USA.

MALOUF, (George Joseph) David; b. 20 March 1934, Brisbane, Qld, Australia. Poet; Novelist. *Education:* BA, University of Queensland, 1954. *Appointments:* Asst Lecturer in English, University of Queensland, 1955–57; Supply Teacher, London, 1959–61; Teacher of Latin and English, Holland Park Comprehensive, 1962; Teacher, St Anselm's Grammar School, 1962–68; Senior Tutor and Lecturer in English, University of Sydney, 1968–77. *Publications:* Poetry: Bicycle and Other Poems, 1970; Neighbours in a Thicket: Poems, 1974; Poems, 1975–1976, 1976; Wild Lemons, 1980; First Things Last, 1981; Selected Poems, 1981; Selected Poems, 1959–1989, 1994. Fiction: Johnno (novel), 1975; An Imaginary Life (novel), 1978; Child's Play (novella), 1981; The Bread of Time to Come (novella), 1981, republished as Fly Away Peter, 1982; Eustace (short story), 1982; The Prowler (short story), 1982; Harland's Half Acre (novel), 1984; Antipodes (short stories), 1985; The Great World (novel), 1990; Remembering Babylon (novel), 1993; The Conversations at Curlow Creek (novel), 1996; Dream Stuff (stories), 2000. Play: Blood Relations, 1988. Opera Libretti: Voss, 1986; Mer de Glace; Baa Baa Black Sheep, 1993. Memoir: Twelve Edmondstone Street, 1985. Editor: We Took Their Orders and Are Dead: An Anti-War Anthology, 1971; Gesture of a Hand (anthology), 1975. *Contributions to:* Four Poets: David Malouf, Don Maynard, Judith Green, Rodney Hall, 1962; Australian; New York Review of Books; Poetry Australia; Southerly; Sydney Morning Herald. *Honours:* Grace Leven Prize for Poetry, 1974; Gold Medals, Australian Literature Society, 1975, 1982; Australian Council Fellowship, 1978; New South Wales Premier's Award for Fiction, 1979; Victorian Premier's Award for Fiction, 1985; New South Wales Premier's Award for Drama, 1987; Commonwealth Writer's Prize, 1991; Miles Franklin Award, 1991; Prix Femina Etranger, 1991; Inaugural International IMPAC Dublin Literary Award, 1996; Newstadt Laureat, 2000. *Address:* 53 Myrtle St, Chippendale, NSW 2008, Australia.

MALTBY, Thomas Clement; b. 18 Aug. 1958, Hove, Sussex, England. Poet; Writer. *Education:* Studied law, University of London. *Publications:* Many poems and fiction. *Contributions to:* Poetry Today; English Poets Society in Edenbridge; Poetry Now, Wales; Poetry Today, Peterborough. *Honours:* Poetry awards. *Memberships:* Poetry Society; Writers' Guild of Great Britain. *Address:* Top Flat, 129 King Charles Rd, Surbiton, Surrey KYB 8PQ, England.

MALTMAN, Kim Rendal; b. 23 Aug. 1950, Canada. Physicist; Poet. *Education:* BSc, Chemistry and Mathematics, University of Calgary; MSc, 1973; PhD, University of Toronto, 1983. *Appointment:* Faculty, York University. *Publications:* Several poems. *Contributions to:* Reviews and journals. *Memberships:* PEN; Writers Union of Canada. *Address:* c/o Dept of Mathematics and Statistics, York University, 4700 Keele St, North York, Ontario M3J 1P3, Canada.

MANDEL, Charlotte; b. 1 April 1925, New York, NY, USA. Poet. *Education:* BA, Brooklyn College; MA, Montclair State University. *Appointment:* Teacher, Poetry Writing, Barnard College Center for Research on Women. *Publications:* The Marriages of Jacob; Keeping Him Alive; The Life of Mary; Doll; A Disc of Clear Water; Sight Lines (poems), 1998. *Honours:* Fellowships, NJ State Council on the Arts; Geraldine E Dodge Foundation Fellow; Kavinoky Award. *Address:* c/o Saturday Press, PO Box 43548, Upper Montclair, NJ 07043, USA.

MANDEL, Oscar; b. 24 Aug. 1926, Antwerp, Belgium (Naturalized US citizen). Prof. of Humanities; Writer; Dramatist; Poet. m. Adriana Schizzano, 1960. *Education:* BA, New York University, 1947; MA, Columbia University, 1948; PhD, Ohio State University, 1951. *Appointments:* Faculty, University of Nebraska, 1955–60; Fulbright Lecturer, University of Amsterdam, 1960–61; Assoc. Prof., 1961–65, Prof. of Humanities, 1965–, California Institute of Technology, Pasadena. *Publications:* Poetry: Simplicities, 1974; Collected Lyrics and Epigrams, 1981. Other: Books of fiction, plays and criticism, 1964–96. *Contributions to:* Scholarly journals. *Memberships:* College Art Asscn; Dramatists Guild; MLA; Société des Auteurs et Compositeurs Dramatiques. *Address:* c/o Division of Humanities and Social Sciences, California Institute of Technology, Pasadena, CA 91125, USA.

MANGANI, Giovanni. See: MANGANO, John Giovanni.

MANGANO, John Giovanni, (Giovanni Mangani); b. 9 Aug. 1953, New Jersey, USA. Artist; Poet; Writer. *Education:* Glassboro State College, 1979–80. *Publications:* Recollections; Le Poesis di Giovanni Mangano. *Contributions to:* Mindy Inquire; Bob Monte Express; World of Dark Shadows; Hoofprints. *Membership:* Atlantic County Historical Society. *Address:* PO Box 255, Hammonton, NJ 08037, USA.

MANHEIM, Werner; b. 17 Feb. 1915, Lissa, Poland (Naturalized US citizen). Prof. (retd); Poet; Pianist. m. Eliane Housiaux, 18 Aug. 1951, deceased. *Education:* BMus, MMus, Cincinnati Conservatory of Music; DFA, Musicology, Chicago Musical College, 1950. *Appointments:* Asst Prof., 1947–54, Research Asst, Kinsey Institute, 1955–58, Asst to Assoc. Prof., 1958–80, Prof., 1980–82, Indiana University. *Publications:* Various poems and monographs. *Honours:* Hon. Doctor of Literature, University of Taiwan, 1983; Golden Poet Awards, 1989, 1990, 1991. *Memberships:* German Haiku Society; International Poets Acad.; United Poets Laureate; World Poetry Society. *Address:* 2906 Hazelwood Ave, Fort Wayne, IN 46805, USA.

MANHIRE, Bill; b. 27 Dec. 1946, Invercargill, New Zealand. University Lecturer; Poet; Writer. *Education:* BA, University of Otago at Dunedin, 1967; MPhil, University College London, 1973. *Appointment:* Lecturer, Victoria University, Wellington, 1973–. *Publications:* Malady, 1970; The Elaboration, 1972; Song Cycle, 1975; How to Take Your Clothes Off at the Picnic, 1977; Dawn/Water, 1980; Good Looks, 1982; Locating the Beloved and Other Stories, 1983; Zoetropes: Poems 1972–82, 1984; The Old Man's Example, 1990; Milky Way Bar, 1991. *Honour:* New Zealand Book Award, 1985. *Address:* Dept of English, Victoria University of Wellington, PO Box 600, Wellington 1, New Zealand.

MANICOM, David Alton; b. 19 July 1960, Ingersoll, Ontario, Canada. Diplomat; Poet. m. Teresa Marquis, 13 Aug. 1983, 2 s., 1 d. *Education:* BA, St Michael's College, University of Toronto, 1983; MA, 1985, PhD, 1989, McGill University. *Appointments:* Lecturer, McGill University, Montréal, 1988–89; Second Secretary, Vice-Consul, Canadian Embassy, Moscow, Russia, 1991–93; First Sec., Canadian High Commission, Islamabad, Pakistan. *Publications:* Sense of Season, 1989; Theology of Swallows, 1991. *Contributions to:* Saturday Night; Malahat Review; Descant, Canada; Shenandoah, USA. *Membership:* Leauge of Canadian Poets. *Address:* PO Box 500, Station A, Ottawa, Ontario K1N 8T7, Canada.

MANN, Christopher Michael, (Zithulele); b. 6 April 1948, Port Elizabeth, South Africa. Poet; Writer; Dramatist. m. Julia Georgina Skeen 10 Dec. 1981, 1 s., 1 d. *Education:* BA, University of the Witwatersrand, 1969; MA, University of Oxford, 1973; MA, University of London, 1974. *Publications:* First Poems, 1977; A New Book of South African Verse (ed. with Guy Butler), 1979; New Shades, 1982; Kites, 1990; Mann Alive (video and book), 1992; South Africans: A Series of Portrait Poems, 1995; Heartlands: A Series of Place Poems, 2002. Plays: The Sand Labyrinth, 2001; Mahoon's Testimony, 1995; The Horn of Plenty: A Series of Painting-Poems, with Julia Skeen (artist), 1997; Frail Care: A Play in Verse, 1997; The Roman Centurion's Good Friday, Cathedral of St Michael and St George, 1999. *Contributions to:* Numerous journals and magazines. *Honours:* Newdigate Prize; Olive Schreiner Award; South African Performing Arts Council Playwright Award; Hon. DLitt, University of Durban-Westville, 1993. *Address:* 19 Frances St, Grahamstown, 6140, South Africa.

MANSELL, Chris; b. 1 March 1953, Sydney, NSW, Australia. Poet; Writer. m. Steven G Sturgess, Dec. 1986, 1 s., 1 d. *Education:* BEc, University of Sydney. *Appointments:* Residencies, Curtin University, 1985, University of Southern Queensland, 1990, K S Prichard Centre, 1992, Bundanon, 1996; Lecturer, University of Wollongong, 1987–89, University of Western Sydney, 1989–91. *Publications:* Delta, 1978; Head, Heart and Stone, 1982; Redshift/Blueshift, 1988; Shining Like a Jinx, 1992; Day Easy Sunlight Fine, 1995; Fickle Brat, 2001; Stalking the Rainbow, 2002. *Contributions to:* Many reviews, quarterlies, and magazines. *Honours:* Amelia Chapbook Award, 1987; Queensland Premier's Prize for Poetry, 1993. *Memberships:* Australian Society of Authors; Poets Union; Women in Publishing. *Literary Agent:* Rachel Skinner, Raftos Management. *Address:* PO Box 94, Berry, NSW 2535, Australia. *E-mail:* writerslink@ozemail.com.au.

MANSON-HERROD, Pettr; b. 22 Sept. 1913. Writer; Poet. *Education:* Durham University. *Publications:* Late and Soon, 1998; And Later, 1999; Later Still, 2000; Last of All, 2000; Caperod'or. Children's books: Children's Volume, 1999; Bruce and Spider; Arthur and Dragon; Gallery Series 'Pictures with Words'; Tale of a Tail. *Contributions to:* Various publications; Haiku contributions. *Membership:* International Society of Poets. *Address:* 2 Clarel Hall Close, Westgate, Tickhill, Nr Doncaster DN11 9NQ, England.

MANWARING, Randle (Gilbert); b. 3 May 1912, London, England. Poet; Writer. m. Betty Violet Rout, 9 Aug. 1941, 3 s., 1 d. *Education:* Private schools; MA, University of Keele, 1982. *Publications:* The Heart of This People, 1954; Satires and Salvation, 1960; Christian Guide to Daily Work, 1963; Under the Magnolia Tree, 1965; Slave to No Sect and Other Poems, 1966; Crossroads of the Year, 1975; Insurance, 1976; From the Four Winds, 1976; In a Time of Unbelief, 1977; The Swifts of Maggiore, 1981; The Run of the Downs, 1984; Collected Poems, 1986; A Study of Hymn Writing and Hymn-singing in the Christian Church, 1990; Some Late Lark Singing, 1992; Love So Amazing, 1995; The Swallow, The Fox and the Cuckoo, 1997; Trade Winds, 2001; From Controversy to Co-Existence, 2002. *Contributions to:* Reviews, quarterlies, and magazines. *Memberships:* Downland Poets, chair., 1981–83; Kent and Sussex Poetry Society; Society of Authors; Society of Sussex Authors. *Address:* Marbles Barn, Newick, East Sussex BN8 4LG, England.

MANZAR. See: MUDDANNA, Kembhavy.

MARCHITTI, Elizabeth; b. 16 March 1931, Paterson, New Jersey, USA. Housewife; Poet. m. John Marchitti, 8 Sept. 1951, 1 s., 3 d. *Education:* Montclair State University, 1981–90. *Publications:* Longing for Water, 1996; Off-Season, 1997; Let Winter Come, 2000. *Contributions to:* Paterson Literary Review; Sensations Magazine. *Honours:* Honorable Mention, Ocean County Maryland Poetry Contest, 1994, Allen Ginsberg Contest, 1995, 1996, Wordsmith Poetry Contest, 1995, 1997; Commendations, Allen Ginsberg Contest, 1998, 2001. *Membership:* Café Poets, founding mem. *Address:* 165 Dewey Ave, Totowa, NJ 07512-2572, USA. *E-mail:* bettypoet1@msn.com.

MARCUS, Mordecai; b. 18 Jan. 1925, Elizabeth, New Jersey, USA. Prof. of Literature and Writing; Poet; Critic. m. Erin J. Gasper, 3 June 1955, 1 s., 1 d. *Education:* BA, Brooklyn College, 1949; MA, New York University, 1950; PhD, University of Kansas, 1958. *Appointments:* Teaching Asst, Rutgers University, 1951–52; Asst Instructor, Instructor, University of Kansas, 1952–58; Instructor, Asst Prof., Purdue University, 1958–65; Assoc. Prof., Prof., University of Nebraska-Lincoln, 1965–. *Publications:* Five Minutes to Noon, 1971; Return from the Desert, 1977; Conversation Basketball, 1980; Talismans, 1981; Restorations, 1984; The Poems of Robert Frost, 1991. Poems: Pursuing the Lost, 1993. *Contributions to:* Shenandoah; South Dakota Review; Kansas Quarterly; Poet Lore; Poet and Critic; Southern Poetry Review; San Jose Studies; Christian Century; Prairie Schooner; Blue Unicorn; North American Review. *Membership:* Robert Frost Society. *Address:* Dept of English, University of Nebraska-Lincoln, Lincoln, NE 68588, USA.

MARGOLIS, William J., (Bimgo, Will Friar); b. 13 Aug. 1927, USA. Poet; Ed.; Publisher. *Education:* BA, Roosevelt University, Chicago, 1950. *Appointments:* Re-Writer, Ed., Wall Street Journal; Ed., Publisher, Mendicant, Mendicant Editions, Miscellaneous Man; Co-Founder, Co-Ed., Beatitude. *Publications:* The Anteroom of Hell, 1957; The Little Love of Our Yearning, 1960; The Eucalyptus Poems, 1974; Rustle and Break, 1987; The Summer Cycles, 1988; A Book of Touch, 1988. *Contributions to:* Numerous reviews, journals, and magazines. *Address:* 1507 Cabrillo Ave, Venice, CA 92091, USA.

MARGOSHES, Dave; b. 8 July 1941, New Brunswick, New Jersey, USA. Writer; Poet. m. Ilya Silbar, 29 April 1963. *Education:* BA, 1963, MFA, 1969, University of Iowa. *Appointments:* Instructor, numerous writers' workshops and creative writing courses; Writer-in-Residence, University of Winnipeg, 1995–96; Saskatoon Public Library, 2001–02. *Publications:* Third Impressions (short stories with Barry Dempster and Don Dickinson), 1982; Small Regrets (short stories), 1986; Walking at Brighton (poems), 1988; Northwest Passage (poems), 1990; Nine Lives (short stories), 1991; Saskatchewan, 1992; Long Distance Calls (short stories), 1996; Fables of Creation (short stories), 1997; Tommy Douglas: Building the New Society (biography) 1999; We who Seek: A Love Story (novella), 1999; I'm Frankie Sterne (novel), 2000; Purity of Absence (poems), 2001. *Contributions to:* Numerous anthologies, journals, and magazines. *Honours:* Canadian Author and Bookman Poem of the Year Award, 1980; Saskatchewan Writers Guild Long Manuscript Award, 1990; Second Prize, League of Canadian Poets' National Poetry Contest, 1991; Stephen Leacock Award for Poetry, 1996. *Address:* 2922 19th Ave, Regina, Saskatchewan S4T 1X5, Canada. *E-mail:* dmargos@sk.sympatico.ca.

MARIANANDA. See: JANSEN, Garfield (Auburn Mariano).

MARIANI, Paul (Louis); b. 29 Feb. 1940, New York, NY, USA. Prof.; Writer; Poet. m. Eileen Spinosa, 24 Aug. 1963, 3 s. *Education:* BA, Manhattan College, 1962; MA, Colgate University, 1964; PhD, Graduate Center, City University of New York, 1968. *Appointments:* Asst Prof., John Jay College of Criminal Justice, 1967–68; Asst Prof., 1968–71, Assoc. Prof., 1971–75, Prof., 1975–, Distinguished University Prof., 1985, University of Massachusetts, Amherst; Robert Frost Fellow, 1980, Faculty, 1982, 1983, 1984, Robert Frost Prof., 1983, Visiting Lecturer, 1986, School of English, Poetry Staff, 1985–96, Bread Loaf Writers' Conference; Dir, The Glen, Colorado Springs, 1995, 1996, 1998; Chair in English, Boston College, 2000–; Poetry Ed., America Magazine, 2000–. *Publications:* Poetry: Timing Devices, 1979; Crossing Cocytus, 1982; Prime Mover, 1985; Salvage Operations: New and Selected Poems, 1990; The Great Wheel, 1996. Other: William Carlos Williams: A New World Naked, 1981; Dream Song: The Life of John Berryman, 1990; Lost Puritan: A Life of Robert Lowell, 1994; The Broken Tower: A Life of Hart Crane, 1999; Thirty Days: On Retreat with the Exercises of St Ignatius, 2002; God and the Imagination: On Poets, Poetry and the Ineffable, 2002 . *Contributions to:* Books and journals. *Honours:* National Endowment for the Humanities Fellowships, 1972–73, 1981–82; New Jersey Writers' Award, 1982; New York Times Notable Books, 1982, 1994, 1999; Nominated, American Book Award in Biography, 1983; Chancellor's Medal, University of Massachusetts, 1984; National Endowment for the Arts Fellowship, 1984; Choice Awards, Prairie Schooner, 1989, 1995; Ohioana Award, 2000; Hon. DHL, Manhattan College, 1998; Hon. DHL, The Elms College, 2001. *Memberships:* Acad. of American Poets; Poetry Society of America. *Address:* Box M, Montague, MA 01351, USA.

MARIE, Charles P., (Mussy Sainte-Agathe); b. 23 Jan. 1939, Nancy, France. Educator; Poet; Writer. *Education:* Licence ès lettres, 1963, Diplôme d'Etudes Supérieures, 1967, Nancy; MA, University of Exeter, 1971; PhD, University of Hull, 1979; CAPES, France, 1989. *Appointments:* Lecturer, Rolle College, Exeter University, 1967–71; Bradford University, 1971–73; Principal Lecturer, Coventry University, 1973–76; Prof. of French, Nigeria, 1977; Visiting Fellow, University of Ulster, 1978–79; Principal Lecturer, Potchefstroom University, 1982–85; Asst Master, Lycée Anna de Noailles, Evian, 1991–. *Publications:* Petit vide-poches, 1973; La Réalité humaine chez Jean Giraudoux, 1975; Virginia Water, 1976; La Mésangette, 1980; Poèmes au Nadir, 1981; Jean Giraudoux aux sources du sens, 1982; Luc Vuagnat dans le Voile d'Isis, 1984; Le Sens sous les mots, 1984; Genève et son Luth: 30 analyses de poètes, 1987; Torches de Lune, 1988; Florilège genevois: Poètes de l'Arbalète

1966–91, 1991; Féminalines au bois, 1992; Mademoiselle d'Ermelo, 1994; De Bergson à Bachelard: Essai de poétique essentialiste, 1995; Dionysos, 1998; Perlesvaus linguisticus, 1999; Le Cycle d'Ishtar ou le langage des eaux, 1999; Question d'Etre, 2002; Les Jardins d'Anne Boleyn, 2002. Other: 18 books in collaboration with other writers, 1978–2001. *Contributions to:* Many anthologies and other publications. *Honours:* Many prizes and medals 1976–98; Poet of the Millennium, International Poets Acad., Chennai, 2000. *Memberships:* Société des Écrivains d'Alsace Lorraine; Société des Poètes Français; Société Suisse des Écrivains; Swiss PEN Club; Institute of Linguists, Society for French Studies, Oxford; Société des Amis de Jean Giraudoux, de Gaston Bachelard; Mem., Institut National Genevois. *Address:* 78 Chemin de la Montagne, 1224 Geneva, Switzerland.

MARITIME, George; b. 19 Feb. 1942, Yonkers, New York, USA. Poet. *Education:* Syracuse University; Sarah Lawrence College. *Appointment:* Dir, Folk Music Hall of Fame. *Publications:* Columbus, 1991; The Cricket's Song; The Story of John Keats, 1992; The Ballad of Christopher Marley, 1994. *Contributions to:* New Press; Herald Statesman. *Honour:* Award, Composers, Artists and Authors of America. *Memberships:* Marlowe Society of America; New York Shelley Society; Melville Society; Marlowe Lives Asscn. *Address:* 44 Cherwing Rd, Bryn Mawr Knolls, Yonkers, NY 10701, USA.

MARKHAM, E(dward) A(rchibald); b. 1 Oct. 1939, Montserrat (British citizen). Ed.; Poet; Writer; Dramatist; Prof. *Education:* University of Wales; University of East Anglia; University of London. *Appointments:* Lecturer, Abraham Moss Centre, Manchester, 1976–78; Asst Ed., Ambit Magazine, London, 1980–; Ed., Artrage, 1985–87, Sheffield Thursday, 1992–; Writer-in-Residence, University of Ulster, Coleraine, 1988–91; Prof., Sheffield Hallam University, 1991–. *Publications:* Poetry: Crossfire, 1972; Mad and Other Poems, 1973; Lambchops, 1976; Philpot in the City, 1976; Love Poems, 1978; Games and Penalities, 1980; Love, Politics and Food, 1982; Human Rites: Selected Poems, 1970–82, 1983; Lambchops in Papua New Guinea, 1985; Living in Disguise, 1986; Towards the End of a Century, 1989; Letter from Ulster and the Hugo Poems, 1993; Misapprehensions, 1995; A Rough Climate, 2002. Plays: The Masterpiece, 1964; The Private Life of the Public Man, 1970; Dropping Out is Violence, 1971; The Windrush Review, 1998; Dreamers, 2001. Short Stories: Something Unusual, 1981; Ten Stories, 1994; Taking the Drawing Room Through Customs: Selected Stories, 2002. Other: A Papua New Guinea Sojourn: More Pleasures of Exile (memoir), 1998; Marking Time (novel) 1999. Editor: Hinterland, 1989; The Penguin Book of Caribbean Short Stories, 1996. *Honours:* C. Day-Lewis Fellowship, 1980–81; Certificate of Honour, Government of Montserrat, 1997. *Address:* c/o Bloodaxe Books Ltd, PO Box 1SN, Newcastle upon Tyne NE99 1SN, England.

MARKHAM, Jehane; b. 12 Feb. 1949, Sussex, England. Poet; Playwright. 3 s. *Education:* Central School of Art, 1969–71. *Publications:* The Captain's Death; Ten Poems, 1993; Virago New Poets, 1993; Twenty Poems, 1999; My Mother, Myself (audio tape), 2001. Radio Plays: More Cherry Cake, 1980; Thanksgiving, 1984; The Bell Jar; Frost in May. Television Play: Nina, 1978. Theatre Plays: One White Day, 1976; The Birth of Pleasure, 1997. *Contributions to:* Women's Press; Longmans Study; Sunday Times; BBC 2 Epilogue; Bananas Literary Magazine; Camden Voices; Independent; Observer; Acorn; Ambit; New Statesman; Cork Literary Review. *Honour:* Winner, Open Book Paradelle Competition, BBC Radio 4, 2002. *Memberships:* Poetry Book Society; Highgate Literary and Scientific Society; Poetry Society; PEN. *Address:* 56 Lady Somerset Rd, London NW5, England.

MARLATT, Daphne (Shirley); b. 11 July 1942, Melbourne, Vic., Australia. Poet; Writer. m. Gordon Alan Marlatt, 24 Aug. 1963, divorced 1970, 1 s. *Education:* BA, English and Creative Writing, University of British Columbia, 1964; MA, Comparative Literature, Indiana University, 1968. *Appointments:* Co-Ed., Tessera (Journal), 1983–91; Special Lecturer in Creative Writing, University of Saskatchewan, 1998–99. *Publications:* Frames of a Story, 1968; Leaf/Leaf/s, 1969; Rings, 1971; Vancouver Poems, 1972; Steveston, 1974; Our Lives, 1975; Steveston Recollected: A Japanese-Canadian History (with M Koizumi), 1975; Zócalo, 1977; Opening Doors: Vancouver's East End (with Carole Itter), 1979; What Matters, 1980; Selected Writing: Net Work, 1980; How Hug a Stone, 1983; Touch to My Tongue, 1984; Double Negative (with Betsy Warland), 1988; Ana Historic, 1988; Salvage, 1991; Ghost Works, 1993; Taken, 1996; Readings from the Labyrinth, 1998; This Tremor Love Is, 2001. *Honours:* Awards and grants. *Membership:* Writers' Union of Canada. *Address:* c/o Writers' Union of Canada, 24 Ryerson Ave, Toronto, Ontario M5T 2P3, Canada.

MARR, William Wei-Yi, (Fei Ma); b. 3 Sept. 1936, China. Engineer (retd); Poet; Ed. m. Jane Jy Chyun Liu, 22 Sept. 1962, 2 s. *Education:* Taipei Institute of Technology, 1957; MS, Marquette University, 1963; PhD, University of Wisconsin, 1969. *Appointments:* Editorial Adviser, The Chinese Poetry International, New World Poetry; Adviser, Chinese Writers Asscn of Greater Chicago, Asscn of Modern Chinese Literature and Arts of North America. *Publications:* In the Windy City, 1975; Selected Poems, 1983; White Horse, 1984; Selected Poems of Fei Ma, 1985; The Galloping Hoofs, 1986; Road, 1987; Selected Short Poems, 1991; Fly Spirit, 1992; Selected Poems, 1994; Autumn Window, 1995; A Microscopic World, 1998; Not All Flowers Need to Bear Fruit,

2000; The Collected Poems of Fei Ma, 2000. *Contributions to:* Periodicals and magazines. *Honours:* Wu Cho Liu Poetry Award, 1982; Li Poetry Trans. Award, 1982, and Poetry Award, 1984. *Memberships:* Chinese Artists Asscn of North America; Illinois State Poetry Society, pres., 1993–95; Li Poetry Society; New Poetry, Beijing, vice pres., 1994–; Poets Club of Chicago. *Address:* 737 Ridgeview St, Downers Grove, IL 60516, USA. *E-mail:* marrfei@aol.com. *Website:* hometown.aol.com/marrfei/bmz.htm.

MARRERO, Melanie. See: MINEO, Melani.

MARRIOTT, David Sylvester; b. 22 Oct. 1963, Nottingham, England. Poet. *Education:* BA, Sussex University, 1983–86. *Appointment:* Lecturer in English. *Publications:* Mortgages; Light; Circles; Woodcutter; Airs and Ligatures; Lative. *Contributions to:* Verse; Avec; Folded Sheets; First Offense; Pearl; La Pagina; Archeus; Poetical Histoires; Scarlet. *Address:* 227 Mayall Rd, London SE24 0PS, England.

MARRODAN, Mario Angel; b. 7 June 1932, Portugalete, Vizcaya, Spain. Lawyer; Critic; Writer; Poet; Ed. m. Mercedes Gómez Estíbaliz, 31 May 1961, 2 s. *Education:* Bachillerato Superior; Licentiate in Law; Philosophy; Letters. *Publications:* Over 300 books, including vols of essays, art criticism, and poetry; 300 poetas cantan a Bilbao, 2000. *Contributions to:* Magazines and journals. *Honours:* Golden Seagull, Royal Basque Society of Friends of the Nation. *Memberships:* Asociación Española de Críticos de Arte; Asociación Española de Críticos Literarios; Asociación Colegial de Escritores de España; International Asscn of Art Critics; Society of Basque Studies; Fraternity of the Béret. *Address:* Apdo de Correos 16, 48920 Portugalete, Vizcaya, Spain.

MARSH, Katherine C.; b. 23 April 1956, Salem, Oregon, USA. Writer; Poet. *Education:* Chemeketa College, 1976, 1986; Linn-Benton College, 1977, 1985–86; Assoc. of Arts, University of Oregon, 1977–78; Writers Digest School, 1995. *Publications:* Voices from the White Noise; My Brother's Keeper (co-author); Demons at My Doorstep (co-author). *Contributions to:* Midwest Poetry Review; Poetic Expressions; The Lucid Stone; Toast; Alpha Beat Press; Poetalk; California State Quarterly. *Honours:* Nashville Newsletter Poetry Awards, 1979, 1981; Newcomer's Award, Society of American Poets, 1994. *Memberships:* Poets and Writers; Poets Guild. *Address:* P O Box 613, Salem, OR 97308, USA.

MARSHALL, Jack; b. 25 Feb. 1937, New York, NY, USA. Writer; Poet. *Education:* Brooklyn Public Schools. *Publications:* The Darkest Continent, 1967; Bearings, 1970; Floats, 1972; Bits of Thirst, 1974; Bits of Thirst and Other Poems and Translations, 1976; Arriving on the Playing Fields of Paradise, 1983; Arabian Nights, 1986; Sesame, 1993. *Address:* 1056 Treat Ave, San Francisco, CA 94110, USA.

MARSHALL, Valerie Ann; b. 23 Sept. 1939, Middlesex, England. Poet. m. Derek, 29 April 1970, 2 s., 1 d. *Appointments:* Private Secretary, The War Office; Senior School Supervisor, 25 years. *Publication:* Starlight Dreams, 1998. *Contributions to:* Anthologies, reviews, quarterlies, journals, magazines, periodicals and newspapers. *Honours:* Ed.'s Choice Awards, 1997, 1998; Showcase Award, 1998. *Address:* 147 Warwick Rd, Scunthorpe, North Lincolnshire DN16 1HH, England.

MARSHBURN, Sandra; b. 6 Jan. 1945, Benton Harbor, Michigan, USA. Assoc. Prof. of English; Poet. m. Robert Marshburn, 10 Sept. 1966, 1 d. *Education:* BA, English, 1969; MA, English, 1972, University of Maryland. *Appointments:* Part-time Instructor, Morris Harvey College, 1974–76; Assoc. Prof., West Virginia State College, 1976–. *Publications:* Controlled Flight, 1990; Undertow, 1992. *Contributions to:* Yankee; Ohio Journal; Writer's Digest; Tar River Poetry; Greensboro Review; Cincinnati Poetry Review; Midwest Quarterly; MacGuffin; West Branch; Devil's Millhopper; Kentucky Poetry Review; Three Rivers Poetry Journal. *Address:* 201 Viking Rd, Charleston, WV 25302, USA.

MARTI, René; b. 7 Nov. 1926, Frauenfeld, Switzerland. Author; Poet. m. Elizabeth Wahrenberger, 13 Oct. 1955, 1 s., 2 d. *Education:* Commercial School, Lausanne; Cambridge Proficiency Class, Polytechnic School, London; Diploma in French and English; Science of Literature and Philosophy, University of Konstanz. *Publications:* Das unauslöschliche Licht, 1954; Dom des Herzens, 1967; Die fünf unbekannten (with others), 1970; Der unsichtbare Kreis, 1975; Weg an Weg, 1979; Besuche dich in der Natur (with Lili Keller), 1983; Gedichte zum Verschenken (with Lili Keller), 1984; Stationen, 1986; Die verbrannten Schreie, 1989; Glib allem ein bisschen Zeit (with Brigitta Weiss), 1993; Rückblicke, 1996; Spatenstich für die Rose (with Magdalena Obergfell), 2001. *Contributions to:* Numerous anthologies, newspapers, magazines, and radio. *Honours:* Several publishing grants; AWMM Lyric Poetry Prize, Luxemburg, 1985. *Memberships:* PEN and other literary organizations; Regensberger Shcriftstellergruppe intern., Turmband Innsbruck, Verband Kath. Schriftsteller Oesterreichs. *Address:* Haus am Herterberg, Haldenstrasse 5, 8500 Frauenfeld, Switzerland.

MARTIN, A. A., or MARTIN, Andy. See: DOWNEY, Martin M.

MARTIN, Angus; b. 6 Feb. 1952, Argyll, Scotland. Postman; Poet. m. Judith Honeyman, 28 March 1986, 3 d. *Publication:* The Larch Plantation. 1990; The Song of the Quern, 1998. *Contributions to:* Weekend Scotsman; Lines Review; Chapman; Poetry Wales; PEN New Poetry; New Writing Scotland; An Canan; Northwords; The Dark Horse. *Honour:* Scottish Arts Council Spring Award. *Address:* 13 Saddell St, Campbeltown, Argyll PA28 6DN, Scotland.

MARTIN, Graham Dunstan; b. 21 Oct. 1932, Leeds, Yorkshire, England. Senior Lecturer; Poet. m. (1) Ryllis Eleanor Daniel, 21 Aug. 1954, 2 s., 1 d., (2) Anne Moone Crombie, 14 June 1969, 2 s. *Education:* Oriel College, Oxford, 1950–54; Manchester University, 1955. *Appointments:* Asst Teacher, various secondary schools, 1956–65; Asst Lecturer, 1965–67, Lecturer, 1967–82, Senior Lecturer, 1982–, Edinburgh University. *Publications:* Remco Campert; Love and Protest; Le Cimetiere Marin; Anthology of Contemporary French Poetry; Louise Labé: Sonnets; J-C Renard: Selected Poems; Jules Laforgue, 1998. *Contributions to:* Lines; London Magazine; Modern Poetry in Translation; Prospice; 2 Plus 2; New Edinburgh Review; Lost Voices of World War One. *Membership:* Society of Antiquaries, Scotland, fellow. *Address:* French Dept, Edinburgh University, 60 George Sq., Edinburgh EH8 9JU, Scotland.

MARTIN, Philip (John Talbot); b. 28 March 1931, Melbourne, Vic., Australia. Senior Lecturer (retd); Poet. *Education:* BA, University of Melbourne, 1958. *Appointments:* Tutor to Senior Tutor in English, University of Melbourne, 1960–62; Lecturer in English, Australian National University, 1963; Lecturer to Senior Lecturer, Monash University, 1964–88. *Publications:* Poetry: Voice Unaccompanied, 1970; A Bone Flute, 1974; From Sweden, 1979; A Flag for the Wind, 1982; New and Selected Poems, 1988. Other: Shakespeare's Sonnets: Self Love and Art (criticism), 1972; Lars Gustafsson: The Stillness of the World Before Bach (trans.), 1988. *Contributions to:* 7 anthologies, 1986–98; Age; Australian; Carleton Miscellany; Helix; Meanjin; New Hungarian Quarterly; Poetry USA; Quadrant; Southerly; TLS. *Address:* 25/9 Nicholson St, Balmain 2041, NSW, Australia.

MARTIN, Ronald. See: DELIUS, Anthony.

MARTIN FUMERO, Graciliano; b. 18 Aug. 1961, Venezuela. Poet; Writer; Teacher. *Education:* Campos Acad., Valencia, Spain. *Contributions to:* Numerous anthologies and periodicals. *Honours:* Several poetry prizes. *Memberships:* International Writers and Artists Asscn; 20th Century Asscn of America.

MARTING, Janet; b. 3 April 1951, Burlington, Vermont, USA. Prof.; Writer; Poet. m. 25 May 1986. *Education:* BA, University of Vermont, 1973; MA, Colorado State University, 1975; PhD, Michigan State University, 1982. *Appointments:* Instructor, Texas Technical University, 1975–78; Asst Prof., Ohio State University, 1982–84; Dir of Composition, 1984–89, Assoc. Prof., 1989–97, Prof., 1997–, University of Akron. *Publications:* The Heart's Geographer, 1979; Making a Living: A Real World Reader, 1993; The Voice of Reflection: A Writer's Reader, 1995; Commitment, Voice and Clarity, 1996; From the Cradle to the Grave: Classic Essays on Age and Aging, 1998; The Family Tree: Classic Essays on Family and Ancestors, 1998. *Contributions to:* Anthologies, reviews and journals. *Honours:* Outstanding Writer, Colorado State University Poetry Contest, 1979; Honourable Mention, Community of Poets Award, Ohio. *Membership:* National Council of Teachers of Writing. *Address:* 373 Greenwood Ave, Akron, OH 44320, USA.

MARTINOVICH BAN, Eva Maria, (Eva Ban); b. 16 March 1934, Brazil. Journalist; Writer; Poet. m. Danilo Martinovich, 13 Jan. 1964, 1 step-s. *Education:* Masters Degree, Cruz Alta Rio Grande Do Sul; University of Curtiba; University of Porto Alegre. *Appointments:* Foreign Correspondent, New York, 1967–79, 1987; Columnist, Ultima Hora. *Publications:* 9 books of poems; 3 books of short stories. *Contributions to:* Many periodicals. *Honours:* 18 Gold Medals; 2 Silver Medals. *Memberships:* International Acad. of Letters; Union of Writers of the State of Rio de Janeiro; Brazilian Press Asscn; Poetry Society of America; International Pen Club. *Address:* Avenida Copacabana 959/503, 22060 Rio de Janeiro, Rio de Janeiro, Brazil.

MARTONE, Michael; b. 22 Aug. 1955, Fort Wayne, IN, USA. Prof.; Writer; Poet. m. Theresa Pappas, 3 April 1984. *Education:* Butler University, Indianapolis, 1973–76; AB, English, Indiana University, 1977; MA, Fiction Writing, Johns Hopkins University, 1979. *Appointments:* Asst Prof., 1980–83, Assoc. Prof., 1983–87, Iowa State University; Ed., Poet and Critic magazine, 1981–86; Contributing Ed., North American Review, 1984–; Briggs-Copeland Lecturer on Fiction, 1987–89, Briggs-Copeland Asst Prof. on Fiction, 1989–91, Harvard University; Assoc. Prof. of English, 1991–96, Syracuse University; Prof., Dir, Program for Creative Writing, 1996–, University of Alabama. *Publications:* Fiction: Alive and Dead in Indiana, 1984; Safety Patrol, 1988; Fort Wayne is Seventh on Hitler's List, 1990; Pensees: The Thoughts of Dan Quayle, 1994; Seeing Eye, 1995; The Blue Guide to Indiana, 2001. Prose Poems: At a Loss, 1977; Return to Powers, 1985; The Sex Lives of the Fantastic Four. Other: The Flatness and Other Landscapes (essays), 1999. Editor: A Place of Sense: Essays in Search of the Midwest, 1988; Townships: Pieces of the Midwest, 1992; The Scribner Anthology of Contemporary Short Fiction, 1999. *Contributions to:* Various books and journals. *Honours:* National Endowment for the Arts Fellowships, 1983, 1988; Margaret Jones Fiction Prize, Black Ice magazine, 1987; Ingram Merrill Foundation Award, 1989; Pushcart Prize, 1990; Second Place, Thin Air Fiction Contest, 1998; Honorable Mention, 32 Pages Chapbook Contest, 1998; Associated Writing Programs Award for Non-Fiction, 1998. *Memberships:* Associated Writing Programs; National Writers Union; PEN. *Address:* PO Box 21179, Tuscaloosa, AL 35402, USA.

MARX, Anne; b. 8 March 1913, Bleicherode, Germany. Poet; Writer; Lecturer; Ed. m. Frederick E Marx, 12 Feb. 1937, 2 s. *Education:* Medical schools; Literary studies, colleges and writers conferences. *Publications:* Hear of Israel, 1975; Face Lifts for All Seasons, 1980; A Further Semester, 1985; Love in Late Season, 1993; The Rest is for Keeps, 2002. *Contributions to:* Anthologies, newspapers, reviews, and magazines. *Honours:* Cecil Hemley Memorial Prize; Greenwood Prize; National League of American Pen Women Prizes; National Federation of State Poetry Society Prizes; Chapbook Publication Awards; Collected papers deposited in New York Public Library Archives. *Memberships:* National League of American Pen Women; Poetry Society of America; Poets and Writers; Acad. of American Poets. *Address:* 315 The Colony, Hartsdale, NY 10530, USA.

MASINI, Donna; b. 13 Dec. 1954, New York, NY, USA. Poet. m. Judd Tully, 28 June 1986. *Education:* BA Honours, English, Classics, Hunter College, 1985; MA, English, Creative Writing, New York University, 1988. *Appointments:* Instructor, English, Creative Writing, New York University, 1988; Instructor, later Asst Prof., English, Creative Writing, Hunter College; Instructor, Creative Writing, Columbia University. *Publications:* That Kind of Danger (poems), 1994; About Yvonne, 1998. *Contributions to:* Paris Review; Georgia Review; Boulevard; Parnassus; Pequod; High Plains Literary Review; Conditions; Thirteenth Noon; Early Ripening; American Women's Poetry, anthology. *Honours:* College Prize, Acad. of American Poets, 1985, 1986; New York Foundation for the Arts Fellowship, 1986; Yaddo Fellow, 1989–91; National Endowment for the Arts Fellowship, 1991; Felix Pollak Poetry Prize, University of Wisconsin, Madison, 1991. *Memberships:* Poets and Writers; Poets House; Associated Writing Programs. *Address:* PO Box 5, Prince Station, New York, NY 10012, USA.

MASON, David (James); b. 11 Dec. 1954, Bellingham, Washington, USA. Assoc. Prof.; Poet; Critic; Writer; Trans. m. Anne Lennox, 16 Oct. 1988, 1 step-d. *Education:* BA, magna cum laude, English, Colorado College, 1978; MA, English, 1986, PhD, English, 1989, University of Rochester. *Appointments:* Visiting Instructor, 1983, 1987, Visiting Prof., 1986, 1987, 1988, 1994, Asst Prof., 1998–, Assoc. Prof., 2000–, Colorado College; Instructor, University of Rochester, 1986–88; Asst Prof., 1989–93, Assoc. Prof., 1993–98, Moorhead State University. *Publications:* Blackened Peaches, 1989; Small Elegies, 1990; The Buried Houses, 1991; Questions at Christmas, 1994; Three Characters from a Lost Home, 1995; The Country I Remember, 1996; Land Without Grief, 1996; Rebel Angeles: 25 Poets of the New Formalism (ed. with Mark Jarman), 1996; Kalamitsi, 1997; The Poetry of Life and the Life of Poetry (essays), 2000; Western Wind: An Introduction to Poetry (co-ed.), 2000. *Contributions to:* Books, reviews, quarterlies, and journals. *Honours:* Nicholas Roerich Poetry Prize, 1991; Alice Fay Di Castagnola Award, Poetry Society of America, 1993; Minnesota Prof. of the Year, Carnegie Foundation for the Advancement of Teaching and Council for Advancement and Support of Education, 1994; Hon. DHL, Colorado College, 1996; Fulbright Artist-in-Residence Fellowship, Greece, 1997. *Address:* 1131 Paradise Valley Dr., Woodland Park, CO 80863, USA.

MASON, H(enry) C(onner), (Logan T Conners); b. 13 March 1952, Portsmouth, Ohio, USA. Poet; Lecturer; Musician; Tutor. 2 s. *Education:* Shawnee State University, Portsmouth. *Appointment:* Ed., Shawnee State University Silhouette. *Contributions to:* Shawnee Silhouette; National Library of Poetry; Shawnee Poetry Review; Bad Haircut Quarterly; Villager; Plowman Anthology. *Honours:* First Prize, National Competition, American Scholastic Press Asscn; Phoenix Writers. *Address:* c/o Shawnee Silhouette, 940 Second St, Portsmouth, OH 45662, USA.

MASON, John Frederick; b. 28 April 1952, London, England. Teacher; Poet. *Education:* Marlborough College, 1964–68; MA, St Catharine's College, 1973. *Appointments:* Faculty, Christ's Hospital, 1973–77, Lady Hawkins School, Kington, 1980–93, University of Åarhus, 1993–. *Publication:* From the Black Square. *Contributions to:* New Democrat; New Welsh Review; Other Poetry: Resurgence. *Memberships:* Poetry Society. *Address:* Paradisuejen 78, 8600 Siliceborg, Denmark.

MASON, Myriam (Adelaide Mosonyi); b. 5 June 1928, Suffolk, England. Writer; Poet. m. Pierre Mosonyi, 1 d. *Education:* Conservatoire Internationale de Musique, 1952–55; Mannes College of Music, New York, 1959–61. *Appointments:* Singing Teacher, Huddersfield College of Music, 1969–70; Tutor, Inner London Education Authority, 1974–89; Part-Time Lecturer, Enfield College, 1976–91. *Publications:* Fiction, poetry and opera libretti. *Memberships:* Poetry Society; Marx Memorial Library; Worker's Music Asscn; Friend, Shakespeare's Globe. *Address:* 6A Fairbourne Rd, London N17 6TP, England.

MASON, Stanley (Allen); b. 16 April 1917, Blairmore, AB, Canada. Ed.; Trans.; Poet; Dramatist. m. Cloris Ielmini, 29 July 1944, 1 d. *Education:* MA English Literature, Oriel College, Oxford, 1938. *Appointments:* Technical Trans., 1943–63; Literary Ed., Graphis Magazine, 1963–83; Ed., Elements Dow Chemical Europe house organ, 1969–75. *Publications:* Modern English Structures (with Ronald Ridout), four vols, 1968–72; A Necklace of Words (poems), 1975; A Reef of Honours (poems), 1983; Send Out the Dove (play) 1986; The Alps, by Albrecht von Haller (trans.), 1987; The Everlasting Snow (poems), 1993; Collected Poems, 1993; A German Treasury (anthology, trans.) 1993–95. *Contributions to:* Many publications. *Honours:* Borestone Mountain Poetry Award; Living Playwright Award. *Address:* Im Zelgli 5, 8307 Effretikon Switzerland.

MASSEY, Alan Randolph Charles; b. 6 June 1932, Berkshire, England Librarian; Poet. m. Gillian Elizabeth Petty, 30 Sept. 1974. *Publications* Trajectories in the Air; The Fire Garden. *Contributions to:* Agenda; Poetry Review; Workshop; Expression. *Membership:* Poetry Society. *Address:* 41 Albany Rd, Windsor, Berkshire SL4 1HL, England.

MASSIMILLA, Stephen T.; b. 31 May 1964, New York, NY, USA. Prof. of Writing; Poet. *Education:* MFA, Columbia University, 1985; BA, magna cum laude, Williams College, 1986. *Appointments:* Ed., Art in America magazine; Instructor in Writing, Columbia University, 1984, 1985; Instructor in Art, School of Visual Arts, 1985, 1986; Prof. of Writing, Barnard College, 1985–; Assoc. Dir, Arthur Danziger Gallery, 1992–. *Publication:* Figure in the Tower, 1996. *Contributions to:* Anthologies and many other publications. *Honours:* Kaufman Prize, 1986; Acad. of America Poets Prizes, 1986, 1996; Semi-Finalist, National Library of Poetry Competition, 1996. *Membership:* Poetry Society of America. *Address:* 55 10th Ave, Sea Cliff, NY 11579, USA.

MAST, Edward; b. 18 Aug. 1954, Los Angeles, CA, USA. Playwright; Poet. *Education:* Bachelor, Liberal Studies, California College at Sonoma, 1976; MFA, Theatre and Playwriting, University of California at Los Angeles, 1978. *Publication:* Suzy and her Husbands, 1996. *Contributions to:* Earthwise; Amaranth Review; Cicada; Point Judith Light; Talking Raven; Snow Monkey; Poets'Corner; Semi-Dwarf Review; Open Bone. *Honour:* Second Place, Still Waters Press Poetry Competition, 1995. *Memberships:* Seattle Playwrights Alliance; Dramatists Guild. *Address:* 520 Third Ave W, No. B, Seattle, WA 98119, USA.

MATEV, Pavel Hristov; b. 6 Dec. 1924, Orizovo, St Zagora, Bulgaria. Poet. m. Louiza Mateva, 8 May 1948, 1 d. *Education:* Graduate, Slavonic Philology, Kliment Ohridski State Univeristy, Sofia. *Appointments:* Sec., Union of Bulgarian Writers, 1958–62; Deputy Chief Ed., Plamuk Magazine, 1962–65; Chief Ed., Septemvri Magazine, 1965–66; Minister of Culture of Bulgaria, 1966–75; Pres., Committe for Bulgarians Abroad, 1975–89. *Publications:* Falling into Rank, 1951; Clear Days, 1953; Duty, 1955; With People's Belief, 1959; Human Alarm, 1960; Time, Homeland, Love, 1962; Pedigree, 1963; Gulls Rest on Waves, 1965; Insights, 1965; Noninsulted Worlds, 1969; One Hundred Poems, 1970; Selected Poems, 1972; Accumulated Silences, 1973; Sever Summer, 1974; Sudden Pauses, 1976; Wounds and Suns, 1978; By the Fire of Fame (essays), 1979; When Birds Fly More Slowly, 1979; Called by Happy Abysses, 1981; I am Tortured by Beauty, 1983; Prophesies, Confessions, two vols, 1984; Heart's Calms, 1985; In the Hour When Shadows Were Born, 1987; Are You a Dream?, 1989; Echo from the Altar, 1992; Dizziness, 1994; Approaching Beauty, 1995; Vigils, 1996; Hushed Time, 1997; Love-Magic Reality, 1997; Transformations, 1998. *Contributions to:* Magazines and periodicals. *Honours:* Dimitro State Prize, 1966; Yavorov Literary Prize, 1973; Literary Prize, City of Bourgas, 1974; Sofia Literary Prize, 1974; Union of Bulgarian Writers Prize, 1978. *Membership:* Union of Bulgarian Writers. *Address:* 21 A. Patriarh Evtimiv Blvd, 1000 Sofia, Bulgaria.

MATHENY, Danny Lee; b. 6 Aug. 1952, San Antonio, Texas, USA. Poet. 1 d. *Contributions to:* Anthologies and other publications. *Honour:* Best Poems of the 90s. *Membership:* International Society of Poets. *Address:* 101 N Bayard St, PO Box 2663, Silver City, NM 88062, USA.

MATHEWS, Harry; b. 14 Feb. 1930, New York, NY, USA. Author; Poet; Ed.; Trans. *Education:* Princeton University; Harvard University; L'École Normale de Musique, Paris. *Publications:* Prose: The Conversions, 1962; The Tlooth, 1966; The Sinking of the Odradek Stadium and Other Novels, 1975; Selected Declarations of Dependence, 1977; Country Cooking and Other Stories, 1980; Cigarettes, 1987; The Orchard (memoirs), 1988; Twenty Lines a Day, 1988; Singular Pleasures, 1988; The American Experience, 1991; Immeasurable Distances (criticism), 1991; The Journalist, 1994; Oulipo Compendium (co-ed.), 1998; Sainte Catherine, 2000. Poetry: The Planisphere, 1974; Trial Impressions, 1977; Armenian Papers, 1987; Out of Bounds, 1989. *Contributions to:* Numerous anthologies, reviews, quarterlies, journals, etc. *Honours:* National Endowment for the Arts Grant, 1982; American Acad. and Institute of Arts and Letters Award, 1991. *Address:* c/o Maxine Groffsky, 2 Fifth Ave, New York, NY 10011, USA.

MATHEWS, Nieves Hayat, (Nieves de Madariaga); b. 3 Dec. 1917, Glasgow, Scotland. Writer; Poet. m. Paul William Mathews, 23 April 1939, 1

s. ,1 d. *Education:* BA, Spanish, French, King's College, University of London. *Publication:* She Died Without a Light, 1956; Francis Bacon: The History of a Character Assassination, 1996. *Contributions to:* Reviews and journals. *Address:* Tecognano, 52040, Montanare di Cortona, Arezzo, Italy.

MATHIAS, Roland Glyn; b. 4 Sept. 1915, Talybont-on-Usk, Breconshire, Wales. Poet; Writer. m. Mary (Molly) Hawes, 4 April 1944, 1 s., 2 d. *Education:* BA, Modern History, 1936, BLitt (by thesis), 1939, MA, 1944, Jesus College, Oxford. *Appointments:* Schoolmaster; Ed., The Anglo-Welsh Review, 1961–76; Extra-Mural Lecturer, University College, Cardiff, 1970–77; Visiting Prof., University of Alabama at Birmingham, 1971. *Publications:* Poetry: Break in Harvest, 1946; The Roses of Tretower, 1952; The Flooded Valley, 1960; Absalom in the Tree, 1971; Snipe's Castle, 1979; Burning Brambles, 1983; A Field at Vallorcines, 1996. Short Stories: The Eleven Men of Eppynt, 1956. Non-Fiction: Whitsun Riot, 1963; Vernon Watkins, 1974; John Cowper Powys as Poet, 1979; A Ride Through the Wood, 1985; Anglo-Welsh Literature: An Illustrated History, 1987; The Collected Short Stories of Roland Mathias, 2001. *Contributions to:* Many literary journals and periodicals. *Honour:* Hon. DHL, Georgetown University, Washington, DC, 1985. *Membership:* Welsh Arts Council, chair., literature committee, 1976–79. *Address:* Deffrobani, 5 Maescelyn, Brecon, Powys LD3 7NL, Wales.

MATHIS-EDDY, Darlene (Fern); b. 19 March 1937, Elkhart, IN, USA. Prof.; Writer; Poet; Ed. m. Spencer Livingston Eddy, 23 May 1964, deceased 1971. *Education:* BA, summa cum laude, Goshen College, 1959; MA, 1961, PhD, 1966, Rutgers University. *Appointments:* Instructor in English, Douglas College, 1962–64; Rutgers University, 1964, 1965, Rutgers University College, 1967; Asst Prof., 1967–71, Assoc. Prof., 1971–75, Prof., 1975–, of English, Poet-in-Residence, 1989–93, Ball State University; Counsulting Ed., Blue Unicorn, 1995–; Founding-Ed., The Hedgerow Press, 1995–. *Publications:* The Worlds of King Lear, 1971; Leaf Threads, Wind Rhymes, 1986; Weathering, 1992. *Contributions to:* Amelia; Barnwood; Blue Unicorn; Bitterroot; Cottonwood; Dog River Review; Forum; Green River Review; Pebble; Snowy Egret; BSU Forum; The Anne Miniver Broadside Series, 1982; The Trumpet Vine Broadside Series, 1995. *Honours:* Fellowships. *Memberships:* American League of Pen Women; Midwest Writers' Workshop. *Address:* c/o Dept of English, Ball State University, Muncie, IN 47306, USA.

MATSON, Clive; b. 13 March 1941, Los Angeles, CA, USA. Poet; Playwright; Teacher. *Education:* Undergraduate work, University of Chicago, 1958–59; MFA, Poetry, School of the Arts, Columbia University. *Publications:* Mainline to the Heart, 1966; Space Age, 1969; Heroin, 1972; On the Inside, 1982; Equal in Desire, 1983; Hourglass, 1987; Breath of Inspiration (essay), 1987; Let the Crazy Child Write, 1998. *Contributions to:* Anthologies and journals. *Honour:* Graduate Writing Fellowship, Columbia University, 1987–88. *Address:* 472 44th St, Oakland, CA 94609, USA.

MATSON, Suzanne Marie; b. 12 Nov. 1959, Portland, Oregon, USA. Writer; Prof. of English; Poet. m. Joseph Donnellan, 15 June 1991, 3 s. *Education:* BA, Portland State University, Oregon, 1981; MA, 1983, PhD, 1987, University of Washington. *Appointments:* Asst Prof. of English, 1988–94, Assoc. Prof. of English, 1994–2002, Prof. of English, 2002–, Boston College. *Publications:* Sea Level, 1990; Durable Goods, 1993; The Hunger Moon (novel), 1997; A Trick of Nature (novel), 2000. *Contributions to:* American Poetry Review; Poetry; Harvard Review; Shenandoah; Indiana Review; Poetry Northwest; Seattle Review; Southern Poetry Review; New England Review. *Honours:* Young Poet's Prize, Poetry Northwest, 1983; Acad. of American Poets Prize at the University of Washington, 1986. *Membership:* Associated Writing Programs. *Address:* c/o Dept of English, Boston College, Chestnut Hill, MA 02167, USA. *E-mail:* suzanne.matson@bc.edu.

MATTHIAS, John (Edward); b. 5 Sept. 1941, Columbus, Ohio, USA. Prof.; Poet; Writer; Trans. m. Diana Clare Jocelyn, 27 Dec. 1967, 2 c. *Education:* BA, Ohio State University, 1963; MA, Stanford University, 1966; Postgraduate Studies, University of London, 1966–67. *Appointments:* Asst Prof., 1967–73, Assoc. Prof., 1973–80, Prof., 1980–, University of Notre Dame; Visiting Fellow in Poetry, 1976–77, Assoc., 1977–, Clare Hall, Cambridge; Visiting Prof., Skidmore College, 1978, University of Chicago, 1980. *Publications:* Bucyrus, 1971; 23 Modern Poets (ed.), 1971; Turns, 1975; Crossing, 1979; Five American Poets (ed.), 1979; Contemporary Swedish Poetry (trans. with Goran Printz-Pahlson), 1979; Barthory and Lermontov, 1980; Northern Summer: New and Selected Poems, 1984; David Jones: Man and Poet, 1989; Tva Dikter, 1989; A Gathering of Ways, 1991; Reading Old Friends, 1992; Selected Works of David Jones, 1993; Swimming at Midnight: Selected Shorter Poems, 1995; Beltane at Aphelion: Collected Longer Poems, 1995. *Contributions to:* Numerous anthologies, reviews, quarterlies, and journals. *Honours:* Fulbright Grant, 1966; Swedish Institute Trans. Award, 1977–78; Columbia University Trans. Award, 1978; Ingram Merrill Foundation Awards, 1984, 1990; Society of Midland Authors Poetry Award, 1986; Society for the Study of Midwestern Literature Poetry Prize, 1986; Slobodan Janovic Literary Prize, 1989; George Bogin Memorial Award, Poetry Society of America, 1990; Lilly Endowment Grant, 1991–92; Ohio Library Asscn Poetry Award, 1996. *Memberships:* American Literary Trans Asscn; PEN American Center; Poetry Society of

America. *Address:* c/o Dept of English, University of Notre Dame, Notre Dame, IN 46556, USA.

MAUGHAN, Jill; b. 18 Jan. 1958, Newcastle upon Tyne, England. Writer; Poet. *Education:* BA, Communication Studies, Sunderland University, 1984. *Publication:* Ghosts at Four O'Clock, 1986. *Contributions to:* Anthologies, newspapers and magazines. *Honours:* First Prize, Newcastle Evening Chronicle Poetry Competition, 1984; Eric Gregory Award, 1987; Northern Arts Writer's Awards, 1987, 1990; Tyrone Guthrie Prize, 1989. *Address:* 3 Prospect Terrace, Plawsworth, Chester-le-Street, County Durham DH2 3LF, England. *E-mail:* jill&jill51@fsnet.co.uk.

MAURER, Susan; b. 30 Oct. 1940, California, USA. Poet. *Education:* AB, Barnard, 1962; MSW, St Louis University, 1972. *Publications:* By the Blue Light of the Morning Glory, 1997; Fire Island (anthology), 1997; Coming Home (anthology), 1997; Help Yourself (anthology). *Contributions to:* American Voice; Virginia Quarterly Review; Orbis; Virginia Quarterly Review; Crazy Horse; Salzburg Review; Brooklyn Review; Gare du Nord. *Address:* 210 E 15th St, New York, NY 10003, USA.

MAWER, Charles E.; b. 1 Feb. 1969, Haslemere, Surrey, England. Poet. *Education:* Lady Margaret Hall, Oxford University. *Publications:* Down the Backs of Sofas; Learning Gumboot; Poetry Now South; Young Words. *Contributions to:* Poetry Nottingham; Envoi; Iota; Iron; People's Poet; First Time; Old Police Station; Surrey Advertiser; Oxford Literary Magazine. *Honours:* Major Award Winner, Young Writer of the Year; Pick of the Fringe. *Memberships:* Oxford Poetry Society; London Blue Nose Poets; Poetry Society. *Address:* Fernside Cottage, Brook Rd, Wormley, Nr Godalming, Surrey GU8 5UA, England.

MAXTON, Hugh, (William John McCormack); b. 15 Sept. 1947, Dublin, Ireland. Poet; Literary Historian. m. Sheelagh Grayson, 9 Jan. 1971, separated 1999, 1 s. *Education:* BA, MA, Trinity College, 1967–71; DPhil, New University of Ulster, 1971–74. *Appointment:* Prof. of Literary History and Head of English, Goldsmiths College, University of London. *Publications:* Collections: Stones, 1970; The Noise of the Fields, 1976; Jubilee for Renegades, 1982; At the Protestant Museum, 1986; The Engraved Passion, 1991; Swift-Mail, 1992. Memoir: Waking, An Irish Protestant Upbringing, 1997. *Honours:* Poetry Book Society Choice; Hungarian Ministry of Culture Prize for Trans. *Membership:* Aosdána; RSA. *Address:* 38 Agamemnon Rd, West Hampstead, London NW6 1EN, England.

MAXWELL, Glyn (Meurig); b. 7 Nov. 1962, Welwyn Garden City, Hertfordshire, England. Poet; Writer; Reviewer; Ed. *Education:* BA, English, Worcester College, Oxford, 1985; MA, Creative Writing, Boston University, Massachusetts, 1988. *Publications:* Tale of the Mayor's Son (poems), 1990; Out of the Rain (poems), 1992; Gnyss the Magnificent: Three Verse Plays, 1993; Blue Burneau (novel), 1994; Rest for the Wicked (poems), 1995; The Breakage, 1998; Time's Fool, 2001. *Contributions to:* Reviews, journals, and magazines. *Honours:* Poetry Book Society Choice, 1990, and Recommendation, 1992; Short-listed, John Llewellyn Rhys Memorial Prize, 1991; Eric Gregory Award, 1991; Somerset Maugham Award, 1993. *Memberships:* PEN; Poetry Society. *Address:* c/o Bloodaxe Books, PO Box 1SN, Newcastle upon Tyne NE99 1SN, England.

MAXWELL, Patricia Anne, (Jennifer Blake, Maxine Patrick, Patricia Ponder, Elizabeth Trehearne); b. 9 March 1942, Winn Parish, LA, USA. Writer; Poet. m. Jerry R Maxwell, 1 Aug. 1957, 2 s., 2 d. *Appointment:* Writer-in-Residence, University of Northeastern Louisiana. *Publications:* Over 40 novels, including: Love's Wild Desire, 1977; Tender Betrayal, 1979; The Storm and the Splender, 1979; Golden Fancy, 1980; Embrace and Conquer, 1981; Royal Seduction, 1983; Surrender in Moonlight, 1984; Midnight Waltz, 1985; Fierce Eden, 1985; Royal Passion, 1986; Prisoner of Desire, 1986; Southern Rapture, 1987; Louisiana Dawn, 1987; Perfume of Paradise, 1988; Love and Smoke, 1989; Spanish Serenade, 1990; Joy and Anger, 1991; Wildest Dreams, 1992; Arrow to the Heart, 1993; Shameless, 1994; Silver-Tongued Devil, 1996; Tigress, 1996; Garden of Scandal, 1997. *Contributions to:* Anthologies and periodicals. *Honours:* Best Historical Romance Novelist of the Year, 1985; Reviewer's Choices, 1984, 1995, Romantic Times; Golden Treasure Award, Romance Writers of America, 1987; Romance Hall of Fame, Affaire de Coeur, 1995; Frank Waters Award for Writing Excellence, 1997. *Memberships:* National League of American Pen Women; Romance Writers of America. *Literary Agent:* Richard Curtis Assocs Inc. *Address:* PO Box 9218, Quitman, LA 71268, USA.

MAY, Brian James; b. 7 Jan. 1945. Teacher (retd); Poet. m. 29 July 1967, 1 s., 2 d. *Education:* BA, 1957; MA, 1971; PGCE, 1973; MA, Education, 1991. *Contributions to:* Orbis; Illuminations; Christ's College Magazine; Times Educational Supplement; Poetry Now. *Membership:* College of Teachers, fellow. *Address:* 3 Holte Dr., Sutton Coldfield, Birmingham B75 6PR, England.

MAYER, Bernadette; b. 12 May 1945, New York, NY, USA. Poet; Writer. 1 s., 2 d. *Education:* New School for Social Research, New York City. *Appointments:* Resident Dir, St Mark's Poetry Project, Greenwich Village, 1980–84; Various workshops. *Publications:* Ceremony Latin, 1964; Story, 1968; Moving, 1971;

The Basketball Article (with Anne Waldman), 1975; Memory, 1975; Studying Hunger, 1975; Poetry, 1976; Eruditio Ex Memoria, 1977; The Golden Book of Words, 1978; Midwinter Day, 1982; Incidents Reports Sonnets, 1984; Utopia, 1984; Mutual Aid, 1985; The Art of Science Writing (with Dales Worsley), 1989; Sonnets, 1989; The Formal Field of Kissing, 1990; A Bernadette Mayer Reader, 1992; The Desires of Mothers to Please Others in Letters, 1994. *Contributions to:* Anthologies. *Address:* c/o Hard Press Inc, PO Box 184, West Stockbridge, MA 01266, USA.

MAYER, Gerda (Kamilla); b. 9 June 1927, Karlovy Vary, Czechoslovakia (Naturalized British citizen). Poet. m. Adolf Mayer, 3 Sept. 1949. *Education:* BA, Bedford College, London, 1963. *Publications:* Oddments, 1970; Gerda Mayer's Library Folder, 1972; Poet Tree Centaur: A Walthamstow Group Anthology (ed.), 1973; Treble Poets 2, 1975; The Knockabout Show, 1978; Monkey on the Analyst's Couch, 1980; The Candy Floss Tree, 1984; March Postman, 1985; A Heartache of Grass, 1988; Time Watching, 1995; Bernini's Cat, 1999. *Contributions to:* Anthologies and other publications. *Memberships:* Poetry Society; Society of Authors. *Address:* 12 Margaret Ave, Chingford, London E4 7NP, England.

MAYER-KOENIG, Wolfgang; b. 28 March 1946, Vienna, Austria. Poet; Writer; Ed.; University Prof.; Industrial Dir. *Education:* Universities of Vienna, Saarbrücken, and Los Angeles. *Publications:* Sichtbare Pavilions, 1969; Stichmarken, 1970; Texte und Bilder, 1972; Sprache-Politik-Aggression, 1975; Texte und Zeichnungen, 1975; Psychologie und Literatursprache, 1976; Language-Politics-Agression, 1977; Italienreisen Goethes, 1978; Robert Musils Moglichkeitsstil, 1979; In den Armen unseres Waerters, 1980; Chagrin non dechiffré, 1986; A Hatalom bonyolult Angyala, 1988; Underestimated Deep, 1989; A Complicated Angel, 1989; Responsibility of Writing: Contributions to a Modern Grammar, 1990; Risks of Writing, 1991; Verzögerung des Vertrauens, 1995; Colloquios nel Cuarto, 1996; Fire and Ice, 1996; Mirror Wading, 1996; Verkannte Tiefe, 1996; Grammatik der Modernen Poesie, 1996; Behind Desires Deficits, 1997; Confessions of an Angry Loving European, 1999. *Contributions to:* Various publications. *Honours:* Theodor Körner Prize for Poetry, 1974; officer Order of Merit, Egypt, 1974; Austrian Cross of Honour for Science and Arts, 1976; Cross of Honour, Lower Austria, 1982; Commander Order of St Agatha, San Marino, 1982; Golden medal of merit, International ARC, 1983; Ordre du Mérite Africain, 1983; Chevalier des Arts et des Lettres, France, 1987; Golden cross Order of Eagle of Tyrol, 1988; Papal Lateran Cross, first class; Grand Cross of Honour, Government of Carinthia, 1993; Cross of merit first class of Lilienfeld, 1984; Cross of Merit of Greek Orthodox Papal Patriarch of Alexandria, Egypt; Star of Peace, Rome, Italy; Premio Prometeo Aureo Lazio, Vienna Art Foundation prize; New Century Award. *Membership:* Acad. Tiberina; Acad. Burckhardt St Gallen; Acad. Consentina; Acad. Europa; Board mem., Austrian Writers' Asscn; PEN; Vice-pres., Robert-Musil Archive Asscn, 1975–. *Address:* Hernalser Guertel 41, 1170 Vienna, Austria.

MAYHAR, Ardath, (Frank Cannon, Frances Hurst, John Killdeer); b. 20 Feb. 1930, Timpson, Texas, USA. Writer; Poet. m. Joe E Mayhar, June 1958. *Education:* Self-educated. *Publications:* Over 40 books, including: How the Gods Wove in Kyrannon, 1979; Soul Singer of Tyrnos, 1981; Runes of the Lyre, 1982; Lords of the Triple Moons, 1983; The World Ends in Hickory Hollow, 1985; A Place of Silver Silence, 1987; Texas Gunsmoke, 1988; Far Horizons, 1994; Island in the Swamp, 1994; Hunters of the Plains, 1995; High Mountain Winter, 1996. *Contributions to:* Quarterlies and magazines. *Honours:* Awards and prizes for fiction and poetry. *Memberships:* SFWA; Western Writers of America. *Address:* 533 CR 486, Chireno, TX 75937, USA. *E-mail:* ardathm@netdot.com. *Website:* netdot.com/ardathm/.

MAYNE, Seymour; b. 18 May 1944, Montréal, QC, Canada. Prof. of English; Poet; Writer; Ed.; Trans. *Education:* BA, Honours, English, McGill University, 1965; MA, English and Creative Writing, 1966, PhD, 1972, University of British Columbia. *Appointments:* Lecturer, University of British Columbia, 1972; Lecturer, 1973, Asst Prof., 1973–78, Assoc. Prof., 1978–85, Prof. of English, 1985–, University of Ottawa; Visiting Prof., 1979–80, Visiting Prof. and Scholar, 1983–84, 1992, Writer-in-Residence, 1987–88, Hebrew University of Jerusalem; Visiting Prof., Concordia University, Montréal, 1982–83, University of La Laguna, Spain, 1993; Adjunct Research Prof., Carleton University, 2002–; Contributing Ed., 1982–90, Poetry Ed., 1990–95, Viewpoints; Contributing Ed., Tel-Aviv Review, 1989–96, Poet Lore, 1992–, Jerusalem Review, 1997–; Founder-Consulting Ed., Bywords, 1990–, Graffito, 1994–. *Publications:* That Monocycle the Moon, 1964; Tiptoeing on the Mount, 1965; From the Portals of Mouseholes, 1966; Manimals, 1969; Mouth, 1970; For Stems of Light, 1971; Face, 1971; Name, 1975; Diasporas, 1977; The Impossible Promised Land: Poems New and Selected, 1981; Children of Abel, 1986; Diversions, 1987; Six Ottawa Poets (with others), 1990; Killing Time, 1992; The Song of Moses and Other Poems, 1995; Five-O'Clock Shadows (with others), 1996; Dragon Trees, 1997; City of the Hidden, 1998; Carbon Filter, 1999; Light Industry, 2000. Other: Ed. or co-ed. of 13 books, 1968–97; Trans. or co-trans. of eight books, 1974–98. *Contributions to:* Anthologies, books, journals, reviews, and quarterlies. *Honours:* Numerous grants and fellowships; Chester Macnaghten First Prize in Creative Writing, 1962; J I Segal Prize in English-French Literature, 1974; York Poetry Workshop Award, 1975; American Literary

Trans Asscn Poetry Trans. Award, 1990; Jewish Book Committee Prize, 1994; Louis L Lockshin Memorial Award, 1997; Fuerstenberg-Aaron Prize, 2000. *Address:* c/o Dept of English, Faculty of Arts, University of Ottawa, PO Box 450, Station A, Ottawa, Ontario K1N 6N5, Canada.

MAYO, Wendell; b. 16 Aug. 1953, Corpus Christi, TX, USA. Asst Prof. of Creative Writing and Literature; Writer; Poet. m. Deborah Masonis, 22 Dec 1982. *Education:* BS, 1975, PhD, 1991, Ohio State University; BA, University of Toledo, 1980; University of Houston, 1984–85; MFA, Vermont College, 1988. *Appointments:* Asst Prof. of English, Indiana University-Purdue University Fort Wayne, 1991–94; Asst Prof., then Assoc. Prof. of Creative Writing and Literature, University of Southwestern Louisiana, Lafayette, 1994–96; Asst Prof. of Creative Writing and Literature, Bowling Green State University, Ohio, 1996–. *Publications:* Centaur of the North (short stories), 1996; In Lithuanian Wood (novel); B Horror and Other Stories, 1999; Giesmininkas (short stories). *Contributions to:* Various reviews, quarterlies and magazines, including: Harvard Review; Prairie Schooner; Western Humanities Review; Missouri Review; New Letters; The Yale Review; North American Review; Threepenny Review; Anthologies, including: City Wilds; 100% Pure Florida Fiction. *Honours:* Fellow, Millay Colony for the Arts, 1992; Master Fellow, Indiana Arts Commission, 1992; Yado Fellow, 1992, 1994, 1996; Fellow, Edward F. Albee Foundation, 1993; First Prize for Fiction, Mississippi Valley Review, 1995, New Delta Review, 1996; Premio Aztlan, University of New Mexico, 1997; National Endowment for the Arts, 2001; Fulbright Grant, 2002. *Memberships:* Associated Writing Programs; Society for the Study of Midwestern Literature. *Address:* 210 Liberty Hi St, PO Box 153, Haskins, OH 43525, USA. *E-mail:* wmayo@bgnet.bgsu.edu.

MAYORAL, Irene; b. 23 Oct. 1930, Madrid, Spain. Poet; Writer. m. (1) Antonio Valcárcel, 20 July 1950, deceased, 1 s., 1 d., (2) Justo González, 18 June 1974, deceased. *Education:* BA, Isabel la Católica Institute and Lope de Vega Institute; Music, Singing, Reciting and Performance, Madrid Conservatoire. *Appointments:* Active Mem., American Culture Institute, Mexico, 1994; Dir, Aula Literaria 2000, Guadalajara Centre, Madrid, 1997; Congresswoman, University Parliament for Security and Peace, 1998; Mem. of Exec. Council, Parliament Journalists Corps, Diplomatic Distinctive, 1998; Head, Exec. Councillors, St Lukas Acad., Germany, 1998. *Publications:* Huellas en la soledad, 1989; Cartas para una voz, 1991; Velázquez y yo, 1992; Esa mirada de Abir desde el Islám, 1993; Africa: Diario de una misionera, 1994; Te estoy (por mayoralas), 1995; De guerras y niños tatuados, 1997; Antología mínima, 1998; Manzanares de la Mancha y yo, 1999; Ven, habitemos en la imaginación, 2001. *Contributions to:* Various Spanish periodicals. *Honours:* Hon. Academician, Felgueiras Cultural Centre, Portugal, 1991; Baronessa delle Arti, Italy, 1994; Rossone d'Oro, Crisalide Universal, Italy, 1994; German Arts '98 International Poetry Prize, St Kukas Acad.; Prof. h.c., St Lukas Acad., 1998; Hon. Mem., CCI, Santa Monica, USA; Dame Commander, Order of St Monica, England, 1998; Countess of Dernek, Germany, 1998; Salvador Rueda Prize, Madrid, 1999. *Memberships:* Asociación Prometeo de Poesía, Madrid, 1989; Asociación Colegial de Escritores de España, Madrid, 1990; Asociación Iberoamericana de Poesía, 1993; Asociación de Escritores y Artistas Españoles, Madrid, 1994. *Address:* c/ Galileo 2, 2° A, 28015 Madrid, Spain.

MAYRÖCKER, Friederike; b. 20 Dec. 1924, Vienna, Austria. Author; Poet; Dramatist. *Education:* Teacher of English training. *Appointment:* Teacher of English, 1946–69. *Publications:* Larifari: Ein konfuses Buch, 1956; Tod durch Musen: Poetische Texte, 1966; Minimonsters Traumlexikon: Texte in Prosa, 1968; Fantom Fan, 1971; Je un umwölkter gipfel: Erzählung, 1973; Das Licht in der Landschaft, 1976; Fast ein Frühling des Markus M., 1976; Heiligenanstalt, 1978; Die Abschiede, 1980; Magische Blätter, Vols I–IV, 1983–87, Vol. V, 1999; Reuse durch die Nacht, 1984; Das Herzzerreissende der Dinge, 1985; Winterglück: Gedichte, 1982–85, 1986; Mein Herz mein Zimmer mein Name, 1988; Stilleben, 1991; Lection, 1994; Notizen auf einem Kamel, 1996; Das zu Sehende, das zu Hörende, 1997; Brütt oder die Seufzenden Gärten, 1998; Benachbarte Metalle, 1998; Mein Arbeitstirol (poems). *Contributions to:* Journals and magazines. *Honours:* Great Austrian State Prize, 1982; Friedrich-Hölderlin Prize, 1993; Great Literature Prize, Bavarian Acad. of Fine Arts, Munich, 1996; Else-Lasker-Schüler Prize, 1996; Meersburger Droste Prize, 1997; Georg Buchner Prize, 2001. *Memberships:* Several Austrian and German literary asscns. *Address:* Zentagasse 16/40, 1050 Vienna, Austria.

MAZZARO, Jerome (Louis); b. 25 Nov. 1934, Detroit, Michigan, USA. Prof. of English and Comparative Literature (retd); Poet; Writer; Ed. *Education:* AB, Wayne University, 1954; MA, University of Iowa, 1956; PhD, Wayne State University, 1963. *Appointments:* Instructor, University of Detroit, 1958–61; Ed., Fresco, 1960–61, Modern Poetry Studies 1970–79; Asst Prof., State University of New York College at Cortland, 1962–64; Asst Ed., North American Review, 1963–65, Noetics, 1964–65; Prof. of English and Comparative Literature, State University of New York at Buffalo, 1964–96; Contributing Ed., Salmagundi, 1967–97, American Poetry Review, 1972–, Italian-American, 1974–88; Poetry Ed., Helios, 1977–79. *Publications:* The Achievement of Robert Lowell, 1939–1959, 1960; Juvenal: Satires (trans.), 1965; The Poetic Themes of Robert Lowell, 1965; Changing the Windows (poems), 1966; Modern American Poetry (ed.), 1970; Transformation in the Renaissance English Lyric, 1970; Profile of Robert Lowell (ed.), 1971; Profile of William Carlos Williams (ed.), 1971; William Carlos Williams: The Later Poetry, 1973; Postmodern American Poetry, 1980; The Figure of Dante: An Essay on the 'Vita Nuova', 1981; The Caves of Love (poems), 1985; Rubbings (poems), 1985; John Logan: The Collected Poems (ed. with Al Poulin), 1989; John Logan: The Collected Fiction (ed.), 1991; Mind Plans: Luigi Pirandello's Theatre, 2000; Robert Lowell and Ovid, 2001; War Games (fiction), 2001. *Contributions to:* Reference works, books and journals. *Honours:* Guggenheim Fellowship, 1964–65; Hadley Fellowship, 1979–80. *Memberships:* Dante Society of America; Mark Twain Society. *Address:* 392 Central Park W, Apt. 11J, New York, NY 10025, USA.

MEAD, Matthew; b. 12 Sept. 1924, Buckinghamshire, England. Poet. *Appointment:* Ed., Satis Magazine, Edinburgh, 1960–62. *Publications:* A Poem in Nine Parts, 1960; Identities, 1964; Kleinigkeiten, 1966; Identities and Other Poems, 1967; Penguin Modern Poets 16 (with Harry Guest and J Beeching), 1970; In the Eyes of the People, 1973; Minusland, 1977; The Midday Muse, 1979; A Roman in Cologne, 1986. *Address:* c/o Anvil Press, 69 King George St, London SE10 8PX, England.

MEANLEY, Deborah Ann, (Harriet Hendren); b. 5 July 1940, Ewell, Surrey, England. Psychiatrist (retd); Poet. m. 24 Feb. 1968, 1 s., 3 d. *Education:* MBBS, London, 1965; LRCP, MRCS, Royal Free Hospital School of Medicine, University of London, 1965. *Appointments:* House Surgeon, Royal Free Hospital, 1966; General Practitioner's Asst, London and North Lincolnshire, 1967–79; Clinical Medical Officer, Scunthorpe Health District, 1979–84; Senior House Physician, Registrar in Psychiatry, Asst Psychiatrist, 1984–98. *Publication:* Mother's Prickly Poems and More..., 1997. *Contributions to:* 5 anthologies. *Honours:* First Place, Humorous Verse, North Lincolnshire Drama Festival, 1996; First Prize, North Lincolnshire Drama Festival, 1997; Special Commendation in Poet of the Year, 1998; Award of Excellence, National Open Poetry Competition, 1998. *Address:* The Old Orchard, Tunnel Rd, Wrawby, Brigg DN20 8SF, England.

MECKEL, Christoph; b. 12 June 1935, Berlin, Germany. Author; Poet; Graphic Artist. *Education:* Studied Graphic Art, Freiburg, Paris, Munich. *Publications:* Manifest der Toten, 1960; Im Land der Umbramauten, 1961; Wildnisse, 1962; Die Drummheit liefert uns ans Messer: Zeitgespräch in zehn Sonetten (with Volker von Törne), 1967; Bockshorn, 1973; Wen es angeht, 1974; Komödie der Hölle, 3 vols, 1979, 1984, 1987; Suchbild: Über meinen Vater, 1980; Ein roter Faden, 1983; Das Buch Jubal, 1987; Das Buch Shiralee, 1989; Von den Luftgeschäften der Poesie, 1989; Die Messingstadt, 1991; Gesang vom unterbrochenen Satz, 1995. *Honours:* Rainer Maria Rilke Prize, 1979; Georg Trakl Prize, 1982; Literature Prize, Kassel, 1993. *Memberships:* Acad. of Science and Literature, Mainz; Akademie für Sprache und Dichtung eV, Darmstadt; PEN. *Address:* Kulmbacherstr 3, 10777 Berlin, Germany.

MEEK, Jay; b. 23 Aug. 1937, Grand Rapids, Michigan, USA. Prof.; Poet. m. Martha George, 29 Aug. 1966, 1 d. *Education:* BA, University of Michigan, 1959; MA, Syracuse University, 1965. *Appointments:* Faculty, Wake Forest University, 1977–80, Sarah Lawrence College, 1980–82; Assoc. Prof., Massachusetts Institute of Technology, 1982–83; Writer-in-Residence, Memphis State University, 1984; Prof., University of North Dakota, 1985–. *Publications:* The Week the Dirigible Came, 1976; Drawing on the Walls, 1980; Earthly Purposes, 1984; Stations, 1989; Windows, 1994; Headlands: New and Selected Poems, 1997. *Contributions to:* Journals and magazines. *Honours:* National Endowment for the Arts Award, 1972–73; Guggenheim Fellowship, 1985–86; Bush Artist Fellowship, 1989. *Address:* c/o Dept of English, University of North Dakota, Box 7209, University Station, Grand Forks, ND 58202, USA.

MEHTA, Vikram. See: ANZRANNII, Avikm Axim.

MEIDINGER-GEISE DRIPGIE, Ingeborg Lucie; b. 16 March 1923, Berlin, Germany. Writer; Poet; Dramatist. *Education:* DPhil. *Publications:* Over 50 works, including novels, stories, poems, essays, criticism, and radio plays. *Contributions to:* Various publications. *Honour:* Hans Sachs Drama Prize, 1976; International Mölle Literary Prize, Sweden, 1979. *Memberships:* Die Kogge, chair., 1967–88; PEN. *Address:* Schobertweg 1a, 91056 Erlangen, Germany.

MEIER, Herbert; b. 29 Aug. 1928, Solothurn, Switzerland. Writer; Poet; Playwright; Trans. m. Yvonne Haas, 23 Sept. 1954, 2 s., 1 d. *Appointments:* Chefdramaturg, Schauspielhaus, Zürich, 1977–82; Writer-in-Residence, University of Southern California at Los Angeles, 1986. *Publications:* Gedichte und Märchen; Siebengestirn; Dem Unbekannten Gott; Elf Strassengesange; Sequenzen; Gli Spaziali; Vier Gedichte; Drei Gedichte; Aufbreche, Reisen von dorther, 1998. *Contributions to:* Literatur und Kunst. *Memberships:* Schweiz Schriftstellerverband; PEN. *Address:* Appenzeller Strasse 73, CH 8049 Zürich, Switzerland.

MEINKE, Peter; b. 29 Dec. 1932, New York, NY, USA. Prof. of Literature (retd); Poet; Writer. m. Jeanne Clark, 14 Dec. 1957, 2 s., 2 d. *Education:* AB, Hamilton College, 1955; MA, University of Michigan, 1961; PhD, University of

Minnesota, 1965. *Appointments:* Asst Prof., Hamline University, St Paul, Minnesota, 1961–66; Prof. of Literature and Dir of the Writing Workshop, Eckerd College, St Petersburg, FL, 1966–93; Fulbright Senior Lecturer, University of Warsaw, 1978–79; Visiting Distinguished Writer, University of Hawaii, 1993, University of North Carolina, Greensboro, 1996; Fellow, Le Château de Lavigny, Switzerland, 1998; Several Writer-in-residencies. *Publications:* Lines from Neuchâtel, 1974; The Night Train and the Golden Bird, 1977; The Rat Poems, 1978; Trying to Surprise God, 1981; The Piano Tuner, 1986; Underneath the Lantern, 1987; Night Watch on the Chesapeake, 1987; Far from Home, 1988; Liquid Paper: New and Selected Poems, 1991; Scars, 1996; Campocorto, 1996; The Shape of Poetry, 1999; Zinc Fingers, 2000; Greatest Hits, 2001. *Contributions to:* Periodicals. *Honours:* First Prize, Olivet Sonnet Competition, 1966; National Endowment for the Arts Fellowships, 1974, 1989; Gustav Davidson Memorial Award, 1976, Lucille Medwick Memorial Award, 1984, Emily Dickinson Award, 1992, Poetry Society of America; Flannery O'Connor Award, 1986; Paumanok Poetry Award, 1993; Master Artist's Fellowship, Fine Arts Work Center, Provincetown, 1995. *Memberships:* Acad. of American Poets; Poetry Society of America. *Address:* 147 Wildwood Lane SE, St Petersburg, FL 33705, USA.

MELEAGROU, Evie; b. 28 May 1930, Nicosia, Cyprus. Author; Poet. m. Dr John Meleagrou, MD, 26 Nov. 1952, 1 s., 2 d. *Education:* Diplome de la Literature Française, Athenaeum Institute, Athens; BA, University of London. *Appointments:* Producer, Literary Programmes, CBC, 1952–55; Ed., Cyprus Chronicles, 1960–72; Secretary, Cyprus Chronicles Cultural Centre, 1960–74; Cyprus Representative, World Writers Conference, 1965. *Publications:* Solomon's Family, 1957; Anonymous City, 1963; Eastern Mediterranean, 1969; Conversations with Che, 1970; Penultimate Era, 1981; Persona is the Unknown Cypriot Woman (literary essays and poetry), 1993; The Virgin Plunge in the Ocean Depths (short stories and novels), 1993; Cyprus Chronaca (historical essays), 1974–1992, 1993; Other: Trans. *Honours:* Severian Literary Prize, 1945; First Pancyprian Prize Short Story Competition, 1952; Pancyprian Novella Competition, 1957; Cyprus National Novel Awards, 1970, 1982; Panhellenic National Novel Award, 1982. *Memberships:* Cyprus Chronicles Cultural Centre, general secretary; Cyprus Cultural Asscn of Women, general secretary; First Cypriot Writers Asscn, secretary, 1961–70; Asscn of Greek Writers, Athens; Cyprus State Literary Awards Committee, 1969–79. *Literary Agent:* Dodoni Publishing House, 3 Asklipios St, Athens, 10679, Greece. *Address:* 22 Messolongi St, Nicosia, Cyprus.

MELFI, Mary; b. 10 June 1951, near Rome, Italy. Author; Poet; Dramatist. m. George Nemeth, 17 May 1975, 2 s. *Education:* BA, Loyola College, Concordia University, 1973; MLS, McGill University, 1977. *Publications:* The Dance, the Cage and the Horse (poems), 1976; A Queen Is Holding a Mummified Cat (poems), 1982; A Bride in Three Acts (poems), 1983; A Dialogue with Masks (novella), 1985; The O Canada Poems, 1986; A Season in Beware (poems), 1989; Infertility Rites (novel), 1991; Ubu: The Witch Who Would Be Rich (children's novel), 1994; Sex Therapy (play), 1996; Painting Moments, Art, AIDS and Nick Palazzo (ed.), 1998; Stages: Selected Poems, 1998; Office Politics (poems), 1999. *Contributions to:* Many reviews, quarterlies and journals. *Honours:* Canada Council Arts Grants, 1981–82, 1982–83; Québec Arts Council Grants, 1993–94, 1996–97; Canadian Heritage Grant, 1995. *Address:* 5040 Grand Blvd, Montréal, QC H3X 3S2, Canada.

MELITAS, Roula. See: POLLARD Roula.

MELLOR, Robin Frederick; b. 16 Nov. 1944, South Wales. Poet; Children's Writer. m. Frances Anne Mellor, 13 June 1988, 2 s., 1 step-s., 1 step-d. *Education:* BEd, London University, 1975. *Appointments:* Teacher, 1967–80; Head Teacher, 1980–91. *Contributions to:* Many anthologies and other publications. *Memberships:* Poetry Society; Society of Authors. *Address:* 51 Bush Rd, Cuxton, Rochester, Kent ME2 1LS, England.

MELTZER, David; b. 17 Feb. 1937, Rochester, New York, USA. Poet; Writer; Teacher; Ed.; Musician. m. Christina Meyer, 1958, 1 s., 3 d. *Education:* Los Angeles City College, 1955–56; University of California at Los Angeles, 1956–57. *Appointments:* Ed., Maya, 1966–71; Tree magazine and Tree Books, 1970–; Faculty, Graduate Poetics Program, 1980–, Chair, Undergraduate Writing and Literature Program, Humanities, 1988–, New College of California, San Francisco. *Publications:* Poetry: Poems (with Donald Schenker), 1957; Ragas, 1959; The Clown, 1960; Station, 1964; The Blackest Rose, 1964; Oyez!, 1965; The Process, 1965; In Hope I Offer a Fire Wheel, 1965; The Dark Continent, 1967; Nature Poem, 1967; Santamaya (with Jack Shoemaker), 1968; Round the Poem Box: Rustic and Domestic Home Movies for Stan and Jane Brakhage, 1969; Yesod, 1969; From Eden Book, 1969; Abulafia Song, 1969; Greenspeech, 1970; Luna, 1970; Letters and Numbers, 1970; Bronx Lil/Head of Lilian S A C, 1970; 32 Beams of Light, 1970; Knots, 1971; Bark: A Polemic, 1973; Hero/Lil, 1973; Tens: Selected Poems 1961–1971, 1973; The Eyes, the Blood, 1973; French Broom, 1973; Blue Rags, 1974; Harps, 1975; Six, 1976; Bolero, 1976; The Art, the Veil, 1981; The Name: Selected Poetry 1973–1983, 1984; Arrows: Selected Poetry 1957–1992, 1994. Fiction: Orf, 1968; The Agency, 1968; The Agent, 1968; How Many Blocks in the Pile?, 1968; Lovely, 1969; Healer, 1969; Out, 1969; Glue Factory, 1969; The Martyr, 1969; Star, 1970; The Agency Trilogy, 1994. Other: We All Have Something to

Say to Each Other: Being an Essay Entitled 'Patchen' and Four Poems, 1962; Introduction to the Outsiders, 1962; Bazascope Mother, 1964; Journal of the Birth, 1967; Isla Vista Notes: Fragmentary, Apocalyptic, Didactic Contradictions, 1970; Two-way Mirror: A Poetry Note-Book, 1977. Editor: Journal for the Protection of All Beings 1 and 3 (with Lawrence Ferlinghetti and Michael McClure), 2 vols, 1961, 1969; The San Francisco Poets, 1971, revised as Golden Gate, 1976; Birth: An Anthology, 1973; The Secret Garden: An Anthology in the Kabbalah, 1976; Death, 1984; Reading Jazz: The White Invention of Jazz, 1993; Writing Jazz, 1997. Honours: Council of Literary Magazine Grants, 1972, 1981; National Endowment for the Arts Grants, 1974, 1975; Tombstone Award for Poetry, James Ryan Morris Memorial Foundation, 1992. Address: Box 9005, Berkeley, CA 94709, USA.

MEMMOTT, David R.; b. 10 Dec. 1948, Grand Rapids, MI, USA. Ed.; Writer; Poet. m. Susan A. Memmott, 14 Sept. 1974, 1 d. Education: BA, Eastern Oregon State University, 1977. Appointments: Man. Ed., 1986–90, Contributing Ed., 1990, 1997, Ice River: Magazine of Speculative Writing. Publications: Alpha Gallery: Selections from the Fantastic Small Press (poetry ed.), 1991; House on Fire: Poetry and Collage, 1992; The Larger Earth: Descending Notes of a Grounded Astronaut (poems), 1996; Within the Walls of Jericho (poems), 1998; Shadow Bones (short stories), 1999. Honours: Co-ordinating Council of Literary Magazines Grant, 1988; Oregon Arts Commission Grants, 1988, 1989; Nominee, Pushcart Prizes, 1989, 1996, 1998, 1999; Fishtrap Fellow, 1990; Rhysling Award, 1990; Nominee, Oregon Book Award for Poetry, 1992, 1996, 1998; Literary Arts Inc Fellowships, 1995, 2000. Memberships: Council for Literature of the Fantastic; Institute for Noetic Sciences. Address: 1003 Y Ave, PO Box 3235, La Grande, OR 97850, USA.

MENASHE, Samuel; b. 16 Sept. 1925, New York, NY, USA. Poet. Education: BA, Queen's College, Flushing, New York, 1947; Doctoral d'Université, Sorbonne, University of Paris, 1950. Publications: The Many Named Beloved, 1961; No Jerusalem But This, 1971; Fringe of Fire, 1973; To Open, 1974; Collected Poems, 1986; Penguin Modern Poets 7, 1996. Contributions to: Periodicals. Honour: Longview Foundation Award, 1957. Membership: PEN. Address: 75 Thompson St, Apt 15, New York, NY 10012, USA.

MENEBROKER, Ann Reynolds, (Ann R. Bauman); b. 30 March 1936, Washington, DC, USA. Poet. m. (1) Jerrol P Bauman, 25 Oct. 1952, (2) Wayne L Menebroker, 23 May 1964, 1 s., 2 d. Publications: Various poems. Contributions to: Anthologies and periodicals. Membership: Sacramento Poetry Center. Address: 2738 Fourth Ave, Sacramento, CA 95818, USA.

MENEZES, Ruth Gwendolen Ballard Francesca Borges de; b. 1 Jan. 1910, Watsonville, CA, USA. Writer; Poet. m. Joaquim de Menezes Jr, 12 May 1931, deceased 1984, 1 s., 1 d. Education: Humboldt State University, 1926–27; San Francisco State University, 1956–57; Jesuit University of San Francisco, 1956–63. Publications: Thunder in Spring, 1924; Woman Songs, 1981; Love Ascending, 1987; The Heart's Far Cry, 1996. Contributions to: Many magazines, including: The Catholic World; America; Voices; St Anthony's Newsletter. Honours: First Place, National Contest of Catholic Magazines and Newspapers; Grand Prize, Sparrowgrass Poetry Forum Contest, 1997. Address: 6124 Buckingham Parkway, No. 102, Culver City, CA 90230, USA.

MENTZER, G(eorge Speraw), (George Schiller Mentzer); b. 10 Feb. 1923, Annville, Pennsylvania, USA. Poet. m. Catherine Jane Shay, 10 Dec. 1943, 2 s., 1 d. Education: Diploma, International School, 1950; Diploma, Air University, 1958; ThB, International Seminary, 1990. Contributions to: Anthologies and periodicals. Honours: Golden Poet Award, 1985; Silver Poet Award, 1989; Honourable Mention, 1990. Memberships: American Poetry Asscn; Great Lakes Poetry Asscn; National Arts Society; World Poetry Asscn. Address: 616 Renova Ave, Lebanon, PA 17042, USA.

MENZIES, Rosemary Laura; b. 8 March 1939, Auckland, New Zealand. Teacher; Peace Activist; Poet; Writer. m. Robert Gordon Menzies, 8 May 1967, 2 d. Education: Diploma, Physical Education, Otago University, 1958; Diploma, Teaching, New Zealand, 1964; Diploma, English Language Teaching, Auckland University, 1989. Appointments: Contributor, Co-ordinator, Weekly Live Poetry Scene, Auckland, 1983–; Tutor, Auckland Language Schools and Carrington Polytechnic, 1994–; Tutor, Auckland University of Technology; Mem., International Peace Journey to Sarajevo and Mostar, 1995–96; Independent journeys to Bosnia as writer and voluntary humanitarian worker, 1996–99. Publications: I Asked the Moon, 1981; The Globe Tapes (co-ed.), 2 vols, 1985; Whitewave and Undertow, 1986; To Where the Bare Earth Waits, 1988; Poems for Bosnia, 1995; New Poems for Bosnia, 1997; Omarska Camp, 1997. Contributions to: Various publications. Honour: Public Speaking Cup, Auckland City Council, 1985. Memberships: PEN New Zealand; Writers-in-Schools; Hon. Mem., Rotary Club of Downtown Auckland; Hon. Mem., Bosnian Cultural Centre, Zagreb. Address: 21 Wernham Pl., Birkenhead, Auckland 10, New Zealand.

MENZIES, Trixie (Te Arama) Thelma; b. 16 Aug. 1936, Wellington, New Zealand. Poet. m. (1) William Stewart, 31 Dec. 1958, (2) Barry Charles Menzies, 14 May 1979, 1 s., 2 d. Education: BA, Auckland University College, 1957; MA, Honours, Auckland University, 1979. Publications: Uenuku, 1986; Papakainga,

1988; Rerenga, 1992. Contributions to: Anthologies, newspapers, journals and magazines. Honours: Co-Winner, PEN Award for Best First Book of Poetry, 1987; Finalist, New Zealand Book Awards in Poetry, 1993. Memberships: Nga Puna Waihanga (New Zealand Maori Writers and Artists Society); New Zealand Society of Authors; Te Ha (Maori Writers Group); Waiata Koa (Maori Women Writers and Artists Collective). Address: PO Box 87-082, Meadowbank, Auckland, New Zealand.

MEO, Franca; b. 16 Dec. 1939, Treviso, Italy. Poet; Writer; Trans. m. Piero Giacomini, 21 July 1961, 2 s., 1 d. Education: Diploma, Foreign Languages and Literature. Publications: Penso a un'ora piu tenue, 1960; Ariete trevisane, 1961; Ci troviamo umili, 1966; Sapere d'essere vivi, 1972; Il sole negli occhi, 1978; Doni d'amore, 1979; Questa vita questo amore, 1982; Amore e disamore, 1986; Come abbiamo potuto dimenticare il paradiso?, 1989; Storie di oggetti e di donne, 1990. Contributions to: 4 anthologies, including A Heart Beating in Space, 1997. Address: Via Gian Maria Maszzucchelli 2, 25080 Ciliverghe (BS), Italy.

MEREDITH, Christopher (Laurence); b. 15 Dec. 1954, Tredegar, Wales. Writer; Poet; Senior Lecturer. m. V. Smythe, 1 Aug. 1981, 2 s. Education: BA, Philosophy and English, University College Wales, Aberystwyth, 1976. Appointment: Senior Lecturer, University of Glamorgan. Publications: Poetry: This, 1984; Snaring Heaven, 1990. Fiction: Shifts, 1988; Griffri, 1991. Contributions to: Literary magazines in Wales, England and USA. Honours: Eric Gregory Award, 1984; Welsh Arts Council Young Writer's Prize, 1985 and Fiction Prize, 1989; Short-listed, Book of the Year Award, 1992. Membership: Yr Academi Gymreig, English language section. Address: c/o Seren Books, Wyndham St, Bridgend, Mid Glamorgan, Wales.

MEREDITH, Jennifer Margaret, (Jenni Meredith, Tonos); b. 8 Oct. 1949, Middlesex, England. Journalist; Cartoonist; Animator; Poet; Arts Administrator. m. Tony Meredith, 10 April 1970, 1 s. Education: Diploma, Fine Art, Hammersmith-Chelsea Art College. Appointments: Founder, Snowball Press, 1991; Editorial Asst, Disability Arts Magazine, 1992–93; Dir, Snow Tracks Productions, 1995–. Publication: Snow Ewes Crowing Over Split Snails, 1991. Other: Through the Pane (animated concrete poetry video), 1995. Contributions to: Anthologies, magazines, BBC Radio Three. Memberships: Poetry Society; Federation of Worker Writers and Community Publishers; Founder, Write to Belong, National Postal Forum of Disabled Writers, 1992. Address: 7 Marine Parade, Dovercourt, Essex CO12 3JX, England.

MEREDITH, Joseph Edward; b. 6 Jan. 1948, Philadelphia, Pennsylvania, USA. Teacher; Writing Consultant; Poet. m. Jeanne M Koenig, 5 Aug. 1972, 1 s., 1 d. Education: BA, La Salle University, 1970; MA, University of Florida, 1974. Appointments: Lecturer, English, 1974–90, Dir, Writing Center, 1979–90, Poet-in-Residence, La Salle University, Philadelphia, 1988–90; Pres., Meredith Assocs, Corporate Writing Consultants, 1990–; Adjunct Prof., Camden County College, Blackwood, NJ, 1991–94; Rutgers University, NJ, 1994–. Publication: Hunter's Moon, 1993. Contributions to: American Scholar; Threepenny Review; Southwest Review; Four Quarters, Philadelphia; Kansas Quarterly; Florida Quarterly; Painted Bride Quarterly, Philadelphia. Honours: Mary Elinor Smith Prize, 1984; Hart Crane Award, 1986; Corcoran Prizes, 1990, 1991, 1992. Address: 4625 Oakland St, Philadelphia, PA 19124, USA.

MEREDITH, William (Morris); b. 9 Jan. 1919, New York, NY, USA. Poet; Prof. of English (retd). Education: AB, Princeton University, 1940. Appointments: Instructor in English and Woodrow Wilson Fellow in Writing, Princeton University, 1946–50; Assoc. Prof. in English, University of Hawaii, 1950–51; Assoc. Prof., 1955–65, Prof. in English, 1965–83, Connecticut College, New London; Instructor, Bread Loaf School of English, Middlebury College, Vermont, 1958–62; Consultant in Poetry, Library of Congress, Washington, DC, 1978–80. Publications: Poetry: Love Letters from an Impossible Land, 1944; Ships and Other Figures, 1948; The Open Sea and Other Poems, 1958; The Wreck of the Thresher and Other Poems, 1964; Winter Verse, 1964; Year End Accounts, 1965; Two Pages from a Colorado Journal, 1967; Earth Walk: New and Selected Poems, 1970; Hazard, the Painter, 1975; The Cheer, 1980; Partial Accounts: New and Selected Poems, 1987. Non-Fiction: Reasons for Poetry and the Reason for Criticism, 1982; Poems Are Hard to Read, 1991. Editor: Shelley: Poems, 1962; University and College Poetry Prizes, 1960–66, 1966; Eighteenth-Century Minor Poets (with Mackie L Jarrell), 1968; Poets of Bulgaria (with others), 1985. Translator: Guillaume Apollinaire: Alcools: Poems, 1898–1913, 1964. Honours: Yale Series of Younger Poets Award, 1943; Harriet Monroe Memorial Prize, 1944; Rockefeller Foundation Grants, 1948, 1968; Oscar Blumenthal Prize, 1953; National Institute of Arts and Letters Grant, 1958, and Loines Prize, 1966; Ford Foundation Fellowship, 1959–60; Van Wyck Brooks Award, 1971; National Endowment for the Arts Grant, 1972, and Fellowship, 1984; Guggenheim Fellowship, 1975–76; International Vaptsarov Prize for Literature, Bulgaria, 1979; Los Angeles Times Prize, 1987; Pulitzer Prize in Poetry, 1988. Memberships: Acad. of American Poets, chancellor; National Institute of Arts and Letters. Address: 6300 Bradley Ave, Bethseda, MD 20817, USA.

MERRILL, Christopher (Lyall); b. 24 Feb. 1957, Northampton, MA, USA. Poet; Writer; Ed.; Trans.; Prof. of English. m. Lisa Ellen Gowdy, 4 June 1983, 2

d. *Education:* BA, Middlebury College, 1979; MA, University of Washington at Seattle, 1982. *Appointments:* Teaching Fellow, University of Utah, 1983–87; Dir, Santa Fe Writer's Conference, 1987–90; Founder-Dir, Taos Conference on Writing and the Natural World, 1987–92, Santa Fe Literary Center, 1988–92; General Ed., Peregrine Smith Poetry Series, 1987–; Adjunct Prof., Santa Fe Community College, 1988–90; Adjunct Faculty, Northwest Writing Institute, Lewis and Clark College, 1993–95; Faculty, Open Society Institute, University of Sarajevo, 1995; William H. Jenks Chair in Contemporary Letters, College of the Holy Cross, 1995–2000; Visiting Lecturer, Chatham College, 1999–2000; Prof. of English, 2000, Dir, International Writing Program, 2000–, University of Iowa. *Publications:* Workbook (poems), 1988; Fevers and Tides (poems), 1989; The Forgotten Language: Contemporary Poets and Nature (ed.), 1991; From the Faraway Nearby: Georgia O'Keefe as Icon (ed. with Ellen Bradbury), 1992; The Grass of Another Country: A Journey Through the World of Soccer, 1993; Watch Fire (poems), 1994; The Old Bridge: The Third Balkan War and the Age of the Refugee, 1995; What Will Suffice: Contemporary American Poets on the Art of Poetry (ed. with Christopher Buckley), 1995; The Forest of Speaking Trees: An Essay on Poetry, 1996; Your Final Pleasure: An Essay on Reading, 1996; Only the Nails Remain: Scenes from the Balkan Wars, 1999; Brilliant Water (poems), 2001. *Contributions to:* Many periodicals. *Honours:* Sherman Brown Neff Fellowship, University of Utah, 1986–87; John Ciardi Fellow in Poetry, Bread Loaf Writers' Conference, 1989; Pushcart Prize in Poetry, 1990; Ingram Merrill Foundation Award in Poetry, 1991; Readers' Choice Award in Poetry, Prairie Schooner, 1992; Peter I. B. Lavan Younger Poets Award, Acad. of American Poets, 1993; Trans. Award, Slovenian Ministry of Culture, 1997. *Memberships:* Acad. of American Poets; Authors' Guild; PEN American Center. *Address:* 216 McLean St, Iowa City, IA 52242, USA.

MERRIN, Jeredith; b. 9 April 1944, California, USA. Prof. of English; Writer; Poet. 1 d. *Education:* BS, Iowa State University, 1968; MA, San Jose State University, 1978; PhD, University of California at Berkeley, 1987. *Appointments:* Instructor, Gifted Program, University of California at Berkeley, 1983–85; Asst Prof., 1987–93, Assoc. Prof., 1993–97, Prof. of English, 1997–, Ohio State University, Columbus; Presenter, workshops and poetry readings. *Publications:* An Enabling Humility: Marianne Moore, Elizabeth Bishop, and the Uses of Tradition, 1990; Shift (poems), 1996; In the Minor Key (poetry criticism), 1999. *Contributions to:* Books, anthologies, reviews, quarterlies and journals. *Honours:* Lilly Foundation Fellow, 1988–89; Regdale Artists Colony Residencies, 1990, 1991, 1996; Fellow, Skidmore College, 1993; Elizabeth Gee Award for Research on Women, 1993; National Endowment for the Humanities Grants, 1995, 1997; Finalist, Lambda Literary Award, 1997. *Address:* c/o Dept of English, Ohio State University, 164 W 17th Ave, Columbus, OH 43210, USA.

MERRY, Rosemary Elisabeth; b. 22 Feb. 1925, Soham, Cambridgeshire, England. Social Worker (retd); Poet. m. Ian W. Merry, 22 Nov. 1947, 1 d. *Education:* University of Nottingham. *Publications:* A Crack in a Wall, 1993; Behind the Lines, 1997. *Contributions to:* Anthologies, magazines and journals. *Honours:* Highly Commended, Library of Avalon Open Competition, 1996, 1997, Surrey and Wey Poets Open Poetry Competition, 1998; Second Prize, Poetry Digest Competition, 1997; First Prize, Manifold Human Rights Competition, 1999; Society of Women Writers and Journalists Joyce Grenfell Memorial Scholarship for Poetry, 2001. *Membership:* Society of Women Writers and Journalists; Suffolk Book League. *Address:* Farmgate Cottage, Wicks Lane, Earl Stonham, Suffolk IP14 5HL, England.

MERWIN, W(illiam) S(tanley); b. 30 Sept. 1927, New York, NY, USA. Poet; Dramatist; Writer; Trans. m. Diane Whalley, 1954. *Education:* AB, Princeton University, 1947. *Appointments:* Playwright-in-Residence, Poet's Theatre, Cambridge, Massachusetts, 1956–57; Poetry Ed., The Nation, 1962; Assoc., Theatre de la Citié, Lyons, 1964–65; Special Consultant in Poetry, Library of Congress, Washington, DC, 1999. *Publications:* Poetry: A Mask for Janus, 1952; The Dancing Bears, 1954; Green with Beasts, 1956; The Drunk in the Furnace, 1960; The Moving Target, 1963; The Lice, 1967; Three Poems, 1968; Animae, 1969; The Carrier of Ladders, 1970; Signs, 1971; Writings to an Unfinished Accompaniment, 1973; The First Four Books of Poems, 1975; Three Poems, 1975; The Compass Flower, 1977; Feathers from the Hill, 1978; Finding the Islands, 1982; Opening the Hand, 1983; The Rain in the Trees, 1988; Selected Poems, 1988; Travels, 1993; The Vixen, 1996; The Folding Cliffs, 1998. Plays: Darkling Child (with Dido Milroy), 1956; Favor Island, 1957; The Gilded West, 1961; adaptations of 5 other plays. Other: A New Right Arm, n.d.; Selected Translations 1948–1968, 1968; The Miner's Pale Children, 1970; Houses and Travellers, 1977; Selected Translations 1968–1978, 1979; Unframed Originals: Recollections, 1982; Regions of Memory: Uncollected Prose 1949–1982, 1987; The Lost Upland, 1993. Editor: West Wind: Supplement of American Poetry, 1961; The Essential Wyatt, 1989. Translator: 19 books, 1959–89. *Honours:* Yale Series of Younger Poets Award, 1952; Bess Hokin Prize, 1962; Ford Foundation Grant, 1964; Harriet Monroe Memorial Prize, 1967; PEN Trans. Prize, 1969; Rockefeller Foundation Grant, 1969; Pulitzer Prize in Poetry, 1971; Acad. of American Poets Fellowship, 1973; Shelley Memorial Award, 1974; National Endowment for the Arts Grant, 1978; Bollingen Prize, 1979; Aiken Taylor Award, 1990; Maurice English Award, 1990; Dorothea Tanning Prize, 1994; Lenore Marshall Award, 1994; Ruth Lilly Poetry Prize, 1998. *Memberships:*

Acad. of American Poets; American Acad. of Arts and Letters. *Address:* c/o Georges Borchardt Inc, 136 E 57th St, New York, NY 10022. USA.

MESTAS, Jean-Paul; b. 15 Nov. 1925, Paris, France. Poet; Writer; Trans. m. Christiane Schoubrenner, 23 Dec. 1977, 2 s., 1 d. *Education:* BA, 1947, LLB, 1947, Institute of Political Studies, Paris. *Publications:* Various poems, essays, and trans, 1965–95. *Contributions to:* Many anthologies and periodicals. *Honours:* Excellence in Poetry, International Poet, New York, 1982; Premio de la Cultura, Palermo, 1991; Prix Marcel Beguey, Bergerac, 1992. *Memberships:* International Acad., Madras, fellow; International Poetry, Korea; International Writers and Artists, board of research.

METZGER, Deena; b. 17 Sept. 1936, New York, NY, USA. Writer; Poet; Playwright; Teacher; Healer. m. (1) H Reed Metzger, 26 Oct. 1957, (2) Michael Ortiz Hill, 20 Dec. 1987, 2 s. *Education:* BA, Brooklyn College; MA, University of California; PhD, International College, Los Angeles. *Appointments:* Prof., Los Angeles Valley College, 1966–69, 1973–74, 1975–79; Faculty, California Institute of the Arts, 1970–75; International Lecturer, Teacher of Writing, Supervision and Training of Healers in the Ethical, Creative and Spiritual Aspects of Healing, 1997–. *Publications:* Skin Shadows/Silence, 1976; Dark Milk, 1978; The Book of Hags, 1978; The Axis Mundi Poems, 1981; What Dinah Thought, 1989; Looking for the Face of God, 1989; A Sabbath Among the Ruins, 1992; Writing for Your Life: A Guide and Companion to the Inner Worlds, 1992; Tree: Essays and Pieces (co-ed.), 1997; Intimate Nature: Women's Bond with Animals (co-ed.), 1998. *Address:* PO Box 186, Topanga, CA 90290, USA.

MEWSHAW, Michael; b. 19 Feb. 1943, Washington, DC, USA. Author; Poet. m. Linda Kirby, 17 June 1967, 2 s. *Education:* MA, 1966, PhD, 1970, University of Virginia. *Appointments:* Instructor, 1970, Visiting Writer, 1989–91, University of Virginia; Asst Prof. of English, University of Massachusetts, 1970–71; Asst Prof. to Assoc. Prof. of English, University of Texas, Austin, 1973–83; Visiting Artist, 1975–76, Writer-in-Residence, 1977–78, American Acad., Rome. *Publications:* Fiction: Man in Motion, 1970; Waking Slow, 1972; The Troll, 1974; Earthly Bread, 1976; Land Without Shadow, 1979; Year of the Gun, 1984; Blackballed, 1986; True Crime, 1991. Non-Fiction: Life for Death, 1980; Short Circuit, 1983; Money to Burn: The True Story of the Benson Family Murders, 1987; Playing Away: Roman Holidays and Other Mediterranean Encounters, 1988; Ladies of the Court: Grace and Disgrace on the Women's Tennis Tour, 1993. *Contributions to:* Newspapers and magazines. *Honours:* Fulbright Fellowship, 1968–69; William Rainey Fellowship, 1970; National Endowment for the Arts Fellowship, 1974–75; Carr Collins Awards for Best Book of Non-Fiction, 1980, 1983; Guggenheim Fellowship, 1981–82; Book of the Year Award, Tennis Week, 1993. *Memberships:* PEN; Society of Fellows of the American Acad. in Rome; Texas Institute of Letters; US Tennis Writers Asscn. *Address:* c/o William Morris Agency, 1350 Sixth Ave, New York, NY 10019, USA.

MEYER, Lynn. See: SLAVITT, David R(ytman).

MEYER, Margaret, (Maggi H. Meyer); b. 1 Feb. 1916, Fargo, North Dakota, USA. Poet; Ed. m. William C Meyer, 27 May 1938, divorced 1947, 1 s. *Education:* University of California at Los Angeles. *Appointments:* Ed., Poetalk, 1979–90. *Publications:* Mix With Love, 1977; Body and Soul, 1978; More, 1979; And More, 1980; It Came With Me, 1981; Sign of No Time, 1982; How is it?, 1983; Changing, 1984; Maggi: 3 Faces of Poetry, 1988; In Thrall, 1992; Et Cetera, 1995; Come Along, 1998; Thursdays, 2001. *Contributions to:* Many anthologies, reviews and quarterlies. *Honours:* Many. *Memberships:* Bay Area Poets Coalition; Renegades. *Address:* 1527 Virginia St, Berkeley, CA 94703, USA.

MEZEY, Katalin; b. 30 May 1943, Budapest, Hungary. Poet; Writer; Journalist; Trans. m. Janos Olah, 1 March 1971, 2 s., 1 d. *Education:* Philology, German Literature, University of Zürich, 1964; Philology, Hungarian Literature and Adult Education, Eötvös Lorand University, Budapest. *Appointments:* Founder-Ed., Szephalom Konyvumuhely, publishers, 1989–; Secretary, 1987–92, General Secretary, 1992–, Trade Union of Hungarian Writers. *Publications:* 11 books, 1970–94. *Address:* Pesthidegkut 2 pf 5, Budapest 1286, Hungary.

MEZEY, Robert; b. 28 Feb. 1935, Philadelphia, Pennsylvania, USA. Poet; Prof. of English. m. Olivia Simpson, 14 July 1963, 1 s., 2 d. *Education:* Kenyon College, 1951–53; BA, University of Iowa, 1959; Graduate Study, University of Iowa and Stanford University, 1960–62. *Appointments:* Asst Prof., Western Reserve University; Prof., Franklin and Marshall College; Asst Prof., Fresno State University; Assoc. Prof., University of Utah; Full Prof., Pomona College, 1976–99. *Publications:* The Lovemaker, 1961; White Blossoms, 1965; A Book of Dying, 1970; The Door Standing Open: New and Selected Poems, 1970; Couplets, 1976; Small Song, 1978; Selected Translations, 1982; Evening Wind, 1987; Collected Poems, 2000. *Contributions to:* Poetry; New Yorker; Partisan Review; Kenyon Review; Raritan; Paris Review; Hudson Review; Antaeus; New York Review of Books, New Criterion; Yale Review. *Honours:* Robert Frost Prize, 1952; Stegner Writing Fellowship, 1960; Lamort Award; Ingram Merrill Fellowships, 1973, 1989; Guggenheim Fellowship, 1977; Poetry

Award, National Institute and Acad. of Arts and Letters, 1982; National Endowment for the Arts Fellowship, 1986. *Membership:* Asscn of Literary Scholars and Critics. *Address:* Baldwin House, 137 N College, Claremount, CA 91711, USA.

MF. See: FERRETT, Mabel.

MICHAEL, Christine, (Angela O'Brien); b. 3 March 1944, Nottingham, England. Poet; Writer. 1 s., 1 d. *Education:* Bishop Grosseteste College, 1963–66; Open University, 1974–81; University College, Cork, 1983–86. *Publications:* Several poems, stories and songs. *Contributions to:* Various publications. *Honour:* Lake Aske Memorial Award. *Memberships:* International Songwriters Asscn; International Songwriters Guild; Performing Rights Society. *Address:* 54 Kingswood Rd, West Bridgford, Nottingham NG2 7HS, England.

MICHAELS, Anne; b. 15 April 1958, Toronto, Ontario, Canada. Poet; Novelist; Writer; Teacher of Creative Writing. *Education:* BA, Honours, University of Toronto, 1980. *Appointments:* Many workshops and poetry readings; Teacher of Creative Writing, University of Toronto, 1988–. *Publications:* Poetry: The Weight of Oranges, 1986; Miner's Pond, 1991; Skin Divers, 1999. Fiction: Fugitive Pieces, 1996. *Contributions to:* Numerous anthologies, reviews, and magazines. *Honours:* Epstein Award for Poetry, 1980; Commonwealth Poetry Prize for the Americas, 1986; Canadian Authors' Asscn Award for Poetry, 1991; National Magazine Award for Poetry, 1991; Chapter/Books in Canada First Novel Award, 1997; Trillium Award, 1997; Lannan Prize, 1997; Guardian Fiction Award, 1997; H H Wingate Award, 1997; Orange Prize for Fiction, 1997; Harry Ribalow Award, 1998. *Memberships:* League of Canadian Poets; Writers' Union of Canada. *Address:* c/o McClelland and Stewart Inc, 481 University Ave, Suite 900, Toronto, Ontario M5G 2E9, Canada.

MICHEL, Sandra Seaton; b. 30 Jan. 1935, Hancock, MI, USA. Writer; Poet; Ed. m. Philip R. Michel, 28 July 1956, 3 s., 1 d. *Education:* BA, Stanford University, 1980. *Appointments:* Delaware State Arts Council and National Endowment for the Arts Residency Artist in Creative Writing, 1974–79, 1984–; Ed., Highland Publishing House, 1996–. *Publications:* My Name is Jaybird, 1972; No More Someday, 1973; From the Peninsula South, 1980; Thomas, My Brother, 1981; Visions to Keep, 1990. *Honours:* Distinguished Service Award, Lutheran Community Services Board, Wilmington, 1994–95; First State Writers Poetry Award, 1998. *Memberships:* Society of Children's Book Writers and Illustrators; National League of Pen Women, state pres., 1996–98. *Address:* 3 Lanark Dr., Wilmington, DE 19803, USA. *E-mail:* sandramichel@att.net.

MICU, Liliana Maria, (Liliana Ursu); b. 11 July 1949, Sibiu, Romania. Radio Producer; Poet. m. Dan Micu, 14 Oct. 1979, 1 s. *Education:* BA, Faculty of English, University of Bucharest, 1972. *Publications:* Viata deasupra orasului, 1977; Ordinea Clipelor, 1978; Piata aurarioir, 1980; Zona de Protectie, 1983; Corali, 1986; Port Angeles, 1992; Wingless Victory: Poems from America, 1993; The Sky Behind the Forest (trans. with Tess Gallagher), 1997; Angel Riding a Beast (trans. with Bruce Weigl), 1998. *Contributions to:* Luceafarul; Romania Literara; Transilvania; Steaua; Euphorion; Atheneum; Cronica; Viata Romaneasca; Convorbiri Literare; Secolul XX; Mihai Eminescu; Glasul Natiunii; Viata Noua; Contemporanul; Poetry Wales; Honest Ulsterman; Applegarth Review; Oxford Poetry; European Poetry Review II; Tribune; American Poetry Review; New Yorker; Ohio Review; Gettysburg Review; Hudson Literary Magazine. *Honours:* Prize for Poetry, Luceafarul Literary Magazine, 1976; Prize for Poetry, Romanian Writers Asscn, 1980. *Memberships:* European Asscn for the Promotion of Poetry; Romanian Writers Union; Romanian Journalists Asscn; European Poetry Centre and Cultural Dialogue East West Constant, Noica, Sibui; Fulbright Alumni Asscn. *Address:* Str Dr Victor Babes nr 20, Sector 5, Bucharest 35, Romania.

MIDDLEBROOK, Diane Wood; b. 16 April 1939, Pocatello, ID, USA. Prof. of English Emeritus; Writer; Poet; Biographer. m. (1) Jonathan Middlebrook, 15 June 1963, divorced 1972, 1 d., (2) Carl Djerassi, 21 June 1985. *Education:* Whitman College, Walla Walla, Washington, 1957–58; AB, University of Washington, 1961; MA, 1962, PhD, 1968, Yale University. *Appointments:* Asst Prof., 1966–73, Assoc. Prof., 1974–83, Dir, Center for Research on Women, 1977–79, Assoc. Dean, Undergraduate Studies, 1979–82, Prof. of English, 1983–2002, Chair, Program in Feminist Studies, 1985–88, Howard H and Jessie T Watkins University Prof., 1985–90, Stanford University; Visiting Assoc. Prof., Rutgers University, 1973. *Publications:* Walt Whitman and Wallace Stevens, 1974; Worlds Into Words: Understanding Modern Poems, 1980; Gin Considered as a Demon (poems), 1983; Coming to Light: American Women Poets (ed. with Marilyn Yalom), 1985; Selected Poems of Anne Sexton (ed. with Diana Hume George), 1988; Anne Sexton: A Biography, 1991; Suits Me: The Double Life of Billy Tipton, 1998. *Contributions to:* Books, anthologies and journals, including poems, articles and reviews. *Honours:* Woodrow Wilson Fellowship, 1961; Albert S Cook Memorial Prize for Poetry, 1962, Theron Rockwell Field Prize for Doctoral Dissertation, 1968, Yale University; Acad. of American Poets Prize, 1965; Dean's Award for Distinguished Teaching, 1977, Walter J Gores Award for Excellence in Teaching, 1987, Stanford University; National Endowment for the Humanities Fellowship, 1982–83; Fellow, Bunting

Institute, Radcliffe College, 1982–83, Stanford Humanities Center, 1983–84 Rockefeller Study Center, Bellagio, Italy, 1990; Guggenheim Fellowship 1988–89; Finalist, National Book Award, 1992; Commonwealth Club o California Gold Medal for Non-Fiction, 1992; Hon. DLitt, Kenyon College 1999. *Memberships:* Chadwyck-Healey LION (Literature Online), editorial board, 1997–; Djerassi Resident Artists Program, trustee, 1980–96, chair, board, 1994; Humanities West, advisory board, 1997–; Investigative Reporters and Eds, 1995–; MLA, 1966–; Biographers' Club, London, 1999–; California Classical Asscn, 1999–; International Asscn of University Profs o English, 1999–. *Address:* 1101 Green St, No. 1501, San Francisco, CA 94109, USA.

MIDDLETON, (John) Christopher; b. 10 June 1926, Truro, Cornwall, England. Prof. of Germanic Languages and Literatures Emeritus; Poet; Writer; Trans. 1 s., 2 d. *Education:* BA, Merton College, Oxford, 1951; MA, DPhil, 1954, University of Oxford. *Appointments:* Lecturer, University of Zürich, 1952–55; Lecturer, 1955–65, Senior Lecturer, 1965–66, King's College, University of London; Visiting Assoc. Prof., 1961–62, Prof. of Germanic Languages and Literatures, 1966–98, Prof. Emeritus, 1998–, University of Texas at Austin; Judith E Wilson Lecturer, University of Cambridge, 1992; Poet-in-Residence, W B Yeats Poetry Summer School, Sligo, Ireland, 1993; Various poetry readings. *Publications:* Poetry: Torse 3: Poems 1949–61, 1962; Nonsequences/Selfpoems, 1965; Our Flowers and Nice Bones, 1969; The Lonely Suppers of W V Balloon, 1975; Carminalenia, 1980; 111 Poems, 1983; Two Horse Wagon Going By, 1986; The Balcony Tree, 1992; Some Dogs, 1993; Intimate Chronicles, 1996; The Swallow Diver, 1997; Twenty Tropes for Doctor Dark, 2000; The World Pavillion and Selected Poems, 2001. Prose: Pataxanadu and Other Prose, 1977; Serpentine, 1985; In the Mirror of the Eighth King, 1999. Other: 'Bolshevism in Art' and Other Expository Writings, 1978; The Pursuit of the Kingfisher, 1983; Jackdaw Jiving: Selected Essays on Poetry and Translation, 1998. Translator: Ohne Hass und Fahne (with W Deppe and H Schönherr), 1958; Modern German Poetry, 1910–60 (with Michael Hamburger), 1962; German Writing Today, 1967; Selected Poems, by Georg Trakl, 1968; Selected Letters, by Friedrich Nietzsche, 1969; Selected Poems, by Friedrich Hölderlin and Eduard Mörike, 1972; Selected Poems of Goethe, 1983; Selected Stories, by Robert Walser, 1983; Andalusian Poems (with Leticia Garza-Falcón), 1993; Faint Harps and Silver Voices: Selected Translations, 1999. *Honours:* Sir Geoffrey Faber Poetry Prize, 1964; Guggenheim Fellowship, 1974–75; Deutscher Akademischer Austauschdienst Fellowships, 1975, 1978; National Endowment for the Arts Fellowship, 1980; Schlegel-Tieck Trans. Prize, 1985; Max Geilinger-Stiftung Prize in Anglo-Swiss Cultural Relations, 1987; Soeurette Diehl Fraser Award for Trans., Texas Institute of Letters, 1993: Camargo Foundation Fellow, 1999. *Address:* 1112 W 11th St, No. 201, Austin, TX 78703, USA.

MIDDLETON, Sheena. See: BLACKHALL, Sheena Booth.

MIHAILOVICH, Vasa D.; b. 12 Aug. 1926, Prokuplje, Yugoslavia (Naturalized US citizen, 1956). Prof. of Slavic Languages and Literatures (retd); Writer; Poet. m. Branka, 28 Dec. 1957, 2 s. *Education:* BA, 1956, MA, 1957, Wayne State University; PhD, University of California at Berkeley, 1966. *Appointments:* Instructor, 1961–63, Asst Prof., 1963–68, Assoc. Prof., 1968–75, Prof. of Slavic Languages and Literatures, 1975–95, University of North Carolina at Chapel Hill. *Publications:* Library of Literary Criticism: Modern Slavic Literatures, 2 vols, 1972, 1976; Introduction to Yugoslav Literature, 1973; A Comprehensive Bibliography of Yugoslav Literature in English, 1976; Contemporary Yugoslav Poetry, 1977; Stari i Novi Vilajet, 1977; Bdenja, 1980; Emigranti i Druge Price, 1980; Krugovi na Vodi, 1982; U Tudjem Pristanistu, 1988; Serbian Poetry From the Beginnings to the Present, 1988; Litija Malih Praznika, 1990; Na Brisanom Prostoru, 1994; Bozic u Starom Kraju, 1994; Dictionary of Literary Biography: South Slavic Writers, 2 vols, 1994, 1997; Songs of the Serbian People: From the Collections of Vuk St Karadzic, 1997; Rasejano Slovo/The Scattered Word, 1997; Braca i Druge Price, 1997; Sesta Rukovet, 2002; Elze i Druge Price, 2002. *Contributions to:* Books Abroad/World Literature Today; Saturday Review; Serbian Studies; Slavic and East European Journal; Slavic Review. *Honours:* Serbian PEN Center, 1988; Zlatni Prsten, 1994; Vukova Zaduzbina, 1997; Povelja Rastko Petrovic, 1998; In a Foreign Harbor: Essays in Honour of Vasa D Mihailovich, 2000. *Membership:* Asscn of Writers of Serbia. *Address:* 821 Emory Dr., Chapel Hill, NC 27514, USA. *E-mail:* vamih@aol.com.

MIKHAILUSENKO, Igor Georgiyevich; b. 20 April 1932, Moscow, Russia. Poet; Trans.; Journalist. *Education:* Graduated, Maurice Thorez Foreign Languages Institute, Moscow, 1958; Diploma, Higher Education. *Publications:* Five Poems Seen by the English Queen; It All Began with a UFO, 2001; Tribute to the Millennium, 2001; Memoirs of a Moscow Man, 2001; A Poet's Dreams, 2001; A Peaceful Journey: The USA Through Foreign Eyes, 2001. *Contributions to:* Various anthologies. *Honours:* Badge of Honour, Moscow Peace Committee, 1982; Recognition, United Poets Laureate International, 1987; Ed.'s Award, Fine Arts Press, USA; Laureate Man of Letters, 1997. *Memberships:* International Writers and Artists Asscn; United Poets Laureate International. *Address:* Bolshaya Gruzinskaya St, House 63, Apt 87, Moscow 123056, Russia. *E-mail:* mig@technoserv.ru. *Website:* www.eat2.com/tween/igormikhailusenko.

MILES, John Arthur; b. 24 Aug. 1942, Erith, Kent, England. Poet; Writer. m. Kay Lesley Foster, 18 Feb. 1972, 1 s., 2 d. *Education:* High School Matriculation, Urrbrae Agricultural College, SA, 1960. *Appointments:* Adelaide Festival Writer's Week, 1992; Poetry Ed., Australian Writer, 1994; Varuna Fellow, 1996. *Publications:* Anthology, 1987; Going Down Swinging, 1991; Homecoming, 1993; He Dances, 1994; Harvest, Five Seasons, 1995; Victorian Festival of Writing, 1997; Lost Angry Penguins, 1998. *Contributions to:* Numerous reviews, journals and magazines. *Honours:* 10 literary prizes and/or awards, 1988–95. *Address:* 17 Nunyah Dr., Banksla Park, SA 5091, Australia.

MILES, Simon James; b. 18 Oct. 1956, Birmingham, England. Poet; Writer; Ed. *Appointments:* Tutor in Creative Writing; Various poetry readings and workshops; Ed., The Archangel. *Publication:* Reasons Why, 1990. *Contributions to:* Several publications. *Honour:* Yeats Club Grand Prize, 1986. *Membership:* Initiator, William Blake Congregations. *Address:* 134A Hartley Rd, Redford, Nottingham NG7 3AJ, England.

MILLER, Aine; b. 15 Jan. 1938, Ireland. Poet; Teacher. m. Alexander Miller, 18 April 1960, 1 s., 3 d. *Education:* BA, University College, Cork, 1958; Middlesex Board of Education Teaching Certificate, 1960. *Appointment:* Writer-in-Residence, D.A.T.E. Centre, Dundrum, 1992–. *Publications:* Six for Gold; The Cloverdale Anthology of Irish Poetry; Goldfish in a Baby Bath, 1994; Jumping Off Shadows, 1995; Touchwood, 2000. *Contributions to:* Anthologies, reviews and journals. *Honours:* Hennessy Literary Award, 1987; Patrick Kavanagh Award, 1992; Moore Medallion, 1994; Kilkenney Prize, 1994. *Memberships:* English Literature Society; Poetry Ireland. *Address:* 35 Finsbury Park, Upper Churchtown Rd, Dublin 14, Ireland.

MILLER, Anesa, (Anesa Miller-Pogacar); b. 8 June 1954, Wichita, KS, USA. Writer; Poet; Ed.; Trans.; Educator. m. (1) Timothy Pogacar, 1980, divorced 1990, (2) Jaak Panksepp, 1 May 1991, 2 d. *Education:* BA, Occidental College, 1976; MA, PhD, University of Kansas, 1992. *Appointments:* Instructor in Russian Language and Literature, University of Kansas, 1979–83, Bowling Green State University, Ohio, 1986–94; Ed., Memorial Foundation for Lost Children, 1994–. *Publications:* After the Future: Paradoxes of Postmodernism and Contemporary Russian Culture (trans. and ed.), 1995; Re-Entering the Sign: Articulating New Russian Culture (co-ed.), 1995; A Road Beyond Loss: Three Cycles of Poems and an Epilogue, 1995. *Contributions to:* Periodicals. *Address:* c/o Memorial Foundation for Lost Children, 708 E Wooster, Bowling Green, OH 43402, USA. *E-mail:* jpankse@bgnet.bgsu.edu.

MILLER, David; b. 2 Oct. 1950, Melbourne, Vic., Australia. Research Fellow; Poet. *Education:* BA, History of Ideas, 1981; PhD, English Literature, 1986. *Publications:* The Caryatids, 1975; Primavera, 1979; Losing to Compassion, 1985; Messages, 1989; The Break, 1991; Pictures of Mercy: Selected Poems, 1991; Stromata, 1995; Elegy, 1996; Collected Poems, 1997; Spiritual Letters (1–10), 1997; Art and Disclosure, 1998; Spiritual Letters (1–12), 2000. *Contributions to:* Agenda; First Intensity; Notus; Acts; Stride; Reality Studios; Tel-let; Morning Star Folios; Intimacy; The Poet's Voice; Pearl; Shearsman; Southfields. *Address:* 6 Waynflete House, Union St, London SE1 0LE, England. *E-mail:* katermurr_uk@yahoo.co.uk.

MILLER, Edmund; b. 18 July 1943, New York, NY, USA. Prof.; Poet; Writer. *Education:* BA, summa cum laude, C W Post Campus, Long Island University, 1965; MA, Ohio State University, 1969; PhD, State University of New York at Stony Brook, 1975. *Appointments:* Lecturer, Ohio State University, 1968–69; Instructor, Rockhurst College, 1969–71; Asst Prof., Temple University, 1977–78, Illinois State University, 1979–80; Assoc. Prof., Hofstra University, 1980–81; Asst Prof., 1981–86, Assoc. Prof., 1986–90, Prof., 1990–, Chair., Dept of English, 1993, C W Post Campus, Long Island University. *Publications:* Poetry: Fucking Animals: A Book of Poems, 1973; The Nadine Poems, 1973; Winter, 1975; A Rider of Currents, 1986; The Happiness Cure, and Other Poems, 1993; Leavings, 1995. Non-Fiction: Drudgerie Divine: The Rhetoric of God and Man in George Herbert, 1979; Exercises in Style, 1980; Like Season'd Timber: New Essays on George Herbert (ed. with Robert DiYanni), 1987; George Herbert's Kinships: An Ahnentafel with Annotations, 1993. Fiction: Night Times, 2000. *Contributions to:* Books and journals. *Memberships:* Conference on Christianity and Literature; Lewis Carroll Society of North America; Milton Society of America, life mem.; MLA, life mem. *Address:* c/o Dept of English, C W Post Campus, Long Island University, Brookville, NY 11548, USA. *E-mail:* edmund.miller@liw.edu.

MILLER, E(ugene) Ethelbert; b. 20 Nov. 1950, New York, NY, USA. University Administrator; Poet. m. Denise King, 25 Sept. 1982, 1 s., 1 d. *Education:* BA, Howard University. *Appointments:* Dir, African American Resource Center, Howard University, 1974–; Jessie Ball duPont Scholar, Emory and Henry College, 1996. *Publications:* Andromeda, 1974; The Land of Smiles and the Land of No Smiles, 1974; Migrant Worker, 1978; Season of Hunger/Cry of Rain, 1982; Where are the Love Poems for Dictators?, 1986; First Light, 1994; Beyond the Frontier, 2002. Editor: Synergy: An Anthology of Washington, DC, Black Poetry, 1975; Women Surviving Massacres and Men, 1977; In Search of Color Everywhere, 1994; Fathering Words: The Making of an

African American Writer, 2000. *Contributions to:* Anthologies and National Public Radio; Code Magazine; Black Issues Book Review. *Honours:* Mayor's Art Award for Literature, Washington, DC, 1982; Public Humanities Award, DC Humanities Council, 1988; Columbia Merit Award, 1993; PEN Oakland Josephine Miles Award, 1994; O B Hardison Jr Poetry Prize, 1995; Hon. DLitt, Emory and Henry College, 1996; Stephen Henderson Poetry Award, African American Literature and Culture Society, 1997. *Memberships:* Associated Writing Programs; DC Commission on the Arts and Humanities; Institute for Policy Studies; PEN American Center. *Literary Agent:* Harvey Klinger Inc, 301 W 53rd St, New York, NY 10019, USA. *Address:* PO Box 441, Howard University, Washington, DC 20059, USA. *Website:* www.eethelbertmiller.com.

MILLER, Leslie Adrienne; b. 22 Oct. 1956, Medina, Ohio, USA. Poet; Assoc. Prof. of English. *Education:* BA, English, Stephens College, 1978; MA, English, University of Missouri, 1980; MFA, Creative Writing, Poetry, University of Iowa, 1982; PhD, Literature, Creative Writing, University of Houston, 1991. *Appointments:* Dir, Creative Writing Program, Stephens College, 1983–87; Visiting Writer, University of Oregon, 1990; Assoc. Prof. of English, University of St Thomas, 1991–. *Publications:* Hanging on the Sunburned Arm of Some Homeboy (with Matthew Graham), 1982; No River, 1987; Staying Up for Love, 1990 Ungodliness, 1994; Yesterday Had a Man In It, 1998. *Contributions to:* Anthologies, reviews, quarterlies, and journals. *Honours:* National Endowment for the Arts Fellowship, 1989; John and Becky Moores Fellowship, University of Houston, 1990; Goethe-Institut Cultural Exchange Fellowship, Berlin, 1992; Loft-McKnight Award in Poetry, 1993, and Award of Distinction, 1998. *Memberships:* Associated Writing Programs; MLA; Poetry Society of America; Poets and Writers. *Address:* 168 College Ave S, No. 2, St Paul, MN 55102, USA.

MILLER, Marge; b. 17 Feb. 1948, New York, NY, USA. Human Resources Supervisor; Poet. m. Donald Miller, 22 May 1966, 2 s. *Education:* Human Resources Management, St Joseph's College, Patchogue, New York. *Appointment:* Production Man., Book Mark Literary Review. *Publication:* Fandango, 1987. *Contributions to:* American Poetry Anthology, 1988; Zephyr; Island Women; Prism; Colorado Old Times; Golden Gate Review. *Honours:* Runner-Up, American Poetry Asscn Poetry Contest, 1988; First Prize, Sister Andrea Brown Memorial Award, 1991. *Membership:* Great South Bay Poetry Co-operative. *Address:* 16 Clusterpine St, Medford, NY 11763, USA.

MILLER, Mona Rosa; b. 10 March 1909, London, England. Poet; Writer. m. Henry Miller, 7 Jan. 1928, 1 s., 1 d. *Education:* 3 Diplomas, Royal Acad. of Music, London; 4 Diplomas, Honours, Drawing, Royal Acad. of Arts. *Publications:* She Walks in Beauty, 1973; A Dialogue in Barnes (co-ed.), 1974; Loving, 1974; Fragment of a Dream, 1983; A Passage in Time (anthology), 1996. *Contributions to:* Numerous publications worldwide. *Honours:* Diploma, Companion of Western Europe, 1981; Diploma of Merit, Universita delle Arti, Italy, 1982; Ed.'s Choice Award for Outstanding Achievement in Poetry, 1996. *Memberships:* International Poetry Society, fellow; London Writers Circle Poetry Group; Sean Dornan Manuscript Society Circulators. *Address:* 30 Carmichael Ct, Barnes, London SW13 0HA, England.

MILLIS, Christopher; b. 27 May 1954, Hartford, CT, USA. Writer; Poet; Prof. m. Nina Davis, 30 July 1977, 1 s. *Education:* BA, Wesleyan University, 1976; MA, 1982, PhD, 1988, New York University. *Appointments:* Instructor, New York University, 1981–85; Asst Prof. of Writing, Hobart College, 1986–89; Boston University, 1990–. *Publications:* The Diary of the Delphic Oracle, 1990; The Dark of the Sun, 1994; Impossible Mirrors, 1995. Productions: The Shining House, 1980; Poems for the End of the World, 1982; The Magnetic Properties of Moonlight, 1984. *Contributions to:* Harvard Review; Quarterly; New Letters; Kansas Quarterly; Seneca Review; Hanging Loose; Croton Review; Central Park; and others. *Honours:* New York State Council on the Arts Award, 1984; First Prize, International Poems for Peace Competition, Barcelona, 1985; Fulbright Grant, 1986; Massachusetts Arts Council Award, 1989; National Poetry Competition Award, Jones Foundation, 1990. *Memberships:* Poetry Society of America; MLA. *Address:* 290 Massachusetts Ave, Cambridge, MA 02139, USA.

MILLS, Ralph J(oseph) Jr; b. 16 Dec. 1931, Chicago, IL, USA. Prof. of English Emeritus; Poet; Writer. m. Helen Daggett Harvey, 25 Nov. 1959, 1 s., 2 d. *Education:* BA, Lake Forest College, 1954; MA, 1956, PhD, 1963, Northwestern University; Oxford University, 1956–57. *Appointments:* Instructor, 1959–61, Asst Prof., 1962–65, University of Chicago; Assoc. Prof., 1965–67, Prof. of English, 1967–97, Prof. Emeritus, 1997–, University of Illinois at Chicago. *Publications:* Poetry: Door to the Sun, 1974; A Man to His Shadow, 1975; Night Road, 1978; Living with Distance, 1979; With No Answer, 1980; March Light, 1983; For a Day, 1985; Each Branch: Poems 1976–1985, 1986; A While, 1989; A Window in Air, 1993; In Wind's Edge, 1997; Grasses Standing: Selected Poems, 2000. Other: Contemporary American Poetry, 1965; On the Poet and His Craft: Selected Prose of Theodore Roethke (ed.), 1965; Edith Sitwell: A Critical Essay, 1966; Kathleen Raine: A Critical Essay, 1967; Creation's Very Self: On the Personal Element in Recent American Poetry, 1969; Cry of the Human: Essays on Contemporary American Poetry, 1975. *Contributions to:* Books and journals. *Honours:* English-Speaking Union

Fellowship, 1956–57; Illinois Arts Council Awards for Poetry, 1979, 1983, 1984; Society of Midland Authors Prize for Poetry, 1980; Carl Sandburg Prize for Poetry, 1984; William Carlos Williams Prize, Poetry Society of America, 2002. *Address:* 1451 N Astor St, Chicago, IL 60610, USA.

MILLWARD, Eric (Geoffrey William); b. 12 March 1935, Longnor, Staffordshire, England. Poet. m. Rosemary Wood, 1975. *Education:* Buxton College, Derbyshire, 1946–54. *Publications:* A Child in the Park, 1969; Dead Letters, 1978; Appropriate Noises, 1987. *Honour:* Arts Council Writers Award, 1979. *Address:* 2 Victoria Row, Knypersley, Stoke on Trent, Staffordshire ST8 7PU, England.

MIŁOSZ, Czesław; b. 30 June 1911, Szetejnie, Lithuania (Naturalized US citizen, 1970). Poet; Novelist; Critic; Essayist; Trans.; Prof. of Slavic Languages and Literatures Emeritus. *Education:* M Juris, University of Wilno, 1934. *Appointments:* Programmer, Polish National Radio, Warsaw, 1934–39; Diplomatic Service, Polish Ministry of Foreign Affairs, 1945–50; Visiting Lecturer, 1960–61, Prof. of Slavic Languages and Literatures, 1961–78, Prof. Emeritus, 1978–, University of California at Berkeley. *Publications:* Poetry: Poems, 1940; Poems, 1969; Selected Poems, 1973; Selected Poems, 1976; The Bells in Winter, 1978; The Separate Notebooks, 1984; Collected Poems, 1990; Provinces: Poems 1987–1991, 1991; Facing the River: New Poems, 1995; Roadside Dog, 1998; New and Collected Poems, 1931–2001, 2001. Fiction: The Seizure of Power, 1955; The Issa Valley, 1981. Non-Fiction: The Captive Mind (essays), 1953; Native Realm: A Search for Self-Definition (essays), 1968; The History of Polish Literature, 1969; Emperor of the Earth: Modes of Eccentric Vision, 1977; Nobel Lecture, 1981; Visions From San Francisco Bay, 1982; The Witness of Poetry (lectures), 1983; The Land of Ulro, 1984; The Rising of the Sun, 1985; Unattainable Earth, 1986; Beginning With My Streets: Essays and Recollections, 1992; Striving Towards Being (correspondence), 1997; To Begin Where I Am: Selected Essays, 2001. Editor and Translator: Postwar Polish Poetry: An Anthology, 1965. *Honours:* Prix Littéraire Européen, Les Guildes du Livre, Geneva, 1953; Marian Kister Literary Award, 1967; Guggenheim Fellowship, 1976; Neustadt International Literary Prize, 1978; Nobel Prize for Literature, 1980; National Medal of Arts, 1990; Several hon. doctorates. *Memberships:* American Acad. and Institute of Arts and Letters; American Acad. of Arts and Sciences; American Asscn for the Advancement of Slavic Studies; Polish Institute of Letters and Sciences in America. *Address:* c/o Dept of Slavic Languages and Literatures, University of California at Berkeley, Berkeley, CA 94720, USA.

MILTNER, Robert F.; b. 25 Feb. 1949, Cleveland, Ohio, USA. Writer; Poet; Educator. m.(1) Linda Smith, 1975, divorced 1996, (2) Mari Artzner Wolf, 12 Oct. 1996, divorced 2002, 1 s., 1 d. *Education:* BA, Xavier University, 1971; MEd, John Carroll University, 1987; PhD, Kent State University, 1998. *Appointments:* English Teacher, private religious high schools, Denver, CO, 1975–77, including Dept Head, Parma, Ohio, 1977–87; Co-ordinator for Developmental Education, 1987–93, 1993–95, Instructor in English, 1987–95, Dir, Writing Center, 1990–92, 1995–97, Asst Prof. of English, 1998–, Kent State University, Stark Campus, Canton, Ohio; Instructor in English, Walsh University, Canton, 1993–94. *Publications:* The Seamless Serial Hour (poems), 1993; Against the Simple (poems), 1995; On the Off Ramp (poems), 1996; Ghost of a Chance (poems), 2002; Four Crows on a Phone Line (poems), 2002; A Box of Light (prose poems), 2002; Curriculum materials. *Contributions to:* New York Quarterly; English Journal; Chiron Review; Ohioana Quarterly; Mid-American Review; Birmingham Poetry Review. *Honour:* Wick Poetry Chapbook Award, 1994. *Memberships:* Associated Writing Programs; American Asscn of University Profs. *Address:* PO Box 167, Winesburg, OH 44694, USA. *E-mail:* rmiltner@stark.kent.edu.

MIN ZHENG; b. 18 July 1920, Beijing, China. Prof. of English and American Literature; Poet; Writer; Trans. m. Shi Bai Tong, 19 Jan. 1952, 1 s., 1 d. *Education:* BA, Philosophy, National South-West Associated University, 1943; MA, English Literature, Brown University, Providence, RI, 1952. *Appointments:* Ed., Dept of Trans., Central News Agency, 1945–48; Asst Research Fellow, Chinese Acad. of Social Sciences, 1956–61; Prof. of English and American Literature, Beijing Normal University, 1961–; Visiting Prof., University of California at San Diego, 1985. *Publications:* Poetry: Collected Poems (1942–1947), 1948; Searching for Poetry, 1986; Psychic Pictures, 1991; Morning. I Am Gathering Flowers in the Rain, 1991; Zheng Min's Poems, 1979–1999, 2000. Criticism: A Structural-Poststructural Approach: Language, Culture, Criticism, 1998; Poetry and Philosophy are Close Neighbours: Structural-Poststructural Poetics, 1999. Translator: A Collection of Contemporary American Poetry, 1987. *Contributions to:* Journals and periodicals. *Honours:* Stars Poetry Writing Award, 1982–83; Best Poetry Award, Poetry Monthly and the Writer's Asscn, 1986; Hon. Citizen, San Jose, California, 1986. *Memberships:* Shakespearean Society, Shanghai; Society of Comparative Literature; Writer's Asscn of China. *Address:* c/o Dept of Foreign Languages, Beijing Normal University, Beijing 100875, China. *E-mail:* mzheng@mail.tsinghua.edu.cn.

MINARIK, John Paul; b. 6 Nov. 1947, McKeesport, PA, USA. Poet; Writer; Engineer. m. Susan Kay Minarik, 15 Oct. 1988, 1 s. *Education:* BS, Mechanical Engineering, Carnegie Mellon University, 1970; BA, magna cum laude, English

and Psychology, University of Pittsburgh, 1978. *Appointments:* Engineer, United Steel Corpn, 1966–71; Instructor, Community College of Allegheny County, 1977–83; Teaching Consultant, University of Pittsburgh, 1978–96; Poet-in-the-Schools, Pennsylvania Council on the Arts, 1979–83; Project Engineer-Consultant, Economy Industrial Corpn, 1981–82; Chief Engineer, New Directions, 1989–96; Founder-Ed., Acad. of Prison Arts; Advisory Ed., Greenfield Review Press; Poetry readings. *Publications:* a book, 1974; Patterns in the Dusk, 1978; Past the Unknown, Remembered Gate, 1981; Kicking Their Heels with Freedom (ed.), 1982. *Contributions to:* Over 100 newspapers in the USA; American Ethnic; Backspace; Caprice; Carnegie Mellon Magazine; Confrontation; Gravida; Greenfield Review; Happiness Holding Tank; Hyacinths and Biscuits; Interstate; Joint Conference; Journal of Popular Culture; Mill Hunk Herald; New Orleans Review; Nitty-Gritty; Old Main; Painted Bride Quarterly; Pittsburgh and Tri-State Area Poets; Prison Writing Review; Poetry Society of America Bulletin; Small Pond; Sunday Clothes; Poems read via Monitoradio, Voice of America, WQED-FM, and WYEP, and at Three Rivers Arts Festival and American Wind Symphony. *Honours:* Hon. Mention, PEN Writing Award, 1976–77; Carnegie Magazine Best Book of the Year Citation, 1982; Pushcart Prize Nomination, 1984; Winner, Poetry and Prose Writing Contests, Pennsylvania Dept of Corrections, 1985, 1988. *Membership:* American Society of Mechanical Engineers. *Address:* 1600 Walters Mill Rd, Somerset, PA 15510, USA.

MINEO, Melani, (M. A. Brawn, Melanie Marrero); b. 11 July 1954, Dexter, Maine, USA. Poet; Counselor. m. Thomas Mineo, 3 July 1990, 1 s. *Education:* California Institute of the Arts, 1985–86; BA, magna cum laude, Liberal Arts, 1988, ESL Certification, 1990; Mediator Certification, 1991; PhD Studies. *Contributions to:* Anthologies and other publications. *Honour:* Fourth Place, World of Poetry Contest, 1990. *Memberships:* American Asscn of University Women; Children International. *Address:* 58 Shinnecock Ave, East Quogue, NY 11942, USA.

MING, Chiu Yee or MING, Emily Yau Yee. See: YAU, Emily.

MINGXIA LI, (Zhang Er); b. 15 Sept. 1960, Beijing, China. Scientist; Poet. m. L Schwartz, 7 Feb. 1995. *Education:* Degree in Medicine, 1982; PhD, 1992. *Appointments:* Senior Research Scientist, American Home Product Co; Overseas Correspondent, Journal of Contemporary Foreign Literature. *Contributions to:* China Press, New York; First Line, New York; Epoch Poetry Quarterly, Taiwan; Talisman, New Jersey; Five Fingers Review; Trafika; Journal of Chinese Religion. *Membership:* First Line Poetry Circle. *Address:* 120 Cabrini Blvd, Apt 137, New York, NY 10033, USA.

MINHINNICK, Robert Christopher; b. 12 Aug. 1952. Poet. 1 d. Education: BA, University College of Wales; PGCE. *Publications:* A Thread in the Maze; Native Ground; Life Sentences; The Dinosaur Park; The Looters. *Contributions to:* Planet; Poetry Wales; Western Mail; Pivot; Literary Review; Poetry Book Society Supplement; PEN Anthology. *Honours:* Literature Prize; Eric Gregory Award; John Morgan Award. *Membership:* Welsh Acad. *Address:* 11 Park Ave, Porthcawl, Mid Glamorgan, South Wales.

MINIM, June. See: HANFORD BRUCE, Mary.

MINISH, Geoffrey Roy Greer; b. 10 March 1929, Toronto, ON, Canada. Journalist; Writer; Poet. m. Pauline Marion Addison, 15 June 1987. *Education:* MA, Trinity College, Dublin, 1957. *Appointments:* Police Reporter, Windsor Star, Ontario, 1954–55; Sub-Ed., Reuters, London, 1960–64; Police Reporter, The Daily Colonist, Victoria, BC, 1965; Sub-Ed., Visnews, London, 1966–67; Sub-Ed., Occasional Reporter, Agence France-Presse, Paris, 1967–87. *Publications:* Anthologies: Poems for Peace; Poetry From the Left. *Contributions to:* Irish Times; Jazz Journal International; Melody Maker; Sight and Sound; New Stateman; Orbis; Poetry Now; Guardians of the State; Bare Bones; Breakthru'; Eavesdropper; Omens; Panurge; Peace News; Smiths Knoll; Verse, Britain; Antigonish Review; Fiddlehead; Plowman, Canada; Paris Metro, France; Holy Door; Icarus, Ireland; Creel; Village Voice, USA; 1993 Poets Diary for all Seasons. *Honour:* Co-winner, Paris Metro Competition, 1977. *Memberships:* National Union of Journalists, Life Mem. *Address:* 133 rue St Dominique, 75007 Paris, France.

MINTER, Sheryl Ann; b. 2 Oct. 1960, Huntington, Long Island, New York, USA. Poet. Divorced, 1 s. *Education:* One year, Law College. *Publications:* Poetic Windows, 1993; Visions of Poetry, 1994; Images of Poetry, 1995; Poetic Views, 1995. *Contributions to:* Third Half; Illinois Architectural and Historical Review; Horse People Magazine; Poetic Page; Poetic Eloquence; Poetry in Motion; Oatmeal and Poetry; Night Roses; Simply Words; Anderie; Christian Poets Pen; Pence and Freedom; Messenger; Newsday. *Honours:* Honorable Mention, National Authors Registry, 1994; Fourth Place, Poetic Page, Metaphors, 1995; Honorable Mention, Poetic Page Chapbook Competition, 1995; Honorable Mention, Christian Poets Pen, 1996. *Memberships:* Smithtown Poetry Society, founding mem.; Babylon Citizens Council on the Arts; National Poets Asscn, assoc. mem. *Address:* 9 Fourth St, Nesconset, NY 11767, USA.

MINTY, Judith; b. 5 Aug. 1937, Detroit, Michigan, USA. Writer; Poet. m. Egar Minty, 19 June 1957, 1 s., 2 d. *Education:* BS, Ithaca College, New York; MA, Western Michigan University. *Appointments:* Visiting Poet, Interlochen Centre for the Arts, Syracuse University, University of California, Santa Cruz; Prof. of English, Humbolt State University, 1981–94. *Publications:* Lake Songs and Other Fears, 1974; Yellow Dog Journal, 1979; Letters to My Daughter, 1980; In the Presence of Mothers, 1981; Counting the Losses, 1986; Dancing the Fault, 1991; The Mad Painter Poems, 1996. *Contributions to:* Poetry; Poetry Northwest; Atlantic; New Yorker; Iowa Review; Missouri Review; Barat Review; Five Fingers Review; Small Towner; Ococh Mountain News; Redstart; Hawaii Review; Great Lakes Review; Black Warrior Review; Green River Review; Seneca Review; Sou'wester; New York Quarterly. *Honours:* United States Award, International Poetry Forum, 1973; John Atherton Fellowship to Bread Loaf, 1974; Eunice Tietjens Award, Poetry Magazine, 1974; Michigan Council for the Arts Creative Artists Grants, 1981, 1983; PEN Syndicated Fiction Awards, 1985, 1986; PEN, Mead Foundation California Award, 1986; Villa Montalvo Award for Excellence in Poetry, 1989; Chrales Hackley Distinguished Lectureship, 1996; Hon. Doctorate in Humanities, Michigan Technological University, 1997; Mark Twain Award, Society for the Study of Midwestern Literature, 1998. *Memberships:* PEN; Poets and Writers; Associated Writing Programs; Poetry Society of America. *Address:* 7113 S Scenic Dr., New Era, MI 49446, USA.

MIRZA, Baldev; b. 6 March 1932, Malerkotla, Punjab, India. Teacher; Publisher; Poet. *Education:* MA, English Literature, AMU Aligarh; BEd, AMU Aligarh; BA, Indian Classical Music, Paryag Samiti Allahabad. *Publications:* Shall I Speak Out; Words On Fire; Buddha My Love; Across the Falling Snow; When the Stars Ache; My Nursery Rhymes, 1973. *Contributions to:* Numerous publications worldwide. *Memberships:* Authors Guild of India; International Writers Asscn. *Address:* Kothi Zamirabad, Raghubirpuri, Aligarh UP, India.

MITCHELL, Adrian, (Volcano Jones, Apeman Mudgeon, Gerald Stimpson); b. 24 Oct. 1932, London, England. Poet; Writer; Dramatist; Lyricist. 2 s., 3 d. *Education:* Christ Church, Oxford, 1953–55. *Appointments:* Granada Fellow, University of Lancaster, 1968–70; Fellow, Wesleyan University, 1972; Resident Writer, Sherman Theatre, 1974–75, Unicorn Theatre for Children, 1982–83; Judith Wilson Fellow, University of Cambridge, 1980–81; Fellow in Drama, Nanyang University, Singapore, 1995; Dylan Thomas Fellow, UK Festival of Literature, Swansea, 1995. *Publications:* Plays with Songs, 1995; The Siege, 1996; The Lion, the Witch and the Wardrobe, 1998; Who Killed Dylan Thomas, 1998. *Contributions to:* Newspapers, magazines, and television. *Honours:* Eric Gregory Award; PEN Trans. Prize; Tokyo Festival Television Film Award; Honarary Doctorate, North London University, 1997. *Memberships:* RSL; Society of Authors; Writers Guild. *Address:* c/o Peters, Fraser and Dunlop Group Ltd, Drury House, 34–43 Russell St, London WC2B 5HA, England.

MITCHELL, Felicia; b. 22 Feb. 1956, Sumter, South Carolina, USA. Assoc. Prof. of English; Poet; Writer. m. Barry A Love, 17 March 1989, 1 s. *Education:* BA, 1977, MA, 1980, University of South Carolina; PhD, University of Texas at Austin, 1987. *Appointments:* Asst Prof. to Assoc. Prof. of English; Poetry readings and workshops. *Publications:* Words and Quilts: A Selection of Quilt Poems, 1996; Case Hysterics, 1996. *Contributions to:* Various anthologies, books, reviews and journals. *Honours:* Various grants; Bread Loaf Writers' Conference Scholarship, 1988; Virginia Center for the Creative Arts Fellowship, 1995. *Address:* 29511 Smyth Chapel Raod, Meadowview, VA 24361, USA.

MITCHELL, Jean Tennent; b. 26 Feb. 1945, Glasgow, Scotland. Poet. m. Alan Mitchell, 28 April 1965, 3 d. *Publications:* Lasting Calm (anthology), 1996; A Quiet Storm; The Secret of Twilight; A Blossom of Dreams; The Lyre's Song; The Sleeping Winds; Say Only a Little, Say It Well; A Taste of Life. *Contributions to:* Periodicals, journals, anthologies and magazines. *Honours:* Ed.'s Choice Awards, Poetry Now, 1996, 1997; Ed.'s Choice Award, 1997–98, Honored Poet, 1998, International Library of Poetry; Poet of Merit Medal, International Society of Poets. *Memberships:* International Library of Poetry; Forward Press. *Address:* 10 Claypotts Castle Gdns, Broughty Ferry, Dundee DD5 3JY, Scotland.

MITCHELL, Kenneth (Ronald); b. 13 Dec. 1940, Moose Jaw, Saskatchewan, Canada. Prof.; Writer; Dramatist. m. Jeanne Shami, 23 Aug. 1983, 4 s., 1 d. *Education:* BA, 1965, MA, 1967, University of Saskatchewan. *Appointments:* Instructor, 1967–70, Prof., 1984–, University of Regina; Visiting Prof., University of Beijing, 1980–81, Foreign Affairs College, Beijing, 1986–87. *Publications:* Wandering Rafferty, 1972; The Meadowlark Connection, 1975; Everybody Gets Something Here, 1977; Cruel Tears (co-author), 1977; Horizon: Writings of the Canadian Prairie (ed.), 1977; The Con Man, 1979; Davin, 1979; Sinclair Ross, 1981; Ken Mitchell Country, 1984; Gone the Burning Sun, 1985; Through the Nan Da Gate, 1986; Witches and Idiots, 1990; The Plainsman, 1992; Stones of the Dalai Lama, 1993. *Honours:* Ottawa Little Theatre Prize, 1971; Canadian Authors Asscn Award for Best Canadian Play, 1985; Order of Canada, 1999. *Memberships:* Canadian Asscn of University Teachers;

Playwrights Union of Canada. *Address:* c/o Dept of English, University of Regina, Regina, SK S4S 0A2, Canada.

MITCHELL, Roger (Sherman); b. 8 Feb. 1935, Boston, Massachusetts, USA. Poet; Teacher. 2 d. *Education:* AB, Harvard College, 1957; MA, University of Colorado, 1961; PhD, Manchester University, 1963. *Appointments:* Ed., Minnesota Review, 1973–81; Dir, Writers Conferences, 1975–85, Creative Writing Program, 1978–96, Indiana University. *Publications:* Letters from Siberia, 1971; Moving, 1976; A Clear Space on a Cold Day, 1986; Adirondack, 1988; Clear Pond, 1991; The Word for Everything, 1996; Braid, 1997; Savage Baggage, 2001. *Contributions to:* Periodicals. *Honours:* Abby M Copps Award, 1971; Midland Poetry Award, 1972; Borestone Mountain Award, 1973; PEN Award, 1977; Arvon Foundation Awards, 1985, 1987; National Endowment for the Arts Fellowships, 1986, 2001; Chester H Jones Award, 1987. *Membership:* Associated Writing Programs. *Address:* 1010 E First St, Bloomington, IN 47401, USA.

MNOOKIN, Wendy; b. 1 Nov. 1946, New York, NY, USA. Poet; Writer. m. James Mnookin, 24 May 1970, 2 s., 1 d. *Education:* BA, English, Radcliffe College, 1968; MFA, Writing, Vermont College, 1991. *Publications:* Guenever Speaks, 1991; To Get Here, 1999; What He Took, 2002. *Contributions to:* Reviews, quarterlies, journals and magazines. *Honour:* Poetry Fellowship, National Endowment for the Arts, 1999. *Address:* 40 Woodchester Dr., Chestnut Hill, MA 02467, USA. *E-mail:* wmnookin@post.harvard.edu.

MOAT, John; b. 11 Sept. 1936, India. Author; Poet. m. 1962, 1 s., 1 d. *Education:* MA, Oxford University, 1960. *Publications:* 6d per Annum, 1966; Heorot (novel), 1968; A Standard of Verse, 1969; Thunder of Grass, 1970; The Tugen and the Toot (novel), 1973; The Ballad of the Leat, 1974; Bartonwood (children's), 1978; Fiesta and the Fox Reviews and His Prophecy, 1979; The Way to Write (with John Fairfax), 1981; Skeleton Key, 1982; Mai's Wedding (novel), 1983; Welcombe Overtunes, 1987; The Missing Moon, 1988; Firewater and the Miraculous Mandarin, 1990; Practice, 1994; The Valley (poems and drawings), 1998; 100 Poems, 1998; Rain (short stories), 2000. *Address:* Crenham Mill, Hartland, North Devon EX39 6HN, England.

MOBBERLEY, David Winstone; b. 12 July 1948, Birmingham, England. Poet. Divorced, 1 s. *Publications:* Equilbrium of Forces, 1992; Beneath the Darkness a Light is Shining, 1993; Sacred Journey, 1995. *Contributions to:* Iota; San Fernando Poetry Journal, USA; Envoi; The Plowman Journal; Poetry Now. *Honours:* First Prizes, Plowman Poetry Contest, 1997, 1999; World Record, Greatest Draw of a Flatbow, Commandery Civil War Centre, Worcester, 1999. *Memberships:* Reivers Archery Club, Gordon, Scotland; Friend of the Classic Malts, Glasgow, Scotland. *Address:* 87 Woodthorpe Rd, Kings Heath, Birmingham B14 6EG, England.

MOE, David J.; b. 17 Sept. 1938, Morris, Minnesota, USA. Insurance Broker; Poet. m. Thordis Hammer, 12 June 1965, 2 d. *Education:* BA, University of Minnesota, 1964; MA, San Francisco State University, 1975. *Publications:* Portrait Poems, 1986; Songs of the Soul, 1988; Collected Poems, 1980–90, 1991. *Contributions to:* Anthologies. *Honour:* Hon. DLitt, World Acad. of Arts and Culture, Bangkok, 1988. *Membership:* World Acad. of Arts and Culture. *Address:* 9011 Tournure, Juneau, AK 99801, USA.

MOFFEIT, Tony A.; b. 14 March 1942, Claremont, Oklahoma, USA. Librarian; Poet. *Education:* BSc, Psychology, Oklahoma State University, 1964; MLS, University of Oklahoma, 1965. *Appointments:* Asst Dir, Library, 1980–, Poet-in-Residence, 1986–95, University of Southern Colorado; Dir, Pueblo Poetry Project, 1980–. *Publications:* La Nortenita, 1983; Outlaw Blues, 1983; Shooting Chant, 1984; Coyote Blues, 1985; Hank Williams Blues, 1985; The Spider Who Walked Underground, 1985; Black Cat Bone, 1986; Dancing With the Ghosts of the Dead, 1986; Pueblo Blues, 1986; Boogie Alley, 1989; Luminous Animal, 1989; Poetry is Dangerous, the Poet is an Outlaw, 1995. *Contributions to:* Journals and magazines. *Honours:* Jack Kerouac Award, 1986; National Endowment for the Arts Fellowship, 1992. *Membership:* American Library Asscn. *Address:* 1501 E Seventh, Pueblo, CO 81001, USA.

MOFFETT, Judith; b. 30 Aug. 1942, Louisville, KY, USA. Poet; Writer; Teacher. m. Edward B Irving, 1983. *Education:* BA, Hanover College, IN, 1964; MA, Colorado State University, 1966; University of Wisconsin at Madison, 1966–67; MA, 1970, PhD, 1971, University of Pennsylvania. *Appointments:* Fulbright Lecturer, University of Lund, Sweden, 1967–68; Asst Prof., Behrend College, Pennsylvania State University, 1971–75; Visiting Lecturer, University of Iowa, 1977–78; Visiting Lecturer, 1978–79, Asst Prof., 1979–86, Adjunct Asst Prof., 1986–88, Adjunct Assoc. Prof., 1988–93, Adjunct Prof. of English, 1993–94, University of Pennsylvania. *Publications:* Poetry: Keeping Time, 1976; Whinny Moor Crossing, 1984. Fiction: Pennterra, 1987; The Ragged World, 1991; Time, Like an Ever-Rolling Stream, 1992; Two That Came True, 1992. Other: James Merrill: An Introduction to the Poetry, 1984; Homestead Year: Back to the Land in Suburbia, 1995. *Honours:* Fulbright Grants, 1967, 1973; American Philosophical Society Grant, 1973; Eunice Tiejens Memorial Prize, 1973; Borestone Mountain Poetry Prize, 1976; Levinson Prize, 1976; Ingram

Merrill Foundation Grants, 1977, 1980, 1989; Columbia University Trans. Prize, 1978; Bread Loaf Writers Conference Tennessee Williams Fellowship, 1978; Swedish Acad. Trans. Prize, 1982; National Endowment for the Humanities Trans. Fellowship, 1983; National Endowment for the Arts Fellowship, 1984; Swedish Acad. Trans. Grant, 1993. *Address:* 951 E Laird Ave, Salt Lake City, UT 84105, USA.

MOHAN RAO, Chandramahanti Madan; b. 5 Sept. 1936, Talasamudram, India. Educator; Writer; Poet. *Education:* BA, Honours, 1957; PhD, 1981–82. *Appointments:* Head, Dept of English, Reader, Principal, MRA College, Vizianagram. *Publication:* Occasional Muse (poems), 1994. Other: Criticism. *Contributions to:* Periodicals. *Memberships:* Books and Books, pres.; Indian Society for Commonwealth Studies; PEN India. *Address:* 8-14-70 Maruti, Balajinagar, Vizianagram 3, India.

MOHANTY, Niranjan; b. 12 April 1953, Calcutta, India. Teacher; Poet. m. Jayanti Mohanty, 26 May 1978, 1 s., 1 d. *Education:* BA, 1972; MA, 1974; PhD, 1992. *Appointment:* Senior Fellow, Government of India Dept of Culture, 1994–97; Writing Fellow, International Writing Program, University of Iowa, 1999. *Publications:* Silencing the Words; Oh, This Bloody Game; Considerations; The Golden Voices; Writing in English; Voices; Prayers to Lord Jogannatha, 1994; Life Lines, 1999; On Touching You and Other Poems, 1999. *Contributions to:* Critical Quarterly; Toronto South Asian Review; Illustrated Weekly of India; Indian PEN; Indian Literature; Tandem; Sunstone; Journal of South Asian Literature; 100 Words. *Memberships:* Poetry Time; Poetry; Indian PEN. *Address:* Prof. of English, Dept of English and Other Modern European Languages, Visva-Bharati, Santiniketan, 731 235, India.

MOISA, Christodoulos Evangeli Georgeau; b. 10 Dec. 1948, Lower Hutt, New Zealand. Teacher; Artist; Poet; Writer; Ed. *Education:* Victoria University; Auckland University; Sir John Cass School of Art, London. *Appointments:* Founder-Managing Ed., One-Eye Press; Head of Art, Kapiti College, Raumati, Wellington; Poetry readings and art exhibitions. *Publications:* Several poems. Editor: Various books of New Zealand poets. *Contributions to:* Periodicals. *Honours:* National Poetry Prize, Te Awamutu Rose Festival, 1981; Queen Elizabeth II Arts Council Fellowship, 1983; Whitereia Poetry Prize, 1991. *Membership:* New Zealand PEN, national exec., 1988. *Address:* c/o PEN New Zealand, PO Box 34631, Birkenhead, Auckland 10, New Zealand.

MOJ. See: SOLEIMANI, Faramarz.

MOJIEB-EIMAN, Syed Imam Akhlaqi; b. 1 Aug. 1934, Patna, Azimabad, India. Physician (retd); Poet. m. (1) Afsar Jahan, 1 Aug. 1952, (2) Houda Fadel, 1 Aug. 1967, 1 s., 3 d. *Education:* MD, 1959; BA, 1961; MA, Honours, Persian, 1963; PhD, Honours, Liberal Arts, 1982; DLitt, Honours, Liberal Arts, 1991. *Publications:* Ashk-e-Shab, 1977; Aah-e Sahar, 1984; Iram-e Gham, 1985; Adab-e Asnaf, 1990; Eiman-Aashna, 1991; Gham-Aashna, 1992. *Contributions to:* Many books, newspapers, journals and radio. *Memberships:* Acad. of Letters, Islamabad; Acad. of Letters, London; Progressive Writers Asscn, London; Progressive Writers Asscn, Pakistan; Writers Guild of Great Britain; Writers Guild of Pakistan. *Address:* Eiman-Manzil, 13A, Sector 3, Kheyaban-e-Sir Syed, Rawalpindi, Islamabad, Pakistan.

MOKASHI-PUNEKAR, Shankar; b. 8 May 1928, Dharwad, India. Prof. of English (retd); Poet. m. Girjia Gurunath Hadimani, 24 May 1948, 3 s., 2 d. *Education:* BA, Honours, Mumbai University, 1948; MA, 1953, PhD, 1965, Karnatak University. *Appointments:* Lecturer in English, Lingaraj College, Belgium, 1953–56, Kishinchand Chellam College, Churchgate, Mumbai, 1956–61; Lecturer and Asst Prof., Indian Institute of Technology, Mumbai, 1961–70; Reader in English, Karnatak University, 1970–80; Prof. of English, University of Mysore, 1980–88. *Publications:* The Captive, 1965; The Cycle of Seasons, 1966; The Pretender, 1968; Epistle to Prof David McCutcheon, 1971; Tent Pole, 1987; Parodims, 1989. *Contributions to:* Sunday Times; Writers Workshop Miscellany. *Honours:* Karnatak Sahitya Akadami Award, 1977; Kuvempu V V Trust Award, 1977; Sudha Magazine Prize, 1981; Central Sahitya Akadami Award, 1989. *Memberships:* Central Sahitya Akadami, Delhi; Karnatak State Sahitya Akadami, Bangalore. *Address:* Malmaddi Rd 2, Dharwad 580 007, Karnatak, India.

MOLBJERG, Lis Guri Nostahl; b. 26 July 1920, Copenhagen, Denmark. Government Official (retd); Writer; Poet. m. Hans Molbjerg, 1944, 1 d. *Education:* BA, Public Administration, 1974. *Publications:* Member of the Party (non-fiction), 1995; Two Minutes Silence (poems), 1995. *Contributions to:* Periodicals. *Membership:* Society of Danish Authors. *Address:* Krogerrupgade 593, 2200 Copenhagen, Denmark.

MOLE, John Douglas; b. 12 Oct. 1941, Taunton, Somerset, England. Poet; Critic. m. Mary Norman, 22 Aug. 1968, 2 s. *Education:* MA, Magdalene College, Cambridge, 1964. *Appointments:* Teacher, Haberdashers' School, Elstree, 1964–73; Exchange Teacher, Riverdale School, New York, 1969–70; Head, Dept of English, Verulam School, 1973–81, St Albans School, 1981–98; Poet-in-Residence, Magdalene College, Cambridge, 1996; Visiting Poet, University of Hertfordshire, 1998–; Poet to the City of London, 1999–. *Publications:* Poetry: Feeding the Lake, 1981; In and Out of the Apple, 1984; Homing, 1987; Boo to a

Goose, 1987; The Mad Parrot's Countdown, 1989; Catching the Spider, 1990; The Conjuror's Rabbit, 1992; Depending on the Light, 1993; Selected Poems, 1995; Hot Air, 1996; Copy Cat (for children), 1997; The Dummy's Dilemma, 1999; For the Moment, 2000; The Wonder Dish, 2002. Other: Passing Judgements: Poetry in the Eighties, 1989; Poetry (ed.), 1945–80; Figures of Speech (ed.), 2000. *Contributions to:* Newspapers, reviews, and magazines. *Honours:* Eric Gregory Award, 1970; Signal Award for Outstanding Contribution to Children's Poetry, 1988; Cholmondeley Award, 1994. *Memberships:* Society of Authors; Ver Poets, vice-pres. *Address:* 11 Hill St, St Albans, Hertfordshire AL3 4QS, England. Email: john_mole@bigfoot.com.

MOLINA LOPEZ, Maria Salome; b. 23 Dec. 1960, Albacete, Spain. Painter; Writer; Poet. *Education:* Diploma, International Literature, World Writers Asscn. *Contributions to:* Anthologies and other publications. *Honour:* First Prize, Henry Abattu Medal, Academia des Lettres et des Arts, Perigord, France, 1990. *Memberships:* International Writers and Artists Asscn; Ligue Fraternité Universelles des Poètes et Artistes; World Acad. of Arts and Culture; World Congress of Poets. *Address:* Capitam Gomez Descalzo No. 16, 02002 Albacete, Spain.

MONACELLI-JOHNSON, Linda; b. 31 March 1949, Pittsburgh, Pennsylvania, USA. Poet; Writer; Ed. m. Whitman Johnson, 7 May 1983. *Education:* BA, Saint Mary's College, 1971; MA, Cleveland State University, 1973. *Publications:* Three books. *Contributions to:* Anthologies, reviews, quarterlies and journals. *Memberships:* Big Mama Poetry Troupe; Last Four Strumpets of the Apocalypse. *Address:* 308 W Houghton, Santa Fe, NM 87505, USA.

MONAHAN, Noel; b. 25 Dec. 1949, County Longford, Ireland. Teacher; Poet; Ed. m. Anne O'Leary, 11 Aug. 1976, 3 s. *Education:* BA, St Patrick's College, 1971; H Dip Ed, 1972. *Appointments:* Humanities Co-ordinator, 1976–89, Senior History Teacher, 1976–, St Clare's College; Dir, Temenos Theatre, 1990–92; Co-Ed., Windows Poetry Broadsheets, 1–5, 1992–99, Windows Selection: Poetry and Prose, 1993, Windows Authors and Artists, 1994. *Publications:* Poetry: Opposite Walls, 1991; Snowfire, 1995; Curse of the Birds, 2000; The Funeral Game. Plays: Broken Cups; Half a Vegetable (dramatization of poems by Patrick Kavanagh); A Proverbial Wet Summer; Feathers of Time; Talking Within. Other: Cathal Buí (poems and short stories, co-ed.), 2001. *Contributions to:* Irish Times; Sunday Tribune; Poetry Ireland; Books Ireland; Honest Ulsterman; Poetry Australia; Poetry Scotland; Paterson Literary Review. *Honours:* Winner, Hastings Poetry Festival; Winner, Cootehill Arts Festival; Kilkenny Prize for Poetry, 1992; William Allingham Poetry Award; First Prize, Poetry Ireland/SeaCat National Poetry Awards, 2001; First Prize, P. J. O'Connor RTE Radio Drama Awards, 2001, short-listed 2002. *Memberships:* Irish Writers Union; Poetry Ireland; Poetry Society. *Address:* Auburn, Stragella, Cavan, Co Cavan, Ireland.

MONEYSMITH, Carol Louise Giesbrecht, (Amber Fielding, Sharleigh Reid); b. 28 Nov. 1943, Bismarck, North Dakota, USA. Poet; Writer. m. 17 June 1964, 2 s., 1 d. *Education:* Cosmetology Licence, 1962; Publishing and Editing Diploma, Institute of Children's Literature, 1982; Private Pilot Certification, 1990. *Contributions to:* Anthologies and other publications. *Honours:* Golden Poet Award, 1989, Silver Poet Award, 1990, World of Poetry. *Address:* PO Box 337, Essex, IA 51638, USA.

MONGRAIN, Serg; b. 15 Jan. 1948, Trois Rivières, QC, Canada. Writer; Poet; Photographer. *Education:* Mathematical Université du Québec, 1972. *Publications:* L'Oeil du l'idée, 1988; Le calcul des heures, 1993; L'objet des sens, 1996; Brouillard, 1999; Le Poème déshabillé, 2000; Gladys, 2001. As Photographer: Lis: écris, 1981; L'image titre, 1981; Agrestes, 1988; Québec Kerouak Blues, 1998. Other: Many exhibition catalogues in art. *Contributions to:* Periodicals. *Membership:* Union des écrivains du Québec. *Address:* 994 rue Sainte Cécile, Trois Rivières, QC G9A 1L3, Canada.

MONKS, Philip; b. 22 Aug. 1960, Leigh, Greater Manchester, England. Poet. m. Jennifer Stephens, 2 Sept. 1990, 1 s. *Education:* BA, St Catherine's College, Cambridge, 1981. *Publications:* Wake Up; Nursery Verse. *Contributions to:* Palantir; Argo. *Memberships:* Canon Poets; Poetry Society. *Address:* 96 Melton Rd, Birmingham B14 7ES, England.

MONROY, Lopez Omar Leonico; b. 30 March 1954, Barquito, Chile. Teacher of Spanish; Mining Technician; Poet. m. Lividina Sonia Avila George, 9 Dec. 1977, 2 s., 1 d. *Education:* Mine Technician, Universidad Tecnica del Estado, 1972; Diploma, Chilean University, 1977; National Library of Chile, 1978. *Publications:* Several poems. *Contributions to:* Anthologies and periodicals. *Honours:* Poetry prizes and medals. *Address:* c/o Biblioteca Publica Federico Varela, Chanaral, III Region, Chile.

MONTAG, Tom; b. 31 Aug. 1947, Fort Dodge, IA, USA. Poet; Writer; Ed.; Publisher. *Education:* BA, Dominican College of Racine, 1972. *Appointments:* Ed., Publisher, Monday Morning Press, Milwaukee, 1971–, Margins Books, 1974–. *Publications:* Wooden Nickel, 1972; Twelve Poems, 1972; Measurers, 1972; To Leave This Place, 1972; Making Hay, 1973; The Urban Ecosystem: A Holistic Approach (ed. with F Stearns), 1974; Making Hay and Other Poems,

1975; Ninety Notes Toward Partial Images and Lover Prints, 1976; Concerns: Essays and Reviews: 1977; Letters Home, 1978: The Essential Ben Zen, 1992. *Address:* c/o Sparrow Press, 193 Waldron St, West Lafayette, IN 47906, USA.

MONTAGUE, John (Patrick); b. 28 Feb. 1929, New York, NY, USA. Poet; Writer; Lecturer. *Education:* BA, 1949, MA, 1953, University College, Dublin; Postgraduate Studies, Yale University, 1953–54; MFA, University of Iowa, 1955. *Appointment:* Lecturer in Poetry, University College, Cork. *Publications:* Forms of Exile, 1958; The Old People, 1960; Poisoned Lands and Other Poems, 1961; The Dolmen Miscellany of Irish Writing (ed.), 1962; Death of a Chieftain and Other Stories, 1964; All Legendary Obstacles, 1966; Patriotic Suite, 1966; A Tribute to Austin Clarke on His Seventieth Birthday, 9th May 1966 (ed. with Liam Miller), 1966; Home Again, 1967; A Chosen Light, 1967; Hymn to the New Omagh Road, 1968; The Bread God: A Lecture, with illustrations in Verse, 1968; A New Siege, 1969; The Planter and the Gael (with J Hewitt), 1970; Tides, 1970; Small Secrets, 1972; The Rough Field (play), 1972; The Cave of Night, 1974; O'Riada's Farewell, 1974; The Faber Book of Irish Verse (ed.), 1974; A Slow Dance, 1975; The Great Cloak, 1978; Selected Poems, 1982; The Dead Kingdom, 1984; Mount Eagle, 1989. *Address:* Dept of English, University College, Cork, Ireland.

MONTALVO, Berta Gutiérrez de; b. 11 Dec. 1919, Havana, Cuba. Poet; Writer. m. José R. Montalvo, 1941, deceased 1993, 1 s., 1 d. *Education:* Law, University of Havana. *Publications:* Para mi gaveta (poems), 1989; Miniaturas (poems), 1990; Gotas de Rocío (poems), 1991; El Hombre Olvidado, 1994; Donde se ocultan las sombras (poems), 1995. *Contributions to:* Anthologies, literary magazines and periodicals. *Memberships:* Acad. of Poetry, Miami; Haiku Society of America. *Address:* 3011 SW 11th St, Miami, FL 33135-4707, USA.

MONTE, Joanne; b. 21 Nov. 1955, Newark, New Jersey, USA. Poet; Writer. m. Kenneth F Potenski. *Education:* Montclair State College, 1978; Upsala College, 1980. *Publications:* Shadows for the Noontide, 1999; The World and the Flesh, 2002. *Contributions to:* Poet Lore; Raintown Review; White Pelican Review; Twilight Ending; Black Bear Review; Metverse Muse; Ancient Paths; The Plowman; Bayou; Poetry Motel; Cerberus. *Honours:* John David Johnson Memorial Poetry Award, 1994; Iva Mary Williams Inspirational Poetry Award, 1995; Writer's Digest Award, 1997; Black Bear Review Annual Poetry Award, 1999. *Memberships:* Acad. of American Poets; International Women's Writing Guild. *Address:* 34 E Passaic Ave, Bloomfield, NJ 07003, USA.

MONTEIRO, George; b. 23 May 1932, Cumberland, RI, USA. Prof.; Poet. 1 s., 2 d. *Education:* AB, 1954, PhD, 1964, Brown University; AM, Columbia University, 1956. *Appointments:* Instructor to Prof., Brown University, 1961–. *Publications:* The Coffee Exchange, 1982; Double Weavers Knot, 1990. *Contributions to:* Denver Quarterly; Centennial Review; NEDGE, New England Journal of Medicine; James River Review. *Address:* 59 Woodland Dr., Windham, CT 06280, USA.

MONTGOMERY, Marion H. Jr; b. 16 April 1925, Thomaston, GA, USA. Prof. of English; Writer; Poet. m. Dorothy Carlisle, 20 Jan. 1952, 1 s., 4 d. *Education:* AB, 1950, MA, 1953, University of Georgia; Creative Writing Workshop, University of Iowa, 1956–58. *Appointments:* Asst Dir, University of Georgia Press, 1950–52; Business Man., Georgia Review, 1951–53; Instructor, Darlington School for Boys, 1953–54; Instructor, 1954–60, Asst Prof., 1960–67, Assoc. Prof., 1967–70, Prof. of English, 1970–, University of Georgia; Writer-in-Residence, Converse College, 1963. *Publications:* Fiction: The Wandering of Desire, 1962; Darrell, 1964; Ye Olde Bluebird, 1967; Fugitive, 1974. Poetry: Dry Lightening, 1960; Stones from the Rubble, 1965; The Gull and Other Georgia Scenes, 1969. Non-Fiction: Ezra Pound: A Critical Essay, 1970; T S Eliot: An Essay on the American Magus, 1970; The Reflective Journey Toward Order: Essays on Dante, Wordsworth, Eliot and Others, 1973; Eliot's Reflective Journey to the Garden, 1978; The Prophetic Poet and the Spirit of the Age, Vol. 1, Why Flannery O'Connor Stayed Home, 1980, Vol. II, Why Poe Drank Liquor, 1983, Vol. III, Why Hawthorne Was Melancholy, 1984; Possum, and Other Receipts for the Recovery of 'Southern' Being, 1987; The Trouble with You Innerleckchuls, 1988; The Men I Have Chosen for Fathers: Literary and Philosophical Passages, 1990; Liberal Arts and Community: The Feeding of the Larger Body, 1990; Virtue and Modern Shadows of Turning: Preliminary Agitations, 1990; Romantic Confusions of the Good: Beauty as Truth, Truth Beauty, 1997; Concerning Intellectual Philandering: Poets and Philosophers, Priests and Politicians, 1998; Making: The Proper Habit of Our Being, 1999; The Truth of Things: Liberal Arts and the Recovery of Reality, 1999; Romancing Reality: Homo Viator and the Scandal of Beauty, 2000. *Contributions to:* Anthologies and magazines. *Honours:* Eugene Saxton Memorial Award, 1960; Georgia Writers' Asscn Literary Achievement Award in Poetry, 1970; Earhart Foundation Fellowship, 1973–74; Stanley W. Lindberg Award, 2001. *Address:* PO Box 115, Crawford, GA 30630, USA.

MOONRAKER, Peter. See: PIERCE, Richard Alistair Burnett.

MOORE, Carolyn; b. 17 Oct. 1944, New River, North Carolina, USA. University Teacher (retd); Writer; Book Reviewer; Novelist; Poet. m. John T Travis, 27 Dec. 1968. *Education:* BA, Willamette University, 1966; MA, University of Massachusetts, Amherst, 1968; Postgraduate Studies, San Francisco State University, University of Arizona. *Appointment:* Lecturer in English, Humboldt State University, 1970–88. *Contributions to:* Literature & Belief; Snake Nation Review; The Pen Woman; Poet Pourri; 1989 Roberts Awards, Literary Annual; Cutting Edge Quarterly. *Honours:* Marion Doyle Memorial Poetry Award, 1986–88; First Prize, Literature and Belief Poetry Award, 1988; First Prize, Dr Orville Miller Crowder Award for Free Verse, 1988; First Prize, Mississippi Valley Poetry Award, 1989; First Prize, Roberts Writing Award for Poetry, 1989. *Memberships:* National League of American Pen Women; Connecticut Poetry Society; North Coast Writers. *Address:* 519 Ole Hanson Rd, Eureka, CA 95501, USA.

MOORE, Gerald Ernest; b. 13 Aug. 1926, London, England. Physician; Dentist; Poet; Painter; Writer. m. (1) Irene Maude Dyer, 10 June 1954, deceased, (2) Ruth Anne Marie Kyburz. *Education:* BA, Eltham College; Graduated, Guy's Hospital, 1949; MSc (med), 1970; MGDSRCS, 1980. *Publications:* Poetry: Insect on the Leaf, 1952; Nest of Druids, 1969; Between Silence, 1974; The Singing Dust (co-author), 1976; Collected Poems 1944–1991, 1991; Famine, 1998. Other: The Cuckoo Who Flew Backwards, 1977; Treading in Treacle (autobiography), 1983; Fighting the Developers: A Planning Protest, 1991; Milk and Honey (novel), 2001. *Contributions to:* Various poetry publications and anthologies. *Honours:* Prize, Spirit of London Open Painting Competition, 1981; Associated Independent Publishers' Fiction of the Year Award, 2001. *Membership:* Fellow, Royal Society of Medicine; Proton Poets. *Address:* Tordown House, Swimbridge, Devon EX32 0QY, England. *E-mail:* r-g.moore@virgin.net.

MOORE, Honor; b. 28 Oct. 1945, New York, NY, USA. Poet; Writer. *Education:* BA, cum laude, Radcliffe College; Theatre Administration, Yale School of Drama. *Appointments:* Visiting Scholar, James Madison University, Harrisonburg, Virginia, 1980; Adjunct Prof., New York University, 1980–82; Curator-Cataloguer, Works of Margarett Sargent, 1980–; Poet-in-Residence, Wells College, Aurora, New York, 1991; Co-Curator, Margarett Sargent Retrospective, Wellesley College, 1996. *Publications:* Poetry: Mourning Pictures, 1974; Poem in Four Movements by My Sister Marian, 1978; Placemats, 1981; Memoir, 1988. Other: The White Blackbird: A Life of the Painter Margarett Sargent, 1996. *Contributions to:* Anthologies, reviews and journals. *Honours:* New York State Council on the Arts Grant, 1975; National Endowment for the Arts Fellowship, 1981; Connecticut Commission on the Arts Grant, 1993. *Memberships:* PEN American Centre; Poetry Society of America; Poets and Writers. *Address:* PO Box 305, Kent, CT 06757, USA.

MOORE, Lenard Duane; b. 13 Feb. 1958, Jacksonville, North Carolina, USA. Poet; Writer; Book Reviewer; Workshop Leader; Contest Judge; Teacher; Public Speaker. m. 15 Oct. 1985, 1 d. *Education:* Coastal Carolina Community College, 1976–78; AIT School, 1978; Administrative Specialist Diploma, University of Maryland, 1980–81; North Carolina State University, 1985, 1988–89. *Appointments:* Poet-in-Residence, Mira Mesa Branch Library, San Diego, 1983; Contributing Ed., The Small Press Book Review, 1987–90; Literary Consultant for Humanities Extension OUTREACH Program, North Carolina State University, 1990–; Writer-in-Residence, United Arts Council of Raleigh and Wake County. *Publications:* Poems of Love and Understanding, 1982; The Open Eye, 1985; Poems for Performance; Desert Storm: A Brief History. *Contributions to:* Steppingstones; Pierian Spring; Poetry Canada Review; Frogpond; Pembroke Magazine; St Andrews Review; Painted Bride Quarterly; Haiku Anthology; Kentucky Poetry Review; Writers West. *Honours:* Outstanding Young Man of America, 1984, 1988, 1987, 1989; Winner, Third Black Writer's Competition, North Carolina Writers' Network, 1991. *Memberships:* Poetry Society of America; Acad. of American Poets; North Carolina Writers Network; Haiku Society of America; National Book Critics Circle; Raleigh Writing Alliance; National Federation of State Poetry Societies; World Poetry Society; North Carolina Poetry Society. *Address:* North Carolina Dept of Education, 301 N Wilmington St, Raleigh, NC 27601, USA.

MOORE, Lucien Cowper; b. 20 Aug. 1960, London, England. Antiquarian Book Dealer; Book Searcher; Poet. *Education:* Foundation Business Diploma, Eastbourne College, 1980; Catering Diploma, City and Guilds of London, 1983. *Appointments:* Trust House Forte, 1983–86; Postal Story International, 1986–89; Isoseles World Corporation, 1989–94. *Publications:* Spoken Thoughts, 1987; Splash in the Well, 1990; Reflections From the Weaver's Brook, 1998. *Contributions to:* Live Broadcast on BBC Radio. *Honour:* Styllus Literary Award, Manchester, 1990. *Address:* Fifty Swaines Way, Heathfield, East Sussex, TN21 0AN, England.

MOORE, Miles David; b. 8 March 1955, Lancaster, Ohio, USA. Journalist; Poet. *Education:* BSJ, summa cum laude, Ohio University, 1977; Creative Writing Workshop, George Washington University, 1990. *Publication:* The Bears of Paris, 1995. *Contributions to:* Reviews, quarterlies, journals and magazines. *Honours:* Honourable Mention, Orbis/Rhyme Revival Award, World Order of Narrative Poets, 1988; Rose Lefcowitz Prize, Poet Lore, 1994; Annual Poetry Prize, Potomac Review, 1996. *Memberships:* Federal Poets; National Press Club; Writer's Centre. *Address:* 5913 Mayflower Ct, No. 102, Alexandria, VA 22312, USA.

MOORE, Philip Carl; b. 16 June 1942, Walla Walla, Washington, USA. Poet. m. Gwendolyn Kay, 9 Feb. 1985. *Education:* DeUry Institute of Technology, Phoenix, 1985–87. *Publications:* A Warming of the Heart. *Contributions to:* Poetry Church. *Honour:* Citation, Poets and Patrons Inc, 1997. *Memberships:* Phoenix Poetry Society; Glendale Poetry Society, pres., 1998. *Address:* 8101 N 29th Dr., Phoenix, AZ 85051, USA.

MOORE, Val; b. 14 Oct. 1943, Lincolnshire, England. Teacher; Poet. m. Peter G Moore, 12 Aug. 1972. *Education:* BA, 1980; PGCE, 1981. *Publication:* Fledgling Confidence, 1993. *Contributions to:* Anthologies, reviews and journals. *Honours:* Merit Award, Yorkshire Competition; Second Prize, Tees Valley Writers Competition; Rosemary Arthur Award, 1993. *Address:* 16 Magnolia Close, Branston, Lincoln LN4 1PW, England.

MOORE, Vincent, (Q.E.D.); b. 29 Feb. 1948, Akron, Ohio, USA. Publisher; Poet. *Education:* MFA, Oberlin College, 1963. *Appointment:* Publisher, True So Press. *Publications:* Several poems. *Contributions to:* Many magazines. *Honour:* Silliman Syntax Prize, San Francisco, 1988. *Address:* PO Box 94924, USA.

MOORHEAD, Andrea D.; b. 25 Sept. 1947, Buffalo, New York, USA. Teacher; Poet; Trans. m. Robert Moorhead, 1969. *Education:* BA, Chatham College, 1969. *Appointments:* Ed., Publisher, Osiris International Poetry Journal, Deerfield, Massachusetts; Poet-in-Residence, Deerfield Acad.; Dir, Deerfield Acad. Press. *Publications:* Iris, 1970; Morganstall, 1971; Black Rain, 1975; The Snows of Troy, 1988; Niagara, 1988; Entre nous la neige (with Bonenfant), 1988; Le silence nous entoure, 1992; The Edges of Light, by Hélène Dorion (trans.), 1993; Winter Light, 1994; La blancheur absolue, 1995; The Cavern of History, by Hélène Dorion (trans.), 1996; Do Not Disclose This Word, by Jean Chapdelaine Gagnon (trans.), 1997; From a Grove of Aspen, 1998; Le vert est fragile, 1999. *Contributions to:* New Directions; Sewanee Review; Oasis; Confrontation; Estuaire; St Andrews Review; Abraxas; American Writing; Illinois Review; La Sape. *Honours:* Phillips Poetry Award, 1986; Pushcart Special Mention, 1990–91; Abraxas Journal Award, 1991. *Memberships:* American Asscn of Teachers of French; American Literary Trans Asscn; Poets and Writers. *Address:* PO Box 297, Deerfield, MA 01342, USA.

MOORTHY, Krishna Kopparam, (Sudhakr); b. 10 Dec. 1929, Sunnapagutta, Karnataka, India. Prof. (retd); Writer; Poet. m. Vedavalli, 10 June 1969, 1 s., 1 d. *Education:* BA, Chennai University, 1952; BEd, Andhra University, 1956; MA, English, 1961, MA, History, 1965, Banaras Hindu University; PhD, English. *Publications:* Over 20 works, 1956–96. *Contributions to:* Various periodicals, domestic and foreign. *Membership:* Authors Guild of India. *Address:* 14-61 Padmavathipwam, Tirupati 517503, India.

MORAES, Dominic; b. 19 July 1938, Mumbai, India. Writer; Poet. *Education:* Jesus College, Oxford. *Appointments:* Managing Ed., Asia Magazine, 1972–; Consultant, United Nations Fund for Population Activities, 1973–. *Publications:* A Beginning, 1957; Gone Away, 1960; My Son's Father (autobiography), 1968; The Tempest Within, 1972; The People Time Forgot, 1972; A Matter of People, 1974; Voices for Life (essays), 1975; Mrs Gandhi, 1980; Bombay, 1980; Ragasthan: Splendour in the Wilderness, 1988; Never at Home (autobiography), 1994. Other: Poetry and travel books. *Honour:* Hawthornden Prize, 1957. *Address:* 521 Fifth Ave, New York, NY 10017, USA.

MORALES (MILOHNIC), (Juan) Andres; b. 26 May 1962, Santiago, Chile. Prof. of Classical and Contemporary Spanish Literature; Poet. *Education:* Licenciate in Literature, University of Chile, Santiago, 1984; PhD, Universidad Autonoma, Barcelona, Spain, 1988. *Appointment:* Prof. of Classical and Contemporary Spanish Literature, University of Chile, Santiago, 1988–. *Publications:* Por insulas extranas, 1982; Soliloquio de fuego, 1984; Lazaro siempre llora, 1985; No el azar: Hors du hasard, 1987; Ejercicio del decir, 1988; Verbo, 1991; Vicio de belleza, 1992. *Contributions to:* Many publications, domestic and foreign. *Honours:* Prizes and grants. *Memberships:* International Writers Asscn; Sociedad Chilena de Estudios Literarios; Sociedad de Escritores de Chile. *Address:* Roger de Flor 2900, Depto 122, Las Condes, Santiago de Chile, Chile.

MORAN, Daniel Thomas; b. 9 March 1957, New York, NY, USA. Dentist; Poet. m. Karen, 1 s., 2 d. *Education:* BSc, Biology, State University of New York at Stony Brook, 1979; DDS, Howard University, 1983. *Publications:* Dancing for Victoria, 1991; Gone to Innistree, 1993; Sheltered by Islands, 1995; In Praise of August, 1999; From Hilo to Willow Pond, 2002. *Contributions to:* Newspapers, reviews and quarterlies. *Honour:* Lyceum Award, Suffolk College, 1991. *Membership:* Vice-Pres. Walt Whitman Birthplace Asscn. *Address:* PO Box 2008, Shelter Island, NY 11964, USA. *E-mail:* dkmoran@optonline.net.

MORAND, Evelyn Jane; b. 23 June 1934, Waterford, New York, USA. Business Man.; Poet. m. 30 April 1955, 1 s., 5 d. *Education:* Pima Community College, Tucson, 1979. *Contributions to:* Anthologies. *Honours:* Golden Poet Award, 1989; Silver Poet Award, 1990; Outstanding Achievement in Poetry, 1990. *Address:* 1425 N Dodge Blvd, No. A, Tucson, AZ 85716, USA.

MOREIGN, Rodneigh. See: MOREN, Rodney.

MOREN, Rodney, (Rodneigh Moreign, Moreena Rodd); b. 15 Aug. 1955, Des Moines, IA, USA. Poet. *Honours:* Awards of Merit, 1983, 1984, 1988; Golden Poet Awards, 1988, 1989; Certificate of Honour, World of Poetry, 1990. *Membership:* Parnassus of World Poets. *Address:* 1111 University Ave, Des Moines, IA 50314, USA.

MORENCY, Pierre; b. 8 May 1942, Lauzon, QC, Canada. Poet; Writer; Dramatist; Broadcaster. *Education:* BA, Collège de Lévis, 1963; Licence ès Lettres, Université Laval, Québec, 1966. *Appointments:* Broadcaster; Co-Founder, Estuaire poetry journal. *Publications:* L'ossature, 1972; Lieu de naissance, 1973; Le temps des oiseaux, 1975; Torrentiel, 1978; Effets personnels, 1987; L'oeil américain: Histoires naturelles du Nouveau Monde, 1989; Lumière des oiseaux: Histoires naturelles du Nouveau Monde, 1992; Les paroles qui marchent dans la nuit, 1994; La vie entière, 1996. *Honours:* Prix Alain Grandbois, 1987; Prix Québec-Paris, 1988; Prix Ludger Duvernay, 1991; Prix France Québec, 1992; Chevalier Ordre des Arts et des Lettres de France. *Memberships:* PEN Club; Union des écrivaines et écrivains québécois. *Address:* 155 Ave Laurier, QC G1R 2K8, Canada.

MORENO, Armando; b. 19 Dec. 1932, Porto, Portugal. Prof.; Physician; Writer; Poet; Dramatist. m. Maria Guinot Moreno, 3 Oct. 1987. *Education:* Licentiate in Medicine, 1960; MD, 1972; Aggregation in Medicine, 1984; Licentiate in Literature, 1986. *Publications:* A Chamada (short stories), 1982; As Carreiras, 1982; O Bojador, 1982; Historias Quase Clinicas (short stories), 3 vols, 1982, 1984, 1988; Cais do Sodre (short stories), 1988; O Animal Que deupla Mente, 1993; Contos Oeirenses (short stories), 1994; A Governaçao pela Competencia, 1995. Other: Medical books, poetry, plays and television series. *Contributions to:* Periodicals. *Honours:* Drama and fiction awards. *Memberships:* Many professional and literary organizations. *Address:* Rua Almirante Matos Moreira 7, 2775 Carcavelos, Portugal.

MORGAN, Ariel Celeste Heatherley, (A. Celeste Heatherley, Ariel Wingrave); b. 30 Sept. 1935, Jerusalem, North Carolina, USA. Poet. m. George Tad Morgan, 14 Oct. 1967, 3 s., 1 d. *Education:* Registered Nurse, North Carolina, 1956; BA, English Literature, summa cum laude, University of North Carolina, 1966. *Contributions to:* Many publications.

MORGAN, (Colin) Pete(r); b. 7 June 1939, Leigh, Lancashire, England. Poet; Dramatist. *Appointments:* Creative Writing for Northern Arts, Loughborough University, 1975–77. *Publications:* A Big Hat or What, 1968; Loss of Two Anchors, 1970; Poems for Shortie, 1973; The Grey Mare Being the Better Steed, 1973; I See You on My Arm, 1975; Ring Song, 1977; The Poet's Deaths, 1977; Alpha Beta, 1979; The Spring Collection, 1979; One Greek Alphabet, 1980; Reporting Back, 1983; A Winter Visitor, 1984; The Pete Morgan Poetry Pack, 1984. Plays: Still the Same Old Harry, 1972; All the Voices Going Away, 1979. Television Documentaries. *Honour:* Arts Council of Great Britain Award, 1973. *Address:* c/o Fordon Fraser Publications, Eastcotts Rd, Bedford MK4Z 0JX, England.

MORGAN, Delane D(urstine); b. 30 Sept. 1928, Columbus, Ohio, USA. College Educator; Poet. m. (1) Hal M Morgan, 6 Aug. 1949, (2) Gordon A Thomas, 9 June 1990, 1 s., 2 d. *Education:* AB, Goucher College, 1949; MA, Ohio State University, 1951; PhD, Occidental College, 1972. *Appointments:* Los Angeles Southwest College, 1974; East Los Angeles College, 1975–76; Part-time, Long Beach City College, 1972–83, 1985–98. *Publications:* The Palos Verdes Story (history), 1982; Hat With a Plume, 1983; Moon Cycle (co-author), 1987; Poetry in Small Doses, 1996; Love Songs to an Elusive Male, 1998; Riding on the Wind (poems), 1998; Second Wind (poems), 1998; My Bad Weather Friend, 1999; Nature Walk (poems), 2000; What Never Can Be the Same, 2001; Zooming In, 2001 (poems). *Contributions to:* Flame; Trace; Palos Verdes Review; Prophetic Voices; CQ; Cycloflame; Archer; Parnassus; Jean's Journal; Voices International; Poetry in the Garden, an anthology, 1996; Sips from Foreign Shores (anthology), 1997; The Beach Reporter; Creative Age; Creative Age 2000. *Honours:* Third Prize, Chapparral Poets, 1961; First Prize, Free Verse, 1962. *Memberships:* California State Poetry Society; Surfwriters; Southwest Manuscripters. *Address:* 512 Esplanade, No. 302, Redondo Beach, CA 90277, USA. *E-mail:* dustyent@msn.com.

MORGAN, Edwin (George); b. 27 April 1920, Glasgow, Scotland. Titular Prof. of English Emeritus; Poet; Writer; Trans. *Education:* MA, University of Glasgow, 1947. *Appointments:* Asst Lecturer, 1947–50, Lecturer, 1960–65, Senior Lecturer, 1965–71, Reader, 1971–75, Titular Prof. of English, 1975–80, Prof. Emeritus, 1980–, University of Glasgow; Visiting Prof., University of Strathclyde, 1987–90; Hon. Prof., University College, Wales, 1991–95. *Publications:* Poetry: The Vision of Cathkin Braes, 1952; The Cape of Good Hope, 1955; Starryveldt, 1965; Scotch Mist, 1965; Sealwear, 1966; Emergent Poems, 1967; The Second Life, 1968; Gnomes, 1968; Proverbfolder, 1969; Penguin Modern Poets 15 (with Alan Bold and Edward Brathwaite), 1969; The Horseman's Word: A Sequence of Concrete Poems, 1970; Twelve Songs, 1970; The Dolphin's Song, 1971; Glasgow Sonnets, 1972; Instamatic Poems, 1972; The Whittrick: A Poem in Eight Dialogues, 1973; From Glasgow to Saturn, 1973; The New Divan, 1977; Colour Poems, 1978; Star Gate: Science

Fiction Poems, 1979; Poems of Thirty Years, 1982; Grafts/Takes, 1983; Sonnets from Scotland, 1984; Selected Poems, 1985; From the Video Box, 1986; Newspoems, 1987; Themes on a Variation, 1988; Tales from Limerick Zoo, 1988; Collected Poems, 1990; Hold Hands Among the Atoms, 1991; Sweeping Out the Dark, 1994; Virtual and Other Realities, 1997; Demon, 1999; New Selected Poems, 2000. Other: Essays, 1974; East European Poets, 1976; Hugh MacDiarmid, 1976; Twentieth Century Scottish Classics, 1987; Nothing Not Giving Messages (interviews), 1990; Crossing the Border: Essays in Scottish Literature, 1990; Language, Poetry and Language Poetry, 1990; Evening Will Come They Will Sew the Blue Sail, 1991. Editor: Collins Albatross Book of Longer Poems: English and American Poetry from the Fourteenth Century to the Present Day, 1963; Scottish Poetry 1–6 (co-ed.), 1966–72; New English Dramatists 14, 1970; Scottish Satirical Verse, 1980; James Thomson: The City of Dreadful Night, 1993. Other: Trans. Honours: Cholmondeley Award for Poetry, 1968; Scottish Arts Council Book Awards, 1968, 1973, 1975, 1977, 1978, 1983, 1984, 1991, 1992; Hungarian PEN Memorial Medal, 1972; O.B.E., 1982; Soros Trans. Award, 1985; Poet Laureate of Glasgow, 1999; Queen's Gold Medal for Poetry, 2000. Address: 19 Whittingehame Ct, Glasgow G12 0BG, Scotland.

MORGAN, Emma; b. 17 June 1965, Bristol, Pennsylvania, USA. Poet. Education: BA, Writing, Adult Degree Program, Vermont College, 1995. Appointment: Poet-in-the-Schools, Crocker Farm Elementary School, Amherst, MA, 1995. Publications: Gooseflesh, 1993; A Stillness Built of Motion: Living with Torette's, 1995. Contributions to: Anthologies and other publications. Honours: Winner, WRSI Radio Poetry Contest, 1996; Visiting Writer, Paumanok Poetry Award Series, State University of New York, Farmingdale, 1999. Membership: National Writers' Union. Address: 491 Bridge Rd, Florence, MA 01062, USA.

MORGAN, (George) Frederick; b. 25 April 1922, New York, NY, USA. Poet; Writer; Ed. m. (1) Constance Canfield, 1942 divorced 1957, 6 c., (2) Rose Fillmore, 1957 divorced 1969, (3) Paula Deitz, 1969. Appointments: Founder-Ed., 1947–98, Founder-Ed., 1998–, The Hudson Review; Chair, Advisory Council, Dept of Romance Languages and Literatures, Princeton University, 1973–90. Publications: Poetry: A Book of Change, 1972; Poems of the Two Worlds, 1977; Death Mother and Other Poems, 1978; The River, 1980; Northbook, 1982; Eleven Poems, 1983; Poems, New and Selected, 1987; Poems for Paula, 1995; The Night Sky, 2002; The One Abiding, 2002. Other: The Tarot of Cornelius Agrippa, 1978; The Fountain and Other Fables, 1985. Editor: The Hudson Review Anthology, 1961; The Modern Poets: Outstanding Stories from 'The Hudson Review', 1965. Honour: Chevalier de l'Ordre des Arts et des Lettres, France, 1984; Aiken Taylor Award for Poetry, 2001. Address: c/o The Hudson Review, 684 Park Ave, New York, NY 10021, USA.

MORGAN, Mihangel. See: MORGAN-FINCH, Mihangel Ioan.

MORGAN, Patrick Malcolm Hulbert; b. 8 Oct. 1934, Buenos Aires, Argentina. Business Consultant; Poet. m. Margarita Ozcoidi, 4 Oct. 1968, 2 s. Education: BA, St Andrew's Scots School, Buenos Aires, 1952; Licenciado, Literature, University of Buenos Aires, 1994. Publications: Landfalls and Departures, 1962; The Life's Eternity, 1962; Selected Poems 1960–1990, 1996. Contributions to: Reviews, journals and magazines. Address: Crámer 381 11 8, 1426 Buenos Aires, Argentina.

MORGAN, Robert; b. 3 Oct. 1944, Hendersonville, North Carolina, USA. Prof. of English; Poet; Writer. m. Nancy K Bullock, 1965, 1 s., 2 d. Education: Emory College, Oxford, 1961–62; North Carolina State University, Raleigh, 1962–63; BA, University of North Carolina at Chapel Hill, 1965; MFA, University of North Carolina at Greensboro, 1968. Apointments: Instructor, Salem College, Winston-Salem, North Carolina, 1968–69; Lecturer, 1971–73, Asst Prof., 1973–78, Assoc. Prof., 1978–84, Prof., 1984–92, Kappa Alpha Prof. of English, 1992–, Cornell University. Publications: Poetry: Zirconia Poems, 1969; The Voice in the Crosshairs, 1971; Red Owl, 1972; Land Diving, 1976; Trunk & Thicket, 1978; Groundwork, 1979; Bronze Age, 1981; At the Edge of the Orchard Country, 1987; Sigodlin, 1990; Green River: New and Selected Poems, 1991. Fiction: The Blue Valleys: A Collection of Stories, 1989; The Mountains Won't Remember Us and Other Stories, 1992; The Hinterlands: A Mountain Tale in Three Parts, 1994; The Truest Pleasure, 1995; Gap Creek, 1999; Topsoil Road, 2000; This Rock, 2001; New and Selected Poems, 2003. Non-Fiction: Good Measure: Essays, Interviews and Notes on Poetry, 1993. Honours: National Endowment for the Arts Fellowships, 1968, 1974, 1981, 1987; Southern Poetry Review Prize, 1975; Eunice Tietjins Award, 1979; Jacaranda Review Fiction Prize, 1988; Guggenheim Fellowship, 1988–89; Amon Liner Prize, 1989; James G Hanes Poetry Prize, 1991; North Carolina Award in Literature, 1991; Southern Book Award, 2000. Address: c/o Dept of English, Goldwin Smith Hall, Cornell University, Ithaca, NY 14853, USA.

MORGAN, Robin (Evonne); b. 29 Jan. 1941, Lake Worth, FL, USA. Journalist; Ed.; Writer; Poet. 1 c. Education: Columbia University. Appointments: Ed., Grove Press, 1967–70; Visiting Chair and Guest Prof., New College, Sarasota, FL, 1973; Ed. and Columnist, 1974–87, Ed.-in-Chief, 1989–93, Ms Magazine; Distinguished Visiting Scholar and Lecturer, Rutgers University, 1987. Publications: Sisterhood is Powerful: An Anthology of

Writings from the Women's Liberation Movement (ed.), 1970; Going Too Far: The Personal Chronicle of a Feminist, 1978; The Anatomy of Freedom: Feminism, Physics and Global Politics, 1982; Sisterhood is Global: The International Women's Movement Anthology (ed.), 1984; The Demon Lover: On the Sexuality of Terrorism, 1989; The Word of a Woman: Feminist Dispatches 1968–91, 1992. Fiction: Dry Your Smile: A Novel, 1987; The Mer-Child: A New Legend, 1991. Poetry: Monster, 1972; Lady of the Beasts, 1976; Death Benefits, 1981; Depth Perception: New Poems and a Masque, 1982; Upstairs in the Garden: Selected and New Poems, 1968–88, 1990. Plays: In Another Country, 1960; The Duel, 1979. Contributions to: Magazines and periodicals. Honours: National Endowment for the Arts Grant, 1979–80; Yaddo Grant, 1980; Ford Foundation Grants, 1982, 1983, 1984; Feminist of the Year Award, Fund for a Feminist Majority, 1990. Memberships: Feminist Writers' Guild; Media Women; North American Feminist Coalition; Sisterhood is Global Institute, co-founder. Address: 230 Park Ave, New York, NY 10169, USA.

MORGAN, Walt; b. 22 Dec. 1921, Ledyard, CT, USA. University Prof.; Poet. Education: BSc, 1946, PhD, 1953, University of Connecticut; MSc, George Washington University, Washington, DC, 1949. Appointments: Research Asst, National Cancer Institute; Research Assoc., Columbia University; Asst Prof., University of Tennessee; Assoc. Prof. to Prof., South Dakota State University. Publications: Now and Then, 1982; Down Under, 1983; Hitchin' Around, 1985; Here and There, 1990; What's Good About China, 1992. Contributions to: American Scientist; Argus Leader; Bioscience; Bits and Pieces; Register; Music Journal; Pasque Petals; Pequot Trails. Honours: Best Haiku in South Dakota; Hon. Mention in national contest. Memberships: Bardic Round Table; South Dakota State Poetry Society; National Federation of State Poetry Societies. Address: 1610 First St, Brookings, SD 57006, USA.

MORGAN-FINCH, Mihangel Ioan, (Mihangel Morgan); b. 7 Dec. 1959, Aberdare, Wales. University Lecturer; Writer; Poet. Education: BA, 1990, PhD, 1995, University of Wales. Publications: Diflaniad Fy Fi, 1988; Beth Yw Rhif Ffon Duw, 1991; Hen Lwybr A Storiau Eraill, 1992; Saith Pechod Marwol, 1993; Dirgel Ddyn, 1993; Te Gyda'r Frenhines, 1994; Tair Ochr Geiniog, 1996. Contributions to: Several publications. Honours: Prose Medal, Eisteddfod, 1993; Runner-Up, BBC Wales Arts Award, 1993; Welsh Arts Council Book of the Year short list, 1993–94. Memberships: Gorsedd Beirdd; Ynys Prydain. Address: Porth Ceri, Talybont, Aberystwyth, Dyfed, Wales.

MORGAN-JONES, Rowena. See: FRENCH, Wendy Rowena.

MORIARTY, Marilyn F(rances); b. 6 Jan. 1953, Fort Jackson, SC, USA. Assoc. Prof. of English; Writer; Poet. Education: Certificate in Linguistics, University of Edinburgh, 1975; BA, 1976, MA, 1980, University of Florida; PhD, University of California at Irvine, 1990. Appointments: Instructor in Rhetoric and Composition, Saddleback Community College, Mission Viejo, CA, 1985–86; Fellow, University of California at Irvine, 1991, National Humanities Center, 1994; Asst Prof., 1992–98, Assoc. Prof. of English, 1998–, Hollins University, Roanoke, VA. Publications: Critical Architecture and Contemporary Culture (co-ed.), 1994; Writing Science Through Critical Thinking, 1997; Moses Unchained, 1998. Contributions to: Periodicals. Honours: First Place Award, University of Utah Novella Contest, 1987; Katherine Anne Porter Prize for Fiction, Arts and Humanities Council, Tulsa, 1990; Creative Non-Fiction Prize, Associated Writing Programs, 1996; Peregrine Prize for Short Fiction, Amherst Writers and Artists Press, 1997. Address: PO Box 9535, Hollins University, Roanoke, VA 24020, USA. E-mail: moriarty@hollins.edu.

MORITZ, A(lbert) F(rank); b. 15 April 1947, Niles, Ohio, USA. Poet; Writer. m. Theresa Carrothers, 1 s. Education: BA, 1969, MA, 1971, PhD, 1975, Marquette University. Appointment: Northrop Frye Visiting Lecturer in Poetry, University of Toronto, 1993–94. Publications: Here, 1975; Signs and Certainties, 1979; Music and Exile, 1980; Black Orchid, 1981; The Pocket Canada (with Theresa Moritz), 1982; Canada Illustrated: The Art of Nineteenth-Century Engraving, 1982; Between the Root and the Flower, 1982; The Visitation, 1983; America the Picturesque: The Art of Nineteenth-Century Engraving, 1983; Stephen Leacock: A Biography (with Theresa Moritz), 1987; Song of Fear, 1992; The Ruined Cottage, 1993; Mahoning, 1994; Phantoms in the Ark, 1994. Contributions to: Periodicals. Honours: American Acad. of Arts and Letters Award, 1991; Guggenheim Fellowship, 1993; Ingram Merrill Foundation Fellowship, 1993–94. Address: 31 Portland St, Toronto, ON M5V 2V9, Canada.

MORLEY, David; b. 16 March 1964, Lancashire, England. Scientist; Writer; Poet. Education: BSc, University of Bristol, 1985; PhD, University of London, 1994. Appointments: Arts Council Fellow in Writing, 1995; Dir, Warwick Writing Programme, 1998, Warwick University. Publications: Releasing Stone: A Belfast Kiss; Under the Rainbow; Mandelstam Vonations; The New Poetry; A Static Ballroom; Clearing a Name; Jude the Obscure (ed.), 1999. Contributions to: London Magazine; Encounter; Exile; Antigonish Review; Quarry; Poetry Review; London Review of Books; The New Yorker. Honours: Tyrone Guthrie Award; Eric Gregory Award; Northern Poetry Competition; Poetry Business Competition; Hawthornden Fellowship; Arts Council Writers

Award, 1995; Arts Council Writing Fellowship, 1997. *Address:* Dept of English and Comparative Literary Studies, University of Warwick, Coventry CV4 7AL, England.

MORRICE, (James) Ken(neth Watt); b. 14 July 1924, Aberdeen, Scotland. Psychiatrist; Poet. m. Norah Thompson, 5 July 1948, 1 s., 2 d. *Education:* MB ChB, 1946, MD, 1954, University of Aberdeen; DPM, University of London. *Publications:* Prototype, 1965; Relations, 1979; For all I Know, 1981; Twal Mile Roon, 1985; When Truth is Known, 1986; The Scampering Marmoset, 1990; Selected Poems, 1991; Talking of Michelangelo, 1996. *Contributions to:* Reviews, journals and periodicals. *Honours:* McCash Prize for Scottish Poetry, 1979; Scottish Arts Council Book Award, 1982; Diploma for Excellence, Scottish International Open Poetry Competition, 1986; Deric Bolton Poetry Award, 1996. *Membership:* Fellow, Royal College of Psychiatrists, 1972. *Address:* 30 Carnegie Crescent, Aberdeen AB2 4AE, Scotland.

MORRIS, Jennifer Margaret, (Jenny Morris, Ripon Steel); b. 3 Dec. 1940, Ripon, Yorkshire, England. Poet. m. (1) Christopher George Hook, 17 Aug. 1963, (2) Lawrence Joseph Morris, 16 April 1982, 1 s., 1 d. *Education:* University of Southampton, 1961; BA, Open University, 1989; MPhil, Anglia Polytechnic University, 1999. *Publications:* Urban Space, 1991; The Sin Eater, 1993. *Contributions to:* Several publications. *Honours:* First Prize, Envoi, 1990; Thetford Prize, 1992; First Prize, Literary Review, 1993; David Thomas Writing Award, 1995; Aberystwyth University Prizewinner, 1996; First Prize, The New Writer (Quartos), 1996; First Prize, Norfolk Libraries Week, 1997; NWC Prize, 1998; Third Prize, Faber and Faber/WWW, 1998; Bittern Line, Railways Prizewinner, 1999; Third Prize, BBAC, 1999; Biscuit Prizewinner, 2001. *Memberships:* Norwich Poetry Group; Poetry Society. *Address:* 3 Upton Rd, Norwich, Norfolk NR4 7PA, England.

MORRIS, Stephen; b. 14 Aug. 1935, Smethwick, England. Artist; Poet; Writer. m. 31 Aug. 1963, divorced 1 Jan. 1989, 1 s., 2 d. *Education:* Moseley Art School, 1950–53; Fircroft College, 1958–59; Marie Borgs Folk High School, 1959–60; Cardiff University, 1960–63; Leicester University, 1965–66. *Appointments:* Asst Lecturer, 1967–69, Lecturer, 1969–72, Senior Lecturer, 1972–86, Wolverhampton University; 40 one-man painting exhibitions. *Publications:* Poetry: The Revolutionary, 1972; The Kingfisher Catcher, 1974; Death of a Clown, 1976; The Moment of Truth, 1978; Too Long at the Circus, 1980; Rolling Dice, 1986; To Forgive the Unforgivable, 1997; Twelve, 1998. Other: Lord of Death (play), 1963. *Contributions to:* Guardian; Observer; Peace News; Rolling Stone; Sunday Times; Tribune. *Address:* 4 Rue Las Cours, Aspiran, L'Herault 34800, France.

MORRISON, (Philip) Blake; b. 8 Oct. 1950, Burnley, Lancashire, England. Author; Poet; Dramatist. m. Katherine Ann Drake, 15 July 1976, 2 s., 1 d. *Education:* BA, University of Nottingham, 1972; MA, McMaster University; PhD, University College, London, 1978. *Appointments:* Poetry and Fiction Ed., TLS, 1978–81; Deputy Literary Ed., 1981–86, Literary Ed., The Observer, 1987–89; Literary Ed., The Independent on Sunday, 1990–94. *Publications:* The Movement: English Poetry and Fiction of the 1950s, 1980; Seamus Heaney, 1982; Penguin Book of Contemporary British Poetry (ed. with Andrew Motion), 1982; Dark Glasses (poems), 1984; The Ballad of the Yorkshire Ripper and Other Poems, 1987; The Yellow House (children's book), 1987; And When Did You Last See Your Father? (memoir), 1993; The Cracked Pot: A Play, after Heinrich von Kleist, 1996; As If: A Crime, a Trial, a Question of Childhood, 1997; Too True (essays and stories), 1998; Dr Ox's Experiment (libretto), 1998; Selected Poems, 1999; The Justification of Johann Gutenberg (novel), 2000. *Honours:* Eric Gregory Award, 1980; Somerset Maugham Award, 1984; Dylan Thomas Prize, 1985; E. M. Forster Award, 1988; J. R. Ackerley Prize, 1994. *Membership:* Fellow, RSL. *Address:* 54 Blackheath Park, London SE3 9SJ, England.

MORRISON, Robert Hay; b. 11 May 1915, South Yarra, Melbourne, Australia. Poet; Writer; Trans. m. Anna Dorothea Booth, 20 Sept. 1939, 1 s., 1 d. *Publications:* Lyrics from Pushkin, 1951; Lyric Images, 1954; A Book of South Australian Verse, 1957; Opus 4, 1971; Australia's Russian Poets, 1971; Some Poems of Verlaine, 1972; Australia's Ukrainian Poets, 1973; Leaf-fall, 1974; America's Russian Poets, 1975; Australia's Italian Poets, 1976; In the Ear of Dusk, 1977; The Secret Greenness and Other Poems, 1978; One Hundred Russian Poems, 1979; Ancient Chinese Odes, 1979; Sonnets from the Spanish, 1980; For the Weeks of the Year, 1981; Poems for an Exhibition, 1985; Poems from My Eight Lives, 1989; Poems from Mandelstam, 1990; All I Have is a Fountain, 1995; The Voice of the Hands, 1997. *Contributions to:* Newspapers, reviews, and journals. *Honours:* Prize, International Haiku Contest, 1990; Roberts Memorial Prize, USA, 1994. *Address:* 6 Bradfield St, Burnside, SA 5066, Australia.

MORRISS, Peter; b. 7 Jan. 1940, Chesterfield, England. Poet. m. Joan Margaret, 7 Sept. 1963, 1 s., 1 d. *Contributions to:* Many anthologies and periodicals, 1992–99. *Honours:* Ed.'s Choice Award, International Society of Poets, 1996; Ed.'s Choice Award, International Library of Poetry, 1998. *Membership:* Society of Authors. *Address:* 16 Solway Close, Melton Mowbray, Leicestershire LE13 0EF, England.

MORT, Graham Robert; b. 11 Aug. 1955, Middleton, England. Poet. m Maggie Mort, 12 Feb. 1979, 3 s. *Education:* BA, University of Liverpool, 1977 PGCE, St Martin's College, Lancaster, 1980; PhD, University of Glamorgan 2000. *Appointments:* Creative Writing Course Leader, Open College of the Arts 1989–2000; Project Leader for British Council Crossing Borders mentoring scheme for African writers; Tutor, Lancaster University. *Publications:* A Country on Fire; Into the Ashes; A Halifax Cider Jar; Sky Burial; Snow from the North; Starting to Write; The Experience of Poetry, Storylines; Circular Breathing. *Contributions to:* Numerous literary magazines and journals. *Honours:* First Prizes, Cheltenham Poetry Competition, 1979, 1982; Duncan Lawrie Prizes, Arvon Poetry Competition, 1982, 1992, 1994; Major Eric Gregory Award, 1985; Authors Foundation Award, 1994. *Memberships* Society of Authors; National Asscn of Writers in Education. *Address:* 2 Chapel Lane, Burton-in-Lonsdale, Carnforth, Lancs LA6 3JY, England. *E-mail:* graham.mort@ukonline.co.uk.

MORTIMER, Ian James Forrester; b. 22 Sept. 1967, Kent, England. Curatorial Officer; Poet. *Education:* University of Exeter, 1986–89; University College, London, 1992–93. *Contributions to:* Acumen; Outposts; Stand; Honest Ulsterman; Orbis; Lines Review; Poetry Nottingham. *Membership:* Royal Historical Society, fellow. *Address:* c/o Royal Commission on Historical Manuscripts, Quality House, Quality Ct, Chancery Lane, London WC2A 1HP, England.

MORTIMER, Peter John Granville; b. 17 Dec. 1943, Nottingham, England. Playwright; Poet; Critic; Ed. 1 s. *Education:* BA, Sheffield University, 1968. *Appointment:* Ed., Iron Literary Magazine, 1973–97. *Publications:* The Shape of Bricks; Waiting for History; Utter Nonsense; The Oosquidal; A Rainbow in its Throat; Croak, the King and a Change in the Weather, 1997; I Married the Angel of the North. Editor: Poetry of Perestroika, 1991. *Contributions to:* Stand; Acumen; Honest Ulsterman; Slow Dancer; Echo Room; Prospice; Poetry Anthologies. *Address:* 5 Marden Terrace, Cullercoats, North Shields, Northumberland NE30 4PD, England.

MORTON, Colin Todd; b. 26 July 1948, Toronto, Ontario, Canada. Writer; Poet; Ed. m. Mary Lee Bragg, 30 Aug. 1969, 1 s. *Education:* BA, University of Calgary, 1970; MA, University of Alberta, 1979. *Appointments:* Creative Writing Instructor, Algonquin College, 1993–94; Writer-in-Residence, Concordia College, 1995–96, Connecticut College, 1997. *Publications:* Oceans Apart (novel), 1995; Various poems. *Contributions to:* Anthologies, reviews, and journals. *Honours:* Several poetry and film awards. *Membership:* League of Canadian Poets, Vice-Pres., 2000–01. *Address:* 40 Grove Ave, Ottawa, Ontario K1S 3A6, Canada.

MORTUS, Cynthia; b. 19 May 1942, Canada. Writer; Poet; Teacher; Desktop Publisher. *Education:* BA, 1964; MA, 1966. *Appointments:* Asst Prof., Radford College; Supervisor, Aetna Life and Casualty; Business Owner, Wordware Inc; Freelancer. *Contributions to:* Connecticut River Review; Poem; Spoon River Anthology; Earth's Daughters; Virginia Country; Cotton Boll; Atlanta Review. *Memberships:* MLA; Publication Services Guild. *Address:* PO Box 870574, Stone Mountain, GA 30087, USA.

MOSDELL, Christopher John; b. 9 Nov. 1949, Gainsborough, Lincolnshire, England. Assoc. Prof. of English Literature; Poet; Lyricist. m. Alice Apel Mosdell, 14 Nov. 1978, 2 d. *Education:* MSc, Microbiology, Nottingham University, 1972; MSc, Pathology, Exeter University, 1973. *Appointments:* Lecturer, Dept of English, Waseda University, 1976–; Assoc. Prof. of English Literature, Tokyo International University, 1982–. *Publications:* Equasian, 1983; Ink Music: The Lyrics of Chris Mosdell, 1985; LAA... The Dangerous Opera Begins, 1989; The Oracles of Distraction, 1990; Writing the Riot Act, 1991; The Yelp House, 1991. *Contributions to:* Lyrics and poems to many major publications. *Honours:* Gold Prize for Lyrics, Tokyo Musical Festival, 1984; Yuki Hayashi-Newkirk Poetry Prize, 1987; Tokyo English Literature Award for Poetry, 1987. *Memberships:* Poetry Society of America; English Literature Society of Japan, Tokyo. *Address:* c/o English Literary Society of Japan, 501 Kenkyusha Building, 9 Surugadai 2-chome, Kanda, Chiyoda-ku, Tokyo 101, Japan.

MOSER, Norman Calvin; b. 15 Oct. 1931, Durham, North Carolina, USA. Writer; Poet. m. (1) Hadassah Haskale, 1966, divorced 1971, (2) Yolanda de Jesus Chitinos, 1978, divorced 1983, 1 s., (3) Romelia Avila, 15 March 1991, divorced 1993. *Appointments:* Teacher, Modern Art History, University of Maryland, Ulm, Germany, 1956; Contemporary Literature, University of California, Berkeley, 1967–68, University of Arizona, 1969; Contributing Ed., Grande Ronde Review, 1969–72; Managing Ed., The Gar, 1972–74; Staff Writer, North Carolina Anvil, 1974–75. *Publications:* A Shaman's Songbook, Poems and Tales, 1976; I Live in the South of My Heart, 1980; Open Season, 1980; Shorter Plays and Scenarios, 1981; The Wild Horses and Other Animal Poems, 1983; El Grito del Morte, 1984; South by Southwest (poems), 1988; Illuminations, Pulse and Gar: Anthology of Literature, Politics and Ecology, 1989. *Contributions to:* West Coast Review of Books; Film Quarterly; Performing Arts; Southern Poetry Review; Grand Ronde Review; Manas; Oakland Tribune; Berkeley Works; Blue Unicorn; Abraxas; The Sun; Galley Sail Review; Athena Incognito; Cloud Hidden Friends; Shaman's Drum;

Minotaur; Xylophone; Mind in Motion; In the Company of Poets; Gypsy; JazziMinds. *Honours:* National Foundation for the Arts Cash Award, 1966; Co-ordinating Councl of Literary Magazines Grants to Eds, 1967, 1969, 1974, 1977; Various other honours and awards. *Memberships:* Bay Area Poets Coalition; Bay Area Poets Union; Aid for Afghan Refugees. *Address:* Phoenix Literary Agency, 1731 10th St, No. A, Berkeley, CA 94710, USA.

MOSES, Black. See: THERSON-COFIE, Larweh.

MOSES, Daniel (David); b. 18 Feb. 1952, Ohsweken, Ontario, Canada. Writer; Dramatist; Poet. *Education:* BA, Honours, York University, 1975; MFA, University of British Columbia, 1977. *Appointments:* Instructor in Creative Writing, University of British Columbia, 1990; Instructor in Playwrighting, Graduate Drama Centre, University of Toronto, 1992; Resident Artist, Banff Centre for the Arts, 1993; Writer-in-Residence, University of Western Ontario, 1994, University of Windsor, 1995–96. *Publications:* Plays: The Dreaming Beauty, 1989; Coyote City, 1991; Almighty Voice and His Wife, 1992; The Indian Medicine Shows, 1995. Poetry: Delicate Bodies, 1980; The White Line. Other: An Anthology of Canadian Native Literature in English (co-ed.), 1992. *Honours:* First Prize, Theatre Canada National Playwrighting Competition, 1990; Winner, New Play Centre Playwrighting Competition, 1994. *Memberships:* League of Canadian Poets; Playwrights Union of Canada; Writers' Guild of Canada; Writers' Union of Canada. *Address:* 1 Browning Ave, No. 4, Toronto, ON M4K 1V6, Canada.

MOSS, Stanley David; b. 21 June 1925, New York, NY, USA. Poet; Ed.; Publisher; Private Art Dealer. m. Jane Moss, 2 s. *Education:* Trinity College; Yale University. *Appointments:* Ed., Halycon, Cambridge, New Directions, Botteghe Oscure, Rome; Poetry Ed., Book Week, New American Review, American Review; Ed. and Publisher, The Sheep Meadow Press. *Publications:* The Wrong Angel, 1969; Skull of Adam, 1979; The Intelligence of Clouds, 1989; Asleep in the Garden: New and Selected Poems, 1998. *Contributions to:* New Yorker; TLS; Poetry; American Poetry Review; Nation; New Republic; Tikkun; TriQuarterly; Vanderbilt Review; Sewanee Review; Encounter, London; Observer; New York Times; Poetry International. *Honours:* Rockefeller Fellow, 1968; Columbia University Alumni Fellow. *Memberships:* PEN; Poetry Society of America. *Address:* 5247 Independence Ave, Riverdale, NY 10471, USA.

MOSSHAM, Nat P. See: THOMPSON, Samuel Richard Charles.

MOTION, Andrew (Peter); b. 26 Oct. 1952, London, England. Poet; Author; Prof. of Creative Writing; Poet Laureate of the United Kingdom, 1999–. m. (1) Joanna Jane Powell, 1973, divorced 1983, (2) Janet Elisabeth Dalley, 1985, 2 s., 1 d. *Education:* BA, 1974, MLitt, 1976, University College, Oxford. *Appointments:* Lecturer in English, University of Hull, 1977–81; Ed., Poetry Review, 1980–83; Poetry Ed., 1983–89, Editorial Dir, 1982–87, Chatto and Windus; Prof. of Creative Writing, University of East Anglia, 1995–; Poet Laureate of the United Kingdom, 1999–. *Publications:* Poetry: The Pleasure Steamers, 1978; Independence, 1981; Secret Narratives, 1983; Dangerous Play, 1984; Natural Causes, 1987; Live in a Life, 1991; The Price of Everything, 1994; Salt Water, 1997; Remember This: An Elegy on the Death of HM Queen Elizabeth The Queen Mother, 2002; A Hymn for the Golden Jubilee (poem), 2002; Public Property, 2002. Fiction: The Pale Companion, 1989; Famous for the Creatures, 1991. Other: The Poetry of Edward Thomas, 1981; Philip Larkin, 1982; The Lamberts, 1986; Philip Larkin: A Writer's Life, 1993; William Barnes: Selected Poems (ed.), 1994; Keats, 1997; Wainewright, the Prisoner, 2000; Here to Eternity: An Anthology of Poetry (ed.), 2001. *Contributions to:* Various publications. *Honours:* Arvon/Observer Prize, 1982; Rhys Memorial Prize, 1984; Somerset Maugham Award, 1987; Dylan Thomas Award, 1987; Whitbread Award, 1994; Hon. DLitt, University of Hull, 1996. *Memberships:* Arts Council, chair., 1996–; RSL, fellow. *Address:* 64 Anson Rd, London N7 0AA, England.

MOTT, Elaine; b. 16 Sept. 1946, New York, NY, USA. Writer; Poet. m. Peter H Mott, 5 Jan. 1968, 1 s., 1 d. *Education:* BA, City College of the City University of New York, 1973; MA, English, Creative Writing, 1990, MA, Applied Linguistics, 1992, Queen's College of the City University of New York. *Contributions to:* Croton Review; Pennsylvania Review; Raccoon; Yarrow; Memphis State Review; Cutbank; Madison Review; Cream City Review; Midwest Quarterly; Art and Life; High Plains Literary Review; West Branch; Rhino; Crosscurrents; Green Mountains Review; Brooklyn Review; Nimrod; Primavera; Oxford Magazine. *Honours:* Honourable Mention, Chester H Jones National Poetry Competition, 1984; First Prize, Yarrow Spring Poetry Contest, 1985; Bernard de Voto Scholar, Poetry, Bread Loaf Writers Conference, 1986. *Address:* 8031 210th St, Hollis Hills, NY 11427, USA.

MOTT, Michael (Charles Alston); b. 8 Dec. 1930, London, England. Prof. of English Emeritus; Writer; Poet. m. (1) Margaret Ann Watt, 6 May 1961, deceased 1990, 2 d., (2) Emma Lou Powers, 16 Nov. 1992. *Education:* Diploma, Central School of Arts and Crafts, London; Intermediate Law Degree, Law Society, London; BA, History of Art, London University, Courtauld and Warburg Institutes, London. *Appointments:* Ed., Air Freight, 1954–59, Thames and Hudson publishers, 1961–64; Asst Ed., Adam

International Review, 1956–66, The Geographical Magazine, 1964–66; Poetry Ed., The Kenyon Review, 1966–70; Visiting Prof. and Writer-in-Residence, Kenyon College, 1966–70, State University of New York at Buffalo, 1968, Concordia University, Montréal, QC, 1970, 1974, Emory University, 1970–77, College of William and Mary, 1978–79, 1985–86; Prof. of English, 1980–92, Prof. Emeritus, 1992–, Bowling Green State University. *Publications:* Fiction: The Notebooks of Susan Berry, 1962; Master Entrick, 1964; Helmet and Wasps, 1964; The Blind Cross, 1968. Poetry: Absence of Unicorns, Presence of Lions, 1977; Counting the Grasses, 1980; Corday, 1986; Piero di Cosimo: The World of Infinite Possibility, 1990; Taino, 1992; Woman and the Sea: Selected Poems, 1999. Non-Fiction: The Seven Mountains of Thomas Merton, 1984. *Contributions to:* Journals and newspapers. *Honours:* Governor's Award in Fine Arts, State of Georgia, 1974; Guggenheim Fellowship, 1979–80; Hon. DLitt, St Mary's College, Notre Dame, 1983; Christopher Award, 1984; Ohioana Book Award, 1985; Olscamp Research Award, 1985; Nancy Dasher Book Award, 1985; Fortsam Award, 1999. *Memberships:* Amnesty International; British Lichen Society; RGS. *Address:* 122 The Colony, Williamsburg, VA 23185, USA.

MOULE, Ros; b. 18 March 1941, Swansea, Wales. Lecturer; Poet. 1 s., 1 d. *Education:* BA, University College, Swansea, 1962; PGCE, London Institute of Education, 1963; AMBDA, 2001. *Appointments:* Lecturer, American and European Studies, University of London, 1970–75; English Language and Literature, Kingston College of Further Education, 1975–87; Lecturer, Media Studies, Man. of Dyslexia Support Unit, Swansea College, 1991–2001; Chair, Tibetan Yungdrung Bon Study Centre, 2000–. *Contributions to:* Poetry Wales; Poetry Digest; Merlin; Westwords; Anglo Welsh Review. *Honours:* West Wales Writers' Competition, 1992; Cup Holder, Swansea Writers' Circle, 1991. *Memberships:* West Wales Writers' Umbrella; Swansea Writers Circle. *Address:* 15 Admirals Walk, Sketty, Swansea SA2 8LQ, Wales. *E-mail:* emaho15@aol.com.

MOURE, Erin; b. 17 April 1955, Calgary, AB, Canada. Poet. *Education:* University of Calgary; University of British Columbia. *Publications:* Empire, York Street, 1979; The Whisky Vigil, 1981; Wanted Alive, 1983; Domestic Fuel, 1985; Furious, 1988; WSW (West South West), 1989; Sheepish Beauty, Civilian Love, 1992; The Green World: Selected Poems, 1994; Search Procedures, 1996; A Frame of the Book, 1999; Pillage Laud, 1999; Sheep's Vigil by a Fervent Person, 2001; O Cidadán, 2002. *Contributions to:* Various publications. *Honour:* Governor-General's Award for Poetry, 1988. *Memberships:* League of Canadian Poets; Writers' Union of Canada. *Address:* c/o League of Canadian Poets, 54 Wolseley St, Third Floor, Toronto, Ontario M5T 1A5, Canada.

MUAMBA, Muepu; b. 23 Nov. 1946, Tshilundu, Belgian Congo. Journalist; Writer; Poet. *Education:* Institut St Ferdinand, Jernappes, Belgium. *Publications:* Afrika in eigener Sache (essays with Jochen Klicker and Klaus Paysan), 1980; Devoir d'ingerence, 1988; Moi Qui T'Amour, 1997; Ma Terre d'O, 1999. *Contributions to:* Various anthologies and periodicals. *Memberships:* Maison Africaine de la Poesie internationale, Dakar; Royal African Society, London; Société Française des Gens de Lettres, Paris; Union Internale des Journalistes et de la Presse de la Langue Française, Paris. *Address:* c/o M. Kohlert-Nemeth, Schaumainkal 99, 6000 Frankfurt am Main 70, Germany.

MUDDANNA, Kembhavy, (Satyananda, Manzar); b. 9 Oct. 1920, Rangampet, Gulberga, India. Surgeon (retd); Poet; Writer; Dramatist. m. Anna Purna Devy, 15 May 1955, 2 d. *Education:* MBBS, Osmania, 1948; FCGP, IMA, India, 1968; MCCP, New Delhi, 1992; FCCP, New Delhi, 1994; FUWA, Madras, 1994. *Publications:* (in English) Blue Eyes, 1968; Horizon, 1995; Glimpses of World Literature, 1995; Glimpses of World Philosophy, 1997. *Contributions to:* Various publications. *Honours:* Government of India Awards, 1971, 1973; Mahatma Gandhi Award, Bangalore University, 1985; Rashtra Kavi Kuvempu Award, 1995. *Memberships:* Authors' Guild of India; PEN, Bombay; Poetry Society of India; United Writers Asscn of India. *Address:* 656 Istage, Indiranagar, Bangalore 560038, India.

MUDGEON, Apeman. See: MITCHELL, Adrian.

MUEHL, Lois Baker; b. 29 April 1920, Oak Park, IL, USA. Assoc. Prof. of Rhetoric (retd); Writer; Poet. m. Siegmar Muehl, 15 April 1944, 2 s., 2 d. *Education:* BA, English, Oberlin College, 1941; MA, English, Education, University of Iowa, 1965. *Publications:* My Name is..., 1959; Worst Room in the School, 1961; The Hidden Year of Devlin Bates, 1967; Winter Holiday Brainteasers, 1979; A Reading Approach to Rhetoric, 1983; Trading Cultures in the Classroom (with Siegmar Muehl), 1993; Talkable Tales, 1993. Other: Poems. *Contributions to:* Scholarly journals and to general magazines. *Honours:* Old Gold Creative Fellowship, 1970; Community Service Commendation, Merced, California, 1984; Grand Prize, Poetry Guild Contest, 1997. *Memberships:* Iowa Poetry Asscn; National League of American Pen Women; University Women's Writers Group. *Address:* 430 Crestview Ave, Iowa City, IA 52245, USA.

MUELLER, Lisel; b. 8 Feb. 1924, Hamburg, Germany (Naturalized US citizen, 1945). Poet; Writer; Trans. m. Paul E Mueller, 15 June 1943, 2 d. *Education:* BA, University of Evansville, 1944; Graduate Studies, Indiana

University, 1950–53. *Appointments:* Instructor in Poetry, Elmhurst College, 1969–72; Associated with Poets in the Schools Programme, 1972–77; Visiting Prof., Goddard College and Warren Wilson College, 1977–86. *Publications:* Poetry: Dependencies, 1965; Life of a Queen, 1970; The Private Life, 1976; Voices From the Forest, 1977; The Need to Hold Still, 1980; Second Language, 1986; Waving From Shore, 1989; Alive Together, 1996. Other: Learning to Play by Ear (essays and poetry), 1990. *Contributions to:* Anthologies and journals. *Honours:* Robert M Ferguson Memorial Award, Friends of Literature, 1966; Helen Bullis Awards, 1974, 1977; Lamont Poetry Selection, 1975; Emily Clark Balch Award, 1976; National Book Award, 1981; Hon. Doctorate, Lake Forest College, 1985; National Endowment for the Arts Fellowship, 1990; Carl Sandburg Award, 1990; Pulitzer Prize for Poetry, 1997; Ruth Lilly Poetry Prize, 2002. *Address:* 27240 N Longwood Rd, Lake Forest, IL 60045, USA.

MUELLER, Rosa Anna M.; b. 24 Dec. 1948, Italy. College Instructor in Foreign Languages and Humanities; Poet. m. Robert R Mueller, 27 June 1971, 2 s. *Education:* BA, Spanish, Hunter College; MA, Romance Languages, 1977, PhD, Comparative Literature, 1977, City University of New York. *Appointments:* Morton College, 1982–90; Columbia College, Chicago, 1990; Also taught at American University, George Mason College, Illinois Benedictine College and Brooklyn College. *Contributions to:* Italian Poetry Today; Prairie Light Review; Poetry Now. *Honour:* Silver Poet Award, 1986. *Memberships:* MLA; American Asscn of Teachers of Spanish and Portuguese. *Address:* 106 N Madison, LaGrange, IL 60525, USA.

MÜHRINGER, Doris Agathe Annemarie; b. 18 Sept. 1920, Graz, Austria. Poet; Writer. *Publications:* Gedichte I, 1957, II, 1969, III, 1976, IV, 1984; Tag, mein Jahr (with H. Valencak), 1983; Das hatten die Ratten vom Schatten: Ein Lachbuch, 1989; Reisen wir (poems), 1995; Aber ietzt zögerst etu Späte Gedichte, 1999. *Contributions to:* Numerous literary magazines, domestic and foreign. *Honours:* Georg Trakl Prize, 1954; Award of Achievement, Vienna, 1961; Lyric Prize of Steiermark, 1973; Austrian State Scholarship, 1976; Award of Achievement, Board of Austrian Litera-Mechana, 1984; Grosser Literturpreis des Landes Steiermark, 1985. *Memberships:* Asscn of Austrian Writers; Kogge; PEN; Poium. *Address:* Goldeggasse 1, 1040 Vienna, Austria.

MUIR, Mary. See: TURNER, Stella.

MUJICA, Barbara; b. 25 Dec. 1943, Los Angeles, CA, USA. Prof. of Spanish; Author. m. Mauro E Mujica, 26 Dec. 1966, 1 s., 2 d. *Education:* AB, University of California at Los Angeles, 1964; MA, Middlebury Graduate School, Paris, 1965; PhD, Honours, New York University, 1974. *Appointments:* Teacher of French, University of California at Los Angeles Extension Division, 1963–64; Assoc. Ed. of Modern Languages, Harcourt Brace Jovanovich, New York City, 1966–73; Instructor, 1973–74, Asst Prof. of Romance Languages, 1974, Bernard Baruch College of the City University of New York; Asst Prof., 1974–79, Assoc. Prof., 1979–91, Prof. of Spanish, 1991–, Georgetown University. *Publications:* Scholarly: Readings in Spanish Literature (ed. with Anthony Zahareas), 1975; Calderón's Characters: An Existential Point of View, 1983; Expanding the Curriculum in Foreign Language Classes: Spanish and Contemporary Affairs (with William Cressey and Mark Goldin), 1983; Iberian Pastoral Characters, 1986; Texto y espectáculo: Selected Proceedings of the Symposium on Spanish Golden Age Theater, March, 1987, 1989; Texto y vida: Introducción a la literatura española, 1990; Antología de literatura española, Vol. I, La Edad Media (with Amanda Curry), 1991, Vol. II, Renacimiento y Siglo de Oro, 1991, Vol. III, Siglos XVIII y XIX (with Eva Florensa), 1999; Et in Arcadia Ego: Essays on Death in the Pastoral Novel (with Bruno Damiani), 1990; Texto y vida: Introducción a la literatura hispanoamericana, 1992; Looking at the Comedia in the Year of the Quincentennial (ed. with Sharon Voros), 1993; Premio Nóbel: Once grandes escritores del mundo hispánico (ed.), 1997; Books of the Americas: Reviews and Interviews from Americas Magazine, 1990–1991, 1997; El texto puesto en escena (ed. with Anita Stoll), 2000; Hispanomundo, 2001. Other: The Deaths of Don Bernardo (novel), 1990; Sanchez across the Street (short stories), 1997; Far from My Mother's Home (short stories), 1999; Affirmative Actions (novel), 2001; Frida (novel), 2001. *Contributions to:* Anthologies, scholarly publications and the popular press. *Honours:* Poets and Writers Recognition for Fiction, New York, 1984; Pushcart Prize Nomination for Fiction, 1989; One of Best Fifty Op Ed Pieces of the Decade, New York Times, 1990; Winner, E L Doctorow International Fiction Contest, 1992; Pangolin Prize for Best Short Story of 1998. *Memberships:* American Asscn of Teachers of Spanish and Portuguese; American Asscn of University Profs; American Council on the Teaching of Foreign Languages; Asscn for Hispanic Classical Theater, Board of Dirs; Feministas Unidas; MLA; Washington Independent Writers; Writer's Center; South Atlantic MLA; Golden Age Division, Secretary, 1999, Pres., 2000, PEN International; National Writers Union; Asociación de Escritoras de España y las Américas. *Address:* c/o Dept of Spanish and Portuguese, Georgetown University, Box 571039, Washington, DC 20057, USA.

MUKHOPADHYAY (MUKHERJEE), Vijaya; b. 11 March 1937, Vikrampur, Dhaka, India. Research Fellow in Indology; Poet. m. Sarat Kumar Mukhopadhyay, 4 July 1967, 1 s. *Education:* MA, Sanskrit. *Appointments:* College Lecturer; Research Fellow in Indology, R K Mission Institute of Culture, Gol Park, Calcutta. *Publications:* Amar Prabhur Janya, 1967;

Uranta Manabali, 1970; Jadi Shartaheen, 1971; Bhenge Jay Ananta Badam, 1977; Danrao Tarjani, 1988; Shrestha Kavita, 1990. *Contributions to:* Numerous publications. *Honours:* All-Bengal Poetry Award, Prabaha Sahitya Sankalan, 1975; Prize for Creative Work, Pratisruti Parishad, Calcutta, 1979; Bridge-in-the-Making Award for Literary Excellence, 1995; Various Cultural Programs, USA, Canada and France, 1996–97. *Membership:* PEN, Calcutta. *Address:* Flat 3C-1, 18-3 Gariahat Rd, Calcutta 700 109, India.

MULDOON, Paul (Benedict); b. 20 June 1951, Portadown, County Armagh, Northern Ireland. Poet; Writer; Dramatist; Prof. in the Humanities. *Education:* BA, English Language and Literature, Queen's University, Belfast, 1973. *Appointments:* Producer, 1973–78, Senior Producer, 1978–85, Radio Arts Programmes, Television Producer, 1985–86, BBC Northern Ireland; Judith E Wilson Visiting Fellow, University of Cambridge, 1986–87; Creative Writing Fellow, University of East Anglia, 1987; Lecturer, Columbia University, 1987–88; Lecturer, 1987–88, 1990–95, Dir, Creative Writing Programme, 1993–, Howard G B Clark Prof. in the Humanities, 1998–, Princeton University; Prof. of Poetry, Univerity of Oxford, 1999–04; Writer-in-Residence, 92nd Street Y, New York City, 1988; Roberta Holloway Lecturer, University of California at Berkeley, 1989; Visiting Prof., University of Massachusetts, Amherst, 1989–90, Bread Loaf School of English, 1997–. *Publications:* Poetry: Knowing My Place, 1971; New Weather, 1973; Spirit of Dawn, 1975; Mules, 1977; Names and Addresses, 1978; Immram, 1980; Why Brownlee Left, 1980; Out of Siberia, 1982; Quoof, 1983; The Wishbone, 1984; Meeting the British, 1987; Madoc: A Mystery, 1990; Incantata, 1994; The Prince of the Quotidian, 1994; The Annals of Chile, 1994; Kerry Slides, 1996; New Selected Poems, 1968–94, 1996; Hopewell Haiku, 1997; The Bangle (Slight Return), 1998; Hay, 1998; Poems, 1968–1998, 2001; Moy Sand and Gravel, 2002. Theatre: Monkeys (television play), 1989; Shining Brow (opera libretto), 1993; Six Honest Serving Men (play), 1995; Bandanna (opera libretto), 1999. Essays: To Ireland, I, 2000. Translator: The Astrakhan Cloak, by Nuala Ni Dhomhnaill, 1993; The Birds, by Aristophanes (with Richard Martin), 1999. Editor: The Scrake of Dawn, 1979; The Faber Book of Contemporary Irish Poetry, 1986; The Essential Byron, 1989; The Faber Book of Beasts, 1997. Children's Books: The O-O's Party, 1981; The Last Thesaurus, 1995; The Noctuary of Narcissus Batt, 1997. *Contributions to:* Anthologies and other publications. *Honours:* Eric Gregory Award, 1972; Sir Geoffrey Faber Memorial Awards, 1980, 1991; Guggenheim Fellowship, 1990; T S Eliot Prize for Poetry, 1994; American Acad. of Arts and Letters Award, 1996; Irish Times Poetry Prize, 1997. *Memberships:* Aosdána; Poetry Society of Great Britain, pres., 1996–; RSL, fellow; American Acad. of Arts and Sciences, 2000. *Address:* c/o Faber and Faber, 3 Queen Sq., London WC1N, England.

MULHERN, Maureen; b. 11 May 1957, Birmingham, West Midlands, England. Poet. *Education:* BA, Sarah Lawrence College, 1980; MFA, University of Iowa, 1983. *Publication:* Parallax, 1986. *Honours:* Ruth Lake Memorial Award, Poetry Society of America, 1984; Yaddo Fellowship, 1986. *Memberships:* Poetry Society of America; Acad. of American Poets; PEN America; MLA.

MULISCH, Harry; b. 29 July 1927, Haarlem, Netherlands. Novelist; Poet; Dramatist. *Education:* Haarlem Lyceum. *Publications:* 22 books of fiction, 1952–92, poetry collections and plays. *Honour:* Knight, Order of Orange Nassau, 1977. *Address:* Van Miereveldstraat 1, 1071 DW Amsterdam, Netherlands.

MULLHOLLAND, Theresa. See: CRAIG, Timothy.

MUMFORD, Ruth, (Ruth Dallas); b. 29 Sept. 1919, Invercargill, New Zealand. Poet; Children's Author. *Publications:* Country Road and Other Poems, 1953; The Turning Wheel, 1961; Experiment in Form, 1964; Day Book: Poems of a Year, 1966; Shadow Show, 1968; Song for a Guitar, 1976; Walking on the Snow, 1976; Steps of the Sun, 1979; Collected Poems, 1987. *Contributions to:* Southland Times; New Zealand Listener; Landfall (New Zealand Quarterly); Meanjin (Australian Quarterly); Poetry Australia; Review Magazine of Otago University. *Honours:* Joint Winner, Achievement Award, New Zealand Literary Fund, 1963; Robert Burns Fellowship, Otago University, 1968; Joint Winner, New Zealand Book Award for Poetry, 1977; Buckland Literary Award, 1977; Hon. DLitt, University of Otago, 1978; C.B.E., 1989. *Membership:* PEN New Zealand. *Address:* 448 Leith St, Denedin, New Zealand.

MUNDEN, Paul Warren Austen; b. 21 March 1958, Poole, Dorset, England. Writer; Poet; Composer. m. Clare Elizabeth Mallorie, 31 Oct. 1981, 2 d. *Education:* BA, University of York, 1980. *Appointments:* Vice Chair, National Asscn of Writers in Education, 1991–; Creative Writing Tutor, Hull University, 1991–, Harrogate College, 1992–; Adviser, Yorkshire and Humberside Arts, 1992–. *Publication:* Henderskelfe. *Contributions to:* Country Life; Encounter; Honest Ulsterman; London Magazine; New Statesman and Society; Poetry Review; Spectator. *Honours:* Writers Bursary; Eric Gregory Award. *Memberships:* National Poetry Society; British Film Institute. *Address:* Three Cottages, Bulmer, York YO6 7BW, England.

MUNGOSHI, Charles Muzuva; b. 2 Dec. 1947, Chivhu, Southern Rhodesia. Author; Poet; Dramatist. m. Jesesi Jaboon, 1976, 4 s., 1 d. *Appointments:* Writer-in-Residence, University of Zimbabwe, 1985–87; Visiting Arts Fellow, University of Durham, 1990. *Publications:* Fiction: Makunun'unu Maodzamwoyo, 1970; Coming of the Dry Season, 1972; Waiting for the Rain, 1975; Ndiko Kupindana Kwanazuva, 1975; Some Kinds of Wounds, 1980; Kunyarara Hakusi Kutaura?, 1983; Setting Sun and the Rolling World, 1987; One Day Long Ago: Tales from a Shona Childhood, 1991; Walking Still, 1997. Poetry: The Milkman Doesn't Only Deliver Milk, 1981. Other: The Axe (film), 1999. *Honours:* Several literary awards. *Address:* PO Box 1688, Harare, Zimbabwe.

MUNKSGAARD NIELSEN, Lone; b. 28 March 1968, Ringkøbing, Denmark. Poet; Dramatist; Trans. *Education:* Graduate, High School, 1986. *Publications:* Poetry: Afvikling, 1993; Frasagn, 1994; Lysvendt/Himmelsöjlen, 1995; Iklaedt en andens hud, 1996; Hvis Mine Fingre Kunne Rasle, 1999; Skæbnen og Mig (children's poems), 2000; Når Guderne Taler i Tunger, 2000. Play: Kapitaeler, 1995. *Contributions to:* Periodicals. *Membership:* Danish Writers' Union. *Address:* Lilliendalsvej 26, 2700 Brönshöj, Denmark.

MURA, David (Alan); b. 17 June 1952, Great Lakes, IL, USA. Poet; Writer; Teacher. m. Susan Sencer, 18 June 1983, 1 d. *Education:* BA, Grinnell College, 1974; Graduate Studies, University of Minnesota, 1974–79; MFA, Vermont College, 1991. *Appointments:* Instructor, 1979–85, Assoc. Dir of the Literature Program, 1982–84, Writers and Artists-in-the-Schools, St Paul, Minnesota; Faculty, The Loft, St Paul, Minnesota, 1984–; Instructor, St Olaf College, 1990–91; Visiting Prof., University of Oregon, 1991; Various poetry readings. *Publications:* A Male Grief: Notes on Pornography and Addiction, 1987; After We Lost Our Way (poems), 1989; Turning Japanese, 1991; The Colors of Desire (poems), 1995; Where the Body Meets Memory, 1996. *Contributions to:* Anthologies and magazines. *Honours:* Fanny Fay Wood Memorial Prize, Acad. of American Poets, 1977; US/Japan Creative Artist Fellow, 1984; National Endowment for the Arts Fellowships, 1985, 1993; Discovery/Nation Award, 1987; National Poetry Series Contest, 1988; Pushcast Prize, 1990; Minnesota State Arts Board Grant and Fellowship, 1991; New York Times Notable Book of the Year, 1991; Loft McKnight Award of Distinction, 1992; Lila Wallace Reader's Digest Writers' Award, 1995; Doctor of Humane Letters, Cornell College, 1997. *Memberships:* Asian-American Renaissance Conference; Center for Arts Criticism, pres., 1991–92; Jerome Foundation; Playwright's Center. *Address:* 1920 E River Terrace, Minneapolis, MN 55414, USA.

MURATORI, Fred; b. 30 April 1951, Derby, CT, USA. Reference Librarian; Poet. m. Kathleen Caldwell, 16 June 1990, divorced 1999. *Education:* BA, English, Fairfield University, 1973; MA, Creative Writing 1977, MLS, Information Studies, 1981, Syracuse University. *Appointments:* Instructor, Syracuse University, 1977, 1978–79, 1985–88; Reference Librarian, Cornell University. *Publications:* The Possible, 1988; Despite Repeated Warnings, 1994. *Contributions to:* Best American Poetry; Spectator; New Directions; Formalist; Denver Quarterly; Northwest Review; Poetry Northwest; New England Review; Literary Review; Talisman; Gargoyle; Mississippi Review; Southern Humanities Review; New American Writing; LIT. *Honours:* Creative Writing Fellowship, Syracuse University, 1973–74; Artist's Fellowship, New York Foundation of the Arts, 1990; Constance Saltonstall Foundation Grant in Poetry, 2000. *Address:* 6 Rochester St, Dryden, NY 13053, USA.

MURAWSKI, Elisabeth Anna; b. 27 Sept. 1936, Chicago, IL, USA. Poet. m. 30 Dec. 1961, divorced 1978, 3 s. *Education:* BA, English, DePaul University, 1957; MFA, Creative Writing, George Mason University, 1991. *Appointments:* Language Arts Ed., Society for Visual Education; Rights and Permissions Ed., Scholastic Magazine; Ed., Catholic University Press; Style Ed., Salesian Studies; Training Specialist, US Census Bureau; Adjunct Prof., University of Virginia, 1993–. *Publications:* Moon and Mercury, 1990; Troubled by an Angel (chapbook), 1997. *Contributions to:* New Republic; Grand Street; American Poetry Review; Shenandoah; American Voice; Ohio Review; Ohio Journal; Virginia Quarterly Review; Helicon 9; Madison Review; New Mexico Humanities Review; Phoebe; Commonwealth; Christian Century; Carolina Quarterly; Poet and Critic; Mudfish; Crab Creek Review; Literary Review; Poetry Northwest. *Honours:* Helene Wurlitzer Foundation Grants, Taos, New Mexico, 1988, 1990, 1991, 1993; Washington Writers Publishing House Prize, 1990. *Memberships:* Associated Writing Program; Writers Center. *Address:* 6804 Kenyon Dr., Alexandria, VA 22307, USA.

MURPHY, Clive; b. 28 Nov. 1935, Liverpool, England. Writer; Poet; Compiler; Ed. *Education:* BA, LLB, Trinity College, Dublin, 1958; Solicitor, Incorporated Law Society of Ireland, 1958. *Publications:* Novels: Summer Overtures, 1972; Freedom for Mr Mildew, 1975; Nigel Someone, 1975. Poetry: Sour Grapes, 2000; Cave Canem, 2002. Other: Compiler or ed., 10 autobiographies, 1978–94. *Contributions to:* Anthologies and magazines. *Honour:* Co-Winner, Adam International First Novel Review Competition, 1968. *Memberships:* PEN; RSL, assoc.; Society of Authors. *Address:* 132 Brick Lane, London E1 6RU, England.

MURPHY, Lizz; b. 7 Aug. 1950, Belfast, Northern Ireland. Poet; Writer; Ed. m. Bill Murphy, 21 Sept. 1969, 1 s., 1 d. *Publications:* Do Fish Get Seasick?, 1994; Pearls and Bullets, 1996. *Contributions to:* Anthologies, reviews and journals. *Honours:* Project grants; ANUtech Poetry Prize, 1994. *Memberships:* Australian Capital Territory Writers; Australian Society of Authors; Fellowship of Australian Authors; National Book Council; New South Wales Writers Centre; Poets Union. *Address:* PO Binalong, NSW 2584, Australia.

MURPHY, Merilene M.; b. 20 March 1955, New Rochelle, New York, USA. Writer; Poet. *Education:* Journalism, International Affairs, Iowa State University, 1971–75; Zora Neale Hurston Scholar, 1995; Jack Kerouac School of Disembodied Poetics, Boulder. *Appointments:* Founder, Pres., Telepoetics Inc. *Publication:* Under Peace Rising, 1995. *Contributions to:* Caffeine; Hyena; Trouble; National Poetry Assn's National Collage Poem, 1995. *Honour:* Living History Maker Arts and Entertainment Award, Turning Point Magazine, 1995. *Memberships:* Poetry Society of America; International Black Writers and Artists; Poets and Writers. *Address:* 1939 1/4 W Washington Blvd, Los Angeles, CA 90018, USA.

MURPHY, Richard; b. 6 Aug. 1927, Co Galway, Ireland. Poet; Author. *Education:* BA, MA, 1948, Magdalen College, Oxford; Sorbonne, University of Paris, 1955. *Appointments:* Various visiting positions, including University of Virginia, 1965, University of Reading, 1968, Bard College, Annandale-on-Hudson, New York, 1972–74, Princeton University, 1974–75, University of Iowa, 1976–77, Syracuse University, 1977–78, Catholic University of America, Washington, DC, 1983, Pacific Lutheran University, Tacoma, Washington, 1985, Wichita State University, 1987; Compton Lecturer in Poetry, University of Hull, 1969; O'Connor Prof. of Literature, Colgate University, 1971; Distinguished Visiting Prof., University of Tulsa, 1992–95. *Publications:* The Archaeology of Love, 1955; The Woman of the House, 1959; The Last Galway Hooker, 1961; Sailing to an Island, 1963; The Battle of Aughrim, 1968; High Island, 1974; Selected Poems, 1979; The Price of Stone, 1985; The Mirror Wall, 1989; New Selected Poems, 1989. *Contributions to:* Various periodicals. *Honours:* Several poetry awards. *Membership:* Fellow, RSL. *Address:* Knockbrack, Glenalua Rd, Killiney, Dublin, Ireland.

MURPHY, Sheila Ellen; b. 5 April 1951, Mishawaka, IN, USA. Management Consultant; Poet. *Education:* BA, English and Music, Nazareth College; MA, English, University of Michigan; PhD, Educational Administration and Supervision, Arizona State University. *Appointments:* Asst Prof. of English, Bay de Noc Community College, 1974–76; Doctoral Fellow, Arizona State University, 1976–78; Vice-Pres., 1980–90, Dir, 1990–, Ramada Inc; Exec. Dir, Business and Management Program, University of Phoenix, 1990–93; Pres., Sheila Murphy Assocs, 1993–. *Publications:* Virtuoso Bird, 1981; Memory Transposed into the Key of C, 1983; Loss Prevention Photograph, Some Pencils and a Memory Elastic, 1986; This Stem Much Stronger Than Your Spine, 1989; Sad Isn't the Color of the Dream, 1991; Teth, 1991; Tommy and Neil, 1993; Pure Mental Breath, 1994; A Clove of Gender, 1995; Falling in Love With Your Syntax: Selected and New Poems, 1997; The Indelible Occasion, 2000; The Stuttering of Wings, 2002; Heresiarch, 2002. *Contributions to:* Various publications. *Memberships:* Arizona State Poetry Society; International Society for Performance Improvement; Phoenix Poetry Society; Valley Leadership. *Address:* 3701 E Monterosa, No. 3, Phoenix, AZ 85018, USA.

MURRAY, John E. III; b. 11 Feb. 1973, Jacksonville, IL, USA. Poet; Writer; Teacher. *Education:* BA, Psychology, 1995; BA, English, 1995. *Publications:* Several poems. *Contributions to:* Anthologies and magazines. *Honours:* Honorable Mention and Pres.'s Award, Iliad Press, 1994; Eds' Choice Awards, National Library of Poetry, 1994, 1995; Accomplishment of Merit, Creative Arts and Science Enterprises, 1995. *Memberships:* International Society of Poets; National Authors Registry. *Address:* 2040 Hilltop Rd, Hoffman Estates, IL 60195, USA.

MURRAY, Les(lie Allan); b. 17 Oct. 1938, Nabiac, NSW, Australia. Poet; Writer; Trans. m. 29 Sept. 1962, 3 s., 2 d. *Education:* BA, University of Sydney, 1969. *Apointments:* Co-Ed., Poetry Australia, 1973–80; Poetry Reader, Angus and Robertson Publishers, 1976–91; Literary Ed., Quadrant, 1990–. *Publications:* Poetry: The Ilex Tree (with Geoffrey Lehmann), 1965; The Weatherboard Cathedral, 1969; Poems Against Economics, 1972; Lunch and Counter Lunch, 1974; Selected Poems: The Vernacular Republic, 1976; Ethnic Radio, 1978; The Boys Who Stole the Funeral, 1980; Equanimities, 1982; The People's Otherworld, 1983; Persistence in Folly, 1984; The Australian Year (with Peter Solness), 1986; The Daylight Moon, 1986; Dog Fox Field, 1990; Collected Poems, 1991; The Rabbiter's Bounty, 1992; Translations from the Natural World, 1991; Subhuman Redneck Poems, 1997; Fredy Neptune: A Novel in Verse, 1998; Learning Human: New Selected Poems, 2001. Prose: The Peasant Mandarin, 1978; Blocks and Tackles, 1991; The Paperbark Tree: Selected Prose, 1992; A Working Forest, 1997. Editor: The New Oxford Book of Australian Verse, 1986; Collins Dove Anthology of Australian Religious Verse, 1986; Fivefathers: Five Australian Poets of the Pre-Academic Era, 1994. *Contributions to:* Many publications. *Honours:* Grace Leven Prizes, 1965, 1980, 1990; Cook Bicentennial Prize, 1970; National Book Awards, 1974, 1984, 1985, 1991, 1993; C J Dennis Memorial Prize, 1976; Gold Medal, Australian Literary Society, 1984; New South Wales Premier's Prizes, 1984,

1993; Canada-Australia Award, 1985; Australian Broadcasting Corporation Bicentennial Prize, 1988; National Poetry Award, 1988; Order of Australia, 1989; Victorian Premier's Prize, 1993; Petrarca Preis, Germany, 1995; T S Eliot Prize, 1997; Queen's Gold Medal for Poetry, 1999; Hon. doctorates. *Membership:* Poetry Society of Great Britain, hon. vice-pres. *Address:* c/o Margaret Connolly and Assocs, 16 Winton St, Warrawee, NSW 2074, Australia.

MURRAY, Patrick. See: PATTEN, Bernard M.

MURRAY, Rona Jean; b. 10 Feb. 1924, London, England. University Lecturer (retd); Poet; Dramatist; Writer. m. (1) Gerry Haddon, 10 Feb. 1944, 2 s., 1 d., (2) Walter Dexter, 28 Jan. 1972. *Education:* Mills College, Oakland, CA, 1941–44; BA, 1961, MA, 1968, University of British Columbia; PhD, University of Kent, Canterbury, 1972. *Appointments:* Lecturer, University of British Columbia, 1963–66, Selkirk College, 1968–74, Douglas College, 1974–76, University of Victoria, 1977–84. *Publications:* Poetry: The Enchanted Adder, 1965; The Power of the Dog and Other Poems, 1968; Ootischenie, 1974; Selected Poems, 1974; An Autumn Journal, 1980; Journey, 1981; Adam and Eve in Middle Age, 1984. Other: Blue Ducks Feather and Eagledown (verse play), 1958; One, Two, Three, Alary (play), 1970; The Art of Earth: An Anthology (co-ed.), 1979; Creatures (play), 1980; The Indigo Dress and Other Stories, 1986; Journey Back to Peshawar (memoirs/travel), 1992; Threshold (poems, ed.), 1998; Memory of Elsewhere (autobiography), 2000; Love and Pomegranates (short stories, ed.), 2000. *Contributions to:* Anthologies, reviews, journals, and radio. *Honours:* BC Centennial One Act Play Award, 1958; Macmillan of Canada Creative Writing Award, 1964; Norma Epstein National Award for Creative Writing, 1965; Canada Council Grants, 1976, 1979; Pat Lowther Award, 1982; Commemorative Medal for the 125th Anniversary of the Confederation of Canada, 1992; Arts and Letters Award, Hawthorne Society, 1998. *Address:* 3825 Duke Rd, Victoria, BC V9C 4B2, Canada.

MURTHY, D. Srikantha; b. 14 Jan. 1952, Mysore, India. Geologist; Poet. m. Swarna Murthy, 12 June 1981, 1 s., 1 d. *Education:* BSc; MSc. *Publications:* Just Born; Guest for Joy; East West Winds; East West Voices; Life and Love. *Contributions to:* Samavedana; Poet; Kavita India; Poet International. *Honour:* International Eminent Poet. *Memberships:* Chetana Literary Group; International Poets Acad. *Address:* 251 I Cross Sixth Block, Banashankari Third Stage, Bangalore 560085, India.

MURTI, K. V. S. See: KOTIKALAPUDI, Venkata Suryanarayana Murti.

MUSBACH, Ruth Ann; b. 20 March 1964, Lincoln, Nebraska, USA. Poet; Writer. 1 s. *Education:* Macalester College, 1982–84; Midland Lutheran College, 1985; BA, English and Creative Writing, University of Minnesota, 1987. *Publication:* For Love of Michael, 2 vols, 1991–92. *Contributions to:* American Knight; Coventry News; Our Journey. *Address:* PO Box 130723, St Paul, MN 55113, USA.

MUSGRAVE, Susan; b. 12 March 1951, Santa Cruz, CA, USA (Canadian citizen). Poet; Author. m. (3) Stephen Reid, 1986, 2 d. *Appointments:* Instructor and Writer-in-Residence, University of Waterloo, Ontario, 1983–85; Instructor, Kootenay School of Writing, BC, 1986, Camosun College, Victoria, 1988–; Writer-in-Residence, University of New Brunswick, 1985, University of Western Ontario, 1992–93, University of Toronto, 1995, Victoria School of Writing, 1996, 1998; Writer-in-Electronic-Residence, York University and Writers' Development Trust, 1991–. *Publications:* Poetry: Songs of the Sea-Witch, 1970; Entrance of the Celebrant, 1972; Grave-Dirt and Selected Strawberries, 1973, revised edn as Selected Strawberries and Other Poems, 1977; The Impstone, 1976; Becky Swan's Book, 1978; A Man to Marry, A Man to Bury, 1979; Tarts and Muggers: Poems New and Selected, 1982; Cocktails at the Mausoleum, 1985; The Embalmer's Art: Poems New and Selected, 1991; In the Small Hours of the Rain, 1991; Forcing the Narcissus, 1994; Things That Keep and Do Not Change, 1999; What the Small Day Cannot Hold: Collected Poems, 1970–1985, 2000. Fiction: The Charcoal Burners, 1980; The Dancing Chicken, 1987; Cargo of Orchids, 2000. Other: Great Musgrave, 1989; Clear Cut Words: Writers for Clayoquot (ed.), 1993; Musgrave Landing: Musings on the Writing Life, 1994; Because You Loved Being a Stranger: 55 Poets Celebrate Patrick Lane (ed.), 1994. Children's Books: Gullband (poems), 1974; Hag Head (fiction), 1980; Kestrel and Leonardo (poems), 1990; Dreams Are More Real than Bathtubs (fiction), 1998. *Contributions to:* Many anthologies, reviews, quarterlies, and journals. *Honours:* Many grants; Second Prize, National Magazine Award, 1981; First Prize, B. P. Nichol Poetry Chapbook Award, 1991; Readers' Choice Award, Prairie Schooner, 1993; Vicky Metcalf Short Story Ed.'s Award, 1996. *Memberships:* British Columbia Federation of Writers; Writer's Union of Canada, chair, 1997–98. *Address:* PO Box 2421, Station Main, Sidney, BC V8L 3Y3, Canada.

MUSICK, Martin. See: GILLILAND Brian Keith.

MUSKE-DUKES, Carol (Anne); b. 17 Dec. 1945, St Paul, Minnesota, USA. Poet; Author; Prof. m. David Dukes, 31 Jan. 1983, deceased 9 Oct. 2000, 1 step-s., 1 d. *Education:* BA, English, Creighton University, Omaha, 1967; MA, English, California State University, San Francisco, 1970. *Appointments:* Founder-Writing Program Dir, Art Without Walls, New York, 1971–84; Lecturer, New School for Social Research, New York City, 1975; Asst Prof., University of New Hampshire, 1978–79; Visiting Writer, 1978, Visiting Poet, 1983, 1993, University of California at Irvine; Adjunct Prof., Columbia University, 1979–81; Visiting Poet, Iowa Writers' Workshop, 1980; Jenny McKean Moore Lecturer, George Washington University, 1980–81; Writer-in-Residence, University of Virginia, 1981; Lecturer, 1984–88, Asst Prof., 1989–91, Assoc. Prof., 1991–93, Prof., 1993–, Founder-Dir, PhD Program in Creative Writing and Literature, 1999–, University of Southern California, Los Angeles; Visiting Fiction Writer, University of California, Los Angeles, 1989. *Publications:* Poetry: Camouflage, 1975; Skylight, 1981; Wyndmere, 1985; Applause, 1989; Red Trousseau, 1993; An Octave Above Thunder: Selected and New Poems, 1997. Fiction: Dear Digby, 1989; Saving St Germ, 1993; Life After Death, 2001; Married to the Icepick Killer: A Poet in Hollywood, 2002. Non-Fiction: Women and Poetry (essays), 1997. *Contributions to:* Numerous anthologies and journals. *Honours:* Dylan Thomas Poetry Award, 1973; Pushcart Prizes, 1978, 1988–89, 1992–93, 1998; Alice Fay di Castagnola Award, Poetry Society of America, 1979; Guggenheim Fellowship, 1981; National Endowment for the Arts Grant, 1984; Ingram Merrill Foundation Fellowship, 1988; New York Times Most Notable Book Citation, 1993; Alumni Achievement Award, Creighton University, 1996; Witter Bynner Award, Library of Congress, Washington, DC, 1997–98; Finalist, Los Angeles Times Book Prize, 1998. *Memberships:* Poetry Society of America, West, program dir and pres., 1992–94. *Literary Agent:* Molly Freidrich, Aaron Priest Agency, New York, NY, USA. *Address:* c/o Dept of English, University of Southern California, Los Angeles, CA 90095, USA.

MYCUE, Edward Delehant; b. 21 March 1937, Niagara Falls, New York, USA. Poet; Writer. *Education:* BA, North Texas State University, 1959; Graduate Studies, North Texas State University, Boston University, University of California at Berkeley, University College at Legon, Ghana, 1959–61; International Peoples College, Elsinore, Denmark, 1968–69. *Publications:* Damage Within the Community, 1973; Chronicle, 1974; Root, Route and Range, 1977; Root, Route and Range: The Song Returns, 1979; The Singing Man My Father Gave Me, 1980; Edward, 1987; Poems, 1988; A Grate Country, 1989; Pink Garden/Brown Trees, 1990; Because We Speak the Same Language, 1994; Split: Life is Built from the Inside Out, 1995; Night Boats, 1999. *Contributions to:* Many publications. *Honour:* MacDowell Colony Fellow, 1974. *Memberships:* PEN; Various local guilds and unions. *Address:* PO Box 640543, San Francisco, CA 94164, USA.

MYERS, Jack (Elliot); b. 29 Nov. 1941, Lynn, Massachusetts, USA. Prof. of English; Poet; Writer. m. (1) Nancy, 1967, (2) Willa, 1981, (3) Thea, 1993, 3 s., 1 d. *Education:* BA, English Literature, University of Massachusetts, Boston, 1970; MFA, Poetry Writing, University of Iowa, 1972. *Appointments:* Asst Prof., 1975–81, Assoc. Prof., 1982–88, Prof. of English, 1988–, Dir, Creative Writing Program, 1990–94, Southern Methodist University, Dallas; Poetry Ed., Fiction International, 1978–80, Cimarron Review, 1989–91; Faculty, MFA Program in Writing, Vermont College, 1981–; Distinguished Poet-in-Residence, Wichita State University, 1992; Distinguished Visiting Writer, University of Idaho, 1993; Distinguished Writer-in-Residence, Northeast Louisiana University, 1995. *Publications:* Poetry: Black Sun Abraxas, 1970; Will It Burn, 1974; The Family War, 1977; I'm Amazed That You're Still Singing, 1981; Coming to the Surface, 1984; As Long as You're Happy, 1986; Blindsided, 1993; Human Being, 1997. Other: A Trout in the Milk: A Composite Portrait of Richard Hugo, 1980; New American Poets of the 80s (ed. with Roger Weingarten), 1984; The Longman Dictionary of Poetic Terms, 1985; A Profile of Twentieth-Century American Poetry (ed. with David Wojahn), 1991; New American Poets of the 90s (ed. with Roger Weingarten), 1991; Leaning House Poets, Vol. 1 (ed. with Mark Elliott), 1996; One On One, 1999. *Contributions to:* Anthologies, reviews, quarterlies, journals, and magazines. *Honours:* Acad. of American Poets Award, 1972; Texas Institute of Letters Poetry Awards, 1978, 1993; Yaddo Fellowship, 1978; National Endowment for the Arts Fellowships, 1982–83, 1986–87; Winner, National Poetry Series Open Competition, 1985; Southern Methodist University Author's Award, 1987. *Memberships:* Associated Writing Programs; PEN; Texas Asscn of Creative Writing Teachers; Texas Institute of Letters. *Address:* 6402 Abrams Rd, Dallas, TX 75231, USA.

N

NADAUS, Roland, (Pol-Jean Mervillon); b. 28 Nov. 1945, Paris, France. Writer; Poet. m. Simone Moris, 9 Sept. 1967, 1 d. *Publications:* Maison de Paroles, 1969; Journal: Vrac, 1981; Je ne Tutoie que Dieu et ma femme (poems), 1992; Dictionnaire initiatique de l'orant, 1993; L'homme que tuèrent les mouches, 1996. *Contributions to:* Journals. *Honour:* Prix Gustave Gasser, 1993. *Membership:* PEN Club of France.

NAFTALI, Ben. See: OFFEN Yehuda.

NAGY, Gáspár; b. 4 May 1949, Berbaltavar, Hungary. Poet; Ed. m. Marta Szabo, 4 May 1974, 1 s., 2 d. *Education:* Teacher Training College, Szombathely, 1968–71; Aesthetics, Budapest, 1972–75. *Publications:* Poems: Koronatuz, 1975; Halantekdob, 1978; Foldi pörök, 1982; Kibiztositott beszed, 1987; Aron mondza, 1986; Mulik a Jövönk, 1989; Mosolyelagazas, 1993; Fölös ebrenletem, 1994; Tudom, nagy nyari delutan lesz, 1998; Szabadrabok, 1999; Husz ev a ketezerböl, 2000; Amig fölragyog a jaszol, 2001. Fiction: Augustusban Ludvík Jahn nyomaban, 1995; Kanizsa(var) vissza, 1999. Essays: Zonaidö, 1995. *Contributions to:* Journals, magazines, periodicals and newspapers. *Honours:* Raduoti, 1977; József Attila, 1990; Greve, 1993; Getz Award, 1995; Balassi Prize, 1999; Kossuth Prize, 2000. *Memberships:* Hungarian Writers Asscn, secretary, 1981–85; Hungarian Art Acad., 2000–. *Address:* Felkeszi v 17, 2092 Budakeszi, Hungary.

NAHRA, Nancy Ann; b. 11 May 1947, Bangor, Maine, USA. Poet; Novelist; University Lecturer. m. Willard Sterne Randall, 19 Oct. 1985, 1 d. *Education:* BA, Classics, Colby College, Maine, 1968; MA, Classics, Stanford University, 1971; PhD, Romance Languages, Princeton University, 1989. *Appointments:* Editorial Asst, Random House, New York City, 1971–72; Ed., Speechwriter, Institute of Signage Research, Palo Alto, CA, 1972–77; Lecturer, Ohio State University, University of Vermont, 1978–93; Poet-in-Residence, John Cabot University, Rome, 1996–. *Publications:* Personal Reflections on the Lake, 1987; Not From Around Here, 1990; More Charming, 1995; American Lives (with Willard Sterne Randall), 1997; Forgotton Americans (with Willard Sterne Randall), 1998. *Contributions to:* Best New Poets of 1986; American Poetry Anthology; Art of Poetry: A Treasure of Contemporary Verse; The Poetry of New England, 1999. *Honour:* John Masefield Award, Poetry Society of America, 1987. *Memberships:* Poetry Society of America; Acad. of American Poets; American Society of Eighteenth Century Studies; North American Society for the Study of Jean-Jacques Rousseau; Princeton Club of New York. *Address:* 200 Summit St, Burlington, VT 05401, USA.

NAIDU, Tulsi, (H. Thulasikumari); b. 10 June 1938, Kharagpur, India. Poet; Ed.; Publisher. m. H M Naidu, 31 Dec. 1980. *Education:* BA, English Literature, 1960; PhD, English Literature, 1994. *Publications:* Old Wine in New Bottles, 1993; Resurrection, Book 1, 1993; Sonnet Century, 1995; Ballads and Ballads, 1995; A Nosegay of New Year Poems, 1996; Lyrics and Limericks, 1997. *Contributions to:* Various publications. *Honours:* Several prizes; Michael Madhusudan Award, 1996. *Memberships:* Friend of Indian PEN; United Writers Asscn, life fellow; Writers Forum. *Address:* 21-46/1 Kakani Nagar, NAD Post Office, Visakhapatnam 530009, Andhra Pradesh, India.

NAIK, Vihang; b. 2 Sept. 1969, Surat, India. Teacher; Poet. *Education:* BA, English Literature and Philosophy, 1993, MA, English and Indian Literature, 1995, MS University of Baroda. *Appointments:* Lecturer in English, Smt M.C. Desai Arts and Commerce College, 1996–97, Ambaji Arts College, North Gujarat University, 1997–; Research Assoc., Indian Institute of Advanced Study, 2001. *Publications:* City Times, 1993; Jeevangeet, 2001. Other: Essays; Trans; Articles. *Contributions to:* Indian PEN; Journal of the Poetry Society of India; The Brown Critique; Journal of Indian Writing in English; Kavya Bharti; Poesis; The Scoria; The Quest; Poetry Today; Poetry Time; Revaluations; The Poetry Chain; Replica; Art and Poetry Today; Many Anthologies. *Honours:* Michel Madhusudan Award, 1998; Recognized Poet of the Year, Poesie India International, 2000. *Memberships:* Poetry Society of India; Forum on Contemporary Theory, World Poetry Society, Intercontinental; Poetry Circle, Mumbai; PEN All-India Centre; United Writers' Asscn. *Address:* PO Box 15, Ambaji 385110, North Gujarat, India. *E-mail:* vihangnaik@yahoo.com.

NAIMAN, Anatoly G.; b. 23 April 1936, Leningrad, Russia. Poet; Writer; Trans. m. Galina Narinskaia, 1969, 1 s., 1 d. *Education:* Degree, Organic Chemistry, Leningrad Technological Institute, 1958; Postgraduate Diploma, Screenwriting, Moscow, 1964. *Appointments:* Visiting Prof., Bryn Mawr College, Pennsylvania, 1991; Visiting Fellow, All Souls College, Oxford, 1991–92. *Publications:* Remembering Anna Akhmatova, 1989; The Poems of Anatoly Naiman, 1989; The Statue of a Commander and Other Stories, 1992; Sir, 2001. Other: Various trans into Russian. *Contributions to:* Newspapers and journals. *Honour:* Latvian Union of Writers Trans. Prize, 1981. *Memberships:*

PEN Club, France; Writers Committee, Moscow. *Address:* Dmitrovskoye Schosse 29, fl 56, Moscow, Russia.

NAIR, Yogesh G.; b. 21 March 1966, Trichur, Kerala, India. Management Consultant; Poet. *Education:* Degree, Arts, 1987; MA, Organisational Psychology, 1989; Postgraduate Diploma, University of Mississippi, 1990. *Contributions to:* Anthologies and many journals. *Memberships:* PEN All India Centre; Poetry Society, India. *Address:* 14/85 Refinery Township, PO Jawaharnagar, Baroda 391320, Gujarat, India.

NAIRN, Thom; b. 8 July 1955, Perth, Scotland. Poet; Ed.; Critic; Lecturer. *Education:* MA, Honours, English Literature and Language, 1982, PhD, Scottish Literature, 1991, University of Edinburgh. *Appointments:* Freelance Tutor and Lecturer, Scottish University, and summer schools, 1986–91. *Publications:* The Arts of Alasdair Gray; The Sand Garden; Poems for Bonnie and Josie. Translator: The Complete Poems of George Vafopoulos; Poems, by K. Kyrou; The Simple Method of Three: Architecture of Intimate Space, by A. Stamatis; The Lies of Orestes Cholkiopoulos, by A. Mitson. *Contributions to:* Scotsman; Poetry Wales; Understanding; Chapman; Edinburgh Review, and many more. *Address:* 20A Montgomery St, Edinburgh EH7 5JS, Scotland.

NAKAJIMA, Hojo, (Tani Kukuo); b. 19 March 1935, Fukuoka, Japan. Exec. Adviser; Poet. m. Moto Yasuoka, 13 Dec. 1961, 2 s., 2 d. *Education:* Graduate, Faculty of Law, Kyushu University, 1959. *Appointments:* Chamberlain to the Crown Prince; Master of Ceremonies; Vice-Grand Master of Ceremonies; Special Asst of New Year Poetry Recitation Commission, Imperial Household Agency; Exec. Adviser, Imperial Hotel Ltd; Lecturer of Waka, Bunkyo Gakuin University, Tokyo. *Publications:* Anthologies: Taniguku no Uta, 1990; Yamabiko no Uta, 1991; Amagumo no Uta, 1995; Taniguka wa Utau, 1995; Kyuchu Utakai Hajime, 1995; Shiratori no Uta, 1999. *Contributions to:* Tanka Gendai Magazine; Tanka Shimbun Newspaper; Japan Economic Journal. *Honours:* Commander, Order of the White Rose, Finland, 1986; Grand Officer, Order of Orange Nassau, Netherlands, 1991; Commander, Order of Merit, Portugal, 1993; Grand Officer, Order of the Rio Branco, Brazil, 1996; Commander, Order of National Merit, France, 1996; Grand Officer, Order of the Aztec Eagle of Mexico, Mexico 1997; Hon. DPhil, Clayton University. *Memberships:* Utakai Hajime, committee of IHA, Adviser; Golden Bird Music Society, Kinnotori, adviser. *Address:* 1-14-9-207, Chuo-cho, Meguro-ku, Tokyo, Japan.

NAM CHING TIN. See: WAI MING (OTIS) WONG.

NANGINI, Mary Angela; b. 1 Jan. 1948, Italy. Teacher; Poet; Artist; Theorist. 2 s., 1 d. *Education:* BA, 1971, BEd, 1985, York University, Toronto; BEd, University of Toronto, 1978; MA, University of Connecticut at Storrs, 1988; Doctoral Studies, Ontario Institute for Studies in Education, 1995; MTS, St Augustine Seminary, Toronto, 2000. *Publications:* Woman in Exile (poems), 1991; With a Bang or a Whimper (play, co-author), 1993; My Ontario Beautiful (poems), 1995. *Contributions to:* Anthologies and other publications. *Honour:* Finalist, Rielo Mystical Poetry Prize, 2001. *Memberships:* International Society of Poets; League of Canadian Poets; Pres., Educators of the Gifted in Ontario, 1997–99. *Address:* 42 Brookview Rd, Brampton, Ontario L6X 2V9, Canada.

NANNINI, Gregg; b. 28 June 1961, Detroit, Michigan, USA. Artist; Poet; Ed.; Publisher. *Education:* BA, English, Western Michigan University, Kalamazoo, 1986. *Appointment:* Ed. and Publisher, Kangaroos and Beans, poetry journal, 1990–. *Publications:* The Lost Generation, 1990; Strange Angels, 1993; Pathways, 1994. *Contributions to:* Kangaroos and Beans; Cambio Magazine; Fact Sheet Five; New Hope International; Parnassus of World Poets, 1994; White Wall Review; Magic Mountain; Metro Times; Nocturnal Lyric; National Library of Poetry. *Honour:* Redpath Award for Young Poets, 1990; Knight of Olympoetry. *Memberships:* Artists Against Censorship; Olympoetry. *Address:* 20484 Kinloch, Redford, MI 48240 1115, USA.

NAOMI, French Wallace; b. 17 Aug. 1960, USA. Dramatist; Poet. *Education:* BA, Hampshire College, 1982; MFA, University of Iowa, 1986. *Appointments:* Teacher of Playwriting, University of Iowa, 1990–93; Playwrite-in-Residence, Illinois State University, 1994. *Publications:* Slaughter City (play); In the Heart of America (play); To Dance a Stony Field (poems). *Contributions to:* Reviews, journals, and magazines. *Honours:* The Nation/Discovery Award; Kentucky Arts Council Fellowship; Mobil Playwriting Award; Susan Smith Blackburn Playwriting Award. *Address:* 4575 Highway 6 SE, Iowa City, IA 52240, USA.

NAPELS, Stella. See: VAN DE LAAR, Waltherus Antonius Bernardinus.

NAPIER, (Bernard) Alan; b. 5 June 1945, East Grand Rapids, Michigan, USA. General Man.; Poet. m. Shirley M Elsbury, 5 Sept. 1970, 1 s., 1 d. *Education:* BA, Comparative Literature, Kent State University, 1973.

Contributions to: Reviews, quarterlies, journals and magazines. *Honours:* Finalist, Eve of St Agnes Competition, 1989; National Poetry Competition, 1990. *Memberships:* Acad. of American Poets; Poetry Society of America. *Address:* 3799 Olmsby Dr., Brimfield, OH 44240, USA.

NAPIER, Felicity Anne; b. 15 Dec. 1943, Croydon, Surrey, England. Tutor; Poet; Writer. m. 10 Jan. 1968, 1 d. *Education:* BA, Kingston Polytechnic, 1986; MA, Distinction, Sussex University, 1998. *Contributions to:* Anthologies, reviews and journals. *Honours:* Winner, Redcliffe National Poetry Competition, 1983, Leek Poetry Competition, 1983. *Address:* 10 Sion Row, Twickenham TW1 3DR, England.

NARAYAMA, Fujio; b. 13 June 1948, Iwate, Japan. Writer; Poet. *Education:* Graduate in Drama, Toho Gakuen Junior College, Tokyo, 1970. *Publications:* Manhattan Ballad, 1977; Sanctuary of Evil, 1979; Lay Traps in the Winter, 1981; The Scarred Bullet, 1989; Neverending Night, 1992. *Honours:* Iwate Arts Festival Awards, 1967, 1969; All Yomimono New Writer's Award, 1975. *Memberships:* Japan Writers Asscn; Mystery Writers of America; Mystery Writers of Japan; Sino-Japanese Cultural Exchange Society. *Address:* 2-1-11 Veruzone 2-B, Nukui, Nerima-ku, Tokyo, Japan.

NASH, Susan Smith; b. 2 April 1958, Ardmore, Oklahoma, USA. Geologist; Poet. m. David Nash, 12 Feb. 1982, 1 s. *Education:* BS, 1981, MA, 1989, PhD, 1996, University of Oklahoma. *Publications:* Pornography, 1992; My Love is Apocalypse and Rhinestone, 1993; Veil in the Sand, 1994; Grammar of the Margin Road, 1993; Liquid Babylon, 1994; A Paleontologist's Notebook, 1995; Channel-Surfing the Apocalypse, 1996. *Contributions to:* Washington Review; World Literature Today; Avec; Talisman; Central Park; Another Chicago Magazine; Paper Air. *Honours:* Gertrude Stein Award in Innovative Writing; Goldia Cooksey Prize for Creative Accomplishments. *Address:* 3760 Cedar Ridge Dr., Norman, OK 73072, USA.

NASSAR, Eugene Paul; b. 20 June 1935, Utica, New York, USA. Prof. of English; Writer; Poet. m. Karen Nocian, 30 Dec. 1969, 1 s., 2 d. *Education:* BA, Kenyon College, 1957; Rhodes Scholarship, 1958; MA, Worcester College, Oxford, 1960; PhD, Cornell University, 1962. *Appointments:* Instructor in English, Hamilton College, 1962–64; Asst Prof., 1964–66, Assoc. Prof., 1966–71, Prof. of English, 1971–, Utica College, Syracuse University; Dir, Ethnic Heritage Studies Center. *Publications:* Wallace Stevens: An Anatomy of Figuration, 1965; The Rape of Cinderella: Essays in Literary Continuity, 1970; Selections from a Prose Poem: East Utica, 1971; The Cantos of Ezra Pound: The Lyric Mode, 1975; Wind of the Land: Two Prose Poems, 1979; Essays: Critical and Metacritical, 1983; Illustrations to Dante's Inferno, 1994; A Walk Around the Block: Literary Texts and Social Contexts, 1999. Editor: Several books. *Contributions to:* Various publications. *Honour:* NEA Fellowship, 1972. *Address:* 918 Arthur St, Utica, NY 13501, USA.

NASSAUER, Rudolf; b. 8 Nov. 1924, Frankfurt am Main, Germany. Writer; Poet. *Education:* University of Reading, 1943–45. *Publications:* Poems, 1947; The Holigan, 1959; The Cuckoo, 1962; The Examination, 1973; The Unveiling, 1975; The Agents of Love, 1976; Midlife Feasts, 1977; Reparations, 1981; Kramer's Goats, 1986. *Address:* 51 St James' Gardens, London W11, England.

NATARASAN, Era; b. 8 Dec. 1964, Lalgudi, India. Lecturer in Psychology; Poet. *Education:* Graduate, Physics, 1985; Postgraduate Studies, Psychology, 1988; Diploma, Journalism, 1989. *Contributions to:* Tamil poetry collections and periodicals. *Honour:* Bharati Medal, 1985. *Memberships:* Voice of Tamil Poets; United Writer's Asscn, Chennai; World Poetry Society, USA. *Address:* 23 Renganathan St, Ganeshnagar, Chennai 600032, India.

NATHAN, Leonard (Edward); b. 8 Nov. 1924, Los Angeles, CA, USA. Prof. Emeritus; Poet; Writer; Trans. m. Carol G Nash, 27 June 1949, 1 s., 2 d. *Education:* BA, Highest Honours, 1950, MA, 1951, PhD, 1961, University of California at Berkeley. *Appointments:* Instructor, Modesto Junior College, CA, 1954–60; Prof., 1961–91, Chair., Dept of Rhetoric, 1968–72, Prof. Emeritus, 1991–, University of California at Berkeley. *Publications:* Poetry: Glad and Sorry Seasons, 1963; The Matchmaker's Lament, 1967; The Day the Perfect Speakers Left, 1969; Flight Plan, 1971; Without Wishing, 1973; Coup and Other Poems, 1975; The Likeness: Poems Out of India, 1975; Returning Your Call, 1975; Teachings of Grandfather Fox, 1976; Lost Distance, 1978; Dear Blood, 1980; Holding Patterns, 1982; Carrying On: New and Selected Poems, 1985; The Potato Eaters, 1999. Prose: The Tragic Drama of W B Yeats: Figures in Dance, 1963; The Poet's Work: An Introduction to Czesław Miłosz (with Arthur Quinn), 1991; Diary of a Left-Handed Bird Watcher, 1996. Translator: First Person, Second Person, by 'Agyeya', 1971; Grace and Mercy in Her Wild Hair, by Ramprasad Sen (with Clinton Seely), 1982; Songs of Something Else, by Gunnar Ekelof (with James Larson), 1985; Happy as a Dog's Tail, by Anna Swir (with Czesław Miłosz), 1985; With the Skin, by Aleksander Wat (with Czesław Miłosz), 1989; Talking to My Body, by Anna Swir (with Czesław Miłosz), 1996. *Contributions to:* Reviews, journals, and magazines. *Honours:* Phelan Award for Narrative Poetry, 1955; Longview Foundation Award for Poetry, 1962; Creative Arts Fellowships, University of California, 1963–64, 1973–74; American Institute of Indian Studies Fellowship, 1967–68; National Institute of Arts and Letters Award, 1971; Guggenheim Fellowship, 1976–77;

Commonwealth Club of California, Medals for Poetry, 1976, 1980, 1999. *Address:* 40 Beverly Rd, Kensington, CA 94707, USA.

NAVEH, David; b. 3 June 1922, Manchester, England. Agronomist; Poet. m. 13 Jan. 1956, 2 s. *Education:* Ruppin Agricultural College, Israel. *Publication:* A Rhyme in Time, 1992. *Contributions to:* Periodicals. *Honour:* First Prize for Humour, Reuben Rose International Poetry Competition, 1990. *Memberships:* Israel English Poetry Asscn; Voices Israel. *Address:* Kubbut Kfar Blum, Mobil Post, Upper Galilee 12 150, Israel.

NAVON, Robert; b. 18 May 1954, New York, NY, USA. Ed.; Poet; Writer; Philosopher. *Education:* BA, Lehman College, City University of New York, 1975; MS, State University of New York, Geneseo, 1978; MA studies, New School for Social Research, New York City, 1982–86; PhD candidate, University of New Mexico, 1991–. *Publications:* Patterns of the Universe, 1977; Autumn Songs: Poems, 1983; The Pythagorean Writings, 1986; Healing of Man and Woman, 1989; Harmony of the Spheres, 1991; Cosmic Patterns, Vol. I, 1993; Great Works of Philosophy, 7 vols (ed.). *Honours:* New York State Regents Scholar, 1971; Intern, Platform Asscn, 1980. *Memberships:* Society of Ancient Greek Philosophy; American Philosophical Asscn. *Address:* PO Box 81702, Albuquerque, NM 87198, USA.

NAZKI, Mohammad Farooq; b. 16 Feb. 1940, Madar, Bandipore, Kashmir, India. Civil Servant; Poet; Writer. m. Bilqees Nazki, 19 Oct. 1963, 1 s., 2 d. *Education:* BA, Philosophy, English Literature, History, Persian; Diploma, Indian Music; MA, Urdu, University of Kashmir; Diploma, Television Programme Production, Berlin. *Appointments:* Ed., Daily Mazdoor; Dir, All India Radio, Jammu, Srinagar, and Leh. *Publications:* Poetry: Akhri Khawab Se Pehley (anthology), 1990; Lafz Lafz Nawah, 1994; Naar Hatun Kazil Wanus, 1994; Gaye Rutoon Ke Sathi, 1995; Rashk-E-Urdu, 1996. *Contributions to:* Several publications. *Honours:* Sahitya Akademy Award, 1995; Best Book of Urdu Poetry Award, 1995; Best Book of Kashmiri Poetry Award, 1995. *Membership:* Acad. of Art, Culture and Languages, Jammu and Kashmir. *Address:* 1 Shervani Rd, Srinagar, 190001 Kashmir, India.

NEAL, Herbert. See: EVERS, Jason Harvey.

NEEF, Roger Marie Joseph de; b. 24 June 1941, Wemmel, Belgium. Journalist; Poet. m. Anne-Marie Constance Vanden Wijngaert, 17 Sept. 1977. *Education:* University degree in Contemporary History; University degree in Press and Journalism. *Appointments:* Theatre Critic, BRTN Radio One, 1967–72; Journalist, National Press Agency, Belga, 1972–; Contributor, Literature, Jazz Music and Painting Sections, BRTN, 1977–89. *Publications:* Winterrunen, 1967; Lichaam mijn landing, 1969; De Grote Wolk, 1972; Gestorven Getal, 1977; Gedichten van Licht en Overspel, 1982; De vertelkunst van de bloemen, 1985; De halsband van de duif, 1993; Empty Bed Blues, 1996. *Contributions to:* Nieuw Vlaams Tijdschrift; Dietsche Warande en Belfort; Impuls; De Vlaamse Gids; Kentering; Diogenes. *Honours:* 8 poetry prizes; De Arkprijs van het Vrije Woord, 1978; State Prize for Poetry, 1982–85. *Memberships:* PEN Club Flanders; Asscn of Flemish Authors. *Address:* Hoeve Winterrunen, Lammeneelstraat nr 11, 2220 Heist-op-den-Berg, Belgium.

NEELD, Judith; b. 24 Aug. 1928, Norwood, Massachusetts, USA. Writer; Poet; Ed. m. Richard Neeld, 11 Sept. 1948, 1 s., 1 d. *Education:* Denison University. *Appointments:* Ed., Publisher, Stone Country, magazine of poetry, art and criticism, 1974–90. *Publications:* Scripts for a Life in Three Parts, 1978; Naming the Island, 1988; Sea Fire, 1987; To Fit the Heart Into the Body, 1999. *Contributions to:* Massachusetts Review; Poetry Review; Tar River Poetry; Texas Review; Oxford Magazine; Cincinatti Poetry Review. *Honours:* Emily Dickinson Award, Poetry Society of America, 1985; Bright Hill Press National Poetry Book Award, 1998. *Memberships:* Poetry Society of America; Vineyard Poets. *Address:* PO Box 132, Menemsha, MA 02552, USA.

NEESER, Andreas; b. 25 Jan. 1964, Schlossrued, Switzerland. Teacher; Writer; Poet. *Education:* Graduated, University of Zürich, 1990; Teacher's Diploma, 1994. *Publications:* Schattensprünge (novel), 1995; Treibholz (poems), 1997. *Honours:* Grants. *Memberships:* PEN Switzerland; Swiss Writers Union, Zürich. *Address:* Neugutstrasse 4, 5000 Aargau, Switzerland.

NEILL, William, (Uilleam Neill); b. 22 Feb. 1922, Prestwick, Ayrshire, Scotland. Teacher (retd); Poet; Writer. m. (1), 2 d., (2) Doris Marie Walker, 2 April 1970. *Education:* MA, Honours, University of Edinburgh, 1971; Teacher's Certificate, 1972. *Publications:* Scotland's Castle, 1970; Poems, 1970; Four Points of a Saltire (co-author), 1970; Despatches Home, 1972; Galloway Landscape, 1981; Cnù a Mogail, 1983; Wild Places, 1985; Blossom, Berry, Fall, 1986; Making Tracks, 1991; Straight Lines, 1922; Tales from the Odyssey, 1992; Selected Poems 1969–92, 1994; Caledonian Cramboclink, 2001. *Contributions to:* Various publications, BBC Scotland, and BBC Radio 4. *Honours:* Bardic Crown, National Gaelic MOD, 1969; Sloan Verse Prize, 1970; Grierson Prize, 1970; Scottish Arts Council Book Award, 1985. *Membership:* PEN International, Scottish Branch. *Address:* Burnside, Crossmichael, Castle Douglas, Kirkcudbrightshire DG7 3AP, Scotland.

NELSON, Curtis Scott Jr; b. 28 May 1929, Crowley, LA, USA. Teacher; Poet. m. Elizabeth Elaine Friesen, 30 June 1961, 1 s., 1 d. *Education:* BA, McNeese State College, 1955; MA, Louisiana State University, 1964. *Appointments:* Instructor of English, 1967, Asst Prof. of English, 1969, Assoc. Prof. of English and Counselor in Basic Studies, 1982, McNeese State University. *Publications:* After Summer, 1986; Remnants, 1992; A Biblical Score, 1995; A Baker's Dozen, 1996; Bits and Pieces, 1996; Harvest and Gleanings, 1997; A Gathering of Gnats, 1998. *Contributions to:* The Archer; Newsletter Inago; The Villager; Voices International; Parnassus Literary Journal. *Honours:* First Place, Triton Colleges' All Nation's Poetry Contest, 1980; Second Place, S S Calliope, 1991. *Address:* 977 E Friesen Rd, Lake Charles, LA 70607, USA.

NELSON, Jo; b. 5 Feb. 1946, Del Norte, CO, USA. Teacher; Antiquarian Bookseller; Poet; Writer. *Education:* BA, German, University of Colorado at Boulder, 1968. *Appointment:* Artist-in-Residence, Washington State Arts Commission, 1993–95. *Publication:* Seattle Five Plus One. *Contributions to:* Reviews and journals. *Membership:* Society of Children's Book Writers and Illustrators.

NELSON, Marilyn, (Marilyn Nelson Waniek); b. 26 April 1946, Cleveland, Ohio, USA. Prof. of English; Poet; Trans. 1 s., 1 d. *Education:* BA, University of California at Davis, 1968; MA, University of Pennsylvania, 1970; PhD, University of Minnesota, 1979. *Appointments:* Visiting Asst Prof., Reed College, Portland, Oregon, 1971–72; Asst Prof., St Olaf College, Northfield, Minnesota, 1973–78; Instructor, University of Hamburg, 1977; Asst Prof. to Prof. of English, University of Connecticut at Storrs, 1978–; Faculty, MFA Program, New York University, 1988, 1994, Vermont College, 1991; Elliston Poet-in-Residence, University of Cincinnati, 1994; Writer-in-Residence, Vanderbilt University, 1999; Visiting Prof., US Military Acad., West Point, 2000. *Publications:* For the Body, 1978; The Cat Walked Through the Casserole (with Pamela Espeland), 1984; Mama's Promises, 1985; The Homeplace, 1990; Partial Truth, 1992; Magnificat, 1995; The Fields of Praise: New and Selected Poems, 1997; Carver: A Life in Poems, 2001. *Contributions to:* Books and journals. *Honours:* Kent Fellowship, 1976; National Endowment for the Arts Fellowships, 1981, 1990; Danish Ministry of Culture Grant, 1984; Connecticut Arts Award, 1990; Individual Artist Grant, Connecticut Commission for the Arts, 1990; Finalist in Poetry, National Book Award, 1991, 1997; Annisfield-Wolf Award, 1992; Fulbright Teaching Fellow, 1995; The Poets' Prize, 1999; Contemplative Practices Fellowship, 1999; Finalist in Young Adult Literature, National Book Award, 2001; Boston Globe/Horn Book Award, 2001; Newbery Honor Book, 2002; Coretta Scott King Honor Book, 2002; Flora Stieglitz Strauss Award, 2002; Guggenheim Fellowship, 2001; Poet Laureate, State of Connecticut, 2001–. *Memberships:* Associated Writing Programs; Poetry Society of America; Society for the Study of Multi-Ethnic Literature of the USA; Society for Values in Higher Education. *Address:* c/o Dept of English, University of Delaware, Newark, DE 19716, USA.

NES. See: SAMUELSDOTTIR, Norma Elisabet.

NESBITT, Eleanor Margaret; b. 13 July 1951, Bournemouth, England. University Lecturer; Poet. m. Ram Krishan, 14 July 1990, 1 step-s., 2 step-d. *Education:* MA, Girton College, Cambridge, 1973; PGCE, University of Oxford, 1973–74; MPhil, University of Nottingham, 1980; PhD, University of Warwick, 1995. *Appointments:* Research Fellow, 1986–98, Lecturer, 1998–, University of Warwick. *Contributions to:* Anthologies, including: Break into Print 2, Coventry City Libraries, 1997; Reviews, quarterlies and journals, including: The Friend; University of Warwick Newsletter; Quaker Monthly. *Honour:* Runner-up, Robert Bloomfield Memorial Awards for Rustic Poetry, 1998. *Address:* c/o Institute of Education, University of Warwick, Coventry CV4 7AL, England.

NEVEU, Angéline; b. 2 Sept. 1946, France. Writer; Poet. *Publications:* Synthèse, 1976; Lyrisme télévisé, 1982; Rêve, 1982; Désir, 1985; Le vent se fieau vent, 1994. *Contributions to:* Journals. *Honour:* Bursary, Centre National des Lettres, Paris, 1986. *Membership:* Union des écrivaines et écrivains québecois.

NEVILLE, Tam Lin; b. 2 Nov. 1944, USA. Poet. m. Herbert J Stern, 30 April 1977, 1 d. *Education:* BA, Religion, Temple University, 1968; MFA, Poetry, Vermont College, 1989. *Appointment:* Emerson College, Boston. *Publication:* Journey Lake, 1998. *Contributions to:* American Poetry Review; Ironwood; Massachusetts Review; Indiana Review; Crazyhorse. *Honour:* Individual Artist Fellowship, Indiana Arts Commission, 1990–91. *Address:* 24 Quincy St, Somerville, MA 02143, USA.

NEVZGLIADOVA, Elena Vsevologovna, (Elena Ushakova); b. 2 June 1939, Leningrad, Russia. Poet; Literary Critic. m. Aleksandr Semyonovich Kushner, 1 s. *Education:* Graduate, 1962, PhD, 1974, University of Leningrad. *Publication:* Nochnoe Solntse (A Night Sun), 1991. *Contributions to:* Various publications. *Membership:* Writers' Union. *Address:* Kaluzhskii per 9, Apt 48, St Petersburg 193015, Russia.

NEWCOMB, Robert Wayne; b. 27 June 1933, Glendale, CA, USA. Prof. of Electrical and Computer Engineering; Writer; Poet. m. Sarah E Fritz, 22 May 1954, 1 s., 1 d. *Education:* BS, Purdue University, 1955; MS, Stanford University, 1957; PhD, University of California at Berkeley, 1960. *Appointments:* Asst, Assoc. Prof., Stanford University, 1960–70; Prof. of Electrical Engineering, University of Maryland at College Park, 1970–. *Publications:* Electrical engineering books, all containing some poetry. *Honour:* Endowed the Acad. of American Poets Prize, University of Maryland. *Membership:* Acad. of American Poets. *Address:* c/o Dept of Electrical and Computer Engineering, University of Maryland at College Park, College Park, MD 20742, USA. Email: newcomb@eng.umd.edu. Website: www.ee.umd.edu\newcomb.html.

NEWCOMER, James William; b. 14 March 1912, Gibsonburg, Ohio, USA. College Prof. (retd); Vice Chancellor Emeritus; Writer; Poet. m. 17 Aug. 1946, 1 s., 2 d. *Education:* PhB, Kenyon College; MA, University of Michigan; PhD, University of Iowa. *Publications:* Non-Fiction: Maria Edgeworth the Novelist, 1967; Maria Edgeworth, 1973; The Grand Duchy of Luxembourg, 1984; Lady Morgan the Novelist, 1990; Luxembourg, 1995; The Nationhood of Luxembourg, 1996. Poetry: The Merton Barn Poems, 1979; The Resonance of Grace, 1984. *Contributions to:* Journals and periodicals. *Honours:* Commander, Order of Merit, Hon. Mem., L'Institut Grand-Ducal, Grand Duchy of Luxembourg. *Address:* 1100 Elizabeth Blvd, Fort Worth, TX 76110, USA.

NEWLIN, Margaret Elizabeth Rudd; b. 27 Feb. 1925, New York, NY, USA. College Teacher and Administrator (retd); Poet; Writer. m. Nicholas Newlin, 2 April 1956, 4 s. *Education:* BA, Bryn Mawr College, 1947; PhD, University of Reading, England, 1951. *Publications:* The Fragile Immigrants, 1971; Day of Sirens, 1973; The Snow Falls Upward: Collected Poems, 1976; The Book of Mourning, 1982; Collected Poems 1963–1985, 1986. *Contributions to:* Anthologies and reviews. *Honours:* Gerald and M C Thomas Awards, 1947; National Book Award Nomination, 1976; National Endowment for the Arts Fellowship, 1977; Hon. DLitt, Washington College, 1980. *Membership:* Poetry Society of America. *Address:* Shipley Farm, Secane, PA 19018, USA.

NEWLOVE, John (Herbert); b. 13 June 1938, Regina, Saskatchewan, Canada. Poet. m. Susan Mary Philips, 1966. *Appointments:* Writer-in-Residence, various Canadian institutions, 1974–83; English Ed., Office of the Commissioner of Official Languages, Ottawa, 1986–95. *Publications:* Grave Sirs, 1962; Elephants, Mothers and Others, 1963; Moving in Alone, 1965; Notebook Pages, 1966; Four Poems, 1967; What They Say, 1967; Black Night Window, 1968; The Cave, 1970; Lies, 1972; The Fat Man: Selected Poems 1962–72, 1977; Dreams Surround Us: Fiction and Poetry (with John Metcalf), 1977; The Green Plain, 1981; Three Poems, 1985; The Night the Dog Smiled, 1986; Apology for Absence: Poems Selected and New, 1993. Other: Ed. of various poetry vols. *Honours:* Governor-General's Award for Poetry, 1972; Literary Press Group Award, 1983; Saskatchewan Writers' Guild Founders' Award, 1986; Archibald Lampern Award, 1993. *Address:* Box 71041, RPO L'Esplanade, Ottawa, Ontario K2P 2L9, Canada.

NEWMAN, Leslea; b. 5 Nov. 1955, New York, NY, USA. Writer; Poet; Teacher. *Education:* BS, Education, University of Vermont, 1977; Certificate in Poetics, Naropa Institute, 1980. *Appointment:* Teacher, women's writing workshops. *Publications:* Good Enough to Eat, 1986; Love Me Like You Mean It, 1987; A Letter to Harvey Milk, 1988; Heather Has Two Mommies, 1989; Bubbe Meisehs by Shayneh Maidelehs, 1989; Secrets, 1990; In Every Laugh a Tear, 1992; Writing from the Heart, 1992; Every Woman's Dream, 1994; Fat Chance, 1994; Too Far Away to Touch, 1995; A Loving Testimony: Remembering Loved Ones Lost to AIDS, 1995; The Femme Mystique, 1995; Remember That, 1996; My Lover is a Woman: Contemporary Lesbian Love Poems, 1996; Out of the Closet and Nothing to Wear, 1997; Matzo Ball Moon, 1998; Still Life With Buddy, 1998; Girls Will Be Girls, 2000; Signs of Love, 2000; Cats, Cats, Cats!, 2001; She Loves Me, She Loves Me Not, 2002; Dogs, Dogs, Dogs!, 2002; Runaway Dreidel, 2002; Felicia's Favourite Story, 2002. *Contributions to:* Magazines. *Honour:* Second Place Finalist, Raymond Carver Short Story Competition, 1987; Massachusetts Artists Fellowship in Poetry, 1989; National Endowment for the Arts Fellowship, 1997. *Memberships:* Authors Guild; Authors League of America; Poets and Writers. *Literary Agent:* Elizabeth Harding, Curtis Brown Ltd, 10 Astor Pl., New York, NY 10003, USA. *Address:* PO Box 815, Northampton, MA 01061, USA.

NEWMAN, Michael Philip; b. 27 Nov. 1943, Little Washbourne, England. Poet. m. 10 July 1982, 2 s., 1 d. *Education:* City of Worcester Training College, 1962–65; Hartpury College of Horticulture, 1970–73. *Publications:* 28 Poems, 1964; Blow Hot, Blow Cold, 1966; Paperback Writer, 1980; Poet's World, 1986; Moods and Melodies, 1988; Cotswold Yearbook, 1999; Service for the Living, 1999; The Unquiet Valley, 2000; Clutching Straws in a Hurricane, 2002. *Contributions to:* Many reviews, periodicals and magazines. *Honours:* First Place, Third Half National Ghost Poetry Competition, 1987; First Place, Writers' Rostrum National Poetry Competition Poet of the Year, 1989; First Place, Cheltenham Poetry Society Open Competition, 1990; FAIM Poet of the Year, 1990; Winner, Cheltenham Competitive Festival, 1994, 2000, 2002. *Memberships:* Cheltenham Poetry Society; International Poetry Society; Poetry Foundation. *Address:* 18 Courtiers Dr., Bishops Cleeve, Cheltenham, Gloucestershire GL52 4NU, England.

NEWMAN, Paul Nigel; b. 12 Oct. 1945, Bristol, England. Author; Poet; Ed. *Education:* Weston Super-Mare Technical College, 1960–64; St Paul's College, Cheltenham, 1966–71. *Appointment:* Founder and Ed., Abraxas: A Journal of Literature, Philosophy and Ideas, 1991–. *Publications:* Channel Passage, 1975; The Hill of the Dragon, 1979; Channel Portraits, 1980; Grandeur and Decay, 1981; Somerset Villages, 1986; Bath, 1986; Bristol, 1987; Gods and Graven Images, 1987; Spiders and Outsiders, 1989; The Meads of Love, 1994; Murder as an Antidote for Boredom, 1996; In Many Ways Frogs (poems with A R Lamb,), 1997; Lost Gods of Albion, 1998; A History of Terror, 2000. *Contributions to:* Writers Monthly; Third Stone; British Archaeology; South West Arts; Westwords; Cornish Review; Psychopoetica; Ramraid Extraordinaire; Story Cellar; Dreams from a Strangers Café. *Address:* 57 Eastbourne Rd, St Austell, Cornwall, England.

NI CHUILLEANAIN, Eilean; b. 28 Nov. 1942, Ireland. Lecturer; Writer; Poet. m. Macdara Woods, 27 June 1978, 1 s. *Education:* BA, 1962, MA, 1964, University College, Cork; BLitt, Lady Margaret Hall, Oxford, 1969. *Appointments:* Lecturer in Mediaeval and Renaissance English, Trinity College, Dublin, 1966–; Prof. of American History and Institutions, University of Oxford, 1969–78. *Publications:* Acts and Monuments, 1972; Site of Ambush, 1975; Cork, 1977; The Second Voyage, 1977; The Rose-Geranium, 1981; Irish Women: Image and Achievement (ed.), 1985; The Magdalene Sermon, 1989; The Brazen Serpent, 1994. *Contributions to:* Cyphers Literary Magazine; Journal of Ecclesiastical History; Poems in many magazines. *Honours:* Irish Times Poetry Prize, 1966; Patrick Kavanagh Pize, 1972; O'Shaughnessy Poetry Award, 1992. *Memberships:* Aosdána; Irish Writers Union. *Address:* 2 Quarry Hollow, Headington, Oxford OX3 8JR, England.

NÍ DHOMHNAILL, Nuala (Maire); b. 16 Feb. 1952, St Helens, Lancashire, England. Poet; Dramatist. m. Dogan Leflef, 16 Dec. 1973, 1 s., 3 d. *Education:* BA, English and Irish, 1972, HDipEd, 1973, University College, Cork. *Appointments:* Instructor, Middle East Technical University, Ankara, 1975–80; Writer-in-Residence, University College, Cork, 1992–93; Visiting Prof., New York University, 1998, Villanova University, 2001; John J. Burns Library Visiting Scholar, Boston College, 1998–99. *Publications:* An Dealg Droighinn, 1981; Feár Suaithinseach, 1984; Raven Introductions (with others), 1984; Selected Poems/Rogha Danta, 1986; Pharoah's Daughter, 1990; Feis, 1991; The Astrakhan Cloak, 1992; Jumping Off Shadows: Selected Contemporary Irish Poets (ed. with Greg Delanty), 1995; Cead Aighnis, 1998; In the Heart of Europe: Poems for Bosnia, 1998; The Water Horse, 1999. *Contributions to:* Many anthologies and magazines. *Honours:* Oireachtas Poetry Awards, 1982, 1989, 1990, 1998; Irish Arts Council Awards, 1985, 1988; O'Shaughnessy Poetry Award, Irish-American Foundation, 1988; Ireland Fund Literature Prize, 1991; Gulbenkian Foundation New Horizons Bursary, 1995; Hon. Doctorate, Dublin City University, 1995. *Memberships:* Aosdána; Irish Writers' Union; Poetry Ireland. *Address:* 2 Little Meadow, Pottery Rd, Dun Laoghaire, Co Dublin, Ireland.

NICHOLS, Grace; b. 18 Jan. 1950, Guyana. Writer; Poet. *Education:* University of Guyana, Georgetown. *Publications:* Trust You, Wriggly, 1980; I Is a Long-Memoried Woman, 1983; Leslyn in London, 1984; The Fat Black Woman's Poems, 1984; The Discovery, 1986; Whole of a Morning Sky, 1986; Come On Into My Tropical Garden, 1988; Black Poetry (ed.), 1988; Lazy Thoughts of a Lazy Woman and Other Poems, 1989; Can I Buy a Slice of Sky? (ed.), 1991; No Hickory Dickory Dock (with John Agard), 1991; Give Yourself a Hug, 1994; A Caribbean Dozen (ed.), 1994; SUNRIS, 1996; Asana and the Animals, 1997. *Honours:* Commonwealth Poetry Prize, 1983; Arts Council Bursary, 1988; Guyana Prize for Poetry, 1996. *Address:* c/o Curtis Brown Ltd, Haymarket House, 28/29 Haymarket, London SW1Y 4SP, England.

NICHOLS, Pamela Amber McCurdy; b. 25 June 1956, Columbus, Ohio, USA. Poet. m. Jerry Lee Nichols, 26 June 1974, 1 s., 1 d. *Education:* Nursing degree, 1994. *Publications:* After the Battle, 1979; Touch the Sun, 1982; Lampslight, 1986; Oh Beloved, My Beloved, 1987; For My Persecuted Brethren, 1988; Wedding Song, 1989. *Contributions to:* Magazines. *Honours:* Awards of Merit, 1986, 1987, 1988. *Membership:* National Society of Published Poets. *Address:* 46430 Buckio Rd, Woodsfield, OH 43793, USA.

NICK, Dagmar; b. 30 May 1926, Breslau, Germany. Writer; Poet. *Education:* Psychology and Graphology studies, Munich, 1947–50. *Publications:* Poetry: Martyrer, 1947; Das Buch Hulofernes, 1955; In den Ellipsen des Mondes, 1959; Zeugnis und Zeichen, 1969; Fluchtlinien, 1978; Gezählte Tage, 1986; Im Stillstand der Stunden, 1991; Gewendete Masken, 1996; Trauer ohne Tabu, 1999; Wegmarken, 2000; Liebesgedichte, 2001. Prose: Einladung nach Israel, 1963; Rhodos, 1967; Israel gestern und heute, 1968; Sizilien, 1976; Götterinseln der Ägäis, 1981; Medea, ein Monolog, 1988; Lilith, eine Metamorphose, 1992; Jüdisches Wirken in Breslau, 1998; Penelope, eine Erfahrung, 2000. *Contributions to:* Reviews and periodicals. *Honours:* Liliencron Prize, Hamburg, 1948; Eichendorff Prize, 1966; Roswitha Medal, 1977; Kulturpreis Schlesien des Landes Niedersachsen, 1986; Andreas Gryphius Prize, 1993; Silbermedaille 'München leuchtet' des Landeshauptstadt München, 2001; Jakob-Wassermann-Literaturpreis der Stadt Fürth, 2002. *Memberships:* Asscn of German Writers; PEN Club. *Address:* Kuglmüllerstrasse 22, 80638 Munich, Germany.

NICOL, Michael George; b. 17 Nov. 1951, Cape Town, South Africa. Writer; Poet; Journalist. 1 s., 1 d. *Education:* BA, Honours, University of South Africa, 1993. *Appointments:* Reporter, To The Point, Johannesburg, 1974–76, The Star, Johannesburg, 1976–79; Ed., African Wildlife, Johannesburg, 1979–81; Freelance Journalist, 1981–85; Asst to the Ed., Leadership, Cape Town, 1986–88; Writer, Journalist, 1989–. *Publications:* Among the Souvenirs (poems), 1979; The Powers That Be (novel), 1989; A Good-Looking Corpse (history), 1991; This Day and Age (novel), 1992; This Sad Place (poems), 1993; Horseman (novel), 1994; The Waiting Country (memoir), 1995; The Ibis Tapestry (novel), 1998; Bra Henry (novella for young adults), 1998; The Invisible Line: The Life and Photography of Ken Oosterbroek (biography), 1998. *Contributions to:* The Guardian; New Statesman; London Magazine. *Honour:* Ingrid Jonker Award, 1980.

NIDITCH, B(arry); b. 8 Jan. 1943, Boston, Massachusetts, USA. Poet; Writer. *Education:* Graduated, Boston University, 1965. *Appointment:* Artistic Dir, The Original Theatre. *Publications:* Elements, 1980; Freedom Trail, 1980; A Boston Winter, 1982; A Musical Collection, 1984; Unholy Empire, 1982; Exile, 1986; Ink Dreams, 1986; On the Eve, 1989; Milton: Poems by B Z Niditch, 1992. *Contributions to:* Encounter; Nottingham Poetry Review; Poetry Review; New Letters; Orbis; Writers Forum; New Hope International; International Poetry Review; Takahe; Denver Quarterly; Webster Review; Fiddlehead; Antigonish Poetry Review; Real Liberales; Miorita; Boston Globe; Midstream; Hawaii Review; Minnesota Review; Ariel; Old Hickory Review; Pittsburgh Quarterly. *Honours:* First Prize, Bitterroot International Poetry Journal; Heershe David Badonneh Prize. *Membership:* New England Poetry Club. *Address:* PO Box 1664, Brookline, MA 02146, USA.

NIELSEN, Pia Moeller; b. 5 Dec. 1956, Randers, Denmark. University Drama Teacher; Poet. *Education:* CandPhil, University of Århus, 1985. *Publication:* Hoejsang, 1992. *Contributions to:* Many publications. *Membership:* Danish Writers' Union.

NIEMINEN, Kai Tapani; b. 11 May 1950, Helsinki, Finland. Poet; Trans. m. 1991, 1 d. *Education:* Philosophy and Musicology, 1970–72; Private studies in Japanese, 1971. *Publications:* 14 books of poetry, 1971–97; Several trans from Japanese poetry and drama. *Contributions to:* Various publications. *Honour:* National Literary Awards, Ministry of Culture, 1986, 1990. *Memberships:* Authors Society; Finnish PEN, pres., 1991–94. *Address:* Baggböle 99 A, 07740 Gammelby, Finland.

NIGAM, Jyoti; b. 23 Sept. 1947, New Delhi, India. Poet; Artist. m. P K Nigrm, 1 June 1967, 1 d. *Education:* MA, Painting, Kanpur University, 1972; Diploma in Commercial Arts, 1978, Diploma in Textile Designing, 1982, Delhi Administration. *Appointments:* Lecturer, Vocational Training College, South Extension, New Delhi. *Publications:* Over 200 poems in English. *Contributions to:* Asian Age; Poets International; Replica. *Honours:* Several. *Address:* 40/117 Parade, Kanpur UP 208001, India.

NIGHTINGALE, Barbra Evans; b. 6 Aug. 1949, Chicago, IL, USA. Prof. of English; Poet. m. Preston S Nightingale, 23 Nov. 1977, 1 d. *Education:* BS, Health Administration, 1980; MA, English, 1985; DEd, Education, 1991. *Appointments:* Assoc. Prof., 1983–97, Prof., 1997–, Broward Community College. *Publications:* Lovers Never Die, 1981; Prelude to a Woman, 1986; Lunar Equations, 1993; Florida in Poetry, 1995. *Contributions to:* Kansas Quarterly; The Poet; Cumberlands; Florida Review; Red Light/Blue Light; Visions; Coy Dog Review; Plametto Review; South Florida Poetry Review; Miami Herald; Sun Sentinel; Others. *Honours:* Grand Prize, National Federation of State Poetry Societies, 1991; James L Knight Endowed Teaching Chair, 1997. *Memberships:* Poetry Society of America; Poets and Writers; Acad. of American Poets; National Federation of State Poetry Societies; Florida State Poets; South Florida Poetry Institute; Writer's Voice. *Address:* 2231 N 52nd Ave, Hollywood, FL 33021, USA.

NIGHTRIDER, Johanny. See: BLAZEK, Joseph Lawrence.

NILSEN, Richard Haldor; b. 20 Jan. 1948, Gloversville, New York, USA. Mental Health Dir; Poet. m. Lynda Joy Canary, 23 Aug. 1969, 1 s., 2 d. *Education:* BA, English Literature, Houghton College, New York; MA, English Literature, MFA, Creative Writing, University of Arkansas. *Contributions to:* Magazines and periodicals. *Membership:* Poets and Writers. *Address:* 180 County Highway 142A, Johnstown, NY 12095, USA.

NINI, Taco. See: SEGUI BENNASSAR, Antoni.

NISBET, Jim; b. 20 Jan. 1947, USA. Writer; Poet. *Publications:* Poems for a Lady, 1978; Gnachos for Bishop Berkeley, 1980; The Gourmet (novel), 1980; Morpho (with Alaistair Johnston), 1982; The Visitor, 1984; Lethal Injection (novel), 1987; Death Puppet (novel), 1989; Laminating the Conic Frustum, 1991; Small Apt, 1992; Ulysses' Dog, 1993; Sous le Signe de la Razoir, 1994. *Address:* c/o William Morris Agency, 1350 Avenue of the Americas, New York, NY 10019, USA.

NISHIKAWA, Morio; b. 24 May 1943, Kobe, Japan. Prof. of English and Linguistics; Poet. m. Sumiko Nishikawa, 3 May 1981. *Education:* BA, Kobe University of Foreign Studies, 1967; MA, Osaka University, 1969. *Appointments:* Asst Teacher, 1969–77, Assoc. Prof., 1977–88, Prof., 1988–, Kumamoto University. *Publications:* Han-Getsu (Half Moon), 1980; Gyoka-Soushitsu (Loss of The Songs of Fish), 1983; Kotozute (Message), 1989. *Contributions to:* Ed., poetry periodical, Genzai; Poetry magazine, Shi to Shisou; Newspaper, Kumamoto Nichi-Nichi Shimbun. *Memberships:* Poetry Society; Modern Poetry Forum, Kumamoto, founder, 1987–. *Address:* Dept of English, Kumamoto University, Kyoo-iku-Gakubu, 2-40-1 Kurokami, Kumamoto City 860, Japan.

NITCHIE, George Wilson; b. 19 May 1921, Chicago, IL, USA. Prof. of English Emeritus; Writer; Poet. m. Laura Margaret Woodard, 19 Jan. 1947, 3 d. *Education:* BA, Middlebury College, 1953; MA, 1947, PhD, 1958, Columbia University. *Appointments:* Instructor, 1947–50, Asst Prof., 1950–59, Assoc. Prof., 1959–66, Prof. of English, 1966–86, Chair., Dept of English, 1972–79, Prof. Emeritus, 1986–, Simmons College. *Publications:* Human Values in the Poetry of Robert Frost, 1960; Marianne Moore: An Introduction to the Poetry, 1969. *Contributions to:* Various critical essays in scholarly journals and poems in many publications. *Membership:* American Asscn of University Profs. *Address:* 50 Pleansantview Ave, Weymouth, MA 02188, USA.

NIXON, Colin Harry; b. 9 March 1939, London, England. Poet; Writer. m. Betty Morgan, 2 Sept. 1967, 3 d. *Education:* Diploma, Sociology, University of London, 1968. *Appointments:* Civil Servant, 1960–99; Disablement Resettlement Officer, 1974–83; ACAS Conciliation Officer, 1983–99. *Publications:* Roads, 1975; Geography of Love, 1977; With All Angles Equal, 1980; The Bright Idea, 1983. *Contributions to:* Anthologies, including: Spongers, 1984; Affirming Flame, 1989; Poetry Street 3, 1991; Red Candle Treasury, 1948–1998, 1998; The Art of Haiku 2000, 2000; Periodicals, including: Outposts; Tribune; Countryman; Cricketer. *Honours:* George Camp Memorial Poetry Prizes, 1975, 1983. *Address:* 72 Barmouth Rd, Wandsworth Common, London SW18 2DS, England.

NOBLESS, H. E. See: CRIPPS, Joy Beaudette.

NOCERINO, Kathryn; b. 6 Feb. 1947, New York, NY, USA. Poet; Reviewer; Ed. *Education:* BFA, Cooper Union, 1968; MSW, Hunter College, 1972. *Appointments:* Poetry Reviewer, Home Planet News, WIN; Guest Contributing Ed., Manhattan Poetry Review, 1983–84. *Publications:* Wax Lips, 1980; Candles in the Daytime, 1986; Death of the Plankton Bar and Grill, 1987. *Contributions to:* Abraxas; Contact/II; Telephone; Calliope; Home Planet News; Street; Joe Soap's Canoe, UK. *Memberships:* Poetry Society of America; Poets and Writers. *Address:* 139 W 19th St Apt 2B, New York, NY 10011, USA.

NOGUCHI, Rick; b. 29 June 1967, Los Angeles, CA, USA. Poet. m. Deneen Jenks, 29 Feb. 1966, 1 d. *Education:* BA, California State University at Long Beach; MFA, Arizona State University. *Publications:* The Wave He Caught, 1991; The Ocean Inside Kenji Takezo, 1995. *Address:* c/o University of Pittsburgh Press, 3347 Forbes Ave, Pittsburgh, PA 15261, USA.

NOGUERE, Suzanne; b. 1 Dec. 1947, New York, NY, USA. Poet; Children's Writer. m. Henry Grinberg, 5 June 1983. *Education:* BA, magna cum laude, Philosophy, Barnard College, Columbia University, 1969. *Publications:* Whirling Round the Sun (poems), 1996. Other: Little Koala (children's); Little Raccoon (children's). *Contributions to:* Anthologies, reviews, and journals. *Honours:* Gertrude B. Claytor Memorial Award, Poetry Society of America, 1989; Discovery/The Nation Award, 1996. *Address:* 27 W 96th St, Apt 12B, New York, NY 10025, USA.

NOLAN, William F(rancis), (Frank Anmar, Mike Cahill, F E Edwards, Michael Phillips); b. 6 March 1928, Kansas City, Missouri, USA. Writer; Poet. *Education:* Kansas City Art Institute, 1946–47; San Diego State College, 1947–48; Los Angeles City College, 1953. *Publications:* Numerous books, including: Barney Oldfield, 1961; Phil Hall: Yankee Champion, 1962; Impact 20 (stories), 1963; John Huston: King Rebel, 1965; Sinners and Superman, 1965; Death is for Losers, 1968; Dashiell Hammett: A Casebook, 1969; Alien Horizons (stories), 1974; Hemingway: Last Days of the Lion, 1974; Wonderworlds (stories), 1977; Hammett: A Life on the Edge, 1983; Things Beyond Midnight (stories), 1984; Dark Encounters (poems), 1986; Logan: A Trilogy, 1986; How to Write Horror Fiction, 1990; Six in Darkness (stories), 1993; Night Shapes (stories), 1993. *Address:* c/o Loni Perkins Assocs Literary Agency, 301 W 53rd St, New York, NY 10019, USA.

NONGKYNRIH, Kynpham Singh; b. 4 April 1964, Cherrapunjee, India. Poet. m. Rubina Khongwir, 23 Dec. 1992, 1 s., 2 d. *Education:* MA, English, North Eastern Hills University, 1987–89. *Appointments:* Auditor, Office of the Accountant General, Government of India, Shillong, 1987–90; Lecturer in English, Sankardev College, Shillong, 1990; Publication Officer, North Eastern Hill University, Shillong, 2001. *Publications:* Moments, 1992; The Sieve, 1992. *Contributions to:* Chandrabhaga; Indian Literature; Literature Alive; Poiesis; Kavya Bharati; Femina; New Welsh Review; Swag Mag. *Honour:*

Short-listed, American Poetry Asscn Poetry Contest, 1992, International Library of Poetry. *Memberships:* Poetry Society of India; Shillong Poetry Society, secretary, 1995–. *Address:* 'Neer', Lawmali Rd, Shillong, Meghalaya 793001, India.

NOORIALA, Partow, (Derakhshandeh Haghdoust); b. 11 Nov. 1946, Tehran, Iran. Poet; Literary Critic. m. Mouhamad Ali Sepanlou, divorced, 1 s., 1 d. *Education:* BA, Philosophy, Tehran University, 1970; MS, Social Work Management, Allameh Tabatabai University, 1978. *Appointments:* Human Resource Planner, Ministry of Art and Culture, 1971; Social Worker, Javadieh Welfare Center, Tehran, 1976; Part-time Philosophy Teacher, Tehran University, 1979; First female publisher in Iran, Damaavand Publications, Tehran, 1983; Jury Interviewer, Los Angeles County Superior Court, Jury Division, 1989–. *Publications:* The Share of the Years, 1979; From the Eyes of the Wind, 1987; My Earth Altered, 1993; Two Critiques (collection of book reviews), 1986; Art and Awareness (essays and literary criticism), 1999; Selected Poems, 2000. *Contributions to:* Numerous magazines and journals. *Address:* 1001 Productions, 914 Westwood Blvd, PO Box 583, Los Angeles, CA 90024; 12157 Moorpark St, No. 206, Studio City, CA 91604, USA.

NORDBRANDT, Henrik; b. 21 March 1945, Copenhagen, Denmark. Poet; Writer. *Education:* Oriental, Chinese, Persian, Turkish, and Arabic studies. *Publications:* 18 books of poetry, including several in English trans. *Contributions to:* Journals and magazines. *Honours:* Many literary awards, including: Danish Acad. Prize; Danish Critics' Prize for Best Book of the Year; Life Grant of Honour, Danish State. *Address:* Plaza Santa Cruz 9, 29700 Velez-Malaga, Spain.

NORMAN, John; b. 20 July 1912, Syracuse, New York, USA. Prof. Emeritus; Writer; Poet. m. Mary Lynott, 28 Dec. 1948, 4 d. *Education:* BA, 1935, MA, 1938, Syracuse University; PhD, Clark University, 1942. *Publications:* Edward Gibbon Wakefield: A Political Reappraisal, 1963; Labor and Politics in Libya and Arab Africa, 1965; Life Lines: A Volume of Verse, 1997. *Contributions to:* Anthologies, reference books, and journals. *Honour:* World Poetry Prize, 1991. *Address:* 94 Cooper Rd, John's Pond, Ridgefield, CT 06877, USA.

NORMAN, Thomas. See: HARVEY, Marshall L.

NORRELL, Gregory T.; b. 24 Nov. 1960, Tallahassee, FL, USA. Writer; Poet; Publisher. m. Karen Norrell, 1980, divorced 1995, 1 s., 1 d. *Education:* BS, State University of West Georgia, 1985; PhD, State University of New York at Albany, 1989. *Appointments:* Publisher, Dandelion Press and Dandelion Media, Idaho Falls, 1955–; Owner, Dandelion Studios, Dandelion Multimedia Recording Division. *Publications:* 'Til Death Do Us Part (short stories), 1997; 95 Windows: An Unofficial Poetry Collection from the Microsoft Network, 1997; Amongst the Shadows (poems), 1997; The River of No Return (novel), 1998; Impact (novel), 1999. *Memberships:* Acad. of American Poets; Web Poets Society, founder. *Address:* 1935 E 113 South St, Idaho Falls, ID 83404, USA. *E-mail:* dandelion@dandelion-multimedia.com.

NORRIS, Kathleen; b. 27 July 1947, Washington, DC, USA. Poet; Writer. m. David J Dwyer. *Education:* BA, Bennington College, 1969. *Appointments:* Poet-in-Residence, North Dakota Arts Council, 1979–92; Oblate, Benedictine Order, 1986–. *Publications:* Poetry: Falling Off, 1971; From South Dakota: Four Poems, 1978; The Middle of the World, 1981; How I Came to Drink My Grandmother's Piano: Some Benedictine Poems, 1989; The Year of Common Things, 1990; The Astronomy of Love, 1994; Little Girls in Church, 1995. Other: Dakota: A Spiritual Geography, 1993; The Cloister Walk, 1996; Amazing Grace: A Vocabulary of Faith, 1998; The Quotidian Mysteries, 1998. Editor: Leaving New York: Writers Look Back, 1995. *Contributions to:* Anthologies and periodicals. *Honours:* Big Table Poetry Series Younger Poets Award, 1971; Creative Artists Public Service Programme Grant, New York State, 1972; Fine Arts Work Centre Fellowship, Provincetown, Massachusetts, 1972; Bush Foundation Grant, 1993; Guggenheim Foundation Grant, 1994; Western Libraries Asscn Award, 1995. *Memberships:* National Book Critics Circle; Poetry Society of America. *Address:* PO Box 570, Lemmon, SD 57638, USA.

NORRIS, Ken; b. 3 April 1951, New York, NY, USA. Prof. of Canadian Literature; Poet. 2 d. *Education:* BA, State University of New York at Stony Brook, 1972; MA, Concordia University, 1975; PhD, McGill University, 1980. *Appointment:* Prof. of Canadian Literature, University of Maine, 1985–. *Publications:* Vegetables, 1975; The Perfect Accident, 1978; Autokinesis, 1980; Whirlwinds, 1983; The Better Part of Heaven, 1984; Islands, 1986; Report: Books 1–4, 1988, 8–11, 1993; In the House of No, 1991; Full Sun: Selected Poems, 1992; The Music, 1995; Odes, 1997; Limbo Road, 1998. *Contributions to:* Various reviews, journals, and periodicals. *Honours:* Third Prize, CBC Literary Competition, 1986. *Memberships:* League of Canadian Poets; Writers' Union of Canada. *Address:* c/o Dept of English, University of Maine, 5752 Neville Hall, Room 304, Orono, ME 04469, USA.

NORRIS, Leslie; b. 21 May 1921, Merthyr Tydfil, Wales. Prof.; Poet; Writer. m. Catherine Mary Morgan, 1948. *Education:* MPhil, University of Southampton, 1958. *Appointments:* Principal Lecturer, West Sussex Institute of Education, 1956–74; Prof., Brigham Young University, Provo, Utah, 1981–.

Publications: Tongue of Beauty, 1941; Poems, 1944; The Loud Winter, 1960; Finding Gold, 1964; Ransoms, 1970; Mountains, Polecats, Pheasants and Other Hegies, 1973; Selected Poems, 1986; Collected Poems, 1996. *Contributions to:* Various publications. *Honours:* British Arts Council Award, 1964; Alice Hunt Bartlett Prize, 1969; Cholmondeley Poetry Prize, 1979; Katherine Mansfield Award, 1981. *Memberships:* RSL, fellow; Welsh Acad., fellow. *Address:* 849 S Carterville Rd, Orem, UT 84058, USA.

NORSE, Harold George; b. 6 July 1916, New York, NY, USA. Prof.; Writer; Poet. *Education:* BA, Brooklyn College, 1938; MA, New York University, 1951. *Appointments:* Instructor, Cooper Union College, New York, 1949–52, Lion School of English, Rome, Italy, 1956–57, United States Information Service School, Naples, Italy, 1958–59; Instructor in Creative Writing, San Jose State University, CA, 1973–75; Prof. in Creative Writing, New College of California, 1994–95. *Publications:* The Roman Sonnets of Giuseppe Gioacchino Belli (trans.), 1960; Karma Circuit (poems), 1967; Hotel Nirvana (poems), 1974; Carnivorous Saint (poems), 1977; Mysteries of Magritte (poems), 1984; Love Poems, 1986; Memoirs of a Bastard Angel (autobiography), 1989; Seismic Events (poems), 1993. *Contributions to:* Journals and magazines. *Honours:* National Endowment for the Arts Fellowship, 1974; R H de Young Museum Grant, 1974; Lifetime Achievement Award in Poetry, National Poetry Asscn, 1991. *Membership:* PEN. *Address:* 157 Albion St, San Francisco, CA 94110, USA.

NORTH, Charles Laurence; b. 9 June 1941, New York, NY, USA. Poet; Prof. of English. m. 2 June 1963, 1 s., 1 d. *Education:* BA, Tufts University, 1962; MA, Columbia University, 1964. *Appointment:* Poet-in-Residence, Pace University. *Publications:* Lineups, 1972; Elizabethan and Nova Scotian Music, 1974; Six Buildings, 1977; Leap Year, 1978; Gemini (co-author), 1981; The Year of the Olive Oil, 1989; No Other Way: Selected Prose, 1998; New and Selected Poems, 1999; The Nearness of the Way You Look Tonight, 2001. *Contributions to:* Paris Review; Sulfur; Poetry (Chicago); New American Writing; O-blek; Literary Review; Columbia; United Artists; Transfer; Adventures in Poetry; Pequod; Hanging Loose; Best American Poetry, 1995, 2002. *Honours:* Poets Foundation Award, 1972; National Endowment for the Arts Fellowship, 1979; Fund for Poetry Awards, 1987, 1989, 1998; National Endowment for the Arts Fellowship, 2001. *Membership:* PEN. *Address:* 251 W 92nd St, No. 12E, New York, NY 10025, USA.

NORTH, Michael (Thomas), (Mick North); b. 3 Aug. 1958, Lancaster, England. Arts Man.; Poet. m. Jani Howker, 15 Oct. 1988, 1 s. *Education:* Foundation Course in Art and Design, Wolverhampton Polytechnic, 1977–78; Studies in Fine Art. *Publications:* Throp's Wife, 1986; The Pheasant Plucker's Son, 1990. *Contributions to:* Anthologies, reviews, and magazines. *Honour:* Eric Gregory Award, 1986. *Memberships:* Arvon Foundation at Lumb Bank; Poetry Society; Northern Asscn of Writers in Education. *Address:* The Cottage, Cumwhitton, Carlisle, Cumbria CA4 9EX, England.

NORWOOD, Victor G(eorge) C(harles); b. 21 March 1920, Lincolnshire, England. Poet; Writer; Dramatist. *Appointments:* Managing Dir, Westcliff Literary Agency, 1947–77. *Publications:* The Know-How of Prospecting, 1976; A Guide to General Prospecting, 1977; Walkabout, 1977; Tressidy's Last Case, 1977; Where the River Ends, 1978; Holocaust, 1978; The Beast of Bulgallon, 1978; Diamonds are Forever, 1979; Sapphire Seekers, 1979; Venom, 1980; A Lifetime of Cheating Death, 1980; Miracles of Cardiac Surgery, 1980; Across Australia by Volkswagen, 1980. *Address:* 194 W Common Lane, Westcliff, Scunthorpe DN17 1PD, England.

NOSINOVICH, Rachel; b. 24 June 1931, Buenos Aires, Argentina. Poet. m. Chaim Nosinovich, 14 Feb. 1962, 3 s., 2 d. *Education:* Completed Teacher Training College, Buenos Aires, 1951; Student, Kibbutz Sem Oranim. *Publications:* Poetry: Awakening the Gleam to Come as a Storm, 1984; Walking in the Fields of the Future, 1985; Jewish Songs and Memories, 1985; National Resurrection, 1986; Thistle and Thorn, 1987; Equal Rights, 1987; Between Lights and Shadows, 1988; Our Spiritual Home at its Smallest, 1990; Deserting This Land, 1990; My Folk and My Dreams, 1990; The Floral Children, 1991; The Dread of the Holocaust, 1992; All Became Sand, 1992; My Dream Comes True, 1993. *Address:* Hozaat Saar, Imanuel Blvd 15, POB 26243, Tel-Aviv, Israel.

NOTLEY, Alice; b. 8 Nov. 1945, Bisbee, AZ, USA. Poet; Writer. m. (1) Ted Berrigan, 1972, deceased 1983, 2 s., (2) Douglas Oliver, 10 Feb. 1988. *Education:* BA, Barnard College, 1967; MFA, University of Iowa, 1969. *Publications:* Poetry: 165 Meeting House Lane, 1971; Phoebe Light, 1973; Incidentals in the Days World, 1973; For Frank O'Hara's Birthday, 1976; Alice Ordered Me to be Made: Poems 1975, 1976; A Diamond Necklace, 1977; Songs for the Unborn Second Baby, 1979; When I Was Alive, 1980; Waltzing Matilda, 1981; How Spring Comes, 1981; Three Zero, Turning Thirty (with Andrei Codrescu), 1982; Sorrento, 1984; Margaret and Dusty, 1985; Parts of a Wedding, 1986; At Night the States, 1988; Selected Poems of Alice Notely, 1993. Other: Doctor Williams' Heiresses: A Lecture, 1980; Tell Me Again, 1981; Homer's 'Art', 1990; The Scarlet Cabinet: A Compendium of Books (with Douglas Oliver), 1992. *Contributions to:* Various publications. *Honours:* National Endowment for the Arts Grant, 1979; Poetry Center Award, 1981;

General Electric Foundation Award, 1983; Fund for Poetry Awards, 1987, 1989. *Address:* 101 St Mark's Pl., No. 12A, New York, NY 10009, USA.

NOVAK, Lela. See: NOVAKOVIC, Mileva.

NOVAKOVIC, Mileva, (Lela Novak); b. 7 Sept. 1938, Zagreb, Yugoslavia. Business Man.; Poet. m. Svetozar Novakovic, 21 Feb. 1959, 1 s., 1 d. *Education:* Pitman's College; Premier School of Journalism, London. *Contributions to:* Various anthologies, newspapers, and magazines. *Honours:* Special mentions. *Memberships:* British Acad. of Songwriters, Composers and Authors; Poetry Society; International Society of Poets. *Address:* 39 The Ridgeway, Gunnersbury Park, London W3 8LW, England.

NOYES, Stanley Tinning; b. 7 April 1924, San Francisco, CA, USA. Writer; Poet. m. Nancy Black, 12 March 1949, 2 s., 1 d. *Education:* BA, English, 1950, MA, English, 1951, University of California, Berkeley. *Publications:* No Flowers for a Clown (novel), 1961; Shadowbox (novel), 1970; Faces and Spirits (poems), 1974; Beyond the Mountains (poems), 1979; The Commander of Dead Leaves (poems), 1984; Los Comanches: The Horse People, 1751–1845, 1993; Comanches in the New West: Historic Photographs, 1895–1908, 1999. *Contributions to:* Reviews and quarterlies. *Honour:* MacDowell Fellow, 1967. *Membership:* PEN American Center. *Address:* 634 E Garcia, Santa Fe, NM 87505, USA.

NUMMI, Lassi; b. 9 Oct. 1928, Helsinki, Finland. Author; Poet; Journalist; Literary Ed. m. Pirkko Aho, 22 Feb. 1959, 2 s. *Education:* University of Helsinki, 1948–54. *Publications:* 29 books, 1949–2000, including: Collected Poems, 1978, 1998; Requiem, 1990; Grandfather's Poems, 1999; Mediterranean, 2000. *Contributions to:* Uusi Suomi newspaper; Nykypäivä newspaper. *Honours:* State Literary Prizes, 1950, 1964, 1968, 1978, 1983; Pro Finlandia Medal, 1972; Hon. PhD, 1986; Savonia Prize, 1990; Suometar Journalist Prize, 1990; State Prof. of Art, 1990–95; Hon. DTh, 2000. *Memberships:* Finnish Writers' Union, pres., 1969–72, hon. mem., 1982–; PEN Centre Finland, pres., 1983–88. *Address:* Ulvilantie 11 BA, 00350 Helsinki, Finland.

NUQUI, Efren Banez. See: FERNANDEZ, Querubin D. Jr.

NUTTALL, Jeffrey; b. 8 July 1933, Clitheroe, Lancashire, England. Artist; Writer; Poet; Teacher. Divorced, 5 s., 1 d. *Education:* Intermediate Examination, Arts and Crafts, Hereford School of Art, 1951; NDD, Painting, Special Level, Bath Acad. of Art, Corsham, 1953; ATD, Institute of Education, University of London, 1954. *Appointments:* Lecturer, Bradford College of Art, 1968–70; Senior Lecturer, Leeds Polytechnic, 1970–81; Head, Dept of Fine Arts, Liverpool Polytechnic, 1981–84; Numerous painting exhibitions; Occasional radio and television broadcasts. *Publications:* Poetry: Objects, 1973; Sun Barbs, 1974; Grape Notes/Apple Music, 1979; Scenes and Dubs, 1987; Mad with Music, 1987. Fiction: The Gold Hole, 1968; Snipe's Spinster, 1973; The Patriarchs, 1975; Anatomy of My Father's Corpse, 1976; What Happened to Jackson, 1977; Muscle, 1980; Teeth, 1994. Non-Fiction: King Twist: A Portrait of Frank Randle, 1978; Performance Art, Vol. I, Memoirs, 1979, Vol. II, Scripts, 1979; The Pleasures of Necessity, 1989; The Bald Soprano, 1989. *Contributions to:* Newspapers and journals. *Honour:* Third winner, Novel in a Day Competition, Grovcho Club, 1994. *Address:* 71 White Hart Lane, Barnes, London SW13 0PP, England.

NYE, Robert; b. 15 March 1939, London, England. Poet; Writer; Dramatist; Critic; Trans. m. (1) Judith Pratt, 1959, divorced 1967, 3 s., (2) Aileen Campbell, 1968, 1 d., 1 step-s., 1 step-d. *Education:* Southend High School, Essex. *Appointment:* Poetry Critic, The Times, 1971–96. *Publications:* Poetry: Juvenilia 1, 1961; Juvenilia 2, 1963; Darker Ends, 1969; Agnus Dei, 1973; Two Prayers, 1974; Five Dreams, 1974; Divisions on a Ground, 1976; A Collection of Poems, 1955–1988, 1989; 14 Poems, 1994; Henry James and Other Poems, 1995; Collected Poems, 1995. Fiction: Doubtfire, 1967; Tales I Told My Mother, 1969; Falstaff, 1976; Merlin, 1978; Faust, 1980; The Voyage of the Destiny, 1982; The Facts of Life and Other Fictions, 1983; The Memoirs of Lord Byron, 1989; The Life and Death of My Lord Gilles de Rais, 1990; Mrs Shakespeare: The Complete Works, 1993; The Late Mr Shakespeare, 1998. Plays: Sawney Bean (with William Watson), 1970; The Seven Deadly Sins: A Mask, 1974; Three Plays: Penthesilia, Fugue, and Sisters, 1976. Editor: A Choice of Sir Walter Ralegh's Verse, 1972; William Barnes of Dorset: A Selection of His Poems, 1973; A Choice of Swinburne's Verse, 1973; The English Sermon, 1750–1850, 1976; The Faber Book of Sonnets, 1976; PEN New Poetry 1, 1986; First Awakenings: The Early Poems of Laura Riding (co-ed.), 1992; A Selection of the Poems of Laura Riding, 1994. Other: Trans and children's books. *Contributions to:* The Times; The Scotsman; Periodicals, magazines and journals in the UK and USA. *Honours:* Eric Gregory Award, 1963; Arts Council Bursaries, 1970, 1973; James Kennaway Memorial Award, 1970; Guardian Fiction Prize, 1976; Hawthornden Prize, 1977; Society of Authors travel scholarship, 1991. *Membership:* Fellow, RSL, 1977–. *Address:* c/o Giles Gordon, Curtis Brown, 37 Queensferry St, Edinburgh EH2 4QS, Scotland.

NYSTROM, Debra; b. 12 July 1954, Pierre, South Dakota, USA. Poet; Writer; University Lecturer. *Education:* BA, English, University of South Dakota, 1976; Boston University, 1978–79; MFA, Creative Writing, Goddard College,

1980; Postgraduate Fellowship in Poetry, University of Virginia, 1982–83. *Appointments:* Faculty in Creative Writing, University of Virginia, 1984–. *Publication:* A Quarter Turn, 1991; Torn Sky, 2003. *Contributions to:* Various anthologies, reviews, quarterlies, and journals. *Honours:* Virginia Commission for the Arts Prizes for Poetry, 1987, 1997; Balch Prize for Poetry, Virginia Quarterly Review, 1991; James Boatwight Prizes for Poetry, Shenandoah, 1994, 2000; Borders Books/HEART Prize, 2002. *Memberships:* Associated Writing Programs; Poetry Society of America. *Address:* University of Virginia, Dept of English, 219 Bryan Hall, PO Box 400121, Charlottesville, VA 22904-4121, USA.

O

O FIONNAIN, See: FANNING, Micheal.

OAKES, Philip; b. 31 Jan. 1928, Burslem, Staffordshire, England. Author; Poet. *Appointments:* Scriptwriter, Granada TV and BBC, London, 1958–62; Film Critic, The Sunday Telegraph, London, 1963–65; Asst Ed., Sunday Times Magazine, 1965–67; Arts Columnist, Sunday Times, London, 1969–80; Columnist, Independent on Sunday, London, 1990, Guardian Weekend, London, 1991–. *Publications:* Unlucky Jonah: Twenty Poems, 1954; The Punch and Judy Man (with Tony Hancock), screenplay, 1962; Exactly What We Want (novel), 1962; In the Affirmative (poems), 1968; The God Botherers, US edn as Miracles: Genuine Cases Contact Box 340 (novel), 1969; Married/Singular (poems), 1973; Experiment at Proto (novel), 1973; Tony Hancock: A Biography, 1975; The Entertainers (ed.), 1975; A Cast of Thousands (novel), 1976; The Film Addict's Archive, 1977; From Middle England (memoirs), 1980; Dwellers All in Time and Space (memoirs), 1982; Selected Poems, 1982; At the Jazz Band Ball (memoirs); Shopping for Women (novel), 1994. *Address:* Fairfax Cottage, North Owersby, Lincolnshire LN8 3PX, England.

OANDASAN, William Cortes; b. 17 Jan. 1947, Santa Rosa, CA, USA. Poet; Ed. m. 28 Oct. 1973, 2 d. *Education:* BA, 1974; MA, 1981; MFA, 1984; Instructor's Credential, 1989. *Appointments:* Ed., A Publications, 1976–; Senior Ed., American Indian Culture and Research Journal, 1981–86; Instructor, English Dept, University of Orleans, Louisiana State University, 1988–90. *Publications:* Moving Inland, 1983; Round Valley Songs, 1984; Summer Night, 1989. *Contributions to:* Anthologies, reviews and journals, including: Colorado Review; Southern California Anthology; California Courier; American Indian Culture and Research Journal; Approaches to Teaching World Literature; Harper's Anthology of 20th Century Native American Poetry. *Honours:* Publishing Grant, National Endowment for the Arts, 1977; American Book Award, 1985; Summer Scholar Award for Writers, 1989; Research Council Grant, 1989. *Memberships:* Associated Writing Programs; MLA; Society for the Study of Multi-Ethnic Literatures; Asscn for the Study of American Indian Literatures; National Asscn of Ethnic Studies; Philological Society of the Pacific Coast. *Address:* 3832 W Ave 43, No. 13, Los Angeles, CA 90041, USA.

OATES, Joyce Carol; b. 16 June 1938, Millersport, New York, USA. Author; Dramatist; Poet; Prof.; Publisher. m. Raymond Joseph Smith, 23 Jan. 1961. *Education:* BA, Syracuse University, 1960; MA, University of Wisconsin at Madison, 1961. *Appointments:* Instructor, 1961–65, Asst Prof., 1965–67, University of Detroit; Faculty, Dept of English, University of Windsor, Ontario, Canada, 1967–78; Co-Publisher (with Raymond Joseph Smith), Ontario Review, 1974–; Writer-in-Residence, 1978–81, Prof., 1987–, Princeton University. *Publications:* Fiction: With Shuddering Fall, 1964; A Garden of Earthly Delights, 1967; Expensive People, 1968; Them, 1969; Wonderland, 1971; Do With Me What You Will, 1973; The Assassins: A Book of Hours, 1975; Childwold, 1976; Son of the Morning, 1978; Unholy Loves, 1979; Cybele, 1979; Angel of Light, 1981; Bellefleur, 1980; A Bloodsmoor Romance, 1982; Mysteries of Winterthurn, 1984; Solstice, 1985; Marya: A Life, 1986; You Must Remember This, 1987; Lives of the Twins, 1987; Soul-Mate, 1989; American Appetites, 1989; Because it is Bitter, and Because it is My Heart, 1990; Snake Eyes, 1992; Black Water, 1992; Foxfire, 1993; What I Lived For, 1994; Zombie, 1995; You Can't Catch Me, 1995; First Love: A Gothic Tale, 1996; We Were the Mulvaneys, 1996; Man Crazy, 1997; My Heart Laid Bare, 1998; Come Meet Muffin, 1998; Starr Bright Will Be With You Soon, 1999; Broke Heart Blues, 1999; Blonde, 2000; The Barrens, 2001; Middle Age: A Romance, 2002. Stories: By the North Gate, 1963; Upon the Sweeping Flood and Other Stories, 1966; The Wheel of Love, 1970; Cupid and Psyche, 1970; Marriages and Infidelities, 1972; A Posthumous Sketch, 1973; The Girl, 1974; Plagiarized Material, 1974; The Goddess and Other Women, 1974; Where Are You Going, Where Have You Been?: Stories of Young America, 1974; The Hungry Ghosts: Seven Allusive Comedies, 1974; The Seduction and Other Stories, 1975; The Poisoned Kiss and Other Stories from the Portuguese, 1975; The Triumph of the Spider Monkey, 1976; Crossing the Border, 1976; Night-Side, 1977; The Step-Father, 1978; All the Good People I've Left Behind, 1979; Queen of the Night, 1979; The Lamb of Abyssalia, 1979; A Middle-Class Education, 1980; A Sentimental Education, 1980; Last Day, 1984; Wild Saturday and Other Stories, 1984; Wild Nights, 1985; Raven's Wing, 1986; The Assignation, 1988; Heat and Other Stories, 1991; Where Is Here?, 1992; Haunted Tales of the Grotesque, 1994; Faithless: Tales of Transgression, 2001. Plays: Three Plays: Ontological Proof of My Existence, Miracle Play, The Triumph of the Spider Monkey, 1980; Twelve Plays, 1991; The Perfectionist and Other Plays, 1995. Poetry: Women in Love and Other Poems, 1968; Anonymous Sins and Other Poems, 1969; Love and its Derangements, 1970; Wooded Forms, 1972; Angel Fire, 1973; Dreaming America and Other Poems, 1973; The Fabulous Beasts, 1975; Seasons of Peril, 1977; Women Whose Lives Are Food, Men Whose Lives Are Money, 1978; Celestial Timepiece, 1980; Nightless Nights: Nine Poems, 1981; Invisible Women: New and Selected Poems 1970–1982, 1982; Luxury of Sin, 1984; The

Time Traveller: Poems 1983–1989, 1989. Other: The Edge of Impossibility Tragic Forms in Literature, 1972; The Hostile Sun: The Poetry of D H Lawrence, 1973; New Heaven, New Earth: The Visionary Experience in Literature, 1974; The Stone Orchard, 1980; Contraries: Essays, 1981; The Profane Art: Essays and Reviews, 1983; Funland, 1983; On Boxing, 1987; (Woman) Writer: Occasions and Opportunities, 1988. Editor: Scenes from American Life: Contemporary Short Fiction, 1973; The Best American Short Stories 1979 (with Shannon Ravenel), 1979; Night Walks: A Bedside Companion, 1982; First Person Singular: Writers on Their Craft, 1983; Story Fictions Past and Present (with Boyd Litzinger), 1985; Reading the Fights (with Daniel Halpern), 1988. *Honours:* National Endowment for the Arts Grants, 1966, 1968; Guggenheim Fellowship, 1967; O Henry Awards, 1967, 1973, and Special Awards for Continuing Achievement, 1970, 1986; Rosenthal Award, 1968; National Book Award, 1970; Rea Award, 1990; Heideman Award, 1990; Bobst Lifetime Achievement Award, 1990; Walt Whitman Award, 1995. *Membership:* American Acad. of Arts and Letters. *Address:* 185 Nassau St, Princeton, NJ 08540, USA.

OBARSKI, Marek; b. 2 July 1947, Poznań, Poland. Writer; Poet; Critic; Ed.; Trans. m. Aleksandra Zaworska, 27 March 1982, 2 s., 1 d. *Appointments:* Dir Flowering Grass Theatre, 1974–79, Literary Dept, Nurt magazine, 1985–90; Critic, Art for Child magazine, 1989–90; Ed., 1991–93, Trans., 1993–, Rebis publishing house; Ed., Europe, 1992–94. *Publications:* 10 vols, 1969–97. *Contributions to:* Journals and magazines. *Honours:* Medal of Young Artists, 1984; Stanisław Pietak Award, 1985. *Memberships:* Ecologic Asscn of Creators; Union des Gens de Lettres Polonaises. *Address:* os W1 Lokietka 13 F m 58, 61-616 Poznań, Poland.

O'BRIEN, Angela. See: MICHAEL, Christine.

O'BRIEN, Edna; b. 15 Dec. 1936, Tuamgraney, County Clare, Ireland. Author; Dramatist; Poet. m. 1954, divorced 1964, 2 s. *Education:* Convents; Pharmaceutical College of Ireland. *Publications:* The Country Girls, 1960; The Lonely Girl, 1962; Girls in Their Married Bliss, 1963; August is a Wicked Month, 1964; Casulaties of Peace, 1966; The Love Object, 1968; A Pagan Place, 1970; Night, 1972; A Scandalous Woman, 1974; Mother Ireland, 1976; Johnnie I Hardly Knew You, 1977; Mrs Reinhardt and Other Stories, 1978; Virginia (play), 1979; The Dazzle, 1981; Returning, 1982; A Christmas Treat, 1982; A Fanatic Heart, 1985; Tales for Telling, 1986; Flesh and Blood (play), 1987; Madame Bovary (play), 1987; The High Road, 1988; On the Bone (poems), 1989; Lantern Slides, 1990; Time and Tide, 1992; House of Splendid Isolation, 1994; Down by the River, 1997; James Joyce: A Biography, 1999; In the Forest, 2001. *Honours:* Yorkshire Post Novel Award, 1971; Los Angeles Times Award, 1990; Writers' Guild Award, 1993; European Prize for Literature, 1995. *Address:* David Godwin Assocs, 14 Goodwin Ct, Covent Garden, London WC2N 4LL, England.

O'BRIEN, Mark David; b. 31 July 1949, USA. Poet; Journalist. *Education:* BA, English, University of California, 1982. *Publication:* Breathing, 1990. *Contributions to:* Margin; Sun; St Andrew's Review. *Membership:* Acad. of American Poets. *Address:* 2420 Dwight Way, No. 1, Berkeley, CA 94704, USA.

O'BRIEN, Mary Kathryn; b. 13 Nov. 1954, Houston, Texas, USA. Editorial Man.; Poet. 1 s. *Education:* BA, University of Arizona, Tucson, 1975. *Publications:* Handbook for Poets, 1977; The Legend of Cherokee Clark, 1989. *Contributions to:* Anthologies, reviews, and journals. *Address:* 339 E 94th St, 2F, New York, NY 10128, USA.

O'BRIEN, Sean (Patrick); b. 19 Dec. 1952, London, England. Writer; Poet. *Education:* BA, Honours, English, Selwyn College, Cambridge, 1974; MA, University of Birmingham, 1977; University of Hull, 1976–79; PGCE, University of Leeds, 1981. *Appointments:* Fellow in Creative Writing, University of Dundee, 1989–91; Northern Arts Literary Fellow, 1992–94; Visiting Writer, University of Odense, Denmark, 1996, Hokudai University, Sapporo, Japan, 1997; Lecturer in Writing, Sheffield Hallam University, 1998–; Writer-in-Residence, University of Leeds, 1999. *Publications:* The Indoor Park, 1983; The Frighteners, 1987; Boundary Beach, 1989; HMS Glasshouse, 1991; Ghost Train, 1995; The Deregulated Muse: Essays on Contemporary Poetry in Britain and Ireland, 1998; The Firebox: Poetry in Britain and Ireland after 1945 (ed.), 1998; Downriver, 2001. Plays: Laughter When We're Dead; My Last Barmaid. *Contributions to:* Anthologies, newspapers, reviews, and radio. *Honours:* Eric Gregory Award, 1979; Somerset Maugham Award, 1984; Cholmondeley Award, 1988; Arts Council Writer's Bursary, 1992; E M Forster Award, 1993; Forward Prize, 1995, 2001. *Literary Agent:* Clare Alexander, Gillon Aitken Assocs, 29 Fernshaw Rd, London SW10 0TG, England. *Address:* 15 Connaught Gardens, Forest Hill, Newcastle upon Tyne NE12 8AT, England. *E-mail:* triplepa@cableinet.co.uk.

OBSTFELD, Raymond, (Pike Bishop, Jason Frost, Don Pendleton, Carl Stevens); b. 22 Jan. 1952, Williamsport, Pennsylvania, USA. Asst Prof. of English; Wrier; Poet; Dramatist; Screenwriter. *Education:* BA, Johnston College, University of Redlands, 1972; MA, University of California at Davis, 1976. *Appointments:* Lecturer to Asst Prof. of English, Orange Coast College, 1976–. *Publications:* Fiction: The Golden Fleece, 1979; Dead-End Option, 1980; Dead Heat, 1981; Dead Bolt, 1982; The Remington Factor, 1985; Masked Dog, 1986; Redtooth, 1987; Brainchild, 1987; The Whippin Boy, 1988. As Pike Bishop: Diamondback, 1983; Judgement at Poisoned Well, 1983. As Jason Frost: Warlord series, 1983–85; Invasion USA, 1985. As Don Pendleton: Bloodsport, 1982; Flesh Wounds, 1983; Savannah Swingsaw, 1985; The Fire Eaters, 1986. As Carl Stevens: The Centaur Conspiracy, 1983; Ride of the Razorback, 1984. Poetry: The Cat With Half a Face, 1978. *Contributions to:* Anthologies and other publications. *Membership:* Mystery Writers of America. *Address:* 190 Greenmoor, Irvine, CA 92714, USA.

O'CEIRIN, Cyril; b. 9 Feb. 1934, Ireland. Poet. *Education:* BA, HDipEd. *Publications:* Le hAer's le Fuacht, 1986; Saltair Muir (ed.), 1989. *Contributions to:* Anthologies and periodicals. *Honours:* Several poetry competitions; Bardic Tour of Scotland, 1979; Bard, Inaugural O'Callaghan Clan Gathering, 1988. *Address:* Teach an Atlantaigh, Lios Duin Bhearna, Co an Chlair, Ireland.

O'CONNELL, Richard (James); b. 25 Oct. 1928, New York, NY, USA. Prof. Emeritus; Poet; Trans. *Education:* BS, Temple University, 1956; MA, Johns Hopkins University, 1957. *Appointments:* Instructor, 1957–61, Asst Prof., 1961–69, Assoc. Prof., 1969–86, Senior Assoc. Prof., 1986–93, Prof. Emeritus, 1993–, Temple University; Fulbright Lecturer, University of Brazil, Rio de Janeiro, 1960, University of Navarre, Pamplona, Spain, 1962–63; Guest Lecturer, Johns Hopkins University, 1961–74; Poet-in-the-Schools, Pennsylvania Council for the Arts, 1971–73. *Publications:* From an Interior Silence, 1961; Cries of Flesh and Stone, 1962; New Poems and Translations, 1963; Brazilian Happenings, 1966; Terrane, 1967; Thirty Epigrams, 1971; Hudson's Fourth Voyage, 1978; Temple Poems, 1985; Hanging Tough, 1986; Battle Poems, 1987; Selected Epigrams, 1990; Lives of the Poets, 1990; The Caliban Poems, 1992; RetroWorlds, 1993; Simulations, 1993; Voyages, 1995; The Bright Tower, 1997. Translator: Various works, including: Irish Monastic Poems, 1975; Middle English Poems, 1976; More Irish Poems, 1976; Epigrams from Martial, 1976; The Epigrams of Luxorius, 1984; New Epigrams from Martial, 1991. *Honour:* Contemporary Poetry Press Prize, 1972. *Memberships:* Associated Writing Programs; MLA; PEN. *Address:* 3 West View Dr., Richmond, RI 02892, USA.

Ó'CURRAOIN, Seán; b. Bearna, Connemara, County Galway, Ireland. Chief Trans. in Irish Parliament; Interpreter in Dáil. *Education:* BA, Irish and English, 1961; MA, Irish, 1980. *Appointments:* Linguistic Researcher and Asst Ed. on Ó Dónaill's Irish-English Dictionary. *Publications:* Soilse ar na Dumhchannaí, 1985; Beairtle, 1985; Tinte Sionnaigh (short stories), 1985; De Ghlaschloch an Oileáin (biography of Máirtín O Cadhain), 1987; Iascairín Chloch na Cora, 2000. *Contributions to:* Comhar; Feasta; Innti; Cyphers. *Memberships:* Irish Trans Asscn; Folklore of Ireland Society. *Address:* 18 Ascaill Verbena, Br. Chill Bharróg, Baile Átha Cliath 13, Ireland.

ØDEGÅRD, Knut; b. 6 Nov. 1945, Molde, Norway. Poet; Writer; Critic. m. Thorgerdur Ingólfsdóttir, 2 Aug. 1981, 2 d. *Education:* Theology and Philosophy, University of Oslo; LittD, 1999. *Appointments:* Poetry Critic, Aftenposten newspaper, 1968–; Man. Dir, Scandinavian Centre, Nordens Hus, Reykjavík, 1984–89; Pres., Norwegian Festival of International Literature, 1992–; Consul, Republic of Slovakia, 1995–97; Consul Gen., Republic of Macedonia, 1997–. *Publications:* 24 poetry books, 1967–98, including: Bee-buzz, Salmon Leap, 1968; Cinema Operator, 1991; Ventriloquy, 1994; Selected Poems, 1995; Missa, 1998. Other: Books of prose and essays; Play; Two non-fiction books about Iceland, 1992, 1998. *Honours:* Knighted by Pres. of Iceland, 1987; Norwegian State Scholar for Life, 1989–; Grand Knight Commander, Order of the Icelandic Falcon, 1993; International Order of Merit, 1993; Knight, Norwegian Order of Literature, 1995; Knighted by the King of Norway, 1998. *Memberships:* Acad. of Norwegian Language; Icelandic Society of Authors; Literary Acad. of Romania; Norwegian Literary Council; Norwegian Society of Authors. *Literary Agent:* J. W. Cappelen, Oslo, Norway. *Address:* Chateau Parkv 42, 6400 Molde, Norway. *E-mail:* knut.odegard@moldenett.no.

O'DONNELL, Dennis Gerrard; b. 14 Sept. 1951, Dechmont, West Lothian, Scotland. Schoolmaster; Poet. m. Joan Murphy, 28 Sept. 1972, 1 d. *Education:* MA, Honours, English Language and Literature, University of Edinburgh, 1973; Postgraduate Studies, 1973–76. *Contributions to:* Various publications. *Address:* Almond Lane, The Cross, Blackburn, West Lothian EH47 7QU, Scotland.

O'DONNELL, Mary (Elizabeth Eugenie); b. 3 April 1954, Monaghan, Ireland. Writer; Poet; Critic. m. Martin Nugent, 18 June 1977. *Education:* BA, Honours, German and Philosophy, 1977, Diploma, Higher Education, 1983, Maynooth College. *Appointments:* Writer-in-Residence, University College, Dublin, and County Laois, 1995; Teacher of Creative Writing,

University of Iowa, Summer Writing Programme, Trinity College, Dublin, 1998–2000. *Publications:* Reading the Sunflowers in September (poems), 1990; Strong Pagans and Other Stories, 1991; The Light-Makers (novel), 1992; Spiderwoman's Third Avenue Rhapsody (poems), 1993; Virgin and the Boy (novel), 1996; Unlegendary Heroes (poems), 1998; The Elysium Testament (novel), 1999. *Contributions to:* Anthologies, reviews, quarterlies, and periodicals. *Honours:* Second Prize, Patrick Kavanagh Poetry Award, 1986; Third Prize Runner-Up, Bloodaxe National Poetry Competition, 1987; Allingham Poetry Award, 1988. *Memberships:* Irish Council for Civil Liberties; Poetry Ireland; Poetry Society; Irish PEN. *Address:* Rook Hollow, Newtown Macabe, Maynooth, Co Kildare, Ireland. *E-mail:* construct@compuserve.com.

O'DONOGHUE, (James) Bernard; b. 14 Dec. 1945, Cullen, County Cork, Ireland. University Teacher of English; Poet. m. Heather MacKinnon, 23 July 1977, 1 s., 2 d. *Education:* MA in English, 1968, BPhil in Medieval English, 1971, Lincoln College, Oxford. *Appointments:* Lecturer and Tutor in English, Magdalen College, Oxford; Fellow in English, Wadham College, Oxford, 1995–. *Publications:* Razorblades and Pencils, 1984; Poaching Rights, 1987; The Weakness, 1991; Gunpowder, 1995; Here Nor There, 1999. *Contributions to:* Norton Anthology of Poetry; Poetry Ireland Review; Poetry Review; TLS. *Honours:* Southern Arts Literature Prize, 1991; Whitbread Poetry Award, 1995. *Memberships:* Poetry Society, London, 1984–; Fellow, RSL, 1999; Fellow, English Society, 1999. *Address:* Wadham College, Oxford OX1 3PN, England.

O'DRISCOLL, Ciaran; b. 2 Oct. 1943, Callan, County Kilkenny, Ireland. Lecturer; Poet; Ed. m. Margaret Farrelly, 3 Sept. 1987, 1 s. *Education:* BA, English and Philosophy, University College Cork, 1968; MA, Philosophy, Bedford College, University of London, 1978. *Appointments:* Lecturer, Limerick School of Art and Design; Ed., Limerick Poetry Broad-sheet, 1988–91; Ed., Cyphers, 1992–93. *Publications:* Gog and Magog, 1987; The Poet and His Shadow, 1990; The Myth of the South, 1992; Listening to Different Drummers, 1993; The Old Women of Magione, 1997. *Contributions to:* Ambit; Aquarius; Cyphers; Dedalus Irish Poets (anthology); Die horen (Germany); Fortnight; Hard Lines; Honest Ulsterman; Irish Press; Irish Times; Krino; North Dakota Quarterly; Omens; Orbis; Poetry Ireland Review; Quarry (Canada); Salmon. *Honours:* Bursary in Literature, Irish Arts Council, 1984; James Joyce Literary Millenium Prize, 1989. *Membership:* Limerick Poetry Workshop. *Address:* 5 St Bridget's Ave, New St, Limerick, Ireland.

O'DRISCOLL, Dennis; b. 1 Jan. 1954, Thurles, County Tipperary, Ireland. Ed.; Poet. m. Julie O'Callaghan, 1985. *Education:* University College, Dublin, 1972–75. *Appointments:* Literary Organiser, Dublin Arts Festival, 1977–79; Ed., Poetry Ireland Review, 1986–87. *Publications:* Kist, 1982; Hidden Extras, 1987. Co-Editor: The First Ten Years: Dublin Arts Festival Poetry, 1979. *Honour:* Irish Arts Council Bursary. *Address:* Ketu, Breffni Gate, Church Rd, Dalkey, County Dublin, Ireland.

OERTLI, Cheryl Lyne Gilmore; b. 26 Jan. 1951, St Johns, Michigan, USA. Writer; Poet. m. Leroy Louis Oertli, 19 Oct. 1972, 2 s. *Education:* Graduate, Lansing Community College, 1989. *Contributions to:* Anthologies and magazines. *Honours:* Golden Poet Awards, World of Poetry, 1985–88; Poets of Now Merit Award, 1988. *Memberships:* National Federation of State Poetry Societies; Poetry Society of Michigan; Poetry Study Club; Poets of Now; Writers Cafe, charter mem., 1992–. *Address:* 4523 Sycamore St, Holt, MI 48842, USA.

OFFEN, Yehuda, (Huri Halim, Ben Naftali); b. 4 April 1922, Altona, Germany. Writer; Poet. m. Tova Arbisser, 28 March 1946, 1 d. *Education:* BA, University of London, 1975; MA, Comparative Literature, Hebrew University of Jerusalem, 1978. *Appointments:* Senior Ed., Al Hamishmar, Daily Guardian, 1960–80. *Publications:* L'Lo L'An, 1961; Har Vakhol, 1963; Lo Agadat Khoref, 1969; Nofim P'nima, 1979; B'Magal Sagur (short stories), 1979; N'Vilat Vered, 1983; Shirim Bir'hov Ayaif, 1984; P'Gishot Me'ever Lazman, 1986; Massekhet Av, 1986; Stoning on the Cross Road (short stories), 1988; Who Once Begot a Star, 1990; Silly Soil, 1992; Back to Germany, 1994. *Contributions to:* Various publications. *Honours:* ACUM (Society of Authors, Composers and Eds in Israel) Prizes for Literature, 1961, 1979, 1984; Talpir Prize for Literature, 1979; Efrat Prize for Poetry, 1989. *Memberships:* ACUM (Society of Authors, Composers and Eds in Israel); Hebrew Writers Asscn, Israel; International Acad. of Poets, USA; International Federation of Journalists, Brussels; National Federation of Israeli Journalists; PEN Centre, Israel. *Address:* 8 Gazit St, Tel-Aviv 69417, Israel.

O'FIANNACHTA, Pádraig; b. 20 Feb. 1927, County Kerry, Ireland. Prof. (retd); Poet; Writer; Ed. *Education:* St Patrick's College, Maynooth, 1944–48; BA, 1947, MA, 1955, National University of Ireland; University College, Cork, 1949–50; PhD, Pontifical University, Maynooth. *Appointments:* Lecturer, 1959–60, Prof. of Early Irish and Lecturer in Welsh, 1960–81, Prof. of Modern Irish, 1981–92, St Patrick's College, Maynooth. *Publications:* Ponc, 1966; Ruin, 1969; Feoirlingí Fileata, 1972; Donn Bo, 1976; An Bíobla Naofa (ed. and trans.), 1981; Spaisteoireacht, 1982; Deora De, 1987; Léim An Dá Míle, 1999. *Contributions to:* Various publications. *Honour:* Douglas Hyde Prize for

Literature, 1969; Monsignor, 1998. *Memberships:* Cumann na Sagart; Oireachtas, pres., 1985; Poetry Ireland; Royal Irish Acad. *Address:* Dingle, Tralee, County Kerry, Ireland.

OGDEN, Georgine. See: PROKOPOV, Georgine Lucile Ogden.

OGDEN, Hugh; b. 11 March 1937, Erie, Pennsylvania, USA. Prof.; Poet; Writer. m. Ruth Simpson, 3 March 1960, 1 s., 2 d. *Education:* BA, Haverford College, 1959; MA, New York University, 1961; PhD, University of Michigan, 1967. *Appointments:* Teaching Asst, 1961–65, Instructor, 1965–67, University of Michigan; Asst Prof., 1967–75, Assoc. Prof., 1975–91, Prof., 1991–, Trinity College, Hartford, CT. *Publications:* Looking for History, 1991; Two Road and this Spring, 1993; Windfalls, 1996; Gift, 1998; Natural Things, 1998. *Contributions to:* Reviews, quarterlies, and journals. *Honours:* Connecticut Commission on the Arts Poetry Project Grant, 1990; National Endowment for the Arts Grant, 1993. *Memberships:* Associated Writing Programs; Poetry Society of America; Poets and Writers. *Address:* c/o Dept of English, Trinity College, Hartford, CT 06106, USA.

OGG, Wilson Reid; b. 26 Feb. 1928, Alhambra, CA, USA. Social Scientist; Philosopher; Lawyer; Poet; Lyricist; Educator. *Education:* AB, 1949; JD, 1952, University of California. *Appointments:* Psychology Instructor, US Armed Forces Institute, Taegu, Korea, 1953–54; English Instructor, Taegu English Language Institute, 1954; Trustee Sec., First Unitarian Church of Berkeley, 1957–58; Research Attorney, Continuing Education of the Bar, University of California, 1958–63; Vice-Pres., International House Asscn, 1961–62; Pres., Board Chair., California Society for Physics Study, 1963–65; Private Law Practice, 1955–; Dir of Admissions, International Society for Philosophical Enquiry, 1981–84. *Contributions to:* Various anthologies and journals. *Honours:* Commendation Ribbon W. Medal Pendant; Cultural Doctorate, World University; Hon. DD, University of Life Church, 1969; Hon. Doctorate, Religious Humanities, 1970. *Memberships:* American Mensa; ASCAP; International Acad. of Law and Sciences; New York Acad. of Sciences; San Francisco Bar Asscn. *Address:* Pinebrook at Bret Harte Way, 8 Bret Harte Way, Berkeley, CA 94708, USA. *E-mail:* wilsonogg@alum.calperbelly.org. *Website:* www.wilsonogg.com.

O'GRADY, Desmond James Bernard; b. 27 Aug. 1935, Limerick, Ireland. Poet; Writer; Trans. 1 s., 2 d. *Education:* MA, 1964, PhD, 1982, Harvard University. *Appointments:* Secondary School Teacher, University Prof., 1955–82. *Publications:* Chords and Orchestrations, 1956; Reilly, 1961; Prof. Kelleher and the Charles River, 1964; Separazioni, 1965; The Dark Edge of Europe, 1967; The Dying Gaul, 1968; Off Licence (trans.), 1968; Hellas, 1971; Separations, 1973; Stations, 1976; Sing Me Creation, 1977; The Gododdin (trans.), 1977; A Limerick Rake (trans.), 1978; The Headgear of the Tribe, 1979; His Skaldcrane's Nest, 1979; Grecian Glances (trans.), 1981; Alexandria Notebook, 1989; The Seven Arab Odes (trans.), 1990; Tipperary, 1991; Ten Modern Arab Poets (trans.), 1992; My Fields This Springtime, 1993; Alternative Manners (trans.), 1993; Trawling Tradition: Collected Translations, 1954–1994, 1994; Il Galata Morente, 1996; The Road Taken: Poems, 1956–1996, 1996; The Golden Odes of Love (trans.), 1997; C P Cavafy: Selected Poems (trans.), 1998; The Wandering Celt, 2001; The Battle of Kinsale, 1601, 2002; The Song of Songs (trans.), 2002. Prose Memoirs: Ezra Pound, Patrick Kavanagh, Samuel Beckett, Olga Rudge, Anna Akhmatova. Essays: On poetry, poets, translating poetry. *Contributions to:* Anthologies and magazines. *Membership:* Aosdána. *Address:* Ardback, Kinsale, County Cork, Ireland.

O'GRADY, Tom; b. 26 Aug. 1943, Baltimore, Maryland, USA. Poet; Writer; Dramatist; Trans.; Ed.; Vintner. m. Bronwyn Southworth, 2 s. *Education:* BA, English, University of Baltimore, 1966; MA, English, Johns Hopkins University, 1967; Graduate Studies, English and American Literature, University of Delaware, 1972–74. *Appointments:* Teacher of writing and literature, various colleges and universities, 1966–96; Founder-Ed., The Hampden-Sydney Poetry Review, 1975–; Numerous lectures and poetry readings. *Publications:* Poetry: Unicorn Evils, 1973; Establishing a Vineyard, 1977; Photo-Graphs, 1980; The Farmville Elegies, 1981; In the Room of the Just Born, 1989; Carvings of the Moon, 1992; Sun, Moon, and Stars, 1996. Prose: Shaking the Tree: A Book of Works and Days, 1993; The Same Earth, The Same Sky: New and Selected Poems and Translations, 2002. Editor: The Hampden-Sydney Poetry Anthology, 1990. Other: Trans; Stage and television plays. *Contributions to:* Anthologies, newspapers, journals, and magazines. *Honours:* Leache Prize for Poetry, 1975; Ed.'s Award, Co-ordinating Council of Literary Magazine, 1977; Merit Award, 1977, Mettauer Research Award, 1984, Trustees Award, 1986, Hampden-Sydney College; Virginia Prize for Poetry, 1989; Teacher of the Arts Award, National Foundation for Advancement in the Arts, 1989–90; Virginia Center for the Arts Fellowship Residency, 1995; Henrico Theater Co Prize, 1997. *Address:* c/o Rose Bower Vineyard and Winery, PO Box 126, Hampden-Sydney, VA 23943, USA.

O'HIGGINS, Michael Cecil Patrick; b. 25 Feb. 1935, Dublin, Ireland. Writer; Poet. m. Julie Patricia Bryden, 8 Dec. 1962, divorced 1968. *Education:* Ruskin College; Magdalen College, Oxford. *Publications:* A Whisper on the Wind, 1960; Wells and Other Poems, 1984; An Adventure of the Mind, 1985; Haiku, 1985;

Schizophrenia, 1988; Much Happy Travelling, 1993. *Contributions to:* Anthologies, journals, and magazines. *Honours:* Elmgrant Trust Award, 1963; Mature State Scholarship, Oxford, 1964; South West Arts Literary Award, 1984; Winner, Martha Robinson Poetry Competition, 1988; Friends of Mendip Poetry Award, 1988. *Membership:* Wells Poetry Group, chair., 1985–90. *Address:* 25 Woodbury Ave, Wells, Somerset BA5 2XW, England.

OJAIDE, Tanure; b. 24 April 1948, Okpara Island, Nigeria. Poet; Writer; Prof. of African-American and African Studies. m. Anne Numuoja, 1976, 5 c. *Education:* Certificate, Federal Government College, Warri, 1967; BA, English, University of Ibadan, 1971; MA, Creative Writing, 1979, PhD, English, 1981, Syracuse University. *Appointments:* Teacher of English, Federal Government College, Warri, 1973–75; Lecturer in English and Communication, Petroleum Training Institute, Effurun, 1975–77; Lecturer, 1977–85, Senior Lecturer, 1985–87, Reader, 1987–89, University of Maiduguri; Visiting Johnston Prof. of Third World Literatures, Whitman College, Walla Walla, WA, 1989–90; Asst Prof., 1990–93, Assoc. Prof., 1993–98, Prof. of African-American and African Studies, 1998–, University of North Carolina at Charlotte; National Endowment for the Humanities Prof., Albright College, Reading, PA, 1996–97. *Publications:* Poetry: Children of Iroko and Other Poems, 1973; Labyrinths of the Delta, 1986; The Eagle's Vision, 1987; Poems, 1988; The Endless Song, 1989; The Fate of Vultures and Other Poems, 1990; The Blood of Peace, 1991; Daydream of Ants, 1997; Delta Blues and Home Songs, 1998; Invoking the Warrior Spirit: New and Selected Poems, 1999; Cannons for the Brave, 1999; When It No Longer Matters Where You Live, 1999; In the Kingdom of Songs: A Trilogy of Poems, 1995–2000, 2001. Other: Yono Urhobo: Obe Rerha (with S. S. Ugheteni), 1981; The Poetry of Wole Soyinka, 1994; Poetic Imagination in Black Africa: Essays on African Poetry, 1996; Great Boys: An African Childhood, 1998; The New African Poetry: An Anthology (ed. with Tijan M. Sallah), 1999; Texts and Contexts: Culture, Society, and Politics in Modern African Literature (with Joseph Obi), 2001; God and his Medicine Men: Short Stories, 2002. *Contributions to:* Books, anthologies, magazines and journals. *Honours:* Africa Regional Winner, Commonwealth Poetry Prize, 1987; Overall Winner, BBC Arts and Africa Poetry Award, 1988; Asscn of Nigerian Authors' Portey Prizes, 1988, 1994; All-Africa Okigbo Prizes for Poetry, 1988, 1997; Fellow, Headlands Center for the Arts, Sausalito, CA, 1994; National Endowment for the Humanities Fellowship, 1999–2000; Residency, Bellagio Center for Scholars and Artists, 2001. *Memberships:* African Literature Asscn; African Studies Asscn; Associated Writing Programs; Asscn of Nigerian Authors; International Asscn of University Profs of English; International Black Writers, Charlotte, NC; MLA of America; North Carolina Writers' Network. *Address:* c/o African-American and African Studies Dept, University of North Carolina at Charlotte, Charlotte, NC 28223, USA. *E-mail:* tojadie@email.uncc.edu.

OKARA, Gabriel (Imomotimi Dbaingbain); b. 21 April 1921, Burmodi, Ijaw District, Rivers State, Western Nigeria. Writer; Poet; Publishing Dir. *Education:* Government College, Umuahia. *Appointment:* Dir, Rivers State Publishing House, Port Harcourt, 1972–. *Publications:* The Voice (novel), 1964; Poetry from Africa, 1968; The Fisherman's Invocation, 1978. *Honour:* Commonwealth Poetry Prize, 1979. *Address:* PO Box 219, Port Harcourt, Nigeria.

OKAZAKI, Tadao; b. 7 April 1943, Japan. Physician; Poet. *Education:* MD, Prefectual Medical School, Japan; State University of New York, USA. *Appointments:* Ed., New Cicada, Japan, 1984–. *Publications:* Several haiku. *Contributions to:* Cicada; Modern Haiku; Frogpond; New Cicada. *Honours:* Cicada Prize; Special Mention Award. *Memberships:* Haiku Society of America; Haiku Canada; Canadian Poetry. *Address:* 13 Shimizu Fushiguro, Fukushima 960-05, Japan.

OKOŃ, Zbigniew Waldemar; b. 21 July 1945, Chelm, Poland. Poet; Writer. m. Halina Pioro Maciejweska, 5 Oct. 1969, 2 s., 1 d. *Education:* Marie Curie-Skłodowska University, Lublin, 1968; Warsaw University, 1991. *Publications:* Outlooks and Reflections, 1968; The Soldiers of the Chalk Hills, 1970; Impatience of the Tree, 1979; Intimidation by Twilight, 1986; Calling Up the Darkness, 1987; Taste of Childhood, 1990; In a Halfway, 1996; Grandpa Tudrey's Cavalry, 1997; By the Simple Muse, 2000; The Strophes Written by Heart, 2000; The Mark Left, 2001. *Contributions to:* Journals and magazines. *Honours:* First Prizes, Poetry Competitions, 1964, 1966, 1968, 1974; The Silver Cross of Merit, 1985; Czechowicz Literary Prize, 1987; National Scholarship, Ministry of Culture and Art, 1985; Jaworski Literary Prize, 2001. *Membership:* Union of Polish Literary Men. *Address:* ul Kolejowa 86-19, 22-100 Chelm, Poland.

OKRI, Ben; b. 15 March 1959, Minna, Nigeria (British-Nigerian citizen). Author; Poet. *Education:* Urhobo College, Warri, Nigeria; University of Essex, Colchester. *Appointments:* Broadcaster and Presenter, BBC, 1983–85; Poetry Ed., West Africa, 1983–86; Fellow Commoner in Creative Arts, Trinity College, Cambridge, 1991–93. *Publications:* Flowers and Shadows, 1980; The Landscapes Within, 1982; Incidents at the Shrine, 1986; Stars of the New Curfew, 1988; The Famished Road, 1991; An African Elegy, 1992; Songs of Enchantment, 1993; Astonishing the Gods, 1995; Birds of Heaven, 1995; Dangerous Love, 1996; A Way of Being Free, 1997; Infinite Riches, 1998;

Mental Fight, 1999; In Arcadia, 2002. *Contributions to:* Many newspapers and journals. *Honours:* Commonwealth Prize for Africa, 1987; Paris Review/Aga Khan Prize for Fiction, 1987; Booker Prize, 1991; Premio Letterario Internazionale Chianti-Ruffino-Antico-Fattore, 1993; Premio Grinzane Cavour, 1994; Crystal Award, 1995; Hon. DLitt, Westminster, 1997; Premio Palmi, 2000; O.B.E., 2001; Hon. doctorate, University of Essex, 2002. *Membership:* Society of Authors; Fellow, RSL; Vice-Pres., English Centre, International PEN, 1997–; Board, Royal National Theatre of Great Britain, 1999–. *Address:* c/o Vintage, Random House, 20 Vauxhall Bridge Rd, London SW1 2SA, England.

OLABISI, Adebayo; b. 25 Sept. 1946, Igboho, Nigeria. Teacher; Poet. m. Anne Chizoma Ike, 3 Aug. 1974, 6 s. *Education:* BEd, Honours, University of Ibadan, 1972; MBA, University of Lagos, 1980. *Appointments:* Lecturer, The Polytechnic, Ibadan, 1982–. *Publications:* Flakes of Free Verses; Fusion of Reminiscences. *Contributions to:* Anthologies and other publications. *Honours:* Ed.'s Choice Award, National Library of Poetry, USA, 1994; Nominations, Poet of the Year Award, International Society of Poets, 1995, 1996. *Memberships:* Asscn of Nigerian Authors; International Society of Poets. *Address:* PO Box 253, Saki, Oyo State, Nigeria.

OLAFSSON, Einar; b. 11 Sept. 1949, Reykjavik, Iceland. Writer; Poet. m. Gudbjorg Sveinsdottir, 8 Aug. 1988, 2 s., 1 d. *Education:* Studied literature at University of Oslo, 1976–78; BA, History, University of Iceland, 1984. *Publications:* Litla Stúlkan Og Brúduleikhúsid, 1971; Ljód, 1971; Öll Réttindi Askilin, 1972; Drepa, Drepa (with Dagur Sigurdason), 1974; Augu Vid Gangstétt, 1983; Sólarbasúnan, 1986; Brynjólfur Bjarnason, Pólitisk Ævisaga, 1989; Mánadúfur, 1995. *Membership:* Writers Asscn of Iceland. *Address:* Tronuhjalli 13, 200 Kopavogur, Iceland.

OLAPPAMANNA, Subrahmanian Nambudiripad; b. 10 Jan. 1923, Vellinezhi, India. Poet. m. Sreedevi Olappamanna, 31 Oct. 1953, 3 s., 1 d. *Education:* Government Victoria College, Palakkad, 1944–46. *Appointments:* Vice-Chair., 1972–78, Chair., 1978–84, Kalamandalam Art Centre, Kerala; Dir, Nedungadi Bank Ltd, 1982–90. *Publications:* Various poems, 1947–88. *Contributions to:* Many publications. *Honours:* Best Malayalam Poetry Award, Chennai Government, 1950–51; Kerala Sahitya Akademy Award, 1966; Otakuzhal Award, 1988; National Award, Central Sahitya Akademy, 1989. *Address:* Hari Sree, Jainmedu, Palakkad, 678 012 Kerala, India.

OLDER, Julia D.; b. 25 May 1941, Chicago, IL, USA. Writer; Poet. *Education:* BA, University of Michigan, 1963; Diploma, Conservatorio Arrigo Boito, Parma, Italy, 1966; MFA, Instituto Allende, Mexico, 1971. *Appointments:* Asst Children's Book Ed., Putnam Publishing Co, New York, 1969–70; Column Writer and Poetry Ed., New Hampshire Times, 1974–76; Regular Book Reviewer, New Letters Review of Books, Kansas City, 1989–91. *Publications:* Oonts and Others, 1982; A Little Wild, 1987; Blues for a Black Cat (trans. of Boris Vian), 1992; The Island Queen (novel), 1994; Higher Latitudes (poems), 1995; Selected Writings of Celia Thaxter (ed.), 1997; Tales of the François Vase (verse play for radio), 1998; Hermaphroditus in America (long poem), 2000; City in the Sky, 2001; The Ossabaw Book of Hours, 2001. *Contributions to:* Reviews and magazines. *Honours:* Hopwood Poetry Award, University of Michigan, 1963; Mary Roberts Rinehart Grant for Prose, 1974; Nomination, Pushcart Anthology, 1992; Daniel Varoujan Poetry Prize, New England Poetry Club, 2001. *Memberships:* New Hampshire Writers Project; Maine Writers and Publishers. *Address:* Box 174, Hancock, NJ 03449, USA.

OLDKNOW, Antony; b. 15 Aug. 1939, Peterborough, England. Poet; Literary Trans.; Prof. *Education:* BA, University of Leeds, 1961; Postgraduate Diploma, Phonetics, University of Edinburgh, 1962; PhD, University of North Dakota, USA, 1983. *Appointments:* Ed., Publisher, Scopcraeft Press Inc, 1966–; Travelling Writer, The Great Plains Book Bus, 1979–81; Writer-in-Residence, Wisconsin Arts Board, 1980–83; Poetry Staff, Cottonwood, 1984–87; Prof. of Literature, Eastern New Mexico University, 1987–; Assoc. Ed., Blackwater Quarterly, 1993. *Publications:* Lost Allegory, 1967; Tomcats and Tigertails, 1968; The Road of the Lord, 1969; Anthem for Rusty Saw and Blue Sky, 1975; Consolations for Beggars, 1978; Miniature Clouds, 1982; Ten Small Songs, 1985; Clara d'Ellébeuse (trans.), 1992; The Villages and Other Poems (trans.), 1993. *Contributions to:* Anthologies, reviews, journals, and magazines. *Address:* Dept of Languages and Literature, Eastern New Mexico University, Portales, NM 88130, USA.

OLDS, Sharon; b. 19 Nov. 1942, San Francisco, CA, USA. Poet; Assoc. Prof. *Education:* BA, Stanford University, 1964; PhD, Columbia University, 1972. *Appointments:* Lecturer-in-Residence on Poetry, Theodor Herzl Institute, New York, 1976–80; Adjunct Prof., 1983–90, Dir, 1988–91, Assoc. Prof., 1990–, Graduate Program in Creative Writing, New York University; Fanny Hurst Chair in Literature, Brandeis University, 1986–87; New York State Poet, 1998–2000. *Publications:* Satan Says, 1980; The Dead and the Living, 1984; The Gold Cell, 1987; The Matter of This World: New and Selected Poems, 1987; The Sign of Saturn, 1991; The Father, 1992; The Wellspring, 1996; Blood, Tin, Straw, 1999. *Honours:* Creative Arts Public Service Award, 1978; Madeline Sadin Award, 1978; Guggenheim Fellowship, 1981–82; National Endowment for the Arts Fellowship, 1982–83; Lamont Prize, 1984; National Book Critics

Circle Award, 1985; T S Eliot Prize short list, 1993; Lila Wallace-Reader's Digest Fellowship, 1993–96. *Address:* c/o Dept of English, New York University, 19 University Pl., New York, NY 10003, USA.

O'LEARY, Patsy B(aker); b. 23 Sept. 1937, NC, USA. Writer; Poet; Teacher. m. Denis L. O'Leary, 1962, divorced 1979, 1 d. *Education:* BS, East Carolina College, 1959; MA, California State University at Northridge, 1979. *Appointments:* Instructor in Creative Writing, Pitt Community College, 1980–; Lecturer in English, 1980–81, and Communications, 1990–95, East Carolina University. *Publications:* With Wings as Eagles (novel), 1997; Phoenix (poem); A Voice Heard in Ramah (short story). *Honours:* First Place Awards for article, 1981, 1982, for novel-in-progress, 1981, 1982, for inspirational poem, 1983, Council of Authors and Journalists; First Place Award for short story, Tar Heel Writer's Roundtable, 1984; Award established in her honour, Pitt Community College, 1989. *Memberships:* National Writers' Union; Poets and Writers; North Carolina Writers Network; Southeastern Writers Asscn. *Literary Agent:* Barrie Van Dyck Agency Inc, 217 Spruce St, Philadelphia, PA 19106, USA. *Address:* 310 Baytree Dr., Greenville, NC 27858, USA.

OLEMA. See: ONU, Johnson Olema.

OLIVEIRA, Joanyr de, (Joanir Ferreira de Oliveira); b. 6 Dec. 1933, Aimorés, Brazil. Journalist; Lawyer; Publisher; Writer; Poet. m. 21 March 1959, 4 s. *Publications:* Various works of fiction and poetry, 1957–92. *Contributions to:* Anthologies and other publications. *Honours:* Several poetry prizes and awards, 1961–92. *Address:* SQS 105, Block H, Apt 205, 70344-080, Brasilia, Brazil.

OLIVER, Colin; b. 13 March 1946, Tasburgh, Norfolk, England. Primary School Headteacher; Poet. m. Carole Oliver, 5 Sept. 1968, 1 s., 1 d. *Education:* Education Diploma, University of London Goldsmiths' College. *Appointment:* Headteacher, Wickambrook Primary School, Suffolk, 1985–. *Publications:* In the Open, 1974; Seeing, 1980; Ploughing at Nightfall, 1993; Stepping into Brilliant Air, 1996. *Contributions to:* Guardian; Iron; Lines Review; Middle Way; Oasis; Resurgence; PN Review; Haiku Hundred anthology; Salmon; Smiths Knoll; Staple; Frogmore Papers; Workshop New Poetry; Mountain Path (India). *Memberships:* Poetry Society, UK; British Haiku Society. *Address:* 45 Westfield, Clare, Sudbury, Suffolk, England.

OLIVER, Douglas Dunlop; b. 14 Sept. 1937, Southampton, England. Poet; Novelist; Prosodist. m. (1) Janet Hughes, July 1962, (2) Alice Notley, Feb. 1988, 2 step-s., 2 d. *Education:* BA, Literature, 1975, MA, Applied Linguistics, 1982, University of Essex. *Appointments:* Journalist, newspapers in England, Agence France-Presse, Paris, 1959–72; University Lecturer, Literature, English, various, 1975–; Editorial Board, Franco-British Studies; Co-Ed., Gare du Nord Magazine. *Publications:* Oppo Hectic, 1969; The Harmless Building, 1973; In the Cave of Succession, 1974; The Diagram Poems, 1979; The Infant and the Pearl, 1985; Kind, 1987; Poetry and Narrative in Performance, 1989; Three Variations on the Theme of Harm, 1990; Penniless Politics, 1991; The Scarlet Cabinet (with Alice Notley), 1992; Selected Poems, 1996; Penguin Modern Poets 10, 1996. *Contributions to:* Anthologies including: A Various Art, 1987; The New British Poetry 1968–1988, 1988; Numerous poems, articles, fiction, to magazines and journals. *Honours:* Eastern Arts Grant, 1977; South-East Arts Grant, 1987; Fund for Poetry Grants, 1990, 1991; Judith E. Wilson Lecturer, University of Cambridge, 1995. *Address:* c/o British Institute in Paris, 11 Rue de Constantine, 75007 Paris, France.

OLIVER, Mary; b. 10 Sept. 1935, Cleveland, Ohio, USA. Poet; Educator. *Education:* Ohio State University; Vassar College. *Appointments:* Mather Visiting Prof., Case Western Reserve University, 1980, 1982; Poet-in-Residence, Bucknell University, 1986; Elliston Visiting Prof., University of Cincinnati, 1986; Margaret Banister Writer-in-Residence, Sweet Briar College, 1991–95; William Blackburn Visiting Prof. of Creative Writing, Duke University, 1995; Catharine Osgood Foster Prof., Bennington College, 1996–. *Publications:* No Voyage, and Other Poems, 1963; The River Styx, Ohio, and Other Poems, 1972; The Night Traveler, 1978; Twelve Moons, 1978; Sleeping in the Forest, 1979; American Primitive, 1983; Dream Work, 1986; Provincetown, 1987; House of Light, 1990; New and Selected Poems, 1992; A Poetry Handbook, 1994; White Pine: Poems and Prose Poems, 1994; Blue Pastures, 1995; West Wind, 1997; Rules for the Dance, 1998; Winter Hours, 1999; The Leaf and the Cloud, 2000; What Do We Know, 2002. *Contributions to:* Periodicals in the US and England. *Honours:* Poetry Society of America First Prize, 1962; Devil's Advocate Award, 1968; Shelley Memorial Award, 1972; National Endowment for the Arts Fellowship, 1972–73; Alice Fay di Castagnola Award, 1973; Guggenheim Fellowship, 1980–81; American Acad. and Institute of Arts and Letters Award, 1983; Pulitzer Prize in Poetry, 1984; Christopher Award, 1991; L L Winship Award, 1991; National Book Award for Poetry, 1992; Lannan Literary Award, 1998. *Membership:* PEN. *Address:* c/o Molly Malone Cook Literary Agency, Box 619, Provincetown, MA 02657, USA.

OLIVER, Stephen; b. 5 Dec. 1950, Wellington, New Zealand. Poet; Writer. *Education:* Journalism Diploma, Wellington Polytechnic; Radio New Zealand Broadcasting School. *Publications:* Henwise, 1975; & Interviews, 1978; Autumn Songs, 1978; Letters to James K. Baxter, 1980; Earthbound Mirrors, 1984;

Guardians, Not Angels, 1993; Islands of Wilderness – A Romance, 1996; Election Year Blues, 1999; Unmanned, 1999; Night of Warehouses: Selected Poems 1978–2000. Other: HeadworX (www.headworx.eyes.co.nz), 2001. Contributions to: Numerous international journals, reviews, anthologies and periodicals. Address: PO Box 1661, Strawberry Hills, Sydney, NSW 2012, Australia. E-mail: sao@smartchat.net.au.

OLSEN, David Leslie; b. 13 Dec. 1943, Berkeley, CA, USA. Writer; Poet; Consultant. m. Barbara Gail Schonborn, 17 March 1985, 1 s., 1 d. Education: BA, University of California at Berkeley, 1965; MBA, Golden Gate University, 1983; MA, San Francisco State University, 1987. Appointments: Book Reviewer, Title Pages, 1985–86; English Instructor, De Anza College, Cupertino, CA, 1987; Writer, Ed., LSI Logic Co, 1987–89; Consultant, Schonborn Assocs, 1989–; Editorial Page Columnist, Community Newspapers Co, 1998–. Publication: Greatest Hits (chapbook), 2001. Contributions to: Larcom; Bogg: An Anglo American Journal; Amelia; Western Journal of Medicine; Black Bear; Tomcat; Poetry San Francisco; Homeless Not Helpless; Wrestling with the Angel; Alms House Sampler; Vol No; Pegasus Review; Sunrust; Feelings; Cow in the Road; Poetry Connoisseur; Eve's Legacy; The Literature of Poverty. Honours: Daly City Arts Commisssion Trophy; Poetry First Prizes, Poetry Olympiad. Memberships: Dramatists Guild; Acad. of American Poets; San Francisco Poetry Center. Address: 14 Vine Brook Rd, Westford, MA 01886, USA.

OLSEN, Lance; b. 14 Oct. 1956, USA. Writer; Poet; Critic. m. Andrea Hirsch, 3 Jan. 1981. Education: BA, Honours, University of Wisconsin, 1978; MFA, University of Iowa, 1980; MA, 1982, PhD, 1985, University of Virginia. Appointments: Prof. of Creative Writing and Contemporary Fiction, University of Idaho, 1996–2001; Writer-in-Residence, State of Idaho, 1996–98; Fulbright Scholar, Turku, Finland, 2000. Publications: Ellipse of Uncertainty, 1987; Circus of the Mind in Motion, 1990; Live From Earth, 1991; William Gibson, 1992; My Dates With Franz, 1993; Natural Selections (poems with Jeff Worley), 1993; Scherzi, I Believe, 1994; Tonguing the Zeitgeist, 1994; Lolita, 1995; Burnt, 1996; Time Famine, 1996; Rebel Yell: A Short Guide to Fiction Writing, 1998; Sewing Shut My Eyes, 2000; Freaknest, 2000; Girl Imagined By Chance, 2002. Contributions to: Journals and magazines. Address: PO Box 306, New Meadows, ID 83654, USA.

OLSON, Toby, (Merle Theodore Olson); b. 17 Aug. 1937, Berwyn, IL, USA. Prof. of English; Writer; Poet. Education: BA, English and Philosophy, Occidental College, Los Angeles, 1965; MA, English, Long Island University, 1968. Appointments: Assoc. Dir, Aspen Writers' Workshop, 1964–67; Asst Prof., Long Island University, 1966–74; Faculty, New School for Social Research, New York City, 1967–75; Prof. of English, Temple University, Philadelphia, 1975–2000. Publications: Fiction: The Life of Jesus, 1976; Seaview, 1982; The Woman Who Escaped From Shame, 1986; Utah, 1987; Dorit in Lesbos, 1990; The Pool, 1991; Reading, 1992; At Sea, 1993; Write Letter to Billy, 2000. Poetry: Maps, 1969; Worms Into Nails, 1969; The Hawk-Foot Poems, 1969; The Brand, 1969; Pig's Book, 1970; Vectors, 1972; Fishing, 1973; The Wrestler and Other Poems, 1974; City, 1974; Changing Appearances: Poems 1965–1975, 1975; Home, 1976; Three and One, 1976; Doctor Miriam, 1977; Aesthetics, 1978; The Florence Poems, 1978; Birdsongs, 1980; Two Standards, 1982; Still/Quiet, 1982; Sitting in Gusevik, 1983; We Are the Fire, 1984; Unfinished Building, 1993; Human Nature, 2000. Editor: Writing Talks: Views on Teaching Writing from Across the Professions (with Muffy E A Siegel), 1983. Opera Libretti: Dorit, 1994; Chihuahua, 1999. Contributions to: Numerous anthologies, newspapers, and magazines. Honours: CAPS Award in Poetry, New York State, 1974; Pennsylvania Council on the Arts Fellowship, 1983; PEN/Faulkner Award for Fiction, 1983; Guggenheim Fellowship, 1985; National Endowment for the Arts Fellowship, 1985; Yaddo Fellowships, 1985, 1986; Rockefeller Foundation Fellowship, Bellagio, Italy, 1987; Creative Achievement Award, Temple University, 1990; PENN/Book Philadelphia Award for Fiction, 1990. Address: 275 S 19th St, Philadelphia, PA 19103, USA.

OLUDHE-MACGOYE, Marjorie Phyllis; b. 21 Oct. 1928, Southampton, England (Kenyan Citizen). Writer; Poet; Bookseller. m. D G W Oludhe-Macgoye, 4 June 1960, deceased 1990, 3 s., 1 d. Education: BA, English, 1948, MA, 1953, University of London. Publications: Growing Up at Lina School (children's), 1971; Murder in Majengo (novel), 1972; Song of Nyarloka and Other Poems, 1977; Coming to Birth (novel), 1986; The Story of Kenya (history), 1986; The Present Moment (novel), 1987; Street Life (novella), 1988; Victoria and Murder in Majengo, 1993; Homing In (novel), 1994; Moral Issues in Kenya, 1996; Chira (novel), 1997; The Black Hand Gang (children's), 1997; Make It Sing and Other Poems, 1998. Contributions to: Anthologies, reviews, and journals. Honours: BBC Arts in Africa Poetry Award, 1982; Sinclair Prize for Fiction, 1986. Address: PO Box 70344, Nairobi, Kenya.

O'MALLEY, Martin J. Jr; b. 9 Feb. 1924, Passaic, New Jersey, USA. Teacher (retd); Poet. Education: Teacher's Certificate, New Jersey, 1958; BA, English, Syracuse University, 1959. Publications: The Lun Yu of Kung Fu, 1960; The Tao of Mao Tse-Tung, 1961. Contributions to: Reviews and magazines. Honours: Golden Poet Awards, World of Poetry, 1987–92. Memberships: International Writers and Artists Asscn; National Library of Poetry; World of Poetry; World Poetry, India. Address: 222 Paulison Ave, A-5, Passaic, NJ 07055, USA.

ONDAATJE, (Philip) Michael; b. 12 Sept. 1943, Colombo, Sri Lanka. Poet; Novelist; Dramatist; Teacher; Film Dir. Education: St Thomas' College, Colombo; Dulwich College, London; Bishop's University, Lennoxville, QC, 1962–64; BA, University of Toronto, 1965; MA, Queen's University, Kingston, Ontario, 1967. Appointments: Teacher, University of Western Ontario, 1969–71; Glendon College, York University, Toronto, 1971–; Visting Prof. University of Hawaii, 1979, Brown University, Providence, RI, 1990; Film Dir. Publications: Poetry: The Dainty Monsters, 1967; The Man With Seven Toes, 1969; Left Handed Poems, 1970; Rat Jelly, 1973; Elimination Dance, 1978; There's a Trick with a Knife I'm Learning to Do: Poems, 1963–1978, 1979; Claude Glass, 1979; Tin Roof, 1982; Secular Love, 1984; All Along the Mazinaw, Two Poems, 1986; The Cinnamon Peeler: Selected Poems, 1989; Handwriting, 1998. Fiction: The Collected Works of Billy the Kid, 1970; Coming Through Slaughter, 1976; In the Skin of a Lion, 1987; The English Patient, 1992; Anil's Ghost, 2000. Criticism: Leonard Cohen, 1970. Non-Fiction: Running in the Family, 1982. Editor: The Broken Ark, verse, 1971, revised edn as A Book of Beasts, 1979; Personal Fictions: Stories by Monroe, Wiebe, Thomas, and Blaise, 1977; The Long Poem Anthology, 1979; Brushes With Greatness: An Anthology of Chance Encounters with Greatness (with Russell Banks and David Young), 1989; The Brick Anthology (with Linda Spalding), 1989; From Ink Lake: An Anthology of Canadian Short Stories, 1990; The Faber Book of Contemporary Canadian Short Stories, 1990. Honours: Ralph Gustafson Award, 1965; Epstein Award, 1966; E J Pratt Medal, 1966; Canadian Governor-General's Awards for Literature, 1971, 1980, 1992; W H Smith/Books in Canada First Novel Award, 1977; Canada-Australia Prize, 1980; City of Toronto Arts Award, 1987; Trillium Book Awards, 1987, 1992; Booker McConnell Prize, British Book Council, 1992; Canadian Authors Asscn Author of the Year Award, 1993; Commonwealth Prize (regional), international nomination, 1993; Chianti Ruffino-Antonio Fattore International Literary Prize, 1994; Nelly Sachs Award, 1995; Premio Grinzane Cavour, 1996; Irish Times International Literature Prize, 2001. Address: c/o Ellen Levine Literary Agency, 15 E 26th St, Suite 1801, New York, NY 10010, USA.

O'NEILL, Michael (Stephen Charles); b. 2 Sept. 1953, Aldershot, Hampshire, England. Prof. of English; Writer; Poet; Ed. m. Rosemary Ann McKendrick, 16 July 1977, 1 s., 1 d. Education: BA, English, 1975, DPhil, 1981, Exeter College, Oxford. Appointments: Faculty, 1979–91, Senior Lecturer, 1991–93, Reader, 1993–95, Prof. of English, 1995–, University of Durham; Co-Founder and Ed., Poetry Durham, 1982–94. Publications: The Human Mind's Imaginings: Conflict and Achievement in Shelley's Poetry, 1989; Percy Bysshe Shelley: A Literary Life, 1989; The Stripped Bed (poems), 1990; Auden, MacNeice, Spender: The Thirties Poetry (with Gareth Reeves), 1992; Percy Bysshe Shelley (ed.), 1993; The 'Defence of Poetry' Fair Copies (ed.), 1994; Keats: Bicentenary Readings (ed.), 1997; Fair-Copy Manuscripts of Shelley's Poems in American and European Libraries (ed. with Donald H Reiman), 1997; Romanticism and the Self-Conscious Poem, 1997; Literature of the Romantic Period: A Bibliographical Guide (ed.), 1998. Contributions to: Books and journals. Honours: Eric Gregory Award, 1983; Cholmondeley Award, 1990. Membership: Fellow, English Asscn, 2000–. Address: c/o Dept of English Studies, University of Durham, England.

ONU, Johnson Olema, (Olema); b. 30 Jan. 1957, Nigeria. Airman; Poet. m. Owakoyi Onu, 26 Aug. 1978, 2 s., 4 d. Education: Diploma, Personnel Management, Kaduna Polytechnic, Nigeria, 1984; Advanced Diploma, Public Administration, University of Jos, Nigeria, 1994. Appointment: Asst Chief Clerk, Directorate of Armament, Nigerian Air Force Headquarters, Lagos, Nigeria. Publications: If I Die in the Struggle, 1992; Travails of Freedom, 1996. Contributions to: Newswatch Magazine; Voice Newspaper; Challenge Magazine. Memberships: Asscn of Nigerian Authors; Poetry League, Benue State, Nigeria. Address: Headquarters, Nigerian Air Force, Ministry of Defense, Lagos, Nigeria.

OOKA, Makoto; b. 16 Feb. 1931, Mishima City, Japan. Poet; Author. m. Kaneko Aizawa, 1957, 1 s., 1 d. Education: Degree in Literature, Tokyo National University, 1953. Appointments: Asst Prof., 1965–70, Prof., 1970–87, Meiji University, Tokyo; Prof., National University of Fine Arts and Music, Tokyo, 1988–93; Soshitsu Sen XV Distinguished Lecturer in Japanese Culture and Visiting Fellow, Donald Keene Center of Japanese Culture, Columbia University, 2000. Publications (in English trans.); A String Around Autumn: Selected Poems, 1952–1980, 1982; A Play of Mirrors: Eight Major Poets of Modern Japan (ed. with Thomas Fitzsimmons), 1987; The Colors of Poetry: Essays in Classic Japanese Verse, 1991; Elegy and Benediction: Selected Poems, 1947–1989, 1991; A Poet's Anthology: The Range of Japanese Poetry, 1994; What the Kite Thinks: A Linked Poem (with others), 1994; Taiga (with Taiga Ike and Tadashi Kobayashi), 1994; Beneath the Sleepless Tossing of the Planets: Selected Poems, 1972–1989, 1995; The Poetry and Poetics of Ancient Japan (ed.), 1997; Love Songs from the Man'yoshu: Selections from a Japanese Classic, 2000. Honours: Officier de l'Ordre des Arts et Lettres, France, 1993; Asahi Prize, 1996; Imperial Award, Japanese Art Acad., 1996; Designated 'Person of Cultural Merit', Japanese government, 1997. Memberships: Japan Art Acad.; Japanese PEN, pres., 1989–93; Poetry International, Rotterdam; Poet's Asscn, Japan, pres., 1979–81. Address: 5-11-5 Jindaiji Minami-cho, Chofu-shi, Tokyo 182-0013, Japan.

OPSTAD, Steinar; b. 28 June 1971, Stokke, Norway. Poet. *Education:* Studied Literature and Languages, Universities of Bergen and Oslo. *Publications:* Tavler og bud (Tablets and Commandments), 1996; Den alminnelige, 1998. *Contributions to:* Vagant; Vinduet; Kritikkjournalen; Den Blå Port; Others. *Honour:* Tarjei Vesaas Prize for Best First Book, 1997. *Membership:* Den Norske Forfatterforening.

ORBAN, Otto; b. 20 May 1936, Budapest, Hungary. Poet; Essayist; Trans.; Ed. m. 23 May 1962, 2 s. *Education:* Unfinished university studies. *Appointments:* Senior Ed., Kortars literary magazine, 1981–; Fulbright Poet, Hamline University, St Paul, Minnesota, University of Minnesota, 1987. *Publications:* Poetry: Szegenynek lenni, 1974; Osszegyujott versek, 1986; Egyik oldalarol a masikra fordulel, 1992. Other: Essays and trans. *Honours:* József Attila Prizes, 1973, 1985; Robert Graves literary prize, 1972; Dery Prize, 1986; Radnoti Prize, 1987; Weores Sandor Prize, 1990; Kossuth Prize, 1992. *Memberships:* Hungarian PEN Club, vice-pres., 1989–; Hungarian Writers' Union; Union of Hungarian Journalists. *Address:* Becsi ut 88-90, 1034 Budapest, Hungary.

ORIOL, Jacques, (Jacques F G Vandievoet); b. 1 Oct. 1923, Brussels, Belgium. Geography Teacher (retd); Poet; Essayist; Critic. 1 s. *Education:* Agrégation, secondary school teaching, 1951. *Publications:* Quarantaine, 1983; Dédicaces, 1984; Midi déjè Minuit, 1985; Voyage, 1986; Etat critique, 1987; Poète aujourd'hui, comment dire?, 1989; Demi-deuil, 1990; Dilecta, 1993. *Contributions to:* Books and journals. *Honours:* François Villon Prize, National Asscn of French Writers, 1986; First Prize, Classical Poetry, École de la Loire, Blois, 1989. *Memberships:* Asscn of Belgian Authors; PEN Club, Belgian Section; Union of Walloon Writers and Artists. *Address:* 210 Ave Molière, boite 10, 1060, Brussels, Belgium.

ORME, David John; b. 1 March 1948, Stoke-on-Trent, Staffordshire, England. Poet; Writer; Ed.; Educational Consultant. m. Helen Bird, 15 Aug. 1971, 2 s. *Education:* Certificate of Education, Christ Church College, Canterbury; BA, Open University. *Appointment:* Internet Ed., magic-nation.com. *Publications:* A Fear of Bells, 1982; The Gravedigger's Sandwich, 1992; Heroes and Villains, 1993; A Magic Nation, 2002. *Membership:* Society of Authors. *Address:* 27 Pennington Close, Colden Common, Winchester SO21 1UR, England. *E-mail:* mail@davidorme.co.uk.

ORME-COLLINS, Donna Youngoon, (Morgan Storm); b. 10 Feb. 1970, Wimbledon, England. Poet; Writer. m. Jonathon R Collins, 23 Dec. 1994, 1 d. *Education:* Mount Vernon College, Washington, DC. *Contributions to:* Several publications. *Membership:* Arizona Poetry Society. *Address:* 4925 E Desert Cove, Apt No. 208, Scottsdale, AZ 85254, USA.

ORMSBY, Eric; b. 16 Oct. 1941, Atlanta, GA, USA. Prof.; Poet; Writer. m. Irena Murray, 30 Sept. 1995, 2 s. *Education:* BA, 1971; MA, 1973; MLS, 1978; PhD, 1981. *Appointments:* Curator, Near East Collections, Princeton University, 1977–83; Dir of Libraries, Catholic University, 1983–86; Dir of Libraries, 1986–96, Prof., 1996–, McGill University. *Publications:* Bavarian Shrine, 1990; Coastlines, 1992; For a Modest God: New and Selected Poems, 1997. *Contributions to:* New Republic; New Yorker; Grand Street; Poetry Wales; Poetry Canada; Paris Review; Southern Review; Gettysburg Review; Chelsea. *Honours:* Special Commendation, Cheltenham Poetry Competition, 1987; A M Klein Prize for Poetry, 1991; Ingram Merrill Foundation Award, 1992. *Address:* 2600 Pierre Dupuy, Apt 207, Montréal H3C 3R6, Canada.

ORMSBY, Frank; b. 30 Oct. 1947, Enniskillen County, Fermanagh, Northern Ireland. Poet; Writer; Ed. *Education:* BA, English, 1970, MA, 1971, Queen's University, Belfast. *Appointment:* Ed., The Honest Ulsterman, 1969–89. *Publications:* A Store of Candles, 1977; Poets from the North of Ireland (ed.), 1979; A Northern Spring, 1986; Northern Windows: An Anthology of Ulster Autobiography (ed.), 1987; The Long Embrace: Twentieth Century Irish Love Poems (ed.), 1987; Thine in Storm and Calm: An Amanda McKittrick Ros Reader (ed.), 1988; The Collected Poems of John Hewitt (ed.), 1991; A Rage for Order: Poetry of the Northern Ireland Troubles (ed.), 1992; The Ghost Train, 1995. *Address:* 36 Strathmore Park N, Belfast BT15 5HR, Northern Ireland.

ORR, Gregory (Simpson); b. 3 Feb. 1947, Albany, New York, USA. Prof. of English; Poet; Writer. m. Trisha Winer, 1973, 2 d. *Education:* BA, Antioch College, 1969; MFA, Columbia University, 1972. *Appointments:* Asst Prof., 1975–80, Assoc. Prof., 1980–88, Prof. of English, 1988–, University of Virginia; Poetry Consultant, Virginia Quarterly Review, 1976–; Visiting Writer, University of Hawaii at Manoa, 1982. *Publications:* Poetry: Burning the Empty Nests, 1973; Gathering the Bones Together, 1975; Salt Wings, 1980; The Red House, 1980; We Must Make a Kingdom of It, 1986; New and Selected Poems, 1988; City of Salt, 1995. Non-Fiction: Stanley Kunitz: An Introduction to the Poetry, 1985; Richer Entanglements: Essays and Notes on Poetry and Poems, 1993. *Honours:* Acad. of American Poets Prize, 1970; YM-YWHA Discovery Award, 1970; Bread Loaf Writers Conference Transatlantic Review Award, 1976; Guggenheim Fellowship, 1977; National Endowment for the Arts Fellowships, 1978, 1989; Fulbright Grant, 1983. *Address:* c/o Dept of English, University of Virginia, Charlottesville, VA 22903, USA.

ORSZAG-LAND, Thomas; b. 12 Jan. 1938, Budapest, Hungary. Writer; Poet; Trans. 2 s. *Publications:* Berlin Proposal, 1990; Free Women, 1991; Tales of Matriarchy, 1998. Translator: Bluebeard's Castle, 1988; Splendid Stags, 1992; 33 Poems by Radnoti, 1992; Poems by Mezei, 1995. *Contributions to:* Newspapers and reviews. *Memberships:* Foreign Press Asscn; International PEN, fellow; Royal Institute of International Affairs; Society of Authors. *Address:* PO Box 1213, London, N6 6HZ, England.

ORTIZ, Simon J(oseph); b. 27 May 1941, Albuquerque, New Mexico, USA. Poet; Writer. m. Marlene Foster, Dec. 1981, divorced Sept. 1984, 3 c. *Education:* Fort Lewis College, 1961–62; University of New Mexico, 1966–68; University of Iowa, 1968–69. *Appointments:* Instructor, San Diego State University, 1974, Institute of American Arts, Santa Fe, New Mexico, 1974, Navajo Community College, Tsaile, AZ, 1975–77, College of Marin, Kentfield, CA, 1976–79, University of New Mexico, Albuquerque, 1979–81, Sinte Gleska College, Mission, South Dakota, 1985–86, Lewis and Clark College, Portland, Oregon, 1990; Consulting Ed., Navajo Comunity College Press, Tsaile, 1982–83, Pueblo of Acoma Press, Acoma, New Mexico, 1982–84; Arts Co-ordinator, Metropolitan Arts Commission, Portland, Oregon, 1990. *Publications:* Naked in the Wind (poems), 1971; Going for the Rain (poems), 1976; A Good Journey (poems), 1977; Howbah Indians (short stories), 1978; Song, Poetry, Language (essays), 1978; Fight Back: For the Sake of the People, For the Sake of the Land (poems and prose), 1980; From Sand Creek: Rising in This Heart Which is Our America (poems), 1981; A Poem is a Journey, 1981; The Importance of Childhood, 1982; Fightin': New and Collected Stories, 1983; Woven Stone: A 3-in-1 Volume of Poetry and Prose, 1991; After and Before the Lightning (poems), 1994. Editor: Califa: The California Poetry (co-ed.), 1978; A Ceremony of Brotherhood (co-ed.), 1980; Earth Power Coming (anthology of Native American short fiction), 1983. *Contributions to:* Various anthologies and textbooks. *Honours:* National Endowment for the Arts Discovery Award, 1969, and Fellowship, 1981; Honored Poet, White House Salute to Poetry and American Poets, 1980; New Mexico Humanities Council Humanitarian Award for Literary Achievement, 1989. *Address:* 3535 N First Ave, No. R-10, Tucson, AZ 85719, USA.

ORTT-SAEED, Jocelyn Anne; b. 18 Jan. 1935, Brisbane, Qld, Australia. Writer; Poet; Educator. m. Mohammed Saeed, 19 Sept. 1959, 3 s., 3 d. *Education:* BA, German and Philosophy, University of Queensland; Teaching Diploma in Language and Literature, Bavarian Ministry of Education, 1961. *Publications:* Rainbow of Promise, 1964; Where No Road Goes, 1968; Between Forever and Never, 1971; Selected Poems, 1986; Burning Bush, 1994; With Silence Surrounded, 2000; Silence Goes on Flowering, 2001. *Contributions to:* Newspapers, magazines and journals. *Honours:* Prizes and awards in Australia and the USA. *Memberships:* Human Rights Commission; World Futures Studies; Literacy for Mothers; Fellowship of Australian Writers; Lahore Arts Forum; Quaid-i-Azam Poets' Reading Group, Lahore. *Address:* Stillpoint, 72-H Tagore Rd, Gulberg III, Lahore, Pakistan.

O'RUAIRC, Micheál, (Crom Dubh); b. 26 May 1953, Kerry, Ireland. Writer; Poet. m. Bríd Clifford, 21 April 1984, 1 s. *Education:* BA, HDE, University College Cork, 1974, 1975; MA, Maynooth University, 1991. *Publications:* Fuil Samhraidh, 1987; Humane Killing, 1992; Dán Is Céad On Leitriúch, 1998; Leocó I Liosnacaolbhuí, 1999. *Contributions to:* Irish Times; Irish Literary Supplement; Honest Ulsterman; Poetry Ireland; Innti; Comhar; RTÉ. *Honours:* Duais An Oireachtais, 1987, 1988. *Memberships:* Poetry Ireland; Irish Writers' Union; PEN. *Address:* 4 Garrán an Ulloird, Cúl Mín, Baile Bhlainséir, Baile Atha Cliath 15, Ireland.

OSBORN, Howard Andrew Morris; b. 28 Nov. 1960, Woking, Surrey, England. Writer; Poet. m. Christine Knowles, 22 June 1985. *Education:* BA, Honours, English Language and Literature, University of Manchester, 1983. *Contributions to:* Odyssey; Illuminations; Outposts; The Third Half. *Address:* 2 Asten Buildings, Cowpe, Waterfoot, Rossendale, Lancashire BB4 7DR, England.

OSBORN, Karen; b. 26 April 1954, Chicago, IL, USA. Novelist; Poet. m. Michael Jenkins, 21 May 1983, 2 d. *Education:* BA, cum laude, Hollins College, 1979; MFA, University of Arkansas at Fayetteville, 1983. *Appointments:* Poet, 1979–83, Dir, 1982–83, Arkansas Poetry in the Schools; Instructor of English, Clemson University, 1983–87; Part-time Instructor of English, University of Kentucky, 1988–93; Various workshops and readings. *Publications:* Patchwork, 1991; Between Earth and Sky, 1996; Bloodlines, 1999. *Contributions to:* Numerous anthologies, including: Jumping Pond: Poems and Stories from the Ozarks; Cardinal: A Contemporary Anthology; Hollins Anthology; Poems to numerous periodicals, including: Artemis; Mid American Review; Seattle Review; Tar River Poetry; Embers; Southern Review; Kansas Quarterly; Poet Lore; Passages North; Montana Review; Centennial Review; Wisconsin Review. *Honours:* Hollins Literary Festival Awards for Poetry, for Fiction, 1979; Nancy Thorp Prize for Poetry, 1979; Mary Vincent Long Award, Distinguished Literary Achievement, 1979; Kentucky Foundation for Women Grant, 1991; Al Smith Artists Fellowship Award for Fiction, Kentucky Arts Council, 1991; New York Times Notable Book, 1991. *Address:* c/o Gelfman Shneider, 250 W 57th St, New York, NY 10107, USA.

OSBORNE, Charles (Thomas); b. 24 Nov. 1927, Brisbane, Qld, Australia. Writer; Critic; Poet. *Education:* Griffith University, 1944. *Appointments:* Asst Ed., London Magazine, 1968–66; Asst Literary Dir, 1966–71, Dir, 1971–86, Arts Council of Great Britain; Opera Critic, Jewish Chronicle, 1985–; Chief Theatre Critic, Daily Telegraph, 1986–92. *Publications:* The Gentle Planet, 1957; Swansong, 1968; The Complete Operas of Verdi, 1969; W H Auden: The Life of a Poet, 1980; Letter to W H Auden and Other Poems, 1984; Giving It Way, 1986; The Bel Canto Operas, 1994; The Pink Danube, 1998. *Contributions to:* Anthologies, newspapers and journals. *Honour:* Gold Medal, 1993. *Memberships:* Critics' Circle; PEN; Fellow, RSL. *Address:* 125 St George's Rd, London SE1 6HY, England.

OSERS, Ewald; b. 13 May 1917, Prague, Czechoslovakia. Poet; Writer; Trans. m. Mary Harman, 3 June 1942, 1 s., 1 d. *Education:* University of Prague; BA, Honours, University of London. *Appointment:* Editorial Dir, Babel, 1979–87. *Publications:* Poetry: Wish You Were Here, 1976; Arrive Where We Started, 1995. Translator: Over 130 books, including 39 vols of poetry. *Contributions to:* Magazines. *Honours:* Cyril and Methodius Order, First Class, Bulgaria, 1987; European Poetry Trans. Prize, 1987; Vitezlaw Nezval Medal, Czechoslovakia, 1987; Golden Pen, Macedonia, 1988; Officer's Cross of Merit, Germany, 1991; Order of Merit, Czech Republic, 1997. *Memberships:* International PEN, English Centre, fellow; Poetry Society; RSL, fellow; Society of Authors. *Address:* 33 Reades Lane, Sonning Common, Reading, Berkshire RG4 9LL, England.

OSHEROW, Jacqueline; b. 15 Aug. 1956, Philadelphia, Pennsylvania, USA. Assoc. Prof. of English and Writing; Poet. m. Saul Korewa, 16 June 1985, 2 d. *Education:* AB, magna cum laude, History and Literature, Harvard University, 1978; Satisfied Examiners, Trinity College, Cambridge, 1979; PhD, English Literature, Princeton University, 1990. *Appointment:* Assoc. Prof. of English. *Publications:* Looking for Angels in New York, 1988; Conversations with Survivors, 1994; With a Moon in Transit, 1996. *Contributions to:* New Yorker; TLS; Paris Review; Triquarterly; Partisan Review; Shenandoah; Georgia Review; Denver Quarterly; New Republic; Western Humanities Review. *Honours:* University Chancellor's Medal, University of Cambridge, 1979; Witter Bynner Prize, American Acad. and Institute of Arts and Letters, 1990; John Masefield Memorial Award, 1993; Lucille Medwick Memorial Award, 1995. *Membership:* Poetry Society of America; PEN; Acad. of American Poets. *Address:* Dept of English, 3500 LNCO, University of Utah, Salt Lake City, UT 84112, USA.

O'SIADHAIL, Micheal; b. 12 Jan. 1947, Dublin, Ireland. Poet; Writer. m. Brid Carroll, 2 July 1970. *Education:* BA, 1968, MLitt, 1971, Trinity College, Dublin; University of Oslo, 1968–69. *Appointments:* Lecturer, Trinity College, Dublin, 1969–73; Prof., Dublin Institute for Advanced Studies, 1974–87; Visiting Prof., University of Iceland, 1982; Ed., Poetry Ireland Review, 1989–91; Ireland's Advisory Committee on Cultural Relations, 1990–97. *Publications:* Poetry: Springnight, 1983; The Image Wheel, 1985; The Chosen Garden, 1990; Hail! Madam Jazz: New and Selected Poems, 1992; A Fragile City, 1995; Our Double Time, 1998; Poems 1975–1995, 1999; The Gossamer Wall: Poems in Witness to the Holocaust, 2002. Other: Learning Irish, 1980; Modern Irish, 1989. *Honours:* Irish-American Cultural Prize for Poetry, 1982; Poetry Book of the Year, Sunday Tribune, 1992; Marten Toonder Prize for Literature, 1998. *Memberships:* Aosdána, founder-mem., 1982–; Dublin International Writers' Festival, board mem.; Ireland Literature Exchange, founder-chair., 1992–. *Address:* 5 Trimleston Ave, Booterstown, Co Dublin, Ireland. *Website:* www.osiadhail.com.

OSOFISAN, Femi, (Babafemi Adeyemi Osofisan); b. 16 June 1946, Erunwon, Nigeria. Dramatist; Writer; Poet; University Teacher. *Education:* BA, 1969, PhD, 1974, University of Ibadan. *Appointment:* Faculty, University of Ibadan, 1973–. *Publications:* Many plays, including: You Have Lost Your Fine Face, 1969; Red is the Freedom Road, 1974; A Restless Run of Locusts, 1975; Once Upon Four Robbers, 1978; Farewell to a Cannibal Rage, 1975; Birthdays Are Not for Dying, 1981; The Oriki of a Grasshopper, 1981; No More the Wasted Breed, 1982; Midnight Hotel, 1982; Aringindin and the Nightwatchman, 1989. Fiction: Kolera Kolej, 1975; Cordelia, 1990. Poetry: Minted Coins, 1986; Dreamseeker on Divining Chain, 1993. *Honour:* Fulbright Fellowship, 1986. *Address:* c/o Dept of Theatre Arts, University of Ibadan, Ibadan, Nigeria.

OSTERBERG, Myra Janet, (Myrna Rose); b. 20 Oct. 1931, Salem, South Dakota, USA. Poet. m. (1) Dale D Spicer, 26 March 1951, 2 d., (2) Leland B Osterberg, 7 June 1969, 1 s., 1 d. *Education:* Graduate, St Mary's High School, Salem, South Dakota, 1949. *Publication:* From My Heart, 1968. *Contributions to:* Anthologies and other publications. *Membership:* South Dakota State Poetry Society, chair., annual poetry contest, 1992–. *Address:* PO Box 613, Salem, SD 57058, USA.

OSTRIKER, Alicia Suskin; b. 11 Nov. 1937, New York, NY, USA. Prof. of English and Creative Writing; Poet; Writer. m. Jeremiah P. Ostriker, 2 Dec. 1958, 1 s., 2 d. *Education:* BA, Brandeis University, 1959; MA, 1960, PhD, 1964, University of Wisconsin. *Appointments:* Asst Prof., 1965–68, Assoc. Prof., 1968–72, Prof. of English and Creative Writing, 1972–, Rutgers University. *Publications:* Poetry: Songs, 1969; Once More Out of Darkness and Other Poems, 1974; A Dream of Springtime: Poems, 1970–77, 1978; The Mother-

Child Papers, 1980; A Woman Under the Surface, 1983; The Imaginary Lover, 1986; Green Age, 1989; The Crack in Everything, 1996; The Little Space: Poems Selected and New 1968–1998, 1998. Criticism: Vision and Verse in William Blake, 1965; Writing Like a Woman, 1982; Stealing the Language, 1986; Feminist Revision and the Bible, 1993; The Nakedness of the Fathers: Biblical Visions and Revisions, 1994; Dancing at the Devil's Party: Essays of Poetry, Politics and the Erotic, 2000. *Contributions to:* Professional journals and general publications. *Honours:* National Endowment for the Arts Fellowship, 1977; Guggenheim Fellowship, 1984–85; William Carlos Williams Prize, Poetry Society of America, 1986; Strousse Poetry Prize, Prairie Schooner, 1987; Anna Rosenberg Poetry Award, 1994; Paterson Poetry Prize, 1996; San Francisco State Poetry Center Award, 1997; Bookman News Book of the Year, 1998. *Memberships:* MLA; PEN; Poetry Society of America, board of governors, 1988–91. *Address:* 33 Philip Dr., Princeton, NJ 08540, USA.

OSTROM, Hans (Ansgar); b. 29 Jan. 1954, Grass Valley, CA, USA. Prof. of English; Writer; Poet. m. Jacquelyn Bacon, 18 July 1983, 1 s. *Education:* BA, English, 1975, MA, English, 1979, PhD, English, 1982, University of California at Davis. *Appointments:* Faculty, University of California at Davis, 1977–80, 1981–83; Visiting Lecturer in American Studies, Johannes Gutenberg University, Mainz, 1980–81; Prof. of English, University of Puget Sound, Tacoma, Washington, 1983–; Fulbright Senior Lecturer, University of Uppsala, 1994. *Publications:* The Living Language: A Reader (co-ed.), 1984; Leigh Hunt: A Reference Guide (with Tim Lulofs), 1985; Spectrum: A Reader (co-ed.), 1987; Lives and Moments: An Introduction to Short Fiction, 1991; Three to Get Ready (novel), 1991; Langston Hughes: A Study of the Short Fiction, 1993; Colors of a Different Horse (ed. with Wendy Bishop), 1994; Water's Night (poems with Wendy Bishop), 1994; Genres of Writing: Mapping the Territories of Discourse (ed. with Wendy Bishop), 1997; The Coast Starlight (poems), 1998. *Contributions to:* Books, journals, reviews, and magazines. *Honours:* First Prize, Harvest Awards, University of Houston, 1978; Grand Prize, Ina Coolbrith Memorial Award, 1979; First Prize, Warren Eyster Competition, New Delta Review, 1985; Second Prize, Redbook Magazine Annual Fiction Contest, 1985; John Lantz Fellowship, University of Puget Sound, 1996–97. *Memberships:* American Asscn of University Profs; Conference on College Composition and Communication; MLA; National Book Critics Circle; National Council of Teachers of English. *Address:* c/o Dept of English, University of Puget Sound, Tacoma, WA 98416, USA.

O'SULLIVAN, Declan Patrick; b. 18 Feb. 1967, Plymouth, Devon, England. Poet. *Education:* BA, Public Administration, Leicester Polytechnic, 1991; MPhil, Peace Studies, Trinity College, Dublin, 1992; PhD, Islamic Studies, University of Durham. *Appointments:* Administrator, National Opinion Poll, Oxford Branch, 1994–95; Research and Campaign Asst, Middle East Section, Amnesty International's International Secretariat, London, 1995–96. *Publications:* Poems: Just Visiting, 1997; Empty Voices, Meaningful Words, 1997; Verse From Within, 1997; Cherished Memories, 1997; A Season's Delight, 1998; A New Horizon, 1998; That's Life, 1998; Villanelle Vogue, 1998; Vivid Emotions, 1998. *Contributions to:* Spotlight Poets; Anchor Books Northern Verse, 1999; The Tavistock Wharf Anthology, 1996; Triumph House; Poetry Now; Arrival Press. *Address:* Shincliffe Hall, Hall Lane, Shincliffe, Durham DH1 2SY, England.

O'SULLIVAN, Maggie; b. 20 July 1951, Lincoln, England. Poet. *Publications:* Concerning Spheres, 1982; An Incomplete Natural History, 1984; A Natural History in 3 Incomplete Parts, 1985; Un-Assuming Personas, 1985; Divisions of Labour, 1986; From the Handbook of That and Furriery, 1986; States of Emergency, 1987; Unofficial Word, 1988; In the House of the Shaman, 1993; Ellen's Lament, 1993; Excla (with Bruce Andrews), 1993; That Bread Should Be, 1996; Out of Everywhere (ed.), 1996. *Contributions to:* City Limits; Reality Studios; Poetry Review; Slow Dancer; Writing Women; Angel Exhaust; Archeus; Palpi; Responses; Critical Quarterly; Inkblot; Writing; Sink; Raddle Moon; Ligne; Avec. *Address:* Middle Fold Farm, Colden, Hebden Bridge, West Yorkshire HX7 7PG, England.

O'SULLIVAN, Vincent (Gerard); b. 28 Sept. 1937, Auckland, New Zealand. Poet; Writer; Dramatist; Ed. *Education:* MA, University of Auckland, 1959; BLitt, Lincoln College, Oxford, 1962. *Publications:* In Quiet, 1956; Opinions: Chapters on Gissing, Rolfe, Wilde, Unicorn, 1959; Our Burning Time, 1965; Revenants, 1969; An Anthology of Twentieth Century New Zealand Poetry (ed.), 1970; Bearings, 1973; New Zealand Poetry in the Sixties, 1973; Katherine Mansfield's New Zealand, 1975; New Zealand Short Stories (ed.), 1975; From the Indian Funeral, 1976; James K. Baxter, 1976; Miracle: A Romance, 1976; Butcher & Co, 1977; The Boy, the Bridge, the River, 1978; Brother Jonathan, Brother Kafka, 1980; Dandy Edison for Lunch and Other Stories, 1981; The Rose Ballroom and Other Poems, 1982; The Butcher Papers, 1982; The Oxford Book of New Zealand Writing Since 1945 (ed. with MacDonald P. Jackson), 1983; The Collected Letters of Katherine Mansfield (ed. with Margaret Scott), three vols, 1984–96; Shuriken (play), 1985; Survivals, 1986; The Pilate Tapes, 1986; Poems of Katherine Mansfield (ed.), 1988; Jones and Jones (play), 1989; Billy, 1990; The Snow in Spain, 1990; Palms and Minarets: Selected Stories, 1992; Selected Poems, 1992; The Oxford Book of New Zealand Short Stories (ed.), 1994; Believers to the Bright Coast, 1998. *Honours:* Jessie Mackay Award, 1965; Farmers Poetry Prize, 1967; New Zealand Book Award, 1981. *Address:* Pukeroro, RD 3, Hamilton, New Zealand.

OTTEN, Charlotte F(ennema); b. 1 March 1926, Chicago, IL, USA. Prof. of English (retd); Poet; Writer. m. Robert T Otten, 21 Dec. 1948, 2 s. *Education:* AB, English and American Language and Literature, Calvin College, Grand Rapids, 1949; MA, English and American Language and Literature, 1969, PhD, English Literature and Language, 1971, Michigan State University. *Appointments:* Assoc. Prof. of English, Grand Valley State University, Allendale, Michigan, 1971–77; Lecturer on Women and Literature, University of Michigan Extension Center, 1972; Prof. of English, Calvin College, Grand Rapids, 1977–91. *Publications:* Environ'd with Eternity: God, Poems, and Plants in Sixteenth and Seventeenth Century England, 1985; A Lycanthropy Reader: Werewolves in Western Culture, 1986; The Voice of the Narrator in Children's Literature (ed. with Gary D Schmidt), 1989; English Women's Voices, 1540–1700, 1992; The Virago Book of Birth Poetry, 1993; The Book of Birth Poetry, 1995; January Rides the Wind, 1997; The Literary Werewolf: An Anthology, 2002; Something Sweeter than Honey, 2002. *Contributions to:* Scholarly books and journals and poetry journals. *Honours:* Several grants and fellowships; Roland H Bainton Book Prize in Early Modern Studies Nomination, 1992; Eds' Choice, Booklist, 1997. *Memberships:* Milton Society of America; MLA; Shakespeare Asscn of America; Society for Literature and Science; Society for Textual Scholarship; Society of Children's Book Writers and Illustrators. *Address:* c/o Dept of English, Calvin College, 3201 Burton St SE, Grand Rapids, MI 49546, USA.

OURIN, Viktor A.; b. 3 June 1924, Russia. Poet; Publisher; Ed.; Sculptor. 1 s. *Education:* MLitt, Maxim Gorky Literary Institute, Moscow, 1949. *Appointments:* Pres., Friends of the Globe Poetry Library, 1971–96; Founder, Olympoetry Movement Fund; Ed.-in-Chief, International Magazine of Poetry. *Publications:* Complete Olympoetry Anthologies, 7 vols, 1980–96; Selected Lyrics, 7 vols, 1988–94; Collected Works, 7 vols, 1988–94. *Contributions to:* Numerous anthologies and magazines worldwide. *Honours:* First Prize, Berlin International Festival, 1968; Madhusudan Acad. Best Book Award, Calcutta, 1993; Alexander of Macedon Medal, Asscn of Poets of Greece, 1994. *Memberships:* American Club of Writers; New York Forum of Poets; World Acad. of Arts and Culture; World Congress of Poets. *Address:* 3395 Neptune Ave, No. 124, New York, NY 11224, USA.

OUTRAM, Richard (Daley); b. 9 April 1930, Oshawa, Ontario, Canada. Poet; Publisher. m. Barbara Howard, 13 April 1957. *Education:* BA, Victoria College, University of Toronto, 1953. *Appointment:* Co-Founder (with Barbara Howard), The Gauntlet Press, 1959. *Publications:* Eight Poems, 1959; Exsulate, Jubilate, 1966; Creatures, 1972; Seer, 1973; Thresholds, 1974; Locus, 1974; Turns and Other Poems, 1975; Arbor, 1976; The Promise of Light, 1979; Selected Poems 1960–1980, 1984; Man in Love, 1985; Benedict Abroad, 1988; Hiram and Jenny, 1989; Mogul Recollected, 1993; Around and About the Toronto Islands, 1993; Peripatetics, 1994; Tradecraft, 1994; Eros Descending, 1995. *Honours:* Reading and exibition of his published work, National Library of Canada, 1986; City of Toronto Book Award, 1999. *Memberships:* PEN Canada; Arts and Letters Club of Toronto. *Address:* 226 Roslin Ave, Toronto, Ontario M4N 1Z6, Canada.

OVERY, Clara May. See: BASS, Clara May Overy.

OVESEN, Ellis; b. 18 July 1923, New Effington, South Dakota, USA. Poet; Writer; Artist; Composer. m. Thor Lowe Smith, 27 Aug. 1949, 2 s. *Education:* MA, cum laude, University of Wisconsin, 1948; California Teacher's Credential, San Jose State University, 1962; Extra classes in poetry writing. *Appointments:* Teacher of English, University of Wisconsin, 1946–48, San Jose State University, 1962–63; Teaching Poetry, 1963–90. *Publications:* Gloried Grass, 1970; Haloed Paths, 1973; To Those Who Love, 1974; The Last Hour: Lives Touch, 1975; A Time for Singing, 1977; A Book of Praises, 1977; Beloved I, 1980, II, 1990; The Green Madonna, 1984; The Flowers of God, 1985; The Keeper of the Word, 1985; The Wing Brush, 1986; The Year of the Snake, 1989; The Year of the Horse, 1990. *Contributions to:* Poet India; Los Altos Town Crier; Paisley Moon; Fresh Hot Bread; Samvedana; Plowman. *Honours:* Los Altos Hills Poet, 1976–90; Hon. Doctorate, World Acad. of Arts and Culture, 1986; Dame of Merit, Knights of Malta, 1988; Golden Poet Awards, 1988, 1989, 1991; Research Fellow, 1992. *Memberships:* National Writers Club; California Writers Club; Poetry Society of America; California State Poetry Society. *Address:* Box 482, Los Altos, CA 94023, USA.

OWEN, Eileen; b. 27 Feb. 1949, Concord, New Hampshire, USA. Poet; Writer. m. John D Owen, 19 June 1971. *Education:* BA, Spanish, University of New Hampshire, 1971; BA, English, 1979, MA, Creative Writing, 1981, University of Washington. *Appointment:* Artist-in-Residence, Ucross Foundation, Wyoming, 1984. *Publication:* Facing the Weather Side, 1985. *Contributions to:* Reviews and journals. *Honour:* Honourable Mention, Washington Poets Asscn. *Address:* 18508 90th Ave W, Edmonds, WA 98020, USA.

OWEN, Jan Jarrold; b. 18 Aug. 1940, Adelaide, SA, Australia. Poet; Writer. 2 s., 1 d. *Education:* BA, 1963, University of Adelaide; ALAA, 1970. *Appointments:* Writer-in-Residence, Venice Studio of the Literature Board of the Australian Council, 1989, Tasmanian State Institute of Technology, 1990, Brisbane Grammar School, 1993, Tasmanian Writers Union, 1993, B. R. Whiting Library, Rome, 1994, Rimbun Dahan, Kuala Lumpur, 1997–98. *Publications:* Boy With a Telescope, 1986; Fingerprints on Light, 1990;

Blackberry Season, 1993; Night Rainbows, 1994. *Contributions to:* Newspapers and magazines. *Honours:* Ian Mudie Prize, 1982; Jessie Litchfield Prize, 1984; Grenfell Henry Lawson Prize, 1985; Harri Jones Memorial Prize, 1986; Anne Elder Award, 1987; Mary Gilmore Prize, 1987; Wesley Michel Wright Poetry Prize, 1992. *Membership:* South Australian Writers' Centre.

OWEN, Maureen; b. 6 July 1943, Graceville, Minnesota, USA. Poet. 3 s. *Education:* University of Seattle, 1961–62; San Francisco State College, 1962–64. *Publications:* Country Rush, 1973; No Travels Journal, 1975; A Brass Choir Approaches the Burial Ground/Big Deal, 1977; Hearts in Space, 1980; Amelia Earhart, 1984; Zombie Notes, 1986; Imaginary Income, 1992; Untapped Maps, 1993; American Rush: The Selected Poems of Maureen Owen, 1998. *Contributions to:* Many anthologies and other publications. *Honours:* National Endowment for the Arts Fellowship, 1979–80; American Book Award, Before Columbus Foundation, 1985; Fund for Poetry Awards, 1987, 1990, 1995; Foundation for Contemporary Performance Arts, 1998. *Memberships:* Before Columbus Foundation; Co-ordinating Council of Literary Magazines, vice-chair., board; St Mark's Poetry Project, advisory board. *Address:* 109 Dunk Rock Rd, Guildford, CT 06437, USA.

OWEN, Sue Ann; b. 5 Sept. 1942, Clarinda, IA, USA. Poet; Teacher. m. 29 Aug. 1964. *Education:* BA, University of Wisconsin, 1964; MFA, Goddard College, 1978. *Appointments:* Poet in the Schools, 1980–92; Poetry Instructor, 1992–98; Poet-in-Residence, 1998–, Louisiana State University. *Publications:* Nursery Rhymes for the Dead, 1980; The Book of Winter, 1988; My Doomsday Sampler, 1999. *Contributions to:* Many anthologies, reviews, quarterlies, and journals. *Honours:* Richard Hugo Fellowship, Port Townsend Writers Conference, 1986; Ohio State University Press/Journal Award in Poetry, 1988; Governor's Arts Award for Professional Artist of the Year, 1998. *Memberships:* Poetry Society of America; Associated Writing Programs. *Address:* 2015 General Cleburne Ave, Baton Rouge, LA 70810, USA.

OWENS, Rochelle; b. 2 April 1936, New York, NY, USA. Poet; Dramatist; Critic; Prof.; Trans. m. (1) David Owens, 30 March 1956, divorced 1959, (2) George Economou, 17 June 1962. *Education:* Theatre Arts, New School for Social Research, New York City; University of Montréal, Alliance Française, Paris, New York. *Appointments:* Visiting Lecturer, University of California at San Diego, 1982; Writer-in-Residence, Brown University, 1989; Adjunct Prof., University of Oklahoma at Norman, 1993–; Poet and Playwright-in Residence, Deep South Writers Conference, University of Southwestern Louisiana, 1997. *Publications:* Poetry: Not Be Essence That Cannot Be, 1961; Four Young Lady Poets (with others), 1962; Salt and Core, 1968; I Am the Babe of Joseph Stalin's Daughter: Poems 1961–1971, 1972; Poems From Joe's Garage, 1973; The Joe 82 Creation Poems, 1974; The Joe Chronicles, Part 2, 1979; Shemuel, 1979; French Light, 1984; Constructs, 1985; W C Fields in French Light, 1986; How Much Paint Does the Painting Need, 1988; Black Chalk, 1992; Rubbed Stones and Other Poems, 1994; New and Selected Poems, 1961–1996, 1997; Luca: Discourse on Life and Death, 2001. Plays: Futz and What Came After, 1968; The Karl Marx Play and Others, 1974; Emma Instigated Me, 1976; The Widow and the Colonel, 1977; Mountain Rites, 1978; Chucky's Hunch, 1982; The Passers by Liliane Atlan (trans.), 1993; Plays by Rochelle Owens: Collection of 4 Plays, 2000. Editor: Spontaneous Combustion: Eight New American Plays, 1972. *Contributions to:* Anthologies and journals. *Honours:* Rockefeller Grants, 1965, 1976; Obie Awards, 1965, 1967, 1982; Yale School of Drama Fellowship, 1968; American Broadcasting Corporation Fellowship, 1968; Guggenheim Fellowship, 1971; National Endowment for the Arts Award, 1976; Villager Award, 1982; Franco-Anglais Festival de Poésie, Paris, 1991; Rockefeller Foundation Resident Scholar, Bellagio, Italy, 1993; Oklahoma Centre for the Book Award, 1998. *Memberships:* American Society of Composers, Authors, and Publishers; Dramatists' Guild. *Address:* 1401 Magnolia, Norman, OK 73072, USA.

OXLEY, William; b. 29 April 1939, Manchester, England. Poet; Writer; Trans. m. Patricia Holmes, 13 April 1963, 2 d. *Education:* Manchester College of Commerce, 1953–55. *Publications:* The Dark Structures, 1967; New Workings, 1969; Passages from Time: Poems from a Life, 1971; The Icon Poems, 1972; Sixteen Days in Autumn (travel), 1972; Opera Vetera, 1973; Mirrors of the Sea, 1973; Eve Free, 1974; Mundane Shell, 1975; Superficies, 1976; The Exile, 1979; The Notebook of Hephaestus and Other Poems, 1981; Poems of a Black Orpheus, 1981; The Synopthegms of a Prophet, 1981; The Idea and Its Imminence, 1982; Of Human Consciousness, 1982; The Cauldron of Inspiration, 1983; A Map of Time, 1984; The Triviad and Other Satires, 1984; The Inner Tapestry, 1985; Vitalism and Celebration, 1987; The Mansands Trilogy, 1988; Mad Tom on Tower Hill, 1988; The Patient Reconstruction of Paradise, 1991; Forest Sequence, 1991; In the Drift of Words, 1992; The Playboy, 1992; Cardboard Troy, 1993; The Hallsands Tragedy, 1993; Collected Longer Poems, 1994; Completing the Picture (ed.), 1995; The Green Crayon Man, 1997; No Accounting for Paradise (autobiography), 1999; Firework Planet (children's), 2000; New and Selected Poems, 2001. *Contributions to:* Anthologies and periodicals. *Address:* 6 The Mount, Furzeham, Brixham, South Devon TQ5 8QY, England.

OZICK, Cynthia; b. 17 April 1928, New York, NY, USA. Author; Poet; Dramatist; Critic; Trans. m. Bernard Hallote, 7 Sept. 1952, 1 d. *Education:* BA, cum laude, English, New York University, 1949; MA, Ohio State University, 1950. *Publications:* Trust, 1966; The Pagan Rabbi and Other Stories, 1971; Bloodshed and Three Novellas, 1976; Levitation: Five Fictions, 1982; Art and Ardor: Essays, 1983; The Cannibal Galaxy, 1983; The Messiah of Stockholm, 1987; Metaphor and Memory: Essays, 1989; The Shawl, 1989; Epodes: First Poems, 1992; What Henry James Knew, and Other Essays on Writers, 1994; Portrait of the Artist as a Bad Character, 1996; The Cynthia Ozick Reader, 1996; Fame and Folly, 1996; The Puttermesser Papers, 1997; Quarrel and Quandary (essays), 2000. *Contributions to:* Many anthologies, reviews, quarterlies, journals, and periodicals. *Honours:* Guggenheim Fellowship, 1982; Mildred and Harold Strauss Living Award, American Acad. of Arts and Letters, 1983; Lucy Martin Donnelly Fellow, Bryn Mawr College, 1992; PEN/Spiegel-Diamonstein Award for the Art of the Essay, 1997; Harold Washington Literary Award, City of Chicago, 1997; John Cheever Award, 1999; Lannan Foundation Award, 2000; Many hon. doctorates. *Memberships:* American Acad. of Arts and Letters; American Acad. of Arts and Sciences; Authors' League; Dramatists' Guild; PEN. *Address:* 34 Southview St, New Rochelle, NY 10805, USA.

P

PABISCH, Peter Karl; b. 17 April 1938, Vienna, Austria. Prof. of German and Comparative Literature; Poet. m. Patricia Pabisch, 25 Nov. 1959, 1 d. *Education:* University of Vienna, 1957–61; MA, 1971, PhD, 1974, University of Illinois, Urbana-Champaign. *Appointment:* Prof. of German and Comparative Literature, University of New Mexico, 1972–. *Publications:* Arroyo Seco, 1984; Der Morgen leicht wie eine Feder, 1989; Santa Fe, 1990; Sioux, 1993; Wortort Tarock, 1999. *Contributions to:* Several publications. *Honours:* Verdienstkreuz, First Class, Federal Republic of Germany, 1985; Grosses Ehrenzeichen, Austria, 1986; Pegasus Poetry Award, 1992; Friedestrom-Preis, 2000. *Memberships:* MLA; PEN Austrian Center; PEN Germany Center. *Address:* c/o Dept of Foreign Languages and Literatures, University of New Mexico, Albuquerque, NM 87131, USA.

PACHE, Jean; b. 4 March 1933, Lausanne, Switzerland. Poet; Writer. m. *Education:* Licence es Lettres, University of Lausanne. *Publications:* Poetry: Les Fenetres Simultanées, 1955; Poèmes de l'Autre, 1960; Analogies, 1966; Repères, 1969; Rituels, 1971; L'Oeil Cérémonial, 1975; Le Corps Morcelé, 1977; Lacunaires, 1980; Les Corps Imaginaires, 1983; Les Prunelles Ardentes, 1989; Brûlots parmi les Dunes, 1990; Les Soupirs de la Sainte et les Cris de la Fée, 1991; Théodolite, 1993; Dans L'Oeil du Silence, 1997. Fiction: La Parodie, 1980; Baroques, 1983; Le Fou de Lilith, 1986; La Straniera, 1990; Le Discours Amoureux d'un Commis Voyageur, 1994; Dans l'oeil du Silence (poems), 1997. *Contributions to:* Various publications. *Honours:* Schiller Foundation Prizes, 1967, 1978; Michel Dentan Prize, 1991; Vaudoise Foundation Grand Prize for Poetry, 1993. *Address:* 14 Route du Signal, 1018 Lausanne, Switzerland.

PACK, Robert; b. 29 May 1929, New York, NY, USA. Prof.; Poet; Writer. m. (1) Isabelle Miller, 1950, (2) Patricia Powell, 1961, 2 s., 1 d. *Education:* BA, Dartmouth College, 1951; MA, Columbia University, 1953. *Appointments:* Teacher, Barnard College, 1957–64; Abernathy Prof., Middlebury College, Vermont, 1970–; Dir, Bread Loaf Writers Conferences, 1973–. *Publications:* Poetry: The Irony of Joy, 1955; A Stranger's Privilege, 1959; Guarded by Women, 1963; Selected Poems, 1964; Home from the Cemetery, 1969; Nothing But Light, 1972; Keeping Watch, 1976; Waking to My Name: New and Selected Poems, 1980; Faces in a Single Tree: A Cycle of Monologues, 1984; Clayfield Rejoices, Clayfield Laments: A Sequence of Poems, 1987; Before It Vanishes: A Packet for Prof. Pagels, 1989; Fathering the Map: New and Selected Later Poems, 1993. Other: Wallace Stevens: An Approach to His Poetry and Thought, 1958; Affirming Limits: Essays on Morality, Choice and Poetic Form, 1985; The Long View: Essays on the Discipline of Hope and Poetic Craft, 1991. Editor: The New Poets of England and America (with Donald Hall and Louis Simpson), 1957; Poems of Doubt and Belief: An Anthology of Modern Religious Poetry (with Tom Driver), 1964; Literature for Composition on the Theme of Innocence and Experience (with Marcus Klein), 1966; Short Stories: Classic, Modern, Contemporary (with Marcus Klein), 1967; Keats: Selected Letters, 1974; The Bread Loaf Anthology of Contemporary American Poetry (with Sydney Lea and Jay Parini), 1985; The Bread Loaf Anthology of Contemporary American Short Stories (with Jay Parini), 2 vols, 1987, 1989; Poems for a Small Planet: An Anthology of Nature Poetry (with Jay Parini), 1993. *Honours:* Fulbright Fellowship, 1956; American Acad. of Arts and Letters Grant, 1957; Borestone Mountain Poetry Award, 1964; National Endowment for the Arts Grant, 1968. *Address:* c/o Middlebury College, Middlebury, VT 05742, USA.

PADEL, Ruth; b. 8 May 1946, London, England. Poet; Writer; Journalist. 1 d. *Education:* BA, 1969, PhD, 1976, University of Oxford. *Publications:* Poetry: Alibi, 1985; Summer Snow, 1990; Angel, 1993; Fusewire, 1996; Rembrandt Would Have Loved You, 1998. Non-Fiction: In and Out of the Mind, 1992; Whom Gods Destroy, 1995, Heroes, 2000. *Honours:* Prizes, 1985, 1992, 1994, First Prize, 1996, National Poetry Competition; Poetry Book Society Recommendation, 1993, Choice, 1998, Arts Council Bursary, 1996. *Memberships:* PEN; Royal Zoological Society; Poetry Society; Society of Authors; RSL, fellow. *Address:* c/o A. P. Watt Ltd, 20 John St, London WC1N 2DR, England.

PADGETT, Ron; b. 17 June 1942, Tulsa, Oklahoma, USA. Poet; Writer; Trans. *Publications:* Bean Spasms (co-author), 1967; Great Balls of Fire, 1969; The Adventures of Mr and Mrs Jim and Ron (co-author), 1970; Antlers in the Treetops (co-author), 1970; Toujours l'Amour, 1976; Tulsa Kid, 1979; Triangles in the Afternoon, 1979; How to be a Woodpecker, 1983; How to be Modern Art, 1984; Among the Blacks, 1988; The Big Something, 1990; Supernatural Overtones (co-author), 1990; Ted, 1992; New and Selected Poems, 1995; Creative Reading, 1997; Albanian Diary, 1999; The Straight Line, 2000; Poems I Guess I Wrote, 2001; You Never Know, 2002. Other: Various trans. *Contributions to:* Numerous anthologies, reviews, and periodicals. *Honours:* Boar's Head Poetry Award, Columbia University, 1964; Gotham Bookmart Avant-Garde Poetry Prize, 1964; Poets Foundation Grants,

1964, 1969; Fulbright Fellowship, 1965; American Acad. of Arts and Letters Awards, 1966, 1971, 1999; National Endowment for the Arts Grant, 1976; New York State Council on the Arts Trans. Grant, 1983, Fellowships, 1983, 1986, 1990; Foundation for Contemporary Performance Art, 1996; Officier dans l'ordre des Arts et des Lettres, 2001. *Address:* 342 E 13th St, Apt 6, New York, NY 10003, USA.

PADHY, Pravat Kumar; b. 27 Dec. 1954, India. Geologist; Poet. m. Namita Padhy, 6 March 1983, 2 d. *Education:* MSc, 1979, PhD, Applied Geology; MTech, Mineral Exploration, 1980. *Publication:* Silence of the Seas, 1992. *Contributions to:* Anthologies and periodicals. *Honour:* Certificate of Honour, Writer's Life Line, Canada, 1986. *Address:* 166 HIG Complex, Chandrasekharpur, Sailashri Vihar, Bhubaneshwar, Orissa, India.

PADMANABHAN, Neela; b. 26 April 1938, Trivandrum, India. Engineer (retd); Poet. m. 3 July 1963, 1 s., 3 d. *Education:* BSc, 1956; BSc, Engineering, 1963. *Publications:* Neela Padmanabhan Kavithaikal, 1975; Surrender and Other Poems, 1982; Naa Kaakka, 1984; Peyarilenna, 1993. *Contributions to:* Many publications. *Honours:* Ulloorparameswaraiyer Poetry Award; Rajah Sir Annamalai Chettiar Award; Government of Tamilnadu Award; Tamilannai Prize' Lily Deva Sikamani Award; Tiruppur Tamilsangham Award. *Memberships:* Authors Guild of India; PEN; Poetry Society of India; Sahitya Akademi, Exec. Commitee. *Address:* Nilakant 39/1870 Kuriyathi Rd, Manacaud PO, Thiruvanantha Puram 695009, Kerala, India.

PAGE, Geoff(rey Donald); b. 7 July 1940, Grafton, NSW, Australia. Poet; Writer; Educator. 1 s. *Education:* BA, Honours, DipEd, University of New England, Armidale, NSW. *Appointments:* Head, Dept of English, Narrabundah College, Canberra, 1974–2001; Writer-in-Residence, University of Wollongong, NSW, 1982, Curtin University, 1990, Edith Cowan University, 1993. *Publications:* The Question, 1971; Smalltown Memorials, 1975; Collecting the Weather, 1978; Cassandra Paddocks, 1980; Clairvoyant in Autumn, 1983; Shadows from Wire: Poems and Photographs of Australians in the Great War Australian War Memorial (ed.), 1983; Benton's Conviction, 1985; Century of Clouds: Selected Poems of Guillaume Apollinaire (trans. with Wendy Coutts), 1985; Collected Lives, 1986; Smiling in English, Smoking in French, 1987; Footwork, 1988; Winter Vision, 1989; Invisible Histories, 1990; Selected Poems, 1991; Gravel Corners, 1992; On the Move (ed.), 1992; Human Interest, 1994; Reader's Guide to Contemporary Australian Poetry, 1995; The Great Forgetting, 1996; The Secret', 1997; Bernie McGann: A Life in Jazz, 1998; Collateral Damage, 1999; The Scarring, 1999; Darker and Lighter, 2001; Day after Day: Selected Poems of Salvatore Quasimodo (trans. with R. F. Brissenden and Loredana Nardi-Ford). *Contributions to:* Newspapers and magazines. *Honours:* Australia Council Literature Board Grants, 1974, 1983, 1987, 1989, 1992, 1997, 2000; Queensland Premier's Prize, 1990; Patrick White Literary Award, 2001. *Memberships:* Australian Society of Authors; Australian Teachers Union. *Address:* 8/40 Leahy Close, Narrabundah, ACT 2604, Australia.

PAGE, Jeremy Neil; b. 23 Feb. 1958, Folkestone, Kent, England. Educator; Poet; Ed. *Education:* BA, Honours, French and Theatre Studies, University of Warwick, 1980; French Drama and Theatre History, University of Bristol, 1983; DipRSA, Teaching English as a Foreign Language; Certificates in Counselling. *Appointments:* Ed., The Frogmore Papers, 1983–; Teacher and Trainer, 1984–, Dir of Studies, 1995–, International House, London; Founder, Frogmore Poetry Prize, 1987; Teacher, Academia Britannica, Arezzo, Italy, 1987–88; Series Ed., Crabflower Pamphlets, 1990–. *Publications:* Bliss, 1989; Frogmore Poetry (co-ed.), 1989; Secret Dormitories, 1993. *Contributions to:* Various anthologies and journals. *Honours:* Fourth Prize, Kent and Sussex Poetry Open Competition, 1989; Grand Transcendent Knight Salamander, Acad. of Paraphysical Science, 1992. *Address:* 6 Vernon Rd, Hornsey, London N8 0QD, England.

PAGE, P(atricia) K(athleen); b. 23 Nov. 1916, Swanage, Dorset, England. Writer; Poet; Painter. m. W Arthur Irwin, 16 Dec. 1950, 1 step-s., 2 step-d. *Education:* Studied art with Frank Schaeffer, Brazil, Charles Seliger, New York; Art Students League, New York; Pratt Graphics, New York. *Appointments:* Scriptwriter, National Film Board, Canada, 1946–50; Conducted writing workshops, Toronto, 1974–77; Teacher, University of Victoria, BC, 1977–78. *Publications:* The Sun and the Moon (novel), 1944; As Ten as Twenty, 1946; The Metal and the Flower, 1954; Cry Ararat: Poems New and Selected, 1967; The Sun and the Moon and Other Fictions, 1973; Poems Selected and New, 1974; To Say the Least (ed.), 1979; Evening Dance of the Grey Flies, 1981; The Glass Air (poems, essays, and drawings), 1985; Brazilian Journal (prose), 1988; I-Sphinx: A Poem for Two Voices, 1988; A Flask of Sea Water (fairy story), 1989; The Glass Air: Poems Selected and New, 1991; The Travelling Musicians (children's book), 1991; Unless the Eye Catch Fire (short story), 1994; The Goat That Flew (fairy story), 1994; Hologram: A Book of Glosas, 1994; A Children's Hymn for the United Nations, 1995; The Hidden Room, Collected Poems, 2 vols, 1997; Alphabetical (poem), 1998; Compass Rose (Italian trans. of selected poems), 1998; And Once More Saw the Stars: Four Poems for Two Voices (with Philip Stretford), 2001; A Kind of Fiction (short stories), 2001. *Contributions to:* Journals and magazines. *Honours:* Governor-General's Award for Poetry, 1954; Oscar Blumenthal Award for Poetry, 1974; Officer of the Order of Canada, 1977; National Magazines Gold Award, 1986, and Silver Award, 1990, for Poetry; British Columbia Book Awards, Hubert Evans Prize, 1988; Banff Centre School of Fine Arts National Award, 1989; Subject of National Film Board film Still Waters, 1991; Readers' Choice Award, Prairie Schooner, 1994; Subject of two-part sound feature The White Glass, CBC, 1996; Subject of special issue of Malahat Review, 1997; b p Nichol Chapbook Award, 1998; Companion of the Order of Canada, 1999; Hon. doctorates including: DLitt. University of Toronto, 1998. *Memberships:* PEN International; Writers' Union of Canada; League of Canadian Poets. *Literary Agent:* Kathryn Mulders, TLA Inc, 185–911 Yates St, Victoria, BC V8V 4Y9, Canada. *Address:* 3260 Exeter Rd, Victoria, BC V8R 6A6, Canada. *Website:* www.winchestergalleriesltd.com.

PAGE, S. M. See: MCMASTER, Susan.

PAI CHIU. See: CHIUNG JUNG HO.

PAIN, Margaret; b. 27 March 1922, Woking, Surrey, England. Poet; Ed. *Education:* Business college. *Appointment:* Co-Ed., Weyfarers Magazine, 1978–97. *Publications:* Walking to Eleusis, 1967; No Dark Legend, 1977; A Fox in the Garden, 1979; Shadow Swordsman, 1988. *Contributions to:* Various anthologies, 1972–2000, and other publications. *Honours:* Third Prize, 1977, Eleanor B North Award, First Prize, 1981, Surrey Poetry Centre Open Competition; Joint Third Prize, Lake Aske Memorial Award, 1977; First Prize, New Poetry Competition, 1978; Special Commendation, South East Arts Group Literary Prize, 1985. *Membership:* Surrey Poetry Society and Wey Poets, chair., 1987–94. *Address:* Hilltop Cottage, 9 White Rose Lane, Woking, Surrey GU22 7JA, England.

PAJOR, Johnjoseph; b. 5 Feb. 1948, South Bend, IN, USA. Poet. m. Cass Peters-Pajor, 18 Nov. 1989, 3 s., 1 d. *Education:* Technical colleges; Some university education. *Appointments:* Poetry readings, radio and cable TV broadcasts, 1965–98. *Publications:* Dies Faustus, revised edn, 1976; In Transit, 1978; A Collection of 3, 1979; Auditions, 1979; Traveler, 1979; African Violets, 1989; Challenger, 1990; Sacred Fire, 1990; Chiaroscuro, 1991; Wilderness: Land of the Raining Moon, 1991; A Brave Boy's Journeying, 1994; The Ten Books, 1997. *Contributions to:* Various journals and anthologies. *Honour:* Literary Honorarium, National Poetry Awards, 1978. *Address:* 848 51st St, Port Townsend, WA 98368, USA.

PALACE, Mary. See: COSCIA, Patricia Denise.

PALEY, Grace; b. 11 Dec. 1922, New York, NY, USA. Author; Poet; University Teacher (retd). m. (1) Jess Paley, 20 June 1942, divorced, 1 s., 1 d., (2) Robert Nichols, 1972. *Education:* Hunter College, New York, 1938–39; New York University. *Appointments:* Teacher, Columbia University, Syracuse University, Sarah Lawrence College, City College of the City University of New York. *Publications:* Fiction: The Little Disturbances of Man: Stories of Women and Men at Love, 1968; Enormous Changes at the Last Minute, 1974; Later the Same Day, 1985; The Collected Stories, 1994. Poetry: Long Walks and Intimate Talks (includes stories), 1991; New and Collected Poems, 1992; Begin Again, 2000. *Contributions to:* Books, anthologies and magazines. *Honours:* Guggenheim Fellowship, 1961; National Institute of Arts and Letters Award, 1970; Edith Wharton Citation of Merit as the first State Author of New York, New York State Writers Institute, 1986; National Endowment for the Arts Senior Fellowship, 1987; Vermont Governor's Award for Excellence in the Arts, 1993. *Membership:* American Acad. of Arts and Letters. *Address:* Box 620, Thetford Hill, VT 05074, USA.

PALLANT, Cheryl; b. 8 Jan. 1960, New York, NY, USA. Poet; Ed.; Reviewer. *Education:* BA, MA, Long Island University. *Appointments:* Ed., Real News, 1978–79; Poetry Ed., Loomings, 1979–80, New Southern Literary Messenger, 1985–87; Reviewer, High Performance, 1990–. *Publications:* Pizza; A Neighbourhood Bar. *Contributions to:* Oxford Magzine; Ambit; Crescent Review; Assembling; Gyphas; New Rain; High Perfromance; Beanfast; Loomings; Rag Mag; Contact Quarterly. Memberships: Poets and Writers; Virginia Writers Club; Associated Writing Programs. *Address:* 108 S Colonial Ave, Richmond, VA 23221, USA.

PALLEY, Julian; b. 16 Sept. 1925, Atlantic City, New Jersey, USA. Prof. of Spanish Literature; Poet; Trans. m. Shirley Wilson, 17 Sept. 1950, 4 s. *Education:* BA, Mexico City College, 1950; MA, Spanish, University of Arizona, 1952; PhD, Romance Languages, University of New Mexico, 1958. *Appointments:* Instructor, Rutgers University, 1956–59; Assoc. Prof., Arizona State University, 1959–62, University of Oregon, 1962–66; Prof. of Spanish Literature, University of California at Irvine, 1966–. *Publications:* Spinoza's Stone, 1976; Bestiary, 1987; Pictures at an Exhibition, 1989; Family Portraits,

1994. Other: Several trans. *Contributions to:* Reviews, quarterlies, and journals. *Honours:* Arizona Quarterly Poetry Prize, 1956; Jefferson Poetry Prize, 1976. *Membership:* California State Poetry Society. *Address:* c/o Dep of Spanish and Portuguese, University of California at Irvine, Irvine, CA 92697 USA.

PALM, Marion; b. 6 Aug. 1940, New York, NY, USA. Poet; Writer; Artist Banker; Adjunct Prof. Divorced, 2 s., 1 d. *Education:* Berkeley School o Business; AIS, Normandale Community College, 1976; BA, University o Minnesota, 1978; MS, Bank Street College of Education, 1995. *Publications* Nightingale Day Songs; Alice's Forget-Me-Nots; Islands of the Blest; Passages Riding the West End Express; The Poetry Leaders Guidebook. *Memberships* Poets and Writers. *Address:* 705 41st St, No. 17, New York, NY 11232, USA.

PALMER, Charlene Noel; b. 23 Feb. 1930, Los Angeles, CA, USA. Poet. m. David Palmer, 16 June 1951, 2 s., 2 d. *Education:* University of California at Los Angeles, 1948–52. *Publications:* Long Stems Colored, 1953. *Contributions to:* Anthologies, reviews, quarterlies, and periodicals. *Membership:* Poets and Writers. *Address:* 2310 Calumet St, MI 48503, USA.

PALMER, (George) Michael; b. 11 May 1943, New York, NY, USA. Poet Writer; Trans. m. Cathy Simon, 1972, 1 d. *Education:* BA, French, 1965, MA Comparative Literature, 1967, Harvard University. *Publications:* Plan of the City of O, 1971; Blake's Newton, 1972; C's Songs, 1973; The Circular Gates, 1974; Without Music, 1977; Alogon, 1980; Notes for Echo Lake, 1981; Code o Signals: Recent Writings in Poetics (ed.), 1983; First Figure, 1984; Side Effects, 1985; Flashback, 1988; Sun, 1988; Extreme Measures, 1991; An Alphabet Underground, 1993; Natural Causes, 1994; At Passage, 1995; The Lion Bridge, 1998. Other: Trans; Ed. of books. *Contributions to:* Many anthologies, books and journals. *Address:* 265 Jersey St, San Francisco, CA 94114, USA.

PALMER, Leslie (Howard); b. 25 Jan. 1941, Memphis, Tennessee, USA. Prof. of Literature; Poet; Writer. m. 27 Aug. 1965, 1 s., 1 d. *Education:* BA, University of Memphis, 1962; MA, 1963, PhD, 1966, University of Tennessee, Knoxville. *Appointments:* Instructor, University of Tennessee, 1966–67; Prof. of Literature, University of North Texas, Denton, 1967–. *Publications:* Ten Poems, 1980; A Red Sox Flag, 1983; Ode to a Frozen Dog, and Other Poems, 1992; Artemis' Bow, 1993; The Devil Sells Ice Cream, 1994; The Jim Tom Poems, 1996; The Bryn Mawr Poems, 1998; Swollen Foot, 1999; Disgraceland, 2000; Last Bite, 2001. *Contributions to:* Numerous anthologies, reviews, quarterlies, journals, and magazines. *Honours:* Beaudoin Gemstone Awards, 1962, 1963; Midsouth Poetry Award, 1963; Pushcart Prize Nomination, 1984; Cape Rock Poetry Award, 1990. *Memberships:* Coda; Modern Humanities Research Asscn; MLA; PEN. *Address:* 1905 W Oak, Denton, TX 76201, USA.

PALMIERI, Emilia; b. 23 Sept. 1946, Rome, Italy. Teacher; Poet. m. Kevin Collins, 19 Oct. 1969. *Education:* Diplomas in Foreign Languages, 1964. *Publications:* Sulle Ali Del Vento, 1994; Fra Le Ombre e la Luce, 1996. Other: Se io Fossi (poem accompanied by choir at the Romanian Acad.), 1994. *Contributions to:* Poetry magazines. *Honours:* Numerous Italian poetry awards. *Address:* Via Ettore Pais 11/2, 00162 Rome, Italy.

PALOMINO JIMÉNEZ, Angel; b. 2 Aug. 1929, Toledo, Spain. Writer; Poet. *Education:* Linguistics, Science and Chemistry, Central University, Madrid. *Publications:* Numerous novels, short stories, essays, and poems, 1957–98. *Contributions to:* Journals. *Honours:* International Prize, Press Club, 1966; Miguel de Cervantes National Literary Prize, 1971; Finalist, Planeta Prize, 1977. *Memberships:* International Asscn of Literary Critics; International Federation of Tourism Writers; National Acad. of Gastronomy; Royal Acad. of Fine Arts and Historical Sciences; Spanish Asscn of Book Writers. *Address:* Conde de Penalver 17, 28006 Madrid, Spain.

PALSSON, Sigurdur; b. 30 July 1948, Skinnastadur, Iceland. Writer; Poet; Trans.; Theatre and Television Dir. m. Kristin Johannesdottir, 26 June 1987, 1 s. *Education:* BA, 1967, DUEL libre, 1972, Maitrise libre, 1980, DEA, 1982, Institut d'Etudes Théatrales, Sorbonne, University of Paris; Diploma, Film Direction, CLCF, Paris, 1978. *Publications:* Ljod vega salt, 1975; Ljod vega menn, 1980; Ljod vega gerd, 1982; Ljod namu land, 1985; Ljod namu menn, 1988; Ljod namu vold, 1990; Ljodlinudans, 1993; Ljodlinuskip, 1995; Ljodlinuspil, 1997; Völundarhus, 1997; Parisarhjol, 1998; Ljodtimaskyn, 1999; Einhveri dyrunum, 2000; Blár thrihyrningur, 2000; Ljodtimaleit, 2001. *Contributions to:* Various publications. *Honour:* Chevalier de l'Ordre des Arts et des Lettres, France, 1989. *Memberships:* Alliance Française of Iceland, pres., 1976–77; PEN Club of Iceland, board of dirs, 1983–; Union of Icelandic Theatre Dirs; Writers Union of Iceland, chair., 1984–88. *Address:* Postholf 1160, Mavahlid 38, 121Reykjavík, Iceland.

PANIKER, Ayyappa; b. 12 Sept. 1930, Kavalam, India. Prof. of English (retd); Poet; Writer; Ed.; Trans. m. Sreeparvathy Paniker, 1961, 2 d. *Education:* BA, Honours, Travancore University, 1951; MA, Kerala University, 1959; CTE, Hyderabad, 1966; MA, PhD, 1971, Indiana University. *Appointments:* Lecturer, 1951–73, Reader, 1973–80, Prof. of English and Head, Dept of English, 1980–90, University of Kerala; Chief Ed., Medieval Indian Literature, 1990–94; Birla Fellowship, 1994–96; UNESCO Subcommission for Culture.

Publications: Numerous books, including: Ayyappa Panikerude Kritikal I, 1974, II, 1982, III, 1990; Ayyappa Panikerude Lekhanangal I, 1982, II, 1990; Selected Poems, 1985; Mayakovskiyude Kavitakal, 1987; Gotrayanam, 1989; Avatarikakal, 1993; Medieval Indian Literature (ed.), 1998; Madhyakala Malayala Karuta, 1998. *Contributions to:* Many anthologies, books, reviews, quarterlies, journals, and magazines. *Honours:* Kerala Sahitya Akademi Award, 1975; Kalyani Krishna Menon Prize, 1977; Central Sahitya Akademi Award, 1984; Asan Prize, 1991; Muscat Award, Kerala Cultural Centre, 1992; Sahitya Parishad Award, 1993; Kabir Prize, 1997; Indira Gandhi Fellowship, 1997–99; Gandadhar Meher Award, 1998. *Memberships:* National Book Trust; National Literacy Mission; Sahitya Akademi. *Address:* 111 Gandhi Nagar, Trivandrum 695014, India.

PAOLUCCI, Anne (Attura); b. Rome, Italy. Prof. of English (retd); Poet; Writer; Dramatist; Ed. m. Henry Paolucci. *Education:* BA, English Literature and Creative Writing, Barnard College, 1947; MA, Italian Literature, 1950, PhD, English and Comparative Literature, 1963, Columbia University. *Appointments:* Instructor, 1959–61, Asst Prof., 1961–69, City College of the City University of New York; Fulbright Lecturer, University of Naples, 1965–67; Research Prof., 1969–75, Prof. of English, 1969–97, Chair, Dept of English, 1974–75, 1982–91, Dir, Doctor of Arts Degree Program in English, 1982–96, St John's University, Jamaica, New York; Founder, Publisher, and Ed.-in-Chief, Review of National Literatures, 1970–; Founder-Pres., Council on National Literatures, 1974–. *Publications:* Poetry: Poems Written for Sbek's Mummies, Marie Menken, and Other Important People, Places, and Things, 1977; Riding the Mast Where It Swings, 1980; Gorbachev in Concert (and Other Poems), 1991; Queensboro Bridge (and Other Poems), 1995. Fiction: Eight Short Stories, 1977; Sepia Tones: Seven Short Stories, 1985; Terminal Degrees, 1997. Non-Fiction: Hegel on Tragedy (with Henry Paolucci), 1962; A Short History of American Drama, 1966; Eugene O'Neill, Arthur Miller, Edward Albee, 1967; From Tension to Tonic: The Plays of Edward Albee, 1972; Pirandello's Theater: The Recovery of the Stage for Dramatic Art, 1974; Dante and the 'Quest for Eloquence' in the Vernacular Languages of India (with Henry Paolucci), 1984. Plays: Minions of the Race, 1978; Cipango!, 1986. Editor: Dante's Influence on American Writers, 1977. *Contributions to:* Numerous books, reviews, and journals. *Honours:* Fulbright Scholarship, Italy, 1951–52; Woodbridge Hon. Fellowship, Columbia University, 1961–62; Writer-in-Residence, Yaddo, 1965; ACLS Grant, 1978; Cavaliere, 1986, Commendatore, 1992, Order of Merit, Italy; Gold Medal, Canada, 1991; Hon. Degree in Humane Letters, Lehman College of the City University of New York, 1995. *Memberships:* American Comparative Literature Asscn; City University of New York, board of trustees, 1996–, chair., 1997–; Dante Society of America; Dramatists Guild; Hegel Society of America; International Comparative Literature Asscn; MLA; PEN American Center; Pirandello Society of America, pres., 1972–95; Renaissance Asscn of America; Renaissance Institute of America; Shakespeare Asscn of America; World Centre for Shakespeare Studies. *Address:* 166 25 Powells Cove Blvd, Beechhurst, NY 11357, USA.

PAPAGEORGIOU, Kostas; b. 4 July 1945, Athens, Greece. Poet; Writer; Ed. *Education:* Law Diploma, 1968; Literature, Philology, University of Athens, 1969–72. *Appointment:* Ed., Grammata ke Technes. *Publications:* Several poetry and prose vols, 1966–. *Contributions to:* Various publications. *Membership:* Greek Authors Union. *Address:* Kerasountos 8, 11528 Athens, Greece.

PARADIS, Philip M.; b. 11 Feb. 1951, Connecticut, USA. Prof.; Poet. m. Marjorie H Paradis, 27 May 1978, 1 c. *Education:* BA, Central Connecticut State College, 1976; MA, University of Utah, 1981; PhD, Oklahoma State University, 1984. *Appointments:* Oklahoma State University, 1980–85; Iowa State University, 1985–87, 1990–91; Western Carolina University, 1987–90; Northern Kentucky University, 1992–98. *Publications:* Tornado Alley, 1986; From Gobbler's Knob, 1989; Something of Ourselves, 1994. *Contributions to:* Poetry; American Scholar; Chariton Review; Poet and Critic; Tar River Poetry; Kansas Quarterly; College English; Zone 3; Southern Humanities Review. *Honours:* Acad. of American Poets Prize, 1982; Appalachian Writers Asscn Poetry Award, 1989. *Memberships:* Associated Writing Programs; Acad. of American Poets; National Council of Teachers of English. *Address:* 146 Ridge Hill Dr., Highland Heights, KY41076, USA. *E-mail:* phil.paradis@fuse.net.

PARARA-EFTICHIDOU, Nitsa Pagona; b. 23 July 1928, Athens, Greece. Poet. m. Lazaros Eftichidis, 10 Sept. 1961, 2 s. *Education:* Studies in French and English. *Publications:* Akbokerana and Jieremiades, 1980; Pigolambides and Jieremiades, 1986; Hores-Hores, 1991; Psimithia Jieremiades Haikai, 1996. *Contributions to:* Anthologies, journals and periodicals. *Memberships:* Literary Society of Greek Authors; International Writers' Asscn. *Address:* Riga Fereou 2-AV, Hirakliou, Nea Ionia 14231 Athens, Greece.

PARINI, Jay (Lee); b. 2 April 1948, Pittston, Pennsylvania, USA. Prof. of English; Author; Poet; Literary Critic. m. Devon Stacey Jersild, 21 June 1981, 3 s. *Education:* AB, Lafayette College, 1970; PhD, University of St Andrews, Scotland, 1975. *Appointments:* Faculty, Dartmouth College, 1975–82; Co-Founder, New England Review, 1976; Prof. of English, Middlebury College, 1982–. *Publications:* Fiction: The Love Run, 1980; The Patch Boys, 1986; The

Last Station, 1990; Bay of Arrows, 1992; Benjamin's Crossing, 1997; The Apprentice Lover, 2002. Poetry: Singing in Time, 1972; Anthracite Country, 1982; Town Life, 1988; House of Days, 1988. Other: Theodore Roethke: An American Romantic, 1979; An Invitation to Poetry, 1988; John Steinbeck: A Biography, 1995; Some Necessary Angels (essays), 1998; Robert Frost, 1999. Editor: Gore Vidal: Writer Against the Grain, 1992; The Columbia History of American Poetry, 1993; The Columbia Anthology of American Poetry, 1995; The Norton Book of American Autobiography, 1999. *Address:* Route 1, Box 195, Middlebury, VT 05753, USA.

PARISH, Barbara Lu Shirk; b. 28 Nov. 1942, Lincoln, KS, USA. Poet. m. Harlie Albert Parish Jr, 30 Aug. 1964, 1 d. *Education:* AB, English, Fort Hays State University, 1964; MA, English, 1966, MA, Library Science, 1968, University of Missouri at Columbia. *Appointments:* Adjunct Instructor in Composition and Advanced Composition, State Technical Institute, Memphis, TN, 1997–. *Contributions to:* The Kentucky Book, 1979, Maverick Western Verse, 1994, and other anthologies, reviews, quarterlies, journals, and magazines. *Honours:* Kentucky State Poetry Society Awards, 1972–94. *Memberships:* Kentucky State Poetry Society, Board of Dirs; Writers Club, Louisville. *Address:* 4293 Beechcliff Lane, Memphis, TN 38128, USA.

PARISI, Joseph (Anthony); b. 18 Nov. 1944, Duluth, Minnesota, USA. Ed.; Writer; Poet; Administrator; Consultant. *Education:* BA, Honours, English, College of St Thomas, St Paul, Minnesota, 1966; MA, English, 1967, PhD, Honours, English, 1973, University of Chicago. *Appointments:* Instructor to Asst Prof. of English, Roosevelt University, Chicago, 1969–78; Assoc. Ed., 1976–83, Acting Ed., 1983–85, Ed., 1985–, Poetry Magazine, Chicago; Visiting and Adjunct Asst Prof. of English, University of Illinois at Chicago, 1978–87; Consultant, American Library Asscn, 1980–; Chair, Ruth Lilly Poetry Prize, 1986–, and Fellowships, 1989–; Producer, Writer, and Host, Poets in Person, National Public Radio, 1991; Exec. Dir, Modern Poetry Asscn, 1996–. *Publications:* The Poetry Anthology, 1912–1977: Sixty-five Years of America's Most Distinguished Verse Magazine (ed. with Daryl Hine), 1978; Voices & Visions: Viewer's Guide, 1987; Marianne Moore: The Art of a Modernist (ed.), 1989; Poets in Person: Listener's Guide, 1992. *Contributions to:* Reference books, scholarly journals, and literary publications. *Honours:* Everett Helm Travelling Fellowship, 1999; Guggenheim Fellowship, 2000 Address: 3440 N Lake Shore Dr., Chicago, IL 60657, USA.

PARK, William; b. 6 May 1962, Hillingdon, West London, England. Tutor in Creative Writing; Poet. *Appointments:* Writer-in-Residence, St Martin's College, Lancaster, 1989; Hawthornden Fellowship, 1991. *Publication:* The Gregory Anthology, 1987–90, 1990. *Contributions to:* Oxford Poetry; Poetry Durham; Ambit; Outposts; Poetry Review; Orbis; Iron; Critical Quarterly; Rialto; Acumen; Verse; Bête Noire; Stand. *Honour:* Major Eric Gregory Award, 1990. *Membership:* Poetry Society. *Address:* 25B Dawson Walk, Preston, Lancashire PR1 1NH, England.

PARKER, Jean. See: SHARAT CHANDRA, Gubbi Shankara Chetty.

PARKER, Michael Richard; b. 13 July 1949, Weymouth, Dorset, England. Senior Lecturer in English; Poet; Writer. m. Aleksandra Gajewska, 19 March 1978, 3 d. *Education:* BA, University of Reading, 1970; Certificate of Education, University of Southampton, 1971; MA, University of Lódz, 1979; MPhil, University of Manchester, 1987; PhD, University of Liverpool, 1997. *Appointments:* Asst in English, later Head of English, Ruffwood School; Lecturer in English, University of Lódz, 1977–79; Head of English, St Nicholas RC High School, 1979–86; Head of English, Holy Cross Sixth Form College, 1986–90; Senior Lecturer in English, Liverpool Hope University College, 1990–. *Publications:* Of Old (poems), 1971; One Way Traffic (poems), 1976; Seamus Heaney: The Making of the Poet, 1993. *Contributions to:* Chapter in: The Achievement of Ted Hughes (ed. by Keith Sagar), 1983; Contemporary Writing & National Identity (ed. by Tracy Hill and William Hughes), 1995; Irish Encounters (ed. by Alan Marshall and Neil Sammells), 1998; Poems, trans, articles and reviews in: Outposts; Honest Ulsterman; TLS; Verse; Prism International; PN Review; New Hibernia Review. *Address:* c/o Dept of English, Liverpool Hope University College, Hope Park, Liverpool L16 9JD, England.

PARKIN, Andrew Terence Leonard, (Jiang An Dao); b. 30 June 1937, Birmingham, England. Poet; Critic. m. (1) Christine George, 14 June 1959, 1 s., (2) Françoise Lentsch, 28 April 1990. *Education:* BA, 1961, MA, 1965, Pembroke College, Cambridge; PhD, University of Bristol, 1969. *Appointments:* Ed., Canadian Journal of Irish Studies, 1974–89; Prof. of English, University of British Columbia, Chinese University of Hong Kong. *Publications:* Stage One: A Canadian Scenebook, 1973; The Dramatic Imagination of W. B. Yeats, 1978; Shaw's Caesar and Cleopatra, 1980; Dion Boucicault: Selected Plays, 1987; Dancers in a Web, 1987; Yeats's Herne's Egg, 1991; Yokohama Days, Kyoto Nights, 1991; File on Nichols, 1993; Hong Kong Poems, 1997; The Humanities (ed.), 2001; Shakespeare Global/Local: The Hong Kong Imaginary in Transcultural Production (ed. with K. K. Tam and Terry Yip), 2002. *Contributions to:* Over 100 essays and reviews in scholarly journals; Over 30 radio broadcasts; Two television interviews; 200 poems. *Honours:* Most Distinguished Ed. of a Learned Journal, 1989; Hon. Adviser, Chinese Acad. of

Social Sciences, Beijing, 2000–; Prof. Emeritus, Hon. Senior Tutor, Shaw College, Chinese University of Hong Kong, 2001–. *Memberships:* Canadian Asscn for Irish Studies, hon. life mem.; League of Canadian Poets; MLA of America; Writers' Union of Canada. *Address:* 52 rue du Rendez-vous, Paris 75012, France.

PARKS, Ian; b. 10 Feb. 1959, Yorkshire, England. Poet. *Appointments:* Writing Fellow, North Riding College, Scarborough, 1986–88; Tutor in Creative Writing, Open College of the Arts. *Publications:* Gargoyles in Winter, 1985; Sirens, 1991; A Climb Through Altered Landscapes, 1998. *Contributions to:* Poetry Review; Rialto; Other Poetry; New Welsh Review; Orbis; Outposts; Acumen; Bête Noire; Poetry Wales; New Voices in British Poetry; Poetry (Chicago); The Observer. *Honours:* Yorkshire Arts Asscn Award, 1984; Hawthornden Fellowship, 1991; Travelling Fellowship to USA, 1993; Third Prize, City of Cardiff International Poetry Competition, 1994; First Prize, Cascando Travel Writing Competition, 1995. *Memberships:* Society of Authors; International PEN. *Address:* 72 Doncaster Rd, Mexborough, South Yorkshire, England.

PARQUE, Richard (Anthony); b. 8 Oct. 1935, Los Angeles, CA, USA. Writer; Poet; Teacher. m. Vo Thi Lan, 1 May 1975, 3 s. *Education:* BA, 1958, MA, 1961, California State University, Los Angeles; California State Teaching Credential, 1961; Postgraduate studies, University of Redlands. *Publications:* Sweet Vietnam, 1984; Hellbound, 1986; Firefight, 1987; Flight of the Phantom, 1988; A Distant Thunder, 1989. *Contributions to:* Journals, magazines and newspapers. *Honours:* Bay Area Poets Award, 1989; Viet Nam novels have been placed in the Colorado State University Vietnam War Collection. *Memberships:* Authors' Guild; Acad. of American Poets. *Address:* PO Box 327, Verdugo City, CA 91046, USA.

PARRELLA, Emidio; b. 19 Oct. 1940, Italy. Poet. m. Maria Rosaria, 15 June 1972, 1 s., 1 d. *Education:* Degree in Arts, Federico II University, 1966. *Publications:* Il Pianto degli Angeli, 1961; Ai Confini Della Ragione, 1979; Storia di una Contropoesia, 1982; Un treno qualunque per andare altrove, 1988; Le Parole del quotioliano, 1997; Poeti europei, 1997; Raccontare Poesie Gabrieli, 2000. *Contributions to:* Silarus; Il Settimanale; Orizzonti; Presenza. *Honours:* Premio Borgese, 1981; Premio Taormina; Premio Medusa Aurea, 1986; Premio Katana, 1989; Premio Cervantes, Spain, 2000; Second Prize, Collina dei Canaldoli, Naples, 2000; Second Prize, La Rocca, Città oli San Miniato. *Memberships:* Centro Studi Poesia e Storia delle Poetiche, Rome. *Address:* Via L. Bianchi 16, Naples, Italy.

PARRINDER, (John) Patrick; b. 11 Oct. 1944, Wadebridge, Cornwall, England. Prof. of English; Literary Critic. 2 d. *Education:* Christ's College, 1962–65, Darwin College, 1965–67, Cambridge; MA, PhD, Cambridge University. *Appointments:* Fellow, King's College, Cambridge, 1967–74; Lecturer, 1974–80, Reader, 1980–86, Prof. of English, 1986–, University of Reading. *Publications:* H G Wells, 1970; Authors and Authority, 1977; Science Fiction: Its Criticism and Teaching, 1980; James Joyce, 1984; The Failure of Theory, 1987; Shadows of the Future, 1995. Editor: H G Wells: The Critical Heritage, 1972; Science Fiction: A Critical Guide, 1979; Learning from Other Worlds, 2000. *Contributions to:* London Review of Books; Many academic journals. *Honours:* Pres.'s Award, World Science Fiction, 1987; Leverhulme Major Research Fellowship, 2001–04; Fellow, English Asscn, 2001. *Memberships:* H G Wells Society; Science Fiction Foundation; Society of Authors. *Address:* Dept of English, University of Reading, PO Box 218, Reading, Berkshire RG6 6AA, England. *E-mail:* j.p.parrinder@reading.ac.uk.

PASCALIS, Stratis; b. 4 March 1958, Athens, Greece. Poet; Trans. m. Sophia Phocas, 28 Feb. 1982, 2 d. *Education:* Graduated, Political Science, University of Athens, 1983. *Publications:* 4 vols of poetry, 1977, 1984, 1989, 1991; Several trans. *Contributions to:* Newspapers and magazines. *Honour:* Maris P Ralli Prize, 1977. *Membership:* Society of Greek Writers. *Address:* Diamandidou 36, Palio Psychiko, Athens 15452, Greece.

PASCHEN, Elise Maria; b. 4 Jan. 1959, Chicago, IL, USA. Arts Administrator; Poet. *Education:* BA, Honours, Harvard University, 1982; MPhil, 1984, DPhil, 1988, University of Oxford. *Appointment:* Exec. Dir, Poetry Society of America. *Publications:* Houses: Coasts, 1985; Infidelities, 1996. *Contributions to:* Reviews, journals, and magazines. *Honours:* Lloyd McKim Garrison Medal for Poetry, Harvard University, 1982; Joan Grey Untermyer Poetry Prize, Harvard University/Radcliffe College, 1982; Richard Selig Prize for Poetry, Magdalen College, Oxford, 1984; Nicholas Roerich Poetry Prize, 1996. *Membership:* National Arts Club. *Address:* c/o Poetry Society of America, 15 Gramercy Park, New York, NY 10003, USA.

PASKANDI, Géza; b. 18 May 1933, Szatmarhegy-Viile Satumare, Romania. Writer; Poet; Dramatist; Screenwriter. m. Anna-Maria Seböl, 24 April 1970, 1 d. *Education:* University Bolyai-Kolozsvar-Cluj, 1953–57. *Publications:* Novels, poems, plays, screenplays, and essays. *Contributions to:* Journals and magazines. *Honours:* Romanian Writers Asscn Award, 1970; József Attila Award, Hungary, 1977; Award for Hungarian Art, 1991; Kossuth Prize, Hungary, 1992. *Memberships:* Hungarian Acad. of Arts; Hungarian Writers

Asscn; Moricz Zsigmond Literary Society; PEN Club. *Address:* Nagyszalonta utca 50, 1112 Budapest, Hungary.

PASTAN, Linda; b. 27 May 1932, New York, NY, USA. Poet. m. Ira Pastan, 14 June 1953, 2 s., 1 d. *Education:* BA, Radcliffe College, 1954; MLS, Simmons College, 1955; MA, Brandeis University, 1957. *Appointments:* Staff, Bread Loaf Writer's Conference; Teacher, American University; Poet Laureate of Maryland, 1991–95. *Publications:* A Perfect Circle of Sun, 1971; Aspects of Eve, 1975; On the Way to the Zoo, 1975; The Five Stages of Grief, 1978; Even As We Sleep, 1980; Setting the Table, 1980; Waiting for My Life, 1981; PM/AM: New and Selected Poems, 1982; A Fraction of Darkness, 1985; The Imperfect Paradise, 1988; Heroes in Disguise, 1991; An Early Afterlife, 1995; Carnival Evening: New and Selected Poems 1968–1998, 1998; The Last Uncle, 2002. *Contributions to:* Atlantic Monthly; New Republic; New Yorker; Poetry; Antaeus; Goergia Review; American Scholar; Grand Street; Gettysburg Review; Nation; Prairie Schooner. *Honours:* Dylan Thomas Poetry Award, 1958; National Endowment for the Arts Fellowship, 1972; Maryland Arts Council Grant, 1978; Di Castagnola Award, 1978; Bess Hokin Prize, 1985; Maurice English Award, 1986; Virginia Faulkner Award, 1992; Charity Randall Citation, International Poetry Forum, 1995; Pushcart Prize. *Memberships:* PEN; Poetry Society of America. *Address:* 11710 Beall Mountain Rd, Potomac, MD 20854, USA.

PATCHETT, Angela; b. 28 Oct. 1949, Hitchin, Hertfordshire, England. Psychotherapist; Poet. Divorced, 2 s., 1 d. *Education:* Diploma, Psychotherapy, London. *Publications:* Poems: My New Man, 1996; Love, 1996; I Light a Candle, 1996; My Secret Wish, 1996; A Special Love, 1996; On the Threshold, 1996; My Little Girl, 1996; Peace in the Eye of the Storm, 1996; Golden Treasure, 1996; Ziggie, 1996; The Wounded Man, 1996; Dervishe, 1997; The Awakening, 1997; A Man and a Woman, 1997; The Gift, 1997; The Fullness of My Essence, 1997; Adam, 1997; I Feel Your Gentle Touch, 1997; I Break Free, 1997; A Secret Shared, 1997; I Give You A Gift, 1998; Old Annies, 1998. *Contributions to:* Anthologies, journals, quarterlies and magazines. *Address:* Mimosa Cottage, 9 Springhead, Ashwell, Hertfordshire SG7 5LL, England.

PATEL, Gieve; b. 18 Aug. 1940, Mumbai, India. Physician; Poet; Dramatist; Painter. m. Toni Diniz, 1969, 1 d. *Education:* BSc, St Xavier's College, Mumbai; MBBS, Grant Medical College, Mumbai. *Publications:* Poetry: Poems, 1966; How Do You Withstand, Body, 1976; Mirrored, Mirroring, 1991. Plays: Princes, 1971; Savaksa, 1982; Mister Behram, 1987. *Honours:* Woodrow Wilson Fellowship, 1984; Rockefeller Foundation Fellowship, 1992. *Address:* SE Malabar Apartments, Nepean Rd, Mumbai 400 036, India.

PATERSON, Alistair (Ian), (Ian Hughes); b. 28 Feb. 1929, Nelson, New Zealand. Poet; Writer; Educational Consultant. m. Dec. 1984, 2 s., 3 d. *Education:* BA, University of New Zealand, 1961; Diploma in Education, University of Auckland, 1972. *Appointments:* Royal New Zealand Navy, 1954–74; Dean of General Studies, New Zealand Police, 1974–78; Tertiary Inspector, New Zealand Dept of Education, 1979–89; Educational Consultant, 1990–. *Publications:* Caves in the Hills, 1965; Birds Flying, 1973; Cities and Strangers, 1976; The Toledo Room: A Poem for Voices, 1978; 15 Contemporary New Zealand Poets (ed.), 1980; Qu'appelle, 1982; The New Poetry, 1982; Incantations for Warriors, 1982; Oedipus Rex, 1986; Short Stories from New Zealand (ed.), 1988; How to be a Millionaire by Next Wednesday (novel), 1994. *Contributions to:* Various publications. *Honours:* Fulbright Fellowship, 1977; John Cowie Reid Award, University of Auckland, 1982; Katherine Mansfield Award for Fiction, 1993; New Zealand Creative Writing Grant, 1995. *Memberships:* PEN; Wellington Poetry Society. *Address:* PO Box 9612, Newmarket, Auckland, New Zealand.

PATERSON, Don(ald); b. 30 Oct. 1963, Dundee, Scotland. Musician; Ed.; Poet. *Appointment:* Writer-in-Residence, Dundee University, 1993–95. *Publications:* Nil Nil, 1993; God's Gift to Women, 1997; The Eyes, 1999. *Honours:* Eric Gregory Award, 1990; Arvon/Observer International Poetry Competition, 1993; Forward Poetry Prize, 1993; Scottish Arts Council Book Awards, 1993, 1997, 1999; Geoffrey Faber Memorial Prize, 1998; T S Eliot Prize, 1998. *Address:* c/o Faber and Faber, 3 Queen Sq., London WC1N 3AU, England.

PATERSON, Stuart A.; b. 31 Jan. 1966, Truro, Cornwall, England. Writer; Poet; Ed. *Education:* Stirling University, 1988–92. *Appointments:* Founder-Ed., Spectrum review, 1990–96; Scottish Arts Council Writer-in-Residence, Dumfries and Galloway Region, 1996–98. *Publications:* Mulaney of Larne and Other Poems, 1991; Saving Graces, 1997. *Contributions to:* Anthologies, reviews, newspapers and journals. *Honour:* Eric Gregory Award, 1992; Scottish Arts Council Writer's Bursary, 1993. *Memberships:* Kilmarnock North West Writers Group, founder; Artists for Independence; Scottish Poetry Library; Scottish National Party. *Address:* c/o 2A Leslie Rd, New Farm Loch, Kilmarnock, Ayrshire KA3 7RR, Scotland.

PATEY-GRABOWSKA, Alicja Wanda, (Alicja Wanda Grabowska-Steffen); b. 24 July 1939, Warsaw, Poland. Poet; Teacher; Ed. m. Jan Steffen, 9 Dec. 1978, 1 s. *Education:* MA, Polish Philology, Warsaw

University. *Publications:* From the Circle, 1968; Adam Ewa, 1975; A Tree From the Inside, 1979; A Lullaby, 1981; You and I, 1982; A Wound of the Earth, 1983; Here Am I Women, 1984; Zoo, 1988; Przed Snem, 1990; Imprints of Time, 1997. *Contributions to:* Anthologies, children's books and periodicals. *Honours:* First Prize for Theatrical Play, 1985; Silver Wreath, Accademia Internazionale di Pontzen, Naples, 1989; Award, Accademia La Crisalide, Italy, 1997; Award, Polish Ministry of Culture, 1997. *Memberships:* Society of Authors; Accademia Internazionale di Pontzen, Naples; Academia La Crisalide, Italy. *Literary Agent:* Authors' Agency, ul Grzybowska 32, PO Box 133, 00-950 Warsaw, Poland. *Address:* Orlowicza 6m 30, 00-414 Warsaw, Poland.

PATILIS, Yannis; b. 21 Feb. 1947, Athens, Greece. Teacher of Literature; Poet; Ed.; Publisher. m. Elsa Liaropoulou, 2 s. *Education:* Degree, Law School, 1971, Byzantine and Hellenic Studies, 1977, University of Athens. *Appointments:* Co-Founder and Co-Ed., Nesus journal, 1983–85; Ed. and Publisher, Planodion journal, 1986–. *Publications:* 9 vols of poetry, including collected poems, 1993; Camel of Darkness: Selected Poems of Yannis Patilis 1970–97, 1997. *Contributions to:* Various publications. *Membership:* Society of Greek Writers. *Address:* 25 Gregoroviou St, 111 41, Athens, Greece.

PATNAIK, Swagat Priyadarshi; b. 20 Aug. 1944, Gunupur, India. Government Employee; Poet. m. Swarnalata Patnaik, 18 May 1969, 1 s., 1 d. *Education:* Diploma in Radio Electronics. *Publication:* Queen of English Poetry (poems), 1999. *Contributions to:* Asian Age; Scoria; Poesie India International Magazine. *Honours:* Certificate, Bireswar-Smriti, 1996; First Prize, Poesie International Poetry Competition, 1998. *Membership:* Writers Forum, Ranchi, India. *Address:* QTR 3R-99, PO Charbatia 754028, India.

PATRICK, Joseph. See: SCULLY, James.

PATRICK, Kathleen; b. 15 Aug. 1957, Brookings, South Dakota, USA. Writer. m. Robert Terhaar, 7 July 1983, 1 s., 1 d. *Education:* AA, Worthington Community College; BSc in English, St Cloud University; MA in English, University of Minnesota. *Publications:* Life on the Line, 1992; We Speak for Peace, 1993; I Am Becoming the Woman I've Wanted, 1994; The Unitarian Universalist Poets: A Contemporary American Survey, 1996; Threads of Experience, 1997; Prayers to Protest, 1997. *Contributions to:* Twin Cities; Sing Heavenly Muse; Milkweed Chronicle; Nimrod; Negative Capability; Primavera. *Honours:* Loft McKnight Award in Poetry, 1991; Jerome Arts Foundation Travel Grant, 1993–94; American Book Award, 1995; Honorable Mention, McKnight Award for Distinction, 1996. *Memberships:* The Loft; American Poetry Society. *Address:* 2953 Webster Ave S, St Louis Park, MN 55416, USA.

PATRICK, Maxine. See: MAXWELL, Patricia Anne.

PATRICK, Susan. See: CLARK, Patricia Denise.

PATTEN, Bernard M., (Patrick Murray); b. 23 March 1941, New York, NY, USA. Physician-Neurologist; Poet. m. Ethel Patten, 18 June 1964, 2 s., 1 d. *Education:* AB, summa cum laude, Columbia College; MD, College of Physicians and Surgeons, Columbia University. *Appointments:* Attending Neurologist, Methodist Hospital; Assoc. Prof. of Neurology, Baylor College of Medicine. *Publications:* Numerous. *Contributions to:* Many reviews, magazines and journals. *Honour:* Bay Area Writer's League Prize, 1995. *Memberships:* Modern Poetry Society; World Congress of Poets. *Address:* 1019 Baronridge, Seabrook, TX 77586, USA.

PATTEN, Brian; b. 7 Feb. 1946, Liverpool, England. Poet; Writer. *Appointment:* Regents Lecturer, University of California at San Diego. *Publications:* Poetry: The Mersey Sound: Penguin Modern Poets 10, 1967; Little Johnny's Confession, 1967; The Home Coming, 1969; Notes to the Hurrying Man: Poems, Winter '66–Summer '68, 1969; The Irrelevant Song, 1970; At Four O'Clock in the Morning, 1971; Walking Out: The Early Poems of Brian Patten, 1971; The Eminent Professors and the Nature of Poetry as Enacted Out by Members of the Poetry Seminar One Rainy Evening, 1972; The Unreliable Nightingale, 1973; Vanishing Trick, 1976; Grave Gossip, 1979; Love Poems, 1981; New Volume, 1983; Storm Damage, 1988; Grinning Jack: Selected Poems, 1990; Armada, 1996; The Utterly Brilliant Book of Poetry (ed.), 1998. Editor: Clare's Countryside: A Book of John Clare, 1981. Children's Books: Prose: The Jumping Mouse, 1972; Mr Moon's Last Case, 1975; Emma's Doll, 1976; Jimmy Tag-along, 1988; Grizzelda Frizzle, 1992; Impossible Parents, 1994; Beowulf, a version, 1999; The Story Giant, 2002. Poetry: Gargling With Jelly, 1985; Thawing Frozen Frogs, 1990; The Puffin Book of 20th Century Children's Verse, 1991; The Magic Bicycle, 1993; The Utter Nutters, 1994; The Blue and Green Ark, 1999; Juggling with Gerbils, 2000. *Contributions to:* Journals and newspapers. *Honours:* Special Award, Mystery Writers of America, 1977; Arts Council of England Writers Award, 1998; Freedom of the City of Liverpool, 2001; Hon. Fellowship, John Moore's Univerisity, 2002. *Membership:* Chelsea Arts Club. *Literary Agent:* Rogers, Coleridge and White. *Address:* c/o Rogers, Coleridge & White, 20 Powis Mews, London W11 1JN, England.

PAULIN, Tom, (Thomas Neilson Paulin); b. 25 Jan. 1949, Leeds, Yorkshire, England. Poet; Critic; Lecturer in English Literature. m. Munjiet Kaut Khosa, 1973, 2 s. *Education:* BA, University of Hull; BLitt, Lincoln College, Oxford. *Appointments:* Lecturer, 1972–89, Reader in Poetry, 1989–94, University of Nottingham; G M Young Lecturer in English Literature, University of Oxford, 1994–; Fellow, Hertford College, Oxford, 1994–. *Publications:* Poetry: Theoretical Locations, 1975; A State of Justice, 1977; Personal Column, 1978; The Strange Museum, 1980; The Book of Juniper, 1981; Liberty Tree, 1983; The Argument at Great Tew, 1985; Fivemiletown, 1987; Selected Poems 1972–90, 1993; Walking a Line, 1994; The Wind Dog, 1999; The Invasion Handbook, 2002. Other: Thomas Hardy: The Poetry of Perception, 1975; Ireland and the English Crisis, 1984; The Faber Book of Political Verse (ed.), 1986; Hard Lines 3 (co-ed.), 1987; Minotaur: Poetry and the Nation State, 1992; Writing to the Moment: Selected Critical Essays, 1996; The Day Star of Liberty: William Hazlitt's Radical Style (biography), 1998. *Honours:* Eric Gregory Award, 1978; Somerset Maugham Award, 1978; Faber Memorial Prize, 1982; Fulbright Scholarship, 1983–84. *Address:* c/o Faber and Faber, 3 Queen Sq., London WC1N 3AU, England.

PAUWELS, Rony, (Claude Van de Berge); b. 30 April 1945, Assenede, Belgium. Docent; Writer; Poet. m. Drongen Pauwels, 30 Jan. 1973. *Education:* Royal Conservatory, Ghent. *Appointments:* Docent, Acad. of Arts, Ecklo, Universities of Brussels, Ghent, Louvain, and Bonn. *Publications:* De koude wind du over het zand waeut, 1977; Het bewegen van her hoge gras op de top van de hevvel, 1981; Hiiumaa, 1987; Attu, 1988; Aztlan, 1990. Poetry: De zang van de maskers, 1988; De Mens in der ster, 1991; Het Silhouet, 1993. *Contributions to:* Journals and magazines. *Membership:* Flemish Writers Union. *Address:* Oude Molenstraat 2, 9960 Assenede, Belgium.

PAWLAK, Mark; b. 29 May 1948, Buffalo, New York, USA. Educator; Poet; Ed. m. Mary F Bonina, 21 Aug. 1981, 2 s. *Education:* BS, Physics, Massachusetts Institute of Technology, 1970. *Appointments:* Academic Co-ordinator, The Group School, 1971–74, 1976–80; Poet-in-Residence, Worcester (Massachusetts) Schools, 1974–76; Dir of Mathematics and Skills, University of Massachusetts, Bsoton, 1980–. *Publications:* The Buffalo Sequence, 1978; All The New, 1985; Special Handling, 1993; Smart Like Me: High School Writing Since 1966 (ed. with Dick Lowrie), 1988; Bullseye: Outstanding Poetry and Prose By High School Writers (ed. with Dick Lowrie), 1995. *Contributions to:* Abraxas; Bogg; Compost; Exquisite Corpse; Hanging Loose; Mother Jones: Slipstream; Synarsthetic; Transfer; Worcester Review. *Honours:* Finalist, Massachusetts Artist Fellow, 1987, 1988. *Address:* 44 Thingvalla Ave, Cambridge, MA 02138, USA.

PEACOCK, Molly; b. 30 June 1947, Buffalo, New York, USA. Writer; Poet. m. Michael Groden, 19 Aug. 1992. *Education:* BA, magna cum laude, Harpur College, State University of New York at Binghamton, 1969; MA, Honours, Johns Hopkins University, 1977. *Appointments:* Lecturer, State University of New York at Binghamton, 1975–76, University of Delaware, 1978–79; Writer-in-Residence, Delaware State Arts Council, 1978–81, University of Western Ontario, 1995–96; English Faculty, Friends Seminary, New York City, 1981–87; Visiting Poet, Hofstra University, 1986, Columbia University, 1986, 1992, Carlow College, 1993; Poet-in-Residence, Bucknell University, 1993, Bennington College, 2001; Contributing Writer, House & Garden, 1996–2001; Regents Lecturer, University of California at Riverside, 1998. *Publications:* Poetry: And Live Apart, 1980; Raw Heaven, 1984; Take Heart, 1989; Original Love, 1995; Cornucopia, 2002. Other: Paradise, Piece by Piece (literary memoir), 1998; How to Read a Poem... and Start a Poetry Circle, 1999. Editor: Poetry in Motion: 100 Poems from the Subways and Buses (with Elise Paschen and Neil Neches), 1996; The Private I: Privacy in a Public Age (essays). *Contributions to:* Anthologies, reviews, quarterlies, journals, and magazines. *Honours:* MacDowell Colony Fellowships, 1975–76, 1979, 1982, 1985, 1989; Danforth Foundation Fellowships, 1976–77; Yaddo Fellowships, 1980, 1982; Ingram Merrill Foundation Awards, 1981, 1986; New Virginia Review Fellowship, 1983; PEN/National Endowment for the Arts Fiction Award, 1984; New York Foundation for the Arts Grant, 1985, 1989; National Endowment for the Arts Grant, 1990. *Memberships:* Acad. of American Poets; Associated Writing Programs; PEN; Poetry Society of America, pres., 1989–95. *Address:* 505 E 14th St, No. 3G, New York, NY 10009, USA; 109 Front St E, No. 1041, Toronto, ON M5A 4P7, Canada.

PEACOCKE, M(argaret) R(uth), (Meg Peacocke); b. 5 March 1930, Reading, Berkshire, England. Psychotherapist; Counsellor; Poet. *Education:* Exhibitioner, St Anne's College, Oxford; BA, 1951, MA, 1954, Oxon; Diploma in Counselling, Aston University, 1981. *Publications:* Marginal Land, 1988; Selves, 1995. *Contributions to:* Anthologies, reviews, and magazines. *Honour:* Commendation, National Poetry Competition, 1985, Arvon Poetry Competition, 1987; First Prize, Green Book, 1987; Second Prize, Bury Metro Arts, 1987; Prizes, Peterloo Poets Open Competition, 1986, 1988, 1992, Lancaster Open, 1986, 1988, 1992, Northern Poetry, 1989. *Address:* Dummah Hill, North Stainmore, Kirkby Stephen, Cumbria, England.

PEARCE, Brian Louis; b. 4 June 1933, London, England. Poet; Author; Dramatist; Lecturer. m. Margaret Wood, 2 Aug. 1969, 1 d. *Education:* MA, University College, London. *Appointments:* Examiner in English Literature,

Library Asscn, 1964–70; College Librarian-Senior Lecturer, Richmond upon Thames College, 1977–88; Occasional Lecturer, National Portrait Gallery, London, 1990–; Hon. Librarian, Theological College of Zimbabwe, Bulawayo, 1997–98. *Publications:* Poetry: Selected Poems 1951–1973, 1978; Dutch Comfort, 1985; Gwen John Talking, 1985; Jack O'Lent, 1991; Leaving the Corner: Selected Poems 1973–1985, 1992; Coeli et terra, 1993; Thames Listener: Poems 1949–89, 1993; The Proper Fuss, 1996. Fiction: Victoria Hammersmith, 1987; 'City Whiskers' sequence in The Playing of the Easter Music (with Caws and Caseley), 1996; London Clay, 1991; The Bust of Minerva, 1992; A Man in his Room, 1992; Battersea Pete, 1994; The Servant of his Country, 1994; The Tufnell Triptych, 1997; Tribal Customs, 1997; The Goldhawk Variations, 1999; Willesden Paper, 2002; St Zacchs, 2002. Plays: The Eagle and the Swan, 1966; Shrine Rites, 1990; The Damien Offices, 2000; The Widow of Gozo, 2002. Other: Palgrave: Selected Poems (ed.), 1985; Thomas Twining of Twickenham, 1988; The Fashioned Reed: The Poets of Twickenham from 1500, 1992; Varieties of Fervour: Portraits of Victorian and Edwardian Poets, 1996; *Dame Ethel Walker: An Essay in Reassessment,* 1997; The Palgraves and John Murray: Letters (ed.), 1997; The Idea of Nicodemus: Sermons and Prayers, 2000; Clemo the Poet, 2002. *Contributions to:* Various publications. *Honours:* First Place, Christian Poetry Competition, 1989. *Memberships:* Browning, David Jones, De la Mare, Hopkins, Masefield, Palgrave Societies; PEN; RSA, fellow; RSL. *Address:* The Marish, 72 Heathfield S, Twickenham, Middlesex TW2 7SS, England.

PEASE, Peter Pembroke; b. 15 April 1941, Columbus, Ohio, USA. Procurement Specialist; Poet. m. Julia Feoktistova, 19 July 1996, 2 s., 1 d. *Education:* BA, MA, Wesleyan University, 1963. *Appointments:* US Foreign Service, 1965–70; Political Officer, Economic and Commercial Officer, Jordan, Japan; Arabian American Oil Company, 1970–85; Procurement Specialist, Task Man., World Bank, 1985–. *Publication:* Rostropovich in Red Square, 1996. *Membership:* Acad. of American Poets. *Address:* 1050 N Stuart St, Apt 818, Arlington, VA 22201, USA.

PEASMAIR, Arthur. See: BLACKMAN, Roy Alfred Arthur.

PECK, John (Frederick); b. 13 Jan. 1941, Pittsburgh, Pennsylvania, USA. Poet. m. Ellen Margaret McKee, 1963, divorced, 1 d. *Education:* AB, Allegheny College, Meadville, Pennsylvania, 1962; PhD, Stanford University, 1973. *Appointments:* Instructor, 1968–70, Visiting Lecturer, 1972–75, Princeton University; Asst Prof., 1977–79, Prof. of English, 1980–82, Mount Holyoke College, South Hadley, Massachusetts. *Publications:* Poetry: Shagbark, 1972; The Broken Blockhouse Wall, 1978; Argura, 1993. Other: The Poems and Translations of Hi-Lo, 1991. *Honours:* American Acad. of Arts and Letters Award, 1975, and Rome Fellowship, 1978; Guggenheim Fellowship, 1981. *Address:* c/o Englisches Seminar, Plattenstrasse 47, 8032 Zürich, Switzerland.

PECKENPAUGH, Angela Johnson; b. 21 March 1942, Richmond, Virginia, USA. Assoc. Prof. of English; Performing Poet. m. Bill Peckenpaugh, 27 July 1970, 1 d. *Education:* BA, Denison University, Ohio, 1965; MA, Ohio University, 1967; MFA, Writing, University of Massachusetts, 1978. *Appointments:* Instructor in English, Ohio University; Lecturer in English, University of Wisconsin at Milwaukee; Dir of Development, Milwaukee Institute of Art and Design; Dir, Writing Programmes for Adults, University of Wisconsin Extension; Prof. in English, University of Wisconsin at Whitewater. *Publications:* Letters from Lee's Army, 1979; Discovering the Mandala, 1981; A Book of Charms, 1983; Refreshing the Fey, 1986; Remembering Rivers, 1991; A Heathen Herbal, 1993; Always Improving My Appetite, 1994. *Contributions to:* Anthologies, reviews, quarterlies, and journals. *Honours:* Honourable Mention, Council of Wisconsin Writers; All University Fellowship, University of Massachusetts; Wisconsin Arts Board Grant. *Memberships:* Poetry Society of America; Associated Writing Programs; Wisconsin Fellowship of Poets; Wisconsin Regional Writers. *Address:* 2513 E Webster Pl., Milwaukee, WI 53211, USA.

PEDERSON, Cynthia; b. 11 Sept. 1956, Oklahoma City, Oklahoma, USA. Teacher; Poet. m. Ronald M Pederson, 20 June 1979. *Education:* BA, Honours, magna cum laude, English, Washburn University, Topeka, 1978; MA, Honours, English, University of Kansas, 1983; MFA, Creative Writing, Wichita State University, 1988. *Appointments:* Adjunct Instructor, Washburn University, 1986, Friends University, 1987; Asst Instructor, Wichita State University, 1988; Instructor, Wilkes Community College, 1988–90; Part-Time Instructor, Danville Community College, 1991–. *Publications:* Spoken Across a Distance, 1982; Earthcolors, 1982; Learning a New Landscape, 1987; Fissures, 1993. *Contributions to:* Anthologies, reviews, quarterlies, journals, and magazines. *Honour:* Great Poets Award, Kansas State Poetry Society. *Address:* 1521 College Ave, Topeka, KS 66604, USA.

PEERADINA, Saleem; b. 5 Oct. 1944, Mumbai, India. Prof. of English; Poet. m. Mumtaz Perradina, 11 May 1978, 2 d. *Education:* MA, University of Mumbai, 1969; MA, Wake Forest University, IL, 1973. *Appointments:* Dir, Open Classroom, Sophia College, Mumbai, 1978–84; Asst Prof. to Prof. of English, Siena Heights College, Michigan, 1989–. *Publications:* First Offence, 1980; Group Portrait, 1992. *Contributions to:* Anthologies, quarterlies, and journals. *Honours:* Fulbright Travel Grant, 1971; British Council Writer's Grant, 1983. *Membership:* MLA. *Address:* 343 Anthony Ct, Adrian, MI 49221, USA.

PEGLER, Timothy Stuart; b. 26 Sept. 1967, Tongala, Vic., Australia. Journalist; Poet. *Education:* BA, University of Melbourne, 1988. *Appointments:* Journalist, Suns News Pictorial, 1989–90, Herald-Sun, 1990–91, Weekly Times, 1991–92, Australian Associated Press, 1992, The Age, 1992–97, The Australian, 1998–. *Contributions to:* Anthologies and magazines. *Honours:* Joint Winner, Human Rights Commission, Human Rights (Print Media) Award, 1996; Joint Winner, United Nations Asscn of Australia Children's Rights (Print Media) Award. *Memberships:* Media Entertainment and Arts Alliance. *Address:* 42 Raphael St, Abbotsford, Vic 3067, Australia.

PEIJI MA. See: MAO YANG MA.

PELC, Ryszarda Lidia; b. 20 June 1938, Poland. Poet. m. Karol I Pelc, 24 Sept. 1959, 1 s. *Education:* MA, University of Wrocé aw, 1962. *Publications:* Fascinations: Collected Poems, 1989; The Journey, 1989; Somewhere on the Highway, 1990; Watching Seagulls, 1990; The Winter Symphony, 1990; The Vigil, 1991; Lake Biwa, 1996. *Contributions to:* Anthologies, Polish-American magazines, and print and online periodicals. *Honours:* Golden Poet Awards 1989, 1990; Certificate of Poetic Achievement, Amherst Poetry Society, 1991. *Address:* 19796 Lakeview Dr., Hancock, MI 49930, USA.

PELUFFO, Luisa; b. 20 Aug. 1941, Buenos Aires, Argentina. Writer; Poet. m. Pablo Masllorens, 24 April 1971, 2 s. *Education:* Degree, National Fine Arts School, 1959; Stage Direction, National Drama School, 1975. *Appointments:* Leader, Literary Workshops, San Carlos de Bariloche Municipal Art School, 1985–2002. *Publications:* Poetry: Materia Viva, 1976; Materia de Revelaciones, 1983; La Otra Orilla, 1991; Un Color Inexistente, 2001. Fiction: Conspiraciones, 1982; Tudo Eso Oyes, 1989; La Doble Vida, 1993. *Contributions to:* Anthologies and periodicals. *Honours:* First Prize, Victoria Ocampo Literary Contest, Fundación Banco de la Provincia de Buenos Aires, 1980; Emecé Ediciones First Prize, 1989; Regional First Prize, National Arts Foundation, 1991; Second Prize, Ricardo Rojas National Literary Contest, Municipalidad de la Ciudad de Buenos Aires, 1993; Secretaría de Cultura de la Nación Literary Contest, Regional First Prize, 1996; First Prize, Ediciones Torremozas XVIII Carmen Conde Women's Poetry Contest, Madrid, 2001. *Address:* Palacios 465 (8400), Bariloche, Provincia de Rio Negro, Argentina.

PENDLETON, Don. See: OBSTFELD, Raymond.

PENG XIANG. See: ZHI LI.

PENHA, James W.; b. 1 Feb. 1947, New York, NY, USA. Asst Prof. of English; Poet. *Education:* BA, St John's University, Jamaica, New York, 1967; MA, Pennsylvania State University, 1968; PhD, New York University, 1978. *Appointments:* Founder-Dir, The Learning Community, New York, 1969–76; Asst Dean, 1978–85, Asst Prof. of English, 1990–, St John's University, Jamaica, New York; Dir of Planning, University of Detroit, 1985–86; Head, High School English, Hong Kong International School, 1986–89. *Contributions to:* Anthologies, reviews, quarterlies, journals, and magazines. *Memberships:* Acad. of American Poets; Associated Writing Programs; MLA; National Council of Teachers of English; National Writing Project; Poetry Society of America; Poets and Writers. *Address:* 472 Howard Ave, No. 24A, Staten Island, NY 10301, USA.

PENWARDEN, Andrew John; b. 5 May 1964, London, England. Poet. *Publications:* The Girl from Verona, 1995; The Witchfinder General, 1995; The Eye of the Storm, 1996; The Land is a Song, 1996. *Contributions to:* Numerous publications. *Honours:* Runner-Up, Pamphlets Competition, 1990; Mrs Sunderland Annual Poetry Competition, 1995. *Address:* 77 Eldon Rd, Marsh, Huddersfield, Yorkshire, England.

PERDIDO, Carlos or PERDU, Charles. See: GEROLD, Charles.

PERELMAN, Bob, (Robert Perelman); b. 2 Dec. 1947, Youngstown, OH, USA. Poet; Writer; Assoc. Prof. m. Francie Shaw, 1975, 2 s. *Education:* MA, University of Michigan, 1969; MFA, University of Iowa, 1970; PhD, University of California, 1990. *Appointments:* Ed., Hills magazine, 1973–80; Asst Prof., 1990–95, Assoc. Prof., 1995–, University of Pennsylvania. *Publications:* Braille, 1975; Seven Works, 1978; a.k.a., 1979; Primer, 1981; To the Reader, 1984; The First World, 1986; Writing/Talks (ed.), 1985; Face Value, 1988; Captive Audience, 1988; Virtual Reality, 1993; The Trouble with Genius: Reading Pound, Joyce, Stein, and Zukovsky, 1994; The Marginalization of Poetry: Language Writings and Literary History, 1996; The Future of Memory, 1998. *Address:* c/o Dept of English, University of Pennsylvania, Philadelphia, PA 19104, USA.

PERLMAN, John N(iels); b. 13 May 1946, Alexandria, Virginia, USA. Poet; Teacher. m. Janis Hadobas, 26 May 1967, 1 d. *Education:* BA, Ohio State University, 1969; MS, Iona College, 1981. *Appointments:* Teacher in schools in Minnesota, Georgia, California, New York. *Publications:* Kachina, 1971; Three Years Rings, 1972; Dinner 650 Warburton Avenue, 1973; Notes Toward a Family, 1975; The Hudson: A Weave, 1976; Nicole, 1976; Self Portrait, 1976; Swath, 1978; Homing, 1981; Powers, 1982; A Wake of, 1983; Longtrail, 1985;

Beacons Imaging Within as Promises, 1990; Imperatives of Address, 1992; Anacoustic, 1993. *Honours:* Acad. of American Poets Awards; New York Foundation for the Arts Fellowship; Vanderwater Prize. *Address:* 29 Lynton Pl., White Plains, NY 10606, USA.

PERRIAM, Wendy Angela; b. 23 Feb. 1940, London, England. Writer; Poet. m. (1) 22 Aug. 1964, 1 d., (2) John Alan Perriam, 29 July 1974. *Education:* St Anne's College, Oxford, 1958–61; BA, Honours, History, 1961, MA, 1972, University of Oxford; London School of Economics and Political Science, 1963–64. *Publications:* Absinthe for Elevenses, 1980; Cuckoo, 1981; After Purple, 1982; Born of Woman, 1983; The Stillness, The Dancing, 1985; Sin City, 1987; Devils, for a Change, 1989; Fifty-Minute Hour, 1990; Bird Inside, 1992; Michael, Michael, 1993; Breaking and Entering, 1994; Coupling, 1996; Second Skin, 1998; Lying, 2000; Dreams, Demons and Desire, 2001; Tread Softly, 2002. *Contributions to:* Anthologies, newspapers and magazines. *Memberships:* British Actors Equity Asscn; PEN; Society of Authors. *Address:* c/o Curtis Brown Ltd, Fourth Floor, Haymarket House, 28/29 Haymarket, London SW1Y 4SP, England. *Website:* www.perriam.demon.co.uk.

PERRIE, Walter; b. 5 June 1949, Lanarkshire, Scotland. Poet; Author; Critic. *Education:* MA, Honours, Mental Philosophy, University of Edinburgh, 1975; MPhil, English Studies, University of Stirling, 1989. *Appointments:* Ed., Chapman, 1970–75; Scottish-Canadian Exchange Fellow, University of British Columbia, Canada, 1984–85; Managing Ed., Margin: International Arts Quarterly, 1985–90; Stirling Writing Fellow, University of Stirling, 1991. *Publications:* Metaphysics and Poetry (with Hugh MacDiarmid), 1974; Poem on a Winter Night, 1976; A Lamentation for the Children, 1977; By Moon and Sun, 1980; Out of Conflict, 1982; Concerning the Dragon, 1984; Roads that Move: A Journey Through Eastern Europe, 1991; Thirteen Lucky Poems, 1991; From Milady's Wood and Other Poems, 1997; The Light in Strathearn (poems), 2000. *Contributions to:* Journals and periodicals. *Honours:* Scottish Arts Council Bursaries, 1976, 1983, 1994, and Book Awards, 1976, 1983; Eric Gregory Award, 1978; Ingram Merrill Foundation Award, 1987 Scottish Arts Council Writers Bursary, 1999; Society of Authors Travelling Scholarship, 2000. *Memberships:* PEN, Scotland; Society of Authors. *Address:* 10 Croft Pl., Dunning, Perthshire PH2 0SB, Scotland.

PERRIMAN, Wendy K(aren); b. 9 July 1958, Stamford, Lincolnshire, England. Poet. m. Steven Perriman, 8 Aug. 1981, 1 s. *Education:* BA, Honours, University of Lancaster, 1979; PGCE, University of Bristol, 1980. *Publications:* Collected Experience, 1996; Show and Tell, 1997; Free Fall, 1998. *Contributions to:* Magazines. *Honours:* Honorable Mention, Writer's Digest, 1995, and John David Johnson Memorial Poetry Award, Poet Magazine, 1995. *Memberships:* Acad. of American Poets; International Women's Writing Guild; Poetry Society of America; Modern Poetry Asscn. *Address:* PO Box 53, Madison, NJ 07940, USA.

PERRIN, Arnold; b. 26 Nov. 1932, Lynn, Massachusetts, USA. Ed.; Publisher; Poet. m. Jacquelyn Tucker, 17 Jan. 1953, divorced June 1994, 5 d. *Education:* BE, Plymouth State College of the University of New Hampshire, 1965; Graduate Studies, Dartmouth College, 1966, University of Maine at Augusta, 1987. *Appointments:* Ed.-Publisher, Wings Press; Poetry Ed., New England Sampler. *Publications:* The Wind's Will, 1979; View from Hill Cabin, 1979; The Essentials of Writing Poetry, 1991; Signs and Seasons, 1991; Noah, 1993; Speaking Inuit, 1994; Window, 1998. *Contributions to:* Newspapers, reviews, and journals. *Memberships:* Live Poets Society, Rockland, Maine, board mem.; Maine Writers and Publishers Alliance. *Address:* PO Box 809, Union, ME 04862, USA.

PERRUCCI, Christy Lynn; b. 17 July 1973, Abington, Pennsylvania, USA. Poet. *Education:* Graduate, William Tennent High School, 1991. *Publication:* Seasons of the Heart, Vol. 1, 1996. *Contributions to:* Anthologies and magazines. *Honours:* Many honorable mentions; Third Prize, Poet's Review, 1995; Outstanding Top Twenty, Cameo Awards, 1996. *Address:* 274 Henry Ave, Warminster, PA 18974, USA.

PERRY, Colin Ian Henry; b. 4 July 1955, England. State Registered Chiropodist and Podiatrist; Poet. m. Agnes Myriam Marcelle, 29 July 1989, 1 s. *Education:* BSc, Leicester University; Diploma of Podiatric Medicine. *Publications:* Little Things Mean a Lot, 1976; Sliding Magnets, 1982. *Contributions to:* Another Wing, anthology; Guernsey Press. *Membership:* Poetry Society. *Address:* Eastwood, 9 Mount Row, St Peter Port, Guernsey, Channel Islands.

PERRY, Mary Elizabeth; b. 23 Feb. 1918, New York, NY, USA. Poet; Ed.; Publisher. m. (1) John Perry, 25 June 1939, 3 s., 1 d., (2) Bert Hildebrand, 6 Nov. 1984. *Education:* BS, 1967, MA, Teacher's College, 1970, Columbia University. *Appointments:* Ed., Poetry Magazine, 1986–2002; Poetry Ed., Pen Woman Magazine, 1997–. *Publications:* Olé, Olé, 1990; Gathered Echoes, 1992. *Contributions to:* Anthologies and periodicals. *Honours:* Distinguished Woman of Southern Nevada Citations, 1989–2002; First Prize, National League of American Pen Women Literary Contest, 1995; First Prize, Nevada State Literary Competition, 1996. *Memberships:* National League of American Pen

Women; Poetry Society of America; Poets and Writers; Small Press Center. *Address:* c/o M. E. Hildebrand, PO Box 61324, Boulder City, NV 89006, USA.

PERRY, Ruth; b. 14 Jan. 1938, Baltimore, Maryland, USA. Poet; Lyricist; Writer. Widow, 1 s. *Education:* English, Morgan State College, 1954–57; Cortez Peters Business School, 1960–62. *Contributions to:* Many anthologies and other publications. *Honours:* Many Merit Certificates and Golden Poet Awards, World of Poetry. *Memberships:* International Society of Poets; Poetry Society of America; World of Poetry. *Address:* 6713 Ransome Dr., Baltimore, MD 21207, USA.

PERSON, Stanley Thomas; b. 7 Oct. 1952, Seattle, Washington, USA. Ed.; Poet. m. Frances Louise Schroeder, 17 Feb. 1990. *Education:* BA, Education and English, Western Washington University, 1974; AA, Music, Shoreline Community College. *Appointments:* Ed., Laughing Bear Press, 1976–, Laughing Bear Newsletter, 1976–, Laughing Bear, Literary Magazine, 1976–78; Faculty Adviser, Spindrift, Shoreline Community College, 1977–79. *Contributions to:* Iron; Interstate; Ghost Dance; Nexus; Telephone; Happiness Holding Tank; Rocky Mountain Arsenal of the Arts; Northwest Review; New York Quarterly. *Address:* PO Box 36159, Denver, CO 80236, USA.

PERU, Cass. See: MACLEOD, N(orma) J(ean).

PETERFREUND, Stuart (Samuel); b. 30 June 1945, New York, NY, USA. Prof. of English; Poet. m. (1) Carol Jean Litzler, 12 Sept. 1981, divorced 17 Dec. 1997, 1 d., (2) Christina Sieber, 6 May 2001. *Education:* BA, English, Cornell University, 1966; MFA, Creative Writing, University of California at Irvine, 1968; English Literature and German Language, Columbia University, 1970–71; PhD, English, University of Washington, 1974. *Appointments:* Lecturer, University of Puget Sound, 1975; Asst Prof., University of Arkansas at Little Rock, 1975–78; Asst Prof., 1978–82, Assoc. Prof., 1982–91, Prof. of English and Chair, Dept of English, Northeastern University, 1991–. *Publications:* Poetry: The Hanged Knife and Other Poems, 1970; Harder than Rain, 1977; Interstatements, 1986. Other: William Blake in the Age of Newton: Essays on Literature as Art and Science, 1998; Shelley Among Others: The Play of the Intertext and the Idea of Language, 2002. Editor: Critical Theory and the Teaching of Literature, 1985; Culture/Criticism/Ideology, 1986; Literature and Science: Theory and Practice, 1990. *Contributions to:* Scholarly books, professional journals, poetry anthologies, and reviews. *Honours:* Grants; Fellowships; First Prize in Poetry, Writers' Digest Competition, 1970; Poet-in-Residence, Southern Literary Festival, 1977; First Prize, Worcester County Poetry Asscn Contest, 1989; Third Prize, Abiko Journal Poetry Contest, 1994; Third Prize, Anna Davidson Rosenberg Award for Poems on the Jewish Experience, 1996. *Memberships:* American Society for Eighteenth-Century Studies; British Society for History of Science; Byron Society; History of Science Society; Interdisciplinary Nineteenth-Century Studies; International Asscn for Philosophy and Literature; Keats-Shelley Asscn of America; MLA; Poets and Writers; Society for Literature and Science, pres., 1995–97; Wordsworth-Coleridge Asscn. *Address:* c/o Dept of English, Northeastern University, 406 Holmes Hall, 360 Huntington Ave, Boston, MA 02115, USA.

PETERKIEWICZ, Jerzy; b. 29 Sept. 1916, Fabianki, Poland. Prof. Emeritus of Polish Language and Literature (retd); Poet; Writer; Dramatist. *Education:* University of Warsaw; MA, University of St Andrews, Scotland, 1944; PhD, King's College, London, 1947. *Appointments:* Lecturer, then Reader, 1952–72; Head, Dept of East European Languages and Literature, 1972–77, Prof. of Polish Language and Literature, 1972–79, University of London. *Publications:* Prowincja, 1936; Wiersze i poematy, 1938; Pogrzeb Europy, 1946; The Knotted Cord, 1953; Loot and Loyalty, 1955; Polish Prose and Verse, 1956; Antologia liryki angielskiej, 1958; Future to Let, 1958; Isolation, 1959; Five Centuries of Polish Poetry (with Burns Singer), 1960, revised edn (also with Jon Stallworthy), 1970; The Quick and the Dead, 1961; That Angel Burning at My Left Side, 1963; Poematy Londynskie, 1965; Inner Circle, 1966; Green Flows the Bile, 1969; The Other Side of Silence: The Poet at the Limits of Language, 1970; The Third Adam, 1975; Easter Vigil and Other Poems, by Karol Wojtyla (Pope John Paul II) (ed. and trans.), 1979; Kula magiczna, 1980; Collected Poems, by Karol Wojtyla (Pope John Paul II) (ed. and trans.), 1982; Poezje Wybrane, 1986; Literatura polska w perspektywie europejskiej, 1986; Modlitwy intelektu, 1988; Messianic Prophecy, 1991; In the Scales of Fate, 1993; Wiersze dobrzynskie, 1994; The Place Within: The Poetry of Pope John Paul II (ed. and trans.), 1994; Slowa sa bez Poreczy (Poems 1935–56), 1998; Cyprian Norwid: Poems, Letters, Drawings (ed. and trans. with Christine Brooke-Rose), 2000. *Contributions to:* Numerous periodicals and BBC3. *Honour:* Commander, Polonice Restituta, 1995. *Address:* 7 Lyndhurst Terrace, London NW3 5QA, England.

PETERS, Lenrie; b. 1 Sept. 1932, Bathurst, Gambia. Physician; Poet; Writer. *Education:* BA, Trinity College, Cambridge, 1956; University College Hospital, London. *Appointments:* Surgeon, Victoria Hospital, Gambia, 1969–72; Surgeon in private practice, Gambia, 1972–. *Publications:* Poems, 1964; Satellites, 1967; Katchikali, 1971; Selected Poetry, 1981. Novel: The Second Round, 1965. *Contributions to:* Many anthologies. *Address:* Westfield Clinic, PO Box 142, Banjul, Gambia.

PETERS, Robert Louis; b. 20 Oct. 1924, Eagle River, Wisconsin, USA. Prof. of English; Poet; Writer. Divorced, 3 s., 1 d. *Education:* BA, 1948, MA, 1949, PhD, 1952, University of Wisconsin at Madison. *Appointments:* Instructor, University of Idaho, 1952–53, Boston University, 1953–55; Asst Prof., Ohio Wesleyan University, 1955–58; Assoc. Prof., Wayne State University, 1958–63; Prof. of English, University of California at Riverside, 1963–68, and Irvine, 1968–94. *Publications:* The Drowned Man to the Fish, 1978; Picnic in the Snow: Ludwig of Bavaria, 1982; What Dillinger Meant to Me, 1983; Hawker, 1984; Kane, 1985; Ludwig of Bavaria: Poems and a Play, 1986; The Blood Countess: Poems and a Play, 1987; Haydon, 1988; Brueghel's Pigs, 1989; Poems: Selected and New, 1992; Goodnight Paul: Poems, 1992; Snapshots for a Serial Killer: A Fiction and Play, 1992; Zapped: 3 Novellas, 1993; Nell: A Woman from Eagle River, 1994; Lili Marlene: A Memoir of World War II, 1995; Familial Love: Poems, 2001. Other: Victorians in Literature and Art, 1961; The Crowns of Apollo: Swinburne's Principles of Literature and Art, 1965; The Letters of John Addington Symonds (co-ed.), 3 vols, 1967–69; Letter to a Tutor: The Tennyson Family Letters to Henry Graham Dakyns (ed.), 1988. *Contributions to:* Professional journals. *Honours:* Guggenheim Fellowship, 1966–67; Yaddo, MacDowell Colony, and Ossabaw Island Project Fellowships, 1973–74; National Endowment for the Arts Grant, 1974. *Memberships:* American Society for Aesthetics; PEN; Writer's Guild. *Address:* 9431 Krepp Dr., Huntington Beach, CA 92646, USA.

PETERSON, John. See: BALON, Brett John Steven.

PETERSON, Robert; b. 2 June 1924, Denver, CO, USA. Writer; Poet. 1 d. *Education:* BA, University of California, Berkeley, 1947; MA, San Francisco State College, 1956. *Appointment:* Writer-in-Residence, Reed College, Portland, Oregon, 1969–71. *Publications:* Home for the Night, 1962; The Binnacle, 1967; Wondering Where You Are, 1969; Lone Rider, 1976; Under Sealed Orders, 1976; Leaving Taos, 1981; The Only Piano Player in La Paz, 1985; Waiting for Garbo: 44 Ghazals, 1987; All The Time in the World, 1996. *Honours:* National Endowment for the Arts Grant, 1967; Amy Lowell Travelling Fellowship, 1972–73. *Memberships:* Marin Poetry Society. *Address:* PO Box 417, Fairfax, CA 94978, USA.

PETRIE, Paul James; b. 1 July 1928, Detroit, Michigan, USA. Prof. of English (retd); Poet. m. Sylvia Spencer, 21 Aug. 1954, 1 s., 2 d. *Education:* BA, 1950, MA, 1951, Wayne State University; PhD, University of Iowa, 1957. *Appointments:* Assoc. Prof., Peru State University, 1958–59; Instructor to Prof. of English, University of Rhode Island, 1959–90. *Publications:* Confessions of a Non-Conformist, 1963; The Race With Time and the Devil, 1965; From Under the Hill of Night, 1969; The Academy of Goodbye, 1974; Light From the Furnace Rising, 1978; Not Seeing is Believing, 1983; Strange Gravity, 1985; The Runners, 1988. *Contributions to:* Newspapers, reviews, quarterlies, journals, and magazines. *Honours:* Scholarly Achievement Award, University of Rhode Island, 1983; Catholic Press Award, 1985; Arts Achievement Award, Wayne State University, 1990. *Address:* 200 Dendron Rd, Peace Dale, RI 02879, USA.

PETRUCCI, Mario; b. 29 Nov. 1958, London, England. Research Physicist and Engineer; Teacher; Poet. *Education:* Degree in Physics and Theoretical Physics, 1980, MA, 1983, Selwyn College, Cambridge; Teaching Qualification, London, 1981; PhD, Optoelectronic Materials, University of London, 1989. *Appointments:* Co-Founder, Bound Spiral Magazine; Poet-in-Residence, Imperial War Museum, 1998–99; Arvon Tutor, 1999–. *Publications:* Mr Bass, 1989; Departures, 1989; Shrapnel and Sheets, 1996; Lepidoptera, 1999; Bosco, 1999, 2001; The Stamina of Sheep, 2002. *Contributions to:* Anthologies and periodicals. *Honours:* First Prize, Southwest Poetry Competition, 1991; Winner, London Writers Competition, 1993, West Sussex Competition, 1993, Salisbury Competition, 1993, New London Writers Competition, 1998, Bridport Competition, 1999; Runner-Up, Sheffield Thursday Competition, 1994, Stand Competition, 2000; Poetry Book Society Recommendation, 1986; Irish Times Perpetual Trophy, 1997; Sheffield Thursday Awards, 1997, 1998; Arts Council Writers Award, 2002. *Memberships:* Blue Nose Poets; Writers Inc.; Colours Poetry Group; Friends of Arvon. *Address:* 79 Lincoln Crescent, Bush Hill Park, Enfield, Middlesex EN1 1JZ, England.

PETTET, Simon; b. 6 Nov. 1953, England. Poet. *Education:* BA, University of Essex, 1976; MA, University of London, 1977. *Publications:* Lyrical Poetry, 1988; Conversations with Rudy Burckhardt, 1988; Twenty One Love, 1991; Talking Pictures (with Rudy Burckhardt), 1994; Selected Poems, 1995; The Selected Art Writings of James Schuyler (ed.), 1999; Abundant Treasures (with Duncan Hannah), 2001. *Contributions to:* Numerous magazines. *Address:* 437 E 12th St, Apt 6, New York, NY 10009, USA.

PETTIT, Stephen Lewis Ingham; b. 25 Feb. 1921, England. Poet; Anthologist; Historian. 1 d. *Education:* The College, Brighton; Royal Air Force College, Cranwell. *Publications:* Peregrine Instant; Glories of English; Elusive Muse; Land of the Shining Waters; Discovering, at Last, King Arthur; Master Knot; Platypus in My Pocket; Master Knot; Glories of English; Today Upon the Thought Screen. *Contributions to:* Various anthologies, reviews and journals. *Honours:* Sovereign's Commendation for Valuable Service in the Air; Wilfrid M Appleby Cup; Dr Olive Lamming Memorial Award; Various

certificates of merit and minor prizes. *Memberships:* Poetry Society o Cheltenham, pres.; International Poetry Society, founder-fellow; Isle of Mai Literary Society; Isle of Man Northern Writers Asscn; Royal Institute o Philosophy, London. *Address:* The Old Vicarage, May Hill, Ramsey IM8 2EG Isle of Man.

PETTY, William Henry; b. 7 Sept. 1921, Bradford, Yorkshire, England Educator (retd); Poet. m. Margaret Elaine Bastow, 31 May 1948, 1 s., 2 d *Education:* Peterhouse, Cambridge, 1940–41, 1945; MA, Cantab, 1950; BSc London, 1953; DLitt, Kent, 1983. *Appointments:* Administrative, Teaching an Lecturing posts, London, Doncaster, North and West Ridings of Yorkshire Kent, 1945–73; Chief Education Officer, Kent, 1973–84; Chair. of Govs, Chris Church University College, Canterbury, 1992–94. *Publications:* No Bol Comfort, 1957; Conquest, 1967; Educational Administration (co-author) 1980; Executive Summaries (booklets), 1984–90; Springfield: Pieces of th Past, 1994; Genius Loci (with Robert Roberts), 1995; The Louvre Imperial 1997; Interpretations of History, 2000; No-one Listening, 2002. *Contributions to:* Various anthologies, 1954–2000, reviews, quarterlies and journals. *Honours* Cheltenham Festival of Literature Prize, 1968; Camden Festival of Music an the Arts Prize, 1969; Greenwood Prize, Poetry Society, 1978; Lake Ask Memorial Award, 1980; C.B.E., 1981; Swanage Festival of Literature Prize 1995; Ali Competition Prize, 1995; Kent Federation of Writers Prize, 1995 White Cliffs Prize, 2000. *Membership:* Poetry Society; English Asscn. *Address* Willow Bank, Moat Rd, Headcorn, Kent TN27 9NT, England.

PFEIFFER, Jeanne; b. 13 March 1962, Redwood City, CA, USA. Poet. m Mark D Pfeiffer, 10 Dec. 1981, 2 d. *Education:* Youngstown State University Cleveland State University; Kent State University. *Publications:* A View from the Edge, 1992; And Time Stood Still, 1994; Dusting Off Dreams, 1995. *Contributions to:* Data Highway; Twinsburg Connection. *Honours:* Ed.'s Choice Award, National Poetry Asscn, 1993; Honourable Mention, Hollywood Famous Poets Society, 1995. *Membership:* National Poetry Asscn. *Address* 8227 Clover Lane, Garrestsville, OH 44231, USA.

PHILIP, Marlene Nourbese; b. 3 Feb. 1947, Tobago. Poet; Writer; Lawyer. m Paul Chamberlain, 1978, 3 c. *Education:* BSc, University of the West Indies, 1968; MA, 1970, LLB, 1973, University of Western Ontario. *Publications:* Thorns, 1980; Salmon Courage, 1983; Harriet's Daughter, 1988; She Tries Her Tongue, Her Silence Softly Breaks, 1989; Looking for Livingstone: An Odyssey of Silence, 1991; Frontiers: Essays and Writings on Racism and Culture, 1992; Showing Grit: Showboating North of the 44th Parallel, 1993. *Honours:* Casa de las Americas Prize for Poetry, 1988; Toronto Book Award for Fiction, 1990; Max and Greta Abel Award for Multicultural Literature, 1990; Guggenheim Fellowship, 1990; Toronto Arts Award, 1995. *Address:* c/o Women's Press, 517 College St, Suite 233, Toronto, ON M6G 4A2, Canada.

PHILLIPS, Carl; b. 23 July 1959, Everett, WA, USA. Prof.; Poet; Writer. *Education:* BA, magna cum laude, Greek and Latin, Harvard University, 1981; MA, Latin and Classical Humanities, University of Massachusetts at Amherst, 1983; MA, Creative Writing, Boston University, 1993. *Appointments:* Poet-in-Residence, 1993–94, Asst Prof., 1994–96, Assoc. Prof., 1996–2000, Dir, Writing Program, 1996–98, 2000–, Prof., 2000–, Washington University, St Louis; Visiting Asst Prof., Harvard University, 1995–96; Faculty, Warren Wilson College, 1997–; Visiting Writer-in-Residence, University of Iowa, 1998. *Publications:* In the Blood, 1992; Cortège, 1995; From the Devotions, 1998; Pastoral, 2000; The Tether, 2001; Rock Horror, 2002. *Contributions to:* Many anthologies, reviews, quarterlies and journals. *Honours:* Samuel French Morse Poetry Prize, 1992; Acad. of American Poets Prize, 1993; Guggenheim Fellowship, 1997–98; Witter Bynner Fellowship, 1997–98; Pushcart Prizes, 1998, 2001; Lambda Literary Award in Poetry, 2001; American Acad. of Arts and Letters Award in Literature, 2001; Kingsley Tufts Poetry Prize, 2002. *Memberships:* Acad. of American Poets; Associated Writing Programs; MLA; PEN American Center; Poetry Society of America. *Address:* 1026 Fairmount Ave, St Louis, MO 63139, USA.

PHILLIPS, H(erbert) I(vor Leason); b. 18 March 1913, London, England. Poet; Novelist; Dramatist. m. 28 Sept. 1940, 1 s., 1 d. *Education:* Diploma, Dental Surgery, 1940. *Appointment:* Dentist, 1941–74. *Publications:* Poems, novels, and plays. *Contributions to:* Daily Mail; Envoi; Observer; Outposts; Poetry Review. *Membership:* Poetry Society. *Address:* 15 Sandy Lane, Cheam, Sutton, Surrey SM2 7NU, England.

PHILLIPS, Judith Irene, (Judith Irene Tucker); b. 15 Oct. 1948, Coose Bay, Oregon, USA. Poet; Writer; Cattle Rancher; Antique Dealer. m. John Valis Tucker, 21 Dec. 1982, 1 s. *Education:* Lane Community College. *Publication:* Award Winning Poetry by Judith I Tucker, 1988. *Contributions to:* Over 15 anthologies, 1984–95. *Honours:* Numerous, including 23 Awards of Merit; 6 Golden Poet Awards; 6 Ed.'s Choice Awards; 2 Gold Medals; Silver Poet Award. *Memberships:* Poet International; World Poetry Society. *Address:* 1387 Romie Howard Rd, Yoncalla, OR 97499, USA.

PHILLIPS, Louis; b. 15 June 1942, Lowell, MA, USA. Prof. of Humanities; Writer; Dramatist; Poet. m. Patricia L. Ranard, 26 Aug. 1971, 2 s. *Education:* BA, Stetson University, 1964; MA, University of North Carolina at Chapel Hill,

1965. *Appointment:* Prof. of Humanities, School of Visual Arts, New York, 1977–. *Publications:* The Man Who Stole the Atlantic Ocean, 1971; Theodore Jonathon Wainwright is Going to Bomb the Pentagon, 1973; The Time, the Hour, the Solitariness of the Place, 1986; A Dream of Countries Where No One Dare Live, 1994; The Hot Corner, 1997. *Contributions to:* The Georgia Review; Massachusetts Review; Chicago Review; Regular Columnist for The Armchair Detective; Shakespeare Bulletin. *Literary Agent:* Fifi Oscard Agency. *Address:* 375 Riverside Dr., Apt 14C, New York, NY 10025, USA.

PHILLIPS, Michael. See: NOLAN, William F(rancis).

PHILLIPS, Michael (Joseph); b. 2 March 1937, Indianapolis, IN, USA. Poet. *Education:* Purdue University, 1955–56; University of Edinburgh, 1957–58, 1959–60; Alliance Française, 1958; BA, cum laude, Wabash College, 1959; MA, 1964; PhD, Indiana University. *Appointments:* Lecturer in English, University of Wisconsin, 1970, 1971, Indiana University-Purdue University at Indianapolis, 1973–78; Instructor in English, Free University of Indianapolis, 1973, 1977–79; Visiting Fellow, Harvard University, 1976–77. *Publications:* Poetry: Libretto for 23 Poems, 1968; Kinetics and Concretes, 1971; The Concrete Book, 1971; 8 Page Poems, 1971; Love, Love, Love, 1975; Visual Sequences, 1975; Abstract Poems, 1978; Underworld Love Poems, 1979; Erotic Concrete Sonnets for Samantha, 1979; Selected Love Poems, 1980; Indy Dolls, 1982; Superbeuts, 1983; Selected Concrete Poems, 1986; Dreamgirls, 1989; 11 Poems, 1992; Neon Dolls, 1997; Love Struck, 1998. Other: Edwin Muir, 1979; The Poet as Mythmaker, 1990. *Contributions to:* Numerous anthologies and periodicals. *Memberships:* Acad. of American Poets; American Comparative Literature Asscn; Mensa; MLA; Society for the Study of Midwestern Literature. *Address:* 238 N Smith Rd, Apt 25, Bloomington, IN 47408, USA.

PHILLIPS, Robert (Schaeffer); b. 2 Feb. 1938, Milford, DE, USA. Prof. of English; Poet; Writer. m. Judith Anne Bloomingdale, 16 June 1962, 1 s. *Education:* BA, English, 1960, BA, Communications, 1960, MA, American Literature, 1962, Syracuse University. *Appointments:* Instructor, New School for Social Research, New York City, 1966–68, Belle Levine Arts Center, 1968–69; Poetry Review Ed., Modern Poetry Studies, 1969–73; Prof. of English, 1991–, Dir, Creative Writing Program, 1991–96, John and Rebecca Moores University Scholar, 1998–2003, University of Houston; Poetry Reviewer, Houston Post, 1992–95, Houston Chronicle, 1995–. *Publications:* Poetry: Inner Weather, 1966; The Pregnant Man, 1978; Running on Empty, 1981; Personal Accounts: New and Selected Poems, 1966–1986, 1986; The Wounded Angel, 1987; Face to Face, 1993; Breakdown Lane, 1994; Spinach Days, 2000; The Madness of Art, 2002. Fiction: The Land of the Lost Content, 1970; Public Landing Revisited, 1992; News About People You Know, 2002. Criticism: Aspects of Alice (ed.), 1971; The Confessional Poets, 1973; Denton Welch, 1974; William Goyen, 1978. *Contributions to:* Many anthologies, reviews, quarterlies, and journals. *Honours:* American Acad. and Institute of Arts and Letters Award, 1987; Arents Pioneer Medal, Syracuse University, 1988; Greenwood Award, 1993; New York Times Notable Book of the Year Citation, 1994; Fort Concho Literary Festival Fiction Prize, 1994; Semi-finalist, The Poets' Prize, 1996. *Memberships:* Acad. of American Poets; American PEN Center, board of dirs; Asscn of Literary Scholars and Critics; English-Speaking Union; Friends of Poets and Writers; National Book Critics Circle; Poetry Society of America; South Central MLA; Texas Institute of Letters, councilor. *Address:* c/o Creative Writing Program, Dept of English, University of Houston, Houston, TX 77204, USA.

PHILLIS, Yannis A.; b. 27 March 1950, Greece. Prof.; Poet. m. Nili Boren, 1 s., 1 d. *Education:* Diploma, National Technical University of Athens, 1973; MS, 1978, Engineering Degree, 1979, PhD, 1980, University of California at Los Angeles. *Appointments:* Research Asst, 1977–78, Teaching Assoc., 1978–80, University of California at Los Angeles; Asst Prof., Boston University, 1980–86; Assoc. Prof., 1986–89, Prof., 1989–, Rector, 1993–97, 1999–, Technical University of Crete. *Publications:* Starting in Nafplion, 1975; Arctic Zone, 1976; Zarathustra and the Five Vespers, 1985; Beyond the Symplegades, 1991; Sisyphus, 1998; The Camp, 2000. *Contributions to:* Harbor Review, USA; Beacon Review, USA; Stone Country, USA; Mother Earth International; Kaleidoscope. *Honours:* Ministry of Culture and Sciences, 1976; Best Book Award, Writers Union, Athens, 1986; Rector, Technical University of Crete, 1993–. *Membership:* Poets and Writers, USA; Greek PEN. *Address:* Technical University of Crete, Dept of Production Engineering and Management, Chania 73100, Greece. *E-mail:* phillis@dpem.tuc.gr.

PICANO, Felice; b. 22 Feb. 1944, New York, NY, USA. Writer; Poet. *Education:* BA, cum laude, Queens College, City University of New York, 1960. *Publications:* Smart as the Devil, 1975; Eyes, 1976; Deformity Lover and Other Poems, 1977; The Lure, 1979; Late in the Season, 1980; An Asian Minor, 1981; Slashed to Ribbons in Defense of Love and Other Stories, 1982; House of Cards, 1984; Ambidextrous, 1985; Men Who Loved Me, 1989; To the Seventh Power, 1989; The New Joy of Gay Sex, 1992; Dryland's End, 1995; Like People in History, 1995. *Contributions to:* Men on Men; Violet Quill Reader; Numerous magazines and journals. *Honours:* Finalist, Ernest Hemingway Award; PEN Syndicated Short Fiction Award; Chapbook Award, Poetry Society of America. *Memberships:* PEN Club; Writers Guild of America; Authors Guild; Publishing Triangle. *Address:* 95 Horatio St, No. 423, New York, NY 10014, USA.

PICHASKE, David R(ichard); b. 2 Sept. 1943, Kenmore, NY, USA. Prof. of English; Poet; Writer; Ed. m. (1) Elaine Ezekian, Aug. 1968, divorced 1988, 1 s., 1 d., (2) Michelle Payne, 3 Sept. 1991. *Education:* BA, Wittenberg University, 1965; MA, PhD, 1969, Ohio University. *Appointments:* Assoc. Prof. of English, Bradley Polytechnical Institute, Peoria, IL, 1970–80; Ed., Spoon River Quarterly, 1977–; Prof. of English, Southwest State University, Marshall, MN, 1980–; Senior Fulbright Lecturer, é ódéη, Poland, 1989–91, Rága, Latvia, 1997–98. *Publications:* Beowulf to Beatles: Approaches to Poetry, 1972; Writing Sense: A Handbook of Composition, 1975; Chaucer's Literary Pilgramage: Movement in the Canterbury Tales, 1978; A Generation in Motion: Popular Music and Culture in the 1960's, 1979; Beowulf to Beatles and Beyond: The Varieties of Poetry, 1980; The Poetry of Rock, 1981; The Jubilee Diary: April 10 1980–April 19 1981, 1982; Salem/Peoria, 1883–1982, 1982; Bringing the Humanities to the Countryside: Access to the Humanities in Western Minnesota (ed. with Gerrit Groen), 1985; Tales from Two Rivers (ed. with John E. Halwas), Vol. 4, 1987; Visiting the Father and Other Poems, 1987; Late Harvest: Rural American Writing (ed.), 1991; Poland in Transition, 1989–1991, 1994; Exercises Against Retirement (poems), 1995; Southwest Minnesota: The Land and the People, 2000. *Contributions to:* Reviews, quarterlies and journals. *Memberships:* Asscn for the Study of Literature and the Environment; Society for the Study of Midwest Literature. *Address:* c/o Dept of English, Southwest State University, Marshall, MN 56258, USA.

PICKARD, Tom, (Thomas Marriner Pickard); b. 7 Jan. 1946, Newcastle upon Tyne, England. Writer; Poet; Documentary Film Maker m. Svava Barker, 15 June 1999, 2 s., 1 d. *Appointment:* Arts Council Writer-in-Residence, University of Warwick, 1979–80. *Publications:* High on the Walls, 1967; New Human Unisphere, 1969; The Order of Chance, 1971; Guttersnipe, 1972; Dancing Under Fire, 1973; Hero Dust: New and Selected Poems, 1979; OK Tree, 1980; The Jarrow March, 1982; Custom and Exile, 1985; We Make Ships, 1989; Tiepin Eros: New and Selected Poems, 1994; Fuckwind: New Poems and Songs, 1999; Hole in the Wall: New and Selected Poems, 2001. Other: Television plays and documentaries. *Contributions to:* Chicago Review; London Magazine; Northern Review; Sniper Logic; David Jones Journal, Address: c/o Judy Daish Assocs, 2 St Charles Pl., London W10 6EG, England.

PIERCE, Richard Alistair Burnett, (Peter Moonraker); b. 14 April 1944, Chippenham, Wiltshire, England. Poet; Writer; Photographer. m. 14 May 1978. *Education:* BA, Sociology, University of Bath, 1986; Postgraduate Studies, British Institute, Florence. *Publications:* Emergence, 1961; Soundings, 1962; A Radio for You, 1987. *Contributions to:* Newspapers, periodicals, and journals. *Honours:* Eistedfodd, 1960–61; Runner-Up, Bridport Competition, 1980, Orbis Rhyme Revival, 1990; Prize and Anthology, Bedford Poetry Society, 1988. *Memberships:* Bath Literary Society; Bath Photographic Society; PEN; Poetry Society. *Address:* 8 Wedmore Ave, Chippenham, Wiltshire SN15 1QP, England.

PIERCY, Marge; b. 31 March 1936, Detroit, MI, USA. Poet; Writer; Ed. m. (3) Ira Wood, 2 June 1982. *Education:* BA, University of Michigan, 1957; MA, Northwestern University, 1958. *Appointments:* Poet-in-Residence, University of Kansas, 1971; Distinguished Visiting Lecturer, Thomas Jefferson College and Grand Valley State College, 1975; Staff, Fine Arts Work Center, Provincetown, Massachusetts, 1976–77; Fiction Writer-in-Residence, College of the Holy Cross, Worcester, Massachusetts, 1976, Ohio State University, 1985; Butler Chair of Letters, State University of New York at Buffalo, 1977; Elliston Poet-in-Residence, University of Cincinnati, 1986; Poetry Ed., Tikkun, 1988–96, Lilith, 2000–; DeRoy Distinguished Visiting Prof., University of Michigan, 1992; Ed., Leapfrog Press, 1997–; Bilgray Scholar-in-Residence, University of Arizona, 2001; Numerous readings, workshops and lectures. *Publications:* Poetry: Breaking Camp, 1968; Hard Loving, 1969; 4-Telling (with Bob Hershon, Emmett Jarrett and Dick Lourie), 1971; To Be of Use, 1973; Living in the Open, 1976; The Twelve-Spoked Wheel Flashing, 1978; The Moon is Always Female, 1980; Circles on the Water (selected poems), 1982; Stone, Paper, Knife, 1983; My Mother's Body, 1985; Available Light, 1988; Mars and Her Children, 1992; What are Big Girls Made Of?, 1997; The Art of Blessing the Day, 1999; Early Grrrl, 1999. Fiction: Going Down Fast, 1969; Dance the Eagles to Sleep, 1970; Small Changes, 1973; Woman on the Edge of Time, 1976; The High Cost of Living, 1978; Via, 1980; Braided Lives, 1982; Fly Away Home, 1984; Gone to Soldiers, 1987; Summer People, 1989; He She and It, 1991; The Longings of Women, 1994; City of Darkness, City of Light, 1996; Storm Tide (with Ira Wood), 1998; Three Women, 1999. Non-Fiction: Parti-Colored Blocks for a Quilt (essays), 1982; So You Want to Write: How to Master the Craft of Writing Fiction and the Personal Narrative (with Ira Wood), 2001; Sleeping with Cats (memoir), 2002. *Contributions to:* Anthologies and periodicals. *Honours:* Borestone Mountain Poetry Awards, 1968, 1974; National Endowment for the Arts Award, 1978; Carolyn Kizer Poetry Prizes, 1986, 1990; Sheaffer-PEN/New England Award for Literary Excellence, 1989; Brit ha-Dorot Award, The Shalom Center, 1992; Arthur C. Clarke Award for Best Science Fiction Novel, 1993; American Library Asscn Notable Book Award, 1997; Peterson Poetry Prize, 2000. *Memberships:* Authors' Guild; Authors' League; National Writers' Union; New England Poetry Club; Poetry Society of America. *Address:* c/o Middlemarsh Inc, PO Box 1473, Wellfleet, MA 02667, USA. *E-mail:* hagolem@c4.net.

PIERPOINT, Katherine Mary; b. 16 Aug. 1961, Northampton, England. Writer; Poet. *Education:* BA, Modern Languages, University of Exeter, 1984. *Publication:* Truffle Beds, 1995. *Contributions to:* Independent; New Yorker; Sunday Times. *Honours:* Somerset Maugham Award, 1996; Sunday Times Young Writer of the Year, 1996. *Address:* c/o 18 King St, Canterbury, Kent CT1 2AJ, England.

PIES, Ronald; b. 6 Dec. 1952, Rochester, NY, USA. Physician; Poet. *Education:* BA, Cornell University, 1974; MD, State University of New York Upstate Medical Center, 1978. *Publications:* Poems: Ruach, 1976; Absence, 1976; Voices, 1978; Missing Children, 1986; In Greens, 1990; Riding Down Dark, 1992; Consultation Request, 1992; Feinmann's Books, 1993; The Road Test, 1993; Styx, 1993; Sitting Shiva, 1994; The Camera, 1994; Spellcheck for a Blighted Fetus, 1995; Sedating the Bard, 1995; Yazowitz on Yom Kippur, 1996; Old Ladder Black, 1996; Purple Loosestrife, 1997; Reflections, 1997; Sophie Fein Goldberg Stein, 1997; Summer of the Quiet Son, 1998; Hunting Season; Butterflies, 1998; Cabbage Soup. *Contributions to:* Literary Review; Vital Signs; Nightshade Press; Kaleidoscope; Oasis; New Jersey Review; Voices West; Poetpourri; Comstock Review; Rockhurst Review; Midstream; Stoneflower; Moment. *Address:* c/o Dept of Psychiatry, Tufts University, PO Box 1007, 750 Washington St, Boston, MA 02111, USA.

PIETRASS, Richard Georg; b. 11 June 1946, Lichtenstein, Sachsen, Germany. Poet; Writer; Trans.; Psychologist. m. Erika Schulze, 26 Aug. 1982, deceased 22 Dec. 1993, 2 s., 1 d. *Education:* Diploma, Psychology, Humboldt University, Berlin, 1975. *Publications:* Poesiealbum 82, 1974; Notausgang, 1980; Freiheitsmuseum, 1982; Spielball, 1987; Was mir zum Glück fehlt, 1989; Weltkind, 1990; Letzte Gestalt, 1994; Randlage, 1996; Grenzfriedhof, 1998. *Honours:* Several. *Memberships:* Asscn of German Writers; PEN Germany. *Address:* Schleusinger Strasse 13, 12687 Berlin, Germany.

PILLING, Christopher (Robert); b. 20 April 1936, Birmingham, England. Writer; Poet. m. Sylvia Hill, 6 Aug. 1960, 1 s., 2 d. *Education:* Diplôme d'Études françaises, University of Poitiers; BA, University of Leeds, 1957; Certificate of Education, Loughborough College, 1959. *Appointments:* English Asst, École Normale, Moulins, France, 1957–58; Teacher of French and PE, Wirral Grammar School, Cheshire, 1959–61, King Edward's School for Boys, Birmingham, 1961–62; Teacher of French and Athletics, and House Master, Ackworth School, Yorkshire, 1962–73; Reviewer, TLS, 1973–74; Head of Modern Languages and Housemaster, Knottingley High School, West Yorkshire, 1973–78; Tutor, Dept of Adult Education, University of Newcastle upon Tyne, 1978–80; Head of French, Keswick School, Cumbria, 1980–88. *Publications:* Snakes and Girls, 1970; In All the Spaces on All the Lines, 1971; Foreign Bodies, 1992; Cross Your Legs and Wish, 1994; These Jaundiced Loves, by Tristan Corbière (trans.), 1995; The Lobster Can Wait, 1998; In the Pink, 1999; The Dice Cup, by Max Jacob (trans. with David Kennedy), 2000; The Ghosts of Greta Hall (with Colin Fleming), 2001. *Contributions to:* Books, anthologies, reviews, quarterlies, journals and newspapers. *Honours:* New Poets Award, 1970; Arts Council Grants, 1971, 1977; Kate Collingwood Award, 1983; Northern Arts Writers Award, 1985, and Tyrone Guthrie Centre Residency, 1994; Lauréat du Concours Européen de Création Littéraire, Centre Culturel du Brabant Wallon, Belgium, 1992; European Poetry Trans. Network Residencies, 1995, 1998; European Commission Residency, Collège International des Traducteurs Littéraires, Arles, 1996; Hawthornden Fellowship, 1998; Trans. Residency at the British Centre for Literary Trans., University of East Anglia, 2000; Short-listed, Weidenfeld Trans. Prize, 2001. *Memberships:* Cumbrian Poets, co-founder, sec.; Society of Authors; Trans Asscn; Cercle Édouard et Tristan Corbière; North Cumbria Playwrights; Les Amis de Max Jacob. *Address:* 25 High Hill, Keswick, Cumbria CA12 5NY, England.

PILON, Jean-Guy; b. 12 Nov. 1930, St Polycarpe, QC, Canada. Poet; Writer. m. Denise Viens, 2 s. *Education:* BA, 1951, LLL, 1954, University of Montréal. *Appointments:* Co-Founder and Dir, Liberté, 1959–79. *Publications:* Poetry: La Fiancée du Matin, 1953; Les Cloitres de l'Eté, 1955; L'Homme et le Jour, 1957; La Mouette et le Large, 1960; Recours au pays, 1961; Pour saluer une ville, 1963; Comme eau retenue, 1969; Saisons pour la Continuelle, 1969; Silences pour une souveraine, 1972. Novel: Solange, 1966. *Contributions to:* Various publications. *Honours:* David Prize, 1957; Louise Labé Prize, 1969; France-Canada Prize, 1969; Governor-General's Award for Poetry, 1970; Athanase David Prize, 1984; Officer of the Order of Canada, 1987; Chevalier de l'Ordre national du Québec, 1987; Officer dans l'Ordre des Arts et Lettres, France, 1992. *Memberships:* Académie des lettres du Québec; Royal Society of Canada. *Address:* 5724 Cote St-Antoine, Montréal, QC H4A 1R9, Canada.

PINE, Ana; b. 13 Nov. 1948, Greece. Poet; Ed.; Publisher. 1 s., 2 d. *Education:* Purley School of Commerce and Languages. *Appointments:* Ed., Publisher, Cokefish Literary Magazine, 1989–91, Bouillabaisse Magazine, 1991–. *Publications:* Broken Silence; New Age Women; Sex on the Interstate; July Moon; Concrete Bologna. *Contributions to:* Morris County Magazine; Observer; Tribune; Alpha Beat Soup; Global Tapestry Journal; Connections; Chiron Review; Blue Jacket; Moody Street Irregular; New Hope Gazette; Impetus; Free Lunch; XIB; Shock Box. *Honour:* Alpha Beat Press Poetry Award. *Address:* PO Box 683, Long Valley, NJ 07853, USA.

PINGEL, Martha. See: TAYLOR Velande Pingel.

PINKSTON, Keli; b. 16 May 1940, Colorado, USA. Poet; Writer; Artist. Divorced, 3 s., 1 d. *Education:* Emergency Medical Technician Diploma, 1977; BSc, Art, Missouri Valley College, 1990. *Contributions to:* Many anthologies and periodicals. *Honours:* Many Merit Awards and Golden Poet Awards. *Membership:* Acad. of American Poets. *Address:* Rt 4, Box 451, Rolla, MO 65401, USA.

PINSKER, Sanford; b. 28 Sept. 1941, Washington, Pennsylvania, USA. Prof. of Humanities; Writer; Poet. m. Ann Getson, 28 Jan. 1968, 1 s., 1 d. *Education:* BA, Washington and Jefferson College, 1963; PhD, University of Washington, 1967. *Appointments:* Asst Prof., 1967–74, Assoc. Prof., 1974–84, Prof., 1984–88, Shadek Prof. of Humanities, 1988–, Franklin and Marshall College; Visiting Prof., University of California at Riverside, 1973, 1975; Ed., Academic Questions, 1995–. *Publications:* The Schlemiel as Metaphor: Studies in the Yiddish and American-Jewish Novel, 1971; The Comedy That 'Hoits': An Essay on the Fiction of Philip Roth, 1975; Still Life and Other Poems, 1975; The Languages of Joseph Conrad, 1978; Between Two Worlds: The American Novel in the 1960s, 1978; Philip Roth: Critical Essays, 1982; Memory Breaks Off and Other Poems, 1984; Conversations with Contemporary American Writers, 1985; Whales at Play and Other Poems of Travel, 1986; Three Pacific Northwest Poets: Stafford, Hugo, and Wagoner, 1987; The Uncompromising Fictions of Cynthia Ozick, 1987; Bearing the Bad News: Contemporary American Literature and Culture, 1990; Understanding Joseph Heller, 1991; Jewish-American Literature and Culture: An Encyclopedia (ed. with Jack Fischel), 1992; Jewish-American Fiction, 1917–1987, 1992; Sketches of Spain (poems), 1992; The Catcher in the Rye: Innocence Under Pressure, 1993; Oedipus Meets the Press and Other Tragi-Comedies of Our Time, 1996. *Contributions to:* Artifcles, stories, poems, and reviews in numerous publications. *Honours:* Fulbright Senior Lecturer, Belgium, 1984–85, Spain, 1990–91; Pennsylvania Humanist, 1985–87, 1990–91, 1996–97. *Membership:* National Book Critics Circle, 1995–. *Address:* 700 N Pine St, Lancaster, PA 17603, USA.

PINSKY, Robert (Neal); b. 20 Oct. 1940, Long Branch, New Jersey, USA. Prof. of English; Poet; Writer; Ed.; Trans. m. Ellen Jane Bailey, 30 Dec. 1961, 3 d. *Education:* BA, Rutgers University, 1962; MA, 1965, PhD, 1966, Stanford University. *Appointments:* Asst Prof. of English, University of Chicago, 1966–67; Prof. of English, Wellesley College, 1967–80, University of California at Berkeley, 1980–89, Boston University, 1988–; Poetry Ed., The New Republic, 1978–87, Slate, 1996–; Visiting Lecturer in English, Harvard University, 1980; Poet Laureate of the US, 1997–2000. *Publications:* Landor's Poetry, 1968; Sadness and Happiness, 1975; The Situation of Poetry, 1977; An Explanation of America, 1980; The Separate Notebooks, by Czesław Miłosz (co-trans.), 1984; History of My Heart, 1984; Poetry and the World, 1988; The Want Bone, 1990; The Inferno of Dante, 1995; The Figured Wheel: New and Collected Poems 1966–1996, 1996; The Sounds of Poetry, 1998; The Handbook of Heartbreak, 1998; Jersey Rain, 2000; Americans' Favourite Poems: The Favourite Poem Anthology (ed. with Maggie Dietz), 2000. *Contributions to:* Anthologies and journals. *Honours:* Fulbright Fellowship, 1965; Stegner Fellowship in Creative Writing, 1965; National Endowment for the Humanities Fellowship, 1974; Massachusetts Council for the Arts Award, 1976; Oscar Blumenthal Prize, 1979; American Acad. and Institute of Arts and Letters Award, 1980; Saxifrage Prize, 1980; Guggenheim Fellowship, 1980; Eunice B Tietjens Prize, 1983; National Endowment for the Arts Fellowship, 1984; William Carlos Williams Prize, 1985; Landon Prize in Trans., 1995; Los Angeles Times Book Award, 1995; Shelley Memorial Award, 1996; Ambassador Book Award in Poetry, 1997. *Memberships:* Acad. of American Poets; American Acad. of Arts and Letters; American Acad. of Arts and Sciences. *Address:* c/o Creative Writing Program, Boston University, 236 Bay State Rd, Boston, MA 02215, USA.

PINTER, Harold; b. 10 Oct. 1930, London, England. Dramatist; Writer; Poet. m. (1) Vivien Merchant, 1956, divorced 1980, 1 s., (2) Lady Antonia Fraser, 1980. *Appointments:* Actor, 1949–57; Assoc. Dir, National Theatre, 1973–83. *Publications:* The Caretaker, 1960; The Birthday Party, and Other Plays, 1960; A Slight Ache, 1961; The Collection, 1963; The Lover, 1963; The Homecoming, 1965; Tea Party, and The Basement, 1967; PEN Anthology of New Poems (co-ed.), 1967; Mac, 1968; Landscape, and Silence, 1969; Five Screenplays, 1971; Old Times, 1971; Poems, 1971; No Man's Land, 1975; The Proust Screenplay: A la Recherche du Temps Perdu, 1978; Betrayal, 1978; Poems and Prose, 1949–1977, 1978; I Know the Place, 1979; Family Voices, 1981; Other Places, 1982; The French Lieutenant's Woman and Other Screenplays, 1982; One for the Road, 1984; Collected Poems and Prose, 1986; 100 Poems by 100 Poets (co-ed.), 1986; Mountain Language, 1988; The Heat of the Day, 1989; The Dwarfs, 1990; Party Time, 1991; Moonlight, 1993; 99 Poems in Translation (co-ed.), 1994; Landscape, 1995; Ashes to Ashes, 1996; Various Voices: Prose, Poetry, Politics, 1948–1998, 1999; Celebration, 1999; Cancer Cells (poem), 2002. Other: Many nonpublished stage, film, radio, and television plays. *Honours:* C.B.E., 1966; Shakespeare Prize, Hamburg, 1970; Austrian State Prize for European Literature, 1973; Pirandello Prize, 1980; Donatello Prize, 1982; Giles Cooper Award, 1982; Elmer Holmes Bobst Award, 1984; David Cohen British Literary Prize, 1975; Laurence Olivier Special Award, 1996; Molière d'Honneur, Paris;

Sunday Times Award for Literary Excellence, 1997; BAFTA Fellowship, 1997; Companion of Literature, RSL, 1998; Critics Circle Award for Distinguished Service to the Arts, 2000; Brianza Poetry Prize, Italy, 2000; South Bank Show Award for Outstanding Achievement in the Arts, 2001; S. T. Dupont Golden Pen Award for a Lifetime's Distinguished Service to Literature, 2001; Premio Fiesole ai Maestri del Cinema, Italy, 2001; Laurea ad honorem, University of Florence, 2001; World Leaders Award, Toronto, 2001; Hermann Kesten Medallion for Outstanding Commitment on Behalf of Persecuted and Imprisoned Writers, German PEN, 2001. Many hon. degrees. *Membership:* RSL, fellow. *Address:* c/o Judy Daish Assocs Ltd, 2 St Charles Pl., London W10 6EG, England. *Website:* www.haroldpinter.org.

PIOMBINO, Nicholas, (Nick Piombino); b. 5 Oct. 1942, New York, NY, USA. Psychoanalyst; Poet; Writer. m. Toni Simon, 25 Nov. 1988. *Education:* BA, City College of the City University of New York, 1964; MSW, Fordham University, 1971; Certificate in Psychoanalysis and Psychotherapy, 1982. *Publications:* Poems, 1988; The Boundary of Blur (essays), 1993; Light Street (poems), 1996; Theoretical Objects, 1999. *Contributions to:* Books and journals. *Honours:* New York Foundation for the Arts Fellowship in Poetry, 1992; Postgraduate Center Literary Award, 1994. *Membership:* Acad. of American Poets. *Address:* 680 West End Ave, No. 1F, New York, NY 10025, USA. *E-mail:* npiombino@aaahawk.com. *Website:* epc.buffalo.edu/authors/piombino/.

PIONTEK, Heinz; b. 15 Nov. 1925, Kreuzburg, Silesia, Germany. Poet; Author. m. Gisela Dallman, 1951. *Education:* Theologisch-Philosophische Hochschule, Dillingen. *Publications:* Poetry: Die Furt, 1952; Die Rauchfahne, 1953; Wassermarken, 1957; Mit einer Kranichfeder, 1962; Klartext, 1966; Tot oder lebendig, 1971; Die Zeit der anderen Auslegung, 1976; Früh im September, 1982; Helldunkel, 1987. Fiction: Dichterleben, 1976; Juttas Neffe, 1979; Zeit meines Lebens, 1984; Stunde der Überlebenden, 1989; Goethe unterwegs in Schlesien: Fast ein Roman, 1993. Collections: Die Erzählungen 1950–1970, 1971; Träumen, Wachen, Widerstehen: Aufzeichnungen aus diesen Jahren, 1978; Das Handwerk des Lesens: Erfahrungen mit Buchern und Autoren, 1979; Farbige Schatten, Die Aufzeichnungen, Die Reisepresa, 1984; Feuer im Wind, Die Erzählungen, Die Hörspiele, Eine Komödie, 1985; Werkauswahl: Indianersommer (selected poems), 1990, and Anhalten um eine Hand (selected stories), 1990. *Honours:* Many, including: Tukan Prize, 1971; Georg Büchner Prize, 1976; Werner Egk Prize, 1981. *Membership:* Bavarian Acad. of Fine Arts, Munich. *Address:* Duffer Strasse 97, 8000 Munich 50, Germany.

PIOTROWSKI, Andrzej Stanislaw, (Andrzej Czcibor-Piotrowski); b. 30 Nov. 1931, Lwów, Poland. Poet; Novelist; Trans. m. Lidia Malgorzata Klimczak, 10 Dec. 1977. *Education:* MA, Slavonic Philology, University of Warsaw, 1955. *Publications:* Over 120 trans. vols; More than 15 books, 1956–2002, including a vol. of selected poems, 1991, and two novels, 1999, 2001. *Contributions to:* Many publications. *Honours:* Poetry and Trans. Awards, 1957, 1984; Silver Medal with Ribbon, Czechoslovakia, 1978; P O Hviezdoslav Prize, 1985; V Nezval Prize with Medal, 1988. *Memberships:* Poets Club; Asscn of Polish Writers; Literary Union, Germany. *Address:* ul Chocimska 35m 21, 00-791 Warsaw, Poland.

PITCHES, Douglas Owen; b. 6 March 1930, Exning, Suffolk, England. Poet. m. Barbara Joyce Budgen, 7 Aug. 1954. *Education:* BA, Honours, Open University, 1979. *Publications:* Poems, 1965; Prayer to the Virgin Mary (Chaucer Translation), 1965; Man in Orbit and Down to Earth, 1981; Art Demands Love Not Homage, 1992. *Contributions to:* Orbis; Outposts; Envoi; Tribune; Anthologies: Responding; New Voices; Another Fifth Poetry Book and others. *Address:* 14 Linkway, Westham, Pevensey, East Sussex BN24 5JB, England.

PITCHFORD, Kenneth S(amuel); b. 24 Jan. 1931, Moorhead, Minnesota, USA. Poet; Ed. m. Robin Morgan, 1962, 1 c. *Education:* BA, University of Minnesota, 1952; MA, New York University, 1959. *Appointments:* Writer-in-Residence, Yaddo Colony, 1958; Assoc. Ed., New International Yearbook, 1960–66. *Publications:* The Blizzard Ape, 1958; A Suite of Angels and Other Poems, 1967; Color Photos of the Atrocities, 1973. *Contributions to:* Anthologies and periodicals. *Honours:* Fulbright Fellowship, 1956–57; Eugene Lee-Hamilton Award for Poetry, 1957; Borestone Mountain Award, 1964. *Address:* c/o Purchase Press, PO Box 5, Harrison, NY 10528, USA.

PITT-KETHLEY, (Helen) Fiona; b. 21 Nov. 1954, Edgware, Middlesex, England. Writer; Poet. m. James Plaskett, 1 s. *Education:* BA, Honours, Chelsea School of Art, 1976. *Publications:* London, 1984; Rome, 1985; The Tower of Glass, 1985; Gesta, 1986; Sky Ray Lolly, 1986; Private Parts, 1987; Journeys to the Underworld, 1988; The Perfect Man, 1989; The Misfortunes of Nigel, 1991; The Literary Companion to Sex, 1992; The Maiden's Progress, 1992; Too Hot to Handle, 1992; Dogs, 1993; The Pan Principle, 1994; The Literary Companion to Low Life, 1995; Double Act, 1996; Memo from a Muse, 1999; Red Light Districts of the World, 2000; Baker's Dozen, 2000; My Schooling (autobiography), 2000. *Contributions to:* Numerous newspapers and magazines. *Honour:* Calouste Gulbenkian Award, 1995. *Address:* Lista de Correos, Correos Central, Torrevieja, Alicante, Spain.

PLAICE, Stephen James; b. 9 Sept. 1951, Watford, Hertfordshire, England. m. Marcia Bellamy, 2 c. Writer; Poet; Librettist. *Education:* BA, Honours, German, 1973, MPhil, Comparative Literature, 1979, University of Sussex; University of Marburg, 1972; University of Zürich, 1975. *Appointments:* Writer-in-Residence, H M Prison, Lewes, 1987–94; Artistic Dir, Alarmist Theatre, 1987–; Ed., Printer's Devil, 1990–. *Publications:* Rumours of Cousins, 1983; Over the Rollers, 1992; Misper (libretto), 2000; Zoë (libretto), 2002. *Literary Agent:* Macnaughton Lord 2000 Ltd, 16–18 Douglas St, London SW1P 4PB, England. *Address:* 83 Stanford Rd, Brighton, East Sussex BN1 5PR, England. *Telephone:* (1273) 700849. *E-mail:* cultureshock@pavilion.co.uk.

PLATT, Charles; b. 26 April 1945, London, England. Writer; Poet. 1 d. *Education:* University of Cambridge; London College of Printing. *Publications:* Fiction: The Garbage World, 1967; The City Dwellers, 1970, US edn as Twilight of the City, 1977; Planet of the Voles, 1971; New Worlds 6 (ed. with M. Moorcock), 1973, US edn as New Worlds 5, 1974; New Worlds 7 (ed. with H. Bailey), 1974, US edn as New Worlds 6, 1975; Sweet Evil, 1977; Free Zone, 1989; Soma, 1989; The Silicon Man, 1991. Non-Fiction: Dream Makers: The Uncommon People Who Write Science Fiction, 1980; When You Can Live Twice as Long, What Will You Do?, 1989. Poetry: Highway Sandwiches (with T M Disch and M Hacker), 1970; The Gas, 1970. *Address:* c/o Gollancz, 14 Henrietta St, London WC2E 8QJ, England.

PLATTHY, Jeno; b. 13 Aug. 1920, Hungary. Poet; Writer; Ed.; Publisher. m. Carol Louise Abell, 25 Sept. 1976. *Education:* Peter Pazmany University, Budapest, 1939–42; Jozsef Ferencz University, 1943–44; Catholic University of America, 1963–65. *Appointments:* Ed.-in-Chief, Monumenta Classical Perennia, 1967–84; Exec. Dir, Federation of International Poetry Asscns of UNESCO, 1976–96; Publisher, New Muses, 1976–. *Publications:* Poetry: Numerous vols, 1976–99, including: Odes Européennes, 1986; Asian Elegies, 1987; Nova Comoedia, 3 parts, 1988, 1990, 1991; Elegies Asiatiques, 1991; Paeans, 1993; Prosodia, 1994; Songs of the Soul, 1996; Ultimacy, 1999. Other: Sources on the Earliest Greek Libraries with the Testimonia, 1968; Ch'u Yuan, 1975; The Mythical Poets of Greece, 1985; Bartók: A Critical Biography, 1988; Plato: A Critical Biography, 1990; Near-Death Experiences in Antiquity, 1992; The Duino Elegies of Rilke (trans. and commentary), 1999. *Contributions to:* Various publications. *Honours:* Poet Laureate, World Congress of Poets, 1973; Confucius Award, 1974; Poet Laureate and Pres., International Congress of Poets, 1976; Officier, Ordre des Arts et des Lettres, France, 1992. *Memberships:* Acad. of American Poets; American Society of Composers, Authors and Publishers; Asscn of Literary Critics and Scholars; International PEN Club; International Poetry Society; Literarische Union, Germany. *Address:* 961 W Sled Circle, Santa Claus, IN 47579, USA.

PLEIJEL, Agneta; b. 26 Feb. 1940, Stockholm, Sweden. Writer; Poet; Dramatist. m. Maciej Zaremba, 27 Nov. 1982, 1 d. *Education:* MA, 1970. *Publications:* Novels, poems, and plays. *Contributions to:* Various publications. *Membership:* Swedish PEN Club.

PLUMLY, Stanley (Ross); b. 23 May 1939, Barnesville, Ohio, USA. Poet; Prof. of English. *Education:* BA, Wilmington College, 1961; MA, Ohio University, 1968. *Appointments:* Instructor in Creative Writing, Louisiana State University, 1968–70; Ed., Ohio Review, 1970–75, Iowa Review, 1976–78; Prof. of English, Ohio University, 1970–74, University of Houston, 1979–; Visiting lecturer at several universities. *Publications:* In the Outer Dark, 1970; How the Plains Indians Got Horses, 1973; Giraffe, 1973; Out-of-the-Body Travel, 1977; Summer Celestial, 1983; Boy on the Step, 1989; The Marriage in the Trees, 1997; The New Bread Loaf Anthology of Contemporary American Poetry (ed. with Michael Collier), 1999; Now That My Father Lies Down Beside Me: New and Selected Poems, 1970–2000, 2000. *Contributions to:* Periodicals. *Honours:* Delmore Schwartz Memorial Award, 1973; Guggenheim Fellowhip, 1973; National Endowment for the Arts Grant, 1977. *Address:* c/o Dept of English and Creative Writing, University of Houston, 4800 Calhoun, Houston, TX 77004, USA.

PLUMMER, Pauline; b. 17 Jan. 1947, Liverpool, England. Poet; Teacher. 2 s. *Publications:* Romeo's Cafe, 1992; Palaver, 1998; Demon Straightening, 2000. *Contributions to:* Anthologies, including: Macmillan Poetry for Schools; Forward Book of Poems, 1993; A Hole Like That; Periodicals, including: The Independent; Rialto; Stand; Blade; Scratch; Smoke; Seam; Diamond Twig; Envoi; Pennine Platform; Smiths Knoll; Mslexia; Red Herring; BBC Radio 4; Tyne Tees Television. *Honours:* First Prize, Write Around, Literary Festival Cleveland; Highly Commended, BBC Wildlife & Devon & Exeter Competitions; First Prize, Teesvalley Writer, Tyrone Guthrie Award for Poetry, Northern Arts, 1996; AHRB Award, 2000; Leverhulme Trust Award, 2001; Ignite Award, New Writing Award, 2001. *Membership:* NAWE; Teesside African Arts Asscn. *Address:* 11 Westbourne Rd, Linthorpe, Middlesbrough TS5 5BN, England.

POBO, Kenneth; b. 24 Aug. 1954, Elmhurst, IL, USA. Assoc. Prof. of English; Poet. Partner. *Education:* BA, English, Wheaton College, 1976; MA, English, 1979, PhD, English, 1983, University of Wisconsin, Milwaukee. *Appointments:* Teacher, University of Wisconsin, Milwaukee, 1977–83; Instructor of English, University of Tennessee, 1983–87; Assoc. Prof. of English, Widener University, Chester, Pennsylvania, 1987–. *Publications:* Musing From the Porchlit Sea,

1979; Billions of Lit Cigarettes, 1981; Evergreen, 1985; A Pause Inside Disk, 1986; Ferns on Fire, 1991; Yes, Irises, 1992; Ravens and Bad Bananas, 1996; A Barbaric Yawp on the Rocks, 1997; Cicadas in the Apple Tree, 2000; Ordering: A Season in My Garden, 2001. *Contributions to:* Over 250 magazines published in USA, UK and Canada, including Orbis, Poetry Durham, Mudfish, University of Windsor Review, Hawaii Review, Poem, Grain, Dalhousie Review, West Branch. *Address:* Humanities Division, Widener University, Chester, PA 19013, USA. *E-mail:* kgpobo@enter.net.

PODHORODECKI, Michael. See: LEBIODA, Dariusz Thomas.

POETESS LOUISE. See: WISINSKI, Louise Ann Helen.

POGSON, Patricia. See: HOLLOWAY, Patricia.

POLITO, Robert; b. 27 Oct. 1951, Boston, Massachusetts, USA. Writer; Poet. m. Kristine M Harris, 27 June 1987. *Education:* BA, Boston College, 1973; PhD, Harvard University, 1981. *Appointments:* Faculty, Harvard University, 1976–81, Wellesley College, 1981–89, New York University, 1990–92, New School for Social Research, New York City, 1992–. *Publications:* Fireworks: The Lost Writings of Jim Thompson (ed.), 1988; A Reader's Guide to James Morrill's The Changing Light at Sandover, 1994; Doubles (poems), 1995; Savage Art: A Biography of Jim Thompson, 1995. *Contributions to:* Newspapers and magazines. *Honour:* National Book Critics Circle Award, 1995. *Address:* c/o Writing Program, New School for Social Research, 66 W 12th St, No. 507, New York, NY 10021, USA.

POLKINHORN, Harry; b. 3 March 1945, Calexico, CA, USA. Writer; Poet; Ed.; Trans. m. Armida Romero, 1 March 1986, divorced 1991, 1 d. *Education:* BA, University of California at Berkeley, 1967; MA, English, MA, Art, 1982, San Diego State University; PhD, New York University, 1975. *Publications:* Excisions (poems), 1976; Radix Zero (poems), 1981; Volvox (poems), 1981; El Libro de Calo: Pachuco Slang Dictionary, 1983, revised edn as El Libro de Calo: Chicano Slang Dictionary (co-author), 1986; Travelling with Women (fiction), 1983; Anaesthesia (poems), 1985; Bridges of Skin Money (visual poems), 1986; Summary Dissolution (visual poems), 1988; Jerome Rothenberg: A Descriptive Bibliography, 1988; Lorenia La Rosa: A Travelogue (fiction), 1989; Begging for Remission (poems), 1989; Teraphim (visual poems), 1995; Mount Soledad (poems), 1996; Throat Shadow (poems), 1997; Blueshift (poems), 1998. Other: Ed. or co-ed. of several publications; Trans. *Contributions to:* Periodicals, including: American Book Review; Afterimage; Poetics Journal; Photostatic; Moody Street Irregulars; Smile; Uno Más Uno; Score; Tempus Fugit; La Poire d'Angoisse; Sink; Kaldron. *Address:* PO Box 927428, San Diego, CA 92192, USA. *E-mail:* hpolkinh@mail.sdsu.edu.

POLLARD, Roula, (Roula Melitas); b. 2 Feb. 1948, Greece. Poet; Writer. m. Ian Pollard, 26 July 1982. *Education:* University of Athens, 1967–72; University of Leeds, 1976–77. *Publications:* Presence; Points of Silence; The Birth of Time. *Contributions to:* Many anthologies and other publications. *Memberships:* Greek Writers Guild; National Asscn of Writers in Education; Yorkshire Playwrights. *Address:* The Manor, South Hiendley, Barnsley, South Yorkshire S72 9BS, England.

POLLITT, Katha; b. 14 Oct. 1949, New York, NY, USA. Writer; Poet; Ed. Divorced, 1 c. *Education:* BA, Harvard University, 1972; MFA, Columbia University, 1975. *Appointments:* Literary Ed., 1982–84, Contributing Ed., 1986–92, Assoc. Ed., 1992–, The Nation; Junior Fellow, Council of Humanities, Princeton University, 1984; Lecturer, New School for Social Research, New York City, 1986–90, Poetry Center, 92nd Street YMHA and WYHA, New York City, 1986–95. *Publications:* Antarctic Traveller, 1982; Reasonable Creatures: Essays on Women and Feminism, 1994. *Contributions to:* Journals and periodicals. *Honours:* National Book Critics Circle Award, 1983; I B Lavan Younger Poet's Award, Acad. of American Poets, 1984; National Endowment for the Arts Grant, 1984; Guggenheim Fellowship, 1987; Whiting Fellowship, 1993. *Address:* 317 W 93rd St, New York, NY 10025, USA.

POLLOCK, Michael Dean Odin; b. 23 Nov. 1953, Marysville, CA, USA. Poet; Musician; Composer. 2 s. *Publications:* Bohemian in Babylon, 1988; The Martial Art of Pagan Diaries, 1994; Poems, 1983–1996, 1996. *Contributions to:* Cafe Review; Kerouac Connection; Howling Mantra; Carnival Serpents Tail; Zig Zag; Thrashing Doves; Tomorrow. *Address:* Post Box 841, 121, Reykjavík, Iceland.

PO-NAI CHOU; b. 14 Aug. 1933, Wu Hwa County, Guangzhou Province, China. Ed.; Writer; Poet. m. 21 May 1960, 1 s., 4 d. *Education:* Communication Electronics School of Chinese Air Force, 1955; Taiwan University, 1958, 1959. *Appointments:* Secretary, Literary Ed., Central Daily News, 1977–80; Council Secretary, Cultural Planning and Development, Exec. Yuan, 1981–90; Chair., Chief Ed., World Tribune, 1990–. *Publications:* A Deserted Town; Cool Autumn Again; If Only Because of Lonelines; On Realism; Trends of Literary Thoughts of the 20th Century; A Study on Modern Fiction. *Contributions to:* Central Daily News; United Daily News; World Tribune. *Honours:* Literary Medal and Golden Statue Award, 1970;

Poetry Education Prize, Ministry of Education, China, 1994. *Membership:* Poetry Asscn of China, vice-chair., 1995–. *Address:* 3F3 No. 5, Lane 68, Sanmin Rd, Taipei, China (Taiwan).

PONDER, Patricia. See: MAXWELL, Patricia Anne.

POOK, John; b. 2 Feb. 1942, Neath, Wales. Poet; Ed. *Education:* Degree in English, Queens' College, Cambridge, 1964. *Publications:* That Cornish Facing Door, 1975; Ten Anglo-Welsh Poets, 1975. *Contributions to:* Poetry Wales; Anglo-Welsh Review; Planet; New Hope International; Iota Poetry Quarterly; Pennine Platform; Working Titles; Orbis. *Honours:* Eric Gregory Award, 1971; Welsh Arts Council Bursary, 1978; Prizes, Open Poetry Competitions, Aberystwyth, 1989, City of Lincoln, 1990, Kent and Sussex, 1998. *Address:* c/ o Welsh Arts Council, Museum Place, Cardiff, South Wales.

POOLE, Margaret Barbara, (Peggy Poole, Terry Roche, Margaret Thornton); b. 8 March 1925, Petham, Kent, England. Broadcaster; Poet; Writer. m. Reginald Poole, 10 Aug. 1949, 3 d. *Appointments:* Co-Organiser Jabberwocky; Producer-Presenter, First Heard poetry programme, BBC Radio Merseyside, 1976–88; Poetry Consultant, BBC Network Northwest, 1988–96. *Publications:* Never a Put-up Job, 1970; Cherry Stones and Other Poems, 1983; No Wilderness in Them, 1984; Midnight Walk, 1986; Hesitations, 1990; Trusting the Rainbow, 1994; From the Tide's Edge, 1999. Editor: Windfall, 1994; Poet's England, Cumbria, 1995; Marigolds Grow Wild on Platforms, 1996; Perceptions, 2000. *Contributions to:* Various anthologies and other publications. *Honours:* Runner-Up, Edmund Blunden Memorial Competition, 1979; First Prize, Waltham Forest Competition, 1987; Prizewinner, Lancaster Literature Festival, 1987, 1991; First Prize, Southport Competition, 1989; Prizewinner, LACE Competition, 1992; Sandburg-Livesey Award, 1999; Commended or Highly Commended in various other competitions. *Memberships:* London Writers' Circle; Poetry Society; Society of Women Writers and Journalists. *Address:* 36 Hilbre Ct, West Kirby, Wirral, Merseyside L48 3JU, England.

POOLE, Richard Arthur; b. 1 Jan. 1945, Yorkshire, England. Tutor in English Literature; Poet. m. Sandra Pauline Smart, 18 July 1970, 1 s. *Education:* BA, 1966, MA, 1968, University College of North Wales. *Appointments:* Tutor in English Literature, Coleg Harlech, 1970–; Ed., Poetry Wales, 1992–96. *Publications:* Goings and Other Poems, 1978; Words Before Midnight, 1981; Natural Histories, 1989; Autobiographies and Explorations, 1994. *Contributions to:* Many reviews and journals. *Membership:* Welsh Acad. *Address:* Glan-y-Werydd, Llandanwg, Gwynedd LL46 2SD, Wales.

POPLE, Ian Stewart; b. 25 Oct. 1952, Ipswich, Suffolk, England. Teacher of English; Poet. m. Olivia Michael, 3 Aug. 1990. *Education:* Certificate in Education, Bedford College of Education, 1976; British Council, Athens, Greece, 1986; Diploma, Teacher of English as a Foreign Language, RSA; MSc, University of Aston, 1990. *Publications:* The Same Condemnation, 1989; The Glass Enclosure, 1996; Ways of Reading, 1996; An Introduction to Text and Discourse Analysis, 1998. *Contributions to:* Anthologies, reviews, and periodicals. *Membership:* National Asscn of Writers in Education, national committee. *Address:* 19 Huddersfield Rd, Diggle, Saddleworth, Lancashire OL3 5NU, England.

PORAD, Francine Joy; b. 3 Sept. 1929, Seattle, Washington, USA. Poet; Painter. m. Bernard L Porad, 12 June 1949, 3 s., 3 d. *Education:* BFA, University of Washington, 1976. *Appointments:* Ed., Brussels Sprout haiku journal, 1988–95, Red Moon Anthologies, 1996. *Publications:* Many poetry books, including: Pen and Inklings, 1986; After Autumn Rain, 1987; Free of Clouds, 1989; Round Renga Round, 1990; A Mural of Leaves, 1991; Joy is My Middle Name, 1993; Waterways, 1995; Extended Wings, 1996; Fog Lifting, 1997; Let's Count the Trees (edited by Le Roy Gorman), 1998; Cur*rent, Linked Haiku, 1998; Other Rens, 2000; The Perfect Worry-stone, 2000; Other Rens, Book 2 plus Book 3, 2000; Trio of Wrens, 2000; To Find the Words (anthology, co-ed.). *Contributions to:* Haiku journals worldwide. *Honours:* Cicada Chapbook Award, 1990; International Tanka Awards, 1991, 1992, 1993; First Prize, Poetry Society of Japan International Tanka Competition, 1993; Haiku Society of America Merit Book Awards, 1994, 2000; Haiku Oregon Pen Women Award, 1995. *Memberships:* Asscn of International Renku; Haiku Society of America, pres., 1993–95; National League of American Pen Women. *Address:* 6944 SE 33rd, Mercer Island, WA 98040, USA. *E-mail:* poradf@aol.com.

PORTEOUS, Katrina; b. 4 Sept. 1960, Aberdeen, Scotland. Poet; Writer. *Education:* BA, History, 1982, MA, 1986, Trinity Hall, Cambridge; Harkness Fellowship, University of California at Berkeley and Harvard University, 1982–84. *Appointments:* Creative writing workshops for adult and children in the United Kingdom, Europe and the USA; Poet-in-Residence, King's College School, Cambridge, 1995–97, Shetland Arts Trust, 1996–97, Aldeburgh Poetry Festival, 2002. *Publications:* The Lost Music, 1996; The Wund an' the Wetter, 1999; Turning the Tide (with Keith Pattison and Robert Soden), 2001. Other: Tam Lin (musical, with Alistair Anderson), 2000; Itchydabbers (film-poem), Poetry International, 2000; Lines for Michael Johnson's sculptures, Seaham Harbour, and for Easington Colliery Memorial Garden; Commissions for BBC

Radio 3 and 4. *Contributions to:* Anthologies and other publications. *Honours:* Eisner Prize for Creative Arts, University of California at Berkeley, 1983; Sotheby Prize, Arvon International Poetry Competition, 1987; Eric Gregory Award, 1989; Northern Arts Writers' Awards, 1990, 1992, 1997; Littlewood Arc, Northern Poetry Competition, 1991; Arts Council Writer's Bursary, 1993; Kathleen Blundell Award, 1998. *Memberships:* National Asscn of Writers in Education; Poetry Society; Northumbrian Language Society; Coble and Keelboat Society. *Address:* Windmillsteads, 58 Harbour Rd, Beadnell, Chathill, Northumberland NE67 5BE, England.

PORTER, Jan; b. 24 July 1948, Sandwich, Kent, England. Poet. *Education:* BA, Honours, English and American Literature, University of Kent, Canterbury, 1977. *Publications:* Remember the Time, 1994; Bridging the Gap, 1994; The West in Her Eye, 1995. *Contributions to:* Many publications. *Honours:* Runner-Up, Mexican Hat Dream Competition, 1993; First Prize, Areopagus Poetry Competition, 1993; Third Place and Merit Prize, Queenie Lee Memorial Poetry Competition, 1995. *Address:* Rascals, 1 Barnhill Cottages, Wembley, Middlesex HA9 9BU, England.

PORTER, Peter (Neville Frederick); b. 16 Feb. 1929, Brisbane, Qld, Australia. Poet; Writer; Broadcaster. m. (1) Jannice Henry, 1961, deceased 1974, 2 d., (2) Christine Berg, 1991. *Publications:* Once Bitten, Twice Bitten, 1961; Penguin Modern Poets, 2, 1962; Poems, Ancient and Modern, 1964; A Porter Folio, 1969; The Last of England, 1970; Preaching to the Converted, 1972; After Martial (trans.), 1972; Jonah (with A. Boyd), 1973; The Lady and the Unicorn (with A. Boyd), 1975; Living in a Calm Country, 1975; New Poetry I (co-ed.), 1975; The Cost of Seriousness, 1978; English Subtitles, 1981; Collected Poems, 1983; Fast Forward, 1984; Narcissus (with A. Boyd), 1985; The Automatic Oracle, 1987; Mars (with A. Boyd), 1988; A Porter Selected, 1989; Possible Worlds, 1989; The Chair of Babel, 1992; Millennial Fables, 1995; New Writing (ed. with A. S. Byatt), 1997; The Oxford Book of Modern Verse (ed.), 1997; The Shared Heritage: Australian and English Literature, 1997; The Oxford Book of Modern Australian Verse (ed.), 1997; Dragons in Their Pleasant Palaces, 1997; Collected Poems, 1961–1999, two vols, 1999; Max is Missing, 2001; Saving from the Wreck: Essays on Poetry, 2001. *Contributions to:* Various publications. *Honours:* Duff Cooper Prize, 1983; Hon. DLitt, University of Melbourne, 1985, Loughborough University, 1987; Whitbread Award for Poetry, 1987; Queen's Gold Medal for Poetry, 2002. *Membership:* Fellow, RSL. *Address:* 42 Cleveland Sq., London W2 6DA, England.

PORTOCALA, Radu; b. 27 March 1951, Bucharest, Romania. Writer; Poet; Journalist. m. Delphine Beaugonin, 21 Dec. 1987, 2 d. *Education:* Master of International Relations, Paris, 1986; BA, Romanian, Paris, 1986. *Publications:* Autopsie Du Coup D'Etat Roumain, 1990; Calatorie in Cusca Hidrelor, 1994; La Chute Dans L'Enthousiasme, 1995; Several poetry vols. *Contributions to:* Various publications. *Address:* 7 Rue Du Docteur Roux, 75015, Paris, France.

POTTI, Kesavan Subramanian; b. 30 Aug. 1942, Ayur, Kerala, India. Teacher; Poet. m. Saraswati, 30 Aug. 1973, 2 d. *Education:* MA, English Literature, Indore University, 1969; MPhil, Literature, Mangalore University, 1988. *Appointments:* Lecturer in English, 1969–85; Reader in English, 1985–86; Prof. of English, 1986–; Principal, 1992–. *Publications:* Atmagitam, 1960; Love: Ancient and Modern, 1977; Song of Wisdom, 1987. *Contributions to:* Hindustan Times; Mail; Vedanta Kesari; Youth Karnataka; Deccan Herald; Yuva Bharati; Quest; Poet Eureka; Journal of Indian Writing in English; Poetry Society of India; Malayalam Literary Survey; Kerala Sahitya Akademi Journal; Akashvani; Bhagirath; New Poetry. *Honours:* 3 Awards, Ministry of Education and Culture; Award, NCERT. *Memberships:* World Poetry Society; Poetry Society of India; Asscn for Writers of Children's Literature; Writers' Forum; United Writers Asscn. *Address:* MPM Government First College of Professional and Business Management, Karkala 574104, India.

POULIN, Gabrielle; b. 21 June 1929, St Prosper, QC, Canada. Writer; Poet. *Education:* MA, University of Montréal; DLitt, University of Sherbrooke. *Appointment:* Writer-in-Residence, Ottawa Public Library, 1988. *Publications:* Les Miroirs d'un poète: Image et reflets de Paul Éluard, 1969; Cogne la caboche, 1979, English trans. as All the Way Home, 1984; L'age de l'interrogation, 1937–52, 1980; Un cri trop grand (novel), 1980; Les Mensonges d'Isabelle (novel), 1983; La couronne d'oubli (novel), 1990; Petites fugues pour une saison sèche (poems), 1991; Le livre de déraison (novel), 1994; Mon père aussi était horloger (poems), 1996; Qu'est-ce qui passe ici si tard? (novel), 1998; La vie l'écriture (memoir), 2000. *Contributions to:* Periodicals. *Honours:* Swiss Embassy Prize, 1967; II Arts Council of Canada Grants, 1968–83, 1985; Champlain Literary Prize, 1979; Carleton Literary Prize, Ottawa, 1983; Alliance Française Literary Prize, 1984; Salon du Livre de Toronto Literary Prize, 1994. *Memberships:* Union des écrivaines et écrivains québécois. *Address:* 1997 Ave Quincy, Ottawa, ON K1J 6B4, Canada.

POULTNEY, Sherman King; b. 18 March 1937, USA. Physicist; Poet. 1 s. *Education:* PhD, Physics, Princeton University, 1962. *Appointments:* Asst Prof., University of Maryland, 1964–75; Senior Scientist, Hughes Danbury Optical Systems, 1975–. *Publications:* The Season Transcended, 1, 1990, 2, 1991; The World Transcended, 1993; The World: Not Mine to Keep, 1994; Male and

Female: Not Mine to Keep, 1995; A Greek Diptych, 1995. *Contributions to:* Signal Magazine; Connecticut Writer. *Memberships:* Connecticut League of Writers; Poetry Society of America. *Address:* 24 Spruce Dr., Wilton, CT 06897, USA.

POWELL, D. A.; b. 16 May 1963, Albany, GA, USA. Poet. Divorced. *Education:* BA, 1991, MA, 1993, Sonoma State University; MFA, University of Iowa, 1996. *Publications:* Explosions and Small Geometries, 1991; Con Sequences (co-author), 1993; Tea, 1998. *Honours:* Acad. of American Poets Prize, 1996; Paul Engle Fellow, James Michener Foundation, 1997–98. *Address:* 77 Colson St, San Francisco, CA 94103, USA. *E-mail:* gpcl69a@prodigy.com.

POWELL, (John) Craig; b. 16 Nov. 1940, New South Wales, Australia. Psychoanalyst; Poet. m. Janet Eileen Dawson, 16 Oct. 1965, 2 s., 1 deceased, 1 d. *Education:* MBBS, University of Sydney, 1965. *Publications:* A Different Kind of Breathing, 1966; I Learn by Going, 1968; A Country Without Exiles, 1972; Rehearsal for Dancers, 1978; A Face in Your Hands, 1984; The Ocean Remembers it is Visible, 1989; Minga Street: New and Selected Poems, 1993; Music and Women's Bodies, 2002. *Contributions to:* Reviews, quarterlies, and magazines. *Honours:* Poetry Magazine Award, 1964; Henry Lawson Festival Award, 1969; Mattara Poetry Prize, 1983; Co-Winner, International Poetry Prize, Quarterly Review of Literature, 1989. *Membership:* Poets Union, Sydney. *Address:* 24 Minga St, Ryde, NSW, 2112, Australia. *E-mail:* jcpowell@iprimus.com.au.

POWELL, Joseph E.; b. 22 Jan. 1952, Ellensburg, Washington, USA. Teacher; Poet. *Education:* BA, University of Washington, 1975; MA, 1978; BA, 1982; MFA, University of Arizona, 1981. *Publications:* Counting the Change, 1986; Winter Insomnia, 1993; Getting Here, 1997. *Contributions to:* Christian Science Monitor; Alaska Quarterly Review; Seattle Review; Southern Poetry Review; Hawaii Review. *Honour:* Book Award, Quarterly Review of Literature, 1997. *Memberships:* Audubon Society; Alpine Lakes Protection Society. *Address:* 221 Cross Creek Dr., Ellensburg, WA 98926, USA.

POWELL, Neil (Ashton); b. 11 Feb. 1948, London, England. Writer; Poet. *Education:* BA, English and American Literature, 1969, MPhil, English Literature, 1971, University of Warwick. *Publications:* Suffolk Poems, 1975; At the Edge, 1977; Carpenters of Light, 1979; Out of Time, 1979; A Season of Calm Weather, 1982; Selected Poems of Fulke Greville (ed.), 1990; True Colours: New and Selected Poems, 1991; Unreal City, 1992; The Stones on Thorpeness Beach, 1994; Roy Fuller: Writer and Society, 1995; Gay Love Poetry (ed.), 1997; The Language of Jazz, 1997; Selected Poems, 1998. *Contributions to:* Anthologies, newspapers, reviews, and journals. *Honours:* Eric Gregory Award, 1969; Authors' Foundation Award, 1992. *Memberships:* Poetry Society; Society of Authors. *Address:* c/o Carcanet Press Ltd, Fourth Floor, Conavon Ct, 12–16 Blackfriars St, Manchester M3 5BQ, England.

POWER, Marjorie; b. 31 Oct. 1947, New York, NY, USA. Poet; Homemaker. m. Max Power, 9 Dec. 1979, 1 s. *Education:* BA, English, San Francisco State University, 1969. *Publications:* Living With It, 1983; Tishku, After She Created Men, 1996; Cave Poems, 1998. *Contributions to:* Southern Poetry Review; Atlanta Review; Puerto Del Sol; Semi-Dwarf Review. *Address:* 508 O'Farrell Ave SE, Olympia, WA 98501, USA.

PRAISNER, Wanda S.; b. 15 Dec. 1933, Staten Island, NY, USA. Poet. m. Robert Praisner, 8 July 1961, 3 s., 1 deceased. *Education:* BA, magna cum laude, Early Childhood Education, 1954, MS, Elementary Education, 1957, Wagner College; Columbia University. *Publication:* Broken Jingles and Moon Shells, 1996. *Contributions to:* New York Magazine; Lullwater Review; Atlanta Review; Marlyand Review; Paterson Literary Review; Journal of New Jersey Poets; Out of Season. *Honours:* Second Award, Allen Ginsberg Contest, 1992; First Place, Maryland Poetry Review's Egan Memorial Contest, 1995; New Jersey State Council on the Arts Fellowship, 1995–96; International Merit Award, Atlanta Review, 1997; Provincetown Fine Arts Work Center Scholarships, 1997, 1998, 1999; First Prize for Poetry, College of New Jersey Writers' Conference, 1998. *Memberships:* Acad. of American Poets; Poetry Society of America; South Mountain Poets, NJ, treas.; US Poets, Princeton. *Address:* 34 Ski Hill Dr., Bedminster, NJ 07921, USA.

PRASAD, V. S. Skanda; b. Sept. 1949, Mysore City, India. Bank Exec.; Poet. m. Suman Prasad, May 1980, 1 s. *Education:* MSc, 1970; DBAIM, 1980. *Publications:* Explorations and Reflections, 1978; Songs of Cosmos, 1981; East West Winds, 1982; Indo-Australian Flowers, 1984; Sweet Sixteen, 1987; East West Voices, 1988; Glimpses, 1990; Rising Stars and Moving Horizon, 1991; New Global Voice: An International Anthology of Poetry (ed.), 1994. *Contributions to:* Anthologies and other publications. *Honours:* DLitt, World Acad. of Arts and Culture, 1984; International Eminent Poet's Award, International Poets Acad., Chennai, 1986; Poetry Prize, Tarascon Acad., France, 1992; Pegasus Award, Olympoetry, 1992; Poetry Ed. of the Year, International Writers Asscn, USA, 1995. *Membership:* Chetana Literary Group, pres. *Address:* Kshema Apartments, Corporation Bank Executive Flat, KMC Men's Hostel Rd, Kaprigudda, Mangalore 575001, India.

PRESCOTT, Richard Chambers; b. 1 April 1952, Houston, Texas, USA. Poet; Writer. m. Sarah Elisabeth Grace, 13 Oct. 1981. *Publications:* The Sage, 1975; Moonstar, 1975; Neuf Songes (Nine Dreams), 1976; The Carouse of Soma, 1977; Lions and Kings, 1977; Allah Wake Up, 1978; Night Reaper, 1979; Dragon Tales, 1983; Dragon Dreams, 1986; Dragon Prayers, 1988; Dragon Songs, 1988; Dragon Maker, 1989; Dragon Thoughts, 1990; Tales of Recognition, 1991; Kings and Sages, 1991; Dragon Sight: A Cremation Poem, 1992; Three Waves, 1992; Years of Wonder, 1992; Dream Appearances, 1992; Remembrance, Recognition and Return, 1992; Spare Advice, 1992; The Imperishable, 1993; The Dark Deitess, 1993; Disturbing Delights: Waves of the Great Goddess, 1993; The Immortal: Racopa and the Rooms of Light, 1993; Hanging Baskets, 1993; Writer's Block and Other Gray Matters, 1993; The Resurrection of Quantum Joe, 1993; The Horse and the Carriage, 1993; Kalee Bhava: The Goddess and Her Moods, 1995; Because of Atma, 1995; The Skills of Kalee, 1995; Measuring Sky without Ground, 1996; Kalee: The Allayer of Sorrows, 1996; The Goddess and the God Man, 1996; Living Sakti: Attempting Quick Knowing in Perpetual Perception and Continuous Becoming, 1997; The Mirage and the Mirror, 1998; Inherent Solutions to Spiritual Obscurations, 1999; The Ancient Method, 1999; Quantum Kamakala, 2000. *Contributions to:* Articles and essays to professional publications. *Address:* 8617 188th St SW, Edmonds, WA 98026, USA.

PRESLEY, Frances Elizabeth; b. 30 Aug. 1952, Chesterfield, Derbyshire, England. Policy Officer; Poet. *Education:* BA, American and English Literature, 1975, MPhil, French Poetry, 1986, University of East Anglia; MA, Comparative Literature, University of Sussex, 1976. *Appointments:* Co-ordinator, Islington Poetry Workshop, 1993–; Editorial Adviser, How2, 1998. *Publications:* The Sex of Art, 1988; Hula Hoop, 1993; Linocut, 1997; Automatic Cross Stitch, 2000; Somerset Letters, 2002. *Contributions to:* Journals. *Membership:* Poetry Society. *Address:* 19B Marriott Rd, London N4 3QN, England.

PRESS, Diannamight. See: DRINKARD, Dianna (Phoebe) Phyllis Marcia Salicoff.

PRESS, John Bryant; b. 11 Jan. 1920, Norwich, England. Poet; Writer. m. Janet Crompton, 20 Dec. 1947, 1 s., 1 d. *Education:* Corpus Christi College, Cambridge, England. *Publications:* The Fire and the Fountain, 1955; The Chequer'd Shade, 1958; A Map of Modern English Verse, 1969; The Lengthening Shadows, 1971; John Betjeman, 1974; Poets of World War ll, 1984; A Girl with Beehive Hair, 1986. *Contributions to:* Encounter; Southern Review; Art International. *Honours:* RSL Heinemann Award, 1959; First Prize, Cheltenham Poetry Festival, 1959. *Membership:* RSL, Fellow. *Address:* 5 S Parade, Frome, Somerset BA11 1EJ, England.

PRESS, Karen Michele; b. 3 Nov. 1956, Cape Town, South Africa. Poet. *Education:* BA, 1977, Teaching Diploma, 1980, BA, Honours, African Studies, 1987, University of Cape Town. *Publications:* This Winter Coming, 1986; Bird Heart Stoning the Sea, 1990. *Contributions to:* Anthologies and magazines. *Address:* PO Box 2580, Cape Town 8000, South Africa.

PRICE, (Edward) Reynolds; b. 1 Feb. 1933, Macon, NC, USA. Prof.; Author; Poet; Dramatist. *Education:* AB, Duke University, 1955; BLitt, Merton College, Oxford, 1958. *Appointments:* Faculty, 1958–61, Asst Prof., 1961–68, Assoc. Prof., 1968–72, Prof., 1972–77, James B. Duke Prof., 1977–, Duke University; Writer-in-Residence, University of North Carolina at Chapel Hill, 1965, University of Kansas, 1967, 1969, 1980, University of North Carolina at Greensboro, 1971; Glasgow Prof., Washington and Lee University, 1971; Faculty, Salzburg Seminar, 1977. *Publications:* A Long and Happy Life, 1962; The Names and Faces of Heroes, 1963; A Generous Man, 1966; Love and Work, 1968; Permanent Errors, 1970; Things Themselves, 1972; The Surface of Earth, 1975; Early Dark, 1977; A Palpable God, 1978; The Source of Light, 1981; Vital Provisions, 1982; Private Contentment, 1984; Kate Vaiden, 1986; The Laws of Ice, 1986; A Common Room, 1987; Good Hearts, 1988; Clear Pictures, 1989; The Tongues of Angels, 1990; The Use of Fire, 1990; New Music, 1990; The Foreseeable Future, 1991; Conversations with Reynolds Price, 1991; Blue Calhoun, 1993; Full Moon, 1993; The Collected Stories, 1993; A Whole New Life, 1994; The Promise of Rest, 1995; Three Gospels, 1996; Roxanne Slade, 1998. *Honours:* William Faulkner Foundation Award for Notable First Novel, 1962; Sir Walter Raleigh Awards, 1962, 1976, 1981, 1984, 1986; Guggenheim Fellowship, 1964–65; National Endowment for the Arts Fellowship, 1967–68; National Institute of Arts and Letters Award, 1971; Bellamann Foundation Award, 1972; North Carolina Award, 1977; National Book Critics Circle Award, 1986; Elmer H. Bobst Award, 1988; R. Hunt Parker Award, North Carolina Literary and Historical Society, 1991. *Membership:* American Acad. of Arts and Letters. *Address:* PO Box 99014, Durham, NC 27708, USA.

PRICE, Richard; b. 15 Aug. 1966, Reading, England. Poet; Librarian; Ed.; Writer. m. Jacqueline Canning, 6 Dec. 1990, 2 d. *Education:* BA, English and Librarianship, PhD, University of Strathclyde, Glasgow. *Appointment:* Curator, Modern British Collections, British Library, London, 1992–. *Publications:* Poetry: Sense and a Minor Fever, 1993; Tube Shelter Perspective, 1993; Marks & Sparks, 1995; Hand Held, 1997; Perfume and Petrol Fumes, 1999; Frosted, Melted, 2002. Other: The Fabulous Matter of Fact: The Poetics of Neil M. Gunn, 1991; César Vallejo: Translations, Transformations, Tributes (ed.

with Stephen Watts), 1998; La nouvelle alliance: Influences francophones sur la littérature ecossaise (ed. with David Kinloch), 2000; The Star You Steer By: Basil Bunting and 'British' Modernism (ed. with James McGonigal), 2000; A Boy in Summer (short stories), 2002. *Contributions to:* Comparative Criticism; Independent; Scotland on Sunday; New Writing Scotland; Verse; Poetry Scotland; Parenthesis; Edinburgh Review; Object Permanence. *Memberships:* Asscn of Scottish Literary Studies; Poetry Society, council, 1998–. *Address:* c/o Modern British Collections, British Library, 96 Euston Rd, London NW1 2DB, England.

PRICE, Victor; b. 10 April 1930, Newcastle, County Down, Northern Ireland. Writer; Poet. *Education:* BA, Honours, Modern Languages (French and German), Queen's University, Belfast, 1947–51. *Appointments:* With the BBC, 1956–90, ending as Head of German Language Service. *Publications:* The Death of Achilles, 1963; The Other Kingdom, 1964; Caliban's Wooing, 1966; The Plays of Georg Büchner, 1971; Two Parts Water (poems), 1980. *Contributions to:* Financial Times; Scotsman; BBC World Service; Deutschland Rundfunk; Channel Four. *Address:* 22 Oxford Gardens, London W4 3BW, England.

PRIEST, Lydia Pallmé; b. 13 Sept. 1940, New York, NY, USA. Poet. m. Walter S Priest, 29 Sept. 1965, deceased 10 Jan. 1992, 2 d. *Education:* AB, 1962, AM, 1967, George Washington University; MA, Andover Newton Theological School, 1992. *Appointments:* Publisher-Reporter, Rockport Eagle newspaper, 1972–84; Pastoral Assoc., Salem, Massachusetts, 1985–89; Reading Teacher and Respite Worker, Asscn of Retarded Citizens, 1992–95; Clan Poet, 1997–; Tutor, America Reads Program. *Contributions to:* Anthologies and periodicals. *Honours:* Honourable Mentions, Gloucester Daily Times Poetry Contest, 1995, International Society of Poets' Magazine, 1995, Poet's Corner, 1996, Newburyport Art Asscn Poetry Contest, 1996; Ed.'s Choice Award, National Library of Poetry, 1995. *Membership:* International Society of Poets. *Address:* 72B Bass Ave, Gloucester, MA 01930, USA.

PRINCE, Alison (Mary); b. 26 March 1931, Kent, England. Writer; Poet. m. Goronwy Siriol Parry, 26 Dec. 1957, 2 s., 1 d. *Education:* Beckenham Grammar School; Slade School Diploma, London University; Art Teacher's Diploma, Goldsmith's College. *Appointment:* Fellow in Creative Writing, Jordanhill College, Glasgow, 1988–90. *Publications:* The Doubting Kind (young adults), 1974; How's Business (children's book), 1985; The Ghost Within (supernatural stories), 1987; The Blue Moon Day (children's book), 1989; The Necessary Goat (essays on creativity), 1992; Kenneth Grahame: An Innocent in the Wild Wood (biography), 1994; Having Been in the City (poems), 1994; The Witching Tree (novel), 1996; The Sherwood Hero (children's book), 1996; Magic Dad (children's book), 1997; Fergus, Fabulous Ferret (children's book), 1997; Hans Christian Andersen: The Fan Dancer (biography), 1998; Screw Loose (children's book), 1998; Cat Number Three (children's book), 1999; Dear Del (children's book), 1999; Second Chance (children's book), 2000; A Nation Again (children's book), 2000; Bird Boy (children's book), 2000; Bumble (children's book), 2001; Boojer (children's book), 2002; Oranges and Murder (children's book), 2001; The Fortune Teller (children's book), 2001; My Tudor Queen (children's book), 2001; Turnaround (children's book), 2002. *Contributions to:* Various educational and other journals. *Honours:* Runner-Up for Smarties Prize, 1986; Guardian Children's Fiction Award, 1996; Literary Review Grand Poetry Prize; Scottish Arts Council Awards for Children's Literature, 2001, 2002. *Memberships:* Scottish PEN; Society of Authors. *Address:* Burnfoot, Whiting Bay, Isle of Arran KA27 8QL, Scotland.

PRINCE, F(rank) T(empleton); b. 13 Sept. 1912, Kimberley, Cape Province, South Africa. Prof. of English (retd); Poet. m. Pauline Elizabeth Bush, 10 March 1943, 2 d. *Education:* BA, Balliol College, Oxford, 1934. *Appointments:* Visiting Fellow, Princeton University, USA, 1935–36, All Souls College, Oxford, 1968–69; Lecturer, 1945–55, Reader, 1955–56, Prof. of English, 1957–74, University of Southampton; Clark Lecturer, University of Cambridge, 1972–73; Prof. of English, University of the West Indies, Jamaica, 1975–78; Fannie Hurst Visiting Prof., Brandeis University, Waltham, Massachusetts, 1978–80; Visiting Prof., Washington University, St Louis, 1980–81, Sana'a University, North Yemen, 1981–83; Writer-in-Residence, Hollins College, Virginia, 1984. *Publications:* Poetry: Poems, 1938; Soldiers Bathing and Other Poems, 1954; The Stolen Heart, 1957; The Doors of Stone: Poems, 1938–1962, 1963; Memoirs in Oxford, 1970; Penguin Modern Poets 20 (with John Heath-Stubbs and Stephen Spender), 1971; Drypoints of the Hasidim, 1975; Afterword on Rupert Brooke, 1976; Collected Poems, 1979; The Yuan Chen Variations, 1981; Later On, 1983; Fragment Poetry, 1986; Walks in Rome, 1987; Collected Poems, 1935–92, 1993. Other: The Italian Element in Milton's Verse, 1954. Editor: John Milton: Samson Agonistes, 1957; William Shakespeare: The Poems, 1960; John Milton: Paradise Lost, Books I and II, 1962; John Milton: Comus and Other Poems, 1968. *Contributions to:* Keats Country (poem), PN Review 106, 1995. *Honours:* DLitt, University of Southampton, 1981, University of York, 1982; American Acad. and Institute of Arts and Letters Award, 1982. *Address:* 32 Brookvale Rd, Southampton, Hampshire S017 1QR, England.

PROKOPOV, Georgine Lucile Ogden, (Georgine Ogden); b. 3 Nov. 1925, Middletown, NY, USA. Poet; Writer. m. Theodore S. Prokopov, 4 Oct. 1968, 1 step-s., 2 step-d. *Education:* BA, University of Wisconsin, 1947; MIA, Columbia University, 1949; PhD, University of London, 1958. *Appointments:* Research Writer, US Dept of State, 1951–53; Research Asst, Population Reference Bureau, 1960–64; Research Analyst, Georgetown Research Project, 1965–66; Assoc. Prof., Upper Iowa University, 1967–73; Administrative Aide, Orange County, NY, Exec.'s Office, 1975–77; Data Analyst, Hudson Valley HSA, 1977–81, 1984–86; Dir of Research and Evaluation, Westchester County Dept of Health, 1981–83; Poet Laureate, 1996–2001, Poet Laureate Emeritus, 2002–, Orange County, NY. *Publications:* Orange Poems, 1987; Shawangunk and Catskill Chirpings, 1995. *Contributions to:* Algonquin Quarterly; Voices of the Majestic Sage; Treasures of the Precious Moments; Dreams and Visions; Anthology Five; Anthology Six; Florida State Poets Asscn; National Federation of State Poetry SocietiesAnthology of Prize Poems, 1988. *Honours:* Hon. Mention, Beatrice Branch Memorial Award; Leona Jones Smith Memorial Award. *Address:* 2 Graham Ave, Godeffroy, NY 12739, USA.

PRUNTY, (Eugene) Wyatt; b. 15 May 1947, Humbolt, TN, USA. Prof. of English; Poet; Writer; Ed. m. Barbara Heather Svell, 14 Aug. 1973, 1 s., 1 d. *Education:* BA, University of the South, 1969; MA, Johns Hopkins University, 1973; PhD, Louisiana State University, 1979. *Appointments:* Instructor in English, Louisiana State University, 1978–79; Asst Prof. to Prof. of English, Virginia Polytechnic Institute and State University, 1978–89; Visiting Writer, Washington and Lee University, 1982–83; Visiting Assoc. and Prof., Johns Hopkins University, 1987–89; Prof. of English, University of the South, 1989–. *Publications:* Poetry: Domestic of the Outer Banks, 1980; The Times Between, 1982; What Women Know, What Men Believe, 1986; Balance as Belief, 1989; The Run of the House, 1993; Since the Noon Mail Stopped, 1997; Unarmed and Dangerous: New and Selected Poems, 1999. Other: Fallen from the Symboled World: Precedents for the New Formalism, 1990; Just Let Me Say This About That: A Narrative Poem (ed. with Peter Mayer), 1998; Sewanee Writers on Writing (ed.), 2001. *Contributions to:* Anthologies, reviews, quarterlies and journals. *Honours:* Poetry Prize, Sewanee Review, 1969; Fellow, Bread Loaf Writers' Conference, 1982. *Memberships:* Associated Writing Programs; College English Asscn; English Institute; MLA of America. *Address:* c/o Dept of English, University of the South, Sewanee, TN 37383, USA.

PRUTKOV, Kozma. See: SNODGRASS, W. D.

PRYNNE, J(eremy) H(alvard); b. 24 June 1936, England. Poet. *Education:* Graduate, Jesus College, Cambridge, 1960. *Appointments:* Fellow, University Lecturer, and Librarian, Gonville and Caius College, Cambridge, 1962–. *Publications:* Kitchen Poems, 1968; Day Light Songs, 1968; The White Stones, 1969; Brass, 1971; Into the Day, 1972; Wound Response, 1974; High Pink on Chrome, 1975; News of Warring Clans, 1977; Down Where Changed, 1979; Poems, 1982; The Oval Window, 1983; Bands Around the Throat, 1987; Word Order, 1989; Not-You, 1993; Her Weasles Wild Returning, 1994; For the Monogram, 1997; Red D Gypsum, 1998; Pearls That Were, 1999; Poems, 1999; Triodes, 1999; Unanswering Rational Shore, 2001. *Address:* Gonville and Caius College, Cambridge CB2 1TA, England.

PUGH, Sheenagh; b. 20 Dec. 1950, Birmingham, England. Poet. m. Michael J H Burns, 1977, 1 s., 1 d. *Education:* BA, Honours, University of Bristol, 1971. *Publications:* Crowded by Shadows, 1977; What a Place to Grow Flowers, 1979; Earth Studies and Other Voyages, 1982; Beware Falling Tortoises, 1987; Selected Poems, 1990; Sing for the Taxman, 1993; Id's Hospit, 1997; Stonelight, 1999; The Beautiful Lie, 2002. *Honours:* Cardiff International Literature Festival Prize, 1988; Cholmondeley Award, 1997; Forward Prize, 1998. *Address:* 4C Romilly Rd, Canton, Cardiff CF5 1FH, Wales.

PUNTER, David Godfrey; b. 19 Nov. 1949, London, England. Prof. of English; Writer; Poet. m. Caroline Case, 5 Dec. 1988, 1 s., 2 d. *Education:* BA, 1970, MA, 1974, PhD, 1984, University of Cambridge. *Appointments:* Lecturer in English, University of East Anglia, 1973–86; Prof. and Head of Dept, Chinese University of Hong Kong, 1986–88; Prof. of English, University of Stirling, 1988–2000; Prof. of English, University of Bristol, 2000–. *Publications:* The Literature of Terror, 1980; Blake, Hegel and Dialectic, 1981; Romanticism and Ideology, 1982; China and Class, 1985; The Hidden Script, 1985; Introduction to Contemporary Cultural Studies (ed.), 1986; Lost in the Supermarket, 1987;

Blake: Selected Poetry and Prose (ed.), 1988; The Romantic Unconscious, 1989; Selected Poems of Philip Larkin (ed.), 1991; Asleep at the Wheel, 1997; Gothic Pathologies, 1998; Spectral Readings (ed.), 1999; Selected Short Stories, 1999; Companion to the Gothic (ed.), 2000; Writing the Passions, 2000; Postcolonial Imaginings, 2000. *Contributions to:* Hundreds of articles, essays, and poems in various publications. *Honours:* Fellow, RSA; Fellow, Society of Antiquaries (Scotland); Scottish Arts Council Award; Founding Fellow, Institute of Contemporary Scotland; DLitt, University of Stirling. *Address:* The Coach House, Church Lane, Backwell, Bristol BS48 3JJ, England.

PURDY, James (Amos); b. 17 July 1923, Ohio, USA. Author; Poet; Dramatist. *Education:* University of Chicago; University of Puebla, Mexico. *Publications:* Fiction: Dream Palace, 1956; Malcolm, 1959; The Nephew, 1961; Cabot Wright Begins, 1964; Eustace Chisholm and the Works, 1967; Jeremy's Version, 1970; I Am Elijah Thrush, 1972; The House of the Solitary Maggot, 1974; Color of Darkness, 1974; In a Shallow Grave, 1976; Narrow Rooms, 1978; Mourners Below, 1981; On Glory's Course, 1984; In the Hollow of His Hand, 1986; Candles of Your Eyes, 1986; Garments the Living Wear, 1989; Collected Stories, 1956–1986, 1991; Out with the Stars, 1992; Gertrude of Stony Island Avenue, 1998. Poetry: The Running Sun, 1971; Sunshine Is an Only Child, 1973; Lessons and Complaints, 1978; Sleep Tight, 1979; The Brooklyn Branding Parlors, 1985; Collected Poems, 1990. Plays: Cracks, 1963; Wedding Finger, 1974; Two Plays, 1979; Scrap of Paper, 1981; The Berrypicker, 1981; Proud Flesh, 1981; Gertrude of Stony Island Avenue (novel), 1997. *Honours:* National Institute of Arts and Letters Grant, 1958; Guggenheim Fellowships, 1958, 1962; Ford Foundation Grant, 1961; Morton Dauwen Zabel Fiction Award, American Acad. of Arts and Letters, 1993; Oscar Williams and Gene Durwood Poetry Award, 1995. *Address:* 236 Henry St, New York, NY 11201, USA.

PURI, Rakshat; b. 24 Feb. 1924, Lahore, India. Poet. m. Meenakshi, 12 Nov. 1953, 2 d. *Education:* Graduate in English Literature, Punjab University, Lahore. *Appointments:* Reporter, 1961–68; Columnist and Editorial Writer, 1969–78, Reporter, 1978–87, The Hindustani Times. *Publications:* Poems, 1968; 17 Poems, 1975; In the Chronicles, 1978; Love is His Own Power, 1991. *Contributions to:* Orbis; New Poetry; New Poetry from Oxford; London-Delhi Poetry Quarterly; Resurgence; Journal; Poetry Chronicle; Illustrated Weekly of India. *Address:* 28 Greville Hall, Greville Pl., London NW6 5JS, England.

PURPURA, Lia; b. 22 Feb. 1964, Long Island, New York, USA. Poet; Teacher. m. Jed Gaylin, 1992, 1 s. *Education:* BA, English, Oberlin College, 1986; MFA, Poetry, Iowa Writers Workshop, 1990. *Appointment:* Dept of Writing and Media, Loyola College, Baltimore, Maryland, 1990. *Publications:* The Brighter the Veil, 1996; Taste of Ash and Berliner Tagebuch-Poems of Grzegorz Musial, in press; Trans., poems by Katarzyna Borun-Jagodzinska and Krzysztof Piechowicz. *Contributions to:* Poems to numerous journals including: American Poetry Review; Antioch Review; Denver Quarterly; Ploughshares; Essays and reviews to several journals including: Willow Springs; Verse. *Honours:* Acad. of American Poets Award, 1986; Teaching and Writing Fellowship, University of Iowa Writers Workshop, 1988–90; Fulbright Fellowship, 1991–92; Blue Mountain Center Residency, 1995; First Prize, Visions International Trans. Prize, 1996; Millay Colony Resident Fellow, 1996; Nominated, Pushcart Prize, 1997. *Address:* 323 Radnor Rd, Baltimore, MD 21212, USA.

PYBUS, Rodney; b. 5 June 1938, Newcastle upon Tyne, England. Writer; Poet. m. Ellen Johnson, 24 June 1961, 2 s. *Education:* BA, Honours, Classics, English, MA, 1965, Gonville and Caius College, Cambridge. *Appointments:* Lecturer, Macquarie University, Australia, 1976–79; Literature Officer, Cumbria, 1979–81. *Publications:* In Memoriam Milena, 1973; Bridging Loans, 1976; At the Stone Junction, 1978; The Loveless Letters, 1981; Talitha Cumi, 1985; Cicadas in Their Summers: New and Selected Poems, 1988; Flying Blues, 1994. *Contributions to:* Numerous publications. *Honours:* Alice Hunt Bartlett Award, Poetry Society, 1974; Arts Council Writer's Fellowships, 1982–85; National Poetry Competition Awards, 1984, 1985, 1988; Hawthornden Fellowship, 1988; First Prize, Peterloo Poetry Competition, 1989. *Memberships:* Poetry Society; Society of Authors. *Address:* 21 Plough Lane, Sudbury, Suffolk CO10 2AU, England.

Q

QAZI, Moin; b. 4 April 1956, Nagpur, India. Bank Exec.; Writer; Poet. m. Nahid Qazi, 30 Dec. 1984, 2 s. *Education:* BA, 1977, LLB, 1980, MA, 1989, Nagpur University; PhD, International University, Los Altos, 1992; DLitt, World Acad. of Arts and Culture, 1993. *Publications:* A Wakeful Heart, 1989; The Real Face, 1992; Songs of Innocence, 1994; Voices from a Tinctured Heart, 1997; The Mission of Muhammad. *Contributions to:* Numerous articles and poems in publications worldwide. *Honours:* Poetry commendations and prizes; Michael Madhusudan Poetry Award, 1997. *Membership:* Fellow, Royal Asiatic Society. *Address:* Gandhi Chowk, Sadar, Nagpur, 440 001, India.

QUEFER. See: FERNANDEZ, Querubin D. Jr.

R

RAAB, Lawrence (Edward); b. 8 May 1946, Pittsfield, Massachusetts, USA. Prof. of English; Poet; Writer. m. Judith Ann Michaels, 29 Dec. 1968, 1 d. *Education:* BA, Middlebury College, 1968; MA, Syracuse University, 1972. *Appointments:* Instructor, American University, 1970–71; Lecturer, University of Michigan, 1974; Prof. of English, Williams College, 1976–; Staff, Bread Loaf School of English, 1979–81, Bennington Writer's Conference, 1988, Bread Loaf Writer's Conference, 1994. *Publications:* Poetry: Mysteries of the Horizon, 1972; The Collector of Cold Weather, 1976; Other Children, 1986; What We Don't Know About Each Other, 1993; The Probable World, 2000. *Contributions to:* Many anthologies, scholarly journals, and periodicals. *Honours:* Acad. of American Poets Prize, 1972; National Endowment for the Arts Fellowships, 1972, 1984; Robert Frost Fellowship, Bread Loaf Writer's Conference, 1973; Yaddo Residencies, 1979–80, 1982, 1984, 1986–90, 1994, 1996, 1998; Bess Hokin Prize, Poetry Magazine, 1983; National Poetry Series Winner, 1992; National Book Award Finalist, 1993; MacDowell Colony Residencies, 1993, 1995, 1997, 2000. *Address:* 139 Bulkley St, Williamstown, MA 01267, USA.

RADAVICH, David Allen; b. 30 Oct. 1949, Boston, Massachusetts, USA. Prof.; Poet. m. Anne Ricketson Zahlan, 2 Jan. 1988, 1 step-d. *Education:* BA, 1971, MA, 1974, PhD, 1979, University of Kansas; Graduate work, Simon Fraser University, Vancouver, BC, 1971–72, University of Aberdeen, Scotland, 1974–75. *Appointments:* Asst Instructor, Iowa State University, 1982–84; Asst Prof., Assoc. Prof., Prof., Eastern Illinois University, 1984–. *Publications:* Slain Species, 1980; By the Way: Poems Over the Years, 1998. Other: Nevertheless... (play), 1988; Several chapbooks. *Contributions to:* Albany Review; Amaryllis Review; Chapman; Counterpoint; International Poetry Review; Kansas Quarterly; Louisville Review; Lyric; Lyrical Iowa; Orbis; Other Poetry; Plainsongs; Poet and Critic; Poetpourri; Poetry Nottingham; Poetry Now; Success; TLS; Timarit Mals Og Menninger; Trends; Weyfarers; Willow Review; Zebra; Orbis, 1992; International Quarterly. *Honours:* Third Prize, Kansas Quarterly, 1976; First Prize, Tell-Tale Poetry Competition, 1978; First Prize and Special Prize, International Verse Competition, 1983; Third Prize, Sucess Competition, 1983; Third Prize, Willow Review Competition, 1987; Featured Poet, Rolling Coulter, 1990; Illinois Distinguished Author, 1995. *Memberships:* Poets and Writers; Dramatists Guild; Chicago Alliance for Playwrights; Missouri Asscn of Playwrights. *Address:* 1832 Ashby Dr., Charleston, IL 61920, USA.

RADULESCU, Stella Vinitchi; b. 12 May 1936, Cluj, Romania. Prof. of French; Poet. m. Gheorghe Radulescu, 9 May 1959, 1 d. *Education:* PhD, French, University of Bucharest, 1977; MA, French, University of Illinois, Chicago, 1986. *Appointments:* Asst Prof. of French, University of Bucharest, 1963–83; Lecturer of French, Loyola University, 1986–96, Northwestern University, Evanston, IL, 1990–. *Publications:* Versuri, 1969; Dincolo de Alb, 1972; Risipa unei veri, 1978; Singuratatea Cuvintelor, 1981; Intre Clipa Si Vreme, 2000; Blooming Death, 1989; Blood and White Apples, 1993; My Dream Has Red Fingers, 2000. *Contributions to:* Luceafarul; Limite; Voices International; Pleiades; Bitterroot; Romania Literarà; Vatra; Spout Magazine; California Quarterly; Visions International; Poems of the World; Dream International. *Honour:* Honorable Mention, New Voices, 1993. *Memberships:* Uniunea Scriitorilor, Romania; Acad. of American Poets. *Address:* 5225 N Kenmore 4L, Chicago, IL 60640, USA.

RAE, Jacque. See: SANCHEZ, Jacqueline Rae Rawlson.

RAFFEL, Burton (Nathan); b. 27 April 1928, New York, NY, USA. Distinguished Prof. of Humanities and Prof. of English; Lawyer; Writer; Poet; Ed.; Trans. m. Elizabeth Clare Wilson, 16 April 1974, 3 s., 3 d. *Education:* BA, Brooklyn College, 1948; MA, Ohio State University, 1949; JD, Yale University, 1958. *Appointments:* Lecturer, Brooklyn College, 1950–51; Ed., Foundation News, 1960–63; Instructor, 1964–65, Asst Prof., 1965–66, State University of New York at Stony Brook; Assoc. Prof., State University of New York at Buffalo, 1966–68; Visiting Prof., Haifa University, 1968–69, York University, Toronto, 1972–75, Emory University, 1974; Prof. of English and Classics, University of Texas at Austin, 1969–71; Senior Tutor (Dean), Ontario College of Art, Toronto, 1971–72; Prof. of English, 1975–87, Lecturer in Law, 1986–87, University of Denver; Ed.-in-Chief, Denver Quarterly, 1976–77; Contributing Ed., Humanities Education, 1983–87; Dir, Adirondack Mountain Foundation, 1987–89; Advisory Ed., The Literary Review, 1987–; Distinguished Prof. of Humanities and Prof. of English, University of Southwestern Louisiana, 1989–. *Publications:* Non-Fiction: The Development of Modern Indonesian Poetry, 1967; The Forked Tongue: A Study of the Translation Process, 1971; Introduction to Poetry, 1971; Why Re-Create?, 1973; Robert Lowell, 1981; T S Eliot, 1982; American Victorians: Explorations in Emotional History, 1984; How to Read a Poem, 1984; Ezra Pound: The Prime Minister of Poetry, 1985; Politicians, Poets and Con Men, 1986; The Art of Translating Poetry, 1988; Artists All: Creativity, the University, and the World, 1991; From Stress to Stress: An Autobiography of English Prosody, 1992; The Art of Translating Prose, 1994; The Annotated Milton, 1999. Fiction: After Such Ignorance, 1986; Founder's Fury (with Elizabeth Raffel), 1988; Founder's Fortune (with Elizabeth Raffel), 1989. Poetry: Mia Poems, 1968; Four Humours, 1979; Changing the Angle of the Sun-Dial, 1984; Grice, 1985; Evenly Distributed Rubble, 1985; Man as a Social Animal, 1986; Beethoven in Denver, and other poems, 1999. Other: Numerous trans. *Contributions to:* Professional journals. *Honours:* Frances Steloff Prize for Fiction, 1978; American-French Foundation Trans. Prize, 1991; Several grants. *Membership:* National Faculty. *Address:* 203 S Mannering Ave, Lafayette, LA 70508, USA.

RAGAN, James; b. 19 Dec. 1944, Pennsylvania, USA. Poet; Dramatist; Dir; Prof. m. Debora Ann Skovranko, 29 May 1982, 1 s., 2 d. *Education:* BA, Vincent College, 1966; PhD, Ohio University, 1971. *Appointments:* Prof. and Dir, Professional Writing Program, University of Southern California, 1981–; Visiting Prof., CALTECH, 1989–; Poet-in-Residence, Charles University, Prague, 1993–. *Publications:* In the Talking Hours, 1979; Womb-Weary, 1990; Yevgeny Yevtushenko: The Collected Poems (ed.), 1991; The Hunger Wall, 1995; Lusions, 1996. *Contributions to:* Anthologies, reviews, quarterlies, journals, and magazines. *Honours:* Humanitarian Award, Swan Foundation, Pittsburgh, 1972; National Endowment for the Arts Grant, 1972; Fulbright Fellow, 1985, 1988; Co-Winner, Gertrude Claytor Award, Poetry Society of America, 1987; Hon. Doctorate of Humane Letters, St Vincent College, 1990; Richmond University, London, 2001; Medal of Merit for Poetry, Ohio University, 1990; Telly Award, Poet's Corner, BHTV, 1996; Hon. Mem., Russian Acad. of Arts and Sciences, 1997. *Memberships:* Associated Writing Programs; MLA; Modern Poetry Asscn; PEN; Poetry Society of America; Writers Guild of America, West. *Address:* 1516 Beverwil Dr., Los Angeles, CA 90035, USA.

RAGHUPATHI, Kota Varadarajulu; b. 18 March 1957, Vellore, Tamil Nadu, India. Teacher; Poet. *Education:* MA, English, 1979, MPhil, 1982, PhD, 1997, Sri Venkateswara University, Tirupati; Diploma in Yoga and Naturopathy, Sri Visweswara Yoga Research Centre, Tirupati, 1995. *Publications:* Desert Blooms, 1987; Echoes Silent, 1988; The Images of a Growing Dying City, 1989; Voice Eternal, 1991; Symphonies for the Soul, 1997. *Contributions to:* Many anthologies and journals. *Address:* 7-96 Second Floor, Shanti Nagar, Tirupati 517 502, India.

RAHU, Chethput; b. 28 Jan. 1916, Vellore, North Arcot District, Tamil Nadu, India. Commercial Exec. and Man. (retd); Poet. m. Eashwari Raju, 14 Nov. 1947, 2 s. *Education:* BA, English, 1957. *Publications:* This Modern Age and Other Poems, 1954; No Exit, 1970. *Contributions to:* Anthologies and reviews. *Honours:* Prizewinner, All India Poetry Contests, 1991, 1992. *Membership:* PEN, India. *Address:* 3 Ganga Vihar, 318 Bhalchandra Rd, Matunga, CR, Mumbai 400 019, India.

RAI, K. B.; b. 20 June 1935, Sarai Sidhu, India. Administrator (retd); Poet. m. Umesh Kanta, 29 May 1970, 2 s. *Education:* Matriculation, Punjab University, 1952; BA, Agra University, 1963; MA, English, Delhi University, 1968. *Publications:* Men and Gods and Other Poems, 1985; Miscellany, 1994. *Contributions to:* Various publications. *Memberships:* International Writers and Artists Asscn, USA; Fellow, United Writers Asscn, India. *Address:* BB/18C, First Floor, Janakpuri, New Delhi 110 058, India.

RAIJADA, Rajendrasinh; b. 1 July 1943, Sondarda, India. Educator; Writer; Poet. m. Gulabkumari Raijada, 21 Feb. 1969, 2 s., 1 d. *Education:* BEd, 1973, MA, 1975, Saurashtra University, Rajkot; PhD, Sardar Patel University, Vallabhvidyanaga, 1979. *Appointments:* Language Expert, 1975–82, Central Committee Mem., 1997–2000, Gujarat State Textbook Board, Gandhinagar. *Publications:* Radha Madhav (trans. from Hindi), 1970; Farva avyo chhun (poems), 1976; Gulmahor ni niche (short stories), 1977; Rahasyavad (essays), 1980; Hun, Kali chhokari ane Suraj (poems), 1982; Darsdhan asne Itishas (articles), 1983; Sant Parampara Vimarsh (criticism), 1989; Tantra Sadhana, Maha Panth Ane Anya Lekho (articles), 1993; Pat upasana ane Pratiko num Rahasya (articles), 2002. *Address:* Sondarda, via Kevadra 362227, Gujarat, India.

RAINE, Craig (Anthony); b. 3 Dec. 1944, Shildon, County Durham, England. Poet; Writer. m. Ann Pasternak Slater, 27 April 1972, 3 s., 1 d. *Education:* Honours Degree in English Language and Literature, 1966, BPhil, 1968, Exeter College, Oxford. *Appointments:* Lecturer, Exeter College, Oxford, 1971–72, Lincoln College, Oxford, 1974–75, Christ Church, Oxford, 1976–79; Books Ed., New Review, London, 1977–78; Ed., Quarto, London, 1979–80; Poetry Ed., New Statesman, London, 1981, Faber & Faber, London, 1981–91; Fellow, New College, Oxford, 1991–; Ed., Areté, 1999–. *Publications:* Poetry: The Onion, Memory, 1978; A Journey to Greece, 1979; A Martian Sends a Postcard Home, 1979; A Free Translation, 1981; Rich, 1984; '1953': A Version of Racine's Andromaque, 1990; History: The Home Movie, 1994; Clay: Whereabouts Unknown, 1996; A la recherche du temps perdu, 2000; Collected Poems, 2000. Other: The Electrification of the Soviet Union (libretto), 1986; A Choice of Kipling's Prose (ed.), 1987; Haydn and the Valve Trumpet (essays), 1990; In Defence of T S Eliot (essays), 2000. *Contributions to:* Periodicals. *Honours:* First Prizes, Cheltenham Festival Poetry Competition, 1977, 1978; Prudence Farmer Awards, New Statesman, 1979, 1980; Cholmondeley Award, 1983; Sunday Times Award for Literary Distinction, 1999. *Memberships:* PEN; RSL. *Literary Agent:* David Goodwin Assocs. *Address:* c/o New College, Oxford OX1 3BN, England.

RAINE, Kathleen (Jessie); b. 14 June 1908, London, England. Poet; Critic; Ed.; Trans. m. (1) Hugh Skyes Davies, divorced, (2) Charles Madge, divorced, 1 s., 1 d. *Education:* MA, Girton College, Cambridge, 1929. *Appointment:* Founder, Temenos Acad., 1990. *Publications:* Poetry: Stone and Flower: Poems, 1935–1943, 1943; Living in Time, 1946; The Pythoness and Other Poems, 1948; Selected Poems, 1952; The Year One, 1953; Collected Poems of Kathleen Raine, 1956; The Hollow Hill and Other Poems, 1960–64, 1965; Ninfa Revisited, 1968; Six Dreams and Other Poems, 1968; A Question of Poetry, 1969; The Lost Country, 1971; Three Poems Written in Ireland, 1973; On a Deserted Shore, 1973; The Oracle in the Heart and Other Poems, 1975–1978, 1980; Collected Poems, 1935–1980, 1981; The Presence: Poems, 1984–87, 1988; Living with Mystery: Poems, 1987–1991, 1992; The Collected Poems of Kathleen Raine, 2001. Non-Fiction: Poetry in Relation to Traditional Wisdom, 1958; Blake and England, 1960; Defending Ancient Springs, 1967; The Written Word, 1967; Blake and Tradition, 2 vols, 1968; William Blake, 1970; Faces of Day and Night (autobiography), 1972; Yeats, the Tarot, and the Golden Dawn, 1972; Farewell Happy Fields: Memories of Childhood, 1973; Death-in-Life and Life-in-Death: Cuchulain Comforted and News for the Delphic Oracle, 1974; A Place, a State, 1974; David Jones, Solitary Perfectionist, 1974; The Land Unknown (autobiography), 1975; The Lion's Mouth: Concluding Chapters of Autobiography, 1977; From Blake to a Vision, 1978; David Jones and the Actually Loved and Known, 1978; Blake and the New Age, 1979; Cecil Collins, Painter of Paradise, 1979; What is Man?, 1980; The Human Face of God: William Blake and the Book of Job, 1982; The Inner Journey of the Poet and Other Papers, 1982; Yeats the Initiate: Essays on Certain Themes in the Writings of W B Yeats, 1984; Poetry and the Frontiers of Consciousness, 1985; The English Language and the Indian Spirit: Correspondence between Kathleen Raine and K D Sethna, 1986; India Seen Afar, 1991; Golgonooza, City of Imagination: Last Studies in William Blake, 1991. Editor: Aspects de la littérature anglaise (with Max-Pol Fouchet), 1947; The Letters of Samuel Taylor Coleridge, 1952; Selected Poems and Prose of Coleridge, 1957; Coleridge: Letters, 1969; Selected Writings of Thomas Taylor the Platonist (with George Mills Harper), 1969; A Choice of Blake's Verse, 1974; Shelley, 1974. *Contributions to:* Books and journals. *Honours:* Harriet Monroe Memorial Prize, 1952; Arts Council Award, 1953; Oscar Blumenthal Prize, 1961; Cholmondeley Award, 1970; W. H. Smith Literary Award, 1972; Foreign Book Prize, France, 1979; Queen's Gold Medal for Poetry, 1993. *Address:* 47 Paultons Sq., London SW3, England.

RAJA, P.; b. 7 Oct. 1952, Pondicherry, India. Writer; Poet; Lecturer in English. m. Periyanayaki, 6 May 1976, 2 s., 1 d. *Education:* BA, English, 1973; MA, English Language and Literature, 1975; PhD, Indian Writing in English, 1992. *Publications:* From Zero to Infinity (poems), 1987; Folktales of Pondicherry, 1987; A Concise History of Pondicherry, 1987; Tales of Mulla Nasruddin, 1989; The Blood and Other Stories, 1991; M P Pandit: A Peep Into His Past, 1993; Many Worlds of Manoj Das, 1993; The Best Woman in My Life and Other Stories, 1994; Sudden Tales the Folks Told, 1995; To the Lonely Grey Hair, 1997. Other: Trans. *Contributions to:* Numerous journals. *Honours:* Literary Award, Pondicherry University, 1987; International Eminent Poet Award, Chennai, 1988; Michael Madhusudan Acad. Award, Calcutta, 1991. *Address:* 74 Poincare St, Olandai-Keerapalayam, Pondicherry 605 004, India.

RAJAN, Tilottama; b. 1 Feb. 1951, New York, NY, USA. Prof.; Writer; Poet. *Education:* BA, Honours, Trinity College, Toronto, 1972; MA, 1973, PhD, 1977, University of Toronto. *Appointments:* Asst Prof., Huron College, University of Western Ontario, 1977–80, Asst Prof., 1980–83, Assoc. Prof., 1983–85, Queen's University; Prof., University of Wisconsin at Madison, 1985–90; Prof., 1990–, Dir, Centre for the Study of Theory and Criticism, 1995–, University of Western Ontario. *Publications:* Myth in a Metal Mirror, 1967; Dark Interpreter: The Discourse of Romanticism, 1980; The Supplement of Reading, 1990; Intersections: Nineteenth Century Philosophy and Contemporary Theory, 1995. *Contributions to:* Professional journals. *Honours:* Guggenheim Fellowship, 1987–88; Fellow, Royal Society of Canada, 1994–. *Memberships:* Canadian Comparative Literature Asscn; University of Teachers of English; Keats-Shelley Asscn; MLA of America; North American Society for the Study of Romanticism; Wordsworth-Coleridge Asscn. *Address:* 870 Wellington St, London, Ontario N6A 5S7, Canada.

RAJARAM, A., (Bramharajan); b. 24 April 1953, Salem, Massachusetts. Teacher; Poet. m. 9 Nov. 1981, 1 d. *Education:* MA; MPhil; PhD. *Publications:* Known Eternity; Men Sensitive to Pain; Memory Sculpture; Ancient Heart. *Contributions to:* Poetry Chronicle; Indian Poetry Today; Anuvadha; Indian Express; Book Review; Indian Literature. *Memberships:*

National Poetry Center Bharat Bhavan. *Address:* Dept of English Government Arts College, Ooty 643 002, India.

RAKOVSZKY, Zsuzsa; b. 4 Dec. 1950, Sopron, Hungary. Writer; Poet; Trans. *Education:* Graduate, Faculty of Art, Eötvös University, Budapest, 1975. *Publications:* Joslatok es hataridok, 1981; Tovabb egy hazzal, 1987; Feherfekete, 1991. *Contributions to:* Kortars; Jelenkor; Alfold; Holmi; 2000; New Hungarian Quarterly. *Honours:* Graves Prize, 1980; Dery Prize, 1986; József Attila Prize, 1986. *Memberships:* Hungarian PEN; Hungarian Writer's Asscn. *Address:* Torna u 22, Sopron, Hungary.

RAMKE, Bin; b. 19 Feb. 1947, Port Neches, Texas, USA. Prof. of English; Ed.; Poet. m. 31 May 1967, 1 s. *Education:* Louisiana State University, 1970; MA, University of New Orleans, 1971; PhD, Ohio University, 1975. *Appointments:* Prof. of English, Columbus University, GA, 1976–85, University of Denver, 1985–; Ed., Contemporary Poetry Series, University of Georgia Press, 1984–; Poetry Ed., 1985–, Ed., 1994–, The Denver Quarterly. *Publications:* The Difference Between Night and Day, 1978; White Monkeys, 1981; The Language Student, 1987; The Erotic Light of Gardens, 1989; Massacre of the Innocents, 1995. *Contributions to:* Reviews, quarterlies, and journals. *Honours:* Yale Younger Poets Award, 1977; Texas Institute of Arts and Letters Award for Poetry, 1978; Iowa Poetry Award, 1995. *Memberships:* Associated Writing Programs; National Book Critics Circle; PEN, American Centre. *Address:* c/o Dept of English, University of Denver, Denver, CO 80208, USA.

RAMNEFALK, (Sylvia) Marie Louise; b. 21 March 1941, Stockholm, Sweden. Poet; Literary Critic. *Education:* FK, 1964, FL, 1968, FD, 1974 (Equivalent to PhD, Literature), University of Stockholm. *Appointment:* Literary Critic, several newspapers and magazines. *Publications:* 12 vols in Swedish, 1971–97. *Contributions to:* Various periodicals. *Honours:* Several scholarships. *Memberships:* Several, including Swedish PEN. *Address:* Vastra Valhallavagen 25A, 182 66 Djursholm, Sweden.

RAMON, Renaat; b. 17 Oct. 1936, Bruges, Belgium. Visual Artist; Essayist; Poet. *Publications:* Poetry: Oogseizoen, 1976; Ansichten, 1980; Flandria Fabulata, 1983; Noodweer, 1987; Ongehoorde gedichten, 1997; Qui-vive, 1999; Color-field Poetry, 1999. Essay: Bloemlezing uit de poësie van Jan van der Hoeven, 2000. *Contributions to:* Kruispunt; De Tafel Ronde; Betoel; Radar; Diogenes; Poeziekrant. *Honour:* Trap Award, 1981. *Memberships:* VWS; PEN. *Address:* Betferkerklaan 187, 8200 Bruges, Belgium. *E-mail:* ram.lam@compaqnet.be. *Website:* ramons.web-page.net.

RAMSAY-BROWN, John Andrew, (Jay Ramsay); b. 20 April 1958, Guildford, Surrey, England. Poet; Writer; Ed.; Trans. *Education:* BA, Honours, English Language and Literature, Pembroke College, Oxford, 1980; Foundation Year Diploma in Psycho-synthesis, London Institute, 1987. *Publications:* Psychic Poetry: A Manifesto, 1985; Angels of Fire (co-ed.), 1986; New Spiritual: Selected Poems, 1986; Trwyn Meditations, 1987; The White Poem, 1988; Transformation: The Poetry of Spiritual Consciousness (ed.), 1988; The Great Return, books 1 to 5, 2 vols, 1988; Transmissions, 1989; Strange Days, 1990; Journey to Eden (with Jenny Davis), 1991; For Now (with Geoffrey Godbert), 1991; The Rain, the Rain, 1992; St Patrick's Breastplate, 1992; Tao Te Ching: A New Translation, 1993; I Ching, 1995; Kuan Yin, 1995; Chuang Tzu (with Martin Palmer), 1996; Alchemy: The Art of Transformation, 1996; Earth Ascending: An Anthology of New and Living Poetry (ed.), 1996; Kingdom of the Edge: New and Selected Poems 1980–1998, 1998. *Contributions to:* Periodicals. *Memberships:* College of Psychic Studies, London; Poetry Society; Psychosynthesis Education and Trust, London. *Address:* c/o Susan Mears, The Old Church, Monkton Deverill, near Warminster, Wiltshire BA12 7EX, England.

RAMSEY, Jarold (William); b. 1 Sept. 1937, Bend, Oregon, USA. Prof. Emeritus; Poet; Writer; Dramatist. m. Dorothy Ann Quinn, 16 Aug. 1959, 1 s., 2 d. *Education:* BA, Honours, English, University of Oregon, 1959; PhD, English Literature, University of Washington, 1966. *Appointments:* Acting Instructor, University of Washington, 1962–65; Asst Prof., 1965–70, Assoc. Prof., 1970–80, Prof. 1980–97, Prof. Emeritus 1997–, University of Rochester; Visiting Prof. of English, University of Victoria, BC, 1974, 1975–76. *Publications:* Poetry: The Space Between Us, 1970; Love in an Earthquake, 1973; Dermographia, 1983; Hand-Shadows, 1989. Plays and Libretti: Coyote Goes Upriver (play), 1981; The Lodge of Shadows (cantata with Samuel Adler), 1974. Non-Fiction: Coyote Was Going There: Indian Literature of the Oregon Country, 1977; Reading the Fire: Essays in the Traditional Indian Literature of the Far West, 1983. Editor: Elizabeth and Melville Jacobs, Nehalem Tillamook Tales, 1990; The Stories We Tell: Anthology of Oregon Folk Literature (with Suzi Jones), 1994. *Contributions to:* Anthologies, reviews, quarterlies, and journals. *Honours:* National Endowment for the Arts Grant, 1974, and Fellowship, 1975; Ingram Merrill Foundation Grant, 1975; Don Walker Award for Best Essay on Western Literature, 1978; Helen Bullis Award for Poetry, 1984; Quarterly Review International Poetry Prize, 1989. *Membership:* MLA. *Address:* 5884 NW Highway, No. 26, Madras, OR 97741, USA.

RANA, Pradeep Shumsher; b. 10 July 1960, Thapathali, Nepal. Poet. *Education:* BA, 1978; MA, 1981, 1988; LLB, 1988. *Appointments:* Asst

Lecturer, NC Campus, 1984–89; Lecturer, RM Campus, 1989–91, JM Campus, 1991–92, JJM Campus, 1992–93; Research Officer, CPS, 1989–; Life Deputy Gov., ABIRA, USA, 1997; Vice-Chair., Himalayan Phasant Asscn, Nepal, 2002; Art Advisor, Chinese Poetry International, 2002. *Publications:* An Estimation of Thomas Hardy, 1988; Empty Talk, 1992; Annotated Bibliography on Population and Development in Nepal, 1994; Silent Growth, 1996. *Contributions to:* Periodicals. *Honours:* Special Recording Award, USA, 1992; Hon. Paradoxist Diploma, USA, 1995; MM Acad. Award, India, 1998. *Memberships:* Nepal Profs Asscn; MIDVIN; ABIRA; IWA; FDS; CPS; Nepal Bar Asscn; The Paradoxist Literary Movt Asscn. *Address:* PO Box 3789, Katmandu, Nepal.

RANDALL, Margaret; b. 6 Dec. 1936, New York, NY, USA. Writer; Poet; Photographer; Teacher; Activist. 1 s., 3 d. *Appointments:* Managing Ed., Frontiers: A Journal of Women's Studies, 1990–91; Distinguished Visiting Prof., University of Delaware, 1991; Visiting Prof., Trinity College, Hartford, CT, 1992. *Publications:* Giant of Tears, 1959; Ecstasy is a Number, 1961; Poems of the Glass, 1964; Small Sounds from the Brass Fiddle, 1964; October, 1965; Twenty-Five Stages of My Spine, 1967; Getting Rid of Blue Plastic, 1967; So Many Rooms Has a House But One Roof, 1967; Part of the Solution, 1972; Day's Coming, 1973; With These Hands, 1973; All My Used Parts, Shackles, Fuel, Tenderness and Stars, 1977; Carlota: Poems and Prose from Havana, 1978; We, 1978; A Poetry of Resistance, 1983; The Coming Home Poems, 1986; Albuquerque: Coming Back to the USA, 1986; This is About Incest, 1987; Memory Says Yes, 1988; The Old Cedar Bar, 1992; Dancing with the Doe, 1992; Hunger's Table: The Recipe Poems, 1997. Oral History: Cuban Women Now, 1974; Sandino's Daughters, 1981. Photography: Women Brave in the Face of Danger, 1985; Nicaragua Libre!, 1985. *Contributions to:* Anthologies, reviews, journals, and magazines. *Honours:* First Prizes, Photography, Nicaraguan Children's Asscn, 1983; Creating Ourselves National Art Exhibition, 1992. *Address:* 50 Cedar Hill Rd NE, Albuquerque, NM 87122, USA.

RANGASWAMI, Srinivasa; b. 20 Feb. 1924, Chennai, India. Senior Parliamentary Officer (retd); Poet; Writer. m. Ramapriya Rangaswami, 30 June 1944, 1 s. *Education:* BA, 1944, MA, 1945, English Language and Literature, Chennai University. *Appointments:* Joint Dir, Research and Information Service, Parliament of India, 1952–82; Officer on Special Duty, Institute of Constitutional and Parliamentary Studies, 1983–91. *Publication:* The Wayside Piper. *Contributions to:* Various poetry anthologies and periodicals. *Honours:* SITA Silver Medal, 1938; Mark Hunter Memorial Prize, Presidency College, Chennai, 1944; Michael Madhusadan Award for Poetry, 2000; United Writers' Asscn Lifetime Achievement Award, 2002. *Memberships:* World Poetry Society Intercontinental, Chennai; Poetry Society of India, New Delhi; Writers Forum, Ranchi; All India PEN Centre, Mumbai; Fellowship of the United Writers Asscn, Chennai. *Address:* N/5 Adyar Apartments, Kottur Gardens, Chennai 600 085, India. *Telephone:* (44) 447-1316.

RANSFORD, Tessa; b. 8 July 1938, Mumbai, India. Poet; Writer; Ed. m. (1) Iain Kay Stiven, 29 Aug. 1959, divorced 1986, 1 s., 3 d., (2) Callum Macdonald, 7 Dec. 1989, deceased. *Education:* MA, University of Edinburgh, 1958; Teacher Training, Craiglockhart College of Education, 1980. *Appointments:* Founder, School of Poets, Edinburgh, 1981–; Dir, Scottish Poetry Library, 1984–99; Ed., Lines Review, 1988–99; Freelance Poetry Practitioner and Adviser, 1999–. *Publications:* Light of the Mind, 1980; Fools and Angels, 1984; Shadows from the Greater Hill, 1987; A Dancing Innocence, 1988; Seven Valleys, 1991; Medusa Dozen and Other Poems, 1994; Scottish Selection, 1998; When it Works it Feels Like Play, 1998; Indian Selection, 2000; Natural Selection, 2001. *Contributions to:* Anthologies, reviews, and journals. *Honours:* Scottish Arts Council Book Award, 1980; Howard Sergeant Award for Services to Poetry, 1989; Heritage Society of Scotland Annual Award, 1996; O.B.E., 2000; Society of Authors Travelling Scholarship, 2001; Royal Literary Fund Writing Fellowship, 2001–03. *Memberships:* Fellow, RSA, 1994; Saltire Society, hon. mem., 1993; Scottish International PEN; Scottish Library Asscn, hon. mem., 1999; Scottish Poetry Library, ex-officio hon. mem., 1999. *Address:* 31 Royal Park Terrace, Edinburgh EH8 8JA, Scotland. *Website:* www.scottish-pamphlet-poetry.com/tessa.

RANSOM, Bill; b. 6 June 1945, Puyallup, Washington, USA. Writer; Poet. 1 d. *Education:* BA, University of Washington, 1970. *Appointment:* Poetry-in-the-Schools Master Poet, National Endowment for the Arts, 1974–77. *Publications:* Fiction: The Jesus Incident, 1979; The Lazarus Effect, 1983; The Ascension Factor, 1988; Jaguar, 1990; Viravax, 1993; Burn, 1995. Poetry: Finding True North, 1974; Waving Arms at the Blind, 1975; Last Rites, 1979; The Single Man Looks at Winter, 1983; Last Call, 1984; Semaphore, 1993. Other: Learning the Ropes (poems, essays, and short fiction), 1995. *Contributions to:* Numerous publications. *Honour:* National Endowment for the Arts Discovery Award, 1977. *Memberships:* International Assocation of Machinists and Aerospace Workers; Poetry Society of America; Poets and Writers; Poets, Essayists, and Novelists; SFWA. *Address:* PO Box 284, Grayland, WA 98547, USA.

RANZ-HORMAZABAL, Maria de los Candelas; b. 23 Aug. 1950, Spain. Poet; Writer. m. Augustin Garcia Alonso, 2 s., 1 d. *Education:* Colegio de Religiosas de Duenas, Palencia. *Publications:* Poetry: Al principio del camino, 1962; Como la luz de la aurora, 1982; Petalos de mis rosas, 1983; Mis poemas,

1983; De verso en verso de flor en flor, 1984; Armor incompleto, 1984; Caprichosas protuberancias poéticas, 1986; Alondra-10, 1986; Sonetos, 1994. Other: Pequeñas biografias de grandes personajes, 1982; Desde mi butaca: Crítica de cine, 1982; Conoce usted a..., 1983; Les presento a..., 1983. *Contributions to:* Periodicals. *Honour:* Poetry Prize, Concurso El Paisaje de Dibujo del Centro Cultural Aga, Viscaya, 1974. *Memberships:* Academia O. Jornal de Felgueiras; Asociación Cultural La Marcilla, Léon, founder-sec.; Centro Cultural Literario y Artístico AGA. *Address:* Entre los Rios, 10, 24760 Castrocalbon, Léon, Spain.

RAO, Kanaka Durga. See: DURGA, Kanaka.

RAPOPORT, Janis; b. 22 June 1946, Toronto, Ontario, Canada. Poet; Writer; Dramatist. m. (1), 1 s., 2 d., (2) Douglas Donegani, 20 May 1980, 1 d. *Education:* BA, University of Toronto, 1967. *Appointments:* Assoc. Ed., Tamarack Review, 1970–82; Playwright-in-Residence, Tarragon Theatre, 1974–75; Dir, Ethos Cultural Development Foundation, 1981–; Ed., Ethos magazine, 1983–87; Part-time Instructor, Sheridan College, 1984–86; Writer-in-Residence, St Thomas Public Library, 1987, Beeton Public Library, 1988, Dundas Public Library, 1990, North York Public Library, 1991; Instructor, School of Continuing Studies, University of Toronto, 1988–. *Publications:* Within the Whirling Moment, 1967; Foothills, 1973; Jeremy's Dream, 1974; Landscape (co-ed.), 1977; Dreamgirls, 1979; Imaginings (co-author), 1982; Upon Her Fluent Route, 1992; After Paradise, 1996. *Contributions to:* Anthologies, newspapers, magazines, and radio. *Honours:* Canadian Council Arts Award, 1981–82; AIGA Certificate of Excellence, 1983; New York Dirs Club Award, 1983; Outstanding Achievement Award, American Poetry Asscn, 1986; Toronto Arts Council Research and Development Awards, 1990, 1992; Excellence in Teaching Award for Creative Writing, School of Continuing Studies, University of Toronto, 1998. *Memberships:* League of Canadian Poets; Playwrights' Union of Canada; Writers' Guild of Canada; Writers' Union of Canada. *Address:* c/o Writers' Union of Canada, 24 Ryerson Ave, Toronto, Ontario M5T 2P3, Canada.

RASUL, Juba Abdulazeem Adibun; b. 15 Oct. 1948, Chicago, IL, USA. Poet; Visual and Performing Artist; Human Rights Advocate. 1 d. *Education:* Degrees in Fine Art and Journalism. *Publications:* A Fearless Butterfly, 1995; Talk Izzz Cheap, 1996. *Contributions to:* Haight Asbury Literary Journal; Zam Bomba; Forked Tongue. *Memberships:* Poetry Society of America; Acad. of American Poets. *Address:* 2100 Golden Gate Ave, San Francisco, CA 94118, USA.

RATCH, Jerry; b. 9 Aug. 1944, Chicago, IL, USA. Writer; Poet. m. Sherry Karver, 18 March 1990. *Education:* BA, English, 1967; MFA, Creative Writing, 1970. *Publications:* Puppet X, 1973; Clown Birth, 1975; Osiris, 1977; Chaucer Marginalia, 1979; Hot Weather, 1982; Helen, 1985; Lenin's Paintings, 1987; Light, 1989; Wild Dreams of Reality (novel), 2001. *Contributions to:* Avec; Ironwood; Sonoma Madala; Carolina Quarterly; Washington Review; Contact II; Northeast Journal. *Address:* 6065 Chabot Rd, Oakland, CA 94618, USA.

RATCLIFFE, Eric Hallam; b. 8 Aug. 1918, Teddington, Middlesex, England. Physicist and Information Scientist (retd); Writer; Poet; Ed. *Appointment:* Founder-Ed., Ore, 1955–95. *Publications:* Over 30, including: The Visitation, 1952; The Chronicle of the Green Man, 1960; Gleanings for a Daughter of Aeolus, 1968; Leo Poems, 1972; Commius, 1976; Nightguard of the Quaternary, 1979; Ballet Class, 1986; The Runner of the Seven Valleys, 1990; The Ballad of Polly McPoo, 1991; Advent, 1992; The Golden Heart Man, 1993; Fire in the Bush: Poems, 1955–1992, 1993; William Ernest Henley (1849–1903): An Introduction, 1993; The Caxton of Her Age: The Career and Family Background of Emily Faithfull (1835–1895), 1993; Winstanley's Walton, 1649: Events in the Civil War at Walton-on-Thames, 1994; Ratcliffe's Megathesaurus, 1995; Anthropos, 1995; Odette, 1995; Sholen, 1996; The Millennium of the Magician, 1996; The Brussels Griffon, 1996; Strange Furlongs, 1996; Wellington- A Broad Front, 1998; Capabilities of the Alchemical Mind, 1999; Cosmologia, 2000; Loyal Women, 2000; The Ghost with Nine Fathers, 2001. *Contributions to:* Anthologies and journals. *Honour:* Baron, Royal Order of the Bohemian Crown, 1995. *Address:* 7 The Towers, Stevenage, Hertfordshire SG1 1HE, England.

RATCLIFFE, Stephen; b. 7 July 1948, USA. Poet; Prof. of English; Publisher; Ed. m. Ashley Perdue Ratcliffe, 17 Nov. 1973, divorced 1994, 1 d. *Education:* BA, 1970, PhD, 1978, University of California at Berkeley. *Appointment:* Prof. of English, Mills College, 1984–. *Publications:* Criticism: Campion: On Song, 1981. Poetry: New York Notes, 1983; Distance, 1986; Mobile/Mobile, 1987; Rustic Diversions, 1988; Spaces in the Light said to be where one/comes from, 1992; Selected Letters, 1992; Private, 1993; Present Tense, 1995. *Contributions to:* New American Writing; Tuyoni; Caliban; Temblor; Sulfur; Central Park; Talisman; Avec; OiArs; Transfer; Poetry Project Newsletter; Exemplaria; Chain. *Honours:* Stegner Fellowship in Creative Writing, Stanford University, 1974; Fund for Poetry Awards, 1988, 1991; National Endowment for the Arts Grants, 1991, 1995. *Memberships:* Associated Writing Programs; MLA. *Address:* PO Box 524, Bolinas, CA 94924, USA.

RATH, Sashibhusan; b. 30 May 1955, Kalahandi, India. Senior Man.; Poet. m. Sanghamitra Rath, 6 Dec. 1986, 2 s. *Education:* BSc, Honours with Distinction, MSc, Physics and Astrophysics, Delhi University; Diploma in Social Work, Calcutta University. *Publications:* Essays on Management, 1992; Tributaries, 1999. *Contributions to:* Asian Age; Bridge in Making; Byword; Poetry; Prophetic

Voices; Telegraph. *Honours:* Prajatantra, 1970; Dharitree, 1984. *Memberships:* Friend of PEN, Mumbai; Poetry Society, Delhi. *Address:* D-3/2 Meghahatuburu, West Singhbhum, Bihar 833 223, India.

RATNER, Rochelle; b. 2 Dec. 1948, Atlantic City, New Jersey, USA. Poet; Writer; Ed. m. Kenneth Thorp, 30 March 1990. *Appointments:* Poetry Columnist, Soho Weekly News, 1975–82; Co-Ed., Hand Book, 1976–82; Exec. Ed., American Book Review, 1978–; Small Press Columnist, Library Journey, 1985; Poetry Consultant, Israel Horizons, 1988–97; Ed., New Jersey Online: Reading Room, 1995–96; NBCC Board of Dirs, 1995–. *Publications:* Poetry: A Birthday of Waters, 1971; False Trees, 1973; The Mysteries, 1976; Pirate's Song, 1976; The Tightrope Walker, 1977; Quarry, 1978; Combing the Waves, 1979; Sea Air in a Grave Ground Hog Turns Toward, 1980; Hide and Seek, 1980; Practicing to be a Woman: New and Selected Poems, 1982; Someday Songs, 1992; Zodiac Arrest, 1995. Fiction: Bobby's Girl, 1986; The Lion's Share, 1991. Other: Trying to Understand What It Means to be a Feminist: Essays on Women Writers, 1984; Bearing Life: Women's Writings on Childlessness (ed.), 2000. *Honour:* Susan Koppelman Award, 2000. *Memberships:* Authors Guild; Hudson Valley Writers Guild; National Book Critics Circle; National Writers Union; PEN; Poetry Society of America; Poets and Writers. *Address:* 609 Columbus Ave, Apt 16F, New York, NY 10024, USA.

RATUSHINSKAYA, Irina; b. 4 March 1954, Odessa, Russia. Poet; Writer. m. Igor Geraschenko, 17 Nov. 1979, 2 s. *Education:* Diploma in Physics, University of Odessa. *Appointment:* Visiting Scholar, Northwestern University, Evanston, IL, 1987–88. *Publications:* No I'm Not Afraid, 1986; A Tale of Three Heads, 1986; Beyond the Limit, 1987; Grey is the Colour of Hope, 1988; Pencil Letter, 1988; In the Beginning, 1990; The Odessans, 1996. *Contributions to:* Various anthologies, 1989–95. *Honours:* Poetry International Rotterdam Award, 1986; Ross McWhirter Foundation, 1987; Christopher Award, USA, 1988; Individual Templeton Award, UK, 1993. *Membership:* PEN International, London. *Address:* 15 Crothall Close, London N13 4BN, England.

RAUT-ROY, Satchidananda; b. 13 May 1916, Gurujang, Orissa, India. Writer; Poet. m. Bhudevi Raut-Roy, 1945, 2 s., 2 d. *Education:* Graduated, 1939; Industrial Relations and Social Welfare, Australia and New Zealand, 1952, International Labour Organization, Geneva, 1955. *Appointments:* Founder-Pres., Diganta Museum and Research Centre, Cuttack; Ed., Diganta journal. *Publications:* Chitragriba, 1935; Kavita, 1962; Swagata, 1969. Other: Poems and short stories trans. into English and Russian. *Contributions to:* Anthologies and journals worldwide. *Honours:* Many, including: Award, 1964, Nominated as Fellow, 1996, Central Sahitya Akademi; Soviet Land Nehru Award, 1965; Hon. Doctorates, Andhra University, 1977, Berhampur University, 1978; Honoured with title of Mahalavi, Rourkela, 1985, Cuttack, 1988; G Rath Award, Cuttack, 1996. *Address:* Mission Rd, Cuttack 753 001, Orissa, India.

RAWNSLEY, Irene; b. 20 June 1935, Leeds, Yorkshire, England. Poet. Divorced, 1 s., 1 d. *Education:* Diploma in Education, University of Leeds; MA, University of York. *Publications:* For Children: Ask a Silly Question, 1988; Dog's Dinner, 1990; House of a Hundred Cats, 1995. For Young Teens: Hiding Out, 1996. For Adults: Shall We Gather at the River?, 1990. *Contributions to:* Periodicals, radio, and television. *Honours:* Joint First Prize, Rhyme Revival International, 1987; Prize, Northern Poetry Competition, Littlewood, 1989; Fourth Prize, Peterloo Poetry Competition, 1989; Prize, Poetry Business Competition, 1996. *Memberships:* Poetry Society; Society of Authors. *Address:* 6 Whitefriars Ct, Settle, North Yorkshire BD24 9EA, England.

RAWORTH, Thomas Moore; b. 19 July 1938, London, England. Poet; Writer. m. Valerie Murphy, 4 s., 1 d. *Education:* MA, University of Essex, 1970. *Appointments:* Poet-in-Residence, University of Essex, 1969, Northeastern University, Chicago, 1973–74; King's College, Cambridge, 1977–78; Lecturer, Bowling Green State University, Ohio, 1972–73; Visiting Lecturer, University of Texas, 1974–75, University of Cape Town, 1991, University of San Diego, 1996. *Publications:* The Relation Ship, 1967; The Big Green Day, 1968; A Serial Biography, 1969; Lion, Lion, 1970; Moving, 1971; Act, 1973; Ace, 1974; Common Sense, 1976; Logbook, 1977; Sky Tails, 1978; Nicht Wahr, Rosie?, 1979; Writing, 1982; Levre de Poche, 1983; Heavy Light, 1984; Tottering State: Selected Poems, 1963–83, 1984; Lazy Left Hand, 1986; Visible Shivers, 1987; All Fours, 1991; Catacoustics, 1991; Eternal Sections, 1991; Survival, 1991; Clean and Well Lit: Selected Poems 1987–1995, 1996. *Contributions to:* Periodicals. *Honours:* Alice Hunt Bartlett Prize, 1969; Cholmondeley Award, 1971; International Committee on Poetry Award, New York, 1988. *Membership:* PEN. *Address:* 3 St Philip's Rd, Cambridge CB1 3AQ, England.

RAY, Barnik; b. 21 Jan. 1936, Dhaka, India. College Teacher (retd); Poet; Trans. 2 s., 1 d. *Education:* MA. *Publications:* Anander Marmanita Andhakar, 1972; Nil Dupwrer Bhay, 1972; Sarirer Udihijila Chayay, 1976; He Amar Mrtyu, 1980; Balir Ghari, 1984; Elomelo Chada, 1988; Sudhu Bece Achi, 1995; Dibya Kabitamala o Sundarbaner Elegy, 1998. Other: Several trans. *Contributions to:* Many newspapers, reviews, journals, and magazines. *Memberships:* Asiatic Society of Bengal; Authors Guild; Sanskrit Society. *Address:* Puspa Apartment, 487 Sahid Hemanta Kumar Basu Sarani, Jawpur, Flat 8, Calcutta 700 074, West Bengal, India.

RAY, Bibekananda; b. 24 March 1940, West Bengal, India. Journalist Broadcaster; Poet. m. Bandana Ray, 3 March 1968, 3 d. *Education:* MA English Literature, Presidency College, Calcutta, 1963. *Contributions to:* New Voices, anthology; La Poésie; Sight and Sound. *Honour:* Short-listed, All India Poetry Contest, 1986. *Address:* 26 Newton Rd, No. 07-03, Newton View 307 957 Singapore.

RAY, David (Eugene); b. 20 May 1932, Sapulpa, OK, USA. Prof. of English Emeritus; Poet; Writer. m. Suzanne Judy Morrish, 21 Feb. 1970, 1 s., 3 d. *Education:* BA, 1952, MA, 1957, University of Chicago. *Appointments:* Instructor, Wright Junior College, 1957–58, Northern Illinois University 1958–60; Asst Prof., Reed College, Portland, OR, 1964–66; Lecturer, University of Iowa, 1969–70; Visiting Assoc. Prof., Bowling Green State University, 1970–71; Ed., New Letters Magazine, 1971–85; Prof. of English, 1971–95, Prof. Emeritus, 1995–, University of Missouri, Kansas City; Visiting Prof., Syracuse University, 1978–79, University of Rajasthan, India, 1981–82; Exchange Prof., University of Otago, New Zealand, 1987; Visiting Fellow, University of Western Australia, 1991; Senior Acad. Prof., University of Arizona, 1996–. *Publications:* X-Rays, 1965; Dragging the Main and Other Poems, 1968; A Hill in Oklahoma, 1972; Gathering Firewood: New Poems and Selected, 1974; Enough of Flying: Poems Inspired by the Ghazals of Ghalib, 1977; The Tramp's Cup, 1978; The Farm in Calabria and Other Poems, 1979; The Touched Life, 1982; On Wednesday I Cleaned Out My Wallet, 1985; Elysium in the Halls of Hell, 1986; Sam's Book, 1987; The Maharani's New Wall, 1987; Not Far From the River, 1990; Wool Highways, 1993; Kangaroo Paws, 1995; Heartstones: New and Selected Poems, 1998; Demons in the Diner, 1999; One Thousand Years, 2002. Short Stories: The Mulberries of Mingo, 1978. *Contributions to:* Journals and newspapers. *Honours:* William Carlos Williams Awards, 1979, 1993; PEN Syndicated Fiction Awards, 1982–86; Bernice Jennings Award for Traditional Poetry, Amelia Magazine, 1987; Maurice English Poetry Award, 1988; National Poetry Award, Passaic Community College, 1989; First Prize, Stanley Hanks Memorial Contest, St Louis Poetry Centre, 1990; New England Poetry Club Daniel Varoujan Award, 1996; New Millennium Poetry Award, 1997; Allen Ginsberg Poetry Award, Poetry Centre, Paterson, 1997; Explorations magazine Poetry Award, 1997; Amelia Magazine Long Poem Award, 1998; Richard Snyder Memorial Prize, 1999; Flyway Magazine Poetry Award, 2000; Nuclear Age Peace Foundation Poetry Award, 2001. *Memberships:* Acad. of American Poets; PEN; Poetry Society of America. *Address:* 2033 E 10th St, Tucson, AZ 85719, USA. *E-mail:* djray@gci-net.com. *Website:* www.davidraypoet.com.

RAY, Suzanne Judy; b. 20 Aug. 1939, Sussex, England. m. David E Ray, 21 Feb. 1970. Poet; Writer; Photographer. *Education:* BA Honours, University of Southampton, 1960. *Appointments:* Secretary, Transition Magazine, Kampala, Uganda, 1965–67; Assoc. Ed., New Letters Magazine, 1971–85; Producer, New Letters on the Air, 1982–86; Exec. Dir, The Writer's Place, Kansas City, 1992–95. *Publications:* Pebble Rings, 1980; The Jaipur Sketchbook: Impressions of India, 1991; Pigeons in the Chandeliers, 1993; Fathers: A Collection of Poems (co-ed.), 1997. *Contributions to:* American Voice; Helicon Nine; New Letters; Paterson Literary Review; Poet and Critic; Poetry Review; West Branch; Cream City Review; Harbor Review; Writers Forum; Anthology of Missouri Women Writers; Getting from Here to There; Tanzania on Tuesday. *Membership:* Poetry Society of America. *Address:* 2033 E 10th St, Tucson, AZ 85719, USA.

RAZ, Athar; b. 25 May 1935, India. Teacher; Poet. m. Zahra, 27 Jan. 1970. *Education:* BSc, Honours; MA. *Appointments:* Mathematics Teacher; Pres., Asian Writer's Guild, UK, 1995. *Publications:* The Bud and the Ray; Murgh e Dil; Khanda e Baija; The Yellow Shroud; Life, Like a Candle; Journey into My Existance, 1997. *Contributions to:* Mostly Asian literary magazines in India and Pakistan. *Honours:* Pakistan Writers Guild and Urdu Tarraqui Board Award; Poem of the Year Award, International Poetry Asscn, 1995; Pakistan Pres.'s Award for Children, 1997, for Poetry, 1998. *Address:* 21 Colwood Gardens, Colliers Wood, London SW19 2DS, England.

READING, Peter; b. 27 July 1946, Liverpool, England. Poet. m. (1) Diana Gilbert, 1968, divorced, 1 d., (2) Deborah Jackson, 1996, divorced, (3) Penelope Hamblen, 2002. *Education:* BA, Liverpool College of Art, 1967. *Appointments:* Lecturer, Dept of Art History, Liverpool College of Art, 1968–70; Fellowship, Sunderland Polytechnic, 1981–83; Writer-in-Residence, University of East Anglia, 1997; Lannon Foundation Literary Residency, Texas, 1998–99. *Publications:* Water and Waste, 1970; For the Municipality's Elderly, 1974; The Prison Cell and Barrel Mystery, 1976; Nothing for Anyone, 1977; Fiction, 1979; Tom O'Bedlam's Beauties, 1981; Diplopic, 1983; 5 x 5 x 5 x 5 x 5, 1983; C, 1984; Ukulele Music, 1985; Stet, 1986; Essential Reading, 1986; Final Demands, 1988; Perduta Gente, 1989; Shitheads, 1989; Evagatory, 1992; 3 in 1, 1992; Last Poems, 1993; Eschatological, 1996; Collected Poems 1970–96, 1996; Work in Regress, 1997; Chinoiserie, 1997; O B, 1999; Marfan, 1999; untitled, 2001; Faunal, 2002. *Honours:* Cholmondeley Award for Poetry, 1978; First Dylan Thomas Award, 1983; Whitbread Award for Poetry, 1986; Lannan Foundation Literary Fellowship Award, USA, 1990. *Membership:* RSL, fellow. *Address:* Highgreen, Tarset, Northumberland, NE48 1RP, England.

REANEY, James (Crerar); b. 1 Sept. 1926, South Easthope, Ontario, Canada. Prof.; Poet; Dramatist. m. 29 Dec. 1951, 2 s., 1 d. *Education:* BA, 1948, MA, 1949, University of Toronto. *Appointments:* Faculty, University of Manitoba, Winnipeg, 1948–60; Prof., Middlesex College, University of Western Ontario, 1960–. *Publications:* Poetry: The Red Heart, 1949; A Suit of Nettles, 1958; Twelve Letters to a Small Town, 1962; The Dance of Death at London, 1963; Poems, 1972; Selected Shorter and Longer Poems, 1975–76; Performance Poems, 1990. Plays: Night Blooming Cereus, 1959; The Killdeer, 1960; One Masque, 1960; The Sun and the Moon, 1965; Listen to the Wind, 1966; The Canada Tree, 1967; Genesis, 1968; Masque, 1972; The Donnellys: A Trilogy, 1973–75; Baldoon, 1976; King Whistle, 1979; Antler River, 1980; Gyroscope, 1981; I, the Parade, 1982; The Canadian Brothers, 1983; Alice Through the Looking Glass (adaptation of Lewis Carroll's book), 1994. Opera Libretti: The Shivaree (music by John Beckwith), 1982; Crazy to Kill (music by John Beckwith). Other: The Box Social and Other Stories, 1996. *Contributions to:* Books, journals and periodicals. *Honours:* Governor-General's Awards, 1949, 1958, 1963; University of Alberta Award for Letters, 1974; Order of Canada, 1975. *Memberships:* Asscn of Canadian University Teachers, pres., 1959–60; Playwright's Union of Canada; League of Canadian Poets. *Literary Agent:* Dean Cooke, Danforth Ave, Ste 201, Toronto, ON M4K 1P1, Canada. *Address:* 276 Huvon St, London, ON N6A 3K7, Canada.

RECTIONS, Edward. See: SHEAHAN, Matthew.

RECTOR, Liam; b. 21 Nov. 1949, Washington, DC, USA. Workshop Dir; Poetry Ed.; Poet; Writer. m. Tree Swenson, 1 d. *Education:* MA, Poetry, Writing Seminars, Johns Hopkins University, 1978; MPA, Administration, Kennedy School of Government, Harvard University, 1992. *Appointments:* Dir of Poetry Programs, Folger Shakespeare Library, 1978–80, 1983; Program Assoc., Co-Dir, Acad. of American Poets, 1980–81; Program Specialist, Literature Program, National Endowment for the Arts, 1983–85; Exec. Dir, Associated Writing Programs, 1986–91; Founder and Dir, Bennington Writing Seminars, Dir, Bennington Summer Writing Workshops, Bennington College, 1991–; Poetry Ed., Harvard Magazine, 1994–96; Columnist, American Poetry Review, 2001–; Various poetry readings, lectures and panels at colleges, universities and community centres among others, USA, Ireland, Yugoslavia. *Publications:* The Sorrow of Architecture, 1984; American Prodigal, 1994. Editor: The Day I Was Older: On the Poetry of Donald Hall, 1989. *Contributions to:* Reviews and journals. *Honours:* National Endowment for the Arts Fellowship, 1980; Kenan Grant, Phillips Acad., Andover, Massachusetts, 1982; Postgraduate Fellow, Vermont College, Montpelier, Vermont, 1984; Guggenheim Fellowship, 1985–86. *Memberships:* Associated Writing Programs, board of dirs, 1995–; PEN New England, council and freedom-to-write committee, 1994–. *Address:* 300 E 34th St, No. 3-J, New York, NY 10016, USA.

REDDY, T. Vasudeva; b. 21 Dec. 1943, Mittapalem, India. Lecturer in English; Writer; Poet. m. 5 Nov. 1970, 2 s., 1 d. *Education:* BSc, 1963; MA, English, 1966; PGDTE, 1983; PhD, English, 1985. *Publications:* When Grief Rains (poems), 1982; The Vultures (novel), 1983; The Broken Rhythms (poems), 1987; Jane Austen, 1987; Jane Austen: Matrix of Matrimony, 1987; The Fleeting (poems), 1989. *Contributions to:* Journals and magazines. *Memberships:* International Poets Acad., Madras; World Poetry Society, CA. *Address:* Narasingapuram Post, Via Chandragiri, Pin 517 102, AP, India.

REDGROVE, Peter (William); b. 2 Jan. 1932, Kingston-on-Thames, Surrey, England. Analytical Psychologist; Poet; Writer. m. (1), 1 d., (2) Penelope Shuttle, 2 s., 1 d. *Education:* Queens' College, Cambridge. *Appointments:* Visiting Poet, University of Buffalo, 1961–62; Gregory Fellow in Poetry, University of Leeds, 1962–65; O'Connor Prof. of Literature, Colgate University, 1974–75; Writer-at-Large, North Cornwall Arts, 1988. *Publications:* Poetry: The Collector, 1960; The Nature of Cold Weather, 1961; At the White Monument, 1963; The Force, 1966; Penguin Modern Poets 11, 1968; Work in Progress, 1969; Dr Faust's Sea-Spiral Spirit, 1972; Three Pieces for Voices, 1972; The Hermaphrodite Album (with Penelope Shuttle), 1973; Sons of My Skin: Selected Poems, 1975; From Every Chink of the Art, 1977; Ten Poems, 1977; The Weddings at Nether Powers, 1979; The Apple Broadcast, 1981; The Working of Water, 1984; The Man Named East, 1985; The Mudlark Poems and Grand Buveur, 1986; In the Hall of the Saurians, 1987; The Moon Disposes: Poems 1954–1987, 1987; The First Earthquake, 1989; Dressed as for a Tarot Pack, 1990; Under the Reservoir, 1992; The Laborators, 1993; The Cyclopean Mistress, 1993; My Father's Trapdoors, 1994; Abyssophone, 1995; Assembling a Ghost, 1996; The Best of Redgrove, 1996; Orchard End, 1997; What the Black Mirror Saw, 1997; Selected Poems, 1999. Fiction: In the Country of the Skin, 1973; The Terrors of Dr Treviles (with Penelope Shuttle), 1974; The Glass Cottage, 1976; The Sleep of the Great Hypnotist, 1979; The God of Glass, 1979; The Beekeepers, 1980; The Facilitators, 1982; Tales from Grimm, 1989. Other: Plays for stage, radio and television. Non-Fiction: The Wise Wound (with Penelope Shuttle), 1978; The Black Goddess and the Sixth Sense, 1987; Alchemy for Women (with Penelope Shuttle), 1995. *Honours:* George Rylands' Verse-Speaking Prize, 1954; Poetry Book Society Choices, 1961, 1966, 1979, 1981; 5 Arts Council Awards, 1969–82; Guardian Fiction Prize, 1973; Prudence Farmer Poetry Award, 1977; Cholmondeley Award, 1985; Queen's Gold Medal for Poetry, 1996; Hon. DLitt, University of

Sheffield, 2001. *Membership:* RSL, fellow. *Address:* c/o David Higham Assocs, 5–8 Lower John St, Golden Sq., London W1R 4HA, England.

REECE, Paul Charles; b. 20 June 1960, Manchester, England. Poet; Writer. *Education:* Tameside College, Manchester. *Publications:* Bard Wire Rainbow; The Day Before the Meteor Came. Other: Children's stories. *Contributions to:* Anthologies, newspapers and magazines. *Honour:* Prize, National Peace Foundation Poetry Competition. *Address:* 50 Town Lane, Denton, Manchester M34 1AE, England.

REED, Ishmael (Scott); b. 22 Feb. 1938, Chattanooga, Tennessee, USA. Writer; Poet; Publisher; Ed.; Teacher. m. (1) Priscilla Rose, 1960, divorced 1970, 1 d., (2) Carla Blank-Reed, 1970, 1 d. *Education:* University of Buffalo, 1956–60. *Appointments:* Lecturer, University of California at Berkeley, 1967–, University of Washington, 1969–70, State University of New York at Buffalo, 1975, 1979, University of Arkansas, 1982, Columbia University, 1983, Harvard University, 1987, University of California at Santa Barbara, 1988; Chair. and Pres., Yardbird Publishing Company, 1971–; Dir, Reed Cannon and Johnson Communications, 1973–; Visiting Prof., 1979, Assoc. Fellow, 1983–, Calhoun House, Yale University; Visiting Prof., Dartmouth College, 1980; Co-Founder (with Al Young) and Ed., Quilt Magazine, 1981–; Assoc. Fellow, Harvard University Signet Society, 1987–. *Publications:* Fiction: The Free-Lance Pallbearers, 1967; Yellow Black Radio Broke-Down, 1969; Mumbo-Jumbo, 1972; The Last Days of Louisiana Red, 1974; Flight to Canada, 1976; The Terrible Twos, 1982; Reckless Eyeballing, 1986; The Terrible Threes, 1989; Japanese by Spring, 1993. Poetry: Catechism of a Neoamerican Hoodoo Church, 1970; Conjure: Selected Poems 1963–1970, 1972; Chattanooga, 1973; A Secretary to the Spirits, 1978; New and Collected Poems, 1988. Other: The Rise, Fall and...? of Adam Clayton Powell (with others), 1967; Shrovetide in Old New Orleans, 1978; God Made Alaska for the Indians, 1982; Cab Calloway Stands in for the Moon, 1986; Ishmael Reed: An Interview, 1990; Airin' Dirty Laundry, 1993; Multi-America, 1996. Editor: 19 Necromancers from Now, 1970; Yardbird Reader, 5 vols, 1971–77; Yardbird Lives! (with Al Young), 1978; Calafia: The California Poetry, 1979; Quilt 2-3 (with Al Young), 2 vols, 1981–82; Writin' is Fightin': Thirty-Seven Years of Boxing on Paper, 1988; The Before Columbus Foundation Fiction Anthology: Selections from the American Book Awards, 1980–1990 (with Kathryn Trueblood and Shawn Wong), 1992; The Reed Reader, 2000. *Honours:* National Endowment for the Arts Grant, 1974; Rosenthal Foundation Award, 1975; Guggenheim Fellowship, 1975; American Acad. of Arts and Letters Award, 1975; Michaux Award, 1978. *Membership:* Before Columbus Foundation, pres., 1976–. *Address:* c/o Ellis J Freedman, 415 Madison Ave, New York, NY 10017, USA.

REED, Jeremy; b. 1951, Jersey, Channel Islands. Poet; Writer. *Education:* BA, University of Essex, Colchester. *Publications:* Target, 1972; Saints and Psychotics: Poems 1973–74, 1974; Vicissitudes, 1974; Diseased Near Deceased, 1975; Emerald Cat, 1975; Ruby Onocentaur, 1975; Blue Talaria, 1976; Count Bluebeard, 1976; Jacks in His Corset, 1978; Walk on Through, 1980; Bleecker Street, 1980; No Refuge Here, 1981; A Long Shot to Heaven, 1982; A Man Afraid, 1982; By the Fisheries, 1984; Elegy for Senta, 1985; Skies, 1985; Border Pass, 1986; Selected Poems, 1987; Engaging Form, 1988; The Escaped Image, 1988; Nineties, 1990; Dicing for Pearls, 1990; Red-Haired Android, 1992. Fiction: The Lipstick Boys, 1984; Blue Rock, 1987; Madness: The Price of Poetry, 1990. *Honour:* Somerset Maugham Award, 1985. *Address:* c/o Jonathan Cape Ltd, 20 Vauxhall Bridge Rd, London SW1V 2SA, England.

REED, Judith; b. 18 Feb. 1947, Waycross, GA, USA. Poet; Musician. m., 1 s. *Education:* Georgia Southwestern College, Americus; Christian Writers' Guild Course, La Canada, CA. *Contributions to:* Anthologies, including: American Poetry Anthology, 1987; As a Ship Saileth; Best New Poetry of 1987; If The Birds Can Sing; America at the Millennium, 2000; Would You Still Believe?; Newspapers and journals. *Honours:* Several poetry nominations. *Address:* 110 Silva Terra Dr., Wilmington, NC 28412, USA.

REES, (Mary) Anne; b. 27 Nov. 1952, Norwich, Norfolk, England. Poet; Writer. m. Philip Rees, 4 Jan. 1975, 1 s., 2 d. *Education:* BA, English Language and Literature, Lady Margaret Hall, Oxford, 1974. *Contributions to:* Ambit; Orbis; Rialto; Poetry Wales; Writing Women; Staple; Poetry and Audience; Psychopoetica. *Honour:* Reader's Award, Orbis, 1991; Runner-up, twice, Staple First Editions Annual Competitions. *Address:* 23 Cassiobury Rd, London E17 7JD, England.

REEVE, F(ranklin) D(olier); b. 18 Sept. 1928, Philadelphia, Pennsylvania, USA. Emeritus Prof. of Letters; Writer; Poet; Trans.; Ed. m. Laura C. Stevenson, 7 c. *Education:* PhD, Columbia University, 1958. *Appointments:* Lecturer, Columbia University, 1952–61; Prof. of Letters, Wesleyan University, 1962–2002; Visiting Prof., University of Oxford, 1964, Columbia University, 1988; Visiting Lecturer, Yale University, 1972–86; Ed., Poetry Review, 1982–84. *Publications:* Five Short Novels by Turgenev (trans.), 1961; Anthology of Russian Plays (trans.), 1961, 1963; Aleksandr Blok: Between Image and Idea, 1962; Robert Frost in Russia, 1964; The Russian Novel, 1966; In the Silent Stones, 1968; The Red Machines, 1968; Just Over the Border, 1969; The Brother, 1971; The Blue Cat, 1972; White Colors, 1973; Nightway, 1987; The White Monk, 1989; The Garden (trans.), 1990; Concrete

Music, 1992; The Trouble with Reason (trans.), 1993; A Few Rounds of Old Maid and Other Stories, 1995; The Blue Boat on the St Anne, 1999; The Moon and Other Failures, 1999; A World You Haven't Seen, 2001; The Urban Stampede and Other Poems, 2002. *Contributions to:* Journals and periodicals. *Honours:* American Acad. of Arts and Letters Award, 1970; PEN Syndicated Fiction Awards, 1985, 1986; Golden Rose, New England Poetry Society, 1994. *Memberships:* Pettee Memorial Library, trustee; Marlboro Review, advisory board; New England Poetry Society, board dir. *Address:* PO 14, Wilmington, VT 05363, USA.

REEVE, Richard E.; b. 6 Aug. 1930, London, England. Lecturer; Writer; Poet. m. Amaryllys Lynn Reeve, 24 April 1994, 2 d. *Education:* DLitt, BA, Honours, Diploma. *Publications:* Through a Glass Darkly, 1997; Sentience, 1998; Reflections of the Mind, 1998. *Contributions to:* Anthologies. *Honours:* Pres.'s Award for Literary Excellence, Iliad Press, 1997; Third Place, Kings Lynn Regional Ottakar's Poetry Competition, 1997. *Address:* 5 Trinity Quay, Page Stair Lane, Kings Lynn, Norfolk P30 1NQ, England.

REEVES, Daniel. See: LIDDY, James.

REHM, Pam; b. 21 Oct. 1967, Camp Hill, Pennsylvania, USA. Poet. m. Lew Daly, 27 June 1991, 1 s. *Education:* BA, English, Shippensburg University, Pennsylvania, 1989; MFA, Creative Writing and Poetry, Brown University, RI, 1991. *Publications:* Piecework, 1992; Pollux, 1992; The Garment in Which No One Had Slept, 1993; To Give It Up, 1995. *Contributions to:* Apex of the M; First Intensity; To; Chicago Review; Notus. *Honour:* National Poetry Series Winner, 1994. *Address:* 331 Herkimer St, Buffalo, NY 14213, USA.

REICH, Asher; b. 5 Sept. 1937, Jerusalem, Palestine. Poet; Writer; Ed. *Education:* Literature, University of Jerusalem. *Appointments:* Consulting Ed., Proza Magazine, 1977–79; Ed., The Literary Magazine, Israel, 1979–90. *Publications:* Poetry: 10 vols, 1963–92. Other: Reminiscences of an Amnesiac, 1993. *Contributions to:* Anthologies and journals worldwide. *Honours:* Anna Frank Prize, 1961; 5 Writer's Guild Prizes, 1972–85; Tel-Aviv Prizes, 1973, 1980, 1988; Chounsky Prize, 1977; Iowa International Writing Program Grant, 1985; Israeli Publishers Organization Poetry Prize, 1987; Deutscher Akademischer Austauschdienst Grant, Berlin, 1990. *Memberships:* Hebrew Writer's Asscn; PEN Club, Israel; Writer's Guild.

REID, Alastair; b. 22 March 1926, Whithorn, Wigtonshire, Scotland. Writer; Trans.; Poet. *Education:* MA, University of St Andrews, Scotland, 1949. *Appointments:* Visiting Lecturer at universities in the UK and USA; Staff Writer, Correspondent, New Yorker, 1959–. *Publications:* To Lighten my House, 1953; Oddments, Inklings, Omens, Moments, 1959; Passwords: Places, Poems, Preoccupations, 1963; Mother Goose in Spanish, 1967; Corgi Modern Poets in Focus 3, 1971; Weathering: Poems and Translations, 1978; Whereabouts: Notes on Being a Foreigner, 1987; An Alastair Reid Reader, 1995. Other: Stories for children and trans. from Spanish of Pablo Neruda, Jorge Luis Borges and other writers. *Honour:* Scottish Arts Council Award, 1979. *Address:* c/o New Yorker, 20 W 43rd St, NY 10036, USA.

REID, Sharleigh. See: MONEYSMITH, Carol Louise Giesbrecht.

REIFF, Andrew Edwin, (Eagin Arthur); b. 25 July 1941, Philadelphia, Pennsylvania, USA. Poet; Writer; Teacher. m. Patricia Ruth Carlson, 28 Sep 1979, 2 s., 1 d. *Education:* BS, Drexel University, 1964; MA, University of Iowa, 1966; PhD, University of Texas. *Appointments:* Instructor of English, Fayetteville University, 1966–68; Assoc. Prof. of English, Bishop College, 1981–86; Ed., Red Rose, Dallas, 1983–85. *Publications:* A Calendar of Poems, 1975; The Taliessin Poems, 1983; Native Texans, 1984; Planet 3: Help Send This Book Into Space, 1985; A Poetical Reading of The Psalms of David, 1985; The New Earth of Char Beamish, 1994; A Whale Tale of Dolphy, 1994. *Contributions to:* Several publications. *Address:* 2645 E Willetta, Phoenix, AZ 85008, USA.

REIN, Evgeny Borisovich; b. 29 Dec. 1935, Leningrad, Russia. Poet; Writer. m. Nadejda Rein, 21 Jan. 1989, 1 s. *Education:* Graduated, Mechanical Engineer, Leningrad Technical Institute, 1959. *Publications:* The Names of Bridges, 1984; Shore Line, 1989; The Darkness of Mirrors, 1989; Irretrievable Day, 1991; Counter-Clockwise, 1992; Nezjnosmo, 1993; Selected Poems, 1993; The Prognostication, 1994; The Top-booty, 1995; The Others, 1996; The News Stage of the Life of The Moscow Beau Monde, 1997; Balkony, 1998. *Contributions to:* Russian, European, and US magazines. *Honours:* Peterburg's Prize of Arts, Tsarskoye Selo, 1995; State Prize of Russia Literature and Art, 1996. *Memberships:* Russian Writers Union; Russian PEN Centre. *Address:* 125057 Moscow, Leningradsky Prospect, 75, Apt 167, Russia.

REISS, James; b. 11 July 1941, New York, NY, USA. Prof. of English; Poet; Writer; Ed. m. Barbara Eve Klevs, 21 June 1964, divorced 1995, 2 d. *Education:* BA, English, 1963, MA, English, 1964, University of Chicago. *Appointments:* Instructor, 1965–69, Asst Prof., 1969–73, Assoc. Prof., 1973–81, Prof., 1981–, of English, Miami University, Oxford, Ohio; Visiting Poet and Assoc. Prof. of English, Queens College of the City University of New York, 1975–76; Ed.,

Miami University Press, 1992–; Numerous poetry readings. *Publications:* Self Interviews: James Dickey (co-ed.), 1970; The Breathers (poems), 1974; Express (poems), 1983; The Parable of Fire (poems), 1996; Ten Thousand Good Mornings (poems), 2001. *Contributions to:* Many anthologies and periodicals. *Honours:* First Prizes, Acad. of American Poets, 1960, 1962; MacDowell Colony Fellowships, 1970, 1974, 1976, 1977; Two Borestone Mountain Poetry Awards, 1974; Consuelo Ford Award, 1974, Lucille Medwick Award, 1989, Poetry Society of America; National Endowment for the Arts Fellowship, 1974–75; Bread Loaf Fellowship, 1975; Creative Artists Public Service Awards, New York State Council on the Arts, 1975–76; Ohio Arts Council Grants, 1980, 1981; Nancy Dasher Book Award, College English Asscn of Ohio, 1984; Dorland Mountain Arts Colony Fellow, 1991, 1993, 1999; James Laughlin Award, Acad. of American Poets, 1995; Pushcart Prize, 1996; Pulitzer *Prize in Poetry* nomination, 2002. *Memberships:* Acad. of American Poets; Poetry Society of America. *Address:* c/o Dept of English, 326 Bachelor Hall, Miami University, Oxford, OH 45056, USA.

RENAUD, (Ernest) Hamilton Jacques; b. 10 Nov. 1943, Montréal, QC, Canada. Author; Poet; Trans.; Speaker. 2 s., 1 d. *Appointments:* Critic and Researcher, Radio Canada, 1965–67; Reporter, Metro-Express, Montréal, 1966; Critic, Le Devoir, Montréal, 1975–78; Teacher, Creative Writing Workshop, University of Québec, 1980–89; Spokesman, Equality Party, 1989; Researcher, Senator Jacques Hebert, 1990. *Publications:* 20 books, including: Electrodes (poems), 1962; Le Casse (stories), 1964; Clandestines (novel), 1980; L'espace du Diable (stories), 1989; Les Cycles du Scorpion (poems), 1989; La Constellation du Bouc Emissaire (non-fiction), 1993. *Contributions to:* Various publications. *Address:* 205 Ivy Crescent 3, Ottawa, Ontario K1M 1X9, Canada.

RENNIE, Barbara Muriel; b. 30 June 1930, England. Poet; Writer; Public Speaker. m. Ian Malcolm Rennie, 14 April 1954, 2 s., 2 d. *Education:* BA, Honours External London degree in English, UCSW, Exeter, 1951. *Publications:* The Sky Wandered By, 1983; As If, 1990; The 50-Minute Hour, 1996. *Contributions to:* Orbis; Envoi; Weyfarers; Headlock. *Honours:* Julia Cairns Awards, Society of Women Writers and Journalists; Assoc. Mem., Society of Authors; London Writers' Circle; Phoenix Poets, London; Elmbridge Writers' Workshop, chair, 1982–92. *Address:* 1 New Rd, Stoke Fleming, Dartmouth, Devon TQ6 0NR, England.

REPLANSKY, Naomi; b. 23 May 1918, New York, NY, USA. Poet. *Education:* BA, University of California, Los Angeles, 1956. *Appointment:* Poet-in-Residence, Pitzer College, Claremont, CA, 1981. *Publications:* Ring Song, 1952; Twenty-One Poems, Old and New, 1988; The Dangerous World, New and Selected Poems, 1994. *Contributions to:* Ploughshares; Missouri Review; Nation; Feminist Studies. *Honour:* Nominated for National Book Award, 1952. *Memberships:* PEN American Center; Poetry Society of America. *Address:* 711 Amsterdam Ave, No. 8E, New York, NY 10025, USA.

REPOSA, Carol Jane Coffee; b. 18 Oct. 1943, San Diego, CA, USA. Asst Prof. of English; Poet. m. Richare Eugene Reposa, 30 Dec. 1967, divorced 5 Dec. 1985, 1 s., 1 d. *Education:* BA, 1965, MA, 1968, University of Texas at Austin. *Appointments:* Instructor in English, Memorial High School, 1969, Trinity University, 1980–82; Instructor in English, 1969–70, 1982–89, Asst Prof. of English, 1989–, San Antonio College. *Publication:* At the Border: Winter Lights, 1989. *Contributions to:* Texas Observer; River Sedge; Passages North; Inlet; Pax; San Jose Studies; Trinity Review; Concho River Review; Stone Drum; Descant; Imagine; Artists' Alliance Review; Wind; English in Texas. *Memberships:* Poetry Society of America; National Council of Teachers of English; South Central MLA; Popular Culture Asscn; Council of College Teachers of English; Texas Asscn of Creative Writing Teachers. *Address:* 263 W Hermine, San Antonio, TX 78212, USA.

RETI, Ingrid; b. 16 Sept. 1927, USA. Teacher; Poet. m. Jerry W Hull, 5 Jan. 1991, 1 s., 1 d. *Education:* BA, American Studies, 1971, MA, English, 1975, California State University. *Appointments:* Instructor, California Polytechnic State University, Extended Education, 1982–. *Publications:* Ephemera, 1987; Echoes of Silence, 1989. *Contributions to:* National Forum; Phoenix; Pinehurst Journal; Broomstick; Thirteen; Coffeehouse Poets Quarterly; Perceptions; Iowa Woman; Petroglyph; Portlandia. *Memberships:* Poets and Writers; Steinbeck Research Center. *Address:* 1650 Descanso St, San Luis Obispo, CA 93405, USA.

REVERE, Michael Rigsby; b. 26 July 1951, East Point, GA, USA. Writer; Poet; Musician; Music Teacher. Partner, Judy Revere, 1 s., 1 d. *Education:* Southwestern Community College, Sylva, NC. *Appointments:* Guest lectures, poetry readings and workshops. *Publications:* Spirit Happy (poems), 1974; The Milky Way Poems, 1976; Shotgun Vision (poems), 1977; Fire and Rain (poems), 1998. *Contributions to:* Journals and periodicals. *Address:* 17 Arkansas Trail, Cullowhee, NC 28723, USA. *E-mail:* aluri@netins.net.

REYES, Carlos; b. 2 June 1935, Marshfield, Missouri, USA. Poet; Teacher. m. (1) Barbara Ann Hollingsworth, 13 Sept. 1958, divorced 1973, 1 s., 3 d., (2) Karen Ann Stoner, 21 May 1979, divorced 1992, (3) Elizabeth Atly, 27 Dec. 1993. *Education:* BA, University of Oregon, 1961; MA, ABD, University of Arizona, 1965. *Appointments:* Governor's Advisory Committee on the Arts, Oregon, 1973; Poet to the City of Portland, 1978; Poet-in-Residence, various public schools in Oregon and Washington; Ed., Hubbub, 1982–90, Ar Mhuin Na Muicea (journal of Irish literature, music, current events), 1995. *Publications:* The Prisoner, 1973; The Shingle Weaver's Journal, 1980; At Doolin Quay, 1982; Nightmarks, 1990; A Suitcase Full of Crows, 1995; Poemas de la Isla (trans. of Josefina de la Torre), 2000; Puertas Abiertas/Open Doors (bilingual edn of poems by Edwin Madrid), 2000; Obra Poética Completa de Jorge Carrera Andrade/Complete Poetic Works of Jorge Carrera Andrade (bilingual edn), 2002. *Contributions to:* Various journals and magazines. *Honours:* Oregon Arts Commission Individual Artist Fellowship, 1982; Yaddo Fellowship, 1984; Fundación Valparaíso, Mojácar, Spain, fellow, 1998. *Memberships:* Portland Poetry Festival Inc, board, 1974–84; PEN Northwest, co-chair, 1992–93; Mountain Writers Series, board, 1996–2000. *Address:* 3222 NE Schuyler, Portland, OR 97212, USA.

REYNOLDS, Susan Helen; b. 28 May 1955, Manchester, England. Tutor; Poet. m. Michael John Halstead, 22 Aug. 1981, diss 1990, 1 s., 1 d. *Education:* MA, Lady Margaret Hall, Oxford, 1979. *Contributions to:* Anthologies, reviews, and journals. *Honour:* Third Prize, National Poetry Competition. *Memberships:* English Goethe Society; Oxford University Classical Society; Poetry Society; Women in German Studies. *Address:* 12 Marriott Close, Harefields, Oxford OX2 8NT, England.

RHINE, David; b. 4 Dec. 1950, Lebanon, Pennsylvania, USA. Poet. *Education:* University of Maryland, 1968–72. *Publication:* Poems from a Live Nightmare, 1991. *Contributions to:* Iota Poetry Quarterly; White Rose; Chiron Review; Dan River Anthology; Nihilistic Review; Tucumcari Literary Review; Journal of Sister Moon; Snake River Reflections; Writers Exchange; Brownbag Press; Matic Poetry Quarterly. *Address:* Calder Sq., PO Box 10445, State College, PA 16805, USA.

RIACH, Alan Scott; b. 1 Aug. 1957, Airdrie, Lanarkshire, Scotland. Poet. m. Raewyn Maree Garton, 12 Sept. 1992, 2 s. *Education:* BA, converted to MA, Churchill College, University of Cambridge, 1976–79; PhD, Dept of Scottish Literature, University of Glasgow, 1979–84; University of Waikato, New Zealand. *Appointments:* Lecturer, Advanced Lecturer, Senior Lecturer, Dept of English, University of Waikato, 1990–99. *Publications:* For What It Is, 1988; Hugh MacDiarmid's Epic Poetry, 1991; This Folding Map, 1990; An Open Return, 1991; First and Last Songs, 1995; From the Vision of Hell: An Extract of Dante, 1998. General Editor: The Collected Works of Hugh MacDiarmid, 1992–. *Contributions to:* New Writing Scotland; Poetry New Zealand; Landfall; Sport; Verse; Chapman; Gairfish; Westerly; Island; Poetry Australia; Edinburgh Review; Words. *Memberships:* University of Waikato Scottish Studies Asscn, secretary, 1991–; Asscn for Scottish Literary Studies. *Address:* c/o Dept of English, University of Waikato, PO Box 3105, Hamilton, New Zealand.

RIBBLE, Ronald George; b. 5 May 1937, West Reading, PA, USA. Lecturer in Psychology; Writer; Poet. m. Catalina Valenzuela Torres, 30 Sept. 1961, 2 s., 1 d. *Education:* BS, Electrical Engineering, 1968, MA, Electrical Engineering, 1969, MA, Psychology, 1985, PhD, 1986, Psychology, University of Missouri, Columbia. *Appointments:* Active Duty, US Air Force, 1956–81; Lecturer, University of Texas at San Antonio, 1989; Publisher, Troubadour: Journal of Lyric Poetry, 1997–99. *Contributions to:* 150 poems in various publications, 1986–2000. *Honours:* Honours: Poetry Award, International Platform Asscn, 1995; Roberts Memorial Award for Lyric Poetry, Lyric Journal, 1995; Pushcart nominee, 1999. *Memberships:* Many professional organizations. *Address:* 14024 N Hills Village Dr., San Antonio, TX 78249, USA.

RICARD, Charles; b. 9 Jan. 1922, Gap, France. Writer; Poet. m. J Balmens, 28 July 1951. *Education:* Professeur de Lettres. *Publications:* Fiction: Les puits, 1967; La dernière des révolutions, 1968; A propos d'un piano cassé, 1977; Le Pot-à-Chien, 1979; Alerte rouge aux cités soleils, 1985; Le mercredi des Cendres, 1986; Le Chemin des Oiseaux, 1991; Rédé, 1992; Les Mystères du Villaret, 1993. Poetry: Si j'avais su, 1960; Je voudrais, 1963; Les ombres du chemin, 1964. *Contributions to:* Magazines and journals. *Honours:* Gold Medal, International Competition of Clubs, Côte d'Azur; Gold Medal, International Competition, Lutèce, 1976; Prix Diamant, 1985; Prix du Vimeu, 1986. *Memberships:* Acad. of the French Provinces; Gens de Lettres de France, assoc.; Society of French Poets, assoc. *Address:* 20 rue du Super-Gap, 05000 Gap, France.

RICE, John; b. 12 March 1948, Glasgow, Scotland. Arts Officer; Poet; Writer; Photographer. m. Clare Rice, Oct. 1970, 2 s., 1 d. *Education:* St Michael's College. *Appointments:* Literature Officer, South East Arts; Dir, Kent Literature Festival, Metropole Arts Centre, Folkestone; Cultural Projects Man., Kent County Council; Poet-in-Residence, Isle of Man Literature Festival, Lowdham Book Festival, Nottingham, Sherwood Primary School, Tunbridge Wells, Cornwallis Secondary School, Maidstone. *Publications:* Butterfly Frost; Landscape, Coastscape, Dreamscape: Poetry, Prose and Photographs of Kent; Bears Don't Like Bananas; Dreaming of Dinosaurs; Down at the Dinosaur Fair; The Dream of Night Fishers: Scottish Islands in Poems and Photographs; Odd Kettle of Fish: Scottish Poems (ed.). Other: Scripts, poetry and stories for BBC Television and Radio. *Contributions to:* Periodicals and anthologies. *Membership:* Society of Kent Authors. *Address:* 47 Hendley Dr., Cranbrook,

Kent TN17 3DY, England. *E-mail:* poetjohnrice@hotmail.com. *Website:* www.poetryjohnrice.com.

RICH, Adrienne (Cecile); b. 16 May 1929, Baltimore, Maryland, USA. Prof. of English and Feminist Studies; Poet; Writer. m. Alfred H Conrad, 1953, deceased 1970, 3 s. *Education:* AB, Radcliffe College, 1951. *Appointments:* Visiting Poet, Swarthmore College, 1966–68; Adjunct Prof., Columbia University, 1967–69; Lecturer, 1968–70, Instructor, 1970–71, Asst Prof., 1971–72, Prof., 1974–75, City College of New York; Fannie Hurst Visiting Prof., Brandeis University, 1972–73; Prof. of English, Douglass College, New Brunswick, New Jersey, 1976–78; A D White Prof.-at-Large, Cornell University, 1981–85; Clark Lecturer and Distinguished Visiting Prof., Scripps College, Claremont, CA, 1983; Visiting Prof., San Jose State University, CA, 1985–86; Burgess Lecturer, Pacific Oaks College, Pasadena, CA, 1986; Prof. of English and Feminist Studies, Stanford University, 1986–93; Board of Chancellors, Acad. of American Poets, 1999–. *Publications:* Poetry: A Change of World, 1951; (Poems), 1952; The Diamond Cutters and Other Poems, 1955; Snapshots of a Daughter-in-Law: Poems 1954–1962, 1963; Necessities of Life: Poems 1962–1965, 1966; Selected Poems, 1967; Leaflets: Poems 1965–1968, 1969; The Will to Change: Poems 1968–1970, 1971; Diving into the Wreck: Poems 1971–1972, 1973; Poems Selected and New, 1975; Twenty-One Love Poems, 1976; The Dream of a Common Language: Poems 1974–1977, 1978; A Wild Patience Has Taken Me This Far: Poems 1978–1981, 1981; Sources, 1983; The Fact of a Doorframe: Poems Selected and New 1950–1984, 1984; Your Native Land, Your Life, 1986; Time's Power: Poems 1985–1988, 1989; An Atlas of the Difficult World: Poems 1988–1991, 1991; Collected Early Poems 1950–1970, 1993; Dark Fields of the Republic: Poems 1991–1995, 1995; Midnight Salvage: Poems 1995–1998, 1999; Fox: Poems 1998–2000, 2001. Other: Of Woman Born: Motherhood as Experience and Institution, 1976; Women and Honor: Some Notes on Lying, 1977; On Lies, Secrets and Silence: Selected Prose 1966–1978, 1979; Compulsory Heterosexuality and Lesbian Existence, 1980; Blood, Bread and Poetry: Selected Prose 1979–1985, 1986; What Is Found There: Notebooks on Poetry and Politics, 1993; Arts of the Possible: Essays and Conversations, 2001. *Honours:* Yale Series of Younger Poets Award, 1951; Guggenheim Fellowships, 1952, 1961; American Acad. of Arts and Letters Award, 1961; Bess Hokin Prize, 1963; Eunice Tietjens Memorial Prize, 1968; National Endowment for the Arts Grant, 1970; Shelley Memorial Award, 1971; Ingram Merrill Foundation Grant, 1973; National Book Award, 1974; Fund for Human Dignity Award, 1981; Ruth Lilly Prize, 1986; Brandeis University Creative Arts Award, 1987; Elmer Holmes Bobst Award, 1989; Commonwealth Award in Literature, 1991; Frost Silver Medal, Poetry Society of America, 1992; Los Angeles Times Book Award, 1992; Lenore Marshall/Nation Award, 1992; William Whitehead Award, 1992; Lambda Book Award, 1992; Harriet Monroe Prize, 1994; John D. and Catherine T. MacArthur Foundation Fellowship, 1994; Tanning Prize, 1996; Lannan Foundation Lifetime Achievement Award, 1999; Hon. doctorates. *Address:* c/o W W Norton & Co, 500 Fifth Ave, New York, NY 10110, USA.

RICH, Elaine Sommers; b. 8 Feb. 1926, Plevna, IN, USA. Writer; Poet. m. Ronald L Rich, 14 June 1953, 3 s., 1 d. *Education:* BA, Goshen College, 1947; MA, Michigan State University, 1950. *Appointments:* Instructor, Goshen College, 1947–49, 1950–53, Bethel College, North Newton, KS, 1953–66; Lecturer, International Christian University, Tokyo, 1971–78; Columnist, Mennonite Weekly Review, 1973–; Adviser to International Students, Bluffton College, Ohio, 1979–89; Adjunct Prof. of English, University of Findlay, Ohio, 1990–. *Publications:* Breaking Bread Together (ed.), 1958; Hannah Elizabeth, 1964; Tomorrow, Tomorrow, Tomorrow, 1966; Am I This Countryside?, 1981; Mennonite Women, 1683–1983: A Story of God's Faithfulness, 1983; Spiritual Elegance: A Biography of Pauline Krehbiel Raid, 1987; Prayers for Everyday, 1990; Walking Together in Faith (ed.), 1993; Pondered in Her Heart, 1998. *Contributions to:* Books and journals. *Memberships:* Fellowship of Reconciliation; International League for Peace and Freedom. *Address:* 112 S Spring St, Bluffton, OH 45817, USA.

RICH, Susanna Lippoczy; b. 17 Oct. 1951, USA. Prof. of English; Poet. m. Morton D Rich, 25 May 1980. *Education:* MA, Philosophy, University of North Carolina, Chapel Hill, 1978; PhD, Communications, New York University, 1987; MFA, Warren Wilson College. *Appointments:* Assoc. Prof. of English, Kean College, 1988–; Liberal Arts Co-ordinator, Sussex County College, 1988. *Publication:* The Flexible Writer, 1995. *Contributions to:* Ailanthus; South Coast Poetry Journal; Findings; American Poetry Society of America; South Mountain Poets. *Address:* 31 Maines Lane, Blairstown, NJ 07825, USA.

RICHARDS, Cyndi. See: RICHESON, C(ena) G(older).

RICHARDS, Sonia Elizabeth; b. 3 Feb. 1939, Exeter, Devon, England. Poet. m. Michael John, 30 Nov. 1957, 1 s., 2 d. *Education:* Shorthand, Typing, Bookkeeping, Proof Reading. *Publications:* The Other Side of the Mirror, 1996; Voices in the Heart, 1997; Womens Words, 1997; Quiet Moments', 1997; We Can Achieve Our Dream, 1998; The Ultimate Villanelle Collection, 1998; The Mind Behind the Face, 1998; Crystal Moons, 1999; **Changing Seasons, 1999.** *Honour:* Special Commendation, 1997. *Address:* 67 Iolanthe Dr., Exeter EX4 9DZ, Devon, England.

RICHESON, C(ena) G(older), (Velma Chamberlain, Jessica Jains, Cyndi Richards); b. 11 April 1941, Oregon, USA. Author; Poet. m. Jerry Dale Richeson, 3 June 1961, 2 s. *Education:* AA, Diablo Valley College, 1962; BA, California State University, 1972. *Appointments:* Instructor, Shasta College, CA, 1974–76; Liberty Union High School, Brentwood, CA, 1984–85; Columnist, Anderson Press Weekly Newspaper, CA, 1976–78; Frontier Correspondent, National Tombstone Epitaph, Tucson, 1986–; Book Reviewer, Publishers Weekly, 1994–95. *Contributions to:* Anthologies and periodicals. *Honours:* Several awards. *Memberships:* California Writers Club, pres., 1991–92; Society of Children's Book Writers; Zane Grey's West Society. *Address:* PO Box 268, Knightsen, CA 94548, USA.

RICHTER, Harvena; b. 13 March 1919, Reading, Pennsylvania, USA. University Lecturer (retd); Writer; Poet. *Education:* BA, University of New Mexico, 1938; MA, 1955, PhD, 1966, New York University. *Appointments:* Lecturer, New York University, 1955–66, University of New Mexico, 1969–89. *Publications:* The Human Shore, 1959; Virginia Woolf: The Inward Voyage, 1970; Writing to Survive: The Private Notebooks of Conrad Richter, 1988; The Yaddo Elegies and Other Poems, 1995; Green Girls: Poems Early and Late, 1996; The Innocent Island, 1999; Frozen Light: The Crystal Poems, 2002; The Golden Fountains: Sources of Energy and Life, 2002. *Contributions to:* Magazines and newspapers. *Honours:* Grants and fellowships. *Membership:* Authors' Guild. *Address:* 1932 Candelaria Rd NW, Albuquerque, NM 87107, USA.

RICHTER, Milan; b. 25 July 1948, Bratislava, Czechoslovakia. Writer; Poet; Trans.; Diplomat. m. Adreinna Matejovova, 1 Oct. 1980, 1 s., 1 d. *Education:* German and English Linguistics and Literature, Comenius University, Bratislava, 1967–72; PhD, 1985. *Appointments:* Part-Time Ed., Dotyky Literary Magazine, 1988–89, Revue Svetovej Literatury, 1991; Fulbright Research Scholar, University of California at Los Angeles, 1990; Head, Slovak Embassy, Oslo, 1993. *Publications:* Poetry books in Slovak and German; Trans into Slovak of various writers. *Contributions to:* Anthologies, magazines, and journals. *Address:* Sidlisko 714, CS 900 42 Dunajska Luzna, Slovakia.

RICKETTS, Harry John Dillon; b. 28 May 1950, London, England. University Teacher; Poet; Biographer; Ed. m., 3 s., 1 d. *Education:* Wellington College, Berkshire; BLitt, MA, Trinity College, Oxford. *Appointments:* Junior Lecturer, University of Hong Kong, 1974–77; Tutorial Asst, University of Leicester, 1978–81; Lecturer, Assoc. Prof., 1981–, Victoria University of Wellington, New Zealand. *Publications:* Coming Here, 1989; Coming Under Scrutiny, 1989; How Things Are, 1986; A Brief History of New Zealand Literature, 1986; 13 Ways, 1997; Nothing to Declare: Selected Writings, 1977–97, 1998; The Unforgiving Minute: A Life of Rudyard Kipling, 1999; Plunge, 2001. *Contributions to:* Numerous journals. *Address:* School of English, Film and Theatre, Victoria University of Wellington, Private Bag, Wellington, New Zealand. *E-mail:* harry.ricketts@vuw.ac.nz.

RICKETTS, Mary Jane Gnegy, (Marijane G Ricketts); b. 16 July 1925, Maryland, USA. Poet. m. Aubrey Eugene Ricketts, 9 April 1950, 1 s., 1 d. *Education:* BA, West Virginia Wesleyan College, 1947; Commercial Arts Diploma, Strayer Business College, 1949. *Publications:* Is it the Onion Making Life Pungent?, 1986; The Poets of Ellicott Street, 1989; A Diamond Anthology of Prose and Poetry, 1992. *Contributions to:* Various anthologies and magazines. *Honours:* Prize, First Honourable Mention, Federation of State Poetry Societies, 1986; Literary Award and Grand Prize for Poetry, Byline Magazine, 1986; Prize, 1987, First Prize for Poetry, 1992, Arts Project Renaissance, Washington, DC. *Memberships:* The Writer's Center, Bethesda, MD; Writer's League of Washington; The Poets of Ellicott St. *Address:* 10203 Clearbrook Pl., Kensington, MD 20895, USA. *E-mail:* marijane@ioip.com.

RIEL, Steven Joseph; b. 31 Dec. 1959, Monson, Massachusetts, USA. Librarian; Poet; Ed. *Education:* AB, Georgetown University, 1981; MLS, Simmons College, 1987. *Appointments:* Poetry Ed., RFD, 1987–95; Staff, Harvard University Library, 1987–89, 1993–, Amherst College Library, 1990–93. *Publications:* How to Dream, 1992. *Contributions to:* Anthologies, reviews, and journals. *Address:* PO Box 679, Natick, MA 01760, USA.

RIELLY, Edward James; b. 22 Dec. 1943, Darlington, Wisconsin, USA. Prof. of English; Poet. m. Jeanne Smith, 16 Aug. 1969, 1 s., 1 d. *Education:* BA, Loras College, 1966; MA, 1968, PhD, 1974, University of Notre Dame. *Appointment:* Prof. of English, St Joseph's College. *Publications:* Rain Falling Quietly, 1985; Family Portraits, 1987; The Furrow's Edge, 1987; The Breaking of Glass Horses and Other Poems, 1988; My Struggling Soil, 1994; Anniversary Haiku, 1997; How Sky Holds the Sun, 1998; The Abandoned Farmhouse and Other Haiku, 2000. *Honours:* Finalist, Maine Arts Commission Poetry Chapbook Competition, 1983; Merit Book Awards, Haiku Society of America, 1988; Best of Issue Award, Frogpond, 1990. *Memberships:* Haiku Society of America; Maine Writers and Publishers Alliance. *Address:* 6 Colony Rd, Westbrook, ME 04092, USA.

RIFBJERG, Klaus (Thorvald); b. 15 Dec. 1931, Copenhagen, Denmark. Author; Poet; Dramatist. m. Inge Merete Gerner, 28 May 1955, 1 s., 2 d.

Education: Princeton University, 1950–51; University of Copenhagen 1951–56. *Appointments:* Literary Critic, Information, Copenhagen, 1955–57 Politiken, Copenhagen, 1959–65; Ed.-in-Chief, Vindrosen, 1959–63; Literar, Dir, Gyldendal Publishers, Copenhagen, 1984–92. *Publications:* Over 40 novels 1958–2000, including: Anna (jeg) Anna, 1969, English trans. as Anna (I) Anna 1982; De hellige aber, 1981, English trans. as Witness to the Future, 1987 Poetry: Numerous poems, including: Selected Poems, 1976; Three Poems, 1982 Krigen, 1992, English trans. as War, 1995. Other: Plays, short stories children's books, etc. *Honours:* Aarstrup Medal, 1964; Danish Critics Award, 1965; Grant of Honour, Danish Dramatists, 1966; Danish Acad Award, 1966; Golden Laurels, 1967; Søren Gyldendal Award, 1969; Nordic Council Award, 1970; Grant of Honour, Danish Writers' Guild; 1973; P. H Prize, 1979; Holberg Medal, 1979; H. C. Andersen Prize, 1988; Nordic Prize Swedish Acad., 1999; Hon. doctorates, University of Lund, 1991, University of Odense, 1996. *Membership:* Danish Acad. *Address:* c/o Gyldendal Publishers, ? Klareboderne, 1001 Copenhagen, Denmark.

RILEY, Denise; b. 1948, England. Poet; Philosopher; Trans. *Education:* PhD, Philosophy, University of Sussex. *Publications:* Marxism for Infants, 1977; No Fee: A Line or Two for Free, 1979; Some Poems: 1968–1978 (with Wendy Mulford), 1982; War in the Nursery: Theories of the Child and Mother, 1983; Dry Air, 1985; 'Am I That Name?': Feminism and the Category of 'Women' in History, 1988; Poets on Writing: Britain, 1970–1991 (ed.), 1992; Mop Mop Georgette: New and Selected Poems, 1993; Selected Poems, 2001; The Words of Selves: Identification, Solidarity, Irony, 2001. *Contributions to:* Several publications. *Address:* c/o Cambridge University Press, Cambridge, England.

RINALDI, Nicholas Michael; b. 2 April 1934, New York, NY, USA. Prof.; Writer; Poet. m. Jacqueline Tellier, 29 Aug. 1959, 3 s., 1 d. *Education:* AB, Shrub Oak College, 1957; MA, 1960, PhD, 1963, Fordham University. *Appointments:* Instructor to Asst Prof., St John's University, 1960–65; Lecturer, City University of New York, 1966; Assoc. Prof., Columbia University, 1966; Asst Prof. to Prof., Fairfield University, 1966–; Prof., University of Connecticut, 1972. *Publications:* The Resurrection of the Snails, 1977; We Have Lost Our Fathers, 1982; The Luftwaffe in Chaos, 1985; Bridge Fall Down, 1985; The Jukebox Queen of Malta, 1999. *Contributions to:* Virginia Quarterly Review; Periodicals. *Honours:* Joseph P Slomovich Memorial Award for Poetry, 1979; All Nations Poetry Awards, 1981, 1983; New York Poetry Forum Award, 1983; Eve of St Agnes Poetry Award, 1984; Charles Angoff Literary Award, 1984. *Memberships:* Associated Writing Programs; Poetry Society of America. *Address:* 190 Brookview Ave, Fairfield, CT 06432, USA.

RIOS, Juan; b. 28 Sept. 1914, Lima, Peru. Poet; Dramatist; Critic. m. Rosa Saco, 16 Sept. 1946, 1 d. *Publications:* Cancion de Siempre, 1941; Malstrom, 1941; La Pintura Contemporanea en el Peru, 1946; Teatro, 1961; Ayar Manko, 1963; Primera Antologia Poetica, 1981. *Honours:* National Prizes for Drama, 1946, 1950, 1952, 1954, 1960; National Prizes for Poetry, 1948, 1953. *Membership:* Academia Peruana de la lengua. *Address:* Bajada de Banos 109, Barranco, Lima 04, Peru.

RIO-SUKAN, Isabel del; b. 8 Sept. 1954, Madrid, Spain. Writer; Poet; Trans. m. H B Sukan, 31 July 1981, 2 d. *Education:* Lic Cc Inf, Madrid Central University, 1977; Incorporated Linguist, Institute of Linguists, London, 1985. *Appointments:* Ed., Arts and Literary Programmes, Spanish Section, BBC World Service, 1978–82; Trans., International Maritime Organisation, United Nations Agency, London. *Publications:* BBC Get By in Spanish, 1992; Ciudad del interior, 1993; La duda, 1995. Other: Trans. *Contributions to:* Professional journals. *Honours:* Finalist, Neuvos Narradores Competition, 1994, Premio Icaro, 1995. *Memberships:* Institute of Linguists; Institute of Trans. and Interpreting; Society of Authors; Trans Asscn. *Address:* PO Box 10314, London W14 0FT, England.

RITCHIE, Elisavietta Artamonoff; b. 29 June 1932, Kansas City, Missouri, USA. Writer; Poet; Trans.; Teacher; Ed.; Photographer. m. (1) Lyell Hale Ritchie Jr, 11 July 1953, divorced 2 s., 1 d., (2) Clyde Henri Farnsworth, 22 June 1991. *Education:* Degré Supérieur, Mention Tres Bien, Sorbonne, University of Paris, 1951; Cornell University, 1951–53; BA, University of California at Berkeley, 1954; MA, French Literature, American University, 1976; Advanced Russian courses, Georgetown University. *Appointments:* US Information Agency Visiting Poet, Brazil, 1972, Far East, 1977, Yugoslavia, 1979, Bulgaria, 1979; Founder-Dir, The Wineberry Press, 1983–; Pres., Washington Writers Publishing House, 1986–89; Leader, various creative writing workshops. *Publications:* Timbot, 1970; Tightening the Circle Over Eel Country 1974; A Sheath of Dreams and Other Games, 1976; Moving to Larger Quarters, 1977; Raking the Snow, 1982; The Chattanooga Cycles, 1984; The Problem with Eden, 1985; Flying Time: Stories and Half-Stories, 1992; A Wound-Up Cat and Other Bedtime Stories, 1993; Wild Garlic: The Journal of Maria X, 1995; Elegy for the Other Woman: New and Selected Terribly Female Poems, 1996; The Arc of the Storm, 1998. *Contributions to:* Many anthologies and periodicals. *Honours:* New Writer's Award for Best First Book of Poetry, Great Lakes Colleges Asscn, 1975–76; 4 PEN Syndicated Fiction Awards; 2 Awards, Poetry Society of America. *Memberships:* Amnesty International; PEN; Poetry Society of America; Poets and Writers; Washington Independent

Writers; Writer's Center. *Address:* 3207 Macomb St NW, Washington, DC 20008, USA.

RITTERBUSCH, Dale Edward; b. 12 Jan. 1946, Waukesha, Wisconsin, USA. Prof.; Poet. m. Patricia, 28 Nov. 1981, 1 d. *Education:* AB, 1972, AM, 1975, University of Pennsylvania; MFA, Bowling Green State University, 1985. *Appointments:* Teaching Asst, Dept of American Civilization, University of Pennsylvania, 1973–74; Visiting Lecturer, Dept of English, Community College of Philadelphia, 1975–79; Teaching Fellow, English Dept, Bowling Green State University, 1983–85; Lecturer I, 1985–88, Lecturer, II, 1988–93, Asst Prof., 1993–97, Assoc. Prof., 1997–, Dept of Languages and Literature, University of Wisconsin-Whitewater. *Publication:* Lessons Learned, 1995. *Contributions to:* Anthologies, periodicals, quarterlies and journals. *Honours:* Posner Book-Length Poetry Award, Council for Wisconsin Writers, 1996; Wisconsin Arts Board Grant, 1997; Best Poem, 128th Annual Conference, Wisconsin Acad. of Sciences, Arts and Letters. 1998; Wisconsin Fellowship of Poets' Muse Award, 2002. *Memberships:* Sport Literature Asscn; Popular Culture Asscn; Council for Wisconsin Writers; Wisconsin Fellowship of Poets; Wisconsin Acad. of Sciences, Arts and Letters. *Address:* 206 Spring St, Waukesha, WI 53188, USA.

RIVARD, David; b. 2 Dec. 1953, Fall River, MA, USA. Writer; Poet; Ed. m. Michaela Sullivan, 17 Dec. 1982, 1 d. *Education:* BA, Southeastern Massachusetts University, 1975; MFA, University of Arizona, 1982. *Appointments:* Faculty, Dept of English, Tufts University; Poetry Ed., Harvard Review. *Publications:* Torque, 1988; Wise Poison, 1996; Bewitched Playground, 2000. *Contributions to:* Periodicals. *Honours:* Fine Arts Work Center Fellowships, Provincetown, Massachusetts, 1984–85, 1986–87; National Endowment for the Arts Fellowships, 1986, 1991; Agnes Lynch Starrett Poetry Prize, University of Pittsburgh, 1987; Pushcart Prize, 1994; Massachusetts Cultural Council Fellow, 1994; James Laughlin Award, Acad. of American Poets, 1996; Finalist, Los Angeles Times Poetry Prize, 1997; Finalist, Massachusetts Book Award, 2000; Guggenheim Fellowship, 2001. *Address:* 72 Inman St, Apt A, Cambridge, MA 02139, USA.

RIVARD, Ken J.; b. 30 June 1947, Montréal, QC, Canada. Special Education Teacher; Poet; Writer. m. Micheline Rivard, 19 Sept. 1972, 2 d. *Education:* BEd, University of Montréal, 1970; MEd, McGill University, 1974. *Publications:* Poetry: Kiss Me Down to Size, 1983; Losing His Thirst, 1985; Franie's Desires, 1987. Fiction: Working Stiffs, 1990; If She Could Take All These Men, 1995; Mom, The School Flooded (children's), 1996. *Contributions to:* Anthologies and periodicals. *Memberships:* League of Canadian Poets; Writers Guild of Great Britain. *Address:* 120 Whiteview Pl. NE, Calgary, AB T1Y 1R6, Canada.

RIVERS, Ann; b. 26 Jan. 1939, Texas, USA. Poet. *Education:* BA, 1959. *Appointments:* Ed.-Publisher, SHY, 1974–79; Guest Ed., As-Sharq, 1979; Contributing Ed., Ocarina, 1979–82. *Publications:* Samos Wine, 1987; A World of Difference, 1995; Pilgrimage and Early Poems, 2000. *Contributions to:* Ore; Iotà; Orbis; Poetry Nottingham; Pennine Platform. *Address:* Hydra, GR 180 40 Greece.

RIVES, Janet M.; b. 10 Feb. 1944, Hartford, CT, USA. Prof. of Economics; Poet. *Education:* BA, University of Arizona, 1966; Diplome, Cours de Civilisation Français, Sorbonne, University of Paris, 1965; MA, 1969, PhD, 1971, Duke University. *Appointments:* Asst Prof., Rutgers University, 1970–77; Assoc. Prof., University of Nebraska, Omaha, 1977–84; Assoc. Prof., Prof., University of Northern Iowa, 1984–. *Contributions to:* Anthologies and periodicals. *Memberships:* Iowa Poetry Asscn; Walt Whitman Guild. *Address:* 317 Heritage Rd, Cedar Falls, IA 50613, USA.

RIZVI, I(ftikhar) H(usain); b. 25 June 1936, Bareilly, India. Educator; Poet. m. Anis Fatima Rizvi, 24 Oct. 1966, 1 s., 4 d. *Education:* MA, English, 1956, MA, History, 1970, Agra University; MA, English, Aligarh University, 1968; BEd, Rajasthan University, 1973. *Appointments:* Lecturer in English, 1957–88, Principal, 1988–, Tilak College, Bareilly. *Publications:* Poetry collections in English: Falling Petals, 1975; Unfading Blooms, 1984; Thirsty Pebbles, 1986; Wandering Fragrance, 1988; Wounded Roses Sing, 1993; Snowflakes of Dreams, 1996. Poetry collection in Urdu: Daman-E-Gul, 1991. *Contributions to:* Anthologies and journals worldwide. *Honours:* DLitt, World University, USA, 1982; Second Prize, International Poetry Contest, Brazil, 1987; Honoured by International Poets Acad., USA, 1987, World Poets Congress, Thailand, 1988, Michael Madhusudan Acad., 1989, and others. *Memberships:* International Poets Acad.; Michael Madhusudan Acad., Calcutta. *Address:* Rizvi Manzil, Kanghi Tola, Bareilly 243 003, Uttar Pradesh, India.

ROBBINS, Jerry Leo; b. 10 Dec. 1940, Covington, Tennessee, USA. Poet. m. Joan L Robbins, 16 Oct. 1965, 1 s., 4 d. *Education:* BA, 1964, MA, 1978, Memphis State University. *Appointments:* Writer, Memphis Press Scimitar, 1969–84, University of Kentucky, 1984–89. *Publications:* Early Stuff, 1990; The Heat, 1991. *Contributions to:* Press Scimitar; Pteranodon; Encore; Tennessee Voices; Inside Reporter; Pegasus. *Memberships:* National Federation of State Poetry Societies; Poetry Society of Tennessee; Kentucky Poetry Society. *Address:* 3425 Holwyn Rd, Lexington, KY 40503, USA.

ROBBINS, Richard (Leroy); b. 27 Aug. 1953, Los Angeles, CA, USA. Prof.; Poet; Writer; Ed. m. Candace L Black, 8 Sept. 1979, 2 s. *Education:* AB, English, San Diego State University, 1975; MFA, Creative Writing, University of Montana, 1979. *Appointments:* Co-Ed., Cafeteria, 1971–81, CutBank and SmokeRoot Press, 1977–79, Montana Arts Council anthologies, 1979–81; Writer-in-Residence, Poet-in-the-Schools, Montana Arts Council, 1979–81; Instructor, Moorhead State University, 1981–82, Oregon State University, 1982–84; Prof., Minnesota State University, Mankato, 1984–; Asst Ed., Mankato Poetry Review, 1984–. *Publications:* Where We Are: The Montana Poets Anthology (ed. with Lex Runciman), 1978; Toward New Weather, 1979; The Invisible Wedding, 1984; Famous Persons We Have Known, 2000. *Contributions to:* 13 anthologies, 1978–2000, reviews, quarterlies, and journals. *Honours:* First Prize in Poetry, Branford P Millar Award, Portland Review, 1978; Frontier Award, University of Montana, 1978; Individual Artist Fellowship, Minnesota State Arts Board, 1986; Robert H Winner Memorial Award, Poetry Society of America, 1988; National Endowment for the Arts Fellowship, 1992; McKnight Individual Artist Grants, 1993, 1996, and Fellowship, 1997; Hawthornden Fellowship, 1998; Fellowship, Minnesota State Arts Board, 1999; The Loft Award of Distinction in Poetry, 2000. *Memberships:* Associated Writing Programs; The Loft; Poetry Society of America; Western Literature Asscn. *Address:* c/o Dept of English, Minnesota State University, 230 Armstrong Hall, Mankato, MN 56001, USA.

ROBERTS, John Anthony; b. 2 Jan. 1935, London, England. Civil Servant (retd); Poet. m. Linda Geraldine Cannons, 20 Dec. 1969, 3 s. *Education:* Honours Degree, Classics and English, Trinity College, Cambridge, 1959; Barrister at Law; Diploma, Librarianship, Ealing College of Higher Education, 1978. *Appointments:* Clerk, House of Lords, 1960–61; Teacher, Holmleigh Prep School, 1962–63, Bernard Mizeki College, Rhodesia, 1963–64; Legal Asst, ICL, 1973–76; Clerical Asst, HM Customs and Excise, 1979–92. *Publication:* Suburban Reflections, 1990. *Contributions to:* Success Magazine; Weyfarers; Focus; What's On; Sutton Advertiser. *Honour:* First Prize, Sutton Library 21st Anniversary Poetry Competition. *Memberships:* Guildford Poets; Sutton Society of Civil Service Authors; Sutton Writer's Circle. *Address:* 24 Salisbury Ave, Cheam, Sutton, Surrey SM1 2DJ, England.

ROBERTS, Keith (John Kingston), (Alistair Bevan); b. 10 Sept. 1935, Kettering, Northamptonshire, England. Writer; Poet. *Education:* National Diploma in Design, Northampton School of Art, 1956; Leicester College of Art, 1956–57. *Publications:* Fiction: The Furies, 1966; The Inner Wheel, 1970; Anita, 1970; The Boat of Fate, 1971; Machines and Men, 1973; The Chalk Giants, 1974; The Grain Kings, 1975; Ladies from Hell, 1979; Molly Zero, 1980; Kiteworld, 1985; Kaeti and Company, 1986; The Lordly Ones, 1986; The Road to Paradise, 1988; Tears in a Glass Eye, 1989; The Event, 1989; Winterwood and Other Hauntings, 1989; Kaeti on Tour, 1992. Poetry: A Heron Caught in the Weeds, 1987. Other: Irish Encounters, 1988; The Natural History of PH, 1988. *Address:* c/o Carnell Literary Agency, Danes Croft, Goose Lane, Little Hallingbury, Hertfordshire CM22 7RG, England.

ROBERTS, Leonard, (Len Roberts); b. 13 March 1947, Cohoes, New York, USA. Prof. of English; Poet; Trans. m. 31 Dec. 1981, 2 s., 1 d. *Education:* BA, English, Siena College, 1970; MA, English, University of Dayton, 1972; PhD, English, Lehigh University, 1976. *Appointments:* Prof. of English, Northampton College, 1974–83, 1986–87, 1989–93, 1995–; Visiting Asst Prof., Lafayette College, 1983–85; Visiting Prof., University of Pittsburgh, 1984–; Fulbright Scholar, Janus Pannonius University, Pécs, Hungary, 1988–89, University of Turku, Finland, 1994. *Publications:* Poetry: Cohoes Theater, 1980; From the Dark, 1984; Sweet Ones, 1988; Black Wings, 1989; Learning About the Heart, 1992; Dangerous Angels, 1993; The Million Branches: Selected Poems and Interview, 1993; Counting the Black Angels, 1994; The Trouble-Making Finch, 1998; The Silent Singer: New and Selected Poems, 2001. Translator: The Selected Poems of Sándor Csoóri, 1992. *Contributions to:* Anthologies and journals. *Honours:* Pennsylvania Council on the Arts Writing Awards in Poetry, 1981, 1986, 1987, 1991; National Endowment for the Arts Awards, 1984, 1989; Great Lakes and Prairies Award, 1988; National Poetry Series Award, 1988; Soros Foundation Poetry Trans. Awards, 1989, 1990, 1992, 1997; Guggenheim Fellowship, 1990–91; Pushcart Prize, 1991; Witter Bynner Poetry Trans. Award, 1991–92; Winner, Silverfish Review Chapbook Competition, 1992; First Prize, Wildwood Poetry Contest, 1993; National Endowment for the Humanities Trans. Award, 1999; Pennsylvania Council on the Arts Poetry Award, 2000. *Memberships:* MLA; Pennsylvania Council on the Arts, advisory board, 1990–; Poetry Society of America; Poets and Writers. *Address:* 2443 Wassergass Rd, Hellertown, PA 18055, USA.

ROBERTS, Michèle (Brigitte); b. 20 May 1949, Hertfordshire, England. Author; Dramatist; Poet. m. Jim Latter, 10 Aug. 1991, 2 step-s. *Education:* MA, Somerville College, Oxford, 1967–70; ALA, University College, London, 1971–72. *Appointments:* Poetry Ed., Spare Rib, 1974, City Limits, 1981–83; Visiting Fellow in Creative Writing, University of East Anglia, 1992; Visiting Research Fellow, 1995–96, Visiting Prof., 1996–, University of Nottingham Trent. *Publications:* A Piece of the Night, 1978; The Visitation, 1983; The Wild Girl, 1984; The Mirror of the Mother (poems), 1986; The Book of Mrs Noah, 1987; The Journeywoman (play), 1988; In the Red Kitchen, 1990; Psyche and the Hurricane (poems), 1991; Daughters of the House, 1992; During Mother's

Absence (stories), 1993; Flesh and Blood, 1994; All the Selves I Was (poems), 1995; Child-Lover (play), 1995; Mind Readings, (co-ed.), 1996; Impossible Saints, 1997; Food, Sex and God (essays), 1998; Fair Exchange, 1999; The Looking-Glass, 2000; Playing Sardines, 2001. *Contributions to:* Periodicals. *Honours:* W. H. Smith Literary Award, 1993; Hon. MA, Nene University, 1999. *Memberships:* British Council, chair., literary committee, 1998–; Fellow, RSL. *Address:* c/o Gillon Aitken Assocs, 29 Fernshaw Rd, London SW10 0TG, England.

ROBERTS, Philippa Mary; b. 7 Aug. 1960, Cheltenham, Gloucestershire, England. Writer; Poet. 1 s., 1 d. *Contributions to:* Anthologies and other publications. *Honours:* Highly commended, Waterstones Competition, 1990, Mary and Alfred Wilkins Memorial Competition, 1991, Writer's Viewpoint Magazine Competition, 1995. *Membership:* Cheltenham Shakespeare Society.

ROBERTS, Robert (James); b. 11 Jan. 1931, Penrith, Cumbria, England. Headmaster (retd); Poet. m. Patricia Mary Milbourne, 8 Aug. 1959, 1 s., deceased, 1 d. *Education:* MA, Pembroke College, Cambridge, 1951–55. *Publications:* Amphibious Landings, 1990; First Selection, 1994; Genius Loci, 1995; Second Selection, 1995; Worm's Eye View, 1995; Third Selection, 1996; Fourth Selection, 1997; Fifth Selection, 1998; Flying Buttresses, 1999; Sixth Selection, 1999; Seventh Selection, 2000; Lest We Forget, 2001. *Contributions to:* Spectator; Countryman; Poetry Review; Acumen; Envoi; Orbis; Outposts; Poetry Nottingham; Staple; Westwords; First Time; Iota; Doors; Otter; Nutshell; Literary Review; Poetry Wales; Seam. *Honours:* Many awards. *Address:* Ellon House, Harpford, Sidmouth, Devon EX10 0NH, England.

ROBERTS, Sheila; b. 19 June 1956, Edmonton, London, England. Poet. Divorced, 1 s., 2 d. *Education:* Diploma, Bookkeeping and Accountancy, Open University. *Publications:* Numerous. *Honour:* Best Poem of 1997. *Memberships:* International Library of Poetry; United Society of Poets; Poetry Guild. *Address:* 74 Great Meadow, Northampton NN3 8DF, England.

ROBERTSON, Howard W.; b. 19 Sept. 1947, Eugene, Oregon, USA. Poet. m. Margaret E Collins, 10 Aug. 1991, 2 s., 2 d. *Education:* BA, Russian, 1970, MA, Comparative Literature, 1978, University of Oregon; MSLS, Library Science, University of Southern California, 1975. *Appointments:* Slavic Catalogue Librarian and Bibliographer, University of Oregon, Eugene, 1975–93; Full-time Poet, 1993–. *Publication:* To The Fierce Guard in the Assyrian Saloon, 1987. *Contributions to:* Nest; The Ahsahta Anthology; Literal Latté; Nimrod; Fireweed; Ergo; Croton Review; Yet Another Little Magazine; Yellow Silk; Negative Capability; Pinchpenny; Assembling; Laughing Unicorn; Laughing Bear; Intown; Pacifica. *Honours:* Bumbershoot Writers-in-Performance Award, 1993; Pacifica Award, 1995; Honourable Mention, Wildwood Prize, 1995; Pablo Neruda Award, 1997; Literal Latté Award. 1997. *Membership:* Lane Literary Guild, Lane County, Oregon. *Address:* 854 Martin St, Eugene, OR 97405, USA.

ROBERTSON, Susan Mary; b. 1 Oct. 1952, Cardiff, Wales. Poet; Writer. *Education:* BSc, King's College, London; 1977; Diploma in Media Practice, 1997, LLB, 2001, Birkbeck College, London. *Publications:* Several poems. *Contributions to:* Various publications. *Honour:* International Poet Merit Award, 1998. *Address:* 212 Cheeseman's Terrace, Star Rd, London W14 9XT, England.

ROBERTSON, Thomas John McMeel; b. 10 Jan. 1928, Nagpur, India. Chartered Engineer. m. Maureen Enca, 12 June 1954, 2 s. *Education:* BSc, Mechanical Engineering, University of Glasgow, 1952. *Publications:* Many anthologies, including: National Poetry Anthology, 2000; Rhyme, Rondeau & Villanelle, 2000; Waters Run Deep, 2000; Seasonal Moods, 2000; Lines of Life, 2000; Rhymes from the Heart, 2001; A Captured Moment, 2002. *Memberships:* Institute of Mechanical Engineers; Institute of Patentees & Inventors; Sinodun Writing Group. *Address:* The Poplars, School Lane, Milton, Abingdon, Oxon OX14 4EH, England.

ROBERTSON, William Paul; b. 29 May 1950, Pennsylvania, USA. Teacher of English; Poet. *Education:* BS, English, Mansfield University, 1972. *Appointments:* Teacher of English, Otto Eldred High School, 1973–78, Bradford Area School District, 1978–. *Publications:* Burial Grounds, 1977; Gardez au Froid, 1979; Animal Comforts, 1981; Life After Sex Life, 1983; Waters Boil Bloody, 1990; 1066, 1992; Hearse Verse, 1994; Battle Verse, 1996. *Contributions to:* Champagne Horror; Cobblestone; Glasgow Magazine; Grue; Lable; Midway Review; Pinehurst Journal; Poetic Knight; Psychopoetica; Slipstream; Stride; Standing Stone; 2AM; Vollmond; Wellspring. *Memberships:* Poets and Writers; National Writers Asscn; Genre Writer's Asscn. *Address:* PO Box 14532, Savannah, GA 31416, USA.

ROBINS, Patricia. See: CLARK, Patricia Denise.

ROBINSON, David Bradford; b. 14 April 1937, Richmond, Virginia, USA. Poet; Writer. BS, 1959; MS, Honours, 1961; AA, 1970; BA, 1973; DSc, 1978; PhD, 1979; MA, 1995; JD, 1995. *Publications:* Characteristics of Cesium, 1978; Lyric Treasure One, 1978; Collected Poems, 1987; Praise the Wildnerness: Nineteen Original New Poems to Survival, 1990. *Contributions to:* Anthologies and reviews. *Honours:* Golden Poet Award, 1987; Pegasus Time Capsule

Award, 1991; Albert Einstein Medal, 1994; World Lifetime Achivemen Award, 1996. *Membership:* International Society of Poets. *Address:* PO Bo 1414, Miami Shores, FL 33153, USA.

ROBINSON, Ian; b. 1 July 1934, Prestwich, Manchester, England. Writer Artist. m. Adelheid Armbrüster, 21 Dec. 1959, 1 s., 2 d. *Education:* MA, Orie College, Oxford, 1958. *Appointments:* Ed., Oasis Magazine, 1969–; Publisher Oasis Books, 1970–. *Publications:* Poetry: Accidents, 1974; Three, 1978; Shor Stories, 1979; Maida Vale Elegies, 1983; Journal, 1987; The Invention o Morning, 1997. Prose: Obsequies, 1979; Fugitive Aromas, 1979; Blown Footage, 1980; Dissolving Views, 1986; 26 1/2 Things, 1995; Thunder on the Dew, 2000; A World Elsewhere, 2002; How Do You Spell Bl...gh?, 2002. Graphic Books: The Glacier in the Cupboard, 1995; Landscapes, 2001 Theorems, 2001. *Contributions to:* Prism International; London Magazine Prospice; Poesie Europe; Osiris; Wide Skirt; Fire; Tears in the Fence; Poets Voice; Prop; 10th Muse; Boxon, France; Offerta Speciale, Italy. *Address:* 12 Stevenage Rd, London SW6 6ES, England.

ROCHE, Terry. See: POOLE, Margaret Barbara.

RODD, Moreena. See: MOREN, Rodney.

RODGERS, Carolyn Marie; b. 14 Dec. 1942, Chicago, IL, USA. Prof.; Writer; Poet; Ed. *Education:* BA, Roosevelt University, 1981; MA, University of Chicago, 1983. *Appointments:* Prof. of Afro-American Literature, 1969, Lecturer in English and Co-ordinator of Poetry Workshop, 1970, Columbia College; Poet-in-Residence, University of Washington, 1970, Indiana University, 1974, Roosevelt University, 1983; Founder-Ed., Eden Press, 1991, Rare Form newsletter, 1994–. *Publications:* Paper Soul, 1968; Songs of a Blackbird, 1970; How I Got Ovah, 1976; The Heart as Evergreen, 1978; Translation, 1980; A Little Lower Than the Angels, 1984; Morning Glory, 1989; The Religious Poetry of Carolyn M Rodgers, 1993; Daughters of Africa, 1993; We're Only Human, 1994; A Train Called Judah, 1996; Chosen to Believe, 1996; Salt: The Salt of the Earth, 1999. *Contributions to:* Journals and magazines. *Honours:* National Endowment for the Arts Award, 1970; Conrad Kent Rivers Award, 1970; Society of Midland Authors Award, 1970; Carnegie Writer's Grant, 1980; Television Gospel Tribute, 1982; PEN Grant, 1987. *Memberships:* Gwendolyn Brooks Writing Workshop; Organization of Black American Culture. *Address:* PO Box 804271, Chicago, IL 60680, USA.

RODLEY, Laura; b. 15 Dec. 1955, Wilmington, DE, USA. Poet; Certified Nurse's Aide. m. James J Rodley, 10 April 1982, 1 s., 2 d. *Education:* Adult Degree Program, Norwich University, Brattleboro. *Contributions to:* Massachusetts Review; Prose Poem; Nurturing; Llama Magazine; Juggler's World; Sanctuary; Paragraphs; Earth's Daughters; Albatross; Blueline, Sahara. *Honour:* Second Place, Springfield Library Poetry Contest, Springfield, Massachusetts, 2002. *Membership:* Wild Women's Writers, 1992–. *Address:* PO Box 63, Shelburne Falls, MA 01370, USA.

RODNING, Charles Bernard; b. 4 Aug. 1943, Pipestone, Minnesota, USA. Physician; Surgeon; Poet. m. Mary Elizabeth Lipke Rodning, 3 s. *Education:* BS, Gustavus Adolphus College, 1965; MD, University of Rochester, 1970; PhD, University of Minnesota, 1979. *Contributions to:* Various anthologies, reviews, and journals. *Memberships:* Acad. of American Poets; Alabama State Poetry Society; Eastern Shore Art Asscn; Haiku International Asscn. *Address:* 2441 Fillingim St, Mobile, AL 36617, USA.

RODRIGUES, Louis Jerome; b. 20 July 1938, Chennai, India. Writer; Poet; Trans. m. (1) Malinda Weaving, deceased, 1 s., (2) Josefina Bernet Soler, 6 Oct. 1984, 1 s. *Education:* BA, Honours, English, 1960; MA, Intermediate Histories and Logic, 1962, University of Chennai; MA, MPhil, Anglo-Saxon, 1965–67, University of London; MA, Law and English Tripos, 1971–73, 1977; PhD, University of Barcelona, 1990. *Appointments:* Asst Dir, Benedict, Mannheim, 1977; Dir of Studies, Inlingua, Barcelona, 1978–82; Dir, Phoenix, Barcelona, 1982–87. *Publications:* A Long Time Waiting, 1979; Anglo-Saxon Riddles, 1990; Seven Anglo-Saxon Elegies, 1991; Chiaroscuro, 1991; The Battles of Maldon and Brunanburh, 1991; Anglo-Saxon Verse Runes, 1992; Anglo-Saxon Verse Charms, Maxims and Heroic Legends, 1993; Anglo-Saxon Elegiac Verse, 1994; Anglo-Saxon Didactic Verse, 1995; Three Anglo-Saxon Battle Poems, 1995; Salvador Espriu: Selected Poems (trans.), 1997; Beowulf and the Fight at Finnsburh. *Contributions to:* Various publications. *Honour:* Poetry Trans. Prize, Catholic University of America, Washington, DC, 1993. *Memberships:* International Asscn of Anglo-Saxonists; RSL; Society of Authors, exec. committee mem., 1988–91; Trans. Asscn; American Literary Trans. Asscn. *Address:* 132 Wisbech Rd, Littleport, Ely, Cambridgeshire CB6 1JJ, England.

RODRIGUEZ, Judith (Catherine); b. 13 Feb. 1936, Perth, WA, Australia. Poet; Dramatist; Librettist; Ed.; Lecturer. m. (1) Fabio Rodriguez, 1964, divorced 1981, 4 c., (2) Thomas Shapcott, 1982. *Education:* BA, University of Queensland, Brisbane, 1957; MA, Girton College, Cambridge, 1962; Certificate of Education, University of London, 1968. *Appointments:* Lecturer in External Studies, University of Queensland, Brisbane, 1959–60; Lecturer in English, Philippa Fawcett College of Education, London, 1962–63, University of the West Indies, Jamaica, 1963–65, St Mary's College of Education, Twickenham,

1966–68, Macarthur Institute of Higher Education, Milperra, Sydney, 1987–88; Royal Melbourne Institute of Technology, 1988–89; Victoria College, 1989–92; Teacher of English as a Foreign Language, St Giles School of English, London, 1965–66; Lecturer, 1969–75, Senior Lecturer in English, 1977–85, La Trobe University, Bundoora, Australia; Writer-in-Residence, Rollins College, FL, 1986; Senior Lecturer, Deakin University, 1993–. *Publications:* Poetry: Four Poets, 1962; Nu-Plastik Fanfare Red, 1973 and Other Poems, 1973; Water Life, 1976; Shadow on Glass, 1978; Arapede, 1979; Mudcrab at Gambaro's, 1980; Witch Heart, 1982; Floridian Poems, 1986; The House by Water: Selected and New Poems, 1988; The Cold, 1992. Play: Poor Johanna (with Robyn Archer), 1994. Opera Libretto: Lindy, 1994. Editor: Mrs Noah and the Minoan Queen, 1982; Poems Selected from the Australia's 20th Anniversary Competition (with Andrew Taylor), 1985; Modern Swedish Poetry (with Thomas Shapcott), 1985; Collected Poems of Jennifer Rankin, 1990. *Contributions to:* Numerous publications. *Honours:* Arts Council of Australia Fellowships, 1974, 1978, 1983; Government of South Australia Biennial Prize for Literature, 1978; International PEN Peter Stuyvesant Prize for Poetry, 1981; Mem. of the Order of Australia, 1994; Christopher Brennan Award, Fellowship of Australian Writers, 1994. *Memberships:* Asscn for the Study of Australian Literature Programs; Australian Society of Authors; International PEN; South Pacific Asscn for Commonwealth Language and Literature Studies; Melbourne PEN Centre; Victorian Writer's Centre; Australian Literary Trans' Asscn. *Address:* PO Box 231, Mont Albert, Vic. 3127, Australia.

RODRIGUEZ, Victorino, (Victor Roz); b. 24 Jan. 1923, Cuba. Lecturer; Instructor; Poet. m. 21 Jan. 1966, 1 s., 1 d., deceased. *Education:* University of Madrid, 1957–58; Licenciado en Filosofia, Pedagogia, Filologia Romanica; PhD, University of Southern California at Los Angeles, 1973. *Appointments:* Teacher, Markham High School, 1966–67; College Spanish Instructor, East Los Angeles, 1969–. *Publications:* Cantos de Cantos: Primera Selección, 1969; Segunda Selección, 1972; Tercera Selección, 1973; Cuarta Selección, 1974; Quinta Selección, 1975; Sexta Selección, 1975; Sumas Poeticas, 1990–97; Pinceladas, 1997. *Contributions to:* Clarin Gemma; Americanto; Invitación a la Poesía; Son de Sometos; Suma de Amor; El Alba de América; Vll Antología de Poesía Contemporánea; Anthologies: World Poetry, South Korea; Parnassus of World Poetry, India; Antología de Poesía Contemporánea, Portugal; Antología Planetaria, Italy; Revista Mairena, Puerto Rico; Olympoetry Anthology, New York. *Honour:* Medal and Title of Caballero de la Orden de Isabel la Católica from the King of Spain, 1990. *Memberships:* Liceo Internacional de Cultura; La Cuadratura del Círculo Los Angeles. *Address:* 8335 Scenic Dr. S, San Gabriel, CA 91770, USA.

ROFFMAN, Rosaly DeMaios; b. 1 June 1937, New York, NY, USA. Assoc. Prof. of English; Poet; Writer. m. Bernard Roffman, 31 May 1964, 1 s. *Education:* BA, Honours, Languages and Literature, City College of New York, 1960; MA, English and Asian Studies, University of Hawaii, 1967. *Appointments:* Instructor, City College of New York, University of Hawaii, Gakushuin University, Aoyama Gakuin, Japan; Assoc. Prof., University of Pennsylvania. *Publications:* Wings of the Rainbow, 1979; Once... a Miracle, 1981; Living Inland, 1988; First Decade, 1989; A Gathering of Poets, 1992; Life on the Line: Selections on Healing and Words (co-ed.), 1993; Antologia, 1993; Going to Bed Whole, 1993; Tottering Palaces, 1998; Approximate Messages, 2000. Other: Collaborations with composers. *Contributions to:* Reviews, quarterlies and journals. *Honours:* Distinguished Faculty Award in the Arts, National Endowment for the Humanities, 1990; Witter Bynner Foundation Awards, 1993, 1994; Best Published Poem, Pittsburgh Poetry Society, 1995. *Memberships:* MLA; National Council of Teachers of English; Poetry Society of America; World Congress of Poets. *Address:* 2580 Evergreen Dr., Indiana, PA 15701, USA.

ROGERS, Bertha Kay; b. 2 June 1941, Illinois, USA. Poet; Arts Administrator; Teacher. m. 27 Aug. 1961, divorced 1987, 2 d. *Education:* Iowa Wesleyan College, 1959–61; University of Iowa, 1962–63; Studio and Forum of Scenic Design, New York City, 1983. *Publications:* The Reason of Trees, 1987; Clouds (with R Hart, G Saintiny, and T Young), 1988; Sleeper, You Wake, 1991; For the Girl Buried in the Peat Bog, 1999. *Contributions to:* Reviews, quarterlies, and periodicals. *Honours:* MacDowell Colony, Millay Colony, Hedgebrook Foundation and Hawthornden Castle Residencies, 1994–99. *Memberships:* Poetry Society of America; Poets and Writers. *Address:* Bright Hill Farm, Rd 1, Box 545, Delhi, NY 13753, USA.

ROGERS, Del Marie; b. 11 April 1936, Washington, DC, USA. Poet; Ed. Divorced, 1 s., 2 d. *Education:* BA, Baylor University, 1957; MA, English, Philosophy, 1970, PhD study, Vanderbilt University. *Publications:* Breaking Free, 1977; Close to Ground, 1990. *Contributions to:* Choice; Chicago; Colorado Review; Eighties; Epoch; Ironwood; Kayak; Nation; New Mexico Magazine; Pacific Review; Perspective; Puerto del Sol; Southern Poetry Review; Sun; Texas Observer; Various anthologies. *Honours:* Monetary Prize, 1970; National Endowment for the Arts Fellowships, 1974–75. *Memberships:* Poetry Society of America; Acad. of American Poets; PEN, USA West. *Address:* 4017 Bond St, Rowlett, TX 75088, USA.

ROGERS, Linda (Hall); b. 10 Oct. 1944, Port Alice, BC, Canada. Poet; Writer; Lecturer. m. Rick Van Krugel, 3 s. *Education:* MA, English Literature,

University of British Columbia. *Appointments:* Lecturer, University of British Columbia, University of Victoria, Camosun College, Malaspina College. *Publications:* Some Breath, 1978; Queens of the Next Hot Star, 1981; I Like to Make a Mess, 1985; Witness, 1985; Singing Rib, 1987; Worm Sandwich, 1989; The Magic Flute, 1990; Brown Bag Blues, 1991; Letters from the Doll Hospital, 1992; Hard Candy, 1994; The Half Life of Radium, 1994; Frankie Zapper and the Disappearing Teacher, 1994; Molly Brown is Not a Clown, 1996; Love in the Rainforest (selected poetry), 1996; Heaven Cake, 1997; The Saning, 1999; The Broad Canvas: Portraits of Women Artists (non-fiction), 1999; Say My Name (novel), 2000; Rehearsing the Miracle (poems), 2001; P. K. Page: Essays on Her Work (ed.), 2001; Al Purdy: Essays on His Work (ed.), 2002; Bill Bissett: Essays on His Work (ed.), 2002; The Bursting Test (poems). *Contributions to:* Journals, magazines, and newspapers. *Honours:* Aya Poetry Prize, 1983; Canada Council Arts Awards, 1987, 1990; British Columbia Writers Poetry Prize, 1989; Cultural Services Award, 1990; Alcuin Awards, 1991, 2002; Gov.-Gen.'s Centennial Medal for Poetry and Performance, 1993; Stephen Leacock Awards for Poetry, 1994, 1996; Dorothy Livesay Award for Poetry, 1995; Voices Israel Poetry Award, 1995; Peoples Poetry Award, 1996; Acorn Rukeyser Award, 1999; Cardiff Poetry Prizes, 1999, 2001; Canada's Peoples Poet, 2000; Bridport Poetry Prize, England, 2000; Millennium Award, 2000; Prix Anglais (France), 2000; Petra Kenny Award, 2001. *Memberships:* Federation of British Columbia Writers, pres.; League of Canadian Poets; Society of Canadian Composers; Writers Union of Canada. *Address:* 1235 Styles St, Victoria, BC V9A 3Z6, Canada. *E-mail:* lrogers@pacificoast.net.

ROGERS, Pattiann; b. 23 March 1940, Joplin, Missouri, USA. Writer; Poet. m. John R Rogers, 3 Sep 1960, 2 s. *Education:* BA, English, University of Missouri, 1961; MA, Creative Writing, University of Houston, 1981. *Publications:* The Expectations of Light, 1981; The Tattooed Lady in the Garden, 1986; Legendary Performance, 1987; Splitting and Binding, 1989; Geocentric, 1993; Firekeeper: New and Selected Poems, 1994; Eating Bread and Honey, 1997; Song of the World Becoming: New and Collected Poems, 1981–2001, 2001. *Contributions to:* Hudson Review; Poetry; Georgia Review; New England Review; Gettysburg Review; Poetry Northwest; Indiana Review; TriQuarterly; Western Humanities Review; Pushcart Prize Anthology, numbers 10, 11, 14, 17, 23. *Honours:* Texas Institute of Letters Awards, 1982, 1990; Guggenheim Fellowship, 1984; National Endowment for the Arts Grant, 1988; Lannan Fellowship in Poetry, 1991; Strousse Award in Poetry, 1992; Best American Poetry, 1996; Bock Award, Poetry, 1998. *Address:* 7412 Berkeley Circle, Castle Rock, CO 80104, USA. *E-mail:* pattiannrogers@mindspring.com.

ROGGEMAN, Willem Maurits; b. 9 July 1935, Brussels, Belgium. Poet; Writer. m. Jacqueline Nardi, 1975, 1 s., 1 d. *Education:* University of Ghent. *Appointments:* Critic, Het Laatste Nieuws newspaper, 1959–81; Ed., De Vlaamse Gids, 1970–92. *Publications:* Poetry: Rhapsody in Blue, 1958; Baudelaire Verliefd, 1964; Memoires, 1985; Een Leegte die Verdwijnt, 1985; Al Wie Omkykt is Gezien, 1988; De Uitvinding van de Tederheid, 1994; Geschiedenis, 1998. Fiction: De Centauren, 1963; De Verbeelding, 1966; De belegering van een Luchtkasteel, 1990. Essays: Cesare Pavese, 1961; Beroepsgeheim, 1975. *Contributions to:* Various publications. *Honours:* Dirk Martensprize, 1962; Prize, City of Brussels, 1975; Prize, St Truiden, 1989. *Memberships:* Flemish PEN Centre, secretary, 1968–80; L P Boon Society, pres., 1984–91.

ROGOFF, Jay; b. 21 Feb. 1954, New York, NY, USA. Lecturer in Liberal Studies; Poet. *Education:* BA, English, University of Pennsylvania, 1975; MA, Creative Writing, 1978, Doctor of Arts, English, 1981, Syracuse University. *Appointments:* Teaching Asst, Syracuse University, New York, 1975–80; Asst Prof. of English, LeMoyne College, Syracuse, 1980–85; Academic Adviser, Inmate Higher Education Programme, 1985–95, Lecturer in Liberal Studies, 1993–, Skidmore College, Saratoga Springs, New York. *Publications:* The Cutoff: A Sequence, The Word Works, 1995; First Hand, 1997; How We Came To Stand on That Shore, 2003. *Contributions to:* Agni; Boundary 2; Chicago Review; Double Take; Georgia Review; Hudson Review; Kansas Quarterly; Kenyon Review; Mademoiselle; Minnesota Review; MSS; New Republic; New Review; Nimrod; Partisan Review; Poetry Northwest; Poetry Review; Prairie Schooner; Present Tense; The Progressive; Quarterly West; Rattapallax; Salmagundi; Sewanee Review; Shenandoah; The Southern Review; Stand; Western Humanities Review; Yale Review; Zone 3; Manoa; Paris Review; Formalist; Spitball: Literary Baseball Magazine. *Honours:* Acad. of American Poets Award, 1976; Delmore Schwartz Poetry Prize, 1981; John Masefield Memorial Award, Poetry Society of America, 1982; Finalist, Walt Whitman Award, Acad. of American Poets, 1986, 1992; Fellow, MacDowell Colony, 1989, 1997; Fellow, 1989, Sloan and Solomon Writer in Residence, 1991, Corpn of Yaddo, 1994, 1996, 1998, 2000, 2001; Washington Prize for Poetry, 1994. *Memberships:* Poets and Writers; Associated Writing Programs; Poetry Society of America; Acad. of American Poets; National Book Critics Circle. *Address:* 35 Pinewood Ave, Saratoga Springs, NY 12866, USA. *E-mail:* jrogoff@skidmore.edu.

ROHEKAR, Joel Ezekiel; b. 5 Oct. 1942, Nadiad, Gujarat, India. Teacher; Poet. m. Sudha Rohekar, 22 March 1974. *Education:* BA, 1966; BEd, 1971; MA, 1974. *Publication:* Gomatesham Panamami. *Contributions to:* Anthologies and periodicals. *Honour:* Certificate of Participation with Honour and Excellence,

International Writers and Artists Asscn and Bluffton College, Ohio, 1995; World Peace Conference Award, Rotary International. *Memberships:* International Writers and Artists Asscn, USA; World Poetry Society Intercontinental. *Address:* 164/65 S Sadar Bazaar, Solapur 413 003, Maharashtra, India.

ROHEN, Edward, (Bruton Connors); b. 10 Feb. 1931, Dowlais, South Wales. Poet; Writer; Artist. m. Elizabeth Jarrett, 4 April 1961, 1 d. *Education:* ATD, Cardiff College of Art, 1952. *Appointments:* Art Teacher, Ladysmith High, BC, Canada, 1956–57; Head of Art, St Bonaventures, London, 1958–73, Ilford County High for Boys, Essex, 1973–82. *Publications:* Nightpriest, 1965; Bruised Concourse, 1973; Old Drunk Eyes Haiku, 1974; Scorpio Broadside 15, 1975; Poems/Poemas, 1976; 109 Haiku and One Seppuku for Maria, 1987; Sonnets for Maria Marriage, 1988; Sonnets: Second Sequence for Maria, 1989. *Contributions to:* Anthologies and magazines. *Memberships:* Academician, Centro Cultural Literario e Artistico de o Jornal de Felgeiras, Portugal; Korean War Veterans Writers and Arts Society; Welsh Acad. *Address:* 57 Kinfauns Rd, Goodmayes, Ilford, Essex IG3 9QH, England.

ROLLS, Eric Charles; b. 25 April 1923, Grenfell, NSW, Australia. Writer; Poet. m. (1) Joan Stephenson, 27 Feb. 1954, deceased 1985, 2 s., 1 d., (2) Elaine van Kempen, 1988. *Publications:* Sheaf Tosser, 1967; They All Ran Wild, 1969; Running Wild, 1973; The River, 1974; The Green Mosaic, 1977; Miss Strawberry Verses, 1978; A Million Wild Acres, 1981; Celebration of the Senses, 1984; Doorways: A Year of the Cumberdeen Diaries, 1989; Selected Poetry, 1990; Sojourners, 1993; From Forest to Sea, 1993; Citizens, 1996; A Celebration of Food and Wine (three vols), 1997; Australia: A Biography, Vol. 1, 2000; Visions of Australia, 2002. *Contributions to:* Bulletin; Overland; National Times; Age; Sydney Morning Herald; Independent Monthly; Sun Herald; various others. *Honours:* David Myer Trust Award for Poetry, 1968; Captain Cook Bicentennial Award for Non-Fiction, 1970; John Franklin Award for Children's Books, 1974; Braille Book of the Year, 1975; The Age Book of the Year, 1981; Talking Book of the Year, 1982; Fellow, Australian Acad. of the Humanities, 1985; Australian Creative Fellow, 1991; Order of Australia, 1991; Hon. Doctorate, University of Canberra, 1995. *Memberships:* Australian Society of Authors; National Book Council. *Address:* PO Box 2038, North Haven, NSW 2443, Australia.

ROLOFF, Michael; b. 19 Dec. 1937, Berlin, Germany (Naturalized US citizen, 1952). Playwright; Poet; Writer. *Education:* BA, Haverford College, Pennsylvania, 1958; MA, Stanford University, 1960. *Publications:* Screenplays: Feelings, 1982; Darlings and Monsters, 1983; Graduation Party, 1984. Plays: Wolves of Wyoming, 1985; Palombe Blue, 1985; Schizzohawk, 1986. Poetry: Headshots, 1984; It Won't Grow Back, 1985. Fiction: Darlings and Monsters Quartet, 4 titles, 1986–. Other: Numerous trans from German. *Address:* Box 6754, Malibu, CA 90264, USA.

ROMBOTIS, Anastasios, (Tasos Korfis); b. 12 Oct. 1929, Corfu, Greece. Vice-Admiral (retd); Poet; Writer. m. Helen Moniakis, 5 Feb. 1959, 1 s., 1 d. *Education:* Greece; USA; NATO Defence College, Rome. *Appointments:* Dir, Prosperos book publishers, 1973–, Anacyclisis Literary magazine, 1985–90. *Publications:* Poetry: Diary 1, 1963, 2, 1964, 3, 1968; Diarios, 1971; Handiwork, 1977; Poems, 1983; Pafsilipa, 1987; 153 Graffiti, 1992. Prose: Journey Without Polar Star, 1953; A Desert House, 1973; Knowledge of the Father, 1984. Other: Coexistences, 1982; The Writer Stratis Doukas, 1895–1936, 1988. *Contributions to:* Various magazines. *Honours:* Several awards. *Membership:* Society of Writers. *Address:* Alkiviadou 9, 10439 Athens, Greece.

ROMER, Stephen Charles Mark; b. 20 Aug. 1957, Bishops Stortford, Hertfordshire, England. University Lecturer; Poet. m. Bridget Stevens, 17 July 1982, 1 s. *Education:* Radley College, 1970–74; English Tripos, Double First, Trinity Hall, Cambridge, 1975–78; Harvard University, 1978–79; British Institute, Paris, 1980–81; PhD, Cantab, 1985. *Publications:* The Growing Dark, 1981; Firebird 3, 1985; Idols, 1986; Plato's Ladder, 1992. *Contributions to:* Anthologies, journals, and periodicals. *Honour:* Gregory Award for Poetry, 1985. *Address:* 6 rue de Verneuil, 75007 Paris, France.

ROMTVEDT, David William; b. 7 June 1950, Portland, Oregon, USA. Writer; Poet. m. Margo Brown, 30 May 1987. *Education:* BA, Reed College, 1972. *Appointments:* State Literature Consultant, Wyoming, 1987; Assoc. Prof. of English, Adjunct Assoc. Prof. of American Studies, University of Wyoming. *Publications:* Free and Compulsory for All, 1984; Moon, 1984; Letters from Mexico, 1987; Black Beauty and Kiev the Ukraine, 1987; Crossing the River: Poets of the Western US, 1987; How Many Horses, 1988; A Flower Whose Name I Do Not Know, 1992; Crossing Wyoming, 1992; Certainty, 1996; Windmill: Essays from Four Mile Ranch. *Contributions to:* Paris Review; Canadian Forum; American Poetry Review; Poets and Writers Magazine. *Honours:* Residency Award, 1979, Fellowship, 1987, Tri-National Exchange Fellowship, 1996, National Endowment for the Arts; Pushcart Prize, 1991; National Poetry Series Award, 1991; Wyoming Gov.'s Arts Award, 2000. *Address:* 457 N Main, Buffalo, WY 82834, USA.

RONAN, John Joseph; b. 18 June 1944, San Diego, CA, USA. Prof.; Poet. *Education:* BA, Loyola University, Chicago; MA, University of Illinois, 1969.

Appointments: Asst Prof., 1973–82, Prof., 1982–, Chair., Dept of Media and Communications, North Shore Community College, Danvers; Dir-Producer The Writer's Block, TV series, WNEC-TV, Gloucester. *Publication:* The Catching Self, 1996 *Contributions to:* Ohio Review; New England Quarterly; Greenboro Review; Three Penny Review; Southern Poetry Review; Yankee Magazine; Delaware Literary Review; Louisville Review; New Laurel Review; Epos; Hollins Critic; Andover Review; Lyric; North Essex Review. *Honours:* Scholarship Winner, Bread Loaf Writers Conference, 1975; Finalist Award, Massachusetts Artists Foundation, 1980; Winner, Willury Farm Competition, 1982; Finalist, Morse Competition, 1988; Capricorn Prize, 1991; National Poetry Series, 1992. *Memberships:* Poetry Society of America; Acad. of American Poets; National Federation of State Poetry Societies; National Writers Union. *Address:* Box 5524, Magnolia, MA 01930, USA.

ROOT, William Pitt; b. 28 Dec. 1941, Austin, Texas, USA. Prof.; Poet. m. Pamela Uschuk, 6 Nov. 1988, 1 d. *Education:* BA, University of Washington, 1964; MFA, University of North Carolina at Greensboro, 1966. *Appointments:* Stegman Fellow, Stanford University, 1967–68; Asst Prof., Michigan State University, 1967–68; Visiting Writer-in-Residence, Amherst College, 1971, University of Southwest Louisiana, 1976, Wichita State University, 1976, University of Montana, 1978, 1980, 1982–85, Pacific Lutheran University, 1990; Prof., Hunter College of the City University of New York, 1986–; Poet Laureate of Tuscon, AZ, 1997–. *Publications:* The Storm and Other Poems, 1969; Striking the Dark Air for Music, 1973; A Journey South, 1977; Reasons for Going It on Foot, 1981; In the World's Common Grasses, 1981; Invisible Guests, 1984; Faultdancing, 1986; Trace Elements from a Recurring Kingdom, 1994. *Contributions to:* Magazines and periodicals. *Honours:* Acad. of American Poetry Prize, 1967; Rockefeller Foundation Grant, 1969–70; Guggenheim Fellowship, 1970–71; National Endowment for the Arts Grant, 1973–74; Pushcart Awards, 1977, 1980, 1985; US-UK Exchange Artist, 1978–79; Stanley Kunitz Poetry Award, 1981; Guy Owen Poetry Award, 1984. *Address:* c/o Dept of English, Hunter College of the City University of New York, 695 Park Ave, New York, NY 10021, USA.

ROSA ROMERO, Jaime Benito; b. 25 July 1949, Bellreguard, Valencia, Spain. Prof.; Poet. 2 s. *Education:* Licentiate in Philosophy, University of Valencia, 1974; Licentiate and Doctor in Philology, Sorbonne, University of Paris, 1982. *Publications:* Poetry: Nubes digitales, 1974; Océan Claxon, 1979; La Estación Azul, 1980; Yo Leopardo, 1982; De Rizo Soplo, 1984; Lugar de Polen, 1993; Anthology of Chicano Poetry, 1996; Los Vasos Comunicantes: Antología de Poesiá Chincana, 1999. Fiction: Arlequin en el laberinto, 1986; Las cuatro caras de la piramide negra, 1990; Hilo de Seda, 1995. *Contributions to:* International Poetry Yearbook, University of Colorado, 1987–88. *Membership:* World Congress of Poets. *Address:* C/7 No. 134, Urb Parque Montealcedo, 46190-Riba-roja, Valencia, Spain.

ROSDAHL, Cecilie; b. 15 Dec. 1975, Copenhagen, Denmark. Poet; Writer; Painter. *Publications:* Lykke Laila, 1993; O (poems), 1996. *Address:* Viborggade 49 4 MF, 2100 Copenhagen 0, Denmark.

ROSE, Daniel Asa; b. 20 Nov. 1949, New York, NY, USA. Writer; Essayist; Poet; Ed. m. (1) Laura Love, 30 Nov. 1974, divorced, 2 s., (2) Shelley Roth, 5 Sept. 1993, 2 s. *Education:* AB, Honours, English, Brown University, 1971. *Appointments:* Arts and Culture Ed., The Forward; Travel Columnist, Esquire; Book Reviewer, Vanity Fair; Travel Ed., Madison. *Publications:* Flipping for it, 1987; Small Family with Rooster, 1988; Hiding Places: A Father and His Sons Retrace their Family's Escape from the Holocaust, 2000. Other: Screenplays, poems, stories, reviews and literary essays. *Contributions to:* The New Yorker; The New York Times Magazine; GQ; Esquire; Playboy. *Honours:* O Henry Prize, 1980; PEN Literary Awards, 1987, 1988; Massachusetts Cultural Council Award, 1992. *Address:* 138 Bay State Rd, Renoboth, MA 02769, USA.

ROSE, Margaret. See: ANDERSDATTER, Karla Margaret.

ROSE, Myrna. See: OSTERBERG, Myra Janet.

ROSE, Sue Ruth; b. 25 July 1959, London, England. Trans.; Poet. *Education:* Diplome de Culture Francaise, 1980; BA, Honours, French and English, 1981; Diploma, Bilingual Secretarial Studies, 1985; Diploma, Trans., 1990. *Contributions to:* Anthologies, reviews, and magazines. *Honours:* Eighth Prize, Skoob/Index on Censorship Competition, 1989; Commendation, National Poetry Competition, 1992; Runner-Up, Poetry Business Competition, 1992; Runner-Up, Peterloo Competition, 1998. *Memberships:* Poetry Society; Society of Authors. *Address:* 14 Tyndale Park, Herne Bay, Kent CT6 6BP, England.

ROSEBUD, Milo. See: ARMSTRONG, Terry Lee.

ROSENBAUM, Marek. See: LEBIODA, Dariusz Thomas.

ROSENBERG, Liz; b. 3 Feb. 1956, Glen Cove, New York, USA. Assoc. Prof. of English; Poet; Writer. m. David Bosnick, 2 June 1996, 1 s. *Education:* BA, Bennington College, 1976; MA, Johns Hopkins University, 1978; PhD, Comparative Literature, State University of New York at Binghamton, 1997.

Appointments: Assoc. Prof. of English, State University of New York at Binghamton; Guest Teacher-Poet, various venues; Many poetry readings. *Publications:* The Fire Music (poems), 1987; A Book of Days (poems), 1992; Children of Paradise (poems), 1994; Heart and Soul (novel), 1996; The Invisible Ladder (ed.), 1997; Earth-Shattering Poems (ed.), 1998; These Happy Eyes (prose poems), 1999. *Contributions to:* Many newspapers, reviews, and journals. *Honours:* Kelloggs Fellow, 1980–82; Pennsylvania Council of the Arts Poetry Grant, 1982; Agnes Starrett Poetry Prize, 1987; Claudia Lewis Poetry Prize, 1997; Best Book for Teens Citation, New York Public Library, 1997; Paterson Prizes for Children's Literature, 1997, 1998. *Memberships:* Associated Writing Programs; PEN. *Address:* c/o Dept of English, General Literature, and Rhetoric, State University of New York at Binghamton, PO Box 6000, Binghamton, NY 13902, USA.

ROSENBLATT, Joe, (Joseph Rosenblatt); b. 26 Dec. 1933, Toronto, Ontario, Canada. Poet; Writer; Artist. m. Faye Smith, 13 Oct. 1970, 1 s. *Education:* Central Technical School, Toronto; George Brown College, Toronto. *Appointments:* Ed., Jewish Dialog magazine, 1969–83; Writer-in-Residence, University of Western Ontario, London, 1979–80, University of Victoria, BC, 1980–81, Saskatoon Public Library, Saskatchewan, 1985–86; Visiting Lecturer, University of Rome and University of Bologna, 1987. *Publications:* The Voyage of the Mood, 1960; The LSD Leacock, 1963; The Winter of the Luna Moth, 1968; Greenbaum, 1970; The Bumblebee Dithyramb, 1972; Blind Photographer: Poems and Sketches, 1973; Dream Craters, 1974; Virgins and Vampires, 1975; Top Soil, 1976; Doctor Anaconda's Solar Fun Club: A Book of Drawings, 1977; Loosely Tied Hands: An Experiment in Punk, 1978; Snake Oil, 1978; The Sleeping Lady, 1979; Brides of the Stream, 1984; Escape from the Glue Factory: A Memoir of a Paranormal Toronto Childhood in the Late Forties, 1985; Poetry Hotel: Selected Poems 1963–1985, 1985; The Kissing Goldfish of Siam: A Memoir of Adolescence in the Fifties, 1989; Gridi nel Buio, 1990; Beds and Consenting Dreamers, 1994; The Joe Rosenblatt Reader, 1995; The Voluptuos Gardener: The Collected Art and Writing of Joe Rosenblatt 1973–1996, 1996. *Contributions to:* Many publications. *Honours:* Canada Council Senior Arts Awards, 1973, 1976, 1980, 1987; Ontario Arts Council Poetry Award, 1970; Governor-Generals' Award for Poetry, 1976; British Columbia Book Award for Poetry, 1986. *Address:* 221 Elizabeth Ave, Qualicum Beach, BC V9K 1G8, Canada.

ROSENBLUM, Martin Jack; b. 19 Aug. 1946, Appleton, Wisconsin, USA. Poet; Writer. m. Maureen Rice, 6 Sept. 1970, 2 d. *Education:* BS, 1969, MA, 1971, PhD, 1980, University of Wisconsin. *Appointments:* Guest Lecturer, University of East Anglia, Norwich, England, 1975; Poet-in-Residence, Wisconsin Review, University of Wisconsin at Oshkosh, 1987. *Publications:* Home, 1971; On, 1972; The Werewolf Sequence, 1974; Brite Shade, 1984; Conjuction, 1987; The Holy Ranger: Harley-Davidson Poems, 1989; No Freedom, Honey (CD), 2000; Places To Go (CD), 2001; Spirit Fugitive (CD), 2002. Non-Fiction: Harley-Davidson Inc, 1903–1993: An Historical Overview, 1994; Harley-Davidson Lore, Vol. 1, 1999, Vol. 2, 2000. Other: Down on the Spirit Farm (CD of music and poetry), 1994. *Honour:* Wisconsin Award, Best Poet of 1995. *Address:* 2521 E Stratford Ct, Shorewood, WI 53211, USA.

ROSENSTAND, Peder Tuxen; b. 2 Nov. 1935, Copenhagen, Denmark. Poet; Artist; Painter; Prof. m. Anni Rosenstand, 1960, 3 s., 1 d. *Education:* Royal Danish Acad. of Art, Copenhagen; University of Copenhagen. *Publications:* Osteklokken, 1974; Blik, 1988. Other: Dramatic works for Danish, Norwegian, and Swedish TV; Painting exhibitions held in Denmark, England, Germany, Italy, New York, and Sweden, 1962–94. *Contributions to:* Pinqvinen. *Membership:* Authors Society, Copenhagen. *Address:* G1 Mollerup, 4673 Rodvig Stevns, Tif 53707030, Denmark.

ROSENSTOCK, Gabriel Stefan; b. 29 Sept. 1949, County Limerick, Ireland. Poet; Ed.; Broadcaster; Trans. m. Eithne Ní Chléirigh, 1 s., 3 d. *Publications:* Portrait of The Artist as an Abominable Snowman, 1989; Oráistí, 1991; The Confessions of Henry Hooter the Third, 1992. *Contributions to:* Poetry Ireland Review; Cyphers; Innti; Comhar; Celtic Dawn; Poetry USA; Irish Times; Irland Journal; Die Andere; Krino; Poetry (Chicago); Tratti; Neue Zürcher Zeitung; Akzente; Éire-Ireland; The Literary Review; Cinnamon Review; World Haiku Review. *Honours:* Arts Council Bursary, 1988; Irish-American Cultural Foundation Award, 1989; Various Oireachtas prizes. *Memberships:* Irish Writers' Union; Irish Trans' Asscn; Aosdána (Irish Acad. of Arts and Letters); British Haiku Society; Haiku Society of America. *Address:* 37 Garrán Arnold, Gleann na gCaorach, Contae Atha Cliath, Ireland. *E-mail:* roseng@educ.irlgov.ie.

ROSENWALD, John; b. 25 June 1943, Oak Park, IL, USA. Teacher; Writer; Poet. m. Ann Arbor, 7 Aug. 1976, 1 d. *Education:* BA, 1964, MA, 1965, University of Illinois; PhD, Duke University, 1969. *Appointments:* Assumption College, Worcester, MA, 1969–75; Beloit College, Beloit, Wisconsin, 1976–; Fudan University, Shanghai, 1987, 1990, 1996–97; Nankai University, Tianjin, 1997; Zhejiang University, Hangzhou, 2001–02. *Publication:* Smoking People: Encountering the New Chinese Poetry, 1989. *Contributions to:* Wisconsin Review; Literary Review; Kansas Quarterly; South Carolina Review; Kennebec; Northeast; Paintbrush; Wisconsin Poets' Calendar; Manoa; Talus; Descant. *Honour:* Fulbright Scholarships, 1965–66,

1996–97, 2001–02. *Memberships:* MLA; Editorial Board, Beloit Poetry Journal; Robert Bly's Annual Conference on The Great Mother. *Address:* Granite Rose Farm, Box 389, South Andover, ME 04216, USA.

ROSNER, Martin Calvin; b. 14 May 1932, New York, NY, USA. Physician; Poet. m. Arlene B. Ackerman, 3 July 1955, 2 s., 1 d. *Education:* University College, New York University, 1949–52; State University of New York Downstate Medical College, 1952–56. *Appointments:* Chief, Hypertension Research, Cardiac Therapy Research Unit, Bronx Veterans Administration Hospital, New York, 1962–66; Chief of Cardiology, Asst Dir of Medicine, Jewish Memorial Hospital, New York, 1964–68; Consultant in Cardiology, 1963–, Pascack Valley Hospital, Westwood, NJ. *Publications:* Kings and Jackals, 1960; The Coracle and Other Poems, 1971; Hormones and Hyacinths, 1981; Pilgrim at Sunset, 1997; The Doctor in the Night, 2002. *Contributions to:* New York Times; Stars and Stripes; Voices International; New Jersey Poetry; Essence; Writers Poetry; Journal of the American Medical Asscn; Cape Codder; Hartford Courant; Millennium Portals. *Memberships:* Acad. of American Poets; Poets and Writers; International Acad. of Poetry, founder fellow. *Address:* 234 Vivien Ct, Paramus, NJ 07652, USA.

ROSS, Joe; b. 27 Dec. 1960, Pennsylvania, USA. Poet; Writer; Ed. *Education:* Magna cum laude, Honours Programme, Temple University, 1983. *Appointments:* Literary Ed., Washington Review, 1990–; Poet-in-Residence, Pyramid Atlantic, 1991–; Writer and Worker, John F Kennedy Center for the Performing Arts. *Publications:* Guards of the Heart, 1990; How to Write, or I Used to be in Love With My Jailer, 1992; An American Voyage, 1993; Push, 1994; De-Flections, 1994; Full Silence, 1995. *Contributions to:* Numerous small press poetry magazines. *Membership:* Contemporary Arts Educational Project. *Address:* 1719 South St NW, No. 2, Washington, DC 20009, USA.

ROSS, Kendric. See: MAIN, Gordon Ian.

ROTHENBERG, Jerome (Dennis); b. 11 Dec. 1931, New York, NY, USA. Prof. of Visual Arts and Literature; Poet; Writer. m. Diane Brodatz, 25 Dec. 1952, 1 s. *Education:* BA, City College, New York City, 1952; MA, University of Michigan, 1953. *Appointments:* Prof. of English and Comparative Literature, State University of New York at Binghamton, 1986–88; Prof. of Visual Arts and Literature, University of California at San Diego, 1988–. *Publications:* New Young German Poets, 1959; White Sun, Black Sun, 1960; Technicians of the Sacred, 1968; Poems for the Game of Silence: Selected Poems, 1971; Shaking the Pumpkin, 1972; America: A Prophecy, 1973; Poland/1931, 1974; Revolution of the Word, 1974; A Big Jewish Book, 1977; A Seneca Journal, 1978; Numbers and Letters, 1980; Vienna Blood, 1980; Pre-Faces, 1981; That Dada Strain, 1983; Symposium of the Whole, 1983; 15 Flower World Variations, 1984; A Merz Sonata, 1985; New Selected Poems, 1970–85, 1986; Exiled in the Word, 1989; Khurbn and Other Poems, 1989; Further Sightings and Conversations, 1989; The Lorca Variations, 1994; Gematria, 1994; An Oracle for Delfi, 1995; Poems for the Millennium, two vols, 1995, 1998; Pictures of the Crucifixion, 1996; Seedings and Other Poems, 1996; The Book: Spiritual Instrument, 1996; A Paradise of Poets, 1999; A Book of the Book, 2000; The Case for Memory, 2001. *Contributions to:* Various publications. *Honours:* National Endowment for the Arts Fellowship, 1975; Guggenheim Fellowship, 1976; American Book Award, 1982; Trans. Award, PEN Center, USA West, 1994; Josephine Miles Literary Awards, PEN Oakland, 1994, 1996. *Memberships:* New Wilderness Foundation; PEN International. *Address:* c/o Dept of Visual Arts, University of California at San Diego, La Jolla, CA 92093, USA.

ROTHSCHILD, Anne; b. 16 March 1943, New York, NY, USA. Etcher; Painter; Art Prof.; Poet; Writer. 1 s. *Education:* Graduate School, Columbia University, 1963; Licence es Lettres, Sorbonne, Paris, 1965; Diplome des Beaux-Arts, Geneva, 1973; Certificat d'Aptitude a l'Enseignement, Geneva, 1975. *Appointments:* Prof. of Art History and Art, Geneva, 1968–84; Attaché Littéraire à la Promotion des Lettres Belges à Paris, 1988–90. *Publications:* L'An Prochain a Jerusalem, 1979; L'Errance du Nom, 1982; Sept Branches – Sept Jours, 1983; Sept Figures du Livre, Poems and Aquatints, 1983; Du Desert au Fleuve, Poems and Aquatints, 1986; L'Eau du Marbre, 1987; Le Passeur, 1990; Draperies de l'Oubli, 1990; Le Buisson de Feu (novel), 1992; Les Arbres Voyageurs, 1995. *Contributions to:* Anthologies and other publications. *Honours:* Prix Max-Pol Fouchet, 1983; Grants from Promotion des Lettres Belges, 1983, 1989, 1991; Office Féderal de La Culture, Switzerland, 1984, City of Geneva, 1984, CNL, Paris, 1985, Pro Helvetia, 1985, 1993, Foundation Alain de Rothschild, Paris, 1991. *Address:* 81 Rue Vieille du Temple, 75003 Paris, France.

ROUPCHEV, George; b. 2 Sept. 1957, Sofia, Bulgaria. Poet; Trans. m. Valentina Petkova, 1 d. *Education:* Graduated, Bulgarian Philology, Psychology, Sofia University, 1982. *Publications:* Tired of Miracles, 1982; Relief of the Night Guard, 1986; Tibalt's Death, 1989; The Men of the Night, 1991. *Contributions to:* Magazines. *Honours:* National Prizes for Student Poetry, 1980, 1981, 1982; Sofia University Prize, 1982; Southern Spring Prize, 1983; Union of Bulgarian Trans Prizes, 1992, 1994. *Memberships:* Union of Bulgarian Writers; Union of Bulgarian Trans. *Address:* Christo Maximov Str 20, 1111 Sofia, Bulgaria.

ROUSE, Anne Barrett; b. 26 Sept. 1954, Washington, DC, USA. Poet; Writer. *Education:* BA, History, University of London, 1977. *Appointments:* Dir, Islington Mind, 1992–95; Visiting Writing Fellow, University of Glasgow, 2000–02. *Publication:* Sunset Grill, 1993; Timing, 1997. *Contributions to:* Periodicals. *Honours:* Poetry Book Society Recommendations, 1993, 1997. *Memberships:* Poetry Society; Writers' Guild. *Address:* c/o Bloodaxe Books, PO Box 1SN, Newcastle upon Tyne NE99 1SN, England.

ROWBOTHAM, Colin Hugh; b. 5 June 1949, Manchester, England. Tutor; Poet. m. Maggie Hindley, 1 Sept. 1979, 1 s., deceased, 2 d. *Education:* BA, Honours, English Literature, York University, 1971; PGCE, Manchester College of Education, 1972; RSA Certificate, TEFL II, 1980. *Appointments:* Primary School Teacher, Hackney, 1972–77; Part-time ESL/Adult Literacy Tutor, Bow/Mile End, 1973–77; English Teacher, Engelbert-Kaempfer Gymnasium, Germany, 1977–78; Mem., Marble Arch EFL Co-Operative, 1979–83; Individual Tutor, Hackney, 1983–. *Publications:* Total Recall, 1987; Johnny, 1988. *Contributions to:* Anthologies; Poetry Review; Orbis; Green Book; Outposts; Other Poetry; Staple; New Spokes; Poetry Nottingham; Rites; New Generation; North. *Honours:* First Prize, Lake Aske Memorial Competition, 1984; First Prize, Newbury Festival Competition, 1985; First Prize, Old Bull Arts Centre Competition, 1985; Third Place, Kent and Sussex Poetry Competition, 1992. *Membership:* North Seven Poetry Group, founder-mem. *Address:* 3 Victor Cazalet House, Gaskin St, London N1 2RX, England.

ROWBOTHAM, David Harold; b. 27 Aug. 1924, Toowoomba, Qld, Australia. Poet; Writer. m. Ethel Jessie Matthews, 14 Jan. 1952, 2 d. *Education:* BA, University of Queensland, 1965; MA, 1969. *Appointments:* Commonwealth Literary Fund Lecturer in Australian Literature, 1956, 1961, 1964; Arts Ed., 1970–80, Literary Ed., 1980–87, Brisbane Courier-Mail. *Publications:* Poetry: Ploughman and Poet, 1954;, 1956; Inland, 1958; All the Room, 1964; Bungalow and Hurricane, 1967; The Makers of the Ark, 1970; The Pen of Feathers, 1971; Mighty Like a Harp, 1974; Selected Poems, 1975; Maydays, 1980; New and Selected Poems, 1945–93, 1994; The Ebony Gates: New & Wayside Poems, 1996. Fiction: Town and City, 1956; The Man in the Jungle, 1964. *Contributions to:* Numerous magazines and journals. *Honours:* Grace Leven Prize, 1964; Second Prize for Poetry, New South Wales Captain Cook Bi-Centennary Celebrations Literary Competition, 1970; Emeritus Fellow of Australian Literature, Australia Council, 1989; A.O., 1991. *Memberships:* Australian Society of Authors; Fellowship of Australian Writers. *Address:* 28 Percival Terrace, Holland Park, Brisbane, Qld 4121, Australia.

ROXMAN, (Pia) Susanna (Ellinor); b. 29 Aug. 1946, Stockholm, Sweden. Writer; Poet; Critic. *Education:* BA, University of Lund, 1973; PhD, Comparative Literature, University of Göteborg, 1984; English Literature, King's College, University of London. *Appointment:* Head, Centre of Classical Mythology, University of Lund, 1996–. *Publications:* Riva villor, 1978; Nymferna kommer, 1983; Glöm de döda, 1985; Goodbye to the Berlin Wall, 1991; Broken Angels, 1996; In the Pouring Rain. *Contributions to:* Reviews, quarterlies and journals worldwide. *Honours:* Swedish Authors' Foundation Grant, 1979; Malmöhus County Council Arts Grant, Sweden, 1984; Swedish Balzac Prize, 1990; Special Mention, Open University Poetry Competition, England, 1994; Ed.'s Choice Prize, Marjorie Lees Linn Poetry Award Competition, Elk River Review, USA. *Memberships:* Författarcentrum Syd (Authors' Centre South); Conservatory of American Letters. *Address:* Lagerbrings Vag 5 B, 224 60 Lund, Sweden.

ROZ, Victor. See: RODRIGUEZ, Victorino.

RUBIN, Diana Kwiatkowski; b. 30 Dec. 1958, New York, NY, USA. Poet; Writer. m. Paul Rubin, 4 Jan. 1986, 1 s., 2 d. *Education:* BA, Marymount Manhattan College, 1988; MA, New York University, 1994. *Publications:* Spirits in Exile, 1990; Visions of Enchantment, 1991; Dinosauria, 1995. *Contributions to:* Amelia; Wind; Quest; Fox Cry; Voices International. *Honour:* First Prize, Sparrowgrass Poetry Forum Awards, 1998. *Membership:* Acad. of American Poets. *Address:* PO Box 398, Piscataway, NJ 08855, USA.

RUBIN, Larry Jerome; b. 14 Feb. 1930, Bayonne, New Jersey, USA. Prof. of English; Poet. *Education:* BA, 1951, MA, 1952, PhD, 1956, Emory University. *Appointments:* Instructor, 1956–58, Asst Prof., 1958–65, Assoc. Prof., 1965–73, Prof., 1973–99, English, Georgia Tech University. *Publications:* The World's Old Way, 1963; Lanced in Light, 1967; All My Mirrors Lie, 1975; Unanswered Calls, 1997. *Contributions to:* New Yorker; Harper's Magazine; The Nation; Poetry; Sewanee Review; London Magazine. *Honours:* Reynolds Lyric Award, Poetry Society of America; Annual Award, Poetry Society of America; Smith-Mundt Award; Fulbright Awards; Several grants. *Memberships:* Poetry Society of America; Poetry Society of Georgia. *Address:* Box 15014, Druid Hills Branch, Atlanta, GA 30333, USA.

RUDMAN, Mark; b. 11 Dec. 1948, New York, NY, USA. Poet; Critic; Ed.; Trans.; Adjunct Prof. m. Madelaine Bates, 1 s. *Education:* BA, New School for Social Research, 1971; MFA, Columbia University, 1974. *Appointments:* Poetry and Criticism Ed., 1975–, Ed.-in-Chief, 1984–, Pequod Journal; Writer-in-Residence, University of Hawaii, 1978, State University of New York at Buffalo, 1979, Wabash College, 1979; Adjunct Lecturer, Queens College of

the City University of New York, 1980–81; Lecturer, Parsons School of Design, 1983; Poet-in-Residence and Assoc. Prof., York College, 1984–88; Asst Dir and Adjunct Prof., Graduate Creative Writing Program, New York University, 1986–; Adjunct Prof., Columbia University, 1988–91, 1992–; Poet-in-Residence, State University of New York, Purchase, 1991; Walt Whitman Poet, 1998. *Publications:* In the Neighboring Cell (poems), 1982; The Mystery in the Garden (chapbook), 1985; By Contraries and Other Poems: 1970–1984 Selected and New, 1986; The Ruin Revived (chapbook), 1986; The Nowhere Steps (poems), 1990; Literature and the Visual Arts (ed.), 1990; Diverse Voices: Essays on Poetry, 1993; Rider (poems), 1994; Realm of Unknowing: Meditations on Art, Suicide, Uncertainty, and Other Transformations, 1995; The Millennium Hotel (poems), 1996; Provoked in Venice (poems), 1999; The Killers (poems), 2000; The Couple, 2001. Translator: Square of Angels, by B. Antonych, 1976; My Sister – Life, by Pasternak, 1983. *Contributions to:* Poems and essays in many anthologies and other publications. *Honours:* Acad. of American Poets Award, 1971; PEN Trans. Fellowship, 1976; Yaddo Residencies, 1977, 1983; Ed.'s Award, Co-ordinating Council for Literary Magazines, 1981; Ingram Merrill Foundation Fellowship, 1983–84; Max Hagward Award for Trans., 1984; New York Foundation of the Arts Fellowship, 1988; National Book Critics Circle Award in Poetry, 1994; National Endowment for the Arts Fellowship, 1995; Guggenheim Fellowship, 1996–97. *Memberships:* PEN; Poetry Society of America, board of governors, 1984–88. *Address:* 817 West End Ave, New York, NY 10025, USA.

RUDOLF, Anthony; b. 6 Sept. 1942, London, England. Poet; Writer; Trans. Divorced, 1 s., 1 d. *Education:* BA, Trinity College, Cambridge, 1964; Diploma, British Institute, Paris, 1961. *Appointments:* Co-Founder and Ed., Menard Press, London, 1969; Advisory Ed., Modern Poetry in Translation, 1973–; Adam Lecturer, King's College, London, 1990; Pierre Rouve Memorial Lecturer, Sofia, 2001; Visiting Lecturer, Faculty of Arts and Humanites, University of North London, 2001. *Publications:* The Same River Twice, 1976; After the Dream: Poems 1964–79, 1980; Primo Levi's War Against Oblivion, 1990; Mandorla, 1999; The Arithmetic of Memory, 1999. Other: Trans of poetry. *Contributions to:* Periodicals and newspapers. *Address:* 8 The Oaks, Woodside Ave, London N12 8AR, England.

RUDOLPH, Lee (Norman); b. 28 March 1948, Cleveland, OH, USA. Mathematician; Poet; Writer. *Education:* BA, Princeton University, 1969; PhD, Massachusetts Institute of Technology, 1974. *Publications:* Curses and Songs and Poems, 1974; The Country Changes, 1978. *Contributions to:* Professional journals, anthologies, and periodicals. *Honours:* Several awards. *Memberships:* Alice James Poetry Co-operative; National Writers Union. *Address:* PO Box 251, Adamsville, RI 02801, USA.

RUDY, Dorothy L; b. 27 June 1924, Ohio, USA. Prof. of English and Creative Writing; Poet. m. Willis Rudy, 31 Jan. 1948, 1 s., 2 d. *Education:* BA, Queens College, 1945; MA, Philosophy, Columbia University, 1948. *Appointments:* Prof. of English and Creative Writing, Montclair State University, 1964–88; Lecturer, Fairleigh Dickinson University, 1988–90, 1996–2001, Bergen Community College, 1991–96, YMHA Wayne Humanities Scholar of the Arts, 1993–. *Publications:* Quality of Small and Other Poems, 1971; Psyche Afoot and Other Poems, 1978; Grace Notes to the Measure of the Heart, 1979; Voices Through Time and Distant Places, 1993. *Contributions to:* Passaic Herald News; Letters; Poem; Laurel Review; Just Pulp; Composers; Authors and Artists Quarterly; Scimiter and Song; Bitterroot; Cellar Door; Pet Gazette; Black Buzzard Press. *Honour:* American Poets Fellowship, 1971; New Jersey Literary Society Hall of Fame, 1994; Certificate of Achievement in the Arts, Literature, Contemporary Women's Club of Bergenfield, 1997. *Memberships:* Composers, Authors and Artists of America; Bergen Poets; New York Poetry Forum; Browning Society; New England Small Press Asscn, Women's Board; Scambi International. *Address:* 161 W Clinton Ave, Tenafly, NJ 07670, USA.

RUHM, Gerhard; b. 12 Feb. 1930, Vienna, Austria. Writer; Poet; Dramatist; Composer; Graphic Artist. *Education:* Acad. of Music, Vienna, 1945–51. *Publications:* Literarisches Cabaret (with H Artmann and K Bayer), 1958–59; hosn rosn baa (with H Artmann and F Achleitner), 1959; Kinderoper (with H Artmann and K Bayer), 1964; Gesammelte Gedichte, 1970; Gesammelte Theaterstücke 1954–1971, 1972; Erste Folger Kurzer Hörstücker, 1973; Zweite Folge kurzer Hörstücke, 1975, 1975; wald: ein deutsches requiem, 1983; Allein, verlassen, verloren: 3 Kurzhörspiele zum Thema Angst (with R Hughes and Marie Luise Kaschnitz), 1986; leselieder/visuelle Musik, 1986; botschaft an die zukunft: gesammelte sprechtexte, 1988; Geschlechterdings: Chansons, Romanzen, Gedichte, 1990; Theatertexte, 1990; Mit Messer und Gabel, 1995. *Honours:* Asscn of War Blind Radio Prize, 1983; Great Austrian State Prize, 1991. *Membership:* Acad. of Fine Arts, Hamburg. *Address:* Lochnerstrasse 7, 50674 Cologne, Germany.

RUHMKORF, Peter; b. 25 Oct. 1929, Dortmund, Germany. Poet; Author. m. Eva-Marie Titze. *Education:* German Language and Literature, Psychology, Hamburg. *Appointments:* Writer-in-Residence, University of Texas at Austin, 1969–70; Lecturer, University of Essen, 1974, 1991–92, University of Warwick, England, 1977. *Publications:* Irdisches Vergnügen in g, 1959; Kunstücke: 50 Gedichte nebst einer Anleitung zum Wilderspruch, 1962; Die Jahre die Ihr kennt: Anfälle und Erinnerungen, 1972; Gesammelte Gedichte, 1976;

Strömungslehre I: Poesie, 1978; Haltbar bis Ende, 199, 1979; Auf Wiedersehen in Kenilworth: Ein Märchen in dreizehn Kapiteln, 1980; agar agar: zaurzaurim: Zur Naturgeschichte dees Reims und der menschlichen Anklangsnerven, 1981; Hüter des Misthaufens, 1981; Kleine Fleckenkunde, 1981; Bleib erschütterbar und widersteh, 1984; Dintemann und Schindemann, 1987; Einmalig wie wir alle, 1989; Selbst III/88: Aus der Fassung, 1989; Tabu I: Tagebücher 1989–1991, 1995. *Honours:* Erich Kastner Prize, 1979; Arno Schmidt Prize, 1986; Heinrich Heine Prize, 1988; Georg Buchner Prize, 1993. *Memberships:* Deutsche Akademie für Sprache und Dichtung eV, Darmstadt; Freie Akademie der Künste, Hamburg; PEN. *Address:* Ovelgönne 50, 22605 Hamburg, Germany.

RUIZ, Bernardo; b. 6 Oct. 1953, México, DF, Mexico. Author; Poet. m. Virginia Abrin Batule, 18 Nov. 1978, 2 s. *Education:* BA, Spanish and Latin American Literature, Universidad Nacional Autonoma de Mexico. *Appointments:* Ed., Universidad Autonoma Metropolitana, 1979, Ministry of Labour, 1985–88; Dir, INBA, Centro Nacional de Informacion y Promocion de la Literatura, 1992. *Publications:* Fiction: Viene la Muerte, 1976; La otra orilla, 1980; Olvidar tu nombre, 1982; Vals sins fin, 1982; Los caminos del hotel, 1991. Poetry: El Tuyo, el mismo, 1986; Juego de Cartas, 1992. *Contributions to:* Various publications. *Memberships:* Asociacion de Criticos de Mexico; Asociacion de Escritores de Mexico; Sociedad General de Escritores de Mexico. *Address:* Arizona 94-6, Col Napoles, CP 03810, Mexico DF, Mexico.

RUIZ DE TORRES, Juan; b. 13 July 1931, Madrid, Spain. Poet; Ed.; Publisher. m. Angela Reyes, 1986, 1 s., 2 d. *Education:* Doctor of Industrial Engineering, 1962, Lic Hispanic Phil and Computer Science, University Politenica de Madrid; PhD Studies. *Appointments:* Pres., Ateneo de Cali, Colombia, 1961–65, Ateneo de Grecia, 1970–73, Asociacion Prometeo de Poesia, Madrid, 1980–94; Founder, Ed., and Dir, Carta de la Poesia, Cuadernos de Poesia Nueva, Valor de la Palabra. *Publications:* 21 books in Spanish, 1977–98. *Contributions to:* Periodicals. *Honours:* Medal, Instituto de Cultura Puertorriquena, 1987; Accademico de Merito with Gold Palm, Accademia Internazionale di Pontzen, Naples, 1991. *Memberships:* Asociacion Colegial de Escritores; Asociacion Cultural El Foro de la Encina, founder-pres.; Order de la Encina del Merito Poetico, founder-Grand Master. *Address:* Apartado 007, 28660 Boadilla, Madrid, Spain.

RULEMAN, William Arthur; b. 20 Jan. 1957, Memphis, TN, USA. Prof. of English; Poet. m. Elizabeth Howard Sayle, 8 Oct. 1983, 1 d. *Education:* BA, University of Virginia, 1979; MA, Memphis State University, 1983. *Appointments:* Instructor, Memphis State University, 1983–84, Northwest Missouri State University, 1987–88, Arkansas State University, 1989–90; Graduate Teaching Asst, University of Alabama, 1984–87; Instructor, 1988–89, Graduate Teaching Asst, 1990–94, University of Mississippi; Prof. of English, Tennessee Wesleyan College, 1994–. *Contributions to:* Berkeley Poetry Review; Global Tapestry; Outposts Poetry Quarterly; Peace and Freedom; Poetry and Audience; Psychopoetica. *Honour:* PhD, University of Mississippi, 1994. *Address:* 319 N Jackson St, Athens, TN 37303, USA.

RUMBOLD, Lady Pauline Letitia, (Pauline Tennant); b. 6 Feb. 1929, London, England. Actress; Poet. m. (1) Julian Pitt-Rivers, 1946, (2) Euan Graham, 1954, (3) Sir A Rumbold Baronet, 1974, 1 adopted s. *Appointments:* Stage roles in: Big Top, She Follows Me About, No Medals, The Day After Tomorrow; Films: The Queen of Spades, Great Day. *Publications:* William Barnes Dorset Poems (trans.), 1989; Loaves and Fishes, 1992. *Memberships:* William Barnes Society, vice-chair.; Poetry Book Society; Prayer Book Society; Friend of Leighton House; Chelsea Arts Club. *Address:* Hatch Cottage, Cokers Frome, Dorchester, Dorset DT2 7SD, England.

RUMENS, Carol Ann; b. 10 Dec. 1944, London, England. Writer; Poet. m. David Rumens, 30 July 1965, divorced, 2 d. *Education:* University of London, 1964–65. *Appointments:* Writing Fellow, University of Kent, 1983–85; Northern Arts Writing Fellow, 1988–90; Writer-in-Residence, Queen's University, Belfast, 1991–. *Publications:* A Strange Girl in Bright Colours, 1973; Unplayed Music, 1981; Star Whisper, 1983; Direct Dialling, 1985; Selected Poems, 1987; Plato Park, 1988; The Greening of the Snow Beach, 1988; From Berlin to Heaven, 1990. *Contributions to:* Periodicals. *Honours:* Joint Winner, Alice Hunt Bartlett Prize, 1981; Prudence Farmer Award, 1983; Cholmondeley Award, 1984. *Memberships:* International PEN; RSL, fellow; Society of Authors. *Address:* 100A Tunis Rd, London W12 7EY, England.

RUSS, Earlene (Biff); b. 12 Aug. 1955, Montague, Massachusetts, USA. Poet. m. James L Ure, 14 Dec. 1979. *Education:* AB, Bryn Mawr College, 1978; MFA, Warren Wilson College, 1983. *Publication:* Black Method, 1991. *Contributions to:* Prairie Schooner; Cream City Review; Berkeley Poetry Review; Poetry East; Passages North; Indiana Review; Midwest Quarterly; New Letters Review of Books; Boulevard. *Honour:* Marianne Moore Poetry Prize, 1991. *Membership:* Acad. of American Poets. *Address:* 1517 W Fargo Ave, No. 2 Chicago, IL 60626, USA.

RUSSELL, (Irwin) Peter; b. 16 Sept. 1921, Bristol, England. Poet; Writer; Trans.; Ed. m. (1) Marjorie Alice Bloxam, 1 s., (2) Lana Sue Long, 1 s., 2 d. *Education:* Malvern College; Queen Mary College, London. *Appointments:*

Owner, Pound Press, 1951–56, Grosvenor Bookship, Kent, 1951–58, Gallery Bookshop, London, 1959–63; Ed., Nine magazine, 1949–58, Marginalia newsletter, 1990–; Poet-in-Residence, University of Victoria, BC, 1973–76, Purdue University, 1976–77; Teaching Fellow, Imperial Iranian Acad. of Philosophy, Tehran, 1977–79. *Publications:* Picnic to the Moon, 1944; Omens and Elegies, 1951; Descent: A Poem Sequence, 1952; Three Elegies of Quintilius, 1954; The Spirit and the Body: An Orphic Poem, 1956; Images of Desire, 1962; Dreamland and Drunkeness, 1963; Complaints to Circe, 1963; Visions and Ruins: An Existentialist Poem, 1965; Agamemnon in Hades, 1965; The Golden Chain: Lyrical Poems 1964–1969, 1970; Paysages Légendaires, 1971; The Elegies of Quintilius, 1975; Ephimeron, 1977; Acts of Recognition: Four Visionary Poems, 1978; Theories, 1978; Africa: A Dream, 1981; Elemental Discourses, 1981; Malice Aforethought, 1981; All for the Wolves: Selected Poems 1947–1975, 1984; Teorie e Altre Liriche, 1990; The Image of Woman as a Figure of the Spirit in Christian and Islamic Medieval Poetry, 1992; The Pound Connection, 1992; Poetic Asides: Essays and Addresses on Poetry, 2 vols, 1992–93; Dante and Islam, 1994; The Duller Olive: Poems 1942–1958, 1993; A False Start: London Poems 1959–63, 1993; Berlin Tegel 1964: Poems and Translations, 1994; Venice Poems 1965, 1996; More for the Wolves, 1997; My Wild Heart: Selected Poems 1990–1996, 1997. *Contributions to:* Various publications. *Honours:* Premio Internazionale Le Muse, City of Florence, 1990; Premio Internazionale Dante Alighieri, 1993; Festschrift for his 75th birthday, 1996; Premio Internazionale Succisa Virescit, University of Cassino, 1997; Premio Firenze, 1998. *Address:* 'La Turbina', 52026 Pian di Scò, Arezzo, Italy.

RUSSELL JONES, Selwyn; b. 11 Sept. 1909, Aberfan, Glamorgan, Wales. Poet. m. Grethe Whitehead, 2 Sept. 1939, 1 s., 1 d. *Education:* South Wales and Monmouth School of Art and Cardiff University College, 1927–32 with Oxford Diploma in Art. *Appointments:* Senior Arts Master and Housemaster, Kings School, Macclesfield, 1932–73; Served during World War II as Officer in Intelligence Corps, Middle East. *Publications:* List to Us (co-author), 1982; Directions of the Wind, 1984; Driftwood Odyssey, 1990. *Contributions to:* Anthologies: Changing Islands; Speak to the Hills; This Climbing Game; Arts Council Anthology; Poetry Magazines: New Poetry; Outposts; Orbis; Envoi; Climber. *Honours:* Prizes won at various poetry festivals, including Birmingham and Lancaster, and also in poetry magazine competitions. *Memberships:* Poetry Society; Friend of Arvon Foundation for Poetry. *Address:* Silvaplana, No. 7 Tytherington Park Rd, Macclesfield, Cheshire SK10 2EL, England.

RUSSELL MCMILLAN, Lisa. See: CLARK, Marjorie Russell McMillan.

RUSSO, Albert; b. 26 Feb. 1943, Kamina, Belgian Congo. Writer; Poet. 1 s., 1 d. *Education:* BSc, General Business Administration, New York University. *Appointments:* Co-Ed., Paris Transcontinental and Plurilingual Europe; Mem., Jury, Prix de l'Europe, 1982–, Neustadt International Prize for Literature, 1996. *Publications:* Incandescences, 1970; Eclats de malachite, 1971; La Pointe du diable, 1973; Mosaique New Yorkaise, 1975; Albert Russo: An Anthology, 1987; Sang Mêlé ou ton Fils Léopold, 1990; Le Cap des Illusions, 1991; Futureyes/Dans la nuit bleu-fauve, 1992; Kaleidoscope, 1993; Eclipse sur le Lac Tanganyika, 1994; Venetian Thresholds, 1995; Painting the Tower of Babel, 1996; Zapinette, 1996; Poetry and Peanuts (collection), 1997; Zapinette Video (novel), 1998; Mixed Blood (novel), 1999; Eclipse over Lake Tanganyika (novel), 1999; L'amant de mon père (novel), 2000; Zapinette à New York (novel), 2000. Short Stories: Beyond the Great Water; Unmasking Hearts; The Age of the Pearl, 2001. *Contributions to:* Professional journals and BBC World Service. *Honours:* Willie Lee Martin Short Story Award, 1987; Silver Medal, 1985; British Diversity Award, 1997; AAS Memorial Trophy for Best Overseas Entry in Poetry, 1999. *Memberships:* Asscn of French Speaking Writers; Authors Guild of America; PEN. *Address:* BP 640, 75826 Paris Cedex 17, France. *E-mail:* albert.russo@wanadoo.fr. *Website:* www.albertrusso.com.

RUSSO, Alex(ander Peter); b. 6 Nov. 1922, Atlantic City, New York, USA. Prof. Emeritus; Painter; Writer; Poet. *Education:* Pratt Institute, 1940–42; Swarthmore College, 1946–47; BFA, Columbia University; Postgraduate, Acad. of Fine Arts, Rome, Italy; Doctoral Thesis, Institute of Advanced Fine Arts, 1977–79. *Appointments:* Asst Prof. of Art, Buffalo, 1955–58; Instructor in Graphic Design, Parsons School of Design, 1958–60; Chair., Drawing and Painting, Corcoran School of Art, 1961–70; MFA Thesis Adviser, George Washington University, 1961–70; Prof. and Chair., Art Dept, 1970–90, Prof. Emeritus, 1990–, Hood College, Frederick, MD. *Publications:* Profiles on Women Artists, 1985; Challenge of Drawing, 1987; Vignettes, 1996. *Contributions to:* East Hampton Star; Long Island Quarterly; Heartlight Journal; Arcadia Poetry Anthology. *Membership:* Eastend Poetry Workshop, 1990–. *Address:* PO Box 1377, Wainscott, NY 11975, USA.

RUTHERFORD, Maurice; b. 28 Sept. 1922, Hull, East Yorkshire, England. Technical Writer (retd); Poet. m. Olive Gray, 12 April 1947, 1 s., 1 d. *Education:* Hull College of Commerce, 1936–38. *Appointments:* Asst Ed., Envoi, 1979–91; Ed., Proof, 1984–85; Management Adviser for Literature, Lincolnshire and Humberside Arts, 1986–88. *Publications:* Slipping the Tugs, 1982; This Day Dawning, 1989; Love is a Four-Letter World, 1994; After the Parade, 1996. *Contributions to:* Critical Survey; Dark Horse; London Magazine; Poetry Review; Rialto; Staple; BBC Radio 3; BBC Radio Humberside; Yorkshire TV.

Memberships: Poetry Society; Poetry Book Society; Philip Larkin Society. *Address:* 58 Wheatley Dr., Bridlington, East Yorkshire YO16 6UF, England.

RUTSALA, Vern; b. 5 Feb. 1934, McCall, ID, USA. Writer; Poet; Teacher. m. Joan Colby, 1957, 2 s., 1 d. *Education:* BA, Reed College, 1956; MFA, University of Iowa, 1960. *Publications:* The Window, 1964; Small Songs, 1969; The Harmful State, 1971; Laments, 1975; The Journey Begins, 1976; Paragraphs, 1978; The New Life, 1978; Walking Home from the Icehouse, 1981; Backtracking, 1985; The Mystery of Lost Shoes, 1985; Ruined Cities, 1987; Selected Poems, 1991; Little-Known Sports, 1994. *Contributions to:* New Yorker; Esquire; Poetry; Hudson Review; Harper's; Atlantic; American Poetry Review; Paris Review. *Honours:* National Endowment for the Arts Fellowships, 1974, 1979; Northwest Poetry Prize, 1976; Guggenheim Fellowship, 1982; Carolyn Kizer Poetry Prizes, 1988, 1997; Masters, Fellowship, Oregon Arts Commission, 1990; Hazel Hall Award, 1992; Juniper Prize, 1993; Duncan Lawrie Prize, Arvon Foundation, 1994. *Memberships:* PEN; Poetry Society of America; Associated Writing Programs. *Address:* 2404 NE 24th Ave, Portland, OR 97212, USA.

S

SABA, Rathnam; b. 14 Feb. 1956, Chettinad, India. Poet. m. Valli Saba, 13 Dec. 1985, 1 d. *Education:* BA, English Literature, 1974–77; MA, Philosophy, 1977–79. *Publications:* The Remembrance of a Dead Red Rose, 1974; A Bunch of Flowers (anthology), 1977; Hidden Strength, 1979; Words, Words, Words, 1991. *Contributions to:* Poet; Poetry Time; Poetcrit; International Poets. *Honour:* INTCR National Eminent Poet, International Poets Acad., 1991. *Memberships:* World Acad. of Arts and Culture; International Poets Acad. *Address:* S Rm CT S House, Chettinad, Tamil Nadu S, India.

SABATIER, Robert; b. 17 Aug. 1923, Paris, France. Author; Poet. m. Christiane Lesparre, 1957. *Publications:* Alain et le nègre, 1953; Le marchand de sable, 1954; Le goût de la cendre, 1955; Les fêtes solaires, 1955; Boulevard, 1956; Canard au sang, 1958; St Vincent de Paul; Dédicace d'un navire, 1959; La Sainte-Farce, 1960; La mort du figuier, 1962; Dessin sur un trottoir, 1964; Les poisons délectables, 1965; Le Chinois d'Afrique, 1966; Dictionaire de la mort, 1967; Les châteaux de millions d'années, 1969; Les allumettes suédoises, 1969; Trois sucettes à la menthe, 1972; Noisettes sauvages, 1974; Histoire de la poésie française des origines à nos jours, eight vols, 1975; Icare et autres poèmes, 1976; Les enfants de l'été, 1978; Les fillettes chantantes, 1980; L'oiseau de demain, 1981; Les années secrétes de la vie d'un homme, 1984; David et Olivier, 1986; Lecture, 1987; La souris verte, 1990; Le livre de la déraison souriante, 1991; Olivier et ses amis, 1993; Ecriture, 1993; Le cygne noir, 1995; Le lit de la merveille, 1997; Les masques et le miroir, 1998; Le sourire aux lèvres, 2000. *Honours:* Commandeur, Légion d'honneur; Commandeur, Ordre nationale du Mérite; Commandeur des Arts et des Lettres; Lauréat, Société des gens de lettres, 1961; Grand Prix de Poésie, l'Academie Française, 1969. *Membership:* Académie Goncourt. *Address:* 64 blvd Exelmans, 75016 Paris, France.

SACHIKO, Yoshihara; b. 1932, Tokyo, Japan. Poet. *Education:* Graduated in French Literature, University of Tokyo. *Appointment:* Co-Publisher, Gendai-shi-La Mer poetry periodical, 1983–93. *Publications:* Yônen Rentô, 1964; Natsu no haka, 1964; Hirugao, 1973; Ondine, 1974; Hakkô, 1995. *Honours:* Murou Saisei Prize, 1965; Takami Jun Prize, 1973; Hagiwara Sakuturô Prize, 1995. *Address:* c/o Japan PEN Club, 265 Akasaka Residential Hotel, 9-1-7 Akasaka, Minato-ku, Tokyo 107, Japan.

SACHS, Arieh; b. 24 March 1932, Tel-Aviv, Palestine. Poet. m. Rachel Sachs, 1977, 1 s., 1 d. *Education:* BA, 1952, MA, 1954, Johns Hopkins University; Sorbonne, University of Paris, 1955–56; Fitzwilliam College, Cambridge, 1958–60; PhD, Hebrew University of Jerusalem, 1962. *Publications:* Passionate Intelligence, 1967; Orange Grove, 1976; The Prankster's Decline, 1978; John Berryman's Dream Songs, 1978; The Pink Book, 1982; Alcohol, 1987; Eros, 1987. *Contributions to:* Various publications. *Honours:* Israel Interfaith Prize, 1977; Israel Publishers Asscn Prize, 1986. *Address:* 14 Hamefaked St, Abu Tor, Jerusalem, Israel.

SADIN, Marjorie; b. 5 Sept. 1954, Englewood, New Jersey, USA. Poet. *Education:* Oberlin College, 1975; BA, English Literature, 1977, MA, American Literature, 1983, George Washington University; Trinity College, 1989–92. *Publications:* The Cliff Edge, 1988; The Black Rose, 1996. *Contributions to:* The Little Magazine; Dark Horse, Modern Images; Chiron Review; Disability Press; Minotaur Press. *Honour:* Vivian Nellis Creative Writing Award, 1977. *Membership:* Writers Center, Bethesda, Maryland. *Address:* 1330 New Hampshire Ave NW, No. 818, Washington, DC 20036, USA.

SAENZ, Gil(bert); b. 17 Oct. 1941, Detroit, Michigan, USA. Computer Programmer; Analyst; Poet. *Education:* BA, English Literature, 1969, Accrued 2 years in post-degree studies program, 1980, Wayne State University. *Publications:* Where Love Is, 1988; Colorful Impressions, 1993; Moments In Time, 1995. *Contributions to:* North American Poetry Review; Odessa Poetry Review; El Central. *Honours:* Four Ed.'s Choice Awards; Sixth Place in Love Poems contest, Poetry Press, Pittsburgh, Texas, 1992. *Membership:* Latino Poets Asscn, Detroit. *Address:* 6237 Appoline St, Dearborn, MI 48126, USA.

SAGARIS, Lake; b. 29 Sept. 1956, Montréal, QC, Canada. Writer; Trans.; Journalist; Poet. m. Patricio Lanfranco, 1981, 3 s. *Education:* BFA, Creative Writing, University of British Columbia, 1981. *Publications:* Exile Home (Exilio en la patria), 1986; Circus Love, 1991; Medusa's Children, 1993; After the First Death: A Journey Through Chile, Time and Mind, 1996. *Contributions to:* Anthologies, newspapers, and magazines. *Honours:* Canada Council Awards for Poetry, 1987, Non-Fiction, 1991, 1992; MaClean Hunter Fellowship in Arts Journalism, 1989; Banff Writers' Studio, 1989. *Memberships:* Writers' Union of Canada; Sociedad de Escritores de Chile; Periodical Writers Asscn, Canada; Foreign Press Asscn, Chile, vice-pres., 1990–91.

SAHANI, Dharma Vir; b. 15 March 1936, Kuala Lumpur, Malaysia. Educator; Poet. m. Sudesh D. Sahani, 21 Sept. 1966, 1 d. *Education:* MCom, 1962; MLB,

Arts & Commerce College, Gwalior, India; MA, Economics, 1964; PhD, Nagpur University, India, 1976. *Appointments:* Head, Dept of Business Economics, NMD College, Gondia, 1964–96; Dir, Institute for Economics and Social Sciences Research, Gondia, 1996–. *Contributions to:* Various publications. *Honour:* Michael Madhusudan Award in Poetry, 1998. *Membership:* Poetry Society of India, New Delhi. *Address:* Ram Nagar, Gondia 441614, India.

SAHAY, Akhowri Chittaranjan; b. 2 Jan. 1925, Muzaffarpur, India. Assoc. Prof. of English (retd); Ed.; Poet; Writer. m. Akhowi Priyamvada Sahay, 17 June 1945, 3 s., 1 d. *Education:* BA, Honours, Distinction, 1945, MA, English, 1947, Patna University; MDEH, National University of Electro Homeopathy, Kanpur, 1964; PhD, English, Stanton University, New York, 1985. *Appointments:* Lecturer and Head, Dept of English, Rajendra College, Chapra, 1948–68; Lecturer, L S College, Muzaffarpur, 1968–74; Assoc. Prof. of English, Bihar University, Muzaffarpur, 1974–85; Chief Ed., Kavita India quarterly, 1987–. *Publications:* Poetry: Van Yoothi, 1939; Van Shephali, 1941; Van Geet, 1943; Ajab Desh, 1945; Roots and Branches, 1979; Emerald Foliage, 1981; Pink Blossoms, 1983; Golden Pollens, 1985; Vernal Equinox, 1987; Summer Clouds, 1989. Short Stories for Children: Dick Aur Ostrich, 1946; Motilal Tota, 1948; Rani Sahiba, 1964. Prose: The Rubaiyat and Other Essays, 1980; My Interest in Occultism, 1982. *Contributions to:* Numerous anthologies and journals. *Honours:* Many prizes, medals, and certificates of merit. *Memberships:* International Writers and Artists Asscn, USA; PEN All India Centre; Poetry Society, India and UK; Theosophical Society, Chennai; United Writers Asscn, Chennai; World Poetry Society; Writers Club, Chennai. *Address:* Kavita India House, South-East Chaturbhujasthan, Muzaffarpur 842001, Bihar, India.

SAHU, N. S.; b. 1 Sept. 1939, India. Reader in English; Poet. m. Shanti Sahu, 17 May 1962, 3 s. *Education:* MA, Linguistics, 1970; MA, English Literature, 1973; PhD, Linguistics, 1975; PhD, English, 1978. *Appointments:* Lecturer in English, Dept of Education, Bhilai Steel Plant, Bhilainagar, 1971–79; Lecturer, 1979–92, Reader in English, 1992–, University of Gorakhpur. *Publications:* Aspects of Linguistics, 1982; T S Eliot: The Man as a Poet, Playwright, Prophet and Critic, 1988; A Study of the Works of Matthew Arnold, 1988; Theatre of Protest and Anger, 1988; Toponymy, 1989; Christopher Marlowe and Theatre of Cruelty and Violence, 1990; An Approach to American Literature, 1991; Poems, 1996. *Contributions to:* Various publications. *Memberships:* American Studies Research Centre; International Goodwill Society of India; Linguistic Society of India. *Address:* 11 New Flat, Hirapuri Colony, University Campus, Gorakhpur 273009, India.

SAIL, Lawrence Richard; b. 29 Oct. 1942, London, England. Poet; Writer. m. (1) Teresa Luke, 1966, divorced 1981, 1 s., 1 d., (2) Helen Bird, 1994. *Education:* BA, Honours, Modern Languages, St John's College, Oxford, 1964. *Appointments:* Teacher of Modern Languages, Lenana School, Nairobi, 1966–71, Millfield School, 1973–74, Blundell's School, Devon, 1975–81, Exeter School, 1982–91; Ed., South West Review, 1981–85; Chair., Arvon Foundation, 1990–94; Programme Dir, 1991, Co-Dir, 1999, Cheltenham Festival of Literature; Jury Mem., European (Aristeion) Literature Prize, 1994–96. *Publications:* Opposite Views, 1974; The Drowned River, 1978; The Kingdom of Atlas, 1980; South West Review: A Celebration (ed.), 1985; Devotions, 1987; Aquamarine, 1988; First and Always (ed.), 1988; Out of Land: New and Selected Poems, 1992; Building into Air, 1995; The New Exeter Book of Riddles (co-ed.), 1999; The World Returning, 2002. *Contributions to:* Anthologies, magazines and newspapers. *Honours:* Hawthornden Fellowship, 1992; Arts Council Writer's Bursary, 1993; Fellow, RSL. *Memberships:* Authors' Society; St John's College, Oxford, senior common room; Poetry Society. *Address:* Richmond Villa, 7 Wonford Rd, Exeter, Devon EX2 4LF, England.

SAINTE-AGATHE, Mussy. See: MARIE, Charles P.

ST AUBIN DE TERAN, Lisa (Gioconda); b. 2 Oct. 1953, London, England. Writer; Poet. m. (1) Jaime Terán, 1970, divorced 1981, 1 d., (2) George MacBeth, 1981, divorced 1989, 1 s., (3) Robbie Duff-Scott, 1989, 1 d. *Education:* James Allen's Girls' School, Dulwich. *Publications:* Keepers of the House, 1982; The Slow Train to Milan, 1983; The Tiger, 1984; The High Place, 1985; The Bay of Silence, 1986; Black Idol, 1987; The Marble Mountain, 1989; Off the Rails: A Memoir, 1989; Joanna, 1990; Venice: The Four Seasons, 1992; Nocturne, 1993; A Valley in Italy, 1994; Distant Landscapes, 1995; The Palace, 1998; The Virago Book of Wanderlust and Dreams (ed.), 1998; Southpaw, 1999. *Honours:* Somerset Maugham Award, 1983; John Llewelyn Rhys Award, 1983; Eric Gregory Award for Poetry, 1983. *Address:* c/o Maggie Phillips, Ed Victor Ltd, 6 Bayley St, Bedford Sq., London WC1B 3HB, England.

ST AUBYN, Edward; b. 14 Jan. 1960, London, England. Writer; Poet. *Education:* University of Oxford, 1979–82. *Publications:* Never Mind, 1992;

Bad News, 1992; Some Hope, 1994. *Honour:* Betty Trask Award, 1992. *Address:* c/o Aitken & Stone, 29 Fernshaw Rd, London SW10 0TG, England.

ST CLAIR, Patricia Margaret; b. 2 Oct. 1937, Hatch End, Middlesex, England. Poet. m. 1 s. *Contributions to:* BBC; Lady; Spectator; Various other newspapers and magazines. *Address:* Westwood, 39 Chester Rd, Branksome Park, Poole, Dorset BH13 6DE, England.

ST CYR, Napoleon; b. 8 May 1924, Franklin, New Hampshire, USA. Ed.; Publisher; Poet. *Education:* BA, University of New Hampshire; BS, MA, Certificate of Advanced Study, Fairfield University. *Appointments:* Ed., The Small Pond Magazine of Literature, 1969–; Mem., Advisory Board of Consultants, Small Press Review of Books, 1985–94; Poetry Ed., Cider Mill Press. *Publications:* Pebble Ring, 1966; Stones Unturned, 1967. *Contributions to:* Over 60 journals. *Membership:* Acad. of American Poets. *Address:* PO Box 664, Stratford, CT 06615, USA.

ST GERMAIN, Sheryl; b. 28 July 1954, New Orleans, LA, USA. Poet; Teacher. 1 s. *Education:* BA, English, Southeastern University, 1979; MA, 1982, PhD, Arts and Humanities, 1986, University of Texas at Dallas. *Appointments:* University of Southwestern Louisiana; Knox College; Iowa State University. *Publications:* The Mask of Medusa, 1984; Going Home, 1989; Making Bread at Midnight, 1992; How Heavy the Breath of God, 1994; The Journals of Scheherazade, 1996. Other: Je Suis Cadien (trans of poems by Jean Arceneaux). *Contributions to:* TriQuarterly; Spoon River Poetry Review; Massachusetts Review; Louisiana Literature; Mid-American Review. *Honours:* Ki Davis Award, 1989, 1990; American Literary Review Award, 1990; Dobie-Paisans Fellowship, 1990–91; National Endowment for the Arts Fellowships, 1991, 1996; Distinguished Advocate of the Arts, 2002. *Address:* Iowa State University, 203 Ross Hall, Ames, IA 50011, USA.

SALAMUN, Tomaz; b. 4 July 1941, Zagreb, Yugoslavia. Poet; Writer. m. (1) Marusa Krese, 1969, divorced 1975, (2) Metka Krašovec, 11 April 1979, 1 s., 1 d. *Education:* MA, University of Ljubljana, 1965; University of Iowa, 1971–73. *Appointments:* Asst Curator, Modern Gallery, Ljubljana, 1968–70; Asst Prof., Acad. of Fine Arts, Ljubljana, 1970–73; Workshops, University of Tennessee at Chattanooga, 1987–88, 1996; Visiting Writer, Vermont College, 1988; Consul, Slovenian Cultural Attaché, New York, 1996–97. *Publications:* Turbines: Twenty-One Poems, 1973; Snow, 1973; Poetry: Pesmi (Poems), 1980; Maske (Masks), 1980; Balada za Metka Krašovec, 1981, English trans. as A Ballad for Metka Krašovec, 2001; Analogije svetlobe, 1982; Glas, 1983; Sonet o mleku, 1984; Soy realidad, 1985; Ljubljanska pomlad, 1986; Mera casa, 1987; Ziva rana, zivi sok, 1988; The Selected Poems of Tomaz Salamun, 1988; Otrok in jelen, 1990; Painted Desert: Poems, 1991; The Shepherd, The Hunter, 1992; Ambra, 1994; The Four Questions of Melancholy: New and Selected Poems, 1997; Crni labod, 1997; Knjiga za mojega brata, 1997; Homage to Hat and Uncle Guido and Eliot, 1998; Morje, 1999; Gozd in kelihi, 2000; Feast, 2000; Table, 2002. *Contributions to:* Anthologies and periodicals. *Honours:* Mladost Prize, 1969; Residencies, Yaddo, 1973–74, 1979, 1986, 1989, MacDowell Colony, 1986, Karoly Foundation, Vence, France, 1987, Maisons des écrivains étrangers, Saint-Nazaire, France, 1996, Civitella Ranieri, Umbertide, Italy, 1997, Bogliasco Foundation, 2002; Fulbright Grant, 1986–87; Jenko Prize, 1988; Pushcart Prize, 1994; Prešeren Prize, 1999; Alta Marea Prize, 2002. *Memberships:* PEN; Slovenian Writers' Asscn. *Address:* Dalmatinova 11, 1000 Ljubljana, Slovenia.

SALEMI, Joseph Salvatore; b. 1 Feb. 1948, New York, NY, USA. Teacher; Poet. *Education:* BA, Fordham University, 1968; MA, 1970, PhD, 1986, New York University. *Appointments:* Asst Prof., English, Hunter College, Fordham University; Assoc. Prof., Humanities, New York University. *Publications:* Formal Complaints, 1997; Nonsense Couplets and Other Jeux d'Esprit, 1999; Masquerade, 2002. *Contributions to:* Aileron; Amelia; Artful Dodge; Blue Unicorn; Cumberland Poetry Review; Esprit; Formalist; Hollins Critic; Laurel Review; Maledicta; Paintbrush; Plains Poetry Journal; Poem; Trans.; University Bookman; Edge City Review; Carolina Quarterly; Pivot; Lyric; Ekphrasis; Iambs & Trochees. *Honours:* Classical and Modern Literature Award, 1993; Lane Cooper Dissertation Fellowship, 1983; N. E. H. Seminar Fellowship, 1984. *Memberships:* Asscn of Literary Scholars and Critics; National Asscn of Scholars. *Address:* 220 Ninth St, New York, NY 11215-3902, USA.

SALLAH, Tijan M.; b. 6 March 1958, Banjul, The Gambia. Economist; Poet. *Education:* BA, BS, Berea College, Ohio; MA, PhD, Virginia Technical University. *Appointments:* Asst Prof., University of Pennsylvania, 1987–88; North Carolina Agricultural and Technical University, 1988–89; Economist, World Bank, 1989–. *Publications:* When Africa Was a Young Woman, 1980; Koraland, 1989; New Poets of West Africa (ed.), 1992; Dreams of Dusty Roads, 1992. *Contributions to:* Reviews and journals. *Honour:* Hon. DLitt, World Poetry Society. *Memberships:* African Literature Asscn; World Poetry Society. *Address:* PO Box 124, Banjul, The Gambia.

SALOM, Philip; b. 8 Aug. 1950, Bunbury, WA, Australia. University Lecturer; Poet; Writer. *Education:* BA, 1976; DipEd, 1981, Curtin University. *Appointments:* Tutor and Lecturer, Curtin University, 1982–93; Writer-in-

Residence, Singapore National University, 1989, B. R. Whiting Library/ Studio, Rome, 1992; Lecturer, Murdoch University, 1994–97, Victorian College of the Arts of the University of Melbourne, 2000–01. *Publications:* The Silent Piano, 1980; The Projectionist: Sequence, 1983; Sky Poems, 1987; Barbecue of the Primitives, 1989; Playback, 1991; Tremors, 1992; Feeding the Ghost, 1993; Always Then and Now, 1993; The Rome Air Naked, 1996; New and Selected Poems, 1998; A Creative Life, 2001. *Honours:* Commonwealth Poetry Prizes, 1981, 1987; Western Australian Premier's Prize, 1984, 1988 1992; Australia/New Zealand Literary Exchange Award, 1992; Newcastle Poetry Prize, 1996, 2000. *Address:* PO Box 273, Kerrimuir, Vic. 3129, Australia. *E-mail:* psalom@netspace.net.au.

SALTER, Mary Jo; b. 15 Aug. 1954, Grand Rapids, Michigan, USA. Lecturer; Poet; Ed. m. Brad Leithauser, 1980, 2 d. *Education:* BA, cum laude, Harvard University, 1976; MA, Cambridge University, 1978. *Appointments:* Instructor, Harvard University, 1978–79; Staff Ed., Atlantic Monthly, 1978–80; Poet-in-Residence, Robert Frost Place, 1981; Lecturer in English, 1984–, Emily Dickinson Lecturer in Humanities, 1995–, Mount Holyoke College, South Hadley, Massachusetts; Poetry Ed., The New Republic, 1992–95. *Publications:* Henry Purcell in Japan, 1985; Unfinished Painting, 1989; The Moon Comes Home, 1989; Sunday Skaters: Poems, 1994; A Kiss in Space: Poems, 1999. *Contributions to:* Periodicals. *Honours:* Discovery Prize, The Nation, 1983; National Endowment for the Arts Fellowship, 1983–84; Lamont Prize in Poetry, 1988; Guggenheim Fellowship, 1993; National Book Critics Circle Award Nomination, 1994; Amy Lowell Scholarship, 1995. *Memberships:* International PEN; Poetry Society of America, vice-pres., 1995–. *Address:* c/o Dept of English, Mt Holyoke College, South Hadley, MA 01075, USA.

SAMARAS, Nicholas; b. 1 Aug. 1954, Foxton, Cambridgeshire, England. Teacher; Poet. *Education:* MDiv, MA, 1981, Holy Cross Greek Orthodox Seminary; MFA, Writing, Columbia University, 1985; Doctorate in English and Creative Writing, University of Denver, 1993. *Appointments:* Teaching Asst, Lecturer, 1985, Teaching Fellow, University of Denver; Assoc. Ed., Denver Quarterly. *Publications:* Hands of the Saddlemaker, 1992; Survivors of the Moving Earth, 1998. *Contributions to:* New Yorker; Poetry; Ontario Review; Indiana Review; Missouri Review; Aegean Review; Southeastern Review; Intro 13; Aspect; Quarto; Confrontation; Open Places; Green Mountains Review; South Florida Poetry Review; Contemporary Review; Croton Review; Voices International; Albany Review. *Honours:* Outstanding Literature Award, Quarto Magazine, 1985; New York Foundation for the Arts Fellowship, 1986–87; University of Denver Fellowship, 1989; Chamberlain Prize in Poetry, 1989. *Memberships:* Poetry Society of America; National Arts Club. *Address:* 1874 Kinsmere Dr., New Port Richey, FL 34655, USA.

SAMBERG, Kenneth Franklin; b. 4 May 1945, New York, USA. Poet. *Education:* BA, English, City University of New York, 1967; BA, Anthropology, University of Toronto, 1974. *Contributions to:* Tower; Dalhousie Review; Laomedon Review; Waves; Origins; Antigonish Review; Pierian Spring; UC Review; Poetry WLU; Ariel; Green's Magazine; CBC Anthology; Buffalo Spree; Z Miscellaneous; Pacific Review. *Address:* 1566 Unionport Rd, Bronx, NY 10462, USA.

SAMUELSDOTTIR, Norma Elisabet, (NES); b. 7 Sept. 1945, Scotland. Writer; Poet. m. Sigurdur Jon Olafsson, 7 Nov. 1971, divorced, 1 s., 2 d. *Publications:* The Day Before Last of the Year (novel), 1980; The Tree Outside My Window, 1982; Bruises in the Colours of the Rainbow, 1987, English trans.; The Long Trek, 1990; Over Sensitive, 1991; The Found Key, 1991; The Woman Mountain and the Small Daisies, 1997. *Contributions to:* Newspapers and magazines. *Membership:* Writers Union of Iceland. *Address:* Miklabraut 16, 105 Reykjavik, Iceland.

SANCHEZ, Jacqueline Rae Rawlson, (Jacque Rae); b. 9 Sept. 1946, Jackson, Michigan, USA. Publisher; Poet. m. Arnulfo H. Sanchez, 23 Oct. 1965, 1 s., 4 d. *Education:* Creative Writing, Wayne State University, 1975. *Appointments:* Publisher, The Sounds of Poetry magazine, 1983–; Founder-Dir, Latino Poet's Asscn, 1983; Founder, Annual Poetry Outreach Series, 1996–. *Publications:* Gypsy Melody in the Mist of the Sea, 1982; Running Free and More..., 1982; Mine Eyes Have Seen, 1985; Moses and More..., 1985; Wings of Fire, 1992; The Rising Sun, 1996; Fragmented Patterns: Scattered Rain, 1998; Candy Apple Red, 1998; Lavender and Lace (with Gil Saenz), 1998. *Contributions to:* Anthologies and magazines. *Membership:* Casa de Unidad, board mem., 1988–90. *Address:* c/o The Sounds of Poetry, 2076 Vinewood, Detroit, MI 48216-5506, USA.

SANCHEZ, Sonia; b. 9 Sept. 1934, Birmingham, AL, USA. Prof. of English; Poet; Dramatist; Writer. m. Etheridge Knight, divorced, 2 s., 1 d. *Education:* BA, Hunter College, 1955; New York University, 1959–60; PhD, Wilberforce University, 1972. *Appointments:* Instructor, San Francisco State College, 1967–69; Lecturer, University of Pittsburgh, 1969–70, Rutgers University, 1970–71, Manhattan Community College, 1971–73, City University of New York, 1972; Assoc. Prof., Amherst College, 1972–73, University of Pennsylvania, 1976–77; Assoc. Prof., 1977–79, Prof. of English, 1979–, Temple University. *Publications:* Poetry: Homecoming, 1969; WE a

BaddDDD People, 1970; Liberation Poem, 1970; It's a New Day: Poems for Young Brothas and Sistuhs, 1971; Ima Talken bout the Nation of Islam, 1971; Love Poems, 1973; A Blues Book for Blue Black Magical Women, 1974; I've Been a Woman: New and Selected Poems, 1978; Homegirls and Handgrenades, 1984; Under a Soprano Sky, 1987; Wounded in the House of a Friend, 1995. Plays: The Bronx is Next, 1968; Sister Son/ji, 1969; Dirty Hearts '72, 1973; Uh, Uh: But How Do it Free Us?, 1974. Stories: A Sound Investment, 1980. Other: Crisis in Culture, 1983. Editor: Three Hundred Sixty Degrees of Blackness Comin' at You, 1972; We Be Word Sorcerers: 25 Stories by Black Americans, 1973. Honours: PEN Award, 1969; American Acad. of Arts and Letters Award, 1970; National Endowment for the Arts Award, 1978; Smith College Tribute to Black Women Award, 1982; Lucretia Mott Award, 1984; Before Columbus Foundation Award, 1985; PEN Fellow, 1993. Address: c/o Dept of English, Temple University, Philadelphia, PA 19041, USA.

SANDERS, (James) Ed(ward); b. 17 Aug. 1939, Kansas City, Missouri, USA. Poet; Writer; Singer; Lecturer. m. Miriam Kittell, 5 Oct. 1961, 1 c. Education: BA, New York University, 1964. Appointments: Ed.-Publisher, Fuck You/A Magazine of the Arts, 1962–65; Founder-Lead Singer, The Fugs, satiric folk-rock-theatre group, 1964–69; Owner, Peace Eye Bookstore, New York City, 1964–70; Visiting Prof. of Language and Literature, Bard College, Annadale-on-Hudson, New York, 1979, 1983; Lectures, readings, performances throughout the US and Europe. Publications: Poetry: Poem from Jail, 1963; A Valorium Edition of the Entire Extant Works of Thales!, 1964; King Lord/ Queen Freak, 1964; The Toe Queen Poems, 1964; The Fugs' Song Book (with Ken Weaver and Betsy Klein), 1965; Peace Eye, 1965; Egyptian Hieroglyphics, 1973; 20,000 A.D., 1976; The Cutting Prow, 1981; Hymn to Maple Syrup and Other Poems, 1985; Poems for Robin, 1987; Thirsting for Peace in a Raging Century: Selected Poems 1961–1985, 1987; Hymn to the Rebel Cafe: Poems 1987–1991, 1993; Chekov: A Biography in Verse, 1995. Editor: Poems for Marilyn, 1962. Compiler and Contributor: Bugger: An Anthology of Buttockry, 1964; Despair: poems to come down by, 1964. Fiction: Shards of God: A Novel of the Yippies, 1970; Tales of Beatnik Glory (short stories), 2 vols, 1975, 1990; Fame and Love in New York, 1980. Non-Fiction: The Family: The Story of Charles Manson's Dune Buggy Attack Battalion, 1971; Vote! (with Abbie Hoffman and Jerry Rubin), 1972; Investigative Poetry, 1976; The Z-D Generation, 1981. Other: Musicals: Recordings with The Fugs; Solo recordings. Honours: Frank O'Hara Prize, Modern Poetry Asscn, 1967; National Endowment for the Arts Awards, 1966, 1970, Fellowship, 1987–88; Guggenheim Fellowship, 1983–84; American Book Award, 1988. Memberships: New York Foundation for the Arts; PEN. Address: PO Box 729, Woodstock, NY 12498, USA.

SANDERS, Noah. See: BLOUNT, Roy (Alton) Jr.

SANDERSON, Anne Hilary; b. 13 Jan. 1944, Brighton, England. University Lecturer (semi-retd); Poet; Writer. m. Michael Sanderson, 25 Sept. 1976. Education: BA, 1966, MA, 1970, MLitt, 1978, St Anne's College, Oxford. Appointments: English Lectrice, École Normale Supérieure de Jeunes Filles, University of Paris, 1969–71; Lecturer in European Literature, University of East Anglia, 1972–98. Contributions to: Anthologies and periodicals, including: Poems in Poetry Now; Peace & Freedom; Purple Patch; The Poetry Church, Advance!, Isthmus Triumph Herald; Reflections; Tree Spirit; The Firing Squad; All Year Round; Articles in Studies on Voltaire & The 18th Century; Jeunesse de Racine; Norwich Papers. Honours: Prix Racine, 1969; Third Prize, Hilton House National Open Poetry Awards for Collections, 1998, 1999. Memberships: Asscn of Christian Writers; Norwich Writers' Circle; Playwrights East. Address: Dept of Literature, University of East Anglia, Norwich NR4 7TJ, England.

SANDY, Stephen; b. 2 Aug. 1934, Minneapolis, MN, USA. Poet; Writer; Trans.; College Teacher (retd). m. Virginia Scoville, 1969, 1 s., 1 d. Education: BA, Yale University, 1955; MA, 1959, PhD, 1963, Harvard University. Appointments: Instructor in English, 1963–67, Visiting Prof., 1986, 1987, 1988, Harvard University; Visiting Prof. of English, Tokyo University of Foreign Studies, 1967–68, Brown University, 1968–69; Visiting Prof. of American Literature, University of Tokyo, 1967–68; Lecturer in English, University of Rhode Island, 1969; Mem., Literature Faculty, Bennington College, 1969–2001; National Endowment for the Arts Poet-in-Residence, Y Poetry Center, Philadelphia, 1985; McGee Prof. of Writing, Davidson College, 1994; Various poetry workshops and numerous poetry readings. Publications: Stresses in the Peaceable Kingdom, 1967; Roofs, 1971; End of the Picaro, 1974; The Ravelling of the Novel: Studies in Romantic Fiction from Walpole to Scott, 1980; Flight of Steps, 1982; Riding to Greylock, 1983; To a Mantis, 1987; Man in the Open Air, 1988; The Epoch, 1990; Thanksgiving Over the Water, 1992; Vale of Academe: A Prose Poem for Bernard Malamud, 1996; Marrow Spoon, 1997; The Thread: New and Selected Poems, 1998; Black Box, 1999; Surface Impressions, 2002. Contributions to: Books, anthologies, reviews, quarterlies and journals. Honours: Ingram Merrill Foundation Fellowship, 1985; Vermont College on the Arts Fellowship, 1988; National Endowment for the Arts Creative Writing Fellowship, 1988; Chubb Life America Fellow, MacDowell Colony, 1993; Reader's Digest Residency for Distinguished Writers, 1997; Howard Moss Residency for Poetry, 1998, Yaddo; Senior Fellow in Literature, Fine Arts Work Center, Provincetown,

1998; Rockefeller Foundation Residency, Bellagio Study and Conference Center, 2001. Address: PO Box 276, Shaftsbury, VT 05262, USA.

SANER, Reg(inald Anthony); b. 30 Dec. 1931, Jacksonville, IL, USA. Poet; Writer; Prof. m. Anne Costigan, 16 Aug. 1958, 2 s. Education: BA, St Norbert College, Wisconsin, 1950; MA, 1954, PhD, 1962, University of Illinois at Urbana; Università per Stranieri, Perugia, 1960–61; Università di Firenze, Florence, 1960–61. Appointments: Asst Instructor, 1956–60, Instructor in English, 1961–62, University of Illinois at Urbana; Asst Prof., 1962–67, Assoc. Prof., 1967–72, Prof. of English, 1972–, University of Colorado at Boulder. Publications: Poetry: Climbing into the Roots, 1976; So This is the Map, 1981; Essay on Air, 1984; Red Letters, 1989. Non-Fiction: The Four-Cornered Falcon: Essays on the Interior West and the Natural Scene, 1993; Reaching Keet Seel: Ruin's Echo and the Anasazi, 1998. Contributions to: Poems and essays in numerous anthologies and other publications. Honours: Fulbright Scholar to Florence, Italy, 1960–61; Borestone Mountain Poetry Awards, 1971, 1973; Walt Whitman Award, 1975; National Endowment for the Arts Creative Writing Fellowship, 1976; Pushcart Prize II, 1977–78; Colorado Governor's Award for Excellence in the Arts, 1983; Quarterly Review of Literature Award, 1989; Rockefeller Foundation Resident Scholar, Bellagio, Italy, 1990; Hazel Barnes Award, University of Colorado, 1993; Wallace Stegner Award, Centre of the American West, 1997. Memberships: Dante Society; PEN; Renaissance Society; Shakespeare Asscn. Address: 1925 Vassar, Boulder, CO 80303, USA.

SANFILIP, Thomas; b. 28 June 1952, Chicago, IL, USA. Poet; Writer; Journalist; Teacher. Education: BA, Northern Illinois University, 1975. Publications: By The Hours and The Years, 1974; Myth, 1994. Contributions to: Shore Poetry Anthology; Lyrics of Love; Towers; Ivory Tower; Thalassa; Nit and Wit; Tomorrow; Letter Ex; Walt Whitman Encyclopedia. Address: PO Box 34807, Chicago, IL 60634, USA.

SANFORD, Geraldine A Jones; b. 8 Jan. 1928, Sioux Falls, South Dakota, USA. Poet; Teacher; Editorial Asst. m. Dayton M Sanford, 28 Aug. 1948, 4 s. Education: BA, English and Psychology, Augustana College, 1971; MA, English, University of South Dakota. Appointments: Editorial Asst, South Dakota Review, 1973–; Instructor and Lecturer in English, University of South Dakota, 1978, 1979; Instructor, University of Minnesota, 1979–82; Extension Instructor, University of South Dakota, 1991. Publication: Unverified Sightings From Dakota East. Contributions to: Real Dakota; Vermillion Literary Project; Longneck; Mankato Poetry Review; Prairie Winds; South Dakota Magazine; Yearnings; Poets Portfolio; Spirits from Clay; South Dakota Review; North Country; Rocky Mountain Creative Arts Journal; North Country Anvil; Aspect; Sunday Clothes. Honours: Graduate Student Poetry Award, Unversity of South Dakota, 1976; Gladys Haase Poetry Prize, 1977. Address: 306 W 36th St, Apt 22, Sioux Falls, SD 57105, USA.

SANGUINETI, Edoardo; b. 9 Dec. 1930, Genoa, Italy. Author; Prof. of Italian Literature. m. Luciana Garabello, 1954, 3 s., 1 d. Education: Università degli Studi, Turin. Appointments: Prof. of Italian Literature, University of Salerno, 1968–74, University of Genoa, 1974–2000; Mem., Chamber of Deputies, 1979–83. Publications: Laborintus, 1956; Opus metricum, 1960; Interpretazione de Malebolge, 1961; Tre studi danteschi, 1961; Tra liberty e crepuscolarismo, 1961; Alberto Moravia, 1962; K. e altre cose, 1962; Passaggio, 1963; Capriccio Italiano, 1963; Tripleuno, 1964; Ideologia e linguaggio, 1965; Il realismo di Dante, 1966; Guido Gozzano, 1966; Il Giuoco dell'Oca, 1967; T.A.T., 1969; Teatro, 1969; Poesia Italiana del Novecento, 1969; Il Giuoco del Satyricon, 1970; Orlando Furioso (with L. Ronconi), 1970; Renga (with O. Paz, J. Roubaud and C. Tomlinson), 1971; Storie Naturali, 1971; Wirrwarr, 1972; Catamerone, 1974; Giornalino, 1976; Postkarten, 1978; Giornalino secondo, 1979; Stracciafoglio, 1980; Scartabello, 1981; Segnalibro, 1982; Alfabeto apocalittico, 1984; Quintine, 1985; Scribilli, 1985; Faust, un travestimento, 1985; Novissimum Testamentum, 1986; Smorfie, 1986; La missione del critico, 1987; Bisbidis, 1987; Ghirigori, 1988; Commedia dell'Inferno, 1989; Lettura del Decameron, 1989; Senzatitolo, 1992; Dante reazionario, 1992; Gazzettini, 1993; Per musica, 1993; Opere e introduzione critica, 1993; Malebolge (with E. Baj), 1995; Per una critica dell'avanguardia poetica (with J. Burgos), 1995; Tracce (with M. Lucchesi), 1995; Minitarjetas, 1996; Orlando Furioso, un travestimento ariostesco, 1996; Corollario, 1997; Il mio amore è come una febbra (with S. Liberovici), 1998; Cose, 1999; Sei personaggi.com, 2001; L'amore delle tre melarance, 2001; L'orologio astronomico, 2002. Address: c/o Dept of Italian, Faculty of Letters, University of Genoa, Via Balbi 6, 16126, Genoa, Italy.

SANJUAN, Purificación Martínez de, (Pura Sanjuán); b. 2 April 1945, Verea, Orente, Spain. Poet. m. Oscar Sanjuán y Lubián, 1 Aug. 1974, 2 s. Education: Pianist, 1965; Teacher, 1966; Computer Engineer, 1977; Master of Educational Management, 1989. Appointments: Teacher of Piano, 1966–77, Teacher of Computers, 1977, Chair, 1978–83, Chief of Computers, 1983–92, Pedagogical University. Publications: Lunita trigueña, 1987; Fantasía y vida, 1988; C'est le Mont Saint-Michel, 1988; Erase que se era, 1988; Ventisca, 1989; Verano en el alma, 1989; A corazón abierto, 1989; Enseñar la vida, 1989; Los versos idílicos, 1989; Neblina, nostalgia, llovizna, morriña, 1989; Primera selección, 1990. Memberships: Authors' Asscn; Society of Engineering;

Teachers' Asscn. *Address:* Avda Mediterraneo 38, 4° B, E Laredo, 28007 Madrid, Spain.

SANTOS, Sherod; b. 9 Sept. 1948, Greenville, South Carolina, USA. Prof. of English; Poet; Writer. m. Lynne Marie McMahon, 1 May 1976, 2 s. *Education:* BA, 1971, MA, 1974, San Diego State University; MFA, University of California at Irvine, 1978; PhD, University of Utah, 1982. *Appointments:* Asst Prof., California State University, San Bernardino, 1982–83; Poetry Ed., Missouri Review, 1983–90; Asst Prof., 1983–86, Assoc. Prof., 1986–92, ; Curators' Distinguished Prof. of English, 2001, University of Missouri; External Examiner and Poet-in-Residence, Poets' House, Islandmagee, Northern Ireland, summers 1991–98; Various poetry readings, lectures, and seminars. *Publications:* Begin, Distance, 1981; Accidental Weather, 1982; The New Days, 1986; The Southern Reaches, 1989; The Unsheltering Ground, 1990; The City of Women, 1993; The Pilot Star Elegies, 1998; The Perishing, 2003. *Contributions to:* Anthologies, journals, and magazines. *Honours:* Discovery/The Nation Award, 1978; Pushcart Prizes in Poetry, 1980, and in the Essay, 1994; Oscar Blumenthal Prize, Poetry magazine, 1981; Ingram Merrill Foundation Grant, 1982; Delmore Schwartz Memorial Award, 1983; Robert Frost Poet and Poet-in-Residence, Robert Frost House, Franconia, New Hampshire, 1984; Guggenheim Fellowship, 1984–85; National Endowment for the Arts Grant, 1987; Yaddo Center for the Arts Fellowship, 1987; Chancellor's Award, University of Missouri, 1993; British Arts Council International Travel Grant to Northern Ireland, 1995; National Endowment for the Arts Literature Panel Mem., 1995; Acad. Award in Literature, American Acad. of Arts and Letters, 1999; National Book Award Finalist, 1999; New Yorker Book Award Finalist, 1999; National Book Critics Circle Award in Criticism Finalist, 2001. *Memberships:* Acad. of American Poets; Associated Writing Programs; PEN American Center; Poetry Society of America; Poets and Writers; Robinson Jeffers Society. *Address:* 1238 Sunset Dr., Columbia, MO 65203, USA.

SAPIA, Yvonne; b. 10 April 1946, New York, NY, USA. Prof. of English; Poet; Writer. *Education:* AA, Miami-Dade Community College, 1967; BA, English, Florida Atlantic University, 1970; MA, English, University of Florida, 1976; PhD, English, Florida State University, 1990. *Appointments:* Reporter and Ed., The Village Post newspaper, Miami, 1971–73; Editorial Asst, University of Florida, 1974–76; Resident Poet and Prof. of English, Lake City Community College, FL, 1976–. *Publications:* The Fertile Crescent (poems), 1983; Valentino's Hair (poems), 1987; Valentino's Hair (novel), 1991. *Contributions to:* Anthologies, reviews, and journals. *Honours:* First Place, Anhinga Press Poetry Chapbook Award, 1983; Third Place, Eve of St Agnes Poetry Competition, 1983; National Endowment for the Arts Fellowship, 1986–87; First Place, Morse Poetry Prize, 1987; Second Prize, Cincinnati Poetry Review Poetry Competition, 1989; Third Place, Apalaches Quarterly Long Poem Contest, 1989; First Place, Nilon Award for Excellence in Minority Fiction, 1991. *Address:* 702 S Marsh St, Lake City, FL 32025, USA.

SAPPHIRE. See: LOFTON, Ramona.

SAR PO. See: SHIU-TIEN TU.

SARAH, Robyn; b. 6 Oct. 1949, New York, NY, USA. Poet; Writer. *Education:* BA, 1970, MA, 1974, McGill University; Concours Diploma in Clarinet, Conservatoire de Musique du Québec, 1972. *Publications:* Poetry: Shadowplay, 1978; The Space Between Sleep and Waking, 1981; Three Sestinas, 1984; Anyone Skating On That Middle Ground, 1984; Becoming Light, 1987; The Touchstone: Poems New and Selected, 1992; Questions About the Stars, 1998. Fiction: A Nice Gazebo (stories), 1992; Promise of Shelter (stories), 1997. *Address:* c/o Vehicule Press, PO Box 125, Pl. du Parc Station, Montréal, QC H2W 2M9, Canada.

SARAMAGO, José; b. 16 Nov. 1922, Azinhaga, Portugal. Author; Poet; Dramatist. *Education:* Principally self-educated. *Publications:* Fiction: Manual de Pintura e Caligrafia, 1977, English trans. as Manual of Painting and Calligraphy, 1994; Objecto Quase (short stories), 1978, English trans. as Quasi Object, 1995; Levantado do Chao (Raised from the Ground), 1980; Memorial do Convento, 1982, English trans. as Baltasar and Blimunda, 1987; A Jangada de Pedra, 1986, English trans. as The Stone Raft, 1994; O Ano da Morte de Ricardo Reis, 1984, English trans. as The Year of the Death of Ricardo Reis, 1991; Historia do Cerco de Lisboa (The History of the Siege of Lisbon), 1989; O Evangelho segundo Jesus Cristo, 1991, English trans. as The Gospel According to Jesus Christ, 1994; Ensaio Sobre a Cegueira, 1996, English trans. as Blindness; All the Names, 2000. Other: Poems, plays, diaries, etc. *Contributions to:* Various publications. *Honours:* Several literary awards and prizes, including the Nobel Prize for Literature, 1998. *Address:* Los Topes 3, 35572 Tias, Lanzarote, Canary Islands, Spain.

SARGENT, Robert Strong; b. 23 May 1912, New Orleans, LA, USA. Electrical Engineer; Poet. m. (1) 1 s., 1 d., (2) Mary Jane Barnett, 21 July 1985. *Education:* BS, Electrical Engineering, Mississippi State University, 1993. *Appointments:* Various electrical engineering posts including US Navy and Dept of Defence. *Publications:* Now is Always the Miraculous Time, 1977; A Woman from Memphis, 1979; Aspects of a Southern Story, 1983; Fish Galore, 1989; The Cartographer, 1994. *Contributions to:* Antioch Review; California

Quarterly; College English; Georgia Review; Hollins Critic; Kansas Quarterly Laurel Review; Louisville Review; Mississippi Review; New York Quarterly *Honours:* MacDowell Colony Residency; Virginia Centre for the Creative Art Fellowship. *Memberships:* Poetry Committee for Greater Washington Area pres., 1990; Poetry Society of America. *Address:* 120 Fifth St NE, Washington DC 20002, USA.

SARMENTO, Luis Filipe; b. 12 Oct. 1956, Lisbon, Portugal. Poet; Writer Publisher. m. Maria Leonor Boleo Tome, 27 Nov. 1980. *Publications:* Trilogia da Noite, 1977; Nuvens, 1978; Orquestras e Coreografias, 1987; Galeria de un sonho intranquilo, 1988; Fim de Paisagem, 1988; Fragmentos de Uma conversa de Quarto, 1989; Ex Posicoes, 1989; Boca Barroca, 1990; Matinas, Laudas Vesperas e Completas, 1991; Tinturas Alquimicas, 1995; A Intimidade do Sono 1996. *Contributions to:* Portugal: Journal de Letras; Coloquio Letras; DL; DPO Diario de Noticias; Spain: Agalia; El Sol; Diari. *Memberships:* Associacao Portuguesa de Escritores; PEN Club of Portugal; Asscn Europeene pour la Promocion de la Poesie; Organization Mondiale des Poetes; World Congress of Poets; World Acad. of Arts and Culture. *Address:* Rua Joao de Deus, 64, 2710 Sintra, Portugal.

SAROYAN, Aram; b. 25 Sept. 1943, New York, NY, USA. Writer; Poet: Dramatist. m. Gailyn McClanahan, 9 Oct. 1968, 1 s., 2 d. *Education:* University of Chicago; New York University; Columbia University. *Publications:* Aram Saroyan, 1968; Pages, 1969; Words and Photographs, 1970; The Street: An Autobiographical Novel, 1974; Genesis Angels: The Saga of Lew Welch and the Beat Generation, 1979; Last Rites: The Death of William Saroyan, 1982; William Saroyan, 1983; Trio: Portrait of an Intimate Friendship, 1985; The Romantic, 1988; Friends in the World: The Education of a Writer, 1992; Rancho Mirage: An American Tragedy of Manners, Madness and Murder, 1993; Day and Night: Bolinas Poems 1972–81, 1998; Starting Out in the Sixties (essays), 2001; Artists in Trouble: New Stories, 2001. Other: Staged readings of plays. *Contributions to:* New York Times Book Review; Los Angeles Times Book Review; The Nation; Village Voice; Mother Jones; Paris Review. *Honours:* National Endowment for the Arts Poetry Awards, 1967, 1968. *Membership:* PEN Center USA West, pres., 1992–93. *Address:* 5482 Village Green, Los Angeles, CA 90016, USA.

SAS, Zbigniew; b. 22 April 1954, London, England. Civil Servant; Poet. *Education:* BA, Philosophy, University of Sussex, 1977; Postgraduate Diploma in Criminology, Institute of Criminology, University of Cambridge, 1992; Doctoral Studies, Theology, University of Greenwich, 1994–. *Contributions to:* Veins of Gold, Ore 1954–1995; Interactions; Outposts; Odyssey; New Hope International, Symphony, Weyfarers. *Address:* 10 Upper Holly Hill Rd, Belvedere, Kent DA17 6HJ, England.

SATYAMURTI, Carole; b. 13 Aug. 1939, Bromley, Kent, England. Poet; Writer; Lecturer. *Education:* BA, Honours, London University, 1960; Diploma in Social Work, University of Birmingham, 1965; MA, University of Illinois, 1967; PhD, University of London, 1979. *Appointments:* Lecturer, Principal Lecturer, University of East London, 1968–. *Publications:* Occupational Survival, 1981; Broken Moon (poems), 1987; Changing the Subject (poems), 1990; Striking Distance (poems), 1994; Selected Poems, 1998; Love and Variations (poems), 2000. *Honours:* First Prize, National Poetry Competition, 1986; Arts Council of Great Britain Writers Award, 1988; Cholmondeley Award, 2000. *Address:* 15 Gladwell Rd, London N8 9AA, England.

SATYANANDA. See: MUDDANNA, Kembhavy.

SAUNDERS, Sally Love; b. 15 Jan. 1940, Bryn Mawr, Pennsylvania, USA. Poet; Poetry Therapist; Lecturer; Freelance Writer. *Education:* BS, George Williams College, Downers Grove, IL, 1965; Poetry Writing Course, The New School, 1968–69; Several other courses. *Appointments:* Poetry Therapist, Institute of Pennsylvania Hospital, Philadelphia, University of Louisville, KY; Lectures, teaching at schools and other venues; Appearances on TV and radio; Numerous poetry writing workshops; Poetry readings. *Publications:* Past the Near Meadows, 1961; Pauses, 1978; Fresh Bread, 1982; Random Thoughts, 1992; Patchwork Quilt, 1993; Quiet Thoughts and Gentle Feelings, 1996; Word Pictures, 1998. *Contributions to:* Anthologies and journals. *Honours:* Honourable Mention, New American Poetry Contest, 1988; Silver Poet Award, World of Poetry, 1989; Nutmegger Book Award. *Memberships:* National Writers Club; Press Club of San Francisco; Poets and Writers Guild; Asscn for Poetry Therapy; Poetry Society of America; Acad. of American Poets; American Poetry Center. *Address:* 609 Rose Hill Rd, Broomall, PA 19008, USA (office); 2030 Vallejo St, Apt 501, San Francisco, CA 94123, USA (home).

SAVAGE, Ramona Ruth, (Ruth Hudson-Savage); b. 29 April 1932, Childress, Texas, USA. Writer; Poet; Book Reviewer. m. Martin Thomas Savage, 18 Sept. 1965, 3 s., 1 d. *Education:* University of South Alabama; University of Texas at Arlington; The Teaching Company; Brown University; State University of New York at Geneseo. *Publications:* Voices in the Wind, 1982; Simply Savage (audio cassette), 1992; Savage Whispers, 1999; Texas Tuff, 2000; Windhover, 2001; New Texas, 2002. *Contributions to:* Fort Worth Texas Star Telegram; Poetry Society of Texas, Book of the Year; Borderlands;

Poems of the World; Cloudburst; An Apple a Day; Cruise Control. *Honours:* Anne Pence Davis Award, 1993; Charles Hanna Award, 1996; Fasel Memorial Award, 1999; Alonzo's Art Award, 1999; Counterpoint Prize, 1999; O Graves and T Brown Award, 1999; Poet Laureate, Arlington, TX. *Memberships:* Poets of Tarrant County, pres., 1994–95; Poetry Society of Texas; Student Poetry Awards Network, Poetry Society of Texas; National Federation of Poets; Acad. of American Poets; Poetry Society of America; Founding Pres., New Millennium Poets, Arlington, Texas, 2000. *Address:* 1700 Ocho Rios Ct, Arlington, TX 76012, USA.

SAVAGE, Thomas, (Tom Savage); b. 14 July 1948, New York, NY, USA. Poet; Writer; Critic; Ed. *Education:* BA, English, Brooklyn College of the City University of New York, 1969; MLS, Columbia University School of Library Science, 1980. *Appointments:* Teaching Asst, Naropa Institute School of Poetics, 1975; Ed., Roof Magazine, 1976–78, Gandhabba Magazine, 1981–93; Teacher, Words, Music, Words for Poets and Composers, St Mark's Poetry Project, 1983–85. *Publications:* Personalities, 1978; Filling Spaces, 1980; Slow Waltz on a Glass Harmonica, 1980; Housing Preservation and Development, 1988; Processed Words, 1990; Out of the World, 1991; Political Conditions and Physical States, 1993; Brain Surgery (poems), 1999. *Contributions to:* Magazines and journals. *Honours:* PEN Grant, 1978; Co-ordinating Council of Literary Magazines Grant, 1981–82. *Membership:* Co-ordinating Council of Literary Magazines. *Address:* 622 E 11th St, No. 14, New York, NY 10009, USA.

SAVVAS, Minas; b. 2 April 1939, Athens, Greece. Prof. of English; Poet. m. Angie Savvas, 2 s. *Education:* BA, 1963, MA, English, 1965, University of Illinois; PhD, English, University of California, 1970. *Appointments:* Asst Prof., 1968–72, Assoc. Prof., 1972–75, Prof., 1975–, San Diego State University. *Publications:* Scars and Smiles, 1974; Chronicle of Exile, 1975; The Subterranean Horses, 1977; The House Vacated, 1989; Peculiar Gestures, 2002. *Contributions to:* Chicago Review; Poetry Venture; College English; TriQuarterly; Aegean Review; International Poetry Review; Interim; Footwork; Antioch Review; Seneca Review. *Honours:* Poetry Prize, University of Illinois, 1963, World of Poetry, 1988. *Memberships:* Poets and Writers; PEN International; Modern Greek Studies Asscn. *Address:* Dept of English, San Diego State University, San Diego, CA 92182, USA.

SCALES-TRENT, Judy; b. 1 Oc.t 1940, Winston-Salem, NC, USA. Prof. of Law; Writer; Poet. 1 s. *Education:* BA, French, Oberlin College, 1962; MA, French, Middlebury College, 1967; JD, Northwestern University School of Law, 1973. *Appointments:* Adjunct Faculty, Catholic University Law School, 1983; Prof. of Law, State University of New York at Buffalo, 1984–; Visiting Prof. of Law, St Mary's University School of Law, 1994. *Publications:* Political Campaign Communication: Principles and Practices (co-author), 1983; Notes of a White Black Woman: Race, Color, Community, 1995. *Contributions to:* Anthologies, literary periodicals and law journals. *Honours:* Co-Recipient, 1986, Recipient, 1991–93, Baldy Center for Law and Social Policy Award, State University of New York at Buffalo; William J. Magavern Fellowship, 1993. *Address:* 352 Old Meadow Rd, East Amherst, NY 14051, USA.

SCAMMACCA, Nat; b. 20 July 1924, New York, NY, USA. Prof. of English (retd); Writer; Poet. m. Nina Scammacca, 1948, 1 s., 2 d. *Education:* BA, Literature and Philosophy, Long Island University; MA, Education, New York University; Graduated in Italian, University of Perugia. *Appointments:* Pilot, US Air Force, India-Burma-China theatre, World War II; Social Worker, Italian Board of Guardians; Prof. of English, British College, Palermo; Ed., Third Page, Trapani Nuova newspaper. *Publications:* Two Worlds (novel), 1980; Schammacanat (Italian and English), 1985; Bye Bye America (short stories), 1986; Cricepeo (Italian and English), 3 vols, 1990; Sikano L'Amerikano! (short stories), 1991; Due Poeti Americani (Italian and English, co-author), 1994; The Hump (World War II stories and poems), 1994. Other: Various books and trans. *Contributions to:* Anthologies and periodicals. *Honours:* Air Medal, Bronze Star, US Air Force; Taormina City Poetry Prize, 1978; Premio Letterario Sikania Prize, 1988; VII Premio di Poesia Petrosino Prize, 1991. *Membership:* Poets and Writers, New York City. *Address:* Villa Schammachanat, Via Argenteria KM4, Trapani, Sicily 91100, Italy.

SCANNELL, Vernon; b. 23 Jan. 1922, Spilsby, Lincolnshire, England. Author; Poet. m. 4 Oct. 1954, 3 s., 2 d. *Appointments:* Visiting Poet, Shrewsbury School, 1973–75; Writer-in-Residence, Berinsfield, Oxfordshire, 1975–76; Poet-in-Residence, King's School, Canterbury, 1979. *Publications:* Fiction: The Fight, 1952; The Wound and the Scar, 1953; The Face of the Enemy, 1960; The Big Time, 1967; Ring of Truth, 1983; Feminine Endings, 2000. Poetry: New and Collected Poems, 1980; Winterlude, 1983; Funeral Games, 1987; Soldiering On, 1989; A Time for Fires, 1991; Collected Poems 1950–1993, 1994; The Black and White Days, 1996; Views and Distances, 2000. Non-Fiction: The Tiger and the Rose, 1971; Argument of Kings, 1987; Drums of Morning, Growing Up in the 30's, 1992. *Contributions to:* Newspapers, reviews, and magazines. *Honours:* Heinemann Award for Literature, 1960; Cholmondeley Award for Poetry, 1974. *Membership:* RSL, hon. fellow. *Address:* 51 North St, Otley, West Yorkshire LS21 1AH, England.

SCARFE, Wendy (Elizabeth); b. 21 Nov. 1933, Adelaide, SA, Australia. Writer; Poet. m. Allan Scarfe, 6 Jan. 1955, 4 c. *Education:* BA; BLitt; ATTC.

Publications: Fiction: The Lotus Throne, 1976; Neither Here Nor There, 1978; Laura My Alter Ego, 1988; The Day They Shot Edward, 1991; Miranda, 1998; Fishing for Strawberries, 2001. Poetry: Shadow and Flowers, 1964. With Allan Scarfe: A Mouthful of Petals, 1967; Tiger on a Rein, 1969; People of India, 1972; The Black Australians, 1974; Victims or Bludgers?: Case Studies in Poverty in Australia, 1974; J P: His Biography, 1975; Victims or Bludgers?: A Poverty Inquiry for Schools, 1978; Labor's Titan: The Story of Percy Brookfield, 1878–1921, 1983; All That Grief: Migrant Recollections of Greek Resistance to Fascism, 1941–1949, 1994; Remembering Jayaprakash, 1997; No Taste for Carnage: Alex Sheppard – A Portrait 1913–1997, 1998. *Contributions to:* Overland; Australian Short Stories; Age. *Honours:* With Allan Scarfe, Australia Literature Board Grants, 1980, 1988. *Address:* 8 Bostock St, Warrnambool, Vic. 3280, Australia.

SCARPA, Michael L. See: PENDRAGON, Michael Malefica.

SCHÄFER, Wendel; b. 25 Aug. 1940, Bundenbach, Germany. Headmaster; Poet. m. Dorothee Schäfer, 22 July 1965, 1 s., 1 d. *Education:* University of Koblenz; University of Mainz. *Publications:* Teils heiter – teils wolkig, 1979; Eisgirlanden, 1981; Die Musenflunder, 1982; Herbstspuren, 1983; Die Nacht ist nicht nur schwarz, 1983; Saurer Regen, 1983; Erosionen, 1984; Flügel-schlager, 1985; Guten Morgen Deutschland, 1986; Au den Leib geschrieben, 1988; Bilder kopf und Blumentritt, 1988; Korne im kopf, 1991; Flügel-Spitzen, 1992. *Contributions to:* 40 anthologies; Numerous periodicals. *Honours:* Hafiz Satire Prizes, 1988, 1990. *Memberships:* Forderkreis dt Schriftsteller, Rheinland-Pfalz; Friedrich-Bödecker-Kreis, regional advisory board; Veiband olt Schriftsteller (VS). *Address:* Igelstrasse 2, 56154 Boppard-Buchenau, Germany.

SCHAFFENBURG, Carlos A.; b. 19 Sept. 1919, México, DF, Mexico. Physician; Poet. m. Lila Marie Williams, 28 June 1952, 2 s., 1 d. *Education:* MD, University of Mexico, 1944. *Appointment:* Consultant, National Institutes of Health. *Publications:* Genesis, 1989; Songs Irreverent and Old, 1995. *Contributions to:* Excelsior; Linden Lane Magazine; Oktoberfest; La Nuez. *Memberships:* Poetry Society of America; Acad. of American Poets. *Address:* 5480 Wisconsin Ave, No. 1014, Chevy Chase, MD 20815, USA.

SCHEDLER, Gilbert Walter; b. 11 March 1935, British Columbia, Canada. Prof.; Poet. 1 s., 2 d. *Education:* BA, Concordia College, 1957; BD, Concordia Seminary, 1960; MA, Washington University, 1963; PhD, University of Chicago, 1970. *Appointments:* Instructor, Washington University, 1962–63; Wittenberg University, 1963–64; Prof., Callison College, 1967–75, University of the Pacific, 1975–. *Publications:* Waking Before Dawn, 1978; Making Plans, 1980; That Invisible Wall, 1985; Starting Over, 1992. *Contributions to:* Contemporary Quarterly; California State Poetry Quarterly; Blue Unicorn; Christian Century; California English Journal; Windless Orchard; Gold Dust; Poetry in the Schools; Midwest Chaparral; Minotaur; Western Ohio Journal. *Address:* 1781 Oxford Way, Stockton, CA 95204, USA.

SCHEELE, Roy Martin; b. 10 Jan. 1942, Houston, Texas, USA. Prof. of English; Poet. m. Frances McGill Hazen, 26 June 1965, 2 s. *Education:* AB, Classical Greek, 1965, MA, English, 1971, University of Nebraska; University of Texas, 1965–66. *Appointments:* Instructor of English, University of Tennessee at Martin, 1966–68; Theodor Heuss Gymnasium, Waltrop, Germany, 1974–75; Lecturer in Classics, Creighton University, 1977–79; Visiting Instructor in Classics, University of Nebraska-Lincoln, 1981; Instructor of English as a Second Language, Midwest Institute for International Studies, Doane College, 1982–90; Poet-in-Residence, Assoc. Prof. of English, Doane College, 1990–. *Publications:* Accompanied, 1974; Noticing, 1979; The Sea-Ocean, 1981; Pointing Out the Sky, 1985; The Voice We Call Human, 1991; To See How It Tallies, 1995; Short Suite, 1997; Keeping the Horses, 1998; From the Ground Up: Thirty Sonnets by Roy Scheele, 2000. *Contributions to:* The American Scholar; The Formalist; Poetry; Sewanee Review; Southern Review; Verse. *Honours:* First Prize, Ione Gardner Noyes Poetry Awards, University of Nebraska, 1962; Second Prize, Ione Gardner Noyes Awards, 1964; First Prize, John G Neihardt Poetry Competition, 1983; Co-Winner, Robert Fleissner Award, 1992; Co-Winner, William Wordsworth Award, 1993; Edmund Spenser Award, 1997; Winner, John Joseph Memorial Award, 2000; Author of the Year, Nebraska Literary Heritage Asscn, 2001–2002. *Address:* 2020 S 25th St, Lincoln, NE 68502, USA.

SCHELLING, Andrew; b. 14 Jan. 1953, Washington, DC, USA. Poet; Writer; Trans.; Asst Prof. m. Kristina Loften, 20 Oct. 1980, divorced 1993, 1 d. *Education:* BA, University of California at Santa Cruz, 1975. *Appointment:* Asst Prof., Naropa Institute, Boulder. *Publications:* Claw Moraine (poems), 1987; Dropping the Bow: Poems from Ancient India (trans.), 1991; Ktaadn's Lamp (poems), 1991; For Love of the Dark One: Songs of Mirabai (trans.), 1993; Moon is a Piece of Tea (poems), 1993; The India Book: Essays and Translations from Indian Asia, 1993; Twilight Speech: Essays on Sanskrit and Buddhist Poetics, 1993; Two Immortals (essays), 1994; Disembodied Poetics: Annals of the Jack Kerouac School (co-ed.), 1994; Old Growth: Selected Poems and Notebooks, 1986–1994, 1995; Songs of the Sons and Daughters of Buddha, (co-trans.), 1996; The Kavyayantra Press: A Brief History, 1993–1997, 1997; The Road to Ocosingo, 1998; The Cane Groves of Narmada River: Erotic Poems from Old India (trans.), 1998; Tea Shack Interior: New and Selected Poetry,

2002; Wild Form Savage Grammar (essays), 2003. *Contributions to:* Numerous anthologies and periodicals. *Honour:* Landon Prize in Trans., Acad. of American Poets, 1992. *Address:* 1125 Hartford Dr., Boulder, CO 80305, USA.

SCHEVILL, James (Erwin); b. 10 June 1920, Berkeley, CA, USA. Writer; Poet; Dramatist; Prof. of English Emeritus. m. (1) Helen Shaner, 1942, divorced 1966, 2 d., (2) Margot Blum, 1966. *Education:* BS, Harvard University, 1942; MA, Brown University. *Appointments:* Asst Prof. of Humanities, California College of Arts and Crafts, Oakland, 1951–59; Assoc. Prof. of English, San Francisco State University, 1959–68; Prof. of English, 1968–88, Prof. Emeritus, 1988–, Brown University. *Publications:* Tensions (poems), 1947; The American Fantasies (poems), 1951; Sherwood Anderson: His Life and Work, 1951; High Sinners, Low Angels (musical play), 1953; The Right to Greet (poems), 1956; The Roaring Market and the Silent Tomb (biography of Bern Porter), 1956; The Bloody Tenet (verse play), 1957; Selected Poems 1945–62, 1962; Voices of Mass and Capital A (play), 1962; The Stalingrad Elegies (poems), 1964; The Black President, and Other Plays, 1965; Violence and Glory: Poems 1962–67, 1969; Lovecraft's Follies (play), 1971; Breakout! In Search of New Theatrical Environments, 1972; The Buddhist Car and Other Characters (poems), 1973; The Arena of Ants (novel), 1977; The Mayan Poems, 1978; The American Fantasies: Collected Poems 1945–1982, 1983; Oppenheimer's Chair (play), 1985; Collected Short Plays, 1986; Ambiguous Dancers of Fame: Collected Poems 1945–1986, 1987; Where to Go, What to Do, When You Are Bern Porter: A Personal Biography, 1992; 5 Plays 5, 1993; Winter Channels (poems), 1994; The Complete American Fantasies (poems), 1996; New and Selected Poems, 2000. *Honours:* Ford Foundation Grant, 1960–61; William Carlos Williams Award, 1965; Guggenheim Fellowship, 1981; Centennial Review Poetry Prize, 1985; Hon. DHL, Rhode Island College, 1986; Pawtucket Arts Council Award for Poetry and Theatre, 1987; American Acad. of Arts and Letters Award, 1991. *Address:* 1309 Oxford St, Berkeley, CA 94709, USA.

SCHMIDT, Carl Anthony; b. 20 Sept. 1948, Cleveland, Ohio, USA. Locomotive Engineer; Poet. m. Barbara Lee Uselis, 24 April 1971, 1 s., 1 d. *Publications:* 12 books, including: A Dad for Sale, 1994; Adrift, 1995; Broken Hearted Hummingbirds, 1995; Everyman's Dream, 1995; A Walk Down the Aisle, 1996. *Contributions to:* Anthologies. *Honour:* Award of Merit, 1995. *Address:* 13029 Fairfield Trail, Chesterland, OH 44026, USA.

SCHMIDT, Michael (Norton); b. 2 March 1947, México, DF, Mexico. Poet; Ed.; Trans. m. Claire Harman, 1979, deceased 1989, 2 s., 1 d. *Education:* Harvard University, 1966; BA, Wadham College, Oxford, 1969. *Appointments:* Editorial Dir, Carcanet Press Ltd, 1969–; Senior Lecturer in Poetry, University of Manchester, 1972–98; Ed., PN Review, 1972–; Dir, Writing School, Manchester Metropolitan University, 1998–. *Publications:* Black Buildings, 1969; One Eye Mirror Cold, 1970; Bedlam and the Oakwood, 1970; Desert of Lions, 1972; British Poetry Since 1960 (ed. with G Lindop), 1972; It Was My Tree, 1972; Flower and Song (trans. with E Kissam), 1975; My Brother Gloucester, 1976; Ten British Poets (ed.), 1976; A Change of Affairs, 1978; A Reader's Guide to Fifty Poets (ed.), 2 vols, 1979; The Colonist, 1980, US edn as Green Island, 1982; Eleven British Poets (ed.), 1980; Choosing a Guest: New and Selected Poems, 1983; Some Contemporary Poets of Britain and Ireland (ed.), 1983; The Dresden Gate, 1986; Octavio Paz: On Poets and Others (trans.), 1986; The Love of Strangers, 1988; Modern Poetry, 1989; New Poetries (ed.), 1994; A Calendar of Modern Poetry (ed.), 1994; Selected Poems, 1997; Lives of the Poets, 1998; The Harvill Book of Twentieth-Century Poetry in English, 1999. *Memberships:* Fellow, RSL, 1990; Fellow, The English Asscn, 1999. *Literary Agent:* David Goodwin Assocs. *Address:* Conavon Ct, Fourth Floor, 12–16 Blackfriars St, Manchester M3 5BQ, England.

SCHMIDT-BLEIBTREU, Ellen. See: CONRADI-BLEIBTREU, Ellen.

SCHMITZ, Dennis (Mathew); b. 11 Aug. 1937, Dubuque, IA, USA. Prof. of English; Poet. m. Loretta D'Agostino, 1960, 2 s., 3 d. *Education:* BA, Loras College, Dubuque, IA, 1959; MA, University of Chicago, 1961. *Appointments:* Instructor, Illinois Institute of Technology, Chicago, 1961–62, University of Wisconsin at Milwaukee, 1962–66; Asst Prof., 1966–69, Poet-in-Residence, 1966–, Assoc. Prof., 1969–74, Prof. of English, 1974–, California State University at Sacramento. *Publications:* We Weep for Our Strangeness, 1969; Double Exposures, 1971; Goodwill, Inc, 1976; String, 1980; Singing, 1985; Eden, 1989; About Night: Selected and New Poems, 1993. *Honours:* New York Poetry Center Discovery Award, 1968; National Endowment for the Arts Fellowships, 1976, 1985, 1992; Guggenheim Fellowship, 1978; di Castagnola Award, 1986; Shelley Memorial Award, 1988. *Address:* c/o Dept of English, California State University at Sacramento, 6000 Jay St, Sacramento, CA 95819, USA.

SCHNACKENBERG, Gjertrud; b. 27 Aug. 1953, Tacoma, WA, USA. Poet; Writer. m. Robert Nozick, 5 Oct. 1987, deceased 2002. *Education:* BA, Mount Holyoke College, 1975. *Appointments:* Christensen Fellow, Saint Catherine's College, Oxford, 1997; Visiting Scholaar, Getty Research Institute, J. Paul Getty Museum, 2000. *Publications:* Portraits and Elegies, 1982; The Lamplit Answer, 1985; A Gilded Lapse of Time, 1992; The Throne of Labdacus, 2000; Supernatural Love: Poems 1976–1992, 2000. *Contributions to:* Books and journals. *Honours:* Glascock Awards for Poetry, 1973, 1974; Lavan Younger

Poets Award, Acad. of American Poets, 1983; Rome Prize, American Acad. and Institute of Arts and Letters, 1983–84; Amy Lowell Traveling Prize, 1984–85; Hon. Doctorate, Mount Holyoke College, 1985; National Endowment for the Arts Grant, 1986–87; Guggenheim Fellowship, 1987–88; Acad. Award ir Literature, American Acad. of Arts and Letters, 1998. *Membership:* American Acad. of Arts and Sciences, fellow, 1996. *Address:* c/o Farrar, Straus & Giroux Inc, 19 Union Sq. W, New York, NY 10003, USA.

SCHNEIDER, Myra Ruth; b. 20 June 1936, London, England. Poet; Teacher. m. Erwin Schneider, 10 Nov. 1963, 1 s. *Education:* English Honours Degree London University, 1959. *Appointments:* Teacher, 1964–74; Writing Class Tutor, 1988–; Tutor, Poetry School, 1997–. *Publications:* Fistful of Yellow Hope, 1984; Cat Therapy, 1986; Cathedral of Birds, 1988; Opening the Ice, 1990; Crossing Point, 1991; Exits, 1994; Writing for Self-Discovery (with John Killick), 1998; The Panic Bird, 1998; Insisting on Yellow: New and Selected Poems, 2000; Parents (anthology, co-ed.), 2000. *Contributions to:* Anthologies, reviews, quarterlies, and journals. *Honours:* Merit Prize, Lake Aske Competition, 1990; Commendation, Greenwich, 1991; Second Prize, Bournemouth Open Competition, 1993; Second Prize, Aberystwyth Open Competition, 1993; Second Prize, Thursday Competition, 1996; First Prize, 'Scintilla' Long Poem Competition, 2000. *Membership:* Poetry Library South Bank. *Address:* 130 Morton Way, Southgate, London N14 7AL, England. *E-mail:* myra.sch@ukonline.co.uk. *Website:* www.esch.dircon.co.uk.

SCHOONOVER, Amy Jo; b. 25 April 1937, Illinois, USA. Instructor of English; Poet. m. (1) Boyd McCarty, 2 s., 1 d., (2) Samuel J Zook Jr, 15 July 1972. *Education:* BA, Wittenburg University, 1969; MA, English, 1982, PhD, 1993, West Virginia University. *Appointments:* Poet in the Schools, 1974–; Instructor of English, Urbana University, Ohio, 1986–88, 1992–, Clark State Community College, 1989–91; Ed., Common Threads. *Publications:* Echoes of England, 1975; A Sonnet Sampler, 1979; New and Used Poems, 1988; Threnody, 1994; The Study and Writing of Poetry: American Women Poets Discuss Their Craft (ed.), revised edn, 1995; The Blue Tree, 2000; Amy Jo Schoonover's Greatest Hits, 2001. *Contributions to:* Canonic Mass (Communion Service text), Hymnal Supplement, 1996; Poems in various publications. *Honour:* Poet of the Year, Ohio Poetry Day Asscn, 1988. *Memberships:* Illinois State Poetry Society; National Federation of State Poetry Societies, pres., 1996–98; National League of American Pen Women; Ohio Poetry Day Asscn, contest chair., 1974–87, treasurer, 1988–; Poetry Society of America; Society for the Study of Midwestern Literature; Ohio Poetry Asscn; West Virginia Poetry Society. *Address:* 3520 State Route 56, Mechanicsburg, OH 43044, USA.

SCHOTT, Erika; b. 28 Dec. 1946, New York, NY, USA. Poet; Artist; Teacher. *Education:* AA, Packer Collegiate Institute, 1966; BA, University of Florida, 1968; MA, Arizona State University, 1983. *Contributions to:* Journals and magazines. *Honour:* Honourable Mention and First Prize for Poetry, 1979. *Memberships:* Arizona Poetry Asscn; World Poetry Society. *Address:* 465 Tyende Oui, Flagstaff, AZ 86001, USA.

SCHROEDER, Andreas Peter; b. 26 Nov. 1946, Hoheneggelsen, Germany. Writer; Poet; Trans. m. Sharon Elizabeth Brown, 2 d. *Education:* BA, 1969, MA, 1972, University of British Columbia. *Appointments:* Literary Critic and Columnist, Vancouver Province newspaper, 1968–72; Co-Founder and Ed.-in-Chief, Contemporary Literature in Trans., 1968–83; Lecturer in Creative Writing, University of Victoria, 1974–75, Simon Fraser University, 1989–90; Writer-in-Residence, University of Winnipeg, 1983–84, Fraser Valley College, 1987; Lecturer in Creative Writing, 1985–87, Prof., Maclean Hunter Chair in Creative Non-Fiction, 1993–, University of British Columbia. *Publications:* The Ozone Minotaur, 1969; File of Uncertainties, 1971; UNIverse, 1971; The Late Man, 1972; Stories From Pacific and Arctic Canada (co-ed.), 1974; Shaking it Rough, 1976; Toccata in 'D', 1984; Dust-Ship Glory, 1986; Word for Word: The Business of Writing in Alberta, 1988; The Eleventh Commandment (with Jack Thiessen), 1990; The Mennonites in Canada: A Photographic History, 1990; Carved From Wood: Mission, B.C. 1891–1992, 1992; Scams, Scandals and Skullduggery, 1996; Cheats, Charlatans and Chicanery, 1998; Fakes, Frauds and Flimflammery, 1999. *Contributions to:* Numerous anthologies, newspapers, and magazines. *Honours:* Woodward Memorial Prize for Prose, 1969; Canada Council Grants, 1969, 1971, 1975, 1979, 1986, 1991; National Film Board of Canada Scriptwriting Prize, 1971; Best Investigative Journalism, Canadian Asscn of Journalists, 1990. *Memberships:* Writers Union of Canada; Alliance of Canadian Cinema, Television and Radio Artists; Federation of British Columbia Writers; PEN Club; Saskatchewan Writers' Guild. *Address:* Stag's Leap, 9564 Erickson Rd, Mission, BC V2V 5X4, Canada.

SCHUFF, Karen Elizabeth; b. 1 June 1937, Highland Park, Michigan, USA. Poet. m. Henry Clefton Schuff, 7 Sept. 1955, 1 s., 1 d. *Publications:* Barefoot Philosopher, 1968; Come, Take My Hand, 1968; Of Rhythm and Cake, 1970; Of June I Sing, 1979; Green as April, 1987. *Contributions to:* Many reviews, quarterlies, and journals. *Honours:* First Prize for Poetry Manuscript, Poetry Forum, 1990; Third Prize for American Sonnet, Parnassus, 1990; First Prize for Contemporary Poem, Poetry Society of Michigan, 1993; First Prize, Second Prize for Poetry, Scottsville, Michigan Contest, 1995; Second Prize for Poetry, Monroe County Library System, 1995. *Memberships:* Avalon; Poetry Society of

Michigan; Society for the Study of Midwestern Literature. *Address:* 15310 Windemere St, Southgate, MI 98195, USA.

SCHULER, Robert Jordan; b. 25 June 1939, California, USA. Prof. of English; Poet. m. Carol Forbis, 7 Sept. 1963, 2 s., 1 d. *Education:* BA, Honours, Political Science, Stanford University, 1961; MA, Comparative Literature, University of California, Berkeley, 1965; PhD, English, University of Minnesota, 1989. *Appointments:* Instructor in English, Menlo College, 1965–67; Instructor in Humanities, Shimer College, 1967–77; Prof. of English, University of Wisconsin-Stout, 1978–. *Publications:* Axle of the Oak, 1978; Seasonings, 1978; Where is Dancers' Hill?, 1979; Morning Raga, 1980; Red Cedar Scroll, 1981; Origins, 1981; Floating Out of Stone, 1982; Music for Monet, 1984; Grace: A Book of Days, 1995; Journeys Toward the Original Mind, 1995; The Red Cedar Suite, 1999. *Contributions to:* Anthologies and periodicals, including: Caliban; Northeast; Tar River Poetry; Longhouse; Dacotah Territory; Wisconsin Acad. Review; Wisconsin Review; North Stone Review; Wisconsin Poetry 1991 Transactions; Hummingbird; Abraxas; Lake Street Review; Inheriting the Earth; Mississippi Valley Review; Coal City Review; Gypsy; Imagining Home, 1995; Ekphrasis; Mid-America Poetry Review. *Honour:* Hormel Professorship, 1995; Wisconsin Arts Board Fellowship for Poetry, 1997. *Membership:* Land Use Commission, Town of Menomonie. *Address:* E4549 479th Ave, Menomonie, WI 54751, USA.

SCHULTZ, David; b. 20 Nov. 1934, Paterson, New Jersey, USA. Teacher; Trans.; Poet; Writer. 2 s. *Education:* BA, Brandeis University, 1956; MA, Columbia University, 1961. *Appointments:* High School Teacher, 1958–69; Ed., Trans., 1958–; College Media Center Dir, 1969–82; High School and College Teacher, 1986–. *Contributions to:* Tin Wreath; The Haven; Footsteps; Horizontes; Transition; Poésie USA; Italian Americana. *Membership:* Advanced Writers Group, Queens, New York. *Address:* 162-31 Ninth Ave, Whitestone, NY 11357, USA.

SCHUTTENBERG, Ernest M.; b. 19 Jan. 1933, New York, NY, USA. Prof. of Education (retd); Poet. m. Lois Ann Myers, 20 July 1957, 2 d. *Education:* BA, English Literature, Rutgers University, 1954; MAT, Secondary Education, Yale University, 1955; DEd, Educational Administration, Adult Education, Boston University, 1972. *Appointments:* Teacher of English, Verona High School, NJ, 1955–56; Military Intelligence Specialist, US Army, 1956–59; Teacher of English, Surrattsville High School, MD, 1959–60; Instructor and Institute Dir, Reading Dynamics Institute, Washington, DC and Oakland, CA, 1961–64; Training Administrator, American Airlines, New York, 1964–68; Organization Development Man., Honeywell Information Systems Inc, Boston, MA, 1969–71; Prof. of Education, Cleveland State University, OH, 1972–98. *Publications:* Beijing Spring, 1989; Carmen, 1990; Running Out of Sandwiches, 1997; Qufu Summer, 1997; How B. F. Skinner Taught His Cat To Fly (poems), 2001. *Contributions to:* Reviews, anthologies and magazines. *Address:* 6083 Park Ridge Dr., North Olmsted, OH 44070-4142, USA.

SCHWARTZ, Betsy Robin; b. 1 Feb. 1956, Newark, New Jersey, USA. Poet. *Education:* BA, cum laude, English, Speech, Theatre, Kean College of New Jersey, 1977. *Appointments:* Host and Producer, Off the Page television show and reading series; Many poetry readings. *Publication:* I'm Not Moving Across the River. *Contributions to:* Anthologies, reviews, and journals. *Honours:* First Place, Allen Ginsberg Award, 1992; Duncan Lawrie Prize, Arvon Foundation, 1993. *Membership:* Acad. of American Poets. *Address:* 79 Myrtle Ave, Metuchen, NJ, USA.

SCHWARTZ, Leonard; b. 7 Oct. 1963, New York, NY, USA. Poet. m. Mingxia Li, 2 Nov. 1995. *Education:* BA, Bard College, 1984; MA, Philosophy, Columbia University, 1986. *Appointments:* Instructor, New School for Social Research, 1989–92; Visiting Asst Prof. of English, Bard College, 1992–. *Publications:* Objects of Thought, Attempts at Speech, 1990; Exiles: Ends, 1990; Gnostic Blessing, 1992. *Contributions to:* Denver Quarterly; Talisman; First Intensity; Agni Trafika; Alea; The World; Five Fingers Review. *Honour:* 'New Voices' Selection, Acad. of American Poets, 1993. *Membership:* PEN, New York. *Address:* 561 Hudson St, Box 44, New York, NY 10014, USA.

SCHWARTZ, Lloyd; b. 29 Nov. 1941, New York, NY, USA. Prof. of English; Music Critic; Poet. *Education:* BA, Queens College, City University of New York, 1962; MA, 1963, PhD, 1976, Harvard University. *Appointments:* Classical Music Ed., Boston Phoenix, 1977–; Assoc. Prof. of English, 1982–86, Dir of Creative Writing, 1982–02, Prof. of English, 1986–94, Frederick S. Troy Prof. of English, 1994–; University of Massachusetts, Boston; Classical Music Critic, Fresh Air, National Public Radio, 1987–; Poetry Commentator, TomPaine.com, 2001–. *Publications:* These People, 1981; Elizabeth Bishop and Her Art (ed.), 1983; Goodnight, Gracie, 1992; Cairo Traffic, 2000. *Contributions to:* American Review; Best American Poetry, 1991, 1994; Harvard Magazine; New Republic; New York Times; Partisan Review; Pequod; Ploughshares; Poetry; New Yorker; Slate; The Handbook of Heartbreak; Boulevard; Southwest Review; Atlantic Monthly. *Honours:* ASCAP-Deems Taylor Awards, 1980, 1987, 1990; Daniel Varoujan Prize, 1987; Pushcart Prize, 1987; Somerville Arts Council Grants, 1987, 1989; National Endowment for the Arts Fellowship, 1990; Runner-Up, Gustav Davidson Memorial Award, 1990; Pulitzer Prize in Criticism, 1994. *Memberships:* New England Poetry Club; PEN New England, exec. committee,

1983–98, exec. council, 1998–; Poetry Society of America. *Address:* 27 Pennsylvania Ave, Somerville, MA 02145, USA.

SCHWARTZ, Lynne Sharon; b. 19 March 1939, New York, NY, USA. Author; Poet. m. Harry Schwartz, 22 Dec. 1957, 2 d. *Education:* BA, Barnard College, 1959; MA, Bryn Mawr College, 1961; New York University, 1967–72. *Publications:* Rough Strife, 1980; Balancing Acts, 1981; Disturbances in the Field, 1983; Acquainted with the Night (stories), 1984; We Are Talking About Homes (stories), 1985; The Melting Pot and Other Subversive Stories, 1987; Leaving Brooklyn, 1989; A Lynne Sharon Schwartz Reader: Selected Prose and Poetry, 1992; The Fatigue Artist, 1995; Ruined by Reading: A Life in Books, 1996; In the Family Way, 1999; Face to Face: A Reader in the World, 2000; In Solitary (poems), 2002; A Place to Live and Other Selected Essays of Natalia Ginzburg (trans.), 2002. *Contributions to:* Periodicals. *Honours:* National Endowment for the Arts Fellowships, 1984, 2002; Guggenheim Fellowship, 1985; New York State Foundation for the Arts Fellowship, 1986. *Memberships:* Authors Guild; National Book Critics Circle; National Writers Union; PEN American Centre. *Address:* 50 Morningside Dr., No. 31, New York, NY 10025, USA.

SCHWARTZ, Rhoda Bette Josephson; b. 28 Dec. 1923, New Jersey, USA. Poet; Writer. m. Edward Schwartz, 27 Feb. 1944, deceased 1 d. *Education:* Privately tutored. *Appointments:* Technical Writer, US Veterans Administration; Founding Ed., The American Poetry Review and Pushcart Press. *Publications:* Anthologies: About Women, 1973; Jewish American Literature, 1974; Speaking for Ourselves, 1975; New World's of Literature, I, 1989, II, 1993; Families, 1990. *Contributions to:* Nation; Chicago Review; Kansas Quarterly; Carolina Quarterly; Books; Big Moon. *Honour:* Pushcart Prize, 1976. *Membership:* Patron, Acad. of American Poets. *Address:* 1901 JFK Blvd, Apt 2321, Philadelphia, PA 19103, USA.

SCHWARZ, Daniel Roger; b. 12 May 1941, Rockville Centre, New York, USA. Prof. of English; Writer; Poet. m. (1) Marcia Mitson, 1 Sept. 1963, divorced 1986, 2 s., (2) Marcia Jacobson, 1998. *Education:* BA, Union College, 1963; MA, 1965, PhD, 1968, Brown University. *Appointments:* Asst Prof., 1968–74, Assoc. Prof., 1974–80; Prof., 1980–, Cornell University; Distinguished Visiting Cooper Prof., University of Arkansas at Little Rock, 1988; Citizen's Chair in Literature, University of Hawaii, 1992–93; Visiting Eminent Scholar, University of Alabama, Huntsville, 1996. *Publications:* Disraeli's Fiction, 1979; Conrad: Almayer's Folly to Under Western Eyes, 1980; Conrad: The Later Fiction, 1982; The Humanistic Heritage: Critical Theories of the English Novel from James to Hillis Miller, 1986; Reading Joyce's Ulysses, 1987; The Transformation of the English Novel 1890–1930: Studies in Hardy, Conrad, Joyce, Lawrence, Forster and Woolf, 1989; The Case for a Humanistic Poetics, 1991; Narrative and Representation in the Poetry of Wallace Stevens, 1993; Narrative and Culture (ed. with Janice Carlise), 1994; Joseph Conrad's The Secret Sharer (ed.), 1997; Reconfiguring Modernism: Explorations in the Relationship Between Modern Art and Modern Literature, 1997; Imagining the Holocaust, 1999; Rereading Conrad, 2001. *Contributions to:* Journals. *Honours:* American Philosophical Society Grant, 1981; Dir, 9 National Endowment for the Humanities Summer Seminars for College and High School Teachers Grants, 1984–93; USIA Lecturer and Academic Specialist Lecturer, Australia, 1993; Cyprus, 1999; Cornell University Russell Distinguished Teaching Award, 1998. *Memberships:* International Asscn of University Profs of English; Society for the Study of Narrative Literature; MLA. *Address:* c/o Dept of English, 242 Goldwin Smith Hall, Cornell University, Ithaca, NY 14853, USA. *E-mail:* drs6@cornell.edu. *Website:* www.people.cornell.edu/pages/drs6/.

SCOBIE, Stephen (Arthur Cross); b. 31 Dec. 1943, Carnoustie, Scotland. Prof. of English; Poet; Writer. m. Sharon Maureen, 6 May 1967. *Education:* MA, University of St Andrews, 1965; PhD, University of British Columbia, 1969. *Appointments:* Faculty, 1969–80, Prof., 1980–81, University of Alberta; Prof. of English, University of Victoria, 1981–; Guest Prof. of Canadian Studies, Christian-Albrechts-Universität, Kiel, 1990. *Publications:* Poetry: Babylondromat, 1966; In the Silence of the Year, 1971; The Birken Tree, 1973; Stone Poems, 1974; The Rooms We Air, 1975; Airloom, 1975; Les toiles n'ont peur de rien, 1979; McAlmon's Chinese Opera, 1980; A Grand Memory for Forgetting, 1981; Expecting Rain, 1985; The Ballad of Isabel Gunn, 1987; Dunino, 1988; Remains, 1990; Ghosts: A Glossary of the Intertext, 1990; Gospel, 1994; Slowly Into Autumn, 1995; Willow, 1995; Taking the Gate: Journey Through Scotland, 1996. Other: Leonard Cohen, 1978; The Maple Laugh Forever: An Anthology of Canadian Comic Poetry (co-ed.), 1981; Alias Bob Dylan, 1991. *Contributions to:* Journals and magazines. *Honours:* Governor-General's Award for Poetry, 1980; Fellow, Royal Society of Canada, 1995. *Memberships:* League of Canadian Poets, vice-pres., 1972–74, 1986–88; Victoria Literary Arts Festival Society, pres. *Address:* 4278 Parkside Crescent, Victoria, BC V8N 2C3, Canada.

SCOTT, Allyson G. See: HODDINOTT, Allyson Gray.

SCOTT, Hope. See: McKEEHAN, Mildred Hope.

SCOTT, John A.; b. 23 April 1948, Littlehampton, Sussex, England. University Lecturer; Poet; Writer. *Education:* BA, DipEd, Monash University, Vic., Australia. *Appointments:* Lecturer, Swinburne Institute, 1975–80, Canberra College of Advanced Education, 1980–89, University of Wollongong, NSW, 1989–. *Publications:* The Barbarous Sideshow, 1976; From the Flooded City, 1981; Smoking, 1983; The Quarrel with Ourselves, 1984; Confession, 1984; St Clair, 1986; Blair, 1988; Singles: Shorter Works 1981–1986, 1989; Translation, 1990; What I Have Written, 1993. *Contributions to:* Various publications. *Honours:* Poetry Society of Australia Award, 1970; Mattara Poetry Prize, 1984; Wesley Michel Wright Awards, 1985, 1988; Victorian Premier's Prize for Poetry, 1986; ANA Award, Fellowship of Australian Writers, 1990.

SCOTT, Jonathan (Henry); b. 22 Jan. 1958, Auckland, New Zealand. Historian; Writer; Poet. m. (1) Sara Bennett, 1980, divorced, (2) Lindsey Bridget Shaw, 1986, divorced 1991, (3) Anne Hansel Pelzel, 1995, 1 s., 1 d. *Education:* BA, 1980, BA, 1981, Victoria University of Wellington; PhD, Trinity College, Cambridge, 1986. *Appointments:* Research Fellow, Magdalene College, Cambridge, 1985–87; Lecturer in History, Victoria University of Wellington, 1987–88, University of Sheffield, 1989–91; Fellow and Dir of Studies in History, Downing College, Cambridge, 1991–. *Publications:* Algernon Sidney and the English Republic, 1623–1677, 1988; Algernon Sidney and the Restoration Crisis, 1677–1683, 1991; Harry's Absence: Looking for My Father on the Mountain, 1997; England's Troubles: Seventeenth Century English Political Instability in European Context, 2000. *Contributions to:* Scholarly books and journals, and literary periodicals. *Address:* c/o Dept of History, Downing College, University of Cambridge, Cambridge CB2 1DQ, England.

SCOTT, Peter Dale; b. 11 Jan. 1929, Montréal, QC, Canada. Prof. of English (retd); Poet. m. Ronna Kabatznick, 14 July 1993, 2 s., 1 d. *Education:* BA, 1949, PhD, Political Science, 1955, McGill University; Institut d'Etudes Politiques, Paris, 1950; University College, Oxford, 1950–52. *Appointments:* Lecturer, McGill University, 1955–56; Canadian Foreign Service, Ottawa and Poland, 1957–61; Prof. of Speech, 1961–66, Prof. of English, 1966–94, University of California at Berkeley. *Publications:* Poems, 1952; Rumors of No Law, 1981; Coming to Jakarta, 1988; Listening to the Candle, 1992; Crossing Borders, 1994; Minding the Darkness, 2000. *Contributions to:* Reviews, quarterlies, and periodicals. *Honour:* Dia Art Foundation, 1989. *Address:* c/o Dept of English, University of California at Berkeley, Berkeley, CA 94720, USA.

SCOTT, (Peter) Hardiman; b. 2 April 1920, Norfolk, England. Poet. m. (1) 2 s., (2) 17 June 1966. *Appointments:* Asst News Ed., BBC Midland Region; Reporter, BBC Radio and TV, London; Political Correspondent and Political Ed., BBC. *Publications:* Adam and Eve and Us, 1946; When the Words are Gone, 1972; Part of Silence, 1984; Selected Poems of Sir Thomas Wyatt (ed.) 1996; Where Shadows Fall, 1998. *Contributions to:* Poetry Review; TLS; Orbis; Outposts; Rialto; BBC. *Honour:* O.B.E., 1989. *Memberships:* Poetry Society; Suffolk Poetry Society, pres. *Address:* The Drey, 4 Butchers Lane, Boxford, Suffolk CO10 5DZ, England.

SCOTT, Rosie; b. 22 March 1948, New Zealand (Joint Australian/New Zealand citizen). Writer; Poet. m. 28 Nov. 1987, 2 d. *Education:* MA, English, 1968; Graduate Diploma, Drama, 1984. *Publications:* Flesh and Blood (poems), 1984; Glory Days, 1988; Queen of Love, 1989; Nights with Grace, 1990; Feral City, 1992; Lives on Fire, 1993; Movie Dreams, 1995; The Red Heart (essays), 1999; Faith Singer, 2001. *Contributions to:* Various publications. *Honours:* Sunday Times-Bruce Mason Award, 1986; Australian Writers Fellowship, 1992. *Memberships:* exec. committee, Australian Society of Authors; PEN Australia. *Address:* 21 Darghan St, Glebe, NSW 2037, Australia.

SCOTT, William Neville, (Bill Scott); b. 4 Oct. 1923, Bundaberg, Qld, Australia. Author; Poet. *Publications:* Focus on Judith Wright, 1967; Some People (short stories), 1968; Brother and Brother (verse), 1972; The Continual Singing: An Anthology of World Poetry, 1973; Portrait of Brisbane, 1976; The Complete Book of Australian Folklore, 1976; Bushranger Ballads, 1976; My Uncle and Other People (short stories), 1977; Boori (children's fiction), 1978; Tough in the Old Days (autobiography), 1979; Ned Kelly After a Century of Acrimony (with John Meredith), 1980; The Second Penguin Australian Songbook, 1980; Darkness Under the Hills (children's fiction), 1980; Reading 360 series (The Blooming Queensland Side, On the Shores of Botany Bay, The Golden West, Bound for South Australia, Upon Van Diemen's Land, The Victorian Bunyip), 6 vols, 1981; Australian Bushrangers, 1983; Penguin Book of Australian Humorous Verse, 1984; Shadows Among the Leaves (children's fiction), 1984; The Long and the Short and the Tall (folklore), 1985; Following the Gold (children's poems), 1989; Many Kinds of Magic (short stories), 1990; Hey Rain (cassette, songs and poems), 1992; The Currency Lad (fiction), 1994; Songbird in Your Pocket (cassette, songs and poems), 1994; Pelicans and Chihuahuas (folklore), 1995; The Banshee and the Bullocky (short stories), 1995; Riverbank and Township (poems), 1999; Opal Miner (CD of songs), 1999; Lies, Flies and Strange Big Fish, 2000. *Honours:* Mary Gilmore Award, 1964; Medal of the Order of Australia, 1992; Heritage Award, 1994; Judith Hosier Memorial Award, 2001. *Address:* 157 Pratten St, Warwick, Qld 4370, Australia.

SCULLY, James, (Joseph Patrick); b. 23 Feb. 1937, New Haven, CT, USA. Poet; Trans. m. Arlene Marie Steeves, 10 Sept. 1960, 2 s., 1 d. *Education:* BA 1959, PhD, 1964, University of Connecticut. *Publications:* Modern Poetics (ed.) 1965; The Marches, 1967; Avenue of the Americas, 1971; Santiago Poems, 1975; Scrap Book, 1977; May Day, 1980; Apollo Helmet, 1983; Line Break: Poetry as Social Practice, 1988; Raging Beauty: Selected Poems, 1994. Translator Aechylus' Prometheus Bound (with C J Herington), 1975; Quechua Peoples Poetry (with M A Proser), 1977; Teresa de Jesus' de Repente – All of a Sudden (with Proser and A Scully), 1979. *Contributions to:* Critical Quarterly Leviathan; Massachusetts Review; Arion; Praxis; New Yorker; Minnesota Review; Literatura Chilena en el Exilio; Harvard Magazine; Poetry Review Compages; Alcatraz. *Honours:* Ingram Merrill Foundation Fellowship, 1962–63; Lamont Poetry Award, 1967; Contributors' Prize, Far Point, 1969; Jenny Taine Memorial Award, Massachusetts Review, 1971; Guggenheim Fellowship, 1973–74; National Endowment for the Arts Fellowships, 1976–77, 1990–91; Trans. Award, Islands and Continents, 1980; Award, Bookcover Design, Bookbuilders of Boston, 1983. *Memberships:* PEN; Poetry Society of America. *Address:* 2865 Bryant St, San Francisco, CA 94110, USA.

SCUPHAM, John Peter; b. 24 Feb. 1933, Liverpool, England. Writer; Poet. m. Carola Nance Braunholtz, 6 Aug. 1957, 3 s., 1 d. *Education:* Honours Degree, English, Emmanuel College, Cambridge, 1957. *Appointment:* Founder-Publisher, The Mandeville Press. *Publications:* The Snowing Globe, 1972; Prehistories, 1975; The Hinterland, 1977; Summer Places, 1980; Winter Quarters, 1983; Out Late, 1986; The Air Show, 1989; Watching the Perseids, 1990; Selected Poems, 1990; The Ark, 1994; Night Watch, 1999. *Contributions to:* Anthologies and magazines. *Membership:* RSL, fellow. *Address:* Old Hall, Norwich Rd, South Burlingham, Norfolk NR13 4EY, England.

SEATOR, Lynette; b. 23 March 1929, Chicago, IL, USA. Poet; Writer. m. Gordon Seator, 8 June 1949, 1 s., 3 d. *Education:* BS, 1963, MA, 1965, PhD, 1972, University of Illinois. *Appointments:* Instructor, Western Illinois University, 1966–67; Prof. of Modern Languages, 1967–89, Pixley Prof. of Humanities, 1988, Illinois College; Dir, Poetry Workshop, Jacksonville Correctional Center, IL. *Publications:* After the Light, 1992; Hear Me Out (ed.), 1997; Behind the Wall (Poems), 1999; Speaking through the Bars (ed.), 1999. *Contributions to:* Reviews, quarterlies, and journals. *Honours:* Harry J Dunbaugh Distinguished Prof., 1976; Illinois Arts Council Artist-in-Residence, 1984, 1985; Writer of the Year Award, Lincoln Library, Springfield, IL, 1996. *Memberships:* Illinois Writers, board members, 1983–87, 1993–; Poets and Writers. *Address:* 1609 Mound Ave, Jacksonville, IL 62650, USA.

SEDGWICK, Fred; b. 20 Jan. 1945, Dublin, Ireland. Lecturer in Education; Poet. *Education:* St Luke's College, Exeter; MA, University of East Anglia at Norwich, 1984. *Appointments:* Head of Downing Primary School, Suffolk; Education Lecturer. *Publications:* Really in the Dark, 1980; From Another Part of the Island, 1981; A Garland for William Cowper, 1984; The Living Daylights, 1986; Falernian, 1987; This Way, That Way: A Collection of Poems for Schools (ed.), 1989; Lighting Up Time: On Children's Writing, 1990. *Address:* 1 Mornington Ave, Ipswich, Suffolk IP1 4LA, England.

SEGUI BENNASSAR, Antoni, (A. S. Bocchoritano, Taco Nini); b. 29 April 1927, Port de Pollenca, Balears, Spain. Teacher (retd); Poet. m. 29 Aug. 1953, 2 s. *Education:* Teaching diplomas, 1952, 1958, 1969. *Publications:* Supervivencia de Miguel Costa i Liobera, 1973; L'amor en quart creixent, 1977; Un Llorer per a Costa i Liobera, 1982; Bocchoris i els seus forners, 1985; Poesy of Joan Guiraud, 1985; My Via-Crucis, 1994. *Contributions to:* Anthologies and other publications. *Honours:* Various prizes, 1967–93. *Memberships:* Agrupacion Hispana des Escritores, Mallorca; International Writers and Artists Asscn. USA. *Address:* C Formentor, 2-1er, Apt 197, 07470 Port de Pollenca, Balears, Spain.

SEIDEL, Frederick (Lewis); b. 19 Feb. 1936, St Louis, MO, USA. Poet. m. Phyllis Munro Ferguson, 7 June 1960, divorced 1969, 1 s., 1 d. *Education:* BA, Harvard University, 1957. *Publications:* Final Solutions, 1963; Sunrise: Poems, 1979; Men and Woman: New and Selected Poems, 1984; Poems, 1959–1979, 1989; These Days: New Poems, 1989; My Tokyo: Poems, 1993; Going Fast: Poems, 1998; The Cosmos Poems, 2000; Life on Earth, 2001. *Contributions to:* Paris Review. *Honours:* Lamont Poetry Prize, Acad. of American Poets, 1980; National Book Critics Circle Award for Poetry, 1981; American Poetry Review Poetry Prize, 1981; Guggenheim Fellowship, 1993. *Address:* 251 W 92nd St, New York, NY 10028, USA.

SEIDMAN, Hugh; b. 1 Aug. 1940, New York, NY, USA. Writer; Poet; Teacher. m. Jayne Holsinger, 2 June 1990. *Education:* BS, Mathematics, Polytechnic Institute of Brooklyn, 1961; MS, Physics, University of Minnesota, 1964; MFA, Poetry, Columbia University, 1969. *Appointments:* Faculty, New School for Social Research, New York City, 1976–; Asst Prof., Washington College, 1979; Visiting Lecturer, University of Wisconsin, 1981, Columbia University, 1985; Poet-in-Residence, College of William and Mary, 1982; Visiting Poet, Writers Voice, New York City, 1988. *Publications:* Collecting Evidence, 1970; Blood Lord, 1974; Throne/Falcon/Eye, 1982; People Live, They Have Lives, 1992; Selected Poems 1965–1995, 1995. *Contributions to:* Many publications. *Honours:* Yale Series of Younger Poets Prize, 1969; National Endowment for the Arts Grant, 1970, and Fellowships, 1972, 1985; Yaddo Fellowships, 1972, 1976, 1986; MacDowell Colony Fellowships, 1974, 1975, 1989; Writers Digest Poetry Prize, 1982; New York Foundation for the Arts Poetry Fellowship, 1990. *Memberships:* American PEN; Authors Guild; Authors League; Poetry Society of America. *Address:* 463 West St, No. H-822, New York, NY 10014, USA.

SEIFERLE, Rebecca A.; b. 14 Dec. 1951, Denver, CO, USA. Instructor in English; Poet. m. Phillip Valencia 11 Aug. 1978, 1 s., 2 d. *Education:* BA, English and History, State University of New York, 1982; MFA, Poetry, Warren Wilson College, 1989. *Appointments:* Artist-in-the School, New Mexico, 1986–88; Instructor in English, San Juan College, 1991–. *Publications:* Trilce, by Cesasr Vallejo (trans.), 1992; The Ripped-Out Seam (poems), 1993; The Music We Dance To (poems), 1999; Bitters (poems), 2001. *Contributions to:* Anthologies, reviews, quarterlies, and journals. *Honours:* Santa Cruz Writers Union Award, 1986; Writers Exchange Award, 1990; George Bogin Memorial Award, 1990; Western States Book Award, 2002; Pushcart Prize, 2002. *Memberships:* American Literary Trans Asscn; Associated Writing Programs; Poetry Society of America; Poets and Letters. *Address:* 5602 Terrace, Farmington, NM 87402, USA.

SELLEN, Derek Robert; b. 8 Jan. 1948, Kent, England. Teacher; Poet. m. Therese Hess, 22 March 1975, 2 d. *Education:* BA, English, University of Birmingham, 1969; RSA Diploma in TEFL, 1975; Adult Education Certificate, Open University, 1990. *Appointments:* Lecturer in English, University of Salamanca; Dir of Studies, Stafford House College, Canterbury. *Publication:* The Dog's-Head Coat, 1996. *Contributions to:* Agenda; Sunday Telegraph; Poetry Review; Orbis; South East Arts Review; Poetry South East; Ore; Arvon/Sotheby's Competition Anthology; Megaphone; Iron; Alta; Birmingham Post; New Poetry. *Honours:* Birmingham University Poetry Competition, 1970; Finalist, Cheltenham Festival Competition, 1976; Fourth Place, National Poetry Competition, 1981; Kent Creative Writing Award, 1986; East Kent Poetry Competition, 1988; Open University Open Competition, 1989; Rhyme International, 1989; Finalist, Canterbury Festival Open Competition, 1994. *Membership:* Judge, Thanet Poetry Competition, 1990. *Address:* 5 Lime Kiln Rd, Canterbury, Kent CT1 3QH, England.

SELTZER, Joanne; b. 21 Nov. 1929, Detroit, Michigan, USA. Writer; Poet. m. Stanley Seltzer, 10 Feb. 1951, 1 s., 3 d. *Education:* BA, University of Michigan, 1951; MA, College of St Rose, 1978. *Publications:* Adirondack Lake Poems, 1985; Suburban Landscape, 1988; Inside Invisible Walls, 1989. *Contributions to:* Journals and magazines. *Honours:* All Nations Poetry Contest Award, 1978; World Order of Narrative and Formalist Poets Competitions Prizes, 1986, 1988, 1990, 1992, 1993, 1994, 1997, 1998, 2000; Tucumari Literary Review Poetry Contest Award, 1989; Amelia Islander Magazine Literary Contest Poetry Prize, 1999. *Memberships:* American Literary Trans Asscn; Associated Writing Programs; Poetry Society of America; Poets & Writers. *Address:* 2481 McGovern Dr., Schenectady, NY 12309, USA. *E-mail:* sseltzer1@juno.com.

SENGUPTA, Preety; b. 17 May 1944, Ahmedabad, India. Writer; Poet. m. Chandan Sengupta, 21 June 1975. *Education:* MA, English Literature. *Publications:* Some 18 works. *Contributions to:* Various publications. *Honours:* Several literary awards. *Memberships:* PEN India; Poetry Society of America. *Address:* 15 Stewart Pl., White Plains, NY 10603, USA.

SENIOR, Olive Marjorie; b. 23 Dec. 1941, Jamaica. Writer; Poet. *Education:* BA, Carleton University, 1967. *Publications:* Fiction: Summer Lightning, 1986; Arrival of the Snake-Woman, 1989; Discerner of Hearts, 1995. Poetry: Talking of Trees, 1986; Gardening in the Tropics, 1994. Non-Fiction: A–Z of Jamaican Heritage, 1984; Working Miracles: Women's Lives in the English Speaking Caribbean, 1991. *Honour:* Commonwealth Writers Prize, 1987. *Membership:* Writers' Union of Canada. *Literary Agent:* Watkins Loomis Agency. *Address:* 65 Springmount Ave, Toronto, ON M6H 2Y5, Canada.

SEPAMLA, (Sydney) Sipho; b. 1932, Johannesburg, South Africa. Poet; Writer; Ed. *Education:* Teacher Training. *Appointments:* Ed., New Classic and S'ketsh magazines. *Publications:* Hurry Up To It, 1975; The Blues is You in Me, 1976; The Soweto I Love, 1977; The Root is One, 1979; A Rise on the Whirlwind, 1981; Children of the Earth, 1983; Selected Poems, 1984; Third Generation, 1986; From Gore to Soweto, 1988; Scattered Survival, 1988.

SEQUIERA, Desmond; b. 20 April 1931, Mangalore, India. Poet. *Education:* Intermediate Degree, Arts and Science, Chennai University, 1950; Diploma, Art and Design, Goldsmith's College, London, 1973. *Publication:* Between Times, 1992. *Contributions to:* Anthologies and other publications. *Honours:* Grand Prize, National Library of Poetry, USA; One of Best Poems, Library of Congress, Washington, DC, 1996. *Address:* 13B Granville Park, London SE13 7DY, England.

SEROTE, Mongane Wally; b. 8 May 1944, Johannesburg, South Africa. Poet; Writer. *Education:* MFA, Columbia University, New York, 1979. *Publications:* Poetry: Yakhal-imkomo, 1972; Tsetlo, 1974; No Baby Must Weep, 1975; Behold Mama, Flowers, 1978; The Night Keeps Winking, 1982; Selected Poems, 1982; A Tought Tale, 1987. Novel: To Every Birth its Blood, 1981. *Honour:* Fulbright Scholarship. *Address:* 28 Penton Rd, PO Box 38, London N1 9PR, England.

SERRAS, Dionysis; b. 27 Nov. 1947, Greece. Teacher of Greek Literature; Poet. *Education:* Degree in Greek Literature, Athens University, 1971. *Appointment:* Ed., Eptanisiaka Filla literary magazine, 1995. *Publications:* Double Voices, 1978; Ode to Dionysius Solomos, 1978; Suns and Nails, 1980; Six Writings for Sepheris, 1987; Antidotes for the Bitter Silence, 1990; Bibliographies of Andrea Kalvo and Ugo Foskolo, 1992; The Poetic March of Lula-Valvi Milona, 1993; Drops in Black and White, 1994. *Contributions to:* Zakynthos in the Greek and Foreign Poetry (anthology), 1994; Periodicals, including: Lexi; Nea Estia; Sullogi; Epikera; Periplous; Tetramena; Porphyras. *Membership:* Greek Literary Asscn. *Address:* Yfantourgion 39, Zakynthos 29100, Greece.

SESHADRI, Vijay; b. 13 Feb. 1954, Bangalore, India (Naturalized US citizen). Prof.; Poet; Ed. m. Suzanne Odette Khuri, Aug. 1992, 1 s. *Education:* BA, Oberlin College, 1974; MFA, Columbia University, 1985. *Appointments:* Ed., The New Yorker, 1993–; Prof., Sarah Lawrence College, 1995–. *Publication:* Wild Kingdom (poems), 1996. *Address:* c/o Sarah Lawrence College, 1 Mead Way, Bronxville, NY 10708, USA. *E-mail:* seshadri@amail.s/s.edu.

SETH, Vikram; b. 20 June 1952, Calcutta, India. Poet; Writer. *Education:* BA, 1975, MA, 1978, Corpus Christi College, Oxford; MA, 1977, PhD, 1979, Stanford University; Diploma, Nanjing University, China, 1982. *Publications:* Mappings, 1980; From Heaven Lake: Travels Through Sianking and Tibet, 1983; The Humble Administrator's Garden, 1985; All You Who Sleep Tonight (trans.), 1985; The Golden Gate: A Novel in Verse, 1986; Beastly Tales From Here to There (fables in verse), 1992; Three Chinese Poets (trans.), 1992; A Suitable Boy, 1994; An Equal Music, 1999. *Contributions to:* Reviews and magazines. *Honours:* Guggenheim Fellowships; Thomas Cook Travel Book Award, 1983; Commonwealth Poetry Prize, 1986; W H Smith Literary Award, 1994. *Address:* c/o Giles Gordon, Curtis Brown, 28–29 Haymarket, London SW14 4SP, England.

SEWERYN, Tadeusz. See: LACZKOWSKI, Zdzislaw Tadeusz.

SHAFRIR-STILLMAN, Moshe David; b. 1935, Tel-Aviv, Palestine. Poet; Geologist. m., 3 s. *Education:* BSc, Geology and Chemistry, Hebrew University of Jerusalem; High School Teacher Certificate, Ben Gurion University, Beer Sheba. *Appointments:* Ministry of Agriculture of Israel; Tahal Consulting Engineers; 'Haboker' daily newspaper; Municipality of Ashdod City; Israeli Institute of Productivity; Hana Oil Exploration Co; Shazar High School, Kiryat-Ono; Engineering College of Tel-Aviv University. *Publications:* Belated Rain, 1967; To Ask and To Answer, 1975; The End of the Game, 1983; Presentations, 1989; Belated Loves, 1995; The Promise of Rain, 1995; Poems on Cain and Other Biblical Figures, 2000. Other: Hallelujah (novel, with Daniel Amarilio), 1995. *Contributions to:* Newspapers and periodicals. *Memberships:* Hebrew Writers Asscn of Israel; PEN Centre Israel, treasurer; Organisation of Israeli Teachers; Israel Geological Society; American Asscn of Petroleum Geologists. *Address:* 67 Pinkas St, Tel-Aviv, 62157, Israel. Telephone and Fax: (3) 6058840. *E-mail:* mdss64@hotmail.com.

SHAHAWY, Ahmed Ibrahim el-; b. 12 Nov. 1960, Domyetta, Egypt. Ed.; Poet. *Education:* Graduate, Journalism, Assyot University. *Appointments:* Ed., Alahram Daily, 1986; Asst Managing Dir, Nisf-el-Dunya Weekly, 1990. *Publications:* Two Prayers for Love, 1988; Al Ahadith, 1991; The Book of Love, 1992; The Hadilhs II, 1994; States of the Lover, 1995. *Contributions to:* Al-Akhbar; Rose Al Yussuf; Al-Hayat; Sahab El Kheir; Al Arab; Al She'r; Al Kahera; Poet Lore; Odjak. *Honours:* First Prize, Poetry Contest, Ministry of Culture, Egypt, 1983; Fellowship Certificate in Literary Writing, University of Iowa, USA, 1991; Certificate of Fellows of Literature, Aiwa University, 1991; Special Diploma in Culture and Science, Ionic Centre, Greece, 1994; UNESCO Literary Award, 1995. *Memberships:* Writers and Artists Society; Egyptian Writers Union; International Writing Programme; Press Syndicate. *Address:* Al-Ahram Newspaper, Al-Galaa St, Cairo, Egypt.

SHAKHTINTERNATIONAL. See: KOUL, Chaman Lal.

SHAMBAUGH, (Frances) J(oan) D(ibble); b. 14 March 1928, Michigan, USA. Poet. m. Benjamin Shambaugh, 26 Dec. 1950, 2 s., 1 d. *Education:* AB, Sociology and Education, Duke Women's College, Duke University, 1949; MEd, Lesley College Graduate School. *Publications:* Poems From Lincoln Hill, 1989; She Who Walks With Trees, 1993. *Contributions to:* Lincoln Review; Cottage Press; Anthology From Lincoln Hill. *Honours:* Readings and Presentations at various venues, 1989, 1991. *Memberships:* Poetry Society of America; New England Poetry Society. *Address:* PO Box 552, Hardwick, VT 05843, USA.

SHANGE, Ntozake, (b. Paulette Williams); b. 18 Oct. 1948, Trenton, New Jersey, USA. Poet; Dramatist; Writer; Assoc. Prof. of Drama. 1 d. *Education:* BA, Barnard College, 1970; MA, University of Southern California at Los Angeles, 1973. *Appointments:* Faculty, Sonoma State College, Rohnert Park, CA, 1973–75; Mills College, Oakland, CA, 1975; City College of the City University of New York, 1975, Douglass College, New Brunswick, New Jersey, 1978; Artist-in-Residence, Equinox Theater, Houston, 1981–; Assoc. Prof. of Drama, University of Houston, 1983–. *Publications:* Poetry: Melissa and Smith, 1976; Natural Disasters and Other Festive Occasions, 1977; Happy

Edges, 1978; Some Men, 1981; A Daughter's Geography, 1983; From Okra to Greens, 1984; Ridin' the Moon in Texas: Word Paintings, 1988; The Love Space Demands: A Continuing Saga, 1992. Plays: For Colored Girls Who Have Considered Suicide When the Rainbow is Enuf, 1976; Photograph: Lovers-in-Motion, 1981; Spell #7, 1981; Boogie Woogie Landscapes, 1981. Fiction: Sassafrass: A Novella, 1977; Sassafrass, Cypress and Indigo, 1982; Betsey Brown, 1985; Liliane: Resurrection of the Daughter, 1995. Non-Fiction: See No Evil: Prefaces, Essays and Accounts 1976–1983, 1984. Honours: New York Drama Critics Circle Award, 1977; Obie Awards, 1977, 1980; Columbia University Medal of Excellence, 1981; Guggenheim Fellowship, 1981. Address: c/o St Martin's Press, 175 Fifth Ave, New York, NY 10010, USA.

SHAPCOTT, Jo(anne Amanda); b. 24 March 1953, London, England. Poet. Education: Foundation Scholar, 1972–76, BA, English Literature and Language, 1976, Trinity College, Dublin; St Hilda's College, Oxford, 1976–78; Harkness Fellow, Harvard University, 1978–80. Appointments: Judith E. Wilson Fellow in Creative Writing, University of Cambridge, 1991; Northern Arts Literary Fellow, 1998–2000; Visiting Prof. of Poetry, Newcastle University, 2001–. Publications: Electroplating the Baby, 1988; Phrase Book, 1992; Emergency Kit: Poems for Strange Times, 1996; My Life Asleep, 1998; Her Book: Poems 1988–98, 1998; Tender Taxes, 2001. Contributions to: The Times; Sunday Times; New Statesman; Poetry Review; TLS; Verse; Southern Review. Honours: First Prize, National Poetry Competition, 1981, 1991; Commonwealth Prize, 1988; Poetry Book Society Choice, 1992, 1998; Short-listed, T. S. Eliot Prize, 1998; Forward Prize, 1998. Address: 62a Meadow Rd, London SW8 1PP, England.

SHAPCOTT, Thomas W(illiam); b. 21 March 1935, Ipswich, Qld, Australia. Poet; Novelist; Writer; Prof. of Creative Writing. m. (1) Margaret Hodge, 1960, (2) Judith Rodriguez, 1982, 1 s., 3 d. Education: BA, University of Queensland, 1968. Appointments: Dir, Australia Council Literature Board, 1983–90; Exec. Dir, National Book Council, 1992–97; Prof. of Creative Writing, University of Adelaide, 1997–. Publications: Poetry: Time on Fire, 1961; The Mankind Thing, 1963; Sonnets, 1960–63, 1963; A Taste of Salt Water, 1967; Inwards to the Sun, 1969; Fingers at Air, 1969; Begin with Walking, 1973; Shabbytown Calendar, 1975; 7th Avenue Poems, 1976; Selected Poems, 1978; Make the Old Man Sing, 1980; Welcome!, 1983; Travel Dice, 1987; Selected Poems, 1956–1988, 1989; In the Beginning, 1990; The City of Home, 1995; Chekhov's Mongoose, 2001. Fiction: The Birthday Gift, 1982; White Stag of Exile, 1984; Hotel Bellevue, 1986; The Search for Galina, 1989; Mona's Gift, 1993; Theatre of Darkness, 1998. Plays: The 7 Deadly Sins, 1970. Editor: New Impulses in Australian Poetry (with R Hall), 1967; Australian Poetry Now, 1970; Contemporary American and Australian Poetry, 1975; Poetry as a Creative Learning Process, 1978; The Moment Made Marvellous (anthology), 1998; An Island on Land: Contemporary Macedonian Poetry (ed. and trans. with Ilija Casule), 1999. Contributions to: Newspapers and journals. Honours: Grace Leven Prize, 1961; Sir Thomas White Memorial Prize, 1967; Sidney Myer Charity Trust Awards, 1967, 1969; Churchill Fellowship, 1972; Canada-Australia Literary Prize, 1978; Officer of the Order of Australia, 1989; Hon. DLitt, Macquarie University, 1989; Gold Wreath, Struga International Poetry Festival, 1989; Christopher Brennan Award for Poetry, 1994; NSW Premier's Special Literary Prize, 1996; Michel Wesley Wright Award, 1996; Patrick White Award, 2000. Memberships: Australian Book Review, chair.; Copyright Agency Ltd, chair.; Australian Society of Authors; International PEN. Address: PO Box 231, Mont Albert, Vic. 3127, Australia.

SHAPIRO, Alan; b. 18 Feb. 1952, Boston, MA, USA. Prof.; Poet; Writer; Trans. m. Della Pollock, 7 Sept. 1984. Education: BA, English, Brandeis University, 1974. Appointments: Jones Lecturer in Creative Writing, 1976–79, Visiting Asst Prof., 1981, Stanford University; Lecturer, 1979–85, Assoc. Prof., 1985–88, Prof., 1988–89, Northwestern University; Poet-in-Residence, University of Chicago, 1981, 1986, 1988; Visiting Asst Prof., 1985, Visiting Prof., 1989, of Creative Writing, University of California at Irvine; Visiting Prof. of Creative Writing, Boston University, 1989; Fannie Hurst Poet-in-Residence, Brandeis University, 1989; Prof., University of North Carolina at Greensboro, 1989–94; Hurst Prof. of Creative Writing, Washington University, 1994; Prof., 1995–, Gillian T. Cell Distinguished Term Prof., 2001–, University of North Carolina at Chapel Hill; Richard L. Thomas Prof. of Creative Writing, Kenyon College, 2002. Publications: After the Digging (poems), 1981; The Courtesy (poems), 1983; Happy Hour (poems), 1987; Covenant (poems), 1991; In Praise of the Impure: Poetry and the Ethical Imagination: Essays (1980–1991), 1993; Mixed Company (poems), 1996; The Last Happy Occasion (memoir), 1996; Vigil (memoir), 1997; The Dead Alive and Busy (poems), 2000; Selected Poems, 2000; Song and Dance (poems), 2002; The Ortesteia (trans.), 2002. Contributions to: Many anthologies, reviews, quarterlies and journals. Honours: Wallace Stegner Creative Writing Fellowship, 1975–76; Acad. of American Poets Award, 1976; National Endowment for the Arts Fellowships, 1984–85, 1991; Guggenheim Fellowship, 1985–86; William Carlos Williams Award, Poetry Society of America, 1987; Lila Wallace-Reader's Digest Writers Award, 1991; Pushcart Prize, 1996; Los Angeles Times Book Award in Poetry, 1996; Open Society Institute Arts Fellowship, 1999; Kingsley Tufts Poetry Award, Claremont Graduate University, 2001. Address: 221 E Queen St, Hillsborough, NC 27278, USA.

SHAPIRO, David (Joel); b. 2 Jan. 1947, Newark, New Jersey, USA. Poet; Art Critic; Prof. of Art History. m. Lindsey Stamm, 1970, 1 c. Education: BA, 1968, PhD, 1973, Columbia University; BA, 1970, MA, 1974, Clare College, Cambridge. Appointments: Violinist in various orchestras, 1963–; Instructor and Asst Prof. of English, Columbia University, 1972–80; Visiting Prof. Brooklyn College of the City University of New York, 1979, Princeton University, 1982–83; Visiting Faculty, Cooper Union, New York City, 1980–; Full Prof. of Art History, William Paterson College, Wayne, New Jersey, 1996–. Publications: Poetry: January: A Book of Poems, 1965; Poems from Deal, 1969; A Man Holding an Acoustic Panel, 1971; The Page-Turner, 1973; Lateness, 1977; To an Idea, 1984; House, Blown Apart, 1988; After a Lost Original, 1990. Other: John Ashbery: An Introduction to the Poetry, 1979; Jim Dine: Painting What One Is, 1981; Jasper Johns: Drawings 1954–1984, 1984; Mondrian Flowers, 1990; Alfred Leslie: The Killing Cycle (with Judith Stein), 1991. Honours: Bread Loaf Writers Conference Robert Frost Fellowship, 1965; Ingram Merrill Foundation Fellowship, 1967; Book-of-the-Month Club Fellowship, 1968; Kellett Fellow, Clare College, Cambridge, 1968–70; Creative Artists Public Service Grant, 1974; Morton Dauwen Zabel Award, 1977; National Endowment for the Arts Grant, 1979; National Endowment for the Humanities Fellowships, 1980; Foundation for Contemporary Performance Arts Grant, 1996; Milton Asery Prof., Bard Graduate School of the Arts, 1996. Address: 3001 Henry Hudson Parkway, Riverdale, NY 10463, USA.

SHAPIRO, Harvey; b. 27 Jan. 1924, Chicago, IL, USA. Ed.; Poet. m Edna Kaufman, 23 July 1953, 2 s. Education: BA, Yale University, 1947; MA, Columbia University, 1948. Appointments: Staff, Commentary, 1955–57, The New Yorker, 1955–57; Staff, 1957–64, Deputy Ed., 1983–, New York Times Magazine; Asst Ed., 1964–75, Ed., 1975–83, New York Times Book Review. Publications: The Eye, 1953; The Book, 1955; Mountain Fire Thornbush, 1961; Battle Report, 1966; This World, 1971; Lauds, 1975; Lauds and Nightsounds, 1978; The Light Holds, 1984; National Cold Storage Company: New and Selected Poems, 1988; A Day's Portion, 1994; Selected Poems, 1997. Contributions to: Periodicals. Honour: Rockefeller Grant for Poetry, 1967. Address: c/o The New York Times Magazine, 229 W 43rd St, New York, NY 10036, USA.

SHARE TAN CHEN; b. 21 Nov. 1934, China. Poet; Political Commentator; Author; Journalist. m. 9 Jan. 1961, 4 s., 1 d. Education: Graduate, Shaanxi Normal University, 1962. Publications: China, 1985; Missing, 1989; You Are the Wind, 1989; Shui Tiao Keh Tou, 1990. Contributions to: Chinese News; China Spring; Central Daily News; Square. Memberships: World Acad. of Arts and Culture Inc, Governing Board of the World Congress of Poets; World Brotherhood and Peace Through Poetry; Asscn of Modern Chinese Literature and Arts of North America. Address: 1831 33rd Ave, San Francisco, CA 94122, USA.

SHARMA, Indra Kumar; b. 1 Jan. 1932, Shamli, India. Assoc. Prof. (retd). Poet. m. Sushila Sharma, 1958, 3 s., 1 d. Education: BA, 1953, MA, 1955. Appointments: Lecturer, Maharaja's College, Jaipur, 1956–62; Asst Prof., 1962–83, Assoc. Prof., 1983–91, University of Rajasthan, Jaipur. Publications: The Shifting Sand-Dunes, 1976; The Native Embers, 1986; Dharamsala and Other Poems, 1993; Camel, Cockroach and Captains, 1998. Contributions to: Reviews, quarterlies, and journals. Honours: First Prize and Gold Medal, Skylark International Poetry Competition, 1977; Hon. DLitt, World University, New York, 1979; Honoured by Rajasthan Sahitya Akademi, 1979; Michael Madhusudan Award, 1998. Memberships: Rajasthan Sahitya Akademi; World Poetry Society Intercontinental. Address: 1-27 SFS, Mansarovar, Jaipur 302 020, India.

SHARMA, Maha Nand; b. 11 July 1924, Bulandshahr, India. Reader in English (retd); Poet. m. Krishna Sharma, 7 Dec. 1945, 2 s., 3 d. Education: MA, English Literature, 1950; PhD, 1967. Appointments: Teacher, DAV Inter College, 1950–51; Lecturer in Education, Cornation Hindu College, 1951–52; Lecturer in English, SSV Degree College, 1952; Lecturer in English, 1952–55, Head, Dept of English, 1955–69, AS College; Lecturer in English, 1967–82, Reader in English, 1982–85, Meerut University. Publications: The Pageant of Seasons, 1956; Flowers and Buds, 1984; A Rudraksha Rosary and Other Poems, 1987; A Spiritual Warrior, 1991; Scattered Leaves, 1991; Divine Glimpses, 1996; Gushing Streams, 1996; Flowering of a Lotus, 1998. Contributions to: Kavita India; Metverse Muse; Brainwave. Address: Shiva Kutir D-29, Shastri Nagar, Meerut, UP, India.

SHARMA, Vera; b. 10 Feb. 1926, Mumbai, India. Writer; Poet; Dramatist. m. 10 March 1949, 1 d. Publications: Stories, poems, and plays, including, Aaher (short stories in Marathi trans.), 1996. Contributions to: Various publications. Honours: Short-listed, Commonwealth Poetry Prize, 1982; Several other prizes. Memberships: Asiatic Society of Bombay; PEN, Mumbai. Address: Bhairavi, 106 Sixth Rd, Tilaknagar, Goregaon W, Mumbai, 400 062, India.

SHATTUCK, Roger (Whitney); b. 20 Aug. 1923, New York, NY, USA. Writer; Trans.; Poet; Ed.; Prof. (retd). m. Nora Ewing White, 20 Aug. 1949, 1 s., 3 d. Education: BA, Yale University, 1947. Appointments: Information Officer, Film Section, UNESCO, Paris, 1947–48; Reporter, Chicago Daily News, Paris Office, 1948–49; Asst Trade Ed., Harcourt, Brace & Co, New York City, 1949–50;

Society of Fellows, 1950–53, Instructor in French, 1953–56, Harvard University; Asst Prof., 1956–59, Assoc. Prof. of Romance Languages, 1959–62, Prof. of French and English, 1962–71, Chair. of the Dept of French and Italian, 1968–71, University of Texas at Austin; Commonwealth Prof. of French, University of Virginia, 1974–88; University Prof. and Prof. of Modern Foreign Languages, Boston University, 1988–97; Lecturer at many universities, colleges, art museums and other venues. *Publications:* Non-Fiction: The Banquet Years: The Origins of the Avant-Garde in France, 1885 to World War One, 1958; Proust's Binoculars: A Study of Memory, Time, and Recognition in A La Recherche du Temps Perdu, 1963; Marcel Proust, 1974; The Forbidden Experiment: The Story of the Wild Boy of Aveyron, 1980; The Innocent Eye: On Literature and the Arts, 1984; Forbidden Knowledge: From Prometheus to Pornography, 1996; Candor and Perversion: Literature, Education and the Arts, 1999; Proust's Way: A Field Guide to In Search of Lost Time, 2000. Poetry: Half Tame, 1964. Editor and Translator: René Daumal: Mount Analogue: A Novel of Symbolically Authentic Non-Euclidean Adventures in Mountain Climbing, 1960; The Selected Writings of Guillaume Apollinaire, 1963; Paul Valéry: Occasions (with Frederick Brown), 1970. Editor: The Craft and Context of Translation (with William Arrowsmith), 1961; Selected Writings of Alfred Jarry: Ubu Cuckolded, Exploits and Opinions of Dr Faustroll, Pataphysician, and Other Writings (with Simon Watson Taylor), 1966. Translator: René Daumal: A Fundamental Experiment, 1987. *Contributions to:* Essays, short stories, and poems in various publications. *Honours:* Guggenheim Fellowship, 1958–59; Fulbright Research Fellow, 1958–59; ACLS Research Fellow, 1969–70; National Book Award, 1975; American Acad. and Institute of Arts and Letters Award, 1987; Doctorat honoris causa, University of Orléans, France, 1990. *Memberships:* National Trans. Center, advisory board, 1964–69, chair., 1966–69; National Humanities Faculty, 1972–73; Publications of the MLA, editorial board, 1977–78; American Acad. of Arts and Sciences, 1990–; Asscn of Literary Scholars and Critics, pres., 1995–96. *Address:* 231 Forge Hill Rd, Lincoln, VT 05443, USA.

SHAW, Robert Burns; b. 16 July 1947, Philadelphia, Pennsylvania, USA. Prof. of English; Poet. m. Hilary Olenchuk, 21 June 1969, 1 s., 1 d. *Education:* AB, Harvard College, 1969; MPhil, 1973, PhD, 1974, Yale University Graduate School. *Appointments:* Lecturer in English, Harvard University, 1974–76; Asst Prof., 1976–78, Assoc. Prof., 1980–83, Yale University; Assoc. Prof. of English, 1983–91, Prof. of English, 1991–, Mount Holyoke College. *Publications:* Curious Questions, 1970; In Witness, 1972; Comforting the Wilderness, 1977; The Wonder of Seeing Double, 1988; The Post Office Murals Restored, 1994; Below The Surface, 1999; Solving for X, 2002. *Contributions to:* Poetry; PN Review; Partisan Review; Yale Review; Paris Review; Shenandoah; Kenyon Review; The Hudson Review; The New Criterion. *Honours:* George Dillon Prize, 1970; National Endowment for the Arts Fellowship, 1987; Ingram Merrill Fellowship, 1990; James Boatwright Prize for Poetry, 1992; Hollis Summers Prize, 2002. *Memberships:* Poetry Society of America; Acad. of American Poets; Asscn of Literary Scholars and Critics. *Address:* Dept of English, Mount Holyoke College, South Hadley, MA 01075, USA. *E-mail:* rshaw@mtholyoke.edu.

SHEAHAN, Matthew, (Edward Rections); b. 18 Nov. 1922, New York, NY, USA. Ed.; Poet. m. Mimi Stetson, 14 Oct. 1948, 1 s., 1 d. *Education:* BA, New York University, 1944; MEng, University of Connecticut, 1950. *Appointments:* Teacher of English, Yonkers Public School, 1951–81; Ed., Westchester Poetry Review, 1976–. *Publications:* All Leaves Gone, 1952; Powder, 1957; Reflections, 1960. *Contributions to:* Cooper Letter; Bog Train; Sociatal Commentary; Frish-American Free Voice. *Honours:* Grange Farmhouse Award; University of Georgia Poetry Award. *Address:* 76 Stephenson Terrace, Briarcliff Manor, NY 10105, USA.

SHECK, Laurie; b. 7 Oct. 1953, New York, NY, USA. Prof.; Poet. m. James Peck, 30 May 1981, 1 d. *Education:* BA, Antioch College, 1975; MFA, University of Iowa, 1978. *Appointments:* Lecturer, Asst Prof., 1981–90, Assoc. Prof., 1990–, Rutgers University. *Publications:* Amarenth, 1981; Lo At Night, 1990. *Contributions to:* New Yorker; Nation; Paris Review; New York Times Book Review. *Address:* c/o Dept of English, Murray Hall CAC, Rutgers University, New Brunswick, NJ 08903, USA.

SHEER, Sita; b. 20 July 1920, Turkey. Trans.; Writer; Poet. m. Isaac Sheer, 6 Aug. 1950, 2 d. *Appointments:* Various administrative posts; Sworn Trans., Supreme Court of South Africa. *Contributions to:* Modern Poetry in Trans.; Orbis; Aki Yerushalayim; Jewish Quarterly. *Memberships:* Institute of Trans. and Interpreting; PEN International; PEN South Africa; English PEN; Society of Authors; Trans Asscn; Society of Women Writers and Journalists. *Address:* 26 Fairview Ct, Linksway, Holders Hill Rd, London NW4 1JS, England.

SHEINFELD, Ilan, (Annand Chatergie, Shlomo Dror, Eshed Esh, Ziv Heler); b. 22 April 1960, Israel. Literary Ed.; Poet; Writer. *Education:* BA, 1984, MA, 1986, Hebrew and English Literature, University of Tel-Aviv. *Appointments:* Literary Ed., Al Hamishmar, Hebrew daily, 1981–92; Freelance, Magaaim, 1990–94; Ed., Suzzane Dellal Center of the Arts monthly. *Publications:* The Bewitched Lizard, 1981; The Tongue of Love, 1984; Lines to a Friend in Parting, 1987; It Begins With Love, 1989; Shalom, 1992; Arai, 1992; The Dream Stealers, 1992; Hey Rimona, 1993; Tashlich, 1994;

Karet (poems), 1997; The Poets School (writing manual), 1997; Shedletse (prose), 1998; There Is No Such Bird, Kortsipa (for children), 1998. *Contributions to:* Anthologies and other publications. *Honours:* Berenstein Prize, 1983; Kugel Poetry Prize, Tel-Aviv Literary Fund, 1988; Dov Sadan Prize for Literary Scholars, University of Tel-Aviv, 1988; Publication Grant, Israeli Asscn of Writers and Composers, 1990; Prime Minister's Prize for Writers, 1991. *Memberships:* Hebrew Writers Asscn; Israel Public Relations Asscn; Israeli Asscn of Writers and Composers. *Address:* 21 Kfar Saba St, Neve Tsedek, Tel-Aviv 65147, Israel.

SHEPARD, Neil; b. 29 Jan. 1951, Fitchburg, Massachusetts, USA. Prof. of Literature and Poetry Writing; Poet. m. Kate Riley, 15 Sept. 1990. *Education:* BA, University of Vermont, 1973; MA, Colorado State University, 1976; PhD, Ohio University, 1980. *Appointments:* Instructor, Louisiana State University, 1980–82; Asst Prof. of Creative Writing and Literature, Rider College, New Jersey, 1982–85; Assoc. Prof. of Creative Writing and Literature, 1985–92, Prof. of Literature and Poetry Writing, 1995–, Johnson State College, Vermont; Ed., Green Mountains Review Literary Magazine; Writing Co-ordinator, Vermont Studio Center Artists Colony. *Publications:* Scavenging the Country for a Heartbeat, 1993; I'm Here Because I Lost My Way (poems), 1998. *Contributions to:* Yearbook of American Poetry, 1983; Anthology of Magazine Verse, 1983, 1986, 1993, 1996, 1997, 1998; Antioch Review; Denver Quarterly; Poetry East; Paris Review; Ploughshares; New England Review; TriQuarterly; Boulevard; Notre Dame Review; Ontario Review; Southern Review; AWP Chronicle; Seneca Review; Southwest Review; Western Humanities Review. *Honours:* Poetry Fellowships, New Jersey Council on the Arts, 1984, Pennsylvania Council on the Arts, 1985, Vermont Council on the Arts, 1986; First Book Prize, Mid-List Press, 1992. *Memberships:* Associated Writing Programs; MLA. *Address:* 2051 Clay Hill Rd, Johnson, VT 05656, USA.

SHEPPERSON, Janet Catherine; b. 15 April 1954, Edinburgh, Scotland. Poet. m. Nick Acheson, 22 July 1983. *Education:* MA, Honours, English, 1976, Postgraduate Certificate, Primary Education, 1978, University of Aberdeen. *Appointments:* Writer-in-Schools, Northern Ireland Arts Council; Teacher of Creative Writing. *Publications:* Trio 5 (with Martin Mooney and Dennis Greig), 1987; A Ring With a Black Stone, 1989; Madonna of the Spaces, 1994; The Aphrodite Stone, 1995. *Contributions to:* Anthologies, reviews, magazines, and BBC TV and Schools Radio. *Honours:* Calder Prize for Verse, 1976; Small Prize, Bridport Arts Centre Competition, 1989. *Memberships:* Poetry Ireland; Poetry Society. *Address:* 30 Ravenhill Park, Belfast 6, Northern Ireland.

SHER, Steven Jay; b. 28 Sept. 1949, USA. Writer; Poet. m. Nancy Green, 11 March 1978, 1 s., 1 d. *Education:* BA, City College of the City University of New York, 1970; MA, University of Iowa, 1972; MFA, Brooklyn College of the City University of New York, 1978. *Appointments:* Dir, Creative Writing, Spalding University, 1979–81; Oregon State University, 1981–86, University of North Carolina at Wilmington, 1986–89; Visiting Writer, Western Oregon University, 1991–2002, Willamette University, 1993. *Publications:* Nickelodeon, 1978; Persnickety, 1979; Caught in the Revolving Door, 1980; Trolley Lives, 1985; Man With a Thousand Eyes and Other Stories, 1989; Traveler's Advisory, 1994; Flying Through Glass, 2001; Thirty-Six, 2002; At the Willamette, 2002. Co-Editor: Northwest Variety: Personal Essays by 14 Regional Authors, 1987. *Contributions to:* Anthologies and periodicals. *Honours:* All Nations Poetry Contest, 1977; Weymouth Centre Residency, 1988; North Carolina Writers Network Writers and Readers Series Competition, 1989; Oregon Book Awards Finalist in Poetry, 1994; How the Ink Feels Poetry Contest, 2001. *Membership:* Pres., Willamette Literary Guild, 1992–2002. *Address:* 3930 NW Witham Hill Dr., No. 197, Corvallis, OR 97330, USA.

SHERIFF, Bat-Sheva; b. 28 June 1937, Tel-Aviv, Israel. Prof., Chair., Israel Postal and Philatelic Museum; Poet. m. Mordechai Manfred Segal, 1962, 2 s. *Education:* Teacher's Diploma, University of Tel-Aviv; Graduated, Philosophy and Literature, Hebrew University, Jerusalem. *Appointments:* Teacher, Secondary School, 1956–71; Dir, Cultural Project for Underprivileged Youth in Development Areas, 1971–86; Ed., Monthly Journal for Inspectors, Inspector, Ministry of Education and Culture. *Publications:* Poems, 1956; Not All the Rivers, 1964; Love Poems, 1972; Persuasive Words, 1974; Man That is Honour: Psalm 49, 1978; Festive Poems, 1981; Ashes Instead of Bread, 1982; By Necessity and By Right, 1986; Letters to Bat-Sheva, 1990; Ancient People, 2002. *Contributions to:* Newspapers and periodicals, radio and television broadcasts. *Memberships:* Exec. Committee, Hebrew Writers' Asscn; Press Council of Israel; PEN Israel; Israeli Council of Arts and Culture; Society of Authors, Composers and Music Publishers; International Confederation of Societies of Authors and Composers. *Address:* 10 Emek Rafaim, PO Box 7353, Jerusalem 91072, Israel.

SHERMAN, William David; b. 24 Dec. 1940, Philadelphia, PA, USA. Poet; Writer; Ed.; Publisher. m. Barbara Beaumont, 22 July 1970, divorced 1978. *Education:* BA, Temple University, 1962; MA, 1964, PhD, 1968, State University of New York at Buffalo; Dickinson School of Law, 1974–75. *Publications:* The Landscape of Contemporary Cinema (with Leon Lewis), 1967; The Cinema of Orson Welles, 1967; The Hard Sidewalk, 1974; The Horses of Gwyddno Garanhir, 1976; Mermaids I, 1977; Heart Attack and Spanish Songs in Mandaine Land, 1981; Duchamp's Door, 1983; She Wants to Go to Pago-Pago, 1986; The Tahitian Journals, 1990; A Tale for Tusitala, 1993; From the South Seas, 1997. *Contributions to:* Anthologies and periodicals. *Honour:* Poetry Prize, Royal Albert Hall Reading, 1995. *Address:* 9300 Atlantic Ave, No. 218, Margate, NJ 08402, USA.

SHERWOOD, Andrea Hilary; b. 27 Sept. 1962, Australia. Teacher; Poet. m. Brett A M Graham, 15 Aug. 1987, divorced 1996, 1 d. *Education:* BA, Literature; DipEd, Double Method English; Postgraduate Diploma in Linguistics. *Publications:* One Siren or Another (poems), 1994; Remember the Sound of Footprints (verse narrative), 1996. *Contributions to:* Various publications in Australia and England. *Honours:* Australia Council Literature Board Grant, 1991; Ministry of the Arts Grant, Victoria, 1991; Anne Elder Award for Best First Collection of Poetry in Australia, 1994; Australia Council Literature Board Fellowship, 1996. *Memberships:* Australian Writers; Poet's Union, Five Bells; Victorian Writers Centre. *Address:* 36 Glenlyou Rd, Brunswick, Vic. 3056, Australia.

SHI TANG; b. 28 May 1920, Wenzhou, China. Poet; Writer. m. Chen Alqiu, July 1946, 2 s., 2 d. *Education:* AB, National Zhejiang University. *Appointments:* Research Fellow, Wenzhou Art Research Institute, 1986–. *Publications:* 10 poetry collections, including selected poems, 1993, and selected sonnets, 1993; Several prose vols. *Contributions to:* Various anthologies and periodicals. *Memberships:* Chinese Dramatists Asscn; Chinese Writers Asscn. *Address:* 22-302 Hualiutang New House, Wenzhou, China.

SHIBASAWA, Naoya. See: GOTO, Takahiko.

SHIELA. See: GUJRAL, Shiela.

SHIELDS, Carol Ann; b. 2 June 1935, Oak Park, IL, USA (Naturalized Canadian citizen, 1974). Author; Poet; Dramatist; Prof. Emerita. m. Donald Hugh Shields, 20 July 1957, 1 s., 4 d. *Education:* BA, Hanover College, 1957; MA, University of Ottawa, 1975. *Appointments:* Editorial Asst, Canadian Slavonic Papers, Ottawa, 1972–74; Lecturer, University of Ottawa, 1976–77, University of British Columbia, 1978–90; Prof., 1980–2000, Prof. Emerita, 2000–, University of Manitoba; The Canada Council, 1994–; Chancellor, 1996–2000, Chancellor Emerita, 2000–, Unviersity of Winnipeg. *Publications:* Fiction: Small Ceremonies, 1976; The Box Garden, 1977; Happenstance, 1980; A Fairly Conventional Woman, 1982; Various Miracles (short stories), 1985; Swann: A Mystery, 1987; The Orange Fish (short stories), 1989; A Celibate Season (with Blanche Howard), 1991; The Republic of Love, 1992; The Stone Diaries, 1993; Larry's Party, 1997; Anniversary (with David Williams), 1998; Dressing Up for the Carnival (short stories), 2000; Unless, 2002. Poetry: Others, 1972; Intersect, 1974; Coming to Canada, 1992. Plays: Women Waiting, 1983; Departures and Arrivals, 1984; Anniversary (with David Williamson), 1986; Thirteen Hands, 1993; Fashion Power Guilt (with Catherine Shields), 1995. Other: Scribner's Best of the Fiction Workshops (ed. with John Kulka and Natalie Danford), 1998; Jane Austen (biography), 2001. *Honours:* Canada Council Grants, 1973, 1976, 1978, 1986; Canadian Authors Asscn Fiction Prize, 1976; Canadian Broadcasting Corporation Prizes, 1983, 1984; National Magazine Award, 1985; Arthur Ellis Award, 1987; Governor-General's Award, 1993; National Book Critics Circle Awards, 1994, 1995; Pulitzer Prize in Fiction, 1995; Hon. doctorates, Universities of Ottawa, Winnipeg, Hanover College, BC, 1995, Concordia University, 1998, University of Toronto, 1998, Queen's University, University of Western Ontario, Carleton University, Wilfrid Laurier University, 2000, University of Victoria, Lakehead University, 2001; Lire Magazine Book of the Year, France, 1995; Orange Prize for Fiction, 1998; Order of Canada, 1999; Guggenheim Fellowship, 1999–2000; Charles Taylor Prize, 2002. *Memberships:* Jane Austen Society; PEN; Writers Guild of Manitoba; Writers Union of Canada; Canada Council; Royal Society of Canada. *Address:* 990 Crescent Ave, Victoria, BC V8B 3V3, Canada.

SHIELDS, Michael Joseph; b. 29 Oct. 1938, England. Writer; Trans.; Poet. *Appointments:* Assoc. Ed., Here Now, 1970–73; Ed., Orbis Magazine, 1980–2002; Consultant Ed., International Who's Who in Poetry, seventh edn, 1993–94, International Authors and Writers Who's Who, 13th edn, 1993–94. *Publications:* Helix, 1970; Micashards, Mothwings: Poetry of Forty Years, 1996. Translator: Superfine Powders, by Ichinose, 1991; Offshore Structures, by Clauss, 1991; Submarines of the US Navy, by Terzibaschitsch, 1991; Dubbel, Engineers Handbook, 1992; Fighters of the Luftwaffe, 1992; Bombers of the Luftwaffe, 1993. *Contributions to:* Outposts; Littack; Writer; New Headland; Poetry Nottingham; Reader's Digest; Weekend; Writers News; Publisher; Contemporary Review, Envoi, Seam, Stride. *Honours:* George Eliot Fellowship Trophy, NFA, 1975, 1977, 1979; John Masefield Award, World Order of Narrative Poets, 1987. *Memberships:* Society of Authors; Institute of Information Scientists, fellow; Trans Asscn, chair., 1984–85, 1998–99; Institute of Translating and Interpreting; Royal Over-Seas League. *Address:* 27 Valley View, Primrose, Jarrow, Tyne and Wear NE32 5QT, England. *E-mail:* smkshlds@aol.com.

SHIGEMATSU, Soiku; b. 13 Oct. 1943, Shimizu, Japan. Zen Buddhist Priest; Prof. of American Literature; Poet. *Education:* BA, Tokyo University of Foreign Studies, 1967; MA, English, Kyoto University, 1971. *Appointments:* Lecturer, Shizuoka Women's College, 1972–75, Shizuoka University, 1975–78; Main Priest, Shogenji Zen Temple, 1975–; Assoc. Prof., 1978–88, Prof., 1988– Shizuoka University. *Publications:* A Zen Forest, 1981; A Zen Harvest, 1988 Sun at Midnight (with W S Merwin), 1989; Zen Haiku, 1994. *Contributions to:* American Poetry Review; Talisman. *Honour:* Jerome J Shestack Prize American Poetry Review. *Memberships:* English Literature Society of Japan; American Literature Society of Japan. *Address:* Shogenji Zen Temple, Shogenji-cho, Shimizu-shi, Shizuoka-ken 424-02, Japan.

SHIU-TIEN TU, (Sar Po); b. 28 July 1944, China (Taiwan). Dentist; Poet; Writer; Trans.; Publisher. m. Tseng Chiu-chu, 22 Nov. 1978, 2 s., 1 d. *Education:* DDS, Kaohsiung Medical College, 1970; Postgraduate Studies, Osaka Dental University, 1972–73, University of Osaka, 1973–74, University of Tokyo, 1974–77. *Publications:* Several vols in Chinese; Hollow Shells (English and Chinese), 1990; Trans into Chinese of T. S. Eliot, Paul Valery and Japanese writers. *Contributions to:* Newspapers, reviews, quarterlies and journals. *Honour:* Kaohsiung Literature Prize. *Memberships:* Chinese Children's Literature Asscn; Chinese Literature Asscn; Chinese Poets Asscn; World Acad. of Arts and Culture; World Chinese Poets Asscn. *Address:* 228 Jen Al First St, 80027 Kaohsiung, China (Taiwan).

SHIVKUMAR, Lalitha; b. 6 Sept. 1944, Kumbakonam, India. Poet. m. R Shivkumar, 28 Oct. 1966, 2 s. *Education:* BSc, 1965; MA, 1973; PhD, 1984; PGCTE, 1984; MA, 1986. *Appointments:* Research Scholar, Punjab University, 1973–84; Lecturer, BEL College, Mother Teresa Women's University. *Publications:* Fragance from Crushed Petals, 1996. *Contributions to:* Anthologies and periodicals. *Honour:* Durga Puja Award, 1986. *Membership:* Writer's Forum. *Address:* 39 Visweswarayya St II, Coimbatore 641 038, India.

SHOAF, Richard (Allen); b. 25 March 1948, Lexington, NC, USA. Prof. of English; Poet; Writer; Ed. m. Judith Patricia McNamara, 1975, 1 s., 1 d. *Education:* BA, Wake Forest University, 1970; BA, University of East Anglia, 1972; MA, 1975, PhD, 1977, Cornell University. *Appointments:* Asst Prof. of English, 1977–81, Assoc. Prof. of English, 1982–85, Yale University; Prof. of English, 1986–, Alumni Prof. of English, 1990–93, University of Florida at Gainesville; Founder-Ed., Exemplaria: A Journal of Theory in Medieval and Renaissance Studies, 1989–; Pres., Council of Eds of Learned Journals, 1994–96. *Publications:* Dante, Chaucer, and the Currency of the Word: Money, Images, and Reference in Late Medieval Poetry, 1983; The Poem as Green Girdle: 'Commercium' in Sir Gawain and the Green Knight, 1984; Milton, Poet of Duality: A Study of Semiosis in the Poetry and the Prose, 1985, revised edn, 1993; Troilus and Criseyde (ed.), 1989; Simple Rules (poems), 1991; Chaucer's Troilus and Criseyde – 'Subgit to alle poesye': Essays in Criticism, 1992; The Testament of Love, by Thomas Usk (ed.), 1998; Chaucer's Body: The Anxiety of Circulation in the Canterbury Tales, 2001. *Contributions to:* Reference works, scholarly books and literary journals. *Honours:* National Endowment for the Humanities Fellowships, 1982–83, 1999–2000; Hon. Visiting Scholar, University of Central Florida, 1993. *Memberships:* Acad. of American Poets; Dante Society of America; John Gower Society; Medieval Acad. of America; MLA of America; South Atlantic MLA. *Address:* 4338 Turlington Hall, University of Florida, Gainesville, FL 32611, USA. *E-mail:* ras@ufl.edu.

SHOLL, Elizabeth Neary, (Betsy Sholl); b. 12 June 1945, Lakewood, Ohio, USA. Poet; Teacher. m. John Douglas Sholl, 17 June 1967, 1 s., 1 d. *Education:* BA, Bucknell University, 1967; MA, University of Rochester, 1969; MFA, Vermont College, 1989. *Appointments:* Instructor, Lasell Junior College, Massachusetts Institute of Technology, University of Southern Maine; MFA Faculty, Vermont College, 1993; Visiting Poet, University of Pittsburgh, 1997. *Publications:* Changing Faces, 1974; Appalachian Winter, 1978; Rooms Overhead, 1986; Pick a Card, 1991; The Red Line, 1992; Don't Explain, 1997. *Contributions to:* Field; Ploughshares; Beloit Poetry Journal; Massachusetts Review; Graham House Review; Sojourners; West Branch; Poetry Miscellany. *Honours:* Maine Chapbook Contest, 1991; Poetry Competition, Associated Writing Programs, 1991; Fellowship to Individual Artist, Maine Arts Commission, 1991; NEA Fellowship, 1993; Fellix Pollack Prize, University of Wisconsin, 1997. *Memberships:* Associated Writing Programs; Maine Writers and Publishers Alliance; Maine Arts Commission, literature panel; Alice James Publishing Co-operative. *Address:* 24 Brentwood St, Portland, ME 04103, USA.

SHRADER, Gail; b. 18 April 1955, Fort Chaffee, AR, USA. Publisher; Ed.; Poet. *Education:* Assoc. in Applied Science Degree in Office Management, Seminole Junior College, 1997. *Appointment:* Publisher-Ed., Poetic Expressions. *Contributions to:* Anthologies and periodicals. *Honour:* Shattered Illusions read at memorial service for the victims of the Oklahoma City Bombing, Seminole Junior College. *Address:* Route 1, Box 268, Konawa, OK 74849, USA.

SHUREY, Richard; b. 22 Sept. 1951, Wales. Factory Worker; Poet. m. Christine, 6 May 1972, 2 s., 1 d. *Publications:* Jewels of the Imagination, 1997; By the Light of the Moon, 1997; On Reflection, 1997; Never Forget, 1998; From the Hand of a Poet, 1999; Open Minds, 1999. *Contributions to:* South Wales Echo; Celtic Press; Rhondda Leader. *Honours:* Ed.'s Choice Award for Outstanding Achievement in Poetry, International Library of Poetry, 1997.

Memberships: Poetry Guild. *Address:* 107 Tylacelyn Rd, Penygraig, Tonypandy, Mid Glamorgan CF40 1JR, South Wales.

SHUTTLE, Penelope Diane; b. 12 May 1947, Staines, Middlesex, England. Writer; Poet. m. Peter Redgrove, 16 Sept. 1980, 1 d. *Publications:* Fiction: An Excusable Vengeance, 1967; All the Usual Hours of Sleeping, 1969; Wailing Monkey Embracing a Tree, 1974; The Terrors of Dr Treviles (with Peter Redgrove), 1974; The Glass Cottage, 1976; Rainsplitter in the Zodiac Garden, 1976; The Mirror of the Giant, 1979. Poetry: The Hermaphrodite Album (with Peter Redgrove), 1973; The Orchard Upstairs, 1980; The Child-Stealer, 1983; The Lion From Rio, 1986; Adventures With My Horse, 1988; Taxing the Rain, 1992; Building a City for Jamie, 1996; Selected Poems, 1980–1996, 1998; A Leaf out of His Book, 1999. Psychology and sociology: The Wise Wound: Menstruation and Everywoman (with Peter Redgrove) 1978; Alchemy for Women (with Peter Redgrove), 1995. Numerous pamphlet collections, broadsheets, radio dramas, recordings, readings and television features. *Contributions to:* Various publications. *Honours:* Arts Council Awards, 1969, 1972, 1985; Greenwood Poetry Prize, 1972; E C Gregory Award for Poetry, 1974. *Address:* c/o David Higham Assocs Ltd, 5–8 Lower John St, London W1R 4HA, England.

SIANI, Cosma; b. 29 Nov. 1945, Foggia, Italy. Teacher of English; Poet; Trans. m. Lina Mazzei, 29 March 1979. *Education:* Degree, Istituto Magistrale, San Giovanni Rotondo, Foggia, 1963; Foreign Languages Degree, Istituto Universitario Orientale, Naples, 1971; Ealing College of Higher Education, London, 1980. *Appointments:* Teacher, Elementary, 1965–69, Junior High, 1972–76, High School, 1976–, University of Cassino, 2002–; Pres., 1990–92, Ed., 1990–99, Tesol, Italy. *Publications:* Ciclo Chiuso (poems), 1972; Lingua e Letteratura, 1992; Microletteratura, 1994; La Percezione Sbagliata (poems), 1996; L'Io Diviso; Emigrazione e Letteratura nell'Esperienza di Joseph Tusiani, 1999; Libri all'Indice e Altri, 2001; Dialetto e Poesia nel Gargano, 2002. *Contributions to:* Various anthologies and reviews. *Address:* Via Isole Capo Verde 220, 00121 Lido di Ostia, Rome, Italy.

SIEGEL, Joan I.; b. 14 June 1946, New York, USA. Prof. of English; Poet. m. J R Solonche, 12 Jan. 1992. *Education:* BA, Hunter College, 1967; MA, English Literature, New York University, 1972. *Contributions to:* Commonweal; Literary Review; Yankee; San Jose Studies; Jama; Poet Lore; Hampden-Sydney Poetry Review; Poet and Critic; Wilderness; Interim; The American Scholar; The Literary Review; Northwestern and Mayfield Anthologies. *Honours:* Honourable Mention, Poetry Centre Competition, 1989, Stone Ridge Poetry Society, 1989, 1990; Finalist, Capricorn Poetry Contest, 1992, Anhinga Prize Competition, 1992; First Prize, Anna Davidson Rosenberg Award, 1998. *Address:* PO Box 99, Blooming Grove, NY 10914, USA.

SIEGEL, Lee; b. 22 July 1945, Los Angeles, CA, USA. Prof. of English; Poet; Writer. 1 s. *Education:* BA, University of California at Berkeley, 1967; MFA, Columbia University, 1969; DPhil, University of Oxford, 1975. *Appointments:* Instructor in English, Western Washington University, Bellingham, 1969–72; Prof. of English, University of Hawaii at Manoa, 1976–; Guest Lecturer, University of Oxford, 1985, Collège de France, 1985. *Publications:* Vivisection, 1973; Sacred and Profane Love in Indian Traditions, 1979; Dreams in the Sramanic Traditions (with Jagdish Sharma), 1980; Fires of Love, Waters of Peace: Passion and Renunciation in Indian Culture, 1983; Laughing Matters: Satire and Humour in India, 1987; Sweet Nothings (trans. of the Amarusataka), 1988. *Contributions to:* Reference works, books, journals and periodicals. *Honours:* Senior Fellow, American Institute of Indian Studies and the Smithsonian Institution, 1979, 1983, 1987; Grants, Center for Asian and Pacific Studies, 1981, ACLS and Social Research Council, 1982, 1985, 1987; Presidential Award for Excellence in Teaching, University of Hawaii, 1986. *Address:* c/o Dept of Religion, University of Hawaii at Manoa, 2500 Campus Rd, Honolulu, HI 96822, USA.

SIEGEL, Robert (Harold); b. 18 Aug. 1939, Oak Park, IL, USA. Writer; Poet; Prof. of English. m. Roberta Ann Hill, 19 Aug. 1961, 3 d. *Education:* BA, Wheaton College, 1961; MA, Johns Hopkins University, 1962; PhD, English, Harvard University, 1968. *Appointments:* Asst Prof. of English, Dartmouth College, 1968–75; Lecturer in Creative Writing, Princeton University, 1975–76; McManes Visiting Prof., Wheaton College, 1976; Asst Prof., 1976–79, Assoc. Prof., 1979–83, Prof. of English, 1983–, University of Wisconsin at Milwaukee. *Publications:* Fiction: Alpha Centauri, 1980; Whalesong, 1981; The Kingdom of Wundle, 1982; White Whale, 1991; The Ice at the End of the World, 1994. Poetry: The Beasts and the Elders, 1973; In a Pig's Eye, 1980. *Contributions to:* Anthologies, reviews, quarterlies and journals, including: Poetry; Atlantic Monthly; Cream City Review. *Honours:* University of Wisconsin Grants, 1978, 1984, 1988, 1996; Glatstein Prize, Poetry Magazine, 1977; Ingram Merrill Foundation Award, 1979; National Endowment for the Arts Fellowship, 1980; First Prizes, Society of Midland Authors, 1981, Council for Wisconsin Writers, 1981; Matson Award, Friends of Literature, 1982; Golden Archer Award, School of Library Science, University of Wisconsin at Oshkosh, 1986; Pushcart Prize Nominations, 1991, 1995. *Memberships:* Author's Guild; Associated Writing Programs. *Address:* c/o Dept of English, University of Wisconsin at Milwaukee, Milwaukee, WI 53201, USA.

SIGURSTEINSSON, Gunnar Hersveinn, (Gunnar Hersveinn); b. 28 March 1960, Reykjavík, Iceland. Poet; Writer; Journalist. m. Margaret Guttormsdottir, 30 Dec. 1989, 1 s., 2 d. *Education:* BA, Philosophy, Psychology, 1986, Journalism, 1995, University of Iceland. *Appointments:* College of Armuli, 1986–87; College of Hamrahlid, 1987–88; College of Breidholt, 1988–91; College of Egilsstadir, 1992–94; Journalist, Morgunbladid, 1995–. *Publications:* Gaegjugat, 1987; Tre i husi, 1989; The Dual Nature, 1990; Raincity of Silent Houses, 1993; IF (play), 1993. *Contributions to:* Various publications. *Membership:* Writers Union of Iceland. *Address:* Solheimar 46, 104 Reykjavik, Iceland.

SIKÉLIANOS, Eléni; b. 31 May 1965, Santa Barbara, CA, USA. Poet; Teacher. *Education:* BFA, 1990, MFA, 1991, Naropa Institute; Diplôme de Langue, l'Institut Catholique, Paris, France. *Appointments:* Creative Writing Instructor for the Homeless, California Arts Council Residency Grant, 1991–95; Poet-in-the-Schools, 1991–95; Creative Writing Instructor, San Francisco Art Institute, 1995; Freelance Writing Instructor. *Publications:* To Speak While Dreaming, 1993; Poetics of the X, 1995. *Contributions to:* Various publications and recordings. *Honours:* Ted Berrigan Award, 1990; Gertrude Stein Award for Innovative American Writing, 1995; National Endowment for the Arts Creative Writing Fellowship, 1995. *Address:* 3754 12th Ave, New York, NY 11218-1921, USA.

SILCOCK, Ruth Mary; b. 8 Aug. 1926, Manchester, England. Social Worker (retd); Poet. *Education:* MA, Girton College, Cambridge; Social Science Diploma, Bedford College; Mental Health Certificate, London School of Economics. *Appointments:* Various posts in the field of social work. *Publication:* Mrs Carmichael, 1987. *Contributions to:* Encounter; Spectator; Observer; Poetry Review; among others. *Honours:* Prizes, Lancaster Literary Festival, 1980, Cheltenham Literary Festival, 1982; Duncan Lawrie Prize, Sothebys/Aroon Poetry Competition, 1989. *Memberships:* Society of Authors; Poetry Society. *Address:* Fairhaven, South St, Letcombe Regis near Wantage, Oxon OX12 9JY, England.

SILK, Dennis; b. 10 July 1928, London, England. Poet; Playwright. *Appointments:* Hebrew University of Jerusalem; Freelance Ed. *Publications:* Retrievements: A Jerusalem Anthology, 1968; Fourteen Israeli Poets: A Selection of Modern Hebrew Poetry (with Harold Schimmel), 1976; The Punished Land, 1980; Hold Fast, 1984; William the Wonderkid (plays and theatre writings), 1987; Catwalk and Overpass, 1990; Costigan, 1998; Life Isn't All Bike-Clips, Belinda, 1998. *Contributions to:* TLS; New York Times; Encounter; Harper's; Midstream; American Poetry Review; Conjunctions; Stand; Literary Review; Tel-Aviv Review; Grand Street; Shenandoah; Jerusalem Post; American Voice. *Honours:* Howard Foundation Fellowship, Brown University, 1966; Peter Schwiefert Prize, Israel, 1976. *Memberships:* Asscn of Hebrew Writers in Israel; UNIMA. *Address:* PO Box 8103, German Colony, Jerusalem, Israel.

SILKO, Leslie Marmon; b. 15 March 1948, Albuquerque, New Mexico, USA. Prof. of English; Writer; Poet. 2 s. *Education:* BA, English, University of New Mexico, 1969. *Appointments:* Teacher, University of New Mexico; Prof. of English, University of Arizona at Tucson, 1978–. *Publications:* Fiction: Ceremony, 1977; Almanac of the Dead, 1991; Yellow Woman, 1993; Gardens in the Dunes, 1999. Poetry: Laguna Woman, 1974; Storyteller, 1981. Other: The Delicacy and Strength of Lace: Letters Between Leslie Marmon Silko and James A Wright, 1986; Sacred Water: Narratives and Pictures, 1993. *Honours:* National Endowment for the Arts Grant, 1974; Chicago Review Award, 1974; Pushcart Prize, 1977; John D. and Catherine T. MacArthur Foundation Fellowship, 1983. *Address:* c/o Dept of English, University of Arizona at Tucson, Tucson, AZ 85721, USA.

SILLIMAN, Ron(ald Glenn); b. 8 May 1946, Pasco, Washington, USA. Ed.; Poet. m. (1) Rochelle Nameroff, 1965, divorced 1972, (2) Krishna Evans, 1986, 2 s. *Education:* Merritt College, 1965, 1969–72; San Francisco State College, 1966–69; University of California at Berkeley, 1969–71. *Appointments:* Ed., Tottel's, 1970–81; Dir of Research and Education, Committee for Prisoner Humanity and Justice, San Rafael, CA, 1972–76; Project Man., Tenderloin Ethnographic Research Project, San Francisco, 1977–78; Dir of Outreach, Central City Hospitality House, San Francisco, 1979–81; Lecturer, University of San Francisco, 1981; Visiting Lecturer, University of California at San Diego, La Jolla, 1982; Writer-in-Residence, New College of California, San Francisco, 1982; Dir of Public Relations and Development, 1982–86, Poet-in-Residence, 1983–90, California Institute of Integral Studies, San Francisco; Exec. Ed., Socialist Review, 1986–89; Managing Ed., Computer Land, 1989–. *Publications:* Poetry: Moon in the Seventh House, 1968; Three Syntactic Fictions for Dennis Schmitz, 1971; Crow, 1971; Mohawk, 1973; Nox, 1974; Sitting Up, Standing Up, Taking Steps, 1978; Ketjak, 1978; Tjanting, 1981; Bart, 1982; ABC, 1983; Paradise, 1985; The Age of Huts, 1986; Lit, 1987; What, 1988; Manifest, 1990; Demo to Ink, 1992; Toner, 1992; Jones, 1993; N/O, 1994; Xing, 1996. Other: A Symposium on Clark Coolidge (ed.), 1978; In the American Tree (ed.), 1986; The New Sentence, 1987. *Honours:* Hart Crane and Alice Crane Williams Award, 1968; Joan Lee Yang Awards, 1970, 1971; National Endowment for the Arts Fellowship, 1979; California Arts Council Grants, 1979, 1980; Poetry Center Book Award, 1985. *Address:* 1819 Curtis, Berkeley, CA 94702, USA.

SILLITOE, Alan; b. 4 March 1928, Nottingham, England. Author; Poet; Dramatist. m. Ruth Esther Fainlight, 19 Nov. 1959, 1 s., 1 adopted d. *Appointment:* Visiting Prof. of English, DeMontfort University, Leicester, 1993–97. *Publications:* Fiction: Saturday Night and Sunday Morning, 1958; The Loneliness of the Long-Distance Runner, 1959; The General, 1960; Key to the Door, 1961; The Ragman's Daughter and Other Stories, 1961; The Death of William Posters, 1965; A Tree on Fire, 1967; Guzman Go Home and Other Stories, 1968; A Start in Life, 1970; Travel in Nihilon, 1971; Raw Material, 1972; Men, Women, and Children, 1973; The Flame of Life, 1974; The Widower's Son, 1976; The Storyteller, 1979; The Second Chance and Other Stories, 1981; Her Victory, 1982; The Lost Flying Boat, 1983; Down from the Hill, 1984; Life Goes On, 1985; Out of the Whirlpool, 1987; The Open Door, 1988; The Far Side of the Street, 1988; Last Loves, 1990; Leonard's War: A Love Story, 1991; Snowstop, 1994; Collected Stories, 1995; Alligator Playground, 1997; The Broken Chariot, 1998; The German Numbers Woman, 1999; Birthday, 2001. Poetry: Without Beer or Bread, 1957; The Rats and Other Poems, 1960; A Falling Out of Love and Other Poems, 1964; Shaman and Other Poems, 1968; Love in the Environs of Voronezh and Other Poems, 1968; Canto Two of the Rats, 1973; Storm: New Poems, 1974; Barbarians and Other Poems, 1974; Words Broadsheet Nineteen (with Ruth Fainlight), 1975; Snow on the North Side of Lucifer, 1979; More Lucifer, 1980; Israel: Poems on a Hebrew Theme, 1981; Sun Before Departure, 1984; Tides and Stone Walls, 1986; Collected Poems, 1993. Plays: Three Plays: The Slot Machine, The Interview, Pit Strike, 1978. Other: Road to Volgograd, 1964; Mountains and Caverns: Selected Essays, 1975; The Saxon Shore Way, 1983; Nottinghamshire, 1987; Life Without Armor (autobiography), 1995. *Honours:* Author's Club Prize, 1958; Hawthornden Prize, 1960; Hon. Fellow, Manchester Polytechnic, 1977; Hon. Doctorates, Nottingham Polytechnic, 1990, University of Nottingham, 1994, De Montfort University, Leicester, 1998. *Memberships:* RGS, fellow; Society of Authors; Writers Action Group. *Address:* 14 Ladbroke Terrace, London W11 3PG, England.

SILLS-DOCHERTY, Jonathan John, (John Docherty); b. 7 Jan. 1941, Bowden, Cheshire, England. Humorous Writer; Lyricist; Poet. *Education:* Fielden Park College, West Didsbury, Manchester, 1977; Poetry Workshop, 1981, Extramural Dept, 1986–87, University of Manchester. *Appointments:* Ed., Guardian Society, 1974; Reporter, Dun and Bradstreet, 1975; Proof Reader, Sub-Ed., Biography Compiler, Odd Fellow Magazine. *Publications:* A Walk Around the City and Other Groans, 1969; Words on Paper, 1977; From Bottoms to Tops and Back Again, 1977; Ballads of Fantasy and Reality, 1982; Ballads of Ecstasy and Perspicacity, 1987; Ballads of North West John (with cassette tape), 1987. *Contributions to:* News-Views; House Journal, Mappin and Webb; Sunday Times; Sunday Telegraph; Manchester Evening News; Stretford and Urmston Journal; Daily Mail; Star; Artful Reporter; What's On In Hulme; Dun and Bradstreet Report Magazine; Radio Manchester. *Honours:* Poetry Award, North West Arts, 1978; Double Prizewinner, Tribute for St George's Day, Granada TV, 1978; Various other prizes and awards including, Most Prolific Letter Writer to Manchester Evening News. Memberships:Turner Society; Court School of Dancing; Independent Order of Odd Fellows; Friend, North West Arts, Manchester City Art Gallery; Authors North. *Address:* 43 Cornbrook Park Rd, Old Trafford, Manchester M15 4EH, England.

SILVERMAN, Sherri; b. 19 April 1951, Atlanta, GA, USA. Artist; Writer; Poet. *Education:* BA, Emory University, 1971; MA, Brandeis University, 1974; PhD, The Union Institute, 1996. *Appointments:* Teaching Fellow, Literature Dept, Maharishi International University, Fairfield, IA, 1980; Poet, Teacher, California Poets-in-the-Schools, Santa Barbara, 1985–86; Dir, Santa Fe Poets-in-the-Schools, New Mexico, 1989–92; Adjunct Faculty, University of North Florida, 1993, Florida Community College, 1993; Visiting Faculty, General Honors Program, University of New Mexico, 1996, The Union Institute Graduate School, 1996; Adjunct Faculty, New Mexico Highlands University, 1997, TVI Community College, 1997–98, College of Santa Fe, 1999; Co-Founder and Dir, Santa Fe School of Art and Enlightenment, 1999. *Contributions to:* Crosswinds, New Mexico; Sackbut Review; Reconstructionist; Heaven Bone; Wind Chimes; Santa Fe Spirit Magazine; Salome: A Literary Dance Magazine; Seeds of Unfolding; Art of Living Journal. *Honours:* Grants, Witter Bynner Foundation for Poetry, 1989, 1990. *Membership:* Poets and Writers. *Address:* P O Box 66, Santa Fe, NM 87504, USA.

SIMETRA. See: ANDERSDATTER, Karla Margaret.

SIMIC, Charles; b. 9 May 1938, Belgrade, Yugoslavia (Naturalized US citizen, 1971). Assoc. Prof. of English; Poet; Writer. m. Helen Dubin, 25 Oct. 1965, 1 s., 1 d. *Education:* University of Chicago, 1956–59; BA, New York University, 1967. *Appointments:* Faculty, California State College, Hayward, 1970–73; Assoc. Prof. of English, University of New Hampshire, 1973–. *Publications:* Poetry: What the Grass Says, 1967; Somewhere Among Us a Stone is Taking Notes, 1969; Dismantling the Silence, 1971; White, 1972; Return to a Place Lit by a Glass of Milk, 1974; Biography and a Lament, 1976; Charon's Cosmology, 1977; Brooms: Selected Poems, 1978; School for Dark Thoughts, 1978; Classic Ballroom Dances, 1980; Shaving at Night, 1982; Austerities, 1982; Weather Forecast for Utopia and Vicinity: Poems: 1967–1982, 1983; The Chicken Without a Head, 1983; Selected Poems 1963–1983, 1985; Unending Blues, 1986; The World Doesn't End: Prose Poems, 1989; In the Room We Share,

1990; The Book of Gods and Devils, 1990; Hotel Insomnia, 1992; A Wedding in Hell, 1994; Walking the Black Cat, 1996; Jackstraws: Poems, 1999; Selected Early Poems, 2000. Other: The Uncertain Certainty: Interviews, Essays and Notes on Poetry, 1985; Wonderful Words, Silent Truth, 1990; Dimestore Alchemy, 1992; Unemployed Fortune Teller, 1994; Orphan Factory, 1998; A Fly in the Soup, 2000. Editor: Another Republic: 17 European and South American Writers (with Mark Strand), 1976; The Essential Campion, 1988. Translator: 12 books, 1970–92. *Honours:* PEN Awards, 1970, 1980; Guggenheim Fellowship, 1972; National Endowment for the Arts Fellowships, 1974, 1979; Edgar Allan Poe Award, 1975; American Acad. of Arts and Letters Award, 1976; Harriet Monroe Poetry Award, 1980; Fulbright Fellowship, 1982; Ingram Merrill Foundation Fellowship, 1983; John D. and Catherine T. MacArthur Foundation Fellowship, 1984; Pulitzer Prize in Poetry, 1990; Acad. of American Poets Fellowship, 1998. *Address:* c/o Dept of English, University of New Hampshire, Durham, NH 03824, USA. SIMIC, Goran; b. 20 Oct. 1952, Vlasenica, Yugoslavia. Writer; Poet; Dramatist. m. Amela Simic, 1 April 1982, 2 c. *Education:* University of Sarajevo. *Publications:* Poetry: A Period Next to a Circle, or, A Journey, 1976; Vertigo, 1977; Mandragora, 1982; Sorrow of Sarajevo, 1996; Sprinting from the Graveyard, 1997; Sorrow and Other Poems, 1999; Walking across the Minefield (poems), 1999. Other: Prose, children's plays, radio plays and opera libretti. *Contributions to:* Anthologies, reviews, quarterlies and journals. *Honours:* Several Yugoslav awards; Hellman-Hammet Grant, 1993; Freedom to Write Award, PEN Center West, USA, 1995; Canada Council Grants, 1996, 1998. *Memberships:* PEN Bosnia-Herzegovina, founder-mem.; PEN Canada. *Address:* 57 Milverton Blvd, Toronto, ON M4J 1T5, Canada. *E-mail:* goransimic@utoronto.ca.

SIMMERMAN, Jim; b. 5 March 1952, Denver, CO, USA. Assoc. Prof. of English; Poet. *Education:* BS, Education, 1973, MA, English, 1976, University of Missouri; MFA, Creative Writing, University of Iowa, 1980. *Appointments:* Instructor, 1977–78, Asst Prof., 1983–86, Assoc. Prof. of English and Dir of Creative Writing, 1986–, Northern Arizona University; Editorial Board, Pushcart Prize Series, 1985–. *Publications:* Home, 1983; Bad Weather, 1987; Once Out of Nature, 1989; Moon Go Away, I Don't Love You Anymore, 1994; Yoyo, 1994; Dog Music: Poetry About Dogs (co-ed.), 1996. *Contributions to:* Anthologies and journals. *Honours:* Arizona Commission on the Arts Fellowships for Poetry, 1983, 1987; National Endowment for the Arts Fellowship, 1984; Pushcart Writers Choice Selection, 1984, and Prize, 1985; Fine Arts Work Center Poetry Fellowship, 1984–85; Best of the Small Presses Book Fair Selection, 1990; Hawthornden Fellowship, Scotland, 1996. *Memberships:* Associated Writing Programs, board of dirs, 1992–95, secretary, 1994–95; Rocky Mountain MLA. *Address:* 3601 Mountain Dr., Flagstaff, AZ 86001, USA.

SIMMIE, Lois; b. 11 June 1932, Edam, SK, Canada. Writer; Poet. 2 s., 2 d. *Education:* Saskatchewan Business College, 1951–52; University of Saskatchewan, 1973–77. *Appointments:* Writer-in-Residence, Saskatoon Public Library, 1987–88; Instructor, community colleges. *Publications:* Ghost House, 1976; They Shouldn't Make You Promise That, 1981; Pictures, 1984; Betty Lee Bonner Lives There, 1993; The Secret Lives of Sgt John Wilson: A True Story of Love and Murder, 1995. *Contributions to:* Numerous anthologies and periodicals. *Honours:* Awards and grants. *Memberships:* Asscn of Canadian Television and Radio Artists; Canadian Children's Book Centre; Saskatchewan Writers Guild; Writers' Union of Canada. *Address:* 1501 Cairns Ave, Saskatoon, SK S7H 2H5, Canada.

SIMMS, Michael Arlin, (Michael Garcia-Simms); b. 6 April 1954, Houston, Texas, USA. Instructor of English; Poet. m. Eva Maria Spork, 29 Sept. 1987, 1 s., 1 d. *Education:* Attended School of Irish Studies, 1974; BA, Southern Methodist University, 1976; MFA, University of Iowa, 1978. *Appointments:* Teaching Asst, University of Iowa, 1976–78; Instructor of Rhetoric, Southern Methodist University, 1979–87; Instructor of Communication, CCAC, 1988–; Instructor of English, Duquesne University, 1995–; Contributing Ed., The Pittsburgh Quarterly, 1997–; Poet-in-Residence, Carnegie Mellon University, 1998; Exec. Dir, Autumn House Press, 1998–. *Publications:* Notes on Continuing Light, 1980; Migration, 1985; The Fire-Eater, 1988. *Contributions to:* Southwest Review; Mid-American Review; Blue Buildings; Intro 9; Poets of the West; Telescope; Pittsburgh Poets; Rhetoric Review; Black Warrior Review; West Branch; Pittsburgh Quarterly; Texas Observer; Pittsbugh Post-Gazette; Pittsburgh Tribune; 5 AM. *Honours:* Yaddo Fellowships, 1979, 1980, 1987; National Endowment for the Humanities Fellowship, 1982; Beyond the Classroom Grants, CCAC, 1988, 1989; International Poetry Forum, 1993, 1994, 1995, 1996, 1997, 1998; Heinz Endowments Grant, 2002; Pennsylvania Council on the Arts Grant, 2002. *Address:* 219 Bigham St, Pittsburgh, PA 15211, USA.

SIMON, M(argaret) B(allif), (Marge Simon); b. 12 Sept. 1942, Washington, DC, USA. Poet; Writer. 1 d. *Education:* BA, 1969, MA, 1970, University of Northern Colorado. *Appointment:* Pres., Small Press Writers and Artists Organization, 1988–90. *Publications:* Mystic Hoofbeats (ed.), 1988; Poets of the Fantastic (ed.), 1990; Recursive Angel, 1990; Eonian Variations, 1995. *Contributions to:* Many publications. *Honour:* Rhysling Award, Best Long Poem, 1997. *Memberships:* SF Poetry Asscn, pres., 1994–; HWA, Mem., 1998–. *Address:* 1412 NE 35th St, Ocala, FL 34479, USA.

SIMON, Maurya; b. 7 Dec. 1950, New York, USA. Poet m. Robert Falk, 17 June 1973, 2 d. *Education:* BA, Pitzer College, 1980; MFA, University of California, Irvine, 1984. *Appointment:* University of California, Riverside, 1984–. *Publications:* The Enchanted Room, 1986; Days of Awe, 1989; Speaking in Tongues, 1990; The Golden Labyrinth, 1995; A Brief History of Punctuation, 2002. *Contributions to:* New Yorker; Los Angeles Times; Georgia Review; Grand Street; Hudson Review; Ironwood; Kenyon Review; Literary Review; Michigan Quarterly Review; Missouri Review; Pacific Review; Poetry; Poetry East. *Honours:* First Prize, National Federation of State Poetry Societies, 1984; First Prize, SCCA International Poetry Competition, 1987; Georgia State Poetry Award, 1988; Fulbright, Indo-American Fellowship, 1990. *Memberships:* Acad. of American Poets; Poetry Society of America; Poets and Writers; PEN USA West; MLA; Associated Writing Programs. *Address:* University of California, Riverside, Creative Writing Dept, 900 University Ave, Riverside, CA 92521, USA.

SIMONSUURI, Kirsti Katariina; b. 26 Dec. 1945, Helsinki, Finland. Prof.; Writer; Poet. *Education:* BA, 1968, MA, Honours, 1971, University of Helsinki; PhD, University of Cambridge, England, 1977. *Appointments:* Prof. of Literature, University of Oulu, 1978–81; Senior Research Fellow, Acad. of Finland, 1981–; Visiting Scholar, Harvard University, USA, 1984–86; Visiting Prof., Columbia University, New York City, 1986–88. *Publications:* Homer's Original Genius, 1979; Murattikaide, 1980; Tuntematon Tekija, 1982; Europan Ryosto, 1984. *Contributions to:* World Literature Today; Ploughshares; Horen; Diavaso. *Honours:* J H Erkko Award for Best First Book, 1980; Wolfson Fellowship Award, British Acad., 1981; Fulbright Postdoctoral Fellowship, 1984. *Memberships:* PEN International; Finnish Literature Society; Finland's Writers and Authors; Society for the Promotion of Hellenic Studies; International Society for Eighteenth Century Studies; MLA. *Address:* 67A Sands Point Rd, Port Washington, NY 11050, USA.

SIMPSON, Louis (Aston Marantz); b. 27 March 1923, Kingston, Jamaica (Naturalized US citizen). Prof. Emeritus; Poet; Writer. m. (1) Jeanne Claire Rogers, 1949, divorced 1979, 1 s., 1 d., (3) Miriam Butensky Bachner, 1985. *Education:* BS, 1948, AM, 1950, PhD, 1959, Columbia University. *Appointments:* Instructor, Columbia University, 1953–59, New School for Social Research, New York City, 1955–59; Asst Prof. to Prof. of English, University of California at Berkeley, 1959–67; Prof. of English and Comparative Literature, 1967–91, Distinguished Prof., 1991–93, Prof. Emeritus, 1993–, State University of New York at Stony Brook. *Publications:* Poetry: The Arrivistes: Poems, 1940–49, 1949; Good News of Death and Other Poems, 1955; A Dream of Governors, 1959; At the End of the Open Road, 1963; Selected Poems, 1965; Adventures of the Letter I, 1971; Searching for the Ox, 1976; Armidale, 1979; Out of Season, 1979; Caviare at the Funeral, 1980; The Best Hour of the Night, 1983; People Live Here: Selected Poems, 1949–83, 1983; Collected Poems, 1988; Wei Wei and Other Poems, 1990; In the Room We Share, 1990; There You Are, 1995. Fiction: Riverside Drive, 1962. Other: The New Poets of England and America (ed. with Donald Hall and Robert Pack), 1957; James Hogg: A Critical Study, 1962; An Introduction to Poetry (ed.), 1967; North of Jamaica, 1972; Three on the Tower: The Lives and Works of Ezra Pound, T S Eliot and William Carlos Williams, 1975; A Revolution in Taste: Studies of Dylan Thomas, Allen Ginsberg, Sylvia Plath and Robert Lowell, 1978; A Company of Poets, 1981; The Character of the Poet, 1986; Selected Prose, 1988; Ships Going into the Blue: Essays and Notes on Poetry, 1994; The King My Father's Wreck, 1995; Modern Poets of France: A Bilingual Anthology, 1997. *Contributions to:* Various publications. *Honours:* Prix de Rome, American Acad. in Rome, 1957; Hudson Review Fellowship, 1957; Edna St Vincent Millay Award, 1960; Distinguished Alumni Award, 1960, Medal for Excellence, 1965, Columbia University; Guggenheim Fellowships, 1962, 1970; ACLS Grant, 1963; Pulitzer Prize for Poetry, 1964; Commonwealth Club of California Poetry Award, 1965; American Acad. of Arts and Letters Award, 1976; Institute of Jamaica Centenary Medal, 1980; Jewish Book Council Award for Poetry, 1981; Elmer Holmes Bobst Award, 1987. *Address:* 186 Old Field Rd, Setauket, NY 11733, USA.

SIMPSON, Matt(hew William); b. 13 May 1936, Lancashire, England. Lecturer in English (retd); Poet; Writer. m. Monika Ingrid Weydert, 13 Dec. 1961, 1 s., 1 d. *Education:* CertEd, Liverpool, 1959; MA, Honours, Cantab, 1961. *Appointments:* Lecturer in English, various schools; Poet-in-Residence, Tasmanian Poetry Festival, 1995. *Publications:* Letters to Berlin, 1971; A Skye Sequence, 1972; Watercolour From an Approved School, 1975; Uneasy Vespers, 1977; Making Arrangements, 1982; See You on the Christmas Tree, 1984; Dead Baiting, 1989; An Elegy for the Galosherman: New and Selected Poems, 1990; The Pigs' Thermal Underwear, 1994; To Tasmania with Mrs Meredith, 1993; Catching Up With History, 1995; Matt, Wes and Pete, 1995; On the Right Side of the Earth, 1995; Somewhere Down the Line, 1998; Cutting the Clouds Towards, 1998; Lost Property Box, 1998; Getting There, 2001. *Contributions to:* Reviews, quarterlies, and magazines. *Address:* 29 Boundary Dr., Liverpool L25 0QB, England.

SIMPSON, Mercer Frederick Hampson; b. 27 Jan. 1926, London, England. Senior Lecturer (retd); Poet; Writer. m. Betty Cook, 9 Aug. 1961, 1 d. *Education:* BA, Honours, English, Magdalene College, Cambridge, 1949; Certificate in Education, University of Bristol, 1950; MA, Cantab, 1970; MA, University

College Cardiff, University of Wales, 1975. *Appointments:* Head, Dept of English, Monkton House Independent Boys Grammar School, Cardiff, Wales, 1950–66; Lecturer, Liberal Studies, Senior Lecturer, Dept of Arts and Languages, University of Glamorgan, 1967–81; Ed., BWA Magazine, Welsh Acad., 1986–91; Judge, Welsh Arts Council Literature Awards, 1987; Reader for Publication Grants, Welsh Arts Council, 1987–; Editorial Board, 1992–99, Poetry Ed., 1998–2001, New Welsh Review. *Publications:* East Anglian Wordscapes, 1993; Rain From a Clear Blue Sky, 1994. *Contributions to:* Anthologies, reviews, and journals. *Memberships:* Welsh Acad., exec. committee, 1985–98, council, 1993–98; Poetry Society of Great Britain; PEN Wales, 1994–; Fellow, RSA, 2001. *Address:* 1 Dan-y-Graig, Pantmawr, Cardiff CF4 7HJ, Wales.

SIMPSON, Ronald Albert; b. 1 Feb. 1929, Melbourne, Vic., Australia. Poet. m. Pamela Bowles, 27 Aug. 1951, 1 s., 1 d. *Education:* Trained Primary Teachers' Certificate, 1951; Assoc. Diploma in Fine Art, Royal Melbourne Institute of Technology, 1966. *Appointments:* Teacher, Junior and Secondary Schools, Australia and England, 1951–68; Lecturer, Senior Lecturer, The Chisholm Institute of Technology, Melbourne, Vic., 1968–87; Poetry Ed., The Age, 1988–97. *Publications:* The Walk Along the Beach, 1960; This Real Pompeii, 1964; After the Assassination, 1968; Diver, 1972; Poems from Murrumbeena, 1976; The Forbidden City, 1979; Poems From The Age (ed.), 1979; Selected Poems, 1981; Words for a Journey, 1986; Dancing Table, 1992; The Impossible and Other Poems, 1998; The Midday Clock, 1999. *Honours:* Australia Council for Travel, 1977, Category A Fellowship to write poetry, 1987; Christopher Brennan Award, 1992; The Age Poetry Book of the Year, 1999. *Membership:* Australian Society of Authors. *Address:* 10 Green Gables Ave, Malvern East, Melbourne, Vic. 3148, Australia.

SINASON, Valerie Elaine; b. 17 Dec. 1946, London, England. Child Psychotherapist; Adult Psychoanalyst; Poet; Writer. m.(1) M. Sinason, 19 Jan. 1969, 1 s., 1 d., (2) D. Leevers, 11 May 2002. *Education:* BA, English Language and Literature, 1968, Postgraduate Teaching Certificate, 1969, London University; MACP, Tavistock Clinic, 1983; Qualified to British Psychoanalytic Society, 1999. *Publications:* Inkstains and Stilettos, 1986; Night Shift, 1996. Other: Attachment, Trauma and Multiplicity: Working with Dissociative Identity Disorder, 2002. *Contributions to:* Tribune; Poetry Review; Spare Rib; Ambit; Outposts; Prospice; Arts Council New Poetry; Women's Press; Iron; Omens; PEN; Radio 3 Poetry Now; Thames TV, Angels of Fire; Argo; Wheels; Literary Review; Jewish Chronicle. *Memberships:* Poetry Society; Poetry West Hampstead. *Address:* Tavistock Clinic, 120 Belsize Lane, London NW3 5BA, England.

SINCLAIR, Iain (Macgregor); b. 11 June 1943, Cardiff, Wales. Poet; Writer. m. Anna Hadman, 4 March 1967, 1 s., 2 d. *Education:* Trinity College, Dublin; Courtauld Institute, London. *Publications:* Poetry: Back Garden Poems, 1970; Muscat's Würm, 1972; The Birth Rug, 1973; Lud Heat, 1975; Brown Clouds, 1977; Suicide Bridge, 1979; Fluxions, 1983; Fresh Eggs and Scalp Metal, 1983; Autistic Poses, 1985; Significant Wreckage, 1988; Selected Poems, 1970–87, 1989; Jack Elam's Other Eye, 1992. Fiction: White Chappell, Scarlet Tracings, 1987; Downriver, 1991; Radon Daughters, 1994; Slow Chocolate Autopsy, 1997; Landor's Tower, 2001. Essays: Lights Out for the Territory, 1997; Liquid City, 1998; Rodinsky's Room (with Rachel Lichtenstein), 1999; London Orbital: A Walk Around the M25, 2002. *Address:* 28 Albion Dr., London E8 4ET, England.

SINGER, Davida; b. 31 Oct. 1947, Burlington, Vermont, USA. Poet; Writer; Teacher. *Education:* BA, Writing, Columbia University, 1978; MA, Journalism, New York University, 1991. *Appointments:* Teacher, Writing Workshops; Co-Dir, Poetry Series, Wow Cafe, New York City and Woman Books, New York City. *Publications:* Shelter Island Poems, 1994; Letters to Women, 1994. *Contributions to:* Little Magazine; Feminist Studies; Passager; Amaranth Review; Metis; Write-Poems-Women Anthology; Feminist Review; Chelsea Journal; Mouth-of-the-Dragon; Primavera; Caprice; Sinister Wisdom; Peregrine. *Membership:* Poets and Writers. *Address:* 162 Ninth Ave, No. 2C, New York, NY 10011, USA.

SINGER, Gali-Dana, (Gad Gresin, Adel Kilka); b. 23 April 1962, Leningrad, USSR. *Education:* State Institute of Theatre, Music & Cinematography, Leningrad, 1979–82. *Appointments:* Chief Ed., Literary Magazines: IO, Jerusalem, 1994–95; Dvojetochije (Colon), 1995–96; Dvojetochije-Nekudataim (bi-lingual Russian-Hebrew), 2001–. *Publications:* Collection, 1992; Adel Kilka, From, 1993; To Think: River, 2000; Blind Poems, 2002; Iarusarim Beseiged, 2002. *Contributions to:* 22; Slog; Dvojetochije; Narod i Zemlja; Kamera Chranenija; Targum; Scopus II; Solnechnoje Spletenije; Arion; Helicon; Dimuj; Gag; Chadarim; Alpaim; Siach Meshorerim; 77; R'hov; Mikarov; Shvo; Carmel; The Poems, Fourth International Poet's Festival, Jerusalem. *Honours:* Prize for Literature, Israel Minister of Absorption, 1996; Prize, Poetry 2000. *Memberships:* General Union of Writers in Israel; Jerusalem Literary Club; Dir, the Poetry Seminary, 1993–. *Address:* Zipori St 33, Nachlaot, 94544 Jerusalem, Israel.

SINGER, Lou. See: WISINSKI, Louise Ann Helen.

SINGER, Sarah Beth; b. 4 July 1915, New York, NY, USA. Poet; Writer. m. Leon E Singer, 23 Nov. 1938, 1 s., 1 d. *Education:* BA, New York University, 1934; Graduate Studies, New School for Social Research, New York City, 1960–64. *Appointments:* Teacher, poetry seminars and workshops, 1968–74, 1981–83; Consulting Ed., Poet Lore, 1976–81. *Publications:* After the Beginning, 1975; Of Love and Shoes, 1987; The Gathering, 1992; Filtered Images (anthology), 1992. *Contributions to:* Anthologies, newspapers and journals. *Honours:* Stephen Vincent Benét Narrative Poetry Awards, 1968, 1971; 5 Poetry Society of America Awards, 1972–76; National League of American Penwomen Awards, 1976–92; Washington Poets Asscn Award, 1989; Haiku Award, Brussels Sprouts, 1992. *Memberships:* National League of American Penwomen; Poetry Society of America, vice-pres., 1974–78. *Address:* 2360 43rd Ave E, Seattle, WA 98112, USA.

SINGH, Charu Sheel; b. 15 May 1955, Uttar Pradesh, India. University Prof.; Writer; Poet; Critic. m. Maya Singh, 6 June 1987, 1 s. *Education:* BA, 1974; MA, 1976; PhD, 1978. *Appointments:* Lecturer in English, MBS College, Gangapur, Varanasi, 1977–79; Lecturer, 1979–86, Reader, 1986–96, Prof., 1996–, Kashi Vidyapith University. *Publications:* Some 24 works, including 5 vols of poems in English. *Contributions to:* Various periodicals and journals. *Honours:* British Council Award, 1982–83; Indian Institute of Advanced Study Fellowships, 1993, 1996–97; Maharashtra Dalit Sahitya Akademie Award, 2000. *Memberships:* American Studies Research Centre; Indian PEN. *Address:* B36-20A/36, Brahmanand Nagar, Ext 1, Durga Kund, Varanasi 221 005, India.

SINGH, Karnail; b. 28 June 1935, Heir, India. College Prof.; Poet. m. Shanta Singh, Dec. 1963, 1 s., 2 d. *Education:* BA, Honours, English, 1954; MA, English, 1956; Graduation in French, 1957; Persian, 1958; PhD, 1966. *Appointment:* Prof., Khalsa College, Amritsar, 1961–93. *Publications:* The Open Heart, 1993; The Wounded Muse, 1994; Mysteries of Love, 1996. *Contributions to:* Books and journals. *Membership:* Amritsar Literary Society. *Address:* 83612, Kot Atma Singh, Amritsar, India.

SINGH, Ram Krishna; b. 31 Dec. 1950, Varanasi, India. Teacher; Writer; Poet; Ed. m. Durga, 1 March 1978, 1 s., 1 d. *Education:* BA, University of Gorakhpur, 1970; MA, Banaras Hindu University, 1972; PhD, English, Kashi Vidyapith, 1981. *Appointments:* Lecturer, Royal Bhutan Polytechnic, 1974–76; Faculty, Indian School of Mines, Dhanbad, 1976–; Co-Ed., Creative Forum, 1987–91; General Ed., Creative Forum New Poets' Series, 1992–; Editorial Assoc., Indian Book Chronicle, 1992–; International Journal of Translation, 1992–; Assoc. Ed., Young Poets, 1994–, Indian Journal of Applied Linguistics, 1994–; Indian Ed., The Hearts of the Handmaidens, 1995–, Slugfest, 1997–. *Publications:* Savitri: A Spiritual Epic, 1984; My Silence, 1985; Using Contemporary English Idioms, 1985–86; Sound and Silence (ed.), 1986; Indian English Writing, 1981–1985: Experiments with Expression (ed.), 1987; Using English in Science and Technology, 1988; Memories Unmemoried, 1988; Practising English in Science and Technology, 1990; Flight of Phoenix, 1990; Music Must Sound, 1990; Recent Indian English Poets: Expressions and Beliefs (ed.), 1992; I Do Not Question, 1994; Krishna Scrivinas: The Poet of Inner Aspiration, 1994; My Silence and Other Selected Poems, 1996; General English Practice, 1995; Writing Your Thesis and Research Papers, 1996; Above the Earth's Green, 1997; Psychic Knot: Search for Tolerance in Indian English Fiction, 1998; New Zealand Literature: Some Recent Trends, 1998; Every Stone Drop Pebble, 1999; Multiple-Choice General English for UPSC Competitive Exams, 2001; The Face in All Seasons, 2002. *Contributions to:* Over 140 poetry journals. *Honours:* Hon. DLitt, World Acad. of Arts and Culture, 1984; Eminent Poet and Fellowship, International Poets Acad., Chennai, 1987; Certificates of Excellence, International Writers and Artists Asscn, 1987, 1988; Michael Madhusudan Award, Michael Madhusudan Acad., Calcutta, 1994; Poet of the Year Award, Canadian Alumni of the World University, Toronto, 1996; Peace Museum Award, Ritsumeikan University, Kyoto, 1999; Certificate of Honour and Nyusen Prize, Kumamoto City, Japan, 2000. *Memberships:* International Asscn of Teachers of English as a Foreign Language; International Poets Acad., Chennai; International Writers and Artists Asscn; PEN, Mumbai; World Poetry Society. *Address:* c/o Dept of Humanities and Social Sciences, Indian School of Mines, Dhanbad 826 004, India. *E-mail:* profrksingh@yahoo.com. *Website:* geocities.com\profrksingh\RKSINGH.html.

SINGHA, Aranyak. See: GANGOPADHYAY, Rabi.

SINGINGARROW-SMITH. See: CHRYSTOS, Christina.

SIRR, Peter Anthony; b. 8 June 1960, Ireland. Administrator; Poet. *Education:* BA, English and Irish, 1982, MLitt, English, 1984, Trinity College, Dublin. *Publications:* Marginal Zones, 1984; Talk Talk, 1987; Ways of Falling, 1991. *Contributions to:* Irish Times; Irish Press; Poetry Ireland Review; Poetry Review, London; Oxford Poetry; Ploughshares; Quarry; Anthologies: Penguin Book of Contemporary Irish Poetry; New Younger Irish Poets. *Honours:* Patrick Kavanagh Award, 1982; Listowel Writers Week Poetry Prize, 1983; Bursaries in Literature, Irish Arts Council, 1985, 1988. *Address:* Irish Writers Centre, 19 Parnell Sq., Dublin 1, Ireland.

SISSON, C(harles) H(ubert); b. 22 April 1914, Bristol, England. Poet; Writer; Trans.; Ed.; Civil Servant (retd). m. Nora Gilbertson, 19 Aug. 1937, 2 d. *Education:* BA, University of Bristol, 1934; Postgraduate studies, University of Berlin and Freiburg, 1934–35, Sorbonne, University of Paris, 1935–36. *Appointments:* Asst Principal, 1936–42, Principal, 1945–53, Asst Secretary 1953–62, Undersecretary, 1962–68, Asst Undersecretary of State, 1968–71, Dir of Occupational Safety and Health, 1971–73, Ministry of Labour. *Publications:* Poetry: Poems, 1959; Twenty-One Poems, 1960; The London Zoo, 1961; Numbers, 1965; The Discarnation: Or, How the Flesh Became Word and Dwelt Among Us, 1967; Metamorphoses, 1968; Roman Poems, 1968; In the Trojan Ditch: Collected Poems and Selected Translations, 1974; The Corridor, 1975; Anchises, 1976; Exactions, 1980; Selected Poems, 1981; Night Thoughts and Other Poems, 1983; Collected Poems, 1943–1983, 1984; God Bless Karl Marx!, 1987; Antidotes, 1991; Nine Sonnets, 1991; The Pattern, 1993; What and Who, 1994; Poems: Selected, 1995; Collected Poems, 1998. Fiction: An Asiatic Romance, 1953; Christopher Homm, 1965. Non-Fiction: The Spirit of British Administration and Some European Comparisons, 1959; Art and Action (essays), 1965; Essays, 1967; English Poetry 1900–1950: An Assessment, 1971; The Case of Walter Baghot, 1972; David Hume, 1976; The English Sermon: An Anthology, Vol. 2, 1976; The Avoidance of Literature: Collected Essays, 1978; Anglican Essays, 1983; The Poet and the Translator, 1985; On the Look-Out: A Partial Autobiography, 1989; In Two Minds: Guesses at Other Writers, 1990; English Perspectives: Essays on Liberty and Government, 1992; Is There a Church of England?, 1993. Translator: Versions and Perversions of Heine, 1955; The Poetry of Catullus, 1966; The Poetic Art: A Translation of Horace's 'Ars Poetica', 1975; Lucretius: De Rerum Natura: The Poem on Nature, 1976; Jean de La Fontaine: Some Tales, 1979; Dante Alighieri: The Divine Comedy, 1981; The Song of Roland, 1983; Joachim du Bellay: The Regrets, 1984; Virgil: The Aeneid, 1986; Jean Racine: Britannicus, Phaedra, Athaliah, 1987; Collected Translations, 1996. Editor: David Wright: South African Album, 1976; Jonathan Swift: Selected Poems, 1977; Thomas Hardy: Jude the Obscure, 1979; Philip Mairet: Autobiographical and Other Papers, 1981; Christina Rossetti: Selected Poems, 1984; Jeremy Taylor: Selected Writings, 1990. *Contributions to:* Agenda; London Magazine; London Review of Books; New Criterion; New York Times Review of Books; Poetry Nation Review; Spectator; TLS. *Honours:* Senior Simon Research Fellow, University of Manchester; Fellow, Royal Society of London, 1975; Hon. DLitt, University of Bristol, 1980; Companion of Honour, 1993. *Address:* Moorfield Cottage, The Hill, Langport, Somerset TA10 9PU, England.

SITKA, Warren. See: LEVI, Steven.

SIVAD, Niwles. See: DAVIS, Selwyn Sylvester.

SKAU, Michael; b. 6 Jan. 1944, Illinois, USA. Prof. of English; Poet. *Education:* BA, 1965, MA, 1967, PhD, 1973, University of Illinois. *Appointments:* Asst Prof., 1973–78, Assoc. Prof., 1978–85, Prof. of English, 1985–, Jefferis Chair in English, 1997–2000, University of Nebraska, Omaha. *Publication:* Me and God Poems, 1990. *Contributions to:* Midland Review; Cumberland Poetry Review; Nothwest Review; Kentucky Poetry Review; Prophetic Voices; Sequoia; Paintbrush; Galley Sail Review; Carolina Quarterly; Great River Review; Illuminations; Passaic Review; Blue Unicorn; Minotaur. *Membership:* MLA. *Address:* Dept of English, University of Nebraska, Omaha, NE 68182, USA. *E-mail:* mskau@mail-unomaha.edu.

SKELLINGS, Edmund; b. 12 March 1932, Ludlow, Massachusetts, USA. Prof.; Dir; Poet. m. Louise Skellings, 6 Aug. 1962, 1 d. *Education:* BA, English, University of Massachusetts, 1957; PhD, English, University of Iowa, 1962. *Appointments:* Poet Laureate of Florida, 1980–; Dir, Florida Center for Electronic Communication, Florida Atlantic University. *Publications:* Duels and Duets, 1960; Heart Attacks, 1976; Face Value, 1977; Showing My Age, 1978; Living Proof, 1985; Collected Poems 1958–1998, 1998. *Honours:* Florida Governor's Award in the Arts, 1979; Hon. DFA, International Fine Arts College, 1995; Florida Arts Recognition Award, 1997. *Address:* 220 SE Second Ave, Fort Lauderdale, FL 33301, USA.

SKENE, Kathleen Vera; b. 17 Oct. 1939, Sault Sainte, Marie, Ontario, Canada. Poet. m. G Leigh Skene, 12 March 1960, 1 s., 1 d. *Education:* Sir George Williams University, 1956–57; Diploma, CDN School of Commercial Art, 1959; Poetry Tutorial, 1988–89; Dept for Continuing Education, Oxford, 1993–95. *Publications:* Victoria Poetry Chapbook No. 11 (ed.), 1990; Pack Rat, 1992; Fire Water, 1994; The Uncertainty Factor/As a Rock, 1995. *Contributions to:* Reviews, quarterlies, and journals. *Honours:* Several honourable mentions; Third Prize, Orbis, 1994. *Memberships:* Burnaby Writer's Asscn; East Street Poets; Federation of British Columbia Writers; League of Canadian Poets; Poetry Society. *Address:* Headbury, Old Malthouse Lane, Langton Matravers, Swanage, Dorset BH19 3JA, England.

SKINNER, Jeffrey; b. 8 Dec. 1949, Buffalo, New York, USA. Asst Prof. of English and Creative Writing; Poet. m. Sarah Gorham, 8 May 1982, 2 d. *Education:* BA, Rollins College, 1971; Graduate Studies, University of Bridgeport, 1973–74; MFA, Columbia University, 1978. *Appointments:* Lecturer in English, University of Bridgeport, 1978–86; Lecturer, Norwalk Community College, 1982; Teacher of Creative Writing, Liberation House, 1982–83, Center for Creative Youth, Wesleyan University, 1986–88; Asst Prof. of English, Salisbury State College, Maryland, 1986–88; Asst Prof. of

English and Creative Writing, University of Louisville, 1988–. *Publications:* Late Stars, 1985; A Guide to Forgetting, 1988; Real Toads in Imaginary Gardens, 1991; The Company of Heaven, 1992. *Contributions to:* Anthologies and magazines. *Honours:* Indiana University Writers Conference Fellow, 1973; Colorado Writers Conference Fellow, 1975; MacDowell Colony and Yaddo Colony Guest, 1981; Provincetown Fine Arts Center Fellow, 1981–82; Connecticut Commission on the Arts Grant, 1983; Ingram Merrill Foundation Grant, 1985; National Endowment for the Arts Fellowship, 1987; Book Award, National Poetry Series, 1987. *Address:* 1637 Rosewood Ave, Louisville, KY 40204, USA.

SKINNER, Knute; b. 25 April 1929, St Louis, Missouri, USA. Prof. of English Emeritus; Poet. m. Edna Faye Kiel, 25 March 1978, 3 s. from previous marriages. *Education:* BA, Speech and Drama, University of Northern Colorado, 1951; MA, English, Middlebury College, 1954; PhD, English, University of Iowa, 1958. *Appointments:* Teacher, Boise Senior High School, 1951–54; Teaching Asst, 1954–55, 1956–57, Instructor, 1955–56, 1957–58, 1960–61, University of Iowa; Asst Prof., Oklahoma College for Women, 1961–62; Asst Prof., 1962–63, Lecturer, 1964–71, Assoc. Prof., 1971–73, Prof., 1973–97, Prof. Emeritus, 1997–, Western Washington University. *Publications:* Stranger With a Watch, 1965; A Close Sky Over Killaspuglonane, 1968; Hearing of the Hard Times, 1981; Selected Poems, 1985; Learning to Spell Zucchini, 1988; The Bears and Other Poems, 1991; What Trudy Knows and Other Poems, 1994; The Cold Irish Earth: Selected Poems of Ireland, 1965–1995, 1996; An Afternoon Quiet and Other Poems, 1998; Greatest Hits, 1964–2000, 2001; Stretches, 2002. *Contributions to:* Journals, reviews, periodicals and quarterlies. *Honours:* Fellowship in Creative Writing, National Endowment for the Arts, 1975; Governor's Invitational Writers' Day Certificate of Recognition, State of Washington, 1978. *Memberships:* Washington Poets Asscn; North Clare Writers Group; Irish Writers Union. *Address:* Killaspuglonane, Lahinch, County Clare, Ireland.

SKINNER, Richard; b. 15 July 1950, London, England. Writer; Poet; Counsellor. *Education:* MA, Natural Science, University of Cambridge, 1972; BPhil, CQSW, Social Work, University of Exeter, 1982. *Appointments:* Various posts. *Publications:* Leaping and Staggering, 1988; In the Stillness, 1990; Is the Clock Slow a Little Up, 1990; The Melting Woman, 1993; Still Staggering..., 1995; Echoes of Eckhart, 1998. *Contributions to:* Outposts; Orbit; Acumen; Westwords. *Address:* Little Bystock, Bystock Close, Exeter, Devon EX4 4JJ, England.

SKINNER, Susan; b. 22 Feb. 1935, Charlton, England. Poet. m. 28 Jan. 1964, 2 s., 2 d. *Education:* BA, Honours, French and English, 1955; PGCE, 1956; Certificate in Calligraphy and Bookbinding, 1992. *Publication:* Monet's Garden, 1991. *Contributions to:* Anthologies and periodicals. *Honours:* First Prize, 1987, Second Prizes, 1988, 1990, Julia Cairns Poetry Competition. *Memberships:* Dunford Novelists, founding mem.; Society of Women Writers and Journalists; Southern Writers Conference; Surrey Poetry Centre. *Address:* Bieldside, West Furlong Lane, Hurst Pier Point, Sussex BN6 9RH, England.

SKRZYNECKI, Peter; b. 6 April 1945, Imhert, Germany (Naturalized Australian citizen). Poet; Writer; Lecturer. m. Kate Magrath, 1 s., 2 d. *Education:* University of Sydney. *Appointment:* Lecturer, University of Western Sydney, 1987. *Publications:* Poetry: There, Behind the Lids, 1970; Headwaters, 1972; Immigrant Chronicle, 1975; The Aviary: Poems, 1975–77; The Polish Immigrant, 1982; Night Swim, 1989. Fiction: The Wild Dogs; The Beloved Mountain, 1988. Other: Joseph's Coat: An Anthology of Multicultural Writing, 1985. *Honour:* Captain Cook Bicentenary Award, 1970. *Address:* 6 Sybil St, Eastwood, NSW 2122, Australia.

ŠKVORECKÝ, Josef (Václav); b. 27 Sept. 1924, Náchod, Czechoslovakia (Canadian citizen). Prof. of English Emeritus; Writer; Dramatist; Poet; Ed.; Trans. m. Salivarová Zdenka, 31 March 1958. *Education:* PhD, Charles University, Prague, 1951. *Appointments:* Ed., Anglo-American Dept, Odeon Publishers, Prague, 1953–56, Sixty-Eight Publishers Corpn, Toronto, 1972–95; Asst Ed.-in-Chief, World Literature Magazine, Prague, 1956–59; Visiting Lecturer, 1968, 1970, Writer-in-Residence, 1970, Assoc. Prof., 1971–75, Prof. of English, 1975–90, Prof. Emeritus, 1990–, University of Toronto. *Publications:* Fiction: The Cowards, 1958; The End of the Nylon Age, 1967; Miss Silver's Past, 1969; The Tank Corps, 1969; The Miracle Game, 1972; The Swell Season, 1975; The End of Lieutenant Borůvka, 1975; The Engineer of Human Souls, 1977; The Return of Lieutenant Borůvka, 1980; Dvořák in Love, 1986; The Bride From Texas, 1992; Two Murders in My Double Life, 1996; Short Meeting With Murder (with Z. Škvorecký), 1999; An Inexplicable Story, or the Narrative of Questus Firmus Siculus, 2002. Short Stories: Eight collections, 1964–95. Plays: The New Men and Women, 1977; God in Your House, 1980. Poetry: Do Not Despair, 1979; The Girl From Chicago, 1980. Other: Reading Detective Stories, 1965; They-Which Is We, 1968; A Tall Tale About America, 1970; All the Bright Young Men and Women, 1972; Working Overtime, 1979; Jiri Menzel and the History of the Closely Watched Trains, 1982; Talkin' Moscow Blues, 1988; Headed for the Blues (memoir), 1996. *Contributions to:* Numerous publications. *Honours:* Various hon. doctorates; Neutstadt International Prize for Literature, 1980; Guggenheim Fellowship, 1980; Fellow, Royal Society of Canada, 1984; Governor-General's Award for Fiction, 1984; City of Toronto Book Award,

1985; Echoing Green Foundation Literature Award, 1990; Mem. of the Order of Canada, 1992; Czech State Prize for Literature, 1999. *Memberships:* Authors League of America; Crime Writers of Canada; Czechoslovak Society of Arts and Sciences, hon. mem.; International PEN Club; Mystery Writers of America; Writers' Union of Canada. *Address:* 487 Sackville St, Toronto, Ontario M4X 1T6, Canada.

SLADE, Quilla. See: LEWIS-SMITH, Anne Elizabeth.

SLAVITT, David R(ytman), (David Benjamin, Henry Lazarus, Lynn Meyer, Henry Sutton); b. 23 March 1935, White Plains, New York, USA. Novelist; Poet; Trans.; Lecturer. m. (1) Lynn Nita Meyer, 27 Aug. 1956, divorced 1977, 2 s., 1 d., (2) Janet Lee Abrahm, 16 April 1978. *Education:* BA, magna cum laude, Yale University, 1956; MA, Columbia University, 1957. *Appointments:* Instructor in English, Georgia Institute of Technology, Atlanta, 1957–58; Staff, Newsweek magazine, 1958–65; Asst Prof., University of Maryland, College Park, 1977; Assoc. Prof. of English, Temple University, Philadelphia, 1978–80; Lecturer in English, Columbia University, 1985–86; Lecturer, Rutgers University, 1987–; Lecturer in English and Classics, University of Pennsylvania, 1991–97; Faculty Mem., Bennington College, 2000–; Visiting Professorships; Many university and college poetry readings. *Publications:* Fiction: Rochelle, or Virtue Rewarded, 1966; Anagrams, 1970; ABCD, 1972; The Outer Mongolian, 1973; The Killing of the King, 1974; King of Hearts, 1976; Jo Stern, 1978; The Sacrifice, 1978; Cold Comfort, 1980; Alice at 80, 1984; The Agent, 1986; The Hussar, 1987; Salazar Blinks, 1988; Lives of the Saints, 1989; Turkish Delights, 1993; The Cliff, 1994; Get Thee to a Nunnery: Two Divertimentos from Shakespeare, 1999; Aspects of the Novel: A Novel, 2003. As Henry Sutton: The Exhibitionist, 1967; The Voyeur, 1969; Vector, 1970; The Liberated, 1973; The Proposal, 1980. As Lynn Meyer: Paperback Thriller, 1975. As Henry Lazarus: That Golden Woman, 1976. As David Benjamin: The Idol, 1979. Non-Fiction: Understanding Social Life: An Introduction to Social Psychology (with Paul F Secord and Carl W Backman), 1976; Physicians Observed, 1987; Virgil, 1991; The Persians of Aeschylus, 1998; Three Amusements of Ausonius, 1998; The Book of Lamentations, 2001. Other: Editor: Adrien Stoutenburg: Land of Superior Mirages: New and Selected Poems, 1986; Short Stories Are Not Real Life: Short Fiction, 1991; Crossroads, 1994; A Gift, 1996; Epigram and Epic: Two Elizabethan Entertainments, 1997; A New Pleade: Seven American Poets, 1998; Falling from Silence: Poems, 2001. Translator: The Eclogues of Virgil, 1971; The Eclogues and the Georgics of Virgil, 1972; The Tristia of Ovid, 1985; Ovid's Poetry of Exile, 1990; Seneca: The Tragedies, 1992; The Fables of Avianus, 1993; The Metamorphoses of Ovid, 1994; The Twelve Minor Prophets, 1999; The Voyage of the Argo of Valerius Flaccus, 1999; Sonnets of Love and Death of Jean de Spande, 2001; The Elegies of Propertius, 2001. *Contributions to:* Various other books as well as periodicals. *Honours:* Pennsylvania Council on the Arts Award, 1985; National Endowment for the Arts Fellowship, 1988; American Acad. and Institute of Arts and Letters Award, 1989; Rockefeller Foundation Artist's Residence, 1989. *Address:* 523 S 41st St, Philadelphia, PA 19104, USA.

SLOAN, Mary Margaret, (Margy Sloan); b. 30 June 1946, Washington, DC, USA. Poet; Teacher. m. Larry Casalino, 4 July 1984, 1 d. *Education:* BA, Poetics, Humanities, New College of California, 1986. *Publications:* Infiltration, 1989; The Said Lands, Islands and Premises, 1995; Moving Borders: Three Decades of Innovative Writing by Women (ed.), 1997. *Contributions to:* Talisman; Avec; Five Fingers Review; Ironwood; Acts; How(ever); Raddle Moon; Big Allis; Mirage. *Address:* 45 Stoneman St, San Francisco, CA 94110, USA.

SMALL, Michael Ronald; b. 3 Jan. 1943, Croydon, Surrey, England. Writer; Poet. *Education:* BA, London University; BEd, La Trobe University, Australia; MA, University of Windsor, Canada; Teacher of English as a Foreign Language, RSA, 1972. *Publications:* Her Natural Life and Other Stories, 1988; Film: A Resource Book for Studying Film as Text (with Brian Keyte), 1994; Unleashed: A History of Footscray Football Club (with John Lack, Chris McConville and Damien Wright), 1996; Urangeline: Voices of Carey 1923–1997, 1997. *Contributions to:* Numerous journals and magazines. *Membership:* Victorian Fellowship of Australian Writers. *Address:* 71 Strabane Ave, Box Hill N, Vic. 3129, Australia.

SMALL, Nola Betty; b. 13 Nov. 1936, Australia. Writer; Poet; Dramatist; Artist; Musician. m. John Oliver Small, 30 March 1968, 3 s., 1 d. *Education:* Diploma in Occupational Therapy, Australia, 1954; OT Reg, Canada, 1959; AMus, 1959; OTR, USA, 1960. *Publications:* Various works, 1990–95. *Contributions to:* Many anthologies and magazines. *Honour:* Runner-up, Northam Poetry Festival, Australia, 1974. *Address:* 6 Scotts Ave, Bromley, Kent BR2 0LQ, England.

SMALLSHAW, Judith; b. 10 April 1935, London, England. Poet; Writer. m. John Smallshaw, 27 Sept. 1958, 2 d. *Education:* PNEU, 1939–51. *Publications:* Copper Farthings, 1977; By Fell Tarn and Crag, 1978; An Apple in My Pocket, 1984. *Contributions to:* Newspapers, reviews and journals. *Honours:* Julia Cairns Silver Salvers, 1983, 1984; World Order of Poets, 1987. *Memberships:*

London Writers; Poetry Society; Society of Authors; Society of Women Writers. *Address:* 178 Warren Rd, Banstead, Surrey SM7 1LB, England.

SMARANDACHE, Florentin; b. 10 Dec. 1954, Balcesti, Romania. Mathematician; Educator; Writer; Poet. m. Eleonora Niculescu, 28 May 1977, 2 s. *Education:* MSc, Mathematics and Computer Science, University of Craiova, 1979; PhD, Mathematics, University of Kishinev, 1997. *Publications:* Some 55 books, 1981–2000. *Contributions to:* Several publications. *Honours:* Premiul Special, Concursal National de Proza Scurta Marin Preda, Alexandria, 1982; Prix Special Étranger, Grand Prix de la Ville de Bergerac, France, 1990; Hon. Mention, Le Concours de l'Académie de Lettres et des Arts du Perigord, France, 1990; Hon. DLitt, World Congress of Poets, 1991; Premio della Literature, Goccia di Luna, Italy, 1995; Nomination, Nobel Prize for Literature, 1999. *Memberships:* International Writers' and Artists' Asscn; MLA; Romanian Writers' Asscn; World Acad. of Arts and Culture. *Address:* University of New Mexico, 200 College Rd, Gallup, NM 87301, USA.

SMART, Harry Watson; b. 6 March 1956, Dewsbury, Yorkshire, England. Writer; Poet. m. Catriona Stewart Murray, 4 April 1979, 1 s. *Education:* BSc, Honours, Geography, 1978; PhD, Social Theory, 1984, University of Aberdeen. *Publications:* Pierrot, 1991; Criticism and Public Rationality, 1991; Shoah, 1993. *Contributions to:* Lines Review; Chapman; West Coast Magazine; Outposts; Oxford Poetry; Poetry Review; Agenda; Stand Magazine; TLS. *Honours:* Writer's Bursary, Scottish Arts Council, 1991; Inflatable Dolphin from Ian Duhig, John Hewitt International Summer School, Antrim, 1991. *Memberships:* Scottish Poetry Library, Edinburgh; Poetry Society, London. *Address:* c/o Faber and Faber, 3 Queen Sq., London WC1N 3AU, England.

SMITH, Arthur Edwin; b. 17 April 1948, Stockton, CA, USA. University Prof.; Poet. *Education:* BA, 1970, MA, 1971, San Francisco State University; PhD, University of Houston, 1986. *Appointment:* University of Tennessee. *Publications:* Elegy on Independence Day, 1985; Orders of Affection, 1996; The Late World, 2002. *Contributions to:* New Yorker; North American Review; Chicago Review; Poetry; Nation; Georgia Review; New England Review; Crazyhorse. *Honours:* The Nation – Discovery Award, 1981; National Endowment for the Arts Fellowship, 1984; Agnes Lynch Starrett Poetry Prize, 1985; Norma Farber First Book Award, 1985. *Memberships:* International Society of America; MLA. *Address:* Dept of English, University of Tennessee, Knoxville, TN 37996, USA.

SMITH, Bernard William; b. 3 Oct. 1916, Sydney, NSW, Australia. Art Historian; Critic; Poet. m. (1) Kate Beatrice Hartley Challis, 16 May 1941, 1 s., 1 d., (2) Margaret Patricia Thompson, 30 July 1995. *Education:* BA, University of Sydney, 1952; Warburg Institute, London, England, 1948–50; PhD, Australian National University, 1956. *Appointment:* Category A Literary Fellowship, Australia Council, 1990–91. *Publications:* Place, Taste and Tradition, 1945; European Vision and the South Pacific, 1960; Australian Painting, 1962; The Architectural Character of Glebe, Sydney (with K Smith), 1973; Documents on Art and Taste in Australia, 1975; The Boy Adeodatus, 1984; The Art of Captain Cook's Voyages (with R Joppien), 3 vols, 1985–87; The Death of the Artist as Hero, 1988; The Critic as Advocate, 1989; Imagining the Pacific, 1992; Noel Counitian, 1993; Poems, 1996; Modernism's History, 1998. *Contributions to:* Journals. *Honours:* Co-Recipient, Ernest Scott Prize for History, Melbourne, 1962; Henry Lawson Prize for Poetry, 1964; Hon. LittD, University of Melbourne, 1976, University of Sydney, 1997; Australian National Book Council Prize, Nettie Palmer Prize for Non-Fiction and Talking Book Award, 1984. *Memberships:* Australian Society of Authors; Australian Acad. of the Humanities, pres., 1977–80; Australian Humanities Research Council, secretary, 1962–65; Fellow, Society of Antiquaries; UNESCO Committee for Letters, Australia, 1963–69. *Address:* 168 Nicholson St, Fitzroy, Vic. 3065, Australia.

SMITH, Bob. See: SMITH, R(obert) Lester.

SMITH, Charlie; b. 27 June 1947, Moultrie, GA, USA. Writer; Poet; University Lecturer. m. (1) Kathleen Huber, 16 Sept. 1974, divorced 21 June 1977, (2) Gretchen Mattox, 16 Dec. 1987, divorced 16 Dec. 1997. *Education:* BA, Duke University, 1971; MFA, University of Iowa, 1983. *Appointments:* Lecturer in Humanities and Creative Writing, Princeton University; Writer-in-Residence, University of Alabama, 2000. *Publications:* Fiction: Canaan, 1985; Shine Hawk, 1988; The Lives of the Dead, 1990; Crystal River, 1991; Chimney Rock, 1993; Cheap Ticket to Heaven, 1996. Poetry: Red Roads, 1987; Indistinguishable from the Darkness, 1990; The Palms, 1993; Before and After: Poems, 1995; Heroin and Other Poems, 2000. *Contributions to:* Literary journals and periodicals. *Honours:* Aga Khan Prize, Paris Review, 1983; National Endowment for the Arts Grant, 2000. *Memberships:* Acad. of American Poets; International PEN; Poetry Society of America. *Address:* c/o Maria Carvainis, 1350 Avenue of the Americas, New York, NY 10019, USA.

SMITH, Dave, (David Jeddie Smith); b. 19 Dec. 1942, Portsmouth, Virginia, USA. Poet; Ed.; Prof. of English. m. Deloras Smith, 31 March 1966, 1 s., 2 d. *Education:* BA, Honours, English, University of Virginia, 1965; MA, English, Southern Illinois University, 1969; PhD, English, Ohio University, 1976. *Appointments:* Ed., The Back Door: A Poetry Magazine, 1970–78, The

Southern Review, 1990–; Instructor in English, Western Michigan University, 1973–74; Asst Prof. of English, Cottey College, 1974–75; Asst Prof., 1976–79, Assoc. Prof. of English, 1979–81, Dir of Creative Writing, 1976–81, University of Utah; Poetry Ed., Rocky Mountain Review, 1978–79, University of Utah Press, 1980–90; Visiting Prof. of English, State University of New York at Binghamton, 1980–81; Dir of Poetry, Bennington Writers Conference, Vermont, 1980–87; Assoc. Prof. of English and Dir of Creative Writing, University of Florida, 1981–82; Prof. of English, Virginia Commonwealth University, 1982–90; Prof. of English, 1991–97, Hopkins P Breazeale Prof. of English, 1997–98, Boyd Prof. of English, 1998–, Louisiana State University. *Publications:* Bull Island, 1970; Mean Rufus Throw Down, 1973; The Fisherman's Whore, 1974; Drunks, 1975; Cumberland Station, 1977; In Dark, Sudden With Light, 1977; Goshawk, Antelope, 1979; Blue Spruce, 1981; Dream Flights, 1981; Homage to Edgar Allan Poe, 1981; Onliness (novel), 1981; The Travelling Photographer, 1981; The Pure Clear Word: Essays on the Poetry of James Wright, 1982; In the House of the Judge, 1983; Southern Delights (stories), 1984; Gray Soldiers, 1984; The Morrow Anthology of Younger American Poets (ed.), 1985; The Roundhouse Voices: Selected and New Poems, 1985; Local Assays: On Contemporary American Poetry, 1985; Cuba Night, 1990; The Essential Poe, 1992; Night Pleasures: New and Selected Poems, 1992; Fate's Kite: Poems 1990–1995, 1996; Floating on Solitude: Three Books of Poems, 1997; The Wick of Memory: New and Selected Poems 1970–2000, 2000. *Contributions to:* Anthologies, reviews, and journals. *Honours:* Bread Loaf Fellow, 1975; National Endowment for the Arts Fellowships, 1976, 1980; American Acad. of Arts and Letters Award, 1979; Runner-up, Pulitzer Prizes in Poetry, 1979, 1981; Guggenheim Fellowship, 1981; Ohio University Alumni of the Year, 1985; Lyndhurst Fellowship, 1987–89; Virginia Poetry Prize, 1988. *Memberships:* Associated Writing Programs; Fellowship of Southern Writers; MLA; National Book Critics Circle; PEN; Poetry Society of America; Poetry Society of Virginia; Society for the Study of Southern Literature; Southern MLA. *Address:* 1430 Knollwood Dr., Baton Rouge, LA 70808, USA.

SMITH, Deirdre Armes; b. 29 Sept. 1922, England. Teacher (retd); Poet. m. 9 Aug. 1947, 2 s., 2 d. *Education:* The College, Saffron Walden, Essex. *Publications:* Cycles to the Moon, 1970; Church Bells on a Wet Sunday, 1985; The Real Thing, 1987; Winter Tennis Courts, 1987; Mother of Wales, 1990; With Untold Care, 1991; Invisible Lady, 1996; Scorched Paper From a Bonfire, 1998; Home Of the Wind, 1998. *Contributions to:* Various publications. *Honours:* Poetry read, Radio Merseyside, 1991, Poetry Festival, Maryland, USA, 1992; Finalist, Bard of the Year Competition, University of Leicester, 1993, 1994. *Membership:* Society of Women Writers and Journalists. *Address:* Talgarth, 21 Parr Fold Ave, Worley, Manchester M28 4EJ, England.

SMITH, Francis Joseph; b. 22 May 1920, Ohio, USA. Priest; Prof.; Poet. *Education:* Xavier University, Cincinnati, 1943; MA, Loyola University, Chicago, 1949; MA, University of Oxford, 1961. *Appointments:* Instructor, University of Detroit; Asst Prof., Assoc. Prof., Prof., John Carroll University. *Publications:* First Prelude, 1981; All is a Prize, 1989; Haiku Yearbook, 1991. *Contributions to:* Aethlon; Chicago Poetry Review; New York Quarterly; Samizdat; Snowy Egret; Song; Spoon River Quarterly. *Honour:* First Place, Cuyahoga Writers Workshop. *Memberships:* Poetry Society of America; Poets and Writers; MLA. *Address:* John Carroll University, 20700 N Park Blvd, Schell House, University Heights, OH 44118, USA.

SMITH, Iain Crichton; b. 1 Jan. 1928, Isle of Lewis, Scotland. Poet; Writer. m. Donalda Gillies Smith, 16 July 1977, 2 step-s. *Education:* MA, Honours, English, University of Aberdeen, 1949. *Publications:* Poetry: Thistles and Roses, 1961; The Law and the Grace, 1969; From Bourgeois Land, 1969; Love Poems and Elegies, 1972; Selected Poems, 1982; A Life, 1985; The Village and Other Poems, 1989; Collected Poems, 1992. Fiction: Consider the Lilies, 1968; The Last Summer, 1969; The Black and the Red (short stories), 1973; On the Island (short stories), 1974; The Hermit and Other Stories, 1977. *Contributions to:* Journals and magazines. *Honours:* PEN Poetry Award, 1970; Poetry Society Recommendations, 1972, 1975, 1989, 1992, and Choice, 1984; Commonwealth Poetry Prize, 1986; Saltire Award, 1992; Cholmondeley Award, 1997. *Membership:* RSL, fellow. *Address:* Tigh Na Fuaran, Taynuilt, Argyll, Scotland.

SMITH, James Ronald; b. 12 Feb. 1949, Savannah, GA, USA. Teacher; Poet. m. Anita Delores Quinney, 1 Nov. 1968, 1 s. *Education:* BA, English and Philosophy, 1971; MA, English, 1974; MFA, Creative Writing, 1985; MH, 1994. *Publication:* Running Again in Hollywood Cemetery, 1988. *Contributions to:* Many reviews, quarterlies, and journals. *Honours:* Guy Owen Poetry Award, Southern Review, 1986; Theodore Roethke Poetry Prize, Poetry Northwest, 1989. *Memberships:* Associated Writing Programs; International James Joyce Foundation; MLA; Poetry Society of Virginia; Robert Penn Warren Circle; Virginia Writers Club. *Address:* 616 Maple Ave, Richmond, VA 23226, USA.

SMITH, John Charles; b. 5 April 1924, High Wycombe, Buckinghamshire, England. Poet; Ed. *Appointments:* Joined, 1946, Managing Dir, 1958–71, Christy and Moore Ltd; Ed., Poetry Review. *Publications:* Gates of Beauty and Death, 1948; The Dark Side of Love, 1952; The Birth of Venus, 1954; Excursus in Autumn, 1958; A Letter to Lao Tze, 1973; A Landscape of My Own (selected poems 1948–1982), 1982; Songs for Simpletons, 1984; Poems for Paul

Klee, 1990. *Contributions to:* Windmill; Listener; Saturday Review; New English Review; Poetry Review; Poetry Quarterly; Poetry and Poverty; Modern Reading; New Verse; Northwest Review; Contemporary Review; Tribune; Adam. *Honours:* Adam International Review Prize, 1952; Poetry Book Society Choice, 1958, 1973, and Recommendation, 1965; Borestone Mountain Award, 1971. *Memberships:* Poetry Society, exec. committee; PEN Exec.; Arts Council, copywright panel. *Address:* 529 Emerald Empire, KNSM Eiland, Amsterdam, Netherlands.

SMITH, Ken; b. 4 Dec. 1938, Rudston, England. Poet. 2 s., 2 d. *Education:* BA, University of Leeds, 1963. *Appointments:* Visiting Writer, Clark University, Massachusetts, 1972–73; Yorkshire Arts Writer-in-Residence, University of Leeds, 1976–78; Writer-in-Residence, Kingston Polytechnic, 1979–81; HMP Wormwood Scrubs, 1985–87. *Publications:* Eleven Poems; Frontwards; Anus Mundi; Tales of the Hunter; Grainy Pictures of the Rain; Inside Time; The Heart, The Border; Berlin: Coming in From the Cold; Tender to the Queen of Spain; Wild Root. *Contributions to:* Stand, Klaonica, Beyond Bedlam. *Honours:* Gregory Award; Arts Council of Great Britain Award; Poetry Book Society Recommendation; Lannan Award, 1997; Cholmondeley Award, 1998. *Address:* c/o Bloodaxe Books, PO Box 15N, Newcastle Upon Tyne NE99 1SN, England.

SMITH, Margery; b. 21 March 1916, Nottingham, England. Teacher (retd); Poet; Ed. *Education:* PNEU Teachers Certificate, Charlotte Mason College, Ambleside, 1936. *Appointment:* Ed., L'Umile Pianta, 1972–79. *Publications:* In Our Time, 1941; Still in My Hand, 1964; In Transit, 1981. *Contributions to:* Various anthologies, reviews, and periodicals. *Honours:* Poetry Review Premium Awards, 1938, 1940; Poem included in D-Day Queen Elizabeth II Concert, 1994. *Memberships:* Byron Society; Camden Poetry Group; International Poetry Society, founder-fellow; Nottingham Poetry Society, co-founder, hon. secretary and treasurer; Poetry Society, UK, general council, 1967–69; Poetry Society of America; Shelley Society of New York, hon. mem. *Address:* 12 Springfield Crescent, Horsham, West Sussex RH12 2PP, England.

SMITH, Patricia Clark; b. 14 Feb. 1943, Holyoke, MA, USA. Writer; Poet; Prof. of English. m. (1) Warren S. Smith, 25 Aug. 1964, divorced 1976, 2 s., (2) John F. Crawford, 26 Nov. 1988. *Education:* BA, Smith College, 1964; MA, 1965, PhD, 1970, Yale University. *Appointments:* Lecturer in English, Smith College, 1968–69; Asst Prof. of English, Luther College, Decorah, IA, 1969–71; Asst Prof., 1971–82, Assoc. Prof., 1982–96, Prof. of English, 1996–, University of New Mexico. *Publications:* Talking to the Land (poems), 1979; Changing Your Story (poems), 1990; Western Literature in a World Context (co-ed.), two vols, 1995; As Long as the Rivers Flow: The Stories of Nine Native Americans (co-author), 1996. *Contributions to:* Anthologies and periodicals. *Address:* 2309 Headingly NW, Albuquerque, NM 87107, USA.

SMITH, R(obert) Lester, (Bob Smith); b. 14 June 1928, Long Beach, CA, USA. Naval Officer (retd); Teacher; Pastor; Poet. m. Maroline Havens, 1958, 2 s., 3 d. *Publications:* Bread for the Head, 1989; Psalms of Theophilus, 1990; The Spit'N Image, 1993; Ducks in a Row, 1995; Six Days for Mankind, 1998. *Contributions to:* Reviews and periodicals. *Honours:* Blue Ribbon Awards for Poetry; Roaring Lamb Award, Amy Foundation, Lansing, Michigan. *Address:* PO Box 660, Foreman, AR 71836, USA.

SMITH, Sam(uel David); b. 24 Dec. 1946, Blackpool, England. Poet; Ed. m. (1) Judith Bone, 1970, 1 d., (2) Stephanie Dart, 2 d. *Appointments:* Founder-Ed., Journal of Contemporary Anglo-Scandinavian Poetry, 1995–2000, Original Plus, 1998–, The Journal, 2000–; Co-Ed., River King Poetry Supplement. *Publications:* Poetry: To Be Like John Clare, 1997; Skin and Bones, 1997; Dialogues, 1998; John the Explorer, 1999; pieces, 2001. Fiction: Sister Blister, 1999; Happiness, 2000; The End of Science Fiction, 2000; Paths of Error: Undeclared War, 2001; Paths of Error: Constant Change, 2001; Perceived Histories, 2001; Paths of Error: As Recorded, 2002; Marks, 2002; Porlock Counterpoint, 2002. *Contributions to:* Numerous publications worldwide. *Memberships:* Anglo-Welsh Poetry Society; John Clare Society. *Address:* Flat 3, 18 Oxford Grove, Ilfracombe, Devon EX34 9HQ, England. *Website:* members.aol.com/smithsssj/index.html.

SMITH, Stephen Mark; b. 16 Jan. 1964, Worcestershire, England. Writer; Poet; Lecturer. *Education:* BA, Honours, English, University College Wales, Aberystwyth; PhD studies. *Appointment:* Lecturer in Advanced Creative Writing, Sutton College of Liberal Arts. *Publication:* The Fabulous Relatives, 1993. *Contributions to:* Anthologies and magazines. *Honour:* Eric Gregory Award, 1991. *Address:* 17 Elgin Ct, 12 Bramley Hill, South Croydon CR2 6LT, England.

SMITH, Steven James; b. 25 April 1972, Wellington, Shropshire, England. Writer; Poet. *Education:* English, History and Philosophy, Crestwood Sixth Form College, 1990. *Publications:* My Realm, 1994; Elysian Dreams, 1996; Images of Understanding, 1997; Poetic Expressions, 1999. *Contributions to:* Tops; Helicon; Poetry Now; Anchor Books; White Tower; National Library of Poetry, USA; Edizioni University, Italy; First Time; Reflections. *Honours:* Ed.'s Choice Awards, National Library of Poetry, 1994, 1995, 1996, 1997. *Memberships:* White Tower Writers Asscn; Dreamlands Poetry Group. *Address:* Grafton Ct, Norwood Rd, Cheltenham GL50 2DG, England.

SMITH, Steven Ross; b. 25 June 1945, Toronto, ON, Canada. Writer; Poet. m. J. Jill Robinson, 1 s. *Education:* Diploma in Radio and Television Arts, Ryerson Polytechnic University. *Appointments:* Writer-in-Residence, Wayburn Public Library, 1987–88, Saskatoon, 1996–97. *Publications:* Ritual Murders, 1983; Blind Zone, 1985; Sleepwalkers (with Richard Truhlar), 1987; Transient Light, 1990; Reading My Father's Book, 1995; Fluttertongue, two vols, 1998–99; Ballet of the Speech Organs: Bob Cobbing on Bob Cobbing, 1998. *Contributions to:* Periodicals. *Memberships:* League of Canadian Poets; Saskatchewan Writers' Guild; Writers' Union of Canada. *Address:* 920 Ninth Ave N, Saskatoon, SK S7K 2Z4, Canada. *E-mail:* steven.ross.smith@sk.sympatico.ca.

SMITH, Thomas R.; b. 16 Jan. 1948, Chippewa Falls, Wisconsin, USA. Poet; Ed. m. Krista Lynn Spieler, 19 Oct. 1985. *Education:* University of Wisconsin at River Falls, 1966–70. *Appointments:* Dir, Artspeople of Wisconsin, 1978–81; Asst to the Pres., Natural Resources Corp, 1982–90; Assoc. Ed., Ally Press, 1990–. *Publications:* Keeping the Star, 1988; Walking Swiftly: Writings and Images on the Occasion of Robert Bly's 65th Birthday (ed.), 1992; Horse of Earth, 1994. *Contributions to:* Reviews, quarterlies, and journals. *Honours:* Winner, Milkweed Chronicle Poetry Contest, 1982; Winner, Lake Superior Writers Series, 1984, 1991; Ed.'s Choice, The Spirit That Moves Us Press, 1987. *Address:* 246 Bedford St SE, No. 2, Minneapolis, MN 55414, USA.

SMITH, Vivian (Brian); b. 3 June 1933, Hobart, Tasmania, Australia. Lecturer; Poet; Ed. m. Sybille Gottwald, 15 Feb. 1960, 1 s., 2 d. *Education:* MA, 1955, PhD, 1970, University of Sydney. *Appointments:* Lecturer, University of Tasmania, 1955–66; Literary Ed., Quadrant magazine, Sydney, 1975–90; Reader, University of Sydney, 1982–96. *Publications:* The Other Meaning, 1956; An Island South, 1967; The Poetry of Robert Lowell, 1975; Familiar Places, 1978; Tide Country, 1982; Tasmania and Australian Poetry, 1984; Selected Poems, 1985; New Selected Poems, 1995; Late News, 2000. *Contributions to:* Newspapers and magazines. *Honours:* Grace Leven Prize; New South Wales Premier's Prize, 1983; Patrick White Literary Award, 1997. *Memberships:* Australian Society of Authors; PEN; Australian Acad. of the Humanities, fellow. *Address:* 19 McLeod St, Mosman, NSW 2088, Australia.

SMITH, William Jay; b. 22 April 1918, Winnfield, LA, USA. Prof. of English Emeritus; Poet; Writer. m. (1) Barbara Howes, 1947, divorced 1965, 2 s., (2) Sonja Haussmann, 1966, 1 step-s. *Education:* BA, 1939, MA, 1941, Washington University, St Louis; Institut de Touraine, Tours, France, 1938; Columbia University, 1946–47; Wadham College, Oxford, 1947–48; University of Florence, 1948–50. *Appointments:* Instructor, 1946–47, Visiting Prof., 1973–75, Columbia University; Instructor, 1951, Poet-in-Residence and Lecturer, 1959–64, 1966–67, Williams College; Writer-in-Residence, 1965–66, Prof. of English, 1967–68, 1970–80, Prof. Emeritus, 1980–, Hollins College, Virginia; Consultant in Poetry, 1968–70, Hon. Consultant, 1970–76, Library of Congress, Washington, DC; Lecturer, Salzburg Seminar in American Studies, 1974; Fulbright Lecturer, Moscow State University, 1981; Poet-in-Residence, Cathedral of St John the Divine, New York City, 1985–88. *Publications:* Poetry: Poems, 1947; Celebrating at Dark, 1950; Snow, 1953; The Stork, 1954; Typewriter Birds, 1954; The Bead Curtain: Calligrams, 1957; The Old Man on the Isthmus, 1957; Poems 1947–1957, 1957; Prince Souvanna Phouma: An Exchange Between Richard Wilbur and William Jay Smith, 1963; Morels, 1964; The Tin Can and Other Poems, 1966; New and Selected Poems, 1970; A Rose for Katherine Anne Porter, 1970; At Delphi: For Allen Tate on His Seventy-Fifth Birthday, 19 November 1974, 1974; Venice in the Fog, 1975; Verses on the Times (with Richard Wilbur), 1978; Journey to the Dead Sea, 1979; The Tall Poets, 1979; Mr Smith, 1980; The Traveler's Tree: New and Selected Poems, 1980; Oxford Doggerel, 1983; Collected Translator: Italian, French, Spanish, Portuguese, 1985; The Tin Can, 1988; Journey to the Interior, 1988; Plain Talk: Epigrams, Epitaphs, Satires, Nonsense, Occasional, Concrete and Quotidian Poems, 1988; Collected Poems 1939–1989, 1990; The World Below the Window: Poems 1937–1997, 1998. Also 16 books of poetry for children, 1955–90. Stories: Ho for a Hat!, 1989. Other: The Spectra Hoax, 1961; The Skies of Venice, 1961; Children and Poetry: A Selective Bibliography (with Virginia Haviland), 1969; Louise Bogan: A Woman's Words, 1972; The Streaks of the Tulip: Selected Criticism, 1972; Green, 1980; Army Brat: A Memoir, 1980. Editor: Herrick, 1962; The Golden Journey: Poems for Young People (with Louise Bogan), 1965; Poems from France, 1967; Poems from Italy, 1972; A Green Place: Modern Poems, 1982. *Contributions to:* Journals and magazines. *Honours:* Rhodes Scholar, 1947–48; Ford Foundation Fellowship, 1964; Henry Bellamann Major Award, 1970; National Endowment for the Arts Grant, 1972; National Endowment for the Humanities Grants, 1975, 1989; Gold Medal of Labor, Hungary, 1978; Ingram Merrill Foundation Grant, 1982. *Membership:* American Acad. of Arts and Letters, vice-pres. for literature, 1986–89. *Address:* 63 Luther Shaw Rd, Cummington, MA 01026, USA.

SMITH, Z. Z. See: WESTHEIMER, David.

SMITH, Zadie; b. 27 Oct. 1975, England. Writer; Poet. *Education:* King's College, Cambridge. *Appointment:* Writer-in-Residence, Institute of Contemporary Arts, London. *Publication:* White Teeth (novel), 2000. *Contributions to:* Anthologies and periodicals. *Honour:* Rylands Prize, King's College, London. *Address:* c/o Random House, 20 Vauxhall Bridge Rd, London SW1V 2SA, England.

SMITH-ZERVANOU, Denise; b. 11 March 1951, Athens, Greece. Poet; Ed.; Publisher. 1 d. *Education:* Degree, Honours, French and Greek Literature, Athens University, 1973; Degree, Honours, Philosophy and Psychology, 1979; DEA, Sorbonne, Paris, 1978. *Appointments:* Lecturer in French, Technology Higher University of Athens, 1976–77; Lecturer in Philosophy, University of Edinburgh, 1983–98; Ed., Understanding, 1989–98. *Publications:* The Stone Moon, 1997. Translator: Various Greek writers. *Contributions to:* Magazines and journals. *Address:* 20A Montgomery St, Edinburgh EH7 5JS, Scotland.

SMITHER, Elizabeth Edwina; b. 15 Sept. 1941, New Plymouth, New Zealand. Librarian; Poet. m. Michael Duncan Smither, 31 Aug. 1963. *Education:* University of Victoria and Massey University, 1960; New Zealand Library School, 1962. *Publications:* 12 collections, including: A Cortège of Daughters, 1993; The Tudor Style, 1993; The Lark Quartet, 1997. *Contributions to:* Newspapers, reviews, and literary magazines. *Honours:* Bursaries; Fellowships; New Zealand Book Award; Montana Book Award; Te Mata Poet Laureate, 2001–03. *Membership:* New Zealand Society of Authors. *Address:* 19a Mount View Pl., New Plymouth, New Zealand.

SMOCK, Frederick; b. 23 June 1954, USA. Ed.; Poet. m. Jacqueline Strange, 3 Sept. 1983, 2 s. *Education:* BA, Georgetown College, 1976; MA, University of Louisville, 1978. *Appointments:* Ed., The American Voice; Writer-in-Residence, Bellarmine College. *Publications:* The Muhammad Ali Poems, 1989; 12 Poems, 1991; This Meadow of Time: A Provence Journal, 1995; Garden Court: Poems, 1997. *Contributions to:* Poetry; Poet and Critic; Iowa Review; La Carta de Oliver; Boulevard; Green Mountains Review; Wind; Plainsong; Thinker Review. *Address:* 2267 Speed Ave, Louisville, KY 40205, USA.

SNEYD, Stephen Henry, (Steve Sneyd); b. 20 March 1941, Maidenhead, Berkshire, England. Poet; Writer. m. Rita Ann Cockburn, 13 March 1964, 1 s., 1 d. *Education:* MA; BSc; DipM; CertEd. *Appointments:* UK Columnist, Scavenger's Newsletter, USA, 1984–99; Contributing Ed. on Poetry, Fantasy Commentator magazine, USA, 1992–. *Publications:* The Legerdemain of Changelings, 1979; Two Humps Not One, 1980; Discourteous Self-Service, 1982; Prug Plac Gamma, 1983; Stone Bones (with Pete Presford), 1983; Fifty-Fifty Infinity, 1989; Bad News from the Stars, 1991; At the Thirteenth Hour, 1991; We Are Not Men, 1991; What Time Has Use For, 1992; A Mile Beyond the Bus, 1992; In Coils of Earthen Hold, 1994; A Reason for Staying, 1999; Gestaltmacher, Gestaltmacher, Make Me a Gestalt, 2000; NeoLithon (with John Light), 2001. *Contributions to:* Over 1,000 reviews, quarterlies, journals, and magazines, worldwide; Radio and television. *Honours:* Trend Prize for Peace Poetry, 1967; Northern Star Poetry Prize, 1983; Diploma di Merito, Accademia Italia, 1983; Best Poet, Small Press and Magazine Awards, 1986; Peterson Prize, 1996; First Prize, Starlife Poetry Contest, USA, 1999; Special Prize Diploma, International Cosmopoetry Festival of SARM, Romania, 1999. *Membership:* Science Fiction Poetry Asscn; National Asscn of Writers in Education. *Address:* 4 Nowell Pl., Almondbury, Huddersfield, West Yorkshire HD5 8PB, England.

SNIDER, Clifton M(ark); b. 3 March 1947, Duluth, Minnesota, USA. University Lecturer; Poet; Writer. *Education:* Southern California College, Costa Mesa, 1965–67; BA, cum laude, English, 1969, MA, English, 1971, California State University, Long Beach; PhD, English, University of New Mexico, 1974. *Appointments:* Faculty, California State University, Long Beach, 1974–, Long Beach City College, 1975–. *Publications:* Poetry: Jesse Comes Back, 1976; Bad Smoke Good Body, 1980; Jesse and His Son, 1982; Edwin: A Character in Poems, 1984; Blood & Bones, 1988; Impervious to Piranhas, 1989; The Age of the Mother, 1992; The Alchemy of Opposites, 2000. Other: The Stuff That Dreams Are Made On: A Jungian Interpretation of Literature, 1991; Loud Whisper (novel), 2000; Bare Roots (novel), 2001; Wrestling with Angels: A Tale of Two Brothers (novel), 2001. *Contributions to:* Anthologies, reviews, quarterlies, and journals. *Honours:* Resident Fellow, Yaddo, 1978, 1982, Helene Wurlitzer Foundation of New Mexico, 1984, 1990, 1998, Michael Karolyi Memorial Foundation, Vence, France, 1986, 1987. *Address:* 2719 Eucalyptus Ave, Long Beach, CA 90806, USA. *E-mail:* csnider@csulb.edu. *Website:* www.csulb.edu/~csnider.

SNODGRASS, W. D. (S. S. Gardons, Will McConnell, Kozma Prutkov); b. 5 Jan. 1926, Wilkinsburg, Pennsylvania, USA. Poet; Writer; Dramatist; m. (1) Lila Jean Hank, 6 June 1946, divorced Dec. 1953, 1 d., (2) Janice Marie Ferguson Wilson, 19 March 1954, divorced Aug. 1966, 1 s., (3) Camille Rykowski, 13 Sept. 1967, divorced 1978, (4) Kathleen Ann Brown, 20 June 1985. *Education:* Geneva College, 1943–44, 1946–47; BA, 1949, MA, 1951, MFA, 1953, University of Iowa. *Appointments:* Instructor in English, Cornell University, 1955–57; Instructor, University of Rochester, New York, 1957–58; Asst Prof. of English, Wayne State University, Detroit, 1959–67; Prof. of English and Speech, Syracuse University, New York, 1968–77; Visiting Prof., Old Dominion University, Norfolk, Virginia, 1978–79; Distinguished Prof., 1979–80, Distinguished Prof. of Creative Writing and Contemporary Poetry, 1980–94, University of Delaware, Newark; Various lectures and poetry readings. *Publications:* Poetry: Heart's Needle, 1959; After Experience, 1967; As S S Gardons, Remains: A Sequence of Poems, 1970; The Fuehrer Bunker, 1977; If Birds Build With Your Hair, 1979; D D Byrde Calling Jennie Wrenne, 1984; A Colored Poem, 1986; The House the Poet Built, 1986; A Locked House,

1986; The Kinder Capers, 1986; Selected Poems, 1957–87, 1987; W D's Midnight Carnival (with DeLoss McGraw), 1988; The Death of Cock Robin (with DeLoss McGraw), 1989; Each in His Season, 1994; The Fuehrer Bunker: The Complete Cycle, 1995. Essays: In Radical Pursuit, 1975; After-Images, 1999; To Sound Like Yourself: Essays on Poetry, 2002. Play: The Fuehrer Bunker, 1978. Other: Trans of songs; Selected Translations, 1998. Criticism: De/Compositions: 101 Good Poems Gone Wrong, 2001. *Contributions to:* Essays, reviews, poems to many periodicals. *Honours:* Ingram Merrill Foundation Award, 1958; Longview Foundation Literary Award, 1959; National Institute of Arts and Letters Grant, 1960; Pulitzer Prize in Poetry, 1960; Yaddo Resident Awards, 1960, 1961, 1965; Guinness Poetry Award, 1961; Ford Foundation Grant, 1963–64; National Endowment for the Arts Grant, 1966–67; Guggenheim Fellowship, 1972–73; Government of Romania Centennial Medal, 1977; Hon. DLitt, Allegheny College, 1991; Harold Morton Landon Trans. Award, Acad. of American Poets, 1999. *Memberships:* National Institute of Arts and Letters; Poetry Society of America; International PEN; American Acad. of Arts and Sciences; Marin Sorescu Foundation. *Address:* 3061 Hughes Rd, Erieville, NY 13061, USA.

SNUGGS, Olive, (Annie Hughes); b. 26 Nov. 1924, Coventry, Warwickshire, England. Poet; Writer. m. Frederic Eric Snuggs, 29 Jan. 1944, 1 s., 4 d. *Publications:* Beneath the Southern Cross. *Contributions to:* Anthologies, radio; journals, and magazines. *Honours:* Medallion, Poetry Day Australia, Melbourne Poetry Society; Several competitions. *Memberships:* Enfield Writers' Club; Fellowship of Australian Writers; Melbourne Poetry Society; South Australian Writers Centre; World Poetry Society; Writers Professional Services. *Address:* 6 Jacaranda Dr., Salisbury East, SA, Australia.

SNYDER, Gary (Sherman); b. 8 May 1930, San Francisco, CA, USA. Poet; Writer; Teacher. m., 2 s., 2 step-d. *Education:* BA, Reed College, Portland, Oregon, 1951; Graduate Studies in Linguistics, Indiana University, 1951; Graduate School, Dept of East Asian Languages, University of California, Berkeley, 1953–56; Studied Zen Buddhism and East Asian culture in Japan. *Appointment:* Faculty, University of California, Davis, 1986–. *Publications:* Poetry: Riprap and Cold Mountain Poems, 1959; Myths and Texts, 1960; A Range of Poems, 1966; Three Worlds, Three Realms, Six Roads, 1966; The Back Country, 1968; The Blue Sky, 1969; Regarding Wave, 1970; Manzanita, 1971; Plute Creek, 1972; The Fudo Trilogy: Spell Against Demons, Smokey the Bear Sutra, The California Water Plan, 1973; Turtle Island, 1974; All in the Family, 1975; Songs for Gaia, 1979; Axe Handles, 1983; Left Out in the Rain: New Poems, 1947–1986, 1986; The Practice of the Wild, 1990; No Nature: New and Selected Poems, 1992; Mountains and Rivers Without End, 1996. Prose: Earth House Hold: Technical Notes and Queries to Fellow Dharma Revolutionaries, 1969; The Old Ways: Six Essays, 1977; He Who Hunted Birds in His Father's Village: The Dimensions of a Haida Myth, 1979; The Real Work: Interviews and Talks, 1964–1979, 1980; Passage Through India, 1984; A Place in Space, 1995. *Contributions to:* Anthologies. *Honours:* Scholarship, First Zen Institute of America, 1956; American Acad. of Arts and Letters Award, 1966; Bollingen Foundation Grant, 1966–67; Frank O'Hara Prize, 1967; Levinson Prize, 1968; Guggenheim Fellowship, 1968–69; Pulitzer Prize in Poetry, 1975; Finalist, National Book Award, 1992. *Memberships:* American Acad. of Arts and Letters; American Acad. of Arts and Sciences. *Address:* 18442 Macnab Cypress Rd, Nevada City, CA 95959, USA.

SO SHUN. See: WAI MING (OTIS) WONG.

SOCOLOW, Elizabeth Anne; b. 15 June 1940, New York, NY, USA. Teacher; Poet. m. Robert Socolow, 10 June 1962, divorced 1982, 2 s. *Education:* BA, Vassar College, 1962; MA, 1963, PhD, 1967, Harvard College. *Appointments:* Lecturer, Yale University, 1967–70, Rutgers University, 1981–82; High School Teacher, 1986–88, 1990–91, 1992–; Lecturer in Poetry, Bernard and Vassar Colleges, 1988–90; Adjunct Lecturer in English, University of Michigan, Wayne State University, Lawrence Technological Institute, 1992–; Poetry Ed., Delodings. *Publication:* Laughing at Gravity: Conversations with Isaac Newton, 1988. *Contributions to:* Ploughshares; Poetry East; New England Quarterly; Wayzgoose; The Bridge. *Honours:* Barnard Women's Poetry Series Winner, 1987; Honorable Mentions, Nimrod, 1987, 1990. *Memberships:* MLA; Princeton Research Forum; Society for Literature and Science; US Poets and Writers Co-operative, founding mem. and consultant. *Address:* 29550 Franklin Rd, No. 228, Southfield, MI 48034, USA.

SOERENSEN, Preben Major; b. 14 April 1937, Copenhagen, Denmark. Author; Poet. *Appointment:* Co-Ed., Epoke literary magazine, 1983–85. *Publications:* Ildmesteren, 1965; Vandmandens gilde, 1967; Alfabetets herre, 1970; I vinden begynder samtalerne, 1973; Af en engels erindringer, 1976; Salvatore l'Enigmatico, 1976; Droemmefaengsler, 1978; Genkaldslser, 1980; Nenia, 1981; Rappaccinis have, 1983; Riget uden graenser, 1984; Vilfarelsen og andre fortaellinger, 1985; Skraemmebilleder, 1986; Ansigter og masker, 1987; Soevnen og skyggerne, 1987; Mishandlinger, 1988; Personlige grunde og afgrunde, 1991; Bevaegelser i Moerket 1993; Faldgréber, 1999; Oeksens lyd, 2002. *Contributions to:* Argo; Strand; Gyldendals Magasin; Hvedekorn; Ta; Faelleden; Luftskibet; Continent Scandinavia; Politiken; Jyllands Posten; Epoke; Kriterium; Kritik; Graf; Passage. *Honours:* Three-year fellowship for creative work; Holger Drachmann Prize; Sophus Michaelis Mindelegat;

Herman Bangs Mindelegat; Beatrice Prize; Henrik Pontoppidans Mindelegat; Henrik Nathansens Foedsels-dagslegat; Aage Barfoeds og Frank Lénds legat. *Membership:* Danske skoenlitteraere forfattere. *Address:* Hovvej 2, 5953 Tranekaer, Denmark.

SOHAIL, Khalid; b. 9 July 1952, Pakistan. Psychiatrist; Writer; Poet. *Education:* MBBS, Pakistan, 1974; FRCP(C), Canada, 1982. *Publications:* Discovering New Highways in Life, 1991; From One Culture to Another, 1992; Literary Encounters, 1992; Pages of My Heart (poems), 1993; A Broken Man (stories), 1993; Mother Earth is Sad (fiction), 1999; Encounters With Creativity, Insanity and Spirituality, 1999. *Contributions to:* Anthologies and journals. *Honours:* Rahul Award, Calcutta, 1994. *Memberships:* Fellow, Royal College of Physicians and Surgeons, Canada; Writers' Forum of Canada; Writers' Union of Canada. *Address:* PH6 100 White Oaks Ct, Whitby, ON L1P 1B7, Canada.

SOLANKI, Mahendra; b. 20 April 1956, Nairobi, Kenya. Educator; Poet. m. Hilary Frances Reed, 8 Aug. 1986, 2 d. *Education:* BA, Honours, English, Philosophy, Middlesex Polytechnic, England, 1979. *Publications:* Shadows of My Making: Poems, 1986; Teaching South Asian Literature in Secondary Schools (co-author), 1986; What You Left Behind (poems), 1996; Exercises in Trust, 2001. *Contributions to:* Bazaar; Multicultural Teaching; Other Poetry; Foreword; Leicester Mercury; Others. *Honours:* Major Writers Bursary, 1991–92. *Address:* 73 Lansdowne Rd, Leicester LE2 8AS, England.

SOLEIMANI, Faramarz, (Maziar Aram, F. Bidel, Moj); b. 25 Oct. 1940, Iran. Physician; Poet. m. Mina Atghai, 31 March 1967, 1 s., 2 d. *Education:* MD, Tehran University Medical School, 1967; Anesthesiologist, Mount Sinai Medical School, City University of New York, 1972; Obstetrician and Gynecologist, Hahnman University, Philadelphia, 1975; Obstetric Anesthesiologist, Mount Sinai Medical School, 1993. *Publications:* Lines and Points, 1980; Silently, 1980; Blue Songs, 1980; Reveries, 1988; Persian Songs, 1988; Through Red Throat of Sohrab, 1990; Nimais (The Sea Sings With Nima's Accent), 1995; Havet Sjunger Med Nimas Britning (Swedish), 1997; Gasht-e Dasht, 1999; Nocturnes of Rockgarden, 1999; Green, White and Red, 1999; Nima and Wave and the Sea, 1999; Night of Reveries, 2002. *Contributions to:* Adineh; Donya-Ye Sokhan; Ferdowsi; Bamdad; Fasl-E Gorgan; Iran Honar; Simorgh; Shahrvand; Shenakht; New Censure; Negin; Khat; Roya; Aftab; Assar; Karnameh; Persian Heritage. *Honours:* Ed.'s Choice Award, International Library of Poetry; International Society of Scholars, Hon. Pres., 1998–99. *Memberships:* Iranian Writers Asscn; Iranian Cultural Society, Washington, DC; Seh Shanbeth Literary Group; World Asscn of Medical Eds. *Address:* PO Box 10484, Burke, VA 22009, USA.

SOLER, Dona K.; b. 7 March 1921, Grand Rapids, MI, USA. Poet; Author; Researcher; Artist. 1 d. *Publications:* Several poems, including: What God Hath Put Together; Our Heritage From the Angels; Expose the Dirty Devil; For Love of Henry; Greyball; House of Evil Secrets; Treasure Book of Poetry 1 and 2. *Contributions to:* Anthologies, 1982–2000, including: Our 20th Century's Greatest Poets, Contemporary Poets of America, Whispers in the Wind, Outstanding Poets, 1994–98, Interludes, Whispers, Meditations, Outstanding Poetry Achievements, Moments, Keepsakes, Feelings, Collections, Best of Quill, By the Light of the Moon, American Poetry Annual, Sensations, A Time to be Free, The Road Song, Celebrating the New Millennium, Etchings, Promises, Verses Magazine. *Honours:* First Place Poetry Prizes, World of Poetry, 1991, 1992, 1993; Finalist Award for Poetry, Poetry Acad., 1993; Award, International Society of Poets, 1994; Award, Redwood Acres Fair, 1995–96; Longfellows Literary Award, 1996; Award, Iliad Press Environmental Competition, 1997; Presidential Award for Literary Excellence, The National Authors' Registry, 1997, 1998, 1999 2000. *Address:* 2604 Willo Lane, Costa Mesa, CA 92607, USA.

SOLEYA, Donya. See: STORHOFF, Diana Faye Carmack.

SOLNICKI, Jill Louise Newman; b. 27 March 1945, Toronto, Ontario, Canada. Writer; Poet; Teacher. m. Victor Solnicki, 27 June 1971, 1 s., 1 d. *Education:* BA, University of Toronto, 1966. *Publications:* This Mortal Coil; The Real Me is Gonna Be a Shock: Year in the Life of a Front-line Teacher, 1992. *Contributions to:* Atlantis; Grain; Fiddlehead; Toronto Life; Dandelion; Antigonish Review; Room of Ones Own; New Quarterly; Quarry; Anthology of Magazine Verse and Yearbook of American Poetry. *Memberships:* League of Canadian Poets; Writers' Union of Canada. *Address:* 53 Hillholm Rd, Toronto, Ontario M5P 1M4, Canada.

SOLWAY, David; b. 8 Dec. 1941, Montréal, QC, Canada. Poet; Writer; Trans.; University Lecturer. m. Karin Semmler, 23 April 1980, 1 d. *Education:* BA, 1962, QMA, 1966, McGill University; MA, Concordia University, 1988; MA, University of Sherbrooke, 1996; PhD, Lajos Kossuth University, 1998. *Appointments:* Lecturer in English Literature, McGill University, 1966–67; Dawson College, 1970–71; John Abbot College, 1971–99; Writer-in-Residence, Concordia University 1999–2000; Several visiting university lectureships. *Publications:* Poetry: In My Own Image, 1962; The Crystal Theatre, 1971; Paximalia, 1972; The Egyptian Airforce and Other Poems, 1973; The Road to Arginos, 1976; Anacrusis, 1976; Mephistopheles and the Astronaut, 1979; The

Mulberry Men, 1982; Selected Poetry, 1982; Stones in Winter, 1983; Modern Marriage, 1987; Bedrock, 1993; Chess Pieces, 1999; The Lover's Progress, 2001; The Properties of Things, 2001. Other: Four Montreal Poets (ed.), 1973; Education Lost: Reflections on Contemporary Pedagogical Practice, 1989; The Anatomy of Arcadia, 1992; Lying About the Wolf: Essays in Culture and Education, 1997; Random Walks: Essays in Elective Criticism, 1997; Saracen Island: The Poems of Andreas Karavis (trans.), 2000; An Andreas Karavis Companion, 2000; The Turtle Hypodermic of Sickenpods: Liberal Studies in the Corporate Age, 2001. *Contributions to:* Many anthologies, reviews, quarterlies and journals, including: The Atlantic Monthly; International Journal of Applied Semiotics; Journal of Modern Greek Studies; Canadian Notes and Queries; Books on Canada; The Sewanee Review. *Honours:* QSPELL Award for Poetry, 1988, and for Non-Fiction, 1990; Various Canada Council Grants. *Memberships:* Canadian Writer's Union; International PEN; Union des écrivaines et écrivains québécois. *Address:* 143 Upper McNaughton, Hudson, QC J0P 1H0, Canada.

SOLZHENITSYN, Aleksandr (Isayevich); b. 11 Dec. 1918, Kislovodsk, Russia. Writer; Poet. m. (1) Natalya Reshetovskaya, 27 April 1940, divorced, (2) 1956, divorced 1972, (3) Natalya Svetlova, April 1973, 3 s., 1 step-s. *Education:* Correspondence course in Philology, Moscow Institute of History, Philosophy, and Literature, 1939–41; Degree in Mathematics and Physics, University of Rostock, 1941. *Appointments:* Writer as a youth; Secondary School Teacher; Commander, Soviet Army during World War II; Held in prisons and labour camp, 1945–53; Exiled as a teacher, Kok-Terek, Kazakhstan, 1953–56; Teacher, Mathematics and Physics, Riazan; Exiled from Soviet Union, 1974–94. *Publications:* One Day in the Life of Ivan Denisovich (novella), 1962; For the Good of the Cause (novella), 1963; We Never Make Mistakes (novel), 1963; The First Circle (novel), 1968; Cancer Ward (novel), 2 vols, 1968–69; The Love Girl and the Innocent (play), 1969; Candle in the Wind (play), 1969; The Rights of the Writer, 1969; The Red Wheel (novel cycle), 1971–, including August 1914, October 1916, March 1917, April 1917; Stories and Prose Poems by Aleksandr Solzhenitsyn, 1971; Six Etudes by Aleksandr Solzhenitsyn, 1971; Nobel Lecture by Aleksandr Solzhenitsyn, 1972; A Lenten Letter to Pimen, Patriarch of All Russia, 1972; The Gulag Archipelago, 1918–1956: An Experiment in Literary Investigation, 3 vols, 1974, 1976, 1979; Peace and Violence, 1974; Prussian Nights: Epic Poems Written at the Forced Labor Camp, 1950, 1974; Letter to the Soviet Leaders, 1974; Solzhenitsyn: A Pictorial Autobiography, 1974; The Oak and the Calf (memoir), 1975; Lenin in Zürich, 1975; American Speeches, 1975; From Under the Rubble (with others), 1975; Warning to the West, 1976; A World Split Apart, 1979; The Mortal Danger, 1981; Victory Celebrations: A Comedy in Four Acts and Prisoners: A Tragedy (plays), 1983; Rebuilding Russia: Towards Some Formulations, 1991; The Russian Question Toward the End of the Century, 1995; November 1916: The Red Wheel, Knot 11, 1999. *Honours:* Prix du Meilleur Livre Étranger, France, 1969; Nobel Prize for Literature, 1970; Freedoms Foundation Award, Stanford University, 1976; Many hon. degrees. *Membership:* American Acad. of Arts and Sciences. *Address:* c/o Farrar, Straus & Giroux, 19 Union Sq. W, New York, NY 10003, USA.

SOMARY, Wolfgang; b. 30 July 1932, Zürich, Switzerland. Banker; Poet. m. Gabriela Hennig, 23 Aug. 1958, 2 s., 2 d. *Education:* BA, 1954, MA, 1956, Economics and Political Science, Trinity College, Dublin. *Contributions to:* Anthologies and periodicals. *Memberships:* East India Club, England; Poetry Society, England. *Address:* 62 Gallery Loft, Hopton St, London SE1 9JL, England.

SOMERVILLE, Yvonne. See: MCCLOSKEY, Phil(omena Mary).

SOMLYO, György; b. 28 Nov. 1920, Balatonboglar, Hungary. Writer; Poet. Divorced, 1988, 1 s. *Education:* University of Budapest, 1945–46; Sorbonne, University of Paris, 1947–48. *Appointments:* Dir, Literary Section, Radio Budapest, 1954–55, Arion magazine, 1966–87. *Publications:* 17 books, including novels, poems, and essays, 1977–96. *Contributions to:* Various publications. *Honours:* Many, including: József Attila Prize; Hungarian Writers Asscn Prize; Officier de l'Ordre des Arts et des Lettres, France. *Memberships:* Acad. of Literature and Arts; Asscn of Hungarian Writers; Hungarian PEN. *Address:* Irinyi 3 u 39, Budapest 111, Hungary.

SOMOZA, Joseph Manuel; b. 30 Oct. 1940, Spain. Poet; Prof.; Ed. m. Jill Rosmarie Eggena, 15 June 1963, 2 s., 1 d. *Education:* BA, English, University of Cincinnati, 1963; MA, English, Roosevelt University, 1966; MFA, Creative Writing, University of Iowa, 1973. *Appointments:* Instructor, Texas Western College, 1966–68; Colegio Regional de Cayey, Puerto Rico, 1969–71; Instructor, Asst Prof., and Assoc. Prof., English, New Mexico State University, 1973–95. *Publications:* Greyhound, 1968; Olive Women, 1976; Backyard Poems, 1986; Out of this World, 1990; Sojourner, So To Speak, 1997. *Contributions to:* Beloit Poetry Review; Bloomsbury Review; Blue Mesa Review; Colorado State Review; Floating Island; Greenfield Review; Hanging Loose; Maryland Poetry Review; Rocky Mountain Review; Sou'Wester; Sumac; Three Rivers Poetry Journal; Z Miscellaneous; Writers' Forum; Hammers. *Honour:* Authors of the Pass, El Paso Writers Hall of Fame, 1998. *Membership:* Poets and Writers. *Address:* 1725 Hamiel Dr., Las Cruces, NM 88001, USA.

SONG, Cathy; b. 20 Aug. 1955, Honolulu, HI, USA. Poet; Writer; Teacher. m. Douglas M Davenport, 19 July 1979. *Education:* University of Hawaii at Manoa; BA in English Literature, Wellesley College, 1977; MA in Creative Writing, Boston University, 1981. *Appointments:* Teacher of Poetry, HI, 1987–; Associated with Poets in the Schools programme. *Publications:* Picture Bridge, 1983; Frameless Windows, Squares of Light, 1988; Sister Stew (ed. with Juliet S Kono), 1991; School Figures, 1994. *Contributions to:* Various anthologies and journals. *Honours:* Yale Series of Younger Poets Prize, 1983; Frederick Book Prize for Poetry, 1986; Cades Award for Literature, 1988; Hawaii Award for Literature, 1993; Shelley Memorial Award, Poetry Society of America, 1993. *Address:* PO Box 27262 Honolulu, HI 96827, USA.

SONIAT, Katherine; b. 11 Jan. 1942, Washington, DC, USA. Asst Prof. of English; Poet. *Education:* BA, History, 1964; MA, English, 1984. *Appointments:* Assoc. Prof., Hollins College, Roanoke, Virginia, 1988–90; Asst Prof. of English, Virginia Polytechnic Institute and State University, Blacksburg, 1990–. *Publications:* Notes of Departure, 1985; Winter Toys, 1989; Cracking Eggs, 1990; A Shared Life, 1994. *Contributions to:* Nation; New Republic; Poetry; Kenyon Review; Antioch Review; American Scholar; North American Review; Southern Review; Iowa Review. *Honours:* Cameden Poetry Prize, Walt Whitman Center for the Arts, 1985; Bread Loaf Writers Conference Fellowship, Middlebury College, 1987; Virginia Prize for Poetry, 1989; Edwin Ford Piper Award, University of Iowa Press, 1994. *Memberships:* Acad. of American Poets; Associated Writing Programs. *Address:* Dept of English, Virginia Polytechnic Institute and State University, Blacksburg, VA 24061, USA.

SONNENFELD, Mark; b. 21 Feb. 1956, Newark, NJ, USA. Poet; Writer; Publisher. m. Maryann Approvato, 9 April 1983. *Publications:* 45 chapbooks, 17 audio sound collages. *Contributions to:* Several periodicals. *Address:* 45-08 Old Millstone Dr., East Windsor, NJ 08520, USA.

SONNEVI, Göran; b. 3 Oct. 1939, Lund, Sweden. Poet. m. Kerstin Kronkvist, 1961. *Education:* University of Lund, 1963. *Publications:* Outfört, 1961; Abstrakta dikter, 1963; Ingrepp-modeller, 1965; och nu!, 1967; Det måste gå, 1970; Det oavslutade språket, 1972; Dikter utan ordning, 1973; Det omöjliga, 1975; Språk; Verktyg; Eld, 1979; Små klanger; en röst, 1981; The Economy Spinning Faster and Faster: Poems (in English), 1982; Oavslutade dikter, 1987; Trädet, 1991; A Child is Not a Knife: Selected Poems of Göran Sonnevi (in English), 1993; Mozarts Tredje Hjärna, 1996; Klangernas bok, 1998. *Address:* c/o Swedish Writers Union, PO Box 3157, Drottninggatan 88B, 103 63 Stockholm, Sweden.

SONTAG, Susan; b. 16 Jan. 1933, New York, NY, USA. Writer; Poet; Dramatist. m. Philip Rieff, 1950, divorced 1958, 1 s. *Education:* BA, University of Chicago, 1951; MA, English, 1954, MA, Philosophy, 1955, Harvard University. *Publications:* The Benefactor (novel), 1963; Against Interpretation (essays), 1966; Death Kit (novel), 1967; Trip to Hanoi (essays), 1968; Styles of Radical Will (essays), 1969; On Photography (essays), 1977; Illness as Metaphor (essays), 1978; I, etcetera (stories), 1978; Under the Sign of Saturn (essays), 1980; A Sontag Reader, 1982; AIDS and Its Metaphors (essays), 1989; The Way We Live Now (story), 1991; The Volcano Lover: A Romance, 1992; Alice in Bed: A Play, 1993; Under the Sign of Saturn (poems), 1996; In America (novel), 2000; Women (with Annie Liebowitz), 2000; Where the Stress Falls (essays), 2001. *Contributions to:* Various publications. *Honours:* Rockefeller Foundation Fellowships, 1965, 1974; Guggenheim Fellowships, 1966, 1975; National Book Critics Circle Award, 1978; Officier de l'Ordre des Arts et des Lettres, France, 1984; John D. and Catherine T. MacArthur Foundation Fellowship, 1990–95; Malaparte Prize, Italy, 1992; Hon. doctorates, Columbia University, 1993, Harvard University, 1993; Montblanc Cultural Achievement Award, 1994; National Book Award for Fiction, 2000; Jerusalem Prize, 2001. *Memberships:* American Acad. of Arts and Letters; PEN American Center, pres., 1987–89. *Address:* 250 W 57th St, Suite 2114, New York, NY 10107, USA.

SOO, William. See: KIM, Unsong.

SORESTAD, Glen Allan; b. 21 May 1937, Vancouver, BC, Canada. Writer; Poet. m. Sonia Diane Talpash, 17 Sept. 1960, 3 s., 1 d. *Education:* BEd, 1963, MEd, 1976, University of Saskatchewan. *Appointments:* Elementary School Teacher, 1957–69; Senior English Teacher, 1969–81; Pres., Thistledown Press, 1975–2000. *Publications:* Hold the Rain in Your Hands: Poems Selected and New, 1985; Birchbark Meditations, 1996; West into Night, 1991; Icons of Flesh, 1998; Today I Belong to Agnes, 2000; Leaving Holds Me Here: Selected Poems, 1975–2000, 2001. *Contributions to:* Numerous newspapers, journals, magazines and periodicals. *Honours:* SWG Founders Award; First Poet Laureate of Saskatchewan, 2000. *Memberships:* Asscn of Canadian Publishers; League of Canadian Poets, life mem.; Candian Poetry Asscn; Saskatchewan Writers' Guild; Writers' Union of Canada. *Address:* 108–835 Heritage Green, Saskatoon, SK S7H 5S5, Canada. *E-mail:* g.sorestad@sk.sympatico.ca.

SORRENTINO, Gilbert; b. 27 April 1929, New York, NY, USA. Novelist; Poet; Prof. of English. m. (1) Elsene Wiessner, divorced, (2) Vivian V. Ortiz, 3 c. *Education:* Brooklyn College, 1950–51, 1955–57. *Appointments:* Ed., Publisher, Neon Magazine, New York City, 1956–60; Ed., Grove Press, New York City, 1965–70; Teacher, Columbia University, 1965, Aspen Writers Workshop, 1967 Sarah Lawrence College, 1971–72, New School for Social Research, New York City, 1976–79; Edwin S Quain Prof. of Literature, University of Scranton, 1979 Prof. of English, Stanford University, 1982–99, Emeritus Prof., 1999– *Publications:* Fiction: The Sky Changes, 1966; Steelwork, 1970; Imaginative Qualities of Actual Things, 1971; Splendide-Hotel, 1973; Mulligan Stew, 1979 Aberration of Starlight, 1980; Crystal Vision, 1981; Blue Pastoral, 1983; Odd Number, 1985; Rose Theatre, 1987; Misterioso, 1989; Under the Shadow, 1991 Red the Fiend, 1995; Gold Fools, 2001; Little Casino, 2002. Poetry: The Darkness Surrounds Us, 1960; Black and White, 1964; The Perfect Fiction 1968; Corrosive Sublimate, 1971; A Dozen Oranges, 1976; White Sail, 1977; The Orangery, 1977; Selected Poems, 1958–1980, 1981. Essays: Something Said 1984. Play: Flawless Play Restored: The Masque of Fungo, 1974. Translator Sulpiciae Elegidia/Elegiacs of Sulpicia: Gilbert Sorrentino Versions, 1977 *Contributions to:* Various anthologies and periodicals. *Honours:* Guggenheim Fellowships, 1973–74, 1987–88; Samuel S Fels Award, 1974; Creative Artists Public Service Grant, 1974–75; Ariadne Foundation Grant, 1975; National Endowment for the Arts Grants, 1975–76, 1978–79, 1983–84; John Dos Passos Prize, 1981; Mildred and Harold Strauss Livings, 1982 (declined); American Acad. and Institute of Arts and Letters Award, 1985; Lannan Literary Award for Fiction, 1992. *Membership:* PEN American Center. *Address:* Dept of English, Stanford University, Stanford, CA 94305, USA.

SOTO, Gary; b. 12 April 1952, Fresno, CA, USA. Writer; Poet. m. Carolyn Sadako Oda, 24 May 1975, 1 d. *Education:* BA, California State University at Fresno, 1974; MFA, University of California at Irving, 1976. *Appointments:* Asst Prof., 1979–85, Assoc. Prof. of English and Ethnic Studies, 1985–92, Part-time Senior Lecturer in English, 1992–93, University of California at Berkeley; Elliston Prof. of Poetry, University of Cincinnati, 1988; Martin Luther King/ Cesar Chavez/Rosa Park Visiting Prof. of English, Wayne State University, 1990. *Publications:* Poetry: The Elements of San Joaquin, 1977; The Tale of Sunlight, 1978; Where Sparrows Work Hard, 1981; Black Hair, 1985; Who Will Know Us?, 1990; A Fire in My Hands, 1990; Home Course in Religion, 1992; Neighborhood Odes, 1992; Canto Familiar/Familiar Song, 1994; New and Selected Poems, 1995; Fearless Fernie, 2002. Other: Living Up the Street: Narrative Recollections, 1985; Small Faces, 1986; Lesser Evils: Ten Quartets, 1988; California Childhood: Recollections and Stories of the Golden State (ed.), 1988; A Summer Life, 1990; Baseball in April and Other Stories, 1990; Taking Sides, 1991; Pacific Crossing, 1992; The Skirt, 1992; Pieces of the Heart: New Chicano Fiction (ed.), 1993; Local News, 1993; The Pool Party, 1993; Crazy Weekend, 1994; Jesse, 1994; Boys at Work, 1995; Chato's Kitchen, 1995; Everyday Seductions (ed.), 1995; Summer on Wheels, 1995; The Old Man and His Door, 1996; Snapshots of the Wedding, 1996; Buried Onions, 1997; Nickel and Dime (novel), 2000; Poetry Lover (novel), 2001; Jessie De La Cruz: A Profile of a United Farm Worker (young adult biography), 2002; The Effects of Knut Hamsun on a Fresno Boy (essays), 2002; If the Shoe Fits (picture book), 2002. *Contributions to:* Magazines. *Honours:* Acad. of American Poets Prize, 1975; Discovery/The Nation Prize, 1975; United States Award, International Poetry Forum, 1976; Bess Hokin Prize for Poetry, 1978; Guggenheim Fellowship, 1979–80; National Endowment for the Arts Fellowships, 1981, 1991; Levinson Award, Poetry Magazine, 1984; American Book Award, Before Columbus Foundation, 1985; California Arts Council Fellowship, 1989; Carnegie Medal, 1993; Thomas Rivera Prize, 1996; Hispanic Heritage Award, 1999; Civil Rights Award, National Education Asscn, 1999. *Address:* 43 The Crescent, Berkeley, CA 94708, USA.

SOUSTER, (Holmes) Raymond, (John Holmes); b. 15 Jan. 1921, Toronto, Ontario, Canada. Writer; Poet. m. Rosalia L Geralde, 24 June 1947. *Education:* University of Toronto Schools, 1932–37; Humberside Collegiate Institute, 1938–39. *Publications:* 100 Poems of 19th Century Canada (ed. with D Lochhead), 1974; Sights and Sounds (ed. with R Wollatt), 1974; These Loved, These Hated Lands (ed. with R Wollatt), 1974; The Poetry of W W Campbell (ed.), 1978; The Best-Known Poems of Archibald Lampman (ed.), 1979; Collected Poems of Raymond Souster, 8 vols, 1980–93; Powassan's Drum: Selected Poems of Duncan Campbell Scott (ed. with D Lochhead), 1983; Queen City: Toronto in Poems and Pictures (with Bill Brooks), 1984; Windflower: The Selected Poems of Bliss Carmen (ed. with D Lochhead), 1986; Riding the Long Black Horse, 1993; Old Bank Notes, 1993; No Sad Songs Wanted Here, 1995; Close to Home, 1997; Of Time and Toronto, 2000. *Contributions to:* Magazines. *Honours:* Governor-General's Award for Poetry in English, 1964; Pres.'s Medal, University of Western Ontario, 1967; Centennial Medal, 1967; City of Toronto Book Award, 1979; Silver Jubilee Medal, 1977; Officer of the Order of Canada, 1995. *Membership:* League of Canadian Poets, founding mem. and chair., 1968–72, life mem., 1996–. *Address:* 39 Baby Point Rd, Toronto, Ontario M6S 2G2, Canada.

SOUTHGATE, Christopher Charles Benedict; b. 26 Sept. 1953, Exeter, Devon. Poet; Ed. m. Sandra Joyce Mitchell, 23 June 1981, 1 step-s. *Education:* BA, Honours, Natural Sciences, 1974, MA, PhD, Biochemistry, 1978, University of Cambridge; GMC, South-West Ministerial Training Course, Exeter, 1991. *Publications:* Landscape or Land?, 1989; Annotations, 1991; Stonechat – Ten Devon Poets, 1992; A Love and Its Sounding: Explorations of T S Eliot, 1997; Beyond the Bitter Wind: Poems 1982–2000. *Contributions to:* Envoi; Nexus; Otter; Pen; Prospice; Westwords; Encounter; Outposts; South

Coast Poetry Journal; Crucible; Christian; Company of Poets Anthologies; Collins New Christian Poetry; Critical Survey; Oxford Magazine; Fire; Connections; Swansea Review; Coffee House; Interpreter's House. *Honours:* South West Arts Literature Award, 1985; Iolaire Arts Prize, 1987; Sidmouth Arts Festival Prize, 1991; Southwest Open Poetry Commendation, 1991; Templeton Foundation Award, 1996; Hawthornden Fellowship, 1999. *Memberships:* Poetry Society; Company of Poets; Friends of Arvon Foundation; Society of Authors. *Address:* Parford Cottage, Chagford, Devon TQ13 8JR, England.

SOYINKA, Wole (Akinwande Oluwole); b. 13 July 1934, Isara, Nigeria. Poet; Dramatist; Writer; Prof. *Education:* University of Ibadan; BA, University of Leeds, 1959. *Appointments:* Research Fellow in Drama, 1960–61, Chair., Dept of Theatre Arts, 1969–72, University of Ibadan; Lecturer in English, 1962–63, Prof. in Dramatic Literature, 1972, Prof. of Comparative Literature, 1976–85, University of Ife; Senior Lecturer in English, University of Lagos, 1965–67; Political prisoner, 1967–69; Fellow, Churchill College, Cambridge, 1973–74; Goldwin Smith Prof. of Africana Studies and Theatre, Cornell University, 1988–92; Exiled by the Nigerian military government, 1995. *Publications:* Poetry: Idanre and Other Poems, 1967; Poems from Prison, 1969, revised edn as A Shuttle in the Crypt, 1972; Ogun Abibiman, 1976; Mandela's Earth and Other Poems, 1989. Plays: The Invention, 1955; A Dance of the Forests, 1960; Longi's Harvest, 1966; The Trials of Brother Jero, 1967; The Strong Breed, 1967; Madmen and Specialists, 1970; Before the Blackout, 1971; Camwood on the Leaves, 1973; Collected Plays, 2 vols, 1973, 1974; Death and the King's Horseman, 1975; Opera Wonyosi, 1981; A Play of Giants, 1984; Six Plays, 1984; Requiem for a Futurologist, 1985; From Zia with Love, 1992; A Scourge of Hyacinths, 1992; The Beatification of Area Boy, 1995. Fiction: The Interpreters, 1965; Season of Anomy, 1973. Other: The Man Died: Prison Notes of Wole Soyinka, 1972; Myth, Literature and the African World, 1976; Ake: The Years of Childhood (autobiography), 1981; Art, Dialogue and Outrage, 1988; Isara: A Voyage Around 'Essay', 1989; Ibadan: The Pentelemes Years (memoir), 1994; The Open Sore of a Continent: A Personal Narrative of the Nigerian Crisis, 1996; The Burden of Memory: The Muse of Forgiveness, 1999; Conversations with Wole Soyinka (ed. by Biodun Jeyifo), 2001. Editor: Plays from the Third World: An Anthology, 1971; Poems of Black Africa, 1975. *Honours:* Rockefeller Foundation Grant, 1960; John Whiting Drama Prize, 1966; Jock Campbell Award, 1968; Nobel Prize for Literature, 1986; Distinguished Scholar-in-Residence, New York University, 1999. *Memberships:* International Theatre Institute; Union of Writers of the African Peoples; National Liberation Council of Nigeria. *Address:* c/o Random House Inc, 201 E 50th St, 22nd Floor, New York, NY 10022, USA.

SPAHIU, Xhevahir; b. 1 March 1945, Malind, Skrapar, Albania. Writer; Poet. m. Marjeta Qejvani, 15 July 1972, 2 s. *Education:* University of Tirana. *Publications:* Several poems, 1970–96. *Contributions to:* Anthologies including: An Elusive Eagle Soars, 1993; Anthologie de la poesie albenaise, 1998. *Honours:* NAIM FRASHERI, Order II, 1982; Awards, MIGJENI, 1987, 1991; First Place, Literature National Competition, 1989; Literature National Award, 1994; Velia, National Literary Award, 1996; Winner, National Songs Festivals on Radiotelevision, 1976, 1979, 1989, 1995. *Memberships:* Writers' and Artists' League of Albania, Sec.-Gen., 1993–98, Chair., 1998–; Albanian Helsinki Committee, 1997. *Address:* Dhe Artisteye, Tirana, Albania.

SPANGLE, Douglas Stewart; b. 8 Feb. 1951, Roanoke, Virginia, USA. Ed.; Reviewer; Trans.; Poet. 1 d. *Education:* University of Maryland, Munich Campus, 1968–71; Nicolet Community College, Rhinelander, Wisconsin, 1977–78. *Appointments:* Assoc. Ed., Moose Magazine, 1980–82; Moderator, Poetry/Talk radio programme, 1982–86; Board Mem., Portland Poetry Festival, 1986–88; Assoc. Ed., 1992–95, Senior Ed., 1995–, Rain City Review; Advisory Ed., Anodyne, 1998–99. *Publications:* Homespun: A Tribute to Mary Barnard (ed.), 1994; Initial (poems), 1996; Suite: Lost Things (poems), 1997; Bread and Wine (trans. of Friedrich Hölderlin's Brot und Wein), 1997; 2½ Bridges (poems), 1999; Perseus Pursuing (poem), 2002. *Contributions to:* Anthologies, reviews, and magazines. *Address:* 1304 SE 50th, Portland, OR 97215, USA. *E-mail:* spangle@pdxmex.com.

SPARK, Dame Muriel (Sarah); b. 1 Feb. 1918, Edinburgh, Scotland. Author; Poet. m. S O Spark, 1937, diss, 1 s. *Education:* Heriot Watt College, Edinburgh. *Appointments:* Political Intelligence Dept, British Foreign Office, 1944–45; General Secretary, Poetry Society, 1947–49; Ed., The Poetry Review, 1947–49; Founder, Forum literary magazine. *Publications:* Fiction: The Comforters, 1957; Robinson, 1958; The Go-Away Bird and Other Stories, 1958; Memento Mori, 1959; The Ballad of Peckham Rye, 1960; The Bachelors, 1960; Voices at Play, 1961; The Prime of Miss Jean Brodie, 1961; The Girls of Slender Means, 1963; The Mandelbaum Gate, 1965; Collected Stories I, 1967; The Public Image, 1968; The Very Fine Clock (for children), 1969; The Driver's Seat, 1970; Not to Disturb, 1971; The Hothouse by the East River, 1973; The Abbess of Crewe, 1974; The Takeover, 1976; Territorial Rights, 1979; Loitering with Intent, 1981; Bang-Bang You're Dead and Other Stories, 1982; The Only Problem, 1984; The Stories of Muriel Spark, 1985; A Far Cry from Kensington, 1988; Symposium, 1990; The French Window and the Small Telephone (for children), 1993; Omnibus 1, 1993; Omnibus ll, 1994; Reality and Dreams, 1996; Omnibus III, 1996; Omnibus IV, 1997; Aiding and Abetting,

2000; The Complete Short Stories of Muriel Spark, 2001. Poetry: The Fanfarlo and Other Verse, 1952; Collected Poems l, 1967; Going Up to Sotheby's and Other Poems, 1982. Play: Doctors of Philosophy, 1962. Non-Fiction: Child of Light: A Reassessment of Mary Wollstonecraft Shelley, 1951, revised edn as Mary Shelley, 1987; John Masefield, 1953; Curriculum Vitae (autobiography), 1992; The Essence of the Brontës, 1993. Editor: 1950; Selected Poems of Emily Brontë, 1952; The Bronte Letters, 1954. *Honours:* Prix Italia, 1962; Fellow, RSL, 1963; Yorkshire Post Book of the Year Award, 1965; James Tait Black Memorial Prize, 1966; Hon. doctorates, University of Strathclyde, 1971, University of Edinburgh, 1989, University of Aberdeen, 1995, Heriot-Watt University, 1995, University of St Andrews, 1998, University of Oxford, 1999, University of London, 2001; Hon. Mem., American Acad. of Arts and Letters, 1978; First Prize, FNAC La Meilleur Recueil des Nouvelles Etrangères, 1987; Saltire Scottish Book of the Year Award, 1987; Companion of Literature, 1991; Ingersoll Foundation T S Eliot Award, 1992; Hon. Mem., Fellow, Royal Society of Edinburgh, 1995; D.B.E., 1993; Commandeur de l'Ordre des Arts et des Lettres, France, 1996; David Cohen British Literature Prize, 1997; International PEN Gold Pen Award, 1998; Edmund Campion Award, 2001. *Address:* c/o David Higham Assocs Ltd, 5–8 Lower John St, Golden Sq., London W1R 4HA, England.

SPARROW. See: KNELL, William.

SPARSHOTT, Francis (Edward); b. 19 May 1926, Chatham, Kent, England. Philosopher; Writer; Poet; Prof. of Philosophy (retd). m. Kathleen Elizabeth Vaughan, 7 Feb. 1953, 1 d. *Education:* BA, MA, Corpus Christi College, Oxford, 1950. *Appointments:* Lecturer, 1950–55, Asst Prof., 1955–62, Assoc. Prof., 1962–64, Prof., 1964–91, of Philosophy, University of Toronto. *Publications:* An Enquiry into Goodness and Related Concepts, 1958; The Structure of Aesthetics, 1963; The Concept of Criticism: An Essay, 1967; Looking for Philosophy, 1972; The Theory of the Arts, 1982; Off the Ground: First Steps in the Philosophy of Dance, 1988; Taking Life Seriously: A Study of the Argument of the Nicomachean Ethic, 1994; A Measured Pace: Toward a Philosophical Understanding of the Arts of Dance, 1995; The Future of Aesthetics, 1998. Poetry: A Divided Voice, 1965; A Cardboard Garage, 1969; The Rainy Hills: Verses After a Japanese Fashion, 1979; The Naming of the Beasts, 1979; New Fingers for Old Dikes, 1980; The Cave of Trophonius and Other Poems, 1983; The Hanging Gardens of Etobicoke, 1983; Storms and Screens, 1986; Sculling to Byzantium, 1989; Views from the Zucchini Gazebo, 1994; Home from the Air, 1997; The City Dwellers, 2000. *Contributions to:* Various books and periodicals. *Honours:* ACLS Fellowship, 1961–62; Canada Council Fellowship, 1970–71; Killam Research Fellowship, 1977–78; First Prize for Poetry, CBC Radio Literary Competition, 1981; Centennial Medal, Royal Society of Canada, 1982; Connaught Senior Fellowship in the Humanities, 1984–85; Doctor of Sacred Letters (DLitt Sac), honoris causa, Victoria University, 2000; LLD, h.c., University of Toronto, 2000. *Memberships:* American Philosophical Asscn; American Society for Aesthetics, pres., 1981–82; Canadian Classical Asscn; Canadian Philosophical Asscn, pres., 1975–76; League of Canadian Poets, pres., 1977–78; PEN International, Canadian Centre; Royal Society of Canada, fellow, 1977. *Address:* 50 Crescentwood Rd, Scarborough, Ontario M1N 1E4, Canada.

SPEAKER, William. See: HOLLIDAY, David John Gregory.

SPEER, Laurel; b. 3 March 1940, Los Angeles, CA, USA. Poet; Essayist; Reviewer. m. Donald P Speer, 27 Jan. 1962, divorced 29 May 1987, 2 s., 1 d. *Education:* BA English, University of California at Los Angeles, 1962. *Publications:* Second Thoughts Over Bourget, 1987; Very Frightened Men, 1988; Cold Egg, 1989; Sin, 1990; Grant Drank, 1991; The Destruction of Liars, 1993; Rebecca at the Port Authority, 1994. *Contributions to:* Reviews, quarterlies, and journals. *Honours:* Barbara Deming Memorial Grant, 1989; Arizona State Commission on the Arts Poetry Fellowship, 1991. *Address:* PO Box 12220, Tucson, AZ 85732, USA.

SPELLS, Paula Rae King; b. 19 Oct. 1939, New York, NY, USA. Poet. m. Henry L. Spells, 9 Jan. 1960, 2 s., 2 d. *Publications:* Several poems. *Contributions to:* Anthologies and periodicals. *Honours:* Ed.'s Choice Awards; International Poetry Hall of Fame, 1997. *Membership:* International Society of Poetry. *Address:* 10804 Evans St, Crowley, TX 76036-5100, USA. *E-mail:* yellowrose101939@aol.com.

SPENCE, Alan; b. 5 Dec. 1947, Glasgow, Scotland. Dramatist; Writer; Poet. *Education:* University of Glasgow, 1966–69, 1973–74. *Appointments:* Writer-in-Residence, University of Glasgow, 1975–77, Traverse Theatre, Edinburgh, 1982, University of Edinburgh, 1989–92, University of Aberdeen, 1996–. *Publications:* Plays: Sailmaker, 1982; Space Invaders, 1983; Changed Days, 1991. Fiction: Its Colours They Are Fine (short stories), 1977; The Magic Flute (novel), 1990; Stone Garden (stories), 1995. Poetry: Plop (15 Haiku), 1970; Glasgow Zen, 1981. *Honours:* Scottish Arts Council Book Awards, 1977, 1990, 1996; People's Prize, 1996; TMA Martini Prize, 1996. *Address:* 21 Waverley Park, Edinburgh EH8 8ER, Scotland.

SPENCE, Noel; b. 25 Dec. 1944, Northern Ireland. Film Producer; Poet. m. Heather Gardiner, 12 Aug. 1971, 1 s., 1 d. *Education:* BA, Honours, English

Literature, Queen's University, Belfast, 1968; Diploma in Education. *Appointments:* Head, Dept of English, Victoria College, Belfast, 1973–86; Self-Employed Film Producer, 1986–. *Publications:* Lines and Rhymes, 1995; First Time Out, 1996; A Passage in Time, 1996. *Honour:* Runner-Up, Peer International Poetry Competition, 1996. *Membership:* Concordant Poets Society. *Address:* 22 Drumhirk Rd, Comber, County Down BT23 5LY, Northern Ireland.

SPERANZA, Susan; b. 7 June 1951, New York, NY, USA. Writer; Poet; Teacher. m. Alan Knittel, 15 Feb. 1978. *Education:* BA, Queens College of the City University of New York, 1980. *Publications:* The City of Light; Exile in the Promised Land. *Contributions to:* Literary Journal of Long Island; Cultural Forum. *Honour:* Brook House New Poets Award. *Memberships:* Poetry Society of America; Poetry Project; South Bay Poets Circle. *Address:* c/o Brook House Press, Mills Pond House, PO Box 52, St James, NY 11780, USA.

SPOONER, David Eugene; b. 1 Sept. 1941, West Kirby, Wirral, England. Writer; Poet; Naturalist. m. Marion O'Neil, 9 March 1986, 1 d. *Education:* BA, University of Leeds, 1963; Diploma in Drama, University of Manchester, 1964; PhD, University of Bristol, 1968. *Appointments:* Lecturer, University of Kent, 1968–73, Manchester Polytechnic, 1974–75; Visiting Prof., Pennsylvania State University, 1973–74; Head of Publishing, Borderline Press, 1976–85; Dir, Butterfly Conservation, East Scotland. *Publications:* Unmakings, 1977; The Angelic Fly: The Butterfly in Art, 1992; The Metaphysics of Insect Life, 1995; Insect into Poem: 20th Century Hispanic Poetry, 1999; Creatures of Air: Poetry 1976–2001, 2001; Thoreau's Insects, 2002. *Contributions to:* Iron; Interactions; Tandem; Weighbauk; Revue de Littérature Comparée; Bestia (Fable Society of America); Margin; Corbie Press; Butterfly Conservation News; Butterfly News; Field Studies; Annales Benjamin Constant. *Memberships:* Welsh Acad. Assoc.; Asscn Benjamin Constant; Academic Board, London Diplomatic Acad.; Thoreau Society. *Address:* 96 Halbeath Rd, Dunfermline, Fife KY12 7LR, Scotland. *E-mail:* doctorspooner@lycos.com. *Website:* davidspooner.freeservers.com.

SPRINGER, Nancy; b. 5 July 1948, Montclair, New Jersey, USA. Writer; Poet. m. Joel H Springer, 13 Sept. 1969, divorced 1997, 1 s., 1 d. *Education:* BA, English Literature, Gettysburg College, 1970. *Appointments:* Personal Development Plan Instructor, University of Pittsburgh, 1983–85; Leisure Learning Instructor, York College, Pennsylvania, 1986–91; Education Instructor, Franklin and Marshall College, 1988–; Instructor of Creative Writing, York College of PA, 1997–1999; Writing Popular Fiction Masters' Degree Program, Seton Hill College, 1998–. *Publications:* The Sable Moon, 1981; The Black Beast, 1982; The Golden Swan, 1983; Wings of Flame, 1985; Chains of Gold, 1986; A Horse to Love (children's), 1987; Madbond, 1987; Chance and Other Gestures of the Hand of Fate, 1987; The Hex Witch of Seldom, 1988; Not on a White Horse (children's), 1988; Apocalypse, 1989; They're All Named Wildfire (children's), 1989; Red Wizard (children's), 1990; Colt (children's), 1991; The Friendship Song (children's), 1992; The Great Pony Hassle (children's), 1993; Stardark Songs (poems), 1993; Larque on the Wing, 1994; The Boy on a Black Horse (children's), 1994; Metal Angel, 1994; Music of Their Hooves (children's poems), 1994; Toughing It, 1994; Looking for Jamie Bridger (children's), 1995; Fair Peril, 1996; Secret Star (children's), 1997; I Am Mordred, 1998; Sky Rider (children's), 1999; Plumage, 2000; I Am Morgan Le Fay, 2001; Rowan Hood: Outlaw Girl of Sherwood Forest (children's), 2001; Separate Sisters (children's), 2001; Lionclaw: A Tale of Rowan Hood (children's), 2002. *Contributions to:* Magazines and journals. *Honours:* Distinguished Alumna, Gettysburg College, 1987; Nominee, Hugo Award, 1987; Nominee, World Fantasy Award, 1987; International Reading Asscn Children's Choice, 1988; Joan Fassler Memorial Book Award, 1992; International Reading Asscn Young Adult's Choice, 1993; Edgar Allen Poe Awards, Mystery Writers of America, 1995, 1996; James Tiptree Jr Award, 1995; Carolyn W. Field Award, 1995; Outstanding Pennsylvania Writer Award. *Memberships:* Society of Children's Book Writers and Illustrators; Pennwriters, pres., 1992–93. *Address:* c/o Jean V. Naggar Literary Agency, 216 E 75th St, New York, NY 10021, USA.

SRI, Indu. See: SRINIVASAN, Indira.

SRINIVAS, Krishna, (Kesri); b. 26 July 1913, Sriangam, India. Ed.; Poet. m. Kothai, 8 July 1933. *Education:* BA, Madras University, 1932; DLitt, University of Karachi, 1970. *Appointment:* Ed., World Poetry, 1990–97. *Publications:* Poetical Works, 1986–89, 1990. *Contributions to:* Anthologies and other publication. *Honours:* Several, including: Michael Madhusuden Award, 1995. *Memberships:* Several, including: World Poetry Society Intercontinental. *Address:* 118 Raja St, Dr Seethapathi Nagar, Velachery, Madras 600 042, India.

SRINIVASAN, Indira, (Indu, Indu Sri); b. 30 May 1938, Visakhapatnam, India. Prof.; Poet; Writer; Trans. m. P K Srinivasan, 2 May 1956, 3 s. *Education:* Sangitha Siromani, Chennai University, 1955; Sangitha Vidwan PG Course, 1957; PhD, Distinction, University of California, 1990. *Appointments:* Prof., Guest Lecturer, Vemlateswala University, Tirupathi College of Music and Dance. *Publications:* 3 books. Other: Poems, songs, and trans. *Contributions to:* Various publications. *Honours:* Iyatisai Nadaga Mandin, 1995; UWA Fellowship, 1996; Chennai University Fellowship, 1996; Ravi Fellowship,

1997. *Memberships:* Poetry Society of Krishna Srimivas; United Writer' Asscn, life mem.; World Etamizh Sangam, hon. patron. *Address:* 22-K Soutl Ave, Thiruvanmiyur, Chennai 600 041, Chennai 41, Tamil Nadu, India.

SRIVASTAVA, Rahul Ram Mohan Lal; b. 2 Oct. 1952, Khewali, Varanas Uttar Pradesh, India. Poet; Ed. m. Madhu Srivastava, 18 Feb. 1976, 2 s., 1 d *Education:* MA, Banares Hindu University, Varanasi, 1975; PhD, 1991, DLitt 1995, Vikramshila Hindi Vidyapeeth, Bhagal Pur, Bihar. *Publications:* Over 2(works. *Contributions to:* Various publications. *Honours:* Awards an(fellowships. *Memberships:* Akhandta Sangram Nagrik Samti, pres., 1991–93 Bhartiy Sahitya Kala Parishad, pres., 1993–95; Sri Shankar Vachnalaya Varanasi, chair., 1997; Authors Guild of India, 1999. *Address:* Sahitya Kuteer, Site 2/44, Vikas Puri, New Delhi 18, India.

SRIVATSA. See: CHANDRA SEKHAR, K.

SRNKOVÁ, Mila. See: HAUGOVA, Mila.

STAHL, Jayne Lyn; b. 27 April 1949, New York, NY, USA. College Instructor Poet. *Education:* BA, State University of New York, 1967; MA, San Francisco State University, 1986. *Appointment:* Instructor, Valley College, Queen: College. *Publication:* Stiffest of the Corpse, 1989. *Contributions to:* City Lights Review; Jacaranda; Exquisite Corpse; New York Quarterly; Niagara Review; Pulpsmith; Mouth; Podium; Orange; Echo; Yearbook of Modern Poetry 1976. *Honour:* Acad. of American Poets Award.

STALLWORTHY, Jon (Howie); b. 18 Jan. 1935, London, England. Prof. ol English Literature; Poet; Writer. m. Gillian Waldock, 25 June 1960, 3 c. *Education:* BA, 1958, BLitt, 1961, Magdalen College, Oxford. *Appointments:* Ed., 1959–71, Deputy Academic Publisher, 1974–77, Oxford University Press; Visiting Fellow, All Souls College, Oxford, 1971–72; Ed., Clarendon Press, Oxford, 1972–77; John Wendell Anderson Prof. of English Literature, Cornell University, Ithaca, New York, 1977–86; Reader in English Literature, 1986–92, Prof. of English, 1992–, University of Oxford. *Publications:* Poetry: The Earthly Paradise, 1958; The Astronomy of Love, 1961; Out of Bounds, 1963; The Almond Tree, 1967; A Day in the City, 1967; Root and Branch, 1969; Positives, 1969; A Dinner of Herbs, 1970; Alexander Blok: The Twelve and Other Poems (trans. with France), 1970; Hand in Hand, 1974; The Apple Barrel: Selected Poems, 1955–63, 1974; A Familiar Tree, 1978; The Anzac Sonata: Selected Poems, 1986; The Guest from the Future, 1995; Rounding the Horn: Collected Poems, 1998. Other: Between the Lines: Yeats's Poetry in the Making, 1963; Vision and Revision in Yeats's Last Poems, 1969; The Penguin Book of Love Poetry (ed.), 1973; Wilfred Owen: A Biography, 1974; Poets of the First World War, 1974; Boris Pasternak: Selected Poems (trans. with France), 1982; The Complete Poems and Fragments of Wilfred Owen (ed.), 1983; The Oxford Book of War Poetry (ed.), 1984; The Poems of Wilfred Owen (ed.), 1985; First Lines: Poems Written in Youth from Herbert to Heaney (ed.), 1987; Henry Reed: Collected Poems (ed.), 1991; Louis MacNeice, 1995; Singing School: The Making of a Poet, 1998; Aleksander Blok: Selected Poems (trans. with France), 2000. *Contributions to:* Professional journals. *Honours:* Duff Cooper Memorial Prize, 1974; W. H. Smith Literary Award, 1974; E. M. Forster Award, 1975; Southern Arts Literary Prize, 1995. *Memberships:* British Acad., fellow; RSL, fellow. *Address:* Wolfson College, Oxford OX2 6UD, England.

STAMATIS, Alexander; b. 19 July 1960, Athens, Greece. Writer; Poet; Architect. *Education:* Diploma in Architecture, National Technical University of Athens, 1985; Graduate Diploma in Housing Studies, Architectural Asscn School of Architecture, 1986; MPhil, Social Sciences, 1988; Postgraduate Diploma, Film and Television Studies, 1988. *Publications:* The Corner of the World (poems), 1992; Architecture of the Ultimate Spaces (poems), 1993; A Simple Method of Three, 1995; The Seventh Elephant (novel), 1998; Dense Now (poems), 1998. *Contributions to:* Greek literary magazines. *Honour:* City of Athens Award. *Address:* Vourgaroktonou 8-16, Athens 11471, Greece.

STANBROUGH, Harvey Ernest; b. 19 Nov. 1952, Alamogordo, New Mexico, USA. US Marine (retd); College Instructor; Poet; Ed. m. Mona Griffith, 23 June 1984, 3 s., 2 d. *Education:* BA, English, 1996. *Publications:* Melancholy and Madness, 1993; Partners in Rhyme, 1996; On Love and War and Other Fantasies, 1997. *Contributions to:* Anthologies and other publications. *Address:* 810 S Michigan, Roswell, NM 88201, USA.

STANDING, Sue; b. 14 April 1952, Salt Lake City, Utah, USA. Poet; Teacher. *Education:* AB, Oberlin College, 1974; MA, Boston University, 1977. *Appointments:* Lecturer, Wellesley College, 1979, Massachusetts Institute of Technology, 1993–98; Writer-in-Residence, Wheaton College, Norton, Massachusetts, 1979–; Consultant in Writing, John F Kennedy School of Government, 1981–87. *Publications:* Deception Pass, 1984; Gravida, 1995. *Contributions to:* Reviews, quarterlies, and journals. *Honours:* Grants; Bunting Institute Fellowship, 1979; National Endowment for the Arts Fellowship, 1984. *Membership:* Associated Writing Programs; Poetry Society of America; Poets and Writers. *Address:* c/o Wheaton College, Norton, MA 02766, USA.

STANFORD, Susan Alice Scott; b. 27 Dec. 1951, London, England. Teacher; Poet. m. William Stanford, 24 Sept. 1976, 2 d. *Education:* BA, Monash University, 1972; Dip.Ed, Sydney University, 1975; MEd, Temple University, 1993. *Appointments:* Teacher in schools, colleges and industry. *Publications:* 80 poems, almost 200 Haiku. *Contributions to:* Island; Famous Reporter; Linq; Scarp; Verandah; Southerly; New England Review; Hobo; Social Alternatives; Sidewalk; Frogpond; Modern Haiku; Lynx; Red Moon Anthology; Outside the Flags. *Honours:* Second Prize, Kumamoto International Kusamakura Haiku Competition, 1997; First Prize, Hobo Haiku Competition, 1998; First Prize, Melbourne Poets Union National Poetry Competition, 2000. *Memberships:* Poets Union; Victorian Writers' Centre. *Address:* 37 King Arthur Dr., Glen Waverley, Vic. 3150, Australia.

STANNARD, Glenys Margaret, (Maggi Stannard); b. 21 June 1942, Wales, England. Teacher; Poet. m. Russell Stannard, 25 May 1984, 3 s. *Education:* Art Intermediate, 1959; Certificate Education, 1968; BEd Honours, 1984. *Contributions to:* Speakeasy; Spokes; OU Poets; Poetry Society; Arford Foundation. *Honour:* Second Prize, Speakeasy, 1986. *Memberships:* Poetry Society; OU Poets; Toddington Poets. *Address:* 21 Alwins Field, Linslade, Beds LU7 7UF, England.

STANNARD, Julian Edward; b. 27 May 1962, Kent, England. Lecturer; Poet; Critic. m. Cristina Angela Ramella, 14 July 1991, 2 s. *Education:* BA, Honours, English Medieval Studies, University of Exeter, 1984; PGCE, English, University of Oxford, 1986; MPhil, English Literature, 1993. *Appointments:* Lecturer, English, University of Genoa, Italy, 1986–93; Lecturer in English, University College, Suffolk, 1994–; Secondment, Scuola di Specializzazione and Masters in International Cultural Management, 2002–03. *Publications:* Fleur Adcock in Context: From Movement to Martians, 1997; Rina's War, 2001. *Contributions to:* Nuova Corrente; Quaderni del Dipartmento di Lingue e Letterature Straniere Moderne Università di Genova; PN Review; First Pressings; Reactions 2; Reactions 3; Thumbscrew; Guardian. *Honours:* Crabbe Memorial Winner, 1996, 1997, 1998; National Poetry Prize Commendation, 1998. *Membership:* Postgraduate Asscn, University of Exeter; Exeter College Asscn, University of Oxford; Mary Ward Writing Workshop, London. *Address:* 48 Oxford Rd, Ipswich, Suffolk, England. *E-mail:* julian.stannard@suffolk.ac.uk.

STANNARD, Martin; b. 27 Aug. 1952, Reading, England. Poet. m. Diana, 4 Sept. 1976, 2 s. *Education:* BA, Middlesex Polytechnic, 1984; MA, University College, London, 1985. *Appointment:* Ed., Publisher, Joe Soap's Canoe Poetry Magazine. *Publications:* Half Man Half Hammock Half Marlo Brandon; The Private Life of the Gauze Butterfly; The Lotte Poems; The Flat of the Land; Something Cold and White; The Gracing of Days; Denying England; From a Recluse to a Roving I Will Go. *Contributions to:* New Statesman; London Magazine; Ambit; Slow Dancer; Wide Skirt; Hanging Loose; B City; Panoply. *Address:* 30 Quilter Rd, Felixstowe, Suffolk IP11 7JJ, England.

STARKIE, Stephen; b. 8 Nov. 1954, Bolton, Lancashire, England. Writer; Poet; Minister. m. Nikki Starkie, 22 June 1987, 3 s. *Education:* BA, Humanities, Bolton Institute, 1980; Bolton College, 1992; Teachers Certificate. *Publications:* Several poems, 1974–99. *Contributions to:* Anthologies, reviews and journals. *Address:* 38 Lord St, Kearsley, Bolton BL4 8BE, England.

STARRATT, Thomas; b. 6 Oct. 1952, Holyoke, MA, USA. Teacher; Poet; Writer. m. Patricia Starratt, 7 April 1994, 3 s., 2 d. *Education:* BSc, Plymouth State Teachers College, New Hampshire, 1975; MEd, University of New Hampshire, 1980; Various graduate courses. *Publications:* Nightwatch, 1994; Amsterdam, 1994; Summer on the Lava Plain, 1994; Eye to Your Storm, 1995; Passages, 1995; Excess, 1995; Summer Days, 1995; Amsterdam Revisited, 1995; Washed Up, 1996. *Contributions to:* Professional journals. *Membership:* International Reading Asscn.

STEAD, C(hristian) K(arlson); b. 17 Oct. 1932, Auckland, New Zealand. Poet; Writer; Critic; Ed.; Prof. of English Emeritus. m. Kathleen Elizabeth Roberts, 8 Jan. 1955, 1 s., 2 d. *Education:* BA, 1954, MA, 1955, University of New Zealand; PhD, University of Bristol, 1961; DLitt, University of Auckland, 1982. *Appointments:* Lecturer in English, University of New England, Australia, 1956–57; Lecturer, 1960–61, Senior Lecturer, 1962–64, Assoc. Prof., 1964–67, Prof. of English, 1967–86, Prof. Emeritus, 1986–, University of Auckland; Chair., New Zealand Literary Fund Advisory Committee, 1972–75, New Zealand Authors' Fund Committee, 1989–91; Senior Visiting Fellow, St John's College, Oxford, 1996–97. *Publications:* Poetry: Whether the Will is Free, 1964; Crossing the Bar, 1972; Quesada: Poems 1972–74, 1975; Walking Westward, 1979; Geographies, 1982; Poems of a Decade, 1983; Paris, 1984; Between, 1988; Voices, 1990; Straw Into Gold: Poems New and Selected, 1997; The Right Thing, 2000. Fiction: Smith's Dream, 1971; Five for the Symbol, 1981; All Visitors Ashore, 1984; The Death of the Body, 1986; Sister Hollywood, 1989; The End of the Century at the End of the World, 1992; The Singing Whakapapa, 1994; Villa Vittoria, 1997; The Blind Blonde with Candles in her Hair (stories), 1998; Talking About O'Dwyer, 1999; The Secret History of Modernism, 2001; All Visitors Ashore, 2001. Criticism: The New Poetic: Yeats to Eliot, 1964; In the Glass Case: Essays on New Zealand Literature, 1981;

Pound, Yeats, Eliot and the Modernist Movement, 1986; Answering to the Language: Essays on Modern Writers, 1989; The Writer at Work: Essays by C. K. Stead, 2000; Kin of Place: Essays on 20 New Zealand Writers, 2002. Editor: World's Classics: New Zealand Short Stories, 1966; Measure for Measure: A Casebook, 1971; Letters and Journals of Katherine Mansfield, 1977; Collected Stories of Maurice Duggan, 1981; The New Gramophone Room: Poetry and Fiction (with Elizabeth Smither and Kendrick Smithyman), 1985; The Faber Book of Contemporary South Pacific Stories, 1994. *Contributions to:* Poetry, fiction and criticism to various anthologies and periodicals. *Honours:* Katherine Mansfield Prize, 1960; Nuffield Travelling Fellowship, 1965; Katherine Mansfield Menton Fellowship, 1972; Jessie Mackay Award for Poetry, 1972; New Zealand Book Awards for Poetry, 1972, 1986; Hon. Research Fellow, University College, London, 1977; C.B.E., 1984; New Zealand Book Awards for Fiction, 1985, 1995; Queen Elizabeth II Arts Council Scholarship in Letters, 1988–89; Queen's Medal for services to New Zealand literature, 1990; Fellow, RSL, 1995; Creative New Zealand, mem., 1999; Hon. DLitt, University of Bristol, 2001. *Membership:* New Zealand PEN, chair., Auckland branch, 1986–89, national vice-pres., 1988–90. *Address:* 37 Tohunga Crescent, Auckland 1, New Zealand.

STEADMAN, John Marcellus; b. 25 Nov. 1918, Spartanburg, South Carolina, USA. Prof. of English Emeritus; Research Scholar; Poet. *Education:* AB, 1940, MA, 1941, Emory University; MA, 1948, PhD, 1949, Princeton University. *Appointments:* Instructor in English, Georgia Institute of Technology, 1941–42; Asst Prof. of English, University of North Carolina, 1949–51; Research Assoc. to Senior Research Assoc., Huntington Library, 1962–2002; Prof. of English, 1966–89, Prof. Emeritus, 1989–, University of California at Riverside. *Publications:* Ryoanji Temple and Other Poems, 1993; Reconnaissances, 1995; Winter Harvest, A Retrospective, 1996; In Earnest or Game: A Seriocomic Medley, 1998. *Contributions to:* Emory University Quarterly; Poet Lore; Verse Craft; American Poetry Review; Cithara. *Honours:* Hon. doctorates, Emory University, 1976, St Bonaventure University, 1998. *Address:* 250 S Oak Knoll Ave, Apt 109, Pasadena, CA 91101, USA.

STEEL, Ripon. See: MORRIS, Jennifer Margaret.

STEELE, Timothy Reid; b. 22 Jan. 1948, Vermont, USA. Prof.; Poet; Writer. m. Victoria Lee Erpelding, 14 Jan. 1979. *Education:* BA, Stanford University, 1970; PhD, Brandeis University, 1977. *Appointments:* Jones Lecturer, Stanford University, 1975–77; Lecturer, University of California at Los Angeles, 1977–83, University of California at Santa Barbara, 1986; Prof., California State University, Los Angeles, 1987–. *Publications:* The Color Wheel, 1994; Sapphics and Uncertainties: Poems 1970–86, 1995; The Poems of J V Cunningham (ed.), 1997; All the Fun's in How You Say a Thing, 1999. *Contributions to:* Poetry; Threepenny Review; Paris Review; Greensboro Review; Southern Review; Crosscurrents; New Criterion; Numbers; Spectator; Formalist; PN Review. *Honours:* Stegner Fellowship; Guggenheim Fellowship; Lavan Younger Poets Award; Commonwealth Club of California Medal; PEN Award for Poetry. *Memberships:* PEN; Acad. of American Poets. *Address:* 1801 Preuss Rd, Los Angeles, CA 90035, USA.

STEFANILE, Felix Neil; b. 13 April 1920, New York, NY, USA. Prof. (retd); Poet. m. Selma Epstein, 17 Jan. 1953. *Education:* BA, City University of New York, 1944. *Appointments:* Ed., Publisher, Sparrow Press, 1954–2002; Visiting Poet, Lecturer, 1961–62, Asst Prof., 1962–64, Assoc. Prof., 1964–69, Prof., 1969–87, Purdue University; Chair., Editorial Board, Purdue University Press, 1964–69. *Publications:* If I Were Fire; In That Far Country; The Blue Moustache; Umberto Saba; East River Nocturne; A Fig Tree in America; The Dance at St Gabriel's, 1995; The Country of Absence, 2001. *Contributions to:* New York Sunday Times Book Review; Sewanne Review; Virginia Quarterly Review; Poetry; Parnassus; TriQuarterly; Hudson Review; New York Times. *Honours:* Pushcart Press Prize; Standard Oil of Indiana Foundation Award; Virginia Quarterly Review Emily Clark Balch Award; Nathan Haskell Dole Prize; National Endowment for the Arts Prize; John Ciardi Award for Lifetime Achievement in Poetry, 1997. *Memberships:* Poetry Society of America; American Literary Trans Asscn. *Address:* 103 Waldron St, West Lafayette, IN 47906, USA.

STEFFEN, Jonathon Neil; b. 5 Oct. 1958, London, England. University Teacher; Writer; Poet; Trans. *Education:* MA, English, King's College, Cambridge, 1981. *Appointment:* Teacher, University of Heidelberg. *Publications:* Fiction: In Seville, 1985; Meeting the Majors, 1987; Carpe Diem, 1991; Cleopatra, 1994; The Story of Icarus, 1994; At Breakfast, 1995. Poetry: The Soldier and the Soldier's Son, 1986; German Hunting Party, 1987; The Moving Hand, 1994; The Great Days of the Railway, 1994; Apprentice and Master, 1994; St Francis in the Slaughter, 1995. *Contributions to:* Reviews, quarterlies, and magazines. *Honours:* Harper-Wood Traveling Studentship, 1981–82; Hawthornden Creative Writing Fellowship, 1987. *Address:* Schillerstrasse 16, 69115 Heidelberg, Germany.

STEFFLER, John Earl; b. 13 Nov. 1947, Toronto, Ontario, Canada. Prof. of English Literature; Poet; Writer. m. Shawn O'Hagan, 30 May 1970, 1 s., 1 d. *Education:* BA, University of Toronto, 1971; MA, University of Guelph, 1974.

Publications: An Explanation of Yellow, 1980; The Grey Islands, 1985; The Wreckage of Play, 1988; The Afterlife of George Cartwright, 1991. *Contributions to:* Journals and periodicals. *Honours:* Books in Canada First Novel Award, 1992; Newfoundland Arts Council Artist of the Year Award, 1992; Thomas Raddall Atlantic Fiction Award, 1992; Joseph S Stauffer Prize, 1993. *Memberships:* League of Canadian Poets; PEN; Writers Alliance of Newfoundland and Labrador. *Address:* c/o Dept of English, Memorial University of Newfoundland, Corner Brook, Newfoundland A2H 6PN, Canada.

STEIN, Clarissa Ingeborg, (Sara Cristiens); b. 3 Sept. 1948, Munich, Germany. Ed.; Poet. m. Herbert Stein, 26 May 1981, 1 d. *Education:* Diploma, Bearntenfachhochschule, Herrsching, Bavaria, 1975. *Appointment:* Ed., Papyrus Publishing, 1991–. *Publications:* New Melodies, Neue Melodien, 1992; Notes From My Land, 1993; Billy Tea and Sand Ballet, 1996; In Meinem Land, 1997; Hermit Woman and Butterfly, 2002. *Contributions to:* Journals and magazines in Australia and overseas. *Memberships:* Deakin Literary Society, Deakin University; Society of Women Writers (Victoria); Poetry Australia Foundation; Ballarat Regional Multicultural Council. *Address:* c/o Post Office, Scarsdale, Vic., 3351, Australia.

STEIN, Kevin; b. 1 Jan. 1954, Anderson, IN, USA. Prof. of English; Writer; Poet; Ed. m. Debra Lang, 26 May 1979, 1 s., 1 d. *Education:* BS, summa cum laude, 1976, MA, 1978, Ball State University; MA, Creative Writing, 1982, PhD, American Literature, 1984, Indiana University. *Appointments:* Instructor, Ball State University, 1978–79; Assoc. Instructor, Indiana University, 1980–84; Asst Prof., 1984–88, Assoc. Prof., 1988–94, Prof. of English, 1994–, Caterpillar Prof. of English, 2000–, Bradley University, Peoria, IL; Ed., Illinois Writers Review, 1988–92; Assoc. Poetry Ed., Crazyhorse, 1992–. *Publications:* A Field of Wings (poems), 1986; The Figure Our Bodies Make (poems), 1988; James Wright: The Poetry of a Grown Man, 1988; A Circus of Want (poems), 1992; Bruised Paradise (poems), 1996; Private Poets: Worldly Acts: Public and Private History in Contemporary American Poetry, 1996; Chance Ransom (poems), 2000; Illinois Voices: An Anthology of Twentieth-Century Poetry (ed. with G. E. Murray), 2001. *Contributions to:* Many reviews, quarterlies and journals. *Honours:* Illinois Arts Council Fellowship, 1986; Chapbook Award, Illinois Writers, 1986; Stanley Hanks Chapbook Award, 1988; Frederick Bock Prize for Poetry, 1987; Faculty Mem. of the Year, Bradley University, 1989; National Endowment for the Arts Fellowship, 1991; Devins Award for Poetry, University of Missouri Press, 1992; Indiana Review Poetry Prize, 1998. *Memberships:* Illinois Writers; MLA. *Address:* c/o Dept of English, College of Liberal Arts and Sciences, Bradley University, 1501 W Bradley Ave, Peoria, IL 61625-0258, USA.

STEINER-ISENMANN, Robert; b. 19 May 1955, Basel, Switzerland. Writer; Poet. 1 d. *Education:* Theology, University of Zürich. *Publications:* Gaetano Donizetti: Sein Leben und seine Opern, 1982; Espoirs-hopfnungen (revue), 1988; Windspeil der Leidenschaft (poems), 1994. *Contributions to:* Anthologies, magazines, and journals. *Memberships:* Asscn Suisse des Ecrivains; Asscn Valaisanne des Ecrivains; PEN Club. *Address:* Café de la Rosablanche, 1996 Basse-Nendaz/VS, Switzerland.

STEINMAN, Lisa (Jill) M(alinowski); b. 8 April 1950, Willimantic, CT, USA. Prof. of English; Poet; Writer; Ed. m. James L Shugrue, 23 July 1984. *Education:* BA, 1971, MFA, 1973, PhD, 1976, Cornell University. *Appointments:* Asst Prof., 1976–82, Assoc. Prof., 1982–89, Prof., 1990–93, Kenan Prof. of English, 1993–, Reed College, Portland, Oregon; Poetry Ed., Hubbub Magazine, 1983–. *Publications:* Lost Poems, 1976; Made in America: Science, Technology, and American Modernist Poets, 1987; All That Comes to Light, 1989; A Book of Other Days, 1993; Ordinary Songs, 1996; Masters of Repetition: Poetry, Culture, and Work, 1998. *Contributions to:* Books, anthologies, reviews, quarterlies, and journals. *Honours:* Scholar, Bread Loaf Writers Conference, 1981; Oregon Arts Commission Poetry Fellow, 1983; National Endowment for the Arts Fellowship, 1984; Rockefeller Scholar-in-Residence, 92nd Street Y Poetry Center, 1987; Pablo Neruda Award, Nimrod Magazine, 1987; Outstanding Academic Book, Choice, 1989; Oregon Book Award, Oregon Institute of Literary Arts, 1993; National Endowment for the Humanities Fellowship, 1996. *Memberships:* Associated Writing Programs; MLA; PEN; PEN/Northwest; Poets and Writers; Wallace Stevens Society; William Carlos Williams Society, pres., 1998–2000. *Address:* 5344 SE 38th Ave, Portland, OR 97202, USA.

STEPHEN, Ian; b. 29 April 1955, Stornoway, Isle of Lewis, Scotland. Writer; Poet; Artist. m. Barbara Ziehm, 9 Nov. 1984, 2 s. *Education:* BEd, Distinction, Honours, English, University of Aberdeen, 1980. *Appointment:* Inaugural Robert Louis Stevenson/Christian Salvesen Fellow, Grez-sur-Loing, France, 1995. *Publications:* Malin, Hebrides, Minches, 1983; Varying States of Grace, 1989; Siud an T-Eilean (ed.), 1993; Providence II, 1994; Broad Bay, 1997; Green Waters, 1998; Mackerel and Creamola (short stories), 2001. Other: Numerous exhibitions of poetry/texts with visual arts. *Contributions to:* Scottish, UK, and Australian publications. *Honour:* Scottish Arts Council Bursaries, 1981, 1995; Creative Scotland Award, 2002. *Memberships:* PEN Scotland. *Address:* Last House, 1 Benside, Isle of Lewis HS2 0DZ, Scotland.

STEPHENS, Meic; b. 23 July 1938, Trefforest, Pontypridd, Wales. Journalist; Poet; Writer; Trans.; Ed. m. Ruth Wynn Meredith, 14 Aug. 1965, 1 s., 3 d. *Education:* BA, University College of Wales, Aberystwyth, 1961; University of Rennes, 1960; University College of North Wales, Bangor, 1962. *Appointments:* Literature Dir, Welsh Arts Council, 1967–90; Visiting Prof., Brigham Young University, Provo, Utah, 1991; Lecturer in Journalism, University of Glamorgan, 1994–, Centre for Journalism Studies, Cardiff University, 1998; Prof. of Welsh Writing in English, University of Glamorgan, 2001. *Publications:* New Companion to the Literature of Wales; The Literary Pilgrim in Wales; Welsh Names for Your Children; Illuminations: An Anthology of Welsh Short Prose. *Contributions to:* Various anthologies, reference works, and journals. *Honours:* Hon. MA, DLitt, University of Wales. *Memberships:* Gorsedd of Bards; Welsh Acad. *Address:* 10 Heol Don, Whitchurch, Cardiff, Wales.

STEPHENS, Michael (Gregory); b. 4 March 1946, USA. Writer; Poet; Dramatist. *Education:* BA, 1975, MA, 1976, City College of the City University of New York; MFA, Yale University, 1979. *Appointments:* Lecturer, Columbia University, 1977–91, Princeton University, 1986–91, New York University, 1989–91; Writer-in-Residence and Asst Prof., Fordham University, 1979–85. *Publications:* Fiction: Season at Coole, 1972; Paragraphs, 1974; Still Life, 1978; Shipping Out, 1979; The Brooklyn Book of the Dead, 1994. Poetry: Alcohol Poems, 1972; Tangun Legend, 1978; After Asia, 1993. Other: Circles End (poems and prose), 1982; The Dramaturgy of Style, 1986; Lost in Seoul: And Other Discoveries on the Korean Peninsula, 1990; Jig and Reels, 1992; Green Dreams: Essays Under the Influence of the Irish, 1994. Plays: A Splendid Occasion in Spring, 1974; Off-Season Rates, 1978; Cloud Dream, 1979; Our Father, 1980; R & R, 1984. *Contributions to:* Many newspapers, journals, and magazines. *Honours:* MacDowell Colony Fellowship, 1968; Fletcher Pratt Fellowship, Bread Loaf Writers Conference, 1971; Creative Artists Public Service Fiction Award, 1978; Connecticut Commission on the Arts Grant, 1979; Associated Writing Programs Award in Creative Non-Fiction, 1993. *Memberships:* Associated Writing Programs; PEN; Royal Asiatic Society. *Address:* 520 W 110th St, No. 5-C, New York, NY 10025, USA.

STERN, Gerald; b. 22 Feb. 1925, Pittsburgh, Pennsylvania, USA. Poet; Teacher. m. Patricia Miller, 1952, 1 s., 1 d. *Education:* BA, University of Pittsburgh, 1947; MA, Columbia University, 1949. *Appointments:* Instructor, Temple University, Philadelphia, 1957–63; Prof., Indiana University of Pennsylvania, 1963–67; Somerset County College, New Jersey, 1968–82; Visiting Poet, Sarah Lawrence College, 1977; Visiting Prof., University of Pittsburgh, 1978; Columbia University, 1980; Bucknell University, 1988; New York Universty, 1989; Faculty, Writer's Workshop, University of Iowa, 1982–94; Distinguished Chair, University of Alabama, 1984; Fanny Hurst Prof., Washington University, St Louis, 1985; Bain Swiggert Chair, Princeton University, 1989; Poet-in-Residence, Bucknell University, 1994. *Publications:* The Naming of Beasts and Other Poems, 1973; Rejoicings, 1973; Lucky Life, 1977; The Red Coal, 1981; Paradise Poems, 1984; Lovesick, 1987; Leaving Another Kingdom: Selected Poems, 1990; Two Long Poems, 1990; Bread Without Sugar, 1992; Odd Mercy, 1995; This Time: New and Selected Poems, 1998; Last Blue, 2000; American Sonnets, 2002. *Honours:* National Endowment for the Arts Grants, 1976, 1981, 1987; Lamont Poetry Selection Award, 1977; Governor's Award, Pennsylvania, 1980; Guggenheim Fellowship, 1980; Bess Hokin Award, 1980; Bernard F Connor Award, 1981; Melville Cane Award, 1982; Jerome J Shestack Prize, 1984; Acad. of American Poets Fellowship, 1993; Ruth Lilly Poetry Prize, 1996; National Book Award for Poetry, 1998; New Jersey Poet Laureate. *Address:* 89 Clinton St, Lambertville, NJ 08530, USA.

STERNLICHT, Sanford; b. 20 Sept. 1931, New York, NY, USA. Prof. of English; Literary Critic; Poet. m. Dorothy Hilkert, 7 June 1956, deceased 1977, 2 s. *Education:* BS, State University of New York at Oswego, 1953; MA, Colgate University, 1955; PhD, Syracuse University, 1962. *Appointments:* Instructor, 1959–60, Asst Prof., 1960–62, Assoc. Prof., 1962, Prof. of English, 1962–72, Prof. of Theatre, 1972–86, State University of New York College at Oswego; Leverhulme Foundation Visiting Fellow, University of York, England, 1965–66; Prof. of English, Syracuse University, 1986–. *Publications:* Poetry: Gull's Way, 1961; Love in Pompeii, 1967. Non-Fiction: Uriah Philips Levy: The Blue Star Commodore, 1961; The Black Devil of the Bayous: The Life and Times of the United States Steam-Sloop Hartford (with E M Jameson), 1970; John Webster's Imagery and the Webster Canon, 1974; John Masefield, 1977; McKinley's Bulldog: The Battleship Oregon, 1977; C S Forester, 1981; USF Constellation: Yankee Racehorse (with E M Jameson), 1981; Padraic Colum, 1985; John Galsworthy, 1987; R F Delderfield, 1988; Stevie Smith, 1990; Stephen Spender, 1992; Siegfried Sassoon, 1993; All Things Herriot: James Herriot and His Peaceable Kingdom, 1995; Jean Rhys, 1996; A Reader's Guide to Modern Irish Drama, 1998. Editor: Selected Stories of Padraic Colum, 1985; Selected Plays of Padraic Colum, 1989; In Search of Stevie Smith, 1991; New Plays from the Abbey Theatre 1993–1995, 1996; Chaim Potok: A Critical Companion, 2000; New Plays from the Abbey Theatre, 1996–1998, 2001; A Reader's Guide to Modern American Drama, 2002. *Contributions to:* Books, professional journals and general periodicals. *Honours:* Prizes, fellowships and grants including: Sir Evelyn Wrench English-Speaking Union Travel/Lecture Grants, 1997, 1998, 1999. *Memberships:* MLA; PEN; Poetry Society of America, fellow; Shakespeare Asscn of America; American Conference for Irish Studies. *Address:* 128 Dorset Rd, Syracuse, NY 13210, USA.

STESSEL, Harold Edward; b. 24 April 1939, Dunkirk, New York, USA. Prof. of English; Poet; Writer. m. Elizabeth Victoria Dewey, 23 Aug. 1970, 1 s. *Education:* BA, English, University of North Carolina, 1959; MA, English, University of Chicago, 1960; MA, American Civilization, 1972, PhD, American Civilization, 1980, University of Pennsylvania. *Appointments:* Asst Prof. of English, Grinnell College, 1974–76; Fulbright Lecturer in American Culture, University of Göteborg, Sweden, 1976–79; Asst Prof. of Humanities, State University of New York, 1981–86; Prof. of English, Westfield State College, Massachusetts, 1986–. *Publications:* American Studies, 1975; Ardis Anthology of New American Poetry, 1977. *Contributions to:* Ascent; Beloit Poetry Review; Commonwealth Review; Connecticut River Review; Cottonwood Review; Exile; Hiram Poetry Review; Honest Ulsterman, Northern Ireland; Kansas Quarterly; Minnesota Review; Mississippi Review; Moosehead Review, Canada; MSS; Noiseless Spider; Quarry; St Andrews Review; Slow Motion Review; Southern Poetry Review; Windless Orchard; Xanadu. *Address:* c/o Dept of English, Westfield State College, Westfield, MA 01086, USA.

STÉTIÉ, Salah; b. 1929, Beirut, Lebanon. Poet; Writer; Art Critic; Trans.; Essayist. *Education:* École Supérieure des Lettres de Beyrouth. *Appointments:* Founder and Ed., L'Orient littéraire (The Literary East, magazine), Beirut; Contributor, Les Lettres Nouvelle, Le Mercure de France, La Revue Française, Diogène, Corps écrit; Permanent Representative of Lebanon to UNESCO, Paris; Ambassador to Morocco; Sec.-Gen., Ministry of Foreign Affairs, Beirut; Ambassador to The Netherlands. *Publications:* Carriers of Fire, 1972; Kept Cold Water, 1973; Fragments: Poem, 1973; Andre Pieyre de Mandiargues, 1978; Ur in Poetry, 1980; Inversion of The Tree and Silence, 1980; The Being Headstock, 1983; Aqualine Dove, 1983; Cloud with Voices, 1984; Blind Archer, 1985; Reading of a Woman, 1987; Incidental Clauses, 1989; The Voyages of Alep, 1991; Seven Door Frames With the Danger of Poetry, 1991; The Sword of the Tears, 1992; Light on Light, Or Creative Islam, 1992; Rimbaud, The Eighth Door Frame, 1993; The Interdict, 1993; Nibbio, 1993; Plural Lebanon, 1994; Refraction of the Desire and Desire, 1994; Ground with the Lapse of Memory, 1994; Glares, Fourteen Haiku, 1994; A Crystal Suspense, 1995; Striped Mirror, 1995; Dormition of Snow, 1996; Signs and Monkeys, 1996; The Herb Tea of the Sphinx, 1997; The Ear of the Wall, 1998; Mystical Wine, 1998; Fingers, 1999; Mahomet, 2000; My Cities, 2001; If To Breathe, 2001; The French, The Other Language, 2001; The Voyage of Alep, 2002; also numerous trans of works from Arabic, English and French, including Poems of Djaykoûr, 1983. *Honour:* Grand Prix de la Francophonie, Académie française, 1995. *Membership:* Commission of Terminology of the French Language. *Address:* c/o Editions Fata Morgana, Fontfroide-le-haut, 34980 Saint-Clément-de-Rivière, France.

STEVEN, Kenneth Campbell; b. 25 Nov. 1968, Glasgow, Scotland. Poet; Writer. *Education:* University of Glasgow. *Publications:* The Unborn, 1992; Remembering Peter, 1993; Dan, 1994; The Missing Days (selected poems), 1995; The Boy and the Blue Balloon, 1995; The Pearl Fisher, 1996; The Summer Is Ended, 1997; Splinters, 1997; The Bearer of Gifts, 1998; Poetry: How to Get Published, How to Get Paid; The Poet's Handbook, 2000; Wild Horses, 2002; A Highland Trilogy, 2002; The Song of the Trees, 2002. *Contributions to:* Anthologies, reviews, and journals. *Honours:* Finalist, Scottish Poetry Open Competition, 1986–91; Runner-Up, Michael Bruce Memorial Poetry Competition, 1991, and Staple First Editions Award, 1992; Short-listed, Deo Gloria Award for Fiction, 1992; Saltire Book Award Nomination, 1994; Hawthornden Fellow, 1995. *Address:* 18 Cathedral St, Dunkeld, PH8 0AW, Scotland.

STEVENS, Carl. See: OBSTFELD, Raymond.

STEVENS, Geoffrey; b. 4 June 1942, West Bromwich, England. Chemist; Poet. m. (1) Barbara C Smith, 20 Feb. 1965, 1 d., (2) Geraldine M Wall, 6 July 1996. *Education:* HNC, Chemistry, Wolverhampton Polytechnic. *Appointments:* Dir of Industrial Archaeology, Black Country Society; Ed., Purple Patch Poetry Magazine, 1976–. *Publications:* Ecstasy, 1992; Field Manual for Poetry Lovers, 1992; A Comparison of Myself With Ivan Blatny, 1992; The Surreal Mind Paints Poetry, 1993; The Complacency of the English, 1995; Skin Print, 1995; For Reference Only, 1996; Been There, 1999; Crossing the Tamar, 2001. *Contributions to:* Magazines and periodicals. *Honour:* Award for Service to Poetry, Hastings Poetry Festival, 1997. *Address:* 25 Griffiths Rd, West Bromwich B71 2EH, England.

STEVENS, Jean Marian, (née Baxter); b. 27 July 1928, Newport Pagnell, Buckinghamshire, England. Poet. m. David Richard Stevens, 14 Aug. 1954, 1 s., 2 d. *Education:* Certificate of Education, Hockerill Teacher Training College, Bishops Stortford, Hertfordshire, 1948. *Publications:* Led by Kingfishers, 1980; Impressions, 2002. *Contributions to:* Anthologies, 1975–2000, quarterlies and journals. *Honours:* Dacorum Poet of the Year, Hemel Hempstead Gazette, 1974; Julia Cairns Salver for Poetry, 1974, 1991. *Membership:* Society of Women Writers and Journalists. *Address:* 3 Nettlecroft, Hemel Hempstead, Hertfordshire HP1 1PQ, England.

STEVENS, Peter (Stanley); b. 17 Nov. 1927, Manchester, England (Naturalized Canadian citizen). Emeritus Prof.; Poet; Critic; Ed. m. June Sidebotham, 13 April 1957, 1 s., 2 d. *Education:* BA, Certificate in Education, University of Nottingham, 1951; MA, McMaster University, 1963; PhD, University of Saskatchewan, 1968. *Appointments:* Faculty, Hillfield-Strathallan College, Hamilton, Ontario, 1957–64; Part-time Lecturer, McMaster University, 1961–64; Lecturer and Asst Prof., University of Saskatchewan, 1964–69; Poetry Ed., Canadian Forum, 1968–73, Literary Review of Canada, 1994–; Assoc. Prof., 1969–76, Prof., 1976–96, University of Windsor. *Publications:* Nothing But Spoons, 1969; The McGill Movement (ed.), 1969; A Few Myths, 1971; Breadcrusts and Glass, 1972; Family Feelings and Other Poems, 1974; A Momentary Stay, 1974; The Dying Sky Like Blood, 1974; The Bogman Pavese Tactics, 1977; Modern English-Canadian Poetry, 1978; Coming Back, 1981; Revenge of the Mistresses, 1982; Out of the Willow Trees, 1986; Miriam Waddington, 1987; Swimming in the Afternoon: New and Selected Poems, 1992; Dorothy Livesay: Patterns in a Poetic Life, 1992; Rip Rap: Yorkshire Ripper Poems, 1995; Thinking Into the Dark, 1997; Attending to This World, 1998; States of Mind, 2001; Bread from Stones, 2002. *Contributions to:* Books, reviews, and journals. *Address:* 2055 Richmond St, Windsor, Ontario N8Y 1L3, Canada.

STEVENSON, Anne Katharine; b. 3 Jan. 1933, Cambridge, England. Poet; Writer. m. (1), 2 s., 1 d., (2) Peter David Lucas, 3 Sept. 1987. *Education:* BA, 1954, MA, 1961, University of Michigan. *Publications:* Living in America, 1965; Reversals, 1969; Travelling Behind Glass, 1974; Correspondences, 1974; Enough of Green, 1977; Minute by Glass Minute, 1982; The Fiction Makers, 1985; Winter Time, 1986; Selected Poems, 1987; The Other House, 1990; Four and a Half Dancing Men, 1993; Collected Poems, 1996; Bitter Fame: A Life of Sylvia Plath; 1998; Five Looks at Elizabeth Bishop, 1998; Between the Iceberg and the Ship (literary essays), 1998; Granny Scarecrow, 2000; Hearing with My Fingers, 2002. *Contributions to:* Reviews, journals, and magazines. *Honours:* Fellowships; Major Hopwood Award, 1954; Arts Council Award, 1974; Poetry Book Society Choice, 1985; Athena Award, 1990; Cholmondely Award, Society of Authors, 1997; Northern Rock Foundation Writers Award, 2002. *Memberships:* Poetry Book Society; Poetry Society; RSL, fellow; Society of Authors; Authors Guild, USA. *Address:* 38 Western Hill, Durham, DH1 4RJ, England.

STEWART, Harold Frederick; b. 14 Dec. 1916, Sydney, NSW, Australia. Poet; Writer; Trans. *Education:* University of Sydney. *Appointments:* Broadcaster, Australian Broadcasting Commission; Lecturer, Victorian Council of Adult Education. *Publications:* Poetry: The Darkening Ecliptic (with James McAuley), 1944; Phoenix Wings: Poems 1940–46, 1948; Orpheus and Other Poems, 1956; The Exiled Immortal: A Song Cycle, 1980; By the Old Walls of Kyoto: A Year's Cycle of Landscape Poems with Prose Commentaries, 1981; Collected Poems (with Ern Malley), 1993. Translator: A Net of Fireflies: Japanese Haiku and Haiku Paintings, 1960; A Chime of Windbells: A Year of Japanese Haiku, 1969; Tannisho: Passages Deploring Deviations of Faith (with Bando Shojun), 1980; The Amida Sutra Mandala (with Inagaki Hisao), 1995. *Honours:* Sydney Morning Herald Prize for Poetry, 1951; Australia Council Grant, 1978; Senior Emeritus Writers Fellow, Australia Council, 1982; Christopher Brennan Prize for Poetry, 1988. *Address:* 501 Keifuku Dai-ni Manshon, Yamabana-icho Dacho 7-1, Shugakuin, Sakyo-ku, Kyoto 606, Japan.

STEWART, Lady Mary (Florence Elinor); b. 17 Sept. 1916, Sunderland, England. Writer; Poet. m. Frederick Henry Stewart, 24 Sept. 1945. *Education:* BA, 1938, DipEd, 1939, MA, 1941, University of Durham. *Publications:* Madam, Will You Talk?, 1954; Wildfire at Midnight, 1956; Thunder on the Right, 1957; Nine Coaches Waiting, 1958; My Brother Michael, 1959; The Ivy Tree, 1961; The Moonspinners, 1962; This Rough Magic, 1964; Airs Above the Ground, 1965; The Gabriel Hounds, 1967; The Wind off the Small Isles, 1968; The Crystal Cave, 1970; The Hollow Hills, 1973; Touch Not the Cat, 1976; The Last Enchantment, 1979; The Wicked Day, 1983; Thornyhold, 1988; Stormy Petrel, 1991; The Prince and the Pilgrim, 1995; Rose Cottage, 1997. Children's Fiction: A Walk in Wolf Wood, 1970; The Little Broomstick, 1971; Ludo and the Star Horse, 1974. Poetry: Frost on the Window and Other Poems, 1990. *Contributions to:* Magazines. *Honours:* Frederick Niven Prize, 1971; Scottish Arts Council Award, 1974; Hon. Fellow, Newnham College, Cambridge. *Memberships:* PEN. *Address:* House of Letterawe, Loch Awe, Dalmally, Argyll PA33 1AH, Scotland.

STEWART, Susan; b. 15 March 1952, York, Pennsylvania, USA. Writer; Poet; Educator. *Education:* BA, Dickinson College, 1973; MA, Poetry, Johns Hopkins University, 1975; PhD, Folklore, University of Pennsylvania, 1978. *Appointments:* Asst Prof., 1978–81, Assoc. Prof., 1981–85, Prof. of English, 1985–, Temple University, Philadelphia, Pennsylvania. *Publications:* Nonsense: Aspects of Intertextuality in Folklore and Literature, 1979; Yellow Stars and Ice (poems), 1981; On Longing: Narratives of the Miniature, the Gigantic, the Souvenir, the Collection, 1984; The Hive: Poems, 1987; Crimes of Writing: Problems in the Containment of Representation, 1991; The Forest (poems), 1995. *Honours:* National Endowment for the Arts Grants, 1981–82, 1984, 1988; Pennsylvania Council on the Arts Grants, 1984, 1988, 1989–90; Guggenheim Foundation Fellowship, 1986–87; Georgia Press Second Book Award, 1987; Temple University Creative Achievement Award, 1991; Senior

Scholar, Getty Center for the History of Art and the Humanities, 1995; Lila Wallace-Reader's Digest Writer's Award for Poetry, 1995; Pew Fellowship, 1995. *Address:* c/o Temple University, Dept of English, 1601 N Broad St, University Service Building, Rm 305, Philadelphia, PA 19122-6099, USA.

STEWART, Susan Elisabeth; b. 13 June 1953, Lancaster, England. Poet. *Education:* BA, Honours, University of Kent, 1979. *Appointments:* Writer and Creative Writing Tutor, Schools, Adult Education, 1982–95; Creative Writing Fellowship, University of Stirling, 1994–95; Literature Officer, East Midlands Arts, 1997–. *Publications:* Book of Hours, 1986; Big World, Little World (ed., green anthology for children), 1991; Inventing the Fishes, 1993; A World of Folk Tales (ed.), 1995. *Contributions to:* Various anthologies, reviews, and periodicals. *Honours:* Finalist, TLS/Cheltenham Poetry Competition, 1988; First Prize, Rhyme Revival Competition, Orbis, 1988; Fifth Prize, Peterloo Poets Open Poetry Competition, 1991; Aldeburgh Poetry Festival Prize for Best First Collection, 1993. *Memberships:* Arvon Foundation; Berkshire Literary Festival, steering committee; Poetry Society; Southern Arts. *Address:* c/o Anvil Press Poetry, Neptune House, 70 Royal Hill, London SE10 8RT, England.

STIMPSON, Gerald. See: MITCHELL, Adrian.

STOCK, Norman; b. 14 July 1940, New York, NY, USA. Librarian; Poet. *Education:* BA, Brooklyn College, 1962; MLS, Rutgers University, 1967; MA, English, Hunter College, New York City, 1971. *Publication:* Buying Breakfast for My Kamikaze Pilot, 1994. *Contributions to:* Reviews and quarterlies. *Honours:* New Voice Award in Poetry, YMCA Writers Voice Program, 1984; National Arts Club Scholar in Poetry, 1985, Alan Collins Fellow in Poetry, 1994, Bread Loaf Writers Conference; Poetry Prize, Bennington Writers Workshop, 1988; Tennessee Williams Scholar in Poetry, Sewanee Writers Conference, 1995. *Membership:* Poetry Society of America. *Address:* 11-11 35th Ave, Apt 2P, Jackson Heights, NY 11372, USA.

STOCKER, Stella; b. London, England. Adult Education Lecturer; Reviews Ed.; Poet. m. Victor Stocker, 1 s. *Education:* Queen Mary College, University of London; High Wycombe College of Art and Technology. *Appointments:* Reviews Ed., Orbis, 1990–91; Panel of Eds, Reviews Ed., Weyfarers Poetry Magazine, 1997, 2002–; Creative Writing Tutor; Gives talks on contemporary poetry and organizes poetry and prose workshops; Compiler and Ed. of children's stories in conjunction with the Royal Marsden Hospital. *Contributions to:* Orbis; Envoi; Counterpoint; New Poetry; Outposts; Pennine Platform; Weyfarers; Palantir; Vision On; Keep; Doors; Staple. *Honours:* Special Mentions, 1982, 1990, Second Prizes, 1987, 1991, Third Prize, 1988, Highly Commended, 1997, Surrey Open Competitions; Commendations, Ver Poets Open Competitions, 1988, 1991; Commendation, Kent and Sussex Open Competition, 1992; Adjudicator, Granville Poetry Competition, 1993. *Memberships:* Poetry Society; Surrey Poetry Centre, hon. mem. *Address:* Treetops, 18 Hermitage Rd, Kenley, Surrey CR8 5EB, England.

STOCKS, John Rryan; b. 17 July 1917, Baildon, West Yorkshire, England. Poet; Dramatist. *Education:* University of Leeds, 1945–50. *Publications:* Zodiac; Trouble on Helicon. Plays: After You've Gone, 1972; Victor's Island (and two other one-act plays), 1990. *Contributions to:* Anthologies and periodicals. *Memberships:* Bradford English Society; Poetry Workshop. *Address:* Bradda, 11 Halstead Dr., Near Ilkey, West Yorkshire LS29 6NT, England.

STOKER, Richard; b. 8 Nov. 1938, Castleford, Yorkshire, England. Poet; Composer; Author; Painter. m. (2) Gillian Patricia Watson, 10 July 1986. *Education:* Huddersfield School of Music and School of Art; Royal Acad. of Music, 1958–62; Composition with Nadia Boulanger, Paris, 1962–63; Private study with Eric Fenby and Arthur Benjamin. *Appointments:* Asst Librarian, London Symphony Orchestra, 1962–63; Prof. of Composition, 1963–87, Tutor, 1970–80, Royal Acad. of Music; Ed., The Composer, 1969–80; Composition Teacher, St Paul's School, Hammersmith, London, 1973–76; Magdalene College, Cambridge, 1973–76; Appointed Magistrate, Inner London Commission, 1995–. *Publications:* Portrait of a Town, 1970; Words Without Music, 1975; Strolling Players', 1980; Open Window–Open Door (autobiography), 1985; Between the Lines, 1991; Tanglewood (novel), 1994; Diva (novel), 1997; Collected Short Stories, 1997; Thomas Armstrong: A Celebration, 1998; A Passage of Time, 1999. *Contributions to:* Anthologies, including: Triumph; Spotlight; Strolling Players; American Poetry Society publications; Periodicals, including: Records and Recording; Books and Bookmen; Guardian; Performance; The Magistrate; Poems on internet publications. *Honours:* BBC Music Award, 1952; Eric Coates Award, 1962; Mendelssohn Scholarship, 1962; Dove Prize, 1962; Assoc., 1965, Fellow, 1971, Royal Acad. of Music; Ed.'s Awards, American National Library, 1995, 1996, 1997. *Memberships:* Composers' Guild, exec. committee; Asscn of Professional Composers; Royal Society; Royal Acad. of Music; Magistrates' Asscn; Atlantic Council of the UK, founder mem.; European Atlantic Group; PEN International and English PEN, 1996. *Address:* c/o Ricordi & Co (London) Ltd, 210 New Kings Rd, London SW6 4NZ, England.

STOLOFF, Carolyn; b. 14 Jan. 1927, New York, NY, USA. Poet; Painter; Teacher. *Education:* Dalton School; University of Illinois, 1944–46; BS,

Painting, Columbia University School of General Studies, 1949; Art studies with Xavier Gonzales, Eric Isenburger and Hans Hofmann; Poetry studies with Stanley Kunitz. *Appointments:* Teacher, Manhattanville College, 1957–74; Stephen's College, 1975, Hamilton College, 1985, University of Rochester, 1985. *Publications:* Stepping Out, 1971; In the Red Meadow, 1973; Dying to Survive, 1973; Lighter-Than-Night Verse, 1977; Swiftly Now, 1982; A Spool of Blue: New and Selected Poems, 1983; You Came to Meet Someone Else, 1993. *Contributions to:* Anthologies and journals. *Honours:* MacDowell Colony Residence Grants, 1961, 1962, 1970, 1976; Theodore Roethke Award, Poetry Northwest, 1967; Gale Award for Poetry, 1999; Various awards for oil painting. *Address:* 24 W Eighth St, New York, NY 10011, USA.

STOLTZFUS, Ben Franklin; b. 15 Sept. 1927, Sofia, Bulgaria (US citizen). Writer; Poet; Prof. Emeritus. m. (1) Elizabeth Burton, 20 Aug. 1955, divorced 20 Oct. 1975, 2 s., 1 d., (2) Judith Palmer, 8 Nov. 1975. *Education:* BA, Amherst College, 1949; MA, Middlebury College, 1954; University of Paris, 1955–56; PhD, University of Wisconsin, 1959. *Appointments:* Instructor in French, Smith College, 1958–60; Asst Prof., 1960–65, Assoc. Prof., 1965–66, Prof. of French, Comparative Literature and Creative Writing, 1967–93, Prof. Emeritus, 1993–, University of California at Riverside. *Publications:* Fiction: The Eye of the Needle, 1967; Black Lazarus, 1972; Red, White, and Blue, 1989. Non-Fiction: Alain Robbe-Grillet and the New French Novel, 1964; Georges Chenneviere et l'unanimisme, 1965; Gide's Eagles, 1969; Gide and Hemingway: Rebels Against God, 1978; Alain Robbe-Grillet: The Body of the Text, 1985; Alain Robbe-Grillet: Life, Work, and Criticism, 1987; Postmodern Politics: Nouveau Roman and Innovative Fiction, 1987; Lacan and Literature: Purloined Pretexts (ed.), 1996. *Contributions to:* Numerous journals, quarterlies, reviews and magazines. *Honours:* Fulbright Scholarships, 1955–56, 1963–64; Hon. doctorate, Amherst College, 1974; NAAP Gradiva Award, 1997. *Memberships:* MLA of America; Poets and Writers. *Address:* c/o Dept of Comparative Literature and Foreign Languages, University of California at Riverside, Riverside, CA 92521, USA.

STONE, Gordon Leonard; b. 27 Feb. 1936, Halifax, Nova Scotia, Canada. Prof. (retd); Poet. m. Betty Jean, 10 Aug. 1957, 1 d. *Education:* BSc, Forestry, 1960; MSc, Forestry, 1967; MSc, Adult Education, 1975. *Publications:* In Search of the Source of Light; Insight into the Mind of a Schizophrenic Friend, 1989; Why I Called?; My Journey of Faith with Telecare, 1996. *Address:* 145 Princess Crescent, Sault Ste Marie, Ontario P6B 3P4, Canada.

STONE, Joan Elizabeth; b. 22 Oct. 1930, Port Angeles, Washington, USA. Asst Prof. of English; Poet; Writer. m. James A Black, 30 July 1990, 4 s., 1 d. *Education:* BA, 1970, MA, 1974, PhD, 1976, University of Washington. *Appointments:* Visiting Prof. of Poetry, University of Montana, 1974; Dir, Creative Writing Workshop, University of Washington, 1975; Asst Prof. of English, Colorado College, 1977–. *Publications:* The Swimmer and Other Poems, 1975; Alba, 1976; A Letter to Myself to Water, 1981; Our Lady of the Harbor, 1986. *Contributions to:* Journals and magazines. *Honours:* Acad. of American Poets Awards, 1969, 1970, 1972; Borestone Mountain Award, 1974. *Address:* 312 E Yampa St, Colorado Springs, CO 80903, USA.

STONE, John; b. 7 Feb. 1936, Jackson, Mississippi, USA. Physician; Cardiologist; Prof.; Poet. m. Lu Crymes, 16 Aug. 1958, 2 s. *Education:* BA, Millsaps College, Jackson, 1958; MD, Washington University, 1962; University of Rochester; Emory University. *Appointments:* Asst Prof. to Prof., School of Medicine, Emory University. *Publications:* The Smell of Matches; In All This Rain; Renaming the Streets; In the Country of Hearts. *Contributions to:* New England Review; Shenandoah; Southern Poetry Review; Beloit Poetry Journal; New Orleans Review; Denver Quarterly; Midwest Quarterly; Greenhouse Review; Raven. *Honour:* Literature Award. *Membership:* Mississippi Institute of Arts and Letters. *Address:* c/o Emory University School of Medicine, WHSCAB-1440 Clifton Rd NE, Atlanta, GA 30322, USA.

STOREY, David (Malcolm); b. 13 July 1933, Wakefield, England. Writer; Dramatist; Screenwriter; Poet. m. Barbara Rudd Hamilton, 1956, 2 s., 2 d. *Education:* Diploma, Slade School of Art, 1956. *Publications:* This Sporting Life, 1960; Flight into Camden, 1960; Radcliffe, 1963; Pasmore, 1972; A Temporary Life, 1973; Edward, 1973; Saville, 1976; A Prodigal Child, 1982; Present Times, 1984; Storey's Lives: Poems 1951–1991, 1992; A Serious Man, 1998. *Honours:* Macmillan Fiction Award, 1960; John Llewellyn Memorial Prize, 1960; Somerset Mauhgam Award, 1960; Evening Standard Awards, 1967, 1970; Los Angeles Drama Critics Award, 1969; Writer of the Year Award, Variety Club of Great Britain, 1969; New York Drama Critics Awards, 1969, 1970, 1971; Geoffrey Faber Memorial Prize, 1973; Fellow, University College, London, 1974; Booker Prize, 1976. *Address:* c/o Jonathon Cape Ltd, Random House, 20 Vauxhall Bridge Rd, London SW1V 2SA, England.

STORHOFF, Diana Faye Carmack, (Donya Soleya); b. 10 Sept. 1946, Anderson, IN, USA. Research Scientist; Poet. Divorced, 2 s. *Education:* Bachelor, Chemistry, 1969; MSc, Chemistry, 1973. *Publications:* 8 poems. *Contributions to:* Anthologies and other publications. *Honours:* Ed.'s Choice Certificate, National Library of Poetry; Honorable Mention, Iliad Literary Awards. *Memberships:* International Society of Poetry; Writers Center of Indianapolis. *Address:* 2682 DeShong, Pendleton, IN 46064, USA.

STORM, Morgan. See: ORME-COLLINS, Donna Youngoon.

STOUT, Frances. See: SUNTREE, Susan.

STOUT, Robert Joe; b. 3 Feb. 1938, Scottsbluff, Nebraska, USA. Writer; Poet. m. Maureen Ryan, 14 April 1988, 2 s., 3 d. Education: BA, Mexico City College, 1960. Publications: Miss Sally, 1973; The Trick, 1974; Swallowing Dust, 1974; Moving Out, 1974; The Way to Pinal, 1979; They Still Play Baseball the Old Way, 1994. Contributions to: Nation; Commonweal; Modern Maturity; Notre Dame Magazine; Beloit Poetry Journal; Chicago Tribune Magazine; New Orleans Review; Chic. Address: Caja Postal 220, LaPaz, BCS, CP 23000, Mexico.

STOW, (Julian) Randolph; b. 28 Nov. 1935, Geraldton, WA, Australia; Writer; Poet; Librettist. Education: University of Western Australia, 1956. Appointments: Lecturer in English, University of Leeds, Yorkshire, 1962, 1968–69, University of Western Australia, 1963–64; Harkness Fellow, USA, 1964–66. Publications: A Haunted Land, 1956; The Bystander, 1957; To the Islands, 1958; Tourmaline, 1963; The Merry-Go-Round in the Sea, 1965; Midnite, 1967; Visitants, 1979; The Girl Green as Elderflower, 1980; The Suburbs of Hell, 1984. Poetry: Act One, 1957; Outrider: Poems 1956–62, 1962; A Counterfeit Silence: Selected Poems, 1969; Randolph Stow (omnibus vol. edited by A J Hassall), 1990. Librettos to Music by Peter Maxwell Davies: Eight Songs for a Mad King, 1969; Miss Donnithorne's Maggot, 1974. Honours: Miles Franklin Award, 1958; Britannica-Australia Award, 1966; Grace Leven Prize, 1969; Arts Council of Great Britain Bursary, 1969; Commonwealth Literary Fund Grant, 1974; Patrick White Award, 1979. Address: c/o Sheil Land Assocs, 43 Doughty St, London WC1N 2LF, England.

STRAND, Mark; b. 11 April 1934, Summerside, PE, Canada. Poet; Writer; Prof. m. (1) Antonia Ratensky, 14 Sept. 1961, divorced June 1973, 1 d., (2) Julia Rumsey Garretson, 15 March 1976, 1 s. Education: AB, Antioch College, 1957; BFA, Yale University, 1959; MA, University of Iowa, 1962. Appointments: Instructor, University of Iowa, 1962–65; Fulbright Lecturer, University of Brazil, 1965; Asst Prof., Mount Holyoke College, 1966; Visiting Prof., University of Washington, 1967, University of Virginia, 1977, California State University at Fresno, 1977, University of California at Irvine, 1978, Wesleyan University, 1979–80; Adjunct Prof., Columbia University, 1968–70; Visiting Lecturer, Yale University, 1969–70, Harvard University, 1980–81; Assoc. Prof., Brooklyn College, 1971; Bain Swiggett Lecturer, Princeton University, 1972; Fanny Hurst Prof. of Poetry, Brandeis University, 1973; Prof., 1981–86, Distinguished Prof., 1986–94, University of Utah; Poet Laureate of the USA, 1990–91; Elliot Coleman Prof. of Poetry, Johns Hopkins University, 1994–97; Andrew MacLeish Distinguished Service Prof., University of Chicago. Publications: Poetry: Sleeping With One Eye Open, 1964; Reasons for Moving, 1968; Darker, 1970; The Sargentville Notebook, 1973; The Story of Our Lives, 1973; The Late Hour, 1978; Selected Poems, 1980; The Continuous Life, 1990; Dark Harbor, 1993; Blizzard of One, 1998. Fiction: Mr and Mrs Baby (short stories), 1985. Prose: The Monument, 1978; The Art of the Real, 1983; William Bailey, 1987; Hopper, 1994. Anthologies: The Contemporary American Poets, 1969; New Poetry of Mexico (with Octavio Paz), 1970; Another Republic (with Charles Simic), 1976; The Best American Poetry 1991 (with David Lehman), 1992; The Weather of Words: Poetic Invention, 2000. Translator: Halty Ferguson: 18 Poems from the Quechua, 1971; Rafael Alberti: The Owl's Insomnia (poems), 1973; Carlos Drummond de Andrade: Souvenir of the Ancient World (poems), 1976; Travelling in the Family: The Selected Poems of Carlos Drummond de Andrade, 1986. Children's Books: The Planet of Lost Things, 1982; The Night Book, 1985; Rembrandt Takes a Walk, 1986. Contributions to: Poems, book reviews, art reviews, essays on poetry and painting and interviews in numerous periodicals. Honours: Fulbright Scholarship to Italy, 1960–61; Ingram Merrill Foundation Fellowship, 1966; National Endowment for the Arts Fellowships, 1967–68, 1977–78; Rockefeller Fellowship, 1968–69; Edgar Allan Poe Prize, 1974; Guggenheim Fellowship, 1974–75; National Institute of Arts and Letters Award, 1975; Acad. of American Poets Fellowship, 1979; Writer-in-Residence, American Acad., Rome, 1982; John D. and Catherine T. MacArthur Foundation Fellowship, 1987–92; Utah Governor's Award in the Arts, 1992; Bobbitt National Prize for Poetry, 1992; Bollingen Prize for Poetry, 1993; Pulitzer Prize in Poetry, 1999. Memberships: American Acad. and Institute of Arts and Letters, 1980–; National Acad. of Arts and Sciences, 1995–. Address: Committee on Social Thought, 1130 E 59th St, Chicago, IL 60637, USA.

STRAUB, Peter Francis; b. 2 March 1943, Milwaukee, Wisconsin, USA. Writer. m. 27 Aug. 1966. Education: BA, University of Wisconsin, 1965; MA, Columbia University, 1966. Publications: Open Air (poems), 1972; Marriage, 1973; Julia, 1975; If You Could See Me New, 1977; Ghost Story, 1979; Shadowland, 1980; Floating Dragon, 1983; The Talisman (with Stephen King), 1984; Koko, 1988; Mystery, 1989; Houses Without Doors, 1990; The Throat, 1993; The Hellfire Club, 1996; Mr X, 1999; Magic Terror, 2000; Black House (with Stephen King), 2001. Contributions to: TLS; New Statesman; Washington Post. Honours: British Fantasy Award, 1983; August Derleth Award, 1983; World Fantasy Best Novel Awards, 1988, 1993; Bram Stoker Awards for Best Novel, 1993, 1998, 2000. Memberships: Mystery Writers of America; Horror Writers of America; PEN. Address: 53 W 85th St, New York, NY 10024, USA.

STRAUSS, Botho; b. 2 Dec. 1944, Naumberg-an-der-Saale, Germany. Author; Poet; Dramatist. Education: German Language and Literature, Drama, Sociology, Cologne and Munich. Publications: Bekannte Gesichter, gemischte Gefühle (with T Bernhard and F Kroetz), 1974; Trilogie des Wiedersehens, 1976; Gross und Klein, 1978; Rumor, 1980; Kalldeway Farce, 1981; Paare, Passanten, 1981; Der Park, 1983; Der junge Mann, 1984; Diese Erinnerung an einen, der nur einen Tag zu Gast War, 1985; Die Fremdenführerin, 1986; Niemand anderes, 1987; Besucher, 1988; Kongress: Die Kette der Demütigungen, 1989; Theaterstücke in zwei Banden, 1994; Wohnen Dammern Lügen, 1994; Das Partikular, 2000; Der Narr und seine Frau heute abend in Pancomedia, 2001. Honours: Dramatists' Prize, Hanover, 1975; Schiller Prize, Baden-Württemberg, 1977; Literary Prize, Bavarian Acad. of Fine Arts, Munich, 1981; Jean Paul Prize, 1987; Georg Büchner Prize, 1989. Membership: PEN. Address: Keithstrasse 8, 17877, Berlin, Germany.

STRAUSS, Jennifer; b. 30 Jan. 1933, Heywood, Vic., Australia. Assoc. Prof.; Poet. m. Werner Strauss, 1958, 3 s. Education: BA, University of Melbourne, 1954; University of Glasgow, 1957–58; PhD, Monash University, 1992. Appointments: Senior Lecturer, 1971–92, Assoc. Prof., 1992–, Monash University. Publications: Children and Other Strangers, 1975; Winter Driving, 1981; Middle English Verse: An Anthology (co-ed.), 1985; Labour Ward, 1988; Boundary Conditions: The Poetry of Gwen Harwood, 1992; The Oxford Book of Australian Love Poems (ed.), 1993; Judith Wright, 1995; Tierra del Fuego: New and Selected Poems, 1997; Family Ties: Australian Poems of the Family (ed.), 1998; Oxford Literary History of Australia (co-ed.), 1998. Contributions to: Various publications. Memberships: Premier's Literary Awards Committee; PEN; Asscn for Study of Australian Literature; Australian Society of Authors. Address: 2–12 Tollington Ave, East Malvern, Vic. 3145, Australia.

STROBLOVA, Jana; b. 1 July 1936, Prague, Czechoslovakia. Poet. m. Otakar Hulec, 21 June 1959, 1 s. Education: Charles University, Prague. Publications: Protez, 1958; Kdyby nebylo na sul, 1961; Hostinec u dvou srdci, 1965; Torza, 1969; Uplnek, 1980; Krajina na muri noze, 1984; Carodeni, 1989; Fatamorgany, 1991; Hra na stvoreni sveta, 1991; Slágr o Iásce, 1994; Svetlohry, 1996. Contributions to: 8 anthologies, 1990–95, reviews, and periodicals. Honour: International Poetry Prize, Florence, 1990. Memberships: Czech PEN Club; Writers' Union. Address: Detska 176, 100 00 Prague 10, Czech Republic.

STROFFOLINO, Chris; b. 20 March 1963, Reading, Pennsylvania, USA. Teacher; Poet. Education: BA, English, Philosophy, Albright College, 1986; MA, English, Temple University, 1988; PhD Studies, English, State University of New York, Albany. Appointments: Teacher, Temple University, 1986–88, Dreyel University, 1988–89, Peirce Junior College, 1991–92, University of Massachusetts, 1992–93, State University of New York, Albany, 1994–. Publications: Incidents, 1990; Oops, 1991; Cusps, 1995. Contributions to: American Poetry Review; Sulfer; New American Writing; O-Blok; Avel; Talisman; Calibah; Sun and Moon; Apex of the M; Tin Fish; Painted Bride Quarterly; Long Shot; The Baffler; New York Quarterly. Memberships: Poets and Writers; Hudson Valley Writers Guild. Address: 365B State St, Albany, NY 12210, USA.

STRONG, Eithne; b. 23 Feb. 1923, West Limerick, Ireland. Writer; Poet. m. Rupert Strong, 12 Nov. 1943, 2 s., 7 d. Education: BA, Trinity College, Dublin. Publications: Poetry: Songs of Living, 1965; Sarah in Passing, 1974; Circt Oibre, 1980; Fuil agus Fallat, 1983; My Darling Neighbour, 1985; Flesh the Greatest Sin, 1989; An Sagart Pinc, 1990; Aoife Faoi Ghlas, 1990; Let Live, 1990; Spatial Nosing, 1993; Nobel, 1998. Fiction: Degrees of Kindred, 1979; The Love Riddle, 1993. Short Fiction: Patterns, 1981. Contributions to: Anthologies, journals, and magazines. Memberships: Aosdána; Conradh Na Gaeilge; Irish PEN; Irish Writers Union; Poetry Ireland. Address: 17 Eaton Sq., Monkstown, Dublin, Ireland.

STROUD, Drew McCord, (Ryu Makoto); b. 3 Sept. 1944, USA. University Prof.; Poet. Education: BA, Harvard College, 1966; MA, University of Arizona, 1986. Publications: Lines Drawn Towards, 1980; Poamorio (trans.), 1984; The Hospitality of Circumstance, 1992. Contributions to: New Republic; Christopher Street; Expatriate Review; Mediterranean Review; Printed Matter; Noctiluca; Dilettante; Christian Science Monitor. Honours: Witter Bynner Foundation for Poetry Award, 1983; Grand Prize, Tokyo English Literature Society, 1983. Memberships: Poetry Society of America; Tokyo English Literature Society; Asiatic Society of Japan. Address: Temple University, 1-16-7 Kamiochiai, Shinjuku-ku, Tokyo 161, Japan.

STRPKA, Ivan; b. 30 June 1944, Hlohovec, Czechoslovakia. Geological Researcher; Poet; Writer. m. 4 May 1968, 2 d. Education: Graduated, Spanish Language and Literature, Slovak Language and Literature, Comenius University, Bratislava, 1969. Publications: 10 books, 1968–96. Contributions to: Various literary journals. Honour: Ivan Krasko Prize, 1969. Memberships: Community of Slovak Writers; Lonely Runners Literary Group, founder; PEN Club, Slovakia. Address: Mlynarovicova 20, 851 03 Bratislava, Slovakia.

STUART, Dabney; b. 4 Nov. 1937, Richmond, Virginia, USA. Prof. of English; Ed.; Poet; Writer. m. (3) Sandra Westcott, 1983, 2 s., 1 d. *Education:* AB, Davidson College, North Carolina, 1960; AM, Harvard Universty, 1962. *Appointments:* Instructor, College of William and Mary, Williamsburg, Virginia, 1961–65; Instructor, 1965–66, Asst Prof., 1966–69, Assoc. Prof., 1969–74, Prof., 1974–91, S Blount Mason Prof. of English, 1991–, Washington and Lee University, Lexington, Virginia; Poetry Ed., 1966–76, Ed.-in-Chief, 1988–95, Shenandoah; Visiting Prof., Middlebury College, 1968–69; McGuffey Chair of Creative Writing, Ohio University, 1972; Visiting Poet, University of Virginia, 1981, 1982–83; Poetry Ed., New Virginia Review, 1983. *Publications:* Poetry: The Diving Bell, 1966; A Particular Place, 1969; Corgi Modern Poets in Focus 3, 1971; The Other Hand, 1974; Friends of Yours, Friends of Mine, 1974; Round and Round: A Triptych, 1977; Rockbridge Poems, 1981; Common Ground, 1982; Don't Look Back, 1987; Narcissus Dreaming, 1990; Light Years: New and Selected Poems, 1994; Second Sight: Poems for Paintings by Carol Cloar, 1996; Long Gone, 1996; Settlers, 1999; Strains of the Old Man, 1999. Fiction: Sweet Lucy Wine: Stories, 1992; The Way to Cobbs Creek, 1997; No Visible Means of Support, 2000. Non-Fiction: Nabokov: The Dimensions of Parody, 1978. *Honours:* Dylan Thomas Prize, Poetry Society of America, 1965; Borestone Mountain Awards, 1969, 1974, 1977; National Endowment for the Arts Grant, 1969, and Fellowships, 1974, 1982; Virginia Governor's Award, 1979; Guggenheim Fellowship, 1987–88; Individual Artists Fellowship, Virginia Commission for the Arts, 1996; Residency, Rockefeller Study Centre, Bellagio, Italy, 2000. *Address:* c/o Dept of English, Washington and Lee University, Lexington, VA 24450, USA.

STUART, Derek. See: FOSTER, John Louis.

STUART, (Jessica) Jane; b. 20 Aug. 1942, Ashland, KY, USA. Poet. 2 s. *Education:* AB, Classics, Case Western Reserve University, 1964; MA, Classical Languages, 1967; MA, Italian, 1969, PhD, Italian, 1971, Indiana University. *Publications:* A Year's Harvest, 1956; Eyes of the Mole, 1967; White Barn, 1971; The Wren and Other Poems, 1993; Karnak, 1993; Passage into Time, 1994; White Tock, 1995; Cherokee Lullaby, 1995; Moon Over Miami, 1996; Journeys, 1998; Thunderbolt, 2000; Red Balloon, 2001; Candlelady, 2002; Heart-Shaped Moon, 2002. *Contributions to:* Reviews, quarterlies, and magazines. *Honours:* Various prizes, including Kentucky State Poetry Society Grand Prix, 1992. *Memberships:* Acad. of American Poets; Virginia State Poetry Society; West Virginia Poetry Society; Ohio Poetry Asscn; West Virginia Poetry Society; Missippi Poetry Society; Georgia Poetry Society; Society of American Poets. *Address:* 1000 W-Hollow, Greenup, KY 41144, USA.

STUDEBAKER, William (Vern); b. 21 May 1947, Salmon, ID, USA. Prof.; Writer; Poet. m. Judy Infanger, 23 Aug. 1969, 2 s., 2 d. *Education:* BA, History, 1970, MA, English, 1986, Idaho State University; Law, University of Idaho, 1974–75; Computer Science, Sonoma State University, 1986. *Appointments:* Asst Prof., 1975–, Chair., Dept of English, 1980–82, College of Southern Idaho; Commissioner, Idaho Commission on the Arts, 1981–86; Councilman, Idaho Humanities Council, 1996–. *Publications:* Everything Goes Without Saying, 1978; The Cleaving, 1985; Idaho's Poetry: A Centennial Anthology, 1989; The Rat Lady at the Company Dump, 1990; Where the Morning Lights' Still Blue: Personal Essays About Idaho, 1994; River Religion, 1997; Traveler' in an Antique Land, 1997; Short of a Good Promise, 1999. *Contributions to:* Numerous reviews, quarterlies, and journals. *Address:* 2616 East St, 4000 North St, Twin Falls, ID 83301, USA.

STUDER, Constance Elaine Browne; b. 4 Dec. 1942, Lodi, Ohio, USA. Writer; Poet; Registered Nurse. Divorced, 1 s. *Education:* Nursing Diploma, Toledo Hospital School of Nursing, 1963; BA, Illinois College, 1971; MA, English Literature, Creative Writing, University of Colorado, 1980. *Appointment:* Artist-in-Residence, Poetry, Rocky Mountain Women's Institute, 1987. *Publications:* Womanthology, 1977; Hyperion: Black Sun, New Moon, 1980; Wingbone: Poetry from Colorado, 1986; Toward Solomon's Mountain, 1986. *Contributions to:* Room of Our Own; Eleventh Muse; Kaleidoscope. *Honours:* Ann Woodbury Hafen Prize, 1977; Finalist, Nimrod Poetry Contest, 1986; Third Place, International Kaleidoscope Poetry Contest, 1986; Winner, Embers Poetry Contest, 1986. *Address:* 1617 Parkside Circle, Lafayette, CO 80026, USA.

SUANDI; Author; Performance Poet. *Appointments:* Live art performances; Live art commissions; International performances; Recordings, television and radio work. *Publications:* Style, 1993; Nearly Forty, 1994; There Will Be No Tears, 1996; Akwaaba, 1996; Fire People, 1998; Women at War, 1998; Television Production, 1997. *Honours:* Winston Churchill Fellowship, 1996; O.B.E., 1999. *Memberships:* British Actors Equity Asscn; National Asscn for Writers in Education; Pankhurst Centre; Informal European Theatre Managers. *Address:* 369 Barlow Moor Rd, Manchester M21 7FZ, England. E-mail: baa@baas.demon.co.uk.

SUBRAMANIAM, P. V.; b. 20 Sept. 1936, Trichur, Kerala, India. Accountant; Poet. m. Prema Subramaniam, 17 April 1971, 1 s. *Education:* Degree, Commerce, 1955; Diploma, Administrative Management, 1968. *Publications:* An Executive's Lament, 1993; A Mirror's Verdict, 1995. *Contributions to:*

Various publications. *Memberships:* Mem. Exec. Committee, PEN All India Centre; Poetry Club of India; Life Mem., Poetry Society, India; Founder Trustee, Haiku Society, India; British Haiku Society. *Address:* C-10? Gurukrupa CHS, Cross Rd No. 2, Swami Samarth Nagar, Andheri (West) Mumbai 400 053, India.

SUBRAMANIAN, (Mary) Belinda; b. 6 Sept. 1953, Statesville, North Carolina, USA. Poet; Ed. m. S. Ramnath, 24 Sept. 1977, 2 d. *Education:* BA Regents College, New York, 1987; MA, California State University, Dominguez Hills, 1990. *Appointment:* Ed., Gypsy Magazine and Vergin Press, 1983– *Publications:* Nürnberg Poems, 1983; Heather and Mace, 1985; Eye of the Beast, 1986; Fighting Woman, 1986; Body Parts, 1987; Skin Divers (with Lyn Lifshin), 1988; Halloween, 1989; The Jesuit Poems, 1989; Elephants and Angels, 1991; The Innocents, 1991; A New Geography of Poets, 1992; Finding Reality in Myth, 1996; Notes of a Human Warehouse Engineer, 1998. *Contributions to:* Anthologies, journals, and magazines. *Honour:* Winner, Nerve Cowboy Poetry Contest, 1998. *Address:* PO Box 370322, El Paso, TX 79937, USA.

SUDHAKR. See: MOORTHY, Krishna Kopparam.

SUKNASKI, Andrew; b. 30 July 1942, Wood Mountain, Saskatchewan, Canada. Ed.; Poet. *Education:* University of British Columbia, Vancouver, 1967–68. *Appointment:* Ed., Three Legged Coyote, Wood Mountain, 1982–. *Publications:* This Shadow of Eden, 1970; Circles, 1970; Rose Wayn in the East, 1972; Old Mill, 1972; The Zen Pilgrimage, 1972; Four Parts Sand: Concrete Poems, 1972; Wood Mountain Poems, 1973; Suicide Notes, Booke One, 1973; These Fragments I've Gathered for Ezra, 1973; Leaving, 1974; Blind Man's House, 1975; Leaving Wood Mountain, 1975; Octomi, 1976; Almighty Voice, 1977; Moses Beauchamp, 1978; The Ghosts Call You Poor, 1978; Two for Father, 1978; In the Name of Narid: New Poems, 1981; Montage for an Interstellar Cry, 1982; The Land They Gave Away: Selected and New Poems, 1982; Silk Trail, 1985. *Honour:* Canada Council Grants. *Address:* c/o Thistledown Press, 668 East Pl., Saskatoon, Sasketchewan S7J 2Z5, Canada.

SULLIVAN, Charles; b. 27 May 1933, Massachusetts, USA. Educator; Poet. Divorced, 2 s., 1 d. *Education:* BA, Swarthmore College, 1955; MA, 1968, PhD, 1973, New York University; MPA, Pennsylvania State University, 1978. *Appointments:* Assoc. Dean, Georgetown University, 1989; Pres., American Foundation for the Arts, 1995. *Publications:* America in Poetry, 1988; Imaginary Gardens, 1989; Ireland in Poetry, 1990; Alphabet Animals, 1991; Children of Promise, 1991; The Lover in Winter, 1991; Numbers at Play, 1992; Circus, 1992; Loving, 1993; Cowboys, 1993; American Beauties, 1994; Fathers and Children, 1995; A Woman of a Certain Age, 1995; Imaginary Animals, 1996. *Contributions to:* Various. *Honours:* Various. *Memberships:* American Poetry Society; Acad. of American Poets; Cosmos Club; National Society of Arts and Letters; Folger Poetry Board; Poetry Committee of Greater Washington. *Address:* 1344 Ballantrae Lane, McLean, VA 22101, USA.

SULLIVAN, James (Edward); b. 11 July 1928, Massachusetts, USA. Librarian (retd); Poet. m. Frances Elizabeth Lynch, 11 Aug. 1963, deceased 1976, 1 s., 1 d. *Education:* AB, Honours, Greek, 1948, AM, History, 1950, Boston College. *Appointment:* Dir, Woods Memorial Library, Barre, Massachusetts, 1967–94. *Publication:* In Order of Appearance: 400 Poems by James Sullivan, 1988. *Contributions to:* America; Barre Gazette; Commonweal; Worcester Review. *Honour:* Worcester County Poetry Asscn Award, 1972. *Membership:* Hopkins Society. *Address:* 590 Sunrise Ave, Box 451, Barre, MA 01005, USA.

SULLIVAN, Rosemary; b. 29 Aug. 1947, Montréal, QC, Canada. Prof.; Author; Poet. *Education:* BA, McGill University, 1968; MA, University of Connecticut, 1969; PhD, University of Sussex, 1972. *Appointments:* Faculty, University of Dijon, 1972–73, University of Bordeaux, 1973–74, University of Victoria, BC, 1974–77; Asst Prof., 1977–80, Assoc. Prof., 1980–91, Prof., 1991–, University of Toronto. *Publications:* The Garden Master: The Poetry of Theodore Roethke, 1975; The Space a Name Makes, 1986; By Heart: Elizabeth Smart, a Life, 1991; Blue Panic, 1991; Shadow Maker: The Life of Gwendolyn MacEwan, 1995; The Red Shoes: Margaret Attwood Starting Out, 1998; The Bone Ladder: New and Selected Poems, 2000; Labyrinth of Desire: Women, Passion and Romantic Obsession, 2001; Memory-Making: Selected Essays, 2001. Other: Ed. or Co-Ed. of several books. *Contributions to:* Many journals and magazines. *Honours:* Gerald Lampert Award for Poetry, 1986; Brascan Silver Medal for Culture, National Magazine Awards, 1986; Guggenheim Fellowship, 1992; Governor-General's Award for Non-Fiction, 1995; City of Toronto Book Award, 1995; Non-Fiction Prize, Canadian Authors' Asscn, 1995; Pres.'s Medal for Biography, Columbia University, 1995; Killam Fellow, 1996; Canada Research Chair, 2000; Connaught Fellowship, 2002. *Memberships:* Amnesty International; Toronto Arts Group for Human Rights, founding mem. *Literary Agent:* Westwood Creative Artists. *Address:* c/o Dept of English, University of Toronto, 7 King's College Circle, Toronto, ON M5S 3K1, Canada.

SUMMERTREE, Katonah. See: WINDSOR, Patricia.

SUNTREE, Susan, (Frances Stout); b. 19 May 1946, Los Angeles, CA, USA. Writer; Poet; Prof. m., 1 s., 1 d. *Education:* BA, University of Arizona, 1968; MA, University of Kent, Canterbury, England, 1970. *Appointments:* Arts Reach Artist-in-Residence, University of California, Los Angeles, 1983–85; Santa Monica College, 1984–88; East Los Angeles College, 1989–. *Publications:* Eye of the Womb, 1981; Tulips (trans.), 1991; Wisdom of the East: Stories of Compassion, Inspiration and Love (ed.), 2001. *Contributions to:* Anthologies, including: The Spirit of Writing: Classic and Contemporary Essays Celebrating the Writing Life, 2001; Magazines and journals. *Honours:* California Arts Council Grant, 1978; 18th Street Art Complex, International Exchange Artist to the Netherlands, 1998. *Memberships:* PEN; Poets and Writers. *E-mail:* ssuntree@earthlink.net. *Website:* www.susansuntree.com.

SURVANT, Joseph William; b. 9 Oct. 1942, Kentucky, USA. Prof.; Poet; Writer. m. Jeannie Ashley, 4 Sept. 1965, 2 d. *Education:* BA, University of Kentucky, 1964; MA, 1966, PhD, 1970, University of Delaware. *Appointments:* Instructor, University of Kentucky, 1967–69; Asst Prof. to Prof., Western Kentucky University, 1970–. *Publications:* We Will All Be Changed, 1995; Anne and Alpheus, 1842–1882, 1996; The Presence of Snow in the Tropics, 2001; Rafting Rise, 2002. *Contributions to:* Many reviews and journals. *Honours:* Many, including: Kentucky Arts Council Poetry Fellowship, 1990; Runner-Up, Robert H Winner Prize, Poetry Society of America, 1994; Arkansas Poetry Prize, 1995. *Memberships:* Associated Writing Programs; Poetry Society of America. *Address:* Western Kentucky University, Bowling Green, KY 42101, USA.

SUTHERLAND-SMITH, James Alfred; b. 17 June 1948, Aberdeen, Scotland. University Lecturer; Poet. m. Viera Schlosserova, 5 Sept. 1992, 1 d. *Education:* BA, University of Leeds, 1971; University of Nottingham, 1974; MA, University of East Anglia, 1988. *Appointments:* Teacher, 1974–85; Deputy Head of Education, National Guard Signal Corps Training School, 1985–86; Head of English Language Unit, Qatar Public Telecom Corp, 1986–88; British Council Lecturer, 1989–. *Publications:* Four Poetry and Audience Poets; A Poetry Quintet; Trapped Water; A Singer from Sabiya; Naming of the Arrow; Not Waiting for Miracles; Contemporary Slovak Poets; At the Skin Resort, 1999. *Contributions to:* Ambit; Encounter; Poetry Durham; Poetry Review; Rialto; Stand; TLS; Literary Review; Kansas Quarterly; Cumberland Poetry Review; Review; Prairie Schooner; West Branch; BBC Radio 3; Slovak Television. *Honours:* Eric Gregory Award; National Poetry Competition of Great Britain; Cheltenham Competition; Philips Award; San Jose Studies Poetry Award; Prizewinner, Bridport, Exeter Festival, Stand Poetry. *Memberships:* Poetry Society Reform Movement; Poets Workshop; Society of Authors; Asscn of Literary Trans. *Address:* Lesnicka 18, Solivar, 08005 Presov, Slovak Republic.

SUTTON, Dorothy Moseley; b. 11 Oct. 1938, Todd County, KY, USA. Prof. of English; Poet. m. William Sutton, 2 Sept. 1961, 2 d. *Education:* BA, Georgetown College, 1960; MA, University of Mississippi, 1963; PhD, University of Kentucky, 1981. *Appointment:* Prof., Eastern Kentucky University, 1971–. *Contributions to:* Antioch Review; Southern Review; Prairie Schooner; Virginia Quarterly Review; Poetry Ireland Review and more than a dozen anthologies. *Honours:* Artists Award Fellowship; Robert Frost Scholar in Poetry; Twice Winner, Arts Place Competition; Grolier Award; Tyrone Guthrie Award; Alumni Asscn Teaching Excellence Award, 1998. *Memberships:* Poetry Society of America; Acad. of American Poets; Associated Writing Programs; Poets and Writers. *Address:* 115 Southland Dr., Richmond, KY 40475, USA.

SUTTON, Henry. See: SLAVITT, David R(ytman).

SUTTON, James Hercules; b. 8 Jan. 1943, Boston, MA, USA. Educator; Poet. m. Nancy Sutton, 8 June 1981, 3 s., 3 d. *Education:* BA, English and American Literature, Brown University, 1964; MFA, Creative Writing, 1968, PhD, Higher Education, 1988, University of Iowa. *Appointments:* Legislative Lobbyist, 1975–81, Agency Lobbyist, 1981–87, Instruction and Professional Devt Specialist, 1983–87, Staff Specialist for Policy Devt, 1987–93, Senior Policy Analyst, 1993–, Iowa State Education Asscn. *Publications:* Prometheus, 1995; Harry's Gloom, 1997; The Last Samurai, 1997; Harry's Gloomsday Dictionary, 1997; Harry's 'Love', 2001. *Contributions to:* Reviews, periodicals and journals. *Honours:* Mellen Poetry Prize, 1997; Hon. DFA, Mellen University, 1997. *Membership:* Des Moines Area Writers Network. *Address:* 4324 Kingman Blvd, Des Moines, IA 50311-3418, USA. *E-mail:* jamessutton@juno.com.

SVATEK, Kurt Franz; b. 26 Jan. 1949, Vienna, Austria. Vocational Teacher; Poet; Writer. m. Herma Kurner, 29 June 1973, 1 d. *Education:* Vienna Acad. of Pedagogy; Axel Anderson Acad., Hamburg, Germany. *Publications:* Poetry: Rhapsodie aus leiser Schwermut, 1995; Jahrtausendleben, 1995; Wie weit trägt der Wind schon ein Wort, 1997; Selected Poems (in English trans.), 1997; Written on the Edge, 1998. Fiction: Wir alle haben Troja zerstört, 1989; Bettlerzinken, 1993; Rendezvous mit der Hoffnung, 1994. Other: Von der Weltunordnung, 1993; Auf dem Saumpfad der Zeit, 1995; Tropfen aus dem Ozean der Zeit, 1998. *Contributions to:* Over 100 anthologies, 350 magazines, and 60 journals worldwide. *Honours:* Various prizes and awards, 1987–95. *Memberships:* Der Kreis, Austria; Haiku Society, Germany; International Society of Poets, USA; PEN, Austria. *Address:* Villa Camena, Schwarzauerstrasse 42A, 2624 Breitenau, Austria.

SVOBODA, Terese; b. 5 Sept. 1950, Ogallala, Nebraska, USA. Poet; Writer; Videomaker. m. Stephen M Bull, 18 July 1981, 3 s. *Education:* MFA, Columbia University, 1978. *Appointments:* Rare Manuscript Curator, McGill University, 1969; Co-Producer, PBS-TV series Voices and Visions, 1980–82; Distinguished Visiting Prof., University of Hawaii, 1992; Prof., Sarah Lawrence College, 1993, Williams College, 1998. *Publications:* Poetry: All Aberration, 1985; Laughing Africa, 1990; Mere Mortal, 1995. Fiction: Cannibal, 1995; A Drink Called Paradise, 1999. *Contributions to:* Poems, fiction, essays, and trans to periodicals. *Honours:* Writer's Choice Column Award, New York Times Book Review, 1985; Iowa Prize, 1990; Bobst Prize, 1995. *Memberships:* PEN; Poets and Writers; Poet's House, founding mem. and advisory board mem., 1986–91. *Address:* 335 Concord Dr., Menlo Park, CA 94025, USA.

SWAN, Susan (Jane); b. 9 June 1945, Midland, Ontario, Canada. Novelist; Writer; Poet; Assoc. Prof. of Humanities. m. Barry Haywood, 25 March 1969, divorced, 1 d. *Education:* BA, McGill University, 1967. *Appointment:* Assoc. Prof. of Humanities, 1989–, Roberts Chair in Canadian Studies, 1999–2000, York University, Toronto. *Publications:* Queen of the Silver Blades, 1975; Unfit for Paradise, 1982; The Biggest Modern Woman of the World, 1983; Tesseracts (co-author), 1985; The Last of the Golden Girls, 1989; Language in Her Eye (ed.), 1990; Mothers Talk Back (co-ed.), 1991; Slow Hand, 1992; The Wives of Bath, 1993; Stupid Boys Are Good to Relax With, 1996. *Contributions to:* Many short stories, articles, and poems in various publications. *Memberships:* Writers' Union of Canada; PEN. *Literary Agent:* Westwood Creative Artists. *Address:* 151 Robert St, Apt 2, Toronto, Ontario M5S 2K6, Canada.

SWANBERG, Ingrid; b. 4 Sept. 1947, California, USA. Poet; Ed.; Publisher. m. 27 July 1974, 1 s. *Education:* BA, English, 1970, MA, English, 1973, California State University, Sacramento; MA, Comparative Literature, University of Wisconsin, 1993. *Appointments:* Ed. and Publisher, Ghost Pony Press, 1980–, Abraxas Press Inc, 1981–; Co-Ed. and Co-Curator, D. A. Levy online publication. *Publications:* Flashlights, 1981; Letter to Persephone and Other Poems, 1984; Zen Concrete & Etc (ed.), 1991. *Contributions to:* Northeast; Lips; Wisconsin Acad. Review; Strange Fruit; Osiris; Le Guépard. *Honour:* Winner, First Annual Chapbook Award, Rhiannon Press, 1984. *Address:* 2518 Gregory St, Madison, WI 53711, USA.

SWANGER, David; b. 1 Aug. 1940, New Jersey, USA. Prof.; Poet. m. Lynn Lundstrom, 5 April 1969, 1 s., 2 d. *Education:* BA, Swarthmore College, 1963; MAT, 1964, DEd, 1970, Harvard University. *Appointments:* Asst Prof., Harvard University, 1970–71; Assoc. Prof., 1976–85, Prof. 1985–, University of California, Santa Cruz. *Publications:* The Poem as Process, 1971; Lemming Song, 1976; The Shape of Waters, 1978; Inside the Horse, 1981; Essays in Aesthetic Education, 1991; Family, 1994; The Evolution of Education, 1995; This Waking Unafraid, 1995. *Contributions to:* Georgia Review; Malahat Review; Poetry Northwest; Chariton Review; America Post and Critic; Quarry West; New Letters; Mother Earth News; Negative Capability; Whetstone; Nimrod; Minnesota Review; Cutbank; Tendril; America; Reaper. *Honours:* National Endowment for the Arts Poetry Award, 1989; Foley Award, 1991. *Memberships:* Acad. of American Poets; Poets and Writers. *Address:* Porter College, University of California, Santa Cruz, CA 95064, USA.

SWARD, Robert (Stuart); b. 23 June 1933, Chicago, IL, USA. Poet; Writer; University Lecturer. Partner, Gloria K. Alford, 2 s., 3 d. *Education:* BA, University of Illinois, 1956; MA, University of Iowa, 1958; Postgraduate Studies, Middlebury College, Vermont, 1959–60, University of Bristol, 1960–61. *Appointments:* Poet-in-Residence, Cornell University, 1962–64, University of Victoria, BC, 1969–73, University of California at Santa Cruz, 1987–; Writer-in-Residence, Foothill Writers Conference, summers 1988–; Writer, Writing Programme, Language Arts Dept, Cabrillo College, 1989–2000. *Publications:* Uncle Dog and Other Poems, 1962; Kissing the Dancer and Other Poems, 1964; Half a Life's History: New and Selected Poems 1957–83, 1983; The Three Roberts (with Robert Zend and Robert Priest), 1985; Four Incarnations: New and Selected Poems 1957–91, 1991; Family (with David Swanger, Tilly Shaw and Charles Atkinson), 1994; Earthquake Collage, 1995; A Much-Married Man (novel), 1996; Uncivilizing: A Collection of Poems, 1997; Rosicrucian in the Basement: Selected Poems, 2001; Heavenly Sex: New and Selected Poems, 2002. *Contributions to:* Anthologies, newspapers and magazines; Contributing Ed., Blue Moon Review and other Internet literary publications including Web Del Sol, locus for literary arts. *Honours:* Fulbright Fellowship, 1960–61; Guggenheim Fellowship, 1965–66; D H Lawrence Fellowship, 1966; Djerassi Foundation Residency, 1990; Villa Montalvo Literary Arts Award for Poetry, 1990; Way Cool Site Award, Editing Internet Literary Magazine, 1996. *Memberships:* League of Canadian Poets; Modern Poetry Asscn; National Writers Union, USA, 1985–; Writers Union of Canada. *Address:* PO Box 7062, Santa Cruz, CA 95061-7062, USA. *E-mail:* sward@cruzio.com. *Website:* www.robertsward.com.

SWEDE, George; b. 20 Nov. 1940, Riga, Latvia. Educator; Poet; Writer. m. (1) Bonnie Lewis, 20 June 1964, divorced 1969, (2) Anita Krumins, 23 July 1974, 2 s. *Education:* BA, University of British Columbia, 1964; MA, Dalhousie University, 1965; PhD, Greenwich University, Australia, 2000. *Appointments:* Instructor, Vancouver City College, 1966–67; Instructor, 1968–73, Prof. of Psychology, 1973–, Ryerson University, Toronto; Dir, Poetry and Things,

1969–71; Developmental Psychology, Open College, 1973–75; Poetry Ed., Poetry Toronto, 1980–81; Co-Ed., Writer's Magazine, 1982–90. *Publications:* Poetry: Tell-Tale Feathers, 1978; A Snowman, Headless, 1979; As Far as the Sea Can Eye, 1979; Flaking Paint, 1983; Frozen Breaths, 1983; Tick Bird, 1983; Bifids, 1984; Night Tides, 1984; Time is Flies, 1984; High Wire Spider, 1986; I Throw Stones at the Mountain, 1988; Leaping Lizzard, 1988; Holes in My Cage, 1989; I Want to Lasso Time, 1991; Leaving My Loneliness, 1992; Five O'Clock Shadows (co-author), 1996; My Shadow Doing Something, 1997; Almost Unseen, 2000. Editor: The Canadian Haiku Anthology, 1979; Cicada Voices, 1983; The Universe is One Poem, 1990; There Will Always Be a Sky, 1993; The Psychology of Art: An Experimental Approach, 1994; Tanka Splendour, 1998; Global Haiku: Twenty-Five Poets Worldwide (ed.), 2000. Non-Fiction: The Modern English Haiku, 1981; Creativity: A New Psychology, 1994. Fiction: Moonlit Gold Dust, 1979; Quilby: The Porcupine Who Lost His Quills (with Anita Krumins), 1980; Missing Heirloom, 1980; Seaside Burglaries, 1981; Downhill Theft, 1982; Undertow, 1982; Dudley and the Birdman, 1985; Dudley and the Christmas Thief, 1986. *Contributions to:* Magazines worldwide. *Honours:* Haiku Society of America Book Award, 1980; High/Coo Press Chapbook Competition Winner, 1982; Museum of Haiku Literature Awards, 1983, 1985, 1993; Canadian Children's Book Centre Our Choice Awards, 1984, 1985, 1987, 1991, 1992; Third Place, International Tanka Contest, Poetry Society of Japan, 1990; First Prize, Haiku in English, Mainichi Daily News, 1993; Second Place, Mainichi 125th Anniversary Haiku Contest, 1997; Third Place, Haiku Society of America Henderson Haiku Contest, 1997. *Memberships:* Haiku Canada, co-founder, 1977; Haiku Society of America; League of Canadian Poets; PEN; Writers' Union of Canada. *Address:* 70 London St, Toronto, Ontario M6G 1N3, Canada.

SWEENEY, Matthew; b. 6 Oct. 1952, County Donegal, Ireland. Poet; Writer. m. Rosemary Barber, 1979. *Education:* University College, Dublin, 1979–78; BA, Polytechnic of North London, 1978. *Appointments:* Writer-in-Residence, Farnham College, Surrey, 1984–85; South Bank Centre, 1994–95; Writing Fellowship, University of East Anglia, 1986; Publicist and Events Asst, Poetry Society, 1988–90; Poet-in-Residence, Hereford and Worcester, 1991, National Library for the Blind, 1999; Writer-in-Residence on the Internet, Chadwyck-Healey, 1997–98. *Publications:* A Dream of Maps, 1981; A Round House, 1983; The Lame Waltzer, 1985; The Chinese Dressing Gown, 1987; Blues Shoes, 1989; The Flying Spring Onion, 1992; Cacti, 1992; The Snow Vulture, 1992; Fatso in the Red Suit, 1995; Emergency Kit: Poems for Strange Times (ed. with Jo Shapcott), 1996; Writing Poetry (with John Hartley Williams), 1997; The Bridal Suite, 1997; Penguin Modern Poets 12, 1997; Beyond Bedlam: Poems Written Out of Mental Distress (ed. with Ken Smith), 1997; A Smell of Fish, 2000; Selected Poems, 2002; Fox, 2002. *Honours:* Prudence Farmer Prize, 1984; Cholmondeley Award, 1987; Arts Council Literature Award, 1992; Arts Council of England Writer's Award, 1999. *Address:* 11 Dombey St, London WC1N 3PB, England.

SWEETMAN, David; b. 16 March 1943, Northumberland, England. Writer; Poet. *Education:* University of Durham, 1960–65; BA, University of East Africa, 1966. *Publications:* Looking into the Deep End (poems), 1981; Van Gogh: His Life and His Art, 1990, UK edn as The Love of Many Things: A Life of Vincent Van Gogh, 1990; Mary Renault, 1993; Paul Gauguin: A Complete Life, 1995; A Tribal Fever (fiction), 1996; Explosive Acts: Toulouse-Lautrec, Oscar Wilde, Félix Fénéon, and the Art and Anarchy of the Fin de Siècle, 2000. Other: 12 children's books, 1971–84. *Contributions to:* Anthologies. *Honour:* Prix Michelet, France, 1990. *Address:* c/o Rogers, Coleridge and White, 20 Powis Mews, London W11 1JN, England.

SWENSON, Karen; b. 29 July 1936, New York, NY, USA. Poet. m. Michael Shuter, 27 Nov. 1958, divorced 1970, 1 s. *Education:* BA, Barnard College, 1959; MA, New York University, 1971. *Appointments:* Lecturer, City College of the City University of New York, 1968–76; Poet-in-Residence, Clark University, 1976; Skidmore College, 1977–78; University of Idaho, 1979–80; City College of Fordham, 1982–87. *Publications:* An Attic of Ideals, 1974; East-West, 1980; A Sense of Direction, 1989; The Landlady in Bangkok, 1994; A Daughter's Latitude: New and Selected Poems, 1999. *Contributions to:* Reviews, quarterlies and journals. *Honours:* TransAtlantic Review Poetry Fellowship, Bread Loaf Writers Conference, 1973; National Poetry Series Winner, 1993. *Memberships:* Associated Writing Programs; PEN; Poetry Society of America. *Address:* 25 W 54th St, New York, NY 10019, USA.

SWILKY, Jody; b. 17 Aug. 1951, New York, NY, USA. Poet. m. 17 May 1981, 1 s. *Education:* BA, State University of New York at Geneseo, 1973; MFA, University of Iowa, 1975; DA, State University of New York at Albany, 1989. *Appointments:* Adjunct Lecturer, Hofstra University, 1982–85; Asst Prof., Drake University, 1989–93. *Publication:* A City of Fences, 1978. *Contributions to:* Georgia Review; North American Review; Mid-American Review; Ohio Review; Yale Review; Missouri Review; Chelsea; Poetry Now; New Boston Review. *Membership:* Poets and Writers. *Address:* 213 Prospect Ave, West Des Moines, IA 50265, USA.

SYLVESTER, Janet; b. 5 May 1950, Youngstown, OH, USA. Poet; University Teacher. m. James Vandenberg, 30 June 1973, divorced 1980. *Education:* BA, 1975, MA, 1978, Goddard College; PhD, University of Utah, 1991. *Appointment:*

Faculty, University of South Carolina at Columbia. *Publications:* Tha Mulberry Wine, 1985; A Visitor at the Gate, 1996; The Mark of Flesh, 1997 *Contributions to:* Anthologies, reivews, quarterlies and journals. *Address:* 700 ! Holly St, Columbia, SC 29205, USA. *E-mail:* sylvesterj@garnet.cla.sc.edu.

SYNEK, Jiri (George), (Frantisek Listopad); b. 26 Nov. 1921, Prague Czechoslovakia. University Teacher; Poet; Writer. 1 s., 5 d. *Education:* D Phil. *Publications:* Malelasky, 1945; Slava urknuti, 1945; Vzduch, 1946; Prvn veta, 1946; Boj Venezuela, 1947; Jarmark, 1947; Svoboda a jine ovoce, 1960 Tristao ou a Traiçao de um Intelectual, 1960; Cerny bily nevim, 1973; Conto Carcomidos, 1974; Secos & Molhados, 1982; Estreitamento Progressivo, 1983 Primeiro Testamento, 1985; Mar-Seco-Gelado-Quente, 1986; Os Novos Territórios 1986; Album de Família, 1988; Outubro Oriente, 1992; Biografia de Cristal, 1992 Nastroje Pameti, 1992; Final Rondi, 1992; Blizko Daleko, 1993; Meio Conto, 1993 Oprava houslí a Kytar, 1996; Prvni vety, 1997; Tristan z mesta do mesta, 1998; Krles 1998; Em Chinatown com a Rosa, 2001; Milostná stehováni, 2001; Prísti poezie 2001. *Contributions to:* Czech, Portuguese, American and French newspaper: and reviews. *Honours:* Acad. of Fine Arts, Prague, 1948; Swedish Acad., Lund 1949; Christian Acad., Rome, 1950; Prize, Radio Free Europe, 1952; Critic': Prizes, Lisbon, 1968, 1970, 1980; Doctor honoris causa, CSFR, 1992; Europear Prize, 2000; Franz Kafka Medal, 2000; Czech Prize and Medal of High Merit fo Extraordinary Achievement, 2001. *Memberships:* PEN Club International Society of Portuguese Writers. *Address:* Rua Joao Dias 15, Lisbon 1400 Portugal.

SZABO, Magda; b. 5 Oct. 1917, Hungary. Writer; Dramatist; Poet. m. Tibo Szobotka, 1948. *Education:* Teacher's Certificate, 1940; PhD, Classica Philology. *Appointments:* Teacher, secondary schools, 1940–44, 1950–59. *Publications:* Novels, plays, radio dramas, poems, essays and film scripts. *Honours:* József Attila Prizes, 1959, 1972; Kossuth Prize, 1978; Getz Corporation Prize, 1992. *Memberships:* Acad. of Sciences of Europe; Hungarian Szechenyi Acad. of Arts. *Address:* Julia-utca 3, 1026 Budapest II Hungary.

SZE, Arthur; b. 1 Dec. 1950, New York, USA. Poet; Prof. 1 s. *Education:* BA, University of California, Berkeley, 1972. *Appointment:* Prof., Institute of American Indian Arts, 1984–. *Publications:* The Willow Wind, 1972; Two Ravens, 1976; Dazzled, 1982; River, River, 1987; Archipelago, 1995; The Redshifting Web: Poems 1970–1998, 1998. *Contributions to:* Paris Review; Chelsea; Harvard Magazine; Mother Jones; New Letters; Manoa; Bloomsbury Review; Seattle Review; River Styx; Tendril; Tyuonyi; American Poetry Review; Kenyon Review. *Honours:* Witter Bynner Foundation for Poetry Grants; New Mexico Arts Division Interdisciplinary Grant; National Endowment for the Arts Creative Writing Fellowships; George A and Eliza Gardener Howard Foundation Fellowship; Eisner Prize; Lannan Literary Award for Poetry, 1995; American Book Award, 1996; Guggenheim Fellowship, 1997; Lila Wallace-Reader's Digest Writers' Award, 1997. *Address:* PO Box 457, Santa Fe, NM 87504, USA.

SZIRTES, George (Gabor Nicholas); b. 29 Nov. 1948, Budapest, Hungary. Poet; Writer; Trans. m. Clarissa Upchurch, 11 July 1970, 1 s., 1 d. *Education:* BA, Fine Art, Leeds College of Art: PhD, 2002. *Publications:* The Slant Door, 1979; November and May, 1981; The Kissing Place, 1982; Short Wave, 1984; The Photographer in Winter, 1986; Metro, 1988; Bridge Passages, 1991; Blind Field, 1994; Selected Poems, 1996; The Red All Over Riddle Book (for children), 1997; Portrait of My Father in an English Landscape, 1998; The Budapest File, 2000; An English Apocalypse, 2001. Criticism: Exercise of Power; The Art of Ana Maria Pacheco, 2001; New Writing 10 (co-ed. with Penelope Lively), 2001. Other: Several Hungarian works trans. into English. *Contributions to:* Numerous journals and magazines. *Honours:* Geoffrey Faber Memorial Prize, 1980; Arts Council Bursary, 1984; British Council Fellowship, 1985; Cholmondeley Award, 1987; Dery Prize for Trans., 1991; Decorated, Republic of Hungary, 1991; Short-listed, Whitbread Poetry Award, 1992; European Poetry Trans. Prize, 1995; Short-listed, Forward Prize, 2000; George Cushing Award, 2001; Society of Authors Travelling Scholarship, 2002. *Memberships:* PEN; RSL, fellow. *Address:* 16 Damgate St, Wymondham, Norfolk NR8 0BQ, England.

SZLAFKAY, Attila; b. 22 Feb. 1953, Romania. Librarian; Poet; Trans. m. Tibay Andrea, 9 Feb. 1985, 1 d. *Publications:* Szinkep (anthology), 1984; Mircea Dinescu: Titanic-Valcer, 1989; Matei Visniec: Lavinaban Harsonaval, 1992; Radu Tuculescu: Liftben, 1996; Fordulatra Varva, 1997. *Contributions to:* Polisz; Hid; Hitel; Stadium; Mozgo; Vilag; Elet es Irodalom; Lato; Helikon. *Honours:* Prize, Festival of International Poetry for Trans. of Famous Romanian Poets and Writers Works, 1997. *Memberships:* Several. *Address:* Donati u 3 fsz 3, 1015 Budapest, Hungary.

SZYMBORSKA, Wisława; b. 2 July 1923, Bnin, Poland. Poet; Critic; Trans. *Education:* Jagiellonian University, Kraków, 1945–48. *Appointment:* Editorial Styaff, Zycie Literackie magazine, 1953–81. *Publications:* Dlatego zyjemy (That's Why We Are Alive), 1952; Pytania zadawane sobie (Questioning Oneself), 1954; Wolanie do Yeti (Calling Out to Yeti), 1957; Sól (Salt), 1962; Wiersze wybrane (Selected Verses), 1964; Poezje wybrane (Selected Poems), 1967; Sto pociech (No End of Fun), 1967; Poezje (Poems), 1970; Wszelki wypadek (Could Have), 1972; Wybór wierszy (Selected Verses), 1973; Tarsjusz i inne wiersze (Tarsius and Other Verses), 1976; Wielka liczba (A Large Number), 1977; Poezje wybrane II (Selected Poems II), 1983; Ludzie na moscie (The People on the Bridge), 1986; Wieczór autorski: Wiersze (Authors' Evening: Verses), 1992; Koniec i poczatek (The End and the Beginning), 1993. Poetry in English: Sounds, Feelings, Thoughts: Seventy Poems, 1981; People on a Bridge, 1990; View with a Grain of Sand, 1995. *Contributions to:* Poetry and criticism in various publications. *Honours:* City of Kraków Prize for Literature, 1954; Polish Ministry of Culture Prize, 1963; Goethe Prize, 1991; Herder Prize, 1995; Hon. doctorate, Adam Mickiewicz University, Poznań, 1995; Nobel Prize for Literature, 1996; Polish PEN Club Prize, 1996. *Address:* Ul Królewska 82/89, 30-079 Kraków, Poland.

T

TABER, Roger Noel; b. 21 Dec. 1945, Gillingham, Kent, England. Librarian; Poet; Writer. *Education:* BA, English and American Literature, University of Kent, 1973; Postgraduate Diploma, Library and Information Science, Ealing School of Librarianship, 1975. *Publications:* How Can You Write a Poem When You're Dying of Aids?, 1993; August and Genet, 1996; Visions of the Mind, 1998; Love and Human Remains, 2000; First Person Plural, 2002. *Contributions to:* Numerous poetry magazines and anthologies. *Honours:* Placed in National Competitions. *Address:* Flat C, Hammond House, 45A Gaisford St, London NW5 2EB, England. *E-mail:* rogertab@aol.com. *Website:* hometown.aol.com/rogertab/myhomepage/poetry.html.

TABORSKI, Boleslaw; b. 7 May 1927, Toruń, Poland. Poet; Writer; Trans. m. Halina Junghertz, 20 June 1959, 1 d. *Education:* BA, MA, University of Bristol. *Appointments:* Producer, Polish Section, 1959–89, Ed., Arts in Action, 1985–93, BBC World Service; Visiting Prof., City University of New York, 1982. *Publications:* Poetry: Times of Passing, 1957; Grains of Night, 1958; Crossing the Border, 1962; Lesson Continuing, 1967; Voice of Silence, 1969; Selected Poems, 1973; Web of Words, 1977; For the Witnesses, 1978; Observer of Shadows, 1979; Love, 1980; A Stranger's Present, 1983; Art, 1985; The Stillness of Grass, 1986; Life and Death, 1988; Politics, 1990; Shakespeare, 1990; Goodnight Nonsense, 1991; Survival, 1998; Selected Poems, 1999; Gniezno Door, 2000; A Fragment of Existence, 2002. Criticism: New Elizabethan Theatre, 1967; Byron and the Theatre, 1972; The Inner Plays of Karol Wojtyla, 1989; My Uprising: Then and Now, 1998. Co-Author: Crowell's Handbook of Contemporary Drama, 1971; Polish Plays in Translation, 1983. Other: Numerous trans. *Contributions to:* Various publications. *Honours:* Polish Writers Asscn Abroad Award, 1954; Jurzykowski Foundation Award, New York, 1968; Merit for Polish Culture Badge and Diploma, Warsaw, 1970; Koscielski Foundation Award, Geneva, 1977; SI Witkiewicz ITI Award, Warsaw, 1988; Asscn of Authors Trans. Awards, Warsaw, 1990, 1995; Societé Europeen de Culture Award, Warsaw, 1998; KLIO, History Publishers Award, Warsaw, 1998. *Memberships:* Asscn of Authors, ZAIKS, Warsaw; Asscn of Polish Writers, Warsaw; Council Gallery in the Provinces Foundation, Lublin; Leon Schiller Foundation, hon. committee; Pro Europa Foundation, Warsaw, council mem., 1994–; World Asscn of the Polish Home Army Exservicemen, Warsaw; Polish Shakespeare Society, Gdańsk, 1995; PEN, Warsaw, 2000. *Address:* 66 Esmond Rd, London W4 1JF, England.

TACI, Pano; b. 13 Oct. 1931, Gjirokaster, Albania. Poet. 1 s. *Education:* High General School (Gymnasium) Gjirokastër, Albania, 1954–58. *Publications:* Hija e gjalle, 1963; Blerimi i thinjur, 1993; Dhe vdekja do paguar, 1997; Buzeqeshja e shtirur, 1998; Qirinjte, 1998. *Contributions to:* Rilindja Demokratike; Drita; Rilindja. *Honours:* Ali Kelmendi Prize, 1993; Asdreni Prize, Korce, 1998. *Membership:* Writers and Artists' Asscn of Albania, 1993–. *Address:* Lagja Misto Mame, Rruga, Ferit Xhajko, No. 16, Tirana, Albania.

TADEUSZ, Rozewicz; b. 9 Oct. 1921, Radomsko, Poland. Poet; Dramatist. m. Wiestawa Koztowska, 1949. *Education:* University of Kraków. *Publications:* Several poems and plays. *Contributions to:* Periodicals. *Honours:* State Prizes, 1955, 1956; Literary Prize, City of Kraków, 1959; Prize of the Minister of Culture and Art, 1962; State Prize, First Class, 1966; Prize of the Minister of Foreign Affairs, 1974, 1987; Austrian State Prize for European Literature, 1982; German Literary Award, 1994. *Membership:* Bavarian Acad. of Fine Arts.

TAFDRUP, Pia; b. 29 May 1952, Copenhagen, Denmark. Poet. m. Bo Hakon Jørgensen, 30 June 1978, 2 s. *Education:* BA, University of Copenhagen, 1977. *Publications:* Various poetry vols in Danish, 1981–2002; Two vols in English trans. as Spring Tide, 1989; Queen's Gate, 2001. Other: 2 plays. *Contributions to:* Many journals and anthologies in the UK, USA and Canada. *Honours:* Scholarship for Authors, Danish State Art Foundation, 1984–86; 12 grants, 1986–97; Lifelong Artist's Grant, 1998; Nordic Council Literature Prize, 1999. *Membership:* Danish Acad.; Danish PEN Centre. *Address:* Rosenvaengets Sideallé, 3.2th, 2100 Copenhagen Ø, DK, Denmark.

TAGGART, John Paul; b. 5 Oct. 1942, USA. University Prof.; Poet; Writer; Trans. m. Jennifer A James, 2 d. *Education:* BA, Earlham College, 1965; MA, University of Chicago, 1966; PhD, Syracuse University, 1974. *Appointment:* English Dept, Shippensburg University, 1969–. *Publications:* Dodeka, 1979; Peace on Earth, 1981; Dehiscence, 1983; Loop, 1991; Prompted, 1991; Aeschylus-Fragments (trans.), 1992; Standing Wave, 1993; Remaining In Light (art criticism), 1993; Songs of Degrees (essays), 1994; When the Saints, 1999. *Contributions to:* Hambone; Conjunctions; Northwest Review; Sulfur; Boundary 2; Epoch; Talisman; Chicago Review. *Honours:* Writing Fellowships, National Endowment for the Arts, 1976, 1986; Poetry Prize, Chicago Review, 1980; Frank Stanford Poetry Prize, 1982; Writing Fellowship, Pennsylvania Council on the Arts, 1987; Gertrude Stein Award, 1996. *Address:* 295 E Creek Rd, Newburg, PA 17240, USA.

TAGLIABUE, John; b. 1 July 1923, Cantu, Italy. College Teacher (retd); Poet; Writer. m. Grace Ten Eyck, 11 Sept. 1946, 2 d. *Education:* BA, 1944, MA, 1945, Advanced Graduate Work, 1947–48, Columbia University. *Appointments:* Teacher, American University, Beirut, 1945, State College of Washington, 1946–47, Alfred University, New York, 1948–50, Bates College, Maine 1953–89; Fulbright Lecturer, University of Pisa, 1950–52, University of Tokyo, 1958–60, Fudan University, Shanghai, 1984, University of Indonesia, 1993. *Publications:* Poems, 1959; A Japanese Journal, 1966; The Buddha Uproar, 1970; The Doorless Door, 1970; The Great Day, 1984; New and Selected Poems 1942–97, 1997. *Contributions to:* Journals, magazines, and periodicals. *Memberships:* Acad. of American Poets; PEN; Poetry Society of America. *Address:* Wayland Manor, Apt 412, 500 Angell St, Providence, RI 02906, USA.

TAHID. See: LOCKETT, Reginald Franklin.

TAIT, Andrew; b. 4 Nov. 1958, Wallsend, nr Newcastle upon Tyne, England. Poet; Writer; Music Teacher. *Education:* French Horn, Guildhall School of Music and Drama, 1977–81; PGCE, Bulmershe College, Reading, 1982. *Publications:* Poetry: Damson in Distress; Energy; Robert's Oriental Tea Garden; Thursdays; Robert's Terrible Vision; Autobiography: Me and Peter Beardsley. Other: Poems published elsewhere: Reincarnation, 1998; Super Trouper, 2000. *Contributions to:* Anthologies, including Golden Girl, 2002; Periodicals, including: The Sunday Times; The Independent; Features and interviews in many publications; Television and radio appearances. *Honours:* Winner, Newcastle Chronicle/Bloodaxe Books Poetry Competition; Winner, Iron Press 30th Anniversary Haiku Competition. *Membership:* Morden Tower Poetry Society. *Address:* Flat 4, 30 Clayton Rd, Jesmond, Newcastle upon Tyne NE2 4RQ, England.

TAKACHI, Jun'ichiro; b. 7 March 1939, Tokushima, Japan. Prof.; Poet. *Education:* BA, Tokushima University, 1964; MA, Hiroshima University, 1964; University of Cambridge, 1979–80; Yale University, 1982–83. *Appointments:* Lecturer, Hirosaki University, 1965–70; Asst Prof., 1970–73, Assoc. Prof., 1973–84, Prof., 1984–, Obirin University. *Publications:* Spring and Fall in Cambridge; The Garden of Orpheus; The Summer of Homer; De Construction of Deconstruction; Manna of Love. *Contributions to:* Shigaku; Gendaishi-Techo; Poetry Tokyo; Japan Poetry Review; Eigo Seinen. *Memberships:* Japan Contemporary Anglo American Poetry Society; Japan Poets Asscn; Japan PEN International; International Comparative Literature Asscn. *Address:* 4-19-20 Lions City No. 705, Haramachida, Machida, Japan.

TALBOT, Norman Clare; b. 14 Sept. 1936, Gislingham, Suffolk, England. Poet; Writer; Ed.; Literary Consultant. m., 17 Aug. 1960, 1 s., 2 d. *Education:* BA, University of Durham, 1959; PhD, University of Leeds, 1962. *Appointments:* Lecturer, 1962, Senior Lecturer, 1968–73, Assoc. Prof. of English, 1973–93, University of Newcastle; Ed.-in-Chief, Nimrod Publications, 1964–; Visiting Prof., Yale University, 1967–68, University of East Anglia, 1975–76, University of Århus, 1976, University of Oregon, 1983, University of Leicester, 1984, Linacre College, Oxford, 1987–88, University of Exeter, 1992; Ed., Babel Handbooks, 1980–2001; Ed., Nimrod Literary Consultancy, 1993–; Vice-Pres., 1997–2002, acting Pres., 2002–, Catchfire Press; Poetry Ed., Australian Friend, 1997–2002; Judge, Aurealis Literary Awards, 1998–2000. *Publications:* The Major Poems of John Keats, 1967; Poems for a Female Universe, 1968; Son of a Female Universe (poems), 1971; The Fishing Boy (poems), 1973; Find the Lady (poems), 1978; A Glossary of Poetic Terms, 1980; Where Two Rivers Meet (poems), 1980; The Kelly Haiku (poems), 1985; Contrary Modes (ed.), 1985; Another Site to be Mined: The New South Wales Anthology (ed.), 1986; Spelling English in Australia (with Nicholas Talbot), 1989; Weaving the Heterocosm: An Anthology of British Narrative Poetry (ed.), 1989; Four Zoas of Australia (poems), 1992; Australian Quaker Christmases (poems), 1993; A Moment for Morris (poems), 1996; Australian Skin, Suffolk Bones (poems), 1996; Betwixt Wood-Woman, the Wolf and Bear: The Heroic-Age Romances of William Morris, 1997; Song-Cycle of the Birds, Lake Macquarie (poems), 1998; Myths and Stories, Lies and Truth, 1999; The Book of Changes (poems), 1999; Seamark for the New Millennium (poems, ed.), 2000. *Honours:* E. C. Gregory Award for Poetry, 1965; ACLS Fellowship, 1967–68; City of Lake Macquarie Award for Services to Poetry, 1994. *Memberships:* Mythopoeic Literature Asscn of Australia, life mem., 1978–; Pres., 1988–92, 1993–99, Legal Officer, 2002–, Newcastle Poetry at the Pub; Pres., 1997–98, Legal Officer, 1999–, Newcastle Writers' Centre. *Address:* PO Box 170, New Lambton 2305, NSW, Australia.

TALL, Deborah; b. 16 March 1951, Washington, DC, USA. Prof.; Poet; Writer; Ed. m. David Weiss, 9 Sept. 1979, 2 d. *Education:* BA, English, University of Michigan, 1972; MFA, Creative Writing, Goddard College, 1979. *Appointments:* Asst Prof., Visiting Fellow in Literature, University of Baltimore, 1980–82; Prof., 1982–, Chair., Dept of English, 1992–94, Hobart and William Smith

Colleges; Ed., Seneca Review, 1982–; Writer-in-Residence, Chautauqua Institution, New York, 1998. *Publications:* Eight Colors Wide, 1974; Ninth Life, 1982; The Island of the White Cow: Memories of an Irish Island, 1986; Come Wind, Come Weather, 1988; Taking Note: From Poets' Notebooks (ed. with Stephen Kuusisto and David Weiss), 1991, revised edn as The Poet's Notebook, 1995; From Where We Stand: Recovering a Sense of Place, 1993; Summons, 2000. *Contributions to:* Many anthologies, reviews, quarterlies, journals, and magazines. *Honours:* Kathryn A Morton Prize for Poetry; Yaddo Residencies, 1982, 1984, 1991; Citation of Achievement, Co-ordinating Council of Literary Magazines, 1986; Ingram Merrill Foundation Grant, 1987; MacDowell Colony Residency, 1998. *Memberships:* Acad. of American Poets; Associated Writing Programs; Asscn for the Study of Literature and the Environment; Authors Guild; PEN; Poetry Society of America. *Address:* c/o Dept of English, Hobart and William Smith Colleges, Geneva, NY 14456, USA.

TAMEN, Pedro Mario Alles; b. 1 Dec. 1934, Lisbon, Portugal. Poet. m. Maria Da Graca, 29 Oct. 1981, 2 s., 2 d. *Education:* University of Lisbon, 1957. *Appointments:* Dir, Moraes Publishing House, 1958–75; Asst Ed., Flama Magazine, 1959–62; Trustee, Calouste Gulbenkian Foundation, 1975–2000. *Publications:* Various poems, including the collection Retábulo das Matérias, 2001. *Contributions to:* Various Portuguese and Brazilian publications. *Honours:* Several literary prizes. *Memberships:* Portuguese Asscn of Writers; Portuguese PEN Club. *Address:* R Luis Pastor de Macedo, Lt 25 50 E, 1750-157, Lisbon, Portugal.

TAPNER, Victor; b. 16 Nov. 1950, Watford, Hertfordshire, England. Journalist; Poet. m. Rosalind Matthews, 10 Sept. 1971, 1 s., 1 d. *Education:* MA, University of Glamorgan, 1998. *Appointments:* Night News Ed., Financial Times; Reporter, Ed., various journals. *Publications:* The Icarus Leaf, 1982; Cold Rain, 1988. *Contributions to:* Many publications. *Honours:* Commendations, John Clare Poetry Competition, 1982, 1983, 1984; International Poetry Competition, 1983; Queenie Lee Competition, 1984; All-London Literary Competition, 1987; Prizewinner, Dulwich Festival Competition, 1998; Museum of London/Blue Nose Poets Millennial Poetry Competition; First Prize, Academi Cardiff International Poetry Competition, 2000. *Membership:* Poetry Society. *Address:* 39 Sun St, Billericay, Essex CM12 9LW, England. *E-mail:* victortapner@hotmail.com.

TAPSCOTT, Stephen; b. 5 Nov. 1948, Des Moines, IA, USA. Poet; Teacher. *Education:* BA, University of Notre Dame, 1970; PhD, Cornell University, 1975. *Appointments:* Lecturer in English, University of Kent at Canterbury, England, 1976–77; Teacher, Goddard College, 1976–82; Asst Prof. of English, Massachusetts Institute of Technology, 1977–. *Publications:* Mesopotamia, poems, 1975; Penobscot: Nine Poems, 1983; American Beauty: William Carlos Williams and the Tradition of the Modernist Whitman, 1984; Pablo Neruda: 100 Love Sonnets, (trans.), 1985; Another Body, (poems), 1989. *Address:* 66 Martin St, No. 2, Cambridge, MA 02138, USA.

TARCZYN, Julia. See: DANIELEWSKA, Lucja Zofia.

TARN, Nathaniel; b. 30 June 1928, Paris, France. Poet; Writer; Prof. Emeritus. m. (1), divorced, 2 c., (2) Janet Rodney, 1981. *Education:* BA, 1948, MA, 1952, University of Cambridge; Dipl CFRE, École des Hautes Études, University of Paris; MA, 1952, PhD, 1957, University of Chicago. *Appointments:* Visiting Prof., State University of New York at Buffalo, 1969–70, Princeton University 1969–70, University of Pennsylvania, 1976, Jilin University, China, 1982; Prof. of Comparative Literature, 1970–85, Prof. Emeritus, 1985–, Rutgers University. *Publications:* Poetry: Old Savage/Young City, 1964; Penguin Modern Poets 7 (with Richard Murphy and Jon Silkin), 1966; Where Babylon Ends, 1968; The Beautiful Contradictions, 1969; October: A Sequence of Ten Poems Followed by Requiem Pro Duabus Filiis Israel, 1969; The Silence, 1970; A Nowhere for Vallejo: Choices, October, 1971; Lyrics for the Bride of God, 1975; Narrative of This Fall, 1975; The House of Leaves, 1976; From Alaska: The Ground of Our Great Admiration of Nature (with Janet Rodney), 1977; The Microcosm, 1977; Birdscapes, with Seaside, 1978; The Forest (with Janet Rodney), 1979; Atitlan/Alashka, 1979; The Land Songs, 1981; Weekends in Mexico, 1982; The Desert Mothers, 1984; At the Western Gates, 1985; Palenque: Selected Poems, 1972–1984, 1986; Seeing America First, 1989; The Mothers of Matagalpa, 1989; Flying the Body, 1993; The Architextures, 2000; Three Letters from the City: The St Petersburg Poems 1968–1998, 2000; Selected Poems, 1950–2000, 2002. Non-Fiction: Views from the Weaving Mountain: Selected Essays in Poetics and Anthropology, 1991; Scandals in the House of Birds, 1998. *Honours:* Guinness Prize, 1963; Wenner Gren Fellowships, 1978, 1980; Commonwealth of Pennsylvania Fellowship, 1984; Rockefeller Foundation Fellowship, 1988. *Address:* PO Box 8187, Santa Fe, NM 87504, USA.

TART, Indrek, (Julius Ürt); b. 2 May 1946, Tallinn, Estonia. Physicist; Poet; Literary Critic. m. Aili Arelaid Tart, 7 Feb. 1980, 1 s., 1 d. *Education:* University of Tartu. *Appointments:* Institute of Cybernetics, 1969–80; Institute of Chemical Physics and Biophysics, Estonian Acad. of Sciences, 1980–92; Dir of Information, Estonian National Commission for UNESCO, 1992–93; Tallinn Pedagogical University, 1992–. *Publications:* Haljendav Ruumala, 1981; Väike Luuletaja ja Teised, 1993. Other: Various trans.

Contributions to: Anthologies and other publications. *Honour:* Hon. Fellow in Writing, University of Iowa. *Membership:* Estonian Writers Union. *Address:* Kurni 17-1, Tallinn 0016, Estonia.

TARTLER (TABARAS), Grete; b. 23 Nov. 1948, Bucharest, Romania. Poet; Ed.; Musician. m. Stelian Tabaras, 23 Sept. 1972, 1 d. *Education:* MA, 1972 and 1976; PhD, 1996. *Appointments:* Teacher, 1972–88; Ed., 1988, 1990; Diplomat, 1992–. *Publications:* Apa Vie; Chorale; Hore; Astronomia Ierbii; Substituiri; Achene Zburatoare; Materia Signata; Orient Express. *Contributions to:* Honest Ulsterman; Poetry Review; TLS; Illuminations; Numbers. *Honours:* Awards of Writers Union; Poetry Prize; Award of Poetry Society England. *Memberships:* Writers Union in Romania; PEN. *Address:* Mihai Bravu ur 1, bld 2 Sc A Apt 7, Sector 2, 73261 Bucharest, Romania.

TATE, James (Vincent); b. 8 Dec. 1943, Kansas City, Missouri, USA. Poet; Prof. *Education:* University of Missouri, 1963–64; BA, Kansas State University, 1965; MFA, University of Iowa, 1967. *Appointments:* Instructor in Creative Writing, University of Iowa, 1966–67; Visiting Lecturer, University of California, Berkeley, 1967–68; Poetry Ed., Dickinson Review, 1967–76; Trustee and Assoc. Ed., Pym-Randall Press, 1968–80; Asst Prof. of English, Columbia University, 1969–71; Assoc. Prof., then Prof. of English, 1971–, University of Massachusetts, Amherst; Poet-in-Residence, Emerson College, 1970–71; Assoc. Ed., Barn Dream Press. *Publications:* Poetry: Cages, 1966; The Destination, 1967; The Lost Pilot, 1967; Notes of Woe: Poems, 1968; Camping in the Valley, 1968; The Torches, 1968; Row with Your Hair, 1969; Is There Anything?, 1969; Shepherds of the Mist, 1969; Amnesia People, 1970; Are You Ready Mary Baker Eddy? (with Bill Knot), 1970; Deaf Girl Playing, 1970; The Oblivion Ha-Ha, 1970; Wrong Songs, 1970; Hints to Pilgrims, 1971; Absences, 1972; Apology for Eating Geoffrey Movius' Hyacinth, 1972; Hottentot Ossuary, 1974; Viper Jazz, 1976; Riven Doggeries, 1979; Land of Little Sticks, 1981; Constant Defender, 1983; Reckoner, 1986; Distance from Loved Ones, 1990; Selected Poems, 1991; Worshipful Company of Fletchers, 1993; Shroud of the Gnome, 1997; Memoir of the Hawk: Poems, 2001. Novel: Lucky Darryl, 1977. *Contributions to:* Numerous books and periodicals. *Honours:* Yale Younger Poets Award, 1966; National Institute of Arts and Letters Award, 1974; Massachusetts Arts and Humanities Fellow, 1975; Guggenheim Fellowship, 1976; National Endowment for the Arts Fellowship, 1980; Pulitzer Prize in Poetry, 1992; National Book Award for Poetry, 1994. *Membership:* Acad. of American Poets, board of chancellors, 2001–. *Address:* Dept of English, University of Massachusetts, Amherst, MA 01003, USA.

TATELBAUM, Brenda Loew; b. 1 April 1951, Boston, Massachusetts, USA. Publisher; Poet. m. Ira Rubin Tatelbaum, 23 Aug. 1970, divorced 1983, 1 s., 1 d. *Education:* BA, Boston University, 1971; MA, Brown University, 1973; Cultural Doctorate, World University, 1992. *Publications:* Eden Poems; Life Evolves From Living; Boston Collection of Womens Poetry. *Contributions to:* Journals, magazines and periodicals. *Address:* c/o EIDOS, PO Box 96, Boston, MA 02137, USA.

TAYLOR, Andrew MacDonald; b. 19 March 1940, Warnambool, Vic., Australia. Prof.; Poet; Writer. m. Beate Josephi, 1981, 1 s., 1 d. *Education:* BA, 1961, MA, 1970, University of Melbourne; DLitt, Melbourne, 1998. *Appointments:* Lockie Fellow, University of Melbourne, 1965–68; Lecturer, 1971–74, Senior Lecturer, 1974–91, Assoc. Prof., 1991–1992, University of Adelaide; Prof., Edith Cowan University, 1992–. *Publications:* Reading Australian Poetry, 1987; Selected Poems, 1960–85, 1988; Folds in the Map, 1991; Sandstone, 1995; The Stone Threshold, 2001; Götterdämmerung Café, 2001. *Contributions to:* Newspapers, journals, and magazines. *Honours:* Several prizes and awards; Mem. of the Order of Australia. *Memberships:* Asscn for the Study of Australian Literature; Australian Society of Authors; PEN. *Address:* c/o School of International Cultural and Community Studies, Edith Cowan University, Mount Lawley, WA 6050, Australia.

TAYLOR, Anna; b. 14 July 1943, Preston, Lancashire, England. Teacher; Writer; Poet; Artist; Trans. m. John E Coombes, 22 Dec. 1967, divorced 1982, 1 s. *Education:* BA, Honours, German and English, University of Bristol, 1965; CertEd, University of York, 1967; MA, Sociology of Literature, University of Essex, 1980. *Publications:* FAUSTA, 1984; Cut Some Cords, 1988; Both And: A Triptych, 1996; Out of the Blues, 1997; INTER?, 1998. *Contributions to:* Anthologies and magazines. *Honours:* Short-listed for several prizes. *Memberships:* Writers Guild of Great Britain; Yorkshire Playwrights, Founder-mem. *Address:* 82 Blackhouse Rd, Fartown, Huddersfield, West Yorkshire HD2 1AR, England.

TAYLOR, Brian Dormer; b. 17 Sept. 1946, Dublin, Ireland. Educator; Poet. *Education:* Assoc., London Acad. of Music and Dramatic Art, 1967; BSc, Economics, 1968, CertEd, 1969, LLB, 1974, University of London; MA, Urban Processes, Problems and Policies, Council for National Academic Awards, 1984; LLM, University of Cambridge, 1985. *Appointments:* Lecturer in Government, Kingston College of Further Education, 1970–72; Lecturer, 1972–78, Senior Lecturer in Law, 1978–91, Leicester Polytechnic. *Publication:* Strong Men Cast Shadows Too, 1982. *Contributions to:* Anthologies, reviews and magazines. *Honour:* Winner, Cheltenham Competitive Festival Open Poetry Competition, 1983. *Memberships:* Poetry Society; RSA, Fellow. *Address:* Bod Awel, Gors Ave, Holyhead, Gwynedd LL65 1PB, Wales.

TAYLOR, Bruce; b. 19 Feb. 1947, Somerville, Massachusetts, USA. Prof. of English; Poet; Ed.; Publisher. m. 4 July 1983, 2 s., 1 d. *Education:* BA, English, Bridgewater State College, Massachusetts, 1964; MA, MFA, University of Arkansas, 1972. *Appointments:* Poetry Ed., Transactions: Journal of Wisconsin Acad. of Sciences, Arts and Letters; Ed., Publisher, Upriver Press; Prof. of English, University of Wisconsin, Eau Claire. *Publications:* Everywhere the Beauty Gives Itself Away, 1976; Idle Tacde: Early Poems, 1979; The Darling Poems: A Romance, 1982; This Day, 1992; Why That Man Talks That, 1994. Editor: Eating the Menu, 1974; Upriver, 1979; Upriver 2, 1981; Upriver 3, 1984; Upriver 4, 1990; Wisconsin Poetry, 1991; Higher Learning, 2001. *Contributions to:* Anglican Theological Review; Chicago Review; Formalist; Kansas Quarterly; Light; Literary Review; Little Magazine; Nation; New Orleans Review; New York Quarterly; Northwest Review; Poetry; Rocky Mountain Review; South Coast Poetry Review; Texas Review. *Honours:* Kenneth Patchen Award for Poetry, 1972; Fellowship, Wisconsin Arts Board, 1981; Writer on the Verge of Significant National Distinction, National Endowment for the Arts and Passages North, 1987; Consulting Humanist and Program Scholar, Voices and Visions: Modern American Poets and Their Poetry, 1988; Faculty Sabbatical, Creative Writing, University of Wisconsin, 1992; Bush Artist Fellowship, Bush Foundation, 1993; Hon. Mention, Passager Prize, 1999; Featured Poet, Poetry SuperHighway, 2001; Various other grants and awards. *Memberships:* Associated Writing Programs; Poets, Essayists and Novelists. *Address:* Dept of English, University of Wisconsin, Eau Claire, WI 54702, USA.

TAYLOR, Henry (Splawn); b. 21 June 1942, Loudoun County, Virginia, USA. Prof. of Literature; Poet; Writer. *Education:* BA, University of Virginia, 1965; MA, Hollins College, 1966. *Appointments:* Instructor, Roanoke College, 1966–68; Asst Prof., University of Utah, 1968–71; Contributing Ed., Hollins Critic, 1970–77; Assoc. Prof., 1971–76, Prof. of Literature, 1976–, Co-Dir, MFA in Creative Writing, 1982–, Dir, American Studies Program, 1983–85, American University; Consulting Ed., Magill's Literary Annual, 1972–, Poet Lore, 1976–84; Writer-in-Residence, Hollins College, 1978; Board of Advisers, 1986–, Poetry Ed., 1988–89, New Virginia Review; Distinguished Poet-in-Residence, Wichita State University, 1994; Poet-in-Residence, Randolph-Macon Women's College, 1996; Elliston Poet-in-Residence, University of Cincinnati, 2002. *Publications:* Poetry: The Horse Show at Midnight: Poems, 1966; Breakings, 1971; An Afternoon of Pocket Billiards, 1975; Desperado, 1979; The Flying Change, 1985; Understanding Fiction: Poems 1986–96, 1996; Brief Candles: 101 Clerihews, 2000. Other: Magill's (Masterplots) Literary Annual 1972 (ed. with Frank N. Magill), 1972; Poetry: Points of Departure, 1974; Magill's (Masterplots) Literary Annual 1973 (assoc. ed.), 1974; Magill's (Masterplots) Literary Annual 1974 (assoc. ed.), 1975; The Water of Light: A Miscellany in Honor of Brewster Ghiselin (ed.), 1976; Compulsory Figures: Essays on Recent American Poets, 1992. *Contributions to:* Many books, anthologies, reviews, and journals. *Honours:* Acad. of American Poets Prizes, 1962, 1964; Utah State Institute of Fine Arts Poetry Prizes, co-winner, 1969, winner, 1971; National Endowment for the Arts Fellowships, 1978, 1986; National Endowment for the Humanities Research Grant, 1980–81; Witter Bynner Prize for Poetry, American Acad. and Institute of Arts and Letters, 1984; Pulitzer Prize in Poetry, 1986; Virginia Cultural Laureate Award, 1986; Teacher Recognition, National Foundation for Advancement in the Arts, 1995–96; Michael Braude Light Verse Prize, American Acad. of Arts and Letters, 2002. *Address:* c/o Dept of Literature, American University, Washington, DC 20016, USA.

TAYLOR, John (Benjamin); b. 19 March 1944, London, England. Teacher; Poet. *Education:* Teachers Certificate, 1977. *Publications:* There Were No Lovely Birds, 1974; Three Familiar Birds, 1984; The Manor House, 1988. *Contributions to:* Anthologies, magazines and BBC Radio and TV. *Memberships:* Church of England/Methodist. *Address:* The Manor House, The Popular Press, 12 Chichester Rd, Bognor Regis, West Sussex PO21 2EX, England.

TAYLOR, Kent; b. 8 Nov. 1940, New Castle, Pennsylvania, USA. Writer; Poet. Widower, 1 s. *Education:* BA, Ohio Wesleyan University, 1962. *Appointment:* Medical Research Assoc. *Publications:* Rabbits Have Fled; Late Show at the Starlight Laundry; Driving Like the Sun; Empty Ground; Shit Outside When Eating Berries; Cleveland Dreams; Torn Birds; Late Stations; Fortuitons Mother Fucker; Aleatory Letters; Selected Poems; Night Physics, 2002. *Contributions to:* Many reviews, quarterlies, and magazines. *Address:* 1450 10th Ave, San Francisco, CA 94122, USA.

TAYLOR, Lisa Canter; b. 16 June 1954, Hartford, CT, USA. Writer; Poet. m. Russell Taylor, 8 Aug. 1981, 1 s., 1 d. *Education:* BA, English, 1979; MA, Counseling Psychology, 1981. *Appointments:* Psychotherapist, Family Therapist, 1981–88; Facilitator, writing and creativity workshops, 1981–; Adjunct Faculty, Eastern Connecticut State University, 1988; Writer-in-Residence and Grantwriter, EASTCONN, 2000–. *Publications:* Falling Open, 1994; Safe Love and Other Political Acts, 1995. *Contributions to:* Written with a Spoon Anthology, 1995; XY Files: Poems about the Male Experience Anthology, 1996; Xanadu; Icarus; Midwest Review; Chaminade Literary Review; Kimera; Connecticut River Review. *Honours:* First Prize, National Scholastic Writing Award for Poetry, 1972; Pushcart Prize nomination, 1999; Finalist, John Gilfun

Award, 2000. *Memberships:* Still River Writers; Acad. of American Poets. *Address:* 27 Mulberry Rd, Mansfield Center, CT 06250, USA. *E-mail:* imagine22@earthlink.net.

TAYLOR, Velande Pingel, (Martha Pingel); b. 10 Sept. 1923, New York, NY, USA. Prof. of Literature and Philosophy (retd); Writer; Poet. m. Bert Raymond Taylor Jr, 28 Oct. 1961. *Education:* BA, 1944, MA, 1945, PhD, 1947, Literature and Philosophy; Independent study in art, music, creative writing, poetry and fiction. *Appointments:* Instructor, Paul Smiths College, New York, 1946–47; Asst Prof., East Carolina University, North Carolina, 1947–58; Prof. and Head, Dept of Humanities, Colorado Woman's College, 1958–66; Visiting Prof., St Mary's University, Texas, 1966–69; Prof., Middle Georgia College, 1969–72; Prof. and Writer-in-Residence, Hong Kong Baptist College, 1974–84; Retreat Facilitator in Poetry and Fiction, WordCraft by Lan, 1984–. *Publications:* An American Utilitarian, 1948; Catalyst, 1951; Mood Montage, 1968; Immortal Dancer, 1968; Mode and Muse in a New Generation, 1979; Homilies in the Marketplace 1996; Copper Flowers, 1996; Walking Songs, 1997; Zbyx, 1997; Tales From the Archetypal World, 1998; Flowing Water, Singing Sand, 1999; Between the Lines, 1999; The Zodiac Affair, 2000; Gallery, 2001. *Contributions to:* Anthologies, periodicals, and radio. *Honours:* Certificate, International Mark Twain Society, 1947; Miniature Medal, Order of the Danne Brog, 1951; Certificate, Writer's Digest Rhymed Poetry Contest, 1994. *Membership:* Acad. of American Poets; American Philosophical Asscn. *Address:* 910 Marion St, No. 1008, Seattle, WA 98104, USA.

TELLER, Gayl; b. 17 June 1946, New York, NY, USA. Poet. m. Michael Teller, 14 Aug. 1965, 1 s. *Education:* BA, 1967, MA 1981, Queens College; MA, Columbia University, 1969. *Appointments:* English Teacher, August Martin High School; Adjunct Assoc. Prof., English, Hofstra University; Poetry Teacher, Five Towns Music and Art Foundation; Dir, Poetry Centre, Mid Island Y, New York. *Publications:* At the Intersection of Everyting You Have Ever Loved, 1989; Shorehaven, 1996; Moving Day, 2002. *Contributions to:* Caesura; South Coast Poetry Journal; Moving Out; Long Island Quarterly; Connecticut Writer; Wyoming: The Hub of the Wheel; Bitteroot; Spring; Half Tones to Jubilee; Small Press Review; Phoebe; Dominion Review; Crone's Nest. *Honours:* First Place, Peninsula Library Poetry Award, 1984; Poetry Award, National Federation of State Poetry Societies, 1984; Poetry Award, Artemis Magazine, 1985; First Place, Poetry Award, Pittenbruach Press, 1989; Poetry Award, National League of American Pen Women, 1992; Edgar Allan Poe Prize for Literature, Bronx County Historical Society and Bronx Council on the Arts, 1997. *Memberships:* Poetry Society of America; Long Island Poetry Collective; Poetry Center, 92nd Street Y. *Address:* One Florence Lane, Plainview, NY 11803, USA.

TEMPLETON, Fiona; b. 23 Dec. 1951, Scotland. Theatre Dir; Poet; Writer. *Education:* MA, University of Edinburgh, 1973; MA, New York University, 1985. *Publications:* Elements of Performance Art, 1976; London, 1984; You the City, 1990; Delirium of Interpretations, 1997; Cells of Release, 1997; Hi Cowboy, 1997. *Contributions to:* Anthologies and journals. *Honours:* Grants, fellowships and awards. *Memberships:* New Dramatists; Poets and Writers. *Address:* 100 St Mark's Pl., No. 7, New York, NY 10009, USA.

TEN BERGE, Hans (Cornelis); b. 24 Dec. 1938, Netherlands. Poet; Writer; Ed. *Appointments:* Lecturer, Art Acad., Arnhem; Writer-in-Residence, University of Texas, USA, University College London, England, University of Gronigen, Netherlands; Ed., Raster, Grid, literary journals. *Publications:* Poetry: Gedichten, 3 vols, 1969; White Shaman, 1973; Poetry of the Aztecs, 1972; Va-banque, 1977; Semblance of Reality, 1981; Texas Elegies, 1983; Songs of Anxiety and Despair, 1988; Materia Prima, Poems, 1963–93; Oesters & gestoofde pot (Oysters and Pot Roast), 2001. Fiction: Zelfportret met witte muts, 1985; Het geheim van een oppewekt humeur, 1986; The Home Loving Traveller, 1995; Women, Jealousy and Other Discomforts, 1996; De Jaren in Zeedorp (The Sea-Town Years), 1998. Other: The Defence of Poetry, essays, 1988; Prose books; Books of myths and fables of Arctic peoples; Numerous poetry trans. *Contributions to:* Periodicals. *Honours:* Van der Hoogt Prize, 1968; Prose Prize, City of Amsterdam, 1971; Multatuli Prize, 1987; Contantijn Huÿgens Prize, 1996. *Memberships:* PEN; Society of Dutch Literature. *Address:* c/o Meulenhoff Publishers, PO Box 100, 1000 AC Amsterdam, Netherlands.

TENNANT, Pauline. See: RUMBOLD, Lady Pauline Letitia.

TERENCE, Susan; b. 14 Aug. 1953, Tucson, AZ, USA. Poet; Writer; Teacher; Puppeteer; Actress. *Education:* BA, English Education and Spanish, University of Arizona, Tucson, 1975; MA, Interdisciplinary Arts, San Francisco State University, 1994. *Appointments:* Visiting Artist, Arts in Arizona Towns, 1981–84, Montana Arts Council, 1989–; Poet-in-the-Schools, CA, 1987–. *Contributions to:* Many anthologies, reviews, quarterlies and journals. *Honours:* Second Place, San Francisco Bay Guardian Poetry Contest, 1989; De War's Young Arts Award for Literature, CA, 1990. *Membership:* Poet-in-the-Schools, CA, San Francisco Co-ordinator. *Address:* 2153 Hayes, San Francisco, CA 94117, USA.

TESH, Ruby Nifong; b. 5 Oct. 1917, Winston-Salem, North Carolina, USA. Organ and Piano Teacher; Choir Dir; Poet. m. Luther E Tesh, 27 Sept. 1936, 2 s. *Education:* Winston-Salem Public Schools. *Publications:* Fleeting Inspiration, 1988; Random Thoughts, 1992. *Contributions to:* Anthologies and periodicals. *Honour:* Charter Membership for Outstanding Achievement in Poetry, International Society of Poets. *Address:* 2409 Friedberg Church Rd, Winson-Salem, NC 27127, USA.

THABIT JONES, Peter; b. 18 May 1951, Swansea, Wales. Poet; Writer. m. Hilary, 4 s., 2 d. *Education:* Diploma in Higher Education, University of Wales; Diploma in Office Studies; Higher National Certificate in Leisure/Conservation Management; Postgraduate Certificate in Education (Further and Higher Education). *Appointments:* Ed., SWAG Magazine, 1995–; Chair. and Treasurer, Swansea Writers and Artists Group, 1996–; Tutor, Children's Literature and Poetry, University of Wales, Swansea. *Publications:* Tacky Brow, 1974; The Apprenticeship, 1977; Clocks Tick Differently, 1980; Visitors, 1986; The Cold Cold Corner, 1995; Ballad of Kilvey Hill, 1999; Selected Poems, 2002. *Contributions to:* 2Plus2; Poetry Wales; Poetry Review; Anglo-Welsh Review; Planet; Outposts Poetry Quarterly; Poetry Nottingham; NER/BLQ; Urbane Gorilla; Docks; Cambrensis; Orbis; White Rose; Exile; Iota; Krax; Weyfarers; Western Mail; South Wales Evening Post; Momentum; Asp; Children's poetry included in many anthologies. *Honours:* Eric Gregory Award for Poetry, 1979; Grants, Royal Literary Fund, 1987, Society of Authors, 1987, Welsh Arts Council, 1990; Commendations, National Poetry Competition, 1983, 1988, Bridport Arts Festival, 1984, Welsh Arts Council (prose), 1986, (poems), 1987; Outposts Competition Winner, 1988; Tutor, St Thomas School Workshop for Prince Charles, Swansea, 1995. *Memberships:* Poetry Society, London; Swansea Writers and Artists Group, chair. and treas.; Welsh Acad., full mem., 1995–. *Address:* Dan y Bryn, 74 Cwm Level Rd, Brynhyfryd, Swansea SA5 9DY, Wales.

THAG, Bhagwan; b. 24 Jan. 1955, Hiwarkhed, Buldana District, India. Civil Servant; Poet. m. Parvati Thag, 27 June 1977, 3 d. *Education:* BA, Parat II. *Publications:* Atmapakshi, 1980; Yuddha, 1985; Anuwad, 1985; Modern Marathi Poetry, 6 vols, 1987–90; Vishw Pratibha, 1988; Anarth, 1991; Dalit Poetry Today, 1991. *Contributions to:* Numerous periodicals. *Honours:* Several awards. *Memberships:* Professional organizations. *Address:* c/o Tuka Mhane, Rajarshi Shahunagar Chaitnyawadi, Buldana, Buldana District (MS) 443 001, India.

THAMEZ, Lorraine D.; b. 26 Nov. 1950, Pueblo, CO, USA. Writer; Poet. 2 s., 1 d. *Education:* AA, Literature, 1997. *Appointment:* Poetry Ed., Purgatoire Magazine. *Publications:* Prairie Woman: Dangerous Games; Together Forever; One Heart; One Hand (poems). *Contributions to:* Periodicals. *Memberships:* PEN; Poets and Writers; Western Writers' Guild. *Address:* 121 Chanlon Rd, New Providence, NJ 07974, USA.

THAM-GOLDBERG, Hilary, (Hilary Tham); b. 20 Aug. 1946, Kelang, Malaysia. Writer; Poet. m. Joseph R Goldberg, 16 Feb. 1971, 3 d. *Education:* BA, Honours in English Literature, University of Malaya. *Appointments:* Chair, Coalition for Resettlement of Vietnamese Refugees, 1979–80; Ed.-in-Chief, Word Works; Poetry Ed., Potomac Review, 1992–. *Publications:* No Gods Today, 1969; Paper Boats, 1987; Bad Names for Women, 1989; Tigerbone Wine, 1992; Men and Other Strange Myths, 1994; Lane With No Name: Memoirs and Poems of a Malaysian-Chinese Girlhood, 1997. *Contributions to:* Antietam Review; International Quarterly; Double Take; Palo Alto Review; Excursus; Waterways; Encodings; Delhi-London Quarterly; Poet Lore; Wind; Maryland Poetry Review; Gargoyle; Phoebe; Minimus; Pig Iron. *Honours:* Second Prize, Virginia Poetry, 1978; Third Prize, Paterson Poetry, 1989. *Membership:* New Room Poets, chair and founder, 1982–. *Address:* 2600 N Upshur St, Arlington, VA 22207, USA.

THEÀRLAICH, Sìne Nic. See: BLACKHALL, Sheena Booth.

THÉORET, France; b. 1942, Montréal, QC, Canada. Author; Dramatist; Poet. *Education:* BA, 1968, MA, 1977, University of Montréal; PhD, Études françaises, University of Sherbrooke, 1982. *Publications:* Bloody Mary, 1977, English trans., 1991; Une voix pour Odile, 1978, English trans., 1991; Vertiges, 1979, English trans., 1991; Nécessairement putain, 1980, English trans., 1991; Nous parlerons comme on écrit, 1982; Intérieurs, 1984; Entre raison et déraison, 1987; L'homme qui peignait Staline, 1989, English trans. as The Man Who Painted Stalin, 1991; Étrangeté, l'étreinte, 1992; La fiction de l'ange, 1992; Journal pour mémoire, 1993; Laurence, 1996. *Contributions to:* Anthologies and other publications. *Address:* c/o Union des écrivaines et écrivains québécois, La Maison des écrivains, 3492 Ave Laval, Montréal, QC H2X 3C8, Canada.

THERSON-COFIE, Larweh, (Kwesi Afra, Eddie Cosmos, Black Moses); b. 8 Sept. 1943, Ghana. Journalist; Poet. m. Rebecca Amobea, 30 Oct. 1988, 1 s. *Education:* Ghana Institute of Journalism; University of Ghana. *Appointments:* Staff, 1967–79, Foreign Ed., 1979–84, Special Correspondent, 1984–90, Asst Ed., 1990–92, Deputy Ed. 1992–, The Mirror; Ed., Ghana Year Book, 1976–1993; Dir, Afra Golden Age Publications, 1992. *Publications:* Poets of Our Time; The Golden Swan and Other Tales and Tales of the Kpiti.

Contributions to: The Mirror, 1976–90; Ghana Broadcasting Corpn (radio), 1994–2000; Anthologies and other publications. *Memberships:* Ghana Asscn of Writers; Pan African Writers Asscn; United Poet Laureates League; Vice-Pres., World Poetry Research Institute; Regent and Parnassian Jurist, World Poetry Society; Regent and Fellow, International Poets Acad., India. *Address:* c/ o The Mirror, PO Box 742, Ghana.

THESEN, Sharon; b. 1 Oct. 1946, Tisdale, Saskatchewan, Canada. Poet; Writer. *Education:* BA, 1970, MA, 1974, Simon Fraser University. *Appointments:* Teacher, Capilano College, Vancouver, 1976–92; Poetry Ed., Capilano Review, 1978–89. *Publications:* Artemis Hates Romance, 1980; Radio New France Radio, 1981; Holding the Pose, 1983; Confabulations: Poems for Malcolm Lowry, 1984; The Beginning of the Long Dash, 1987; The Pangs of Sunday, 1990; The New Long Poems Anthology (ed.), 1991; Aurora, 1995; A Pair of Scissors, 2000. *Contributions to:* Various publications. *Address:* c/o League of Canadian Poets, 54 Wolseley St, Third Floor, Toronto, Ontario M5T 1A5, Canada.

THIBAUDEAU, Colleen; b. 29 Dec. 1925, Toronto, Ontario, Canada. Poet; Writer. m. James C Reaney, 29 Dec. 1951, 2 s., 1 d. *Education:* St Thomas Collegiate Institute, 1944; BA, 1948, MA, 1949, University College, University of Toronto; Diploma, l'Université Catholique de l'ouest, Angers, 1951. *Publications:* Poetry: Ten Letters, 1975; My Granddaughters are Combing Out Their Long Hair, 1977; The Martha Landscapes, 1984; The Artemesia Book: Poems Selected and New, 1991; The Patricia Album and Other Poems, 1992. *Contributions to:* Poems and stories in various anthologies. *Membership:* League of Canadian Poets, hon. mem., 1997–; New Democratic Party, life mem. *Address:* 276 Huron St, London, Ontario N6A 2J9, Canada.

THOLANA, Ashok Chakarvarthy; b. 7 May 1959, Hyderabad, India. Poet. m. Sri Vani, 9 May 1987. *Education:* BCom; Postgraduate Diploma in Journalism. *Contributions to:* Newspapers, anthologies and magazines. *Honours:* Poet of the Month, Channel 6 Magazine, 1993, 1997; International Poet of Merit, International Society of Poets, 1995. *Memberships:* Poetry Club of India; New Zealand Poetry Society. *Address:* 16-2-836/L, Plot 39, Madhavnagar Colony, Saidabad, Hyderabad 59, India.

THOM THE WORLD POET. See: WOODRUFF, Thom.

THOMAS, Donald Michael; b. 27 Jan. 1935, Redruth, Cornwall, England. Poet; Writer; Trans. 2 s., 1 d. *Education:* BA, English, MA, New College, Oxford. *Appointment:* Lecturer, Hereford College of Education, 1964–78. *Publications:* Poetry: Penguin Modern Poets 11, 1968; Two Voices, 1968; Logan Stone, 1971; Love and Other Deaths, 1975; The Honeymoon Voyage, 1978; Dreaming in Bronze, 1981; Selected Poems, 1983; Puberty Tree, 1992. Fiction: The Flute Player, 1979; Birthstone, 1980; The White Hotel, 1981; Ararat, 1983; Swallow, 1984; Sphinx, 1986; Summit, 1987; Lying Together, 1990; Flying into Love, 1992; Pictures at an Exhibition, 1993; Eating Pavlova, 1994; Lady with a Laptop, 1996; Alexander Solzhenitsyn, 1998; Charlotte, 2000. Translator: Requiem, and Poem Without a Hero, by Akhmatova, 1976; Way of All the Earth, by Akhmatova, 1979; The Bronze Horseman, by Pushkin, 1982. *Address:* The Coach House, Rashleigh Vale, Tregolis Rd, Truro TR1 1TJ, England.

THOMAS, F(ranklin) Richard; b. 1 Aug. 1940, Evansville, IN, USA. Prof. of American Thought and Language; Poet; Writer. m. Sharon Kay Myers, 2 June 1962, 1 s., 1 d. *Education:* AB, 1963, MA, 1964, Purdue University; PhD, Indiana University, 1970. *Appointments:* Purdue University, 1969–70; Prof., Michigan State University, 1971–; Ed., Centering magazine, 1973–80; Research Assoc., Indiana University, 1978–79. *Publications:* Poetry: Fat Grass, 1970; Alive with You This Day, 1980; Frog Praises Night: Poems with Commentary, 1980; Heart Climbing Stairs, 1986; Corolla, Stamen, and Style, 1986; The Whole Mustery of the Bregn, 1990; Miracles, 1996; Death at Camp Pahoka, 2000. Novel: Prism: The Journal of John Fish, 1992. Criticism: Literary Admirers of Alfred Stieglitz, 1983. Editor: Various books including: The Landlocked Heart: Poems from Indiana, 1980; Americans in Denmark: Comparisons of the Two Cultures by Writers, Artists and Teachers, 1990. *Contributions to:* Numerous journals and magazines. *Honours:* Fulbright Awards, 1974, 1985; MacDowell Colony Fellowship, 1979; Michigan Council for the Arts Award, 1990; National Writing Project Summer Institute Fellow, 1993. *Address:* 2113 La Mer Lane, Haslett, MI 48840, USA.

THOMPSON, Francis George; b. 29 March 1931, Isle of Lewis, Scotland. Senior Lecturer (retd); Poet. m. Margaret Elaine Pullar, 23 April 1960, 1 s., 3 d. *Education:* Fellow, Institution of Incorporated Engineers. *Appointments:* Technical Writer; Technical College Lecturer; Senior Lecturer. *Publications:* Void, 1975; First Light, 1977; Touchlines, 1978; Reflections, 1985. *Contributions to:* Lines Review; Chapman; Prospice; Northwords; Orbis; Words. *Honour:* Hugh McDiarmid Memorial Cup, Scottish Open Poetry Competition, 1979. *Address:* 5 Rathad na Muilne, Stornoway, Isle of Lewis, Scotland.

THOMPSON, Julius Eric; b. 15 July 1946, Vicksburg, Mississippi, USA. Assoc. Prof.; Writer; Poet. *Education:* BS, Alcorn State University, Lorman, Mississippi, 1969; MA, History, 1971, PhD, 1973, Princeton University.

Appointments: Faculty, Jackson State University, Mississippi, 1973–80, Florida Memorial College, 1980–81, State University of New York at Albany, 1983–88, University of Rochester, New York, 1988–89; Assoc. Prof., Southern Illinois University, Carbondale, 1989–96, University of Missouri, Columbia, 1996–. *Publications:* Hopes Tied Up in Promises, 1977; The Anthology of Black Mississippi Poets (ed.), 1988; The Black Press in Mississippi, 1865–1985, 1993; Percy Greene and the Jackson Advocate: The Life and Times of a Radical Conservative Black Newspaperman, 1897–1977, 1994. *Contributions to:* Scholarly journals and general periodicals. *Honours:* Danforth Fellow, 1969–73; Doctoral Award, Ford Foundation, 1972–73; Fulbright Program Award to Zimbabwe, 1987; National Endowment for the Humanities Fellowship, 1994. *Memberships:* Asscn for the Study of Afro-American Life and History; Mississippi Historical Society; Southern Black Cultural Alliance. *Address:* 2803 Yukon Dr., Columbia, MO 65202, USA.

THOMPSON, K. Lloyd; b. 10 Feb. 1945, Jackson, Mississippi, USA. Economist; Physicist; Poet. *Education:* AB, Princeton University, 1966; MSc, London School of Economics, 1967; MA, Stanford University, 1969; PhD, Trinity Hall, University of Cambridge, 1979. *Publication:* Baked Beans, 1994. *Contributions to:* Agenda; Ambit; Argo; Honest Ulsterman; Literature Review; Orbis; Outposts; Poetry Review; TLS. *Honours:* Seatonian Prizes, 1987, 1989, 1990, 1991, 1992. *Memberships:* Judith E Wilson Workshop, University of Cambridge; Poetry Society. *Address:* 4 Napier St, Cambridge CB1 1HS, England.

THOMPSON, Keith; b. 27 Sept. 1947, England. Software Quality Man.; Poet. m. Caroline Ann Thompson, 18 May 1968, 1 d. *Education:* BA, Literature, Open University. *Publications:* Goldmines at Thelnetham, 1991; Jasmine and Honeysuckle Pavilion, 1991; My Affair with Emily, 1991; Pedlar of Dreams, 1993. *Contributions to:* Various anthologies, reviews, magazines and journals. *Honours:* Diploma, Scottish Open Poetry Competition, 1983; Second Prize, Newcastle Brown Ale Poetry Competition, 1992. *Memberships:* Institute of Management Specialists, fellow; Institute of Quality Assurance; British Computer Society; Poetry Society; Open University Poetry Society, chair., 1988–91. *Address:* Bacchus, Hinderclay Rd, Thelnetham, Diss, Suffolk IP22 1JZ, England.

THOMPSON, Lucille, (E Whitney); b. 23 Aug. 1926, Tobago. Poet. m. 19 June 1954, 3 s., 1 d. *Publications:* Pocket Book of Verse; Phoenix. *Contributions to:* Magazine of New Verse; Poetry Press; London Poetry Society. *Memberships:* London Poetry Society; ICA. *Address:* 35 Crown Dale, Upper Norwood, London SE19 3PB, England.

THOMPSON, Rebecca Patricia; b. 14 April 1938, Dover, New Hampshire, USA. Writer; Poet; Ed.; Teacher. m. Ted van Griethuysen, 26 May 1962. *Education:* BA, History and English, University of New Hampshire; MA, Theatre Arts and Speech, Pennsylvania State University, 1960; Aesthetic Realism with Eli Siegel, 1961–78. *Appointments:* Instructor, Pennsylvania State University, 1959–60, Baldwin Center, CT, 1984–86, University of Southern California, 1989; Poetry Instructor, Shakespeare Theatre at the Folger, Washington, DC, 1988–; Various poetry workshops and readings. *Publications:* Essays and poems. *Contributions to:* Anthologies, reviews, quarterlies, journals and magazines. *Membership:* Poetry Society of America. *Address:* 116 Sixth St NE, No. 61, Washington, DC 20002, USA.

THOMPSON, Samuel Richard Charles, (Nat P Mossham); b. 9 Feb. 1968, London, England. Teacher; Poet. *Education:* BA, English, University of Manchester, 1990; Postgraduate Certificate in Education (Primary), Charlotte Mason College of Education. *Appointments:* Teacher; Co-Ed., Muse magazine, 1989. *Publications:* Taken by a Wave, 1992; Fresh Fields, 1993. Criticism: A Linguistic Analysis of The Waste Land, 1989; Music in the Poetry of T S Eliot, 1990; These Fragments I Have Shored Against My Ruins – Poetry in the Primary School, 1991. *Contributions to:* Magazines. *Honours:* Thomas De Quincy Prize, University of Manchester, 1989. *Memberships:* Manchester University Poetry Society, chair, 1990; Poetry Society. *Address:* Tree House, 3 Woodsyre, Sydenham Hill, London SE26 6SS, England.

THOMSON, Charles Geoffrey; b. 6 Feb. 1953, Romford, Essex, England. Poet. m. Andrea Mestanek, 25 Oct. 1974, divorced 1980, 1 s. *Education:* Maidstone College of Art, 1975–79; FFIAD, 1979. *Appointments:* Writer-in-Residence, Borough of Bexley-GLAA, 1985, Stonehouse Hospital, 1989; Poet-in-Residence, Invicta Radio, 1987, Medway Arts Centre, 1988, SCEA Schools, Germany, 1993–95; Poetry Ed., Kent Companion, 1987–88; Artistic Consultant, National Convention of Poets and Small Presses, 1988; Poetry Columnist, Kent Life, 1989–90. *Publications:* The Middle Class, 1982; The Royal Tour, 1983; The End of the Boer War, 1985; The Art of Killing Chickens, 1985; Lunchtime Rhymes, 1988; The Manic Computer, 1990; Something to Sling in Your Shopping Basket, 1991; The Glurgle Gloop, 1992; I'm Brilliant, 1992. *Contributions to:* Radio and television. *Honours:* Southeast Arts Literary Group Award, 1980; First Prize, Woman Royal Wedding Party Competition, 1987; The Forward Book of Poetry, 1993. *Memberships:* Betjeman Society; Medway Poets; National Asscn of Writers in Education, committee mem.; Poetry Society; Society of Authors. *Address:* 1 Bank Mansions, Golders Green Rd, London NW11 8LG, England.

THOMSON, Derick S(mith), (Ruaraidh MacThòmais); b. 5 Aug. 1921, Stornoway, Isle of Lewis, Scotland. Prof. of Celtic (retd); Poet; Writer. m. Carol Galbraith, 1952, 5 s., 1 d. *Education:* MA, University of Aberdeen, 1947; BA, Emmanuel College, Cambridge, 1948. *Appointments:* Asst in Celtic, University of Edinburgh, 1948–49; Lecturer in Welsh, 1949–56, Prof. of Celtic, 1963–91, University of Glasgow; Ed., Gairm Gaelic Literary Quarterly, 1952–2002; Reader in Celtic, University of Aberdeen, 1956–63. *Publications:* An Dealbh Briste, 1951; The Gaelic Sources of Macpherson's 'Ossian', 1952; Eadar Samhradh is Foghar, 1967; An Rathad Cian, 1970; The Far Road and Other Poems, 1971; An Introduction to Gaelic Poetry, 1974; Saorsa agus an Iolaire, 1977; Creachadh na Clarsaich, 1982; The Companion to Gaelic Scotland, 1983; European Poetry in Gaelic Translation, 1990; Smeur an Dochais, 1992; Gaelic Poetry in the Eighteenth Century, 1993; Meall Garbh/The Rugged Mountain, 1995; Mac Mhaighstir Alasdair, Selected Poems, 1996. *Contributions to:* Books, journals and magazines. *Honours:* Publication Awards, Scottish Arts Council, 1971, 1992; Ossian Prize, FVS Foundation, Hamburg, 1974; Saltire Scottish Book of the Year Award, 1983; Hon. DLitt, University of Wales, 1987, University of Aberdeen, 1994. *Memberships:* British Acad., fellow; Glasgow Arts Club; Scottish Gaelic Texts Society, hon. pres.; Royal Society of Edinburgh, fellow; Saltire Society, hon. pres., 1997; Scottish Poetry Library, hon. pres., 1999. *Address:* 15 Struan Rd, Cathcart, Glasgow G44 3AT, Scotland.

THOMSON, Susan Clark; b. 14 Oct. 1966, Scotland. Poet. *Education:* English Literature, University of Edinburgh, 1991–95. *Contributions to:* Frogmore Papers; Third Half; Scratchings; Spokes; Odyssey; First Time; Peace and Freedom; Cokefish (US); Graffiti; Smiths Knoll. *Memberships:* National Poetry Society; Writers News. *Address:* 14 Candlemakers Park, Gilmerton, Edinburgh EH17 8TH, Scotland.

THORBURN, James Alexander; b. 24 Aug. 1923, Martins Ferry, Ohio, USA. Prof. of English and Linguistics Emeritus; Writer; Poet; Trans. m. (1) Lois McElroy, 3 July 1954, 1 s., 1 d., (2) June Yingling, 18 April 1981. *Education:* BA, 1949, MA, 1951, Ohio State University; PhD, Linguistics, Louisiana State University, 1977. *Appointments:* Instructor in English, Louisiana State University, 1961–70; Prof. of English and Linguistics, 1970–89, Prof. Emeritus, 1989–, Southeastern Louisiana University. *Contributions to:* Many anthologies, journals and periodicals. *Honours:* Several. *Memberships:* Numerous professional organizations. *Address:* c/o Southeastern Louisiana University, Hammond, LA 70402, USA.

THORGEIRSSON, Arni Ibsen, (Arni Ibsen); b. 17 May 1948, Stykkisholmur, Iceland. Writer; Dramatist; Poet; Trans.; Teacher. m. Hildur Kristjansdottir, 20 Feb. 1971, 3 s. *Education:* Teacher's Diploma, Icelandic Teachers Training College, 1971; BA, Honours, English and Drama, University of Exeter, England, 1975. *Publications:* Kom, 1975; Samuel Beckett (trans. of prose, plays, and poems), 1987; Vort Skarda Lif, 1990. Other: Several plays. *Contributions to:* Reference books, anthologies, and periodicals. *Honour:* Prize for Writing, Icelandic Writers Fund, 1985. *Memberships:* Icelandic Playwrights Union, executvie committee; Icelandic Writers Fund; Icelandic Writers Union. *Address:* Stekkjarkinn 19, 220 Hafnafjordur, Iceland.

THORN, Howard Stephen; b. 26 May 1929, London, England. Draughtsman; Poet. m. 19 March 1955. *Education:* ONC Mechanical Engineering, Technical College, 1945–50. *Contributions to:* Anthologies, including: Memories of the Millennium, 2000; Poetry Now Southern England, 2000; Christian Perspectives, 2000; Momentous Occasions, 2000; Expressions of Life, 2000; Seasons of Emotion, 2000; Reflections: An Anthology of Contemporary Mystical Poetry, 2000; A Place to Remember, 2001; Where Dreams Are Made, 2001; In Honour Of..., 2001; Poetry Now Southern England, 2002. *Honour:* Semi-finalist, International Society of Poets Competition, 1995. *Memberships:* Authors' Licensing and Collecting Society Ltd, London; International Society of Poets, honoured mem. *Address:* 37 Crossways, Sittingbourne, Kent ME10 4RJ, England.

THORNE, Peter. See: DANIEL, Geoffrey Peter.

THORNTON, Donald Ray; b. 15 Dec. 1936, Winnsborro, LA, USA. Poet; Artist; Teacher. m. Suzannah Smith. *Education:* BA, Art Education, Louisiana Tech University, 1960; MA, Design, Louisiana State University, 1967. MA coursework, University of Southwestern Louisiana, 1988. *Appointments:* Instructor in Art, University of Southwestern Louisiana, 1967–73; Artist-in-Residence, College of Mainland, 1973, 1976. *Publications:* Outcry, 1960; Sounding, 1976; A Walk on Water, 1985; Ascending, 1993; Mentor, 1993. Other: Ed. of several works. *Contributions to:* Various anthologies, reviews, quarterlies and journals. *Address:* 1504 Howard St, New Iberia, LA 70560, USA.

THORNTON, Margaret. See: POOLE, Margaret Barbara.

THORPE, Dobbin. See: DISCH, Thomas M(ichael).

THULASIKUMARI, H. See: NAIDU, Tulsi.

THURIDUR, Gudmundsdottir; b. 16 Nov. 1939, Iceland. Poet. *Education:* Reykjavík City College, 1960; Icelandic Teachers College, 1963. *Publications:* Only One Flower, 1969; Your Cloudy Laughter, 1972; On the Balcony, 1975; And There Was Spring, 1980; The Autumn Told Me, 1985; The Words Grow Around Me, 1989; The Night is Listening to Me, 1994. *Contributions to:* Anthologies, newspapers and periodicals. *Honours:* Literature Awards, Writers Union of Iceland, 1973, 1983, 1991. *Memberships:* Icelandic Authors Asscn; Writers Union of Iceland. *Address:* Asvallagata 40, 101 Reykjavík, Iceland.

THWAITE, Anthony Simon; b. 23 June 1930, Chester, Cheshire, England. Poet; Critic; Writer; Ed. m. Ann Barbara Harrop, 4 Aug. 1955, 4 d. *Education:* BA, 1955, MA, 1959, Christ Church, Oxford. *Appointments:* Visiting Lecturer in English, 1955–57, Japan Foundation Fellow, 1985–86, University of Tokyo; Producer, BBC, 1957–62; Literary Ed., The Listener, 1962–65, New Statesman, 1968–72; Asst Prof. of English, University of Libya, 1965–67; Henfield Writing Fellow, University of East Anglia, 1972; Co-Ed., Encounter, 1973–85; Visiting Prof., Kuwait University, 1974; Chair. of the Judges, Booker Prize, 1986; Dir, 1986–92, Editorial Consultant, 1992–95, André Deutsch, Ltd; Poet-in-Residence, Vanderbilt University, 1992. *Publications:* Poetry: Home Truths, 1957; The Owl in the Tree, 1963; The Stones of Emptiness, 1967; Inscriptions, 1973; New Confessions, 1974; A Portion for Foxes, 1977; Victorian Voices, 1980; Poems 1953–1983, 1984, revised edn as Poems 1953–1988, 1989; Letter from Tokyo, 1987; The Dust of the World, 1994; Selected Poems, 1956–1996, 1997; A Different Country: New Poems, 2000. Other: Contemporary English Poetry, 1959; Japan (with Roloff Beny), 1968; The Deserts of Hesperides, 1969; Poetry Today, 1973; In Italy (with Roloff Beny and Peter Porter), 1974; Twentieth Century English Poetry, 1978; Odyssey: Mirror of the Mediterranean (with Roloff Beny), 1981; Six Centuries of Verse, 1984. Editor: The Penguin Book of Japanese Verse (with Geoffrey Bownas), 1964; The English Poets (with Peter Porter), 1974; New Poetry 4 (with Fleur Adcock), 1978; Larkin at Sixty, 1982; Poetry 1945 to 1980 (with John Mole), 1983; Collected Poems of Philip Larkin, 1988; Selected Letters of Philip Larkin, 1992; Further Requirements: Philip Larkin, 2001. *Honours:* Richard Hillary Memorial Prize, 1968; Fellow, RSL, 1978; Cholmondeley Prize, 1983; Hon. DLitt, University of Hull, 1989; O.B.E., 1990; Fellow, Society of Antiquaries, 2000. *Address:* The Mill House, Low Tharston, Norfolk NR15 2YN, England.

THWAITES, (Stephen) Dane; b. 15 June 1950, Inverell, NSW, Australia. Bookseller; Publisher; Poet. Separated, 1 s. *Education:* BA, English Literature, University of Nebraska, Armidale, 1971. *Publications:* Winter Light, 1983; South China, 1994. *Contributions to:* Various publications. *Honour:* Co-Winner, Mattara Prize, 1987. *Address:* c/o Butterfly Bookshop, Shop 6, Renae's Arcade, Station St, Wentworth Falls, NSW 2782, Australia.

TICE, Arden A., (Hava Arden, Arden Eckles, Arden MacNab); b. 8 March 1938, Lawton, Oklahoma, USA. Psychotherapist; Psychologist; Social Worker; Teacher; Poet. *Education:* BA, English, University of Texas at Austin, 1951; MA, Psychology, Saint Matthew University, Columbus, Ohio, 1971; Graduate Studies, University of New Mexico, Albuquerque, 1968, 1986–87. *Appointments:* Dir, Alcoholism Treatment, Southwest Mental Health Centre, Las Cruces, New Mexico, 1973–74; Instructor in Psychology, El Paso Community College, Texas, 1974–81; Psychotherapist, El Paso, Texas, 1978–88. *Publications:* Take It and Fake the Rest, 1974; Wind in My Fist, 1990; The Augmented Moon, 1991; Looking for the Frontier, 1992; A Naming of Women. *Contributions to:* Reviews and journals. *Membership:* American Asscn of Artist-Therapists. *Address:* PO Box 7403, Albuquerque, NM 87194, USA.

TICE, Bradley Scott; b. 6 Oct. 1959, Palo Alto, CA, USA. Researcher; Poet. *Education:* AA, Liberal Arts 1983, AA, MDL, 1995, De Anza College; BA, History, San Jose State University, 1987; PhD, Chemistry, Fairfax University, 1996. *Appointment:* Researcher, Pacific Language Institute, Cupertino, CA, 1993–. *Publication:* Suburban White (chapbook), 1996. *Contributions to:* Anthologies, including: Crossings, 1995; Inspirations, 1996; A Moment in Time, 1995; Best Poems of 1996; Walk Through Paradise, 1995; Windows of the Soul, 1995; Poems, 1997. *Honours:* Ed.'s Choice Award, 1995, 1996; Third Prize, North American Open Poetry Competition, 1996; Pres.'s Award, 1996. *Address:* PO Box 2214, Cupertino, CA 95015-2214, USA.

TICE, Richard Ellis; b. 29 Nov. 1950, Oakland, CA, USA. Ed.; Publisher; Poet. m. Kathleen Tripp, 9 Oct. 1982, 3 s., 2 d. *Education:* BA, Comparative Literature, Brigham Young University, 1975. *Appointments:* Asst Ed., 1982–86, Assoc. Ed., 1989–, Deseret Book Co, Salt Lake City; Ed.-Publisher, Dragonfly: East-West Haiku Quarterly, 1985–; Asst Ed., Ensign Magazine, 1986–89. *Publication:* Station Stop: A Collection of Haiku and Related Forms, 1986. *Contributions to:* Anthologies, newspapers, and periodicals. *Honours:* First Place, Hart-Larson Poetry Contest, Brigham Young University, 1981; Other awards. *Memberships:* League of Utah Writers; Utah State Poetry Society. *Address:* 5737 Middlewood Ave, Salt Lake City, UT 84118, USA.

TICHY, Susan Elizabeth; b. 25 April 1952, Washington, DC, USA. Assoc. Prof.; Poet. m. Lewis Michael O'Hanlon, 29 Jan. 1982. *Education:* BA, Goddard College, 1976; MA, University of Colorado, 1979; Other coursework at Macalester College, University of California at Berkeley. *Appointments:*

Visiting Assoc. Prof., Ohio University, 1987; Artist-in-Residence, Colorado Council on the Arts and Humanities, 1987–88; Asst Prof., 1988–93, Assoc. Prof., 1993–, George Mason University, Fairfax, Virginia. *Publications:* The Hands in Exile, 1983; A Smell of Burning Starts the Day, 1988. *Contributions to:* Antioch Review; American Voice; Beloit Poetry Journal; Five Fingers Review; Indiana Review; High Plains Literary Review; Tonantzin; Northwest Review; Ploughshares; Sing Heavenly Muse; Black Warrior Review; Guadalupe Review. *Honours:* National Poetry Series, 1983; Eugene Kayden Award, 1985; Pushcart Prize, 1987; National Endowment for the Arts Fellowship, 1988; Nominee, Dewars Performing Arts Award, 1991. *Memberships:* Poets and Writers; Associated Writing Programs; Acad. of American Poets. *Address:* c/o Dept of English, George Mason University, Fairfax, VA 22030, USA.

TIERNEY, Karl Joseph; b. 15 June 1956, Westfield, Massachusetts, USA. Word Processor; Poet. *Education:* BA, English, Emory University, Atlanta, GA, 1980; MFA, Creative Writing (Poetry), University of Arkansas, 1983. *Contributions to:* American Poetry Review; Berkeley Poetry Review; James White Review; Crazyquilt Quarterly; Contact II; Exquisite Corpse; Oregonian; San Francisco Sentinel; Equinox. *Honour:* Finalist, Walt Whitman Award, 1992. *Membership:* PEN (USA, West division), 1989–. *Address:* 6-B Sumner St, San Francisco, CA 94103, USA.

TILL, Christa Maria; b. 23 Jan. 1946, Vienna, Austria. Writer; Poet. m. Hans Heinrich Schiesser, 27 Sept. 1974. *Education:* PhD Studies, University of Vienna. *Publications:* David, David Supermann, 1986; E Wie Emma, 1989; Wiener Altwaren Vendetta, 1995; Wiener Atlanten, 2000. *Contributions to:* Rund um den Kreis, 1996. *Honour:* KOELA, 1978. *Memberships:* I G Autoren, Vienna; Swiss Writers Asscn. *Address:* Fehrenstrasse 12, 8032 Zürich, Switzerland.

TILLINGHAST, Richard (Williford); b. 25 Nov. 1940, Memphis, TN, USA. Prof. of English; Poet; Writer. m. (1) Nancy Walton Pringle, 1965, divorced 1970, (2) Mary Graves, 22 April 1973, 1 s., 1 d. *Education:* BA, University of the South, 1962; MA, 1963, PhD, 1970, Harvard University. *Appointments:* Asst Prof. of English, University of California at Berkeley, 1968–73; Visiting Asst Prof., University of the South, 1979–80; Briggs-Copeland Lecturer, Harvard University, 1980–83; Assoc. Prof., 1983–92, Prof. of English, 1992–, University of Michigan at Ann Arbor; Assoc., Michigan Institute for the Humanities, 1989–90, 1993–94. *Publications:* Poetry: Sleep Watch, 1969; The Knife and Other Poems, 1980; Sewanee in Ruins, 1981; Fossils, Metal, and the Blue Limit, 1982; Our Flag Was Still There, 1984; The Stonecutter's Hand, 1994; Today in the Café Trieste, 1997; Six Mile Mountain, 2000. Other: A Quiet Pint in Kinvara, 1991; Robert Lowell's Life and Work: Damaged Grandeur, 1995; A Visit to the Gallery: The University of Michigan Museum of Art (ed.), 1997. *Contributions to:* Newspapers, reviews, journals and magazines. *Honours:* National Endowment for the Humanities Grant, 1980; Bread Loaf Fellowship, 1982; Millay Colony Residency, 1985; Yaddo Writers' Retreat Residency, 1986; Amy Lowell Travel Fellowship, 1990–91; British Council Fellowship, 1992, and Travel Grant, 1994; Ann Stanford Prize for Poetry, University of Southern California at Los Angeles, 1992. *Address:* c/o Dept of English, University of Michigan at Ann Arbor, Ann Arbor, MI 48109, USA.

TIMONEY JENKIN, Ann; b. 6 July 1933, London, England. Poet. Divorced, 2 s., 1 d. *Education:* University of London; Music, South Australian Institute, 1980. *Appointment:* Music Teacher, Annesley College, Adelaide, 1980–90. *Publication:* Midwinter Light, 1995. *Contributions to:* Anthologies and reviews. *Honour:* Individual Arts Project Grant, South Australian Dept for the Arts and Cultural Heritage. *Memberships:* Australian Society of Authors; Friendly Street Poets. *Address:* 10 Margaret St, Norwood, SA 5067, Australia.

TINKLER, Janet; b. 29 Oct. 1943, Gateshead, England. Poet. m. Derek Tinkler, 8 Oct. 1966, 1 s., 1 d. *Publications:* Autumn, 1996; Dark Days, 1996; Environmental Destruction, 1996; Kingdom of the Condor, 1996; Silhouettes, 1996; Angel, 1998; Euphony of Summer, 1998; Heaven's Breath, 1998; Northern Heritage, 1998; One Small Step, 1998; The Heroine, 1998; The River, 1998; The Wardrobe Mistress, 1998; Tora Tora Tora, 1998. *Contributions to:* Evening Gazette; Exile Magazine. *Honour:* Ed.'s Choice Award, 1997. *Address:* 9 Dorrien Crescent, Ormesby Rd, Middlesborough TS3 7AW, England.

TIPTON, David John; b. 28 April 1934, Birmingham, England. Poet; Writer; Ed.; Trans.; Teacher. m. (1) Ena Hollis, 10 June 1956, (2) Glenys Tipton, Feb. 1975, 2 s., 3 d. *Education:* Certificate of Education, Saltley College, 1959; University of Essex, 1976–77. *Appointments:* Ed., Rivelin Press, 1974–84, Redbeck Press, 1984–. *Publications:* Peru: The New Poetry (trans.), 1970–76; Millstone Grit, 1972; At Night the Cats, by Antonio Cisneros (trans.), 1985; Nomads and Settlers, 1980; Wars of the Roses, 1984; Crossing the Rimac, 1995; Family Chronicle (poems), 1997; Path Through the Canefields (trans. of José Watanabe), 1997; Amulet Against the Evil Eye, 1998; Paradise of Exiles (fiction), 1999; A Mountain Crowned by a Cemetery, by Tulio Nora (trans.), 2001; Nordic Barbarians (fiction), 2002; Medal for Malaya (fiction), 2002. *Contributions to:* Various publications. *Address:* 24 Aireville Rd, Frizinghall, Bradford BD9 4HH, England.

TOBIAS-TURNER, Bessye; b. 10 Oct. 1917, Liberty, Mississippi, USA. Educator (retd); Poet; Lecturer. *Education:* AB, English, Rust College; MA, Literature, MA, Speech, Columbia University; PhD, Literature, World University, 1977. *Appointment:* Dir-Gen., Librae Foundation for the Arts and Culture, 1990–. *Publications:* La Librae: Anthology of Poetry for Living, 1968; Peace and Love, 1972; Laurel Leaves for Bess, 1977. *Contributions to:* Various anthologies, 1979–89. *Honours:* Many, including: Grand Prix Mediterranee, 1983, 1984; Grand Prix Etoiles d'Europa, 1986; Medals, United Poets Laureate International, 1986, 1987. *Memberships:* Acad. of American Poets, assoc.; International Society of Poets, distinguished and assoc. mem.; World Acad. of Arts and Poetry, board mem., 1981; World Congress of Poets. *Address:* 829 Wall St, McComb, MS 39648, USA.

TOBIN, Meryl Elaine, (Meryl Brown Tobin); b. 26 Aug. 1940, Melbourne, Vic., Australia. Writer; Poet. m. Hartley Tobin, 6 Jan. 1962, 2 s., 1 d. *Education:* BA, 1961, DipEd, 1962, University of Melbourne; Diploma of Arts (Professional Writing and Editing), Chisholm Institute of Technical and Further Education, Vic., 2002. *Publications:* Puzzles Galore, 1978; More Puzzles Galore!, 1980; Carloads of Fun, 1983; Exploring Outback Australia, 1988; Puzzleways: Grammar and Spelling, 1990; Animal Puzzle Parade, 1991; Puzzle Round Australia, 1992; Puzzling Cats, 1994; Pets to Puzzle, 1995; Puzzles Ahoy?, 1995; Play with Words, 1996; Lefty, 2000. Other: Many short stories and poems published. *Contributions to:* Numerous publications. *Honours:* 25 awards. *Memberships:* Australian Society of Authors Ltd; Fellowship of Australian Writers (Victoria) Inc.; Society of Women Writers of Victoria Inc; Victorian Writers Centre; Copyright Agency Ltd. *Address:* Ningan, Bass Highway, The Gurdies, Vic., 3984, Australia.

TOLMACHYOV, Vlad; b. 28 Jan. 1962, Leningrad, Russia. Poet; Computer Consultant. m. Jane Maiksaya, 16 July 1988. *Education:* BA, New York University, 1985. *Publications:* The Second Beginning, 1990; Poetry of Vlad Tolmachyov, 1991; Under the Dome of a Carrousel, 1992. *Contributions to:* Anthologies and magazines. *Honours:* First Prize, International Pushkin Society Poetry Competition, 1990; White Aster, Friends of the Globe Poetry, 1991. *Address:* 67 Oxford St, Glen Ridge, NJ 07028, USA.

TOMASEVIC, Bosko; b. 8 May 1947, Becej, Yugoslavia. Poet; Writer. m. (1) Rajka Gnjatic, 24 May 1975, divorced, 2 s., (2) Vera Kureluk, 12 March 1995. *Education:* BA, 1972, MA, 1976, PhD, 1982, University of Belgrade. *Appointment:* Visiting Prof. of Literary Theory, University of Nancy, 1990–92. *Publications:* Cartesian Passage, 1989; Watchman of the Times, 1990; Celan Studies, 1991; Repetition and Difference, 1992; Cool Memories, 1994; Live Coals, 1994; Landscape with Wittgenstein and Other Ruins, 1995; Open Space and Presence, 1995; Plan of the Return, 1996. *Contributions to:* Various publications. *Memberships:* Acad. of Science, New York; European Acad. of Sciences, Arts and Literature; International Comparative Literature Asscn; Martin Heidegger Asscn; PEN Club, France; Société des Gens des Lettres de France. *Address:* rue de St Lambert, Imb 4, Apt 422, 54000 Nancy, France.

TOMAZOS, Criton; b. 13 April 1940, Larnaca, Cyprus. Architect; Artist; Poet; Writer. *Education:* Diploma in Architecture, RIBA, Part II, The Polytechnic, Regent Street, School of Architecture, 1964; Scholarship in Advanced Theatre Design, 1977, and in Advanced Writing for Film and TV, 1982. *Appointments:* Various architectural positions; Founder-Dir, Theatre for Mankind Voluntary Organisation, 1985–; Ed., Journalist, Letters and Arts Page, Parikiaki, 1997–. *Publications:* Poetry: Lovepoem, 1965; Monologue of the Ancient Hero, 1970; Relationships, 1975; Poems of 1960–61, 1976; He Who Left His Fingerprints, 1979; Factory Backyard, 1980; Diaphanies (Transparencies), 1982; Letter to the Returning Astronaut, 1982; Synora Mnemes (Boundaries of Memory), 1987–88; The Visit, 1988; First Explorations, 1989; Tora (Now), 1994. Other: The Gospel of Contemporary Slavery (essay), 1977. *Contributions to:* Numerous anthologies, magazines and journals. *Honours:* Three Hon. Doctorates. *Memberships:* Writers' Guild; Poetry Society; Writers' Forum; Theatre for Mankind; Theatre Writers' Union, committee mem.; New Playwrights' Trust, management committee mem.; Asscn of Greek Scientists/Professional People. *Address:* c/o Environmental Forum, 12 A. Ennis Rd, Finsbury Park, London N4 3HD, England.

TOMLINSON, (Alfred) Charles; b. 8 Jan. 1927, Stoke-on-Trent, Staffordshire, England. Prof. of English Emeritus; Poet; Writer. m. 23 Oct. 1948, 2 d. *Education:* BA, Queens' College, Cambridge; MA, London. *Appointments:* Lecturer, 1956–68, Reader, 1968–82, Prof. of English, 1982–92, Prof. Emeritus, 1992–, Senior Research Fellow, 1996–, University of Bristol; Visiting Prof., University of New Mexico, 1962–63; O'Connor Prof., Colgate University, New York, 1967–68, 1989–90; Visiting Fellow of Humanities, Princeton University, 1981; Lamont Prof., Union College, New York, 1987. *Publications:* Poetry: Relations and Contraries, 1951; The Necklace, 1955; Seeing is Believing, 1958; A Peopled Landscape, 1963; American Scenes, 1966; The Poem as Initiation, 1968; The Way of a World, 1969; Renga, 1970; Written on Water, 1972; The Way In, 1974; The Shaft, 1978; Selected Poems, 1951–74, 1978; The Flood, 1981; Airborn: Hijos del aire, 1981; Notes from New York, 1984; Collected Poems, 1985; The Return, 1987; Annunciations, 1989; The Door in the Wall, 1992; Poemas, 1992; Gedichte, 1994; La insistencia de las cosas, 1994; In Italia, 1995; Jubilation, 1995;

Portuguese Pieces, 1996; The Fox Gallery, 1996; Parole e Acqua, 1997; Selected Poems 1955–97, 1997; The Vineyard Above the Sea, 1999; Luoghi Italiani, 2000. Other: In Black and White, 1976; The Oxford Book of Verse in English Translation (ed.), 1980; Some Americans: A Literary Memoir, 1981; Poetry and Metamorphosis, 1983; Eros Englished: Erotic Poems from the Greek and Latin (ed.), 1991; American Essays: Making it New, 2001. *Contributions to:* Books, professional journals and other publications. *Honours:* Bess Hokin Prize, 1968; Oscar Blumenthal Prize, 1960; Inez Boulton Prize, 1964; Frank O'Hara Prize, 1968; Cheltenham Poetry Prize, 1976; Cholmondeley Poetry Award, 1979; Wilbur Award for Poetic Achievement, 1982; Premio Europeo di Cittadella, Italy, 1991; Bennett Award for Poetry, 1992; Premio Intenazionale Flaiano, 2001; Hon. Fellow, Queens' College Cambridge, 1976–, Royal Holloway College, London, 1991; Hon. doctorates. *Memberships:* Academic and literary organizations. *Address:* Brook Cottage, Ozleworth Bottom, Wotton-under-Edge, Gloucestershire GL12 7QB, England.

TONG, Raymond; b. 20 Aug. 1922, Winchester, Hampshire, England. British Council Admin. (retd); Poet; Writer. m. Mariana Apergis, 16 Nov. 1946. *Education:* BSc, Honours, Economics, 1948, DipEd, 1949, University of London. *Appointments:* Education Officer, Senior Education Officer, Nigeria, 1949–58, Uganda, 1958–61; British Council Administrator, South America, India, Middle East, England, 1961–82. *Publications:* Today the Sun, 1947; Angry Decade, 1950; African Helicon (anthology), 1954; Fabled City, 1960; A Matter of History, 1976; Crossing the Border, 1978; Selected Poems, 1994; Returning Home, 1996. *Contributions to:* Many reviews, quarterlies, and journals in England and overseas. *Memberships:* Poetry Society, life mem.; West Country Writers Asscn. *Address:* 1 Beaufort Rd, Clifton, Bristol BS8 2JT, England.

TONOS. See: MEREDITH, Jennifer Margaret.

TOONA GOTTSCHALK, Elin-Kai; b. 12 July 1937, Tallinn, Estonia. Writer; Poet; Dramatist. m. Donald Frederick Gottschalk, 9 Oct. 1967, 1 s. *Publications:* Puuingel, 1965; Lotukata, 1968; Spielgas Sinise Kausi All, 1973; In Search of Coffee Mountains, 1977; Lady Cavaliers, 1977; Pictures, and DP Camp Child: Poetry in Visions, 1988; Kalevikula Viimne Tutar, 1988; Kolm Valget Tuvi, 1992; Rôomtzzb Tazua Taga Tuld, 2000. *Contributions to:* BBC; Reviews, quarterlies, journals, magazines and Radio Liberty. *Honours:* First Prize, Writer's Review, London, 1966; H Visnapuu Literary Award, World Asscn of Estonians, 1966; Ennu Literary Prize, USA, 1968; First Prize, National Examiner Contest, 1983; First Prize for Non-Fiction and Second Prize for Photo Journalism, National League of American Pen Women; Lauri Literary Prize, 1993. *Memberships:* International PEN, Estonian Branch; International Platform Asscn; National League of American Pen Women; Various Estonian literary asscns. *Address:* 27554 US 19 North, No. 37, Clearwater, FL 33761, USA.

TOPAL, Carine; b. 5 May 1949, New York, NY, USA. Poet. m. Victor Gorsky, 12 July 1987, 1 s. *Education:* BA, Sociology and Anthropology, C W Post College, 1971; MA, Special Education, New York University, 1974. *Publication:* Edging the Nile, 1989. *Contributions to:* Reviews, quarterlies and magazines. *Honours:* Double First Prize, Embers Poetry Contests, 1988; Finalist, Roberts Writing Award, 1990. *Membership:* Acad. of American Poets. *Address:* 25061 Via Bajo Cerro, Laguna Niguel, CA 92677, USA.

TOPP, Vincent; b. 3 Feb. 1973, Radcliffe, North Manchester, England. Poet. *Education:* Media and Video Production, Llandrillo College. *Publications:* Anthologies: Pathways, 1993; Feelings, 1993; Wales, 1995; Living in the 20th Century, 1995; Quiet Moments, 1996; Too Hot to Handle, 1998. *Honour:* Finalist, Poetry Guild National Poetry Contest, 1997. *Address:* 9 Woodland Park, Colwyn Bay LL29 7DS, Wales.

TORREGIAN, Sotère; b. 25 June 1941, USA. Poet; Scholar. Divorced, 2 d. *Education:* Philosophy, Rutgers University. *Appointments:* Instructor, Black American Literature, African Literature and Philosophy, Asst to the Dir, Afro-American Studies, 1969–73, Hon. Visiting Scholar, African and Third World Affairs, 1989–90, Stanford University; Visiting Lecturer, African and Third World Ideology, Art and Literature, University of Santa Clara, CA, 1970–72. *Publications:* Song for Woman, 1965; The Golden Palomino Bites the Clock, 1966; The Wounded Mattress, 1968; City of Light, 1971; The Age of Gold, Poems, 1968–70, 1976; The Young Englishwoman, 1989; AMTRAK-Trek, The Newark Cantos: Always for the First Time: Poems 1995–1998, 1999; The Expanded Age of Gold: Poems 1968–1998, 2002; 'I Must Go' (She Said) 'Because My Pizza's Cold': Selected Works, 1957–99, 2002; Théâtres: Poem-Plays, 1966–2002, 2002. *Contributions to:* Art and Literature, Isère, France; Paris Review; Il Tarocco, Italy; Rutgers Literary Review; Bay Review; Chelsea; Andy Warhol Monster Issue; Mike and Dales's Poetry Journal. *Honours:* Frank O'Hara Award, Modern American Poetry, 1968; Author of the Year, Gotham Book Mart, New York City, 1976. *Address:* c/o Mrs Tatyana Torregian, Porter Green, 999 Porter Ave, No. 28, Stockton, CA 95207-4278, USA.

TOTH, Eva; b. 30 Jan. 1939, Debrecen, Hungary. Writer; Poet. m. Gabor Ambrus, 1 s. *Education:* Hungarian and French Languages and Literatures, 1962, Spanish Language and Literature, 1968, Eötvös Lorand University,

Budapest. *Appointments:* Fellow, International Writing Program, IA, 1982; Ed.-in-Chief, Corvina Press, 1982; Columnist, léj Tükör cultural; Merrill Assoc., St Catherine's College, Oxford, 1989; Fulbright Visiting Prof., University of Georgia, Athens, 1992–93. *Publications:* Egyetlen Értelem, 1977; Hóhatár, 1982; Kámfor Benedek, 1986; Wanted, 1992; Límite de las nieves eternas, 1992; Emlékœos, 1999; Az eltaposotl pillanat, 2000. *Contributions to:* Various anthologies and other publications. *Honours:* Joint Second Prize, Salvatore Quasimodo International Poetry Contest, 1996; Arany Janos Award, Hungarian Writers' Asscn, 1997; Solonai Prize, 2001; József Attila Prize, 2002. *Memberships:* Hungarian PEN Club, vice-pres., 1994; Hungarian Writer's Asscn, foreign secretary, 1990. *Address:* Csalan u 45/B, Fszt 2, 1025 Budapest, Hungary.

TOUSTER-REED, Alison; b. 29 Jan. 1952, Nashville, Tennessee, USA. Teacher; Poet. 1 s., 1 d. *Education:* BA, 1976, MA, 1977, Student, PhD, Vanderbilt University. *Appointment:* Adjunct Prof., Tennessee State University, 1977–78, 1995–. *Publications:* The First Movement, 1976; Bid Me Welcome, 1978. *Contributions to:* Reviews and quarterlies. *Honours:* Acad. of American Poets Prize, 1971; Merrill Moore Award for Literary Promise, 1976; Indiana University Foundation Prize in Poetry, 1977. *Address:* 114 Vaughn Rd, Nashville, TN 37221, USA.

TOWNLEY, Roderick Carl; b. 7 June 1942, New Jersey, USA. Writer; Poet. m. Wyatt Townley, 15 Feb. 1986, 1 s., 1 d. *Education:* AB, Bard College; PhD, Rutgers University, 1972. *Appointments:* Prof. of English, Universidad de Concepcion, Chile, 1978–79; National Editorial Writer, TV Guide, 1980–89; Senior Ed., US magazine, 1989–90; Exec. Dir, The Writers Place, Kansas City, Missouri, 1995–96. *Publications:* The Early Poetry of William Carlos Williams, 1975; Minor Gods (novel), 1977; Three Musicians (poems), 1978; Final Approach (poems), 1986; Night Errands: How Poets Use Dreams, 1998; The Great Good Thing (novel), 2001; Into the Labyrinth (novel), 2002. *Contributions to:* Newspapers and journals. *Honours:* Co-Winner, 1969, First Prize, 1971, Acad. of American Poets; Finalist, Yale Series of Younger Poets, 1976; Fulbright Professorship, Chile, 1978–79; Peregrine Prize in Short Fiction, 1998; Kansas Arts Commission Individual Artist Grant, 2000. *Address:* PO Box 13302, Shawnee Mission, KS 66282, USA.

TOWNLEY, Wyatt; b. 20 Sept. 1954, Kansas City, Missouri, USA. Poet; Teacher. m. Roderick Carl Townley, 15 Feb. 1986, 1 d. *Education:* BFA, Dance, Purchase College, State University of New York, 1977; North Carolina School of the Arts. *Publications:* Perfectly Normal, 1990; The Breathing Field, 2002. *Contributions to:* Reviews and quarterlies. *Honours:* First Presidential Award for Outstanding Achievement, Purchase College, State University of New York, 1977; Finalist, Yale Series of Younger Poets, 1989; Hackney National Literary Award, 1998; Individual Artist Fellowship in Poetry, Kansas Arts Commission, 2002. *Memberships:* Acad. of American Poets; Society of Children's Book Writers and Illustrators; Poetry Society of America. *Address:* PO Box 13302, Shawnee Mission, KS 66282, USA.

TOWNSEND, Ann; b. 5 Dec. 1962, Pittsburgh, Pennsylvania, USA. Assoc. Prof.; Poet. m. David Baker, 19 July 1987, 1 d. *Education:* BA, Denison University, 1985; MA, English, 1987, PhD, English, 1991, Ohio State University. *Appointment:* Asst Prof., 1992–99, Assoc. Prof., 1999–, English, Denison University. *Publications:* Modern Love, 1995; Dimestore Erotics, 1998. *Contributions to:* The Nation; Kenyon Review; TriQuarterly; Southern Review; North American Review. *Honours:* Bread Loaf Scholarship for Poetry, 1991; Nation Prize for Poetry, 1994; Pushcart Prize for Poetry, 1995; Bread Loaf Fellowship in Poetry, 1998. *Memberships:* Associated Writing Programs; Poets and Writers; Acad. of American Poets; Poetry Society of America. *Address:* Dept of English, Denison University, Granville, OH 43023, USA.

TRACHTENBERG, Paul; b. 25 Oct. 1948, Los Angeles, CA, USA. Poet. *Education:* AA, Fullerton Junior College, 1966; California State Polytechnic University, Pomona, 1968. *Publications:* Short Changes for Loretta, 1982; Making Waves, 1986; Ben's Exit, 1993. *Address:* 9431 Krepp Dr., Huntington Beach, CA 92646, USA.

TRACY, James D.; b. 14 Feb. 1938, St Louis, MO, USA. Prof. of History; Writer; Ed. m. Nancy Ann McBride, 6 Sept. 1968, 2 s., 1 d. *Education:* BA, St Louis University, 1959; MA, Johns Hopkins University, 1960; MA, University of Notre Dame, 1961; PhD, Princeton University, 1967. *Appointments:* Instructor in History, University of Michigan, 1964–66; Assoc. Prof. of History, 1966–77, Prof. of History, 1977–, University of Minnesota; Man. Ed., Journal of Early Modern History, 1995–. *Publications:* Erasmus: The Growth of a Mind, 1972; Early Modern European History, 1500–1715 (ed.), 1976; The Politics of Erasmus: A Pacifist Intellectual and His Political Milieu, 1979; True Ocean Found: Paludanus's Letters on Dutch Voyages to the Kara Sea, 1595–1596, 1980; A Financial Revolution in the Habsburg Netherlands: Renten and Renteniers in the Country of Holland, 1515–1565, 1985; Holland Under Habsburg Rule, 1506–1566: The Formation of a Body Politic, 1990; The Rise of Merchant Empires: Long-Distance Trade in the Early Modern World, 1350–1750 (ed.), 1990; The Political Economy of Merchant Empires: State Power and World Trade, 1350–1750 (ed.), 1991; Handbook of European History, 1400–1600: Late Middle Ages, Renaissance, and Reformation (ed. with Thomas A. Brady and Heiko A. Oberman), 1996; Erasmus of the Low Countries, 1996; Europe's Reformations, 1450–1650, 1999; City Wall: The Urban Enceinte in Global Perspective (ed.), 2000. *Contributions to:* Scholarly books and learned journals. *Address:* c/o Dept of History, University of Minnesota, Minneapolis, MN 55455, USA. *E-mail:* tracy001@umn.edu.

TRAKAS, Deno; b. 23 April 1952, USA. Assoc. Prof.; Poet. m. Kathy Jackson, 10 Aug. 1974, 1 s., 1 d. *Education:* BA, 1974; MA, 1976; PhD, 1981. *Appointments:* Prof., Wofford College, 1980–; Instructor, Creative Writing, South California Governors School of the Arts, 1981–. *Publications:* The Shuffle of Wings, 1990; New Southern Harmonies, 1998; Human and Puny, 2001. *Contributions to:* Denver Quarterly; Kansas Quarterly; Louisville Review. *Honour:* Acad. of American Poets Prize. *Address:* Wofford College, 429 N Church St, Spartanburg, SC 29303, USA.

TRANSTRÖMER, Tomas (Gösta); b. 15 April 1931, Stockholm, Sweden. Poet; Psychologist. m. Monica Blach, 1958, 2 d. *Education:* Degree, University of Stockholm, 1956. *Publications:* In English: Twenty Poems, 1970; Night Vision, 1971; Windows and Stones: Selected Poems, 1972; Elegy: Some October Notes, 1973; Citoyens, 1974; Baltics, 1975; Truth Barriers: Poems by Tomas Tranströmer, 1980; How the Late Autumn Night Novel Begins, 1980; Tomas Tranströmer: Selected Poems, 1982; The Wild Marketplace, 1985; Selected Poems of Tomas Tranströmer, 1954–1986, 1987; Collected Poems, 1987; For the Living and the Dead, 1995; The Sorrow Gondola, 1996. *Contributions to:* Periodicals. *Honours:* Aftonbladets Literary Prize, 1958; Bellman Prize, 1966; Swedish Award, International Poetry Forum, 1971; Oevralids Prize, 1975; Boklotteriets Prize, 1981; Petrarca Prize, 1981; Nordic Council Literary Prize, 1990. *Membership:* Swedish Writers Union. *Address:* c/o Swedish Writers Union, Box 3157, Drottninggatan 88B, 103 63 Stockholm, Sweden.

TRANTER, John Ernest; b. 29 April 1943, Cooma, NSW, Australia. Poet. m. 1968, 1 s., 1 d. *Education:* BA, 1970. *Appointments:* Visiting Fellow, 1981, Writer-in-Residence, 1987, Australian National University, Canberra; Writer-in-Residence, New South Wales Institute of Technology, Sydney, 1983, Macquarie University, Sydney, 1985; Rollins College, Winter Park, FL, 1992; Poetry Ed., The Bulletin weekly, Sydney, 1990–93. *Publications:* Parallax, 1970; Dazed in the Ladies Lounge, 1970; Red Movie, 1972; The Blast Area, 1974; The Alphabet Murders, 1975; 100 Sonnets, 1977; The New Australian Poetry (ed.), 1979; Selected Poems, 1982; Gloria, 1986; Under Berlin: New Poems, 1988; The Tin Wash Dish (compiler), 1989; The Penguin Book of Modern Australian Poetry (ed. with Philip Mead), 1991. *Contributions to:* Anthologies, reviews and magazines. *Honours:* Australia Council Literature Board Senior Fellowships and Grants; Kenneth Slessor Prize for Poetry, 1989; Australian Artists Creative Fellowship, 1990. *Address:* PO Box 788, Strawberry Hills, NSW 2008, Australia.

TRAWICK, Leonard M(oses); b. 4 July 1933, Decatur, AL, USA. Prof. of English Emeritus; Poet; Writer; Ed. m. Kerstin Ekfelt, 16 July 1960, 1 s., 1 d. *Education:* BA, University of the South, Sewanee, Tennessee, 1955; MA in English, University of Chicago, 1956; PhD in English, Harvard University, 1961. *Appointments:* Instructor to Asst Prof. of English, Columbia University, 1961–69; Assoc. Prof., 1969–72, Prof. of English, 1972–98, Prof. Emeritus, 1998–, Principal Ed., 1971–98, and Dir, 1990–92, Poetry Center, Cleveland State University; Founding Ed., 1980, Co-Ed., 1983–92, The Gamut journal. *Publications:* Poetry: Beast Forms, 1971; Severed Parts, 1981; Beastmorfs, 1994. Opera Librettos: Spinoza, by Julius Drossin, 1982; The Enchanted Garden, by Klaus G Roy, 1983; Mary Stuart: A Queen Betrayed, by Bain Murray, 1991. Other: Backgrounds of Romanticism: English Philosophical Prose of the Eighteenth Century, 1967; World, Self, Poem (ed.), 1990; German Literature of the Romantic Era and the Age of Goethe (co-ed. and principal trans.), 1993. *Contributions to:* Scholarly books and journals, and to anthologies and magazines. *Honours:* Fulbright Scholarship, University of Dijon, 1956–57; Individual Artist Award, Ohio Arts Council, 1980; Award for Excellence in the Media, Northern Ohio Live, 1990; Co-Recipient, James P Barry Ohioana Award for Editorial Excellence, 1991; Ohioana Poetry Award for Lifetime Achievement in Poetry, 1994. *Address:* c/o Dept of English, Cleveland State University, Rhodes Tower, Room 1815, Cleveland, OH 44115, USA.

TRAYNOR, Shaun; b. 19 July 1941, Northern Ireland. Teacher; Poet; Novelist. 2 d. *Appointment:* Southern Arts Writer-in-Residence, Wiltshire Libraries and Museum Service, 1979–81. *Publications:* The Hardening Ground, 1975; Images in Winter, 1979. Children's Fiction: Hugo O Hugo The Children's Giant; The Giants' Olympics; A Little Man in England; The Lost City of Belfast; The Poolbeg Book of Irish Poetry for Children (ed.), 1997, 1998, 2000. *Contributions to:* TLS; Times Educational Supplement; Independent on Sunday; London Irish Writer; Fortnight; Irish Aquarius Magazine; ILEA News. *Memberships:* Society of Authors; United Arts Club, Dublin. *Address:* 50 Birchwood Rd, London SW17 9BH, England.

TREBORLANG, Robert; b. 19 Dec. 1943, Jerusalem, Palestine. Writer; Poet. m. Moi Moi Cumines, 6 May 1971. *Education:* BA, Language, University of Sydney, 1968. *Publications:* How to Survive in Australia, 1985; How to be Normal in Australia, 1987; Sydney: Discover the City, 1988; How to Make it Big in Australia, 1989; She Vomits Like a Lady, 1991; Staying Sane in Australia, 1991; Men, Women and Other Necessities, 1992; A Hop Through Australia's History, 1993; How to Mate in Australia, 1993; The Little Book of Aussie Wisdom, 1994; The Little Book of Aussie Insults, 1994; The Little Book of Aussie Manners, 1995; It's Not the Pale Moon, 1999; Dancing With Mother, 1999. *Contributions to:* 24 Hours; Australian; Australian Jewish Times. *Honour:* Literature Grant, Australia, 1976. *Memberships:* Australian Journalists Asscn; Entertainment and Arts Alliance. *Address:* PO Box 997, Potts Point, NSW 2011, Australia.

TREHEARNE, Elizabeth. See: MAXWELL, Patricia Anne.

TREMBLAY, Gail Elizabeth; b. 15 Dec. 1945, Buffalo, New York, USA. Poet; Artist; College Teacher. *Education:* BA, Drama, University of New Hampshire, 1967; MFA, Creative Writing, University of Oregon, 1969. *Appointments:* Lecturer, Keene State College, New Hampshire; Asst Prof., University of Nebraska; Faculty, Evergreen State College, Olympia, Washington. *Publications:* Night Gives Woman the Word, 1979; Talking to the Grandfathers, 1980; Indian Singing in 20th Century America, 1990. *Contributions to:* Reviews, quarterlies, and journals. *Honour:* Alfred E Richards Poetry Prize, 1967. *Memberships:* Indian Youth of America, pres.; International Asscn of Art, UNESCO, US National Committee board mem.; Native American Writers Circle of the Americas; Woman's Caucus for Art, board mem., pres. *Address:* c/o Evergreen State College, Olympia, WA 98505, USA.

TREMBLAY, William (Andrew), (Bill Tremblay); b. 9 June 1940, Massachusetts, USA. Prof.; Poet; Writer; Critic. m. Cynthia Ann Crooks, 28 Sept. 1962, 3 s. *Education:* AB, 1962, MA, 1969, Clark University; MFA, University of Massachusetts, 1972. *Appointments:* Asst Prof., Leicester Junior College, 1967–70; Teaching Asst, University of Massachusetts, 1970–72; Instructor, Springfield College, 1972; Prof., Colorado State University, 1973–; Various poetry readings. *Publications:* Poetry: Crying in the Cheap Seats, 1971; The Anarchist Heart, 1977; Home Front, 1978; Second Sun: New and Selected Poems, 1985; Duhamel: Ideas of Order in Little Canada, 1986. Fiction: The June Rise: The Apocryphal Letters of Joseph Antoine Janis, 1994. *Contributions to:* Numerous anthologies, reviews, journals and periodicals. *Honours:* Fulbright-Hays Lecturer, Universidade Nova, Lisbon; National Endowment for the Humanities Grant; National Endowment for the Arts Fellowship, 1985; Pushcart Prize, 1986. *Memberships:* Associated Writing Programs; High Plains Arts Centre. *Address:* 3412 Lancaster Dr., Fort Collins, CO 80523, USA.

TRIBE, David Harold; b. 17 Dec. 1931, Sydney, NSW, Australia. Poet; Writer; Performer. *Education:* Open Scholarship, Fellowship, Medicine, University of Queensland, 1949–54. *Publication:* Why Are We Here?, 1965. *Contributions to:* Numerous anthologies, reviews, magazines, newspapers and radio. *Memberships:* Australian Society of Authors; Poets Union; Poetry Australia Foundation. *Address:* 12/2B Wallaringa Ave, Neutral Bay, NSW 2089, Australia.

TRIPATHY, Sailendra Narayan; b. 22 July 1957, Kendrapara, Orissa, India. College Lecturer; Ed.; Poet. m. Ashoka Tripathy, 11 May 1981, 1 s., 1 d. *Education:* BA, English; MA, English, Ravenshaw College, Cuttange, 1979; PhD Studies. *Publications:* I am Phallic God and Other Poems, 1989; The Trapped Word (ed.), 1989; Love Apples, 1992. *Contributions to:* Anthologies and periodicals. *Memberships:* Asscn of Little Presses, London; Commonwealth Society, life mem. *Address:* c/o Poesie Publications, Shastrinagar, Berhampur 760001, Orissa, India.

TRIPATHY, Upendra; b. 5 Oct. 1956, Kahakapur, India. Public Servant; Poet. m. 2 July 1982, 1 s., 1 d. *Education:* BSc, 1974, BA, Political Science, 1976, Ravanshaw College; MA, Political Science, Jawaharlal Nehru University, New Delhi, 1979. *Publication:* Caged, 1990. *Contributions to:* Anthologies and periodicals. *Address:* c/o Indian Administrative Service, Hassan, Karnataka, India.

TROUPE, Quincy (Thomas Jr); b. 23 July 1943, New York, NY, USA. Poet; Writer; University Instructor. m. Margaret Porter, 4 c. *Education:* BA, Gambling College, 1963; AA, Los Angeles City College, 1967. *Appointments:* Instructor, various colleges and universities; Instructor in Creative Writing and American, African-American and Caribbean Literature, University of California at San Diego; Many poetry readings. *Publications:* Watts Poets: A Book of New Poetry and Essays (ed.), 1968; Embryo Poems, 1967–1971, 1972; Giant Talk: An Anthology of Third World Writings (ed. with Rainer Schulte), 1975; The Inside Story of TV's 'Roots' (ed. with David L. Wolper), 1978; Snakeback Solos: Selected Poems, 1969–1977, 1978; Skulls Along the River (poems), 1984; Soundings, 1988; James Baldwin: The Legacy (ed.), 1989; Miles: The Autobiography (with Miles Davis), 1989; Weather Reports: New and Selected Poems, 1991; Avalanche: Poems, 1996; Choruses: Poems, 1999; Miles and Me, 2000. *Contributions to:* Periodicals. *Honours:* National Endowment for the Arts Award in Poetry, 1978; American Book Awards, 1980, 1990; New York Foundation for the Arts Fellowship in Poetry, 1987. *Membership:* Poetry Society of America. *Address:* c/o University of California at San Diego, Mail Code 0410, 9500 Gilman Dr., La Jolla, CA 92093, USA.

TROWBRIDGE, William; b. 9 May 1941, Chicago, IL, USA. Poet; Ed. m. Waneta Sue Downing, 6 July 1963, 2 s., 1 d. *Education:* BA, 1963, MA, 1965, University of Missouri at Columbia; PhD, Vanderbilt University, 1975. *Appointments:* Instructor, University of Missouri at Columbia, 1966; Vanderbilt University, 1970; Asst Prof. to Distinguished University Prof. Northwest Missouri State University, 1971–98; Co-Ed., The Laurel Review, 1986–99; Asst Ed., The Georgia Review, 2000; Assoc. Ed., The Laurel Review, 2001. *Publications:* The Book of Kong, 1986; Enter Dark Stranger, 1989; O Paradise, 1995; Flickers, 2000; The Four Seasons, 2002. *Contributions to:* Poetry; Georgia Review; Kenyon Review; Southern Review; Gettysburg Review, and many others. *Honours:* Acad. of American Poets Prize, 1970; Bread Loaf Writers Conference Scholarship, 1981; Yaddo Fellowship, 1992. *Address:* 907 S Dunn St, Maryville, MO 64468, USA.

TRUCK, Robert-Paul (Count); b. 3 May 1917, Calais, France. Poet; Critic; Historian. m. Jeanne Brogniart, 24 July 1942, 1 d. *Education:* Baccalaureat, 1935; French Naval School, 1938. *Publications:* Poetry: Heures folles, 1938; Au bord de la Nuit, 1948; Intersignes, 1953; Vertiges, 1989; Bois des Iles, 1992; Marche des Rois, 1993; Cicatrices, 1995. Non-Fiction: Médecins de la Honte (with Betty Truck), 1975; Mengele, l'ange de la mort (with Betty Truck), 1976. *Contributions to:* Anthologies and other publications. *Honours:* Various medals, diplomas, certificates, etc. *Memberships:* Accademia Leonardo da Vinci; Institut Académique de Paris; International Acad. of Poets; Société des Poètes Français; World Literary Acad. *Address:* Varouna, 49 Rue de Lhomel, 62600 Berck-Plage, France.

TRUE, Michael; b. 8 Nov. 1933, Oklahoma City, Oklahoma, USA. Prof. of English; Writer; Poet. m. Mary Patricia Delaney, 12 April 1958, 3 s., 3 d. *Education:* BA, University of Oklahoma, 1955; MA, University of Minnesota, 1957; PhD, Duke University, 1964; Postdoctoral Study, Harvard Divinity School, 1968; Columbia University, 1976–77. *Appointments:* Founding Ed., Worcester Review, 1973; Prof. of English, Assumption College, 1974–97; Poetry Ed., English Journal, 1976; Visiting Prof. of American Literature, Nanjing University, China, 1984–85, 1989; Sheffer Visiting Prof. of Religion, Colorado College, 1988, 1990, 1993; Contributing Ed., Spectrum, 1988–98; Fulbright Lecturer, American Literature, India, 1997–98. *Publications:* Homemade Social Justice, 1982; Justice-Seekers, Peacemakers: 32 Portraits in Courage, 1985; Ordinary People: Teaching Values in the Family, 1991; Worcester Area Writers, 1680–1980, 1987; To Construct Peace: 30 More Justice-Seekers, Peacemakers, 1992; Daniel Berrigan: Poetry, Drama, Prose (ed.), 1988; An Energy Field More Intense Than War: The Nonviolent Tradition and American Literature, 1995; Frontiers of Nonviolence (ed. with Chaiwat Satha-Anand), 1998. *Contributions to:* Worcester Review; Peacework; College Composition and Communication; Poetry International (China); Worcester Magazine; Contemporary Poets; Friends Journal. *Honour:* Teacher of the Year, Massachusetts Council of Teachers of English, 1976; Peace Teacher of the Year, Consortium on Peace Research, Education and Development, 1996; Lifetime Achievement Award, Peace Studies Asscn, 1998; Gandhi Award, 2002. *Memberships:* Worcester Poetry Asscn Inc, co-founder; International Peace Research Asscn. *Address:* 4 Westland St, Worcester, MA 01602, USA.

TSALOUMAS, Dimitris; b. 13 Oct. 1921, Leros, Greece. Poet; Ed.; Trans. 2 s., 2 d. *Appointments:* Teacher, Victorian schools, 1958–82; Writer-in-Residence, University of Oxford, University of Melbourne, Queensland University, La Trobe University. *Publications:* Resurrection, 1967; Triptych for a Second Coming, 1974; Observations for a Hypochondriac, 1974; The House with the Eucalyptus, 1975; The Sick Barber and Other Characters, 1979; The Book of Epigrams, 1981; The Observatory: Selected Poems, 1983; Falcon Drinking: The English Poems, 1988; Portrait of a Dog, 1991; The Barge, 1993; Six Improvisations On the River, 1995; The Harbour, 1998; Stoneland Harvest, 1999; New and Selected Poems, 2000. *Honours:* Australia Council Grant and Fellowship; National Book Council Award, 1983; Wesley M. Wright Prize for Poetry, 1994; Patrick White Award, 1994; John Bray Poetry Award, Adelaide Festival, 2000; Australia Council Emeritus Award, 2002. *Address:* 72 Glenhuntly Rd, Elwood, Vic. 3184, Australia.

TSCHABOLD, Matthias; b. 16 April 1956, Lausanne, Switzerland. Poet. m. Anne-Marie Haddad, 8 May 1986. *Education:* Licence en Théologie, University of Lausanne, 1980; Licence és Lettres, 1993, Pedagogical Diploma, 1997, University of Zürich. *Publications:* La Depossession, 1981; Le Transfuge, 1992; L'Heure du Tigre, 1999. *Contributions to:* Journals. *Membership:* Société Suisse des écrivains. *Address:* Zweiackerstrasse 41, 8053 Zürich, Switzerland.

TSCHUMI, Jean-Raymond; b. 21 Oct. 1953, Switzerland. Poet; Teacher. m. Hélène Veyre, 19 May 1994, 3 d. *Education:* Licence ès Lettres, University of Lausanne, 1979. *Publications:* Résurgences, 1990; L'Été Disloqué, 1994; Un an a Vif, 1996. *Contributions to:* Anthologies and periodicals. *Honour:* Prix Claude Sernet, France, 1991. *Memberships:* Asscn Vaudoise des Écrivains; Swiss Writers' Asscn. *Address:* Chemin du Village 1, 1012 Lausanne, Switzerland.

TUCKER, Judith Irene. See: PHILLIPS, Judith Irene.

TUCKER, Martin; b. 8 Feb. 1928, Philadelphia, Pennsylvania, USA. Prof. of English; Writer; Poet. *Education:* BA, 1949, PhD, 1963, New York University; MA, University of Arizona, 1954. *Appointments:* Faculty, Long Island University, 1956–; Ed., Confrontation magazine, 1970–. *Publications:* Modern British Literature (ed.), Vols I–IV, 1967–76; Africa in Modern Literature, 1967; The Critical Temper (ed.), Vols I–V, 1970–89; Joseph Conrad, 1976; Homes of Locks and Mysteries (poems), 1982; Literary Exile in the United States, 1991; Sam Shepard, 1992; Attention Spans (poems), 1997; Modern American Literature (ed.), 1997. *Contributions to:* Professional journals and general periodicals. *Honours:* National Endowment for the Arts/Co-ordinating Council and Literary Magazine Awards for Editorial Distinction, 1976, 1984; English-Speaking Union Award, 1982. *Memberships:* African Literature Asscn; African Studies Asscn; Authors Guild; MLA; National Book Critics Circle; PEN, exec. board, 1973–96; Poetry Society of America. *Address:* 4540 Gulf of Mexico Dr., Longboat Key, FL 34228, USA.

TULLOS, Frances Sue; b. 15 Dec. 1945, Orange, Texas, USA. Poet. *Education:* BA, English and Sociology, 1969, MA, English and History, 1970, University of Texas at Austin; PhD, Contemporary American Literature, Texas Tech University, 1977. *Publication:* A Pink Disregard for Decorum, 1989. *Contributions to:* Reivews, journals and magazines. *Honours:* Best Poetry Award, Dialogue Magazine, 1976; Jean Kennedy Shriver Award, Excellence in Performing Arts, 1979; First Places, 1980, 1981, Second Place, 1982, South Plains Writers Asscn Poetry Contest. *Membership:* National Federation of State Poetry Societies. *Address:* 506 W Healey, Apt 4, Champaign, IL 61820, USA.

TUNNICLIFFE, Stephen; b. 22 May 1925, Wakefield, Yorkshire, England. Poet; Writer. m. Hilary Katharine Routh, 5 Aug. 1949, 3 s. *Education:* BA, Honours, English, 1951, MA, Distinction, English, 1965, University of London; Certificate of Education, Institute of Education, 1952. *Publications:* English in Practice (with Geoffrey Summerfield), 1971; Reading and Discrimination (with Denys Thompson), 1979; Poetry Experience: Teaching and Writing Poetry in Secondary Schools, 1984; Building and Other Poems, 1993. Other: Libretti for John Joubert: The Martyrdom of St Alban; The Raising of Lazarus; The Magus; The Prisoner; The Wayfarers; Wings of Faith; For Francis Routh: Circles. *Contributions to:* Reviews and journals. *Membership:* Society of Authors. *Address:* Clairmont, The Square, Clun, Shropshire SY7 8JA, England.

TURCO, Lewis Putnam, (Wesli Court); b. 2 May 1934, Buffalo, New York, USA. Writer; Poet. m. Jean Cate Houdlette, 16 June 1956, 1 s., 1 d. *Education:* BA, English, University of Connecticut, 1959; MA, English, University of Iowa, 1962. *Appointments:* Instructor, Fenn College, 1960–64; Founding Dir, Poetry Center, 1961–64, Cleveland State University; Asst Prof., Hillsdale College, Michigan, 1964–65; Asst Prof., 1965–68, Assoc. Prof., 1968–71, Dir, Writing Arts, 1969–95, Prof., 1971–96, State University of New York College at Oswego; Visiting Prof., State University of New York College at Potsdam, 1968–69; Bingham Poet-in-Residence, University of Louisville, 1982; Writer-in-Residence, Ashland University, Ohio, 1991. *Publications:* First Poems, 1960; The Book of Forms: A Handbook of Poetics, 1968; Awaken, Bells Falling: Poems 1959–67, 1968; The Inhabitant, 1970; Pocoangelini: A Fantography and Other Poems, 1971; Poetry: An Introduction, 1973; Seasons of the Blood, 1980; The Airs of Wales, 1981; American Still Lifes, 1981; The Compleat Melancholick, 1985; The New Book of Forms, 1986; Visions and Revisions of American Poetry, 1986; A Maze of Monsters, 1986; The Shifting Web: New and Selected Poems, 1989; Dialogue, 1989; The Public Poet, 1991; Emily Dickinson, Woman of Letters, 1993; Bordello, 1996; A Book of Fears, 1998; Shaking the Family Tree (memoirs), 1998; The Book of Literary Terms, 1999; The Green Maces of Autumn, 2002. *Contributions to:* New Yorker; Nation; Poetry; Orbis; Carleton Miscellany; Sewanee Review; Tri-Quarterly; Ploughshares; Formalist; Atlantic; Hudson Review; New Republic; Saturday Review; Ontario Review; Kenyon Review; Southern Review; Massachusetts Review. *Honours:* Resident Fellowships, Yaddo, 1959, 1977; Acad. of American Poets Prize, University of Iowa, 1960; Bread Loaf Poetry Fellow, 1961; Chapbook Award, American Weave Press, 1962; Helen Bullis Prize, Poetry Northwest, 1972; First Poetry Award, Kansas Quarterly, Kansas Arts Commission, 1984–85; Pres.'s Award, State University of New York College, Oswego, 1985; Winner, Chapbook Competition, Silverfish Review, 1989; First Place, Chapbook Competition, Cooper House, 1990; Bordighera Bilingual Poetry Bookshop Prize, 1997; Hon. LHD, Ashland University, 2000. *Address:* c/o Mathom, PO Box 161, Dresden, ME 04342, USA.

TURK, Eugene M. See: YICTOVE.

TURNBULL, Gael Lundin; b. 7 April 1928, Edinburgh, Scotland. Poet; Former Medical Practitioner. m. (1) Jonnie May Draper, 1952, 3 d., (2) Pamela Jill Iles, 1983. *Education:* BA, University of Cambridge, 1948; MD, University of Pennsylvania, 1951. *Publications:* A Trampoline, 1968; Scantlings, 1970; A Gathering of Poems, 1950–80, 1983; A Year and a Day, 1985; A Winter Journey, 1987; While Breath Persist, 1992; For Whose Delight, 1995; A Rattle of Scree, 1997; Transmutations, 1997; Might a Shape of Words, 2000. *Contributions to:* Numerous journals and magazines. *Honour:* Alice Hunt Bartlett Award, 1969. *Address:* 12 Strathearn Pl., Edinburgh EH9 2AL, Scotland.

TURNER, Alberta Tucker; b. 22 Oct. 1919, New York, NY, USA. Prof. Emerita; Poet; Writer. m. William Arthur Turner, 9 April 1943, 1 s., 1 d. *Education:* BA, Hunter College, New York City, 1940; MA, Wellesley College, Massachusetts, 1941; PhD, Ohio State University, 1946. *Appointments:* Lecturer to Prof., 1964–90, Dir, Poetry Center, 1964–90, Prof. Emerita, 1990–, Cleveland State University; Assoc. Ed., Field, Contemporary Poetry and Poetics, 1970–. *Publications:* Poetry: Need, 1971; Learning to Count, 1974; Lid and Spoon, 1977; A Belfry of Knees, 1983; Beginning with And: New and Selected Poems, 1994. Other: 50 Contemporary Poets: The Creative Process (ed.), 1977; Poets Teaching (ed.), 1981; To Make a Poem, 1982; 45 Contemporary Poems: The Creative Process (ed.), 1985; Responses to Poetry, 1990; Tomorrow is a Tight Fist, 2001. *Contributions to:* Journals and magazines. *Honours:* MacDowell Colony Fellowship, 1985; Cleveland Arts Prize, 1985; Ohio Poetry Award, 1986; Ohio Governor's Award for Arts in Education, 1988. *Memberships:* Milton Society of America; PEN American Center. *Address:* 482 Caskey Ct, Oberlin, OH 44074, USA.

TURNER, Brian (Lindsay); b. 4 March 1944, Dunedin, New Zealand. Poet; Writer. 1 s. *Appointments:* Managing Ed., John McIndoe Ltd, Dunedin, 1975–83, 1985–86; Writer-in-Residence, University of Canterbury, 1997. *Publications:* Poetry: Ladders of Rain, 1978; Ancestors, 1981; Listening to the River, 1983; Bones, 1985; All That Blue Be, 1989; Beyond, 1992; Timeless Land, 1995; Taking Off, 2001. Other: Images of Coastal Otago, 1982; New Zealand High Country: Four Seasons, 1983; Opening Up (with Glenn Turner), 1987; The Last River's Song, 1989; The Guide to Trout Fishing in Otago, 1994; Lifting the Covers (with Glenn Turner), 1998; On the Loose (with Josh Kronfeld), 1999; New Zealand Photographers (with Scott Freeman), 2000; Meads (with Colin Meads), 2002; Somebodies and Nobodies, 2002. *Honours:* Commonwealth Poetry Prize, 1978; Robert Burns Fellowship, 1984; John Crowe Reid Memorial Prize, 1985; New Zealand Book Award for Poetry, 1993; Scholarship in Letters, 1994. *Address:* Main Rd, Oturehua, Central Otago, New Zealand.

TURNER, Frederick; b. 19 Nov. 1943, East Haddon, Northamptonshire, England. Prof. of Arts and Humanities; Writer; Poet. m. Mei Lin Chang, 25 June 1966, 2 s. *Education:* BA, 1965, MA, 1967, BLitt, 1967, English Language and Literature, University of Oxford. *Appointments:* Asst Prof. of English, University of California, Santa Barbara, 1967–72; Assoc. Prof. of English, Kenyon College, 1972–85; Ed., Kenyon Review, 1978–83; Visiting Prof. of English, University of Exeter, 1984–85; Founders Prof. of Arts and Humanities, University of Texas at Dallas, Richardson, 1985–. *Publications:* Shakespeare and the Nature of Time, 1971; Between Two Lives, 1972; The Return, 1979; The New World, 1985; The Garden, 1985; Natural Classicism, 1986; Genesis: An Epic Poem, 1988; Rebirth of Value, 1991; Tempest, Flute and Oz, 1991; April Wind, 1991; Beauty, 1991; Foamy Sky: The Major Poems of Miklos Radnoti (trans. with Zsuzanna Ozsváth), 1992; The Culture of Hope, 1995; The Ballad of the Good Cowboy, 1997; Hadean Eclogues, 1999; Shakespeare's Twenty-First Century Economics: The Morality of Love and Money, 1999; The Iron-Blue Vault: Selected Poems of Attila József (trans. with Zsuzsanna Ozsváth), 1999. *Contributions to:* Journals and periodicals. *Honours:* Ohioana Prize for Editorial Excellence, 1980; Djerassi Foundation Grant and Residency, 1981; Levinson Poetry Prize, 1983; Missouri Review Essay Prize, 1986; PEN Golden Pen Award, 1992; Milan Fust Prize, 1996. *Membership:* PEN. *Address:* 2668 Aster Dr., Richardson, TX 75082, USA.

TURNER, Martin Vernon Lawrence; b. 9 Feb. 1948, London, England. Educational Psychologist; Poet. m. Farah, 9 Aug. 1981, 2 d. *Education:* BA, University of Exeter, 1975; PGCE, St Lukes College, Exeter, 1976; MSc, University of Strathclyde, 1978; MA, University of Kent, 1988. *Appointment:* Educational Psychologist, Motherwell, Lanarkshire, 1978–79; Newham, 1979–84; Senior Educational Psychologist, Croydon, 1984–91; Head of Psychology, Dyslexia Institute, Staines, 1991–. *Publication:* Trespass. *Contributions to:* Ashes; Litmus; Poetry Durham; Wasafiri; Other Poetry; Poetry Book Society Anthology; Sepia; Poetry World; Comparative Criticism. *Honour:* Kent Literature Festival National Poetry Competition. *Membership:* Poetry Society. *Address:* 120 Gravel Hill, Croydon CR0 5BF, England.

TURNER, Stella, (Harriet Hill, Mary Muir); b. 6 Feb. 1918, Melbourne, Vic., Australia. Cellist and Teacher (retd); Poet. m. Stanley John Turner, 2 s., 1 deceased. *Education:* Matriculation, 1936. *Appointments:* Various poetry readings. *Publications:* Books From the Dandenongs, 1984; Season of Gold, 1986; Dance Suite, 1988; The Seasons, 1989; Sounds and Music (music book for children), 1989; Lost Valley, 1993; 25 Wild Flowers of the Dandenongs, 1996; Fuchsias at Six, 1998. *Contributions to:* Various publications. *Honours:* Several commendations; Charles Meeking Prize for Women Poets, 1983; Co-Winner, Henry Lawson Award, 1985; Australia Day Medallion, 1991. *Membership:* Society of Women Writers of Australia. *Address:* Terrigal, 24 Church St, Emerald, Vic. 3782, Australia.

TUROW, David; b. 3 April 1963, Kiev, Ukraine. Poet. *Education:* BA, New York University; Graduate Certificate in Communications, Pace University. *Publication:* The Awakening. *Contributions to:* Anthologies and periodicals. *Honours:* Several Golden Poet Awards, National Society of Poetry; Knight, 1994, Order of Pegasus, 1995, Consul General, Olympoetry.

TURPIN, Janet. See: CRAIG, Timothy.

TUSIANI, Joseph; b. 14 Jan. 1924, Foggia, Italy (Naturalized US citizen, 1956). Prof. (retd); Writer; Poet. *Education:* Dottore in Lettere, summa cum laude, University of Naples, 1947. *Appointments:* Chair., Italian Dept, College of Mount St Vincent, 1948–71; Lecturer in Italian, Hunter College, New York City, 1950–62; Visiting Assoc. Prof., New York University, 1956–64, City University of New York, 1971–83; NDEA Visiting Prof. of Italian, Connecticut State College, 1962; Prof., Herbert H Lehman College, New York City, 1971–83. *Publications:* Dante in Licenza, 1952; Two Critical Essays on Emily Dickinson, 1952; Melos Cordis (poems in Latin), 1955; Odi Sacre: Poems, 1958; The Complete Poems of Michelangelo, 1960; Lust and Liberty: The Poems of Machiavelli, 1963; Tasso's Jerusalem Delivered (verse trans.), 1970; Italian Poets of the Renaissance, 1971; The Age of Dante, 1973; Tasso's Creation of the World, 1982; Rosa Rosarum (poems in Latin), 1984; In Exilio Rerum (poems in Latin), 1985; La Parola Difficile, 3 vols, 1988, 1991, 1992; Carmina Latina, 1994; Leopardi's Canti (trans.), 1994; Le Poesie Inglesi di G A Borgese, 1995; Pulci's Morgante (verse trans.), 1998; Dante's Lyric Poems, 1998; Radicitus (poems in Latin), 2000; Ethnicity, 2000; Two Languages, Two Lands (proceedings of an international convention on his work), 2000. *Contributions to:* Books and journals. *Honours:* Greenwood Prize for Poetry, 1956; Cavaliere ufficiale, Italy, 1973; Leone di San Marco Award, 1982; Joseph Tusiani Scholarship Fund founded in his honour, Lehman College, 1983; Congressional Medal of Merit, 1984; Progresso Medal of Liberty, 1986; Outstanding Teacher Award, American Asscn of Teachers of Italian, 1987; Renoir Literary Award, 1988; Festschrift published in his honour, 1995; Enrico Fermi Award, 1995; National Endowment for the Humanities Fellowship, 1998; Fiorello La Guardia Award, 1998; Governor's Award for Excellence, 2000; Premio Puglia, 2000. *Memberships:* Catholic Poetry Society of America; Poetry Society of America. *Address:* 308 E 72nd St, New York, NY 10021, USA.

TUWHARE, Hone; b. 21 Oct. 1922, Kaikohe, New Zealand. Poet. *Education:* Seddon Memorial and Otahuhu Technical Colleges, Auckland, 1939–41. *Publications:* No Ordinary Sun, 1964; Come Rain Hail, 1970; Sapwood and Milk, 1972; Something Nothing, 1973; Making a Fist of it, 1978; Selected Poems, 1980; Year of the Dog, 1982; Mihi: Collected Poems, 1987; Deep River Talk, 1994. *Honour:* New Zealand Award for Achievement, 1965. *Address:* c/o John McIndoe Ltd, 51 Crawford St, PO Box 694, Dunedin, New Zealand.

TWICHELL, Chase; b. 20 Aug. 1950, New Haven, CT, USA. Poet; Writer; Teacher; Publisher. m. Russell Banks, 25 Aug. 1989. *Education:* BA, Trinity College, 1973; MFA, University of Iowa, 1976. *Appointments:* Ed., Pennyroyal Press, 1976–85; Assoc. Prof., University of Alabama, 1985–88; Lecturer, Princeton University, 1990–2000; Assoc. Faculty, Goddard College, 1996–98, Warren Wilson College, 1999–; Ed., Ausable Press, 1999–. *Publications:* Northern Spy, 1981; The Odds, 1986; Perdido, 1991; The Practice of Poetry (co-ed.), 1992; The Ghost of Eden, 1995; The Snow Watcher, 1998. *Contributions to:* Antaeus; Field; Georgia Review; Nation; New England Review; New Yorker; Ohio Review; Ontario Review; Paris Review; Ploughshares; Poetry Review; Southern Review; Yale Review. *Honours:* National Endowment for the Arts Fellowships, 1987, 1993; Guggenheim Fellowship, 1990; Artists Foundation Fellowship, Boston, 1990; New Jersey State Council on the Arts Fellowship, 1990; American Acad. of Arts and Letters Award, 1994; Alice Fay Di Castagnola Award, Poetry Society of America, 1997. *Address:* c/o Ellen Levine Literary Agency, 15 East St, Suite 1801, New York, NY 10010, USA.

TYRRELL, Richard; b. 19 June 1959, Dublin, Ireland. Arts Man.; Poet. *Education:* BSc, 1981; MA, 1989. *Appointments:* Festival Dir, Worldlinks Readers and Writers Festival, 1988–89; Asst Dir, QMW Launch, 1989–92; Business Development Man., Brunel University, 1992–. *Publication:* Happy Hour Conversation, 1991. *Contributions to:* Irish Press; New Statesman; Poetry Reviewer; London Magazine; Ambit; Outposts; Other Poetry; Independent; Guardian; TLS. *Memberships:* Society of Authors; Poetry Society, chair., 1993–94. *Address:* 23 Earlsmead Rd, London NW10 5QD, England.

U

UHRMAN, Esther; b. 7 July 1921, New London, CT, USA. Social Worker (retd); Artist; Poet; Writer; Dramatist. *Education:* BA, Traphagen School of Fashion, New York City, 1955; AA, Technical College, 1974; MA, Cornell University, 1976; PhD, Danzig University, 1977. *Publications:* From Canarsie to Masada (novel), 1978; 2057 (radio play), 1984; Mitras the Second (novel), 1988; Various poems. *Contributions to:* Anthologies and magazines. *Honours:* Third Place, Podiker Essay Award, 1968; Golden Windmill Radio Drama Contest Award, 1971; Diploma di Benemerenza Allavivlta, 1972; Diplome d'Honneur des Beaux Arts, IAG Cultural Exchange Between Nations, 1976; Diploma di Benemerenza Acad. Leonardo da Vinci for Poetry, 1980; Finalist, Dentsu Award, Tokyo, 1985. *Memberships:* International Acad. of Poets, founding fellow; Koret Living Library, University of San Francisco. *Address:* 1655 Flatbush Ave, Apt C 106, New York, NY 11210, USA.

ULMER, James Kenneth; b. 2 Sept. 1954, Plainfield, New Jersey, USA. College Prof.; Poet. m. Robin Kozak, 15 Aug. 1985. *Education:* AB, Honours in English, Gettysburg College, 1976; MA, English, University of Washington, 1981; PhD, English, Creative Writing, University of Houston, 1988. *Appointments:* Instructor, 1986–88, Writer-in-Residence, 1988–, Houston Baptist University, Texas. *Contributions to:* New Yorker; Antioch Review; Poetry; Black Warrior Review; Cincinnati Poetry Review; New Criterion; North American Review; Journal; Intro; Missouri Review; Gulf Coast; Poetry Northwest; Seattle Review; Quarterly West; Three Rivers Poetry Journal; Mississippi Valley Review; Virginia Quarterly Review; Nimrod; Boulevard; Under 35: The New Generation of American Poets. *Honours:* Joan Grayston Poetry Prize, 1981; Acad. of American Poets Prizes, 1981, 1985; Henry Hoyns Fellowship in Poetry, University of Virginia, 1981–82; Pablo Neruda Poetry Prize, 1985; National Graduate Fellowship Program Fellow, 1986–87; PEN Southwest Discovery Prize for Poetry, 1987; Artist's Residency, MacDowell Colony, 1988; Creative Artists Program Grant, Cultural Arts Council, Houston, 1989. *Memberships:* Poetry Society of America; Associated Writing Programs; MLA. *Address:* Dept of Languages, Houston Baptist University, 7502 Fondren Rd, Houston, TX 77074, USA.

UNDERWOOD, Juliana Ruth; b. 8 Feb. 1938, San Bernardino, CA, USA. Counselor; Poet. m. Arthur Underwood, deceased, 1 s. *Education:* BA, Music, California State University; PhD, Psychology, University of Humanistic Studies, San Diego. *Contributions to:* Anthologies, 1996–98. *Address:* 618 Soda Creek Dr., Evergreen, CO 80439, USA.

UNGER, Barbara; b. 2 Oct. 1932, New York, NY, USA. Prof. of English and Creative Writing; Poet. m. (1), 2 d., (2) Theodore Kiichiro Sakano, 31 July 1987. *Education:* BA, 1954, MA, 1957, City College of New York. *Appointment:* Prof. of English and Creative Writing, Rockland Community College, State University of New York, 1969–. *Publications:* Basement: Poems 1959–63, 1975; The Man Who Burned Money, 1980; Inside the Wind, 1986; Learning to Foxtrot, 1989; Dying for Uncle Ray and Other Stories, 1990; Blue Depression Glass, 1991. *Contributions to:* Journals and magazines. *Honours:* Bread Loaf Scholar, 1978; National Poetry Competition Award, 1982; Ragdale Foundation Fellowships, 1985, 1986; Goodman Award in Poetry, 1989; Anna Davidson Rosenberg Award for Poems on the Jewish Experience, 1990; Djerassi Foundation Literature Residency, 1991; J. H. G. Roberts Writing Award in Poetry, 1991. *Membership:* Poetry Society of America. *Address:* 101 Parkside Dr., Suffern, NY 10901, USA.

UPDIKE, John (Hoyer); b. 18 March 1932, Shillington, PA, USA. Author; Poet. m. (1) Mary Entwistle Pennington, 26 June 1953, divorced 1977, 2 s., 2 d., (2) Martha Ruggles Bernhard, 30 Sept. 1977, 3 step-c. *Education:* BA, Harvard University, 1954; Ruskin School of Drawing and Fine Art, Oxford, 1954–55. *Publications:* Fiction: The Poorhouse Affair, 1959; The Same Door, 1959; Rabbit, Run, 1960; Pigeon Feathers and Other Stories, 1962; The Centaur, 1963; Of the Farm, 1965; The Music School, 1966; Couples, 1968; Bech: A Book, 1970; Rabbit Redux, 1971; Museums and Women and Other Stories, 1972; A Month of Sundays, 1975; Marry Me: A Romance, 1976; The Coup, 1979; Too Far to Go: The Maples Stories, 1979; Problems and Other Stories, 1979; Your Lover Just Called: Stories of Joan and Richard Maple, 1980; Rabbit is Rich, 1981; Bech is Back, 1982; The Witches of Eastwick, 1984; Roger's Version, 1986; Trust Me: Short Stories, 1987; S, 1988; Rabbit at Rest, 1990; Memories of the Ford Administration, 1992; Brazil, 1994; The Afterlife and Other Stories, 1994; Toward the End of Time, 1997; Bech at Bay, 1998; Gertrude and Claudius, 2000; Licks of Love, 2000. Poetry: The Carpenter Hen and Other Tame Creatures, 1958; Telephone Poles and Other Poems, 1963; Midpoint and Other Poems, 1969; Seventy Poems, 1972; Tossing and Turning, 1977; Sixteen Sonnets, 1979; Jester's Dozen, 1984; Facing Nature, 1985; Collected Poems, 1953–1993, 1993; Americana, 2001. Non-Fiction: Picked Up Pieces, 1975; Hugging the Shore: Essays and Criticism, 1983; Just Looking: Essays on Art, 1989; Self-Consciousness: Memoirs, 1989; Odd Jobs, 1991; A Century of Arts and Letters (ed.), 1998; More Matter: Essays and Criticism, 1999. Play: Buchanan Dying, 1974. *Contributions to:* Many publications. *Honours:* Guggenheim

Fellowship, 1959; National Book Award for Fiction, 1966; Prix Médicis Étranger, 1966; O. Henry Awards for Fiction, 1966, 1991; MacDowell Medal for Literature, 1981; Pulitzer Prizes in Fiction, 1982, 1991; National Book Critics Circle Awards for Fiction, 1982, 1991, and for Criticism, 1984; PEN/ Malamud Memorial Prize, 1988; National Medal of Arts, 1989. *Memberships:* American Acad. of Arts and Letters; American Acad. of Arts and Sciences. *Address:* c/o Alfred A. Knopf Inc, 299 Park Ave, New York, NY 10171, USA.

UPTON, Lee; b. 2 June 1953, St Johns, MI, USA. Prof. of English; Poet; Writer. m. Eric Jozef Ziolkowski, 31 March 1989, 2 d. *Education:* BA, Journalism, Michigan State University, 1978; MFA, English, University of Massachusetts at Amherst, 1981; PhD, English, State University of New York at Binghamton, 1986. *Appointments:* Visiting Asst Prof., 1986–87, Asst Prof., 1988–92, Assoc. Prof., 1992–98, of English, Prof. of English and Writer-in-Residence, 1998–, Lafayette College; Asst Prof., Grand Valley State University, 1987–88. *Publications:* Poetry: The Invention of Kindness, 1984; Sudden Distances, 1988; No Mercy, 1989; Approximate Darling, 1996; Civilian Histories, 2000. Criticism: Jean Garrigue: A Poetics of Plenitude, 1991; Obsession and Release: Rereading the Poetry of Louise Bogan, 1996; The Muse of Abandonment: Origin, Identity and Mastery in Five American Poets, 1998. *Contributions to:* Numerous reviews, quarterlies, journals and periodicals. *Honours:* Poetry prizes. *Memberships:* MLA; National Council of Teachers of English; Poetry Society of America. *Address:* c/o Dept of English, Lafayette College, Easton, PA 18042, USA.

URIEL, Gila, (b. Olga Krengel-Stamm), (Tella Vivian); b. 23 Jan. 1913, Kraków, Poland. Administrator (retd); Poet; Writer; Trans. *Education:* Herzlia College, Tel-Aviv, 1931; High School of Law and Economics, Tel-Aviv, 1933; London School of Economics and Political Science, 1939; UNPA Fellow, England and Wales, 1953. *Appointments:* Dir, Mayor's Parlour, Tel-Aviv, 1933–53; Dir, Efficiency and Training Dept, Tel-Aviv Municipality, 1954–74. *Publications:* Yearning: English and Hebrew Poems, 1975; City Management, 1983; Municipal Trifles, 1988; The Poet's World: An Anthology, 1992; The World of the Poetess: An Anthology, 1995; Three Generations: A Family Saga, 1995; The Heart's Thread: Poems, 1997; The Golden Days: Tel-Aviv's 90th Anniversary, 1999; Irony of Fate (short stories), 1999. Other: Pearls of World Poetry (trans.); Broadcasts in UK and Israel, 1966. *Contributions to:* Reviews and radio. *Membership:* Co-founder of PADM Institute, Tel-Aviv. *Address:* 9 Prague St, Tel-Aviv YAFO 63477, Israel.

URSELL, Geoffrey; b. 14 March 1943, Moose Jaw, SK, Canada. Writer; Dramatist; Poet; Composer. m. Barbara Sapergia, 8 July 1967. *Education:* BA, 1965, MA, 1966, University of Manitoba; PhD, University of London, 1973. *Appointments:* Lecturer, 1975–79, Special Asst Prof. in English, 1980–81, 1982–83, University of Regina; Writer-in-Residence, Saskatoon Public Library, 1984–85. *Publications:* Number One Northern: Poetry from Saskatchewan (co-ed.), 1977; The Tenth Negative Pig (co-author), 1980; The Running of the Deer (play), 1981; Black Powder (musical), 1982; Saskatchewan Gold (ed.), 1982; Trap Lines (poems), 1982; Perdue, or, How the West Was Lost (novel), 1984; Sky High: Stories from Saskatchewan, 1988; Way Out West (short stories), 1989; The Look-Out Tower (poems), 1989; Due West (ed.), 1996. Other: Various unpublished stage plays and radio plays. *Contributions to:* Periodicals. *Honours:* Several prizes and awards. *Memberships:* Asscn of Canadian Television and Radio Artists; Guild of Canadian Playwrights; Playwrights Canada. *Address:* 2226 MacTavish St, Regina, SK S4T 3X2, Canada.

URSU, Liliana. See: MICU, Liliana Maria.

ÜRT, Julius. See: TART, Indrek.

USHA, P. (Usha Jayan); b. 23 Oct. 1951, Vallicodu, Kottayam, India. Librarian; Poet. m. K Jayachandran Nair, 25 Nov. 1976, 1 s., 1 d. *Education:* MA, English Language and Literature, 1973; Postgraduate Diploma, Russian, 1981; MLISc, 1984; DCE - Diploma in Creative Writing in English, 1995. *Appointment:* Asst Librarian. *Publication:* Ripples: A Collection of Poems, 1997. *Contributions to:* School Man; Indian Express; Poet; International Poets; The Quest; Mosaic; Poems '97. *Memberships:* World Poetry Society Intercontinental, Chennai; Writer's Forum, Ranchi; Kochi Sahitya Vedi, exec. mem. *Address:* Asst Librarian, University Library, Cochin University of Science and Technology, Kochi 682 022, Kerala, India.

USHAKOVA, Elena. See: NEVZGLIADOVA, Elena Vsevologovna.

UTLEY, Steven; b. 10 Nov. 1948, Fort Knox, KY, USA. Writer; Poet. *Education:* Middle Tennessee State University, Murfreesboro, TN. *Publications:* Lone Star Universe (ed. with Geo W. Proctor), 1976; Ghost Seas (short stories), 1997; This Impatient Ape (poems), 1998; Career Moves of the Gods (poems), 2000. *Contributions to:* Asimov's Science Fiction; Poetry Today;

Cyclo-Flame; Galaxy; Shayol; New Dimensions; Bachy; Fly by Night; Cthulhu Calls; SumerMorn. *Address:* 113 Kentwell Dr., Smyrna, TN 37167, USA.

UZEIL-FARCHI, Rachel; b. 31 July 1937, Tel-Aviv, Palestine. Journalist; Poet; Writer. m. David Farchi, 31 March 1957, 1 s. *Education:* Diploma, Drama Teacher. *Publications:* A Sheep in the Streets of Jerusalem, 1974; 4 Poets, 1977; A Woman Gave a Man a Bubble, 1986; Flying Balloons Between East and West, 1991. *Contributions to:* Anthologies, journals and radio. *Memberships:* Israeli Writers Society; Voices, Israel. *Address:* Heller St 7/27, Givat Mordechi, Jerusalem 93710, Israel.

V

VACIK, Milos; b. 21 June 1922, Kozlany, Czechoslovakia. Journalist; Poet. m. (1) Eva, 27 March 1943, (2) Drahomira, 24 Feb. 1967, 2 s., 2 d. *Education:* Literature and Philosophy, Charles University, Prague, 1947. *Appointments:* Journalist, Pres. of the Cultural Section of the Union of Liberated Political Prisoners, 1945; Ed.-in-Chief, MIR Publishing House, 1947; Journalist, Literary Critic, 1950; Prohibition of Publishing, 1969–89; Journalist, Pres. of the Weekly New Books (Nové Knihy), 1990. *Publications:* Kralovstvi (Kingdom), 1943; Mala Kalvarie (Small Calvary), 1946; Sonety z Opusteneho Nadrazi (Sonnets from a Desolate Train Station), 1947; Zeme Jistotna (Land of Certainty), 1949; Zahrada na dva Zamky (Garden Double-Locked), 1983; Nemilostna a Milostna (Unloved and Loved), 1990; Ctyri krahujci (Four Sparrow-hawk), 1991; Kriky Narky Ticha (Cries, Laments, Silences), 1995; Ty jsi ten sad (You are that Orchard), 1996; Rapsodie hraná na strepy (Rhapsody Played on the Sherds), 1999. *Contributions to:* List Mladych; Blok; Rudé Pravo; Impuls; Nové Knihy; Listy; Tvar; Razgledi; Sodobnost (Slovenija); Nouvel Art de Français (France). *Honours:* Czechoslovak War Cross, 1939; Annual Publishers Award, Melantrich Publishing House, 1990. *Memberships:* Union of Czechoslovak Writers; Writers Guild; Czech Centre of International PEN. *Address:* Cukrovarnicka 8, 16200 Prague 6, Czech Republic.

VAGGE, Ornello, (Lionello Grifo); b. 10 Aug. 1934, Rome, Italy. Poet; Writer; Trans. *Education:* PhD, Political and Social Sciences, Brussels, 1958. *Publications:* Many poems and short stories, 1980–97. *Contributions to:* Numerous anthologies, journals and magazines. *Honours:* Communaute Europeenne des Journalistes Prize, Malta, 1972; Commenda della Repubblica Italiana, Rome, 1973; Genti e Paesi Prize for Poetry, La Spezia, Regione Liguria and Dante Alighieri Society, 1990; Trofeo Letterario Biellese di Poesia, 1994; Premio Internazionale Lerici PEA, 1995. *Memberships:* International Society of Poets; Italian Society of Authors and Publishers; Ordine Nazionale Giornalisti Italiani; Società Dante Alighieri; World Literary Acad. *Address:* c/o Blue Jay Press, Apdo Correos 32, 30380 La Manga del Mar Menor, Spain.

VAJDI, Shadab; b. 27 July 1937, Shiraz, Iran. Poet. m. Lotfali Khonji, 25 June 1972, 1 d. *Education:* BA, Persian Literature, 1958, MA, Social Sciences, 1973, Tehran University; PhD, Linguistics, London University, 1976. *Appointments:* Teacher, Persian Literature, Rezashah High School, Tehran; Producer, Persian Section, BBC World Service, England; Chief Examiner for Persian GCSE, London and East Anglia Examination Board; Vice-pres., Iran PEN Centre (in exile), 1997–98; Teacher, Persian Language and Literature, School of Oriental and African Studies, University of London. *Publications:* A Bend in the Alley, 1961; A Song for Little Hands, 1968; To the Memory of the Thirst of Southern Mountain Slopes, 1982; Closed Circuit, 1989. Poetry: Another Day, 1992; Under Rain Fall, 1995. Translator: Inside the Third World, by Paul Harrison, 1987; Return to China, by Ling Heng, 1991. *Contributions to:* Various publications. *Membership:* Poetry Society; Iranian Writers' Asscn (in exile). *Address:* 31 Sevington Rd, London NW4 3RY, England.

VALENCAK, Hannelore; b. 23 Jan. 1929, Donawitz, Austria. Writer; Poet. m. (2) Viktor Mayer, 28 April 1962, 1 s. *Education:* PhD, Physics, University of Graz. *Publications:* Fiction: Die Hohlen Noahs, 1961; Ein Fremder Garten, 1964; Zuflucht hinter der Zeit, 1967; Vorhof der Wirklichkeit, 1972; Das magische Tagebuch, 1981. Other: Various short stories, poems and books for young people. *Contributions to:* Many publications. *Honours:* National Advancement Award, 1957; Peter Rosegger Prize, Styria, 1966; Austrian Children's Book Prize, 1977; Amade Prize, Monaco, 1978. *Memberships:* Austrian PEN Club; Austrian Writers Union. *Address:* Schwarzspanierstrasse 15/2/8, 1090 Vienna, Austria.

VALENTINE, Jean; b. 27 April 1934, Chicago, IL, USA. Poet; Teacher. m. James Chace, 1957, divorced 1968, 2 d. *Education:* BA, Radcliffe College, 1956. *Appointments:* Teacher, Swarthmore College, 1968–70, Barnard College, 1968, 1970, Yale University, 1970, 1973–74, Hunter College of the City University of New York, 1970–75, Sarah Lawrence College, Columbia University, 1974–. *Publications:* Dream Barker and Other Poems, 1965; Pilgrims, 1969; Ordinary Things, 1974; Turn, 1977; The Messenger, 1979; Home, Deep, Blue: New and Selected Poems, 1988; Night Lake, 1992; The River at Wolf, 1992; The Under Voice: Selected Poems, 1995; Growing Darkness, Growing Light, 1997; The Cradle of the Real Life, 2000. *Honours:* Yale Series of Younger Poets Award, 1965; National Endowment for the Arts Grant, 1972; Guggenheim Fellowship, 1976. *Address:* c/o Dept of Writing, Columbia University, New York, NY 10027, USA.

VALGARDSON, W(illiam) D(empsey); b. 7 May 1939, Winnipeg, Manitoba, Canada. Writer; Poet; Dramatist; Prof. Divorced, 1 s., 1 d. *Education:* BA, United College, 1961; BEd, University of Manitoba, 1966; MFA, University of Iowa, 1969. *Appointments:* Assoc. Prof., 1970–74, Prof., 1974–, University of Victoria, BC; Fiction Ed., Canadian Author, 1996–. *Publications:* Bloodflowers, 1973; God is Not a Fish Inspector, 1975; In the Gutting Shed, 1976; Red Dust, 1978; Gentle Sinners, 1980; The Carpenter of Dreams, 1986; What Can't Be Changed

Shouldn't Be Mourned, 1990; The Girl With the Botticelli Face, 1992; Thor, 1994; Sarah and the People of Sand River, 1996; Garbage Creek, 1997. *Contributions to:* Magazines. *Honours:* Books in Canada First Novel Award, 1980; Ethel Wilson Literary Prize, 1992; Mr Christie Prize, 1995; Vicky Metcalf Short Story Award, 1998. *Address:* 1908 Waterloo Rd, Victoria, BC V8P 1J3, Canada.

VAN DE BERGE, Claude. See: PAUWELS, Rony.

VAN DE LAAR, Waltherus Antonius Bernardinus, (Stella Napels, Victor Vroomkoning); b. 6 Oct. 1938, Boxtel, Netherlands. Poet; Writer. 1 s., 1 d. *Education:* MA, Philosophy, Dutch Linguistics and Literature, 1978; Degree in Philosophy, 1990. *Appointments:* Teacher, Interstudie teachers' training college, Arnhem, 1977–83; Co-Ed., Kirtisch Literatur Lexicon, 1981–. *Publications:* De einders tegemoet, 1983; De laatste dingen, 1983; Circuit des souvenirs, 1984; Klein museum, 1987; Groesbeek Tijdrit, 1989; Echo van een echo, 1990; Oud zeer, 1993; Een zucht als bluchtig eerbetoon, 1995; Lippendienst, 1997; Ysbeerbestaan, 1999; Verloren Spraak, 2000. *Contributions to:* Magazines and periodicals. *Honour:* Pablo Neruda Prize, 1983. *Membership:* Lira. *Address:* Aldenhof, 70-17, 6537 DZ Nijmegen, Netherlands.

VAN DER HOEVEN, Jan; b. 3 Nov. 1929, Bruges, Belgium. Poet; Trans. m. Palm Margaret, 16 July 1965, 1 s., 2 d. *Education:* University of Ghent, 1964. *Publications:* Projekjie Schrjven; Te Woord Staan; Lecina Je Land; Elementair; Hagel En Blank; Anarchipel; Knoop Voor Knoop; Light Verse. *Contributions to:* Diagram; De Tafelronde; Radar; Diogenes; NVT; De Vlaamse Gids; Yang; Kentering; Kunst Van Nu. *Honours:* Merendree Poetry Prize; Knokke; Trap; Harelbeke. *Memberships:* Society of Flemish Writers; Society of West Writers. *Address:* Brieversweg 89, 8310 Bruges, Belgium.

VAN DUYN, Mona (Jane); b. 9 May 1921, Waterloo, IA, USA. Poet; Writer; Critic; Ed.; Reviewer; Lecturer. m. Jarvis A Thurston, 31 Aug. 1943. *Education:* BA, Iowa State Teachers College, 1942; MA, State University of Iowa, 1943. *Appointments:* Reviewer, Poetry magazine, 1944–70; Instructor in English, State University of Iowa, 1945, University of Louisville, 1946–50; Founder-Ed. (with Jarvis A Thurston), Perspective: A Quarterly of Literature, 1947–67; Lecturer in English, 1950–67, Adjunct Prof., 1983, Visiting Hurst Prof., 1987, Washington University, St Louis; Poetry Adviser, College English, 1955–57; Lecturer, Salzburg Seminar in American Studies, 1973; Poet-in-Residence, Bread Loaf Writing Conferences, 1974, 1976; Poet Laureate of the USA, 1992–93; Numerous poetry readings. *Publications:* Valentines to the Wide World: Poems, 1959; A Time of Bees, 1964; To See, To Take, 1970; Bedtime Stories, 1972; Merciful Disguises: Poems Published and Unpublished, 1973; Letters From a Father and Other Poems, 1982; Near Changes: Poems, 1990; Lives and Deaths of the Poets and Non-Poets, 1991; If It Be Not I: Collected Poems, 1992; Firefall, 1993. *Contributions to:* Many anthologies; Poems, criticism, reviews, and short stories in various periodicals. *Honours:* Eunice Tietjens Memorial Prize, 1956; National Endowment for the Arts Grants, 1966–67, 1985; Harriet Monroe Memorial Prize, 1968; Hart Crane Memorial Award, 1968; First Prize, Borestone Mountain Awards, 1968; Bollingen Prize, 1970; National Book Award for Poetry, 1971; Guggenheim Fellowship, 1972–73; Loines Prize, National Institute of Arts and Letters, 1976; Fellow, Acad. of American Poets, 1981; Sandburg Prize, Cornell College, 1982; Shelley Memorial Award, Poetry Society of America, 1987; Ruth Lilly Prize, 1989; Pulitzer Prize in Poetry, 1991. *Memberships:* Acad. of American Poets, board of chancellors, 1985–99; National Institute of Arts and Letters. *Address:* 7505 Teasdale Ave, St Louis, MO 63130, USA.

VAN SOMEREN, Gretta June; b. 20 July 1968, Chickishae, Oklahoma, USA. Pianist; Music Teacher; Poet. m. Jay A Van Someren, 4 Aug. 1990, 1 d. *Education:* BM Certificate to teach choral and general music, 1991. *Contributions to:* Anthologies, 1996–97, magazines and journals. *Memberships:* National Poet's Asscn; UAPAA. *Address:* 2357 20th St, Rice Lake, WI 54868, USA.

VAN SPANCKEREN, Kathryn; b. 14 Dec. 1945, Kansas City, Missouri, USA. Prof.; Poet; Ed. m. Stephen Breslow, 26 June 1976, 1 s. *Education:* BA, English, Folklore and Mythology, University of California at Berkeley, 1967; MA, English Literature, Brandeis University, 1968; MA, English Literature, 1969, PhD, English and American Literature, 1976, Harvard University. *Appointments:* Teaching Fellow, Harvard University, 1970–73; Asst Prof., Wheaton College, Massachusetts, 1974–79; Program Dir and Co-ordinator, Co-ordinating Council of Literary Magazines, New York City, 1979–80; Asst Prof. to Prof., University of Tampa, 1982–; Poetry Ed., Tampa Review, 1988–. *Publications:* Mountains Hidden in Mountains, 1992; Salt and Sweet Water, 1993; Outline History of American History, 1997. *Contributions to:* Anthologies, reviews, quarterlies and journals. *Honours:* Honourable Mentions. *Memberships:* Margaret Atwood Society, past pres.; MLA, past pres.; Open Window Literature Asscn; Poetry Society of America; Poets and Writers. *Address:* 93 Martinique Ave, Tampa, FL 33606, USA.

VAN WINCKEL, Nance; b. 24 Oct. 1951, Roanoke, VA, USA. Poet; Writer; Prof. m. Robert Fredrik Nelson, 1985. *Education:* BA, University of Wisconsin, Milwaukee, 1973; MA, University of Denver, 1976. *Appointments:* Instructor in English, Marymount College, Salina, KS, 1976–79; Assoc. Prof. of English and Dir, Writing Program, Lake Forest College, IL, 1979–90; Assoc. Prof. to Prof. of English, Eastern Washington University, Cheney, 1990–; Faculty, Vermont College, 2000–. *Publications:* The Twenty-Four Doors: Advent Calendar Poems, 1985; Bad Girl, with Hawk (poems), 1988; Limited Lifetime Warranty (short stories), 1994; The Dirt (poems), 1994; Quake (short stories), 1997; After a Spell (poems), 1998; Curtain Creek Farm (short stories), 2000. *Contributions to:* Many periodicals. *Honours:* Illinois Arts Council Fellowships, 1983, 1985, 1987, 1989; National Endowment for the Arts Fellowships, 1988, 2001; Society of Midland Authors Poetry Award, 1989; Gordon Barber Award, Poetry Society of America, 1989; Northwest Institute Grants, 1991, 1993, 1994; Paterson Fiction Prize, 1998; Washington State Artists Trust Literary Award in Fiction, 1998; Washington State Gov.'s Award for Literature, 1999. *Address:* c/o Graduate Creative Writing Program, Eastern Washington University, Cheney, WA 99004, USA.

VANCE, Andrea Elois; b. 20 March 1961, Louisville, KY, USA. Poet; Playwright. *Education:* Psychology, Jefferson Community College, Louisville, 1979–81; BA, Communications and Psychology, University of Louisville, 1983. *Publication:* Holding On, 2000. Other: Performed at the Kentucky Centre for the Arts, 1990; Poem recited, Actor's Theatre, Louisville, 1995; Performed at the Carnegie Centre for Literary and Learning in Lexington, KY, 1999. *Contributions to:* Anthologies and periodicals. *Honour:* Golden Poet Award, World of Poetry, 1988. *Membership:* National League of American Pen Women. *Address:* 1487 Olive St, Louisville, KY 40210, USA.

VANDO (HICKOK), Gloria; b. 21 May 1936, New York, NY, USA. Poet; Publisher; Ed. m. (1) Maurice Peress, 2 July 1955, 1 s., 2 d., (2) William Harrison Hickok, 4 Oct. 1980. *Education:* BA, Texas A & I College, Corpus Christi, 1975; Graduate Studies, Southampton College, Long Island University, New York. *Appointments:* Founding Publisher, ed., Helicon Nine Editions, 1977–. *Publications:* Caprichos, 1987; Promesas: Geography of the Impossible, 1993; Touching the Fire: Fifteen Poets of Today's Latino Renaissance (anthology), 1998; Spud Songs: An Anthology of Potato Poems (co-ed.), 1999; Shadows and Supposes: Poems, 2002. *Contributions to:* Cottonwood Magazine, Gloria Vando Issue, Summer 1994; Kenyon Review; Western Humanities Review; Seattle Review; New Letters, Carolina Quarterly. *Honours:* Poetry Fellowship, Kansas Arts Commission, 1989–91; Kansas Gov.'s Arts Award, 1991; Billee Murray Denny Prize, 1991; Thorpe Menn Book Award, 1994; River Styx International Poetry Award, second place, 1997; Poetry Society of America's Alice Fay Di Castagnola Award, 1998. *Memberships:* PEN International; Poetry Society of America; Writers' Place, Kansas City, Missouri, co-founder; Cockefair Chair., University of Missouri-Kansas City, board; Clearing House for Midcontinent Foundations, art chair., 1988–90; Midwest Center for the Literary Arts Inc, board vice-pres.; Acad. of American Poets. *Address:* c/o Helicon Nine Editions, PO Box 22412, Kansas City, MO 64113, USA.

VANIČEK, Zdenák, (Alois Bocek); b. 24 June 1947, Chlumec, Czechoslovakia. Diplomat; Prof.; Poet; Writer. m. Nadya Jankovska, 2 s., 1 d. *Education:* BA, College of Economics, Prague, 1972; MA, LLD, Charles University, Prague, 1979; PhD, Diplomatic Acad., Prague, 1981 *Appointments;* Czechoslovak Diplomatic Service, 1972–91; Prof. of International Relations and Law, 1993–; Pres., Czech Asscn of Competitive Communications, 1999–. *Publications:* The Theory and the Practice of British Neo-Conservatism, 1988; Amidst the Ruins of Memories, 1990; To the Ends of the Earth, 1992; On the Edge of Rain, 1994; Under the Range of Mountains of Five Fingers, 1996; Seven Thousand Years Chiselled in Limestone, 1996; Amidst Memory's Ruins (mid-life poetry 1988–1998), 1999; Whereupon He Was Arrested (short stories), 2002. *Contributions to:* Newspapers and magazines. *Honours:* Pontifical Medal, 1990; Masaryk Award, Acad. of Arts, 1997; Karel Hynek Mácha Prize for Poetry, 1998. *Memberships:* Poetry Society, England; RSL. *Address:* Heémanova 10/1087, 170 00 Prague 7, Czech Republic.

VANNELLI, Maria Antonietta; b. 10 Dec. 1946, Livorno, Italy. Journalist; Poet. m. Franco Petri, 3 June 1967, separated, 2 s. *Education:* Diploma as Teacher of French. *Appointments:* Journalist with newspapers and television. *Publications:* Un giorno una vita, 1976; Saudade, 1980; La donna di vetro, 1984; Una zattera di liberta, 1991. *Contributions to:* Various publications. *Honours:* Several prizes. *Memberships:* Centro Studi e Storia delle Poetiche; Gruppo Internazionale di Lettura. *Address:* Via Piastelli 115, 55043 Lido di Camaiore, Lucca, Italy.

VARJU, Livia; b. Eger, Hungary. International Civil Servant (retd); Poet; Writer; Ed.; Trans. *Publications:* Swissericks (co-author), 1991. *Contributions to:* Sheep Don't Go to School, 1999; Anthologies and other publications. *Honour:* Gold Medal for trans. of Hungarian poetry into English, Arpad Acad., Cleveland, 1988. *Memberships:* Various writers' groups in Geneva. *Address:* 4 chemin du Repos, 1213 Petit-Lancy, Geneva, Switzerland.

VASSILIEVA, Larissa; b. 23 Nov. 1935, Kharkov, Russia. Writer; Poet. m Oleg Vassiliev, 19 Jan. 1957, deceased 1993, 1 s. *Education:* Graduated, Dept c Philology, University of Moscow, 1958. *Publications:* Poetry: Linen Moon, 1968 Fire-fly, 1969; The Goose-foot, 1970; Blue Twilight, 1970; Encounter, 1974; A Rainbow of Snow, 1974; Meadows, 1975; Light in the Window, 1978; Russiar Names, 1980; Foliage, 1980; Fireflower, 1981; Selected Poetry, 1981; Grove 1984; Mirror, 1985; Moskvorechie, 1985; Lantern, 1985; Waiting for You in the Sky, 1986; Selected Works, 2 vols, 1989; Strange Quality, 1991. Other: Prose and essays. *Contributions to:* Literary Gazette; Literary Russia; Pravda Ogonyok; Novyi Mir; Yunost; Nash Sovremennik; Druzhba Narodov Krestyanka; Komsomolskaya Pravda. *Honours:* Moscow Komsomol Prize 1971; Order of Merit, 1971, 1980; Order of Friendship of People, 1984 *Memberships:* Union of Russian Writers; League of Woman Writers, pres Address: 8 Usievicha Str, Apt 86, Moscow 125319, Russia.

VAUGHAN WILLIAMS, Ursula, (Ursula Wood); b. 15 March 1911, Malta. Poet; Writer; Librettist. m. (1) Michael Forrester Wood, 24 May 1933, deceased 1942, (2) Ralph Vaughan Williams, 7 Feb. 1953, deceased 1958. *Education:* Private. *Publications:* No Other Choice, 1941; Fall of Leaf, 1944; Need for Speech, 1948; Silence and Music, 1959; Aspects, 1984; Collected Poems. Other: Libretti for operas and cantatas by various composers. *Address:* 66 Gloucester Crescent, London NW1 7EG, England.

VÁZQUEZ DÍAZ, René; b. 7 Sept. 1952, Caibarien, Cuba. Writer; Poet; Trans. *Education:* Polish Language, Univerity of Łódź; Swedish Language, University of Lund. *Appointment:* Review Writer, Swedish Journal. *Publications:* La Era Imaginaria; Querido Traidor; La Isla Del Cundeamor; El últiom Concierto; Difusos Mapas. *Contributions to:* Sydsvenska Dagladet; Bonniers; El País; El Urogallo; Geo; El Nuevo Herald. *Honour:* Fellowships. *Memberships:* Swedish Union of Writers; Swedish PEN Club. *Address:* Albert Bonniers Forlag, Box 3159, 103-63 Stockholm, Sweden.

VEGA, Janine Pommy; b. 5 Feb. 1942, Jersey City, New Jersey, USA. Poet; Writer; Performer; Lecturer; Teacher. *Education:* MFA Equivalency. *Appointments:* Poet in the Schools, 1975–88; Dir, Incisions/Arts, 1988–2003, Mad Dogs of Trieste, 2000, Alternative Literary Programs in the Schools, 1991–, Teachers and Writers, 1995–. *Publications:* Poems to Fernando, 1968; Morning Passage, 1976; Here at the Door, 1978; Journal of a Hermit, 1979; The Bard Owl, 1980; Apex of the Earth's Way, 1984; Drunk on a Glacier Talking to Flies, 1988; Island of the Sun, 1991; Threading the Maze, 1992; Red Bracelets, 1994; The Road to Your House is a Mountain Road, 1995; Tracking the Serpent, 1997. *Contributions to:* Anthologies and periodicals. *Honours:* Operating Grant, New York State Council on the Arts, 1988–2003; Heaven Bone Chapbook Competition, 1994. *Memberships:* PEN, Prison Writers Committee; Poets and Writers. *Address:* Box 162, Bearsville, NY 12409, USA.

VEGE, Nageswara Rao; b. 18 Jan. 1932, Peda, India. Physician; Surgeon; Poet; Writer. *Education:* BA, Andhra University; MD, University of Parma. *Publications:* Poetry: Pace e Vita, 1963; Life and Love, 1965; Santi Priya, 1966; The Light of Asoka, 1970; Peace and Love, 1981; Templi Trascurati, 1983; The Best of Vege, 1992. Other: 100 Opinions of Great Men on Life, 1992. *Contributions to:* Newspapers and magazines. *Honours:* Giuseppe Ungaretti Award, 1982; Grand Prix Mediterranee, 1982; Schiller Award, 1985; Greenwood Poetry Forum Award, 1985; La Ballata Award, 1991; Viareggio Award, 1992. *Memberships:* International PEN; Italian Writers Asscn; Scrittori della Svizzera Italiana; Swiss Writers Asscn; World Doctors Writers Asscn.

VELARDE, Damian John; b. 29 Aug. 1938, Liverpool, England. Teacher; Poet. m. Eileen Power, 28 July 1964, 1 s., 1 d. *Education:* BSc, University of Liverpool, 1960; BA, Open University, 1976; Diploma, Art Education, Birmingham, 1979. *Appointments:* Teacher of Biology and Art, Liverpool; Head of Biology, Sheffield, 1964–. *Contributions to:* Poetry and Audience; Poetry Nottingham; Pen to Paper; New Welsh Review. *Honours:* Likely Literature Festival; Work included in collection of contemporary Yorkshire Poetry, 1984. *Memberships:* Poetry Society. *Address:* The Orchard, 60A Dore Rd, Dore, Sheffield S17 3QB, England.

VELASCO, Lola (García); b. 19 Oct. 1961, Madrid, Spain. Writer; Poet; Critic. *Education:* Literary studies. *Publications:* Le Frente de Una Mujer Oblicua, 1986; El Sueno de las Piedras, 1987; La Cometa o las Manos Sobre el Papel, 1992. *Contributions to:* Anthologies, newspapers, and magazines. *Honours:* Finalist, Hiperion Prize, 1986; Nominee, Icaro Prize, 1990. *Address:* c/o Costanilla de Santiago 2, 401lz, 28013 Madrid, Spain.

VENABLES, Roger Evelyn Cavendish; b. 4 March 1911, Varna, Bulgaria. Poet; Writer. *Education:* Beaumont and Christ Church, Oxford; MA, University of Oxford. *Publications:* Poetry: Combe, 1942; Images of Power, 1960; The Night Comes, 1961; Leaves and Seasons, 1961; Forebodings, 1963; Farewell to Combe, 1974; Bari, 1974; The Cornish Hundreds, 1980; Leaflets, 1986; Memories and Forebodings, 1991; The Hooting Carn, 1993. Other: D: Portrait of a Don, 1967. *Honour:* Bard of Cornish Gorseth, 1984. *Memberships:* Lancashire Authors Asscn; St Just and Pendeen Old Cornwall Society, past pres. *Address:* Atlanta, Pendeen, Penzance, Cornwall, England.

VENEZIANO, Patricia Joan Morse; b. 4 April 1931, Waterbury, CT, USA. Educator; Librarian; Poet. m. Santo Veneziano, 20 Feb. 1965. *Education:* Fordham University, 1942–54; University of Connecticut, 1956–58; Southeast Connecticut State University, 1959–62. *Contributions to:* Waterbury Republican-American; Naugatuck Daily News, CT. *Membership:* Connecticut Poetry Society. *Address:* 170 Hillside Ave, No. 3-H, Waterbury, CT 06710, USA.

VERILLI, Joseph; b. 2 May 1952, Bridgeport, CT, USA. Poet. m. Janet Ochs, 21 Nov. 1981. *Education:* Graduate, Kolbe High School, 1970. *Publications:* It's Always Been '71, 1996; Manifesto, 1997; Modern Love, 1999. *Contributions to:* Anthologies, 1993–95, and numerous other publications. *Honours:* Ed.'s Choice Awards, National Library of Poetry, 1993, 1994, 1995; Second Place, Distinguished Poet Awards, Sparrowgrass Poetry Forum, 1994; Second Place and Honourable Mention, Poetic Page, 1995. *Membership:* Connecticut Poetry Society. *Address:* 115 Washington Ave, Apt GH, Bridgeport, CT 06604, USA.

VERNON, Annette Robyn. See: CORKHILL, Annette Robyn.

VERTREACE-DOODY, Martha Modena; b. 24 Nov. 1945, Washington, DC, USA. Prof. of English; Poet; Writer. *Education:* BA, English, District of Columbia Teachers College, 1967; MA, English, 1972, MPH, 1973, Roosevelt University; MS, Religious Studies, Mundelein College, 1982. *Appointments:* Instructor, 1976–85, Asst Prof., 1986–90, Poet-in-Residence, 1986–, Assoc. Prof. of English, 1991–, Distinguished Prof., 1995–96, Kennedy-King College; Asst Adjunct Prof. of English, Rosary College, 1982–83; Co-Ed., Rhino; Ed., Class Act. *Publications:* Second House from the Corner, 1986; Kelly in the Mirror, 1993; Under a Cat's-Eye Moon, 1994; Oracle Bones, 1994; Cinnabar, 1995; Light Caught Bending, 1995; Maafa: When Night Becomes a Lion, 1996; Smokeless Flame, 1998; Second Mourning, 1998; Dragon Lady: Tsukimi, 1999. *Contributions to:* Anthologies, reviews, quarterlies and journals. *Honours:* First Prizes, Salute to the Arts Poetry Contest, Triton College, 1985, 1986, 1987, 1990; Excellence in Professional Writing, Harcourt Brace Jovanovich, 1986; Roberts Writing Awards, 1990; Hawthornden Fellowship, Scotland, 1992; Poetry Fellow, Writers Centre, Dublin, 1993; Significant Illinois Poet, 1993; National Endowment for the Arts Grant, 1993; Writers Fellowship, Illinois Arts Council, 1993. *Memberships:* Illinois State Poetry Society; National Federation of State Poetry Societies; Poets Study Club; Society of Midland Authors; Society of Writers of Children's Literature. *Address:* 5232 S Greenwood Ave, Chicago, IL 60615, USA.

VETTESE, Raymond John; b. 1 Nov. 1950, Angus, Scotland. Teacher; Poet. m. Maureen Elizabeth Vettese, 13 May 1972. *Education:* Montrose Acad., 1961–67; Dundee College of Education, 1972–75. *Publications:* Four Scottish Poets; The Right Noise and Other Poems; A Keen New Air, 1995. *Contributions to:* Reviews, quarterlies and journals. *Honours:* Scotsman Prize for Best First Book, Saltire Society; William Soutar Writers Fellowship. *Memberships:* Scots Language Resource Center; Scots Language Society; Scottish PEN. *Address:* 9 Tayock Ave, Montrose, Angus, Tayside DD10 9AP, Scotland.

VIDAL, Francisco Cervantes; b. 7 April 1938, Queretoro, Mexico. Journalist; Publisher; Poet. *Publications:* Los varones senalados/La materia del tributo, 1971; Esta sustanicia amarga, 1972; Cantado para nadie, 1982; Heridas que se alternan, 1985; Los husesos peregrinos, 1986; El canto del abismo (with Joan Boldo i Climent), 1987; Relatorio sentimental, 1987; Materia de Distintos Lais, 1987; El Libro de Nicole, 1992. *Contributions to:* Various publications. *Honours:* Guggenheim Fellowship, 1977–78; Villaurrotia Prize for Poetry, 1982; Heriberto Frias, Queretoro, 1986; Officer of the Order of Rio Branco, Brazil. *Address:* Eve Central, Lazaro Cordenas 12, 0600 Mexico DF, Hotel Cosmos, Mexico.

VIDALES IBARRA, Aura Maria; b. 11 July 1958, Mexico. Poet; Journalist. m. José Salvador Guerrero, 11 Dec. 1990, 1 s., 1 d. *Education:* Licentiate in Journalism, Escuela Carlos Septien Garcia, 1984. *Publications:* Ensueno, 1979; Estalactitas, 1984; Balada para un viento suave, 1987; Ventanas vacias, 1990. *Contributions to:* Anthologies, newspapers, reviews and journals. *Honour:* Scholarship, National Council for Culture and Arts, 1990. *Address:* Ingenieros Militares 94, Colonia Periodista, Mexico DF 11220, Mexico.

VIDOR, Vassillil. See: BARRIERE, William J.

VIERECK, Peter (Robert Edwin); b. 5 Aug. 1916, New York, NY, USA. Historian; Poet; Prof. m. (1) Anya de Markov, June 1945, divorced May 1970, 1 s., 1 d., (2) Betty Martin Falkenberg, 30 Aug. 1972. *Education:* BS, 1937, MA, 1939, PhD, 1942, Harvard University; Graduate Study as a Henry Fellow, Christ Church, Oxford, 1937–38. *Appointments:* Instructor, Tutor, Harvard University, 1946–47; Asst Prof. of History, 1947–48, Visiting Lecturer in Russian History, 1948–49, Smith College, Northampton, Massachusetts; Assoc. Prof., 1948–55, Prof. of Modern European and Russian History, 1955–65, Mount Holyoke Alumnae Foundation Chair of Interpretive Studies, 1965–79, William R Kenan Chair of History, 1979–, Mount Holyoke College; Whittal Lecturer in Poetry, Library of Congress, Washington, DC, 1954, 1963; Fulbright Prof. in American Poetry and Civilization, University of Florida, 1955; Elliston Chair and Poetry Lecturer, University of Cincinnati, 1956; Visiting Lecturer, University of California at Berkeley, 1957, 1964, City College of the City University of New York, 1964; Visiting Research Scholar in Russian for the Twentieth Century

Fund, 1962–63; Dir, Poetry Workshop, New York Writers Conferences, 1965–67. *Publications:* History: Metapolitics: From the Romantics to Hitler, 1941, revised edn as Metapolitics: The Roots of the Nazi Mind, 1961; Conservatism Revisited: The Revolt Against Revolt, 1815–1949, 1949, second edn as Conservatism Revisited and the New Conservatism: What Went Wrong?, 1962; Shame and Glory of the Intellectuals: Babbitt, Jr Versus the Rediscovery of Values, 1953; The Unadjusted Man: A New Hero for Americans: Reflections on the Distinction Between Conserving and Conforming, 1956; Inner Liberty: The Stubborn Grit in the Machine, 1957; Conservatism from Burke and John Adams till 1982: A History and an Anthology, 1982. Poetry: Terror and Decorum: Poems 1940–1948, 1948; Strike Through Mask: Lyrical Poems, 1950; The First Morning: New Poems, 1952; Dream and Responsibility: The Tension Between Poetry and Society, 1953; The Persimmon Tree, 1956; The Tree Witch: A Poem and a Play (First of All a Poem), 1961; New and Selected Poems, 1932–1967, 1967; Archer in the Marrow: The Applewood Cycles of 1967–1987, 1987; Tide and Continuities: Last and First Poems, 1995–1938, 1995. *Contributions to:* Monographs, essays, reviews and poems to numerous periodicals. *Honours:* Pulitzer Prize in Poetry, 1949; Rockefeller Foundation Research Grant, 1958; Guggenheim Fellowship, 1959–60; National Endowment for the Humanities Senior Research Fellowship, 1969; Poetry Award, Massachusetts Artists Foundation, 1978; Sadin Prize, New York Quarterly, 1980; Golden Rose Award, 1981, Varoujan Poetry Prize, 1983, New England Poetry Club; Ingram Merrill Foundation Fellowship in Poetry, 1985. *Memberships:* American Committee for Cultural Freedom, exec. committee; American Historical Asscn; Committee for Basic Education, charter mem.; Oxford Society; PEN. *Address:* 12 Silver St, South Hadley, MA 01075, USA.

VIERU, Grigore Pavel; b. 14 Feb. 1935, Moldova. Writer; Poet. m. Vieru Raisa Tudor, 8 June 1959, 2 s. *Education:* Romanian Language, Chisinau Pedagogic Institute. *Publications:* Various poetry collections and children's books. *Contributions to:* Reviews and journals. *Honours:* Moldova State laureate, 1979; Romanian Acad. Nominee for the Nobel Prize for Literature, 1992. *Memberships:* Moldova Writer's Union; Romanian Acad. of Science, hon. mem. *Address:* Chisinau str Nicolae Iorga 7 ap 10, Moldova, Romania.

VIJAY BHANU, A. K., (Chaarithra); b. 10 July 1930, Ayyampalayam, Dindigul Q M District, Tamil Nadu, India. Civil Servant (retd); Advocate; Poet. m. Gnana Soundhari, 18 Oct. 1956, 2 s., 1 d. *Education:* BA, Honours, Economics; MA, Economics; Bachelor of Law; DLitt, World University. *Appointments:* Various government positions. *Publications:* In English: Silvern Waters, 1987; Revels, 1987; Wood-Nymphs, 1988; Flute, 1988; Ecstasy, 1988; Mystic Rocks, 1988; Goddess, 1989; Honey Comb, 1989; Shadows, 1989. *Contributions to:* Indian journals in English. *Address:* Pearl Castle, S 106, Main Rd, Anna Nagar, Chennai 40, India.

VILLA, Carlo; b. 3 Oct. 1931, Rome, Italy. Journalist; Writer; Poet. *Education:* Graduate. *Appointments:* Dir, Centro Sistema Bibliotecario Cittadino; Secretary-General, Centro Internazionale Eugenio Montale; Book Reviewer and Scriptwriter, RAI TV; Italian Correspondent, Radio Televisione Svizzera Italiana. *Publications:* Poetry: Fiera Letteraria, 1959; Il privilegio di essere vivi, 1962; Solo sperando nauseati, 1963; Siamo esseri antichi, 1964; Gorba, 1972; Le maestà delle finte, 1977; Polvere di miele, 1980; Infanzia del dettato, 1981; Come la rosa al naso, 1984; Corpo a Cuore, 1985; Cento di questi fogli, 1989; Pochades, 1992; L'Apparenza, 1993; Simboli eroici, 1993; Consumato amore, 1994; Pas de deux, 1994; L'infinito è un quadrato senz'angoli, 1995; Dedicamenta, 1999; Roba da gatti; Pelle d'anima; L'amore per l'anima del podice, 2000; A piel di sogno, 2001; L'osadi inefistofele, 2002. Fiction: La nausea media, 1964; I sensi lunghi, 1967; Deposito celeste, 1970; L'isola in bottiglia, 1972; Muore il padrone, 1978; Mandrake, Arcivescovo di Salem, 1982; Morte per Lucro, 1988; Pan di patata, 1995; Analità, 1998. Essays: Il figlio assurdo, 1972; Guida alla lettura di Vasco Pratolini, 1973; L'Eros nella poesia italiana del '900, 1981; Roma su strada, 1984; La vie consolari romane, 1995; Eros violato, 1999; Lector in tabula, 2002. *Contributions to:* Various newspapers and magazines. *Membership:* International PEN Club. *Address:* Via Virginia Agnelli 24, 00151 Rome, Italy.

VINCENT, Elizabeth, (Za); b. 20 Nov. 1940, Amersham, Buckinghamshire, England. Poet. m. Michael Vincent, 19 Sept. 1959, 2 s. *Education:* Teachers Certificate in Education, with distinction, 1972; BEd, University of London, 1973. *Appointments:* Senior Teacher, Primary Education, Sutton, Surrey, 1973–90; Lecturer, Literacy Campaign, Croydon, 1975–78; Lecturer in Communications, Erith, 1977. *Publications:* Blue Apples, 1958; Green Apples, 1959; The Bride, 1960; Tactical Navigators 1, 1961; Cunt Art Can't, 1962; Mirrors, 1963; Maryelisa, 1969; Beached; Ruiad. *Address:* Rowans, 20 Byron Close, N Heath Lane, Horsham, West Sussex RH12 5PA, England.

VIRGO, Crescent. See: BALACHANDRAN, Kannaiya.

VIRGO, Seán; b. 1940, Mtarfa, Malta. Writer; Poet. *Education:* BA, University of Nottingham. *Publications:* Fiction: White Lies and Other Fictions, 1979; Through the Eyes of a Cat: Irish Stories, 1983; Selakhi, 1987; Wormwood, 1989; White Lies... Plus Two, 1990; Waking in Eden, 1990; The Scream of the Butterfly, 1996; Poetry: Sea Change, 1971; Pieces for the Old Earth Man, 1973; Island (with Paul and Lutia Lauzon), 1975; Kiskatinaw Songs (with

Susan Musgrave), 1977; Deathwatch on Skidegate Narrows, 1979; Selected Poems, 1992. *Membership:* League of Canadian Poets. *Address: c/o* League of Canadian Poets, 54 Wolseley St, Suite 204, Toronto, ON M5T 1A5, Canada.

VISHAL, Vijay; b. 17 Oct. 1949, Mirzajaan, District of Gurdaspur, Punjab, India. College Teacher of English; Poet. m. Vipan Sharma, 2 March 1976, 2 s., 2 d. *Education:* BA, 1969; MA, English, 1971; University Grants Commission Summer Institute in English Language Teaching for College Teachers, 1973; Refresher Course in English (Phonetics and Spoken English), Central Institute of English and Foreign Languages Regional Centre, Lucknow, 1983. *Appointments:* Lecturer in English, Head, Dept of English, GGDSD College, Baijnath, 1971. *Publications:* Speechless Messages, 1992; Parting Wish, 2001. Other: Poems in Hindi and English broadcast on radio and television. *Contributions to:* Poetry Journal; Skylark; Canopy; The Quest; New Quest; Poetcrit; Kavita India; Rock Pebbles; Rambag; The Young Poet; Indian Book Chronicle; Poets International; Brain Wave; Newspapers, including: The Tribune; Indian Express; Trigart Times; Himachal Reporter; Radical Thought; Hindi Newspapers: Punjab Kesari; Veer Partaap; Dainik Tribune. *Memberships:* Poetry Society of India; Press Sec., S. D. Pritinidhi Sabba Punjab; Organizing Sec., S. D. Mahavir Dal Punjab, GGDSD Education Board; Religious, social and educational organizations in North India. *Address:* Mannan House, Preet Nagar, Baijnath 176125, Distt. Kangra, Himachal Pradesh, India. *Telephone:* (1894) 63165.

VISSER, Audrae Eugenie; b. 3 June 1919, Hurley, South Dakota, USA. Poet. 1 s. *Education:* AA, Black Hills State University, Spearfish, South Dakota, 1942; BS, South Dakota University, Brookings, 1948; MA, University of Denver, 1954. *Appointment:* Ed., Pasque Petals, South Dakota Poetry Magazine, 1998– Publications: Rustic Roads, 1961; Poems for Brother Donald, 1974; Meter for Momma, 1974; Poems for Pop, 1976; South Dakota, 1980; Country Cousin, 1986; Pheasant Flights, 1989; Grass Roots Poetry, 1991; Prairie Poetry, 1998. *Contributions to:* Various publications. *Honours:* South Dakota State Poet Laureate, 1974; Centennial Poet, South Dakota State Poetry Society, 1989; Woman of Achievement in Fine Arts, General Federation of Women's Clubs, South Dakota, 1990. *Memberships:* National League of American Pen Women, Black Hills Branch; South Dakota State Poetry Society; Western Women in the Arts, South Dakota. *Address:* 710 Elk St, Elkton, SD 57026, USA.

VIVIAN, Tella. See: URIEL, Gila.

VIZENOR, Gerald (Robert); b. 22 Oct. 1934, Minneapolis, Minnesota, USA. Author; Poet; Prof. of Native American Literature. m. (1) Judith Helen Horns, Sept. 1959, divorced 1968, 1 s., (2) Laura Jane Hall, May 1981. *Education:* BA, University of Minnesota, 1960. *Appointments:* Lecturer, 1976–80, Prof. of Native American Literature, 1990–, Richard and Rhoda Goldman Distinguished Prof. of American Studies, 2000–02, University of California at Berkeley; Prof., University of Minnesota, 1980–85, University of California at Santa Cruz, 1987–90; Resident Scholar, School of American Research, Santa Fe, 1985–86; David Burr Chair of Letters, Prof., University of Oklahoma, 1990–91. *Publications:* Thomas James White Hawk, 1968; Summer in the Spring: Anishinaable Lyric Poems and Stories, 1970; The Everlasting Sky: New Voices from the People Named the Chippewa, 1972; Tribal Scenes and Ceremonies, 1976, revised edn as Crossbloods: Bone Courts, Bingo, and Other Reports, 1990; Darkness in Saint Louis Bearheart (novel), 1978, revised edn as Bearheart: The Heirship Chronicles, 1990; Wordarrows: Indians and Whites in the New Fur Trade, 1978; Earthdivers: Tribal Narratives on Mixed Descent, 1983; The People Named the Chippewa: Narrative Histories, 1983; Matsushima: Pine Islands (collected haiku poems), 1984; Griever: An American Monkey King in China (novel), 1986; Touchwood: A Collection of Ojibway Prose (ed.), 1987; The Trickster of Liberty: Tribal Heirs to a Wild Baronage (novel), 1988; Narrative Chance: Postmodern Discourse on Native American Literatures (ed.), 1989; Interior Landscapes: Autobiographical Myths and Metaphors, 1990; Landfill Meditation (short stories), 1991; The Heirs of Columbus (novel), 1991; Dead Voices: Natural Agonies in the New World (novel), 1993; Manifest Manners: Postindian Warriors of Survivance (critical essays), 1994; Shadow Distance: A Gerald Vizenor Reader, 1994; Native American Literature (ed.), 1995; Hotline Healers: An Almost Browne Novel, 1997; Fugitive Poses: Native American Indian Scenes of Absence and Presence, 1998; Postindian Conversations, 1999; Cranes Arise (haiku). 1999; Raising the Moon Vines (haiku), 1999; Chancers (novel), 2000. *Contributions to:* Numerous books, journals, and periodicals. *Honours:* New York Fiction Collective Award, 1986; American Book Award, 1988; California Arts Council Artists Fellowship in Literature, 1989; Josephine Miles Awards, PEN Oakland, 1990, 1996; Doctor of Humane Letters, Macalester College, 1999. *Address: c/o* American Studies, 301 Campbell Hall, University of California at Berkeley, Berkeley, CA 94720, USA.

VOGELSANG, Arthur; b. 31 Jan. 1942, Baltimore, Maryland, USA. Poet; Ed. m. Judith Ayers, 14 June 1966. *Education:* BA, University of Maryland, 1965; MA, Johns Hopkins University, 1966; MFA, University of Iowa, 1970. *Appointment:* Ed., The American Poetry Review, 1973–. *Publications:* A Planet, 1983; Twentieth Century Women, 1988; Cities and Towns, 1996. *Honours:* National Endowment for the Arts Fellowships in Poetry, 1976, 1985,

1995; California Arts Council Grant, 1995; Juniper Prize, 1995. *Address:* 1730 N Vista St, Los Angeles, CA 90046, USA.

VOIGT, Ellen Bryant; b. 9 May 1943, Danville, Virginia, USA. Poet; College Teacher. m. Francis G W Voigt, 5 Sept. 1965, 1 s., 1 d. *Education:* BA, Converse College, Spartanburg, South Carolina, 1964; MFA, University of Iowa, 1966. *Appointments:* Faculty, Iowa Wesleyan College, 1966–69, Goddard College, 1969–79, Massachusetts Institute of Technology, 1979–82, Warren Wilson College, 1981–. *Publications:* Claiming Kin, 1976; The Forces of Plenty, 1983; The Lotus Flowers, 1987; Two Trees, 1992; Kyrie, 1996; The Flexible Lyric, 2001; Shadow of Heaven, 2002. *Contributions to:* Reviews, quarterlies, and journals. *Honours:* National Endowment for the Arts Fellowship, 1975; Guggenheim Fellowship, 1978; Pushcart Prizes, 1983, 1987; Honorable Mention, The Poets' Prize, 1987; Emily Clark Balch Award, 1987; Hon. Doctor of Letters, Converse College, 1989; Haines Award for Poetry, Fellowship of Southern Writers, 1993; Finalist, National Book Critics Circle Award, 1996; Acad. of American Poets Fellowship, 2001. *Address:* PO Box 16, Marshfield, VT 05658, USA.

VOINOVICH, Vladimir (Nikolaievich); b. 26 Sept. 1932, Dushanbe, Russia. Author; Poet. m. (1) Valentina, 1 s., 1 d., (2) Irina, 1 d. *Education:* Pegagogical Institute, Moscow. Publications (in English trans.): The Life and Extraordinary Adventures of Private Ivan Chonkin, 1977; The Ivankiad: The Tale of the Writer Voinovich's Installation in His New Apartment, 1977; In Plain Russian: Stories, 1979; Pretender to the Throne: The Further Adventures of Private Ivan Chonkin, 1981; The Anti-Soviet Soviet Union, 1986; Moscow 2042, 1987; The Fur Hat, 1989. *Honour:* Ford Foundation Grant, 1982. *Memberships:* Bavarian Acad. of Fine Arts; Mark Twain Society, hon. mem.; PEN, France. *Address:* Hans Carossastr 5, 8035 Stockdorf, Germany.

VOLDSETH, Beverly Ann; b. 23 Oct. 1935, Sioux Falls, South Dakota, USA. Teacher; Poet; Writer; Publisher. Ed. m. Robert R Allers, 26 June 1958, 3 d. *Education:* BA, English and Speech, 1957. *Appointments:* Teaching positions; Publisher and Ed., Black Hat Press. *Publications:* Absorb the Colors, 1984; I Am Becoming the Woman I Wanted, 1994; Tremors, Vibrations, 1995. *Contributions to:* Various publications. *Honour:* Lake Superior Writers Series Award, 1995. *Memberships:* The Loft; Northfield Womens Poets; Poets and Writers. *Address:* Box 12, 508 Second Ave, Goodhue, MN 55027, USA.

VOLK, Patricia (Gay); b. 16 July 1943, New York, NY, USA. Writer. m. Andrew Blitzer, 21 Dec. 1969, 1 s., 1 d. *Education:* BFA, cum laude, Syracuse University, 1964; Académie de la Grande Chaumière, Paris; School of Visual Arts, New York; New School, New York; Columbia University. *Appointments:* Copywriter to Senior Vice-Pres., Doyle Dane Bernbach Inc, 1969–88; Adjunct Instructor in Fiction, Yeshiva College, 1991; Columnist, Newsday, 1995–96. *Publications:* The Yellow Banana, 1985; White Light, 1987; All it Takes, 1990; Stuffed: Adventures of a Restaurant Family, 2001. *Contributions to:* Many publications. *Honours:* Stephen E. Kelly Award, 1983; Yaddo Fellowships, 1983, 1999; MacDowell Colony Fellowships, 1984, 2000. *Memberships:* Authors' Guild; PEN. *Address: c/o* Gloria Loomis, 133 E 35th St, New York, NY 10016, USA.

VOLKOW, Veronica; b. 26 April 1955, Mexico. Writer; Poet; Trans.; Art Critic. *Education:* Licentiate, Spanish Literature, 1978; MA, Comparative Literature, Columbia University, New York, 1981. *Publications:* La Sibila de Cumas, 1974; Litoral de Tinta, 1979; El Inicio, 1983; Diario de Sudafrica, 1988; Los Caminos, 1989. *Contributions to:* Vuelta; Sabado; Revista de la UNAM; La Jornada; Poesie 89. *Honours:* Salvador Novo Fellowship, 1977; International Writers Programme, 1985; Fellowship, Centro Mexicano de Escritores, 1991. *Address:* Cerro del Vigilante 191, Col Romero de Terreros, CP 04320, Mexico DF, Mexico.

VOLLMAR, James Anthony; b. 8 Jan. 1952, Wellingborough, Northamptonshire, England. Writer; Poet; Playwright. m. *Education:* Queen Mary College, University of London, 1970–72. *Appointment:* Founder, Ed., Greylag Press, 1977–. *Publications:* Circles and Spaces; Orkney Poems; Hoy: The Seven Postcards; Warming the Stones; Explorers Log Book. *Contributions to:* Agenda; Iron; Oasis; Joe Soaps Canoe; Ally; Pacific Quarterly; Ambit. *Membership:* Writers' Guild of Great Britain. *Address:* 7 Moreton Way, Kingsthorpe, Northampton NN2 8PD, England.

VOS, Ida; b. 13 Dec. 1931, Gröningen, The Netherlands. Author; Poet. m. Henk Vos, 3 April 1956, 2 s., 1 d. *Education:* Teacher training certificates, 1950, 1952. *Publications:* Wie niet weg is wordt Gezien, 1981, English trans. as Hide and Seek, 1991; Anna is er nog, 1986, English trans. as Anna Is Still There, 1993; Dansen op de brig can Avignon, 1989, English trans. as Dancing on the Bridge at Avignon, 1995; The Key is Lost, 2000. Other: Several other books and poems in Dutch. *Contributions to:* Periodicals. *Honours:* Many Dutch literary prizes. *Membership:* Dutch Writers' Asscn. *Address:* Dr Wibautlaan 6G, Rijswijk 2285XY, The Netherlands.

VROOMKONING, Victor. See: VAN DE LAAR, Waltherus Antonius Bernardinus.

W

WADDINGTON-FEATHER, John Joseph; b. 10 July 1933, Keighley, Yorkshire, England. Anglican Priest; Poet; Writer; Publisher. m. Sheila Mary Booker, 23 July 1960, 3 d. *Education:* BA, University of Leeds, 1954; PGCE, Keele, 1974; Ordination Certificate, Church of England, 1977. *Appointments:* Co-Ed., Orbis, 1971–80; Teacher, Shrewsbury Sixth Form College, 1981–83, Khartoum University, 1984–85; Hon. Chaplain, HM Prisons, 1977–; Chaplain, Prestfelde School, 1985–96; Dir, Feather Books; Ed., Poetry Church Magazine, Poetry Church Anthology, 1997–2002. *Publications:* Collection of Verse, 1964; Of Mills, Moors and Men, 1966; Garlic Lane, 1970; Easy Street, 1971; One Man's Road, 1977; Quill's Adventures in the Great Beyond, 1980; Tall Tales from Yukon, 1983; Khartoum Trilogy and Other Poems, 1985; Quill's Adventures in Wasteland, 1986; Quill's Adventures in Grozzieland, 1988; Six Christian Monologues, 1990; Six More Christian Poems, 1994; Shropshire, 1994; Feather's Foibles, 1995; Wild Tales from the West, 1999; The Museum Mystery, 1999; The Bradshaw Mystery, 2000; The Marcham Mystery, 2002; Yorkshire Dialect, 2002; Legends of Americaola, 2002; Grundy and Feather Hymn Series, Part I, 2002. *Contributions to:* Journals and magazines. *Honours:* Brontë Society Prize, 1966; Cyril Hodges Poetry Award, 1974; Carnegie Medal Nomination, 1988; Burton Prize, 1999. *Memberships:* Brontë Society, council mem., 1994–2000; RSA, fellow; Yorkshire Dialect Society; J. B. Priestley Society, chair., 1998–. *Address:* Fair View, Old Coppice, Lyth Bank, Shrewsbury, Shropshire SY3 0BW, England.

WAGNER-MARTIN, Linda; b. 18 Aug. 1936, St Marys, Ohio, USA. Prof. of English and Comparative Literature; Poet; Writer. *Education:* BA, Honours, English, 1957, MA, English, 1959, PhD, English, 1963, Bowling Green State University. *Appointments:* Instructor and Asst Prof., Bowling Green State University, 1961–66; Asst Prof., Wayne State University, 1966–68; Asst Prof. to Prof., Michigan State University, 1968–87; Hanes Prof. of English and Comparative Literature, University of North Carolina at Chapel Hill, 1988–. *Publications:* The Poems of William Carlos Williams: A Critical Study, 1964; Denise Levertov, 1967; Intaglios: Poems, 1967; The Prose of William Carlos Williams, 1970; Phyllis McGinley, 1971; Hemingway and Faulkner: Inventors/ Masters, 1975; Ernest Hemingway: A Reference Guide, 1977; William Carlos Williams: A Reference Guide, 1978; Dos Passos: Artist as American, 1979; American Modern: Selected Essays in Fiction and Poetry, 1980; Songs for Isadora: Poems, 1981; Ellen Glasgow; Beyond Convention, 1982; Sylvia Plath: A Biography, 1987; The Modern American Novel, 1914–1945, 1989; Wharton's The House of Mirth: A Novel of Admonition, 1990; Plath's the Bell Jar: A Novel of the Fifties, 1992; Telling Women's Lives: The New Biography, 1994; 'Favored Strangers': Gertrude Stein and Her Family, 1995; Wharton's The Age of Innocence: A Novel of Ironic Nostalgia, 1996; The Mid-Century American Novel, 1935–1965, 1997; Sylvia Plath: A Literary Life, 1999. Editor: William Faulkner: Four Decades of Criticism, 1973; Ernest Hemingway: Five Decades of Criticism, 1974; T S Eliot, 1976; 'Speaking Straight Ahead': Interviews with William Carlos Williams, 1976; Robert Frost: The Critical Heritage, 1977; Denise Levertov: In Her Own Province, 1979; Joyce Carol Oates: Critical Essays, 1979; Sylvia Plath: Critical Essays, 1984; Ernest Hemingway: Six Decades of Criticism, 1987; New Essays on Hemingway's The Sun Also Rises, 1987; Sylvia Plath: The Critical Heritage, 1988; Anne Sexton: Critical Essays, 1989; Denise Levertov: Critical Essays, 1991; The Oxford Companion to Women's Writing in the United States (with Cathy N Davidson), 1995; The Oxford Book of Women's Writing in the United States, 1995; New Essays to Faulkner's Go Down, Moses, 1996; Ernest Hemingway: Seven Decades of Criticism, 1998; Festchrift for Frederick Eckman (with David Adams), 1998; The Historical Guide to Ernest Hemingway, 1999. *Contributions to:* Scholarly books and journals. *Honours:* Guggenheim Fellowship, 1975–76; Bunting Institute Fellow, 1975–76; Rockefeller Foundation Fellow, Bellagio, Italy, 1990; Fellow, Institute for the Arts and Humanities, University of North Carolina, 1992; National Endowment for the Humanities Senior Fellowship, 1992–93; Teacher-Scholar Award, College English Asscn, 1994; Visiting Distinguished Prof., Emory University, 1994; Citation for Exceptional Merit, House of Representatives, Ohio, 1994; Brackenridge Distinguished Prof., University of Texas at San Antonio, 1998. *Memberships:* Ellen Glasgow Society, pres., 1982–87; Ernest Hemingway Foundation and Society, pres., 1993–96; MLA; Society for the Study of Midwestern Literature, pres., 1974–76; Society for the Study of Narrative Technique, pres., 1988–89. *Address:* c/o Dept of English, 3520 University of North Carolina at Chapel Hill, Chapel Hill, NC 27599, USA.

WAGONER, David (Russell); b. 5 June 1926, Massillon, Ohio, USA. Prof. of English; Poet; Author. m. (1) Patricia Parrott, 1961, divorced 1982, (2) Robin Heather Seyfried, 1982. *Education:* BA, Pennsylvania State University, 1947; MA, Indiana University, 1949. *Appointments:* Instructor, DePauw University, 1949–50, Pennsylvania State University, 1950–53; Asst Prof., 1954–57, Assoc. Prof., 1958–66, Prof. of English, 1966–, University of Washington, Seattle; Ed., Poetry Northwest, 1966–; Elliston Prof. of Poetry, University of Cincinnati, 1968. *Publications:* Poetry: Dry Sun, Dry Wind, 1953; A Place to Stand, 1958;

Poems, 1959; The Nesting Ground, 1963; Staying Alive, 1966; New and Selected Poems, 1969; Working Against Time, 1970; Riverbed, 1972; Sleeping in the Woods, 1974; A Guide to Dungeness Spit, 1975; Travelling Light, 1976; Collected Poems, 1956–1976, 1976; Who Shall be the Sun?: Poems Based on the Love, Legends, and Myths of Northwest Coast and Plateau Indians, 1978; In Broken Country, 1979; Landfall, 1981; First Light, 1983; Through the Forest: New and Selected Poems, 1977–1987, 1987; Traveling Light: Collected and New Poems, 1999. Fiction: The Man in the Middle, 1954; Money, Money, Money, 1955; Rock, 1958; The Escape Artist, 1965; Baby, Come on Inside, 1968; Where Is My Wandering Boy Tonight?, 1970; The Road to Many a Wonder, 1974; Tracker, 1975; Whole Hog, 1976; The Hanging Garden, 1980. Editor: Straw for the Fire: From the Notebooks of Theodore Roethke 1943–1963, 1972. *Honours:* Guggenheim Fellowship, 1956; Ford Foundation Fellowship, 1964; American Acad. of Arts and Letters Grant, 1967; National Endowment for the Arts Grant, 1969; Morton Dauwen Zabel Prize, 1967; Oscar Blumenthal Prize, 1974; Fels Prize, 1975; Eunice Tietjens Memorial Prize, 1977; English-Speaking Union Prize, 1980; Sherwood Anderson Prize, 1980; Pacific Northwest Booksellers Award, 2000. *Membership:* Acad. of American Poets, chancellor, 1978. *Address:* 5416 154th Pl. SW, Edmonds, WA 98026, USA.

WAHLBECK, Jan-Christer; b. 10 July 1948, Vasa, Finland. Psychologist; Family Therapist; Poet; Writer. m. Liisa Ryyppö, 1 Dec. 1978, 1 s., 2 d. *Education:* MA, 1976; Advanced Family Therapist, 1988; Organizational Consultant, 1988. *Publications:* Poetry: Steg På Hållplatsen, 1977; Bussen Stannar Bakom Hörnet, 1979; Mognadens Opera, 1981; Katastrof Efter Katastrof, 1984; Bilen Och Lidelserna, 1991; Huset Och Luftens Musik, 1993. Fiction: Näckrosor Och Bränt Vatten, 1983; Pojken Och Korpen, 1988. *Honour:* Villa Biaudet Fellowship, 1985–88. *Membership:* Finlandsswede Union of Writers. *Address:* Brunnsgatan 12, 06100 Borgå, Finland.

WAI MING (OTIS) WONG, (Nam Ching Tin, So Shun, Wong Chung); b. 21 Aug. 1954, Hong Kong. Civil Servant; Ed.; Poet; Critic. m. Lee Shu Hing, 6 March 1976, 3 s. *Education:* Diploma in English Language and Literature, Shue Yan College, 1981; MA, Chinese Language and Literature, Suzhou University, 2000. *Appointments:* Ed., Poetry, 1976–84, Shi Bi-Monthly, 1989–94, 1997–98; Ed.-in-Chief, Overseas Poetry Series, 1991–. *Publications:* Modern Poetry: East and West (ed.), 1981; Aesculus Chinensis, 1991; Modern Chinese Poetry Anthology (ed.), 1995; On Poets and Poetry, 1999. *Contributions to:* Various publications. *Honour:* International Order of Merit. *Memberships:* Hong Kong Archaeological Society; Shih Feng Asscn; Shi Bi-monthly Asscn. *Address:* PO Box 50431, Sai Ying Pun Post Office, Hong Kong.

WAINWRIGHT, Jeffrey; b. 19 Feb. 1944, Stoke on Trent, England. Poet; Dramatist; Trans.; Prof. m. Judith Batt, 22 July 1967, 1 s., 1 d. *Education:* BA, 1965, MA, 1967, University of Leeds. *Appointments:* Asst Lecturer, Lecturer, University of Wales, 1967–72; Visiting Instructor, Long Island University, 1970–71; Senior Lecturer, 1972–99, Prof., 1999–, Manchester Metropolitan University; Northern Theatre Critic, The Independent, 1988–99. *Publications:* Poetry: The Important Man, 1970; Heart's Desire, 1978; Selected Poems, 1985; The Red-Headed Pupil, 1994; Out of the Air, 1999. Other: Trans of various plays into English. *Contributions to:* Anthologies; BBC Radio; Many periodicals. *Honour:* Judith E Wilson Visiting Fellow, 1985. *Address:* 11 Hesketh Ave, Didsbury, Manchester M20 2QN, England.

WAKOSKI, Diane; b. 3 Aug. 1937, Whittier, CA, USA. Poet; Prof. of English. m. Robert J Turney, 14 Feb. 1982. *Education:* BA, English, University of California at Berkeley, 1960. *Appointments:* Poet-in-Residence, Prof. of English, 1975–, University Distinguished Prof., 1990–, Michigan State University; Many visiting writer-in-residencies. *Publications:* Poetry: Coins and Coffins, 1962; Discrepancies and Apparitions, 1966; The George Washington Poems, 1967; Inside the Blood Factory, 1968; The Magellanic Clouds, 1970; The Motorcycle Betrayal Poems, 1971; Smudging, 1972; Dancing on the Grave of a Son of a Bitch, 1973; Virtuoso Literature for Two and Four Hands, 1975; Waiting for the King of Spain, 1976; The Man Who Shook Hands, 1978; Cap of Darkness, 1980; The Magician's Feastletters, 1982; The Collected Greed, 1984; The Rings of Saturn, 1986; Emerald Ice: Selected Poems 1962–1987, 1988; Medea the Sorceress, 1991; Jason the Sailor, 1993; The Emerald City of Las Vegas, 1995; Argonaut Rose, 1998; The Butcher's Apron: New and Selected Poems, 2000. Criticism: Towards a New Poetry, 1980. *Contributions to:* Anthologies and other publications. *Honours:* Cassandra Foundation Grant, 1970; Guggenheim Fellowship, 1972; National Endowment for the Arts Grant, 1973; Writer's Fulbright Award, 1984; Michigan Arts Council Grant, 1988; William Carlos Williams Prize, 1989; Distinguished Artist Award, Michigan Arts Foundation, 1989. *Memberships:* Author's Guild; PEN; Poetry Society of America. *Address:* 607 Division St, East Lansing, MI 48823, USA.

WALCOTT, Derek (Alton); b. 23 Jan. 1930, Castries, St Lucia. Poet; Dramatist; Visiting Prof. m. (1) Fay Moyston, 1954, divorced 1959, 1 s., (2) Margaret Ruth Maillard, 1962, divorced, 2 d., (3) Norline Metivier, 1982. *Education:* St Mary's College, Castries, 1941–47; BA, University of the West Indies, Jamaica, 1953. *Appointments:* Teacher, St Mary's College, Castries, 1947–50, 1954, Grenada Boy's Secondary School, St George's, 1953–54, Jamaica College, Kingston, 1955; Feature Writer, Public Opinion, Kingston, 1956–57; Founder-Dir, Little Carib Theatre Workshop, later Trinidad Theatre Workshop, 1959–76; Feature Writer, 1960–62, Drama Critic, 1963–68, Trinidad Guardian, Port-of-Spain; Visiting Prof., Columbia University, 1981, Harvard University, 1982, 1987; Asst Prof. of Creative Writing, 1981, Visiting Prof., 1985–, Brown University. *Publications:* Poetry: 25 Poems, 1948; Epitaph for the Young: XII Cantos, 1949; Poems, 1951; In a Green Night: Poems 1948–1960, 1962; Selected Poems, 1964; The Castaway and Other Poems, 1965; The Gulf and Other Poems, 1969; Another Life, 1973; Sea Grapes, 1976; The Star-Apple Kingdom, 1979; Selected Poems, 1981; The Fortunate Traveller, 1981; The Caribbean Poetry of Derek Walcott and the Art of Romare Bearden, 1983; Midsummer, 1984; Collected Poems 1948–1984, 1986; The Arkansas Testament, 1987; Omeros, 1989; Collected Poems, 1990; Poems 1965–1980, 1992; Derek Walcott: Selected Poems, 1993; Tiepolo's Hounds, 2000. Plays: Cry for a Leader, 1950; Senza Alcun Sospetto or Paolo and Francesca, 1950; Henri Christophe: A Chronicle, 1950; Robin and Andrea or Bim, 1950; Three Assassins, 1951; The Price of Mercy, 1951; Harry Dernier, 1952; The Sea at Dauphin, 1954; Crossroads, 1954; The Charlatan, 1954; The Wine of the Country, 1956; The Golden Lions, 1956; Ione: A Play with Music, 1957; Ti-Jean and His Brothers, 1957; Drums and Colours, 1958; Malcochon, or, The Six in the Rain, 1959; Jourmard, or, A Comedy till the Last Minute, 1959; Batai, 1965; Dream on Monkey Mountain, 1967; Franklin: A Tale of the Islands, 1969; In a Fine Castle, 1970; The Joker of Seville, 1974; O Babylon!, 1976; Remembrance, 1977; The Snow Queen, 1977; Pantomime, 1978; Marie Laveau, 1979; The Isle is Full of Noises, 1982; Beef, No Chicken, 1982; The Odyssey: A Stage Version, 1993. Non-Fiction: The Antilles: Fragments of Epic Memory: The Nobel Lecture, 1993; What the Twilight Says (essays), 1998. *Honours:* Rockefeller Foundation Grants, 1957, 1966, and Fellowship, 1958; Arts Advisory Council of Jamaica Prize, 1960; Guinness Award, 1961; Ingram Merrill Foundation Grant, 1962; Borestone Mountain Awards, 1964, 1977; Heinemann Awards, RSL, 1966, 1983; Cholmondeley Award, 1969; Eugene O'Neill Foundation Fellowship, 1969; Gold Hummingbird Medal, Trinidad, 1969; Obie Award, 1971; O.B.E., 1972; Guggenheim Fellowship, 1977; Welsh Arts Council International Writers Prize, 1980; John D. and Catherine T. MacArthur Foundation Fellowship, 1981; Los Angeles Times Book Prize, 1986; Queen's Gold Medal for Poetry, 1988; Nobel Prize for Literature, 1992. *Memberships:* American Acad. of Arts and Letters, hon. mem.; RSL, fellow. *Address:* 165 Duke of Edinburgh Ave, Diego Martin, Trinidad and Tobago.

WALDMAN, Anne; b. 2 April 1945, Millville, New Jersey, USA. Poet; Lecturer; Performer; Ed. *Education:* BA, Bennington College, 1966. *Appointments:* Ed., Angel Hair Magazine, 1965–, The World, 1966–78; Asst Dir, Poetry Project, St Marks Church In-the-Bowery, 1966–68; Dir, Poetry Project, New York City, 1968–78; Founder-Dir, Jack Kerouac School of Disembodied Poetics, Naropa Institute, Boulder, CO; Poetry readings and performance events worldwide. *Publications:* Journals and Dreams, 1976; First Baby Poems, 1983; Makeup on Empty Space, 1984; Invention, 1985; Skin Meat Bones, 1985; Blue Mosque, 1987; The Romance Thing, 1987–88; Helping the Dreamer: New and Selected Poems, 1966–1988; Iovis, 1993; Troubairitz, Kill or Cure, 1994; Iovis, Book II, 1996. Editor: The World Anthology, 1969; Another World, 1971; Nice to See You: Homage to Ted Berrigan, 1991; In and Out of This World: An Anthology of the St Marks Poetry Project, 1992; The Beat Book, 1996. *Contributions to:* Various publications. *Honours:* National Endowment for the Arts Grant, 1980; Achievement in Poetry Award, Bennington College Alumni, 1981. *Memberships:* Committee for International Poetry; PEN Poetry Society of America. *Address:* c/o The Naropa Institute, 2130 Arapahoe Ave, Boulder, CO 80302, USA.

WALDROP, Rosmarie; b. 24 Aug. 1935, Kitzingen-am-Main, Germany. Poet; Writer; Trans.; Ed.; Publisher. m. Keith Waldrop, 20 Jan. 1959. *Education:* University of Wurzburg, 1954–56; University of Aix-Marseille, 1956–57; University of Freiburg, 1957–58; MA, 1960, PhD, 1966, Comparative Literature, University of Michigan. *Appointments:* Wesleyan University, 1964–70; Co-Ed. and Co-Publisher (with Keith Waldrop), Burning Desk Press, 1968–; Visiting Assoc. Prof., Brown University, 1977–78, 1983, 1990–91; Visiting Lecturer, Tufts University, 1979–81. *Publications:* Poetry: The Aggressive Ways of the Casual Stranger, 1972; The Road Is Everywhere or Stop This Body, 1978; When They Have Senses, 1980; Nothing Has Changed, 1981; Differences for Four Hands, 1984; Streets Enough to Welcome Snow, 1986; The Reproduction of Profiles, 1987; Shorter American Memory, 1988; Peculiar Motions, 1990; Lawn of Excluded Middle, 1993; A Key Into the Language of America, 1994; Another Language: Selected Poems, 1997; Split Infinites, 1998; Reluctant Gravities, 1999. Fiction: The Hanky of Pippin's Daughter, 1986; A Form/ of Taking/ It All, 1990. Essays: Against Language?, 1971; The Ground Is the Only Figure: Notebook Spring, 1996, 1997. Other: Various poetry chapbooks and trans. *Honours:* Major Hopwood Award in Poetry, 1963; Alexander von Humboldt Fellowships, 1970–71, 1975–76;

Howard Foundation Fellowship, 1974–75; Columbia University Trans. Center Award, 1978; National Endowment for the Arts Fellowships, 1980, 1984; Governor's Arts Award, RI, 1988; Fund for Poetry Award, 1990; PEN/Book-of-the-Month Club Citation in Trans., 1991; Deutscher Akademische Austauschdienst Fellowship, Berlin, 1993; Harold Morton Landon Trans. Award, 1994; Chevalier des Arts et des Lettres, France, 1999; Lila Wallace Reader's Digest Writer's Award, 1999–2001; Chevalier des Arts et Lettres 1999. *Membership:* PEN. *Address:* 71 Elmgrove Ave, Providence RI 02906 USA.

WALKER, Alice (Malsenior); b. 9 Feb. 1944, Eatonton, GA, USA. Author Poet. m. Melvyn R Leventhal, 17 March 1967, divorced 1976, 1 d. *Education:* BA, Sarah Lawrence College, 1966. *Appointments:* Writer-in-Residence and Teacher of Black Studies, Jackson State College, 1968–69, Tougaloo College 1970–71; Lecturer in Literature, Wellesley College, 1972–73; University o Massachusetts at Boston, 1972–73; Distinguished Writer, Afro-American Studies Dept, University of California at Berkeley, 1982; Fannie Hurst Prof of Literature, Brandeis University, 1982; Co-Founder and Publisher, Wild Trees Press, Navarro, CA, 1984–88. *Publications:* Once, 1968; The Third Life of Grange Copeland, 1970; Five Poems, 1972; Revolutionary Petunias and Other Poems, 1973; In Love and Trouble, 1973; Langston Hughes: American Poet, 1973; Meridian, 1976; Goodnight, Willie Lee, I'll See You in the Morning 1979; You Can't Keep a Good Woman Down, 1981; The Color Purple, 1982; In Search of Our Mother's Gardens, 1983; Horses Make a Landscape Look More Beautiful, 1984; To Hell With Dying, 1988; Living by the Word: Selected Writings, 1973–1987, 1988; The Temple of My Familiar, 1989; Her Blue Body Everything We Know: Earthling Poems, 1965–1990, 1991; Finding the Green Stone, 1991; Possessing the Secret of Joy, 1992; Warrior Marks (with Pratibha Parmar), 1993; Double Stitch: Black Women Write About Mothers and Daughters (with others), 1993; Everyday Use, 1994; By the Light of My Father's Smile, 1998; The Way Forward is with a Broken heart, 2000. Editor: I Love Myself When I'm Laughing... And Then Again When I'm Looking Mean and Impressive, 1979. *Honours:* Bread Loaf Writer's Conference Scholar, 1966: Ingram Merrill Foundation Fellowship, 1967; McDowell Colony Fellowships, 1967, 1977–78; National Endowment for the Arts Grants, 1969, 1977; Richard and Hinda Rosenthal Pound Award, American Acad. and Institute of Arts and Letters, 1974; Guggenheim Fellowship, 1977–78; Pulitzer Prize for Fiction, 1983; American Book Award, 1983; O Henry Award, 1986; Nora Astorga Leadership Award, 1989; Freedom to Write Award, PEN Center, West, 1990; Hon. doctorates. *Address:* c/o Wendy Weil Agency Inc, 232 Madison Ave, Suite 1300, New York, NY 10016, USA.

WALKER, J. Brenda; b. 15 April 1934, Liverpool, England. Poet; Trans.; Publisher. m. Jolyon William Wilsone Walker, 28 July 1956, deceased Nov. 1995, 2 s., 3 d. *Education:* Teacher's Certificate, Hull, 1964; BA, Honours, English Literature, 1977, MA, Educational Psychology, 1981, University of Keele. *Appointments:* Senior Lecturer, Avery Hill College of Education, 1970–76; Head Teacher, London Borough of Waltham Forest, 1976–87; Dir, Forest Books, 1988–. *Publications:* Mind Games, 1989; Night Train, 1994. Other: Poetry trans and co-trans/transformations from Romanian, Bulgarian, Urdu, Hindi and Arabic, 1984–96. *Contributions to:* Numerous newspapers and magazines worldwide. *Honours:* New Venture Award, Women in Publishing, 1987; Howard Sargant Award for Services to Poetry, 1990; Romanian Writers Union Award for Translating and Publishing, 1990. *Memberships:* Poetry Society; Society of Authors. *Address:* 20 Forest View, Chingford, London E4 7AY, England.

WALKER, Jeanne Murray; b. 27 May 1944, Parkers Prairie, Minnesota, USA. Prof. of English; Poet; Dramatist; Writer. m. E Daniel Larkin, 16 July 1983, 1 s., 1 d. *Education:* BA, Wheaton College, IL, 1966; MA, Loyola University, Chicago, 1969; PhD, University of Pennsylvania, 1974. *Appointments:* Asst Prof. of English, Haverford College, Pennsylvania; Prof. of English, University of Delaware. *Publications:* Poetry: Nailing Up the Home Sweet Home, 1980; Fugitive Angels, 1985; Coming Into History, 1990; Stranger Than Fiction, 1992; Gaining Time, 1997. Other: 8 plays, 1990–2001. *Contributions to:* Numerous reviews, quarterlies, journals, and periodicals including: Poetry, Shenandoah, Prairie Schooner; American Poetry Review; The Nation; Georgia Review; The Kenyon Review. *Honours:* Delaware Humanities Council Grant, 1979; Delaware Arts Council Grant, 1981; 6 Pennsylvania Council on the Arts Fellowships, 1983–2001; Prairie Schooner/ Strousse Award, 1988; Winner, Washington National Theatre Competition, 1990; Colladay Award for Poetry, 1992; Fellow, Center for Advanced Studies, 1993; National Endowment for the Arts Fellowship, 1994; Lewis Prizes for New Plays, Brigham Young Theatre, 1995, 1997; Stagetime Award, PEW Fellow in the Arts, 1998. *Memberships:* Dramatists' Guild; PEN; Poets and Writers. *Address:* c/o Dept of English, 127 Memorial Hall, University of Delaware, Newark, DE 19716, USA.

WALKER, Ted; b. 28 Nov. 1934, Lancing, England. Poet; Writer; Prof. Emeritus. m. (1) Lorna Ruth Benfell, 11 Aug. 1956, deceased 1987, 2 s., 2 d., (2) Audrey Joan Hicks, 8 July 1988. *Education:* MA, St John's College, Cambridge, 1956. *Appointments:* Prof. of Creative Writing and English Literature, 1971–92, Prof. Emeritus, 1992–, New England College, Arundel. *Publications:* Fox on a Barn Door (poems); The Solitaries (poems); The Night

Bathers (poems); Gloves to the Hangman (poems); Burning the Ivy (poems); The Lion's Cavalcade (children's verse); The High Path (autobiography); In Spain (travel); You've Never Heard Me Sing (short stories); Hands at a Live Fire (selected poems); The Last of England (autobiography); Grandad's Seagulls (children's verse); Mangoes on the Moon (poems), 1999; He Danced with a Chair (short stories), 2001. *Contributions to:* The New Yorker; Atlantic Monthly; McCall's; The London Magazine; Spectator; New Statesman; Virginia Quarterly. *Contributions to:* Reviews, quarterlies and magazines. *Honours:* Eric Gregory Award; Cholmondeley Award; Hon. DLitt, University of Southampton, 1995. *Membership:* Fellow, RSL. *Address:* 7 The Village, 03728 Alcalali, Alicante, Spain.

WALKER, Wendy Alison; b. 25 Jan. 1951, New York, NY, USA. Writer; Poet. m. Tom La Farge, 26 Nov. 1982. *Education:* AB, cum laude, Harvard University, 1972; MA, Teachers College, Columbia University, 1974. *Appointment:* Adjunct Assoc. Prof. of Writing, Hofstra University, 1995–2000. *Publications:* The Sea-Rabbit, or, The Artist of Life, 1988; The Secret Service, 1992; Stories Out of Omarie, 1995. *Contributions to:* Conjunctions; Parnassus: Poetry in Review; Ironwood; Fiction International; Chain; Facture. *Honours:* IAFA Crawford Award, 1994; Gertrude Stein Award, 1994–95; National Book Award Nominee, 1995. *Membership:* PEN. *Address:* 855 West End Ave, No. 6A, New York, NY 10025, USA. *E-mail:* wwalker102@aol.com.

WALKER MURRAY, Jeanne; b. 27 May 1944, Parkers Prairie, Minnesota, USA. Prof. of English; Poet; Writer. m. 16 July 1983, 1 s., 1 d. *Education:* BA, English, Wheaton College, IL; MA, English, Loyola University, Chicago; PhD, English, University of Pennsylvania, Philadelphia. *Appointments:* Asst Prof., English, Haverford College, Pennsylvania; Prof., English, University of Delaware, Newark. *Publications:* Nailing Up The Home Sweet Home, 1980; Fugitive Angels, 1985; Coming Into History, 1990; Stranger Than Fiction, 1992; Gaining Time, 1998. *Contributions to:* American Scholar; Arizona Quarterly; American Poetry Review; Aspen Anthology; Ariel; Poetry Miscellany; Jawbone; Carolina Quarterly; Chicago Tribune; Christian Science Monitor; Cimarron Review; Chariton Review; Critical Quarterly; Georgia Review; Southern Humanities Review; Iowa Review; Kenyon Review; Louisville Review; Lyric; Massachusetts Review; Milkweed Chronicle; Descant; Northwest Review; Christian Century; New England Review; Nantucket Review; Wascona Review; Poet and Critic; 2 Plus 2: Poetry Now; St Andrews Review; Pennsylvania Review; Kansas Quarterly; Seattle Review; Poetry; Shenendoah; Painted Bride Quarterly; Whetstone; Boulevard; Partisan Review. *Honours:* Fellowship, Delaware Arts Council, 1980; Fellowships, Pennsylvania Council on the Arts, 1984, 1987, 1989, 1991; Strousse Award, Best Sequence of Poems, Prairie Schooner, 1988; Fellow, Center for Advanced Studies, 1993; NEA Fellowship, 1994; Pew Fellow in the Arts, 1998. *Memberships:* PEN; Poets and Writers; American Poetry Center; Dramatists Guild; Chrysostom Society. *Address:* University of Delaware, Newark, DE 19711, USA.

WALLACE, Naomi (French); b. 17 Aug. 1960, Kentucky, USA. Poet; Dramatist; Writer. m. Bruce McLeod, 3 d. *Education:* BA, Hampshire College, 1982; MFA, University of Iowa, 1986. *Publications:* To Dance a Stony Field (poems), 1995; Slaughter City (play), 1996; Birdy (play), 1997; One Flea Spare (play), 1997. *Honours:* Obie Award, Village Voice; Susan Smith Blackburn Award; Discovery Award, The Nation; Fellowship of Southern Writers Award. *Address:* PO Box 750, Prospect, KY 40059, USA.

WALLACE, Ronald William; b. 18 Feb. 1945, Cedar Rapids, IA, USA. Poet; Prof. of English. m. Margaret Elizabeth McCreight, 3 Aug. 1968, 2 d. *Education:* BA, College of Wooster, 1967; MA, 1968, PhD, 1971, University of Michigan. *Appointments:* Dir of Creative Writing, University of Wisconsin, Madison, 1975–; Series Ed., Brittingham Prize in Poetry, 1985–; Dir, Wisconsin Institute for Creative Writing, 1986–. *Publications:* Henry James and the Comic Form, 1975; Installing the Bees, 1977; Cucumbers, 1977; The Last Laugh, 1979; The Facts of Life, 1979; Plums, Stones, Kisses and Hooks, 1981; Tunes for Bears to Dance to, 1983; God Be With the Clown, 1984; The Owl in the Kitchen, 1985; People and Dog in the Sun, 1987; Vital Signs, 1989; The Makings of Happiness, 1991; Time's Fancy, 1994; The Uses of Adversity, 1998; Quick Bright Things, 2000. *Contributions to:* New Yorker; Atlantic; Nation; Poetry; Southern Review; Poetry Northwest. *Honours:* Hopwood Award for Poetry, 1970; Council for Wisconsin Writers Awards, 1978, 1979, 1984, 1985, 1986, 1988; Helen Bullis Prize in Poetry, 1985; Robert E Gard Award for Excellence in Poetry, 1990; Posner Poetry Prize, 1992; Gerald A Bartell Award in the Arts, 1994; Felix Pollak Prof. of Poetry. *Memberships:* Poets and Writers; Associated Writing Programs. *Address:* Dept of English, University of Wisconsin, Madison, WI 53706, USA.

WALLACE-CRABBE, Chris(topher Keith); b. 6 May 1934, Richmond, Vic., Australia. Prof. of English; Poet; Writer. m. (1) Helen Margaret Wiltshire, 1957, 1 s., 1 d., (2) Marianne Sophie Feil, 1979, 2 s. *Education:* BA, 1956, MA, 1964, University of Melbourne. *Appointments:* Reader in English, 1976–88, Prof. of English, 1988–, University of Melbourne. *Publications:* Poetry: No Glass Houses, 1956; The Music of Division, 1959; Eight Metropolitan Poems, 1962; In Light and Darkness, 1964; The Rebel General, 1967; Where the Wind Came, 1971; Act in the Noon, 1974; The Shapes of Gallipoli, 1975; The Foundations of

Joy, 1976; The Emotions Are Not Skilled Workers, 1979; The Amorous Cannibal and Other Poems, 1985; I'm Deadly Serious, 1988; Selected Poems 1956–1994, 1995. Novel: Splinters, 1981. Other: Melbourne or the Bush: Essays on Australian Literature and Society, 1973; Author! Author!, 1999. Editor: Vols of Australian poetry. *Honours:* Masefield Prize for Poetry, 1957; Grace Levin Prize, 1986; Dublin Prize, 1987; Christopher Brennan Award, 1990; Age Book of the Year Prize, 1995. *Address:* c/o Dept of English, University of Melbourne, Melbourne, Vic. 3052, Australia.

WALLENSTEIN, Barry; b. 13 Feb. 1940, New York, NY, USA. Poet; Prof. of English. m. Lorna Harbus, 19 March 1978, 1 s., 1 d. *Education:* BA, 1962, MA, 1963, PhD, 1972, New York University. *Appointments:* Prof. of English, City College of the City University of New York, 1965–; Exchange Prof., University of Paris, 1981, Polytechnic of North London, 1987–88; Writer-in-Residence, University of North Michigan, 1993. *Publications:* Poetry: Beast is a Wolf with Brown Fire, 1977; Roller Coaster Kid, 1982; Love and Crush, 1991; The Short Life of the Five Minute Dancer, 1993; A Measure of Conduct, 1999. Criticism: Visions and Revisions: An Approach to Poetry, 1971. *Contributions to:* Anthologies, reviews, quarterlies, and journals. *Honours:* City University of New York Research Fund Grant; MacDowell Colony Residency Fellowship. *Memberships:* Acad. of American Poets; Poets and Writers; Poets House. *Address:* 340 Riverside Dr., New York, NY 10025, USA.

WALSER, Martin; b. 24 March 1927, Wasserburg, Bodensee, Germany. Writer; Playwright; Poet. m. Käthe Jehle, 1950, 4 d. *Education:* Theologisch-Philosophische Hochschule, Regensburg; DPhil, University of Tübingen. *Publications:* Ehen in Philippsburg, 1957; Halbzeit, 1960; Das Einhorn, 1966; Fiction, 1970; Die Gallistlische Krankheit, 1972; Der Sturz, 1973; Jenseits der Liebe, 1976; Ein fliehendes Pferd, 1978; Seelenarbeit, 1979; Das Schwanenhaus, 1980; Brief an Lord Liszt, 1982; Brandung, 1985; Dorle und Wolf, 1987; Jagd, 1988; Die Verteidigung der Kindheit, 1991; Ohne einander, 1993; Finks Krieg, 1996; Ein springender Brunnen, 1998; Tod Eines Kritikers, 2002. Short Stories: Ein Flugzeug über dem Haus, 1955; Lügengeschichten, 1964. Plays: Der Abstecher, 1961; Eiche und Angora, 1962; Überlebensgross Herr Krott, 1963; Der schwarze Schwan, 1964; Die Zimmerschlacht, 1967; Ein Kinderspiel, 1970; Das Sauspiel, 1975; In Goethe's Hand, 1982; Die Ohrfeige, 1986; Das Sofa, 1992; Kaschmir in Parching, 1995. Essays: Beschreibung einer Form, Versuch über Franz Kafka, 1961; Erfahrungen und Leseerfahrungen, 1965; Heimatkunde, 1968; Wie und wovon handelt Literatur, 1973; Wer ist ein Schriftsteller, 1978; Selbstbewusstsein und Ironie, 1981; Messmers Gedanken, 1985; Über Deutschland reden, 1988; Vormittag eines Schriftstellers, 1994. Poetry: Der Grund zur Freude, 1978. *Honours:* Group 47 Prize, 1955; Hermann-Hesse Prize, 1957; Gerhart-Hauptmann Prize, 1962; Schiller Prize, 1980; Büchner Prize, 1981; Friedenspreis des Deutschen Buchhandels, 1998; Grasses Bundesverdienstkreuz mit Stern. *Address:* 88662 Überlingen-Nussdorf, Zum Hecht 36, Germany. *Telephone:* (7551) 4131. *Fax:* (7551) 68494.

WALTER, Colin; b. 23 Sept. 1940, Maidstone, Kent, England. Educator; Writer; Poet. m. Cheryl Anne Osborne, 2 Oct. 1965, 2 d. *Education:* BEd, Honours, 1972, MA, 1976, University of London. *Publications:* Inhabiting Poetry: A Formal Contribution to the Debate Upon Teaching Poetry, 1988; An Early Start to Poetry, 1989; Introduction to BP Teacher: Poetry Resources Files for Primary and Secondary Schools, 1992. *Contributions to:* Educational journals. *Honours:* Fellow, RSA; Fellow, College of Preceptors. *Membership:* Poetry Society. *Address:* 59 The Highway, Chelsfield, Near Orpington, Kent BR6 9DQ, England.

WALTER, Hugo; b. 12 March 1959, Philadelphia, Pennsylvania, USA. College Prof. *Education:* BA, Princeton University, 1981; PhD in Literature, Yale University, 1985; MA, Old Dominion University, 1989; PhD in Humanities, Drew University, 1996. *Appointments:* Instructor, Yale University, 1983–85; Asst Prof., Rhodes College, 1986–87; University of Missouri, 1987–88; Washington and Jefferson College, 1989–92, Fairleigh Dickinson University, 1992–96; Asst Prof. of Humanities, GMI Engineering and Management Institute, 1996–. *Publications:* Amber Blossoms and Evening Shadows, 1990; Golden Thorns of Light and Sterling Silhouettes, 1991; Waiting for Babel: Prophecies of Sunflower Dreams, 1992; Along the Maroon-Prismed Threshold of Bronze-Pealing Eternity, 1992; The Light of the Dance is the Music of Eternity, 1993; Dusk-Gloaming Mirrors and Castle- Winding Dreams, 1994; Amaranth-Sage Epiphanies of Dusk-Weaving Paradise, 1995. *Memberships:* American Asscn of Poets; International Society of Poets. *Address:* Dept of Humanities, GMI Engineering Institute, 1700 W Third Ave, Flint, MI 48504, USA.

WALWICZ, Ania; b. 19 May 1951, Swidnica, Poland (Naturalized Australian citizen). Poet; Dramatist; Writer; Artist. *Education:* Diploma in Education, University of Melbourne, 1984; Diploma and Graduate Diploma, Victorian College of the Arts. *Appointments:* Writer-in-Residence, Deakin University and Murdoch University, 1987–88. *Publications:* Writing, 1982; Boat, 1989. Plays: Girlboytalk, 1986; Dissecting Mice, 1989; Elegant, 1990; Red Roses, 1992; Telltale, 1994. *Contributions to:* 85 anthologies. *Honours:* Australian Council Literature Board grants, and Fellowship, 1990; New Writing Prize, Victorian Premier's Literary Awards, 1990. *Address:* Unit 40, 26 Victoria St, Melbourne, Vic. 3065, Australia.

WANDOR, Michelene Dinah; b. 20 April 1940, London, England. Writer; Poet; Dramatist; Critic; Musician. m. Edward Victor, 1963, divorced, 2 s. *Education:* BA, Honours, English, Newnham College, Cambridge, 1962; MA, Sociology of Literature, University of Essex, 1976; LTCL, DipTCL, Trinity College of Music, London, 1993; MMus, University of London, 1997. *Appointment:* Poetry Ed., Time Out Magazine, 1971–82; Senior Lecturer, University of North London, 1998. *Publications:* Cutlasses and Earrings (ed. and contributor), 1977; Carry on Understudies, 1981; Upbeat, 1981; Touch Papers, 1982; Five Plays, 1984; Gardens of Eden, 1984; Routledge, 1986; Look Back in Gender, 1987; Guests in the Body, 1987; Drama 1970–1990, 1993; Gardens of Eden Revisited, 1999; Post-War British Drama: Looking Back in Gender, 2000. *Contributions to:* Periodicals. *Honour:* International Emmy, 1987. *Membership:* Society of Authors. *Address:* 71 Belsize Lane, London NW3 5AU, England.

WANIEK, Marilyn Nelson. See: NELSON, Marilyn.

WANSBROUGH, David James; b. 15 April 1948, New Zealand. Writer; Poet; Painter. m. Roslyn Jones, 5 s., 2 d. *Education:* DipEd, Auckland Teacher's College, 1971; LicTheol, 1980, PhL, 1981, Seminary of St Basil, Australia; DD, Collegium Sancti Spiritus, 1992; DTh, St Ephrems Institute, 1995. *Appointments:* Dir, Australian Institute of Contemporary Studies, 1979–81; Exec. Dir, later Deputy Chair., Gavemer Foundation Ltd, 1985–; Exec. Dir, Arunta Group of Cos, 1987–; Chair., Neemoil Australia Pty Ltd, 1990–93; Dir, Scitec Communications Corpn, 1991–92; Visiting Prof., M. V. Lomonosov College, Moscow State University, 1993–; Visiting Lecturer, Institute for Pedagogical Innovations of the Russian Acad. for Education, 1996; Australia Society Inaugural Lecture, 1999; Lecture, Lenin Library, Moscow, 2000. *Publications:* On the Lip of the Pit, 1980; Seeing Through, 1981; Poetry for a Human-Centered Education, 1985; Word Weaving, 1987; A Pillar of Salt?, 1988; At the Edge of Darkness, 1989; Festivals, Seasons and The Southern Sun, 1991; Moscow: Journey into the Heart, 1993; Dreams, Delights, Fears, Fragments, 1996; Christianity: An Impulse of East and West, 1997; Whispers, 2000; Bulgarkov's Migraine, 2001. *Honours:* Hon. Resurgent Prisoner, Parramatta Gaol, 1975; Alfred Nobel Commemmorative Medal, 1988; Medal, Albert Einstein International Acad., 1991; Hon. DLitt, Academie des Sciences, Humaines Universelles, 1992; International Order of Merit, 1992; Diplome D'Honneur, Institut des Affaires Internationalis, 1993; Poetry Cup, New South Wales Writers' Centre, 1993. *Memberships:* Australia Society, hon. life mem.; China Education Centre, University of Sydney, patron; International Acad. of Poets, fellow; Live Poets Society; Poets' Union; Regenisis Therapeutic Community, patron; World Literary Acad., life fellow. *Address:* PO Box 424, St Leonards, NSW 2065, Australia.

WARD, David John; b. 4 Nov. 1949, Northampton, England. Poet. m. Frieda Nyahoe, 26 May 1972, 3 s., 1 d. *Education:* BA, Honours, English, University of Lancaster. *Appointments:* Co-ordinator, Windows Poetry Project; Ed., Smoke, poetry magazine. *Publications:* Jambo, 1993; Candy and Jazzz, 1994; Tracts, 1996. *Contributions to:* Poetry Review; Transatlantic Review; Poetry Wales; University of Toronto Review; Die Horen, Germany. *Memberships:* University of Lancaster Literary Society, chair; Nemo Poets, Northampton; John Clare Society; Halewood Arts Asscn, secretary. *Address:* 22 Roseheath Dr., Halewood, Merseyside L26 9UH, England.

WARD, John Hood; b. 16 Dec. 1915, Newcastle upon Tyne, England. Civil Service Senior Principal (retd); Writer; Poet. m. Gladys Hilda Thorogood, 27 July 1940, 1 s., 2 d. *Education:* Royal Grammar School, Newcastle, 1925–33. *Appointment:* Senior Principal, Dept of Health and Social Security, –1978. *Publications:* A Late Harvest, 1982; The Dark Sea, 1983; A Kind of Likeness, 1985; The Wrong Side of Glory, 1986; A Song at Twilight, 1989; Grandfather Best and the Protestant Work Ethic, 1991; Tales of Love and Hate, 1993; The Brilliance of Light, 1994; Winter Song, 1995; Selected Poems, 1968–95, 1996. *Contributions to:* Anthologies and periodicals. *Honours:* Imperial Service Order, 1977; Poetry Prize, City of Westminster Arts Council, 1977; Open Poetry Prize, Wharfedale Music Festival, 1978; Lancaster Festival Prizes, 1982, 1987, 1988, 1989, 1994, 1995; First Prize, Bury Open Poetry Competition, 1987; First Prizes, High Peak Open Competition, 1988, 1989; First Prize, May and Alfred Wilkins Memorial Prize, 1995. *Memberships:* Manchester Poets; Society of Civil Service Authors.

WARD, John Powell; b. 28 Nov. 1937, Suffolk, England. Poet. m. Sarah Woodfull Rogers, 16 Jan. 1965, 2 s. *Education:* BA, University of Toronto, 1959; BA, 1961, MA, 1969, University of Cambridge; MSc, Economics, University of Wales, 1969. *Appointments:* Lecturer in Education, 1963–84, Lecturer in English, 1985–86, Senior Lecturer in English, 1986–88, Hon. Research Fellow, 1988–, University of Wales, Swansea; Ed., Poetry Wales, 1975–80. *Publications:* The Other Man, 1970; The Line of Knowledge, 1972; From Alphabet to Logos, 1972; Things, 1980; To Get Clear, 1981; The Clearing, 1984; A Certain Marvellous Thing, 1993; Genesis, 1996; Late Thoughts in March, 1999. *Contributions to:* Reviews, quarterlies, journals, magazines, and BBC Radio 3 and 4. *Honours:* Poetry Prize, Welsh Arts Council, 1985; Fellow, Welsh Acad., 2000. *Address:* Ct Lodge, Horton Kirby, Dartford, Kent DA4 9BN, England.

WARDENÆR, Torild; b. 30 Nov. 1951, Stavanger, Norway. Poet; Writer; Playwright. 1 s. *Education:* BEd, 1982; University Degrees in Communication, Art History, Literature, 1989–93; Writers' Acad., Skrivekunstakademiet i Hordaland, 1992–93. *Publications:* Poetry: I Pionertiden (In the Pioneer Time), 1994; Null Komma to Lux (Zero Point Two Lux), 1995; Houdini til Minne (In Memory of Houdini), 1997; Døgndrift, 1998, English trans. as The Drift of Days and Nights, 1999; Titanporten, 2001, English trans. as The Titan Gate, 2001. Plays: Sebramannen (The Zebra-man), 1998; Ikke et hvilket som helst intermezzo (Not an Ordinary Intermezzo), 1998; Drømmekasper (Kasper the Dreamer), 1999. Translator: Gnomens liksvøp, by James Tate; Selected Poems in Translation, by James Tate. Other: Collaborations with musicians, actors, visual artists and photographers; Readings, book days, festivals, television and radio appearances. *Contributions to:* Literary magazines and anthologies. *Honours:* Debut Prize, H. Aschehoug Eco, 1994; Brageprisen nomination, 1995; Herman Wildenvey Poetry Prize, 1997; Mats Wiel Nygaards Award, 1997; Fundación Valparaíso Grant, Spain, 1997; Norwegian Authors' Union Scholarships, 1995–2002; Halldis Moren Vesaas Prize, 1998; Fellowship Award, International Writers' Retreat, Hawthornden Castle, Scotland, Writer-in-Residence, 1999; Three-year Stipendium, Norwegian Authors' Union, 1999; Council of Stavanger Cultural Prize, 1999; H. A. Benneches Stipendium for skjønlitterært Forfatterskab, Norsk Videnskapsakademi, 1999. *Memberships:* Norwegian Authors' Union; PAN Poetry Society, board mem., 1995–. *Address:* Ordfører Scheies gt. 24, 4085 Hundvåg, Norway. *Telephone:* 51549693. *E-mail:* twardena@c2i.net. *Website:* kunst.no/torild/.

WARDMAN, Gordon Arthur; b. 16 Feb. 1948, England. Poet. m. Susan Connor, 25 Nov. 1972, 1 s., 1 d. *Education:* BA, Oriel College, Oxford, 1970; CQSW, University of Kent, 1972. *Publications:* Crispins Spur, 1985; Reparations, 1987; High Country Hank, 1993; The Newfoundland Cantos, 1994; Trolleytown, 1996; Smaller Thoughts, 1999; Harlowski, 1999; Caedmon, 2001. *Contributions to:* Numerous anthologies and magazines. *Address:* 86 Greenhills, Harlow, Essex CM20 3SZ, England.

WARNER, Francis, (Robert Le Plastrier); b. 21 Oct. 1937, Bishopthorpe, Yorkshire, England. Poet; Dramatist; Fellow; Tutor. m. (1) Mary Hall, 1958, divorced 1972, 2 d., (2) Penelope Anne Davis, 1983, 1 s., 1 d. *Education:* Christ's Hospital; London College of Music; BA, MA, St Catharine's College, Cambridge. *Appointments:* Supervisor in English, St Catharine's College, Cambridge, 1959–65; Staff Tutor in English, Cambridge University Board of Extra-Mural Studies, 1963–65; Fellow and Tutor, 1965–99, Fellow Librarian, 1966–76, Dean of Degrees, 1984–, Vice-Master, 1987–89, Emeritus Fellow, 1999–, St Peter's College, Oxford; University Lecturer, 1965–99, Pro-Proctor, 1989–90, 1996–97, 1999–2000, University of Oxford. *Publications:* Poetry: Perennia, 1962; Early Poems, 1964; Experimental Sonnets, 1965; Madrigals, 1967; The Poetry of Francis Warner, 1970; Lucca Quartet, 1975; Morning Vespers, 1980; Spring Harvest, 1981; Epithalamium, 1983; Collected Poems 1960–84, 1985; Nightingales: Poems 1985–96, 1997; Cambridge, 2001; Oxford, 2002. Plays: Maquettes: A Trilogy of One-Act Plays, 1972; Requiem: Part 1, Lying Figures, 1972, Part 2, Killing Time, 1976, Part 3, Meeting Ends, 1974; A Conception of Love, 1978; Light Shadows, 1980; Moving Reflections, 1983; Living Creation, 1985; Healing Nature: The Athens of Pericles, 1988; Byzantium, 1990; Virgil and Caesar, 1993; Agora: An Epic, 1994; King Francis First, 1995; Goethe's Weimar, 1997; Rembrandt's Mirror, 1999. Editor: Eleven Poems by Edmund Blunden, 1965; Garland, 1968; Studies in the Arts, 1968. *Contributions to:* Anthologies and journals. *Honours:* Messing International Award, 1972; Benemerenti Silver Medal, Knights of St George, Constantinian Order, Italy, 1990; Foreign Academician, Acad. of Letters and Arts, Portugal, 1993; Hon. Fellow, St Catherine's College, Cambridge, 1999. *Address:* St Peter's College, Oxford OX1 2DL, England; St Catherine's College, Cambridge, CB2 1RL, England.

WARNER, Val; b. 15 Jan. 1946, Middlesex, England. Writer; Poet. *Education:* BA, Somerville College, Oxford, 1968. *Appointments:* Writer-in-Residence, University College, Swansea, 1977–78, University of Dundee, 1979–81. *Publications:* These Yellow Photos, 1971; Under the Penthouse, 1973; The Centenary Corbiere (trans.), 1975; The Collected Poems and Prose of Charlotte Mew (ed.), 1981; Before Lunch, 1986; Tooting Idyll, 1998. *Contributions to:* Many journals and periodicals. *Honours:* Gregory Award for Poetry, 1975; Third Prize, Lincolnshire Literature Festival Poetry Competition, 1995. *Memberships:* PEN; RSL, fellow. *Address:* c/o Carcanet Press Ltd, Conavon Ct, Fourth Floor, 12–16 Blackfriars St, Manchester M3 5BQ, England. *E-mail:* valwarner@etce.freeserve.co.uk.

WARREN, Celia Rosemary; b. 17 Jan. 1953, England. Poet; Writer. m. Raymond John Albert Kenneth Warren, 20 Sept. 1975, 1 s., 1 d. *Education:* Certificate of Education, Loughborough College of Education, 1974. *Publications:* Pathways Series: A Fishy Tale, 1994; Meg's Mad Magnet, 1996; Skittles and Skullbone: The Skeletons, 1996; Fairground Toast and Buttered Fun, 1996; Damien and the Alien Socks, 1998; Where Oak Birds Sing, 2000; Scholastic Poetry Workshop KS1 (series ed. and author), 2000; Never Sit on a Squid, 2001; The Ant and the Dove (retold in verse), 2001; Vikings Don't Wear Pants (with Roger Stevens), 2001. *Contributions to:* Anthologies and periodicals; Online publications. *Honour:* Short-listed, Lichfield Prize, 1995.

Membership: Lichfield and District Writers. *Address:* 133 Gillway Lane, Tamworth, Staffordshire B79 8PN, England.

WARREN, James E(dward); b. 11 Dec. 1908, Atlanta, GA, USA. Teacher (retd); Writer; Poet. *Education:* BA, 1930, MAT, 1941, Emory University; Diploma, Yale Summer School, 1960. *Publications:* This Side of Babylon, 1938; Against the Furious Men, 1946; Selected Poems, 1967; Collected Poems, 1980; Poems of Lovett, 1986. Other: 12 poetry chapbooks, 1964–89. *Contributions to:* Many reviews, quarterlies, and journals. *Honours:* Poetry Society of America Prize, 1937; Barrow Prizes, Poetry Society of Georgia, 1945, 1947; Leitch Prize, Poetry Society of Virginia, 1967; Literary Achievement Award, Georgia Writers Asscn, 1967; Aurelia Austin Writer of the Year Award, Atlanta Writers Club, 1968; Governor's Award, GA, 1980. *Memberships:* Acad. of American Poets; Cum Laude Society; Georgia Writers Asscn; Poetry Society of America. *Address:* St Anne's Terrace, Apt 309, 3100 Northside Parkway NW, Atlanta, GA 30327, USA.

WARREN, Rosanna; b. 27 July 1953, Fairfield, CT, USA. Assoc. Prof. of English; Poet; Writer. m. Stephen Scully, 1981, 2 d., 1 step-s. *Education:* BA, summa cum laude, Yale University, 1976; MA, Johns Hopkins University, 1980. *Appointments:* Asst Prof., Vanderbilt University, 1981–82; Visiting Asst Prof., 1982–88, Asst Prof., 1989–95, Assoc. Prof. of English, 1995–, Boston University; Poetry Consultant and Contributing Ed., Partisan Review, 1985–; Poet-in-Residence, Robert Frost Farm, 1990. *Publications:* The Joey Story, 1963; Snow Day, 1981; Each Leaf Shines Separate, 1984; The Art of Translation: Voices from the Field (ed.), 1989; Stained Glass, 1993; Eugenio Montale's Cuttlefish Bones (ed.), 1993; Euripides' Suppliant Women (trans. with Stephen Scully), 1995; Eugenio Montale's Satura (ed.), 1998. *Contributions to:* Many journals and magazines. *Honours:* National Discovery Award in Poetry, 92nd Street YMHA-YWCA, New York City, 1980; Yaddo Fellow, 1980; Ingram Merrill Foundation Grants, 1983, 1993; Guggenheim Fellowship, 1985–86; ACLS Grant, 1989–90; Lavan Younger Poets Prize, 1992, and Lamont Poetry Prize, 1993, Acad. of American Poets; Lila Wallace Writers' Fund Award, 1994; Witter Bynner Prize in Poetry, American Acad. of Arts and Letters, 1994; May Sarton Award, New England Poetry Club, 1995. *Memberships:* Acad. of American Poets, board of chancellors, 1999–; MLA; American Literary Trans Asscn; Asscn of Literary Scholars and Critics; PEN. *Address:* c/o University Profs Program, Boston University, 745 Commonwealth Ave, Boston, MA 02215, USA.

WARSH, Lewis; b. 9 Nov. 1944, New York, NY, USA. Poet; Writer; Publisher; Teacher. m. Bernadette Mayer, Nov. 1975, 1 s., 2 d. *Education:* BA, 1966, MA, 1975, City College of the City University of New York. *Appointments:* Co-Founder and Co-Ed., Angel Hair magazine and Angel Hair Books, New York City, 1966–77; Co-Ed., Boston Eagle, Massachusetts, 1973–75; Teacher, St Marks in the Bowery Poetry Project, 1973–75; Co-Founder and Publisher, United Artists magazine and United Artists Books, New York, 1977–; Lecturer, Kerouac School of Disembodied Poetics, Boulder, CO, 1978, New England College, 1979–80, Queens College, 1984–86, Farleigh Dickinson University, 1987–; Adjunct Assoc. Prof., Long Island University, 1987–. *Publications:* Poetry: The Suicide Rates, 1967; Highjacking: Poems, 1968; Moving Through Air, 1968; Chicago (with Tom Clark), 1969; Dreaming as One: Poems, 1971; Long Distance, 1971; Immediate Surrounding, 1974; Today, 1974; Blue Heaven, 1978; Hives, 1979; Methods of Birth Control, 1982; The Corset, 1986; Information from the Surface of Venus, 1987; A Free Man, 1991; Avenue of Escape, 1995. Other: Part of My History (autobiography), 1972; The Maharajah's Son (autobiography), 1977; Agnes and Sally (fiction), 1984. *Honours:* Poet's Foundation Award, 1972; Creative Artists Public Service Award in Fiction, 1977; National Endowment for the Arts Grant in Poetry, 1979; Co-ordinating Council of Literary Magazines Ed.'s Fellowship, 1981. *Address:* 701 President St, No. 1, New York, NY 11215, USA.

WASSERMAN, Rosanne; b. 29 Nov. 1952, Kentucky, USA. Poet; Publisher; Prof.; Ed. m. Eugene Daniel Richie, 12 June 1977, 1 s. *Education:* BA, 1974; MFA, 1976; PhD, 1986. *Appointments:* Ed., Metropolitan Museum of Art, 1974–91, The Groundwater Press, 1976–99; Poet in Public Schools, 1986–91; Assoc. Prof., USMMA, 1986–99. *Publications:* Apple Perfume, 1989; The Lacemakers, 1992; No Archive on Earth, 1995; Other Selves, 1999. *Contributions to:* Best American Poetry; Sulfur; Broadway; Numbers; Talus; Bad Henry Review; Mudfish; Caliban; Joe Soaps Canoe; Private; Gambit; American Letters and Commentary; Poetry New York. *Honours:* New York Foundation for the Arts Fellowship; Indiana University Writers Conference Award. *Membership:* PEN. *Address:* PO Box 704, Hudson, NY 12534, USA.

WASSMO, Herbjorg; b. 6 Dec. 1942, Myre i Vesteralen, Norway. Writer; Poet. *Publications:* Fiction: Huset med den blinde glassveranda, 1981, English trans. as The House With the Blind Glass Windows, 1987; Det stumme rommet, 1983; Hudlos himmel, 1986; Dinas bok, 1989, English trans. as Dina's Book, 1994; Lykkens sonn, 1992; Reiser: Fire Fortellinger, 1995. Poetry: Vingeslag, 1976; Flotid, 1977; Lite gront bilde i stor bla ramme, 1991. *Contributions to:* Periodicals. *Honours:* Norwegian Critics' Award, 1982; Nordic Council Literature Prize, 1987.

WASTIE, Heather Ann; b. 18 Oct. 1955, Stourbridge, England. Musician; Writer; Poet. m. Mark Edward Wastie, 10 April 1982. *Education:* BA, Maths/ Music, Birmingham University, 1974–77. *Publication:* Until I Saw Your Foot, 1997. *Contributions to:* Raw Edge Magazine. *Honours:* Winner, Poetry Digest Love Competition, 1996; Second Prize Poetry Digest, Gold Sprint Competition, 1997. *Address:* 25 Hailstone Close, Rowley Regis, B65 8LJ, England.

WATADA, Terry; b. 6 July 1951, Toronto, ON, Canada. Writer; Dramatist; Poet; Ed.; Musician. m. Tane Akamatsu, 1989, 1 s. *Education:* BA, 1974, BEd, 1978, University of Toronto; MA, York University, 1975. *Publications:* Asian Voices: Stories from Canada, Korea, China, Vietnam and Japan (ed.), 1992; The Tale of the Mask (play), 1995; Face Kao: Portraits of Japanese Canadians Interned During World War II (ed.), 1996; Bukkyo Tozen: A History of Jodo Shinshu Buddhism in Canada, 1996; A Thousand Homes (poems), 1997; Daruma Days (stories), 1997; Collected Voices: An Anthology of Asian North American Periodical Writing (ed.), 1997. Other: Unpublished plays. *Contributions to:* Periodicals. *Honours:* William P. Hubbard Award for Race Relations, City of Toronto, 1991; Gerald Lampert Memorial Award, League of Canadian Poets, 1995; First Prize in Poetry, Moon Rabbit Review Fiction and Poetry Contest, 1996. *Address:* 6 Wildwood Cres., Toronto, ON M4L 2K7, Canada. *E-mail:* tanea@ibm.net.

WATERMAN, Andrew (John); b. 28 May 1940, London, England. Senior Lecturer in English; Poet. Divorced, 1 s. *Education:* BA, English, University of Leicester, 1966; Worcester College, Oxford, 1966–68. *Appointments:* Lecturer, 1968–78, Senior Lecturer in English, 1978–97, University of Ulster, Coleraine, Northern Ireland. *Publications:* Living Room, 1974; From the Other Country, 1977; Over the Wall, 1980; Out for the Elements, 1981; The Poetry of Chess (ed.), 1981; Selected Poems, 1986; In the Planetarium, 1990; The End of the Pier Show, 1995; Collected Poems 1959–1999, 2000. *Contributions to:* Anthologies, journals and periodicals. *Honours:* Poetry Book Society Choice, 1974 and Recommendation, 1981; Cholmondeley Award for Poetry, 1977; Arvon Poetry Competition Prize, 1981. *Address:* 5 Guernsey Rd, Norwich NR3 1JJ, England.

WATERS, Chocolate; b. 21 Jan. 1949, Aberdeen, Maryland, USA. Poet; Writer; Designer. *Education:* BA, Lock Haven State College, Pennsylvania, 1971. *Publications:* To the Man Reporter from The Denver Post, 1975; Take Me Like a Photograph, 1977; Charting New Waters, 1980; Ladies & Gentlemen: The Hudson Pier Poets, 2002; Stand Up Poetry, 2002; Chocolate Waters Uncensored (CD), 2002. *Contributions to:* Various anthologies, reviews, and journals. *Honours:* Outstanding Journalist Achievement Award, Mt Joy Bulletin, 1967; Second Place Awards, Colorado Press Women, Denver, 1975; Honourable Mention, Passaic County Community Collge Contest, New Jersey, 1988; Finalist, Roberts Writing Awards Contest, Pittsburg, KS, 1990; Barbara Deming Memorial Fund Grant, 1990; First Place, Poetry Contest, Poetry Arts Project, 1990, 1991; Hon. Mentions and Third Place Award, National Federation of State Poetry Societies, 1993–94; New York Foundation for the Arts Fellowship in Poetry, 1995; Hon. Mentions, Short Poetry Contest, 2000. *Memberships:* Acad. of American Poets; National Federation of State Poetry Societies; Poetry Society of America. *Address:* 415 W 44th St, No. 7, New York, NY 10036, USA. *E-mail:* c-w@chocolate.waters.com. *Website:* www.chocolate-waters.com.

WATSON, John Richard; b. 15 June 1934, Ipswich, England. Prof. of English; Writer; Poet. m. Pauline Elizabeth Roberts, 21 July 1962, 1 s., 2 d. *Education:* BA, 1958, MA, 1964, Magdalen College, Oxford; PhD, University of Glasgow, 1966. *Appointments:* Asst, then Lecturer, University of Glasgow, 1962–66; Lecturer, then Senior Lecturer, University of Leicester, 1966–78; Prof. of English, 1978–99, Public Orator, 1989–99, University of Durham. *Publications:* A Leicester Calendar, 1976; Everyman's Book of Victorian Verse (ed.), 1982; Wordsworth's Vital Soul, 1982; Wordsworth, 1983; English Poetry of the Romantic Period, 1789–1830, 1985; The Poetry of Gerard Manley Hopkins, 1986; Companion to Hymns and Psalms, 1988; A Handbook to English Romanticism, 1992; The English Hymn, 1997; An Annotated Anthology of Hymns, 2002. *Contributions to:* Scholarly and literary journals. *Honours:* Matthew Arnold Memorial Prize, Oxford University, 1961; Ewing Prize, Glasgow University, 1962; Prize, Stroud Festival, 1971; Prize, Suffolk Poetry Society, 1975. *Memberships:* Charles Wesley Society; International Asscn of University Profs of English; Modern Humanities Research Asscn. *Address:* Stoneyhurst, 27 Western Hill, Durham DH1 4RL, England.

WATSON, Larry; b. 1947, USA. Writer; Poet. *Publications:* In a Dark Time (novel), 1980; Leaving Dakota (poems), 1983; Montana 1948 (novel), 1993; Justice (novel), 1995; White Crosses (novel), 1997. *Honours:* National Education Asscn Creative Writing Fellowship, 1987; Milkweed National Fiction Prize, 1993. *Address:* c/o Milkweed Editions, 430 First Ave N, Suite 400, Minneapolis, MN 55401, USA.

WATSON, Lynn; b. 5 June 1948, Woodland, CA, USA. Teacher; Writer; Poet. *Education:* University of California at Berkeley, 1966–68; BA, English, Sonoma State University, 1975; MFA, Fiction Writing, University of Iowa, 1977. *Appointments:* Teacher, University of Iowa, College of the Desert, Sonoma State University, Santa Rosa Junior College. *Publications:* Alimony or Death of the Clock (novel), 1981; Amateur Blues (poems), 1990; Catching the Devil (poems), 1995. *Contributions to:* Journals and periodicals. *Honours:* First Place, National Poetry Asscn, 1990; Honorable Mention, World of Poetry Contest, 1991. *Membership:* California Poets-in-the-Schools. *Address:* PO Box 1253, Occidental, CA 95465, USA.

WATSON, Scott Harrison, (Zenmai); b. 22 March 1954, Philadelphia, PA, USA. Prof. of English; Poet. m. Morie Chiba, 27 Dec. 1981, 2 s. *Education:* College of William and Mary, Williamsburg, VA, 1972–75; BA, Ursinus College, PA, 1979; MA, University of Delaware, 1982. *Appointments:* Prof. of English, Tohoku Gakuin University, Japan, 1986–; Dir, Bookgirl Press; Ed., Bongos of the Lord poetry magazine; Organizer, Universe-City of Poetry poetry readings, Sendai, Japan. *Publication:* Poetry: First Poems, 1979; From: The Women of Japan (chapbook), 1991; With/In (chapbook), 1993; Morie's Book (chapbook), 1995; Here (chapbook), 1996; Forager (chapbook), 1998; Urban Aboriginal (chapbook), 1999; Born (chapbook), 2001; No Vision Will Tell: Selected Poems 1992–2002, 2002. Other: Many trans of Japanese poetry; Essays. *Contributions to:* Anthologies, including: Poesie Yaponesia, 2000; Periodicals and newspapers, including: Hummingbird; Longhouse; Persimmons; Lift; Haiku Quarterly; Shearsman; Kater Murr's Press; Brobdingnagian Times; Edge; Blue Jacket; Seien; Printed Matter; Poetry Nippon; Living Room; Stroker; New Observer; Literary reviews and journals. *Memberships:* Sendai Modern Poetry Salon; Poetry Society of Japan; World Congress of Poets; Japan English-American Modern Poetry Society. *Address:* 3-13-16 Tsurugaya-higashi, Miyagino-ku, Sendai, 983-0826, Japan. *Telephone:* (22) 252-8194. *E-mail:* swbgp@izcc.tohoku-gakuin.ac.jp.

WATTS, Anthony; b. 3 Feb. 1941, Wimbledon, England. Library Asst; Poet. m. Dorothy May Clarke, 18 May 1966, 1 s., 3 d. *Appointment:* Somerset County Library, 1959–. *Publication:* Strange Gold, 1991. *Contributions to:* Outposts; PEN; Thames Poetry; Orbis; Envoi; Iron; New Poetry; Poetry Northampton; The Rialto. *Honours:* Arvon Foundation Prize, 1982; Lake Aske Memorial Award, 1978; Edmund Blunden Memorial Competition Prize, 1979; Michael Johnson Memorial Prize, 1979; Scottish Open Poetry Competition, 1981; Arvon Foundation Prize, 1982. *Address:* Flat 1, Camden Rd, Bridgwater, Somerset TA6 3HD, England.

WAYMAN, Tom, (Thomas Ethan Wayman); b. 13 Aug. 1945, Hawkesbury, Ontario, Canada. Poet; Writer; University Teacher. *Education:* BA, Honours, English, University of British Columbia, 1966; MFA, English and Creative Writing, University of California at Irvine, 1968. *Appointments:* Instructor, Colorado State University, Fort Collins, 1968–69; Writer-in-Residence, University of Windsor, Ontario, 1975–76, University of Alberta, Edmonton, 1978–79, Simon Fraser University, Burnaby, BC, 1983; Asst Prof., Wayne State University, Detroit, 1976–77; Faculty, David Thompson University Centre, Nelson, BC, 1980–82; Banff School of Fine Arts, AB, 1980, 1982, Kwantlen College, Surrey, BC, 1983, 1988–89, Kootenay School of Writing, Vancouver, 1984–87, Victoria School of Writing, BC, 1996, Kwantlen University College, Surrey, BC, 1998–2000; Prof., Okanagan College, Kelowna, BC, 1990–91, 1993–95; Faculty, 1991–92, Co-Head, Writing Studio, 1995–98, Kootenay School of the Arts, Nelson, BC; Asst Prof., University of Calgary, 2002–; Presidential Writer-in-Residence, University of Toronto, 1996. *Publications:* Poetry: Waiting for Wayman, 1973; For and Against the Moon, 1974; Money and Rain, 1975; Free Time, 1977; A Planet Mostly Sea, 1979; Living on the Ground, 1980; Introducing Tom Wayman: Selected Poems 1973–80, 1980; The Nobel Prize Acceptance Speech, 1981; Counting the Hours, 1983; The Face of Jack Munro, 1986; In a Small House on the Outskirts of Heaven, 1989; Did I Miss Anything?: Selected Poems 1973–1993, 1993; The Astonishing Weight of the Dead, 1994; I'll Be Right Back: New & Selected Poems 1980–1996, 1997; The Colours of the Forest, 1999. Non-Fiction: Inside Job: Essays on the New Work Writing, 1983; A Country Not Considered: Canada, Culture, Work, 1993. Editor: Beaton Abbot's Got the Contract, 1974; A Government Job at Last, 1976; Going for Coffee, 1981; East of Main: An Anthology of Poems from East Vancouver (with Calvin Wharton), 1989; Paperwork, 1991; The Dominion of Love: An Anthology of Canadian Love Poems, 2001. *Contributions to:* Anthologies and magazines. *Honours:* A J M Smith Prize, Michigan State University, 1976; First Prize, National Bicentennial Poetry Awards, San Jose, 1976; Several Canada Council Senior Arts Grants. *Memberships:* Associated Writing Programs; Federation of British Columbia Writers. *Address:* PO Box 163, Winlaw, BC V0G 2J0, Canada. *E-mail:* appledot@netidea.com. *Website:* www.library.utoronto.ca/www/canpoetry/wayman.

WAYS, C. R. See: BLOUNT, Roy (Alton) Jr.

WEARNE, Alan Richard; b. 23 July 1948, Melbourne, Vic., Australia. Poet; Verse and Prose Novelist. *Education:* BA, Latrobe University, 1973; DipEd, Rusden, 1977. *Publications:* Public Relations, 1972; New Devil, New Parish, 1976; The Nightmarkets, 1986; Out Here, 1987; Kicking in Danger, 1997; The Lovemakers, Book One, 2001. *Honours:* National Book Council Award, 1987; Gold Medal, Asscn for the Study of Australian Literature, 1987; New South Wales Premier's Prize for Poetry, 2002; Kenneth Slessor Award, 2002; New South Wales Premier's Prize Book of the Year, 2002. *Literary Agent:* Bryson Agency Australia Pty Ltd, PO Box 226, Flinders Lane PO, Melbourne, Vic. 8009, Australia. *Address:* c/o Faculty of Creative Arts, University of Wollongong, Wollongong, NSW 2015, Australia.

WEAVER, Roger Keys; b. 2 Feb. 1935, Portland, Oregon, USA. Emeritus Prof of English; Poet. m. Sharron Beckett, 2 s. *Education:* BA, 1957, MFA, 1967, University of Oregon; MA, University of Washington, 1962. *Appointments:* Asst Prof., Assoc. Prof., Full Prof. of English, Oregon State University, Corvallis, 1962–. *Publications:* The Orange and Other Poems, 1978; Twenty-One Waking Dreams, 1985; Traveling on the Great Wheel, 1990; Standing on Earth, Throwing These Sequins at the Stars, 1994. *Contributions to:* Massachusetts Review; North American Review; Nimrod; Greenfield Review; Dog River Review; Colorado Quarterly; Northwest Review; Fireweed. *Honours:* Oregon State Poetry Awards Bicentennial, 1976; Tucson Poetry Contest, 1978; Prof. Emeritus, 1997. *Memberships:* Acad. of American Poets; Willamette Literary Guild. *Address:* 712 NW 13th St, Corvallis, OR 97330, USA.

WEBB, Bernice Larson; b. 1934, Ludell, KS, USA. Prof. (retd); Consultant; Poet; Writer. m. Robert MacHardy Webb, 14 July 1961, 1 s., 1 d. *Education:* AB, 1956, MA, 1957, PhD, 1961, University of Kansas; University of Aberdeen, Scotland, 1959–60. *Appointments:* Asst Instructor, University of Kansas, 1958–59, 1960–61; Asst Prof., 1961–67, Assoc. Prof., 1967–80, Prof., 1980–87, Consultant, 1987–, University of Southwestern Louisiana; Ed., Cajun Chatter, 1964–66, The Magnolia, 1967–71, Louisiana Poets, 1970–89; Book Reviewer, Journal of American Culture, 1980–87, Journal of Popular Culture, 1980–87. *Publications:* The Basketball Man, 1973; Beware of Ostriches, 1978; Poetry on the Stage, 1979; Lady Doctor on a Homestead, 1987; Two Peach Baskets, 1991; Spider Webb, 1993; Born to Be a Loser (with Johnnie Allen), 1993; Mating Dance, 1996; From Acorn ro Oakbourne, 1998. *Contributions to:* Various publications. *Honours:* Many poetry awards and prizes. *Memberships:* Deep South Writers Conference, board mem.; Louisiana State Poetry Society, pres., 1978–79, 1981–82; South Central College English Asscn, pres., 1986–87. *Address:* 159 Whittington Dr., Lafayette, LA 70503, USA.

WEBB, Phyllis; b. 8 April 1927, Victoria, BC, Canada. Poet; Writer. *Education:* BA, University of British Columbia, Vancouver, 1949; McGill University, Montréal. *Appointment:* Adjunct Prof., University of Victoria, BC, 1989–93. *Publications:* Poetry: Trio (with G Turnbull and Eli Mandel), 1954; Even Your Right Eye, 1956; The Sea is Also a Garden, 1962; Naked Poems, 1965; Phyllis Webb Selected Poems, 1954–1965, 1971; Wilson's Bowl, 1980; Sunday Water: Thirteen Anti Ghazals, 1982; The Vision Tree: Selected Poems, 1982; Water and Light: Ghazals and Anti Ghazals, 1984; Hanging Fire, 1990. Other: Talking (essays), 1982; Nothing But Brush Strokes: Selected Prose, 1995. *Honours:* Canada Council Awards; Governor-General's Award for Poetry, 1982; Officer of the Order of Canada, 1992. *Address:* 128 Menhinick Dr., Salt Spring Island, BC V8K 1W7, Canada.

WEBSTER, Leonard, (Len Webster); b. 6 July 1948, Birmingham, England. Poet; Writer. m. Emorn Puttalong, 26 Nov. 1985. *Education:* BEd, University of Warwick, 1973; MA, Modern English and American Literature, University of Leicester, 1976; Poetry Society Adult Verse Speaking Certificate, 1977; Dip RSA TEFLA, 1983; MA, Linguistics, University of Birmingham, 1988. *Appointments:* Journalist, Birmingham Post and Mail, 1965–68, Coventry Evening Telegraph, 1973–74; Teacher, Oldbury High School, 1976–77, Tarsus American College, Turkey, 1977–78, King Edward VI Grammar School, Handsworth, Birmingham, 1978–84; Lecturer, Ministry of Education, Singapore, 1984–87, 1988–94, City College, Handsworth, Birmingham, 1996–. *Publications:* Behind the Painted Veil, 1972; Beneath the Blue Moon, 1992; Hell-Riders, 1994; Flight From the Sibyl, 1994. *Memberships:* Poetry Society; Society of Authors. *Address:* c/o 48 Marshall Rd, Warley, West Midlands B68 9ED, England. *Website:* home.freeuk.com/castlegates/webster.htm.

WEDDE, Ian; b. 17 Oct. 1946, Blenheim, New Zealand. Writer; Poet; Dramatist; Trans. m. Rosemary Beauchamp, 1967, 3 s. *Education:* MA, University of Auckland, 1968. *Appointments:* Poetry Reviewer, London magazine, 1970–71; Writer-in-Residence, Victoria University, Wellington, 1984; Art Critic, Wellington Evening Post, 1983–90. *Publictions:* Fiction: Dick Seddon's Great Drive, 1976; The Shirt Factory and Other Stories, 1981; Symmes Hole, 1986; Survival Arts, 1988. Poetry: Homage to Matisse, 1971; Made Over, 1974; Pathway to the Sea, 1974; Earthly: Sonnets for Carlos, 1975; Don't Listen, 1977; Spells for Coming Out, 1977; Castaly, 1981; Tales of Gotham City, 1984; Georgicon, 1984; Driving Into the Storm: Selected Poems, 1988; Tendering, 1988; The Drummer, 1993; The Commonplace Odes, 2001. Plays: Stations, 1969; Pukeko, 1972; Eyeball, Eyeball, 1983; Double or Quit: The Life and Times of Percy TopLiss, 1984. Editor: The Penguin Book of New Zealand Verse (with Harvey McQueen), 1986; Now See Hear!: Art, Language, and Translation (with G Burke), 1990. *Address:* 118-A Maidavale Rd, Roseneath, Wellington, New Zealand.

WEDGE, John Francis Newdigate; b. 13 July 1921, London, England. Banker (retd); Poet. m. Laura Jacqueline Roberts, 10 Oct. 1946, 1 s., 2 d. *Contributions to:* Anthologies: Poems from the Forces; Poems of the Second World War; The Terrible Rain; Verse of Valour; In Time of War; Poetry Pot Pourri; Echoes of War; Poetry Review; Literary Review. *Address:* 23 Talbot Rd, Carshalton, Surrey SM5 3BP, England.

WEIGL, Bruce; b. 27 Jan. 1949, Lorain, OH, USA. Distinguished Prof.; Poet; Writer; Ed.; Trans. m. Jean Kondo, 1 s., 1 d. *Education:* BA, Oberlin College, 1974; MA, University of New Hampshire, 1975; PhD, University of Utah, 1979. *Appointments:* Instructor in English, 1975–76, Distinguished Prof., 2000–, Lorain County Community College; Asst Prof. of English, University of Arkansas at Little Rock, 1979–81, Old Dominion University, Norfolk, 1981–86; Assoc. Prof. to Prof. of English, Pennsylvania State University at University Park, 1986–2000. *Publications:* Poetry: Like a Sack Full of Old Quarrels, 1976; Executioner, 1977; A Romance, 1979; The Monkey Wars, 1984; Song of Nepalm, 1988; What Saves Us, 1992; Sweet Lorain, 1996; Archeology of the Circle: New and Selected Poems, 1999; The Circle of Hanh: A Memoir, 2000. Editor: The Giver of Morning: On the Poetry of Dave Smith, 1982; The Imagination as Glory: The Poetry of James Dickey (with T. R. Hummer), 1984; Charles Simic: Essays on the Poetry, 1996; Writing Between the Lines: An Anthology on War and Its Social Consequences (with Kevin Bowen), 1997; Mountain River: Vietnamese Poetry from the Wars, 1948–1993: A Bilingual Collection (with Kevin Bowen and Nguyan Ba Chung), 1998. *Contributions to:* Anthologies, reviews, quarterlies and journals. *Honours:* American Acad. of Poets Prize, 1979; Pushcart Prizes, 1980, 1985; Bread Loaf Writers' Conference Fellowship, 1981; National Endowment for the Arts Grant, 1988. *Address:* c/o Division of Arts and Humanities, Lorain County Community College, Elyria, OH 44035, USA.

WEILD, Desney. See: JESSENER, Stephen.

WEINFIELD, Henry (Michael); b. 3 Jan. 1949, Montréal, QC, Canada. Assoc. Prof. in Liberal Studies; Poet; Writer; Trans. *Education:* BA, City College of New York, 1970; MA, State University of New York, Binghamton, 1973; PhD, City University of New York, 1985. *Appointments:* Lecturer, State University of New York, Binghamton, 1973–74; Adjunct Lecturer, Lehman College, 1974–77, Baruch College, 1979–81, City College of New York, 1982–83; Adjunct Lecturer, 1983–84, Special Lecturer, 1984–91, New Jersey Institute of Technology; Asst Prof., 1991–96, Assoc. Prof., 1996–, in Liberal Studies, University of Notre Dame. *Publications:* Poetry: The Carnival Cantata, 1971; In the Sweetness of New Time, 1980; Sonnets Elegiac and Satirical, 1982. Other: The Poet Without a Name: Gray's Elegy and the Problem of History, 1991; The Collected Poems of Stéphane Mallarmé, (trans. and commentator), 1995; The Sorrows of Eros and Other Poems, 1999. *Contributions to:* Articles, poems, trans in many publications. *Honours:* Co-ordinating Council of Literary Magazines Award, 1975; National Endowment for the Humanities Fellowship, 1989. *Address:* Program of Liberal Studies, University of Notre Dame, Notre Dame, IN 46556, USA.

WEISS, Theodore (Russell); b. 16 Dec. 1916, Reading, PA, USA. Poet; Writer; Ed.; Publisher; Prof. Emeritus. m. Renée Karol, 6 July 1941. *Education:* BA, Muhlenberg College, 1938; MA, 1940, Postgraduate Studies, 1940–41, Columbia University. *Appointments:* Instructor in English, University of Maryland at College Park, 1941, University of North Carolina at Chapel Hill, 1942–44; Yale University, 1944–46; Ed. and Publisher, Quarterly Review of Literature, 1943–; Asst Prof., 1946–52, Assoc. Prof., 1952–55, Prof. of English, 1955–68, Bard College; Lecturer, New School for Social Research, 1955–56, YMHA, New York, 1965–67; Visiting Prof. of Poetry, Massachusetts Institute of Technology, 1961–62; Resident Fellow in Creative Writing, 1966–67, Prof. of English and Creative Writing, 1968–87, William and Annie S. Paton Prof. of Ancient and Modern Literature, 1977–87, Prof. Emeritus, 1987–, Princeton University; Ed., poetry series, Princeton University Press, 1974–78; Fannie Hurst Visiting Prof. of Literature, Washington University, St Louis, 1978; Poet-in-Residence, Monash University, Melbourne, Australia, 1982; Visiting Instructor, Institute for Advanced Study, Princeton, 1986–87, 1987–88, Villa Serbelloni, Bellagio, Italy, 1989; Prof. of English, Cooper Union, 1988; Guest Lecturer, Peking University, Shanghai University, China, 1991. *Publications:* Poetry: The Catch, 1951; Outlanders, 1960; Gunsight, 1962; The Medium, 1965; The Last Day and the First, 1968; The World Before Us: Poems, 1950–70, 1970; Fireweeds, 1976; Views and Spectacles: Selected Poems, 1978; Views and Spectacles: New and Selected Shorter Poems, 1979; Recoveries, 1982; A Slow Fuse, 1984; From Princeton One Autumn Afternoon: Collected Poems of Theodore Weiss, 1950–1986, 1987; A Sum of Destructions, 1994; Selected Poems, 1995. Other: Selections from the Notebooks of Gerard Manley Hopkins (ed.), 1945; The Breath of Clowns and Kings: Shakespeare's Early Comedies and Histories, 1971; The Man from Porlock: Selected Essays, 1982. *Contributions to:* Anthologies, quarterlies, reviews and journals. *Honours:* Fellow, Ford Foundation, 1953–54, Ingram Merrill Foundation, 1974–75, Guggenheim Foundation, 1986–87; Hon. Fellow, Ezra Stiles College, Yale University; Wallace Stevens Award, 1956; National Foundation for Arts and Humanities Grant, 1967–68; Hon. DLitt, Muhlenberg College, 1968, Bard College, 1973; Brandeis University Creative Arts Award, 1977; Shelley Memorial Award, Poetry Society of America, 1989; Co-Winner (with Renée Weiss), PEN Club Special Achievement Award, 1997; Oscar Williams and Gene Derwood Award, 1997. *Membership:* Poetry Society of America. *Address:* 26 Haslet Ave, Princeton, NJ 08540-4914, USA. *Telephone:* (609) 921-6976.

WEISSBORT, Daniel; b. 1 May 1935, London, England. Prof.; Poet; Trans.; Ed. *Education:* BA, Queen's College, Cambridge, 1956. *Appointment:* Co-Founder (with Ted Hughes), Modern Poetry in Translation, 1965–83; Prof.,

University of Iowa, 1980–. *Publications:* The Leaseholder, 1971; In an Emergency, 1972; Soundings, 1977; Leaseholder: New and Collected Poems, 1965–85, 1986; Inscription, 1990; Lake, 1993. Other: Ed. and trans. of Russian literature. *Honour:* Arts Council Literature Award, 1984. *Address:* c/o Dept of English, University of Iowa, Iowa City, IA 52242, USA.

WELBURN, Ron; b. 30 April 1944, Pennsylvania, USA. Assoc. Prof. of English; Poet; Writer. m. Cheryl T Donohue, 16 Oct. 1988, 2 s., 1 d. *Education:* BA, Lincoln University, 1968; MA, University of Arizona, 1971; PhD, New York University, 1983. *Appointments:* Asst Prof., Syracuse University, 1970–75, Western Connecticut State University, 1983–92; Co-ordinator, Jazz Oral History Project, Institute of Jazz Studies, Rutgers University, Newark, 1980–83; Assoc. Prof. of English, University of Massachusetts at Amherst, 1992–. *Publications:* The Look in the Night Sky, 1978; Heartland, 1981; Council Decisions, 1991. *Contributions to:* Anthologies, reviews, quarterlies, and journals. *Honours:* Silver Poetry Award; Certificate of Recognition for Contributing to the Literary Legacy of Langston Hughes. *Address:* c/o Dept of English, University of Massachusetts at Amherst, Amherst, MA 01003, USA.

WELCH, Don; b. 3 June 1932, Hastings, NE, USA. University Prof. (retd); Poet. m. Marcia Lee Zorn, 14 June 1953, 2 s., 4 d. *Education:* BA, Kearney State College, 1954; MA, University of Northern Colorado, 1958; PhD, University of Nebraska, 1965. *Appointments:* Martin Distinguished Prof. of English, 1981–89, Reynolds Distinguished Prof. of Poetry, 1990–97, University of Nebraska at Kearney. *Publications:* Dead Horse Table, 1975; Handwork, 1978; The Rarer Game, 1980; The Keeper of Miniature Deer, 1986; The Platte River, 1992; Carved By Obadiah Verity, 1993; Fire's Tongue in the Candle's End, 1996; A Brief History of Feathers, 1996; Inklings, 2001. *Contributions to:* Prairie Schooner; Georgia Review; Tendril; Pacific Review; Laurel Review; Tar River Poetry; Epoch; Southern Humanities Review. *Honours:* Pablo Neruda Prize for Poetry, 1980; Blue Unicorn First Prize for Poetry, 1983, 1987; Nebraska Review First Prize for Poetry, 1987; Elkhorn Review Prize for Poetry, 1989. *Address:* 611 W 27th St, Kearney, NE 68847, USA.

WELCH, James; b. 1940, Browning, Montana, USA. Writer; Poet. m. Lois M Welch. *Education:* Northern Montana College; BA, University of Montana. *Publications:* Fiction: Winter in the Blood, 1974; The Death of Jim Loney, 1979; Fool's Crow, 1986; The Indian Lawyer, 1990; The Heartsong of Charging Elk, 2000. Poetry: Riding the Earthboy 40, 1971. Non-Fiction: Killing Custer: The Battle of the Little Bighorn and the Fate of the Plains Indians (with Paul Stekler), 1994. Editor: Richard Hugo: The Real West Marginal Way: A Poet's Autobiography (with Ripley S Hugg and Lois M Welch), 1986. *Contributions to:* Periodicals. *Honours:* National Endowment for the Arts Grant, 1969; Los Angeles Times Book Prize, 1987; Pacific Northwest Booksellers Asscn Book Award, 1987. *Address:* 2321 Wylie St, Missoula, MT 59802, USA.

WELCH, Jennifer. See: BOSVELD, Jennifer Miller.

WELCH, Liliane; b. 20 Oct. 1937, Luxembourg. Prof. of French Literature; Poet; Writer. m. Cyril Welch, 1 d. *Education:* BA, 1960, MA, 1961, University of Montana; PhD, Pennsylvania State University, 1964. *Appointments:* Asst Prof., East Carolina University, 1965–66, Antioch College, Ohio, 1966–67; Asst Prof., 1967–71, Assoc. Prof., 1971–72, Prof. of French Literature, 1972–, Mount Allison University. *Publications:* Emergence: Baudelaire, Mallarmé, Rimbaud, 1973; Winter Songs, 1973; Syntax of Ferment, 1979; Assailing Beats, 1979; October Winds, 1980; Brush and Trunks, 1981; From the Songs of the Artisans, 1983; Manstoma, 1985; Rest Unbound, 1985; Word-House of a Grandchild, 1987; Seismographs: Selected Essays and Reviews, 1988; Fire to the Looms Below, 1990; Life in Another Language, 1992; Von Menschen und Orten, 1992; Dream Museum, 1995; Fidelities, 1997; Frescoes: Travel Pieces, 1998; The Rock's Stillness (poems), 1999; Unlearning Ice (poems), 2001; Untethered in Paradise (prose and poems), 2002. *Contributions to:* Professional and literary journals. *Honours:* Alfred Bailey Prize, 1986; Bressani Prize, 1992; Membre Correspondant de L'Institut Grand Ducal de Luxembourg, 1998. *Memberships:* Asscn of Italian-Canadian Poets; Federation of New Brunswick Writers; League of Canadian Poets; Letzebuerger Schriftsteller Verband; Writers' Union of Canada. *Address:* Box 1652 Sackville, New Brunswick E4L 1G6, Canada.

WELCH, Robert; b. 25 Nov. 1947, Cork, Ireland. Prof. of English; Writer; Poet; Ed. m. Angela Welch, 30 June 1970, 3 s. *Education:* BA, 1968, MA, 1971, National University of Ireland; PhD, University of Leeds, 1974. *Appointments:* Lecturer, University of Leeds, 1971–73, 1974–84, University of Ife, Nigeria, 1973–74; Visiting Lecturer, National University of Ireland, 1982; Prof. of English, 1984–, Head, Dept of English, Media and Theatre Studies, 1984–94, Dir, Centre for Irish Literature and Bibliography, 1994–, University of Ulster; Founder-General Ed., Ulster Editions and Monographs, 1988–. *Publications:* Irish Poetry from Moore to Yeats, 1980; The Way Back: George Moore's The Untilled Field and The Lake (ed.), 1982; A History of Verse from the Irish, 1789–1897, 1988; Literature and the Art of Creation: Essays in Honour of A. N. Jeffares (co-ed.), 1988; Muskerry (poems), 1991; Irish Writers and Religion (ed.), 1991; Changing States: Transformations in Modern Irish Writing, 1993; W. B. Yeats: Irish Folklore, Legend, and Myth (ed.), 1993; The Kilcolman

Notebook (novel), 1994; The Oxford Companion to Irish Literature (ed.), 1996; Irish Myths, 1996; Patrick Falvin: New and Selected Poems (co-ed.), 1996; Groundwork (novel), 1997; Secret Societies (poems), 1997; Tearmann (novel), 1997; The Blue Formica Table (poems), 1998; A History of the Abbey Theatre, 1998; The Plays and Poems of J. M. Synge, 1999; The Concise Companion to Irish Literature, 2000. *Contributions to:* Books and periodicals. *Honours:* Visiting Fellow, St John's College, Oxford, 1986; Grants, Leverhulme Trust, 1989, Community Relations Council, 1990, British Acad., 1996; Critics Award, O'Reachtas, 1996. *Address:* 34 Station Rd, Portstewart, Co Derry BT55 7DA, Northern Ireland.

WELDON, Maureen. See: GARSTON, Maureen Beatrice Courtnay.

WELLMAN, Donald; b. 7 July 1944, Nashua, New Hampshire, USA. Poet; Teacher; Ed. m. (1), 1 s., (2) Irene Turner, 2 Jan. 1982, 1 d. *Education:* BA, University of New Hampshire, 1967; MA, 1972, DA, 1974, University of Oregon. *Appointments:* Prof. and Chair, Humanities Division, Daniel Webster College, Nashua, New Hampshire; Ed., OARS Inc. *Publications:* The House in the Fields, 1992; Fields, 1995. *Contributions to:* Tyuonyi; Puckerbruch Review; Interstate; Zone; Adz; Polis; Boundary-2; Tamarisk; Hyperion; MC; New Maine Writing; Main Review; Generator; Sagetrieb. *Address:* 21 Rockland Rd, Weare, NH 03281, USA. *E-mail:* wellman@dwc.edu.

WELLS, Alan Richard; b. 27 Nov. 1948, New Zealand. Composer; Music Critic; Poet. *Education:* University of Canterbury, 1970–71; Victoria University of Wellington, 1973–75, 1982–87, 1991–92. *Appointments:* Secretary, Amnesty International, 1976–77; Asst Librarian, IHC, 1985–88; Music Critic, New Zealand, 1989–; Judge, New Zealand Poetry Society International Haiku Contest, 1996. *Contributions to:* Several anthologies, quarterlies, and journals. *Honours:* Runner-Up, New Zealand Poetry Society Competition; First Equal, New Zealand Poetry Society Haiku Contest. *Membership:* New Zealand Poetry Society. *Address:* Box 27080, Upper Willis St, Wellington, New Zealand.

WELLS, John David; b. 18 Aug. 1964, Newbury, Berkshire, England. Research Assoc.; Writer; Poet. *Education:* BA, History, 1986, MA, 1990, University of Cambridge. *Appointments:* Research Officer, Location Register of English Literary Manuscripts and Letters, University of Reading, 1987–90; Research Assoc., University of Cambridge, 1994–. *Publications:* Ambion Hill, 1987; Le Pavillon Des Trois Soeurs, 1991; Samuel Taylor Coleridge: Four Letters to Anna and Basil Montagu (ed.), 1995; The Princely Hong: Jardine Matheson, Hong Kong, and Eastern Trade (with Mark Nicholls), 1997. *Honours:* Eric Gregory Award, 1990; Northern Poets Award, 1991; Hawthornden Fellowship, 1991. *Membership:* Society of Archivists, 1994–. *Address:* 6 Porter End, Pyle Hill, Newbury, Berkshire RG14 7JP, England.

WELLS, Peter; b. 12 Jan. 1919, London, England. Writer; Poet. m. (1) Elisabeth Vander Meulen, deceased 1967, 1 daugher, (2) Gillian Anne Hayes-Newington, 1988. *Education:* Diploma, Social Studies, University of London, 1970; Certificate, Psychiatric Social Work, University of Manchester, 1973. *Publications:* Poetry Folios (co-ed.), 1942–46, 1951; Poems (retrospective collection), 1997; Six Poems (with illustrations), 1998. *Contributions to:* Anthologies and periodicals, including: Poetry (London); Poetry (Chicago); View; New English Weekly; Quarterly Review of Literature; The Dublin Magazine. *Memberships:* PEN; Society of Authors. *Address:* Model Farm, Linstead Magna, Halesworth, Suffolk, England.

WELLS, Robert; b. 17 Aug. 1947, Oxford, England. Poet; Trans. *Education:* King's College, Cambridge, 1965–68. *Appointments:* Teacher, University of Leicester, 1979–82. *Publications:* Shade Mariners (with Dick Davis and Clive Wilmer), 1970; The Winter's Task: Poems, 1977; The Georgics, by Virgil (trans.), 4 vols, 1981; Selected Poems, 1986; The Idylls, by Theocritus (trans.), 1988. *Contributions to:* Anthologies.

WENDT, Albert; b. 27 Oct. 1939, Apia, Western Samoa. Prof. of English; Writer; Poet; Dramatist. 1 s., 2 d. *Education:* MA, History, Victoria University, Wellington, 1964. *Appointments:* Prof. of Pacific Literature, University of the South Pacific, Suva, Fiji, 1982–87; Prof. of English, University of Auckland, 1988–. *Publications:* Fiction: Sons for the Return Home, 1973; Pouliuli, 1977; Leaves of the Banyan Tree, 1979; Ola, 1990; Black Rainbow, 1992. Short Stories: Flying-Fox in a Freedom Tree, 1974; The Birth and Death of the Miracle Man, 1986; The Best of Albert Wendt's Short Stories, 1999. Plays: Comes the Revolution, 1972; The Contract, 1972. Poetry: Inside Us the Dead: Poems 1961–74, 1975; Shaman of Visions, 1984; Photographs, 1995. *Honours:* Landfall Prize, 1963; Wattie Award, 1980; Commonwealth Book Prize, South East Asia and the Pacific, 1991; Companion of the New Zealand Order of Merit, 2001. *Address:* c/o Dept of English, University of Auckland, Private Bag, Auckland, New Zealand.

WERNER, Judith; b. 26 Oct. 1941, New York, NY, USA. Poet; Writer. m. William Werner, 16 Aug. 1975, 1 s., 1 d. *Education:* AB, Barnard College, Columbia University, 1962. *Appointment:* Senior Ed., Rattapallax, 1999–2002. *Contributions to:* Books, anthologies, reviews, quarterlies, and journals. *Honours:* Lenore Marshall Poetry Prize, 1962; Acad. of American Poets Prize,

Columbia University, 1963; Best of Issue Prize, The Lyric, 1992; Ronald J Kemski Prize, 1993. *Memberships:* Poetry Society of America; Poet's House. *Address:* 24 Joralemon St, Apt E 125, Brooklyn, NY 11201, USA.

WERNER-KING, Janeen Anne; b. 30 Dec. 1958, Edmonton, AB, Canada. Teacher; Poet. m. Robert W King, 11 July 1981. *Education:* BEd, Distinction, University of Alberta; MA, English, University of Calgary. *Appointments:* English Teacher, Clover Bar School, AB, 1981–85, University of Calgary, 1987, Wetaskiwin Composite High School, 1989–91, Our Lady of Peace School, AB, 1991–; English Dept Head, Bishop Grandin Senior High, 1996. *Publication:* Bending Light: A Chapbook Anthology, 1993. *Contributions to:* Orbis; Dandelion; Ariel; Other Voices; Secrets from the Orange Couch; SansCrit; Canadian Broadcasting Corporation Alberta Anthology; Skylines; Eclectic Muse; Alberta Poetry Yearbook; Whetstone; Contemporary Verse 2. *Honours:* Literary Awards Competition, Edmonton Journal, 1980, 1985; Galbraith Publishing Poetry Contest, 1989. *Memberships:* Celebration of Women in the Arts, literary chair, 1990–92; Writers Guild of Alberta, mem.-at-large; Calgary Writers Asscn; Calgary Stroll of Poets Co-ordinator, 1993–95. *Address:* 7944 Ave NW, Suite 71, Calgary, AB T3B 4J3, Canada.

WERNICH, Von. See: KNELL, William.

WEST, Colin Edward; b. 21 May 1951, Epping, Essex, England. Writer; Poet; Illustrator. *Education:* MA, Royal College of Art, 1975. *Publications:* Not to Be Taken Seriously, 1982; A Step in the Wrong Direction, 1984; It's Funny When You Look at It, 1984; A Moment in Rhyme, 1987; What Would You Do With A Wobble-Dee-Woo?, 1988; I Bought My Love a Tabby Cat, 1988; Between the Sun, the Moon and Me, 1990; The Best of West, 1990; Long Tales, Short Tales and Tall Tales, 1995; The Big Book of Nonsense, 2001. *Memberships:* Childrens' Writers' Group; Society of Authors. *Address:* 14 High St, Epping, Essex CM16 4AB, England. *E-mail:* post@colinwest.com. *Website:* www.colinwest.com.

WEST, Kathleene; b. 28 Dec. 1947, Genoa, Nebraska, USA. Prof. of English; Poet; Ed. *Education:* BA, 1967, PhD, 1986, University of Nebraska; MA, University of Washington, 1975. *Appointments:* Assoc. Prof. of English, New Mexico State University, 1987–; Poetry Ed., Puerto del Sol, 1995–. *Publications:* Land Bound, 1977; Water Witching, 1984; Plainswoman, 1985; The Farmer's Daughter, 1990. *Contributions to:* Reviews, quarterlies, and journals. *Honour:* Fulbright Scholar, Iceland, 1983–85. *Memberships:* Associated Writing Programs; Barbara Pym Society; PEN. *Address:* c/o Dept of English, Box 3001, New Mexico State University, Las Cruces, NM 88003, USA.

WESTERMAN, Lyn; b. 9 Dec. 1949, Sussex, England. Actor; Poet. Divorced 1986, 1 d. *Appointments:* Creative Writing Tutor, WEA, RACC, London School of Journalism; Publicity Chair, Women Writers Network; Hosted LBC Phone-In on Creative Writing; BBC Woman's Hour; Viva Radio. *Publications:* The Dybbuk of Delight, 1995; Jumping the Gap, 1996; Future Fiction (audio tapes), 1998. *Contributions to:* Envoi; Tandem; Poetry Nottingham; Atomic Shadows; Perceptions; Poetry Now. *Honours:* Second Prize, Woodmans Press, 1993; Winner, Barnet Open Poetry Competition, 1994; Poems on London Buses, 1994–95; Winner, Beehive Press, 1995. *Memberships:* Poetry Society; Poetry Library; Women Writers' Network; RNA; Society of Women Writers and Journalists; Equity; Mensa. *Address:* 207 Cannon Lane, Pinner, Middlesex HA5 1HZ, England.

WESTHEIMER, David, (Z. Z. Smith); b. 11 April 1917, Houston, TX, USA. Writer; Poet. m. Doris Rothstein Kahn, 9 Oct. 1945, 2 s. *Education:* BA, Rice Institute, Houston, 1937. *Publications:* Summer on the Water, 1948; The Magic Fallacy, 1950; Watching Out for Dulie, 1960; This Time Next Year, 1963; Von Ryan's Express, 1964; My Sweet Charlie, 1965; Song of the Young Sentry, 1968; Lighter Than a Feather, 1971; Over the Edge, 1972; Going Public, 1973; The Aulia Gold, 1974; The Olmec Head, 1974; Von Ryan's Return, 1980; Rider on the Wind, 1984; Sitting it Out, 1992; The Great Wounded Bird (poems), 2000. *Honour:* Texas Review Press Poetry Prize, 2000. *Memberships:* Authors Guild; PEN; California Writers' Club; Retd Officers' Asscn; Writers' Guild of America West; Acad. of American Poets. *Address:* 11722 Darlington Ave, No. 2, Los Angeles, CA 90049, USA.

WESTON, Joanna Mary; b. 20 Jan. 1938, England. Poet. m. Robert John Weston, 20 May 1967, 3 c. *Education:* MA, University of British Columbia, 1969. *Publications:* Seasons, 1993; All Seasons, 1996. Other: The Willow Tree Girl (online), 2002. *Contributions to:* Magazines and periodicals. *Memberships:* Cedar Creek Writers; League of Canadian Poets; Saskatchewan Writers' Guild; Sans Nom Poets. *Address:* 1960 Berger Rd, Shawnigan Lake, BC V0R 2W0, Canada. *E-mail:* weston@islandnet.com.

WEVILL, David (Anthony); b. 15 March 1935, Yokohama, Japan. Lecturer; Poet. m. Assia Gutman, 1960. *Education:* BA, Caius College, Cambridge, 1957. *Appointment:* Lecturer, University of Texas, Austin. *Publications:* Penguin Modern Poets, 1963; Birth of a Spark, 1964; A Christ of the Ice Floes, 1966; Firebreak, 1971; Where the Arrow Falls, 1973; Other Names for the Heart: New and Selected Poems, 1964–84, 1985; Figures of Eight, 1987. Other: Trans. of Hungarian poetry. *Address:* Dept of English, University of Texas at Austin, Austin, TX 78712, USA.

WHALLEY, Dorothy, (Dorothy Cowlin); b. 16 Aug. 1911, Grantham, Lincolnshire, England. Teacher (retd); Writer; Poet. m. R H Whalley, 12 April 1941, 1 d. *Education:* BA, University of Manchester, 1929–31. *Appointments:* Asst Teacher, St John's, Heaten Mersey, Stockport, and Junior School, Flixton, Lancashire. *Publications:* The Sound of Rain, 1991; Winter Rooks (poems), 1998. *Contributions to:* Envoi; Pennine Platform; Pennine Ink; Airings; Hybrid; Iota; Moonstone; Psychopoetica; New Hope International; Rialto; The Dalesman. *Honours:* Yorkshire TV Competition, 1993; Area Winner, Faber & Faber/Ottakars Bookshops competition. *Membership:* Scarborough Poetry Workshop. *Address:* 14 Littledale, Pickering, North Yorkshire YO18 8PS, England.

WHALLON, William; b. 24 Sept. 1928, Richmond, IN, USA. Poet; Writer. *Education:* BA, McGill University, 1950. *Appointments:* Fellow, Center for Hellenic Studies, 1962; Fulbright Prof. in Comparative Literature, University of Bayreuth, 1985. *Publications:* A Book of Time (poems), 1990; Giants in the Earth (ed.), 1991; The Oresteia / Apollo & Bacchus (scenarios), 1997. *Address:* 1655 Walnut Heights, East Lansing, MI 48823, USA.

WHEATCROFT, John Stewart; b. 24 July 1925, Philadelphia, Pennsylvania, USA. Prof.; Writer; Poet. m. (1) Joan Mitchell Osborne, 10 Nov. 1952, divorced 1974, 2 s., 1 d., (2) Katherine Whaley Warner, 14 Nov. 1992. *Education:* BA, Bucknell University, 1949; MA, 1950, PhD, 1960, Rutgers University. *Publications:* Poetry: Death of a Clown, 1963; Prodigal Son, 1967; A Voice from the Hump, 1977; Ordering Demons, 1981; The Stare on the Donkey's Face, 1990; Random Necessities, 1997. Fiction: Edie Tells, 1975; Catherine, Her Book, 1983; The Beholder's Eye, 1987; Killer Swan, 1992; Mother of All Loves, 1994; Trio with Four Players, 1995; The Education of Malcolm Palmer, 1997. Other: Slow Exposures (stories), 1986; Our Other Voices (ed.), 1991. *Contributions to:* New York Times; New York Times Book Review; Hartford Courant; Herald Tribune; Harper's Bazaar; Mademoiselle; Yankee; Many literary magazines. *Honours:* Alcoa Playwriting Award, 1966; National Educational Television Award, 1967; Yaddo Fellowships, 1972, 1985; MacDowell Colony Fellowship, 1973; Fellowships, Virginia Center for the Creative Arts, 1976, 1978, 1980, 1982. *Address:* R R No. 1, PO Box 5, Lewisburg, PA 17837, USA.

WHEATLEY, Jeffery John; b. 31 May 1933, Epsom, Surrey, England. Business Economist; Poet. m. Jean Margaret Tyson, 15 March 1958, 2 s., 1 d. *Education:* BSc, Economics, London School of Economics and Political Science, 1956; Hon. Fellow, Telecommunications Engineering Staff College, 1990. *Appointments:* Independent Consultant, 1990–98; Reviewer, Orbis, 1991–96. *Publications:* As the Hard Red Sand, 1979; Prince Arthur, 1981. *Contributions to:* An Idea of Bosnia; Chapman; Christian Poetry; Counterpoint; Incept; Iron; Juju; Linq; Orbis; Ore; Pennine Platform; Poetry NZ; Periaktos, Poets' England; Poets' Voice; Voices; Voices of Israel; Voices of Surrey; Weyfarers. *Honour:* First Prize, Maze Poetry Competition, 1992. *Memberships:* Surrey Poetry Centre, vice-chair.; Weyfarers, panel ed., Guildford Poets Press; Poetry Society. *Address:* 9 Copse Edge, Elstead, Godalming, Surrey GU8 6DJ, England.

WHEATLEY, Margery Patience; b. 4 Sept. 1924, Berkshire, England. Teacher (retd); Poet. m. David Irvine Wanklyn, 6 April 1948, 1 s., 2 d. *Education:* BA, McGill University, Montréal, 1946. *Appointment:* Teacher of Creative Writing, Thomas More Institute for Adult Education, Montréal. *Publications:* A Hinge of Spring, 1986; Good-bye to the Sugar Refinery, 1989. *Contributions to:* Various anthologies, 1986–95, reviews, quarterlies, and journals. *Honour:* First Prize, Kingston Arts Council Literary Award, 1991. *Memberships:* Feminist Caucus, chair, 1988–90; League of Canadian Poets; Poetry Society, London; Writers' Union of Canada. *Address:* 33 Riverside Dr., Kingston, Ontario K7L 4V1, Canada.

WHEELER, Dennis R.; b. 1 Jan. 1948, North Bend, Oregon, USA. Law Enforcement Officer; Poet. m. Dorothy Beyerle, 13 March 1971, 2 s. *Education:* Assoc. Arts Degree, San Bernardino Valley College, 1976. *Appointments:* Law Enforcement Officer, various agencies in South Dakota and California, 1970–; Patrol Sergeant, Rialto Police Dept, Rialto, CA. *Publications:* A Family Affair; A Family Affair II. *Contributions to:* Mobridge Tribune; Mobridge, South Dakota. *Honours:* Ed.'s Choice Award, National Library of Poetry, 1996; Certificate, Famous Poet, Famous Poets Society, 1996. *Memberships:* International Society of Poets; Famous Poets Society. *Address:* 1148 E Sonora, San Bernardino, CA 92404, USA.

WHEELER, Griffith Sylvia; b. 30 May 1930, Kansas, USA. Assoc. Prof. of English; Poet. Divorced, 2 s., 1 d. *Education:* University of Kansas, 1968; University of Missouri, 1971. *Appointments:* Assoc. Ed., BkMk Press, 1971–77; Poet-in-Schools, KS, 1971–88; Assoc. Prof. of English, University of South Dakota, 1977–. *Publications:* Counting Back; Dancing Along; This Fool History; This Can't Go On Forever; City Limits; The Masters (play), 1995. *Contributions to:* Reviews, quarterlies, and journals. *Honours:* Witter Bynner Foundation Award; Third Prize, Seaton Award; FMCT Midwestern Playwrights Award; Gwendolyn Brooks Poetry Prize; South Dakota Arts Council Individual Artist Award. *Memberships:* Poets and Writers; Society for the Study of Midwestern Literature. *Address:* c/o Dept of English, University of South Dakota, Vermillion, SD 57069, USA.

WHEELER, Susan; b. 16 July 1955, Pittsburgh, Pennsylvania, USA. Poet. m., 2 c. *Education:* BA, Bennington College, 1977; University of Chicago, 1979–81. *Appointments:* Vermont Council on the Arts; Art Institute of Chicago; Rutgers University, 1995–95; MFA Program, New School University, 1996–; New York University, 1997–99; Princeton University, 1999–. *Publications:* Bag o' Diamonds, 1993; Smokes, 1998; Source Codes, 2001. *Contributions to:* Boston Review; Massachusetts Review; The New Yorker; Paris Review; The Best American Poetry Anthologies (five edns since 1988). *Honours:* Roberts Writing Award; Grolier Poetry Prize; Wurlitzer Foundation Award; New York Foundation for the Arts Fellowships, 1993, 1997; Norma Farber First Book Award, Poetry Society of America, 1994; Four Way Books Award, 1996; Guggenheim Fellowship, 1999; Witter Bynner Award for Poetry, American Acad. of Arts and Letters, 2002. *Membership:* Poetry Society of America; Acad. of American Poets; PEN, council mem., 1998–. *Agent:* Bill Clegg, Burnes & Clegg, 1133 Broadway, No. 1020,, New York, NY 10010, USA. *Telephone:* (212) 331-9880. *Website:* www. susanwheeler.net.

WHIPPLE, George; b. 24 May 1927, St John, NB, Canada. Poet. *Education:* Vancouver Teacher's College, 1953. *Publication:* Life Cycle, 1984; Passing Through Eden, 1991; Hats Off to the Sun, 1996. *Contributions to:* Poetry Canada Review; Canadian Forum; Fiddlehead; Writers Market (USA); Candleabrum (UK); Antigonish Review. *Memberships:* League of Canadian Posts; Writers' Union of Canada. *Address:* 2004-4390 Grange St, St Burnaby, BC V5H 1P6, Canada.

WHITE, Gail (Brockett); b. 1 April 1945, Florida, USA. Poet; Ed. m. 27 March 1967. *Education:* BA, Stetson University, 1967. *Appointments:* Ed., Piedmont Literary Review. *Publications:* Sibyl & Sphinx; Rockhill Press; The Price of Everything; Irreverent Parables; Fishing for Leviathan; A Formal Feeling Comes. *Contributions to:* American Scholar; Southern Poetry Review; Lyric; Plains Poetry Journal; South Carolina Review; South Coast Poetry Journal; Christian Century; Outposts; Descant; University of Windsor Review; Room of Ones Own; Kalliope; New Laurel Review; Negative Capability; Western Humanities Review. *Honours:* Bernard Meredith Award; Virginia Prize; Seneca Award. *Address:* 1017 Spanish Moss Lane, Breaux Bridge, LA 70517, USA.

WHITE, Howard; b. 18 April 1945, Abbotsford, BC, Canada. Writer; Poet; Ed.; Publisher. 2 s. *Appointments:* Founder, Ed., Publisher, Peninsula Voice, 1969–74; Ed., Raincoast Chronicles, 1972–; Founder, Pres., Publisher, Harbour Publishing, 1974–. *Publications:* Raincoast Chronicles (ed.), five vols, 1975, 1983, 1987, 1990, 1994; A Hard Man to Beat: The Story of Bill White, Labour Leader, Historian, Shipyard Worker, Raconteur: An Oral History (co-author), 1983; The Men There Were There, 1983; The New Canadian Poets (ed.), 1985; Spilsbury's Coast: Pioneer Years in the Wet West (co-author), 1987; The Accidental Airline, 1988; Writing in the Rain (essays and poetry), 1990; Ghost in the Gears, 1993; The Sunshine Coast: From Gibsons to Powell River, 1996. *Contributions to:* Periodicals. *Honours:* Eaton's British Columbia Book Award, 1976; Career Award for Regional History, Canadian History Asscn, 1989; Stephen Leacock Medal for Humour, 1990; Roderick Haig Brown Award, 1995. *Membership:* Asscn of Book Publishers of British Columbia, pres., 1988–90. *Address:* PO Box 219, Madeira Park, BC VON 2H0, Canada.

WHITE, James P(atrick); b. 28 Sept. 1940, Wichita Falls, TX, USA. Prof.; Writer; Poet; Dramatist; Ed.; Trans. m. Janice Lou Turner, 11 Sept. 1961, 1 s. *Education:* BA, University of Texas at Austin, 1961; MA, History, Vanderbilt University, 1963; MA, Creative Writing, Brown University, 1973. *Appointments:* Asst Prof., 1973–74; Assoc. Prof., 1974–77, University of Texas of the Permian Basin at Odessa; Ed., Sands literary review, 1974–78; Visiting Prof., University of Texas at Dallas, 1977–78; Founder-Ed., Texas Books in Review, 1977–79; Dir, Masters in Professional Writing, University of Southern California at Los Angeles, 1979–82; Mem., International Editorial Board, Translation Review, 1980–; Dir of Creative Writing, 1982–, Prof., 1987–, University of South Alabama. *Publications:* Fiction: Birdsong, 1977; The Ninth Car (with Anne Rooth), 1978; The Persian Oven, 1985; Two Novellas: The Persian Oven and California Exit, 1987; Clara's Call (in Two Short Novels, with R. V. Cassill), 1992. Poetry: Poetry, 1979; The Great Depression (with Walter Feldman), 1997. Editor: Clarity: A Text on Writing (with Janice White), 1982; Where Joy Resides: A Christopher Isherwood Reader (with Don Bachardy), 1989; Black Alabama: An Anthology of Contemporary Black Alabama Fiction Writers, 1998. *Contributions to:* Anthologies, reviews, quarterlies, journals, newspapers and magazines. *Honours:* Guggenheim Fellowship, 1988–89; Dean's Lecturer, University of South Alabama, 1990. *Memberships:* Alabama Writer's Forum; Associated Writing Programs; Christopher Isherwood Foundation, dir; Gulf Coast Asscn of Creative Writing Teachers, founder-pres., 1993; Texas Asscn of Creative Writing Teachers, founder-pres., 1974–78. *Address:* PO Box 428, Montrose, AL 36559, USA.

WHITE, John Austin; b. 27 June 1942, England. Canon; Writer; Poet. *Education:* BA, Honours, University of Hull; College of the Resurrection, Mirfield. *Appointments:* Asst Curate, St Aidan's Church, Leeds, 1966–69; Asst Chaplain, University of Leeds, 1969–73; Asst Dir, Post Ordination Training, Dioceses of Ripon, 1970–73; Chaplain, Northern Ordination Course, 1973–82; Canon of Windsor, 1982–; Warden, St George's House, 2000–.

Publications: A Necessary End: Attitudes to Death (with Julia Neuberger), 1991; Nicholas Ferrar: Materials for a Life (with L R Muir), 1997; Phoenix in Flight (with Thetis Blacker). *Contributions to:* Various publications. *Membership:* Fellow, RSA. *Address:* 8 The Cloisters, Windsor Castle, Berkshire SL4 1NJ, England.

WHITE, Jon (Ewbank) Manchip; b. 22 June 1924, Cardiff, Glamorganshire, Wales. Writer; Poet; Prof. of English (retd). m. Valerie Leighton, 2 c. *Education:* St Catharine's College, Cambridge, 1942–43, 1946–50; Open Exhibitioner in English Literature; MA, Honours, English, Prehistoric Archaeology, and Oriental Languages (Egyptology), and University Diploma in Anthropology. *Appointments:* Story Ed., BBC-TV, London, 1950–51; Senior Exec. Officer, British Foreign Service, 1952–56; Independent Author, 1956–67, including a period as screenwriter for Samuel Bronston Productions, Paris and Madrid, 1960–64; Prof. of English, University of Texas, El Paso, 1967–77; Lindsay Young Prof. of English, University of Tennessee, Knoxville, 1977–94. *Publications:* Fiction: Mask of Dust, 1953; Build Us a Dam, 1955; The Girl from Indiana, 1956; No Home But Heaven, 1957; The Mercenaries, 1958; Hour of the Rat, 1962; The Rose in the Brandy Glass, 1965; Nightclimber, 1968; The Game of Troy, 1971; The Garden Game, 1973; Send for Mr Robinson, 1974; The Moscow Papers, 1979; Death by Dreaming, 1981; The Last Grand Master, 1985; Whistling Past the Churchyard, 1992. Poetry: Dragon and Other Poems, 1943; Salamander and Other Poems, 1945; The Rout of San Romano, 1952; The Mountain Lion, 1971. Other: Ancient Egypt, 1952; Anthropology, 1954; Marshal of France: The Life and Times of Maurice, Comte de Saxe, 1962; Everyday Life in Ancient Egypt, 1964; Diego Velázquez, Painter and Courtier, 1969; The Land God Made in Anger: Reflections on a Journey Through South West Africa, 1969; Cortés and the Downfall of the Aztec Empire, 1971; A World Elsewhere: One Man's Fascination with the American Southwest, 1975; Everyday Life of the North American Indians, 1979; What to do When the Russians Come: A Survivors' Handbook (with Robert Conquest), 1984; The Journeying Boy: Scenes from a Welsh Childhood, 1991. *Memberships:* Texas Institute of Letters, 1970; Welsh Acad., 1995. *Address:* 5620 Pinellas Dr., Knoxville, TN 37919, USA.

WHITE, June; b. 11 June 1930, Somerset, England. Poet. m. Alan White, 8 March 1954. *Education:* Secretarial Training College. *Publications:* The Living Land; Woodpecker Morning. *Contributions to:* Northants & Beds Life; Writer Magazine; Writers Own Magazine; Clover International Poetry Anthology; Lilac & English Tea; Salopeot Poetry Anthology; She Magazine. *Honours:* John McMahon Trophy; Joyce McKay Trophy; Salopian Poetry Society Winner; Writers Review Poetry Competition Winner; Writers Own Magazine Poetry Competition Winner. *Membership:* Salopian Poetry Society. *Address:* Sequoia 5 Taylors Ride, Leighton Buzzard, Bedfordshire LU7 7JN, England.

WHITE, Kenneth; b. 28 April 1936, Glasgow, Scotland. Prof. of 20th Century Poetics; Poet; Writer. m. Marie Claude Charfut. *Education:* MA, University of Glasgow, 1959; University of Munich; University of Paris. *Appointments:* Lecturer in English, Institut Charles V, Paris, 1969–83; Prof. of 20th Century Poetics, Sorbonne, University of Paris, 1983–. *Publications:* Poetry: Wild Coal, 1963; En Toute Candeur, 1964; The Cold Wind of Dawn, 1966; The Most Difficult Area, 1968; A Walk Along the Shore, 1977; Mahamudra, 1979; Le Grand Rivage, 1980; Terre de diament, 1983; Atlantica: Mouvements et meditations, 1986; L'esprit nomade, 1987; The Bird Bath: Collected Longer Poems, 1989; Handbook for the Diamond Country: Collected Shorter Poems 1960–1990, 1990. Fiction: Letters from Gourgounel, 1966; Les Limbes Incandescents, 1978; Le Visage du vent d'Est, 1980; La Route Bleue, 1983; Travels in the Drifting Dawn, 1989; Pilgrim of the Viod, 1994. Other: Essays. *Contributions to:* Various publications. *Honour:* Grand Prix de Rayonnement, French Acad., 1985. *Address:* Gwenved, Chemin du Goaquer, 22560 Trebeurden, France.

WHITE, W(illiam) Robin(son); b. 12 July 1928, Kodaikanal, South India. Author; Poet. m. Marian Biesterfeld, 3 Feb. 1948, deceased 8 March 1983, 2 s., 1 d. *Education:* BA, Yale University, 1950; Bread Loaf Fellow, Middlebury College, 1956; Stegner Creative Writing Fellow, Stanford University, 1956–57; MA, California State Polytechnic University, 1991. *Appointments:* Ed.-in-Chief, Per-Se International Quarterly, Stanford University Press, 1965–69; Instructor, Photojournalism, 1973, Dir, Creative Writing Seminar, 1984, Mendocino Art Center; Lecturer, Scripps College, 1984; Fiction Ed., West-word literary magazine, 1985–90; Instructor, University of California, Los Angeles, 1985–; Research Reader, The Huntington Library, 1985–86; Lecturer, Writing Programme and CompuWrite, California State Polytechnic University, 1985–93. *Publications:* House of Many Rooms, 1958; Elephant Hill, 1959; Men and Angels, 1961; Foreign Soil, 1962; All In Favor Say No, 1964; His Own Kind, 1967; Be Not Afraid, 1972; The Special Child, 1978; The Troll of Crazy Mule Camp, 1979; Moses the Man, 1981; The Winning Writer, 1997. *Contributions to:* Journals and magazines. *Honours:* Harper Prize, 1959; O Henry Prize, 1960; Co-ordinating Council of Literary Magazines Award, 1968; Distinguished Achievement Award, Educational Press, 1974; Spring Harvest Poetry Awards, 1992, 1994, 1995; Ed.'s Choice Awards, Poetry, 1998, 2000; California State Polytechnic University Golden Leaves Award, 2000; New Century Writers Award, 2000. *Memberships:* Authors Guild; California State Poetry Society. *Address:* 1940 Fletcher Ave, South Pasadena, CA 91030, USA.

WHITEHEAD, Anthony Keith; b. 21 June 1937, Dewsbury, Yorkshire, England. Christian Evangelist; Poet. m. Iris Theresa Smith, 26 Dec. 1958, 2 s. *Education:* City and Guilds Full Technological Certificate in Pattermaking, 1958; BA, Economics, 1971; Postgraduate Certificate in Education, 1972; MPhil, 1978; Certification in Religious Studies, University of Cambridge, 1989. *Publications:* People and Employment, 1981; Prophetic Verse, 1993; Another Counsellor, 1995; Times and Seasons, 1999. *Contributions to:* Reviews, journals, newspapers and magazines. *Address:* Emmaus, 94 Nunn's Lane, Purston, West Yorkshire WF7 5HH, England.

WHITEHOUSE, Anne Cherner; b. 30 Jan. 1954, Alabama, USA. Writer; Poet. m. Stephen Whitehouse, 24 June 1979, 1 d. *Education:* BA, Harvard University, 1976; MFA, Columbia University, 1979. *Publication:* The Surveyor's Hand. *Contributions to:* New England Review; American Voice; Black Warrior Review; Alaska Quarterly Review; Buffalo Spree; New York Times Book Review; Miami Herald; Baltimore Sun; Los Angeles Times; Forward; Atlanta Journal and Constitution. *Honour:* Acad. of American Poets. *Memberships:* Poetry Society of America; Acad. of American Writers; Columbia University Seminar on Latin America. *Address:* 340 Riverside Dr., New York, NY 10025, USA.

WHITMAN, Ruth (Bashein); b. 28 May 1922, New York, NY, USA. Poet; Ed.; Trans.; Teacher. m. (1) Cedric Whitman, 13 Oct. 1941, divorced 1958, 2 d., (2) Firman Houghton, 23 July 1959, divorced 1964, 1 s., (3) Morton Sacks, 6 Oct. 1966. *Education:* BA, Radcliffe College, 1944; MA, Harvard University, 1947. *Appointments:* Editorial Asst, 1941–42, Educational Ed., 1944–45, Houghton Mifflin Co, Boston; Freelance Ed., Harvard University Press, 1945–60; Poetry Ed., Audience magazine, 1958–63; Dir, Poetry Workshop, Cambridge Center for Adult Education, 1964–68, Poetry in the Schools Program, Massachusetts Council on the Arts, 1970–73; Scholar-in-Residence, Radcliffe Institute, 1968–70; Instructor in Poetry, Radcliffe College, 1970–, Harvard University Writing Program, 1979–84; Writer-in-Residence and Visiting Lecturer at various colleges and universities; Many poetry readings. *Publications:* Blood and Milk Poems, 1963; Alain Bosquet: Selected Poems (trans. with others), 1963; Isaac Bashevis Singer: The Seance (trans. with others), 1968; The Marriage Wig, and Other Poems, 1968; The Selected Poems of Jacob Glatstein (ed. and trans.), 1972; The Passion of Lizzie Borden: New and Selected Poems, 1973; Poetmaking: Poets in Classrooms (ed.), 1975; Tamsen Donner: A Woman's Journey, 1975; Permanent Address: New Poems, 1973–1980, 1980; Becoming a Poet: Source, Process, and Practice, 1982; The Testing of Hanna Senesh, 1986; The Fiddle Rose: Selected Poems of Abraham Sutzkever (trans.), 1989; Laughing Gas: Poems New and Selected, 1963–1990, 1991; Hatsheput, Speak to Me, 1992. *Contributions to:* Anthologies and periodicals. *Honours:* MacDowell Colony Fellowships, 1962, 1964, 1972–74, 1979, 1982; Kovner Award, Jewish Book Council of America, 1969; Guiness International Poetry Award, 1973; National Endowment for the Arts Grant, 1974–75; John Masefield Award, 1976; Senior Fulbright Fellowship, 1984–85; Urbanarts Award, 1987. *Memberships:* Authors Guild; Authors League of America; New England Poetry Club; PEN; Poetry Society of America. *Address:* 40 Tuckerman Ave, Middletown, RI 02840, USA.

WHITNEY, E. See: THOMPSON, Lucille.

WHITTEN, Leslie H(unter) Jr; b. 21 Feb. 1928, Jacksonville, FL, USA. Writer; Poet; Journalist. m. Phyllis Webber, 11 Nov. 1951, 3 s., 1 d. *Education:* BA, English and Journalism, Lehigh University. *Publications:* Progeny of the Adder, 1965; Moon of the Wolf, 1967; Pinion, The Golden Eagle, 1968; The Abyss, 1970; F. Lee Bailey, 1971; The Alchemist, 1973; Conflict of Interest, 1976; Washington Cycle (poems), 1979; Sometimes a Hero, 1979; A Killing Pace, 1983; A Day Without Sunshine, 1985; The Lost Disciple, 1989; The Fangs of Morning, 1994; Sad Madrigals, 1997; Moses: The Lost Book of the Bible, 1999. *Contributions to:* Newspapers and literary magazines. *Honours:* Doctor, Humane Letters, Lehigh University, 1989; Journalistic Awards; Edgerton Award, American Civil Liberties Union. *Address:* 114 Eastmoor Dr., Sliver Spring, MD 20901, USA.

WICHERT, Sabine; b. 8 June 1942, Germany. University Teacher; Poet. *Education:* Universities in Frankfurt, Marburg, Berlin, Mannheim, London and Oxford. *Appointment:* Lecturer, 1971–97, Senior Lecturer, 1997–, Queen's University, Belfast. *Publications:* Northern Ireland Since 1945, 1991; Miranda, 1993; Tin Drum Country, 1995. *Contributions to:* Irish Press; Poetry Ireland Review; Fortnight; Honest Ulsterman; Filmdirections; Raven Introductions; Cyphers; Sunday Tribune; Gown Literary Supplement; Poetry Nottingham; Orbis; Salmon; Big Spoon; Windows Selection; Rustic Rub; Scratch; Envoi; Day by Day; Acumen; Spark; WP Monthly; Writing Women. *Honour:* Short-listed, Hennessy Sunday Tribune Award. *Membership:* Poetry Society. *Address:* 63 Vauxhall Park, Stranmillis, Belfast BT9 5HB, Northern Ireland.

WICKS, Susan Jane; b. 24 Oct. 1947, Kent, England. Tutor; Writer; Poet. m. John Collins, 7 April 1973, 2 d. *Education:* BA Honours, French, University of Hull, 1971; DPhil, University of Sussex, 1975. *Appointments:* University of Dijon, 1974–76; Asst Lecturer, French, University College, Dublin, 1976–77; Part-time Tutor, University of Kent Centre, Tonbridge, 1983–. *Publications:* Singing Underwater, 1992; Open Diagnosis, 1994; Driving My Father (prose),

1995. *Contributions to:* TLS; Observer; LRB; Poetry Review; London Magazine; Ambit; Poetry Durham; Poetry Wales; Poetry East; Women's Review of Books; Orbis; The New Yorker. *Honours:* Residency, Hedgebrook, Washington State, 1991; Aldeburgh Poetry Festival Prize, 1992; Ragdale Residency, IL, 1992; Residency, Virginia Centre for the Creative Arts, 1994. *Memberships:* Poetry Society; Kent and Sussex Poetry Society. *Address:* c/o University of Kent Centre, Avebury Ave, Tonbridge, Kent TN9 1TG, England.

WIEDER, Laurance; b. 28 June 1946, New York, NY, USA. Writer; Poet. m. Andrea Korotky Wieder, 1 d. *Education:* BA, Columbia University, 1968; MA, Cornell University, 1970. *Publications:* Man's Best Friend, 1982; The Coronet of Tours, 1972; No Harm Done, 1975; Duke: The Poems as told to..., 1990; Full Circle, 1990; The Last Century: Selected Poems, 1992; Chapters into Verse: Poetry in English Inspired by the Bible, 1993; King Solomon's Garden: Poems and Art Inspired by the Old Testament, 1994; The Red Sea Haggadah, 1995; The Poets' Book of Psalms, 1995; Chapters into Verse: A Selection of..., 2002. *Contributions to:* Scripsi; Pequod; Boulevard; New Yorker; Pataphysics; Partisan Review; Poetry; Columbia Review; Columbia College Today; Paris Review; Epoch; First Things; Chronicles; The Christian Century; Books and Culture; The Weekly Standard; Commonweal. *Honour:* Ingram Merrill Foundation Grant in Poetry, 1974. *Address:* 114 Oak St, Patchogue, NY 11772, USA. *E-mail:* mosesmuses@redsea.com.

WIER, Dara; b. 30 Dec. 1949, New Orleans, LA, USA. Poet; Prof. m. (1) Allen Wier, 2 April 1969, divorced 1983, (2) Michael Pettit, 1 Sept. 1983, divorced 1990, 1 s., 1 d. *Education:* Louisiana State University, 1967–70; BS, Longwood College, 1971; MFA, Bowling Green State University, 1974. *Appointments:* Instructor, University of Pittsburgh, 1974–75; Instructor, 1975–76, Asst Prof., 1977–80, Hollins College; Assoc. Prof., 1980–85, Dir of Graduate Studies, 1980–82, Dir of Writing Program, 1983–84, University of Alabama at Tuscaloosa; Assoc. Prof., 1985–96, Prof., 1996–, Dir., MFA programmes for poets and writers, 1985–91, 1992–94, 1997–98, University of Massachusetts at Amherst; Visiting poet at various colleges and universities. *Publications:* Blood, Hook, and Eye, 1977; The 8-Step Grapevine, 1981; All You Have in Common, 1984; The Book of Knowledge, 1988; Blue for the Plough, 1992; Our Master Plan, 1997; Voyages in English, 2001; Hatona Pond, 2002. *Contributions to:* Anthologies and periodicals. *Honours:* National Endowment for the Arts Fellowship, 1980; Guggenheim Fellowship, 1993–94; Jerome Shostack Award, American Poetry Review, 2001; Pushcart Prize, 2002. *Memberships:* Associated Writing Programs, pres., 1981–82; Authors Guild; Authors League of America; PEN; Poetry Society of America. *Address:* 504 Montague Rd, Amherst, MA 01002, USA.

WIG, Neelima; b. 8 March 1963, Jalandhar, Punjab, India. Writer; Poet; Designer. m. Sunil Mohan Wig, 30 Jan. 1982, 2 s. *Education:* BA Hons, English, Jalandhar City, Punjab; LLB, Lucknow University, India. *Publications:* Moments, Madness & Me, 1984; The Distant Echo, 1989; Among the Stars, 1996. *Contributions to:* The Northern News; The Hindu. *Memberships:* Samwaad; The Poetry Society, India. *Address:* A22/12 DLF Qutub Enclave, Phasse I Gurgaon, Haryana, India.

WIGHT, Jane (Alison); b. 24 Nov. 1935, Wangford, Suffolk, England. Lecturer; Poet; Writer. *Education:* MA, University of St Andrews, 1959; BA, University of Reading, 1965. *Appointment:* Part-time Lecturer, Extra-Mural Studies, University of Reading, 1977–94. *Publications:* Poetry: Place and Time, 1978; Thinking in Sentences, 1980; Contour and Cover, 1981; Catching the Sun, 1984; Point the Courses of the Stars, 1986; Linking Islands, 1988; Try Number Seven, 1989; Irregular Measure, 1991; After Image, 1993; Unlatch the Gate, 1996; Wing-Span, 2000. Other: Brick Building... to 1550, 1972; Mediaeval Floor Tiles, 1975; The Best Part of the Day, by May Ivimy (ed.), 1992; Waiting for the Echo (ed., anthology), 1994. *Contributions to:* Anthologies and periodicals. *Memberships:* Norwich Poetry Group, committee mem.; Ver Poets, St Albans. *Address:* 91 Bury St, Norwich, Norfolk NR2 2DL, England.

WIKHOLM-OSTLING, Gungerd Helen; b. 14 Oct. 1954, Karis, Finland. Writer; Poet; Journalist. m. Tom Seth Ostling, 14 Sept. 1990, 2 d. *Education:* Svenska Social-Och Kommunalhögskolan, Helsingor, 1974–77. *Appointment:* Cultural Journalist, Finnish Broadcasting Co, 1977–. *Publications:* Poetry: Torplandet, 1982; Aria, 1987; Anhalter, Svarta Och Roda, 1990; Ur Vattnets Arkiv, 1993; Stora Dagen, Lilla Natten, 1995. *Contributions to:* Periodicals. *Honours:* Svenska Litteratursällskapet, 1988; Langmanska Fonden, 1993. *Membership:* Finlands Svenska Forfattareforening. *Address:* Kilavägen 29 A3, Karis, Finland.

WILBER, Richard A.; b. 4 Sept. 1948, St Louis, Missouri, USA. Prof. of Journalism; Writer; Poet; Ed. m. Robin Smith, 16 March 1984, 1 s., 1 d. *Education:* BA, English and Journalism, 1970, MFA, English, 1976, DEd, 1996, Southern Illinois University. *Appointments:* Assoc. Ed., The Midwest Motorist, 1970–76; Prof. of Journalism, Florida State College, 1980–88, University of South Florida, 1988–96, Southern Illinois University, 1988–; Ed., Fiction Quarterly, 1988–. *Publication:* To Leuchars, 1997. *Contributions to:* Reviews, quarterlies and journals. *Memberships:* SFWA; Textbook Authors Asscn. *Address:* 210 Isle Dr., St Pete Beach, FL 33706, USA.

WILBUR, Richard (Purdy); b. 1 March 1921, New York, NY, USA. Poet; Writer; Trans.; Ed.; Prof. m. Mary Charlotte Hayes Ward, 20 June 1942, 3 s., 1 d. *Education:* AB, Amherst College, 1942; AM, Harvard University, 1947. *Appointments:* Asst Prof. of English, Harvard University, 1950–54; Assoc. Prof. of English, Wellesley College, 1955–57; Prof. of English, Wesleyan University, 1957–77; Writer-in-Residence, Smith College, 1977–86; Poet Laureate of the USA, 1987–88; Visiting Lecturer at various colleges and universities. *Publications:* Poetry: The Beautiful Changes and Other Poems, 1947; Ceremony and Other Poems, 1950; Things of This World, 1956; Poems, 1943–1956, 1957; Advice to a Prophet and Other Poems, 1961; The Poems of Richard Wilbur, 1963; Walking to Sleep: New Poems and Translations, 1969; Digging to China, 1970; Seed Leaves: Homage to R F, 1974; The Mind-Reader: New Poems, 1976; Seven Poems, 1981; New and Collected Poems, 1988. For Children: Loudmouse, 1963; Opposites, 1973; More Opposites, 1991; A Game of Catch, 1994; Runaway Opposites, 1995; Bone Key and Other Poems, 1998; Mayflies, 2000. Non-Fiction: Anniversary Lectures (with Robert Hillyer and Cleanth Brooks), 1959; Emily Dickinson: Three Views (with Louise Bogan and Archibald MacLeish), 1960; Responses: Prose Pieces, 1953–1976, 1976; The Catbird's Song, 1997. Editor: Modern American and Modern British Poetry (with Louis Untermeyer and Karl Shapiro), 1955; A Bestiary, 1955; Poe: Complete Poems, 1959; Shakespeare: Poems (with Alfred Harbage), 1966; Poe: The Narrative of Arthur Gordon Pym, 1974; Witter Bynner: Selected Poems, 1978. Translator: Molière: The Misanthrope, 1955; Molière: Tartuffe, 1963; Molière: The School for Wives, 1971; Molière: The Learned Ladies, 1978; Racine: Andromache, 1982; Racine: Phaedra, 1986; Molière: The School for Husbands, 1992; Molière: Amphitryon, 1995; Molière: Don Juan, 2000; Molière: The Bungler, 2000. *Honours:* Harriet Monroe Memorial Prizes, 1948, 1978; Oscar Blumenthal Prize, 1950; Guggenheim Fellowships, 1952–53, 1963–64; Prix de Rome Fellowship, American Acad. of Arts and Letters, 1954; Edna St Vincent Millay Memorial Award, 1957; Pulitzer Prizes in Poetry, 1957, 1989; National Book Award for Poetry, 1957; Ford Foundation Fellowship, 1960; Bollingen Prizes, 1963, 1971; Brandeis University Creative Arts Award, 1971; Shelley Memorial Award, 1973; Drama Desk Award, 1983; Chevalier, Ordre des Palmes Académiques, 1983; Los Angeles Times Books Prize, 1988; Gold Medal for Poetry, American Acad. and Institute of Arts and Letters, 1991; Edward Mac Dowell Medal, 1991; National Medal of Arts, 1994. *Memberships:* Acad. of American Poets, chancellor; American Acad. of Arts and Letters, pres., 1974–76, chancellor, 1976–78, 1980–81; American Acad. of Arts and Sciences; ASCAP; Authors League of America; Dramatists' Guild; MLA, hon. fellow. *Address:* 87 Dodwells Rd, Cummington, MA 01206, USA.

WILD, Peter; b. 25 April 1940, Northampton, Massachusetts, USA. Prof. of English; Poet; Writer. m. (1) Sylvia Ortiz, 1966, (2) Rosemary Harrold, 1981. *Education:* BA, 1962, MA, 1967, University of Arizona; MFA, University of California at Irvine, 1969. *Appointments:* Asst Prof., Sul Ross State University, Alpine, Texas, 1969–71; Asst Prof., 1971–73, Assoc. Prof., 1973–79, Prof. of English. 1979–, University of Arizona; Contributing Ed., High Country News, 1974–; Consulting Ed., Diversions, 1983–. *Publications:* Poetry: The Good Fox, 1967; Sonnets, 1967; The Afternoon in Dismay, 1968; Mica Mountain Poems, 1968; Joining Up and Other Poems, 1968; Mad Night with Sunflowers, 1968; Love Poems, 1969; Three Nights in the Chiricahuas, 1969; Poems, 1969; Fat Man Poems, 1970; Term and Renewals, 1970; Grace, 1971; Dilemma, 1971; Wild's Magical Book of Cranial Effusions, 1971; Peligros, 1972; New and Selected Poems, 1973; Cochise, 1973; The Cloning, 1974; Tumacacori, 1974; Health, 1974; Chihuahua, 1976; The Island Hunter, 1976; Pioneers, 1976; The Cavalryman, 1976; House Fires, 1977; Gold Mines, 1978; Barn Fires, 1978; Zuni Butte, 1978; The Lost Tribe, 1979; Jeanne d'Arc: A Collection of New Poems, 1980; Rainbow, 1980; Wilderness, 1980; Heretics, 1981; Bitteroots, 1982; The Peaceable Kingdom, 1983; Getting Ready for a Date, 1984; The Light on Little Mormon Lake, 1984; The Brides of Christ, 1991; Easy Victory, 1994. Other: Pioneer Conservationists of Western America, 2 vols, 1979, 1983; Enos Mills, 1979; Clarence King, 1981; James Welch, 1983; Barry Lopez, 1984; John Haines, 1985; John Nicholas, 1986; The Saguaro Forest, 1986; John C Van Dyke: The Desert, 1988; Alvar Núñez Cabeza de Vaca, 1991; Ann Zwinger, 1993. Editor: New Poetry of the American West (with Frank Graziano), 1982. *Honours:* Writer's Digest Prize, 1964; Hart Crane and Alice Crane Williams Memorial Fund Grant, 1969; Ark River Review Prize, 1972; Ohio State University Pres.'s Prize, 1982. *Address:* 1547 E Lester, Tucson, AZ 85719, USA.

WILDHAGEN, Dorothy Mabel, (Dorcas); b. 8 July 1942, New York, NY, USA. Poet. m. Charles B Wildhagen, 5 Oct. 1968, deceased 1975. *Education:* Mandl Medical Assts School, 1960; City College of the City University of New York, 1960–61; Spiritual Development Program, 1986. *Publication:* The Eighth of July: Poetry by Dorcas, 1996. *Contributions to:* Anthologies and periodicals. *Honours:* 2 Awards, Ed.'s Choice Award, National Library of Poetry, 1995. *Memberships:* Kentucky State Poetry Society; Sparrowgrass Poetry Forum. *Address:* 3119 Bailey Ave, Bronx, NY 10463, USA.

WILDWOOD, James. See: HANF, James Alphonso.

WILEY, Valerie; b. 7 April 1954, Philadelphia, Pennsylvania, USA. Poet; Patient Advocate. *Education:* Temple University; Newspaper Institute. *Publications:* Poetry Okayval, 1982; He's a Prince, 1994; Would You Stand Up, 1996. *Contributions to:* Anthologies, newspapers, magazines, radio, and television. *Honour:* Danae, 1976. *Memberships:* Clover Leaf Poetry Society; PCA; Philadelphia Library. *Address:* 1655 N Allison St, Philadelphia, PA 19131, USA.

WILKINSON, Rosemary Regina Challoner; b. 21 Feb. 1924, New Orleans, LA, USA. Poet; Writer. m. Henry Bertram Wilkinson, 15 Oct. 1949, 3 s., 1 d. *Education:* San Francisco State University; Livre University, Pakistan. *Appointments:* Teacher; Lecturer; Poetry Readings. *Publications:* Angels and Poetry, 1992; Cambrian Zephyr, 1993; My Plea (English/Russian), 2000; Selected Verses (English/Mandarin), 2001; Sing in the Wind with Love, 2002; Blessing of Poetry (English/French), 2002 . *Contributions to:* Various publications. *Honours:* Many awards and fellowships. *Memberships:* Acad. of American Poets; Authors League of America; National League of American Pen Women; Poetry Society, London; Poetry Society of America. *Address:* 3146 Buckeye Ct, Placeville, CA 95667, USA.

WILL, Frederic; b. 4 Dec. 1928, New Haven, CT, USA. University Pres.; Poet. *Education:* AB, Indiana University, 1949; PhD, Yale University, 1954. *Appointments:* Instructor in Classics, Dartmouth College, 1953–55; Asst Prof. of Classics, Pennsylvania State University, 1954–59, University of Texas, 1960–64; Assoc. Prof. of English and Comparative Literature, 1964–66, Prof. of Comparative Literature, 1966–71, University of Iowa; Prof. of Comparative LIterature, University of Massachusetts at Amherst, 1971–84; Pres., Mellen University, 1995–; Visiting Lecturer in poetry and criticism at many colleges and universities; Many poetry readings. *Publications:* Intelligible Beauty in Aesthetic Thought: From Winckelmann to Victor Cousin, 1958; Mosaic and Other Poems, 1959; A Wedge of Words (poems), 1962; Kostes Palamas: The Twelve Words of the Gypsy (trans.), 1964; Hereditas: Seven Essays on the Modern Experience of the Classical (ed.), 1964; Metaphrasis: An Anthology from the University of Iowa Trans. Workshop, 1964–65 (ed.), 1965; Flumen Historicum: Victor Cousin's Aesthetic and Its Sources, 1965; Literature Inside Out: Ten Speculative Essays, 1966; Planets (poems), 1966; Kostes Palamas: The King's Flute (trans.), 1967; From a Year in Greece, 1967; Archilochos, 1969; Herondas, 1972; Brandy in the Snow (poems), 1972; Theodor Adorno: The Jargon of Authenticity (trans. with Knut Tarnowski), 1973; The Knife in the Stone, 1973; The Fact of Literature, 1973; Guatemala, 1973; Botulism (poems), 1975; The Generic Demands of Greek Literature, 1976; Belphagor, 1977; Epics of America (poems), 1977; Our Thousand Year Old Bodies: Selected Poems, 1956–1976, 1980; Shamans in Turtlenecks: Selected Essays, 1984; The Sliced Dog, 1984; Entering the Open Hole, 1989; Recoveries, 1993. *Contributions to:* Many poems and articles in various periodicals. *Honours:* Fulbright Grants, 1950–51, 1955, 1956–57, 1975–76, 1980–81; ACLS Grant, 1958; Voertman Poetry Awards, Texas Institute of Letters, 1962, 1964; Bollingen Foundation Grant; National Endowment for the Arts Grant. *Address:* 617 7th St NW, Mount Vernon, IA 52314, USA.

WILLI RED BEAR. See: KERR, Kathryn Ann.

WILLIAMS, Alberta Norine, (Sonia Davis); b. 22 April 1908, Olds, AB, Canada. Poet; Author; Songwriter. m. Billy D Williams, 4 Sept. 1928, 1 s., 1 d. *Education:* Business College, Fayetteville, AR, 1921; Pueblo Community College, 1960; Writer's Digest and Will Heideman Correspondence Courses. *Publications:* Pearls of a Lady, 1976; Potpourri of a Poet, 1992; Prairie Bird, 1994. *Contributions to:* Many publications. *Honours:* Inducted, International World Writers Hall of Fame, 1997; Diamond-Homer Award, 1999. *Memberships:* Daughters of the American Revolution; Green Horn Valley Art Society; Verses of the Valley; National League of American Pen Women; Foundation of Women's Clubs, Rye. *Address:* 2538 County Rd, 660, Rye, CO 81069, USA.

WILLIAMS, C(harles) K(enneth); b. 4 Nov. 1936, Newark, New Jersey, USA. Poet; Prof. m. Catherine Justine Mauger, April 1975, 1 s., 1 d. *Education:* BA, University of Pennsylvania, 1959. *Appointments:* Visiting Prof., Franklin and Marshall College, Lancaster, Pennsylvania, 1977, University of California at Irvine, 1978, Boston University, 1979–80; Prof. of English, George Mason University, 1982; Visiting Prof., Brooklyn College, 1982–83; Lecturer, Columbia University, 1982–85; Holloway Lecturer, University of California at Berkeley, 1986; Prof., Princeton University, 1996–. *Publications:* A Day for Anne Frank, 1968; Lies, 1969; I Am the Bitter Name, 1972; The Sensuous President, 1972; With Ignorance, 1977; The Women of Trachis (co-trans.), 1978; The Lark, the Thrush, the Starling, 1983; Tar, 1983; Flesh and Blood, 1987; Poems 1963–1983, 1988; The Bacchae of Euripides (trans.), 1990; A Dream of Mind, 1992; Selected Poems, 1994; The Vigil, 1997; Poetry and Consciousness (selected essays), 1998; Repair (poems), 1999; Misgivings, A Memoir, 2000; Love About Love, 2001. *Contributions to:* Akzent; Atlantic; Carleton Miscellany; Crazyhorse; Grand Street; Iowa Review; Madison Review; New England Review; New Yorker; Seneca Review; Transpacific Review; TriQuarterly; Yale Review; Threepenny Review. Honours; Guggenheim Fellowship; Pushcart Press Prizes, 1982, 1983, 1987; National Book Critics Circle Award, 1983; National Endowment for the Arts Fellowship, 1985; Morton Dauwen Zabel Prize, 1988; Lila Wallace Writers Award, 1993; Berlin Prize Fellowship, 1998; PEN Voelker Prize, 1998; Pulitzer Prize for Poetry, 2000; Los Angeles Times Book Prize, 2000. *Memberships:* PEN; American Acad. of Arts and Sciences. *Address:* 82 Rue d'Hauteville, 75010 Paris, France.

WILLIAMS, Faith; b. 15 April 1941, New York, NY, USA. Teacher; Librarian; Poet. m. Stephen Fain Williams, 11 June 1966, 3 s., 2 d. *Education:* BA, Radcliffe College, 1963; PhD, Columbia University, 1973; Master of Library Science, Catholic University of America, 1992. *Contributions to:* Poet Lore; Nimrod; Kansas Quarterly; Bogg; Bridge. *Memberships:* Poets and Writers, New York; Writer's Center, Bethesda, Maryland. *Address:* 3768 McKinley St NW, Washington, DC 20015, USA.

WILLIAMS, Heathcote; b. 15 Nov. 1941, Helsby, Cheshire, England. Playwright; Poet. *Appointment:* Assoc. Ed., Transatlantic Review, New York and London. *Publications:* The Local Stigmatic, 1967; AC/DC, 1970; Remember the Truth Dentist, 1974; The Speakers, 1974; Very Tasty: A Pantomime, 1975; An Invitation to the Official Lynching of Abdul Malik, 1975; Anatomy of a Space Rat, 1976; Hancock's Last Half-Hour, 1977; Playpen, 1977; The Immortalist, 1977; At It, 1982; Whales, 1986. Poetry: Whale Nation, 1988; Falling for a Dolphin, 1988; Sacred Elephant, 1989; Autogeddon, 1991. Other: The Speakers, 1964; Manifestoes, Manifestern, 1975; Severe Joy, 1979; Elephants, 1983. *Honour:* Evening Standard Award, 1970. *Address:* c/o Curtis Brown, Haymarket House, 28–29 Haymarket, London SW1Y 4SP, England.

WILLIAMS, Herbert Lloyd; b. 8 Sept. 1932, Aberystwyth, Wales. Writer; Poet; Dramatist. m. Dorothy Maud Edwards, 13 Nov. 1954, 4 s., 1 d. *Publications:* The Trophy, 1967; A Lethal Kind of Love, 1968; Battles in Wales, 1975; Come Out Wherever You Are, 1976; Stage Coaches in Wales, 1977; The Welsh Quiz Book, 1978; Railways in Wales, 1981; The Pembrokeshire Coast National Park, 1987; Stories of King Arthur, 1990; Ghost Country, 1991; Davies the Ocean, 1991; The Stars in Their Courses, 1992; John Cowper Powys, 1997; Looking Through Time, 1998; A Severe Case of Dandruff, 1999; Voices of Wales, 1999; The Woman in Back Row, 2000; Punters, 2002. Television Dramas and Documentaries: Taff Acre, 1981; A Solitary Mister, 1983; Alone in a Crowd, 1984; Calvert in Camera, 1990; The Great Powys, 1994; Arouse All Wales, 1996. Radio Dramas: Doing the Bard, 1986; Bodyline, 1991. Adaptations: A Child's Christmas in Wales, 1994; The Citadel, 1997. *Contributions to:* Reviews and journals. *Honours:* Welsh Arts Council Short Story Prize, 1972, and Bursary, 1988; Aberystwyth Open Poetry Competition, 1990; Hawthornden Poetry Fellowship, 1992; Rhys Davies Short Story Award, 1995. *Memberships:* Welsh Acad., fellow; Welsh Union of Writers; Society of Authors; William Barnes Society. *Address:* 63 Bwlch Rd, Fairwater, Cardiff CF5 3BX, Wales. *E-mail:* h.williams13@ntlworld.com. *Website:* www.herbert-williams,co.uk.

WILLIAMS, Hugo (Mordaunt); b. 20 Feb. 1942, Windsor, Berkshire, England. Writer; Critic; Poet. m. Hermine Demoriane, 12 Oct. 1966, 1 d. *Education:* Eton College, 1955–60. *Appointments:* Asst Ed., London Magazine, 1961–69; Television Critic, New Statesman, 1982–87; Theatre Critic, Sunday Correspondent, 1989–90; Film Critic, Harpers & Queen, 1993–99. *Publications:* Symptoms of Loss, 1965; All the Time in the World, 1966; Sugar Daddy, 1970; Some Sweet Day, 1975; Love Life, 1979; No Particular Place to Go, 1981; Writing Home, 1985; Self-Portrait with a Slide, 1990; Dock Leaves, 1994; Billy's Rain, 2000; Curtain Call: 101 Portraits in Verse (ed.), 2001. *Contributions to:* Newspapers and periodicals. *Honours:* Eric Gregory Award, 1965; Cholmondeley Award, 1970; Geoffrey Faber Memorial Prize, 1979; T S Eliot Prize, 1999. *Membership:* RSL. *Address:* 3 Raleigh St, London N1 8NW, England.

WILLIAMS, John A(lfred); b. 5 Dec. 1925, Jackson, Mississippi, USA. Writer; Journalist; Poet; Educator. m. (1) Carolyn Clopton, 1947, divorced, 2 s., (2) Lorrain Isaac, 5 Oct. 1965, 1 s. *Education:* BA, Syracuse University, 1950; Graduate School, 1951. *Appointments:* Ed. and Publisher, Negro Market Newsletter, 1956–57; Contributing Ed., Herald-Tribune Book Week, 1963–65, American Journal, 1972–74, Politicks, 1977, Journal of African Civilizations, 1980–88; Lecturer, College of the Virgin Islands, 1968, City College of the City University of New York, 1968–69; Visiting Prof., Macalester College, 1970, University of Hawaii, 1974, Boston University, 1978–79, University of Houston, 1994, Bard College, 1994–95; Regents Lecturer, University of California at Santa Barbara, 1972; Guest Writer, Sarah Lawrence College, 1972–73; Distinguished Prof., LaGuardia Community College of the City University of New York, 1973–79; Distinguished Visiting Prof., Cooper Union, 1974–75; Prof., Rutgers University, 1979–93; Exxon Visiting Prof., New York University, 1986–87. *Publications:* Fiction: The Angry Ones, 1960, revised edn as One for New York, 1975; Night Song, 1961; Sissie, 1963; The Man Who Cried I Am, 1967; Sons of Darkness, Sons of Light, 1969; Captain Blackman, 1972; Mothersill and the Foxes, 1975; The Junio Bachelor Society, 1976; !Click Song, 1982; The Berhama Account, 1985; Jacob's Ladder, 1987; Clifford's Blues, 1999. Libretto: Vanqui, premier, 1999. Poetry: Safari West, 1998. Non-Fiction: Africa: Her History, Lands and People, 1963; The Protectors, 1964; This Is My Country Too, 1965; The Most Native of Sons: A Biography of Richard Wright, 1970; The King God Didn't Save: Reflections on the Life and Death of Martin Luther King, Jr., 1970; Flashbacks: A Twenty-Year Diary of Article Writing, 1975; Minorities in the City, 1975; If I Stop I'll Die: The Comedy and Tragedy of Richard Pryor (with Dennis A Williams), 1991. Editor or Co-Editor: The Angry Black, 1962, revised edn as Beyond the Angry Black, 1967; Amistad 1, 1970; Amistad 2, 1971; Y'Bird, 1978; Introduction to Literature, 1985; Street Guide to African Americans in Paris,

1992; Approaches to Literature, 1994; Bridges: Literature Across Cultures, 1994. *Contributions to:* Anthologies, journals, reviews, and magazines. *Honours:* National Institute of Arts and Letters Award, 1962; Centennial Medal, 1970, Hon. DLitt, 1995, Syracuse University; Richard Wright-Jacques Roumain Award, 1973; National Endowment for the Arts Award, 1977; Hon. Doctor of Literature, Southeastern Massachusetts University, 1978; American Book Awards, Before Columbus Foundation, 1983, 1998; New Jersey State Council on the Arts Award, 1985; Michael Award, New Jersey Literary Hall of Fame, 1987; Distinguished Writer Award, Middle Atlantic Writers, 1987; J A Williams Archive established, University of Rochester, 1987; Carter G Woodson Award, Mercy College, 1989; National Literary Hall of Fame, 1998. *Memberships:* Authors Guild; Poets and Writers; PEN. *Literary Agent:* Barbara Hogenson, 165 West End Ave, New York, NY 10024, USA. *Address:* 693 Forest Ave, Teaneck, NJ 07666, USA.

WILLIAMS, John Hartley; b. 7 Feb. 1942, England. Poet; Lecturer. m. Gizella Horvat, 7 March 1970, 1 d. *Education:* BA, Honours, English, University of Nottingham, 1965; MPhil, English and Education, University of London, 1974; Certificate in Phonetics, University College, London, 1974. *Appointment:* Lecturer, Free University of Berlin, 1976–. *Publications:* Hidden Identities, 1982; Bright River Yonder, 1987; Cornerless People, 1990; Double, 1994; Ignoble Sentiments, 1995; Teach Yourself Writing Poetry (with Matthew Sweeney), 1997; The Scar in the Stone, edited by Chris Agee (contributing trans. to poems from Serbo-Croatian), 1998; Spending Time with Walter, 2001. *Contributions to:* Anthologies, reviews, and journals. *Honours:* First Prize, Arvon International Poetry Competition, 1983; Poetry Book Recommendation, 1987; Short-listed, T. S. Eliot Prize, 1997. *Membership:* Poetry Society. *Address:* 18 Jenbacherweg, 12209, Berlin, Germany.

WILLIAMS, Merryn; b. 9 July 1944, Devon, England. Writer; Poet; Ed. m. John Hemp, 14 April 1973, 1 s., 1 d. *Education:* BA, 1966, PhD, 1970, University of Cambridge. *Appointments:* Lecturer, Open University, 1970–71; Ed., The Interpreter's House, 1996–; Ed., Wilfrid Owen Asscn newsletter. *Publications:* The Bloodstream, 1989; Selected Poems of Federico García Lorca, 1992; Wilfred Owen, 1993; The Sun's Yellow Eye, 1997; The Latin Master's Story, 2000; In the Spirit of Wilfrid Owen (ed., anthology), 2002. *Contributions to:* Reviews, quarterlies, journals, and magazines. *Memberships:* Open University Poets; Welsh Acad. *Address:* 10 Farrell Rd, Wootton, Bedfordshire MK43 9DU, England. *E-mail:* hemp@cranfield.ac.uk.

WILLIAMS, Miller; b. 8 April 1930, Hoxie, AR, USA. Prof.; University Press Dir; Writer; Poet. m. (1) Lucille Day, 29 Dec. 1951, 1 s., 2 d., (2) Jordan Hall, 1969. *Education:* BS, Arkansas State College, 1950; MS, University of Arkansas, 1952. *Appointments:* Founder-Ed., 1968–70, Advisory Ed., 1975–, New Orleans Review; Prof., University of Arkansas, 1971–; Dir, University of Arkansas Press, 1980–97. *Publications:* A Circle of Stone, 1964; Southern Writing in the Sixties (with J W Corrington), 2 vols, 1966; So Long at the Fair, 1968; Chile: An Anthology of New Writing, 1968; The Achievement of John Ciardi, 1968; The Only World There Is, 1968; The Poetry of John Crowe Ransom, 1971; Contemporary Poetry in America, 1972; Halfway from Hoxie: New and Selected Poems, 1973; How Does a Poem Mean? (with John Ciardi), 1974; Railroad (with James Alan McPherson), 1976; Why God Permits Evil, 1977; A Roman Collection, 1980; Distraction, 1981; Ozark, Ozark: A Hillside Reader, 1981; The Boys on Their Bony Mules, 1983; Living on the Surface: New and Selected Poems, 1989; Adjusting to the Light, 1992; Points of Departure, 1995; The Ways We Touch (poems), 1997; Some Jazz a While: Collected Poems, 1999; The Lives of Kelvin Fletcher: Stories Mostly Short, 2002. *Contributions to:* Various publications. *Honours:* Henry Bellaman Poetry Award, 1957; Bread Loaf Fellowship in Poetry, 1961; Fulbright Lecturer, 1970; Prix de Rome, American Acad. of Arts and Letters, 1976; Hon. Doctor of Humanities, Lander College, 1983; National Poets Prize, 1992; John William Corrington Award for Excellence in Literature, Centenary College, LA, 1994; American Acad. of Arts and Letters Award, 1995; Hon. LHD, Hendrix College, 1995; Inaugural Poet, Presidential Inauguration, 1997. *Address:* 1111 Valley View Dr., Fayetteville, AR 72701, USA.

WILLIAMS, Tyrone; b. 24 Feb. 1954, Detroit, Michigan, USA. Assoc. Prof.; Poet. *Education:* BA, 1977; MA, 1983; PhD, 1992. *Appointments:* Teaching Asst, Wayne State University, 1979–83; Prof., Xavier University, 1983–. *Publication:* Convalescence. *Contributions to:* Kenyon Review; Obsidian; Colorado Review; World; Transfer. *Honours:* Finalist, National Poetry Service; Second Prize, Poet Hunt; First Prize, Topkins Poetry Award. *Address:* 2217 Victory Parkway, C-1, Cincinnati, OH 45206, USA.

WILLIAMS-WITHERSPOON, Kimmika L. H.; b. 7 Jan. 1959, Pennsylvania, USA. Playwright; Poet; Performance Artist. m. Darrell V. Witherspoon, 11 July 1992, 2 d. *Education:* BA, Journalism, Howard University, 1980; MFA, Playwriting, Temple University, 1996; Graduate Certificate in Women's Studies, 1996. *Appointments:* Future Faculty Fellow, Anthropology Dept, Temple University. *Publications:* God Made Men Brown, 1982; It Ain't Easy To Be Different, 1986; Halley's Comet, 1988; Envisioning a Sea of Dry Bones, 1990; Epic Memory: Places and Spaces I've Been, 1995; Signs of the Times: Culture Gap, 1999. *Contributions to:* Women's Words; Sunlight on the Moon. *Honours:* Playwrights Exchange Grants, 1994, 1996. *Memberships:* Poets and

Prophets; Poets and Writers. *Address:* c/o Temple University, 219 Tomlinson Hall, Philadelphia, PA 19122, USA.

WILLIAMSON, Greg; b. 26 June 1964, Columbus, Ohio, USA. Teacher; Poet. *Education:* BA, Vanderbilt University, 1986; MA, University of Wisconsin, 1987; MA, Johns Hopkins University, 1989. *Appointment:* Lecturer, Johns Hopkins University. *Publication:* Silent Partner, 1995. *Contributions to:* Yale Review; Poetry; Partisan Review; New Republic; Formalist; Paris Review; Southwest Review; New Criterion; Tennessee Quarterly. *Honour:* Nicholas Roerich Poetry Prize, 1995. *Membership:* Acad. of American Poets. *Address:* 5704 Lofthill Ct, Alexandria, VA 22303, USA.

WILLOUGHBY, Katrina Agness; b. 8 March 1948, New Zealand. Librarian; Poet. m. 1 s., 1 d. *Education:* Central Hawkes Bay College. *Publications:* A Green Dreaming; 10 Each. *Contributions to:* Journals and magazines. *Memberships:* PEN; Poetry Society.

WILMER, Clive; b. 10 Feb. 1945, Harrogate, Yorkshire, England. Lecturer; Writer; Poet; Trans.; Broadcaster. m. Diane Redmond, 12 Sept. 1971, divorced 1986, 1 s., 1 d. *Education:* BA, English, 1967, MA, 1970, King's College, Cambridge. *Appointments:* Visiting Prof. in Creative Writing, University of California at Santa Barbara, 1986; Ed., Numbers, 1986–90; Presenter, Poet of the Month series, BBC Radio 3, 1989–92; Mikimoto Memorial Ruskin Lecturer, University of Lancaster, 1996; Research Fellow and Poet-in-Residence, Anglia Polytechnic University, 1998–2002; Assoc. Teaching Officer, Sidney Sussex and Fitzwilliam Colleges, Cambridge, 1999–2002. *Publications:* Poetry: The Dwelling Place, 1977; Devotions, 1982; Of Earthly Paradise, 1992; Selected Poems, 1995; The Falls, 2000. Translator: Forced March, by Miklós Radnóti (with G. Gömöri), 1979; Night Song of the Personal Shadow, by György Petri (with G. Gömöri), 1991; My Manifold City, by George Gömöri, 1996; Eternal Monday by György Petri (with G. Gömöri), 1999. Editor: Thom Gunn: The Occasions of Poetry, 1982; John Ruskin: Unto This Last and Other Writings, 1985; Dante Gabriel Rossetti: Selected Poems and Translations, 1991; William Morris: News From Nowhere and Other Writings, 1993; Poets Talking: The 'Poet of the Month' Interviews from BBC Radio 3, 1994; Cambridge Observed: An Anthology (ed. with Charles Moseley), 1998; Donald Davie: With the Grain, 1998; The Life and Work of Miklós Radnóti: Essays (ed. with George Gömöri), 1999. *Contributions to:* Many reviews, newspapers, quarterlies and journals. *Honours:* Cambridge University Chancellor's Medal for an English Poem, 1967; Writer's Grant, Arts Council of Great Britain, 1979; Author's Foundation Grant, 1993; Hon. Fellowship, Anglia Polytechnic University, 1997; Hungarian PEN Club Memorial Medal for Trans., 1998; Short-listed for Weidenfeld Trans. Prize, 2000. *Membership:* Companion of the Guild of St George, 1995. *Literary Agent:* A. M. Heath and Co Ltd, 79 St Martin's Lane, London WC2N 4AA, England. *Address:* 57 Norwich St, Cambridge CB2 1ND, England.

WILNER, Eleanor; b. 29 July 1937, Ohio, USA. Poet; Teacher. m. Robert Weinberg, 1 d. *Education:* BA, 1959; MA, 1964; PhD, 1971. *Appointments:* Teacher, Morgan State University, Goucher College, Temple University, Japan; Poet-in-Residence, University of Chicago, University of Iowa, University of Hawaii, Northwestern University, 1997, University of Utah, 1999; Assoc. Ed., Calyx: A Journal of Art and Literature by Women; Faculty, MFA Program for Writers, Warren Wilson College, 1999. *Publications:* Maya, 1979; Shekhinah, 1984; Sarah's Choice, 1989; Otherwise, 1993; Reversing the Spell: New and Selected Poems, 1998. *Contributions to:* Beloit Poetry Journal; Chicago Review; Kenyon Review; New Republic; New Yorker; Southwest Review; Boulevard, Poetry; Prairie Schooner. *Honours:* John D. and Catherine T. MacArthur Foundation Fellowship; Pennbook Philadelphia Award; Pennsylvania Council on the Arts Fellowship; National Endowment for the Arts Creative Writing Grant; Juniper Prize. *Memberships:* PEN; Associated Writing Programs. *Address:* 324 S 12th St, Philadelphia, PA 19107, USA.

WILOCH, Thomas; b. 3 Feb. 1953, Detroit, Michigan, USA. Poet; Writer; Ed. m. Denise Gottis, 10 Oct. 1981. *Education:* BA, Wayne State University, 1978. *Appointments:* Associated with Gale Group 1977–; Pres., Manuscript Unlimited Inc., 2000–; Content Man., Poe Central website, 2001–02. Columnist, Retrofuturism, 1991–93, Photo Static, 1993–94; Book Reviewer, Anti-Matter Magazine, 1992–94, Sentimentalist, 2002–, Green Man Review, 2002–. *Publications:* Stigmata Junction, 1985; Paper Mask, 1988; The Mannikin Cypher, 1989; Tales of Lord Shantih, 1990; Decoded Factories of the Heart, 1991; Night Rain, 1991; Narcotic Signature, 1992; Lyrical Brandy, 1993; Mr Templeton's Toyshop, 1995; Neon Trance, 1997. *Contributions to:* Over 200 magazines. *Honours:* Nominations, Pushcart Prize, 1988, 1990, Rhysling Award, 1992, 1996. *Membership:* Asscn of Literary Scholars and Critics. *Address:* PMB 226, 42015 Ford Rd, Canton, MI 48187, USA. *E-mail:* mssunltd@postmark.net.

WILSON, Allison; b. 14 March 1953, York, South Carolina, USA. Prof.; Poet. m. Rodger E Wilson, 9 April 1971. *Education:* BA, Winthrop College, 1971; MS, 1972, MAT, 1973 Jackson State University; Ed D, Columbia University Teachers College, 1979. *Appointments:* Lecturer, 1979–80, Asst Prof., 1980–86, Assoc. Prof., 1986–93, Prof., 1993–, Jackson State University. *Contributions to:* Bucks County Panorama; Independent Review; Journal of the Mississippi Poetry Society. *Honours:* First Prize, Independent Review Competition; Jackson George Regional Library Competition; Mississippi Poetry Society Award; Writers Unlimited Award; Many Honorable Mentions. *Memberships:* Mississippi Poetry Society; Mississippi Writers Club; MLA. *Address:* Dept of English and Modern Foreign Languages, Jackson State University, Jackson, MS 39217, USA.

WILSON, Edwin James (Peter); b. 27 Oct. 1942, Lismore, NSW, Australia. Poet. m. Cheryl Lillian Turnham, 1 Sept. 1975, 2 s., 1 d. *Education:* BSc, University of New South Wales. *Publications:* Banyan, 1982; Royal Botanic Gardens, 1982; Liberty, Egality, Fraternity, 1984; The Dragon Tree, 1985; Discovering the Domain, 1986; Wild Tamarind, 1987; Falling Up into Verse, 1989; Songs of the Forest, 1990; The Rose Garden, 1991; The Wishing Tree, 1992; The Botanic Verses, 1993; Chaos Theory, 1997; Cosmos Seven: Selected Poems, 1967–1997, 1998; The Mullumbimby Kid: A Portrait of the Poet as a Child, 2000; Cedar House, 2001; Asteroid Belt, 2002. *Contributions to:* Australian Folklore; Poetry Australia. *Membership:* New South Wales Poets Union. *Address:* PO Box 32, Lane Cove, NSW 2066, Australia.

WILSON, Frances Jean; b. 8 July 1937, Wiltshire, England. Teacher; Poet. m. Harry Wilson, April 1963, 1 s., 1 d. *Education:* BA, Honours, English Literature, University College, London, 1958; Diploma in Education, Goldsmiths College, London, 1959. *Appointments:* Leader, writing workshops, colleges, and WEA, 1980–96. *Publications:* Where the Light Gets In, 1992; Close to Home, 1993. *Contributions to:* Reviews and journals. *Honours:* Prizes, Lace Open Competition, 1987, Orbis Rhyme International Competition, 1987, 1991, Staple Summer Competition, 1987, 1988, 1995, Ver Poets Poemcard Competition, 1988, 1989, Lancaster Competition, 1990, 1992, National Poetry Competition, 1991, Lake Aske Open, 1995. *Memberships:* Poetry Society; Ware Poetry Group, co-founder and organiser, 1991–. *Address:* 52 Watton Rd, Ware, Hertfordshire SG11 0AT, England.

WILSON, Gina; b. 1 April 1943, Abergele, North Wales. Children's Writer; Poet. *Education:* MA, University of Edinburgh, 1965; Mount Holyoke College, 1965–66. *Appointments:* Asst Ed., Scottish National Dictionary, 1967–73, Dictionary of the Older Scottish Tongue, 1972–73. *Publications:* Cora Ravenwing, 1980; A Friendship of Equals, 1981; The Whisper, 1982; All Ends Up, 1984; Family Feeling, 1986; Just Us, 1988; Polly Pipes Up, 1989; I Hope You Know, 1989; Jim Jam Pyjamas, 1990; Wompus Galumpus, 1990; Riding the Great White, 1992; Prowlpuss, 1994; Ignis, 2001. *Honours:* Frogmore Poetry Prize, 1997; Annual Lace Poetry Prize, 1999. *Address:* 24 Beaumont St, Oxford OX1 2NP, England.

WILSON, Jim C., (James Crawford Wilson); b. 16 July 1948, Edinburgh, Scotland. Writer; Poet. m. Mik Kerr, 21 Aug. 1971. *Education:* MA, English Language and Literature, University of Edinburgh, 1971. *Appointments:* Lecturer in English, Telford College, Edinburgh, 1972–81; Writer-in-Residence, Stirling District, 1989–91; Creative Writing Tutor, University of Edinburgh, 1994–; Royal Literary Fund Writing Fellow, Napier University, Edinburgh, 2001–02, Office of Lifelong Learning, University of Edinburgh, 2002–03. *Publications:* The Loutra Hotel, 1988; Cellos in Hell, 1993. *Contributions to:* Anthologies, including: A Book of Scottish Verse; Such Strange Joy; New Writing Scotland; 100 Major Modern Poets; Present Poets; Six Twentieth Century Poets; Periodicals, journals and newspapers, including: Acumen; Stand; Rialto; Outposts; Chapman; Orbis; Scotsman; Glasgow Herald; Encounter. *Honours:* Scottish Arts Council Writer's Bursaries, 1987, 1994; First Prize, Scottish International Open Poetry Competition, 1987; First Prizes, Swanage Arts Festival Literary Competition, 1988, 1989, 1997; Hugh MacDiarmid Trophy, 1997. *Membership:* Scottish PEN. *Address:* 25 Muirfield Park, Gullane, East Lothian EH31 2DY, Scotland. *Telephone:* (1620) 842167. *Website:* www.rlf.org.uk.

WILSON, Keith; b. 26 Dec. 1927, Clovis, New Mexico, USA. Poet; Writer. m. Heloise Brigham, 15 Feb. 1958, 1 s., 4 d. *Education:* BS, US Naval Acad., 1950; MA, University of New Mexico, 1956. *Publications:* Homestead, 1969; Thantog: Songs of a Jaguar Priest, 1977; While Dancing Feet Shatter the Earth, 1977; The Streets of San Miguel, 1979; Retablos, 1981; Stone Roses: Poems from Transylvania, 1983; Meeting at Jal (with Theodore Enslin), 1985; Lion's Gate: Selected Poems 1963–1986, 1988; The Wind of Pentecost, 1991; Graves Registry, 1992; The Way of the Dove, 1994; Bosque Redoudo: The Enclosed Grove, 2000. *Contributions to:* Journals. *Honours:* National Endowment for the Arts Fellowship; Fulbright-Hays Fellowship; D H Lawrence Creative Writing Fellowship. *Address:* 1500 S Locust St, No. C-21, Las Cruces, NM 88001, USA.

WILSON, Steve; b. 30 March 1960, Fort Sill, Oklahoma, USA. Prof. of English; Poet. m. Nancy Effinger, 31 July 1982, 2 s. *Education:* BA, Letters, University of Oklahoma, 1982; MA, English, Texas Christian University, 1984; MFA, Creative Writing, Wichita State University, 1987. *Appointments:* English Faculty, 1987, MFA Faculty, 1992–, Southwest Texas State University. *Publications:* Allegory Dance, 1991; The Singapore Express, 1994; A Fulbrighter's Experiences in Romania: Thought and Action, 1998. Editor: The Anatomy of Water: A Sampling of Contemporary American Prose Poetry, 1992. *Contributions to:* New American Writing; Asylum Annual; Midwest Quarterly; The Literary Review; Envoi; Negative Capability; Descant; The Prose Poem: An

International Journal; Yankee Magazine; New Letters; New Orleans Review Oasis. *Honours:* National Endowment fot the Arts Grant, 1992; Fulbrigh Scholar in Creative Writing, Romania, 1994–95, in American Literature and Creative Writing, Slovenia, 2002. *Memberships:* Fulbright Asscn, Texas Asscr of Creative Writing Teachers. *Address:* Dept of English, Southwest Texas State University, San Marcos, TX 78666, USA.

WILTON-JONES, Anne Mary, (Áine an Caipín, Anni Wilton-Jones); b. 8 April 1949, Bromborough, Wales. Performance Poet; Lecturer. 2 s., 5 d *Education:* DSRT, 1969, DSRR, 1970, School of Radiography, Southampton BA, Open University, 1994; PGCE, E and T, 1999; Cert SEN, 2000, UCWN *Publications:* Bridges, 1999; This is... Salem, 1999; Fresh Voices For Younger Listeners, 2000; Anam Cara (CD), 2001; Light Touch, 2002. *Contributions to* Newspapers and journals. *Address:* Ty Beirdd, 53 Church St, Ebbw Vale, NP2: 6BG Wales. *E-mail:* annipoetry@yahoo.co.uk.

WINANS, A(llan) D.; b. 12 Jan. 1936, San Francisco, CA, USA. Equal Opportunity Specialist; Civil Rights Investigator (retd); Poet. *Education:* BA San Francisco State University. *Publications:* In Memoriam; Regan Psalms Further Adventures of Crazy John; North Beach Poems; ORG Minus One; All the Graffiti on all the Bathroom Walls in the World Can't Hide These Scars o: Mine; Straws of Sanity; Crazy John Poems; Carmel Clowns; This Land Isn't My Land; The Charles Bukowski/Second Coming Years, 1996; San Francisco Streets, 1997; America, 1998; Looking for an Answer, 1998; From Pussy to Politics, 1999; Scar Tissue, 1999; North Beach Revisited, 2000; 13 Jazz Poems 2000; City Blues, 2001; I Kiss the Feet of Angels, 2001; The Holy Grail, 2002; A Bastard Child With No Place to Go, 2002. *Contributions to:* City Lights Journal Kansas Quarterly; Beat Scene; New York Quarterly; Confrontation; Chiron Review; Beatitude; Haight Ashbury Quarterly; NIK; Nexus; Rattle; Split Shift; Southern; Ocean Review; Stance. *Honours:* San Francisco Arts and Letters Fund, Literarty Achievement Award, 1983; Many grants. *Membership:* PEN. *Address:* PO Box 31249, San Francisco, CA 94131, USA.

WINCH, Terence Patrick; b. 1 Nov. 1945, New York, NY, USA. Poet; Ed.; Musician. m. Susan Francis Campbell, 8 Nov. 1981, 1 s. *Education:* BA, Iona College, 1967; MA, Fordham University, 1968. *Appointment:* Head of Publications, National Museum of the American Indian, Smithsonian Institution, Washington, DC. *Publications:* Luncheonette Jealousy, 1975; Nuns, 1976; The Attachment Sonnets, 1981; Irish Musicians/American Friends, 1986; Contenders, 1989; The Great Indoors (poems), 1995; The Drift of Things (poems), 2001. Other: Hard New York Days (music recording), 1995. *Contributions to:* New Republic; Brooklyn Review; Saint Mark's Poetry Project Newsletter; Exquisite Corpse; American Poetry Review; Little Magazine; Shiny; New American Writing; Harvard Magazine; Paris Review; Western Humanities Review. *Honours:* Yaddo Fellowship, 1975; American Book Award, 1986; National Endowment for the Arts Fellowship, 1992. *Address:* 10113 Greeley Ave, Silver Spring, MD 20902, USA.

WINDER, Barbara Dietz; b. 14 Oct. 1927, New York, NY, USA. Prof. (retd). Poet. m. Alvin E Winder, 21 June 1949, 2 s., 2 d. *Education:* BA, University of Chicago, 1950; MFA, University of Massachusetts, 1971; DA, State University of New York at Albany, 1981. *Publication:* Pinochle Under the Stars. *Contributions to:* Anthologies, reviews, quarterlies, and journals. *Honours:* Golden Poet Award, World of Poetry; New Letters Award; City of Hartford 350th Anniversary Prize; Hans S Bodenheimer Award; Arts/Wayland Laurel Award; Wildwood Poetry Prize. *Address:* 81 Old Mystic St, Arlington, MA 02174, USA.

WINDORQUILL, Marcus Ivan. See: INDERMILL, Marilyn.

WINDSOR, Patricia, (Colin Daniel, Katonah Summertree); b. 21 Sept. 1938, New York, NY, USA. Writer; Poet; Lecturer; Teacher. 1 s., 1 d. *Appointments:* Faculty, Institute of Children's Literature, University of Maryland Writers Institute; Ed.-in-Chief, The Easterner, Washington, DC; Co-Dir, Wordspring Literary Consultants; Dir, Summertree Studios, Savannah; Instructor, Creative Writing, Armstrong Atlantic University, Savannah. *Publications:* The Summer Before, 1973; Something's Waiting for You, Baker D, 1974; Home is Where Your Feet Are Standing, 1975; Mad Martin, 1976; Killing Time, 1980; The Sandman's Eyes, 1985; The Hero, 1988; Just Like the Movies, 1990; The Christmas Killer, 1991; The Blooding, 1996; The House of Death, 1996. *Contributions to:* Anthologies and magazines. *Honours:* American Library Asscn Best Book Award, 1973; Outstanding Book for Young Adults Citation, New York Times, 1976; Edgar Allan Poe Award, Mystery Writers of America, 1986. *Memberships:* Authors Guild; Childrens Book Guild; International Writing Guild; Mystery Writers of America; Poetry Society of Georgia; Savannah Storytellers. *Address:* c/o Writers House, 21 W 26th St, New York, NY 10010, USA.

WINDSOR, Penny Anne; b. 21 Dec. 1946, England. Writer; Poet; Teacher. *Education:* Teaching Certificate, 1971; BEd, 1972; Diploma in Community Work, 1980. *Appointments:* Teacher, Rochdale LEA, 1972–73; Teacher, West Glamoragon LEA, 1973–76; Co-ordinator, Youth Enterprise, Swansea, 1980–87; Writer-in-Residence, Open Learning Centres, West Glamorgan, 1991, Centre for the Visually Impaired, West Glamorgan, 1995; Creative

Writing and Literature Tutor, University of Wales, Swansea, 1996–2002. *Publications:* Heroines; Running Wild; Dangerous Women, 1987; Like Oranges, 1989; Love is a Four Letter Word; Crashing the Moon, 1994; Curses and Dances, 1996; When Dreams were Screams, 1998; One Enchanted Glance, 2001. *Contributions to:* New Statesman; Spare Rib; Poetry Wales; New Welsh Review; Other Poetry; Tribune; Ore; New Hope International; Orbis; Tears in the Fence; Rustic Rub. *Honours:* Grant, RSL, 1988–91; Grant, Society of Authors, 1992; Grant, 1993, Irma Chilton Award for Children's Literature, 2000, Welsh Arts Council. *Memberships:* Welsh Acad.; Writers on Tour (Academi); Lyricist: Performing Right Society. *Address:* Riverside, 11A Heol Aman, Glanaman, Ammanford, Carmarthenshire SA18 2AW, Wales.

WINFIELD, Frances; b. 29 Nov. 1932, Birmingham, England. Poet. m. Peter Winfield, 27 July 1956, 1 s. *Education:* Various language courses. *Publications:* Numerous poems in anthologies. *Honours:* Runner-Up Prize and Special Commendation, Hilton House National Poet of the Year, 1996; Third Prize and two Special Commendations, H. H. Poet of the Year, 1998; Runner-Up Individual and Collection, Poet of the Year, 1998. *Membership:* Hilton House Fraternity of Poets. *Address:* The Cottage, Wythes Lane, Fishtoft, Boston, Lincs PE21 9RY, England.

WINFREE, Marie Davis; b. 6 Oct. 1939, Johnston, North Carolina, USA. Poet; Writer. m. Ted Harold Winfree, 18 June 1955, 2 s. *Education:* Ddr, Walters University of North Carolina, 1981; Methodist College, 1984; Community College, North Carolina, 1986. *Publications:* New Voices; Southern Images; A Time to Listen (exec. ed.); Rainey Days and Sardine Tins. *Contributions to:* Anthologies and magazines. *Honours:* Third Prize, World Poets Award, 1980; 2 Arts Service Awards, 1991; Fortner's Honours Award, 1995. *Memberships:* Dickens Group; Network; North Carolina Poetry Society; Writers Ink Guild. *Address:* 3109 Phillie Circle, Fayetteville, NC 28306, USA.

WINGRAVE, Ariel. See: MORGAN, Ariel Celeste Heatherley.

WIRZ, Mario; b. 3 Dec. 1956, Germany. Poet. *Education:* Acad. for Acting and Theatre, Berlin. *Appointments:* Actor, Dir. *Publications:* Dream Hair, 1982; All There Night Steps, 1984; Calling the Wolves, 1993; The Heart of This Hour, 1997. *Contributions to:* Tages Spiegel; Neves Deutchland; Freitag; Neve Jevtsche Literatur. *Honours:* First Prize, PEN Club, 1991; Förderpreis of Brandenburg, 1997. *Memberships:* PEN; Deutscher Schriffsteller Verband. *Address:* Altenbraker str 17, 12053 Berlin, Germany.

WISEMAN, Christopher (Stephen); b. 31 May 1936, Hull, Yorkshire, England. Prof. of English (retd); Poet; Writer. m. Jean Leytem, 1 Jan. 1963, 2 s. *Education:* BA, 1959, MA, 1962, University of Cambridge; PhD, University of Strathclyde, 1971. *Appointments:* Asst to Prof. of English, University of Calgary, 1969–97. *Publications:* Waiting for the Barbarians, 1971; The Barbarian File, 1974; Beyond the Labyrinth: A Study of Edwin Muir's Poetry, 1978; The Upper Hand, 1981; An Ocean of Whispers, 1982; Postcards Home: Poems New and Selected, 1988; Missing Persons, 1989; Remembering Mr Fox, 1995; Crossing the Salt Flats, 1999. *Contributions to:* Reviews, quarterlies, journals, and magazines. *Honours:* Writers Guild of Alberta Poetry Award, 1988; Alberta Achievement Award for Excellence in Writing, 1988; Alberta Poetry Awards, 1988, 1989. *Memberships:* League of Canadian Poets; Writers Guild of Alberta. *Address:* 8 Varwood Pl. NW, Calgary, AB T3A 0C1, Canada.

WISINSKI, Louise Ann Helen, (Poetess Louise, Lou Singer); b. 7 Nov. 1947, Milwaukee, Wisconsin, USA. *Education:* Graduate, Notre Dame High School. *Publications:* At Day's End, 1994; Today's Great Poems, 1994. *Contributions to:* Sophomore Jinx, 1994; Allusive Images, 1994. *Honours:* Ed.'s Choice Award, National Library of Poetry, 1994; Award of Recognition, Famous Poets Society, 1995. *Address:* 1132 S 57th St, West Allis, Wisconsin 53214, USA.

WITT, Harold Vernon; b. 6 Feb. 1923, Santa Ana, CA, USA. Writer; Poet; Ed. m. Beth Hewitt, 8 Sept. 1948, 1 s., 2 d. *Education:* BA, 1943, BLS, 1953, University of California at Berkeley; MA, University of Michigan, 1947. *Appointments:* Co-Ed., California State Poetry Quarterly, 1976, Blue Unicorn, 1977–; Consulting Ed., Poet Lore, 1976–91. *Publications:* The Death of Venus, 1958; Beasts in Clothes, 1961; Now Swim, 1974; Suprised by Others at Fort Cronkhite, 1975; Winesburg by the Sea, 1979; The Snow Prince, 1982; Flashbacks and Reruns, 1985; The Light at Newport, 1992; American Literature, 1994. *Contributions to:* Journals and periodicals. *Honours:* Hopwood Award, 1947; Phelan Award, 1960; First Prize, San Francisco Poetry Centre Poetic Drama Competition, 1963; Emily Dickinson Award, Poetry Society of America, 1972; Various awards, World Order of Narrative Poets. *Address:* 39 Claremont Ave, Orinda, CA 94563, USA.

WITTEN, Anne Rubicam; b. 4 Nov. 1942, Washington, USA. Poet; Prof. *Education:* BA, University of Colorado; Boston University. *Appointments:* Visiting Prof., University of Maine; Lecturer, University of New England. *Publications:* Stone Stone Water; Touch Touch Touch; O Star. *Honours:* Colorado Portfolio Poetry Prize; American Institute of Graphic Arts Award; PEN Grant. *Memberships:* Poets and Writers; Maine Writers and Publishers Alliance; Union of Maine Visual Artists. *Address:* 15 Adams St, Peaks Island, ME 04108, USA.

WOERDEHOFF, Valorie Anne Breyfogle, (Valorie Anne Broadhurst); b. 5 July 1954, Kansas City, MO, USA. Dir of Marketing; Poet. m. Thomas Alan Woerdehoff, 5 July 1986, 3 s., 2 d. *Education:* AA, College of Lake County, 1979; BA, Loras College, 1982. *Appointments:* Community Relations Officer, Clinton Community College, 1984; Dir, University Relations, University of Dubuque, 1984–92; Dir, Publications, 1994–96, Assoc. Dir, Institutional Marketing, 1996–98, Dir, Institutional Marketing, 1998–, Loras College. *Publication:* Fourfront. *Contributions to:* Cottonwood Review; Frog Pond; Spoon River Quarterly; Wind Chimes; Cape Rock; Brussels Sprout; Iowa Woman; Modern Haiku; Woodnotes; 100 Words; Cicada; Haiku Moment: An Anthology of North American Haiku, 1882–1992; Haiku Seasons; How to Haiku, 2002. *Honours:* Grant to Artists, Iowa Arts Council; National Endowment for the Arts; First Place, Hawaii Education Asscn International Haiku Contest, 1995; First Place, Haiku Poets of Northern California Rengay Contest, 1995; Literary Artist of the Year, River Arts Network, 1996; First Place, National League of American Pen Women (Palomar Branch), International Poetry Contest, 1996. *Memberships:* Haiku Society of America; Poets and Writers; Dubuque Writers Guild. *Address:* 3246 St Anne Dr., Dubuque, IA 52001, USA.

WOESSNER, Warren (Dexter); b. 31 May 1944, Brunswick, New Jersey, USA. Attorney; Ed.; Poet; Writer. m. Iris Freeman, 6 Jan. 1990. *Education:* BA, Cornell University, 1966; PhD, 1971, JD, 1981, University of Wisconsin. *Appointments:* Founder, Ed., and Publisher, 1968–81, Senior Ed., 1981–, Abraxas Magazine; Board of Dirs, 1988–92, Pres., 1989–92, Coffee House Press; Contributing Ed., Pharmaceutical News. *Publications:* The Forest and the Trees, 1968; Landing, 1974; No Hiding Place, 1979; Storm Lines, 1987; Clear to Chukchi, 1996. *Contributions to:* Anthologies, magazines and periodicals. *Honours:* National Endowment for the Arts Fellowship, 1974; Wisconsin Arts Board Fellowships, 1975, 1976; Loft-McKnight Fellow, 1985; Minnesota Voices, Competition for Poetry, 1986. *Address:* 34 W Minnehaha Parkway, Minneapolis, MN 55419, USA.

WOIWODE, Larry (Alfred); b. 30 Oct. 1941, Carrington, ND, USA. Writer; Poet. m. Carole Ann Peterson, 21 May 1965, 4 c. *Education:* University of Illinois at Urbana-Champaign, 1959–64. *Appointments:* Writer-in-Residence, University of Wisconsin at Madison, 1973–74; Prof., Wheaton College, 1981, 1984; Visiting Prof., 1983–85, Prof. and Dir of the Creative Writing Program, 1985–88, State University of New York at Binghamton; Various workshops and readings at many colleges and universities. *Publications:* Fiction: What I'm Going to Do, I Think, 1969; Beyond the Bedroom Wall: A Family Album, 1975; Poppa John, 1981; Born Brothers, 1988; The Neumiller Stories, 1989; Indian Affairs: A Novel, 1992; Silent Passengers: Stories, 1993. Poetry: Even Tide, 1975. Non-Fiction: Acts, 1993; The Aristocrat of the West: Biography of Harold Schafer, 2000; What I Think I Did: A Season of Survival in Two Acts (autobiography), 2000. *Contributions to:* Books, anthologies, reviews, periodicals, journals, etc. *Honours:* Notable Book Award, American Library Asscn, 1970; William Faulkner Foundation Award, 1970; Guggenheim Fellowship, 1971–72; Fiction Award, Friends of American Writers, 1976; Hon. doctorates, North Dakota State University, 1977, Geneva College, 1997; Fiction Award, 1980, Medal of Merit, 1995, American Acad. of Arts and Letters; Aga Khan Literary Prize, Paris Review, 1990; Book Award of Short Fiction, Louisiana State University/Southern Review, 1990; John Dos Passos Prize, 1991; Poet Laureate of North Dakota, 1995. *Address:* c/o Basic Books, 10 E 53rd St, New York, NY 10022, USA.

WOLVERTON, Terry; b. 23 Aug. 1954, Cape Canaveral, FL, USA. Writer; Poet. *Education:* BA, Thomas Jefferson College, 1977. *Publications:* Black Slip, 1992; Mystery Bruise, 1999. *Contributions to:* Numerous anthologies and periodicals. *Honours:* University of Detroit New Poets Award, 1973; Selected Poet, Poetry on the Buses Competition, Santa Monica Arts Foundation, 1987; Vesta Award in Literature, Woman's Building, 1991; Nomination, Best Lesbian Poetry, Lambda Book Award, 1993; First Place Winner, Sheila-Na-Gig Second Annual Poetry Contest, 1994; Honourable Mention, Poetry in the Windows Competition, Arroyo Arts Collective, 1995; Movers and Shakers Award for Women Writers, Southern California Library for Social Research, 1995; California Arts Council Artist Fellowship in Poetry, 2002. *Memberships:* Board of Dirs, PEN Center, USA West; Los Angeles Poetry Festival Advisory Board. *Address:* 4022 Fountain Ave, Suite 202, Los Angeles, CA 90029, USA.

WONG CHUNG. See: WAI MING (OTIS) WONG.

WOOD, Francis James, (Frank Wood); b. 12 Nov. 1925, Preston, Lancashire, England. Teacher (retd); Poet. m. Margaret Marie-Therese Aspinwall, 7 May 1953, 1 s. *Education:* Certificate of Education, Dudley College of Education, 1959; Advanced Diploma in English Studies, University of Leeds, 1971. *Contributions to:* Anthologies, journals, and periodicals. *Honours:* Prizes, Rhyme Revival International Poetry Competition, 1985, Crabbe Memorial Competition, 1985, 1989, Red Candle Press Poetry Competition, 1986, Red Candle Press Mark Wild Memorial Competition, 1986, Kent and Sussex Poetry Society Open Poetry Competition, 1988. *Memberships:* Poetry Society; Suffolk Poetry Society. *Address:* 20A Lynwood Ave, Felixstowe, Suffolk IP11 9HS, England.

WOOD, Marguerite Noreen; b. 27 Sept. 1923, Ipswich, Suffolk, England. Physiotherapist; Poet. m. Douglas James Wood, 12 April 1947, 1 s., 1 d. *Education:* Chartered Physiotherapist, 1944; BA, Honours, Open University, 1982. *Appointment:* Justice of the Peace, 1968–93. *Publications:* Stone of Vision, 1964; Windows Are Not Enough, 1971; Crack Me The Shell, 1975; A Line Drawn in Water, 1980; A Wall Cracks, 1993; The Day's Canvas, 1998. *Contributions to:* Anthologies and magazines. *Honours:* Various. *Memberships:* Suffolk Poetry Society; Poetry Society; Magistrates' Asscn. *Address:* Sandy Hill, Sandy Lane, Woodbridge, Suffolk IP12 4DJ, England.

WOOD, Renate; b. 5 Feb. 1938, Berlin, Germany. Poet. m. William B Wood, 30 June 1961, 2 s. *Education:* PhD, Stanford University, 1970; MFA Program for Writers, Warren Wilson College, North Carolina, 1985. *Appointments:* Lecturer, University of Colorado, Boulder, 1985–91; Faculty, Program for Writers, Warren Wilson College, North Carolina. *Publications:* Points of Entry, 1981; Raised Underground, 1991; The Patience of Ice, 2000. *Contributions to:* American Poetry Review; Massachusetts Review; New England Review; TriQuarterly; Virginia Review; Seneca Review; Prairie Schooner; Ploughshares. *Honours:* Nominee, Colorado Governor's Award for Excellence in the Arts, 1982; Grant, Colorado Council on the Arts, 1995. *Memberships:* Associated Writing Programs; Acad. of American Poets. *Address:* 1900 King Ave, Boulder, CO 80302, USA.

WOOD, Susan; b. 31 May 1946, Commerce, Texas, USA. Poet. m. Cliff L Wood, 2 June 1967, divorced 1982, 1 s., 1 d. *Education:* BA, East Texas State University, 1968; MA, University of Texas at Arlington, 1970; Graduate Studies, Rice University, 1973–75. *Publications:* Bazaar, 1981; Campo Santo, 1990. *Contributions to:* Newspapers and periodicals. *Address:* c/o Maxine Groffsky Literary Agency, 2 Fifth Ave, New York, NY 10011, USA.

WOOD, Ursula. See: VAUGHAN WILLIAMS, Ursula.

WOOD, Wendy; b. 9 Feb. 1957, Ohio, USA. Poet. *Education:* BA, Bennington College, 1983. *Contributions to:* Bad Henry Review; New Voices; New Observations; Pearl; Thirst; Telephone. *Honours:* Grant Escandalar; Acad. of American Poets College Prize Winner; George Bogin Memorial Award, Poetry Society of America. *Memberships:* Poets and Writers. *Address:* PO Box 7333, JAF Station, New York, NY 10011, USA.

WOODBRIDGE, Norma (Barnabas); b. 21 April 1931, Flushing, New York, USA. Teacher of Piano and English; Poet. *Education:* University of Pennsylvania, 1952; BS, Temple University, 1958. *Publications:* African Realities, African Dreams; Resting Places; Meditations of a Modern Pilgrim; Dear Child; Joy in the Morning; Conversations with God. *Contributions to:* New Jersey Poetry Society Anthology; The Princeton Packet. *Honours:* Fellowship to Yaddo Writing Colony; Honorable Dectorate. *Memberships:* National League of American Pen Women; New Jersey Poetry Society; ASCAP; Garden State Storytellers League; Christian Writers Fellowship. *Address:* 2606 Zoysie Lane, North Fort Myers, FL 33917, USA.

WOODBURY, Sara Jorgenson, (SJW); b. 15 Oct. 1944, Wisconsin, USA. Poet. m. Lon E Woodbury, 23 Aug. 1967, divorced, 1 s., 2 d. *Education:* University of Wisconsin, 1961; University of Idaho, 1962–67; University of Washington, 1971; Eastern Washington University, 1978. *Publications:* Selected Poems; Sketches; Air of Dream; Shadows; Collected Works; Contrasts; Poetry Sampler, All These Years; Still Window Profiles; Edge of Night; Ways of Silence; A Field, A Mountain. *Contributions to:* Nostoc; Archer; Philadelphia Poets; Poetalk; Poetry Peddlar; Hemispheres; Metropolis; Lazer; Tight; Cokefish; Broken Street; Felicity; Wide Open; SOPA Review; Quill Books; Cripes; Red Owl; Ruby; Westbury Anthology; Quest; Poetic Realm; Pegasus. *Honour:* Certificate of Excellence. *Memberships:* Spokane Open Poets Asscn; Pacific Northwest Writers Conference; Lake Hills Jaycees; PEN West USA. *Address:* PO Box 676, Spokane, WA 99210, USA.

WOODCOCK, Joan; b. 6 Feb. 1908, Bournemouth, Dorset, England. Poet; Artist; Genealogist. m. Alexander Neville Woodcock, 18 Sept. 1937, 2 s., 1 d. *Publications:* The Wandering Years, 1990; Borrowing From Time, 1992; Stabbed Awake, 1994. *Contributions to:* Anthologies and journals. *Memberships:* British Haiku Society; Calne Writers' Circle; National Federation of State Poetry Societies, USA; Peterloo Poets; Poetry Society; Various genealogical organizations. *Address:* 6 Hudson Rd, Malmesbury, Wiltshire SN16 0BS, England.

WOODFORD, Bruce Powers; b. 22 Sept. 1919, Astoria, Oregon, USA. Writer; Poet; Prof. (retd). m. Xanta Grisogono, 19 Nov. 1955, 1 d. *Education:* BA, 1948, MA, 1949, PhD, 1958, University of Denver. *Publications:* Twenty-One Poems and a Play, 1958; Love and Other Weathers, 1966; A Suit of Four, 1973; Indiana, Indiana, 1976; The Edges of Distance, 1977. *Contributions to:* Arizona Quarterly; New Mexico Quarterly Review; Colorado Quarterly; Four Quarters; Uroboros; Wind; Stone; West Ham Review; Quartet. *Honours:* Foley Best Short Stories List of Distinction, 1948, 1949. *Membership:* American Poetry Society. *Address:* 140 Mesa Vista, Santa Fe, NM 87501, USA.

WOODHOUSE, Jennifer May (Jena); b. 11 Aug. 1949, Rockhampton, Qld, Australia. Writer; Poet. 1 s., 1 d. *Education:* BA, Russian Language and Literature, University of Queensland, 1976; Diploma in Education, 1983. *Appointment:* Examiner in English, University of Cambridge Local Examinations Syndicate, Athens, 1997–. *Publications:* Eros in Landscape, 1989; Passenger on a Ferry, 1994. *Contributions to:* Anthologies, newspapers and periodicals. *Honours:* John Shaw Neilson Award for Poetry, 1987; Rothmans Foundation Poetry Prize, 1988; Charles Meeting Poetry Prize, 1989. *Address:* Dimitriou Soutsou 48, Ambelokipi 115-10, Athens, Greece.

WOODROW, Philip James; b. 4 Sept. 1957, Surrey, England. Nurse; Poet. m. 1 Sept. 1984. *Education:* BA, Literature, 1979, MA, Victorian Literature, 1980, University of Essex. *Appointment:* Ed., Eavesdropper, 1989–91. *Publications:* Matin Songs, 1979; Boudicca, 1982; Post from Armageddon, 1987; A Cloud of Distress, 1989; Kind of Light, 1995; Allusions, 1996; Before Silence, 1996; In Different Voices, 1997; Portraits and Landscapes, 1998. *Contributions to:* Reviews and journals. *Memberships:* National Poetry Society, life mem.; Tennyson Society; Vertical Images, founder, 1986, co-ordinator, 1986–89; Margate Poetry Festival Society, chair., 1998–. *Address:* 30 York St, Broadstairs, Kent, England.

WOODRUFF, Thom, (Thom the World Poet); b. 14 June 1949, Brisbane, Qld, Australia. Poet. m. Wendy A Woodruff, 23 Dec. 1993. *Education:* BA, University of Queensland, 1967–69; LLB, 1970–72; Dip Ed, University of Melbourne, 1973. *Appointments:* Guest performance, Kansas City School of Performing Arts, 1993; Poet-in-Residence, Charles University, 1994; Poet on Tour, Arts Council of Wales, 1994–95; Featured Performer, Cheltenham Literature Festival, 1995–96. *Publications:* My Father's Son, 1991; Goddess, 1992; Strawberries, 1993; Redemption Poems, 1994; Romance!, 1995; Austin TX, 1995; Moon!, 1995; The Book of Thom, 1996; Persian Limes, 1996; Diamonds, 1996. *Contributions to:* Chronicle; Coreys; La Mama Poetica; Poesia y Calle. *Honours:* 9 Times Poet of the Week, Chronicle, 1994–96. *Memberships:* Austin International Poetry Festival, programmer; Austin Poets at Large. *Address:* 5003 Lark Cove, Austin, TX 78745, USA.

WOODS, Gregory Karl Waverling; b. 4 Jan. 1953, Egypt. Prof. of Lesbian and Gay Studies; Poet. *Education:* BA, 1974; MA, 1975; PhD, 1983. *Appointments:* Lector, University of Salerno, 1980–84; Lecturer, Crewe and Alsager College of Higher Education, 1985–90; Lecturer, 1990–95, Reader in Lesbian and Gay Studies, 1995–98, Prof., 1998–, Nottingham Trent University; International Advisory Board, European Gay Review; Editorial Board, PerVersions; Dir, East Midland Arts, 2000–02. *Publications:* We Have the Melon, 1992; Articulate Flesh: Male Homo-eroticism and Modern Poetry, 1987; This Is No Book: A Gay Reader, 1994; A History of Gay Literature: The Male Tradition, 1998; May I Say Nothing, 1998; The District Commissioner's Dreams, 2002. *Contributions to:* Reviews, quarterlies, journals, and periodicals. *Honour:* Third Prize, Skoob/Index on Censorship Poetry Competition, 1989; East Midlands Arts Writers Bursary, 1997; Hawthornden Fellowship, 1999; AHRB Study-leave Award, 2001–02. *Membership:* English Asscn, founding fellow, 2000. *Address:* c/o Dept of English and Media Studies, Nottingham Trent University, Clifton Lane, Nottingham NG11 8NS, England.

WOODS, Simon Andrew; b. 5 Sept. 1952, London, England. Arts Administrator; Poet. *Education:* BA, Honours, Law, 1978; Diploma in Publishing, 1982; BA, Honours, Fine Art, 1992. *Publication:* The Leopard, 1981. *Contributions to:* Ambit; Poetry Review; Stand. *Membership:* Poetry Society. *Address:* 69 Ericson Close, Wandsworth, London SW18 1SQ, England.

WOODWARD, Gerard; b. 1961, United Kingdom. Poet; Writer. *Publications:* Poetry: Householder, 1991; After the Deafening, 1994; Island to Island, 1999; Healing Fountain, 2003. Fiction: August, 2001. *Honours:* Somerset Maugham Award, 1992; Short-listed for J. L. Rhys Award; Nominated for Whitbread Prize, 2001. *Address:* c/o Chatto and Windus Ltd, 20 Vauxhall Bridge Rd, London SW1V 2SA, England.

WOOLFOLK, Miriam R. Lamy; b. 14 Feb. 1926, Louisville, KY, USA. Poet; Ed. m. (1) 1944, divorced 1964, 1 s., 3 d., (2), Patch G Woolfolk, 8 Aug. 1968, 2 step-d., 1 deceased. *Appointments:* Ed., Lexington Art League Newsletter, 1975–79, Reaching Poetry Journal, 1978–88, Kentucky State Poetry Society Newsletter, 1985–90, Pegasus Journal, 1992–. *Publications:* Poems by a Kentuckian for Anyone; Seasons; One Plus One; Sunshine and Thunder; For the Birds; Thoughts and Visions; Reflections & Other Poems; A Stitch in Time. *Contributions to:* Anthologies, reviews, quarterlies, journals, and magazines. *Honours:* Special Recognition, Alabama Poetry Society National Contest; West Virginia Haiku Poetry Award; Mainichi Daily News Award; Pres.'s Award, Kentucky State Poetry Society. *Memberships:* Kentucky State Poetry Society, pres., 1985; Kentucky Watercolor Society, charter mem.; Lexington Art League, life mem.; National Federation of State Poetry Societies. *Address:* 3289 Hunting Hills Dr., Lexington, KY 40515, USA.

WORLEY, Jeff Robert; b. 10 July 1947, Wichita, KS, USA. Ed.; Writer; Poet. m. Linda Kraus, 10 Jan. 1982. *Education:* BA, 1971, MFA, 1975, Wichita State University. *Appointments:* Instructor, University of Cincinnati, 1983–84; Asst Prof., Pennsylvania State University, 1984–86; Assoc. Ed., 1986–97, Ed., 1997–

Odyssey Magazine. *Publications:* Other Heart, 1991; Natural Selections, 1993; The Only Time There Is, 1995. *Contributions to:* Poetry Northwest; College English; Chicago Review; Prairie Schooner; Literary Review; Threepenny Review; Three Rivers Poetry Journal; Malahat Review; New York Quarterly; Anthology of Magazine Verse and Yearbook of American Poetry. *Honours:* Seaton First Award, Kansas Quarterly; First Prize, Cincinnati Poetry Review; National Endowment for the Arts Fellowship, 1991; Al Smith Fellowship, 1997. *Address:* 136 Shawnee Pl., Lexington, KY 40503, USA.

WRIGHT, A(mos) J(asper III); b. 3 March 1952, Gadsden, AL, USA. Medical Librarian; Writer; Poet. m. Margaret Dianne Vargo, 14 June 1980, 1 s., 1 d. *Education:* BA, Auburn University, 1973; MLS, University of Alabama, 1983. *Publications:* Frozen Fruit (poems), 1978; Right Now I Feel Like Robert Johnson (poems), 1981; Criminal Activity in the Deep South, 1800–1930, 1989. *Contributions to:* Medical journals, anthologies, reviews, quarterlies, and magazines. *Memberships:* Anaesthesia History Asscn; Medical Library Asscn. *Address:* 119 Pintail Dr., Pelham, AL 35124, USA.

WRIGHT, C(arolyn) D.; b. 6 Jan. 1949, Mountain Home, AR, USA. Poet; Prof. m. Forrest Gander, 3 April 1983, 1 s. *Education:* BA, Memphis State University, 1971; MFA, University of Arkansas, 1976. *Appointments:* Prof. of English and Creative Writing, Brown University, 1983–; State Poet of Rhode Island, 1994–. *Publications:* Terrorism, 1979; Translations of the Gospel Back Into Tongues, 1981; Further Adventures with God, 1986; String Light, 1991; Just Whistle, 1993; The Lost Roads Project: A Walk-in Book of Arkansas, 1994; The Reader's Map of Arkansas, 1994; Tremble, 1996; Deepstep Come Shining, 1998. *Contributions to:* American Letters and Commentary; BRICK; Conjunctions; Sulfur. *Honours:* National Endowment for the Arts Fellowships, 1981, 1987; Witter Bynner Prize for Poetry, 1986; Guggenheim Fellowship, 1987; Mary Ingraham Bunting Fellowship, 1987; General Electric Award for Younger Writers, 1988; Whiting Writers Award, 1989; Rhode Island Governor's Award for the Arts, 1990; Lila Wallace/Reader's Digest Writers Award, 1992; University of Arkansas Distinguished Alumni Award, 1998; Lannan Literary Award, 1999; Artist Award, Foundation for Contemporary Performance Art, 1999; Lange-Taylor Prize, Center for Documentary Studies, 2000. *Membership:* PEN, New England, Council Mem. *Address:* 351 Nayatt Rd, Barrington, RI 02806, USA.

WRIGHT, Charles (Penzel); b. 25 Aug. 1935, Pickwick Dam, Tennessee, USA. Poet; Writer; Teacher. m. Holly McIntire, 6 April 1969, 1 s. *Education:* BA, Davidson College, 1957; MFA, University of Iowa, 1963; Postgraduate Studies, University of Rome, 1963–64. *Appointments:* Faculty, University of California at Irvine, 1966–83, University of Virginia, 1983–. *Publications:* Grave of the Right Hand, 1970; Hard Freight, 1973; Bloodlines, 1975; China Trace, 1977; Southern Cross, 1981; Country Music, 1982; The Other Side of the River, 1984; Zone Journals, 1988; The World of the 10,000 Things, 1990; Chickamauga, 1995; Black Zodiac, 1997; Appalachia, 1998; Negative Blue: Selected Later Poems, 2000; A Short History of the Shadow. *Contributions to:* Numerous journals and magazines. *Honours:* Edgar Allan Poe Award, Acad. of American Poets, 1976; PEN Trans. Award, 1979; National Book Award for Poetry, 1983; Brandeis Book Critics Circle Award, 1998; Pulitzer Prize for Poetry, 1998. *Memberships:* Acad. of American Poets, board of chancellors, 1999–2002; American Acad. of Arts and Letters; Fellowship of Southern Writers; American Acad. of Arts and Sciences; PEN American Centre. *Address:* 940 Locust Ave, Charlottesville, VA 22901, USA.

WRIGHT, Christopher. See: WRIGHT, Kit.

WRIGHT, David, (John Murray); b. 1920, England. Writer; Poet. *Appointments:* Staff Mem., Sunday Times, 1941–47; Ed., Nimbus, 1955–56, X Magazine, 1959–62; Gregory Fellow in Poetry, University of Leeds, 1965–67. *Publications:* The Forsaken Garden; Moral Stories; Monologue of a Deaf Man; Seven Victorian Poets; Poems; A Portrait and a Guide; Nerve Ends, A South African Album; A View of the North; The Penguin Book of Everyday Verse; The Canterbury Tales; Deafness. *Address:* c/o A D Peters Ltd, 10 Buckingham St, Adelphi, London WC2N 6BU, England.

WRIGHT, George T(haddeus); b. 17 Dec. 1925, Staten Island, New York, USA. Prof. Emeritus; Author; Poet. m. Jerry Honeywell, 28 April 1955. *Education:* BA, Columbia College, 1946; MA, Columbia University, 1947; University of Geneva, 1947–48; PhD, University of California, 1957. *Appointments:* Teaching Asst, 1954–55, Lecturer, 1956–57, University of California; Visiting Asst Prof., New Mexico Highlands University, 1957; Instructor-Asst Prof., University of Kentucky, 1957–60; Asst Prof., San Francisco State College, 1960–61; Assoc. Prof., University of Tennessee, 1961–68; Fulbright Lecturer, University of Aix-Marseilles, 1964–66, University of Thessaloniki, 1977–78; Visiting Lecturer, University of Nice, 1965; Prof., 1968–89, Chair., English Dept, 1974–77, Regents' Prof., 1989–93, Regents' Prof. Emeritus, 1993–, University of Minnesota. *Publications:* The Poet in the Poem: The Personae of Eliot, Yeats and Pound, 1960; W H Auden, 1969; Shakespeare's Metrical Art, 1988; Aimless Life: Poems 1961–1995, 1999; Hearing the Measures: Shakespearean and Other Inflections, 2002. Editor: Seven American Literary Stylists from Poe to Mailer: An Introduction, 1973. *Contributions to:* Articles, reviews, poems and trans in many periodicals and

books. *Honours:* Guggenheim Fellowship, 1981–82; National Endowment for the Humanities Fellowship, 1984–85; William Riley Parker Prizes, MLA, 1974, 1981. *Memberships:* Minnesota Humanities Comission, 1985–88; MLA; Shakespeare Asscn of America. *Address:* 2617 W Crown King Dr., Tucson, AZ 85741, USA.

WRIGHT, Jay; b. 25 May 1934, Albuquerque, NM, USA. Poet; Dramatist. *Education:* BA, University of California at Berkeley, 1961; Union Theological Seminary, New York; MA, Rutgers University, 1967. *Publications:* The Homecoming Singer, 1971; Soothsayers and Omens, 1976; Dimensions of History, 1976; The Double Invention of Komo, 1980; Explications/Interpretations, 1984; Selected Poems of Jay Wright, 1987; Elaine's Book, 1988; Boleros, 1991; Transfigurations: Collected Poems, 2000. *Honours:* American Acad. and Institute of Arts and Letters Award; Guggenheim Fellowship; MacArthur Fellowship; Ingram Merrill Foundation Award; National Endowment for the Arts Grant; Fellowship, Acad. of American Poets, 1996; Fellow, American Acad. of Arts and Sciences; Lannan Literary Award for Poetry, 2000; L. L. Winship/PEN Award, 2001; Anisfield-Wolf Lifetime Achievement Award, 2002. *Address:* PO Box 381, Bradford, VT 05033, USA.

WRIGHT, Kit, (Christopher Wright); b. 1944, Kent, England. Poet. *Education:* New College, Oxford. *Appointments:* Education Secretary, Poetry Society, London, 1970–75; Fellow Commoner in Creative Arts, Trinity College, Cambridge, 1977–79. *Publications:* Treble Poets 1 (with Stephen Miller and Elizabeth Maslen), 1974; The Bear Looked Over the Mountain, 1977; Arthur's Father, 4 vols, 1978; Rabbiting On and Other Poems, 1978; Hot Dog and Other Poems, 1981; Prof. Potts Meets the Animals of Africa, 1981; Bump Starting the Hearse, 1983; From the Day Room, 1983; Cat Among the Pigeons, 1987; Poems 1974–1984, 1988; Real Rags and Red, 1988; Short Afternoons, 1989; Funnybunch, 1993; Tigerella, 1994. *Honours:* Alice Hunt Bartlett Prize; Geoffrey Faber Memorial Award; Hawthornden Prize; W H Heinemann Award. *Address:* Viking Kestrel, 27 Wrights Lane, London W8 5TZ, England.

WRIGHT, Linda Jayne; b. 2 March 1963, Derby, England. Writer; Poet. m. 3 Oct. 1986, 1 d. *Publications:* Nature's Song, 1996; A Palatable Puzzle, 1996;' Charlotte, 1997; Portrait of an Old Master, 1997; The Tempest, 1997; The Illicit Agreement, 1997; Relics of Egypt, 1997; Kiss of the Vampire, 1997; Eventide, 1997; Visions of the Countryside, 1997; A Rose Without Thorns, 1997. *Honours:* First Prize, First Impressions, Vol. 25, 1996; 2 Ed.'s Choice Awards, International Library of Poetry, 1997. *Address:* 28 Eggesford Rd, Stenson Fields, Derby DE24 3BH, England.

WRIGHT, Michael George Hamilton; b. 16 Oct. 1927, Leigh on Sea, Essex, England. Librarian (retd); Poet. m. Mary Margaret Hill, 26 March 1988. *Education:* BA, 1952, MA, 1954, St Catharine's College, Cambridge; North Western Polytechnic, London, 1955; FLA, 1967; FCLIP, 2002. *Publications:* Ancestral Voices, 1979; Mosaic of the Air, 1997. *Contributions to:* Outposts Poetry Quarterly; Orbis; Acumen; Envoi; Iota; Weyfarers; Westwords; Understanding; Candelabrum; Poet's Voice; Links. *Honour:* Third Place, Farnborough Festival of the Arts. *Memberships:* RMAS Literary Society; Shirley Society; Friends of Shakespeare's Globe; Jane Austen Society; Basingstoke Poets. *Address:* Calliope, Parkstone Dr., Camberley, Surrey GU15 2PA, England.

WRIGLEY, Robert; b. 27 Feb. 1951, East St Louis, IL, USA. College Prof.; Poet. m. Kim Barnes, 1983, 2 s., 1 d. *Education:* BA, Southern Illinois University, 1974; University of Montana, 1976. *Appointments:* Poet-in-Residence, Prof., Lewis Clark State College, ID, 1977–90; Richard Hugo Poet-in-Residence, University of Montana, 1990; Acting Dir, MFA Program, University of Oregon, 1990–91. *Publications:* Moon In a Mason Jar, 1986; What My Father Believed, 1991; In the Bank of Beautiful Sins, 1995. *Contributions to:* Poetry; Kenyon Review; Shenandoah; Georgia Review; New England Review; Poetry Northwest; Virginia Quarterly Review. *Honours:* National Endowment for the Arts Fellowship; Idaho Arts Commission Grant; Celia Wagner Award; Richard Hugo Memorial Award; Frederick Bock Prize; Poet Laureate of Idaho. *Memberships:* Acad. of American Poets; Associated Writing Programs; Poetry Society of America. *Address:* RRI, Box 96W4, Lenore, ID 83541, USA.

WRZOS, Lucja. See: DANIELEWSKA, Lucja Zofia.

WU, Dahan or WU, Jin. See: DU, Yunxie.

WURM, Franz; b. 16 March 1926, Prague, Czechoslovakia (British citizen). Writer. m. Barbara M. Z'Graggen, 1 June 1992. *Education:* BA, MA, Queen's College, Oxford. *Appointments:* Head of Third Program, German Swiss Radio, Zürich, 1966–69; Dir, Feldenkrais Institute, Zürich, 1974–. *Publications:* Anmeldung, 1959; Vorgang, 1962; Anker und Unruh, 1964; Vier Gedichte, 1965; Brehy v zádech, 1974; Acht Gedichte in Faksimile, 1975; Hundstage, 1986; In diesem Fall, 1989; Dirzulande, 1990; Nachbemerkungen zu Feldenkrais, 1995; 53 Gedichte, 1996; König auf dem Dach, 1997; Orangenblau, 1998. *Contributions to:* Neue Zürcher Zeitung; Akzente; Neue Rundschau; Literatur and Kritik; Neue Deutsche Literatur. *Memberships:* PEN; Hölderlin Gesellschaft, Tübingen; Franz Kafka Society, Prague. *Address:* Flühgasse 35, 8008 Zürich, Switzerland.

WURSTER, Michael; b. 8 Aug. 1940, Illinois, USA. Poet. *Education:* BA, Dickinson College, 1962. *Appointments:* Founder, Co-Dir, Pittsburgh Poetry Exchange, 1974–; Consultant, Facilitator, Acad. of Prison Arts, 1979–83; Co-ordinator, Carson Street Gallery Poetry Series, 1986–88; Mem., Literature Panel, Pennsylvania Council on the Arts, 1990–; Poet-in-Residence, Sweetwater Arts Center, 1990. *Publication:* The Cruelty of the Desert, 1989. *Contributions to:* 5 AM; Pittsburgh Quarterly; Poetry; Canada Review; Wind; Interstate; Bassettown Review; Galley Sail Review; Golden Triangle; Flipside; Greenfield Review; Pig Iron; Northern Red Oak; Religious Humanism; Chapter Voice; Fourth World Forum; Sunrust. *Honours:* Pittsburgh Award; Most Valuable Player Award. *Memberships:* Pittsburgh Poetry Exchange; Acad. of American Poets; Poetry Society of America; Canadian Poetry Asscn. *Address:* 159 S 16th St, Pittsburgh, PA 15203, USA.

WUZZLE Mrs. See: FERRETT, Mabel.

WYLIE, Betty Jane; b. 21 Feb. 1931, Winnipeg, MB, Canada. Writer; Dramatist; Poet. m. William Tennent Wylie, 2 s., 2 d. *Education:* BA, 1950, MA, 1951, University of Manitoba. *Appointments:* Bunting Fellow, Radcliffe College, 1989–90; Writer-in-Residence, Metro Toronto Library, York Branch, 2001. *Publications:* Over 35 books. Other: Many plays. *Contributions to:* Periodicals. *Honours:* Several awards. *Memberships:* Playwrights' Union of Canada; Writers' Union of Canada. *Address:* c/o Writers' Union of Canada, 24 Ryerson Ave, Toronto, ON M5T 2P3, Canada.

WYNAND, Derk; b. 12 June 1944, Bad Suderode, Germany. Prof.; Poet; Writer; Trans.; Ed. m. Eva Kortemme, 8 May 1971. *Education:* BA, 1966, MA, 1969, University of British Columbia. *Appointments:* Visiting Lecturer, 1969–73, Asst Prof. to Prof., 1973–, Chair, Dept of Creative Writing, 1987–90, 1996–99, University of Victoria; Ed., The Malahat Review, 1992–98. *Publications:* Locus, 1971; Snowscapes, 1974; Pointwise, 1979; One Cook, Once Dreaming, 1980; Second Person, 1983; Fetishistic, 1984; Heatwaves, 1988; Airborne, 1994; Door Slowly Closing, 1995; Closer to Home, 1997; Dead Man's Float, 2001. *Honours:* The Malahat Review named Magazine of the Year, 1995; Honourable Mention, BP Nichol Chapbook Award, 1995. *Address:* c/o Dept of Writing, University of Victoria, PO Box 3045, Victoria, BC V8W 3P4, Canada.

Y

YANG, Lian; b. 22 Feb. 1955, Bern, Switzerland. Poet. m. Liu You Hong, 19 Oct. 1989. *Appointments:* Writer, Central Broadcasting, 1977–88; Visiting Scholar, Auckland University, 1989–90, Sydney University, 1992–93; Writer-in-Residence, Berlin, 1990–91; Fellowship, Amherst College, USA, 1993–94; Poet-in-Residence, Akademie Schloss Solitude. *Publications:* Li Hun, 1985; Huang Hun, 1986; Pilgerfahrt, 1986; In Symmetry with Death, 1988; Huang, 1989; Ren de Zijue, 1989; Masks and Crocodile, 1990; The Death in Exile, 1990; Yi, 1991; Gedichte, 1992; Gui Hua, 1994; Non-Person Singular, 1994; Geisterreden, 1995; Where the Sea Stands Still, 1995; Der Ruhepunkt des Meeres, 1996; Yang Lian's Works, 1982–1997, 1998; Where the Sea Stands Still: New Poems, 1999. *Contributions to:* TLS; World Apart; Wild Peony; Die Zeit; Die Tageszeitung. *Honour:* Chinese Poetry Reader's Choice, 1986. *Memberships:* Survivors Poetry Club, founder; Today Literature Research Society, councillor. *Address:* 22 Carlton Mansions, Holmleigh Rd, London N16 5PX, England.

YANKEVICH, Leo, (Leo Jankiewicz); b. 30 Oct. 1961, Pennsylvania, USA. Teacher; Poet. m. Danuta Katarzyna Kaminska, 14 Sept. 1989, 2 s. *Education:* BA, History and Polish Literature, Alliance College, Cambridge Springs, Pennsylvania, 1984; Jagiellonian University, Kraków, Poland, 1984–85, 1988, 1989. *Appointments:* Teacher of English, Gliwice, Poland, 1989–; Ed. and Publisher, Mandrake Poetry Magazine, 1993–. *Publications:* The Light at the End of the World and Other Poems, 1992; Several poetry vols in Polish. *Contributions to:* Various publications in Poland and abroad. *Address:* ul Wielkiej Niedzwiedzicy 35/8, 44-117 Gliwice, Poland.

YANXIANG SHAO, (Han Yeping); b. 10 June 1933, Beijing, China. Poet. m. Xie Wenxiu, 27 Jan. 1957, 1 s., 1 d. *Education:* L'Universite Franci-Chinoise, 1948–49. *Appointments:* Ed., correspondent, Radio Beijing, 1949; Detained in labour camp, 1966–77; Rehabilitated, 1978; Deputy Ed.-in-Chief, Shikan magazine, 1978. *Publications:* Singing of the City of Beijing, 1951; Going to the Faraway Place, 1955; To My Comrades, 1956; The Campfire in August, 1956; A Reed-pipe, 1957; Love Songs to History, 1980; At the Faraway Place, 1981; In Full Blossom Lake Flowers, 1983; Flower Late in Blossom, 1984; Collection of Long Lyrics, 1985; Essays Written at Mornings and Evenings, 1986; 100 Articles with Sorrows and Joys, 1986; There's Joy, There's Sorrow, 1988; Written in Little Honeycomb, 1992; Selected Poems, 1992; Catch That Butterfly, 1993; Rewriting The Bible, 1993; One Cup, 1993; Multum in Parvo, 1994; The Essay Workshop, 1994; Hot Thoughts and Cold Words, 1995; Beyond Pain, 1995; Laugh at Yourself, 1996; Essays by Shao Yanxiang, 3 vols: Notes on History, Notes on Men, Notes on Dreams, 1997. *Address:* 48-1108 Huawei Beili, Beijing 100021, China.

YAOS-KEST, Itamar; b. 3 Aug. 1934, Hungary. Poet; Author. m. Hanna Mercazy, 21 Aug. 1958, 1 s., 1 d. *Education:* BA, University of Tel-Aviv. *Appointment:* Founder, Eked Publishing House, 1958. *Publications:* 15 books, 1959–92. *Contributions to:* Magazines. *Honours:* Herzel Prize, 1972; Talpir Prize, 1984; Lea Goldberg Prize, 1990; Prime Minister's Prize, 1993. *Membership:* Asscn of Hebrew Writers. *Address:* Merian Hahashunonout 25, Tel-Aviv, Israel.

YATES, J(oel) Michael; b. 10 April 1938, Fulton, Missouri, USA (Naturalized Canadian citizen). Poet. *Education:* MA, University of Michigan, 1961. *Appointments:* Teacher at universities of Michigan, Ohio, British Columbia, Arkansas and Texas at Dallas, 1976–77; Sales Representative, Mitchell Press, 1978–. *Publications:* Spital of Mirrors, 1967; Hunt in an Unmapped Interior and Other Poems, 1967; Canticle for Electronic Music, 1967; Parallax, 1968; The Great Bear Lake Meditations, 1970; New and Selected Poems, 1973; Breath of the Snow Leopard, 1974; The Qualicum Physics, 1975; Fugue Brancusi, 1983; The Queen Charlotte Island Meditations, 1983; Selected Shorter Lyrics, 1984; Schedules of Silence: The Collected Longer Poems, 1986. Editor: Light Like a Summons: Five Poets, 1989; Contemporary Poetry of British Columbia (co-ed.), 1970–72. *Honours:* Canada Council Grants and Senior Arts Awards.

YAU, Emily, (Chiu Yee Ming, Emily Yau Yee Ming, Yee Ming); b. 12 Dec. 1940, China. Scholar; Poet; Trans.; Ed. *Education:* BA, South China Normal University. *Appointments:* Asst, South China Teachers College, 1962–78; Lecturer, South China Normal University, 1978–88; Senior Lecturer, Hong Kong Shue Yan College, 1989–90; Ed. and Consultant, National Poetry Asscn, 1990–. *Publications:* Dandelion; Li Qing's Poems; Selected Foreign Poems of the 1980's. *Contributions to:* Anthologies, reviews, quarterlies, and journals. *Honours:* Awards and prizes. *Memberships:* Chinese Modern Literature and Arts Asscn; International Writers and Artists Asscn; National Poetry Asscn; World Congress of Poets; World of Poetry. *Address:* c/o National Poetry Asscn, Fort Mason Center, Building D, Second Floor, San Francisco, CA 94123, USA.

YEVTUSHENKO, Yevgeny Aleksandrovich; b. 18 July 1933, Stanzia Zima, Siberia, Russia. Poet; Writer. m. (1) Bella Akhmadulina, divorced, (2) Galina Semyonovna, 1 c. *Education:* Gorky Literary Institute, 1951–54. *Publications:* (in English trans.) Poetry: The Poetry of Yevgeny Yevtushenko, 1953–1965, 1965; Bratsk Station, The City of Yes and the City of No, and Other New Poems, 1970; Kazan University and Other New Poems, 1973; From Desire to Desire, 1976; Invisible Threads, 1982; Ardabiola, 1985; Almost at the End, 1987; The Collected Poems, 1952–1990, 1991. Other: A Precocious Autobiography, 1963; Wild Berries (novel), 1984; Divided Twins: Alaska and Siberia, 1988. *Honours:* Order of the Red Banner of Labour; USSR State Prize, 1984. Memberships; International PEN; Union of Russian Writers. *Address:* c/o Union of Russian Writers, ul. Vorovskogo 52, Moscow, Russia.

YICTOVE, (Eugene M. Turk); b. 28 Feb. 1946, New Orleans, LA, USA. Teacher; Poet. 1 d. *Education:* Fine Arts Major, Xavier University, New Orleans, LA, 1967. *Appointments:* Poet in the Schools, Geraldine Dodge Foundation, 1990–95; Host, Poetry Series, Local Cable TV, 1992–95 and Knitting Factory, New York. *Publications:* No Big Thing, 1967; D J Soliloquy, 1988; Tributes, 1993; Contributions and Other Poems of Love, 1994. *Contributions to:* Essence Magazine; Rant. *Address:* 2832 St Bernard Ave, New Orleans, LA 70128, USA.

YORICK. See: IVENS, Michael William.

YOSHIMASU, Gozo; b. 22 Feb. 1939, Tokyo, Japan. Poet; Essayist; Lecturer. m. Marilia, 17 Nov. 1973. *Education:* BA, Keio University, 1963. *Appointments:* Chief Ed., Sansai Finer Arts magazine, 1964–69; Fulbright Visiting Writer, University of Iowa, 1970–71; Poet-in-Residence, Oakland University, Rochester, MI, 1979–81; Lecturer, Tama Art University, 1984–; Visiting Lecturer at various institutions; Many poetry readings around the world. *Publication:* A Thousand Steps and More: Selected Poems and Prose, 1964–1984 (in English trans.), 1987. *Contributions to:* Anthologies and periodicals. *Honours:* Takami Jun Prize, 1971; Rekitei Prize, 1979; Hanatsubaki Modern Poetry Prize, 1984. *Memberships:* Japan PEN Club; Japan Writers' Asscn. *Address:* 1-215-5 Kasumi-cho, Hachioji City 192, Japan.

YOSHIMURA, Ikuyo; b. 5 Jan. 1944, Kyoto, Japan. Prof.; Writer; Poet. m. Hitoshige Yoshimura, 1 s., 1 d. *Education:* BA, English Literature, Doshisha University, 1966; MA, Comparative Literature and Culture, Aichigakuin University, 1993. *Appointment:* Prof., Ogaki Junior Women's College. *Publications:* A Small Picture, 1966; Introduction to Haiku in English, 1989; At the Riverside, 1990; Renaissance of the Works of R. H. Blyth, 1995; The Life of R. H. Blyth, 1996; Spring Thunder, 1996. *Contributions to:* Periodicals. *Honours:* Haiku Four Seasons Award, Newsweek, 1989; Aichi Prefecture Prize for Haiku in English, 1990; Special Merit Book Award, Australia Day Council, 1991. *Address:* 1–3 Oonawaba, 4-chome, Gifu 500-8889, Japan.

YOUNG, Al(bert James); b. 31 May 1939, Ocean Springs, MS, USA. Writer; Poet. m. Arline June Belch, 1963, 1 s. *Education:* University of Michigan, 1957–61; Stanford University, 1966–67; BA, University of California at Berkeley, 1969. *Appointments:* Jones Lecturer in Creative Writing, Stanford University, 1969–74; Writer-in-Residence, University of Washington, Seattle, 1981–82; Co-Founder (with Ishmael Reed) and Ed., Quilt magazine, 1981–. *Publications:* Fiction: Snakes, 1970; Who is Angelina?, 1975; Sitting Pretty, 1976; Ask Me Now, 1980; Seduction by Light, 1988. Poetry: Dancing, 1969; The Song Turning Back into Itself, 1971; Some Recent Fiction, 1974; Geography of the Near Past, 1976; The Blues Don't Change: New and Selected Poems, 1982; Heaven: Collected Poems 1958–1988, 1989; Straight No Chaser, 1994; The Sound of Dreams Remembered, 2001. Other: Bodies and Soul: Musical Memoirs, 1981; Kinds of Blue: Musical Memoirs, 1984; Things Ain't What They Used to Be: Musical Memoirs, 1987; Mingus/Mingus: Two Memoirs (with Janet Coleman), 1989; Drowning in the Sea of Love: Musical Memoirs, 1995. *Honours:* National Endowment for the Arts Grants, 1968, 1969, 1974; Joseph Henry Jackson Award, San Francisco Foundation, 1969; Guggenheim Fellowship, 1974; Pushcart Prize, 1980; Before Columbus Foundation Award, 1982.

YOUNG, Elizabeth (Ann), (Lady Kennet); b. 14 April 1923, London, England. Writer; Poet. m. Wayland Hilton Young, 2nd Baron Kennet, 24 Jan. 1948, 1 s., 5 d. *Education:* MA, Oxford University. *Publications:* Old London Churches (with Wayland Hilton Young), 1956; Time is as Time Does (poems), 1958; Quiet Enjoyment: Arms Control and Police Forces for the Ocean (ed. with Ritchie Calder), 1971; A Farewell to Arms Control?, 1972; London's Churches (with Wayland Hilton Young), 1986; Northern Lazio (with Wayland Hilton Young), 1990. *Contributions to:* Anthologies and other publications on arms control, maritime affairs, and architectural conservation. *Honour:* European Federation Tourist Press Overall Prize, 1990. *Address:* 100 Bayswater Rd, London W2 3HJ, England.

YOUNG, Gary; b. 8 Sept. 1951, Santa Monica, CA, USA. Poet; Artist. m. Margaret Orenstein, 18 April 1986, 2 s. *Education:* BA, University of California at Santa Cruz, 1973; MFA, University of California at Irvine, 1975. *Appointments:* Instructor, University of California at Santa Cruz, Gavilan College; Staff Writer, The Sun; Vice-Pres., AE Foundation; Ed., Greenhouse Review Press. *Publications:* Hands; Six Prayers; In the Durable World; The Dream of a Moral Life; Then It Happens, 1996; My Place Here Below, 1996; Days, 1997; The Geography of Home: California's Poetry of Place, 1999; Braver Deeds, 1999; No Other Life, 2002. *Contributions to:* American Poetry Review; Antaeus; Poetry; Nation; New England Journal of Medicine; Antioch Review; Missouri Review; Denver Quarterly; Kenyon Review; Poetry. *Honours:* Ludwig Vogelstein Foundation Grant; John Ciardi Fellowship; James D Phelan Award; National Endowment for the Humanities Fellowship; National Endowment for the Arts Fellowship. *Memberships:* Poetry Society of America; Jackalope Society; AE Foundation. *Address:* 3965 Bonny Doon Rd, Santa Cruz, CA 95060, USA.

YOUNG, Gloria. See: ARMSTRONG, Naomi Young.

YOUNG, Ian George; b. 5 Jan. 1945, London, England. Poet; Writer; Ed. *Appointments:* Dir, Catalyst Press, 1969–80, TMW Communications, 1990–. *Publications:* Poetry: White Garland, 1969; Year of the Quiet Sun, 1969; Double Exposure, 1970; Cool Fire, 1970; Lions in the Stream, 1971; Some Green Moths, 1972; The Male Muse, 1973; Invisible Words, 1974; Common-or-Garden Gods, 1976; The Son of the Male Muse, 1983; Sex Magick, 1986. Fiction: On the Line, 1981. Non-Fiction: The Male Homosexual in Literature, 1975; Overlooked and Underrated, 1981; Gay Resistance, 1985; The AIDS Dissidents, 1993; The Stonewall Experiment, 1995; The AIDS Cult, 1997; The AIDS Dissidents: A Supplement, 2001; Autobibliography, 2001. *Honours:* Several Canada Council and Ontario Arts Council Awards. *Membership:* International Psychohistory Asscn. *Address:* 2483 Gerrard St E, Scarborough, ON M1N 1W7, Canada. *E-mail:* iyoung@arvotek.net.

YOUNG, Patricia (Rose); b. 7 Aug. 1954, Victoria, BC, Canada. Poet. m. Terence Young, 27 May 1974, 1 s., 1 d. *Education:* BA, University of Victoria, 1983. *Appointment:* Lecturer in Creative Writing, University of Victoria, 1985–91. *Publications:* Travelling the Floodwaters, 1983; Melancholy Ain't No Baby, 1985; All I Ever Needed Was a Beautiful Room, 1987; The Mad and Beautiful Mothers, 1989; Those Were the Mermaid Days, 1991; More Watery Still, 1993; Ruin & Beauty: New and Selected Poems, 2000. *Honours:* Many Canada Council grants; First Prize for Poetry, British Columbia Federation of Writers, 1988; British Columbia Book Prize for Poetry, 1988; National Magazine Silver Award for Poetry, 1988; Second Prize for Poetry, CBC Literary Competition, 1988; Co-Winner, 1989, Winner, 1993, League of Canadian Poets National Poetry Competition; Pat Lowther Memorial Award for Poetry, 1990. *Membership:* League of Canadian Poets. *Address:* 130 Moss St, Victoria, BC V8V 4M3, Canada.

YUAN LU, (Liu Ban-jiu); b. 8 Nov. 1922, Huangpi, Hubei, China. Ed.; Poet; Writer; Trans. m. Lou Hui, 12 Dec. 1944, 2 s., 2 d. *Education:* BA, Foreign Literature, National Fu Tan University, Chungking, 1944. *Publications:* Many poems, some in trans., 1942–98. *Contributions to:* Anthologies and journals, both domestic and foreign. *Honour:* National Poetry Prize, Chinese Writers Asscn, 1986; Rainbow Trans. Award, Luxun Literary Prize, 1998; Golden Wreath Award, Strega Poetry Evenings in Macedonia, 1998. *Memberships:* Chinese Writers Asscn; Chinese Trans Asscn; National Foreign Literature Institute; PEN Club, China Centre; International Asscn for Germanic Studies; Goethe Gesellschaft, Weimar. *Address:* c/o Peoples' Literature Publishing House, 166 Chao Nei St, Beijing 100705, China.

YUASA, Nobuyuki; b. 10 Feb. 1932, Hiroshima, Japan. Prof. Emeritus; Poet; Trans. m. Shigeko Yuasa, 20 March 1967, 2 d. *Education:* BA, English, University of Hiroshima, 1954; MA, English, University of California at Berkeley, 1956. *Appointments:* Lecturer, 1961–65, Assoc. Prof., 1965–92, Prof., 1982–95; Prof. Emeritus, 1995–, University of Hiroshima. *Publications:* Several poems. Translator: Various vols, including John Donne's Complete Poetry, 1996. *Contributions to:* Various publications. *Membership:* British Haiku Society. *Address:* 1-1-10 Waseda, Ushita, Higashiku, Hiroshima 732, Japan.

YUDKIN, Leon Israel; b. 8 Sept. 1939, England. University Lecturer; Writer. m. Meirah Goss, 29 Sept. 1967. *Education:* BA, 1960, MA, 1964, University of London. *Appointments:* Asst Lecturer, Lecturer, University of Manchester, 1966–; Lecturer, University College, London, 1996; Visiting Prof., University of Paris VIII, 2000. *Publications:* Isaac Lamdan: A Study in Twentieth-Century Hebrew Poetry, 1971; Meetings with the Angel (co-ed.), 1973; Escape into Siege, 1974; U. Z. Greenberg: On the Anvil of Hebrew Poetry, 1980; Jewish Writing and Identity in the Twentieth Century, 1982; 1948 and After: Aspects of Israeli Fiction, 1984; Modern Hebrew Literature in English Translation (ed.), 1986; Agnon: Texts and Contexts in English Translation (ed.), 1988; Else Lasker-Schüler: A Study in German-Jewish Literature, 1990; Beyond Sequence: Current Israeli Fiction and Its Context, 1992; The Israeli Writer and the Holocaust (ed.), 1993; The Other in Israeli Literature (ed.), 1993; A Home Within: Varities of Jewish Expression in Modern Fiction, 1996; Public Crisis and Literary Response: Modern Jewish Literature, 2001. *Contributions to:* Various publications. *Honour:* DLitt, University of London, 1995. *Address:* 51 Hillside Ct, 409 Finchley Rd, London NW3 6HQ, England.

YVONNE. See: CHISM-PEACE, Yvonne.

Z

ZAHNISER, Ed(ward DeFrance); b. 11 Dec. 1945, Washington, DC, USA. Writer; Poet; Ed. m. Ruth Christine Hope Deuwel, 13 July 1968, 2 s. *Education:* BA, Greenville College, IL, 1967; Officers' Basic Course, Defence Information School, 1971. *Appointments:* Poetry Ed., The Living Wilderness Magazine, 1972–75; Founding Ed., Some of Us Press, Washington, DC, 1972–75; Arts Ed., Good News Paper, 1981–; Ed., Arts and Kulchur, 1989–91; Assoc. Poetry Ed., Antietam Review, 1992–. *Publications:* The Ultimate Double Play (poems), 1974; I Live in a Small Town (with Justin Duewel-Zahniser), 1984; The Way to Heron Mountain (poems), 1986; Sheenjek and Denali (poems), 1990; Jonathan Edwards (artist book), 1991; Howard Zahniser: Where Wilderness Preservation Began: Adirondack Wilderness Writings (ed.), 1992; A Calendar of Worship and Other Poems, 1995. *Contributions to:* Anthologies and periodicals. *Honours:* Woodrow Wilson Fellow, 1967; First and Second Prize in Poetry, West Virginia Writers Annual Competitions, 1989, 1991, 1992; Second Prize, Essay, 1995. *Address:* c/o Atlantis Rising, PO Box 955, Shepherdstown, WV 25443-0955, USA.

ZAMBARAS, Vassilis; b. 1 May 1944, Revmatia, Messenias, Greece. Teacher of English as a Second Language; Poet. m. Eleni Nezi, Oct. 1980, 1 s., 1 d. *Education:* BA, English, 1970, MA, English, 1972, University of Washington, Seattle. *Publications:* Sentences, 1976; Aural, 1984. *Contributions to:* How the Net is Gripped: Selection of Contemporary American Poetry, 1992; Poetry Northwest; Madrona; West Coast Review; Wisconsin Review; Assay; Edge; Text; Smoot Drive Press; Rialto; Shearsman; Southeastern Review; Southern Poetry Review; Longhouse; Intermedio; Workshop; Falcon; Klinamen; Apopeira. *Honours:* Harcourt, Brace and Jovanovich Poetry Fellowship to the University of Colorado, Boulder, 1970; University of Washington Poetry Prizewinner, 1972. *Address:* 21 K Fotopoulou, Meligalas 24002, Messenias, Greece.

ZAPATA, Miguel-Angel; b. 27 June 1955, Peru. Writer; Poet; Prof. of Spanish. m. Janice Lynn Kincaid, 4 Feb. 1982, 1 s., 2 d. *Education:* BA, Universidad Nacional Mayor de San Marcos, Lima, Peru, 1979; BA, California State University, 1985; MA, University of California at Santa Barbara, 1989. *Appointments:* Co-Ed., Codice, Journal of Poetry, and Tabla de Poesia Actual. *Publications:* Partida y ausencia, 1984; Periplos de abandonado, 1986; Imagenes los Juegos, 1987; Poemas para violin y orquesta, 1991. *Contributions to:* Various publications. *Honour:* First Prize, Juegos Red-Tap, Lima, Peru, 1977. *Membership:* MLA of America. *Address:* 7418 Rupert Ave, St Louis, MO 63117, USA.

ZAPPALA, Simonetta; b. 18 June 1937, Rome, Italy. Poet; Trans. *Education:* Lower Certificate English Language; Proficiency, English Language and Literature. *Publications:* Forsele Parole; Il mio Nomednon e Niente Chesospiro; Fiabe; Voce Umanda; Poesied Amore; Rime Piccine; Il Marealla Porta. *Contributions to:* Tempo; Corriere Della Sera; Voce Umana; Fiabe. *Honours:* Premarosa Poetry Prize; Gold Medal, Centewario of Dante Festival; First Prize, Citta Eterna Festival. *Memberships:* Italian Authors' and Eds' Guild; Italian Writers Guild; Eugenio Montale Movement; English Poetry Society. *Address:* Viariccardo Zandonai 75, Rome 00194, Italy.

ZARIN, Cynthia Rebecca; b. 9 July 1959, New York, NY, USA. Writer; Poet. m. 24 Jan. 1988, 1 d. *Education:* AB, Radcliffe College, 1981; MFA, Columbia University, 1984. *Appointments:* Lecturer, Yale College, Princeton College; Staff Writer, New Yorker Magazine. *Publications:* The Swordfish Tooth; Fire Lyric, 1993. *Contributions to:* New Yorker; New Republic; New Criterion; Yale Review; Paris Review; Grand Street. *Honours:* Ingram Merrill Foundation Award; Fellowship, Corporation of Yaddo; Fellowship, MacDowell Colony. *Memberships:* Poetry Society of America; Authors Guild. *Address:* c/o The New Yorker Magazine, 20 W 43rd St, New York, NY 10036, USA.

ZAVATSKY, Bill; b. 1 June 1943, Brideport, CT, USA. Teacher of English; Poet; Trans. m. Phyllis Geffen, 1968, divorced 1991. *Education:* BA, Comparative Literature, Columbia University, 1974; MFA, Writing, Columbia University School of the Arts, 1974. *Appointments:* Teacher, Poetry Writing Workshops, Teachers and Writers Collaborative, 1971–86; Instructor in Creative Writing, University of Texas at Austin, 1977–79; Teacher of English, Trinity School, New York City, 1987–. *Publications:* Theories of Rain and Other Poems, 1975; The Poems of A O Barnabooth by Valery Larbaud (trans. with Ron Padgett), 1977; The Whole World Catalogue 2 (ed. with Ron Padgett), 1977; For Steve Royal and Other Poems, 1985; Earthlight: Poems of André Breton (trans. with Zack Rogow), 1993. *Contributions to:* Reviews and periodicals. *Honours:* Creative Artistis Public Service Fellowship, 1976; Columbia University Trans. Center Award, 1977; National Endowment for the Arts Fellowship in Poetry, 1979. *Membership:* PEN. *Address:* 100 W 92nd St, No. 9D, New York, NY 10025, USA.

ZAWADIWSKY, Christina; b. 8 July 1950, USA. Poet; Journalist; Writer; Art Critic; Television Producer. *Education:* BFA, University of Wisconsin, 1974. *Appointments:* Contributing Ed., Pushcart Prize annual literary anthology, 1977–; Freelance Journalist, 1980–; Originator, Interviewer, Producer, Where the Waters Meet Television Series, 1991–. *Publications:* The World at Large, 1978; Sleeping with the Enemy, 1980; The Hand on the Head of Lazarus, 1986; I Began to Dream, 1996; What Will Be, 1997; Isolation, 1998; Desperation, 1998. *Contributions to:* Reviews and periodicals. *Honours:* Best Arts Television Programming Series in the USA and Canada, National Federation of Local Cable Programmers, 1992, and National Alliance for Community Media, 1995; Art Futures Award, 1997. *Memberships:* Inner City Arts Council; Milwaukee Press Club; National Alliance for Community Media Task Force, panel mem.; National Women's Museum; Poets and Writers; Wisconsin Artists in All Media; Walter's Point Center for the Arts, advisory board, 1999. *Address:* 1641 N Humboldt Ave, Milwaukee, WI 53202, USA.

ZEIGER, Lila; b. 6 Dec. 1927, USA. Teacher; Poet; Writer. m. David Zeiger, 24 Nov. 1949, 1 s., 1 d. *Education:* MA, Cornell University, 1949; MLS, Pratt Institute, 1957. *Appointment:* Writing Consultant, Aids Day Treatment Program, 1988–. *Publication:* The Way to Castle Garden, 1982. *Contributions to:* Reviews, quarterlies, journals, magazines and anthologies. *Honours:* Small Press Tour de Force Award, 1977; MacDowell Colony Fellowships, 1977, 1979, 1983; Claytor Award, 1978, Hemley Award, 1979, Kreymborg Award, 1980, Poetry Society of America; CAPS Grant, New York State, 1983–84; Witter Bynner Foundation Grant, 1990–91. *Memberships:* Poetry Society of America; Poets and Writers. *Address:* PO Box 4518, Great Neck, NY 11023, USA.

ZEMANEK, Alicja; b. 2 Aug. 1949, Bielsko-Biaé a, Poland. Scientist; Poet. m. Bogdan Zemanek, 30 July 1981. *Education:* PhD, 1977, Jagiellonian University. *Appointments:* Assoc. Prof., 1990–2000, Prof., 2000–, Jagiellonian University. *Publications:* Egzotyczny ogród na Wesoé ej, 1986; Listopad w Bibliotece, 1988; Dzieé w którym zniknáé am, 1990; Wakacje w Krakowie, 1991; Podobni do zagajnika olch, 1993; Modlitwa do táczy, 1996; écieé¥ki Ogrodu Botanicznego, 2000; Medytacje o zmierzchu, 2001. *Contributions to:* Periodicals. *Memberships:* Polskie Towarzystwo Botaniczne; British Society for the History of Science; Society for the History of Natural History; Zwiázek Literatów Polskich. *Address:* ul Kopernika 27, 31 501 Kraków, Poland. *E-mail:* zemaneka@ib.uk.edu.pl.

ZENIS, Sarah; b. 10 Jan. 1925, Lynn, Massachusetts, USA. Poet; Writer. *Education:* Boston University, 1945; Brandeis University, 1950; Brooklyn College, 1960; New School for Social Research, New York City, 1970. *Appointments:* Poetry By Telephone, outreach for the homebound, 1997–; Poetry Workshop, 1998 *Publications:* Leaders in Poetry for You and Me, 1993; Twilight Echoes (poems), 2002. *Contributions to:* East Coast Writers Anthology; Becoming; Echo; Gotham Memo; Innovators; International Center. *Honours:* Third Place, National Poetry Contest; Special Honour, North Shore Jewish Historical Society. *Memberships:* National Writers Club; World Federalist Publicist; New York Poetry Forum; Bread Loaf Writers Conference; Katherine Engel Senior Center; Lambs Club. *Address:* 146 W 79th St, New York, NY 10024, USA.

ZENOFON, Fonda; b. 31 Aug. 1953, Greece (Naturalized Australian citizen). Variety Entertainer; Writer; Poet. *Appointments:* Founder, Brunswick Poetry Workshop; Poet Laureate, Brunswick City (First Official Poetry Body in Victoria). *Publications:* 3 poetry books; 1 play. *Contributions to:* Anthologies, reviews, journals, and magazines. *Honour:* Diploma and Fellowship, International Poets Acad. *Address:* 7 Mountfield St, Brunswick, Vic. 3056, Australia.

ZEPHANIAH, Benjamin (Obadiah Iqbal); b. 15 April 1958, Birmingham, England. Poet; Dramatist; Writer. m. Amina Iqbal Zephaniah, 17 March 1990. *Appointments:* Writer-in-Residence, Africa Arts Collective, Liverpool, 1989, Hay-on-Wye Literature Festival, 1991, Memphis State University, Tennessee, 1991–95. *Publications:* Fiction: Face, 1999; Refugee Boy, 2001. Poetry: Pen Rhythm, 1980; The Dread Affair, 1985; Inna Liverpool, 1988; Rasta Time in Palestine, 1990; City Psalms, 1992; Talking Turkeys, 1994; Funky Chickens, 1996; Propa Propaganda, 1996; School's Out, 1997; We Are Britain, 2002; Too Black, Too Strong, 2002; The Little Book of Vegan Poems, 2002. Plays: Playing the Right Tune, 1985; Job Rocking, 1987; Delirium, 1987; Streetwise, 1990; The Trial of Mickey Tekka, 1991. Radio Plays: Hurricane Dub, 1988; Our Teacher's Gone Crazy, 1990. Television Play: Dread Poets Society. *Contributions to:* Periodicals, radio, television, and recordings. *Honours:* Literary Chair Nominations, Cambridge, 1987, Oxford, 1989; BBC Young Playwrights Festival Award, 1988; Hon. Doctorate, University of North London, 1998. *Memberships:* Musicians' Union; Equity; Performing Rights Society; ALCS. *Address:* c/o Sandra Boyce Management, 1 Kingsway House, Albion Rd, London N16 0TA, England. *Website:* www.benjaminzephaniah.com.

ZHANG ER. See: MINGXIA LI.

ZHI LI, (Peng Xiang); b. 27 April 1962, Beijing, China. Trans.; Ed.; Poet. *Education:* Chinese Social University, 1982–86; University of Beijing, 1985. *Publications:* Several poems. *Contributions to:* Various anthologies and other publications in USA, Japan, Israel, India, UK, and other nations. *Honour:* Prize, World New Ancient Poetry Contest, 1994. *Memberships:* Contemporary Poetry Society, Hong Kong; DHP Society, Taiwan; World Acad. of Arts and Culture; World Poetry Society. *Address:* 168 Lang Run Yuan, University of Beijing, Beijing 100871, China.

ZIELINSKI, Christopher Thomas; b. 7 Nov. 1950, London, England. Poet; Publisher; Ed.; Trans. m. Diana Vivien Trimmer, 28 July 1973, 2 s. *Education:* BSc, Dundee University, 1971; MSc, Canfield Institute of Technology, 1977. *Appointment:* Dir, Health and Biomedical Information, World Health Organization, Geneva. *Publications:* Sculled; Artificial Respiration; The Real Canary. *Contributions to:* Magazines. *Honours:* Second Prize, New Poetry Quarterly Competition; Third Prize, Alice Hunt Bartlett Competition. *Memberships:* Council of Biology Eds; European Asscn of Science Eds; International Federation of Scholarly Book Publishers; Middle East Asscn of Science Eds; Poetry Society. *Address:* c/o World Health Organization, MH1 EMRO, Ave Appia, 1211 Geneva, Switzerland.

ZITHULELE. See: MANN, Christopher Michael.

ZOGRAFOU, Marina; b. 9 March 1937, Komotini, Greece. Poet; Writer; Painter. *Education:* High School of Economics; Piano; Certificate, Higher School of Telecommunications for Execs. *Publications:* 10 books, including poetry and prose, some trans. into French and English. *Contributions to:* Various anthologies, reviews, and periodicals. *Honours:* Hellenic Society of Writers Award; Nobel Prize for Literature Nomination, 1997. *Memberships:* Society of Greek Arts and Culture; Society of Greek Writers; United Writers of the World; World Acad. of Arts and Culture; World Poetry Society. *Address:* 46 Hestionos St, Thrakomakedones, 13671 Athens, Greece.

ZOLLER, James Alexander; b. 7 Nov. 1948, Laramie, Wyoming, USA. College Teacher; Poet; Writer. m. Donna Dean, 20 June 1970, 3 s., 1 d. *Education:* BA, History, University of New Hampshire, 1971; MA, English/ Creative Writing, San Francisco State University, 1973; DA, State University of New York, Albany, 1984. *Publication:* Simple Clutter (poems), 1998. *Contributions to:* Antaeus; Blueline; Greenfield Review; Kudzu; Other Poetry; Oxford Magazine; HIS; Kentucky Poetry Review; Christianity and Literature; English Record; Zone 3; Spree. *Memberships:* National Council of Teachers of English; Associated Writing Programs. *Address:* 9800 Seymour St, Houghton, NY 14744, USA.

ZOLYNAS, Al(girdas Richard Johann); b. 1 June 1945, Dornbirn, Austria. Prof. of English and Literature; Poet; Writer. m. 24 June 1967. *Education:* BA, University of Illinois, 1966; MA, 1969, PhD, 1973, University of Utah. *Appointments:* Instructor, Asst Prof., Writer-in-Residence, Southwest State University, Marshall, MN; Lecturer, Weber State College, Ogden, UT, San Diego State University. *Publications:* The New Physics, 1979; 4 Petunia Avenue, 1987; Men of Our Time: An Anthology of Male Poetry in Contemporary America (ed. with Fred Moramarco), 1992; Under Ideal Conditions, 1994. *Contributions to:* Various anthologies, reviews, quarterlies and journals. *Honour:* San Diego Book Award for Best Poetry, 1994. *Membership:* Poets and Writers. *Address:* 2380 Viewridge Pl., Escondido, CA 92026, USA.

ZUCKER, Jack S.; b. 23 Jan. 1935, USA. Teacher of English; Poet; Ed. m. Helen Zucker, 19 Aug. 1959, 2 d. *Education:* BA, City College of New York, 1957; MA, New York University, 1961. *Appointments:* Dept of Rhetoric, Oakland University, Rochester, Michigan, 1964–; Ed., The Bridge literary magazine. *Publications:* Beginnings, 1981; From Manhattan, 1985.

Contributions to: Esquire; Poetry Northwest; Literary Review; Southern Poetry Review; Trace; Webster Review; Permaforst. *Honour:* John Masefield Award, 1977. *Address:* 14050 Vernon St, Oak Park, MI 48237, USA.

ZWICKY, Jan; b. 10 May 1955, Calgary, AB, Canada. Poet; Philosopher. *Education:* BA, University of Calgary, 1976; MA, 1976, PhD, 1981, University of Toronto. *Appointments:* Teacher, University of Waterloo, 1981, 1984, 1985, Princeton University, 1982, University of Western Ontario, 1989, University of Alberta, 1992, University of New Brunswick, 1994, 1995, University of Victoria 1996–; Ed., Brick Books. *Publications:* Wittgenstein Elegies, 1986; The New Room, 1989; Lyric Philosophy, 1992; Songs for Relinquishing the Earth, 1998. *Honours:* Gov.-Gen.'s Award for Poetry, 1999.

ZWICKY, (Julia) Fay; b. 4 July 1933, Melbourne, Vic., Australia. Poet; Ed. m. (1) Karl Zwicky, 1957, 2 c., (2) James Mackie, 1990. *Education:* BA, University of Melbourne, 1954. *Appointments:* Senior Lecturer in English, University of Western Australia, 1972–87; Assoc. Ed., Westerly, 1973–95. *Publications:* Isaac Babel's Fiddle, 1975; Quarry: A Selection of Western Australian Poetry (ed.), 1981; Kaddish and Other Poems, 1982; Journeys: Poems by Judith Wright, Rosemary Dobson, Gwen Harwood, Dorothy Hewett (ed.), 1982; Seven Hostages and Other Stories, 1983; The Lyre in the Pawnshop: Essays on Literature and Survival, 1974–84, 1986; Procession: Youngstreet Poets 3 (ed.), 1987; Ask Me, 1990; Poems 1970–1992, 1993; The Gatekeeper's Wife, 1997. *Honours:* New South Wales Premier's Award, 1982; Western Australian Premier's Awards, 1987, 1991, 1999. *Address:* 30 Goldsmith Rd, Claremont, WA 6010, Australia.

ZYCH, Adam Alfred; b. 28 July 1945, Czestochowa, Poland. Psychologist; Gerontologist; Poet; Trans. m. 24 Dec. 1969, 3 s. *Education:* MA, Acad. of Catholic Theology, Warsaw, 1971; PhD, Institute for Educational Research, Warsaw, 1975; Habilitation, University of Gdańsk, 1984. *Appointments:* Lecturer/Adjunct in Psychology and Pedagogics, University of Pedagogy, Kielce, 1975–86; Visiting Prof., University of Giessen, University of Vienna and European Viadrina University of Frankfurt/Oder, 1987–94; Asst Prof. 1987–90, Prof. of Pedagogics, 1990–, Vice Dean of Pedagogical Faculty, 1996–2002, Higher Pedagogical School, Kielce; Visiting Scholar, Buehler Center on Aging, Northwestern University, Chicago, 1991–92. *Publications:* Most/The Bridge; Na mojej ziemi byl Oswiecim/Auschwitz Was in My Land, 2 vols, 1987, 1993; Psalmy emigracyjne/Emigrant's Psalms; Odlot jest us nas/ Departure is in us; Auschwitz-Gedichte, 2 vols, 2001; Czlowiek wobec starosci: Szkice z gerontologii spolecznej/Man and Old Age: Essays in Social Gerontology, 1995; Wiersze wybrane/Selected Poems, 1997; Jestem zakochany. Wiersze i przeklady/I an in Love: Poems and Translations, 1999; The Auschwitz Poems: An Anthology, 1999; Slownik gerontologii spolecznej/ Dictionary of Social Psychology, 2001. *Contributions to:* Wspolczesnosc; Kultura; Wiez; Tygodnik Kulturalny; Zycie i Mysl; Nowiny Kurier; Nowy Dziennik; Kurier Zachodni; Zycie; Relax; Bialy Orzel; Moderne polnische Lyrik; Holocaust Poetry, 1995; Parnassus of World Poets, 1997; Kalejdoskop Tygodnia; Anthology Olympoetry, 1994, 1998. *Honours:* Gold Medal, 1984, Silver Medal, 1986 Gilded Medal 1989, Académie Internationale de Lutèce, Paris; Order of the Pegasus, Olympoetry Movement, Greece, 1994; Gold Cross of Merit, Poland, 1996; City of Auschwitz Medal, 2000. *Address:* ul Sienkiewicza 42 m 6, 25-507 Kielce, Poland. *E-mail:* aazych@poczta.onet.pl/.

ZYDANOWICZ, Janina Regina, (Pobóg); b. 25 May 1916, Warsaw, Poland. Architect; Painter; Poet. *Education:* Diploma, Engineer-Architect MSc, Engineering College, Faculty of Architecture, Warsaw; Acad. of Fine Arts, Warsaw, 1950–54. *Contributions to:* Various anthologies, 1979–98, and other publications. *Honours:* Various prizes, medals, diplomas, and awards, 1979–96. *Memberships:* Académie Internationale de Lutèce, Paris; Accademia Internazionale Leonardo da Vinci, Rome; Associazione Siciliana per le Lettere e le Arti, Palermo; International Arts Guild, Monaco. *Address:* Grotthera 11A/3, 00-785 Warsaw, Poland.

PART TWO

Appendices

APPENDIX A: A SUMMARY OF POETIC FORMS AND RHYME SCHEMES

Rhymes are represented by small letters: thus 'a' represents the first rhyme of poem (e.g. red), and is repeated wherever that rhyme appears again (e.g. led, bread, said, etc). The second rhyme of the poem is represented by the letter 'b', and so on.

Where a whole line is repeated, a capital letter is used. If a single word or line is used as a refrain throughout the poem, a capital R is used. Where the refrain consists of part of a line, the R is placed in brackets immediately before the rhyming letter of the line in which it appears (e.g. (R) a b a b R means that part of the final line of the poem appears again at the end of a four-line stanza as a refrain).

These are very condensed details, and refer only to the rhyme scheme of the poem. For further information, you should consult a dictionary of poetic forms such as *The Poets' Manual and Rhyming Dictionary*, by Frances Stillman (Thames & Hudson), from which many of these forms are taken.

SONNET

(i) Shakespearian or English: abab cdcd efef gg

(ii) Petrarchan or Italian: abba abba cde cde (or cdc dcd)

(iii) Spenserian: abab bcbc cdcd ee

(iv) Miltonic: rhyme scheme as Italian but no break

Many other sonnet variants exist; see e.g. Shelley 'Ozymandias' and Mason Sonnet.

VILLANELLE

$A_1bA_2abA_1abA_2abA_1abA_2abA_1A_2$

Here the first and third lines rhyme and are repeated as marked, hence A_1 and A_2.

BALLADE

(i) Eight-line ababbcbC ababbcbC ababbcbC bcbC

(ii) Ten-line ababbccdcD ababbccdcD ababbccdcD ccdcD

(iii) Seven-line ababbcC ababbcC ababbcC ababbcC

There are other ballade variants, such as the double ballade, with six stanzas.

TERZA RIMA

aba bcb cdc... xyx yy

OTTAVA RIMA

abababcc... (stanza continued ad lib)

RHYME ROYAL

ababbcc... (stanza continued ad lib)

RONDEAU, RONDEL

(i) Rondeau (R) aabba aabR aabbaR (or (R) abbaabR ababa)

(ii) Rondeau of Villon (R) abba abR abbaR

(iii) Rondel ABbaabABabbaAB (or ABabbaABabababAB)

(iv) Rondel (13-line) ABba abAB abbaA

(v) Roundel abaB bab abaB (or abaR bab abaR)

(vi) Chaucerian Roundel Abb abA abbA

(vii) Rondeau Redouble $(R)A_1B_1A_2B_2abbA_1abaB_1babA_2abaB_2ababR$

(viii) Rondelet AbAabbA

TRIOLET

ABaAabAB

PANTOUM

$A_1B_1A_2B_2B_1C_1B_2C_2C_1D_1C_2D_2\ldots X_1A_2X_2A_1$

The first and third lines appear reversed in the last stanza: the poem may be as long as needed.

SESTINA

Basically an unrhymed form, it is nevertheless included in rhymed poetry because it uses repeated words. The end words of each six-line stanza are repeated in varying patterns, as follows:

123456 615243 364125 532614 451362 246531 plus three-line envoi using repeated words in the middle and ends of the lines as follows: 2 - 54 - 36 - 1

Rhymed sestinas also exist in various forms.

ODE

Many 'odes' of no particular form exist, but Keats used a rhyme scheme ababcdecde.

RUBAI OR QUATRAIN

Best know from Fitzgerald's version of Omar Khayyam, stanzas rhyme aaba.

ENGLYN

A Welsh syllabic form consisting of 30 syllables arranged in lines as follows:

10, 6, 7, 7

The sixth syllable rhymes with the ends of the last three lines (i.e. syllables 16, 23 and 30).

LIMERICK

Mainly humorous form rhyming aabba.

GLOSA

Spanish 14th–15th Century form in various rhyme schemes and metres, featuring an introductory quatrain followed by four stanzas, each of which ends with one of the lines of the quatrain and comments on (glosses) it.

APPENDIX B:
POETRY AWARDS AND PRIZES

The following list covers main poetry prizes, organizations offering awards and prizes, and, where applicable, recent winners. Conditions and availability of prizes and awards often change with little notice and the most recent situation should be ascertained by direct application to the sponsoring organization.

Academy of American Poets Fellowship: 584 Bdwy, Suite 1208, New York, NY 10012, USA. Fellows are elected each year by majority vote of the Academy's Board of Chancellors. No applications are accepted. Each Fellow is awarded a stipend of US $35,000. Winner: Ellen Bryant Voigt, 2001.

Aldeburgh Poetry Festival Prize: Aldeburgh Poetry Festival, Goldings, Goldings Lane, Leiston, Suffolk IP16 4EB, England. Tel. (1728) 830631. Awarded annually for the best first full collection of poetry published in the United Kingdom and the Republic of Ireland in the preceding 12 months. Submissions are accepted from publishers or individual poets. Winners are announced at the opening event of the festival. Prize: £500 and invitation to participate at the following year's festival. Winner: Beyond Calling Distance by Esther Morgan, 2001.

Atlanta Review Poetry Competition: Poetry 2001–International Poetry Competition, PO Box 8248, Atlanta, GA 31106, USA. Annual competition run by Atlanta Review, a leading US literary journal. Approximately 5,000 entrants from 30 countries participate. All entries are considered for publication in a special autumn issue. Prizes: Gold (US $2,000), Silver ($500) and Bronze ($250) prizes, plus 50 International Merit awards.

Benson Medal: Royal Society of Literature, c/o Royal Literary Fund, Fleet St, London EC4A 3EA, England. E-mail: rslit@aol.com. Periodical award to a well-regarded writer of poetry, fiction or biography. Submissions are not accepted. Winner: Christopher Fry, 2000.

Bollingen Prize in Poetry: Beinecke Rare Book and Manuscript Library, Yale University Library, PO Box 208240, New Haven, CT 06520, USA. Biennial award for the best book of poetry by an American during the preceding two years. No applications accepted. Prize: US $50,000. Winner: Louise Glück, 2001.

Bremen Literature Prize: Bremen City Council, Freie Hansestadt Bremen, Rembertiring 9–11, Senator für Bildung, Wissenschaft und Kunst, 28195 Bremen, Germany. Annual award to German-speaking writers and poets. Prize: DM 15,000.

Bridport Prize: The Bridport Prize Secretary, Coneygarth, Coneygar Park, Bridport, Dorset DT6 3BA, England. Website: www.bridportprize.org.uk. f. 1973. Awarded for original poems of not more than 42 lines, and short stories between 1,000 and 5,000 words. Entries must be written in English and must not have been previously published or broadcast, nor entered in any other competition. Prizes: (In each category) First prize £3,000; Second prize £1,000; Third prize £500; 10 supplementary prizes of £50. Winners, Poetry 2001: The Dying and the Light by Rowland Molony (first), Myself and W. B.Yeats Fall Out with One Another by Rosaleen Croghan (second), Compulsory Showers by Simon Crowcroft (third).

Witter Bynner Foundation for Poetry: PO Box 10169, Santa Fe, NM 87504, USA. Annual award for poetry-related projects. Prize: US $25,000.

Caine Prize for African Writing: 2 Drayson Mews, London W8 4LY, England(20) 7376-0440(20) 7398-3728. E-mail: caineprize@jftaylor.com. f. 2000. Annual award to a fictional work or narrative poem (minimum of 3,000 words) by an African writer, published in English anywhere in the world in the previous two years. Prize: $15,000. Winner: Discovering Home by Binyavanga Wainaina, 2002.

Canadian Authors' Association Literary Awards: PO Box 419, Campbellford, ON K0L 1L0, Canada. Several annual awards, including fiction, short story, biography, Canadian history, poetry, drama, and body of work. Poetry Award for full-length English-language work by a Canadian author. Prize: C $2,500 and a silver medal. Winner: Credo by Carmine Starnoi, 2001.

Giosué Carducci Prize: University of Bologna, Via Zamboni 33, 40100 Bologna, Italy. Annual award for poetry, monographs and essays on poetry and poets. Prize: 1.5m. lire.

Cholmondeley Awards for Poets: Society of Authors, 84 Drayton Gdns, London SW10 9SB, England. Tel. (20) 7373-6642. Fax (20) 7373-5768. E-mail: authorsoc@writers.org.uk. The annual non-competitive award is for work generally, not for a specific book, and submissions are not required. Prize: £8,000 (shared). Winners, 2001: Ian Duhig, Paul Durcan, Kathleen Jamie, Grace Nichols.

Duff Cooper Prize: Artemis Cooper, 54 St Maur Rd, London SW6 4DP, England. Tel. (20) 7736-3729. Fax (20) 7731-7638. Annual award to a literary work in the field of history, biography, politics or poetry, published in the previous year. Prize: £3,000 and a presentation copy of Duff Cooper's autobiography Old Men Forget. Winner: John Maynard Keynes by Robert Skidelsky, 2000.

County of Cardiff International Poetry Competition: Welsh Academy, Third Floor, Mount Stuart House, Mount Stuart Sq., Cardiff CF1 6DQ, Wales. Annual award for unpublished poems of up to 50 lines written in English. Prize: £5,000.

Daily Telegraph Arvon International Poetry Competition: 11 Westbourne Cres., London W2 3DB, England. Biennial poetry competition run by the Daily Telegraph, for poems of any length written in English, not previously published or broadcast. Prizes: First prize of £5,000 with at least 15 other prizes. Winner: Ararat by Henry Shukman, 2000.

T. S. Eliot Prize: Poetry Book Society, Book House, 45 East Hill, London SW18 2QZ, England. Tel. (20) 8870-8403. Fax (20) 8877-1615. E-mail: info@poetrybooks.co.uk. Website: www.poetrybooks.co.uk. Annual award for the best new collection of poetry, over 32 pages in length, published in the United Kingdom and the Republic of Ireland, at least 75% of which must have been previously unpublished in book form. Prize: £10,000. Winner: The Beauty of the Husband by Anne Carson, 2001.

English Academy of Southern Africa: PO Box 124, Witwatersrand 2050, South Africa. Awards the Thomas Pringle Awards and the Olive Schreiner Prizes.

Geoffrey Faber Memorial Prize: Faber and Faber Ltd, 3 Queen Sq., London WC1N 3AU, England. Tel. (20) 7465-0045. Fax (20) 7465-0043. E-mail: belinda.matthews@faber.co.uk. f. 1963. Annual award in memory of the founder and first Chairman of Faber and Faber, with prizes in alternate years for a volume of verse or prose fiction first published in the United Kingdom in the previous two years. Eligible writers must be under 40 years of age at the time of publication, a citizen of the United Kingdom, the Republic of Ireland, the Commonwealth or South Africa. Prize: £1,000. Winner: The Hiding Place by Trezza Azzopardi, 2001.

Forward Prizes for Poetry: c/o Coleman Getty PR, 126–130 Regent St, London W1R 5FE, England. Tel. (20) 7439-1783. Fax (20) 7439-1784. E-mail: pr@colmangettypr.co.uk. Three annual awards for poems in English, written by a citizen of the United Kingdom or the Republic of Ireland. Prizes: Best Collection of Poetry (£10,000); Waterstones Prize for Best First Collection of Poetry (£5,000); Tolman Cunard Prize for Best Single Poem (£1,000). Winners, 2001: Best Collection: Downriver by Sean O'Brien; Best First Collection: Panoramic Lounge Bar by John Stammers; Best Single Poem: The Lammas Hireling by Ian Duhig.

Frogmore Poetry Prize: Frogmore Press, 42 Morehall Ave, Folkestone, Kent CT19 4EF, England. Website: www.frogmorepress.co.uk. f. 1987. Awarded for unpublished poems of no more than 40 lines, written in English. Prizes: First prize 200 guineas and a lifetime subscription to The Frogmore Papers; Runners-up prizes of 50 and 25 guineas, each with a lifetime subscription to The Frogmore Papers; ten short-listed poems are published in the September issue of The Frogmore Papers. Winner: Gerald Watts, 2001.

Mary Gilmore Award: Association for the Study of Australian Literature, Dept of English, University College, ADFA, Campbell, ACT 2600, Australia. Awarded for a first book of poetry published in the preceding year. No nominations are required. Prize: $ A1,000. Winner: Memory Shell Five by Lucy Dougan, 2000.

Eric Gregory Trust Fund Award: Society of Authors, 84 Drayton Gdns, London SW10 9SB, England. Tel. (20) 7373 6642. Fax (20) 7373 5768. E-mail: authorsoc@writers.org.uk. Annual award for poets aged under 30 who are likely to benefit from more time given to writing. Prize: £25,000 (shared). Winners, 2001: Ross Cogan, Mathew Holis, Helen Ivory, Andrew Pideux, Owen Sheers, Dan Wyke.

Griffin Poetry Prize: The Griffin Trust for Excellence in Poetry, 6610 Edwards Blvd, Mississauga, ON L5T 2V6, Canada. Tel. (905) 565-5993. E-mail: info@griffinpoetryprize.com. Website: www.griffinpoetryprize.com. f. 2000. The Griffin Trust awards two annual literary awards for collections of poetry published in English during the preceding year, one to a living Canadian poet and the other to a living poet from any country. Prizes: C $40,000 each. Winners, 2001: Glottal Stop: 101 Poems by Paul Celan (International Prize); Men in the Off Hours by Anne Carson (Canadian Prize).

Ingersoll Prizes: Ingersoll Foundation, 934 N Main St, Rockford, IL 61103, USA.

International Prize for Poetry: La Maison Internationale de la Poésie, Chaussée de Wavre 150, 1050 Brussels, Belgium. Biennial prize awarded by an international jury. No submissions. Prize: 150,000 Belgian Francs.

Irish Times Irish Literature Prizes: Irish Times Ltd, 10–16 D'Olier St, Dublin 2, Ireland. Tel. (1) 679-2022. Fax (1) 679-3910. Biennial awards to books in five categories: international fiction; Irish fiction; Irish non-fiction; Irish poetry; and Irish language, chosen from nominations (no submissions). For the Irish poetry award, poets must be Irish by birth or be an Irish citizen. Prize: IR £27,500 (shared). Winner: Opened Ground by Seamus Heaney, 1999.

Gerald Lampert Award: League of Canadian Poets, 54 Wolseley St, Toronto, ON M5T 1A5, Canada. Tel. (416) 504-1657. Fax (416) 504-0096. E-mail: league@poets.ca. Website: www.poets.ca. Annual award recognizing the best first book of poetry published by a Canadian in the preceding year. Prize: C $1,000. Winner: Light Falls Through You by Anne Simpson, 2001.

Harold Morton Landon Translation Award: Academy of American Poets, 584 Bdwy, Suite 1208, New York, NY 10012, USA. Tel. (212) 274-0343. Fax (212) 274-9427. f. 1976. Annual award to the translator of a published translation of poetry from any language into English. Publishers may submit eligible books. Prize: US $1,000. Winners, 2001: Clayton Eshleman for Trilce by César Vallejo, and Edward Snow for Duino Elegies by Rainer Maria Rilke.

James Laughlin Award: Academy of American Poets, 584 Bdwy, Suite 1208, New York, NY 10012, USA. f. as Lamont Poetry Selection. Annual award to support the publication of an American poet's second volume of poetry. Only manuscripts already under contract with publishers are considered. Publishers are invited to submit manuscripts by American poets who have already published one volume of poems in a standard edition. Prize: US $5,000. Winner: Miracles and Mortifications by Peter Johnson, 2001.

Grace Leven Prize for Poetry: c/o Perpetual Trustee Company Ltd, 39 Hunter St, Sydney, NSW 2000, Australia. Award of $ A200 in recognition of the best volume of poetry published in the previous year. Poets must be Australian by birth, or naturalized Australians resident in the country for over 10 years.

Ruth Lilly Poetry Prize: c/o Modern Poetry Association, 60 W Walton St, Chicago, IL 60610, USA. Annual award to a US poet whose accomplishments warrant extraordinary recognition. Prize: US $100,000. Winner: Lisel Mueller, 2002.

Dorothy Livesay Poetry Prize: West Coast Book Prizes Society, 1033 Davie St, Suite 700, Vancouver, BC V6E 1M7, Canada. Regional award for poets resident in the area for over three years. Prize: C $2,000.

Mail on Sunday / John Llewellyn Rhys Prize: Book Trust, Book House, 45 East Hill, London SW18 2QZ, England. Tel. (20) 8516-2972. Fax (20) 8516-2978. f. 1942. Award for works of fiction, non-fiction, drama or poetry written in English and published in the United Kingdom in that year. Writers must be under 35 years old and a citizen of the United Kingdom or the Commonwealth. Prizes: First prize £5,000; £500 to each of five short-listed authors. Winner: Leadville by Edward Platt, 2000.

Lenore Marshall Poetry Prize: Academy of American Poets, 584 Bdwy, Suite 1208, New York, NY 10012, USA. Tel. (212) 274-0343. Fax (212) 274-9427. f. 1975. Annual award recognizes the most outstanding book of poetry published in the USA in the previous year. Publishers are invited to submit books. Prize: US $10,000. Winner: Selected Poems by Fanny Howe, 2001.

National Book Awards: National Book Awards Foundation, 260 Fifth Ave, 4th Floor, New York, NY 10001, USA. Website: www.nationalbook.org. f. 1950. Annual award to living American writers in four categories (fiction, non-fiction, poetry and young people's literature). Prizes: US $10,000 for each category; short-listed works $1,000. Winner, Poetry: Poems Seven: New and Complete Poetry by Alan Dugan, 2001.

National Book Critics Circle Awards: 400 N Broad St, Philadelphia, PA 19103, USA. Website: www.bookcritics.org. Annual award for excellence in biography, criticism, fiction, non-fiction and poetry by American authors, published for the first time in the previous year. Nominated by members. Prize: Scroll and citation. Winner, Poetry: Albert Goldbarth, 2001.

National Poetry Competition: Poetry Society, 22 Betterton St, London WC2H 9BU, England. Annual award for an unpublished poem of up to 40 lines by anyone over the age of 18. Prizes: First £3,000; Second £500; Third £250. Winners, 2000: Ian Duhig (first); Candy Neubert (second); Alex Barr (third).

Neustadt International Prize for Literature: World Literature Today, University of Oklahoma, 110 Monnet Hall, Norman, OK 73019, USA. Biennial award recognizing outstanding achievement of a living author, in fiction, poetry or drama written in English, French and/or Spanish. No applications are accepted. Prize: US $40,000, a replica of an eagle feather cast in silver and a certificate. Winner: Alvaro Mutis, 2002.

New Criterion Poetry Prize: 850 Seventh Ave, Suite 400, New York, NY 10019, USA. Website: www.newcriterion.com. Award for a previously unpublished collection of poems. Prize: US $3,000 and publication of the winning collection.

Newcastle Poetry Prize: Coal River Press, 246 Parry St, Newcastle West, NSW 2302, Australia. Tel. (49) 611696. Fax (49) 623959. E-mail: npp@artshunter.com.au. Website: www.artshunter.com.au. Annual awards for Australian poets. There are three sections: the Open Section, the New Media award for innovation in poetry production and presentation, and a special prize for a Newcastle poet. Prizes: $ A8,000 (Open Section); $2,000 (New Media).

Nova Poetica Open Poetry Competition: 14 Pennington Oval, Lymington, Hampshire SO41 8BQ, England. Prizes: First £300; runners-up prizes.

Observer National Children's Poetry Competition: Observer Magazine, Chelsea Bridge House, Queenstown Rd, London SW8 4NN, England.

Outposts Poetry Competition: c/o Hippopotamus Press, 22 Whitewell Rd, Frome, Somerset BA11 4EL, England. Annual award for unpublished works of not more than 40 lines. Prize: £1,000.

Peterloo Poets Open Poetry Competition: Sand Lane, Calstock, Cornwall PL18 9QX, England. Tel. (1822) 833473. Fax (1822) 833989. E-mail: poets@peterloo.fsnet.co.uk. Website: www.peterloopoets.co.uk. Annual award for unpublished poems in English of not more than 40 lines. Prizes: First £4,000; runners-up prizes. Winner: Jem Poster, 2001.

Poetry Life Open Poetry Competition: 14 Pennington Oval, Lymington, Hampshire SO41 8BQ, England. Prizes: First £500; runners-up prizes.

Premio Hispanoamericano de Poesía Sor Juana Inés de la Cruz: Centro Cultural de México, Los Yoses 4a., Entrada 250 S, PO Box 10107-1000, San José, Costa Rica. Open to all writers in Spanish living in Latin America. The award is given to a previously unpublished collection of poems of no more than 60 pages, which has not won any prizes. Prize: US $3,000, a Diploma and publication of the work by the Consejo Nacional para la Cultura y las Artes de México.

Premio Letterario Internazionale di Poesia Ulivo d'Oro: LIDH Italia, c/o ONMPIC, Via Lieni 48, Torino 10155, Italy. Tel. 1128-4218. Fax 1128-4218. f. 1983.

Premio Octavio Paz de Poesía y Ensayo: Fundación Octavio Paz, Francisco Sosa 383, Col. Barrio de Santa Catarina, 04000 Mexico City, DF, Mexico. Tel. (5) 659-5797. Fax (5) 554-9705. Website: www.fundacionpaz.org.mx. An annual award for a poet or essayist with the artistic, intellectual and critical qualities of great poets or essayists, inscribed in the modern tradition that Octavio Paz represented. Prize: Diploma and US $100,000. Winner: Juan Goytisolo, 2001.

Prijs der Nederlandse Letteren (Prize for Dutch Letters): Nederlandse Taalunie, Stadhoudersplantsoen 2, 2517 JL The Hague, Netherlands. A prize to celebrate writers in the Dutch language, with categories for prose, poetry, essays and drama. Prize: f 30,000 every three years.

Thomas Pringle Award: English Academy of Southern Africa, PO Box 124, Wits 2050, South Africa. Tel. (11) 717-9339. E-mail: engac@cosmos.wits.ac.za. Website: www.englishacademy.co.za. f. 1962. Annual award to honour achievements in five different categories: reviews, educational articles, literary articles, short stories or one act plays, and poetry, with three categories honoured each year. Prize: R2,000 for each category. Winners, 2001: Shaun de Waal, Rodrik Wade, Nicole Geslin, Peter Merrington, Shabbir Banoobhia.

Pulitzer Prize for American Poetry: Columbia University, New York, NY 10027, USA. Joseph Pulitzer (1847–1911), publisher of The New York World, endowed the Pulitzer Prizes in a bequest to Columbia University. The prize for American Poetry was established in 1922 and is awarded annually by the President of Columbia University on the recommendation of the Pulitzer Prize Board. Prize: (Poetry) US $3,000. Winner: Practical Gods by Carl Dennis, 2002.

Queen's Gold Medal for Poetry: Buckingham Palace, London, England. The King's Gold Medal for Poetry was instituted by King George V in 1933 at the suggestion of the then Poet Laureate, John Masefield. It became the Queen's Gold Medal for Poetry on the accession to the throne of Queen Elizabeth II in 1952. The Medal is given for a book of verse published in the English language, but translations of exceptional merit may be considered. Since 1985 subjects in Commonwealth Monarchies have been eligible for consideration. A small committee, under the chairmanship of the Poet Laureate, selects the winner. This choice is approved by the Queen and the Medal is presented at Buckingham Palace. It is not awarded every year. Winner: Michael Longley, 2001.

Raiziss/De Palchi Translation Award: Academy of American Poets, 584 Bdwy, Suite 1208, New York, NY 10012, USA. Website: www.poets.org. f. 1995. Book and fellowship awards, given in alternating years, recognizing outstanding translations of modern Italian poetry into English. No applications are accepted for the book prize, but submissions for the fellowship are accepted. Prizes: US $5,000 book prize; $20,000 fellowship, with a residency at the American Academy in Rome. Winners: Book Prize: Stephen Sartarelli for Songbook: The Selected Poems of Umberto Saba, 2001; Fellowship: Emanuel di Pasquale for Sharing a Trip: Selected Poems by Silvio Ramat, 2000.

Royal Society of Literature Award under the W. H. Heinemann Bequest: Royal Society of Literature, 1 Hyde Park Gdns, London W2 2LT, England. Annual award to works written in English and published in the previous year. Prize: £5,000. Winner: Night of Stone: Death and Memory in Russia by Catherine Merridale, 2000.

Olive Schreiner Prize: English Academy of Southern Africa, PO Box 124, Wits 2050, South Africa. Tel. (11) 717-9339. E-mail: engac@cosmos.wits.ac.za. Website: www.englishacademy.co.za. f. 1964.

Annual award to honour new talent for excellence in prose, poetry and drama. Winners are chosen by a panel of experts. Prize: R5,000 and an illuminated certificate. Winner, Poetry: Shaun de Waal, 2002.

Stand International Poetry Competition: Stand Magazine, 179 Wingrove Rd, Newcastle upon Tyne NE4 9DA, England. Award for an original poem of no longer than 500 lines, written in English, not previously published or broadcast. Prize: First £1,500; Runners-up prizes totalling £1,000. Winner: Vona Groarke, 2001.

Wallace Stevens Award: Academy of American Poets, 584 Bdwy, Suite 1208, New York, NY 10012, USA. Tel. (212) 274-0343. Fax (212) 274-9427. f. 1994 as the Tanning Prize. Annual award recognizing outstanding and proven mastery in the art of poetry. No submissions are accepted. Prize: US $150,000. Winner: John Ashbery, 2001.

Sunday Times Young Writer of the Year: The Awards Secretary, The Society of Authors, 84 Drayton Gdns, London SW10 9SB, England. Tel. (20) 7373-6642. Fax (20) 7373-5768. E-mail: authorsoc@writers.org.uk. Annual award to a writer under the age of 35 for a work of fiction, non-fiction or poetry published in the previous year. The author must be a citizen of the United Kingdom. Prize: £5,000.

Kingsley Tufts Poetry Prize: Poetic Gallery for the Kingsley and Kate Tufts Poetry Awards, Claremont Graduate University, 160 E 10th St, Harper East B7, Claremont, CA 91711-6165, USA. Tel. (909) 621-8974. Website: www.cgu.edu/tufts/. f. 1992–93. The Kingsley Tufts Poetry Prize is an annual award for a work by an emerging poet. The Kate Tufts Discovery Award is an annual award for a first or very early work by a promising poet. Prize: US $100,000 (Kingsley Tufts Poetry Prize); $10,000 (Kate Tufts Discovery Award). Winner, Kingsley Tufts Poetry Prize: The Tether by Carl Phillips, 2002.

Whitbread Book of the Year and Literary Awards: Booksellers' Association, Minster House, 272 Vauxhall Bridge Rd, London SW1V 1BA, England. Tel. (20) 7834-5477. Fax (20) 7834-8812. Website: www.whitbread-bookawards.co.uk. f. 1971. Annual awards to promote and increase good English literature in each of five categories: novel, first novel, biography, children's novel and poetry. Entries are submitted by publishers and the authors must have been resident in the United Kingdom or the Republic of Ireland for at least three years. One category winner is then voted Whitbread Book of the Year by the panel of judges. Prizes: £25,000 (Book of the Year); £5,000 (Poetry). Winner, Poetry: Bunny by Selima Hill, 2001.

Whiting Writers' Awards: Mrs Giles Whiting Foundation, 1133 Avenue of the Americas, New York, NY 10003, USA. Annual awards presented to emergent writers in recognition of their writing achievement and future promise in four categories: fiction, poetry, non-fiction and play. Prize: US $35,000. Winners, Poetry 2001: Joel Brouwer, Jason Sommer.

Walt Whitman Award: Academy of American Poets, 584 Bdwy, Suite 1208, New York, NY 10012, USA. f. 1975. Annual award for an eminent American poet who has not yet published a book of poetry in a standard edition. Prize: US $5,000, publication of the winner's first book and a one-month residency of the Vermont Studio Center. Winner: Notes from the Divided Country by Sue Kwock Kim, 2002.

APPENDIX C: POETRY ORGANIZATIONS

For organizations of more general interest to writers, see Appendix B of the International Who's Who of Authors and Writers.

AUSTRALIA

Australian Haiku Society—HaikuOz: 44 Bayside Dr., Lauderdale, Tasmania 7021; tel. (03) 6248-8496; e-mail haikuoz@yahoo.com; website users.mullum.com.au/jbird/ahs_about.html; f. 2000; promotes haiku within Australia; Contact Officer Lyn Reeves.

OZpoet: website www.ozpoet.asn.au; resources for poets and those interested in poetry; f.1999; Editor Gillian Savage.

Poetry Australia Foundation: PO Box U34, Wollongong University 2500; e-mail kpretty@uow.edu.au; website paf.scriptmania.com.

Poetry Society of Australia: PO Box N110, Grosvenor St, Sydney, NSW 2000; website www.ozpoeticsociety.com; Publs: New Poetry (quarterly); also poems, articles, reviews, notes and comments, interviews.

BELGIUM

European Association for the Promotion of Poetry: European Poetry House, 'The Seven Sleepers', J. P. Minckelsstraat 168, 3000 Leuven.

European Poetry Library: Blidjde Inkommststrasse 9, 3000 Leuven.

Haikoe Centrum Vlaanderen—HCV: Willy Vande Walle, Waaienbergstraat 14, 3090 Overijse; promotes Haiku poetry in Belgium.

Maison Internationale de la Poésie: 150 Chaussée de Wavre, Brussels 1050; tel. (2) 511-9122; fax (2) 511-5383; e-mail maison.intpoesie@ .profor.be; website www.maison-int-poesie.cfwb.be; f. 1955.

BRAZIL

Movimento Internacional Poetrix: PO Box 8622, Salvador, Bahia 41857-970; tel. (71) 9935-3500; e-mail poetrix@bol.com.br; website poetrix.vila.bol.com.br.

CANADA

Canadian Authors' Association: 275 Slater St, Suite 500, Ottawa, ON K1P 5H9.

Canadian Poetry Association: PO Box 22571, St George Postal Outlet, 264 Bloor St W, Toronto, ON M5S 1V8; website www.mirror.org/groups/ cpa/.

Haiku Canada: 51 Graham W, Napanee, ON K7R 2J6; website www.atreide.net/rendezvous/haikucanada; f. 1978.

League of Canadian Poets: 54 Wolseley St, Suite 204, Toronto, ON M5T 1A5; tel. (416) 504-1657; fax (416) 504-0096; e-mail league@poets.ca; website www.poets.ca.

THE PEOPLE'S REPUBLIC OF CHINA

China Poetry Society: 17 Beibingmasi Lane, Dongcheng District, Beijing 100009.

Chinese Poetry Association: 1 Xilou Lane, Yonghe Palace St, Beijing 100007; tel. (10) 640-72207; e-mail miusi@263.net; f. 1996; aims to unite poets throughout the country and to encourage new poets.

FRANCE

Association Internationale 'La Porte des Poètes': 128 rue Saint Maur, Paris 75011; tel. 1 43 38 24 29; fax 1 43 38 24 29; f. 1986.

Interational Parliament of Writers: PO Box 63, 67068 Strasbourg Cédex.

Maison International des Poètes et des Ecrivains: 5 rue du Pelicot, St Malo 35400; tel. 2 99 40 28 77; f. 1990.

Poètes sans frontières: 8 ave du Levant, Fitou 11510; tel. 4 68 45 70 18; website perso.wanadoo.fr/l-etrave/; f. 1993.

Société des Poètes Français: Hôtel de Massa, 38 rue du Fb Saint-Jacques, Paris 75014; tel. 1 40 46 99 82; website www .societedespoetesfrancais.asso.fr; f. 1902; lectures, prizes, defending interests of members; publishes quarterly bulletin.

GERMANY

German Haiku Society—Deutschen Haiku-gesellschaft: 49424 Goldenstedt, Lutten; tel. and fax (04441) 83897; e-mail haiku-dhg@kulturserver-nds.de; website haiku-dhg.kulturserver-nds.de.

LiteraturWerkstatt Berlin, section Lyrikline: c/o LiteraturWerkstatt Berlin, Majakowskiring 46/48, Berlin 13156; tel. and fax (30) 4852-4530; e-mail mail@lyrikline.org; website www.lyrikline.org; f. 1999.

INDIA

Poetry Society of India: L-67A Malviya Nagar, New Delhi 110 017.

World Poetry Society Intercontinental: 118 Raja St, Velacheri, Chennai 600 042, Tamil Nadu.

IRELAND

Irish Writers' Centre: 19 Parnell Sq., Dublin 1; tel. (1) 872-1302; e-mail iwc@iol.ie; website www.writerscentre.ie.

Poetry Ireland (Eigse Eireann): Bermingham Tower, Upper Yard, Dublin Castle, Dublin 2; tel. (1) 6714632; fax (1) 6714634; e-mail poetry@iol.ie; organization promoting and supporting poetry in Ireland; organizes tours, readings and the National Poetry Competition; Publs: Poetry Ireland Review (quarterly magazine) and bi-monthly newsletter; Dir Joseph Woods.

JAPAN

Association of Haiku Poets: Haiku Bungakukan Bldg, 3-28-10 Hyakunin-cho, Shinjuku-ku, Tokyo 169-8521; tel. (3) 3367-6621; fax (3) 3367-665; Chair. Shugyo Takaha.

Association of International Renku—AIR: Shinku Fukuda, Tadashi Kondô, Kanagawa; e-mail yeiko@peach.ocn.ne.jp; website www.ignoramus .nu/renku/index.shtml; Contact Eiko Yachimoto.

Haiku International Association: 9-1-7-914 Alaska, Minato-ku, Tokyo 107; f. 1989; Hon. Pres. Sono Uchida.

Japan Poets Association: c/o Eiji Kikai, 3-16-1 Minami, Azabu, Minato-ku, Tokyo 105; cultivates the mutual friendship among poets.

Japan Tanka Poets' Club: 408 Ebisu-Mansion, 1-2-1 Ebisu-Nishi, Shibuya-ku; website www.yk.rim.or.jp/~kajin/.

MEXICO

Poesía Virtual: 53510 Mexico City, DF; tel. (5) 351-0479; e-mail webmaster@poesiavirtual.com; website poesiavirtual.com; f. 2001.

THE NETHERLANDS

Haiku Kring Nederlande—HKN: Max Verhaart, Spoermekerlaan 30, 5237 Hertogenbosch.

Poetry International Foundation: William Boothlaan 4, 3012 VJ Rotterdam; tel. (10) 282-2777; fax (10) 282-2775; e-mail poetry@luna.nl; organizes annual poetry festival.

NEW ZEALAND

New Zealand Poetry Society: 58 Cecil Road, Wadestown, Wellington; Editor Cyril Childs.

SPAIN

Associació d'Escriptors en Llengua Catalana—AELC: Canuda 6, 5°, Barcelona 08002; tel. (93) 302-7828; fax (93) 412-5873; e-mail info@aelc.es; website www.escriptors.com; f. 1976.

Aula de Poesia de Barcelona: Passeig de la Vall d'Hebron 171, Barcelona 08035; tel. (93) 403-5096; e-mail apdeb@d5.ub.es; website www.ub.es/aulapoesiabarcelona; f. 1991.

Fundación Federico García Lorca: Calle Pinar 23, Madrid 28006; tel. (91) 562-1899; e-mail ffgl@garcia-lorca.org; website www.garcia-lorca.org; f. 1984.

SWEDEN

Swedish Haiku Society: Kai Falkman, S - UD 103 39 Stockholm; tel. (08) 4055371; fax (08) 7231176; e-mail kaj.falkman@foreign.ministry.se.

THE UNITED KINGDOM

Academi—The Welsh National Literature Promotion Agency and Society for Writers: Third Floor, Mount Stuart House, Mount Stuart Sq., Cardiff CF1 6DQ, Wales; tel. (29) 2047-2266; fax (29) 2049-2930; e-mail post@academi.org; website www.academi.org; Writers' organization responsible for literary activity in Wales; Sponsors the Cardiff International Poetry Competition; Chief Exec. Peter Finch.

The Arvon Foundation: 2nd Floor, 42A Buckingham Palace Rd, London SW1W 0RE; tel. (20) 7931-7611; fax (20) 7963-0961; website www.arvonfoundation.org; organizes writing courses for poetry, fiction, stage drama, television and radio; Chair. Prudence Skene.

Association of Small Press Poets: 7 Pincott Pl., London SE4 2ER; tel. (20) 7277-8831; fax (8707) 403511; e-mail robooth@gofornet.co.uk; website www.smallpresspoets.co.uk; Co-ordinator Ruth Booth.

British Haiku Society: Lenacre Ford, Woolhope, Hereford HR1 4RF; tel. (1432) 860328; website www.britishhaikusociety.org; f. 1990; Promotes the appreciation and writing of haiku, senyru, tanka, haibun and renga; Administers annual James W. Hackett Award, the Sasakawa prize and the Nobuyuki Yuasa International English Haibun Contest; Gen. Sec. David Walker.

International Poets, Playwrights, Essayists, Editors and Novelists Association—PEN: 9–10 Charterhouse Bldgs, Goswell Rd, London EC1M 7AT; tel. (20) 7253-4308; fax (20) 7253-5711; e-mail intpen@dircon.co.uk; f. 1921; International Pres. Homero Aridjis.

National Poetry Foundation: 27 Mill Rd, Fareham, Hants PO16 0TH; tel. (1329) 822218; publishes first poetry collections; organization encourages new writers; Publs: Pause magazine.

Northern Poetry Library: Central Library, The Willows, Morpeth, Northumberland NE61 1TA; tel. (1670) 534524; fax (1670) 534513; e-mail amenities@northumberland.gov.uk; books and magazines for loan, and access to text database of English poetry; postal loans available.

Poetry Association of Scotland: 38 Dovecot Rd, Edinburgh EH12 7LE, Scotland.

Poetry Book Society—PBS: Book House, 45 East Hill, London SW18 2QZ; tel. (20) 8870-8403; fax (20) 8877-1615; website www.poetrybooks.co.uk; f. 1953 by T. S. Eliot; Provides information about poetry from publishers in the United Kingdom and Ireland; Runs the annual T. S. Eliot Prize for the best collection of new poetry; Dir. Clare Brown.

Poetry Can: Unit 11, Kuumba Project, 20-22 Hepburn Rd, Bristol BS2 8UD; tel. (117) 9426976; fax (117) 9441478; e-mail hester@poetrycan.demon.co.uk; website www.poetrycan.demon.co.uk; f. 1995; poetry development agency in Bristol and Bath; Dir Hester Cockcroft.

Poetry Library: Royal Festival Hall, Level 5, South Bank Centre, London SE1 8XX; tel. (20) 7921-0943; fax (20) 7921-0939; e-mail info@poetrylibrary.org.uk; website www.poetrylibrary.org.uk; f. 1953 to support and promote modern British poetry; includes all 20th Century poetry in English and a collection of all poetry magazines published in the United Kingdom; arranges functions and provides an information service; approx. 80,000 vols.; Librarian Mary Enright.

Poetry London: 1A Jewel Rd, London E17 4QU; tel. (20) 8521-0776; fax (20) 8521-0776; e-mail editors@plondon.demon.co.uk; website www.poetrylondon.co.uk; poetry magazine; Poetry Editor Pascale Petit.

Poetry Society: 22 Betterton St, London WC2H 9BU; tel. (20) 7420-9880; fax (20) 7240-4818; e-mail poetrysoc@dial.pipex.com; website www.poetrysociety.org.uk; f. 1909; operates a series of seminars and training courses, education services and a library service, and administers the National Poetry Competition; Publs: Poetry Review (quarterly magazine) and Poetry News (newsletter); Chair. Richard Price.

Scottish Poetry Library: 5 Crichton's Close, Canongate, Edinburgh EH8 8DT, Scotland; tel. (131) 557-2876; poetry books, tapes and magazines can be borrowed in person or by post; provides specialist lists and bibliographies; Dir Robyn Marsack.

Second Light: 9 Greendale Close, London SE22 8TG; e-mail dilys_wood@lineone.net; promotes and supports women's poetry; Dir Dilys Wood.

Society of Authors: 84 Drayton Gdns, London SW10 9SB.

Ver Poets: Haycroft, 61–63 Chiswell Green Lane, St Albans, Herts AL2 3AL; promotes poetry and helps poets through information, events and publications; holds regular competitions, including the annual Ver Poets Open Competition.

World Haiku Club: Leys Farm, Rousham, Bicester, Oxfordshire OX6 3RA; tel. (1869) 340261; fax (1869) 340619; e-mail aminetoxford@cwcom.net; website www.come.to/worldhaiku/; f. 1998; organizes World Haiku Festival; Chair. and Founder Susumu Takiguchi.

THE UNITED STATES OF AMERICA

Academy of American Poets: 588 Bdwy, Suite 1203, New York, NY 10012-3210; tel. (212) 274-0343; fax (212) 274-9427; website www.poets.org; f. 1934; sponsors the James Laughlin Award, the Walt Whitman Award, the Harold Morton Landon Translation Award, the Tanning Prize, the Raiziss/de Palchi Translation Award and annual college poetry prizes; workshops, classes and literary historical walking tours; awards fellowships to American poets for distinguished poetic achievement.

American Academy of Arts and Letters: 633 W 155th St, New York, NY 10032, USA.

American Society of Composers, Authors and Publishers—ASCAP: 1 Lincoln Plaza, New York, NY 10023.

Council of Literary Magazines and Presses: 154 Christopher St, Suite 3C, New York, NY 10014.

Federation of International Poetry Associations: PO Box 579, Santa Claus, IN 47579.

Haiku Society of America: PO Box 2461, Winchester, VA 22604; website www.hsa-haiku.org; f. 1968; promotes the appreciation of Haiku in English.

International Poetry Forum: 4415 Fifth Ave, Pittsburgh, PA 15213.

Ingram Merrill Foundation: 104 E 40th St, Suite 302, New York, NY 10016, USA.

Modern Poetry Association: 60 W Walton St, Chicago, IL 60610; tel. (312) 255-3703; e-mail poetry@poetrymagazine.org; website www.poetrymagazine.org; f. 1941; publishes annual poetry magazine.

National Federation of State Poetry Societies—NFSPS: 2736 Creekwood Lane, Fort Worth, TX 76123; website www.nfsps.com; f. 1959; educational and literary organization; societies of members in 40 states (2001).

National Poetry Association: PO Box 173, Bayport, MN 55003.

National Poetry Foundation: University of Maine, 5752 Neville Hall, Orono, ME 04469-5752; tel. (207) 581-3813; website www.ume.maine.edu/~npf/; f.1971.

PEN American Center: 568 Bdwy, New York, NY 10012-3225; tel. (212) 334-1660; fax (212) 334-2181; e-mail pen@pen.org; website www.pen.org; Sec. Michael Roberts.

Poetry Project: St Mark's Church, 131 E 10th S At Second Ave, New York, NY 10003.

Poetry Society of America—PSA: 15 Gramercy Park, New York, NY 10003; tel. (212) 254-9628; website www.poetrysociety.org; f. 1910; organization dedicated to the promotion of poets and poetry; sponsors readings, lectures and contests; houses the Van Voorhis Library; administers annual PSA Award.

Poets and Writers Inc: 72 Spring St, New York, NY 10012; national non-profit information centre for those interested in contemporary American literature; publishes a directory of American poets and fiction writers and sponsors readings and workshop programmes.

Poets' House: 72 Spring St, Second Floor, New York, NY 10012; tel. (212) 431-7920; e-mail info@poetshouse.org; website www.poetshouse.org; literary center and poetry archive.

Theodore Roethke Memorial Foundation: 11 W Hannum Blvd, Saginaw, MI 48602.

Science Fiction Poetry Association: 6075 Bellevue Dr., North Olmsted, OH 44070; e-mail dragontea@earthlink.net; website dm.net/~bejay/sfpa.htm; f. 1978.

Tanka Society of America: 248 Beach Park Blvd, Foster City, CA 94404; website www.millikin.edu/haiku/global/tankasociety.html; Pres. Michael Dylan Welch.

World Academy of Arts and Culture: 3146 Buckeye Ct, Placerville, CA 95667.

World Haiku Association—WHA: PO Box 2461, Winchester, VA 22604; website www.epiphanous.org/wha/; f. 2000; Contact Jim Kacian, Max Verhart.

YUGOSLAVIA

Haiku Association of South-Eastern Europe—HASEE: Jasminka Nadaskic Diordievic, 11300 Smederevo, Radnicka 1; e-mail dior@sezampro.yu; website web.wanadoo.be/tempslibres/hasee.html; network of haiku poets in South-Eastern European countries.

APPENDIX D: POETRY PUBLISHERS

AUSTRALIA

Five Islands Press: PO Box U34 Wollongong University; tel. (02) 4271 5292; fax (02) 4272 7292; e-mail kpretty@uow.edu.au; website www.5islands.1earth.net; specializes in contemporary Australian poetry.

Little Esther Books: South Australian Publishing Ventures & Futures Inc, PO Box 8091, Station Arcade, Adelaide, SA 5000; fax (8) 8211-7323; website www.eaf.asn.au/otis/otismai1.html.

Salt Publishing: PO Box 202, Applecross, WA 6153; e-mail cnewman@saltpublishing.com; poetry, drama and experimental fiction.

Spinifex Press: PO Box 212, 504 Queensberry St, North Melbourne, Vic. 3051; tel. (3) 9329-6088; fax (3) 9329-9238; e-mail world@spinifexpress.co.au; website www.spinifexpress.com.au.

Thylazine Publishing Australia: PO Box 645, Harbord, NSW 2096; e-mail coralhull@thylazine.org; website www.thylazine.org; f. 2000; Exec. Editor Coral Hull.

Vagabond Press: PO Box 80, Newtown, NSW 2042; e-mail lizbo22@hotmail.com.

AUSTRIA

Poetry Salzburg: University of Salzburg, Dept of English and American Studies, Akademiestr. 24, 5020 Salzburg; e-mail wolfgang.goertschacher@sbg.ac.at; website www.poetrysalzburg.com.

CANADA

Black Moss Press: 2450 Byng Rd, Windsor, ON N8W 3E8; tel. (519) 252-2551; fax (519) 253-7809; e-mail bfox@blackmosspress.on.ca; Contact C. H. Gervais.

Delirium Press: 5352 Ave du Parc, Apt 36, Montreal, QC H2V 4G8.

Hidden Brook Press: 412–701 King St W, Toronto, ON M5V 2W7; tel. (416) 504-3966; e-mail writers@hiddenbrookpress.com; Contact Richard M. Grove.

House of Anansi Press: 895 Don Mills Rd, 400–402 Park Centre, Toronto, ON M3C 1W3; website www.anansi.ca; poetry, fiction, literary criticism and non-fiction; Publisher Martha Sharpe.

Housepress: 1339 19th Ave NW, Calgary, AB; e-mail housepress@home.com; website www.housepress.ca.

Thistledown Press Ltd: 633 Main St, Saskatoon, SK S7H 0J8; website www.thistledown.sk.ca; poetry and fiction by Canadian writers.

GERMANY

Elfenbein Verlag: Pappelallee 3–4, 10437 Berlin; tel. (30) 4432 -7769; fax (30) 4432-7780; website www.elfenbein-verlag.de; publishes Portuguese, German and Czech literature and poetry.

INDIA

Abhinav Publications: E37 Hauz Khas, New Delhi 110016; tel. (11) 656-6387; fax (11) 685-7009; e-mail shakti@nde.vsnl.net.in; website www.abhinavexport.com.

Ananda Publishers: 45 Beniatola Lane, Calcutta 700 009; tel. (33) 241-4352; fax (33) 225-3240; e-mail ananda@cal3.vsnl.net.in.

Bahri Publications: 997a Street No. 9, PO Box 4453, Gobindpuri, Kalkaji, New Delhi 110019; tel. (11) 644-5710; fax (33) 644-8606; e-mail bahrius@del6.vsnl.net.in; website www.bahripublications.org.

D. C. Books: Kottayam, Kerala 686001; tel. (481) 563-114; fax (481) 564-758; e-mail dcbooks@sancharnet.in; website www.dcbooks.com.

Kitabghar: 24 Ansari Rd, Darya Ganj, New Delhi 110002; tel. (11) 328-1244; fax (11) 327-1844; e-mail kitabghar@bplnet.com.

Parimal Prakashan: Parimal Bldg, Khadkeshwar, Aurangabad 431001; tel. (240) 323-887.

Shipra Publications: 115A, 3rd Floor, Vikas Marg, Shakarpur, Delhi 110092; tel. (11) 220-0954; fax (11) 245-8662; e-mail shiprapub@satyam.net.in.

IRELAND

Cló Iar-Chonnachta: Indreabhán, Connemara, Galway; tel. (91) 593307; fax (91) 593362.

Collins Press: Carey's Lane, The Huguenot Quarter, Cork; tel. (21) 271346; fax (21) 275489.

Dedalus Poetry Press: 24 The Heath, Cypress Downs, Dublin 6.

Gallery Press: Loughcrew, Oldcastle, Co Meath.

Hard Pressed Poetry: 37 Grosvenor Ct, Templeville Rd, Templeogue, Dublin 6.

Lilliput Press: 4 Rosemount Terrace, Arbour Hill, Dublin 7; tel. (1) 6711647; fax (1) 6711647.

Marmara Press: 3 Sweetmount Dr., Dundrum, Dublin 14; e-mail b.kennedy@esatclear.ie.

Mercier Press Ltd: PO Box 6, 5 French Church St, Cork; tel. (21) 275040; fax (21) 274969.

New Island Books: 2 Brookside, Dundrum Rd, Dublin 14.

Salmon Publishing Ltd: Cliffs of Moher, Co Clare; e-mail info@salmonpoetry.com; website www.salmonpoetry.com.

Wild Honey Press: 16a Ballyman Rd, Bray, Co Wicklow; e-mail suantrai@iol.ie; website www.wildhoneypress.com.

SOUTH AFRICA

Jonathan Ball Publishers: PO Box 33977, Jeppestown, 2043; tel. (11) 622-2900; fax (11) 622-7610.

Barefoot Press: PO Box 532, Auckland Park 2006; website www.pix.za/barefoot.press/bareinfo.htm; features South African poets; Man. Editor Roy Blumenthal.

David Phillip Publishers: PO Box 23408, Claremont, Cape Town, 7735; tel. (21) 674-4136; fax (21) 674-3358; e-mail info@dpp.co.za; website www.dpp.co.za.

SPAIN

Point: Ithaca, Apdo 119, 03590 Altea; tel. (96) 5842350; fax (96) 6882767; e-mail elpoeta@point-editions.com; website www.point-editions.com; f. 1984 as Poetry International; multilingual publisher of contemporary poetry; Dir Germain Droogenbroodt.

THE UNITED KINGDOM

Anchor Books: 1–2 Wainman Rd, Woodston, Peterborough PE2 7BU; tel. (1733) 230746; fax (1733) 230751; e-mail pete@forwardpress.co.uk; poetry imprint of the Forward Press.

Anvil Press Poetry Ltd: Neptune House, 70 Royal Hill, London SE10 8RT; tel. (20) 8469-3033; fax (20) 8469-3363; Editorial Dir Peter Jay.

Arc Publications: Shaw Wood Road, Todmorden, Lancashire OL14 6DA; tel. (1706) 812338; fax (1706) 818948; contemporary poetry from new and established national and international writers; Editor Tony Ward.

Aural Images: Alan White, 5 Hamilton St, Astley Bridge, Bolton, Lancs BL1 6RT.

Beyond the Cloister Publications: Hugh Hellicar, Flat 1, 14 Lewes Cres., Brighton, East Sussex BN2 1FH; tel. (1273) 676019.

Blackwater Press: PO Box 5115, Leicester LE2 8ZD; tel. (116) 2238703.

Bloodaxe Books Ltd: Highgreen, Tarset, Northumberland NE48 1RP; tel. (1434) 240500; fax (1434) 240505; e-mail editor@bloodaxebooks .demon.co.uk; website www.bloodaxebooks.com; Editor Neil Astley.

Jonathan Cape: Random House, 20 Vauxhall Bridge Rd, London SW1V 2SA; tel. (20) 7840-8576; fax (20) 7233-6117.

Carcanet Press: 4th Floor, Conavon Ct, Blackfriars St, Manchester M3 5BQ; tel. (161) 8348730; fax (161) 8320084; e-mail pnr@carcanet.u-net.com; website www.carcanet.co.uk.

Chatto & Windus: Random House, 20 Vauxhall Bridge Rd, London SW1V 2SA; tel. (20) 7840-8400; fax (20) 7233-6117; e-mail enquiries@randomhouse.co.uk; website www.randomhouse.co.uk.

Community of Poets Press: Thyme Cottage, Bogshole Lane, Whitstable CT5 3AT; e-mail bennetta.artco@virgin.net; website www.artistspress .co.uk.

Creation Books: 4th Floor, 72–80 Leather Lane, London EC1N 7TR; tel. (20) 7430-9878; fax (20) 7242-5527; e-mail info@creationbooks.com; website www.creationbooks.com.

Diehard Poetry: 3 Spittal St, Edinburgh EH3 9DY.

Dionysia Press Ltd: 20a Montgomery St, Edinburgh EH7 5JS; tel. (131) 478-0927; fax (131) 478-2572.

Enitharmon Press: 26B Caversham Rd, London NW5 2DU; tel. (20) 7482-5967; fax (20) 7284-1787; e-mail books@enitharmon.co.uk; website www.enitharmon.co.uk; Dir Stephen Stuart-Smith.

Envoi Poets Press: Pen Ffordd, Newport, Pembrokeshire SA42 0QT.

Faber and Faber Ltd: 3 Queen's Sq., London WC1N 3AU; tel. (20) 7465-0045; e-mail contact@faber.co.uk; website www.faber.co.uk.

Flambard Press: Stable Cottage, East Fourstones, Hexham, Northumberland NE47 5DY; tel. (1434) 674360; fax (1434) 674178; e-mail signatur@dircon.co.uk.

Forward Press: Remus House, Coltsfoot Dr., Woodston, Peterborough PE2 9JX; tel. (1733) 890099; fax (1733) 313524.

Frogmore Press: 18 Nevill Rd, Lewes, East Sussex BN7 1PF; Poetry by new and established writers.

Granta Books: 2–3 Hanover Yard, Noel Rd, London N1 8BE; tel. (20) 7704-9776; fax (20) 7704-0474; website www.granta.com; f. 1989; Publishing Dir Neil Belton.

Greylag Press: 7 Moreton Way, Kingsthorpe, Northampton NN2 8PD.

Robert Hale Ltd: Clerkenwell House, 45–47 Clerkenwell Green, London EC1R 0HT; tel. (171) 2512661; fax (171) 4904958.

Hearing Eye Publications: c/o 99 Torriano Ave, Kentish Town, London NW5 2RX; e-mail hearing_eye@torriano.org; website www.torriano.org/hearing_eye/.

William Heinemann: Random House, 20 Vauxhall Bridge Rd, London SW1V 2SA; tel. (20) 7840-8733; fax (20) 7233-6127; e-mail enquiries@randomhouse.co.uk; website www.randomhouse.co.uk.

Hilton House Publishers: Hilton House, 39 Long John Hill, Norwich NR1 2JP; tel. and fax (1603) 449845.

Hippopotamus Press: 22 Whitewell Rd, Frome, Somerset BA11 4EL; tel. (1373) 466653; fax (1373) 466653.

Hutchinson: Random House, 20 Vauxhall Bridge Rd, London SW1V 2SA; tel. (20) 7840-8564; fax (20) 7233-6127; e-mail enquiries@randomhouse.co.uk; website www.randomhouse.co.uk.

Katabasis: 10 St Martins Close, London NW1 0HR; tel. and fax (20) 7485-3830; e-mail katabasis@katabasis.co.uk; website www.katabasis.co.uk; English and bilingual editions of Latin American poetry.

K. T. Publications (Kite Books): 16 Fane Close, Stamford, Lincolnshire PE9 1HG; tel. (1780) 754193.

Lateral Moves Press (Poetry): 5 Hamilton St, Astley Bridge, Bolton, Lancs BL1 6RJ; tel. (1204) 596369.

Ligden Publishers: 34 Lineacre, Grange Park, Swindon, Wiltshire SN5 6DA; tel. and fax (1793) 875941; e-mail david.pike@virgin.net; linked to the Ligden Poetry Society and Pulsar poetry magazine.

Odyssey Poets: Coleridge Cottage, Nether Stowey, Somerset TA5 1NQ; tel. (1278) 732662; first collections, booklets, full collections.

Other Press: 19 Marriott Rd, London N4 3QN; tel. (20) 7272-9023; e-mail fpresley@compuserve.com; experimental women's poetry.

Oxford University Press: Walton St, Oxford OX2 6DP; e-mail enquiry@oup.co.uk; website www.oup.co.uk.

Yvonne Parsons Publishing: 21 Park Rd, Bramcote, Nottingham NG9 3LA; tel. (115) 9168714.

Partners in Poetry: 289 Elmwood Ave, Feltham, Middlesex TW13 7QB tel. (20) 8751-8652.

Penguin Books Ltd: 80 Strand, London WC2R 0RL; website www.penguin.co.uk.

Peterloo Poets: 2 Kelly Gdns, Calstock, Cornwall PL18 9SA; tel. (1822 833473; Poetry Editor Harry Chambers.

Picador: 25 Eccleston Place, London SW1W 9NF; website www.panmacmillan.com/picador/.

Poetical Histories: Peter Riley Books, 27 Sturton St, Cambridge CB1 2QG.

Poetry Business: The Studio, Byram Arcade, Westgate, Huddersfield West Yorkshire HD1 1ND; tel. (1484) 434840; fax (1484) 426566; e-mail edit@poetrybusiness.co.uk; website www.poetrybusiness.co.uk; f. 1986 publishes under Smith/Doorstop imprint; Dirs Peter Sansom, Janet Fisher.

Poetry Monthly Press: 39 Cavendish Rd, Long Eaton, Nottingham NG10 4HY; tel. (115) 9461267; e-mail martinholroyd@compuserve.com.

Poetry Now: Remus House, Coltsfoot Dr., Woodston, Peterborough PE2 9JX; tel. (1733) 890099; fax (1733) 313524; e-mail forward_press@compuserve.com.

Polygon at Edinburgh: 22 George Sq., Edinburgh EH8 9LF, Scotland; tel. (131) 6504223; website www.eup.ed.ac.uk.

Profile Books: 58A Hatton Garden, London EC1N 8LX; tel. (20) 7404-3001; fax (20) 7404-3003; e-mail info@profilebooks.co.uk; website www.profilebooks.co.uk.

Random House: Random House, 20 Vauxhall Bridge Rd, London SW1V 2SA; tel. (20) 7840-8000; fax (20) 7821-7387; website www.randomhouse .co.uk.

Reality Street Editions: 4 Howard Ct, Peckham Rye, London SE15 3PH; tel. (20) 7639-7297; e-mail info@realitystreet.co.uk; website freespace .virgin.net/reality.street/; Publisher Ken Edwards.

Red Candle Press: 9 Milner Rd, Wisbech, Cambridgeshire PE13 2LR; tel. (1945) 581067.

Robson Books Ltd: 10 Blenheim Ct, Brewery Rd, London N7 9NT; tel. (20) 7700-7444; fax (20) 7700-4552.

Salt Publishing: PO Box 937, Great Wilbraham, Cambridge CB1 5JX; e-mail cemery@saltpublishing.com; website www.geocities.com/SoHo/Square/1664/index.html; non-profit publisher of poetry and poetics.

Saqi Books: 26 Westbourne Grove, London W2 5RH; tel. (20) 7221-9347; fax (20) 7229-7492; website www.alsaqibookshop.com; f. 1984.

Secker & Warburg: Random House, 20 Vauxhall Bridge Rd, London SW1V 2SA; tel. (20) 7840-8570; fax (20) 7233-6117; e-mail enquiries@randomhouse.co.uk; website www.randomhouse.co.uk.

Seren: First and Second Floors, 38–40 Nolton St, Bridgend CF31 3BN, Wales; tel. (1656) 663018; fax (1656) 649226; e-mail enquiries@seren.force9.co.uk; website www.seren-books.com.

Smith/Doorstop Books: The Studio, Byram Arcade, Westgate, Huddersfield, West Yorkshire HD1 1ND; tel. (1484) 434840; fax (1484) 426566; e-mail poetbus@pop3.potel.org.uk; contemporary poetry books, pamphlets and cassettes.

Tarantula Publications: 14 Vine St, Salford, Manchester M7 3PG; tel. (161) 792-4593; fax (161) 792-4593.

Vintage: Random House, 20 Vauxhall Bridge Rd, London SW1V 2SA; tel. (20) 7840-8573; fax (20) 7233-6117; e-mail enquiries@randomhouse.co.uk; website www.randomhouse.co.uk.

Virago Press: Time Warner Books UK, Brettenham House, Lancaster Pl., London WC2E 7EN; tel. (20) 7911-8000; fax (20) 7911-8100; e-mail virago.press@timewarnerbooks.co.uk; website www.virago.co.uk.

Women's Press: 34 Great Sutton St, London EC1V 0LQ; tel. (20) 7251-3007; fax (20) 7608-1938; e-mail sales@the-womens-press.com; website www.the-womens-press.com.

Zum Zum Books: Neil Oram, Goshem, Bunlight, Drumnadrochit, Invernessshire IV3 6AH; tel. (1456) 450402.

THE UNITED STATES OF AMERICA

Alice James Books: 238 Main St, Farmington, ME 04938; tel. (207) 778-7071; website www.umf.maine.edu/~ajb/; emphasizes the work of New England poets.

Big Bridge Press: 2000 Hwy 1, Pacifica CA 94044; e-mail poezine@bigbridge.org; Editor Michael Rothenberg.

Black Sparrow Press: 24 10th St, Santa Rosa, CA 95401; tel. (707) 579-4011; fax (707) 579-0567; e-mail books@blacksparrowpress.com; website www.blacksparrowpress.com; avant-garde poetry and fiction.

Cadmus Editions: PO Box 126, Tiburon-Belvedere, CA, 94920; tel. (707) 762-0510; website www.cadmus-editions.com; literary fiction, non-fiction and poetry.

Copper Canyon Press: PO Box 271, Bldg 313, Fort Worden State Park, Port Townsend WA 98368; tel. (360) 385-4925; fax (360) 385-4985; e-mail joseph@coppercanyonpress.org; website www.coppercanyonpress.org.

Distant Frontier Press: PO Box 5031, Dept W, South Hackensack, New Jersey 07606; e-mail contestdirector@historyonline.net; website www.historyonline.net/poetcont.htm; poetry with history themes.

Duration Press: 117 Donahue St, Suite 32, Sausalito 94965; tel. (415) 332-8041; e-mail info@durationpress.com; website www.durationpress .com; f. 1997; pamphlets of contemporary world poetry in English translation.

Floating Bridge Press: PO Box 18814, Seattle, WA 98118; e-mail ppereira5@aol.com; website www.scn.org/arts/floatingbridge/; f. 1994; non-profit literary arts organization to recognize and promote Washington State poets; organizes annual Poetry Chapbook Award.

Ludlow Press: PO Box 2612, New York, NY 10009; e-mail mailing@ludlowpress.com; website www.ludlowpress.com.

Mayapple Press: PO Box 5473, Saginaw, MI 48603-0473; website www.mayapplepress.com; f. 1978 by poet and editor Judith Kerman; specializes in Great Lakes Regional poetry and poetry by women.

O Books: 5729 Clover Dr., Oakland, CA 94618-1622; fax (510) 601-9588; contemporary poetry and essays and plays by poets.

Oberlin College Press: 10 N Professor St, Oberlin, OH 44074-1095; tel. (440) 775-8408; fax (440) 775-8124; e-mail oc.press@oberline.edu; website www.oberlin.edu/~ocpress/; contemporary poetry and poetics.

Orchises Press: PO Box 20602, Alexandria, VA 22320-1602; website mason.gmu.edu/~rlathbur/index.html; specializes in poetry and reprints; Editor Roger Lathbury.

Pudding House Publications: 60 N Main St, Johnstown, OH 43031; tel. (740) 967-6060; website www.puddinghouse.com; poetry anthologies.

Sarabande Books: 2234 Dundee Rd, Suite 200, Louisville, KY 40205; tel. (502) 458-4028; fax (502) 458-4065; website www.sarabandebooks.org; non-profit press; poetry, essays and short fiction.

Sherman Asher Publishing: PO Box 2853, Santa Fe, NM 87504; website www.shermanasher.com.

Six Gallery Press—6GP: PO Box 601, Geneva OH 44041-0601; e-mail sixgallerypress@usa.net; website www.sixgallerypress.com.

Story Line Press: Three Oaks Farm, PO Box 1240, Ashland, OR 97520-0055; tel. (541) 512-8792; website www.storylinepress.com; independent, non-profit press.

Talisman Publishers Inc: Talisman House, PO Box 896, Greenfield, MA 01302; website www.talismanpublishers.com; poetry, fiction, theory and criticism.

Time Being Press: St Louis, MO; website www.timebeing.com; contemporary American poetry; Dir Jane Goldberg.

Word Press: PO Box 541106, Cincinnati, OH 45254-1106; tel. (513) 474-3761; fax (513) 474-9034; e-mail connect@wordtechweb.com; website www.word-press.com.

Zoo Press: PO Box 22990, Lincoln, NE 68542; tel. (402) 770-8104; fax (402) 328-2803; e-mail editors@zoopress.org; website www.zoopress.org; publishes works of emerging poets and playwrights.

APPENDIX E: POETS LAUREATE OF THE UNITED KINGDOM

The Royal Office of Poet Laureate of the United Kingdom commenced with a pension granted to Ben Jonson by King James I in 1616. Following Jonson's death in 1637, Sir William D'Avenant was awarded a pension for his services to the crown as poet. Upon D'Avenant's death in 1668, the Royal Office of Poet Laureate was officially established with the appointment of John Dryden.

The Laureateship has become the award for eminence in poetry and is filled automatically when vacant. It was originally an appointment for life, Dryden being the only Poet Laureate to lose the office when he refused to take the oath of allegiance in the wake of the Revolution of 1688. However, with the appointment of the new Poet Laureate in 1999, the tenure was altered to 10 years with an annual emolument of £5,000. The role of the Poet Laureate was expanded to include raising the profile of poetry in the United Kingdom.

The Poets Laureate of the United Kingdom with dates of service:

1668–88	*John Dryden*
1688–92	*Thomas Shadwell*
1692–1715	*Nahum Tate*
1715–18	*Nicholas Rowe*
1718–30	*Laurence Eusden*
1730–57	*Colley Cibber*
1757–85	*William Whitehead*
1785–90	*Thomas Warton*
1790–1813	*Henry James Pye*
1813–43	*Robert Southey*
1843–50	*William Wordsworth*
1850–96	*Alfred, Lord Tennyson*
1896–1913	*Alfred Austin*
1913–30	*Robert Bridges*
1930–67	*John Masefield*
1968–72	*C. Day-Lewis*

APPENDIX F: POETS LAUREATE OF THE UNITED STATES OF AMERICA

The position of Poet Laureate of the United States of America was authorized by the US Senate in 1985 as an adjunct to the Consultant for Poetry of the Library of Congress in Washington, DC. The position is a salaried one but requires no ceremonial verse.

The Poets Laureate of the United States of America with dates of service:

1986–87	*Robert Penn Warren*
1987–88	*Richard Wilbur*
1988–90	*Howard Nemerov*
1990–91	*Mark Strand*
1991–92	*Joseph Brodsky*
1992–93	*Mona Van Duyn*
1993–95	*Rita Dove*
1995–97	*Robert Hass*
1997–2000	*Robert Pinsky*
2000–01	*Stanley Kunitz*
2001–	*Billy Collins*

APPENDIX G:
LITERARY FIGURES OF THE PAST

Aakjaer, Jeppe (1866–1930), Danish novelist and poet, author of the novel Vredens børn, et tyendes saga (Children of Wrath: A Hired Man's Saga, 1904) and the poetry collection Rugens sange (Songs of the Rye, 1906).

Abasiyanik, Sait Falik (1907–54), Turkish short-story writer.

Abbey, Edwin (1927–89), American novelist and essayist.

Abbott, George (1887–1995), prominent American theatre director, dramatist and writer.

Abbott, Lyman (1835–1922), American clergyman, writer and editor.

'Abd al-Ghanī (ibn Ismā'īl) an-Nābulusī (1641–1731), Syrian mystic, writer and poet.

Abdülhak Hâmid (Tarhan) (1852–1937), Turkish poet and dramatist.

Abdullah bin Abdul Kadir, Munshi (1796–1854), Malaysian writer.

Abe Kōbō (actually Abe Kimifuṣa) (1924–1993), Japanese novelist, short-story writer and dramatist, best known for his novel Suna no omna (1962; English trans. as The Woman in the Dunes, 1964).

Abelard, Peter (1079–1144), French philosopher, theologian and poet, author of the controversial Sic et non (Yes and No) and Theologia, the latter being condemned as heretical.

Abell, Kjeld (1901–1961), Danish dramatist and social critic.

Abercrombie, Lascelles (1881–1938), English poet and critic.

Abert, Anna Amalie (1906–1996), German music scholar, author of the important Geschichte der Oper (History of Opera, 1994).

Abhdisho bar Berikha or Ebedjesus of Nisibus (died 1318), Syrian Christian theologian and poet, particularly remembered for his Margaritha vitae (The Pearl of Life).

Abrabanel, Isaac ben Judah (1437–1508), Spanish Jewish statesman and writer on religion.

Abraham, Gerald (Ernest Heal) (1904–1988), English music scholar.

Abrahams, Israel (1858–1925), English Jewish scholar, esteemed for his Jewish Life in the Middle Ages (1896).

Abū al'Atāhiya (actually Abū Ishāq Ismā'īl ibn al-Qāsim ibn Suwayd ibn Kaysān) (748–825), Arab poet, author of the ascetic poems the Zuhdīat.

Abu Madi, Iliya (c.1890–1957), Arab-American journalist and poet.

Abū Nuwās or Nu'ās (actually Abu Nuwas al-Hāsan ibn Hāni' al-Hakamī) (c.755–c.814), Arab poet who extolled the life of unrestricted pleasure.

Abu Rishah, 'Umar (1910–1990), Syrian poet and diplomat.

Abū Tammām (Habīb ibn Aws) (804–c.845), Arab poet, best remembered as editor of the anthology Hamāsah.

Accius or Attius, Lucius (170–c.86 BC), Roman dramatist, poet and writer.

Accursio or Accorsi, Mariangelo (c.1480–1546), Italian poet, critic and translator, especially admired for his satiric dialogues.

Acevedo Díaz, Eduardo (1851–1924), Uruguayan politician and writer whose finest work was the novel Soledad (Solitude, 1894).

Achilles Tatius (2nd Century), Greek writer whose Leucippe and Cleitophon presaged the development of the novel.

Ackerely, J(oseph) R(andolph) (1896–1967), English writer and editor.

Ackermann, Louise-Victorine (née Choquet) (1813–1890), French poet, best known for her Poésies, premières poésies, poésies philosophiques (Poetry, First Poetry, Philosophical Poetry, 1874).

Ackland, Rodney (1908–1991), English dramatist.

Aconcio or Aconzio, Giacomo (1492–c.1566), Italian-born English writer on religious toleration, author of the Satanae stratagematum (Stratagems of Satan, 1562).

Acosta, Joaquín (c.1800–1852), Colombian statesman, scientist and historian who wrote a history of 16th-Century New Granada (1848).

Acosta, José de (1539–1600), Spanish Jesuit theologian and missionary, author of De procuranda indoru salute (1588) and the Historia natural y moral de las Indias (1590; English trans. as Natural and Moral History of the Indies, 1604).

Acosta, Uriel (actually Gabriel da Costa) (c.1585–1640), Portuguese Jewish philosopher who championed natural law and reason over revealed religion; committed suicide.

Acropolites, George (1217–1282), Byzantine statesman, scholar and poet.

Acton, Sir Harold Mario Mitchell (1904–1994), English writer and poet.

Acton, Lord (actually John Emerich Edward Dalberg Acton, 1st Baron and 8th Baronet Acton) (1834–1902), English historian and philosopher, an advocate of Christian liberalism.

Adalbéron (died 1030), Frankish bishop and poet who was known as Ascelin, Asselin and the 'Old Traitor'.

Adam de la Halle (c.1247–c.1287), French trouvère poet and composer who was also known as Adan le Bossu (Adan the Hunchback) although he was not a hunchback.

Adam, Paul (1862–1920), French novelist.

Adamic, Louis (1899–1951), Yugoslav-born American writer.

Adamnan, Saint (c.628–704), Irish abbot and scholar who was also known as Adomnan or Eunan, author of the hagiography Vita S Columbae.

Adamov, Arthur (1908–1970), Russian-born French dramatist, writer and poet, a principal figure in the Theatre of the Absurd; committed suicide.

Adams, Alice (1926–1999), American novelist and short-story writer, best known for her novel Superior Women (1984).

Adams, Andy (1859–1935), American novelist and short-story writer of the Old West.

Adams, Brooks (1848–1927), American historian, author of Law of Civilization and Decay (1895) and The Theory of Social Revolutions (1913); brother of Charles Francis Adams Jr and Henry (Brooks) Adams.

Adams, Charles Follen (1842–1918), American poet of humorous verse.

Adams, Charles Francis Jr (1835–1915), American writer; brother of Brooks Adams and Henry (Brooks) Adams.

Adams, Charles Kendall (1835–1902), American historian.

Adams, Douglas (Noël) (1952–2001), English writer who became best known for his science fiction novel, The Hitchiker's Guide to the Galaxy (1978).

Adams, Henry (Brooks) (1838–1918), eminent American historian, author of the History of the United States During the Administrations of Thomas Jefferson and James Monroe (nine vols, 1889–91), Mont-Saint-Michel and Chartres (1904) and the classic autobiography The Education of Henry Adams (1907); brother of Brooks Adams and Charles Francis Adams Jr.

Adams, Herbert Baxter (1850–1901), American historian and educator.

Adams, James Truslow (1878–1949), American historian, author of The Founding of New England (1921), Revolutionary New England (1923) and New England in the Republic (1926), and general editor of the Dictionary of American History (1940).

Adams, John (1704–1740), American clergyman, scholar and poet.

Adams, John Turvill (1805–1882), American novelist, particularly known for his The Lost Hunter (1856) and The White Chief Among the Red Men; or, Knight of the Golden Melice (1859).

Adams, Léonie (Fuller) (1899–1988), American poet who excelled in metaphysical verse.

Adams, Samuel Hopkins (1871–1958), American journalist and writer who often wrote under the name Warner Fabian.

Adams, Sarah (née Flower) (1805–1848), English poet, best remembered for her hymn Nearer, My God, To Thee (1840).

Adams, William Taylor (1822–1897), American writer and editor who wrote many children's books under the name Oliver Optic.

Addams, Jane (1860–1935), famous American social reformer, pacifist and writer; was co-winner of the Nobel Prize for Peace (1931).

Addison, Joseph (1672–1719), noted English essayist, poet, dramatist and statesman, author of the poem The Campaign (1705) and founder, with Richard Steele, of The Spectator.

Ade, George (1866–1944), American writer and dramatist who was particularly admired for his humorous Fables in Slang (1899).

Adelard of Bath (12th Century), English scholastic philosopher.

Adenet le Roi (c.1240–c.1300), French poet and musician who was known as Roi Adam, Li Rois Adenes, Adan le Menestrel and Adam Rex Menestrallus.

Adler, Alfred (1870–1937), Austrian psychiatrist, known for his writings on individual psychiatry.

Adler, Cyrus (1863–1940), American Jewish scholar, educator and editor.

Adler, Felix (1851–1933), German-born American educator and writer, founder of the Ethical Movement.

Adler, Mortimer J(erome) (1902–2001), American philosopher, writer and editor.

Adorno, Theodor (actually Theodor Wiesengrund) (1903–1969), influential German social philosopher, music sociologist and writer.

Ady, Endre (1877–1919), Hungarian poet.

AE (actually George Williams Russell) (1867–1935), Irish poet, editor and essayist, especially known for his mystical poetry.

Aelian, Claudius (c.170–235), Roman writer, author of De animalium natura and Varia historia.

Aelianus (2nd Century), Greek military writer who was also known as Aelianus Tacticus and Aelian, author of taktiké theória (Tactical Theory, 106).

Aelred or Ailred or Aethelred or Ethelred of Rievaulx, Saint (c.1110–1167), notable English Cistercian abbot and writer whose most important work was De spirituali amicitia (On Spiritual Friendship).

Aeschylus (525–456 BC), Greek dramatist, celebrated as the father of the tragic drama.

Aesop (6th Century BC), legendary Greek writer of fables.

Affre, Denis-Auguste (1793–1848), French Roman Catholic prelate and writer on theological and philosophical subjects.

Africanus, Sextus Julius (c.180–c.250), Roman Christian historian and biblical scholar, author of the historical treatise Chronographiai (5 vols, 221).

Agar, Herbert (Sebastian) (1897–1980), American historian and critic.

Agassiz, Louis (1807–1873), Swiss-born American naturalist, geologist and teacher, author of such important studies as Recherches sur les poissons fossiles (Research on Fossil Fishes, 1833–43), Études sur les glaciers (1840), Lake Superior (1850) and Contributions to the Natural History of the United States (1857–62).

Agate, James (Evershed) (1877–1947), notable English critic, diarist, essayist and novelist.

Agathias (c.536–c.582), Byzantine poet and historian, best known for his love poems and epigrams.

Agathon (c.445–c.400 BC), Greek dramatist.

Agee, James (1909–1955), admired American writer, critic, poet and screenwriter, especially remembered for his novel A Death in the Family (published 1957).

Agnon, Shmuel Yosef (actually Samuel Josef Czaczkes) (1888–1970), celebrated Polish-born Hebrew novelist and short-story writer; was co-winner of the Nobel Prize for Literature (1966).

Agoult, Marie (-Catherine-Sophie-) de Flavigny, Comtesse d' (1805–1876), French writer who wrote under the name Daniel Stern, perhaps best remembered as the mistress of Franz Liszt.

Agreda, María de (actually María Fernández Coronel) (1602–1665), Spanish abbess and mystic who was known as Sister María de Jesús, author of The Mystical City of God (1670).

Agricola, Johann (actually Johann Schneider) (1494–1566), German Protestant theologian and reformer who was an exponent of antinomianism.

Agrippa von Nettesheim, Heinrich Cornelius (1486–1535), controversial German theologian, philosopher and physician, author of De occulta philosophia and Of the Vanitie and Uncertaintie of Artes and Sciences (published 1569).

Aguilar, Grace (1816–1847), English poet, novelist and writer on Jewish history and religion, author of the novel Home Influence (1847).

Agustini, Delmira (1886–1914), talented Uruguayan poet, author of El libro blanco (The White Book, 1907), Cantos de la mañana (Songs of Tomorrow, 1910), Los calices vacios (Empty Chalices, 1913) and Los astros de abismo (Stars of the Abyss, 1924); murdered by her estranged husband.

Ahmad Khan, Sir Sayyid (1817–1898), Indian Muslim educator and writer on religion.

Ahmed Haşim (1884–1933), gifted Turkish poet of Symbolist verse, author of such poetry collections as Göl saatleri (The Hours of the Lake, 1921) and Göl kuslari (The Birds of the Lake).

Ahmed Yesevi or Yasavi (died 1166), notable Turkish poet and Sūfī (Muslim mystic).

Ahmedi, Taceddin (actually Taceddin or Taj al-Dīn Ibrahim ibn Hizr Ahmedi) (c.1334–1413), esteemed Anatolian poet, particularly admired for his Iskendername (The Book of Alexander).

Ahmet Paşa Bursali (c.1497), Turkish poet, the first great classicist of Ottoman poetry who was especially esteemed for his odes and lyrics.

Aho, Juhani (actually Johannes Brofeldt) (1861–1921), Finnish novelist and short-story writer.

Aicard, (François-Victor-) Jean (1848–1921), French poet, novelist and dramatist.

Ai Quing (actually Jiang Haicheng) (1910–1996), Chinese poet who chronicled the Communist era of his homeland in nationalistic and folk-flavoured works.

Aiken, Conrad (Potter) (1889–1973), prominent American poet, novelist, short-story writer and critic.

Aiken, George L. (1830–1876), American actor and dramatist.

Aimard, Gustave (actually Olivier Gloux) (1818–1883), French novelist who was widely successful in his day.

Ainslie, Hew (1792–1878), Scottish-born American poet, known for his dialect poems.

Ainsworth, William Harrison (1805–1882), English novelist and editor, best remembered for his novel Jack Sheppard (1839).

Aistis, Jonas (actually Jonas Aleksandravichius) (1904–1973), Lithuanian-born American poet and essayist.

Akenside, Mark (1721–1770), English poet and physician, best known for his poem The Pleasures of the Imagination (1744).

Akers, Elizabeth (Chase) (1832–1911), American journalist and poet, author of the poem Rock Me To Sleep (1860), which appeared under the name Florence Percy.

Akhmatova, Anna (actually Anna Andreievna Gorenko) (1889–1966), Russian poet whose mastery of her craft was acknowledged in spite of her difficulties with the Soviet regime throughout her career.

Akhtal, al- (actually **Ghiyāth ibn Ghawth ibn as-Salt al-Akhtal**) **(c.640–710),** renowned Arab poet.

Akiba ben Joseph (c.40–c.135), important Jewish rabbinic scholar, known for his refinement of the biblical interpretation of Midrash; was martyred.

Akindynos, Gregorios (c.1300–c.1349), Byzantine monk, theologian and poet who was condemned as a heretic.

Akins, Zoë (1886–1958), American dramatist and novelist.

Aksakov, Sergei (Timofeievich) (1791–1859), notable Russian novelist, essayist and poet, author of the classic novels Semeynaya khronika (1856; English trans. as Chronicles of a Russian Family, 1924), Vospominaniya (1856; English trans. as The Autobiography of a Russian Schoolboy, 1917) and Detskie gody bagrova-vnuka (1858; English trans. as Years of Childhood, 1916).

Akutagawa Ryūnosuke (1892–1927), admired Japanese short-story writer, dramatist and poet who wrote under the names Chokodo Shujin and Gaki.

Alabaster, William (1567–1640), English mystic, poet and scholar who wrote the Latin tragedy Roxana (1597).

Alain (actually **Émile-Auguste Chartier) (1868–1951),** French philosopher and writer.

Alain de Lille or **Alanus de Insulis (c.1128–1202),** renowned French theologian and poet who was acclaimed as the 'universal doctor', author of the theological works The Art of the Catholic Faith, Treatise Against Heretics and Maxims of Theology, and the poems Plaint of Nature and Anticlaudianus.

Alain-Fournier (actually **Henri-Alban Fournier) (1886–1914),** French writer, author of the classic novel Le Grand Meaulnes (1913; English trans. as The Lost Domain, 1959); killed in World War I.

Alamanni, Luigi (1495–1556), Italian poet.

Alarcón, Pedro Antonio de (1833–1891), Spanish journalist, poet and novelist, author of the novel El sombrero de tres picos (1874; English trans. as The Three-Cornered Hat, 1918).

Alas, Leopoldo (1852–1901), Spanish critic, novelist and short-story writer who wrote under the name Clarín (i.e. bugle), admired for his naturalistic novels La regenta (The Professor's Wife, 1884–85) and Su único hijo (An Only Son, 1890).

Albers, Josef (1889–1976), German-born American painter, theorist and poet, author of Poems and Drawings (1958).

Alberti, Leon Battista (1404–1472), versatile Italian poet, scholar and architect, author of books in various fields, including Della Famiglia (On the Family), Della pittura (On Painting, 1435) and De re aedificatoria (Ten Books on Architecture, 1452).

Alberti, Rafael (1902–1999), Spanish poet, dramatist and writer, especially celebrated for his La arboleda perdida (1942; English trans. as The Lost Grove, 1976).

Albertus Magnus, Saint (c.1200–80), celebrated Swabian theologian and scholastic philosopher who was an authority on Aristotle.

Albinovanus Pedo (1st Century), Roman poet.

Albright, W(illiam) F(oxwell) (1891–1971), notable American biblical archaeologist who wrote several books in his field.

Alcaeus (c.620–c.580 BC), Greek poet.

Alcman (7th Century), Greek poet.

Alcott, (Amos) Bronson (1799–1888), American educational reformer, philosopher and writer; father of Louisa May Alcott.

Alcott, Louisa May (1832–1888), American novelist, short-story writer and poet, author of the children's classic Little Women (1868–69); daughter of (Amos) Bronson Alcott.

Alcuin (c.732–804), Anglo-Latin cleric, educator, writer and poet.

Aldanov, Mark Aleksandrovich (actually **Mark Aleksandrovich Landau) (1889–1957),** Russian-born French, later American, novelist and essayist.

Aldhelm (c.639–709), notable English bishop, writer and poet.

Aldington, Richard (actually **Edward Godfree Aldington) (1892–1962),** English poet, novelist, biographer, essayist and translator; husband of Hilda Doolittle.

Aldrich, Bess Streeter (1881–1954), American novelist.

Aldrich, Thomas Bailey (1836–1907), American poet, short-story writer, essayist, dramatist and editor, remembered for the prose works The Story of a Bad Boy (1870) and Marjorie Daw and Other People (1873) and for several poetry collections.

Aleandro, Girolamo (1480–1542), Italian Roman Catholic cardinal scholar and poet, a determined opponent of the Protestant Reformation.

Aleardi, Aleardo, Conte (actually **Gaetano Aleardi) (1812–1878),** Italian poet and politician.

Alecsandri, Vasile (c.1819–1890), Romanian poet, dramatist and diplomat.

Aleixandre, Vicente (1898–1984), noted Spanish poet; won the Nobel Prize for Literature (1977).

Alemán, Mateo (1547–c.1614), Spanish novelist who wrote the early picaresque novel Guzmán de Alfarache (2 parts, 1599, 1604; English trans. as The Spanish Rogue, 1622).

Alembert, Jean Le Rond d' (1717–1783), French mathematician, scientist, philosopher and writer who, with Diderot, edited the famous Encyclopédie; illegitimate son of Claudine-Alexadrine Guérin de Tencin.

Alencar, José (Martiniano) de (1829–1877), Brazilian journalist and novelist, esteemed for his novels O Guarany (The Guarani Indian, 1857) and Iracema (1865).

Alexander, Cecil Frances (née Humphreys) (1818–1895), Irish poet and hymnist, best known for her All Things Bright and Beautiful, Once in Royal David's City and There is a Green Hill Far Away.

Alexander, Samuel (1859–1938), English philosopher, author of Space, Time and Deity (1920).

Alexander Aetolus (flourished c.280 BC), Greek poet.

Alexandra of Aphrodisias (flourished c.200), Greek philosopher who wrote on Aristotle, the soul and the mind.

Alexander of Hales (c.1177–1245), English theologian and philosopher, known as Doctor Irrefragabilis to the scholastics.

Alexander Polyhistor (actually **Lucius Cornelius Alexander Polyhistor) (died c.35 BC),** Greek historian, geographer and philosopher.

Alexis (c.375–c.275 BC), Greek dramatist.

Alexis, Willibald (actually **Georg Wilhelm Heinrich Haring) (1798–1871),** German novelist, short-story writer, dramatist and poet, best known for his historical novels.

Alfieri, Vittorio, Conte (1749–1803), Italian dramatist and poet whose works presaged the Risorgimento.

Alfred, William (1922–1999), American dramatist and educator, best remembered for his play Hogan's Goat (1965).

Algarotti, Francesco (1712–1764), learned Italian writer on the arts and sciences.

Alger, Horatio (1834–1899), American writer of 'rags to riches' stories.

Alger of Liège or **Alger of Cluny** or **Algerus Magister (c.1060–c.1131),** French Roman Catholic priest and writer on religious subjects.

Algren, Nelson (1909–1981), American novelist and essayist, author of the novels The Man with the Golden Arm (1949) and A Walk on the Wild Side (1956).

Alkabetz, Solomon ben Moses ha-Devi (c.1505–1574), Jewish Kabbalist poet who wrote Lekha dodi (Come, My Beloved), which is traditionally recited each Friday evening to begin the Sabbath in Jewish synagogues.

Allen, (Charles) Grant (Blairfindie) (1848–1899), Canadian philosopher and novelist.

Allen, Frederick Lewis (1890–1954), American writer.

Allen, James Lane (1849–1925), American novelist, short-story writer and essayist.

Allen, Paul (1775–1826), American poet and writer.

Allen, William (1784–1868), American educator and historian.

Allen, (William) Hervey (1889–1949), American novelist, biographer and short-story writer, author of the novel Anthony Adverse (1933).

Allibone, Samuel Austin (1816–1889), American lexicographer, editor of the valuable A Critical Dictionary of English Literature and British and American Authors (3 vols, 1858–71).

Allingham, Margery (Louise) (1904–1966), admired English detective-story writer, creator of the detective Albert Campion.

Allingham, William (1824–1889), Irish poet, particularly remembered for The Fairies (1850).

Allston, Joseph Blyth (1833–1904), American poet, author of Stack Arms, written while he was a Union prisoner during the American Civil War.

Allston, Washington (1779–1843), American painter, poet and novelist, author of The Sylphs of the Seasons with Other Poems (1813) and the Gothic novel Monaldi (1841).

Almeida, José Valentin Fialho de (1857–1911), Portuguese short-story writer and political pamphleteer.

Almeida, Manuel Antônio de (1831–1861), Brazilian journalist, writer and translator who wrote the first novel of his homeland Memórias de um Sargento de Milícias (Memoirs of a Militia Sergeant, 1854–55); died in a shipwreck.

Almqvist, Carl Jonas Love (1793–1866), important Swedish novelist, short-story writer, dramatist, poet and musician, author of such notable books as Amorina (c.1821; published 1839) and Drottningens juvelsmycke (The Queen's Diamond Ornament, 1834).

Alonso, Dámaso (1898–1990), Spanish poet, literary critic, scholar and translator.

Alsop, Richard (1761–1815), American poet, particularly known for his light verse.

Altenburg, Peter (c.1862–1919), Austrian poet.

Althusius or Althaus, Johannes (1557–1638), Dutch Calvinist political theorist, author of the Politica methodice digesta atque exemplis sacris et profanis illustrata (1603).

Amado, Jorge (1912–2001), Brazilian writer, author of such novels as Terras do sem fim (1942; English trans. as The Violent Land, 1965), Gabriela, cravo e canela (1958; English trans. as Gabriela, Clove and Cinnamon, 1962) and Dona Flor e seus dois maridos (1966; English trans. as Dona Flor and Her Two Husbands, 1969).

Ambler, Eric (1909–1998), English writer, best known for his thrillers.

Ambros, August Wilhelm (1816–1876), Austrian music scholar who wrote the important Geschichte der Musik (History of Music, 5 vols, 1862–82).

Ambrose or Ambroise d'Evereux (12th Century), Norman poet who wrote a chronicle of the Third Crusade.

Ambrose of Camaldoni (1386–1439), Italian ecclesiastic, scholar and patristic translator.

Ambrose, Saint (c.339–397), famous Roman Catholic bishop, writer and hymnist.

Ames, William (1576–1633), English Puritan theologian, author of such works as Medulla Theologiae (1623; English trans. as The Marrow of Sacred Divinity, 1642) and De Conscientia et Ejus Jure vel Casibus (1623; English trans. as Conscience, 1639).

Ames, Winthrop (1870–1937), American theatre producer, manager, director and dramatist.

Amhurst, Nicholas (1697–1742), English editor, political pamphleteer and poet of a satirical bent.

Amichai, Yehuda (1924–2000), Notable German-born Israeli poet and writer.

Amiel, Henri Frédéric (1821–1881), Swiss writer whose finest achievement was his Journal intime (1847–81).

'Āmilī , Muhammad ibn Husayn Bahā' ad-Dīn, al- (c.1546–c.1622), significant Shi'ite Muslim theologian, mathematician, astronomer and writer.

Ami Ali, Sayyid (1849–1928), Indian-born English Muslim leader, jurist and writer, author of The Critical Examination of the Life and Teachings of Mohammed (1873) and The Spirit of Islam (1891).

Amīr Khosrow (1253–1325), notable Indian poet and historian who wrote in the Persian language.

Amis, Sir Kingsley (William) (1922–1995), English novelist, poet and critic who established his reputation with his first novel Lucky Jim (1954).

Ammons, A(rchie) R(andolph) (1926–2001), American poet and scholar whose Collected Poems (1971) and Garbage (1993) won critical accolades.

Amory, Cleveland (1917–1998), American writer and animal rights advocate.

Amory, Thomas (c.1691–1788), Irish writer, best known for The Life and Opinions of John Buncle, Esq. (2 vols, 1756, 1766).

Ampère, Jean-Jacques (-Antoine) (1800–1864), French philologist and historian, author of such noted works as Histoire littéraire de la France avant la douzième siècle (History of French Literature before the Twelfth Century, 3 vols, 1839–40), Histoire de la formation de la langue française (History of the Development of the French Language, 1841) and L'Histoire romaine à Rome (Roman History in Rome, 4 vols, 1861–64).

'Amr ibn Kulthum (6th Century), Arab poet who wrote a famous pre-Islamic ode.

Amrouche, Jean (1906–1962), Algerian poet who wrote the poetry collections Cendres (1934) and Étoile secrète (1937).

Amyot, Jacques (1513–1593), French Roman Catholic bishop and scholar, known for his translations of classical writers.

Anacreon (c.582–c.485 BC), celebrated Greek poet, renowned for his satires and love poems.

Anchieta, José de (1534–1597), notable Portuguese Jesuit scholar, poet and dramatist, author of the famous poem De beata virgine dei matre Maria (The Blessed Virgin Mary).

Ancillon, Charles (1659–1715), French-born German educator, jurist and historian.

Ancillon, David (1617–1692), French Protestant pastor and theologian who wrote the Traité de la tradition (Treatise on Tradition, 1657).

Ancillon, Johann Peter Friedrich (1767–1837), German statesman, historian and political philosopher, author of Tableau des révolutions du système politique de l' Europe depuis le XVe Siécle (View of European Political Revolutions since the Fifteenth Century, 4 vols, 1803–05).

Andersen, Hans Christian (1805–1875), famous Danish writer, dramatist and poet, renowned the world over for his superb fairy tales.

Anderson, Tryggve (1866–1920), Norwegian novelist and short-story writer, particularly admired for his short-story collection I cancelliraadens dage (In the days of the Chancery Counsellor, 1897).

Anderson, Maxwell (1888–1959), American dramatist and poet, especially remembered for his play Winterset (1935).

Anderson, Poul (William) (1926–2001), American writer of science fiction novels, including Brain Wave (1954), Tau Zero (1970), A Midsummer Tempest (1974), The Boat of a Million Years (1989) and Genesis (2000).

Anderson, Sherwood (1876–1941), American writer, poet and editor who made his mark with the short-story collection Winesburg, Ohio (1919).

Andersson, Dan(iel) (1888–1920), Swedish poet and writer, author of the poetry collections Kolarhistorier (Charcoal Burner's Tales, 1914) and Kolvaktarens visor (Charcoal Watcher's Songs, 1915).

Andrade, (José) Oswald de (Souza) (1890–1954), Brazilian political radical, poet, dramatist and novelist.

Andrade, Mário (Raul) de (Morais) (1893–1945), Brazilian poet, novelist and critic.

Andrea de Barberino (c.1370–c.1432), Italian writer and compiler of epic tales.

Andreas-Salomé, Lou (1861–1937), German novelist and writer.

Andreini, Giovambattista (c.1576–c.1654), Italian actor, dramatist and poet, best known for the play L'adamo (1613).

Andrewes, Lancelot (1555–1626), English Anglican theologian and preacher, best known for his anti-Roman Catholic apologetics.

Andrews, Charles McLean (1863–1943), American historian, author of the Colonial Period of American History.

Andrews, Roy Chapman (1884–1960), American naturalist, explorer and writer.

Andreyev, Leonid (Nikolaievich) (1871–1919), Russian novelist, short-story writer and dramatist.

Andrić, Ivo (1892–1975), Serbo-Croatian novelist and short-story writer; won the Nobel Prize for Literature (1961).

Andrieux, François (-Guillaume-Jean-Stanislas) (1759–1833), French dramatist, poet and politician who won his finest success with the play Les Etourdis (The Scatterbrained, 1787).

Andrzejewski, Jerzy (1909–1983), Polish novelist, short-story writer and political dissident who opposed the Nazi occupation during World War II and the Communist regime in later years, particularly remembered for his novel Popiół I diament (Ashes and Diamonds, 1948).

Aneirin (6th Century), Welsh poet, author of Y Gododdin.

Angell, Sir Norman (1874–1967), English economist and peace crusader who wrote the anti-war tome The Great Illusion (1910); won the Nobel Prize for Peace (1933).

Angilbert (c.740–814), Frankish prelate and poet.

Angiolieri, Cecco (c.1260–c.1312), esteemed Italian poet who excelled in comic verse.

Anouilh, Jean (-Marie-Lucien-Pierre) (1910–1987), French dramatist whose output detailed the duality of good and evil in the human condition.

Anscombe, G(ertrude) E(lizabeth) M(argaret) (1919–2001), English philosopher whose conversion to Roman Catholicism led her to embrace many of the Church's moral and philosophical teachings.

Anselm of Canterbury, Saint (c.1033–1109), Italian-born English theologian and Archbishop of Canterbury, founder of Scholasticism, who wrote such important works as Monologium (1077) and Cur Deus homo? (Why Did God Become Man?, 1098).

Anselm of Laon or Anselme de Laon (died 1117), French theologian and scholastic, author of Interlinear Glosses, a commentary on the Vulgate Bible.

Anselme of the Virgin Mary, Father (actually Pierre de Guibours) (1625–1694), French friar and genealogist who wrote the valuable Histoire généalogique et chronologique de la maison royale de France, des pairs, des grands officiers de la courrone, et de la maison du roy et des anciens barons du royaume (Genealogical and Chronological History of the Royal House of France, the Peers, the Grand Officers of the Crown, and of the Royal House and the Ancient Barons of the Realm, 2 vols, 1674).

Anstey, Christopher (1724–1805), English poet, author of the epistolary novel in verse The New Bath Guide; or, Memoirs of the B–R–D Family (1766).

Anstey, F (actually Thomas Anstey Guthrie) (1856–1934), English novelist and short-story writer, best known for his fantastic novel Vice Versa (1882).

Antar (actually l'Antarah ibn Shaddād al-Absi) (6th Century), famous Arab warrior and poet who wrote one of the 7 Golden Odes.

Anthony of Tagrit (9th Century), Syrian Orthodox theologian, writer and poet.

Anthony, Katharine (Susan) (1877–1965), American biographer who became best known for her controversial study of Charles and Mary Lamb in The Lambs (1945).

Anthony, Susan B(rownell) (1820–1906), notable American woman suffrage leader and lecturer who, with Elizabeth Cady Stanton and Matilda Joslyn Gage, wrote The History of Woman Suffrage (4 vols, 1881–1902).

Antimachus of Colophon (flourished c.400 BC), Greek poet and grammarian, author of the epic Thebais.

Antin, Mary (actually Mary Antin Grabau) (1881–1949), Russian-born American writer who wrote From Polotsk to Boston (1899), The Promised Land (1912) and They Who Knock at Our Gates (1914).

Anvarī (actually Awhad ad-Dīn 'Ali ibn Vāhid ad-Dīn Muhammad Khāvarānī) (c.1126–c.1189), Persian poet, especially esteemed for his odes and lyrics.

Anyte (3rd Century BC), renowned Greek poet who was acclaimed as a 'female Homer'.

Anzengruber, Ludwig (1839–1889), Austrian dramatist and novelist, particularly noted for his comic plays.

Apollinaire, Guillaume (actually Wilhelm Apollinaris de Kostrowitzki) (1880–1918), significant Italian-Polish poet of the French avant-garde.

Apollinaris the Apologist, Saint (flourished 2nd Century), Roman Catholic bishop who wrote the Defense of the Faith (c.175).

Apollinaris or Apollinarius the Younger (c.310–c.390), Roman Catholic bishop who was declared a heretic for his Incarnation of the Word.

Apollodorus of Athens (flourished 140 BC), Greek scholar, author of Chronicle of Greek History.

Apollodorus of Carystus (3rd Century BC), Greek dramatist.

Apollonius of Rhodes (b. c.295 BC), notable Greek poet and grammarian, author of the celebrated epic poem the Argonautica.

Appel, Benjamin (1907–1979), American novelist, short-story writer and poet.

Appian of Alexandria (2nd Century), Greek historian who chronicled the Roman conquests from the Republic down to his own era.

Appleton, Thomas Gold (1812–1884), American poet and essayist, brother-in-law of Henry Wadsworth Longfellow.

Apuleius, Lucius or Apuleius of Madaura (c.124–c.171), notable Greek writer, philosopher and rhetorician, celebrated for his prose narrative Metamorphoses, better known as The Golden Ass.

Aqqad, 'Abbas Mahmud al- (1889–1964), Egyptian writer, poet and critic.

Aragon, Louis (1897–1982), French poet, novelist, essayist, editor and Marxist political activist.

Arany, János (1817–1882), Hungarian poet, essayist and translator, author of the epic trilogy Toldi (1847), Toldi szerelme (Toldi's Love 1848–79) and Toldi estéje (Toldi's Evening, 1854).

Aratus (c.315–c.245 BC), Greek poet who wrote the noted poem on astronomy Phaenomena.

Arbuckle, James (died 1742), Irish poet and essayist.

Arbuthnot, John (1667–1735), Scottish physician, writer and poet, well known for his wit and satirical writings.

Archer, William (1856–1924), English drama critic, dramatist, essayist and translator.

Archias, Aulus Licinius (b. c.120 BC), Greek poet.

Archilochus of Paros (714–676 BC), renowned Greek poet, famous for his command of satire.

Arciniegas Angueyra, Germán (1900–1999), Colombian historian, novelist, essayist and diplomat.

Arendt, Hannah (1906–1975), German-born American political scientist and philosopher, author of the important study Origins of Totalitarianism (1951).

Aretino, Pietro (1492–1556), Italian poet, writer and dramatist, known for his Sonetti lussuriosi (1524).

Arévalo Martínez, Rafael (1884–1975), Guatemalan novelist and short-story writer.

Argens, Jean-Baptiste de Boyer, Marquis d' (1703–1771), French nobleman and philosopher who was a determined freethinker.

Argensola, Lupercio Leonardo de (1559–1613), Spanish dramatist and poet.

Arguedas, Alcides (1879–1946), Bolivian politician, sociologist, novelist and historian.

Arguedas, José María (1911–1969), Peruvian novelist and short-story writer; committed suicide.

Aribau, Buenaventura Carles (1798–1862), Catalan economist, editor, writer and poet, author of the noted poem Oda a la patria (Ode to the Fatherland, 1832).

Ariosto, Ludovico (1474–1533), famous Italian poet and dramatist, author of the poem Orlando furioso (1502–33).

Arishima Takeo (1878–1923), Japanese novelist; committed suicide.

Aristides (2nd Century), Greek Christian philosopher and apologist who wrote the Apology for the Christian Faith, the earliest such work extant.

Aristophanes (c.450–c.388 BC), Greek dramatist who was a master of comedic invention.

Aristotle (384–322 BC), august Greek philosopher, logician and scientist whose writings profoundly influenced the course of intellectual history.

Arland, Marcel (1899–1986), French novelist, short-story writer, critic and essayist.

Arlen, Michael (actually Dikran Kouyoumdjian) (1895–1956), Bulgarian-born English novelist of Armenian descent, author of the novel The Green Hat (1924).

Arlt, Roberto (1900–1942), Argentine novelist, short-story writer and dramatist who championed the novel of the absurd.

Arminius, Jacobus (actually Jacob Harmensen or Hermansz) (1560–1609), Dutch Protestant minister and theologian who opposed the Calvinist view of predestination.

Armstrong, John (1709–1779), Scottish physician and poet, particularly known for his didactic and satirical poetry.

Arnauld, Antoine (1612–1694), French theologian and philosopher, known as the Great Arnauld, a prominent figure in the heretical Jansenist movement; brother of Robert Arnauld d'Andilly.

Arnauld d'Andilly, Robert (1589–1674), French Jansenist hermit, poet and translator; brother of Antoine Arnauld.

Arnaut, Daniel (12th Century), Provençal poet.

Arndt, Ernst Moritz (1769–1860), revered German patriot, writer and poet who was known as Father Arndt.

Arniches (y Barrera), Carlos (1866–1943), Spanish dramatist, admired for his comic plays.

Arnim, Achim von (actually Karl Joachim Friedrich Ludwig von Arnim) (1781–1831), German folklorist, novelist, short-story writer, dramatist and poet, best remembered for his collaboration with Clemens Brentano on the edition of folk poetry Des Knaben Wunderhorn (The Youth's Magic Horn, 1805); husband of Bettina von Arnim.

Arnim, Bettina von (actually Elisabeth Katharina Ludovica Magdalena Brentano) (1785–1859), renowned German writer, sculptor and musician, one of the major figures in German Romanticism; wife of Achim von Arnim.

Arnobius the Elder (4th Century), African Christian apologist, author of Adversus nationes (Against the Pagans, 7 vols, c.303).

Arnold, Denis (Midgley) (1926–1986), English music scholar.

Arnold, Sir Edwin (1832–1904), English editor, poet and translator, best known for his blank verse setting The Light of Asia, or the Great Renunciation (1879).

Arnold, George (1834–1865), American poet and humourist.

Arnold, Matthew (1822–1888), eminent English poet and critic, author of the poetical vols Empedocles on Etna, and Other Poems (1852) and New Poems (1867), and the critical vols Essays in Criticism (2 series, 1865, 1888) and Culture and Anarchy (1869).

Arnow, Harriette (1906–1986), American novelist.

Aron, Raymond (-Claude-Ferdinand) (1905–1983), notable French philosopher, sociologist and journalist.

Arp, Jean or Hans (1887–1966), significant French sculptor, painter and poet of the avant-garde.

Artaud, Antonin (1896–1948), French dramatist, poet and actor, creator of the Surrealist 'Theatre of Cruelty'.

Artybashev, Mikhail Petrovich (1878–1927), Russian writer whose output expressed his preoccupation with pessimism and immorality, best remembered for his novel Sanin (1907).

Asachi, Gheorghe (c.1788–c.1869), Romanian short-story writer and poet.

Asan, Kumaran (1873–1924), Indian poet who espoused social reform.

Asbjørnsen, Peter Christian (1812–1885), Norwegian folklorist who, with Jørgen Engebretsen Moe, edited the influential collection Norske folkeeventyr (Norwegian Folk Tales, 1841).

Asch, Nathan (1902–1964), Polish-born American novelist and short-story writer; son of Sholem Asch.

Asch, Sholem or Shalom (1880–1957), prominent Polish-born American novelist, dramatist and writer; father of Nathan Asch.

Ascham, Roger (1515–1568), English Humanist scholar, best known for The Scholemaster (published 1570).

Ásgrímsson, Eysteinn (c.1310–1361), Icelandic monk and poet, author of the sacred poem Lilja (The Lily).

A'shā-, al- (the Blind) (actually Maymūn ibn Qays al-A'shā) (c.569–c.625), Arab poet.

Ashton-Warner, Sylvia (Constance) (1908–1984), New Zealand novelist, short-story writer and poet.

Asimov, Isaac (1920–1992), Russian-born American biochemist and writer, author of many science fiction and science books.

Astafyev, Viktor Petrovich (1924–2001), Russian novelist of the realist persuasion who chronicled the desperate lives of villagers and of the World War II generation.

Asturias, Miguel Angel (1899–1974), esteemed Guatemalan writer, poet and diplomat, author of the novel Hombres de maíz (Men of Corn, 1949); won the Nobel Prize for Literature (1967).

Aśvaghosa (c.80–c.150), famous Indian philosopher, poet and dramatist who is considered the father of Sanskrit drama.

Athanasius, Saint (c.293–373), Egyptian Roman Catholic bishop and theologian who was a determined opponent of the Arian heresy, author of Four Orations Against the Arians and The Life of St Antony.

Atherton, Gertrude (Franklin) (1857–1948), American novelist, short-story writer and essayist.

Atkinson, (Justin) Brooks (1894–1984), American critic, journalist and writer.

Attaway, William (1911–1986), American novelist.

Atterbom, Per Daniel Amadeus (1790–1855), Swedish poet and literary historian whose masterwork was the poetic fairy-tale play Lyckalighetens ö (The Isle of Bliss, 1824–27).

Atterbury, Francis (1663–1732), English Anglican bishop and polemical writer of force and distinction.

Aubignac, François Hédelin, Abbé d' (1604–1676), French critic, dramatist, writer and translator, author of the important study La Pratique de théâtre (1657; English trans. as The Whole Art of the Stage, 1684).

Aubigné, Theodore-Agrippa d' (1552–1630), famous French Huguenot soldier, poet, historian and polemical writer, author of the poem the Tragiques (7 cantos, 1577–1616).

Aubrey, John (1626–1697), English antiquarian and writer, particularly known for his biographical works.

Auden, W(ystan) H(ugh) (1907–1973), English-born American poet, librettist and essayist.

Audiberti, Jacques (1899–1965), French poet, dramatist and novelist.

Audubon, John James (1785–1851), notable French-born American naturalist and artist who excelled in the depiction of every known species of North American birds, best known for his The Birds of America (4 vols, 1827–38).

Auerbach, Berthold (1812–1882), German novelist.

Auerbach, Erich (1892–1957), German-born American scholar of Romance literatures and languages.

Auezov, Mukhtar (1897–1961), Kazakh writer.

Augier, (Guillaume-Victor-) Émile (1820–1889), French dramatist, best remembered for his collaboration with Jules Sandeau on the play Le Gendre de Monsieur Poirier (1854).

Augustine of Hippo, Saint (354–430), Roman Catholic bishop and theologian, celebrated for such works as De doctrina Christiana (Christian Instruction, 397–428), Confessiones (The Confessions, c.400) and De civitate Dei (The City of God, 413–426).

Aukrust, Olav (1883–1929), Norwegian poet, best known for his mystical Himmelvarden (Cairn of Heaven, 1916).

Aulard, François-Alphonse (1849–1928), French historian who was an authority on the French Revolution.

Aulnoy or Aunoy, Marie-Catherine Le Jumel de Barneville, Comtesse d' (c.1650–1705), French novelist and fairy-tale writer whose own life of adventure equalled her fiction.

Aurobindo, Sri (actually Sri Aurobindo Ghose) (1872–1950), Indian seer, philosopher, nationalist, poet and dramatist.

Aury, Dominique (1907–1998), French writer and translator who wrote the erotic best-seller Histoire d'O (1954) under the name Pauline Réage.

Auslander, Joseph (1897–1965), American poet and writer; husband of Audrey Wurdemann.

Ausonius, Decimus Magnus (c.310–c.395), Latin poet and rhetorician.

Austen, Jane (1775–1817), English novelist of the classic works Sense and Sensibility (1811), Pride and Prejudice (1813), Mansfield Park (1814), Emma (1815–16) and Northanger Abbey and Persuasion (published posthumously, 1817–18).

Austin, Alfred (1835–1913), English journalist and poet; became Poet Laureate of the United Kingdom (1896).

Austin, John (1790–1859), English jurist, author of The Province of Jurisprudence Determined (1832).

Austin, J(ohn) L(angshaw) (1911–1960), English philosopher.

Austin, Mary (née Hunter) (1868–1934), American novelist, short-story writer and essayist.

Austin, William (1778–1841), American lawyer, politician and writer, remembered for his tale Peter Rugg, the Missing Man (1824).

Avallone, Michael (Angelo Jr) (1924–1999), American writer.

Avenarius, Richard (Heinrich Ludwig) (1843–1896), German philosopher, best known for his Kritik der reinen Erfahrung (2 vols, 1888, 1900).

Aventinus (actually Johannes Turmair) (1477–1534), German Humanist and historian who wrote the important Annales Boiorum (Bavarian Annals, 1517–21).

Averröes (1126–1198), Islamic religious philosopher, jurist and physician.

Avicenna (980–1037), Islamic philosopher, scientist and physician, author of the Book of Healing and the Canon of Medicine.

Avvakum Petrovich (c.1620–1682), famous Russian clergyman and writer, leader of the Old Believers in opposition to the Russian Orthodox Church and author of a celebrated autobiography; was condemned and burned at the stake.

Ayala y Herrera, Adelardo Lopez de (1828–1879), Spanish dramatist and politician whose most successful play was Consuelo (1878).

Ayer, Sir A(lfred) J(ules) (1910–1989), eminent English philosopher, author of such significant works as Language, Truth and Logic (1936), The Problem of Knowledge (1956), Philosophy and Language (1960) and The Concept of a Person and Other Essays (1963).

Aymé, Marcel (1902–1967), French novelist, short-story writer, dramatist and essayist.

Ayrer, Jakob (1543–1605), German dramatist.

Ayton or Aytoun, Sir Robert (1570–1638), Scottish poet who wrote English, Latin, Greek and French verse.

Aytoun, William Edmondstoune (1813–1865), Scottish poet and writer.

Azaïs, Pierre-Hyacinthe (1766–1845), French philosopher and writer, author of Des compensations dans les destinées humaines (3 vols, 1809), and Système universel (8 vols, 1809–12).

Azeglio, Massimo Taparelli, Marchese d' (1798–1866), Italian statesman, writer and painter who was a principal figure in the Risorgimento.

Azevedo, Aluízio (1857–1913), Brazilian novelist and diplomat.

Azorin (actually José Martínez Ruiz) (1874–1967), Spanish writer and critic.

Azuela, Mariano (1873–1952), Mexican novelist of social protest.

Baader, Franz Xaver von (1765–1841), German Roman Catholic mystic and theologian who espoused the cause of ecumenism in his writings.

Bābā Tāher (c.1000–c.1056), illustrious Persian poet who was known as 'Oryān (the Naked) since he may have been a Muslim mystic.

Babbitt, Irving (1865–1933), notable American critic and teacher, founder of the New Humanism of Neohumanism.

Babel, Isaac (Emmanuilovich) (1894–1941), prominent Russian writer who lost favour with the Stalinist regime; died in a prison camp in Siberia.

Babits, Mihály (1883–1941), Hungarian poet, novelist, essayist and translator.

Babrius (c.2nd Century), Greek writer of fables.

Bacchelli, Riccardo (1891–1985), Italian novelist, poet, dramatist and critic, well known for his novel trilogy Il mulino del Po (1938–40; English trans. as The Mill on the Po, 3 vols, 1952–55).

Bacchylides (5th Century BC), Greek poet of a lyric nature; nephew of Simonides of Ceas.

Bachaumont, François Le Coigneux de (1624–1702), French poet who, with Chapelle, wrote the satirical Voyage (1663).

Bacheller, Irving (Addison) (1859–1950), American journalist and novelist, author of such novels as Eben Holden: A Tale of the North Country (1900) and D'ri and I (1901).

Bachman, John (1790–1874), American Lutheran minister and naturalist who collaborated with John James Audubon on several vols and was the author of The Unity of the Human Race (1850) and A Defense of Luther and the Reformation (1853).

Bachofen, Johann Jakob (1815–1887), Swiss jurist and anthropologist, author of the significant social anthropological study Das Mutterrecht (Mother Right, 1861).

Backus, Isaac (1724–1806), American Baptist preacher and historian who wrote A History of New England, With Particular Reference to the Denomination of Christians Called Baptists (3 vols, 1777–96).

Bacon, Delia (Salter) (1811–1859), American writer and dramatist who attempted to prove that Shakespeare's plays were not by the Bard of Avon in her Philosophy of the Plays of Shakespeare Unfolded (1857); died insane.

Bacon, Francis, Baron Verulam, Viscount St Albans (1561–1626), famous English lawyer, courtier, statesman, philosopher and writer, author of Novum Organum (1620).

Bacon, Leonard (1887–1954), American poet, admired for his vol. Sunderland Capture (1940).

Bacon, Peggy (Margaret Fuller) (1895–1987), American artist and poet.

Bacon, Roger (c.1220–1292), celebrated English philosopher, known as the Doctor Mirabilis, author of the Opus majus, Opus minus and Opus tertium.

Baconthorpe, John (c.1290–c.1346), English theologian and philosopher, known as John Bacon, Johannes de Baconthorpe, Johannes de Anglicus and Doctor Resolutus, especially appreciated for his commentaries on Aristotle and Averroës.

Badā'ūnī, 'Abd al-Qādir (1540–c.1615), Indo-Persian historian who wrote copiously on Muslim subjects.

Baeck, Leo (1873–1956), German-born English Reform rabbi and theologian who suffered numerous arrests and survived a Nazi concentration camp, author of a major vol. on the essence of Judaism (1905).

Bagehot, Walter (1826–1877), English journalist, economist, political analyst and sociologist, author of The English Constitution (1867), Physics and Politics (1872) and Lombard Street (1873).

Baggesen, Jens (Immanuel) (1764–1826), Danish writer and poet, particularly admired for his prose vol. Labyrinten (The Labyrinth, 1792–93).

Bagnold, Enid (Algerine), Lady Roderick Jones (1889–1981), English novelist and dramatist, author of the novel National Velvet (1935) and the enormously successful play The Chalk Garden (1956).

Bagritsky (Dzyubin), Eduard Georgievich (1895–1934), Russian poet who championed the Soviet order.

Bahā' ad-Dīn Zuhayr (actually Abū al-Fadl Zuhayr ibn Muhammad al-Muhallabī) (1186–1258), Arab poet, known for his odes and love poems.

Bahār, Mohammad Taqī (1885–1951), Iranian poet, writer and translator.

Bahr, Hermann (1863–1934), Austrian writer and dramatist.

Baïf, Jean-Antoine de (1532–1589), inventive French poet, much esteemed for his Mimes, enseignemens et proverbes (Mimes, Lessons and Proverbs, 1576).

Bailey, Nathan or Nathaniel (died c.1742), English philologist and lexicographer.

Bailey, Philip James (1816–1902), English poet, author of Festus (1838–89).

Bailey, Samuel (1791–1870), English economist and philospher whose most significant works were Essays on the Formation and Publication of Opinions (1821), A Critical Dissertation on the Nature, Measures, and Causes of Value (1825) and Essays on the Pursuit of Truth, on the Progress of Knowledge, and on the Fundamental Principle of All Evidence and Expectation (1829).

Baillie, Joanna (1762–1851), Scottish dramatist and poet, author of Fugitive Verses (1790) and Plays on the Passions (3 vols, 1798–1812).

Baillie, Lady Grizel (1665–1746), Scottish poet who became best known for her songs.

Baillie, Robert (1599–1662), Scottish Presbyterian minister and scholar.

Bain, Alexander (1818–1903), Scottish philosopher, particularly known for his studies in psychology and for his work Logic (2 vols, 1870).

Baines, Thomas (1822–1875), English artist, explorer, naturalist and writer, author of Explorations in South-West Africa (1864).

Bainville, Jacques (1879–1936), French historian who wrote perceptive books on French, German and British history.

Baius, Michael (1513–1589), Belgian theologian who was also known as Michael Bajus and Michel de Bay.

Baker, Augustine (1575–1641), English Benedictine monk who wrote on ascetic and mystical theology.

Baker, Benjamin A (1818–1890), American dramatist, best remembered for his melodrama A Glance at New York (1848).

Baker, Carlos (Heard) (1909–1987), American literary scholar, critic and novelist who was an authority on Shelley and Hemingway.

Baker, Dorothy (1907–1968), American novelist.

Baker, Leonard (Stanley) (1931–1984), American journalist and writer of biographies and historical books.

Baker, Ray Stannard (1870–1946), American journalist, essayist and biographer who often wrote under the name David Grayson, author of Woodrow Wilson: Life and Letters (8 vols, 1927–39).

Baker, Sir Richard (c.1568–1645), English writer and translator who wrote A Chronicle of the Kings of England (1643).

Baker, William Mumford (1825–1883), American Presbyterian minister and writer, author of the novel Inside: A Chronicle of Secession (1866), which he wrote under the name George F Harrington.

Bakhtin, Mikhail Mikhailovich (1895–1975), Russian philosopher of language and literature.

Bâkî (actually Mahmud Abdülbâkî) (1526–1600), Arab poet who excelled in lyric poetry.

Bakunin, Mikhail Alexandrovich (1814–1876), noted Russian anarchist and political writer who was a principal opponent of Karl Marx.

Balādhurī, al- (actually Ahmad ibn Yahyā al-Balādhurī) (died c.892), Arab historian who chronicled the founding of the Arab Muslim empire (English trans. as The Origins of the Islamic State, 1916–24).

Balaguer y Circera, Victor (1824–1901), Spanish poet, historian and politician.

Balassi or Balassa, Bálint (1554–1594), esteemed Hungarian poet who was admired for his lyric gifts.

Balbín, Bohuslav (1621–1688), Czech historian.

Balbo, Cesare, Conte (1789–1853), Italian poltician and writer, best remembered for his Delle speranze d'Italia (The Hopes of Italy, 1844).

Balbuena, Bernardo de (c.1562–1627), Spanish Roman Catholic bishop and poet.

Balch, Emily Greene (1867–1961), American sociologist, political scientist, economist and pacifist; was co-winner of the Nobel Prize for Peace (1946).

Balchin, Nigel (Martin) (1908–1970), English novelist, particularly admired for The Small Back Room (1943) and Mine Own Executioner (1945).

Baldwin, Faith (1893–1978), American writer and poet.

Baldwin, James (Arthur) (1924–1987), provocative American novelist, short-story writer, dramatist and essayist of the black experience.

Baldwin, James Mark (1861–1934), American philosopher and psychologist who wrote Genetic Logic (3 vols, 1906–11).

Bale, John (1495–1563), prominent English Protestant bishop, antiquarian, polemical writer and dramatist, author of one of the earliest English history plays Kynge Johan.

Balestier, (Charles) Wolcott (1861–1891), English novelist and short-story writer; brother-in-law of (Joseph) Rudyard Kipling.

Ball, Hugo (1886–1927), German critic, writer and dramatist who wrote the studies Kritik der deutschen Intelligenz (1919) and Die Flucht aus der Zeit (1927).

Ballanche, Pierre-Simon (1776–1847), French philosopher, author of Du sentiment considéré dans ses rapports avec la littératures et les arts (Sentiment Considered in Its Relationship to Literature and the Arts, 1801).

Ballantyne, Robert Michael (1825–1894), Scottish writer, particularly known for The Coral Island (1858).

Ballou, Adin (1803–1890), American writer on religious subjects, author of Practical Christian Socialism (1854) and Primitive Christianity and Its Corruptions (1870).

Ballou, Hosea (1771–1852), American Universalist pastor, theologian, essayist and hymnist who wrote An Examination of the Doctrine of Future Retribution (1834); father of Maturin Murray Ballou.

Ballou, Maturin Murray (1820–1895), American writer, publisher and editor who often wrote under the name Lieutenant Murray; son of Hosea Ballou.

Balmes, Jaime Luciano (1810–1848), Spanish writer on religion, politics and philosophy.

Balmont, Konstantin Dmitrievich (1867–1943), Russian poet, essayist and translator.

Baluze, Étienne (1630–1718), French scholar, particularly known as an historian and editor.

Balzac, Honoré de (1799–1850), French writer who elevated the form of the novel to an exalted position through his extraordinary series of works he described as La Comédie humaine (The Human Comedy).

Balzac, Jean-Louis Guez de (1597–1654), French writer and critic, especially admired for his writings published under the title Lettres (1624 et seq.).

Bamford, Samuel (1788–1872), English radical reformer and poet.

Bàn, Donnchadh (1724–1812), Scottish writer who was also known as Duncan MacIntyre.

Bancroft, George (1800–1891), prominent American politician and historian who wrote the exhaustive History of the United States (10 vols, 1834–74).

Bancroft, Hubert Howe (1832–1918), American historian who oversaw the publication of a vast history of the American West (39 vols, 1874–92).

Bandeira (Filho), Manuel (Carneiro de Sousa) (1886–1968), eminent Brazilian poet, literary historian, educator and translator.

Bandelier, Adolph (Francis Alphonse) (1840–1914), Swiss-born American anthropologist and archaeologist who was known for his studies of Native American cultures of the US and of Aztec culture of Mexico.

Bandello, Matteo (1485–1561), Italian-born French writer and Roman Catholic bishop, author of the notable series of 214 stories in his Novelle (4 vols, 1554–73).

Bang, Herman (1857–1912), Danish novelist, poet, dramatist and critic.

Banim, John (1798–1842), Irish novelist, short-story writer, dramatist and poet who often collaborated with his brother Michael Banim.

Banim, Michael (1796–1874), Irish novelist and short-story writer, a frequent collaborator with his brother John Banim.

Banning, Margaret Culkin (1891–1982), American novelist.

Bannister, Nathaniel Harrington (1813–1847), American dramatist, best remembered for his Putnam (1844).

Banville, (Étienne-Claude-Jean-Baptiste-) Théodore (-Faullain) de (1823–1891), admired French poet and dramatist, esteemed for the poetry collection Les Odes funambulesques (1857).

Bar, François de (1538–1606), French scholar and Roman Catholic prior who was known for his work on church history and law.

Baradooni, Abdullah al- (1929–1999), Yemeni poet and writer.

Barahona de Soto, Luis (c.1548–1595), Spanish poet, author of Primera parte de la Angélica (The First Part of the Angélica, 1586), better known as Las lagrimas de Angélica (The Tears of Angélica).

Baranauskas, Antanas (1835–1902), Lithuanian Roman Catholic bishop and poet, author of the esteemed poem Anykščiu šilelis (1858–59; English trans. as The Forest of Anykščiai, 1956).

Barante, Amable-Guillaume-Prosper Brugiere, Baron de (1782–1866), French statesman, historian , biographer and translator, author of Histoire des ducs de Bourgogne (History of the Dukes of Burgundy, 1824–28).

Baratynsky or Boratynsky, Yevgeny (Abramovich) (1800–1844), important Russian poet, a master of philosophical poetry.

Barbauld, Anna Laetitia (née Aikin) (1743–1825), English poet and writer.

Barbey d'Aurevilly, Jules-Amédée (1808–1889), French novelist, short-story writer and critic, particularly esteemed for his short-story collection Les Diaboliques (1874; English trans. as Weird Women, 1900).

Barbon, Nicholas (c.1640–1698), English economist whose writings presaged those of Adam Smith.

Barbon, Praise-God (c.1596–1680), English sectarian preacher and writer who became known as Barebone and Barebones, the latter prompting the naming of the Puritan Barebones Parliament.

Barbour or Barbere or Barbier, John (c.1325–1395), Scottish poet, scholar and prelate who wrote the national epic The Actes and Life of the most Victorious Conqueror, Robert Bruce King of Scotland (20 vols, 1376), popularly known as The Bruce.

Barbusse, Henri (1873–1935), French writer and poet, author of the World War I novel Le Feu (1916; English trans. as Under Fire, 1917).

Barclay, Alexander (c.1476–1552), Scottish poet who wrote The Shyp of Folys of the Worlde (1509), an adaptation of Brant's Das Narrenschiff.

Barclay, John (1582–1621), Scottish writer and poet, known for his book Euphormionis Lusinini Satyricon (1603–07), and the Latin poem the Argenis (1621).

Barclay, Robert (1648–1690), Scottish Quaker and writer, author of the Theses Theologicae (1675) and the Apology for the True Christian Divinity (1678), the latter a classic exposition of Quaker beliefs.

Bardesanes or Bardaisan or Bar Dausān (154–c.222), Syrian Christian Gnostic writer and hymnist.

Bardi, Giovanni de', Count of Vernio (1534–1612), Italian nobleman, music and art patron, composer and writer, influential in the development of opera and author of Discorso mandato a Caccini sopra la Musica Antica (Discourse to Caccini on Ancient Music, 1580).

Baretti, Giuseppe (Marc' Antonio) (1719–1789), Italian-born English critic and lexicographer, editor of A Dictionary of the English and Italian Languages (1760).

Barham, Richard Harris (1788–1845), English churchman and poet, best remembered for his humorous collections The Ingoldsby Legends (1840, 1842, 1847).

Bar Hebraeus (1226–1286), Syrian scholar and chief prelate of the Eastern Jacobite Church, best known for his encyclopedia Hē'wath hekkmthā (The Butter of Wisdom).

Baring, Maurice (1874–1945), English writer, dramatist, biographer, critic, poet and translator.

Baring-Gould, Sabine (1834–1924), English writer and churchman, author of the hymns Onward, Christian Soldiers and Now the Day is Over.

Barker, George (Granville) (1913–1991), English poet and novelist who wrote the poems Calamiterror (1937) and The True Confession of George Barker (1950).

Barker, James Nelson (1784–1858), American dramatist, best known for his play Superstition (1824).

Barlow, Joel (1754–1812), American poet and writer, author of The Vision of Columbus (1787; revised as the epic poem The Columbiad, 1807) and the mock-heroic poem The Hasty Pudding (1796).

Barnard, Lady Anne (née Lindsay) (1750–1825), Scottish writer of the well-known ballad Auld Robin Gray (1771).

Barnave, Antoine (-Pierre-Joseph-Marie) (1761–1793), French politician who was a leading figure in the Revolution but whose advocacy of a constitutional monarchy led to his imprisonment and execution, author of the significant book Introduction à la révolution française (1792), written during his incarceration.

Barnes, Barnabe (c.1569–1609), English poet, writer and dramatist, remembered for his poetry collection Parthenophil and Parthenophe (1593).

Barnes, Charlotte Mary Sanford (1818–1863), American dramatist, known for her melodramas Octavia Bragaldi (1837, published 1848) and The Forest Princess (1848).

Barnes, Djuna Chappell (1892–1982), American novelist, short-story writer, dramatist, poet and illustrator.

Barnes, Ernest William (1874–1953), English Anglican bishop and pacifist, known for his liberal views in such writings as Scientific Theory and Religion (1933) and The Rise of Christianity (1947).

Barnes, Harry Elmer (1889–1968), American sociologist and historian.

Barnes, Margaret Ayer (1896–1967), American novelist and dramatist, especially admired for her novel Years of Grace (1930); sister of Janet Ayer Fairbank.

Barnes, Robert (1495–1540), English prior who became an advocate of Lutheranism, author of A Supplication to Henry VII (1531), Vitae Romanorum Pontificum (Lives of the Roman Pontiffs, 1535) and Confession of Faith (1540); was condemned as a heretic and burned.

Barnes, William (1801–1886), English poet and priest, known for his dialect poems.

Barnfield, Richard (1574–1627), English poet of pastoral verse.

Baroja, Pío (1872–1956), eminent Spanish novelist and short-story writer, author of the trilogy La lucha por la vida (1904; English trans. as The Struggle for Life, 1922–24) and the vast Memorias de un hombre de accion (Memoirs of a Man of Action, 22 vols).

Baronius, Caesar (1538–1607), Italian historian and apologist of the Roman Catholic Church who wrote the well-known Annales Ecclesiastici (12 folios, 1588–1607).

Barr, Amelia Edith (Huddleston) (1831–1919), English-born American novelist.

Barr, Stringfellow (1897–1982), American educator and writer.

Barrès, (Auguste-) Maurice (1862–1923), French novelist, essayist and politician.

Barrie, Sir James (Matthew) (1860–1937), English dramatist and novelist, creator of the ever-youthful Peter Pan.

Barros, João de (c.1496–1570), Portuguese government official, historian and Orientalist who was known as the Portuguese Livy.

Barros Arana, Diego (1830–1907), Chilean historian, educator and diplomat, author of the Historia jeneral de Chile (General History of Chile, 16 vols, 1884–1902).

Barrow, Henry (c.1550–1593), English lawyer and Congregationalist reformer, author of A True Description out of the Word of God, of the Visible Church (1589) and A Brief Discovery of the False Church (1590); was imprisoned and hanged for his advocacy of Separatism.

Barry, Philip (1896–1949), American dramatist, much esteemed for such plays as White Wings (1926), Hotel Universe (1930), Here Come the Clowns (1938) and The Philadelphia Story (1939).

Bar-Salibi, Jacob (died 1171), Turkish-born bishop of the Jakobite (Monophysite) Church, theologian and poet.

Bartas, Guillaume de Salluste, Seigneur (1544–1590), French soldier, diplomat and poet who wrote the poem La Semaine (1578).

Barth, Heinrich (1821–1865), German geographer and explorer, author of the important Travels and Discoveries in North and Central Africa (5 vols, 1857–58).

Barth, Karl (1886–1968), renowned Swiss Protestant theologian, author of Die kirchliche Dogmatik (1932 et seq.; English trans. as The Church Dogmatics, 13 vols, 1936–69).

Barth, Paul (1858–1922), German philosopher and sociologist who wrote studies on Hegel and his followers (1896) and on the philosophy of history of sociology (1897).

Barthélemy, Jean-Jacques (1716–1795), French scholar and writer, best remembered for his novel Le Voyage du jeune Anacharsis en Grèce, dans le milieu du quatrième siècle avant l' ère vulgaire (1788; English trans. as Travels of Anacharsis the Younger in Greece, 1791).

Barthélemy-Saint-Hilaire, Jules (1805–1895), French journalist, statesman, scholar, writer and translator.

Barthelme, Donald (1931–1989), American novelist and short-story writer.

Barthes, Roland (1915–1980), French writer, literary theorist and semiologist who was a central figure in the Structuralist movement.

Bartholomaeus Anglicus or Bartholomew the Englishman (13th Century), English Franciscan scholar and compiler of the notable encyclopedia De proprietatibus rerum (On the Properties of Things).

Bartoli, Daniello (1608–1685), Italian Jesuit scholar, particularly remembered for his Dell'huomo de lettere (The Learned Man).

Bartoli, Matteo Giulio (1873–1946), Italian linguist, founder of neolinguistics or areal linguistics.

Bashshar ibn Burd (died c.784), Muslim poet.

Basil of Ancyra (died c.364), Greek bishop and theologian.

Basil the Great, Saint (c.329–379), celebrated Roman Catholic bishop and theologian who was a leading opponent of the Arian heresy.

Basile, Giambattista (c.1575–1632), Italian soldier, public official, poet and writer, author of the folk-tale collection Lo cunto di li cunti (1634; English trans. as The Pentamerone, 1932).

Basin, Thomas (1412–1491), French Roman Catholic bishop and historian.

Basnage, Jacques (1653–1723), French Huguenot minister, historian and diplomat.

Bassani, Giorgio (1916–2000), Italian writer and poet whose best-known work was the novel Il giardino dei Finzi-Contini (1962; English trans. as The Garden of the Finzi Continis).

Basselin, Olivier (c.1400–1450), French poet.

Bassett, John Spencer (1867–1928), American historian.

Basso, (Joseph) Hamilton (1904–1964), American writer, best known for his novels of Southern society.

Bastian, Adolf (1826–1905), German ethnologist who wrote the important study Der Mensch in der Geschichte (Man in History, 3 vols, 1860).

Bastiat, (Claude-) Frédéric (1801–1850), French journalist, economist and politician who opposed Socialism and Communism.

Bataille, (Félix-) Henry (1872–1922), French dramatist, best remembered for his play La Femme nue (The Nude Woman, 1908).

Bate, Walter Jackson (1918–99), American literary scholar who wrote authoritative biographies of John Keats (1963) and Samuel Johnson (1977).

Bateman, Sidney Frances (1823–1881), American actress and dramatist who wrote the play of social satire Self (1856).

Bates, Arlo (1850–1918), American novelist, short-story writer and poet.

Bates, Ernest Sutherland (1879–1939), American writer.

Bates, H(erbert) E(rnest) (1905–74), English novelist and short-story writer.

Bates, Katherine Lee (1859–1929), American educator, writer and poet, celebrated for her patriotic poem America the Beautiful (1893).

Bateson, F(rederick Noel) W(ilse) (1901–78), English scholar, critic and editor.

Batsányi, János (1763–1845), Hungarian poet who won fame for his political verse.

Baty, (Jean-Baptiste-Marie-) Gaston (1885–1952), French dramatist, appreciated for his Dulcinée (1938).

Batyushkov, Konstantin (Nikolaievich) (1787–1855), Russian poet of elegiac verse whose career was aborted by insanity.

Baudelaire, Charles (Pierre) (1821–1867), French poet renowned for his collection Les Fleurs du mal (1857).

Baudouin, François (1520–c.1574), French theologian and historian, a pioneer in legal history.

Baudouin de Courtenay, Jan Niecislaw (1845–1929), Polish linguist, author of the study Versuch einer Theorie phonetischer Alternationer (Essay on a Theory of Phonetic Alternation, 1895).

Bauer, Bruno (1809–1882), German theologian and historian who espoused a radical interpretation of the New Testament.

Bauernfeld, Eduard von (1802–1890), Austrian dramatist who had great success with his politically-tinged drawing-room comedies.

Baum, L(yman) Frank (1856–1919), American writer of the land of Oz books.

Baum, Vicki (actually Hedwig Baum) (1888–1960), Austrian-born American novelist and screenwriter, best known for her novel Menschen im Hotel (1929; English trans. as Grand Hotel, 1931).

Baumbach, Rudolf (1840–1905), German poet of the vagabond tradition.

Baumgarten, Alexander Gottlieb (1714–1762), important German philosopher who made the study of aesthetics a special branch of philosophical discourse, author of the influential study Aesthetica (2 vols, 1750, 1758).

Baumgarten, Hermann (1825–1893), German historian.

Baumgarten, Siegmund Jakob (1706–1757), German theologian of rationalist proclivities.

Baur, Ferdinand Christian (1792–1860), German theologian and church historian who founded the Protestant Tübingen school of biblical criticism.

Baxter, Andrew (c.1686–1750), Scottish philosopher who espoused a metaphysical rationalism, author of An Enquiry Into the Nature of the Human Soul (1733; Appendix, 1750) and Matho, sive cosmotheoria puerilis (1738).

Baxter, James K(eir) (1926–1972), New Zealand poet, dramatist and critic.

Baxter, Richard (1615–1691), notable English Puritan minister and theologian who wrote numerous works, including Aphorismes of Justification (1649) and an autobiography Reliquiae Baxterianae or Mr Richard Baxter's Narrative of the Most Memorable Passages of his Life and Times (published 1696).

Bayle, Pierre (1647–1706), French scholar and philosopher, compiler of the noted Dictionnaire historique et critique (2 vols, 1695, 1697).

Baylebridge, William (actually Charles William Blocksidge) (1883–1942), Australian poet and short-story writer.

Bayly, Nathaniel Thomas Haynes (1797–1839), English poet and dramatist who won popularity as the author of various songs.

Baylor, Frances Courtenay (1848–1920), American novelist.

Bazin, Hervé (actually Jean-Pierre Hervé-Bazin) (1911–1996), prominent French novelist, short-story writer and poet; great-nephew of René (-François-Nicolas-Marie) Bazin.

Bazin, René (-François-Nicolas-Marie) (1853–1932), French novelist who became an upholder of traditional values; great-uncle of Hervé Bazin.

Beach, Joseph Warren (1880–1957), American critic and poet.

Beach, Rex (Ellingwood) (1877–1949), American novelist.

Beals, Carleton (1893–1981), American journalist, novelist and biographer.

Beard, Charles A(ustin) (1874–1948), eminent American historian who wrote the important study An Economic Interpretation of the Constitution of the United States (1913); husband of Mary R(itter) Beard.

Beard, Mary R(itter) (1876–1958), American historian; wife of Charles A(ustin) Beard.

Beardsley, Aubrey (Vincent) (1872–1898), English illustrator, writer and poet, author of the erotic The Story of Venus and Tannhauser (published 1907).

Beattie, James (1735–1803), Scottish poet and essayist who wrote the poem The Minstrel (2 parts, 1771, 1774).

Beatus Rhenanus (1485–1547), German Humanist scholar, writer and editor who was known as Beatus Bild.

Beauchamp, Alphonse de (1767–1832), French historian and biographer.

Beauchemin, Neree (1850–1931), French-Canadian poet and physician.

Beaulieu, Michel (1941–1985), French-Canadian poet and writer.

Beaumarchais, Pierre-Augustin Caron de (1732–1799), French dramatist, remembered for his Le Barbier de Seville (1775; English trans. as The Barber of Seville, 1776), and Le Mariage de Figaro (1784; English trans. as The Marriage of Figaro, 1785), plays set to music as celebrated operas respectively by Rossini and Mozart.

Beaumont, Francis (c.1584–1616), English dramatist who collaborated with John Fletcher on a series of notable plays, among them Phylaster (1610) and The Maides Tragedy (1611); brother of Sir John Beaumont.

Beaumont, Sir John (1583–1627), English poet who introduced the heroic couplet to English verse, author of the extensive poem The Crown of Thornes (12 vols); brother of Francis Beaumont.

Beauvoir, Roger de (actually Edouard Roger de Bully) (1809–1866), French novelist.

Beauvoir, Simone de (1908–1986), influential French writer, philosopher and political activist, especially known for her espousal of Existentialism.

Bebey, Francis (1929–2001), Cameroonian novelist, poet, composer and musician.

Beccaria, Cesare Bonesana, Marchese di (1738–1794), Italian scholar who wrote on criminal law and economics, author of the influential study Dei delletti e delle pene (1764; English trans. as Crimes and Punishments, 1880).

Becher, Johannes Robert (1891–1958), German poet, critic and editor of a Marxist persuasion.

Bechtel, Friedrich (1855–1924), German classical scholar.

Becker, Carl L(otus) (1873–1945), American historian, author of The Beginnings of the American People (1915), The Eve of the Revolution (1918), The Declaration of Independence (1922) and The Heavenly City of the Eighteenth-Century Philosophers (1932).

Becker, Jürek (1937–1997), German novelist.

Becker, Wilhelm Adolf (1796–1846), German archaeologist who wrote such works as Gallus (1838), Charikles (1840) and Handbuch der romischen Altertumer (Handbook of Roman Antiquities, 5 vols, 1843–68).

Beckett, Samuel (Barclay) (1906–1989), celebrated Irish dramatist, writer, poet and critic, particularly known for his play En attendant Godot (1952; English trans. as Waiting for Godot, 1954) and the prose trilogy Molloy (1951), Malone meurt (1951; English trans. as Malone Dies, 1956) and L'Innomable (1953; English trans. as The Unnamable, 1958); won the Nobel Prize for Literature (1969).

Beckford, William (c.1760–1844), English writer of an eccentric nature, author of the classic Gothic novel Vathek (1786).

Becque, Henry-François (1837–1899), French dramatist and critic, known for his naturalist plays Les Corbeaux (1882; English trans. as The Vultures, 1913) and La Parisienne (1885).

Becquer, Gustavo Adolfo (1836–1870), Spanish writer and poet, best remembered for his poems of troubadour love.

Beddoes, Thomas Lovell (1803–1849), English poet and physiologist, author of Death's Jest-Book, or, The Fool's Tragedy (1825–49); committed suicide.

Bede or Baeda or Bede the Venerable, Saint (c.672–735), significant Anglo-Saxon theologian and historian, author of the invaluable Historia ecclesiastica gentis Anglorum (Ecclesiastical History of the English People, 732).

Bedier, (Charles-Marie-) Joseph (1864–1938), French scholar, known for his Le Roman de Tristan et Iseult (1900) and Les Légendes epiques (4 vols, 1908–21).

Bedil, Mirza (actually Mirza 'abd-ul-Qadir ibn 'abd-ul-Khaliq Arlas Bedil) (1644–1721), Indian Muslim poet, known for his prolific mystical poems.

Bedny, Demyan (actually Yefim Alexseievich Pridvorov) (1885–1945), Russian poet who wrote on Soviet themes while displaying a satirical streak.

Beebe, Charles William (1877–1962), American biologist, naturalist, explorer and writer.

Beecher, Catharine E(sther) (1800–1878), American educator, social reformer and writer, daughter of Lyman Beecher and sister of Henry Ward Beecher and Harriet Beecher Stowe.

Beecher, Henry Ward (1813–1887), controversial American Congregationalist minister, writer and editor of pronouced liberal views, son of Lyman Beecher and brother of Catharine E(sther) Beecher and Harriet Beecher Stowe.

Beecher, Lyman (1775–1863), American Presbyterian minister, writer and editor; father of Catharine E(sther) Beecher, Henry Ward Beecher and Harriet Beecher Stowe.

Beer, Patricia (1924–99), English poet and writer.

Beer, Thomas (1889–1940), American novelist and short-story writer.

Beerbohm, Sir (Henry) Max(imilian) (1872–1956), English critic, essayist and caricaturist, known for his wit.

Beers, Ethel Lynn (1827–1879), American poet and writer, best remembered for her poem The Picket-Guard (1861), later known as All Quiet Along the Potomac.

Beets, Nicolaas (1814–1903), Dutch pastor, writer and poet, author of the collection Camera obscura (1839).

Behan, Brendan (Francis) (1923–1964), provocative Irish dramatist and poet, best known for his play The Hostage (1958).

Behn, Aphra (1640–1689), English dramatist, poet and writer, known as the Incomparable Astrea, author of the novel Oroonoko (1688).

Behrman, S(amuel) N(athaniel) (1893–1973), American dramatist and writer.

Bein, Albert (1902–1963), American novelist and dramatist.

Beke, Charles Tilstone (1800–1874), English biblical scholar and geographer, author of Origines Biblicae, or Researches in Primeval History (1834), An Essay on the Nile and Its Tributaries (1847) and The Sources of the Nile (1860).

Bekker, August Immanuel (1785–1871), German classical scholar and editor.

Belasco, David (1853–1931), American theatre producer and dramatist, especially remembered for his Madame Butterfly (1900) and The Girl of the Golden West (1905) which were set to music as operas by Puccini.

Belinsky, Vissarion (Grigorievich) (1811–1848), influential Russian literary critic.

Belknap, Jeremy (1744–1798), American Congregationalist minister and historian who wrote a History of New Hampshire (3 vols, 1784, 1791, 1792), and American Biography (2 vols, 1794, 1798).

Bell, Gertrude Margaret Lowthian (1868–1926), English traveller and writer.

Bellamy, Edward (1850–1898), American novelist, short-story writer, essayist and journalist, author of the Utopian novel Looking Backward, 2000–1887 (1888).

Bellamy, Joseph (1719–1790), American writer of theological pamphlets, best known for his True Religion Delineated (1750).

Bellarmine, Saint Robert (actually Roberto Francesco Romolo Bellarmino) (1542–1621), Italian Roman Catholic cardinal and theologian who was a vigorous opponent of the Protestant Reformation, author of Disputationes de controversiis Christiane fidei adversus huius temporis haereticos (Lectures Concerning the Controversies of the Christian Faith Against the Heretics of This Time, 1586–93).

Bellay, Guillaume du, Seigneur de Langey (1491–1543), French soldier and historian who wrote the Ogdoades (only fragments extant; published 1905) and Épitome de l'antiquité des Gaules et de France (Abridgment of the Early Times of Gaul and France, 1556).

Bellay, Jean du (c.1492–1560), French Roman Catholic cardinal, diplomat and poet.

Bellay, Joachim du (c.1522–1560), French poet and writer, a principal figure in the literary group known as the Pléiade and author of its manifesto La Defense et illustration de la langue française (1549; English trans. as The Defence and Illustration of the French Language, 1939).

Belleau, Rémy (1528–1577), French poet, scholar and translator, especially esteemed for his poetic portraits in miniature.

Bellecour (actually Jean-Claude-Gilles Colson) (1725–1778), French actor and dramatist, remembered for his play Les Fausses Apparences (The False Appearances, 1761).

Bellenden or Ballenden or Ballentyne or Ballantyne or Bannatyne, John (16th Century), Scottish canon, poet and translator.

Belli, Giuseppe Gioacchino (1791–1863), provocative Italian poet, particularly admired for his numerous sonnets.

Bellman, Carl Michael (1740–1795), esteemed Swedish poet, dramatist and composer.

Bello, Andrés (1781–1865), Venezuelan poet and scholar, known for his two poems Silvas americanas (1826–27).

Belloc, (Joseph-Pierre) Hilaire (1870–1953), French-born English poet, historian and essayist.

Bely, Andrei (actually Boris Nikolaievich Bugaiev) (1880–1934), Russian novelist, poet and critic, a leading Symbolist.

Bemelmans, Ludwig (1898–1962), Austrian-born American novelist, short-story writer and painter.

Bémont, Charles (1848–1939), French scholar who wrote on European and English medieval subjects.

ben Asher, Aaron ben Moses (10th Century), Jewish rabbinic scholar who made important critical notations on the Bible.

Benavente y Martínez, Jacinto (1866–1954), notable Spanish dramatist whose most celebrated play was Los intereses creados (1907; English trans. as The Bonds of Interest); won the Nobel Prize for Literature (1922).

Benchley, Nathaniel (1915–1981), American humourist, novelist, dramatist and screenwriter; son of Robert (Charles) Benchley.

Benchley, Robert (Charles) (1889–1945), American humourist, drama critic, essayist and actor; father of Nathaniel Benchley.

Benda, Julien (1867–1956), French novelist and philosopher, author of the novel L'Ordination (1911; English trans. as The Yolk of Pity, 1913), and the philosophical tome La Trahison des clercs (1927; English trans. as The Treason of the Intellectuals, 1928).

Benedict, Ruth (née Fulton) (1887–1948), American anthropologist who wrote such studies as Patterns of Culture (1934), Race, Science and Politics (1940) and The Chrysanthemum and the Sword (1946).

Benedictsson, Victoria (1850–1888), Danish novelist and short-story writer who wrote under the name Ernst Ahlgren; committed suicide.

Benediktsson, Einar (1864–1940), Icelandic poet, author of 5 vols of Symbolic poetry (1897, 1906, 1913, 1921, 1930).

Benefield, (John) Barry (1877–1956), American novelist and short-story writer.

Benét, Stephen Vincent (1898–1943), American poet, novelist and short-story writer, author of the well-known poem John Brown's Body (1928); brother of William Rose Benét.

Benét, William Rose (1886–1950), American poet and critic; brother of Stephen Vincent Benét and husband of Elinor Wylie.

Benet Goita, Juan (1927–1993), Spanish novelist, short-story writer , essayist and translator.

Benezet, Anthony (1713–1784), French-born American teacher and writer.

Benfey, Theodor (1809–1881), German comparative language scholar, known especially for his Sanskrit studies.

Bengel, J(ohann) A(lbrecht) (1687–1752), German Lutheran theologian who was esteemed for his New Testament studies.

Bengtsson, Frans Gunnar (1894–1954), Swedish poet, novelist, biographer and essayist.

Benivieni, Girolamo (1453–1542), Italian poet.

Benjamin, Park (1809–1864), American editor, publisher and poet.

Benjamin, Walter (1892–1940), German literary critic who was compelled to leave his homeland after the Nazis came to power in 1933; committed suicide to avoid arrest by the Gestapo.

Benlowes, Edward (1602–1676), English poet, best remembered for his Theophila or Loves Sacrifice (1652).

Benn, Gottfried (1886–1956), significant German poet and essayist whose initial Expressionist style of pessimism gave way in later years to a pragmatic mode of expression.

Bennett, Emerson (1822–1905), American novelist and short-story writer.

Bennett, (Enoch) Arnold (1867–1931), English novelist, dramatist, critic and essayist, whose most notable novel was The Old Wives' Tale (1908).

Bennett, John (1865–1956), American writer, best known for the boys' book Master Skylark (1897).

Benoît de Sainte-Maure (12th Century), French poet, author of the Roman de Troie.

Benserade, Isaac de (c.1612–1691), French poet, librettist and dramatist.

Benson, A(rthur) C(hristopher) (1862–1925), English biographer, critic, diarist and poet, especially remembered for his famous poem Land of Hope and Glory; son of E(dward) W(hite) Benson and brother of E(dward) F(rederic) Benson and R(obert) H(ugh) Benson.

Benson, E(dward) F(rederic) (1867–1940), English novelist and biographer, author of the Dodo and Lucia series of novels; son of E(dward) W(hite) Benson and brother of A(rthur) C(hristopher) Benson and R(obert) H(ugh) Benson.

Benson E(dward) W(hite) (1829–1896), English Anglican priest, Archbishop of Canterbury and writer; father of A(rthur) C(hristopher), E(dward) F(rederic) and R(obert) H(ugh) Benson.

Benson, R(obert) H(ugh) (1871–1914), English novelist, writer and poet; son of E(dward) W(hite) Benson and brother of A(rthur) C(hristopher) Benson and E(dward) F(rederic) Benson.

Benson, Sally (actually Sara Mahala Redway Smith Benson) (1900–1972), American writer.

Bentham, Jeremy (1748–1831), notable English Utilitarian philosopher whose most celebrated work was An Introduction to the Principles of Morals and Legislation (1789).

Bentivoglio, Guido (1579–1644), Italian Roman Catholic cardinal, diplomat and historian.

Bentley, Arthur F(isher) (1870–1957), American political scientist and philosopher, particularly remembered for The Process of Government: A Study of Social Pressures (1908).

Bentley, Edmund Clerihew (1875–1956), English journalist, writer and poet, inventor of the clerihew, a humorous verse form, and author of the classic detective story Trent's Last Case (1913).

Bentley, Phyllis (1894–1977), English novelist and critic, author of the novel Inheritance (1932).

Bentley, Richard (1662–1742), eminent English classical scholar.

Béranger, Pierre-Jean de (1780–1857), French poet and writer, author of satirical and witty poems.

Berberova, Nina Nikolaievna (1901–1993), Russian-born American novelist and short-story writer.

Berceo, Gonzalo de (c.1195–c.1264), Spanish poet, known for his devotional works.

Berchet, Giovanni (1783–1851), Italian poet, a formative figure in the development of Romantic poetry in his homeland.

Bercovici, Konrad (1882–1961), Romanian-born American novelist and short-story writer.

Berenson, Bernard (1865–1959), Lithuanian-born American art critic, author of the important study Italian Painters of the Renaissance (1952).

Berent, Wacław (1873–1940), Polish novelist who wrote such works as Próchno (Rotten Wood, 1903) and Ozimina (Winter Corn, 1911).

Bergbom, Kaarlo (1843–1906), Finnish writer.

Berger, Gaston (1896–1960), French philosopher.

Bergman, Bo Hjalmar (1869–1967), Swedish poet, novelist, short-story writer and critic.

Bergman, Hjalmar Fredrik Elgérus (1883–1931), admired Swedish novelist, short-story writer, dramatist and poet, particularly esteemed for his novels Markurells i Wadköping (1919; English trans. as God's Orchid, 1924), Farmor och vår Herre (1921; English trans. as Thy Rod and Thy Staff, 1937) and Chefen Fru Ingeborg (1924; English trans. as The Head of the Firm, 1936).

Bergson, Henri-Louis (1859–1941), prominent French philosopher, especially known for his study L'Évolution créatice (1907); won the Nobel Prize for Literature (1927).

Berkeley, George (1685–1753), English philosopher and Anglican bishop, author of An Essay Towards a New Theory of Vision (1709), A Treatise Concerning the Principles of Human Knowledge (1710), Three Dialogues Between Hyals and Philonous (1713) and De Motu (1721).

Berkenhead, Sir John (1617–1679), English journalist, writer and poet, particularly remembered for his wit displayed in his newsbook Mercurius Aulicus (1643–45).

Berlin, Sir Isaiah (1909–1997), respected Latvian-born English historian and philosopher.

Berlin, Isaiah ben Judah Loeb (1725–1799), Hebrew scholar, respected for his talmudic studies.

Berlioz, (Louis-) Hector (1803–1869), French composer, author of Grand traité d'instrumentation et d'orchestration modernes (1843) and the autobiography Mémoires de Hector Berlioz (1870).

Bernanos, Georges (1888–1948), French novelist and essayist whose finest work was the novel Journal d'un curé de campagne (1936; English trans. as The Diary of a Country Priest, 1937).

Bernard, Jean-Jacques (1888–1972), French dramatist and writer whose play Martine (1922) was a notable example of the 'drama of the unexpressed'.

Bernard, Tristan (actually Paul Bernard) (1866–1947), French dramatist, novelist, journalist and lawyer, best known for his works in a light vein.

Bernard, William Bayle (1807–1875), American dramatist.

Bernard de Ventadour (12th Century), Provençal poet, noted for his love poems.

Bernard of Chartres (c.1080–c.1130), French philosopher who espoused Platonic Idealism.

Bernard of Cluny or Bernard of Morlaix (c.1100–c.1150), French monk, poet and hymnist, author of the satirical poem De comtemptu mundi (On Condemning the World, c.1140).

Bernardes, Padre Manuel (1644–1710), Portuguese writer.

Bernardin de Saint-Pierre, Jacques-Henri (1737–1814), French writer, best known for Paul et Virginie (1788).

Bernardino of Siena, Saint (1380–1444), famous Italian Franciscan preacher and theologian.

Berners, John Bourchier, 2nd Baron (c.1469–1533), English statesman, writer and translator.

Berners, Lord (Sir Gerald Hugh Tyrwhitt-Wilson, Baronet) (1883–1950), English composer, writer and painter of an eccentric disposition.

Bernhard, Thomas (1931–1989), Austrian novelist, dramatist and poet.

Berni, Francesco (c.1497–1535), Italian poet and translator, especially admired for his satirical poems.

Bernstein, Henry (-Léon-Gustave-Charles) (1876–1953), French dramatist who delineated the evils of anti-Semitism and Nazism in plays of distinction.

Berquin, Arnaud (c.1749–1791), French writer.

Berr, Henri (1863–1954), French historian and philosopher who edited the mammoth cooperative study L'Évolution de l'Humanité (65 vols, 1920–54).

Berrigan, Ted (actually Edmund Berrigan Jr) (1934–1983), American poet, dramatist and writer who became known for his experimentation.

Berryman, John (1914–1972), notable American poet and novelist particularly admired for such works in verse as Homage to Mistres Bradstreet (1956), 77 Dream Songs (1964), Berryman's Sonnets (1967 and His Toy, His Dream, His Rest (1968); committed suicide.

Bertaut, Jean de Caen (1552–1611), French Roman Catholic bishop an poet.

Bertholet, Alfred (1868–1951), Swiss Protestant Old Testament an religious scholar.

Bertolucci, Attilio (1911–2000), Italian poet, critic and translator.

Bertrand, Louis (–Jacques-Napoléon) (1807–1841), French poet wh was known as Aloysius Bertrand and who introduced the prose poem t his homeland in Gaspard de la Nuit (Gaspard of the Night, 1842).

Berwisńki, Ryszard Wincenty (1819–1879), Polish political radical poet and writer.

Berzsenyi, Dániel (1776–1836), Hungarian poet who wrote the patriotic A magyarokhoz (To the Hungarians), Fohász (Prayer) and various elegies

Besant, Sir Walter (1836–1901), English novelist, critic, editor and philanthropist.

Bessarion John (actually Basil Bessarion) (1403–1472), Byzantine Roman Catholic cardinal and scholar, author of In calumniatorem Platonis (Against the Calumniator of Plato).

Besseler, Heinrich (1900–1969), German music scholar who wrote the important study Die Musik des Mittelaters und der Renaissance (The Music of the Middle Ages and the Renaissance, 1931).

Bessenyei, György (c.1746–1811), Hungarian writer.

Beti, Mongo (1932–2001), Cameroonian novelist and writer on politics.

Betjeman, Sir John (1906–1984), English poet and writer; became Poet Laureate of the United Kingdom (1972).

Betti, Ugo (1892–1953), Italian dramatist whose collected works were published posthumously (1955).

Beveridge, Albert J(eremiah) (1862–1927), American politician and biographer, author of a Life of John Marshall (4 vols, 1916–19) and an unfinished Life of Abraham Lincoln (2 vols, 1928).

Beyer, Absalon Pederssøn (1528–1575), Norwegian Lutheran scholar.

Beza, Theodore (actually Théodore de Bèze) (1519–1605), French-born Swiss Calvinist theologian, educator, writer, translator and poet, author of Histoire ecclésiastique des Églises réformées au royaume de France (Ecclesiastical History of the Reformed Church in the Kingdom of France, 1580).

Bezrûc, Petr (actually Vladimir Vasek) (1867–1958), Czech poet who won distinction for his Silesian verse.

Bhartrhari (c.570–c.651), important Hindu poet and philosopher, author of the vol. on the philosophy of language Vākyapadīya (Words in a Sentence).

Bhasa (2nd or 3rd Century), Sanskrit dramatist.

Bhavabhūti (8th Century), Indian dramatist and poet.

Bialik, Hayyim Nahman (1873–1934), Hebrew poet, short-story writer, editor and translator.

Bibaud, Michel (1782–1857), French-Canadian poet, historian and editor.

Bickerstaffe, Isaac (c.1735–c.1812), Irish dramatist.

Biddle, John (1615–1662), English theologian who was known as the father of English Utilitarianism, author of the controversial Twelve Arguments Against the Deity of the Holy Ghost (c.1644); died in prison.

Biel, Gabriel (c.1420–1495), German theologian, philosopher and economist, acclaimed as the last great scholastic.

Bierce, Ambrose (Gwinnett) (1842–c.1914), American newspaperman and short-story writer who excelled as a wit and satirist.

Bigelow, John (1817–1911), American journalist, diplomat and writer.

Biggers, Earl (Derr) (1884–1933), American journalist, novelist and dramatist, creator of the Chinese detective Charlie Chan.

Bilderdijk, Willem (1756–1831), Dutch poet and philologist, best known for his unfinished epic poem De ondergang der eerste wareld (The Destruction of the First World, 1810).

Bilfinger, Georg Bernhard (1693–1750), German scholar who wrote on many subjects ranging from philosophy and theology to botany and physics.

Billetdoux, François (1927–1991), French dramatist who followed an avant-garde path.

Billinger, Richard (1893–1965), Austrian poet and novelist.

Billings, Josh (actually Henry Wheeler Shaw) (1818–1885), American journalist, writer and lecturer who became popular as a humourist.

Bing Xin (actually Hsieh Wan-Ying) (1900–1999), Chinese short-story writer and poet.

Binkis, Kazys (1893–1942), Lithuanian poet, dramatist and editor.

Binney, Thomas (1798–1874), English Congregationalist minister, writer and poet.

Binyon, (Robert) Laurence (1869–1943), English poet, dramatist, art historian and translator, author of the classic study Painting in the Far East (1908) and the esteemed elegy For the Fallen (1914).

Bion (flourished 100 BC), Greek poet.

Bion of Borysthenes (c.325–c.255 BC), Greek philosopher, reputedly the creator of the Cynic diatribe.

Biondo, Flavio or Flavius Blondus (1392–1463), Italian historian who wrote the important studies Historiarum ab inclinatione Romanorum imperii decades (Decades of History from the Deterioration of the Roman Empire, 1439–53, published 1483) and Italia illustrata (1448–58, published 1474).

Bioy Casares, Adolfo (1914–1999), Argentine writer, editor and publisher.

Birch, Thomas (1705–1766), English historian and biographer.

Bird, Robert Montgomery (1806–1854), American dramatist, novelist and literary editor.

Birmingham, George A (actually James Owen Hannay) (1865–1950), Irish Protestant clergyman and novelist.

Birney, (Alfred) Earle (1904–1995), Canadian poet, writer, dramatist and critic.

Birrell, Augustine (1850–1933), English politician and writer, author of the essay collections Obiter Dicta (2 vols, 1884, 1887).

Bīrūnī, al- (actually Abū Arrayhān Muhammad ibn Ahmad al-Būrūnī) (973–1048), famous Arab scholar whose learning embraced many disciplines.

Bishop, Elizabeth (1911–1979), American poet and short-story writer, esteemed for the poetry collections North & South (1946; revised edition as North & South: A Cold Spring, 1955) and Questions of Travel (1965).

Bishop, John Peale (1892–1944), American poet, novelist and critic.

Bishop, Morris (Gilbert) (1893–1973), American poet of light verse.

Bissell, Richard (Pike) (1913–1977), American novelist and dramatist whose first novel, 7 ½ Cents (1953), was reworked as the Broadway musical The Pajama Game (1954).

Bitzius, Albert (1797–1854), admired Swiss novelist, short-story writer and pastor who wrote under the name Jeremias Gotthelf.

Bjørneboe, Jens (Ingvald) (1920–1976), Norwegian novelist, dramatist, poet and essayist.

Bjørnson, Bjørnstjerne Martinius (1832–1910), eminent Norwegian poet, novelist, dramatist, editor and poltician, author of Norway's National Anthem Ja, vi elsker dette landet (Yes, We Love This Land Forever); won the Nobel Prize for Literature (1903).

Black, Charles Lund Jr (1915–2001), American legal scholar who was an authority on constitutional law.

Black, Max (1909–1988), Azerbaijanian-born American philosopher who wrote extensively on numerous subjects.

Black, William (1841–1898), Scottish novelist.

Blackburn, Paul (1926–1971), American poet.

Blackburn, Thomas (1916–1977), English poet, writer and critic.

Blacklock, Thomas (1721–1791), Scottish poet who was known as the 'blind bard'.

Blackmore, Sir Richard (1654–1729), English physician, poet and writer.

Blackmore R(ichard) D(oddridge) (1825–1900), English novelist, poet and translator, best remembered for his novel Lorna Doone (1869).

Blackmur, R(ichard) P(almer) (1904–1965), American critic and poet.

Blackstone, Sir William (1723–1780), eminent English jurist, author of the classic Commentaries on the Laws of England (4 vols, 1765–69).

Blackwell, John (1797–1840), Welsh poet and writer who wrote under the name Alun.

Blackwell, Thomas, the Younger (1701–1757), Scottish classical scholar.

Blackwood, Algernon Henry (1869–1951), English novelist and short-story writer of mystery and supernatural tales.

Blair, Robert (1699–1746), Scottish poet and preacher who wrote the well-known poem The Grave (1743).

Blake, William (1757–1827), famous English poet, writer, painter, engraver and mystic, renowned for such poetry collections as Songs of Innocence (1789) and Songs of Experience (1794), and the prose vol. The Marriage of Heaven and Hell (1790–93).

Blanco Fombona, Rufino (1874–1944), Venezuelan literary historian, poet, short-story writer, novelist and essayist.

Blanchard, Brand (1892–1987), American philosopher who espoused the cause of rationalism and idealism in his writings.

Blasco Ibáñez, Vicente (1867–1928), Spanish novelist, journalist and politician who won distinction with his novel Los Cuatro Jinetes del Apocalipsis (1916; English trans. as The Four Horsemen of the Apocalypse, 1918).

Blavatsky, Helena Petrovna (née Hahn) (1831–1891), Russian spiritualist and writer, co-founder of the Theosophical Society and author of The Secret Doctrine (2 vols, 1888).

Bleecker, Ann Eliza (1752–1783), American writer and poet, remembered for her epistolary novel The History of Maria Kittle (published 1797).

Blessington, Marguerite, Countess of (1789–1849), Irish writer, best known for her novel Grace Cassidy, or The Repealers (1833) and for her non-fiction works Conversations of Lord Byron (1843), The Idler in Italy (1839–40) and The Idler in France (1841).

Blest Gana, Alberto (1830–1920), admired Chilean novelist whose notable works included Durante la Reconquista (During the Reconquest, 1897) and Los transplados (The Uprooted, 1905).

Bleuler, Eugen (1857–1939), influential Swiss psychiatrist, a pioneering figure in the study of schizophrenia.

Blicher, Steen Steensen (1782–1848), Danish poet and short-story writer, author of the fine poetry collection Traekfuglene (Birds of Passage, 1838).

Bloch, Ernst (1885–1977), German philosopher who propounded an independent Marxist course which he described as the 'philosophy of hope', author of Das Prinzip Hoffnung (The Hope Principle, 3 vols, 1954–59).

Bloch, Jean-Richard (1884–1947), French journalist, essayist, novelist and dramatist who espoused the Marxist cause.

Bloch, Marc (Léopold Benjamin) (1886–1944), French historian, author of the major studies Les Rois Thaumaturges: Étude sur le caractère surnaturel attribué à la puissance royale, particulièrement en France et en Angleterre (The Royal Touch: Sacred Monarchy and Scrofula in France and England, 1924), Les Caractères originaux de l'histoire rurale française (The Basic Characteristics of French Rural History, 1931) and La Société féodale (The Feudal Society, 1939); during World War II, he was a member of the French Resistance, was captured and executed.

Bloch, Robert (Albert) (1917–1994), American writer who became best known for his works of suspense and horror, particularly Psycho (1959).

Blok, Alexander Alexandrovich (1880–1921), notable Russian poet and dramatist of the Symbolist movement, especially known for his ode Skify (Scythians, 1918).

Blom, Eric (Walter) (1888–1959), English writer on music and lexicographer.

Blondel, Georges (1856–1948), French historian.

Blondel, Maurice (Édouard) (1861–1949), French philosopher, author of L'action (1893), La Pensée (Thought, 2 vols, 1934) and Exigences philosophiques du Christianisme (The Philosophical Demands of Christianity, 1950).

Blondel de Nesle (12th Century), French trouvère.

Blood, Benjamin Paul (1822–1919), American philosopher and poet whose output reflected his worldview as a mystic.

Bloom, Allan (David) (1930–1992), American philosopher, essayist and translator who gained wide recognition as a trenchant critic of higher education in the US.

Bloomfield, Leonard (1887–1949), American linguist whose book Language (1933) proved influential in the development of structurual linguistics.

Bloomfield, Robert (1766–1823), English poet, author of The Farmer's Boy (1800), Rural Tales, Ballads and Songs (1802) and The Banks of Wye (1811).

Blosius, Franciscus Ludovicus (1506–1566), Belgian-born French Benedictine monastic reformer and theologian.

Bloy, Léon (1846–1917), French novelist, critic and Roman Catholic polemicist.

Blume, Friedrich (1893–1975), German music scholar and lexicographer.

Blunck, Hans Friedrich (1888–1961), German poet and novelist.

Blunden, Edmund Charles (1896–1974), English poet, critic and scholar, well respected for his book Undertones of War (1928) and the collection Poems of Many Years (1957).

Blunt, Lady Anne Isabella Noel, Baroness Wentworth (1837–1917), English writer; wife of Wilfrid Scawen Blunt.

Blunt, Wilfred Scawen (1840–1922), English poet and traveller; husband of Lady Anne Isabella Noel Blunt, Baroness Wentworth.

Blyth, Edward (1810–1873), English naturalist whose 'localizing principle' anticipated Charles Darwin's theory of organic evolution through natural selection.

Boas, Franz (1858–1942), significant German-born American anthropologist whose studies ranged from Native American cultures to linguistics.

Bobrzýnski, Michal (1849–1935), Polish historian and politician.

Bocage, Manoel Maria Barbosa du (1765–1805), Portuguese poet and translator who displayed a fine gift for writing sonnets.

Boccaccio, Giovanni (1313–1375), celebrated Italian poet and writer whose stories in the Decameron (c.1328–53) are renowned the world over.

Boccage, Marie Anne Fiquet du (née Le Page) (1710–1802), French poet.

Boccalini, Traiano (1556–1613), Italian writer, author of Ragguagli di Parnasso (2 parts, 1612–13) and Pietra del paragone politico (published 1614), both of which were published in an English trans. as Advertisements from Parnassus in two centuries with the Politicke Touchstone (1656), and Commentarii sopra Cornelio Tacito (Comments upon Cornelius Tacitus).

Bochart, Samuel (1599–1667), French reformed Church pastor and scholar.

Bodel, Jehan (c.1167–1210), French jongleur, poet and dramatist who wrote the first miracle play in France Jeu de Saint Nicholas (The Play of Saint Nicholas).

Bodenheim, Maxwell (1893–1954), American poet, novelist and dramatist; was murdered.

Bodenstedt, Friedrich Martin von (1819–1892), German poet, writer, critic and translator.

Bodin, Jean (1530–1596), French philosopher, best remembered for his Six Livres de la République (1576; English trans. as The Six Bookes of a Commonweale, 1606).

Bodmer, Johann Jakob (1698–1783), Swiss literary scholar and poet.

Boece or Boethius, Hector (c.1465–c.1536), Scottish historian, author of Scotorum historiae a prima gentis origine (1527; English trans. as The hystory and croniklis of Scotland, c.1536).

Boethius, Anicius Manlius Severinus (c.480–524), Roman theologian, philosopher and statesmen who wrote the famous De consolatione philosophiae while in prison; was executed for treason and magic.

Bogan, Louise (1897–1970), esteemed American poet and critic whose poetry followed along Metaphysical lines.

Bogdanovich, Ippolit Fyodorovich (1743–1803), Russian poet.

Bogusławski, Wojciech (1757–1829), Polish actor, theatre director and dramatist, well known for his comic plays.

Böhme, Jakob (1575–1624), German philosopher who embraced mysticism.

Böhmer, Johann Friedrich (1795–1863), German historian.

Bohomolec, Franciszek (1720–1784), Polish Jesuit priest, dramatist, linguist and editor.

Bohtlingk, Otto von (1815–1904), German language scholar and lexicographer.

Boiardo, Matteo Maria, Conte (c.1441–1494), Italian poet, author of the unfinished Orlando innamorato (c.1476–94).

Boie, Heinrich Christian (1744–1806), German poet and editor.

Boileau (-Despréaux), Nicolas (1636–1711), French poet and critic, master of satirical and epistolary writing.

Boisrobert, François Le Metel, Seigneur de (1589–1662), French churchman and dramatist who became best known for his wit and blasphemies at court.

Boito, Arrigo (actually Enrico Giuseppe Giovanni Boito) (1842–1918), Italian composer and poet who wrote the libretto to his own opera Mefistofele (1868), as well as to Verdi's operas Otello and Falstaff.

Bojer, Johan (1872–1959), Norwegian novelist, best remembered for Den store hunger (1916; English trans. as The Great Hunger, 1918) and Folk ved sjøen (1929; English trans. as Folk by the Sea, 1931).

Bokenam or Bokenham, Osbern (c.1392–c.1447), English writer, author of Legends of Holy Women.

Boker, George Henry (1823–1890), American poet, dramatist and diplomat, known for his sonnets and the verse tragedy Francesca da Rimini (1855).

Boldrewood, Rolf (actually Thomas Alexander Browne) (1826–1915), English-born Australian novelist and short-story writer, author of the novels Robbery Under Arms (1888) and Miner's Right (1890).

Böll, Heinrich (1917–1985), notable German novelist and short-story writer; won the Nobel Prize for Literature (1972).

Bolland or Bollandus, Jean (1596–1665), Belgian Jesuit historian who was the principal compiler of the Acta Sanctorum (2 parts, 1643, 1658), a collection of the lives of the Christian saints.

Bolt, Robert (Oxton) (1924–1995), English dramatist, particularly remembered for his play A Man for All Seasons (1960).

Bolton or Boulton, Edmund (c.1575–c.1633), English historian, antiquarian and poet, some of whose fine poems were included in the miscellany Englands Helicon (1600).

Bolton, Herbert Eugene (1870–1953), American historian who specialized in the study of the history of the Western hemisphere.

Bolyai, Farkas (1775–1856), Hungarian mathematician, poet, dramatist and composer.

Bonald, Louis-Garbriel-Ambroise, Vicomte de (1754–1840), French statesman and political philosopher who espoused the royalist cause.

Bonar, Horatius (1808–1889), Scottish Presbyterian minister, poet, hymnist and writer, author of Faith and Hope (1857–66).

Bonaventure, Saint (c.1217–1274), noted Italian Roman Catholic theologian, minister general of the Franciscan Order and cardinal bishop of Albano.

Boncompagno da Signa (c.1165–c.1240), Italian writer who became well known for his writings on rhetoric.

Boner or Bonerius, Ulrich (14th Century), Swiss Dominican monk and writer, remembered for his verse fables Der Edelstein (The Precious Stone).

Bongars, Jacques, Seigneur de Bauldry and de la Chesnaye (1554–1612), French diplomat and classical scholar, author of Gosta Dei per Francos (God's Work Through the Franks), a compilation of accounts of the Crusades.

Bonhoeffer, Dietrich (1906–1945), notable German Protestant theologian who became an opponent of the Nazi regime; implicated in the plot to assassinate Hitler, he was imprisoned and executed.

Bonivard François (c.1494–1570), Swiss patriot and historian, author of the Chroniques de Genève (History of Geneva, 1542–51, published 1831).

Bonnet, Charles (1720–1793), Swiss naturalist and philosopher.

Bonstetten, Karl Viktor von (1745–1832), Swiss writer.

Bontempelli, Massimo (1878–1960), Italian poet, novelist, dramatist and critic.

Bontemps, Arna (Wendell) (1902–1973), American writer who chronicled the black experience in books of fiction and non-fiction.

Bonvesin de la Riva (c.1240–c.1315), Italian writer and poet, best known for his Libro delle tre scritture (Book of the Three Writings, 1274).

Boorde or Borde, Andrew (c.1490–1549), English physician and writer, author of the first guidebook to Europe Fyrst Boke of the Introduction of Knowledge (1548).

Bopp, Franz (1791–1867), learned German linguist who wrote the major study Vergleichende Grammatik des Sanskrit, Zend, Griechischen, Lateinischen, Litthauischen, Altslawischen, Gotischen und Deutschen (Comparitive Grammar of Sanskrit, Zend, Greek, Latin, Lithuanian, Old Slavic, Gothic and German, 6 parts, 1833–52).

Borel, Petrus (actually Joseph-Pierre Borel) (1809–59), French poet, novelist and critic who was also known as Borel d'Hauterive.

Borgen, Johan (Collet Müller) (1902–79), Norwegian novelist, short-story writer, dramatist and essayist who was particularly acclaimed for the novel trilogy Lillelord (1955), De mørke kilder (The Dark Springs, 1956) and Vi har ham nå (Now We Have Him, 1957), all three of which appeared in an English trans. as Lillelord (1982).

Borges, Jorge Luis (1899–1986), Argentine poet, short-story writer and essayist.

Borowski, Tadeusz (1922–1951), Polish short-story writer.

Borron or Boron, Robert de (12th–13th Century), French poet who wrote the trilogy Joseph d'Arimathie, Merlin and Perceval.

Bosanquet, Bernard (1848–1923), English philosopher who espoused Hegelian principles, author of The Philosophical Theory of the State (1899).

Bosboom-Toussaint, Anna (1812–1846), Dutch writer.

Boscán Almogáver, Juan (Catalan name Joan Boscà Almugàver) (c.1487–1542), Catalan poet who helped to introduce Italian verse forms into Spain.

Bosch (Gaviño), Juan (1909–2001), Dominican politician and writer.

Bosquet, Alain (actually Anatole Bisk) (1919–98), Russian-born French poet, novelist and critic.

Bossert, Helmuth Theodor (1889–1961), German philologist and archaeologist, author of Geschichte des Kunstgewerbes aller Völker und Zeiten (History of the Arts and Crafts of All People and Times, 6 vols, 1928–35).

Bossuet, Jacques-Bénigne (1627–1704), French Roman Catholic bishop and writer, remembered especially for his political treatises.

Boswell, James (1740–1795), famous English biographer and diarist, author of the celebrated Life of Johnson (2 vols, 1791).

Botev, Khristo (1848–1876), Bulgarian patriot and poet; died in the Bulgarian uprising against Turkish rule.

Botta, Carlo Giuseppe Guglielmo (1766–1837), Italian-born French politician and historian.

Botta, Paul-Émile (1802–1870), Italian archaeologist, a pioneering figure in the study of ancient Mesopotamia.

Bottome, Phyllis (1884–1963), English novelist and short-story writer, author of the novels Private Worlds (1934) and The Mortal Storm (1937).

Bottomely, Gordon (1874–1948), English poet and dramatist who wrote Poems of Thirty Years (1925).

Boucher, Jonathan (1738–1804), English clergyman, writer and philologist who supported the royalist cause in America.

Boucher (de Crèvecoeur) de Perthes, Jacques (1788–1868), French archaeologist, author of Antiquités celtiques et antédiluviennes (Celtic and Antediluvian Antiquities, 3 vols, 1847–64).

Boucicault, Dion (actually Dionysius Lardner Boursiquot) (1820–1890), Irish-born American dramatist.

Boufflers, Stanislas-Jean, Chevalier de (1738–1815), French writer, poet and soldier who wrote the well-known picaresque romance Aline, reine de Golconde (Aline, Queen of Golconda).

Boulainvilliers, Henri, Comte de (1658–1722), French historian, particularly esteemed for his État de la France (3 vols, 1727–28).

Bouilhet, Louis (1821–1869), French poet and dramatist.

Boulle, Pierre (1912–1994), French novelist, best remembered for Le Pont de la rivière Kwaï (1952; English trans. as The Bridge on the River Kwai, 1954).

Bourdieu, Pierre (1930–2002), French sociologist who became well known through his writings and activism as a trenchant critic of capitalist society.

Bourget, Paul (-Charles-Joseph) (1852–1935), French poet, novelist and critic, best known for his novel Le Disciple (1889).

Bourne, Randolph Silliman (1886–1918), American critic, essayist and pacifist.

Boursalt, Edme (1638–1701), French poet, dramatist and novelist.

Bousset, Wilhelm (1865–1920), German New Testament scholar and theologian, author of Die Religion des Judentums im neutestamentlichen (späthellenistischen) Zeitalter (The Religion of the Jews in the New Testament [late Hellenistic] Era, 1903).

Boutens, Pieter Cornelis (1870–1943), Dutch poet and classical scholar who espoused mysticism.

Bouterwek, Friedrich (1766–1828), German philosopher and critic who wrote on various subjects, among them Kantian logic, religion, aesthetics and literature.

Bowdich, Thomas Edward (1791–1824), English traveller and writer.

Bowdler, Thomas (1754–1825), English physician and man of letters whose expurgation of Shakespeare's works was immortalized in the word 'bowdlerize'.

Bowen, Catherine (Shober) Drinker (1897–1973), American biographer and essayist.

Bowen, Elizabeth (Dorothea Cole) (1899–1973), highly regarded Irish novelist and short-story writer.

Bowen, Marjorie (actually Gabrielle Margaret Vere née Campbell Long) (1886–1952), English novelist, dramatist and biographer.

Bower, Walter (1385–1449), Scottish historian who wrote the Scotichronicon (16 vols, 1441–47).

Bowers, Edgar (1924–2000), American poet, a master of formalist verse.

Bowles, Jane (1917–1973), American novelist, short-story writer and dramatist, author of the avant-garde novel Two Serious Ladies (1943).

Bowles, Paul (Frederic) (1910–99), American writer, poet and composer, author of the novel The Sheltering Sky (1949).

Bowles, William Lisle (1762–1850), English churchman, poet and critic whose works presaged the Romantic era of verse.

Bowra, Sir (Cecil) Maurice (1898–1971), English critic and scholar.

Bowring, Sir John (1792–1872), English politician, diplomat and writer.

Boyd, Ernest (1887–1946), Irish-born American critic, writer and translator.

Boyd, James (1888–1944), American novelist and poet, expecially remembered for his novels Drums (1925) and Marching On (1927).

Boyd, Martin (à Beckett) (1893–1972), Australian novelist and poet, particularly known for his novel The Montforts (1928).

Boyd, Thomas (Alexander) (1898–1935), American novelist, short-story writer and biographer, author of the novels Through the Wheat (1923) and In Time of Peace (1935).

Boye, Karin Maria (1900–1941), Swedish poet and novelist, especially known for her novels Kris (Crisis, 1934) and Kallocain (1940); committed suicide.

Boyesen, Hjalmar Hjorth (1848–1895), Norwegian-born American writer and poet.

Boyle, Kay (1902–1992), American poet, essayist and novelist.

Boyle, Robert (1627–1691), English chemist and philosopher, author of The Sceptical Chemyist (1661) and The Origin of Forms and Qualities (1666).

Boylesve, René (actually René-Marie-Auguste Tardiveau) (1867–1926), French novelist who won distinction with his novels of Touraine series.

Braak, Menno ter (1902–1940), trenchant Dutch critic; committed suicide.

Braaten, Oskar (1881–1939), Norwegian novelist, dramatist, journalist and editor.

Brace, Gerald Warner (1901–1978), American novelist and critic.

Brackenridge, Hugh Henry (1748–1816), American lawyer, jurist and novelist, author of Modern Chivalry (1792–1815).

Bracton or Bratton, Henry de (died 1268), English jurist, known for his De legibus et consuetudinibus Angliae (On the Laws and Customs of England, c.1250).

Bradbury, Sir Malcolm (Stanley) (1932–2000), English novelist, critic and educator, author of novels such as Eating People is Wrong (1959), The History of Man (1975), Rates of Exchange (1983), Dr Criminale (1992) and To the Hermitage (2000).

Braddon, Mary Elizabeth (1837–1915), English novelist and poet, author of sensational novel Lady Audley's Secret (3 vols, 1862).

Bradford, Gamaliel (1863–1932), American biographer, poet, novelist and dramatist.

Bradford, Roark (1896–1948), American writer, author of Ol' Man Adam an' His Chillun (1928), which Marc Connelly adapted as the play The Green Pastures.

Bradford, William (1590–1657), English-born American governor of the Plymouth Colony and author of the invaluable History of Plymouth Plantation, 1620–47.

Bradley, A(ndrew) C(ecil) (1851–1935), English critic and scholar, known for his Shakespearean studies.

Bradley, F(rancis) H(erbert) (1846–1924), eminent English philosopher, author of the important vol. Appearance and Reality: A Metaphysical Essay (1893).

Bradstreet, Anne (Dudley) (c.1612–1672), pioneering English-born American poet, particularly admired for her collection The Tenth Muse Lately Sprung Up in America (1650).

Bradwardine, Thomas (c.1290–1349), English theologian and archbishop of Cantebury, author of De Causa Dei contra Pelagium (1344).

Brady, Cyrus Townsend (1861–1920), American Episcopal clergyman and prolific novelist.

Brady, Nicholas (1659–1726), Irish churchman and poet, author, with Nahum Tate, of a New Version of the Psalms (1696).

Braga, (Joaquim) Téofilo (Fernandes) (1843–1924), Portuguese scholar, poet and statesman who wrote the valuable História do Romantismo em Portugal (History of Romanticism in Portugal, 1880).

Brahm, Otto (1856–1912), German critic and theatre director.

Brainard, John Gardiner Calkins (1796–1828), American poet, writer and editor.

Braine, John (Gerard) (1922–1986), English novelist, author of Room at the Top (1957) and Life at the Top (1962).

Braithwaite, R(ichard) B(evan) (1900–1990), English philosopher who wrote Scientific Explanation (1955).

Braithwaite, William (Stanley Beaumont) (1878–1962), American poet, writer and editor.

Bramah, Ernest (actually Ernest Bramah Smith) (c.1869–1942), English short-story writer, creator of the blind detective Max Carrados.

Branagan, Thomas (1774–1843), Irish-born American writer and poet.

Branch, Anna Hempstead (1875–1937), American poet and dramatist

Brand, Max (actually Frederick Faust) (1892–1944), American novelist, author of Destry Rides Again (1930) and the Dr Kildare series.

Brandão, Frei António (1584–1637), Portuguese historian.

Brandes, (Carl) Edvard (Cohen) (1847–1931), Danish critic and politician; brother of Georg (Morris Cohen) Brandes.

Brandes, Georg (Morris Cohen) (1842–1927), noted Danish critic and scholar of a radical disposition, author of Hovedstrømninger i det 19de aarhundredes litteratur (1871–87; English trans. as Main Currents in 19th Century Literature, 1901–05), Danske digtere (Danish Poets, 1877) Det moderne gjennembruds maend (Men of the Modern Break-Through 1883), Friedrich Nietzsche (1909) and Sagnet om Jesus (1925; English trans. as Jesus, a Myth, 1926).

Brandr, Abbot Jónsson (died 1264), Icelandic abbot and writer.

Brandt, Geerhardt (1626–1685), Dutch historian and biographer.

Brandys, Kazimierz (1916–2000), Polish novelist and essayist whose masterpiece was the novel Wariacje pocztowe (Postal Variations, 1972).

Branner, Hans Christian (1903–1966), Danish novelist, short-story writer and dramatist.

Brant, Sebastian (c.1458–1521), German poet, author of the satirical Das Narrenschiff (1494; English trans. as The Ship of Fools, 1509).

Brantôme, Pierre (de Bourdeille, Abbé and Seigneur) de (c.1540–1614), French soldier and writer, best known for an account of his life and times (published 1665–66).

Brathwait, Richard (1588–1673), English poet and writer, author of the Latin poem Barnabees Journal (1638), which he wrote under the name Corymbaeus.

Braudel, (Paul Achille) Fernand (1902–85), French historian whose important works included La Méditerranée et le monde méditerranéen à l'époque de Philippe II (The Mediterranean and the Mediterannean World in the Age of Philip II, two vols, 1949) and Civilisation matérielle, économie et capitalisme, 15e–18e siècle (Civilization and Capitalism, 15th–18th Century, three vols, 1968, 1979, 1979).

Braun, Lily (née von Kretschman) (1865–1916), German feminist, pacifist, socialist and novelist.

Brautigan, Richard (1935–1984), American writer and poet.

Breasted, James Henry (1865–1935), American archaeologist and historian.

Brébeuf, Saint Jean de (1593–1649), French Jesuit missionary and writer.

Brecht, Bertolt (actually Eugen Berthold Friedrich Brecht) (1898–1956), celebrated German dramatist and poet, master of the modern theatre.

Bredero, Gerbrand Adriaenszoon (1585–1618), Dutch poet and dramatist.

Bregendahl, Marie (1867–1940), Danish novelist, author of En dødsnat (1912; English trans. as A Night of Death, 1931).

Bréhier, Émile (1876–1952), French philosopher who espoused rationalism.

Bréhier, Louis (1868–1951), French historian and archaeologist.

Breitinger, Johann Jakob (1701–1776), Swiss critic and scholar, author of the Critische Dichtkunst (1740).

Bremer, Fredrika (1801–1865), Swedish novelist and reformer, a prominent figure in the movement for women's rights.

Brenan, (Edward Fitz-) Gerald (1894–1987), English writer who became best known for his books on Spanish subjects.

Brennan, Christopher (John) (1870–1932), Australian poet and critic.

Brentano, Clemens (1778–1842), important German poet, novelist and folklorist who, with Achim von Arnim, collaborated on the notable edition of folk poetry Des Knaben Wunderhorn (The Youth's Magic Horn, 1805); uncle of Franz Brentano.

Brentano, Franz (1838–1917), German philosopher, author of Psychologie vom empirischen Standpunkte (Psychology from an Empirical Standpoint, 1874), Untersuchungen zur Sinnespsychologie

(Inquiry into Sense Psychology, 1907) and Von der Klassifikation der psychischen Phänomene (On the Classification of Psychological Phenomena, (1911); nephew of Clemens Brentano.

Bresslau, Harry (1848–1926), German historian and paleographer.

Breton, André (1896–1966), famous French poet, essayist, critic and editor, a leading proponent of Surrealism.

Breton, Nicholas (c.1553–c.1625), English poet and writer, particularly appreciated for his poem The Passionate Shepheard (1604).

Bretón de los Herreros, Manuel (1796–1873), Spanish dramatist and poet.

Bretschneider, Carl Gottlieb (1776–1848), German Protestant theologian who wrote an important study on New Testament literature Probabilia (Probables, 1820).

Breuer, Josef (1842–1925), Austrian physician and physiologist whose work anticipated psychoanalysis, co-author with Freud of Studien über Hysterie (1895).

Breuil, Henri-Édouard-Prosper (1877–1961), eminent French archaeologist who wrote numerous studies on prehistoric cave paintings.

Brewster, Henry B (1850–1908), American writer.

Březina, Otakar (1868–1929), influential Czech poet who wrote 5 vols of poetry (1895, 1896, 1897, 1899, 1901).

Bridel, Philippe-Sirice (1757–1845), Swiss writer, philologist and poet.

Bridges, Robert (Seymour) (1844–1930), notable English poet, dramatist and critic; became Poet Laureate of the United Kingdom (1913); father of Elizabeth Daryush.

Bridie, James (actually Osborne Henry Mavor) (1888–1951), Scottish dramatist who won popularity with his comedies.

Brieux, Eugène (1858–1932), French dramatist, known for his realist plays.

Briggs, Charles Augustus (1841–1913), American Old Testament scholar who championed the cause of higher criticism.

Brighouse, Harold (1882–1958), English dramatist and novelist, best known for his play Hobson's Choice (1916).

Brightman, Edgar Sheffield (1884–1953), American philosopher.

Brinig, Myron (1900–1991), American novelist.

Brink, Bernhard ten (1841–1892), Dutch literary scholar, author of Geschichte der englischen Literatur (2 vols, 1877–93; English trans. as History of English Literature, 1883–93).

Brinnin, John Malcolm (1916–1998), American poet, biographer and critic.

Brinton, Crane (1898–1968), American writer.

Brito, Frei Bernardo de (1568–1617), Portuguese historian.

Brittain, Vera Mary (1893–1970), English pacifist, feminist and writer.

Brizieux, Julien Auguste Pélage (1803–1858), French poet.

Broad, C(harles) D(unbar) (1887–1971), English philosopher.

Broch, Hermann (1886–1951), notable Austrian writer, known for such works as Die Schlafwandler (1931–32; English trans. as The Sleepwalkers, 1932), Der Tod des Virgil (1945; English trans. as The Death of Virgil, 1945) and Der Versucher (The Bewitchment, published 1953).

Brochu, André (1942–2000), Canadian writer, poet and critic.

Brockes, Barthold Heinrich (1680–1747), German poet who extolled the world of nature.

Brod, Max (1884–1968), Austrian poet, dramatist, novelist, essayist and biographer.

Brodkey, Harold (actually Aaron Roy Weintraub) (1930–1996), American novelist and short-story writer.

Brodsky, Joseph (Alexandrovich) (1940–1996), prominent Russian-born American poet whose reputation was secured as an exile in the West; won the Nobel Prize for Literature (1987) and was Poet Laureate of the US (1991–92).

Broglie, (Jacques-Victor-) Albert, 4th Duc de (1821–1901), French statesman and writer.

Broke or Brooke, Arthur (died 1563), English poet and writer, author of the poem The Tragicall Historye of Romeus and Juliet (1562), which served as the basis of Sheakspeare's Romeo and Juliet.

Brome, Alexander (1620–1666), English poet who excelled in writing drinking songs and satirical witticisms attacking the Rump Parliament.

Brome, Richard (died c.1652), English dramatist, best remembered for The Northern Lasse (c.1629).

Bromfield, Louis (1896–1956), American novelist and essayist, particularly known for his series of novels entitled Escape.

Broniewski, Władysław (1897–1962), Polish poet.

Bronowski, Jacob (1908–74), Polish-born English mathematician and writer, author of The Common Sense of Science (1951), Science and Human Values (1956), and the Identity of Man (1965).

Brontë, Anne (1820–1849), English novelist and poet, author of the novel Agnes Grey (1848); sister of Charlotte and Emily Jane Brontë.

Brontë, Charlotte (1816–1855), English novelist and poet who wrote the classic novel Jane Eyre (1847); sister of Anne and Emily Jane Brontë.

Brontë, Emily Jane (1818–1848), English poet and novelist, author of the fine Gondal poems and the classic novel Wuthering Heights (1847); sister of Anne and Charlotte Brontë.

Bronzino, Il (actually Agnolo or Angiolo di Cosimo) (1503–1572), Italian painter and poet.

Brook, Barry S(helley) (1918–1997), American music scholar.

Brook, (Bernard) Jocelyn (1908–1966), English poet and novelist.

Brooke, Frances (1724–1789), English writer, dramatist and translator.

Brooke, Henry (c.1703–1783), Irish novelist, dramatist and poet, author of the poem Universal Beauty (1728) and the novel The Fool of Quality (1765–70).

Brooke, Rupert (Chawner) (1887–1915), admired English poet, beloved for his sonnet collection 1914 (1915); died in World War I.

Brooks, Charles T(imothy) (1813–1883), American clergyman, translator and poet.

Brooks, Cleanth (1906–1994), American critic, a prominent figure in the New Criticism.

Brooks, Gwendolyn (1917–2000), American poet and writer whose works depicted the black experience in such poetry collections as Annie Allen (1949), Riot (1969), and To Disembark (1982).

Brooks, Maria Gowen (c.1794–1845), American poet and dramatist who was known as Maria of the West.

Brooks, Phillips (1835–1893), American Episcopal clergyman who wrote the celebrated hymn O Little Town of Bethlehem (1868).

Brooks, Van Wyck (1886–1963), American literary historian and biographer, especially known for The Flowering of New England, 1815–1865 (1936).

Broome, William (1689–1745), English scholar and poet.

Brophy, Brigid (Antonia) (1929–1995), English novelist, dramatist and writer.

Brosses, Charles de (1709–1777), French magistrate and scholar, author of Lettres sur Herculaneum (1750).

Brougham, John (1814–1880), Irish-born American actor, dramatist and theatre manager.

Broughton, Rhoda (1840–1920), English novelist.

Broun, Heywood (Campbell) (1888–1939), American journalist and critic of liberal views.

Brown, Alice (1857–1948), American novelist, short-story writer and dramatist.

Brown, Charles Brockden (1771–1810), pioneering American novelist, known as the father of the American novel for his Wieland (1798).

Brown, George Mackay (1921–1996), Scottish poet and writer.

Brown, Harry (Peter McNab Jr) (1917–1986), American writer and poet.

Brown, John (1715–1766), English Anglican clergyman, philosopher and dramatist.

Brown, John (1810–1882), Scottish physician and essayist, remembered for his Horae Subsecivae (3 vols, 1858–82).

Brown, John Mason (1900–1969), American drama critic and biographer.

Brown, Raymond E(dward) (1928–1998), American Roman Catholic biblical scholar and priest, author of The Birth of the Messiah (1977) and The Death of the Messiah (1994).

Brown, Sterling A(llan) (1901–1989), American poet and critic.

Brown, Thomas (1663–1704), English poet and translator, particularly remembered for his satirical bent.

Brown, T(homas) E(dward) (1830–1897), English poet.

Brown, William Hill (1765–1793), American novelist and dramatist, author of the epistolary novel Power of Sympathy, or the Triumph of Nature Founded in Truth (1789).

Brown, William Wells (c.1816–1884), American writer and poet, author of Clotelle, or, The President's Daughter (1853).

Brown, Isaac Hawkins (1705–1760), English poet who was known for his wit, author of the parody A Pipe of Tobacco and the more serious Du Animi Immortalitate (On the Immortality of the Soul, 1754).

Browne, J(ohn) Ross (1821–1875), American writer, author of fiction and travel books.

Browne, Sir Thomas (1605–1682), eminent English writer and physician who wrote Religio Medici (1642) and Pseudodoxis Epidemica, or, Enquiries into Very many received Tenets, commonly presumed truths (1646).

Browne, William (c.1591–c.1645), English poet, admired for such works as Britannia's Pastorals (1613) and The Inner Temple Masque (c.1614).

Brownell, W(illiam) C(rary) (1851–1928), American critic and editor.

Browning, Elizabeth Barrett (1806–1861), English poet famous for such works as Sonnets from the Portuguese (1850) and Aurora Leigh (1857); wife of Robert Browning.

Browning, Robert (1812–1889), renowned English poet, author of Christmas-Eve and Easter-Day (1850), Men and Women (1855), Dramatis Personae (1864), The Ring and the Book (1868–69) and Dramatic Idyls (2 parts, 1879, 1880); husband of Elizabeth Barrett Browning.

Brownson, Orestes Augustus (1803–1876), liberal American clergyman, editor, poet and writer, author of books on subjects ranging from religion and philosophy to science and political reform.

Brú, Hedin (actually Hans Jakob Jacobsen) (1901–1987), Faeroese novelist whose finest work was Fedgar à ferd (The Old Man and His Sons, 1940).

Bruce, Michael (1746–1767), Scottish poet, admired for his Elegy Written in Spring (published 1770).

Brucioli, Antonio (c.1499–1566), Italian scholar and translator, best known for his translation of the Bible into Italian (1532) which led to his imprisonment by the Inquisition.

Bruckberger, Raymond-Léopold (1907–1998), French Roman Catholic priest and writer who embraced secularism.

Brugmann, (Friedrich) Karl (1849–1919), important German linguist, author of the Grundiss der vergleichenden Grammatik der Indogermanischen Sprachen (Outline of the Comparative Grammar of Indo-Germanic Languages, 5 vols, 1886–93).

Brugsch, Heinrich Karl (1827–1894), German Egyptologist who edited a monumental hieroglyphic-demotic dictionary (1867–82).

Brun, Johan Nordahl (1745–1816), Norwegian bishop, hymnist, dramatist and politician, author of the first Norwegian National Anthem For Norge, kjaempers fødeland (For Norway, Land of Heroes, 1771).

Brunetière, Ferdinand (1849–1906), French critic and literary historian.

Brunhoff, Jean de (1899–1937), French writer and illustrator who won success with his series of Babar books for children.

Bruni, Leonardo (c.1370–1444), Italian scholar who was also known as Leonardo Aretino, author of the Historiarum Florentini populi libri XII (12 Books of Florentine Histories, published 1610).

Brunner, (Heinrich) Emil (1889–1966), significant Swiss theologian who was a determined exponent of Neo-orthodoxy in opposition to liberal theology.

Bruno, Giordano (1548–1600), notable Italian philosopher, mathematician and scientist; burned as a heretic by the Inquisition.

Brunschvicg, Léon (1869–1944), important French philosopher, author of the influential La Modalité du jugement (1897), a dissertation setting forth his Idealism.

Brusewitz, Axel (Karl Adolf) (1881–1950), Swedish political scientist, an authority on the constitutional history of his homeland.

Bryan, Sir Francis (died 1550), English soldier, courtier and poet, called the 'vicar of hell' by Oliver Cromwell.

Bryant, Sir Arthur (Wynne Morgan) (1899–1985), English historian and biographer who was especially admired for his biography of Samuel Pepys (three vols, 1933, 1935, 1938).

Bryant, William Cullen (1794–1878), prominent American poet and journalist whose poem Thanatopsis (1817) became an American classic.

Bryce, James, 1st Viscount (1838–1922), English politician, diplomat and historian, author of The Holy Roman Empire (1864) and The American Commonwealth (3 vols, 1888).

Brydges, Sir Samuel Egerton (1762–1837), English bibliogrpher and writer.

Bryher (actually Annie Winifred Ellerman) (1894–1983), English novelist, poet and critic who was admired for her historical fiction.

Bryusov, Valeri Yakovlevich (1873–1924), Russian poet, novelist, dramatist, critic and translator.

Brzozowski, Stanisław (1878–1911), Polish writer.

Buber, Martin (1878–1965), notable Austrian-born Jewish philosopher who became well known for his ethical and theological dialogue Ich und Du (1923; English trans. as I and Thou, 1937).

Buchan, John, 1st Baron Tweedsmuir (1875–1940), Scottish statesman and writer.

Buchanan, Dugald (1716–1768), Scottish writer.

Buchanan, George (1506–1582), Scottish scholar and poet.

Buchanan, Robert Williams (1841–1901), English poet, novelist and dramatist who wrote under the name Thomas Maitland.

Bucher, (Adolf) Lothar (1817–1892), German government official and writer.

Büchner, Georg (1813–1837), German dramatist whose works anticipated Expressionism, author of Dantons Tod (Danton's Death, 1835), Leonce und Lena (1836) and Woyzeck (1836), the latter set as the libretto to Alban Berg's opera Wozzeck.

Büchner, Ludwig (1824–1899), German physician and philosopher who embraced materialism in his well-known vol. Kraft und Stoff (1855; English trans. as Force and Matter, 1870).

Buck, Pearl (née Sydenstricker) (1892–1973), admired American writer who secured her reputation with the novel The Good Earth (1931); won the Nobel Prize for Literature (1938).

Bucke, Richard Maurice (1837–1902), Canadian biographer.

Buckingham, George Villiers, 2nd Duke of (1628–1687), English politician and writer, principally remembered for his dissolute life.

Buckingham, James Silk (1786–1855), English traveller and writer.

Buckle, Henry Thomas (1821–1862), English historian who wrote the unfinished History of Civilization in England (2 vols, 1857, 1861).

Budé, Guillaume (1467–1540), French scholar, diplomat and royal librarian who was known for his Greek classical studies.

Budge, Sir (Ernest Alfred Thompson) Wallis (1857–1934), English Orientalist and museum curator, known for his studies in Egyptian and Assyrian antiquities.

Budgell, Eustace (1686–1737), English writer.

Buero Vallejo, Antonio (1916–2000), Spanish dramatist.

Bufalino, Gesualdo (1920–1996), Italian writer, poet and translator.

Buffier, Claude (1661–1737), noted French philosopher, historian and philologist, best remembered for the Traité des vérités premiéres et de la source de nos jugements (Treatise on First Truths and on the Source of Our Judgements, 1724).

Buffon, Georges-Louis-Leclerc, Comte de (1707–1788), French naturalist, author of the significant Histoire naturelle, générale et particuliére (36 vols, 1749–88).

Bugge, (Elseus) Sophus (1833–1907), Norwegian philologist who published a critical edition of the Poetic Edda of 13th-Century Iceland (1891 et seq.).

Bühler, Karl (1879–1963), German linguist and psychologist.

Buhturī, al- (actually Abū 'Ubādah al-Walīd ibn 'Ubayd Allāh al-Buhturī) (821–897), Arab poet, best known for his panegyrics.

Bukharin, Nikolai Ivanovich (1888–1938), Russian revolutionary, politician and Marxist theoretician and economist; executed during the Stalinist purges.

Bukowski, Charles (1920–1994), American poet, novelist and screenwriter whose underground career made him a literary cult figure.

Bulfinch, Thomas (1796–1867), American writer, author of The Age of Fable (1855), The Age of Chivalry (1858) and Oregon and Eldorado (1866).

Bulgakov, Mikhail (Afanasievich) (1891–1940), Russian novelist, short-story writer and dramatist.

Bulgakov, Sergei Nikolaievich (1871–1944), Russian Orthodox theologian and economist, a proponent of the philosophical-theological system known as sophiology (after the Greek word sophia, i.e. wisdom).

Bulgaris, Eugenius (1716–1806), Greek Orthodox theologian and scholar.

Bull, Olaf (Jacob Martin Luther) (1883–1933), Norwegian poet.

Bullett, Gerald (William) (1893–1958), English novelist, biographer, critic and poet.

Bullinger, Heinrich (1504–1575), prominent Swiss Protestant pastor and writer, author of Reformationsgeschichte (History of the Reformation, published 1838–40).

Bultmann, Rudolf (Karl) (1884–1976), influential German theologian who applied Existentialist philosophical principles in his effort to 'demythologize' the New Testament.

Bunce, Oliver Bell (1828–1890), American dramatist, writer and editor.

Bunin, Ivan Alexseievich (1870–1953), noted Russian poet, short-story writer and novelist; won the Nobel Prize for Literature (1933).

Bunner, Henry Cuyler (1855–1896), American poet, novelist and editor.

Bunting, Basil (1900–1985), English poet who espoused the cause of Modernism.

Bunyan, John (1628–1688), famous English Puritan minister and writer, author of the classic The Pilgrim's Progress (2 parts, 1678, 1684), as well as the admired Grace Abounding to the Chief of Sinners (1666) and The Holy War (1682).

Burckhardt, Jakob (Christoph) (1818–1897), eminent Swiss historian of art and culture.

Bürger, Gottfried August (1747–1794), esteemed German poet and translator, one of the principal figures in the development of Romantic ballad literature in his homeland.

Burgess, Anthony (actually John Anthony Burgess Wilson) (1917–1993), notable English novelist, critic and composer who secured his literary reputation with the novel A Clockwork Orange (1962).

Burgess, Gelett (Frank) (1866–1951), American poet, writer and artist, best known for his humorous poem The Purple Cow.

Burgon, John William (1813–1888), English churchman, scholar and poet, author of the poem Petra (1845).

Burgoyne, John (1722–1792), English general and dramatist whose most popular play was The Heiress (1786).

Buridian, Jean or Joannes Buridanus (1300–1358), French logician, philosopher and theologian, one of the leading Aristotelians of his era.

Burk, John Daly (c.1775–1808), Irish-born American dramatist and writer.

Burke, Edmund (1729–1797), Irish-born English statesman and political theorist, author of the classic Reflections on the Revolution in France (1790).

Burke, Kenneth (Duva) (1897–1993), American critic and poet.

Burnet, Gilbert (1643–1715), Scottish Anglican bishop and historian who wrote History of the Reformation in England (3 vols, 1679–1714) and History of My Own Time (2 vols, published 1723, 1734).

Burnett, Frances Eliza (née Hodgson) (1849–1924), English-born American novelist and dramatist, best known for her successful novel Little Lord Fauntleroy (1886).

Burnett, W(illiam) R(iley) (1899–1982), American novelist.

Burney, Charles (1726–1814), famous English music scholar, author of a General History of Music (4 vols, 1776–89); father of Fanny Burney.

Burney, Fanny (actually Frances Burney, later Madame D'Arblay) (1752–1840), English novelist and letter writer, author of the classic novel of manners Evelina, or a Young Lady's Entrance into the World (1778); daughter of Charles Burney.

Burns, John Horne (1916–1953), American novelist.

Burns, Robert (1759–1796), celebrated Scottish poet, master of the folk tradition of his native land.

Burroughs, Edgar Rice (1875–1950), American writer, creator of Tarzan.

Burroughs, John (1837–1921), American naturalist and essayist.

Burroughs, William S(eward) (1914–1997), experimental American novelist who influenced the writers of the Beat generation.

Burt, (Maxwell) Struthers (1882–1954), American writer.

Burton, Sir Richard (Francis) (1821–1890), colourful English explorer, linguist,writer and poet who prepared unexpurgated editions of such erotic works as The Kama Sutra (1883), the Arabian Nights (1885–88) and The Perfumed Garden (1886).

Burton, Robert (1577–1640), English Anglican clergyman and scholar who wrote the classic The Anatomy of Melancholy (1621).

Bury, J(ohn) B(agnell) (1861–1927), English classical scholar, historian and editor.

Busch, Wilhelm (1832–1908), German painter and poet.

Busembaum or Busenbaum, Hermann (1600–1668), German Jesuit theologian, author of the famous Medulla Theologiae Moralis, Facili ac Perspicua Methodo Resolvens Casus Conscientiae ex Variis Probatisque Auctoribus Concinnata (The Heart of Moral Theology, an Easy and Perspicacious Method Resolving the Claims of Conscience Compiled from Various Worthy Authors, c.1645).

Bushnell, Horace (1802–1876), American Congregational minister and theologian, author of God in Christ (1849), Christ in Theology (1851), Nature and the Supernatural (1858), The Vicarious Sacrifice (1866) and Forgiveness and Law (1874).

Būsīrī, al- (actually Sharaf ad-Dīn Muhammad ibn Sa'īd al-Būsīrī as-Sanhājī) (c.1212–c.1295), Arab poet who wrote the celebrated poem al-Burdah (English trans. as The Poem of the Mantle).

Busken Huet, Conrad (1826–1886), noted Dutch critic, author of the classic study Het land van Rembrandt (The Country of Rembrandt, 1882–84).

Buson (actually Taniguchi Buson) (1716–1783), Japanese poet and painter who was known as Yosa Buson.

Bussy, Roger de Rabutin, Comte de (1618–1693), infamous French libertine and writer who was known as Bussy-Rabutin, author of the scandalous tales Histoire amoureuse des Gaules (1665).

Butler, Alban (1710–1773), English Roman Catholic priest and historian who wrote the celebrated The Lives of the Fathers, Martyrs, and Other Principal Saints (4 vols, 1756–59).

Butler, Ellis Parker (1869–1937), American writer of a humorous turn.

Butler, (Frederick) Guy (1918–2001), South African poet, dramatist and writer.

Butler, James (c.1755–1842), English-born American writer, best remembered for his novel Fortunes's Foot-ball, or, The Adventures of Mercutio (1797–98).

Butler, Joseph (1692–1752), English Anglican bishop and philosopher, author of the notable Sermons on Human Nature (1726) and The Analogy of Religion, Natural and Revealed, to the Constitution and Course of Nature (1736).

Butler, Nicholas Murray (1862–1947), prominent American educator, internationalist and writer; was co-winner of the Nobel Prize for Peace (1931).

Butler, Samuel (1612–1680), notable English poet whose mastery of satire was revealed in his Hudibras (3 parts, 1663, 1664, 1678).

Butler, Samuel (1835–1902), English novelist, essayist and critic, author of the novels Erewhon (1872) and The Way of All Flesh (published 1903).

Buysse, Cyriel (1859–1932), Dutch novelist and dramatist, a prominent figure of the Flemish naturalist school.

Buzurg, 'Alavī (1904–97), Persian novelist and short-story writer who spent many years in East Germany.

Buzzati, Dino (1906–1972), esteemed Italian novelist, short-story writer and dramatist, especially known for his Kafkaesque themes.

Byles, Mather (1707–1788), American clergyman, theologian and poet.

Bynner, Edwin Lassetter (1842–1893), American lawyer and writer, best known for his novel Agnes Surriage (1886).

Bynner, (Harold) Witter (1881–1968), American poet and writer who displayed a fine command of both lyrical and satirical writing.

Byrd, William (1674–1744), American planter, satirist and diarist whose writings were published posthumously and revealed him as a literary figure of merit.

Byrne, Donn (1889–1928), American writer and poet.

Byrom, John (1692–1763), English poet and hymnist, best remembered for his hymn Christians Awake! Salute the Happy Morn.

Byron, Lord (actually George Gordon Byron, 6th Baron Byron) (1788–1824), celebrated English poet, self-created 'Byronic hero' of the Romantic age and advocate of political liberty, author of such famous works as Childe Harold's Pilgrimage (4 cantos, 1812, 1816, 1818), Manfred (1817) and Don Juan (1819–24).

Caballero, Fernán (actually Cecilia Böhl de Faber) (1796–1877), German-Spanish novelist whose most noted novel was La gaviota (1849; English trans. as The Seagull, 1867).

Cabanis, Pierre-Jean-Georges (1757–1808), French philosopher and physiologist, particularly known for his Rapports du physique et du moral de l'homme (Relations of the Physical and the Moral in Man, 1802).

Cabasilas, Saint Nicolas (c.1320–1390), notable Greek Orthodox lay theologian who wrote the important Commentary on the Divine Liturgy and Life of Christ.

Cabasilas, Nilus (c.1298–c.1363), Greek Orthodox metropolitan and theologian, author of De processione Spiritus Sancti (On the Procession of the Holy Spirit).

Cabell, James Branch (1879–1958), American writer and critic, best remembered for his novel Jurgen (1919).

Cabet, Étienne (1788–1856), French-born American Socialist whose novel Voyage en Icarie (1840) espouses his thoughts on the ideal society.

Cable, George Washington (1844–1925), American novelist, short-story writer, essayist and reformer.

Cabral de Melo Neto, João (1920–99), Brazilian poet, writer and diplomat.

Cabrol, Fernand (1855–1937), French Benedictine monk and writer, particularly known for his Livre de la prière antique (1900; English trans. as Liturgical Prayer, 1922).

Cadalso or Cadahlso y Vázquez, José de (1741–1782), Spanish writer, poet and dramatist, author of the books Cartas marruecas (Moroccan Letters, 1793) and Noches lúgubres (Sombre Nights, 1798).

Caecilius (1st Century), Greek rhetorician.

Caecilius, Statius (c.219–166 BC), Roman poet.

Caedmon (7th Century), Anglo-Saxon monk and poet.

Caesar, (Gaius) Julius (100–44 BC), Roman general and dictator who wrote Commentarii de bello Gallico (52–51 BC; English trans. as The Gallic War, 1917) and Commentarii de bello civili (c.45 BC; English trans. as The Civil Wars, 1914); was assassinated.

Caesarius of Heisterbach (c.1170–c.1240), German preacher and writer, author of the Dialogus Miraculorum (c.1219–23), several books on miracles and a life of Saint Engelbert.

Caffaro di Caschifellone (b. c.1080–1166), Italian soldier, statesman and crusader who chronicled the First Crusade and 12th-Century Genoa.

Cahan, Abraham (1860–1951), Russian-born American journalist and writer.

Cain, James M(allahan) (1892–1977), American novelist and short-story writer, best known for his novels The Postman Always Rings Twice (1934), Double Indemnity (1936) and Mildred Pierce (1941).

Caine, Sir (Thomas Henry) Hall (1853–1931), English novelist.

Caird, Edward (1835–1908), English philosopher, author of A Critical Account of the Philosophy of Kant (1877), The Critical Philosophy of Immanuel Kant (2 vols, 1889), The Evolution of Religion (2 vols, 1893) and The Evolution of Theology in the Greek Philosophers (2 vols, 1904).

Caird, John (1820–1898), Scottish Presbyterian minister and theologian who wrote An Introduction to the Philosophy of Religion (1880) and The Fundamental Ideas of Christianity (2 vols, 1899).

Cairnes, John Elliott (1823–1875), Irish economist, author of Some Leading Principles of Political Economy Newly Expounded (1874).

Caius, John (1510–1573), English physician and writer.

Cajetan or Cajetanus (c.1648–1534), notable Roman Catholic theologian who took the Dominican name Tommaso de Vio, author of a major commentary on the Summa theologiae of Saint Thomas Aquinas.

Calderon de la Barca, Pedro (1600–1681), eminent Spanish dramatist and poet, especially known for his play La hija del aire (The Daughter of Air, 1653).

Caldwell, Erskine (Preston) (1903–1987), prominent American novelist and short-story writer, especially known for his novels Tobacco Road (1932), God's Little Acre (1933) and Trouble in July (1940).

Caldwell, (Janet) Taylor (1900–1985), English-born American novelist.

Calef, Robert (1648–1719), American merchant who wrote a trenchant attack on the perpetrators of the Salem witchcraft trials in his More Wonders of the Invisible World (1700).

Callaghan, Morley (Edward) (1903–1990), Canadian novelist and short-story writer.

Callimachus (c.305–c.240 BC), Greek poet and scholar, author of the famous elegy Aetia (Causes, c.270 BC).

Callinus (7th Century BC), Greek poet.

Calpurnius Siculus, Titus (2nd Century), Roman poet of several pastoral eclogues.

Calverley, Charles Stuart (1831–1884), English poet and translator whose gift of parody was revealed in such vols as Verses and Translations (1862) and Fly Leaves (1872).

Calvert, George Henry (1803–1889), American writer, dramatist and poet.

Calverton, V(ictor) F(rancis) (actually George Goetz) (1900–1940), American critic and editor who embraced Marxist principles.

Calvin, John (1509–1564), French Protestant reformer and theologian, author of the famous Institutes (1536).

Calvino, Italo (1923–1985), Italian novelist and short-story writer.

Calvus, Gaius Licinius Macer (82–c.47 BC), Roman poet and orator.

Calzabigi, Raniero (Simone Francesco Maria) di (1714–1795), Italian poet and music theorist who wrote the librettos for Gluck's operas Orfeo ed Euridice (1762), Alceste (1767) and Paride ed Elena (1770).

Cambridge, Ada (1844–1926), English-born Australian novelist and poet.

Cambridge, Richard Owen (1717–1802), English poet and essayist, author of the mock epic poem The Scribleriad.

Camden, William (1551–1623), English antiquarian who wrote a topographical survey of England in his Britannia (1586).

Camerarius, Joachim (1500–1574), German Lutheran theologian and classical scholar.

Cameron, (John) Norman (1905–1953), Scottish poet.

Cammaerts, Émile (1878–1953), Belgian-born English poet and writer.

Camões, Luís (Vaz) de (c.1524–1580), renowned Portuguese poet, author of the famous epic Os Lusíadas.

Campanella, Tommaso (actually Giovanno Domenico Campanella) (1568–1639), Italian philosopher and poet who wrote the socialistic tome La Città del Sole (The City of the Sun, 1602) during his imprisonment by the Inquisition (1599–1626).

Campbell, Alexander (1788–1866), Irish-born American Protestant clergyman, writer and co-founder of the Disciples of Christ or Christian Church.

Campbell, Bartley (1843–1888), American dramatist, best remembered for My Partner (1879).

Campbell, George (1719–1796), English writer.

Campbell, (Ignatius) Roy(ston Dunnachie) (1901–1957), admired South African poet, writer and translator who excelled in lyric poetry; died in an automobile accident.

Campbell, John W(ood Jr) (1910–71), American writer who is generally recognized as the father of modern science fiction.

Campbell, Joseph (1879–1944), Irish poet who wrote some of his poems under his Irish name Seosamh MacCathmhaoil.

Campbell, Joseph (1904–1987), American writer and editor who became best known for his exploration of mythology.

Campbell, Thomas (1777–1844), Scottish poet and writer, particularly remembered for such poems as The Pleasures of Hope (1799), The Battle of the Baltic, Hohenlinden, The Soldier's Dream and Ye Mariners of England.

Campbell, William Wilfred (1861–1918), Canadian churchman, poet and writer, author of Lake Lyrics and Other Poems (1889).

Campe, Joachim Heinrich (1746–1818), German educator and writer.

Camphuysen, Dirk Rafaëlszoon (1586–1627), Dutch poet who wrote on religious themes.

Campion, Thomas (1567–1620), English physician, poet, theorist and composer, author of both English and Latin poems.

Campoamor y Campoosorio, Ramón de (1817–1901), Spanish poet who became known for his epigrams.

Camus, Albert (1913–1960), French novelist, short-story writer, dramatist and essayist who pondered what he considered to be the absurdity of the human dilemma; won the Nobel Prize for Literature (1957); died in an automobile accident.

Canby, Henry Seidel (1878–1961), American critic, biographer and editor.

Cane, Melville H(enry) (1879–1980), American lawyer, poet and writer.

Canetti, Elias (1905–1994), notable Bulgarian novelist and dramatist; won the Nobel Prize for Literature (1981).

Canfield (Fisher), Dorothy (1879–1958), American novelist and short-story writer.

Canisius, Saint Peter or Petrus Kanis (1521–1597), Dutch Jesuit scholar who was a vigorous opponent of Protestantism.

Canitz, Friedrich Rudolf, Freiherr von (1654–1699), German poet whose satires helped to introduce classical values to German letters.

Cankar, Ivan (1876–1918), Slovenian writer, poet and dramatist.

Cannon, Charles James (1800–1860), American dramatist, poet and writer.

Cano, Melchor (c.1509–1560), Spanish Roman Catholic bishop and theologian, author of De locis theologicis.

Canth, Minna (actually Ulrika Vilhelmina née Johnsson Canth) (1844–1897), Finnish novelist, short-story writer and dramatist.

Cantwell, Robert (Emmett) (1908–1978), American novelist and biographer.

Čapek, Karel (1890–1938), Czech novelist, short-story writer, dramatist and essayist.

Capella, Martianus Minneus Felix (4th–5th Century), North African poet and writer.

Capgrave, John (1393–1464), English theologian, historian and biographer.

Capito, Wolfgang Fabricius (actually Wolfgang Köpfel) (1478–1541), Alsatian Protestant reformer and Old Testament scholar.

Capote, Truman (1924–1984), American novelist, short-story writer and dramatist.

Cappel, Louis or Ludovicus Capellus (1585–1658), French theologian and Hebrew scholar, author of the significant Critica Sacra (1650).

Capponi, Gino, Marchese (1792–1876), Italian statesman and writer, author of the important Storia della republicca di Firenze (History of the Rupublic of Florence, 1875).

Capréolus, Jean (c.1380–1444), French theologian and philosopher, best known for his defence of Saint Thomas in his Defensiones (4 vols, 1409–32).

Capuana, Luigi (1839–1915), Italian novelist, short-story writer, dramatist and critic.

Caragiale, Ion Luca (1852–1912), Romanian dramatist and short-story writer.

Carducci, Giosuè (1835–1907), prominent Italian poet and scholar; won the Nobel Prize for Literature (1906).

Carew, Richard (1555–1620), English poet, antiquarian and translator.

Carew, Thomas (c.1594–c.1639), English poet who wrote the finely-crafted A Rapture.

Carey, Henry (c.1687–1743), English poet, dramatist and composer, particularly known for his ballad Sally in Our Alley (1737).

Carey, Henry Charles (1793–1879), American economist and sociologist; son of Matthew Carey.

Carey, Matthew (1760–1839), Irish-born American journalist and writer; father of Henry Charles Carey.

Carey, William (1761–1834), English Baptist missionary, grammarian, lexicographer and translator.

Carleton, Henry Guy (1856–1910), American dramatist, best remembered for his farces.

Carleton, William (1794–1869), Irish novelist and short-story writer.

Carleton, Will(iam McKendree) (1845–1912), American poet who wrote ballads of farm and city life.

Carlile, Richard (1790–1843), English journalist, well known as an advocate of radical causes.

Carlini, Armando (1878–1959), Italian philosopher, author of such books as La vita dello spirito (The Life of the Spirit, 1921), La metafisica di Aristotele (The Metaphysics of Aristotle, 1928), La religiosita dell'arte e della filosofia (The Religiousness of Art and Philosophy, 1934) and Alla ricerca di me stesso (On the Research of Myself, 1951).

Carlyle, Thomas (1795–1881), noted Scottish essayist and historian, author of The French Revolution (1837).

Carman, (William) Bliss (1861–1929), Canadian-born American poet and writer who was esteemed for his love poems.

Carmer, Carl (Lamson) (1893–1976), American writer and editor.

Carnap, Rudolf (1891–1970), German-born American empiricist philospher and logician who wrote such significant books as Der logische Aufbau der Welt (1928; English trans. as The Logical Structure of the World, 1967), Logische Syntax der Sprache (1934; English trans. as The Logical Syntax of Language, 1937), Meaning and Necessity (1947) and Logical Foundations of Probability (1950).

Caro, Annibale (1507–1566), Italian poet, dramatist and translator, particularly known for his Lettere familiare (Familiar Letters, published 1572–74) and translation of Virgil's Aeneid (published 1581).

Carossa, Hans (1878–1956), German novelist and poet, best remembered for his autobiographical novels.

Carpenter, Edward (1844–1929), English Socialist, writer and poet.

Carpentier (y Valmont), Alejo (1904–80), Cuban novelist, journalist, musicologist and government official whose most important work was the novel Los pasos perdidos (1953; English trans. as The Lost Steps, 1956).

Carr, E(dward) H(allett) (1892–1982), English political scientist and historian, author of A History of Soviet Russia (10 vols, 1950–78).

Carr, Emily (1871–1945), Canadian painter and writer.

Carr, John Dickson (1906–77), American writer of detective fiction.

Carranza, Bartolomé de (1503–1576), Spanish Roman Catholic archbishop and theologian who wrote the Quattuor controversiae (Four Controversies, 1546) and Comentarios sobre el catechismo christiano (Commentaries on the Christian Catechism, 1558), the latter causing his imprisonment by the Inquisition (1559–1576).

Carrasquilla, Tomás (1858–1940), Colombian novelist and short-story writer.

Carillo y Sotomayor, Luis (c.1583–1610), Spanish poet, esteemed for his Fábula de Acis y Galatea (published 1611).

Carroll, Lewis (actually Charles Lutwidge Dodgson) (1832–1898), famous English writer, poet, logician and mathematician, celebrated for his nonsense verse and for his classic books Alice's Adventures in Wonderland (1865) and Through the Looking-Glass and What Alice Found There (1871).

Carryl, Charles Edward (1842–1920), American financier, writer and poet; father of Guy Wetmore Carryl.

Carryl, Guy Wetmore (1873–1904), American novelist, short-story writer and poet; son of Charles Edward Carryl.

Carson, Rachel (Louise) (1907–1964), American biologist and writer on science, author of The Sea Around Us (1951) and Silent Spring (1962).

Carter, Angela (Olive née Stalker) (1940–1992), English novelist, poet and essayist.

Carter, Elizabeth (1717–1806), English poet and translator.

Cartland, Dame Barbara (Hamilton) (1901–2000), Prolific English writer of romance novels whose books sold over 1,000m. copies.

Carton de Wiart, Henri (-Victor), Comte (1869–1951), Belgian statesman, jurist, novelist and essayist.

Cartwright, Peter (1785–1872), American Methodist preacher whose career was the subject of his interesting Autobiography (1857), The Backwoods Preacher (1858) and Fifty Years as a Presiding Elder (1871).

Cartwright, William (1611–1643), English preacher, dramatist and poet.

Caruthers, William Alexander (1802–1846), American novelist.

Carver, Jonathan (1710–1780), American explorer who left an account of his explorations in his Travels Through the Interior Parts of North America in the Years 1766, 1767, 1768 (1778).

Carver, Raymond (1938–88), American poet and short-story writer.

Cary, Alice (1820–1871), American poet and writer; sister of Phoebe Cary.

Cary, (Arthur) Joyce (Lunel) (1888–1957), Irish-born English novelist and short-story writer, especially known for his novel trilogies Herself Surprised (1941), To Be a Pilgrim (1942) and The Horse's Mouth (1944) and A Prisoner of Grace (1952), Except the Lord (1953) and Not Honour More (1955).

Cary, Henry Francis (1772–1844), English biographer and translator who became best known for his blank verse translation of Dante's Divine Comedy (1814).

Cary, Pheobe (1824–1871), American poet and hymnist; sister of Alice Cary.

Casa, Giovanni Della (1503–1556), Italian Roman Catholic bishop, poet and translator.

Casal, Julián del (1863–1893), Cuban poet.

Casanova, Giovani Giacomo, Chevalier de Seingalt (1725–1798), outrageous Italian adventurer, writer and poet whose life as a libertine was recounted in his infamous autobiography Histoire de ma vie (English trans. as History of My Life, 1966 et seq.).

Casaubon, Isaac (1559–1614), French-born English scholar who prepared editions of and commentaries on ancient writers.

Case, Shirley Jackson (1872–1947), Canadian-born American theologian, author of Jesus: A New Biography (1927).

Cash, W(ilbur) J(oseph) (1900–41), American journalist and writer, author of The Mind of the South (1941); committed suicide.

Cassill, R(onald) V(erlin) (1919–2002), American novelist, short-story writer and editor.

Cassiodorus (actually Flavius Magnus Aurelius Cassiodorus) (c.490–c.585), Italian monk, statesman and historian.

Cassirer, Ernst (1874–1945), German philosopher who espoused neo-Kantian principles, author of the important study Die Philosophie der symbolischen Formen (3 vols, 1923–29; English trans. as The Philosophy of Symbolic Forms, 1953–57).

Cassola, Carlo (1917–1987), Italian novelist and short-story writer.

Cassou, Jean (1897–1986), French poet, novelist and art critic.

Castaneda, Carlos (1925–1998), Peruvian-born American writer.

Castelar y Ripoll, Emilio (1832–1899), Spanish statesman, novelist and historian.

Castelli, Ignaz Franz (1781–1862), Austrian poet.

Castelo Branco, Camilo (1825–1890), notable Portuguese novelist, particularly remembered for his Amor de Perdicao (Fatal Love, 1862); committed suicide.

Castelvetro, Ludovico (c.1505–1571), Italian scholar, critic and translator, known for his edition of Aristotle's Poetics (1570).

Casti, Giovanni Battista (1724–1803), Italian poet and librettist, particularly remembered for his verse satires Poema tartaro (Tartar Poem, 1787) and Gli animali parlanti (1802; English trans. as The Court and Parliament of Beasts, 1819).

Castiglione, Baldassaré (1478–1529), Italian courtier and diplomat, author of Il libro del cortegiano (1528; English trans. as The Courtyer, 1561).

Castilho, António Feliciano de (1800–1875), esteemed Portuguese poet, critic and translator.

Castillejo, Cristóbal de (c.1490–1550), Spanish poet who wrote the erotic Sermón de amores (1542).

Castillo Solorzano, Alonso de (1584–c.1648), Spanish novelist, short-story writer and dramatist.

Castillo y Saavedra, Antonio del (1616–1668), Spanish painter, sculptor and poet.

Castro, Eugénio de (1869–1944), Portuguese poet who won distinction as his country's leading Symbolist with his Oaristos (1890) and Horas (1891).

Castro, Rosalía de (1837–1885), Spanish poet and novelist in the Galician language, author of the poems Cantares gallegos (1863) and Follas novas (1880), in Galician, and En las orillas del Sar (1884), in Castilian.

Castro Alves, Antônio de (1847–1871), Brazilian poet who espoused the abolitionist cause and thus became known as the 'poet of the slaves'.

Castro y Bellvís, Guillén (1569–1631), Spanish dramatist, best remembered for his Las mocedades del Cid (c.1599).

Cather, Willa (Sibert) (1873–1947), American novelist whose works included O Pioneers! (1913), My Ántonia (1918), One of Ours (1922) and Death Comes for the Archbishop (1927).

Catherwood, Mary (Hartwell) (1847–1902), American writer.

Catlin, George (1796–1872), American artist and writer.

Cato, Marcus Porcius (234–149 BC), eminent Roman statesman, orator and writer who was also known as Cato the Censor and Cato the Elder.

Cato, Publius Valerius (b. c.100 BC), Roman poet and writer.

Cats, Jacob (1577–1660), Dutch statesman and poet, beloved by his countrymen and known as 'Father Cats'.

Cattaneo, Carlo (1801–1869), Italian scholar and writer, a leading figure in the Risorgimento.

Cattell, James McKeen (1860–1944), American psychologist, writer and editor.

Catton, (Charles) Bruce (1899–1978), American historian, especially admired for his Mr Lincoln's Army (1951), Glory Road (1952) and A Stillness at Appomattox (1953).

Catullus, Gaius Valerius (c.84–c.54 BC), celebrated Roman poet, a master of lyric verse whose love poems and satirical works are exemplary.

Cauldwell, Sarah (1939–2000), English novelist who won wide success with her well-crafted mysteries.

Cavafy, Constantine (actually Konstantínos Pétrou Kaváfis) (1863–1933), noted Greek poet whose output reflected his stance as a skeptic.

Cavalcanti, Guido (c.1255–1300), Italian poet, esteemed for his love poems and ballads.

Cavendish, George (c.1499–c.1561), English biographer who wrote The Life and Death of Cardinal Wolsey (published 1641).

Cawein, Madison (Julius) (1865–1914), American poet.

Caxton, William (c.1422–1491), significant English publisher and translator.

Caylus, Anne-Claude-Phillipe de Tubières, Comte de (1692–1765), French archaeologist, engraver and writer.

Cecco d'Ascoli (actually Francesco Stabili) (1269–1327), Italian astrologer, poet and writer; was condemned as a heretic and burned at the stake.

Cecil, Lord (Edward Christian) David Gascoyne (1902–1986), English critic and biographer.

Cela (Trulock), Camilo José (1916–2002), Spanish novelist, poet and essayist, author of La familia de Pascual Duarte (1942); won the Nobel Prize for Literature (1989).

Celan, Paul (actually Paul Antschel) (1920–1970), Romanian-born French poet who won considerable distinction in Germany after World War II; committed suicide.

Céline, Louis Ferdinand (actually Loius-Ferdinand Destouches) (1894–1961), French novelist who secured his reputation with his Voyage au bout de la nuit (1932; English trans. as Journey to the End of Night, 1934).

Cellini, Benvenuto (1500–1571), famous Italian sculptor, goldsmith and writer, author of a celebrated autobiography (1730).

Celsus, Aulus Cornelius (1st Century), Roman writer on medicine, author of the famous De medicina (English trans., 1945–48).

Celtis or Celtes, Conradus (German name Conrad Pickel) (1459–1508), German scholar and poet who was known as Der Erzhumanist (The Archumanist).

Cendrars, Blaise (actually Frédéric Louis Sauser) (1887–1961), Swiss novelist and poet, author of such poems as Les Pâques à New York (Easter in New York, 1912) and La prose du Transsiberien et de la petite Jehanne de France (The Prose of the Trans-Siberian and of Little Jehanne of France, 1913).

Centlivre, Susannah (1669–1723), English actress and dramatist.

Cervantes (Saavedra), Miguel de (1547–1616), Spanish novelist, short-story writer, dramatist and poet, author of the novel Don Quixote de la Mancha (2 parts, 1605, 1615), one of the supreme masterpieces of world literature.

Cesarotti, Melchiorre (1730–1808), Italian poet, critic, essayist and translator.

Céspedes, Pablo de (1538–1608), Spanish poet, writer, painter, sculptor and architect.

Céspedes y Meneses, Gonzalo de (c.1585–1638), Spanish writer, author of Poema Trágica del Español Gerardo, y Desengaño del Amor Lasciuo (1615–17; English trans. as Gerardo the Unfortunate Spaniard, or a Patterne for Lasciuious Lovers, 1622).

Cetina, Gutierre de (c.1520–c.1557), Spanish poet who wrote the notable Ojos claros.

Ceva, Tommaso (1648–1737), Italian mathematician and poet, author of the poem Jesus Puer (Child Jesus, 1690).

Cevdet Paşa, Ahmed (1822–1895), Turkish statesman, historian and poet.

Chaadaiev, Pietr Yakovlevich (c.1794–1856), Russian writer who wrote a biting critical assessment of Russian history and culture in his Lettres Philosophiques (Philosophical Letters, 1827–31).

Chacel, Rosa (Clotilde Cecilia María del Carmen) (1898–1994), Spanish novelist and poet.

Chadwick, H(ector) Munro (1870–1947), English philologist and historian.

Chafee, Zechariah, Jr (1885–1957), American legal scholar and champion of civil liberties, author of Free Speech in the United States (1941).

Chalcocondyles or Chalcondyles, Laonicus (c.1423–c.1490), Byzantine historian who wrote the important Historiarum demonstrationes.

Chalkhill, John (died 1642), English poet, author of Thealma and Clearchus (published 1683).

Challoner, Richard (1691–1781), English Roman Catholic churchman who wrote The Garden of the Soul (1740), a revision of the Reims-Douai version of the Bible (1749–50) and Meditations for Every Day of the Year (1753).

Chalmers, Alexander (1759–1834), noted Scottish editor and biographer.

Chalmers, George (1742–1825), Scottish lawyer, historian and antiquarian.

Chalmers, Thomas (1780–1847), Scottish Presbyterian preacher, theologian, social reformer and writer, author of On the Adaptation of External Nature to the Moral and Intellectual Constitution of Man (1833).

Chamberlain, Houston Stewart (1855–1927), English-born German political philosopher and writer on music who espoused Pan-German ideas of Aryan national and racial superiority.

Chamberlayne, William (1619–1689), English physician and poet, author of Love's Victory (1658), Pharonnida (1659) and England's Jubilee (1660).

Chambers, Sir E(dmund) K(erchever) (1866–1954), English literary scholar and biographer.

Chambers, Ephraim (c.1680–1740), English encyclopedist who published the Cyclopaedia, or Universal Dictionary of Arts and Sciences (1728).

Chambers, R(aymond) W(ilson) (1874–1942), English literary scholar.

Chambers, Robert (1802–1871), Scottish publisher and writer, co-founder with his brother William (1800–1883) of W and R Chambers Ltd.

Chamfort, Sébastien-Roch Nicolas (1740–1794), French dramatist and writer who won renown for his wit; was a victim of the Reign of Terror.

Chamisso, Adelbert von (actually Louis-Charles-Adélaïde Chamisso de Boncourt) (1781–1838), important French-born German poet, writer and scientist, author of Frauenliebe und Leben (Women's Love and Life), set to music by Robert Schumann, and the story Peter Schlemihls wundersame Geschichte (1814; English trans. as Peter Schlemihl's Remarkable Story, 1927).

Champfleury (actually Jules-François-Félix Husson) (1821–1889), French novelist and journalist who was an exponent of Realism.

Champollion, Jean-François (1790–1832), significant French historian and linguist, the founder of scientific Egyptology and a pioneering figure in the elucidation of Egyptian hieroglyphics; brother of Jacques-Joseph Champollion-Figeac.

Champollion-Figeac, Jacques-Joseph (1778–1867), French librarian, paleographer and historian; brother of Jean-François Champollion.

Chandler, Elizabeth Margaret (1807–1834), American poet who championed the antislavery cause in verse.

Chandler, Raymond (Thornton) (1888–1959), American writer who created the private detective Philip Marlowe.

Chang Ping-lin (1868–1936), Chinese Nationalist revolutionary, Confucian scholar, writer and poet.

Chang Tsai (1020–1077), Chinese philosopher, author of the Cheng-meng (Correct Discipline for Beginners).

Chang Tzu-p'ing (1893–c.1947), Chinese writer.

Channing, Edward (1856–1931), American historian whose major work was the History of the United States (6 vols, 1905–25).

Channing, William Ellery (1780–1842), prominent American clergyman, social reformer and writer, known as the 'apostle of Unitarianism'; uncle of William Ellery and William Henry Channing.

Channing, William Ellery (1818–1901), American poet of the Transcendentalist school; nephew of William Ellery Channing.

Channing, William Henry (1810–1884), American Christian Socialist, editor and writer; nephew of William Ellery Channing the elder.

Chapais, Sir (Joseph Amable) Thomas (1858–1946), Canadian lawyer, public official and historian.

Chapelain, Jean (1595–1674), French critic and poet.

Chaplin, Sid(ney) (1916–86), English novelist and short-story writer.

Chapman, George (c.1559–1634), English dramatist, poet and translator, known for his translations of Homer's Iliad (1598–1611) and Odyssey (1616), and for the poem Euthymiae and Raptus, or The Teares of Peace (1609).

Chapman, John Jay (1862–1933), American poet, dramatist and critic who was active as a political reformer.

Chapone, Hester (née Mulso) (1727–1801), English writer.

Char, René (1907–1988), esteemed French poet who wrote finely-crafted verse of an economical austerity.

Charbonneau, Jean (1875–1960), French-Canadian poet, translator and lawyer.

Chariton (2nd Century), Greek writer who wrote the novel Chaereas and Callirhoe.

Charles, Duc d'Orléans (1394–1465), French poet of both French and English verse.

Charnay, Claude-Joseph-Désiré (1828–1915), French explorer and archaeologist, author of Les Anciennes Villes du Nouveau Monde (1885; English trans. as The Ancient Cities of the New World, 1887).

Charriére, Isabelle Agnès Élizabeth de (1740–1805), Dutch-born Swiss novelist, particularly remembered for her Lettres neuchâteloises (1784) and Caliste, ou lettres écrites de Lausanne (1786).

Charron, Pierre (1541–1603), important French Roman Catholic theologian who espoused a form of Skepticism in his Les Trois Vérités (The Three Truths, 1593) and De la sagesse (1601; English trans. as On Wisdom, 1697).

Charteris, Leslie (actually Leslie Charles Bowyer Yin) (1907–1993), Chinese-English novelist who created Simon Templar or the Saint, the chief figure in a long and successful series of mystery-adventure novels.

Chartier, Alain (c.1385–c.1433), French poet, writer and courtier, best known for his La Belle Dame sans merci and Livre des quatre dames (c.1415).

Chase, Mary Coyle (1907–1981), American dramatist whose best known play was Harvey (1944).

Chase, Mary Ellen (1887–1973), American novelist and scholar, especially admired for her novels Mary Peters (1934) and Silas Crockett (1935).

Chasles, (Victor-Euphémien-) Philarète (1798–1873), French scholar and writer.

Chassignet, Jean-Baptiste (1578–1620), French poet.

Chastellain, Georges (c.1410–1475), Burgundian historian, essayist, dramatist and poet, author of the history Chronique des ducs de Bourgogne.

Chateaubriand (actually François-René de Chateaubriand, Vicomte de (1768–1848), prominent French writer and statesman, esteemed for his prose epics and his autobiography Mémoires d'outre-tombe (Memoirs from Beyond the Tomb).

Châtalet, Gabrielle-Émile Le Tonnelier de Breteuil, Marquise du (1706–1749), French philosopher and scientist who wrote Institutions de physique (Institutions of Physics, 1740), Response à lettre de Mairan sur la question des forces vives (Response to Mairan's Letter on the Question of Vital Forces, 1741) and Dissertation sur la nature et la propagation du feu (Dissertation on the Nature and Propagation of Fire, 1744).

Chatterjee, Bankim Chandra or Bankim-Chandra Cattopadhyay (1838–1894), important Indian novelist, especially esteemed for his Krishnakanter Uil (1878).

Chatterton, Thomas (1752–1770), gifted English poet who wrote the 'Rowley' poems, forgeries he attributed to a mythical 15th Century monk he dubbed Thomas Rowley; committed suicide.

Chatwin, (Charles) Bruce (1940–1989), English traveller and writer.

Chaucer, Geoffrey (c.1343–1400), English poet, celebrated throughout the world for his masterpieces Troilus and Criseyde and The Canterbury Tales.

Chaudhuri, Nirad Chandra (1897–1999), Indian writer, author of The Autobiography of an Unknown Indian (1951), A Passage to England (1959) and Thy Hand, Great Anarch (1987).

Chauncy, Charles (1705–1787), American clergyman and writer who espoused Universalism in the last years of his career.

Chayefsky, Paddy (1923–1981), American dramatist whose Marty (1953) was a pioneering effort in television drama.

Cheever, John (1912–1982), American novelist and short-story writer.

Chekov, Anton (Pavlovich) (1860–1904), famous Russian short-story writer and dramatist.

Chelčický, Peter (c.1390–c.1460), Czech writer on religious and political subjects whose Sít Víry (Net of the Faith, 1440) led to the blossoming of the religious sect of the Bohemian Brethren.

Chemnitz or Kemnitz, Martin (1522–1586), German Protestant churchman and theologian.

Cheng Chen-to (1898–1958), Chinese literary historian; died in an airplane crash.

Cheng Ch'iao (1108–1166), notable Chinese historian, author of T'ung chih (General Treatises).

Chénier, André (-Marie) de (1762–1794), illustrious French poet author of Hermes, L'Invention and Suzanne; was guillotined at the close of the Reign of Terror; brother of Marie-Joseph-Blaise de Chénier.

Chénier, Marie-Joseph-Blaise de (1764–1811), French poet, dramatist and politician; brother of André (Marie) de Chénier.

Chernyshevsky, Nikolai Gavrilovich (1828–1889), Russian journalist and writer.

Chéruel, (Pierre-) Adolphe (1809–1891), French historian who wrote the valuable Histoire de France pendant la minorité de Louis XIV (History of France During the Youth of Louis XIV, 4 vols, 1879–1880) and Histoire de France sous le ministère de Mazarin, 1651–1661 (History of France Under the Ministry of Mazarin, 1651–1661, 3 vols, 1882).

Chesnut, Mary Boykin (Miller) (1823–1886), American diarist whose diary was published as A Diary from Dixie (1905; complete text, 1981).

Chesnutt, Charles W(addell) (1858–1932), American novelist, short-story writer and essayist.

Chester, George Randolph (1869–1924), American journalist and writer, particularly remembered for his Get-Rich-Quick Wallingford (1908).

Chesterfield, Philip Dormer Stanhope, 4th Earl of (1694–1773), English statesman and diplomat who wrote the celebrated Letters to His Son and Letters to His Godson.

Chesterton, G(ilbert) K(eith) (1874–1936), famous English critic, novelist, short-story writer, essayist and poet, creator of the detective-priest Father Brown.

Chettle, Henry (c.1560–c.1607), English dramatist and pamphleteer.

Chevalier, Jules (1824–1907), French Roman Catholic priest and writer, founder of the Missionarii Sacratissimi Cordis Jesu (Missionaries of the Sacred Heart of Jesus).

Chevalier, Ulysse (1841–1923), French Roman Catholic priest and scholar who prepared valuable bibliographical works on medieval history.

Cheyney, Peter (actually Reginald Evelyn Peter Southouse-Cheyney) (1896–1951), English writer and poet, author of crime novels.

Chiabrera, Gabriello (1552–1638), Italian poet who introduced the poetical epistle to his homeland in his Lettere Famigliari.

Ch'i Ju-shan (1876–1962), Chinese dramatist and scholar.

Chikamatsu Monzaemon (actually Sugimori Nobumori) (1653–1724), Japanese dramatist.

Child, Francis J(ames) (1825–1896), American literary scholar.

Child, Lydia Maria (née Francis) (1802–1880), American writer, reformer and Abolitionist.

Childe, V(ere) Gordon (1892–1957), Australian prehistorian who wrote the important studies The Dawn of European Civilization (1925) and The Danube in Prehistory (1929).

Childers, Robert Erskine (1870–1922), Irish nationalist and writer, author of the spy story The Riddle of the Sands (1903); his republican sympathies led to his execution.

Chillingworth, William (1602–1644), English theologian who wrote The Religion of the Protestants a safe way to Salvation (1637).

Chivers, Thomas Holley (1809–1858), American poet, writer and dramatist.

Chocano, José Santos (1875–1934), Peruvian revolutionary and poet who espoused the cause of South American nationalism; was murdered by a former friend.

Choerilus (5th Century BC), Greek poet.

Choniates, Michael (c.1140–c.1222), Byzantine archbishop and scholar.

Choniates, Nicetas (c.1140–1213), notable Byzantine statesman, historian and theologian.

Chopin, Kate (née O'Flaherty) (1850–1904), American writer, poet and essayist.

Choromański, Michał (1904–72), Polish novelist and dramatist.

Chou Tun-i (1017–1073), important Chinese philosopher who was also known as Chou Lien-Hsi, founder of the Neo-Confucian school.

Chrétien de Troyes (12th Century), celebrated French poet, inventor of the courtly romance.

Christie, Dame Agatha (Mary Clarissa née Miller) (1890–1976), famous English novelist and dramatist, renowned as a writer of mysteries.

Christine de Pisan (1364–c.1430), gifted Italian poet, writer and translator.

Chrysander, (Karl Franz) Friedrich (1826–1901), German music scholar and editor.

Chrysippus (c.280–c.206 BC), Greek philosopher.

Chrysoloras, Manuel (c.1353–1415), Greek scholar and translator.

Chrysostom, Saint John (c.347–407), Greek Roman Catholic preacher, archbishop and writer, author of commentaries on New Testament writings.

Chubb, Thomas (1679–1747), English writer of Deist tracts.

Chu Hsi (1130–1200), Chinese philosopher, author of the Ssu shu (Four Books).

Chulkov, Mikhail Dmitrievich (c.1743–1792), Russian novelist.

Chumnus, Nicephorus (1250–1327), Byzantine stateman and scholar.

Church, Benjamin (1734–1776), American writer of political essays.

Church, Richard (Thomas) (1893–1972), English poet, novelist and essayist.

Churchill, Charles (1731–1764), English poet, best known for The Apology (1761) and The Rosciad (1761).

Churchill, Randolph Frederick Edward Spencer (1911–1968), English journalist and writer; son of Sir Winston (Leonard Spencer) Churchill.

Churchill, Winston (1871–1947), American novelist, author of such works as Richard Carvel (1899), The Crisis (1901), and The Crossing (1904).

Churchill, Sir Winston (Leonard Spencer) (1874–1965), English statesman, orator amd writer who wrote histories of World War II and of the English-speaking peoples; won the Nobel Prize for Literature (1953); father of Randolph Frederick Edward Spencer Churchill.

Churchyard, Thomas (c.1520–1604), English writer and poet.

Ch'ü Yüan (c.343–c.289 BC), illustrious Chinese poet.

Ciardi, John (Anthony) (1916–1985), American poet, essayist and translator.

Cibber, Colley (1671–1757), prominent English poet, dramatist, actor and theatre manager, best known for his sentimental comedies; became Poet Laureate of the United Kingdom (1730); father of Theophilus Cibber.

Cibber, Theophilus (1703–1758), English actor and dramatist; son of Colley Cibber.

Cicero, (Marcus Tullius) (106–43 BC), Roman statesman, orator, scholar and writer.

Cieza de León, (Pedro de) (1518–1560), Spanish historian, author of the valuable Crónica del Perú.

Cigoli, Ludovico (Cardi da) (1559–1613), Italian painter, architect and poet.

Cinna, Gaius Helvius (1st Century BC), Roman poet who wrote the epic Smyrna.

Cinnamus, John (12th Century), Byzantine historian.

Cino da Pistoia (actually Cino dei Sighibuldi) (c.1270–c.1336), Italian jurist, poet and writer.

Claes, Ernest (André Jozef) (1885–1968), Flemish novelist and short-story writer.

Clampitt, Amy (1920–1994), American poet.

Clanvowe, Sir John (died 1391), English diplomat, courtier and poet, author of The Two Ways.

Clapp, Henry (1814–1875), American journalist and writer who wrote under the name Figaro.

Clare, Ada (actually Jane McElheney) (1836–1874), American poet, writer and actress.

Clare, John (1793–1864), English poet, author of Poems Descriptive of Rural Life and Scenery (1820), The Shepherd's Calendar, with Village Stories, and Other Poems (1827), and The Rural Muse (1835).

Clarendon, Edward Hyde, 1st Earl of (1609–1674), English statesman and historian who wrote the History of the Rebellion and Civil Wars in England.

Clark, Alan (Kenneth McKenzie) (1928–99), English historian and politician, especially remembered for his provocative Diaries (1993).

Clark, Charles Heber (1841–1915), American journalist, novelist and short-story writer who wrote under the name Max Adeler.

Clark, Francis Edward (1851–1927), American Congregational clergyman and writer.

Clark, John Bates (1847–1938), American economist, author of the Philosophy of Wealth (1886) and The Distribution of Wealth (1899).

Clark, Kenneth Mackenzie, Lord (1903–1983), English art historian and writer.

Clark, Lewis Gaylord (1808–1873), American magazine editor and writer, author of Knick-Knacks from an Editor's Table (1852); brother of Willis Gaylord Clark.

Clark, Walter van Tilburg (1909–1971), American novelist and short-story writer, best remembered for his novel The Ox-Bow Incident (1940).

Clark, Willis Gaylord (1808–1841), American magazine editor and writer; brother of Lewis Gaylord Clark.

Clarke, Austin (1896–1974), Irish poet and dramatist.

Clarke, Charles Cowden (1787–1877), English editor and critic; husband of Mary Victoria Cowden Clarke.

Clarke, James Freeman (1810–1888), American Unitarian minister, theologian, writer and editor.

Clarke, Marcus (Andrew Hislop) (1846–1881), English-born Australian novelist and short-story writer, particularly known for his novel For the Term of His Natural Life (1874).

Clarke, Mary Victoria Cowden (1809–1898), English editor and critic; wife of Charles Cowden Clarke.

Clarke, McDonald (1798–1842), American poet, dubbed the 'mad poet of Broadway', author of the collection Elixir of Moonshine by the Mad Poet (1822).

Clarke, Samuel (1675–1729), prominent English theologian and philosopher who expounded rational theological views in such vols as A Demonstration of the Being and Attributes of God (1705), A Discourse Concerning the Unchangeable Obligations of Natural Religion (1706) and Scripture Doctrine of the Trinity (1712).

Clarkson, Laurence (1615–1667), English religious pamphleteer, author of the autobiography The Lost Sheep Found (1660).

Clauberg, Johann (1622–1665), German philosopher and theologian who wrote such important works as Defensio Cartesiana (1652), Initatio philosophi (1655), Exercitationes centum de cognitione Dei et nostri (One Hundred Exercises on the Knowledge of God and Ourselves, 1656) and Corporis et animae in homine conjunctio (On the Joining of the Body and Soul in Man, 1663).

Claudel, Paul (-Louis-Charles-Marie) (1868–1955), French poet, essayist and dramatist, author of Cinq Grandes Odes (1910) and the play Le Soulier de satin (1924; English trans. as The Satin Slipper, 1931).

Claudian (actually Claudius Claudianus) (c.370–c.404), Roman poet who was celebrated for his epic verse.

Claudius, Matthias (1740–1815), German poet and editor, known for his Der Mond ist aufgegangen (The Moon has Risen).

Clausewitz, Carl von (1780–1831), notable German general and military strategist, author of the celebrated Von Kriege (On War).

Claussen, Sophus (Niels Christen) (1865–1931), Danish poet and writer, a leading figure in the Symbolist movement.

Clavell, James (1924–1994), English-born American novelist and screenwriter, author of such novels as Tai-Pan (1966), Shogun (1975) and Noble House (1981).

Clavell, John (1603–1642), English highwayman who wrote the metrical autobiography Recantation of an ill led life (1628).

Clavijo y Fajardo, José (1730–1806), Spanish naturalist, writer and editor.

Cleland, John (1709–1789), English journalist, dramatist and writer, author of the pornographic novel Fanny Hill, or, Memoirs of a Woman of Pleasure (1748–49).

Cleland, William (c.1661–1689), Scottish poet; died defending Dunkeld against the Jacobite rebels.

Clemens, Jeremiah (1814–1865), American novelist.

Clement of Alexandria, Saint (c.150–c.213), prominent Greek Roman Catholic theologian.

Clemo, Jack (actually Reginald John Clemo) (1916–1994), English poet and writer.

Clermont-Ganneau, Charles (1846–1923), French biblical archaeologist who was known for his Études d'archéologie orientale (Studies in Eastern Archaeology, 2 vols, 1880, 1897).

Cleveland, John (1613–1658), noted English poet, known for his Royalist verse.

Clifford, Sir Hugh Charles (1866–1941), English civil servant and writer.

Clifford, John (1836–1923), English Baptist minister, social reformer and writer.

Clifford, William Kingdon (1845–1879), English mathematician and philosopher.

Clifford, William (1772–1799), American poet.

Clive, Caroline Archer (1801–1873), English novelist and poet, particularly known for her novel Paul Ferroll (1855); died in a fire.

Clough, Arthur Hugh (1819–1861), English poet who wrote such admired works as The Bothie or Tober-na-Vuolich (1848), Amours de Voyage (1858) and Dipsychus (published 1865).

Coates, Robert M(yron) (1897–1973), American novelist and short-story writer.

Coatsworth, Elizabeth (Jane) (1893–1986), American poet and writer.

Cobb, Irving S(hrewsbury) (1876–1944), American journalist and writer who became best known for his humorous output.

Cobb, Joseph B(eckham) (1819–1858), American writer.

Cobb, Sylvanus Jr (1823–1887), American novelist and short-story writer.

Cobbett, William (1763–1835), English journalist and writer.

Cocceius, Johannes (1603–1669), German Reformed Church theologian and biblical scholar.

Cochlaeus, Johannes (1479–1552), German Roman Catholic priest and theologian who became one of the principal opponents of Lutheranism.

Cockburn, Alicia or Alison (née Rutherford) (1713–1794), Scottish poet, author of The Flowers of the Forest.

Cockburn, Catharine (née Trotter) (1679–1749), English dramatist, poet and writer.

Cocteau, Jean (1889–1963), famous French poet, librettist, novelist, critic, actor, film director and painter.

Codrington, R(obert) H(enry) (1830–1922), English Anglican priest and anthropologist.

Coffin, Charles Carleton (1823–1896), American journalist and writer.

Coffin, Henry Sloane (1877–1954), American Presbyterian minister, educator and writer.

Coffin, Robert P(eter) T(ristram) (1892–1955), American poet and writer.

Coggleshall, William Turner (1824–1867), American journalist, critic and writer.

Cohen, Hermann (1842–1918), German philosopher.

Cohen, Matt (1942–99), Canadian novelist and short-story writer.

Cohen, Morris Raphael (1880–1947), American philosopher.

Cohen, Octavus Roy (1891–1959), American writer.

Coke, Sir Edward (1552–1634), English jurist and politician who wrote on legal subjects.

Coke, Thomas (1747–1814), English Methodist bishop and writer.

Colden, Cadwallader (1688–1776), Scottish-born American politician and writer on various subjects, including the History of the Five Indian Nations (1727), Explication of the First Causes of Action in Matter, and, of the Causes of Gravitation (1745) and on philosophy, science and medicine in Plantae Coldenghamiae (1749, 1751).

Cole, Fay-Cooper (1881–1961), American anthropologist.

Cole, G(eorge) D(ouglas) H(oward) (1889–1959), English economist, author of A History of Socialist Thought (1953–58).

Cole, Thomas (1801–1848), English-born American writer and poet.

Colenso, John William (1814–1883), English Anglican bishop and mathematician who became highly controversial for his liberal religious views.

Coleridge, (David) Hartley (1796–1849), English poet and writer, particularly esteemed for his sonnets; son of Samuel Taylor Coleridge.

Coleridge, Mary (1861–1907), English poet, novelist and essayist whose sonnets were much admired; great-great-niece of Samuel Taylor Coleridge.

Coleridge, Samuel Taylor (1772–1834), renowned English poet and critic, celebrated for the originality and beauty revealed in such poems as Ode to France (1796), The Rime of the Ancient Mariner (1798), Ode to Dejection (1802), Christabel (1816) and Kubla Khan (1816), and for the insight he brought to his literary criticism in his Biographia Literaria (1817); father of Sara Coleridge.

Coleridge, Sara (1802–1852), English translator, editor, writer and poet; daughter of Samuel Taylor Coleridge.

Colet, John (c.1466–1519), English theologian and scholar.

Colet, Louise (née Revoil) (1810–1876), French poet and novelist, particularly known for her novel Lui (Him, 1859).

Colette, (Sidonie-Gabrielle) (1873–1954), famous French novelist.

Collett, Camilla (née Wergeland) (1813–1895), Norwegian novelist who wrote the notably successful Amtmandens dottre (The Governor's Daughter, 1855).

Collier, Arthur (1680–1732), English philosopher and theologian, author of the Clavis Universalis (Universal Key, 1713), A Specimen of True Philosophy (1730) and Logology (1732).

Collier, Jeremy (1650–1726), English nonjuring bishop who became best known for his attack on the contemporary theatre in his Short View of the Immorality and Profaneness of the English Stage (1698).

Collier, John (1708–1786), English poet who wrote satirical and humorous verse under the name Tim Bobbin.

Collingwood, R(obin) G(eorge) (1889–1943), English historian and philosopher who wrote such works as Speculum Mentis (1924), The Archaeology of Roman Britain (1930), Essay on Philosophical Method (1933), An Essay on Metaphysics (1940) and The Idea of History (published 1946).

Collins, Anthony (1676–1729), English philosopher whose most important work was A Discourse of Free-thinking (1713).

Collins, William (1721–1759), English poet who revealed a special talent for lyrical expression.

Collins, (William) Wilkie (1824–1889), English writer, a master of the mystery-story genre, whose notable works included The Woman in White (1860) and The Moonstone (1868).

Collis, John Stewart (1900–1984), English writer and biographer.

Collitz, Hermann (1855–1935), German-born American linguist who was known for his studies on Indo-European languages.

Colluthus of Lycopolis (6th Century), Greek poet.

Colman, Benjamin (1673–1747), American clergyman and poet.

Colman, George, the Elder (1732–1794), English dramatist and theatre manager, best remembered for his comedies; father of George Colman the Younger.

Colman, George, the Younger (1762–1836), English dramatist, poet and theatre manager, particularly successful with his comic play John Bull (1803); son of George Colman the Elder.

Colonna, Vittoria (1492–1547), Italian poet.

Colton, John (1889–1946), American dramatist.

Colton, Walter (1797–1851), American writer.

Colum, Padraic (1881–1972), Irish poet, dramatist and writer.

Columban or Columbanus, Saint (c.543–615), Irish Roman Catholic abbot, missionary, writer and poet.

Columbus, Samuel (1642–1679), Swedish poet and writer.

Columella, Lucius Junius Moderatus (1st Century), Roman soldier and farmer who wrote De re rustica (12 vols).

Colvin, Sir Sidney (1845–1927), English literary and art critic.

Colwin, Laurie E (1944–1992), American novelist and short-story writer.

Combe, William (1741–1823), English writer and poet, author of the poem Tour of Dr Syntax in Search of the Picturesque (1812).

Comenius, John Amos (actually Jan Ámos Komenský) (1592–1670), Moravian educational reformer and religious leader, author of the influential Janua Linguarum Reserata (1631; English trans. as The Gates of Tongues Unlocked and Opened, 1637).

Comestor, Petrus (died 1179), French writer, author of the Historia Scholastica.

Comfort, Alex(ander) (1920–2000), English physician, writer and poet, author of the celebrated guide to sex The Joy of Sex (1972).

Commager, Henry Steele (1902–1998), prominent American historian and educator.

Commynes, Philippe de (c.1447–1511), French statesman and chronicler who wrote the notable Mémoires (published 1524).

Compagni, Dino (c.1255–1324), Italian public official and historian, author of a valuable history of Florence Cronica delle cose occorrenti ne' tempi suoi (published 1726).

Compton-Burnett, Dame Ivy (1884–1969), esteemed English novelist.

Comte, (Isidore-) Auguste (-Marie-François-Xavier) (1798–1857), French philosopher who founded sociology and Positivism, author of the Cours de philosophie positive (6 vols, 1830–42) and the Système de politique positive (4 vols, 1851–54).

Condillac, Étienne Bonnot de (1715–1780), influential French philosopher, logician, psychologist, economist and writer who wrote such important works as Essai sur l'origine des connaissances humaines (Essay on the Origin of Human Knowledge, 1746) and Traité des sensations (Treatise on Sensation, 1754).

Condon, Richard (Thomas) (1915–1996), American novelist.

Condorcet, (Marie-Jean-Antoine-Nicolas de Caritat), Marquis de (1743–1794), French philosopher and educational reformer whose most important work was the Esquisse d'un tableau historique des progrès de l'esprit humain (Sketch for a Historical Picture of the Progress of the Human Mind, published 1795).

Confucius (actually K'ung Ch'iu) (551–479 BC), Chinese philosopher, political theorist, teacher and writer who is know in China as K'ung-Fu-Tzu, K'ung-Tzu and Chung-Ni; grandfather of Tzu Ssu.

Congreve, Richard (1818–1899), English philosopher and writer who founded the Church of Humanity on positivist principles.

Congreve, William (1670–1729), English dramatist and poet, especially esteemed for his plays The Old Bachelor (1691), The Double Dealer (1693), Love for Love (1695) and The Way of the World (1700).

Conkling, Grace Hazard (1878–1958), American poet who surveyed the beauty of nature.

Connelly, Marc(us Cook) (1890–1980), American journalist and dramatist, best remembered for his play Green Pastures (1930), based on Roark Bradford's Ol' Man Adam an' His Chillun.

Connolly, Cyril (Vernon) (1903–1974), English critic, essayist and writer.

Connor, Ralph (actually Charles William Gordon) (1860–1937), Canadian Presbyterian minister and novelist.

Conrad, Joseph (actually Józef Teodor Konrad Korzeniowski) (1857–1924), prominent Polish-born English novelist and short-story writer, author of such works as Lord Jim (1900), Nostromo (1904), The Secret Agent (1907) and Under Western Eyes (1911).

Conrart, Valentin (1603–1675), French grammarian and one of the principal figures of the Académie Française.

Conroy, Jack (actually John Wesley Conroy) (1899–1990), American novelist and editor.

Conscience, Hendrik (1812–1883), Flemish novelist, one of the masters of Flemish romanticism.

Considerant, Victor-Prosper (1808–1893), French Socialist theoretician, editor and writer, author of Destinee sociale (1834–38).

Constable, Henry (1562–1613), English poet who was known for his sonnets.

Constant (de Rebecque), (Henri-) Benjamin (1767–1830), Swiss-born French novelist and political writer, best known for his novels Adolphe (1816) and Cecile (1951).

Contarini, Gasparo (1483–1542), Italian Roman Catholic cardinal, theologian, scholar and diplomat who advocated church reform and dialogue with the Lutherans.

Conway, Anne Finch, Viscountess (1631–1679), English philosopher of the metaphysical school.

Conway, Moncure Daniel (1832–1907), American Unitarian minister, Abolitionist and writer, author of the Life of Thomas Paine (2 vols, 1892) and an Autobiography (1904).

Conwell, Russell Herman (1843–1925), American lawyer, Baptist minister, educator, writer and lecturer.

Cook, Ebenezer (18th Century), American poet who wrote the satirical The Sot-Weed Factor.

Cook, Eliza (1818–1889), English poet.

Cook, George Cram (1873–1924), American novelist, dramatist and poet; husband of Susan Glaspell.

Cook, Mark (1933–1994), English-born Canadian dramatist.

Cooke, John Esten (1830–1886), American novelist and short-story writer; brother of Philip Pendleton Cooke.

Cooke, Philip Pendleton (1816–1850), American poet and critic who wrote the poem Florence Vane (1840); brother of John Esten Cooke.

Cooke, Rose (née Terry) (1827–1892), American writer and poet.

Cookson, Dame Catherine (Ann) (1906–1998), English novelist.

Coolbrith, Ina (Donna) (1842–1928), American poet who became known for her lyric sentiment.

Cooley, Charles Horton (1864–1929), American sociologist, author of Human Nature and the Social Order (1902), Social Organization (1909) and Social Process (1918).

Coolidge, William Augustus Brevoort (1850–1926), American historian and mountaineer.

Coomaraswamy, Ananda Kentish (1877–1947), Ceylonese-English historian of the fine arts of India.

Cooper, Giles (Stannus) (1918–1966), Irish dramatist who won notable success for his radio and television plays.

Cooper, James Fenimore (1789–1851), American novelist who wrote the classic Leatherstocking Tales in The Pioneers (1823), The Last of the Mohicans (1826), The Prairie (1827), The Pathfinder (1840) and The Deerslayer (1841); father of Susan Fenimore Cooper.

Cooper, John M(ontgomery) (1881–1949), American Roman Catholic priest, ethnologist and sociologist.

Cooper, Myles (1735–1785), English-born American Anglican clergyman, educator and writer whose Loyalist writings forced him to return to England in 1775.

Cooper, Peter (1791–1883), American inventor, financier and philanthropist who wrote Ideas for a Science of Good Government (1883).

Cooper, Susan Fenimore (1813–1894), American writer; daughter of James Fenimore Cooper.

Cooper, Thomas (c.1517–1594), English bishop and writer.

Cooper, Thomas (1759–1839), English-born American scholar and educator, particularly remembered for his political pamphlets and Political Essays (1799).

Cooper, Thomas (1805–1892), English writer and poet who espoused the Chartist cause in his verse epic The Purgatory of Suicides (1843–44), written during his imprisonment for sedition.

Coornhert, Dirk Volkertszoon (1522–1590), Dutch poet, dramatist, writer and translator.

Copernicus, Nicolaus (1473–1543), Polish astronomer whose De Revolutionbus (1543) proposed the theory that the earth and other planets move in orbits around the sun, a theory which eventually supplanted the Ptolemaic geocentric theory.

Coppard, A(lfred) E(dgar) (1878–1957), English short-story writer and poet.

Coppée, François (1842–1908), French poet, writer and dramatist, author of the poetry collection Les Humbles (1872).

Copway, George (1818–c.1863), American Ojibway Indian chief, Wesleyan missionary and writer.

Corbet, Richard (1582–1635), English Anglican bishop and poet.

Corbett, Sir Julian Stafford (1854–1922), English naval historian.

Corbière, Tristan (actually Edouard Joachim Corbière) (1845–1875), French poet who excelled in realist verse.

Corbusier, Le (actually Charles-Édouard Jeanneret) (1887–1965), celebrated French architect, city planner, painter, sculptor and writer.

Cordemoy, Geraud de (c.1620–1684), French historian and philosopher.

Cordemoy, J-L de (1631–1731), French abbot and writer.

Cordovero, Moses ben Jacob (1522–1570), renowned Jewish rabbi and philosopher of the Kabbala.

Corelli, Marie (actually Mary Mackay) (1855–1924), English novelist who won success with her Barabbas: A Dream of the World's Tragedy (1893), The Sorrows of Satan (1895) and The Murder of Delicia (1896).

Corippus, Flavius Cresconius (6th Century), significant African-born Latin poet who wrote the Johannis (8 vols) and In laudem Justini (4 vols).

Corle, Edwin (1906–1956), American writer.

Corneille, Pierre (1606–1684), French dramatist who was acclaimed as the father of French comedic and tragic writing for the stage; brother of Thomas Corneille.

Corneille, Thomas (1625–1709), esteemed French dramatist; brother of Pierre Corneille.

Cornelius, (Carl August) Peter (1824–1874), German composer and writer.

Cornford, Frances (Crofts) (1886–1960), English poet; mother of John Cornford.

Cornford, John (1915–1936), English poet who died in the Loyalist cause in the Spanish Civil War; son of Frances (Crofts) Cornford.

Cornutus, Lucius Annaeus (1st Century), Roman philosopher of the Stoic school.

Cornyshe, William (died 1523), English composer, poet and dramatist.

Corso, Gregory (Nunzio) (1930–2001), American poet, writer and dramatist who was a prominent figure in the Beat movement.

Cortázar, Julio (1914–84), Argentine novelist and short-story writer, author of the experimental novel Rayuela (1963; English trans. as Hopscotch, 1966).

Côrte-Real, Jerónimo (1533–1588), Portuguese poet.

Cory, William Johnson (1823–1892), English poet.

Coryate, Thomas (c.1577–1617), English traveller and writer.

Cosin, John (1594–1672), respected English Anglican bishop, theologian and liturgist.

Cosmas (6th Century), Egyptian merchant, traveller, theologian and geographer, author of the famous treatise Topographia Christiana (c.535–547).

Cosmas of Prague (c.1045–1125), Bohemian historian.

Costa, Isaäc da (1798–1860), Dutch poet and writer.

Costain, Thomas B(ertram) (1885–1965), Canadian-born American writer, particularly remembered for The Black Rose (1945) and The Silver Chalice (1952).

Coster, Charles-Théodore-Henri de (1827–1879), prominent Belgian novelist, author of La Légende et les aventures héroïques, joyeuses, et glorieuses d'Ulenspiegel et de Lamme Goedzak au pays de Flandres et ailleurs (1867; English trans. as The Glorious Adventures of Ty Ulenspiegl, 1943).

Costin, Miron (1633–1691), Moldavian historian and poet; father of Niculae Costin.

Costin, Niculae (1672–1745), Moldavian historian and editor; son of Miron Costin.

Cotton, Charles (1630–1687), English poet, writer and translator.

Cotton, John (1582–1652), English-born American Puritan leader and writer.

Coubertin, Pierre, Baron de (1863–1937), French scholar and educator who is best remembered for his resusitation of the Olympic Games in 1896.

Couperus, Louis Marie Anne (1863–1923), highly regarded Dutch novelist, best remembered for his Eline vere (1889).

Courier, Paul-Louis (1772–1825), French classical scholar; was murdered by his unfaithful wife's lover.

Cournot, Antoine-Augustin (1801–1877), French economist and mathematician.

Court, Antoine (1695–1760), French-born Swiss Reformed Church minister and writer.

Court de Gébelin (1725–1784), French philologist and writer, author of the important Le Monde primitif, analysé et comparé avec le monde moderne (1773–84).

Courteline, Georges (actually Georges-Victor-Marcel Moinaux) (1858–1929), French writer and dramatist.

Courthope, William John (1842–1917), English critic who wrote the History of English Poetry (6 vols, 1895–1910).

Cousin, Victor (1792–1867), prominent French philosopher, historian and educational reformer.

Cousins, Norman (1912–1990), American editor and writer.

Cousteau, Jacques (-Yves) (1910–1997), French naval officer, ocean explorer, writer and film producer.

Couturat, Louis (1868–1914), French philosopher and logician, author of L'Infinie mathématique (1896).

Covarrubias, Miguel (1904–1957), Mexican painter, anthropologist and writer.

Coventry, Francis (1725–1754), English curate and writer, best known for the satirical work The History of Pompey the Little, or the Life and Adventures of a Lap-Dog 1751).

Coverdale, Miles (c.1487–1569), English bishop, writer and translator who translated the first printed English Bible (1535).

Coward, Sir Noel (Peirce) (1899–1973), famous English actor, dramatist, writer and composer.

Cowl, Jane (actually Grace Bailey) (1883–1950), American actress and dramatist.

Cowley, Abraham (1618–1667), admired English poet and essayist whose most significant work was the unfinished epic poem the Davideis (c.1640).

Cowley, Hannah (née Parkhouse) (1743–1809), English dramatist.

Cowley, Malcolm (1898–1989), American critic, social historian, poet and editor.

Cowper, William (1731–1800), English poet, celebrated for such works as The Task (1785), Yardley Oak (1791) and The Castaway (1796).

Cox, Sir George W(illiams) (1827–1902), English mythologist.

Cox, Jacob Dolson (1828–1900), American politician and historian, author of the important Military Reminiscences of the Civil War (2 vols, 1900).

Cozzens, Frederick Swartwout (1818–1869), American writer who wrote under the name Richard Hayrwarde.

Cozzens, James Gould (1903–1978), notable American novelist, author of Men and Brethren (1936), Ask Me Tomorrow (1940), Guard of Honor (1948) and By Love Possessed (1957).

Crabbe, George (1754–1832), English poet who was admired for The Village (1783), The Parish Register (1807), The Borough (1810) and Tales of the Hall (1819).

Craddock, Charles Egbert (actually Mary Noailles Murfree) (1850–1922), American short-story writer.

Crafts, William (1787–1826), American lawyer, orator, essayist, poet and critic.

Craig, Edward Gordon (actually Edward Henry Gordon Godwin) (1872–1966), English actor, artist, theatre director and designer, and writer, author of The Art of the Theatre (1905; revised edition as On the Art of the Theatre, 1911) and Towards a new Theatre (1913).

Craigie, Sir William Alexander (1867–1957), English philologist and lexicographer.

Craik, Dinah Maria Murlock (1826–1887), English novelist, short-story writer, essayist and poet.

Cram, Ralph Adams (1863–1942), American architect and writer who wrote such works as The Ministry of Art (1914), The Nemesis of Mediocrity (1918) and The End of Democracy (1937).

Cranch, Christopher Pearse (1813–1892), American clergyman, Transcendentalist and poet.

Crane, (Harold) Hart (1899–1932), important American poet, author of White Buildings (1926) and The Bridge (1930); committed suicide.

Crane, Ronald (Salmon) (1886–1967), American critic.

Crane, Stephen (1871–1900), American novelist, short-story writer and poet, especially admired for his prose writings Maggie: A Girl of the Streets (1893) and The Red Badge of Courage (1895), and the poetry collection War is Kind (1899).

Cranmer, Thomas (1489–1556), prominent English prelate and Archbishop of Canterbury who prepared The Book of Common Prayer; was condemned as a heretic and burned at the stake.

Crantor (4th–3rd Century BC), Greek philosopher.

Crapsey, Adelaide (1878–1914), American poet who invented the metrical form known as cinquains.

Crashaw, Richard (c.1613–1649), admired English poet, author of the collection Carmen Deo Nostro (Hymn to Our Lord, published 1652).

Crates (flourished 450–470 BC), Greek actor and dramatist.

Cratinus (c.519–c.420 BC), famous Greek dramatist who was acclaimed as a master of the comedy.

Craven, Frank (1880–1945), American actor, producer and dramatist.

Crawford, Francis Marion (1854–1909), American novelist, short-story writer and dramatist.

Crawford, Isabelle Valancy (1850–1887), Irish-born Canadian poet who was esteemed for her landscape verse.

Crawford, John Wallace (1847–1917), American frontier scout and poet, author of such works as The Poet Scout (1879) and The Broncho Book (1908).

Crébillon, Claude-Prosper Jolyot, Sieur de (1707–1777), French novelist; son of Prosper Jolyot Crébillon.

Crébillon, Prosper Jolyot (actually Prosper Jolyot Crais-Billon), Sieur de (1674–1762), French dramatist, best remembered for his tragedy Rhadamiste et Zénobie (1711); father of Claude-Prosper Jolyot Crébillon.

Creel, George (Edward) (1876–1953), American journalist and writer.

Creighton, James Edwin (1861–1924), Canadian-born American philosopher of the Idealist school.

Creighton, Mandell (1843–1901), English Anglican bishop and historian, author of the notable History of the Papacy during the period of the Reformation (5 vols, 1882–94).

Crémazie, (Joseph) Octave (1827–1879), French-Canadian poet, acclaimed as the father of French-Canadian poetry.

Crescas, Hasdai (ben Abraham) (1340–1410), Spanish philosopher, Talmudic scholar and rabbi.

Cressy, Hugh Paulin (c.1605–1674), English Benedictine monk, historian, writer and editor who was known as Serenus Cressy.

Creutz, Gustav Philip (1731–1785), Swedish diplomat and poet.

Creuzer, Georg Friedrich (1771–1858), German philologist and historian whose most significant work was the Symbolik und Mythologie der alten Völker besonders der Griechen (Symbolism and Mythology of the Ancients, Especially the Greeks, 4 vols, 1810–12).

Crèvecoeur, Michel-Guillaume-Jean de (1735–1813), French-born American writer and naturalist who was known as Hector Saint-John de Crèvecoeur and J Hector St John, author of the essay collection Letters from an American Farmer (1782; revised edition as Lettres d'un cultivateur Américain, 1784).

Crichton, James (1560–1582), Scottish adventurer, scholar and poet, widely known as the Admirable Crichton.

Crichton Smith, Iain (1928–1998), esteemed Scottish poet, novelist and dramatist.

Crisp, Samuel (1707–1783), English writer.

Critias (c.480–c.403 BC), Greek poet, orator, statesman and philosopher.

Critobulos of Imbros (15th Century), Byzantine historian.

Critolaus (2nd Century BC), Greek philosopher.

Croce, Benedetto (1866–1952), Italian philosopher and historian.

Crockett, Samuel Rutherford (1860–1914), Scottish novelist.

Croft, Sir Herbert (1751–1816), English writer.

Crofts, Freeman Willis (1879–1957), Irish writer, a master of detective fiction.

Croker, Thomas Crofton (1798–1854), Irish antiquarian who published collections of tales and songs.

Croly, George (1780–1860), Irish Anglican clergyman, writer and poet, particularly known for his novel Salathiel (1828).

Croly, Herbert David (1869–1930), American magazine editor and political philosopher, author of the influential The Promise of American Life (1909); son of Jane Cunningham Croly.

Croly, Jane Cunningham (1829–1901), English-born American journalist and writer; mother of Herbert David Croly.

Cronin, A(rchibald) J(oseph) (1896–1981), English physician and novelist, author of Hatters Castle (1931), The Stars Look Down (1935), The Citadel (1937) and The Keys of the Kingdom (1942).

Cros, (Émile-Hortensius-) Charles (1842–1888), French poet and inventor, best known for his Symbolist work Le Coffret de santal (The Sandalwood Chest, 1873).

Cross, F(rank) L(eslie) (1900–1968), English theologian and ecumenist, editor of The Oxford Dictionary of the Christian Church (1957).

Crothers, Rachel (1878–1958), American dramatist and director, particulary known for her plays A Man's World (1909) and He and She (1911).

Crothers, Samuel McChord (1857–1927), American Presbyterian minister and essayist.

Crotus Rubianus (actually Johann Jäger) (c.1480–c.1539), German Roman Catholic priest, author of an Apologia (1531).

Crousaz, Jean-Pierre de (1663–1750), Swiss theologian and philosopher.

Crouse, Russel (1893–1966), American dramatist, author of such plays as Life with Father (in collaboration with Howard Lindsay, 1939), State of the Union (1945) and Life with Mother (1948).

Crowe, Sir Joseph Archer (1825–1896), English journalist, diplomat and art historian.

Crowley, Aleister (actually Edward Alexander Crowley) (1875–1947), English Satanist and poet, the self-described 'Beast from the Book of Revelation'.

Crowley, Robert (c.1518–1588), English Puritan churchman, social reformer, writer and poet.

Crowne, John (c.1640–c.1703), English dramatist.

Crucé, Émeric (c.1590–1648), French writer who was a pioneering figure in advocating international arbitration in his Le nouveau Cynée (1623; English trans. as The New Cyneas of Émeric Crucé, 1909).

Cruden, Alexander (1701–1770), English writer, best known for his concordance to the King James Version of the Bible.

Cruz, Sor Juana Inés de la (actually Juana Inés de Asbaje) (1651–1695), notable Mexican poet, dramatist, nun and scholar.

Cruz, Ramón de la (1731–1794), Spanish dramatist.

Cruz e Silva, António Dinis da (1731–1799), Portuguese poet who wrote the satirical O Hissope (c.1772).

Csokonai Vitéz, Mihály (1773–1805), illustrious Hungarian poet and dramatist who wrote the first Hungarian comic epic Dorottya (1804).

Ctesias (flourished 400 BC), Greek physician and historian.

Cuadra, Pablo Antonio (1912–2002), Nicaraguan poet and journalist.

Cudworth, Ralph (1617–1688), English theologian and philosopher of the Cambridge Platonist school, author of The True Intellectual System of the Universe: The First Part: Wherein All the Reason and Philosophy of Atheism is Confuted and its Impossibility Demonstrated (1678) and A Treatise Concerning Eternal and Immutable Morality (published 1731).

Cueva, Juan de la (c.1543–1610), Spanish poet and dramatist.

Cujas, Jacques (1522–1590), French jurist and classical scholar.

Cullen, Countee (1903–1946), gifted American poet of the Harlem Renaissance, noted for his Copper Sun (1927), The Ballad of the Brown Girl (1928), The Black Christ and Other Poems (1929) and The Medea and Some Poems (1935).

Culverwel, Nathanael (c.1618–1651), English philosopher of the Empiricist school, best remembered for his An Elegant and Learned Discourse of the Light of Nature (published 1652).

Cumberland, Richard (1631–1718), English Anglican bishop, theologian and philosopher, author of De Legibus Naturae, Disquisitio Philosophica (1672; English trans. as A Philosophical Enquiry into the Laws of Nature, 1750).

Cumberland, Richard (1732–1811), English dramatist and writer who wrote such plays as The Brothers (1769), The West Indian (1771), The Fashionable Lover (1772), The Jew (1794) and The Wheel of Fortune (1795).

Cummings, Bruce Frederick (actually Wilhelm Nero Pilate Barbellion) (1889–1919), English journalist, naturalist and writer, author of The Journal of a Disappointed Man (1919), Enjoying Life and Other Literary Remains (1919) and A Last Diary (published 1920).

Cummings, e. e. (actually Edward Estlin Cummings) (1894–1962), notable American poet, writer and painter, renowned for his inventive verse.

Cummins, Maria Susanna (1827–1866), American novelist who wrote the successful The Lamplighter (1854).

Cumont, Franz (-Valéry-Marie) (1868–1947), Belgian archaeologist and philologist.

Cunha, Euclides da (1866–1909), Brazilian journalist and writer, author of the classic Os Sertões (1902; English trans. as Rebellion in the Backlands, 1944); was murdered.

Cunningham, Allan (1784–1842), Scottish poet and writer, best remembered for his sea shanty A Wet Sheet and a Flowing Sea.

Cunningham, J(ames) V(incent) (1911–1985), American poet.

Cunningham, William (1849–1919), Scottish economist and churchman, author of The Growth of English Industry and Commerce (1882).

Cunninghame Graham, R(obert) B(ontine) (1852–1936), English writer and traveller.

Cuoco or Coco, Vincenzo (1770–1823), Italian historian and novelist, author of the Saggio storico sulla rivoluzione di Napoli (Historical Essay on the Neapolitan Revolution, 3 vols, 1800) and the novel Platone in Italia (Plato in Italy, 1804); died insane.

Curel, François, Vicomte di (1854–1928), French dramatist and novelist.

Curnow, (Thomas) Allen (Monro) (1911–2001), New Zealand poet, dramatist, critic and editor.

Curtis, George Ticknor (1812–1894), American lawyer and writer.

Curtis, George William (1824–1892), American journalist, editor and writer.

Curtis, Lionel George (1872–1955), English public administrator and writer who promoted the cause of world federation in his Civitas Dei (3 vols, 1934–37).

Curtius, Ernst (1814–1896), German archaeologist and historian; brother of Georg Curtius.

Curtius, Georg (1820–1885), German linguist, an authority on Greek linguistics; brother of Ernst Curtius.

Curwood, James Oliver (1878–1927), American journalist and novelist.

Curzon, Lord (actually George Nathaniel Curzon, 1st Marquess Curzon of Kedleston) (1859–1925), English statesman and writer.

Cushing, Frank Hamilton (1857–1900), American ethnologist and archaeologist.

Custis, George Washington Parke (1781–1857), American dramatist and writer, author of Recollections and Private Memoirs of Washington (published 1859); grandson of Martha Washington.

Cuvier, Georges (Jean-Leopold-Nicolas-Frédéric), Baron (1769–1832), eminent French zoologist and statesman, founder of comparative anatomy and paleontology.

Cydones, Demetrius (c.1324–c.1398), renowned Byzantine scholar, theologian and statesman; brother of Prochorus Cydones.

Cydones, Prochorus (c.1330–c.1369), Byzantine Eastern Orthodox monk, theologian and linguist; brother of Demetrius Cydones.

Cynddelw Brydydd Mawr (12th Century), noteworthy Welsh poet who was called Cynddelw the Great Poet, most likely an allusion to his physical stature.

Cynewulf (c. 8th Century), Anglo-Saxon poet.

Cyrano de Bergerac, Savinien (1619–1655), French writer and dramatist who became best known for his satire.

Czechowicz, Józef (1903–1939), Polish poet; killed during the early days of the German invasion of Poland.

Da Ponte, Lorenzo (actually Emanuele Conegliano) (1749–1838), famous Italian poet who wrote the librettos for Mozart's operas Le Nozze di Figaro (The Marriage of Figaro, 1786), Don Giovanni (1787) and Così fan tutte (Women Are Like That, 1790).

Dabrowska, Maria (1889–1965), Polish novelist, short-story writer and critic, particularly known for her novel cycle Noce i dnie (Nights and Day, 4 vols, 1932–34).

Dach, Simon (1605–1659), German poet, best remembered for his Der Mensch hat nichts so eigen (Man Has Nothing of His Own).

Dacier, André (1651–1722), French classical scholar and translator; husband of Anne (née Lefebvre) Dacier.

Dacier, Anne (née Lefebvre) (1654–1720), French classical scholar and translator, author of Des causes de la corruption goût (Of the Causes of the Corruption of Taste, 1714); wife of André Dacier.

Dafydd ab Edmwnd (15th Century), Welsh poet who excelled in love lyrics, elegies and eulogies.

Dafydd ap Gwilym (c.1320–c.1380), renowned Welsh poet, a master of bardic verse.

Dafydd Nanmor (15th Century), Welsh poet who was admired for his odes.

Dagerman, Stig (1923–1954), Swedish novelist, short-story writer and dramatist; committed suicide.

Dahl, Roald (1916–1990), English writer, dramatist and poet, best known for his children's works.

Dahlberg, Edward (1900–1977), American novelist, critic and poet.

Dahlgren, Karl Fredrik (1791–1844), Swedish poet, novelist, dramatist and preacher.

Dahlhaus, Carl (1928–1989), learned German music scholar.

Dahlmann, Friedrich (Christoph) (1785–1860), German historian who wrote the Geschichte der englischen Revolution (History of the English Revolution, 1844) and Geschichte der französischen Revolution (History of the French Revolution, 1845).

Dahn, (Julius Sophus) Felix (1834–1912), German historian, poet, novelist and dramatist.

Dalin, Olof von (1709–1763), Swedish historian, dramatist and poet.

Dallán Forgaill (6th Century), Irish poet.

Daly, (John) Augustin (1838–1899), American dramatist and theatre manager, author of Under the Gaslight (1867), Horizon (1871) and Divorce (1871).

Daly, Thomas Augustine (1871–1948), American journalist and poet.

Damascius (c.480–c.550), Greek philosopher of the Neoplatonist school, author of Aporiai kai lyseis peri ton proton archon (English trans. as Problems and Solutions About the First Principles, 1889).

Damian, Saint Peter (1007–1072), Italian Roman Catholic cardinal and theologian.

Dampier, William (1652–1715), English buccaneer who wrote A New Voyage Round the World (1697).

Dana, Charles A(nderson) (1819–1897), American journalist, editor and writer.

Dana, Richard Henry (1787–1879), American poet and critic; father of Richard Henry Dana.

Dana, Richard Henry (1815–1882), American lawyer and writer, author of the novel Two Years Before the Mast (1840); son of Richard Henry Dana.

Dancourt, Florent Carton (1661–1725), French actor and dramatist, creator of the French comedy of manners.

Dane, Clemence (actually Winifred Ashton) (1888–1965), English novelist and dramatist.

Daniel, Gabriel (1649–1728), French Jesuit historian who wrote the notable Histoire de France depuis l'établissement de la monarchie française (1713).

Daniel, Samuel (c.1562–1619), admired English poet, dramatist and writer.

Daniel, Yuly (Markovich) (1925–1988), Russian writer and poet who suffered imprisonment for 'slandering' the Soviet Union (1965–69).

Daniels, Jonathan (Worth) (1902–1981), American journalist and writer; son of Josephus Daniels.

Daniels, Josephus (1862–1948), American editor, newspaper publisher and diplomat; father of Jonathan (Worth) Daniels.

Danielsson, Olof August (1852–1933), Swedish classical scholar and comparative linguist.

Danilevsky, Nikolai Yakovlevich (1822–1865), Russian naturalist and philosopher, author of Rossiya i Evropa (Russia and Europe, published 1869).

D'Annunzio, Gabriele (1863–1938), prominent Italian poet, novelist, short-story writer, dramatist and political adventurer.

Dantas, Julio (1876–1962), Portuguese poet, dramatist and short-story writer.

Dante (Alighieri) (1265–1321), Italian poet, celebrated for his Divina Commedia (Divine Comedy), one of the supreme achievements in world literature.

Dantiscus, Johannes (actually Jan Flachsbinder) (1485–1548), German writer and poet who wrote in Latin.

Dareste de la Chavanne, Antoine (-Elisabeth-Cléophas) (1820–1882), French historian who wrote the valuable Histoire de France (9 vols, 1865–79).

Dargan, Olive Tilford (1869–1968), American dramatist, poet and writer.

Darío, Rubén (actually Félix Rubén García Sarmiento) (1867–1916), significant Nicaraguan poet, journalist and diplomat, acclaimed for his Azul (Blue, 1888), Prosas profanas y otros poemas (Profane Hymns and Other Poems, 1896) and Cantos de vida y esperanza (Songs of Life and Hope, 1905).

Darley, George (1795–1846), Irish poet, writer, critic and mathematician, remembered for his poetry collection The Errors of Ecstasie (1822) and the unfinished epic Nepenthe (1835).

Darmesteter, Arsene (1846–1888), French language and literary scholar; brother of James Darmesteter.

Darmesteter, James (1849–1894), French Orientalist; brother of Arsene Darmesteter.

Darrow, Clarence (Seward) (1857–1938), prominent American lawyer, lecturer, debater and writer.

Darwin, Charles (Robert) (1809–1882), celebrated English naturalist, author of the influential work On the Origin of Species by Means of Natural Selection (1859); son of Erasmus Darwin.

Darwin, Erasmus (1731–1802), English physician and poet; father of Charles Robert Darwin.

Daryush, Elizabeth (1887–1977), English poet; daughter of Robert (Seymour) Bridges.

Das, Jibananda (1899–1954), Bengali poet.

Dasgupta, S(urendra) N(ath) (1885–1952), Indian philosopher who was the author of the valuable History of Indian Philosophy (five vols, 1922–55).

Dass, Petter (1647–1707), Norwegian pastor and poet, particularly admired for his Nordlands trompet (published 1739; English trans. as The Trumpet of Nordland, 1954).

Datta or Dutt, Michael Madhusudan (1824–1873), notable Indian poet and dramatist, a master of Bengali literature.

Daubenton or D'Aubenton, Louis-Jean-Marie (1716–1800), French naturalist whose most important work was the Histoire naturelle (1794–1804).

Däubler, Theodor (1876–1934), German poet and writer.

Daudet, Alphonse (1840–1897), French poet, novelist and short-story writer; father of (Alphonse-Marie-) Léon Daudet.

Daudet, (Alphonse-Marie-) Léon (1867–1942), French journalist and novelist; son of Alphonse Daudet.

Daukantas, Simanas (1793–1864), pioneering Lithuanian historian.

Daunou, Pierre-Claude-François (1761–1840), French statesman and historian.

D'Avenant or Davenant, Sir William (1606–1668), notable English poet and dramatist; became Poet Laureate of the United Kingdom (1638).

Davenport, Christopher (1598–1680), English Franciscan priest and theologian, author of Deus, Natura, Gratia (1634).

Davenport, John (1597–1670), English-born American noncomformist pastor and writer.

David, Ferenc (1510–1579), Transylvanian Unitarian preacher and theologian.

Davidescu, Nicolae (1888–1954), Romanian poet and novelist.

Davidson, Donald (Grady) (1893–1968), American poet and essayist.

Davidson, John (1857–1909), Scottish poet, dramatist and novelist; committed suicide.

Davidson, Thomas (1840–1900), Scottish-born American philosopher.

Davie, Donald (Alfred) (1922–1995), English poet and critic, a leading figure in the anti-Romantic group known as the Movement.

Davies, John (c.1565–1618), English poet, best known for his love sonnets and the religious treatise Microcosmos (1603).

Davies, Sir John (1569–1626), English poet and statesman, author of Orchestra, or a Poem of Dancing (1596), Hymnes of Astraea in Acrosticke Verse (1599) and Nosce teipsum (Know Thyself, 1599).

Davies, Samuel (1723–1761), American Presbyterian preacher and hymnist.

Davies, William Henry (1871–1940), Welsh poet and writer whose early years as a tramp earned him the title of the 'tramp poet'.

Davies, (William) Robertson (1913–1995), eminent Canadian novelist, dramatist and critic.

Davila, Enrico Caterino (1576–1631), Italian historian, author of the well-known Historia delle guerre civili di Francia (1630); was murdered.

Davis, Andrew Jackson (1826–1910), American Spiritualist who became known as the 'Poughkeepsie Seer', author of Principles of Nature, Her Devine Revelations, and a Voice to Mankind (1847) and The Great Harmonia (1850).

Davis, Clyde Brion (1894–1962), American novelist.

Davis, Elmer (Holmes) (1890–1958), American journalist, broadcaster and writer.

Davis, H(arold) L(enoir) (1896–1960), American writer and poet.

Davis, Idris (1905–1953), Welsh poet.

Davis, John (1775–1854), English sailor and novelist.

Davis, Owen (1874–1956), American dramatist, author of The Detour (1921) and Icebound (1923).

Davis, Rebecca (Blaine) Harding (1831–1910), American novelist and short-story writer; mother of Richard Harding Davis.

Davis, Richard Harding (1864–1916), American journalist, novelist and short-story writer; son of Rebecca (Blaine) Harding Davis.

Davis, William Stearns (1877–1930), American scholar and novelist.

Dawes, Rufus (1803–1859), American writer and poet.

Dawson, William (1704–1752), English-born American poet.

Day, Clarence (Shepard) (1874–1935), American writer who gained enormous success with his autobiographical works God and My Father (1932), Life With Father (1935) and Life With Mother (published 1936).

Day, John (1574–c.1640), English dramatist, best remembered for The Parliament of Bees (c.1607).

Day-Lewis, C(ecil) (1904–1972), admired Irish poet, critic, detective-story writer and translator; became Poet Laureate of the United Kingdom (1968).

Dazai Osamu (actually Tsushima Shuji) (1909–1948), esteemed Japanese writer, a master of the short story; committed suicide.

De Amicis, Edmondo (1846–1908), Italian writer and poet, particularly known for his children's tale Cuore (1886; English trans. as The Heart of a Boy, 1960).

De Casseres, Benjamin (1873–1945), American journalist, critic, essayist and poet.

De Dominis, Marco Antonio (c.1566–1624), Dalmatian theologian and churchman whose writings cost him favour with both the Roman Catholic and Anglican churches.

De Jong, David (Cornel) (1905–1967), Dutch-born American writer and poet.

De Kruif, Paul (1890–1971), American writer.

De la Mare, Walter (John) (1873–1956), admired English poet and novelist who won favour with both children and adults.

de la Roche, Mazo (1885–1961), Canadian novelist and dramatist.

De Leon, Daniel (1852–1914), American journalist, writer and Marxist.

De Mille, James (1836–1880), Canadian novelist, short-story writer and poet.

De Morgan, William Frend (1839–1917), English ceramic artist and novelist.

De Quille, Dan (actually William Wright) (1829–1898), American journalist who became known for his humorous writing.

De Quincey, Thomas (1785–1859), English critic and essayist, author of the classic Confessions of an English Opium Eater (1822).

De Ste. Croix, Geoffrey (Ernest Maurice) (1910–2000), English historian of a Marxist persuasion, author of The Origins of the Peloponnesian War (1972) and The Class Struggle in the Ancient World (1982).

De Sanctis, Francesco (1817–1883), influential Italian literary scholar who wrote the valuable Storia della letteratura italiana (1870).

De Smet, Pierre Jean (1801–1873), Belgian-born American Jesuit missionary and writer who was active in Indian mission work.

De Vere, Aubrey Thomas (1814–1902), Irish poet and writer.

De Vinne, Theodore L(ow) (1828–1914), American scholar who wrote works on typography.

De Voto, Bernard (Augustine) (1897–1955), American critic, historian and novelist.

De Vries, Peter (1910–1993), American novelist and short-story writer.

De Wette, Wilhelm Martin Leberecht (1780–1849), German theologian who employed the principles of historical criticism to the Pentateuch.

Dearmer, Geoffrey (1893–1996), English poet whose collection A Pilgrim's Song was published in his 100th year.

Debelyanov, Dimcho (1887–1916), Bulgarian poet.

Debs, Eugene V(ictor) (1855–1926), American labour organizer, Socialist, editor and writer.

Déchelette, Joseph (1862–1914), French archaeologist and writer.

Decker, Sir Matthew, Baronet (1679–1749), English merchant and writer on trade, commerce and taxation.

Deeping, (George) Warwick (1877–1950), English novelist, particularly known for his Sorrell and Son (1925).

Deering, Nathaniel (1791–1881), American editor and dramatist.

Deffand, Marie de Vichy-Chamrond, Marquise du (1697–1780), French woman of letters, best remembered for her Correspondance inédite (published 1809).

Defoe, Daniel (actually Daniel Foe) (1660–1731), famous English writer and journalist, author of the celebrated The Life and Strange and Surprising Adventures of Robinson Crusoe (1719).

DeForest, John William (1826–1906), American novelist who espoused the cause of realism in such works as Miss Ravenel's Conversion from Secession to Loyalty (1867), Kate Beaumont (1872), Honest John Vane (1875), Playing the Mischief (1875) and The Bloody Chasm (1881).

Dehmel, Richard (1863–1920), notable German poet whose works anticipated Expressionism.

Deken, Agatha (actually Aagje Deken) (1741–1804), Dutch novelist and poet who collaborated with Elisabeth Wolff-Bekker on the earliest Dutch novel Sara Burgerhart (1782), and on Willem Leevend (8 vols, 1784–85).

Dekker, Thomas (c.1572–c.1632), important English dramatist and writer, particularly esteemed for his play The Shomakers Holiday (1600).

Delafield, E M (actually Edmée Elizabeth Monica Dashwood) (1890–1943), English novelist, journalist and magistrate.

Delafosse, Maurice (1870–1926), French language scholar.

Deland, Margaret (ta Wade née Campbell) (1857–1945), American writer and poet.

Delano, Alonzo (c.1802–1874), American writer who was know for his humorous works and his travel account Life on the Plains and Among the Diggings (1854).

Delany, Martin R(obinson) (1812–1885), American writer.

Delavigne, Jean François Casimir (1793–1843), French dramatist.

Delblanc, Sven (1931–92), Swedish novelist.

Delbrück, Berthold (1842–1922), learned German linguist who founded the study of the comparative syntax of the Indo-European languages.

Delbrück, Hans (1848–1929), German military historian and politician.

Deledda, Grazia (1875–1936), Italian novelist of the verismo school; won the Nobel Prize for Literature (1926).

Delehaye, Hippolyte (1859–1941), Belgian Jesuit, priest and scholar who became an authority on the saints of the Roman Catholic Church.

Delille, Jacques, Abbé (1738–1813), French poet and translator.

Delisle, Léopold Victor (1826–1910), French scholar.

Dell, Floyd (1887–1969), American journalist, novelist, dramatist and poet.

Delmedigo, Elijah (c.1460–c.1497), Candian philosopher and translator who was known for his criticism of the Kabbala; great-grandfather of Joseph Solomon Delmedigo.

Delmedigo, Joseph Solomon (1591–1655), Candian scientist and philosopher who defended the Kabbala; great-grandson of Elijah Delmedigo.

Deloney, Thomas (c.1563–1600), English writer and poet, particularly known for his story collection The Gentle Craft (2 parts, 1597–98).

Delvig, Anton Antonovich, Baron von (1798–1831), Russian poet.

Demetrius Chalcondyles (1424–1511), Greek-born Italian scholar.

Demetrius of Lacon (2nd Century BC), Greek philosopher of the Epicurean school.

Deming, P(hilander) (1829–1915), American writer.

Demochares (c.355–c.270 BC), Greek orator, statesman and historian who was the nephew of the Greek statesman Demosthenes.

Democritus (c.460–c.370 BC), notable Greek philosopher.

Demolder, Eugene (1862–1919), Belgian novelist and short-story writer.

Dempster, Thomas (c.1579–1625), Scottish poet.

Denck, Hans (c.1495–1527), German theologian and reformer who embraced Anabaptism.

Denham, Sir John (1615–1669), Irish poet, author of The Sophy (1641) and Cooper's Hill (1642).

Denifle, Heinrich Seuse (1844–1905), Austrian Dominican priest and church historian.

Denis, Maurice (1870–1943), French artist, theorist and writer of the Symbolist school.

Dennie, Joseph (1768–1812), American essayist and poet.

Dennis, John (1657–1734), English critic, poet and dramatist, particularly remembered for his quarrel with Alexander Pope over the role of passion in poetry.

Dennis, Nigel (Forbes) (1912–1989), English journalist, critic, novelist and dramatist.

Densmore, Frances (1867–1957), American ethnologist who wrote important works on the life and culture of the American Indian.

Densuşianu, Ovid (1873–1938), Romanian folklorist, philologist and poet whose poetry appeared under the name Ervin.

Derby, George Horatio (1823–1861), American army officer and writer, particularly known for his wit.

Dereme, Tristan (actually Phillippe Huc) (1889–1941), French poet.

Derleth, August (William) (1909–1971), American novelist and poet.

Dermoût, Maria (actually Helena Antonia Maria Elisabeth Dermoût-Ingermann) (1888–1962), Dutch novelist and short-story writer.

Déroulède, Paul (1846–1914), French poet, dramatist and politician who espoused nationalist themes.

Derozio, Henry Louis Vivian (1809–1831), Indian poet, best known for his sonnets.

Derzhavin, Gavril (Romanovich) (1743–1816), renowned Russian poet, a master of lyricism.

Desbordes-Valmore, Marceline (1786–1859), French poet and writer.

Descartes, René (1596–1650), French mathematician and philosopher, author of Discours de la méthode (1637), Méditations philosophiques (1641), Principia philosophiae (1644) and Traité des passions de l' âme (1649).

Deschamps (de Saint-Amand), Émile (1791–1871), French poet and librettist who championed Romanticism.

Deschamps, Eustache (c.1346–c.1406), French poet and writer, author of the earliest treatise on poetry in French L'Art de dictier (1392).

Desgabets, Robert (1620–1678), French Benedictine theologian and philosopher of the Cartesian school.

Deshoulières, Antoinette Ligier de la Garde (1638–1694), French poet.

Desmarets de Saint-Sorlin, Jean (1595–1676), French writer, poet, dramatist and government official who became best known as a Christian apologist.

Desmoulins, Camille (1760–1794), prominent French journalist and pamphleteer who defended the cause of the moderate democratic forces; was guillotined.

Desnos, Robert (1900–1945), esteemed French poet, a leading figure in Symbolist circles; a member of the Resistance during World War II, he was imprisoned by the Nazis and died a few days after his liberation by American troops.

Des Périers, Bonaventure (c.1500–c.1544), French writer, poet and translator whose freethinking sentiments in his Cymbalum Mundi (1537) earned him many enemies.

Desportes, Philippe (1546–1606), French courtier, poet and translator.

DesRochers, Alfred (1901–1978), French-Canadian poet and writer.

Desrosiers, Leo-Paul (1896–1967), French-Canadian writer.

Dessoir, Max (1867–1947), German aesthetician and philosopher.

Destouches, Philippe Néricault (1680–1754), French dramatist whose finest play was Le Glorieux (1732; English trans. as The Conceited Count, 1923).

Deus, João de (1830–1896), admired Portuguese poet who excelled in lyric verse.

Deutsch, Babette (1895–1982), American poet, novelist and critic.

Deutscher, Isaac (1907–1967), Polish-born English historian and biographer.

D'Ewes, Sir Simonds (1602–1650), English antiquarian and diarist.

Dewey, John (1859–1952), influential American philosopher, psychologist and educator, one of the leading figures in the Pragmatic school.

Dewey, Melvil (1851–1931), American librarian who developed the Dewey Decimal System of Classification for cataloging library collections.

Dexippus, Publius Herennius (c.210–c.270), Roman historian and statesman.

Deyssel, Lodewijk van (actually Karel Joan Lodewijk Alberdingk Thijm) (1864–1952), Dutch critic and writer.

Dhlomo, R(olfus) R(eginald) R(aymond) (1901–71), South African journalist and novelist who wrote in both Zulu and English, author of the first novel in English by a Zulu writer, An African Tragedy (1928).

Di Donato, Pietro (1911–1992), American writer.

Diadochus of Photice (5th Century), Greek theologian, mystic and bishop, author of the Hekaton Kephalaia Gnostika (The Hundred Chapters, or Maxims, of Knowledge).

Diaper, William (1685–1717), English poet.

Díaz del Castillo, Bernal (1492–c.1581), Spanish soldier and writer, author of the Historia verdadera de la conquista de la Nueva España (published 1632).

Dibdin, Charles (1745–1814), English composer, writer, actor and theatre manager; uncle of Thomas Frognall Dibdin.

Dibdin, Thomas Frognall (1776–1847), English bibliographer and librarian, author of the Introduction to the Knowledge of Rare and Valuable Editions of the Greek and Latin Classics (1802) and Bibliomania (1809); nephew of Charles Dibdin.

Dibelius, Martin (1883–1947), noted German New Testament scholar who wrote Die Formgeschichte des Evangeliums (1919; English trans. as From Tradition to Gospel, 1934).

Dicaearchus (flourished 320 BC), Greek philosopher, author of the Bios Hellados (Life of Greece).

Dicey, Albert Venn (1835–1922), English jurist who wrote the Introduction to the Study of the Law of the Constitution (1885).

Dick, Philip K(indred) (1928–82), American writer of science fiction.

Dickens, Charles (John Huffam) (1812–1870), English novelist; great-grandfather of Monica Enid Dickens.

Dickens, Monica Enid (1915–1992), English novelist; great-granddaughter of Charles (John Huffam) Dickens.

Dickenson, John (16th Century), English writer and poet.

Dickey, James (Lafayette) (1923–1997), American poet and novelist, admired for his poetry collection Buckdancer's Choice (1965) and the novel Deliverance (1970).

Dickinson, Emily (Elizabeth) (1830–1886), American poet.

Dickinson, John (1732–1808), American statesman and writer who became known as the 'penman of the Revolution'.

Dickson, Gordon (Rupert) (1923–2001), Canadian-born American writer of science fiction.

Dicuil (9th Century), Irish monk, grammarian and geographer who wrote the valuable De mensura orbis terrae (Concerning the Measurement of the World).

Diderot, Denis (1713–1784), eminent French philosopher of the materialist school and chief editor of the famous Encyclopédie (1745–72).

Didymus Chalcenterus (c.80–10 BC), Greek scholar.

Didymus the Blind (c.313–c.398), Egyptian Roman Catholic theologian, best known for his treatise on the Holy Spirit.

Dietzgen, Joseph (1828–1888), German-born American democratic Socialist.

Dieulafoy, Marcel-Auguste (1844–1920), French archaeologist who wrote L'Art antique de la Perse (The Ancient Art of Persia, 5 vols, 1884–89) and L'Acropole de Suse (The Acropolis of Susa, 1890–92).

Diez, Friedrich Christian (1794–1876), German language scholar who was an authority on Romance languages.

Digby, Sir Kenelm (1603–1665), English courtier, diplomat, philosopher and scientist, author of Of the Nature of Bodies (1644) and Of the Nature of Mans soule (1644).

Dillmann, (Christian Friedrich) August (1823–1894), German biblical scholar.

Dillon, George (1906–1968), American poet and translator.

Dilthey, Wilhelm (1833–1911), German philosopher who advocated a distinct methodology for the humanities.

Dīnawarī, al- (actually Abū Hanīfah Ahmad ibn Dā' ūd al-Dīnawarī) (c.815–895), Persian astronomer, botanist and historian.

Dinesen, Isak (actually Karen Christence Dinesen, Baroness Blixen-Finecke) (1885–1962), Danish short-story writer.

Dingelstedt, Franz Ferdinand, Freiherr von (1814–1881), German poet and dramatist who was known for his political satire.

Dinis, Júlio, (actually Joaquim Guilherme Gomes Coelho) (1839–1871), Portuguese novelist, poet and dramatist, best remembered for the novel As Pupilas do Senhor Reitor (The Pupils of the Dean, 1867).

Dio or Dion Cassius (actually Dio Cassius Cocceianus) (c.150–235), Roman administrator and historian.

Dio Chrysostom (c.40–c.112), celebrated Greek rhetorician and philosopher.

Diocles (4th Century BC), Greek physician and philosopher.

Diodati, Giovanni (1576–1649), Swiss Calvinist pastor, biblical translator and writer.

Diodore of Tarsus (c.330–c.390), Syrian Christian bishop and theologian.

Diodorus Siculus (1st Century BC), Greek historian who wrote the valuable Bibliotheca historica.

Diogenes Laërtius (3rd Century), Greek writer, author of the significant Peri bion dogmaton kai apophthegmaton ton en philosophia eudakimé santon (English trans. as Diogenes Laertius: Lives of Eminent Philosophers, 1925).

Diogenes of Apollonia (5th Century BC), Greek philosopher.

Dionysius Exiguus (c.500–c.560), Scythian-born Italian Roman Catholic theologian, mathematician, astronomer and translator, reputed inventor of the Christian calendar.

Dionysius of Halicarnassus (flourished c.20 BC), Greek historian and literary scholar.

Dionysius Telmaharensis or Dionysius of Tell Mahre (died 845), Syrian patriarch of the Jacobite Christian Church, author of The Chronicles or The Annal.

Dionysius the Carthusian (c.1402–1471), Flemish Roman Catholic theologian and mystic who wrote De contemplatione.

Diop, Birago Ismael (1906–1989), Senegalese poet and writer.

Diop, David (1927–1960), French-born West African poet who championed the cause of African independence; died in an airplane crash.

Diphilus (4th Century BC), Greek poet.

D'Israeli, Isaac (1766–1848), English writer, best remembered for his Curiosities of Literature (5 vols, 1791–1823); father of the statesman Benjamin Disraeli.

Dixon, Richard Watson (1833–1900), English poet and church historian.

Dixon, Roland B(urrage) (1875–1934), American cultural anthropologist, author of The Racial History of Man (1923) and The Building of Cultures (1928).

Dixon, Thomas (1864–1946), American novelist and dramatist, best known for his espousal of white supremacy in his novel The Clansman (1905), which served as the basis of D W Griffith's classic film The Birth of a Nation (1915).

Djilas, Milovan (1911–1995), Yugoslav politician, writer, poet and translator whose early espousal of Marxism was replaced with unremitting disdain in such works as The New Class (1957), Conversations with Stalin (1962) and The Unperfect Society (1969).

Długosz, Jan (1415–1480), Polish diplomat and historian who wrote the important Historiae Poloicae (12 vols, 1455–80).

Dobell, Sydney Thompson (1824–1874), English poet whose works became well known under the name Sydney Yendys.

Dobie, Charles Caldwell (1881–1943), American novelist and short-story writer.

Dobie, J(ames) Frank (1888–1964), American writer.

Doblin, Alfred (1878–1957), German novelist and essayist.

Dobrolyubov, Nikolai (Alexandrovich) (1836–1861), Russian critic who espoused the principles of the radical intelligentsia.

Dobrovský, Josef (1753–1829), Austro-Hungarian language scholar and antiquarian, author of the important Geschichte der böhmischen Sprache und Litteratur (History of the Bohemian Language and Literature, 1792).

Dobson, (Henry) Austin (1840–1921), English poet, biographer and essayist of distinction.

Dodd, C(harles) H(arold) (1884–1973), English New Testament scholar and theologian.

Doddridge, Philip (1702–1751), English Dissenting minister, writer and hymnist, author of The Rise and Progress of Religion in the Soul (1745).

Doderer, Heimito von (1896–1966), Austrian novelist, best known for his acclaimed novel Die Dämonen (The Demons, 1956).

Dodge, Mary Abigail (1833–1896), American writer who wrote under the name Gail Hamilton.

Dodge, Mary (Elizabeth) Mapes (1831–1905), American editor and writer of children's works, best remembered for her Hans Brinker, or, The Silver Skates (1865).

Dodsley, Robert (1703–1764), English poet, dramatist and publisher.

Does, Johan van der (1545–1609), Dutch statesman, poet and historian.

Doesburg, Theo van (actually Christian Emil Marie Küpper) (1883–1931), Dutch painter, decorator, art theorist and poet.

Dole, Nathan Haskell (1852–1935), American writer, poet, editor and translator.

Dolet, Étienne (1509–1546), French Humanist, scholar and printer whose fierce intellectual independence resulted in conflicts with the authorities and eventual condemnation and burning at the stake.

Döllinger, Johann Joseph Ignaz von (1799–1890), German church historian and theologian who opposed the doctrine of papal infallibility in his Der Papst und das Konzil (The Pope and the Council, 1869), was excommunicated and became a defender of the Old Catholic Churches.

Domett, Alfred (1811–1887), English poet and politician who served as Prime Minister of New Zealand (1862–63).

Donatus, Aelius (4th Century), celebrated Roman grammarian and teacher.

Donelaitis or Duonelaitis, Kristijonas (1714–1780), Lithuanian poet and Lutheran pastor, the first to employ hexameters in Lithuanian verse in his Metai (published 1818; English trans. as The Seasons, 1967).

Donnay, Maurice (-Charles) (1859–1945), French dramatist and writer.

Donne, John (1572–1631), English poet, writer and Anglican churchman and preacher, a Metaphysical poet whose poetry was complemented by his prose work Devotions upon Emergent Occasions (1624) and his sermons.

Donnelly, Ignatius (1831–1901), American politician and novelist.

Donoso, José (1924–96), Chilean novelist and short-story writer whose masterpiece was the novel El obsceno pájaro de la noche (1970; English trans. as The Obscene Bird of Night, 1973).

Donoso Cortes, Juan, Marquis de Valdegamas (1809–1853), Spanish diplomat and writer.

Dooley, Thomas Anthony (1927–1961), American physician, lecturer and writer who became known as the 'jungle doctor' for his efforts to relieve medical distress in Southeast Asia.

Doolittle, Hilda (1886–1961), American poet and novelist who wrote under the name H. D., an exponent of Imagism; wife of Richard Aldington.

Dorat or Daurat, Jean (1508–1588), important French poet and scholar who excelled in both Greek and Latin verse.

Dorris, Michael (Anthony) (1945–1997), American writer and poet; committed suicide.

Dorsey, George Amos (1868–1931), American anthropologist.

Dositheos (1641–1707), Greek Orthodox churchman and theologian.

Dos Passos, John (Roderigo) (1896–1970), eminent American novelist, poet and dramatist, author of the sweeping prose trilogy U.S.A. (The 42nd Parallel, 1930; 1919, 1932; The Big Money, 1936).

Dostoyevsky, Fyodor (Mikhailovich) (1821–1881), Russian novelist and short-story writer, author of such works as Zapiski iz myortvogo doma (Notes From the House of the Dead, 1861–62), Prestupleniye i nakazaniye (Crime and Punishment, 1866), Idiot (The Idiot, 1868–69), Besy (The Devils, 1871–72) and Bratya Karamazovy (The Brothers Karamazov, 1879–80).

Doughty, Charles Montague (1843–1926), English traveller and poet, best remembered for his Travels in Arabia Deserta (1888).

Douglas, Alfred Bruce, Lord (1870–1945), English poet.

Douglas, Gawin or Gavin (1474–1522), Scottish bishop, political figure, poet and translator, noted for his translation of Virgil's Aeneid.

Douglas, George (actually George Douglas Brown) (1869–1902), Scottish novelist.

Douglas, (George) Norman (1868–1952), English novelist and essayist.

Douglas, Keith Castellain (1920–1944), talented English poet; died in World War II.

Douglas, Lloyd C(assel) (1877–1951), American Lutheran clergyman and novelist, author of the works Magnificent Obsession (1929) and The Robe (1942).

Douglas-Home, William (1912–1992), English dramatist and writer.

Douglass, Frederick (actually Frederick Augustus Washington Bailey) (1817–1895), famous American Abolitionist, orator, writer and public official whose escape from slavery to eminence was captured in his autobiography (1845, new version as My Bondage and My Freedom, 1855 and final version as Life and Times of Frederick Douglass, 1882).

Dowden, Edward (1843–1913), Irish critic, biographer and poet who distinguished himself particularly as a Shakespearean scholar.

Dowson, Ernest Christopher (1867–1900), English poet, short-story writer and dramatist, a principal figure in the so-called Decadents movement in poetry, especially admired for his Verses (1896) and Decorations (1899).

Doyle, Sir Arthur Conan (1859–1930), noted Scottish writer, creator of the celebrated master detective Sherlock Holmes.

Doyle, Sir Francis Hastings Charles, 2nd Baronet (1810–1888), English poet who was known for his ballads.

Dozy, Reinhart Pieter (Anne) (1820–1883), Dutch historian.

Drachmann, Holger Henrik Herholdt (1846–1908), major Danish poet, writer and dramatist.

Dracontius, Blossius Aemilius (5th Century), famous African Christian Latin poet.

Drake, Benjamin (1795–1841), American writer; brother of Daniel Drake.

Drake, Daniel (1785–1852), American physician, educator and writer; brother of Benjamin Drake.

Drake, Joseph Rodman (1795–1820), American poet who collaborated with Fitz-Greene Halleck on the satirical poems the Croaker Papers.

Drayton, Michael (1563–1631), significant English poet, author of the collections Polyolbion (1612) and Poems (1619).

Dreiser, Theodore (Herman Albert) (1871–1945), important American novelist, essayist and poet, best known for his naturalistic novels Sister Carrie (1900), the trilogy The Financier (1912), The Titan (1914) and The Stoic (1947), and An American Tragedy (1925).

Dresser, Horatio (1866–1954), American writer.

Drieu La Rochelle, Pierre (1893–1945), French novelist and essayist; a convert to Nazism, he committed suicide.

Drinkwater, John (1882–1937), English poet, dramatist and critic.

Drost, Aernoust (1810–1834), Dutch novelist and short-story writer.

Droste-Hülshoff, Annette Elisabeth von (1797–1848), German poet and writer, renowned for her mastery of refined classicism.

Droysen, Johann Gustav (1808–1884), German historian and politician who wrote the unfinished Geschichte der preussischen Politik (14 vols, 1855–86).

Drummond, Henry (1786–1860), English banker, politician, writer and angel (bishop) of the Catholic Apostolic Church.

Drummond, William (1585–1649), Scottish poet and writer who was known as William Drummond of Hawthornden.

Drummond, William Henry (1854–1907), French-Canadian poet of humorous verse in dialect.

Drummond de Andrade, Carlos (1902–87), Brazilian poet, journalist and writer.

Drury, Allen (Stuart) (1918–1998), American writer, best known for his novel Advise and Consent (1959).

Dryden, John (1631–1700), celebrated English poet, dramatist, critic and translator whose works presaged the neo-Classical movement; was Poet Laureate of the United Kingdom (1668–88).

Duane, William (1760–1835), American journalist and writer.

Du Bois, W(illiam) E(dward) B(urghardt) (1868–1963), influential American sociologist, civil rights advocate, writer and editor whose controversial career ended with his espousal of Marxism.

Du Bos, Charles (1882–1939), French critic whose writings on both French and English literature were notable.

Du Camp, Maxime (1822–1894), French poet, novelist and journalist.

Du Cange, Charles du Fresne, Sieur (1610–1688), French scholar, especially renowned for his studies in historical linguistics in his Glossarium ad Scriptores Mediae et Infimae Latinitatis (A Glossary for Writers of Middle and Low Latin, 1678) and Glossarium ad Scriptores Mediae et Infimae Graecitatis (A Glossary for Middle and Low Greek, 1688).

Du Casse, Isidore-Lucien (1846–1870), French poet who wrote under the name Comte de Lautréamont.

Du Casse, Pierre-Emmanuel-Albert, Baron (1813–1893), French soldier, military historian and editor.

Du Chaillu, Paul Belloni (1835–1903), French explorer and writer, best remembered for his Explorations and Adventures in Equatorial Africa (1861).

Du Maurier, Dame Daphne (1907–1989), English novelist and dramatist, best remembered for her novel Rebecca (1938); granddaughter of George (Louis Palmella Busson) Du Maurier.

Du Maurier, George (Louis Palmella Busson) (1834–1896), French-born English illustrator and writer; grandfather of Dame Daphne Du Maurier.

Du Ponceau, Pierre Étienne (1760–1844), French-born American writer and lawyer who wrote on such subjects as the law, government and philology.

du Pont de Nemours, Pierre Samuel (1739–1817), French economist.

Du Toit, Jakob Daniel (1877–1953), Afrikaans pastor, biblical scholar and poet.

Dube, John Langalibalele (1871–1946), South African minister, educator, journalist and writer, author of the first novel published by a Zulu in the native tongue Insila ka Shaka (1930; English trans. as Jeqe, the Bodyservant of King Shaka, 1951).

Dubé, Rodolphe (1905–1985), French-Canadian poet, essayist and philosopher who wrote under the name François Hertel.

Dubnow, Simon (1860–1941), eminent Russian Jewish historian whose greatest work was the expansive Weltgeschichte des jüdischen Volkes (World History of the Jewish People, 10 vols, 1925–29).

Dubois, Jean-Antoine (1765–1848), French Roman Catholic priest and educator who left an account of his missionary activities in India (1817).

Dubus, Andre (1936–99), American writer, particularly known for his short-story collection Dancing After Hours (1996).

Duche, Jacob (1737–1798), American Anglican clergyman and writer, author of Observations or Caspipina's Letters (1774) and Discourses on Various Subjects (1779).

Duchesne, André (1584–1640), significant French historian and geographer.

Duchesne, Jacques (1897–1971), French theatre director, manager and dramatist.

Duchesne, Louis-Marie-Olivier (1843–1922), French Roman Catholic priest and church historian, author of the Histoire ancienne de l'église chrétienne (Early History of the Christian Church, 4 vols, 1905–25).

Ducis, Jean-François (1733–1816), French poet and dramatist, particularly known for his tragic plays Oedipe che Admète (Oedipus at Admetus, 1778) and Abufar (1795).

Duck, Stephen (1705–1756), English poet and churchman; committed suicide.

Ducommun, Élie (1833–1906), French editor, writer and peace activist; won the Nobel Prize for Peace (1902).

Dudek, Louis (1918–2001), Canadian poet, author of works such as Europe (1955), En México (1958) and Atlantis (1967).

Dudintsev, Vladimir Dmitrievich (1918–1998), Russian writer, best remembered for his dissident novel Ne khelbom yedinim (1957; English trans. as Not by Bread Alone).

Dudley, Edmund (c.1462–1510), English minister of King Henry VII and author of the political allegory The Tree of Commonwealth (1509); was convicted of treason and executed.

Dudley, Sir Robert (1574–1649), English sailor and engineer who wrote Dell'Arcano del mare (Concerning the Secret of the Sea, 3 vols, 1646–47).

Dudo of Saint-Quentin (c.960–c.1042), French historian, author of De moribus et actis primorum Normannaie ducum.

Dufresnoy, Charles-Alphonse (1611–1665), French painter, writer on art and poet.

Duganne, Augustine Joseph Hickey (1823–1884), American poet and writer.

Dugdale, Sir William (1605–1686), notable English antiquarian and scholar.

Dugonics, András (1740–1818), Hungarian writer.

Duhamel, Georges (1884–1966), eminent French novelist and poet highly regarded for his novel cycles Vie et aventures de Salavin (5 vols, 1920–32; English trans. as Salavin, 1936) and Chronique des Pasquier (10 vols, 1933–44).

Duhem, Pierre-Maurice-Marie (1861–1916), French physicist and philosopher.

Dühring, Karl Eugen (1833–1921), German philosopher and political economist, a leading exponent of Positivism.

Dujardin, Édouard (-Émile-Louis) (1861–1949), French novelist, poet, dramatist and critic, author of the first novel to utilize the interior monologue Les Lauriers sont coupés (1888; English trans. as We'll to the Woods No More, 1938).

Dumas, Alexandre (Davy de la Pailleterie) (1802–1870), famous French writer and dramatist who was know as Dumas père, author of such celebrated novels as Les Trois Mousquetaires (The Three Musketeers, 1844), Vingt Ans après (Twenty Years After, 1845), Le Comte de Monte Cristo (The Count of Monte Cristo, 1845), Dix Ans plus tard ou le Vicomte de Bragelonne (Ten Years Later, or, The Vicomte de Bragelonne, 1848–50) and La Tulipe noire (The Black Tulip, 1850); father of Alexandre Dumas fils.

Dumas, Alexandre (1824–1895), French dramatist and writer who was known as Dumas fils, author of the novel La Dame aux camelias (1848; adapted as a play, 1852), which inspired Verdi's opera La traviata (1853); son of Alexandre Dumas père.

Dumont, Fernand (1927–1997), French-Canadian sociologist, essayist and poet.

Dunash ben Labrat (c.920–c.990), Hebrew poet, grammarian and polemicist, the first to employ Arabic metres in his verse.

Dunbar, Paul Laurence (1872–1906), American poet and novelist, some of whose poems in black dialect were included in his collection Lyrics of Lowly Life (1896).

Dunbar, William (c.1460–c.1530), Scottish poet and priest, renowned for The Thrissil and the Rois (1503) and The Lament for the Makaris (c.1507).

Duncan, Robert (Edward) (1919–1988), American poet, writer and dramatist.

Duncan, Ronald (Frederick Henry) (1914–82), English dramatist, poet and writer.

Dunlap, William (1766–1839), American dramatist, writer and painter.

Dunne, Finley Peter (1867–1936), American journalist who created the humorous wit Mr Dooley.

Dunnett, Dorothy (1923–2001), Scottish writer and portrait painter who became best known for her novels The Lymond Chronicles (six vols) and The House of Niccolò (eight vols).

Dunsany, Edward (John Moreton Drax Plunkett), 18th Baron (1878–1957), Irish poet, novelist and dramatist.

Duns Scotus, John (c.1266–1308), eminent Scottish Franciscan philosopher and Scholastic theologian who was known as Doctor Subtilis, author of the celebrated Quaestiones quodlibetales.

Dunster, Henry (1609–1659), English-born American Baptist minister, scholar and educator.

Dupin, Louis Ellies (1657–1719), French church historian, author of the Nouvelle Bibliothèque des auteurs ecclésiastiques (New Library of Ecclesiastical Writers, 58 vols, 1686–1704).

Dupuy, Eliza Ann (1814–1881), American writer.

Dupuy, Pierre (1582–1651), French historian and royal librarian.

Duran, Profiat (actually Isaac ben Moses Ha-Levi) (c.1350–c.1415), French Jewish philosopher and grammarian who wrote a satirical attack on Christianity in his 'Al tehi ka-'avotekha (Be Not Like Thy Fathers, c.1396).

Duran, Simeon ben Zemah (1361–1444), Spanish Jewish rabbi and Talmudic scholar.

Durand, Guillaume (c.1230–1296), French Roman Catholic prelate and scholar, particularly known for his Speculum iudiciale (1271–76) and Rationale divinorum officiorum (c.1289).

Durandus of Saint-Pourçain (c.1270–1334), French Roman Catholic bishop, theologian and philosopher who opposed the ideas of St Thomas Aquinas.

Durant, Wil(liam James) (1885–1981), American writer who wrote such studies as The Story of Philosophy (1926) and The Story of Civilization (10 vols, 1935–67).

Durão, José de Santa Rita (c.1737–1784), Brazilian poet, author of the epic Caramúru (1781).

Duras, Marguerite (actually Marguerite Donnadieu) (1914–1996), admired French novelist and screenwriter, especially known for her screenplay Hiroshima mon amour (1959) and the novel L'Amant (1984; English trans. as The Lover, 1984).

D'Urfé, Honoré (1567–1625), French novelist who wrote L'Astrée (4 vols, 1607–27).

D'Urfey, Thomas (1653–1723), English dramatist and songwriter, particularly remembered for his satirical bent.

Durkheim, Émile (1858–1917), influential French social scientist who helped to establish sociology in his homeland.

Durrell, Lawrence (George) (1912–1990), esteemed English poet, novelist, dramatist and critic, highly regarded for his novel in four parts Justine (1957), Balthazar (1958), Mountolive (1958) and Clea (1960), all four published as The Alexandria Quartet (1962).

Dürrenmatt, Friedrich (1921–1990), famous Swiss dramatist and novelist, one of the masters of experimental theatre in the 20th Century.

Dutton, Geoffrey Piers Henry (1922–1998), Australian novelist, poet, critic, publisher and activist, best known for his novel Queen Emma of the South Seas (1976).

Duun, Olav (1876–1939), Norwegian novelist who wrote the notable series of works Juvikfolke (The People of Juvik, 1918–23).

Duvergier de Hauranne, Jean (1581–1643), French Roman Catholic abbot and theologian who founded the Jansenist movement in opposition to the Jesuits.

Duyckinck, Evert Augustus (1816–1878), American editor, critic and biographer who, with his brother George, published the Cyclopaedia of American Literature (2 vols, 1855, supplement 1866).

Duyckinck, George Long (1823–1863), American editor, critic and biographer who, with his brother Evert, published the Cyclopaedia of American Literature (2 vols 1855, supplement 1866).

Dwight, John S(ullivan) (1813–1893), noted American music critic who edited Dwight's Journal of Music (1852–81).

Dwight, Theodore (1764–1846), American editor, writer and poet; brother of Timothy and father of Theodore Dwight.

Dwight, Theodore (1796–1866), American editor and writer; son of Theodore Dwight.

Dwight, Timothy (1752–1817), American clergyman, educator, writer and poet; brother of Theodore Dwight.

Dyce, Alexander (1798–1869), Scottish editor and lexicographer.

Dyer, Sir Edward (1543–1607), English courtier and poet.

Dyer, John (1699–1757), Welsh poet and painter, known for such poems as Grongar Hill (1726), The Ruins of Rome (1740) and The Fleece (1757).

Eames, Wilberforce (1855–1937), American scholar and bibliographer.

Earle, Alice Morse (1853–1911), American historian.

Earle or Earles, John (c.1601–1665), English Anglican clergyman, writer and translator, best known for his Micro-cosmographie, Or, A Peece of the World Discovered; in Essays and Characters (1628).

Eastburn, James Wallis (1797–1819), English-born American Episcopal clergyman, poet and hymnist.

Eastlake, Charles Lock (1836–1906), English meseologist and writer on art who wrote Hints on Household Taste in Furniture, Upholstery and Other Details (1868), Lectures on Decorative Art and Art Workmanship (1876) and Our Square and Circle (1895).

Eastman, Charles Alexander (1858–1939), American physician and writer, author of various books dealing with his Indian heritage.

Eastman, Mary H(enderson) (1818–1880), American writer whose Aunt Phillis's Cabin, or, Southern Life as It Is (1852) was a reply to Uncle Tom's Cabin.

Eastman, Max (Forrester) (1883–1969), American poet, writer, editor and political radical who later espoused conservatism.

Ebbinghaus, Hermann (1850–1909), German psychologist who wrote Grundzüge der Psychologie (Principles of Psychology, 1902) and Abriss der Psychologie (Summary of Psychology, 1908).

Eberhard, Johann August (1739–1809), German philosopher and lexicographer, a proponent of empericism.

Ebert, Karl Egon (1801–1882), Bohemian poet, author of the national epic Vlasta (1829).

Ebner-Eschenbach, Marie, Freifrau von (1830–1916), Austrian novelist, best known for her Das Gemeindekind (1887; English trans. as The Child of the Parish, 1893).

Eça de Queirós, José Maria de (1845–1900), renowned Portuguese novelist and diplomat, author of O Crime do Padre Amaro (1875; English trans. as The Sin of Father Amaro, 1962), O Primo Basílio (1878; English trans. as Cousin Bazilio, 1953), Os Maias (1888; English trans. as The Maias, 1965) and A Cidade e as Serras (1901; English trans. as The City and the Mountains, 1955).

Echegaray y Eizaguirre, José (1832–1916), eminent Spanish dramatist, mathematician and statesman; co-winner of the Nobel Prize for Literature (1904).

Echeverría, Esteban (1809–1851), Argentine poet.

Eck, Johann (1486–1543), prominent German Roman Catholic theologian and polemicist, a leading figure of the Counter-Reformation.

Eckermann, Johann Peter (1792–1854), German writer, best remembered for his Gespräche mit Goethe in den letzten Jahren seines Lebens, 1823–32 (Conversations with Goethe in the Last Years of His Life, 1832–32, 3 vols, 1836–48).

Eddy, Mary Baker (1821–1910), American religious leader who founded Christian Science and wrote Science and Health (1875; revised edition as Science and Health with Key to the Scriptures).

Edel, (Joseph) Leon (1907–1997), esteemed American literary scholar and biographer.

Edgeworth, Maria (1767–1849), admired Anglo-Irish writer, author of the novels Castle Rackrent (1800) and Tales of Fashionable Life (6 vols, 1809–12); daughter of Richard Lovell Edgeworth.

Edgeworth, Richard Lovell (1744–1817), English inventor and educator who collaborated with his daughter on the tome Practical Education; father of Maria Edgeworth.

Edmer or Eadmer (c.1060–c.1128), English monk, author of Historia novorum in Anglia (c.1115) and Vita Anselmi (c.1124).

Edmonds, Walter D(umaux) (1903–1998), American novelist and short-story writer, best remembered for his classic novel Drums Along the Mohawk (1936).

Edmund, Saint (c.1175–1240), noted English scholar and Archbishop of Canterbury who was known as Edmund of Abingdon, author of Speculum ecclesia (English trans., 1905).

Edwards, Jonathan (1703–1758), famous American Protestant preacher, theologian and philosopher who inspired the religious revival known as the 'Great Awakening'; grandson of Solomon Stoddard.

Edwards, Sir Owen Morgan (1858–1920), Welsh scholar and educator.

Edwards, Richard (1524–1566), English poet, dramatist and composer.

Edwards, Thomas Charles (1837–1900), Welsh Separatist churchman and educator.

Edwards Bello, Joaquín (1888–1968), Chilean journalist and novelist.

Eeden, Frederik Willem van (1860–1932), Dutch physician, writer, poet, dramatist and translator.

Eekhoud, Georges (1854–1927), Belgian novelist and poet.

Effen, Justus van (1684–1735), Dutch journalist and essayist.

Egan, Pierce (1772–1849), English writer on sports.

Eggleston, Edward (1837–1902), American writer and editor, best known for his novel The Hoosier Schoolmaster (1871); brother of George Cary Eggleston.

Eggleston, George Cary (1839–1911), American journalist and writer; brother of Edward Eggleston.

Egill Skallagrímsson (c.910–990), celebrated Icelandic poet.

Eguren, José María (1874–1942), Peruvian poet and critic.

Ehrenburg, Ilya (Grigorievich) (1891–1967), prominent Russian journalist and writer of the Soviet era.

Ehrenfels, Christian, Freiherr von (1859–1932), Austrian philosopher who gave the term Gestalt to psychology and wrote the important System der Werttheorie (Sytem of Value Theory, 2 vols, 1897–98).

Ehrlich, Eugen (1862–1922), Austro-Hungarian legal scholar, author of Grundlegung der Soziologie des Rechts (1913; English trans. as Fundamental Principles of the Sociology of Law, 1936).

Eichendorff, Joseph, Freiherr von (1788–1857), important German poet, novelist and critic, one of the principal Romantic lyricists of his homeland.

Eichhorn, Johann Gottfried (1752–1827), German biblical scholar, Orientalist and educator.

Eichrodt, Walther (1890–1978), German biblical scholar who wrote the major study Theologie des Alten Testaments (Theology of the Old Testament, two vols, 1933, 1935).

Eilhart von Oberge (12th Century), German poet who wrote the epic Tristant.

Einhard or Eginhard (c.770–840), German scholar who wrote a valuable study of Charlemagne and the Carolingian Empire Vita Caroli Magni (c.830).

Eiseley, Loren (Corey) (1907–1977), American anthropologist, writer and poet.

Ekelöf, (Bengt) Gunnar (1907–1968), Swedish poet and essayist.

Ekelund, Vilhelm (1880–1949), Swedish poet and essayist.

Ekkehard I the Elder (c.910–973), Swiss teacher, monk, poet and hymnist, the reputed author of the Latin heroic poem Waltharius (c.930).

Ekkehard IV (c.980–c.1069), Swiss teacher, writer, poet and musician, one of the major authors of the Casus Sancti Galli (The Events of St Gall).

Ekrem Bey, Recaizade Mahmud (1847–1914), Turkish writer, poet, dramatist, critic and translator.

Eldad (ben Mahli) ha-Dani (9th Century), Jewish traveller and philologist.

Eleazar ben Azariah (1st Century), rabbinic scholar.

Eleazar ben Judah (ben Kalonymos) of Worms (c.1160–1238), German rabbi, scholar and mystic who was also known as Eleazar Rokeah.

Eliade, Mircea (1907–1986), eminent Romanian-born American historian of religions, author of the important studies Traité d'histoire des religions (1949; English trans. as Patterns of Comparative Religion, 1958), Le Mythe de l'éternel retour (1949; English trans. as The Myth of the Eternal Return, 1954) and Le Chamanisme et les techniques archaïques de l'extase (1951; English trans. as Shamanism: Archaic Techniques of Ectasy, 1964).

Eliezer ben Hyrcanus (1st–2nd Century), Palestinian scholar.

Eliezer ben Yehuda (1858–1923), Israeli novelist.

Eliot, Charles W(illiam) (1834–1926), American educator and writer.

Eliot, George (actually Mary Ann Evans) (1819–1880), English novelist and poet, author of Adam Bede (1859), The Mill on the Floss (1860), Silas Marner (1861), Romola (1862–63), Middlemarch (1871–72) and Daniel Deronda (1876).

Eliot, John (1604–1690), English-born American Puritan preacher and missionary, known as the 'Apostle to the Indians' for his translation of the Bible into the Algonkian language (1661–63).

Eliot, T(homas) S(tearns) (1888–1965), celebrated American-born English poet, dramatist and critic, especially known for such poetry as Prufrock and Other Observations (1917), The Waste Land (1922) and Four Quartets (1935), and the plays Murder in the Cathedral (1935) and The Cocktail Party (1950); won the Nobel Prize for Literature (1948).

Elizabeth (1843–1916), Romanian queen consort, writer and poet who wrote under the name Carmen Sylva.

Elkin, Stanley (Lawrence) (1930–1995), American novelist and short-story writer.

Ellerman, (Annie) Winifred (1894–1983), English arts patroness, novelist and poet who wrote under the name Bryher.

Elliott, George P(aul) (1918–1980), American novelist, short-story writer and essayist.

Elliott, Maud Howe (1854–1948), American writer who collaborated with her sister Laura E Richards on a biography of their mother Julia Ward Howe (1915).

Ellis, Edward S(ylvester) (1840–1916), American writer of enormously successful dime novels.

Ellis, George (1753–1815), English poet and translator who excelled in satirical verse.

Ellis, (Henry) Havelock (1859–1939), English physician, essayist and editor whose study of human sexuality resulted in his Studies in the Psychology of Sex (7 vols, 1897–1928).

Ellison, Ralph (Waldo) (1915–1994), American novelist and essayist esteemed for his novel Invisible Man (1952).

Ellmann, Richard (1918–1987), notable American literary scholar and biographer.

Elskamp, Max (1862–1931), esteemed Belgian poet, one of the finest representatives of the Symbolist movement of his day.

Elsschot, Willem (actually Alfons de Ridder) (1882–1960), Belgian novelist.

Elstob, Elizabeth (1683–1756), English writer on Anglo-Saxon subjects.

Éluard, Paul (actually Eugène Grindel) (1895–1952), significant French poet of the Surrealist movement.

Eluttaccan (16th Century), Indian Malayalam poet.

Elyot, Sir Thomas (c.1490–1546), English philosopher and lexicographer.

Elytis, Odysseus (actually Odysseus Alepoudhelis) (1911–1996), noted Greek poet, especially admired for his To Axion Esti (1959; English trans. as The Axion Esti, 1967); won the Nobel Prize for Literature (1979).

Embury, Emma Catherine (1806–1863), American novelist and poet.

Emden, Jacob Israel (actually Jacob ben Zebi) (1697–1776), eminent Danish rabbi and Talmudic scholar who was known as Yaabetz, an acronym based on his given name.

Emerson, Ralph Waldo (1803–1882), famous American poet, essayist, lecturer and champion of Transcendentalism, one of the most significant figures in American literary history.

Emery, Gilbert (actually Emery Bemsley Pottle) (1875–1945), American dramatist who was best known for his play The Hero (1921).

Eminescu, Mihail (actually Mihail Eminovici) (1850–1889), esteemed Romanian poet and writer.

Emlyn, Thomas (1663–1741), English Presbyterian minister and writer.

Empedocles (c.490–430 BC), Greek philosopher, poet, physiologist and statesman.

Empson, Sir William (1906–1984), English critic and poet, author of the important critical study Seven Types of Ambiguity (1930).

Emre, Yunus (c.1250–c.1321), significant Turkish mystic and poet.

Emser, Hieronymus (1478–1527), German theologian, biblical translator, essayist and Roman Catholic priest who became an opponent of Lutheranism.

Encina, Juan del (c.1468–c.1530), Spanish poet, dramatist, composer and Roman Catholic priest.

Enckell, Rabbe (Arnfinn) (1903–74), Finnish poet, dramatist and critic.

Endō Shūsaku (1923–96), Japanese writer and dramatist, particularly admired for his novels Chimmoku (Silence, 1966) and Samurai (1980).

Enfantin, Barthélemy-Prosper (1796–1864), French social reformer and writer, one of the principal figures of the St Simonian movement.

Engels, Friedrich (1820–1895), influential German-born English philosopher who collaborated with Karl Marx in developing Communist theory.

Engle, Paul (Hamilton) (1908–1991), American poet and writer.

English, Thomas Dunn (1819–1902), American poet and dramatist, best remembered for his poem Ben Bolt.

Ennius, Quintus (c.239–169 BC), illustrious Roman poet and dramatist, the acknowledged father of Roman literature who introduced the hexameter into Latin verse.

Ennodius, Magnus Felix (c.473–521), Italian poet, writer, rhetorician and bishop.

Enríquez Gómez, Antonio (actually Enríquez de Pax) (1602–c.1662), Spanish dramatist and poet.

Eötvös, József, Baron (1813–1871), prominent Hungarian novelist, short-story writer, statesman and educator.

Ephorus (c.405–330 BC), Greek historian who wrote the first universal history.

Ephraem or Aphrem Syrus, Saint (c.306–373), important Syrian Christian theologian, poet and hymnist who left a large output of works.

Epicharmus (c.530–440 BC), Greek poet.

Epicurus (341–270 BC), notable Greek philosopher whose writings have only been preserved in fragments.

Epimenides (6th Century BC), Cretan poet and priest.

Épinay, Louise-Florence-Pétronille Tardieu d'Esclavelles, Dame de La Live d' (1726–1783), French writer who became best known for her literary salon.

Epiphanius, Saint (c.315–403), significant Christian theologian and bishop, author of a work on heresies Panarium (374–77).

Episcopius, Simon (1583–1643), Dutch theologian.

Equiano, Olaudah (c.1750–1797), African-born English Abolitionist whose early years as a slave and later as a free man were depicted in his autobiography The Interesting Narrative of the Life of Olaudah Equiano, or Gustavus Vassa, the African (1789).

Erasmus, Desiderius (c.1466–1536), Dutch Humanist and scholar.

Erastus, Thomas (actually Thomas Lüber, Lieber or Liebler) (1524–1583), Swiss physician and writer on religion, author of a treatise on excommunication Explicatio gravissimae quaestionis (Explication of the Gravest Question, published 1589).

Eratosthenes of Cyrene (c.276–c.194 BC), Greek astronomer and poet who is generally believed to have been the first to have measured the circumference of the Earth; committed suicide.

Ercilla y Zúñiga, Alonso de (1533–1594), Spanish poet, author of the expansive epic La Araucana (3 parts, 1569, 1578, 1589).

Erckmann-Chatrian (actually Emile Érckmann [1822–1899] and Louis-Alexandre Chatrian [1826–1890], French novelists who collaborated on a series of successful regional novels.

Erigena, John Scotus (810–877), Irish philosopher, theologian and translator.

Erikson, Erik H(omburger) (1902–94), German-born American psychoanalyst and writer who wrote widely on history, politics and culture.

Erinna (4th Century BC), Greek poet, author of The Distaff.

Erlingsson, Thorsteinn (1858–1914), Icelandic poet who wrote the collections Thyrnar (Thorns, 1897) and Eidurinn (The Oath, 1913).

Ermoldus Nigellus (790–838), French scholar and poet.

Ernesti, Johann August (1707–1781), German philologist and theologian.

Ernst, Paul (Karl Friedrich) (1866–1933), German short-story writer, essayist, poet and dramatist.

Ervine, St John (Greer) (1883–1971), Irish dramatist, novelist, biographer and essayist.

Escobar y Mendoza, Antonio (1589–1669), Spanish Jesuit preacher and theologian.

Esenin, Sergei (Alexandrovich) (1895–1925), Russian poet; committed suicide.

Espinel, Vicente (Martínez) (1550–1624), Spanish Roman Catholic priest, writer, poet and musician.

Espinosa, Pedro de (1578–1650), Spanish poet and editor, best known for his poem Fábula del Genil and the important anthology Flores de poetas ilustres de España (Flowers From the Illustrious Poets of Spain, 1605).

Espronceda (y Delgado), José de (1808–1842), Spanish poet who espoused Romanticism.

Esquiros, Henri Alphonse (1814–1876), French poet, writer and politician.

Estaunié, Edouard (1862–1942), French novelist.

Estébanez Calderón, Serafín (1799–1867), Spanish writer and poet who wrote under the name of El Solitario.

Estienne, Charles (died c.1564), French writer; brother of Robert Estienne.

Estienne, Henri (1528–1598), French scholar and printer; son of Robert Estienne.

Estienne, Robert (1503–1559), French scholar and printer; father of Henri Estienne.

Etherege, Sir George (c.1635–1692), English dramatist and poet who created the Restoration comedy of manners with The Comical Revenge, or, Love in a Tub (1664), She wou'd if she cou'd (1668) and The Man of Mode, or, Sir Fopling Flutter (1676).

Ethier-Blais, Jean (1925–1995), French-Canadian writer, poet and critic.

Eucken, Rudolf Christoph (1846–1926), German philosopher of Idealism; won the Nobel Prize for Literature (1908).

Eudemos of Rhodes (4th Century BC), Greek philosopher.

Eugenikos, John (15th Century), Byzantine theologian, scholar and poet, author of the famous ode Oratorio for the Great City which he wrote in the wake of the Muslim capture of Constantinople in 1453.

Eugenikos, Markus (c.1392–1445), Greek Orthodox churchman and theologian.

Euhemerus (300 BC), Greek mythographer who wrote a work on popular myths.

Eumenius (3rd Century), Roman orator who wrote the Oratio pro instaurondis scholis (Oration on the Restoration of Schools).

Eunapius (c.345–c.420), Greek historian, author of a valuable work on the lives of the philosophers and Sophists (English trans., 1922).

Euphorion (c.275–c.220 BC), Greek poet and grammarian.

Eupolis (5th Century BC), famous Greek dramatist.

Eurelius, Gunno (actually Gunno Dahlstierna) (1661–1709), Swedish writer.

Euripides (c.484–406 BC), Greek dramatist, a master of the tragedy.

Eusden, Laurence (1688–1730), English poet who was often the victim of the satirical arrows of Alexander Pope; became Poet Laureate of the United Kingdom (1718).

Eusebius of Caesarea (c.260–c.340), celebrated Christian bishop and church historian, author of an important ecclesiastical history (10 vols).

Eusebius of Dorylaeum (5th Century), prominent Christian bishop and theologian who opposed Nestorianism in his Contestatio.

Eustathius of Thessalonica (c.1100–c.1194), learned Greek Orthodox churchman and scholar.

Euthymius I (c.834–917), Byzantine Orthodox monk, churchman and theologian.

Euthymius of Tŭrnovo (c.1317–c.1402), Byzantine Orthodox churchman and scholar.

Euthymius the Hagiorite (c.955–1028), Georgian Orthodox churchman and scholar.

Evagrius Ponticus (346–399), Christian mystic and theologian.

Evans, Augusta Jane (1835–1909), American novelist who wrote St Elmo (1867).

Evans, Caradoc (actually David Evans) (1878–1945), Welsh novelist and short-story writer.

Evans, Charles (1850–1935), American bibliographer.

Evans, Donald (1884–1921), American poet, journalist and music critic; committed suicide.

Evans, Evan (1731–1788), Welsh scholar, critic and poet.

Evans, George Henry (1805–1856), American journalist and writer.

Evans, Sir John (1823–1908), English antiquarian and numismatist who helped to found prehistoric archaeology.

Evans, Nathaniel (1742–1767), American Anglican clergyman and poet.

Evans-Pritchard, E(dward) E(van) (1902–1973), English social anthropologist.

Evelyn, John (1620–1706), English writer and diarist.

Everett, Alexander Hill (1790–1847), American editor, writer, poet and diplomat.

Everett, Edward (1794–1865), American orator, lecturer and statesman.

Everson, William (1912–1994), esteemed American poet who, as a Dominican lay bother, wrote under the name Brother Antoninus.

Ewald, Heinrich (Georg August) von (1803–1875), German theologian and Orientalist, author of the important Geschichte des Volkes Israel (7 vols, 1843–59).

Ewald, Johannes (1743–1781), Danish poet and writer, a master of lyric poetry.

Ewart, Gavin (Buchanan) (1916–1995), English poet who was especially known for his light verse.

Ewing, A(lfred) C(yril) (1899–1973), English philosopher.

Eximenis, Francesc (c.1340–1409), Catalonian writer.

Eybeschütz, Jonathan (1690–1764), Danish rabbi who became well known for his views on the Talmud and Kabbala.

Eymeric or Eymerich, Nicholas (c.1320–1399), Spanish Roman Catholic theologian and zealous grand inquisitor, author of Directorium inquisitorium (1376).

Eysenck, Hans J(ürgen) (1916–1997), German-born English psychologist who was known for his controversial theories on intelligence and personality.

Faber, Frederick William (1814–1863), English Roman Catholic theologian and hymnist, best remembered for his hymns Hark! Hark, My Soul and My God, How Wonderful Thou Art.

Fabius Pictor, Quintus (200 BC), Roman historian.

Fabre, Émile (1869–1955), French dramatist.

Fabre, Ferdinand (1827–1898), French novelist.

Fabre d'Églantine, Philippet (-François-Nazaire) (1750–1794), French dramatist and poet, author of the famous comedy Le Philente de Molière (1790); was guillotined.

Fadeyev, Alexander Alexandrovich (1901–1956), Russian novelist and Communist theoretician who was a leading figure during the Stalinist era; in the wake of the denunciation of the Stalinist regime, he committed suicide.

Fadiman, Clifton (Paul) (1904–99), American critic, editor, essayist and anthologist.

Faesi, Robert (1883–1972), Swiss writer, poet, dramatist and critic who was particularly admired for his novel trilogy Die Stadt der Väter (The City of the Fathers), Die Stadt der Freiheit (The City of Freedom) and Die Stadt des Friedens (The City of Peace), published between 1941 and 1952.

Faguet, Émile (1847–1916), French literary critic and historian who wrote the Politiques et moralistes du dixneuvième siècle (3 vols, 1891–1900).

Fagunwa, D(aniel) O (1910–1963), esteemed Nigerian novelist in the Yoruba language.

Fain, Agathon-Jean-François, Baron (1778–1837), important French historian who wrote the invaluable Manuscrit de 1814, contenant l'histoire des six derniers mois du règne de Napoléon (Notebook of 1814, Relating the History of the Last Six Months of Napoleon's Reign, 1823).

Fairbairn, Andrew Martin (1838–1912), English Congregationalist minister, theologian and educator.

Fairbank, Janet Ayer (1879–1951), American novelist and short-story writer; sister of Margaret Ayer Barnes.

Fairfax, Edward (c.1575–1635), English poet and translator.

Fairfield, Sumner Lincoln (1803–1844), American poet and writer.

Fakhr ad-Dīn ar-Rāzī (actually Abū 'Abd Allāh Muhammad ibn 'Umar ibn al-Husayn Fakhr ad-Dīn-Rāzī) (1149–1209), noted Muslim theologian and scholar.

Falconer, William (1732–1769), English poet, seaman and lexicographer, author of the poem The Shipwreck (1762; revised 176 and 1769); ironically he died in the sinking of the frigate Aurora.

Falkberget, Johan Petter (actually Johan Petter Lillebakken) (1879–1967), Norwegian novelist.

Falke, Gustav (1853–1916), German poet and novelist.

Falkland, Lucius Cary, 2nd Viscount (1610–1643), English royalist writer on theology and poet; died in the Battle of Newbury.

Falkner, J(ohn) Meade (1858–1932), English novelist, antiquarian and poet.

Falkner, William Clark (1825–1889), American writer, army officer lawyer and railroad builder; great-grandfather of William Faulkner.

Fanon, Frantz (Omar) (1925–1961), Martinique psychoanalyst and social philosopher who was known for his espousal of the cause of national liberation of colonial peoples.

Fanshaw, Sir Richard, Baronet (1608–1666), English diplomat, poet and translator.

Fante, John (1909–1983), American novelist and screenwriter.

Fārābī, al- (actually Muhammad ibn Muhammad ibn Tarkhān ibn Uzalagh al- Fārābī) (c.878–c.950), celebrated Muslim philosopher who advocated that the state should be ruled by the philosopher.

Farazdaq, al- (actually Hammān ibn Ghālib al-Farazdaq) (c.641–c.729), notable Arab poet who excelled in satirical poems.

Fardd, Eben (actually Ebenezer Thomas) (1802–1863), Welsh poet and hymnist.

Farel, Guillaume (1489–1565), significant French-born Swiss Protestant reformer and preacher.

Fargue, Léon-Paul (1876–1947), French poet and essayist.

Faria y Sousa, Manuel de (1590–1649), Portuguese poet.

Farini, Luigi Carlo (1812–1866), Italian physician, statesman and historian.

Farjeon, Eleanor (1881–1965), English poet and writer.

Farley, Harriet (1817–1907), American writer.

Farnol, (John) Jeffery (1878–1952), English novelist.

Farquhar, George (1678–1707), prominent Irish dramatist whose mastery of comedic invention was revealed in such plays as The Recruiting Officer (1706) and The Beaux Stratagem (1707).

Farrar, Frederic William (1831–1903), English churchman, philologist and writer, author of the novel Eric, or, Little by Little (1858) and the theological tomes The Witness of History to Christ (1871) and Life of Christ (1874).

Farrell, J(ames) G(ordon) (1935–1979), English novelist, admired for his Troubles (1970), The Siege of Krishnapur (1973) and The Singapore Grip (1978).

Farrell, James T(homas) (1904–1979), noted American novelist, essayist and poet, best known for his novel trilogy Young Lonigan (1932), The Young Manhood of Studs Lonigan (1934) and Judgment Day (1935).

Farrokhī (died 1037), Persian poet.

Faulkner, William (actually William Harrison Falkner) (1897–1962), celebrated American novelist, short-story writer, essayist and poet, author of such important novels as The Sound and the Fury (1929), As I Lay Dying (1930), Light in August (1932), Absalom, Absalom! (1936), The Hamlet (1940), Intruder in the Dust (1948), The Town (1957) and The Mansion (1959); won the Nobel Prize for Literature (1950); great-grandson of William Clark Falkner.

Fauriel, Claude (-Charles) (1772–1844), French literary scholar and writer.

Fauset, Jessie Redmond (1882–1961), American novelist who depicted the black experience.

Favart, Charles-Simon (1710–1792), French dramatist and theatre director, best known for his Bastien et Bastienne (1753), which Mozart set as an opera, and Les Trois Sultanes (1761).

Fawcett, Edgar (1847–1904), American novelist, dramatist and poet.

Fawkes, Francis (1720–1777), English poet and translator.

Fay, András (1786–1864), Hungarian poet, dramatist and novelist.

Fay, Sidney Bradshaw (1876–1967), American historian who wrote the important Origins of the World War (2 vols, 1928).

Fay, Theodore Sedgwick (1807–1898), American diplomat, writer and poet.

Fearing, Kenneth (1902–1961), American poet and novelist.

Featley, Daniel (actually Daniel Fairclough) (1582–1645), English Anglican priest and polemicist who was imprisoned for his support of the royalist cause by the Puritan government.

Fechner, Gustav Theodor (1801–1887), German physicist and philosopher, one of the principal figures in the development of psychophysics, author of Zend-Avesta: Oder über de Dinge des Himmels und des Jenseits (1851; English trans. as Zend-Avesta: On the Things of Heaven and the Hereafter, 1882) and Elements der Psychophysik (2 vols, 1860; English trans. as Elements of Psychophysics, 1966).

Federer, Heinrich (1866–1928), Swiss novelist of Christian themes.

Fedin, Konstantin Alexandrovich (1892–1977), Russian novelist.

Feijóo y Montenegro, Benito Jerónimo (1676–1764), Spanish Benedictine philosopher and theologian.

Feith, Rhijnivs (1753–1824), Dutch poet, novelist and critic.

Fell, John (1625–1686), English Anglican priest, writer and editor.

Felltham, Owen (c.1602–1668), English essayist and poet, best remembered for his book of essays Resolves Divine, Morall, and Politicall (1623).

Felton, Cornelius Conway (1807–1862), American classical scholar.

Fénelon, François de Salignac de la Mothe- (1651–1715), notable French Roman Catholic archbishop, mystical theologian, pedagogue and writer.

Fenestella (c.40 BC–c.25 AD), Latin poet and annalist.

Feng Kuei-fen (1809–1874), Chinese scholar who advocated the adoption of Western technology to meet the challenge of the West in his Chiao-pin-lu k'ang-i (Protest from the Chiao-pin Studio).

Feng Meng-lung (1574–1645), Chinese writer.

Fenollosa, Ernest F(rancisco) (1853–1908), American Orientalist and educator who wrote the valuable studies An Outline History of Ukiyo-3 (1901) and Epochs of Chinese and Japanese Art (published 1912).

Fenton, Elijah (1683–1730), English poet and translator, esteemed for his Poems on Several Occasions (1717).

Feraoun, Mouloud (1913–62), Algerian novelist whose support of the Algerian independence movement resulted in his assassination.

Ferber, Edna (1887–1968), American novelist, short-story writer and dramatist.

Ferdowsī or Firdausī (actually Abū ol-Qāsem Mansūr) (c.935–c.1020), Persian poet who wrote the national epic Shāh-nāmeh (Book of Kings).

Ferenczi, Sándor (1873–1933), Hungarian psychoanalyst.

Ferguson, Adam (1723–1816), Scottish philosopher and historian.

Ferguson, Sir Samuel (1810–1886), Irish poet.

Fergusson, Harvey (1890–1971), American novelist.

Fergusson, Robert (1750–1774), admired Scottish poet, best known for his Auld Reekie.

Fernald, Chester Bailey (1869–1938), American writer and dramatist.

Fernández, Lucas (c.1474–1542), Spanish dramatist and composer.

Fernández de Lizardi, José Joaquín (1776–1827), Mexican editor and novelist, author of the first picaresque novel of Spanish America El periquillo sarniento (1816; English trans. as The Itching Parrot, 1941).

Fernández de Moratín, Leandro (1760–1828), eminent Spanish dramatist and poet, a master of satire.

Ferrari, Giuseppe (1811–1876), Italian historian and political philosopher.

Ferreira, António (1528–1569), gifted Portuguese poet of classical verse who was known as the Horace of his homeland.

Ferreira, Manuel (1917–92), Portuguese literary scholar, novelist and short-story writer.

Ferreira, Virgílio (1916–1996), Portuguese novelist and essayist.

Ferreira de Castro, José Maria (1898–1974), Portuguese journalist and novelist.

Ferrero, Guglielmo (1871–1942), Italian historian.

Ferrier, James Frederick (1808–1864), Scottish philosopher.

Ferrier, Susan Edmonstone (1782–1854), Scottish novelist, author of Marriage (1818), The Inheritance (1824) and Destiny, or, The Chief's Daughter (1831).

Ferril, Thomas Hornsby (1896–1988), American journalist, writer and poet.

Ferron, Jacques (1921–1985), French-Canadian writer and dramatist.

Fessenden, Thomas Green (1771–1837), American journalist, writer and poet who wrote under the name Christopher Caustic.

Fet, Afanasy Afanaseivich (1820–1892), prominent Russian poet and translator whose works greatly influenced the later Symbolists.

Fetis, François-Joseph (1784–1871), eminent Belgian music theorist, historian and critic, compiler of the monumental Biographie universelle des musiciens et bibliographie générale de la musique (8 vols, 1833–44).

Feuchtwanger, Lion (1884–1958), German-born American novelist and dramatist.

Feuerbach, Ludwig Andreas (1804–1872), influential German philosopher and theologian who espoused the cause of humanistic atheism in his Das Wesen des Christenhums (The Essence of Christianity, 1841).

Feydeau, Georges (-Léon-Jules-Marie) (1862–1921), French dramatist who excelled in the writing of farces.

Fichte, Johann Gottlieb (1762–1814), German philosopher of Idealism.

Ficino, Marsilio (1433–1499), Italian philosopher, theologian, linguist and translator, author of the Liber de Christiana religione (Book on the Christian Religion, 1474) and Theologia Platonica (Platonic Theology, 1482).

Fick, August (1833–1916), German linguist who was an authority on Indo-European languages.

Ficke, Arthur Davison (1883–1945), American poet.

Ficker, Julius von (1826–1902), German jurist and historian.

Field, Eugene (1850–1895), American journalist and poet, known as the 'poet of childhood' for such works as Little Boy Blue and Dutch Lullaby (Wynken, Blynken and Nod); brother of Roswell Martin Field.

Field, Joseph M (1810–1856), American actor, theatre manager and journalist.

Field, Rachel (Lyman) (1894–1942), American writer.

Field, Roswell Martin (1851–1919), American journalist and music and drama critic; brother of Eugene Field.

Fielding, Henry (1707–1754), celebrated English novelist and dramatist, author of An Apology for the Life of Mrs Shamela Andrews (1741), The Life of Mr Jonathan Wild the Great (1743) and The History of Tom Jones, a Foundling (1749); brother of Sarah Fielding.

Fielding, Sarah (1710–1768), English novelist; sister of Henry Fielding.

Fields, Annie Adams (1834–1915), American poet; wife of James T(homas) Fields.

Fields, James T(homas) (1817–1881), American publisher, poet and writer, co-founder of the publishing firm Ticknor and Fields; husband of Annie Adams Fields.

Fiennes, Celia (1662–1741), English traveller and writer.

Figueiredo, Antero de (1866–1953), Portugese novelist and essayist.

Figueroa, Francisco de (1536–c.1620), Spanish poet.

Figueroa, John (Joseph Maria) (1920–99), Jamaican writer and poet.

Figulus, Publius Migidius (1st Century BC), Roman savant and writer.

Filarete (actually Antonio di Pietro Averlino or Averulino) (c.1400–c.1469), Italian architect, sculptor and writer.

Filelfo, Francesco (1398–1481), Italian scholar and poet.

Filicaia, Vincenzo da (1642–1707), Italian poet who was known for his patriotic sonnets.

Filmer, Sir Robert (c.1588–1653), English philosopher, a champion of monarchial statecraft in his Patriarcha, or the Natural Power of Kings (c.1638).

Finch, Francis Miles (1827–1907), American lawyer, judge, educator and poet, best remembered for his poem Nathan Hale in his collection The Blue and the Gray and Other Verses (published 1909).

Finch, Robert (Duer Claydon) (1900–1995), American-born Canadian literary scholar, poet, painter and musician.

Finkel, Nathan Tzevi ben Moses (1849–1927), Jewish scholar, religious philosopher and educator.

Finlay, George (1799–1875), English historian, author of The Hellenic Kingdom and the Greek Nation (1836), Greece Under the Romans (2 vols, 1836), History of the Byzantine and Greek Empires (2 vols, 1854) and History of the Greek Revolution (2 vols, 1861).

Finney, Charles Grandison (1792–1875), American Protestant evangelist and educator who wrote Lectures on Revivals (1835) and Lectures on Systematic Theology (1847).

Fiore Pasquale (1837–1914), Italian jurist who was known as an authority on international law.

Fiorelli, Giuseppe (1823–1896), Italian archaeologist, author of Descrizione di Pompei (Description of Pompeii, 1875).

Firbank, (Arthur Annesley) Ronald (1886–1926), English novelist.

Firenzuola, Angolo (1493–1543), Italian writer.

Firishtah (c.1570–c.1620), celebrated Muslim Indian writer who was also known as Muhammad Qāsim Hindūshāh.

Fischart, Johann (1546–1590), German writer, famous for his satirical works.

Fischer, Fritz (1908–99), German historian, author of Griff nach der Weltmacht: Die Kriegszielpolitik das kaiserlichen Deutschland 1914–18 (1961; English trans. as Germany's Aims in the First World War, 1967).

Fischer, Kuno (actually Ernst Kuno Berthold) (1824–1907), German philosopher, author of System der Logik und Metaphysik (System of Logic and Metaphysics, 1852).

Fischer von Erlach, Johann Bernhard (1656–1723), Austrian architect, sculptor and architectural historian.

Fisher, Herbert Albert Laurens (1865–1940), English historian, educator and government official who wrote The History of Europe (3 vols, 1935).

Fisher, Irving (1867–1947), American economist, author of The Purchasing Power of Money (1911).

Fisher, Saint John (1469–1535), notable English Roman Catholic prelate and theologian who opposed the Supremacy Act of 1534; was condemned for treason and executed.

Fisher, M(ary) F(rances) K(ennedy) (1908–1992), American writer.

Fisher, Vardis (Alvero) (1895–1968), American novelist, short-story writer and essayist.

Fiske, Harrison Grey (1861–1942), American dramatist and theatre manager.

Fiske, John (1842–1901), American historian and philosopher, particularly known for his The Outlines of Cosmic Philosophy (1874), Darwinism and Other Essays (1879), The Destiny of Man Viewed in the Light of His Origin (1884), The Critical Period of American History, 1783–1789 (1888) and The Beginnings of New England (1889).

Fitch, Nathan (1733–1799), American clergyman and writer, author of the Historical Discourse (1776) and The Moral Monitor (published 1801).

Fitch, (William) Clyde (1865–1909), American dramatist.

Fitts, Dudley (1903–1968), American poet and translator.

Fitzgerald, Edward (1809–1883), English poet and translator, admired for his translation of quatrains from the Rubáiyát of Omar Khayyám (1859).

Fitzgerald, F(rancis) Scott (Key) (1896–1940), famous American novelist, short-story writer, essayist and poet whose life epitomised the jazz age; husband of Zelda Fitzgerald.

Fitzgerald, Penelope Mary (1916–2000), English writer.

FitzGerald, Robert David (1902–1985), highly regarded Australian poet.

Fitzgerald, Robert Stuart (1910–1985), American poet, translator and critic.

Fitzgerald, Zelda (1899–1948), American novelist, author of Save Me the Waltz (1932); wife of F(rancis) Scott (Key) Fitzgerald.

Fitzhugh, George (1806–1881), American lawyer, journalist and writer who espoused the cause of slavery in his Sociology for the South (1854) and Cannibals All! (1857).

FitzRalph, Richard (c.1295–1360), English Roman Catholic archbishop and scholar, author of Defensio Curatorum and De Pauperie Salvatoris.

Flach, (Jacques-) Geoffroi (1846–1919), French jurist and historian who wrote Les Origines de l'anciennce France (4 vols, 1886–1917).

Flacius, Matthias (1520–1575), prominent Italian-born German Lutheran reformer, church historian and theologian who wrote the important Centuriae Magdeburgenses (Magdeburg Centuries, 1574).

Flanagan, Thomas (James Bonner) (1923–2002), American novelist who was especially esteemed for his novel trilogy The Year of the French (1979), The Tenants of Time (1988) and The End of the Hunt (1994).

Flandrau, Charles Macomb (1871–1938), American journalist and writer.

Flanner, Janet (1892–1978), American journalist and writer who wrote under the name Genêt.

Flatman, Thomas (1637–1688), English painter and poet.

Flaubert, Gustave (1821–1880), celebrated French novelist, author of the acclaimed Madame Bovary (1857).

Flavin, Martin (Archer) (1883–1967), American dramatist and novelist.

Flecker, James Elroy (actually Herman Elroy Fleckner) (1884–1915), English poet and dramatist, particularly known for his poem The Golden Journey to Samarkand (1913) and the verse play Hassan (published 1922).

Flecknoe, Richard (c.1600–c.1678), Irish poet and dramatist.

Fleetwood, William (1656–1723), English Anglican bishop, preacher and economist, remembered for his Four Sermons (1712).

Fleming, Ian (Lancaster) (1908–1964), English novelist, creator of James Bond, the British secret service agent 007; brother of (Robert) Peter Fleming.

Fleming , Paul (1609–1640), German poet, renowned for his sonnets.

Fleming, (Robert) Peter (1907–1971), English journalist and travel writer; brother of Ian (Lancaster) Fleming.

Fletcher, Alice Cunningham (1838–1923), American anthropologist.

Fletcher, Giles, the Elder (c.1548–1611), English poet; father of Giles Fletcher the Younger and Phineas Fletcher.

Fletcher, Giles, the Younger (c.1585–1623), admired English poet, author of Christs Victorie, and Triump in Heaven, and Earth, over, and after death (1610); son of Giles Fletcher the Elder, brother of Phineas Fletcher and cousin of John Fletcher.

Fletcher, John (1579–1625), notable English dramatist who collaborated with Francis Beaumont on a series of fine plays; cousin of Giles Fletcher the Younger and Phineas Fletcher.

Fletcher, John Gould (1886–1950), American poet and essayist.

Fletcher, Phineas (1582–1650), English poet, particularly esteemed for his expansive poem The Purple Island (1633); brother of Giles Fletcher the Younger and cousin of John Fletcher.

Flewelling, Ralph Tyler (1871–1960), American philosopher of Idealism, author of The Person (1952).

Flexner, Abraham (1866–1959), American educator.

Flint, F(rank) S(tewart) (1885–1960), English poet and translator, an admired Imagist.

Flint, Timothy (1780–1840), American Protestant clergyman, novelist, biographer and historian.

Flodoard (c.893–966), French chronicler.

Florence, William Jermyn (1831–1891), American actor, dramatist and songwriter.

Flórez (de Setién y Huidobro), Enrique (1702–1773), Spanish historian.

Florio, John (c.1553–c.1625), English lexicographer and translator who was also known as Giovanni Florio.

Florus, Publius Annius (1st–2nd Century), Roman historian and poet.

Florens, Gustave (1838–1871), French scholar and radical who, as a prominent figure in the Paris Commune, lost his life soon thereafter.

Fludd or Flud, Robert (1574–1637), English physician and mystical philosopher, author of Apologia Compendiaria Fraternitatem de Rosea Croce (Brief Apology for the Fraternity of the Rosy Cross, 1616).

Flügel, Gustav Lebrecht (1802–1870), German scholar in Arab studies.

Focillon, Henri-Joseph (1881–1943), French art historian and critic.

Fogazzaro, Antonio (1842–1911), Italian novelist, short-story writer, dramatist and poet, especially admired for his novel Piccolo mondo antico (1896; English trans. as The Little World of the Past, 1962).

Folengo, Teofilo (actually Girolamo Folengo) (1491–1544), pre-eminent Italian macaronic poet whose greatest work was his Baldus (4 versions, 1517, 1521, 1539–40, 1552).

Folger, Peter (1617–1690), American poet, author of A Looking Glass for the Times (1676); grandfather of Benjamin Franklin.

Follen, August Adolf Ludwig (1794–1855), German political radical and poet whose output reflected political and Romantic themes.

Follen, Charles (actually Karl Theodor Christian Follen) (1795–1840), German-born American political liberal, educator and Unitarian minister; husband of Eliza Lee Cabot Follen.

Follen, Eliza Lee Cabot (1787–1860), American political liberal, writer and poet; wife of Charles Follen.

Folquet de Marseille or Marseilla (c.1160–1231), Provençal poet and bishop.

Fonseca, Pedro de (1528–1599), Portuguese philosopher.

Fontane, Theodor (1819–1898), notable German novelist, drama critic and poet whose masterpiece was the novel Vor dem Sturm (Before the Storm, 1878).

Fontanes, Louis, Marquis de (1757–1821), French journalist, writer and poet.

Fontenelle, Bernard Le Bovier, Sieur de (1657–1757), prominent French scientist and writer, best remembered for his Entretiens sur la pluralite des mondes (A Plurality of Worlds, 1688).

Fonvizin, Denis Ivanovich (1774–1792), Russian dramatist whose Nedorosl (The Minor, 1783) is recognised as the first great Russian drama.

Foote, Mary Hallock (1847–1938), American novelist.

Foote, Samuel (1720–1777), English actor and dramatist who was known for his wit.

Forberg, Friedrich Karl (1770–1848), German philosopher of Idealism.

Forbes, Esther (1891–1967), American novelist and biographer.

Forbes, James (1871–1938), American dramatist.

Ford, Ford Madox (actually Ford Hermann Hueffer) (1873–1939), English novelist, editor, critic and poet, author of such notable novels as The Good Soldier (1915), Some Do Not (1924), No More Parades (1925), A Man Could Stand Up (1926) and Last Post (1928).

Ford, John (1586–c.1639), esteemed English dramatist, particularly known for such plays as The Broken Heart, The Lover's Melancholy, Perkin Warbeck and 'Tis Pitty Shees a Whore.

Ford, Paul Leicester (1865–1902), American novelist and scholar; was murdered by his disinherited brother Malcolm Ford; brother of Worthington Chauncey Ford.

Ford, Richard (1796–1858), English writer, author of the well known A Handbook for Travellers in Spain (1845).

Ford, Worthington Chauncey (1858–1941), American librarian and editor; brother of Paul Leicester Ford.

Forester, C(ecil) S(cott) (actually Cecil Lewis Troughton Smith) (1899–1966), English novelist and journalist who created the admiral Horatio Hornblower.

Forkel, Johann Nikolaus (1749–1818), eminent German music scholar who wrote the first biography of J S Bach (1802).

Formstecher, Solomon (1808–1889), German Jewish rabbi and Idealist philosopher, best known for his Die Religion des Geistes (The Religion of the Spirit, 1841).

Forner, Juan Pablo (1756–1797), Spanish literary critic and poet who excelled in polemical works of a biting satire.

Förster, Bernhard (1843–1889), German writer who espoused anti-Semitic views; husband of Elizabeth Förster-Nietzsche.

Forster, E(dward) M(organ) (1879–1970), noted English novelist, essayist and critic, best remembered for his novels Howards End (1910) and A Passage To India (1924).

Forster, Georg (actually Johann Georg Adam Forster) (1754–1794), German explorer and scientist who wrote the important A voyage round the world (1777), an account of his travels with Capt. James Cook.

Forster, John (1812–1876), English journalist, editor, biographer and essayist, author of the valuable The Life of Dickens (1872–74).

Förster-Nietzsche, Elizabeth (1846–1935), German executrix and biographer of her brother Friedrich Wilhelm Nietzsche whose efforts were marred by sloppy editing and outright forgery; husband of Bernhard Förster.

Forsyth, Peter Taylor (1848–1921), Scottish Congregationalist minister and theologian, especially known for his The Person and Place of Jesus Christ (1909).

Fort, Paul (1872–1960), French poet, dramatist and editor, author of numerous ballads.

Fortescue, Sir John (c.1385–c.1479), English jurist who wrote the famous treatise De laudibus legum Angliae (In Praise of the Laws of England, c.1470).

Fortiguerra, Niccòlo (1674–1735), Italian poet and Roman Catholic prelate who wrote the satirical epic Il Ricciardetto (published 1738).

Fortunatus, Venantius (Honorius Clemantianus) (c.540–c.600), Italian poet and Roman Catholic bishop, admired for his Latin poems and hymns.

Foscolo, Ugo (actually Niccòlo Foscolo) (1778–1827), Italian poet, novelist, dramatist and critic, author of the patriotic poem Dei sepolcri (Of the Sepulchres, 1807).

Fosdick, Harry Emerson (1878–1969), American Protestant clergyman and writer who espoused a liberal theology.

Foss, Sam Walter (1858–1911), American journalist and poet, remembered for the poem The House by the Side of the Road.

Foster, Hannah Webster (1759–1840), American writer, author of the novel The Coquette (1797).

Foucault, Michel (1926–84), French philosopher, literary critic and historian who was a leading figure in the Structuralist movement.

Foucher, Simon (1644–1696), French philosopher.

Fouque, Friedrich Heinrich Karl de la Motte, Baron (1777–1843), German novelist and dramatist, best known for his fairy tale Undine (1811).

Fourier, (François-Marie-) Charles (1772–1837), French social theorist.

Fowler, Francis George (1870–1918), English grammarian and lexicographer; brother of Henry Watson Fowler.

Fowler, Henry Watson (1858–1933), English grammarian and lexicographer, compiler of A Dictionary of Modern English Usage (1926); brother of Francis George Fowler.

Fowler, William Warde (1847–1921), English historian.

Fox, John (William) Jr (1862–1919), American writer.

Fox, Sir William (1812–1893), English politician and writer.

Foxe, John (1516–1587), English Protestant reformer, preacher and martyrologist, author of the celebrated Commentarii rerum in ecclesia gestarum (1554; English trans. as Actes and Monuments of these Latter and Perilous Dayes, 1563), better known as The Book of Martyrs.

Foy, Maximilien (-Sébastien) (1775–1825), French military leader, statesman and writer.

Fracastoro, Girolamo or Hieronymus Fracastorius (c.1478–1553), illustrious Italian physician, astronomer, geologist and poet, proponent of the germ theory of disease.

France, Anatole (actually Jacques-Anatole-François Thibault) (1844–1924), French novelist and critic; won the Nobel Prize for Literature (1921).

Francis, Sir Philip (1740–1818), Irish-born English politician and pamphleteer.

Francis of Meyronnes or Franciscus de Mayronis (c.1285–c.1329), notable French Franciscan philosopher, theologian and monk who championed the realist system of John Duns Scotus.

Francis of Sales, Saint (1567–1622), French Roman Catholic bishop and theologian.

Franck, Sebastian (c.1499–c.1542), German Protestant reformer and theologian who espoused a radical anti-dogmatic theology, author of Chronica: Zeitbuch und Geschichtsbibel (Chronica: Time Book and Historical Bible, 1531).

Francke, August Hermann (1663–1727), German Protestant religious leader, educator and social reformer who championed Pietism.

Francke, Kuno (1855–1930), German-born American historian.

Frank, Anne (1929–1945), German Jewish victim of the Nazi Holocaust whose diary brought her posthumous fame; died in the Bergen-Belsen concentration camp.

Frank, Leonhard (1882–1961), prominent German poet and novelist, a leading proponent of Expressionism.

Frank, Waldo (David) (1889–1967), American novelist and critic.

Frankau, Gilbert (1884–1952), English novelist.

Frankel, Zacharias (1801–1875), German rabbi and theologian who founded a religious system which presaged the advent of Conservative Judaism.

Frankfort, Henri (1897–1954), Dutch-born American archaeologist who was a leading authority on comparative studies of Egypt and Mesopotamia.

Frankfurter, Felix (1882–1965), influential Austrian-born American legal scholar, educator and jurist.

Frankl, Ludwig, Ritter von Hochwart (1810–1893), Austrian poet.

Franklin, Benjamin (1706–1790), famous American statesman, inventor, scientist, publisher and writer.

Franko, Ivan Yakovlevich (1856–1916), Ukrainian scholar and writer.

Franzén, Frans Mikael (1772–1847), Finnish-Swedish poet whose output presaged the Romantic movement in Sweden.

Fraser, James Baillie (1783–1856), Scottish traveller and writer, best known for his works on his travels in Persia.

Fraşeri, Şemseddin Sami (1850–1904), Turkish scholar, lexicographer, novelist and dramatist.

Frauenstadt, Julius (1813–1879), German philosopher.

Fraunce, Abraham (c.1558–c.1633), English poet and writer.

Frazer, Sir James George (1854–1941), eminent Scottish anthropologist, folklorist and classical scholar, author of The Golden Bough: A Study in Magic and Religion (1890).

Fréchette, Louis-Honoré (1839–1908), French-Canadian poet, dramatist and writer.

Frederic, Harold (1856–1898), American journalist and novelist, best known for his novel The Damnation of Theron Ware (1896).

Fredro, Alexander (1793–1876), Polish dramatist who excelled in comedic invention.

Freeman, Douglas Southall (1886–1953), American newspaper editor and biographer, author of major studies of Robert E Lee (4 vols, 1934–35) and George Washington (6 vols, 1948–54).

Freeman, Edward Augustus (1823–1892), English historian.

Freeman, John (1880–1929), English poet.

Freeman, Joseph (1897–1965), American critic and novelist who espoused Marxist views.

Freeman, Mary (Eleanor) Wilkins (1852–1930), American novelist and short-story writer.

Freeman, Richard Austin (1862–1943), English novelist and short-story writer, creator of the pathologist-detective John Thorndyke.

Frege, (Friedrich Ludwig) Gottlob (1848–1925), eminent German mathematician and philosopher who was known as a learned mathematical logician.

Freiligrath, (Hermann) Ferdinand (1810–1876), German poet, translator and advocate of democracy in his homeland.

French, Alice (1850–1934), American novelist and short-story writer who wrote under the name Octave Thanet.

Freneau, Philip (Morin) (1752–1832), prominent American poet, essayist and editor who was known as the 'poet of the American Revolution'.

Frenssen, Gustav (1863–1945), German novelist who excelled in regionalist fiction.

Frere, John (1740–1807), English antiquarian who helped to found prehistoric archaeology.

Frere, John Hookham (1769–1846), English diplomat, poet and translator.

Freshfield, Douglas William (1845–1934), English mountaineer, explorer, geographer and writer.

Freud, Anna (1895–1982), Austrian-born English child psychoanalyst; daughter of Sigmund Freud.

Freud, Sigmund (1856–1939), renowned Austrian physician and neurologist who founded psychoanalysis, author of the influential study Die Traumdeutung (1899; English trans. as The Interpretation of Dreams, 1953); father of Anna Freud.

Frey, Adolf (1855–1920), Swiss poet, novelist and biographer.

Friedland, Valentin (1490–1556), German educator.

Friedlander, Ludwig Heinrich (1824–1909), German historian who wrote the valuable Darstellungen aus der Sittengeschichte Roms (Representations from Roman Cultural History, 3 vols, 1864–71).

Fries, Jakob Friedrich (1773–1843), German philosopher, author of the significant tome Neue oder anthropologische Kritik der venunft (3 vols, 1807).

Frings, Ketti (1910–1981), American novelist and dramatist.

Frisch, Max (Rudolf) (1911–1991), significant Swiss novelist and dramatist, author of such masterworks as the plays Don Juan oder die Liebe zur Geometrie (Don Juan, or the Love of Geometry, 1953), Biedermann und die Brandstifter (1958; English trans. as The Fire Raisers, 1962) and Andorra (1962), and the novels Stiller (1954; English trans. as I'm Not Stiller, 1958), Homo Faber (195), Montauk (1975), Der Mensch erscheint im Holozän (Man in the Holocene, 1979) and Blaubart (Bluebeard, 1982).

Frobenius, Leo (Viktor) (1873–1938), German explorer and ethnologist, noted especially for his studies of culture.

Fröding, Gustaf (1860–1911), Swedish poet who was esteemed for his mastery of lyricism.

Froebel, Friedrich (Wilhelm August) (1782–1852), German educator and writer, founder of kindergarten education.

Frohschammer, Jakob (1821–1893), German Roman Catholic priest and philosopher whose liberal views led to his excommunication.

Froissart, Jean (c.1333–c.1400), famous French historian and poet, author of the valuable Chronicles.

Fromentin, Eugéne (1820–1876), French writer and painter.

Fromm, Erich (1900–1980), influential German-born American psychoanalyst and social philosopher.

Frommel, Gaston (1862–1906), Swiss Protestant theologian and philosopher.

Frost, Robert (Lee) (1874–1963), famous American poet whose finely-honed and subtle verse placed him among the principal poets in American literary annals.

Frothingham, Octavius Brooks (1822–1895), American Unitarian and writer.

Froude, James Anthony (1818–1894), English historian and biographer, author of a biography of Thomas Carlyle (4 vols, 1882–84); brother of Richard Hurrell Froude.

Froude, Richard Hurrell (1803–1836), English writer and poet; brother of James Anthony Froude.

Frugoni, Carlo Innocenzo (1692–1768), Italian poet, librettist and translator.

Frye, (Herman) Northrop (1912–1991), Canadian literary scholar and writer.

Fujita Tōko (1806–1855), Japanese scholar and politician; died in an earthquake.

Fujiwara Nobuzane (1176–c.1265), famous Japanese painter, courtier and poet.

Fujiwara Sadaie (1162–1241), august Japanese poet, theorist and critic who was generally known as Fujiwara Teika.

Fujiwara Seika (1561–1619), Japanese philosopher of the Neo-Confucian school.

Fukuchi Genichiro (1841–1906), Japanese dramatist and publisher.

Fukuzawa Yukichi (1835–1901), Japanese writer, educator and publisher who embraced the cause of introducing Western ideas to his homeland.

Fulbert of Chartes, Saint (c.960–1028), French Roman Catholic bishop and poet.

Fulcher of Chartres (c.1059–c.1127), French chaplain and chronicler who wrote a valuable account of the First Crusade in his Gesta Francorum Jherusalem peregrinantium (3 parts, 1101, 1106, 1124–27).

Fulgentius, Fabius Planciades (5th–6th Century), African Christian Latin writer.

Fulgentius of Ruspe, Saint (c.462–c.527), African Roman Catholic bishop and writer who was a vigorous opponent of Arianism.

Fuller, Andrew (1754–1815), English Baptist minister and theologian.

Fuller, Henry Blake (1857–1929), American novelist, short-story writer, poet, dramatist, critic and editor.

Fuller, J(ohn) F(rederick) C(harles) (1878–1966), prominent English Army officer, military theoretician and historian, author of A Military History of the Western World (3 vols, 1954–56).

Fuller, Roy (Broadbent) (1912–1991), English poet and novelist.

Fuller, (Sarah) Margaret (1810–1850), American writer and critic.

Fuller, Thomas (1608–1661), prominent English preacher and scholar, author of The Holy State and The Profane State (1642), The church-history of Britain, with the history of the University of Cambridge (1655) and The History of the Worthies of England (published 1662).

Fung Yu-lan (1895–1990), Chinese philosopher of idealism, author of a valuable history of Chinese philosophy (two vols, 1934).

Furetière, Antoine (1619–1688), noted French novelist and lexicographer whose penchant for satire made him many enemies, compiler of the Dictionnaire universel (published 1690).

Furnas, J(oseph) C(hamberlain) (1905–2001), American social historian and writer.

Furness, Horace Howard (1833–1912), American scholar who prepared variorum editions of 20 plays of Shakespeare.

Furnivall, Frederick James (1825–1910), English literary scholar, a specialist in textual criticism.

Furphy, Joseph (1843–1912), Australian novelist and poet who wrote under the name Tom Collins, especially known for his novel Such is Life (1903).

Fuseli, Henry (actually Johann Heinrich Füssli) (1741–1825), Swiss-born English painter and writer.

Fustel de Coulanges, Numa-Denis (1830–1889), French historian, author of La Cité antique (1864).

Futabatei Shimei (actually Tatsunosuke Hasegawa) (1864–1909), Japanese novelist and translator, best known for his novel Ukigomo (1889).

Fux, Johann Joseph (1660–1741), famous Austrian musician, composer and theorist who wrote the classic counterpoint treatise Gradus ad Parnassum (1725).

Fuzûlî, (Mehmed) (c.1495–1556), celebrated Turkish poet of classical verse.

Gabelentz, Hans Conon von der (1807–1874), German linguist, ethnologist and government official.

Gaboriau, Émile (1832–1873), French novelist who excelled in the detective novel.

Gadamer, Hans-Georg (1900–2002), German philosopher whose book Truth and Method (1975) confirmed his reputation as one of the principal advocates of hermeneutics of his era.

Gadda, Carlo Emilio (1893–1973), Italian novelist, short-story writer and essayist, author of the celebrated novel Quer pasticciaccio brutto de via Merulana (1957; English trans. as That Awful Mess on Via Merulana, 1965).

Gaddis, William (Thomas) (1922–1998), significant American novelist of a satiric bent, author of The Recognitions (1955), JR (1975), Carpenter's Gothic (1985) and A Frolic of His Own (1994).

Gagern, Hans Christoph, Freiherr von (1766–1852), German politician and writer.

Gaimar, Geoffrei (12th Century), Norman writer, author of L'Estoire des Engleis.

Gaius (2nd Century), Roman jurist who wrote the important Institutiones (4 vols, c.161).

Gale, Zona (1874–1938), American writer and poet, especially remembered for his novel Miss Lulu Bett (1920).

Galiani, Ferdinando (1728–1787), Italian economist.

Gâlib Dede (actually Mehmed es' Ad) (1757–1799), significant Turkish poet whose masterpiece was Hüsn ü Aşk (Beauty and Love).

Galien, Joseph (1699–1762), French Roman Catholic friar, theologian and philosopher.

Galileo (Galilei) (1564–1642), Italian mathematician, astronomer and physicist whose championship of unfettered intellectual inquiry led to a major conflict with the Roman Catholic Church.

Gallagher, William Davis (1808–1894), American editor and poet.

Galland, Antoine (1646–1715), French scholar, particularly remembered for his adaptation of Near Eastern tales as Mille et une nuits (1704–17; English trans. as The Thousand and One Nights, 1706).

Gallegos (Freire), Rómulo (1884–1969), Venezuelan novelist, short-story writer and politician who served briefly as president of his homeland (1948) but was ousted in a military coup.

Gallitzin, Demetrius Augustine (1770–1840), Dutch-born American Roman Catholic priest and polemicist.

Gallus, Gaius Cornelius (c.70–26 BC), famous Roman soldier and poet, admired for his elegies; committed suicide.

Galsworthy, John (1867–1933), noted English novelist, dramatist and poet, best known for his series of novels collectively known as The Forsyte Saga (1906 et seq.); won the Nobel Prize for Literature (1932).

Galt, John (1779–1839), Scottish novelist, especially esteemed for his The Ayrshire Legatees (1820), The Annals of the Parish (1821), Sir Andrew Wylie (1822), The Provost (1822), The Entail (1823) and Lawrie Todd (1830).

Galton, Sir Francis (1822–1911), English explorer, anthropologist and eugenicist, author of Hereditary Genius (1869) and Inquiries into Human Faculty (1883).

Gálvez, Manuel (1882–1962), Argentine novelist and biographer, particularly known for his novel La maestra normal (The Schoolmistress, 1914).

Gama, (José) Basílio da (1740–1795), Brazilian poet who wrote the epic O Uruguai (1769).

Gamow, George (1904–1968), Russian-born American nuclear physicist, cosmologist and writer.

Ganivet y García, Angel (1865–98), Spanish essayist and novelist; committed suicide.

Gans, Eduard (1798–1839), German jurist, author of Das Erbrecht in weltgeschichtlicher Entwicklung (Historical Development of Inheritance Law, 4 vols, 1824–35) and Vorlesungen über die Geschichte der Letzten fünfzig Jahre (Lectures on the History of the Last Fifty Years, 1833–34).

Garbett, Cyril Forster (1875–1955), English Anglican archbishop and writer.

Garborg, Arne Evenson (1851–1924), Norwegian novelist, poet, dramatist and essayist.

Garção, Pedro António Correia (1724–1772), esteemed Portugese poet who championed Neoclassical ideals.

García Calderón, Francisco (1883–1953), Puruvian diplomat and writer.

García de le Huerta, Vicente (Antonio) (1734–1787), Spanish dramatist, poet and critic, best known for his play Raquel (1778).

García Gutiérrez, Antonio (1813–1884), Spanish dramatist and poet, particularly admired for his play El trovador (The Troubadour, 1836).

García Lorca, Federico (1898–1936), Spanish poet and dramatist; as a supporter of the Loyalist government, he was shot by nationalist forces at the outbreak of the Spanish Civil War.

Gardiner, Samuel Rawson (1829–1902), English historian who wrote on the English Civil War.

Gardner, Erle Stanley (1889–1970), American writer and lawyer, creator of the famous lawyer-detective Perry Mason.

Gardner, Dame Helen Louise (1908–1986), English critic and scholar.

Gardner, Isabella (Stewart) (1915–1981), American poet whose output revealed a fine lyric talent.

Gardner, John (Champlin Jr) (1933–1982), American writer, biographer, critic and poet who wrote the epic poem Jason and Medeia (1973).

Garin-Mikailovsky, Nikolai Georgievich (1852–1906), Russian writer.

Garioch, Robert (actually Robert Garioch Sutherland) (1909–1981), Scottish poet, writer and translator.

Garis, Howard R(oger) (1873–1962), American writer, creator of the children's story character Uncle Wiggley.

Garland, (Hannibal) Hamlin (1860–1940), American writer, especially known for his autobiographical 'Middle Border' series.

Garland, John (c.1180–c.1272), English grammarian and poet, also known as Johannes de Garlandia, was a major figure in the development of medieval Latin literature.

Garneau, François-Xavier (1809–1866), French-Canadian historian, author of the Histoire du Canada (History of Canada, 1845–52); great-grandfather of Hector de Saint-Denys Garneau.

Garneau, Hector de Saint-Denys (1912–1943), French-Canadian poet; great-grandson of François-Xavier Garneau.

Garnett, Constance (1862–1946), English translator of the Russian classics; wife of Edward Garnett and mother of David Garnett.

Garnett, David (1892–1981), English writer and critic; son of Constance and Edward Garnett.

Garnett, Edward (1868–1936), English novelist, dramatist and critic; husband of Constance Garnett and father of David Garnett.

Garnett, Richard (1835–1906), English poet, biographer, writer, translator and editor.

Garnier, Robert (c.1545–1590), esteemed French dramatist and poet who was much appreciated for his fine tragedies.

Garrett, João Baptista da Silva Leitão de Almeida (1799–1854), illustrious Portuguese poet, dramatist, novelist, journalist and statesman, the preeminent representative of the Romantic movement in his homeland.

Garrick, David (1717–1779), prominent English actor, producer, dramatist and poet.

Garrigue, Jean (1914–1972), American poet.

Garrison, William Lloyd (1805–1879), famous American journalist and Abolitionist.

Garro, Elena (1920–1998), Mexican writer and dramatist.

Garrod, Dorothy Annie Elizabeth (1892–1968), English archaeologist, author of The Stone Age of Mount Carmel (2 vols, 1937, 1939).

Garros, Pey de (c.1530–1585), Provençal poet.

Garshin, Vsevolod Mikhailovich (1855–88), Russian short-story writer; committed suicide.

Garstang, John (1876–1956), English archaeologist, particularly known for his studies of the history of Asia Minor and Palestine.

Garth, Sir Samuel (1661–1719), English poet, physician and freethinker, author of the burlesque poem The Dispensary (1699).

Gary, Romain (actually Romain Kacew) (1914–80), Lithuanian-born French diplomat and writer, author of the novels L' éducation européenne (1945; English trans. as Nothing Important Ever Dies, 1960) and Les racines du ciel (1956; English trans. as The Roots of Heaven, 1958).

Gascoigne, George (c.1525–1577), admired English poet and writer.

Gascoyne, David (Emery) (1916–2001), English poet, writer, critic and translator who championed Surrealism.

Gaskell, Elizabeth Cleghorn (née Stevenson) (1810–1865), English novelist, short-story writer and biographer.

Gaspé, Philippe Aubert de (1781), French-Canadian writer, author of the classic novel Les Anciens Canadiens (The Canadians of Old, 1863).

Gasprinski, Ismail (1851–1914), Russian journalist and writer who was also known as Ismail Gaspirali.

Gasquet, Francis Neil Aidan (1846–1929), English Roman Catholic cardinal and historian, author of studies on monastic history.

Gassendi, Pierre (1592–1655), French scientist, mathematician and philosopher who espoused Epicureanism.

Gaster, Moses (1856–1939), Romanian-born English Jewish scholar and Zionist.

Gatto, Alfonso (1909–1976), Italian poet.

Gaunilo, Count (11th Century), French Benedictine monk, author of Liber pro insipiente (In Defense of the Fool), which questioned St Anselm's ontological argument for the existence of God.

Gautier, (Émile-Théodore-) Léon (1832–1897), French literary historian.

Gautier, Théophile (1811–1872), notable French poet, novelist and critic, champion of Romanticism, later of Naturalism.

Gautier d'Arras (died 1185), French writer of romances.

Gautier de Metz (13th Century), French clerk and poet who was also known as Gossuin de Metz.

Gay, John (1685–1732), famous English poet and dramatist, author of the celebrated ballad opera The Beggar's Opera (1728) and the admired poem Trivia, or the Art of Walking the Streets of London (1716).

Gay, John (1699–1745), English biblical scholar and philosopher.

Gay, (Marie-Françoise-) Sophie (Nichault de Lavalette) (1776–1852), French writer and dramatist.

Gayarré, Charles Étienne Arthur (1805–1895), American historian and novelist, best known for his History of Louisiana (4 vols, 1851–66) and Philip II of Spain (1866).

Geber (14th Century), influential Spanish alchemist and metallurgist.

Geddes, Alexander (1737–1802), Scottish Roman Catholic priest, linguist and biblical scholar.

Geddes, Sir Patrick (1854–1932), Scottish biologist and sociologist who, with John Arthur Thomson, wrote The Evolution of Sex (1889).

Geibel, (Franz) Emanuel (August von) (1815–1884), German poet, dramatist and translator.

Geiger, Abraham (1810–1874), eminent German Jewish theologian, author of the important study Urschrift und Übersetzungen der Bibel in ihrer Abhängigkeit von der innern Entwicklung des Judentums (the Original Text and the Translations of the Bible; Their Dependence on the Inner Development of Judaism, 1857).

Geiger, Theodor Julius (1891–1952), German-born Danish sociologist, best known for his studies on social stratification and mobility.

Geijer, Erik Gustaf (1783–1847), Swedish poet, historian, philosopher and theorist.

Geisel, Theodor Seuss (1904–91), American writer and illustrator of children's books who wrote under the name of Doctor Seuss.

Gélinas, Gratien (1909–99), Canadian actor, director, producer and dramatist.

Gellert, Christian Fürchtegott (1715–1769), German poet and writer, best remembered for his tales Fabeln und Erzählungen (Fables and Tales, 1746–48) and Geistliche Oden und Lieder (spiritual Odes and Songs, 1757).

Gellhorn, Martha Ellis (1908–1998), American journalist and novelist.

Gellius, Aulus (2nd Century), Latin writer, author of the Noctes atticae (Attic Nights).

Gellu, Naum (1915–2001), Romanian poet and dramatist of the Surrealist persuasion.

Gemistus Plethon, George (c.1355–c.1451), Byzantine philosopher and scholar of influence on the development of Italian Renaissance philosophical discourse.

Genesius, Joseph (10th Century), Byzantine historian.

Genet, Jean (1910–1986), important French poet, dramatist and novelist, a leading figure in the Theatre of the Absurd and the Theatre of Hatred.

Genlis, Stéphanie Du Crest de Saint-Aubin, Comtesse de (1746–1830), French children's writer.

Gennadius I of Constantinople, Saint (died 471), Byzantine patriach and theologian.

Gennadius II Scholarios (c.1405–c.1472), notable Greek Orthodox patriarch and theologian, particularly known for his Aristotelian polemics.

Gennadius of Marseilles (5th Century), French priest and theologian, author of the invaluable De viris illustribus (On Famous Men).

Genovesi, Antonio (1712–1769), Italian philosopher and economist who wrote Disciplinarum Metaphysicarum Elementa (Elements of the Discipline of Metaphysics, 5 vols, 1743–52), Delle lezioni di commercio (Lectures on Commerce, 1765) and Universae Christianae Theologiae Elementa (published 1771).

Gentile, Giovanni (1875–1944), prominent Italian philosopher, educator, editor and politician who embraced Fascism; was executed by the partisans.

Gentili, Alberico (1552–1608), significant Italian jurist, author of De jure belli libri tres (1598; English trans. as Three Books on the Law of War, 1933).

Gentz, Friedrich von (1764–1832), noted German journalist and political philosopher.

Geoffrey de Vinsauf (12th–13th Century), English rhetorician who wrote Nova Poetria and Summa de Coloribus Rhetoricis.

Geoffrey of Monmouth (died 1155), English cleric and chronicler, author of the fanciful Historia Regum Britanniae (c.1137).

Geometres, John (10th Century), Byzantine bishop and poet who was also known as John Kyriotes.

George, Henry (1839–1897), American land reformer and economist whose Progress and Poverty (1879) urged the adoption of the single tax.

George, Stefan (1868–1933), signifciant German poet, writer and translator, a master of lyric writing.

George of Trebizond (1396–1486), learned Byzantine scholar, especially noted for his Aristotelian studies.

George the Monk (actually Georgios Hamartolos) (9th Century), Byzantine historian.

George the Pisidian (actually Georgios Pisides) (7th Century), Byzantine cleric, historian and poet.

George the Syncellus (8th Century), Byzantine historian.

Gerard, Alexander (1728–1795), English theologian and philosopher, particularly known for his writings on aesthetics.

Gerard, John (1545–1612), English herbalist who wrote The Herball, or generall historie of plantes (1597).

Gerard of Cremona (c.1114–1187), Spanish scholar.

Gerhard, Johann (1582–1637), eminent German Lutheran theologian, author of the celebrated Loci Theologici (9 vols, 1610–22).

Gerhardie, William Alexander (actually William Alexander Gerhardi) (1895–1977), English novelist.

Gérin-Lajoie, Antoine (1824–1882), French-Canadian writer.

Gerlach, Hellmut von (1866–1935), German journalist and politician who espoused pacifism and opposed German nationalism.

Gerlache, Étienne-Constantin, Baron de (1785–1871), Belgian statesman and historian.

Germanus I, Saint (c.634–c.732), Byzantine patriarch and theologian.

Germanus II (c.1175–1240), Byzantine patriarch and theologian.

Gerould, Gordon Hall (1877–1953), American literary scholar and novelist; husband of Katharine Fullerton Gerould.

Gerould, Katherine Fullerton (1879–1944), American novelist and short-story writer; wife of Gordon Hall Gerould.

Gershom ben Judah (c.960–c.1035), famous French-born German Jewish scholar.

Gerson, Jean de (1363–1429), French Roman Catholic theologian who was also known as Jean de Charlier.

Gerstäcker, Friedrich (1816–1872), German adventurer and writer who described his various travels in various nations of the world in many books.

Gerstenberg, Heinrich Wilhelm von (1737–1823), German poet, critic and theorist, author of bardic verse and the tragedy Ugolino (1768).

Gervase of Canterbury (c.1141–c.1210), English monk and chronicler who was also known as Gervasius Dorobornensis.

Gervase of Tilbury (c.1152–c.1220), English scholar and courtier, author of the Otia imperialia.

Gesenius, (Heinrich Friedrich) Wilhelm (1786–1842), eminent German biblical scholar and philologist.

Gesner, Johann Matthias (1691–1761), notable German classical philologist.

Gessner, Salomon (1730–1788), versatile Swiss poet, writer, translator, painter and etcher.

Geulincx, Arnold (1624–1669), influential Dutch metaphysician and logician.

Gevers, Marie (actually Maria Theresia Carolina Fanny Gevers) (1883–1975), Belgian novelist and poet.

Geyl, Pieter (1887–1966), Dutch historian.

Gezelle, Guido (1830–1899), prominent Flemish poet, writer and churchman, a master of lyric poetry.

Ghālib, Mīrzā Asadullāh Khān (1797–1869), gifted Indian poet and writer in the Persian language.

Ghassaniy, Muyaka bin Haji al- (1776–1840), Kenyan poet in the Swahili language.

Ghazālī, al- (actually Abū Hāmid Muhammad ibn Muhammad at-Tūsī al-Ghazālī) (1058–1111), Persian Muslim jurist and theologian whose Ihyā' 'ulūm ad-dīn (The Revival of the Religious Sciences) gained acceptance for Sūfism in orthodox Islam.

Ghelderode, Michel de (1898–1962), avant-garde Belgian dramatist.

Ghosh, Girish Chandra (1844–1912), Bengali dramatist.

Giannone, Pietro (1676–1748), Italian historian who wrote the significant study Il triregno, ossia del regno del cielo, della terra, e del papa (The Triple Crown, or the Reign of Heaven, Earth, and the Pope).

Gibbon, Edward (1737–1794), English historian, celebrated for his masterpiece The History of the Decline and Fall of the Roman Empire (6 vols, 1776–88).

Gibbon, Lewis Grassle (actually James Leslie Mitchell) (1901–1935), Scottish writer, particularly esteemed for his novel trilogy Sunset Song (1932), Cloud Howe (1933) and Grey Granite (1934).

Gibbons, Stella (Dorothea) (1902–89), English novelist, short-story writer and poet, best remembered for her novel Cold Comfort Farm (1932).

Gibbs, Wolcott (1902–1958), American drama critic.

Gibran or Jibran, Khalil (actually Jubrān Khalīl Jubrān) (1883–1931), Lebanese essayist, novelist, poet and artist whose works in both Arabic and English reflected his preoccupation with religion and mysticism.

Gibson, Wilfred Wilson (1878–1962), English poet and dramatist.

Giddings, Franklin H(enry) (1855–1931), American sociologist, author of Studies in the Theory of Human Society (1922).

Gide, André (Paul Guillaume) (1869–1951), eminent French poet, novelist, dramatist and critic; won the Nobel Prize for Literature (1947).

Giedion, Sigfried (1888–1968), Swiss art historian.

Gierke, Otto Friedrich von (1841–1921), German legal philosopher.

Giesebrecht, (Friedrich) Wilhelm (Benjamin) von (1814–89), German historian, author of Geschichte der deutschen Kaiserzeit (History of the German Imperial Age, six vols, 1855–95).

Gieseler, Johann Karl Ludwig (1792–1854), German Protestant church historian who wrote the Lehrbuch der Kirchengeschichte (Textbook of Church History, 5 vols, 1824–57).

Gifford, Edward W(inslow) (1887–1959), American anthropologist, archaeologist and ethnologist.

Gifford, William (1756–1826), English editor, scholar and poet.

Gikatilla, Joseph (1248–c.1305), Spanish Kabbalist writer.

Gilbert, Sir W(illiam) S(chwenck) (1836–1911), English dramatist and librettist, famous for his collaboration with the composer Sir Arthur Sullivan on a celebrated series of operettas.

Gilbreth, Frank (Bunker Jr) (1911–2001), American journalist and writer, co-author of the memoirs Cheaper by the Dozen (1948) and Belles on Their Toes (1950).

Gilchrist, Alexander (1828–1861), English biographer; husband of Anne (née Burrow) Gilchrist.

Gilchrist, Anne (née Burrow) (1828–1885), English biographer and essayist; wife of Alexander Gilchrist.

Gildas (died 570), English historian, author of De excidio et conquestu Britanniae (The Ruin of Britain, c.546).

Gildersleeve, B(asil) L(anneau) (1831–1924), American classical scholar.

Giles, H A (1845–1935), English Orientalist.

Gilfillan, George (1813–1878), Scottish Dissenting minister, literary critic and editor.

Gill, (Arthur) Eric (Rowan) (1882–1940), English typographic designer, engraver, sculptor and writer.

Gill, Brendan (1914–1997), American critic and writer.

Gill, Francis James (1856–1912), Australian anthropologist.

Gilles li Muisis (1272–1352), French abbot, poet and chronicler who was also known as Le Muiset.

Gillespie, George (1613–1648), Scottish churchman and polemicist.

Gillette, William Hooker (1855–1937), American actor and dramatist, best remembered for his appearance in his own play Sherlock Holmes (1899).

Gilman, Caroline Howard (1794–1888), American writer and poet.

Gilman, Charlotte Perkins (1860–1935), American novelist and short-story writer.

Gilmore, Dame Mary Jane (1865–1962), Australian poet and writer.

Gilpin, William (1724–1804), English writer.

Gilpin, William (1813–1894), American soldier, politician and editor.

Gil Polo, Gaspar (c.1535–1591), Spanish poet who won distinction for his Diana enamorada (1564).

Gilson, Étienne (-Henry) (1884–1978), French historian of medieval philosophy, a champion of Thomism.

Giner de los Ríos, Francisco (1839–1915), Spanish philosopher, literary critic and educator.

Ginsberg, Allen (1926–1997), famous American poet, a central figure in the Beat and counterculture movements.

Ginsburg, Christian David (1831–1914), Polish-born English Hebrew and biblical scholar, an authority on the Masorah.

Ginzburg, Louis (1873–1953), Lithuanian-born American Jewish scholar.

Ginzburg, Natalia (1916–1991), prominent Italian novelist, dramatist and essayist.

Gioberti, Vincenzo (1801–1852), Italian philosopher and politician whose writings reflected his Christian beliefs, author of Del primato morale e civile degli italiano (On the Moral and Civil Primacy of the Italian Race, 1843) and Del rinnovamento civile d'Italia (On the Civil Renewal of Italy, 1851).

Giono, Jean (1895–1970), French novelist and poet.

Giordani, Pietro (1774–1848), Italian writer and patriot.

Giovannitti, Arturo (1884–1959), Italian-born American poet remembered for his condemnation of the American prison system in Arrows in the Gale (1914).

Gippius, Zinaida (Nikolaievna) (1869–1945), Russian poet, dramatist, writer and essayist; wife of Dmitri Sergeievich Merezhkovsky.

Giraldi, Giambattista (1505–1573), Italian dramatist, writer and poet who was also known as Cinzio or Cinthio after his academic name Cynthius.

Giraldus Cambrensis (c.1146–1223), Welsh historian who opposed Anglo-Saxon authority over the Welsh church and who was also known as Gerald of Wales and Gerald de Barri.

Girard, Jean-Baptiste (1765–1850), Swiss educator who was also known as Père Girard and Père Grégoire.

Girardin, Émile de (1806–1881), prominent French journalist.

Giraudoux, (Hyppolyte-) Jean (1882–1944), noted French novelist, dramatist, essayist and poet.

Giry, (Jean-Marie-Joseph-) Arthur (1848–1899), French historian, particularly known for his studies of the Middle Ages.

Gissing, George Robert (1857–1903), English novelist, best remembered for his New Grub Street (1891) and The Private Papers of Henry Ryecroft (1903).

Gittings, Robert William Victor (1911–1992), English poet, biographer and dramatist.

Giusti, Giuseppe (1809–1850), Italian poet and writer, a master of political satire.

Giustiniani, Agostino (1479–1536), Italian aristocrat, Dominican priest, statesman and scholar who excelled in Eastern studies.

Giustiniani, Leonardo (1338–1446), Italian aristocrat, statesman, scholar and poet whose Canzoni o strambotti d'amore (Songs of Fine Tunes of Love) served as the model for the giustiniane form of love poems.

Giustiniani, Pompeo (1569–1616), Italian soldier and historian who was also known as Braccio di Ferro (Iron Arm) in reference to the mechanical arm he wore after he lost his arm in battle.

Gjellerup, Karl Adolph (1857–1919), Danish poet and novelist; was co-winner of the Nobel Prize for Literature (1917).

Glaber, Radulfus (c.985–c.1047), French monk and chronicler.

Gladden, Washington (1836–1918), American Congregationalist minister, journalist, writer and poet whose poem O Master, Let Me Walk With Thee became a well-known hymn.

Gladkov, Fyodor Vasilievich (1883–1958), Russian novelist whose writings followed the tenets of Socialist Realism.

Glanvill or Glanvil, Joseph (1636–1680), English scholar, author of The Vanity of Dogmatizing, or Confidence in Opinions (1661), Plus Ultra or the Progress and Advancement of Knowledge Since the Days of Aristotle (1668) and Essays on Several Important Subjects (1676).

Glanville or Glanvil or Glanvill, Ranulf de (died 1190), English justiciar or chief minister to Henry II, reputed author of Tractatus de legibus et consuetudinibus regni Angliae (Treatise on the Laws and Customs of the Kingdom of England, c.1188).

Glapthorne, Henry (c.1610–c.1643), English poet and dramatist.

Glareanus, Henricus (actually Heinrich Loris) (1488–1563), Swiss scholar, poet and music theorist, author of the music treatise Dodecachordon (1547).

Glasgow, Ellen (Anderson Gholson) (1873–1945), esteemed American novelist and short-story writer, best known for her novels Virginia (1913), Barren Ground (1925) and The Sheltered Life (1932).

Glaspell, Susan (1882–1948), American novelist, short-story writer and dramatist, particularly remembered for her play Alison's House (1930).

Glassco, John (1909–1981), Canadian writer, poet and translator.

Glatigny, (Joseph-) Albert-Alexandre (1839–1873), French poet who adhered to Parnassian precepts.

Gleim, Johann Wilhelm Ludwig (1719–1803), German poet.

Glen, William (1789–1826), Scottish poet, author of the Jacobite lament Wae's me for Prince Charlie.

Glover, Richard (1712–1785), English politician and poet, best known for his ballad Admiral Hosier's Ghost (1740).

Glycas, Michael (12th Century), Byzantine historian, theologian and poet.

Glyn, Sir Anthony (actually Geoffrey Davson) (1922–1998), English novelist, author of The Dragon Variation (1969); grandson of Elinor Glyn.

Glyn, Elinor (1864–1943), English novelist, best remembered for her Three Weeks (1907); grandmother of Sir Anthony Glyn.

Gneist, Rudolf von (1816–1895), German jurist, politician and legal theorist, author of Englische Verfassungsgeschichte (1882; English trans. as The History of the English Constitution, 1886).

Gobat, Charles-Albert (1834–1914), Swiss politician, administrator, philanthropist and writer; was co-winner of the Nobel Prize for Peace (1902).

Gobineau, Joseph-Arthur, Comte de (1816–1882), French diplomat, writer and ethnologist, author of the influential Essai sur l'inégalité des races humains (4 vols, 1853–55; English trans. as Essay on the Inequality of Human Races, 1967).

Godden, (Margaret) Rumer (1907–1998), English writer.

Godefroy, Denis (1549–1622), French legal scholar who wrote Corpus juris civilis (1583).

Gödel, Kurt (1906–1978), Austro-Hungarian mathematical logician and philosopher.

Godfrey, Thomas (1736–1763), American poet who wrote in the style of the Cavalier poets.

Godfrey of Fontaines (c.1249–c.1306), French philosopher and theologian who espoused Aristotelian principles.

Godfrey of Saint-Victor (c.1125–1194), important French philosopher, theologian, poet and monk, author of Microcosmus and Fons philosophiae, notable works of the early medieval Christian Humanist movement.

Godin, Gérald (1938–1994), French-Canadian poet and writer.

Godkin, E(dwin) L(awrence) (1831–1902), Irish-born American journalist and editor.

Godley, A(lfred) D(enis) (1856–1925), English scholar and poet.

Godolphin, Sidney (1610–1643), English poet; died defending the Royalist cause.

Godwin, Edward William (1833–1886), English architect, designer and writer.

Godwin, Francis (1562–1633), English bishop, historian and writer, best known for his tale The Man in the Moone, or a Discourse of a Voyage Thither by Domingo Gonsales, the Speedy Messenger (published 1638).

Godwin, Mary Wollstonecraft (1759–1797), English writer and champion of women's rights; wife of William Godwin.

Godwin, William (1756–1836), English political and social philosopher, freethinker and writer, author of An Enquiry Concerning Political Justice and Its Influence on General Virtue and Happiness (1793); husband of Mary Wollstonecraft Godwin.

Goeje, Michael Jan de (1836–1909), Dutch scholar, an authority on Arabic subjects.

Goetel, Ferdynand (1890–1960), Polish novelist and essayist.

Goethe, Johann Wolfgang von (1749–1832), German poet, dramatist, painter, scientist and philosopher whose Faust (2 parts, 1808, 1832) stands as one of the supreme achievements of world literature.

Gogarty, Oliver Joseph St John (1878–1957), English surgeon, novelist and poet.

Gogol, Nikolai (Vasilievich) (1809–1852), renowned Russian writer and dramatist, celebrated for his novel Dead Souls (1842).

Góis, Damião de (1502–1574), learned Portugese scholar.

Gökalp, Ziya (actually Mehmed Ziya) (c.1875–1924), Turkish sociologist, writer and poet, a leading figure in the nationalist movement of his homeland.

Gold, Michael (actually Irwin Granich) (1893–1967), American editor, writer and dramatist who espoused Marxism.

Goldenweiser, Alexander (Alexandrovich) (1880–1940), Ukranian-born American anthropologist.

Goldfaden, Abraham (actually Abraham Goldenfoden) (1840–1908), Russian Hebrew and Yiddish poet and dramatist, generally acknowledged as the creator of Yiddish theatre and opera.

Golding, Louis (1895–1958), English novelist, short-story writer, essayist and poet.

Golding, Sir William (Gerald) (1911–1993), eminent English novelist, particularly admired for his Lord of the Flies (1954); won the Nobel Prize for Literature (1983).

Goldman, Emma (1869–1940), Lithuanian-born American anarchist, social reformer and writer.

Goldman, James (1927–1998), American novelist, dramatist and screenwriter, best known for his screenplay The Lion in Winter (1968).

Goldoni, Carlo (1707–1793), Italian dramatist who excelled in realistic comic plays.

Goldschmidt, Adolph (1863–1944), German art historian.

Goldschmidt, Meïr Aron (1819–1887), Danish novelist and short-story writer.

Goldsmith, Oliver (1730–1774), gifted Irish essayist, writer, dramatist and poet, especially esteemed for his poems The Traveller (1764) and The Deserted Village (1770), the novel The Vicar of Wakefield (1766) and the play She Stoops to Conquer (1773).

Gollancz, Israel (1864–1930), English scholar and editor who was known for his medieval and Shakespearean studies.

Gomarus or Gommer, Franciscus (1563–1641), French-born Dutch Calvinist theologian, one of the leading opponents of Arminianism.

Gombrich, Sir E(rnst) H(ans Josef) (1909–2001), Austrian-born English art historian who wrote the classic study The Story of Art (1950).

Gombrowicz, Witold (1904–1969), Polish novelist and short-story writer.

Gómez de Avellaneda, Gertrudis (1814–1873), celebrated Spanish dramatist, poet and writer, and Romanticist.

Gómez de la Serna, Ramón (1888–1963), Spanish writer and poet whose poetic greguerías (confused noise) influenced avant-garde writers in Europe and Latin America.

Gomperz, Theodor (1832–1912), Austrian classical philologist and philosopher, author of Griechische Denker: Eine Geschichte der antiken Philosophie (2 vols, 1893, 1902; English trans. as Greek Thinkers: A History of Ancient Philosophy, 4 vols, 1901–12).

Gonçalves Crespo, António Cândido (1846–1883), Portuguese poet.

Gonçalves de Magalhães, Domingos José (1811–1882), Brazilian poet, remembered for his Suspiros Poéticos e Saudades (Poetic Sighs and Longings, 1836).

Goncalves Dias, Antonio (1823–1864), Brazilian poet and scholar, author of the poem Song of Exile (1843); died in a shipwreck.

Goncharov, Ivan Alexandrovich (1812–1891), Russian novelist who wrote Obyknovennaya istoriya (1847; English trans. as A Common Story, 1917), Oblomov (1859; English trans., 1954) and Obryv (1869; English trans. as The Precipice, 1915).

Goncourt, Edmond (-Louis-Antoine Huot) de (1822–1896), French writer whose close collaboration with his brother produced the celebrated Journal (1851 et seq.) and the famous novel Germinie (1864); brother of Jules (-Alfred Huot) de Goncourt.

Goncourt, Jules (-Alfred Huot) de (1830–1870), French writer, a close collaborator with his brother on the celebrated Journals (1851 et seq.) and the famous novel Germinie (1864); brother of Edmond (-Louis-Antoine Huot) de Goncourt.

Góngora y Argote, Luis de (1561–1627), significant Spanish poet who became known for his complex style known as Gongorism.

Gonzaga, Tomás António (1744–1810), Portuguese poet who won distinction for his love poetry Marília de Dirceu (1792).

González Martínez, Enrique (1871–1952), Mexican poet, physician and diplomat.

González Prada, Manuel (1844–1919), Peruvian poet.

Gooch, George Peabody (1873–1968), English historian.

Goodman, Paul (1911–1972), American essayist, short-story writer, dramatist and poet, principally known for his antiestablishment views.

Goodnow, Frank J(ohnson) (1859–1939), American political scientist and educator.

Goodrich, Samuel Griswold (1793–1860), American writer and poet, best remembered for his many children's books he wrote under the name Peter Parley.

Goodrich or Goodricke, Thomas (c.1480–1554), English bishop and biblical translator.

Goodspeed, Edgar J(ohnson) (1871–1962), American biblical scholar, translator and linguist.

Goodwin, William Watson (1831–1912), American classical scholar.

Googe, Barnabe (1540–1594), English poet, known for his Eclogues (1563) and Cupido Conquered.

Gordin, Jacob (1853–1909), Yiddish dramatist.

Gordon, Aaron David (1856–1922), Russian-born Zionist and essayist.

Gordon, Adam Lindsay (1833–1870), Australian poet who won popularity with his ballads.

Gordon, Caroline (1895–1981), American novelist and short-story writer.

Gordon, Judah Leib (1830–1892), Lithuanian-born Russian Hebrew poet, essayist, novelist and short-story writer who was also known as Leon Gordon.

Gore, Catherine Grace Frances (née Moody) (1799–1861), English novelist, short-story writer and dramatist.

Gore, Charles (1853–1932), English Anglican bishop and theologian who espoused liberal views.

Gorges, Sir Arthur (1557–1625), English courtier and poet.

Georgias of Leontini (c.483–c.376 BC), Greek philosopher and rhetorician.

Gorky, Maxim (actually Aleksei Maximovich Peshkov) (1868–1936), famous Russian novelist and short-story writer.

Gorman, Herbert S(herman) (1893–1954), American biographer and novelist.

Görres, (Johann) Joseph von (1776–1848), notable German writer and journalist, particularly known for his expansive Christliche Mystic (Christian Mysticism, 4 vols, 1836–42).

Gorter, Herman (1864–1927), Dutch poet, author of Mei (May, 1889), Verzen (1890) and Pan (1916).

Goślicki, Wawrzyniec (c.1530–1607), Polish Roman Catholic bishop and diplomat who championed liberalism in his De optimo senatore (1568; English trans. as The Accomplished Senator, 1733).

Gosse, Sir Edmund William (1849–1928), English poet, literary historian, critic and translator.

Gossen, Herman Heinrich (1810–1858), German economist.

Gosson, Stephen (1554–1624), English dramatist who became known for his Puritan attacks on the stage.

Gottfried von Strassburg (13th Century), famous German poet and scholar, author of the German version of Tristan und Isolde (c.1210).

Gottschalk or Gottescalc or Godescalchus of Orbais (c.803–c.868), German monk, theologian and poet.

Gottsched, Johann Christoph (1700–1766), German literary theorist, critic and dramatist.

Gould, Edward Sherman (1805–1885), American writer.

Gould, Stephen Jay (1941–2002), American paleontologist, evolutionary biologist and writer, author of many books on science, including the award-winning The Mismeasure of Man (1981).

Gourgaud, Gaspard (1783–1852), French soldier and historian.

Gourmont, Jean de (1877–1928), French writer and poet; brother of Rémy de Gourmont.

Gourmont, Rémy de (1858–1915), French essayist, poet, novelist and dramatist; brother of Jean de Gourmont.

Gower, John (c.1330–1408), notable English poet, author of Confessio amantis, Speculum meditantis and Vox clamantis.

Goyen, (Charles) William (1915–1983), American novelist, short-story writer and dramatist.

Gozzi, Carlo, Conte (1720–1806), important Italian poet, dramatist and writer, particularly successful for his fairy-tale plays.

Gozzi, Gasparo, Conte (1713–1786), Italian journalist, critic, writer and poet.

Gqoba, William Wellington (1840–1888), Bantu poet and philologist.

Grabbe, Christian Dietrich (1801–1836), German dramatist and poet whose works presaged Expressionism.

Graça Aranha, José Pereira da (1868–1931), Brazilian novelist and diplomat, best known for his novel Canaã (1902; English trans. as Canaan, 1920).

Gracián (y Morales), Baltasar (1601–1658), Spanish Jesuit philosopher and writer, author of the philosophical novel El criticón (3 parts, 1651, 1653, 1657; English trans. as The Critic, 1681).

Grade, Chaim (1910–82), Yiddish poet, novelist and short-story writer.

Grady, Henry Woodfin (1850–1889), American journalist and orator.

Graebner, (Robert) Fritz (1877–1934), German ethnologist who wrote Methode der Ethnologie (Method of Ethnology, 1911) and Das Weltbild der Primitiven (The World View of the Primitives, 1924).

Graetz, Heinrich (1817–1891), Polish-born German historian, author of the Geschichte der Juden von den altesten Zeiten bis auf die Gegenwart (11 vols, 1853–76; abridged English trans. as History of the Jews from Oldest Times to the Present, 1891–92).

Graevius, Johann (actually Johann Georg Greffe) (1632–1703), Dutch scholar and antiquarian.

Graham, William Sydney (1918–1986), esteemed Scottish poet.

Grahame, James (1765–1811), Scottish poet.

Grahame, Kenneth (1859–1932), Scottish writer, best known for his children's classic The Wind in the Willows (1908).

Grainger, James (c.1721–1766), English physician and poet, author of the didactic poem Sugar Cane (1764).

Gramsci, Antonio (1891–1937), Italian politician, journalist, critic and writer, founder of the Italian Communist Party (1921).

Grand, Sarah (actually Frances Elizabeth Bellenden McFall née Clarke) (1854–1943), English novelist who wrote The Heavenly Twins (1893) and The Beth Book (1897).

Grandbois, Alain (1900–1975), French-Canadian poet, biographer and short-story writer.

Grandgent, Charles Hall (1862–1939), American linguist who was an authority on Vulgar Latin and Dante.

Grange, John (c.1557–1611), English novelist, author of The Golden Aphroditis (1577).

Granovsky, Timofei Nikolaievich (1813–1855), Russian historian.

Grant, Anne (née MacVicar) (1755–1838), Scottish poet and essayist.

Grant, George (1918–1988), Canadian philosopher.

Grant, James (1822–1887), English soldier and writer.

Grant, Robert (1852–1940), American jurist, novelist, essayist and poet.

Granville-Barker, Harley (1877–1946), influential English dramatist, theater producer and critic.

Gratian (c.1100–c.1158), significant Italian monk and legal scholar who was also known under his academic name of Magister Gratianus.

Graves, Richard (1715–1804), English novelist and poet, best remembered for his novel The Spiritual Quixote, or the Summer's Ramble of Mr Geoffry Wildgoose (1772).

Graves, Robert (van Ranke) (1895–1985), English poet, novelist, essayist and critic.

Gray, Asa (1810–1888), American botanist, author of the standard Manual of the Botany of the Northern United States, from New England to Wisconsin and South to Ohio and Pennsylvania Inclusive (1848).

Gray, David (1838–1861), Scottish poet.

Gray, John Henry (1866–1934), English churchman and poet.

Gray, Thomas (1716–1771), sublime English poet, celebrated for his Elegy Written in a Country Churchyard (1751).

Grayson, William J(ohn) (1788–1863), American lawyer, politician, writer and poet who championed slavery in his expansive didactic poem The Hireling and the Slave (1854).

Grazzini, Anton Francesco (1503–1584), Italian poet, dramatist and storyteller who was known as Il Lasca (The Roach).

Gréban, Arnoul (1420–1471), French dramatist, author of the famous sacred play Mystere de la Passion (c.1453).

Greeley, Horace (1811–1872), American newspaper editor, a prominent figure in the antislavery and Radical Republican movements.

Green, Alice Sophia Amelia (actually Alice Sophia Amelia Stopford) (1847–1929), Irish historian.

Green, Anna Katharine (1846–1935), American writer of detective novels.

Green, Henry (actually Henry Vincent Yorke) (1905–1973), English novelist and industrialist.

Green, John Richard (1837–1883), English historian, author of a Short History of the English People (1874).

Green, Julien (actually Julian Green) (1900–1998), American-born French writer, dramatist and memoirist.

Green, Matthew (1697–1737), English poet who wrote The Spleen (1737).

Green, Paul (Eliot) (1894–1981), American dramatist and novelist, best remembered for his play In Abraham's Bosom (1927).

Green, T(homas) H(ill) (1836–1882), English philosopher and political theorist, author of Prolegomena to Ethics (published 1883) and Lectures on the Principles of Political Obligation (published 1885–88).

Greenberg, Samuel Bernard (1893–1917), American poet who revealed a fine talent for lyric expression.

Greene, Asa (1789–c.1837), American physician, journalist and novelist.

Greene, (Henry) Graham (1904–1991), eminent English novelist, short-story writer, biographer, dramatist and essayist.

Greene, Robert (c.1558–1592), English dramatist and writer, especially admired for his blank verse romantic comedies.

Greenwood, Walter (1903–1974), English novelist and dramatist, best known for his novel Love on the Dole (1933).

Greg, Sir Walter Wilson (1875–1959), English literary scholar and bibliographer.

Gregoras, Nicephorus (1295–1360), important Byzantine scholar, philosopher and theologian, author of a monumental Byzantine history (37 vols).

Gregory, Horace (Victor) (1898–1982), American poet, essayist, editor and translator; husband of Marya Zaturenska.

Gregory, Isabella Augusta (née Persse), Lady (1852–1932), Irish writer, dramatist and translator.

Gregory Narekatzi, Saint (951–1001), Armenian theologian and poet who espoused mysticism, also known as Gregory Narek.

Gregory of Nyssa, Saint (c.335–c.394), Bishop and theologian who was the principal defender of Trinitarianism of his era.

Gregory of Rimini (c.1299–1358), influential Italian philosopher and theologian who was a proponent of a moderate Nominalist worldview.

Gregory of Sinai (c.1299–1346), Greek Orthodox monk, theologian and mystic who was also known as Gregory Sinaites.

Gregory of Tours, Saint (actually Georgius Florentius) (c.538–c.595), notable French Roman Catholic bishop and writer, particularly known for his history of the Franks and the lives of the church fathers.

Gregory Thaumaturgus, Saint (c.213–c.270), Greek Roman Catholic bishop and theologian who wrote a famous exposition of his faith.

Greiff, León de (1895–1976), Colombian poet.

Grein, Jack Thomas (actually Jacob Thomas Grein) (1862–1935), Dutch-born English critic, theater manager and dramatist.

Grenfell, Julian (1888–1915), English poet who was admired for his Into Battle (1915); died in World War I.

Gresset, Jean-Baptiste-Louis (1709–1777), French poet and dramatist, author of the celebrated comic narrative poem Ver-Vert (1734).

Gressmann, Hugo (1877–1927), German Old Testament scholar.

Greville, Sir Fulke, 1st Baron Brooke (1554–1628), English writer, poet, dramatist and courtier; was murdered by a manservant.

Grévin, Jacques (1538–1570), French poet, dramatist and physician.

Grey, Zane (1872–1939), American novelist of popular tales of the Old West.

Griboyedov, Alexander Sergeievich (1795–1829), Russian dramatist who won distinction with his comic play Gore ot uma (1822–24; English trans. as Wit Works Woe, 1933).

Grieg, (Johan) Nordahl Brun (1902–1943), Norwegian poet, dramatist and novelist; as a member of the Resistance, he died when his airplane was shot down by the Germans in World War II.

Grierson, Sir George Abraham (1851–1941), English linguist.

Grierson, Sir Herbert John Clifford (1866–1960), English literary scholar.

Griffin, Gerald (1803–1840), Irish novelist, poet and dramatist, best remembered for his novel The Collegians (1829).

Griffith, Arthur (1872–1922), prominent Irish journalist and nationalist leader who served as president of the Irish Republic (1922).

Griffiths, Ann (née Thomas) (1776–1805), Welsh hymnist.

Grignon, Claude-Henri (1894–1978), esteemed French-Canadian journalist and novelist who wrote under the name Valdombre, author of the novel Un Homme et son péché (A Man and His Sin, 1933).

Grigoriev, Apollon (Alexandrovich) (1822–1864), Russian critic and poet.

Grigson, Geoffrey (Edward Harvey) (1905–1985), English poet, editor and critic.

Grillparzer, Franz (1791–1872), Austrian dramatist and poet whose tragic plays rank among the august creations of Austrian literature.

Grimald or Grimoald, Nicholas (1519–c.1562), English poet, dramatist and translator.

Grimké, Angelina Emily (1805–1879), American pamphleteer and lecturer who was active in the antislavery movement; sister of Sarah Moore Grimké.

Grimké, Sarah Moore (1792–1873), American pamphleteer and lecturer who was known for her antislavery views; sister of Angelina Emily Grimké.

Grimm, Friedrich Melchior, Baron von (1723–1807), German critic.

Grimm, Hans (1875–1959), German writer, particularly known for his Pan Germanist novel Volk ohne Raum (People without Space, 1926).

Grimm, Jacob Ludwig Carl (1785–1863), famous German folklorist who, with his brother, collected the classic Kinder- und Hausmärchen (1812–22), best known as Grimm's Fairy Tales; brother of Wilhelm Carl Grimm.

Grimm, Wilhelm Carl (1786–1859), famous German folklorist who collaborated with his brother on the classic Kinder- und Hausmärchen (1812–22), better known as Grimm's Fairy Tales; brother of Jacob Ludwig Carl Grimm.

Grimmelshausen, Hans Jacob Christoph (c.1622–1676), German novelist, author of the renowned satirical Simplicissimus series of novels (1669 et seq.).

Grimshaw, Beatrice (Ethel) (1871–1953), Irish traveller and writer.

Grin or Grinovsky, Alexander Stepanovich (1880–1932), Russian writer, best known for his short stories.

Gringore or Gringoire, Pierre (c.1475–c.1538), French poet and dramatist.

Gripenberg, Bertel Johan Sebastian, Baron (1878–1947), Finnish poet and writer who wrote in Swedish.

Griswold, Rufus Wilmot (1815–1857), American journalist, critic and editor.

Grober, Gustav (1844–1911), German scholar and medievalist.

Grocyn, William (c.1446–1519), English scholar.

Groen van Prinsterer, Guillaume (1801–1876), Dutch Protestant politician, religious writer and historian.

Gronovius, Johannes Fredericus (1611–1671), Dutch Latinist.

Grosseteste, Robert (c.1175–1235), English Roman Catholic bishop and scholar.

Grossi, Tommaso (1791–1853), Italian poet, best remembered for his I Lombardi all prima crociata (1826).

Grosvenor, Gilbert H(ovey) (1875–1966), American geographer, writer and editor.

Grote, George (1794–1871), English historian, author of a History of Greece (12 vols, 1846–56).

Grotefend, Georg Friedrich (1775–1853), German educator and language scholar who wrote the important Neue Beiträge zur Erläuterung der persepolitanischen Keilschrift (New Contributions to a Commentary on the Persepolitan Cuneiform Writing, 1837).

Groth, Klaus (1819–1899), German poet and writer, admired for his poetry collection Quickborn (1853).

Grotius, Hugo (1583–1645), Dutch jurist, scholar and poet, author of the celebrated De Jure Belli ac Pacis (On the Law of War and Peace, 1625), a fundamental work in the development of international jurisprudence.

Groulx, Lionel-Adolphe (1878–1967), French-Canadian historian and novelist whose fiction appeared under the name Alonié de Lestres.

Grout, Donald J(ay) (1902–1987), American music scholar.

Grove, Frederick Philip (1871–1948), Canadian novelist and essayist.

Grove, Sir George (1820–1900), renowned English music and biblical lexicographer, celebrated for his expansive Dictionary of Music and Musicians (4 vols, 1879–89).

Gruber, Johann Gottfried (1774–1851), German archaeologist, literary historian and encylopedist.

Gruffydd, William John (1881–1954), Welsh poet, scholar and editor.

Grün, Anastasius (actually Anton Alexander, Graf von Auersperg) (1806–1876), Austrian statesman, poet and translator.

Grundtvig, N(ikolai) F(rederik) S(everin) (1783–1872), Danish bishop, theologian, historian, poet and hymnist.

Gryphius, Andreas (actually Andreas Greif) (1616–1664), important German poet and dramatist, a master of lyric expression.

Guardini, Romano (1885–1968), Italian-born German Roman Catholic theologian.

Guarini, (Giovanni) Battista (1538–1612), Italian poet, author of the celebrated Il pastor fido (The Faithful Shepherd, 1590).

Guarino Veronese (c.1372–1460), Italian classical scholar who was also known as Guarino da Verona.

Gudmundsson, Kristmann (1902–1983), noted Icelandic novelist.

Gudmundsson, Tómas (1901–1983), Icelandic poet.

Guedalla, Philip (1889–1944), English historian and biographer.

Guérin, Charles (1873–1907), French poet who championed Symbolism.

Guérin, Eugénie de (1805–1848), talented French poet and writer; sister of (Georges-) Maurice de Guérin.

Guérin, (Georges-) Maurice (1810–1839), gifted French poet and writer; brother of Eugénie de Guérin.

Guernes de Pont-Sainte-Maxence (12th Century), French scholar, author of Vie de saint Thomas Becket (c.1174).

Guerrazzi, Francesco Domenico (1804–1873), Italian politician and historical novelist.

Guest, Edgar A(lbert) (1881–1959), English-born American poet who wrote A Heap o' Livin' (1916).

Guevara, Antonio de (c.1481–1545), Spanish court preacher and writer, author of Reloj de príncipes o libro aureo del emperador Marco Aurelio (1529; English trans. as The Golden Boke of Marcus Aurelius, 1535).

Guèvremont, Germain (née Grignon) (1900–1968), French-Canadian novelist, known for her Le Survenant (1945; English trans. as The Outlander, 1950) and Marie-Dedace (1947; English trans. as Monk's Reach, 1950).

Gui or Guy, Bernard (c.1261–1331), Dominican bishop, historian and inquisitor.

Guicciardini, Francesco (1483–1540), Italian statesman and historian.

Guidi, Alessandro (1650–1712), Italian poet, an exponent of classical ideals.

Guido delle Colonne (c.1215–c.1290), Italian jurist, writer and poet, author of the Historia destructionis Troiae (History of the Destruction of Troy, 1287).

Guillaume de Champeaux (c.1070–1121), French Roman Catholic bishop, theologian and philosopher.

Guillaume de Lorris (13th Century), French poet who wrote the Roman de la Rose, a work completed by Jean de Meun.

Guillén, Jorge (1893–1984), Spanish poet of an experimental bent.

Guillén (Batista), Nicolás (1902–89), Cuban poet of social protest who became an ardent supporter of the Castro dictatorship.

Guimarães, Bernardo (da Silva) (1825–1884), Brazilian poet, dramatist and novelist.

Guimarães Rosa, João (1908–1967), Brazilian novelist and short-story writer.

Guimerá, Angel (1847–1924), Catalan dramatist and poet, especially remembered for his play Terra baixa (1896; English trans. as Martha of the Lowlands, 1914).

Guiney, Louise Imogen (1861–1920), American poet and essayist.

Guinizelli, Guido (13th Century), Italian poet.

Güiraldes, Ricardo (1886–1927), Argentine novelist and poet, best known for his novel Don Segundo Sombra (1926).

Guiterman, Arthur (1871–1943), American poet and journalist of a humorous turn.

Guitry, Sacha (1885–1957), French dramatist and actor who won acclaim for his mastery of improvisation.

Guittone d'Arezzo (c.1235–1294), Italian poet and writer, particularly known for his amorous and sacred poetry.

Guizot, François (-Pierre-Guillaume) (1787–1874), prominent French politician and historian who espoused the cause of conservative constitutional monarchist principles.

Gumilev, Nikolai Stepanovich (1886–1921), Russian poet who was a leading figure in Acmeist circles.

Gumplowicz, Ludwig (1838–1909), influential Polish-born Austrian sociologist and legal philosopher, known for his cyclical theory of history.

Gundisalvo, Domingo (12th Century), Spanish Roman Catholic archdeacon, philosopher and linguist.

Gundulić, Ivan (1589–1638), Croatian poet and dramatist, author of the epic poem Osman (1626).

Gunkel, (Johann Friedrich) Hermann (1862–1932), noted German Old Testament scholar, a prominent advocate of form criticism.

Gunnarsson, Gunnar (1889–1975), Icelandic novelist and short-story writer.

Gunning, Susannah (c.1740–1800), English novelist and poet.

Güntekin, Reşat Nuri (1892–1956), Turkish novelist who won distinction with his Çalikuşu (1922; English trans. as The Autobiography of a Turkish Girl, 1949).

Gunter, Archibald Clavering (1847–1907), English-born American novelist, best remembered for his Mr Barnes of New York (1887).

Günther, Johann Christian (1695–1723), German poet who was a master of lyric expression.

Gunther, John (1901–1970), American journalist and writer.

Gunzburg, David (1857–1910), Russian Jewish scholar.

Guo Moruo (actually Kuo K'ai-Chen) (1892–1978), Chinese scholar, writer, dramatist and poet who played a major role in the cultural life of Communist China.

Gurney, Edmund (1847–1888), English philosopher.

Gurney, Ivor (Bertie) (1890–1937), English poet and composer whose gassing during military service in World War I led to his confinement in a mental institution.

Gurney, Joseph John (1788–1847), English Quaker and theologian.

Gurwitsch, Aron (1901–1973), Lithuanian-born American philosopher.

Gustafson, Ralph Barker (1909–1995), admired Canadian poet who wrote finely-crafted verse.

Guthrie, A(lfred) B(ertram) Jr (1901–1991), American novelist and short-story writer.

Gutiérrez Nájera, Manuel (1859–1895), Mexican poet and writer.

Gutiérrez Solana, José (1886–1947), Spanish painter and writer.

Guto'r Glyn (15th Century), Welsh poet.

Gutzkow, Karl (Ferdinand) (1811–1878), influential German novelist and dramatist, one of the leading representatives of the social novel in his homeland.

Guyon, Jeanne-Marie de la Motte (née Bouvier) (1648–1717), French mystic and writer who extolled Quietism.

Guzmán, Martín Luis (1887–1976), Mexican novelist.

Gvadányi, József (1725–1801), Hungarian writer.

Gwalchmai ap Meilyr (c.1140–c.1180), Welsh poet.

Gyllenborg, Gustaf Fredrik, Count (1731–1808), Swedish poet, particularly remembered for his Menniskjans Elände (Misery of Man, 1762).

Gyöngyösi, István (1620–1704), Hungarian poet.

Haanpaa, Pentti (1905–1955), Finnish writer.

Habberton, John (1842–1921), American journalist and writer, best known for his novel Helen's Babies (1876).

Haberl, Franz Xaver (1860–1910), German music scholar.

Habington, William (1605–1654), English poet, best remembered for his Castara (1634).

Haddad, Malek (1927–78), Algerian poet and novelist.

Haddon, Alfred Cort (1855–1940), English anthropologist.

Hāfez (actually Mohammad Shams od-Dīn Hāfez) (c.1325–c.1389), famous Persian poet, a master of lyric expression.

Hāfiz Ibrāhīm, Muhammad (1872–1932), Egyptian poet and writer, known as the poet of the Nile.

Hāfiz-i Abrū (actually 'Abd Allāh ibn Lutf Allāh ibn 'Abd ar-Rashīd al-Bihdādīnī Hāfiz-i Abrū) (died 1430), important Persian historian.

Hafner, Philipp (1731–1764), Austrian dramatist.

Hafstein, Hannes (Petursson) (1861–1922), Icelandic politician and poet.

Hagalin, Gudmundur G(íslason) (1898–1985), Icelandic novelist, short-story writer and essayist.

Hagedorn, Friedrich von (1708–1754), admired German poet, author of Versuch in poetischen Fabeln und Erzählungen (Attempt at Poetic Fables and Tales, 1738) and Oden und Lieder (Odes and Songs, 3 vols, 1742–52).

Hagedorn, Hermann (1882–1964), American writer and poet.

Hägerström, Axel (Anders Theodor) (1868–1939), Swedish philosopher who championed phenomenological and conceptual analysis.

Haggard, Sir H(enry) Rider (1856–1925), English novelist who wrote King Solomon's Mines (1886) and She (1887).

Hagiwara Sakutarō (1886–1942), Japanese poet.

Hahn-Hahn, Ida, Gräfin von (1805–1880), German novelist, travel writer and poet, best known for her novel Gräfin Faustine (1841).

Hai ben Sherira (939–1038), Bablonian Talmudic scholar.

Haidari, Buland al- (1926–1996), Iraqi poet of Kurdish descent, an exponent of free verse.

Hake, Edward (16th Century), English poet who wrote the satirical Newes out of Powless Churcheyarde.

Hakīm, Tawfīq (Husayn) al- (1898–1987), major Egyptian writer and dramatist.

Hakluyt, Richard (c.1552–1616), English geographer and writer, particularly known for The principall Navigations, Voiages and Discoveries of the English nation (1589).

Hakuin (1685–1768), Japanese Buddhist priest, artist and writer, a leading figure in the restoration of Zen Buddhism in his homeland.

Halberstam, Hayyim ben Leibush (1793–1876), controversial Hasidic rabbi and Talmudic scholar.

Haldane, Elizabeth Sanderson (1862–1937), Scottish social welfare worker, reformer, writer and translator; sister of John Scott Haldane and Richard Burdon Haldane.

Haldane, J(ohn) B(urdon) S(anderson) (1892–1964), English-born Indian scientist and writer of Scottish descent; son of John Scott Haldane.

Haldane, John Scott (1860–1936), Scottish physiologist and philosopher; brother of Elizabeth Sanderson Haldane and Richard Burdon Haldane, and father of J(ohn) B(urdon) S(anderson) Haldane.

Haldane, Richard Burdon, 1st Viscount (1856–1928), Scottish politician and philosopher; brother of Elizabeth Sanderson Haldane and John Scott Haldane.

Hale, Edward Everett (1822–1909), American clergyman and writer, author of the famous story 'The Man Without a Country' (1863); brother of Lucretia Peabody Hale and grandfather of Nancy Hale.

Hale, Horatio (Emmons) (1817–1896), influential American anthropologist who wrote the major study The Iroquois Book of Rites (1883).

Hale, Sir John (Rigby) (1923–99), English historian, author of the authoritative study The Civilization of Europe in the Renaissance (1993).

Hale, Lucretia Peabody (1820–1900), American writer, author of The Peterkin Papers (1880) and The Last of the Peterkins, with Others of Their Kin (1886); sister of Edward Everett Hale.

Hale, Sir Matthew (1609–1676), eminent English scholar, an authority on the development of English common law.

Hale, Nancy (1908–1988), American novelist and short-story writer; granddaughter of Edward Everett Hale.

Hale, Sarah Josepha (Buell) (1788–1879), American writer, dramatist and poet, best known for her children's poem Mary Had a Little Lamb (1830).

Halévy, Élie (1870–1937), French historian, author of Histoire du peuple anglais au XIXe siècle (3 vols, 1913–23; English trans. as A History of the English People in the Nineteenth Century, 1949–51).

Halévy, Leon (actually Leon Levi) (1802–1883), French poet, novelist, historian and translator.

Haley, Alex (Palmer) (1921–1992), American writer, best remembered for the chronicle Roots (1976).

Haliburton, Hugh (actually James Logie Robertson) (1846–1922), Scottish poet and essayist.

Haliburton, Thomas Chandler (1796–1865), Canadian writer, creator of the satirical character Sam Slick.

Halid Ziya Ushakligil (1865–1945), Turkish novelist and short-story writer whose most famous work was the novel Ashk-i Memnu (1900).

Halide Edib Adivar (1883–1964), Turkish feminist and novelist, especially celebrated for her novel Ateşten gömlek (Shirt of Fire, 1922).

Halifax, Charles Montague, 1st Earl of (1661–1715), English statesman and poet who collaborated with Matthew Prior on The Town and Country Mouse (1687), a parody of Dryden's The Hind and The Panther.

Halifax, George Savile, 1st Marquess of (1633–1695), English statesman and political writer who became known as 'The Trimmer' for his neutral political stance.

Hall, Basil (1788–1844), English naval officer and traveller.

Hall, Baynard Rush (1798–1863), American Presbyterian minister and writer.

Hall or Halle, Edward (c.1498–1547), English historian, author of the important chronicle The Union of the Two Noble and Illustre Famelies of Lancastre and Yorke (1542).

Hall, G(ranville) Stanley (1844–1924), American psychologist, influential for his pioneering studies in child psychology and educational psychology.

Hall, James (1793–1868), American judge, banker, editor and writer who was especially admired for his works on the American frontier.

Hall, James Norman (1887–1951), American novelist, essayist and poet.

Hall, Joseph (1574–1656), English Anglican bishop, philosopher, poet and writer, author of the political satire Virgidemairum (A Harvest of Blows, 6 vols, 1597–1602).

Hall, (Marguerite) Radclyffe (1886–1943), English poet and novelist, best known for the uproar she created over the subject of lesbianism in her novel The Well of Loneliness (1928).

Hall, Robert (1764–1831), English Baptist minister, social reformer and writer.

Hallāj, al- (actually Abū al-Mughīth al Husayn ibn Mansūr al Hallāj) (858–922), Persian preacher and writer of Islamic mysticism (Sūfism); was crucified by his opponents.

Hallam, Arthur Henry (1811–1833), English poet and essayist; son of Henry Hallam.

Hallam, Henry (1777–1859), English historian; father of Arthur Henry Hallam.

Halleck, Fitz-Greene (1790–1867), American poet, best known for his satirical and Romantic verse and for his collaboration with Joseph Rodman Drake on the 'Croaker Papers'.

Hallgrímsson, Jónas (1807–1845), admired Icelandic poet who excelled in Romantic expression.

Hall-Stevenson, John (1718–1785), English poet , particularly known for his satirical bent.

Halliwell-Phillipps, James Orchard (actually James Orchard Halliwell) (1820–1889), English scholar who was an authority on Shakespeare.

Halper, Albert (1904–1984), American novelist and short-story writer.

Halpine, Charles Graham (1829–1868), Irish-born American army officer who wrote a humorous account of the Civil War in The Life and Adventures... of Private Miles O'Reilly (1864).

Hamadānī (actually 'Alī ibn Shihāb ad-Dīn ibn Muhammad Hamadānī) (1314–1385), Persian mystic theologian.

Hamadhānī, al- (actually Badī' az-Zamān Abū al-Fadl Ahmad ibn al-Husayn al-Hamadānī) (969–1008), Arab writer and poet.

Hamann, Johann Georg (1730–1788), German philosopher , a leading proponent of fideism.

Hamdānī, al- (actually Abūmuhammad al-Hasan ibn Ahmad al-Hamdānī) (c.893–c.945), Arab poet, grammarian, historian, astronomer and geographer.

Hamerling, Robert (actually Rupert Johann Hammerling) (1830–1889), Austrian poet, dramatist and writer, esteemed for his epic poems.

Hamilton, Alexander (1755–1804), prominent American politician who, with James Madison and John Jay, collaborated on the classic essays The Federalist (1787–88); killed in a duel with Aaron Burr.

Hamilton, (Anthony Walter) Patrick (1904–1962), English dramatist and novelist.

Hamilton, Charles Harold St John (1876–1961), English writer of numerous books for boys.

Hamilton, (Robert) Ian (1938–2001), English poet, biographer, critic and editor.

Hamilton, William (c.1665–1751), Scottish poet who was known as William Hamilton of Gilbertfield.

Hamilton, William (1704–1754), Scottish Jacobite patriot and poet who was known as William Hamilton of Bangour.

Hamilton, Sir William, Baronet (1788–1856), Scottish philosopher and educator.

Hamilton, Sir William Rowan (1805–1865), notable English mathematician and amateur poet.

Hammer-Purgstall, Joseph, Freiherr von (1774–1856), Austrian diplomat and writer.

Hammett, Samuel Adams (1816–1865), American writer of frontier humour who used the name Philip Paxton.

Hammett, (Samuel) Dashiell (1894–1961), American writer, creator of the hard-boiled genre of detective fiction.

Hammon, Jupiter (c.1720–c.1800), American slave poet of religious verse.

Hammond Innes, Ralph (1913–98), English writer, best remembered for his novel The Wreck of the 'Mary Deare' (1956).

Hamsun, Knut (actually Knut Petersen) (1859–1952), prominent Norweigan novelist, poet and dramatist whose support of the Nazi occupation of his homeland earned him the title of traitor and imprisonment in his old age; won the Nobel Prize for Literature (1920).

Hanley, James (1901–1985), Irish novelist, short-story writer and dramatist.

Hanotaux, (Albert-Auguste-) Gabriel (1853–1944), French politician, diplomat and historian.

Hansberry, Lorraine (1930–1965), American dramatist whose A Raisin in the Sun (1959) was the first play by a black woman produced on Broadway.

Hansen, Martin (Jens) Alfred (1909–1955), Danish novelist.

Hanslick, Eduard (1825–1904), famous Austrian music critic of Czech descent, known for his withering criticism and defense of conservative ideals.

Hansson, Ola (1860–1925), Swedish poet, writer and critic.

Han Yong-un (1879–1944), Korean Buddhist priest, political leader and poet who was also known as Manhae, author of the fine poetry collection Nimuich'immuk (The Silence of the Lover).

Han Yü (768–824), Chinese writer and poet who was also known as Han Wen-Kung and whose works presaged Neo-Confucianism.

Hapgood, Hutchins (1869–1944), American journalist and writer; brother of Norman Hapgood.

Hapgood, Norman (1868–1937), American editor and writer; brother of Hutchins Hapgood.

Harben, William Nathaniel (1858–1919), American novelist and short-story writer.

Har Dayal (1884–1939), Indian revolutionary leader and scholar.

Harden, Maximilian Felix Ernst (actually Felix Ernst Witkowski) (1861–1927), German political journalist of extreme nationalist, and then radical socialist, views.

Hardouin, Jean (1646–1729), French Jesuit scholar.

Hardy, Alexandre (c.1572–c.1632), French dramatist and actor.

Hardy, Arthur Sherburne (1847–1930), American novelist, short-story writer and poet.

Hardy, Thomas (1840–1928), English novelist, poet and dramatist, particularly admired for his series of 'Wessex' novels.

Hardyng, John (1378–c.1465), English writer who wrote the verse vol. The Chronicle of John Hardyng (1440–57).

Hare, Augustus William (1792–1834), English biographer and travel writer; brother of Julius Charles Hare.

Hare, Julius Charles (1795–1855), English writer and translator; brother of Augustus William Hare.

Hare, Richard M(ervyn) (1919–2002), English moral philosopher, author of The Language of Morals (1952), Freedom and Reason (1963), Essays on the Moral Concepts (1972), Moral Thinking (1981), Essays on Political Morality (1989), Essays on Religion and Education (1992) and Objective Prescriptions and Other Essays (1999).

Harington, Sir John (1561–1612), English courtier, writer, poet and translator who became well known for his wit.

Harīrī, al- (actually Abū Muhammad al-Qāsim ibn 'Alī al-Harīrī) (1054–1122), Arab scholar and government official who wrote the famous collection of tales the Magamat (English trans. as The Assemblies of al-Harīrī, 1867, 1898).

Harishchandra (1850–1885), important Indian poet, dramatist, journalist and critic who was also known as Bharatendu, often hailed as the father of modern Hindi.

Harizi, Judah ben Solomon (c.1170–c.1235), Spanish Hebrew poet and translator.

Harland, Henry (1861–1905), American novelist and short-story writer.

Harnack, Adolf (Karl Gustav) von (1851–1930), eminent German church historian and theologian.

Harper, Edith Alice Mary (1884–1947), English poet who wrote under the name Anna Wickham.

Harper, Francis Ellen Watkins (1825–1911), American poet and writer who championed the cause of her black compatriots.

Harper, William Rainey (1856–1906), American scholar and educator who wrote studies on Semitic languages and the Bible.

Harpocration, Valerius (2nd Century), Greek grammarian.

Harpur, Charles (1813–1868), Australian poet.

Harrington or Harington, James (1611–1677), English political philosopher, best known for The Commonwealth of Oceana (1656).

Harriot or Hariot, Thomas (1560–1621), English mathematician and astronomer, author of A Briefe and True Report of the New Found Land of Virginia (1588).

Harris, Alexander (1805–1874), English writer, best known for his Settlers and Convicts, or, Recollections of Sixteen Years' Labour in the Australian Backwoods (1847).

Harris, Benjamin (flourished 1673–1716), English bookseller and writer, author of The Protestant Tutor (1679; revised edition as The New England Primer, c.1690) and publisher of the first American newspaper (1690), which was suppressed by the Boston authorities after one edition.

Harris, Frank (actually James Thomas Harris) (1856–1931), Irish journalist and writer, best known for his candid autobiography My Life and Loves (3 vols, 1923–27).

Harris, George Washington (1814–1869), American writer who was known for his humorous tales.

Harris, Joel Chandler (1848–1908), American writer, creator of the famous Uncle Remus.

Harris, John (1820–1884), English poet whose works reflected his love of Cornish landscapes.

Harris, Maxwell Henley (1921–1995), Australian poet, editor and publisher.

Harris, Thomas Lake (1823–1906), English-born American poet of a mystical turn.

Harris, William Torrey (1835–1909), American educator, philosopher and lexicographer.

Harris, Zellig S(abbetai) (1909–92), Russian-born American structural linguist, author of Methods in Structural Linguistics (1951).

Harrison, Constance Cary (1843–1920), American novelist, short-story writer and essayist.

Harrison, Frederic (1831–1923), English writer.

Harrison, Henry Sydnor (1880–1930), American novelist, author of Queed (1911) and V. V.'s Eyes (1913).

Harrison, William (1534–1593), English historian, especially remembered for his Description of England (1577).

Harry or Henry the Minstrel (15th Century), Scottish poet, author of The Acts and Deeds of the Illustrious and Valiant Champion Sir William Wallace, Knight of Elderslie (1488), a historical romance in verse.

Harsdörfer, Georg Philipp (1607–1658), German poet and theorist.

Hart, Frances Noyes (1890–1943), American writer, best known for her detective novels.

Hart, Heinrich (1855–1906), German critic, poet, short-story writer and dramatist; brother of Julius Hart.

Hart, Joseph (1798–1855), American lawyer, journalist and writer.

Hart, Julius (1859–1930), German critic, poet, short-story writer and dramatist; brother of Heinrich Hart.

Hart, Moss (1904–1961), American dramatist who collaborated with George S Kaufman on the notably successful plays You Can't Take It With You (1936) and The Man Who Came To Dinner (1939).

Harte, (Francis) Bret(t) (1836–1902), American poet, editor and short-story writer.

Hartleben, Otto Erich (1864–1905), German dramatist, poet and short-story writer.

Hartley, David (1705–1757), English physician and philosopher, author of Observations on Man, His Frame, His Duty, and His Expectations (2 vols, 1749).

Hartley, L(eslie) P(oles) (1895–1972), English novelist, short-story writer and critic.

Hartlib, Samuel (c.1600–1662), German-born English educator, reformer and writer, particularly known for his utopian treatise Macaria (1641).

Hartmann, (Carl) Sadakichi (1869–1944), American art critic, writer, dramatist and poet of German-Japanese descent.

Hartmann, (Karl Robert) Eduard von (1842–1906), German philosopher, author of Die Philosophie des Unbewussten (3 vols, 1870; English trans. as The Philosophy of the Unconscious, 1884).

Hartmann, Nicolai (1882–1950), Latvian-born German philosopher who wrote Ethik (1926; English trans. as Ehtics, 3 vols, 1932), Die Philosophie des deutschen Idealismus (The Philosophy of German Idealism, 2 vols, 1923, 1929) and Neue Wege der Ontologie (1942; English trans. as New Ways of Ontology, 1953).

Hartmann von Aue (c.1170–1215), German poet, admired for his Der arme Heinrich.

Hartshorne, Charles (1897–2000), American process philosopher and theologian.

Hartzenbusch, Juan Eugenio (1806–1880), Spanish dramatist, poet and editor.

Harvey, Gabriel (c.1545–1630), learned English writer, poet and university don.

Harvey, Sir (Henry) Paul (1869–1948), English literary scholar and diplomat.

Harvey, William Hope (1851–1936), American writer who wrote under the name Coin Harvey as an advocate of bimetallism.

Harwood, Edward (1729–1794), English biblical scholar.

Hasan of Delhi (died 1328), Persian poet.

Haşdeu, Bogdan Petriceicu (1836–1907), Romanian language and historical scholar.

Hašek, Jaroslav (1883–1923), Czech writer and poet, best remembered for his famous unfinished novel series Osudy dobrého vojáka Švejka za světové války (4 vols, 1920–23; English trans. as The Good Soldier Schweik, 1930).

Hasenclever, Walter (1890–1940), German dramatist and poet who espoused Expressionism; a pacifist, he commited suicide while confined in a French internment camp.

Hashar, Agha (1876–1935), Parsi dramatist.

Haskins, Charles Homer (1870–1937), American medieval scholar, author of the important study Norman Institutions (1918).

Hassall, Christopher Vernon (1912–1963), English poet, dramatist, librettist and biographer.

Hassān ibn Thābit (c.563–c.674), Arab poet who was known for his defense of the Prophet Muhammad.

Hasselt, André-Henri-Constant van (1806–1874), notable Dutch-born Belgian poet, especially esteemed for his epic Les Quatre Incarnations du Christ (1863).

Hatano Seiichi (1877–1950), Japanese scholar who wrote on Christianity and Western philosophy.

Hauch, Johannes Carsten (1790–1872), Danish poet, dramatist and novelist.

Hauff, Wilhelm (1802–1827), German poet and writer of fairy stories.

Hauge, Alfred (1915–86), Norwegian novelist and poet.

Haughton, William (c.1575–1605), English dramatist.

Haupt, Moritz (1808–1874), German philologist.

Hauptmann, Gerhart (Johann Robert) (1862–1946), German dramatist and novelist; won the Nobel Prize for Literature (1912).

Haushofer, Karl (Ernst) (1869–1946), German army officer who espoused geopolitics in various writings; commited suicide.

Häusser, Ludwig (1818–1867), German journalist and historian.

Havighurst, Walter (Edwin) (1901–1994), American writer.

Havlíček, Karel (1821–1856), Czech journalist, writer and poet who excelled in satirical effusions.

Hawes, Stephen (c.1475–c.1525), English poet, author of The Passetyme of Pleasure (1509).

Hawker, R(obert) S(tephen) (1803–1875), English poet, remembered for his ballads.

Hawkes, John (Clendennin Burne Jr) (1925–1998), American novelist of the avant-garde.

Hawkesworth, John (c.1715–1773), English writer, dramatist and poet.

Hawkins, Sir John (1719–1789), notable English music scholar, author of A General History of the Science and Practice of Music (5 vols, 1776).

Hawkins or Hawkyns, Sir Richard (c.1560–1622), English seaman who wrote an account of his adventures in Observations in His Voyage into the South Sea (1622).

Hawthorne, Julian (1846–1934), American writer; son of Nathaniel Hawthorne.

Hawthorne, Nathaniel (1804–1864), renowned American novelist and short-story writer whose masterpiece was the novel The Scarlet Letter (1850); father of Julian Hawthorne.

Hay, Sir Gilbert (15th Century), Scottish priest, translator and poet who was also known as Sir Gilbert of the Haye.

Hay, John (Milton) (1838–1905), American diplomat, writer and poet who collaborated with John Nicolay on a major biography of Abraham Lincoln (10 vols, 1890).

Hayashi Fumiko (actually Miyata Fumiko) (1904–1951), Japanese novelist.

Hayashi Razan (actually Hayashi Nobukatsu) (1583–1657), important Japanese neo-Confucian scholar who became known for his historical writings and poems.

Hayashi Shihei (1738–1793), Japanese military scholar.

Hayden, Robert (1913–1980), American poet.

Haydon, Benjamin Robert (1786–1846), English painter and writer, author of an autobiography (published 1847).

Hayek, Friedrich (August) von (1899–1992), German economist; won the Nobel Prize for Economic Science (1974).

Hayes, Alfred (1911–1985), English-born American writer.

Hayford, Harrison (1916–2001), American literary scholar, an authority on Herman Melville and editor of his collected works (1965 et seq.).

Hayley, William (1754–1820), English poet, dramatist, essayist and biographer.

Hayne, Paul Hamilton (1830–1886), esteemed American poet, particularly admired for his collection Legends and Lyrics (1872).

Hayward, Abraham (1801–1884), English essayist and biographer.

Hayward, Sir John (c.1564–1627), English historian.

Haywood, Eliza (née Fowler) (c.1693–1756), English novelist who wrote a series of works of a scandalous nature.

Hazard, Paul Gustave Marie Camille (1878–1944), French literary historian.

Hazlitt, William (1778–1830), notable English essayist, celebrated for his Table Talk (1821) and The Plain Speaker (1826).

Head, Bessie (actually Bessie Amelia Emery) (1937–1986), South African-born Botswanan novelist and short-story writer.

Headlam, Arthur Cayley (1862–1947), English Anglican bishop and biblical scholar, author of the Doctrine of the Church and Christian Reunion (1920).

Hearn, (Patricio) Lafcadio (Tessima Carlos) (1850–1904), Irish-Greek writer, translator and teacher.

Hearne, Thomas (1678–1735), English historian and antiquarian.

Heath, James Ewell (1792–1862), American writer.

Heavysege, Charles (1816–1876), English-born Canadian poet and writer.

Hebbel, (Christian) Friedrich (1813–1863), noted German dramatist and poet whose masterpiece was the play Gyges und sein Ring (Gyges and His Ring, 1854).

Heber, Reginald (1773–1826), English churchman, poet, hymnist and translator.

Hébert, Anne (1916–2000), Canadian poet, novelist and dramatist.

Hébert, Jacques-René (1757–1794), prominent French political journalist and advocate of the sans-culottes during the Revolution; was guillotined.

Hebreo, León (actually Judah Abrabanel) (c.1460–c.1521), Spanish philosopher and physician, author of the Dialoghi di amore.

Hecataeus of Miltus (6th–5th Century BC), Greek writer.

Hecht, Ben (1894–1964), American novelist, dramatist and screenwriter.

Heckewelder, John Gottlieb Ernestus (1743–1823), English-born American Moravian missionary to the Indians who wrote two accounts of his activities (1819, 1820).

Hedāyat, Sādeq (1903–1951), Persian writer and scholar; commited suicide.

Hedberg, Olle (1899–1974), Swedish novelist.

Hedge, Frederic Henry (1805–1890), American Unitarian minister, writer and translator.

Hegel, Georg Wilhelm Friedrich (1770–1831), German philosopher, author of the Phänomenologie des Geistes (1807; English trans. as The Phenomenology of Mind, 1931), Wissenschaft der Logik (2 vols, 1812, 1816; English trans. as the Science of Logic, 1969), Encyklopädie der philosophischen Wissenschaften im Grundrisse (1817; partial English trans. as Encyclopaedia of the Philosophical Sciences in Outline, 1970) and Grundlinien der Philosophie des Rechts (1821; English trans. as The Philosophy of Right, 1942).

Hegesippus, Saint (2nd Century), Greek Christian historian who wrote The Memoirs (c.180).

Heggen, Thomas (Orlo) (1919–1949), American writer, best remembered for his novel Mister Roberts (1946).

Heiberg, Gunnar (1857–1929), eminent Norweigan dramatist who excelled as an Expressionist.

Heiberg, Johan Ludvig (1791–1860), major Danish dramatist, poet, historian and critic; son of Peter Andreas Heiberg.

Heiberg, Peter Andreas (1758–1841), Dansih political radical, poet and dramatist; father of Johan Ludvig Heiberg.

Heidegger, Johann Heinrich (1633–1698), Swiss Reformed theologian and educator whose Formula Consensus Helvetici (Swiss Formula of Concord, 1675) called for a reconciliation between Swiss Reformed and Lutheran adherents.

Heidegger, Martin (1889–1976), famous German philosopher who was a leading figure in the development of Existentialism, author of the influential Sein und Zeit (1927; English trans. as Being and Time, 1962).

Heidenstam, (Carl Gustaf) Verner von (1859–1940), prominent Swedish poet and writer; won the Nobel Prize for Literature (1916).

Heijermans, Herman (1864–1924), Dutch writer and dramatist.

Heiler, (Johann) Friedrich (1892–1967), German religious writer, author of Das Gebet (1918; abridged English trans. as Prayer, 1932), Der Katholizismus (1923), Urkirche und Ostkirche (1937; revised edition as Die Ostkirchen, 1971) and Erscheinungsformen und Wesen der Religion (1961).

Heine, Heinrich (1797–1856), famous German poet, essayist and champion of democratic ideals, especially renowned for his poetry collections Buch der Lieder (Book of Songs, 1827) and Neue Gedichte (New Poems, 1844).

Heinlein, Robert A(nson) (1907–1988), American writer, a master of science fiction.

Heinrich von Melk (12th Century), German poet, the first to write in a satirical vein in such works as Von des Tôdes gehugede (Remembrance of Death or Momento Mori, c.1150–60) and Vom Priesterleben (About Priestly Life).

Heinrich von Morungen (died 1222), German Minnesinger who espoused the cause of love in his poetry.

Heinse, Johann Jakob Wilhelm (1746–1803), German novelist and art critic, especially esteemed for his novels Ardinghello und die glückseligen Inseln (Ardinghell and the Blessed Islands, 1787) and Hildegard von Hohenthal (1795–96).

Heinsius or Heins, Daniël (1580–1655), Dutch scholar and poet.

Heinsius, Nicolaus (1602–1681), Dutch Latinist and philologist.

Heisenberg, Werner (Karl) (1901–1976), eminent German physicist and philosopher who discovered the uncertainty principle in quantum mechanics; won the Nobel Prize for Physics (1932).

Heissenbüttel, Helmut (1921–1996), German novelist and poet of avant-garde persuasion.

Hektorović, Petar (1487–1572), Dalmatian poet.

Helgesen, Paul (c.1485–c.1535), Danish Carmelite monk, humanist and Roman Catholic apologist.

Heliodorus (3rd Century), Greek novelist who wrote the Aethiopica.

Hellanicus (5th Century BC), Greek historian.

Hellens, Franz (actually Frédéric van Ermengem) (1881–1972), Belgian novelist and poet.

Heller, Hermann (1891–1933), German political scientist whose works delineated the central role of the state in society but who nevertheless opposed Nazism.

Heller, Joseph (1923–99), American writer, best known for his novel Catch-22 (1961).

Heller, Yom Tov Lipmann ben Nathan ha-Levi ben Wallerstein (1579–1654), German Jewish scholar.

Hellman, Lillian (Florence) (1905–1984), American dramatist whose output reflected her deep attachments as an unreconstructed leftist.

Hellström, (Erik) Gustaf (1882–1953), Swedish journalist, novelist and critic.

Helmold of Bosau (c.1120–c.1178), German Roman Catholic priest and historian.

Helper, Hinton Rowan (1829–1909), American writer who, although a Southerner, attacked slavery in his The Impending Crisis of the South: How to Meet It (1857) but later wrote racist tracts advocating the deportation of blacks.

Helvétius, Claude-Adrien (1715–1771), prominent French philosopher who was a proponent of hedonism in his controversial De l'esprit (On the Mind, 1758).

Hélyot, Hippolyte (actually Pierre Hélyot) (1660–1716), French Franciscan monk and historian who wrote the important Histoire des ordres monastiques, religieux et militaires, et des congrégations séculières de l'un et de l'autre sexe (8 vols, 1714–19; completed by Père Maximilien Bullot).

Hemacandra (1088–1172), celebrated Indian writer and Jain sage who was also known as Hemacandra Sūri, Candradeva, Cangadeva and Somacandra.

Hemans, Felicia Dorothea (née Browne) (1793–1835), English poet, particularly known for her Casabianca.

Hemingway, Ernest (Miller) (1899–1961), celebrated American novelist, short-story writer and poet, admired for such novels as The Sun Also Rises (1926), A Farewell to Arms (1929), For Whom the Bell Tolls (1940) and The Old man and the Sea (1952); won the Nobel Prize for Literature (1954); commited suicide.

Hémon, Louis (1880–1913), French writer, author of the novel Maria Chapdelaine (published 1915); died in a train accident.

Hemsterhuis, Franciscus (1721–1790), Dutch philosopher and aesthetician.

Henderick, Burton J(esse) (1870–1949), American journalist and historian.

Henderson, Alexander (c.1583–1646), Scottish Presbyterian clergyman and writer, a champion of the presbyterian form of church government and an opponent of Charles I.

Henderson, Alice Corbin (1881–1949), American poet.

Hengstenberg, Ernst Wilhelm (1802–1869), German Lutheran theologian, known as a defender of Christian orthodoxy.

Henley, William Ernest (1849–1903), prominent English critic, editor, poet and dramatist.

Henne am Rhyn, Otto (1828–1914), Swiss journalist and historian, author of the massive Allgemeine Kulturgeschichte (Universal History of Civilization, 8 vols, 1877–1908).

Henri, Adrian (Maurice) (1932–2000), English poet, writer, dramatist and painter.

Henry, O. (actually William Sidney Porter) (1862–1910), American short-story writer.

Henry of Ghent (c.1217–1293), celebrated Belgian philosopher and theologian who was known as Doctor Solemnis and as one of the major opponents of St Thomas Aquinas.

Henry of Huntingdon (c.1084–1155), English archdeacon who compiled the Historia Anglorum.

Henryson, Robert (c.1425–c.1508), Scottish poet, particularly known for The Testament of Cresseid.

Henson, Herbert Hensley (1863–1947), English Anglican bishop and writer who was known for his liberal views.

Henty, George Alfred (1832–1902), English writer.

Hentz, Caroline Lee (1800–1856), American novelist and short-story writer; wife of Nicolas Marcellus Hentz.

Hentz, Nicolas Marcellus (1797–1856), French-born American novelist; husband of Caroline Lee Hentz.

Heracleitus (c.540–c.480 BC), Greek philosopher.

Herbart, Johann Friedrich (1776–1841), German philosopher and educator.

Herbert, Sir A(lan) P(atrick) (1890–1971), English politician, novelist, dramatist and poet.

Herbert, George (1593–1633), admired English poet and churchman, one of the finest metaphysical poets of devotion; brother of Edward Herbert, 1st Baron Herbert of Cherbury.

Herbert, Henry William (1807–1858), English-born American writer.

Herbert (Brundage), John (1926–2001), Canadian dramatist who was best known for his play Fortune and Men's Eyes (1967).

Herbert, Zbigniew (1924–1998), Polish poet and essayist.

Herbert of Cherbury, Edward Herbert, 1st Baron (1582–1648), noted English courtier, soldier, diplomat, philosopher, historian and poet, called the father of English Deism; brother of George Herbert.

Herbst, Josephine (Frey) (1892–1969), American writer.

Herculano de Carvalho e Araújo, Alexandre (1810–1877), eminent Portuguese historian, author of the História de Portugal (History of Portugal, four vols, 1846–53).

Herczeg, Ferenc (1863–1954), Hungarian novelist and dramatist.

Herder, Johann Gottfried von (1744–1803), influential German critic, theologian, philosopher and poet.

Heredia, José María (1803–1839), Cuban poet; cousin of José María de Heredia.

Heredia, José María de (1842–1905), Cuban-born French poet, especially esteemed for his sonnets; cousin of José María Heredia.

Herford, Oliver (1863–1935), English-born American writer, poet, dramatist and illustrator.

Hergenröther, Joseph (1824–1890), German theologian and church historian.

Hergesheimer, Joseph (1880–1954), American novelist, short-story writer and biographer, particularly remembered for his novels The Three Black Pennys (1917), Java Head (1919) and Balisand (1924).

Herlihy, James Leo (1927–1993), American novelist and dramatist.

Herling, Gustaw (1919–2000), Polish writer who was best known for his searing memoir, A World Apart (1951), in which he related his imprisonment in a Soviet labour camp.

Herman de Valenciennes (12th Century), French priest, writer and poet.

Hermann, Eduard (1869–1950), German linguist.

Hermann, (Johann) Gottfried (Jakob) (1772–1848), German classical scholar.

Hermann von Reichenau (1013–1054), Swabian chronicler, poet, composer, astronomer and mathematician who was also known as Hermmanus Contractus and Hermann the Lame.

Hermes, Georg (1775–1831), German Roman Catholic theologian who was a proponent of rational necessity as a basis of Christian faith.

Hermesianax (c.300–c.250 BC), Greek poet, admired for his elegies.

Hernández, José (1834–1886), Argentine poet, a master of gaucho poetry.

Hernández, Miguel (1910–42), Spanish poet and dramatist; a member of the Communist Party and a combatant in the Spanish Civil War, he died in a Nationalist prison.

Herndon, William Henry (1818–1891), American lawyer, best remembered for his partnership in law with Abraham Lincoln, author with Jesse W Weik of Herndon's Lincoln: The True Story of a Great Life (3 vols, 1889).

Herne, James A (actually James Ahern) (1839–1901), American dramatist, best known for his play Shore Acres (1892).

Herodas or Herondas (3rd Century BC), Greek poet who wrote mimes, a short verse form depicting the life of the lowly.

Herodes Atticus (actually Lucius Vibullius Hipparchus Tiberius Claudius Atticus Herodes) (c.101–177), famous Greek orator and writer.

Herodian (3rd Century), Syrian historian who wrote on the Roman Empire.

Herodianus, Aelius (2nd Century), Greek grammarian and writer who was also known as Herodianus Technicus.

Herodotus (c.484–c.425 BC), illustrious Greek historian, known as the father of history.

Héroët, Antoine (c.1492–1568), Fernch poet and Roman Catholic bishop.

Herrera, Fernando de (c.1534–1597), notable Spanish poet, historian and translator who earned the name El Divino.

Herrera y Reissig, Julio (1875–1910), Uruguayan poet.

Herrera y Tordesillas, Antonio de (1559–1625), Spanish historian.

Herrick, Robert (1591–1674), admired English poet and cleric, a master of lyric expression.

Herrick, Robert (1868–1938), American novelist and short-story writer.

Herriot, Édouard (1872–1957), prominent French politician and writer.

Herrmann, (Johann) Wilhelm (1846–1922), German protestant theologian, author of Der Verkehr des Christen mit Gott (1886; English trans. as The Communion of the Christian With God, 1895) and Ethik (1901).

Hersey, John (Richard) (1914–1993), American novelist, short-story writer and essayist.

Herskovits, Melville J(ean) (1895–1963), American anthropologist.

Hertling, Georg (Friedrich), Graf von (1843–1919), German philosopher and statesman.

Hertz, Henrik (actually Heyman Hertz) (1797–1870), Danish poet and dramatist.

Hertz, Joseph Herman (1872–1946), Hungarian-born English rabbi, Zionist and writer, author of A Book of Jewish Thoughts (1920).

Hervey, James (1714–1758), English clergyman and poet.

Hervey of Ickworth, John Hervey, Baron (1696–1743), English politician who wrote the valuable Memoirs of the Reign of George the Second (published 1848).

Hervieu, Paul-Ernest (1857–1915), French novelist, short-story writer and dramatist.

Herwegh, Georg (1817–1875), German poet who played an active role in the revolutionary events of 1848.

Herzen, Alexander (Ivanovich) (1812–1870), influential Russian journalist and political thinker who espoused socialism as the path to freedom in his homeland.

Herzog, Isaac Halevi (1888–1959), Polish-born Israeli rabbi and scholar.

Herzog, Johann Jakob (1805–1882), German Protestant theologian, editor of the Realencyklopädie für protestantische Theologie und Kirche (22 vols, 1854–68).

Heschel, Abraham Joshua (1907–1972), German-born American Jewish theologian and philosopher.

Hesiod (8th Century BC), Greek poet, known for his didactic Theogony and Works and Days.

Hess, Moses (actually Moritz Hess) (1812–1875), German journalist, socialist and Zionist who influenced the thought of Marx and Engels.

Hesse, Hermann (1877–1962), eminent German-born Swiss novelist and poet who became widely known for such novels as Demian (1919), Der Steppenwolf (1927), Narziss und Goldmund (1930; English trans. as Death and the Lover, 1932), Die Morgenlandfahrt (1932; English trans. as Journey to the East, 1956) and Das Glasperlenspiel (1943; English trans. as Magister Ludi, 1949); won the Nobel Prize for Literature (1946).

Hesychius of Alexandria (5th Century), Greek lexicographer.

Hesychius of Jerusalem, Saint (died c.450), Eastern Orthodox theologian and biblical commentator.

Hesychius of Miletus (6th Century), Byzantine historian and biographer.

Hetherington, (Hector) Alastair (1919–99), English journalist and writer.

Hewat, Alexander (c.1745–1829), Scottish-born American Presbyterian clergyman who wrote An Historical Account of the Rise and Progress of the Colonies of South Carolina and Georgia (2 vols, 1779).

Hewlett, Maurice Henry (1861–1923), English poet, novelist and essayist, author of the poem The Song of the Plow (1916).

Heyer, Georgette (1902–1974), English novelist and detective-story writer.

Heyerdahl, Thor (1914–2002), Norwegian ethnologist and explorer whose Kon-Tiki (1947) and Ra (1969–70) expeditions were attempts to prove the possibility of transoceanic contacts between ancient civilizations, and which were related to his books Kon-Tiki (1950) and The Ra Expeditions (1971).

Heylyn, Peter (1600–1662), English Anglican polemicist and historian.

Heym, Georg (1887–1912), German poet of the Expressionist school.

Heym, Stefan (real name Helmut Flieg) (1913–2001), German writer whose works included Hostages (1942), The Crusaders (1948), The Day Marked X (1953; definitive version as Fünf Tage in Juni, 1974), Der König David Bericht (1972), The Queen Against Defoe (1974), Ahasver (1981) and Radek (1995).

Heyne, Christian Gottlob (1729–1812), German philologist.

Heyse, Paul Johann Ludwig von (1830–1914), notable German novelist and short-story writer; won the Nobel Prize for Literature (1910).

Heyward, (Edwin) Dubose (1885–1940), American novelist, dramatist and poet who collaborated with his wife Dorothy Heyward (1890–1961) on the novel Porgy (1925), later made famous as Gershwin's opera Porgy and Bess (1935).

Heywood, Jasper (1535–1598), English Jesuit priest, poet and translator.

Heywood, John (c.1497–1580), English dramatist and poet, especially known for his satirical verse allegory The Spider and the Flie (1556).

Heywood, Thomas (c.1574–1641), English actor and dramatist.

Hiärne, Urban (1641–1724), Swedish dramatist and poet.

Hibbert, Eleanor Alice (c.1906–1993), prolific English romance novelist who wrote under various pseudonyms, including Victoria Holt and Jean Plaidy.

Hichens, Robert Smythe (1864–1950), English novelist, especially remembered for his satirical The Green Carnation (1894).

Hickes, George (1642–1715), noted English scholar and non-juring divine, an authority on Anglo-Saxon subjects.

Hicks, Elias (1748–1830), American Quaker preacher and Abolitionist, author of Observations on the Slavery of the Africans and Their Descendants (1811).

Hicks, Granville (1901–1982), American novelist and critic.

Hierocles (6th Century), Byzantine grammarian, author of the valuable Synekdemos.

Hierocles of Alexandria (5th Century), Greek philosopher.

Higden or Higdon, Ranulf (c.1280–1364), English monk and writer, best known for his Polychronicon (c.1350).

Higgins, Alexander Pearce (1865–1935), English lawyer and writer, especially remembered for his works on international and maritime law and history.

Higgins, Frederick Robert (1896–1941), Irish poet.

Higgins, George V(incent) (1939–99), American writer of crime novels.

Higgins, Matthew James (1810–1868), English journalist and essayist who was known as Jacob Omnium.

Higginson, Francis (1586–1630), English-born American nonconformist clergyman, author of the journal New-Englands Plantation (1630; first complete edition, 1891).

Highsmith, Patricia (1921–1995), American mystery novelist and short-story writer.

Highwater, Jamake (c.1941–2001), American writer, poet and lecturer.

Higuchi Ichiyō (actually Higuchi Natsuko) (1872–1896), talented Japanese novelist and poet whose finest work was his novel Takekurabe (1895; English trans. as Growing Up, 1956).

Hikmet, Nazim (1902–1963), significant Turkish poet of a Marxist persuasion, also known as Nazim Hikmet Ran.

Hilarius (12th Century), French poet and scholar who wrote in Latin and French.

Hildegard von Bingen (1098–1179), famous German abbess, mystic, composer and poet.

Hildreth, Richard (1807–1865), American jurist, writer and historian, particularly known for his novel The Slave, or, Memoirs of Archy Moore (1836) and his History of the United States (6 vols, 1849–52).

Hill, Aaron (1685–1750), English poet, dramatist and essayist.

Hill G(eorge) B(irkbeck Norman) (1835–1903), English biographer and editor.

Hill, John (c.1716–1775), English writer and botanist.

Hill, Rowland (1744–1833), English evangelist and writer.

Hillebrand, Karl (1829–1884), German historian and essayist.

Hillel (flourished 1st Century BC–1st Century AD), celebrated Jewish sage and Talmudic scholar.

Hillel ben Samuel (c.1220–c.1295), Jewish physician, Talmudic scholar and philosopher.

Hillhouse, James Abraham (1789–1841), American poet, author of romantic verse dramas.

Hillī, al- (actually Jamāl ad-Dīn Hasan ibn Yūsuf ibn 'Alī ibn Muthahhar al-Hillī) (1250–1325), Arab theologian who was known for his valuable writings on Shi'ite doctrines.

Hillyer, Robert (Silliman) (1895–1961), American poet, novelist and critic.

Hilton, James (1900–1954), English novelist, author of the highly successful Lost Horizon (1933), Goodbye Mr Chips (1934) and Random Harvest (1941).

Hilton, Walter (c.1340–1396), famous English mystic, author of The Scale of Perfection and the Mixed Life.

Himerius (c.315–c.386), Greek rhetorician.

Himes, Chester (Bomar) (1909–1984), American novelist and short-story writer.

Hincmar of Reims (c.806–882), noted French Roman Catholic archbishop, canon lawyer and theologian.

Hindus, Maurice (Gerschon) (1891–1969), Russian-born American writer.

Hinman, Charlton (1911–1977), English scholar, an authority on Shakespeare's texts.

Hippel, Theodor Gottlieb von (1741–1796), German writer.

Hippias of Elis (5th Century BC), Greek philosopher who wrote on various subjects, discoverer of the quadratrix in mathematics.

Hippocrates (c.460–c.377 BC), celebrated Greek physician, revered as the father of medicine.

Hippolytus of Rome, Saint (c.170–c.235), Roman Catholic theologian, first antipope and martyr, author of Philosophumena (Refutation of All Heresies).

Hipponax (6th Century BC), Greek poet.

Hiraga Gennai (c.1728–1779), Japanese philosopher.

Hirsch, Samson Raphael (1808–1888), important German Jewish theologian, founder of Trennungsorthodoxie (Separatist Orthodoxy) or Neo-Orthodoxy.

Hirsch, Samuel (1815–1889), German-born American Jewish rabbi and philosopher, a proponent of radical Reform Judaism.

Hirst, Henry Beck (1817–1874), American poet of an eccentric nature.

Hirt, Hermann (1865–1936), German linguist, author of Indogermanische Grammatik (Indo-European Grammar, 7 vols, 1921–37).

Hirtius, Aulus (c.90–43 BC), Roman soldier and writer; died in battle.

Hishām ibn (Muhammad) al-Kalbī (c.746–c.820), Arab scholar and poet.

Hitchcock, Enos (1744–1803), American clergyman and writer, author of the novel Memoirs of the Bloomsgrove Family (1790).

Hjärne, Harald Gabriel (1848–1922), Swedish historian and politician.

Hjartarson, Snorri (1906–1986), Icelandic poet.

Hobart, John Henry (1775–1830), American Episcopal bishop and writer, a defender of orthodox religious and social views.

Hobbes, John Oliver (actually Mrs Pearl 'Mary Teresa' Craigie) (1867–1906), English novelist and essayist.

Hobbes, Thomas (1588–1679), English philosopher, author of such major works as the trilogy De Cive (Concerning Citizenship, 1642), De Corpore (Concerning Body, 1655) and De Homine (Concerning Man, 1658), and Human Nature, or, The Fundamental Elements of Policie (1650), De Corpore Politico, or, The Elements of Law, Moral and Politick (1650), Leviathan, or, The Matter, Forme, and Power of a Commonwealth, Ecclesiasticall and Civil (1651) and The Questions Concerning Liberty, Necessity, and Chance (1656).

Hobhouse, Leonard Trelawny (1864–1929), English sociologist and philosopher.

Hobson, John Atkinson (1858–1940), English economist and writer.

Hobson, Laura Zametkin (1900–1986), American novelist, best known for her Gentleman's Agreement (1947).

Hoby, Sir Thomas (1530–1566), English diplomat and translator, particularly remembered for his influential translation of Castiglione's Il cortegiano as The Courtyer of Count Baldesser Castillo (1561).

Hoccleve or Occleve, Thomas (c.1368–c.1450), English poet.

Hocking, William Ernest (1873–1966), American philosopher of the Idealist school.

Hodge, Charles (1797–1878), prominent American biblical scholar, author of Systematic Theology (3 vols, 1871–73).

Hodgson, Ralph (Edwin) (1871–1962), English poet, best known for his The Bull (1913).

Hodgson, Shadworth Holloway (1832–1912), English philosopher.

Hoel, Sigurd (1890–1960), Norwegian novelist, best remembered for his Veien til verdens ende (Road to the World's End, 1933).

Hoen, Cornelius (16th Century), Dutch theologian.

Hoffer, Eric (1902–1983), American longshoreman and philosopher, author of such books as The True Believer (1951), The Ordeal of Change (1963), Reflections on the Human Condition (1972) and Before the Sabbath (1979).

Hoffman, Charles Fenno (1806–1884), American editor, writer and poet whose career was aborted by insanity in 1849.

Hoffmann, August Heinrich (1798–1874), German poet, historian and philologist who wrote under the name Hoffmann von Fallersleben; his Deutschland, Deutschland über Alles (1841) was made the National Anthem of Germany (1922).

Hoffmann, E(rnst) T(heodor) A(madeus) (actually Ernst Theodor Wilhelm Hoffman) (1776–1822), German writer, composer, music critic and caricaturist, especially known for his collections of tales of the supernatural and fantastic in Die Serapionsbrüder (4 vols, 1819–21) and Die Lebensanischten des Katers Murr (2 vols, 1820, 1822).

Hoffmann, Heinrich (1809–1874), German physician and writer, known for his chldren's classic Struwwelpeter (Shock-head Peter, 1847).

Hofmannsthal, Hugo von (1874–1929), Austrian poet, dramatist and essayist who wrote the librettos for several operas by Richard Strauss.

Hoffmannswaldau, Christian Hofmann von (1617–1679), German poet and writer, remembered for his collection Heldenbriefe (Heroes' Letters, 1663).

Hofmeister, Sebastian (1476–1533), Swiss religious reformer.

Hofstadter, Richard (1916–70), American historian, author of The Age of Reform (1955) and Anti-Intellectualism in American Life (1963).

Hogarth, David George (1862–1927), English archaeologist and diplomat.

Hogg, James (1770–1835), Scottish poet and writer who was known as the Ettrick Shepherd after his birthplace, author of the poetry collection The Queen's Wake (1813).

Hogg, Thomas Jefferson (1792–1862), English writer, especially known for his The Life of Shelley (2 vols, 1858), the biography of his friend Percy Bysshe Shelley.

Holbach, Paul Henri Dietrich, Baron d' (actually Paul Henri Dietrich) (1723–1789), French philosopher and encyclopedist whose Système de la nature (System of Nature, 1770) vigorously championed atheism and materialism.

Holberg, Ludwig, Baron (1684–1754), Norwegian scholar and writer, duly regarded as the founder of both Norwegian and Danish letters.

Holbrook, Josiah (1788–1854), American educational reformer.

Holbrook, Stewart H(all) (1893–1964), American journalist and historian.

Holcot, Robert (died 1349), English Dominican and writer, author of Moralitates Historiarum.

Holcroft, Thomas (1745–1809), English actor, dramatist, journalist and novelist, especially remembered for his Memoirs (published 1816).

Holder, Alfred Theophil (1840–1916), Austrian language scholar.

Hölderlin, (Johann Christian) Friedrich (1770–1843), German poet, a master of the ode and elegy.

Holdheim, Samuel (1806–1860), German rabbi and theologian, author of the influential vol. of Reform Judaism Über die Autonomie der Rabbinen (The Autonomy of the Rabbis).

Holinshed, Raphael (died c.1580), English chronicler and translator, author of the Chronicles of England, Scotlande and Irelande (2 vols, 1577).

Holland, Edwin Clifford (c.1794–1824), American poet, best remembered for his Odes, Naval Songs, and Other Occasional Poems (1813).

Holland, Henry Scott (1847–1918), English Anglican theologian and philosopher.

Holland, Josiah Gilbert (1819–1881), American editor, writer and poet who wrote under the name Timothy Titcomb.

Holland, Philemon (1552–1637), English translator of Greek and Latin classics.

Holland, Sir (Thomas) Erskine (1835–1926), English legal scholar who wrote the valuable Elements of Jurisprudence (1880).

Holland, Vyvyan Oscar Beresford (actually Vyvyan Oscar Beresford Wilde) (1886–1967), English writer and translator; son of Oscar (Fingal O'Flahertie Wills) Wilde.

Holley, Marietta (1836–1926), American humorist who wrote under the name Josiah Allen's Wife.

Hollister, Gideon Hiram (1817–1881), American lawyer and writer.

Holme, Constance (1881–1955), English novelist.

Holmes, Abiel (1763–1837), American Congregationalist minister and writer, author of The Annals of America; father of Oliver Wendell Holmes.

Holmes, John (Clellon) (1926–1988), American poet, novelist and essayist.

Holmes, May Jane (Hawes) (1825–1907), American novelist, best known for her Lena Rivers (1856).

Holmes, Oliver Wendell (1809–1894), prominent American poet, writer and physician, particularly admired for his collection of poems and essays The Autocrat of the Breakfast Table (1858); son of Abiel Holmes and father of Oliver Wendell Holmes Jr.

Holmes, Oliver Wendell Jr (1841–1935), American jurist, legal historian and philosopher; son of Oliver Wendell Holmes.

Holmes, William Henry (1846–1933), American archaeologist and artist.

Holste, Luc (1596–1661), German classical scholar.

Holt, Edwin B(issell) (1873–1946), American psychologist and philosopher, author of The Concept of Consciousness (1914), The Freudian Wish and Its Place in Ethics (1915) and Animal Drive and the Learning Process (1931).

Holtby, Winifred (1898–1935), English journalist and novelist, especially admired for her novel South Riding (published 1936).

Holtei, Karl von (1798–1880), German actor, poet and novelist.

Hölty, Ludwig Heinrich Christoph (1748–1776), talented German poet who excelled in lyric expression.

Holtzmann, Heinrich Julius (1832–1910), German Protestant theologian.

Holub, Emil (1847–1902), Austro-Hungarian naturalist and traveller.

Holub, Miroslav (1923–1998), Czech poet, writer and immunologist.

Holz, Arnold (1863–1929), German poet, dramatist and critic.

Home, Henry, Lord Kames (1696–1782), Scottish jurist, landowner and writer, author of Elements of Criticism (1762) and Sketches of the History of Man (1774).

Home, John (1722–1808), Scottish dramatist, best remembered for his play Douglas (1756).

Homer (8th Century BC), legendary Greek poet, reputedly the author of the epics the Iliad and the Odyssey.

Honda Toshiaki (1744–1821), Japanese scholar who devoted himself to the study of Western culture.

Hone, William (1780–1842), English writer and bookseller, well known for his satirical bent.

Hontheim, Johann Nikolaus von (1701–1790), German historian and theologian who, under the name Justinus Febronius, wrote the controversial De Statu Ecclesia et Legitima Potestate Romani Pontificis (Concerning the State of the Church and the Legitimate Power of the Roman Pope, 1763).

Hood, Thomas (1799–1845), admired English poet and editor, a master of humorous verse; father of Tom Hood.

Hood, Tom (actually Thomas Hood) (1835–1874), English novelist, poet and artist; son of Thomas Hood.

Hooft, Pieter Corneliszoon (1581–1647), renowned Dutch poet, dramatist and writer, author of the monumental Nederlandse historien (20 vols, 1642).

Hook, Sidney (1902–1989), American philosopher and educator, best remembered for his fervent advocacy of democratic socialism as an alternative to totalitarianism.

Hook, Theodore Edward (1788–1841), English poet, dramatist and novelist.

Hooker, Richard (c.1554–1600), English Anglican theologian, author of the famous treatise Of the Laws of Ecclesiastical Polity (Vols 1–5, 1593–97, Vols 6 and 8, 1648, Vol. 7, 1662).

Hooper, Johnson Jones (1815–1862), American writer, newspaper editor and lawyer, creator of the backwoods frontiersman Captain Simon Suggs.

Hooton, Earnest A(lbert) (1887–1954), American anthropologist.

Hope, A(lec) D(erwent) (1907–2000), Australian poet, essayist and critic.

Hope, Anthony (actually Sir Anthony Hope Hawkins) (1863–1933), English writer, author of the novel The Prisoner of Zenda (1894).

Hope, Laurence (actually Adela Florence née Cory Nicolson) (1865–1904), English poet.

Hope, Thomas (1769–1831), English designer and writer, a champion of the Regency style.

Hopkins, Gerard Manley (1844–1889), English poet and Jesuit priest who employed what he described as 'sprung thythm' in his most notable creative efforts, among them The Wreck of the Deutschland (1876), Pied Beauty (1877) and The Windhover (1877).

Hopkins, Lemuel (1750–1801), American physician and poet.

Hopkins, Mark (1802–1887), American educator and philosopher.

Hopkins, Pauline (1859–1930), American writer, best remembered for her Contending Forces: A Romance Illustrative of Negro Life North and South (1900).

Hopkins, Samuel (1721–1803), American Congregationalist minister and theologian, author of The System of Doctrines Contained in Divine Revelation (1793).

Hopkinson, Francis (1737–1791), American statesman, writer, poet and composer; great-grandfather of Francis Hopkinson Smith.

Hopwood, Avery (1882–1929), American dramatist.

Horace (actually Quintus Horatius Flaccus) (65–8 BC), Roman poet whose satires, odes and epodes stand as monuments of world literature.

Horapollon (5th Century), Greek-Egyptian writer, author of Hieroglyphica.

Hornbostel, Erich Moritz von (1877–1935), notable Austrian music scholar, an authority on non-European music.

Horgan, Paul (1903–1995), American writer.

Horman, William (c.1458–1535), English educator, author of Vulgaria.

Horne, Richard Henry (1802–1884), English poet who wrote the allegorical epic Orion (1843).

Horney, Karen (nèe Danielsen) (1885–1952), German-born American psychoanalyst, author of New Ways in Psychoanalysis (1939), Our Inner Conflicts (1945) and Neurosis and Human Growth (1950).

Hornung, E(rnest) W(illiam) (1866–1921), English novelist.

Horovitz, Frances (née Hooker) (1938–1983), English actress, broadcaster and poet.

Horowitz, Isaiah ben Abraham ha-Levi (c.1565–1630), Jewish rabbi, mystic and philosopher.

Horsley, John (c.1685–1732), English antiquarian, author of Britannia Romana: Or the Roman Antiquities of Britain.

Horsley, Samuel (1733–1806), Welsh Anglican bishop, theologian and scientist who was a defender of orthodox views.

Hort, Fenton J(ohn) A(nthony) (1828–1892), English New Testament scholar.

Hortensius, Quintus (114–50 BC), Roman orator, writer and poet, author of the epic on the Social War Annales.

Horton, George Moses (c.1798–c.1880), American poet who was born a slave but revealed a talent for writing love poems.

Horváth, Ödön Edmund Josef von (1901–38), Hungarian novelist and dramatist.

Hosius, Stanislaus (actually Stanisław Hozjusz) (1504–1579), Polish Roman Catholic cardinal and theologian, author of the famous Confessio catholicae fidei Christiana (Christian Confession of Catholic Faith).

Hoskyns, Sir Edwyn Clement (1884–1937), English Anglican biblical scholar and theologian, especially noted for his Fourth Gospel (2 vols, published 1940).

Hosmer, William H(owe) C(uyler) (1814–1877), American lawyer and poet.

Hotman, François (1524–1590), French jurist and humanist scholar who was also known as Sieur de Villiers Saint-Paul.

Hotson, Leslie (1897–1992), Canadian literary scholar.

Hough, Emerson (1857–1923), American journalist and writer.

Hough, Richard (Alexander) (1922–99), English writer.

Houghton, Richard Monckton Milnes, 1st Baron (1809–1885), English poet, writer and politician.

Houghton, (William) Stanley (1881–1913), English dramatist.

Household, Geoffrey (Edward West) (1900–1988), English novelist, especially known for his Rogue Male (1939) and Rogue Justice (1982).

Housman, A(lfred) E(dward) (1859–1936), English poet and scholar, admired for his poetry collections A Shropshire Lad (1896) and Last Poems (1922); brother of Laurence Housman.

Housman, Laurence (1865–1959), English artist, dramatist, poet and writer, particularly known for his play Victoria Regina (1934); brother of A(lfred) E(dward) Housman.

Hout, Jan van (1542–1609), Dutch humanist theorist, historian, poet and translator.

Hovedon or Howden, Roger of (died c.1201), English chronicler.

Hovey, Richard (1864–1900), American poet, dramatist and translator.

Howard, Blanche Willis (1847–1898), American novelist, author of Guenn: A Wave on the Breton Coast (1883).

Howard, Bronson (Crocker) (1842–1908), American dramatist, best known for his Saratoga (1870).

Howard, Sir Robert (1626–1698), English dramatist and poet.

Howard, Sidney (Coe) (1891–1939), American dramatist, author of They Knew What They Wanted (1924), The Silver Cord (1926) and Yellow Jack (in collaboration with Paul de Kruif, 1934).

Howe, E(dgar) W(atson) (1853–1937), American journalist, novelist and essayist best known for his novel The Story of a Country Town (1883).

Howe, Irving (1920–1993), American literary and social critic.

Howe, John (1630–1705), English Puritan minister and writer.

Howe, Julia Ward (1819–1910), American poet, writer, dramatist and social reformer, celebrated author of the patriotic poem The Battle Hymn of the Republic (1862); sister of Samuel Ward and mother of Maud Howe Elliott.

Howe, M(ark) A(ntony) De Wolfe (1864–1960), American poet, writer and editor.

Howell, James (c.1594–1666), Welsh writer, author of the Epistolae Ho-Elianae (4 vols, 1645–55).

Howell, Thomas (16th Century), English poet.

Howells, William Dean (1837–1920), eminent American novelist, short-story writer, essayist, poet and editor.

Howes, Barbara (1914–1994), American poet and writer.

Hoyle, Sir Fred (1915–2001), English astrophysicist and writer who wrote authoritative works on science and engaging science fiction novels.

Hoyt, Charles Hale (1860–1900), American dramatist of popular farces.

Hrabal, Bohumil (1914–1997), Czech writer.

Hrdlička, Aleš (1869–1943), Czech-born American anthropologist.

Hrosvitha or Roswitha (c.935–1000), German nun and poet.

Hrozný, Bedřich (1879–1952), Bohemian archaeologist and language scholar.

Hsi K'ang (223–262), Chinese Taoist philosopher, alchemist and poet whose scandalous thought and conduct resulted in his execution by order of the Emperor.

Hsin Ch'i-chi (1140–1207), Chinese soldier and poet.

Hsiung Fo-hsi or Hsiung Fu-His (1900–1965), Chinese dramatist, one of the principal creators of drama for the peasantry.

Hsiung Shih-li (1885–1968), Chinese philosopher who developed a philosophical system which embraced Buddhist, Confucian and Western elements.

Hsü Chih-mo (1896–1931), Chinese poet and essayist who wrote under the names Nan-Hu and Shih-Che; died in an airplane crash.

Huang Tsung-hsi (1610–1695), notable Chinese scholar, author of the Ming-i tai-fang lu (A Plan for the Prince, 1662) and Ming-ju-hsüeh-an (Survey of Ming Confucianists, 1676).

Huang Tsun-hsien (1848–1905), Chinese poet, writer and government official.

Hubbard, Elbert (Green) (1856–1915), American editor, publisher and writer; died in the sinking of the 'Lusitania'.

Hubbard, Frank McKinney (1868–1930), American journalist and caricaturist, creator of the humorous and shrewd character Abe Martin.

Hubmaier, Balthasar (1485–1528), German Anabaptist preacher and theologian; condemned as a heretic and burned at the stake.

Hucbald (c.840–930), important Flemish music theorist, composer and monk.

Huchel, Peter (1903–1981), German poet.

Hudson, W(illiam) H(enry) (1841–1922), English writer, naturalist and ornithologist, particularly remembered for his novel Green Mansions (1904).

Huerta, Vicente García de (1730–1787), Spanish poet and critic.

Huet, Pierre-Daniel (1630–1721), French Roman Catholic bishop, scientist and scholar, especially known for his Censura Philosophiae Cartesiane (Criticisms of the Philosophy of Descartes, 1689) and Nouveaux memoires pour servir a l'histoire (New Memoires in the Service of History, 1692).

Hügel, Baron Friedrich von (1852–1925), German-born English Roman Catholic theologian and philosopher.

Hughes, Hugh Price (1847–1902), English Wesleyan Methodist leader and writer.

Hughes, (James Mercer) Langston (1902–1967), American poet, dramatist and short-story writer, one of the principal figures in the Harlem Renaissance.

Hughes, John Ceiriog (1832–1887), Welsh poet and folklorist who wrote under the names Ceiriog and Syr Meurig Grynswth.

Hughes, Richard (Arthur Warren) (1900–1976), English novelist, poet and dramatist, especially known for his novel A High Wind in Jamaica (1929).

Hughes, Rupert (1872–1956), American writer and dramatist.

Hughes, Ted (actually Edward James Hughes) (1930–1998), English poet and writer; Poet Laureate of the United Kingdom (1984–1998); husband of Sylvia Plath.

Hughes, Thomas (1822–1896), English jurist and novelist, author of Tom Brown's School Days (1857).

Hugh of Saint-Victor (1096–1141), famous French scholar, theologian and mystic.

Hugo, Joseph-Léopold-Sigisbert (1773–1828), French general and writer.

Hugo, Richard (Franklin) (1923–1982), American poet and essayist.

Hugo, Victor (Marie) (1802–1885), celebrated French poet, novelist and dramatist, author of the classic novels Notre Dame de Paris (1831) and Les Misérables (1862).

Huidobro, Vicente (1893–1948), Chilean poet, writer and theorist of avant-garde persuasion.

Huizinga, Johan (1872–1945), eminent Dutch historian, author of Herfsttij der middeleeuwen (1919; English trans. as The Waning of the Middle Ages, 1924), Erasmus (1924), In de schaduwen van Morgen (1935; English trans. as In the Shadow of Tomorrow, 1936) and Homo Ludens (1938).

Hull, Clark L(eonard) (1884–1952), influential American psychologist who wrote Aptitude Testing (1928), Hypnosis and Suggestibility (1933), Mathematico-Deductive Theory of Rote Learning (1940), Principles of Behavior (1943) and A Behavior System (1952).

Hulme, T(homas) E(rnest) (1883–1917), English poet, critic and philosopher who was a gifted Imagist; died in World War I.

Humbert of Silva Candida (c.1000–1061), French Roman Catholic cardinal, legate and theologian.

Humboldt, (Friedrich Wilhelm Karl Heinrich) Alexander von (1769–1859), German explorer and scientist, author of the important treatise Kosmos.

Humboldt, (Karl) Wilhelm, Freiherr von (1767–1835), eminent German language scholar, philosopher and diplomat who wrote the valuable study Über den Dualis (On the Dual, 1828).

Hume, Alexander (c.1560–1609), Scottish poet, best known for his O the Day Estival and Epistle to Maister Gilbert Mont-Crief.

Hume, David (1711–1776), renowned Scottish philosopher, historian, economist and essayist, author of A Treatise of Human Nature (3 vols, 1739–40), An Enquiry Concerning Human Understanding (1748), An Enquiry Concerning the Principles of Morals (1751) and The History of England (6 vols, 1754–62).

Humphrey, George (1889–1966), English psychologist.

Humphreys, David (1752–1818), American poet.

Humphries, (George) Rolfe (1894–1969), American poet and translator.

Huneker, James Gibbons (1860–1921), American music and literary critic.

Hung Shen (1893–1955), Chinese dramatist and film maker.

Hunt, (Isobel) Violet (1866–1942), English novelist.

Hunt, (James Henry) Leigh (1784–1859), English poet, critic, journalist and essayist.

Hunter, Sir William Wilson (1840–1900), Scottish writer.

Hurd, Richard (1720–1808), English Anglican bishop and scholar, author of the influential Letters on Chivalry and Romance (1762).

Hurdis, James (1763–1801), English poet, best known for The Village Curate (1788).

Hurst, Fannie (1889–1968), American novelist, dramatist and screenwriter.

Hurston, Zora Neale (1903–1960), American novelist and short-story writer.

Hüseyin Rahmi Gürpinar (1864–1944), Turkish novelist.

Husserl, Edmund (1859–1938), important Moravian-born German philosopher, founder of phenomenology.

Hutcheson, Francis (1694–1746), prominent Irish-born Scottish Presbyterian minister and philosopher who wrote Inquiry into the Original of Our Ideas of Beauty and Virtue (1725), An Essay on the Nature and Conduct of the Passions and Affections, with Illustrations upon the Moral Sense (1728) and System of Moral Philosophy (2 vols, published 1755).

Hutchins, Robert M(aynard) (1899–1977), American educator who was a champion of the liberal arts in higher education.

Hutchinson, Alfred (1924–72), South African writer who wrote a compelling autobiography Road to Ghana (1960), which related his imprisonment in 1952 for his opposition to apartheid and his escape from his homeland.

Hutchinson, R(ay) C(oryton) (1907–1975), English novelist.

Hutchinson, (William) Bruce (1901–1992), Canadian journalist and novelist.

Hutten, Ulrich von (1488–1523), German knight, patriot, writer and poet.

Hutton, John Henry (1885–1968), English anthropologist.

Hutton, Richard Holt (1826–1897), English journalist and essayist.

Huxley, Aldous (Leonard) (1894–1963), esteemed English novelist, essayist and poet, author of the classic novel Brave New World (1932); grandson of Thomas Henry Huxley and brother of Sir Julian Sorell Huxley.

Huxley, Sir Julian Sorell (1887–1975), English biologist and writer; grandson of Thomas Henry Huxley and brother of Aldous (Leonard) Huxley.

Huxley, Thomas Henry (1825–1895), renowned English scientist, humanist and writer; grandfather of Aldous (Leonard) Huxley and Sir Julian Sorell Huxley.

Huygens, Constantijn (1596–1687), Dutch scholar and poet.

Huysmans, Joris-Karl (actually Charles Huysmans) (1848–1907), notable French novelist and art critic, author of the important novels À vau-l'eau (1882; English trans. as Down Stream, 1927), À rebours (1884; English trans. as Against the Grain, 1922), Là-bas (1891; English trans. as Down There, 1924) and En Route(1895).

Hviezdoslav (actually Pavol Országh) (1849–1921), pioneering Slovak poet.

Hyde, Charles Cheney (1873–1952), American scholar of international law and diplomacy.

Hyde, Douglas (1860–1949), prominent Irish scholar who wrote under the name An Craoibhin Aoibhinn and who served as the first president of Ireland (1938–45).

Hyginus, Gaius Julius (1st Century), Latin scholar.

Hyndman, Henry Mayers (1842–1921), English Marxist, author of The Evolution of Revolution (1920).

Hypatia (c.370–415), famous Egyptian mathematician and philosopher; was killed by a mob of fanatical Christians.

Hyslop, James (1798–1827), Scottish poet.

Hywel ab Owain Gwynedd (died 1170), Welsh warrior-prince and poet.

Iamblichus (c.250–c.330), Syrian philosopher of the Neoplatonic school.

Ibarbourou, Juana de (actually Juanita Fernández Morales) (1895–1979), Uruguayan poet.

Ibn 'Abbād (actually Abū 'Abd Allāh Muhammad ibn Abī Ishāq Ibrāhīm an-Nafzī al- Himyarī ar-Rundī) (1333–1390), Spanish-born Arab mystic and theologian of Sūfism.

ibn Abī ar-Rijāl, Ahmad (ibn Sālih) (1620–1681), Yemeni scholar and theologian.

Ibn al-Abbār (actually Abū 'Abd Allāh Muhammad al-Qudā'ī) (1199–1260), Spanish Muslim historian and theologian who was also known for his humour and satire.

Ibn al'Arabī (actually Muhyi ad-Dīn Abū 'Abd Allāh Muhammad ibn 'Alī ibn Muhammad ibn al-'Arabī al-Hātimī at-Tā'ī ibn al'Arabī) (1165–1240), famous Spanish Muslim mystic philosopher and poet who used the literary name Abu Bakr.

Ibn al-Athīr (actually Abū al-Hasan 'Alī 'Izz ad-Dīn ibn al-Athīr) (1160–1233), Arab historian.

Ibn al-Farid (actually Sharaf ad-Dīn Abū Hafs 'Umar ibn al-Fārid) (c.1181–1235), revered Egyptian Muslim poet who was regarded as a saint during his lifetime.

Ibn al-Jawzī (actually 'Abd ar-Rahmān ibn 'Alī ibn Muhammad Abū al-Farash ibn al-Jawzī) (1126–1200), prominent Iraqi theologian, preacher and scholar who championed the cause of Islamic orthodoxy.

Ibn al-Muqaffa' (died c.756), Muslim writer.

Ibn 'Alqāmah (11th Century), Arab historian.

Ibn al-Walīd (c.1215), Yemenite Isma'ili theologian.

Ibn al-Warrāq (died 861), Muslim theologian.

Ibn 'Aqil (actually Abū al-Wafā' 'Alī ibn 'Aqīl ibn Muhammad ibn 'Aqīl ibn Ahmad al-Baghdādī az-Zafarī) (1040–1119), notable Iraqi Islamic theologian and scholar.

Ibn Bābawayh (actually Abū Ja'far Muhammad ibn Abū al-Hasan 'Ali ibn Husayn ibn Mūsā al-Qummī) (c.923–991), influential Persian Islamic theologian of Shī'ism.

Ibn Battūtah (actually Abū 'Abd Allāh Muhammad ibn 'Abd Allāh al-Lawātī Attanjī ibn Battūtah) (1304–c.1368), famous Arab traveller who wrote the celebrated Rihlah, an account of his extensive travels.

Ibn Dā'ud (died 910), Muslim theologian and poet.

ibn Daud, Abraham (c.1110–c.1180), Spanish Jewish physician and historian, author of Emuna rama (Exalted Faith) and Sefer ha-Kabbala (The Book of Tradition).

Ibn Durayd (actually Abū Bakr Muhammad ibn al-Hasan ibn Durayd al-Azdī) (c.837–933), Arab philologist and poet.

ibn Ezra, Abraham ben Meir (c.1090–1164), important Spanish Jewish biblical scholar, philosopher, grammarian, astronomer and poet.

ibn Ezra, Moses (ben Jacob ha-Sallab) (c.1060–c.1139), Spanish Hebrew poet and critic, a master of both sacred and secular verse.

Ibn Falaquera (c.1225–c.1295), Spanish Jewish philosopher and translator.

Ibn Gabirol (actually Solomon ben Yehuda ibn Gabirol) (c.1021–c.1070), Spanish Jewish poet and Neoplatonic philosopher.

Ibn Hāni' (died 973), Spanish Muslim poet.

Ibn Hazm (actually Abū Muhammad 'Alī ibn Ahmad ibn Sa'īd ibn Hazm) (994–1064), celebrated Spanish Muslim writer, jurist, historian and theologian.

Ibn Ishāq (actually Muhammad ibn Ishāq ibn Yasār ibn Khiyār) (704–767), Iraqi biographer of the Prophet Muhammad.

ibn Janāh, Abū al-Walīd Marwān (c.990–c.1050), learned Spanish Hebrew grammarian and lexicographer.

Ibn Kathīr (actually 'Imād ad-Dīn Ismā'il ibn 'Umar ibn Kathīr) (c.1300–1373), noted Syrian historian and theologian, author of the valuable al-Bidayah wa-an-nihayah (The Beginning and the End, 14 vols), a history of Islam.

Ibn Khafājah (died 1138), Spanish Muslim poet.

Ibn Khaldūn (actually Abū Zayd 'Abd ar-Rahmān ibn Khaldūn) (1332–1406), Arab historian whose most important work was the Muqaddimah (Introduction to History).

Ibn Kullāb (died c.864), Muslim theologian.

Ibn Miskawayh (actually Abū 'Ali Ahmad ibn Muhammad ibn Ya'qūb Miskawayh) (c.930–1030), Arab philosopher and historian.

Ibn Qutaybah (actually Abū Muhammad 'Abd Allāh ibn Muslim al-Dīnawarī ibn Qutaybah) (828–889), esteemed Arab writer.

Ibn Quzmān (died 1160), Spanish Muslim poet.

ibn Shem Tov, Joesph ben Shem Tov (c.1400–c.1460), Spanish Jewish philosopher and court physician, author of Kevod Elohim (The Glory of God, 1442).

Ibn Tufayl (actually Muhammad ibn 'Abd al-Malik ibn Muhammad ibn Muhammad ibn Tufayl al-Qaysī) (c.1110–c.1185), Spanish philosopher and physician, author of Risālat Hayy ibn Takzān (c.1175; English trans. as The Improvement of Human Reason, 1708).

ibn Zabara, Joesph ben Meir (12th Century), Spanish Jewish writer.

Ibn Zaydūn (died 1071), Spanish Muslim poet.

Ibsen, Henrik (Johan) (1828–1906), Norwegian dramatist and poet of incalculable importance in the development of modern drama, renowned for such plays as Brand (1866), Peer Gynt (1867), A Doll's House (1879), Ghosts (1881) and Hedda Gabler (1890).

Ibycus (6th Century BC), Greek poet.

Icaza (Coronel), Jorge (1906–78), Ecuadorean novelist and dramatist whose works depicted the oppressed lives of his nation's Indian peoples.

Idelsohn, Abraham Zevi (1882–1938), Latvian music scholar and composer, an authority on Jewish music.

Idrīs, Yūsuf (1929–1991), Egyptian writer and dramatist.

Idrīsī, (Abū 'Abd Allāh Muhammad) al- (1100–1165), Arab geographer and scientist who wrote valuable works on geography.

Iffland, August Wilhelm (1759–1814), notable German actor, dramatist and theatre manager, especially admired for his sentimental and comic plays.

Ignatius, Saint (c.35–c.107), esteemed Christian bishop whose letters were highly influential; was martyred by the Roman authorities.

Ignatow, David (1914–1997), American poet.

Ihara or Ibara Saikaku (1642–1693), celebrated Japanese poet and novelist.

Iio Sōgi (1421–1502), famous Japanese poet and Buddist monk, a master of renga (linked verse).

Ilf, Ilya (Arnoldovich) (1897–1937), Russian writer who collaborated with Yevgeny Petrov on the successful novels Dvenadtsat stulyev (1928; English trans. as The Twelve Chairs, 1961) and Zolotoy telyonok (1931; English trans. as The Little Golden Calf, 1962).

Imber, Naphtali Herz (1865–1909), Hebrew poet.

Immanuel ben Solomon (c.1260–c.1328), significant Hebrew poet and biblical scholar, author of both sacred and secular verse of high merit.

Immermann, Karl Leberecht (1796–1840), German dramatist and novelist.

Imru' al-Qays (ibn Hujr) (died c.550), illustrious Arab poet.

Inchbald, Elizabeth (née Simpson) (1753–1821), English novelist, dramatist and actress, best remembered for her novels A Simple Story (1791) and Nature and Art (1796).

Inge, William (Motter) (1913–1973), American dramatist and novelist.

Inge, William Ralph (1860–1954), English Anglican dean and writer.

Ingelow, Jean (1820–1897), English poet and novelist, particularly known for a vol. of Poems (1863).

Ingemann, Bernhard Severin (1789–1862), Danish poet and novelist.

Ingersoll, Charles Jared (1782–1862), American politician, writer and poet.

Ingersoll, Robert G(reen) (1833–1899), American politician, orator and writer who became particularly well known for his advocacy of agnosticism.

Ingraham, Joesph Holt (1809–1860), American Episcopal clergyman and writer, best known for his historical and religious romances; father of Prentiss Ingraham.

Ingraham, Prentiss (1834–1904), American writer and dramatist who wrote over 600 dime novels; son of Joesph Holt Ingraham.

Ingram, John Kells (1823–1907), Irish scholar and economist.

Inoue Enryō (1859–1919), Japanese philosopher and educator who developed a nationalistic Buddhist doctrine.

Inoue Tetsujirō (1855–1944), Japanese philosopher.

Ionesco, Eugène (1909–1994), famous Romanian-born French dramatist and writer who profoundly influenced modern drama as the creator of the 'Theatre of the Absurd'.

Iorga, Nicolae (1871–1940), prominent Romanian historian and statesman; was assassinated.

Iqbāl, Muhammad (1876–1938), Indian poet and philosopher, author of the extensive Persian poem Asrār-ekhūdī (The Secrets of the Self, 1915).

Ireland, John (c.1435–c.1500), Scottish theologian, diplomat and writer, author of The Meroure of Wyssdome (1490).

Irenaeus, Saint (c.130–c.200), Roman Catholic theologian and bishop, author of Adversus haereses (Against Heresies, c.180).

Iriarte y Oropesa, Tomas de (1750–1791), Spanish poet, writer and translator.

Irving, John Treat (1812–1906), American writer; nephew of Washington Irving.

Irving, Peter (1771–1838), American writer; brother of Washington Irving and William Irving.

Irving, Pierre Munro (1803–1876), American lawyer and writer; son of William Irving and nephew of Washington Irving.

Irving, Washington (1783–1859), American writer whose most famous work was The Sketch Book (1820); brother of Peter Irving and William Irving.

Irving, William (1766–1821), American poet; father of Pierre Munro Irving and brother of Peter Irving and Washington Irving.

Irwin, Wallace (Admah) (1875–1959), American poet, journalist and novelist; brother of Will(iam Henry) Irwin.

Irwin Will(iam Henry) (1873–1948), American journalist, writer and dramatist; brother of Wallace (Admah) Irving.

Irzykowski, Karol (1873–1944), Polish writer.

Isaac of Antioch (died 460), notable Syrian poet and writer who was also known as Isaac the Great.

Isaac of Nineveh (died c.700), Syrian monk, bishop and theologian who was also known as Isaac the Syrian.

Isaac of Stella (c.1100–c.1178), famous English-born French monk, theologian and philosopher, author of the Epistola de anima ae Alcherum (Letter to Alcher on the Soul).

Isaacs, Jorge (1837–1895), Colombian novelist and poet, especially admired for his novel María (1867).

Isherwood, Christopher (actually Christopher William Bradshaw-Isherwood) (1904–1986), English-born American novelist, short-story writer, essayist, poet and dramatist, particularly remembered for his novels Mr Norris Changes Trains (1935) and Goodbye to Berlin (1939).

Ishikawa Takuboku (actually Ishikawa Hajime) (1885–1912), Japanese poet and writer.

Isidore of Kiev (c.1385–1463), Greek Orthodox patriarch of Russia, Roman Catholic cardinal, scholar and theologian.

Isidore of Seville, Saint (c.560–636), Spanish Roman Catholic archbishop, theologian and scholar.

Isla (y Rojo), José Francisco de (1703–1781), Spanish Jesuit and writer who wrote the satirical and controversial Fray Gerundio (1758), a book condemned by the Inquisition.

Isocrates (436–338 BC), celebrated Greek rhetorician and writer who espoused the cause of Greek unification in the face of Persian hegemony; committed suicide.

Israeli, Isaac ben Solomon (c.833–c.933), famous Jewish physician and philosopher.

Issa (actually Kobayashi Issa) (1763–1827), Japanese poet who wrote much of his work under the name Kobayashi Yataró.

Italus, John (11th Century), Byzantine philosopher and court official, a proponent of Platonism.

Itó Jinsai (1627–1705), Japanese philosopher, author of Gómójigi (1683), a commentary on the analects of the Chinese philosophers Confucius and Mencius.

Itó Tógai (1670–1736), Japanese philosopher of the Confucian school.

Ivanov, Viacheslav Ivanovich (1866–1949), Russian poet, philosopher and scholar, a noted Symbolist.

Ivanov, Vsevolod Viacheslavoch (1895–1963), Russian writer.

Ivo of Chartres, Saint (c.1040–1116), French Roman Catholic bishop and canonist.

Izumi Kyóka (actually Izumi Kyotaro) (1873–1939), Japanese short-story writer.

Jabayev, Jambul (1846–1945), Kazakh poet.

Jablonski, Daniel Ernst (1660–1741), German Protestant theologian.

Jabotinsky, Vladimir (1880–1940), prominent Russian Zionist, journalist and writer, leader of the Zionist Revisionist movement.

Jacinto, António (actually António Jacinto do Amaral Martins) (1924–1991), Angolan poet and Marxist anticolonial leader who often wrote under the name Orlando Tavora.

Jackson, A(braham) V(alentine) Williams (1862–1937), American scholar of Indo-Iranian languages and Iranian religion.

Jackson, Charles (Reginald) (1903–1968), American writer, best remembered for his novel The Lost Weekend (1944).

Jackson, Cyril (1746–1819), English Anglican clergyman, classics scholar and educator.

Jackson, Helen (Maria) Hunt (née Fiske) (1831–1885), American novelist and poet, particularly esteemed for her novel Ramona (1884).

Jackson, Shirley (Hardie) (1916–1965), American novelist and short-story writer.

Jackson, William (1730–1803), English composer and writer on music.

Jackson, William (c.1737–1795), English clergyman and radical journalist who supported various revolutionary causes; arrested and convicted of treason, he committed suicide.

Jacob, Max (1876–1944), noted French poet and writer who was especially known for his Surrealist and lyrical poetry; died in a concentration camp.

Jacob, Violet (née Kennedy-Erskine) (1863–1946), Scottish poet and novelist.

Jacobi, Friedrich Heinrich (1743–1819), important German philosopher who espoused the philosophy of feeling as an alternative to Rationalism.

Jacobi, Johann Georg (1740–1814), German poet.

Jacob of Edessa (c.640–708), Syrian theologian and scholar.

Jacob of Serugh or Sarug (451–521), Syrian Roman Catholic bishop, writer and poet.

Jacobs, Harriet A (1813–1897), American memoirist whose account of her years as a slave were recorded in her Incidents in the Life of a Slave Girl: Written by Herself (1861), published under the name Linda Brent.

Jacobs, Joesph (1854–1916), Australian folklorist and writer.

Jacobs, W(illiam) W(ymark) (1863–1943), English short-story writer, author of the classic horror story 'The Monkey's Paw' (1902).

Jacobsen, Jens Peter (1847–1885), Danish novelist, short-story writer and poet, creator of the Naturalist movement in Denmark.

Jacobus de Voragine (c.1229–1298), Italian Roman Catholic archbishop and writer, author of the Legenda aurea (Golden Legend), a religious chronicle.

Jacopone daTodi (actually Jacopo dei Benedetti) (c.1230–1306), admired Italian poet, reputed author of the celebrated sacred Latin poem Stabat mater dolorosa, which later became a part of the Roman Catholic liturgy.

Jacotot, Jean-Joseph (1770–1840), influential French educator whose pedagogical ideas were delineated in his Enseignement universel (Universal Teaching Method, 1823).

Jaeger, Hans Henrik (1854–1910), Norwegian novelist whose Fra Kristiania-Bohêmen (From the Christiania Bohemian, 1885) caused a scandal for its frank treatment of sexuality and was confiscated by the authorities as pornographic.

Jaeger, Werner (1888–1961), German classical scholar.

Jafri, Ali Sardar (1913–2000), Indian poet and writer.

Jagannātha Dās (16th Century), Indian poet.

Jago, Richard (1715–1781), English poet, author of the extensive topographical poem Edge-hill (1767).

Jāhiz, al- (actually Abū 'Uthmān 'Amr ibn Bahr ibn Mahbūb al-Jāhiz) (c.776–c.868), celebrated Arab theologian and writer.

Jahn, Otto (1813–1869), German philologist, archaeologist and music scholar, especially known for his valuable biography of Mozart (4 vols, 1856–59).

Jakobson, Roman (1896–1982), influential Russian-born American linguist, one of the principal figures in the structural linguistics movement that became known as the Prague school.

Jalāl ad-Dīn ar-Rūmī (1207–1273), foremost Sūfi Muslim poet in the Persian language.

Jamalzadeh, Mohammad Ali (1892–1997), Persian writer of fiction and non-fiction.

James, E(dwin) O(liver) (1888–1972), English anthropologist.

James, Henry, Sr (1811–1882), American philosopher of theological concerns; father of Henry James and William James.

James, Henry (1843–1916), illustrious American novelist, short-story writer and critic, author of such classic works as The Portrait of a Lady (1881), The Bostonians (1886), The Spoils of Poynton (1897), The Wings of the Dove (1902), The Ambassadors (1903) and The Golden Bowl (1904); son of Henry James Sr and brother of William James.

James, Marquis (1891–1955), American biographer and writer.

James, William (1842–1910), eminent American philosopher and psychologist of the Pragmatist school, author of the important studies The Principles of Psychology (1890) and The Varieties of Religious Experience (1902); son of Henry James Sr and brother of Henry James.

James, Will(iam Roderick) (1892–1942), American writer and illustrator of books on the Old West.

Jameson, Anna Brownell (1794–1860), English biographer, historian, critic and essayist.

Jameson, (Margaret) Storm (1891–1986), English novelist, poet, biographer and essayist.

Jāmī (actually Mowlanā Nū r od-Dīn 'abd Orrahmān ebn Ahmad) (1414–1492), celebrated Persian poet, scholar and mystic.

Jammes, Francis (1868–1938), French poet, novelist and short-story writer.

Jandl, Ernst (1925–2000), Austrian poet and dramatist who was especially known for his experimental works.

Janet, Pierre (-Marie-Felix) (1859–1947), French psychologist and neurologist, author of The Major Symptoms of Hysteria (1907).

Janin, Jules-Gabriel (1804–1874), French journalist, writer and essayist.

Janowitz, Morris (1919–88), American sociologist and political scientist.

Janssen, Johannes (1829–1891), German Roman Catholic historian, author of the important but controversial Geschichte des deutschen Volkes seit dem Ausgang des Mittelalters (History of Germany from the Close of the Middle Ages, 8 vols, 1876–94).

Janvier, Thomas Allibone (1849–1913), American writer.

Jaques-Dalcroze, Emile (1865–1950), Swiss music educator and composer of French descent, creator of eurythmics, a method of rythmic training.

Jarīr (ibn 'Atīyah ibn al-Khatafā) (c.650–c.729), illustrious Arab poet.

Jarnés (y Millán), Benjamín (1888–1949), Spanish novelist.

Jarrell, Randall (1914–1965), esteemed American poet, novelist and critic.

Jarry, Alfred (1873–1907), French dramatist, novelist and poet whose controversial play Ubu roi (1896) is considered the first drama of the Theatre of the Absurd.

Jarves, James Jackson (1818–1888), American art collector, critic and writer.

Jasmin, Jacques (actually Jacques Boé) (1798–1864), French poet of dialect verse.

Jaspers, Karl (Theodor) (1883–1969), eminent German philosopher, a principal exponent of Existentialism and author of the important vol. Philosophie (1932).

Jastrun, Mieczysław (1903–83), Polish poet and essayist.

Jaucourt, Louis de (1704–1799), French scholar.

Jawahri, Mohammed Mahdi al- (1900–1997), Iraqi poet.

Jean d'Arras (15th Century), French trouvère.

Jean de Meun or Meung (c.1240–c.1300), French poet who completed Guillaume de Lorris's allegorical poem the Roman de la rose (c.1280).

Jean le Bel (c.1290–1370), Belgian canon, soldier and writer, author of the chronicle Vrayes Chroniques.

Jebb, Sir Richard Claverhouse (1841–1905), esteemed English classical scholar.

Jeda Bin (1874–1916), Japanese poet and scholar.

Jefferies, (John) Richard (1848–1887), English naturalist, novelist and essayist.

Jeffers, (John) Robinson (1887–1962), notable American poet who was known for his bitter indictment of his era.

Jefferson, Thomas (1743–1826), American statesman, 3rd president of the US (1801–09), author of A Summary View of the Rights of British America (1774), The Declaration of Independence (1776) and Notes on the State of Virginia (1784).

Jeffery, Francis, Lord (1773–1850), Scottish judge and literary critic, editor of The Edinburgh Review (1803–29).

Jellinek, Adolf (1821–1893), Moravian Jewish rabbi and scholar.

Jellinek, Georg (1851–1911), German philosopher, author of Die socialethische Bedeutung von Recht, Unrecht und Strafe (The Social-Ethical Significance of Right, Wrong, and Punishment, 1878), Die Erklärung der Menschen- und Bürgerrechte (1895; English trans. as The Declaration of the Rights of Man and of Citizens, 1901) and Allgemeine Staatslehre (General Theory of the State, 1900).

Jennings, Elizabeth (Joan) (1926–2001), English poet of such volumes as Recoveries (1964), The Mind Has Mountains (1966), Lucidities (1970), Moments of Grace (1979), Tributes (1989), Familiar Spirits (1994) and A Spell of Words (1997).

Jennings, Gary (1928–99), American novelist.

Jensen, Johannes V(ilhelm) (1873–1950), eminent Danish novelist, poet and essayist, especially esteemed for his 6 novels published under the general title Den lange rejse (1908–22; English trans. as The Long Journey, 1922–24; won the Nobel Prize for Literature (1944).

Jensen, Wilhelm (1837–1911), German poet and novelist.

Jenyns, Soame (1704–1787), English politician and poet.

Jerome, Saint (actually Eusebius Hieronymus) (c.345–420), renowned biblical scholar, celebrated for his Latin translation of the Bible.

Jerome, Jerome K(lapka) (1859–1927), English writer and dramatist.

Jerome of Prague (c.1365–1416), Czech philosopher and theologian.

Jerrold, Douglas William (1803–1857), English journalist and dramatist, best remembered for his play Black-Eyed Susan (1829) and the vol. of prose Curtain Lectures (1846); father of William Blanchard Jerrold.

Jerrold, William Blanchard (1826–1884), English journalist, dramatist, biographer and essayist; son of Douglas William Jerrold.

Jespersen, (Jens) Otto (Harry) (1860–1943), Danish linguist who was a leading authority on English grammar and author of the valuable Modern English Grammar (7 vols, 1909–49).

Jesse, F(riniwyd) Tennyson (1889–1958), English novelist and dramatist; grand niece of Alfred Lord Tennyson.

Jevons, William Stanley (1835–1882), English logician and economist, author of the Theory of Political Economy (1871) and Principles of Science (1874).

Jewel, John (1522–1571), prominent English Anglican bishop and apologist, particularly known for his Apologia pro Ecclesia Anglicana (Defence of the Anglican Church, 1562).

Jewett, Sarah Orne (1849–1909), American writer and poet, best known for her prose vol. The Country of the Pointed Firs (1896).

Jewsbury, Geraldine Endsor (1812–1880), English writer.

Jhering, Rudolf von (1818–1892), German legal scholar who wrote the important studies Geist des römischen Rechts (The Spirit of the Roman Law, 4 vols, 1852–65) and Der Zweck im Recht (2 vols, 1877, 1833; English trans. as Law As a Means to an End, 1924).

Jien (actually Fujiwara Dokai) (1145–1225), Japanese historian and Buddist monk, author of the Gukanshó (c.1220).

Jīlī, al- (actually 'Abd al-Karīm Qutb ad-Dīn ibn Ibrāhīm al-Jīlī) (1365–c.1424), Arab mystic who propounded an elaborate doctrine of the perfect man in his al-Insān al-Kāmil fi ma'rifat al-awākhir wa (partial English trans. as Studies in Islamic Mysticism, 1921).

Jiménez, Juan Ramón (1881–1958), admired Spanish poet and writer, especially known for his free verse; won the Nobel Prize for Literature (1956).

Jippensha Ikku (1765–1831), Japanese writer.

Jirásek, Alois (1851–1930), noted Czech novelist, especially admired for his Temno (Darkness, 1915).

Jnānadeva or Jnāneśvara (1275–1296), Indian poet, a master of the Mahārāshtrian school of mystical poets; committed suicide.

Joachim, Harold Henry (1868–1938), English philosopher.

Joachim of Fiore (c.1133–c.1201), Italian mystic, biblical commentator and theologian.

Joad, C(yril) E(dwin) M(itchinson) (1891–1953), English philosopher who was known for his advocacy of rationalism.

Jocelin de Brakelond (12th–13th Century), English Benedictine monk who wrote the Cronica (English trans., 1949).

Jochelson, Vladimir Ilich (1855–1937), Russian ethnographer and linguist.

Jöcher, Christian Gottlieb (1694–1758), German scholar and lexicographer.

Jochumsson, Matthías (1835–1920), Icelandic poet, dramatist translator and clergyman, author of the National Anthem of Iceland.

Jodelle, Étienne (1532–1573), French poet and dramatist.

Johann von Tepl or Saaz (c.1350–c.1415), Bohemian writer, author of the famous Der Ackermann aus Böhmen (c.1400; English trans. as Death and the Ploughman, 1947).

John Climacus, Saint (c.579–c.649), Byzantine monk, author of the celebrated Climax tou paradeisou (The Ladder of Divine Ascent).

John of Ávila, Saint (c.1499–1569), Spanish Roman Catholic preacher and reformer who wrote the celebrated treatise Audi filia (Listen, Daughter).

John of Damascus, Saint (c.645–749), Syrian monk, preacher and theologian who was also known as Johannes Damascenus.

John of Ephesus (c.507–c.586), Syrian Roman Catholic bishop and historian whose Monophysite views led to his banishment late in life, author of an ecclesiastical history and of a lives of the Eastern saints.

John of Fordun (14th Century), Scottish chronicler who wrote a history of Scotland.

John of Guildford (14th Century), English writer on heraldry.

John of Jandun (c.1286–1328), French scholar who wrote commentaries on Aristotle.

John of Jerusalem (c.356–417), Roman Catholic bishop and theologian who upheld the Platonistic tradition of Alexandria.

John of Kronstadt (actually Ivan Ilich Sergeiev) (1829–1909), Russian Orthodox priest and writer.

John of Mirecourt (14th Century), French Cistercian monk, philosopher and theologian who was a leading proponent of nominalism and voluntarism.

John of Odzun (650–729), Armenian Orthodox churchman and theologian.

John of Paris (c.1255–1306), French Dominican monk, theologian and philosopher who was also known as Jean Quidort and Johannes de Soardis, author of the controversial treatises De potestate regia et papali (On Royal and Papal Powers, c.1302) and Determinatio (1304).

John of St Thomas (actually John Poinsot) (1589–1644), notable Portuguese theologian and philosopher of the Thomist school, particularly known for his Cursus Philosophicus (Course in Philosophy, 9 vols, 1632–36) and Cursus Theologicus (Course in Theology, 7 vols, 1637–44).

John of Salisbury (c.1117–1180), English Roman Catholic bishop and theologian, author of the Policraticus (1159), Metalogicon (1159) and Historia pontificalis (1163).

John of Scythopolis (6th Century), Byzantine bishop and theologian who was known for his writings on Christ and for his commentaries on Neoplatonism.

John of the Cross, Saint (actually Juan de Yepes y Alvarez) (1542–1591), revered Spanish Roman Catholic mystic, reformer and poet, celebrated for such works as the Cántico espiritual (Spiritual Canticle) and Noche oscura del alma (Dark Night of the Soul).

John Scholasticus or John of Antioch (c.503–577), Syrian theologian, ecclesiastical jurist and patriarch.

Johnson, B(ryan) S(tanley William) (1933–1973), English novelist of the experimental school; committed suicide.

Johnson, Charles (1679–1748), English dramatist.

Johnson, Charles Spurgeon (1893–1956), American sociologist and educator who wrote valuable studies on the black experience and race relations.

Johnson, Edward (1598–1672), English-born American settler who wrote a Puritan account of the founding of New England (1654).

Johnson, (Emily) Pauline (1862–1913), Canadian Indian poet and writer who wrote under her Indian name Tekahionwake, best remembered for her poem The Song my Paddle Sings.

Johnson, Eyvind (1900–1976), noted Swedish novelist and short-story writer, particularly admired for his novel Strändernas svall (1946; English trans. as Return to Ithaca, 1952); was co-winner of the Nobel Prize for Literature (1974).

Johnson, Gisle (1822–1894), Norwegian Lutheran theologian.

Johnson, James Weldon (1871–1938), prominent American educator, civil rights advocate, poet, writer and anthologist of black culture.

Johnson, Lionel Pigot (1867–1902), English poet and critic who was known for his poem By the Statue of King Charles at Charing Cross.

Johnson, Louis Albert (1924–1988), New Zealand poet.

Johnson, Owen (McMahon) (1878–1952), American writer; son of Robert Underwood Johnson.

Johnson, Pamela Hansford (1912–1981), English novelist and critic.

Johnson, Richard (1573–c.1659), English writer, particularly known for his romance The Most Famous of the Seaven Champions of Christendome (3 parts, 1596, 1608, 1616).

Johnson, Robert Underwood (1853–1937), American poet and editor; father of Owen (McMahon) Johnson.

Johnson, Ronald (1935–98), American poet whose masterwork was the extensive ARK (1980–96).

Johnson, Samuel (1696–1772), American Anglican churchman and philosopher, author of Ethics Elementa (1746; revised edition as Elementa Philosophica, 1752).

Johnson, Samuel (1709–1784), celebrated English writer, critic, essayist, lexicographer and poet.

Johnson, Uwe (1934–1984), German novelist and essayist.

Johnston, Annie Fellows (1863–1931), American writer of children's stories.

Johnston, Arthur (1587–1641), Scottish poet and physician.

Johnston, Mary (1870–1936), American writer.

Johnston, Richard Malcom (1822–1898), American writer, best known for his humorous stories.

Johnston, (William) Denis (1901–1984), English dramatist, writer and critic.

Johnstone, Charles (c.1719–1800), English journalist and writer, author of Chrysal, or the Adventures of a Guinea (1760–65), The History of Arsaces, Prince of Betlis (1774), The Pilgrim (1775) and John Juniper (1781).

Joinville, François-Ferdinand-Phillippe-Louis-Marie d'Orléans, Prince de (1818–1900), French naval officer and writer on military subjects.

Joinville, Jean, Sire de (c.1224–1317), French court official who wrote the celebrated Histoire de saint-Louis (c.1270–1309; published 1547).

Jókai, Mór (1825–1904), Hungarian novelist.

Jokl, Norbert (1877–1942), Austrian linguist, an authority on the Albanian language.

Jomini, (Antoine-) Henri, Baron de (1779–1869), French general and military historian who wrote the important Précis de l'art de la guerre (1838; English trans. as Summary of the Art of War, 1868).

Jonas, Justus (1493–1555), German Protestant reformer, legal scholar and translator who helped to draft the Ausburg Confession.

Jones, (Alfred) Ernest (1897–1958), Welsh psychoanalyst and biographer of Freud.

Jones, Daniel (1881–1967), English linguist and phonetician.

Jones, David (Michael) (1895–1974), English poet, writer and artist, particularly esteemed for his novel In Parenthesis (1937) and the religious poem The Anathemata (1952).

Jones, Ernest (1819–1869), English poet, a leader of the Chartrist movement and author of the epic TheRevolt of Hindostan.

Jones, Henry Arthur (1851–1929), English dramatist.

Jones, Howard Mumford (1892–1980), American writer, dramatist and poet.

Jones, Hugh (c.1670–1760), American minister, mathematician and historian, author of The Present State of Virginia (1724).

Jones, James (1921–1977), American writer, best remembered for his novel From Here to Eternity (1951).

Jones, James Athearn (1791–1854), American writer, poet and editor.

Jones, John Beauchamp (1810–1866), American journalist and novelist, best remembered for his realistic Civil War novel A Rebel War Clerk's Diary (1866).

Jones, Joseph Stevens (1809–1877), American physician, actor, theatre manager and dramatist.

Jones, Owen (1809–1874), English designer, architect and writer who wrote The Grammer of Ornament (1856), a valuable study of Western and Eastern design motifs.

Jones, Rufus Matthew (1863–1948), American Quaker philosopher, author of many books on Christian mysticism and Quakerism.

Jones, Thomas Gwynn (1871–1949), Welsh poet and scholar.

Jones, Sir William (1746–1794), English jurist and Orientalist, author of the standard tome Essay on the Law of Bailments (1781).

Jonker, Ingrid (1933–1965), South African novelist.

Jonson, Ben(jamin) (1572–1637), famous English dramatist, poet and critic, particularly known for his plays Volpone (1606) and The Alchemist (1610).

Jónsson, Arngrímur (1568–1648), important Icelandic historian who was known as Arngrímur the Learned.

Jónsson, Finnur (1704–1759), Icelandic bishop and historian.

Jónsson, Hjálmar (1796–1875), Icelandic poet of satirical verse who was known as Bólu-Hjálmar.

Jordan A(rchibald) C (1906–1968), South African novelist and educator, best known for his novel Ingqumbo Yeminyanya (The Wrath of the Ancestors, 1940), a story of Xosa life.

Jordan, David Starr (1851–1931), American educator, philosopher and naturalist.

Jordan, Thomas (c.1612–c.1685), English poet, dramatist and Royalist pamphleteer, best remembered for A Royal Arbour of Loyall Poesie (1664) and A Nursery of Novelties in Variety of Poetry.

Jordanes (6th Century), Goth historian who wrote in Latin, author of the valuable De origine actibusque Getarum (On the Origin and Deeds of the Getae, 551).

Jørgensen, (Jens) Johannes (1866–1956), Danish novelist, poet and biographer.

Joris, David (c.1501–1556), highly controversial Anabaptist leader, mystic visionary and prophet, author of the Wonder Boeck (Wonder Book, 2 parts, 1542, 1551); was posthumously condemned as a heretic, his body exhumed and burned at the stake (1559).

Joesph ben Jacob ibn Tzaddik (1075–1149), Spanish Jewish philosopher and poet.

Joesph of Volokolamsk, Saint (actually Joesph Panin) (1439–1515), influential Russian monk and theologian who opposed Western humanistic elements in Christian faith and practice.

Josephson, Matthew (1899–1978), American biographer and writer.

Josephus, Flavius (actually Joesph ben Matthias) (c.37–c.100), notable Jewish historian and priest, author of a valuable history of the Jewish war (75–79) and antiquities of the Jews (93).

Joubert, Joesph (1754–1824), French writer.

Jovanović, Slobodan (1869–1958), Serbian statesman and scholar.

Jouve, Pierre–Jean (1887–1976), French poet, novelist and critic.

Jovellanos, Gaspar Melchor de (1744–1811), Spanish stateman and scholar.

Joveyni , Ata Malek (actually 'Alā' od-Dīn 'Ata Malek Joveyni) (1226–1283), notable Persian historian, author of the valuable Tarikh-i jehan-gusha (1252–56; English trans. as A History of the World Conqueror, 1958).

Jovius, Paulus (1483–1552), Italian historian and biographer who was also known as Paolo Giovio.

Jowett, Benjamin (1817–1893), English classical scholar, especially noted for his translations of Plato.

Joyce, James (Augustine Aloysius) (1882–1941), Irish novelist, short-story writer and poet whose novels Ulysses (1922) and Finnegan's Wake (1939) changed the course of modern literature.

Joyce, Patrick Weston (1827–1914), Irish writer.

József, Attila (1905–1937), Hungarian poet who espoused the cause of Marxism.

Juan Yüan (1764–1849), Chinese scholar and government official.

Jud, Jakob (1882–1952), Swiss linguist who was an authority on Romance languages.

Jud, Leo (1482–1542), Swiss Protestant reformer and biblical scholar who translated the Bible into German (c.1535).

Judah, Samuel B(enjamin) H(elbert) (1804–1876), American lawyer, writer and poet.

Judah ben Samuel (died 1217), German Jewish mystic and one of the leading figures in Hasidism, principal author of the treatise Sefer Hasidim (Book of the Pious, published 1538).

Judah ha-Levi (actually Yeduha ben Shemuel ha-Levi) (c.1075–1141), important Jewish Hebrew poet and philosopher.

Judah ha-Nasi (c.135–c.220), Palestinian Jewish scholar and patriarch, an interpreter of the Jewish Oral Law, a part of which he preserved as the Mishna (Teaching).

Judd, Charles Hubbard (1873–1946), American psychologist and educator.

Judd, Sylvester (1813–1853), American Unitarian minister and writer, author of the novels Margaret (1845) and Richard Edney and the Governor's Family (1850), and the epic Philo, an Evangeliad (1850).

Judson, Adoniram (1788–1850), American Baptist misionary and linguist who translated the Bible into Burmese and edited a Burmese dictionary; husband of Emily (Chubbuck) Judson.

Judson, E(dward) Z(ane) C(arroll) (1823–1886), American adventurer and writer, creator of the so-called dime novels which he wrote under the name Ned Buntline.

Judson, Emily (Chubbuck) (1817–1854), American writer and poet who wrote under the name Fanny Forester; wife of Adoniram Judson.

Julian of Eclanum (c.386–454), Apulian Christian theologian who espoused Pelagian views.

Julian of Norwich (c.1342–c.1417), English Roman Catholic mystic and anchoress, celebrated for her Showings or Revelation(s) of Divine Love.

Jung, Carl (Gustav) (1875–1961), renowned Swiss psychologist and psychiatrist, founder of analytic psychology and author of the study Wandlungen und Symbole der Libido (1912; English trans. as The Psychology of the Unconscious, 1921).

Jünger, Ernst (1895–1998), German novelist and essayist whose espousal of militarism gave way to an ardent anti-militarism during the Nazi regime.

Jungmann, Josef (1773–1847), Czech linguist and writer.

Jung-Stilling, Johann Heinrich (1740–1817), German writer who became best known for his autobiography Heinrich Stillings Leben (Heinrich Stilling's Life, 5 vols, 1806).

Junius, Franciscus (1589–1677), German-born English language and literary scholar.

Junod, Henri Alexandre (1863–1934), Swiss Protestant missionary and anthropologist.

Junot, Laure, Duchesse d'Abrantès (actually Laure Permon) (1784–1838), French memoirist, author of Mémoires sur Napoléon, la Révolution, le Consulat, L'Empire et la Restauration (English trans., 8 vols, 1831–35).

Junqueiro, Abílio Manuel Guerra (1850–1923), prominent Portuguese poet.

Jurjānī, al- (actually Abū Bakr 'Abd al-Qāhir ibn 'Abd ar-Rahmān al-Jurjānī) (died 1078), Arab philologist and literary scholar.

Jurjānī, al- (actually 'Alī ibn Muhammad al-Jurjānī) (1339–1413), Persian theologian and scholar.

Justin Martyr, Saint (c.100–c.165), famous Christian apologist, author of two Apologies and the Dialogue with Trypho; after refusing to sacrifice to the Roman gods, he was scourged and beheaded.

Juvenval (actually Decimus Junius Juvenalist) (c.55–c.128), celebrated Roman poet of satirical verse.

Kabīr (1440–1518), Indian mystic and poet who espoused the cause of unity between Hindu and Muslim worldviews.

Kačić Miošić, Andrija (c.1704–1760), Croatian poet.

Kaden-Bandrowski, Juliusz (1885–1944), Polish novelist and short story writer.

Kafka, Franz (1883–1924), famous Czech-born Austrian novelist and short-story writer, author of the classic novels Der Prozess (published 1925; English trans. as The Trial, 1937) and Das Schloss (published 1926; English trans. as The Castle, 1930).

Kagawa Toyohiko (1888–1960), Japanese Christian social reformer and writer.

Kah-ge-ga-gah-bowh, Chief or George Copway (1818–1863), Canadian-born American chief of the Ojibway tribe, writer and poet, author of the epic poem The Ojibway Conquest, a Tale of the Northwest (1850).

Kahn, Gustave (1859–1936), prominent French poet and critic, one of the earliest and most effective writers of vers libre.

Kaibara Ekiken (actually Atsunobu) (1630–1714), Japanese philosopher, botanist and travel writer.

Kailas, Uuno (1901–1933), Finnish writer.

Kaiser, Georg (1878–1945), German dramatist who wrote notable Expressionist works for the stage.

Kakinomoto Hitomaro (7th–8th Century), revered Japanese poet.

Kaler, James Otis (1848–1912), American writer of works for boys who wrote under the name James Otis.

Kālidāsa (5th Century), Indian poet and dramatist writing in Sanskrit.

Kalīm, Abū Tālib (died 1651), Indian Muslim poet.

Kallas, Aino (1878–1956), Finnish writer.

Kallen, H(orace) M(eyer) (1882–1974), American cultural and political philosopher.

Kalm, Peter (1716–1779), Swedish scientist and traveller who left a valuable account of his visit to America (3 vols, 1753–61).

Kálvos, Andréas Ioannídis (1792–1869), Greek poet who was known for his patriotic odes (2 fascicles, 1824, 1826).

Kamal, Sufia (1911–99), Bangladeshi writer, poet and feminist.

Kamban, Gudmundur (Jonsson Hallgrimsson) (1888–1945), Icelandic novelist and dramatist whose masterpiece was the historical novel Skáholt (four vols, 1930–32); suspected of Nazi sympathies, he was accidentally shot and killed when Danish resistance forces attempted to arrest him for questioning in Copenhagen.

Kames, Henry Home, Lord (1696–1782), English jurist and philosopher, author of the notable Elements of Criticism (3 vols, 1762).

Kamo Chōmei (c.1155–1216), Japanese poet and critic, a master of vernacular verse.

Kämpfer, Engelbert (1651–1716), German traveller who wrote accounts of his travels to Persia and Japan.

Kanagaki Robun (actually Bunzó Nozaki) (1829–1874), Japanese writer.

Kanakadāsa (16th Century), Indian mystical poet.

Kane, Sarah (1970–99), English dramatist; committed suicide.

K'ang Yu-wei (1858–1927), Chinese scholar and reformer.

Kanik, Orhan Veli (1914–50), Turkish poet.

Kanin, Garson (1912–99), American dramatist, writer and theatre director.

Kant, Immanuel (1724–1804), German philosopher of Idealism, author of the influential treatises Kritik der reinen Vernunft (Critique of Pure Reason, 1781), Kritik der practischen Vernunft (Critique of Practical Reason, 1788) and Kritik der Urthielskraft (Critique of Judgement, 1790).

Kantor, MacKinlay (1904–1977), American novelist and short-story writer.

Kantorowicz, Hermann (1877–1940), Polish legal scholar.

Kaplan, Mordecai Menahem (1881–1983), Lithuanian-born American rabbi, educator and theologian, founder of the liberal Reconstructionist movement in Judaism.

Karadić, Vuk Stefanović (1787–1864), Serbian scholar who was an authority on the language and folk literature of his country.

Karamzin, Nikolai Mikhailovich (1766–1826), influential Russian historian, journalist and poet, author of the Istoriya gosudarstva rossiyakogo (History of the Russian State, 12 vols, 1816–29).

Karaosmanoğlu, Yakup Kadri (1889–1974), Turkish novelist and poet.

Karavelov, Lyuben Stoychev (1834–1879), Bulgarian writer and revolutionary.

Karelitz, Avraham Yeshayahu (ben Shmazyahn Joseph) (1878–1953), Jewish scholar who was an authority on the Halakha.

Kariotákis, Kóstas (1896–1928), Greek poet.

Karkavítsas, Andréas (1860–1922), Greek novelist and short-story writer.

Karlfeldt, Erik Axel (1864–1931), admired Swedish poet; was posthumously awarded the Nobel Prize for Literature (1931).

Karlstadt, Andreas Rudolf Bodenstein von (c.1480–1541), German Protestant theologian who was an early supporter of Lutheranism but later espoused more radical views in various tracts.

Kármán, József (1769–1795), Hungarian writer.

Karo or Caro or Qaro, Joesph ben Ephraim (1488–1575), Jewish scholar who prepared the last great codification of Jewish law in his Bet Yosef (House of Joseph), which he condensed in his Shulhan 'arukh (The Prepared Table).

Kaschnitz (-Weinberg), Marie Luise (von) (1901–74), German poet, novelist and dramatist.

Kasprowicz, Jan (1860–1926), admired Polish poet and translator.

Kassák, Lajos (1887–1967), Hungarian poet and novelist who championed radical political ideas.

Kästner, Erich (1899–1974), German poet and novelist who was known for his satire but also for his writings for children.

Katayev, Valentin (Petrovich) (1897–1986), Russian novelist and dramatist.

Kateb Yacine (1929–89), Algerian poet, novelist and dramatist.

Katkov, Mikhail Nikiforovich (1818–1887), influential Russian journalist of reactionary views.

Katō Hiroyuki (1836–1916), Japanese writer, political theorist and educator who helped to introduce Western ideas into his homeland.

Katona, József (1791–1830), Hungarian dramatist and lawyer, author of the important play Bánk bán (1821).

Kaufman, George S(imon) (1889–1961), American dramatist who collaborated with others on such plays as Of Thee I Sing (1931), You Can't Take it With You (1936) and The Man who Came to Dinner (1939).

Kautilya (actually Cānakya) (flourished 300 BC), Hindu statesman and philosopher who wrote Artha-sastra (English trans., 1926), a famous treatise on statecraft.

Kautsky, Karl (1854–1938), German Marxist journalist and political theorist who opposed Bolshevism.

Kavanagh, Patrick Joesph (1905–1967), respected Irish poet, novelist and critic, best known for his poem The Great Hunger (1942).

Kawabata Yasunari (1899–1972), esteemed Japanese novelist; won the Nobel Prize for Literature (1968).

Kawakami Hajime (1879–1946), Japanese poet and Marxist theorist.

Kawatake Mokuami (1816–1893), Japanese dramatist of the Kabuki theatre.

Kaye-Smith, (Emily) Shelia (1887–1956), English novelist.

Kaygusuz Abdal (15th Century), Turkish poet of Sufism.

Kazakov, Yuri Pavlovich (1927–82), Russian writer.

Kazantzákis, Níkos (1885–1957), Greek novelist, dramatist, essayist, poet and translator, best known for the epic poem The Odyssey, a Modern Sequel (1938) and the novel Zorba the Greek (1946).

Kazin, Alfred (1915–1998), esteemed American literary critic.

Kazinczy, Ferenc (1759–1831), Hungarian writer and poet.

Keane, Molly (actually Mary Nesta Skrine) (1904–1996), Irish novelist and dramatist.

Keating, Geofferey (c.1570–c.1644), Irish writer.

Keats, John (1795–1821), celebrated English poet, a master of lyric expression, renowned for his Lamia and Other Poems (1820), which included such masterworks as The Eve of St Agnes, Lamia, On a Grecian Urn, On Melancholy, To Autumn, To a Nightingale and To Psyche.

Keble, John (1792–1866), English Anglican priest, theologian and poet, founder of the Oxford Movement of the Church of England for the restoration of high-church principles.

Keckley, Elizabeth (1827–1907), American memoirist whose account of her years as a dressmaker to the wealthy and famous was published in the valuable Behind the Scenes, or, Thirty Years a Slave and Four Years in the White House (1868).

Keeler, Ralph Olmstead (1840–1873), American journalist and novelist.

Keenan, Henry Francis (1850–1928), American writer whose novel The Money-Makers (1885) was published anonymously.

Kees, Weldon (1914–1955), American poet, painter, jazz pianist and composer.

Keith, George (c.1638–1716), Scottish-born American Quaker, later Anglican clergyman and writer.

Kelland, Clarence Budington (1881–1964), American novelist and short-story writer.

Keller, Ferdinand (1800–1881), Swiss archaeologist and prehistorian.

Keller. Gottfried (1819–1890), Swiss novelist, short-story writer and poet whose finest work was the novel Der grüne Heinrich (1854–55; revised version, 1879–80; English trans. as Green Henry, 1960).

Keller, Helen Adams (1880–1968), famous American writer and lecturer who triumphed over her being born blind, deaf, and mute.

Kellermann, Bernhard (1879–1951), German journalist and novelist, best remembered for his novel Der Tunnel (1913; English trans. as The Tunnel , 1915).

Kelley, Edith Summers (1884–1956), Canadian-born American novelist.

Kellgren, Johan Henrik (1751–1795), important Swedish poet and journalist whose masterpiece was the poem Den Nya Skapelsen, eller inbillningensvärld (The New Creation, or the World of the Imagination, 1790).

Kellogg, Elijah (1813–1901), American Congregationalist minister and writer of children's books.

Kelly, George (Edward) (1887–1974), American dramatist, actor and director, author of The Torch-Bearers (1922), The Show Off (1924) and Craig's Wife (1925).

Kelly, Hugh (1739–1777), English dramatist, critic and journalist.

Kelly, Jonathan Falconbridge (c.1817–1855), American journalist and writer who became known for his humor.

Kelsen, Hans (1881–1973), Austrian-born American legal philosopher who was particularly known for his writings on international law.

Kemal, (Mehmed) Namik (1840–1888), significant Turkish writer and poet who helped to Westernize the literature of his homeland.

Kemalpaşazâde (c.1468–1534), renowned Turkish historian and poet.

Kemble, Fanny (actually Frances Ann Kemble) (1809–1893), English actress, writer, dramatist and poet.

Kemble, John Mitchell (1807–1857), English historian and philologist.

Kemény, Zsigmond, Baron (1814–1875), Hungarian journalist and novelist.

Kemp, Harry (actually Hibbard Kemp) (1883–1960), American poet, writer and dramatist who was known as the 'tramp poet'.

Kempe, Margery (c.1373–c.1440), English religious mystic who was known for her dictated autobiography (c.1435; published 1936).

Ken, Thomas (1637–1711), English Anglican bishop and hymnist, author of the hymns Awake, My Soul, and With the Sun and Glory to Thee, My God, This Night.

Kendall, George Wilkins (1809–1867), American journalist and writer.

Kendall, Henry (1839–1882), leading Australian poet.

Kennan, George (1845–1924), American traveller and writer.

Kennedy, Charles Rann (1871–1950), English dramatist.

Kennedy, John Pendleton (1795–1870), American writer and politician.

Kennedy, Margaret, Lady Davies (1896–1967), English novelist, critic and biographer.

Kennedy, Walter (c.1460–c.1508), Scottish poet of secular and sacred verse.

Kenneth, Saint (c.515–c.599), Irish Roman Catholic abbot, missionary and poet.

Kent, James (1763–1847), American legal scholar and jurist, author of the influential Commentaries on American Law (4 vols, 1826–30).

Kent, Rockwell (1882–1971), American writer, painter and illustrator.

Kenyon, John S(amuel) (1874–1959), American phonetician.

Kephart, Horace (1862–1931), American naturalist.

Ker, William Paton (1855–1923), English literary scholar.

Kerner, Justinus Andreas Christian (1786–1862), German poet, writer and physician.

Kerouac, Jack (actually Jean-Louis Kerouac) (1922–1969), prominent American novelist and poet, a leading figure in the Beat movement who was best known for his novel On the Road (1957).

Kerr, Walter Francis (1913–1996), influential American drama critic.

Kesey, Ken (Elton) (1935–2001), American writer who won fame as a counterculturalist, author of the novels One Flew Over the Cuckoo's Nest (1962), Sometimes a Great Notion (1964) and Sailor Song (1992).

Keshub Chunder Sen (1838–1884), Hindu religious reformer and writer.

Ketteler, Wilhelm Emmanuel, Freiherr von (1811–1877), German Roman Catholic bishop and social reformer.

Key, Ellen (Karolina Sofia) (1849–1926), Swedish essayist who espoused various liberal causes.

Key, Francis Scott (1779–1843), American lawyer and poet, author of The Star-Spangled Banner (1814), which was officially adopted as the US National Anthem (1931).

Key, V(aldimer) O(rlando) Jr (1908–1963), American political scientist.

Keyes, Frances Parkinson (1885–1970), American writer of romantic historical novels.

Keyes, Sydney Arthur Kilworth (1922–1943), English poet; died in World War II.

Keynes, Sir Geoffrey Langdon (1887–1982), English literary scholar, bibliographer and surgeon; son of John Neville Keynes and brother of J(ohn) M(aynard) Keynes.

Keynes, J(ohn) M(aynard), 1st Baron Keynes of Tilton (1883–1946), influential English economist, author of A General Theory of Employment, Interest, and Money (1936); son of John Neville Keynes and brother of Sir Geoffery Langdon Keynes.

Keynes, John Neville (1852–1949), English philosopher and economist; father of Sir Geoffrey Langdon and J(ohn) M(aynard) Keynes.

Keyserling, Hermann Alexander, Graf (1880–1946), German philosopher, especially remembered for his Das Reisetagebuch eines Philosophen (1919; English trans. as The Travel Diary of a Philosopher, 1925).

Khalīl ibn Ahmad, al- (actually Abū 'Abd ar-Rahman al-Khalīl ibn Ahmad ibn 'Amr ibn Timīn al-Farāhidi al-Azdī al-Yuhmadī) (c.718–c.788), Arab philologist and lexicographer.

Khansā, al- (actually Tumādir Bint 'Amr ibn al-Hārith ibn Ash Sharīd) (died c.631), celebrated Arab poet of elegies.

Khāqānī (actually Afzal od-Dīn Bādel Ebrāhim ebn 'Alī Khāqānī Shīrvānī) (c.1106–c.1185), Persian poet who excelled in writing court poems, epigrams and satires.

Khashhāl Khān Khatak (died 1689), Afgan soldier and poet.

Kheraskov, Mikhail Matveievich (1733–1807), Russian poet who wa known for his epics.

Khlebnikov, Velemir Vladimirovich (actually Vikto Vladimirovich Khlebnikov) (1885–1922), influential Russian poe founder of the Russian Futurist movement.

Khomyakov, Aleksei Stepanovich (1804–1860), Russian poet and la theologian of the Orthodox Church who was a principal figure in th Slavophile movement.

Khwāndamīr, Ghiyās ad-Dīn Muhammad (c.1475–c.1535), Persia historian.

Kickham, Charles Joseph (1826–1882), Irish poet and novelist especially remembered for his espousal of Irish nationalism.

Kidder, Alfred V(incent) (1885–1963), American archaeologist, autho of the Introduction to the Study of Southwestern Archaeology (1924).

Kielland, Alexander (1849–1906), noted Norwegian novelist, short story writer and dramatist.

Kierkegaard, Søren (Aabye) (1813–1855), renowned Danish religiou philosopher whose Existentialist world view was explicated in such important works as Enten-Eller: Et Livs Fragment (1843:English trans as Either/Or: A Fragment of Life, 1944), Frygt og Baeven (1843; English trans. as Fear and Trembling, 1939), Gjentagelsen (1843; English trans as Repetition, 1942), Philosophiske Smuler, eller en Smule Philosoph (1844; English trans. as Philosophical Fragments, or a Fragment o Philosophy, 1936), Begrebet Angest (1844; English trans. as The Concept of Dread, 1944), Stadier paa Livets vei (1845; English trans. as Stages on Life's Way, 1940), Kjerlighedens Gjerninger (1847; English trans. as Works of Love, 1946) and Sygdommen til Døden (1849; English trans. as The Sickness unto Death, 1941).

Kikuchi Kan (1888–1948), Japanese dramatist, novelist and publisher.

Killligrew, Henry (1613–1700), English dramatist; brother of Thomas Killigrew the elder and Sir William Killigrew.

Killigrew, Thomas, the elder (1612–1683), English dramatist; father o Thomas Killigrew the younger and brother of Henry Killigrew and Sir William Killigrew.

Killigrew, Thomas, the younger (1657–1719), English dramatist; son of Thomas Killigrew the elder.

Killigrew, Sir William (c.1606–1695), English dramatist; brother of Henry Killigrew and Thomas Killigrew the elder.

Kilmer, (Alfred) Joyce (1886–1918), American poet who wrote the famous Trees (1913); died in World War I; husband of Aline Kilmer.

Kilmer, Aline (1888–1941), American poet; wife of (Alfred) Joyce Kilmer.

Kilpi, Volter (1874–1939), Finnish novelist who became best known for his novel Alastalon salissa (In the Parlour at Alastalo, 1933).

Kilvert, (Robert) Francis (1840–1879), English clergyman and diarist.

Kimball, Richard Burleigh (1816–1892), American lawyer and novelist.

Kimhi, David (c.1160–c.1235), celebrated Jewish scholar of the Hebrew language; son of Joseph Kimhi and brother of Moses Kimhi.

Kimhi, Joseph (c1105–c.1170), Jewish grammarian, biblical scholar and poet; father of David and Moses Kimhi.

Kimhi, Moses (died c.1190), Jewish grammarian; son of Joesph Kimhi and brother of David Kimhi.

Kim Man-jung (17th Century), Korean writer.

Kinck, Hans E(rnst) (1865–1926), Norwegian novelist, short-story writer, dramatist and essayist, particularly remembered for his novel Sneskavlen brast (The Avalanche Broke, 3 vols, 1918–19).

Kindī, Ya'qūb ibn Ishāq as-Sabah, al (died c.870), important Arab Islamic philosopher.

King, Charles (1844–1933), American army officer and writer.

King, Clarence (1842–1901), American geologist and writer.

King, Grace Elizabeth (1851–1932), American novelist and short-story writer.

King, Henry (1592–1669), English Anglican bishop and poet, author of Poems, Elegies, Paradoxes and Sonets (1657), in which is found his celebrated Exequy to his Matchless never to be forgotten friend.

King, Martin Luther, Jr (1929–1968), famous American Baptist preacher, civil rights leader and writer; won the Nobel Prize for Peace (1964); was assassinated.

King, Thomas Starr (1824–1864), American Unitarian minister and writer.

King, William (1663–1712), English poet and writer.

King-Hall, (William Richard) Stephen, Baron (1893–1966), English writer and editor.

Kinglake, Alexander William (1809–1891), English traveller and writer, best known for his Eothen: or traces of travel brought home from the East (1844).

Kingo, Thomas (Hansen) (1634–1703), esteemed Danish poet, hymnist and clergyman.

Kingsley, Charles (1819–1875), noted English Anglican clergyman, novelist, essayist and poet; brother of George Henry Kingsley and Henry Kingsley.

Kingsley, George Henry (1827–1892), English physician and traveller, author of South Sea Bubbles (1872); brother of Charles and Henry Kingsley.

Kingsley, Henry (1830–1876), English novelist, particularly remembered for his Ravenshoe (1861) and The Hillyars and the Burtons (1865); brother of Charles and George Henry Kingsley.

Kingsley, Mary Henrietta (1862–1900), English traveller, author of Travels in West Africa (1897) and West African Studies (1899).

Kingsley, Sidney (actually Sidney Kirshner) (1906–1995), American dramatist and actor.

Kingsmill, Hugh (actually Hugh Kingsmill Lunn) (1889–1949), English novelist, biographer and critic.

Kingston, W(illiam) H(enry) G(iles) (1814–1880), English writer of stories for boys.

Kinkel, Gottfried (1815–1882), German poet who was active in the revolutionary uprisings of 1848 and escaped from prison to live abroad in exile.

Kino Tsurayuki (died c.945), Japanese nobleman, court official and poet.

Kinsey, Alfred Charles (1894–1956), American zoologist who wrote the controversial studies Sexual Behavior in the Human Male (1948) and Sexual Behavior in the Human Female (1953).

Kipling, (Joseph) Rudyard (1865–1936), famous English poet, novelist and short-story writer, particularly remembered for his children's classics The Jungle Books (1894–95) and Kim (1901); won the Nobel Prize for Literature (1907); brother-in-law of (Charles) Wolcott Balestier.

Kirby, William (1817–1906), English-born Canadian writer, best known for his classic novel The Golden Dog (1877).

Kireyevsky, Ivan Vasilievich (1806–1856), Russian critic and editor.

Kirkland, Caroline Stansbury (1801–1864), American writer; granddaughter of Joseph Stansbury and mother of Joseph Kirkland.

Kirkland, Joseph (1830–1894), American novelist, author of Zury: The Meanest Man in Spring County (1887), The McVeys (1888) and The Captain of Company Z (1891); son of Caroline Stansbury Kirkland.

Kirkwood, James (1924–1989), American writer, co-author of the musical A Chorus Line (1975).

Kirst, Hans Helmut (1914–1989), German novelist, particularly remembered for Die Nacht der Generale (1962; English trans. as The Night of the Generals, 1963).

Kisfaludy, Károly (1788–1830), Hungarian dramatist, a leading figure in the Romantic movement in his homeland.

Kisfaludy, Sándor (1772–1844), Hungarian writer.

Kitabatake Chikafusa (1292–1354), Japanese warrior and statesman who wrote the important treatise Jinnō shōtōki (Record of the Legitimate Succession of the Divine Emperors, 1339).

Kitchin, Clifford Henry Benn (1895–1967), English novelist, short-story writer and barrister.

Kittel, Rudolf (1853–1929), German Old Testament scholar.

Kittredge, George Lyman (1860–1941), eminent American literary scholar and critic, an authority on Shakespeare, Chaucer and Malory.

Kivi, Aleksis (actually Aleksis Stenvall) (1834–1872), important Finnish novelist, dramatist and poet, duly recognised as the father of the Finnish novel and drama.

Kjellen, (Johan) Rudolf (1864–1922), Swedish political scientist who coined the term geopolitics and wrote the treatise Staten som lifs-form (The State as a Life-Form, 1918–19).

Klabund (actually Alfred Henschke) (1890–1928), German poet, dramatist and novelist, a prominent Expressionist.

Klaczko, Julian (1825–1906), Lithuanian journalist and literary critic.

Klaj or Clajust, Johann (1616–1656), German poet.

Klaproth, Heinrich Julius (1783–1835), German Orientalist and explorer, author of the valuable Asia polyglotta nebst Sprachatlas (Asia Polyglotta with Language Atlas, 1823).

Klein, A(braham) Moses (1909–1972), esteemed Canadian poet and writer whose works reflect his Talmudic studies.

Klein, Charles (1867–1915), American dramatist who was best known for his sentimental plays The Auctioneer (1901) and The Music Master (1904).

Klein, Melanie (née Reizes) (1882–1960), influential Austrian-born English psychoanalyst who specialized in child therapy, author of The Psychoanalysis of Children (1932).

Kleist, (Bernd) Heinrich (Wilhelm) von (1777–1811), important German dramatist, writer and poet; committed suicide.

Kleist, Ewald Christian von (1715–1759), German poet, much admired for his Der Früling (The Spring, 1749); died from wounds sustained in the battle of Kundersdorf.

Klemm, Gustav Friedrich (1802–1867), noted German anthropologist, author of Allgemeine Kulturgeschichte der Menschheit (General Cultural History of Mankind, 10 vols, 1843–52) and Allgemeine Kulturwissenschaft (General Science of Culture, 2 vols, 1854–55).

Kleutgen, Joseph (1811–1883), German Jesuit philosopher.

Klinger, Friedrich Maximilian von (1752–1831), German dramatist and novelist, a prominent figure in the Sturm und Drang movement.

Klonowic, Sebastian (Fabian) (c.1545–1602), Polish poet who wrote both Polish and Latin verse.

Kloos, Willem Johan Theodor (1859–1938), Dutch poet and critic whose sonnets were admired.

Klopstock, Friedrich Gottlieb (1724–1803), eminent German poet of lyric refinement, author of Des Messias (The Messiah, 1749–73) and various odes.

Kluckhohn, Clyde (Kay Maben) (1905–1960), American anthropologist who wrote Navaho Witchcraft (1944) and Mirror for Man (1949).

Klyuchevsky, Vasily Osipovich (1841–1911), Russian historian whose work was marked by a regard for sociological principles.

Knapp, Samuel Lorenzo (1783–1838), American essayist.

Knebel, Karl Ludwig von (1744–1834), German poet who was highly esteemed for his sonnets.

Kneeland, Abner (1774–1844), American Universalist minister and freethinker.

Knigge, Adolf Franz Friedrich, Freiherr von (1752–1796), German novelist.

Knight, Charles (1791–1873), English publisher and writer.

Knight, G(eorge Richard) Wilson (1897–1985), English literary scholar and critic, especially known for his Shakespearian studies.

Knight, Sarah Kemble (1666–1727), American teacher and buisnesswoman who wrote an interesting travel journal (published 1825).

Knighton, Henry (died c.1396), English chronicler.

Knolles, Richard (c.1550–1610), English historian, author of a Generall Historie of the Turkes, from the first beginning of that Nation (1603).

Knowles, James Sheridan (1784–1862), English actor and dramatist.

Knowles, Sir James Thomas (1831–1908), English editor and architect.

Knowles, John (1926–2001), American writer who won notable success with his novel A Separate Peace (1959).

Knox, Edmund George Valpy (1881–1971), English essayist, humorist and editor who, as Evoe, served as editor of Punch (1932–49); brother of Ronald Arbuthnott Knox.

Knox, John (c.1513–1572), Scottish Protestant Reformation leader, author of the History of the Reformation of Religioun within the realme of Scotland (published 1587).

Knox, Ronald Arbuthnott (1888–1957), English Roman Catholic theologian, writer and translator of the Bible; brother of Edmund George Valpy Knox.

Knudtzon, Jørgen Alexander (1854–1917), Norwegian Oriental scholar.

Knayazhnin, Yakov Borisovich (1742–1791), Russian writer.

Kobayashi Takiji (1903–1933), Japanese writer and political radical.

Kober, Arthur (1900–1974), Polish-born American dramatist and writer.

Koch, Kenneth (Jay) (1925–2002), American poet, dramatist and writer.

Koch, Martin (1882–1940), Swedish novelist, best known for his Arbetare (Workers, 1912), Timmerdalen (Timber Valley, 1913) and Guds vackra värld (God's Beautiful World, 1916).

Kochanowska, Jan (1530–1584), significant Polish poet and dramatist, renowned for his poems Treny (1580; English trans. as Laments, 1920).

Kochowski, Wespazjan (1633–1700), Polish poet and historian, remembered for his poetic epic Psalmodia polska (Polish Psalmody, 1695).

Kock, Charles-Paul de (1793–1871), French novelist.

Kōda Rohan (actually Kōda Shigeyuki) (1867–1947), Japanese novelist and essayist.

Koeber, Raphael von (1842–1923), Russian philosopher.

Koeppen, Wolfgang (1906–1996), German novelist and essayist.

Koestler, Arthur (1905–1983), Hungarian-born English journalist, novelist and critic, particularly known for his novel Darkness at Noon (1940); committed suicide.

Koffka, Kurt (1886–1941), German-born American psychologist whose pioneering work in Gestalt psychology was elaborated in his Gestalt Psychology (1929) and Principles of Gestalt Psychology (1935).

Kogălniceanu, Mihail (1817–1891), Romanian political reformer and historian.

Koghbatzi, Eznik (5th Century), Armenian writer.

Kohler, Josef (1849–1919), German philosopher.

Kohler, Kaufmann (1843–1926), German-born American Jewish rabbi and theologian of Reform Judaism, author of Jewish Theology Systematically and Historically Considered (1918).

Köhler, Wolfgang (1887–1967), German-born American psychologist who was a major figure in the development of Gestalt psychology, author of the influential Intelligenzprüfungen an Menschenaffen (1917; English trans. as The Mentality of Apes, 1924).

Kohut, Alexander (1842–1894), Hungarian-born American Jewish rabbi and scholar.

Kokoschka, Oskar (1886–1980), Austrian-born English painter and writer.

Kolcsey, Ferenc (1790–1838), Hungarian poet, critic and politician, author of the Hungarian National anthem.

Koldewey, Robert (1855–1925), German architect and archaeologist.

Kollár, Ján (1793–1852), Slovak pastor and poet, author of the epic poem Slávy dcera (The Daughter of Slava).

Kołłataj, Hugo (1750–1812), Polish Roman Catholic priest, educator and politician who advocated radical reform in the structure of Polish society.

Koltsov, Aleksie Vasilievich (1809–1842), Russian poet.

Komroff, Manuel (1890–1974), American novelist and short-story writer.

Konarski, Stanisław (1700–1773), Polish Roman Catholic priest and writer on historical and political subjects.

Konopnicka, Maria (actually Maria Wasiłowska) (1842–1910), admired Polish short-story writer and poet, remembered especially for her poetic cycle Italia (Italy, 1901).

Konrad von Würzburg (c.1225–1287), German poet who upheld the cause of a dying chivalry.

Kook, Abraham Isaac (1865–1935), Latvian mystic, Zionist, chief rabbi of Palestine and essayist.

Kopisch, August (1799–1853), Polish poet and painter.

Koppers, Wilhelm (1886–1961), German-born Austrian Roman Catholic priest and cultural anthropologist.

Koraïs, Adamántios (1748–1833), influential Greek scholar of humanistic ideals.

Körner, (Karl) Theodor (1791–1813), German poet and dramatist especially known for his patriotic play Zriny (1812).

Korolenko, Vladimir Galaktionovich (1853–1921), Russian short story writer and journalist.

Korsch, Karl (1886–1961), German political philosopher and Marxist theoretician.

Korzybski, Alfred (Habdank Skarbek) (1879–1950), Polish-born American scientist and philosopher, author of Science and Sanity: An Introduction to Non-Aristotelian Systems and General Semantics (1933).

Kosinski, Jerzy (Nikodem) (1933–1991), Polish-born American novelist, especially known for The Painted Bird (1965); committed suicide.

Kosovel, Srečko (1904–1926), Slovenian writer.

Kosztolányi, Dezso (1885–1936), admired Hungarian poet, novelist, short-story writer and critic, author of the novel Édes Anna (1926; English trans. as Wonder Maid, 1947).

Kotlyarevsky, Ivan (1769–1838), Ukrainian writer, best known for the Eneyida (1798), a burlesque-travesty of Virgil's Aeneid.

Kotsyubinsky, Mikhaylo (1864–1913), Ukrainian novelist and short story writer.

Kotzebue, August (Friedrich Ferdinand) von (1761–1819), prominent German dramatist, writer and court official in Russia, denounced as a traitor to the German fatherland for his service in Russia, he was assassinated by a member of a radical student group.

Kovalevskaya, Sofia (1850–1891), Russian mathematician and novelist.

Kowatake Mokuami (1816–1893), Japanese dramatist of the Kabuki theatre.

Kraemer, Hendrik (1880–1965), Dutch theologian.

Kráľ, Janko (1822–1876), notable Slovak poet.

Krasicki, Ignacy (1735–1801), Polish poet, writer and Roman Catholic archbishop.

Krasiński, Zygmunt, Count (1812–1859), esteemed Polish poet and dramatist.

Kraszewski, Jósef Ignacy (1812–1887), Polish novelist, poet, dramatist, historian and critic.

Kraus, Karl (1874–1936), Austrian writer, dramatist, poet and editor.

Krause, Herbert (1905–1976), American writer and poet.

Krause, Karl Christian Friedrich (1781–1832), German philosopher.

Kretschmer, Ernst (1888–1964), German psychiatrist, particularly known for his controversial treatise Körperbau und Charakter (1921; English trans. as Physique and Character, 1925).

Kretschmer, Paul (1866–1956), German-born Austrian classical linguist.

Kretzer, Max (1854–1941), German novelist of the Expressionist school.

Kreutzwald, F(riedrich) Reinhold (1803–1882), Estonian physician, folklorist and poet who compiled and contributed original verse to the national epic poem the Kalevipoeg (The Son of Kalevi, 1857–61).

Krėvė-Mickievičius, Vincas (1882–1954), leading Lithuanian poet, dramatist and philologist who was also known as Vincas Kreve.

Kreymborg, Alfred (1883–1966), American poet and dramatist.

Krige, (Mattheus) Uys (1910–1987), South African journalist, novelist, dramatist and poet who wrote in both Afrikaans and English.

Kristensen, (Aage) Tom (1893–1974), Danish poet, novelist and critic.

Kristensen, W(ilhelm) Brede (1867–1953), Norwegian-born Dutch historian who was known for his studies in religious symbolism.

Krianić, Juraj (1618–1683), Croatian Roman Catholic priest and scholar who was a leading advocate of Pan-Slavism in Russia.

Krleža, Miroslav (1893–1981), Croatian novelist and dramatist.

Krochmal, Nachman (1785–1840), Polish Jewish scholar and philosopher, author of the notable More nevukhe ha-zman (The Guide for the Perplexed of Our Time).

Kroeber, A(lfred) L(ouis) (1876–1960), American cultural anthropologist, author of Anthropology (1923), Configurations of Culture Growth (1945) and The Nature of Culture (1952).

Kropotkin, Pyotr Alexeievich (1842–1921), prominent Russian revolutionary and anarchist theoretician.

Kruczkowski, Leon (1900–1962), Polish writer.

Krumbacher, Karl (1856–1909), German scholar, an authority on Byzantine culture.

Krünitz, Johann Georg (1728–1796), German philosopher, physician and encyclopaedist.

Krusenstjerna, Agnes von (1894–1940), Swedish novelist.

Krŭst'o, Krustyu (1866–1910), Bulgarian writer.

Krutch, Joseph Wood (1893–1970), American drama critic and naturalist.

Krylov, Ivan Andreievich (1769–1844), Russian writer who won distinction for his fables in verse.

Kuan Han-ch'ing (c.1241–c.1320), Chinese dramatist.

Kudirka, Vincas (1858–1899), Lithuanian journalist, writer and patriot, author of the Lithuanian National Anthem.

Kugler, Franz (1808–1854), German historian.

Kuhn, (Franz Felix) Adalbert (1812–1881), German language scholar and folklorist who was an authority on the Indo-European peoples.

Kuhn, Thomas S(amuel) (1922–1996), American philosopher, author of the important study The Structure of Scientific Revolutions (1962).

Kūkai (actually Kobo Daishi) (774–835), Japanese Buddist saint, philosopher, poet, artist and calligrapher, founder of the Shingon (True Word) school of Buddhism.

Külpe, Oswald (1862–1915), German psychologist and philosopher, author of Gundriss der Psychologie (1893; English trans. as Outlines of Psychology, 1895) and Die Realisierung (Realization, 3 vols, 1912–23).

Kumazawa Banzan (1619–1691), Japanese philosopher who espoused the cause of political liberalism.

Kume Masao (1891–1952), Japanese novelist and dramatist.

Kunanbayev, Abai Ibragim (1845–1904), Kazakh writer.

Kuncewicz(owa), Maria (1899–1989), Polish novelist, short-story writer, essayist and dramatist.

Kung-sun Lung (c.320–c.250 BC), Chinese philosopher.

Kuo Hsi (11th Century), renowned Chinese artist and essayist.

Kuo Hsiang (died 312), Chinese philosopher and government official, reputed author of the Chuang-tzu, a fundamental work of Taoism.

Kupala, Yanka (1882–1942), Belorussian writer.

Kuprin, Alexander Ivanovich (1870–1938), Russian novelist and short-story writer.

Kürenberger (12th Century), Austrian Minnesinger, the earliest known by name, who also was called the Knight of Kurenberg.

Kurz, Hermann (1813–1873), German novelist, journalist, translator and editor, especially esteemed for his novels Schillers Heimatjahre (Schiller's Homeland Years, 1843) and Der Sonnenwirt (The Proprietor of the Sun Inn, 1855), and for his Erzählungen (Tales, 1858–63).

Kuwaki Genyoku (1874–1946), Japanese philosopher who espoused Kantian principles.

Kuyper, Abraham (1837–1920), Dutch Protestant theologian and politician.

Kuznetsov, Anatoli Vasilievich (1929–79), Russian writer, author of the autobiographical novel Baby Yar (1966; uncensored version, 1970), which described the Nazi and Soviet depredations in the Ukraine.

Kvaran, Einar Hjörleifsson (1859–1938), Icelandic journalist, novelist, short-story writer, dramatist and poet.

Kyd, Thomas (1558–1594), English dramatist, author of The Spanish Tragedie (1592), the first revenge play of the Elizabethan era.

Kyne, Peter B(ernard) (1880–1957), American writer.

Labadie, Jean de (1610–1674), French Protestant theologian who espoused pietism.

Labé, Louise (Charly Perrin) (c.1524–1566), French poet, admired for her sonnets.

Labeo, Marcus Antistius (died c.10), famous Roman jurist and writer on the law.

Labiche, Eugène-Marin (1815–1888), French dramatist who excelled in light comedies.

Labourche, Henry Du Pré (1831–1912), English journalist and politician who was known as Labby.

Labriola, Antonio (1843–1904), Italian philosopher who was known for his exposition of Marxism.

La Bruyère, Jean de (1645–1696), French writer, author of the satirical Les Caractères ou les moeurs de ce siècle (The Characters or the Manners of this Age, 1688).

La Calprenède, Gautier de Costes, Seigneur de (c.1610–c.1663), French writer.

La Chaussée, Pierre-Claude Nivelle de (1692–1745), French dramatist.

Lachmann, Karl (Konrad Friedrich Wilhelm) (1793–1851), notable German classical scholar who advanced the cause of textual criticism.

Laclos, Pierre (-Ambroise-François) Choderlos de (1741–1803), French soldier and novelist, author of the classic Les Liaisons dangereuses (1782; English trans. as Dangerous Acquaintances, 1924).

Lacordaire, (Jean-Baptiste-) Henri (1802–1861), French Roman Catholic ecclesiastic and writer.

Lacretelle, Jacques de (1888–1985), French novelist whose finest work was Sabine (1932).

Lacretelle, Jean-Charles-Dominique de (1766–1855), French journalist and historian who was known as Lacretelle le Jeune.

Lactantius (actually Lucius Caecilius Firmianus Lactantius) (c.240–c.320), Roman Christian apologist, author of the Divine Institutiones (The Divine Precepts).

La Curne de Sainte-Pelaye, Jean-Baptiste de (1697–1781), French medievalist and lexicographer.

Lacy, Ernest (1863–1916), American dramatist and poet.

Ladd, George Trumbull (1842–1921), American philosopher and experimental psychologist.

Ladd, Joseph Brown (1764–1786), American physician and poet, remembered for The Poems of Arouet (1786).

Ladd, William (1778–1841), American writer and lecturer on world peace.

La Farge, Christopher (1897–1956), American writer, poet, painter and architect; grandson of John La Farge.

La Farge, John (1835–1910), American artist and writer; grandfather of Christopher and Oliver (Hazard Perry) La Farge.

La Farge, Oliver (Hazard Perry) (1901–1963), American ethnologist and writer; grandson of John La Farge.

La Farina, Giuseppe (1815–1863), Italian revolutionary leader and writer of the Risorgimento movement.

La Fayette, Maire-Madeleine (Pioche de la Vergne), Comtesse de (1634–1693), French novelist, author of La Princesse de Clèves (1678).

Laffitte, Pierre (1823–1903), French philosopher who espoused positivism.

La Flesche, Francis (1857–1932), American ethnologist whose heritage as a native American is delineated in his memoir The Middle Five (1900).

La Flesche, Susette (Indian name Bright Eyes) (1854–1903), American writer and lecturer who was an activist on behalf of native American causes.

Lafontaine, Henri-Marie (1854–1943), Belgian lawyer and advocate of international peace; won the Nobel Prize for Peace (1913).

La Fontaine, Jean de (1621–1695), eminent French poet and writer, celebrated for his Fables choisies mises en vers (12 vols, 1668–94).

La Forge, Louis de (17th Century), French philosopher of the Cartesian school.

Laforgue, Jules (1860–1887), gifted French poet, a leading exponent of vers libre and Symbolism.

Lagerkvist, Pär (Fabian) (1891–1974), Swedish novelist, poet and dramatist whose most celebrated work was the novel Barabbas (1950); won the Nobel Prize for Literature (1951).

Lagerlöf, Selma (Ottiliana Lovisa) (1858–1940), famous Swedish novelist and short-story writer; won the Nobel Prize for Literature (1909).

Lagrange, Marie-Joseph (1855–1938), French Roman Catholic theologian and biblical scholar.

La Guma, Alex (1925–85), South African novelist, author of A Walk in the Night (1962), And a Threefold Cord (1964), The Stone-Country (1965), In the Fog of the Season's End (1972) and Time of the Butcherbird (1979).

La Harpe, Jean-François de (1739–1803), French poet, dramatist and critic.

Lahbabi, Mohammed Aziz (1922–1993), Moroccan philosopher, writer, critic and poet.

La Hontan, Louis-Armand de Lom d'Arce, Baron de (1666–1715), French soldier and writer.

Laidlaw, William (1780–1845), Scottish poet.

Lajpat Rai, Lala (1865–1928), Indian politician and writer, a prominent figure in the anti-British nationalist movement and Hindu supremacist.

Lake, Kirsopp (1872–1946), English biblical scholar.

Lalic, Ivan (1931–1996), Serbian poet.

La Marche, Olivier de (c.1425–1502), French historian and poet.

Lamarck, Jean-Baptiste Pierre Antoine de Monet, Chevalier de (1744–1829), famous French naturalist, author of Philosophie Zoologique (1809).

Lamartine, Alphonse (Marie Louis) de (1790–1869), prominent French poet, historian and statesman, very much admired for his poetry collection Méditations poétiques (1820).

Lamb, Charles (1775–1834), noted English essayist, critic and poet, esteemed for his Essays of Elia (1823) and The Last Essays of Elia (1833); brother of Mary Ann Lamb.

Lamb, Mary Ann (1764–1847), English writer; sister of Charles Lamb.

Lambert, Johann Heinrich (1728–1777), German mathematician, astronomer, physicist and philosopher.

Lambert of Hersfeld (1025–c.1088), learned German scholar, author of the valuable Annales Hersveldenses (c.1078; published 1525).

Lamennais, (Hughes-) Félicité (-Robert de) (1782–1854), French Roman Catholic priest and philosopher who championed political liberalism.

La Mettrie, Julian Offroy de (1709–1751), French physician and philosopher who espoused the cause of materialism and atheism.

Lamontague-Beauregard, Blanche (1889–1958), French-Canadian poet of distinction.

La Mothe Le Vayer, François de (1588–1672), French philosopher who was known as a committed skeptic.

La Motte, Antoine Houdar de (1672–1731), French poet and dramatist.

L'Amour, Louis (Dearborn) (actually Louis Dearborn LaMoore) (1908–1988), American novelist and short-story writer of a prolific output.

Lampedusa, Giuseppe Tomasi Di (1896–1957), Italian writer, best known for his novel Il gattopardo (The Leopard, 1956).

Lampman, Archibald (1861–1899), prominent Canadian poet.

Lamprecht, Karl Gottfried (1856–1915), eminent German historian, author of the exhaustive Deutsche Geschichte (German History, 12 vols, 1891–1901).

Lancaster, Sir Osbert (1908–1986), English cartoonist and writer who was especially esteemed for his books on architecture.

Lancelot, Claude (c.1615–1695), French language scholar.

Lanciani, Rodolfo Amadeo (1847–1929), Italian archaeologist and topographer who wrote important works on ancient Rome.

Landau, Ezekiel (1713–1793), Polish Jewish rabbi, author of a valuable book on the Halakha.

Lander, Richard Lemon (1804–1834), English explorer who left interesting accounts of his travels in West Africa.

Landon, Letitia Elizabeth (1802–1838), English poet and novelist who was known as L.E.L.

Landon, Melville de Lancey (1839–1910), American journalist and writer who wrote under the name Eli Perkins.

Landor, Robert Eyres (1781–1869), English dramatist and poet, brother of Walter Savage Landor.

Landor, Walter Savage (1775–1864), English poet and writer; brother of Robert Eyres Landor.

Landstad, Magnus Brostrup (1802–1880), Norwegian clergyman, poet and hymnist.

Lang, Andrew (1844–1912), esteemed Scottish writer and poet who excelled in writing fairy-tales.

Lange, Friedrich Albert (1828–1875), German philosopher and socialist, a noted materialist.

Langer, František (1888–1965), Czech physician, dramatist and short-story writer.

Langer, Susanne K(nauth) (1895–1985), American philosopher, author of Philosophy in a New Key: A Study in the Symbolism of Reason, Rite and Art (1942).

Langhorne, John (1735–1779), English poet and translator, best known for The Country Justice (3 parts, 1774–77).

Langland, William (c.1330–c.1400), English poet, reputed author of the famous Vision of William concerning Piers the Plowman.

Langlois, Charles-Victor (1863–1929), French scholar, an authority on the Middle Ages.

Langtoft, Peter (died c.1307), Anglo-Norman poet and churchman, author of a chronicle in alexandrines.

Languet, Hubert (1518–1581), French writer and diplomat.

Lanier, Emilia (née Bassano) (1569–1645), Italian-born English poet.

Lanier, Sidney (1842–1881), American poet, writer and composer.

Lanigan, George Thomas (1845–1886), Canadian-born American journalist and poet who was known for his wit.

Lanman, Charles Rockwell (1850–1941), American Sanskrit scholar and editor who compiled the Sanskrit Reader (1884).

La Noue, François de (1531–1591), French soldier and writer, author of the Discours politiques et militaires (1587).

Lansel, Peider (1863–1943), Italian poet, short-story writer and textual scholar who edited anthologies of Raeto-Romance works.

Lanzi, Luigi (1732–1810), Italian art historian, archaeologist and antiquarian.

Lao-tzu (6th Century BC), celebrated Chinese philosopher of Taoism.

Larbaud, Valery-Nicolas (1881–1957), French novelist, short-story writer and critic.

Larcom, Lucy (1824–1893), American Abolitionist and poet.

Lardner, Ring(gold Wilmer) (1885–1933), American short-story writer.

Larivey, Pierre de (c.1540–1619), French dramatist and canon.

Larkin, Philip (Arthur) (1922–1985), admired English poet, dramatist and essayist, particularly esteemed for his poetry collections The Less Deceived (1955) and The Whitsun Weddings (1964).

La Roche, Sophie von (née Gutermann) (1731–1807), German novelist, author of the much admired Geschichte des Fräuleins von Sternheim (1771; English trans. as History of Lady Sophia Sternheim, 1776).

La Rochefoucauld, (François, Duc de) (1613–1680), French writer who excelled in his Maximes (1665), a form of epigram.

La Rochefoucauld-Liancourt, François-Alexandre-Frederic, Duc de (1747–1827), French educator, social reformer and writer.

Laromiguière, Pierre (1756–1837), French philosopher, especially known for his Leçons de philosophie (Lessons on Philosophy, 1815–18).

Larousse, Pierre (-Athanase) (1817–1875), French grammarian, lexicographer and encyclopaedist, especially known for his Grand Dictionnaire universel du XIXe siècle (15 vols, 1866–76; supplements, 1878, 1890).

Larra (y Sanchez de Castro), Mariano José de (1809–1837), Spanish poet and writer, known for his satirical bent.

Larreta, Enrique Rodríguez (1875–1961), Argentine novelist, author of the well-known La Gloria de Don Ramiro (The Glory of Don Ramiro, 1908).

Larsen, Nella (1891–1964), American novelist.

La Sale or La Salle, Antoine de (c.1386–c.1460), French writer, best remembered for his Le Petit Jehan de Saintré (c.1456).

Lascaris, John (c.1445–c.1535), Greek scholar and diplomat.

Las Casas, Bartolomé de (1474–1566), Spanish missionary and historian, author of the famous Historia de las Indias.

Las Cases, Emmanuel (-Augustin-Dieudonné-Joseph), Comte de (1766–1842), French government official and politician who wrote an account of the last days of Napoleon in his Memorial de St Helene (1823).

Lashley, Karl S(pencer) (1890–1958), American psychologist, author of Brain Mechanisms and Intelligence (1929).

Lasker-Schüler, Else (1869–1945), German poet, novelist, short-story writer and dramatist who excelled in poetic lyricism.

Laski, Harold J(oseph) (1893–1950), influential English political scientist who championed the cause of socialism.

Lasswell, Harold D(wight) (1902–1978), important American political scientist who was an authority on power relationships in the political arena.

La Taille, Jean de (c.1540–c.1607), French poet and dramatist.

Lathrop, George Parsons (1851–1898), American writer; husband of Rose Hawthorne, later Mother Alphonsa Lathrop.

Lathrop, Mother Alphonsa (originally Rose Hawthorne) (1851–1926), American writer, poet and Roman Catholic nun; wife of George Parsons Lathrop.

Latimer, Hugh (c.1485–1555), notable English Protestant reformer and preacher; was burned at the stake during the reign of the Catholic queen Mary Tudor.

Latini, Brunetto (c.1220–c.1294), Italian politician and scholar.

Lattimore, Owen (1900–1989), American educator, government official and writer whose Ordeal by Slander (1950) was an account of his experience as a target of the McCarthy investigation into alleged Communist activities in the US government; brother of Richmond (Alexander) Lattimore.

Lattimore, Richmond (Alexander) (1906–1984), American poet, critic and translator; brother of Owen Lattimore.

Laud, William (1573–1645), English statesman and archbishop of Canterbury (1633–45); was accused of treason in the House of Commons, tried, found guilty and beheaded.

Laughlin, James (1914–1997), American publisher, writer and poet, founder of the innovative New Directions publishing firm.

Laugier, Marc-Antoine (1713–1769), French historian.

Laurence, Margaret (actually Jean Margaret Wemys) (1926–1987), Canadian novelist and short-story writer, author of the novels The Stone Angel (1964), A Jest of God (1966), The Fire-Dwellers (1969) and The Diviners (1974).

Laurent, François (1810–1887), Belgian legal scholar and historian, particularly esteemed for his monumental Études sur l'historie de l'humanitè (Studies on the History of Humanitié, 18 vols, 1861–70).

Lautréamont, Comte de (actually Isidore-Lucien Ducasse) (1846–1870), French poet whose works were marked by a penchant for violent expression.

Lavater, Johann Kaspar (1741–1801), Swiss physiognomist, pastor, patriot, poet and writer.

Lavin, Mary (1912–1996), Irish-born American short-story writer.

Lavisse, Ernest (1842–1922), French scholar.

Lavrov, Pyotr (Lavrovich) (1823–1900), Russian philosopher of socialism.

Law, William (1686–1761), English writer on Christian subjects.

Lawless, Emily (1845–1913), Irish novelist and poet.

Lawrence, D(avid) H(erbert) (1885–1930), famous English novelist, short-story writer, essayist and poet who was especially known for his themes of social and sexual liberation, most candidly in his novel Lady Chatterly's Lover (1928).

Lawrence, George Alfred (1827–1876), English novelist, best remembered for his Guy Livingstone (1857).

Lawrence, Josephine (1890–1978), American writer.

Lawrence, T(homas) E(dward) (1888–1935), renowned English adventurer and writer who was known as Lawrence of Arabia, author of The Seven Pillars of Wisdom (1926).

Lawson, Henry (Archibald) (1867–1922), Australian short-story writer and poet.

Lawson, James (1799–1880), Scottish-born American poet and dramatist.

Lawson, John Howard (1895–1977), American dramatist.

Lawson, Thomas W(illiam) (1857–1925), American stockbroker and writer, best remembered for his muckraking articles and his novel Friday, the Thirteenth (1907).

Laxness, Halldór (Kiljan) (actually Halldór Kiljan Gudjónsson) (1902–1998), Icelandic novelist, poet and dramatist who espoused socialist themes; won the Nobel Prize for Literature (1955).

Layamon (13th Century), English poet and priest, author of the romance-chronicle the Brut (c.1200).

Layard, Sir Austen Henry (1817–1894), English archaeologist, diplomat and politician who wrote the well-known Discoveries in the Ruins of Nineveh and Babylon (1853).

Laye, Camara (1924–1980), notable Guinean writer, author of the novels L'Enfant noir (1953; English trans. as The Dark Child, 1954), Le Regard du roi (1954; English trans. as The Radiance of the King, 1956) and Dramouss (1966; English trans. as A Dream of Africa, 1968).

Lazarus, Emma (1849–1887), American poet, writer and translator, best known for her poem The New Colossus (1883), which was inscribed on the Statue of Liberty in New York harbour.

Lazarus, Moritz (1824–1903), prominent German Jewish philosopher and psychologist, particularly known for his opposition to anti-Semitism and as founder of comparative psychology.

Lea, Henry Charles (1825–1909), American historian who was especially known for his studies on the history of the Roman Catholic Church.

Lea, Homer (1876–1912), American soldier who predicted the Japanese attack on the US some 30 years in advance in his The Valor of Ignorance (1909).

Leacock, Stephen Butler (1869–1944), admired English-born Canadian writer who won extraordinary success as a humorist.

Leake, William Martin (1777–1860), English soldier, topographer and antiquarian, author of Travels in the Morea (1830) and Travels in Northern Greece (1835).

Leakey, L(ouis) S(eymour) B(azett) (1903–1972), famous English archaeologist and anthropologist.

Leal, António Duarte Gomes (1848–1921), Portuguese poet and political pamphleteer, best known for his poetry collection Claridades do sul (Bright Lights of the South, 1875).

Lear, Edward (1812–1888), English artist, writer and poet who excelled in nonsense versification.

Leavis, F(rank) R(aymond) (1895–1978), influential English literary and social critic.

Leblanc, Maurice(-Marie-Émile) (1864–1941), French novelist and short-story writer who became best known for his crime fiction.

Le Bon, Gustave (1841–1931), French social psychologist, author of Les loi psychologiques de l'évolution des peuples (1894; English trans. as The Psychology of Peoples, 1898), La psychologie des foules (1895; English trans. as The Crowd, 1896) and La révolution française et la psychologie des révolutions (1912; English trans. as The Psychology of Revolution, 1913).

Le Braz, Anatole (1859–1926), French folklorist, novelist and poet.

Lechón, Jan (actually Leszek Serafinowicz) (1899–1956), Polish poet, editor and diplomat; committed suicide.

Lecky, William Edward Hartpole (1838–1903), Irish historian, author of a History of England in the Eighteenth Century (1878–90).

Leclerc, Jean (1657–1736), Swiss-born Dutch biblical scholar and encyclopaedist.

Le Conte, Joseph (1823–1901), American naturalist who espounsed the theories of Darwin and Lyell.

Leconte de Lisle, Charles-Marie-René (1818–1894), French poet and translator, a leading figure among the Parnassians.

Ledgwidge, Francis (1891–1917), Irish poet; died in World War 1.

Ledru-Rollin, Alexandre-Auguste (1807–1874), French lawyer and writer on politics who played a major role in bringing universal suffrage to his homeland.

Lee, Eliza Buckminster (c.1788–1864), American writer and translator.

Lee, Harriet (1757–1851), English novelist and dramatist; sister of Sophia Lee.

Lee, Nathaniel (c.1649–1692), English dramatist who became best known for his tragedies.

Lee, Sir Sidney (actually Solomon Lazarus Levi) (1859–1926), English scholar and lexicographer, particularly known for his Shakespearian studies.

Lee, Sophia (1750–1824), English novelist and dramatist; sister of Harriet Lee.

Lee, Vernon (actually Violet Paget) (1856–1935), English essayist, dramatist and novelist.

Leech, Margaret (Kernochan) (1893–1974), American novelist and biographer.

Leeuw, Gerardus van der (1890–1950), Dutch Reformed theologian and historian.

Le Fanu, Joseph Sheridan (1814–1873), Irish novelist and short-story writer who was known for his supernatural tales, especially In a Glass Darkly (1872).

Lefebvre, Georges (1874–1959), French historian.

Lefèvre d' Étaples, Jacques (c.1455–1536), French scholar, theologian and biblical translator.

Le Gallienne, Richard (1866–1947), English writer and poet.

Legare, Hugh Swinton (1797–1843), American lawyer, politician and writer.

Leggett, William (c.1802–1839), American journalist and writer.

Le Grand, Antoine (died 1699), French-born English Franciscan and philosopher.

Lehmann, Rosamond Nina (1901–1990), English novelist; sister of (Rudolph) John (Frederick) Lehmann.

Lehmann, (Rudolph) John (Frederick) (1907–1987), English poet, novelist, editor and publisher; brother of Rosamond Nina Lehmann.

Lehtonen, Joel (1881–1934), Finnish writer.

Leibniz, Gottfried Wilhelm (1646–1716), German philosopher and mathematician.

Leighton, Robert (1611–1684), English-born Scottish Presbyterian minister and writer.

Leino, Eino (actually Armas Eino Leopold Lönnbohm) (1878–1926), notable Finnish poet, novelist and translator, especially esteemed for his lyric poetry.

Leipoldt, C(hristiaan Frederik) Louis (1880–1947), South African dramatist, writer, poet and physician who wrote in Afrikaans.

Leiris, Michel (Julien) (1901–1990), French anthropologist, writer and poet.

Leisewitz, Johann Anton (1752–1806), German dramatist, best known for his Julius von Tarent (1776).

Leland, Charles Godfrey (1824–1903), American poet who wrote various works under the name Hans Breitmann, including numerous ballads.

Leland, John (1691–1766), English-born Irish Noncomformist minister and polemicist.

Lelewel, Joachim (1786–1861), Polish scholar and patriot.

Lemaire de Belges, Jean (1473–1525), Flemish poet and historian.

Le Maistre, Antoine (1608–1658), French writer on religion, founder of the Jansenists.

Le Maistre de Sacy, Isaac-Louis (1613–1684), French theologian and biblical translator.

Lemaître, Georges (1894–1966), Belgian astronomer and cosmologist who originated the big-bang theory of the creation of the universe.

Lemaître, (François-Élie-) Jules (1853–1914), French critic, writer and dramatist.

Lemay, (Léon-) Pamphile (1837–1918), French-Canadian poet and writer.

Lemercier, (Louise-Jean) Népomucéne (1771–1840), French poet and dramatist.

Lemnius, Simon (actually Margadant Lemnius) (c.1505–1550), German poet and scholar.

Lemonnier, (Antoine-Louis-) Camille (1844–1913), Belgian novelist, short-story writer and art critic.

Lemprière, John (died 1824), English classical scholar, author of the standard Bibliotheca Classica.

Lenau, Nikolaus (actually Nikolaus Franz Niembsch von Strehlenau) (1802–1850), Austrian poet.

Lenin, V(ladmir) I(lich) (actually Vladimir Ilich Ulyanov) (1870–1924), Russian Communist revolutionary and Marxist theoretician, founder and ruthless dictator of the Soviet Union.

Lennep, Jacob van (1802–1868), Dutch novelist and poet.

Lenngren, Anna Maria (née Malmstedt) (1754–1817), esteemed Swedish poet who was known for her fine craftsmanship.

Lennox, Charlotte (née Ramsay) (1720–1804), English novelist, author of The Female Quixote (1752).

Lenormand, Henri-René (1882–1951), French dramatist.

Lenormant, François (1837–1883), French archaeologist and numismatist.

Lenz, Hermann (1913–1998), esteemed German novelist and poet.

Lenz J(akob) M(ichael) R(einhold) (1751–1792), German poet and dramatist.

Lenz, Wilhelm von (1809–1883), Russian music scholar of German descent, especially remembered for his study of the three periods of Beethoven's creative life (2 vols, 1852).

Leo Africanus (c.1485–c.1554), Spanish traveller who left the interesting account Descrittione dell' Africa (1550; English trans. as A Geographical Historie of Africa, 1600).

León, Luis de (1527–1591), celebrated Spanish writer and poet whoes masterwork was the prose vol. De los nombres de Cristo (1583–85; published 1631).

Leonard, William Ellery (1876–1944), American poet, translator and critic.

Leonidas of Tarentum (3rd Century BC), Greek poet.

Leonov, Leonid (Maksimovich) (1899–1994), Russian novelist and dramatist.

Leonowens, Anna Harriette (née Crawford) (1834–1914), Welsh writer, author of The English Governess at the Siamese Court (1870) and The Romance of the Harem (1872).

Leontius of Byzantium (c.485–c.543), Byzantine monk and theologian whose major treatise was Libri tres contra Nestorianos et Eutychianos (Three Books Against the Nestorians and the Eutychians).

Leopardi, Giacomo (1798–1837), Italian lyric poet, scholar and philosopher.

Leopold, Aldo (1887–1948), American conservationist.

Leopold, Carl Gustaf (1756–1829), Swedish poet who served the courts of Gustav III and Gustav IV, particularly remembered for his ode Försynen (Providence, 1793).

Leopold, Jan Hendrik (1865–1925), Dutch poet whose finest work was the epic Cheops (1915).

Léotard, (Ange-) Philippe (1940–2001), French actor, chanssonier and poet.

Lepsius, Karl Richard (1810–1884), eminent German Egyptologist who played a major role in establishing scientific archaeology.

Lermontov, Mikhail (Yurievich) (1814–1841), important Russian novelist, poet and dramatist, author of the famous novel Geroy nashego vremeni (1840; English transalation as A Hero of Our Time, 1964); died in a duel.

Lerner, Max(well Allan) (1902–1992), Russian-born American political scientist, essayist and editor.

Lernet-Holenia, Alexander (1897–1976), Austrian novelist, dramatist and poet.

Leroux, Gaston (1868–1927), French novelist whose best known work was Le fantôme de l'opéra (The Phantom of the Opera, 1910).

Leroux, Pierre (1797–1871), French philosopher, economist, journalist and politician who championed socialism.

LeRoy, Edouard (1870–1954), French philosopher.

Lesage or Le Sage, Alain-René (1668–1747), French novelist and dramatist, best known for his classic picaresque novel Histoire de Gil Blas de Santillane (3 parts, 1715, 1724 1735).

Leskien, August (1840–1916), German linguist who was an authority on Baltic and Slavic linguistics.

Leskov, Nikolai Semyonovich (1831–1895), notable Russian short-story writer and novelist who wrote under the name Stebnitski.

Leslie or Lesley, John (1527–1596), Scottish Roman Catholic bishop and historian, author of De origine, moribus et rebus gestis Scotorum (1578).

Leśmian, Bolesław (actually Bolesław Lesman) (1878–1937), admired Polish poet who was the first in his homeland to embrace Symbolism and Expressionism.

Lessing, Gotthold Ephraim (1729–1781), celebrated German dramatist, poet, critic and scholar, author of such major works as the treatise Laokoon, oder über die Grenzen der Malerei und Poesie (Laocoon, or on the Limits of Painting and Poetry, 1766) and the plays Miss Sara Sampson (1755), Minna von Barnhelm (1767), Emilia Galotti (1772) and Nathan der Weise (Nathan the Wise, 1779).

L'Estrange, Sir Roger (1616–1704), English journalist, pamphleteer and translator.

Lethaby, William Richard (1857–1931), English writer and architect.

Leuba, J(ames) Henry (1868–1946), American psychologist.

Leucippus (5th Century BC), Greek philosopher.

Lever, Charles James (1806–1872), Irish novelist and editor.

Leverson, Ada (1862–1933), English novelist.

Levertin, Oscar Ivar (1862–1906), Swedish literary historian and poet, author of the admired poem Kung Salomo och Morolf (King Solomon and Morolf, 1905).

Levertov, Denise (1923–1997), English-born American poet, essayist and radical political activist.

Levi, Carlo (1902–1975), Italian writer, journalist and painter, especially remembered for his novel Cristo si è fermato a Eboli (1945; English trans. as Christ Stopped at Eboli, 1947).

Levi, Peter (1931–2000), English classical scholar, poet, writer and translator.

Levi, Primo (1919–1987), Italian writer and poet who wrote accounts of his imprisonment in the Auschwitz concentration camp in Se questo è un uomo (If This is a Man, 1947) and La regua (The Truce, 1963), and an acclaimed vol. of stories in Il sistema periodico (The Periodic Table, 1975).

Lévi, Sylvain (1863–1935), French Orientalist and lexicographer.

Levi ben Gershom (1288–1344), French mathematician, philosopher, astronomer and Talmudic and biblical scholar.

Levin, Hanoch (1943–99), Israeli dramatist whose works engendered controversy for their critical examination of political and social themes.

Levin, Meyer (1905–81), American writer.

Levita, Elijah (actually Eliyahu ben Asher Ha-Levi Ashkenazi) (1469–1549), German-born Jewish grammarian.

Levitsky, Ivan (actually Ivan Nechuv) (1838–1918), Ukrainian novelist.

Lévy-Bruhl, Lucien (1857–1939), French philosopher, author of La Morale et la science des moeurs (1903; English trans. as Ethics and Moral Science, 1905) and Les fonctions mentales dans les sociétés primitives (1910; English trans. as How Natives Think, 1926).

Lewald, Fanny (1811–1889), German novelist.

Lewes, George Henry (1817–1878), English philosopher, scientist, critic, dramatist and editor.

Lewin, Kurt (1890–1947), German-born American social psychologist who followed Gestalt principles.

Lewis, Alfred Henry (c.1858–1914), American writer, best known for his books on the Southwest.

Lewis, Alun (1915–1944), Welsh poet and short-story writer; died in World War II.

Lewis, Charles Bertran (1842–1924), American writer of a humorous bent who wrote under the name M. Quad.

Lewis, C(larence) I(rving) (1883–1964), American philosopher, author of Symbolic Logic (with Cooper Harold Langford, 1932), An Analysis of Knowledge and Valuation (1947) and The Ground and Nature of the Right (1955).

Lewis, C(live) S(taples) (1898–1963), notable English scholar, novelist and Christian apologist, especially admired for his Screwtape Letters (1942) and his children's stories in the Chronicles of Narnia series.

Lewis, David K(ellogg) (1941–2001), American philosopher, author of Counterfactuals (1973) and On the Plurality of Worlds (1986).

Lewis, Sir George Cornewall (1806–1863), English statesman and writer.

Lewis, (Harry) Sinclair (1885–1951), prominent American novelist and essayist, particularly known for his novels Babbitt (1922), Arrowsmith (1925) and Elmer Gantry (1927); won the Nobel Prize for Literature (1930).

Lewis, Janet (1899–1998), American writer and poet.

Lewis, Matthew Gregory (1775–1818), English novelist and dramatist, best known for his Gothic novel The Monk (1796).

Lewis, (Percy) Wyndham (1882–1957), English artist and writer.

Lewis, Sarah Anna (1824–1880), American poet who, as 'Estelle', became the friend and benefactor of Poe.

Lewis, Saunders (1893–1985), Welsh dramatist, poet, novelist, essayist and critic.

Lewis Glyn Cothi or Llywelyn y Glyn (15th Century), Welsh poet.

Lewisohn, Ludwig (1882–1955), German-born American novelist and critic, best remembered for his novel The Case of Mr. Crump (1926).

Leyden, John (1755–1811), Scottish poet and Orientalist, particularly known for his ballads.

Lezama Lima, José (1910–76), Cuban poet, novelist and essayist.

L'Hospital, Michel de (1507–1573), French statesman and scholar.

Lhote, André (1885–1962), French painter, sculptor and writer.

Liang Ch'en-yü (1510–1580), Chinese dramatist.

Liang Ch'i-ch'ao (1873–1929), Chinese scholar.

Liang Shih-ch'iu (1902–87), Chinese literary scholar, writer and translator.

Liang Shu-ming (1893–1988), Chinese philosopher.

Libanius (314–393), Greek philosopher and rhetorician.

Li Chih (1527–1602), Chinese philosopher.

Li Ch'ing-chao (1081–c.1142), Chinese poet, the foremost female poet of China.

Liddell, Henry George (1811–1898), English lexicographer and historian, co-editor of the standard Greek-English Lexicon (1843).

Liddell Hart, Sir Basil (Henry) (1895–1970), English military historian, biographer and strategist.

Liddon, Henry Parry (1829–1890), English Anglican priest and theologian, a principal figure in the Oxford Movement.

Lidner, Bengt (1757–1793), Swedish dramatist and poet, a leading figure in the Romantic movement in his homeland.

Lie, Jonas (Lauritz Idemil) (1833–1908), Norwegian novelist, poet and dramatist, author of the notable novel Familien paa Gilje (1883; English trans. as The Family at Gilje, 1920).

Lieber, Francis (1800–1872), German-born American political philosopher, historian and encyclopaedist, founder and first editor of the Encyclopaedia Americana (13 vols, 1829–33).

Liebling, A(bbott) J(oseph) (1904–1963), American journalist and writer.

Liebmann, Otto (1840–1912), German philosopher.

Lietzmann, Hans (1875–1942), learned German Lutheran church historian, author of Geschichte der alten Kirche (4 vols, 1932–44; English trans. as A History of the Early Church, 4 vols, 1937–51).

Lightfoot, John (1602–1675), English biblical and rabbinic scholar.

Lightfoot, Joseph Barber (1828–1889), English Anglican churchman, scholar and reformer.

Ligne, Charles-Joseph, Prince de (1735–1814), Belgian nobleman and court official who left valuable accounts of his era in his memoirs and correspondence (34 vols, 1795–1811).

Liguori, Saint Alfonso Maria de' (1696–1787), notable Italian Roman Catholic moral theologian, author of the famous Theologia moralis (1748).

Li Ho (791–817), gifted Chinese poet.

Likhachev, Dimitri (Sergeievich) (1906–99), Russian literary scholar who was an authority on Russian medieval literature.

Lilburne, John (c.1614–1657), controversial English political agitator and pamphleteer whose leadership of the democratic movement known as the Levellers cost him many imprisonments.

Liliencron, (Friedrich Adolf Axel) Detlev, Freiherr von (1844–1909), German poet, novelist and dramatist.

Lillo, George (1693–1739), influential English dramatist who presaged the bourgeois drama in his The London Merchant, or The History of George Barnwell (1731).

Lily, William (c.1468–1522), English classical grammarian.

Lima, Jorge de (1895–1953), Brazilian poet and novelist.

Lima Barreto, Afonso Henriques de (1881–1922), Brazilian writer.

Linacre, Thomas (c.1460–1524), English physician and classical scholar who became a Roman Catholic priest late in life.

Lincoln, Joseph C(rosby) (1870–1944), American novelist and short-story writer.

Lincoln, Victoria (1904–1981), American novelist and short-story writer.

Lincoln W(illiam) Bruce (1938–2000), American historian who wrote various studies on Russia of the Imperial and Communist eras.

Lindbergh, Anne Spencer Morrow (1906–2001), American aviator and writer, author of North to the Orient (1935), Listen! The Wind (1938), The Steep Ascent (1944) and Gift from the Sea (1955).

Lindegren, Erik (Johan) (1910–1968), Swedish poet of the experimental school.

Linderman, Frank Bird (1869–1938), American writer and poet.

Lindgren, Astrid (1907–2002), Swedish writer and poet of the Pippi Longstocking stories.

Lindsay, (Nicholas) Vachel (1879–1931), American poet, best known for his General Booth Enters Into Heaven and Other Poems (1913) and The Congo and Other Poems (1914); committed suicide.

Lindsay, Norman (Alfred William) (1879–1969), Australian artist and novelist.

Lindsey, Ben(jamin) B(arr) (1869–1943), American judge, legal and social reformer and writer.

Lingard, John (1771–1851), English Roman Catholic priest and historian, author of The Antiquities of the Anglo-Saxon Church (1806) and History of England (1819–30).

Link, Arthur S(tanley) (1920–1998), American historian, author of an exhaustive biography of Woodrow Wilson and editor of his papers.

Linklater, Eric (1889–1974), Scottish novelist.

Linn, John Blair (1777–1804), American clergyman and poet who wrote The Death of Washington (1800).

Linnaeus, Carolus (actually Carl von Linné) (1707–1778), noted Swedish botanist and explorer.

Linnankoski, Johannes (actually Vihtori Peltonen) (1869–1913), Finnish novelist who was active in the movement for independence from Russia.

Lins do Rêgo, José (1901–1957), Brazilian novelist.

Linton, Ralph (1893–1953), American cultural anthropologist, author of The Study of Man (1936), The Cultural Background of Personality (1945) and The Tree of Culture (published 1955).

Linton, William James (1812–1897), English wood engraver, writer and poet who was active in the Chartist movement.

Li Po (701–762), Chinese poet whose works celebrated an unrestrained joy of life and nature.

Lin Yü-tang (1895–1976), Chinese writer.

Lippard, George (1822–1854), American writer and dramatist who was also active in social reform.

Lippincott, Sara Jane (Clarke) (1823–1904), American journalist, poet and essayist who wrote under the name Grace Greenwood.

Lippman, Walter (1889–1974), influential American political commentator and writer.

Lipps, Theodor (1851–1914), German psychologist, author of the study Ästhetik (Aesthetics, 2 vols, 1903, 1906).

Lipsius, Justus (1547–1606), Belgian classical scholar.

Lipsius, Richard Adelbert (1830–1892), German Protestant theologian who wrote Philosophie und Religion (1885).

Li Shang-yin (813–858), admired Chinese poet.

Li-Shih-chen (16th Century), Chinese scholar, compiler of the Pents'ao kang-mu (Great Pharmacopoeia).

Lispector, Clarice (1925–77), Brazilian novelist and short-story writer.

Lissauer, Ernst (1882–1937), German poet and dramatist whose World War I poem Hassgesang gegen England (1914) won acclaim in his homeland for its refrain 'Gott strafe England'.

Lista (y Aragón), Alberto (1775–1848), Spanish poet and critic, the leading representative of Neoclassicism in his homeland in his day.

Lister, Thomas Henry (1800–1842), English novelist.

Littell, William (1768–1824), American writer on the law and satirical essayist.

Littré, Maximilien-Paul-Emilé (1801–1881), eminent French language scholar, lexicographer and philosopher, editor of the celebrated Dictionnaire de la langue française (4 vols, 1863–73).

Liu E or Liu O (1857–1909), Chinese novelist.

Liu Hsiang (1st Century), Chinese writer.

Liu Hsieh (465–522), Chinese writer.

Liutprand of Cremona (c.920–c.972), Italian Roman Catholic bishop, diplomat and historian.

Liu Tsung-yüan (773–819), Chinese poet and writer.

Livesay, Dorothy (Kathleen May) (1909–1996), Canadian poet whose output reflected her preoccupation with feminist and political issues.

Livingstone, David (1813–1873), Scottish missionary and explorer who wrote accounts of his African journeys.

Livingstone, Sir Richard Winn (1880–1960), English classical scholar.

Livius Andronicus, Lucius (c.284–c.204 BC), celebrated Roman poet and dramatist, founder of epic Latin poetry and drama.

Livy (actually Titus Livius) (c.62 BC–17 AD), Roman historian.

Li Yü or Li Hou-Chu (937–978), famous Chinese poet and last emperor of the Southern T'ang dynasty (937–975); was poisoned by order of his successor.

Llewellyn, Richard (actually Richard Dafydd Vivian Llewellyn Lloyd) (1906–1983), Welsh novelist and dramatist, author of How Green Was My Valley (1939).

Lloyd, Henry Demarest (1847–1903), American journalist who was a proponent of social reform.

Llull, Ramon (c.1235–1316), celebrated Catalan theologian, mystic and poet who was known as the 'enlightened doctor'.

Llwyd, Morgan (1619–1659), Welsh Puritan writer, author of the classic Llyfr y Tri Aderyn (The Book of the Three Birds, 1653).

Locke, Alain (LeRoy) (1886–1954), American philosopher, critic and writer, the principal figure in the Harlem Renaissance.

Locke, David Ross (1833–1888), American journalist and writer who won fame as a humorist under the name Petroleum V Nasby.

Locke, John (1632–1704), renowned English philosopher whose most profound works were An Essay Concerning Human Understanding (1690) and Two Treatises of Government (1690).

Locker-Lampson, Frederick (1821–1895), English poet who was especially remembered for his witty verse.

Lockhart, John Gibson (1794–1854), English critic, novelist and biographer, author of the classic Life of Sir Walter Scott (1837–38).

Lockridge, Ross (Franklin Jr) (1914–1948), American writer who wrote the highly regarded novel Raintree County (1948); committed suicide.

Lockwood, Ralph Ingersoll (1798–c.1858), American writer, author of the novels Rosine Laval (1833) and The Insurgents (1835).

Lodge, Thomas (c.1557–1625), English dramatist, writer and poet, known for his poetry collections Scillaes Metamorphosis (1589) and A Fig for Momus (1595), and the romance Rosalynde (1590).

Lofft, Capel (1751–1824), English poet, writer and lawyer.

Lofting, Hugh (1886–1947), English-born American children's writer and poet, particularly known for his classic stories concerning Dr Dolittle.

Logan, Cornelius Ambrosius (1806–1853), American dramatist, actor and theatre manager who wrote popular farces; father of Olive Logan.

Logan, James (1674–1751), Irish-born American politician and scholar.

Logan, John (1748–1788), Scottish poet, dramatist and churchman.

Logan, Olive (1839–1909), American actress, writer and dramatist; daughter of Cornelius Ambrosius Logan.

Loisy, Alfred Firman (1857–1940), influential French biblical scholar and philosopher of religion, one of the principal figures in Roman Catholic modernist circles.

Lo-Johansson, (Karl) Ivar (1901–1990), Swedish novelist and short-story writer, known for his depiction of proletarian life.

Lo Kuan-chung (c.1330–1400), celebrated Chinese novelist who wrote the classic San kuo chih yen-i (English trans. as Romance of the Three Kingdoms, 1925).

Lomax, Alan (1915–2002), American ethnomusicologist and writer who was an authority on American folk, blues and jazz genres.

Lombroso, Cesare (1835–1909), Italian criminologist, author of L'uomo delinquente (The Criminal Man, 1876).

Lomonosiv, Mikhail Vasilievich (1711–1765), important Russian scientist, literary scholar and poet.

London, Jack (actually John Griffith London) (1876–1916), American novelist and short-story writer, author of Call of the Wild (1903), The Sea Wolf (1904), White Fang (1906), The Iron Heel (1907) and Burning Daylight (1910).

Lonergan, Bernard (1904–1984), Canadian Roman Catholic philosopher.

Long, John Luther (1851–1927), American novelist, dramatist and librettist.

Longfellow, Henry Wadsworth (1807–1882), American poet, particularly known for Evangeline (1847), The Song of Hiawatha (1855) and The Courtship of Miles Standish (1858), as well as the collection Tales of a Wayside Inn (1863), which included his classic Paul Revere's Ride; brother of Samuel Longfellow and brother-in-law of Thomas Gold Appleton.

Longfellow, Samuel (1819–1892), American Unitarian clergyman, hymnist and writer; brother of Henry Wadsworth Longfellow.

Longhi, Alessandro (1733–1813), Italian painter, etcher and biographer.

Longinus (1st Century), Greek literary critic, reputed author of the treatise On the Sublime.

Longstreet, Augustus Baldwin (1790–1870), American educator and writer, best known for Georgia Scenes, Characters, and Incidents (1835).

Longus (2nd–3rd Centuries), Greek writer, author of the famous Daphnis and Chloe.

Lönnrot, Elias (1802–1884), Finnish folklorist and philologist, compiler of the Kalevala (1835), Finland's national epic.

Lonsdale, Frederick Leonard (1881–1954), English dramatist.

Loos, Anita (1893–1981), American dramatist and writer, best known for her play Gentlemen Prefer Blonds (1925).

Looy, Jacobus van (1855–1930), Dutch writer and painter.

Lopes, Fernão (c.1380–c.1460), Portuguese historian.

López, Luis Carlos (1883–1950), Colombian poet.

López de Ayala, Pedro (1332–1407), Spanish poet and historian, author of the valuable Cronicas and the poem Rimado de palacio.

López de Ayala y Herrera, Adelardo (1828–1879), esteemed Spanish dramatist.

López Velarde, Ramón (1888–1921), Mexican poet and essayist who was an influential figure in avant-garde circles.

López y Fuentes, Gregorio (1895–1966), Mexican novelist.

Lord, John (Walter Jr) (1917–2002), American writer, best remembered for his A Night to Remember (1955), an account of the sinking of the Titanic in 1912.

Lord, William Wilberforce (1819–1907), American clergyman and poet.

Lorde, Audre (1934–1992), American poet and writer who espoused feminism.

Lorimer, James (1818–1890), Scottish philosopher who wrote on natural law.

Lorris, Guillaume de (13th Century), French poet.

Lossky, Nicolai Onufriyevich (1870–1965), Russian philosopher.

Lot, Ferdinand (1866–1952), learned French historian who was an authority on the early Middle Ages.

Lothrop, Harriet Mulford Stone (1844–1924), American writer of children's books who wrote under the name Margaret Sidney.

Loti, Pierre (actually Louis-Marie-Julien Viaud) (1850–1923), French novelist.

Lotichius, Petrus Secundus (1528–1560), notable German poet.

Lotze, Rudolf Hermann (1817–1881), German philosopher, author of Metaphysik (1841) and Logik (1843).

Lounsbury, Thomas Raynesford (1838–1915), American literary scholar.

Louvet (de Couvray), Jean-Baptiste (1760–1797), French writer and politician, best remembered for his erotic novel Les Amours du chevalier de Faublas (1787–90).

Louÿs, Pierre (actually Pierre Louis) (1870–1925), French novelist and poet, best known for his prose poems Chansons de Bilitis (1894) and the novels Aphrodite (1896) and La Femme et le pantin (1898; English trans. as Woman and Puppet, 1908).

Love, Alfred Henry (1830–1913), American Quaker and pacifist.

Lovecraft, H(oward) P(hillips) (1890–1937), America writer and poet, a cult figure among science fiction aficionados.

Lovejoy, Arthur O(ncken) (1873–1962), American philosopher, author of The Revolt Against Dualism (1930) and The Great Chain of Being: A Study of the History of an Idea (1936).

Lovelace, Richard (1618–1657), noted English poet and soldier whose To Althea, from Prison (1642) includes the unforgettable lines Stone walls do not a prison make/Nor iron bars a cage, written while he was imprisoned for his championship of the Royalist cause.

Lover, Samuel (1797–1868), Irish painter, novelist and songwriter.

Lovett, Robert Morss (1870–1956), American literary scholar, novelist and dramatist.

Lowell, Abbott Lawrence (1856–1943), American educator, author of Conflicts of Principle (1932) and At War with Academic Tradition in America (1934); brother of Amy Lowell.

Lowell, Amy (1874–1925), American poet and critic, a prominent Imagist; sister of Abbott Lawrence Lowell.

Lowell, James Russell (1819–1891), prominent American poet, critic and diplomat; brother of Robert Traill Spence Lowell and husband of Maria White Lowell.

Lowell, Maria White (1821–1853), American poet, author of the Abolitionist poem Africa; wife of James Russell Lowell.

Lowell, Robert Traill Spence (1816–1891), American novelist and poet; brother of James Russell Lowell.

Lowell, Robert (Traill Spence Jr) (1917–1977), American poet, dramatist and translator, especially admired for such poetry collections as Lord Weary's Castle (1946), Mills of the Kavanaughs (1951), Life Studies (1959), For the Union Dead (1964), Near the Ocean (1967) and Notebook 1967–68 (1969); great-grandnephew of James Russell Lowell.

Lowes, John Livingston (1867–1945), American literary scholar.

Lowie, Robert H(arry) (1883–1957), American anthropologist, author of Primitive Society (1920), The History of Ethnological Theory (1937) and Social Organization (1948).

Lowndes, Marie Adelaide Belloc (1868–1947), English novelist and dramatist.

Lowry, (Clarence) Malcolm (1909–1957), English novelist, short-story writer and poet whose most significant work was the novel Under the Volcano (1947).

Lowth or Louth, Robert (1710–1787), English Anglican bishop and literary scholar.

Loy, Mina (actually Mina Gertrude Lowy) (1882–1966), English-born American poet who excelled in free verse.

Lubbock, Percy (1879–1965), English critic and biographer.

Lucan (actually Marcus Annaeus Lucanus) (39–65), Roman poet whose only surviving work is the epic Bellum civile or Pharsalia; committed suicide after the failure of Piso's conspiracy against the emperor Nero.

Lucaris, Cyril (actually Kyrillos Loukaris) (1572–1638), Greek Orthodox patriarch of Constantinople and theologian.

Lucas, E(dward) V(errall) (1868–1938), English journalist and essayist.

Lucas, F(rank) L(aurence) (1894–1967), English literary scholar, poet and translator.

Luce, Clare Boothe (1903–1987), American dramatist and public official, best remembered for her plays The Women (1936) and Kiss the Boys Goodbye (1938).

Lucena, João de (1549–1600), Portuguese writer.

Luchaire, (Denis-Jean-) Achille (1846–1908), French historian, author of important studies of the Capetians and of a biography of Innocent III (6 vols, 1904–08).

Lu Chi (261–303), notable Chinese writer, critic, poet and government official; was executed after plotting against the emperor.

Lu Chiu-yüan (1139–1193), Chinese philosopher of the Neo-Confucian school who was also known as Lu Hsiang-Shan.

Lucian (c.120–c.181), Greek satirist and rhetorician.

Lucidor, Lasse (actually Lars Johansson) (1638–1674), Swedish poet.

Lucifer (died c.370), Bishop of Cagliari, Sardinia and theologian who was the most vigorous opponent of the Arian heresey.

Lucilius, Gaius (c.180–c.103 BC), Roman poet, reputed creator of the political satire.

Lucretius (actually Titus Lucretius Carus) (c.99–55 BC), admired Roman poet and philosopher, author of the famous poem De rerum natura (On the Nature of Things).

Ludlow, Fitz Hugh (1836–1870), American writer, best known for his The Hasheesh Eater (1857), which was based on his own expieriences of drug addiction.

Ludlum, Robert (1927–2001), American writer of suspense novels.

Ludwig, Emil (1881–1948), German biographer, dramatist and poet.

Ludwig, Otto (1813–1865), German novelist, dramatist and critic.

Lugones, Leopoldo (1874–1938), prominent Argentine poet, writer and critic; committed suicide.

Luhan, Mabel Dodge (1879–1962), American writer.

Lu Hsün (actually Chou Shu-Jen) (1881–1936), Chinese writer and essayist.

Lukács, György (1885–1971), Hungarian Marxist philosopher, writer and critic.

Lukas, J(ay) Anthony (1933–1997), American journalist and writer; committed suicide.

Łukasiewicz, Jan (1878–1956), Polish philosopher.

Lukens, Henry Clay (1838–c.1900), American journalist and writer who often wrote under the name Erratic Enrique.

Lummis, Charles Fletcher (1859–1928), American writer and poet.

Lunacharsky, Anatoli Vasilievich (1875–1933), Russian writer and politician.

Lundkvist, Artur Nils (1906–1991), Swedish writer, poet and translator.

Lupus of Ferrières or Loup de Ferrières (c.805–c.862), French scholar who was also known as Lupus Servatus.

Luther, Martin (1483–1546), German Protestant reformer, biblical scholar and linguist, the central figure in the Protestant Reformation in Germany.

Lutterell, John (died 1335), English theologian.

Luttrell, Henry (c.1765–1851), English poet known for his light verse.

Luxemburg, Rosa (1871–1919), Polish-born German revolutionary and Marxist polemicist; was murdered.

Luyken, Jan (1649–1712), Dutch poet and lithographer who embraced mysticism, author of Jezus en de ziel (Jesus and the Soul, 1678).

Lu Yu (1125–1210), Chinese poet of a prolific output of some 20,000 poems, of which some 9,000 are extant.

Luzel, François-Marie (1821–1895), French writer, historian and critic.

Luzzatto, Moshe Hayyim (1707–1747), Italian Jewish writer, dramatist, poet and cabalist.

Luzzatto, Samuel David (1800–1865), Italian Jewish writer and scholar who was known as Shedal.

Lyall, Sir Alfred Comyn (1835–1911), English writer and poet.

Lyall, Edna (actually Ada Ellen Bayly) (1857–1903), English novelist whose espousal of liberal political causes informed most of her output.

Lydgate, John (c.1370–c.1450), English monk and poet.

Lyly, John (c.1554–1606), English novelist, dramatist and poet, known as the Euphuist after his novel Euphues (2 parts, 1578, 1580).

Lynch, Benito (1885–1951), Argentine novelist and short-story writer.

Lynd Helen (née Merrell) (1896–1982), American sociologist who collaborated with her husband on Middletown: A Study in Contemporary American Culture (1929) and Middletown in Transition: a Study in Cultural Conflicts (1937); wife of Robert Staughton Lynd.

Lynd, Robert Staughton (1892–1970), American sociologist who collaborated with his wife on Middletown: A Study in Contemporary American Culture (1929) and Middletown in Transition: A Study in Cultural Conflicts (1937).

Lynd, Sylvia (née Dryhurst) (1888–1952), English poet and short-story writer.

Lyndsay or Lindsay, Sir David (c.1490–c.1555), Scottish poet, dramatist and courtier whose satirical gift was displayed in his morality play Ane Satyre of the Thrie Estaits (1540).

Lyon, Harris Merton (1883–1916), American journalist, critic and writer.

Lyotard, Jean-François (1924–1998), French philosopher.

Lyte, Henry Francis (1793–1847), Scottish poet and hymnist who wrote the famous hymn Abide With Me.

Lyttelton, George, 1st Baron (1709–1773), English politician, writer and poet.

Lytton, Edward George Earle Bulwer-Lytton, 1st Baron (1803–1873), English novelist, dramatist, essayist, poet and politician.

Lytton, (Edward) Robert Bulwer-Lytton, 1st Earl of (1831–1891), English poet, dramatist and statesman who wrote under the name Owen Meredith.

Ma'arrī, al- (actually Abū al-'Alā' Ahmad ibn 'Abd Allāh al-Ma'iarrī) (973–1057), illustrious Arab poet.

Maas, Peter (1929–2001), American writer.

Mabillon, Jean (1632–1707), learned French scholar and monk, especially influential in the development of paleography.

Mably, Gabriel Bonnet de (1709–1785), French philosopher.

McAlmon, Robert (1896–1956), American poet and writer of the 'lost generation'.

Macarius (c.1482–1564), Russian Orthodox prelate and scholar.

Macarius Magnes (5th Century), Eastern Orthodox bishop and Christian apologist, author of Apokritikos e monogenes pros Hellenas (Response of the Only-Begotten to the Greeks, 5 vols, c.400).

Macarius the Egyptian (c.300–c.390), Egyptian monk and ascetic, one of the principal figures in the development of Christian monasticism.

MacArthur, Charles (1895–1956), American dramatist and screenwriter.

M'Carthy, Justin (1830–1912), Irish novelist, historian and politician.

McCarthy, Mary (Therese) (1912–1989), prominent American critic, novelist and memoirist.

Macaulay, Catherine (1731–1791), English historian, author of a History of England (8 vols, 1763–83).

Macaulay, Dame (Emilie) Rose (1881–1958), English writer, poet and critic.

Macaulay, Thomas Babington (1800–1859), noted English historian, author of a History of England (5 vols, 1849–61).

McAuley, James Phillip (1917–76), Australian poet and writer.

MacBeth, George Mann (1932–1992), Scottish poet and novelist.

MacCaig, Norman Alexander (1910–1996), Scottish poet, a master of his craft.

MacCarthy, Sir (Charles Otto) Desmond (1877–1952), English literary critic.

MacCarthy, Denis Florence (1817–1882), Irish poet and writer.

McConnell, Francis John (1871–1953), American Methodist bishop, educator, social reformer and writer.

McCosh, James (1811–1894), Scottish-born American philosopher and educator.

McCoy, Horace (1897–1955), American novelist and screenwriter.

McCrae, Hugh (Raymond) (1876–1958), Australian poet, writer and actor.

McCullers, Carson (Smith) (1917–1967), admired American novelist, short-story writer and dramatist, author of the novels The Heart is a Lonely Hunter (1940) and A Member of the Wedding (1946), and the novelette The Ballad of the Sad Café (1951).

McCulloch, John R(amsay) (1789–1864), Scottish-born English economist and statistician.

McCutcheon, George Barr (1866–1928), American novelist.

MacDiarmid, Hugh (actually Christopher Murray Grieve) (1892–1978), Scottish poet, the principal figure in the Scottish renaissance.

MacDonagh, Donagh (1912–1968), Irish poet, dramatist and balladeer, son of Thomas MacDonagh.

MacDonagh, Thomas (1878–1916), prominent Irish poet, critic and nationalist who was executed for his role in the Easter Rising; father of Donagh MacDonagh.

MacDonald, Alexander (c.1700–c.1780), Scottish-Gaelic poet who wrote under the name Alasdair Mac Mhaighstir Alasdair.

Macdonald, Dwight (1906–1982), American literary and political essayist.

Macdonald, George (1824–1905), Scottish poet and novelist.

MacDonald, John (c.1620–1716), Scottish-Gaelic poet.

MacDonald, John D(ann) (1916–1986), American writer of mystery novels and science fiction of mass appeal.

Macdonald, Ross (actually Kenneth Millar) (1915–1983), American novelist and essayist.

McDougall, William (1871–1938), English-born American psychologist, author of Introduction to Social Psychology (1908), Body and Mind: A History and Defense of Animism (1911) and The Group Mind (1920).

MacDowell, Katherine Sherwood (Bonner) (1849–1883), American writer who wrote under the name Sherwood Bonner.

Macedo, José Agostinho de (1761–1831), Portuguese poet, critic and pamphleteer.

McFee, William (Morley Punshon) (1881–1966), English-born American writer and poet.

McGee, Thomas D'Arcy (1825–1868), Irish-born Canadian poet, writer and politician.

Macghill-Eathain, Somhairle (1911–1996), Scottish poet of Gaelic verse who also wrote under the name Sorley Maclean and Samuel Maclean.

MacGill, Patrick (1890–1963), Irish novelist and poet.

MacGillivray, James Pittendrigh (1856–1938), Scottish sculptor and poet.

McGinley, Phyllis (1905–1978), American poet and writer.

McGonagall, William (1830–1902), Scottish poet and novelist.

MacGrath, Harold (1871–1932), American writer of the romance genre.

Mach, Ernst (1838–1916), Austrian physicist and philosopher.

Mácha, Karel Hynek (1810–1836), talented Czech poet, author of the classic epic Máj (May, 1836).

Machado de Assis, Joaquim Maria (1839–1908), esteemed Brazilian poet, novelist and short-story writer.

Machado y Ruiz, Antonio (1875–1939), Spanish poet and writer; brother of Manuel Machado y Ruiz.

Machado y Ruiz, Manuel (1874–1947), Spanish poet and writer; brother of Antonio Machado y Ruiz.

Machaut, Guillaume de (c.1300–1377), celebrated French composer and poet.

Machen, Arthur (actually Arthur Llewellyn Jones) (1863–1947), Welsh novelist, short-story writer, essayist and translator.

Machen, John Gresham (1881–1937), American Presbyterian scholar.

McHenry, James (1785–1845), Irish-born American poet and novelist.

Machiavelli, Niccolò (1469–1527), renowned Italian statesman and writer, author of the famous political treatise Il principe (The Prince, 1513).

Ma Chih-yüan (14th Century), Chinese dramatist and poet.

MacInnes, Colin (1914–1976), English novelist.

MacInnes, Tom (actually Thomas Robert Edward McInnes) (1867–1951), Canadian writer and poet.

McIntyre, Duncan (actually Donnchad Bàn Macan t-Saoir) (1724–1812), Scottish-Gaelic poet.

MacIver, Robert Morrison (1882–1970), Scottish-born American sociologist, political scientist and educator.

McKay, Claude (1890–1948), Jamaican-born American novelist and poet.

McKay, (George Cadogan) Gardner (1932–2001), American actor, dramatist and novelist.

MacKaye, (James Morrison) Steele (1842–1894), American dramatist, actor, theatre manager and inventor; father of Percy (Wallace) MacKaye.

MacKaye, Percy (Wallace) (1875–1956), American poet and dramatist; son of (James Morrison) Steele MacKaye.

Macken, Walter (1915–1967), Irish novelist and dramatist.

McKenney, Ruth (1911–1972), American writer, best known for My Sister Eileen (1938).

Mackenzie, Sir (Edward Morgan) Compton (1883–1972), English novelist, biographer, essayist and poet.

Mackenzie, Henry (1745–1831), Scottish novelist, poet, dramatist and editor, best remembered for his novel The Man of Feeling (1771).

Mackintosh, Sir James Brunlees (1765–1832), Scottish physician, philosopher and barrister.

Macklin, Charles (actually Charles McLaughlin) (c.1700–1797), Irish actor and dramatist.

McLachlan, Alexander (1818–1896), Scottish-born Canadian poet, especially remembered for his poems in Scots dialect.

MacLean, Alistair (1922–1987), Scottish novelist of thrillers who also wrote under the name Ian Stuart.

McLean, Sarah Pratt (1856–1935), American novelist and short-story writer.

McLellan, Isaac (1806–1899), American poet.

MacLennan, (John) Hugh (1907–1990), Canadian novelist and essayist.

Macleod, Mary or Mairi Nighean Alasdair Rudaidh (c.1615–c.1706), Scottish-Gaelic poet.

MacLeish, Archibald (1892–1982), eminent American poet, dramatist, government official and educator, particularly admired for his poem Conquistador (1932) and the verse drama J. B. (1958).

McLuhan, (Herbert) Marshall (1911–80), Canadian communications theorist best remembered for his study The Medium Is the Message: An Inventory of Effects (with Quentin Fiore, 1967).

McMaster, John Bach (1852–1932), American historian, author of a history of the US (9 vols, 1883–1927).

MacNeice, (Frederick) Louis (1907–1963), Irish poet and critic.

MacNeill, John Gordon Swift (1849–1926), Irish politician and historian.

Macpherson, James (1736–1796), Scottish poet who 'translated' the epic verse of the legendary poet and warrior 'Ossian'.

Macready, William Charles (1793–1873), English actor, theatre manager and diarist.

Macrobius, Ambrosius Theodosius (5th Century), Latin grammarian and philosopher, author of the Saturnalia.

McTaggart, John McTaggart Ellis (1866–1925), English philosopher who espoused an atheistic idealism.

Madách, Imre (1823–1864), Hungarian poet who wrote the admired poetic drama Az ember tragediája (1861; English trans. as The Tragedy of Man, 1933).

Madariaga y Rojo, Salvador de (1886–1978), Spanish writer, dramatist and poet.

Mādhavācārya (c.1296–c.1386), Hindu statesman and philosopher.

Madhva (c.1199–c.1278), Hindu philosopher who was also known as Anandatīrtha and Pūrnaprajna.

Madison, James (1751–1836), American statesman and 4th President of the US (1809–17), author of many of the papers in The Federalist (1787–88) and of the invaluable Journal of the Federal Convention (3 vols, 1840).

Madox, Thomas (1666–1726), English legal antiquarian and historian.

Madvig, Johan Nicolai (1804–1886), Danish classical scholar and government official.

Maerlant, Jacob van (1225–1291), Dutch poet and translator.

Maeterlinck, Maurice (Polydore-Marie-Bernard) (1862–1949), notable Belgian dramatist, poet and writer, best remembered for his celebrated Symbolist play Pelléas et Mélisande (1892); won the Nobel Prize for Literature (1911).

Maevius (1st Century), Roman poet.

Maeztu y Whitney, Ramiro de (1875–1936), Spanish political writer whose views led to his execution by the Republican government during the Spanish Civil War.

Maffei, Francesco Scipione, Marchese di (1675–1755), Italian dramatist, poet and scholar, particularly known for his verse tragedy Merope (1713).

Maginn, Willliam (1793–1842), Irish journalist, writer and poet.

Magnus, Johannes (actually Johan Mansson) (1488–1544), Swedish Roman Catholic archbishop and historian; brother of Olaus Magnus.

Magnus, Olaus (actually Olaf Mansson) (1490–1557), Swedish Roman Catholic archbishop and historian; brother of Johannes Magnus.

Magnússon, Jón (c.1610–1696), Icelandic parson who wrote a fantastic account of his reputed sufferings at the hands of 'sorcerers' in his Píslarsaga (Passion Story).

Mahan, Alfred Thayer (1840–1914), American naval officer and historian, author of The Influence of Sea Power upon History, 1660–1783 (1890), The Influence of Sea Power upon the French Revolution and Empire, 1793–1812 (1892) and The Interest of America in Sea Power, Present and Future (1897).

Mahony, Francis Sylvester (1804–1866), Irish journalist and poet who wrote under the name of Father Prout.

Mailáth, János, Count (1786–1855), Hungarian historian; committed suicide.

Maillet, Andrée (1921–1996), French-Canadian journalist, novelist, short-story writer, poet and dramatist.

Maimbourg, Louis (1610–1686), French Jesuit and historian.

Maimon, Salomon (c.1754–1800), Polish Jewish philosopher who was known for his skepticism and citicism of Kantian precepts.

Maimonides, Moses (1135–1204), Spanish Jewish philosopher, jurist and physician.

Maine, Sir Henry (James Sumner) (1822–1888), English jurist and legal historian who was a primary figure in the development of comparative law.

Maine de Biran (actually Marie-François-Pierre Gonthier de Biran) (1766–1824), French statesman and philosopher of the empirical school.

Maiorescu, Titu (1840–1917), Romanian writer.

Mairet, Jean (1604–1686), French dramatist who excelled in the classical genre.

Maironis (actually Jonas Mačiulis) (1862–1932), Lithuanian poet of distinction.

Maistre, Joseph de (1753–1821), French government official and polemicist who became well known for his rigorous defense of conservative principles of church and state.

Maitland, Fredric William (1850–1906), English legal historian who collaborated with Sir Fredrick Pollock on the classic study The History of English Law Before Time of Edward I (2 vols, 1895).

Maitland, Sir Richard (1496–1586), Scottish poet, anthologist, lawyer and statesman who was also known as Lord Lethington.

Maitland, Thomas (1841–1901), English poet and novelist who wrote under the name Robert Buchanan.

Major, Charles (1856–1913), American novelist best remembered for his When Knighthood was in Flower (1898).

Malalas, John (c.491–c.578), Byzantine chronicler.

Malamud, Bernard (1914–1986), American novelist and short-story writer.

Malaparte, Curzio (actually Kurt Erich Suckert) (1898–1957), important Italian journalist, novelist, short-story writer and dramatist who at first was a confirmed supporter of Fascism but later became one of its leading opponents.

Malcolm X (actually Malcom Little) (1925–1965), controversial American Black Muslim militant whose dictated The Autobiography of Malcolm X (1965) proved influential; was murdered.

Malczewski, Antoni (1793–1826), Polish poet.

Malebranche, Nicolas (1638–1715), French Roman Catholic priest, theologian and philosopher of the Cartesian school, author of De la recherche de la vérité (3 vols, 1647–78; English trans. as Search after Truth, 1694–95) and Traité de la nature et de la grâce (1680; English trans. as Treatise of Nature and Grace, 1695).

Malherbe, Daniel François (1881–1969), South African novelist, dramatist and poet in Afrikaans.

Malherbe, François de (1555–1628), French poet, critic and translator.

Mālik ibn Anas (actually Abū 'Abd Allāh Mālik ibn Anas ibn al-Hārith al-Asbahī) (c.715–795), Muslim theologian.

Malinowski, Bronisław (1884–1942), eminent Polish anthropologist, the pioneering figure in the development of social anthropology.

Mallarmé, Stéphane (1842–1898), famous French poet and writer of the Symbolist movement, renowned for his poems Herodiade (1864) and L'Après-midi d'un Faune (1865).

Mallea, Eduardo (1903–82), Argentine novelist, short-story writer and essayist.

Mallet, David (actually David Malloch) (c.1705–1765), Scottish poet and dramatist.

Mallock, William Hurrell (1849–1923), English writer and poet.

Malmström, Bernhard Elis (1816–1865), Swedish poet and critic.

Malone, Dumas (1892–1986), American historian and lexicographer, author of a major biography of Thomas Jefferson (6 vols, 1948–81).

Malone, Edmond (1741–1812), Irish-born English scholar, best known for his Shakespearian studies.

Malone, Kemp (1889–1971), American philologist who wrote extensively on linguistics and literature.

Malory, Sir Thomas (died 1471), English writer, author of the celebrated Morte Darthur (published 1485).

Malraux, André(-Georges) (1901–1976), prominent French novelist, art historian and government official.

Malthus, Thomas Robert (1766–1834), English economist and demographer, best known for his An Essay on the Principle of Population (1798).

Maltz, Albert (1908–1985), American novelist, dramatist and screenwriter.

Mameli, Goffredo (1827–1849), Italian poet and patriot; died while defending Rome against the French.

Mammeri, Mouloud (1917–89), Algerian novelist and dramatist.

Manasseh ben Israel (1604–1657), Jewish rabbi and scholar in the Kabbala.

Manasses, Constantine (died 1187), Byzantine metropolitan, poet and writer.

Mandel, Eli(as Wolf) (1922–1992), Canadian poet, critic and editor.

Mandelkern, Solomon (1846–1902), Hebrew poet and grammarian.

Mandelstam, Osip (Yemilievich) (1891–1938), Russian poet, critic and translator who died a victim of Stalin's tyranny.

Mander, Karel van (1548–1606), Belgian painter, poet and writer.

Mandeville, Bernard de (1670–1733), Dutch-born English writer and philosopher, author of The Fable of the Bees: Private Vices, Publick Benefits (1714).

Mandeville, Sir John (14th Century), English writer, reputed author of The Voyage and Travels of Sir John Mandeville.

Manetti, Gianozzo (1396–1459), Italian scholar and orator.

Manfalūtī Mustafā Lutfial (1876–1924), Egyptian short-story writer and essayist.

Mangan, James Clarence (1803–1849), Irish poet and translator.

Mangoaela, Z(akea) D(olphin) (1883–1963), South African writer and folklorist.

Mānikkavācakar (c. 9th Century), Indian mystic and poet who wrote in Tamil.

Manilius, Marcus (1st Century), Roman poet of didactic verse.

Maning, Frederick (Edward) (1811–1883), Irish-born New Zealand judge and writer.

Mankiewicz, Herman (Jacob) (1897–1953), American journalist, dramatist and screenwriter.

Mankowitz, (Cyril) Wolf (1924–1998), English novelist, dramatist and screenwriter.

Manley, Mary de la Riviere (1663–1724), English witer, especially remembered for her Secret Memoirs... of Several Persons of Quality (1709).

Mann, Gottfried Angelo (1909–1994), German historian; son of Thomas Mann.

Mann, Heinrich (1871–1950), German novelist and essayist; brother of Thomas Mann.

Mann, Horace (1796–1859), influential American educator who was the pioneering figure in public education in his homeland.

Mann, Thomas (1875–1955), renowned German novelist and essayist, author of such important novels as Buddenbrooks (1900), Der Zauberberg (1924; English trans. as The Magic Mountain, 1927), Joseph und seine Brüder (4 vols, 1933–43; English trans. as Joseph and His Brothers, 1948) and Doktor Faustus (1947); won the Nobel Prize for Literature (1929); brother of Heinrich Mann and father of Gottfried Angelo Mann.

Manner, Eeva Liisa (1921–95), Finnish poet and dramatist.

Mannheim, Karl (1893–1947), German born English sociologist who wote Ideologie und Utopie (1929; English trans. as Ideology and Utopia: An Introduction to the Sociology of Knowledge, 1936) and Freedom, Power, and Democratic Planning (published 1950).

Manning, Henry Edward (1808–1892), English Roman Catholic cardinal, archbishop of Westminster and polemicist.

Manning, Olivia (1908–1980), English novelist and short-story writer, author of The Balkan Trilogy (The Great Fortune, 1960, The Spoilt City, 1962 and Friends and Heroes, 1965) and The Levant Trilogy (The Danger Tree, 1977, The Battle Lost and Won, 1978 and The Sum of Things, 1980).

Mannyng of Brunne, Robert (c.1283–c.1327), English poet who wrote the poem Handlying Synne and the fictional chronicle Story of England.

Manrique, Gómez (c.1415–1490), Spanish soldier, politician, dramatist and poet.

Manrique, Jorge (c.1440–1479), Spanish poet whose most notable work was his Coplas por la muerte de su padre (Stanzas for the Death of his Father).

Mansel, Henry Longueville (1820–1871), English Anglican Priest, theologian and philosopher.

Mansfield, Katherine (actually Kathleen Mansfield Beauchamp) (1888–1923), New Zealand short-story writer.

Mantoo, Saadat Hussan (1912–1955), Pakistani writer.

Mantuan or Mantuanus (actually Johannes Baptista Spagnolo) (1448–1516), Spanish friar and poet who won distinction for his Latin eclogues.

Manuel, Don Juan (1282–c.1348), Spanish nobleman and writer, especially known for his Libro del Conde Lucor (The Book of Count Lucor, 1323–35).

Manuel, Niklas (1484–1530), Swiss soldier, statesman, painter and writer.

Manutius, Aldus (1449–1515), important Italian scholar, printer and editior.

Manutius, Aldus, the Younger (1547–1597), Italian scholar and printer.

Manzoni, Alessandro (1785–1873), Italian novelist, poet and statesman, author of the famous novel I promessi sposi (1825–27; English trans. as The Betrothed, 1951).

Mao Ch'ang (flourished 145 BC), Chinese scholar.

Mao Dun (actually Shen Te-Hung) (1896–1981), Chinese novelist.

Map or Mapes, Walter (c.1140–c.1209), Anglo-Norman churchman, writer and poet, author of the miscellany De nugis curialium (Of Courtiers' Trifles).

Mapu, Abraham (1808–1867), Russian writer, author of the first Hebrew novel, Ahavat Ziyyon (1853; English trans. as Annou: Prince and Peasant, 1887).

Marasco, Robert (1936–1998), American dramatist and novelist, author of the play Child's Play (1970).

Marat, Jean-Paul (1743–1793), French politician, journalist and physician who espoused radical policies during the French Revolution; was assassinated.

Marbeck or Marbecke, John (c.1505–1585), English composer, organist and writer on theology, compiler of the first published concordance of the English Bible (1550) and composer of the liturgical music in The Booke of Common Praier Noted (1550).

Marcabru or Marcabrun (12th Century), Provençal poet.

Marcel, Gabriel(-Honoré) (1889–1971), French philosopher of the Existentialist school, author of the Journal métaphysique (1927; English trans. as Metaphysical Journal, 1952), Être et avoir (1935; English trans. as Being and Having, 1949), Homo Viator (1945) and Le Mystère de l' étre (2 vols, 1951; English trans. as The Mystery of Being, 2 vols, 1951).

Marcello, Benedetto (1686–1739), Italian composer and writer.

March, Ausiàs (1397–1459), important Catalan poet.

March, Francis Andrew (1825–1911), American language scholar and lexicographer whose most important work was A Comparative Grammar of the Anglo-Saxon Language (1870).

March, William (actually William Edward March Campbell) (1893–1954), American novelist and short-story writer.

Marchand, Leslie A(lexis) (1900–99), American literary scholar who was an authority on Byron.

Marcion (died c.160), Christian heretic and theologian who rejected the Old Testament outright and espoused the view of the centrality of the gospel of love in the New Testament.

Marcus Aurelius (Antoninus) (26–180), Roman emperor, author of the celebrated Meditations.

Marcuse, Herbert (1898–1979), German-born American philosopher of the Marxist persuasion who wrote One Dimensional Man (1964), Essay on Liberation (1969), Counter Revolution and Revolt (1972) and The Aesthetic Dimension (1978).

Marechal, Leopoldo (1900–70), Argentine writer and critic whose most important work was the novel Adán Buenosayres (1948).

Maréchal, Pierre-Sylvain (1750–1803), French poet and writer, known for his antireligious views.

Marett, R(obert) R(anulph) (1866–1943), English anthropologist who was especially known for his studies of primitive religion.

Margoliouth, David Samuel (1858–1940), English Anglican churchman and Arabic scholor.

Margueritte, Paul (1860–1918), French novelist; brother of Victor Margueritte.

Margueritte, Victor (1866–1942), French novelist; brother of Paul Margueritte.

Margunios, Maximus (died 1602), Greek Orthodox bishop, theologian and scholor.

Mariana, Juan de (1536–1624), Spanish historian, author of the important Historia general de España (General History of Spain, 1601).

Marianus Scotus (actually Molbrigte, 'Servant of Bridget') (1028–c.1083), Irish chronicler who wrote a history of the world.

Marie de France (12th Century), French poet who created the lai Breton, a form of verse narrative.

Mariette, Auguste (-Ferdinand-François) (1821–1881), French archaeologist who wrote on the early era of the history of Egypt.

Marinetti, Filippo Tommaso (Emilio) (1876–1944), influential Italian poet, dramatist and writer who founded Futurism.

Marini or Marino, Giambattista (1569–1625), Italian poet, creator of the elborate Baroque style known as marinismo.

Maritain, Jacques (1882–1973), eminent French philosopher of the Thomist school, author of Art et scolastique (1920; English translaton as Art and Scholasticism, 1930), Distinguer pour unir, ou les degrés du savoir (1932; English trans. as The Degrees of Knowledge, 1937), Frontières de la poésie et autres essais (1935; English trans. as Art and Poetry, 1943) Humanisme intégral (1936; English trans. as True Humanism, 1938) and La Philosophie morale... (1960; English trans. as Moral Philosophy, 1964).

Marius Victorinus, Gaius (died c.364), Roman Christian philosopher and rhetorician.

Marivaux, Pierre (Carlet de Chamblain de) (1688–1763), important French dramatist and writer, especially significant for his comic plays.

Markham, Edwin (actually Charles Edward Anson Markham) (1852–1940), American poet, best remembered for The Man with the Hoe and Other Poems (1899) and Lincoln and Other Poems (1901).

Markham, Gervase or Jervis (c.1568–1637), English writer, dramatist and poet.

Markoe, Peter (c.1752–1792), Danish West Indies-born American dramatist, poet and writer.

Marković, Svetozar (1846–1875), Serbian socialist and political writer.

Mark the Hermit (c. 5th Century), Christian ascetic and theologian, author of Contra Nestorianos (Against the Nestorians).

Marlowe, Christopher (1564–1593), celebrated English dramatist and poet; died in a tavern brawl.

Marmion, Shackerley (1603–1639), English dramatist and poet.

Mármol, José (Pedro Crisólogo) (1817–1871), Argentine poet and novelist.

Marmontel, Jean-François (1723–1799), French poet, dramatist, writer and critic, best known for his autobiographical Mémoires d'un père (Memoirs of a Father, 1804).

Marnix van Sint Aldegonde, Philips van (1540–1598), Dutch theologian, translator and poet.

Marot, Clément (c.1496–1544), French poet and translator who transformed Italian literary forms into new French ones of notable distinction.

Marpurg, Friedrich Wilhelm (1718–1795), German writer on music and composer.

Marquand, J(ohn) P(hillip) (1893–1960), American writer, admired for The Late George Apley (1937) and as creator of the Japanese detective Mr Moto.

Marqués, René (1919–79), Puerto Rican dramatist, short-story writer and critic.

Marquis, Don(ald Robert Perry) (1878–1937), American journalist, novelist, dramatist and poet.

Marryat, Frederick (1792–1848), English naval officer and novelist.

Marsh, Dame (Edith) Ngaio (1899–1982), New Zealand writer of detective fiction.

Marsh, Sir Edward Howard (1872–1953), English literary scholar and art collector.

Marsh, George Perkins (1801–1882), American diplomat, scholar and conservationist, author of the memorable Man and Nature (1864).

Marshall, Alfred (1842–1924), English economist, author of Principles of Economics (1890).

Marshall, Tom (1938–1993), Canadian poet, novelist and essayist.

Marsilius of Padua (c.1280–c.1343), influential Italian political philosopher who wrote Defensor pacis (Defender of Peace).

Marsman, Hendrik (1899–1940), Dutch poet and critic; died in the sinking of a ship during World War II.

Marston, John (1576–1634), English dramatist, poet and churchman, a satirist whose most important work was the play The Malcontent (1604).

Marston, John Westland (1819–1890), English dramatist and critic; father of Philip Bourke Marston.

Marston, Philip Bourke (1850–1887), English poet and short-story writer; son of John Westland Marston.

Martí (y Pérez), José Julian (1853–1895), famous Cuban patriot, poet and essayist; died in battle.

Martial (actually Marcus Valerius Martial) (38–c.103), celebrated Roman poet who was unmatched in his mastery of the epigram.

Martianus Capella or Marcian (5th Century), African writer, author of De Nuptiis Philologiae et Mercurii.

Martin, (Bon-Louis-) Henri (1810–1883), French historian and politician, best known for his Histoire de France (15 vols, 1833–36) and Histoire de France depuis 1789 jusqu' à nos jours (History of France from 1789 to Our Time, 6 vols, 1878–83).

Martin, Gregory (c.1540–1582), English Roman Catholic biblical scholar, translator of the Latin Vulgate Bible into English.

Martin, Sir Theodore (1816–1909), Scottish writer and translator who collaborated with W E Aytoun on the 'Bon Gaultier' ballads (1845).

Martin du Gard, Roger (1881–1958), eminent French novelist and dramatist, author of the 8–part novel cycle Les Thibault (1922–40; English trans. as The World of the Thibaults, 1939–41); won the Nobel prize for Literature (1937).

Martín Gaite, Carmen (1925–2000), Spanish writer, poet and translator.

Martín-Santos, Luis (1924–64), Spanish psychiatrist and novelist; died in an automobile accident.

Martineau, Harriet (1802–1876), English writer who wrote widely on social, economic and historical subjects; sister of James Martineau.

Martineau, James (1805–1900), English Unitarian theologian and philosopher who espoused liberal views on the authority of Scripture; brother of Harriet Martineau.

Martínez de la Rosa (Berdejo Gómez y Arroyo), Francisco de Paula (1787–1862), Spanish statesman, dramatist and poet, author of the play La conjuracion de Venecia (The Conspiracy of Venice).

Martínez Estrada, Ezequiel (1895–1964), Argentine writer.

Martínez Sierra, Gregorio (1881–1947), Spanish dramatist, writer and poet.

Martini, Giovanni Battista (1706–1784), notable Italian music theorist and composer who was known as Padre Martini.

Martinson, Harry Edmund (1904–1978), Swedish poet and novelist; was co-winner of the Nobel Prize for Literature (1974); husband of Moa Martinson (1929–40).

Martinson, Moa (actually Helga Swartz) (1890–1964), Swedish novelist; wife of Harry Edmund Martinson (1929–40).

Martyn, Edward (1859–1923), Irish dramatist.

Martyn, John (1699–1768), English botanist, writer and translator, best known for his translations of Virgil.

Marulić, Marko (1450–1524), Croatian philosopher and poet.

Marvell, Andrew (1621–1678), English poet and writer, one of the most gifted of the metaphysicians, author of the poems To His Coy Mistress, The Nymp Complaining for the Death of Her Faun and A Poem upon the Death of His Late Highness the Lord Protector (1658), and the prose works The Rehearsal Transposed (2 Parts, 1672–73) and An Account of the Growth of Popery and Arbitrary Government (1677).

Marx, Karl (Heinrich) (1818–1883), German-born English political economist and philosopher whose radical advocacy of revolutionary change made him the central figure in the development of socialism, author of the Manifest der kommunistischen Partei (1848; English trans. as the The Communist Manifesto, 1930) and Das Kapital (3 vols, 1867, 1885, 1894; English trans. as Capital: A Critique of Political Economy, 3 vols, 1886, 1907, 1909).

Masamune Hakuchō (actually Masamune Tadao) (1879–1962), prominent Japanese critic and writer.

Masaoka Shiki (actually Masaoka Tsunenori) (1867–1902), admired Japanese poet and essayist who brought renewed life to the haiku and tanka.

Masefield, John (1878–1967), English poet and writer, especially known for such poetical works as Salt-Water Ballads (1902), The Everlasting Mercy (1911), Dauber (1913) and Reynard the Fox (1919); became Poet Laureate of the United Kingdom (1930).

Mason, A(lfred) E(dward) W(oodley) (1865–1948), English novelist whose best known work was The Four Feathers (1902).

Mason, John Mitchell (1770–1829), American Protestant minister and educator.

Mason, William (1725–1797), English poet and churchman.

Maspero, Gaston (-Camille-Charles) (1846–1916), French archaeologist who wrote Causeries d' Égypte (1907; English trans. as New Light on Ancient Egypt, 1908).

Massey, Gerald (1828–1907), English mystic, poet and writer.

Massinger, Philip (1583–1640), notable English dramatist and poet, especially admired for his play A New Way to Pay Old Debts (c.1621).

Massingham, Harold John (1888–1952), English writer and biographer.

Masson, Frédéric (1847–1923), French historian who wrote on Napoleon and his era.

Masterman, C(harles) F(rederick) G(urney) (1874–1927), English politician and writer.

Masters, Edgar Lee (1869–1950), esteemed American poet and writer, highly regarded for his poems in Spoon River Anthology (1915) and The New Spoon River (1924).

Masuji, Ibuse (1898–1993), Japanese novelist and short-story writer.

Mather, Cotton (1663–1728), learned American Puritan minister and scholar who wrote numerous books on a vast number of subjects; son of Increase Mather and father of Samuel Mather.

Mather, Increase (1639–1723), prominent American Puritan minister, diplomat, educator and writer; son of Richard Mather.

Mather, Richard (1596–1669), English-born American Puritan minister and writer; father of Increase Mather.

Mather, Samuel (1706–1785), American Protestant minister and writer; son of Cotton Mather.

Mathews, Cornelius (1817–1889), American editor, dramatist, novelist and poet.

Mathews, Shailer (1863–1941), American religious educator and writer, one of the principal figures in the social gospel movement.

Mathias, Thomas James (c.1754–1835), English writer, best remembered for his anonymously published The Pursuits of Literature (2 parts, 1794, 1797).

Matiez, Albert (1874–1932), French historian who wrote on the French Revolution.

Matos Guerra, Gregório de (1633–1696), Brazilian poet who was known for his satirical verse.

Matsunaga Teitoku (1571–1653), Japanese poet who created the Teimon school of haiku poetry.

Matsuo Bashō (actually Matsuo Munefusa) (1644–1694), Japanese poet, the foremost master of haiku poetry.

Matteson, Johann (1681–1764), important German writer on music and lexicographer.

Matthews, (James) Brander (1852–1929), American drama critic, essayist, novelist and educator.

Matthews, William (Procter) (1942–1997), American poet.

Matthiessen, F(rancis) O(tto) (1902–1950), American literary biographer and essayist.

Matthisson, Friedrich von (1761–1831), German poet.

Matto de Turner, Clorinda (1854–1909), Peruvian novelist, dramatist and poet, best known for her novel Aves sin nido (1889; English trans. as Birds Without a Nest, 1904).

Ma Tuan-lin (13th Century), important Chinese historian.

Maturin, Charles Robert (1782–1824), Irish clergyman, novelist and dramatist, author of the famous gothic novel Melmoth the Wanderer (1820).

Maugham, Robin (actually Robert Cecil Romer Maugham, 2nd Viscount Maugham of Hartfield) (1916–81), English novelist, dramatist, travel writer and memoirist who gained notoriety with his novel The Servant (1948); nephew of W(illiam) Somerset Maugham.

Maugham, W(illiam) Somerset (1874–1965), admired English novelist, short-story writer and dramatist, author of the novels Of Human Bondage (1915), The Moon and Sixpence (1919), Cakes and Ale (1930), and The Razor's Edge (1944); uncle of Robin Maugham.

Maupassant, (Henry-René-Albert-) Guy de (1850–1893), French short-story writer.

Mauriac, Claude (1914–1996), French novelist, dramatist and critic; son of François Mauriac.

Mauriac, François (1885–1970), French novelist, essayist, poet and dramatist; won the Nobel Prize for Literature (1952); father of Claude Mauriac.

Maurice, Furnley (actually Frank Leslie Thompson Wilmot) (1881–1942), admired Australian poet who won accolades for his poem To God: From the Warring Nations (1917) and the collections Eyes of Vigilance (1920) and Melbourne Odes (1934).

Maurice, (John) Fredrick Denison (1805–1872), influential English Anglican theologian and Christian socialist, author of The Kingdom of Christ (1838), Theological Essays (1853) and Social Morality (1869).

Maurois, André (actually Emile Herzog) (1885–1967), eminent French biographer, essayist and novelist.

Mauropus, John (11th Century), Byzantine ecclesiastic, scholar and poet.

Maurras, Charles (1868–1952), prominent French writer, political theorist and poet whose support of the Vichy regime during World War II led to his arrest in 1944 and imprisonment until his release shortly before his death.

Mauss, Marcel (1872–1950), French sociologist and anthropologist, author of Essai sur le don (1925; English trans. as The Gift, 1954).

Mauthner, Fritz (1849–1923), Bohemian-born German drama critic, novelist and philosopher who espoused skepticism.

Maximus the Confessor, Saint (c.580–662), notable Byzantine theologian.

Maximus the Greek (1480–1556), Greek Orthodox monk and scholar who translated the Scriptures into Russian.

Max Müller, Fredrich (1823–1900), German-born English philologist who was known for his studies on comparative mythology and comparative religions; son of Wilhelm Müller.

Maxwell, Gavin (1914–1969), Scottish novelist, poet and painter.

Maxwell, William (actually William Maxwell Keepers Jr) (1908–2000), American writer and editor.

May, Karl (Friedrich) (1842–1912), German writer, best known for his books for young people.

May, Rollo Reece (1909–1994), American psychologist and writer who developed existential psychotherapy.

May, Samuel Joseph (1797–1871), Americn Unitarian minister and writer who was active in many liberal social and political causes of his era.

May, Thomas (1595–1650), English dramatist, poet, historian and translator.

Mayakovsky, Vladimir (Vladimirovich) (1893–1930), famous Russian poet and dramatist; committed suicide.

Mayer, Hans Heinrich (1907–2001), German literary scholar who wrote significant studies on Martin Luther, Johann Wolfgang von Goethe, Friedrich von Schiller, Richard Wagner, Georg Büchner, Thomas Mann, Bertolt Brecht and Friedrich Dürrenmatt.

Mayhew, Experience (1673–1758), American Protestant preacher, writer and translator, especially known for his work among the Indians of New England; grandson of Thomas Mayhew and father of Jonathan Mayhew.

Mayhew, Jonathan (1720–1766), American Protestant preacher and polemicist who was known for his championship of liberal religious and political views; son of Experience Mayhew.

Mayhew, Thomas (c.1621–1657), American Protestant missionary to the Indians who collaborated with John Eliot on several tracts; grandfather of Experience Mayhew.

Maynard, François (c.1582–1646), French poet.

Mayo, Frank (1839–1896), American actor and dramatist.

Mayo, (George) Elton (1880–1949), Australian-born American psychologist who was known for his studies in industrial sociology.

Mayo, William Starbuck (1811–1895), American novelist, short-story writer and physician.

Mayr, Michael (1864–1922), Austrian historian and statesman.

Mayrhofer, Johann (1787–1836), Austrian poet.

Mazzini, Giuseppe (1805–1872), Italian revolutionary and political writer who espoused the cause of Italian republicanism.

Mead, George Herbert (1863–1931), American philosopher who was known as a pragmatist.

Mead or Mede, Joseph (1586–1638), English Anglican biblical scholar.

Mead, Margaret (1901–1979), prominent American anthropologist.

Medhurst, Walter Henry (1796–1857), English Anglican missionary and Oriental linguist.

Medina, Bartolome dé (1528–1580), Spanish Dominican theologian.

Medina, José Toribio (1852–1930), Chilean scholar and statesman who prepared important bibliographical vols.

Medwall, Henry (15th Century), English churchman and dramatist whose Fulgens and Lucrece was the first secular play in English.

Megasthenes (c.350–c.290 BC), Greek historian and diplomat, author of the Indika, a history of India.

Mehmet Fuat Köprülü (1890–1966), Turkish scholar and statesman who was also known as Köprülüzade.

Mehring, Franz (1846–1919), German radical journalist and historian, author of the important tomes Geschichte der deutschen Sozialdemocratie (History of German Social Democracy, 4 vols, 1897–98) and Karl Marx: Geschichte seines Lebens (Karl Marx: History of his Life, 1918).

Meiklejohn, Alexander (1872–1964), English-born American philosopher and educator.

Meillet, Antoine (1866–1936), French linguist.

Meinecke, Fredrich (1862–1954), German historian, author of Idee der Staatsräson in der neueren Geschichte (1924; English trans. as Machiavellism: The Doctrine of Raison d'Etat and Its Place in Modern History, 1957) and Die deutsche Katastrophe (1946; English trans. as The German Catastrophe, 1950).

Meinhold, Johann Wilhelm (1797–1815), German pastor, poet and dramatist.

Meinong, Alexius (1853–1920), Austrian philosopher and psychologist, author of Über Annahmen (On Assumptions, 1902).

Meireles, Cecília (1901–1964), esteemed Brazilian poet, particularly known for her Espectros (Visions, 1919) and Viagem (Journey, 1939).

Meiri, Menahem ben Solomon (1249–1316), Jewish Talmudic scholar.

Meir of Rothenburg or Meir ben Baruch (c.1215–1293), German Jewish scholar who was an authority on the Talmud.

Mei Sheng (died 140 BC), Chinese poet.

Mela, Pomponius (1st Century), important Roman geographer, author of the classic De situ orbis (A Description of the World, c.43).

Melanchthon, Philipp (1497–1560), notable German Protestant reformer, theologian and scholar who wrote the Confession of Augsburg of the Lutheran Church (1530).

Meleager (1st Century BC), Greek poet, admired for his elegies and epigrams.

Meléndez Valdés, Juan (1754–1817), Sapnish poet and politician, esteemed for his lyric poetry.

Meletios Pegas (1549–1601), Greek Orthodox patriarch of Alexandria and theologian.

Meletius of Antioch (c.310–381), Armenian theologian and bishop of Antioch, a principal figure in the anti-Arian movement.

Meletus (4th Century BC), Greek poet.

Melito of Sardis (2nd Century), important Greek theologian and bishop of Sardis who influenced his successors of the Christian faith.

Mellen, Grenville (1799–1841), American writer and poet.

Melo, Francisco Manuel de (1608–1666), Portuguese soldier, historian, literary critic and poet.

Melville, Andrew (1545–1622), Scottish Protestant reformer and scholar, one of the principal figures of the Scottish Reformed Church and its adoption of presbyteries.

Melville, Herman (1819–1891), American writer and poet whose masterpiece was the novel Moby Dick (1851).

Melville, James (1556–1614), Scottish Presbyterian reformer, educator and diarist.

Mena, Juan de (1411–1456), Spanish poet, author of El laberinto de fortuna or Las trescientas (1444).

Ménage, Gilles (1613–1692), French scholar.

Menahem ben Saruq (c.910–c.970), Spanish Jewish lexicographer and poet, compiler of the first dictionary in Hebrew.

Menander (342–292 BC), Greek dramatist, master of comedic writing.

Menander Protector (6th Century), Byzantine historian.

Ménard, Louis-Nicolas (1822–1901), French scholar, novelist and poet.

Mencius (c.371–c.289 BC), Chinese philosopher of orthodox Confucianism.

Mencken, H(enry) L(ouis) (1880–1956), iconoclastic American journalist, critic and essayist.

Mendele Mokher Sefarim (actually Shalom Jacob Broyde or Abramovich) (1835–1917), important Russian Jewish writer who was the central figure in the development of the modern Yiddish and Hebrew narrative literary genres and of modern written Hebrew.

Mendelssohn, Moses (1729–1786), German Jewish philosopher and biblical scholar, author of Phadon, oder über die Unsterblichkeit der Seele (Phaedo, or on the Immortality of the Soul, 1767).

Mendès, Catulle (1843–1909), French poet, dramatist and writer.

Mendes, Murilo (1901–75), Brazilian poet and diplomat.

Menen, Aubrey (actually Salvator Aubrey Clarence Menen) (1912–1989), English novelist and essayist.

Menéndez Pidal, Ramón (1869–1968), Spanish scholar who was known for his philological and literary studies.

Menéndez y Pelyao, Marcelino (1856–1912), eminent Spanish scholar and poet.

Menger, Karl (1840–1921), Austrian economist.

Menken, Adah Isaacs (actually Dolores Adios Fuertes) (c.1835–1868), American actress and poet.

Menno Simons (1496–1561), Dutch Anabaptist leader and writer on religion whose followers became known as Mennonites.

Menzel, Wolfgang (1798–1873), German literary critic, poet and historian.

Mera, Juan León (1832–1894), Ecuadorian novelist.

Mercati, Michele (1541–1593), Italian naturalist and physician.

Mercer, Cecil William (1885–1960), English novelist who wrote under the name Dornford Yates.

Mercer, David (1928–80), English dramatist.

Mercier, Désiré-Joseph (1851–1926), Belgian Roman Catholic cardinal, philosopher and educator, one of the principal figures in the revival of Thomism.

Mercier, Louis-Sébastien (1740–1814), French dramatist who was known for his middle-class tragedies.

Merck, Johann Heinrich (1741–1791), German writer and critic.

Meredith, George (1828–1909), notable English novelist and poet.

Meres, Francis (1565–1647), English churchman who brought out Palladis Tamia: Wits Treasury (1598), a vol. devoted to Elizabethan poetry.

Merezhkovski, Dmitri Sergeievich (1865–1941), Russian novelist, poet and critic; husband of Zinaida (Nikolaievna) Gippius.

Mérimée, Prosper (1803–1870), prominent French novelist, short-story writer, dramatist and scholar.

Merle d'Aubingé, Jean-Henri (1794–1872), important Swiss church historian, author of the Histoire de la Réformation du seiziéme siécle (5 vols, 1835–53; English trans. as History of the Great Reformation of the Sixteenth-Century, 1838–41) and Histoire de la Réformation en Europe au temps de Calvin (History of the Reformation in Europe at the Time of Calvin, 8 vols, 1863–78).

Merleau-Ponty, Maurice (1908–1961), French philosopher, particularly known for his La Structure du comportement (1942; English trans. as The Structure of Behavior, 1965) and Phenomenologie de la perception (1945; English trans. as Phenomenology of Perception, 1962).

Merrill, James Ingram (1926–1995), eminent American poet whose output was highly esteemed for its mastery of lyric and epic writing.

Merill, Stuart Fitzrandolph (1863–1915), American poet, author of the Symbolist masterwork Une Voix dans la foule (1909).

Merriman, Brian (1747–1805), Irish-Gaelic poet, known for his satirical and erotic mock-heroic epic Cúirt an Mheánin Oidhche (The Midnight Court, c.1786).

Merriman, Henry Seton (actually Hugh Stowell Scott) (1862–1903), English writer.

Mersenne, Marin (1588–1648), notable French mathematician, philosopher and theologian, especially known for his work on prime numbers.

Merton, Thomas (1915–1968), American Trappist monk, writer and poet.

Mesrob, Saint (actually Mashtots) (c.350–c.439), Armenian monk, theologian and linguist who translated the Bible into Armenian.

Metastasio, Pietro (actually Pietro Antonio Domenico Bonaventura Trapassi) (1698–1782), famous Italian poet who wrote the librettos for many operas.

Metcalf, Paul (1917–99), American writer, poet and dramatist.

Meteren, Emanuel von (1535–1612), Flemish historian.

Metge, Bernat or Bernardo (1350–1413), Catalan poet, author of Lo Somni (1398).

Metlitzki, Dorothee (1914–2001), German-born American literary scholar who was an authority on medieval English and Arabic literature, and on the writings of Herman Melville.

Metochites, George (c.1240–c.1328), Byzantine scholar and theologian; father of Theodore Metochites.

Metochites, Theodore (c.1260–1332), Byzantine statesman and scholar; son of George Metochites.

Metraux, Alfred (1902–1963), Swiss anthropologist.

Metrophanes Kritopoulos (1589–1639), Greek Orthodox patriarch of Alexandria, Egypt and theologian.

Meun, Jean de (c.1250–1305), French poet and translator.

Mew, Charlotte Mary (1869–1928), English poet and short-story writer; committed suicide.

Meyer, Adolf (1866–1950), Swiss-born American psychiatrist.

Meyer, Conrad Ferdinand (1825–1898), esteemed Swiss poet, novelist and short-story writer, especially admired for his novel Jürg Jenatsch, (1875–76).

Meyer, Eduard (1855–1930), German historian.

Meyer, Joseph (1796–1856), German industrialist, publisher and writer.

Meyer, Jürgen Bona (1829–1897), German philosopher of the Empiricist school.

Meyer, Kuno (1858–1919), German language scholar who was an authority on Celtic languages.

Meyer, (Marie-) Paul (-Hyacinthe) (1840–1917), French literary and language scholar.

Meyer, Michael (Leverson) (1921–2000), English writer, dramatist and translator who wrote biographies of Ibsen and Strindberg.

Meyer-Lübke, Wilhelm (1861–1936), Swiss-born German language scholar.

Meynell, Alice (Christiana Gertrude née Thompson) (1847–1922), English essayist and poet.

Michaud, Joseph (1767–1839), French journalist and historian.

Michaux, Henri (1899–1984), Belgian poet and painter.

Michel, Louise (1830–1905), French anarchist, poet and writer.

Michelangelo (actually Michelangelo di Lodovico Buonarroti Simoni) (1475–1564), Italian sculptor, painter, architect and poet.

Michelet, Jules (1798–1874), eminent French historian who wrote the expansive Histoire de France (1833–67).

Michels, Robert (1876–1936), German sociologist and economist, author of the important study Zur Soziologie des Parteiwesens in der modernen Demokratie (1911; English trans. as Political Parties: A Sociological Study of the Oligarchical Tendencies of Modern Democracy, 1962).

Michener, James A(lbert) (1907–1997), American novelist, author of such works as Tales of the South Pacific (1947), Hawaii (1959) and Texas (1985).

Miciński, Tadeusz (1873–1918), Polish writer.

Mickiewicz, Adam (Bernard) (1798–1855), renowned Polish poet who was acclaimed as the national poet of Poland.

Middleton, Conyers (1683–1750), English writer, particularly remembered for his A Free Inquiry into the Miraculous Powers which are supposed to have subsisted in the Christian Church (1749).

Middleton, Thomas (c.1570–1627), English dramatist, writer and poet, especially known for his plays Women beware Women (c.1621) and The Changeling (with William Rowley; 1622).

Middleton, T(homas) F(anshaw) (1769–1822), English Anglican missionary and bishop of Calcutta, author of The Doctrine of the Greek Article Applied to the Criticism and Illustration of the New Testament (1808).

Mi Fei (actually Mi Fu) (1051–1107), Chinese calligrapher, artist, scholar, poet and critic.

Mifflin, Lloyd (1846–1921), American poet who was known for his sonnets.

Mignet, François (-Auguste-Marie) (1796–1884), French historian.

Mikhailovsky, Nikolai Konstantinovich (1842–1904), Russian sociologist and political writer, the principal figure in the narodnik (populist) movement.

Miki Kiyoski (1897–1945), Japanese Marxist philosopher.

Mikszáth, Kálmán (1847–1910), Hungarian novelist and short-story writer.

Miles, George Henry (1824–1871), American writer, dramatist and poet.

Miles, Josephine (1911–1985), American poet and critic.

Milescu, Nicolae (1626–1708), Russian scholar, translator and traveller.

Milič of Kroměři, Jan (c.1305–1374), Czech Roman Catholic theologian, ascetic and religious reformer.

Mill, James (1773–1836), influential English philosopher, historian and economist of the Utilitarian school, author of a History of British India (3 vols, 1817); father of John Stuart Mill.

Mill, John Stuart (1806–1873), English philosopher and political economist of the Utilitarian school, author of A System of Logic (1843), Principles of Political Economy (1848), On Liberty (1859) and Considerations on Representative Government (1861); son of James Mill.

Millay, Edna St Vincent (1892–1950), prominent American poet and dramatist whose admired poetry collections included Renascence and Other Poems (1917), Second April (1921), The Harp Weaver and Other Poems (1923), The Buck in the Snow (1928), Fatal Interview (1931) and Wine from These Grapes (1934).

Miller, Henry (Valentine) (1891–1980), provocative American novelist, short-story writer and essayist whose preoccupation with candid sexual themes made him one of the most controversial writers of his era.

Miller, Hugh (1802–1856), English journalist, geologist and poet; committed suicide.

Miller, Jason (1939–2001), American dramatist, screenwriter, actor and director, author of the award-winning play That Championship Season (1971).

Miller, Joaquin (actually Cincinnatus Hiner (Heine) Miller) (1837–1913), American poet and journalist, best remembered for his poetry collection Songs of the Sierras (1871).

Miller, Perry (Gilbert Eddy) (1905–1963), American literary scholar.

Miller, William (1810–1872), Scottish poet, known for his Wee Willi Winkie.

Millin, Sarah Gertrude (née Liebson) (1889–1968), Lithuanian-bor South African novelist and essayist, author of the notable novels God' Step-Children (1924) and Mary Glenn (1925).

Mills, C(harles) Wright (1916–1962), American sociologist.

Milman, Henry Hart (1791–1868), English poet and historian.

Milne, A(lan) A(lexander) (1882–1956), English writer and poet wh was enormously successful in writing verse for children, especiall Winnie-the-Pooh (1926).

Milnes, (Richard) Monckton, Baron Houghton (1809–1885), Englis biographer, historian, literary scholar, editor and poet.

Milton, John (1608–1674), English poet and religious and politica polemicist, celebrated for his epic poem Paradise Lost (1667) and it sequel Paradise Regained (1671).

Milyukov, Pavel Nikolaievich (1859–1943), Russian statesman anc historian who espoused liberal democracy but was compelled to go intc exile after the Bolshevik Revolution of 1917.

Mimnermus (c.600 BC), Greek poet.

Mir, Pedro (1913–2000), Dominican poet.

Mīrā Bāī (c.1450–c.1547), Hindu mystic and poet.

Mirabeau, Victor Riqueti, Marquis de (1715–1789), French politica economist.

Mirbeau, Octave (-Henri-Marie) (1850–1917), French novelist anc dramatist.

Mīrkhwānd (actually Muhammad ibn Khāvandshāh ibn Mahmūd) (1433–1498), Persian historian.

Miró (Ferrer), Gabriel (1879–1930), Spanish novelist, short-story writer and essayist.

Miron, Gaston (1928–1996), French-Canadian poet.

Mirsky, D S (actually Prince Dmitri Petrovich Sviatopolk-Mirsky) (1890–1939), Russian literary critic and historian.

Mishima Yukio (actually Kimitake Miraoka) (1925–1970), provocative Japanese novelist and short-story writer who probed the conflicts between Japanese and Western traditions; committed suicide.

Misrama, Suryamal (1872–1952), Indian poet.

Mistral, Frédéric (1830–1914), esteemed French poet and short-story writer, author of the narrative poems Mirèio (1859), Calendau (1867), Nerto (1884) and Lou Pouèmo dóu Rose (1897); was co-winner of the Nobel Prize for Literature (1904).

Mistral, Gabriela (actually Lucila Godoy Alcayaga) (1889–1957), admired Chilean poet who espoused the cause of Modernism; won the Nobel Prize for Literature (1945).

Mitchel, John (1815–1875), Irish-born American nationalist and journalist, best known for his Jail Journal, or Five Years in British Prisons (1854).

Mitchell, Donald Grant (1822–1908), American writer who wrote under the names Ik Marvel and Ike Marvel.

Mitchell, John Ames (1845–1918), American editor, novelist and artist.

Mitchell, Joseph (1908–1996), American journalist and writer.

Mitchell, Langdon (Elwyn) (1862–1935), American dramatist and essayist; son of S(ilas) Weir Mitchell.

Mitchell, Margaret (1900–1949), American novelist who wrote Gone with the Wind (1936).

Mitchell, S(ilas) Weir (1829–1914), American physician, writer and poet, best known for his novel Hugh Wynne, Free Quaker (1897); father of Langdon (Elwyn) Mitchell.

Mitchell, Wesley Clair (1874–1948), American economist who was an authority on business cycles.

Mitchell, W(illiam) O(rmond) (1914–1998), notable Canadian writer and dramatist.

Mitford, Jessica (Lucy) (1917–1996), English-born American journalist and writer who was known for her muckracking proclivities; sister of Nancy (Freeman) Mitford.

Mitford, John (1781–1859), English clergyman, writer and poet.

Mitford, Mary Russell (1787–1855), English poet, dramatist and writer.

Mitford, Nancy (Freeman) (1904–1973), English novelist and biographer; sister of Jessica (Lucy) Mitford.

Mitford, William (1744–1827), English historian, author of a History of Greece (1785–1810).

Mitre, Bartolomé (1821–1906), notable Argentine soldier, statesman, journalist, writer, poet and translator.

Moberg, (Carl Artur) Vilhelm (1898–1973), Swedish novelist and dramatist.

Mocatta, Frederic David (1828–1905), English Jewish philanthropist, bibliophile and historian, author of The Jews of Spain and Portugal and the Inquisition (1877).

Mochnacki, Maurycy (1804–1834), influential Romanian literary critic.

Modena, Leone (1571–1648), Italian rabbi, preacher, poet and scholar.

Moe, Jørgen Engebretsen (1813–1882), Norwegian poet and folklorist who, with Peter Christian Asbjørnsen, collaborated on the important collection Norske folkeeventyr (Norwegian Folk Tales, 1841).

Moeller, Philip (1880–1958), American dramatist.

Moeller van den Bruck, Arthur (1876–1925), influential German cultural critic whose book Das Dritte Reich (The Third Reich, 1923) was adopted by the Nazi regime as the description of its totalitarian regime; committed suicide.

Moffat, James (1870–1944), Scottish biblical scholar and translator.

Moffat, Robert (1795–1883), English missionary and biblical translator who was active in Africa.

Mofolo, Thomas (Mokopu) (1877–1948), notable South African novelist who wrote in the Sesotho language, author of Moeti oa Bochabela (1906; English trans. as The Traveller to the East, 1934), Pitseng (At the Pot, 1910) and Chaka (1925; English trans. as Chaka: A Historical Romance, 1931).

Mogila, Peter (1596–1646), Russian Orthodox monk, theologian and metopolitan of Kiev.

Möhler, Johann Adam (1796–1838), German Roman Catholic priest and church historian who advocated unity between Catholics and Protestants, author of Die Einheit in der Kirche (Unity in the Church, 1825), Symbolik (1832; English trans. as On the Creeds, 1843) and Neue Untersuchung der Lehrgegensätze zwischen Katholiken und Protestanten (New Examination of the Doctrinal Differences Between Catholics and Protestants, 1834).

Moir, David Macbeth(1798–1851), Scottish physician and poet who wrote under the name Delta.

Moleschott, Jacob (1822–1893), Dutch physiologist and philosopher, best known for his study Kreislauf des Lebens (Circuit of Life, 1852).

Molesworth, Mary Louisa (née Stewart) (1839–1921), English novelist and writer of children's books under the name Ennis Graham.

Molesworth, Robert, 1st Viscount (1656–1725), English diplomat and political writer.

Molière (actually Jean-Baptiste Poquelin) (1622–1673), French dramatist and poet, author of such celebrated plays as L'École des femmes (1662; English trans. as The School for Wives, 1948), Tartuffe (1664; English trans. as The Imposter, 1950), Le Bourgeois Gentilhome (1670; English trans. as The Prodigal Snob, 1952) and Le Malade Imaginaire (1673; English trans. as The Imaginary Invalid, 1925).

Molina, Luis de (1535–1600), important Spanish Jesuit theologian who wrote the significant tome Concordia liberi arbitrii cum gratiae donis (The Union of Free Will and Divine Grace, 1588).

Molinet, Jean (1435–1507), French poet and writer.

Molinos, Miguel de (1628–1696), Spanish Roman Catholic priest and theologian whose Guia espiritual (Spiritual Guide, 1675) espoused an extreme form of Quietism; was arrested by the Holy Office, tried, condemned and died in prison.

Møller, Poul Martin (1794–1838), Danish writer and poet, best known for his novel En dansk students eventyr (The Adventures of a Danish Student, 1824).

Molnár, Ferenc (1878–1952), Hungarian dramatist, novelist and short-story writer.

Molyneux, William (1656–1698), English philosopher.

Mommsen, Theodor (1817–1903), eminent German historian, author of the Römische Geschichte (4 vols, 1854–85; English trans. as The History of Rome, 4 vols, 1862–75); won the Nobel Prize for Literature (1902).

Monboddo, James Burnett, Lord (1714–1799), Scottish jurist and anthropologist, author of the tome Of the Origin and Progress of Language (6 vols, 1773–92).

Moneta, Ernest Teodoro (1833–1918), Italian journalist and pacifist; was co-winner of the Nobel Prize for Peace (1907).

Monette, Paul (1945–1995), American writer and poet, particularly remembered for his autobiographies Borrowed Time: An AIDS Memoir (1988) and Becoming a Man: Half a Life Story (1992).

Monk, Maria (c.1817–1850), American writer who created a scandal with her Awful Disclosures (1836) and Further Disclosures (1837), accounts of alleged terrors in a Montreal convent which were later proved to be fabrications.

Monluc, Blaise de Lasseran-Massencôme, Seigneur de (c.1500–1577), French soldier who wrote a valuable autobiography entitled Commentaires (1592; English trans. as Commentaries, 1674).

Monnier, Henri (1805–1877), French caricaturist and dramatist.

Monod, Adolphe (-Louis-Frédéric) Théodore (1802–1856), notable French Reformed pastor and theologian of Swiss descent.

Monod, Gabriel (-Jean-Jacques) (1844–1912), French historian.

Monrad, Marcus Jakob (1816–1897), Norwegian philosopher.

Monro, H(arold) E(dward) (1879–1932), English publisher, editor and poet.

Monroe, Harriet (1860–1936), American poet, critic and editor.

Monsarrat, Nicholas (actually John Turney) (1910–1979), English novelist, best remembered for The Cruel Sea (1951).

Montagu, Basil (1770–1851), English barrister, writer and poet.

Montagu, Elizabeth (née Robinson) (1720–1800), prominent English woman of letters and writer, a leading figure among the 'bluestockings'.

Montagu, Lady Mary Wortley (1689–1762), notable English letter writer, essayist, poet, feminist and traveller.

Montagu, (Montague Francis) Ashley (1905–99), English-born American anthropologist and writer.

Montagu or Montague, Richard (1577–1641), English Anglian bishop and theologian who championed the cause of a middle way in the disputes between Calvinist and Roman Catholic doctrines.

Montague, Charles Edward (1867–1928), English journalist, novelist and short-story writer.

Montaigne, Michel (Eyquem) de (1533–1592), celebrated French essayist who created the form of the essay in his famous Essais (3 vols, 1580–88).

Montale, Eugenio (1896–1981), eminent Italian poet, writer, editior and translator; won the Nobel Prize for Literature (1975).

Montalembert, Charles (-Forbes-René) de (1810–1870), French politician and historian who opposed both church and state absolutism.

Montalvo, Juan (1832–1889), Ecuadoran essayist and writer.

Montausier, Charles de Saint-Marie, Duc de (1610–1690), French soldier, poet and writer.

Montchrestien, Antoine de (c.1575–1621), French economist and dramatist.

Montefiore, Claude Joseph Goldsmid (1858–1938), English Jewish theologian, Reform leader and philanthropist.

Monteiro Lobato, José Bento (1883–1948), Brazilian writer and publisher.

Montelius, (Gustav) Oscar (Augustin) (1843–1921), Swedish archaeologist.

Montemayor or Montemor, Jorge de (c1520–c.1561), Portuguese-born Spanish writer and poet whose Diana (c.1559) was the first Spanish pastoral novel.

Montesquieu, (Charles-Louis de Secondat, Baron de la Brède et de) (1689–1755), illustrious French political philosopher, author of Lettres persanes (1721; English trans. as Persian Letters, 1721), Considérations sur les causes de la grandeur des Romains et de leur décadence (1734; English trans. as Reflections on on the Rise and Fall of the Roman Empire, 1734), L'Esprit des lois (1748; English trans. as The Spirit of Laws, 1750) and Defense de l'Esprit des lois (1750).

Montessori, Maria (1870–1952), influential Italian educator who developed the Montessori method of education, author of Il metodo della pedagogia scientifica (1909; English trans. as The Montessori Method, 1912), The Secret of Childhood (1936), To Educate the Human Potential (1948) and La mente assorbente (1949; English trans. as The Absorbent Mind, 1949).

Montet, Pierre (1885–1966), French archaeologist who was a prominent Egyptologist.

Montfaucon, Bernard de (1655–1741), esteemed French patristic scholar, paleographer and archaeologist.

Montgomerie, Alexander (c.1545–c.1611), Scottish poet whose major work was the allegorical The Cherry and the Slae (1597).

Montgomery, James (1771–1854), Scottish poet, hymnist and journalist.

Montgomery, Lucy Maude (1874–1942), Canadian novelist, author of Anne of Green Gables (1908).

Montgomery, Robert (1807–1855), English preacher and poet.

Montherlant, Henry (-Marie-Joseph-Millon) de (1896–1972), French novelist and dramatist, particularly known for his novel-cycle Les Jeunes Filles (1936), Pitie pour les femmes (1936), Le Demon du bien (1937) and Les Lepreuses (1939), all of which were published in an English trans. as The Girls: A Tetralogy of Novels (2 vols, 1968); committed suicide.

Monti, Vincenzo (1754–1828), Italian poet and translator.

Montrose, James Graham, 5th Earl and 1st Marquess of (1612–1650), English general and poet who espoused the Royalist cause; following his defeat at Carbisdale, he was hanged.

Montúfar y Rivera Maestre, Lorenzo (1823–1898), Guatemalan statesman and histiorian who espoused liberalism, author of the expansive Reseña Historica de Centro America (17 vols, 1878–88).

Moodie, Susanna Strickland (1803–1885), English-born Canadian pioneer, best remembered for her Roughing It in the Bush; or, Life in Canada (1852).

Moody, William Vaughn (1869–1910), American dramatist and poet, best known for his plays The Great Divide (1906) and The Faith Healer (1909).

Moore, Clement Clarke (1779–1863), American biblical scholar and poet who wrote the celebrated poem A Visit from St Nicholas (1822), better known as 'Twas the Night Before Christmas.

Moore, Edward (1712–1757), English dramatist, writer and poet, best remembered for his play The Gamester (1753).

Moore, George (Augustus) (1852–1933), Irish novelist and short-story writer, particularly admired for his novel Esther Waters (1894) and the autobiographical trilogy Hail and Farewell (Ave, 1911, Salve, 1912 and Vale, 1914).

Moore, G(eorge) E(dward) (1873–1958), English philosopher of the Idealist school, author of Principia Ethica (1903), Philosophical Studies (1922) and Some Main Problems of Philosophy (1953); brother of T(homas) Sturge Moore.

Moore, George Foot (1851–1931), American biblical scholar, theologian and Orientalist who wrote Judaism in the First Centuries of the Christian Era (3 vols, 1927–30).

Moore, George Henry (1823–1892), American historian; brother of (Horatio) Frank(lin) Moore.

Moore, (Horatio) Frank(lin) (1828–1904), American historian; brother of George Henry Moore.

Moore, John Bassett (1860–1947), American scholar of international law.

Moore, John Trotwood (1858–1929), American novelist and poet; father of Merrill Moore.

Moore, Julia A (1847–1920), American poet and writer who was known as the 'Sweet Singer of Michigan'.

Moore, Marianne (Craig) (1887–1972), American poet, essayist and editor.

Moore, Merrill (1903–1957), American psychiatrist and poet; son of John Trotwood Moore.

Moore, Thomas (1779–1852), renowned Irish poet and composer, author of Irish Melodies (1807–34), Lallah Rookh (1817) and The Loves of the Angels (1823).

Moore, T(homas) Sturge (1870–1944), English poet, critic and wood engraver; brother of G(eorge) E(dward) Moore.

Mooris, Willie (1934–99), American editor and writer.

Morand, Paul (1888–1976), French diplomat, novelist and short-story writer who collaborated with the Vichy regime.

Morant, Harry Harbord (1865–1902), English-born Australian adventurer and poet; executed by firing squad for murderous actions he committed during the Boer War.

Morante, Elsa (1918–85), Italian novelist, short-story writer and poet.

Morata, Olympia (1526–1555), Italian poet and scholar.

Moravia, Alberto (actually Alberto Pincherle) (1907–1990), prominent Italian novelist and short-story writer.

More, Hannah (1745–1833), English writer and educator of the poor.

More, Henry (1614–1687), English poet and philosopher who was a leading figure among the Cambridge Platonists.

More, Paul Elmer (1864–1937), American literary scholar who espoused the New Humanism until turning to Christianity late in life.

More, Sir Thomas or Saint Thomas More (1477–1535), eminent English scholar and statesman, author of the classic political vol. Utopia (1516); as a Roman Catholic, he refused to accept King Henry VIII as head of the Church of England and was beheaded.

Moréas, Jean (actually Yannis Papadiamantopoulos) (1856–1910), Greek-born French poet who first embraced Symbolism but later became a champion of Greek and Latin classicism.

Morellet, André (1727–1819), French economist and writer, author of Mémoires sur le XVIIIe siècle et la Révolution (published 1821).

Morelly (18th Century), French philosopher who wrote the Utopian Code de la nature (1755), a trenchant attack on private property.

Moreto (y Cabaña), Agustín (1618–1669), Spanish dramatist.

Morford, Henry (1823–1881), American journalist, novelist and poet.

Mogan, Charles (Langbridge) (1894–1958), English novelist, dramatist and critic.

Morgan, Lady (née Sydney Owenson) (1776–1859), English writer and poet.

Morgan, Lewis Henry (1818–1881), American ethnologist and anthropologist, author of Ancient Society, or Researches in the Lines of Human Progress from Savagery through Barbarism to Civilization (1877).

Morgan, William (c.1545–1604), Welsh Anglican bishop who translated the Bible into Welsh.

Morgenstern, Christian (1871–1914), German poet who wrote nonsense verse imbued with esoteric meaning.

Morgenthau, Hans J(oachim) (1904–1980), German-born American political scientist and historian.

Móricz, Zsigmond (1879–1942), notable Hungarian novelist and short-story writer.

Morier, James Justinian (c.1780–1849), English diplomat and writer, author of The Adventures of Hajji Baba of Ispahan (1824).

Mörike, Eduard Friedrich (1804–1875), celebrated German poet and writer, one of the foremost lyric poets of Germany.

Morin, Jean (1591–1659), French Roman Catholic theologian.

Morin, Paul (d'Equilly) (1889–1963), French-Canadian poet.

Mori Ogai (actually Mori Rintarō) (1862–1922), important Japanese writer who extolled the Samurai code.

Morison, James (1816–1893), Scottish theologian who founded the Evangelical Union and espoused universalism.

Morison, Samuel Eliot (1887–1976), eminent American historian and biographer, author of biographies of Columbus (1942) and John Paul Jones (1959) and the official history of US naval operations (14 vols, 1947–60).

Morison, Stanley (1889–1967), English scholar who devoted himself to the study of printing.

Moritz, Karl Philipp (1757–1793), German novelist and aesthetician who was especialy admired for his autobiographical novels Anton Reiser (4 vols, 1785–90) and Andreas Hartknopf (1786).

Morley, Christopher (Darlington) (1890–1957), American novelist, essayist and poet.

Morley, Henry (1822–1894), English journalist, editior and biographer.

Morley, Henry Parker, Lord (1476–1556), English courtier, diplomat, writer and translator.

Morley, John, 1st Viscount Morley of Blackburn (1838–1923), English politician, essayist and biographer.

Morley, Thomas (c.1557–1602), notable English composer, organist and theorist, author of the treatise A Plaine and Easie Introduction to Practicall Musicke (1597).

Mornay, Philippe de, Seigneur du Plessis-Marly (1549–1623), French diplomat and political and religious polemicist.

Morris, George Pope (1802–1864), American journalist and poet, best remembered for his poem Woodman, Spare that Tree (1830).

Morris, Sir Lewis (1833–1907), Welsh poet, dramatist and barrister.

Morris, Richard (Brandon) (1904–1989), American historian.

Morris, William (1834–1896), English craftsman, socialist, poet and writer.

Morris, Wright (Marion) (1910–1998), American novelist, short-story writer, essayist and photographer.

Morris-Jones, Sir John (1864–1929), Welsh scholar, poet and translator.

Morrison, Arthur (1863–1945), English novelist and short-story writer.

Morrison, Robert (1782–1834), English Presbyterian minister, missionary and translator who collaborated with William Milne on a translation of the Bible into Chinese.

Morrison, Theodore (1901–1988), American novelist and poet.

Morrow, Honoré Willsie (1880–1940), American novelist.

Morse, Jedidiah (1761–1826), American Congregational minister and geographer; father of Samuel F(inley) B(resse) Morse.

Morse, Samuel F(inley) B(reese) (1791–1872), American inventor of the electric telegraph, artist and memoirist; son of the Jedidiah Morse.

Morsztyn, Jan Andrzej (1613–1693), Polish writer.

Morsztyn, Zbigniew (1627–1689), Polish writer.

Mortillet, (Louis-Laurent-Marie) Gabriel de (1821–1898), French archaeologist.

Mortimer, Penelope (Ruth Fletcher) (1918–99), English writer, author of the novel The Pumpkin Eater (1962) and the controversial biography Queen Elizabeth: A Life of the Queen Mother (1986).

Morton, Charles (c.1627–1698), English-born American Puritan clergyman and writer on religion, logic and science.

Morton, George (1585–1624), English Puritan leader, author of an account of the Plymouth Plantation in New England (1622); father of Nathaniel Morton.

Morton, John Maddison (1811–1891), English dramatist; son of Thomas Morton.

Morton, Nathaniel (1613–1686), English-born American Puritan leader, author of a history of New England as New Englands Memorial (1669), a work owing much to other writers; father of George Morton.

Morton, Sarah Wentworth (1759–1846), American writer and poet.

Morton, Thomas (c.1590–1647), English-born American trader and adventurer, author of New English Canaan (1637).

Morton, Thomas (c.1764–1838), English dramatist; father of John Maddison Morton.

Mosca, Gaetano (1858–1941), Italian jurist and political theorist, author of Elementi di scienza politica (1896; English trans. as The Ruling Class, 1939).

Moscherosch, Johann Michael (1601–1699), German Lutheran statesman and writer whose satirical gifts were revealed in his Wunderliche und wahrhafftige Gesichte Philanders von Sittewald (Peculiar and True Visions of Philanders von Sittewald, 1641–43).

Moschopoulos, Manuel (13th–14th Century), Byzantine scholar.

Moschus (flourished 150 BC), Greek poet and grammarian.

Moschus, John (c.550–619), Byzantine monk and writer, author of the Pratum Spirituale (The Spiritual Meadow) which dealt with spirtual experiences.

Mościcki, Ignacy (1867–1946), Polish politician, scholar and scientist who served as president of Poland (1926–39).

Möser, Justus (1720–1794), German political essayist and poet whose output presaged the Sturm und Drang movement.

Moses (ben Shem Tov) de Leon (1250–1305), Spanish Jewish Kabbalist, reputedly the author of the Sefer ha-zohar (The Book of Splendour), a celebrated vol. of Jewish mysticism.

Mosheim, Johann Lorenz von (1694–1755), German Lutheran theologian and church historian.

Moss, Howard (1922–1987), American poet, editor, essayist, reviewer and dramatist.

Motherwell, William (1797–1835), Scottish journalist and poet.

Motley, John Lothrop (1814–1877), American diplomat and historian, author of The Rise of the Dutch Republic (1856).

Motley, Willard (1912–1965), American novelist and short-story writer.

Moto-ori Norinaga (1730–1801), notable Japanese literarary scholar.

Mott, Frank Luther (1886–1964), American scholar of journalism.

Motteux, Peter Anthony (1660–1718), English jouralist, dramatist and translator.

Motteville, Françoise Bertaut, Dame de (c.1621–1689), French memorialist, author of the Mémoires (1723).

Mottley, John (1692–1750), English dramatist and biographer.

Mottram, R(alph) H(ale) (1883–1971), English novelist.

Mo-tzu (c.470–c.391 BC), Chinese philosopher.

Moulton, (Ellen) Louise Chandler (1835–1908), American poet and writer.

Mourao-Ferreira, David (1927–1996), Portuguese writer and poet.

Mourning Dove (actually Hum-Ishu-Ma) (1888–1936), native American novelist and storyteller, author of the novel Cogewea the Half-Blood: A Depiction of the Great Montana Cattle Range (1927).

Mowatt, Anna Cora (née Ogden) (1819–1870), American actress and dramatist, best remembered for her satirical play Fashion (1845).

Moxon, Edward (1801–1858), English publisher, bookseller and poet.

Moyes, (Gertrude) Patricia (1923–2000), Irish-born English writer of detective fiction.

Mqhayi, Samuel E(dward) K(rune) (1875–1945), South African poet, writer and translator.

Mubārak, 'Alī Pasha (c.1823–1893), Egyptian writer and educator.

Mubarrad, al- (actually Abū al-'Abbās Muhammad ibn Yazīd) (826–898), Arab literary scholar and grammarian.

Muggleton, Lodowick (1609–1698), English Puritan religious leader who espoused an anti-Trinitarian heresy with his cousin John Reeve in A Transcendent Spiritual Treatise upon Several Heavenly Doctrines (1652) and A Divine Looking-Glass (1656).

Muhammad ibn Falāh (c.1400–1461), Persian Muslim theologian who founded the Musha'sha sect of Shī'ism, author of the Kalam al-mahdi (The Words of the Mahdi).

Muhāsibī, al- (actually Abū Allāh al-Harith ibn Asad al-'Anazī al-Muhāsibī) (c.781–857), Iraqi Muslim mystic of the Sūfi sect.

Muir, Edwin (1887–1959), prominent Scottish poet, critic and translator, particularly known for his poetry vols The Voyage (1946) and The Labyrinth (1949).

Muir, John (1838–1914), American naturalist and writer.

Mukammas, David al- (actually David Abū Sulaymān ibn Marwān ar-Raqqī al-Mukammas) (10th Century), Jewish philosopher.

Mulcaster, Richard (c.1530–1611), English schoolmaster, author of two vols on education, Positions (1581) and The Elementarie (1582).

Mulford, Clarence E(dward) (1883–1956), American writer of Westerns, creator of Hopalong Cassidy.

Mulford, Prentice (1834–1891), American journalist and essayist.

Mulla Sadra (c.1571–1640), Persian philosopher.

Müller, Friedrich (1749–1825), German poet, dramatist and painter who was known as Friedrich Maler (i.e. Painter).

Müller, Friedrich (1834–1898), Bohemian philologist.

Müller, Georg Elias (1850–1934), German experimental pyschologist.

Müller, Heiner (1929–1996), German dramatist and writer.

Müller, Johannes von (1752–1809), significant Swiss historian, author of the Geschichten Schweizerischer Eidgenossenschaft (1786–1808).

Müller, Karl Otfried (1797–1840), German scholar who devoted himself to the study of ancient Greece, author of Geschichten hellenischer Stamme und Stadte (History of Greek Cities and Peoples, 1820).

Müller, Sophus Otto (1846–1934), Danish paleontologist.

Müller, Wilhelm (1794–1827), admired German poet whose Die Schöne Müllerin (The Fair Maid of the Mill, 1821) and Die Winterreise (The Winter Journey, 1821) inspired the great song cycles by Schubert.

Multatuli (actually Eduard Douwes Dekker) (1820–1887), notable Dutch novelist, best known for his Max Havelaar (1860).

Mumford, Lewis (1895–1990), American social critic and writer.

Mun, Thomas (1571–1641), English economist who published a cogent treatise on the balance of trade theory in his A Discourse of Trade, from England unto the East Indies (1621).

Munby, Arthur Joseph (1828–1910), English poet and diarist.

Munch, Peter Andreas (1810–1863), Norwegian historian, author of Det norske Folks Historie (The History of the Norwegian People, 1852–63).

Munday, Anthony (c.1560–1633), esteemed English poet, dramatist, pamphleteer and translator.

Müneccim Başî (actually Derviş Ahmet Dede ibn Lutfullah) (1631–1702), Ottoman historian who wrote a universal history.

Munford, Robert (c.1730–1784), American dramatist, poet and translator; father of William Munford.

Munford, William (1775–1825), American poet, writer and translator; son of Robert Munford.

Munk, Kaj Harald Leininger (1898–1944), Danish priest, patriot and dramatist who wrote the plays En Idealist (1928; English trans. as Herod the King, 1955), Cant (1931), Ordet (1932; English trans. as The Word, 1955) and Han sidder ved Smeltediglen (1938; English trans. as He Sits at the Melting-Pot, 1944); was murdered by the Nazis.

Munro, Hector Hugh (1870–1916), Scottish short-story writer who wrote under the name Saki.

Munshi, Kanaiyalal (1887–1971), Indian novelist.

Münster, Sebastian (1489–1552), Important German Hebrew scholar, author of the influential Cosmographia (Cosmography, 1544).

Münsterberg, Hugo (1863–1916), German-born American psychologist and philosopher.

Munthe, Axel Martin Fredrik (1857–1949), Swedish physician, psychiatrist and writer, author of the autobiographical account The Story of San Michele (1929).

Müntzer, Thomas (c.1489–1525), German Protestant Reformer and polemicist whose radical views culminated in his leadership of the Peasants' Revolt (1524–25); was executed.

Muralt, Béat-Louis de (1665–1749), Swiss writer of a Pietist persuasion.

Murasaki Shikibu (c.978–c.1026), famous Japanese court lady and writer, author of the celebrated novel Genji monogatari (English trans as The Tale of Genji, 1935).

Muratori, Lodovico Antonio (1672–1750), oustanding Italian scholar who wrote the important Antiquitates Italicae Medii Aevi (Antiquities of the Italian Middle Ages, 6 vols, 1738–42).

Murdoch, Frank Hitchcock (1843–1872), American actor and dramatist.

Mure, Sir William (1594–1657), Scottish poet.

Muretus (actually Marc-Antoine Muret) (1526–1585), French poet and scholar.

Murfree, Mary Noailles (1850–1922), American novelist and short-story writer.

Murger, (Louis-) Henri (1822–1861), French writer and poet who was known for his novel Scènes de la vie bohème (1847–49), which inspired operas by Leoncavallo and Puccini.

Murillo, Gerardo (1875–1964), Mexican painter and writer.

Muris, Johannes de (c.1300–c.1351), significant French music theorist, astronomer and mathematician.

Murner, Thomas (1475–1537), German Franciscan friar and poet who was known for his satirical poetry.

Muro Kyūsō (1658–1734), prominent Japanese Confucian scholar and government official.

Murphy, Arthur (1727–1805), English barrister, journalist, actor and dramatist.

Murray, Charles (1864–1941), Scottish poet.

Murray, (George) Gilbert (Aimé) (1866–1957), English scholar who made effective translations of the ancient Greek dramatists.

Murray, Sir James (Augustus Henry) (1837–1915), English lexicographer who edited the New English Dictionary on Historical Principles (1884–1915), later known as the Oxford English Dictionary.

Murray, John (1741–1815), English-born American preacher and writer who founded Universalism; husband of Judith Murray.

Murray, John Courtney (1904–1967), American Roman Catholic priest and theologian.

Murray, Judith (1751–1820), American writer and poet who wrote under the name Constantia; wife of John Murray.

Murray, Lindley (1745–1826), American-born English Quaker minister and grammarian.

Murry, John Middleton (1889–1957), influential English editor, critic, essayist and poet.

Musaeus (5th–6th Century), Greek poet, author of Hero and Leander.

Musaus, Johann Karl August (1735–87), German writer of satirical fairy tales.

Musil, Robert Edler von (1880–1942), Austrian writer and dramatist, author of the unfinished expansive novel Der Mann ohne Eigenschaften (1930–32: English trans. as The Man Without Qualities, 1953–60).

Muslim ibn al-Hajjāj (actually Abū al-Husayn Muslim ibn al-Hajjāj al-Qushayrī) (c.817–875), Islamic scholar.

Mussato, Albertino (1261–1329), noted Italian statesman, historian and poet.

Musset, (Louis-Charles-) Alfred de (1810–1857), eminent French poet and dramatist, a leading Romanticist.

Mutanabbī, al- (actually Abū at-Tayyib Ahmad ibn Husayn al-Mutanabbī) (915–965), famous Arab poet who led an adventurous life; was murdered by bandits.

Muáková, Johanna (1830–1899), Czech novelist who wrote under the name Karolina Světlá.

Myers, Ernest James (1844–1921), English poet and translator; brother of F(rederic) W(illiam) H(enry) Myers.

Myers, F(rederic) W(illiam) H(enry) (1843–1901), English poet, critic and essayist; brother of Ernest James Myers.

Myers, L(eopold) H(amilton) (1881–1944), English novelist who wrote the tetralogy The Near and the Far East (1929), Prince Jali (1931), The Root and the Flower (1935) and The Pool of Vishnu (1940).

Myers, Peter Hamilton (1812–1878), American lawyer and novelist.

Myres, Sir John Linton (1869–1954), English historian and anthropologist who was known for his studies of ancient history.

Nabbes, Thomas (1605–41), English dramatist and poet.

Nābighad, an- (actually an-Nābighah adh-Dhubyāni) (7th Century), Arab poet.

Nabokov, Vladimir (Vladimirovich) (1899–1977), notable Russian-born American novelist and poet, author of the famous novel Lolita (1955).

Nadel, S(iegfried) F(rederick) (1903–1956), English anthropologist, author of The Foundations of Social Anthropology (1951) and Theory of Social Structure (published 1958).

Naevius, Gnaeus (c.270–c.199 BC), important Roman poet and dramatist, creator of the fabulae praetextas (historical play).

Nagai Kafū (actually Nagai Sōkichi) (1879–1959), Japanese novelist.

Nagarjuna (c.150–c.250), Indian Buddhist monk and philosopher who founded the Madhyamika (Middle Path) school.

Nagel, Ernest (1901–85), Bohemian-born American philosopher, author of Logic Without Metaphysics (1957) and The Structure of Science (1961).

Nahman of Bratslav, Rabbi (1772–1811), Hasidic writer.

Naidu, Sarojini (née Chattopadhyay) (1879–1949), prominent Indian feminist, politician and poet, known as the 'Nightingale of India', author of the poetry collections The Golden Threshold (1905) and The Bird of Time (1912).

Naima, Mustafa (1655–1716), Turkish historian who wrote Tarih (English trans. as Annals of the Turkish Empire from 1591–1659 of the Christian Era, 1832).

Naipaul, Shiva (1945–1985), West Indian novelist.

Nairne, Carolina (née Oliphant), Baroness (1766–1845), English poet and songwriter.

Nakae Chōmin (actually Nakae Tokusuke) (1847–1901), Japanese writer.

Nakae Tōju (1608–1648), Japanese Neo-Confucian scholar.

Naka Michiyo (1851–1908), Japanese historian.

Nalbandean, Mikael (1829–1866), Armenian writer.

Nałkowska, Zofia (1884–1954), Polish writer.

Nāmdev (c.1270–c.1350), notable Indian poet and saint.

Namier, Sir Lewis Bernstein (1888–1960), English historian who wrote the influential tome The Structure of Politics at the Accession of George III (1929).

Namiki Gohei (1747–1808), Japanese dramatist of the Kabuki theater.

Namiki Shōzō I (18th Century), Japanese dramatist.

Namiki Shōzō II (died 1807), Japanese dramatist and writer.

Namora, Fernando Goncalves (1919–1989), Portuguese poet, writer and physician.

Napier, John (1550–1617), Scottish mathematician and writer on theology.

Napier, Sir William Francis Patrick (1785–1860), English general and historian, particularly known for his History of the War in the Peninsula... (6 vols, 1828–40).

Narayan, R. K. (actually Rasipuram Krishnaswami Narayanswami) (1906–2001), gifted Indian novelist and short-story writer whose most acclaimed work was the novel The Guide (1958).

Nardi, Jacopo (1476–c.1564), Italian statesman, historian, dramatist and translator, author of the Istoria della citta' di Firenze (History of the City of Florence, 1582).

Nariño, Antonio (1765–1823), Colombian revolutionary and writer.

Naruszewicz, Adam (Stanisław) (1733–1796), Polish historian and poet.

Nasby, Petroleum V(esuvius) (actually David Ross Locke) (1833–1888), American journalist who was known for his satirical bent.

Nascimento, Francisco Manuel do (1734–1819), Portuguese poet who embraced the cause of Romanticism and wrote under the name Filinto Elisio.

Nāser-e Khosrow (actually Abū Mo' īn Nāser-e Khosrow al-Marvāzī al-Qubādiyānī) (1004–c.1075), renowned Persian poet and Islamic theologian of the Shī'ah sect.

Nash, (Frederic) Ogden (1902–1971), American poet, a master of wit.

Nashe or Nash, Thomas (1567–c.1601), English writer, dramatist, poet and political pamphleteer, author of the first English picaresque novel The unfortunate traveller, or The Life of Jack Wilton (1594).

Natalis, Alexander (actually Alexandre Noel) (1639–1724), French theologian and historian who advocated the restriction of papal hegemony, author of Selecta historiae ecclesiaticae capita (Selected Chapters of Ecclesiastical History, 24 vols, 1676–86; revised edition as Historia ecclesiastica veteris et novi testamenti (Ecclesiastical History of the Old and New Testaments), 8 vols, 1699).

Nathan, George Jean (1882–1958), American drama critic, editor and writer.

Nathan, Robert (Gruntal) (1894–1985), American novelist, poet and dramatist.

Natorp, Paul (1854–1924), German philosopher of the Neo-Kantian school.

Natsume Sōseki (actually Natsume Kinosuke) (1867–1916), Japanese novelist, author of Wagahai-wa Neko-de aru (1906; English trans. as I Am a Cat, 1961), Botchan (1906; English trans. as Master Darling, 1918) and Kusamakura (1906: English trans. as The Three-Cornered World, 1965).

Naughton, William (John Francis) (1910–1992), Irish dramatist, novelist and short-story writer.

Naumann, Friedrich (1860–1919), German politician and theorist.

Nava'i, (Mir) Ali Shir (1441–1501), Turkish poet and scholar.

Nayler or Naylor, James (1618–1660), English Quaker preacher and writer.

Nazor, Vladimir (1876–1949), Croatian poet.

Nazzām, Ibrāhīm an- (actually Abū Ishāq Ibrāhīm ibn Sayyār Hanī' an-Nazzām) (c.775–c.845), Iraqi Muslim theologian, jurist, historian and poet.

Neal, Daniel (1678–1743), English Nonconformist minister and historian.

Neal, John (1793–1876), American novelist, critic and poet.

Neal, Joseph Clay (1807–1847), American journalist and writer who was known for his humour.

Neale, J(ohn) M(ason) (1818–1866), English hymnist, historian and translator, author of The History of the Holy Eastern Church (1847–73).

Nearing, Scott (1883–1983), American economist and environmentalist, especially remembered for his exposition of the counterculture in Living the Good Life (1954).

Nedham or Needham, Marchamont (1620–1678), English journalist who was the principal author of Mercurius Britanicus (1643–46).

Nedim, Ahmed (1681–1730), celebrated Turkish poet, a master of lyricism.

Nefi'i of Erzurum (actually Ömer) (died 1636), famous Turkish poet who was renowned as a satirist and panegyrist.

Negri, Ada (1870–1945), Italian poet and short-story writer.

Neidhart von Reuenthal (c.1180–c.1250), German poet, creator of hofische Dorfpoesie (courtly village poetry).

Neihardt, John G(neisenau) (1881–1973), American poet and writer.

Nekrasov, Nikolai Alexeievich (1821–1878), Russian poet and journalist.

Nekrasov, Viktor Platonovich (1911–1987), Russian novelist, short-story writer and essayist whose dissident views led him to emigrate to France in 1974.

Nelligan, Émile (1897–1941), French-Canadian poet.

Nelson, Leonard (1882–1927), German philosopher.

Nemerov, Howard (1920–1991), admired American poet, writer and essayist; was Poet Laureate of the US (1988–90).

Nemesianus, Marcus Aurelius Olympius (3rd Century), Roman poet.

Nemesius of Emesa (4th Century), Christian bishop of Emesa, apologist and philosopher who wrote Peri physeos anthropou (On the Nature of Man).

Nemirovich-Danchenko, Vladimir Ivanovich (1858–1943), Russian dramatist, novelist and theatre producer who co-founded the celebrated Moscow Art Theatre.

Nennius (c.800), Welsh antiquarian.

Nepos, Cornelius (c.100–c.25 BC), Roman historian and biographer.

Neruda, Pablo (actually Neftalí Ricardo Reyes Basoalto) (1904–1973), prominent Chilean poet and diplomat; won the Nobel Prize for Literature (1971).

Nerval, Gerárd de (actually Gérárd Labrunie) (1808–1855), French writer and poet who wrote both Symbolic and Surrealist verse; dissipation and insanity led him to commit suicide.

Nervo, Amado (actually Juan Crisóstomo Ruiz de Nervo) (1870–1919), Mexican poet and diplomat, a principal figure in the Modernist movement of Spanish-American literature.

Nesbit, E(dith) (1858–1924), English writer, best remembered for her children's books.

Nesimi, Seyyid Imadeddin (died c.1418), renowned Turkish poet who wrote mystic verse.

Neşri (actually Hüseyn ibn Eyne Beg) (died c.1520), Turkish historian.

Nestor (c.1056–1113), Russian monk and hagiographer.

Nestroy, Johann Nepomuk Eduard Ambrosius (1801–1862), Austrian dramatist of comic plays.

Neto, (Antônio) Agostinho (1922–1979), Angolan physician, revolutionary and poet who served as the first president of the People's Republic of Angola (1975–79).

Neurath, Otto (1882–1945), German philosopher and sociologist.

Nevā'ī, Alī Shīr (1441–1501), noted Turkish poet and scholar.

Nevins, Allan (1890–1971), American historian.

Newbolt, Sir Henry John (1862–1938), English poet and historian, particularly remembered for his patriotic and sea lyrics.

Newcastle, Margaret, Duchess of (1623–1673), English poet, dramatist and writer; wife of William Cavendish, 1st Duke of Newcastle.

Newcastle, William Cavendish, 1st Duke of (1592–1676), English poet and dramatist; husband of Margaret, Duchess of Newcastle.

Newell, Peter (1862–1924), American writer and illustrator who was best known for his humour.

Newell, Robert Henry (1836–1901), American journalist, writer and poet whose humorous effusions often appeared under the name Orpheus C Kerr, a pun on the words 'office seeker'.

Newman, John Henry (1801–1890), eminent English Anglican churchman, later Roman Catholic cardinal, writer and poet who was a major figure in the Oxford Movement.

Newton, A(lfred) Edward (1863–1940), American book collector, writer and dramatist.

Newton, Sir Charles Thomas (1816–1894), English archaeologist.

Newton, Sir Isaac (1643–1727), English physicist and mathematician, author of the important vols Principia (1687) and Opticks (1704).

Newton, John (1725–1807), English Evangelical leader, hymnist and letter writer.

Nexø, Martin Andersen (1869–1954), Danish writer who championed the lot of the downtrodden of society and embraced Communism, author of the novels Pelle erobreren (4 vols, 1906–10; English trans. as Pelle the Conqueror, 1913–16), Ditte mennskebarn (5 vols, 1917–21; English trans. as Ditte, Daughter of Man, 1920–22) and Midt i en Jaerntid (1929: English trans. as In God's Land, 1933).

Nezāmi (actually Elyās Yūsof Nezāmi Ganjavī) (c.1141–c.1207), Persian poet.

Nguyen Du (actually Nguyen-Du Thanh-Hien) (1765–1820), notable Vietnamese poet, author of the national epic Kim Van Kieu (English trans., 1968).

Niceforo, Alfredo (1876–1960), Italian sociologist, criminologist and statistician, best known for his theory of the dual ego in man's being as delineated in his L'io profondo e le sue maschere (The Deep Ego and Its Masks, 1949).

Nicephorus I, Saint (c.758–829), Greek Orthodox theologian, historian and patriarch of Constantinople.

Nicephorus, Callistus Xanthopoulos (c.1256–c.1335), Byzantine historian, writer and poet.

Nicetas of Remesiana (5th Century), Greek Christian bishop theologian and composer.

Nicetas Stethatos (c.1000–c.1080), Byzantine monk, mystic and theologian, the leading champion of Greek Orthodoxy in opposition to Roman Catholic doctrine.

Nicholas III (11th Century), Byzantine theological scholar and Orthodox patriarch of Constantinople.

Nicholas of Autrecourt (c.1300–c.1350), influential French philosopher and theologian whose Skepticism led to his condemnation as a heretic by Pope Clement VI in 1346.

Nicholas of Clémanges (actually Nicolas Poillevilain) (c.1363–1437), French theologian, scholar and poet who was a leading advocate of ecclesiastical reform in the face of church corruption.

Nicholas of Cusa (1401–1464), important German Roman Catholic cardinal, scientist and philosopher, author of De docta ignorantia (On Learned Ignorance, 1440), in which he declared that the attainment of the full knowledge of God and the universe was impossible.

Nicholas of Damascus (1st Centry BC), Greek historian and philosopher.

Nicholas of Hereford (died c.1420), English theologian who was a leading champion of the Lollard reform movement in the Roman Catholic Church, a movement he later denounced.

Nicholas of Lyra (c.1270–1349), learned French theologian of the Franciscans who published the first biblical commentary in his expansive Postillae perpetuae in universam S. Scripturam (Commentary Notes to the Universal Holy Scripture, 50 vols).

Nichols, John (1745–1826), English printer, antiquarian and biographer.

Nichols, Robert Malise Bowyer (1893–1944), English poet and dramatist.

Nicholson, Meredith (1866–1947), American novelist, short-story writer, essayist and poet.

Nicholson, Reynold Alleyne (1868–1945), English Orientalist, author of the valuable Literary History of the Arabs (1907).

Nicodemus the Hagiorite (1748–1809), Greek Orthodox monk and theologian.

Nicol, Davidson (Sylvester Hector Willoughby) (1924–94), Sierra Leonean physician, diplomat, writer and poet who sometimes wrote under the name Abioseh Nicol.

Nicolai, Christoph Friedrich (1733–1811), German writer, journalist and bookseller.

Nicolay, John George (actually Johann Georg Nicolai) (1832–1901), German-born American biographer who collaborated with John Hay on a major biography of Abraham Lincoln (10 vols, 1890).

Nicole, Pierre (1625–1695), French theologian, best remembered for his polemical writings championing Jansenism.

Nicoletti, Paolo (14th–15th Century), Italian philosopher.

Nicolson, Sir Harold (George) (1886–1968), English diplomat, writer, biographer and critic; husband of Victoria Sackville-West.

Niebuhr, Barthold Georg (1776–1831), influential German historian who was a pioneering figure in the use of source criticism, author of Römische Geschichte (3 vols, 1811–32; English trans. as History of Rome, 1828–42).

Niebuhr, Carsten (1733–1815), German traveller who was the only survivor of the first scientific expedition to Arabia, which he recounted in two vols (1772, 1774).

Niebuhr, (Helmut) Richard (1894–1962), American theologian, author of The Meaning of Revelation (1941), Christ and Culture (1951) and Radical Monotheism and Western Civilization (1960); brother of Reinhold Niebuhr.

Niebuhr, Reinhold (1892–1971), influential American theologian and writer on ethical, social and political subjects, author of The Nature and Destiny of Man (2 vols, 1941, 1943); brother of (Helmut) Richard Niebuhr.

Nielsen, Morten (1922–1944), esteemed Danish poet; as a member of the resistance to the German occupation of his homeland, he was killed by the Nazis.

Niemcewicz, Julian Ursyn (1758–1841), Polish dramatist, writer, poet and translator.

Niemöller, (Fredrich Gustav Emil) Martin (1892–1984), courageous German Protestant pastor and theologian who opposed the Nazi regime and survived years in concentration camps, author of Vom U-Boot zur Kanzel (1934; English trans. as From U-Boat to Concentration Camp, 1939).

Nietzsche, Friedrich Wilhelm (1844–1900), German philosopher, scholar and critic who wrote such important works as Die Geburt der Tragödie (1872; English trans. as The Birth of Tragedy, 1968), Also sprach Zarathustra (parts 1–3, 1883–84, part 4, 1891; English trans. as Thus Spake Zarathustra, 1954), Jenseits von Gut und Böse (1886; English trans. as Beyond Good and Evil, 1968) and Zur Genealogie der Moral (1887; English trans. as On the Genealogy of Morals, 1968).

Nifo, Agostino (c.1473–c.1539), Italian philosopher and Christian apologist who wrote Tractatus de immortalitate animae contra Pomponatium (Treatise on the Immortality of the Soul Against Pomponazzi, 1581).

Nijhoff, Martinus (1894–1953), Danish poet who was known as a master of his craft.

Nijlen, Jan van (1884–1965), Flemish poet.

Niles, Samuel (1674–1762), American Congregationalist clergyman, historian and polemicist.

Nims, John Frederick (1913–99), American poet, writer and translator.

Nin, Anaïs (1903–1977), French-born American novelist, short-story writer and diarist.

Nishi Armane (1829–1897), Japanese philosopher.

Nishida Kitarō (1870–1945), important Japanese philosopher who assimilated Western thought with non-Western ideas.

Nishiyama Sōin (1605–1682), Japanese poet.

Nithard (c.790–844), Frankish count and historian.

Niven, Frederick John (1878–1944), Scottish novelist, essayist and poet.

Noailles, Anna (-Élisabeth, Princess Brancovan, Comtesse Mathieu) de (1876–1933), French poet and novelist who was called 'Princesses des lettres' of France.

Nōami (1397–1494), Japanese poet, painter and art critic who was also known as Shinnō.

Nobre, António (1867–1900), Portuguese poet, remembered for his So (Alone, 1892).

Nock, Albert Jay (1870–1945), American writer and essayist who expounded on a wide variety of subjects.

Nodier, Charles (1780–1844), French writer.

Noel, Roden Berkely Wriothesley (1834–1894), English poet.

Noguchi, Yone (1875–1947), Japanese poet.

Nöldeke, Theodor (1836–1930), German language scholar and historian who was an authority on Semitic languages and Islamic history.

Noma Hiroshi (1915–91), Japanese novelist and essayist.

Nonius Marcellus (c.5th Century), African Latin grammarian and lexicographer, compiler of De compendiosa doctrina.

Nonnus (5th Century), Greek poet who was admired for his epic Dionysiaca.

Noot, Jonker Jan van der (c.1540–c.1596), Dutch poet, author of the epic Olympiados.

Nordal, Sigurour (Jóhannesson) (1886–1974), Icelandic scholar, poet and short-story writer.

Nordau, Max (actually Max Simon Sudfeld) (1849–1923), Austro-Hungarian writer, dramatist, poet, Zionist and physician, best known for his controversial polemical vol. Die conventionellen Lügen der Kulturmenschheit (1883; English trans. as The Conventional Lies of Our Civilization, 1884).

Nordenflycht, Hedvig Charlotta (1718–1763), Swedish poet who was esteemed for her love poems.

Nordenskiöld, (Nils) Erland (Herbert) (1877–1932), important Swedish ethnologist and archaeologist who was an authority on the culture of the South American Indians.

Nordhoff, Charles (1830–1901), German-born American journalist and writer; grandfather of Charles Bernard Nordhoff.

Nordhoff, Charles Bernard (1887–1947), American novelist who collaborated with James N Hall on Mutiny on the Bounty (1932), Men Against the Sea (1934) and Pitcairn's Island (1934); grandson of Charles Nordhoff.

Nordström, Ludvig Anselm (1882–1942), Swedish writer.

Norris, (Benjamin) Frank(lin) (1870–1902), American novelist, short-story writer and essayist; brother of Charles G(ilman) Norris.

Norris, Charles G(ilman) (1881–1945), American novelist; brother of (Benjamin) Frank(lin) Norris and husband of Kathleen Norris.

Norris, John (1657–1711), English poet and philosopher, author of An Essay towards the Theory of the Ideal or Intelligible World (1701–04).

Norris, Kathleen (1880–1966), American novelist; wife of Charles G(ilman) Norris.

North, Christopher (actually John Wilson) (1785–1854), Scottish writer.

North, Roger (1653–1734), English lawyer and biographer.

North, Sir Thomas (1535–c.1603), English translator, especially known for his translation from the French of Jacques Amyot's version of Plutarch's Lives of the Noble Grecians and Romans (1579).

Norton, Andrews (1786–1853), American biblical scholar, author of The Evidences of the Genuineness of the Gospels (3 vols, 1837, 1844) and Internal Evidences of the Genuineness of the Gospels (1855); father of Charles Eliot Norton.

Norton, Caroline Elizabeth Sarah (née Sheridan) (1808–1877), Irish poet and novelist; granddaughter of Richard Brinsley Sheridan.

Norton, Charles Eliot (1827–1908), American scholar and educator; son of Andrews Norton.

Norton, John (1606–1663), English-born American Puritan leader and scholar.

Norton, Thomas (1532–1584), English dramatist and poet who, with Thomas Sackville, wrote the earliest English tragedy Gorboduc (1561).

Norwid, Cyprian Kamil (1821–1883), Polish poet and writer.

Nossack, Hans Erich (1901–1977), German novelist, poet and dramatist.

Nostradamus (1503–1566), celebrated French astrologer and physician whose prophecies were published in the vol. Centuries (1555).

Noth, Martin (1902–1968), German biblical scholar.

Nott, Henry Junius (1797–1837), American jurist and writer, author of the picaresque Novelettes of a Traveller, or, Odds and Ends from the Knapsack of Thomas Singularity, Journeyman Printer (1834).

Novalis (actually Friedrich Leopold, Freiherr von Hardenberg) (1772–1801), significant German poet, writer and theorist, known as the 'Prophet of Romanticism'.

Novatian (c.200–c.258), Roman theologian and 2nd antipope who was known for his rigorist doctrine; excommunicated and probably martyred during the reign of Emperor Valerian.

Novikov, Nikolai Ivanovich (1744–1818), Russian writer, philanthropist and Freemason whose enlightened views led to his imprisonment by Empress Catherine II the Great in 1792; was released by Emperor Paul in 1796.

Nowell, Alexander (c.1507–1602), English Anglican priest, scholar and dean of St Paul's Cathedral in London, author of the catechism of the Church of England (in the Prayer Book, 1549, supplemented 1604).

Noyes, Alfred (1880–1958), English poet and dramatist, best known for his lyric style of poetry.

Noyes, John Humphrey (1811–1886), American socio-religious idealist who espoused a doctrine of perfectionism, author of Bible Communism (1848) and History of American Socialisms (1870).

Nozick, Robert (1938–2002), American philosopher whose writings included Anarchy, State and Utopia (1981), The Examined Life (1989) and The Nature of Rationality (1993).

Numenius of Apamea (2nd Century), Greek philosopher.

Núñez, Rafael (1825–1894), Colombian politician, writer and poet.

Núñez de Arce, Gaspar (1832–1903), Spanish poet, dramatist and statesman.

Nye, Bill (actually Edgar Wilson Nye) (1850–1896), American journalist and writer who was known for his humorous bent.

Oakes, Urian (c.1631–1681), American clergyman and poet.

Obradović, Dositej (1742–1811), Serbian writer and translator.

O'Brian, Patrick (actually Richard Patrick Russ) (1914–2000), English novelist who won acclaim for his vivid depiction of seafaring life during the Napoleonic era.

O'Brien, Fitz-James (c.1828–1862), Amerian writer, dramatist and poet whose tales presage modern science fiction; died of wounds sustained as a Union soldier in the Civil War.

O'Brien, Flann (actually Brian Ó Nuallain) (1911–1966), Irish novelist, dramatist and columnist, author of the novel At Swim-Two Birds (1939).

Ó Bruadair, Dáibhidh (c.1625–1698), compelling Irish-Gaelic poet.

Obstfelder, Sigbjørn (1866–1900), Norwegian poet of a refined Symbolist persuasion.

O'Casey, Sean (1880–1964), Irish dramatist.

Ockham, William of (c.1285–c.1349), important English Roman Catholic Scholastic philosopher who was excommunicated for his opposition to unlimited papal authority.

O'Clery, Michael (1575–1643), Irish historian.

O'Connor, Edwin (1918–1968), American writer, particularly remembered for The Last Hurrah (1956) and The Edge of Sadness (1961).

O'Connor, Frank (actually Michael O'Donovan) (1903–1966), Irish novelist, short-story writer, dramatist and translator.

O'Connor, (Mary) Flannery (1925–1964), notable American novelist and short-story writer, especially admired for her novels Wise Book (1952) and The Violent Bear it Away (1960).

O'Connor, William Douglas (1832–1889), American journalist and writer, best remembered for his profile of Walt Whitman in The Good Gray Poet (1866).

Odell, George C(linton) D(ensmore) (1866–1949), American literary scholar.

Odell, Jonathan (1737–1818), American poet and writer who vociferously championed the Loyalist cause during the American Revolution.

Odets, Clifford (1906–1963), American dramatist of social protest, author of Paradise Lost (1935), Waiting for Lefty (1935), Awake and Sing (1935) and Golden Boy (1937).

Odiorne, Thomas (1769–1851), American poet, author of The Progress of Refinement (1792).

Odoric of Pordenone (c.1286–1331), Italian Franciscan friar and traveller who wrote an account of his travels in China.

O'Dowd, Bernard Patrick (1866–1953), Australian poet.

Odum, Howard Washington (1884–1954), American sociologist, author of Rainbow Round My Shoulder: The Blue Trail of Black Ulysses (1928).

Oecolampadius, John (actually Johannes Huszgen) (1482–1531), prominent Swiss Protestant Reformer, preacher and patristic scholar.

Oehlenschläger, Adam Gottlob (1779–1850), notable Danish poet and dramatist who was hailed as the national poet of Denmark.

Oertel, Hanns (1868–1952), German linguist, an authority on Sanskrit.

O'Faolain, Sean (actually Sean Whelan) (1900–1991), Irish writer, biographer and essayist.

O'Flaherty, Liam (1896–1984), Irish novelist and short-story writer.

Ofterdingen, Heinrich von (12th–13th Century), celebrated German Minnesinger.

Ogburn, William Fielding (1886–1959), American sociologist.

Ogden, Charles Kay (1889–1957), English linguist and writer who created Basic English for the international use of English.

Ogilby, John (1600–1676), Scottish-born English printer, poet and translator.

Ogilvie, James (1775–1820), Scottish-born American writer, best known for his Philosophical Essays (1816); committed suicide.

O'Grady, Standish James (1846–1928), Irish novelist and literary historian.

Ogyū Sorai (1666–1728), Japanese scholar of Chinese culture who was a major figure in Confucianism.

O'Hara, Frank (1926–1966), American poet and critic.

O'Hara, John (Henry) (1905–1970), American novelist and short-story writer.

O'Hara, Theodore (1820–1867), American journalist and poet.

O'Higgins, Harvey (Jerrold) (1876–1929), Canadian-born American writer.

Okada, John (1923–1971), American dramatist, author of the Nisei antiwar play No-No Boy (1957).

Okamoto Kidō (1872–1939), Japanese dramatist of the Kabuki theater.

Okawa Shūmei (1886–1957), Japanese political scientist who espoused the cause of ultra-nationalism.

Oken, Lorenz (1779–1851), German naturalist.

Okigbo, Christopher (1932–1967), Nigerian poet; died in the fight for Biafran independence from Nigeria.

Okudzhava, Bulat Shalovich (1924–1997), Russian poet, writer and folksinger.

Ólafsson, Eggert (1726–1768), Icelandic poet and antiquarian.

Ólafsson, Stefan (1620–1688), Icelandic poet.

Olcott, Henry Steel (1832–1907), American lawyer and writer who was a co-founder of the Theosophical Society and author of the Buddhist Catechism (1881).

Oldham, John (1653–1683), English poet and translator.

Oldmixon, John (c.1673–1742), English historian, dramatist and poet.

Old Moore, Francis Moore (1657–1714), English astrologer and physician, author of the famous Vox Stellarum, an Almanac for 1701 with astrological observations (1700).

Oldys, William (1696–1761), English biographer and editor.

Olesha, Yuri (Karlovich) (1899–1960), Russian writer.

Oliphant, Laurence (1829–1888), English mystic, traveller and writer.

Oliphant, Margaret (née Wilson) (1828–1897), Scottish novelist and biographer.

Oliveira Martins, Joaquim Pedro de (1845–1894), Portuguese writer and biographer.

Ollivier, Émile (1825–1913), French statesman and writer, author of L'Empire liberal (The Liberal Empire, 17 vols).

Olmedo, José Joaquín (1780–1847), Ecuadoran statesman and poet, especially esteemed for his patriotic odes.

Olmsted, Frederick Law (1822–1903), American landscape architect, conservationist and travel writer.

Olson, Charles (John) (1910–1970), American poet, writer, dramatist and essayist, particularly known for his avant-garde poetry.

Olson, Elder (James) (1909–1992), American poet and critic.

Oman, John Wood (1860–1939), English Presbyterian theologian, author of The Natural and the Supernatural (1931).

Omar Khayyam (actually Gheyás od-Dín Abú ol-Fath 'Umar ebn Ebrahim ol-Khayyámí) (c.1048–1122), renowned Persian poet, mathematician and astronomer whose Ruba'iyat (Quatrains) are celebrated the world over.

Oña, Pedro de (c.1570–c.1643), Chilean poet.

O'Neill, Eugene (Gladstone) (1888–1953), important American dramatist and poet, author of such plays as Beyond the Horizon (1920), Anna Christie (1922), Strange Interlude (1928), Long Day's Journey into Night (1941) and The Iceman Cometh (1946); won the Nobel Prize for Literature (1936).

Onetti, Juan Carlos (1909–1994), Uruguayan-born Spanish novelist, short-story writer and essayist.

Onions, C(harles) T(albut) (1873–1965), English grammarian and lexicographer.

Onions, (George) Oliver (1873–1961), English novelist and short-story writer.

Opie, Amelia (née Alderson) (1769–1853), English novelist and poet, author of the novel Father and Daughter (1801).

Opie, Peter Mason (1918–1982), English writer and folklorist.

Opitz (von Boberfeld), Martin (1597–1639), Silesian poet and theorist who introduced Renaissance poetic theories to Germany.

Oppen, George (1908–1984), American poet who was the preeminent figure of the Objectivist school of verse.

Oppenheim, E(dward) Phillips (1866–1946), English novelist and short-story writer.

Oppenheim, James (1882–1932), American poet.

Oppenheim, Lassa Francis Lawrence (1858–1919), German-born English jurist and pedagogue, author of International Law: A Treatise (2 vols, 1905–06).

Orage, Alfred Richard (actually Alfred James Orage) (1873–1934), English editor and writer who championed the cause of guild socialism.

Orchard, William Edwin (1877–1955), English Roman Catholic priest and writer, author of The Temple (1913) and Sancta Sanctorum (1955).

Orczy, Baroness (Emmuska) (1865–1947), Hungarian-born English novelist, best remembered for The Scarlet Pimpernel (1905).

Orderic Vitalis (1075–c.1142), English monk and historian, author of the Historia ecclesiastica (c.1108–41).

O'Reilly, John Boyle (1844–1890), Irish-born American journalist and poet who was known as an advocate of Irish republicanism.

Oresme, Nicole d' (c.1325–1382), French Roman Catholic bishop and scholar, especially known for his opposition to Aristotelian thought.

Orhan Veli Kanik (1914–1950), admired Turkish poet.

Origen (c.185–c.254), Egyptian biblical scholar, theologian and writer, author of De Principiis (4 vols), an influential work on Christian doctrine.

Ørjasaeter, Tore (1886–1968), Norwegian poet.

Orkan, Władysław (actually Franciszek Smreczyński) (1875–1930), Polish poet and writer.

Ormond, John (1923–1900), Welsh poet and filmmaker.

Orosius, Paulus (5th Century), Christian theologian and apologist, author of Historiarum adversus paganos libra VII (English trans. as Seven Books of Histories Against the Pagans, 1936).

Orrery, Roger Boyle, 1st Earl of (1621–1679), Irish statesman, poet and dramatist.

Orsi, Paolo (1859–1935), Italian archaeologist who was an authority on Sicilian culture.

Ors y Rovira, Eugenio d' (1882–1954), Spanish novelist, essayist and art critic.

Ortega y Gasset, José (1883–1955), Spanish philosopher who espoused humanism.

Ortelius, Abraham (1527–1598), Belgian cartographer and antiquarian who published the earliest modern atlas in his Theatrum orbis terrarum (1570; English version as Theatre of the Whole World, 1606).

Ortese, Anna Maria (1914–1998), Italian writer.

Ortigão, José Duarte Ramalho (1836–1915), Portuguese journalist and essayist.

Orton, Joe (actually John Kingsley Orton) (1933–1967), English dramatist, author of the black comedy Loot (1965; revised version 1966); was murdered by his gay lover.

Orwell, George (actually Eric Arthur Blair) (1903–1950), notable English writer and critic, author of the satirical masterpieces Animal Farm (1945) and Nineteen Eighty-four (1949).

Orzeszkowa, Eliza (actually Eliza Pawłowska) (1841–1910), Polish novelist and short-story writer.

Osborn, Henry Fairfield (1857–1935), American paleontologist and museum curator, author of From the Greeks to Darwin (1894) and Origin and Evolution of Life (1917).

Osborn, Laughton (c.1809–1878), American writer, poet and dramatist.

Osborne, John (James) (1929–1994), significant English dramatist, author of Look Back in Anger (1956), The Entertainer (1957), Luther (1961), Inadmissible Evidence (1964), A Patriot for me (1965), West of Suez (1971) and Watch it Come Down (1976).

Osbourne, (Samuel) Lloyd (1868–1947), American novelist and dramatist.

Osgood, Frances Sargent (Locke) (1811–1850), American poet of sentimental verse.

O'Shaughnessy, Arthur (William Edgar) (1844–1881), English poet, best known for his Ode (We Are the Music-makers) (1874).

O'Sheel, Shaemas (1886–1954), American poet, particularly remembered for They Went Forth to Battle, But They Always Fell.

Oshio Heihachirō (1796–1837), Japanese philosopher of the Confucian school.

Osiander, Andreas (actually Andreas Hosemann) (1498–1552), German Protestant theologian and reformer.

Osler, Sir William (1849–1919), Canadian physician, author of the standard textbook The Principles and Practice of Medicine (1892).

Osnovyanenko, Gritsko (actually Grigory Fyodorovich Kvitka) (1778–1843), Ukrainian writer.

Osorio da Fonseca, Jeronimo (1506–1580), Portuguese historian.

Ossietzky, Carl von (1888–1938), German journalist and pacifist who was first imprisoned during the Weimar regime (1931–32) and later the Nazi regime (1933–38); won the Nobel Prize for Peace (1935).

Ostaijen, Paul van (1896–1928), Belgian poet, writer and critic who was a major figure in avant-garde circles.

Ostenso, Martha (1900–1963), Norwegian-born American writer.

Ostrogorsky, Moisey (Yakovlevich) (1854–1919), Russian political scientist who was an early authority on the role of democracy and political parties.

Ostrovksy, Alexander Nikolaievich (1823–1886), celebrated Russian dramatist, a master of realistic drama.

Ostrovksy, Nikolai (1904–1936), Russian writer.

Otis, James (1725–1783), American politician and polemicist.

Otto, Rudolf (1869–1937), eminent German theologian, philosopher and historian, author of Das Heilige (1917; English trans. as The Idea of the Holy, 1923), West-Östliche Mystik (1926; English trans. as Mysticism East and West, 1932), Die Gnadenreligion Indiens und das Christentum (1930; English trans. as India's Religion of Grace and Christianity, 1930) and Reich Gottes und Menschensohn (1934; English trans. as The Kingdom of God and the Son of Man, 1938).

Otto of Freising (c.1111–1158), German Roman Catholic bishop and historian, especially known for his world history Chronica sive historia de duabus civitatibus.

Otway, Thomas (1652–1685), notable English dramatist and poet, author of the esteemed poem The Poet's Complaint of His Muse (1680) and the play Venice Preserved, or a Plot Discovered (1682).

Ouida (actually Maria Louise Ramé) (1839–1908), English novelist.

Ouspensky, Paul (1878–1947), Russian philosopher.

Outremeuse, Jean d' (1338–1399), Belgian writer, author of La Geste de Liège and Ly Myreru des Histors.

Ou-yang Hsiu (1007–1072), Chinese statesman, poet and historian.

Overbury, Sir Thomas (1581–1613), English courtier, poet and essayist whose involvement in political intrigue led to his slow poisoning in the Tower of London.

Øverland, Arnulf (1889–1968), Norwegian poet and socialist who survived incarceration in a Nazi concentration camp to become one of his homeland's most respected literary figures.

Ovid (actually Publius Ovidius Naso) (43 BC–17 AD), famous Roman poet, author of the celebrated Ars Armatoria (Art of Love) and Metamorphoses.

Owain Cyfeiliog (c.1130–c.1197), Welsh warrior-prince and poet who was known for his poem Hirlas Owain (The Drinking Horn of Owain).

Owen, Alun (Davies) (1925–94), Welsh dramatist.

Owen, Daniel (1836–1895), prominent Welsh novelist, short-story writer, essayist and poet.

Owen, Goronwy (1723–1769), Welsh clergyman and poet who espoused the cause of classicism in Welsh Literature.

Owen, John (c.1563–1622), English poet of Latin epigrams.

Owen, Sir Richard (1804–1892), English anatomist and paleontologist who was a strident critic of Darwin's theory of evolution.

Owen, Robert (1771–1858), Welsh manufacturer, reformer and utopian socialist, author of A New View of Society (1813); father of Robert Dale Owen.

Owen, Robert Dale (1801–1877), Welsh-born American politician, reformer and writer; son of Robert Owen.

Owen, Wilfred (1893–1918), English poet who wrote such memorable works as the Anthem for Doomed Youth and Dulce et Decorum Est; died in battle in France a week before the Armistice ending World War I.

Oxenford, John (1812–1877), English dramatist and critic.

Oxenstierna, Johan Gabriel (1750–1818), Swedish writer.

Oxford, Edward de Vere, 17th Earl of (1560–1604), English courtier, poet and dramatist.

Ozaki Kōyō (actually Ozaki Tokutarō) (1867–1903), significant Japanese novelist, poet and essayist, author of the highly regarded novel Konjiki yasha (1897–1902; English trans. as The Gold Demon, 1917).

Ozanam, Antoine-Frédéric (1813–1853), French historian.

Paavolainen, Olavi (1903–1964), Finnish writer.

Pacatus Drepanius, Latinius or Latinus (4th Century), Gallo-Roman public official, orator and poet.

Pacheco, Francisco (1564–1654), Spanish painter and scholar, author of the valuable Arte de la pintura (1649).

Pachymeres, Georges (1242–c.1310), Byzantine scholar who wrote on various subjects, from theology to history.

Pacuvius, Marcus (220–c.130 BC), Roman dramatist who was celebrated for his tragedies.

Padilla, Heberto (1932–2000), Cuban poet whose volume Fuera del juego (1968) led to his imprisonment , the banning of his writings and his eventual exile from his homeland.

Page, Thomas Nelson (1853–1922), American writer, essayist and biographer.

Page, Walter Hines (1855–1918), American journalist, publisher, diplomat and writer.

Pagninus, Santes (1470–1536), Italian Dominican scholar who prepared a Latin version of the Hebrew Bible (1528).

Pagnol, Marcel Paul (1895–1974), French writer, and film producer and director.

Paine, Albert Bigelow (1861–1937), American biographer, novelist, dramatist and editor.

Paine, Robert Treat (1773–1811), American poet, best remembered for The Invention of Letters (1795), The Ruling Passion (1796) and Adams and Liberty (1798).

Paine, Thomas (1737–1809), famous and controversial American political and religious pamphleteer, author of Common Sense (1776), the Crisis papers (1776–83), Rights of Man (1791) and Age of Reason (1794).

Painter, William (c.1540–1594), English writer, author of the collection of tales known as The Palace of Pleasure (1566).

Pais, Ettore (1856–1939), Italian historian who wrote an expansive history of the Roman Republic (1898–1931).

Pal, Bipin Chandra (1858–1932), Indian journalist who championed the cause of nationalism.

Palacio Valdés, Armando (1853–1938), Spanish novelist.

Palacký, František (1798–1876), important Bohemian historian and politician, author of a major history of the Czech nation as Geschichte von Böhmen (5 vols, 1836–67).

Palamás, Kostís (1859–1943), Greek poet, short-story writer and critic.

Palés Matos, Luis (1898–1959), Puerto Rican poet and lyricist.

Paley, William (1743–1805), influential English Anglican priest, Utilitarian philosopher and writer, best known for his teleological argument for the existence of God in his Natural Theology (1802).

Palfrey, John Gorham (1796–1881), American Unitarian clergyman, writer and editor.

Palgrave, Sir Francis (actually Francis Cohen) (1788–1861), English barrister, antiquarian and historian who was particularly known as a medievalist; father of Francis Turner Palgrave and William Gifford Palgrave.

Palgrave, Francis Turner (1824–1897), English critic and poet, editor of the well-known anthology The Golden Treasury of English Songs and Lyrics (1861); son of Sir Francis Palgrave and brother of William Gifford Palgrave.

Palgrave, William Gifford (1826–1888), English Jesuit missionary who left an account of a journey to Arabia in his Narrative of a Year's Journey through Central and Eastern Arabia (1865); son of Sir Francis Palgrave and brother of Francis Turner Palgrave.

Palissy, Bernard (1510–1589), French potter, scientist and writer, author of a notable series of lectures on natural history as Discours admirables (1580; English trans. as Admirable Discourses, 1957); as a Huguenot, he was imprisoned in 1588 and died in the Bastille in Paris.

Palladius (c.363–c.425), Galitian Roman Catholic monk, bishop and historian, author of a history of early monasticism in his so-called Lausiac History (c.420).

Pallas, Peter Simon (1741–1811), German naturalist, author of the Reise durch verschiedene Provinzen des russischen Reichs (Journey Through the Various Provinces of the Russian Empire, 3 vols, 1771–76).

Palma, Ricardo (1833–1919), Peruvian writer and poet.

Palmer, Edward H(enry) (1840–1882), English Orientalist, linguist, writer, poet and traveller, was ambushed and killed while in service to the British government in Egypt.

Palmer, (Edward) Vance (1885–1959), leading Australian novelist, short-story writer and dramatist.

Palmer, George Herbert (1842–1933), American philosopher.

Palmer, Joel (1810–1881), American pioneer who wrote an account of his trek to Oregon in his Journal of Travels Over the Rocky Mountains (1847).

Palmer, Ray (1808–1887), American Congregationalist minister and hymnist.

Palomino (de Castro y Velasco), Antonio (1655–1726), Spanish painter and scholar, author of the valuable Museo pictorico y escala optica (1715–24).

Paltock, Robert (1697–1767), English writer, author of the romance The Life and Adventures of Peter Wilkins, A Cornishman (1751).

Paludan-Müller, Frederik (1809–1876), Danish poet who wrote the epic Adam Homo (2 parts, 1841, 1848).

Pan Chao (45–c.115), Chinese scholar, essayist and poet who was especially known for her labours as a chronicler of Chinese history.

Panduro, Leif (1923–77), Danish novelist and dramatist.

Panizzi, Sir Anthony (actually Antonio Genesio Maria Panizzi) (1797–1879), Italian-born English librarian and literary scholar who championed the cause of the unification of Italy.

Panneton, Philippe (1895–1960), French-Canadian novelist and short-story writer who wrote under the name Ringuet.

Pannonius, Janus (1434–1472), Hungarian poet.

Panofsky, Erwin (1892–1968), German-born American art historian.

Papadiamadis, Alexandros (1851–1911), Greek writer.

Papias (c.50–130), bishop of Hierapolis and theologian whose Expositions of the Oracles of the Lord is only extant in fragments but remains valuable for the light shed on the early Christian church.

Papini, Giovanni (1881–1956), prominent Italian journalist, critic, novelist and poet.

Papinian (actually Aemilius Papinianus) (c.140–212), Roman jurist who was known for his writings on the law, especially his Quaestiones and Responsa; was executed by order of the Emperor Caracalla.

Pappus of Alexandria (4th Century), Greek geometer who wrote the valuable Synagoge (Collection, c.340) on mathematics.

Paquet, Louis-Adolphe (1859–1942), Canadian writer.

Paracelsus (actually Philippus Aureolus Theophrastus Bombast von Honenheim) (1493–1541), famous Swiss physician and alchemist who first delineated the importance of chemistry in medicine, author of Die grosse Wundartzney (Great Surgery Book, 1536).

Paramanuchit, Prince (1791–1852), prince patriarch of the Siamese Buddhist Church, writer and poet who was also known as Prince Paramanujita Jinorasa.

Parandowski, Jan (1895–1978), Polish writer, essayist and translator.

Paráskhos, Akhilléfs (1838–1895), Greek poet who was a champion of Romanticism.

Pardo Bazán, Emilia, Condesa de (1852–1921), Spanish novelist, short-story writer and critic.

Pareto, Vilfredo (1848–1923), influential Italian economist and sociologist, author of the Cours d'Économie Politique (1896–97), Manuale d'economia politica (1906) and Tratto di sociologia generale (1916; English trans. as Mind and Society, 1963).

Parini, Giuseppe (1729–1799), Italian writer and poet, admired for his Horatian odes and his satiric poem Il giorno (4 vols, 1763, 1765, 1801, 1801).

Paris, (Bruno-Paulin-) Gaston (1839–1903), learned French philologist.

Paris, Matthew (died 1259), English Benedictine monk and historian.

Parish, Elijah (1762–1825), American Congregationalist minister and writer.

Park, Robert Ezra (1864–1944), American sociologist.

Parke, John (1754–1789), American poet and translator, author of the anonymous vol. The Lyric Works of Horace... to Which are Added, a Number of Original Poems... (1786).

Parker, Dorothy (Lee née Rothschild) (1893–1967), notable American short-story writer, poet and critic who was especially famous for her telling wit.

Parker, Eric (actually Frederick Moore Searle) (1870–1955), English journalist, editor and writer.

Parker, Sir (Horatio) Gilbert (1862–1932), Canadian-born English novelist and short-story writer.

Parker, Jane Marsh (1836–1913), American novelist.

Parker, Theodore (1810–1860), American Unitarian theologian, scholar and social reformer.

Parkinson, C(yril) Northcote (1909–1993), English historian who was admired as much for his witticisms as his scholarly writings.

Parkman, Francis (1823–1893), American historian who wrote extensively on the settlement of North America.

Parmenides (5th Century BC), Greek philosopher.

Parnell, Thomas (1679–1718), Irish poet and churchman, author of An Elegy to an Old Beauty, The Hermit, Hymn to Contentment and The Night Piece of Death.

Parr, Samuel (1747–1825), English Latin scholar and writer.

Parrington, Vernon L(ouis) (1871–1929), important American literary historian.

Parrish, Anne (1888–1957), American novelist.

Parry, Sir C(harles) Hubert H(astings) (1848–1918), English composer, teacher and writer on music.

Parry, Milman (1902–1935), American literary scholar who was an authority on Homer.

Parsons, Elsie (Worthington) Clews (1875–1941), American sociologist and anthropologist who wrote authoritative works on the Indians of the southwestern US.

Parsons, Robert (1546–1610), English Jesuit and religious polemicist.

Parsons, Talcott (1902–79), American sociologist.

Parsons, Thomas William (1819–1892), American translator, writer and poet.

Parton, James (1822–1891), English-born American biographer and writer.

Pascal, Blaise (1623–1662), French mathematician, physicist and religious philosopher, author of the celebrated Pensées (1670).

Pascal, Carlo (1866–1926), Italian Latin scholar.

Pasch, Georg (1661–1707), German philosopher and mathematician.

Paschasius Radbertus, Saint (c.785–c.860), influential French Roman Catholic abbot and theologian, author of De corpore et sanguine Christi (Concerning Christ's Body and Blood, c.832).

Pascoli, Giovanni (1855–1912), Italian poet and scholar.

Pasolini, Pier Paolo (1922–1975), Italian poet, novelist, critic and film director; was murdered.

Pasquier, Étienne (1529–1615), French lawyer, scholar and poet, author of the expansive Recherches de la France (1560–c.1610).

Passerat, Jean (1534–1602), French poet.

Pasternak, Boris (Leonidovich) (1890–1960), renowned Russian poet, novelist and translator whose celebrated novel Dr Zhivago (1957) stands as an indictment of the Bolshevik Revolution of 1917; won the Nobel Prize for Literature (1958) but was compelled by the Soviet government to refuse it.

Pastor, Ludwig Freiherr von (1854–1928), eminent German church historian, author of the monumental Geschichte der Päpste seit dem Ausang des Mittelalters (16 vols, 1886–1933; English trans. as The History of the Popes from the Close of the Middle Ages, 40 vols, 1891–1954).

Pastorius, Francis Daniel (1651–c.1720), German-born American lawyer, writer and poet.

Patchen, Kenneth (1911–1972), American poet, novelist, dramatist, painter and graphic designer who was known for his experimental works.

Pater, Walter Horatio (1839–1894), English critic and essayist.

Paterson, A(ndrew) B(arton) (1864–1941), Australian journalist, poet and short-story writer, author of the celebrated song Waltzing Matilda (1917).

Patmore, Coventry (Kersey Dighton) (1823–1896), English poet and essayist, best known for his epic novel in verse The Angel in the House (2 vols, 1854, 1856) and The Victories of Love (2 vols, 1860, 1863).

Paton, Alan (Stewart) (1903–1988), notable South African writer and liberal politician, author of the famous novel Cry, the Beloved Country (1948).

Pattee, Fred Lewis (1863–1950), American literary scholar.

Patten, William Gilbert (1866–1945), American writer who wrote numerous works under the name Burt L Standish.

Pattison, Mark (1813–1884), English scholar.

Paul, Elliot (Harold) (1891–1958), American novelist.

Paul, Saint (actually Saul) (died c.63), seminal Jewish-born Christian Apostle and theologian, author of several major books of the New Testament.

Paul of Aegina (c.625–c.690), Greek physician and medical encyclopaedist, compiler of the Epitomae medicae libri septem.

Paul the Deacon (c.720–c.799), Italian historian and poet who wrote the valuable Historia Langobardorum (History of the Lombards).

Paulding, James Kirke (1778–1860), American novelist, dramatist and government official.

Paulinus of Nola, Saint (actually Meropius Pontius Anicius Paulinus) (353–431), significant Latin Christian poet and bishop.

Paulsen, Friedrich (1846–1908), German philosopher of spiritual moralism.

Paulus, H(einrich) E(berhard) G(ottlob) (1761–1851), German theologian and Orientalist.

Pauly, August von (1796–1845), German classical philologist.

Pausanias (2nd Century), Greek traveller and geographer, author of an important guide to the ancient ruins of his homeland.

Paustovsky, Konstantin (Georgievich) (1892–1968), Russian writer.

Pavese, Cesare (1908–1950), Italian novelist, poet, critic and translator; committed suicide.

Pawlikowska-Jasnorzewska, Maria (1893–1945), Polish poet.

Payn, James (1830–1898), English novelist, poet, essayist and editor.

Payne, John Howard (1791–1852), influential American dramatist and actor, particularly known for his Brutus, or The Fall of Tarquin (1818).

Paz, Octavio (1914–1998), eminent Mexican poet and essayist; won the Nobel Prize for Literature (1990).

Pázmány, Péter (1570–1637), Hungarian statesman and theologian.

Paz Soldán, Mariano Felipe (1821–1886), Peruvian statesman, historian and geographer.

p'Bitek, Okot (1931–82), Ugandan poet, novelist and anthropologist.

Peabody, Andrew Preston (1811–1893), American Unitarian minister and writer.

Peabody, Elizabeth Palmer (1804–1894), American educator and writer who was active in the Transcendentalist movement.

Peabody, Josephine Preston (1874–1922), American dramatist and poet.

Peacham, Henry (c.1576–c.1643), English writer, author of the Compleat Gentleman (1622).

Peacock, Thomas Love (1785–1866), English novelist and poet, especially remembered for his novel Nightmare Abbey (1818).

Peake, Mervyn Laurence (1911–1968), English novelist, poet and artist, especially known for his novel trilogy Titus Groan (1946), Gormenghast (1950) and Titus Alone (1959).

Peale, Rembrandt (1778–1860), American painter and writer, author of Notes on Italy (1831) and Portfolio of an Artist (1839).

Peano, Giuseppe (1858–1932), important Italian mathematician who was a major figure in the development of symoblic logic.

Pearse, Patrick Henry (1879–1916), Irish nationalist, poet, short-story writer and dramatist; as commander-in-chief of the insurgent forces in the failed Easter Rising, he was executed.

Pearson, Edmund (Lester) (1880–1937), American librarian, bibliophile and writer.

Pearson, (Edward) Hesketh (Gibbons) (1887–1964), English biographer.

Pearson, John (1613–1686), English bishop and theologian, author of the classic Exposition of the Creed (1659).

Pearson, Karl (1857–1936), notable English mathematician and philosopher of science, author of the classic The Grammar of Science (1892).

Pease, Edward Reynolds (1857–1955), English writer who was a founder and leading figure of the Fabian Society.

Peattie, Donald Culross (1898–1964), American writer.

Peck, George Wilbur (1840–1916), American journalist and writer of humorous works, especially known for his collected articles in Peck's Bad Boy and His Pa (1883).

Peck, Harry Thurston (1856–1914), American scholar and critic; committed suicide.

Peck, John Mason (1789–1858), American Baptist preacher missionary, journalist and writer.

Pecock, Reginald (c.1393–1461), prominent Welsh bishop and theologian who was charged with heresy in 1457, removed from his bishopric and confined for his remaining days.

Pedersen, Christiern (c.1480–1554), Danish scholar.

Pedersen, Holger (1857–1953), learned Danish linguist.

Pedersen, Johannes Peder Ejler (1883–1951), Danish Old Testament scholar and Semitic philologist.

Pedrell, Felipe (1841–1922), disinguished Spanish music scholar and composer.

Peele, George (1556–1596), important English dramatist and poet.

Pegler, Westbrook (1894–1969), American journalist who was known for his outspoken conservative views.

Peglotti, Francesco Balducci (14th Century), Italian commercial agent who wrote a valuable account of trade and travel of his era.

Péguy, Charles Pierre (1873–1914), French nationalist, publisher and poet; died in World War I.

Peirce, Charles Sanders (1839–1914), American scientist, logician and philosopher.

Pekkanen, Toivo (1902–1957), Finnish writer.

Pelagius (c.354–c.420), Christian monk and theologian who was condemned and excommunicated for his insistence upon the human role in spiritual salvation, which became known as Pelagianism.

Peletier, Jacques (1517–1582), French poet, writer and critic who was also known as Peletier du Mans.

Pellico, Silvio (1789–1854), Italian patriot, poet and dramatist, particularly known for his memoirs Le mie prigioni (1832; English trans. as My Prisons, 1853), which related his experience as a political prisoner.

Pelloutier, Fernand (1867–1901), French labour organizer and theorist of the anarcho-syndicalist movement.

Pembroke, Mary Herbert, Countess of (1561–1621), esteemed English patroness of the arts and learning and translator; sister of Sir Philip Sidney and Sir Robert Sidney.

Penn, William (1644–1718), English Quaker and founder of the American Commonwealth of Pennsyslvania, author of The Sandy Foundation Shaken (1668), No Cross, No Crown (1669) and Some Fruits of Solitude (1693).

Pennant, Thomas (1726–1798), important English naturalist whose tome British Zoology (1766) was highly influential.

Pennell, Joseph (1857–1926), American etcher, lithographer and writer.

Pennell, Joseph Stanley (1908–1963), American journalist, novelist and poet.

Penry, John (1559–1593), Welsh Puritan polemicist.

Pepe, Guglielmo (1783–1855), Italian soldier and memoirist.

Pepys, Samuel (1633–1703), English government official and diarist whose diary (1660–69) stands as a literary classic.

Percival, James Gates (1795–1856), American poet and chemist.

Percy, Thomas (1729–1811), English bishop, antiquarian and scholar, particularly known for his compilation of ballads Reliques of Ancient English Poetry (1765).

Percy, Walker (1916–1990), American novelist and essayist.

Pereda, José Mariá de (1833–1906), esteemed Spanish novelist.

Perelman, S(idney) J(oseph) (1904–1979), American dramatist and writer.

Peretz, Isaac Leib (c.1851–1915), Polish poet, dramatist and writer, one of the leading Yiddish figures of his era.

Pérez de Ayala, Ramón (1880–1962), Spanish novelist, short-story writer, poet, essayist and critic.

Pérez de Guzmán, Fernán (c.1378–c.1460), august Spanish historian and poet whose Mar de historias brought him posthumous fame as the Spanish Plutarch.

Pérez de Hita, Ginés (c.1544–c.1619), Spanish novelist.

Pérez Galdós, Benito (1843–1920), Spanish novelist, author of the classic Fortunata y Jacinto (4 vols, 1886–87).

Perkins, Frederic Beecher (1828–1899), American journalist, writer and librarian; nephew of Henry Ward Beecher.

Perkins, Lucy Fitch (1865–1937), American writer of children's books.

Perkins, William (1558–1602), English Puritan theologian.

Perl, Joseph (1773–1839), Russian Jewish writer.

Perrault, Charles (1628–1703), French writer and poet who became well known for his children's fairy-tales.

Perron, (Charles) Edgar du (1899–1940), Dutch writer, poet and critic.

Perry, Bliss (1860–1954), American literary scholar and writer.

Perry, Ralph Barton (1876–1957), American philosopher of the Realist persuasion.

Perry, Thomas Sergeant (1845–1928), American critic, writer and translator.

Perry, W(illiam) J(ames) (1868–1949), English anthropologist who argued for a diffusionist theory of culutral development.

Perse, Saint-John (actually Marie-René-Auguste-Alexis Léger) (1887–1975), notable French poet and diplomat; won the Nobel Prize for Literature (1960).

Persius (actually Aulus Persius Flaccus) (34–62), esteemed Roman poet who excelled in his satires.

Pessanha, Camilo (1867–1926), Portuguese poet who espoused Symbolism.

Pessoa, Fernando António Nogueira (1888–1935), Portuguese poet, writer and critic.

Pestalozzi, Johann Heinrich (1746–1827), Swiss educational reformer and writer, author of the novel Leonard and Gertrude (4 vols, 1781–87).

Peter, Hugh (1598–1660), English Independent minister and writer who was active in Cromwellian circles; following the Restoration, he was executed.

Peter Lombard (c.1100–1160), famous Italian Roman Catholic theologian and bishop of Paris, author of the celebrated Sententiarum libri quator (Books of Four Sentences, c.1155–58).

Peter of Blois (c.1135–c.1212), French poet and writer.

Peterkin, Julia (Mood) (1880–1961), American novelist, especially remembered for her Scarlet Sister Mary (1928).

Peters, Samuel Andrew (1735–1826), notorius American Anglican clergyman, Loyalist and polemicist.

Petersen, Nis (1897–1943), Danish poet and novelist.

Peterson, Charles Jacobs (1819–1887), American writer, editor and publisher.

Petofi, Sándor (1823–1849), celebrated Hungarian poet and revolutionary; died in the Battle of Segesvár.

Petrarch (actually Francesco Petrarca) (1304–1374), Italian poet and scholar, renowned for the extraordinary beauty of his lyricism.

Petri, Sir (William Matthew) Flinders (1853–1942), eminent English archaeologist and Egyptologist.

Petronious Arbiter (1st Century), famous Roman writer and poet, reputed author of the first Western European novel the Satyricon; committed suicide.

Petrov, Yevgeny (Petrovich) (actually Yevgeny Katayev) (1907–1942), Russian writer who collaborated with Ilya Ilf on a series of satirical short stories and novels; was killed while serving as a correspondent during the defense of Sevastopol during World War II.

Petrus Aureoli (c.1280–1322), French archbishop and Franciscan philosopher who was a critic of the theory of knowledge as expounded by Duns Scotus and Saint Thomas Aquinas.

Pétrus Ky (1837–1898), Vietnamese scholar and statesman.

Pettazzoni, Raffaele (1883–1959), Italian historian of religions.

Pettie, George (c.1548–1589), English writer, author of A petite Pallace of Pettie his pleasure (1576).

Petty, Sir William (1623–1687), English political economist and statistician, particularly known for his Treatise of Taxes and Contributions (1662).

Pétursson, Hallgrímur (1614–1674), significant Icelandic poet whose mastery was revealed in his Passiusalmar (Hymns of the Passion, 1666).

Pevsner, Sir Nikolaus Bernhard Leon (1902–1983), German-born English art historian.

Pfefferkorn, Johannes (Joseph) (1469–1524), German-born Jewish Christian convert and polemicist.

Pfleiderer, Otto (1839–1908), German Protestant theologian and religious historian.

Phaedo or Phaedon (flourished 400 BC), Greek philosopher who wrote on ethics and dialectics.

Phaedrus (c.15 BC–c.50 AD), Roman poet who won fame for his didactic fables.

Phelps, William Lyon (1865–1943), American literary scholar and critic.

Philaret (actually Vasili Mikhailovich Drozdov) (1782–1867), Russian Orthodox metropolitan of Moscow, theologian and scholar.

Philemon (c.368–c.264 BC), Greek dramatist, a major figure in Athenian New Comedy.

Philes, Manuel (13th–14th Century), Byzantine poet.

Philetas of Cos (c.330–c.270 BC), Greek poet and grammarian.

Philip, John (1775–1851), controversial Scottish clergyman and missionary to South Africa, author of Researches in South Africa (1826).

Philipon, Charles (1806–1862), French caricaturist, lithographer, journalist and writer who was a master of political satire.

Philippe, Charles-Louis (1874–1909), French novelist, known for his depictions of the downtrodden elements of society.

Philips, Ambrose (1674–1749), English poet and dramatist, best remembered for his collection of Pastorals (1710).

Philips, John (1676–1709), English poet and writer, best known for his poems Blenheim (1705), The Splendid Shilling (1705) and Cyder (1708).

Philips, Katherine (née Fowler) (1631–1664), English poet who was known as Orinda.

Philistus (c.430–356 BC), Greek historian.

Phillips, David Graham (1867–1911), American novelist, dramatist and essayist; was murdered by a lunatic.

Phillips, Edward (1630–c.1696), English editor, biographer and writer; brother of John Phillips and nephew of John Milton.

Phillips, John (1631–1706), English poet, writer and translator; brother of Edward Phillips and nephew of John Milton.

Phillips, Stephen (1864–1915), English actor, poet and dramatist.

Phillips, Wendell (1811–1884), American reformer, orator and polemicist, one of the principal figures in the Abolitionist movement.

Phillpotts, Eden (1862–1960), English novelist, dramatist, poet and essayist.

Philo of Alexandria (c.13 BC–c.50 AD), celebrated Egyptian-born Jewish philosopher and theologian.

Philodemus (c.110–c.35 BC), Greek poet and philosopher of the Epicurean school.

Philoponus, John (6th Century), important Greek Christian theologian, philosopher and literary scholar who was known as John the Grammarian.

Philostorgius (c.368–c.433), Byzantine historian of the Arian persuasion, author of a church history (only fragments extant).

Philostratus, Flavius (c.170–c.245), Greek writer; father-in-law of Philostratus the Lemmian.

Philostratus the Lemmian (2nd–3rd Century), Greek writer; son-in-law of Flavius Philstratus and grandfather of Philostratus the Younger.

Philostratus the Younger (3rd Century), Greek writer; grandson of Philostratus the Lemmian.

Philotheus Coccinus (c.1300–1379), prominent Byzantine monk, theologian and patriarch of Constantinople who was the leader of the opposition to the union of the Greek Orthodox Church with the Roman Catholic Church.

Philoxenus of Mabbug (c.440–c.523), Syrian Christian theologian, bishop and writer who was a principal figure in the Jacobite Monophysite church.

Phocylides (flourished 500 BC), Greek poet who was known for his aphorisms.

Phrynichus (flourished 500 BC), Greek dramatist of tragedies.

Phrynichus (flourished c.400 BC), Greek dramatist of the Old Comedy.

Phrynichus Arabius (2nd Century), Greek grammarian and rhetorician.

Piaget, Jean (1896–1980), notable Swiss physchologist, an authority on child psychology.

Picabia, Francis Martinez de (1879–1953), French painter, illustrator, designer and writer.

Piccolomini, Alessandro (1508–1578), Italian writer.

Picken, Ebenezer (1769–1816), Scottish poet.

Pickering, John (1777–1846), American lawyer and philologist who was a learned authority on various North American Indian languages.

Pico della Mirandola, Giovanni, Conte (1463–1494), Italian philosopher and scholar of the Platonist school.

Pictet de Rochemont, Charles (1755–1824), Swiss statesman and writer.

Pierpont, John (1785–1866), American Unitarian clergyman and poet, author of Airs of Palestine (1816) and The Anti-Slavery Poems of John Pierpont (1843).

Pigou, Arthur Cecil (1877–1959), influential English economist, author of The Economics of Welfare (1920).

Pike, Albert (1809–1891), American lawyer, poet and writer who was a controversial Confederate commander during the Civil War and later a leading figure in Masonic circles in the South.

Pike, Mary Hayden (Green) (1824–1908), American novelist, best known for her anti-slavery novels Ida May (1854) and Caste (1856).

Pillai, Thakazhi Sivasankara (1912–99), Indian novelist and short-story writer.

Pillsbury, Parker (1809–1898), American Abolitionist, woman suffrage leader and editor, author of Acts of the Anti-Slavery Apostles (1883).

Pilnyak, Boris (Andreievich) (actually Boris Andreievich Vogau) (1894–c.1938), Russian novelist and short-story writer of the Symbolist persuasion; denounced as a reactionary by the Stalinist regime, he disappeared from the scene in the wake of the Great Purge.

Pindar (actually Pindaros) (c.522–c.440 BC), celebrated Greek poet, renowned for his superlative odes.

Pindemonte, Giovanni (1751–1812), Italian politician, poet and dramatist; brother of Ippolito Pindemonte.

Pindemonte, Ippolito (1753–1828), Italian writer, poet and translator; brother of Giovanni Pindemonte.

Pinel, Philippe (1745–1826), significant French physician who was a pioneering figure in the development of psychiatry.

Pinero, Sir Arthur Wing (1855–1934), English dramatist.

Pinget, Robert (1919–1997), Swiss-born French novelist and dramatist.

Pinkney, Edward Coote (1802–1828), American poet.

Pinski, David (1872–1959), Russian-born Israeli Yiddish writer and dramatist.

Pinto, Fernão Mendes (c.1510–1583), Portuguese adventurer who left a classic account of his travels in Asia in his Peregrinaçam (1614).

Piozzi, Hester Lynch (née Salusbury) (1741–1821), Welsh writer and poet who was known as Mrs Thrale, the friend of Samuel Johnson.

Pirandello, Luigi (1867–1936), Italian dramatist, novelist and short-story writer; won the Nobel Prize for Literature (1934).

Pirenne, Henri (1862–1935), notable Belgian historian who was an authority on the Middle Ages and Belgian history.

Pires, José Augusto Neves Cardoso (1925–1998), Portuguese writer.

Pirmez, Octave (1832–1883), Belgian essayist, author of Pensées e maximes (Thoughts and Maxims, 1862) and Heures de philosophi (Hours of Philosophy, 1873).

Piron, Alexis (1689–1773), French poet and dramatist, especially admired for his play La Métromanie.

Pirro, André (Gabriel Edme) (1869–1943), influential French music scholar.

Pirrotta, Nino (actually Antonino Pirrotta) (1908–1998), Italian music scholar.

Pisarev, Dmitri Ivanovich (1840–1868), Russian social philosopher and literary critic who was the leading nihilist of his era.

Pisemsky, Alexie Feofilaktovich (1820–1881), Russian novelist and dramatist, particularly known for his novel Tysyacha dush (A Thousand Souls, 1858) and his play Gorkaya sudbina (A Bitter Lot, 1859).

Pithou, Pierre (1539–1596), French lawyer and historian.

Pitoëff, Georges (1886–1939), Russian-born French actor, producer and dramatist.

Pitt-Rivers, Augustus Henry Lane-Fox (1827–1900), English army officer and archaeologist, known as the father of British archaeology.

Pius II, Pope (actually Aeneas Silvius Piccolomini) (1405–1464), Italian scholar, statesman and pope (1458–64).

Pixérécourt, (René-Charles-) Guilbert de (1773–1844), French dramatist.

Plaatje, Solomon Tshekiso (1877–1932), South African journalist, politician, linguist and writer.

Place, Francis (1771–1854), English radical reformer, author of Illustrations and Proofs of the Principle of Population (1822).

Planché, James Robinson (1796–1880), English dramatist, librettist and translator of Huguenot descent.

Planudes, Maximus (1260–c.1310), Greek Orthodox theologian and scholar.

Platen-Hallermünde, August, Graf von (1796–1835), esteemed German poet, dramatist and scholar who upheld classical precepts.

Plath, Sylvia (1932–1963), American poet and novelist, author of The Bell Jar; wife of Ted Hughes; committed suicide.

Plato (c.427–c.347 BC), Greek philosopher, author of a series of celebrated dialogues addressing the central issues of philosophy.

Platonov, Andrei Paltonovich (1899–1951), Russian writer.

Platonov, Sergei Fyodorovich (1860–1933), Russian historian who was an authority on 16th and 17th century Russian history.

Platter, Thomas (1499–1582), Swiss scholar and writer, author of an important autobiography.

Plautus, Titus Maccius (c.254–184 BC), renowned Roman dramatist, a master of comic drama.

Plekhanov, Georgi Valentinovich (1856–1918), Russian Marxist theorist.

Plessner, Helmuth (1892–1985), German philosopher who played a leading role in the development of philosophical anthropology.

Plievier, Theodor (1892–1955), German novelist who won success with his trilogy Stalingrad (1945), Moskau (1952) and Berlin (1954).

Pliny the Elder (actually Gaius Plinius Secundus) (23–79), Roman naturalist and writer, author of the famous Historia naturalis; uncle of Pliny the Younger.

Pliny the Younger (actually Gaius Plinius Caecilius Secundis) (c.61–c.113), Roman writer and government official, author of a series of celebrated letters; nephew of Pliny the Elder.

Plomer, William (Charles Franklyn) (1903–1973), South African poet, writer, librettist, memoirist and editor.

Plotinus (205–270), influential Roman philosopher, the father of Neoplatonist thought.

Plumb, Sir John (Harold) (1911–2001), English historian who was particularly noted for his writings on 18th-century English social and political history.

Plutarch (46–c.120), Greek biographer and writer, author of the celebrated Bioi paralleloi (English trans. as Plutarch's Lives).

Po Chü-i (772–846), eminent Chinese poet who was esteemed for the direct appeal of his verse.

Pobedonostsev, Konstantin Petrovich (1827–1907), Russian government official and political philosopher who upheld conservative principles.

Pocci, Franz, Graf von (1807–1876), German writer of children's books.

Poe, Edgar Allan (1809–1849), brilliant American poet and writer whose poetic genius was equalled in his prose by his mastery of the macabre.

Poggio (actually Gian Francesco Poggio Bracciolini) (1380–1459), important Italian Humanist scholar and calligrapher.

Poincaré, (Jules-) Henri (1854–1912), French mathematician, theoretical astronomer and philosopher of science.

Pokorny, Julius (1887–1970), learned Czech-born Swiss linguist and lexicographer, editor of the standard Indogermanisches etymologisches Wörterbuch (Indo-European Etymological Dictionary, 2 vols, 1948, 1969).

Pokrovsky, Mikhail Nicolaievich (1868–1932), Russian historian and government official who became widely known for his Marxist interpretation of Russian history.

Polidoúri, Maria (1905–1930), Greek poet.

Politian (actually Angelo Poliziano) (1454–1494), Italian poet and scholar, especially renowned for his poem Stanze per la giostra del Magnifico Giuliano de' Medici (1475–78).

Pollard, A(lbert) F(rederick) (1869–1948), English historian who was particularly esteemed for his studies in Tudor history.

Pollard, Alfred William (1859–1944), English literary scholar.

Pollard, (Joseph) Percival (1869–1911), German-born English, later American, critic, writer and dramatist.

Pollio, Gaius Asinius (76 BC–4 AD), Roman historian, orator and poet.

Pollock, Channing (1880–1946), American journalist, drama critic, dramatist and writer.

Pollock, Sir Frederick, 3rd Baronet (1845–1937), English legal scholar.

Pollux, Julius (2nd Century), Egyptian writer, author of an Onomasticon, a Greek thesaurus of terms.

Polo, Marco (1254–1324), famous Italian merchant and adventurer who left a celebrated account of his travels to Asia as Il milione (English trans. as The Travels of Marco Polo, 1958).

Polotsky, Simeon (actually Samuil Yemelyanovich Petrovsky-Sitnianovich) (1629–1680), Byelorussian monk, scholar and writer.

Polybius (c.200–c.118 BC), Greek historian who chronicled the rise of Rome to world mastery in his histories.

Polycarp, Saint (2nd Century), Greek Christian bishop of Smyrna and theologian, author of the significant Letter to the Philippians; was martyred for his faith.

Pomfret, John (1667–1702), English churchman and poet, author of The Choice (1700).

Pomponazzi, Pietro (1462–1525), Italian philosopher of the Aristotelian school, author of the Tractatus de immortalitate animae (1516), Apologia (1518), Defensorium (1519), De incantationibus (published 1556) and De fato (published 1567).

Ponce de Léon, Luis (1527–1591), Spanish monk, scholar and poet.

Ponge, Francis (1899–1988), French poet.

Ponsard, François (1814–1867), French dramatist.

Pontano, Giovanni or Gioviano (c.1422–1503), Italian government offical, writer and poet.

Pontoppidan, Erik (1698–1764), Danish-Norwegian Lutheran bishop and theologian.

Pontoppidan, Henrik (1857–1943), admired Danish novelist and short-story writer; was co-winner of the Nobel Prize for Literature (1917).

Poole, Ernest (1880–1950), American writer.

Poole, John (c.1786–1872), English dramatist, poet and essayist.

Poole, William Frederick (1821–1894), American librarian and bibliographer.

Poore, Benjamin Perley (1820–1887), American journalist and writer.

Popa, Vasko (1922–1991), Serbian poet.

Pope, Alexander (1688–1744), famous English poet and translator, a master of satire, renowned for such works as the Essay on Criticism (1711), The Rape of the Lock (1712–14), The Dunciad (1728) and An Essay on Man (1733–34).

Popper, Sir Karl (Raimund) (1902–1994), notable Austrian-born English philosopher of science and politics, author of Logik der Forschung (1934; English trans. as The Logic of Scientific Discovery, 1959), The Open Society and Its Enemies (1945), The Poverty of Historicism (1957) and A World of Propensities (1990).

Popple, William (1701–1764), English dramatist.

Porphyry (actually Malchus) (c.234–c.305), Syrian-born Roman philosopher of the Neoplatonist school.

Porson, Richard (1759–1808), learned English classical scholar.

Porta, Carlo (1776–1821), Italian poet.

Porta, Giambattista della (c.1535–1615), Italian philosopher and scientist, author of Magia naturalis (4 vols, 1558).

Porter, Anna Maria (1780–1832), English poet and novelist; sister of Jane Porter.

Porter, Eleanor Hodgman (1868–1920), American writer of children's novels, creator of Pollyanna, the 'glad girl'.

Porter, Hal (1911–1984), Australian novelist, short-story writer, dramatist and poet.

Porter, Henry (16th Century), English dramatist.

Porter, Jane (1776–1850), English writer who won notable success for her Thaddeus of Warsaw (1803); sister of Anna Maria Porter.

Porter, Katherine Anne (1890–1980), esteemed American novelist, short-story writer and essayist, author of the story collection Pale Horse, Pale Rider (1939) and the novel Ship of Fools (1962).

Porter, Noah (1811–1892), American philosopher, author of The Human Intellect (1868).

Porter, Roy (1946–2002), English historian whose important studies included English Society in the Eighteenth Century (1982), A Social History of Madness (1987), London: A Social History (1994), The Greatest Benefit to Mankind: A Medical History (1998) and Enlightenment: Britain and the Creation of the Modern World (2000).

Porto-Riche, Georges de (1849–1930), French dramatist of the realist school of psychological drama.

Poseidonius (c.135–c.50 BC), Greek philosopher of the Stoic school.

Post, Emily (née Price) (1872–1960), American writer who became best known as an arbiter of social behaviour via her Etiquette: The Blue Book of Social Usage.

Post, Sir Laurens Jan van der (1906–1996), South African novelist and memoirist.

Potgieter, Everhardus Johannes (1808–1875), Dutch writer and poet.

Potocki, Wacław (1625–c.1697), Polish poet, author of the epic Wojna chocimska (The Chocim Ward) and many fine epigrams.

Potok, Chaim (1929–2002), American writer who was admired for his novels and short stories.

Pott, August (Friedrich) (1802–1887), significant German linguist who was one of the principal figures in the development of Indo-Europen linguistic studies.

Potter, Dennis Christopher George (1935–1994), English dramatist.

Potter, (Helen) Beatrix (1866–1943), English writer of children's books.

Potter, Paul Meredith (1853–1921), English-born American dramatist, author of The Ugly Duckling (1890).

Pound, Ezra (Weston Loomis) (1885–1972), American poet, critic and translator, author of the challenging epic Cantos.

Pound, Louise (1872–1958), American scholar of linguistics, folklore and balladry; sister of Roscoe Pound.

Pound, Roscoe (1870–1964), American jurist, botanist and educator; brother of Louise Pound.

Powdermaker, Hortense (1900–1970), American cultural anthropologist.

Powell, Anthony (Dymoke) (1905–2000), English writer, author of the expansive novel series A Dance to the Music of Time (12 vols, 1959–75).

Powell, (John) Enoch (1912–1998), controversial English politician and scholar.

Powers, J(ames) F(arl) (1917–99), American novelist and short-story writer.

Powys, John Cowper (1872–1963), English novelist, poet and essayist; brother of Llewelyn and T(heodore) F(rancis) Powys.

Powys, Llewelyn (1884–1939), English journalist and writer; brother of John Cowper and T(hedore) F(rancis) Powys.

Powys, T(heodore) F(rancis) (1875–1953), English novelist and short-story writer; brother of John Cowper and Llewelyn Powys.

Praed, Winthrop Mackworth (1802–1839), English poet and politician.

Praetorius, Michael (1571–1621), German composer and music theorist, author of the monumental Syntagma musicum (3 vols, 1614–18).

Prati, Giovanni (1815–1884), Italian writer and poet.

Pratolini, Vasco (1913–1991), Italian novelist and short-story writer.

Pratt, E(dwin) J(ohn) (1883–1964), Canadian poet whose masterpiece was the expansive Brébeuf and His Brethren (12 vols, 1940).

Pratt, Samuel Jackson (1749–1814), English poet, writer and dramatist who wrote under the name Courtney Melmoth.

Praz, Mario (1896–1982), Italian literary scholar and critic.

Preil, Gabriel (1911–1993), admired Estonian-born American poet who excelled in writing Hebrew poetry.

Prem Chad (actually Dhanpat Rai Srivastana) (1880–1936), Indian novelist and short-story writer.

Prentice, George Dennison (1802–1870), American editor and poet.

Prescott, William Hickling (1796–1859), American historian, author of the History of the Conquest of Mexico (3 vols, 1843) and History of the Conquest of Peru (2 vols, 1847).

Prešeren, France (1800–1849), important Slovenian poet of the Romantic era.

Preston, Margaret Junkin (1820–1897), American poet and writer.

Preuss, Hugo (1860–1925), German political theorist and legal scholar.

Prevert, Jacques(-Henri-Marie) (1900–1977), French poet and screenwriter.

Prévost (d'Exiles, Antoine-François), Abbé (1697–1763), French novelist, author of the celebrated Histoire du Chevalier des Grieux et de Manon Lescaut (1731), which inspired operas by Massenet and Puccini.

Prévost, (Eugène-) Marcel (1862–1941), French novelist, best remembered for his Les Demi-Vierges (The Half-Virgins, 1894).

Price, H(enry) H(abberley) (1899–1984), English philosopher, author of Perception (1932).

Price, Richard (1723–1791), English Dissenter and philosopher, author of the Review of the Principal Questions and Difficulties in Morals (1758) and Observations on the Nature of Civil Liberty, the Principles of Government, and the Justice and Policy of the War with America (1776).

Price-Mars, Jean (1876–1970), Haitian physician, government official, ethnologist and historian.

Prichard, Harold Arthur (1871–1947), English philosopher of the Oxford intuitionist school of moral philosophy, author of Kant's Theory of Knowledge (1909), Duty and Interest (1928), Moral Obligation (published 1949) and Knowledge and Perception (published 1950).

Prichard, James Cowles (1786–1848), English physician and ethnologist who wrote the Eastern Origin of the Celtic Nations (1831), Researches as to the Physical History of Man (5 vols, 1836–47) and Natural History of Man (1843).

Prichard, Rhys (c.1579–1644), Welsh vicar and poet, author of the Canwyll y Cymry (The Welshman's Candle).

Priestley, J(ohn) B(oynton) (1894–1984), prominent English novelist dramatist and essayist.

Priestley, Joseph (1733–1804), English-born American clergyman scientist and political theorist.

Prime, Benjamin Youngs (1733–1791), American poet.

Prince, Morton (Henry) (1854–1929), American physician and psychologist.

Prince, Thomas (1687–1758), American Congregationalist clergyman and writer, author of the Chronological History of New England in the Form of Annals (1736) and The Christian History (1744–45).

Pingle, Thomas (1789–1834), Scottish-South African writer and poet.

Prior, Matthew (1664–1721), notable English poet and diplomat especially admired for his telling wit.

Priscian (actually Priscianus Caesariensis) (6th Century), influential Latin grammarian, author of the classic Institutiones grammaticae.

Priscillian (c.340–385), Spanish Christian bishop and heretic who was the first to be executed for his beliefs.

Pritchett, Sir V(ictor) S(awdon) (1900–1997), esteemed English literary critic, biographer, essayist, novelist and short-story writer.

Probus, Marcus Valerius (1st Century), Latin grammarian and literary critic.

Proclus (c.410–485), Greek philosopher of the Neoplatonic school.

Procter, Adelaide Ann (1825–1864), English poet who wrote under the name Mary Berwick and who won special recognition for her Legends and Lyrics (1858–60) and The Lost Chord, the latter set to music by Sir Arthur Sullivan; daughter of Bryan Walker Procter.

Procter, Bryan Walker (1787–1874), English poet who wrote under the name Barry Cornwall; father of Adelaide Ann Procter.

Prokopovich, Feofan (1681–1736), Russian Orthodox theologian, writer, poet, dramatist and archbishop of Novgorod who collaborated with Czar Peter I the Great in westernizing his homeland.

Prokosch, Frederic (1908–1989), American writer.

Propertius, Sextus (c.48–c.15 BC), Roman poet who was known for his elegiac effusions to his mistress Cynthia.

Prosper of Aquitaine, Saint (c.390–c.463), influential Latin Christian polemicist who upheld the teachings of Saint Augustine.

Protagoras (c.485–c.410 BC), celebrated Greek philosopher of the Sophist persuasion.

Proud, Joseph (1745–1826), English Baptist churchman and hymnist, a prominent figure in Swedenborgian circles.

Proudhon, Pierre–Joseph (1809–1865), French Socialist polemicist whose theory of mutualist economic organization influenced the development of radical and anarchist ideas.

Proust, Marcel (1871–1922), French novelist, essayist and critic, author of the celebrated novel series À la recherche du temps perdu (1913–27; English trans. as Remembrance of Things Past, 1924–70).

Prouty, Olive Higgins (1882–1974), American novelist, best known for her Stella Dallas (1922).

Prudentius, Aurelius Clemens (348–c.406), esteemed Christian Latin poet, author of the acclaimed Psychomachia (The Contest of the Soul, 405).

Prynne, William (1600–1669), prominent English Puritan pamphleteer whose polemical writings led to conflicts with both the monarchy and the parliamentarians, author of the classic Histrio Mastix: The Players Scourge, or, Actors tragoedie (1633).

Prys-Jones, Arthur Glyn (1888–1987), eminent Welsh poet.

Psellus, Michael (Constantine) (1018–c.1078), Byzantine statesman, theologian and philosopher.

Psichari, Ernest (1883–1914), French novelist; died in World War I.

Psicharis, Ioannis (1854–1929), Greek writer.

Pufendorf, Samuel von (1632–1694), German scholar who wrote an important treatise on natural law in his De Jure Naturae et Gentium Libri Octo (1672).

Puig, Manuel (1932–1990), Argentine novelist and screenwriter, best remembered for his novel El beso de la mujer araña (1976; English trans. as Kiss of the Spider Woman, 1979).

Pulci, Luigi (1432–1484), Italian poet, author of the burlesque epic in Tuscan dialect Morgante or Morgante Maggiore (c.1460–83).

Purchas, Samuel (c.1577–1626), English compiler of books on travel and discovery.

Pusey, E(dward) B(ouverie) (1800–1882), English Anglican scholar and theologian who was a prominent figure in the Oxford Movement.

Pushkin, Alexander (Sergeievich) (1799–1837), Russian poet, writer and dramatist who was acclaimed as the national poet of Russia; died in a duel defending his wife's honour.

Putnam, Samuel (1892–1950), American literary scholar and translator who was an authority on Romance literatures.

Putrament, Jerzy (1910–1986), Polish journalist, novelist and poet.

Puttenham, George (c.1529–1590), English courtier and most likely the author of the Arte of English Poesie (1589), a pioneering study in the field of criticism.

Pyat, (Aimé-) Félix (1810–1889), French journalist, dramatist and political radical.

Pyle, Ernie (actually Ernest Taylor Pyle) (1900–1945), famous American journalist and war correspondent; killed while covering the Okianawa campaign against the Japanese in the closing days of World War II.

Pyle, Howard (1853–1911), American illustrator, painter and writer, best known for his children's books.

Pym, Barbara Mary Crampton (1913–1980), English novelist.

Pyrrho (c.360–c.270 BC), famous Greek philosopher who originated Skepticism.

Pythagoras (c.580–c.500 BC), Greek philosopher and mathematician.

Qabbani, Nizar (1923–1998), prominent Syrian poet.

Quarles, Francis (1592–1644), English poet and writer, author of the poetry vols Emblemes (1635) and Hieroglyphikes of the life of Man (1638).

Quasimodo, Salvatore (1901–1968), notable Italian poet, critic and translator; won the Nobel Prize for Literature (1959).

Queffélec, Henri (1910–1992), French novelist.

Queneau, Raymond (1903–1976), French poet, novelist and essayist.

Quennell, Sir Peter (Courtney) (1905–1993), English poet, writer, critic, editor and translator.

Quental, Antero Tarquínio de (1842–1891), Portuguese poet, leading figure in the postromantic movement in Portugal; committed suicide.

Querido, Israël, (1874–1932), Dutch novelist of the naturalist school.

Quesnay, François (1694–1774), French economist, author of Tableau economique (1758).

Quesnal, Pasquier (1634–1719), French theologian who championed the Jansenist cause and wrote the controversial tome Nouveau Testament en français avec des réflexions morales (New Testament in French and Thoughts on Morality, 1692).

Quetelet, (Lambert) Adolphe (Jacques) (1796–1874), French mathematician, astronomer, sociologist and statistician, author of Sur l'homme (1835; English trans. as A Treatise on Man and the Development of His Faculties, 1842).

Quevedo y Villegas, Francisco Gómez de (1580–1645), Spanish writer and poet who excelled in satirical expression.

Quicherat, Jules (-Étienne-Joseph) (1814–1882), French archaeologist and scholar.

Quidde, Ludwig (1858–1941), German historian and politician who espoused the cause of pacifism.

Quiller-Couch, Sir Arthur Thomas (1863–1944), English poet, novelist, essayist and critic who wrote under the name Q.

Quincy, Edmund (1808–1877), American Abolitionist and writer; son of Josiah Quincy.

Quincy, Josiah (1772–1864), American politician, educator and writer; father of Edmund Quincy.

Quine, Willard Van Orman (1908–2000), American philosopher of the radical empiricist school, author of From a Logical Point of View (1953), Word and Object (1960) and Pursuit of Truth (1990).

Quinet, Edgar (1803–1875), French philosopher, historian and poet who championed political liberalism.

Quintana, Manuel José (1772–1857), Spanish poet, writer, critic and dramatist who was crowned the national poet of Spain by Queen Isabella (1855).

Quintilian (actually Marcus Fabius Quintilianus) (c.35–c.97), Roman writer, best known for his classic exposition on rhetoric Institutio oratoria.

Quintus Smyrnaeus (4th Century), Greek poet of epic verse.

Quiroga, Horacio (1878–1937), Uruguayan-born Argentine writer who excelled in the short story; committed suicide.

Raabe, Wilhelm (1831–1910), German novelist.

Rab, Gusztáv (1901–1966), Hungarian novelist.

Rabanus Maurus (c.780–856), German Benedictine abbot, archbishop and theologian who was known as the Praeceptor Germaniae (Teacher of Germany).

Rabbula (c.350–c.435), Syrian theologian and bishop of Edessa.

Rabéarivelo, Jean-Joseph (1901–1937), Madagascar poet who wrote in French; committed suicide.

Rabelais, François (c.1483–1553), famous French writer and physician whose mastery of biting satire was revealed in his classic Gargantua and Pantagruel (four vols, 1532, 1535, 1546, 1552).

Racan, Honorat de Bueil, Seigneur de (1589–1670), French poet, best known for his Stances sur la retraite (c.1618).

Racine, Jean (1639–1699), French dramatist and poet, a master of the tragic play.

Racine, Louis (1692–1763), French poet.

Radcliffe, Ann (née Ward) (1764–1823), English novelist of Gothic tales of terror, most notably The Mysteries of Udolpho (1794) and The Italian (1797).

Radcliffe-Brown, A(lfred) R(eginald) (1881–1955), English social anthropologist.

Raden, Adjeng Kartini (1879–1904), Japanese poet.

Radhakrishnan, Sarvepalli (1888–1975), Indian scholar and statesman who wrote on philosophy and religion.

Radiguet, Raymond (1903–1923), gifted French novelist and poet, author of Le Diable au corps (1923; English trans. as The Devil in the Flesh, 1932).

Radin, Max (1880–1950), Polish-born American writer.

Radin, Paul (1883–1959), significant Polish-born American anthropologist, author of Primitive Man as Philosopher (1927), Method and Theory of Ethnology (1933) and Primitive Religion (1938).

Radischev, Alexander Nikolaievich (1749–1802), Russian nobleman and writer, author of Puteshestvie iz Peterburga v Moskvu (1790; English trans. as A Journey from St Petersburg to Moscow, 1958) whose indictment of social injustice led to his banishment to Siberia; committed suicide.

Radlov, Vasili (actually Wilhelm Radloff) (1837–1919), German-born Russian scholar who was particularly known for his linguistic studies.

Rădulescu, Eliade (1802–1872), Romanian writer.

Raffi (actually Hakob Meliq-Hakobian) (1835–1888), Armenian novelist and short-story writer.

Rafinesque, Constantine Samuel (1783–1840), Turkish-born American naturalist and writer.

Rāghavānka (13th Century), Indian poet.

Raghunātha Siromani (c.1475–c.1550), Indian philosopher and logician.

Rahbek, Knud Lyne (1760–1830), Danish poet, dramatist, critic and editor.

Rahner, Karl (1904–1984), German Roman Catholic theologian.

Rahv, Philip (1908–1973), Russian-born American literary critic and editor.

Raimund, Ferdinand (1790–1836), Austrian dramatist.

Rainis (actually Jānis Pliekšāns) (1865–1929), leading Latvian poet and dramatist.

Rainolds, John (1549–1607), English scholar.

Rakovski, Georgi Sava (1821–1867), Bulgarian revolutionary and writer.

Raleigh or Ralegh, Sir Walter (1554–1618), famous English courtier, navigator and poet; was beheaded for treason.

Raleigh, Sir Walter (Alexander) (1861–1922), English critic and essayist.

Ralph of Coggeshall (13th Century), English monk and chronicler.

Rāmānuja (c.1017–c.1137), Indian theologian and philsopher of Hinduism.

Ramatirtha (actually Tirath Rama) (1873–1906), Indian religious leader of Hinduism.

Rameau, Jean-Philippe (1683–1764), renowned French composer and music theorist.

Ramos, Graciliano (1892–1953), Brazilian novelist.

Ramsay, Allan (1686–1758), Scottish poet, best known for The Gentle Shepherd, a Pastoral Comedy (1725).

Ramsey, Frank Plumpton (1903–1930), English philosopher and mathematician.

Ramsey, Ian Thomas (1915–1972), English bishop of Durham and philosopher.

Ramus, Petrus (1515–1572), French philosopher and logician, author of Aristotelicae animadversiones (1543), Dialecticae partitiones (1543), Dialectique (1550) and Dialecticae libri duo (1556); after converting to Protestantism, he was subjected to persecution and finally was murdered by hired assassins.

Ramusio, Giovanni Battista (1485–1557), Italian geographer and compiler of travel writings.

Ramuz, Charles-Ferdinand (1878–1947), esteemed Swiss novelist.

Rand, Ayn (1905–1982), Russian-born American novelist, dramatist and essayist, author of the well-known novels The Fountainhead (1943) and Atlas Shrugged (1957).

Randall, James Ryder (1839–1908), American poet who extolled the Confederacy.

Randall, John Herman Jr (1899–1980), American historian and philosopher, author of The Western Mind (2 vols, 1924; revised edition as The Making of the Modern Mind, 1926) and Career of Philosophy in Modern Times (2 vols, 1962, 1965).

Randall-MacIver, David (1873–1945), English archaeologist and anthropologist.

Randolph, Thomas (1605–1635), English poet and dramatist.

Rands, William Brighty (1823–1882), English journalist and writer, best remembered for his vol. of children's verse Lilliput Levee (1864).

Rank, Otto (1884–1939), Austrian psychoanalyst, author of Der Mythus von der Geburt des Helden (1909; English trans. as The Myth of the Birth of the Hero, 1914) and Das Inzest-Motiv in Dichtung und Sage (The Incest Motive in Poetry and Saga, 1912).

Ranke, Leopold von (1795–1886), eminent German historian who left unfinished a history of the world (9 vols, 1881–88).

Ransom, John Crowe (1888–1974), American poet, critic and editor.

Ransome, Arthur (Mitchell) (1884–1967), English journalist and writer, best known for his adventure novels for children.

Raoul de Houdenc (13th Century), French poet and musician, author of the notable Méraugis de Portlesguez.

Rascoe, (Arthur) Burton (1892–1957), American critic, writer and editor.

Rashdall, Hastings (1858–1924), English theologian, philosopher and historian.

Rashi (acronym for Rabbi Shlomo Yitzhaqi) (1040–1105), French rabbi and commentator on the Bible and Talmud.

Rashīd ad-Dīn (1247–1318), Persian statesman and historian, author of a universal history.

Rashīd Ridā, (Muhammad) (1865–1935), Syrian Muslim scholar.

Rask, Rasmus (Kristian) (1787–1832), important Danish language scholar who helped to develop comparative linguistics.

Raspe, Rudolph Erich (1737–1794), German adventurer and writer, best known for his tales of the adventures of the fictional Baron Munchhausen.

Rastell, John (c.1475–1536), English printer, barrister and dramatist; father of William Rastell.

Rastell, William (1508–1565), English printer, barrister and writer; son of John Rastell.

Rathenau, Walther (1867–1922), German industrialist, statesman and political philosopher; was assassinated by nationalist extremists.

Ratramnus (9th Century), French Roman Catholic priest and theologian.

Rattigan, Sir Terence (Mervyn) (1911–1977), English dramatist and screenwriter.

Ratzel, Friedrich (1844–1904), German geographer and ethnographer who originated the theory of Lebensraum (living space).

Rauschenbusch, Walter (1861–1918), American clergyman and theologian, a principal figure in the Social Gospel movement.

Ravaisson-Mollien, Jean-Gaspard-Félix Lacher (1813–1900), French philosopher.

Raven, Simon (Arthur Noël) (1927–2001), English writer, author of the 10-vol. series of novels Alms for Oblivion (1964–76) and the seven-vol. series of novels The First-Born of Egypt (1984–92).

Rawlings, Marjorie Kinnan (1896–1953), American writer, best known for her novel The Yearling (1938).

Ray, John (1627–1705), English naturalist whose most significant work was the Historia Plantarum (3 vols, 1686–1704).

Raynal, Guillaume-Thomas, Abbé de (1713–1796), French writer and polemicist.

Raynouard, François-Juste-Marie (1761–1836), French poet, dramatist and philologist.

Rāzī, ar- (actually Abū Bakr Muhammad ibn Zakarīyā) (c.865–c.928), famous Persian alchemist, physician and Muslim philosopher.

Read, Sir Herbert (Edward) (1893–1968), English poet, critic and writer.

Read, Opie (Percival) (1852–1939), American journalist and writer.

Read, Thomas Buchanan (1822–1872), American poet and painter.

Reade, Charles (1814–1884), prominent English novelist, particularly known for The Cloister and the Hearth (1861); uncle of William Winwood Reade.

Reade, William Winwood (1838–1875), English explorer and novelist; nephew of Charles Reade.

Realf, Richard (1834–1878), English-born American poet; committed suicide.

Rebreanu, Liviu (1885–1943), Romanian novelist.

Reclus, (Jean-Jacques-) Élisée (1830–1905), French geographer and anarchist, author of the monumental Nouvelle Géographie universelle; La Terre et les hommes (19 vols, 1876–94).

Redfield, Robert (1897–1958), American cultural anthropologist.

Redi, Francesco (1626–1698), Italian physician and poet, author of Bacco in Toscana (1685).

Redpath, James (1833–1891), Scottish-born American journalist and reformer who was a leading Abolitionist.

Redlich, Joseph (1869–1936), Austrian statesman and historian.

Rée, Paul (1849–1901), German philosopher.

Reed, Henry (1914–1986), English poet, dramatist and translator.

Reed, Isaac (1742–1807), English bibliophile, editor and biographer.

Reed, John (1887–1920), American Marxist revolutionary, writer and poet, apologist for the 1917 Bolshevik Revolution is his book Ten Days That Shook the World (1919).

Reed, Sampson (1800–1880), American Swedenborgian clergyman and writer, author of Observations on the Growth of the Mind (1826).

Reese, Lizette Woodworth (1856–1935), American poet, remembered for her Tears (1899).

Reeve, Clara (1729–1807), English novelist, best remembered for The Champion of Virtue: A Gothic Story (1777), reprinted as The Old English Baron (1778).

Regino von Prüm (10th Century), German cleric and chronicler, author of the Chronicon (published 1521).

Regio, José (1901–1969), esteemed Portuguese poet, novelist, dramatist and critic.

Regis, Pierre-Sylvan (1632–1707), French philosopher of the Cartesian school.

Regnard, Jean-François (1655–1709), French dramatist who excelled in comedic invention.

Régnier, Henri (-François-Joseph) de (1864–1936), admired French poet, novelist and critic, a proponent of Symbolism.

Régnier, Mathurin (1573–1613), gifted French poet and critic, noted especially for his satirical mastery in his poem Macette (1609).

Rehberg, August Wilhelm (1757–1836), German political theorist.

Reichenbach, Hans (1891–1953), German-born American philosopher, author of Elements of Symbolic Logic (1947) and The Rise of Scientific Philosophy (1951).

Reid, Forrest (1875–1947), Irish novelist and critic.

Reid, Thomas (1710–1796), Scottish philosopher of the common sense school.

Reid, (Thomas) Mayne (1818–1883), Irish-born American novelist.

Reid, Whitelaw (1837–1912), American journalist, diplomat and politician.

Reimarus, Hermann Samuel (1694–1768), influential German philosopher who was a leading Deist, author of the Apologie oder Schutzschrift für die vernunftigen Verehrer Gottes (Apologia or Defense for the Rational Reverers of God).

Reinkens, Josef Hubert (1821–1896), German Roman Catholic bishop and scholar who became the first bishop of the Old Catholic Church.

Reinmar von Hagenau (12th–13th Century), German poet.

Reiske, Johann Jakob (1716–1774), learned German scholar, an authority on Arabic and Greek literature.

Remarque, Erich Maria (1898–1970), German-born American novelist, best known for his Im Westen nichts Neues (1929; English trans. as All Quiet on the Western Front, 1929).

Remizov, Alexei (Mikhailovich) (1877–1957), Russian writer of the Symbolist school.

Renan, (Joseph-)Ernest (1823–1892), French religious historian, philosopher and scholar.

Renard, Jules (1864–1910), French writer and dramatist, best remembered for his Poil de carotte (1894; English trans. as Carrots, 1946), a prose work based on his bitter childhood.

Renart, Jean (13th Century), French writer.

Renault, Mary (actually Mary Challans) (1905–1983), English novelist, best known for her historical fiction.

René of Provence, Duc d'Anjou and Comte de Provence (1408–1480), French writer and poet.

Renn, Ludwig (actually Arnold Friedrich Vieth von Golssenau) (1889–1979), German novelist, best known for his novel Krieg (War, 1928).

Renouvier, Charles-Bernard (1815–1903), French philosopher who espoused a neocritical idealist philosophy.

Repplier, Agnes (1858–1950), American essayist and biographer.

Resende, Garcia de (c.1470–1536), Portuguese poet, writer and editor.

Restif, Nicolas-Edme (1734–1806), French novelist who was also known as Restif de la Bretonne.

Retz, Jean-François-Paul de Gondi, Cardinal de (1613–1679), French churchman and political adventurer who was a leading figure in the Fronde, especially known for his classic Mémoires (published 1715).

Reuchlin, Johannes (1455–1522), notable German classical scholar, author of De Rudimentis Hebraicis (On the Fundamentals of Hebrew, 1506) and the satirical Epistolae obscurorum virorum (Letters of the Obscure Men, 1515–17).

Reuter, Fritz (1810–1874), admired German novelist whose finest work was Ut mine Stromtid (During My Apprenticeship, 1862–64).

Reverdy, Pierre (1889–1960), French poet who embraced Cubism and later Surrealism.

Revius, Jacobus (1586–1658), admired Dutch theologian and poet of the Calvinist persuasion, particularly known for his sonnet collection on Christ.

Revueltas, José (1914–76), Mexican novelist, short-story writer and political activist.

Rexroth, Kenneth (1905–1982), American poet, essayist, critic, translator and painter.

Reyes, Alfonso (1889–1959), Mexican poet, writer, scholar and diplomat.

Reymont, Władysław Stanisław (1867–1925), Polish novelist and short-story writer; won the Nobel Prize for Literature (1924).

Reynolds, John Hamilton (1796–1852), English poet and writer, particularly admired for his poems in The Garden of Florence (1821).

Reynolds, Sir Joshua (1723–1792), famous English painter and writer on aesthetics.

Reznikoff, Charles (1894–1976), American poet of the Objectivist school.

Rezzori, Gregor von (1914–1998), Austrian novelist and memoirist.

Rhianus (3rd Century BC), Greek poet and scholar.

Rhigas, Konstantinos (1760–1798), Greek poet and revolutionary; as organizer of the anti-Turkish revolutionary movement in Vienna, he was betrayed and killed.

Rhodes, Eugene Manlove (1869–1934), American novelist who excelled in the depiction of the Old West.

Rhodes, James Ford (1848–1927), American historian, author of a History of the United States from the Compromise of 1850 (7 vols, 1893–1906) and a History of the Civil War (1917).

Rhys, Ernest Percival (1859–1946), English editor, writer and poet.

Rhys, Jean (actually Ella Gwendolen Rees Williams) (c.1890–1979), West Indies novelist and short-story writer.

Rhys, Siôn Dafydd (1534–c.1609), Welsh physician and grammarian.

Ribeiro, Aquilino (Gomes) (1885–1963), Portuguese writer.

Ribeiro, Bernardim (c.1482–1552), Portuguese poet and writer who helped to reinvigorate Portuguese literature.

Ribeiro Couto, Rui (1898–1963), Brazilian diplomat, poet and short-story writer.

Ricardo, David (1772–1823), English economist, author of On the Principles of Political Economy and Taxation (1817).

Ricardo (Leite), Cassiano (1895–1974), Brazilian poet, essayist and critic.

Rice, Alice (Caldwell) Hegan (1870–1942), American novelist and short-story writer, best known for her Mrs Wiggs of the Cabbage Patch (1901); wife of Cale Young Rice.

Rice, Cale Young (1872–1943), American poet and dramatist; husband of Alice (Caldwell) Hegan Rice.

Rice, Elmer (actually Elmer Reizenstein) (1892–1967), American dramatist, novelist and essayist.

Rice, James (1843–1882), English novelist and journalist.

Rich, Barnabe (1542–1617), English soldier and writer.

Richard of Saint-Victor (died 1173), Scottish theologian who wrote classic works on mysticism in his Benjamin major and Benjamin minor.

Richards, I(vor) A(rmstrong) (1893–1979), English poet and critic.

Richards, Laura Elizabeth (1850–1943), American biographer and children's writer.

Richards, (Thomas Franklin) Grant (1872–1948), English publisher and writer.

Richardson, Dorothy Miller (1873–1957), English novelist, acclaimed for her novel series Pilgrimage.

Richardson, Henry Handel (actually Ethel Florence Lindesay Richardson) (1870–1946), English novelist, author of the trilogy The Fortunes of Richard Mahony (Australia Felix, 1917, The Way Home, 1925, and Ultima Thule, 1929).

Richardson, John (1796–1852), Canadian novelist, author of Écarté (1829) and Wacousta (1832).

Richardson, Samuel (1689–1761), English novelist who wrote Pamela, or, Virtue Rewarded (1740), Clarissa, or, The History of a Young Lady (1747–48) and The History of Sir Charles Grandison (1753–54).

Richepin, Jean (1849–1926), French poet, dramatist and novelist.

Richler, Mordecai (1931–2001), Canadian writer and dramatist who was particularly known for his novels The Apprenticeship of Duddy Kravitz (1959), Cocksure (1968), St Urbain's Horseman (1971) and Solomon Gursky Was Here (1989).

Richmond, Legh (1772–1827), English divine and writer, best known for his The Diaryman's Daughter (1809).

Richter, Conrad (Michael) (1890–1968), American novelist and short-story writer.

Richter, Johann Friedrich (1763–1825), famous German writer and poet who also wrote under the name Jean Paul, renowned for his novels Hesperus (1795) and Titan (1800–03).

Ricket, Heinrich (1863–1936), German philosopher of neo-Kantian persuasion.

Ricketson, Daniel (1813–1898), American poet.

Rickword, Edgell (1898–1982), English poet and critic.

Ridge, John Rollin (1827–1867), American journalist, writer and poet who wrote under the name Yellow Bird, a translation of his Cherokee name.

Ridge, Lola (1871–1941), Irish-born American poet who was esteemed for her Symbolist verse.

Riding, Laura (actually Laura Reichenthal) (1901–1991), American poet, novelist and critic.

Ridler, Anne (Barbara Bradby) (1912–2001), English poet, librettist, editor and translator whose poetry reflected her high regard for the Metaphysical poets of the 17th Century.

Ridley, James (1736–1765), English cleric and writer, author of the Tales of the Genii (1764).

Ridley, Nicholas (c.1500–1555), English Protestant Reformation leader and theologian; was condemned as a heretic and burned at the stake.

Riegl, Alois (1858–1905), Austrian scholar.

Riehl, Alois (1844–1924), Austrian philosopher of the Kantian school.

Riehl, Wilhelm Heinrich (1823–1897), German historian, author of Die Naturgeschichte des deutschen Volkes als Grundlage einer deutschen Social Politik (The Natural Law of the German People as a Foundation of German Social Politics, 4 vols, 1851–69).

Riemann, (Karl Wilhelm Julius) Hugo (1849–1919), German music scholar and lexicographer.

Riggs, Lynn (1899–1954), American poet and dramatist.

Rigord (c.1150–c.1207), French monk and chronicler.

Riis, Jacob August (1849–1914), Danish-born American journalist, photographer, social reformer and writer, best known for his account of slum life in New York City in How the Other Half Lives (1890).

Riley, (Isaac) Woodbridge (1869–1933), American philosopher.

Riley, James Whitcomb (1849–1916), American poet, known as the 'Hoosier poet', who won acclaim for his dialect poems.

Rilke, Rainer Maria (1875–1926), Austrian poet, celebrated for his Duineser Elegien (1922) and Die Sonnette an Orpheus (1923).

Rimbaud, (Jean-Nicolas-) Arthur (1854–1891), celebrated French poet, author of Les Illuminations (1886).

Rin-chen-bzang-po (958–1055), Tibetan scholar and translator of Buddhist texts.

Rinehart, Mary Roberts (1876–1958), American novelist and dramatist, best known for her mysteries.

Rinuccini, Ottavio (1562–1621), Italian poet.

Ripley, George (1802–1880), prominent American reformer, journalist, literary critic, writer and encyclopedist, the founder of the utopian Brook Farm.

Ripley, W(illiam) Z(ebina) (1867–1941), American anthropologist and economist.

Ritchie, Anne Isabella Thackeray, Lady (1837–1919), English novelist and essayist; daughter of William Makepeace Thackeray.

Ritschl, Albrecht (1822–1889), influential German Protestant theologian, author of Die christliche Lehre von der Rechtfertigung und Versöhnung (3 vols, 1870–74; English trans. as The Christian Doctrine of Justification and Reconciliation, 1872–1900).

Ritschl, F(riedrich) W(ilhelm) (1806–1876), German classical scholar.

Ritson, Joseph (1752–1803), English literary scholar who was known as much for his eccentric nature as for his learning; died insane.

Ritsos, Yannis (1909–1990), Greek poet who championed the cause of Marxism.

Rivarol, Antoine, Comte de (1753–1801), French journalist and epigrammatist whose claim to nobility is doubtful, especially known for his satirical bent.

Rive, Richard Moore (1931–1989), South African novelist and short-story writer; was murdered.

Rivera, José Eustasio (1889–1928), notable Colombian novelist and poet, author of the famous novel La voragine (1924; English trans. as The Vortex, 1935).

Rivers, W(illiam) H(alse) R(ivers) (1864–1922), English medical psychologist and anthropologist.

Rives, Amélie (1863–1945), American novelist, poet and dramatist.

Rivet, Paul (1876–1958), French ethnologist.

Rivière, Jacques (1886–1925), French writer, critic and editor.

Rizal, José (actually José Rizal y Mercado) (1861–1896), Filipino physician, patriot, writer and poet; was arrested, tried for sedition and executed by the military.

Robbins, Harold (actually Francis Kane) (1916–1997), American writer best remembered for his novel The Carpetbaggers (1961).

Robert de Torigni (c.1110–1186), French abbot and chronicler.

Robert of Avesbury (14th Century), English historian.

Robert of Gloucester (13th Century), English chronicler.

Roberts, Sir Charles G(eorge) D(ouglas) (1860–1943), eminent Canadian poet, writer and editor.

Roberts, Elizabeth Madox (1881–1941), American novelist, short-story writer and poet, best remembered for her novel The Great Meadow (1930).

Roberts, Kate (1891–1985), Welsh novelist, short-story writer and dramatist.

Roberts, Kenneth (Lewis) (1885–1957), American writer, particularly known for his historical novels.

Roberts, Michael William Edward (1902–1948), English poet, critic and editor.

Robertson, Morgan Andrew (1861–1915), American writer.

Robertson, Thomas William (1829–1871), English dramatist, producer and director.

Robertson, William (1721–1793), Scottish historian and Church of Scotland leader, author of the authoritative work The History of the Reign of the Emperor Charles the Fifth (1769), and History of America (2 vols, 1777).

Robinson, Edward (1794–1863), American biblical scholar who specialized in the geography of the Bible.

Robinson, Edwin Arlington (1869–1935), esteemed American poet who was especially known for his naturalism and lyricism.

Robinson, (Esmé Stuart) Lennox (1886–1958), Irish dramatist and editor.

Robinson, Henry Crabb (1775–1867), English diarist and conversationalist.

Robinson, Henry Wheeler (1872–1945), English Nonconformist Baptist theologian and Old Testament scholar.

Robinson, James Harvey (1863–1936), influential American historian, author of The New History (1912) and The Mind in the Making (1921).

Robinson, John (c.1575–1625), English Puritan minister and writer, particularly known for his A Justification of Separation from the Church of England (1610).

Robinson, Rowland Evans (1833–1900), American writer.

Robinson, Solon (1803–1880), American writer.

Roblès, Emmanuel (François) (1914–1995), Algerian-born French novelist and dramatist of Spanish descent.

Rochester, John Wilmot, 2nd Earl of (1647–1680), notable English poet and courtier, admired for his love poems and his satirical writings.

Rod, Édouard (1857–1910), Swiss writer and critic.

Rode, Helge (1870–1937), Danish poet, novelist, dramatist and essayist who was the principal figure in the antirationalist movement in Denmark.

Rodenbach, Albrecht (1856–1880), Belgian poet who was a major figure in the revival of Flemish letters.

Rodo, José Enrique (1872–1917), important Uruguayan philosopher and essayist.

Rodrigues Lobo, Francisco (1580–1622), Portuguese poet and writer who espoused pastoral themes.

Roe, E(dward) P(ayson) (1838–1888), American novelist, best known for his Barriers Burned Away (1872).

Roe, Sir Thomas (c.1581–1644), English diplomat and memoirist.

Roethke, Theodore (1908–1963), esteemed American poet and essayist, particularly known for his poetry collection The Waking (1953).

Roger of Wendover (died 1236), English monk and chronicler, author of Flores historiarum.

Rogers, James Edwin Thorold (1825–1890), English clergyman, economist and politician, best known for his tome on inflation A History of Agriculture and Prices in England (1866–67).

Rogers, John (c.1500–1555), English Protestant reformer and biblical editor; was burned as a heretic.

Rogers, Samuel (1763–1855), English poet who wrote The Pleasures of Memory (1792).

Rogers, Will (actually William Penn Adair Rogers) (1879–1935), American humorist, actor and writer; was killed in an airplane crash.

Roget, Peter Mark (1779–1869), English physician and philologist, compiler of the famous Thesaurus of English Words and Phrases (1852).

Róheim, Géza (1891–1953), Hungarian-born American psychoanalyst and ethnologist, author of Animism, Magic, and the Divine King (1930), Psychoanalysis and Anthropology (1950), The Gates of the Dream (1952) and Magic and Schizophrenia (published 1955).

Rojas, Fernando de (c.1465–1541), Spanish writer, best known for his novel Celestina (1499).

Rojas, Manuel (Sepúlveda) (1896–1973), Chilean novelist and short-story writer.

Rojas Villandrando, Agustin de (1572–c.1635), Spanish writer, author of the picaresque novel El viaje entretenido (The Pleasant Voyage).

Rojas Zorrilla, Francisco do (1607–1648), Spanish dramatist, particularly remembered for his Del rey abajo, ninguno (Below the King, No One).

Roland Holst-van der Schalk, Henriëtte Goverdina Anna (1869–1952), Dutch poet, biographer and socialist.

Rolfe, Frederick William (Serafino Austin Lewis Mary) (1860–1913), English writer who wrote under the name Baron Corvo, especially admired for his Hadrian the Seventh (1904) and The Desire and Pursuit of the Whole (published 1934).

Rolland, Romain (1866–1944), renowned French novelist, dramatist and essayist; won the Nobel Prize for Literature (1915).

Rolle, Richard (actually Richard Rolle de Hampole) (c.1300–1349), English poet and writer on mystical subjects.

Rolli, Paolo Antonio (1687–1765), Italian librettist, poet and translator.

Rölvaag, Ole (Edvart) (1876–1931), Norwegian-born American novelist, author of the esteemed Giants in the Earth (1927).

Romains, Jules (actually Louis-Henri-Jean Farigoule) (1885–1972), French novelist, dramatist and poet whose masterpiece was the epic prose cycle Les Hommes de bonne volonte (27 vols, 1932–46; English trans. as Men of Good Will, 14 vols, 1933–46).

Romani, Felice (1788–1865), Italian librettist and writer.

Romer, Alfred Sherwood (1894–1973), American paleontologist.

Romero, José Rubén (1890–1952), Mexican novelist, poet and diplomat.

Ronsard, Pierre de (1524–1585), celebrated French poet who excelled in the ode and sonnet.

Roosevelt, Theodore (1858–1919), famous American explorer, soldier, writer, politician and 26th president of the US (1901–09), author of the much esteemed The Winning of the West (4 vols, 1889–96).

Roquebrune, Robert Laroque de (1889–1978), French-Canadian novelist, short-story writer and memoirist.

Ros, Amanda McKittrick (née Anna Margaret McKittrick) (1860–1939), Irish novelist.

Rosa, Salvator (1615–1673), Italian painter, etcher, poet, actor and musician.

Roscoe, William (1753–1831), English lawyer, banker, botanist, scholar and poet, much admired for his study Life of Lorenzo de' Medici (1795) and for his children's verse.

Roscommon, Wentworth Dillon, 4th Earl of (c.1633–1685), English poet and critic.

Rose, Aquila (c.1695–1723), English-born American poet and typographer.

Rose, Valentin (1829–1916), German scholar, best known for his work on Aristotle.

Rosegger, Peter (1843–1918), Austrian poet and novelist, particularly known for his novels Die Schriften des Waldschulmeisters (1875; English trans. as The Forest Schoolmaster, 1901) and Waldheimat (1877; English trans. as The Forest Farm, 1912).

Rosenberg, Harold (1906–78), American writer, poet and art critic.

Rosenberg, Isaac (1890–1918), English poet and artist who excelled in 'trench' poetry; died in World War I.

Rosenfeld, Morris (1862–1923), Russian-born American poet of Yiddish verse.

Rosenstein, Nils von (1752–1824), Swedish writer.

Rosenstock-Huessy, Eugen (1888–1973), German writer.

Rosenzweig, Franz (1886–1929), German philosopher who espoused a religious Existentialist worldview.

Rosmini-Serbati, Antonio (1797–1855), Italian Roman Catholic priest, theologian and philosopher, author of the Nuovo saggio sull' origine delle idee (3 vols, 1830; English trans. as The Origin of Ideas, 1883–84) and Massime di perfezione Cristiana (1830; English trans. as Maxims of Christian Perfection, 1849).

Ross, Alan (1922–2001), Englist poet and editor.

Ross, Alexander (1699–1784), Scottish poet and songwriter, best known for his pastoral The Fortunate Shepherdess (1768).

Ross, Edward (Alsworth) (1866–1951), American sociologist, author of Social Control (1901).

Ross, Harold (Wallace) (1892–1951), American editor, founder and editor of the influential magazine The New Yorker (1925–51).

Ross, (James) Sinclair (1908–1996), Canadian novelist and short-story writer, particularly admired for his novel As for Me and My House (1941).

Ross, Sir W(illiam) D(avid) (1877–1971), Scottish philosopher of the rationalistic moral persuasion, author of The Right and the Good (1930) and Foundations of Ethics (1939).

Ross, William (1762–1790), Scottish poet.

Rossetti, Christina Georgina (1830–1894), admired English poet, author of Goblin Market (1862) and Prince's Progress and Other Poems (1866); daughter of Gabriele Pasquale Rossetti and sister of Dante Gabriel and William Michael Rossetti.

Rossetti, Dante Gabriel (actually Gabriel Charles Dante Rossetti) (1828–1882), famous English poet, translator and painter, celebrated for such poems as The Blessed Damozel (1850) and The House of Life (1881); son of Gabriele Pasquale Rossetti and brother of Christina Georgina and William Michael Rossetti.

Rossetti, Gabriele Pasquale (1783–1854), Italian-born English poet and writer; father of Christina Georgina, Dante Gabriel and William Michael Rossetti.

Rossetti, William Michael (1829–1919), English literary and art critic; son of Gabriele Pasquale Rossetti and brother of Christina Georgina and Dante Gabriel Rossetti.

Rostand, Edmond (1868–1918), French poet and dramatist, author of the famous play Cyrano de Bergerac (1897).

Rosten, Leo (Calvin) (1908–1997), Polish-born American writer, particularly known for The Education of H*Y*M*A*N K*A*P*L*A*N (1937).

Rostovzeff, Michael Ivanovich (1870–1952), learned Russian-born American archaeologist who was an authority on ancient Greece and Rome.

Rota, Gian-Carlo (1932–99), Italian-born American mathematician, philosopher and writer.

Roth, Henry (1906–1995), Austrian-born American novelist and short-story writer, particularly remembered for his novel Call It Sleep (1934).

Rothe, Richard (1799–1867), German Lutheran theologian of Idealism, especially known for his works on the church and state, and on ethics.

Rotimi, (Emmanuel Gladstone) Ola(wale) (1938–2000), Nigerian dramatist and theatre director.

Rotrou, Jean de (1609–1650), important French dramatist of the Neoclassical school.

Rougemont, Denis de (1906–1985), Swiss cultural historian and writer.

Rouget de Lisle, Claude-Joseph (1760–1836), French poet and writer, author of the words and composer of the music of the French National Anthem La Marseillaise (1792).

Roumain, Jacques (1907–1944), Haitian writer.

Roumanille, Joseph (1818–1891), French poet and writer.

Rouquette, Adrien Emmanuel (1813–1887), American poet and writer; brother of François Dominique Rouquette.

Rouquette, François Dominique (1810–1890), American poet; brother of Adrien Emmanuel Rouquette.

Rourke, Constance (Mayfield) (1885–1941), American writer.

Rousseau, Jean-Baptiste (1671–1741), French dramatist and poet, especially known for his epigrams.

Rousseau, Jean-Jacques (1712–1778), celebrated Swiss philosopher, political theorist and writer, author of the famous autobiography Confessions (published 1782).

Rousselot, Jean-Pierre (1846–1924), French phonetician and linguist.

Routh, Martin Joseph (1755–1854), English educator, scholar and editor.

Rovere, Richard (Halworth) (1915–1979), American journalist and writer, especially known for his writings on politics.

Rowe, Nicholas (1674–1718), eminent English dramatist, poet, editor and translator; became Poet Laureate of the United Kingdom (1715).

Rowlands, Samuel (c.1570–c.1630), English poet and writer of a satirical turn.

Rowley, Samuel (16th–17th Century), English dramatist.

Rowley, William (c.1585–1626), English dramatist and actor.

Rowntree, Benjamin Seebohm (1871–1954), English philanthropist and sociologist.

Rowse, A(lfred) L(eslie) (1903–1997), English poet, biographer and historian.

Rowson, Susanna (Haswell) (c.1762–1824), English-born American writer and poet.

Roy, D L (1863–1913), Bengali dramatist.

Roy, Gabrielle (1909–1983), esteemed French-Canadian novelist and short-story writer.

Roy, (Joseph) Camille (1870–1943), French-Canadian critic and literary historian.

Royce, Josiah (1855–1916), prominent American philosopher of Idealism.

Royer-Collard, Pierre-Paul (1763–1845), French statesman and philosopher.

Royle, Edwin (Milton) (1862–1942), American dramatist, best remembered for The Squaw Man (1905).

Rozanov, Vasili Vasilievich (1856–1919), Russian writer.

Rozhdestvensky, Robert Ivanovich (1932–1994), Russian poet.

Rucellai, Giovanni (1475–1525), Italian poet and dramatist, author of the didactic poem Le api (The Bees, published 1539).

Rückert, Friedrich (1788–1866), admired German poet and scholar whose moving poems Kindertotenlieder (Songs on the Death of Children) were set to music by Gustav Mahler.

Rudbeck, Olof (1630–1702), Swedish scientist and writer.

Rudd, Steele (actually Arthur Hoey Davis) (1868–1935), Australian novelist, short-story writer and dramatist.

Rudnicki, Adolf (1912–1990), Polish writer.

Rudolf von Ems (c.1200–c.1254), important Austrian poet of epic verse.

Rueda, Lope de (c.1510–1565), Spanish actor and dramatist.

Rufinus, Tyrannius (c.345–c.410), Italian priest, theologian, writer and translator.

Ruiz, Juan (c.1283–c.1350), Spanish poet who wrote the classic Libro de buen amor (1330; English trans. as The Book of Good Love, 1933).

Ruiz de Alarcón (y Mendoza), Juan (c.1581–1639), Mexican-born Spanish dramatist.

Rukeyser, Muriel (1913–1980), American poet, writer, dramatist and translator.

Rulfo, Juan Pérez (1918–1986), Mexican writer.

Rulhière, Claude-Carloman (1734–1791), French historian and poet.

Rumilly, Robert (1897–1983), French-Canadian historian, author of the expansive Histoire de la province de Québec (41 vols, 1940–63).

Rumpf, Georg Eberhard (1627–1702), German naturalist.

Runciman, Sir (James Cochran) Steven(son) (1903–2000), English historian who wrote the authoritative studies A History of the Crusades (three vols, 1951–54) and The Fall of Constantinople, 1453 (1965).

Runeberg, Johan Ludvig (1804–1877), eminent Finnish poet and dramatist, author of Vårt land (Our Land), which was adopted as the Finnish National Anthem.

Runius, Johan (1679–1713), Swedish poet.

Runyon, (Alfred) Damon (1884–1946), American journalist, columnist and short-story writer.

Rushworth, John (c.1612–1690), English historian, author of the Historical Collections of Private Passages of State (1659–1701).

Ruskin, John (1819–1900), eminent English writer, art critic and lecturer, especially known for Modern Painters (1843), The Seven Lamps of Architecture (1849) and The Stones of Venice (1851–53).

Russell, Bertrand (Arthur William), 3rd Earl (1872–1970), celebrated English logician, philosopher and pacifist; won the Nobel Prize for Literature (1950).

Russell, Irwin (1853–1879), American poet who wrote in black dialect.

Russell, Lord John, 1st Earl (1792–1878), English statesman and writer.

Russell, Thomas (1762–1788), English poet, much admired for his Sonnets and Miscellaneous Poems (published 1789).

Rutebeuf (13th Century), French trouvère.

Rutherford, Mark (actually William Hale White) (1831–1913), English novelist and critic.

Rutilius Namatianus Claudius (5th Century), Roman poet, author of the elegy De reditu suo.

Ruysbroeck, Jan van (1293–1381), Flemish Roman Catholic mystic and writer, author of the famous Die Chierheit der gheesteliker Brulocht (1350; English trans. as The Spiritual Espousals, 1952).

Ruzzante (actually Angelo Beolco) (1502–1542), Italian actor and dramatist.

Ryan, Abram Joseph (1838–1886), American poet and Roman Catholic priest whose espousal of the Confederate cause led him to be dubbed the 'Tom Moore of Dixie'.

Rybakov, Anatoly (1911–1998), Russian novelist, author of Children of the Arbat (1987).

Rydberg, (Abraham) Viktor (1828–1895), Swedish writer and poet.

Ryle, Gilbert (1900–1976), influential English philosopher of the Oxford school, author of The Concept of Mind (1949), Dilemmas (1954) and Plato's Progress (1966).

Rymer, Thomas (c.1643–1713), English historian and literary critic.

Sa'adia ben Joseph (882–942), Egyptian Jewish philosopher and polemicist, author of an Arabic translation of the Old Testament.

Saavedra Fajardo, Diego da (1584–1648), Spanish diplomat and writer, author of the Idea de un Príncipe político cristiano (1640).

Saavedra Lamas, Carlos (1878–1959), Argentine jurist and writer on international law; won the Nobel Prize for Peace (1936).

Saavedra (Ramírez de Baquendano), Ángel de, Duque de Rivas (1791–1865), prominent Spanish dramatist and poet, especially known for his play Don Alvaro, o la fuerza del sino (1835).

Saba, Umberto (actually Umberto Poli) (1883–1957), Italian poet.

Sabatier, (Louis-) Auguste (1839–1901), French Protestant theologian who espoused liberal views in biblical criticism.

Sabine, Lorenzo (1803–1877), American historian.

Sable, Madeleine de Souvre, Marquise de (1599–1678), French writer.

Sabzevari, Haji Hadi (c.1797–1878), notable Persian philosopher and poet.

Sá-Carneiro, Mário de (1890–1916), talented Portuguese poet, novelist and short-story writer.

Sacchetti, Franco (c.1330–1400), Italian poet and writer.

Sachs, Curt (1881–1959), German-born American music historian.

Sachs, Hans (1494–1576), celebrated German poet, dramatist and writer who was the inspiration for Wagner's opera Die Meistersinger von Nürnberg.

Sachs, Nelly (Leonie) (1891–1970), German-born Swedish poet and dramatist; was co-winner of the Nobel Prize for Literature (1966).

Sackler, Howard (1929–1982), American dramatist and poet.

Sackville, Charles, Lord Buckhurst, later 6th Earl of Dorset (1638–1706), English courtier and poet.

Sackville, Thomas, 1st Earl of Dorset and Baron Buckhurst (1536–1608), English statesman, poet and dramatist, author of the play The Tragedie of Gorboduc (in collaboration with Thomas Norton, 1561) and the poetry collection A Myrroure for Magistrates (1563).

Sackville-West, Victoria (Mary) (1892–1962), English poet and writer; wife of Sir Harold (George) Nicolson.

Sade, Marquis de (actually Donatien-Alphonse-François Sade) (1740–1814), infamous French libertine, writer and dramatist whose sexual perversions led to the coinage of the word sadism.

Sadeddin, Hoca (1536–1599), Turkish historian.

Sá de Miranda, Francisco de (1481–1558), Portuguese poet, author of Cartas (verse epistles), satires and the eclogue Basto.

Sa'dī (c.1213–1292), Persian poet and writer, author of the classic vols Būstān (The Garden, 1257) and Golestān (The Rose Garden, 1258).

Sadleir, Michael (actually Michael Sadler) (1888–1957), English bibliographer and novelist.

Sadoveanu, Mihail (1880–1961), Romanian novelist and short-story writer.

Saemundr, Sigfússon (1056–1133), Icelandic chieftan, priest and chronicler.

Šafařík, Pavel Josef (1795–1861), Czech philologist and archaeologist.

Sagan, Carl (Edward) (1934–1996), prominent American astronomer, exobiologist and writer who was a popularizer of science via books and television.

Sahagun, Bernardino de (c.1490–1590), Spanish Roman Catholic missionary and historian of New Spain.

Sa'ib (died 1677), Persian poet.

Saigyó (1118–1190), Japanese Buddhist priest and poet who excelled in writing in the tanka form.

Saint-Amant, (Marc-) Antonio Girard, Sieur de (c.1594–1661), French poet, especially esteemed for his Albion (1643), Rome ridicule (1649) and Moïse sauve (Moses Rescued, 1653).

Saint-Denis, Michel (actually Jacques Duchesne) (1897–1971), French actor, director and dramatist.

Saint-Évremond, Charles de Marguetel de Saint-Denis, Seigneur de (c.1613–1703), French writer and poet.

Saint-Exupéry, Antoine (-Marie-Roger) de (1900–1944), notable French aviator and writer; died in World War II.

Saint-Martin, Louis-Claude de (1743–1803), French philosopher and poet who espoused illuminism.

Saint-Pierre, Charles-Irénée Castel, Abbé de (1658–1743), French reformer and writer who was known for his controversial and utopian ideas.

Saint-Réal, César Vichard, Abbé de (1639–1692), French writer.

Saint-Simon, (Claude-) Henri (de Rouvroy, Comte) de (1760–1825), influential French social thinker and socialist, author of Opinions littéraires, philosophiques et industrielles (1825) and Le Nouveau Christianisme (1825).

Saint-Simon, Louis de Rouvroy, Duc de (1675–1755), French writer who wrote the Mémoires.

Sainte-Beuve, Charles-Augustin (1804–1869), famous French critic, writer and poet.

Saintine, Joseph Xavier (1798–1865), French dramatist, poet and writer.

Sainstbury, George Edward Bateman (1845–1933), eminent English literary critic and historian.

Sait Faik Abasiyanik (1907–1954), Turkish writer.

Saitō Mokichi (1882–1953), Japanese poet.

Sakai Hōitsu (actually Tadanao) (1761–1828), Japanese painter and poet.

Salesbury, William (c.1520–c.1584), Welsh lexicographer and translator, best known for his translation of the New Testament into Welsh (1567).

Salimbene di Adam (1221–c.1290), Italian Franciscan friar and historian.

Salinas (y Serrano), Pedro (1891–1951), Spanish poet, dramatist, essayist and scholar.

Salis-Seewis, Johann Gaudenz, Freiherr von (1762–1834), Swiss poet.

Salkey, (Felix) Andrew (Alexander) (1928–1995), Panamanian novelist, short-story writer and dramatist.

Sallust (actually Gaius Sallustius Crispus) (c.86–c.35 BC), Roman historian and politician.

Salmasius, Claudius (actually Claude de Saumaise) (1588–1653), learned French classical scholar.

Salten, Felix (actually Siegmund Salzmann) (1869–1945), Austrian theatre critic and novelist, especially remembered for his Bambi (1923).

Saltus, Edgar (Evertson) (1855–1921), American novelist and short-story writer.

Saltykov, Mikhail Yevgrafovich (1826–1889), Russian novelist who was especially known for his mastery of satire.

Salutati, (Lino) Coluccio (di Piero) (1331–1406), Italian public official, writer and poet.

Samain, Albert Victor (1844–1910), French poet.

Samaniego, Félix Mariá (1745–1801), Spanish poet who was known for his children's fables.

Samuel, Herbert Louis, 1st Viscount (1870–1963), English politician and philosopher.

Samuel ha-Nagid (actually Abu Ibrahim Samuel ben Joseph Halevi ibn Nagdela) (993–1056), Spanish Jewish warrior, statesman, scholar and poet.

Sanā'ī (actually Abu al-Majd Majdud ibn Adam) (c.1050–1131), notable Persian poet of Islam, esteemed for his Hadiqeh ol-haqiqat (The Enclosed Garden of Truth).

Sanawbari, as- (died 945), Arab poet.

Sanborn, Franklin Benjamin (1831–1917), American Abolitionist and biographer.

Sanches or Sanchez, Francisco (c.1550–c.1623), Spanish physician and philosopher of Skepticism.

Sánchez, Luis Alberto (1900–1994), Peruvian politician, writer and poet.

Sanchuniathon (c.14th Century BC), Phoenician writer.

Sand, George (actually Amandine-Aurore-Lucile née Dupin Dudevant) (1804–1876), celebrated French novelist, short-story writer and dramatist who was equally celebrated for her numerous liaisons.

Sanday, William (1843–1920), English New Testament scholar.

Sandburg, Carl (August) (1878–1967), American poet, biographer, novelist and folklorist.

Sandeau, Léonard-Sylvain-Julien (1811–1883), French novelist and dramatist, best known for his novel Mademoiselle de la Seiglière (1848) and his liaison with George Sand.

Sandeman, Robert (1718–1771), Scottish-born American Protestant leader and writer, particularly known for Some Thoughts on Christianity (1764).

Sandemose, Aksel (1899–1965), Danish-born Norwegian novelist of an experimental turn.

Sanders, Lawrence (1920–1998), American writer, best remembered for his suspense thriller The Anderson Tapes (1970).

Sanders, Nicholas (c.1530–1581), English Roman Catholic scholar and polemicist, author of a valuable history of the English Reformation written in Latin (English trans. as The Rise and Growth of the Anglican Schism, 1877).

Sanderson, John (1783–1844), American writer, particularly known for his Sketches of Paris: In Familiar Letters to His Friends (1838).

Sandoz, Mari (1896–1966), American writer.

Sands, Robert C(harles) (1799–1832), American journalist, writer and poet.

Sandys, George (1578–1664), significant English poet, traveller and government official, especially important for his contribution to the development of the heroic couplet.

Sandys, John Edwin (1844–1922), English classical historian.

Sanger, Margaret (née Higgins) (1883–1966), American birth-control advocate and writer.

Śankara (c.700–c.750), celebrated Hindu philosopher and theologian.

Śankaradeva (died 1568), Indian poet.

Śankardeb (1449–1569), Indian poet of religious verse.

Sannazzaro, Jacopo (1456–1530), admired Italian poet, author of the first pastoral romance Arcadia (1504).

Sansom, William (1912–1976), English novelist and short-story writer.

Santayana, George (actually Jorge Agustín Nicolás Ruiz de Santayana) (1863–1952), Spanish philosopher, critic, writer and poet.

Santillana, Iñigo López de Mendoza, Marqués de (1398–1458) notable Spanish poet of pastoral lyrics.

Sanudo, Marino (1466–1536), Italian historian whose diary is of historical value.

Sapir, Edward (1884–1939), Polish-born American linguist and anthropologist who was an authority on North American Indian languages, author of the important study Language (1921).

Sapper (actually Herman Cyril McNeile) (1888–1937), English soldier and writer who wrote the highly successful thriller Bull-Dog Drummond (1920).

Sappho or Psappho (c.610–c.580 BC), celebrated Greek poet, renowned for her sensual love poems.

Sarasin, Jean-François (1614–1654), French poet who was known for his fine craftsmanship and for introducing the burlesque genre to France via Italy.

Sardou, Victorien (1831–1908), prominent French dramatist.

Sarett, Lew (1888–1954), American poet.

Sargent, Epes (1813–1880), American journalist, writer and poet.

Sargent, Lucius Manlius (1786–1867), American writer and antiquarian.

Sargent, Winthrop (1825–1870), American historian.

Sargeson, Frank (actually Norris Frank Davey) (1903–82), New Zealand novelist and short-story writer.

Sarkar, Sir Jadunath (1870–1958), Indian historian.

Sarkia, Kaarlo (1902–1945), Finnish writer.

Sarmiento, Domingo Faustino (1811–1888), Paraguayan statesman, educator and writer.

Saroyan, William (1908–1981), American writer and dramatist.

Sarpi, Paolo (actually Pietro Soave Polano) (1552–1623), Italian scholar who defended Venice's republican form of government against papal hegemony.

Sarton, George Alfred Leon (1884–1956), Belgian-born English, later American historian of science.

Sarton, May (actually Eléanore Marie Sarton) (1912–1995), American poet who became a cult figure in feminist circles.

Sartoris, Adelaide (née Kemble) (c.1814–1879), English singer and writer.

Sartre, Jean-Paul (1905–1980), famous French philosopher, novelist, dramatist, critic and political activist; won the Nobel Prize for Literature (1964) but, in characteristic fashion, refused it.

Sassoon, Siegfried (Lorraine) (1886–1967), eminent English poet and novelist, especially admired for his antiwar poems.

Satō Haruo (1892–1964), Japanese poet, novelist and critic.

Sauppe, Hermann (1809–1893), German philologist.

Saussure, Ferdinand de (1857–1913), influential Swiss linguist.

Savage, Philip Henry (1868–1899), American poet.

Savage, Richard (c.1697–1743), English poet, remembered for his dissolute life and the poem The Wanderer (1729).

Savard, Félix-Antoine (1896–1982), French-Candian poet and writer.

Savigny, Friedrich Karl von (1779–1861), German jurist who was an influential figure in the development of private international jurisprudence.

Savile, Sir Henry (1549–1622), English scholar who was a leading figure in the work on the King James Version of the Bible.

Saxe, John Godfrey (1816–1887), American poet who wrote light verse.

Saxo Grammaticus (12th–13th Century), Danish historian who wrote the first major history of Denmark in his Gesta Danorum.

Sayat-Nova (actually Aruthin Sayadian) (1712–1795), Armenian poet who was known for his love songs.

Sayce, Archibald H(enry) (1845–1933), English language scholar and archaeologist who made important contributions to the study of ancient Near Eastern history.

Sayers, Dorothy L(eigh) (1893–1957), admired English scholar, writer and translator, especially known for her detective fiction featuring Lord Peter Wimsey.

Scaevola, Quintus Mucius (died 82 BC), significant Roman public official who founded the scientific study of Roman jurisprudence which he systematized in 80 vols.

Scaliger, Joseph Justus (1540–1609), French philologist and historian of Italian descent, author of the important study Opus de emendatione tempore (1583); son of Julius Caesar Scaliger.

Scaliger, Julius Caesar (1484–1558), Italian-born French classical scholar; father of Joseph Justus Scaliger.

Scarron, Paul (1610–1660), notable French novelist, poet and dramatist, best known for his realistic novel Le Roman comique (The Comic Novel, 2 vols, 1651, 1657).

Scève, Maurice (c.1501–c.1564), French poet, author of the cycle Délie, objet de plus haute vertu (Délie, Object of Highest Virtue, 1544).

Schaepman, Hermanus Johannes Aloysius Maria (1844–1903), Dutch Roman Catholic priest, politician, writer and poet.

Schaff, Philip (1819–1893), Swiss-born American theologian and church historian, author of a History of the Christian Church (12 vols, 1883–93).

Schäffle, Albert (1831–1903), German economist and sociologist.

Schaukal, Richard (1874–1942), Austrian poet who embraced Symbolism.

Schechter, Solomon (1847–1915), Romanian-born American Jewish scholar and leader, a noted authority on the Talmud.

Scheffel, (Joseph) Viktor von (1826–1886), German poet and novelist.

Scheffler, Johannes (1624–1677), Polish mystic, Roman Catholic polemicist and poet who wrote under the name Angelus Silesius.

Scheler, Max (1874–1928), German philosopher who espoused Phenomenological views.

Schelling, Friedrich (Wilhelm Joseph von) (1775–1854), important German philosopher of Idealism.

Schendel, Arthur (François-Émile) van (1874–1946), Dutch novelist and short-story writer.

Schenker, Heinrich (1868–1935), influential Austrian music theorist.

Scherer, Wilhelm (1841–1886), German philologist and literary historian.

Schickele, René (1883–1940), admired Alsatian poet, dramatist and novelist, a master of Expressionism.

Schiller, Ferdinand Canning Scott (1864–1937), German-born English philosopher of Pragmatism.

Schiller, (Johann Christoph) Friedrich (von) (1759–1805), German dramatist, poet, theorist and writer, author of the celebrated dramatic trilogy Wallenstein (1796–99) and the famous poem An die Freude (Ode to Joy), the latter immortalized in the finale of Beethoven's 9th Symphony.

Schiltberger, Hans (actually Johann Schiltberger) (1380–c.1440), German traveller who left an interesting account of his travels.

Schimper, Carl Friedrich (1803–1867), German naturalist and poet.

Schlegel, August Wilhelm von (1767–1845), esteemed German critic, translator and editor, a pioneering figure in the Romantic movement; nephew of Johann Elias Schlegel and brother of (Karl Wilhelm) Friedrich von Schlegel.

Schlegel, Johann Elias (1719–1749), German writer and critic; uncle of August Wilhelm von and (Karl Wilhelm) Friedrich von Schlegel.

Schlegel, (Karl Wilhelm) Friedrich von (1772–1829), German critic, editor and linguist, one of the principal figures in the development of Romanticism; nephew of Johann Elias Schlegel and brother of August Wilhelm von Schlegel.

Schleicher, August (1821–1868), influential German linguist.

Schleiermacher, Friedrich (Ernst Daniel) (1768–1834), German Protestant theologian and scholar, author of Reden über die Religion (1799; English trans. as Religion: Speeches to its Cultured Despisers, 1893) and Der christliche Glaube nach den Grundsätzen der evangelischen Kirche im Zusammenhang dargestellet (1821–22).

Schlesinger, Arthur Meier (1888–1965), American historian who was known for his studies in social and urban history.

Schleyer, Johann Martin (1831–1912), German bishop and proponent of the international language Volapük.

Schlick, Moritz (1882–1936), influential German-born Austrian philosopher who espoused Logical Empiricism, author of Fragen der Ethik (1930; English trans. as Problems of Ethics, 1939), Grundzüge der Naturphilosophie (published 1948; English trans. as Philosophy of Nature, 1949) and Natur und Kultur (published 1952); was murdered by a deranged student.

Schliemann, Heinrich (1822–1890), important German archaeologist, particularly known for his excavations of ancient Troy.

Schlosser, Friedrich (1776–1861), German historian, best remembered for his Weltgeschichte für das deutsche Volk (World History for the German People, 18 vols, 1854–56).

Schlözer, A(ugust) L(udwig) (1735–1809), German historian.

Schmidt, Arno (Otto) (1914–1979), German writer known for his experimental output.

Schmidt, Johannes (1843–1901), German linguist.

Schmidt, Wilhelm (1868–1954), German Roman Catholic priest and anthropologist , author of Der Ursprung der Gottesidee (The Origin of the Idea of God, 12 vols, 1912–55) and Ursprung und Werden der Religion (1930; English trans. as The Origin and Growth of Religion, 1931).

Schmitt, Gladys (1909–1972), American novelist.

Schmoller, Gustav von (1838–1917), German economist who wrote on economic history.

Schmucker, S(amuel) S(imon) (1799–1873), American Lutheran theologian and educator.

Schnitzler, Arthur (1862–1931), Austrian dramatist, novelist, short-story writer and physician.

Scholem, Gershom (1897–1982), German-born Israeli scholar who was an authority on the Kabbala and Jewish mysticism.

Schönherr, Karl (1867–1943), Austrian dramatist and short-story writer.

Schopenhauer, Arthur (1788–1860), German philosopher whose most important work in metaphysics was his Die Welt als Wille und Vorstellung (1819; English trans. as The World as Will and Idea, 1883–86).

Schorer, Mark (1908–1977), American literary scholar, novelist and short-story writer.

Schreiner, Olive (Emilie Albertina) (1855–1920), South African novelist, short-story writer and activist, especially known for her novel The Story of an African Farm (1883), published under the name Ralph Iron.

Schrieke, Bertram (1890–1945), Dutch anthropologist.

Schröder, Ernst (1841–1902), German logician and mathematician.

Schröder, Friedrich Ludwig (1744–1816), German actor, theatre manager and dramatist.

Schubart, Christian Friedrich Daniel (1739–1791), German poet.

Schuchardt, Hugo (1842–1927), German philologist.

Schücking , Levin (1814–1883), German novelist.

Schumpeter, Joseph (Alois) (1883–1950), influential Moravian-born American economist and sociologist, author of Capitalism, Socialism, and Democracy (third edition, 1950).

Schurz, Carl (1829–1906), prominent German-born American reformer, journalist, writer and politician.

Schuyler, George (1895–1977), American journalist and writer, author of Black No More (1931) and Black and Conservative (1966).

Schuyler, James (Marcus) (1923–1991), American poet, dramatist and writer.

Schwartz, Delmore (1913–1966), American poet, critic, writer and dramatist.

Schwartz, Eduard (1858–1940), German classical philologist.

Schweitzer, Albert (1875–1965), celebrated Alsatian theologian, philosopher, organist, music scholar and missionary physician; won the Nobel Prize for Peace (1952).

Schwenckfeld (von Ossig), Kaspar (1489–1561), German Protestant preacher, theologian and writer who founded the controversial movement known as the Reformation of the Middle Way.

Schwitters, Kurt (1887–1948), German artist and poet of the Dada school.

Sciascia, Leonardo (1921–89), Italian novelist, short-story writer, dramatist and essayist.

Scogan, Henry (c.1361–1407), English poet.

Scollard, Clinton (1860–1932), American poet and writer.

Scorza, Manuel (1928–83), Peruvian novelist, poet and political activist.

Scot, Michael (c.1175–c.1235), Scottish astrologer, wizard, mathematician and translator.

Scott, Alexander (c.1525–c.1585), Scottish poet.

Scott, Cyril (Meir) (1879–1970), English composer and poet.

Scott, Duncan Campbell (1862–1947), Canadian poet.

Scott, Evelyn (1893–1963), American novelist and poet.

Scott, F(rancis) R(eginald) (1899–1985), notable Canadian poet, socialist, educator and authority on constitutional law; son of Frederick George Scott.

Scott, Frederick George (1861–1944), Canadian archdeacon, poet, writer and social activist; father of F(rancis) R(eginald) Scott.

Scott, Geoffrey (1883–1929), English poet and biographer.

Scott, Michael (1789–1835), Scottish writer.

Scott, Paul Mark (1920–1978), English novelist, author of the 'Raj Quartet' series The Jewel in the Crown (1966), The Day of the Scorpion (1968), The Towers of Silence (1971) and A Division of the Spoils (1975).

Scott, Sir Walter (1771–1832), renowned Scottish novelist and poet, creator of the historical novel and author of Guy Mannering (1815), Old Mortality (1816), The Heart of Midlothian (1818) and Redgauntlet (1824).

Scott, William Bell (1811–1890), English poet, artist and art critic.

Scott, Winfield Townley (1910–1968), American poet.

Scribe, (Augustin-) Eugène (1791–1861), French dramatist.

Scudder, Horace Elisha (1838–1902), American editor, novelist and biographer.

Scudéry, George de (1601–1667), French dramatist and critic; brother of Magdeleine de Scudéry.

Scudéry, Magdeleine de (1607–1701), French poet and novelist who was best known as Sapho; sister of George de Scudéry.

Scylitzes, John (11th Century), Byzantine historian, author of the Synopsis historiarum.

Sealsfield, Charles (actually Karl Postl) (1793–1864), Moravian-born Swiss journalist and writer who left valuable accounts of his travels in the US.

Seaman, Sir Owen (1861–1936), English poet and editor.

Sebald, W(infried) G(eorg) (1944–2001), German-born English scholar, writer and poet, author of Schwindel, Gefühle (1990; English trans. as Vertigo, 1999), Die Ausgewanderten (1992; English trans. as The Emigrants, 1996), Die Ringe des Saturn (1995; English trans. as The Rings of Saturn, 1998) and Austerlitz (2001).

Seccomb, John (1708–1792), American clergyman and poet.

Seckendorff, Veit Ludwig von (1626–1692), German statesman and historian.

Sedaine, Michel-Jean (1719–1797), French dramatist, best known for his comedy Le Philosophe sans le savoir (1765; English trans. as The Duel, 1772).

Sedgwick, Anne Douglas (1873–1935), American novelist and short-story writer.

Sedgwick, Catharine Maria (1789–1867), American writer; sister-in-law of Susan (Ridley) Sedgwick.

Sedgwick, Susan (Ridley) (c.1789–1867), American writer; sister-in-law of Catharine Maria Sedgwick.

Sedley, Sir Charles (1639–1701), English courtier, poet and dramatist, best remembered for his debauchery and wit at court.

Sedulius Scottus (9th Century), Irish poet and scholar.

Seeger, Alan (1888–1916), American poet who wrote the celebrated I Have a Rendezvous with Death (1916); died in World War I.

Seeley, Sir John Robert (1834–1895), English historian, particularly esteemed for The Expansion of England in the Eighteenth Century (1883).

Seers, Eugène (1865–1945), French-Canadian poet and critic who wrote under the name Louis Dantin.

Seferiades, Georgios (1900–1971), prominent Greek poet, essayist and diplomat who wrote under the name George Seferis; won the Nobel Prize for Literature (1963).

Seghers, Anna (actually Netti Radványi) (1900–1983), German novelist and short-story writer.

Ségur, Sophie Rostopchine, Comtesse de (1799–1874), Russian-born French writer of children's stories.

Sei Shōnagon (c.966–c.1013), Japanese diarist and poet, known for her wit at the imperial court.

Seifert, Jaroslav (1901–1986), Czech poet; won the Nobel Prize for Literature (1984).

Selden, John (1584–1654), English politician, antiquarian, Orientalist and writer.

Seldes, Gilbert (Vivian) (1893–1970), American journalist, drama critic, writer and editor.

Seligman, C(harles) G(abriel) (1873–1940), English anthropologist.

Selincourt, Ernest de (1870–1943), English literary scholar and critic.

Selvon, Samuel Dickson (1923–1994), Trinidadian-born Canadian writer, especially admired for his novel The Lonely Londoners (1956).

Semler, Johann Salomo (1725–1791), German Lutheran theologian who played an important role in the development of biblical textual criticism.

Semper, Gottfried (1803–1879), notable German architect and writer on art.

Sempill, Sir James (1566–1625), Scottish poet who wrote the satirical A picktooth for the Pope, or the packman's paternoster.

Sempill, Robert (c.1530–1595), English poet who was known for his wit and satire.

Sempill, Robert (c.1595–c.1665), Scottish poet.

Sénac, Jean (1926–73), Algerian poet who supported his country's fight against French colonial rule; was assassinated.

Sénancour, Étienne Pivert de (1770–1846), French novelist, author of the notable Obermann (1804).

Senart, Émile (1847–1928), French Sanskrit scholar.

Sender, Ramón José (1902–82), Spanish-born American novelist.

Seneca the Younger (actually Lucius Annaeus Seneca) (c.4 BC–65 AD), celebrated Roman philosopher, statesman and dramatist whose verse tragedies proved highly influential; committed suicide after the failure of Piso's conspiracy against the emperor Nero.

Senghor, Léopold (Sédar) (1906–2001), Senagalese poet, writer and statesman who was the leading representative of the black cultural movement known as négritude and who served as President of Senegal (1960–80).

Senior, Nassau William (1790–1864), English economist, author of An Outline of the Science of Political Economy (1836).

Šenoa, August (1838–1881), Croatian novelist, dramatist, poet, critic and editor.

Sep Szarzyński, Mikołaj (1550–81), Polish poet.

Serafimovich, Alexander (1863–1949), Russian writer.

Serao, Matilde (1856–1927), Italian journalist and novelist.

Sergeant, John (1622–1707), English Roman Catholic priest and polemicist.

Sergius of Resaina (died 536), Syrian Christian theologian, scholar and physician.

Serlio, Sebastiano (1475–1554), Italian architect, painter and theorist, particularly known for his influential treatise Tutte l'opere d'architettura.

Sérusier, (Louis-) Paul (-Henri) (1865–1927), French painter and theorist of the Postimpressionist school who spent his last years as a mystic.

Servetus, Michael (actually Miguel Serveto) (c.1511–1553), Spanish theologian and physician whose antiTrinitarian views in his De Trinitatis Erroribus Libri VII (1531) and Christianismi Restitutio (1553) riled both Roman Catholics and Protestants; was burned at the stake as a heretic by the Protestants.

Service, Robert W(illiam) (1874–1958), English-born Canadian poet and novelist.

Servius (4th Century), Latin grammarian who wrote an important commentary on Virgil.

Seton, Anya (c.1904–1990), American novelist; daughter of Ernest Thompson Seton.

Seton, Ernest Thompson (1860–1946), English-born American naturalist and writer; father of Anya Seton.

Settle, Elkanah (1648–1724), English dramatist.

Severian (4th–5th Century), Syrian theologian and bishop of Gabala who became a leading opponent of John Chrysostom.

Severus (c.465–538), learned Greek monk, theologian and patriarch of Antioch.

Sévigné, Marie de Rabutin-Chantal, Marquise de (1626–1696), French writer and epistolar.

Sewall, Samuel (1652–1730), English-born American merchant, judge, writer and diarist.

Seward, Anna (1747–1809), English poet and writer, author of the novel Louisa (1784).

Sewell, Anna (1820–1878), English writer who wrote Black Beauty (1877).

Sexton, Anne (née Harvey) (1928–1974), admired American poet who excelled in imagist verse; committed suicide.

Sextus Empiricus (3rd Century), Greek philosopher and historian.

Seyfeddin, Omer (1884–1920), Turkish writer.

Şeyhi or Sheykhi, Sinan (died 1428), Turkish poet.

Seymour-Smith, Martin (1928–1998), English literary critic, biographer, poet and editor.

Shaaban, Robert (1911–1962), Swahili poet and writer.

Shaara, Michael (Joseph Jr) (1929–1988), American writer.

Shabestarī, (Sa'd od-Dīn) Mahmūd (c.1250–c.1320), Persian mystic who wrote the classic Golshan-e rāz (English trans. as The Mystic Rose Garden, 1880) on Sūfism.

Shadwell, Thomas (c.1642–1692), prominent English dramatist and poet, especially remembered for his comedies of manners; became Poet Laureate of the United Kingdom (1688).

Shaffer, Anthony (Joshua) (1926–2001), English dramatist and writer who scored a notable success in the theatre with his Sleuth (1970).

Shaftesbury, Anthony Ashley Cooper, 3rd Earl of (1671–1713), English politician and philosopher, author of Characteristicks of Men, Manners, Opinions, Times (1711).

Shakespeare, William (1564–1616), immortal English dramatist and poet, celebrated the world over as one of the supreme geniuses of literature.

Shao Yung (1011–1077), important Chinese philosopher of Neo-Confucian idealism.

Shapiro, Karl (actually Carl Jay) (1913–2000), American poet and writer.

Sharaf ad-Dīn 'Ali Yazdī (died 1454), Persian historian.

Sha 'rānī, ash-I (actually 'abd al-Wahhāb ibn Ahmad) (1492–1565), Egyptian scholar and mystic.

Sharp, Cecil (James) (1859–1924), English folk song and dance collector and editor.

Sharp, Granville (1735–1813), English scholar and philanthropist.

Sharp, William (1855–1905), Scottish writer, biographer, essayist and poet who wrote under the name Fiona Macleod.

Shaw, George Bernard (1856–1950), famous Irish dramatist, essayist, critic and socialist, author of such notable plays as Caesar and Cleopatra (1901), Man and Superman (1903), Major Barbara (1905) and Saint Joan (1923); won the Nobel Prize for Literature (1925).

Shaw, Irwin (1913–1984), American writer, dramatist and essayist.

Shawqī, Ahmad (1868–1932), Egyptian poet and dramatist.

Shcherbatov, Mikhail Mikhailovich (1733–90), Russian historian.

Shchervatskoy, Fyodor Ippolitovich (1866–1942), learned Russian linguist and philosopher who was an authority on Buddhist philosophy.

Shebbeare, John (1709–1788), English pamphleteer and writer who was twice imprisoned for libel.

Sheffield, John, 3rd Earl of Mulgrave, later 1st Duke of Buckingham and Normanby (1648–1721), English statesman and essayist.

Sheldon, Charles M(onroe) (1857–1946), American preacher and writer, best known for his novel In His Steps (1896).

Sheldon, Edward (Brewster) (1886–1946), American dramatist, author of The Nigger (1909), The Boss (1911) and Romance(1913).

Shelley, Mary Wollstonecraft (née Godwin) (1797–1851), English novelist, poet and dramatist, best remembered for her novel Frankenstein, or the Modern Prometheus (1818); wife of Percy Bysshe Shelley.

Shelley, Percy Bysshe (1792–1822), celebrated English poet of extraordinary gifts and a writer of provocative prose, author of the renowned poem Prometheus Unbound (1819–20); drowned when his boat was capsized in a squall in Italy; husband of Mary Wollstonecraft (née Godwin) Shelley.

Shelton, Frederick William (1815–1881), American Episcopal clergyman and writer.

Shen Ts'ung-wen (1902–1988), Chinese writer, poet and dramatist who suffered persecution under the Communist regime.

Shenstone, William (1714–1763), English poet, best known for The Judgement of Hercules (1741) and The Schoolmistress (1742).

Shepard, Odell (1884–1967), American writer, critic and poet.

Shepard, Thomas (1605–1649), English-born American Calvinist preacher and writer, author of The Sincere Convert (1641).

Shepherd, William Robert (1871–1934), American historian who was especially known for his writings on Latin America.

Sheridan, Frances (1724–1766), English novelist, particularly remembered for The Memoirs of Miss Sydney Biddulph (1761); mother of Richard Brinsley (Butler) Sheridan.

Sheridan, Richard Brinsley (Butler) (1751–1816), famous Irish dramatist, impresario and politician, author of such plays as The Rivals (1775), The Duenna (1775) and The School for Scandal (1777); son of Frances Sheridan, grandson of Thomas Sheridan and grandfather of Caroline Elizabeth Sarah (née Sheridan) Norton.

Sheridan, Thomas (1687–1738), English schoolmaster and translator; grandfather of Richard Brinsley (Butler) Sheridan.

Sherlock, Thomas (1678–1761), English Anglican bishop and writer, author of A Trial of the Witnesses of the Resurrection of Jesus (1729); son of William Sherlock.

Sherlock, William (1641–1707), English churchman, dean of St Paul's and controversial writer, author of A Practical Discourse concerning Death (1689); father of Thomas Sherlock.

Sherman, Frank Dempster (1860–1916), American poet who often wrote under the name Felix Carmen.

Sherman, Stuart P(ratt) (1881–1926), American literary critic and essayist.

Sherriff, R(obert) C(edric) (1896–1975), English dramatist, screenwriter and novelist, author of the highly successful play Journey's End (1929).

Sherwood, Mary Martha (1775–1851), English writer of children's books.

Sherwood, Robert E(mmet) (1896–1955), American dramatist, author of The Petrified Forest (1935), Idiot's Delight (1936), Abe Lincoln in Illinois (1939) and There Shall Be No Night (1941).

Shevchenko, Taras Grigorievich (1814–1861), renowned Ukrainian poet and writer.

Shiga Naoya (1883–1971), Japanese writer, author of the novel Anya Kōro (Road Through the Dark Night, 1921–37).

Shillaber, Benjamin Penhallow (1814–1890), American writer of a humorous bent.

Shimazaki Tōson (actually Shimazaki Haruki) (1872–1943), Japanese poet and novelist.

Shinran (1173–1262), influential Japanese Buddhist reformer and philosopher.

Shirer, William L(awrence) (1904–1993), American journalist and writer.

Shirley, James (1596–1666), English poet and dramatist, famous for such plays as The Wittie Faire One (1628), The Traytor (1631), The Lady of Pleasure (1635) and The Cardinal (1641); died in the Great Fire of London.

Shishkov, Alexander Semyonovich (1754–1841), Russian writer and statesman.

Shlonsky, Abraham (1900–1973), Ukrainian-born Israeli poet, editor and translator, creator of the Symbolist movement in Israel.

Sholem Aleichem (actually Sholem Yakov Rabinowitz) (1859–1916), famous Ukrainian-born American novelist, short-story writer and dramatist who wrote in Yiddish.

Sholokhov, Mikhail (Alexandrovich) (1905–1984), prominent Russian writer who was a proponent of socialist realism; won the Nobel Prize for Literature (1965).

Shorey, Paul (1857–1934), American scholar who was an authority on ancient Greek poetry and philosophy.

Shorthouse, Joseph Henry (1834–1903), English novelist, author of John Inglesant (1881).

Shotwell, James Thomson (1874–1965), American historian and diplomat who was an authority on international relations.

Shute, Nevil (actually Nevil Shute Norway) (1899–1960), Australian novelist, best known for On the Beach (1957).

Sickel, Theodor von (1826–1908), German historian who was an authority on the early middle ages.

Sidgwick, Henry (1838–1900), important English philosopher of Utilitarian views, author of Methods of Ethics (1874).

Sidney, Sir Philip (1554–1586), English poet, writer, statesman and military leader, author of Arcadia, Astrophel and Stella and The Defence of Poesie; died from wounds sustained in an attack on a Spanish convoy; brother of Mary Herbert Pembroke and Sir Robert Sidney.

Sidney, Sir Robert (1563–1626), English statesman and poet; brother of Mary Herbert Pembroke and Sir Philip Sidney.

Sidonius Apollinaris, Saint (actually Gaius Sollius) (c.430–c.483), Gallic-Roman poet who was canonized by the Roman Catholic Church.

Sienkiewicz, Henryk (1846–1916), eminent Polish novelist who wrote under the name Litwos, author of the trilogy Ogniem i mieczem (With Fire and Sword, 1884), Potop (The Deluge, 1886) and Pan Wołodyjowski (1887–88), and for Quo Vadis? (1896); won the Nobel Prize for Literature (1905).

Sigebert of Gembloux (c.1030–1112), Belgian Benedictine monk and chronicler.

Siger of Brabant (c.1240–c.1282), Belgian philosopher who espoused a radical Aristotelianism.

Sigonio, Carlo (1524–1584), Italian historian who was particularly known for his studies of ancient Greece.

Sigourney, Lydia Huntley (1791–1865), American poet of sentimental verse.

Sigurjónsson, Jóhann (1880–1919), notable Icelandic dramatist and poet, author of the play Fjalla-Eyvindur (1911; English trans. as Eyvind of the Hills, 1916).

Sikelianós, Angelos (1884–1951), esteemed Greek poet who won distinction for his lyricism.

Silius Italicus (actually Tiberius Catius Asconius Silius Italicus) (25–101), Roman poet and politican, author of the epic Punica; committed suicide.

Sill, Edward Rowland (1841–1887), American poet and writer who often used the name Andrew Hedbrooke.

Sillanpää, Frans Eemil (1888–1964), Finnish novelist and short-story writer; won the Nobel Prize for Literature (1939).

Silone, Ignazio (actually Secondo Tranquilli) (1900–1978), prominent Italian novelist and short-story writer whose early advocacy of socialism, and then Communism gave way to a Christian worldview.

Silva, Antônio José da (1705–1739), gifted Brazilian-born Portuguese dramatist whose Jewish heritage led to his persecution and death at the hands of the Inquisition.

Silva, José Asuncion (1865–1896), notable Colombian poet; committed suicide.

Simenon, Georges (–Joseph-Christian) (1903–1989), Belgian-French novelist and short-story writer whose output was prolific.

Simeon, Charles (1759–1836), English Anglican clergyman and biblical expositor.

Simeon of Durham (11th–12th Century), English monk and chronicler.

Simmel, Georg (1858–1918), German sociologist and philosopher.

Simmons, James (Stewart Alexander) (1933–2001), Irish poet, writer and editor.

Simms, William Gilmore (1806–1870), eminent American novelist, short-story writer, poet and critic who was most appreciated for his historical novels.

Simon, Herbert A(lexander) (1916–2001), American social scientist.

Simon, Jules (-François) (1814–1896), French political leader and theorist.

Simon, Richard (1638–1712), French biblical scholar whose works presaged modern critical methods.

Simonides of Ceas (c.556–c.468 BC), Greek poet and epigrammatist; uncle of Bacchylides.

Simplicius of Cilicia (6th Century), Greek philosopher.

Simrock, Karl Joseph (1802–1876), German literary scholar and poet.

Şinasi, Ibrahim (1826–1871), Turkish writer, dramatist and poet.

Sinclair, Catherine (1800–1864), Scottish writer of children's books.

Sinclair, Isaak von (1775–1815), German diplomat, philosopher and poet.

Sinclair, Sir Keith (1922–93), New Zealand historian and poet.

Sinclair, May (actually Mary Amelia St Clair Sinclair) (1863–1946), English novelist.

Sinclair, Upton (Beall) (1878–1968), American novelist and socialist, best remembered for his novel The Jungle (1906).

Singer, Isaac Bashevis (1904–1991), admired Polish-born American novelist and short-story writer; won the Nobel Prize for Literature (1978).

Singer, Israel Joshua (1893–1944), Polish-born American novelist and dramatist.

Singmaster, Elsie (1879–1958), American novelist.

Sinyavsky, Andrei (Donatovich) (1925–1997), prominent Russian novelist, short-story writer and dissident who often wrote under the name Abram Tertz.

Siôn Cent (c.1367–c.1430), Welsh poet.

Sirhindī, Shaykh Ahmad (1564–1624), Indian mystic and theologian of orthodox Islam.

Siringo, Charles (1855–1928), American writer who was best known for his autobiography A Texas Cowboy, or Fifteen Years on the Hurricane Deck of a Spanish Pony (1885) and Lone Star Cowboy (1919).

Sismondi, Jean-Charles-Léonard Simonde de (1773–1842), Swiss economist and historian, author of the influential Historie des républiques italiennes du moyen âge (16 vols, 1809–18; English trans. as History of the Italian Republics in the Middle Ages, 1831).

Sitwell, Dame Edith (Louisa) (1887–1964), esteemed English poet and writer whose notable works included Façade (1923), Gold Coast Customs (1929), Street Songs (1942), Green Song (1944), Song of the Cold (1945),

Gardeners and Astronomers (1953) and The Outcasts (1962); sister of Sir (Francis) Osbert (Sacheverell) 5th Baronet Sitwell, and Sir Sacheverell, 6th Baronet Sitwell.

Sitwell, Sir (Francis) Osbert (Sacheverell), 5th Baronet (1892–1969), prominent English poet and writer; brother of Dame Edith (Louisa) Sitwell and Sir Sacheverell, 6th Baronet Sitwell.

Sitwell, Sir Sacheverell, 6th Baronet (1897–1988), notable English writer, art critic and poet; brother of Dame Edith (Louisa) Sitwell and Sir (Francis) Osbert (Sacheverell), 5th Baronet Sitwell.

Siwertz, (Per) Sigfrid (1882–1970), Swedish novelist and short-story writer.

Sjöberg, Birger (1885–1929), innovative Swedish poet of modernism.

Skarga, Piotr (actually Piotr Skarga Poweski) (1536–1612), Polish Jesuit preacher and writer.

Skeat, W(alter) W(illiam) (1835–1912), English literary editor of Old and Middle English literature.

Skeffington, Sir Lumley St George (1771–1850), English dramatist.

Skelton, John (c.1460–1529), English poet, a master of political and religious satire and creator of the poetic form known as Skeltonics.

Skelton, Robin (1925–1997), English-born Canadian poet, writer, translator, visual artist and occultist.

Skinner, B(urrhus) F(rederic) (1904–1990), significant American behavioral psychologist, author of Walden Two (1948).

Skinner, Constance Lindsay (1879–1939), Canadian-born American writer.

Skinner, Cornelia Otis (1901–1979), American actress and writer.

Skram, Amalie (née Alver) (1847–1905), Norwegian novelist of the Naturalist school.

Slauerhoff, Jan Jacob (1898–1936), Dutch poet of pessimistic verse.

Slaughter, Frank (Gill) (1908–2001), American physician and writer who wrote more than 55 best-selling novels.

Slaveyko, Pencho Petkov (1866–1912), Bulgarian poet, essayist and translator; son of Petko Rachev Slaveykov.

Slaveyko, Petko Rachev (1827–1895), Bulgarian poet, journalist and politician; father of Pencho Petkov Slaveykov.

Sleidanus, Johannes (1506–1556), German historian who wrote an account of the Protestant Reformation.

Slessor, Kenneth (Adolf) (1901–1971), Australian poet and journalist, author of the notable poem Beach Burial.

Slonimsky, Nicolas (actually Nikolai Leonidovch Slonimsky) (1894–1995), Russian-born American music scholar and lexicographer whose learning was complemented by a penchant for witty asides.

Słowacki, Juliusz (1809–1849), famous Polish poet and dramatist, a leading proponent of Romanticism.

Small, Albion (Woodbury) (1854–1926), American sociologist who became best known for his writings on political science and economics.

Smalley, George Washburn (1833–1916), American journalist and writer.

Smart, Christopher (1722–1771), English poet and translator, particularly known for A Song to David (1763).

Smedley, Francis Edward (1818–1864), English editor and novelist.

Smellie, William (c.1740–1795), Scottish natural historian, writer and translator, was the compiler of the first edition of the Encyclopaedia Britannica (1768–71).

Smet, Pierre-Jean de (1801–1873), Belgian-born American Jesuit missionary and writer who became a friend of Indian tribes of the western US.

Smiles, Samuel (1812–1904), Scottish writer, best remembered for his didactic Self-Help, with Illustrations of Character and Conduct (1859).

Smith, Adam (1723–1790), Scottish philosopher and economist, author of the celebrated study An Inquiry into the nature and causes of the Wealth of Nations (1776).

Smith, Alexander (1830–1867), Scottish poet and essayist.

Smith, A(rthur) J(ames) M(arshall) (1902–1980), Canadian poet, critic and editor.

Smith, Betty (Wehner) (1904–1972), American novelist.

Smith, Chard Powers (1894–1977), American writer and poet.

Smith, Charles Henry (1826–1903), American writer of humorous works who wrote under the name Bill Arp.

Smith, Charlotte (née Turner) (1749–1806), English novelist, short-story writer and poet.

Smith, Elihu Hubbard (1771–1798), American physician, writer and poetry anthologist.

Smith, Elizabeth Oakes (1806–1893), American novelist, short-story writer and essayist; wife of Seba Smith.

Smith, Francis Hopkinson (1838–1915), American writer and illustrator; grandson of Francis Hopkinson.

Smith, George (1840–1876), English archaeologist, author of the Chaldean Account of Genesis (1876).

Smith, Sir George Adam (1856–1942), Scottish preacher and Semitic scholar who was a leading proponent of the higher criticism of the Old Testament.

Smith, Horatio (Horace) (1779–1849), English novelist, dramatist and poet, collaborated with his brother James on Rejected Addresses (1812) and Horace of London (1813).

Smith, James (1775–1839), English writer, collaborated with his brother Horatio (Horace) on Rejected Addresses (1812) and Horace of London (1813).

Smith, John (c.1580–1631), famous English adventurer, explorer, writer and cartographer, the principal organizer of Jamestown, Virginia, the first permanent English settlement in North America.

Smith, Lillian (Eugenia) (1897–1966), American writer.

Smith, (Lloyd) Logan Pearsall (1865–1946), American essayist, writer and poet.

Smith, Margaret Bayard (1778–1844), American novelist.

Smith, Preserved (1880–1941), American historian, author of The Age of the Reformation (1920).

Smith, Richard Penn (1799–1854), American dramatist and writer.

Smith, Samuel Francis (1808–1895), American clergyman, poet and writer.

Smith, Samuel Stanhope (1750–1819), American clergyman, educator and scholar.

Smith, Seba (1792–1868), American journalist and writer who was known for his creation of the humorous Major Jack Downing; husband of Elizabeth Oakes Smith.

Smith, Sol(omon Franklin) (1801–1869), American actor, theater manager, lawyer, editor and writer.

Smith, Stevie (actually Florence Margaret Smith) (1902–1971), English poet and novelist.

Smith, Sydney (1771–1845), prominent English clergyman and essayist.

Smith, Sydney Goodsir (1915–1975), New Zealand-born Scottish poet and critic.

Smith, Thorne (1892–1934), American writer who was known as a humorist.

Smith, William (1727–1803), Scottish-born American Episcopal clergyman and educator who was a champion of conservative views.

Smith, William (1728–1793), American-born English lawyer, historian and chief justice of Canada (1786–93).

Smith, Sir William (1813–1893), English classical scholar and lexicographer.

Smith, William Robertson (1846–1894), Scottish Semitic scholar and encyclopaedist, editor-in-chief of the Encyclopaedia Britannica and author of Lectures on the Religion of the Semites (1889).

Smith, Winchell (1871–1933), American actor, theatre director and dramatist.

Smollett, Tobias (George) (1721–1771), notable Scottish novelist, author of The Adventures of Roderick Random (1748), The Adventures of Peregrine Pickle (1751), The Adventures of Sir Launcelot Greaves (1762) and The Expedition of Humphry Clinker (1771).

Smyth, John (died 1612), English Nonconformist minister who championed the cause of religious libertarianism.

Snelling, William Joseph (1804–1848), American journalist, reformer and writer.

Snellman, Johan Vilhelm (1806–1881), prominent Finnish statesman and philosopher.

Snider, Denton Jaques (1841–1925), American scholar, writer and poet.

Snoilsky, Carl Johan Gustaf, Count (1841–1903), Swedish poet of social and political themes.

Snorri Sturluson (1179–1241), Icelandic chieftan, historian and poet, author of the Prose Edda, a handbook on poetics; was killed by order of King Haakon IV of Norway; uncle of Sturla Thordarson.

Snow, C(harles) P(ercy), Baron Snow of Leicester (1905–1980), prominent English writer, scientist and government official, especially known for his 'Strangers and Brothers' novels (11 vols) and for The Two Cultures and the Scientific Revolution (1959).

Snow, (Charles) Wilbert (1884–1977), American poet.

Sōami (1472–1525), influential Japanese painter, art critic and poet.

Socé, Ousmane (Diop) (1911–74), Senagalese writer, poet and diplomat.

Sōchō (1448–1532), Japanese poet.

Socinus, Faustus (actually Fausto Paolo Sozzini) (1539–1604), Italian theologian whose anti-Trinitarian views brought him into conflict with the Inquisition, author of De sacrae scripturae auctoritate (1570), De Jesu Christo servatore (1594) and Christianae religionis institutio (unfinished); nephew of Laelius Socinus.

Socinus, Laelius (actually Lelio Francesco Maria Socini) (1525–1562), Italian theologian of anti-Trinitarian beliefs; uncle of Faustus Socinus.

Socrates (c.470–399 BC), famous Greek philosopher who was a major influence on Plato and Aristotle; was indicted for impiety, found guilty and compelled to take his own life by hemlock poisoning.

Socrates Scholasticus (380–c.450), Byzantine historian who wrote the important Historia ecclesiastica (7 vols).

Soden, Hermann, Feiherr von (1852–1914), German biblical scholar who was known for his studies on the New Testament.

Söderberg, Hjalmar Erik Fredrik (1849–1941), Danish novelist, short-story writer and critic.

Söderblom, Nathan (1866–1931), Swedish Lutheran archbishop and scholar who was particularly known for his studies in comparative religion; won the Nobel Prize for Peace (1930).

Södergran, Edith (Irene) (1892–1923), significant Finnish poet, founder of the modernist movement of Finnish poets who wrote in Swedish.

Soga, Tiyo (1829–1871), South African minister, hymnist, translator, journlist and anthologist, a pioneering figure in Xosa literary circles.

Sohlman, (Per) August (Ferdinand) (1824–1874), Swedish journalist who was a prominent figure in the Pan-Scandinavian movement.

Sokolow, Nahum (1861–1936), Polish Jewish writer and Zionist.

Solís y Ribadeneyra, Antonio de (1610–1686), Spanish poet and dramatist.

Solomós, Dhionísios, Count (1798–1857), Greek poet.

Solon (c.640–559 BC), renowned Greek lawgiver and poet.

Soloukhin, Vladimir Alexeievich (1924–1997), Russian writer and poet.

Solovyov, Vladimir Sergeievich (1853–1900), Russian mystic and philosopher.

Somerville, William (1675–1742), English poet.

Sommer, Ferdinand (1875–1962), German linguist who was an authority on Hittite and classical languages.

Sommo, Judah Leone ben Isaac (actually Yeuda Sommo) (1527–1592), Italian dramatist and writer on the theatre, author of the first Hebrew drama Tzahut bedihuta de-qiddushin (An Eloquent Comedy of Marriage, 1550).

Sophocles (c.496–406 BC), Greek dramatist, author of the celebrated Oedipus Rex.

Sophron of Syracuse (4th Century BC), Greek poet.

Sophronius (c.560–638), Syrian monk, theologian and patriarch of Jerusalem.

Sordello (c.1200–c.1268), famous Italian adventurer and poet.

Sorel, Georges (-Eugène) (1847–1922), French socialist and writer, author of Réflexions sur la violence (1908; English trans. as Reflections on Violence, 1914).

Sorell, Walter (1905–1997), Austrian-born American writer on the theatre and dance.

Sørensen, Villy (1929–2001), Danish writer, literary critic, philosopher, editor and translator.

Sorge, Reinhard Johannes (1892–1916), German dramatist of expressionist plays.

Sorley, Charles Hamilton (1895–1915), Scottish poet; died in World War I.

Sorokin, Pitirim A(lexandrovich) (1889–1968), Russian-born American sociologist, author of Social and Cultural Dynamics (4 vols, 1937–41), Man and Society in Calamity (1942) and Altruistic Love (1950).

Soromenho, Fernando Monteiro de Castro (1910–68), Angolan novelist whose opposition to Portuguese colonial rule compelled him to flee his homeland.

Sorsky, Saint Nil (actually Nikolai Maykov) (1433–1508), Russian monk, mystic and writer.

Soupault, Philippe (1897–1990), French poet, novelist and essayist.

Sousa, Frei Luís de (actually Manuel de Sousa Coutinho) (1555–1632), Portuguese Dominican monk and chronicler of the order in his História de São Domingos (3 vols, 1623, 1662, 1678).

Soutar, William (1898–1943), Scottish poet and diarist.

South, Robert (1634–1716), English Anglican preacher of a sarcastic bent, author of Animadversions (1690).

Southern, Sir Richard (William) (1912–2001), English historian who wrote such valuable works as The Making of the Middle Ages (1953), Western Views of Islam in the Middle Ages (1962) and Scholastic Humanism and the Unification of Europe (two vols, 1995, 2000).

Southerne, Thomas (1660–1746), Irish dramatist who wrote The Fatal Marriage (1694) and Oroonoko (1696).

Southery, Robert (1774–1843), notable English poet and writer, especially admired for his prose; became Poet Laureate of the United Kingdom (1813).

Southwell, Robert (1561–1595), English poet and Jesuit priest, author of The Burning Babe and St Peters Complaynt; was martyred.

Southworth E(mma) D(orothy) E(liza) N(evitte) (1819–1899), American novelist.

Soútsos, Aléxandros (1803–1863), important Greek poet who was the creator of Greek Romantic verse.

Sozomen (c.400–c.450), Greek church historian.

Spalatin, Georg (actually Georg Burkhardt) (1484–1545), German historian and Humanist who was a leading figure in the Reformation.

Sparks, Jared (1789–1866), American historian and educator.

Spearman, Charles E(dward) (1863–1945), English psychologist, author of The Nature of 'Intelligence' and the Principles of Cognition (1923) and The Abilities of Man (1927).

Spedding, James (1808–1881), English editor and writer, author of Evenings with a Reviewer (1848) and editor of The Works of Francis Bacon (7 vols, 1857–59).

Speed, John (c.1552–1629), English historian and cartographer.

Spegel, Haquin (1645–1714), Swedish historian.

Spelman, Sir Henry (c.1564–1641), English antiquarian and historian who was known for his studies in ecclesiastical and legal history.

Spence, (James) Lewis Thomas Chalmers (1874–1955), Scottish poet and anthropologist.

Spence, Joseph (1699–1768), English clergyman, scholar and anecdotist.

Spence, Thomas (1750–1814), English reformer and poet who was an advocate of the socialization of land.

Spencer, Herbert (1820–1903), eminent English philosopher who was a leading evolutionist, author of The Synthetic Philosophy (The Principles of Psychology, 1855, The Principles of Sociology, 3 vols, 1876–96 and The Principles of Ethics, 2 vols, 1892–93) and The Man versus the State (1884).

Spender, Sir Stephen (Harold) (1909–1995), English poet and critic, one of the most influential figures of the Oxford generation.

Spener, Philipp Jakob (1635–1705), influential German Lutheran theologian and reformer who was a major figure in the Pietist movement, author of Pia Desideria (1675; English trans. as Pious Desires, 1964).

Spengler, Oswald (1880–1936), important German philosopher of history, author of Der Untergang des Abendlandes (2 vols, 1918, 1922; English trans. as The Decline of the West, 1926–28).

Spenser, Edmund (1552–1599), English poet who wrote the celebrated masterpiece The Faerie Queene (6 parts, 1590–96),

Speusippus (died c.338 BC), Greek philosopher.

Speyer, Leonora (1872–1956), American poet.

Sphrantzes, George (15th Century), Byzantine monk and historian.

Spicer, Jack (1925–1965), American poet.

Spieghel, Henric Laurenszoon (1549–1612), gifted Dutch poet, author of the Hertspiegel (Heartmirror).

Spielhagen, Friedrich von (1829–1911), German novelist and dramatist, author of the novels Problematische Naturen (4 vols, 1861; English trans. as Problematic Characters, 1869) and Sturmflut (3 vols, 1877; English trans. as The Breaking of the Storm, 1877).

Spingarn, J(oel) E(lias) (1875–1939), American poet and critic.

Spinoza, Benedict (1632–1677), Dutch philosopher and religious expositor of the Rationalist school, author of the Tractatus Theologico-Politicus (1670), Tractatus de Intellectus Emendatione (1677) and Ethica in Ordine Geometrico Demonstrata (1677; English trans. as Ethics, 1894).

Spitta, (Julius August) Philipp (1841–1894), eminent German music scholar, author of a major study of Johann Sebastian Bach (2 vols, 1873, 1880).

Spitteler, Carl (Friedrich Georg) (1845–1924), imaginative Swiss poet and novelist.

Spofford, Harriet (Elizabeth) Prescott (1835–1921), American novelist, short-story writer and poet.

Spottiswoode, Alicia Ann, Lady John Scott (1810–1900), Scottish poet and songwriter, author of Annie Laurie and Durrisdeer.

Sprague, Charles (1791–1875), American poet.

Sprat, Thomas (1635–1713), English Anglican bishop, dean, historian and poet.

Sprigg, Christopher St John (1907–1937), English critic, poet and novelist of a Marxist persuasion who often wrote under the name Christopher Caudwell; died in the Spanish Civil War.

Spring, Howard (1889–1965), American novelist, best known for O Absalom! (1938).

Spurgeon, Caroline (1869–1942), English literary scholar who was known for her stylistic analysis of Shakespeare.

Spurgeon, C(harles) H(addon) (1834–1892), English Baptist minister and writer.

Spyri, Johanna (née Heusser) (1829–1901), Swiss writer, author of the children's classic Heidi (2 vols, 1880–81).

Squier, Ephraim George (1821–1888), American journalist, diplomat and archaeologist.

Squire, Sir J(ohn) C(ollings) (1884–1958), English critic, editor, poet and dramtist.

Ssu-ma Ch'ien (c.145–c.85 BC), Chinese historian, astronomer and calendar reformer.

Ssu-ma Hsiang-ju (179–117 BC), important Chinese poet who was a master of descriptive verse.

Ssu-ma Kuang (1019–1086), Chinese statesman, scholar and poet.

Stace, W(alter) T(erence) (1886–1967), English philosopher.

Stacpoole, H(enry) de Vere (1863–1951), English novelist, particularly remembered for The Blue Lagoon (1908).

Stackton, David (Derek) (1923–1968), American novelist.

Staël, Madame de (actually Anne-Louise-Germaine Necker) (1766–1817), significant French novelist and critic, especially known for her writings on the Romantic movement.

Staff, Leopold (1878–1957), Polish poet, dramatist and translator.

Stafford, Jean (1915–1979), American novelist.

Stagnelius, Erik Johan (1793–1823), Swedish poet of Romanticism.

Stallings, Laurence (1894–1968), American novelist, dramatist and screenwriter.

Stammler, Rudolf (1856–1938), German legal philosopher.

Stangerup, Henrik (1937–1998), Danish writer and film director.

Stanley, Arthur Penrhyn (1815–1881), English historian and biographer.

Stanley, Sir Henry Morton (1841–1904), Welsh explorer and journalist, author of In Darkest Africa (1890) and Through South Africa (1898).

Stanley, Thomas (1625–1678), English writer, poet and translator, author of The History of Philosophy (1655–62).

Stansbury, Joseph (1742–1809), English-born American poet who defended the Loyalist cause during the American Revolution; grandfather of Caroline Stansbury Kirkland.

Stanton, Elizabeth Cady (1815–1902), prominent American suffragist, reformer and writer.

Stanton, Frank Lebby (1857–1927), American poet.

Stanyhurst, Richard (1547–1618), Irish historian and poet.

Stapledon, (William) Olaf (1886–1950), English writer who became particularly known for his science fiction novels, most notably Last and First Men (1930).

Stark, Dame Freya (1893–1993), English travel writer and photographer.

Staszic, Stanisław (Wawrzyniec) (1755–1826), Polish political writer, poet and translator.

Statius, Publius Papinius (c.45–96), Roman poet, admired for his Silvae and Thebaïs.

Stead, Christina Ellen (1902–1983), Australian novelist, best known for The Man Who Loved Children (1940).

Stead, Robert J(ames) C(ampbell) (1880–1959), Canadian writer and poet.

Stead, W(illiam) T(homas) (1849–1912), English journalist and reformer; died in the sinking of the Titanic.

Stedman, Edmund Clarence (1833–1908), American poet, essayist, critic and banker.

Steegmuller, Francis (1906–1994), American biographer, critic, novelist, editor and translator.

Steele, Sir Richard (1672–1729), Irish essayist, journalist, dramatist and politician.

Steele, Wilbur Daniel (1886–1970), American novelist, short-story writer and dramatist.

Steendam, Jacob (c.1616–c.1672), Dutch poet.

Steevens, George (1736–1800), English editor who collaborated with Samuel Johnson in editing the plays of Shakespeare (10 vols, 1773).

Stefánsson, David (1895–1964), Icelandic poet, novelist and dramatist.

Stefansson, Vilhjalmur (1879–1962), Canadian explorer, ethnologist and writer.

Steffen, Albert (1884–1963), Swiss novelist and dramatist.

Steffens, Henrik (1773–1845), Norwegian-born German philosopher and scientist.

Steffens, (Joseph) Lincoln (1866–1936), American journalist, lecturer and writer, one of the most prominent members of the muckrakers.

Stegner, Wallace (Earle) (1909–1993), notable American writer and poet who was one of the leading lights in avant-garde circles.

Stein, Charlotte von (née von Schardt) (1742–1827), German writer, best known for her close relationship with Goethe.

Stein, Edith (1891–1942), German-born Jewish Roman Catholic convert, nun and philosopher who took the name Teresa Benedicta of the Cross, author of the treatise Studie über Joannes a Cruce: Kreuzwswissenschaft (published 1950; English trans. as The Science of the Cross, 1955); was arrested by the Nazis as a non-Catholic Aryan and put to death at the Auschwitz concentration camp.

Stein, Gertrude (1874–1946), famous American writer and poet, one of the principal avant-garde literary figures of her era; sister of Leo Stein.

Stein, Leo (1872–1947), American writer; brother of Gertrude Stein.

Stein, Sir (Mark) Aurel (1862–1943), Hungarian-born English archaeologist and geographer.

Steinbeck, John (Ernst) (1902–1968), prominent American novelist and short-story writer whose masterpiece was The Grapes of Wrath (1939); won the Nobel Prize for Literature (1962).

Steiner, Rudolf (1861–1925), Austrian-born Swiss scientist, educator, artist and writer who founded the spiritual movement known as anthroposophy.

Steinheim, Solomon Ludwig (1789–1866), German philosopher who was known for his writings on Jewish religious philosophy.

Steinschneider, Moritz (1816–1907), German scholar.

Stendahl (actually Marie-Henri Beyle) (1783–1842), famous French novelist, author of the celebrated Le Rouge et le noir (1830; English trans. as The Red and the Black, 1926) and La Chartreuse de Parme (1839; English trans. as The Charterhouse of Parma, 1925).

Stephansson, Stephan G (actually Stefán Guomundarson) (1853–1927), gifted Icelandic-born Canadian poet who was much esteemed for his collection Andvökur (Sleepless Nights, 1909–38).

Stephen, Sir James (1789–1859), English colonial administrator and historian, author of Essays in Ecclesiastical Biography (1849) and Lectures on the History of France (1851); father of Sir James Fitzjames Stephen and Sir Leslie Stephen.

Stephen, Sir James Fitzjames (1829–1894), English colonial administrator, judge and writer, author of a General View of the Criminal Law of England (1863), Liberty, Equality, Fraternity (1873) and History of the Criminal Law of England (1883); son of Sir James Stephen, brother of Sir Leslie Stephen and father of James Kenneth Stephen.

Stephen, James Kenneth (1859–1892), English journalist and poet, author of Lapsus Calami (1891) and Quo Musa Tendis (1891); son of Sir James Fitzjames Stephen; died insane.

Stephen, Sir Leslie (1832–1904), English editor, essayist and biographer, author of The Playground of Europe (1871), History of English Thought in the 18th Century (1876) and English Literature and Society in the Eighteenth Century (1904), and editor of the Dictionary of National Biography (1882–91); son of Sir James Stephen, brother of Sir James Fitzjames Stephen and father of Virginia Woolf.

Stephens, Alfred George (1865–1933), Australian journalist and literary critic.

Stephens, Ann Sophia (1810–1886), American writer, best known for her dime novel Malaeska:The Indian Wife of the White Hunter (1860).

Stephens, James (1882–1950), Irish poet, novelist and short-story writer.

Stephens, John Lloyd (1805–1852), American traveller and archaeologist.

Sterling, George (1869–1926), American poet and writer; committed suicide.

Sterling, James (c.1701–1763), Irish-born American poet and dramatist.

Sterling, John (1806–1844), Scottish essayist, novelist and poet.

Stern, Richard Martin (1915–2001), American writer.

Sterne, Laurence (1713–1768), famous Irish-born novelist and clergyman, author of the celebrated The Life and Opinions of Tristram Shandy (9 vols, 1759–67).

Sternheim, (Wilhelm Adolf) Carl (1878–1942), German dramatist.

Stesichorus (c.630–c.554 BC), Greek poet who was known for his Calyce, Daphnis and Rhadine.

Stevens, Abel (1815–1897), American Methodist clergyman and historian of his church.

Stevens, James (Floyd) (1892–1971), American novelist and short-story writer.

Stevens, Wallace (1879–1955), American poet.

Stevenson, Robert Louis (1850–1894), Scottish novelist, essayist, literary critic and poet, author of the classic novels Treasure Island (1881), Kidnapped (1886), The Strange Case of Dr. Jekyll and Mr. Hyde (1886) and Black Arrow (1888).

Steward, Julian (1902–1972), influential American anthropologist, author of Theory of Culture Change: The Methodology of Multilinear Evolution (1955).

Steward, Donald (Ogden) (1894–1980), American writer, dramatist and screenwriter.

Stewart, Douglas (Alexander) (1913–1985), New Zealand-born Australian poet, dramatist, writer and critic.

Stewart, Dugald (1753–1828), Scottish philosopher, author of Elements of the Philosophy of the Human Mind (3 vols, 1792, 1814, 1827).

Stewart, George R(ippey) (1895–1980), American writer and educator.

Stewart, J(ohn) I(nnes) M(ackintosh) (1906–1994), Scottish novelist, short-story writer and literary critic who often wrote under the name Michael Innes.

Stickney, (Joseph) Trumbull (1874–1904), American poet.

Stiernhielm, Georg (Olofson) (1598–1672), august Swedish poet and linguist, one of the principal figures in the development of Swedish poetry.

Stifter, Adalbert (1805–1868), esteemed Austrian novelist and short-story writer.

Stiles, Ezra (1727–1795), American Congregational minister, educator and scholar; grandson of Edward Taylor.

Stillingfleet, Edward (1635–1699), English Anglican bishop and scholar.

Stilo Praeconinus, Lucius Aelius (c.154–74 BC), Roman literary scholar.

Stirling, Sir William Alexander, 1st Earl of (c.1576–1640), Scottish courtier, statesman and poet.

Stirner, Max (actually Johann Kaspar Schmidt) (1806–1856), German philosopher who espoused anti-statist views, author of Der Einzige und sein Eigentum (1845; English trans. as The Ego and His Own, 1907).

Stockton, Frank R (actually Francis Richard Stockton) (1834–1902), American novelist and short-story writer.

Stoddard, Charles Warren (1843–1909), American writer and poet.

Stoddard, Richard Henry (1825–1903), American poet, critic and essayist.

Stoddard, Solomon (1643–1729), American Congregational clergyman and polemicist; grandfather of Jonathan Edwards.

Stoddard, William Osborn (1835–1925), American writer who wrote a biography of Abraham Lincoln (1884) and numerous books for boys.

Stoker, Bram (actually Abraham Stoker) (1847–1912), Irish novelist and short-story writer, author of the celebrated horror novel Dracula (1897).

Stolberg, Christian, Count of (1748–1821), German poet and translator; brother of Friedrich Leopold, Count of Stolberg.

Stolberg, Friedrich Leopold, Count of (1750–1819), German poet, dramatist and translator; brother of Christian, Count of Stolberg.

Stone, Barton Warren (1772–1844), American Protestant clergyman and writer, one of the principal figures in the founding of the religious denomination known as the Disciples of Christ.

Stone, Irving (1903–1989), American writer of fictionalized biographies.

Stone, John Augustus (1800–1834), American actor and dramatist.

Stone, Samuel (1602–1663), English-born American Nonconformist clergyman.

Stone, William Leete (1792–1844), American journalist and writer; father of William Leete Stone Jr.

Stone, William Leete Jr (1835–1908), American journalist and writer; son of William Leete Stone.

Stong, Phil(ip Duffield) (1899–1957), American writer, journalist and screenwriter.

Stopes, Marie (Charlotte Carmichael) (1880–1958), English palaeobotanist, dramatist and poet who became best known as a pioneering crusader for birth control.

Storm, (Hans) Theodor Woldsen (1817–1888), German writer and poet, an exponent of the novella.

Storni, Alfonsina (1892–1938), Argentine poet, particularly esteemed for his El dulce daño (The Sweet Injury, 1918); committed suicide.

Story, Isaac (1774–1803), American poet and writer.

Story, Joseph (1779–1845), influential American jurist and legal scholar who served as an associate justice of the US Supreme Court (1811–45).

Story, William Wetmore (1819–1895), American sculptor and poet.

Stout, George Frederick (1860–1944), English psychologist and philosopher, author of Analytic Psychology (2 vols, 1896), Manual of Psychology (1899) and Mind and Matter (1931).

Stort, Rex (Todhunter) (1886–1975), American novelist, creator of the famous detective Nero Wolfe.

Stow, John (1525–1605), English antiquarian, author of the celebrated Survey of London (1598).

Stowe, Calvin Ellis (1802–1886), American religious scholar and educator; husband of Harriet (Elizabeth) Beecher Stowe.

Stowe, Harriet (Elizabeth) Beecher (1811–1896), American writer and poet who wrote the famous novel Uncle Tom's Cabin or, Life Among the Lowly (1852); daughter of Lyman Beecher, sister of Catherine E(sther) and Henry Ward Beecher, and wife of Calvin Ellis Stowe.

Stowell, William Scott, Baron (1745–1836), English judge who influenced the doctrines of admiralty law.

Strabo (c.64 BC–c.24 AD), important Greek geographer and historian.

Strachey, (Evelyn) John (St Loe) (1901–1963), English politician and writer who first embraced Communism but later espoused Socialism.

Strachey, (Giles) Lytton (1880–1932), English biographer and critic, best known for his Eminent Victorians (1918) and Queen Victoria (1921).

Strachwitz, Moritz (Karl Wilhelm Anton), Graf von (1822–1847), German poet who was admired for his Lieder eines Erwachenden (Songs of Awakening, 1842) and Neue Gedichte (New Poems, published 1848).

Strangford, Percy Clinton, 6th Viscount (1780–1855), English diplomat and poet, author of Poems from the Portuguese of Camoens (1803).

Straparola, Giovan Francesco (16th Century), Italian writer, author of the novelle Piacevoli Notti (Pleasant Nights, 2 vols, 1550, 1553).

Strashimirov, Anton (1872–1937), Bulgarian writer who espoused realism in his works.

Stratemeyer, Edward (1863–1930), American writer of fiction for boys and girls.

Stratton-Porter, Gene(va) (1863–1924), American writer of fiction for girls, best remembered for Freckles (1904) and A Girl of the Limberlost (1909).

Strauss, David Friedrich (1808–1874), influential but controversial German Protestant theologian, philosopher and writer who espoused the 'myth theory' of the life of Christ, author of Das Leben Jesu kritisch bearbeitet (2 vols, 1835–36; English trans. as The Life of Jesus, Critically Examined, 1846) and Der alte und neue Glaube (1872; English trans. as The Old and the New, 1873).

Strauss, Leo (1899–1973), German-born American political philosopher, author of On Tyranny (1948) and Natural Right and History (1950).

Street, Alfred Billings (1811–1881), American lawyer, librarian and poet.

Streeter, Edward (1891–1976), American writer.

Streeter, Burnett Hillman (1874–1937), English theologian and biblical scholar, author of The Four Gospels: A Study of Origins (1924) and The Primitive Church (1929).

Streitberg, Wilhelm (August) (1864–1925), German historical linguist.

Stretton, Hesba (actually Sarah Smith) (1832–1911), English Writer.

Streuvels, Stijn (actually Frank Lateur) (1871–1969), Belgian novelist and short-story writer who wrote in Flemish.

Strickland, Agnes (1796–1874), English biographer, poet and children's writer, author of Lives of the Queens of England (in collaboration with her sister Elizabeth, 12 vols, 1840–48) and Lives of the Queens of Scotland and English Princesses (8 vols 1850–59).

Strindberg, (Johan) August (1849–1912), famous Swedish dramatist, novelist and short-story writer who influenced the development of modern drama via such plays as Fadren (1887; English trans. as The Father, 1899), Fröken Julie (1888; English trans. as Miss Julie, 1918), Creditörer (1890; English trans. as Creditors, 1914), Drömspelet (1902; English trans. as A Dream Play, 1929) and Spöksonaten (1907; English trans. as The Ghost Sonata, 1916).

Strode, William (c.1599–1645), English Puritan leader, politician and poet who opposed the policies of King Charles I and served 11 years in prison.

Strong, Josiah (1847–1916), American Congregationalist minister and writer who espoused the social gospel.

Strong, L(eonard) A(lfred) G(eorge) (1896–1958), English novelist and poet.

Strong, William Duncan (1899–1962), American anthropologist who was known for his studies of Indian cultures of the Americas.

Strubberg, Friedrich Armand (1806–1889), German writer whose years in the US as a frontiersman informed his novels.

Strutt, Joseph (1749–1802), English antiquarian, writer, artist and engraver.

Strype, John (1643–1737), English historian and biographer who was known for his studies of ecclesiastical subjects.

Stuart, Daniel (1766–1846), English journalist.

Stuart, Ruth (McEnery) (1849–1917), American writer.

Stubbes or Stubbs, Philip (16th Century), English Puritan pamphleteer, author of The Anatomie of Abuses (1583) and A Christal Glasse for Christian Women (1591).

Stubbs, John (c.1541–1590), English pamphleteer, author of The Discoverie of a Gaping Gulf whereinto England is like to be Swallowed (1579), a protest against the marriage of the Queen to the brother of the French Queen, which resulted in his imprisonment and loss of his right hand.

Stubbs, William (1825–1901), eminent English historian who was an authority on English medieval history.

Stuckenberg, Viggo (1863–1905), Danish poet.

Stukeley, William (1687–1765), English antiquarian and physician, author of Itinerarium Curiosum (Observant Itinerary, 1724).

Stumpf, Carl (1848–1936), German philosopher and psychologist.

Stumpf, Johannes (1500–1578), Swiss religious reformer, theologian and chronicler.

Sturgeon, Thoeodore (Hamilton) (1918–1985), American novelist and short-story writer who was known for his fantasy and science fiction.

Sturgis, Howard (Overing) (1855–1920), American novelist, best known for his Belchamber (1904).

Sturla Thórdason (actually Sturla Pórdarson) (c.1214–1284), Icelandic historian, author of the Íslendinga saga.

Sturt, Charles (1795–1869), Australian explorer who left vivid accounts of his expeditions in Two Expeditions into the Interior of Southern Australia, 1828–31 (1833) and Narrative of an Expedition into Central Australia (1849).

Sturt, George (1863–1927), English writer who often wrote under the name George Bourne.

Suárez, Francisco (1548–1617), Spanish Roman Catholic theologian and philosopher, author of Disputationes Metaphysicae (1597) and De Ligibus (1612).

Suckling, Sir John (1609–1642), English courtier, poet and dramatist who was admired for his lyric gifts.

Suckow, Ruth (1892–1960), American novelist and short-story writer.

Sudermann, Hermann (1857–1928), German novelist and dramatist who espoused Naturalism.

Sue, Eugène (1804–1857), French writer who won enormous success for his novels depicting the underside of life.

Sue Sumii (1902–1997), Japanese novelist and social reformer.

Suess, Eduard (1831–1914), Austrian geologist, author of the important Das Antlitz der Erde (1885– 1909; English trans. as The Face of the Earth, 1904–25).

Suetonius (actually Gaius Suetonius Tranquillus) (c.69–c.140), Roman biographer and historian, author of the famous De vita Caesarum (English trans. as The Twelve Caesars, 1957).

Suhrawardi, as- (actually Shihāb ad-Dīn Yahyā ibn Habāsh ibn Amīrak) (c.1155–1191), important Islamic mystic theologian and philosopher who was one of the principal representatives of the illuminative movement.

Sukenik, Eliezar Lipa (1889–1953), Israeli archaeologist who was an authority on the Dead Sea Scrolls.

Süleyman Çelebi (died 1429), celebrated Turkish poet, author of the renowned poem on the life of Muhammad Mevlûd-i Nebi or Mevlûd-i Peygamberi (English trans. as Hymn on the Prophet's Nativity, 1943).

Sullivan, Frank (actually Francis John Sullivan) (1892–1976), American writer and poet of a humorous disposition.

Sullivan, Harry Stack (1892–1949), influential American psychiatrist.

Sullivan, Mark (1874–1952), American journalist and writer, author of Our Times: The United States 1900–1925 (six vols, 1926–35).

Sully Prudhomme (actually René-François-Armand Prudhomme) (1839–1907), French poet and writer of the Parnassian movement; won the first Nobel Prize for Literature (1901).

Sumarokov, Alexander Petrovich (c.1718–1777), Russian poet and dramatist.

Sumner, William Graham (1840–1910), American sociologist and economist who espoused social Darwinism, author of Folkways (1907).

Supervielle, Jules (1884–1960), Uruguayan-born French poet, dramatist and writer.

Surrey, Henry Howard, Earl of (1517–1547), English courtier and poet; was executed for treason.

Surtees, Robert Smith (1803–1864), English novelist, creator of the famous comic figure Mr Jorrocks.

Suso, Heinrich (actually Heinrich von Berg) (c.1295–1366), famous German Catholic mystic who was a principal figure in the Gottesfreunde (Friends of God) movement, author of Das Büchlein der Wahrheit (c.1326) and Das Büchlein der ewigen Weisheit (c.1328), which were translated into English as Little Book of Eternal Wisdom and Little Book of Truth (1953).

Sutherland, Efua Theodora (1924–1996), Ghanian dramatist, poet and writer.

Sutter, David (1811–1880), Swiss-born French sculptor, painter, engraver, aesthetician, writer and musician.

Suttner, Bertha Félicie Sophie (née Kinsky von Chinic und Tettau), Baroness von (1843–1914), Austrian novelist and pacifist, author of the novel Die Waffen nieder! (1889; English trans. as Lay Down Your Arms!, 1892).

Su Tung-P'o (actually Su Shih) (1036–1101), important Chinese painter, calligrapher, poet, philosopher and statesman.

Suyūtī, as- (actually Abū al-Fadl 'Abd ar-Rahman ibn Abī Bakr Jalāl ad-Dīn as Suyūtī) (1445–1505), Egyptian writer.

Suzuki, D(aisetsu) T(eitaro) (1870–1966), learned Japanese Buddhist scholar.

Světlá, Karolina (actually Johanna Muzáková) (1830–1899), Czech novelist.

Svevo, Italo (actually Ettore Schmitz) (1861–1928), important Italian novelist and short-story writer whose masterpiece was La coscienza di Zeno (1923; English trans. as Confessions of Zenog 1930); was killed in an automobile accident.

Swadesh, Morris (1909–1967), American linguist.

Swados, Harvey (1920–1972), American novelist and short-story writer.

Swanton, John Reed (1873–1958), important American anthropologist and ethnohistorian who was an authority on the North American Indians.

Swedberg, Jesper (1653–1735), Swedish theologian, bishop and writer; father of Emanuel Swedenborg.

Swedenborg, Emanuel (actually Emanuel Swedberg) (1688–1772), celebrated Swedish scientist, theologian, philosopher and mystic, author of the Principia Rerum Nauralium (Principles of Natural Things, 1734); son of Jesper Swedberg.

Sweet, Henry (1845–1912), English phonetician.

Swenson, May (1927–1989), American poet of experimental verse.

Swift, Jonathan (1667–1745), celebrated Irish writer, poet and churchman who was a master of satire, author of the classic novel Gulliver's Travels (1726).

Swinburne, Algernon Charles (1837–1909), English poet, writer, critic and dramatist, particularly known for his Poems and Ballads (2 vols, 1866, 1878) and Songs before Sunrise (1871).

Swinnerton, Frank (1884–1982), English novelist and critic.

Swinton, William (1833–1892), Scottish-born American journalist and writer who wrote important accounts of the US Civil War.

Sybel, Heinrich von (1817–1895), German historian,

Sylvain, George (1865–1925), Haitian writer.

Sylvester, János (16th Century), pioneering Hungarian poet, grammarian and translator of the New Testament.

Sylvester, (Anthony) David (Bernard) (1924–2001), influential English art critic.

Sylvester, Joshua (1563–1618), English merchant, translator and poet.

Syme, Sir Ronald (1903–1989), English historian who distinguished himself in studies of ancient Rome.

Symeon, Saint (c.949–1022), Byzantine monk, mystic and theologian who was known as Symeon the New Theologian.

Symmachus, Quintus Aurelius (c.345–c.402), Roman statesman, orator and writer who was a determined foe of Christianity.

Symmachus Ben Joseph (3rd Century), Jewish writer.

Symonds, John Addington (1840–1893), prominent English writer, biographer, poet and translator, especially known for his important study Renaissance in Italy (7 vols, 1875–86).

Symons, A(lphonse) J(ames) A(lbert) (1900–1941), English bibliographer, bibliophile and biographer; brother of Julian (Gustave) Symons.

Symons, Arthur (William) (1865–1945), Welsh critic and poet.

Symons, Julian (Gustave) (1912–1995), English novelist and critic; brother of (A)lphonse (J)ames (A)lbert Symons.

Synesius of Cyrene (c.370–413), Christian bishop and philosopher of Neoplatonism.

Synge, (Edmund) John Millington (1872–1909), influential Irish dramatist, especially admired for The Playboy of the Western World (1907).

Széchenyi, István, Count (1791–1860), Hungarian reformer and writer whose last years were marred by insanity; committed suicide.

Szulc, Tad(eusz Witold) (1926–2001), Polish-born American journalist and writer.

Tabb, John B(anister) (1845–1909), American poet.

Tabarī, at- (actually Abū Ja'far Muhammed ibn Jarīr at-Tabarī) (c.839–923), Islamic scholar.

Tacitus, Cornelius (c.56–c.120), Roman historian, orator and public official, author of the celebrated Historiae (English trans. as The Histories, 1964) and Annals (ab excessu divi Augusti) (English trans. as The Annals of Imperial Rome, 1956).

Taggard, Genevieve (1894–1948), American poet.

Tagore, Debendranath (1817–1905), Indian Hindu religious reformer, philosopher and writer.

Tagore, Rabindranath (1861–1941), Indian poet, novelist and philosopher; won the Novel Prize for Literature (1913).

Taha Hussein (1889–1973), Egyptian novelist, short-story writer, essayist and critic.

Thatāwī, Rifa'ah Rāfi' at- (1801–1873), Egyptian educator, scholar and writer.

Tai Chen or Tai Tung-Yüan (1724–1777), Chinese philosopher of the empiricist persuasion.

Taine, Hippolyte (-Adolphe) (1828–1893), notable French philosopher and historian, author of the expansive Les Origines de la France contemporaine (The Origins of Contemporary France, 6 vols, 1876–93).

Tait, Archibald Campbell (1811–1882), English Anglican archbishop of Canterbury and writer.

Taj, Imtiaz Ali (1900–1970), Urdu dramatist.

Takahama Kyoshi (1874–1959), Japanese philosopher.

Takayana Rinjirō (1871–1902), Japanese philosopher who wrote under the name Chogyū.

Takemoto Gidayū (1651–1714), Japanese writer.

Takizawa Bakin (1767–1848), Japanese novelist.

Talfourd, Sir Thomas Noon (1795–1854), English judge, politician, literary critic and writer.

Taliaferro, Harden (1818–1875), American Baptist minister, editor and writer.

Tallemant des Réaux, Gédéon (1619–1692), French biographer.

Tam, Jacob ben Meir (1100–1171), French Jewish scholar who was an authority on the Talmud,

Tamayo y Baus, Manuel (1829–1898), Spanish dramatist.

Tamenaga Shunsui (1790–1842), Japanese writer.

Tam'si, Tchicaya U (1931–1988), Congolese poet, novelist and dramatist.

Tanabe Hajime (1885–1962), Japanese philosopher.

Tanaka Odō (1867–1932), Japanese philosopher.

T'ang Yin (1470–1523), admired Chinese painter and poet.

Tanhum ben Joseph (13th Century), Jewish rabbinic scholar.

Tanizaki Jun-ichirō (1886–1965), important Japanese novelist, author of Tade Kuu mushi (1929; English trans. as Some Prefer Nettles, 1955), Sasame-yuki (1943–48; English trans. as The Makioka Sisters, 1957) and Fūten Rōjin Nikki (1961–1962; English trans. as The Diary of a Mad Old Man, 1965).

Tannahill, Robert (1774–1810), Scottish poet and song-writer; committed suicide.

Tannhäuser (c.1200–c.1270), famous German Minnesinger who was the inspiration for Wagner's opera of the same name.

T'an Ssu-t'ung (1865–1898), Chinese philosopher.

T'ao Ch'ien (365–427), Chinese poet.

Tarafah (actually Tarafah' Amr ibn al-'Abd ibn Sufyān ibn Mālik ibn Dubay'ah al-Bakrī ibn Wā'il) (6th Century), celebrated Arab Poet.

Taranātha (16th Century), Tibetan historian of Buddhism.

Tarbell, Ida M(inerva) (1857–1944), American journalist and writer of the muckraking school.

Tarde, Gabriel (actually Jean-Gabriel de Tarde) (1843–1904), French sociologist and criminologist.

Tarkington, (Newton) Booth (1869–1946), admired American novelist and dramatist, particularly remembered for his novels The Magnificent Ambersons (1918) and Alice Adams (1921).

Tarlton, Richard (died 1588), English actor, dramatist and ballad writer who gained fame as the court jester of Queen Elizabeth I.

Tarnowski, Jan, Count (1488–1561), Polish soldier and writer on war.

Tasso, Bernardo (1493–1569), Italian poet and courtier who was known for his epic Amadigi (1560); father of Torquato Tasso.

Tasso, Torquato (1544–1595), Italian poet, author of the celebrated epic Gerusaleme liberata (1581; English trans. as Jerusalem Liberated, 1884); son of Bernardo Tasso.

Tassoni, Alessandro (1565–1635), Italian writer, literary critic and poet, best known for his mock-heroic satiric poem La Secchia rapita (1622; English trans. as La Secchia Rapita, or the Rape of the Bucket, 1825).

Tate, (John Orley) Allen (1899–1979), American poet, novelist, biographer and editor.

Tate, Nahum (1652–1715), Irish poet and dramatist; became Poet Laureate of the United Kingdom (1692).

Tatian (c.120–173), Syrian Christian apologist who was best known for his Greek and Syriac version of the four canonical Gospels.

Tausen, Hans (1494–1561), influential Danish religious reformer and language scholar who converted from Roman Catholicism to Lutheranism.

Tavares, Eugénio (de Paulo) (1867–1930), Cape Verdean poet.

Tawney, Richard Henry (1880–1962), important English economic historian, author of The Acquisitive Society (1920) and Religion and the Rise of Capitalism (1926).

Tayama Katai (1871–1930), Japanese novelist who was one of the principal exponents of Naturalism.

Taylor, A(lan) J(ohn) P(ercivale) (1906–1990), English historian.

Taylor, Ann (1782–1866), English poet of children's verse; sister of Jane Taylor.

Taylor, Edward (1644–1729), English-born American pastor, physician and poet; grandfather of Ezra Stiles.

Taylor, Elizabeth (née Coles) (1912–1975), English novelist and short-story writer, especially known for her novels A Wreath of Roses (1950) and Mrs Palfrey at the Claremont (1972).

Taylor, Graham (1851–1938), American writer on religious and social subjects.

Taylor, Sir Henry (1800–1886), English poet, dramatist and writer.

Taylor, (James) Bayard (1825–1878), American novelist, poet, dramatist, translator and diplomat.

Taylor, Jane (1783–1824), English writer of children's verse; sister of Ann Taylor.

Taylor, Jeremy (1613–1667), English Anglican clergyman and writer, author of The Rule and Exercises of Holy Living (1650) and The Rule and Exercises of Holy Dying (1651).

Taylor, John (1580–1653), English poet, pamphleteer and journalist who became known as the 'waterpoet'.

Taylor, John (1753–1824), American politician and theorist.

Taylor, Peter (Hillsman) (1917–1994), American novelist, short-story writer and dramatist.

Taylor, Thomas (1758–1835), English classical scholar, philosopher and mathematician.

Taylor, Tom (1817–1800), English dramatist.

Taylor, William (1765–1836), English literary critic, essayist and translator.

Teale, Edwin Way (1899–1980), American journalist and writer, best known for his studies on nature and ecology.

Teasdale, Sara (1884–1933), esteemed American poet who was especially admired for her lyrical gifts as revealed in such vols as Sonnets to Duse and Other Poems (1907), Rivers to the Sea (1915), Love Songs (1917), Flame and Shadow (1920), Dark of the Moon (1926) and Strange Victory (1933); committed suicide.

Teggart, Frederick J(ohn) (1870–1946), Irish-born American historian, author of Prolegomena to History (1916), The Processes of History (1918) and Theory of History (1925).

Tegnér, Esaias (1782–1846), admired Swedish poet and bishop.

Teilhard de Chardin, Pierre (1881–1955), important French Roman Catholic philosopher and palaeontologist who attempted to fuse Christianity and science, author of the major study Le Phénomène humain (1938–40; English trans. as The Phenomenon of Man, 1959).

Teirlinck, Hermann (Louis-Cesar) (1879–1967), Flemish novelist, short-story writer, dramatist, poet and essayist.

Teixeira de Pascoais (actually Joaquim Pereira Teixeira de Vasconcelos) (c.1878–1952), Portuguese poet and philosopher.

Telesio, Bernardino (1509–1588), Significant Italian philosopher and natural scientist of the empiricist school whose most important work was De natura juxta propria principia (On Nature According to Its Own Principles, 9 vols, 1585).

Temple, Frederick (1821–1902), English Anglican archbishop of Canterbury and educational reformer, author of the controversial essay The Education of the World (1860); father of William Temple.

Temple, Sir William (1628–1699), English statesman, diplomat and essayist.

Temple, William (1881–1944), English Anglican archbishop of Canterbury, ecumenical leader, social reformer and writer; son of Frederick Temple.

Tench, Watkin (c.1758–1833), English Army officer and writer, author of A Narrative of the Expedition to Botany Bay (1789), Complete Account of the Settlement at Port Jackson (1793) and Letters Written in France to a Friend in London (1796).

Tencin, Claudine-Alexandrine Guérin de (1682–1749), French novelist who wrote Mémoires du Comte de Comminges (1735); mother of Jean Le Rond d'Alembert.

Tennant, Frederick Robert (1866–1957), English theologian and philosopher whose most important work was Philosophical Theology (2 vols, 1928, 1930).

Tennant, Kylie (1912–88), Australian novelist and dramatist.

Tennant, William (1784–1848), Scottish poet and scholar.

Tenney, Tabitha (Gilman) (1762–1837), American writer, author of the novel Female Quixotism (1801).

Tennyson, Alfred, Lord (1809–1892), famous English poet, celebrated for his Poems (2 vols 1833, 1842), Poems Chiefly Lyrical (1830), In Memoriam (1850) and Crossing the Bar (1889); became Poet Laureate of the United Kingdom (1850); brother of Frederick Tennyson and Charles Tennyson Turner.

Tennyson, Frederick (1807–1898), English poet; brother of Alfred, Lord Tennyson, and Charles Tennyson Turner.

Tennyson Turner, Charles (1808–1879), English poet; brother of Alfred, Lord Tennyson, and Frederick Tennyson.

Tenreiro, Francisco José (de Vasques) (1921–63), São Toméan poet and critic.

Terence (actually Publius Terentine Afer) (185–c.159 BC), notable Greek dramatist who was admired for his comic plays.

Teresa of Avila, Saint (actually Teresa de Cepeda y Ahumada) (1515–1582), famous Spanish Roman Catholic mystic, reformer, writer and poet.

Terhune, Albert Payson (1872–1942), American novelist and short-story writer; son of Mary Virginia Terhune.

Terhune, Mary Virginia (1830–1922), American writer who wrote under the name Marion Harland; mother of Albert Payton Terhune.

Terman, Lewis M(adison) (1877–1956), American psychologist who was known for his studies on human intelligence and for coining the term IQ (Intelligence Quotient).

Terpander (c.700–645 BC), Greek poet.

Tertullian (actually Quintus Septimus Florens Tertullianus) (c.157–c.225), significant Latin Christian theologian and writer who broke from orthodoxy and founded his own strict Christian sect.

Tetens, Johannes Nikolaus (1736–1807), German philosopher and scholar of Empiricism, author of the Philosophische Versuche über die menschliche Natur und ihre Entwickelung (Philosophical Experiment on Human Nature and Its Development, 1777).

Tetmajer (-Przerwa), Kazimierz (1865–1940), Polish poet and short-story writer.

Tevfik Fikret (actually Mehmed Tevfik) (1867–1915), Turkish poet who was the most important figure in modern Turkish verse.

Tey, Josephine (actually Elizabeth Mackintosh) (1897–1952), English novelist and dramatist who was particularly known for her detective novels.

Thābit ibn Qurrah (c.836–901), Syrian mathematician, physician and philosopher.

Thackeray, William Makepeace (1811–1863), prominent English writer, editor and poet, best remembered for his novels Vanity Fair (1847–48) and The History of Henry Esmond, Esq (1848–50); father of Anne Isabella Thackeray, Lady Ritchie.

Thara Saikaku (1642–1693), Japanese poet.

Tharaud, Jean (1877–1952), French writer who collaborated with his brother Jérôme on many books.

Tharaud, Jérôme (1874–1953), French writer who collaborated with his brother Jean on many books.

Thatcher, Benjamin Bussey (1809–1840), American antislavery leader and writer.

Thaxter, Celia (Laighton) (1835–1894), American poet.

Thayer, Alexander Wheelock (1817–1897), American music scholar who wrote a major biography of Beethoven in German as Ludwig van Beethovens Leben (5 vols, 1866–1908); definitive English trans. as Thayer's Life of Beethoven, 1964).

Thayer, William Roscoe (1859–1923), American biographer and historian.

Theobald, Lewis (1688–1744), English scholar, poet, essayist and dramatist.

Theocritus (c.310–250 BC), famous Greek poet, especially admired for his idylls.

Theodore, Saint (c.602–690), Cilian-born English archbishop of Canterbury whose rulings on church matters appeared as the Poenitentiale.

Theodore Ascidas (died 558), Eastern Orthodox monk, archbishop and theologian who espoused the cause of Platonism.

Theodore bar Konai (9th Century), Syrian scholar who prepared annotations on the Syriac Bible.

Theodore of Mopsuestia (c.350–c.428), celebrated Antiochene theologian and biblical exegete.

Theodore of Rhaithu (6th Century), German monk and theologian.

Theodore of Studios, Saint (759–826), monk, monastic reformer, polemicist and poet who was an opponent of the Iconoclasts.

Theodoret of Cyrrhus (c.393–c.458), Christian theologian, bishop and writer.

Theodorus Lector (6th Century), Greek church historian.

Theodosius of Alexandria (6th Century), Turkish-born theologian and patriarch of Alexandria.

Theodosius the Deacon (10th Century), Byzantine poet and historian.

Theodotion (2nd Century), Greek Jewish scholar.

Theodotus (flourished c.100 BC), Egyptian Jewish writer.

Theodotus of Ancyra (died c.446), Byzantine theologian and bishop of Ancyra.

Theodulf of Orléans (750–821), French prelate, theologian and poet.

Theodurus Abu Qurrah (c.750–c.825), Syrian Orthodox bishop and theologian.

Theognis (5th Century BC), Greek poet who was known for his elegies.

Theognostos (9th Century), Byzantine monk, theologian and chronicler.

Theognostus of Alexandria (3rd Century), Greek theologian and writer.

Theoleptus of Philadelphia (c.1250–c.1326), Greek Orthodox theologian, writer and metropolitan of Philadelphia.

Theophanes the Confessor (c.752–c.818), Byzantine monk, theologian and chronicler.

Theophilus (5th Century), Greek Orthodox theologian and patriarch of Alexandria.

Theophilus (12th Century), German monk, author of De diversis artibus.

Theophrastus (c.372–c.287), Greek philosopher.

Theophylactus of Ochrida (c.1050–c.1109), Greek Orthodox theologian, language scholar and archbishop.

Theophylactus Simocattes (7th Century), Byzantine historian.

Theotokás, Yorgos (1906–66), Greek novelist and dramatist.

Theotókis, Konstantínos (1872–1923), Greek novelist.

Thériault, Yves (1915–1983), prominent French-Canadian novelist, short-story writer and dramatist.

Thespis (6th Century BC), Greek poet who is generally considered the creator of Greek tragedy.

Theuriet, André (1833– 1907), French poet and novelist.

Thibaut IV (1201–1253), celebrated French trouvère.

Thibaut, Anton Friedrich Justus (1772–1840), German jurist and legal philosopher.

Thierry, (Jacques-Nicolas-) Augustin (1795–1856), French historian who wrote on the Middle Ages.

Thierry de Chartres (c.1100–c.1150), French philosopher, theologian and encyclopaedist.

Thiers, (Louis-) Adolphe (1797–1877), French statesman and historian.

Thirkell, Angela (Margaret) (1890–1961), English novelist.

Thirwall, Connop (1797–1875), English churchman, historian and translator.

Thomas (12th Century), Anglo-Norman poet.

Thomas, Albert (1878–1932), French statesman and historian.

Thomas, Augustus (1857–1934), American dramatist.

Thomas, Dylan (Marlais) (1914–1953), notable Welsh poet and writer who was especially admired for his poems Fern Hill (1946) and A Refusal to Mourn the Death by Fire of a Child in London (1946), and the play Under Milk Wood (1953).

Thomas, Edith Matilda (1854–1925), American poet.

Thomas, Frederick William (1806–1866), American novelist and poet.

Thomas, Isaiah (1749–1831), American printer, publisher and editor who wrote the valuable History of Printing in America (2 vols, 1810).

Thomas, Norman (Mattoon) (1884–1968), American socialist, reformer and writer.

Thomas, (Philip) Edward (1878–1917), English poet and writer; died in World War 1.

Thomas, William (1832–1878), Welsh clergyman, author of the unfinished Y Storm (1856; English trans. as The Storm, 1938).

Thomas, William Isaac (1863–1947), American sociologist and psychologist.

Thomas à Kempis (actually Thomas Hemerken) (c.1379–1471), celebrated German monk and scholar, reputed author of the famous Imitatio Christi (Imitation of Christ).

Thomas Aquinas, Saint (c.1224–1274), Italian Roman Catholic theologian and philosopher who wrote the influential Summa contra gentiles (c.1258–64; English trans. as On the Truth of the Catholic Faith, 1955) and Summa theologiae (c.1265–73).

Thomas the Rhymer or Thomas Rymour of Erceldoune (c.1220–c.1297), Scottish prophet and poet.

Thomasius, Christian (1655–1728), German educator and philosopher.

Thomes, William Henry (1824–1895), American writer.

Thompson, Daniel Pierce (1795–1868), American novelist.

Thompson, Sir D'Arcy Wentworth (1860–1948), Scottish zoologist and classical scholar.

Thompson, Denman (1833–1911), American actor and dramatist.

Thompson, Dorothy (1894–1961), American journalist and writer.

Thompson, Edward Herbert (1856–1935), American archaeologist, author of People of the Serpent (1932).

Thompson, E(dward) P(almer) (1924–1993), English historian.

Thompson, Flora Jane (née Timms) (1876–1947), English writer and poet.

Thompson, Francis (1859–1907), esteemed English poet and writer, especially remembered for his poem The Hound of Heaven.

Thompson, (James) Maurice (1844–1901), American writer, best known for his novel Alice of Old Vincennes (1900).

Thompson, James Reuben (1823–1873), American editor, poet and writer.

Thompson, R(eginald) Campbell (1876–1941), English archaeologist and Oriental scholar.

Thompson, Vance (Charles) (1863–1925), American writer, dramatist and poet.

Thompson, William Tappan (1812–1882), American writer who was known for his humour.

Thompson, Zadock (1796–1856), American historian and naturalist.

Thoms, William John (1803–1885), English antiquarian and writer.

Thomsen, Christian Jürgensen (1788–1865), Danish archaeologist.

Thomsen, Wilhelm (1842–1927), Danish philologist.

Thomson, Sir Charles Wyville (1830–1882), Scottish naturalist, author of The Depths of the Sea (1873).

Thomson, James (1700–1748), Scottish poet who presaged the Romantic movement in such well-known pieces as The Seasons (1730), Rule Britannia (1740) and The Castle of Indolence (1748).

Thomson, James (1834–1882), Scottish poet who wrote under the name Bysshe Vanolis or BV, best remembered for The City of Dreadful Night (1874).

Thomson, Sir John Arthur (1861–1933), English naturalist.

Thomson, Joseph (1858–1895), Scottish geologist, naturalist and explorer who wrote on his travels in eastern Africa.

Thomson, Mortimer Neal (1831–1875), American writer who was known for his humour.

Thórarensen, Bjarni Vigfússon (1786–1841), Icelandic poet, a pioneering figure in the Romantic movement in Iceland.

Thorarensen, Jakob (1886–1972), Icelandic poet and short-story writer.

Thoreau, Henry David (1817–1862), famous American essayist and poet, celebrated for the classic prose works Civil Disobedience (1849) and Walden, or Life in the Woods (1854).

Thorgilsson, Ari (c.1067–1148), Icelandic writer.

Thorild, Thomas (actually Thomas Thorén) (1759–1808), Swedish poet and critic.

Thorláksson, Gudbrandur (1541–1627), Icelandic Lutheran bishop and scholar.

Thorndike, Edward Lee (1874–1949), American psychologist who was a leading figure in educational psychology.

Thornton, William (1759–1828), West Indies-born American writer.

Thoroddsen, Jón (1818–1868), Icelandic novelist and poet.

Thorpe, Rose Hartwick (1850–1939), American writer.

Thorpe, Thomas B(angs) (1815–1878), American writer and painter who was known as a humorist.

Thorsteinsson, Steingrímur (Bjarnason) (1831–1913), Icelandic poet and translator.

Thou, Jacques-Auguste de (1553–1617), French statesman, historian and bibliophile who was a pioneering figure in the field of scientific history.

Thucydides (5th Century BC), Greek historian who wrote a celebrated history of the Peloponnesian War.

Thurber, James (Grover) (1894– 1961), American writer and artist who was admired for his humour.

Thurlow, Edward, 2nd Baron (1781–1829), English writer and poet.

Thurneysen, Rudolf (1857–1940), Swiss linguist.

Thurnwald, Richard (1869–1954), Austrian anthropologist and sociologist.

Thurstone, L(ouis) L(eon) (1887–1955), American psychologist.

Thwaites, Reuben Gold (1853–1913), American historian.

Tibullus, (Albius) (c.55–c.19 BC), admired Roman poet who was a master of the elegy.

Tichener, Edward Bradford (1867–1927), English-born American psychologist.

Tickell, Thomas (1686–1740), English poet and translator.

Ticknor, George (1791–1871), American historian.

Tieck, (Johann) Ludwig (1773–1853), prominent German writer, critic, editor and poet.

Tiele, Cornelis Petrus (1830–1902), Dutch theologian and historian who was an influential figure in the development of the study of comparative religion.

Tiernan, Mary Spear (1836–1891), American novelist.

Tietjens, Eunice (Strong Hammond) (1884–1944), American poet, novelist, editor and translator.

Tikhonov, Nikolai Semyonovich (1896–1979), Russian poet and writer.

Tilak, Bal Gangadhar (1856–1920), notable Indian nationalist leader and scholar.

Tillemont, (Louis-) Sebastien Le Nain de (1637–1698), French historian.

Tillich, Paul (Johannes Oskar) (1886–1965), influential German-born American theologian and philosopher, author of the expansive Systematic Theology (3 vols, 1951–63).

Tillotson, John (1630–1694), English Anglican churchman who served as archbishop of Canterbury and became widely known for his popular sermons.

Tillyard, E(ustace) M(andeville) W(etenhall) (1889–1962), English literary scholar and critic.

Tilton, Theodore (1835–1907), American journalist, writer and poet.

Timaeus (c.356–c.260 BC), Greek historian.

Timmermans, Felix (1886–1947), admired Flemish novelist.

Timon of Phlius (c.325–c.235 BC), Greek philosopher and poet who was known for his scepticism.

Timrod, Henry (1828–1867), gifted American poet who became known as the 'Laureate of the Confederacy'.

Tinctoris, Johannes (c.1435–1511), important Franco-Flemish music theorist and lexicographer, editor of the first dictionary of musical terms (1495).

Tirmidhī, at- (actually Abū 'Isā Muhammad ibn 'Isā ibn Sawrah ibn Shaddād at-Tirmidhī) (9th Century), Arab scholar.

Tirso de Molina (actually Gabriel Téllez) (c.1584–1648), renowned Spanish dramatist, a master of both tragic and comic genres.

Tischendorf, (Lobegott Friedrich) Konstantin von (1815–1874), influential German biblical scholar who was a major figure in biblical textual criticism.

Titchener, Edward Bradford (1867–1927), English-born American experimental psychologist, author of the major study Experimental Psychology (4 vols, 1901–05).

Tocqueville, Alexis (Charles-Henri-Clérel) de (1805–1859), French political scientist, historian and politician, author of the classic De la democratie en Amérique (2 vols, 1835, 1840; English trans. as Democracy in America, 1945).

Todd, Mabel Loomis (1856–1932), American writer and poet.

Todi, Jacopone da (c.1230–1306), Italian poet who excelled in religious verse.

Todorov, Petko (1879–1916), Bulgarian writer.

Tokuda Shūsei (actually Tokuda Sueo) (1871–1943), Japanese novelist of the Naturalist school.

Tokugawa Mitsukuni (1628–1700), Japanese lord and historian, author of the important Dai Nihon shi (History of Great Japan).

Tokutomi Rōka (actually Tokutomi Tetsujirō) (1868–1927), Japanese novelist; brother of Tokutomi Sohō.

Tokutomi Sohō (actually Tokutomi Ichirō) (1863–1957), Japanese journalist and historian who wrote the major study Kinsei Nihon Kokuminshi (A History of the Japanese People in Modern Times, 1918–46); brother of Tokutomi Rōka.

Toland, John (1670–1722), prominent Irish freethinker and controversial writer, particularly known for his Christianity not Mysterious (1695).

Tolentino de Almeida, Nicolau (1740–1811), notable Portuguese poet who was a master of satire.

Tolkien J(ohn) R(onald) R(eul) (1892–1973), English scholar and writer, particularly known for his work as a linguist and as the author of the famous fantasy trilogy The Lord of the Rings (1954–55).

Tollens, Hendrik (1780–1856), Dutch poet, author of the national hymn of the Netherlands Wien Neerlandsch Bloed.

Toller, Ernst (1893–1939), German poet and dramatist who embraced Marxism; committed suicide as an exile in the US.

Tolman, Edward C(hace) (1886–1959), American psychologist, author of Purposive Behavior in Animals and Men (1932).

Tolson, Melvin B(eaunorus) (1898–1966), American poet, writer and dramatist.

Tolstoy, Alexei Konstantinovich, Count (1817–1875), Russian dramatist, poet and novelist; distant relative of Leo Tolstoy.

Tolstoy, Alexei Nikolaievich (1883–1945), Russian novelist and short-story writer.

Tolstoy, Leo (actually Lev Nokolaievich, Count Tolstoy) (1828–1910), Russian novelist, thinker and social reformer, author of the celebrated novels Voyna i mir (1865–69; English trans. as War and Peace, 1952) and Anna Karenina (1875–77).

Tomasi di Lampedusa, Giuseppe (1896–1957), Italian novelist who gained posthumous renown via his novel Il gattopardo (The Leopard, 1958).

Tominaga Nakamoto (18th Century), Japanese philosopher.

Tomkis, Thomas (c.1580–c.1634), English dramatist.

Tomlinson, H(enry) M(ajor) (1873–1958), English novelist and essayist.

Tompson, Benjamin (1642–1714), American poet.

Tönnies, Ferdinand Julius (1855–1936), German sociologist, author of Gemeinschaft und Gesellschaft (1887; English trans. as Community and Society, 1957).

Tooke, John Horne (1736–1812), English radical politician and linguist.

Toole, John Kennedy (1937–1969), American writer, author of the novel A Confederacy of Dunces (published 1980); committed suicide.

Toomer, Jean (1894–1967), American writer and poet.

Topelius, Zacharias (1818–1898), Finnish novelist, short-story writer and poet.

Töpffer, Rodolphe (1799–1846), Swiss artist, writer and politician.

Torga, Miguel (actually Adolfo Correia da Rocha) (1907–1995), Portuguese poet, dramatist and diarist.

Torrence, (Frederic) Ridgely (1875– 1950), American poet, dramatist and journalist.

Torrente Ballester, Gonzalo (1910–99), Spanish novelist, dramatist and literary critic.

Torres Bodet, Jaime (1902–74), Mexican poet, novelist and statesman; committed suicide.

Torres Naharro, Bartolomé de (c.1484–c.1525), Spanish dramatist.

Torres Villarroel, Diego de (c.1693–1770), Spanish mathematician, writer and poet, author of the celebrated picaresque memoirs the Vida (1743).

Torrey, Bradford (1843–1912), American essayist.

Torrey, Charles Cutler (1863–1956), notable American biblical scholar.

Tory, Geoffroy (c.1480–c.1533), French publisher, printer, orthographer, engraver and writer.

Totheroh, Dan (1895– 1976), American dramatist.

Tourgée, Albion W(inegar) (1838–1905), American writer.

Tourneur, Cyril (c.1575–1626), English dramatist and poet, known for his plays The Revenger's Tragedie (1607) and The Atheist's Tragedie, or the Honest Man's Revenge (1611).

Toussaint, François-Vincent (c.1715–1772), French writer.

Tout, Thomas Frederick (1855–1929), English historian.

Tovey, Sir Donald Francis (1875–1940), esteemed English music scholar.

Townley, James (1714–1778), English dramatist.

Townsend, Edward Waterman (1855–1942), American writer.

Townsend, George Alfred (1841–1914), American journalist, writer, poet and dramatist who wrote under the name Gath.

Townsend, Mary Ashley (Van Voorhis) (1832–1901), American novelist.

Townshend, Aurelian (c.1583–c.1643), English dramatist and poet.

Toynbee, Arnold (Joseph) (1889–1975), notable English historian, author of the expansive and controversial tome A Study of History (12 vols, 1934–61); father of (Theodore) Philip Toynbee.

Toynbee, (Theodore) Philip (1916–1981), English writer and editor; son of Arnold (Joseph) Toynbee.

Tozzer, Alfred M(arston) (1877–1954), American anthropologist and archaeologist, author of Social Origins and Social Continuities (1925).

Tradescant, John (1608–1662), English naturalist.

Traherne, Thomas (1637–1674), admired English writer and poet who espoused mysticism.

Traill, Catherine Parr Strickland (1802–1899), English-born Canadian writer who was known for her books on nature and for her children's books.

Traill, Henry Duff (1842–1900), English journalist, editor, critic, biographer and poet.

Train, Arthur (Cheney) (1875–1945), American lawyer, public official and writer.

Trakl, Georg (1887–1914), influential Austrian poet of the Expressionist school who was known for his haunting poems of decline and death.

Tranter, Nigel Godwin (1909–2000), Scottish historian and novelist who wrote a series of Western novels under the name Nye Tregold.

Traubel, Horace (1858–1919), American writer.

Traven, B (probably Otto Feige) (c.1882–1969), mysterious German-born Mexican novelist and short-story writer who veiled his life in legend and wrote under the name Traven Torsvan.

Travers, Ben (1886–1980), English novelist and dramatist.

Travers, P(amela) L(yndon) (actually Helen Lyndon Goff) (1899–1996), Australian-born English writer, best known for her children's book Mary Poppins (1934).

Trease, (Robert) Geoffrey (1909–1998), English writer, best known for his children's historical novels.

Trediakovsky, Vasily Kirillovich (1703–1769), Russian theorist and poet.

Treece, Henry (1911–1966), Welsh novelist and poet.

Treitschke, Heinrich von (1834–1896), German historian, author of the Deutsche Geschichte im 19. Jahrhundert (5 vols, 1879–94; English trans. as Treitschke's History of Germany in the Nineteenth Century, 7 vols 1915–19).

Trelawny, Edward John (1792–1881), English adventurer and writer, author of Adventures of a Younger Son (1831) and Recollections of the Last Days of Shelley and Byron (1858; revised edition as Records of Shelley, Byron and the Author, 1878).

Trench, Frederick Herbert (1865–1923), Irish poet.

Trench, Richard Chenevix (1807–1886), Irish prelate, philologist and poet.

Trendelenburg, Freidrich Adolf (1802–1872), German philosopher and philologist, author of Naturrecht auf dem Grunde der Ethik (Natural Law on the Basis of Ethics, 1860).

Tressel, Robert (c.1870–1911), Irish writer who wrote under the name Robert Noonan, author of the novel The Ragged Trousered Philanthropists (published 1914).

Trevelyan, Sir George Otto, 2nd Baron (1838–1928), English statesman and historian.

Trevelyan, G(eorge) M(acaulay) (1876–1962), English historian.

Trevisa, John of (c.1340–1402), English translator.

Triclinius, Demetrius (14th Century), important Byzantine scholar who edited the works of the ancient Greek poets.

Trilling, Diana (Rubin) (1905–1996), esteemed American critic and writer; wife of Lionel Trilling.

Trilling, Lionel (1905–1975), American critic and novelist; husband of Diana (Rubin) Trilling.

Trimmer, Sarah (née Kirby) (1741–1810), English writer of children's books.

Tripp, John (1926–1986), Welsh poet.

Trissino, Gian Giorgio (1478–1550), notable Italian poet, philologist and dramatist, author of the epic poem L'Italia liberata dai Goti (Italy Liberated from the Goths, 1547–48).

Tristan l'Hermite (c.1601–1655), significant French dramatist and poet who was also known as François l'Hermite, one of the principal figures in the creation of French classical drama.

Troeltsch, Ernst (1865–1923), learned German scholar, author of Die Soziallehren der christlichen Kirchen und Gruppen (1912; English trans. as The Social Teaching of the Christian Churches, 1931).

Trogus, Pompeius (1st Century BC), Roman historian.

Trollope, Anthony (1815–1882), notable English novelist, especially esteemed for his series of 'Barsetshire' novels; son of Frances Trollope.

Trollope, Frances (1780–1863), English writer; mother of Anthony Trollope.

Trotsky, Leon (actually Lev Davidovich Bronstein) (1879–1940), Russian Communist revolutionary and theorist; was assassinated on order of Stalin while in exile in Mexico.

Trotter, Wilfred (Batten Lewis) (1872–1939), English physician and sociologist, best known for his influential study Instincts of the Herd in Peace and War (1916).

Trowbridge J(ohn) T(ownsend) (1827–1916), American writer and poet.

Trubar, Primoz (1508–1586), Austrian theologian.

Trumbo, Dalton (1905–1976), American novelist and screenwriter, best remembered for his novel Johnny Got His Gun (1939).

Trumbull, Benjamin (1735–1820), American Congregationalist clergyman and historian.

Trumbull, John (1750–1831), American lawyer, judge and poet.

Trumbull, John (1756–1843), American painter, architect and writer.

Truth, Sojourner (actually Isabella Van Wagener) (c.1797–1883), famous American evangelist, Abolitionist and suffragist who was born a slave but was set free to pursue an active life as a reformer, 'author' of the dictated vol. The Narrative of Sojourner Truth (1851).

Ts'ao Chan (c.1715–1763), Chinese writer who was also known as Ts'ao Hsüeh-Ch'in, author of the celebrated novel Hung lou meng (Dream of the Red Chamber).

Ts'ao Chih (192–232), Chinese poet, a master of lyricism.

Tschudi, Gilg (1505–1572), Swiss scholar and chronicler, author of the valuable Chronicon Helveticum (Swiss Chronicle, 2 vols, 1734, 1736).

Tseng-tzu (505–c.436 BC), Chinese philosopher who was also known as Tseng Ts'an.

Tsou Yen (340–c.260 BC), Chinese philosopher.

Tsubouchi Shōyō (actually Tsubouchi Yūzō) (1859–1935), notable Japanese novelist, dramatist, critic and translator.

Tsuruya Namboku (1755–1829), Japanese dramatist of the Kabuki theatre.

Tsvetayeva (Efron), Marina Ivanovna (1892–1941), Russian poet and writer; committed suicide.

Tuchman, Barbara (Wertheim) (1912–1989), American historian, author of The Guns of August (1962) and Stilwell and the American Experience in China, 1911–1945 (1971).

Tucker, George (1775–1861), American historian, author of a Life of Thomas Jefferson (2 vols, 1837) and a History of the United States (4 vols, 1856–57).

Tucker, Nathaniel Beverley (1784–1851), American lawyer and writer who wrote under the name Edward William Sidney, author of the novels George Balcombe (1836) and The Partisan Leader (1836).

Tucker, St George (1752–1827), American jurist and writer.

Tuckerman, Frederick Goddard (1821–1873), American poet.

Tuckerman, Henry Theodore (1813–1871), American writer, essayist and biographer.

Tudor, William (1779–1830), American editor and writer.

Tu Fu (712–770), Chinese poet.

Tully, Jim (1888–1947), American novelist and short-story writer.

Tully, Richard Walton (1877–1945), American dramatist.

Tulsīdās (1543–1623), famous Indian poet who wrote the Rāmcaritmānas (The Holy Lake of Rama's Deeds).

Tung Chung-shu (c.179–c.104 BC), Chinese scholar who played a significant role in making Confucianism the state cult of China.

Tunstall, Cuthbert (1474–1559), English Anglican theologian and bishop of Durham.

Tunström, Göran (1938–2000), Swedish novelist, dramatist and poet.

Tupper, Martin Farquhar (1810–1889), English writer and poet, best known for his collection of verse Proverbial Philosophy (4 parts, 1838–76).

Turberville or Turbervile, George (c.1540–c.1596), English poet and translator, a pioneer of blank verse.

Turell, Jane (Colman) (1708–1735), American poet.

Turgenev, Ivan (Sergeievich) (1818–1883), celebrated Russian novelist, short-story writer, dramatist and poet, author of such notable works as the play Mesyats v derevne (1855; English trans. as A Month in the Country, 1933) and the novels Rudin (1856), Dvoryanskoye gnezdo (1859; English trans. as Home of the Gentry, 1970), Nakanune (1860; English trans. as On the Eve, 1950) and Otsy i deti (1862; English trans. as Fathers and Sons, 1950).

Turnbull, George (1698–1748), English philosopher, author of the Treatise on Ancient Painting (1739) and Principles of Moral and Christian Philosophy (2 vols, 1740).

Turner, Frederick Jackson (1861–1932), significant American historian, author of the essays The Significance of History (1891) and Problems in American History (1892), and the studies The Frontier in American History (1920) and The Significance of Sections in American History (1932).

Turner J(oseph) M(allord) W(illiam) (1775–1851), English painter who also wrote poetry.

Turner, Ralph E(dmund) (1893–1964), American cultural historian.

Turner, Sharon (1768–1847), English historian, best known for his literary studies.

Turner, Walter James Redfern (1889–1946), Australian poet, novelist and critic.

Tūsī, Nasīr ad-Dīn at- (1201–1274), Persian philosopher, scientist and mathematician.

Tusser, Thomas (c.1524–1580), English poet and writer on agriculture.

Tutuola, Amos (1920–1997), notable Nigerian novelist and short-story writer.

Tuwim, Julian (1894–1953), Polish poet who was admired for his lyric gifts.

Twain, Mark (actually Samuel Langhorne Clemens) (1835–1910), celebrated American writer, journalist and lecturer, renowned for his pointed humour and for such classics as The Adventures of Tom Sawyer (1876) and The Adventures of Huckleberry Finn (1885).

Twardowski, Samuel (1600–1661), Polish writer.

Twichell, Joseph Hopkins (1838–1918), American Congregationalist clergyman and writer.

Twysden, Sir Roger (1597–1672), English political pamphleteer and constitutional historian, author of the Historiae Anglicanae Scriptores X (1652), Certaine Considerations upon the Government of England (1655) and An Historical Vindication of the Church of England (1657).

Tyard, Pontus de (c.1522–1605), French poet, writer and churchman.

Tyler, Moses Coit (1835–1900), American literary historian, author of the important studies History of American Literature, 1607–1765 (2 vols, 1878) and Literary History of the American Revolution (2 vols, 1897).

Tyler, Royall (1757–1826), American lawyer, jurist, dramatist and poet, author of the first American comedy The Contrast (1787).

Tylor, Sir Edward Burnett (1832–1917), eminent English anthropologist who wrote the significant study Primitive Culture (1871).

Tynan, Katharine (1861–1931), Irish poet and novelist.

Tynan, Kenneth Peacock (1927–1980), English drama critic and essayist.

Tyndale, William (c.1494–1536), English biblical translator and Protestant martyr; was condemned as a heretic and burned at the stake.

Tyndall, John (1820–1893), English physicist and writer.

Tyrrell, George (1861–1909), Irish Roman Catholic priest and theologian of the Modernist persuasion.

Tyrtaeus (7th Century BC), Greek poet.

Tyrwhitt, Thomas (1730–1786), English literary scholar and editor.

Tytler, Patrick Fraser (1791–1849), Scottish lawyer and historian.

Tyutchev, Fyodor (Ivanovich) (1803–1873), Russian poet and writer.

Tzara, Tristan (1896–1963), influential Romanian-born French poet and essayist, founder of the Dada movement.

Tzetzes, John (12th Century), Byzantine poet and scholar.

Tzu Ssu (483–402 BC), Chinese philosopher, author of the classic Doctrine of the Mean; grandson of Confucius.

Uchimura Kanzō (1861–1930), Japanese religious philosopher and writer who founded his own Japanese Christian Church.

Udall, Nicholas (c.1505–1556), English dramatist and translator, author of the comic play Ralph Roister Doister (c.1553).

Ueda Akinari (actually Ueda Senjiro) (1734–1809), Japanese writer and poet.

Ugarte, Manuel (1878–1951), Argentine writer, best known for his short stories and for his opposition to what he described as the imperialism of El coloso del norte (The Colossus of the North), i.e. the USA.

Ugttenbogaert, Johannes (1557–1644), Dutch theologian.

Uhland, (Johann) Ludwig (1787–1862), German poet and essayist who was especially admired for the lyricism of his verse.

Ukrainka, Lesya (actually Larisa Petrovna Kosach-Kvitka) (1871–1913), Ukrainian poet who excelled in both lyric and dramatic verse.

Ulfilas (c.311–c.382), famous Christian missionary, bishop, writer and translator who is reputed to have created the Gothic alphabet and prepared the earliest translation of the Bible into a Germanic language.

Ulloa, Antonio de (1716–1795), Spanish scientist, naval officer, government official and writer.

Ulpian (actually Domitius Ulpianus) (died 228), Roman jurist and writer on the law.

'Umar ibn Abī Rabī'ah (actually 'Umar ibn 'Abd Allāh ibn Abī Rabī'ah al-Makhzūmī) (644–c.715), celebrated Arab poet of amatoric verse.

'Umarī, al- (actually Shihāb ad-Dīn Ahmad ibn Fadl Allāh al-'Umarī) (1301–1349), Syrian scholar who was an authority on Mamluk history.

Unamuno (y Jugo), Miguel de (1864–1936), notable Spanish scholar, novelist and short-story writer, author of the study Del sentimiento trágico de la vida (1913; English trans. as The Tragic Sense of Life in Men and in Peoples, 1921) and the novel San Manuel bueno, mártir (1931).

Underhill, Evelyn (1875–1941), English mystic, poet and novelist, best remembered for her studies Mysticism (1911), The Mystic Way (1913) and Worship (1936).

Underhill, John (c.1597–1672), American military leader who wrote an account of his role in the war against the Pequot Indians in Newes from America (1638).

Underwood, Francis Henry (1825–1894), American novelist, editor and lawyer.

Undset, Sigrid (1882–1949), eminent Norwegian novelist whose most important achievement was her trilogy Kristan Lavransdatter (1920–22); won the Nobel Prize for Literature (1928).

Ungaretti, Giuseppe (1888–1970), Italian poet, founder of the Hermetic movement.

Unruh, Fritz von (1885–1970), admired German dramatist, novelist and poet, a prominent Expressionist.

Untermeyer, Jean Starr (1886–1970), American poet, wife of Louis Untermeyer.

Untermeyer, Louis (1885–1977), American poet, writer, critic and translator; husband of Jean Starr Untermeyer.

Updike, Daniel Berkeley (1860–1941), American printer and scholar.

Upfield, Arthur William (1888–1964), English-born Australian novelist, short-story writer and essayist.

Upham, Charles Wentworth (1802–1875), American Unitarian minister and writer.

Uppdal, Kristofer (1878–1961), Norwegian novelist and poet, author of the expansive proletarian novel Dansen gjenom skuggeheimen (The Dance Through the World of Shadows, 10 vols, 1911–24).

Urquhart, Sir Thomas (1611–1660), learned Scottish writer, poet and translator.

Usakligil, Halid Ziya (1866–1945), Turkish novelist, dramatist and essayist, particularly admired for his novel Mavi ve siyah (The Blue and the Black, 1897).

Usāmah ibn Munqidh (died 1188), Arab writer who wrote a celebrated autobiography.

Usk, Thomas (died 1388), English writer, author of The Testament of Love.

Usman dan Fodio (actually 'Uthmān ibn Fūdī) (1754–1817), Arab mystic, reformer and philosopher, author of the treatise Bayan wujub al-hijrah (1806).

Uspensky, Gleb (Ivanovich) (1843–1902), Russian writer; committed suicide.

Ussher, James (1581–1656), Irish scholar, theologian and Anglican archbishop of Armagh.

Uttley, Alison (1884–1976), English writer of children's books.

Vacarius (c.1117–c.1199), Italian-born English scholar of civil and canon law.

Vācaspati Miśra (9th Century), Hindu philosopher.

Vadianus, Joachim (actually Joachim von Watt) (1484–1551), Swiss Protestant reformer, preacher and historian.

Vaihinger, Hans (1852–1933), German philosopher, author of Die Philosophie des Als Ob (1911; English trans. as The Philosophy of 'As If', 1924).

Vaillant, George C(lapp) (1901–1945), American anthropologist and archaeologist.

Vair, Guillaume du (1556–1621), important French philosopher who espoused a form of Christian Stoicism.

Vajiravudh (1881–1925), king of Siam (1910–25), dramatist, writer and translator.

Vala, Katri (1901–1944), Finnish poet.

Valaorítis, Aristotelís (1824–1879), Greek poet and statesman who wrote with patriotic fervor.

Valdés, Alfonso de (c.1490–1532), Spanish court official and scholar, brother of Juan de Valdés.

Valdés, Juan de (c.1498–1541), Spanish-born Italian court official and scholar; brother of Alfonso de Valdés.

Valencia, Guillermo (1873–1943), prominent Colombian statesman and poet.

Valentine, David Thomas (1801–1869), American antiquarian.

Valentinus (2nd Century), Egyptian religious philosopher of the Gnostic persuasion.

Valera y Alcalá Galiano, Juan (1824–1905), Spanish novelist.

Valerius Flaccus, Gaius (1st Century), Roman poet who wrote his own version of the Argonautica, much of which was based on the work of Apollonius Rhodius.

Valerius Maximus (1st Century), Roman historian and moralist, author of the Factorum et dictorum memorabilium libri ix (Nine Books of Memorable Deeds and Sayings).

Valéry, (Ambroise-)Paul(-Tous-Saint-Jules) (1871–1945), French poet, writer and dramatist.

Valla, Lorenzo (1407–1457), influential Italian philosopher and literary critic who espoused Humanism.

Vallabha (1479–1531), Hindu philosopher.

Valle, Pietro della (1586–1652), Italian traveller who left important accounts of his travels to Persia and India.

Vallée-Poussin, Louis de la (1869–1938), French scholar.

Valle-Inclán, Ramón María del (1869–1936), esteemed Spanish novelist, dramatist and poet.

Vallejo, César (1893–1938), Peruvian poet.

Vallentine, Benjamin Bennaton (1843–1926), English-born American journalist and dramatist.

Vallès, Jules(-Louis-Joseph) (1832–1885), French journalist, novelist and Socialist.

Vallières, Pierre (1938–1998), Canadian writer, best remembered for his Les Negres blancs d'Amerique (1968; English trans. as White Niggers of America, 1971).

Valverde, José María (1926–1996), eminent Spanish poet, literary historian and translator.

Van Dine, S S (actually Willard Huntington Wright) (1888–1939), American literary critic and writer, creator of the detective Philo Vance.

Van Doren, Carl (Clinton) (1885–1950), American literary critic, biographer and novelist; brother of Mark (Albert) Van Doren.

Van Doren, Mark (Albert) (1894–1972), American poet, writer and literary critic; brother of Carl (Clinton) Van Doren.

Van Druten, John (William) (1901–1957), English-born American dramatist and novelist.

Van Dyke, Henry (1852–1933), American Presbyterian minister, short-story writer, essayist and poet.

Van Dyke, John C(harles) (1856–1932), American writer.

Van Gennep, Arnold (1873–1957), French ethnographer and folklorist.

Van Loon, Hendrik Willem (1882–1944), Dutch-born American writer.

Van Vechten, Carl (1880–1964), American novelist and music and drama critic.

Vanbrugh, Sir John (1664–1726), English architect and dramatist.

Vančura, Vladislav (1891–1942), Czech writer.

Vane, (Vane) Sutton (1888–1963), English dramatist, author of Outward Bound (1923).

Vane, Sutton (actually Vane Sutton-Vane) (1888–1963), English dramatist who scored a notable success with his play Outward Bound (1923).

Vaptsarov, Nikola (1909–1942), Bulgarian writer and poet.

Varāhamihira (505–587), Indian philosopher, astronomer and mathematician.

Varenius, Bernhardus (actually Bernhard Varen) (1622–c.1650), German geographer, author of Geographia generalis (1650).

Varnhagen von Ense, Karl August (1785–1858), German diplomat, writer and biographer.

Varro, Marcus Terentius (116–27 BC), renowned Roman scholar and poet who excelled as a satirist.

Varro, Publius Terentius (c.82–37 BC), Roman poet.

Varthema, Lodovico de (c.1470–c.1510), Italian adventurer and traveller, author of Itinerario de Ludouico de Varthema Bolognese (1510; English trans. as Travels of Ludovico di Varthema, 1863).

Vasari, Giorgio (1511–1574), Italian painter, architect and writer, author of the important Le Vite de' più eccellenti architetti, pittori, et scultori italiani (The Lives of the Most Eminent Italian Architects, Painters and Sculptors, 1550).

Vasconcelos, Jorge Ferreira de (1515–1585), Portuguese dramatist.

Vasconcelos, José (1882–1959), Mexican educator, politician, philosopher, essayist and memoirist.

Vasubandhu (4th Century), Indian philosopher and logician.

Vattel, Emmerich de (1714–1767), Swiss jurist, author of Le Droit des gens (The Law of Nations, 1758).

Vaugelas, Claude Favre, Baron de Perouges, Seigneur de (1585–1650), French grammarian.

Vaughan, Henry (c.1621–1695), esteemed English poet, writer and physician who found inspiration in religious themes; brother of Thomas Vaughan.

Vaughan, Thomas (c.1621–1666), English poet and writer who often wrote under the name Eugenius Philalethes; brother of Henry Vaughan.

Vaughan, William (1577–1641), Welsh poet and colonizer.

Vauquelin de La Fresnaye, Jean, Sieur des Yveteaux (1536–c.1607), French magistrate and poet who introduced satirical literature to France.

Vauvenargues, Luc de Clapiers, Marquis de (1715–1747), French essayist and moralist.

Vaux, Thomas, 2nd Baron (1510–1556), English poet.

Vazov, Ivan Minchev (1850–1921), Bulgarian poet, dramatist, novelist and short-story writer.

Veblen, Thorstein (Bunde) (1857–1929), American economist and social scientist, author of The Theory of the Leisure Class (1899) and The Theory of Business Enterprise (1904).

Vedāntadeśika (1268–1370), Indian theologian, philosopher and writer.

Vedder, Elihu (1836–1923), American painter, illustrator and writer.

Vedel, Anders Sørensen (1542–1616), Danish historian, ballad collector and translator.

Vega, Garcilaso de la (1503–1536), gifted Spanish poet who was a master of lyricism.

Vega, Garcilaso de la (1539–1616), notable Spanish historian.

Vega Carpio, Lope Félix de (1562–1635), Spanish dramatist and poet who was also known as Lope de Vega.

Veitch, John (1829–1894), Scottish poet and scholar.

Veldeke, Heinrich von (12th Century), German poet.

Vélez de Guevara, Luis (1579–1644), Spanish poet, dramatist and novelist.

Velichkov, Konstantin (1855–1907), Bulgarian writer.

Velikovsky, Immanuel (1895–1979), Russian-born American writer who became well known for his unorthodox theories of cosmogony and history.

Venette, Jean de (c.1308–c.1369), French chronicler and poet, author of a valuable Latin chronicle of his era.

Venn, John (1834–1923), English logician and writer.

Vercors (actually Jean-Marcel Bruller) (1902–1991), French novelist, dramatist, essayist and artist-engraver.

Verde, (José Joaquim) Césario (1855–1886), Portuguese poet.

Verga, Giovanni (1840–1922), eminent Italian novelist who founded the verismo school of Italian novelists.

Vergerio, Pietro Paolo (1498–1565), influential Italian educator and theorist.

Vergil, Polydore (c.1470–1555), Italian scholar, author of the important Anglicae historia libri XXVI (Twenty-Six Books of English History, 1546 et seq.).

Verhaeren, Émile (1855–1916), renowned Belgian poet who wrote in French.

Veríssimo, Érico Lopes (1905–75), Brazilian novelist, critic and literary historian.

Verlaine, Paul (1844–1896), French poet, celebrated for his La Bonne Chanson (1870), Romances sans paroles (1872) and Sagesse (1880).

Vermigli, Pietro Martire (1500–1562), prominent Italian religious reformer and theologian.

Verne, Jules (1828–1905), French novelist of science fiction.

Verner, Karl (Adolf) (1846–1896), Danish linguist.

Verplanck, Gulian Crommelin (1786–1870), American lawyer, politician, journalist and writer.

Verri, Pietro, Conte (1728–1797), Italian government official, journalist and writer.

Verschaeve, Cyriel (1874–1949), Belgian writer.

Vertue, George (1684–1756), English engraver and antiquarian who left valuable notes on the history of the arts.

Verwey, Albert (1865–1937), notable Dutch poet and literary historian.

Very, Jones (1813–1880), American mystic and poet; brother of Lydia Louise Ann Very.

Very, Lydia Louise Ann (1823–1901), American poet; sister of Jones Very.

Vesaas, Tarjei (1897–1970), Norwegian novelist, short-story writer and poet.

Vestdijk, Simon (1898–1971), Dutch novelist and poet.

Veuillot, Louis (1813–1883), French novelist, biographer, polemicist and poet.

Vian, Boris (1920–1959), French novelist, dramatist and poet.

Viau, Théophile de (1590–1626), French poet and dramatist.

Vicente, Gil (c.1465–c.1536), significant Portuguese dramatist and poet.

Vico, Giambattista (1668–1744), influential Italian philosopher, author of the important Scienza Nuova (1721–22).

Victor, Frances Fuller (1826–1902), American poet and writer.

Victor, Metta Victoria (1831–1886), American writer.

Victor, Sextus Aurelius (4th Century), Roman historian.

Victorinus, Gaius Marius (4th Century), Christian theologian.

Victorinus of Pettau (died c.304), Latin Christian writer and martyr.

Vida, Marco Girolamo (c.1480–1566), Italian poet who was known as the 'Christian Virgil'.

Vidalín, Jón Thorkelsson (1666–1720), Icelandic Lutheran bishop and writer.

Vidyasagar, Isvar Chandra (1820–1891), Hindu educator, social reformer and writer.

Vieira, António (1608–1697), Portuguese Jesuit missionary, diplomat and writer.

Vielé-Griffin, Francis (actually Egbert Ludovicus Viele) (1864–1937), American-born French poet who embraced Symbolism.

Viereck, George Sylvester (1884–1962), German-born American writer, poet and dramatist.

Vierkandt, Alfred Ferdinand (1867–1953), German sociologist.

Vigfússon, Gudbrandur (1827–1889), learned Icelandic scholar who was an authority on Old Norse.

Vigny, Alfred de (1797–1863), French poet, dramatist and writer, one of the principal Romanticists of his era.

Vikélas, Dimítrios (1835–1908), Greek poet.

Vilakazi, Benedict Wallet (1906–1947), South African Zulu poet and writer.

Villagrá, Gaspar Pérez de (c.1555–c.1620), Spanish explorer and poet.

Villani, Giovanni (c.1275–1348), Italian chronicler, author of the expansive Cronica (12 vols, c.1308 et seq.).

Villard, Henry (actually Ferdinand Heinrich Gustav Hilgard) (1835–1900), German-born American journalist and financier; father of Oswald Garrison Villard.

Villard, Oswald Garrison (1872–1949), American journalist, editor and publisher; son of Henry Villard.

Villegas, Esteban Manuel de (1589–1669), Spanish poet, best known for his Poesías eróticas y amatorias (1617–18).

Villehardouin, Geoffroi de (c.1150–c.1213), French Marshal of Champagne and chronicler, author of an account of the Fourth Crusade, Histoire de l'empire de Constantinople (c.1209), of which he was a prominent leader.

Villena, Enrique de (c.1384–1434), Spanish writer.

Villiers de l'Isle-Adam, Jean-Marie-Mathias-Philippe-Auguste, Comte de (1838–1889), notable French poet, dramatist and writer, particularly known for his play Axël (1886).

Villon, François (actually François de Montcorbier or de Logos) (1431–c.1463), French poet and criminal, author of Le Lais (The Legacy; also known as Le Petit Testament) and Le Testament (also known as Le Grand Testament).

Vinal, Harold (1891–1965), American poet.

Vincent of Beauvais (c.1190–1264), celebrated French scholar, author of the important encyclopedia Speculum majus (Great Mirror).

Vincent of Lérins, Saint (died c.449), Christian priest, monk and theologian who wrote an attack on the doctrine of predestination in his Commonitoria (Memoranda, c.435).

Viner, Charles (1678–1756), English legal scholar, author of A General Abridgement of Law and Equity (23 vols, 1742–53).

Vinet, Alexandre-Rodolphe (1797–1847), Swiss theologian and writer who founded the Free Church of French-speaking Switzerland.

Vinje, Aasmund Olafson (1818–1870), Norwegian journalist and poet.

Vinogradoff, Sir Paul (Gavrilovich) (1854–1925), Russian-born English legal scholar, author of the valuable Villeinage in England (1892).

Viollet-le-Duc, Eugène-Emmanuel (1814–1879), eminent French architect and writer of the Gothic Revival, author of the Dictionnaire raisonné de l'architecture française du XIe au XVIe siècle (1854–68) and Dictionnaire raisonné du mobilier français de l'époque carlovingienne à la Rénaissance (1858–75).

Virgil or Vergil (actually Publius Vergilius Maro) (70–19 BC), Roman poet whose masterpiece was the unfinished Aeneid (c.30–19 BC).

Vir Singh, Bhai (1872–1957), significant Sikh theologian, writer and poet.

Vischer, Friedrich Theodor (1807–1887), German literary critic and aesthetician.

Vise, Jean Donneau de (1638–1710), French writer and publisher.

Visscher, Ann Roemers (c.1583–1651), Dutch poet; daughter of Roemer Visscher.

Visscher, Roemer (1547–1620), Dutch poet; father of Ann Roemers Visscher.

Viśvanātha (17th Century), Indian philosopher.

Vital, Hayyim ben Joseph (c.1542–1620), Jewish Kabbalist scholar.

Vitoria, Francisco de (1486–1546), esteemed Spanish Roman Catholic theologian.

Vitruvius (actually Marcus Vitruvius Pollio) (1st Century BC), Roman architect and engineer who wrote the famous treatise De architectura.

Vitry, Philippe de (1291–1361), French Roman Catholic bishop, diplomat, writer, poet and composer.

Vittorini, Elio (1908–1966), prominent Italian novelist, literary critic and translator, particularly known for his novel Conversazione in Sicilia (1941; English trans. as Conversation in Sicily, 1948).

Vivekananda (1862–1902), Hindu philosopher and social reformer.

Vives, Juan Luis (1492–1540), Spanish scholar who wrote De anima et vita libri tres (Three Books on the Soul and Life, 1538).

Vivien, Renée (actually Pauline Tarn) (1877–1909), French poet.

Vizetelly, Frank (actually Francis Horace Vizetelly) (1864–1938), English-born American philologist and lexicographer.

Vodnik, Valentin (1758–1819), Slovenian writer.

Voetius, Gisbertus (1589–1676), Dutch Reformed theologian, Semitic scholar and writer.

Vogelsang, Karl, Freiherr von (1818–1890), German-born Austrian Roman Catholic social reformer and writer who espoused a romantic form of Socialism.

Vogt, Nils Collett (1864–1937), Norwegian novelist and poet.

Voigt, Georg (1827–1891), German historian.

Voiture, Vincent (1597–1648), French poet and letter writer.

Volkelt, Johannes (1848–1930), German philosopher.

Volney, Constantin-François de Chasseboeuf, Comte de (1757–1820), French historian and philosopher, particularly known for his Les Ruines, ou méditations sur les révolutions des empires (1791; English trans. as The Ruins: or A Survey of the Revolutions of Empires, 1795).

Voltaire (actually François-Marie Arouet) (1694–1778), French dramatist, writer and poet, champion of free inquiry and a master satirist in his Candide, ou l'Optimisme (1759).

Von Arnim, Elizabeth (actually Mary Annette Beauchamp) (1866–1941), Australian novelist.

Vondel, Joost van den (1587–1679), notable Dutch dramatist and poet, author of the dramatic trilogy Lucifer (1654), Adam in ballingschap (1664) and Noah (1667).

Vörösmarty, Mihály (1800–1855), important Hungarian poet and dramatist, author of the famous fairy play Csongor és Tünde (1830).

Vorse, Mary Heaton (1874–1966), American novelist.

Voss, Johann Heinrich (1751–1826), German poet and translator.

Vossius (actually Gerhard Johannes Voss) (1577–1649), important Dutch theologian.

Vossius, Isaac (1618–1689), Dutch scholar.

Voynich, Ethel Lillian (née Boole) (1864–1960), Irish novelist, best known for The Gadfly (1897).

Vrichlický, Jaroslav (actually Emil Frída) (1853–1912), Czech poet, dramatist and translator.

Vulpius, Christian August (1762–1827), German novelist, best remembered for Rinaldo Rinaldini, der Rauberhauptmann (Rinaldo Rinaldini, the Robber Captain, 3 vols, 1797–1800).

Vyazemsky, Prince Pyotr Andreievich (1792–1878), Russian poet.

Wace, Robert (c.1115–c.1183), Anglo-Norman poet, author of the Roman de Brut (1155) and the Roman de Rou (1160–74).

Wach, Joachim (1898–1955), learned German Protestant theologian and scholar.

Wackenroder, Wilhelm Heinrich (1773–1798), significant German critic and writer of Romanticism.

Wackernagel, Jacob (1853–1938), Swiss linguist who was known for his authoritative works on Sanskrit.

Waddell, Helen Jane (1889–1965), English scholar and translator.

Waddell, Lawrence Austine (1854–1938), English Orientalist and archaeologist.

Waddington, William Henry (1826–1894), French politician, diplomat and scholar.

Wade, Sir Thomas Francis (1818–1895), English Sinologist.

Wagner, Adolph (1835–1917), German economist.

Wägner, Elin (1882–1949), Swedish novelist.

Wain, John (Barrington) (1925–1994), English writer, poet, dramatist and critic.

Waitz, Georg (1813–1886), German constitutional historian.

Waitz, Theodor (1821–1864), German psychologist and anthropologist.

Walafrid Strabo (c.808–849), German Benedictine abbot, theologian and poet.

Waley, Arthur (actually Arthur David Schloss) (1889–1966), English poet, scholar and translator.

Walī Allāh, Shāh (c.1702–1762), influential Indian Islamic theologian.

Walker, David (1785–1830), black American Abolitionist who called upon slaves to take up arms for their freedom in his pamphlet Appeal... to the Colored Citizens of the World (1829).

Walker, Francis Amasa (1840–1897), American economist and statistician.

Wallace, Alfred Russel (1823–1913), Welsh naturalist, author of Contributions to the Theory of Natural Selection (1870).

Wallace, Horace Binney (1817–1852), American lawyer and essayist.

Wallace, Irving (1916–1990), American writer.

Wallace, Lew(is) (1827–1905), American soldier, lawyer, diplomat, novelist and poet, best remembered for his novel Ben Hur: A Tale of the Christ (1880).

Wallace (Richard Horatio) Edgar (1875–1932), English novelist and dramatist, best known for his detective fiction.

Wallace, William Ross (1819–1881), American lawyer and poet, author of The Hand That Rocks the Cradle.

Wallack, Lester (actually John Johnstone Wallack) (1820–1888), American actor, dramatist and theater manager.

Wallant, Edward Lewis (1926–1962), American writer and graphic artist.

Wallas, Graham (1858–1932), English educator and sociologist, author of The Great Society (1914).

Waller, Edmund (1606–1687), English poet, best remembered for his celebrated Go, lovely Rose!

Waller, Max (actually Maurice Warlomont) (1866–1895), Belgian poet and editor.

Waller, Willard Walter (1899–1945), notable American sociologist, author of the important study The Sociology of Teaching (1932).

Wallis, Wilson D(allam) (1886–1970), American anthropologist who wrote Messiahs: Christian and Pagan (1918) and Messiahs: Their Role in Civilization (1943).

Walpole, Horace, 4th Earl of Oxford (actually Horatio Walpole) (1717–1797), English writer and collector who wrote voluminous letters and the Gothic novel The Castle of Otranto (1765).

Walpole, Sir Hugh (Seymour) (1884–1941), New Zealand novelist, dramatist and critic.

Walras, (Marie-Esprit-) Léon (1834–1910), French-born Swiss economist, author of the important study Éléments d'économie politique pure (1874–77; English trans. as Elements of Pure Economics).

Walsh, Robert (1784–1859), American journalist and writer.

Walsh, William (1663–1708), English poet.

Walsingham, Thomas (died c.1422), English Benedictine monk and chronicler.

Waltari, Mika (Toimi) (1908–79), Finnish novelist.

Walter, Eugene (1874–1941), American dramatist.

Walter, Thomas (1696–1725), American Congregationalist minister, writer and poet.

Walther, Carl Ferdinand Wilhelm (1811–1887), German-born American Lutheran theologian and writer of conservative views.

Walther von der Vogelweide (c.1170–c.1230), illustrious German poet whose subjects ranged from religion to love.

Walton, Izaak (1593–1683), English writer, best known for his classic The Compleat Angler, or the Contemplative Man's Recreation (1653).

Walwyn, William (mid-17th Century), English religious and political pamphleteer who was a leader of the Levellers.

Wang An-shih (1021–1086), Chinese statesman, poet and writer.

Wang Ch'ung (27–c.100), Chinese philosopher who espoused a rationalistic naturalism.

Wang Fu-chih (1619–1692), Chinese scholar and poet.

Wang Ruowang (1918–2001), Chinese writer whose trenchant criticism of first the Nationalist and then the Communist regimes led to frequent periods of incarceration.

Wang Shih-chen (1526–1590), Chinese historian.

Wang Shih-fu (c.1250–c.1337), Chinese dramatist.

Wang Wei (699–759), renowned Chinese poet and painter.

Wang Yang-ming (1472–1529), important Chinese philosopher of the Neo-Confucianist school.

Wang Ying-lin (1223–1292), Chinese scholar.

Wanley, Humfrey (1672–1726), English palaeographer, author of the standard catalogue of Anglo-Saxon manuscripts (1705); son of Nathaniel Wanley.

Wanley, Nathaniel (1634–1680), English divine and poet; father of Humfrey Wanley.

Warburg, Amy (1866–1929), German art historian.

Warburton, Eliot (actually Bartholomew Eliott George Warburton) (1810–1852), Irish traveller and writer, particularly known for The Crescent and the Cross, or, Romance and Realities of Eastern Travel (1845).

Warburton, William (1698–1779), English Anglican bishop and writer, author of The Alliance Between Church and State (1736) and The Divine Legation of Moses (2 vols, 1737, 1741).

Ward, Artemus (actually Charles Farrar Browne) (1838–1867), American lecturer and writer of a humorous turn.

Ward, Elizabeth Stuart Phelps (1844–1911), American novelist, short-story writer and poet.

Ward, Mrs Humphry (née Mary Augusta Arnold) (1851–1920), English novelist, best remembered for her Robert Elsmere (1888).

Ward, James (1843–1925), English psychologist and philosopher, author of Psychological Principles (1918).

Ward, Lester Frank (1841–1913), American sociologist, author of Dynamic Sociology (2 vols, 1883).

Ward, Nathaniel (c.1578–1652), English Puritan minister, writer and poet.

Ward, Ned (actually Edward Ward) (1667–1731), English poet who wrote the satirical A Trip to New England (1699).

Ward, Plumer (actually Robert Ward) (1765–1846), English lawyer, politician and writer.

Ward, Samuel (1814–1884), American journalist and writer; brother of Julia Ward Howe.

Ward, William George (1812–1882), English theologian and writer who was a radical member of the Oxford Movement.

Ware, Henry (1764–1845), American Unitarian clergyman and polemicist; father of William Ware.

Ware, William (1797–1852), American Unitarian clergyman and novelist; son of Henry Ware.

Warner, Anna Bartlett (1827–1915), American writer of children's novels who wrote under the name Amy Lothrop; sister of Susan Bogert Warner.

Warner, Charles Dudley (1829–1900), American novelist and essayist.

Warner, Rex (Ernest) (1905–1986), English poet, novelist, critic and translator.

Warner, Susan Bogert (1819–1885), American writer of children's novels who wrote under the name Elizabeth Wetherell; sister of Anna Bartlett Warner.

Warner, Sylvia Townsend (1893–1978), English novelist and poet.

Warner, William (c.1558–1609), English poet, writer and translator.

Warner, W(illiam) Lloyd (1898–1970), American anthropologist.

Warren, Caroline Matilda (c.1787–1844), American writer.

Warren, John Byrne Leicester, Baron de Tabley (1835–1895), English poet and dramatist.

Warren, Mercy Otis (1728–1814), American writer and poet.

Warren, Robert Penn (1905–1989), notable American novelist and poet; was the first Poet Laureate of the US (1986–87).

Warren, Samuel (1807–1877), English novelist, author of Passages from the Diary of a Late Physician (1832–38), Ten Thousand a Year (1840–41) and Now and Then (1847).

Warton, Joseph (1722–1800), English classical scholar and critic; son of Thomas Warton, and brother of Thomas Warton, the Poet Laureate.

Warton, Thomas (c.1688–1745), English poet; father of Joseph and Thomas Warton.

Warton, Thomas (1728–1790), English critic and poet; became Poet Laureate of the United Kingdom (1785); son of Thomas Warton and brother of Joseph Warton.

Washburne, Elihu B (1816–1887), American politician and historian.

Washington, Booker T(aliaferro) (1856–1915), prominent American reformer, educator and writer, author of the famous autobiography Up From Slavery (1901).

Wassermann, Jakob (1873–1934), notable German novelist, especially remembered for Der Fall Maurizius (1928; English trans. as The Maurizius Case, 1929).

Wast, Hugo (actually Gustavo Martínez Zuviría) (1883–1962), prominent Argentine novelist and short-story writer.

Watkins, Vernon Phillips (1906–1967), Welsh poet.

Watson, John B(roadus) (1878–1958), influential American psychologist, author of Behavior: An Introduction to Comparative Psychology (1914), Psychology from the Standpoint of a Behaviorist (1919) and Behaviorism (1925).

Watson, Sir (John) William (1858–1935), English poet, best known for his April, April, Laugh Thy Girlish Laughter.

Watson, Richard (1737–1816), English Anglican bishop and writer, author of Apology for Christianity (1776) and Apology for the Bible (1796).

Watson, Thomas (c.1557–1592), English poet and translator who was admired for his sonnets.

Watsuji Tetsurō (1889–1960), Japanese philosopher and historian.

Watt, Robert (1774–1819), Scottish bibliographer, compiler of the valuable Bibliotheca Britannica, or a General Index to British and Foreign Literature (published 1824).

Watts, Alan (1915–1973), English-born American Zen Buddhist and writer.

Watts, Alaric Alexander (1797–1864), English journalist and poet.

Watts, Isaac (1647–1748), notable English Nonconformist minister, hymnist and poet, especially known for his hymns O God, Our Help in Ages Past and When I Survey the Wondrous Cross.

Watts, Mary S(tanbery) (1868–1958), American novelist.

Watts-Dunton, Walter Theodore (1832–1914), English poet and critic.

Waugh, Alec (actually Alexander Raban Waugh) (1898–1981), English novelist and travel writer; brother of Evelyn (Arthur St John) Waugh.

Waugh, Auberon (Alexander) (1939–2001), English writer and journalist who became best known for his caustic views on politics and society; son of Evelyn (Arthur St John) Waugh.

Waugh, Evelyn (Arthur St John) (1903–1966), English novelist, author of Brideshead Revisited (1945); brother of Alec Waugh and father of Auberon (Alexander) Waugh.

Weaver, John V(an) A(lstyn) (1893–1938), American poet, writer and dramatist.

Webb, Beatrice (née Potter) (1858–1943), influential English social and economic reformer and historian; wife of Sidney Webb.

Webb, Charles Henry (1834–1905), American journalist, writer and poet.

Webb, Clement Charles Julian (1865–1954), English scholar.

Webb, Mary Gladys (née Meredith) (1881–1927), English writer and poet.

Webb, Sidney (1859–1947), influential English social and economic reformer and historian; husband of Beatrice (née Potter) Webb.

Webb, Walter Prescott (1888–1963), American historian.

Weber, Max (1864–1920), German sociologist and political economist, author of Die protestantische Ethik und der Geist des Kapitalismus (1904–05; English trans. as The Protestant Ethic and the Spirit of Capitalism, 1930).

Webster, Daniel (1782–1852), American orator and statesman whose speeches and writings comprise 18 vols (1903).

Webster, Jean (1876–1916), American writer of children's novels.

Webster, John (c.1580–1625), English dramatist and poet, author of the celebrated plays The White Divel (1612) and The Duchess of Malfi (1623).

Webster, Noah (1758–1843), American lexicographer, compiler of the American Spelling Book (1783) and the American Dictionary of the English Language (1828).

Wechsberg, Joseph (1907–1983), Czech-born American journalist and novelist.

Wedekind, Frank (1864–1918), influential German dramatist and actor whose works presaged the Theatre of the Absurd.

Wedgwood, Dame (Cicely) Veronica (1910–1997), eminent English historian, especially known for her studies The Thirty Years War (1938) and William the Silent (1944).

Weems, Mason Locke (1759–1825), American clergyman, book agent and writer of popular but unscholarly biographies of George Washington and Francis Marion, known as Parson Weems.

Weidenreich, Franz (1873–1948), German-born American anatomist and physical anthropologist who was known for his important studies on prehistoric man.

Weidman, Jerome (1913–1998), American novelist and dramatist.

Weil, Simone (1909–1943), French Roman Catholic mystic, philosopher and member of the Resistance during World War II, author of the famous La Pesanteur et la grâce (published 1947; English trans. as Gravity and Grace, 1952).

Weinheber Josef (1892–1945), gifted Austrian poet.

Weininger, Otto (1880–1903), Austrian philosopher who wrote Geschlecht und Charakter (1903; English trans. as Sex and Character, 1906); committed suicide.

Weiss, Bernhard (1827–1918), German Protestant theologian.

Weiss, John (1818–1879), American Unitarian minister, writer and translator.

Weiss, Peter (Ulrich) (1916–1982), German dramatist and novelist, best known for his plays Marat/Sade (1964) and Die Ermittlung (1965; English trans. as The Investigation, 1966).

Wei Yüan (1794–1856), Chinese historian and geographer.

Welch, (Maurice) Denton (1917–1948), English painter and novelist, author of Maiden Voyage (1943) and In Youth's Pleasure (1944).

Weld, Theodore Dwight (1803–1895), American Abolitionist and pamphleteer.

Weld, Thomas (1595–1661), English Congregationalist minister and writer.

Welhaven, Johan Sebastian Cammermeyer (1807–1873), Norwegian poet and critic.

Wellesley, Dorothy Violet (née Ashton), Duchess of Wellington (1889–1956), English poet.

Wellhausen, Julius (1844–1918), eminent German old Testament scholar.

Wells, Charles Jeremiah (c.1800–1879), English poet who wrote the verse play Joseph and his Brethren: A Scriptural Drama (1824) under the name H L Howard.

Wells, David Ames (1828–1898), American writer on science and economics.

Wells, H(erbert) G(eorge) (1866–1945), notable English novelist, short-story writer and popular historian.

Welty, Eudora (Alice) (1909–2001), American writer, author of Delta Wedding (1946), The Ponder Heart (1954), Losing Battles (1970) and The Optimist's Daughter (1972).

Wendell, Barrett (1855–1921), American literary scholar and biographer.

Wenker, Georg (1852–1911), German linguist.

Wen T'ing-yün (c.818–870), Chinese poet.

Weores, Sandor (1913–1989), Hungarian poet who was esteemed for his lyricism.

Werfel, Franz (1890–1945), German poet, dramatist and novelist, best known for his novels Die vierzig Tage des Musa Dagh (1933; English trans. as The Forty Days of Musa Dagh, 1934) and Das Lied von Bernadette (1941; English trans. as The Song of Bernadette, 1942).

Wergeland, Henrik Arnold (1808–1845), Norwegian poet, dramatist and patriot.

Werner, M(orris) R(obert) (1897–1981), American journalist and writer.

Wertheimer, Max (1880– 1943), influential German psychologist and philosopher who founded Gestalt psychology.

Wescott, Glenway (1901–1987), American writer.

Wesendonck, Mathilde (1828–1902), German poet, writer and dramatist whose affair with the composer Richard Wagner prompted him to compose the Wesendonck Lieder.

Wesley, Charles (1707–1788), famous English Methodist clergyman and hymnist; brother of John Wesley.

Wesley, John (1703–1791), celebrated English clergyman and evangelist, founder of the Methodist church; brother of Charles Wesley.

Wessel, Johan Herman (1742–1785), Norwegian-born Danish poet and dramatist who was a master of wit.

Wessely, Naphtali Herz (1725–1805), German Jewish Haskala poet.

West, Dorothy (1907–1998), American writer, best known for her novel The Wedding (1995).

West, Jessaymn (1907–1984), American writer and poet.

West, Morris (Langlo) (1916–99), Australian novelist and dramatist.

West, Nathanael (actually Nathan Weinstein) (1903–1940), American novelist who was a master of satire; died in an automobile accident.

West, Dame Rebecca (actually Cicely Isabel Fairfield) (1892–1983), English journalist, novelist and critic.

West, Richard (1716–1742), English poet.

Westcott, Edward Noyes (1846–1898), American banker and writer, author of the posthumously published novel David Harum: A Story of American Life (1898).

Westermann, Diedrich (1875–1956), German scholar who was an authority on African culture and anthropology.

Westermarck, Edward (Alexander) (1862–1939), important Finnish sociologist, anthropologist and philosopher, author of significant studies on the history of human marriage (1891) and the origin and development of moral ideas (2 vols, 1906, 1908).

Westlake, John (1828–1913), influential English international lawyer and social reformer, author of the pioneering Treatise on Private International Law (1858).

Wetzstein, Johann Gottfried (1815–1905), German Orientalist.

Wexley, John (1907–1985), American dramatist.

Weyman, Stanley John (1855–1928), English novelist.

Weymouth, Richard Francis (1822–1902), English philologist, biblical scholar and translator.

Wharton, Edith (Newbold née Jones) (1862–1937), prominent American novelist, short-story writer and poet who was best known for her writings about upper-class society.

Whately, Richard (1787–1863), English Anglican archbishop of Dublin, educator and social reformer.

Wheatley, Dennis Yates (1897–1977), English novelist who wrote works dealing with the occult.

Wheatley, Phillis (c.1753–1784), African-born American poet, author of Poems on Various Subjects, Religious and Moral (1773).

Wheaton, Henry (1795–1848), American maritime jurist, diplomat and writer, author of the standard Elements of International Law (1836).

Wheelock, John Hall (1886–1978), American poet and writer.

Wheelwright, John (c.1592–1679), English-born American Congregationalist clergyman, author of Mercurius Americanus (1645).

Whetstone, George (1550–1587), English dramatist, poet and writer, best known for his play Promos and Cassandra (1578).

Whewell, William (1794–1866), English philosopher, historian, essayist poet and translator, author of the History of Scientific Ideas (2 vols, 1858), Novum Organon Renovatum (1858) and On the Philosophy of Discovery (1860).

Whichcote, Benjamin (1609–1683), English philosopher who was a leading figure among the Cambridge Platonists.

Whipple, Edwin Percy (1819–1886), American literary critic and lecturer.

Whistler, James (Abbott) McNeill (1834–1903), American artist and art theorist.

Whiston, William (1667–1752), English Anglican priest, mathematician and writer who espoused Arian sentiments and became a General Baptist.

Whitcher, Francis Miriam (1814–1852), American writer who was known for her humorous sketches in colloquial dialect.

White, Andrew Dickson (1832–1918), American historian and educator.

White, Antonia (1899–1979), English novelist and translator.

White, Edward Lucas (1866–1934), America novelist.

White, E(lwyn) B(rooks) (1899–1985), esteemed American essayist and poet.

White, Gilbert (1720–1793), English naturalist, author of the Natural History and Antiquities of Selborne (1789).

White, Henry Kirke (1785–1806), English poet.

White, Joseph Blanco (actually José Maria Blanco y Crespo) (1775–1841), Spanish-born English journalist, writer and poet.

White, Patrick (Victor Martindale) (1912–1990), prominent Australian novelist, short-story writer and dramatist; won the Nobel Prize for Literature (1973).

White, Richard Grant (1821–1885), American literary, music and art critic.

White, Stewart Edward (1873–1946), American novelist.

White, Terence de Vere (1912–1994), Irish critic, writer, historian and biographer.

White T(erence) H(anbury) (1906–1964), English novelist and social historian.

White, Theodore H(arold) (1915–1986), American journalist, novelist and dramatist.

White, William Allen (1868–1944), American journalist, novelist, short-story writer and biographer.

Whitefield, George (1714–1770), prominent English evangelist and pamphleteer.

Whitehead, Alfred North (1861–1947), English mathematician and philosopher, author of Principia Mathematica (in collaboration with Bertrand Russell; 3 vols, 1910–13).

Whitehead, Charles (1804–1862), English poet, novelist and dramatist.

Whitehead, Paul (1710–1774), English poet.

Whitehead, William (1715–1785), English poet and dramatist; became Poet Laureate of the United Kingdom (1757).

Whitgift, John (c.1530–1604), English archbishop of Canterbury and writer.

Whiting, John Robert (1917–1963), English dramatist.

Whitlock, Brand (1869–1934), American novelist, writer on politics and biographer.

Whitman, Albery Allson (1851–1901), American clergyman and writer.

Whitman, Sarah Helen (Power) (1803–1878), American poet.

Whitman, Walt(er) (1819–1892), famous American poet, essayist and journalist, celebrated for his liberating poems in Leaves of Grass (1855).

Whitney, William Dwight (1827–1894), learned American linguist who wrote the standard Sanskrit Grammar (1879).

Whittier, John Greenleaf (1807–1892), prominent American poet, journalist and Abolitionist whose Quaker faith informed his poetry.

Whorf, Benjamin Lee (1897–1941), American linguist.

Whyte-Melville, George John (1821–1878), English novelist.

Whythorne, Thomas (1528–1596), English composer and poet.

Wicksell, (Johan Gustaf) Knut (1851–1926), Swedish economist.

Wicquefort, Abraham de (17th Century), Dutch historian.

Widdemer, Margaret (1884–1978), American poet, novelist and short-story writer.

Widmann, Joseph Viktor (1842–1911), German poet, dramatist, writer, critic and editor.

Wied, Gustav (Johannes) (1858–1914), Danish dramatist, novelist and poet.

Wieland, Christoph Martin (1733–1813), German poet, writer and translator.

Wienberg, Ludolf (1802–1872), German writer.

Wiggin, Kate Douglas (1856–1923), American writer, best known for her children's book Rebecca of Sunnybrook Farm (1903).

Wigglesworth, Michael (1631–1705), English-born American poet and clergyman, author of the first American epic The Day of Doom (1662).

Wigmore, John Henry (1863–1943), American legal scholar who wrote the authoritative Treatise on the Anglo-American System of Evidence in Trials at Common Law (10 vols, 1904–05).

Wilamowitz-Moellendorff, Ulrich von (1848–1931), learned German classical scholar.

Wilberforce, Samuel (1805–1873), prominent English Anglican bishop and writer who played a significant role in the preservation of the Oxford Movement; son of William Wilberforce.

Wilberforce, William (1759–1833), notable English politician and philanthropist who championed the abolition of slavery, author of A Practical View of the Prevailing Religious System of Professed Christians (1797); father of Samuel Wilberforce.

Wilcox, Carlos (1794–1827), American Congregationalist minister and poet, admired for his didactic poem The Age of Benelovence.

Wilcox, Ella (née Wheeler) (1850–1919), American journalist and poet.

Wilde, Jane Francesca, Lady (1826–1896), Irish poet, known as Speranza.

Wilde, Oscar (Fingal O'Flahertie Wills) (1854–1900), celebrated Irish wit, dramatist, poet, novelist and essayist, author of the famous comic play The Importance of Being Earnest (1895); father of Vyvyan Oscar Beresford Holland.

Wilde, Richard Henry (1789–1847), Irish-born American poet, lawyer and politician.

Wildenbruch, Ernst von (1845–1909), prominent German dramatist, novelist and poet.

Wildenvey, Herman (actually Herman Portaas) (1886–1959), Norwegian poet.

Wilder, Laura Ingalls (1867–1957), American writer of children's books, especially remembered for her Little House on the Prairie (1935).

Wilder, Thornton (Niven) (1897–1975), prominent American dramatist and novelist, author of the famous play Our Town (1938).

Wildgans, Anton (1881–1932), Austrian poet and dramatist.

Wilkes, John (1725–1797), English journalist and politician who was a champion of liberty in spite of repeated expulsions from Parliament.

Wilkie, William (1721–1772), English scholar and poet, author of the epic poem The Epigoniad (9 vols, 1757).

Wilkins, John (1614–1672), English Anglican bishop and scientist.

Willard, Emma (Hart) (1787–1870), American educator and poet, author of Rocked in the Cradle of the Deep (1831).

Willard, Francis (Elizabeth Caroline) (1839–1898), American educator, reformer and writer, founder of the National Women's Christian Temperance Union; aunt of Josiah Flint Willard.

Willard, Josiah Flint (1869–1907), American writer who wrote under the name of Josiah Flynt; nephew of Francis (Elizabeth Caroline) Willard.

Willard, Samuel (1640–1707), American Congregationalist clergyman and educator whose collected writings were published posthumously as the Compleat Body of Divinity (1726).

Willems, Jan Frans (1793–1846), Flemish philologist, poet, dramatist and essayist.

William de la Mare (died c.1290), important English Christian philosopher and biblical scholar, author of a critique of Thomas Aquinas in the Correctorium fratris Thomae (Corrective of Brother Thomas, 1278).

William of Auvergne (c.1181–1249), French philosopher and theologian who wrote the expansive Magisterium divinale (The Divine Teaching, 7 vols, 1223–40).

William of Auxerye (c.1150–1231), French philosopher and theologian whose most important work was the Summa super quattuor libros sententiarum (Compendium of the Four Books of Sentences, 4 vols, 1215–20).

William of Conches (c.1100–1154), French philosopher of the scholastic school.

William of Hirsau (died 1091), German Benedictine abbot and scholar.

William of Malmesbury (c.1095–1143), important English historian who wrote major accounts of English political and ecclesiastical history.

William of Moerbeke (c.1215–c.1286), Belgian Roman Catholic archbishop of Corinth and classical scholar, especially known for his Latin translations of ancient Greek philosophers.

William of Newburgh (1136–c.1198), English historian, author of the Historia rerum Anglicarum (History of English Events, c.1197).

William of Saint-Amour (c.1200–1272), French philosopher and theologian, a determined opponent of the mendicant religious orders.

William of Saint-Thierry (c.1085–1148), notable Belgian Roman Catholic monk, mystic and theologian.

William of Tyre (c.1130–1185), Syrian politician, churchman and historian of French descent, author of an important history of medieval Palestine as Historia rerum in partibus transmarinis gestarum.

Williams, Anna (1706–1783), English poet and writer.

Williams, Ben Ames (1889–1953), American novelist and short-story writer.

Williams, Charles (Walter Stansby) (1886–1945), English poet and writer.

Williams, Edward (1747–1826), Welsh poet, creator of the 14th-Century poet Dafydd ap Gwilym and the works attributed to him.

Williams, (George) Emlyn (1905–1987), Welsh actor and dramatist.

Williams, George Washington (1849–1891), American historian who wrote important studies on his race, including a History of the Negro Race in America (1883) and A History of the Negro Troops in the War of Rebellion (1888).

Williams, Helen Maria (1762–1827), English poet.

Williams, Isaac (1802–1865), English theologian and poet.

Williams, John (1761–1818), English-born American poet, dramatist and biographer who became best known for his searing satires under the name Anthony Pasquin.

Williams, Raymond Henry (1921–1988), English critic and novelist.

Williams, Roger (c.1603–1683), English-born American colonist and writer, best known as a passionate defender of religious liberty and as author of The Bloudy Tenent of Persecution (1644).

Williams, Tennessee (actually Thomas Lanier Williams) (1911–1983), American dramatist, short-story writer and poet, admired for such notable plays as The Glass Menagerie (1944), A Street Car Named Desire (1947), Summer and Smoke (1948) and Cat on a Hot Tin Roof (1955).

Williams, Waldo (1904–1971), Welsh poet.

Williams, William Carlos (1883–1963), eminent American poet and writer, especially admired for his Pictures from Brueghel, and Other Poems (1962).

Williamson, Henry (1895–1977), English novelist.

Willingham, Calder (Baynard Jr) (1922–1995), American novelist, short-story writer and screenwriter.

Willis, N(athaniel) P(arker) (1806–1867), American poet, writer and dramatist; brother of Sara Payson Willis.

Willis, Sara Payson (1811–1872), American writer who wrote under the name Fanny Fern; sister of N(athaniel) P(arker) Willis.

Wills, William Gorman (1828–1891), Irish dramatist, novelist and poet.

Wilson, Alexander (1766–1813), American ornithologist and poet.

Wilson, Sir Angus (Frank Johnstone) (1913–1991), noted English novelist and short-story writer.

Wilson, Edmund (1895–1972), prominent American critic, essayist, novelist, poet and dramatist.

Wilson, Frank Percy (1889–1963), English literary scholar.

Wilson, Harriet (1808–c.1870), American writer whose Our Nig: Sketches from the Life of a Free Black, in a Two-Story White House, North, Showing That Slavery's Shadows Fall Even There (1859) was the first novel by an African-American.

Wilson, Harriette (née Dubochet) (1786–1846), English courtesan and writer, best known for her Memoirs of Harriette Wilson, written by herself (1825).

Wilson, Harry Leon (1867–1939), American novelist and dramatist.

Wilson, James (1742–1798), Scottish-born American lawyer, jurist and political theorist.

Wilson, James (1805–1860), English economist.

Wilson, John (c.1591–1667), English-born American Congregationalist minister and poet.

Wilson, John (1785–1854), Scottish philosopher who wrote under the name Christopher North.

Wilson, John Cook (1849–1915), English philosopher.

Wilson, (John) Dover (1881–1969), English literary scholar, especially known for his Shakespearean studies.

Wilson, Thomas (c.1525–1581), English statesman and writer, author of The Rule of Reason (1551) and The Art of Retorique (1553).

Winchilsea, Anne Finch (née Kingsmith), Countess of (1661–1720), English poet.

Winckelmann, Johann (Joachim) (1717–1768), influential German archaeologist and art historian, author of the seminal Geschichte der Kunst des Alterthums (History of the Art of theAncients, 1764).

Winckler, Hugo (1863–1913), German archaeologist and historian.

Windelband, Wilhelm (1848–1915), German philosopher.

Wing, Donald Goddard (1904–1972), American scholar and bibliographer.

Winslow, Edward (1595–1655), English-born American Puritan leader and writer who helped to found the Plymouth colony in Massachusetts, author of the Glorious Progress of the Gospel Amongst the Indians in New England (1649).

Winslow, Thyra Samter (1893–1961), American drama critic and short-story writer.

Winsor, Justin (1831–1897), American librarian and historian.

Winstanley, Gerrard (c.1609–c.1661), English agrarian leader and pamphleteer who espoused communist sentiments in his The Law of Freedom in a Platform (1652).

Winter, William (1836–1917), American drama critic, biographer, writer and poet.

Winter, Zikmund (1846–1912), Czech writer.

Winterich, John T(racy) (1891–1970), American writer on literary subjects.

Winters, (Arthur) Yvor (1900–1968), American critic and poet.

Winthrop, John (1588–1649), English-born American political leader and writer who served as the first governor of the Massachusetts Bay Colony, author of a valuable Journal (published 1790).

Winthrop, Theodore (1828–1861), American novelist.

Wireker, Nigel (12th Century), English churchman who wrote Burnellus or Speculum Stultorum, a satire on monks.

Wirth, Louis (1897–1952), German-born American sociologist.

Wirt, William (1772–1834), American lawyer, politician and writer.

Wise, Henry Augustus (1819–1869), American naval officer and writer whose novels were published under the name Harry Gringo.

Wise, John (1652–1725), American clergyman and pamphleteer who became known for his espousal of democratic rights.

Wiseman, Nicholas Patrick Stephen (1802–1865), English Roman Catholic cardinal and writer, particularly known for his scholarly tome Horae Syriaeae (Syrian Seasons, 1827) and the novel Fabiola (1854).

Wishart, William (c.1692–1753), Scottish churchman and philosopher.

Wister, Owen (1860–1938), American writer, best known for his novel The Virginian (1902).

Witelo (c.1225–c.1275), Polish scientist and philosopher.

Wither, George (1588–1667), English writer and poet.

Witherspoon, John (1723–1794), Scottish-born American Presbyterian minister, educator and writer.

Witkiewicz, Stanisław Ignacy (1885–1939), Polish novelist and dramatist.

Wittgenstein, Ludwig (Josef Johann) (1889–1951), eminent Austrian-born English philosopher who was particularly known for his theories on logic and the philosophy of language.

Wittlin, Józef (1896–1976), Polish-born American poet, novelist and essayist.

Wivallius, Lars (1605–1669), Swedish adventurer and poet.

Wodehouse, Sir P(elham) G(renville) (1881–1975), prominent English-born American novelist, short-story writer, dramatist and poet, creator of the celebrated manservant Jeeves.

Woestijne, Karel van de (1878–1929), Flemish poet, famous for his mastery of Symbolic expression in his De modderen man (The Man of Mud, 1920).

Wolcot, John (1738–1819), English poet and writer who wrote satirical works under the name Peter Pindar.

Wolf, Friedrich August (1759–1824), German classical philologist.

Wolfe, Charles (1791–1823), Irish churchman and poet, known for The Burial of Sir John Moore at Corunna (1817).

Wolfe, Humbert (1885–1940), English poet and critic.

Wolfe, Thomas (Clayton) (1900–1938), important American novelist, author of Look Homeward Angel (1929), Of Time and the River (1935) and You Can't Go Home Again (published 1940).

Wolff, Christian, Freiherr von (1679–1754), influential German philosopher, scientist and scholar who was a leading exponent of Rationalism.

Wolff-Bekker, Elizabeth (1738–1804), Dutch writer who collaborated with Agatha Deken on the first Dutch novel, Sara Burgerhart (1782).

Wölfflin, Heinrich (1864–1945), Swiss aesthetician and art historian, author of the significant study Kunstgeschichtliche Grundbegriffe (1915; English trans. as Principles of Art History, 1932).

Wolfram von Eschenbach (c.1170–c.1220), famous German poet who wrote the epic Parzival (1200–10).

Wollaston, William (1659–1724), English philosopher of the Rationalist school, author of The Religion of Nature Delineated (1724).

Wollstonecraft, Mary (1759–1797), English writer on controversial subjects, particularly known for A Vindication of the Rights of Woman; mother of Mary Wollstonecraft Shelley.

Wood, Anthony (1632–1695), English antiquarian who became known as Anthony à Wood, author of the valuable Athenae Oxonienses (1691–92).

Wood, Charles Erskine Scott (1852–1944), American poet, especially known for his Heavenly Discourse (1927) and Earthly Discourse (1937).

Wood, Ellen (née Price) (1814–1887), English novelist who was known as Mrs Henry Wood, author of East Lynne (1861).

Wood, Sarah Sayward Barrell Keating (1759–1855), American writer who had notable success with her Gothic romances.

Woodberry, George Edward (1855–1930), American critic and poet.

Woodcock, George (1912–1995), Canadian poet, critic, writer, dramatist and editor.

Woodhull, Victoria Claflin (1838–1927), controversial American reformer and polemicist who championed causes ranging from socialism to free love.

Woodson, Carter G(odwin) (1875–1950), American historian who wrote important studies on black history.

Woodward, C(omer) Vann (1908–99), American historian, author of The Strange Career of Jim Crow (1955), The Burden of Southern History (1960) and Thinking Back: The Perils of Writing History (1986).

Woodward, W(illiam) E (1874–1950), American writer.

Woodworth, Samuel (1785–1842), American journalist, poet and dramatist.

Woolf, (Adeline) Virginia (née Stephen) (1882–1941), famous English novelist and critic; daughter of Sir Leslie Stephen and wife of Leonard (Sidney) Woolf; committed suicide.

Woolf, Leonard (Sidney) (1880–1969), English writer, publisher and internationalist; husband of (Adeline) Virginia (née Stephen) Woolf.

Woollcott, Alexander (Humphreys) (1887–1943), American critic and essayist.

Woolley, Sir (Charles) Leonard (1880–1960), English archaeologist.

Woolman, John (1720–1772), American Quaker leader, Abolitionist and writer, author of a celebrated Journal (published 1774).

Woolner, Thomas (1826–1892), English poet and sculptor.

Woolsey, Theodore Dwight (1801–1889), American scholar and educator.

Woolson, Constance Fenimore (1840–1894), American novelist and short-story writer; grandniece of James Fenimore Cooper.

Woolston, Thomas (1670–1733), controversial English Deist whose writings led to his imprisonment and death in prison.

Worcester, Joseph Emerson (1784–1865), American lexicographer, compiler of the Dictionary of the English Language (1860).

Wordsworth, Christopher (1807–1885), English Anglican churchman, biblical scholar and hymnist; nephew of William Wordsworth.

Wordsworth, Dorothy (1771–1855), English writer, best known for her posthumously published Alfoxden Journal 1798 (1941) and Grasmere Journals 1800–03 (1941); sister of William Wordsworth.

Wordsworth, William (1770–1850), English poet, celebrated for his Lyrical Ballads (1798) and The Prelude (1805); became Poet Laureate of the United Kingdom (1843); brother of Dorothy Wordsworth.

Worsaae, Jens Jacob Asmussen (1821–1885), pioneering Danish archaeologist who wrote the important study Danmarks Oldtid oplyst Oldsager og Gravhøie (1843; English trans. as The Primeval Antiquities of Denmark, 1849).

Wotton, Sir Henry (1568–1639), English poet and diplomat, best remembered for his You Meaner Beauties of the Night.

Wotton, William (1666–1727), English scholar.

Wrede, William (1859–1906), German New Testament scholar, author of Das Messiasgeheimnis in der Evangelein (1901).

Wren, P(ercival) C(hristopher) (1885–1941), English novelist and short-story writer.

Wright, Austin Tappan (1883–1931), American educator and writer, author of the Utopian novel Islandia (published 1942).

Wright, Chauncey (1830–1875), American mathematician and philosopher.

Wright, Frances (1795–1852), Scottish-born American freethinker and writer.

Wright, Frank Lloyd (1869–1959), famous American architect and writer on architecture.

Wright, Harold Bell (1872–1944), American novelist.

Wright, James (Arlington) (1927–1980), American poet.

Wright, Judith (1915–2000), Australian poet and writer who won distinction with her poetry collections The Moving Image (1946) and Woman to Man (1949).

Wright, L(aurali) R(ose) (1939–2001), Canadian writer of crime novels.

Wright, (Philip) Quincy (1890–1970), American political scientist who was best known as an authority on international law.

Wright, Richard (Nathaniel) (1908–1960), important black American novelist and short-story writer, author of the novel Native Son (1940).

Wright, Thomas (1711–1786), English philosopher.

Wright, Thomas (1810–1877), English antiquarian.

Wroth, L(awrence) C(ounselman) (1884–1970), American historian.

Wu Ch'eng-en (c.1500–c.1582), Chinese novelist and poet.

Wu Ching-tzu (1701–1754), Chinese novelist, author of the classic satirical novel Ju-lin wai-shih (c.1750; English trans. as The Scholars).

Wulfstan (died 1023), English archbishop of York and writer, best known for his homilies.

Wuolijok, Hella (1886–1954), Finnish writer.

Wurdemann, Audrey (1911–1960), American poet; wife of Joseph Auslander.

Wuttke, Heinrich (1818–1876), German historian.

Wyat or Wyatt, Sir Thomas (1503–1542), English courtier and poet who introduced the sonnet, the italian ottava rima and terza rima, and the French rondeau into English poetry.

Wycherley, William (1640–1716), English dramatist, best known for The Country-Wife (1675).

Wycliffe, John (c.1330–1384), English philosopher, theologian and religious reformer.

Wylie, Elinor (Morton Hoyt) (1885–1928), American poet and writer; wife of William Rose Benét.

Wyndham, John (actually John Benyon Harris) (1903–1969), English science fiction writer.

Wynne (o Lasynys), Ellis (1671–1734), Welsh clergyman and writer, author of the classic Gweledigaetheu y Bardd Cwsc (Visions of the Sleeping Bard, 1703).

Wyntoun, Andrew of (c.1350–c.1423), Scottish chronicler, known for the valuable Orygynale Cronykil.

Wyspiański, Stanisław (1869–1907), eminent Polish poet, dramatist and painter.

Xenarchus (1stt Century BC), Greek philosopher.

Xenocrates (died 314 BC), Greek philosopher.

Xenophanes (c.560–c.478 BC), Greek poet and philosopher.

Xenophon (431–c.350 BC), Greek historian, author of the Anabasis, the Hellenica and the Memorabilia.

Xenopoulos, Gegorios (1867–1951), Greek writer.

Yamabe Akahito (8th Century), Japanese poet.

Yananoue Okura (c.660–c.733), important Japanese poet.

Yáñez, Agustín (1904–80), Mexican novelist, short-story writer and politician.

Yang Chu (440–c.360 BC), Chinese philosopher.

Yang Hsien-chih (6th Century), Chinese writer.

Yang Hsiung (c.53 BC–18 AD), Chinese poet and philosopher.

Ya'qūbī, al- (actually Ahmad ibn Abū Ya'qūb ibn Ja'far ibn Wahb ibn Wādih al-Ya'qūbī) (died 897), Arab historian and geographer.

Yates, Dornford (actually Cecil William Mercer) (1885–1960), English writer.

Yates, Dame Frances Amelia (1899–1981), English scholar who was an authority on Renaissance studies.

Yates, Edmund Hodgson (1831–94), English journalist and novelist.

Yavorov, Peyo (actually Peyo Kracholov) (1877–1914), Bulgarian poet and dramatist who founded the Symbolist movement in his homeland; committed suicide.

Yāzījī, Nāsīf (1800–1871), Lebanese literary scholar.

Yearsley, Ann (née Cromartie) (1752–1806), English poet, novelist and dramatist.

Yeats, William Butler (1865–1939), celebrated Irish poet, dramatist and writer; won the Nobel Prize for Literature (1923).

Yen Jo-Chü (1636–1704), important Chinese historian.

Yen Yüan (1635–1704), notable Chinese philosopher who propounded a pragmatic form of Confucianism.

Yerby, Frank (Garvin) (1916–1991), American novelist.

Yerkes, Robert M(earns) (1876–1956), American psychologist who was a pioneering figure in the development of animal psychology.

Yesenin, Sergei Alexandrovich (1895–1925), Russian poet; committed suicide.

Yezierska, Anzia (1885–1970), Russian-born American novelist and short-story writer.

Yokomitsu Riichi (1898–1947), noted Japanese writer who was also known as Yokomitsu Toshikazu.

Yonge, Charlotte Mary (1823–1901), English novelist, particularly remembered for The Heir of Redclyffe (1853).

Yosano Akiko (1878–1942), esteemed Japanese poet who was also known as Ho Sho.

Yoshida Kenkō (actually Urabe Kaneyoshi) (1283–1350), Japanese poet and essayist.

Yoshikawa Eiji (actually Yoshikawa Hidetsugu) (1892–1962), Japanese novelist.

Young, Douglas (1913–1973), Scottish poet, dramatist and translator.

Young, Edward (1683–1765), admired English poet, dramatist and critic, author of The Complaint or Night Thoughts on Life, Death and Immortality (1742–45).

Young, Francis Brett (1884–1954), English novelist, short-story writer and poet.

Young, Marguerite Vivian (1909–1995), American novelist and poet.

Young, Stark (1881–1963), American critic, poet, writer and dramatist.

Yourcenar, Marguerite (actually Marguerite de Crayencour) (1903–1987), Belgian-born French novelist and poet.

Yovkov, Yordan Stefanovich (1880–1937), Bulgarian novelist, short-story writer and dramatist.

Yüan Chi (210–263), notable Chinese poet.

Yü Ta-fu (1896–1945), Chinese writer.

Zaehner, R(obert) C(harles) (1913–74), English historian of religion.

Zagoskin, Mikhail Nikolaievich (1789–1852), Russian writer.

Zahn, Ernst (1867–1952), Swiss writer.

Zalygin, Sergei Pavlovich (1913–2000), Russian writer and editor.

Zamyatin, Yevgeny Ivanovich (1884–1937), Russian novelist and dramatist.

Zangwill, Israel (1864–1926), English novelist, poet, dramatist and essayist.

Zapolska, Gabriela (actually Maria Gabriela Korwin-Piotrowska) (1857–1921), Polish novelist and dramatist.

Zarlino, Gioseffo (1517–1590), Italian composer and writer on music.

Zaturenska, Marya (1902–1982), Russian-born American poet; wife of Horace (Victor) Gregory.

Zayas y Sotomayor, Mariá de (1590–c.1650), Spanish novelist.

Zeami Motokiyo (1363–1443), celebrated Japanese dramatist.

Zélide (actually Isabella van Tuyll van Serooskerken) (1740–1805), Dutch novelist.

Zell, Matthew (1477–1548), German Protestant reformer and writer.

Zeno, Apostolo (1668–1750), Italian poet.

Zeno of Citium (c.335–c.263 BC), Greek philosopher, founder of Stoicism.

Zeno of Elea (c.495–c.430 BC), Greek philosopher and mathematician.

Zeromski, Stefan (1864–1925), Polish novelist, dramatist and poet.

Zhukovsky, Vasily Andreievich (1783–1852), notable Russian poet and translator.

Zimorowic, Bartłomej (1597–1677), Polish poet.

Zittel, Karl Alfred, Ritter von (1839–1904), German paleontologist.

Znaniecki, Florian Witold (1882–1958), Polish-born American sociologist.

Zola, Émile (-Édouard-Charles-Antoine) (1840–1902), famous French novelist and critic who created the Naturalist movement in literature.

Zollinger, Albin (1895–1941), Swiss poet and novelist.

Zonares, John (12th Century), Byzantine historian.

Zorrilla de San Martín, Juan (1855–1931), Uruguayan poet, known for his epic Tabare (1886).

Zorrilla y Moral, José (1817–1893), Spanish poet and dramatist.

Zouche, Richard (1590–1661), English jurist whose Juris et judicii fecialis (1650) was a pioneering treatise on international law.

Zrínyi, Miklós (1620–1664), Hungarian statesman, military leader, poet and writer, author of the famous epic poem Szigeti Veszedelem (1645–46; English trans. as The Peril of Sziget, 1955).

Zuckmayer, Carl (1896–1977), German-born American dramatist and poet.

Zugsmith, Leane (1903–1969), American novelist.

Zuhayr (ibn Abī Sulmā Rabī'ah ibn Rīyāh al-Muzanī) (c.520–c.609), renowned Arab poet.

Zukofsky, Louis (1904–1978), American poet, author of the provocative and vast poem A (1927–78).

Zumpt, Karl Gottlob (1792–1849), German philologist.

Zunz, Leopold (1794–1886), German Jewish literary historian.

Zunzunegui, Juan Antonio de (1901–82), Spanish novelist and short-story writer.

Zweig, Arnold (1887–1968), German writer, best known for his novel Der Streit um den Sergeanten Grischa (1927; English trans. as The Case of Sergeant Grischa, 1927).

Zweig, Stefan (1881–1942), Austrian-born English poet, novelist, short-story writer and translator; committed suicide.

Zwingli, Huldrych (1484–1531), Swiss Protestant reformer and theologian; died in battle.

*For Product Safety Concerns and Information please contact
our EU representative GPSR@taylorandfrancis.com Taylor & Francis
Verlag GmbH, Kaufingerstraße 24, 80331 München, Germany*

T - #0060 - 270225 - C0 - 280/208/27 [29] - CB - 9781857431599 - Gloss Lamination